FEATURE FILMS

FEATURE FILMS

A Directory of Feature Films on 16mm and
Videotape Available for Rental, Sale, and Lease

Eighth Edition

Compiled and Edited
under the Direction of
James L. Limbacher

R. R. Bowker Company
New York & London, 1985

Published by R. R. Bowker Co.
205 East Forty-second Street, New York, NY 10017
Copyright © 1985 by James L. Limbacher

All rights reserved. Reproduction of this work,
in whole or in part, without written permission
of the publisher is prohibited.

International Standard Book Number: 0-8352-1929-1
International Standard Serial Number: 0071-4100
Library of Congress Catalog Card Number: 68-58279

Printed and bound in the United States of America

CONTENTS

CONTENTS

FOREWORD

This eighth edition of *Feature Films* lists 22,205 feature films and videotapes available for rental, sale, and lease from the best-known distributors. It eliminates the need of film people to comb through hundreds of catalogs to find the availability of specific titles for booking or purchasing. In an effort to provide the most comprehensive index for features, this edition includes an estimated 95 percent of all features generally available in the United States and from major Canadian sources.

Since the last edition there have been major changes in film and videotape distribution. At least half a dozen major companies have merged while the field saw the disappearance of another dozen more. Because of the astronomical growth of the videotape field, video versions of Hollywood features have been eliminated, unless they are available exclusively through the distributors. Videotape versions, however, *are* listed for documentaries and educational features that would not be available at videotape centers.

The eighth edition updates all of the features of earlier editions—a directors index, a foreign-language index, a list of film reference works, and a complete list of film companies and distributors by alphabetical code and classified by geographical areas. Many film catalogs themselves feature an index of actors and their films.

Opinions vary regarding the definition of a "feature film," but this publication has always followed the rule that any film over one 16mm reel long or running 48 minutes or more is a "feature." There are one or two exceptions in the case of a classic film, which the editor feels should be included, even though it might run for a shorter time.

"Exclusive distribution" is a term that pertains to the major companies that have exclusive rights to many films. Firms such as MGM/UA Entertainment and Films Incorporated have exclusive rights to most titles in their catalogs. In a few cases, they might sublease some of their material to other distributors. Several companies, such as Walt Disney and Columbia, lease films to a group of rental agencies.

As mentioned earlier, almost every feature in this edition has a video counterpart. There are several sources for videotape and videodisc lists and the following two books may be consulted for a reasonably complete title list of video materials: *Video Source Book* (National Video Clearinghouse, Box 3, Syosset, NY 11791) and *The Videolog: Programs for General Interest and Entertainment* (Esselte Video, Box 978, Edison, NJ 08817).

The phaseout of regular and super 8mm films is seen in this new edition and there are very few titles still listed. They have become a "special order" item.

There are always the legendary titles that are not available. *Annie Get Your Gun* is owned by Irving Berlin and *1984* and *The Manchurian Candidate* were withdrawn by the producers. The good news is that five previously withdrawn Alfred Hitchcock films have been reissued theatrically by Universal and will be available for viewing again.

Rights to films often change when lease agreements expire and are picked up by other distributors. A few titles disappear and cannot be replaced because the print materials have been lost, stolen, deteriorated, or destroyed. In other cases, prints have been returned to Europe when American rights expired.

This publication cannot be responsible for distribution changes and withdrawals that are not reported by the distributors or that occur after the deadline for this edition. The editor would be grateful if distributors and users would report changes so supplements and new editions can be amended. The quarterly supplements to this publication appear in *Sightlines* magazine, available free to members of the Educational Film Library Association (EFLA) and on a subscription basis from EFLA (45 John St., Suite, 301, New York, NY 10038).

Since motion pictures and video formats are classified as copyrighted materials, only the copyright owner or licensed distributor may legally present them to the public for rental, lease, or sale. This directory has been compiled from the distributors' printed catalogs and supplementary lists supplied by them, and neither the editor nor the publisher is responsible for the listing of any unauthorized distribution of any title. Furthermore, this publication cannot guarantee either the condition of any individual print or its exact running time. Books listed in the section on Film Reference Works were consulted to check basic information on many films, especially when data were lacking in the distributors' catalogs.

This directory has been compiled for reference and booking purposes only—not for advertising. No distributor paid to have its films listed. Any omissions, changes, or corrections submitted to the editor will be checked and included in subsequent editions, which appear on a more or less biennial basis.

We hope you find this latest edition valuable and useful.

JAMES L. LIMBACHER

PREFACE

The users of *Feature Films: A Directory of Feature Films on 16mm and Videotape Available for Rental, Sale, and Lease* can access information in the Main Index and Serials Index to 22,205 feature films available in various formats. When available, each entry in these indexes includes the following: title, alternate title, translated title, number of parts, part number, version, series title and subtitle, original title, current and original languages (if other than English), cast, director, release date, producer or country of origin, special information (anamorphic, documentary, etc.), number of items, running time, sound statement, size/format, color/B&W, dubbing/narration statement, and distributor. Double features are not listed.

The Directors Index includes 17,822 films arranged alphabetically under 4,570 directors' names. A page reference guides the user to the Main or Serials Indexes where full information can be found. The Foreign-Language Films Index lists 1,436 films alphabetically under 43 foreign languages. The Film Reference Works section includes an alphabetical bibliography with a subject classification.

Distributors' names are abbreviated. A key to these abbreviations can be found in the Film Companies and Distributors section on page 725. Entries in this section are arranged alphabetically by the abbreviation used in the feature film entry, including full name, address, and telephone number. Immediately following are film companies and distributors classified by six major areas: New York, the East, the Midwest, the South, the West, and Canada.

ACQUISITION OF DATA

Feature Films: A Directory of Feature Films on 16mm and Videotape Available for Rental, Sale and Lease was produced from data stored on magnetic tape, edited by computer programs, and set in type by computer-controlled videocomposition.

Our acquisition efforts included two mailings to more than 240 film companies and distributors throughout the United States and Canada. Consistent information is provided for each film and was prepared primarily from materials collected directly from these mailing efforts.

This edition of *Feature Films* includes Main and Serials Indexes with information on 22,205 films, Directors Index, Foreign-Language Index, Film Reference Works, and Film Companies and Distributors with an area directory to those companies.

Many people at the R. R. Bowker Company made contributions in preparing this publication. Emilia Tomaszewski, Manager, New Database Development and Production, worked under the direction of Peter Simon, Vice President, Data Services Division, on designing this first database version of *Feature Films*. Product development support was received from Gary Ink, Executive Editor, Book Publishing Division. Special thanks are extended to Jane Tiarsmith, Project Manager, for her editorial and ongoing contributions. Additional thanks for their special contributions go to Michael Gold, Applications Manager; Philip Pan, Applications Manager; Penelope Davis, Programmer/Analyst; and Jack Murphy, Computer Operator Specialist.

The R. R. Bowker Company (A Xerox Information Company) has made a concerted effort in collecting and editing the data included in *Feature Films: A Directory of Feature Films on 16mm and Videotape Available for Rental, Sale, and Lease,* Eighth Edition. The Bowker Company, therefore, does not assume and hereby disclaims any liability to any party for any loss or damage caused by errors or omissions in *Feature Films,* Eighth Edition, whether such errors or omissions result from negligence, accident, or any other cause.

We welcome and appreciate the comments and suggestions of our users so that future editions may be even more useful.

MAIN INDEX

A-Haunting We Will Go. Stan Laurel & Oliver Hardy. Directed by Jim Jacobs. 1942. Fox. 67 min. Sound. 16mm B&W. *Rental:* Films Inc & Inst Cinema.

A is for Atom B Is for Bomb. 1980. 58 min. Videotape *Rental:* PBS Video. *Sale:* PBS Video.

A. K. A. Cassius Clay: Muhammed Ali, A. K. A. Cassius Clay. Directed by Jim Jacobs. 1970. United Artists. (Documentary). 79 min. Sound. 16mm Color. *Rental:* MGM United.

A. L. A. Satellite Seminar on Copyright. 1979. ALA. (Lecture). 120 min. Videotape Color. *Rental:* PBS Video. *Sale:* PBS Video.

A la Biena de Dios. Spain. (Cast unlisted). 82 min. Sound. 16mm B&W. *Rental:* Film Classics.

A la Brava: Prison & Beyond. 1974. (Documentary). 54 min. 16mm Color. *Rental:* U Cal Media. *Sale:* U Cal Media. *Sale:* U Cal Media, Videotape version.

A la Luz de un Fosforo. Span. Mexico. (Cast unlisted). 85 min. Sound. 16mm B&W. subtitles. *Rental:* Film Classics.

A las Buenos Dios. Span. 1953. Spain. (Cast unlisted). 85 min. Sound. 16mm B&W. subtitles. *Rental:* Film Classics.

A. M. Klein: The Poet As Landscape. Directed by David Kaufman. 1978. Carousel. (Documentary). Sound. 16mm Color. *Sale:* Carousel Films. *Sale:* Carousel Films, Videotape version.

A Nous la Liberte. Raymond Cordy, Henri Marchand & Paul Oliver. Directed by Rene Clair. Fr. 1931. France. 87 min. Sound. 16mm B&W. subtitles. *Rental:* Budget Films, Corinth Films, Films Inc, Images Film, Iowa Films & Kit Parker. *Lease:* Corinth Films. *Sale:* Cinema Eight, Glenn Photo, Festival Films, Natl Cinema, Reel Images & Images Film. *Sale:* Tamarelles French Film, Festival Films & Images Film, Videotape version.

A Propos de Nice. Directed by Jean Vigo. 1930. 28 min. Sound. 16mm B&W. *Rental:* Films Inc.

A Tout Prendre *see* Take It All.

Aaron Loves Angela. Kevin Hooks & Moses Gunn. Directed by Gordon Parks Jr. 1975. Columbia. 99 min. Sound. 16mm Color. *Rental:* Budget Films, Cine Craft, Swank Motion & Westcoast Films. *Rental:* Swank Motion, Videotape version.

Aaron Slick from Punkin' Creek. Alan Young, Dinah Shore & Robert Merrill. Directed by Claude Binyon. 1952. Paramount. 95 min. Sound. 16mm Color. *Rental:* Films Inc.

Abandon Ship! Tyrone Power, Lloyd Nolan & Stephen Boyd. Directed by Richard Sale. 1957. Columbia. 90 min. Sound. 16mm B&W. *Rental:* Budget Films, Charard Motion Pics, Film Ctr DC, Films Inc, Images Film, Inst Cinema, Modern Sound, Roas Films, Welling Motion Pictures & Wholesome Film Ctr. *Rental:* Budget Films, 100 mins. version.

Abandoned Children, The *see* Ninos Abandonados.

Abba: The Movie. Directed by Lasse Hallstrom. 1979. Warners. (Anamorphic). 90 min. Sound. 16mm Color. *Rental:* Swank Motion, Twyman Films & Williams Films.

Abbott & Costello Go to Mars. Bud Abbott & Lou Costello. Directed by Charles Lamont. 1953. Universal. 77 min. Sound. 16mm B&W. *Rental:* Williams Films.

Abbott & Costello in Hollywood. Bud Abbott & Lou Costello. Directed by S. Sylvan Simon. 1945. MGM. 83 min. Sound. 16mm B&W. *Rental:* MGM United. *Rental:* MGM United, Videotape version.

Abbott & Costello in Society. Bud Abbott & Lou Costello. Directed by Jean Yarbrough. 1944. Universal. 75 min. Sound. 16mm B&W. *Rental:* Swank Motion.

Abbott & Costello in the Foreign Legion. Bud Abbott & Lou Costello. Directed by Charles Lamont. 1950. Universal. 78 min. Sound. 16mm B&W. *Rental:* Swank Motion & Williams Films.

Abbott & Costello in the Navy. Bud Abbott & Lou Costello. Directed by Arthur Lubin. 1941. Universal. 74 min. Sound. 16mm B&W. *Rental:* Swank Motion.

Abbott & Costello in the White House. Bud Abbott & Lou Costello. 1953. Colgate Comedy Hour. 60 min. Sound. Super 8 B&W. *Sale:* Reel Images.

Abbott & Costello Meet Captain Kidd. Bud Abbott, Lou Costello & Charles Laughton. Directed by Charles Lamont. 1953. Warners. 70 min. Sound. 16mm B&W. *Rental:* Arcus Film, Budget Films, Cine Craft, Films Inc, Williams Films, Roas Films, Welling Motion Pictures & Wholesome Film Ctr. *Rental:* Budget Films, Maljack & Welling Motion Pictures, *Lease:* Video Comm, Color version. *Rental:* Maljack, Salz Ent & Video Comm, Videotape version.

Abbott & Costello Meet Dr. Jekyll & Mr. Hyde. Bud Abbott & Lou Costello. Directed by Charles Lamont. 1953. Universal. 77 min. Sound. 16mm B&W. *Rental:* Swank Motion. *Rental:* Swank Motion, Videotape version.

Abbott & Costello Meet Frankenstein. Orig. Title: Brain of Frankenstein. Bud Abbott & Lou Costello. Directed by Charles Barton. 1948. Universal. 82 min. Sound. 16mm B&W. *Rental:* Swank Motion. *Rental:* Swank Motion, Videotape version.

Abbott & Costello Meet the Invisible Man. Bud Abbott & Lou Costello. Directed by Charles Lamont. 1951. Universal. 82 min. Sound. 16mm B&W. *Rental:* Williams Films.

Abbott & Costello Meet the Keystone Kops. Bud Abbott & Lou Costello. Directed by Charles Lamont. 1955. Universal. 79 min. Sound. 16mm B&W. *Rental:* Swank Motion.

Abbott & Costello Meet the Killer. Bud Abbott & Lou Costello. Directed by Charles Barton. 1949. Universal. 82 min. Sound. 16mm B&W. *Rental:* Williams Films.

Abbott & Costello Meet the Mummy. Bud Abbott & Lou Costello. Directed by Charles Lamont. 1955. Universal. 79 min. Sound. 16mm B&W. *Rental:* Swank Motion.

1

Abdication, The. Peter Finch & Liv Ullmann. Directed by Anthony Harvey. 1974. Universal. 103 min. Sound. 16mm Color. *Rental:* Swank Motion.

Abdication, The. 1978. Media Guild. (Documentary). 86 min. Sound. 16mm Color. *Rental:* Media Guild. *Sale:* Media Guild. *Sale:* Media Guild, Videotape version.

Abduction, The. Judith-Marie Bergan & Leif Erickson. Directed by Joseph Zito. 1975. Venture. 100 min. Sound. 16mm Color. *Rental:* Films Inc.

Abductors, The. Victor McLaglen & Fay Spain. Directed by Andrew V. McLaglen. 1957. 80 min. Sound. 16mm B&W. *Rental:* Ivy Films. *Sale:* Rep Pic Film.

Abe Lincoln: Freedom Fighter. Andrew Prine, Brock Peters & Whit Bissell. Directed by Jack Hively. 1979. NBC. 53 min. 16mm Color. *Sale:* Lucerne Films & Welling Motion Pictures. *Sale:* Lucerne Films, Videotape version.

Abe Lincoln in Illinois. Raymond Massey, Gene Lockhart & Ruth Gordon. Directed by John Cromwell. 1940. RKO. 110 min. Sound. 16mm B&W. *Rental:* Films Inc. *Lease:* Films Inc.

Abe Lincoln of Ninth Avenue *see* Streets of New York.

Abel Gance: The Charm of Dynamite. Directed by Kevin Brownlow. 1968. Britain. (Documentary). 52 min. Sound. 16mm B&W. *Rental:* U Mich Media & Images Film. *Sale:* Images Film.

Abilene Town. Randolph Scott, Lloyd Bridges & Ann Dvorak. Directed by Edwin L. Marin. 1946. United Artists. 89 min. Sound. 16mm B&W. *Rental:* Budget Films, Classic Film Mus, Mogulls Films & Willoughby Peer. *Sale:* Cinema Concepts & Reel Images, Super 8 sound version.

Abilene Trail. Whip Wilson. Directed by Lewis D. Collins. 1951. Monogram. 64 min. Sound. 16mm B&W. *Rental:* Hurlock Cine.

Abominable Dr. Phibes, The. Vincent Price & Joseph Cotten. Directed by Robert Fuest. 1971. Britain. 93 min. Sound. 16mm Color. *Rental:* Images Film, Video Comm, Welling Motion Pictures & Wholesome Film Ctr.

Abominable Snowman, The. Forrest Tucker & Peter Cushing. Directed by Val Guest. 1957. (Anamorphic). 93 min. Sound. 16mm B&W. *Rental:* Films Inc.

Abortion & the Law. 1965. CBS. 54 min. Sound. 16mm B&W. *Rental:* BYU Merid & Mass Media. *Sale:* Carousel Films.

Abortion at Will in the First Twelve Weeks. 1971. NET. (Documentary). 57 min. Sound. 16mm B&W. *Rental:* Indiana AV Ctr. *Sale:* Indiana AV Ctr.

Abortion of the Human Race. 50 min. Sound. 16mm Color. *Rental:* Gospel Films.

About Face. William Tracy & Joe Sawyer. Directed by Kurt Neumann. 1942. United Artists. 50 min. Sound. 16mm B&W. *Rental:* Budget Films.

About Time. 56 min. Sound. 16mm Color. *Rental:* Utah Media.

Above & Beyond. Robert Taylor & Eleanor Parker. Directed by Melvin Frank. MGM. 122 min. Sound. 16mm B&W. *Rental:* MGM United.

Above Us the Earth. Directed by Karl Francis. 1977. Britain. (Cast unlisted). 90 min. Sound. 16mm Color. *Rental:* Museum Mod Art. *Lease:* Museum Mod Art.

Abraham Kaplan. 1967. NET. (Documentary). 59 min. Sound. 16mm B&W. *Rental:* Indiana AV Ctr. *Sale:* Indiana Av Ctr.

Abraham Lincoln. Walter Huston, Una Merkel & Lucille La Verne. Directed by D. W. Griffith. 1930. United Artists. 81 min. Sound. 16mm B&W. *Rental:* A Twyman Pres, Alba House, Classic Film Mus, Em Gee Film Lib, Film Classics, Images Film, Inst Cinema, Killiam Collect, Kit Parker, Mogulls Films, Wholesome Film Ctr & Budget Films. *Sale:* Classic Film Mus & Natl Cinema. *Rental:* Killiam Collect, Tinted version. *Rental:* Ivy Films, *Sale:* Ivy Films, Super 8 version. *Sale:* Em Gee Film Lib, Videotape version. *Rental:* Films Inc, 83 min. version.

Abraham's Sacrifice. Gene Barry & Andrew Duggan. Directed by Jack Hively. 1979. United Artists. 50 min. Sound. 16mm Color. *Rental:* Budget Films. *Sale:* Lucerne Films. *Sale:* Lucerne Films, Videotape version.

Absence of Malice, An. Paul Newman, Sally Field & Bob Balaban. Directed by Sydney Pollack. 1983. Columbia. 116 min. Sound. 16mm Color. *Rental:* Swank Motion. *Rental:* Swank Motion, Videotape version.

Absent-Minded Professor, The. Fred MacMurray, Nancy Olson, Keenan Wynn & Robert Stevenson. 1961. Disney. 96 min. Sound. 16mm B&W. *Rental:* Buchan Pic, Cine Craft, Cousino Visual Ed, Williams Films, Bosco Films, Disney Prod, Elliot Film Co, Film Ctr DC, Film Pres, Films Inc, MGM United, Modern Sound, Newman Film Lib, Roas Films, Swank Motion, Twyman Films, U of IL Film, Welling Motion Pictures & Westcoast Films. *Rental:* Williams Films, Videotape version.

Absolute Quiet. Irene Hervey & Lionel Atwill. Directed by George B. Seitz. 1936. MGM. 71 min. Sound. 16mm B&W. *Rental:* MGM United.

Abysses, Les. Francine Berge & Colette Berge. Directed by Nico Papatakis. Fr. 1963. 90 min. Sound. 16mm B&W. subtitles Eng. *Rental:* Films Inc.

AC-DC: Let There Be Rock. Directed by Eric Dionysius & Eric Mistler. 1980. Warners. 95 min. Sound. 16mm Color. *Rental:* Swank Motion.

Acadia, Acadia. 1974. Canada. (Documentary). 75 min. Sound. 16mm B&W. subtitles. *Sale:* Natl Film CN.

Acapulco Gold. Marjoe Gortner & Robert Lansing. Directed by Burt Brinckerhoff. 1976. Mar Vista. 92 min. Sound. 16mm Color. *Rental:* Twyman Films.

Accattone. Franco Citti & Franca Pasut. Directed by Pier Paolo Pasolini. Ital. 1961. 120 min. Sound. 16mm B&W. subtitles. *Rental:* Films Inc.

Accident. Dirk Bogarde & Stanley Baker. Directed by Joseph Losey. 1967. Britain. 105 min. Sound. 16mm Color. *Rental:* Film Inc.

Accident Investigation. 1972. Motorola. (Documentary). 66 min. Sound. 16mm Color. *Rental:* BYU Media.

Accidents Will Happen. Ronald Reagan & Gloria Blondell. Directed by William Clemens. 1938. Warners. 62 min. Sound. 16mm B&W. *Rental:* MGM United.

Accomplice. Richard Arlen & Veda Ann Borg. Directed by Walter Colmes. 1946. PRC. 68 min. Sound. 16mm B&W. *Sale:* Classics Assoc NY.

Accoralada. Span. 1950. Mexico. (Cast unlisted). 90 min. Sound. 16mm B&W. *Rental:* Film Classics.

According to Mrs. Hoyle. Spring Byington. Directed by Jean Yarbrough. 1951. Monogram. 60 min. 16mm B&W. *Rental:* Hurlock Cine.

Accursed, The. Sir Donald Wolfit. Directed by Michael McCarthy. 1958. Britain. 78 min. Sound. 16mm B&W. *Rental:* Hurlock Cine.

Accused of Murder. David Brian & Vera Ralston. Directed by Joseph Kane. 1956. Republic. 74 min. Sound. 16mm B&W. *Rental:* Ivy Films. *Sale:* Rep Pic Film.

Ace Eli and Rodger of the Skies. Cliff Robertson & Eric Shea. Directed by Bill Sampson. 1973. Fox. 92 min. Sound. 16mm Color. *Rental:* Films Inc. *Rental:* Films Inc, Anamorphic version.

Ace High. Eli Wallach & Terence Hill. Directed by Giuseppe Collizzi. 1968. Britain. 120 min. Sound. 16mm Color. *Rental:* Films Inc.

Ace in the Hole *see* Big Carnival, The.

Ace of Aces. Ralph Bellamy & Richard Dix. Directed by Merian C. Cooper. 1934. RKO. 74 min. Sound. 16mm *Rental:* RKO General Pics.

Ace of Cactus Range. Art Mix. Directed by Malon Andrus. 1924. Standard. 45 min. Silent. 16mm B&W. *Rental:* Film Classics. *Sale:* Film Classics. *Sale:* Film Classics, Silent 8mm version.

Ace of Clubs. Al Hoxie. Directed by J. P. McGowan. 1926. Rayart. 60 min. Silent. 16mm B&W. *Rental:* Film Classics. *Sale:* Film Classics. *Sale:* Film Classics, Silent 8mm version.

Aces & Eights. Tim McCoy. Directed by Sam Newfield. 1936. Puritan. 70 min. Sound. 16mm B&W. *Rental:* Budget Films. *Sale:* Video Comm, Videotape version.

Aces High. Malcolm McDowell, Peter Firth & Christopher Plummer. Directed by Jack Gold. 1976. Britain. 103 min. Sound. 16mm Color. *Rental:* Films Inc & Westcoast Films.

Achievers, The. 1978. Young Peoples Specials. (Documentary). 50 min. Sound. 16mm Color. *Sale:* Young People Media.

Across One-Hundred & Tenth Street. Anthony Quinn & Yaphet Kotto. Directed by Barry Shear. 1972. United Artists. 102 min. Sound. 16mm Color. *Rental:* MGM United.

Across the Bridge. Rod Steiger. Directed by Ken Annakin. 1958. Britain. 103 min. Sound. 16mm B&W. *Rental:* Budget Films, Films Inc, Learning Corp Am, Twyman Films & U of IL Film. *Sale:* Learning Corp Am.

Across the Frontiers. 1975. Britain. (Documentary). 52 min. Sound. 16mm Color. *Rental:* Iowa Films & U of IL Film.

Across the Pacific. Humphrey Bogart & Mary Astor. Directed by John Huston. 1942. Warner. 86 min. Sound. 16mm B&W. *Rental:* MGM United.

Across the Plains. Jack Randall. Directed by Spencer G. Bennett. 1939. Monogram. 60 min. Sound. 16mm B&W. *Rental:* Hurlock Cine.

Across the Rio Grande. Jimmy Wakely. Directed by Oliver Drake. 1949. Monogram. 55 min. Sound. 16mm B&W. *Rental:* Hurlock Cine.

Across the Silence Barrier. 1977. Nova. (Documentary). 57 min. Sound. 16mm B&W. *Rental:* U of IL Film & U Mich Media.

Across the Wide Missouri. Clark Gable & Ricardo Montalban. Directed by William A. Wellman. 1951. MGM. 79 min. Sound. 16mm Color. *Rental:* MGM United.

Across the World with Mr. & Mrs. Martin Johnson. 1930. Taking Picture Epics. (Documentary). 70 min. Sound. 16mm B&W. *Rental:* Film Classics & Film Ctr DC.

Act Now. 1972. KQED. 60 min. Sound. 16mm Color. *Rental:* Film Wright. *Sale:* Film Wright.

Act of Abortion, An. 1972. Britain. (Documentary). 60 min. Sound. 16mm B&W. *Rental:* Time-Life Multimedia. *Sale:* Time-Life Multimedia.

Act of Agression, An. Catherine Deneuve & Jean-Louis Trintignant. Directed by Gerard Pires. Fr. 1975. France. 94 min. Sound. 16mm Color. subtitles. *Rental:* J Green Pics.

Act of Congress, An. Directed by Charles Guggenheim. 1979. Learning Corp. (Documentary). 58 min. Sound. 16mm Color. *Rental:* Iowa Films, Kent St U Film, Learning Corp Am, Syracuse U Film, U Cal Media, U Mich Media & Utah Media. *Sale:* Learning Corp Am. *Rental:* Learning Corp Am, *Sale:* Learning Corp Am, Videotape version.

Act of Love, An. Kirk Douglas & Dany Robin. Directed by Anatole Litvak. 1953. United Artists. 105 min. Sound. 16mm B&W. *Rental:* MGM United.

Act of Murder, An. Fredric March & Florence Eldredge. Directed by Michael Gordon. 1948. Universal. 90 min. Sound. 16mm B&W. *Rental:* Swank Motion.

Act of the Heart, An. Genevieve Bujold & Donald Sutherland. Directed by Paul Almond. 1970. Universal. 103 min. Sound. 16mm Color. *Rental:* Swank Motion.

Act of Vengeance, An: The Violator. Jo Ann Harris & Peter Brown. Directed by Bob Kelljan. 1974. American International. 90 min. Sound. 16mm Color. *Sale:* Swank Motion.

Act of Violence. Robert Ryan & Janet Leigh. Directed by Fred Zinnemann. 1949. MGM. 75 min. Sound. 16mm B&W. *Rental:* Bosco Films & MGM United.

Act One. George Hamilton & Jason Robards. Directed by Dore Schary. 1963. Warners. 110 min. Sound. 16mm B&W. *Rental:* Cine Craft, Films Inc, Welling Motion Pictures & Willoughby Peer.

Action for Slander. Clive Brook. Directed by Tim Whelan. 1937. 84 min. 16mm *Rental:* A Twyman Pres.

Action in Arabia. Virginia Bruce & George Sanders. Directed by Leonide Moguy. 1944. RKO. 75 min. Sound. 16mm B&W. *Rental:* Films Inc. *Lease:* Films Inc.

Action in the North Atlantic. Humphrey Bogart & Raymond Massey. Directed by Lloyd Bacon. 1943. Warners. 127 min. Sound. 16mm B&W. *Rental:* MGM United.

Action of the Tiger. Van Johnson & Martine Carol. Directed by Terence Young. 1957. MGM. (Anamorphic). 93 min. Sound. 16mm Color. *Rental:* MGM United.

Action: The October Crisis of 1970. Directed by Robin Spry. 1975. Canada. (Documentary). 87 min. Sound. 16mm Color. *Rental:* U Cal Media & Natl Film CN. *Sale:* Natl Film CN.

Activator One. 1971. Canada. 59 min. Sound. 16mm B&W. *Rental:* Natl Film CN. *Sale:* Natl Film CN.

Activity Group Therapy. 1950. S. R. Slavson. (Documentary). 56 min. Sound. 16mm B&W. *Rental:* U Cal Media.

Actor, The. 1968. ABC. (Documentary). 54 min. Sound. 16mm Color. *Rental:* Budget Films, Syracuse U Film & U Mich Media.

Actors and Sin. 2 pts. Edward G. Robinson, Marsha Hunt, Eddie Albert & Jenny Hecht. Directed by Ben Hecht. 1952. United Artists. 90 min. Sound. 16mm B&W. *Rental:* Budget Films.

Actor's Revenge, The. Kazuo Hasegawa & Ayako Wakao. Directed by Kon Ichikawa. Jap. 1963. Japan. 114 min. Sound. 16mm Color. subtitles. *Rental:* New Yorker Films.

Actress, The. Spencer Tracy & Jean Simmons. Directed by George Cukor. 1953. MGM. 90 min. Sound. 16mm B&W. *Rental:* MGM United.

Acupuncture Anaesthesia. 1976. China. (Documentary). 50 min. Sound. 16mm Color. *Rental:* Asia Film Library & Grove. *Sale:* Grove.

Acute Myocardial Infarction: Unit Three, Diagnosis. 1977. 50 min. Sound. Videotape B&W. *Sale:* Natl AV Ctr.

Acute or Chronic Respiratory Failure. 1968. US Government. (Documentary). 90 min. Sound. 16mm B&W. *Sale:* Natl AV Ctr.

Ada. Susan Hayward & Dean Martin. Directed by Daniel Mann. 1961. MGM. (Anamorphic). 108 min. Sound. 16mm Color. *Rental:* MGM United.

Adalen Thirty-One. Peter Schmidt, Anita Bjork & Kerstin Tidelius. Directed by Bo Widerberg. Swed. 1969. Sweden. (Anamorphic). 114 min. Sound. 16mm Color. subtitles. *Rental:* Films Inc.

Adam & Evalyn. Stewart Granger & Jean Simmons. Directed by Harold French. 1948. Britain. 70 min. Sound. 16mm B&W. *Rental:* Mogulls Films.

Adam at Six A.M. Michael Douglas & Lee Purcell. Directed by Robert Sheerer. 1970. National General. 90 min. Sound. 16mm Color. *Rental:* Swank Motion.

Adam Clayton Powell: An Autobiographical Documentary. 1977. WABC. (Documentary). 58 min. Sound. 16mm Color. *Rental:* Phoenix Films. *Sale:* Phoenix Films. *Sale:* Phoenix Films, Videotape version.

Adam Had Four Sons. Warner Baxter & Ingrid Bergman. Directed by Gregory Ratoff. 1941. Columbia. 82 min. Sound. 16mm B&W. *Rental:* Kit Parker. *Sale:* Tamarelles French Film, Videotape version.

Adam Two. Directed by Jan Lenica. 1976. Phoenix. (Animated). 73 min. Sound. 16mm Color. *Rental:* La Inst Res Ctr & Phoenix Films. *Sale:* Phoenix Films.

Adam's Rib. Spencer Tracy & Katharine Hepburn. Directed by George Cukor. 1949. MGM. 101 min. Sound. 16mm B&W. *Rental:* MGM United. *Rental:* MGM United, Videotape version.

Adam's Woman. Beau Bridges & Jane Merrow. Directed by Philip Leacock. 1968. Australia. 115 min. Sound. 16mm Color. *Rental:* Cine Craft, Films Inc & Mogulls Films.

Addicted, The. 1958. CBS. (Documentary). 52 min. Sound. 16mm B&W. *Rental:* Macmillan Films. *Sale:* Macmillan Films.

Addio Fratello Crudele *see* Tis a Pity She's a Whore.

Address Unknown. Paul Lukas & Mady Christians. Directed by William Cameron Menzies. 1944. Columbia. 73 min. Sound. 16mm B&W. *Rental:* Kit Parker.

Adelaide. Ingrid Thulin & Jean Sorel. Directed by Jean-Daniel Simon. 1968. France. 86 min. Sound. 16mm subtitles. *Rental:* Films Inc.

Adieu Philippine. Yveline Cery. Directed by Jacques Rozier. Fr. 1961. France. 111 min. Sound. 16mm B&W. *Rental:* New Yorker Films.

Adios Amigo. Fred Williamson, Richard Pryor & James Brown. Directed by James Brown. 1976. Atlas. 87 min. Sound. 16mm Color. *Rental:* Films Inc.

Adios, Sabata. Yul Brynner. Directed by Frank Kramer. 1971. United Artists. 109 min. Sound. 16mm Color. *Rental:* MGM United.

Adland. 1973. WTTW. (Documentary). 60 min. Sound. Videotape B&W Color. *Sale:* Electro Art. *Sale:* Electro Art, Videotape version.

Admirable Crichton, The. Kenneth More & Sally Ann Howes. Directed by Lewis Gilbert. 1957. Britain. 94 min. Sound. 16mm B&W. *Rental:* Films Inc & Wholesome Film Ctr.

Admiral Ushakov. Ivan Pereverzev. Directed by Mikhail Romm. Rus. 1953. Russia. 106 min. Sound. 16mm B&W. subtitles. *Rental:* Corinth Films.

Admiral Was a Lady, The. Edmond O'Brien, Wanda Hendrix & Rudy Vallee. Directed by Albert S. Rogell. 1950. United Artists. 85 min. Sound. 16mm B&W. *Rental:* Budget Films.

Adolph Hitler. 1963. Wolper. (Documentary). 52 min. Sound. 16mm B&W. *Rental:* Films Inc. *Sale:* Films Inc.

Adoption. Kati Berek & Laszlo Szabo. Directed by Marta Meszaros. Hungarian. 1975. Hungary. 89 min. Sound. 16mm B&W. subtitles. *Rental:* Films Inc.

Adorable Cheat. Lila Lee. Directed by Burton King. 1928. Chesterfield. 72 min. Sound. 16mm B&W. *Rental:* Mogulls Films & Willoughby Peer. *Rental:* Mogulls Films, Silent 8mm version.

Adorable Julia. Lilli Palmer & Charles Boyer. Directed by Alfred Weidenmann. Fr. 1964. France. 94 min. Sound. 16mm B&W. subtitles. *Rental:* Budget Films, Kit Parker & Video Comm. *Rental:* Video Comm, Videotape, English dubbed version.

Adorable Menteuse. Marina Vlady & Macha Meril. Directed by Michel Deville. Fr. 1962. France. 120 min. Sound. 16mm B&W. subtitles. *Rental:* French Am Cul.

Adrift. Paula Pritchett & Rade Markovic. Directed by Jan Kadar. Czech. 1970. Czechoslovakia. 105 min. Sound. 16mm Color. subtitles. *Rental:* Films Inc.

Advance to the Rear. Glenn Ford, Melvyn Douglas & Stella Stevens. 1964. MGM. (Anamorphic). 97 min. Sound. 16mm B&W. *Rental:* MGM United.

Adventure. Clark Gable & Greer Garson. Directed by Victor Fleming. 1946. MGM. 126 min. Sound. 16mm B&W. *Rental:* MGM United.

Adventure Girl. Joan Lowell. Directed by J. Van Beuren. 1934. RKO. 76 min. Sound. 16mm *Rental:* RKO General Pics.

Adventure in Baltimore. Shirley Temple & John Agar. Directed by Richard Wallace. 1949. RKO. 89 min. Sound. 16mm B&W. *Rental:* Films Inc.

Adventure in Bokhara. Lev Sverdlin. Directed by Yakov Protazanov. 1943. 85 min. Sound. 16mm B&W. subtitles. *Rental:* Corinth Films.

Adventure in Capri. Elke Sommer. Ger. 1962. Germany. 82 min. Sound. 16mm B&W. dubbed. *Sale:* Natl Cinema.

Adventure in the Hopfields. Mandy Miller & Melvyn Hayes. Directed by John Guillermin. 1954. Britain. 60 min. Sound. 16mm B&W. *Rental:* Lucerne Films.

Adventure in Washington. Herbert Marshall & Virginia Bruce. Directed by Alfred E. Green. 1941. Columbia. 86 min. Sound. 16mm B&W. *Rental:* Inst Cinema & Welling Motion Pictures.

Adventure Island. Rory Calhoun & Rhonda Fleming. Directed by Peter Stewart. 1947. Paramount. 67 min. Sound. 16mm B&W. *Rental:* Film Ctr DC.

Adventurer of Tortuga, The. Guy Madison & Nadia Gray. Ital. 1964. Italy. 100 min. Sound. 16mm Color. dubbed. *Rental:* Westcoast Films.

Adventurers, The. Bekim Fehmiu, Charles Aznavour & Alan Badel. Directed by Lewis Gilbert. 1970. Paramount. 171 min. Sound. 16mm Color. *Rental:* Films Inc.

Adventurers of a Brown Man in Search of Civilization. Directed by James Ivory. 1972. Britain. (Documentary). 56 min. Sound. 16mm Color. *Rental:* Film Images. *Sale:* Film Images.

Adventures in Manhattan. Joel McCrea, Reginald Owen & Jean Arthur. Directed by Edward Ludwig. 1937. Columbia. 76 min. Sound. 16mm B&W. *Rental:* Bosco Films & Kit Parker.

Adventures in Silverado. William Bishop & Forrest Tucker. Directed by Phil Karlson. 1948. Columbia. 75 min. Sound. 16mm B&W. *Rental:* Inst Cinema & Modern Sound.

Adventures of a Rookie. Alan Carney & Wally Brown. Directed by Leslie Goodwins. 1943. RKO. 64 min. Sound. 16mm B&W. *Rental:* Films Inc.

Adventures of A Young Man *see* Hemingway's Adventures of a Young Man.

Adventures of Bullwhip Griffin, The. Roddy McDowall, Suzanne Pleshette & Karl Malden. Directed by James Neilson. 1967. Disney. 111 min. Sound. 16mm Color. *Rental:* Bosco Films, Cine Craft, Disney Prod, Elliot Film Co, Film Ctr DC, Film Pres, Films Inc, MGM United, Modern Sound, Newman Film Lib, Roas Films, Swank Motion, Twyman Films, U of IL Film, Welling Motion Pictures, Westcoast Films & Williams Films.

Adventures of Captain Fabian, The. Errol Flynn & Vincent Price. Directed by William Marshall. 1951. Republic. 100 min. Sound. 16mm B&W. *Rental:* Ivy Films. *Lease:* Rep Pic Film.

Adventures of Captain Marvel. Tom Tyler & Frank Coghlan. Directed by William Witney. 1941. Republic. 217 min. Sound. 16mm B&W. *Rental:* Ivy Films.

Adventures of Casanova, The. Turhan Bey & Arturo de Cordova. Directed by Roberto Gavaldon. 1948. Eagle Lion. 83 min. Sound. 16mm B&W. *Sale:* Classics Assoc NY.

Adventures of Chico, The. Directed by Stacy Woodward & Horace Woodward. Span. 1938. Mexico. (Documentary). 55 min. Sound. 16mm B&W. *Rental:* Film Classics & Ivy Films. *Sale:* Intl Film & Classic Assoc NY. *Rental:* Budget Films, Charard Motion Pics, Mogulls Films & Twyman Films, *Sale:* Classics Assoc NY, Intl Film & Rep Pic Film, English narrated version.

Adventures of Danny Boy, The *see* Danny Boy.

Adventures of Dobie Gillis, The. Bobby Van & Debbie Reynolds. Directed by Don Weis. 1953. MGM. 73 min. Sound. 16mm B&W. *Rental:* MGM United. *Rental:* MGM United, Videotape version.

Adventures of Don Coyote, The. Richard Martin & Frances Rafferty. Directed by Reginald Le Borg. 1947. United Artists. 65 min. Sound. 16mm B&W. *Rental:* Ivy Films.

Adventures of Don Juan, The. Errol Flynn & Viveca Lindfors. Directed by Vincent Sherman. 1949. Warners. 110 min. Sound. 16mm Color. *Rental:* MGM United.

Adventures of Frontier Fremont, The. Dan Haggerty & Denver Pyle. Directed by Richard Freidenberg. 1979. Sunn. 102 min. Sound. 16mm Color. *Rental:* Modern Sound & Williams Films. *Sale:* Lucerne Films. *Sale:* Lucerne Films & Williams Films, Videotape version.

Adventures of Gallant Bess, The. Cameron Mitchell & Fuzzy Knight. Directed by Lew Landers. 1948. Eagle Lion. 72 min. Sound. 16mm Color. *Rental:* Alba House, Budget Films, Charard Motion Pics & Mogulls Films.

Adventures of Gerard, The. Peter McEnery, Eli Wallach & Jack Hawkins. Directed by Jerzy Skolimowski. 1970. United Artists. 91 min. Sound. 16mm Color. *Rental:* MGM United.

Adventures of Hajji Baba, The. John Derek & Elaine Stewart. Directed by Don Weis. 1954. Fox. 93 min. Sound. 16mm Color. *Rental:* Films Inc.

Adventures of Huckleberry Finn, The. Eddie Hodges & Tony Randall. Directed by Michael Curtiz. 1960. MGM. 107 min. Sound. 16mm Color. *Rental:* MGM United. *Lease:* Films Inc. *Rental:* Films Inc, Anamorphic, Color version. *Rental:* MGM United, Videotape version.

Adventures of Huckleberry Finn, The. Forrest Tucker & Brock Peters. Directed by Jack Hively. 1979. Viacom. 103 min. Sound. 16mm Color. *Rental:* Budget Films & Modern Sound. *Sale:* Lucerne Films. *Sale:* Lucerne Films, Videotape version.

Adventures of Huckleberry Finn, The. Mickey Rooney & Rex Ingram. Directed by Richard Thorpe. 1939. 91 min. 16mm B&W. *Rental:* MGM United.

Adventures of Jane Arden, The. William Gargan & Rosella Towne. Directed by Terry Morse. 1939. Warners. 58 min. Sound. 16mm B&W. *Rental:* MGM United.

Adventures of Juan Quin Quin, The. Julio Martinez & Julio Garcia Espinosa. Span. 1975. Cuba. (Anamorphic). 113 min. Sound. 16mm B&W. *Rental:* New Cinema, Cinema Guild & Natl Films CN. *Sale:* Cinema Guild. *Rental:* New Cinema, French Subtitled version.

Adventures of Marco Polo, The. Gary Cooper, Sigrid Gurie & Basil Rathbone. Directed by Archie Mayo. 1938. Goldwyn. 104 min. Sound. 16mm B&W. *Rental:* Films Inc.

Adventures of Mark Twain, The. Fredric March & Alexis Smith. Directed by Irving Rapper. 1944. Warners. 130 min. Sound. 16mm B&W. *Rental:* MGM United.

Adventures of Martin Eden, The. Glenn Ford & Claire Trevor. Directed by Sidney Salkow. 1942. Columbia. 88 min. Sound. 16mm B&W. *Rental:* Film Classics, Mogulls Films & Film Ctr DC.

Adventures of Michael Strogoff. Akim Tamiroff, Anton Walbrook & Fay Bainter. Directed by George Nicholls. 1937. RKO. 80 min. Sound. 16mm B&W. *Rental:* Mogulls Films.

Adventures of Mr. Wonderbird, The. Trans. Title: Bergere Et le Ramoneur, La. Directed by Pierre Grimault. Fr. 1952. France. (Animated). 72 min. Sound. 16mm Color. dubbed. *Rental:* Cine Craft, Films Inc & Wholesome Film Ctr.

Adventures of Neeka, The. Robert Rockwell, Jed Allen & Lassie. Wrather. 75 min. Sound. 16mm Color. *Rental:* Roas Films, Modern Sound & Williams Films.

Adventures of Pinocchio, The. Directed by Jesse Vogel. 1978. (Animated). 92 min. Sound. 16mm Color. *Rental:* Films Inc, Modern Sound & Williams Films.

Adventures of Prince Achmed, The. Directed by Lotte Reiniger. Ger. 1927. Germany. (Animated, Musical Score Only). 65 min. Sound. 16mm Color. *Rental:* Em Gee Film Lib. *Sale:* Carman Ed Assoc. *Sale:* Carman Ed Assoc, Color version.

Adventures of Robin Hood, The. Errol Flynn & Olivia de Havilland. Directed by Michael Curtiz. 1938. Warners. 102 min. Sound. 16mm Color. *Rental:* MGM United. *Rental:* MGM United, Videotape version.

Adventures of Robinson Crusoe, The. Dan O'Herlihy, James Fernandez & Felipe De Alba. Directed by Luis Bunuel. 1954. Mexico. 100 min. Sound. 16mm Color. *Rental:* Alba House, Budget Films, Films Inc & Twyman Films.

Adventures of Rusty, The. Ted Donaldson. Directed by Paul Burnford. 1945. Columbia. 66 min. Sound. 16mm B&W. *Rental:* Welling Motion Pictures.

Adventures of Sadie, The. Joan Collins & Hermione Gingold. Directed by Noel Langley. 1955. Fox. 88 min. Sound. 16mm Color. *Rental:* Budget Films, Films Inc & Video Comm. *Lease:* Video Comm. *Rental:* Video Comm, *Lease:* Video Comm, Videotape version.

Adventures of Scaramouche, The. Gerard Barray & Gianna Maria Canale. Directed by Antonio Issai Isamendi. Ital. 1964. Italy. 98 min. Sound. 16mm Color. dubbed. *Rental:* Films Inc.

Adventures of Sherlock Holmes, The. Basil Rathbone, Nigel Bruce & Ida Lupino. Directed by Alfred M. Werker. 1939. Fox. 85 min. Sound. 16mm B&W. *Rental:* Budget Films, Films Inc, Images Film, Kit Parker, Learning Corp Am, Modern Sound, Twyman Films, U of IL Film, Westcoast Films & Williams Films. *Sale:* Learning Corp Am.

Adventures of Sherlock Holmes' Smarter Brother, The. Gene Wilder & Madeline Kahn. Directed by Gene Wilder. 1976. Fox. 91 min. Sound. 16mm Color. *Rental:* Films Inc & Williams Films.

Adventures of Sinbad. 82 min. Sound. 16mm B&W. *Rental:* Westcoast Films.

Adventures of Tartu, The. Robert Donat & Valerie Hobson. Directed by Harold S. Bucquet. 1943. MGM. 103 min. Sound. 16mm B&W. *Rental:* Budget Films & MGM United.

Adventures of Tarzan, The. Elmo Lincoln & Louise Lorraine. Directed by Robert Hill. 1921. Artclass. 70 min. Silent. 16mm B&W. *Rental:* Ivy Films, Kerr Film, Kit Parker, Video Comm & Westcoast Films. *Sale:* Blackhawk Film. *Rental:* Ivy Films, *Sale:* Blackhawk Films, Super 8, silent version. *Rental:* Video Comm, Videotape version.

Adventures of Teenage Scientists. 1983. Nova. (Documentary). 57 min. Sound. 16mm Color. *Rental:* U Cal Media & Time-Life Multimedia. *Sale:* Time-Life Multimedia.

Adventures of the Masked Phantom, The. Monte Rawlins & Betty Burgess. Directed by Charles Abbott. 1938. 60 min. Sound. 16mm *Rental:* Budget Films.

Adventures of the Texas Kid, The. Hugh Hooker & Pamela Blake. 60 min. Sound. 16mm B&W. *Rental:* Budget Films.

Adventures on the New Frontier. 1965. Time-Life. (Documentary). 54 min. Sound. 16mm B&W. *Rental:* Time-Life Multimedia. *Sale:* Time-Life Multimedia.

Adventurous Blonde. Glenda Farrell & Barton MacLane. Directed by Frank McDonald. 1937. Warners. 61 min. Sound. 16mm B&W. *Rental:* MGM United.

Adversary, The. Dhritiman Chatterjee & Joyshree Roy. Directed by Satyajit Ray. Bengali. 1971. Bengal. 110 min. Sound. 16mm B&W. subtitles. *Rental:* Films Inc.

Advise & Consent. Henry Fonda, Charles Laughton & Don Murray. Directed by Otto Preminger. 1962. Columbia. 139 min. Sound. 16mm B&W. *Rental:* Arcus Film, Budget Films, Corinth Films, Bosco Films, Films Inc, Images Film, Ivy Films, Modern Films, Modern Sound, Natl Film CN, Newman Film Lib, Swank Motion, U of IL Film, Video Comm, Welling Motion Pictures, Westcoast Films, Wholesome Films Ctr, Williams Films, Willoughby Peer & Kit Parker. *Rental:* Corinth Films, Films Inc, Kit Parker & Twyman Films, Anamorphic version.

Aelita. Valentina Kuinzh & Nikolai Tseretelli. Directed by Yakov Protazanov. Rus. 1924. Russia. 90 min. Silent. 16mm B&W. subtitles Eng. *Rental:* Films Inc.

Aerograd: Frontier. Directed by Alexander Dovzhenko. Rus. 1935. Russia. (Documentary). 81 min. Sound. 16mm B&W. *Rental:* Museum Mod Art. *Lease:* Museum Mod Art.

Affair Blum, The. Hans Christian Blech & Gisela Trowe. Directed by Erich Engel. Ger. 1948. Germany. 109 min. Sound. 16mm B&W. subtitles. *Rental:* Films Inc.

Affair in Havana. John Cassavetes & Raymond Burr. Directed by Laslo Benedek. 1957. Allied Artists. 77 min. Sound. 16mm B&W. *Rental:* Ivy Films.

Affair in Reno. Alan Hale Jr. & John Lund. Directed by R. G. Springsteen. 1956. Republic. 75 min. Sound. 16mm B&W. *Rental:* Ivy Films.

Affair in the Air. 1978. PBS. (Documentary). 59 min. Videotape Color. *Rental:* PBS Video. *Sale:* PBS Video.

Affair in Trinidad. Glenn Ford & Rita Hayworth. Directed by Vincent Sherman. 1952. Columbia. 98 min. Sound. 16mm B&W. *Rental:* Cine Craft, Films Inc & Kit Parker.

Affair of States. Lilli Palmer, Curt Jurgens & Daniel Gelin. Directed by Sammy Drechsel. 1966. Austria, France & Germany. 94 min. Sound. 16mm Color. dubbed. *Rental:* Video Comm.

Affair of the Skin, An. Viveca Lindfors & Kevin McCarthy. Directed by Ben Maddow. 1963. 142 min. Sound. 16mm B&W. *Rental:* Films Inc.

Affair to Remember, An. Cary Grant, Deborah Kerr & Richard Denning. Directed by Leo McCarey. 1957. Fox. 114 min. Sound. 16mm Color. *Rental:* Williams Films, Films Inc, Twyman Films & Welling Motion Pictures. *Rental:* Films Inc, Anamorphic version.

Affair with a Stranger. Jean Simmons & Victor Mature. Directed by Roy Rowland. 1953. RKO. 87 min. Sound. 16mm B&W. *Rental:* Films Inc.

Affaire Est Dans le Sac, L'. Jean-Paul Dreyfus. Directed by Pierre Prevert. Fr. 1932. France. 45 min. Sound. 16mm B&W. subtitles. *Rental:* Images Film. *Lease:* Images Film. *Sale:* Festival Films. *Sale:* Festival Films, Videotape version.

Affairs of a Rogue, The. Jean-Pierre Aumont & Joan Hopkins. Directed by Alberto Cavalcanti. 1949. Columbia. 95 min. Sound. 16mm B&W. *Rental:* Kit Parker.

Affairs of Annabel, The. Lucille Ball & Jack Oakie. Directed by Ben Stoloff. 1939. RKO. 68 min. Sound. 16mm *Rental:* RKO General Pics.

Affairs of Cappy Ricks, The. Walter Brennan & Lyle Talbot. Directed by Ralph Staub. 1937. Republic. 61 min. Sound. 16mm B&W. *Rental:* Ivy Films.

Affairs of Geraldine, The. James Lydon & Johnny Sands. Directed by George Blair. 1946. Republic. 68 min. Sound. 16mm B&W. *Rental:* Ivy Films.

Affectionately Yours. Dennis Morgan, Merle Oberon & Rita Hayworth. Directed by Lloyd Bacon. 1941. Warners. 88 min. Sound. 16mm B&W. *Rental:* MGM United.

Afghanistan: Naim & Jabar. 1975. AUFS. (Documentary). 50 min. Sound. 16mm Color. *Rental:* Syracuse U Film.

Africa. 1967. Africa. (Documentary). 60 min. Sound. 16mm B&W. *Rental:* U Cal Media.

Africa Adventure. 1954. RKO. (Documentary). 64 min. Sound. 16mm Color. *Rental:* Films Inc.

Africa in Search of Itself. 1978. Britain. (Documentary). 53 min. Sound. 16mm Color. *Rental:* U of IL Film.

Africa Screams. Bud Abbott, Lou Costello & Hillary Brooke. Directed by Charles Barton. 1949. United Artists. 79 min. Sound. 16mm B&W. *Rental:* Alba House, Budget Films, Cine Craft, Classic Film Mus, Em Gee Film Lib, Film Ctr DC, Films Inc, Roas Films, Westcoast Films & Wholesome Film Ctr. *Sale:* Natl Cinema, Super 8 version. *Sale:* Festival Films, Videotape version.

Africa Speaks. Directed by Walter Futter. 1930. Columbia. (Documentary). 70 min. Sound. 16mm B&W. *Sale:* Morcraft Films.

Africa-Texas Style. Hugh O'Brian & John Mills. Directed by Andrew Marton. 1967. Paramount. 109 min. Sound. 16mm Color. *Rental:* Ivy Films, Modern Sound & Westcoast Films. *Lease:* Rep Pic Film.

Africa: The Hidden Frontiers. 1964. NET. (Documentary). 60 min. Sound. 16mm B&W. *Rental:* Indiana AV Ctr. *Lease:* Indiana AV Ctr.

African, The see Roots.

African Adventure. Directed by Marty Stouffer. 1973. Africa. (Documentary). 93 min. Sound. 16mm Color. *Rental:* Films Inc, Video Comm & Westcoast Films. *Lease:* Video Comm. *Rental:* Video Comm, *Lease:* Video Comm, Videotape version.

African Adventure. Directed by Robert C. Ruark. 1950. RKO. (Documentary). 64 min. Sound. *Rental:* RKO General Pics.

African Fury see Cry the Beloved Country.

African Manhunt. Myron Healey & Karin Booth. Directed by Seymour Friedman. 1955. Republic. 70 min. Sound. 16mm B&W. *Rental:* Modern Sound.

African Queen, The. Katharine Hepburn, Humphrey Bogart & Robert Morley. Directed by John Huston. 1951. United Artists. 105 min. Sound. 16mm Color. *Rental:* Arcus Film, Budget Films, Cine Craft, Films Inc, Images Film, Inst Cinema, Ivy Films, Macmillan Films, Modern Sound, Newman Film Lib, New Cinema, Swank Motion, Syracuse U Film, Twyman Films, Video Comm, Welling Motion Pictures, Westcoast Films, Wholesome Film Ctr & Willoughby Peer. *Lease:* Macmillan Films.

African Religions: Zulu Zion. 1977. Britain. (Documentary). 52 min. Sound. 16mm Color. *Rental:* Time-Life Multimedia. *Sale:* Time-Life Multimedia. *Sale:* Time-Life Multimedia, Videotape version.

African Safari. Ronald E. Shanin & Bambuti Pygmies. Directed by Ronald E. Shanin. 1970. Crown. (Documentary). 98 min. Sound. 16mm Color. *Rental:* Budget Films, Films Inc, Macmillan Films, Syracuse U Film & Westcoast Films. *Lease:* Macmillan Films. *Rental:* Video Comm, Videotape version.

African Sanctus. 1976. Britain. (Documentary). 50 min. Sound. 16mm Color. *Rental:* Films Inc. *Sale:* Films Inc. *Sale:* Films Inc, Videotape version.

African Treasure *see* Bomba & the African Treasure.

Africane Orestes *see* Notes for an African Orestes.

Africa's Defiant White Tribe. Directed by Robert Rogers. 1977. NBC. (Documentary). 50 min. Sound. 16mm Color. *Rental:* Films Inc & U Mich Media. *Sale:* Films Inc. *Sale:* Films Inc, Videotape version.

After a Million. Kenneth McDonald. Directed by Jack Nelson. 1926. Sunset. 60 min. Silent. 8mm B&W. *Rental:* Mogulls Films.

After Hours with Art Hodes. 5 pts. 1982. Indiana U.. (Performance). 145 min. Videotape Color. *Rental:* Indiana Av Ctr. *Sale:* Indiana Av Ctr.

After Mein Kampf. 1940. Britain. (Documentary). 45 min. Sound. 16mm B&W. *Sale:* Morcraft FIlms. *Sale:* Morcraft Films, Super 8 sound version.

After Mr. Sam. Directed by Arthur Hommond. 1975. Canada. (Documentary). 77 min. Sound. 16mm Color. *Rental:* U Cal Media & Natl Film CN. *Sale:* Natl Film CN & U Cal Media, Videotape version.

After That Crocodile! Xerox. (Cast unlisted). 57 min. Sound. 16mm B&W. *Sale:* Xerox Films.

After the Axe. Directed by Sturla Gunnarsson. 1981. 56 min. 16mm Color. *Rental:* Natl Film CN & U Cal Media. *Sale:* Natl Film CN, *Rental:* Natl Film CN, Videotape version.

After the Dance. Nancy Carroll & George Murphy. Directed by Leo Bulgakov. 1935. Columbia. 70 min. Sound. 16mm B&W. *Rental:* Kit Parker.

After the Fox. Peter Sellers & Victor Mature. Directed by Vittorio De Sica. 1966. United Artists. 103 min. Sound. 16mm Color. *Rental:* MGM United.

After the Miracle. 1966. NET. (Documentary). 60 min. Sound. 16mm B&W. *Rental:* U Cal Media.

After the Thin Man. William Powell & Myrna Loy. Directed by W. S. Van Dyke II. 1936. MGM. 112 min. Sound. 16mm B&W. *Rental:* MGM United.

After Tonight. Gilbert Roland & Constance Bennett. Directed by Merian C. Cooper. 1933. RKO. 71 min. Sound. 16mm *Rental:* RKO General Pics.

Aftermath, The: How the Mighty Are Fallen. 1976. Britain. (Documentary). 52 min. Sound. 16mm Color. *Rental:* Time-Life Multimedia. *Sale:* Time-Life Multimedia. *Sale:* Time-Life Multimedia, Videotape version.

Aga Khan, The. 1965. Time-Life. (Documentary). 54 min. Sound. 16mm B&W. *Rental:* Time-Life Multimedia. *Sale:* Time-Life Multimedia.

Against a Crooked Sky. Richard Boone & Stewart Petersen. Directed by Earl Bellamy. 1976. Doty-Dayton. 90 min. Sound. 16mm Color. *Rental:* Swank Motion.

Against All Flags. Errol Flynn & Maureen O'Hara. Directed by George Sherman. 1952. Universal. 83 min. Sound. 16mm Color. *Rental:* Williams Films.

Against All Odds *see* Kiss & Kill.

Against All Odds. Jeff Bridges, Rachel Ward & James Woods. Directed by Taylor Hackford. 1984. Columbia. 125 min. Sound. 16mm Color. *Rental:* Swank Motion.

Against Wind & Tide: A Cuban Odyssey. Directed by Jim Burroughs. 1981. Filmakers Library. (Documentary). 55 min. Sound. 16mm Color. *Rental:* Film Makers. *Sale:* Film Makers.

Agatha. Dustin Hoffman & Vanessa Redgrave. Directed by Michael Apted. 1979. Warners. 98 min. Sound. 16mm Color. *Rental:* Swank Motion, Twyman Films & Williams Films.

Age d'Or, L'. Gaston Modot. Directed by Luis Bunuel. Fr. 1930. France. 60 min. Sound. 16mm B&W. subtitles. *Rental:* Corinth Films.

Age of Anxiety, The. 1962. CBS. (Documentary). 52 min. Sound. 16mm B&W. *Rental:* Macmillan Films & Syracuse U Film. *Sale:* Macmillan Films.

Age of Ballyhoo, The. 1976. Gould. (Documentary). 52 min. Sound. 16mm Color. *Rental:* Budget Films & U of IL Film. *Sale:* Lucerne Films. *Sale:* Lucerne Films, Videotape version.

Age of Consent, The. James Mason & Helen Mirren. Directed by Michael Powell. 1969. Australia. 98 min. Sound. 16mm B&W. *Rental:* Kit Parker.

Age of Daydreaming, The. Andras Balint & IIona Beres. Directed by Istvan Szabo. Hungarian. 1964. Hungary. 97 min. Sound. 16mm B&W. subtitles Eng. *Rental:* Films Inc.

Age of Exploration, The. 10 pts. 1976. Britain. (Documentary). 520 min. Sound. 16mm Color. *Rental:* Time-Life Multimedia. *Sale:* Time-Life Multimedia. *Rental:* Time-Life Multimedia, *Sale:* Time-Life Multimedia, Videotape version.

Age of Indiscretion, The. Paul Lukas & Madge Evans. Directed by Edward Ludwig. 1935. MGM. 80 min. Sound. 16mm B&W. *Rental:* MGM United.

Age of Infidelity *see* Death of a Cyclist.

Age of Kennedy, The. 1967. NBC. (Documentary). 98 min. 16mm B&W. *Rental:* McGraw-Hill Films, Syracuse U Film, U Mich Media & U Nev AV Ctr. *Sale:* McGraw-Hill Films.

Age of Kennedy, Part II, The: The Presidency. 1967. NBC. 52 min. Sound. 16mm B&W. *Rental:* Iowa Films & U Mich Media.

Age of the Composer, The. 1980. Canada. (Documentary). 57 min. Sound. 16mm Color. *Rental:* Budget Films & Time-Life Multimedia. *Sale:* Time-Life Multimedia. *Sale:* Time-Life Multimedia, Videotape version.

Age of the Individual, The. 1980. Canada. (Documentary). 57 min. Sound. 16mm Color. *Rental:* Budget Films & Time-Life Multimedia. *Sale:* Time-Life Multimedia. *Sale:* Time-Life Multimedia, Videotape version.

Age of the Medici, The. Marcello Di Falco. Directed by Roberto Rossellini. 1973. Italy. 252 min. Sound. 16mm Color. dubbed. *Rental:* Films Inc.

Agee. Directed by Ross Spears. 1978. First Run. (Documentary). 88 min. Sound. 16mm Color. *Rental:* First Run.

Ageless Mozart, The. 1965. Saudek. (Documentary). 60 min. Sound. 16mm B&W. *Rental:* IQ Film. *Sale:* IQ Film.

Agence Barnett, L'. Directed by Jean-Pierre Decourt. Fr. 1971. France. 55 min. Sound. 16mm Color. *Rental:* Films Inc.

Agent Eight & Three Quarters. Dirk Bogarde & Robert Morley. Directed by Ralph Thomas. 1965. Britain. 98 min. Sound. 16mm Color. *Rental:* Cousino Visual Ed.

Agent for Panic. Brad Newman & Eric Douglas. 1964. Majestic. 96 min. Sound. 16mm B&W. *Rental:* Films Inc.

Agent from H.A.R.M. Mark Richman & Wendell Corey. Directed by Gerd Oswald. 1966. Universal. 84 min. Sound. 16mm Color. *Rental:* Swank Motion.

Agentes Del Su Grupo, Los. Span. 1950. Mexico. 90 min. Sound. 16mm B&W. *Rental:* Film Classics.

Ages of Man, The. Sir John Gielgud. 1966. CBS. 104 min. Sound. 16mm B&W. *Rental:* A Cantor & McGraw-Hill Films. *Sale:* A Cantor, Arcus Film & McGraw-Hill Films.

Aggie Appleby. Betty Furness & William Gargan. Directed by Mark Sandrich. 1934. 73 min. Sound. 16mm *Rental:* RKO General Pics.

Aggression: The Explosive Emotion. 1975. PBS. (Documentary). 59 min. Sound. 16mm Color. *Rental:* Indiana AV Ctr, Syracuse U Film & U Cal Media. *Sale:* Indiana AV Ctr.

Aging: The Methuselah Syndrome. 1982. WGBH. 57 min. Sound. 16mm Color. *Rental:* U Mich Media.

Agitator, The. William Hartnell & Mary Morris. Directed by John Harlow. 1946. Britain. 95 min. Sound. 16mm B&W. *Rental:* Ivy Films. *Sale:* Rep Pic Film.

Agony & the Ecstasy, The. Rex Harrison & Charlton Heston. Directed by Sir Carol Reed. 1965. Fox. (Anamorphic). 123 min. Sound. 16mm Color. *Rental:* Films Inc. *Rental:* Films Inc, Anamorphic version.

Aguirre, the Wrath of God. Klaus Kinski & Ray Guerra. Directed by Werner Herzog. Ger. 1973. Germany. 94 min. Sound. 16mm Color. subtitles. *Rental:* New Cinema & New Yorker Films.

Ah, Wilderness. Wallace Beery & Lionel Barrymore. Directed by Clarence Brown. 1935. MGM. 101 min. Sound. 16mm B&W. *Rental:* MGM United.

Ahynung: Two Korean Families. East Long Prod. 59 min. Sound. 16mm Color. *Rental:* U Mich Media.

Aida. Sophia Loren & Lois Maxwell. Directed by Clemente Fracassi. Ital. 1953. Italy. 96 min. Sound. 16mm B&W. *Rental:* Corinth Films.

Ain't Misbehavin'. Nell Carter, Andre DeShields & Armelia McQueen. Directed by Don Mischer. 1985. Columbia. 97 min. Sound. 16mm Color. *Rental:* Swank Motion.

Ain't No Time for Glory. Gene Barry, Barry Sullivan & Richard Jaeckel. 1957. CBS. (Kinescope). 70 min. Sound. 16mm B&W. *Rental:* Bosco Films.

Air Devils, The. John Randolph, Chris Beaumont, Louise Latham & James Carroll Jordan. Sunn. 50 min. Sound. 16mm Color. *Rental:* Williams Films. *Sale:* Lucerne Films. *Sale:* Lucerne Films & Williams Films, Videotape version.

Air Force. John Garfield & Gig Young. Directed by Howard Hawks. 1943. Warners. 124 min. Sound. 16mm B&W. *Rental:* MGM United.

Air Hostess. Evelyn Knapp & Thelma Todd. Directed by Albert S. Rogell. 1933. Columbia. 65 min. Sound. 16mm B&W. *Rental:* Kit Parker.

Air Mail. Pat O'Brien & Ralph Bellamy. Directed by John Ford. 1932. 83 min. Sound. 16mm B&W. *Rental:* Swank Motion.

Air Patrol *see* Happy Landing.

Air Pollution: Take a Deep Deadly Breath. 1968. ABC. (Documentary). 54 min. Sound. 16mm Color. *Rental:* McGraw-Hill Films & Syracuse U Film. *Sale:* McGraw-Hill Films.

Air Raid Wardens. Stan Laurel & Oliver Hardy. Directed by Edward Sedgwick. 1943. MGM. 67 min. Sound. 16mm B&W. *Rental:* MGM United.

Air Strike. Richard Denning & Jason Robards. Directed by Cy Roth. 1955. Lippert. 69 min. Sound. 16mm B&W. *Rental:* Ivy Films. *Sale:* Rep Pic Film.

Airplane! Peter Graves, Lloyd Bridges & Robert Hays. Directed by Jim Abrahams, Jerry Zucker & David Zucker. 1980. Paramont. 88 min. Sound. 16mm Color. *Rental:* Films Inc.

Airplane II: The Sequel. Robert Hays & Julie Hagerty. Directed by Ken Finkleman. 1982. Paramount. 85 min. Sound. 16mm Color. *Rental:* Films Inc.

Airport. Burt Lancaster & Dean Martin. Directed by George Seaton. 1970. Universal. 137 min. Sound. 16mm Color. *Rental:* Swank Motion.

Airport '79 *see* Concorde.

Airport Nineteen Seventy-Five. Charlton Heston & Karen Black. Directed by Jack Smight. 1974. Universal. 107 min. Sound. 16mm Color. *Rental:* Swank Motion, Anamorphic version.

Airport Seventy-Seven. Jack Lemmon & Lee Grant. Directed by Jerry Jameson. 1977. Universal. 113 min. Sound. 16mm Color. *Rental:* Swank Motion. *Rental:* Swank Motion, Anamorphic version.

Akibiyori *see* Late Autumn.

Akran. Robert Ohlrich & Pat Myers. Directed by Richard Myers. 1969. Richard Myers. 118 min. Sound. 16mm B&W. *Rental:* Canyon Cinema & New Line Cinema.

Akrobat Scho-o-on. Charlie Rivel & Clara Tabody. Directed by Wolfgang Staudte. Ger. 1943. Germany. 111 min. Sound. 16mm B&W. subtitles. *Rental:* Trans-World Films.

Akropolis. Directed by Jerzy Grotowski. Pol. 1967. (Cast unlisted). 60 min. Sound. 16mm B&W. subtitles. *Rental:* A Cantor. *Sale:* A Cantor.

Aku-Aku. 1960. Artfilm. (Documentary). 85 min. Sound. 16mm Color. *Rental:* Janus Films.

Al Capone. Rod Steiger & James Gregory. Directed by Richard Wilson. 1959. Allied Artists. 105 min. Sound. 16mm B&W. *Rental:* Hurlock Cine.

Al Fateh. Ital. Italy. (Documentary). 80 min. Sound. 16mm B&W. narrated Eng. *Rental:* CA Newsreel.

Al Jennings of Oklahoma. Dan Duryea & Gale Storm. Directed by Ray Nazarro. 1951. 98 min. Sound. 16mm Color. *Rental:* Cine Craft. *Lease:* Time-Life Multimedia.

Alabama Connection, The. 1977. Penn State. (Documentary). 59 min. Sound. 16mm Color. *Rental:* Penn St AV Serv. *Sale:* Penn St AV Serv. *Rental:* Penn St AV Serv, *Sale:* Penn St AV Serv, Videotape version.

Aladdin & His Lamp. Patricia Medina & John Sands. Directed by Lew Landers. 1952. Monogram. 67 min. Sound. 16mm Color. *Rental:* Hurlock Cine.

Aladdin & His Magic Lamp. 1968. Childhood. (Cast unlisted). 85 min. Sound. 16mm Color. dubbed. *Rental:* Westcoast Films.

Aladdin & the Wonderful Lamp. FoxKids. Directed by Sidney Franklin & Chester M. Franklin. 1917. Fox. 45 min. Silent. 16mm B&W. *Rental:* Mogulls Films.

Aladdin's Lamp. 1965. Famous Fantasies. (Puppets). 90 min. Sound. 16mm Color. *Rental:* Bosco Films & Film Ctr DC.

Alakazam the Great. 1961. Japan. (Animated). 87 min. Sound. 16mm Color. dubbed. *Rental:* Arcus Film, Budget Films, Cine Craft, Charard Motion Pics, Cousino Visual Ed, Kerr Film, Newman Film Lib, Roas Films, Video Comm, Welling Motion Pictures, Westcoast Films, Wholesome Film Ctr, Williams Films & Willoughby Peer.

Alambrista. Domingo Ambriz, Trinidad Silva, Linda Gillin & Ned Beatty. Directed by Robert M. Young. 1976. Bobwin-Filmhaus. 110 min. Sound. 16mm Color. *Rental:* Cinema Five.

Alamo, The. John Wayne & Richard Widmark. Directed by John Wayne. 1960. United Artists. 161 min. Sound. 16mm Color. *Rental:* Arcus Film, Budget Films, MGM United & Westcoast Films. *Rental:* MGM United, Videotape version.

Alan King Goes to Queens College. 1979. Verve. 58 min. Videotape Color. *Rental:* Films Inc.

Alaska. Dean Jagger & John Carradine. Directed by George Archainbaud. 1944. Monogram. 76 min. Sound. 16mm B&W. *Rental:* Hurlock Cine.

Alaska. 1967. National Geographic. (Documentary). 51 min. Sound. 16mm Color. *Rental:* Films Inc, Syracuse U Film & Wholesome Film Ctr. *Sale:* Films Inc.

Alaska Patrol. Richard Travis & Helen Wescott. Directed by Jack Bernhard. 1949. Film Classics. 61 min. Sound. 16mm B&W. *Rental:* Films Inc & Mogulls Films.

Alaska Seas. Robert Ryan & Jan Sterling. Directed by Jerry Hopper. Paramount. 78 min. Sound. 16mm B&W. *Rental:* Films Inc.

Alaska: The Closing Frontier. 1978. 58 min. Sound. Videotape *Rental:* PBS Video. *Sale:* PBS Video.

Alaskan Earthquake, The. 1965. 45 min. Sound. 16mm B&W. *Rental:* Natl AV Ctr.

Alaskan Safari. Directed by Ron Hayes & Bev Hayes. 1971. American National. (Documentary). 120 min. Sound. 16mm Color. *Rental:* Films Inc, Video Comm & Budget Films. *Rental:* Video Comm, *Lease:* Video Comm, Videotape version.

Albert R. N: Break to Freedom. Robert Beatty, Anthony Steel & Jack Warner. Directed by Lewis Gilbert. 1953. 88 min. Sound. 16mm B&W. *Rental:* Charard Motion Pics.

Albert Schweitzer. Directed by Jerome Hill. 1957. De Rochement. (Documentary). 80 min. Sound. 16mm Color. .

Albert Shanker: Teacher Power. 1973. WNET. (Documentary). 58 min. Sound. 16mm Color. *Rental:* WNET Media. *Sale:* WNET Media.

Alcatraz Island. Ann Sheridan & John Litel. Directed by William McGann. 1937. Warners. 64 min. Sound. 16mm B&W. *Rental:* MGM United.

Alcohol & College Youth: Adolescence & Alcohol. 1965. University of California. (Documentary). 52 min. Sound. 16mm B&W. *Rental:* U Cal Media. *Sale:* U Cal Media.

Alcoholism & Drug Dependence: Parts 1-3. 1980. 125 min. Sound. Videotape Color. *Rental:* Natl AV Ctr.

Aleko. Directed by Sergei Sidelyev. Rus. 1953. Russia. (Cast Unlisted). 61 min. Sound. 16mm B&W. subtitles. *Rental:* Corinth Films.

Alex & the Gypsy. Jack Lemmon & Genevieve Bujold. Directed by John Korty. 1976. Fox. 99 min. Sound. 16mm Color. *Rental:* Films Inc.

Alex in Wonderland. Donald Sutherland & Ellen Burstyn. Directed by Larry Tucker & Paul Mazursky. 1970. MGM. 109 min. Sound. 16mm B&W. *Rental:* MGM United. *Rental:* MGM United, Videotape version.

Alexander Calder: Engineer in Space. 1966. NET. (Documentary). 59 min. Sound. 16mm B&W. *Rental:* Indiana AV Ctr. *Sale:* Indiana AV Ctr.

Alexander Hamilton. George Arliss & Doris Kenyon. Directed by John Adolfi. 1931. Warners. 71 min. Sound. 16mm B&W. *Rental:* MGM United.

Alexander Nevsky. Nikolai Cherkasov. Directed by Sergei Eisenstein & D. L. Vassilev. Rus. 1938. Russia. 109 min. Sound. 16mm B&W. *Rental:* Budget Films, Corinth Films, Films Inc, Em Gee Film Lib, Ivy Films, Images Film, Janus Films, Kit Parker, Macmillian, Museum Mod Art, Natl Film Video, U of IL Film & Westcoast Films. *Sale:* Classic Film Mus, Festival Films, Images Film, Natl Film, Reel Images & Natl Cinema. *Lease:* Macmillan Films & Corinth Films. *Sale:* Morcraft Films, Super 8 sound version. *Sale:* Festival Films, Ivy Films, Video Comm, Tamarelles French Film & Images Film, Videotape version.

Alexander the Great. Richard Burton & Fredric March. Directed by Robert Rossen. 1956. United Artists. 135 min. Sound. 16mm Color. *Rental:* MGM United.

Alexander the Second of Russia. Romy Schneider & Curt Jurgens. Ger. 100 min. Sound. 16mm Color. dubbed. *Rental:* Bosco Films.

Alexander: Very Happy Alexander. Philippe Noiret & Marlene Jobert. Directed by Yves Robert. Fr. 1969. France. 94 min. Sound. 16mm Color. subtitles. *Rental:* Cinema Five. *Lease:* Cinema Five.

Alexander Von Humboldt. Directed by Fred Burnley. 1977. (Cast unlisted). 49 min. Sound. 16mm Color. *Rental:* Time-Life Multimedia. *Sale:* Time-Life Multimedia. *Sale:* Time-Life Multimedia, Videotape version.

Alexander William Doniphan. Peter Lawford. Directed by Paul Stanley. 1965. Saudek. 50 min. Sound. 16mm B&W. *Rental:* IQ Films & U of IL Film. *Sale:* IQ Films. *Sale:* IQ Films, Spanish dubbed version.

Alfie. Michael Caine, Shelley Winters & Millicent Martin. Directed by Lewis Gilbert. 1966. Paramount. 114 min. Sound. 16mm Color. *Rental:* Films Inc.

Alfred Hitchcock Trilogy *see* Three by Hitchcock.

Alfred the Great. David Hemmings & Michael York. Directed by Clive Donner. 1969. MGM. (Anamorphic). 122 min. Sound. 16mm Color. *Rental:* MGM United.

Alfredo, Alfredo. Dustin Hoffman, Stefania Sandrelli & Carla Gravina. Directed by Pietro Germi. Ital. 1973. Italy. 98 min. Sound. 16mm Color. subtitles. *Rental:* Films Inc.

Algeria: What Price Freedom?. 1966. NET. 54 min. Sound. 16mm B&W. *Rental:* Indiana AV Ctr. *Lease:* Indiana AV Ctr.

Algiers. Charles Boyer, Hedy Lamarr, Sigrid Gurie & Peter Lorre. Directed by John Cromwell. 1939. United Artists. 95 min. Sound. 16mm B&W. *Rental:* Budget Films, Classic Film Mus, Em Gee Film Lib, Kit Parker, Maljack, Mogulls Films, Video Comm & Wholesome Film Ctr. *Sale:* Classic Film Mus, Cinema Concepts, Festival Films & Glenn Photo. *Sale:* Glenn Photo & Reel Images, Super 8 sound version. *Sale:* Cinema Concept, Festival Films, Video Comm & Tamarelles French Film, Videotape version.

Ali Baba & the Forty Thieves. Jon Hall, Maria Montez & Turhan Bey. Directed by Arthur Lubin. 1944. Universal. 87 min. Sound. 16mm Color. *Rental:* Swank Motion.

Ali Baba Goes to Town. Eddie Cantor & Tony Martin. Directed by David Butler. 1937. Fox. 81 min. Sound. 16mm B&W. *Rental:* Films Inc.

Ali, Fear Eats the Soul. Brigitte Mira. Directed by Rainer Werner Fassbinder. Ger. 1974. West Germany. 94 min. Sound. 16mm Color. subtitles. *Rental:* New Yorker Films.

Ali: Skill, Brains & Guts. (Cast Unlisted). Videotape *Sale:* Vidamerica.

Ali vs. Spinks. 1978. Universal. (Documentary). 64 min. Sound. 16mm Color. *Rental:* Swank Motion & Wholesome Film Ctr.

Alias a Gentleman. Wallace Beery & Tom Drake. Directed by Harry Beaumont. 1948. MGM. 76 min. Sound. 16mm B&W. *Rental:* MGM United.

Alias Billy the Kid. Sunset Carson & Peggy Stewart. Directed by Thomas Carr. 1946. Republic. 69 min. Sound. 16mm B&W. *Rental:* Ivy Films. *Sale:* Rep Pic Film.

Alias Bulldog Drummond. Sir Ralph Richardson, Jack Hulbert & Fay Wray. Directed by Walter Forde. 1935. 65 min. Sound. 16mm B&W. *Rental:* Film Classics.

Alias French Gertie. Bebe Daniels & Ben Lyon. Directed by George Archainbaud. 1934. RKO. 71 min. Sound. 16mm *Rental:* RKO General Pics.

Alias the Bad Man. Ken Maynard. Directed by Phil Rosen. 1931. Tiffany. 66 min. Sound. 16mm B&W. *Sale:* Cinema Concepts. *Sale:* Video Comm, Videotape version.

Alias the Champ. Robert Rockwell & Audrey Long. Directed by George Blair. 1949. Republic. 60 min. Sound. 16mm B&W. *Rental:* Ivy Films. *Sale:* Rep Pic Film.

Alias the Doctor. Richard Barthelmess & Marian Marsh. Directed by Michael Curtiz. 1932. Warners. 62 min. Sound. 16mm B&W. *Rental:* MGM United.

Alibi. Orig. Title: Perfect Alibi, The. Chester Morris & Mae Busch. Directed by Roland West. 1929. United Artists. 90 min. Sound. 16mm B&W. *Rental:* A Twyman Pres & Twyman Films.

Alibi Ike. Joe E. Brown. Directed by Ray Enright. 1935. Warners. 72 min. Sound. 16mm B&W. *Rental:* MGM United.

Alice Adams. Katharine Hepburn, Fred MacMurray & Fred Stone. Directed by George Stevens. 1935. RKO. 99 min. Sound. 16mm B&W. *Rental:* Films Inc. *Sale:* Tamarelles French Film, Videotape version.

Alice Cooper & Friend in Concert. 50 min. Videotape Color. *Sale:* Cinema Concepts.

Alice Doesn't Live Here Anymore. Ellen Burstyn, Diane Ladd & Kris Kristofferson. Directed by Martin Scorsese. 1975. Warners. 113 min. Sound. 16mm Color. *Rental:* Films Inc, Swank Motion, Twyman Films & Williams Films. *Rental:* Swank Motion, Videotape version.

Alice in the Cities. Directed by Wim Wenders. Ger. 1974. Germany. (Cast unlisted). 110 min. Sound. 16mm B&W. subtitles. *Rental:* Liberty Co.

Alice in Wonderland. 1914. Maienthau. (Cast unlisted). 60 min. Silent. 16mm B&W. *Sale:* Film Classics.

Alice in Wonderland. Alice Savoy. Directed by W. W. Young. 1915. Nonpareil. 45 min. Silent. 16mm B&W. *Rental:* Budget Films & Em Gee Film Lib. *Sale:* Natl Cinema.

Alice in Wonderland. 1927. Pathe. (Cast Unlisted). 60 min. Silent. 16mm B&W. *Rental:* Mogulls Films.

Alice in Wonderland. W. C. Fields & Gary Cooper. Directed by Norman Z. McLeod. 1933. Paramount. 79 min. Sound. 16mm B&W. *Rental:* Williams Films.

Alice in Wonderland. 1951. Disney. (Animated). 75 min. Sound. 16mm Color. *Rental:* Cousino Visual Ed, Disney Prod, Films Inc, Swank Motion & Twyman Films. *Rental:* Swank Motion, Videotape version.

Alice in Wonderland. Kristine de Bell. Directed by Bud Townsend. 1977. General National. 75 min. Sound. 16mm Color. *Rental:* New Line Cinema.

Alice of Wonderland in Paris. Directed by Gene Deitch. 1968. Childhood. (Animated). 70 min. Sound. 16mm Color. *Rental:* Films Inc, Newman Film Lib, Westcoast Films, Welling Motion Pictures, Wholesome Film Ctr & Williams Films. *Rental:* Westcoast Films, 52 mins. version.

Alice, Sweet Alice. Linda Miller & Brooke Shields. Directed by Alfred Sole. 1977. Allied Artists. 108 min. Sound. 16mm Color. *Rental:* Hurlock Cine.

Alice's Adventures in Wonderland. Michael Crawford, Sir Ralph Richardson & Fiona Fullerton. Directed by William Sterling. American National. 96 min. Sound. 16mm Color. *Rental:* Budget Films, Films Inc, Maljack, Natl Film Video, Video Comm, Westcoast Films & Willimas Films. *Lease:* Video Comm. *Rental:* Video Comm, Videotape version.

Alice's Restaurant. Arlo Guthrie & Pat Quinn. Directed by Arthur Penn. 1969. 110 min. Sound. 16mm Color. *Rental:* MGM United. *Sale:* Tamarelles French Film, Videotape version.

Alicia. Directed by Victor Casaus. Span. 1976. (Documentary). 75 min. Sound. 16mm Color. subtitles. *Rental:* Unifilm. *Sale:* Unifilm.

Alien. Tom Skerritt, Sigourney Weaver & John Hurt. Directed by Ridley Scott. 1979. Fox. 124 min. Sound. 16mm Color. *Rental:* Films Inc. *Rental:* Films Inc, Anamorphic version.

Alienist, The. Directed by Nelson Pereira dos Santos. Port. 1970. (Cast Unlisted). 80 min. Sound. 16mm Color. *Rental:* New Yorker Films.

Alien's Place, The. Directed by Rudolf Van den Berg. 1979. 87 min. 16mm *Rental:* Icarus Films. *Sale:* Icarus Films.

Alimony. Martha Vickers & John Beal. Directed by Alfred Zeisler. 1949. Eagle Lion. 70 min. Sound. 16mm B&W. *Rental:* Charard Motion Pics & Mogulls Films.

Allinsky Went to War *see* Saul Alinsky Went to War.

Ali's Last Fight. 1978. (Documentary). 67 min. Sound. 16mm Color. *Rental:* Twyman Films & Westcoast Films. *Rental:* Williams Films, 90 min. version.

Alison's Birthday. Joanne Samuel & Lou Brown. 99 min. Sound. Videotape Color. *Sale:* Vidamerica.

All About Eve. Bette Davis, George Sanders & Anne Baxter. Directed by Joseph L. Mankiewicz. 1950. Fox. 130 min. Sound. 16mm B&W. *Rental:* Films Inc.

All American Co-Ed. Frances Langford & Noah Beery Jr. Directed by LeRoy Prinz. 1961. Hal Roach. 60 min. Sound. 16mm B&W. *Rental:* Wholesome Film Ctr.

All at Sea. Sir Alec Guinness. Directed by Charles Frend. 1958. 87 min. Sound. 16mm B&W. *Rental:* MGM United.

All at Sea. Gary Smith. Directed by Ken Fairbairn. 1972. Britain. 60 min. Sound. 16mm Color. *Sale:* Lucerne Films.

All Cops Are? Martin Potter & Julia Foster. Directed by Sidney Hayers. Britain. 87 min. Sound. 16mm B&W. *Rental:* Cinema Five.

All Fall Down. Eva Marie Saint & Warren Beatty. Directed by John Frankenheimer. 1962. MGM. 111 min. Sound. 16mm B&W. *Rental:* MGM United. *Rental:* MGM United, Videotape version.

All in a Night's Work. Dean Martin & Shirley MacLaine. Directed by Joseph Anthony. 1961. Paramount. 94 min. Sound. 16mm Color. *Rental:* Films Inc. *Rental:* Ivy Films, *Sale:* Blackwood Films, Super 8 sound version. *Rental:* Williams Films, Videotape version.

All Mine to Give: The Day They Gave the Babies Away. Cameron Mitchell & Glynis Johns. Directed by Allen Reisner. 1958. Universal. 102 min. Sound. 16mm Color. *Rental:* Arcus Film, Budget Films, Bosco Films, Films Inc, Maljack, Natl Film CN, Roas Films, Video Comm, Welling Motion Pictures & Westcoast Films. *Lease:* Video Comm. *Sale:* Natl Film CN. *Rental:* Maljack & Video Comm, *Lease:* Video Comm, Videotape version.

All My Babies. Directed by George Stoney. 1952. George Stoney. (Documentary). 55 min. Sound. 16mm B&W. *Rental:* BYU Media, Iowa Films, Museum Mod Art, U Cal Media & U Mich Media.

All My Sons. Edward G. Robinson & Burt Lancaster. Directed by Irving Reis. 1948. Universal. 92 min. Sound. 16mm B&W. *Rental:* Swank Motion & Williams Films.

All Neat in Black Stockings. Victor Henry & Susan George. Directed by Christopher Morahan. 1969. National General. 99 min. Sound. 16mm Color. *Rental:* Swank Motion.

All Night Long. Betsy Blair & Richard Attenborough. Directed by Basil Dearden. 1963. Britain. 91 min. Sound. 16mm B&W. *Rental:* Ivy Films & Swank Motion.

All Nudity Shall Be Punished. Directed by Arnaldo Jabor. Port. 1973. 102 min. Sound. 16mm Color. subtitles. *Rental:* New Yorker Films.

All Over Town. Olson & Johnson. Directed by James W. Horne. 1937. Republic. 62 min. Sound. 16mm B&W. *Rental:* Classic Film Mus & Ivy Films. *Sale:* Cinema Concepts & Rep Pic Film.

All Quiet on the Western Front. Lew Ayres & Louis Wolheim. Directed by Lewis Milestone. 1930. Universal. 103 min. Sound. 16mm B&W. *Rental:* Swank Motion. *Rental:* Swank Motion, Videotape version.

All Quiet on the Western Front. Richard Thomas, Ernest Borgnine & Ian Holm. Directed by Delbert Mann. 1979. ITC. 116 min. Sound. 16mm Color. *Rental:* Swank Motion.

All Round Reduced Personality, The. Helke Sander. Directed by Helke Sander. Ger. 1977. Germany. 98 min. Sound. 16mm B&W. *Rental:* Cinema Guild & Unifilm. *Sale:* Cinema Guild & Unifilm.

All Screwed Up. Trans. Title: Tutto A Posto E Niente In Ordine. Luigi Diberti & Linda Polito. Directed by Lina Wertmuller. Ital. 1974. Italy. 95 min. Sound. 16mm Color. subtitles. *Rental:* New Line Cinema.

All That Heaven Allows. Jane Wyman & Rock Hudson. Directed by Douglas Sirk. 1949. Universal. 89 min. Sound. 16mm Color. *Rental:* Swank Motion.

All That Jazz. Roy Scheider. Directed by Bob Fosse. 1979. Columbia/Fox. 120 min. Sound. 16mm Color. *Rental:* Swank Motion.

All that Money can Buy *see* Devil & Daniel Webster.

All the Brothers Were Valiant. Robert Taylor & Stewart Granger. Directed by Richard Thorpe. 1953. MGM. 93 min. Sound. 16mm Color. *Rental:* MGM United.

All the Fine Young Cannibals. Robert Wagner & Natalie Wood. Directed by Michael Anderson. 1960. MGM. 122 min. Sound. 16mm Color. *Rental:* MGM United. *Rental:* MGM United, Anamorphic color version. *Rental:* MGM United, Videotape version.

All the Kids Like That: Tommy's Story. 1974. Westinghouse. (Documentary). 50 min. Sound. 16mm Color. *Rental:* Edupac & NYU Film Lib. *Sale:* Edupac.

All the King's Horses. 1983. WMAQ. (Documentary). 54 min. Sound. Videotape Color. *Sale:* Films Inc.

All the King's Horses & All the King's Men. 1963. Hearst. (Documentary). 50 min. Sound. 16mm B&W. *Sale:* King Features.

All the King's Men. Broderick Crawford & Mercedes McCambridge. Directed by Robert Rossen. 1949. Columbia. 109 min. Sound. 16mm B&W. *Rental:* Arcus Film, Budget Films, Bosco Films, Cine Craft, Charard Motion Pics, Film Ctr DC, Films Inc, Images Film, Inst Cinema, Ivy Films, Kerr Film, Kit Parker, Modern Sound, Natl Film Lib, Natl Film Video, Newman Film Lib, Roas Films, Swank Motion, Twyman Films, U of IL Film, Welling Motion Pictures, Westcoast Films, Wholesome Film Ctr & Williams Films, Videotape version.

All the Loving Couples. Norman Alden. Directed by Mack Bing. 1969. UMC. 81 min. Sound. 16mm Color. *Rental:* Swank Motion.

All the Marbles. Peter Falk, Vicki Fredrick & Laureen Landon. Directed by Robert Aldrich. 1981. MGM. 112 min. Sound. 16mm Color. *Rental:* MGM United. *Rental:* MGM United, Videotape version.

All the President's Men. Robert Redford & Dustin Hoffman. Directed by Alan J. Pakula. 1976. Warners. 136 min. Sound. 16mm Color. *Rental:* Swank Motion. *Rental:* Swank Motion, Videotape version.

All the Right Moves. Tom Cruise & Craig T. Nelson. Directed by Michael Chapman. 1983. Columbia. 90 min. Sound. 16mm Color. *Rental:* Films Inc. *Sale:* Tamarelles French Film, Videotape version.

All the Right Noises. Tom Bell & Olivia Hussey. Directed by Gerry O'Hara. 1971. Britain. 92 min. Sound. 16mm Color. *Rental:* Film Makers.

All the Way, Boys. Terence Hill & Bud Spencer. Directed by Giuseppe Collizzi. Ital. 1973. Italy. 105 min. Sound. 16mm Color. dubbed. *Rental:* Films Inc. *Rental:* Films Inc, Anamorphic color version.

All the Way Home. Jean Simmons, Robert Preston & Michael Kearney. Directed by Alex Segal. 1963. Paramount. 103 min. Sound. 16mm B&W. *Rental:* Films Inc. *Sale:* Glenn Photo, Super 8 sound version. *Rental:* Video Comm, Videotape version.

All the World Wondered *see* Last Mile.

All the Young Men. Alan Ladd, Sidney Poitier & James Darren. Directed by Hall Bartlett. 1960. Columbia. 87 min. Sound. 16mm Color. *Rental:* Budget Films, Cine Craft, Charard Motion Pics, Film Ctr DC, Films Inc, Inst Cinema, Modern Sound, Roas Films & Twyman Films.

All These Women. Eva Dahlbeck, Harriet Anderson & Bibi Anderson. Directed by Ingmar Bergman. Swed. 1964. Sweden. 80 min. Sound. 16mm Color. subtitles. *Rental:* Janus Films, Films Inc & New Cinema.

All This & Heaven Too. Bette Davis & Charles Boyer. Directed by Anatole Litvak. 1940. Warners. 143 min. Sound. 16mm B&W. *Rental:* MGM United.

All This & World War II. Leo Sayer & Helen Reddy. Directed by Susan Winslow. 1976. Fox. 99 min. Sound. 16mm Color. *Rental:* Films Inc.

All Through the Night. Humphrey Bogart & Conrad Viedt. Directed by Vincent Sherman. 1942. Warners. 107 min. Sound. 16mm B&W. *Rental:* MGM United.

Allegheny Uprising: The First Rebel. John Wayne & Claire Trevor. Directed by William A. Seiter. 1939. RKO. 81 min. Sound. 16mm B&W. *Rental:* Films Inc. *Sale:* Blackhawk Films, Super 8 sound version.

Allegro Non Troppo. Orig. Title: Bruno Bozzetto Music. Directed by Bruno Bozzetto. Ital. 1976. Italy. (Animated). 70 min. Sound. 16mm Color. *Rental:* New Line Cinema. *Rental:* Films Inc, Videotape version.

Allen Case, The. US Government. (Documentary). 75 min. Sound. 16mm B&W. *Sale:* Natl AV Ctr. *Rental:* Natl AV Ctr.

Allergy to Love. 1979. 60 min. Sound. videotape Color. *Rental:* Iowa Films.

Alliance for Progress. Roberto Carnagui & Carlos del Burgo. Directed by Julio Luduena. Span. 1972. Argentina. 104 min. Sound. 16mm B&W. *Rental:* Unifilm. *Sale:* Unifilm.

Allies: The End of the War. 1976. Britain. (Documentary). 52 min. Sound. 16mm Color. *Rental:* Time-Life Multimedia. *Sale:* Time-Life Multimedia. *Sale:* Time-Life Multimedia, Videotape version.

Alligator. Robert Forster & Michael Gazzo. Directed by Lewis Teague. 1980. Group I. 92 min. Sound. 16mm Color. *Rental:* Swank Motion. *Rental:* Swank Motion, Videotape version.

Alligator Named Daisy, An. Donald Sinden & Diana Dors. Directed by J. Lee Thompson. 1957. Britain. 84 min. Sound. 16mm B&W. *Rental:* Cousino Visual Ed.

All's Well That Ends Well. Celia Johnson & Ian Charleson. 1980. Britain. 141 min. Videotape Color. *Rental:* Iowa Films.

Almost a Bride: A Kiss for Corliss. Shirley Temple & David Niven. Directed by Richard Wallace. 1949. United Artists. 85 min. Sound. 16mm B&W. *Rental:* Budget Films.

Almost a Gentleman. James Ellison & Helen Wood. Directed by Leslie Goodwins. 1939. RKO. 65 min. Sound. 16mm *Rental:* RKO General Pics.

Almost Angels. Peter Weck, Hans Holt, Vincent Winter & Sean Scully. Directed by Steve Previn. Ger. 1962. Germany. 93 min. Sound. 16mm Color. dubbed. *Rental:* Buchan Pic, Bosco Films, Cousino Visual Ed, Disney Prod, Elliot Film Co, Film Ctr DC, Films Inc, Films Pres, MGM United, Modern Sound, Newman Film Lib, Roas Films, Swank Motion, Twyman Films, Welling Motion Pictures, Westcoast Films & Williams Films.

Almost Human *see* It's a Dog's Life.

Almost Perfect Affair, An. Keith Carradine, Monica Vitti & Raf Vallone. Directed by Michael Ritchie. 1979. Paramount. 93 min. Sound. 16mm Color. *Rental:* Films Inc.

Almost Summer. Bruno Kirby & Didi Conn. Directed by Martin Davidson. 1978. Universal. 89 min. Sound. 16mm Color. *Rental:* Swank Motion.

Aloha, Bobby & Rose. Paul LeMat & Dianne Hull. Directed by Floyd Mutrux. 1976. Columbia. 89 min. Sound. 16mm Color. *Rental:* Films Inc, Ivy Films, Natl Film Video, Swank Motion, Westcoast Films & Welling Motion Pictures.

Aloha: No Greater Love. Ben Lyon & Alan Hale. Directed by Albert S. Rogell. 1930. Tiffany. 90 min. Sound. 16mm B&W. *Rental:* Mogulls Films.

Aloma of the South Seas. Dorothy Lamour & Jon Hall. Directed by Alfred Santell. 1941. Paramount. 77 min. Sound. 16mm Color. *Rental:* Swank Motion.

Alone in the Midst of the Land. 1970. NBC. (Documentary). 52 min. Sound. 16mm Color. *Rental:* Films Inc & Twymam Films. *Sale:* Films Inc.

Alone in the Streets. Carlo Tamberlani & Brunella Bovo. Directed by Silvio Siano. Ital. 1955. Italy. 80 min. Sound. 16mm B&W. subtitles Eng. *Rental:* Films Inc.

Alone: May 1940-May 1941. Directed by Hugh Raggett. (World at War Ser.). : Pt. 4.). 1973. Media Guild. (Documentary). 52 min. Sound. 16mm Color. *Rental:* Media Guild. *Sale:* Media Guild. *Sale:* Media Guild, Videotape version.

Along Came Jones. Gary Copper & Loretta Young. Directed by Stuart Heisler. 1945. United Artists. 90 min. Sound. 16mm B&W. *Rental:* MGM United.

Along the Navajo Trail. Roy Rogers. Directed by Frank McDonald. 1945. Republic. 65 min. Sound. 16mm B&W. *Rental:* Ivy Films. *Sale:* Rep Pic Film.

Along the Oregon Trail. Monte Hale & Adrian Booth. Directed by R. G. Springsteen. 1947. Republic. 64 min. Sound. 16mm B&W. *Rental:* Ivy Films.

Along the Rio Grande. Tim Holt & Ray Whitley. Directed by Bert Gilroy. 1941. RKO. 64 min. Sound. 16mm *Rental:* RKO General Pics.

Along the Sundown Trail. Bill Stage Boyd. Directed by Peter Stewart. 1942. PRC. 59 min. Sound. 16mm B&W. *Rental:* Budget Films & Mogulls Films.

Alpha Beta. Albert Finney & Rachel Roberts. Directed by Anthony Page. 1976. Britain. 70 min. Videotape Color. *Sale:* Cinema Concepts & Video Lib.

Alphabet Conspiracy, The. 1959. Bell Telephone. (Animated). 60 min. Sound. 16mm Color. *Rental:* BYU Media & Utah Media.

Alphabet Murders, The. Tony Randall & Anita Ekberg. Directed by Frank Tashlin. 1966. MGM. 90 min. Sound. 16mm B&W. *Rental:* MGM United.

Alphaville. Eddie Constantine, Anna Karina & Akim Tamiroff. Directed by Jean-Luc Godard. Fr. 1965. 100 min. Sound. 16mm B&W. subtitles. *Rental:* Budget Films, Images Film, New Cinema & New Yorker Films. *Sale:* Reel Images & Festival Films. *Lease:* Images Film. *Sale:* Festival Films, Videotape version.

Altar of Fire. 1976. Univ of Calif Extension Media. 45 min. Sound. 16mm Color. *Rental:* U Mich Media.

Alte und der Junge Konig, Der. Trans. Title: Making of a King, The. Emil Jannings. Directed by Hans Steinhoff. Ger. 1935. Germany. 92 min. Sound. 16mm B&W. subtitles. *Rental:* Trans-World Films. *Rental:* Trans-World Films, Subtitled version.

Altered States. William Hurt, Blair Brown & Bob Balaban. Directed by Ken Russell. 102 min. Sound. 16mm Color. *Rental:* Swank Motion. *Rental:* Swank Motion, Videotape version.

Alternate Solutions: Part Two. 52 min. Sound. 16mm Color. *Rental:* MTI Tele.

Alternative, The. Directed by Fred G. Thorne. 1968. Fred G. Thorne. (Documentary). 50 min. Sound. 16mm Color. *Rental:* Canyon Cinema.

Alternative Lifestyles in California: West Meets East. 1977. Britain. (Documentary). 52 min. Sound. 16mm Color. *Rental:* U Cal Media, Videotape version.

Alternatives for Learning. 1974. 52 min. Sound. 16mm Color. *Rental:* U Mich Media.

Alvarez Kelly. Williams Holden & Richard Widmark. Directed by Edward Dmytryk. 1966. Columbia. 116 min. Sound. 16mm Color. *Rental:* Arcus Film, Bosco Films, Budget Films, Charad Motion Pics, Cinema, Cine Craft, Kerr Film, Modern Sound, Roas Films, Westcoast Films & Wholesome Film Ctr.

Alvin Ailey: Memories & Visions. Directed by Stan Lathan. 1974. WNET. (Documentary). 54 min. Sound. 16mm Color. *Rental:* Budget Films, La Inst Res Ctr, Phoenix Films, Syracuse U Film & U Cal Media. *Sale:* Phoenix Films. *Sale:* Phoenix Films, Videotape version.

Always a Bride. Rosemary Lane & George Reeves. Directed by Noel Smith. 1940. Warners. 58 min. Sound. 16mm B&W. *Rental:* MGM United.

Always Another Wave. 1967. Lawrence-Wolf. (Documentary). 56 min. Sound. 16mm Color. *Rental:* Films Inc & Kerr Film.

Always for Pleasure. 1977. Les Blank. (Documentary). 58 min. Sound. 16mm Color. *Rental:* Canyon Cinema, U Cal Media & Unifilm. *Sale:* Unifilm.

Always in My Heart. Kay Francis & Walter Huston. Directed by Jo Graham. 1942. Warners. 92 min. Sound. 16mm B&W. *Rental:* MGM United.

Always Leave 'Em Laughing. Milton Berle & Virginia Mayo. Directed by Roy Del Ruth. 1949. Warners. 116 min. Sound. 16mm B&W. *Rental:* MGM United.

Amant de Lady Chatterley, L' *see* Lady Chatterley's Lover.

Amante Para Dos. Alberto Olmedo, Tato Bores & Maria Casan. Span. Spain. 95 min. Sound. Videotape Color. *Sale:* Tamarelles French Film.

Amants, Les *see* Lovers.

Amarcord. Magali Noel. Directed by Federico Fellini. Ital. 1974. Italy. 127 min. Sound. 16mm Color. subtitles. *Rental:* Films Inc.

Amateur, The. John Savage & Christopher Plummer. Directed by Charles Jarrott. 1982. Fox. 111 min. Sound. 16mm Color. *Rental:* Films Inc.

Amateur Night at City Hall: The Story of Frank L. Rizzo. Directed by Robert Mugge. 1978. Direct Cinema. (Documentary). 75 min. Sound. 16mm Color. *Rental:* Direct Cinema. *Sale:* Direct Cinema. *Sale:* Direct Cinema, Videotape version.

Amazing Adventure, The. Cary Grant & Mary Brian. Directed by Alfred Zeisler. 1936. Grand National. 70 min. Sound. 16mm B&W. *Sale:* Classic Film Mus, Natl Cinema & Reel Images. *Rental:* Budget Films. *Rental:* Budget Films, 80 mins. version. *Sale:* Tamarelles French Film, Videotape version.

Amazing Colossal Man, The. Glenn Langan & Cathy Downs. Directed by Bert I. Gordon. 1957. American International. 89 min. Sound. 16mm B&W. *Rental:* Films Inc & Westcoast Films.

Amazing Dobermans, The. Fred Astaire, Barbara Eden & James Franciscus. Directed by Byron Chudnow. 1976. Golden. 94 min. Sound. 16mm Color. *Rental:* Modern Sound, Swank Motion & Wholesome Film Ctr.

Amazing Dr. Clitterhouse, The. Edward G Robinson & Humphrey Bogart. Directed by Anatole Litvak. 1938. Warners. 87 min. Sound. 16mm B&W. *Rental:* MGM United.

Amazing Equal Pay Show, The. 1974. Britain. (Cast unlisted). 50 min. Sound. 16mm Color. *Rental:* Women Movies.

Amazing Grace. Moms Mabley, Slappy White & Moses Gunn. Directed by Stan Lathan. 1974. United Artists. 99 min. Sound. 16mm Color. *Rental:* Films Inc, MGM United & Welling Motion Pictures.

Amazing Grace. Directed by Allan Miller. 1976. Allan Miller. (Documentary). 58 min. Sound. 16mm Color. *Rental:* Pyramid Film & Budget Films. *Sale:* Pyramid Film. *Rental:* Pyramid Film, *Sale:* Pyramid Film, Videotape version.

Amazing Mr. Blunden, The. Laurence Naismith & Diana Dors. 1974. Britain. 90 min. Sound. 16mm Color. *Rental:* Bosco Films, Budget Films & Films Inc. *Rental:* Williams Films, 8mm version. *Rental:* Budget Films, 99 min. version.

Amazing Mr. Williams, The. Melvyn Douglas & Joan Blondell. Directed by Alexander Hall. 1939. Columbia. 90 min. Sound. 16mm B&W. *Lease:* Time-Life Multimedia.

Amazing Mr. X, The. Turhan Bey & Lynn Bari. Directed by Bernard Vorhaus. 1948. Eagle Lion. 79 min. Sound. 16mm B&W. *Rental:* Budget Films & Mogulls Films.

Amazing Nellie Bly, The *see* Nellie Bly.

Amazing Quest of Mr. Ernest Bliss. Cary Grant & Ralph Richardson. Directed by Alfred Zeisler. 80 min. 16mm *Rental:* A Twyman Pres.

Amazing Transparent Man, The. Douglas Kennedy & Marguerite Chapman. Directed by Edgar G. Ulmer. 1960. American International. 58 min. Sound. 16mm B&W. *Rental:* Films Inc.

Amazing World of Ghosts, The. Directed by Wheeler Dixon. 1979. Gold Key. (Documentary). 96 min. Sound. 16mm Color. *Rental:* Gold Key.

Amazing World of Psychic Phenomena, The. Directed by Richard Guenette. 1979. Sunn. (Documentary). 95 min. Sound. Videotape Color. *Sale:* Vidamerica & Williams Films. *Sale:* Lucerne Films. *Sale:* Lucerne Films & Williams Films, Videotape version.

Amazon, The. 1967. National Geographic. (Documentary). 52 min. Sound. 16mm Color. *Rental:* Films Inc, Natl Geog, Syracuse U Film & Wholesome Film Ctr. *Sale:* Natl Geog. *Sale:* Natl Geog, Videotape version.

Amazon Quest. Tom Neal & Carole Mathews. Directed by S. K. Seeley. 1949. Film Classics. 75 min. Sound. 16mm B&W. *Rental:* Ivy Films. *Sale:* Rep Pic Film.

Amazons of Rome. Louis Jourdan & Sylvia Sims. Directed by Carlo Bragaglia. 1963. France-Italy. 93 min. Sound. 16mm Color. dubbed. *Rental:* MGM United.

Ambition. 1981. CTW. (Cast unlisted). 60 min. Sound. Videotape Color. *Rental:* PBS Video. *Sale:* PBS Video.

Ambush. Robert Taylor & Arlene Dahl. Directed by Sam Wood. 1949. MGM. 90 min. Sound. 16mm B&W. *Rental:* MGM United.

Ambush At Cimarron Pass. Scott Brady & Clint Eastwood. Directed by Jodie Copelan. 1958. Fox. (Anamorphic). 73 min. Sound. 16mm B&W. *Rental:* Ivy Films. *Sale:* Rep Pic Film.

Ambush Trail, The. Bob Steele. Directed by Harry Fraser. 1946. PRC. 59 min. Sound. 16mm B&W. *Sale:* Classics Assoc NY.

Ambush Valley. Bob Custer. Directed by Bernard B. Ray. 1936. Reliable. 60 min. Sound. 16mm B&W. *Rental:* Mogulls Films.

Ambushers, The. Dean Martin, Senta Berger & Janice Rule. Directed by Henry Levin. 1967. Columbia. 102 min. Sound. 16mm Color. *Rental:* Arcus Film, Budget Films, Cine Craft, Films Inc, Inst Cinema, Modern Sound, Video Comm, Welling Motion Pictures, Westcoast Films & Wholesome Film Ctr.

America. Lionel Barrymore, Carol Dempster & Neil Hamilton. Directed by D. W. Griffith. 1924. United Artists. 173 min. Silent. 16mm B&W. *Rental:* A Twyman Pres & Museum Mod Art. *Rental:* Killiam Collect & Twyman Films, 95 min. sound, tinted, with musical score version, Videotape version. *Rental:* Ivy Films, *Sale:* Blackhawk Films, Super 8 silent version. *Sale:* Blackhawk Films, Silent 8mm version.

America. 13 pts. 1972. Britain. (Documentary). 676 min. Sound. 16mm Color. *Rental:* BYU Media & U Cal Media.

America: A More Abundant Life. 1972. Britain. (Documentary). 52 min. Sound. 16mm Color. *Rental:* Kent St U Film & Utah Media.

America America. Stathis Giallelis & Linda Marsh. Directed by Elia Kazan. 1963. Warners. 168 min. Sound. 16mm B&W. *Rental:* Swank Motion.

America & the Americans. 1968. NBC. (Documentary). 51 min. Sound. 16mm Color. *Rental:* Iowa Films, McGraw-Hill Films & U of IL Film. *Sale:* McGraw-Hill Films.

America at the Movies. 1976. American Film Institute. (Documentary). 116 min. Sound. 16mm Color. *Rental:* Cinema Five.

America Between the Great Wars. 1978. Blackhawk. (Documentary, tinted sequences). 60 min. Videotape *Sale:* Blackhawk Films.

America Black & White. 1981. NBC. 52 min. Sound. 16mm Color. *Rental:* U Mich Media.

America Comes of Age. 1950. Film Classic Exchange. (Documentary, musical score only). 50 min. Sound. 16mm B&W. narrated. *Rental:* Film Classics. *Sale:* Film Classics. *Rental:* Film Classics, Videotape version.

America: Domesticating a Wilderness. 1972. Britain. (Documentary). 52 min. Sound. 16mm Color. *Rental:* Kent St U Film, Syracuse U Film & Utah Media.

America Goes Over. (Documentary). 75 min. Silent. 16mm B&W. *Sale:* Blackhawk Films. *Sale:* Blackhawk Films, Super 8 silent version. *Sale:* Blackhawk Films, Silent 8mm version.

America: Gone West. 1972. Britain. (Documentary). 52 min. Sound. 16mm Color. *Rental:* Kent St U Film, OK AV Ctr, Syracuse U Film & Utah Media.

America: Home Away from Home. 1972. Britain. (Documentary). 52 min. Sound. 16mm Color. *Rental:* Kent St U Film, Syracuse U Film & Utah Media.

America: Huddled Masses. 1972. Britain. (Documentary). 52 min. Sound. 16mm Color. *Rental:* Kent St U Film, OK AV Ctr, Syracuse U Film & Utah Media.

America: Inventing a Nation. 1972. Britain. (Documentary). 52 min. Sound. 16mm Color. *Rental:* Kent St U Film, OK AV Ctr, Syracuse U Film & Utah Media.

America Is Hard to See. Directed by Emile De Antonio. 1969. EYR. (Documentary). 101 min. Sound. 16mm B&W. *Rental:* New Cinema & New Yorker Films.

America Lost & Found. Directed by Lance Bird & Tom Johnson. 1980. Media Study-Buffalo. (Documentary). 59 min. Sound. 16mm B&W. *Rental:* Direct Cinema. *Sale:* Direct Cinema. *Sale:* Direct Cinema, Videotape version.

America: Making a Revolution. 1972. Britain. (Documentary). 52 min. Sound. 16mm Color. *Rental:* Kent St U Film, Syracuse U Film & Utah Media.

America: Money on the Land. 1972. Britain. (Documentary). 52 min. Sound. 16mm Color. *Rental:* Kent St U Film, OK AV Ctr, Syracuse U Film & Utah Media, Videotape version.

America: New Found Land. 1972. Britain. (Documentary). 52 min. Sound. 16mm Color. *Rental:* Kent St U Film, Syracuse U Film & Utah Media.

America on the Road. 58 min. Sound. Videotape *Rental:* PBS Video. *Rental:* PBS Video.

America: The Arsenal. 1972. Britain. (Documentary). 52 min. Sound. 16mm Color. *Rental:* Kent St U Film, Syracuse U Film & Utah Media, Videotape version.

America: The First Impact. 1972. Britain. (Documentary). 52 min. Sound. 16mm Color. *Rental:* Kent St U Film & Utah Media, Videotape version.

America: The Promise Fulfilled & the Promise Broken. 1972. Britain. (Documentary). 52 min. Sound. 16mm Color. *Rental:* Kent St U Film, OK AV Ctr & Utah Media, Videotape version.

America Works When Americans Work. 1980. NBC. (Documentary). 78 min. Sound. 16mm Color. *Rental:* Films Inc, Syracuse U Film, U of IL Film & U Mich Media. *Sale:* Films Inc. *Sale:* Films Inc, Videotape version.

America-Edge of Abundance see Edge of Abundance.

America's Crises: The Emotional Dilemma see Emotional Dilemma.

America's Crises: The Parent see Parents.

American Adventure, An: The Rocket Pilot. 1981. NBC. (Documentary). 77 min. Sound. 16mm Color. *Rental:* Films Inc. *Sale:* Films Inc, Videotape version.

American Alcoholic, The. 1968. NBC. (Documentary). 54 min. Sound. 16mm Color. *Rental:* U of IL Film, McGraw-Hill Films & Roas Films. *Sale:* McGraw-Hill Films.

American Aristocracy. Douglas Fairbanks & Jewel Carmen. Directed by John Emerson. 1916. Fine Arts-Triangle. 60 min. Silent. 16mm B&W. *Rental:* Em Gee Film Lib & Film Images. *Sale:* Blackhawk Films. *Rental:* Ivy Films, *Sale:* Blackhawk Films, Super 8 silent version. *Sale:* Blackhawk Films, Silent 8mm version.

American Art in the Sixties. 1975. Blackwood. (Documentary). 57 min. Sound. 16mm Color. *Rental:* Blackwood Films. *Sale:* Blackwood Films.

American Ballet: Eliot Feld, Artistic Director. 1971. Blackwood. (Dance). 58 min. Sound. 16mm Color. *Rental:* Blackwood Films. *Sale:* Blackwood Films.

American Ballet Theater. 1976. WNET. (Documentary). 58 min. Videotape Color. *Rental:* WNET Media. *Sale:* WNET Media.

American Ballet Theater: A Closeup in Time. Directed by Jerome Schnur. 1973. Cantor. (Dance). 90 min. Sound. 16mm Color. *Rental:* A Cantor. *Sale:* A Cantor.

American Condition, The. 3 pts. 1976. ABC. (Documentary). 49 min. Sound. 16mm Color. *Rental:* McGraw-Hill Films. *Sale:* McGraw-Hill Films. *Rental:* McGraw-Hill Films, *Sale:* McGraw-Hill Films, Videotape version.

American Cowboy, The see Cowboy.

American Empire. Richard Dix & Preston Foster. Directed by William McGann. 1942. United Artists. 72 min. Sound. 16mm B&W. *Rental:* Budget Films, Classic Film Mus, Learning Corp Am & Mogulls Films. *Sale:* Cinema Concepts & Learning Corp Am.

American Family, An. 12 pts. 1973. WNET. (Documentary). 720 min. Videotape Color. *Rental:* WNET Media.

American Fashion: Rags to Riches. 1980. NBC. (Documentary). 52 min. Videotape Color. *Rental:* Films Inc & Iowa Films. *Sale:* Films Inc.

American Foreign Policy. 6 pts. 1968. NBC. (Documentary). 120 min. Sound. 16mm B&W. *Rental:* Films Inc. *Sale:* Films Inc.

American Foreign Policy: Where Are We Going. 1973. WNET. (Interview). 60 min. Videotape Color. *Rental:* WNET Media. *Sale:* WNET Media.

American Friend, The. Bruno Ganz & Dennis Hopper. Directed by Wim Wenders. Ger. 1977. Germany. 127 min. Sound. 16mm Color. subtitles. *Rental:* New Cinema & New Yorker Films.

American Game, The. Directed by Jay Freund & David Wolf. 1979. World-Northal. (Documentary). 85 min. Sound. 16mm Color. *Rental:* Corinth Films.

American Gigolo. Richard Gere & Lauren Hutton. Directed by Paul Schrader. 1980. Paramount. 117 min. Sound. 16mm Color. *Rental:* Films Inc.

American Graffiti. Richard Dreyfuss & Ron Howard. Directed by George Lucas. 1973. Universal. 109 min. Sound. 16mm Color. *Rental:* Swank Motion. *Rental:* Swank Motion, Anamorphic version. *Rental:* Swank Motion, Videotape version.

American Guerrilla in the Philippines, An. Tyrone Power, Micheline Presle & Tom Ewell. Directed by Fritz Lang. 1950. Fox. 105 min. Sound. 16mm B&W. *Rental:* Films Inc.

American Hero, An see Knute Rockne.

American Highlands, The. 1979. PBS. (Documentary). 58 min. Videotape Color. *Rental:* PBS Video. *Sale:* PBS Video.

American Hot Wax. Tim McIntire, Jay Leno & Laraine Newman. Directed by Floyd Mutrux. 1978. Paramount. 98 min. Sound. 16mm Color. *Rental:* Films Inc.

American Image, The. 1967. NBC. (Documentary). 54 min. Sound. 16mm Color. *Sale:* McGraw-Hill Films & Utah Media.

American in Paris, An. Gene Kelly & Leslie Caron. Directed by Vincente Minnelli. 1951. MGM. 113 min. Sound. 16mm Color. *Rental:* MGM United. *Rental:* MGM United, Videotape version.

American Jewish Writer, The. 1968. Anti-Defamation League. 60 min. Sound. 16mm B&W. *Rental:* ADL. *Sale:* ADL.

American Madness. Walter Huston & Pat O'Brien. Directed by Frank Capra. 1932. Columbia. 78 min. Sound. 16mm B&W. *Rental:* Corinth Films & Swank Motion.

American Military Strength: Second to None. 1978. ABC. 51 min. Sound. 16mm Color. *Rental:* MTI Tele & Syracuse U Film. *Sale:* MTI Tele. *Sale:* MTI Tele, Videotape version.

American Music: From Folk to Jazz to Pop. 1967. ABC. (Documentary). 51 min. Sound. 16mm B&W. *Rental:* McGraw-Hill Films, Syracuse U Film, U of IL Film & U Mich Media. *Sale:* McGraw-Hill Films.

American Plains Indian: End of the Trail. 1967. 53 min. Sound. 16mm B&W. *Rental:* Iowa Films & Utah Media.

American Pop. Directed by Ralph Bakshi. 1981. Columbia. (Animated). 97 min. Sound. 16mm Color. *Rental:* Swank Motion.

American Presidency, The. 1980. NBC. (Documentary). 82 min. Sound. 16mm Color. *Rental:* Films Inc. *Sale:* Films Inc. *Rental:* Films Inc, *Sale:* Films Inc, Videotape version.

American Revolution, The. 2 pts. 1972. IQ. (Documentary). 49 min. Sound. 16mm Color. *Rental:* OK AV Ctr. *Sale:* Learning Corp Am.

American Revolution of '63, The. 1963. ABC. (Documentary). 180 min. Sound. 16mm B&W. *Rental:* Xerox Films. *Sale:* Xerox Films.

American Revolution Two. 1975. Film Group. (Documentary). 80 min. Sound. 16mm B&W. *Rental:* Vision Quest. *Sale:* Vision Quest.

American Romance, An. Brian Donlevy & Ann Richards. Directed by King Vidor. 1944. MGM. 122 min. Sound. 16mm Color. *Rental:* MGM United.

American Samoa: Paradise Lost. 1969. NET. (Documentary). 55 min. Sound. 16mm B&W. *Rental:* U Cal Media, Color version.

American Schools: Flunking the Test. 1976. ABC. (Documentary). 52 min. Sound. 16mm Color. *Rental:* McGraw-Hill Films & Syracuse U Film. *Sale:* McGraw-Hill Films. *Sale:* McGraw-Hill Films, Videotape version.

American Soldier, The. Rainer Werner Fassbinder & Margarethe Von Trotta. Directed by Rainer Werner Fassbinder. Ger. 1970. Germany. 80 min. Sound. 16mm B&W. subtitles. *Rental:* New Yorker Films.

American Tragedy, An. Sylvia Sidney & Phillips Holmes. Directed by Josef Von Sternberg. 1931. Paramount. 95 min. Sound. 16mm B&W. *Rental:* Swank Motion & Williams Films.

American Werewolf in London, An. David Naughton, Jenny Agutter & Griffin Dunne. Directed by John Landis. 97 min. Sound. 16mm Color. *Rental:* Swank Motion. *Rental:* Swank Motion, Videotape version.

American Wilderness, The. 1971. NBC. (Documentary). 53 min. Sound. 16mm Color. *Rental:* Films Inc, Ryramid Film, U Cal Media & U Mich Media. *Sale:* Films Inc. *Sale:* Films Inc, Videotape version.

American Woman in the Twentieth Century, The. 1963. Wolper. (Documentary). 50 min. Sound. 16mm B&W. *Rental:* Films Inc & Syracuse U Film. *Sale:* Films Inc. *Sale:* Films Inc, Videotape version.

American Woman: The Portraits of Courage. Patricia Neal & Joan Hackett. Directed by Robert Deubel. 1975. Concepts Unlimited. 53 min. Sound. 16mm Color. *Rental:* McGraw-Hill Films, SD AV Ctr, Syracuse U Film, U Cal Media & U Mich Media. *Sale:* McGraw-Hill Films.

American"Ism": Joe McCarthy. 1979. Films Inc. 90 min. Sound. 16mm Color. *Rental:* Syracuse U Film.

Americanization of Emily, The. James Garner & Julie Andrews. Directed by Arthur Hiller. 1964. MGM. 115 min. Sound. 16mm B&W. *Rental:* MGM United.

Americano, The. Douglas Fairbanks. Directed by John Emerson. 1917. Fine Arts-Triangle. 50 min. Silent. 16mm B&W. *Rental:* Em Gee Film Lib, Film Classics & Ivy Films. *Sale:* Blackhawk Films & Film Classics. *Rental:* Film Classics, Videotape version.

Americano, The. Glenn Ford & Frank Lovejoy. Directed by William Castle. 1955. RKO. 85 min. Sound. 16mm Color. *Rental:* Budget Films & Ivy Films. *Lease:* Rep Pic Film.

Americans on Everest. 1965. National Goegraphic. (Documentary). 50 min. Sound. 16mm Color. *Rental:* Budget Films, BYU Media, Pyramid Film, Syracuse U Film, Utah Media & New Cinema. *Sale:* Pyramid Film. *Sale:* Pyramid Film, *Rental:* Pyramid Film, Videotape version.

Americartune. Directed by Tim Blaskovich. 1978. 86 min. Sound. 16mm Color. *Rental:* Canyon Cinema.

America's Pop Collector. Directed by E. J. Vaughn & John Scott. 1974. Cinema Five. (Documentary). 72 min. Sound. 16mm Color. *Rental:* Cinema Five & Museum Mod Art. *Lease:* Cinema Five.

America's Wonderlands: The National Parks. 1968. National Geographic. (Documentary). 53 min. Sound. 16mm Color. *Rental:* Natl Geog. *Sale:* Natl Geog. *Sale:* Natl Geog, Videotape version.

Americathon. John Ritter, Harvey Korman & Chief Dan George. Directed by Neil Israel. 1979. United Artists. 85 min. Sound. 16mm Color. *Rental:* MGM United & Swank Motion.

Amherst. 1975. Canada. (Documentary). 50 min. Sound. 16mm Color. *Rental:* B Raymond. *Sale:* B Raymond.

Amico, Un. (Cast unlisted). 50 min. Sound. 16mm Color. *Rental:* Films Inc.

Amish, The: A People of Preservation. 1976. Gateway. (Documentary). 52 min. Sound. 16mm Color. *Rental:* La Inst Res Ctr & Ency Brit Ed. *Sale:* Ency Brit Ed. *Sale:* Ency Brit Ed, Videotape version avail. version.

Amities Particuliers, Les: This Special Friendship. Directed by Jean Delannoy. 1964. France. 99 min. Sound. Videotape B&W. *Sale:* Tamarelles French Film.

Amityville Horror. James Brolin & Margot Kidder. Directed by Stuart Rosenberg. 1979. A. I. P.. 117 min. Sound. 16mm Color. *Rental:* Williams Films, Images Film, Swank Motion, Welling Motion Pictures & Wholesome Film Ctr.

Amityville II: The Possession. James Olson, Burt Young & Rutanya Alda. Directed by Damiano Damiani. 104 min. Sound. 16mm Color. *Rental:* Williams Films.

Amok Time. William Shatner & Leonard Nimoy. Directed by Joseph Pevney. 1967. Star Trek. 50 min. Sound. 16mm Color. *Sale:* Reel Images & Roas Films. *Sale:* Reel Images, Super 8 sound version.

Among the Wild Chimpanzees. 59 min. Sound. 16mm Color. *Rental:* Natl Geog. *Sale:* Natl Geog. *Sale:* Natl Geog, Videotape version.

Amore, L'. Trans. Title: Human Voice, The. 2 pts. Anna Magnani. Directed by Roberto Rossellini. Ital. 1948. Italy. 69 min. Sound. 16mm B&W. subtitles. *Rental:* Films Inc & Roas Films.

Amorous Adventures of Moll Flanders, The. Kim Novak, Angela Lansbury & Richard Johnson. Directed by Terence Young. 1965. Paramount. 126 min. Sound. 16mm Color. *Rental:* Films Inc.

Amsterdam Kill. Robert Mitchum, Richard Egan & Keye Luke. Directed by Robert Clouse. 1978. Columbia. 90 min. Sound. 16mm Color. *Rental:* Arcus Film, Budget Films, Modern Sound, Swank Motion, Twyman Films, Westcoast Films & Williams Films.

Amsterdam Travel Diary. 1966. NET. (Documentary). 59 min. Sound. 16mm B&W. *Rental:* Indiana AV Ctr. *Sale:* Indiana AV Ctr.

Amy. Jenny Agutter & Barry Newman. Directed by Vincent McEveety. 1981. Disney. 100 min. Sound. 16mm B&W. *Rental:* Films Inc.

Ana & the Wolves. Geraldine Chaplin & Fernando Fernan-Gomez. Directed by Carlos Saura. Span. 1973. Janus. 100 min. Sound. 16mm Color. subtitles Eng. *Rental:* Films Inc.

Ana Mario. Span. 1945. Spain. (Documentary). 87 min. Sound. 16mm B&W. *Rental:* Film Classics.

Anais Observed. Directed by Robert Snyder. 1974. Cornerstone. (Documentary). 87 min. Sound. 16mm Color. *Rental:* A Cantor. *Sale:* A Cantor.

Analysis of Nucleon: Nucleon Scattering Experiments. 1961. US Government. (Documentary). 50 min. Sound. 16mm Color. *Sale:* Natl AV Ctr.

Anarchism in America. 75 min. Sound. 16mm Color. *Rental:* Cinema Guild.

Anastasia. Ingrid Bergman, Yul Brynner & Helen Hayes. Directed by Anatole Litvak. 1956. Fox. 105 min. Sound. 16mm Color. *Rental:* Films Inc. *Rental:* Films Inc, Anamorphic color version.

Anatahan. Skemi Negishi. Directed by Josef Von Sternberg. Jap. 1953. Japan. 92 min. Sound. 16mm B&W. narrated Eng. *Rental:* Twyman Films. *Sale:* Twyman Films.

Anatomy of a Crisis. 1980. Penn. 60 min. Sound. 16mm Color. *Rental:* Ency Brit Ed. *Sale:* Ency Brit Ed. *Rental:* Iowa Films, *Sale:* Ency Brit Ed, Videotape verison version.

Anatomy of a Hit. 1964. NET. (Documentary). 90 min. Sound. 16mm B&W. *Rental:* U Cal Media.

Anatomy of a Murder. James Stewart, Lee Remick & Ben Gazzara. Directed by Otto Preminger. 1959. Columbia. 161 min. Sound. 16mm B&W. *Rental:* Arcus Film, Bosco Films, Budget Films, Cine Craft, Film Ctr DC, Films Inc, Inst Cinema, Kit Parker, Modern Sound, Natl Film Video, Roas Films, U of IL Film, Video Comm, Welling Motion Pictures, Westcoast Films, Wholesome Film Ctr & Williams Films.

Anatomy of a Volcano. 1980. Britain. (Documentary). 57 min. Sound. 16mm Color. *Rental:* Iowa Films.

Anchors Aweigh. Frank Sinatra & Gene Kelly. Directed by George Sidney. 1945. MGM. 103 min. Sound. 16mm Color. *Rental:* MGM United.

Ancient Egypt. Directed by Brian Brake. 1970. Time Life. (Documentary). 51 min. Sound. 16mm Color. *Rental:* U Cal Media & U Mich Media. *Rental:* U Cal Media & U Mich Media, Videotape version. *Rental:* U Cal Media & U Mich Media, Spanish language version.

Ancient Mariners. 58 min. Sound. Videotape *Rental:* PBS Video. *Sale:* PBS Video.

Ancient World: Egypt. 1955. New York University. (Documentary). 66 min. Sound. 16mm Color. *Rental:* BYU Media.

Ancient World: Greece. 1955. New York University. (Documentary). 66 min. Sound. 16mm Color. *Rental:* BYU Media.

And Away We Go. 1964. Wolper. (Documentary). 50 min. Sound. 16mm B&W. *Rental:* Films Inc. *Sale:* Films Inc. *Sale:* Films Inc, Videotape version.

And God Created Woman. Brigitte Bardot & Curt Jurgens. Directed by Roger Vadim. 1956. France. (Anamorphic). 91 min. Sound. 16mm Color. *Rental:* Corinth Films.

And Hope to Die. Robert Ryan & Jean-Louis Trintignant. Directed by Rene Clement. 1972. France. 99 min. Sound. 16mm Color. *Rental:* Films Inc.

And Justice for All. Al Pacino, Jack Warden & John Forsythe. Directed by Norman Jewison. 119 min. Sound. 16mm Color. *Rental:* Swank Motion. *Rental:* Swank Motion, Videotape version.

And Millions Will Die. Richard Basehart & Leslie Nielsen. 1974. Allied Artists. 97 min. Color. *Sale:* Blackhawk Films.

And No Bells Ring. 1960. (Documentary). 57 min. Sound. 16mm Color. *Rental:* SD AV Ctr & U of IL Film.

And Now for Something Completely Different. Monty Python. Directed by Ian MacNaughton. 1971. Britain. 89 min. Sound. 16mm Color. *Rental:* Swank Motion.

And Now Miguel. Directed by Joseph Krumgold. 1953. US Government. (Documentary). 60 min. Sound. 16mm B&W. *Rental:* Wholesome film Ctr.

And Now Miguel. Guy Stockwell & Pat Cardi. Directed by James B. Clark. 1966. Universal. 95 min. Sound. 16mm Color. *Rental:* Swank Motion.

And Now My Love. Marthe Keller & Charles Denner. Directed by Claude Lelouch. Fr. 1974. France. 121 min. Sound. 16mm Color. subtitles. *Rental:* Swank Motion.

And Now the Screaming Starts. Peter Cushing & Herbert Lom. Directed by Roy Ward Baker. 1973. Cinerama. 87 min. Sound. 16mm Color. *Rental:* Film Pres, Modern Sound & Swank Motion.

And Now Tomorrow. Protestant. (Documentary). 80 min. Sound. 16mm B&W. *Rental:* Welling Motion Pictures.

And One Was Beautiful. Laraine Day & Robert Cummings. Directed by Robert B. Sinclair. 1940. MGM. 70 min. Sound. 16mm B&W. *Rental:* MGM United.

And Quiet Flows the Don. Ellinia Bystritskaya. Directed by Sergei Gerassimov. Rus. 1957. Russia. 107 min. Sound. 16mm B&W. subtitles. *Rental:* Corinth Films. *Rental:* Corinth Films, 243 mins version.

And Should We Die. 1967. Brigham Young. (Documentary). 50 min. Sound. 16mm Color. *Rental:* BYU Media.

And So They Were Married. Melvyn Douglas & Mary Astor. Directed by Elliott Nugent. 1936. Columbia. 75 min. Sound. 16mm B&W. *Rental:* Kit Parker.

And So They Were Married: Johnny Doesn't Live Here Anymore. Simone Simon & Robert Mitchum. Directed by Joe May. 1944. Monogram. 79 min. Sound. 16mm B&W. *Rental:* Kit Parker.

And Suddenly It's Murder. Trans. Title: Crime Ne Paie Pas, Le. Alberto Sordi, Vittorio Gassman & Sylvana Mangano. Directed by Mario Camerini. 1960. Italy. (Anamorphic). 90 min. Sound. 16mm B&W. dubbed. *Rental:* Swank Motion.

And Suddenly You Run *see* Terror at Midnight.

And the Heavens Were Taken by Storm *see* Y el Cielo Fue Tomado Por Asalto.

And the Meek Shall Inherit the Earth. 1971. NET. (Documentary). 59 min. Sound. Color. *Rental:* Indiana AV Ctr. *Sale:* Indiana Av Ctr.

And the Rich Shall Inherit the Earth. 1974. Westinghouse. (Documentary). 50 min. Sound. 16mm Color. *Rental:* Edupac & NYU Flim Lib. *Sale:* Edupac.

And the Ship Sails On. Freddie Jones, Barbara Jefford & Victor Poletti. Directed by Federico Fellini. 1985. Columbia. 128 min. Sound. 16mm Color. *Rental:* Swank Motion.

And Then There Were None. Orig. Title: Ten Little Indians. Barry Fitzgerald, Walter Huston & Roland Young. Directed by Rene Clair. 1945. Fox. 101 min. Sound. 16mm B&W. *Rental:* Arcus Film, Buchan Pic, Budget Films, Bosco Films, Em Gee Film Lib, Films Inc, Images Film, Ivy Films, Kit Parker, Maljack, Modern Sound, Roas Films, Video Comm, Welling Motion Pictures, Westcoast Films & Wholesome Film Ctr. *Lease:* Video Comm. *Rental:* Video Comm, *Lease:* Video Comm, Videotape version.

And There Came a Man see Man Named John.

And Who Shall Feed This World? 1975. NBC. (Documentary). 48 min. Sound. 16mm Color. *Rental:* Films Inc, SD AV Ctr, Syracuse U Film, U Cal Media & U of IL Film. *Sale:* Films Inc. *Sale:* Films Inc, Videotape version.

Anderson Platoon, The. Directed by Pierre Schoendorffer. Fr. 1967. France. (Documentary). 65 min. Sound. 16mm B&W. narrated Eng. *Rental:* Iowa Films, Films Inc, Syracuse U Film, U Cal Media & U Nev Ctr. *Sale:* Films Inc. *Sale:* Films Inc, Videotape version.

Anderson Tapes, The. Sean Connery, Dyan Cannon & Martin Balsam. Directed by Sidney Lumet. 1971. Columbia. 98 min. Sound. 16mm Color. *Rental:* Arcus Film, Budget Films, Cine Craft, Bosco Films, Film Ctr DC, Films Inc, Images Film, Natl Film Video, Swank Motion, Welling Motion Pictures, Westcoast Films & Wholesome Film Ctr.

Andreas Schluter. Heinrich George & Dorothea Wieck. Directed by Herbert Maisch. Ger. 1942. Germany. 84 min. Sound. 16mm B&W. subtitles. *Rental:* Trans-World Films.

Andrei Rublev. Anatoli Solonitzine & Ivan Lapitkov. Directed by Andrei Tarkovsky. Rus. 1966. Columbia. (Anamorphic, color sequence). 185 min. Sound. 16mm subtitles. *Rental:* Corinth Films.

Andrew Johnson. Walter Matthau. Directed by Alexander Singer. (Profiles in Courage Ser.). 1965. Saudek. 50 min. Sound. 16mm B&W. *Rental:* Syracuse U Film, U of IL Film & U Mich Media. *Sale:* IQ Films. *Sale:* IQ Films, Spanish dubbed version.

Andrew Young Remembers Martin Luther King. 1979. WNET. (Documentary). 58 min. Videotape Color. *Rental:* WNET Media. *Sale:* WNET Media.

Androcles & the Lion. Jean Simmons, Victor Mature & Alan Young. Directed by Chester Erskine. 1952. RKO. 93 min. Sound. 16mm B&W. *Rental:* Janus Films.

Andromeda Strain, The. David Wayne, Kate Reid & Arthur Hill. Directed by Robert Wise. 1971. Universal. 130 min. Sound. 16mm Color. *Rental:* Swank Motion. *Rental:* Swank Motion, Videotape version.

Andy Hardy Comes Home. Mickey Rooney & Patricia Breslin. Directed by Howard Koch. 1958. MGM. 80 min. Sound. 16mm B&W. *Rental:* MGM United.

Andy Hardy Gets Spring Fever. Mickey Rooney & Ann Rutherford. Directed by W. S. Van Dyke. 1939. MGM. 85 min. Sound. 16mm B&W. *Rental:* MGM United.

Andy Hardy Meets a Debutante. Mickey Rooney & Judy Garland. Directed by George B. Seitz. 1940. MGM. 89 min. Sound. 16mm B&W. *Rental:* MGM United.

Andy Warhol. 1975. Blackwood. (Documentary). 53 min. Sound. 16mm Color. *Rental:* Blackwood Films. *Sale:* Blackwood Films.

Andy Warhol's Bad. Carroll Baker & Susan Tyrrell. Directed by Jed Johnson. 1976. New World. 110 min. Sound. 16mm Color. *Rental:* Films Inc.

Andy Warhol's Dracula. Udo Kier & Joe Dallesandro. Directed by Paul Morrissey. 1974. Bryanston. 106 min. Sound. 16mm Color. *Rental:* Swank Motion.

Andy Warhol's Frankenstein. Joe Dallesandro & Monique Van Vooren. Directed by Paul Morrissey. 1974. Bryanston. 95 min. Sound. 16mm Color. *Rental:* Swank Motion.

Angel. Cliff Gorman & Susan Tyrrell. Directed by Robert O'Neil. 1985. Warners. 92 min. Sound. 16mm Color. *Rental:* Swank Motion. *Rental:* Swank Motion, Videotape version.

Angel & Sinner. Trans. Title: Boule De Suif. Fr. 1946. France. (Cast Unlisted). 90 min. Sound. 16mm subtitles. *Rental:* Film Classics.

Angel & the Badman, The. John Wayne & Gail Russell. Directed by James Edward Grant. 1947. Republic. 101 min. Sound. 16mm *Rental:* Budget Films, Classic Film Mus, Em Gee Film Lib, Ivy Films, Kit Parker, Modern Sound & Natl Film Video. *Sale:* Festival Films & Glenn Photo. *Lease:* Rep Pic Film. *Sale:* Reel Images, Festival Films & Tamarelles French Film, Videotape version.

Angel Baby. George Hamilton & Salome Jens. Directed by Paul Wendkos. 1961. Allied Artists. 98 min. Sound. 16mm B&W. *Rental:* Hurlock Cine.

Angel City. Ralph Waite & Paul Winfield. Directed by Philip Leacock. 1980. CBS. 105 min. Sound. 16mm Color. *Rental:* Twyman Films.

Angel Comes to Brooklyn, An. Robert Duke & Charles Kemper. Directed by Leslie Goodwins. 1946. Republic. 70 min. Sound. 16mm B&W. *Rental:* Ivy Films.

Angel Face. Jean Simmons, Robert Mitchum & Mona Freeman. Directed by Otto Preminger. 1953. RKO. 90 min. Sound. 16mm B&W. *Rental:* Films Inc.

Angel From Texas, The. Eddie Albert & Jane Wyman. Directed by Ray Enright. 1940. Warners. 69 min. 16mm B&W. *Rental:* MGM United.

Angel in Ebony. 45 min. Sound. 16mm Color. *Rental:* Gospel Films.

Angel in Exile. John Carroll & Adele Mara. Directed by Philip Ford. 1948. Republic. 90 min. Sound. 16mm B&W. *Rental:* Ivy Films.

Angel in My Pocket. Andy Griffith. Directed by Alan Rafkin. 1968. Universal. 90 min. Sound. 16mm Color. *Rental:* Williams Films. *Rental:* Williams Films, Anamorphic Color version.

Angel Levine, The. Harry Belafonte & Zero Mostel. Directed by Jan Kadar. 1970. United Artists. 114 min. Sound. 16mm Color. *Rental:* MGM United, Welling Motion Pictures, Westcoast Films, Wholesome Film Ctr & Budget Films.

Angel on My Shoulder. Paul Muni, Claude Rains & Anne Baxter. Directed by Archie Mayo. 99 min. Sound. 16mm *Rental:* Budget Films, Classic Film Mus, Ivy Films, Natl Film Video, Video Comm & Welling Motion Pictures. *Sale:* Cinema Concepts, Reel Images & Morcraft Films. *Sale:* Morcraft Films, Super 8 version. *Sale:* Cinema Concepts, Ivy Films, Video Comm & Tamarelles French Film, Videotape version.

Angel on the Amazon, The: Drums Along the Amazon. George Brent, Vera Ralston & Brian Ahern. Directed by John H. Auer. 1948. Republic. 97 min. Sound. 16mm B&W. *Rental:* Ivy Films. *Sale:* Rep Pic Film.

Angel Passes over Brooklyn, An see Man Who Wagged His Tail.

Angel Street see Gaslight.

Angel Unchained. Don Stroud & Luke Askew. Directed by Lee Madden. 1970. American International. 86 min. Sound. 16mm Color. *Rental:* Budget Films & Westcoast Films.

Angel Wore Red, The. Ava Gardner & Dick Bogarde. Directed by Nunnally Johnson. 1960. MGM. 99 min. Sound. 16mm B&W. *Rental:* MGM United.

Angela. Dennis O'Keefe. Directed by Dennis O'Keefe. 1955. 80 min. 16mm *Rental:* A Twyman Pres.

Angela Davis: Portrait of a Revolutionary. Directed by Yolande Du Luart. 1971. New Yorker. (Documentary). 60 min. Sound. 16mm B&W. *Rental:* New Yorker Films.

Angela: Fireworks Womam. Quality X. 85 min. Videotape Color. *Sale:* Quality X Video.

Angele. Fernandel. Directed by Marcel Pagnol. Fr. 1934. France. Sound. 16mm B&W. subtitles. *Rental:* Images Film.

Angelitos Negros *see* Little Dark Angels.

Angelo. Renato Baldine. Directed by Francesco De Robertis. Ital. 1957. Italy. 95 min. Sound. 16mm B&W. subtitles. *Rental:* Inst Cinema.

Angelo My Love. Angelo Evans, Michael Evans & Steve Tsigonoff. Directed by Robert Duvall. 1983. 115 min. Sound. 16mm Color. *Rental:* New Yorker Films.

Angels Brigade. Jack Palance & Sylvia Anderson. Directed by Greydon Clark. 1979. Arista. 87 min. Sound. 16mm Color. *Rental:* Films Inc.

Angels Hard As They Come. Janet Wood, Scott Glenn & Charles Dierkop. Directed by Joe Viola. 1971. New World. 90 min. Sound. 16mm Color. *Rental:* Films Inc.

Angels in the Outfield. Paul Douglas & Janet Leigh. Directed by Clarence Brown. 1951. MGM. 99 min. Sound. 16mm B&W. *Rental:* MGM United.

Angels of Darkness. Linda Darnell & Anthony Quinn. Ital. 1957. Italy. 84 min. Sound. 16mm B&W. dubbed. *Rental:* Mogulls Films.

Angels on Wheels. Romy Schneider & Henri Duval. 1951. NTA. 88 min. Sound. 16mm Color. dubbed. *Rental:* Ivy Films.

Angels One-Five. Jack Hawkins & Dulcie Gray. Directed by George More O'Ferrall. 1952. Britain. 98 min. Sound. 16mm B&W. *Rental:* Mogulls Films.

Angels Over Broadway. Rita Hayworth & Dougals Fairbanks Jr. Directed by Ben Hecht. 1945. Columbia. 76 min. Sound. 16mm B&W. *Rental:* Cine Craft, Kit Parker, Swank Motion & Welling Motion Pictures.

Angels Wash Their Faces. Ronald Reagan & Ann Sheridan. Directed by Ray Enright. 1939. Warner. 86 min. Sound. 16mm B&W. *Rental:* MGM United.

Angels with Broken Wings. Sidney Blackmer. Directed by Bernard Vorhaus. 1941. Republic. 54 min. Sound. 16mm B&W. *Rental:* Ivy Films. *Sale:* Rep Pic Film.

Angels with Dirty Faces. James Cagney & Humphrey Bogart. Directed by Michael Curtiz. 1938. Warner. 97 min. Sound. 16mm B&W. *Rental:* MGM United.

Anger Magick Lantern Cycle. Kenneth Anger. 158 min. Sound. 16mm B&W Color. *Rental:* Filmmakers Coop.

Anger Within, The. 1982. 90 min. Sound. Videotape Color. *Rental:* Iowa Films.

Anges du Peche, Les. Renee Faure & Jany Holt. Directed by Robert Bresson. Fr. 1943. 80 min. Sound. 16mm B&W. subtitles Eng. *Rental:* Films Inc.

Angi Vera. Directed by Pal Gabor. Hungarian. 1979. 96 min. Sound. 16mm Color. subtitles. *Rental:* New Yorker Films.

Angiography As a Diagnostic Procedure. 1968. US Government. (Documentary, Kinescope). 90 min. Sound. 16mm B&W. *Sale:* Natl Av Ctr.

Angola: The People Have Chosen. Directed by Herbert Risz. 1975. Congo. (Documentary). 50 min. Sound. 16mm Color. *Rental:* Tricontinental Film. *Sale:* CA Newsreel.

Angola: Victory of Hope. Directed by Jose Massip. Span. 1977. Cuba. (Documentary). 72 min. Sound. 16mm Color. subtitles. *Rental:* Cinema Guild. *Sale:* Cinema Guild.

Angry Breed, The. Jan Sterling, James MacArthur & William Windom. Directed by David Commons. 1968. Commonwealth United. 89 min. Sound. 16mm Color. *Rental:* Films Inc, Ivy Films, Kerr Film, Rep Pic Film & Video Comm.

Angry God, The. Directed by Herbert Jean De Grasse. 1973. 67 min. Sound. 16mm Color. *Rental:* Canyon Cinema.

Angry Hills, The. Robert Mitchum & Stanley Baker. Directed by Robert Aldrich. 1959. MGM. 89 min. Sound. 16mm B&W. *Rental:* MGM United. *Rental:* MGM United, Anamorphic version.

Angry Joe Bass. Henry Bal & Holly Mershon. TV. 87 min. Sound. 16mm Color. *Rental:* Williams Films.

Angry Red Planet, The. Gerald Mohr, Les Tremayne & Nora Hayden. Directed by Ib Melchior. 1960. American International. 83 min. Sound. 16mm Color. dubbed. *Rental:* Budget Films, Westcoast Films, Wholesome Film Ctr & Willoughby Peer.

Angry Silence, The. Richard Attenborough & Pier Angeli. Directed by Guy Green. 1960. Britain. 95 min. Sound. 16mm B&W. *Rental:* Corinth Films.

Angry Voices of Watts, The. 1968. NBC. (Documentary). 50 min. Sound. 16mm B&W. *Rental:* Films Inc. *Sale:* Films Inc. *Sale:* Films Inc, Videotape version.

Animal Crackers. Marx Brothers. Directed by Victor Heerman. 1930. Paramount. (Sepia tone). 97 min. Sound. 16mm *Rental:* Swank Motion. *Sale:* Blackhawk Films, *Rental:* Swank Motion, Videotape version.

Animal Farm. Directed by John Halas & Joy Batchelor. 1955. Britain. (Animated). 75 min. Sound. 16mm Color. *Rental:* Bosco Films, Budget Films, Em Gee Film Lib, Images Film, Janus Films, Kit Parker, La Inst Res Ctr, Natl Film Video, Phoenix Films, Roas Films, Syracuse U Film, Liberty Co, U of IL Film, Viewfinders, Welling Motion Pictures, Westcoast Films & Wholesome Film Ctr. *Sale:* Natl Cinema, Phoenix Films, Reel Images & Texture Film. *Sale:* Phoenix Films, Tamarelles French Film & Texture Film, Videotape version.

Animal Imposters. 1983. Nova Series. (Documentary). 57 min. Sound. 16mm Color. *Rental:* U Cal Media.

Animal Kingdom, The. Ann Harding & Leslie Howard. Directed by Edward H. Griffith. 1932. RKO. 90 min. Sound. 16mm B&W. *Rental:* Classic Film Mus. *Sale:* Classic Film Mus.

Animal Olympians. 1981. Britain. (Documentary). 50 min. Sound. 16mm Color. *Rental:* Films Inc & Syracuse U Film. *Sale:* Films Inc. *Rental:* Films Inc, *Sale:* Films Inc, Videotape version.

Animals, The. Trans. Title: Les Animaux. Directed by Frederic Rossif. Fr. 1964. France. (Documentary). 80 min. Sound. 16mm narrated Eng. *Rental:* French Am Cul. *Rental:* Films Inc, Color version.

Animals, The. Directed by Myriam Alaux & Victor Schonfeld. Slick Pics. (Documentary). 136 min. Sound. 16mm Color. *Rental:* Cinema Guild.

Animals Nobody Loved, The. 59 min. Sound. 16mm Color. *Rental:* Natl Geog. *Sale:* Natl Geog. *Rental:* Syracuse U Film, *Sale:* Natl Geog, Videotape version.

Animation: The Beginning. Budget. (Animated Anthology). 50 min. Silent. 16mm B&W. *Rental:* Budget Films. *Sale:* Cinema Concepts.

Ann & Eve. Gio Petre & Marie Liljedahal. Directed by Arne Mattsson. 1970. Sweden. 89 min. Sound. 16mm Color. dubbed. *Rental:* Films Inc.

Anna & the King of Siam. Irene Dunne, Rex Harrison & Lee J. Cobb. Directed by John Cromwell. 1946. Fox. 140 min. Sound. 16mm B&W. *Rental:* Films Inc.

Anna Christie. Blanche Sweet & William Russell. Directed by John Griffith Wray. 1923. Ince. 75 min. Silent. 16mm B&W. *Rental:* Em Gee Film Lib & Museum Mod Art. *Sale:* Museum Mod Art.

Anna Christie. Greta Garbo & Marie Dressler. Directed by Clarence Brown. 1930. MGM. 90 min. Sound. 16mm B&W. *Rental:* MGM United.

Anna Karenina. Greta Garbo & Fredric March. Directed by Clarence Brown. 1935. MGM. 94 min. Sound. 16mm B&W. *Rental:* MGM United.

Anna Karenina. Tatyana Samoiliva. Directed by Alexander Zharkhi. Rus. 1968. Russia. 105 min. Sound. 16mm Color. dubbed. *Rental:* Ivy Films.

Anna Karenina. Rus. 1974. Russia. (Dance, anamorphic). 81 min. Sound. 16mm Color. subtitles. *Rental:* Corinth Films.

Anna Lucasta. Paulette Goddard & John Ireland. Directed by Irving Rapper. 1949. Columbia. 86 min. Sound. 16mm B&W. *Rental:* Bosco Films.

Annabel Takes a Tour. Lucille Ball & Jack Oakie. Directed by Lew Landers. 1939. 67 min. Sound. 16mm *Rental:* RKO General Pics.

Annabelle Lee. 1924. American. (Cast unlisted). 65 min. Silent. 16mm B&W. *Rental:* Film Classics. *Sale:* Film Classics.

Annapolis: Branded a Coward. Johnny Mack Brown. Directed by Christy Cabanne. 1928. Pathe. 60 min. Silent. 16mm B&W. *Rental:* Film Classics & Mogulls Films. *Sale:* Film Classics. *Sale:* Film Classics, Silent 8mm version.

Annapolis Salute. Van Heflin & Marsha Hunt. Directed by Christy Cabanne. 1935. RKO. 65 min. Sound. 16mm Color. *Rental:* RKO General Pics.

Annapolis Story, The: The Blue & the Gold. Orig. Title: Blue & the Gold, The. John Derek & Diana Lynn. Directed by Don Siegel. 1955. Allied Artists. 81 min. Sound. 16mm Color. *Rental:* Hurlock Cine.

Annapurna. Directed by Marcel Ichac. Fr. 1952. France. (Documentary). 57 min. Sound. 16mm B&W. narrated Eng. *Rental:* Films Inc & Macmillan Films. *Sale:* Macmillan Films. *Rental:* Macmillan Films, *Sale:* Macmillan Films, Color version.

Anne Boleyn. Keith Michell. 1976. Britain. 90 min. Videotape Color. *Rental:* Films Inc. *Sale:* Films Inc.

Anne Hutchinson. Wendy Hiller. Directed by Cyril Ritchard. (Profiles in Courage Ser.). 1965. Saudek. 50 min. Sound. 16mm B&W. *Rental:* BYU Media, Mass Media, Syracuse U Film & U Mich Media. *Sale:* IQ Film. *Sale:* IQ Film, Spanish Dubbed version.

Anne Of Cleves. Keith Michell. 1976. Britain. 90 min. Videotape Color. *Rental:* Films Inc. *Sale:* Films Inc.

Anne of Green Gables. Anne Shirley & Tom Brown. Directed by George Nicholls Jr. 1935. RKO. 79 min. Sound. 16mm *Rental:* RKO General Pics.

Anne of the Thousand Days. Richard Burton & Genevieve Bujold. Directed by Charles Jarrott. 1969. Universal. 145 min. Sound. 16mm Color. *Rental:* Swank Motion. *Rental:* Swank Motion, Anamorphic version.

Anne of Windy Poplars. Anne Shirley. Directed by Jack Hively. 1940. RKO. 86 min. Sound. 16mm B&W. *Rental:* Films Inc.

Annee Derniere a Marienbad, L' *see* Last Year at Marienbad.

Annie. Albert Finney, Carol Burnett & Aileen Quinn. Directed by John Huston. 1985. Columbia. 128 min. Sound. 16mm Color. *Rental:* Swank Motion. *Rental:* Swank Motion, Videotape version.

Annie Hall. Woody Allen & Diane Keaton. Directed by Woody Allen. 1978. United Artists. 93 min. Sound. 16mm Color. *Rental:* MGM United. *Rental:* MGM United, Videotape version.

Annie Oakley. Barbara Stanwyck & Preston Foster. Directed by George Stevens. 1935. RKO. 88 min. Sound. 16mm B&W. *Rental:* Films Inc. *Sale:* Tamarelles French Film, Videotape version.

Anniversary, The. Bette Davis. Directed by Roy Ward Baker. 1968. Britain. 95 min. Sound. 16mm Color. *Rental:* Films Inc.

Anonymous Venetian, The. Tony Musante & Florinda Bolkan. Directed by Enrico Salerno. 1970. Italy. 92 min. Sound. 16mm Color. *Rental:* Hurlock Cine.

Anoop & the Elephant. Jimmy Edwards. Directed by David Eady. 1974. Britain. 45 min. Sound. 16mm Color. *Rental:* Janus Films. *Sale:* Janus Films & Sterling Ed Film.

Another Dawn. Errol Flynn & Kay Francis. Directed by William Dieterle. 1937. Warners. 73 min. Sound. 16mm B&W. *Rental:* MGM United.

Another Face. Brian Donlevy & Phyllis Brooks. Directed by Wesley Ruggles. 1936. RKO. 70 min. Sound. 16mm *Rental:* RKO General Pics.

Another Language. Helen Hayes & Robert Montgomery. Directed by Edward H. Griffith. 1936. MGM. 77 min. Sound. 16mm B&W. *Rental:* MGM United.

Another Man, Another Chance. James Caan & Genevieve Bujold. Directed by Claude Lelouch. 1977. United Artists. 129 min. Sound. 16mm Color. *Rental:* MGM United.

Another Man's Boots. Francis Ford. Directed by William James Craft. 1922. Aywon. 60 min. Silent. 8mm B&W. *Rental:* Mogulls Films.

Another Part of the Forest. Fredric March & Ann Blyth. Directed by Michael Gordon. 1948. Universal. 108 min. Sound. 16mm B&W. *Rental:* Swank Motion.

Another Thin Man. William Powell & Myrna Loy. Directed by W. S. Van Dyke. 1939. MGM. 102 min. Sound. 16mm B&W. *Rental:* MGM United.

Another Time, Another Place. Lana Turner, Sean Connery & Barry Sullivan. Directed by Lewis Allen. 1958. Paramount. 95 min. Sound. 16mm *Rental:* Films Inc.

Ansel Adams: Photographer. Directed by John Huszar. 1981. (Documentary). 60 min. Sound. 16mm Color. *Rental:* A Cantor. *Sale:* A Cantor.

Antarctic Crossing. 1959. Britain. (Documentary). 49 min. Sound. 16mm Color. *Rental:* Budget Films & Film Images. *Lease:* Film Images.

Antarctica. 1978. Indiana U. (Documentary). 57 min. Sound. 16mm Color. *Rental:* Iowa Films, Indiana Av Ctr & U Cal Media. *Sale:* Indiana Av Ctr.

Antarctica: Ninety Degrees Below. 1976. 58 min. Sound. Videotape *Rental:* PBS Video. *Sale:* PBS Video.

Anthology of Italian Cinema: 1896-1926. Italy. (Anthology). 152 min. Sound. 16mm B&W. narrated Eng. *Rental:* Museum Mod Art.

Anthology of Italian Cinema: 1929-1943. Italy. (Anthology). 189 min. Sound. 16mm B&W. narrated English. *Rental:* Museum Mod Art.

Anthony Adverse. Fredric March & Olivia De Havilland. Directed by Mervyn Leroy. 1936. Warners. 141 min. Sound. 16mm B&W. *Rental:* MGM United.

Anthony & Cleopatra. 1913. Italy. 61 min. Silent. 16mm B&W. *Rental:* A Twyman Pres.

Anthony Burgess's Rome. 1978. Learning Corp.. (Documentary). 50 min. Sound. 16mm Color. *Rental:* Kent St U Film & Learning Corp Am. *Sale:* Learning Corp Am.

Anthropology on Trial. 1983. Nova. (Documentary). 57 min. Sound. 16mm Color. *Rental:* U Cal Media & Time-Life Multimedia.

Antigone. Irene Papas. Directed by George Tzavellas. Gr. 1962. Greece. 88 min. Sound. 16mm B&W. subtitles. *Rental:* Macmillan Films. *Lease:* Macmillan Films.

Antonia, a Portrait of a Woman. Directed by Judy Collins & Jill Godmilow. 1974. Phoenix. (Documentary). 58 min. Sound. 16mm Color. *Rental:* Budget Films, Images Film, Phoenix Films, Syracuse U Film, U Cal Media & U Mich Media. *Sale:* Phoenix Films. *Sale:* Phoenix Films, Videotape version.

Antonio. 1973. Saga. (Cast unlisted). 81 min. Sound. 16mm Color. *Rental:* Modern Sound & Welling Motion Pictures. *Sale:* Salz Ent.

Antonio das Mortes. Mauricio Do Valle & Odete Lara. Directed by Glauber Rocha. 1969. Brazil. 100 min. Sound. 16mm Color. subtitles. *Rental:* Grove. *Sale:* Grove.

Antony & Cleopatra. Antonio Novelli & Josephine Trimble. 1913. Italy. 61 min. Silent. 16mm B&W. *Rental:* Em Gee Film Lib & Film Classics. *Sale:* Morcraft Films. *Sale:* Film Classics & Morcraft Films, Silent 8mm version. *Rental:* Film Classics, Videotape version.

Antony & Cleopatra. Jane Lapotaire & Colin Blakely. 1980. Britain. 171 min. Videotape Color. *Rental:* Iowa Films & Time-Life Multimedia. *Sale:* Time-Life Multimedia.

Anxiety: The Endless Crisis. 1975. WNET. (Documentary). 60 min. Sound. 16mm Color. *Rental:* Indiana Av Ctr, Iowa Films & Syracuse U Film. *Sale:* Indiana Av Ctr.

Any Gun Can Play. Trans. Title: Vado, l'Ammazzo E Torno. Gilbert Roland & Edd Byrnes. Directed by Enzo G. Castellari. Ital. 1968. Italy. 92 min. Sound. 16mm Color. dubbed. *Rental:* Budget Films, Kerr Film & Video Comm.

Any Man's Woman: No Escape. Trans. Title: La Piege. 1959. France. (Cast unlisted). 98 min. Sound. 16mm B&W. dubbed. *Rental:* Ivy Films.

Any Number Can Play. Clark Gable & Alexis Smith. Directed by Mervyn Leroy. 1949. MGM. 112 min. Sound. 16mm B&W. *Rental:* MGM United.

Any Which Way You Can. Clint Eastwood, Sondra Locke & Ruth Gordon. Directed by Buddy Van Horn. 115 min. Sound. 16mm Color. *Rental:* Swank Motion. *Rental:* Swank Motion, Videotape version.

Anybody's Child: Dyslexia Defined. 1975. MPC. (Documentary). 48 min. Sound. 16mm Color. *Rental:* U Cal Media.

Anyone Can Play. Trans. Title: Dolci Signore, Le. David Hemmings, Michael York & Virna Lisi. Directed by Luigi Zampa. 1968. Italy. (Anamorphic). 122 min. Sound. 16mm Color. dubbed. *Rental:* Films Inc.

Anyplace but Here. 1978. CBS. (Documentary). 50 min. Sound. 16mm Color. *Rental:* Iowa Films, Syracuse U Film, U Cal Media & U Mich Media. *Sale:* Carousel Films. *Sale:* Carousel Films, Videotape version.

Anything for a Thrill. Frankie Darro & Kane Richmond. Directed by Leslie Goodwins. 1937. Ambassador. 65 min. Sound. 16mm B&W. *Sale:* Blackhawk Films. *Sale:* Blackhawk Films, Super 8 Sound version.

Anything Goes. Bing Crosby, Jeanmaire & Donald O'Connor. Directed by Robert Lewis. 1956. Paramount. 106 min. Sound. 16mm Color. *Rental:* Films Inc.

Anything Goes. Ethel Merman, Frank Sinatra & Bert Lahr. 1956. NBC. (Kinescope). 60 min. Sound. 16mm *Sale:* Reel Images. *Sale:* Reel Images, Videotape version. *Sale:* Reel Images, Super 8 Sound version.

Anzio. Robert Mitchum, Peter Falk & Earl Holliman. Directed by Edward Dmytryk. 1968. Columbia. 124 min. Sound. 16mm Color. *Rental:* Films Inc, Inst Cinema, Modern Sound, Roas Films & Westcoast Films.

Apache, The. Burt Lancaster, Jean Peters & Charles Bronson. Directed by Robert Aldrich. 1954. United Artists. 68 min. Sound. 16mm Color. *Rental:* MGM United & Westcoast Films. *Rental:* MGM United, Videotape version.

Apache Ambush. Bill Williams & Tex Ritter. Directed by Fred F. Sears. 1955. Columbia. 68 min. Sound. 16mm B&W. *Rental:* Inst Cinema.

Apache Chief. Alan Curtis, Tom Neal & Russell Hayden. Directed by Frank McDonald. 1949. Lippert. 75 min. Sound. 16mm B&W. *Rental:* Budget Films & Westcoast Films.

Apache Gold. Lex Barker. Directed by Harold Reinl. 80 min. Sound. 16mm Color. *Rental:* Welling Motion Pictures.

Apache Kid, The. Don Barry & Lynn Merrick. Directed by George Sherman. 1941. Republic. 54 min. Sound. 16mm B&W. *Rental:* Ivy Films.

Apache Rose. Roy Rogers & Dale Evans. Directed by William Witney. 1947. Republic. 54 min. Sound. 16mm B&W. *Rental:* Ivy Films. *Sale:* Natl Cinema, Rep Pic Film & Nostalgia Merchant, Videotape version.

Apache Territory. Rory Calhoun & Barbara Bates. Directed by Ray Nazarro. 1958. Columbia. 85 min. Sound. 16mm Color. *Rental:* Inst Cinema, Modern Sound, Film Ctr DC & Westcoast Films.

Apache Trail, The. Donna Reed & Lloyd Nolan. Directed by Richard Thorpe. 1942. MGM. 66 min. Sound. 16mm B&W. *Rental:* MGM United.

Apache Uprising. Rory Calhoun, Corinne Calvet & John Russell. Directed by R. G. Springsteen. 1966. Paramount. 90 min. Sound. 16mm Color. *Rental:* Films Inc. *Rental:* Films Inc, Anamorphic version.

Apache War Smoke. Gilbert Roland & Glenda Farrell. Directed by Harold Kress. 1952. MGM. 67 min. Sound. 16mm B&W. *Rental:* MGM United.

Apache Warrior. Keith Larsen & Jim Davis. Directed by Elmo Williams. 1957. Fox. (Anamorphic). 73 min. Sound. 16mm B&W. *Rental:* Ivy Films. *Sale:* Rep Pic Film.

Apache Woman. Lloyd Bridges & Joan Taylor. Directed by Roger Corman. 1955. American International. 83 min. Sound. 16mm Color. *Rental:* Swank Motion.

Apache's Last Battle, The. Lex Barker & Guy Madison. 1966. Germany. 108 min. Sound. 16mm Color. dubbed. *Rental:* Westcoast Films.

Aparajito. Pinaki Sen Gupta & Kanu Bannerjee. Directed by Satyajit Ray. Bengali. 1956. Bengal. 108 min. Sound. 16mm B&W. subtitles Eng. *Rental:* Budget Films & Films Inc.

Apartment, The. Jack Lemmon & Shirley MacLaine. Directed by Billy Wilder. 1960. United Artists. 125 min. Sound. 16mm B&W. *Rental:* MGM United. *Rental:* MGM United, Videotape version.

Apartment for Peggy. Jeanne Crain & William Holden. Directed by George Seaton. 1948. Fox. 99 min. Sound. 16mm B&W. *Rental:* Films Inc.

Ape, The. Boris Karloff & Maris Wrixon. Directed by William Nigh. 1940. Monogram. 62 min. Sound. 16mm B&W. *Sale:* Cinema Concepts.

Ape Man, The. Orig. Title: Lock Your Doors. Bela Lugosi, Wallace Ford & Louise Currie. Directed by William Beaudine. 1943. Monogram. 64 min. Sound. 16mm *Rental:* Budget Films, Classic Film Mus, Films Inc, Ivy Films, Mogulls Films, Video Comm & Wholesome Film Ctr. *Sale:* Cinema Concepts. *Rental:* Vidamerica & Video Comm, Videotape version.

Ape Man of the Jungle. Ralph Hudson & Rita Clein. Directed by Carlos Velo. 1964. American International. 63 min. Sound. 16mm B&W. dubbed. *Rental:* Films Inc.

Ape Woman, The. Ugo Tognazzi & Annie Girardot. Directed by Marco Ferreri. Ital. 1964. Embassy. 92 min. Sound. 16mm B&W. subtitles. *Rental:* Films Inc.

Apocalypse Now. Martin Sheen & Robert Duvall. Directed by Francis Ford Coppola. 1979. United Artists. 153 min. Sound. 16mm Color. *Rental:* MGM United. *Rental:* MGM United, Anamorphic version.

Apocalypse Three Sixteen. Myron van Brundt. Directed by Martin Chariot. 1967. Martin Charlot. Sound. 16mm B&W. *Rental:* Canyon Cinema.

Apollo & Dionysus: Two Fundamental Human Alternatives. 1977. Miami-Dade. (Documentary). 60 min. Sound. Videotape Color. *Rental:* Films Inc. *Sale:* Films Inc.

Apology for Murder. Hugh Beaumont & Ann Savage. Directed by Sam Newfield. 1945. PRC. 66 min. Sound. 16mm B&W. *Sale:* Classics Assoc NY.

Appalachia: Rich Land, Poor People. 1969. NET. (Documentary). 59 min. Sound. 16mm B&W. *Rental:* Iowa Films, Indiana AV Ctr, New Time Films & U Cal Media. *Sale:* Indiana Av Ctr & New Time Films.

Appaloosa, The. Marlon Brando & Anjanette Comer. Directed by Sidney J. Furie. 1966. Universal. 98 min. Sound. 16mm Color. *Rental:* Twyman Films.

Appalshop Show, The. Directed by Bill Richardson & Herb E. Smith. 1977. Appalshop. (Anthology). 90 min. Sound. 16mm Color. *Rental:* Appals.

Apparition, The. Directed by Larry Jordan. 1976. 50 min. Sound. 16mm Color. *Rental:* Canyon Cinema.

Appearance & Reality. Directed by Michael Chanan. 1972. Oxford U.. (Interviews). 60 min. Sound. 16mm Color. *Rental:* New Yorker Films.

Applause. Helen Morgan. Directed by Rouben Mamoulian. 1929. Paramount. 80 min. Sound. 16mm B&W. *Rental:* Museum Mod Art & Swank Motion.

Apple Dumpling Gang, The. Don Knotts, Tim Conway & Bill Bixby. Directed by Norman Tokar. 1975. Disney. 101 min. Sound. 16mm Color. *Rental:* Bosco Films, Buchan Pic, Cine Craft, Disney Prod, Elliot Film Co, Film Ctr DC, Films Inc, MGM United, Newman Film Lib, Roas Films, Swank Motion, Twyman Films, Welling Motion Pictures, Westcoast Films & Williams Films. *Rental:* Williams Films, Videotape version.

Apple Dumpling Gang Rides Again, The. Tim Conway, Don Knotts & Tim Matheson. Directed by Vincent McEveety. 1979. Disney. 89 min. Sound. 16mm Color. *Rental:* Bosco Films, Disney Prod, Film Ctr DC, Film Pres, Films Inc, MGM United, Modern Sound, Roas Films, Swank Motion, Twyman Films, U of IL Film, Welling Motion Pictures, Westcoast Films & Williams Films. *Rental:* Williams Films, Videotape version.

Apple War, The. Max Von Sydow. Directed by Tage Danielsson. Swed. 1973. Sweden. 102 min. Sound. 16mm Color. subtitles. *Rental:* New Line Cinema & Specialty Films.

Appointment, The. Omar Sharif & Anouk Aimee. Directed by Sidney Lumet. 1970. MGM. 136 min. Sound. 16mm Color. *Rental:* MGM United.

Appointment in Berlin. George Sanders & Gale Sondergaard. Directed by Alfred E. Green. 1943. Columbia. 77 min. Sound. 16mm B&W. *Rental:* Kit Parker.

Appointment in Honduras. Ann Sheridan & Glenn Ford. Directed by Jacques Tourneur. 1953. RKO. 79 min. Sound. Super 8 Color. *Sale:* Cinema Concepts.

Appointment in Tokyo. 1950. U.S. Government. (Documentary). 56 min. Sound. 16mm B&W. *Rental:* Natl AV Ctr.

Appointment with Crime. William Hartnell & Herbert Lom. Directed by John Harlow. 1947. Britain. 91 min. Sound. 16mm B&W. *Rental:* Ivy Films.

Appointment with Danger. Alan Ladd, Phyllis Calvert & Paul Stewart. Directed by Lewis Allen. 1951. Paramount. 89 min. Sound. 16mm B&W. *Rental:* Films Inc.

Appointment with Murder. John Calvert. Directed by Jack Bernhard. 1948. Film Classics. 72 min. Sound. 16mm B&W. *Sale:* Classics Assoc NY.

Appointment with Venus *see* Island Rescue.

Apprenti Salaud, L. Robert Lamoureaux & Christine Dojoux. Directed by Michel Deville. Fr. France. 85 min. Sound. 16mm Color. subtitles. *Rental:* French Am Cul.

Apprenticeship of Duddy Kravitz, The. Richard Dreyfuss, Jack Warden & Randy Quaid. Directed by Ted Kotcheff. 1974. Canada. 121 min. Sound. 16mm Color. *Rental:* Films Inc.

Approach to Inpatient & Outpatient Services in a VA Hospital, An: Long Version. 1982. 60 min. Sound. Videotape *Sale:* Natl AV Ctr.

April Fool. Alex Carr, Nat Carr & Baby Peggy. Directed by Nat Ross. 1926. Chadwick. 70 min. Silent. 16mm B&W. *Rental:* Em Gee Film Lib & Mogulls Films.

April Fools, The. Jack Lemmon & Catherine Deneuve. Directed by Stuart Rosenberg. 1969. National General. 98 min. Sound. 16mm Color. *Rental:* Swank Motion.

April is the End of Summer. 1967. NET. (Documentary). 54 min. Sound. 16mm B&W. *Rental:* Indiana AV Ctr. *Lease:* Indiana AV Ctr.

April Love. Pat Boone & Shirley Jones. Directed by Henry Levin. 1957. Fox. (Anamorphic). 99 min. Sound. 16mm Color. *Rental:* Films Inc.

April Romance. Richard Tauber. Directed by Paul L. Stein. 1937. MGM. 80 min. Sound. 16mm B&W. *Rental:* Mogulls Films.

April Showers. Jack Carson & Ann Sothern. Directed by James V. Kern. 1948. Warners. 94 min. Sound. 16mm B&W. *Rental:* MGM United.

Apu Trilogy, The *see* World of Apu.

Arabella. Virna Lisi & Margaret Rutherford. Directed by Mauro Bolognini. 1969. Italy. 91 min. Sound. 16mm Color. *Rental:* Swank Motion.

Arabesque. Gregory Peck & Sophia Loren. Directed by Stanley Donen. 1966. Universal. 118 min. Sound. 16mm Color. *Rental:* Williams Films. *Rental:* Williams Films, Anamorphic Color version.

Arabian Adventure. Christopher Lee & Milo O'Shea. Directed by Kevin Connor. 1979. Britain. 98 min. Sound. 16mm Color. *Rental:* Swank Motion.

Arabian Nights. Jon Hall, Sabu & Maria Montez. Directed by John Rawlins. 1942. Universal. 86 min. Sound. 16mm Color. *Rental:* Swank Motion.

Arabian Nights. Ninette Davoli, Franco Citti & Ines Pellegrini. 1974. 136 min. Sound. 35mm Color. *Rental:* MGM United.

Aranyer Din Ratri *see* Days & Nights in the Forest.

Araucanians of Ruca Choroy. Directed by Jorge Preloran. 1974. Argentina. (Documentary). 50 min. Sound. 16mm Color. *Rental:* Phoenix Films. *Sale:* Phoenix Films. *Sale:* Phoenix Films, Videotape version.

Arbitration: The Truth of the Matter. 48 min. Sound. 16mm Color. *Rental:* Iowa Films.

Arch of Triumph. Ingrid Bergman, Charles Boyer & Charles Laughton. Directed by Lewis Milestone. 1948. United Artists. 120 min. Sound. 16mm B&W. *Rental:* Ivy Films. *Lease:* Rep Pic Film.

Arctic Flight. Wayne Morris & Lola Albright. Directed by Lew Landers. 1952. Monogram. 78 min. Sound. 16mm B&W. *Rental:* Hurlock Cine.

Arctic Four. Directed by James de B. Domville. 1975. Canada. (Documentary). 58 min. Sound. 16mm Color. *Rental:* Natl Film CN. *Sale:* Natl Film CN.

Arctic Fury. Del Cambre & Eve Miller. Directed by Norman Dawn. 1950. RKO. (Documentary). 61 min. Sound. 16mm *Rental:* RKO General Pics.

Are Husbands Necessary? Betty Field & Ray Milland. Directed by Norman Taurog. 1942. Paramount. 79 min. Sound. 16mm B&W. *Rental:* Swank Motion.

Are Parents People? Betty Bronson, Florence Vidor & Adolphe Menjou. Directed by Mal St. Clair. 1925. Paramount. 60 min. Silent. 16mm B&W. *Rental:* Em Gee Film Lib & Willoughby Peer, Silent 8mm version.

Are These Our Children? Ben Alexander & Rochelle Hudson. Directed by Wesley Ruggles. 1932. RKO. 83 min. Sound. 16mm *Rental:* RKO General Pics.

Are These Our Parents? Helen Vinson & Lyle Talbot. Directed by William Nigh. 1944. Monogram. 79 min. Sound. 16mm B&W. *Rental:* Hurlock Cine.

Are We Making a Good Peace? 1975. Britain. (Documentary). 52 min. Sound. 16mm Color. *Rental:* U Of IL Film. *Rental:* U Of IL Film, Videotape version.

Are You Doing This for Me, Doctor, or am I Doing It for You? 1975. Britain. (Documentary). 52 min. Sound. 16mm Color. *Rental:* Films Inc, Syracuse U Film & U Mich Media. *Sale:* Films Inc. *Rental:* Films Inc, *Sale:* Films Inc, Videotape version.

Are You Listening? Directed by Harry Beaumont. 1932. MGM. (Cast unlisted). 80 min. Sound. 16mm B&W. *Rental:* MGM United.

Are You Now or Have You Ever Been? Liza Minnelli. 1978. Cinema Concepts. 100 min. Videotape Color. *Sale:* Cinema Concepts.

Arena. Gig Young & Jean Hagen. Directed by Richard Fleischer. 1953. MGM. 71 min. Sound. 16mm Color. *Rental:* MGM United.

Arena, The. Pam Grier. Directed by Steve Carver. 1975. New World. 85 min. Sound. 16mm Color. *Rental:* Films Inc.

Argentine Nights. The Andrews Sisters & The Ritz Brothers. Directed by Albert S. Rogell. 1940. Universal. 75 min. Sound. 16mm B&W. *Rental:* Swank Motion.

Argyle Secrets, The. William Gargan & Marjorie Lord. Directed by Cy Endfield. 1948. Film Classics. 63 min. Sound. 16mm B&W. *Rental:* Charard Motion Pics.

Aria for an Athlete. Directed by Filip Bajon. Pol. 1980. 108 min. Sound. 16mm Color. subtitles Eng. *Rental:* New Yorker Films.

Ariane. Elizabeth Bergner & Percy Marmont. Directed by Paul Czinner. 1931. Germany. 90 min. Sound. 16mm B&W. subtitles. *Rental:* Janus Films.

Arise, My Love. Claudette Colbert & Ray Milland. Directed by Mitchell Leisen. 1940. Paramount. 110 min. Sound. 16mm B&W. *Rental:* Swank Motion.

Aristocats, The. Directed by Wolfgang Reitherman. 1970. Disney. (Animated). 78 min. Sound. 16mm Color. *Rental:* Disney Prod, Film Ctr DC & Films Inc.

Aristophanes: Women In Power. 1976. Films for the Humanities. (Documentary). 60 min. Sound. 16mm Color. *Rental:* Films Human & U Of IL Film. *Sale:* Films Human.

Arizona. William Holden & Jean Arthur. Directed by Wesley Ruggles. 1940. Columbia. 130 min. Sound. 16mm B&W. *Rental:* Films Inc & Roas Films. *Rental:* Bosco Films, 122 mins. version.

Arizona Bushwackers. Howard Keel, Scott Brady & Yvonne De Carlo. Directed by Lesley Selander. 1968. Paramount. (Anamorphic). 86 min. Sound. 16mm Color. *Rental:* Films Inc.

Arizona Cowboy. Rex Allen & Teala Loring. Directed by R. G. Springsteen. 1949. Republic. 67 min. Sound. 16mm B&W. *Rental:* Ivy Films. *Sale:* Rep Pic Film.

Arizona Days. Bob Custer. Directed by J. P. McGowan. 1929. Syndicate. 50 min. Silent. Videotape B&W. *Sale:* Video Comm.

Arizona Days. Tex Ritter. Directed by John English. 1937. Grand National. 60 min. Sound. 16mm B&W. *Sale:* Natl Cinema. *Sale:* Reel Images & Video Comm, Videotape version.

Arizona Frontier. Tex Ritter. Directed by Al Herman. 1940. Monogram. 55 min. Sound. 16mm B&W. *Rental:* Hurlock Cine.

Arizona Gang Busters. Orig. Title: Gang Busters. Tim McCoy. Directed by Peter Stewart. 1940. PRC. 57 min. Sound. 16mm B&W. *Rental:* Film Classics.

Arizona Gunfighter. Bob Steele. Directed by Sam Newfield. 1937. Republic. 60 min. Sound. 16mm B&W. *Rental:* Ivy Films & Mogulls Films.

Arizona Kid, The. Roy Rogers & Gabby Hayes. Directed by Joseph Kane. 1939. Republic. 54 min. Sound. 16mm B&W. *Rental:* Ivy Films. *Sale:* Rep Pic Film.

Arizona Legion. Chill Wills & George O'Brien. Directed by David Howard. 1939. RKO. 58 min. Sound. 16mm *Rental:* RKO General Pics.

Arizona Manhunt. Michael Chapin & Eilene Janssen. Directed by Fred C. Brannon. 1951. Republic. 55 min. Sound. 16mm B&W. *Rental:* Ivy Films. *Sale:* Rep Pic Film.

Arizona Raiders. Buster Crabbe & Marsha Hunt. Directed by James Hogan. 1936. Paramount. 54 min. Sound. 16mm B&W. *Rental:* Budget Films & Video Comm. *Sale:* Video Comm, Videotape version.

Arizona Ranger. Tim Holt & Steve Brodie. Directed by John Rawlins. 1948. RKO. 63 min. Sound. 16mm *Rental:* Films Inc.

Arizona Stagecoach. Range Busters. Directed by S. Roy Luby. 1942. Monogram. 60 min. Sound. 16mm B&W. *Sale:* Morcraft Films.

Arizona Territory. Whip Wilson. Directed by Wallace Fox. 1950. Monogram. 56 min. Sound. 16mm B&W. *Rental:* Hurlock Cine.

Arizona Terror. Ken Maynard. Directed by Phil Rosen. 1931. Tiffany. 60 min. Videotape B&W. *Sale:* Video Comm.

Arizona Terrors. Don Barry & Lynn Merrick. Directed by George Sherman. 1941. Republic. 56 min. Sound. 16mm B&W. *Rental:* Ivy Films.

Arizona Whirlwind. Bob Steele. Directed by Robert Tansey. 1944. Monogram. 60 min. Sound. 16mm B&W. *Rental:* Budget Films, MGM United & Mogulls Films.

Arizonian, The. Margot Grahame & Steve Brodie. Directed by Charles Vidor. 1935. RKO. 75 min. Sound. 16mm *Rental:* RKO General Pics.

Ark II. Filmation. 66 min. Sound. 16mm Color. *Rental:* Williams Films.

Arkansas Judge. Spring Byington & Pauline Moore. Directed by Frank McDonald. 1941. Republic. 72 min. Sound. 16mm B&W. *Rental:* Ivy Films.

Arlo's Gang: Arlo Guthrie, Steve Goodman & Hoyt Axton. 1980. Verve. (Concert). 58 min. Videotape Color. *Rental:* Films Inc.

Arming of the Earth, The. 58 min. Sound. Videotape *Rental:* PBS Video. *Sale:* PBS Video.

Armored Attack *see* North Star.

Armored Car Robbery. Charles McGraw & Adele Jergens. Directed by Richard Fleischer. 1950. RKO. 68 min. Sound. 16mm B&W. *Rental:* Films Inc.

Armored Command. Howard Keel & Tina Louise. Directed by Byron Haskin. 1961. Allied Artists. 99 min. Sound. 16mm B&W. *Rental:* Hurlock Cine.

Arms & the Woman *see* Mr. Winkle Goes to War.

Arms & the Man: Helden. Orig. Title: Helden. O. W. Fischer, Lisolette Pulver & Kurt Kasznar. Directed by Franz Peter Wirth. 1958. Germany. 93 min. Sound. 16mm Color. dubbed. *Rental:* Films Inc.

Army Bound. Stanley Clements. Directed by Paul Landres. 1952. Monogram. 61 min. Sound. 16mm B&W. *Sale:* Reel Images. *Rental:* Hurlock Cine.

Army Camp, An. Directed by Joris Ivens & Marceline Loridan. 1980. Cinema Perspectives. (Documentary). 57 min. Sound. 16mm Color. *Rental:* Cinema Arts.

Army Girl. Orig. Title: Last of the Cavalry, The. Preston Foster & Neil Hamilton. Directed by George Nicholls Jr. 1938. Republic. 80 min. Sound. 16mm B&W. *Rental:* Ivy Films. *Sale:* Rep Pic Film.

Army-Navy Screen Magazine Highlights. 1945. US Government. (Documentary). 52 min. Sound. 16mm B&W. *Sale:* Natl AV Ctr. *Sale:* Natl AV Ctr, videotape version.

Army of Lovers. Directed by Rosa Von Praunheim. 1980. (Documentary). 90 min. Sound. 16mm Color. *Rental:* Canyon Cinema.

Army Surgeon. Kent Taylor & Jane Wyatt. Directed by Edward Sutherland. 1943. RKO. 63 min. Sound. 16mm *Rental:* RKO General Pics.

Army Wives. Elyse Knox & Rick Vallin. Directed by Phil Rosen. 1945. Monogram. 68 min. Sound. 16mm B&W. *Rental:* Hurlock Cine.

Arnelo Affair, The. George Murphy & John Hodiak. Directed by Arch Oboler. 1947. MGM. 87 min. Sound. 16mm B&W. *Rental:* MGM United.

Arnold. Stella Stevens & Roddy McDowall. Directed by George Fenady. 1974. Cinerama. 95 min. Sound. 16mm Color. *Rental:* Swank Motion.

Around the World. Kay Kayser. Directed by Allan Dwan. 1943. RKO. 81 min. Sound. 16mm B&W. *Rental:* Films Inc.

Around the World in 80 Days. David Niven, Cantinflas & Shirley MacLaine. Directed by Michael Anderson. Rel. 1956. United Artists. 140 min. Sound. 16mm Color. *Rental:* Swank Motion.

Around the World in Eighty Minutes. Douglas Fairbanks. Directed by Victor Fleming & Douglas Fairbanks. 1931. United Artists. 78 min. Sound. 16mm B&W. *Rental:* Museum Mod Art.

Around the World Under the Sea. Orig. Title: Longest Hunt, The. Lloyd Bridges & Shirley Eaton. Directed by Andrew Marton. 1966. MGM. 110 min. Sound. 16mm Color. *Rental:* Ivy Films & MGM United. *Sale:* Rep Pic Film.

Arousers, The. Tab Hunter & Cheri Latimer. Directed by Curtis Hanson. 1976. New World. 87 min. Sound. 16mm Color. *Rental:* Films Inc.

Arrangement, The. Kirk Douglas, Deborah Kerr & Faye Dunaway. Directed by Elia Kazan. 1969. Warners. 126 min. Sound. 16mm Color. *Rental:* Films Inc, Twyman Films, Welling Motion, Williams Films & Willoughby Peer.

Arrest Bulldog Drummmond. John Howard & Heather Angel. Directed by James Hogan. 1939. United Artists. 57 min. Sound. 16mm B&W. *Rental:* Budget Films.

Arrestation d'Arsene Lupin, Le. George Descrieres. Directed by Jean-Pierre Decourt. Fr. 1971. France. 55 min. Sound. 16mm Color. subtitles. *Rental:* French Am Cul.

Arrivederci, Baby. Tony Curtis, Rosanna Schiaffino & Lionel Jeffries. Directed by Ken Hughes. 1967. Paramount. (Anamorphic). 105 min. Sound. 16mm Color. *Rental:* Films Inc.

Arrow in the Dust. Sterling Hayden & Coleen Gray. Directed by Lesley Selander. 1954. Allied Artists. 80 min. Sound. 16mm Color. *Rental:* Hurlock Cine.

Arrowhead. Charlton Heston, Jack Palance & Katy Jurado. Directed by Charles Marquis Warren. 1953. Paramount. 105 min. Sound. 16mm Color. *Rental:* Films Inc.

Arsenal. Semyon Svashenko. Directed by Alexander Dovzhenko. Rus. 1929. Russia. 95 min. Silent. 16mm B&W. *Rental:* Budget Films, Em Gee Film Lib, Kit Parker, Museum Mod Art & Corinth Films. *Sale:* Reel Images & Glenn Photo. *Rental:* Ivy Films, *Sale:* Glenn Photo & Reel Images, Super 8 Silent version. *Sale:* Tamarelles French Film, Videotape version.

Arsene Lupin. John Barrymore, Lionel Barrymore & Karen Morley. Directed by Jack Conway. 1932. MGM. 84 min. Sound. 16mm B&W. *Rental:* MGM United.

Arsene Lupin Contre Sherlock Holmes. George Descrieres. Directed by Jean-Pierre Decourt. Fr. 1971. France. 55 min. Sound. 16mm Color. *Rental:* French Am Cul.

Arsenic & Old Lace. Cary Grant & Priscilla Lane. Directed by Frank Capra. 1944. Warners. 108 min. Sound. 16mm B&W. *Rental:* MGM United.

Arson for Hire. Steve Brodie. Directed by Thor Brooks. 1959. Allied Artists. 67 min. Sound. 16mm B&W. *Rental:* Ivy Films. *Sale:* Rep Pic Film.

Arson, Inc. Robert Lowery & Anne Gwynne. Directed by William Berke. 1949. Lippert. 65 min. Sound. 16mm B&W. *Rental:* Film Ctr DC & Mogulls Films.

Arson Racket Squad. Robert Livingston & Jackie Moran. Directed by Joseph Kane. 1938. Republic. 54 min. Sound. 16mm B&W. *Rental:* Ivy Films. *Sale:* Classics Assoc NY.

Arson Squad. Robert Armstrong. Directed by Lew Landers. 1945. PRC. 63 min. Sound. 16mm B&W. *Rental:* Inst Cinema. *Sale:* Rep Pic Film & Classics Assoc NY.

Art & Craft. 1975. Cineproduzione. (Documentary). 55 min. Sound. 16mm Color. *Rental:* B Raymond. *Sale:* B Raymond.

Art & Politics. 1974. UCV. (Documentary). 60 min. Videotape B&W. *Rental:* U Comm Video. *Sale:* U Comm Video.

Art in Revolution. 1972. Britain. (Documentary). 50 min. Sound. 16mm Color. *Rental:* Films Inc. *Sale:* Films Inc. *Sale:* Films Inc, Videotape version.

Art of Being Fully Human, The. 1979. PBS. (Documentary). 58 min. Videotape Color. *Rental:* PBS Video & Syracuse U Film. *Sale:* PBS Video.

Art of Collecting, The. 1967. NBC. (Documentary). 52 min. Sound. 16mm Color. *Rental:* McGraw-Hill Films & Syracuse U Film. *Sale:* McGraw-Hill Films.

Art of Etching, The. 1960. Argonaut. (Documentary). 52 min. Sound. 16mm Color. *Rental:* BYU Media.

Art of Hitting .300, The. Charley Lau. Videotape Color. *Rental:* Best Film & Video.

Art of James McMullan, The. 45 min. Sound. 16mm Color. *Rental:* Utah Media.

Art of Living, The: Coping with Death. 1977. Miami-Dade. (Documentary). 60 min. Sound. Videotape Color. *Rental:* Films Inc. *Sale:* Films Inc.

Art of Living, The: What Is Happiness?. 1977. Miami-Dade. (Documentary). 60 min. Sound. Videotape Color. *Rental:* Films Inc. *Sale:* Films Inc.

Art of Living, The: What Is Love?. 1977. Miami-Dade. (Documentary). 60 min. Sound. Videotape Color. *Rental:* Films Inc. *Sale:* Films Inc.

Art of Love, The. Dick Van Dyke & James Garner. Directed by Norman Jewison. 1965. Universal. (Documentary). 98 min. Sound. 16mm Color. *Rental:* Swank Motion.

Art of the Potter, The. Directed by David Outerbridge. 1972. Phoenix. (Documentary). 50 min. Sound. 16mm Color. *Rental:* Budget Films, La Inst Res Ctr, Museum Mod Art, Phoenix Films, U Cal Media, U of IL Film & U Mich Media. *Sale:* Phoenix Films. *Sale:* Phoenix Films, Videotape version.

Art of Worldly Wisdom, The. 1979. 55 min. Sound. 16mm Color. *Rental:* Canyon Cinema.

Art Pepper: Notes from a Jazz Survivor. 1982. 48 min. Sound. 16mm Color. *Sale:* Festival Films. *Sale:* Festival Films, Videotape version.

Art School. 60 min. Videotape Color. *Sale:* Videx Home Lib.

Arterial Pressure in the Cat. 1980. McGill. 80 min. Sound. 16mm *Rental:* Syracuse U Film.

Arthritis. 1980. US Government. (Lecture). 60 min. Videotape Color. *Sale:* Natl AV Ctr.

Arthur. Dudley Moore & Liza Minnelli. Directed by Steve Gordon. 1981. Orion. 100 min. Sound. 16mm Color. *Rental:* Films Inc.

Arthur Penn Nineteen Hundred & Twenty Two: Theme & Variants. Directed by Robert Hughes. 1970. Audio Film Classics. (Documentary). 86 min. Sound. 16mm Color. *Rental:* Films Inc, Macmillan Films, Syracuse U Film, Texture Film, U Mich Media & Willoughby Peer. *Sale:* Texture Film. *Sale:* Texture Film, Videotape version.

Artist Was a Woman, The. 1981. ABC. (Documentary). 58 min. Sound. 16mm Color. *Rental:* MTI Tele.

Artpark People. Directed by Michael Blackwood. 1977. Blackwood. (Documentary). 53 min. Sound. 16mm Color. *Rental:* Blackwood Films. *Lease:* Blackwood Films.

Artur Rubinstein Love of Life see Love of Life.

Arvelo Esta Loco, El. Walter Brennan & Ed Wynn. Directed by Robert Stevenson. 1967. Disney. 90 min. Sound. 16mm Color. dubbed. *Rental:* Twyman Films.

As If It Were Yesterday. Directed by Myriam Abramowicz & Esther Hoffenberg. 1980. Belgium. (Documentary). 85 min. Sound. 16mm B&W. *Rental:* Cinema Five.

As Long As the Rivers Run. 1971. American Documentary. (Documentary). 60 min. Sound. 16mm Color. *Rental:* Icarus Films & CA Newsreel. *Sale:* Icarus Films.

As Long As We're Together. 1979. PBS. (Documentary). 58 min. Videotape Color. *Rental:* PBS Video. *Sale:* PBS Video.

As the Earth Turns. Jean Muir & Donald Woods. Directed by Alfred E. Green. 1934. Warners. 73 min. Sound. 16mm B&W. *Rental:* MGM United.

As the Twig Is Bent: How Our Children Learn. 1973. WNET. (Documentary). 58 min. Sound. 16mm Color. *Rental:* B Raymond. *Sale:* B Raymond, Videotape version.

As We With Candles Do. 1980. Broadcasting & Film Comm. (Documentary). 60 min. Sound. Videotape Color. *Lease:* CC Films & Natl Churches Christ.

As You Desire Me. Greta Garbo, Melvyn Douglas & Erich Von Stroheim. Directed by George Fitzmaurice. 1932. MGM. 71 min. Sound. 16mm Color. *Rental:* MGM United.

As You Like It. Rose Coghlan, Maurice Costello & James Morrison. Directed by J. Stuart Blackton & James Young. 1912. Vitagraph. 60 min. Silent. 8mm B&W. *Sale:* Film Classics. *Rental:* Film Classics, Videotape version.

As You Like It. Elizabeth Bergner, Laurence Olivier & Henry Ainley. Directed by Paul Czinner. 1936. Britain. 98 min. Sound. 16mm B&W. *Rental:* Budget Films, Em Gee Film Lib, Films Inc, Images Film, Ivy Films, Janus Films, Kit Parker, Modern Sound, Natl Film Video, Film Images, Twyman Films, U Cal Media, Video Comm & Westcoast Films. *Sale:* Blackhawk Films, Festival Films & Reel Images. *Rental:* Maljack & Video Comm, Videotape version.

As You Like It. Helen Mirren & Richard Pasco. 1979. Britain. 150 min. Videotape Color. *Rental:* Iowa Films.

As You Were. William Tracy & Joe Sawyer. Directed by Fred Guiol. 1951. Lippert. 60 min. Sound. 16mm B&W. *Rental:* Budget Films & Mogulls Films.

As Young As We Are. Robert Harland & Pippa Scott. Directed by Bernard Girard. 1958. Paramount. 76 min. Sound. 16mm B&W. *Rental:* Films Inc.

As Young As You Feel. Monty Woolley & Thelma Ritter. Directed by Harmon Jones. 1951. Fox. 77 min. Sound. 16mm B&W. *Rental:* Films inc.

Asante Market Women. 1982. Britain. (Documentary). 52 min. Sound. Videotape Color. *Rental:* Film Makers. *Sale:* Film Makers.

Asbestos: A Lethal Legacy. 1981. 57 min. Color. *Rental:* Educ Media CA.

Asbestos: The Way to Dusty Death. 1978. ABC. (Documentary). 48 min. Sound. 16mm Color. *Rental:* U of IL Film. *Sale:* MTI Tele, Videotape version.

Ascenseur Pour l'Echaufaud see Frantic.

Ascent of Man: World within Worlds. 1974. 52 min. Sound. 16mm Color. *Rental:* Iowa Films.

Ash Wednesday. Elizabeth Taylor & Henry Fonda. Directed by Larry Peerce. 1973. Paramount. 99 min. Sound. 16mm Color. *Rental:* Films Inc.

Ashes & Diamonds. Trans. Title: Wajda Trilogy. Zbigniew Cybulski, Eva Krzyzewska & Adam Pawlikowski. Directed by Andrzej Wajda. Pol. 1959. Poland. 99 min. Sound. 16mm B&W. subtitles. *Rental:* Films Inc & Janus Films.

Ashes of Vengeance. Norma Talmadge. Directed by Frank Lloyd. *Rental:* A Twyman Pres.

Asi No Hay Cama Que Aguante. Jorge Porcel & Moria Casan. Spain. 100 min. Sound. Videotape Color. subtitles. *Sale:* Tamarelles French Film.

Asia: The Japanese. 1969. (Documentary). 52 min. Sound. 16mm Color. *Rental:* Budget Films.

Asian Insight: Hong Kong/Singapore. Directed by Arch Nicholson. 1976. Australia. (Documentary). 53 min. Sound. 16mm Color. *Rental:* Aust Info Serv. *Sale:* Aust Info Serv.

Asian Insight: Indonesia. Directed by Arch Nicholson. 1976. Australia. (Documentary). 53 min. Sound. 16mm Color. *Rental:* Aust Info Serv. *Sale:* Aust Info Serv.

Asian Insight: Japan. Directed by Arch Nicholson. 1976. Australia. (Documentary). 52 min. Sound. 16mm Color. *Rental:* Aust Info Serv. *Sale:* Aust Info Serv.

Asian Insight: Malaysia. Directed by arch Nicholson. 1976. Australia. (Documentary). 52 min. Sound. 16mm Color. *Rental:* Aust Info Serv. *Sale:* Aust Info Serv.

Asian Insight: Thailand. Directed by Arch Nicholson. 1976. Australia. (Documentary). 52 min. Sound. 16mm Color. *Rental:* Aust Info Serv. *Sale:* Aust Info Serv.

Asian Insight: The Philippines. Directed by Arch Nicholson. 1976. Australia. (Documentary). 52 min. Sound. 16mm Color. *Rental:* Aust Info Serv. *Sale:* Aust Info Serv.

Asian Summit Nineteen Seventy-Seven. 1977. Malaysia. (Documentary). 55 min. Sound. 16mm Color. *Rental:* Malaysia Emb.

Ask Any Girl. Shirley MacLaine & David Niven. Directed by Charles Walters. 1958. MGM. 98 min. Sound. 16mm Color. *Rental:* MGM United. *Rental:* Films Inc, Anamorphic, color version.

Asking for Trouble. Max Miller. Directed by Oswald Mitchell. 1949. Britain. 50 min. Sound. 16mm B&W. *Rental:* Ivy Films.

Asmat: Cannibals of New Guinea. 1983. Films Inc. 56 min. Sound. 16mm Color. *Rental:* Syracuse U Film.

Aspects of Jewish Theology. 2 pts. Anti-Defamation League. (Documentary). 60 min. Sound. 16mm B&W. *Rental:* ADL. *Sale:* ADL.

Asphalt Jungle, The. Sterling Hayden & Marilyn Monroe. Directed by John Huston. 1950. MGM. 112 min. Sound. 16mm B&W. *Rental:* MGM United. *Rental:* MGM United, Videotape version.

Asphyx, The. Robert Stephens. Directed by Peter Newbrook. 1970. Paragon. 98 min. Sound. 16mm Color. *Rental:* Budget Films, Films Inc, Kerr Film, Video Comm & Westcoast Films. *Sale:* Video Lib, Videotape version.

Assailant, The see Swedish Wedding Night.

Assassin, The. Directed by Roderick Bradley. 1967. Roderick Bradley. (Experimental). 77 min. Sound. 16mm B&W. *Rental:* Canyon Cinema.

Assassin for Hire. Ronald Howard. Directed by Michael McCarthy. 1951. Britain. 60 min. Sound. 16mm B&W. *Rental:* Video Comm. *Rental:* Video Comm, Videotape version.

Assassin Lives at Number Twenty One. Pierre Fresnay & Suzy Delair. Directed by Henri-Georges Clouzot. 1942. 82 min. Sound. 16mm B&W. *Rental:* Films Inc.

Assassin of Youth. Directed by Elmer Clifton. 1935. McCarthy. (Cast unlisted). 80 min. Sound. 16mm B&W. *Rental:* Budget Films, Classic Film Mus, Educ Media CA & Kit Parker. *Sale:* Reel Images.

Assassination, The. Tetsuro Tamba & Shima Iwashita. Directed by Masahiro Shinoda. Jap. 1964. Shochiku. 105 min. Sound. 16mm Color. subtitles Eng. *Rental:* Films Inc.

Assassination Bureau, The. Oliver Reed, Diana Rigg & Telly Savalas. Directed by Basil Dearden. 1969. Paramount. 110 min. Sound. 16mm Color. *Rental:* Films Inc.

Assassination of President Kennedy, The. 80 min. Sound. 16mm Color. *Rental:* Budget Films, Phoenix Films & Syracuse U Film. *Sale:* Phoenix Films. *Sale:* Phoenix Films, Videotape version.

Assassination of Trotsky, The. Richard Burton & Alain Delon. Directed by Joseph Losey. 1973. Cinerama. 105 min. Sound. 16mm Color. *Rental:* Swank Motion.

Assault. Knut Pettersen. Directed by Lasse Forsberg. Swed. 1971. Sweden. 103 min. Sound. 16mm B&W. subtitles. *Rental:* New Line Cinema. *Sale:* New Line Cinema.

Assault of Innocence. Videotape Color. *Sale:* Videx Home Lib.

Assault on a Queen. Frank Sinatra, Virna Lisi & Tony Franciosa. Directed by Jack Donohue. 1966. Paramount. 105 min. Sound. 16mm Color. *Rental:* Films Inc. *Rental:* Films Inc, Anamorphic color version.

Assault on Life. 1967. Britain. (Documentary). 50 min. Sound. 16mm B&W. *Rental:* BYU Media.

Assault on Precinct Thirteen. Austin Stoker, Darwin Joston & Laurie Zimmer. Directed by John Carpenter. 1977. Turtle. 91 min. Sound. 16mm Color. *Rental:* Budget Films, Films Inc & Wholesome Film Ctr.

Assemblage. 1972. KQED. (Ballet). 60 min. Sound. 16mm Color. *Rental:* Film Wright. *Sale:* Film Wright.

Assessment & Case Planning. 1979. 45 min. Sound. Videotape Color. *Rental:* Iowa Films.

Assigned to Danger. Gene Raymond & Noreen Nash. Directed by Budd Boetticher. 1948. Eagle Lion. 66 min. Sound. 16mm B&W. *Sale:* Classics Assoc NY.

Assignment in Brittany. Jean-Pierre Aumont & Susan Peters. Directed by Jack Conway. 1943. MGM. 96 min. Sound. 16mm B&W. *Rental:* MGM United.

Assignment in China see State Dept. File Six Hundred Forty-Nine.

Assignment: India. 1967. NBC. (Documentary). 57 min. Sound. 16mm B&W. *Rental:* Films Inc. *Sale:* Films Inc.

Assignment K. Stephen Boyd & Camilla Sparv. Directed by Val Guest. 1968. Columbia. 97 min. Sound. 16mm Color. *Rental:* Modern Sound, Welling Motion Pictures & Westcoast Films.

Assignment: Outer Space. Archie Savage & Rik Van Nutter. 1962. American International. 79 min. Sound. 16mm Color. *Rental:* Charard Motion Pics, Films Inc & Rep Pic Film.

Assignment: Paris. Dana Andrews & George Sanders. Directed by Robert Parrish. 1952. Columbia. 85 min. Sound. 16mm B&W. *Rental:* Cine Craft, Charard Motion Pics, Films Inc & Inst Cinema.

Assignment Skybolt. Directed by Gregg Tallas. 109 min. 16mm Color. *Rental:* BF Video.

Assignment to Kill. Patrick O'Neal & Joan Hacket. Directed by Sheldon Reynolds. 1968. Britain. 99 min. 16mm Color. *Rental:* Cine Craft & Films Inc.

Assunta Spina. Francesca Bertini. Directed by Gustavo Serena. 1915. Italy. 66 min. Silent. 16mm B&W. *Rental:* Museum Mod Art.

Asteroid & the Dinosaur, The. 1980. WGBH. (Documentary). 57 min. Sound. 16mm Color. *Rental:* Time-Life Multimedia. *Sale:* Time-Life Multimedia. *Sale:* Time-Life Multimedia, Videotape version.

Astonished Heart, The. Noel Coward & Celia Johnson. Directed by Anthony Fisher & Anthony Darnborough. 1950. Britain. 92 min. Sound. 16mm B&W. *Rental:* Budget Films.

Astounding She-Monster, The: Mysterious Invader. Robert Clarke & Kenne Duncan. Directed by Ronnie Ashcroft. 1957. American International. 60 min. Sound. 16mm B&W. *Rental:* Films Inc & Westcoast Films.

Astro Zombies. Wendell Corey & John Carradine. Directed by Ted V. Mikels. 1967. Harris. 83 min. Sound. 16mm Color. *Rental:* Budget Films & Video Comm.

Asya. Elena Koreneva. Directed by Josef Kheifits. Rus. 1978. Russia. 97 min. Sound. 16mm Color. subtitles. *Rental:* Corinth Films.

Asylum. 1974. Insight. (Documentary). 95 min. Sound. 16mm Color. *Rental:* U CAL Media & U Mich Media.

Asylum: House of Crazies. Peter Cushing, Herbert Lom & Charlotte Rampling. Directed by Roy Ward Baker. 1972. Britain. 100 min. Sound. 16mm Color. *Rental:* Film Pres, Modern Sound & Swank Motion.

At Five Past Five. Directed by Kamar Vasudev. India. 66 min. Sound. 16mm B&W. *Rental:* Films Inc.

At Gunpoint. Fred MacMurray & Dorothy Malone. Directed by Alfred M. Werker. 1958. Allied Artists. 81 min. Sound. 16mm B&W. *Rental:* Ivy Films. *Sale:* Rep Pic Film. *Rental:* Hurlock Cine, *Lease:* Rep Pic Film, Color version.

At Long Last Love. Burt Reynolds, Cybill Shepherd & Madeline Kahn. Directed by Peter Bogdanovich. 1975. Fox. 118 min. Sound. 16mm Color. *Rental:* Films Inc.

At Sword's Point. Cornel Wilde & Maureen O'Hara. Directed by Lewis Allen. 1952. RKO. 81 min. Sound. 16mm Color. *Rental:* Films Inc.

At the Circus. Marx Brothers. Directed by Edward Buzzell. 1939. MGM. 87 min. Sound. 166mm B&W. *Rental:* MGM United. *Rental:* MGM United, Videotape version.

At the Earth's Core. Doug McClure & Peter Cushing. Directed by Kevin Connor. 1976. American International. 90 min. Sound. 16mm Color. *Rental:* Welling Motion Pictures & Westcoast Films.

At the Edge of History: A Conversation with William Irwin Thompson. 1979. WNET. (Documentary). 58 min. Sound. Videotape Color. *Rental:* WNET Media. *Sale:* WNET Media.

At the Front in North Africa. 1943. Army. (Documentary). 79 min. Sound. 16mm B&W. *Rental:* Budget Films & Natl AV Ctr. *Rental:* Budget Films, 45 mins. version.

At the Stroke of Nine. Patricia Dainton & Lance Comfort. 1957. 71 min. 16mm *Rental:* A Twyman Pres.

At the Table. 1974. 45 min. Sound. 16mm *Rental:* Natl AV Ctr.

At the Winter Sea Ice Camp. 3 pts. Directed by Quentin Brown. 1967. 102 min. 16mm B&W. *Rental:* National Film CN & U Cal Media.

At War With the Army. Dean Martin, Jerry Lewis & Mike Kellin. Directed by Hal Walker. 1950. Paramount. 100 min. Sound. 16mm B&W. *Rental:* Films Inc. *Rental:* Budget Films, 72 mins. version.

Atalante, L'. Michel Simon & Dita Parlo. Directed by Jean Vigo. Fr. 1934. France. 82 min. Sound. 16mm B&W. subtitles. *Rental:* Budget Films, Classic Film Mus, Em Gee Film Lib, Films Inc, Images Film, Kit Parker & Macmillan Films. *Sale:* Cinema Concepts & Reel Images. *Sale:* Cinema Concepts, Videotape version. *Sale:* Tamarelles French Film, Videotape version.

Atencingo. Directed by Eduardo Maldonado. Span. 1974. Mexico. (Cast unlisted). 58 min. Sound. 16mm Color. subtitles. *Rental:* CA Newsreel & Tricontinental Film. *Sale:* Tricontinental Film.

Athena. Jane Powell & Debbie Reynolds. Directed by Richard Thorpe. 1954. MGM. (Documentary). 96 min. Sound. 16mm Color. *Rental:* MGM United.

Atlantic. Franklin Dyall & Madeleine Carroll. Directed by E. A. Dupont. 1929. Britain. 95 min. Sound. 16mm B&W. *Sale:* Reel Images. *Sale:* Tamarelles French Film, Videotape version.

Atlantic Adventure. Harry Langdon, Nancy Carroll & Lloyd Nolan. Directed by Albert S. Rogell. 1935. Columbia. 70 min. Sound. 16mm B&W. *Rental:* Twyman Films.

Atlantic City. Constance Moore, Louis Armstrong & Paul Whiteman. Directed by Ray McCarey. 1944. Republic. 87 min. Sound. 16mm B&W. *Sale:* Rep Pic Film.

Atlantic City. Burt Lancaster, Susan Sarandon & Kate Reid. Directed by Louis Malle. 1981. Paramount. 103 min. Sound. 16mm Color. *Rental:* Films Inc.

Atlantic Flight. Dick Merrill & Milburn Stone. Directed by William Nigh. 1937. Monogram. 60 min. Sound. 16mm B&W. *Rental:* Mogulls Films.

Atlantide, L'. Fritz Kortner & Lucie Mannheim. Directed by E. A. Dupont. Ger. 1932. Germany. 95 min. Sound. 16mm B&W. subtitles. *Rental:* Images Film & Janus Films. *Sale:* Glenn Photo.

Atlantis: The Lost Continent. Anthony Hall & Joyce Taylor. Directed by George Pal. 1961. MGM. 90 min. Sound. 16mm Color. *Rental:* MGM United.

Atlas. Michael Forest. Directed by Roger Corman. 1961. Allied Artists. 80 min. Sound. 16mm Color. *Rental:* Hurlock Cine.

Atoll K *see* Utopia.

Atom Age Vampire. Albert Luao. 1961. Italy. 86 min. Sound. 16mm B&W. dubbed. *Sale:* Salz Ent.

Atomic Brain, The. Orig. Title: Monstrosity. Erika Peters, Judy Bamber & Frank Gerstle. Directed by Joseph V. Mascelli. 1964. Emerson. 65 min. Sound. 16mm B&W. *Rental:* Films Inc & Ivy Films.

Atomic Cafe, The. Directed by Kevin Rafferty, Jayne Loader & Pierce Rafferty. 1982. 88 min. Sound. 16mm Color. *Rental:* New Yorker Films. *Rental:* Direct Camera, Videotape version.

Atomic City. Gene Barry & Lydia Clarke. Directed by Jerry Hopper. 1952. Paramount. 85 min. Sound. 16mm B&W. *Rental:* Films Inc.

Atomic Kid, The. Mickey Rooney & Hal March. Directed by Leslie Martinson. 1954. Republic. 86 min. 16m B&W. *Sale:* Natl Telefilm.

Atomic Man, The. Gene Nelson & Faith Domergue. Directed by Ken Hughes. 1956. Allied Artists. 78 min. 16mm B&W. *Rental:* Hurlock Cine.

Atomic Physics. 5 pts. 1948. Atomic Energy Commission. (Documentary). 90 min. Sound. 16mm B&W. *Rental:* Natl AV Ctr.

Atomic Submarine, The. Arthur Franz & Dick Foran. Directed by Spencer G. Bennett. 1959. Allied Artists. (Documentary). 73 min. Sound. 16mm B&W. *Rental:* Modern Sound & Video Comm. *Sale:* Cinema Concepts, Super 8 sound version.

Atonement, The. 1971. Canada. (Documentary). 51 min. Sound. 16mm Color. *Rental:* Films Inc, Natl Film CN, Syracause U Film & U Cal Media. *Sale:* Films Inc. *Sale:* Films Inc, Videotape version.

Atonement of Gosta Berling *see* Story of Gosta Berling.

Atragon. Tadao Takashima, Yu Fujiki & Yoko Fujiyama. Directed by Inoshiro Honda. Jap. 1965. Japan. 90 min. Sound. 16mm Color. dubbed. *Rental:* Kerr Film & Wholesome Film Ctr.

Atrocities of the Orient. Linda Estrella & Fernando Royo. 1959. Philippines. 80 min. Sound. 16mm B&W. *Rental:* Budget Films. *Sale:* Morcraft Films.

Attack! Jack Palance & Lee Marvin. Directed by Robert Aldrich. 1956. United Artists. 107 min. Sound. 16mm B&W. *Rental:* MGM United.

Attack from Outer Space. 1979. Gold Key. (Documentary). 96 min. Sound. 16mm Color. *Rental:* Gold Key.

Attack from the Sea. Ivan Pereverzev. Directed by Mikhail Romm. 1953. 93 min. Sound. 16mm B&W. subtitles. *Rental:* Corinth Films.

Attack in the Pacific. 1945. Army. (Documentary). 50 min. Sound. 16mm B&W. *Rental:* Natl Av Ctr.

Attack of the Crab Monsters. Richard Garland & Pamela Duncan. Directed by Roger Corman. 1957. Allied Artists. 70 min. Sound. 16mm *Rental:* Hurlock Cine.

Attack of the Fifty Foot Woman, The. Allison Hayes & William Hudson. Directed by Nathan Hertz. 1958. Allied Artists. 65 min. Sound. 16mm B&W. *Rental:* Hurlock Cine.

Attack of the Giant Leeches, The: Demons of the Swamp. Ken Clark, Yvette Vickers & Jan Shepard. 1959. American International. 62 min. Sound. 16mm B&W. *Rental:* Films Inc.

Attack of the Iron Cost. Lloyd Bridges. Directed by Paul Wendkos. 1968. United Artists. 89 min. Sound. 16mm Color. *Rental:* MGM United.

Attack of the Killer Tomatoes. David Miller, George Wilson & Sharon Taylor. Directed by John De Bello. 86 min. Sound. 16mm Color. *Rental:* Swank Motion. *Rental:* Swank Motion, Videotape version.

Attack of the Kung Fu Girls. 1974. China. 90 min. Sound. 16mm Color. dubbed. *Rental:* Budget Films, Films Inc & Westcoast Films.

Attack of the Mushroom People, The. 1964. 89 min. Sound. 16mm Color. *Rental:* Ivy Films.

Attack of the Puppet People. John Agar, John Hoyt & John Kennedy. 1958. Gordon. 78 min. Sound. 16mm B&W. *Rental:* Films Inc.

Attack of the Robots. Eddie Constantine & Fernando Rey. Directed by Jess Franco. 1960. American International. 85 min. Sound. 16mm B&W. *Rental:* Films Inc.

Attica. Directed by Cinda Firestone. 1973. Tricontinental. (Documentary). 90 min. Sound. 16mm B&W. *Rental:* New Cinema, U Mich Media & Unifilm. *Sale:* Unifilm.

Attica. George Grizzard & Roger E. Mosley. Directed by Marvin J. Chomsky. 1980. ABC. 96 min. Sound. 16mm Color. *Rental:* U of IL Film, Videotape version.

Au Dela Des Grilles *see* Walls of Malapaga.

Au Hasard Balthazar. Anne Wiazemsky & Francois Lafarge. Directed by Robert Bresson. Fr. 1966. France. 95 min. Sound. 16mm B&W. subtitles. *Rental:* New Line Cinema.

Au Pays de l'Eau Tranquille. Jacques Fabri. Directed by Jean-Pierre Decourt. Fr. 1975. France. 52 min. Sound. 16mm Color. subtitles. *Rental:* French Am Cul. *Rental:* French Am Cul, Videotape version.

Audio-Lingual Techniques for Teaching Foreign Languages: French. 1962. U. S. Government. (Lecture). 66 min. Sound. 16mm B&W. *Sale:* Natl Av Ctr.

Audio-Lingual Techniques for Teaching Foreign Languages: German. 1962. U. S. Government. (Lecture). 60 min. Sound. 16mm B&W. *Rental:* BYU Media. *Sale:* Natl Av Ctr.

Audio-Lingual Techniques for Teaching Foreign Languages: Russian. 1962. U. S. Government. (Lecture). 66 min. Sound. 16mm B&W. *Sale:* Natl AV Ctr.

Audrey Rose. Anthony Hopkins & Marsha Mason. Directed by Robert Wise. 1977. United Artists. 113 min. Sound. 16mm Color. *Rental:* MGM United.

Audubon. 1970. NET. (Documentary). 58 min. Sound. 16mm Color. *Rental:* Indiana AV Ctr. *Lease:* Indiana AV Ctr. *Sale:* Indiana AV Ctr, Videotape version.

August & July. Directed by Murray Markowitz. 1972. Canada. (Documentary). 90 min. Sound. 16mm Color. *Rental:* New Cinema.

Augustina de Aragon. Aurora Bautista. Span. 1953. Spain. 90 min. Sound. 16mm B&W. subtitles. *Rental:* Film Classics. *Rental:* Film Classics, Videotape version.

Augustine. 1979. Canada. (Documentary). 57 min. Sound. 16mm Color. *Rental:* Kent St U Film.

Augustine of Hippo. Dary Berkani. Directed by Roberto Rossellini. 1972. 120 min. Sound. 16mm B&W. *Rental:* Films Inc.

Aunt Clara. Margaret Rutherford & Ronald Shiner. Directed by Anthony Kimmins. 1953. Britain. 84 min. Sound. 16mm B&W. *Rental:* Charard Motion Pics.

Auntie Mame. Rosalind Russell, Forrest Tucker & Coral Browne. Directed by Morton Da Costa. 1958. Warners. 143 min. Sound. 16mm Color. *Rental:* Buchan Film, Cine Craft, Films Inc, Inst Cinema, Modern Sound, Twyman Films, Video Comm, Williams Films & Willoughby Peer. *Rental:* Twyman Films, Anamorphic version.

Auschwitz & the Allies. 1982. Britain. 110 min. Sound. 16mm B&W. *Rental:* Films Inc.

Aussi Longue Absence, Une. Alida Valli. Directed by Henri Colpi. Fr. 1961. France. 105 min. Sound. 16mm B&W. subtitles. *Rental:* French Am Cul.

Australia at War: 1914-1918. Australia. (Documentary). 63 min. Sound. 16mm B&W. *Rental:* Aust Info Serv. *Sale:* Aust Info Serv.

Australia: The Luck Country. 1979. 58 min. Sound. Videotape *Rental:* PBS Video. *Sale:* PBS Video.

Australia: The Timeless Land. 1968. National Geographic. (Documentary). 53 min. Sound. 16mm Color. *Rental:* Natl Geog. *Sale:* Natl Geog. *Sale:* Natl Geog, Videotape version.

Australia's Animal Mysteries. 59 min. Sound. 16mm Color. *Rental:* Natl Geog. *Sale:* Natl Geog. *Sale:* Natl Geog, Videotape version.

Autobiography of a Princess. James Mason. Directed by James Ivory. 1975. Cinema Five. 60 min. Sound. 16mm Color. *Rental:* Corinth Films & Cinema Five. *Sale:* New Cinema.

Autobiography of Miss Jane Pittman, The. Cicely Tyson, Barbara Chaney & Richard Dysart. Directed by John Korty. 1974. CBS. 107 min. Sound. 16mm Color. *Rental:* Arcus Film, Budget Films, Cine Craft, Film Ctr DC, Film Pres, Films Inc, Inst Cinema, Images Film, Kent St U Film, Kit Parker, Mass Media, Modern Sound, Newman Film Lib, Roas Films, Swank Motion, Syracuse U Film, Twyman Films, U Mich Media, U of IL Film, Welling Motion Pictures, Westcoast Films & Wholesome Film Ctr. *Sale:* Learning Corp Am. *Lease:* Learning Corp Am. *Sale:* Learning Corp Am, Videotape version.

Automation. 1957. CBS. (Documentary). 84 min. Sound. 16mm B&W. *Rental:* BYU Media & McGraw-Hill Films. *Sale:* McGraw-Hill Films.

Automobiles: The Great Love Affair. 1966. CBS. (Documentary). 54 min. Sound. 16mm B&W. *Rental:* McGraw-Hill Films & U Mich Media. *Sale:* McGraw-Hill Films.

Autopsy Techniques & Restoration. 72 min. Sound. 16mm Color. *Rental:* Iowa Films.

Autumn Across America, with Edward Tiel. 1970. Xerox. (Documentary). 50 min. Sound. 16mm Color. *Rental:* Cinema Guild, NYC Film Lib, Syracuse U Film & Xerox Films. *Sale:* Xerox Films.

Autumn Afternoon, An. Chishu Ryu. Directed by Yasujiro Ozu. Jap. 1962. Japan. 112 min. Sound. 16mm Color. subtitles. *Rental:* New Yorker Films.

Autumn Leaves. Joan Crawford & Cliff Robertson. Directed by Robert Aldrich. 1956. 108 min. Sound. 16mm B&W. *Rental:* Bosco Films, Budget Films, Kit Parker & Welling Motion Pictures.

Autumn of the Kohayagawa Family, The *see* End of Summer.

Autumn Sonata. Ingrid Bergman & Liv Ullmann. Directed by Ingmar Bergman. 1978. New World. 97 min. Sound. 16mm Color. *Rental:* Films Inc & New Cinema.

Available Light. Directed by Kevin Burke. 1971. Kevin Burke. (Documentary). 90 min. Sound. 16mm Color. *Rental:* New Line Cinema. *Sale:* New Line Cinema.

Avalanche. Bruce Cabot & Roscoe Karnes. Directed by Irving Allen. 1946. PRC. 70 min. Sound. 16mm B&W. *Sale:* Classics Assoc NY.

Avalanche. Wally Bosco. Directed by Frederic Goode. 1978. Britain. 56 min. Sound. 16mm Color. *Sale:* Lucerne Films.

Avalanche. Rock Hudson, Mia Farrow & Robert Forster. Directed by Corey Allen. 1978. New World. 91 min. Sound. 16mm Color. *Rental:* Films Inc.

Avalanche Express. Lee Marvin & Robert Shaw. Directed by Mark Robson. 1979. Fox. (Anamorphic). 88 min. Sound. 16mm Color. *Rental:* Films Inc.

Avanti! Jack Lemmon & Juliet Mills. Directed by Billy Wilder. 1973. United Artists. 144 min. Sound. 16mm Color. *Rental:* MGM United.

Ave Maria. 1920. Bavaria. (Cast unlisted). 45 min. Silent. 16mm B&W. *Rental:* Film classics.

Avenger of the Seven Seas. Richard Harrison. 1960. Italy. 94 min. Sound. 16mm Color. dubbed. *Rental:* Westcoast Films.

Avenging Conscience, The. Henry B. Walthall & Blanche Sweet. Directed by D. W. Griffith. 1914. Biograph. 84 min. Silent. 16mm B&W. *Rental:* Em Gee Film Lib, Kit Parker & Museum Mod Art. *Sale:* Festival Films & Glenn Photo. *Rental:* Ivy Films, Super 8 silent version.

Avenging Rider, The. Tim Holt & Cliff Edwards. Directed by Bert Gilroy. 1943. RKO. 85 min. Sound. 16mm *Rental:* RKO General Pics.

Avenging Stranger, The *see* God's Country & the Woman.

Avenging Warriors of Shaolin, The. Lu Feng. 97 min. Sound. 16mm *Rental:* WW Enter. *Rental:* WW Enter, Videotape version.

Aventuras de Cucuruchito y Pinocchio, Las. Elvira Gonsalo. Directed by Carlos Vesar Jr. Span. Mexico. Sound. 16mm B&W. *Rental:* Film Classics.

Aventuras de Joselito y Pulgarcito, Las. Joselito Pulgarcito. Directed by Rene Cardona. Span. 1961. Mexico. 93 min. Sound. 16mm Color. *Rental:* Twyman Films.

Avenue of the Americas. Directed by Jorge Reyes. 1976. Pueblo. 82 min. Sound. 16mm Color. subtitles. *Rental:* New Line Cinema & Cinema Guild.

Average Woman, The. Pauline Garon & Harrison Ford. Directed by Christy Cabanne. 1924. Burr. 65 min. Silent. 8mm B&W. *Rental:* Em Gee Film Lib.

Aviator's Wife, The. Directed by Eric Rohmer. Fr. 1980. 104 min. Sound. 16mm Color. subtitles. *Rental:* New Yorker Films.

Avventura, L'. Monica Vitti. Directed by Michelangelo Antonioni. Ital. 1961. Italy. 145 min. Sound. 16mm B&W. subtitles. *Rental:* Films Inc. *Sale:* Festival Films, Films Inc, New Cinema & Reel Images. *Sale:* Festival Films, Videotape version.

Awakening, The. Anna Magnani & Eleonora Rossi Drago. Directed by Mario Camerini. 1958. 97 min. Sound. 16mm B&W. *Rental:* Films Inc.

Awakening, The. Charlton Heston & Susannah York. Directed by Mike Newell. 1980. Orion. 100 min. Sound. 16mm Color. *Rental:* Films Inc.

Away All Boats. Jeff Chandler & George Nader. Directed by Joseph Pevney. 1956. Universal. 116 min. Sound. 16mm Color. *Rental:* Swank Motion.

Away We Go. 1964. Wolper. 50 min. Sound. 16mm B&W. *Rental:* Films Inc. *Sale:* Films Inc.

Away with All Pests. 1972. Blue Bus. (Documentary). 58 min. Sound. 16mm B&W. *Rental:* Unifilm. *Sale:* Unifilm.

Awful Dr. Orloff, The. Howard Vernon. Directed by Jess Franco. 1964. Spain. 80 min. Sound. 16mm B&W. dubbed. *Rental:* Ivy Films.

Awful Truth, The. Irene Dunne, Cary Grant & Ralph Bellamy. Directed by Leo McCarey. 1937. Columbia. 92 min. Sound. 16mm B&W. *Rental:* Arcus Film, Bosco Films, Budget Films, Films Inc, Images Film, Ivy Films, Kit Parker, Modern Sound, Natl Film Video, Swank Motion, Twyman Films, Welling Motion Pictures & Wholesome Film Ctr.

Axe, The. Jack Canon, Frederick Friedel & Leslie Lee. 66 min. Sound. 16mm Color. *Rental:* BF Video.

Azafatas con Permiso. Span. 1950. Mexico. (Cast unlisted). 90 min. Sound. 16mm B&W. *Rental:* Film Classics.

B. F. Skinner & Behavior Change. Directed by Phillip R. Blake. 1975. McGraw Hill. (Documentary). 48 min. Sound. 16mm Color. *Rental:* Iowa Films, McGraw-Hill Films & U of IL Film. *Sale:* McGraw-Hill Films. *Rental:* Iowa Films, Videotape version.

B. F.'s Daughter. Barbara Stanwyck & Van Heflin. Directed by Robert Z. Leonard. 1948. MGM. 108 min. Sound. 16mm B&W. *Rental:* MGM United.

B Must Die. Patricia Neal & Burgess Meredith. 1973. Spain. 94 min. Sound. 16mm Color. *Rental:* Hurlock Cine.

B. S., I Love You. Peter Kastner & Joanna Barnes. Directed by Steven Hilliard Stern. 1971. Fox. 99 min. Sound. 16mm Color. *Rental:* Films Inc.

Baba. Directed by Yilmaz Guney. Turkish. 1974. Turkey. (Documentary). 95 min. Sound. 16mm Color. subtitles. *Rental:* Icarus Films. *Sale:* Icarus Films.

Babbitt. Guy Kibbee & Aline MacMahon. Directed by William Keighley. 1934. Warners. 74 min. Sound. 16mm B&W. *Rental:* MGM United.

Babe Ruth Story, The. William Bendix & Claire Trevor. Directed by Roy Del Ruth. 1948. Allied Artists. 107 min. Sound. 16mm B&W. *Rental:* Hurlock Cine. *Rental:* Bosco Films, 90 mins version.

Babes in Arms. Mickey Rooney & Judy Garland. Directed by Busby Berkeley. 1939. MGM. 91 min. Sound. 16mm B&W. *Rental:* MGM United.

Babes in Bagdad. Paulette Goddard & John Boles. Directed by Edgar G. Ulmer. 1952. United Artists. 79 min. Sound. 16mm B&W. *Rental:* Willoughby Peer.

Babes in the Woods. Directed by Charles Franklin. 1917. Fox. (Cast unlisted). 59 min. Silent. 16mm B&W. *Rental:* Em Gee Film Lib. *Sale:* Glenn Photo. *Sale:* Glenn Photo, Super 8 silent version. *Sale:* Glenn Photo, Silent 8 mm version.

Babes in Toyland. Ray Bolger, Tommy Sands & Annette Funicello. Directed by Jack Donohue. 1961. Disney. 100 min. Sound. 16mm Color. *Rental:* Bosco Films, Cine Craft, Disney Prod, Elliot Film Co, Film Ctr DC, Film Pres, MGM United, Modern Sound, Newman Film Lib, Roas Films, Swank Motion, Twyman Films, U of Il Film & Welling Motion Pictures.

Babes in Toyland *see* March of the Wooden Soldiers.

Babes on Broadway. Mickey Rooney & Judy Garland. Directed by Busby Berkeley. 1941. MGM. 118 min. Sound. 16mm B&W. *Rental:* MGM United.

Babette Goes to War. Brigitte Bardot & Jacques Charrier. Directed by Christian-Jaque. Fr. 1959. France. 103 min. Sound. 16mm Color. dubbed. *Rental:* Cine Craft & Films Inc.

Babies for Sale. Rochelle Hudson & Glenn Ford. Directed by Charles Barton. 1940. Columbia. 64 min. Sound. 16mm B&W. *Rental:* Kit Parker.

Babo Seventy-Three. Taylor Mead. Directed by Robert Downey. 1964. Robert Downey. (Color sequences). 60 min. Sound. 16mm B&W. *Rental:* Canyon Cinema.

Baboona *see* Bride of the Beast.

Baby, The. Ruth Roman & Anjanette Comer. Directed by Ted Post. 1972. Scotia. 86 min. Sound. 16mm Color. *Rental:* Budget Films.

Baby & the Battleship, The. John Mills & Richard Attenborough. Directed by Jay Lewis. 1957. 96 min. Sound. 16mm Color. *Rental:* Budget Films.

Baby Blue Marine. Jan-Michael Vincent & Glynnis O'Connor. Directed by John Hancock. 1976. Columbia. 90 min. Sound. 16mm Color. *Rental:* Budget Films, Kit Parker, Modern Sound, Natl Film Video, Swank Motion, Welling Motion Pictures & Westcoast Films.

Baby Face. Barbara Stanwyck, George Brent & John Wayne. Directed by Alfred E. Green. 1933. Warners. 70 min. Sound. 16mm B&W. *Rental:* MGM United.

Baby Face Harrington. Charles Butterworth, Eugene Pallette & Una Merkel. Directed by Raoul Walsh. 1935. MGM. 61 min. Sound. 16mm B&W. *Rental:* MGM United.

Baby, It's You. Rosanna Arquette & Vincent Spano. Directed by John Sayles. 1983. Paramount. 105 min. Sound. 16mm Color. *Rental:* Films Inc.

Baby Love. Ann Lynn & Keith Barron. Directed by Alastair Reid. 1969. Embassy. 98 min. Sound. 16mm Color. *Rental:* Films Inc.

Baby Maker, The. Barbara Hershey & Sam Groom. Directed by James Bridges. 1970. National General. 109 min. Sound. 16mm Color. *Rental:* Swank Motion.

Baby Oil. 60 min. Videotape Color. *Sale:* Videx Home Lib.

Baby, the Rain Must Fall. Steve McQueen & Lee Remick. Directed by Robert Mulligan. 1965. Columbia. 100 min. Sound. 16mm B&W. *Rental:* Budget Films, Cine Craft, Films Inc, Kit Parker, Modern Sound, Video Comm & Wholesome Film Ctr.

Babysitter, The. Patricia Wymer. Directed by Don Henderson. 1969. Crown. 76 min. Sound. 16mm B&W. *Rental:* Video Comm. *Lease:* Video Comm. *Rental:* Video Comm, *Lease:* Video Comm, Videotape version.

Bach Transmogrified. 1969. CBS. (Documentary). 54 min. Sound. 16mm B&W. *Rental:* Iowa Films & McGraw-Hill Films. *Sale:* McGraw-Hill Films.

Bachelor & the Bobby Soxer, The. Cary Grant, Myrna Loy & Shirley Temple. Directed by Irving Reis. 1947. RKO. 95 min. Sound. 16mm B&W. *Rental:* Films Inc. *Sale:* Blackhawk Films, Videotape version.

Bachelor Apartment. Irene Dunne & Mae Murray. Directed by Lowell Sherman. 1931. RKO. 77 min. Sound. 16mm B&W. *Rental:* Films Inc.

Bachelor Bait. Stuart Erwin, Rochelle Hudson & Pert Kelton. Directed by George Stevens. 1934. RKO. 75 min. Sound. 16mm B&W. *Sale:* Blackhawk Films.

Bachelor Flat. Richard Beymer & Tuesday Weld. Directed by Frank Tashlin. 1961. Fox. 91 min. Sound. 16mm Color. *Rental:* Films Inc. *Rental:* Films Inc, Anamorphic color version.

Bachelor Girls *see* Bachelor's Daughters.

Bachelor in Paradise. Bob Hope & Lana Turner. Directed by Jack Arnold. 1961. MGM. 109 min. Sound. 16mm B&W. *Rental:* MGM United. *Rental:* MGM United, Anamorphic color version.

Bachelor Mother. Ginger Rogers & David Niven. Directed by Garson Kanin. 1939. RKO. 80 min. Sound. 16mm B&W. *Rental:* Film Inc. *Sale:* BlackhawkFilms & Tamarelles French Film, Videotape version.

Bachelor Party. Don Murray & E. G. Marshall. Directed by Delbert Mann. 1957. United Artists. 93 min. Sound. 16mm B&W. *Rental:* MGM United.

Bachelor's Daughters. Orig. Title: Bachelor Girls. Adolphe Menjou & Ann Dvorak. Directed by Andrew Stone. 1946. United Artists. 88 min. Sound. 16mm B&W. *Rental:* Budget Films, Inst Cinema & Ivy Films.

Back & Forth. Directed by Michael Snow. 1969. Canada. (Experimental). 52 min. Sound. 16mm Color. *Rental:* Museum Mod Art.

Back Door to Hell. Jimmie Rodgers & Jack Nicholson. Directed by Monte Hellman. 1964. Fox. 68 min. Sound. 16mm B&W. *Rental:* Films Inc.

Back from Eternity. Robert Ryan & Rod Steiger. Directed by John Farrow. 1956. RKO. 98 min. Sound. 16mm B&W. *Rental:* Budget Films, Kit Parker, Video Comm & Westcoast Films. *Lease:* Video Comm. *Rental:* Video Comm, *Lease:* Video Comm, Videotape version.

Back from the Dead. Peggie Castle & Arthur Franz. Directed by Charles Marquis Warren. 1957. Fox. 81 min. Sound. 16mm B&W. *Rental:* Ivy Films. *Sale:* Rep Pic Film.

Back in Circulation. Pat O'Brien & Joan Blondell. Directed by Ray Enright. 1937. Warners. 82 min. Sound. 16mm B&W. *Rental:* MGM United.

Back in the Saddle. Gene Autry. Directed by Lew Landers. 1941. Republic. 54 min. Sound. 16mm B&W. *Rental:* Ivy Films. *Sale:* Rep Pic Film.

Back of Beyond. Directed by John Heyer. 1954. Australia. (Documentary). 66 min. Sound. 16mm B&W. *Rental:* Films Inc, Viewfinders & Texture Film. *Sale:* Texture Film. *Sale:* Texture Film, Videotape version.

Back Pay. Montagu Love & Corinne Griffith. Directed by William A. Seiter. 1930. Warners. 77 min. Sound. 16mm B&W. *Rental:* MGM United.

Back Roads. Sally Field & Tommy Lee Jones. Directed by Martin Ritt. 94 min. Sound. 16mm Color. *Rental:* Swank Motion. *Rental:* Swank Motion, Videotape version.

Back Street. Susan Hayward & John Gavin. Directed by David Miller. 1961. Universal. 107 min. Sound. 16mm Color. *Rental:* Cousino Visual Ed & Swank Motion.

Back Street. Irene Dunne & John Boles. Directed by John M. Stahl. 1932. Universal. 100 min. Sound. 16mm B&W. *Rental:* Swank Motion.

Back Street. Margaret Sullavan & Charles Boyer. Directed by Robert Stevenson. 1941. Universal. 89 min. Sound. 16mm B&W. *Rental:* Swank Motion.

Back Streets of Paris. Andre Clement & Paul Meurisse. Directed by Marcel Blistene. 1948. France. 94 min. Sound. 16mm B&W. *Rental:* Films Inc.

Back to Bataan. John Wayne & Anthony Quinn. Directed by Edward Dmytryk. 1945. RKO. 97 min. Sound. 16mm B&W. *Rental:* Films Inc. *Sale:* Blackhawk Films, Videotape version.

Back to God's Country. Nell Shipman. Directed by David Hartford. 1919. Canada. 70 min. Silent. 16mm B&W. *Rental:* Museum Mod Art. *Lease:* Museum Mod Art.

Back to God's Country. Rock Hudson & Hugh O'Brian. Directed by Joseph Pevney. 1953. Universal. 78 min. Sound. 16mm Color. *Rental:* Swank Motion.

Back to Kampuchea. Directed by Martin Duckworth. 1982. First Run. 57 min. Sound. 16mm Color. *Rental:* First Run. *Lease:* First Run.

Back Track. Ida Lupino, Neville Brand & James Drury. 1969. NBC. 95 min. Sound. 16mm Color. *Rental:* Swank Motion.

Back Trail. Johnny Mack Brown. Directed by Christy Cabanne. 1948. Monogram. 54 min. Sound. 16mm B&W. *Rental:* Welling Motion Pictures.

Back Wards to Back Streets. 1982. WNET. (Documentary). 60 min. Sound. 16mm Color. *Rental:* Films Inc.

Backbone of Night, The. 1980. Cosmos. (Documentary). 60 min. Sound. 16mm Color. *Rental:* Films Inc. *Sale:* Films Inc. *Sale:* Films Inc, Videotape version.

Backfire. Jack Hoxie. Directed by Alvin J. Neitz. 1922. Sunset. 60 min. Silent. 8mm B&W. *Sale:* Film classics.

Backfire. Jean Seberg & Jean-Paul Belmondo. Directed by Jean Becker. 1956. France. 105 min. Sound. 16mm B&W. dubbed. *Rental:* Cine Craft, Film Ctr DC & Modern Sound.

Background to Danger. George Raft & Brenda Marshall. Directed by Raoul Walsh. 1943. Warners. 80 min. Sound. 16mm B&W. *Rental:* MGM United.

Backlash. Richard Widmark & Donna Reed. Directed by John Sturges. 1956. Universal. 84 min. Sound. 16mm Color. *Rental:* Swank Motion.

Backstairs. Henny Porten & William Dieterle. Directed by Leopold Jessner & Paul Leni. Ger. 1921. Germany. (Tinted). 40 min. Silent. 16mm *Rental:* Em Gee Film Lib, Film Images & Kit Parker. *Sale:* Cinema Concepts, Film Images & Reel Images.

Backstreet Six, The. 80 min. Sound. 16mm Color. *Rental:* Phoenix Films. *Sale:* Phoenix Films. *Sale:* Phoenix Films, Videotape version.

Bacterial Endocarditis. 1972. 60 min. Sound. 16mm B&W. *Sale:* Natl AV Ctr.

Bacterial Meningitis. 1972. 45 min. Sound. 16mm B&W. *Sale:* Natl AV Ctr.

Bad & the Beautiful, The. Lana Turner & Kirk Douglas. Directed by Vincente Minnelli. 1952. MGM. 118 min. Sound. 16mm B&W. *Rental:* MGM United. *Rental:* MGM United, Videotape version.

Bad Blonde *see* Flanagan Boy.

Bad Blonde. Barbara Peyton & Tony Wright. Directed by Reginald Le Borg. 80 min. Sound. 16mm B&W. *Rental:* Budget Films.

Bad Boy *see* Story of Danny Lester.

Bad Boys. Directed by Alan Raymond & Susan Raymond. 1978. PBS. (Documentary). 120 min. Sound. 16mm B&W. *Rental:* Direct Cinema. *Sale:* Direct Cinema. *Sale:* Direct Cinema, Videotape version.

Bad Boys. Sean Penn & Reni Santoni. Directed by Richard Rosenthal. 1982. Universal. 123 min. Sound. 16mm Color. *Rental:* Swank Motion.

Bad Boys. Yukio Yamada & Hirokaza Yoshitake. Directed by Susumi Hani. Jap. 1960. Japan. 90 min. Sound. 16mm B&W. subtitles Eng. *Rental:* Films Inc.

Bad Bunch, The. Greydon Clark & Aldo Ray. Directed by Greydon Clark. 1976. Dimension. 85 min. Sound. 16mm Color. *Sale:* Salz Film.

Bad Company. Trans. Title: Mauvaises Frequentations, Les. Jean-Pierre Leaud. Directed by Jean Eustache. Fr. 1964. France. 83 min. Sound. 16mm B&W. subtitles. *Rental:* New Yorker Films.

Bad Company. Jeff Bridges. Directed by Robert Benton. 1972. Paramount. 93 min. Sound. 16mm B&W. *Rental:* Films Inc.

Bad Company. Rolf Kempf & Clay Borris. Directed by Peter Wronski. 1979. Canada. 76 min. Sound. 16mm Color. *Rental:* Natl Film CN. *Sale:* Natl Film CN.

Bad Company. Frank MacHugh & Ricardo Cortez. Directed by Tay Garnett. 1932. RKO. 75 min. Sound. 16mm *Rental:* RKO General Pics.

Bad Day at Black Rock. Spencer Tracy & Robert Ryan. Directed by John Sturges. 1955. MGM. 81 min. Sound. 16mm B&W. *Rental:* MGM United. *Rental:* MGM United, Color version. *Rental:* Films Inc, Anamorphic B&W version. *Rental:* Films Inc, Anamorphic color version.

Bad for Each Other. Charlton Heston & Lizabeth Scott. Directed by Irving Rapper. 1953. Columbia. 83 min. Sound. 16mm B&W. *Rental:* Kit Parker.

Bad Georgia Road. Gary Lockwood & Carol Lynley. Directed by John C. Broderick. 1977. Dimension. 85 min. Sound. 16mm Color. *Rental:* Welling Motion Pictures & Williams Films. *Sale:* Salz Ent.

Bad Guy, The. Bruce Cabot & Virginia Grey. Directed by Edward L. Cahn. 1937. MGM. 67 min. Sound. 16mm B&W. *Rental:* MGM United.

Bad Little Angel, The. Virginia Weidler & Gene Reynolds. Directed by William Thiele. 1939. MGM. 72 min. Sound. 16mm B&W. *Rental:* MGM United.

Bad Lord Byron. Dennis Price & Joan Greenwood. Directed by David McDonald. 1952. Britain. 85 min. Sound. 16mm B&W. *Rental:* Budget Films.

Bad Man from Big Bend. Directed by Carl Shrum. 1948. Astor. 60 min. Sound. 16mm B&W. *Rental:* Mogulls Films.

Bad Man of Deadwood. Roy Rogers. Directed by Joseph Kane. 1941. Republic. 54 min. Sound. 16mm B&W. *Rental:* Budget Films & Ivy Films. *Sale:* Rep Pic Film.

Bad Men of Tombstone. Broderick Crawford & Barry Sullivan. Directed by Kurt Neumann. 1948. Allied Artists. 80 min. Sound. 16mm B&W. *Rental:* Budget Films & Hurlock Cine.

Bad News Bears, The. Walter Matthau, Tatum O'Neal & Vic Morrow. Directed by Michael Ritchie. 1976. Paramount. 102 min. Sound. 16mm Color. *Rental:* Films Inc.

Bad News Bears Go to Japan, The. Tony Curtis, Jackie Earle Haley & Matthew Anton. Directed by John Berry. 1978. Paramount. 102 min. Sound. 16mm Color. *Rental:* Films Inc.

Bad News Bears in Breaking Training, The. William Devane, Clifton James & Jackie Earle Haley. Directed by Michael Pressman. 1977. Paramount. 99 min. Sound. 16mm Color. *Rental:* Films Inc.

Bad One, The. Delores Del Rio & Edmund Lowe. Directed by George Fitzmaurice. 1930. United Artists. 70 min. Sound. 16mm B&W. *Rental:* Film classics.

Bad Penny. 1978. Quality X. 83 min. Videotape Color. *Sale:* Quality X Video.

Bad Seed, The. Nancy Kelly, Patty McCormack & Henry Jones. Directed by Mervyn LeRoy. 1956. Warners. 129 min. Sound. 16mm B&W. *Rental:* Williams Films, Films Inc, Mogulls Films, Swank Motion & Twyman Films.

Bad Sister. Bette Davis & Conrad Nagel. Directed by Hobart Henley. 1931. Universal. 68 min. Sound. 16mm B&W. *Rental:* Swank Motion.

Bad Timing- A Sensual Obsession. Theresa Russell & Art Garfunkel. Directed by Nicholas Roeg. 1980. Britain. (Anamorphic). 122 min. Sound. 16mm Color. *Rental:* Corinth Films & WW Enter. *Rental:* Corinth Films & WW Enter, Videotape version.

Baddest Daddy in the World, The. Directed by Fred Haines. 1972. Switzerland. (Documentary). 52 min. Sound. 16mm B&W. *Rental:* New Yorker Films.

Badge of Honor. Buster Crabbe & Ruth Hall. Directed by Spencer G. Bennett. 1934. Mayfair. 65 min. Sound. 16mm B&W. *Rental:* Modern Sound.

Badge of Marshall Brennan, The. Jim Davis & Arleen Whalen. Directed by Albert C. Gannaway. 1957. Allied Artists. 76 min. Sound. 16mm B&W. *Rental:* Ivy Films. *Sale:* Rep Pic Film.

Badge Three Hundred & Seventy-Three. Robert Duvall, Verna Bloom & Henry Darrow. Directed by Howard Koch. 1973. Paramount. 116 min. Sound. 16mm B&W. *Rental:* Films Inc.

Badlanders, The. Alan Ladd & Ernest Borgnine. Directed by Delmer Daves. 1958. MGM. 87 min. Sound. 16mm Color. *Rental:* MGM United. *Rental:* MGM United, Anamorphic color version.

Badlands. Martin Sheen & Sissy Spacek. Directed by Terrence Malick. 1974. Warners. 95 min. Sound. 16mm Color. *Rental:* Swank Motion. *Rental:* Swank Motion, Videotape version.

Badlands. Noah Beery & Robert Barrat. Directed by Lew Landers. 1939. RKO. 70 min. Sound. 16mm B&W. *Rental:* RKO General Pics.

Badlands of Montana. Rex Reason & Beverly Garland. Directed by Daniel B. Ullman. 1957. Fox. 75 min. Sound. 16mm B&W. *Rental:* Ivy Films. *Sale:* Rep Pic Film.

Badman's Gold. Johnny Carpenter. Directed by Robert Tansey. 1951. United Artists. 58 min. Sound. 16mm B&W. *Rental:* Westcoast Films.

Badman's Territory. Randolph Scott & Ann Richards. Directed by Tim Whelan. 1946. RKO. 97 min. Sound. 16mm B&W. *Rental:* Films Inc.

Badmen of Missouri. Dennis Morgan & Jane Wyman. Directed by Ray Enright. 1941. Warners. 71 min. Sound. 16mm B&W. *Rental:* MGM United.

Bags of Life. 1981. Britain. 50 min. Sound. 16mm Color. *Rental:* Films Inc. *Sale:* Films Inc. *Sale:* Films Inc, Videotape version.

Bahia. Antonio Pitanga & Mira Fonseca. Directed by Marcel Camus. Port. New Line Cinema. 90 min. Sound. 16mm Color. subtitles. *Rental:* New Line Cinema.

Bailout at Forty-Three Thousand. John Payne & Paul Kelly. Directed by Francis D. Lyon. 1957. United Artists. 78 min. Sound. 16mm B&W. *Rental:* MGM United.

Baiser Voles *see* Stolen Kisses.

Bait, The. Diana Napier & John Bentley. Directed by Frank Richardson. 1950. Britain. 72 min. Sound. 16mm B&W. *Rental:* Film Classics.

Bait. Cleo Moore & Hugo Haas. Directed by Hugo Haas. 1954. 79 min. Sound. 16mm B&W. *Rental:* Kit Parker.

Baker's Hawk. Clint Walker & Burl Ives. Directed by Lyman Dayton. 1976. Doty/Dayton. 98 min. Sound. 16mm Color. *Rental:* Modern Sound & Swank Motion.

Baker's Wife, The. Trans. Title: Femme Du Boulanger, La. Raimu & Ginette Leclerc. Directed by Marcel Pagnol. Fr. 1938. France. 120 min. Sound. 16mm B&W. subtitles. *Sale:* Reel Images.

Bakhtiari Migration, The. 1973. Anthony-David. (Documentary). 52 min. Sound. 16mm Color. *Rental:* Films Inc & Iowa Films. *Sale:* Films Inc. *Sale:* Films Inc, Videotape version.

Baking Desert, The. 55 min. Color. *Rental:* EMC.

Bal, Le. Directed by Ettore Scola. 1983. France. 112 min. Sound. Videotape Color. *Sale:* Tamarelles French Film.

Bal Tabarin. Muriel Lawrence & Steve Brodie. Directed by Philip Ford. 1951. Repulic. 84 min. 16mm B&W. *Rental:* Ivy Films. *Sale:* Rep Pic Film.

Balalaika. Nelson Eddy & Ilona Massey. Directed by Reinhold Schunzel. 1939. MGM. 102 min. Sound. 16mm B&W. *Rental:* MGM United.

Balancing Act. 1979. Body in Question. (Documentary). 60 min. Videotape Color. *Rental:* Films Inc. *Sale:* Films Inc.

Balboa. Frank Latimore & Joseph Briggs. Directed by J. M. Elias. Ital. 1964. Italy. 92 min. Sound. 16mm Color. dubbed. *Rental:* Video Comm.

Balcony, The. Shelley Winters & Peter Falk. Directed by Joseph Strick. 1963. Embassy. 84 min. Sound. 16mm B&W. *Rental:* Budget Films & U Cal Media.

Balearic Caper, The. Jacques Sernac & Daniela Bianchi. Fr. & Ital. 1966. France-Italy. 93 min. Sound. 16mm Color. dubbed. *Rental:* Westcoast Films.

Ball of Fire. Gary Cooper, Barbara Stanwyck & Oscar Homolka. Directed by Howard Hawks. 1941. Goldwyn. 111 min. Sound. 16mm B&W. *Rental:* Films Inc.

Ballad of a Bounty Hunter. James Philbrook & Pearl Cristal. Span. Spain. 92 min. Sound. 16mm Color. dubbed. *Rental:* Films Inc & Westcoast Films. *Rental:* Westcoast Films, 80 mins version.

Ballad of a Gunfighter. Marty Robbins. Directed by Bill Ward. 1965. Parade. 84 min. Sound. 16mm Color. *Rental:* Ivy Films.

Ballad of a Soldier. Vladimir Ivashev, Shanna Prokhorenko & Antonia Maximova. Directed by Grigori Chukrai. Rus. 1960. Russia. 89 min. Sound. 16mm B&W. subtitles. *Rental:* Budget Films, Corinth Films, Em Gee Film Lib, Films Inc, Images Film & Kit Parker. *Sale:* Cinema Concepts, Festival Films, Reel Images & Images Film. *Lease:* Corinth Films. *Sale:* Festival Films, Images Film & Tamarelles French Film, Videotape version.

Ballad of Gregorio Cortez, The. Edward James Olmos & James Gammon. Directed by Robert M. Young. 1983. Embassy. 100 min. Sound. 16mm Color. *Rental:* Films Inc.

Ballad of Josie, The. Doris Day & Peter Graves. Directed by Andrew V. McLaglen. 1968. Universal. 102 min. Sound. 16mm Color. *Rental:* Williams Films.

Ballad of Smokey the Bear, The. 1969. UPA. (Animated). 57 min. Sound. 16mm Color. *Rental:* Buchan Pic, Cine Craft, Charard Motion Pics, Films Inc, Inst Cinema, Newman Film Lib, Welling Motion Pictures & Westcoast Films.

Ballerina. Violette Verdy & Romney Brent. Fr. 1953. France. 78 min. Sound. 16mm B&W. *Rental:* MGM United & Natl Telefilm.

Ballet of Romeo & Juliet, The. Galina Ulanova. 1954. Russia. 96 min. Sound. 16mm Color. narrated Eng. *Rental:* Corinth Films, Films Inc & Macmillan Films. *Lease:* Macmillan Films.

Balloon Safari. Directed by Alan Root. 1981. Benchmark. (Documentary). 55 min. Sound. 16mm Color. *Rental:* Benchmark Films, Iowa Films, Syracuse U Film, U Cal Media & U of IL Film. *Sale:* Benchmark Films. *Sale:* Benchmark Films, 8mm version avail. version.

Ballot Blackmail: Gangs, Inc.. Alan Ladd & Joan Woodbury. Directed by Phil Rosen. Fr. 1941. PRC. 72 min. Sound. 16mm B&W. *Rental:* Mogulls Films & Video Comm.

Baltic Deputy. Directed by Alexander Zharki. Rus. 1937. Russia. 95 min. Sound. 16mm B&W. subtitles. *Rental:* Corinth Films.

Baltimore Bullet, The. James Coburn & Omar Sharif. Directed by Robert Ellis Miller. 1980. Embassy. 103 min. Sound. 16mm Color. *Rental:* Films Inc.

Balzac. Fr. France. (Cast unlisted). 60 min. Sound. 16mm B&W. *Rental:* French Am Cul.

Bam: Beyond Baikal. 30 min. Sound. 16mm Color. *Rental:* First Run.

Bambi. Directed by David Hand. 1942. Disney. (Animated). 70 min. Sound. 16mm Color. *Rental:* Buchan Pic, Disney Prod, Films Inc, Swank Motion & Twyman Films.

Bambole. Monica Vitti, Elke Sommer & Gina Lollobrigida. Directed by Mauro Bolognini, Franco Rossi, Luigi Comencini & Dino Risi. 1965. France-Italy. 111 min. Sound. 16mm B&W. dubbed. *Rental:* Kit Parker.

Bamboo Blonde, The. Frances Langford. Directed by Anthony Mann. 1946. RKO. 67 min. Sound. 16mm B&W. *Rental:* Films Inc & RKO General Pics.

Bamboo Gods & Iron Men. James Iglehart. Directed by Cesar Gallardo. 1973. Philippines. 88 min. Sound. 16mm Color. dubbed. *Rental:* Swank Motion.

Bamboo Prison, The. Brain Keith & Robert Francis. Directed by Lewis Seiler. 1954. Columbia. 80 min. Sound. 16mm B&W. *Rental:* Charard Motion Pics, Films Inc, Inst Cinema & Modern Sound.

Bamboo Saucer. John Erickson & Dan Duryea. Directed by Frank Telford. 1967. NTA. 95 min. Sound. 16mm Color. *Rental:* Ivy Films. *Sale:* Rep Pic Film.

Bambuti: Wild Animals. Directed by Michael Grzimek. 1959. Germany. (Documentary). 61 min. Sound. 16mm Color. *Rental:* Ivy Films.

Banana Boat, The. Hayley Mills, Doug McClure & Lionel Jeffries. Directed by Sidney Hayers. Britain. 82 min. Sound. 16mm Color. *Rental:* Arcus Film & Modern Sound.

Banana Peel. Jeanne Moreau & Jean-Paul Belmomdo. Directed by Marcel Ophuls. Fr. 1965. France. 97 min. Sound. 16mm B&W. subtitles. *Rental:* Films Inc.

Bananas. Woody Allen & Louise Lasser. Directed by Woody Allen. 1971. United Artists. 82 min. Sound. 16mm Color. *Rental:* MGM United. *Rental:* MGM United, Videotape version.

Band of Outsiders. Anna Karina & Claude Brasseur. Directed by Jean-Luc Godard. Fr. 1964. France. 95 min. Sound. 16mm B&W. subtitles Eng. *Rental:* Budget Films & Corinth Films. *Sale:* Festival Films, Reel Images & Tamarelles French Film. *Sale:* Festival Films & Tamarelles French Film, Videotape version.

Band Plays On, The. Robert Young & Betty Furness. Directed by Russell Mack. 1934. MGM. 88 min. Sound. 16mm B&W. *Rental:* MGM United.

Band Wagon, The. Fred Astaire & Cyd Charisse. Directed by Vincente Minnelli. 1953. MGM. 111 min. Sound. 16mm Color. *Rental:* MGM United. *Rental:* MGM United, Videotape version.

Bandit & the Princess, The. Helmut Lohner & Peter Weck. Directed by Franz Antel. Ger. 1953. Germany. 100 min. Sound. 16mm Color. dubbed. *Rental:* Creative Film.

Bandit General *see* Torch.

Bandit King of Texas, The. Allan Lane. Directed by Fred C. Brannon. 1949. Republic. 60 min. Sound. 16mm B&W. *Rental:* Ivy Films. *Sale:* Rep Pic Film.

Bandit of Sherwood Forest, The. Cornel Wilde & Anita Louise. Directed by George Sherman & Henry Levin. 1946. Columbia. 87 min. Sound. 16mm Color. *Rental:* Cine Craft & Williams Films.

Bandit of Zhobe, The. Victor Mature & Anthony Newley. Directed by John Gilling. 1959. Columbia. 80 min. Sound. 16mm Color. *Rental:* Inst Cinema, Westcoast Films & Welling Motion Pictures.

Bandit Queen, The. Barbara Britton & Willard Parker. Directed by William Berke. 1950. Lippert. 68 min. Sound. 16mm B&W. *Rental:* Budget Films.

Bandit Ranger, The. Tim Holt & Cliff Edwards. Directed by Bert Gilroy. 1943. RKO. 60 min. Sound. 16mm *Rental:* RKO General Pics.

Bandit Trail, The. Tim Holt & Ray Whitley. Directed by Bert Gilroy. 1942. RKO. 60 min. Sound. 16mm *Rental:* RKO General Pics.

Bandits of Dark Canyon, The. Allan Lane. Directed by Philip Ford. 1948. Republic. 59 min. Sound. 16mm B&W. *Rental:* Ivy Films. *Sale:* Rep Pic Film & Nostalgia Merchant.

Bandits of Orgosolo, The. Michele Cessu. Directed by Vittorio De Seta. Ital. 1964. Italy. Sound. 16mm B&W. subtitles. *Rental:* Janus Films. *Sale:* Morcraft Films, Videotape version.

Bandits of the Badlands. Sunset Carson. Directed by Thomas Carr. 1945. Republic. 54 min. Sound. 16mm B&W. *Rental:* Ivy Films. *Sale:* Rep Pic Film.

Bandits of the West. Allan Lane. Directed by Harry Keller. 1953. Republic. 54 min. Sound. 16mm B&W. *Rental:* Ivy Films. *Sale:* Rep Pic Film.

Bandolero. Dean Martin & James Stewart. Directed by Andrew V. McLaglen. 1968. Fox. (Anamorphic). 106 min. Sound. 16mm Color. *Rental:* Films Inc.

Bang Bang Kid, The. Guy Madison, Tom Bosley & Sandra Milo. Directed by Stanley Prager. Ital. & Span. 1968. Italy-Spain. 92 min. Sound. 16mm Color. dubbed. *Rental:* Films Inc.

Bang Bang, You Got It. Quality X. 80 min. Videotape Color. *Sale:* Quality X Video.

Bang! Bang! You're Dead! Tony Randall & Senta Berger. Directed by Don Sharp. 1966. American International. 92 min. Sound. 16mm Color. *Rental:* Charard Motion Pics, Ivy Films & Video Comm.

Bang the Drum Slowly. Michael Moriarty, Robert de Niro & Vincent Gardenia. Directed by John Hancock. 1973. Paramount. 96 min. Sound. 16mm Color. *Rental:* Wholesome Film Ctr & Budget Films.

Banjo. Sharyn Moffet & Jacqueline White. Directed by Richard Fleischer. 1947. RKO. 68 min. Sound. 16mm B&W. *Rental:* Films Inc.

Banjo on My Knee. Barbara Stanwyck & Joel McCrea. Directed by John Cromwell. 1936. Fox. 105 min. Sound. 16mm B&W. *Rental:* Films Inc.

Bank Dick, The. W. C. Fields. Directed by Edward Cline. 1940. Universal. 73 min. Sound. 16mm B&W. *Rental:* Swank Motion.

Bank Holiday. Margaret Lockwood & John Lodge. Directed by Sir Carol Reed. 1938. Britain. 86 min. Sound. 16mm B&W. *Rental:* Janus Films.

Bank Robbery *see* Renegades of the Rio Grande.

Bank Shot. George C. Scott & Sorrell Booke. Directed by Gower Champion. 1974. United Artists. 83 min. Sound. 16mm Color. *Rental:* MGM United.

Banking on the Brink. 1983. NBC. (Documentary). 52 min. Sound. Videotape Color. *Sale:* Films Inc.

Banks & the Poor. 1971. NET. (Documentary). 59 min. Sound. 16mm B&W. *Rental:* U Cal Media & Indiana AV Ctr. *Sale:* Indiana AV Ctr.

Bannerline. Keefe Brasselle & Lionel Barrymore. Directed by Don Weis. 1951. MGM. 81 min. Sound. 16mm B&W. *Rental:* MGM United.

Banning. Robert Wagner & Jill St. John. Directed by Ron Winston. 1967. Universal. 102 min. Sound. 16mm Color. *Rental:* Swank Motion.

Banquet of Life. 1966. NET. (Documentary). 69 min. Sound. 16mm B&W. *Rental:* Indiana AV Ctr. *Lease:* Indiana AV Ctr.

Banzai: Japan 1931-1942. Directed by Hugh Raggett. (World at War Ser.). : Pt. 6.). 1975. Media Guild. (Documentary). 52 min. Sound. 16mm Color. *Rental:* Media Guild. *Sale:* Media Guild. *Sale:* Media Guild, Videotape version.

Baobab: Portrait of a Tree. 1973. Alan Root. (Documentary). 53 min. Sound. 16mm Color. *Rental:* U Cal Media, McGraw-Hill Films & U Mich Media. *Sale:* McGraw-Hill Films.

Baptism of Fire. 1940. US Government. (Documentary). 51 min. Sound. 16mm B&W. *Rental:* Budget Films, Em Gee Film Lib & Kit Parker. *Sale:* Festival Films & Natl Cinema. *Sale:* Festival Films, Videotape version.

Bar Mitzvah Boy. Jeremy Steyn, Maria Charles & Bernard Spear. 1980. Time-Life Films. 75 min. Sound. 16mm Color. *Rental:* Roas Films.

Bar Twenty. William Boyd. Directed by Lesley Selander. 1943. United Artists. 60 min. Sound. 16mm B&W. *Sale:* Glenn Photo. *Lease:* Cinema Concepts, Super 8 sound version. *Sale:* Em Gee Film Lib, Videotape version.

Bar Twenty Justice. William Boyd & Gabby Hayes. Directed by Lesley Selander. 1938. Paramount. 70 min. Sound. 16mm B&W. *Lease:* Cinema Concepts. *Rental:* Budget Films.

Bar Twenty Rides Again. William Boyd. Directed by Howard Bretherton. 1935. Paramount. 60 min. Sound. 16mm B&W. *Rental:* Budget Films.

Bar Z Badmen. Johnny Mack Brown. Directed by Sam Newfield. 1936. Republic. 60 min. Sound. 16mm B&W. *Rental:* Ivy Films. *Sale:* Rep Pic Film.

Barabbas. Anthony Quinn, Silvana Mangano & Arthur Kennedy. Directed by Richard Fleischer. 1962. Columbia. 144 min. Sound. 16mm Color. *Rental:* Alba House, Arcus Film, Bosco Films, Buchan Pic, Budget Films, Cine Craft, Charard Motion Pics, Film Ctr DC, Film Pres, Films Inc, Modern Sound, Natl Film Video, Roas Films, Twyman Films, Video Comm & Welling Motion Pictures.

Baraka X-Seventy-Seven. Sylva Koscina. 1968. Italy. 93 min. Sound. 16mm Color. dubbed. *Rental:* Westcoast Films.

Barbara Broadcast. 1977. Quality X. 87 min. Videotape Color. *Sale:* Quality X Video.

Barbara Frietchie. Florence Vidor & Edmund Lowe. Directed by Lambert Hillyer. 1924. PDC. 85 min. Sound. 16mm B&W. *Sale:* Cinema Concepts.

Barbarella. Jane Fonda, John Philip Law & David Hemmings. Directed by Roger Vadim. 1968. Paramount. (Anamorphic). 98 min. Sound. Color. *Rental:* Films Inc. *Sale:* Blackhawk Films & Cinema Concepts, Videotape version.

Barbarian, The. Monroe Salisbury, Jane Novak & Alan Hale. Directed by Donald Crisp. 1921. Pioneer. 55 min. Silent. 16mm B&W. *Sale:* Morcraft Films. *Rental:* MGM United.

Barbarian & the Geisha, The. John Wayne & Sam Jaffe. Directed by John Huston. 1958. Fox. 104 min. Sound. 16mm Color. *Rental:* Films Inc, Inst Cinema & Willoughby Peer.

Barbarosa. Willie Nelson & Gary Busey. Directed by Fred Schepisi. 1982. Australia. 90 min. Sound. 16mm Color. *Rental:* Swank Motion.

Barbarosa: June-December 1941. Directed by Hugh Raggett. (World at War Ser.). : Pt. 5). 1974. Media Guild. (Documentary). 52 min. Sound. 16mm Color. *Rental:* Media Guild & U Cal Media. *Sale:* Media Guild. *Sale:* Media Guild, Videotape version.

Barbary Coast. Walter Brennan, Miriam Hopkins & Edward G. Robinson. Directed by Howard Hawks. 1935. Goldwyn. 90 min. Sound. 16mm B&W. *Rental:* Films Inc & Swank Motion.

Barbary Coast Gent. Wallace Beery & Binnie Barnes. Directed by Roy Del Ruth. 1944. MGM. 87 min. Sound. 16mm B&W. *Rental:* MGM United.

Barber of Seville, The. Trans. Title: Figaro. Tito Gobbi & Ferruccio Tagliavini. Directed by Camillo Mastrocinque. Ital. 1955. Italy. 100 min. Sound. 16mm B&W. narrated Eng. *Rental:* Mogulls Films & Trans-World Films.

Barber of Seville, The. 1975. Britain. (Opera). 54 min. Sound. 16mm Color. *Rental:* Centron Films. *Sale:* Centron Films.

Barefoot Boy. Jackie Moran & Marcia Mae Jones. Directed by Karl Brown. 1938. Monogram. 75 min. Sound. 16mm B&W. *Rental:* Alba House.

Barefoot Contessa, The. Humphrey Bogart & Ava Gardner. Directed by Joseph L. Mankiewicz. 1954. United Artists. 128 min. Sound. 16mm Color. *Rental:* MGM United. *Rental:* MGM United, Videotape version.

Barefoot Doctors of Rural China, The. Directed by Diane Li. 1975. Diane Li. (Documentary). 52 min. Sound. 16mm Color. *Rental:* Cambridge Doc, U of IL Film & U Mich Media. *Sale:* Cambridge Doc. *Sale:* Cambridge Doc, Videotape version.

Barefoot Executive, The. Kurt Russell, Joe Flynn & Harry Morgan. Directed by Robert Butler. 1971. Disney. 96 min. Sound. 16mm Color. *Rental:* Bosco Films, Buchan Pic, Cine Craft, Disney Prod, Elliot Film Co, Film Ctr DC, Film Pres, Films Inc, MGM United, Newman Film Lib, Roas Films, Swank Motion, Twyman Films, U of IL Film, Welling Motion Pictures & Westcoast Films.

Barefoot in the Park. Robert Redford, Jane Fonda & Charles Boyer. Directed by Gene Saks. 1967. Paramount. 106 min. Sound. 16mm Color. *Rental:* Films Inc.

Barefoot Mailman, The. Robert Cummings & Terry Moore. Directed by Earl McEvoy. 1951. Columbia. 83 min. Sound. 16mm B&W. *Rental:* Inst Cinema & Welling Motion Pictures.

Bargain, The. Williams S. Hart. Directed by Thomas H. Ince. 1914. New York. 75 min. Silent. 16mm B&W. *Rental:* Em Gee Film Lib & Film Images. *Sale:* Film Images.

Barkleys of Broadway, The. Fred Astaire & Ginger Rogers. Directed by Charles Walters. 1949. MGM. 109 min. Sound. 16mm Color. *Rental:* MGM United.

Barnaby & Me. Sid Caesar & Juliet Mills. Directed by Norman Panama. 1979. Australia. 90 min. Sound. 16mm Color. *Rental:* Modern Sound & Twyman Films.

Barnet: The Child. 1971. Sweden. (Documentary). 48 min. Sound. 16mm Color. *Rental:* Intl Film, Iowa Films & Syracuse U Film. *Sale:* Intl Film.

Barnyard Follies. Joan Woodbury & Carl Switzer. Directed by Frank McDonald. 1940. Republic. 68 min. Sound. 16mm B&W. *Rental:* Ivy Films.

Baron Blood. Joseph Cotten & Elke Sommer. Directed by Mario Bava. Ital. 1972. Italy. 90 min. Sound. 16mm Color. dubbed. *Rental:* Swank Motion.

Baron Del Terror, El *see* Brainiac.

Baron Munchhausen. Hans Albers & Brigitte Horney. Directed by Josef Von Baky. Ger. 1943. Germany. 110 min. Sound. 16mm Color. subtitles. *Rental:* Kit Parker.

Baron of Arizona, The. Vincent Price & Ellen Drew. Directed by Samuel Fuller. 1950. 93 min. Sound. 16mm *Rental:* Budget Films.

Baron's Africa War, The. Rod Cameron. Directed by Spencer G. Bennett. 1966. Republic. 100 min. Sound. 16mm B&W. *Rental:* Ivy Films. *Sale:* Rep Pic Film.

Barquero. Lee Van Cleef & Warren Oates. 1970. United Artists. 108 min. Sound. 16mm Color. *Rental:* MGM United.

Barravento. Orig. Title: Turning Wind, The. Atila Iorio. Directed by Glauber Rocha. Port. 1962. Brazil. 76 min. Sound. 16mm B&W. subtitles. *Rental:* New Yorker Films. *Sale:* New Yorker Films.

Barres. Fr. France. 60 min. Sound. 16mm B&W. *Rental:* French Am Cul. *Rental:* French Am Cul, Videotape version.

Barretts of Wimpole Street, The. Norma Shearer & Charles Laughton. Directed by Sidney Franklin. 1934. MGM. 111 min. Sound. 16mm B&W. *Rental:* MGM United.

Barretts of Wimpole Street, The. Sir John Gielgud & Jennifer Jones. Directed by Sidney Franklin. 1957. MGM. (Anamorphic). 105 min. 16mm Color. *Rental:* MGM United. *Rental:* MGM United, Videotape version.

Barricade. Alice Faye & Warner Baxter. Directed by Gregory Ratoff. 1939. Fox. 71 min. Sound. 16mm B&W. *Rental:* Films Inc.

Barrier. Jan Nowicki & Joanna Szczerbic. Directed by Jerzy Skolimowski. Pol. 1966. Janus. 84 min. Sound. 16mm B&W. subtitles Eng. *Rental:* Films Inc.

Barrier of the Law. Rossano Brazzi & Lea Padovani. 1950. Italy. 81 min. Sound. 16mm B&W. dubbed. *Rental:* Films Inc.

Barrier, The: The Great Barrier. Richard Arlen & Lilli Palmer. Directed by Milton Rosmer. 1937. Britain. 90 min. Sound. 16mm B&W. *Rental:* Mogulls Films.

Barry Lyndon. Ryan O'Neal & Marisa Berenson. Directed by Stanley Kubrick. 1976. Warners. 185 min. Sound. 16mm Color. *Rental:* Swank Motion.

Bas Fonds, Les see Lower Depths.

Baseball World of Joe Garagiola, The. 2 pts. 1975. NBC. (Documentary). 48 min. Sound. 16mm Color. *Rental:* Modern Talking.

Bashful Bachelor, The. Lum & Abner. Directed by Mal St. Clair. 1942. RKO. 77 min. Sound. 16mm B&W. *Rental:* Budget Films, Inst Cinema & Mogulls Films.

Bashful Elephant, The. Mollie Mack & Helmut Schmid. Directed by Dorrell McGowan & Stuart McGowan. 1962. Germany. 82 min. Sound. 16mm B&W. dubbed. *Rental:* Hurlock Cine.

Basic Autopsy Procedure. 1971. U.S. Government. (Documentary). 51 min. Sound. 16mm Color. *Sale:* Natl AV Ctr.

Basic Diagnostic & Treatment Procedures in Ophthalmology. 1975. 54 min. videotape B&W. *Sale:* Natl AV Ctr.

Basic English by Video. 90 min. Sound. Videotape Color. *Sale:* Tamarelles French Film.

Basic French by Video. 90 min. Sound. Videotape Color. *Sale:* Tamarelles French Films.

Basic Influencing Skills, Part I. 1975. 56 min. Sound. Videotape B&W. *Rental:* Iowa Films.

Basic Influencing Skills: Part Two. 1975. 56 min. Sound. Videotape B&W. *Rental:* Iowa Films.

Basic Training. Directed by Frederick Wiseman. 1971. Zipporah. (Documentary). 89 min. Sound. 16mm B&W. *Rental:* Zipporah Films. *Lease:* Zipporah Films, Videotape version.

Basingstoke: Runcorn British New Towns. 1975. Canada. (Documentary). 87 min. Sound. 16mm Color. *Rental:* Natl Film CN. *Sale:* Natl Film CN.

Basis for Human Dignity, The. 50 min. Sound. 16mm Color. *Rental:* Gospel Films.

Basket of Crabs, A. Pierre Michael. Directed by Joseph Lisbona. Fr. 1960. France. 88 min. Sound. 16mm B&W. *Rental:* Films Inc.

Basketball Fix, The. John Ireland & Vanessa Brown. Directed by Felix Feist. 1951. Realart. 70 min. Sound. 16mm B&W. *Rental:* Mogulls Films.

Bastardo, El. Joan Jose. Directed by Ramon Peon. Span. Spain. Sound. 16mm B&W. *Rental:* Film Classics.

Bat, The. Vincent Price, Agnes Moorehead & Gavin Gordon. Directed by Crane Wilbur. 1959. Allied Artists. 80 min. Sound. 16mm B&W. *Rental:* Films Inc.

Bat People, The. Stewart Moss. Directed by Jerry Jameson. 1974. American International. 91 min. Sound. 16mm Color. *Rental:* Swank Motion.

Bataan. Robert Taylor & George Murphy. Directed by Tay Garnett. 1943. MGM. 110 min. Sound. 16mm B&W. *Rental:* MGM United.

Bataan, the Forgotten Hell. 1983. NBC. (Documentary). 52 min. Sound. Videotape Color. *Sale:* Films Inc.

Bath Waters. 1980. Britain. (Documentary). 50 min. Sound. 16mm Color. *Rental:* Films Inc. *Sale:* Films Inc. *Sale:* Films Inc, Videotape version.

Bathing Beauty. Esther Williams & Red Skelton. Directed by George Sidney. 1944. MGM. 101 min. Sound. 16mm Color. *Rental:* MGM United.

Batman. Adam West, Burt Ward & Lee Meriwether. Directed by Leslie Martinson. 1967. Fox. 105 min. Sound. 16mm Color. *Rental:* Films Inc & Williams Films.

Batmen of Africa. Clyde Beatty. Directed by B. Reeves Eason & Joseph Kane. 1949. Republic. 100 min. Sound. 16mm B&W. *Rental:* Ivy Films. *Sale:* Rep Pic Film.

Baton de Ancla. Antonio Casal. Directed by Ramon Torrado. Span. Mexico. Sound. 16mm B&W. subtitles. *Rental:* Film Classics.

Battered. 1978. 98 min. Sound. 16mm Color. *Rental:* Learning Corp Am. *Lease:* Learning Corp Am. *Sale:* Learning Corp Am, *Sale:* Learning Corp Am, Videotape version.

Battered Child, The. 1969. NET. (Documentary). 59 min. Sound. 16mm B&W. *Rental:* Indiana AV Ctr, Iowa Films, NYU Film Lib, U Cal Media, U of IL Film & U Mich Media. *Sale:* Indiana AV Ctr & Natl AV Ctr.

Battered Wives. 1979. 45 min. Sound. 16mm Color. *Rental:* Learning Corp Am & Syracuse U Film.

Battle at Apache Pass, The. Jeff Chandler & John Lund. Directed by Lesley Selander. 1952. Universal. 85 min. Sound. 16mm Color. *Rental:* Swank Motion.

Battle at Bloody Beach, The. Audie Murphy & Gary Crosby. Directed by Herbert Coleman. 1961. Fox. (Anamorphic). 80 min. Sound. 16mm B&W. *Rental:* Willoughby Peer.

Battle Beneath the Earth, The. Kerwin Mathews. Directed by Montgomery Tully. 1968. MGM. 92 min. Sound. 16mm Color. *Rental:* MGM United. *Rental:* MGM United, Anamorphic color version.

Battle Beyond the Sun, The. Orig. Title: Nebo Zowet. Andy Stewart. Directed by Thomas Colchart. 1963. American International. 67 min. Sound. 16mm Color. *Rental:* Films Inc.

Battle Circus. Humphrey Bogart & June Allyson. Directed by Richard Brooks. 1953. MGM. 90 min. Sound. 16mm B&W. *Rental:* MGM United.

Battle Cry. Van Heflin, Aldo Ray & Mona Freeman. Directed by Raoul Walsh. 1955. Warners. 148 min. Sound. 16mm Color. *Rental:* Films Inc, Ivy Films & Video Comm.

Battle Flame. Scott Brady & Robert Blake. Directed by R. G. Springsteen. 1959. Allied Artists. 75 min. Sound. 16mm B&W. *Rental:* Hurlock Cine.

Battle for Cassino. 1972. Peter Batty. (Documentary). 50 min. Sound. 16mm Color. *Rental:* Budget Films & Time-Life Multimedia. *Sale:* Time-Life Multimedia.

Battle for Music, The. Sir Adrian Boult & Constant Lambert. Directed by Don Taylor. 1948. Britain. 100 min. Sound. 16mm B&W. *Rental:* Ivy Films.

Battle for New Britain, The. 1944. 46 min. Sound. 16mm B&W. *Rental:* Natl AV Ctr.

Battle for Siberia, The. Varvara Miasnikova. Directed by Georgy Vassiliev. Rus. Russia. 90 min. Sound. 16mm B&W. subtitles. *Rental:* Corinth Films.

Battle for the Planet of the Apes, The. Roddy McDowall & Claude Akins. Directed by J. Lee Thompson. 1973. Fox. (Anamorphic). 86 min. Sound. 16mm Color. *Rental:* Films Inc.

Battle Hell: Yangtse Incident. Richard Todd & William Hartnell. Directed by Michael Anderson. 1956. Britain. 84 min. Sound. 16mm B&W. *Rental:* Budget Films, Ivy Films, Modern Sound & Roas Films, Super 8 sound version.

Battle Hymn. Rock Hudson & Martha Hyer. Directed by Douglas Sirk. 1956. Universal. 111 min. Sound. 16mm Color. *Rental:* Swank Motion.

Battle in Outer Space, The. Kyoko Anzai & Koreya Senda. Directed by Inoshiro Honda. 1960. Japan. 90 min. Sound. 16mm Color. dubbed. *Rental:* Cine Craft, Film Ctr DC, Films Inc, Inst Cinema & Modern Sound.

Battle of Algiers, The. Jean Martin, Yacef Saadi & Brahim Haggiag. Directed by Gillo Pontecorvo. Ital. 1966. Italy. 123 min. Sound. 16mm B&W. subtitles. *Rental:* U Cal Media, Classic Film Mus, Films Inc & New Cinema. *Sale:* Tamarelles French Film, Videotape version.

Battle of Britain. Directed by Frank Capra. 1943. War Department. (Documentary). 55 min. Sound. 16mm B&W. *Rental:* Maljack & Trans-World Films. *Sale:* Cinema Concepts, Natl AV Ctr & Reel Images. *Rental:* Natl AV Ctr & Video Comm, Videotape version.

Battle of Britain, The. 1964. Wolper. (Documentary). 55 min. Sound. 16mm B&W. *Rental:* Films Inc, Iowa Films, Natl AV Ctr & U Mich Media. *Sale:* Festival Films & Films Inc. *Sale:* Festival Films & Films Inc, Videotape version. *Rental:* Natl AV Ctr, 55 mins. version.

Battle of Britain, The. Michael Caine, Trevor Howard, Sir Laurence Olivier. Directed by Guy Hamilton. 1969. United Artists. (Anamorphic). 132 min. Sound. 16mm B&W. *Rental:* MGM United.

Battle of Chile, The. 2 pts. Directed by Patricio Guzman. Span. 1973. Chile-Cuba. (Documentary). 191 min. Sound. 16mm B&W. subtitles Eng. *Rental:* New Yorker Films & Unifilm. *Sale:* Unifilm.

Battle of China, The. Directed by Frank Capra. 1944. War Department. (Documentary). 65 min. Sound. 16mm B&W. *Rental:* Iowa Films, Maljack, Natl AV Ctr & Trans-World Films. *Sale:* Museum Mod Art & Natl Av Ctr. *Sale:* Natl AV Ctr, Videotape version.

Battle of Culloden, The. Orig. Title: Culloden. Directed by Peter Watkins. 1966. Britain. (Documentary). 72 min. Sound. 16mm B&W. *Rental:* U Cal Media, Films Inc, Images Film, U Mich Media & Syracuse U Film. *Sale:* Films Inc. *Rental:* Films Inc, *Sale:* Films Inc, Videotape version.

Battle of East St. Louis, The. 1970. 46 min. Sound. 16mm B&W. *Rental:* Iowa Films & U Mich Media.

Battle of Gallipoli see Tell England.

Battle of Neretva, The. Yul Brynner & Sergei Bondarchuk. Directed by Veljko Bulajic. 1962. Commonwealth United. 102 min. Sound. 16mm Color. dubbed. *Rental:* Budget Films & Rep Pic Film. *Sale:* Rep Pic Film. *Rental:* Films Inc & Ivy Films, Anamorphic version. *Sale:* Tamarelles French Film, Videotape version.

Battle of Newburgh, The. 1963. NBC. (Documentary). 54 min. Sound. 16mm B&W. *Rental:* Iowa Films, McGraw-Hill Films, Syracuse U Film, U Cal Media, U Mich Media, U Nev AV Ctr & Utah Media. *Sale:* McGraw-Hill Films.

Battle of Rogue River, The. George Montgomery & Richard Denning. Directed by William Castle. 1954. Columbia. 71 min. Sound. 16mm Color. *Rental:* Arcus Film, Film Ctr DC, Film Serv, Inst Cinema, Modern Sound & Roas Films.

Battle of Russia. Directed by Anatole Litvak. 1943. War Department. (Documentary). 83 min. Sound. 16mm B&W. *Rental:* Budget Films, Iowa Films, Maljack, Natl AV Ctr & Trans-World Films. *Sale:* Natl AV Ctr & New Cinema. *Sale:* Blackhawk Films & Natl AV Ctr, Videotape version.

Battle of the Amazons, The. Lincoln Tate & Paola Tedesco. Directed by Al Bradley. 1973. Italy. 92 min. Sound. 16mm Color. dubbed. *Rental:* Swank Motion.

Battle of the Baritones, The. (Anthology). 89 min. Sound. Videotape B&W. *Sale:* Reel Images.

Battle of the Bulge, The. 1970. Britain. (Documentary). 50 min. Sound. 16mm Color. *Rental:* Time-Life Multimedia. *Sale:* Time-Life Multimedia.

Battle of the Commandoes, The. Jack Palance. 1969. Italy. 96 min. Sound. 16mm Color. dubbed. *Rental:* Ivy Films, Rep Pic Film & Video Comm. *Lease:* Rep Pic Film.

Battle of the Coral Sea, The. Cliff Robertson & Gia Scala. Directed by Paul Wendkos. 1959. Columbia. 87 min. Sound. 16mm B&W. *Rental:* Inst Cinema & Westcoast Films.

Battle of the Mods, The. Ricky Shayne & Joachim Fuchsberger. Directed by Franco Montemurro. 1968. Germany. 94 min. Sound. 16mm Color. dubbed. *Rental:* Video Comm.

Battle of the Pacific, The: The Setting Sun. 1950. 50 min. Sound. 16mm *Rental:* Budget Films.

Battle of the River Plate, The see Pursuit of the Graf Spee.

Battle of the Sexes, The. Peter Sellers, Constance Cummings & Robert Morley. Directed by Charles Crichton. 1960. Britain. 88 min. Sound. 16mm B&W. *Rental:* Budget Films & Kino Intl. *Sale:* Kino Intl. *Lease:* Kino Intl.

Battle of the Westlands, The. Directed by Carol Mon Pere & Sandra Nichols. 1980. PBS. (Documentary). 59 min. Videotape Color. *Rental:* Museum Mod Art & PBS Video. *Sale:* PBS Video.

Battle of the Worlds, The. Claude Rains & Bill Carter. Directed by Anthony Dawson. 1965. Britain. 90 min. Sound. 16mm Color. *Rental:* Welling Motion Pictures, Westcoast Films & Willoughby Peer.

Battle Shock: A Woman's Devotion. Ralph Meeker & Janice Rule. Directed by Paul Henried. 1956. Republic. 88 min. Sound. 16mm B&W. *Rental:* Ivy Films.

Battle Stations. John Lund & William Bendix. Directed by Lewis Seiler. 1956. Columbia. 81 min. Sound. 16mm B&W. *Rental:* Buchan Pic, Inst Cinema & Westcoast Films.

Battle Zone. John Hodiak & Stephen McNally. Directed by Lesley Selander. 1962. Allied Artists. 82 min. Sound. 16mm B&W. *Rental:* Hurlock Cine.

Battlefield. William Shatner & Leonard Nimoy. Directed by Frank Gorshin. 1967. Star Trek. 52 min. Sound. 16mm Color. *Sale:* Reel Images. *Sale:* Reel Images, Super 8 sound version.

Battleground. Van Johnson & John Hodiak. Directed by William A. Wellman. 1949. MGM. 117 min. Sound. 16mm B&W. *Rental:* MGM United.

Battleground Washington: Politics of Pressure. 1979. ABC. (Documentary). 52 min. Sound. 16mm Color. *Sale:* MTI Tele & Syracuse U Film. *Sale:* MTI Tele. *Sale:* MTI Tele, Videotape version.

Battles of Chief Pontiac. Lex Barker & Helen Wescott. Directed by Felix Feist. 1953. Realart. 70 min. Sound. 16mm B&W. *Rental:* Cine Craft.

Battlestar Galactica. Lorne Greene, Dirk Benedict & Richard Hatch. Directed by Richard A. Colla. 1978. Universal. 125 min. Sound. 16mm Color. *Rental:* Swank Motion & Twyman Films.

Battling Bellhop, The *see* Kid Galahad.

Battling Bunyan. Wesley Barry. Directed by Richard Thorpe. 1924. Associated Exhibitors. 60 min. Silent. 16mm B&W. *Sale:* Blackhawk Films & E Finney. *Rental:* Ivy Films, Super 8 silent version. *Sale:* Blackhawk Films, Silent 8mm version.

Battling Butler, The. Buster Keaton & Sally O'Neill. Directed by Buster Keaton. 1926. MGM. 103 min. Silent. 16mm B&W. *Rental:* A Twyman Pres.

Battling Fool, The. William Fairbanks II. Directed by W. S. Van Dyke. 1924. Goldwyn. 44 min. Silent. 16mm B&W. *Rental:* Film Classics & Mogulls Films. *Sale:* Film Classics. *Rental:* Film Classics, *Sale:* Film Classics, Silent 8mm version.

Battling Hoofer, The *see* Something to Sing About.

Battling Marshal, The. Sunset Carson. 1948. Astor. 60 min. Videotape B&W. *Rental:* Video Comm. *Sale:* Video Comm.

Battling Orioles. Glenn Tryon & Noah Young. Directed by Ted Wilde & Fred Guiol. 1924. Pathe. 70 min. Silent. 16mm B&W. *Rental:* Em Gee Film Lib. *Sale:* Glenn Photo. *Sale:* Glenn Photo, Super 8 silent version.

Bawdy Adventures of Tom Jones, The. Trevor Howard & Terry-Thomas. Directed by Cliff Owen. 1976. Universal. 88 min. Silent. 16mm Color. *Rental:* Twyman Films.

Baxter! Patricia Neal & Scott Jacoby. Directed by Lionel Jeffries. 1972. National General. 100 min. Sound. 16mm Color. *Rental:* Swank Motion.

Bay of Angels. Jeanne Moreau. Directed by Jacques Demy. Fr. 1962. France. 85 min. Sound. 16mm B&W. subtitles. *Rental:* Films Inc & Kit Parker.

Bay of Blood. 84 min. Sound. Videotape Color. *Rental:* Maljack.

Bay of Pigs. Directed by Manuel Herrera. 1973. Cuba. (Anamorphic, Documentary). 110 min. Sound. 16mm B&W. *Rental:* Cinema Guild. *Sale:* Cinema Guild.

Bay of St. Michel, The. Orig. Title: Operation Mermaid. Keenan Wynn & Ronald Howard. Directed by John Ainsworth. 1961. Britain. 86 min. Sound. 16mm B&W. *Rental:* Westcoast Films.

Bayahihan Philippine Dance Company. 1962. Philippines. (Documentary). 50 min. Sound. 16mm Color. *Rental:* U of IL Film.

Bayley Scales of Infant Development. 2 pts. 1975. Inst. of Human Development. (Lecture). 100 min. Sound. 16mm B&W. *Rental:* U Cal Media.

Be Careful How You Wish *see* Incredible Mr. Limpet.

Be Glad Then America. 1977. Penn State. (Documentary). 60 min. Silent. Videotape Color. *Rental:* Penn St AV Serv. *Sale:* Penn St AV Serv.

Be Yourself. Fannie Brice & Robert Armstrong. Directed by Thornton Freeland. 1930. United Artists. 67 min. Sound. 16mm B&W. *Rental:* Budget Films & Mogulls Films. *Sale:* Blackhawk Films. *Sale:* Blackhawk Films, Super 8 sound version.

Beach Ball. Edd Byrnes & Chris Noel. Directed by Len Weinrib. 1965. Paramount. 83 min. Sound. 16mm Color. *Rental:* Films Inc.

Beach Blanket Bingo. Frankie Avalon, Annette Funicello & Deborah Walley. Directed by William Asher. 1965. American International. 98 min. Sound. 13mm Color. *Rental:* Films Inc & Westcoast Films.

Beach Party. Frankie Avalon, Annette Funicello & Bob Cummings. Directed by William Asher. 1963. American International. 100 min. Sound. 16mm Color. *Rental:* Cinc Craft, Charard Motion Pics, Films Inc, Westcoast Films & Wholesome Film Ctr.

Beach Red. Cornel Wilde. Directed by Cornel Wilde. 1967. United Artists. 103 min. Sound. 16mm Color. *Rental:* MGM United.

Beachcomber, The. Charles Laughton & Elsa Lanchester. Directed by Erich Pommer. 1939. Britain. 88 min. Sound. 16mm B&W. *Rental:* A Twyman Pres, Budget Films, Classic Film Mus, Kit Parker, Mogulls Films, Westcoast Films & Wholesome Film Ctr. *Sale:* Classic Film Mus & Reel Images. *Sale:* Cinema Concepts, Videotape version.

Beachcomber, The *see* Vessel of Wrath.

Bears & I, The. Patricia Wayne, Chief Dan George & Andrew Duggan. Directed by Bernard McEveety. 1975. Disney. 88 min. Sound. 16mm Color. *Rental:* Buchan Pic, Bosco Films, Disney Prod, Elliot Film Co, Film Pres, Films Inc, MGM United, Modern Sound, Newman Film Lib, Roas Films, Swank Motion, Twyman Films, U of IL Film, Welling Motion Pictures, Westcoast Films & Williams Films.

Beartooth: Bearheart of the Northwest. Marshall Reed, Joey Young & Fritz Feld. Directed by Rand Brooks. 1964. Medallion. 90 min. Sound. 16mm Color. *Rental:* Films Inc.

Beast, The. 80 min. Sound. Videotape Color. *Rental:* Maljack Productions

Beast from Twenty Thousand Fathoms. Paul Christian, Paula Raymond & Cecil Kellaway. Directed by Eugene Lourie. 1953. Warners. 80 min. Sound. 16mm B&W. *Rental:* Films Inc, Ivy Films, Twyman Films, Video Comm & Willoughby Peer.

Beast Must Die, The. Calvin Lockhart & Peter Cushing. Directed by Paul Annett. 1974. Cinerama. 93 min. Sound. 16mm Color. *Rental:* Modern Sound & Swank Motion.

Beast of Budapest, The. Greta Thyssen. Directed by Harmon Jones. 1958. Allied Artists. 74 min. Sound. 16mm B&W. *Rental:* Hurlock Cine.

Beast of Hollow Mountain, The. Guy Madison & Patricia Medina. Directed by Edward Nassour & Ismael Rodriguez. 1956. United Artists. (Anamorphic). 79 min. Sound. 16mm Color. *Rental:* MGM United.

Beast of the City, The. Jean Harlow, Walter Huston & Wallace Ford. Directed by Charles Brabin. 1932. MGM. 87 min. Sound. 16mm B&W. *Rental:* MGM United.

Beast with a Million Eyes, The. Paul Birch & Lorna Thayer. Directed by David Kramarsky. 1956. American International. 78 min. Sound. 16mm B&W. *Rental:* Films Inc.

Beast with Five Fingers, The. Robert Alda & Peter Lorre. Directed by Robert Florey. 1946. Warners. 88 min. Sound. 16mm B&W. *Rental:* MGM United.

Beast Within, The. Ronny Cox, Bibi Besch & Paul Clemens. Directed by Philippe Mora. 1982. 98 min. Sound. 16mm Color. *Rental:* MGM United. *Rental:* MGM United, Videotape version.

Beastmaster, The. Marc Singer & Tanya Roberts. Directed by Don Coscarelli. 1982. MGM-UA. 118 min. Sound. 16mm Color. *Rental:* MGM United. *Rental:* MGM United, Videotape version.

Beat Girl. Christopher Lee, Noelle Adam & David Farar. Directed by Edmond Greville. 1961. Britain. 80 min. Sound. 16mm B&W. *Rental:* Budget Films & Video Comm. *Lease:* Video Comm. *Rental:* Video Comm, *Lease:* Video Comm, Videotape version.

Beat the Band. Frances Langford & Ralph Edwards. Directed by John H. Auer. 1947. RKO. 67 min. Sound. 16mm B&W. *Rental:* Films Inc.

Beat the Deva. 1979. Kit Parker. (Animated). 91 min. Sound. 16mm Color. *Rental:* Kit Parker.

Beat the Devil. Humphrey Bogart, Jennifer Jones & Robert Morley. Directed by John Huston. 1954. United Artists. 94 min. Sound. 16mm B&W. *Rental:* Budget Films, Cine Craft, Films Inc, Images Film, Kit Parker, Natl Film Video, Swank Motion, Twyman Films, U of IL Film, Welling Motion Pictures, Westcoast Films & Wholesome Film Ctr. *Rental:* Budget Films, 100 mins. version.

Beatles at Shea Stadium, The. Japan. (Documentary). 65 min. Sound. 16mm Color. *Rental:* Budget Films & Natl Film Video. *Rental:* Glenn Photo. *Sale:* Video Comm, Videotape version.

Beatrix Potter: A Private World. 1978. (Documentary). 42 min. Sound. 16mm Color. *Rental:* A Cantor. *Sale:* A Cantor.

Beau Bandit. Mitchell Lewis & Doris Kenyon. Directed by Lambert Hillyer. 1930. RKO. 68 min. Sound. 16mm *Rental:* RKO General Pics.

Beau Brummel. John Barrymore & Mary Astor. Directed by Harry Beaumont. 1924. Warners. 95 min. Silent. 16mm B&W. *Rental:* Budget Films, Em Gee Film Lib, Film Classics, Films Inc, Kerr Film & Willoughby Peer. *Sale:* Film Classics, Glenn Photo & New Cinema. *Rental:* Ivy Films, *Sale:* Glenn Photo, Super 8 silent version.

Beau Brummel. Stewart Granger & Elizabeth Taylor. Directed by Curtis Bernhardt. 1954. MGM. 111 min. Sound. 16mm Color. *Rental:* MGM United.

Beau Geste. Ronald Colman, Neil Hamilton & Mary Brian. Directed by Herbert Brenon. 1926. Paramount. 109 min. Silent. 16mm B&W. *Rental:* Museum Mod Art.

Beau Geste. Gary Cooper & Ray Milland. Directed by William A. Wellman. 1939. Paramount. 114 min. Sound. 16mm B&W. *Rental:* Swank Motion & Williams Films.

Beau Geste. Guy Stockwell & Doug McClure. Directed by Douglas Heyes. 1966. Universal. 105 min. Sound. 16mm Color. *Rental:* Swank Motion.

Beau Ideal. Loretta Young & Ralph Forbes. Directed by Herbert Brenon. 1931. RKO. 79 min. Sound. 16mm *Rental:* RKO General Pics.

Beau James. Bob Hope, Vera Miles & Paul Douglas. Directed by Melville Shavelson. 1957. Paramount. 105 min. Sound. 16mm Color. *Rental:* Films Inc.

Beau Revel. Lewis Stone, Florence Vidor & Lloyd Hughes. Directed by John Griffith. 1921. Paramount. 85 min. Silent. 16mm B&W. *Sale:* Blackhawk Films. *Rental:* Ivy Films, *Sale:* Blackhawk Films, Super 8 silent version.

Beau Serge, Le. Gerard Blain & Jean-Claude Brialy. Directed by Claude Chabrol. Fr. 1958. France. 97 min. Sound. 16mm B&W. subtitles. *Rental:* Corinth Films.

Beaubourg. Directed by Denis Pastle. 1980. 52 min. Sound. 16mm Color. *Rental:* A Cantor. *Sale:* A Cantor.

Beauhunks. Stan Laurel & Oliver Hardy. Directed by James W. Horne. 1932. Hal Roach. 45 min. Sound. 16mm B&W. *Rental:* Budget Films, Em Gee Film Lib, Films Inc, Kerr Film, Modern Sound, Twyman Films & Westcoast Films. *Sale:* Blackhawk Films. *Sale:* Blackhawk Films, Super 8 sound version.

Beaumarchais. France. 60 min. Sound. 16mm B&W. *Rental:* French Am Cul. *Rental:* French Am Cul, Videotape version.

Beautiful Baby Boy, But, A. 58 min. Sound. Videotape *Rental:* PBS Video. *Sale:* PBS Video.

Beautiful Blonde from Bashful Bend, The. Betty Grable & Cesar Romero. Directed by Preston Sturges. 1949. Fox. 76 min. Sound. 16mm B&W. *Rental:* Films Inc.

Beautiful Blue & Red Danube, The. 1967. ABC. (Documentary). 53 min. Sound. 16mm Color. *Rental:* McGraw-Hill Films, Syracuse U Film & U of IL Film. *Sale:* McGraw-Hill Films.

Beautiful But Broke. Joan Davis, Jane Frazee & John Hubbard. Directed by Charles Barton. 1944. Columbia. 80 min. Sound. 16mm B&W. *Rental:* Newman Film Lib & Welling Motion Pictures.

Beautiful But Dangerous *see* She Couldn't Say No.

Beautiful But Dangerous *see* She Couldn't Say No.

Beauty & the Bandit. Gilbert Roland. Directed by William Nigh. 1946. Monogram. 80 min. Sound. 16mm B&W. *Rental:* Video Comm. *Rental:* Video Comm, *Sale:* Video Comm, Videotape version.

Beauty & the Beast. Trans. Title: Belle et la Bete, La. Jean Marais & Josette Day. Directed by Jean Cocteau. Fr. 1946. France. 90 min. Sound. 16mm B&W. subtitles. *Rental:* Janus Films.

Beauty & the Beast. Joyce Taylor & Mark Damon. Directed by Edward L. Cahn. 1969. United Artists. 77 min. Sound. 16mm Color. *Rental:* Films Inc & MGM United.

Beauty & the Beast. Robert Gladstein & Linda Meyer. 1969. ABC. (Ballet). 50 min. Sound. 16mm Color. *Rental:* Films Inc.

Beauty & the Boss. Warren William & Marian Marsh. Directed by Roy Del Ruth. 1932. Warners. 66 min. Sound. 16mm B&W. *Rental:* MGM United.

Beauty, Bonny, Daisy, Violet, Grace, & Geoffrey Morton. 1974. Britain. (Documentary). 60 min. Sound. 16mm Color. *Rental:* B Raymond, Media Guild & U of IL Film. *Sale:* B Raymond & Media Guild. *Sale:* Media Guild, Videotape version.

Beauty for Sale. Madge Evans & Otto Kruger. Directed by Richard Boleslawski. 1933. MGM. 88 min. Sound. 16mm B&W. *Rental:* MGM United.

Because He's My Friend. Karen Black & Keir Dullea. Directed by Ralph Nelson. 1979. Canada. 93 min. Sound. 16mm Color. *Rental:* Modern Sound & Twyman Films.

Because of Him. Deanna Durbin & Franchot Tone. Directed by Richard Wallace. 1946. Universal. 88 min. Sound. 16mm B&W. *Rental:* Swank Motion.

Because of You. Loretta Young & Jeff Chandler. Directed by Joseph Pevney. 1952. Universal. 95 min. Sound. 16mm B&W. *Rental:* Swank Motion.

Because They're Young. Dick Clark & Tuesday Weld. Directed by Paul Wendkos. 1960. Columbia. 102 min. Sound. 16mm B&W. *Rental:* Arcus Film, Cine Craft, Modern Sound, Roas Films & Welling Motion Pictures.

Because You're Mine. Mario Lanza & Doretta Morrow. Directed by Alexander Hall. 1952. MGM. 103 min. Sound. 16mm Color. *Rental:* MGM United.

Becket. Richard Burton & Peter O'Toole. Directed by Peter Glenville. 1964. 148 min. Sound. 16mm Color. *Sale:* Festival Films & Maljack. *Sale:* Festival Films, Videotape version.

Becky Sharp. Miriam Hopkins & Alan Mowbray. Directed by Rouben Mamoulian. 1935. RKO. 80 min. Sound. 16mm B&W. *Rental:* Ivy Films, Mogulls Films & Rep Pic Film. *Sale:* Classics Assoc NY. *Rental:* Classic Film Mus, *Sale:* Classic Film Mus, Color version. *Sale:* Cinema Concepts, Videotape version.

Bed & Board. Jean-Pierre Leaud. Directed by Francois Truffaut. Fr. 1971. France. Sound. 16mm Color. subtitles. *Rental:* Corinth Films, Swank Motion & Twyman Films.

Bed & Sofa. Trans. Title: Tretya Meshchanskaya. Ludmilla Semyonova & Nikolai Batalov. Directed by Abram Room. 1926. Russia. 85 min. Silent. 16mm B&W. *Rental:* Budget Films, Corinth Films, Em Gee Film Lib, Kit Parker & Museum Mod Art. *Sale:* Festival Films & Reel Images. *Rental:* Ivy Films, Super 8 silent version. *Sale:* Festival Films & Tamarelles French Film, Videotape version.

Bed of Roses. Joel McCrea & Constance Bennett. Directed by Gregory La Cava. 1933. RKO. 67 min. Sound. 16mm *Rental:* RKO General Pics.

Bed Sitting Room, The. Rita Tushingham & Mona Washbourne. Directed by Richard Lester. 1969. Britain. 90 min. Sound. 16mm Color. *Rental:* MGM United.

Bedazzled. Peter Cook & Dudley Moore. Directed by Stanley Donen. 1967. Fox. (Anamorphic). 107 min. Sound. 16mm Color. *Rental:* Films Inc.

Bedelia. Margaret Lockwood & Ian Hunter. Directed by Lance Comfort. 1947. Britain. 92 min. Sound. 16mm B&W. *Rental:* Video Comm.

Bedeviled. Anne Baxter & Steve Forrest. Directed by Mitchell Leisen. 1955. MGM. 85 min. Sound. 16mm B&W. *Rental:* MGM United.

Bedford Incident, The. Richard Widmark, Sidney Poitier & James MacArthur. Directed by James B. Harris. 1965. Columbia. 102 min. Sound. 16mm B&W. *Rental:* Arcus Film, Budget Films, Cine Craft, Film Ctr DC, Images Film, Ivy Films, Kit Parker, Modern Sound, Natl Film Video, Newman Film Lib, Welling Motion Pictures, Westcoast Films & Wholesome Films Ctr.

Bedknobs & Broomsticks. Angela Lansbury, David Tomlinson & Roddy McDowall. Directed by Robert Stevenson. 1971. Disney. 117 min. Sound. 16mm Color. *Rental:* Bosco Films, Cine Craft, Disney Prod, Elliot Film Co, Film Ctr DC, Film Pres, Films Inc, MGM United, Modern Sound, Roas Films, Twyman Films, Welling Motion Pictures & Westcoast Films.

Bedlam. Boris Karloff, Anna Lee & Billy House. Directed by Mark Robson. 1946. RKO. 88 min. Sound. 16mm B&W. *Rental:* Films Inc.

Bedroom Bandit, The. Orig. Title: Swashbuckler, The. Jean-Paul Belmondo. Directed by Jean-Paul Rappeneau. Fr. 1975. France. 100 min. Sound. 16mm Color. subtitles. *Rental:* J Green Pics.

Bedroom Bedlam. 60 min. Videotape Color. *Sale:* Videx Home Lib.

Bedside. Warren William & Jean Muir. Directed by Robert Florey. 1934. Warners. 65 min. Sound. 16mm B&W. *Rental:* MGM United.

Bedside Manner *see* Her Favorite Patient.

Bedtime for Bonzo. Ronald Reagan, Diana Lynn & Walter Slezak. Directed by Frederick De Cordova. 83 min. Sound. 16mm B&W. *Rental:* Swank Motion. *Rental:* Swank Motion, Videotape version.

Bedtime Story. Loretta Young & Fredric March. Directed by Alexander Hall. 1941. Columbia. 90 min. Sound. 16mm B&W. *Rental:* Welling Motion Pictures.

Bedtime Story. Maurice Chevalier & Helen Twelvetrees. Directed by Norman Taurog. 1933. Paramount. 89 min. Sound. 16mm B&W. *Rental:* Swank Motion.

Beethoven. Trans. Title: Grand Amour de Beethoven. Harry Bauer. Directed by Abel Gance. Fr. 1937. France. 115 min. Sound. 16mm B&W. subtitles. *Rental:* Films Inc & Images Film.

Beethoven: Ordeal & Triumph. 1967. ABC. (Documentary). 51 min. Sound. 16mm Color. *Rental:* McGraw-Hill Films, Syracuse U Film, U of IL Film & U Mich Media. *Sale:* McGraw-Hill Films.

Beethoven, Sonata in A Flat, Opus 110. 1980. PBS. (Concert). 59 min. Videotape Color. *Rental:* PBS Video. *Sale:* PBS Video.

Beethoven, Sonata in C Minor, Opus 111. 1980. PBS. (Concert). 59 min. Videotape Color. *Rental:* PBS Video. *Sale:* PBS Video.

Beethoven, Sonata in E Flat, Opus 109. 1980. PBS. (Concert). 58 min. Videotape Color. *Rental:* PBS Video. *Sale:* PBS Video.

Beethoven, Symphony No. 1. 1980. PBS. (Concert). 60 min. Videotape Color. *Rental:* PBS Video. *Sale:* PBS Video.

Beethoven, Symphony No. 2. 1980. PBS. (Concert). 60 min. Videotape Color. *Rental:* PBS Video. *Sale:* PBS Video.

Beethoven, Symphony No. 3. 1980. PBS. (Concert). 60 min. Videotape Color. *Rental:* PBS Video. *Sale:* PBS Video.

Beethoven, Symphony No. 4. 1980. PBS. (Concert). 60 min. Videotape Color. *Rental:* PBS Video. *Sale:* PBS Video.

Beethoven, Symphony No. 5. 1980. PBS. (Concert). 60 min. Videotape Color. *Rental:* PBS Video. *Sale:* PBS Video.

Beethoven, Symphony No. 6. 1980. PBS. (Concert). 60 min. Videotape Color. *Rental:* PBS Video. *Sale:* PBS Video.

Beethoven, Symphony No. 7. 1980. PBS. (Concert). 60 min. Videotape Color. *Rental:* PBS Video. *Sale:* PBS Video.

Beethoven, Symphony No. 8. 1980. PBS. (Concert). 60 min. Videotape Color. *Rental:* PBS Video. *Sale:* PBS VIdeo.

Beethoven, Symphony No. 9. 1980. PBS. (Concert). 90 min. Videotape Color. *Rental:* PBS Video. *Sale:* PBS Video.

Before & After. Patty Duke & Bradford Dillman. Directed by Kim Friedman. 1980. CBS. 105 min. Sound. SD Color. *Rental:* Twyman Films.

Before Dawn. Stuart Erwin & Warner Oland. Directed by Merian C. Cooper. 1933. RKO. 62 min. Sound. 16mm *Rental:* RKO General Pics.

Before Hindsight. Directed by Jonathan Lewis. 1978. Britain. (Documentary). 78 min. Sound. 16mm B&W. *Rental:* Liberty Co & Museum Mod Art. *Sale:* Museum Mod Art.

Before I Die. (Cast unlisted). 70 min. Sound. 16mm B&W. *Rental:* Bosco Films.

Before I Hang. Boris Karloff & Evelyn Keyes. Directed by Nick Grinde. 1940. Columbia. 60 min. Sound. 16mm B&W. *Rental:* Kit Parker.

Before I Wake. Jean Kent. Directed by Al Rogell. 1955. 80 min. 16mm *Rental:* A Twyman Pres.

Before Need. Directed by Gunvor Nelson & Dorothy Wiley. 1979. 75 min. Sound. 16mm Color. *Rental:* Canyon Cinema.

Before the Mountain Was Moved. Directed by Robert K. Sharpe. 1970. McGraw-Hill. (Documentary). 58 min. Sound. 16mm Color. *Rental:* McGraw-Hill Films, Syracuse U Film, U Cal Media, U of IL Film & U Mich Media. *Sale:* McGraw-Hill Films.

Before the Nickelodeon: The Early Cinema of Edwin S. Porter. Directed by Charles Musser. 1982. Museum of Modern Art. (Documentary). 60 min. Sound. 16mm Color. *Rental:* First Run & Museum Mod Art. *Sale:* Museum Mod Art.

Before the Revolution. Francesco Barilli. Directed by Bernardo Bertolucci. Ital. 1962. Italy. 115 min. Sound. 16mm B&W. subtitles. *Rental:* New Yorker Films.

Before the White Man Came. 1920. Arrow. (Documentary, musical score only). 50 min. Sound. 16mm B&W. *Rental:* Film Classics, Mogulls Films & Utah Media. *Sale:* Film Classics. *Rental:* Film Classics, Videotape version.

Before Winter Comes. David Niven & Anna Karina. Directed by J. Lee Thompson. 1969. Britain. 108 min. Sound. 16mm Color. *Rental:* Charard Motion Pics, Films Inc, Modern Sound & Welling Motion Pictures.

Beggar at the Gates. Directed by Paul Steele. 1968. WBZ. (Documentary). 60 min. Sound. 16mm Color. *Rental:* Natl Churches Christ. *Sale:* Natl Churches Christ.

Beggars in Ermine. Betty Furness, Lionel Atwill & H. B. Walthall. Directed by Phil Rosen. 1935. Monogram. 70 min. Sound. 16mm B&W. *Rental:* Mogulls Films.

Beggars' Opera, The. Sir Laurence Olivier, Hugh Griffith & Dorothy Tutin. Directed by Peter Brook. 1953. Warners. 94 min. Sound. 16mm Color. *Rental:* Films Inc, Inst Cinema, Twyman Films & Willoughby Peer.

Beginning of the War. 1939. (Documentary). 70 min. Sound. 16mm B&W. *Rental:* Film Classics. *Rental:* Film Classics, Videotape version.

Beginning or the End. Brian Donlevy & Robert Walker. Directed by Norman Taurog. 1947. MGM. 110 min. Sound. 16mm B&W. *Rental:* MGM United.

Beginning to End. Jack MacGowran. Directed by Lewis Freedman. 1970. KCET. 58 min. Sound. 16mm Color. *Rental:* Grove. *Sale:* Grove.

Beguiled, The. Clint Eastwood & Geraldine Page. Directed by Don Siegel. 1971. Universal. 109 min. Sound. 16mm Color. *Rental:* Swank Motion.

Behave Yourself. Shelley Winters & Farley Granger. Directed by George Beck. 1951. RKO. 81 min. Sound. 16mm B&W. *Rental:* Budget Films & Video Comm. *Rental:* Video Comm, *Lease:* Video Comm, Videotape version.

Behavior Control. 58 min. Sound. Videotape *Rental:* PBS Video. *Sale:* PBS Video.

Behavior Management. 65 min. Sound. 16mm B&W. *Rental:* U Mich Media.

Behavior Therapy with an Autistic Child. 1964. 45 min. Sound. 16mm B&W. *Rental:* U Mich Media.

Behind Green Lights. William Gargan & Carole Landis. Directed by Otto Brower. 1946. Fox. 70 min. Sound. 16mm B&W. *Rental:* Films Inc.

Behind Locked Doors. Trans. Title: Human Gorilla, The. Richard Carlson & Lucille Bremer. Directed by Budd Boetticher. 1948. Eagle Lion. 62 min. Sound. 16mm B&W. *Sale:* Classics Assoc NY, Super 8 sound version.

Behind Locked Doors. Eve Reeves, Joyce Denner & Daniel Garth. 79 min. 16mm Color. *Rental:* BF Video.

Behind Office Doors. Mary Astor & Ricardo Cortez. Directed by Melville Brown. 1931. RKO. 82 min. Sound. 16mm *Rental:* RKO General Pics.

Behind Stone Walls. Eddie Nugent & Robert Elliot. Directed by Frank R. Strayer. 1932. Mayfair. 60 min. Sound. 16mm B&W. *Rental:* Modern Sound.

Behind the Door see Man with Nine Lives.

Behind the Eight Ball. Ritz Brothers. Directed by Edward Cline. 1942. Universal. 60 min. Sound. 16mm B&W. *Rental:* Swank Motion.

Behind the Front. Wallace Beery, Raymond Hatton & Mary Brian. Directed by Edward Sutherland. 1926. Paramount. 50 min. Silent. 16mm B&W. *Rental:* Em Gee Film Lib.

Behind the Great Wall. Directed by Carlo Lizzani. 1959. China. (Documentary). 96 min. Sound. 16mm Color. narrated Eng. *Rental:* Willoughby Peer.

Behind the Green Door. Marilyn Chambers. 1972. Mitchell Bros. 72 min. Videotape Color. *Sale:* Videx Home Lib.

Behind the Headlines. Lee Tracy & Paul Guilfoyle. Directed by Richard Rosson. 1937. RKO. 58 min. Sound. 16mm *Rental:* RKO General Pics.

Behind the Mask. Sir Michael Redgrave & Vanessa Redgrave. Directed by Brian Desmond-Hurst. 1958. Britain. 85 min. Sound. 16mm B&W. *Rental:* Liberty Co & Video Comm.

Behind the Mask. 1975. Britain. (Documentary). 52 min. Sound. 16mm Color. *Rental:* U Cal Media, U of IL Film, Iowa Films & U Mich Media.

Behind the News. Lloyd Nolan & Robert Armstrong. Directed by Joseph Santley. 1940. Republic. 73 min. Sound. 16mm B&W. *Rental:* Ivy Films & Mogulls Films. *Sale:* Rep Pic Film.

Behind the Rising Sun. Robert Ryan & Merle Oberon. Directed by Jacques Tourneur. 1943. RKO. 87 min. Sound. 16mm *Rental:* RKO General Pics.

Behind the Scenes at Disney Studios. Alan Ladd & Frances Gifford. Directed by Alfred M. Werker. 1941. Disney. 72 min. Sound. 16mm B&W. *Rental:* Bosco Films, Elliot Film Co, Film Inc, Welling Motion Pictures & Westcoast Films.

Behold a Pale Horse. Gregory Peck, Anthony Quinn & Omar Sharif. Directed by Fred Zinnemann. 1964. Columbia. 122 min. Sound. 16mm B&W. *Rental:* Budget Films, Cine Craft, Corinth Films, Bosco Films, Film Ctr DC, Films Inc, Images Film, Kerr Film, Modern Sound, Twyman Films, Video Comm, Westcoast Films & Wholesome Film Ctr.

Being There. Peter Sellers, Melvyn Douglas & Shirley MacLaine. Directed by Hal Ashby. 1979. United Artists. 130 min. Sound. 16mm Color. *Rental:* MGM United & Swank Motion. *Rental:* Swank Motion, Videotape version.

Being Two Isn't Easy. Trans. Title: Watashi Wa Nisai. Hiroo Suzuki & Kumeko Urabe. Directed by Kon Ichikawa. Jap. 1962. Japan. 72 min. Sound. 16mm B&W. subtitles. *Rental:* Films Inc & Janus Films.

Being with John F. Kennedy. Directed by Robert Drew. 1983. Nancy Dickerson. 100 min. Sound. Color. *Rental:* Direct Cinema. *Sale:* Direct Cinema. *Sale:* Direct Cinema, Videotape version.

Bekenntnisse der Hockstaplers see Confessions of Felix Krull.

Bel Ami. Quality X. 90 min. Videotape Color. *Sale:* Quality X Video.

Bela Lugosi Meets a Brooklyn Gorilla. Orig. Title: Boys from Brooklyn, The. Duke Mitchell & Sammy Petrillo. Directed by William Beaudine. 1952. Realart. 74 min. Sound. 16mm B&W. *Sale:* Natl Cinema.

Belated Flowers. Olga Zhizneva. Directed by Abram Room. Rus. 1972. Russia. 100 min. Sound. 16mm Color. subtitles. *Rental:* Corinth Films.

Believe! 57 min. Sound. 16mm Color. *Lease:* Gospel Films. *Rental:* Gospel Films, *Lease:* Gospel Films, Videotape version.

Believe in Me. Michael Sarrazin & Jacqueline Bisset. Directed by Stuart Hageman. 1971. MGM. 88 min. Sound. 16mm Color. *Rental:* MGM United.

Bell' Antonio. Marcello Mastroianni & Claudia Cardinale. Directed by Mauro Bolognini. Ital. 1960. Italian. 101 min. Sound. 16mm B&W. subtitles Eng. *Rental:* Films Inc.

Bell, Book & Candle. James Stewart, Kim Novak & Jack Lemmon. Directed by Richard Quine. 1958. Columbia. 103 min. Sound. 16mm Color. *Rental:* Arcus Film, Bosco Films, Budget Films, Cine Craft, Corinth Films, Film Ctr DC, Films Inc, Kerr Film, Kit Parker, Natl Film Video, Twyman Films, Video Comm & Wholesome Film Ctr.

Bell for Adano, A. John Hodiak & Gene Tierney. Directed by Henry King. 1945. Fox. 104 min. Sound. 16mm B&W. *Rental:* Films Inc.

Bellboy, The. Jerry Lewis. Directed by Jerry Lewis. 1960. Paramount. 72 min. Sound. 16mm B&W. *Rental:* Films Inc.

Belle. Jean-Luc Bideau. Directed by Andre Delvaux. Fr. 1973. Belgium. 93 min. Sound. 16mm Color. subtitles. *Rental:* New Yorker Films.

Belle Americaine, La. Orig. Title: What a Chassis! Robert Dhery & Colette Brosset. Directed by Robert Dhery. Fr. 1961. France. 100 min. Sound. 16mm B&W. subtitles. *Rental:* Budget Films. *Sale:* Tamarelles French Film, Videotape version.

Belle Apparence, La. Anouk Simard. Directed by Denyse Benoit. Fr. 1978. Canada. 90 min. Sound. 16mm Color. subtitles. *Rental:* Natl Film CN. *Sale:* Natl Film CN.

Belle de Jour. Catherine Deneuve & Jean Sorel. Directed by Luis Bunuel. Fr. 1968. France. 100 min. Sound. 16mm Color. subtitles. *Rental:* Films Inc.

Belle et la Bete, La see Beauty & the Beast.

Belle le Grand. Vera Ralston & John Carroll. Directed by Allan Dwan. 1950. Republic. 90 min. Sound. 16mm B&W. *Rental:* Ivy Films. *Sale:* Rep Pic Film.

Belle of Amherst, The. Julie Harris. 1979. Sunrise. 89 min. Sound. 16mm Color. *Rental:* IFEX & Twyman Films.

Belle of New York, The. Fred Astaire & Vera-Ellen. Directed by Charles Walters. 1952. MGM. 82 min. Sound. 16mm Color. *Rental:* MGM United.

Belle of Old Mexico. Estellita Rodriguez. Directed by R. G. Springsteen. 1949. Republic. 70 min. Sound. 16mm B&W. *Rental:* Ivy Films. *Sale:* Rep Pic Film.

Belle of the Yukon. Randolph Scott & Dinah Shore. Directed by William A. Seiter. 1944. RKO. 84 min. Sound. 16mm B&W. *Rental:* MGM United.

Belle Starr's Daughter. George Montgomery & Ruth Roman. Directed by Lesley Selander. 1948. Fox. 85 min. Sound. 16mm B&W. *Rental:* Charard Motion Pics & Westcoast Films.

Belles of St. Trinian's, The. Alastair Sim, Joyce Grenfell & George Cole. Directed by Frank Launder. 1955. Britain. 90 min. Sound. 16mm B&W. *Rental:* Corinth Films.

Belles on Their Toes. Jeanne Crain & Myrna Loy. Directed by Henry Levin. 1952. Fox. 89 min. Sound. 16mm B&W. *Rental:* Films Inc.

Bellissima. Anna Magnani & Walter Chiari. Directed by Luchino Visconti. Ital. 1951. Italy. 90 min. Sound. 16mm B&W. subtitles. *Rental:* Cinema Guild.

Bells, The. Lionel Barrymore & Boris Karloff. Directed by James Young. 1926. Chadwick. 75 min. Silent. 16mm B&W. *Rental:* Em Gee Film Lib & E Finney.

Bells Are Ringing. Judy Holliday & Dean Martin. Directed by Vincente Minnelli. 1960. MGM. 127 min. Sound. 16mm Color. *Rental:* MGM United. *Rental:* Films Inc, Anamorphic color version. *Rental:* MGM United, Videotape version.

Bells of Capistrano, The. Gene Autry. Directed by William Morgan. 1942. Republic. 54 min. Sound. 16mm B&W. *Rental:* Ivy Films & Westcoast Films.

Bells of Coronado, The. Roy Rogers. Directed by William Witney. 1950. Republic. 67 min. Sound. 16mm B&W. *Rental:* Ivy Films. *Sale:* Rep Pic Film & Nostalgia Merchant. *Sale:* Nostalgia Merchant, Color version.

Bells of Rosarita, The. Roy Rogers. Directed by Frank McDonald. 1945. Republic. 54 min. Sound. 16mm B&W. *Rental:* Ivy Films. *Sale:* Cinema Concepts, Rep Pic Film & Nostalgia Merchant. *Sale:* Blackhawk Films, Super 8 sound version.

Bells of St. Mary's, The. Bing Crosby & Ingrid Bergman. Directed by Leo McCarey. 1945. RKO. 126 min. Sound. 16mm B&W. *Rental:* Arcus Film, Budget Films, Cine Craft, Ivy Films, Film Ctr DC, Welling Motion Pictures & Westcoast Films. *Sale:* Rep Pic Film.

Bells of San Angelo, The. Roy Rogers. Directed by William Witney. 1947. Republic. 54 min. Sound. 16mm B&W. *Rental:* Ivy Films. *Sale:* Rep Pic Film & Nostalgia Merchant.

Bells of San Fernando, The. Donald Woods & Gloria Warren. Directed by Terry Morse. 1947. Screen Guild. 60 min. Sound. 16mm B&W. *Rental:* Westcoast Films. *Rental:* Bosco Films, 70 mins. version.

Belonging. 1978. Community series. 89 min. 16mm Color. *Sale:* Aust Info Serv. *Rental:* Aust Info Serv.

Beloved Brat. Bonita Granville & Dolores Costello. Directed by Arthur Lubin. 1938. Warners. 62 min. Sound. 16mm B&W. *Rental:* MGM United.

Beloved Enemy. Merle Oberon, Brian Aherne & David Niven. Directed by H. C. Potter. 1936. Goldwyn. 86 min. Sound. 16mm B&W. *Rental:* Films Inc.

Beloved Infidel. Deborah Kerr & Gregory Peck. Directed by Henry King. 1959. Fox. (Anamorphic). 108 min. Sound. 16mm Color. *Rental:* Films Inc.

Beloved Rogue, The. John Barrymore & Conrad Veidt. Directed by Alan Crosland. 1927. United Artists. (Tinted Musical Score only). Silent. 16mm B&W. *Rental:* Budget Films, Em Gee Film Lib, Ivy Films, Standard Film & Willoughby Peer. *Sale:* Blackhawk Films & Glenn Film. *Rental:* Ivy Films, *Sale:* Blackhawk Films & Glenn Photo, Super 8 silent version. *Sale:* Glenn Photo, Silent 8mm version.

Below the Border. Buck Jones & Tim McCoy. Directed by Howard Bretherton. 1942. Monogram. 55 min. Sound. 16mm B&W. *Rental:* Hurlock Cine. *Sale:* Cinema Concepts, Natl Cinema & Reel Images.

Below the Deadline. Barbara Worth & Frank Leigh. Directed by J. P. McGowan. 1921. Asher. 72 min. Silent. 8mm B&W. *Rental:* Modern Sound.

Below the Deadline. Warren Douglas. Directed by William Beaudine. 1940. Monogram. 65 min. Sound. 16mm B&W. *Rental:* Hurlock Cine.

Below the Sahara. Directed by Armand Denis. 1953. RKO. (Documentary). 65 min. Sound. 16mm Color. *Rental:* Films Inc.

Below the Surface. Hobart Bosworth & Lloyd Hughes. Directed by Irvin Willat. 1920. Paramount. 74 min. Silent. 16mm B&W. *Rental:* Em Gee Film Lib & Ivy Films. *Sale:* Blackhawk Films. *Sale:* Blackhawk Films, Super 8 silent version. *Sale:* Blackhawk Films, Silent 8mm version.

Below Zero. 1971. Canada. (Documentary). 107 min. Sound. 16mm Color. *Rental:* Natl Film CN. *Sale:* Natl Film CN.

Belstone Fox, The. Eric Porter & Rachel Roberts. Directed by James Hill. 1978. Britain. 88 min. Sound. 16mm Color. *Rental:* Twyman Films.

Belvedere Rings the Bell see Mr. Belvedere Rings the Bell.

Ben. Lee Harcourt Montgomery & Arthur O'Connell. Directed by Phil Karlson. 1973. Cinerama. 95 min. Sound. 16mm Color. *Rental:* Film Pres, Modern Sound, Swank Motion, Westcoast Films & Wholesome Film Ctr.

Ben Franklin. Directed by Jack Hively. 1979. Viacom. (Cast unlisted). 97 min. Sound. 16mm Color. *Sale:* Lucerne Films.

Ben-Hur. Ramon Navarro & Francis X. Bushman. Directed by Fred Niblo. 1926. MGM. 128 min. Silent. 16mm B&W. *Rental:* MGM United.

Ben-Hur. Charlton Heston & Jack Hawkins. Directed by William Wyler. 1959. MGM. (Anamorphic). 213 min. Sound. 16mm Color. *Rental:* MGM United. *Rental:* MGM United, Videotape version.

Bend of the River. Orig. Title: Where the River Bends. James Stewart & Rock Hudson. Directed by Anthony Mann. 1952. Universal. 91 min. Sound. 16mm Color. *Rental:* Williams Films.

Beneath the Frozen World. 1977. Metro media. (Documentary). 52 min. Sound. 16mm Color. *Rental:* Churchill Films.

Beneath the Planet of the Apes. Charlton Heston, James Franciscus & Kim Hunter. Directed by Ted Post. 1970. Fox. (Anamorphic). 95 min. Sound. 16mm Color. *Rental:* Films Inc, Twyman Films, Welling Motion Pictures, Westcoast Films & Williams Films.

Beneath the Twelve-Mile Reef. Robert Wagner & Terry Moore. Directed by Robert Webb. 1953. Fox. (Anamorphic). 102 min. Sound. 16mm Color. *Rental:* Budget Films & Films Inc.

Beneath the Valley of the Ultravixens. Francesca Natividad. Directed by Russ Meyer. 1979. Meyer. 93 min. Sound. 16mm Color. *Rental:* Corinth Films.

Beneath Western Skies. Robert Livingston. Directed by Spencer G. Bennett. 1944. Republic. 60 min. Sound. 16mm B&W. *Rental:* Ivy Films. *Sale:* Rep Pic Film.

Benedict Arnold. Directed by Walter Gutman. 1974. 105 min. Sound. 16mm Color. *Rental:* Canyon Cinema.

Bengal Brigade. Rock Hudson & Arlene Dahl. Directed by Laslo Benedek. 1954. Universal. 87 min. Sound. 16mm B&W. *Rental:* Swank Motion.

Bengal Tiger. Barton MacLane, Warren Hull & June Travis. Directed by Louis King. 1936. Warners. 60 min. Sound. 16mm B&W. *Rental:* MGM United.

Bengal Tiger, The. Directed by Richard Martin. 1972. India. (Documentary). 91 min. Sound. 16mm Color. *Rental:* Films Inc, Video Comm & Westcoast Films. *Lease:* Video Comm. *Rental:* Video Comm, *Lease:* Video Comm, Videotape version.

Bengazi. Richard Conte & Victor McLaglen. Directed by John Brahm. 1955. RKO. 79 min. Sound. 16mm B&W. *Rental:* Budget Films & Video Comm. *Lease:* Video Comm. *Rental:* Video Comm, Videotape version.

Benito Cereno. Trans. Title: Old Glory, The. Roscoe Lee Browne & Lester Rawlins. 1965. NET. 105 min. Sound. 16mm B&W. *Rental:* BYU Media.

Benjamin B. Lindsey. Orig. Title: Benjamin Barr Lindsey. George Grizzard. Directed by Robert Gist. 1965. Saudek. 50 min. Sound. 16mm B&W. *Rental:* IQ Film. *Sale:* IQ Film. *Rental:* IQ Film & U Mich Media, *Sale:* IQ Film, Spanish dubbed version.

Benjamin Banneker: The Man Who Loved the Stars. Phoenix. (Documentary). 58 min. Sound. 16mm Color. *Rental:* Iowa Films & Phoenix Films. *Sale:* Phoenix Films. *Sale:* Phoenix, Videotape version.

Benjamin Barr Lindsey *see* Benjamin B. Lindsey.

Benji. Deborah Walley, Edgar Buchanan & Peter Breck. Directed by Joe Camp. 1974. Mulberry Square. 85 min. Sound. 16mm Color. *Rental:* Films Inc, Modern Sound, Swank Motion & Williams Films.

Benny Goodman Story, The. Steve Allen & Donna Reed. Directed by Valentine Davies. 1955. Universal. 117 min. Sound. 16mm Color. *Rental:* Swank Motion & Williams Films.

Ben's Mill. 1981. PBS. (Documentary). 60 min. Videotape Color. *Rental:* Iowa Films & PBS Video. *Sale:* PBS Video.

Berenice. Marcelle Ranson & Jacques Dacqmine. Directed by Jean Kerchbron. Fr. France. 90 min. Sound. 16mm B&W. *Rental:* French Am Cul.

Bergere Et le Ramoneur, La *see* Adventures of Mr. Wonderbird.

Berlin Alexanderplatz. Hanna Schygulla. Directed by Rainer Werner Fassbinder. Ger. 1983. 900 min. Sound. 16mm Color. subtitles. *Sale:* Festival Films. *Sale:* Festival Films, Videotape version.

Berlin Correspondent. Dana Andrews & Virginia Gilmore. Directed by Eugene Forde. 1942. Fox. 70 min. Sound. 16mm B&W. *Rental:* Films Inc.

Berlin Express. Merle Oberon, Robert Ryan & Paul Lukas. Directed by Jacques Tourneur. 1948. RKO. 86 min. Sound. 16mm B&W. *Rental:* Films Inc. *Lease:* Films Inc.

Berlin: Kaiser to Khrushchev. 1964. Wolper. (Documentary). 55 min. Sound. 16mm B&W. *Rental:* Films Inc & Wholesome Film Ctr. *Sale:* Films Inc. *Sale:* Films Inc, Videotape version.

Berlin: Symphony of a Great City. Directed by Walter Ruttmann. 1927. Germany. (Experimental). 53 min. Sound. 16mm B&W. *Rental:* Budget Films, Em Gee Film Lib, Images Film, Kit Parker, Museum Mod Art & Film Images. *Sale:* Festival Films, Natl Cinema, Film Images, Reel Images & Images Film. *Rental:* Ivy Films, *Sale:* Blackhawk Films, Glenn Photo & Reel Images, Super 8 silent version. *Sale:* Blackhawk Films, Silent 8mm version. *Sale:* Festival Films & Images Film, Videotape version.

Berlioz Takes a Trip. 1969. CBS. 53 min. Sound. 16mm B&W. *Rental:* Mcgraw-Hill Films. *Sale:* McGraw-Hill Films.

Bermuda Mystery, The. Preston Foster & Ann Rutherford. Directed by Ben Stoloff. 1944. Fox. 65 min. Sound. 16mm B&W. *Rental:* Films Inc.

Bermuda Triangle, The. Directed by Richard Freidenberg. 1979. Sunn. (Documentary). 95 min. Sound. 16mm Color. *Rental:* Syracuse U Film, Westcoast Films & Williams Films. *Sale:* Lucerne Films. *Sale:* Lucerne Films & Williams Films, Videotape version.

Bernadette, Messenger of the Blessed Virgin Mary. 1929. France. (Documemtary, musical score only). 79 min. Silent. 16mm B&W. *Rental:* Film Classics.

Bernadottes, The. Directed by Victor Vicas. 1972. AIF. (Documentary). 60 min. Sound. Videotape B&W. *Sale:* Americas Films. *Sale:* Vidamerica. *Sale:* Americas Films, Spanish version.

Bernice Bobs Her Hair. Shelly Duvall & Bud Cort. Directed by Joan Micklin Silver. 1977. Learning in Focus. 48 min. Sound. 16mm Color. *Rental:* Iowa Films, Kent St U Film, SD AV Ctr, Syracuse U Film, U of IL Film, U Mich Media & Utah Media. *Sale:* Perspect Film. *Sale:* Perspect Film, Videocassette version.

Bernstein on Beethoven. 1974. Amberson. (Concert). 158 min. Videotape Color. *Rental:* Time-Life Multimedia. *Sale:* Time-Life Multimedia.

Bernstein: Verdi's Requiem. 1974. Amberson. (Concert). 100 min. Videotape Color. *Rental:* Time-Life Multimedia. *Sale:* Time-Life Multimedia.

Berserk! Orig. Title: Circus of Blood. Joan Crawford & Ty Hardin. Directed by Jim O'Connolly. 1968. Columbia. 96 min. Sound. 16mm Color. *Rental:* Bosco Films, Budget Films, Cine Craft, Ivy Films, Modern Sound, Natl Film Video & Westcoast Films.

Bertolucci Shoots Nineteen Hundred. Burt Lancaster. Directed by Gianni Amelio. 1977. Italy. (Documentary). 60 min. Sound. 16mm Color. *Rental:* Budget Films, Films Inc & Texture Film. *Sale:* Texture Film. *Sale:* Texture Film, Videotape version.

Besieged Majority, The. 1970. NBC. (Documentary). 53 min. Sound. 16mm Color. *Rental:* BYU Media, Films Inc, Syracuse U Film & U Mich Media. *Sale:* Films Inc. *Sale:* Films Inc, Videotape version.

Best Damn Fiddler from Calabogie to Kaladar, The. 1969. Canada. (Documentary). 49 min. Sound. 16mm B&W. *Rental:* Natl Film CN & U Mich Media. *Sale:* Natl Film CN.

Best Downhill Racer in the World, The. 1982. 51 min. Sound. Videotape *Rental:* PBS Video. *Sale:* PBS Video.

Best Foot Forward. Lucille Ball & June Allyson. Directed by Edward Buzzell. 1943. MGM. 95 min. Sound. 16mm B&W. *Rental:* MGM United.

Best Friends. Burt Reynolds & Goldie Hawn. Directed by Norman Jewison. 1983. Warners. 116 min. Sound. 16mm Color. *Rental:* Swank Motion. *Rental:* Swank Motion, Videotape version.

Best House in London, The. David Hemmings & Joanna Pettit. Directed by Philip Saville. 1969. MGM. 97 min. Sound. 16mm Color. *Rental:* MGM United.

Best I Can Be, The. 1979. PBS. (Documentary). 59 min. Videotape Color. *Rental:* PBS Video. *Sale:* PBS Video.

Best Little Whorehouse in Texas, The. Burt Reynolds, Dolly Parton & Dom DeLuise. Directed by Colin Higgins. 1985. Universal. 114 min. Sound. 16mm Color. *Rental:* Swank Motion. *Rental:* Swank Motion, Videotape version.

Best Man, The. Henry Fonda & Cliff Robertson. Directed by Franklin Schaffner. 1964. United Artists. 102 min. Sound. 16mm B&W. *Rental:* MGM United.

Best Man Wins, The. Orig. Title: Celebrated Jumping Frog, The. Edgar Buchanan & Anna Lee. Directed by John Sturges. 1948. Columbia. 80 min. Sound. 16mm B&W. *Rental:* Kit Parker.

Best of Enemies, The. David Niven, Alberto Sordi & Harry Andrews. Directed by Guy Hamilton. 1962. Columbia. 104 min. Sound. 16mm Color. *Rental:* Buchan Pic, Cine Craft, Films Inc, Kerr Film, Modern Sound, Roas Films, Welling Motion Pictures, Westcoast Films & Wholesome Film Ctr.

Best of Everything, The. Stephen Boyd & Joan Crawford. Directed by Jean Negulesco. 1959. Fox. (Anamorphic). 122 min. Sound. 16mm Color. *Rental:* Films Inc.

Best of Groucho, The. Marx Groucho & Guests. 130 min. Sound. Videotape *Rental:* WW Enter.

Best of Midnight Blue, The. 1976. Screw. (Adult anthology). 120 min. Sound. Videotape Color. *Sale:* Cinema Concepts & Video Lib.

Best of New Cinema, The. 1969. Janus. ((Adult anthology)). 108 min. Sound. 16mm B&W Color. *Rental:* Janus Films.

Best of the Badmen, The. Robert Ryan & Claire Trevor. Directed by William D. Russell. 1951. RKO. 84 min. Sound. 16mm Color. *Rental:* Films Inc.

Best of the First New York Erotic Film Festival, The. 1972. New Line Cinema. (Adult anthology). 110 min. Sound. 16mm B&W Color. *Rental:* New Line Cinema.

Best of the New York Festival of Women's Films, The. 1973. New Line Cinema. (Adult Anthology). Sound. 16mm B&W Color. *Rental:* New Line Cinema. *Sale:* New Line Cinema, Videotape version.

Best of the Second Annual Erotic Film Festival, The. New Line Cinema. (Adult anthology). Videotape Color. *Sale:* New Line Cinema.

Best of Times, the Worst of Times, The. Directed by Brian Nolan. 1973. Canada. (Documemtary). 57 min. Sound. 16mm Color. *Rental:* Natl Film CN. *Sale:* Natl Film CN.

Best Things in Life Are Free, The. Gordon MacRae & Dan Dailey. Directed by Michael Curtiz. 1956. Fox. 104 min. Sound. 16mm Color. *Rental:* Films Inc. *Rental:* Films Inc, Anamorphic color version.

Best Way, The. Patrick Dewaere & Christine Pascal. Directed by Claude Miller. New Line Cinema. 85 min. Sound. 16mm Color. *Rental:* New Line Cinema.

Best Years of Our Lives, The. Fredric March, Myrna Loy & Harold Russell. Directed by William Wyler. 1946. Goldwyn. 170 min. Sound. 16mm B&W. *Rental:* Films Inc, Ivy Films, Macmillian Films, Syracuse U Film & Video Comm. *Lease:* Macmillan Films.

Bete Humaine, La. Trans. Title: Human Beast, The. Jean Gabin & Simone Simon. Directed by Jean Renoir. Fr. 1938. France. 90 min. Sound. 16mm B&W. subtitles. *Rental:* Budget Films, Corinth Films, Em Gee Film Lib, Images Film, Iowa Films, Ivy Films, Kit Parker, U Cal Media & Video Comm. *Sale:* Cinema Concepts, Festival Films, Glenn Photo, Reel Images & Images Film. *Sale:* Festival Films, Images Film & Tamarelles French Film, Videotape version. *Rental:* Westcoast Films, 82 mins. version.

Bethune. Directed by John Kemeny. 1964. Canada. (Documentary). 59 min. Sound. 16mm B&W. *Rental:* McGraw-Hill Films, Museum Mod Art & Natl Film CN. *Sale:* McGraw-Hill Films, Museum Mod Art & Natl Film CN. *Sale:* Natl Film CN, *Rental:* Natl Film CN, Viseotape version.

Betrayal. Jeremy Irons & Ben Kingsley. Directed by David Jones. 1983. Fox. 95 min. Sound. 16mm Color. *Rental:* Films Inc.

Betrayal from the East. Nancy Kelly & Lee Tracy. Directed by William Berke. 1945. RKO. 82 min. Sound. 16mm *Rental:* RKO General Pics.

Betrayed. Orig. Title: When Strangers Marry. Robert Mitchum & Kim Hunter. Directed by William Castle. 1944. Monogram. 67 min. Sound. 16mm B&W. *Rental:* Hurlock Cine.

Betrayed. Clark Gable & Lana Turner. Directed by Gottfried Reinhardt. 1954. MGM. 108 min. Sound. 16mm Color. *Rental:* MGM United.

Betrayed, The *see* Fraulein Doktor.

Betsy, The. Sir Laurence Olivier & Katherine Ross. Directed by Daniel Petrie. 1978. Allied Artists. 125 min. Sound. 16mm Color. *Rental:* Hurlock Cine. *Sale:* Tamarelles French Film, Videotape version.

Betsy Ross. Alice Brady & Frank May. Directed by William A. Brady. 1917. Peerless-World. 60 min. Silent. 8mm B&W. *Rental:* Mogulls Films.

Bettelstudent, Der. Ger. 1936. Germany. 95 min. Sound. 16mm B&W. subtitles. *Rental:* Trans-World Films. *Rental:* Trans-World Film, Unsubtitled version.

Better a Widow. Virna Lisi & Peter McEnery. Directed by Duccio Tessari. 1969. Italy. 105 min. Sound. 16mm Color. dubbed. *Rental:* Swank Motion.

Better Active Today Than Radioactive Tomorrow. 1975. Gladitz-Teldok. (Documentary). 65 min. Sound. 16mm Color. *Rental:* Green Mt. *Sale:* Green Mt.

Better Late Than Never. David Niven & Maggie Smith. Directed by Bryan Forbes. 1983. Warners. 95 min. Sound. 16mm Color. *Rental:* Swank Motion.

Betty Boop Scandals of 1974. Directed by Max Fleischer. 1974. Crystal. (Animated Anthology). 112 min. Sound. 16mm B&W. *Rental:* Ivy Films.

Betty Boop's Goodies. Directed by Max Fleischer. 1974. Paramount. (Animated anthology). 84 min. Sound. 16mm B&W. *Rental:* Ivy Films.

Betty Coed. Jean Porter & Shirley Mills. Directed by Arthur Dreifuss. 1946. Columbia. 70 min. Sound. 16mm B&W. *Rental:* Bosco Films & Kit Parker.

Between a Rock & a Hard Place. Directed by Kenneth Fink. First Run. (Documentary). 59 min. Sound. 16mm Color. *Rental:* First Run. *Lease:* First Run.

Between Fighting Men. Ken Maynard. Directed by Forrest Sheldon. 1933. World Wide. 60 min. Sound. 16mm B&W. *Sale:* Reel Images.

Between Heaven & Hell. Robert Wagner & Terry Moore. Directed by Richard Fleischer. 1956. Fox. (Anamorphic). 93 min. Sound. 16mm Color. *Rental:* Films Inc.

Between Men. Johnny Mack Brown. Directed by Robert N. Bradbury. 1935. Supreme. 60 min. Sound. 16mm B&W. *Sale:* Reel Images. *Sale:* Reel Images, Super 8 sound version.

Between Men. Directed by Will Roberts. 1979. United Documentary. (Documentary). 57 min. Sound. 16mm Color. *Rental:* United Doc Film. *Sale:* United Doc Film.

Between September & May. 1978. Poland. (Documentary). 90 min. Sound. 16mm Color. narrated Eng. *Rental:* Polish People.

Between the Lines. John Heard & Lindsay Crouse. Directed by Joan Micklin Silver. 1977. Silver. 101 min. Sound. 16mm Color. *Rental:* Ivy Films.

Between Time & Eternity. Lilli Palmer. Directed by Arthur Maria Rabenalt. 1960. Germany. 98 min. Sound. 16mm Color. dubbed. *Rental:* Modern Sound.

Between Time & Timbuktu. Bob & Ray & Kevin McCarthy. Directed by Kurt Vonnegut. 1971. Kurt Vonnegut. 90 min. Sound. 16mm Color. *Rental:* New Cinema & New Line Cinema. *Sale:* New Line Cinema. *Sale:* New Line Cinema, Videotape version.

Between Two Women. Franchot Tone & Virginia Bruce. Directed by George B. Seitz. 1937. MGM. 89 min. Sound. 16mm B&W. *Rental:* MGM United.

Between Two Worlds. John Garfield & Eleanor Parker. Directed by Edward A. Blatt. 1944. Warners. 112 min. Sound. 16mm B&W. *Rental:* MGM United.

Beware. Directed by Bud Pollard. 1946. Astor. 60 min. Sound. 16mm B&W. *Rental:* Budget Films. *Sale:* Natl Cinema.

Beware My Lovely. Ida Lupino & Robert Ryan. Directed by Harry Horner. 1952. RKO. 77 min. Sound. 16mm B&W. *Rental:* Ivy Films. *Sale:* Rep Pic Film.

Beware of a Holy Whore. Lou Castel & Eddie Constantine. Directed by Rainer Werner Fassbinder. Ger. 1970. Germany. 103 min. Sound. 16mm Color. subtitles. *Rental:* New Yorker Films.

Beware of Blondie. Penny Singleton & Arthur Lake. Directed by Edward Bernds. 1950. Columbia. 75 min. Sound. 16mm B&W. *Rental:* Video Comm. *Lease:* King Features.

Beware of Children. Orig. Title: No Kidding. Leslie Philips & Geraldine McEwen. Directed by Gerald Thomas. 1961. Britain. 87 min. Sound. 16mm B&W. *Rental:* Budget Films & Films Inc.

Beware of Ladies. Donald Cook & George Meeker. Directed by Irving Pichel. 1937. Republic. 54 min. Sound. 16mm B&W. *Rental:* Ivy Films. *Sale:* Rep Pic Film.

Beware, Spooks! Joe E. Brown. Directed by Edward Sedgwick. 1939. Columbia. 68 min. Sound. 16mm B&W. *Rental:* Films Inc & Welling Motion Pictures.

Beware! The Blob! see Son of Blob.

Beyond a Reasonable Doubt. Dana Andrews & Joan Fontaine. Directed by Fritz Lang. 1956. RKO. 80 min. Sound. 16mm B&W. *Rental:* Budget Films, Charard Motion Pics, Ivy Films, Kit Parker, Video Comm, Westcoast Films & Wholesome Film Ctr. *Sale:* Video Comm, Videotape version.

Beyond & Back. Directed by James L. Conway. 1979. Sunn. (Documentary). 95 min. Sound. 16mm Color. *Rental:* Williams Films. *Sale:* Lucerne Films. *Sale:* Lucerne Films, Videotape version.

Beyond Bengal. 1934. Showmen's. (Documentary). 65 min. Sound. 16mm B&W. *Rental:* Wholesome Film Ctr. *Sale:* Natl Cinema.

Beyond Cubism. Directed by Ray Witlin. 1977. Blackwood. (Documentary). 58 min. Sound. 16mm Color. *Rental:* Blackwood Films. *Lease:* Blackwood Films.

Beyond Death's Door. Tom Hallick, Howard Platt, Jo Ann Harris & Bethel Leslie. Directed by Henning Schellerup. 1980. Sunn. 82 min. Sound. 16mm Color. *Rental:* Modern Sound & U of IL Film. *Sale:* Lucerne Films. *Sale:* Lucerne Films, Videotape version.

Beyond Fear. Michel Bouquet. 1975. France. 92 min. Sound. Videotape Color. *Sale:* Cinema Concepts.

Beyond Glory. Alan Ladd & Donna Reed. Directed by John Farrow. 1948. Paramount. 92 min. Sound. 16mm B&W. *Rental:* Swank Motion.

Beyond Good & Evil. Dominique Sanda, Robert Powell & Erland Josephson. Directed by Liliana Cavani. 1980. Italy. 126 min. Sound. 16mm Color. subtitles. *Rental:* Films Inc.

Beyond Mombasa. Cornel Wilde & Donna Reed. Directed by George Marshall. 1957. Columbia. 90 min. Sound. 16mm Color. *Rental:* Charard Motion Pics, Film Ctr DC, Modern Sound, Welling Motion Pictures & Westcoast Films.

Beyond Reasonable Doubt. David Hemmings & John Hargreaves. Directed by John Laing. 1980. New Zealand. (p). 108 min. Sound. Videotape Color. *Sale:* Tamarelles French Film & Vidamerica.

Beyond the Blue Horizon. Dorothy Lamour & Richard Denning. Directed by Alfred Santell. 1942. Paramount. 76 min. Sound. 16mm B&W. *Rental:* Swank Motion.

Beyond the Curtain. Richard Greene & Eva Bartok. Directed by Compton Bennett. 1960. Britain. 88 min. Sound. 16mm B&W. *Rental:* Ivy Films.

Beyond the Door. Juliet Mills & Richard Johnson. Directed by Oliver Hellman. 1977. Film Ventures. 100 min. Sound. 16mm Color. *Rental:* Swank Motion.

Beyond the Forest. Bette Davis & Joseph Cotten. Directed by King Vidor. 1949. Warners. 96 min. Sound. 16mm B&W. *Rental:* MGM United.

Beyond the Last Frontier. Eddie Dew. Directed by Howard Bretherton. 1943. Republic. 60 min. Sound. 16mm B&W. *Rental:* Ivy Films. *Sale:* Rep Pic Film.

Beyond the Law. Lane Chandler & Robert Frazer. Directed by J. P. McGowan. 1930. Raytone. 60 min. Sound. 16mm B&W. *Sale:* Natl Cinema.

Beyond the Law see Californian.

Beyond the Law Blue. Rip Torn & Norman Mailer. Directed by Norman Mailer. 1971. Norman Mailer. 100 min. Sound. 16mm B&W. *Rental:* New Line Cinema. *Sale:* New Line Cinema.

Beyond the Limit. Richard Gere & Michael Caine. Directed by John Mackenzie. 1983. Paramount. 103 min. Sound. 16mm Color. *Rental:* Films Inc.

Beyond the Mainstream: Post Modern Dancers. 1980. WNET. (Dance). 60 min. Sound. 16mm Color. *Rental:* Films Inc. *Sale:* Films Inc, Videotape version.

Beyond the Milky Way. 1980. Britain. (Documentary). 57 min. Sound. 16mm Color. *Rental:* Time-Life Multimedia & Utah Media. *Sale:* Time-Life Multimedia. *Sale:* Time-Life Multimedia, Videotape version.

Beyond the Pecos. Rod Cameron & Eddie Dew. Directed by Lambert Hillyer. 1945. Universal. 59 min. Sound. 16mm B&W. *Rental:* Budget Films.

Beyond the Poseidon Adventure. Michael Caine, Sally Field & Telly Savalas. Directed by Irwin Allen. 1979. Warners. 114 min. Sound. 16mm Color. *Rental:* Swank Motion & Williams Films. *Rental:* Williams Films, Videotape version.

Beyond the River *see* Bottom of the Bottle.

Beyond the Rockies. Tom Keene & Rochelle Hudson. Directed by Fred Allen. 1932. RKO. 54 min. Sound. 16mm *Rental:* RKO General Pics.

Beyond the Sacramento. Orig. Title: Power of Justice. William Elliott & Evelyn Keyes. Directed by Lambert Hillyer. 1940. Columbia. 90 min. Sound. 16mm B&W. *Rental:* Newman Film Lib.

Beyond the Time Barrier. Robert Clarke. Directed by Edgar G. Ulmer. 1960. American International. 75 min. Sound. 16mm B&W. *Rental:* Films Inc.

Beyond the Valley of the Dolls. Dolly Read & Cynthia Myers. Directed by Russ Meyer. 1970. Fox. (Anamorphic). 109 min. Sound. 16mm Color. *Rental:* Films Inc.

Beyond This Place *see* Web of Evidence.

Beyond Tomorrow. Richard Carlson & Jean Parker. Directed by Edward Sutherland. 1940. RKO. 90 min. Sound. 16mm B&W. *Rental:* Alba House, Budget Films, Classic Film Mus, Inst Cinema, Ivy Films, Mogulls Films, Video Comm & Welling Motion Pictures.

Beyond Utopia: Changing Attitudes in American Architecture. Directed by Michael Blackwood. 16mm *Rental:* Blackwood. *Sale:* Blackwood.

Beyond Victory. Bill Boyd & James Gleason. Directed by John Robertson. 1932. RKO. 73 min. Sound. 16mm *Rental:* RKO General Pics.

Bhowani Junction. Ava Gardner & Stewart Granger. Directed by George Cukor. 1956. MGM. 110 min. Sound. 16mm Color. *Rental:* MGM United. *Rental:* MGM United, Anamorphic color version. *Rental:* MGM United, Videotape version.

BIBA. 60 min. Sound. 16mm Color. *Rental:* Alden.

Bible, The. Michael Parks & Richard Harris. Directed by John Huston. 1966. Fox. 154 min. Sound. 16mm Color. *Rental:* Films Inc & Twyman Films. *Rental:* Films Inc, Anamorphic version.

Biches, Les. Stephanie Audran & Jean-Louis Trintignant. Directed by Claude Chabrol. 1968. 97 min. Sound. 16mm Color. *Rental:* Films Inc.

Bicycle Compliance Test. 1976. 45 min. Sound. 16mm *Rental:* Natl AV Ctr.

Bicycle Thief, The. Lamberto Maggiorani & Enzo Staiola. Directed by Vittorio De Sica. Ital. 1949. Italy. 87 min. Sound. 16mm B&W. subtitles. *Rental:* Corinth Films & Films Inc. *Lease:* Corinth Films.

Bidone, Il *see* Swindle.

Big Bad Mama. Angie Dickinson & William Shatner. Directed by Steve Carver. 1974. New World. 87 min. Sound. 16mm Color. *Rental:* Films Inc.

Big Bad Wolf, The. 1966. American International. 53 min. Sound. 16mm Color. narrated Eng. *Rental:* Cine Craft, Films Inc, Macmillan Films, Video Comm & Welling Motion Pictures. *Lease:* Macmillan Films.

Big Band Cavalcade, The. 1979. PBS. 49 min. Videotape Color. *Rental:* PBS Video. *Sale:* PBS Video.

Big Blast, The. 1962. Gospel. (Documentary). 60 min. Sound. 16mm Color. *Rental:* Roas Films.

Big Boodle, The. Orig. Title: Night in Havana, A. Errol Flynn & Gia Scala. Directed by Richard Wilson. 1957. United Artists. 83 min. Sound. 16mm B&W. *Rental:* MGM United.

Big Bounce, The. Leigh Taylor-Young & Ryan O'Neal. Directed by Alex March. 1969. Warners. 102 min. Sound. 16mm Color. *Rental:* Swank Motion.

Big Boy. Al Jolson & Noah Beery. Directed by Alan Crosland. 1930. Warners. 69 min. Sound. 16mm B&W. *Rental:* MGM United.

Big Brawl, The. Jackie Chan & Jose Ferrer. Directed by Robert Clouse. 1980. Warners. 95 min. Sound. 16mm Color. *Rental:* Williams Films.

Big Broadcast of 1932, The. George Burns & Gracie Allen. Directed by Frank Tuttle. 1932. Paramount. 97 min. Sound. 16mm B&W. *Rental:* Swank Motion.

Big Broadcast of 1936, The. Jack Oakie, George Burns & Gracie Allen. Directed by Norman Taurog. 1935. Paramount. 97 min. Sound. 16mm B&W. *Rental:* Swank Motion.

Big Broadcast of 1937, The. Jack Benny & Martha Raye. Directed by Mitchell Leisen. 1936. Paramount. 102 min. Sound. 16mm B&W. *Rental:* Swank Motion.

Big Broadcast of 1938, The. W. C. Fields & Martha Raye. Directed by Mitchell Leisen. 1938. Paramount. 91 min. Sound. 16mm B&W. *Rental:* Swank Motion.

Big Brown Eyes. Cary Grant & Joan Bennett. Directed by Raoul Walsh. 1936. Paramount. 78 min. Sound. 16mm B&W. *Rental:* Swank Motion.

Big Bus, The. Joseph Bologna & Stockard Channing. Directed by James Frawley. 1976. Paramount. 88 min. Sound. 16mm Color. *Rental:* Films Inc.

Big Business Girl. Loretta Young & Joan Blondell. Directed by William A. Seiter. 1931. Warners. 75 min. Sound. 16mm B&W. *Rental:* MGM United.

Big Calibre. Bob Steele. Directed by Robert N. Bradbury. (Bob Steele Westerns). 1935. United Artists. 60 min. Sound. 16mm B&W. *Rental:* Budget Films.

Big Caper, The. Rory Calhoun & Mary Costa. Directed by Robert Stevens. 1957. United Artists. 80 min. Sound. 16mm B&W. *Rental:* MGM United & Newman Film Lib.

Big Carnival, The. Orig. Title: Ace in the Hole. Kirk Douglas & Jan Sterling. Directed by Billy Wilder. 1951. Paramount. 112 min. Sound. 16mm B&W. *Rental:* Films Inc.

Big Cat, The. Preston Foster & Lon McCallister. Directed by Phil Karlson. 1949. Eagle Lion. 75 min. Sound. 16mm Color. *Rental:* Budget Films. *Sale:* Morcraft Films. *Sale:* Morcraft Films, Super 8 sound version.

Big Cats, The. 1974. National Geographic. (Documentary). 52 min. Sound. 16mm Color. *Sale:* Natl Geog. *Rental:* Natl Geog. *Sale:* Natl Geog, Videotape version.

Big Chance, The. Mickey Rooney & Merna Kennedy. Directed by Al Herman. 1933. Eagle. 70 min. Sound. 16mm B&W. *Sale:* Morcraft Films. *Sale:* Morcraft Films, Super 8 sound version.

Big Chase, The. Glen Langan & Adele Jergens. Directed by Arthur Hilton. 1954. Lippert. 60 min. Sound. 16mm B&W. *Rental:* Budget Films.

Big Chill, The. Glenn Close & William Hurt. Directed by Lawrence Kasdan. 1983. Columbia. 104 min. Sound. 16mm Color. *Rental:* Swank Motion. *Sale:* Tamarelles French Film, Videotape version.

Big Circus, The. Victor Mature & Rhonda Fleming. Directed by Joseph Newman. 1959. Allied Artists. 109 min. Sound. 16mm Color. *Rental:* Hurlock Cine.

Big City, The. Spencer Tracy & Luise Rainer. Directed by Frank Borzage. 1937. MGM. 79 min. Sound. 16mm B&W. *Rental:* MGM United.

Big City, The. Margaret O'Brien, Danny Thomas & Robert Preston. Directed by Norman Taurog. 1948. MGM. 103 min. Sound. 16mm B&W. *Rental:* Films Inc & MGM United.

Big City *see* Skyscraper Wilderness.

Big City *see* Grande Cidade.

Big Day, The *see* Jour de Fete.

Big City *see* Reou-Takh.

Big City Blues. Joan Blondell & Humphrey Bogart. Directed by Mervyn LeRoy. 1932. Warners. 63 min. Sound. 16mm B&W. *Rental:* MGM United.

Big City 1980. 1960. CBS. (Documentary). 52 min. Sound. 16mm B&W. *Rental:* U of IL Film & Syracuse U Film. *Sale:* Carousel Films.

Big Clock, The. Orig. Title: Under the Clock. Ray Milland & Charles Laughton. Directed by John Farrow. 1948. Paramount. 95 min. Sound. 16mm B&W. *Rental:* Williams Films.

Big Combo, The. Cornel Wilde & Richard Conte. Directed by Joseph Lewis. 1955. Allied Artists. 89 min. 16mm B&W. *Rental:* Hurlock Cine.

Big Corporation, The. 2 Pts. 1976. Britain. (Documentary). 60 min. Sound. 16mm Color. *Rental:* Films Inc, OK AV Ctr, Syracuse U Film, U Cal Media, U of IL Film & Utah Media. *Sale:* Films Inc. *Sale:* Films Inc, Videotape version.

Big Country, The. Gregory Peck & Jean Simmons. Directed by William Wyler. 1958. United Artists. 166 min. Sound. 16mm Color. *Rental:* MGM United, Westcoast Films, Wholesome Film Ctr & Budget Films.

Big Deal, The *see* Blondie's Big Deal.

Big Deal on Madonna Street. Marcello Mastroianni & Toto. Directed by Mario Monicelli. 1960. Italy. 91 min. Sound. 16mm B&W. *Rental:* Films Inc. *Sale:* Cinema Concepts & Natl Cinema. *Sale:* Tamarelles French Film, Videotape version.

Big Dig, The. 1973. TV Ltd. (Documentary). 54 min. Sound. 16mm Color. *Rental:* U Cal Media.

Big Doll House, The. Pam Grier & Judy Brown. Directed by Jack Hill. 1971. New World. 93 min. Sound. 16mm Color. *Rental:* Films Inc.

Big Fella. Paul Robeson. Directed by J. Elder Wills. 1937. 75 min. 16mm *Rental:* A Twyman Pres.

Big Fight, The. Orig. Title: Joe Palooka in the Big Fight. Joe Kirkwood & Leon Errol. Directed by Cy Endfield. 1949. Monogram. 70 min. Sound. 16mm B&W. *Rental:* Mogulls Films.

Big Fix, The. James Brown & Sheila Ryan. Directed by James Flood. 1947. PRC. 63 min. Sound. 16mm B&W. *Sale:* Classics Assoc NY.

Big Fix, The. Richard Dreyfuss & Susan Anspach. Directed by Jeremy Paul Kagan. 1978. Universal. 113 min. Sound. 16mm Color. *Rental:* Swank Motion.

Big Frame, The. Mark Stevens & Jean Kent. Directed by David MacDonald. 1953. RKO. 67 min. Sound. 16mm B&W. *Rental:* Films Inc.

Big Freeze, The. Orig. Title: On Thin Ice. Tony Sailor. 1961. Comet. 90 min. Sound. 16mm Color. *Rental:* Ivy Films.

Big Game, The. Stephen Boyd & France Nuyen. Directed by Ray Milland. 1972. Gold Key. 95 min. Sound. 16mm Color. *Rental:* Budget Films & Video Comm. *Lease:* Video Comm. *Rental:* Video Comm, *Lease:* Video Comm, Videotape version.

Big Game, The. Andy Devine & James Gleason. Directed by Pandro S. Berman. 1937. RKO. 73 min. Sound. 16mm *Rental:* RKO General Pics.

Big Game America. 1974. NFL. (Documentary). 60 min. Videotape Color. *Rental:* Iowa Films & Time-Life Multimedia. *Sale:* Time-Life Multimedia.

Big Gundown, The. Lee Van Cleef & Tomas Milian. Directed by Sergio Sollima. 1968. Columbia. 90 min. Sound. 16mm Color. dubbed. *Rental:* Cine Craft, Inst Cinema, Kerr Film, Welling Motion Pictures & Westcoast Films.

Big Hand for the Little Lady, A. Joanne Woodward, Henry Fonda & Jason Robards. Directed by Fielder Cook. 1966. Warners. 95 min. Sound. 16mm Color. *Rental:* Charard Motion Pics, Films Inc, Inst Cinema, Swank Motion, Welling Motion Pictures & Willoughby Peer.

Big Hangover, The. Elizabeth Taylor & Van Johnson. Directed by Norman Krasna. 1950. MGM. 82 min. Sound. 16mm B&W. *Rental:* MGM United.

Big Heart, The *see* Miracle on Thirty-Fourth Street.

Big Heat, The. Glenn Ford, Lee Marvin & Gloria Grahame. Directed by Fritz Lang. 1953. Columbia. 90 min. Sound. 16mm B&W. *Rental:* Budget Films, Cine Craft, Films Inc, Images Film, Kit Parker, Swank Motion, Twyman Films, U of IL Film, Welling Motion Pictures, Westcoast Films, Wholesome Film Ctr & Willoughby Peer. *Rental:* Swank Motion, Videotape version.

Big Henry & the Polka Dot Kid. Ned Beatty & Estelle Parsons. Directed by Richard Marquand. 1977. Learning Corp. 51 min. Sound. 16mm Color. *Rental:* Learning Corp Am. *Sale:* Learning Corp Am. *Sale:* Learning Corp Am, *Rental:* Learning Corp Am, Videotape version.

Big House, The. Chester Morris & Wallace Beery. Directed by George Hill. 1930. MGM. 84 min. Sound. 16mm B&W. *Rental:* MGM United.

Big House for Girls. Maureen O'Sullivan & Betty Compson. Directed by Alan Crosland. 1932. United Artists. 62 min. Sound. 16mm B&W. *Rental:* Films Inc.

Big Hunt, The. Directed by George Sherwood. 1969. Gold Key. (Documentary). 90 min. Sound. 16mm Color. *Rental:* Video Comm. *Lease:* Video Comm. *Rental:* Video Comm, *Lease:* Video Comm, Videotape version.

Big If, The: Interferon. 1980. Britain. (Documentary). 50 min. Sound. 16mm Color. *Rental:* Films Inc & Syracuse U Film. *Sale:* Films Inc. *Sale:* Films Inc, Videotape version.

Big Jack. Wallace Beery & Richard Conte. Directed by Richard Thorpe. 1949. MGM. 85 min. Sound. 16mm B&W. *Rental:* MGM United.

Big Jake. John Wayne & Maureen O'Hara. Directed by George Sherman. 1971. Cinema Center. 110 min. Sound. 16mm Color. *Rental:* Cine Craft, Swank Motion, Westcoast Films & Williams Films.

Big Jim McClain. John Wayne & James Arness. Directed by Edward Ludwig. 1952. Warners. 90 min. Sound. 16mm B&W. *Rental:* Swank Motion.

Big Knife, The. Jack Palance & Rod Steiger. Directed by Robert Aldrich. 1955. United Artists. 111 min. Sound. 16mm B&W. *Rental:* MGM United.

Big Land, The. Orig. Title: Stampeded. Alan Ladd, Virginia Mayo & Edmond O'Brien. Directed by Gordon Douglas. 1957. Warners. 93 min. Sound. 16mm Color. *Rental:* Budget Films, Films Inc, Natl Film Video, Video Comm & Westcoast Films. *Lease:* Video Comm. *Rental:* Video Comm, *Lease:* Video Comm, Videotape version.

Big Leaguer, The. Edward G. Robinson & Vera-Ellen. Directed by Robert Aldrich. 1953. MGM. 71 min. Sound. 16mm B&W. *Rental:* MGM United.

Big Lever, The: Party Politics in Leslie County, Kentucky. Directed by Frances Morton. 1983. Appalshop. (Documentary). 53 min. Sound. 16mm Color. *Rental:* Appals. *Sale:* Appals.

Big Lift, The. Paul Douglas & Montgomery Clift. Directed by George Seaton. 1950. Fox. 119 min. Sound. 16mm B&W. *Rental:* Films Inc.

Big Mouth, The. Jerry Lewis, Harold J. Stone & Susan Bay. Directed by Jerry Lewis. 1967. Columbia. 107 min. Sound. 16mm Color. *Rental:* Arcus Film, Buchan Pic, Budget Films, Charard Motion Pics, Cine Craft, Film Ctr DC, Film Pres, Films Inc, Modern Sound, Natl Film Video, Newman Film Lib, Twyman Films, Welling Motion Pictures, Westcoast Films, Wholesome Film Ctr, Williams Films & Willoughby Peer.

Big News. Robert Armstrong & Carole Lombard. Directed by Gregory La Cava. 1929. Pathe. 70 min. Sound. 16mm B&W. *Rental:* Mogulls Films.

Big Night, The. John Barrymore Jr. & Preston Foster. Directed by Joseph Losey. 1951. United Artists. 75 min. Sound. 16mm B&W. *Rental:* MGM United.

Big Night, The. Randy Sparks, Dick Foran & Venetia Stevenson. Directed by Sidney Salkow. 1960. Paramount. 74 min. Sound. 16mm B&W. *Rental:* Films Inc.

Big Noise, The. Guy Kibbee & Marie Wilson. Directed by Frank McDonald. 1936. Warners. 58 min. Sound. 16mm B&W. *Rental:* MGM United.

Big Noise, The. Stan Laurel & Oliver Hardy. Directed by Mal St. Clair. 1944. Fox. 74 min. Sound. 16mm B&W. *Rental:* Films Inc, Inst Cinema & Willoughby Peer.

Big Parade, The. John Gilbert & Renee Adoree. Directed by King Vidor. 1925. MGM. (Music & sound effects only). 125 min. Sound. 16mm B&W. *Rental:* MGM United.

Big Parade of Comedy *see* MGM's Big Parade of Comedy.

Big Punch, The. Wayne Morris & Gordon MacRae. Directed by Sherry Shourds. 1948. Warners. 80 min. Sound. 16mm B&W. *Rental:* MGM United.

Big Rascal. Bruce Li. 93 min. Sound. 16mm Color. *Rental:* Best Film & Video.

Big Red. Walter Pidgeon, Gilles Payant & Emile Genest. Directed by Norman Tokar. 1962. Disney. 89 min. Sound. 16mm Color. *Rental:* Bosco Films, Buchan Pic, Cine Craft, Cousino Visual Ed, Elliot Film Co, Film Ctr DC, Films Inc, MGM United, Modern Sound, Newman Film Lib, Roas Films, Swank Motion, Twyman Films, U of IL Film, Welling Motion Pictures, Westcoast Films & Williams Films.

Big Search, The *see* East of Kilimanjaro.

Big Shakedown, The. Ricardo Cortez, Bette Davis & Glenda Farrell. Directed by John Francis Dillon. 1934. Warners. 61 min. Sound. 16mm B&W. *Rental:* MGM United.

Big Shot, The. Humphrey Bogart & Irene Manning. Directed by Lewis Seiler. 1942. Warners. 82 min. Sound. 16mm B&W. *Rental:* MGM United.

Big Shot, The. Maureen O'Sullivan & Eddie Quillan. Directed by Ralph Murphy. 1932. RKO. 66 min. Sound. 16mm *Rental:* RKO General Pics.

Big Shot, The. Guy Kibbee & Gordon Jones. Directed by Edward Killy. 1937. RKO. 60 min. Sound. 16mm *Rental:* RKO General Pics.

Big Show, The. Gene Autry. Directed by Mack V. Wright. 1936. Republic. 54 min. Sound. 16mm B&W. *Rental:* Budget Films & Ivy Films. *Sale:* Cinema Concepts, Natl Cinema & Reel Images, Videotape version.

Big Show, The. Esther Williams & Cliff Robertson. Directed by James B. Clark. 1961. Fox. (Anamorphic). 113 min. Sound. 16mm Color. *Rental:* Willoughby Peer.

Big Sky, The. Kirk Douglas & Dewey Martin. Directed by Howard Hawks. 1952. RKO. 122 min. Sound. 16mm B&W. *Rental:* Films Inc. *Lease:* Films Inc.

Big Sleep, The. Humphrey Bogart & Lauren Bacall. Directed by Howard Hawks. 1946. Warners. 114 min. Sound. 16mm B&W. *Rental:* MGM United.

Big Sleep, The. Robert Mitchum & Sarah Miles. Directed by Michael Winner. 1978. United Artists. 114 min. Sound. 16mm B&W. *Rental:* MGM United. *Sale:* Festival Films. *Sale:* Festival Films & Tamarelles French Film, Videotape version.

Big Stakes. H. B. Warner. Directed by Clifford S. Elfelt. 1922. East Coast. 73 min. Silent. 16mm B&W. *Rental:* Em Gee Film Lib. *Sale:* Glenn Photo. *Sale:* Glenn Photo, Super 8 silent version.

Big Stampede, The. John Wayne & Noah Beery. Directed by Tenny Wright. 1932. Warners. 54 min. Sound. 16mm B&W. *Rental:* MGM United.

Big Steal, The. Robert Mitchum & Jane Greer. Directed by Don Siegel. 1949. RKO. 70 min. Sound. 16mm B&W. *Rental:* Films Inc.

Big Store, The. Marx Brothers & Margaret Dumont. Directed by Charles Reisner. 1941. MGM. 80 min. Sound. 16mm B&W. *Rental:* MGM United.

Big Street, The. Henry Fonda & Lucille Ball. Directed by Irving Reis. 1942. RKO. 88 min. Sound. 16mm B&W. *Rental:* Films Inc. *Lease:* Films Inc.

Big Thrill, The *see* High Gear.

Big Timber. Roddy McDowell & Jeff Donnell. Directed by Jean Yarbrough. 1950. Monogram. 73 min. Sound. 16mm B&W. *Rental:* Budget Films.

Big Time. Christopher Joy & Jayne Kennedy. Directed by Andrew Georgias. 1978. Filmways. 94 min. Sound. 16mm B&W. *Rental:* Films Inc.

Big Time Operators, The *see* Smallest Show on Earth.

Big Wave, The. Sessue Hayakawa. Directed by Ted Danielewski. 1961. Japan. 71 min. Sound. 16mm B&W. dubbed. *Rental:* Hurlock Cine.

Big Wednesday. Jan-Michael Vincent, William Katt & Gary Busey. Directed by John Milius. 1979. Warners. 125 min. Sound. 16mm Color. *Rental:* Swank Motion, Twyman Films.

Big Wheel, The. Mickey Rooney & Thomas Mitchell. Directed by Edward Ludwig. 1949. United Artists. 92 min. Sound. 16mm B&W. *Rental:* Budget Films, Charard Motion Pics, Film Ctr DC, Video Comm & Welling Motion Pictures. *Lease:* Video Comm. *Rental:* Video Comm, *Lease:* Video Comm, Videotape version.

Big Wheels & Sailor. 1981. Britain. (Cast unlisted). 57 min. Sound. 16mm Color. *Sale:* Lucerne Films. *Rental:* Lucerne Films.

Bigamist, The. Ida Lupino, Edmond O'Brien & Joan Fontaine. Directed by Ida Lupino. 1953. Filmakers. 80 min. Sound. 16mm B&W. *Rental:* Ivy Films & Kit Parker. *Sale:* Rep Pic Film.

Bigfoot. John Carradine & James Craig. Directed by Robert F. Slatzer. 1970. Ellman. 94 min. Sound. 16mm Color. *Rental:* Budget Films & Video Comm.

Bigger Splash, A. David Hockney. Directed by Jack Hazan. 1975. Britain. 105 min. Sound. 16mm Color. *Rental:* New Line Cinema & Direct Cinema.

Bigger Than Life. James Mason, Walter Matthau & Barbara Rush. Directed by Nicholas Ray. 1956. Fox. 95 min. Sound. 16mm Color. *Rental:* Films Inc.

Biggest Bundle of Them All, The. Vittorio De Sica & Robert Wagner. Directed by Ken Annakin. 1968. MGM. 110 min. Sound. 16mm Color. *Rental:* MGM United. *Rental:* Films Inc, Anamorphic color version.

Biggest Jewish City in the World, The. (Destination America Ser.). 52 min. Sound. 16mm Color. *Rental:* Media Guild. *Sale:* Media Guild. *Sale:* Media Guild, Videotape version.

Bighorn. 1972. Stouffer. (Documentary). 52 min. Sound. 16mm Color. *Rental:* Budget Films.

Bighorn, with John Denver. 1975. LCA. 52 min. Sound. 16mm Color. *Rental:* Syracuse U Film.

Bigorne, Caporal de France, La. Francois Perier & Rossana Podesta. Directed by Robert Darene. Fr. 1957. France. 87 min. Sound. 16mm Color. subtitles. *Rental:* French Am Cul. *Rental:* French Am Cul, Videotape version.

Bikini Beach. Frankie Avalon, Annette Funicello & Don Rickles. Directed by William Asher. 1964. American International. 100 min. Sound. 16mm Color. *Rental:* Cine Craft, Westcoast Films & Wholesome Film Ctr.

Bikini Paradise. Janette Scott & Alexander Knox. Directed by Gregg Tallas. 1967. Allied Artists. 88 min. Sound. 16mm Color. *Rental:* Hurlock Cine.

Bill *see* Crainquebille.

Bill & Coo. Directed by Dean Riesner. 1947. Republic. (All bird cast). 61 min. Sound. 16mm Color. *Rental:* Budget Films.

Bill Cracks Down. Orig. Title: Men of Steel. Grant Withers & Beatrice Roberts. Directed by William Nigh. 1937. Republic. 54 min. Sound. 16mm B&W. *Rental:* Ivy Films. *Sale:* Rep Pic Film.

Billie. Patty Duke & Warren Berlinger. Directed by Don Weis. 1965. United Artists. (Anamorphic). 87 min. Sound. 16mm Color. *Rental:* MGM United, Modern Sound, Westcoast Films & Williams Films.

Billion Dollar Brain. Michael Caine & Karl Malden. Directed by Ken Russell. 1967. United Artists. 108 min. Sound. 16mm Color. *Rental:* MGM United.

Billion Dollar Bubble. Sam Wanamaker & James Woods. Directed by Brian Gibson. 1977. Britain. 60 min. Sound. 16mm Color. *Rental:* Films Inc & Syracuse U Film. *Sale:* Films Inc. *Rental:* Films Inc, *Sale:* Films Inc, Videotape version.

Billion Dollar Hobo. Tim Conway, Will Geer & Eric Weston. Directed by Stuart McGowan. 1978. International Picture Show. 96 min. Sound. 16mm Color. *Rental:* Buchan Pic, Films Inc, MGM United, Modern Sound, Twyman Films & Williams Films.

Billy Boy. Duane Bobick & Kin Braden. 94 min. 16mm Color. *Rental:* BF Video.

Billy Budd. Terence Stamp, Peter Ustinov & Robert Ryan. Directed by Peter Ustinov. 1962. Allied Artists. 123 min. Sound. 16mm B&W. *Rental:* Hurlock Cine.

Billy Crystal. 1980. Verve. (Performance). 58 min. Videotape Color. *Rental:* Films Inc.

Billy in the Lowlands. Directed by Jan Egleson. First Run. (Cast unlisted). 88 min. Sound. 16mm Color. *Rental:* First Run. *Lease:* First Run.

Billy Joel. Home Run. (Concert). 59 min. Videotape Color. *Sale:* Time-Life Multimedia.

Billy Liar. Tom Courtenay & Julie Christie. Directed by John Schlesinger. 1963. Britain. 96 min. Sound. 16mm B&W. *Rental:* Budget Films & Images Film. *Rental:* Images Film, Anamorphic B&W version.

Billy Rose's Jumbo. Orig. Title: Jumbo. Doris Day & Stephen Boyd. Directed by Charles Walters. 1962. MGM. 121 min. Sound. 16mm Color. *Rental:* MGM United. *Rental:* MGM United, Anamorphic color version.

Billy the Kid. Johnny Mack Brown & Wallace Beery. Directed by King Vidor. 1930. MGM. 98 min. Sound. 16mm B&W. *Rental:* MGM United.

Billy the Kid. Robert Taylor & Brian Donlevy. Directed by David Miller. 1941. MGM. 94 min. Sound. 16mm Color. *Rental:* MGM United.

Billy the Kid in Santa Fe. Bob Steele. Directed by Sherman Scott. 1941. PRC. 66 min. Sound. 16mm B&W. *Sale:* Natl Cinema.

Billy the Kid in Texas. Bob Steele. Directed by Peter Stewart. 1940. PRC. 55 min. Sound. 16mm B&W. *Sale:* Cinema Concepts & Natl Cinema.

Billy the Kid Returns. Orig. Title: Return of Billy the Kid, The. Roy Rogers. Directed by Joseph Kane. 1938. Republic. 54 min. Sound. 16mm B&W. *Rental:* Ivy Films. *Sale:* Cinema Concepts, Natl Cinema & Rep Pic Film.

Billy the Kid Trapped. Buster Crabbe. Directed by Sherman Scott. 1942. PRC. 59 min. Sound. 16mm B&W. *Sale:* Natl Cinema.

Billy the Kid vs. Dracula. John Carradine & Virginia Christine. Directed by William Beaudine. 1966. Embassy. 72 min. Sound. 16mm Color. *Rental:* Films Inc.

Billy the Kid's Smoking Guns *see* Smoking Guns.

Billy the Kid's Law & Order. Orig. Title: Law & Order. Buster Crabbe. Directed by Sherman Scott. 1942. PRC. 60 min. Sound. 16mm B&W. *Sale:* Natl Cinema.

Billy Two Hats. Gregory Peck & Desi Arnaz Jr. Directed by Ted Kotcheff. 1974. United Artists. 99 min. Sound. 16mm Color. *Rental:* MGM United.

Billy Wilder. 1978. American Film Institute. (Lecture). 55 min. Sound. Videotape Color. *Sale:* Am Film Inst.

Bim. Directed by Albert Lamourisse. 1952. France. 49 min. Sound. 16mm B&W. dubbed. *Rental:* French Am Cul, McGraw-Hill Films & Wholesome Film Ctr. *Sale:* McGraw-Hill Films.

Bingo Long Traveling All-Stars & Motor Kings, The. Billy Dee Williams & James Earl Jones. Directed by John Badham. 1976. Universal. 111 min. Sound. 16mm Color. *Rental:* Swank Motion.

Biography. Gertrude Lawrence & Kevin McCarthy. Directed by Donald Davis. 1950. (Kinescope). 60 min. Sound. 16mm B&W. *Rental:* Budget Films.

Biography of a Bachelor Girl. Ann Harding & Robert Montgomery. Directed by Edward H. Griffith. 1935. MGM. 84 min. Sound. 16mm B&W. *Rental:* MGM United.

Biography of a Baseball Rookie. 1964. 55 min. Sound. 16mm B&W. *Rental:* Syracuse U Film.

Biography of a Cancer. 1960. CBS. (Documentary). 54 min. Sound. 16mm B&W. *Sale:* Carousel.

Biography of a Missile. 1960. CBS. (Documentary). 54 min. Sound. 16mm B&W. *Sale:* Carousel.

Biography of a Rookie. 1961. Wolper. (Documentary). 50 min. Sound. 16mm B&W. *Rental:* Budget Films & Films Inc. *Sale:* Films Inc. *Sale:* Films Inc, Videotape version.

Biological Effects of Ionizing Radiation. 1977. 85 min. videotape *Sale:* Natl AV Ctr.

Biological Transformation of Energy. 1961. US Government. (Documentary). 54 min. Sound. 16mm Color. *Rental:* SD AV Ctr. *Sale:* Natl AV Ctr.

Biquefarre. Directed by Georges Rouquier. Fr. 1983. 90 min. Sound. 16mm Color. subtitles Eng. *Rental:* New Yorker Films.

Birch Interval. Eddie Albert & Rip Torn. Directed by Delbert Mann. 1976. Gamma III. 104 min. Sound. 16mm Color. *Rental:* Swank Motion.

Birchwood. Daniel Olbrychski. Directed by Andrzej Wajda. 1970. Poland. 99 min. Sound. 16mm Color. subtitles. *Rental:* Films Inc.

Bird Man of Alcatraz. Burt Lancaster & Karl Malden. Directed by John Frankenheimer. 1962. United Artists. 146 min. Sound. 16mm B&W. *Rental:* MGM United. *Rental:* MGM United, Videotape version.

Bird of Paradise. Joel McCrea & Dolores Del Rio. Directed by King Vidor. 1932. RKO. 81 min. Sound. 16mm B&W. *Rental:* Budget Films, Classic Film Mus, Em Gee Film Lib, Kit Parker & Video Comm. *Sale:* Festival Films & Reel Images. *Sale:* Cinema Concepts, Super 8 sound version. *Sale:* Cinema Concepts, Festival Films & Reel Images, Videotape version.

Bird of Paradise. Louis Jourdan & Debra Paget. Directed by Delmer Daves. 1951. Fox. 100 min. Sound. 16mm Color. *Rental:* Films Inc.

Bird With the Crystal Plumage, The. Tony Musante & Suzy Kendall. Directed by Dario Argento. 1970. Italy. 98 min. Sound. 16mm Color. *Rental:* Budget Films & Film Ctr DC.

Birds, The. Rod Taylor & Tippi Hedren. Directed by Alfred Hitchcock. 1963. Universal. 119 min. Sound. 16mm Color. *Rental:* Swank Motion. *Rental:* Swank Motion, Videotape version.

Birds & the Bees, The. George Gobel, Mitzi Gaynor & David Niven. Directed by Norman Taurog. 1956. Paramount. 94 min. Sound. 16mm Color. *Rental:* Films Inc.

Birds Do It. Soupy Sales, Tab Hunter & Arthur O'Connell. Directed by Andrew Marton. 1966. Columbia. 95 min. Sound. 16mm Color. *Rental:* Cine Craft, Films Inc, Modern Sound, Westcoast Films & Welling Motion Pictures.

Birds in Peru. Jean Seberg & Maurice Ronet. Directed by Romain Gary. 1968. France. 93 min. Sound. 16mm Color. *Rental:* Swank Motion.

Birds of a Feather *see* Cage Aux Folles II.

Birds, the Bees & the Italians, The. Virna Lisi. Directed by Pietro Germi. 1967. Italy. 115 min. Sound. 16mm B&W. dubbed. *Rental:* Swank Motion.

Birgitt Hass Must Be Killed. Trans. Title: Il Faut Tuer Birgitt Hass. Philippe Noiret & Jean Rochefort. Directed by Laurent Heynemann. Fr. 1982. France. 105 min. Sound. Videotape Color. *Sale:* Tamarelles French Films.

Birth. Directed by Arthur Barron. 1968. PBS. (Documentary). 72 min. Sound. 16mm B&W. *Rental:* U Cal Media.

Birth. 1971. Family of Man. (Documentary). 50 min. Sound. 16mm Color. *Rental:* Films Inc. *Sale:* Films Inc. *Rental:* Films Inc, *Sale:* Films Inc, Videotape version.

Birth. Directed by Sam Pillsbury. 1977. Media Insights. (Documentary). 57 min. Sound. 16mm Color. *Rental:* Films Inc. *Sale:* Films Inc. *Sale:* Films Inc, Videotape version.

Birth Control. 1968. NET. (Documentary). 60 min. Sound. 16mm B&W. *Rental:* Indiana AV Ctr.

Birth Control & the Law. 1962. CBS. (Documentary). 51 min. Sound. 16mm B&W. *Rental:* Mass Media & U Mich Media. *Sale:* Carousel Films.

Birth of a Brain. 1983. 57 min. Sound. 16mm Color. *Rental:* U Cal Media.

Birth of a Legend. Directed by Dick Robinson. 1966. (Documentary). 96 min. Sound. 16mm Color. *Rental:* Films Inc & Video Comm. *Lease:* Video Comm.

Birth of a Nation, The. Lillian Gish & Henry B. Walthall. Directed by D. W. Griffith. 1915. Epoch. 180 min. Silent. 16mm B&W. *Rental:* A Twyman Pres, Budget Films, Films Inc, U Cal Media, Charard Motion Pics, Em Gee Film Lib, Iowa Films, Ivy Films, Janus Films, Killiam Collect, Kit Parker, Pyramid Wholesome Film Ctr & Westcoast Films. *Sale:* Cinema Concepts, Glenn Photo, Images Film, Morcraft Films, Reel Images & Pyramid Film. *Sale:* Festival Films, Silent tinted 169 min. version. *Rental:* Budget Films, Em Gee Film Lib, Inst Cinema, Images Film, Janus Films, Museum Mod Art & SD AV Ctr, *Sale:* Cinema Concepts & Twyman Films, 129 min. version. *Rental:* Budget Films, Em Gee Film Lib, Museum Mod Art, Kit Parker & Natl Cinema, *Sale:* Festival Films, Tinted & Music 129 min. version. *Rental:* Natl Film Video, *Sale:* MGM United, Silent 102 min. version. *Rental:* Blackhawk Films, Super 8 sound tinted version. *Sale:* Cinema Concepts & Morcraft Films, Super 8 silent version. *Sale:* Morcraft Films, Super 8 silent tinted version. *Sale:* Blackhawk Films, Cinema Concepts, Em Gee Film Lib, Natl Film Video, Pyramid Film, Video Lib & Video Comm, Videotape version. *Sale:* Cinema Concepts & Festival Films, Tinted videotape version. *Rental:* Em Gee Film Lib & Westcoast Films, *Sale:* Festival Films, 129 min. Tinted version. *Rental:* Em Gee Film Lib & Natl Cinema, 134 min. Tinted version. *Sale:* Festival Films, 129 min. version. *Sale:* Glenn Photo, 201 min. Silent Tinted version. *Rental:* Westcoast Films, 173 mins version.

Birth of Soviet Cinema, The. 1972. Russia. (Documentary). 49 min. Sound. 16mm B&W. *Rental:* BYU Media, Films Human, U of IL Film & U Mich Media. *Sale:* Films Human. *Sale:* Films Human, Videotape version.

Birth of the Blues, The. Bing Crosby & Mary Martin. Directed by Victor Schertzinger. 1941. Paramount. 85 min. Sound. 16mm B&W. *Rental:* Swank Motion.

Birth of the Talkies, The: 1927-1929. Directed by Armand Panigel. France. (Documentary). 60 min. Sound. 16mm B&W. subtitles. *Rental:* French Am Cul.

Birth with R. D. Laing. Directed by Sam Pillsbury. 1977. Media Insights. (Documentary). 57 min. Sound. 16mm Color. *Rental:* Films Inc. *Sale:* Films Inc. *Sale:* Films Inc, Videotape version.

Birthday Party, The. Robert Shaw, Patrick Magee & Dandy Nichols. Directed by William Friedkin. 1968. Britain. 127 min. Sound. 16mm Color. *Rental:* Films Inc.

Biscuit Eater, The. Billy Lee. Directed by Stuart Heisler. 1940. Paramount. 83 min. Sound. 16mm B&W. *Rental:* Swank Motion.

Bishop Misbehaves, The. Edmund Gwenn & Maureen O'Sullivan. Directed by E. A. Dupont. 1935. MGM. 87 min. Sound. 16mm B&W. *Rental:* MGM United.

Bishop Murder Case, The. Basil Rathbone & Roland Young. Directed by Nick Grinde. 1930. MGM. 80 min. Sound. 16mm B&W. *Rental:* MGM United.

Bishop's Wife, The. Orig. Title: Cary & the Bishop's Wife. Cary Grant, Loretta Young & David Niven. Directed by Henry Koster. 1947. Goldwyn. 109 min. Sound. 16mm B&W. *Rental:* Films Inc.

Bit of an Experience, A. 1970. Britain. (Documentary). 69 min. Sound. 16mm B&W. *Rental:* Time-Life Multimedia. *Sale:* Time-Life Multimedia.

Bitch, The *see* Scarlet Street.

Bite the Bullet. Gene Hackman & Candice Bergen. Directed by Richard Brooks. 1975. Columbia. 131 min. Sound. 16mm Color. *Rental:* Arcus Film, Budget Films, Cine Craft, Film Ctr DC, Ivy Films, Modern Sound, Natl Film Video, Roas Films, Swank Motion, Twyman Films, Twyman Films, U of IL Film, Welling Motion Pictures, Westcoast Films, Wholesome Film Ctr & Images Film. *Rental:* Images Film, Anamorphic version. *Sale:* Tamarelles French Film, Videotape version.

Bitter Cane. Directed by Jacques Arcelin. 75 min. Sound. 16mm Color. *Rental:* Cinema Guild.

Bitter Creek. Bill Elliott & Beverly Garland. Directed by Thomas Carr. 1954. Allied Artists. 79 min. Sound. 16mm B&W. *Rental:* Hurlock Cine.

Bitter Sweet. Anna Neagle & Carl Linden. Directed by Herbert Wilcox. 1933. Britain. 95 min. Sound. 16mm B&W. *Rental:* Budget Films. *Sale:* Reel Images & Morcraft Films. *Sale:* Reel Images, Super 8 sound version.

Bitter Sweet. Jeanette MacDonald & Nelson Eddy. Directed by W. S. Van Dyke II. 1940. MGM. 94 min. Sound. 16mm B&W. *Rental:* MGM United.

Bitter Tea of General Yen, The. Barbara Stanwyck, Nils Asther & Walter Connolly. Directed by Frank Capra. 1933. Columbia. 89 min. Sound. 16mm B&W. *Rental:* Budget Films, Films Inc, Images Film, Kit Parker, Swank Motion, Twyman Films, Welling Motion Pictures, Westcoast Films, Wholesome Film Ctr & Williams Films.

Bitter Tears of Petra Von Kant, The. Margit Carstensen. Directed by Rainer Werner Fassbinder. Ger. 1972. Germany. 124 min. Sound. 16mm Color. subtitles. *Rental:* New Yorker Films.

Bitter Victory. Richard Burton, Curt Jurgens & Ruth Roman. Directed by Nicholas Ray. 1958. Columbia. (Anamorphic). 83 min. Sound. 16mm B&W. *Rental:* Films Inc, Kit Parker, Swank Motion & Welling Motion Pictures.

Biwak in Winter. 1940. Germany. (Cast unlisted). 80 min. Sound. 16mm B&W. *Rental:* Film Classics. *Rental:* Film Classics, Videotape version.

Bizarre. Directed by Anthony Balch. 1971. Anthony Balch. (Cast unlisted). 92 min. Sound. 16mm Color. *Rental:* New Line Cinema. *Sale:* New Line Cinema.

Bizarre, Bizarre. Trans. Title: Drole de Drame. Louis Jouvet & Michel Simon. Directed by Marcel Carne. Fr. 1937. France. 90 min. Sound. 16mm B&W. subtitles. *Rental:* Budget Films, Em Gee Film Lib, Kit Parker & Westcoast Films. *Sale:* Festival Films, Glenn Photo, Natl Cinema & Reel Images. *Sale:* Festival Films & Tamarelles French Film, Videotape version.

Black American Dream, The. 1971. Britain. (Documentary). 65 min. Sound. 16mm Color. *Rental:* Films Inc & U Cal Media. *Sale:* Films Inc. *Rental:* Films Inc, *Sale:* Films Inc, Videotape version.

Black & Blue. Black Sabbath & Blue Oyster Cult. Directed by Jay Dubin. 1981. 91 min. Sound. 16mm Color. *Rental:* MGM United. *Rental:* MGM United, Videotape version.

Black & White in Color. Jacques Spiesser. Directed by Jean-Jacques Annaud. 1976. Allied Artists. 91 min. Sound. 16mm Color. *Rental:* Corinth Films.

Black & White Together. 1969. NET. (Documentary). 58 min. Sound. 16mm B&W. *Rental:* Indiana AV Ctr. *Sale:* Indiana AV Ctr.

Black Angels. Des Roberts. 1970. Merrick. 92 min. Sound. 16mm Color. *Rental:* Budget Films.

Black Arrow, The. Louis Hayward & Janet Blair. Directed by Gordon Douglas. 1948. Columbia. 55 min. Sound. 16mm B&W. *Rental:* Films Inc, Welling Motion Pictures & Westcoast Films.

Black Arrow, The. 1972. Australia. (Animated). 60 min. Sound. 16mm Color. *Rental:* Budget Films & Williams Films. *Sale:* Inst Cinema.

Black Athlete, The. 1980. Pyramid. (Documentary). 58 min. Sound. 16mm Color. *Rental:* Budget Films, U Cal Media & Pyramid Film. *Sale:* Pyramid Film. *Sale:* Pyramid Film, *Rental:* Pyramid Film, Videotape version.

Black Battalion, The. Jar Mares. Directed by Vlad Cek. 1958. Sound. 16mm B&W. *Rental:* Films Inc.

Black Beauty. Directed by David Smith. 1921. Vitagraph. (Cast unlisted). 60 min. Silent. 16mm B&W. *Rental:* Film Classics. *Sale:* Film Classics.

Black Beauty. Esther Ralston. Directed by Phil Rosen. 1933. Monogram. 77 min. Sound. 16mm B&W. *Rental:* Film Classics.

Black Beauty. Mona Freeman. Directed by Max Nosseck. 1946. Fox. 74 min. Sound. 16mm B&W. *Rental:* FIlms Inc. *Lease:* Films Inc.

Black Beauty. Mark Lester, Walter Slezak & Ursula Glas. Directed by James Hill. 1971. Paramount. 106 min. Sound. 16mm Color. *Rental:* Films Inc.

Black Belly of the Tarantula, The. Claudine Auger. Directed by Paolo Cavara. 1972. Italy. 98 min. Sound. 16mm Color. dubbed. *Rental:* MGM United.

Black Belt Jones. Jim Kelly. Directed by Robert Clouse. 1974. United International. 95 min. Sound. 16mm Color. dubbed. *Rental:* Films Inc.

Black Bird, The. Lon Chaney. Directed by Tod Browning. 1926. MGM. 75 min. Silent. 16mm B&W. *Rental:* Films Inc.

Black Bird, The. George Segal, Lionel Stander & Stephane Audran. Directed by David Giler. 1975. Columbia. 122 min. Sound. 16mm Color. *Rental:* Arcus Film, Budget Films, Film Ctr DC, Films Inc, Images Film, Inst Cinema, Ivy Films, MGM United, Modern Sound, Swank Motion, Twyman Films, Welling Motion Pictures, Westcoast Films & Williams Films.

Black Book, The. Robert Cummings & Arlene Dahl. Directed by Anthony Mann. 1949. Eagle Lion. 89 min. Sound. 16mm B&W. *Rental:* Budget Films, Kit Parker & Mogulls Films.

Black Caesar. Fred Williamson & Art Lund. Directed by Larry Cohen. 1972. American International. 92 min. Sound. 16mm Color. *Rental:* Swank Motion.

Black Castle, The. Richard Greene & Boris Karloff. Directed by Nathan Juran. 1952. Universal. 81 min. Sound. 16mm B&W. *Rental:* Swank Motion.

Black Cat, The. Orig. Title: House of Doom, The. Boris Karloff & Bela Lugosi. Directed by Edgar G. Ulmer. 1934. Universal. 65 min. Sound. 16mm B&W. *Rental:* Swank Motion.

Black Cat, The. Basil Rathbone & Bela Lugosi. Directed by Albert S. Rogell. 1941. Universal. 70 min. Sound. 16mm B&W. *Rental:* Swank Motion.

Black Cat, The. Patrick Magee & David Warbek. 92 min. Sound. Videotape *Rental:* WW Enter.

Black Chapel, The. Peter Van Eyck & Dawn Addams. 1962. Germany. 88 min. Sound. 16mm B&W. dubbed. *Rental:* Bosco Films & Westcoast Films.

Black Christmas. Olivia Hussey & Keir Dullea. Directed by Bob Clark. 1974. Warners. 100 min. Sound. 16mm Color. *Rental:* Swank Motion, Twyman Films & Williams Films.

Black Culture in America *see* Black Roots.

Black Cyclone. Guinn Williams. Directed by Fred W. Jackman. 1925. Pathe. 70 min. Silent. 16mm B&W. *Rental:* Film Classics. *Sale:* Film Classics, Silent 8mm version.

Black Dawn *see* Dawn to Dawn.

Black Devils of Kali. Orig. Title: Mystery of the Black Jungle. Lex Barker. 1955. Republic. 72 min. Sound. 16mm B&W. *Rental:* Charard Motion Pics.

Black Doll, The. Nan Grey & Donald Woods. Directed by Otis Garrett. 1938. Universal. 65 min. Sound. 16mm B&W. *Rental:* Budget Films, Ivy Films & Video Comm. *Rental:* Video Comm. *Rental:* Video Comm, Videotape version.

Black Dragon of Manzanar, The. Rod Cameron & Constance Worth. Directed by William Witney. 1943. Republic. 100 min. Sound. 16mm B&W. *Rental:* Ivy Films. *Sale:* Rep Pic Film.

Black Dragons. Bela Lugosi & Clayton Moore. Directed by William Nigh. 1942. Monogram. 65 min. Sound. 16mm B&W. *Rental:* Budget Films, Classic Film Mus, Em Gee Film Lib, Ivy Films & Rep Pic Film. *Sale:* Rep Pic Film.

Black Duke, The. Cameron Mitchell & Gloria Milland. Directed by Pino Mercanti. 1962. Italy. 105 min. Sound. 16mm B&W. dubbed. *Sale:* Natl Cinema.

Black Eagle of Santa Fe, The. Brad Harris & Tony Kendall. 1966. Italy. 86 min. Sound. 16mm Color. dubbed. *Rental:* Westcoast Films.

Black Eye, The. Fred Williamson & Rosemary Forsyth. Directed by Jack Arnold. 1974. Warners. 98 min. Sound. 16mm Color. *Rental:* Swank Motion & Williams Films.

Black Fantasy. Directed by Lionel Rogosin. 1974. Rogosin. (Experimental). 78 min. Sound. 16mm Color. *Rental:* Icarus Films. *Sale:* Icarus Films.

Black Fox, The. Directed by Richard Kaplan & Louis Clyde Stoumen. 1962. Capri. (Documentary). 89 min. Sound. 16mm B&W. *Sale:* Texture Film.

Black Friday. Boris Karloff & Bela Lugosi. Directed by Arthur Lubin. 1940. Universal. 70 min. Sound. 16mm B&W. *Rental:* Swank Motion.

Black Fury. Paul Muni & Akim Tamiroff. Directed by Michael Curtiz. 1935. Warners. 95 min. Sound. 16mm B&W. *Rental:* MGM United.

Black G. I., The 1970. NET. (Documentary). 55 min. Sound. 16mm B&W. *Rental:* Indiana AV Ctr & U Cal Media. *Sale:* Indiana AV Ctr.

Black Girl. Mbissine Therese Diop. Directed by Ousmane Sembene. Senegalese. 1965. Senegal. 60 min. Sound. 16mm B&W. subtitles. *Rental:* New Cinema & New Yorker Films.

Black Girl. Brock Peters, Leslie Uggams & Claudia McNeil. Directed by Ossie Davis. 1973. Cinerama. 107 min. Sound. 16mm B&W. *Rental:* Swank Motion.

Black Glove, The. Alex Nichol & Eleanor Summerfield. Directed by Terence Fisher. 1954. Lippert. 84 min. Sound. 16mm B&W. *Rental:* Bosco Films & Budget Films.

Black God, White Devil. Trans. Title: Deus E O Biabo Na Terra Do Sol. Yona Magalhase & Geraldo Del Ray. Directed by Glauber Rocha. 1963. Brazil. 120 min. Sound. 16mm B&W. subtitles. *Rental:* Hurlock Cine.

Black Gold. Anthony Quinn & Katherine DeMille. Directed by Phil Karlson. 1947. Allied Artists. 92 min. Sound. 16mm B&W. *Rental:* Budget Films & Hurlock Cine.

Black Gunn. Jim Brown & Martin Landau. Directed by Robert Hartford-Davis. 1972. Columbia. 97 min. Sound. 16mm Color. *Rental:* Budget Films, Cine Craft, Swank Motion & Westcoast Films.

Black Hand, The. Gene Kelly & J. Carroll Naish. Directed by Richard Thorpe. 1950. MGM. 92 min. Sound. 16mm B&W. *Rental:* MGM United.

Black Hills. Eddie Dean. Directed by Ray Taylor. 1947. Eagle Lion. 58 min. Sound. 16mm B&W. *Sale:* Classics Assoc NY.

Black Hills Ambush. Allan Lane. Directed by Harry Keller. 1952. Republic. 54 min. Sound. 16mm B&W. *Rental:* Ivy Films. *Sale:* Rep Pic Film & Nostalgia Merchant.

Black Hills Express. Don Barry. Directed by John English. 1943. Republic. 55 min. Sound. 16mm B&W. *Rental:* Ivy Films. *Sale:* Rep Pic Film & Nostalgia Merchant.

Black History: Lost, Stolen or Strayed. 1968. CBS. (Documentary). 55 min. Sound. 16mm Color. *Rental:* ADL, Budget Films, BYU Media, Iowa Films, La Inst Res Ctr, NYU Film Lib, Syracuse U Film, U Cal Media & U Mich Media. *Sale:* Phoenix Films. *Rental:* Twyman Films, *Sale:* Phoenix Films, Color version. *Sale:* Phoenix Films, Videotape version.

Black Hole, The. Maximilian Schell, Anthony Perkins & Yvette Mimieux. Directed by Gary Nelson. 1979. Disney. 97 min. Sound. 16mm Color. *Rental:* Bosco Films, Elliot Film Co, Film Ctr DC, Film Pres, Films Inc, MGM United, Modern Sound, Roas Films, Swank Motion, Twyman Films, U of IL Film, Welling Motion Pictures, Westcoast Films & Williams Films. *Rental:* Williams Films, Videotape version.

Black Holes of Gravity. 1978. Britain. (Documentary). 56 min. Sound. 16mm Color. *Rental:* Films Inc, Iowa Films & U of IL Film. *Sale:* Films Inc. *Rental:* Films Inc, *Sale:* Films Inc, Videotape version.

Black Island. 1980. Britain. (Cast unlisted). 58 min. Sound. 16mm Color. *Sale:* Lucerne Films.

Black Jack. Georg Stanford Brown & Brandon De Wilde. Directed by William T. Naud. 1973. American International. 87 min. Sound. 16mm Color. *Rental:* Swank Motion.

Black King. Orig. Title: Harlem Hot Shot. Directed by Bud Pollard. 1933. Metropolitan. (Cast unlisted). 70 min. Sound. 16mm B&W. *Rental:* Budget Films.

Black Knight, The. Alan Ladd & Patricia Medina. Directed by Tay Garnett. 1954. Columbia. 85 min. Sound. 16mm Color. *Rental:* Arcus Film, Cine Craft, Film Ctr DC, Modern Sound & Williams Films.

Black Lash. Lash LaRue. Directed by Ron Ormond. 1952. Realart. 55 min. Sound. 16mm B&W. *Rental:* Budget Films. *Sale:* Morcraft Films. *Rental:* Westcoast Films, 60 mins. version.

Black Legion, The. Humphrey Bogart & Ann Sheridan. Directed by Archie Mayo. 1936. Warners. 83 min. Sound. 16mm B&W. *Rental:* MGM United.

Black Like Me. James Whitmore, Will Geer & Roscoe Lee Brown. Directed by Carl Lerner. 1964. Continental. 110 min. Sound. 16mm B&W. *Rental:* Budget Films & Kino Intl. *Sale:* Kino Intl. *Lease:* Kino Intl.

Black Magic. Orig. Title: Cagliostro. Orson Welles & Akim Tamiroff. Directed by Gregory Ratoff. 1944. United Artists. 105 min. Sound. 16mm B&W. *Rental:* Budget Films & Kit Parker.

Black Magic *see* Meeting at Midnight.

Black Mama, White Mama. Pam Grier & Margaret Markov. Directed by Eddie Romero. 1973. American International. 87 min. Sound. 16mm Color. *Rental:* Swank Motion.

Black Man's Land No. One. 1975. Films Inc. 51 min. Sound. 16mm Color. *Rental:* Syracuse U Film.

Black Man's Land: No. Three. 1975. Films inc. 51 min. Sound. 16mm Color. *Rental:* Syracuse U Film.

Black Man's Land: No. Two. 1975. Films Inc. 51 min. Sound. 16mm Color. *Rental:* Syracuse U Film.

Black Marble, The. Robert Foxworth, Paula Prentiss & Harry Dean Stanton. Directed by Harold Becker. 1980. Embassy. 113 min. Sound. 16mm Color. *Rental:* Films Inc.

Black Market Babies. Ralph Morgan. Directed by William Beaudine. 1945. Monogram. 71 min. Sound. 16mm B&W. *Rental:* Hurlock Cine.

Black Market Rustlers. Range Busters. Directed by S. Roy Luby. 1943. Monogram. 60 min. Sound. 16mm B&W. *Rental:* Budget Films & Modern Sound.

Black Midnight. Roddy McDowell. Directed by Budd Boetticher. 1949. Monogram. 66 min. Sound. 16mm B&W. *Rental:* Hurlock Cine.

Black Moon. Joe Dallesandro. Directed by Louis Malle. Fr. 1975. France. 92 min. Sound. 16mm Color. *Sale:* Films Inc, Subtitled version.

Black Mountain Stage. Tim McCoy. 1940. 60 min. Sound. 16mm B&W. *Rental:* Mogulls Films.

Black Narcissus. Deborah Kerr, Flora Robson & Jean Simmons. Directed by Michael Powell & Emeric Pressburger. 1947. Britain. 101 min. Sound. 16mm Color. *Rental:* Arcus Film, Budget Films, Films Inc, Images Film, Janus Films, Kit Parker, Learning Corp Am, Twyman Films & Williams Films. *Sale:* Learning Corp Am.

Black Oak Conspiracy, The. Jesse Vint & Seymour Cassel. Directed by Bob Kelljan. 1977. New World. 92 min. Sound. 16mm Color. *Rental:* Films Inc.

Black Orchid, The. Sophia Loren, Anthony Quinn & Ina Balin. Directed by Martin Ritt. 1959. Paramount. 95 min. Sound. 16mm B&W. *Rental:* Films Inc.

Black Orpheus. Marpessa Dawn, Bruno Melo & Lourdes De Oliveira. Directed by Marcel Camus. 1960. Brazil. 103 min. Sound. 16mm Color. subtitles. *Rental:* Films Inc, Janus Films & New Cinema. *Rental:* Janus Films, Dubbed version.

Black Panther, The. Rose Chiang Hung. Directed by Wang Ping. Chinese. 1965. China. 110 min. Sound. 16mm Color. subtitles. *Rental:* Films Inc.

Black Pearl, The. Gilbert Roland, Carl Anderson & Emilio Rodriquez. Columbia. 90 min. Sound. 16mm Color. *Rental:* Williams Films.

Black Perspective on the News: KKK & American Nazi Party Leaders. 1979. PBS. (Documentary). 59 min. Videotape Color. *Rental:* PBS Video. *Sale:* PBS Video.

Black Peter. Ladislav Jakim & Pavla Martinkova. Directed by Milos Forman. 1964. 85 min. Sound. 16mm B&W. *Rental:* Films Inc.

Black Pirate, The. Douglas Fairbanks & Billie Dove. Directed by Albert Parker. 1926. United Artists. 95 min. Silent. 16mm B&W. *Rental:* A Twyman Pres, Budget Films, Classic Film Mus, Creative Film, Em Gee Film Lib, Film Images, Ivy Films, Kerr Film, Kit Parker, Film Images, Video Comm, Westcoast Films, Welling Motion Pictures & Willoughby Peer. *Sale:* Blackhawk Films, Cinema Concepts & Griggs Movie. *Rental:* Video Comm & Welling Motion Pictures, *Sale:* See-Art Films, Sound 16mm version. *Rental:* Killiam Collect & New Cinema, Tinted version. *Rental:* Ivy Films, *Sale:* Blackhawk Films, Super 8 silent version. *Rental:* Video Comm, Videotape version. *Rental:* Bosco Films & Westcoast Films, 50 mins. version. *Rental:* Films Inc, 80 mins. version.

Black Pirate, The. Anthony Dexter. Directed by Allen H. Miner. 1954. Lippert. 80 min. Sound. 16mm B&W. *Rental:* Film Classics & Film Ctr DC.

Black Power in Dixie. 2 pts. 1969. Holt, Rinehart & Winston. (Documentary). 60 min. Sound. 16mm B&W. *Sale:* Phoenix Films.

Black Power, White Backlash. 1966. CBS. (Documentary). 50 min. Sound. 16mm B&W. *Rental:* CBS Inc.

Black Raven, The. George Zucco & Wanda McKay. Directed by Sam Newfield. 1943. PRC. 64 min. Sound. 16mm B&W. *Rental:* Budget Films, Films Inc & Video Comm. *Sale:* Cinema Concepts.

Black River. Sergio Corrieri & Nelson Villagra. Directed by Manuel Perez. Span. 1977. Cuba. 135 min. Sound. 16mm Color. subtitles. *Rental:* Tricontinental Film.

Black Rodeo. Woody Strode & Muhammed Ali. Directed by Jeff Kanew. 1972. Cinerama. 87 min. Sound. 16mm Color. *Rental:* Swank Motion. *Rental:* Swank Motion, Anamorphic color version.

Black Room, The. Boris Karloff & Marian Marsh. Directed by Roy William Neill. 1935. Columbia. 70 min. Sound. 16mm B&W. *Rental:* Cine Craft & Welling Motion Pictures.

Black Roots. Orig. Title: Black Culture in America. Directed by Lionel Rogosin. 1970. Rogosin. (Documentary). 61 min. Sound. 16mm Color. *Rental:* Inst Cinema. *Sale:* Inst Cinema.

Black Rose, The. Tyrone Power & Orson Welles. Directed by Henry Hathaway. 1950. Fox. 120 min. Sound. 16mm Color. *Rental:* Films Inc.

Black Sabbath. Boris Karloff, Susy Andersen & Jacqueline Soussard. Directed by Mario Bava. 1964. American International. 99 min. Sound. 16mm Color. *Rental:* Budget Films, Cine Craft, Ivy Films, Roas Films, Video Comm, Welling Motion Pictures, Westcoast Films & Willoughby Peer.

Black Samson. Rockne Tarkington. Directed by Charles Bail. 1974. Warners. 88 min. Sound. 16mm Color. *Rental:* Swank Motion, Twyman Films & Williams Films.

Black Shadows on a Silver Screen. 1976. Gould. (Documentary). 53 min. Sound. 16mm Color. *Rental:* Budget Films, U of IL Film, Utah Media & Westcoast Films. *Sale:* Lucerne Films. *Sale:* Lucerne Films, Videotape version.

Black Shampoo. John Daniels & Tanya Boyd. Directed by Greydon Clark. 1975. World Amusement. 83 min. Sound. 16mm Color. *Sale:* Salz Ent.

Black Shield of Falworth, The. Tony Curtis & Julie Adams. Directed by Rudolph Mate. 1954. Universal. 100 min. Sound. 16mm Color. *Rental:* Williams Films.

Black Spurs. Rory Calhoun, Terry Moore & Linda Darnell. Directed by R. G. Springsteen. 1965. Paramount. 81 min. Sound. 16mm Color. *Rental:* Films Inc.

Black Stallion, The. Mickey Rooney & Kelly Reno. Directed by Carroll Ballard. 1979. United Artists. 118 min. Sound. 16mm Color. *Rental:* MGM United. *Rental:* MGM United, Videotape version.

Black Stallion *see* Return of Wildfire.

Black Stallion Returns, The. Kelly Reno, Vince Spano & Terri Garr. 1982. United Artists. 103 min. Sound. 16mm Color. *Rental:* MGM United. *Rental:* MGM United, Videotape version.

Black Star. Filmation. (Animated). 66 min. Sound. 16mm Color. *Rental:* Williams Films.

Black Sunday. Bruce Dern, Robert Shaw & Marthe Keller. Directed by John Frankenheimer. 1977. Paramount. 145 min. Sound. 16mm Color. *Rental:* Films Inc.

Black Swan, The. Tyrone Power & Maureen O'Hara. Directed by Henry King. 1942. Fox. 85 min. Sound. 16mm B&W. *Rental:* Films Inc.

Black Tent, The. Anthony Steele & Donald Sinden. Directed by Brian Desmond-Hurst. 1957. Britain. 85 min. Sound. 16mm B&W. *Rental:* Cousino Visual Ed.

Black Thursday. Christine Pascal. Directed by Michael Mitrani. Fr. 1974. France. 90 min. Sound. 16mm Color. subtitles. *Rental:* Films Inc.

Black Tide. John Ireland & Derek Bond. 1956. Britain. 79 min. Sound. 16mm B&W. *Rental:* Ivy Films & Video Comm. *Rental:* Video Comm, Videotape version.

Black Tide. 1978. Nova. (Documentary). 59 min. Sound. 16mm Color. *Rental:* Time-Life Multimedia. *Sale:* Time-Life Multimedia. *Sale:* Time-Life Multimedia, Videotape version.

Black Tights. Directed by Terence Young. 1962. Roland Petit. 120 min. Sound. 16mm Color. *Rental:* Dance Film Archive.

Black Veil for Lisa, A. John Mills & Luciana Paluzzi. Directed by Massimo Dellamano. 1969. Landau. 88 min. Sound. 16mm Color. dubbed. *Rental:* Ivy Films & Rep Pic Film. *Lease:* Rep Pic Film.

Black Whip, The. Hugh Marlowe & Coleen Gray. Directed by Charles Marquis Warren. 1956. Fox. 79 min. Sound. 16mm B&W. *Rental:* Ivy Films. *Sale:* Rep Pic Film.

Black Widow, The. Ginger Rogers & Van Heflin. Directed by Nunnally Johnson. 1954. Fox. 95 min. Sound. 16mm Color. *Rental:* Films Inc.

Black Widow, The. Bruce Edwards, Carol Forman & Ramsay Ames. Directed by Spencer G. Bennett & Fred C. Brannon. 1947. Republic. 176 min. Sound. 16mm B&W. *Rental:* Ivy Films. *Sale:* Cinema Concepts, Videotape version.

Black Windmill, The. Michael Caine & Donald Pleasence. Directed by Don Siegel. 1974. Universal. 106 min. Sound. 16mm Color. *Rental:* Swank Motion.

Black Woman, The. 1970. NET. (Documentary). 52 min. Sound. 16mm B&W. *Rental:* Indiana AV Ctr & U Mich Media. *Sale:* Indiana AV Ctr.

Black World. 2 Pts. 1968. CBS. (Documentary). 55 min. Sound. 16mm B&W. *Rental:* Budget Films, OK AV Ctr, NYU Film Lib, U Cal Media & U Mich Media. *Sale:* Phoenix Films. *Sale:* Phoenix Films, Color version.

Black Zoo. Michael Gough & Jeanne Cooper. Directed by Robert Gordon. 1963. Allied Artists. 88 min. Sound. 16mm Color. *Rental:* Hurlock Cine.

Blackamoor of Peter the Great, The. Alexei Petrenko & Vladimir Visotsky. Directed by Alexander Mitta. 1978. 99 min. Sound. 16mm Color. *Rental:* Corinth Films.

Blackbeard the Pirate. Robert Newton & Linda Darnell. Directed by Raoul Walsh. 1952. RKO. 98 min. Sound. 16mm Color. *Rental:* Films Inc.

Blackbeard's Ghost. Peter Ustinov, Dean Jones & Suzanne Pleshette. Directed by Robert Stevenson. 1968. Disney. 107 min. Sound. 16mm Color. *Rental:* Disney Prod, Film Pres, Films Inc, Modern Sound, Roas Films, Swank Motion, Twyman Films, Welling Motion Pictures & Williams Films.

Blackboard Jungle, The. Glen Ford & Anne Francis. Directed by Richard Brooks. 1955. MGM. 101 min. Sound. 16mm B&W. *Rental:* MGM United. *Rental:* MGM United, Videotape version.

Blackenstein. 1973. L. F. G.. (Cast unlisted). 87 min. Videotape Color. *Sale:* Cinema Concepts.

Blackie. 1965. Time-Life. (Documentary). 54 min. Sound. 16mm B&W. *Rental:* Time-Life Multimedia. *Sale:* Time-Life Multimedia.

Blackjack Ketchum, Desperado. Howard Duff & Victor Jory. Directed by Earl Bellamy. 1956. Columbia. 76 min. Sound. 16mm Color. *Lease:* Time-Life Multimedia.

Blackmail. Anny Ondra & Sara Allgood. Directed by Alfred Hitchcock. 1929. Britain. 86 min. Sound. 16mm B&W. *Rental:* Budget Films, Classic Film Mus, Em Gee Film Lib, Films Inc, Inst Cinema, Ivy Films, Janus Films, Kit Parker, Museum Mod Art, Video Comm, Westcoast Films, Wholesome Film Ctr & Images Film. *Sale:* Classic Film Mus, Cinema Concepts, Festival Films, Glenn Photo, Natl Cinema, Reel Images & Images Film. *Sale:* Cinema Concepts, Festival Films, Glenn Photo, Video Comm & Tamarelles French Film, Videotape version.

Blackmail. William Marshall & Adele Mara. Directed by Lesley Selander. 1947. Republic. 71 min. Sound. 16mm B&W. *Rental:* Ivy Films.

Blackmail. Edward G. Robinson & Ruth Hussey. Directed by H. C. Potter. 1939. MGM. 81 min. Sound. 16mm B&W. *Rental:* MGM United.

Blackmailers, The. Manuel Benitez. 1960. Spain. 86 min. Sound. 16mm Color. dubbed. *Rental:* Ivy Films.

Blackout. Dane Clark & Belinda Lee. Directed by Terence Fisher. 1954. Lippert. 87 min. Sound. 16mm B&W. *Rental:* Budget Films & Bosco Films.

Blackout. Jim Mitchum & Robert Carradine. Directed by Eddie Matalon. 1978. New World. 90 min. Sound. 16mm Color. *Rental:* Films Inc.

Blacks, Blues, Black! 10 pts. 1979. PBS. (Documentary). 600 min. Videotape Color. *Rental:* PBS Video. *Sale:* PBS Video.

Blacula. William Marshall, Denise Nicholas & Vonetta McGee. Directed by William Crain. 1972. American International. 92 min. Sound. 16mm Color. *Rental:* Welling Motion Pictures.

Blade. John Marley & William Prince. Directed by Ernest Pintoff. 1972. Joseph Green. 90 min. Sound. 16mm Color. *Rental:* J Green Pics.

Blade Runner. Harrison Ford, Rutger Hauer & Sean Young. Directed by Ridley Scott. 124 min. Sound. 16mm Color. *Rental:* Swank Motion. *Rental:* Swank Motion, Videotape version.

Blake. 1979. Canada. (Documentary). 57 min. Sound. 16mm Color. *Rental:* Kent St U Film.

Blanche Fury. Valerie Hobson & Stewart Granger. Directed by Marc Allegret. 1948. Britain. 93 min. Sound. 16mm Color. *Rental:* Budget Films.

Blancheville Monster. Joan Hills & Richard Davis. Directed by Alberto De Martino. 1964. American International. 89 min. Sound. 16mm B&W. dubbed. *Rental:* Films Inc.

Blast. Billy Dee Williams, Raymond St. Jacques, Pamela Jones & Oscar Williams. 1976. New World. 85 min. Sound. 16mm Color. *Rental:* Films Inc.

Blaze of Noon. William Holden & Anne Baxter. Directed by John Farrow. 1947. Paramount. 91 min. Sound. 16mm B&W. *Rental:* Swank Motion.

Blazing Across the Pecos. Orig. Title: Under Arrest. Charles Starrett. Directed by Ray Nazarro. 1948. Columbia. 55 min. Sound. 16mm B&W. *Rental:* Budget Films.

Blazing Barriers. Junior Coughlin. Directed by Aubrey Scotto. 1937. Monogram. 60 min. Sound. 16mm B&W. *Rental:* Mogulls Films.

Blazing Bullets. Johnny Mack Brown. Directed by Wallace Fox. 1951. Monogram. 51 min. Sound. 16mm B&W. *Rental:* Hurlock Cine.

Blazing Forest, The. John Payne. Directed by Edward Ludwig. 1952. Paramount. 90 min. Sound. 16mm B&W. *Rental:* Budget Films, Video Comm & Willoughby Peer.

Blazing Frontier. Buster Crabbe. Directed by Sam Newfield. 1943. PRC. 61 min. Sound. 16mm B&W. *Rental:* Mogulls Films.

Blazing Guns. Hoot Gibson & Ken Maynard. Directed by Robert Tansey. 1943. Monogram. 60 min. Sound. 16mm B&W. *Rental:* MGM United & Mogulls Films.

Blazing Saddles. Mel Brooks & Madeline Kahn. Directed by Mel Brooks. 1974. Warners. 93 min. Sound. 16mm Color. *Rental:* Swank Motion. *Rental:* Swank Motion, Videotape version.

Blazing Sixes. Dick Foran. Directed by Noel Smith. 1937. Warners. 55 min. Sound. 16mm B&W. *Rental:* MGM United.

Bleak Moments, Loving Moments. Anna Raitte & Eric Allen. Directed by Mike Leigh. 1975. Autumn. 110 min. Sound. 16mm Color. *Rental:* Film Images.

Bleak Morning. Rufina Nifontova. Directed by Grigori Roshal. 1959. Russia. 120 min. Sound. 16mm B&W. *Rental:* Corinth Films.

Bless the Beasts & Children. Billy Mumy, Barry Robins & Miles Chapin. Directed by Stanley Kramer. 1971. Columbia. 106 min. Sound. 16mm Color. *Rental:* Arcus Film, Bosco Films, Budget Films, Cine Craft, Films Inc, Inst Cinema, Ivy Films, Kerr Film, Kit Parker, Modern Sound, Natl Film Video, Newman Film Lib, Roas Films, Twyman Films, U of IL Film, Video Comm, Welling Motion Pictures, Westcoast Films, Wholesome Film Ctr, Williams Films & Willoughby Peer.

Bless This House. Sidney James & Diana Coupland. Directed by Gerald Thomas. Britain. 95 min. Sound. 16mm B&W. *Rental:* Cinema Five.

Blessed Event. Lee Tracy & Mary Brian. Directed by Roy Del Ruth. 1932. Warners. 83 min. Sound. 16mm B&W. *Rental:* MGM United.

Blind Adventure. Ralph Bellamy & Robert Armstrong. Directed by Merian C. Cooper. 1933. RKO. 60 min. Sound. 16mm *Rental:* RKO General Pics.

Blind Alibi. Richard Dix & Paul Guilfoyle. Directed by Lew Landers. 1938. RKO. 61 min. Sound. 16mm *Rental:* RKO General Pics.

Blind Alley. Ralph Bellamy, Chester Morris & Ann Dvorak. Directed by Charles Vidor. 1939. Columbia. 71 min. Sound. 16mm B&W. *Rental:* Kit Parker.

Blind Bird. 45 min. Sound. 16mm Color. *Rental:* McGraw-Hill Films & Syracuse U Film.

Blind Husbands. Erich Von Stroheim. Directed by Erich Von Stroheim. 1919. Universal. 68 min. Silent. 16mm B&W. *Rental:* Budget Films, Creative Films, Em Gee Film Lib, Film Images, Films Inc, Images Film, Ivy Films, Kit Parker, Museum·Mod Art, Swank Motion, Video Comm & Westcoast Films. *Sale:* Festival Films, Glenn Photo, Images Film, Natl Cinema, Film Images & Reel Images. *Sale:* Tamarelles French Film, *Rental:* Video Comm, Videotape version. *Rental:* Kit Parker, 16mm 92 min. version.

Blind Man's Bluff. 1979. Britain. (Cast unlisted). 59 min. Sound. 16mm Color. *Sale:* Lucerne Films. *Rental:* Lucerne Films.

Blindfold. Rock Hudson & Claudia Cardinale. Directed by Philip Dunne. 1967. Universal. 102 min. Sound. 16mm Color. *Rental:* Swank Motion.

Blindfolded Eyes. Geraldine Chaplin. Directed by Carlos Saura. 1978. Janus. 100 min. Sound. 16mm Color. subtitles. *Rental:* Films Inc.

Blindman. Tony Anthony & Ringo Starr. Directed by Ferdinando Baldi. 1972. Fox. (Anamorphic). 105 min. Sound. 16mm Color. *Rental:* Films Inc.

Bliss of Mrs. Blossom. Shirley MacLaine, Richard Attenborough & James Booth. Directed by Joseph McGrath. 1968. Paramount. 93 min. Sound. 16mm Color. *Rental:* Films Inc.

Blithe Spirit. Rex Harrison, Constance Cummings & Kay Hammond. Directed by David Lean. 1945. Britain. 96 min. Sound. 16mm Color. *Rental:* Budget Films, Films Inc, Images Film, Kit Parker, Learning Corp Am, Twyman Films, U of IL Film & Welling Motion Pictures. *Sale:* Learning Corp Am.

Blitzkrieg Bop. CBGB. (Concert). 60 min. Sound. 16mm Color. *Rental:* Ivy Films.

Blob, The. Steve McQueen, Aneta Corseaut & Olin Howlin. Directed by Irvin Yeaworth Jr. 1958. Paramount. 85 min. Sound. 16mm Color. *Rental:* Films Inc.

Block Busters. East Side Kids. Directed by Wallace Fox. 1944. Monogram. 63 min. Sound. 16mm B&W. *Rental:* Ivy Films, Modern Sound & Video Comm. *Rental:* Video Comm. *Rental:* Ivy Films, Videotape version.

Block Signal. Ralph Lewis & Jean Arthur. Directed by Frank O'Connor. 1926. Gothan. 70 min. Silent. 16mm B&W. *Rental:* Mogulls Films. *Sale:* Blackhawk Films, Silent 8mm version.

Blockade. Henry Fonda & Madeline Carroll. Directed by William Dieterle. 84 min. 16mm B&W. *Rental:* Budget Films, Films Inc, Learning Corp Am & Video Comm. *Sale:* Learning Corp Am.

Blocked Trail. Tom Tyler & Bob Steele. Directed by Elmer Clifton. 1943. Republic. 56 min. Sound. 16mm B&W. *Rental:* Ivy Films. *Sale:* Rep Pic Film & Nostalgia Merchant.

Blockheads. Stan Laurel, Oliver Hardy & Billy Gilbert. Directed by John G. Blystone. 1938. Hal Roach. 65 min. Sound. 16mm B&W. *Rental:* Alba House, Budget Films, Cine Craft, Em Gee Film Lib, Films Inc, Inst Cinema, Kit Parker, Lewis Film, Modern Sound, Mogulls Films, Newman Film Lib, Film Images, Roas Films, Twyman Films, Westcoast Films, Wholesome Film Ctr & Willoughby Peer. *Sale:* Blackhawk Films. *Sale:* Blackhawk Films, Super 8 sound version.

Blodiga Tiden, Das *see* Mein Kampf.

Blond Cheat. Joan Fontaine & Cecil Kellaway. Directed by Joseph Santley. 1938. RKO. 62 min. Sound. 16mm *Rental:* RKO General Pics.

Blond Crazy. Orig. Title: Larceny Lane. James Cagney, Joan Blondell & Ray Milland. Directed by Roy Del Ruth. 1931. Warners. 82 min. Sound. 16mm B&W. *Rental:* MGM United.

Blonde Bait. Orig. Title: Women Without Men. Beverly Michaels & Richard Travis. Directed by Elmo Williams. 1956. Associated. 71 min. Sound. 16mm B&W. *Rental:* Ivy Films. *Sale:* Rep Pic Film.

Blonde Bandit, The. Dorothy Patrick & Gerald Mohr. Directed by Harry Keller. 1950. Republic. 60 min. Sound. 16mm B&W. *Rental:* Ivy Films. *Sale:* Rep Pic Film.

Blonde Bombshell *see* Bombshell.

Blonde Comet. Virginia Vale & Barney Oldfield. Directed by William Beaudine. 1941. PRC. 67 min. Sound. 16mm B&W. *Rental:* Mogulls Films.

Blonde Fever. Mary Astor & Philip Dorn. Directed by Richard Whorf. 1944. MGM. 69 min. Sound. 16mm B&W. *Rental:* MGM United.

Blonde for a Day. Hugh Beaumont & Kathryn Adams. Directed by Sam Newfield. 1946. PRC. 68 min. Sound. 16mm B&W. *Sale:* Classics Assoc NY.

Blonde in Bondage. 1957. DCA. (Cast unlisted). 90 min. Sound. 16mm B&W. *Rental:* Ivy Films.

Blonde Inspiration. John Shelton & Virginia Grey. Directed by Busby Berkeley. 1941. MGM. 72 min. Sound. 16mm B&W. *Rental:* MGM United.

Blonde Venus. Marlene Dietrich, Herbert Marshall & Cary Grant. Directed by Josef Von Sternberg. 1932. Paramount. 88 min. Sound. 16mm B&W. *Rental:* Museum Mod Art, Swank Motion & Twyman Films, 97 min. version.

Blondes at Work. Glenda Farrell & Carole Landis. Directed by Frank McDonald. 1938. Warners. 63 min. Sound. 16mm B&W. *Rental:* MGM United.

Blondes for Danger. Gordon Harker. Directed by Jack Raymond. 1932. 16mm *Rental:* A Twyman Pres.

Blondie. Penny Singleton & Arthur Lake. Directed by Frank R. Strayer. 1939. Columbia. 75 min. Sound. 16mm B&W. *Rental:* Video Comm & Westcoast Films. *Lease:* King Features.

Blondie Brings Up Baby. Penny Singleton & Arthur Lake. Directed by Frank R. Strayer. 1940. Columbia. 75 min. Sound. 16mm B&W. *Rental:* Modern Sound & Video Comm. *Lease:* King Features.

Blondie for Victory. Penny Singleton & Arthur Lake. Directed by Frank R. Strayer. 1941. Columbia. 75 min. Sound. 16mm B&W. *Rental:* Video Comm. *Lease:* King Features.

Blondie Goes Latin. Orig. Title: Conga Swing. Penny Singleton & Arthur Lake. Directed by Frank R. Strayer. 1941. Columbia. 75 min. Sound. 16mm B&W. *Rental:* Video Comm. *Lease:* King Features.

Blondie Goes to College. Orig. Title: Boss Said No, The. Penny Singleton & Arthur Lake. Directed by Frank R. Strayer. 1942. Columbia. 75 min. Sound. 16mm B&W. *Rental:* Video Comm. *Lease:* King Features.

Blondie Has Servant Trouble. Penny Singleton & Arthur Lake. Directed by Frank R. Strayer. 1940. Columbia. 75 min. Sound. 16mm B&W. *Rental:* Modern Sound & Video Comm. *Lease:* King Features.

Blondie Hits the Jackpot. Penny Singleton & Arthur Lake. Directed by Edward Bernds. 1950. Columbia. 75 min. Sound. 16mm B&W. *Rental:* Modern Sound & Video Comm. *Lease:* King Features.

Blondie in Society. Orig. Title: Henpecked. Penny Singleton & Arthur Lake. Directed by Frank R. Strayer. 1941. Columbia. 75 min. Sound. 16mm B&W. *Rental:* Modern Sound, Video Comm & Westcoast Films. *Lease:* King Features.

Blondie in the Dough. Penny Singleton & Arthur Lake. Directed by Abby Berlin. 1948. Columbia. 75 min. Sound. 16mm B&W. *Rental:* Modern Sound & Video Comm. *Lease:* King Features.

Blondie Johnson. Joan Blondell & Chester Morris. Directed by Ray Enright. 1933. Warners. 67 min. Sound. 16mm B&W. *Rental:* MGM United.

Blondie Knows Best. Penny Singleton & Arthur Lake. Directed by Edward Bernds. 1947. Columbia. 75 min. Sound. 16mm B&W. *Rental:* Modern Sound & Video Comm. *Lease:* King Features.

Blondie Meets the Boss. Penny Singleton & Arthur Lake. Directed by Frank R. Strayer. 1939. Columbia. 75 min. Sound. 16mm B&W. *Rental:* Video Comm. *Lease:* King Features.

Blondie of the Follies. Marion Davies & Robert Montgomery. Directed by Edmund Goulding. 1932. MGM. 90 min. Sound. 16mm B&W. *Rental:* MGM United.

Blondie on a Budget. Penny Singleton & Arthur Lake. Directed by Frank R. Strayer. 1940. Columbia. 75 min. Sound. 16mm B&W. *Rental:* Video Comm. *Lease:* King Features.

Blondie Plays Cupid. Penny Singleton & Arthur Lake. Directed by Frank R. Strayer. 1941. Columbia. 75 min. Sound. 16mm B&W. *Rental:* Modern Sound & Video Comm. *Lease:* King Features.

Blondie Take a Vacation. Penny Singleton & Arthur Lake. Directed by Frank R. Strayer. 1939. Columbia. 75 min. Sound. 16mm B&W. *Rental:* Video Comm. *Lease:* King Features.

Blondie's Anniversary. Penny Singleton & Arthur Lake. Directed by Abby Berlin. 1948. Columbia. 75 min. Sound. 16mm B&W. *Rental:* Modern Sound & Video Comm. *Lease:* King Features.

Blondie's Big Deal. Orig. Title: Big Deal, The. Penny Singleton & Arthur Lake. Directed by Edward Bernds. 1949. Columbia. 75 min. Sound. 16mm B&W. *Rental:* Modern Sound & Video Comm. *Lease:* King Features.

Blondie's Big Moment. Penny Singleton & Arthur Lake. Directed by Abby Berlin. 1947. Columbia. 75 min. Sound. 16mm B&W. *Rental:* Modern Sound & Video Comm. *Lease:* King Features.

Blondie's Blessed Event. Orig. Title: Bundle of Trouble, A. Penny Singleton & Arthur Lake. Directed by Frank R. Strayer. 1942. Columbia. 75 min. Sound. 16mm B&W. *Rental:* Video Comm. *Lease:* King Features.

Blondie's Hero. Penny Singleton & Arthur Lake. Directed by Edward Bernds. 1950. Columbia. 75 min. Sound. 16mm B&W. *Rental:* Modern Sound & Video Comm. *Lease:* King Features.

Blondie's Holiday. Penny Singleton & Arthur Lake. Directed by Abby Berlin. 1975. Columbia. 75 min. Sound. 16mm B&W. *Rental:* Modern Sound & Video Comm. *Lease:* King Features.

Blondie's Lucky Day. Penny Singleton & Arthur Lake. Directed by Abby Berlin. 1946. Columbia. 75 min. Sound. 16mm B&W. *Rental:* Video Comm. *Lease:* King Features.

Blondie's Reward. Penny Singleton & Arthur Lake. Directed by Abby Berlin. 1948. Columbia. 75 min. Sound. 16mm B&W. *Rental:* Modern Sound & Video Comm. *Lease:* King Features.

Blondie's Secret. Penny Singleton & Arthur Lake. Directed by Edward Bernds. 1948. Columbia. 75 min. Sound. 16mm B&W. *Rental:* Modern Sound & Video Comm. *Lease:* King Features.

Blood & Black Lace. Cameron Mitchell & Eva Bartok. Directed by Mario Bava. 1965. Italy. 88 min. Sound. 16mm Color. dubbed. *Rental:* Ivy Films, Video Comm, Welling Motion Pictures & WilloughbyPeer.

Blood & Roses. Mel Ferrer, Elsa Martinelli & Annette Vadim. Directed by Roger Vadim. 1961. Paramount. 74 min. Sound. 16mm Color. *Rental:* Films Inc.

Blood & Sand. Rudolph Valentino, Nita Naldi & Lila Lee. Directed by Fred Niblo. 1922. Paramount. 113 min. Silent. 16mm B&W. *Rental:* Budget Films, Classic Film Mus, Em Gee Film Lib, Film Images, Ivy Films, Kerr Film, Kit Parker, Museum Mod Art, Swank Motion, Video Comm, Welling Motion Pictures & Willoughby Peer. *Sale:* Glenn Photo. *Rental:* Video Comm & Welling Motion Pictures, *Sale:* Blackhawk Films & See-Art Films, Sound 16mm version. *Rental:* Killiam Collect & New Cinema, Sound 16mm tinted, music & narration only version. *Sale:* Blackhawk Films, Super 8 sound version. *Rental:* Video Comm, *Sale:* Blackhawk Films, Videotape version. *Rental:* Ivy Films, *Sale:* Blackhawk Films & Glenn Photo, Super 8 silent version. *Rental:* A Twyman Pres, 90 min. version.

Blood & Sand. Tyrone Power, Rita Hayworth & Linda Darnell. Directed by Rouben Mamoulian. 1941. Fox. 123 min. Sound. 16mm B&W. *Rental:* Films Inc.

Blood & Sand: War in the Sahara. Directed by Sharon Sopher. 1982. First Run. (Documentary). 58 min. Sound. 16mm Color. *Rental:* First Run. *Lease:* First Run.

Blood & Steel. Helen Holmes & William Desmond. Directed by J. P. McGowan. 1925. Independent. 60 min. Silent. 16mm B&W. *Rental:* Em Gee Film Lib. *Sale:* Glenn Photo, Super 8 silent version. *Sale:* Em Gee Film Lib, Silent 8mm version.

Blood Arrow. Scott Brady & Phyllis Coates. Directed by Charles Marquis Warren. 1958. Fox. 78 min. Sound. 16mm B&W. *Rental:* Ivy Films & Westcoast Films. *Sale:* Rep Pic Film.

Blood Bath see Track of the Vampire.

Blood Beach. David Huffman, Mariana Hill & John Saxon. Directed by Jeffrey Bloom. 1981. Viacom. 95 min. Sound. 16mm Color. *Rental:* Williams Films.

Blood Beast Terror, The. Peter Cushing & Robert Flemyng. Directed by Vernon Sewell. 1967. Britain. 88 min. Sound. 16mm Color. *Rental:* Budget Films, Inst Cinema & Roas Films.

Blood for a Silver Dollar. Montgomery Wood & Evelyn Stewart. 1965. Italy. 92 min. Sound. 16mm Color. dubbed. *Rental:* Modern Sound.

Blood from the Mummy's Tomb. Andrew Keir, Valerie Leon & James Villiers. Directed by Seth Holt. 1972. Britain. 94 min. Sound. 16mm Color. *Rental:* Images Film.

Blood Is My Heritage *see* Blood of Dracula.

Blood Mania. Peter Carpenter. Directed by Robert O'Neil. 1971. Crown. 88 min. Sound. 16mm Color. *Rental:* Budget Films & Video Comm. *Lease:* Video Comm. *Rental:* Video Comm, *Lease:* Video Comm, Videotape version.

Blood Money. George Bancroft & Judith Anderson. Directed by Rowland Brown. 1933. Fox. 75 min. Sound. 16mm B&W. *Rental:* Films Inc.

Blood of a Poet. Directed by Jean Cocteau. Fr. 1932. France. (Experimental). 58 min. Sound. 16mm B&W. subtitles. *Rental:* Budget Films, Classic Film Mus, Corinth Films, Em Gee Film Lib, Films Inc, Iowa Films, Ivy Films, Macmillan Films, Maljack, Syracuse U Film, Texture Film, U Cal Media, Video Comm & Images Film. *Sale:* Classic Film Mus, Cinema Concepts, Festival Films, Films Inc, Glenn Photo, Images Film, Natl Cinema & Reel Images. *Rental:* Ivy Films, Super 8 silent version. *Rental:* Ivy Films, *Sale:* Festival Films, Tamarelles French Film & Texture Film, Videotape version. *Rental:* Texture Film, *Sale:* Texture Film, 55 min version.

Blood of Dracula. Orig. Title: Blood Is My Heritage. Sandra Harrison & Louise Lewis. Directed by Herbert L. Strock. 1957. American International. 70 min. Sound. 16mm B&W. *Rental:* Budget Films.

Blood of Dracula's Castle. Paula Raymond, John Carradine & Gene Shane. Directed by Al Adamson. 1969. Crown. 84 min. Sound. 16mm Color. *Rental:* Films Inc, Ivy Films, Film Ctr DC, Video Comm, Westcoast Films & Welling Motion. *Rental:* Video Comm, Videotape version.

Blood of Jesus. Spencer Williams. Directed by Spencer Williams. 1941. 78 min. Sound. 16mm B&W. *Rental:* Budget Films, Film Classics & Standard Film. *Rental:* Film Classics, Videotape version.

Blood of the Condor, The. Directed by Jorge Sanjines. Span. 1970. Bolivia. (Documentary). 72 min. Sound. 16mm B&W. subtitles. *Rental:* New Yorker Films & Unifilm. *Sale:* Unifilm, 72 mins. version.

Blood of the Vampire. Sir Donald Wolfit & Barbara Shelley. Directed by Henry Cass. 1958. Britain. 87 min. Sound. 16mm Color. *Rental:* Arcus Film, Budget Films, Modern Sound, Roas Films & Williams Films.

Blood on the Arrow. Dale Robertson & Martha Hyer. Directed by Sidney Salkow. 1964. Allied Artists. 92 min. Sound. 16mm Color. *Rental:* Hurlock Cine. *Rental:* Video Comm, Videotape version.

Blood on the Balcony. Directed by Roberto Rossellini. 1963. Italy. (Documentary). 92 min. Sound. 16mm B&W. narrated Eng. *Rental:* Charard Motion Pics.

Blood on the Moon. Robert Mitchum & Barbara Bel Geddes. Directed by Robert Wise. 1948. RKO. 88 min. Sound. 16mm B&W. *Rental:* Films Inc.

Blood on the Mountain. 1974. Mark IV. (Cast unlisted). 71 min. Sound. 16mm Color. *Rental:* G Herne.

Blood on the Sun. James Cagney & Sylvia Sidney. Directed by Frank Lloyd. 1945. United Artists. 94 min. Sound. 16mm B&W. *Rental:* Budget Films & Corinth Films. *Sale:* Reel Images.

Blood Relations. (Body in Question Series). (Documentary). 60 min. Videotape Color. *Rental:* Films Inc & Syracuse U Film. *Sale:* Films Inc.

Blood Rose, The. Phillipe Lemaire & Annie Duperey. Directed by Claude Mulot. 1970. France-Italy. 92 min. Sound. 16mm Color. dubbed. *Rental:* Hurlock Cine. *Sale:* Blackhawk Films, Videotape version.

Blood-Spattered Bride, The. 84 min. Sound. Videotape Color. *Rental:* Maljack Productions.

Blood Transfusions: Benefits & Risks. 1980. US Government. (Documentary). 60 min. Videotape Color. *Sale:* Natl AV Ctr.

Blood Wedding. 1981. 72 min. Sound. 16mm Color. *Rental:* Films Inc.

Bloodbrothers. Richard Gere & Paul Sorvino. Directed by Robert Mulligan. 1978. Warners. 116 min. Sound. 16mm Color. *Rental:* Swank Motion & Twyman Films.

Bloodhounds of Broadway. Mitzi Gaynor & Scott Brady. Directed by Harmon Jones. 1952. Fox. 90 min. Sound. 16mm Color. *Rental:* Films Inc.

Bloodline *see* Sidney Sheldon's Bloodline.

Bloodlust. Robert Reed. Directed by Ralph Brooke. 1962. Crown International. 68 min. Sound. 16mm B&W. *Rental:* Video Comm & Willoughby Peer. *Lease:* Video Comm. *Rental:* Video Comm, *Lease:* Video Comm, Videotape version.

Bloodrage: Never Pick Up a Stranger. Ian Scott, Lawrence Tierney & Judith Marie Bergan. 86 min. 16mm Color. *Rental:* BF Video.

Bloody Mama. Shelley Winters, Pat Hingle & Don Stroud. Directed by Roger Corman. 1970. American International. 70 min. Sound. 16mm Color. *Rental:* Budget Films, Films Inc & Film Ctr DC.

Bloody Vampire, The. Trans. Title: Vampiro Sangriento. Carlos Agosti & Begona Palacios. Directed by Miguel Morayta. 1961. Mexico. 98 min. Sound. 16mm dubbed Spanish. *Rental:* Budget Films.

Blossoms in the Dust. Greer Garson & Walter Pidgeon. Directed by Mervyn LeRoy. 1941. MGM. 99 min. Sound. 16mm Color. *Rental:* MGM United.

Blot, The. Claire Windsor & Louis Calhern. Directed by Lois Weber. 1921. Lois Weber Prod. 104 min. Silent. 16mm B&W. *Rental:* Budget Films, Em Gee Film Lib, Images Film & Museum Mod Art. *Sale:* Glenn Photo, Reel Images & Images Film. *Sale:* Glenn Photo & Reel Images, Super 8 silent version.

Blow for Blow. Trans. Title: Coup Pour Coup. Directed by Marin Karmitz. Fr. 1972. France. (Cast unlisted). 89 min. Sound. 16mm Color. subtitles. *Rental:* Unifilm. *Sale:* Unifilm.

Blow Hot, Blow Cold. Rosemary Dexter, Bibi Andersson & Gunnar Bjornstrand. Directed by Florestano Vancini. 1969. Italy. 92 min. Sound. 16mm Color. dubbed. *Rental:* Swank Motion.

Blow Out. John Travolta, Nancy Allen & John Lithgow. Directed by Brian De Palma. 1981. USA. 107 min. Sound. 16mm Color. *Rental:* Images Film & Swank Motion. *Rental:* Images Film, Anamorphic version.

Blow Up. David Hemmings & Vanessa Redgrave. Directed by Michelangelo Antonioni. 1967. MGM. 108 min. Sound. 16mm Color. *Rental:* Films Inc & MGM United.

Blow Your Own Trumpet. Michael Crawford. Directed by Cecil Musk. 1959. Britain. 56 min. Sound. 16mm B&W. *Sale:* Lucerne Films.

Blowing Wild. Gary Cooper & Barbara Stanwyck. Directed by Hugo Fregonese. 1953. Warners. 92 min. Sound. 16mm B&W. *Rental:* Corinth Films.

Bloxham Tapes, The. 1978. Britain. (Documentary). 48 min. Sound. 16mm Color. *Rental:* U of IL Film, Films Inc & SD AV Ctr. *Sale:* Films Inc. *Rental:* Films Inc, *Sale:* Films Inc, Videotape version.

Blue. Terence Stamp, Karl Malden & Ricardo Montalban. Directed by Silvio Narizzano. 1968. Paramount. (Anamorphic). 113 min. Sound. 16mm Color. *Rental:* Films Inc.

Blue & the Gold, The *see* Annapolis Story.

Blue Angel, The. Marlene Dietrich, Emil Jannings & Kurt Gerron. Directed by Josef Von Sternberg. Ger. 1930. Germany. 93 min. Sound. 16mm B&W. subtitles. *Rental:* A Twyman Pres, Budget Films, Classic Film Mus, Creative Film, Films Inc, Em Gee Film Lib, Images Film, Ivy Films, Janus Films, Kerr Film, Kit Parker, La Inst Res Ctr, Natl Film Video, Roas Films, Swank Motion, Syracuse U Film, Twyman Films, U Cal Media, Welling Motion Pictures, Wholesome Film Ctr & Willoughby Peer. *Sale:* Cinema Concepts, Festival Films, Griggs Movie, Glenn Photo, Images Film, Natl Cinema & Reel Images. *Rental:* Museum Mod Art, Unsubtitled version. *Rental:* Ivy Films, *Sale:* Ivy Films, Super 8 sound version. *Sale:* Cinema Concepts, Festival Films, Ivy Films, Video Comm, Tamarelles French Film & Images Film, Videotape version. *Rental:* Welling Motion Pictures, 87 mins version. *Rental:* A Twyman Pres, Dubbed English version.

Blue Angel, The. May Britt & Curt Jurgens. Directed by Edward Dmytryk. 1959. Fox. (Anamorphic). 107 min. Sound. 16mm Color. *Rental:* Films Inc & Westcoast Films. *Sale:* Reel Images. *Rental:* Westcoast Films, 87 mins. version.

Blue Bird, The. Shirley Temple & Spring Byington. Directed by Walter Lang. 1940. Fox. 88 min. Sound. 16mm Color. *Rental:* Films Inc.

Blue Bird, The. Elizabeth Taylor & Cicely Tyson. Directed by George Cukor. 1976. Fox. 97 min. Sound. 16mm Color. *Rental:* Williams Films.

Blue Blazes Rawden. William S. Hart. Directed by William S. Hart & Lambert Hillyer. 1918. Artcraft. 70 min. Silent. 16mm B&W. *Rental:* Budget Films, Creative Film & Em Gee Film Lib. *Sale:* Glenn Photo & Natl Cinema. *Rental:* Ivy Films, *Sale:* Glenn Photo, Super 8 silent version. *Rental:* Em Gee Film Lib, *Sale:* Glenn Photo & Morcraft Films, Silent 8mm version.

Blue Blood. George Walsh. Directed by Scott R. Dunlap. 1925. Chadwick. 84 min. Silent. 8mm B&W. *Rental:* Mogulls Films.

Blue Blood. Bill Williams & Jane Nigh. Directed by Lew Landers. 1951. Monogram. 72 min. Sound. 16mm B&W. *Rental:* Hurlock Cine & Newman Film Lib.

Blue Collar. Richard Pryor, Harvey Keitel & Yaphet Kotto. Directed by Paul Schrader. 110 min. Sound. 16mm Color. *Rental:* Swank Motion. *Rental:* Swank Motion, Videotape version.

Blue Collar Trap, The. 1972. NBC. (Documentary). 51 min. Sound. 16mm Color. *Rental:* Films Inc, Iowa Films, Syracuse U Film, U Cal Media, U Mich Media & Utah Media. *Sale:* Films Inc. *Sale:* Films Inc, Videotape version.

Blue Country. Brigitte Fossey & Jacques Sernas. Directed by Jean-Charles Tacchella. Fr. 1978. Quartet. 104 min. Sound. 16mm Color. subtitles. *Rental:* Films Inc. *Sale:* Tamarelles French Film, Videotape version.

Blue Dahlia, The. Alan Ladd & Veronica Lake. Directed by George Marshall. 1946. Paramount. 99 min. Sound. 16mm B&W. *Rental:* Swank Motion & Williams Films.

Blue Denim. Brandon De Wilde & Carol Lynley. Directed by Philip Dunne. 1959. Fox. 89 min. Sound. 16mm B&W. *Rental:* Films Inc. *Rental:* Films Inc, Anamorphic B&W version.

Blue Gardenia, The. Anne Baxter, Richard Conte & Ann Sothern. Directed by Fritz Lang. 1953. Warners. 91 min. Sound. 16mm B&W. *Rental:* Kit Parker.

Blue Grass of Kentucky. Bill Williams & Jane Nigh. Directed by William Beaudine. 1950. Monogram. 72 min. Sound. 16mm B&W. *Rental:* Budget Films & Hurlock Cine.

Blue Hawaii. Elvis Presley & Angela Lansbury. Directed by Norman Taurog. 1961. Paramount. 101 min. Sound. 16mm Color. *Rental:* Films Inc. *Sale:* Blackhawk Films & Cinema Concepts, Super 8 sound version.

Blue Hotel, The. David Warner. Directed by Jan Kadar. 1977. Learning in Focus. 54 min. Sound. 16mm Color. *Rental:* Iowa Films, Kent St U Film, SD AV Ctr, Syracuse U Film, U of IL Film, U Mich Media & Utah Media. *Sale:* Perspect Film. *Sale:* Perspect Film, Videotape version.

Blue Lagoon, The. Jean Simmons & Donald Houston. Directed by Frank Launder. 1949. Britain. 101 min. Sound. 16mm Color. *Rental:* Budget Films & Kit Parker.

Blue Lagoon, The. Brooke Shields & Christopher Atkins. Directed by Randal Kleiser. 1980. Columbia. 104 min. Sound. 16mm Color. *Rental:* Swank Motion. *Rental:* Swank Motion, Videotape version.

Blue Lamp, The. Dirk Bogarde & Jack Warner. Directed by Basil Dearden. 1951. Britain. 84 min. Sound. 16mm B&W. *Rental:* Janus Films.

Blue Light, The. Leni Riefenstahl. Directed by Leni Riefenstahl. Ger. 1932. Germany. 90 min. Sound. 16mm B&W. subtitles. *Rental:* Budget Films, Em Gee Film Lib & Janus Films.

Blue Max, The. George Peppard, James Mason & Ursula Andress. Directed by John Guillermin. 1966. Fox. (Anamorphic). 156 min. 16mm Color. *Rental:* Films Inc.

Blue Mountain Skies. Gene Autry. Directed by B. Reeves Eason. 1939. Republic. 54 min. Sound. 16mm B&W. *Rental:* Ivy Films.

Blue Murder at St. Trinian's. Joyce Grenfell, Terry-Thomas & Alastair Sim. Directed by Frank Launder. 1958. Britain. 86 min. Sound. 16mm B&W. *Rental:* Corinth Films.

Blue Skies. Bing Crosby & Fred Astaire. Directed by Stuart Heisler. 1946. Paramount. 104 min. Sound. 16mm Color. *Rental:* Williams Films.

Blue Steel. John Wayne. Directed by Robert N. Bradbury. 1934. Monogram. 54 min. Sound. 16mm B&W. *Rental:* Ivy Films & Mogulls Films. *Sale:* Classics Assoc NY & Rep Pic Film. *Sale:* Video Comm, Videotape version.

Blue Suede Shoes. Bill Haley. 90 min. Sound. Videotape *Rental:* WW Enter.

Blue Summer. Dorcey Hollingsworth. 80 min. Sound. 16mm Color. *Sale:* Morcraft Films. *Sale:* Morcraft Films, Super 8 sound version. *Sale:* Morcraft Films, Videotape version.

Blue Sunshine. Zalman King & Deborah Winters. Directed by Jeff Lieberman. 1977. Cinema. 97 min. Sound. 16mm Color. *Rental:* Films Inc.

Blue Surf-Ari. Directed by Milton Blair. 1967. Britain. (Documentary). 90 min. Sound. 16mm Color. *Rental:* Bosco Films, Budget Films, Films Inc, Video Comm, Westcoast Films, Welling Motion Pictures & Willoughby Peer.

Blue Thunder. Roy Scheider, Warren Oates & Malcolm McDowell. Directed by John Badham. 1983. Columbia. 115 min. Sound. 16mm Color. *Rental:* Swank Motion. *Rental:* Swank Motion, Videotape version.

Blue Veil, The. Jane Wyman & Charles Laughton. Directed by Curtis Bernhardt. 1951. RKO. 114 min. Sound. 16mm B&W. *Rental:* Bosco Films, Budget Films, Video Comm & Wholesome Film Ctr.

Blue Water, White Death. Peter Gimbel, Rodney Jonklas & Peter A. Lake. Directed by Peter Gimbel. 1971. Cinema Center. (Documentary). 100 min. Sound. 16mm Color. *Rental:* Cine Craft, Films Inc, Swank Motion, Twyman Films & Williams Films. *Rental:* Swank Motion, Anamorphic color version.

Blue, White & Perfect. Lloyd Nolan & Mary Beth Hughes. Directed by Herbert I. Leeds. 1942. Fox. 78 min. Sound. 16mm B&W. *Rental:* Films Inc.

Blue Winter. Christiane Levesque. Directed by Andre Blanchard. 1978. Canada. 81 min. Sound. 16mm Color. subtitles. *Rental:* Natl Film CN. *Sale:* Natl Film CN.

Bluebeard. John Carradine & Jean Parker. Directed by Edgar G. Ulmer. 1944. PRC. 74 min. Sound. 16mm B&W. *Rental:* Bosco Films, Budget Films, Ivy Films, Kit Parker, Mogulls Films & Westcoast Films. *Sale:* Classic Film Mus, Classics Assoc NY, Festival Films, Natl Cinema, Rep Pic Film & Reel Images, Super 8 sound version. *Sale:* Festival Films, Videotape version.

Bluebeard. Richard Burton & Raquel Welch. Directed by Edward Dmytryk. 1973. Cinerama. 125 min. Sound. 16mm Color. *Rental:* Swank Motion.

Bluebeard's Eighth Wife. Gary Cooper & Claudette Colbert. Directed by Ernst Lubitsch. 1938. Paramount. 80 min. Sound. 16mm B&W. *Rental:* Swank Motion.

Bluebeard's Ten Honeymoons. George Sanders & Corinne Calvet. Directed by W. Lee Wilder. 1959. Allied Artists. 93 min. Sound. 16mm B&W. *Rental:* Cinema Concepts & Hurlock Cine.

Blueprint for Murder, A. Joseph Cotten & Jean Peters. Directed by Andrew Stone. 1953. Fox. 76 min. Sound. 16mm B&W. *Rental:* Films Inc.

Blueprint for Robbery. J. Pat O'Malley, Robert J. Wilkie & Robert Gist. Directed by Jerry Hopper. 1961. Paramount. 88 min. Sound. 16mm B&W. *Rental:* Films Inc.

Blueprints in the Bloodstream. 1978. Britain. (Documentary). 49 min. Sound. 16mm Color. *Rental:* Kent St U Film & U of IL Film.

Blues Brothers, The. John Belushi & Dan Aykroyd. Directed by John Landis. 133 min. Sound. 16mm Color. *Rental:* Swank Motion. *Rental:* Swank Motion, Videotape version.

Blues for a Red Planet. 1980. Cosmos. 60 min. Sound. 16mm Color. *Rental:* Films Inc. *Sale:* Films Inc. *Rental:* Films Inc, *Sale:* Films Inc, Videotape version.

Blues for Lovers. Ray Charles, Tom Bell & Mary Peach. Directed by Paul Henried. 1966. Britain. 89 min. Sound. 16mm B&W. *Rental:* Films Inc.

Blume in Love. George Segal. Directed by Paul Mazursky. 1973. Warners. 115 min. Sound. 16mm Color. *Rental:* Swank Motion & Twyman Films.

Blumen Aus Nizza. Trans. Title: Flowers of Nice, The. Erna Sack & Paul Kemp. Directed by Augusto Genina. Ger. 1936. Germany. 80 min. Sound. 16mm B&W. *Rental:* Mogulls Films.

Boabab: Portrait of a Tree. 1974. 53 min. Sound. 16mm Color. *Rental:* Iowa Films.

Boardinghouse Blues. Moms Mabley & Dusty Fletcher. Directed by Josh Binney. 1948. 90 min. Sound. 16mm B&W. *Rental:* Budget Films.

Boardwalk. Ruth Gordon & Lee Strasberg. Directed by Stephen F. Verona. 1979. Atlantic. 100 min. Sound. 16mm Color. *Rental:* Ivy Films.

Boat is Full, The. Curt Bois & Renate Steiger. Directed by Markus Imhoof. 1980. QFI. 100 min. Sound. 16mm Color. *Rental:* Films Inc.

Boatniks, The. Robert Morse, Stephanie Powers & Phil Silvers. Directed by Norman Tokar. 1970. Disney. 100 min. Sound. 16mm Color. *Rental:* Cine Craft, Disney Prod, Film Ctr DC, Films Inc, MGM United, Modern Sound, Roas Films, Swank Motion, Twyman Films & Williams Films.

Bob & Carol & Ted & Alice. Natalie Wood, Elliott Gould, Robert Culp & Dyan Cannon. Directed by Paul Mazursky. 1969. Columbia. 104 min. Sound. 16mm Color. *Rental:* Budget Films, Cine Craft, Films Inc, Inst Cinema, Ivy Films, Kit Parker, Natl Film Video, Swank Motion, Twyman Films, U of IL Film, Welling Motion Pictures, Westcoast Films & Wholesome Film Ctr.

Bob le Flambeur. Isabel Corey & Roger Duchense. Directed by Jean-Pierre Melville. 1981. France. 100 min. Sound. 16mm B&W. subtitles. *Rental:* Swank Motion. *Rental:* Swank Motion, Videotape version.

Bob Mathias Story, The. Orig. Title: Flaming Torch, The. Bob Mathias & Ward Bond. Directed by Francis D. Lyon. 1955. Allied Artists. 80 min. Sound. 16mm B&W. *Rental:* Hurlock Cine.

Bobbie Jo & the Outlaw. Marjoe Gortner & Lynda Carter. Directed by Mark L. Lester. 1976. American International. 89 min. Sound. 16mm Color. *Rental:* Swank Motion.

Bobbikins. Shirley Jones & Max Bygraves. Directed by Robert Day. 1960. Fox. 89 min. Sound. 16mm B&W. *Rental:* Modern Sound, Anamorphic B&W version.

Bobby Breen Festival. RKO. (Anthology). 75 min. Sound. 16mm B&W. *Rental:* Alba House.

Bobby Darin & Friends. Bobby Darin, Bob Hope & Joanie Summers. 1961. NBC. 52 min. Sound. Videotape B&W. *Sale:* Reel Images.

Bobby Deerfield. Al Pacino & Marthe Keller. Directed by Sydney Pollack. 1977. Columbia. 124 min. Sound. 16mm Color. *Rental:* Swank Motion, Twyman Films & Williams Films. *Rental:* Swank Motion, Videotape version.

Bobby Ware Is Missing. Neville Brand & Arthur Franz. Directed by Thomas Carr. 1955. Allied Artists. 66 min. Sound. 16mm B&W. *Rental:* Hurlock Cine.

Bobwhite Through the Year. Soil Conservation Service. (Documentary). 50 min. Sound. 16mm Color. *Rental:* SD AV Ctr, U of IL Film & U Mich Media.

Body & Soul. John Garfield & Lilli Palmer. Directed by Robert Rossen. 1947. United Artists. 104 min. Sound. 16mm B&W. *Rental:* Budget Films, Ivy Films, Kit Parker & Westcoast Films. *Lease:* Rep Pic Film. *Sale:* Ivy Films, Super 8 sound version.

Body & Soul. 2 pts. 1968. CBS. (Documentary). 52 min. Sound. 16mm B&W. *Rental:* NYU Film Lib. *Sale:* Phoenix Films. *Sale:* Phoenix Films, Color version.

Body & Soul. Leon Isaac Kennedy, Jane Kennedy & Muhammad Ali. Directed by George Bowers. 100 min. Sound. 16mm Color. *Rental:* Swank Motion.

Body & Soul. Paul Robeson. Directed by Oscar Micheaux. 1925. 80 min. 16mm *Rental:* A Twyman Pres.

Body Business. 1983. Embassy. (Documentary). 60 min. Sound. 16mm Color. *Rental:* Films Inc. *Sale:* Films Inc. *Sale:* Films Inc, Videotape version.

Body Disappears, The. Jane Wyman & Jeffrey Lynn. Directed by D. Ross Lederman. 1941. Warners. 72 min. Sound. 16mm B&W. *Rental:* MGM United.

Body Heat. William Hurt, Kathleen Turner & Richard Crenna. Directed by Lawrence Kasdan. 1985. Ladd Company. 118 min. Sound. 16mm Color. *Rental:* Swank Motion. *Rental:* Swank Motion, Videotape version.

Body in Question No. 6: Balancing Act. 1980. Films Inc. 60 min. Sound. 16mm *Rental:* Syracuse U Film.

Body in Question No. 7: Breathlessness. 1980. Films Inc. 60 min. Sound. 16mm *Rental:* Syracuse U Film.

Body Snatcher, The. Boris Karloff, Bela Lugosi & Henry Daniell. Directed by Robert Wise. 1945. RKO. 77 min. Sound. 16mm B&W. *Rental:* Films Inc. *Lease:* Films Inc.

Body Stealers, The *see* Thin Air.

Bodyguard. Lawrence Tierney & Priscilla Lane. Directed by Richard Fleischer. 1948. RKO. 62 min. Sound. 16mm B&W. *Rental:* Films Inc.

Boeing, Boeing. Tony Curtis & Jerry Lewis. Directed by John Rich. 1966. Paramount. 102 min. Sound. 16mm Color. *Rental:* Films Inc.

Boesman & Lena. Athol Fugard. Directed by Ross Devenish. 1973. South Africa. (English dialog). 102 min. Sound. 16mm Color. *Rental:* New Yorker Films.

Bogota, One Day. 1978. 90 min. Sound. Videotape *Rental:* PBS Video. *Sale:* PBS Video.

Boheme, La. Lillian Gish. Directed by King Vidor. 1926. MGM. 90 min. Silent. 16mm B&W. *Rental:* Films Inc.

Bohemian Girl, The. Stan Laurel & Oliver Hardy. Directed by James W. Horne. 1936. Hal Roach. 75 min. Sound. 16mm B&W. *Rental:* Budget Films, Em Gee Film Lib, Film Ctr DC, Films Inc, Ivy Films, Kit Parker, Modern Sound, Roas Films, Swank Motion, Twyman Films, Westcoast Films & Willoughby Peer. *Sale:* Blackhawk Films. *Sale:* Blackhawk Films, Super 8 sound version. *Rental:* Williams Films, 70 min. version.

Boiling Point. Hoot Gibson. Directed by George Melford. 1932. Allied. 67 min. Sound. 16mm B&W. *Sale:* Video Comm. *Sale:* Video Comm, Videotape version.

Bold Caballero, The. Robert Livingston & Heather Angel. Directed by Wells Root. 1936. Republic. 69 min. Sound. 16mm B&W. *Rental:* Ivy Films. *Sale:* Rep Pic Film.

Bold Frontierman, The. Allan Lane. Directed by Philip Ford. 1948. Republic. 60 min. Sound. 16mm B&W. *Rental:* Ivy Films. *Sale:* Rep Pic Film & Nostalgia Merchant.

Bold Men, The. 1965. Wolper. (Documentary). 50 min. Sound. 16mm B&W. *Rental:* Films Inc. *Sale:* Films Inc. *Sale:* Films Inc, Videotape version.

Bold New Approach, A. 1966. Mental Health. (Documentary). 62 min. Sound. 16mm B&W. *Rental:* U of IL Film.

Bolero. Carole Lombard & George Raft. Directed by Wesley Ruggles. 1934. Paramount. 85 min. Sound. 16mm B&W. *Rental:* Swank Motion.

Bolidos de Acero. Span. 1950. Mexico. (Cast unlisted). 90 min. Sound. 16mm B&W. *Rental:* Film Classics.

Bologna: An Ancient City for a New Society. 1975. Canada. (Documentary). 57 min. Sound. 16mm Color. *Rental:* Natl Film CN. *Sale:* Natl Film CN.

Bolshevism on Trial. Robert Frazer. Directed by Harley Knowles. 1919. Select. 85 min. Silent. 16mm B&W. *Sale:* Blackhawk Films. *Rental:* Ivy Films, *Sale:* Blackhawk Films, Super 8 silent version. *Sale:* Blackhawk Films, Silent 8mm version.

Bomb, The. Directed by Hugh Raggett. 1974. Britain. (Documentary). 60 min. Sound. 16mm Color. *Rental:* U CaL Media.

Bomb, The. 1945. 55 min. Sound. 16mm Color. *Rental:* U Mich Media.

Bomb, The: February-September 1945. (World at War Ser.). : Pt. 24.). 1973. Media Guild. (Documentary). 52 min. Sound. 16mm Color. *Rental:* Media Guild. *Sale:* Media Guild. *Sale:* Media Guild, Videotape version.

Bomb for a Dictator, A. Pierre Fresnay & Michel Auclair. Directed by Alex Joffe. 1960. France. 73 min. Sound. 16mm B&W. dubbed. *Rental:* Welling Motion Pictures.

Bomba & the African Treasure. Orig. Title: African Treasure. Johnny Sheffield. Directed by Ford Beebe. 1951. Monogram. 70 min. Sound. 16mm B&W. *Rental:* Hurlock Cine.

Bomba & the Elephant Stampede. Orig. Title: Elephant Stampede, The. Johnny Sheffield. Directed by Ford Beebe. 1951. Monogram. 71 min. Sound. 16mm B&W. *Rental:* Hurlock Cine.

Bomba & the Hidden City. Johnny Sheffield. Directed by Ford Beebe. 1949. Monogram. 71 min. Sound. 16mm B&W. *Rental:* Hurlock Cine.

Bomba & the Jungle Girl. Johnny Sheffield. Directed by Ford Beebe. 1951. Monogram. 70 min. Sound. 16mm B&W. *Rental:* Hurlock Cine.

Bomba & the Lion Hunters. Johnny Sheffield. Directed by Ford Beebe. 1950. Monogram. 75 min. Sound. 16mm B&W. *Rental:* Hurlock Cine.

Bomba & the Lost Volcano. Johnny Sheffield. Directed by Ford Beebe. 1950. Monogram. 76 min. Sound. 16mm B&W. *Rental:* Cine Craft, Film Ctr DC & Hurlock Cine.

Bomba on Panther Island. Orig. Title: Panther Island. Johnny Sheffield. Directed by Ford Beebe. 1950. Monogram. 71 min. Sound. 16mm B&W. *Rental:* Budget Films & Hurlock Cine.

Bomba, the Jungle Boy. Johnny Sheffield. Directed by Ford Beebe. 1949. Monogram. 71 min. Sound. 16mm B&W. *Rental:* Hurlock Cine.

Bombardier. Robert Ryan, Eddie Albert & Randolph Scott. Directed by Richard Wallace. 1943. RKO. 99 min. Sound. 16mm *Rental:* Films Inc.

Bombay Talkie. Shashi Kapoor & Jennifer Kendal. Directed by James Ivory. 1970. India. 112 min. Sound. 16mm Color. *Rental:* Corinth Films, Films Inc & New Yorker Films.

Bomber's Moon. George Montgomery & Annabella. Directed by Charles Fuhr. 1943. Fox. 70 min. Sound. 16mm B&W. *Rental:* Films Inc.

Bombshell. Orig. Title: Blonde Bombshell. Jean Harlow, Lee Tracy & Frank Morgan. Directed by Victor Fleming. 1933. MGM. 91 min. Sound. 16mm B&W. *Rental:* MGM United.

Bon Anniversaire. Fr. France. 50 min. Sound. 16mm Color. subtitles. *Rental:* U Mich Media.

Bon Voyage, Charlie Brown & Don't Come Back. 1980. Paramount. (Animated). 76 min. Sound. 16mm Color. *Rental:* Films Inc.

Bonaparte & the Revolution. Albert Dieudonne. Directed by Abel Gance. Fr. 1971. France. (Color sequences). 235 min. Sound. 16mm B&W. subtitles. *Rental:* Images Film. *Lease:* Images Film.

Bonapartes, The. Directed by Victor Vicas. 1972. AIF. (Documentary). 60 min. Sound. 16mm B&W. *Sale:* Americas Films. *Sale:* Americas Films, Spanish version.

Bonheur, Le. Jean-Claude Drouet & Claire Drouet. Directed by Agnes Varda. 1965. France. 85 min. Sound. 16mm Color. subtitles. *Rental:* Janus Films & Films Inc. *Rental:* Video Comm, Dubbed version.

Bonhoeffer. 1978. Canada. (Documentary). 57 min. Sound. 16mm Color. *Rental:* Kent St U Film.

Bonjour Amour. Pas Meynier & Guihaine Dubos. Directed by Roger Andrieux. Fr. New Line Cinema. 90 min. Sound. 16mm Color. subtitles. *Rental:* New Line Cinema.

Bonjour Tristesse. Deborah Kerr, David Niven & Jean Seberg. Directed by Otto Preminger. 1958. Columbia. (Color sequence). 94 min. Sound. 16mm B&W. *Rental:* Budget Films, Corinth Films, Films Inc, Modern Sound, Natl Film Video & Welling Motion Pictures. *Rental:* Corinth Films & Kit Parker, Anamorphic version.

Bonne Soupe, La. Annie Giradot & Gerard Blain. Directed by Robert Thomas. Fr. 1964. France. (Anamorphic). 97 min. Sound. 16mm B&W. subtitles. *Rental:* Films Inc.

Bonnes Causes, Les. Bourvil, Marina Vlady, Virna Lisi & Pierre Brasseur. Directed by Christian-Jaque. Fr. 1963. France. 120 min. Sound. 16mm B&W. subtitles. *Rental:* French Am Cul.

Bonnie & Clyde. Warren Beatty & Faye Dunaway. Directed by Arthur Penn. 1967. Warners. 111 min. Sound. Videotape Color. *Sale:* Festival Films.

Bonnie Parker Story, The. Dorothy Provine, Jack Hogan & Richard Bakalyan. Directed by William Witney. 1958. American International. 81 min. Sound. 16mm B&W. *Rental:* Budget Films & Film Ctr DC.

Bonnie Prince Charlie. David Niven, Margaret Leighton & Jack Hawkins. Directed by Anthony Kimmins. 1948. Britain. 118 min. Sound. 16mm B&W. *Rental:* Budget Films & Roas Films.

Bonnie Scotland. Stan Laurel & Oliver Hardy. Directed by James W. Horne. 1935. Hal Roach. 80 min. Sound. 16mm B&W. *Rental:* Budget Films, Em Gee Film Lib, Films Inc, Inst Cinema, MGM United, Modern Sound & Wholesome Film Ctr.

Bono Medicines. 1981. White Pine. (Documentary). 72 min. Sound. 16mm Color. *Rental:* Iowa Films.

Bonzo Goes to College. Maureen O'Sullivan & Edmund Gwenn. Directed by Frederick De Cordova. 1952. Universal. 98 min. Sound. 16mm B&W. *Rental:* Swank Motion.

Boogie Man Will Get You, The. Boris Karloff, Peter Lorre & Larry Parks. Directed by Lew Landers. 1942. Columbia. 70 min. Sound. 16mm B&W. *Rental:* Bosco Films & Kit Parker.

Book of Numbers. Raymond St. Jacques & Freda Payne. Directed by Raymond St. Jacques. 1973. Embassy. 81 min. Sound. 16mm Color. *Rental:* Swank Motion.

Books Under Fire. Directed by Arnold Bennett & Grady Watts. 1982. Public Media. (Documentary). 58 min. Sound. 16mm Color. *Rental:* Films Inc & U Cal Media. *Sale:* Films Inc. *Sale:* Films Inc, Videotape version.

Boom! Elizabeth Taylor & Richard Burton. Directed by Joseph Losey. 1968. Universal. 110 min. Sound. 16mm Color. *Rental:* Swank Motion.

Boom Town. Clark Gable, Spencer Tracy, Claudette Colbert & Hedy Lamarr. Directed by Jack Conway. 1940. MGM. 120 min. Sound. 16mm B&W. *Rental:* MGM United.

Boomerang. Dana Andrews & Lee J. Cobb. Directed by Elia Kazan. 1947. Fox. 88 min. Sound. 16mm B&W. *Rental:* Films Inc & Twyman Films.

Boot, Das. Directed by Wolfgang Peterson. 1981. 145 min. Sound. Videotape Color. dubbed. *Sale:* Festival Films.

Boot Hill Bandits. Range Busters. Directed by S. Roy Luby. 1942. Monogram. 59 min. Sound. 16mm B&W. *Rental:* Budget Films.

Boot Polish. Rattan Kumar. Directed by Prakash Arora. Hindi. 1958. India. 100 min. Sound. 16mm B&W. subtitles. *Rental:* Inst Cinema.

Boothill Brigade. Johnny Mack Brown. Directed by Sam Newfield. 1937. Republic. 60 min. Sound. 16mm B&W. *Rental:* Ivy Films.

Boots & Saddles. Gene Autry. Directed by Joseph Kane. 1937. Republic. 54 min. Sound. 16mm B&W. *Rental:* Budget Films & Ivy Films. *Sale:* Cinema Concepts, Super 8 sound version. *Sale:* Video Comm, Videotape version.

Boots Malone. William Holden & Stanley Clements. Directed by William Dieterle. 1952. Columbia. 103 min. Sound. 16mm B&W. *Rental:* Bosco Films, Cine Craft, Charard Motion Pics, Film Ctr DC & Newman Film Lib.

Boots of Destiny. Ken Maynard. Directed by Arthur Rosson. 1937. Grand National. 60 min. Videotape B&W. *Sale:* Video Comm.

Border, The. Jack Nicholson, Harvey Keitel & Valerie Perrine. Directed by Tony Richardson. 1982. 107 min. Sound. 16mm Color. *Rental:* Swank Motion.

Border Badmen. Buster Crabbe. Directed by Sam Newfield. 1945. PRC. 59 min. Sound. 16mm B&W. *Sale:* Classics Assoc NY.

Border Bandits. Johnny Mack Brown. Directed by Lambert Hillyer. 1946. Monogram. 60 min. Sound. 16mm B&W. *Rental:* Hurlock Cine & Mogulls Films.

Border Buckaroos. Dave O'Brien & James Newill. Directed by Oliver Drake. 1943. PRC. 60 min. Sound. 16mm B&W. *Rental:* Lewis Film.

Border Cafe. John Beal & J. Carol Naish. Directed by Lew Landers. 1937. RKO. 67 min. Sound. 16mm *Rental:* RKO General Pics.

Border Confirmed, The: The Treaty of Washington. 1968. Canada. (Documentary). 58 min. Sound. 16mm B&W. *Rental:* Natl Film CN. *Sale:* Natl Film CN.

Border Feud. Lash LaRue. Directed by Ray Taylor. 1947. PRC. 54 min. Sound. 16mm B&W. *Sale:* Classics Assoc NY.

Border G-Man. George O'Brien & Ray Whitley. Directed by Bert Gilroy. 1938. RKO. 60 min. Sound. 16mm *Rental:* RKO General Pics.

Border Incident. Ricardo Montalban & George Murphy. Directed by Anthony Mann. 1949. MGM. 92 min. Sound. 16mm B&W. *Rental:* MGM United.

Border Marshal. Tim McCoy. 60 min. Sound. 16mm B&W. *Rental:* Mogulls Films.

Border Menace. Bill Cody. Directed by Jack Nelson. 60 min. Sound. 16mm B&W. *Rental:* Budget Films. *Sale:* Morcraft Films.

Border Outlaws. Spade Cooley. 1950. Eagle-Lion. 65 min. Videotape B&W. *Sale:* Video Comm. *Sale:* Video Comm, Videotape version.

Border Patrol. William Boyd & Robert Mitchum. Directed by Lesley Selander. 1943. United Artists. 54 min. Sound. 16mm B&W. *Lease:* Cinema Concepts. *Sale:* Cinema Concepts, Super 8 sound version.

Border Phantom. Bob Steele. Directed by S. Roy Luby. 1937. Republic. 60 min. Sound. 16mm B&W. *Rental:* Ivy Films & Willoughby Peer. *Sale:* Cinema Concepts & Natl Cinema.

Border Rangers. Don Barry & Robert Lowery. Directed by William Berke. 1950. Lippert. 59 min. Sound. 16mm B&W. *Rental:* Westcoast Films.

Border River. Joel McCrea & Yvonne De Carlo. Directed by George Sherman. 1954. Universal. 80 min. Sound. 16mm B&W. *Rental:* Swank Motion.

Border Saddlemates. Rex Allen. Directed by William Witney. 1952. Republic. 67 min. Sound. 16mm B&W. *Rental:* Ivy Films. *Sale:* Rep Pic Film.

Border Sheriff. Jack Hoxie. 1925. Universal. 55 min. Silent. 16mm B&W. *Rental:* Em Gee Film Lib.

Border Street. J. Leszczynski & Maria Broniewska. Directed by Aleksander Ford. 1948. 110 min. Sound. 16mm B&W. *Rental:* Corinth Films.

Border Treasure. Tim Holt & Jane Nigh. Directed by George Archainbaud. 1951. RKO. 60 min. Sound. 16mm *Rental:* RKO General Pics.

Border Vengeance. Jack Perrin. Directed by Harry S. Webb. 1925. Aywon. 60 min. Silent. 16mm B&W. *Sale:* Select Film.

Border Vigilantes. William Boyd. Directed by Derwin Abrahams. 1941. Paramount. 54 min. Sound. 16mm B&W. *Lease:* Cinema Concepts. *Sale:* Natl Cinema.

Borderland. William Boyd. Directed by Nate Watt. 1937. Paramount. 65 min. Sound. 16mm B&W. *Rental:* Newman Film Lib.

Borderline. Paul Robeson & Kenneth MacPherson. 1930. 60 min. 16mm *Rental:* A Twyman Pres.

Bordertown. Bette Davis, Paul Muni & Margaret Lindsay. Directed by Archie Mayo. 1935. 90 min. Sound. 16mm B&W. *Rental:* MGM United.

Bordertown Gunfighters. Bill Elliott. Directed by Howard Bretherton. 1943. Republic. 56 min. Sound. 16mm B&W. *Rental:* Ivy Films. *Sale:* Rep Pic Film & Nostalgia Merchant.

Bordertown Trail. Sunset Carson. Directed by Lesley Selander. 1944. Republic. 55 min. Sound. 16mm B&W. *Rental:* Ivy Films. *Sale:* Rep Pic Film.

Borgia Stick, The. Don Murray & Fritz Weaver. Directed by David Lowell Rich. 1967. Universal. 100 min. Sound. 16mm Color. *Rental:* Swank Motion.

Boris Godunov. Alexander Pirogov. Directed by Vera Stroyeva. Rus. 1954. Russia. 105 min. Sound. 16mm Color. subtitles. *Rental:* Corinth Films. *Lease:* Corinth Films. *Rental:* Corinth Films, *Lease:* Corinth Films, Videotape version.

Born Again. Dean Jones, Anne Francis & Dana Andrews. Directed by Irving Rapper. 1978. Embassy. 110 min. Sound. 16mm Color. *Rental:* Films Inc.

Born Chinese. 1965. Britain. (Documentary). 57 min. Sound. 16mm B&W. *Rental:* Time-Life Multimedia. *Sale:* Time-Life Multimedia. *Rental:* Time-Life Multimedia, *Sale:* Time-Life Multimedia, Videotape version.

Born for Trouble. Van Johnson & Faye Emerson. Directed by B. Reeves Eason. 1942. Warners. 67 min. Sound. 16mm B&W. *Rental:* MGM United.

Born Free. Bill Travers, Virginia McKenna & Geoffrey Keen. Directed by James Hill. 1966. Columbia. 95 min. Sound. 16mm Color. *Rental:* Arcus Film, Bosco Films, Buchan Pic, Budget Films, Cine Craft, Charard Motion Pics, Film Ctr DC, Film Pres, Films Inc, Hurlock Cine, Inst Cinema, Kerr Film, Modern Sound, Natl Film Video, Newman Film Lib, Roas Films, Syracuse U Film, Twyman Films, U of IL Film , Video Comm, Welling Motion Pictures, Westcoast Films, Wholesome Film Ctr, Williams Films & Willoughby Peer.

Born in Flames. 1983. 90 min. Sound. 16mm Color. *Rental:* First Run.

Born Innocent. Linda Blair, Kim Hunter & Richard Jaeckel. Directed by Donald Wrye. 1975. Tomorrow Entertainment. 99 min. Sound. 16mm Color. *Rental:* Budget Films, Kent St U Film, Kit Parker, Learning Corp Am, Syracuse U Film, Twyman Films & U of IL Film. *Lease:* Learning Corp Am.

Born Losers. Tom Laughlin, Jane Russell & Elizabeth James. Directed by T. C. Frank. 1967. American International. 112 min. Sound. 16mm Color. *Rental:* Welling Motion Pictures & Westcoast Films.

Born of Fire. 59 min. Sound. 16mm Color. *Rental:* Natl Geog. *Sale:* Natl Geog. *Sale:* Natl Geog, Videotape version.

Born to Battle. Bill Cody & Barbara Luddy. Directed by Alvin J. Neitz. 1927. Pathe. 65 min. Silent. 16mm B&W. *Sale:* Blackhawk Films. *Rental:* Ivy Films, *Sale:* Blackhawk Films, Super 8 silent version. *Sale:* Blackhawk Films, Silent 8mm version.

Born to Battle. Tom Tyler. Directed by Harry S. Webb. 1935. Commodore. 60 min. Sound. 16mm B&W. *Rental:* Mogulls Films.

Born to Be Bad. Joan Fontaine & Robert Ryan. Directed by Nicholas Ray. 1950. RKO. 94 min. Sound. 16mm B&W. *Rental:* Films Inc & RKO General Pics.

Born to Be Wild. Ralph Byrd & Ward Bond. Directed by Joseph Kane. 1938. Republic. 54 min. Sound. 16mm B&W. *Rental:* Ivy Films. *Sale:* Rep Pic Film.

Born to Buck. Directed by Casey Tibbs. 1968. Pandora. (Documentary). 94 min. Sound. 16mm Color. *Rental:* Budget Films, Video comm & Westcoast Films. *Lease:* Video Comm. *Rental:* Video Comm, *Lease:* Video Comm, Videotape version.

Born to Dance. Eleanor Powell. Directed by Roy Del Ruth. 1936. MGM. 106 min. Sound. 16mm B&W. *Rental:* MGM United.

Born to Kill. Warren Oates. Directed by Monte Hellman. 1974. New World. 85 min. Sound. 16mm Color. *Rental:* Films Inc.

Born to Kill. Walter Slezak & Claire Trevor. Directed by Robert Wise. 1947. RKO. 92 min. Sound. 16mm *Rental:* RKO General Pics.

Born to Love. Joel MacCrea & Constance Bennett. Directed by Paul L. Stein. 1932. RKO. 99 min. Sound. 16mm *Rental:* RKO General Pics.

Born to Speed. Johnny Sands & Terry Austin. Directed by Edward L. Cahn. 1947. PRC. 61 min. Sound. 16mm B&W. *Rental:* Ivy Films & Lewis Film. *Sale:* Classics Assoc NY & Rep Pic Film.

Born to the Saddle. Leif Erickson & Donald Woods. Directed by William Beaudine. 1954. Astor. 74 min. Sound. 16mm B&W. *Rental:* Budget Films & Ivy Films.

Born to Win. George Segal, Karen Black & Paula Prentiss. Directed by Ivan Passer. 1971. United Artists. 90 min. Sound. 16mm Color. *Rental:* MGM United.

Born Yesterday. Judy Holliday, Broderick Crawford & William Holden. Directed by George Cukor. 1950. Columbia. 103 min. Sound. 16mm B&W. *Rental:* Arcus Film, Bosco Films, Budget Films, Films Inc, Images Film, Kit Parker, Modern Sound, Natl Film Video, Twyman Films, U of IL Film, Welling Motion Pictures, Wholesome Film Ctr & Williams Films.

Borneo. Directed by Martin Johnson & Osa Johnson. 1937. Fox. (Documentary). 75 min. Sound. 16mm B&W. *Rental:* Budget Films, Em Gee Film Lib & Mogulls Films. *Sale:* Glenn Photo & Natl Cinema.

Borroka. 1974. Spain. (Documentary). 55 min. Sound. 16mm Color. *Rental:* Tricontinental Film.

Borrowed Trouble. William Boyd. Directed by George Archainbaud. 1948. United Artists. 60 min. Sound. 16mm B&W. *Sale:* Cinema Concepts.

Borsalino. Alain Delon & Jean-Paul Belmondo. Directed by Jacques Deray. 1970. France. 125 min. Sound. 16mm Color. dubbed. *Rental:* Films Inc.

Bosambo see Sanders of the River.

Boss, The. John Payne. Directed by Byron Haskin. 1956. United Artists. 89 min. Sound. 16mm B&W. *Rental:* MGM United.

Boss, The. Orig. Title: Boss Nigger. Fred Williamson & D'Urville Martin. Directed by Jack Arnold. 1975. Dimension. (Anamorphic). 90 min. Sound. 16mm Color. *Rental:* Williams Films. *Sale:* Salz Ent.

Boss Foreman. Orig. Title: Caught in the Act. Henry Armetta & Iris Meredith. Directed by Jean Yarbrough. 1941. PRC. 70 min. Sound. 16mm B&W. *Rental:* Alba House.

Boss Nigger see Boss.

Boss of Hangtown Mesa, The. Johnny Mack Brown. Directed by Joseph Lewis. 1942. Universal. 56 min. Sound. 16mm B&W. *Rental:* Swank Motion & Budget Films.

Boss of Rawhide, The. James Newill. Directed by Elmer Clifton. 1944. PRC. 60 min. Sound. 16mm B&W. *Rental:* Mogulls Films.

Boss Said No, The see Blondie Goes to College.

Boston Blackie. Chester Morris & Lloyd Corrigan. Directed by Arthur Dreifuss. 67 min. Sound. 16mm B&W. *Rental:* Bosco Films.

Boston Blackie Booked on Suspicion. Chester Morris, Lloyd Corrigan & Lynn Merrick. Directed by Arthur Dreifuss. 1945. Columbia. 67 min. Sound. 16mm B&W. *Rental:* Kit Parker.

Boston Blackie's Chinese Venture. Chester Morris. Directed by Seymour Freidman. 1949. Columbia. 59 min. Sound. 16mm B&W. *Rental:* Wholesome Film Ctr.

Boston Blackie's Rendezvous. Chester Morris, George E. Stone & Nina Foch. Directed by Arthur Dreifuss. 1945. Columbia. 65 min. Sound. 16mm B&W. *Rental:* Bosco Films & Kit Parker.

Boston Strangler. Tony Curtis, Henry Fonda & George Kennedy. Directed by Richard Fleischer. 1968. Fox. 120 min. Sound. 16mm Color. *Rental:* Films Inc. *Rental:* Films Inc, Anamorphic color version.

Botany Bay. Alan Ladd, James Mason & Patricia Medina. Directed by John Farrow. 1953. Paramount. 94 min. Sound. 16mm Color. *Rental:* Films Inc.

Bottom of the Bottle, The. Orig. Title: Beyond the River. Van Johnson & Joseph Cotten. Directed by Henry Hathaway. 1956. Fox. (Anamorphic). 88 min. Sound. 16mm Color. *Rental:* Films Inc.

Bottom of the Oil Barrel, The. 1973. Films Inc. (Documentary). 50 min. Sound. 16mm Color. *Rental:* Films Inc. *Sale:* Films Inc. *Sale:* Films Inc, Videotape version.

Boucher, Le. Orig. Title: Butcher, The. Stephane Audran & Jean Yanne. Directed by Claude Chabrol. Fr. 1972. France. 93 min. Sound. 16mm Color. subtitles. *Rental:* Swank Motion. *Rental:* Swank Motion, Anamorphic version, Dubbed version.

Bouchon de Cristal, Le. George Descrieres. Directed by Jean-Pierre Decourt. 1971. France. 55 min. Sound. 16mm Color. *Rental:* French Am Cul.

Boudu Saved from Drowning. Michel Simon. Directed by Jean Renoir. Fr. 1932. France. 87 min. Sound. 16mm B&W. subtitles. *Rental:* Budget Films, Images Film, Ivy Films, Iowa Films, Kit Parker & Utah Media. *Sale:* Festival Films, Glenn Photo, Natl Cinema, Reel Images & Images Film. *Sale:* Festival Films, Images Film & Tamarelles French Film, Videotape version. *Rental:* Utah Media, 77 mins. version.

Boulder Dam. Ross Alexander & Patricia Ellis. Directed by Frank McDonald. 1936. Warners. 70 min. Sound. 16mm B&W. *Rental:* MGM United.

Boule De Suif see Angel & Sinner.

Boulevard Nights. Richard Yniquez, Danny De La Paz & Marta Du Bois. Warners. 102 min. Sound. 16mm Color. *Rental:* Williams Films.

Boum, La. Sophie Marceau & Claude Brasseur. Directed by Claude Pinoteau. 1983. France. 109 min. Sound. Videotape Color. *Sale:* Tamarelles French Films. *Rental:* Swank Motion.

Bouncin' Britches. 1979. PBS. (Documentary). 59 min. Videotape Color. *Rental:* PBS Video. *Sale:* PBS Video.

Bound for Freedom. Directed by David A. Tapper. 1976. Tapper. 90 min. Sound. 16mm Color. *Rental:* Films Inc, Syracuse U Film & U of IL Film. *Sale:* Films Inc. *Sale:* Films Inc, Videotape version.

Bound for Glory. David Carradine & Ronny Cox. Directed by Hal Ashby. 1976. United Artists. 146 min. Sound. 16mm Color. *Rental:* MGM United.

Boundless Seas, The. 1980. Western Audio Visual. (Documentary). 50 min. Sound. 16mm Color. *Rental:* SD AV Ctr.

Bounty Experiment, The. 1981. 50 min. 16mm Color. *Sale:* Aust Info Serv. *Rental:* Aust Info Serv.

Bounty Hunter, The. Reynaldo Miravalles. Directed by Sergio Giral. Span. 1976. Cuba. 95 min. Sound. 16mm Color. subtitles. *Rental:* Tricontinental Film.

Bounty Killer, The. Dan Duryea, Rod Cameron & Richard Arlen. Directed by Spencer G. Bennett. 1965. Embassy. 92 min. Sound. 16mm Color. *Rental:* Films Inc.

Bourbons of Spain, The. Directed by Victor Vicas. 1972. AIF. (Documentary). 60 min. Sound. 16mm B&W. *Sale:* Americas Films. *Sale:* Americas Films, Spanish dubbed version.

Bourgeois Gentilhomme, Le see Would-Be Gentleman.

Bout de Souffle, A see Breathless.

Bowery, The. Wallace Beery & George Raft. Directed by Raoul Walsh. 1933. Fox. 90 min. Sound. 16mm B&W. *Rental:* Films Inc.

Bowery at Midnight. Bela Lugosi. Directed by Wallace Fox. 1942. Monogram. 63 min. Sound. 16mm B&W. *Rental:* Ivy Films, Mogulls Films & Video Comm. *Rental:* Video Comm, Videotape version.

Bowery Blitzkrieg. East Side Kids. Directed by Wallace Fox. 1941. Monogram. 61 min. Sound. 16mm B&W. *Rental:* Roas Films. *Sale:* Reel Images & Morcraft Films. *Sale:* Morcraft Films, Super 8 sound version. *Sale:* Morcarft Films, Videotape version.

Bowery Bombshell. Bowery Boys. Directed by Phil Karlson. 1946. Monogram. 65 min. Sound. 16mm B&W. *Rental:* Modern Sound.

Bowery Boy. Dennis O'Keefe & Louise Campbell. Directed by William Morgan. 1940. Republic. 54 min. Sound. 16mm B&W. *Rental:* Ivy Films. *Sale:* Rep Pic Film.

Bowery Buckaroos. Bowery Boys. Directed by William Beaudine. 1947. Monogram. 70 min. Sound. 16mm B&W. *Rental:* Mogulls Films.

Bowery Champs. Bowery Boys. Directed by William Beaudine. 1944. Monogram. 65 min. Sound. 16mm B&W. *Rental:* Classic Film Mus, Ivy Films, Modern Sound & Video Comm. *Rental:* Video Comm, Videotape version.

Bowery to Broadway. Maria Montez & Jack Oakie. Directed by Charles Lamont. 1944. Universal. 94 min. Sound. 16mm B&W. *Rental:* Swank Motion.

Boxcar Bertha. Barbara Hershey, David Carradine & Barry Primus. Directed by Martin Scorsese. 1972. USA. 92 min. Sound. 16mm Color. *Rental:* Images Film.

Boxer, The. Robert Blake & Ernest Borgnine. Directed by Franco Prosperi. 1971. Italy. 70 min. Sound. 16mm Color. *Rental:* Bosco Films & New Cinema.

Boy. Fumio Watanabe. Directed by Nagisa Oshima. Jap. 1969. Japan. (Anamorphic). 97 min. Sound. 16mm Color. subtitles. *Rental:* New Yorker Films.

Boy, a Girl & a Dog, A. Orig. Title: Lucky. Sharyn Moffitt & Harry Davenport. Directed by Herbert Kline. 1946. Film Classics. 75 min. Sound. 16mm B&W. *Rental:* Alba House, Budget Films & Mogulls Films.

Boy & His Dog, A. Don Johnson. Directed by L. Q. Jones. 1975. JAF. 91 min. Sound. 16mm Color. *Rental:* Films Inc. *Rental:* Films Inc, Anamorphic version.

Boy Cried Murder, The. Veronica Hurst & Phil Brown. Directed by George Breakston. 1966. Britain. 86 min. Sound. 16mm Color. *Rental:* Cousino Visual Ed & Swank Motion.

Boy, Did I Get a Wrong Number. Bob Hope & Phyllis Diller. Directed by George Marshall. 1966. United Artists. 99 min. Sound. 16mm Color. *Rental:* MGM United.

Boy Friend, The. Twiggy & Christopher Gable. Directed by Ken Russell. 1971. Britain. 109 min. Sound. 16mm Color. *Rental:* MGM United.

Boy from Indiana, The. Lon McCallister & Billie Burke. Directed by John Rawlins. 1950. Eagle Lion. 66 min. Sound. 16mm B&W. *Sale:* Rep Pic Film.

Boy Meets Girl. James Cagney, Pat O'Brien & Marie Wilson. Directed by Lloyd Bacon. 1938. Warners. 86 min. Sound. 16mm B&W. *Rental:* MGM United.

Boy Named Charlie Brown, A. Directed by Bill Melendez. 1969. National General. 85 min. Sound. 16mm Color. *Rental:* Films Inc, Inst Cinema, Swank Motion, Twyman Films & Williams Films.

Boy Named Terry Egan, A. 1973. CBS. (Documentary). 53 min. Sound. 16mm B&W. *Rental:* Iowa Films, Syracuse U Film & U of IL Film. *Sale:* Carousel Films. *Rental:* U Cal Media, *Sale:* Carousel Films, Color version.

Boy of Two Worlds, A. Orig. Title: Paw. Jimmy Sherman & Edwin Adolphson. Directed by Astrid Henning-Jensen. 1960. Denmark. 88 min. Sound. 16mm Color. dubbed. *Rental:* Budget Films, Film Ctr DC, Films Inc, Welling Motion Pictures & Westcoast Films.

Boy on a Dolphin. Alan Ladd & Sophia Loren. Directed by Jean Negulesco. 1957. Fox. 111 min. Sound. 16mm Color. *Rental:* Films Inc. *Rental:* Films Inc, Anamorphic color version. *Sale:* Blackhawk Films, Magnetic Video & Video Lib, Videotape version.

Boy or Girl: Should the Choice Be Ours?. 58 min. Sound. Videotape *Rental:* PBS Video. *Sale:* PBS Video.

Boy Slaves. Anne Shirley & Alan Baxter. Directed by Pandro S. Berman. 1939. RKO. 72 min. Sound. 16mm *Rental:* RKO General Pics.

Boy Ten Feet Tall, A. Edward G. Robinson & Fergus MacClelland. Directed by Alexander MacKendrick. 1964. Britain. 89 min. Sound. 16mm Color. *Rental:* Films Inc & Wholesome Film Ctr.

Boy, What a Girl! Directed by Arthur Leonard. 1945. Herald. (All Black Cast). 60 min. Sound. 16mm B&W. *Rental:* Em Gee Film Lib.

Boy Who Caught a Crook, The. Wanda Hendrix & Don Beddoe. Directed by Edward L. Cahn. 1961. United Artists. 72 min. Sound. 16mm B&W. *Rental:* MGM United.

Boy Who Cried Werewolf, The. Kerwin Matthews & Elaine Devry. Directed by Nathan Juran. 1973. Universal. 93 min. Sound. 16mm Color. *Rental:* Swank Motion.

Boy Who Loved Horses, The. Stig Wilner. 1961. Denmark. 90 min. Sound. 16mm B&W. dubbed. *Rental:* Films Inc, Macmillan Films & Wholesome Film Ctr. *Lease:* Macmillan Films.

Boy Who Never Was, The. 1981. Britain. (Cast unlisted). 58 min. Sound. 16mm Color. *Sale:* Lucerne Films.

Boy Who Stole a Million, The. Maurice Reyna. Directed by Charles Crichton. 1960. Paramount. 64 min. Sound. 16mm B&W. *Rental:* Films Inc.

Boy With Glasses, The. Directed by Tuhichi Uno. 1969. Japan. (Cast unlisted). 45 min. Sound. 16mm B&W. dubbed. *Rental:* McGraw-Hill Films. *Sale:* McGraw-Hill Films.

Boy with Green Hair, The. Robert Ryan & Pat O'Brien. Directed by Joseph Losey. 1949. RKO. 82 min. Sound. 16mm *Rental:* RKO General Pics.

Boys & Other Strangers, The. (Adult). 60 min. Videotape Color. *Sale:* Vydio Philms.

Boys from Brazil, The. Sir Laurence Olivier, Gregory Peck & James Mason. Directed by Franklin Schaffner. 1978. Fox. 124 min. Sound. 16mm Color. *Rental:* Films Inc, Twyman Films & Williams Films. *Rental:* Williams FIlms, Videotape version.

Boys from Brooklyn, The *see* Bela Lugosi Meets a Brooklyn Gorilla.

Boys from Syracuse, The. Alan Jones, Joe Penner & Martha Raye. Directed by Edward Sutherland. 1940. Universal. 73 min. Sound. 16mm B&W. *Rental:* Swank Motion.

Boys in Company C, The. Stan Shaw & Andrew Stevens. Directed by Sidney J. Furie. 1978. Columbia. 125 min. Sound. 16mm Color. *Rental:* Swank Motion. *Rental:* Swank Motion, Videotape version.

Boys in Conflict. 1969. Harvard Medical School. (Documentary). 72 min. Sound. 16mm B&W. *Rental:* U Cal Media.

Boys in the Band, The. Kenneth Nelson, Cliff Gorman & Leonard Frey. Directed by William Friedkin. 1970. Cinema Center. 120 min. Sound. 16mm Color. *Rental:* Films Inc, Inst Cinema & Swank Motion. *Rental:* Swank Motion, Videotape version.

Boys' Night Out. Kim Novak & James Garner. Directed by Michael Gordon. 1962. MGM. 115 min. Sound. 16mm Color. *Rental:* MGM United. *Rental:* MGM United, Anamorphic color version.

Boys of Paul Street, The. Anthony Kemp. Directed by Zoltan Fabri. 1969. Hungary. 104 min. Sound. 16mm Color. dubbed. *Rental:* Films Inc.

Boys of Summer, The. Videotape *Sale:* Vidamerica.

Boys of the City. Bowery Boys. Directed by Joseph Lewis. 1940. Monogram. 63 min. Sound. 16mm B&W. *Rental:* Budget Films, Modern Sound & Newman Film Lib. *Sale:* Natl Cinema. *Sale:* Cinema Concepts, Super 8 sound version. *Sale:* Cinema Concepts, Videotape version.

Boys' Ranch. Butch Jenkins & James Craig. Directed by Roy Rowland. 1946. MGM. 97 min. Sound. 16mm B&W. *Rental:* MGM United.

Boys' Town. Spencer Tracy & Mickey Rooney. Directed by Norman Taurog. 1938. MGM. 94 min. Sound. 16mm B&W. *Rental:* MGM United.

Boys' Prison *see* Johnny Holiday.

Bozarts *see* We Are All Picasso!.

Brady's Escape. John Savage & Kelly Reno. Directed by Pal Gabor. 92 min. Sound. Videotape Color. *Sale:* Vidamerica.

Brain, The. David Niven, Eli Wallach & Jean-Paul Belmondo. Directed by Gerard Oury. 1969. Paramount. 100 min. Sound. 16mm Color. *Rental:* Films Inc.

Brain Eaters, The. Edwin Nelson & Joanna Lee. Directed by Bruno Ve Sota. 1958. American International. 61 min. Sound. 16mm B&W. *Rental:* Films Inc.

Brain from Planet Arous, The. 1958. 70 min. Sound. 16mm B&W. *Rental:* Ivy Films.

Brain of Frankenstein *see* Abbott & Costello Meet Frankenstein.

Brain That Wouldn't Die, The. Jason Evers, Virginia Leith & Adele Lamont. Directed by Joseph Green. 1963. American International. 81 min. Sound. 16mm B&W. *Rental:* Films Inc. *Sale:* Festival Films. *Sale:* Festival Films, Videotape version.

Brainiac, The. Trans. Title: Baron Del Terror, El. Abel Salazar & Ariadne Welter. Directed by Chano Urueta. 1960. Mexico. 77 min. Sound. 16mm dubbed Spanish. *Rental:* Budget Films.

Brainstorm. Natalie Wood & Christopher Walken. Directed by Douglas Trumbull. 1983. MGM-UA. 106 min. Sound. 16mm Color. *Rental:* MGM United. *Rental:* MGM United, Videotape version.

Brainwashing. 1968. CBS. (Documentary). 52 min. Sound. 16mm B&W. *Rental:* Macmillan Films & Syracuse U Film. *Lease:* Macmillan Films.

Bramble Bush, The. Richard Burton & Barbara Rush. Directed by Daniel Petrie. 1960. Warners. 103 min. Sound. 16mm Color. *Rental:* Swank Motion.

Branches. Bill Weidner & Connie Brady. Directed by Ed Emschwiller. 1971. Cornell U. 103 min. Sound. 16mm B&W. *Rental:* New Line Cinema. *Sale:* New Line Cinema.

Brand New Life, A. Cloris Leachman & Martin Balsam. Directed by Sam O'Steen. 1974. CBS. 72 min. Sound. 16mm Color. *Rental:* Budget Films, Kent St U Film, Learning Corp Am, Modern Sound, Syracuse U Film, Twyman Films, U Cal Media, U of IL Film, Westcoast Films & Wholesome Film Ctr. *Lease:* Learning Corp Am.

Brand of Fear. Jimmy Wakely. Directed by Oliver Drake. 1949. Monogram. 55 min. Sound. 16mm B&W. *Rental:* Hurlock Cine.

Brand of Hate. Bob Steele. Directed by Lewis D. Collins. 1934. Steiner. 63 min. Sound. 16mm B&W. *Rental:* Budget Films.

Brand of the Devil. James Newill. Directed by Harry Fraser. 1944. PRC. 62 min. Sound. 16mm B&W. *Sale:* Morcraft Films & Reel Images. *Sale:* Reel Images & Morcraft Films, Super 8 sound version.

Brand X. Taylor Mead & Abbie Hoffman. Directed by Win Chamberlin. 1970. CMB. 77 min. Sound. 16mm Color. *Rental:* New Cinema & New Line Cinema.

Branded. Buck Jones. Directed by D. Ross Lederman. 1931. Columbia. 60 min. Sound. 16mm B&W. *Sale:* Cinema Concepts.

Branded. Alan Ladd, Mona Freeman & Charles Bickford. Directed by Rudolph Mate. 1950. Paramount. 94 min. Sound. 16mm B&W. *Rental:* Films Inc. *Rental:* Films Inc, Color version.

Branded Men. Ken Maynard. Directed by Phil Rosen. 1931. Tiffany. 60 min. Sound. 16mm B&W. *Sale:* Video Comm.

Branded Woman. Norma Talmadge. Directed by Albert Parker. 1920. 16mm *Rental:* A Twyman Pres.

Brandy in the Wilderness. Directed by Stanton Kaye. 1968. Stanton Kaye. (Cast unlisted). 74 min. Sound. 16mm B&W. *Rental:* New Line Cinema.

Brannigan. John Wayne, Richard Attenborough & Judy Geeson. Directed by Douglas Hickox. 1975. United Artists. (Anamorphic). 111 min. Sound. 16mm Color. *Rental:* Budget Films, MGM United, Welling Motion Pictures & Westcoast Films. *Rental:* MGM United, Videotape version.

Brasher Doubloon, The. George Montgomery & Nancy Guild. Directed by John Brahm. 1947. Fox. 72 min. Sound. 16mm B&W. *Rental:* Films Inc.

Brass Bottle, The. Tony Randall & Burl Ives. Directed by Harry Keller. 1964. Universal. 89 min. Sound. 16mm Color. *Rental:* Williams Films.

Brass Legend, The. Hugh O'Brien & Nancy Gates. Directed by Gerd Oswald. 1956. United Artists. 79 min. Sound. 16mm B&W. *Rental:* MGM United.

Brass Target, The. Sophia Loren & George Kennedy. Directed by John Hough. 1978. MGM. 111 min. Sound. 16mm Color. *Rental:* MGM United.

Bravados, The. Gregory Peck & Joan Collins. Directed by Henry King. 1958. Fox. 99 min. Sound. 16mm Color. *Rental:* Films Inc.

Brave Bulls, The. Mel Ferrer, Anthony Quinn & Eugene Iglesias. Directed by Robert Rossen. 1951. Columbia. 108 min. Sound. 16mm B&W. *Rental:* Bosco Films, Kit Parker & Budget Films. *Rental:* Kit Parker, 114 min. version.

Brave Little Tailor, The. 1972. (Cast unlisted). 81 min. Sound. 16mm Color. *Rental:* Films Inc.

Brave One, The. Michel Ray. Directed by Irving Rapper. 1956. RKO. (Anamorphic). 100 min. Sound. 16mm Color. *Rental:* Films Inc.

Brave Rifles, The. Arthur Kennedy. 51 min. Sound. 16mm B&W. *Rental:* Westcoast Films.

Braveheart. Rod La Rocque & Tyrone Power Sr. Directed by Alan Hale. 1926. PDC. 60 min. Silent. 16mm B&W. *Rental:* Em Gee Film Lib, Film Classics, Modern Sound & Mogulls Films. *Sale:* Glenn Photo. *Rental:* Em Gee Film Lib & Mogulls Films, *Sale:* Film Classics & Glenn Photo, Silent 8mm version.

Bravo Guerreiro, O. Directed by Joaquin Pedro De Andrade. Port. 1969. Brazil. (Ballet). 80 min. Sound. 16mm B&W. subtitles. *Rental:* New Yorker Films.

Brazil. Tito Guizar & Virginia Bruce. Directed by Joseph Santley. 1944. Republic. 91 min. Sound. 16mm B&W. *Rental:* Ivy Films.

Brazil: The Gathering Millions. 1965. NET. (Documentary). 60 min. Sound. 16mm B&W. *Rental:* BYU Media & Indiana AV Ctr.

Brazil: The Rude Awakening. 1967. CBS. (Documentary). 54 min. Sound. 16mm B&W. *Rental:* McGraw-Hill Films. *Sale:* McGraw-Hill Films.

Brazil: The Take Off Point. 1964. NET. (Documentary). 60 min. Sound. 16mm B&W. *Rental:* Indiana AV Ctr.

Brazilian Connection, The. 60 min. Sound. 16mm Color. *Rental:* Cinema Guild.

Bread & Chocolate. Nino Manfredi & Anna Karina. Directed by Franco Brusati. Ital. 1978. Italy. 111 min. Sound. 16mm Color. subtitles. *Rental:* Cinema Five, Corinth Films, World Northal & WW Enter. *Rental:* WW Enter, Videotape version.

Break in the Circle, A. Forrest Tucker & Eva Bartok. Directed by Val Guest. 1957. Fox. 69 min. Sound. 16mm B&W. *Rental:* Films Inc.

Break of Hearts. Katharine Hepburn & Charles Boyer. Directed by Philip Moeller. 1935. RKO. 80 min. Sound. 16mm B&W. *Rental:* Films Inc. *Lease:* Films Inc.

Breakdown. Ann Richards & William Bishop. Directed by Edmond Angelo. 1952. Realart. 75 min. Sound. 16mm B&W. *Rental:* Budget Films.

Breaker Morant. Edward Woodward & Jack Thompson. Directed by Bruce Beresford. 1979. New World-QFI. 107 min. Sound. 16mm Color. *Rental:* Films Inc.

Breakfast at Sunrise. Constance Talmadge. Directed by Malcolm St. Clair. 1927. 16mm *Rental:* A Twyman Pres.

Breakfast at Tiffany's. Audrey Hepburn, George Peppard & Mickey Rooney. Directed by Blake Edwards. 1961. Paramount. 115 min. Sound. 16mm Color. *Rental:* Films Inc.

Breakfast for Two. Barbara Stanwyck & Herbert Marshall. Directed by Alfred Santell. 1937. RKO. 65 min. Sound. 16mm *Rental:* RKO General Pics.

Breakfast in Hollywood. Billie Burke & ZaSu Pitts. Directed by Harold Schuster. 1946. United Artists. 100 min. Sound. 16mm B&W. *Rental:* Mogulls Films.

Breakheart Pass. Charles Bronson & Ben Johnson. Directed by Tom Gries. 1976. United Artists. 95 min. Sound. 16mm Color. *Rental:* Budget Films, MGM United, Westcoast Films & Welling Motion Pictures & Wholesome Film Ctr.

Breaking Away. Dennis Christopher, Dennis Quaid & Daniel Stern. Directed by Peter Yates. 1979. Fox. 99 min. Sound. 16mm Color. *Rental:* Films Inc.

Breaking Free. 1981. Australia. (Documentary). 50 min. Sound. 16mm Color. *Rental:* MTI Tele. *Sale:* MTI Tele.

Breaking Point, The. Bo Svenson & Robert Culp. Directed by Bob Clark. 1976. Fox. 92 min. Sound. 16mm Color. *Rental:* Films Inc.

Breaking the Ice. Bobby Breen & Charles Ruggles. Directed by Edward Cline. 1938. RKO. 88 min. Sound. 16mm B&W. *Rental:* Alba House & Roas Films. *Sale:* Reel Images, Videotape version.

Breaking the Sound Barrier. Sir Ralph Richardson & Ann Todd. Directed by David Lean. 1952. Britain. 109 min. Sound. 16mm B&W. *Rental:* Films Inc & Willoughby Peer.

Breaking the Trade Barrier. 1962. CBS. (Documentary). 54 min. Sound. 16mm B&W. *Rental:* McGraw-Hill Films, U of IL Film & U Mich Media. *Sale:* McGraw-Hill Films.

Breaking Up. Lee Remick. Directed by Delbert Mann. 1978. Susskind. 90 min. Videotape Color. *Sale:* Time-Life Multimedia.

Breaking with Old Ideas. 1975. (Documentary). 120 min. Sound. 16mm Color. *Rental:* Canyon Cinema.

Breakout. Charles Bronson, Randy Quaid & Robert Duvall. Directed by Tom Gries. 1975. Columbia. 96 min. Sound. 16mm Color. *Rental:* Arcus Film, Bosco Films, Budget Films, Cine Craft, Film Ctr DC, Films Inc, Ivy Films, Kit Parker, Modern Sound, Natl Film Video, Roas Films, Swank Motion, Welling Motion Pictures, Westcoast Films & Williams Films.

Breast Cancer. 1980. US Government. (Documentary). 60 min. Sound. Videotape Color. *Sale:* Natl AV Ctr.

Breath of Scandal, A. Sophia Loren, John Gavin & Maurice Chevalier. Directed by Michael Curtiz. 1960. Paramount. 98 min. Sound. 16mm Color. *Rental:* Films Inc.

Breathing Together: Revolution of the Electric Family. Directed by Morley Markson. 1971. Morley Markson. (Documentary). 88 min. Sound. 16mm B&W. *Rental:* New Cinema & New Line Cinema. *Sale:* New Line Cinema. *Sale:* New Line Cinema, Videotape version.

Breathless. Trans. Title: Bout de Souffle, A. Jean-Paul Belmondo & Jean Seberg. Directed by Jean-Luc Godard. 1959. France. 89 min. Sound. 16mm Color. *Rental:* Images Film, Ivy Films & New Yorker Films. *Sale:* Festival Films, Natl Cinema & Reel Images. *Lease:* Images Film. *Rental:* Festival Films, *Sale:* Tamarelles French Film, Videotape version.

Breathless. Richard Gere & Valerie Kaprisky. Directed by Jim McBride. 1983. Orion. 100 min. Sound. 16mm Color. *Rental:* Films Inc.

Breed of the Border. Bob Steele. Directed by Robert N. Bradbury. 1933. Monogram. 60 min. Sound. 16mm B&W. *Rental:* Mogulls Films.

Breed of the West. Wally Wales. Directed by Alvin J. Neitz. 1930. Big Four. 57 min. Sound. 16mm B&W. *Sale:* Natl Cinema.

Breezy. William Holden & Kay Lenz. Directed by Clint Eastwood. 1974. Universal. 105 min. Sound. 16mm Color. *Rental:* Swank Motion & Twyman Films.

Brementown Musicians. Directed by Raimer Geis. 1950. Childhood. (Cast unlisted). 58 min. Sound. 16mm Color. dubbed. *Rental:* Films Inc, Roas Films, Westcoast Films & Willoughby Peer.

Brendan Behan: The Man Behind the Myth. 1974. Britain. 52 min. Sound. 16mm Color. *Rental:* Time-Life Multimedia.

Brendan Voyage, The. 1979. Britain. (Documentary). 57 min. Sound. 16mm Color. *Rental:* Films Inc. *Sale:* Films Inc. *Rental:* Films Inc, *Sale:* Films Inc, Videotape version.

Brewster McCloud. Bud Cort & Sally Kellerman. Directed by Robert Altman. 1970. MGM. 101 min. Sound. 16mm Color. *Rental:* MGM United. *Rental:* MGM United, Anamorphic version.

Brewster's Millions. Dennis O'Keefe & June Havoc. Directed by Allan Dwan. 1945. Small. 79 min. Sound. 16mm B&W. *Rental:* Mogulls Films.

Brian's Song. James Caan, Billy Dee Williams & Judy Pace. Directed by Buzz Kulik. 1971. Screen Gems. 75 min. Sound. 16mm Color. *Rental:* Arcus Film, Budget Films, Film Ctr DC, Film Pres, Films Inc, Inst Cinema, Ivy Films, Kent St U Film, Kit Parker, Learning Corp Am, Mass Media, Modern Sound, Newman Film Lib, Roas Films, Swank Motion, Syracuse U Film, Twyman Films, U Cal Media, U of IL Film, U Mich Media, Video Comm, Welling Motion Pictures, Westcoast Films, Wholesome Film Ctr & Williams Films. *Lease:* Learning Corp Am. *Rental:* Learning Corp Am & Swank Motion, *Lease:* Learning Corp Am, Videotape version.

Bribe, The. Robert Taylor & Ava Gardner. Directed by Robert Z. Leonard. 1949. MGM. 98 min. Sound. 16mm B&W. *Rental:* MGM United.

Bridal Intrigue. 60 min. Videotape Color. *Sale:* Videx Home Lib.

Bridal Suite. Annabella & Robert Young. Directed by William Thiele. 1939. MGM. 70 min. Sound. 16mm B&W. *Rental:* MGM United.

Bride & the Beast, The. Charlotte Austin & Lance Fuller. Directed by Adrian Weiss. 1958. Allied Artists. 78 min. Sound. 16mm B&W. *Rental:* Budget Films & Hurlock Cine.

Bride by Mistake. Laraine Day & Alan Marshall. Directed by Richard Wallace. 1943. RKO. 80 min. Sound. 16mm B&W. *Rental:* Films Inc.

Bride Came C.O.D., The Bette Davis & James Cagney. Directed by William Keighley. 1941. Warners. 92 min. Sound. 16mm B&W. *Rental:* MGM United.

Bride Comes Home, The. Claudette Colbert & Fred MacMurray. Directed by Wesley Ruggles. 1935. Paramount. 85 min. Sound. 16mm B&W. *Rental:* Swank Motion.

Bride Goes Wild, The. Van Johnson & June Allyson. Directed by Norman Taurog. 1948. MGM. 97 min. Sound. 16mm B&W. *Rental:* MGM United.

Bride of Frankenstein, The. Boris Karloff & Elsa Lanchester. Directed by James Whale. 1935. Universal. 75 min. Sound. 16mm B&W. *Rental:* Swank Motion.

Bride of the Andes, The. Sachiko Hadari. Directed by Susumi Hani. Jap. 1966. Japan. 102 min. Sound. 16mm Color. subtitles. *Rental:* Film Images.

Bride of the Beast. Orig. Title: Baboona. Directed by Martin Johnson. 1935. Fox. (Documentary). 75 min. Sound. 16mm B&W. *Rental:* Modern Sound. *Sale:* Blackhawk Films & Morcraft Films. *Sale:* Blackhawk Films, Super 8 sound version.

Bride of the Monster. Bela Lugosi. 1956. Banner. 67 min. Sound. 16mm B&W. *Rental:* Budget Films & Ivy Films. *Sale:* Festival Films, Videotape version.

Bride Walks Out, The. Barbara Stanwyck & Robert Young. Directed by Leigh Jason. 1936. RKO. 81 min. Sound. 16mm *Rental:* RKO General Pics.

Bride with a Dowry. V. Vasilieva. Directed by T. Lukashevich & B. Ravenskikh. 1953. Russia. 118 min. Sound. 16mm B&W. *Rental:* Corinth Films.

Bride Wore Black, The. Jeanne Moreau & Jean-Claude Brialy. Directed by Francois Truffaut. Fr. 1968. France. 107 min. Sound. 16mm Color. subtitles. *Rental:* MGM United.

Bride Wore Boots, The. Barbara Stanwyck & Robert Cummings. Directed by Irving Pichel. 1946. Paramount. 86 min. Sound. 16mm B&W. *Rental:* Swank Motion.

Bride Wore Red, The. Joan Crawford & Franchot Tone. Directed by Dorothy Arzner. 1937. MGM. 103 min. Sound. 16mm B&W. *Rental:* MGM United.

Brides Are Like That. Ross Alexander & Anita Louise. Directed by William McGann. 1936. Warners. 67 min. Sound. 16mm B&W. *Rental:* MGM United.

Brides of Dracula. Peter Cushing. Directed by Terence Fisher. 1960. Britain. 85 min. Sound. 16mm Color. *Rental:* Swank Motion & Williams Films.

Bridge, The. Gunther Hoffman. Directed by Bernhard Wicki. 1960. Germany. 102 min. Sound. 16mm B&W. subtitles. *Rental:* Hurlock Cine. *Rental:* Hurlock Cine, Dubbed version.

Bridge, The. 1981. CTW. (Cast unlisted). 60 min. Sound. 16mm Color. *Rental:* Indiana AV Ctr. *Sale:* Indiana AV Ctr. *Rental:* PBS Video, *Sale:* PBS Video, Videotape version.

Bridge at Remagen, The. 2 pts. 1945. Army. (Documentary). 56 min. Sound. 16mm B&W. *Rental:* Natl AV Ctr.

Bridge at Remagen, The. George Segal & Ben Gazzara. Directed by John Guillermin. 1969. United Artists. 115 min. Sound. 16mm Color. *Rental:* MGM United.

Bridge of Adam Rush, The. 1975. ABC. (Cast unlisted). 47 min. Sound. 16mm Color. *Rental:* D Wilson, Kent St U Film, U of IL Film & U Mich Media, Videotape version.

Bridge of San Luis Rey, The. Lynn Bari, Francis Lederer & Nazimova. Directed by Rowland V. Lee. 1944. United Artists. 92 min. Sound. 16mm B&W. *Sale:* Classics Assoc NY.

Bridge on the River Kwai, The. Sir Alec Guinness, William Holden & Jack Hawkins. Directed by David Lean. 1957. Columbia. 161 min. Sound. 16mm Color. *Rental:* Arcus Film, Bosco Films, Buchan Pic, Budget Films, Cine Craft, Corinth Films, Film Ctr DC, Film Pres, Films Inc, Hurlock Cine, Ivy Films, Kerr Film, Kit Parker, Modern Sound, Natl Film Video, Newman Film Lib, Roas Films, Swank Motion, Twyman Films, U of IL Film, Video Comm, Welling Motion Pictures, Westcoast Films, Wholesome Film Ctr, Williams Films & Willoughby Peer. *Rental:* Corinth Films, Images Film, Kit Parker & Twyman Films, Anamorphic version. *Rental:* Swank Motion, Videotape version.

Bridge That Spanned the World, The. 1978. 58 min. Sound. Videotape *Rental:* PBS Video. *Sale:* PBS Video.

Bridge to the Sun, A. Carroll Baker & James Shigeta. Directed by Etienne Perier. 1961. MGM. 113 min. Sound. 16mm B&W. *Rental:* MGM United.

Bridge Too Far, A. Robert Redford & Sean Connery. Directed by Sir Richard Attenborough. 1977. United Artists. (Anamorphic). 176 min. Sound. 16mm Color. *Rental:* MGM United. *Rental:* MGM United, Videotape version.

Bridges at Toko-Ri, The. William Holden, Grace Kelly & Fredric March. Directed by Mark Robson. 1955. Paramount. 103 min. Sound. 16mm Color. *Rental:* Films Inc.

Brief Encounter. Celia Johnson, Trevor Howard & Stanley Holloway. Directed by David Lean. 1946. Britain. 99 min. Sound. 16mm B&W. *Rental:* Budget Films, Films Inc, Images Film, Kit Parker, Learning Corp Am, Twyman Films & U of IL Film. *Sale:* Learning Corp Am.

Brief Encounter. Richard Burton & Sophia Loren. Directed by Alan Bridges. 1974. ITC. 90 min. Sound. 16mm Color. *Rental:* Swank Motion.

Brief Lives. Roy Dotrice. Directed by Patrick Garland. 1968. Britain. 90 min. Sound. 16mm Color. *Rental:* Arcus Film.

Brief Moment. Carole Lombard & Gene Raymond. Directed by David Burton. 1933. Columbia. 70 min. Sound. 16mm B&W. *Rental:* Bosco Films & Kit Parker.

Brief Vacation, A. Florinda Bolkan, Renato Salvatori & Daniel Quenaud. Directed by Vittorio De Sica. Ital. 1975. Italy. 106 min. Sound. 16mm Color. subtitles. *Rental:* Films Inc.

Brig, The. Warren Finnerty & Jim Anderson. Directed by Jonas Mekas. 1964. Jonas Mekas. 68 min. Sound. 16mm B&W. *Rental:* Canyon Cinema.

Brigadoon. Gene Kelly & Cyd Charisse. Directed by Vincente Minnelli. 1954. MGM. 108 min. Sound. 16mm Color. *Rental:* MGM United. *Rental:* MGM United, Anamorphic color version. *Rental:* MGM United, Videotape version.

Brigand, The. Anthony Dexter, Jody Lawrence & Anthony Quinn. Directed by Phil Karlson. 1952. Columbia. 94 min. Sound. 16mm Color. *Rental:* Kit Parker.

Brigham Young: Frontiersman. Tyrone Power, Linda Darnell & Dean Jagger. Directed by Henry Hathaway. 1940. Fox. 110 min. Sound. 16mm B&W. *Rental:* Films Inc & Twyman Films.

Bright College Years. Directed by Peter Rosen. 1971. Embassy. (Documentary). 52 min. Sound. 16mm Color. *Rental:* Films Inc.

Bright Eyes. Shirley Temple. Directed by David Butler. 1934. Fox. 83 min. Sound. 16mm B&W. *Rental:* Films Inc.

Bright Leaf. Gary Cooper & Patricia Neal. Directed by Michael Curtiz. 1950. Warners. 110 min. Sound. 16mm B&W. *Rental:* Swank Motion.

Bright Lights. Orig. Title: Funny Face. Dorothy Mackail & Frank Fay. Directed by Michael Curtiz. 1931. Warners. 72 min. Sound. 16mm B&W. *Rental:* MGM United.

Bright Lights. Joe E. Brown, Ann Dvorak & Patricia Ellis. Directed by Busby Berkeley. 1935. Warners. 86 min. Sound. 16mm B&W. *Rental:* MGM United.

Bright Road. Dorothy Dandridge & Harry Belafonte. Directed by Gerald Mayer. 1953. MGM. 69 min. Sound. 16mm B&W. *Rental:* MGM United.

Bright Victory. Arthur Kennedy & Julie Adams. Directed by Mark Robson. 1951. Universal. 97 min. Sound. 16mm B&W. *Rental:* Swank Motion.

Brighton Rock. Richard Attenborough & Hermione Baddeley. Directed by John Boulting. 1947. Britain. 91 min. Sound. 16mm B&W. *Rental:* Corinth Films.

Brighton Strangler, The. John Loder & June Duprez. Directed by Max Nosseck. 1944. RKO. 67 min. Sound. 16mm B&W. *Rental:* Films Inc.

Brighty of the Grand Canyon. Joseph Cotten, Pat Conway & Dick Foran. Directed by Norman Foster. 1966. Stephen Booth. 85 min. Sound. 16mm Color. *Rental:* Arcus Film, Buchan Pic, Budget Films, Charard Motion Pics, Film Ctr DC, Film Pres, Films Inc, Ivy Films, Kerr Film, Modern Sound, Newman Film Lib, Roas Films, Syracuse U Film, Twyman Films, Welling Motion Pictures, Westcoast Films, Wholesome Film Ctr & Williams Films. *Lease:* Salz Ent.

Brigida Criminal. Jose Svarez. Directed by Ignacio Iquino. Span. 1953. Spain. 78 min. Sound. 16mm B&W. subtitles. *Rental:* Film Classics.

Brimstone. Walter Brennan & Rod Cameron. Directed by Thomas Williamson. 1949. Republic. 90 min. Sound. 16mm B&W. *Rental:* Ivy Films. *Sale:* Rep Pic Film.

Brimstone & Treacle. Sting, Denholm Elliot & Joan Plowright. Directed by Richard Loncraine. 1983. Britain. 85 min. Sound. 16mm Color. *Rental:* MGM United. *Rental:* MGM United, Videotape version.

Bring Back My Bonnie. 1982. Filmmakers. (Documentary). 51 min. Sound. 16mm Color. *Rental:* U Cal Media.

Bring 'em Back Alive. Frank Buck. Directed by J. Van Beuren. 1933. RKO. (Documentary). 70 min. Sound. 16mm *Rental:* RKO General Pics.

Bring Me the Head of Alfredo Garcia. Warren Oates & Gig Young. Directed by Sam Peckinpah. 1974. United Artists. 112 min. Sound. 16mm Color. *Rental:* Film Ctr DC, MGM United, Welling Motion Pictures & Budget Films.

Bring Your Smile Along. Frankie Laine & Constance Towers. Directed by Blake Edwards. 1955. Columbia. 83 min. Sound. 16mm Color. *Rental:* Modern Sound & Welling Motion Pictures.

Bringing Up Baby. Cary Grant, Katharine Hepburn & Charles Ruggles. Directed by Howard Hawks. 1938. MGM. 102 min. Sound. 16mm B&W. *Rental:* Films Inc. *Lease:* Films Inc.

Brink of Life. Eva Dahlbeck & Ingrid Thulin. Directed by Ingmar Bergman. Swed. 1957. Sweden. 100 min. Sound. 16mm B&W. subtitles. *Rental:* Janus Films. *Sale:* Reel Images.

Brink's Job, The. Peter Falk & Peter Boyle. Directed by William Friedkin. 1978. Universal. 103 min. Sound. 16mm Color. *Rental:* Swank Motion.

Bristle Face. Brian Keith, Jeff Donnell & Wallace Ford. 1970. Disney. 64 min. Sound. 16mm Color. *Rental:* Buchan Pic, Cine Craft, Film Ctr DC, Disney Prod, Films Inc, Newman Film Lib, Roas Films & U of IL Film.

Britannia Hospital. Leonard Rossiter & Malcolm McDowell. Directed by Lindsay Anderson. 1983. Britain. 116 min. Sound. 16mm Color. *Rental:* MGM United. *Rental:* MGM United, Videotape version.

British Agent. Leslie Howard, Kay Francis & William Gargan. Directed by Michael Curtiz. 1934. Warners. 81 min. Sound. 16mm B&W. *Rental:* MGM United.

British Intelligence. Orig. Title: Enemy Agent. Boris Karloff & Margaret Lindsay. Directed by Terry Morse. 1940. Warners. 62 min. Sound. 16mm B&W. *Rental:* MGM United.

Brivele der Mamen, A. Lucy Gehrman & Misha Gehrman. Directed by Joseph Green. Yiddish. 1939. Poland. 90 min. Sound. 16mm B&W. subtitles. *Rental:* Films Inc.

Broad-Minded. Joe E. Brown, Ona Munson & Bela Lugosi. Directed by Mervyn LeRoy. 1931. Warners. 73 min. Sound. 16mm B&W. *Rental:* MGM United.

Broadway Babies. Alice White & Sally Eilers. Directed by Mervyn LeRoy. 1929. Warners. 89 min. Sound. 16mm B&W. *Rental:* MGM United.

Broadway Drifter. George Walsh. Directed by Bernard McEveety. 1927. Excellent. 70 min. Silent. 16mm B&W. *Sale:* Film Classics.

Broadway Gondolier. Dick Powell, Joan Blondell & Adolphe Menjou. Directed by Lloyd Bacon. 1935. Warners. 98 min. Sound. 16mm B&W. *Rental:* MGM United.

Broadway Hostess. Phil Regan & Winnie Shaw. Directed by Frank McDonald. 1935. Warners. 68 min. Sound. 16mm B&W. *Rental:* MGM United.

Broadway Limited. Marjorie Woodworth & Victor McLaglen. Directed by Gordon Douglas. 1941. Hal Roach. 50 min. Sound. 16mm B&W. *Rental:* Mogulls Films.

Broadway Melody. Orig. Title: Broadway Melody of 1929. Anita Page & Bessie Love. Directed by Harry Beaumont. 1929. MGM. 110 min. Sound. 16mm B&W. *Rental:* MGM United.

Broadway Melody of 1929 *see* Broadway Melody.

Broadway Melody of 1936. Jack Benny, Eleanor Powell & Robert Taylor. Directed by Roy Del Ruth. 1936. MGM. 110 min. Sound. 16mm B&W. *Rental:* MGM United.

Broadway Melody of 1938. Judy Garland & George Murphy. Directed by Roy Del Ruth. 1938. MGM. 105 min. Sound. 16mm B&W. *Rental:* MGM United.

Broadway Melody of 1940. Fred Astaire, Eleanor Powell & George Murphy. Directed by Norman Taurog. 1940. MGM. 102 min. Sound. 16mm B&W. *Rental:* MGM United.

Broadway Musketeers. Ann Sheridan, Marie Wilson & Margaret Lindsay. Directed by John Farrow. 1938. Warners. 62 min. Sound. 16mm B&W. *Rental:* MGM United.

Broadway Serenade. Jeanette McDonald & Lew Ayres. Directed by Robert Z. Leonard. 1939. MGM. 114 min. Sound. 16mm B&W. *Rental:* MGM United.

Broadway Thru a Keyhole. Constance Cummings & Russ Columbo. Directed by Lowell Sherman. 1933. Fox. 90 min. Sound. 16mm B&W. *Rental:* Films Inc.

Broadway to Cheyenne. Rex Bell. Directed by Harry Fraser. 1932. Monogram. 60 min. Sound. 16mm B&W. *Rental:* Mogulls Films. *Sale:* Reel Images. *Sale:* Reel Images, Super 8 sound version.

Broadway to Hollywood. Frank Morgan & Jackie Cooper. Directed by Willard Mack. 1933. MGM. 85 min. Sound. 16mm B&W. *Rental:* MGM United.

Broken Arrow. James Stewart, Jeff Chandler & Debra Paget. Directed by Delmer Daves. 1950. Fox. 93 min. Sound. 16mm Color. *Rental:* Films Inc.

Broken Barrier. Kay Ngarimu & Terence Bayler. Directed by Roger Mirams & John O'Shea. 1951. 71 min. 16mm *Rental:* A Twyman Pres.

Broken Blossoms. Richard Barthelmess, Donald Crisp & Lillian Gish. Directed by D. W. Griffith. 1919. Griffith. 92 min. Silent. 16mm B&W. *Rental:* Budget Films, Classic Film Mus, Em Gee Film Lib, Kerr Film, Kit Parker, Museum Mod Art, Twyman Films, Utah Media & Willoughby Peer. *Sale:* Cinema Concepts, Festival Films, Griggs Movie & Reel Images. *Rental:* Museum Mod Art, Tinted version. *Rental:* Killiam Collect & Museum Mod Art, Tinted, musical score only, 16mm & 76 min. version. *Rental:* Ivy Films, Super 8 silent version. *Rental:* Budget Films, 88 min version. *Sale:* Festival Films, 68 min. version. *Sale:* Festival Films, 68 min. Videotape version.

Broken Hearts of Broadway. Johnny Moore & Johnny Walker. Directed by Irving Cummings. 1923. Cummings. 90 min. Silent. 16mm B&W. *Sale:* Blackhawk Films. *Rental:* Ivy Films, *Sale:* Blackhawk Films, Super 8 silent version. *Sale:* Blackhawk Films, Silent 8mm version.

Broken Hill. 1967. Broken Hill Smelters. (Documentary). 51 min. Sound. 16mm Color. *Rental:* Modern Talking.

Broken Jug, The *see* Zerbrochene Krug.

Broken Lance. Spencer Tracy & Richard Widmark. Directed by Edward Dmytryk. 1954. Fox. (Anamorphic). 96 min. Sound. 16mm Color. *Rental:* Films Inc.

Broken Land. Kent Taylor & Jody McCrea. Directed by John Bushelman. 1962. Fox. 60 min. Sound. 16mm Color. *Rental:* Films Inc.

Broken Lullaby. Orig. Title: Man I Killed, The. Lionel Barrymore & Nancy Carroll. Directed by Ernst Lubitsch. 1932. Paramount. 77 min. Sound. 16mm B&W. *Rental:* Museum Mod Art & Swank Motion.

Broken Silence. Zeena Keefe & J. Barney Sherry. Directed by Del Henderson. 1922. Pine Tree. 65 min. Silent. 16mm B&W. *Sale:* E Finney.

Broken Strings. Clarence Muse. 1940. International Roadshows. 80 min. Sound. 16mm B&W. *Rental:* Standard Film.

Broken Treaty at Battle Mountain. Directed by Joel L. Freedman. 1974. Soho. (Documentary). 60 min. Sound. 16mm Color. *Rental:* Cinema Guild. *Sale:* Cinema Guild.

Bronco Billy. Clint Eastwood & Sondra Locke. Directed by Clint Eastwood. 1980. Warners. 119 min. Sound. 16mm Color. *Rental:* Swank Motion & Williams Films. *Rental:* Swank Motion, Videotape version.

Bronco Bullfrog. Del Walker & Anne Gooding. Directed by Barney Platts-Mills. 1971. Britain. 86 min. Sound. 16mm B&W. *Rental:* New Cinema.

Bronco Buster. John Lund & Scott Brady. Directed by Budd Boetticher. 1952. Universal. 81 min. Sound. 16mm Color. *Rental:* Swank Motion.

Bronx Is Burning, The. 1974. Britain. (Documentary). 52 min. Sound. 16mm Color. *Rental:* Time-Life Multimedia. *Sale:* Time-Life Multimedia. *Rental:* Time-Life Multimedia, *Sale:* Time-Life Multimedia, Videotape version.

Bronze Buckaroo, The. Herbert Jeffrey & Artie Young. Directed by Richard C. Kahn. 1938. 60 min. Sound. 16mm *Rental:* Budget Films.

Brood, The. Oliver Reed & Samantha Eggar. Directed by David Cronenberg. 1979. New World. 90 min. Sound. 16mm Color. *Rental:* Films Inc.

Brooklyn Bridge. Directed by Ken Burns. 1982. Florentine. (Documentary). 58 min. Sound. 16mm Color. *Rental:* Direct Cinema. *Sale:* Direct Cinema. *Sale:* Direct Cinema, Videotape version.

Brooklyn Orchid. Majorie Woodworth & William Bendix. Directed by Kurt Neumann. 1942. Hal Roach. 50 min. Sound. 16mm B&W. *Rental:* Mogulls Films.

Broth of a Boy. Barry Fitzgerald & Abbey Players. Directed by George Pollack. 1958. 77 min. 16mm *Rental:* A Twyman Pres.

Brother, Cry for Me. Anthony Caruso & Larry Pennell. Directed by William White. 1970. International Center. 95 min. Sound. 16mm Color. *Rental:* Video Comm.

Brother John. Sidney Poitier, Will Geer & Beverly Todd. Directed by James Goldstone. 1971. Columbia. 94 min. Sound. 16mm Color. *Rental:* Arcus Film, Cine Craft, Film Ctr DC, Films Inc, Inst Cinema, Kerr Film, Modern Sound, Natl Film Video, Video Comm, Welling Motion Pictures, Westcoast Films & Willoughby Peer.

Brother of the Wind. Directed by Dick Robertson. 1972. Sunn International. (Documentary). 90 min. Sound. 16mm Color. *Rental:* Arcus Film, Bosco Films, Budget Films, Cine Craft, Films Inc, Kerr Film, Maljack, Roas Films, Video Comm, Westcoast Films, Wholesome Film Ctr & Williams Films. *Lease:* Video Comm. *Rental:* Video Comm, *Lease:* Video Comm, Videotape version.

Brother Orchid. Edward G. Robinson & Humphrey Bogart. Directed by Lloyd Bacon. 1940. Warners. 91 min. Sound. 16mm B&W. *Rental:* MGM United.

Brother Rat. Ronald Reagan & Eddie Albert. Directed by William Keighley. 1938. Warners. 89 min. Sound. 16mm B&W. *Rental:* MGM United.

Brother Rat & a Baby. Jane Wyman, Ronald Reagan, Eddie Albert & Priscilla Lane. Directed by Ray Enright. 1940. Warners. 87 min. Sound. 16mm B&W. *Rental:* MGM United.

Brother Sun, Sister Moon. Sir Alec Guinness, Judi Bowker & Graham Faulkner. Directed by Franco Zeffirelli. 1973. Paramount. 120 min. Sound. 16mm Color. *Rental:* Films Inc.

Brotherhood, The. Kirk Douglas, Alex Cord & Susan Srasberg. Directed by Martin Ritt. 1968. Paramount. 98 min. Sound. 16mm Color. *Rental:* Films Inc.

Brotherhood of Death, The. Roy Jefferson & Mike Thomas. Directed by Bill Berry. 1976. Cinema Shares. 82 min. Sound. 16mm Color. *Rental:* Films Inc.

Brotherhood of Satan, The. Strother Martin, Ahna Capri & Alvy Moore. Directed by Bernard McEveety. 1971. Columbia. 92 min. Sound. 16mm Color. *Rental:* Budget Films, Cine Craft, Film Ctr DC, Films Inc, Modern Sound, Roas Films, Welling Motion Pictures, Westcoast Films & Willoughby Peer.

Brotherly Love. Peter O'Toole & Susannah York. Directed by J. Lee Thompson. 1970. MGM. 112 min. Sound. 16mm Color. *Rental:* MGM United.

Brothers. Barbara Bedford & Cornelius Keefe. Directed by Scott Pembroke. 1926. Rayart. 65 min. Silent. 16mm B&W. *Sale:* Mogulls Films, Silent 8mm version.

Brothers. Orig. Title: Bruder. Directed by Werner Hochbaum. 1929. Germany. (Musical score & effects only). 63 min. Sound. 16mm B&W. *Rental:* Museum Mod Art.

Brothers. Bernie Casey, Vonetta McGee & Ron O'Neal. Directed by Arthur Barron. 1977. Warners. 104 min. Sound. 16mm Color. *Rental:* Films Inc, Swank Motion, Twyman Film & Williams Films.

Brothers & Sisters in Concert. Curtis Mayfield. Directed by Stan Lathan. 1973. Paramount. 90 min. Sound. 16mm Color. *Rental:* Films Inc.

Brothers in the Saddle. Tim Holt & Richard Martin. Directed by Lesley Selander. 1949. RKO. 60 min. Sound. 16mm B&W. *Rental:* Budget Films.

Brothers Karamazov, The. Yul Brynner & Maria Schell. Directed by Richard Brooks. 1958. MGM. 146 min. Sound. 16mm Color. *Rental:* MGM United. *Rental:* MGM United, Videotape version.

Brothers Karamazov, The. Mikhail Oulinov. Directed by Ivan Pyriev. Rus. 1972. Russia. 154 min. Sound. 16mm Color. subtitles. *Rental:* Corinth Films.

Brothers O'Toole, The. John Astin, Pat Carroll & Hans Conried. Directed by Richard Erdman. 1973. American National. 94 min. Sound. 16mm Color. *Rental:* Arcus Film, Budget Films, Films Inc, Video Comm, Westcoast Films & Williams Films. *Lease:* Video Comm. *Rental:* Video Comm, *Lease:* Video Comm, Videotape version.

Brothers Rico, The. Richard Conte & Dianne Foster. Directed by Phil Karlson. 1957. Columbia. 81 min. Sound. 16mm B&W. *Rental:* Budget Films, Bosco Films, Inst Cinema, Kit Parker & Williams Films.

Browning Version, The. Sir Michael Redgrave, Jean Kent & Bill Travers. Directed by Anthony Asquith. 1951. Britain. 90 min. Sound. 16mm B&W. *Rental:* Budget Films, Images Film, Janus Films, Kit Parker, Learning Corp Am, Twyman Films & U of IL Film. *Sale:* Learning Corp Am.

Brubaker. Robert Redford, Yaphet Kotto & Jane Alexander. Directed by Stuart Rosenberg. 1980. Fox. 124 min. Sound. 16mm Color. *Rental:* Films Inc & Williams Films. *Rental:* Williams Films, Videotape version.

Bruce & Shao-Lin Kung-Fu: The Fierce Boxer & Bruce. 85 min. Sound. 16mm Color. *Rental:* Best Films & Video Corp..

Bruce Lee, His Last Days. Li Hsiu Hsien & Betty Ting Pei. 91 min. Sound. 16mm *Rental:* WW Enter. *Rental:* WW Enter, Videotape version.

Bruce Lee, Superdragon. Directed by Shih Ti. 1974. Cinema Shares. (Documentary). 90 min. Videotape Color. *Sale:* Blackhawk Films.

Bruce Lee: The Man & the Myth. Orig. Title: Bruce Lee, the True Story. Bruce Li & Linda Herst. Directed by Ng See Yuen. 1978. Hong Kong. 104 min. Sound. 16mm Color. *Rental:* Films Inc & Modern Sound.

Bruce Lee, the True Story *see* Bruce Lee.

Bruce Lee's Game of Death. Orig. Title: Game of Death. Bruce Lee, Gig Young & Dean Jagger. Directed by Robert Clouse. 1979. Columbia. 102 min. Sound. 16mm Color. *Rental:* Bosco Films, Budget Films, Cine Craft, Cine Craft, Films Inc, Modern Sound, Twyman Films, Welling Motion Pictures, Wholesome Film Ctr, Williams Films, Bosco Films, Swank Motion & Westcoast Films.

Bruce the Super Hero: Eighteen Weapons of Kung-Fu. Bruce Lee. 90 min. Sound. 16mm Color. .

Bruce vs. Bill. Bruce Lee. 90 min. Sound. 16mm Color. *Rental:* BF Video.

Bruder *see* Brothers.

Bruges. Directed by Mary Norman. 1978. International Film Bureau. (Documentary). 58 min. Sound. 16mm Color. *Rental:* Intl Film. *Sale:* Intl Film.

Bruges: Story of a Medieval City. 1977. 59 min. Sound. 16mm Color. *Rental:* Utah Media.

Bruno Bozzetto Music *see* Allegro Non Troppo.

Brush & Barre: The Life & Work of Toulouse-Lautrec. Directed by Linda Fowler. 1980. U. of California. (Documentary). 59 min. Sound. 16mm Color. *Rental:* U Cal Media. *Sale:* U Cal Media. *Sale:* U Cal Media, Videotape version.

Brushfire. John Ireland, Everett Sloane & Jo Morrow. Directed by Jack Warner Jr. 1962. Paramount. 80 min. Sound. 16mm Color. *Rental:* Films Inc.

Brutalization of Franz Blum, The. Burkhard Driest. Directed by Reinhard Hauff. Ger. 1975. Germany. 108 min. Sound. 16mm Color. *Rental:* New Yorker Films.

Brute & the Beast, The. Franco Nero. Directed by Lucio Fulci. 1968. Italy. 87 min. Sound. 16mm Color. dubbed. *Rental:* Westcoast Films.

Brute Force. Burt Lancaster & Hume Cronyn. Directed by Jules Dassin. 1947. Universal. 96 min. Sound. 16mm B&W. *Rental:* Ivy Films.

Brute Island. Harry Carey. Independent. 50 min. Silent. 16mm B&W. *Rental:* Em Gee Film Lib, Mogulls Films & Willoughby Peer.

Brute Machine, The. 1979. Body in Question. (Documentary). 60 min. Videotape Color. *Rental:* Films Inc & Syracuse U Film. *Sale:* Films Inc.

Brute Man, The. Rondo Hatton & Tom Neal. Directed by Jean Yarbrough. 1946. PRC. 60 min. Sound. 16mm B&W. *Sale:* Classics Assoc NY.

Bruto, El. Directed by Luis Bunuel. Span. 1952. 83 min. 16mm B&W. subtitles Eng. *Rental:* New Yorker Films.

Buccaneer, The. Yul Brynner, Charlton Heston & Claire Bloom. Directed by Anthony Quinn. 1958. Paramount. 119 min. Sound. 16mm Color. *Rental:* Films Inc.

Buccaneer's Girl. Yvonne De Carlo & Philip Friend. Directed by Frederick De Cordova. 1950. Universal. 77 min. Sound. 16mm Color. *Rental:* Swank Motion.

Buchanan Rides Alone. Randolph Scott, Craig Stevens & Barry Kelley. Directed by Budd Boetticher. 1958. Columbia. 78 min. Sound. 16mm Color. *Rental:* Budget Films, Bosco Films, Films Inc, Images Film, Kit Parker, Modern Sound, Film Ctr DC & Welling Motion Pictures.

Buck & the Preacher. Sidney Poitier, Harry Belafonte & Ruby Dee. Directed by Sidney Poitier. 1972. Columbia. 102 min. Sound. 16mm Color. *Rental:* Arcus Film, Buchan Pic, Budget Films, Cine Craft, Film Ctr DC, Films Inc, Inst Cinema, Modern Sound, Newman Film Lib, Natl Film Video, Roas Films, Swank Motion, Welling Motion Pictures & Westcoast Films.

Buck Benny Rides Again. Jack Benny. Directed by Mark Sandrich. 1940. Paramount. 86 min. Sound. 16mm B&W. *Rental:* Swank Motion.

Buck Rogers in the Twenty-Fifth Century. Gil Gerard & Pamela Hensley. Directed by Daniel Haller. 1979. Universal. 89 min. Sound. 16mm Color. *Rental:* Swank Motion & Twyman Films. *Rental:* Swank Motion, Videotape version.

Buckaroo Sheriff of Texas. Hugh O'Brien & Michael Chapin. Directed by Philip Ford. 1950. Republic. 60 min. Sound. 16mm B&W. *Rental:* Ivy Films. *Sale:* Rep Pic Film.

Bucket of Blood, A. Dick Miller, Anthony Carbone & Barboura Morris. Directed by Roger Corman. 1959. American International. 66 min. Sound. 16mm B&W. *Rental:* Ivy Films & Video Comm.

Buckley vs. Galbraith. American World. 60 min. Sound. 16mm B&W. *Rental:* BYU Media.

Buckskin. Barry Sullivan & Joan Caulfield. Directed by Michael Moore. 1968. Paramount. 97 min. Sound. 16mm Color. *Rental:* Films Inc.

Buckskin Frontier. Orig. Title: Iron Road, The. Richard Dix & Jane Wyatt. Directed by Lesley Selander. 1943. United Artists. 75 min. Sound. 16mm B&W. *Rental:* Alba House, Films Inc & Learning Corp Am. *Sale:* Learning Corp Am.

Bucktown, U. S. A. Fred Williamson & Pam Grier. Directed by Arthur Marks. 1975. American International. 94 min. Sound. 16mm Color. *Rental:* Swank Motion.

Budaya: The Performing Arts of Indonesia. 1979. PBS. (Dance). 59 min. Sound. Videotape Color. *Rental:* PBS Video. *Sale:* PBS Video.

Buddenbrooks. Liselotte Pulver & Najda Tiller. Directed by Alfred Weidenmann. Ger. 1959. Germany. 205 min. Sound. 16mm B&W. subtitles. *Rental:* Films Inc.

Buddhism. 1956. NET. (Documentary). 60 min. Sound. 16mm B&W. *Rental:* BYU Media, Syracuse U Film & Indiana AV Ctr.

Buddhism: Footprints of the Buddha India. 1978. Britain. (Documentary). 52 min. Sound. 16mm Color. *Rental:* U Cal Media.

Buddhism: The Land of the Disappearing Buddha-Japan. 1977. Britain. (Documentary). 52 min. Sound. 16mm Color. *Rental:* U Cal Media.

Buddy Buddy. Jack Lemmon, Walter Matthau & Paula Prentiss. Directed by Billy Wilder. 1981. 96 min. Sound. 16mm *Rental:* MGM United. *Rental:* MGM United, Videotape version.

Buddy Holly Story, The. Gary Busey, Don Stroud & Charles Martin Smith. Directed by Steve Rash. 1978. Columbia. 113 min. Sound. 16mm Color. *Rental:* Arcus Film, Budget Films, Images Film, Kit Parker, Swank Motion, Welling Motion Pictures, Westcoast Films & Wholesome Film Ctr. *Rental:* Swank Motion, Videotape version.

Buffalo Bill. Joel McCrea, Maureen O'Hara & Linda Darnell. Directed by William A. Wellman. 1944. Fox. 90 min. Sound. 16mm Color. *Rental:* Films Inc.

Buffalo Bill. Gordon Scott & Mario Brega. Directed by Mario Costa. 1965. Italy. 88 min. Sound. 16mm Color. dubbed. *Rental:* Charard Motion Pics & Films Inc.

Buffalo Bill & the Indians, or Sitting Bull's History Lesson. Paul Newman. Directed by Robert Altman. 1976. United Artists. 123 min. Sound. 16mm Color. *Rental:* MGM United.

Buffalo Bill in Tomahawk Territory. Clayton Moore & Chief Thundercloud. Directed by Bernard B. Ray. 1952. United Artists. 67 min. Sound. 16mm B&W. *Rental:* Budget Films.

Buffalo Bill on the U. P. Trail. Roy Stewart. Directed by Frank S. Mattison. 1926. Sunset. 60 min. Silent. 16mm B&W. *Rental:* Em Gee Film Lib, Film Classics & Willoughby Peer.

Buffalo Bill Rides Again. Richard Arlen & Jennifer Holt. Directed by Bernard B. Ray. 1947. Screen Guild. 90 min. Sound. 16mm B&W. *Rental:* Budget Films, Film Classics, Welling Motion Pictures & Westcoast Films.

Buffalo Stampede. Randolph Scott & Buster Crabbe. Directed by Henry Hathaway. 1933. Paramount. 60 min. Sound. 16mm B&W. *Rental:* Budget Films. *Sale:* Reel Images & Morcraft Films. *Sale:* Reel Images & Morcraft Films, Super 8 sound version.

Bug. Orig. Title: Hephaestus Plague, The. Bradford Dillman. Directed by Jeannot Szwarc. 1975. Paramount. 99 min. Sound. 16mm Color. *Rental:* Films Inc.

Bugle Sounds, The. Wallace Beery & Marjorie Main. Directed by S. Sylvan Simon. 1942. MGM. 101 min. Sound. 16mm B&W. *Rental:* MGM United.

Bugles in the Afternoon. Ray Milland & Forrest Tucker. Directed by Roy Rowland. 1952. Warners. 85 min. Sound. 16mm Color. *Rental:* Corinth Films.

Bugs Bunny Road Runner Movie, The. Directed by Chuck Jones. 1979. Warners. (Animated). 98 min. Sound. 16mm Color. *Rental:* Swank Motion. *Rental:* Swank Motion, Videotape version.

Bugs Bunny, Superstar. Bugs Bunny & Daffy Duck. Directed by Larry E. Jackson. 1976. Hare Raising. (Anthology). 90 min. Sound. 16mm Color. *Rental:* MGM United.

Bugs Bunny's Third Movie: One Thousand & One Rabbit Tales. 1983. Warners. (Animated). 90 min. Sound. 16mm Color. *Rental:* Swank Motion.

Bugsy Malone. Jodie Foster & Scott Baio. Directed by Alan Parker. 1976. Paramount. 93 min. Sound. 16mm Color. *Rental:* Films Inc.

Build My Gallows High *see* Out of the Past.

Building a Kayak. 2 pts. Directed by Quentin Brown. 1967. 65 min. 16mm B&W. *Rental:* Natl Film CN.

Building Bodies. 1980. Britain. (Documentary). 58 min. Sound. 16mm Color. *Rental:* Films Inc. *Sale:* Films Inc.

Building for the Future. 45 min. Sound. 16mm Color. *Rental:* Utah Media.

Building of the Bomb, The. 1967. Britain. (Documentary). 72 min. Sound. 16mm B&W. *Rental:* Time-Life Multimedia & Iowa Films. *Sale:* Time-Life Multimedia.

Building of the Capitol. 1976. Gould. (Documentary). 53 min. Sound. 16mm Color. *Rental:* Lucerne Films. *Sale:* Lucerne Films. *Sale:* Lucerne Films, Videotape version.

Building of the Earth. 1983. 55 min. Color. *Rental:* U Cal Media.

Built-In Blackout. 1969. PBS. (Documentary). 49 min. Sound. 16mm B&W. *Rental:* Indiana AV Ctr. *Sale:* Indiana AV Ctr.

Bulldog Courage. Tim McCoy & Lois January. Directed by Sam Newfield. 1935. Puritan. 55 min. Sound. 16mm B&W. *Sale:* Video Comm.

Bulldog Drummond at Bay. John Lodge. Directed by Norman Lee. 1937. Paramount. 70 min. Sound. 16mm B&W. *Rental:* Classic Film Mus. *Sale:* Classic Film Mus.

Bulldog Drummond at Bay. Ron Randell & Anita Louise. Directed by Sidney Salkow. 1947. Columbia. 70 min. Sound. 16mm B&W. *Rental:* Bosco Films.

Bulldog Drummond Comes Back. Orig. Title: Bulldog Drummond Strikes Again. John Howard & Heather Angel. Directed by Louis King. 1937. Paramount. 70 min. Sound. 16mm B&W. *Rental:* Budget Films & Classic Film Mus. *Sale:* Classic Film Mus & Morcraft Films.

Bulldog Drummond Escapes. Reginald Denny & E. E. Clive. Directed by James Hogan. 1937. Paramount. 70 min. Sound. 16mm B&W. *Rental:* Budget Films, Classic Film Mus, Janus Films & Westcoast Films. *Sale:* Morcraft Films.

Bulldog Drummond in Africa. John Howard & Heather Angel. Directed by Louis King. 1938. Paramount. 70 min. Sound. 16mm B&W. *Rental:* Classic Film Mus. *Sale:* Classic Film Mus.

Bulldog Drummond Strikes Again *see* Bulldog Drummond Comes Back.

Bulldog Drummond Strikes Back. Ron Randell & Gloria Henry. Directed by Frank McDonald. 1947. Columbia. 65 min. Sound. 16mm B&W. *Rental:* Bosco Films.

Bulldog Drummond's Bride. John Howard. Directed by James Hogan. 1939. Paramount. 65 min. Sound. 16mm B&W. *Rental:* Budget Films & Classic Film Mus. *Sale:* Classic Film Mus.

Bulldog Drummond's Peril. John Howard & Heather Angel. Directed by James Hogan. 1938. Paramount. 70 min. Sound. 16mm B&W. *Rental:* Budget Films & Classic Film Mus. *Sale:* Classic Film Mus.

Bulldog Drummond's Revenge. John Howard & Heather Angel. Directed by Louis King. 1937. Paramount. 70 min. Sound. 16mm B&W. *Rental:* Classic Film Mus & Westcoast Films. *Sale:* Classic Film Mus. *Rental:* Westcoast Films, 60 mins. version.

Bulldog Drummond's Secret Police. John Howard & Heather Angel. Directed by James Hogan. 1939. Paramount. 70 min. Sound. 16mm B&W. *Rental:* Budget Films, Classic Film Mus & Westcoast Films. *Sale:* Classic Film Mus. *Rental:* Westcoast Films, 55 mins. version.

Bulldog Edition. Orig. Title: Lady Reporter. Ray Walker & Regis Toomey. Directed by Charles Lamont. 1936. Republic. 54 min. Sound. 16mm B&W. *Rental:* Ivy Films. *Sale:* Rep Pic Film.

Bulldog Jack. Jack Hulbert & Sir Ralph Richardson. Directed by Walter Forde. 1937. Britain. 73 min. Sound. 16mm B&W. *Rental:* Budget Films, Em Gee Film Lib & Janus Films. *Sale:* Glenn Photo. *Sale:* Glenn Photo, Super 8 sound version.

Bullet Code. George O'Brien & Virginia Vale. Directed by David Howard. 1940. RKO. 58 min. Sound. 16mm *Rental:* RKO General Pics.

Bullet for a Badman. Darren McGavin & Audie Murphy. Directed by R. G. Springsteen. 1964. Universal. 80 min. Sound. 16mm Color. *Rental:* Swank Motion.

Bullet for Joey, A. Edwards G. Robinson & George Raft. Directed by Lewis Allen. 1955. United Artists. 85 min. Sound. 16mm B&W. *Rental:* MGM United.

Bullet for Pretty Boy, A. Fabian. Directed by Larry Buchanan. 1970. American International. 88 min. Sound. 16mm B&W. *Rental:* Films Inc & Westcoast Films.

Bullet in the Flesh. Rod Cameron. 1963. 85 min. Sound. 16mm Color. *Rental:* Films Inc.

Bullet Is Waiting, A. Jean Simmons & Rory Calhoun. Directed by John Farrow. 1954. Columbia. 82 min. Sound. 16mm Color. *Rental:* Maljack. *Lease:* Maljack. *Lease:* Maljack, Videotape version.

Bullet Scars. Regis Toomey & Adele Longmire. Directed by D. Ross Lederman. 1942. Warners. 59 min. Sound. 16mm B&W. *Rental:* MGM United.

Bullet Train. Sonny Chiba. 119 min. Sound. 16mm *Rental:* WW Enter. *Rental:* WW Enter, Videotape version.

Bullets & Saddles. Orig. Title: Vengeance in the Saddle. Ray Corrigan. Directed by Anthony Marshall. 1943. Monogram. 60 min. Sound. 16mm B&W. *Rental:* Film Ctr DC & Modern Sound.

Bullets Don't Argue. Rod Cameron & Dick Palmer. 1965. Italy. 96 min. Sound. 16mm Color. dubbed. *Rental:* Video Comm & Westcoast Films.

Bullets for O'Hara. Roger Pryor & Anthony Quinn. Directed by William K. Howard. 1941. Warners. 50 min. Sound. 16mm B&W. *Rental:* MGM United.

Bullets or Ballots. Edward G. Robinson & Humphrey Bogart. Directed by William Keighley. 1936. Warners. 81 min. Sound. 16mm B&W. *Rental:* MGM United.

Bullfight. Directed by Pierre Braunberger. 1956. Spain. (Documentary). 76 min. Sound. 16mm B&W. *Rental:* Budget Films.

Bullfighter & the Lady, The. Robert Stack & Gilbert Roland. Directed by Budd Boetticher. 1950. Republic. 87 min. Sound. 16mm B&W. *Rental:* Budget Films & Ivy Films. *Lease:* Rep Pic Film.

Bullfighters, The. Stan Laurel & Oliver Hardy. Directed by Mal St. Clair. 1945. Fox. 62 min. Sound. 16mm B&W. *Rental:* Films Inc.

Bull's Eye War, The. 1980. Britain. (Documentary). 50 min. Sound. 16mm Color. *Rental:* Films Inc & Syracuse U Film. *Sale:* Films Inc. *Rental:* Films Inc, *Sale:* Films Inc, Videotape version.

Bullwhip. Guy Madison & Rhonda Fleming. Directed by Harmon Jones. 1958. Allied Artists. 80 min. Sound. 16mm Color. *Rental:* Ivy Films. *Lease:* Rep Pic Film. *Rental:* Ivy Films, Anamorphic color version.

Bunco Squad. Robert Sterling & Ricardo Cortez. Directed by Herbert I. Leeds. 1950. RKO. 67 min. Sound. 16mm B&W. *Rental:* Films Inc.

Bundle of Joy. Debbie Reynolds & Eddie Fisher. Directed by Norman Taurog. 1956. RKO. 98 min. Sound. 16mm Color. *Rental:* Arcus Film, Bosco Films, Modern Sound, Video Comm & Welling Motion Pictures. *Lease:* Video Comm. *Rental:* Video Comm, Videotape version.

Bundle of Trouble, A *see* Blondie's Blessed Event.

Bungala Boys. Directed by Jim Jeffrey. 1961. Australia. (Cast unlisted). 61 min. Sound. 16mm Color. *Sale:* Lucerne Films.

Bunker Bean. Lucille Ball & Hedda Hopper. Directed by William Hamilton. 1936. RKO. 67 min. Sound. 16mm *Rental:* RKO General Pics.

Bunny Lake is Missing. Carol Lynley, Keir Dullea, Sir Laurence Olivier & Noel Coward. Directed by Otto Preminger. 1965. Columbia. 107 min. Sound. 16mm B&W. *Rental:* Bosco Films, Budget Films, Corinth Films, Films Inc, Kerr Film, Modern Sound, Swank Motion, Welling Motion Pictures, Westcoast Films & Wholesome Film Ctr. *Rental:* Corinth Films & Kit Parker, Anamorphic version.

Bunny O'Hare. Bette Davis & Ernest Borgnine. Directed by Gerd Oswald. 1971. American International. 91 min. Sound. 16mm Color. *Rental:* Swank Motion.

Buona Sera, Mrs. Campbell. Gina Lollobrigida & Phil Silvers. Directed by Melvin Frank. 1968. United Artists. 111 min. Sound. 16mm Color. *Rental:* Film Ctr DC, MGM United, Westcoast Films & Welling Motion Pictures.

Burden & the Glory of John F. Kennedy, The. 1964. CBS. (Documentary). 52 min. Sound. 16mm B&W. *Rental:* Budget Films, Syracuse U Film & U Mich Media. *Sale:* Carousel Films.

Burden of Dreams, The. Directed by Les Blank. 1982. Les Blank. (Documentary). 94 min. Sound. 16mm Color. *Rental:* Flower Films. *Sale:* Flower Films.

Burden of Truth, The. 1958. United Steel Workers. (Cast unlisted). 67 min. Sound. 16mm B&W. *Rental:* Utah Media.

Bureau of Missing Persons. Bette Davis, Pat O'Brien & Lewis Stone. Directed by Roy Del Ruth. 1933. Warners. 73 min. Sound. 16mm B&W. *Rental:* MGM United.

Burglar, The. Dan Duryea & Jayne Mansfield. Directed by Paul Wendkos. 1957. Columbia. 120 min. Sound. 16mm B&W. *Rental:* Kit Parker.

Burglars, The. Trans. Title: Casse, Le. Jean-Paul Belmondo & Dyan Cannon. Directed by Henri Verneuil. 1972. Columbia. (Anamorphic). 120 min. Sound. 16mm Color. dubbed. *Rental:* Arcus Film, Kerr Film & Welling Motion Pictures.

Buried Alive. Roland Young & Lillian Gish. Directed by Arthur Hopkins. 1933. Paramount. 67 min. Sound. 16mm B&W. *Rental:* Em Gee Film Lib. *Sale:* Classic Film Mus.

Buried Alive. Robert Wilcox & Beverly Roberts. Directed by Victor Halperin. 1940. PRC. 75 min. Sound. 16mm B&W. *Rental:* Video Comm. *Sale:* Cinema Concepts. *Rental:* Video Comm, Videotape version.

Burke & Wills. Directed by Anthony Armstrong-Jones. 1977. Britain. (Cast unlisted). 52 min. Sound. 16mm Color. *Rental:* Time-Life Multimedia. *Sale:* Time-Multimedia. *Rental:* Time-Life Multimedia, *Sale:* Time-Life Multimedia, Videotape version.

Burks of Georgia, The. Directed by Albert Maysles & David Maysles. 1976. Group W. (Documentary). 59 min. Sound. 16mm Color. *Rental:* U Cal Media, Iowa Films, U Mich Media & Syracuse U Film. *Sale:* Carousel Films. *Sale:* Carousel Films, Videotape version.

Burma: Buddhism & Neutralism. 1957. McGraw-Hill. (Documentary). 55 min. Sound. 16mm B&W. *Rental:* U Mich Media.

Burmese Harp, The. Orig. Title: Harp of Burma. Shoji Yasui & Rentara Mikuni. Directed by Kon Ichikawa. Jap. 1956. Japan. 116 min. Sound. 16mm B&W. subtitles. *Rental:* Budget Films & Films Inc.

Burn! Marlon Brando. Directed by Gillo Pontecorvo. 1970. United Artists. 112 min. Sound. 16mm Color. *Rental:* MGM United.

Burn 'em Up Barnes. Johnny Hines & J. Barney Sherry. Directed by George Beranger. 1921. Burr. 65 min. Silent. 16mm B&W. *Sale:* Blackhawk Films. *Sale:* Blackhawk Films, Silent 8mm version.

Burn 'em Up O'Connor. Dennis O'Keefe & Cecelia Parker. Directed by Edward Sedgwick. 1939. MGM. 70 min. Sound. 16mm B&W. *Rental:* MGM United.

Burn, Witch, Burn. Orig. Title: Night of the Eagle. Janet Blair & Peter Wyngarde. Directed by Sidney Hayers. Britain. 90 min. Sound. 16mm B&W. *Rental:* Budget Films, Ivy Films, Video Comm, Westcoast Films, Wholesome Film Ctr & Willoughby Peer.

Burning Arrows *see* Captain John Smith & Pocahontas.

Burning Cross, The. Hank Daniels & Virginia Patton. Directed by Walter Colmes. 1947. Screen Guild. 79 min. Sound. 16mm B&W. *Rental:* Ivy Films.

Burning Gold. William Boyd & Irene Ware. Directed by Sam Newfield. 1935. Winchester. 65 min. Sound. 16mm B&W. *Rental:* Wholesome Film Ctr.

Burnout. Mark Schneider & Robert Louden. Directed by Graham Meech-Burkestone. 1979. Crown. 90 min. Sound. 16mm Color. *Rental:* Films Inc.

Burnt Offerings. Bette Davis, Karen Black & Oliver Reed. Directed by Dan Curtis. 1973. United Artists. 116 min. Sound. 16mm Color. *Rental:* Films Inc, MGM United & Welling Motion Pictures.

Bury Me Dead. June Lockhart & Cathy O'Donnell. Directed by Bernard Vorhaus. 1947. Eagle Lion. 70 min. Sound. 16mm B&W. *Sale:* Classics Assoc NY.

Bus, The. Directed by Haskell Wexler. 1965. Harrison. 62 min. Sound. 16mm B&W. *Rental:* Films Inc.

Bus Ride Through the Night. 1969. (Cast unlisted). 50 min. Sound. 16mm B&W. *Sale:* Japan Society. *Sale:* Japan Society, Color version. *Sale:* Japan Society, Subtitled version. *Sale:* Japan Society, Videotape version.

Bus Stop. Orig. Title: Wrong Kind of Girl. Marilyn Monroe & Don Murray. Directed by Joshua Logan. 1956. Fox. 94 min. Sound. 16mm Color. *Rental:* Films Inc, Twyman Films & Williams Films. *Rental:* Films Inc, Anamorphic color version. *Rental:* Williams Films, Videotape version.

Bush Country Adventure. Chips Rafferty. 1947. Australia. 64 min. Sound. 16mm B&W. *Rental:* Inst Cinema & Wholesome Film Ctr.

Bush Mama. Directed by Haile Gerima. 1975. Tricontinental. (Documentary). 96 min. Sound. 16mm B&W. *Rental:* Unifilm. *Sale:* Unifilm.

Bush Pilot. Jack La Rue & Rochelle Hudson. Directed by Stanley Campbell. 1947. Screen Guild. 67 min. Sound. 16mm B&W. *Rental:* Mogulls Films.

Bushbaby, The. Margaret Brooks & Louis Gossett. Directed by John Trent. 1970. MGM. 100 min. Sound. 16mm Color. *Rental:* MGM United.

Busher, The. Charles Ray, Colleen Moore & John Gilbert. Directed by Jerome Storm. 1919. Paramount. 45 min. Silent. 8mm B&W. *Sale:* Blackhawk Films.

Bushmen of the Kalahari. 1974. National Geographic. (Documentary). 52 min. Sound. 16mm Color. *Sale:* Natl Geog. *Rental:* Iowa Films & Natl Geog. *Sale:* Natl Geog, Videotape version.

Bushwackers, The. Orig. Title: Rebel, The. Dorothy Malone & John Ireland. Directed by Rod Amateau. 1951. Realart. 60 min. Sound. 16mm B&W. *Rental:* Budget Films.

Business of America, The. 1984. 45 min. Sound. 16mm Color. *Rental:* U Mich Media.

Business of Extinction, The. 1978. 58 min. Sound. Videotape *Rental:* PBS Video. *Sale:* PBS Video.

Busing: Some Voices from the South. 1977. Edupac. (Documentary). 50 min. Sound. 16mm Color. *Rental:* Edupac. *Sale:* Edupac.

Busses Roar. Richard Travis, Eleanor Parker & Julie Bishop. Directed by D. Ross Lederman. 1942. Warners. 60 min. Sound. 16mm B&W. *Rental:* MGM United.

Buster & Billie. Jan-Michael Vincent & Pamela Sue Martin. Directed by Daniel Petrie. 1974. Columbia. 98 min. Sound. 16mm Color. *Rental:* Budget Films, Films Inc, Ivy Films, Kit Parker, Swank Motion, Welling Motion Pictures, Westcoast Films & Wholesome Film Ctr.

Buster Keaton Rides Again. Directed by John Spotton. 1965. Canada. (Documentary). 55 min. Sound. 16mm B&W. *Rental:* Budget Films, Kit Parker, Natl Film CN, McGraw-Hill Films, Syracuse U Film, U Cal Media, U Mich Media & Westcoast Films. *Sale:* McGraw-Hill Films & Natl Film CN.

Buster Keaton Story, The. Donald O'Connor & Rhonda Fleming. Directed by Sidney Sheldon. 1957. Paramount. 91 min. Sound. 16mm B&W. *Rental:* Films Inc.

Buster Keaton: The Great Shorts. Ivy. (Anthology). 55 min. Videotape B&W. *Sale:* Ivy Films.

Bustin' Loose. Richard Pryor & Cicely Tyson. Directed by Oz Scott. 1981. Universal. 94 min. Sound. 16mm Color. *Rental:* Swank Motion. *Rental:* Swank Motion, Videotape version.

Busting. Elliot Gould & Robert Blake. Directed by Peter Hyams. 1974. United Artists. 92 min. Sound. 16mm Color. *Rental:* MGM United, Westcoast Films, Welling Motion Pictures & Wholesome Film Ctr.

Busy Body, The. Sid Caesar & Robert Ryan. Directed by William Castle. 1967. Paramount. (Anamorphic). 101 min. Sound. 16mm Color. *Rental:* Films Inc.

But Is This Progress? 1974. NBC. (Documentary). 51 min. Sound. 16mm Color. *Rental:* Films Inc & U Mich Media. *Sale:* Films Inc. *Sale:* Films Inc, Videotape version.

But Not for Me. Clark Gable & Carroll Baker. Directed by Walter Lang. 1959. Paramount. 105 min. Sound. 16mm B&W. *Rental:* Films Inc.

But Not in Vain. Raymond Lovell. Directed by Edmond Greville. 1952. 74 min. 16mm *Rental:* A Twyman Pres.

But the Flesh Is Weak. Robert Montgomery & C. Aubrey Smith. Directed by Jack Conway. 1932. MGM. 82 min. Sound. 16mm B&W. *Rental:* MGM United.

But Then, She's Betty Carter. Directed by Michelle Parkerson. 1980. Women Make Movies. (Documentary). 53 min. Sound. 16mm Color. *Rental:* Women Movies. *Sale:* Women Movies.

But What If the Dream Comes True? 1972. CBS. (Documentary). 52 min. Sound. 16mm Color. *Rental:* Iowa Films, Roas Films & U Mich Media. *Sale:* Carousel Films.

Butch & Sundance: The Early Days. William Katt & Tom Berenger. Directed by Richard Lester. 1979. Fox. 107 min. Sound. 16mm Color. *Rental:* Films Inc.

Butch Cassidy & the Sundance Kid. Paul Newman & Robert Redford. Directed by George Roy Hill. 1969. Fox. (Anamorphic). 112 min. Sound. 16mm Color. *Rental:* Films Inc.

Butcher, The see Boucher.

Butcher, Baker, Nightmare Maker. Bo Svenson & Jimmy McNichol. Directed by William Asher. 1980. Comworld. 96 min. Sound. 16mm Color. *Rental:* Swank Motion.

Butler's Dilemma, The. Hermione Gingold. Directed by Leslie Hiscott. 1944. Britain. 72 min. Sound. 16mm B&W. *Rental:* Ivy Films. *Sale:* Rep Pic Film.

Butley. Alan Bates. Directed by Harold Pinter. 1973. AFT. 129 min. Sound. 16mm Color. *Rental:* Films Inc.

Butterfield Eight. Elizabeth Taylor & Laurence Harvey. Directed by Daniel Mann. 1960. MGM. 109 min. Sound. 16mm Color. *Rental:* MGM United. *Rental:* MGM United, Anamorphic color version. *Rental:* MGM United, Videotape version.

Butterflies Are Free. Goldie Hawn, Edward Albert & Eileen Heckart. Directed by Milton Katselas. 1972. Columbia. 109 min. Sound. 16mm Color. *Rental:* Arcus Film, Bosco Films, Buchan Pic, Budget Films, Cine Craft, Films Inc, Images Film, Inst Cinema, Ivy Films, Natl Film Video, Swank Motion, Twyman Films, U of IL Film, Welling Motion Pictures, Westcoast Films & Williams Films, Videotape version.

Butterflies in Perspective. 1981. Britain. (Documentary). 108 min. Sound. 16mm Color. *Rental:* Films Inc. *Sale:* Films Inc. *Rental:* Films Inc, *Sale:* Films Inc, Videotape version.

Butterfly Affair, The. Claudia Cardinale & Stanley Baker. Directed by Jean Herman. 1970. France-Italy. 100 min. Sound. 16mm Color. *Rental:* Swank Motion.

Buy Low, Sell High. 1966. Canada. (Documentary). 58 min. Sound. 16mm B&W. *Sale:* Natl Film CN. *Rental:* Natl Film CN.

Buzzy Rides the Range see Western Terror.

Bwana Toshi. Kiyoshi Atsumi & Tsutomu Shimomoto. Directed by Susumi Hani. Jap. 1965. Toho. 115 min. Sound. 16mm B&W. subtitles Eng. *Rental:* Films Inc.

By a Jury of His Peers. 1979. PBS. (Documentary). 59 min. Videotape Color. *Rental:* PBS Video. *Sale:* PBS Video.

By Any Other Name. William Shatner & Leonard Nimoy. 1968. Star Trek. 52 min. Sound. 16mm Color. *Sale:* Morcraft Films. *Sale:* Morcraft Films, Super 8 sound version.

By Candlelight. Elissa Landi & Paul Lucas. Directed by James Whale. 1934. Universal. 70 min. Sound. 16mm B&W. *Rental:* Swank Motion.

By Hook or by Crook *see* I Dood It.

By Right of Purchase. Norma Talmadge. Directed by Charles Miller. 1918. 16mm *Rental:* A Twyman Pres.

By the Blood of Others. Mariangela Melato. Directed by Marc Simenon. Fr. France. 90 min. Sound. 16mm Color. subtitles. *Rental:* J Green Pics. *Sale:* Tamarelles French Film, Videotape version.

By the Law. Trans. Title: Po Zakonu. Sergei Komarov. Directed by Lev Kuleshov. 1926. Russia. 85 min. Sound. 16mm B&W. *Rental:* Budget Films, Em Gee Film Lib, Kit Parker & Museum Mod Art. *Sale:* Glenn Photo. *Sale:* Glenn Photo, Super 8 silent version.

By the People. Directed by Bill Mahin. 1970. Film Images. (Documentary). 81 min. Sound. 16mm B&W. *Rental:* Film Images. *Sale:* Film Images.

By Your Leave. Betty Grable & Gene Lockhart. Directed by Pandro S. Berman. 1935. RKO. 82 min. Sound. 16mm *Rental:* RKO General Pics.

Bye, Bye Birdie. Dick Van Dyke & Janet Leigh. Directed by George Sidney. 1963. Columbia. 111 min. Sound. 16mm Color. *Rental:* Arcus Film, Bosco Films, Budget Films, Cine Craft, Charard Motion Pics, Film Pres, Films Inc, Inst Cinema, Kit Parker, Natl Film Video, Newman Film Lib, Roas Films, Twyman Films, U of IL Film, Welling Motion Pictures, Westcoast Films, Wholesome Film Ctr & Willoughby Peer. *Rental:* Kit Parker, Anamorphic version.

Bye, Bye Braverman. George Segal & Alan King. Directed by Sidney Lumet. 1968. Warners. 94 min. Sound. 16mm Color. *Rental:* Arcus Film.

Bye, Bye Brazil. Jose Wilker. Directed by Carlos Diegues. 1980. Unifilm. 110 min. Sound. 16mm Color. *Rental:* New Yorker Films.

Bye, See You Monday: Au Revoir, A Lundi. Miou Miou. Directed by Maurice Dugowson. Fr. 1979. Canada. 110 min. Sound. 16mm Color. subtitles. *Rental:* Natl Film CN. *Sale:* Natl Film CN.

C. C. & Company. Ann-Margaret & Joe Namath. Directed by Seymour Robbie. 1970. Embassy. 94 min. Sound. 16mm B&W. *Rental:* Films Inc.

C-Man. Dean Jagger & John Carradine. Directed by Joseph Lerner. 1949. Film Classics. 80 min. Sound. 16mm B&W. *Rental:* Mogulls Films.

Ca Ira *see* Thermidor.

Caballo del Pueblo, El. Span. 1950. Mexico. (Cast unlisted). 90 min. Sound. 16mm B&W. *Rental:* Film Classics.

Cabaret. Liza Minnelli & Joel Gray. Directed by Bob Fosse. 1972. Allied Artists. 123 min. Sound. 16mm Color. *Rental:* Hurlock Cine.

Cabeza Viviente, La *see* Living Head.

Cabezas Cortadas. Directed by Glauber Rocha. Port. 1970. Brazil. (Cast unlisted). 90 min. Sound. 16mm Color. *Rental:* New Yorker Films.

Cabin in the Cotton. Richard Barthelmess & Bette Davis. Directed by Michael Curtiz. 1932. Warners. 79 min. Sound. 16mm B&W. *Rental:* MGM United.

Cabin in the Sky. Ethel Waters & Lena Horne. Directed by Vincente Minnelli. 1943. MGM. 100 min. Sound. 16mm B&W. *Rental:* MGM United.

Cabinet of Caligari, The. Dan O'Herlihy & Glynis Johns. Directed by Roger Kay. 1962. Fox. (Anamorphic). 104 min. Sound. 16mm B&W. *Rental:* Films Inc.

Cabinet of Dr. Caligari, The. Werner Krauss, Conrad Veidt & Lil Dagover. Directed by Robert Weine. 1920. Germany. 72 min. Sound. 16mm B&W. *Rental:* Willoughby Peer, Creative Film, Film Images, Images Film, Ivy Films, Iowa Films, Janus Films, Kerr Film, Kit Parker, Maljack, Natl Film Video, SD AV Ctr, Swank Motion, Syracuse U Film, U Cal Media, U Mich Media, Utah Media, Westcoast Films & Wholesome Film Ctr. *Sale:* Cinema Concepts, Griggs Movie, Images Film, Natl Cinema & Reel Images. *Rental:* Budget Films, Em Gee Film Lib, Films Inc, Mogulls Films, Museum Mod Art, Twyman Films, Video Comm, Wholesome Film Ctr & Classic Film Mus, *Sale:* Em Gee Film Lib, Glenn Photo & Classic Film Mus, Silent 16mm version. *Sale:* Reel Images, Super 8 sound version. *Rental:* Ivy Films, *Sale:* Blackhawk Films, Em Gee Film Lib & Glenn Photo, Super 8 silent version. *Rental:* Em Gee Film Lib, Maljack & Video Comm, *Sale:* Images Film & Tamarelles French Film, Videotape version. *Rental:* Utah Media, 92 mins. version. *Sale:* Festival Films, *Rental:* A Twyman Pres, 52 min. sound 16mm version. *Sale:* Festival Films, 52 min. Videotape version.

Cabiria. Almirante Manzini. Directed by Giovanni Pastrone. 1914. Italy. 116 min. Silent. 16mm B&W. *Rental:* Museum Mod Art.

Cactus Flower. Ingrid Bergman & Walter Matthau. Directed by Gene Saks. 1969. Columbia. 103 min. Sound. 16mm Color. *Rental:* Arcus Film, Buchan Pic, Bosco Films, Budget Films, Cine Craft, Films Inc, Ivy Films, Modern Sound, Natl Film Video, Newman Film Lib, Twyman Films, Video Comm, Welling Motion Pictures, Westcoast Films, Wholesome Film Ctr & Willoughby Peer.

Cactus in the Snow. Richard Thomas & Mary Layne. Directed by Martin Zweiback. 1972. General. 90 min. Sound. 16mm Color. *Rental:* Hurlock Cine.

Cactus Kid, The. Jack Perrin. 1934. Commodore. 60 min. Sound. 16mm B&W. *Rental:* Mogulls Films.

Caddie. Helen Morse & Jack Thompson. Directed by Donald Crombie. 1981. Australia. 102 min. Sound. 16mm Color. *Rental:* Ivy Films.

Caddy, The. Jerry Lewis & Dean Martin. Directed by Norman Taurog. 1953. Paramount. 95 min. Sound. 16mm B&W. *Rental:* Films Inc. *Sale:* Morcraft Films, Super 8 sound version.

Caddyshack. Bill Murray & Chevy Chase. Directed by Harold Ramis. 1980. Orion. 107 min. Sound. 16mm Color. *Rental:* Films Inc.

Cadets on Parade. Freddie Bartholomew & Jimmy Lydon. Directed by Lew Landers. 1942. Columbia. 80 min. Sound. 16mm B&W. *Rental:* Mogulls Films.

Caesar & Cleopatra. Vivien Leigh & Claude Rains. Directed by Gabriel Pascal. 1946. Britain. 127 min. Sound. Videotape Color. *Sale:* Films Inc, Janus Films & Vidamerica.

Cafe Colon. Maria Felix & Pedro Armendariz. Directed by Benito Alazraki. Span. 1960. Mexico. 81 min. Sound. 16mm B&W. *Rental:* Trans-World Films.

Cafe Hostess. Preston Foster & Ann Dvorak. Directed by Sidney Salkow. 1939. Columbia. 63 min. Sound. 16mm B&W. *Rental:* Kit Parker.

Cage aux Folles, La. Ugo Tognazzi & Michel Serrault. Directed by Edouard Molinaro. Fr. 1979. 91 min. 16mm Color. subtitles. *Rental:* MGM United. *Rental:* MGM United, Videotape version.

Cage Aux Folles II, La. Orig. Title: Birds of a Feather. Ugo Tognazzi & Michel Serrault. Directed by Edouard Molinaro. Fr. 1981. France. 99 min. Sound. 16mm Color. subtitles. *Rental:* MGM United. *Rental:* MGM United, Videotape version.

Cage of Evil. Ronald Foster. Directed by Edward L. Cahn. 1960. United Artists. 70 min. Sound. 16mm B&W. *Rental:* MGM United.

Cage of Gold. Jean Simmons & David Farrar. Directed by Basil Dearden. 1951. Britain. 80 min. Sound. 16mm B&W. *Rental:* Janus Films.

Caged Fury. Buster Crabbe & Richard Denning. Directed by William Berke. 1948. Paramount. 60 min. Sound. 16mm B&W. *Rental:* Bosco Films.

Caged Heat. Barbara Steele. Directed by Jonathan Demme. 1974. New World. 83 min. Sound. 16mm Color. *Rental:* Films Inc.

Caged Women. Trans. Title: Maison Des Femmes, La. Eva Dahlbeck. Directed by Hampe Faustman. Swed. 1952. Sweden. 89 min. Sound. 16mm B&W. subtitles. *Rental:* Film Classics.

Cagliostro see Black Magic.

Cahill, United States Marshall. John Wayne & Gary Grimes. Directed by Andrew V. McLaglen. 1973. 103 min. Sound. Videotape Color. *Sale:* Tamarelles French Films.

Cain & Mabel. Clark Gable & Marion Davies. Directed by Lloyd Bacon. 1936. Warners. 89 min. Sound. 16mm B&W. *Rental:* MGM United.

Caine Mutiny, The. Humphrey Bogart, Jose Ferrer & Van Johnson. Directed by Edward Dmytryk. 1954. Columbia. 125 min. Sound. 16mm Color. *Rental:* Arcus Film, Bosco Films, Buchan Pics, Budget Films, Cine Craft, Charard Motion Pics, Film Ctr DC, Film Pres, Films Inc, Hurlock Cine, Images Film, Ivy Films, Kit Parker, Modern Sound, Natl Film Video, Roas Films, Swank Motion, Syracuse U Film, Twyman Films, U of IL Film, Video Comm, Welling Motion Pictures, Westcoast Films, Wholesome Film Ctr & Williams Films.

Cairo. Jeanette MacDonald & Robert Young. Directed by W. S. Van Dyke II. 1942. MGM. 101 min. Sound. 16mm B&W. *Rental:* MGM United.

Cairo. Richard Johnson & George Sanders. Directed by Wolf Rilla. 1963. Britain. 91 min. Sound. 16mm B&W. *Rental:* MGM United.

Calamity Jane. Doris Day & Howard Keel. Directed by David Butler. 1953. Warners. 101 min. Sound. 16mm Color. *Rental:* Charard Motion Pics, Films Inc, Modern Sound & Twyman Films.

Calamity the Cow. John Moulder-Brown. Directed by David Eastman. 1963. Britain. 55 min. Sound. 16mm B&W. *Sale:* Lucerne Films.

Calcutta. Directed by Louis Malle. Hindi. 1969. India. (Documentary). 115 min. Sound. 16mm Color. subtitles. *Rental:* Budget Films, Images Film, Pyramid Film, Swank Motion, Twyman Films, U of IL Film & Willoughby Peer. *Sale:* Images Film, Pyramid Film & Twyman Films. *Sale:* Tamarelles French Film, Videotape version.

Calendar Girl. Gail Patrick & Victor McLaglen. Directed by Allan Dwan. 1947. Republic. 88 min. Sound. 16mm B&W. *Rental:* Ivy Films. *Sale:* Rep Pic Film.

California. Ray Milland & Barbara Stanwyck. Directed by John Farrow. 1946. Paramount. 98 min. Sound. 16mm B&W. *Rental:* Swank Motion.

California Conquest. Cornel Wilde & Teresa Wright. Directed by Lew Landers. 1952. Columbia. 79 min. Sound. 16mm Color. *Rental:* Welling Motion Pictures.

California Dreaming. Glynnis O'Connor & Seymour Cassel. Directed by John Hancock. 1979. American International. 92 min. Sound. 16mm Color. *Rental:* Swank Motion.

California Firebrand. Monte Hale. Directed by Philip Ford. 1946. Republic. 63 min. Sound. 16mm B&W. *Rental:* Ivy Films. *Sale:* Rep Pic Film.

California Gold Rush. Bill Elliott. Directed by R. G. Springsteen. 1946. Republic. 54 min. Sound. 16mm B&W. *Rental:* Ivy Films & Rep Pic Film. *Sale:* Rep Pic film, Videotape version.

California Gold Rush. John Dehner & Henry Jones. Directed by Jack Hively. 1979. Viacom. 98 min. Sound. 16mm Color. *Rental:* Williams Films & Modern Sound. *Sale:* Lucerne Films. *Sale:* Lucerne Films, 48 min. version. *Sale:* Lucerne Films, 98 or 48 min. Videotape version. *Rental:* Williams Films, 98 min. Videotape version.

California in Forty Nine. Neva Gerber & Ed Cobb. Directed by Jacques Jaccard. 1925. Arrow. 60 min. Silent. 8mm B&W. *Sale:* Morcraft Films.

California in 1878 see Fightin' Thru.

California Joe. Don Barry. Directed by Spencer G. Bennett. 1943. Republic. 55 min. Sound. 16mm B&W. *Rental:* Ivy Films. *Sale:* Rep Pic Film.

California Mail. Dick Foran. Directed by Noel Smith. 1936. Warners. 56 min. Sound. 16mm B&W. *Rental:* MGM United.

California Passage. Forrest Tucker. Directed by Joseph Kane. 1950. Republic. 90 min. Sound. 16mm B&W. *Rental:* Ivy Films. *Sale:* Rep Pic Film.

California Reich, The. Directed by Walter F. Parkes & Keith Critchlow. 1976. RBC. 60 min. Sound. 16mm Color. *Rental:* Films Inc.

California Split. George Segal, Elliott Gould & Gwen Welles. Directed by Robert Altman. 1974. Columbia. 108 min. Sound. 16mm Color. *Rental:* Arcus Film, Cine Craft, Corinth Films, Films Inc, Inst Cinema, Ivy Films, Natl Film Video, Syracuse U Film, Twyamn Films, U of IL Film, Welling Motion Pictures, Westcoast Films, Wholesome Film Ctr, Budget Films & Kit Parker. *Rental:* Corinth Films, Kit Parker, Twyman Films & Images Film, Anamorphic version.

California Straight Ahead. Reginald Denny & Gertrude Olmstead. Directed by Harry Pollard. 1925. Universal. 80 min. Silent. Super 8 B&W. *Sale:* Cinema Concepts.

California Straight Ahead. John Wayne & Louise Latimer. Directed by Arthur Lubin. 1937. Universal. 67 min. Sound. 16mm B&W. *Rental:* Swank Motion.

California Suite. Alan Alda, Jane Fonda, Maggie Smith & Walter Matthau. Directed by Herbert Ross. 1978. Columbia. 103 min. Sound. 16mm Color. *Rental:* Arcus Film, Budget Films, Films Inc, Images Film, Modern Sound, Swank Motion, Twyman Films, Welling Motion Pictures & Wholesome Films Ctr. *Rental:* Swank Motion, Videotape version.

California Trail. Buck Jones. Directed by Lambert Hillyer. 1933. Columbia. 60 min. Sound. 16mm B&W. *Rental:* Willoughby Peer.

Californian, The. Orig. Title: Beyond the Law. Ricardo Cortez & Marjorie Weaver. Directed by Gus Meins. 1937. Fox. 77 min. Sound. 16mm B&W. *Rental:* Mogulls Films.

Caligari's Cure. Directed by Tom Palazzolo. 1982. 70 min. Sound. 16mm Color. *Rental:* Canyon Cinema.

Caligula. Malcom McDowell & Teresa Ann Savoy. Directed by Bob Guccione. 1979. 143 min. Sound. Videotape Color. *Sale:* Tamarelles French Film.

Call Harry Crown *see* Ninety-Nine & Forty-Four One-Hundred Percent Dead.

Call Her Savage. Clara Bow & Gilbert Roland. Directed by John Francis Dillon. 1932. Fox. 88 min. Sound. 16mm B&W. *Rental:* Films Inc.

Call Him Mr. Shatter. Stuart Whitman & Peter Cushing. Directed by Michael Carreras. 1975. Embassy. 90 min. Sound. 16mm Color. *Rental:* Films Inc.

Call It a Day. Olivia De Havilland & Ian Hunter. Directed by Archie Mayo. 1937. Warners. 89 min. Sound. 16mm B&W. *Rental:* MGM United.

Call It Murder. Orig. Title: Midnight. Humphrey Bogart & Henry Hull. Directed by Chester Erskine. 1934. Guaranteed. 72 min. Sound. 16mm B&W. *Rental:* Budget Films, Classic Film Mus & Video Comm. *Sale:* Blackhawk Films, Classic Film Mus & Morcraft Films. *Sale:* Blackhawk Films & Video Comm, Super 8 sound version. *Sale:* Blackhawk Films, Videotape version.

Call Me Bwana. Bob Hope & Anita Ekberg. Directed by Gordon Douglas. 1963. United Artists. 103 min. Sound. 16mm Color. *Rental:* MGM United.

Call Me Genius. Orig. Title: Rebel, The. Tony Hancock. Directed by Robert Day. 1961. Britain. 105 min. Sound. 16mm Color. *Rental:* Films Inc.

Call Me Madam. Ethel Merman & Donald O'Connor. Directed by Walter Lang. 1953. Fox. 115 min. Sound. 16mm Color. *Rental:* Films Inc.

Call Me Mister. Betty Grable & Dan Dailey. Directed by Lloyd Bacon. 1951. Fox. 96 min. Sound. 16mm Color. *Rental:* Films Inc.

Call Northside Seven Seven-Seven. James Stewart & Lee J. Cobb. Directed by Henry Hathaway. 1948. Fox. 111 min. Sound. 16mm B&W. *Rental:* Films Inc.

Call of the Blood. Lea Padovani. Directed by John Clements. 1948. 88 min. 16mm *Rental:* A Twyman Pres.

Call of the Canyon. Gene Autry. Directed by Joseph Santley. 1942. Republic. 54 min. Sound. 16mm B&W. *Rental:* Ivy Films. *Sale:* Blackhawk Films. *Sale:* Blackhawk Films, Super 8 sound version. *Sale:* Blackhawk Films, Videotape version.

Call of the Flesh. Ramon Navarro & Dorothy Jordan. Directed by Charles Brabin. 1930. MGM. 100 min. Sound. 16mm B&W. *Rental:* MGM United.

Call of the Forest. Ken Curtis & Robert Lowery. Directed by John F. Link. 1949. Lippert. 75 min. Sound. 16mm B&W. *Rental:* Alba House, Budget Films & Willoughby Peer.

Call of the Klondike. Dorothy Dawn & Gaston Glass. Directed by Oscar Apfel. 1926. Rayart. 45 min. Silent. 16mm B&W. *Rental:* Mogulls Films & Willoughby Peer.

Call of the Klondike. Kirby Grant & Anne Gwynne. Directed by Frank McDonald. 1950. Monogram. 70 min. Sound. 16mm B&W. *Rental:* Hurlock Cine.

Call of the Navajo. 1952. Films of Christ. (Cast Unlisted). 45 min. Sound. 16mm Color. *Rental:* Roas Films.

Call of the Prairie. William Boyd. Directed by Howard Bretherton. 1936. Paramount. 64 min. Sound. 16mm B&W. *Lease:* Cinema Concepts.

Call of the Ring, The *see* Duke Comes Back.

Call of the Rockies. Sunset Carson. Directed by Lesley Selander. 1944. Republic. 56 min. Sound. 16mm B&W. *Rental:* Ivy Films. *Sale:* Rep Pic Film.

Call of the Savage *see* Savage Fury.

Call of the South Seas. William Henry & Adele Mara. Directed by John English. 1944. Republic. 60 min. Sound. 16mm B&W. *Rental:* Ivy Films.

Call of the Wild. Clark Gable & Loretta Young. Directed by William A. Wellman. 1935. United Artists. 78 min. Sound. 16mm B&W. *Rental:* Films Inc & Twyman Films. *Rental:* Westcoast Films, 102 mins. version.

Call of the Wild, The. Charlton Heston & Michele Mercier. Directed by Ken Annakin. 1972. 102 min. Sound. 16mm Color. *Rental:* Budget Films.

Call of the Yukon. Richard Arlen. Directed by B. Reeves Eason. 1938. Republic. 75 min. Sound. 16mm B&W. *Rental:* Ivy Films. *Sale:* Rep Pic Film.

Call Out the Marines. Victor Mature & Edmund Lowe. Directed by Frank Ryan. 1942. RKO. 69 min. Sound. 16mm B&W. *Rental:* Films Inc.

Call the Mesquiteers. Orig. Title: Outlaws of the West. Robert Livingston, Ray Corrigan & Max Terhune. Directed by John English. 1938. Republic. 54 min. Sound. 16mm B&W. *Rental:* Ivy Films. *Sale:* Rep Pic Film.

Call to Arms. 1981. 50 min. Sound. 16mm Color. *Rental:* U Mich Media.

Callan. Edward Woodward. Directed by Don Sharp. 1974. Britain. 106 min. Sound. 16mm Color. *Rental:* Budget Films. *Sale:* Natl Cinema.

Callaway Went Thataway. Orig. Title: Star Said No, The. Fred MacMurray & Dorothy McGuire. Directed by Norman Panama & Melvin Frank. 1951. MGM. 82 min. Sound. 16mm B&W. *Rental:* MGM United.

Called Back. Franklin Dyall. Directed by Reginald Denham & Jack Harris. 1933. Britain. 50 min. Sound. 16mm B&W. *Rental:* Ivy Films.

Calling All Husbands. Ernest Truex & George Tobias. Directed by Noel Smith. 1940. Warners. 64 min. Sound. 16mm B&W. *Rental:* MGM United.

Calling All Marines. Don Barry & Helen Mack. Directed by John H. Auer. 1940. Republic. 71 min. Sound. 16mm B&W. *Rental:* Ivy Films.

Calling Bulldog Drummond. Walter Pidgeon & Margaret Leighton. Directed by Victor Saville. 1951. MGM. 80 min. Sound. 16mm B&W. *Rental:* MGM United.

Calling Dr. Death. Lon Chaney Jr. & J. Carroll Naish. Directed by Reginald Le Borg. 1943. Universal. 68 min. Sound. 16mm B&W. *Rental:* Swank Motion.

Calling Dr. Gillespie. Lionel Barrymore & Donna Reed. Directed by Harold S. Bucquet. 1942. MGM. 84 min. Sound. 16mm B&W. *Rental:* MGM United.

Calling Dr. Kildare. Lew Ayres & Lionel Barrymore. Directed by Harold S. Bucquet. 1939. MGM. 86 min. Sound. 16mm B&W. *Rental:* MGM United.

Calling Homicide. Bill Elliott. Directed by Edward Bernds. 1956. Allied Artists. 61 min. Sound. 16mm B&W. *Rental:* Hurlock Cine.

Calling of Dan Matthews, The. Richard Arlen & Donald Cook. Directed by Phil Rosen. 1936. Columbia. 70 min. Sound. 16mm B&W. *Rental:* Mogulls Films.

Calling Philo Vance. James Stephenson. Directed by William Clemens. 1940. Warners. 62 min. Sound. 16mm B&W. *Rental:* MGM United.

Calling Wild Bill Elliott. Bill Elliott. Directed by Spencer G. Bennett. 1943. Republic. 55 min. Sound. 16mm B&W. *Rental:* Ivy Films. *Sale:* Rep Pic Film & Nostalgia Merchant.

Calm Prevails Over the Country. Directed by Peter Lilienthal. Ger. 1976. Germany. (Cast unlisted). 100 min. Sound. 16mm Color. subtitles. *Rental:* New Yorker Films.

Calm Yourself. Robert Young & Madge Evans. Directed by George B. Seitz. 1935. MGM. 71 min. Sound. 16mm B&W. *Rental:* MGM United.

Calmos *see* Femmes Fatales.

Calypso Joe. Herb Jeffries & Angie Dickinson. Directed by Edward Dein. 1957. Allied Artists. 76 min. Sound. 16mm B&W. *Rental:* Hurlock Cine.

Camelot. Richard Harris, Vanessa Redgrave & Franco Nero. Directed by Joshua Logan. 1967. Warners. 158 min. Sound. 16mm Color. *Rental:* Swank Motion & Williams Films. *Rental:* Swank Motion, Anamorphic color version. *Rental:* Swank Motion, Videotape version.

Camels & the Pitjantjara. 1971. Australia. (Documentary). 57 min. Sound. 16mm Color. *Rental:* U Cal Media. *Sale:* U Cal Media.

Camels West *see* Southwest Passage.

Camera Buff. Jerzy Stuhr. Directed by Krzysztof Kieslowski. Pol. 1980. Poland. 112 min. Sound. 16mm Color. subtitles. *Rental:* New Yorker Films.

Cameraman, The. Buster Keaton & Marceline Day. Directed by Edward Sedgwick. 1928. MGM. 69 min. Silent. 16mm B&W. *Rental:* MGM United.

Camille. Rudolph Valentino & Alla Nazimova. Directed by Ray Smallwood. 1921. MGM. 63 min. Silent. 16mm B&W. *Rental:* MGM United. *Rental:* MGM United, Videotape version.

Camille. Greta Garbo & Robert Taylor. Directed by George Cukor. 1936. MGM. 108 min. Sound. 16mm B&W. *Rental:* MGM United.

Camille. Norma Talmadge. Directed by Fred Niblo. 1927. 80 min. 16mm *Rental:* A Twyman Pres.

Camisards, Les. Jacques Debary. Directed by Rene Allio. Fr. 1970. France. 120 min. Sound. 16mm Color. subtitles. *Rental:* French Am Cul.

Camouflage. Piotr Garlicki. Directed by Krzysztof Zanussi. Pol. 1976. Poland. 106 min. Sound. 16mm Color. subtitles. *Rental:* Cinema Five.

Campbell's Kingdom. Dirk Bogarde & Stanley Baker. Directed by Ralph Thomas. 1958. Britain. 102 min. Sound. 16mm Color. *Rental:* Learning Corp Am. *Sale:* Learning Corp Am.

Campeon Soy Yo, El. Span. 1950. Mexico. (Cast unlisted). 90 min. Sound. 16mm B&W. *Rental:* Film Classics.

Campesinos, Los: The Farmers of Mexico. 1976. PBS. (Documentary). 60 min. Sound. 16mm Color. *Rental:* WNET Media. *Sale:* WNET Media. *Sale:* WNET Media, Videotape version.

Campus Honeymoon. Lyn Wilde & Adele Mara. Directed by Richard Sale. 1948. Republic. 63 min. Sound. 16mm B&W. *Rental:* Ivy Films. *Sale:* Rep Pic Film.

Campus Knights. Raymond McKee & Shirley Palmer. 1929. Chesterfield. 72 min. Silent. 16mm B&W. *Rental:* Mogulls Films.

Campus Sleuth. Freddie Stewart & June Preisser. Directed by Will Jason. 1949. Monogram. 64 min. Sound. 16mm B&W. *Rental:* Hurlock Cine.

Can-Can. Frank Sinatra & Shirley MacLaine. Directed by Walter Lang. 1960. Fox. 130 min. Sound. 16mm Color. *Rental:* Films Inc & Williams Films. *Rental:* Films Inc, Anamorphic color version.

Can Heironymus Merkin Ever Forget Mercy Humppe & Find True Happiness? Anthony Newley & Joan Collins. Directed by Anthony Newley. 1969. Britain. 104 min. Sound. 16mm Color. *Rental:* Swank Motion.

Canada & the American Revolution. 1968. Canada. (Documentary). 57 min. Sound. 16mm B&W. *Rental:* Natl Film CN. *Sale:* Natl Film CN.

Canada in Crisis. 1966. NET. (Documentary). 59 min. Sound. 16mm B&W. *Rental:* Indiana AV Ctr. *Sale:* Indiana AV Ctr.

Canadian Pacific. Randolph Scott & Nancy Olsen. Directed by Edwin L. Marin. 1949. Fox. 81 min. Sound. 16mm B&W. *Rental:* Alba House, Budget Films, Cine Craft, Film Ctr DC, Lewis Film & Newman Film Lib, Super 8 sound version.

Canadians, The. Robert Ryan & Teresa Stratas. Directed by Burt Kennedy. 1961. Fox. 85 min. Sound. 16mm Color. *Rental:* Inst Cinema. *Rental:* Willoughby Peer, Anamorphic color version.

Canadienses, Los. 1976. Canada. (Documentary). 58 min. Sound. 16mm Color. *Rental:* Natl Film CN. *Sale:* Natl Film CN.

Canal Zone. Chester Morris & Harriet Hillard. Directed by Lew Landers. 1942. Columbia. 79 min. Sound. 16mm B&W. *Rental:* Kit Parker.

Canal Zone. Directed by Frederick Wiseman. 1977. Zipporah. (Documentary). 174 min. Sound. 16mm B&W. *Rental:* Zipporah Films.

Cancer & the Environment. 1980. US Government. (Documentary). 60 min. Videotape Color. *Sale:* Natl AV Ctr.

Cancer Detective of Lin Xian, The. 1980. Britain. 57 min. Sound. 16mm Color. *Rental:* Time-Life Multimedia. *Sale:* Time-Life Multimedia. *Sale:* Time-Life Multimedia, Videotape version.

Cancer Is the Next Frontier. 1970. NBC. (Documentary). 53 min. Sound. 16mm Color. *Rental:* Films Inc, U Mich Media & NYU Film Lib. *Sale:* Films Inc. *Sale:* Films Inc, Videotape version.

Cancer Treatment. 1980. US Government. (Documentary). 60 min. Sound. Videotape Color. *Sale:* Natl AV Ctr.

Cancer War, The. 1983. Document Associates. (Documentary). 60 min. Sound. 16mm Color. *Rental:* Cinema Guild. *Sale:* Cinema Guild. *Sale:* Cinema Guild, Videotape version.

Cancer: What Is It?. US Government. 60 min. Videotape Color. *Sale:* Natl AV Ctr.

Candidate for a Killing. Anita Ekberg & Fernando Rey. 1969. G. G. P.. 96 min. Sound. 16mm Color. *Rental:* Budget Films, Ivy Films & Video Comm. *Rental:* Video Comm, Videotape version.

Candide. Jean Pierre Cassel. Directed by Pierre Cardinal. 1960. France. 60 min. Sound. 16mm B&W. *Rental:* French Am Cul. *Rental:* Budget Films, Dubbed version.

Candide. Frank Finlay. 1976. Britain. 95 min. Sound. 16mm Color. *Rental:* Time-Life Multimedia. *Sale:* Time-Life Multimedia. *Rental:* Time-Life Multimedia, *Sale:* Time-Life Multimedia, Videotape version.

Candles at Nine. Jessie Matthews & John Stuart. Directed by John Harlow. 1944. Britain. 83 min. Sound. 16mm B&W. *Rental:* Ivy Films.

Candleshoe. Helen Hayes, Jodie Foster & David Niven. Directed by Norman Tokar. 1977. Disney. 101 min. Sound. 16mm Color. *Rental:* Bosco Films, Buchan Pic, Disney Prod, Elliot Film Co, Film Ctr DC, Film Pres, Films Inc, MGM United, Modern Sound, Roas Films, Swank Motion, Twyman Films, U of IL Film, Welling Motion Pictures, Westcoast Films & Williams Films.

Candy. Ewa Aulin & Marlon Brando. Directed by Christian Marquand. 1968. ABC. 122 min. Sound. 16mm Color. *Rental:* Films Inc.

Candy Man. George Sanders & Leslie Parrish. Directed by Herbert J. Leder. 1968. Allied Artists. 97 min. Sound. 16mm Color. *Rental:* Video Comm.

Candy Stripe Nurses. Candice Rialson & Robin Mattson. Directed by Allan Holleb. New World. 79 min. Sound. 16mm Color. *Rental:* Films Inc.

Cannery Row. Nick Nolte, Debra Winger & Audra Lindley. Directed by David S. Ward. 1982. 120 min. Sound. 16mm Color. *Rental:* MGM United. *Rental:* MGM United, Videotape version.

Cannibal Attack. Johnny Weissmuller. Directed by Lee Sholem. 1954. Columbia. 69 min. Sound. 16mm Color. *Rental:* Bosco Films & Inst Cinema.

Cannibal Girls. Eugene Levy & Andrea Martin. Directed by Ivan Reitman. 1973. American International. 84 min. Sound. 16mm Color. *Rental:* Swank Motion.

Cannon for Cordoba, A. George Peppard, Raf Vallone & Peter Duell. 1970. United Artists. (Anamorphic). 104 min. Sound. 16mm Color. *Rental:* MGM United.

Cannon Serenade. Vittorio De Sica & Folco Lulli. Directed by Wolfgang Staudte. 1966. Italy. 90 min. Sound. 16mm Color. dubbed. *Rental:* Video Comm.

Cannonball. David Carradine & Bill McKinney. Directed by Paul Bartel. 1976. New World. 93 min. Sound. 16mm Color. *Rental:* Films Inc.

Cannonball Run, The. Burt Reynolds & Roger Moore. Directed by Hal Needham. 1981. Fox. 97 min. Sound. 16mm Color. *Rental:* Films Inc & Swank Motion.

Canon City. Scott Brady & Jeff Corey. Directed by Crane Wilbur. 1948. Eagle Lion. 82 min. Sound. 16mm B&W. *Rental:* Budget Films.

Can't Help Singing. Deanna Durbin & Robert Paige. Directed by Frank Ryan. 1944. Universal. 89 min. Sound. 16mm Color. *Rental:* Swank Motion.

Can't It Be Anyone Else? 1980. Pyramid. (Documentary). 54 min. Sound. 16mm Color. *Rental:* Pyramid Film & U Cal Media. *Sale:* Pyramid Film. *Sale:* Pyramid Film, *Rental:* Pyramid Film, Videotape version.

Cantata de Chile. Nelson Villagra & Shenda Roman. Directed by Humberto Solas. Span. 1976. Cuba. 119 min. Sound. 16mm Color. subtitles. *Rental:* Tricontinental Merchant.

Canterbury Tales, The. Franco Citti & Laura Betti. Directed by Pier Paolo Pasolini. 1972. Italy. 111 min. Sound. 16mm Color. subtitles. *Rental:* MGM United.

Canterville Ghost, The. Charles Laughton & Margaret O'Brien. Directed by Jules Dassin. 1944. MGM. 95 min. Sound. 16mm B&W. *Rental:* MGM United.

Cantor's Son, The. Moishe Oysher & Judith Abarbanel. Directed by Ilya Motyleff. Yiddish. 1937. Israel. 90 min. Sound. 16mm B&W. subtitles Eng. *Rental:* Films Inc.

Canyon Ambush. Johnny Mack Brown. Directed by Lewis D. Collins. 1952. Monogram. 53 min. Sound. 16mm B&W. *Rental:* Hurlock Cine.

Canyon City. Don Barry. Directed by Spencer G. Bennett. 1943. Republic. 56 min. Sound. 16mm B&W. *Rental:* Ivy Films.

Canyon Crossroads. Phyllis Kirk & Richard Basehart. Directed by Alfred M. Werker. 1955. United Artists. 83 min. Sound. 16mm B&W. *Rental:* Budget Films & MGM United.

Canyon Raiders. Whip Wilson. Directed by Lewis D. Collins. 1951. Monogram. 54 min. Sound. 16mm B&W. *Rental:* Hurlock Cine.

Canyon River. George Montgomery & Marcia Henderson. Directed by Harmon Jones. 1956. Allied Artists. 80 min. Sound. 16mm Color. *Rental:* Hurlock Cine.

Cape Canaveral Monster. Scott Peters. Directed by Phil Tucker. 1960. Max A. Alexander. 71 min. Sound. 16mm B&W. *Rental:* Ivy Films.

Cape Fear. Gregory Peck & Robert Mitchum. Directed by J. Lee Thompson. 1962. Universal. 106 min. Sound. 16mm B&W. *Rental:* Swank Motion.

Caper of the Golden Bulls. Stephen Boyd & Yvette Mimieux. Directed by Russell Rouse. 1967. Embassy. 104 min. Sound. 16mm Color. *Rental:* Films Inc.

Capone. Harry Guardino & Ben Gazzara. Directed by Steve Carver. 1975. Fox. 101 min. Sound. 16mm Color. *Rental:* Films Inc & Williams Films.

Cappy Ricks Returns. Robert McWade & Ray Walker. Directed by Mack V. Wright. 1935. Republic. 69 min. Sound. 16mm B&W. *Rental:* Ivy Films.

Caprice. Doris Day & Richard Harris. Directed by Frank Tashlin. 1967. Fox. (Anamorphic). 98 min. Sound. 16mm Color. *Rental:* Films Inc.

Capricious Summer. Rudolf Hrusinsky & Vlastimil Brodsky. Directed by Jiri Menzel. 1968. 78 min. Sound. 16mm Color. *Rental:* Films Inc.

Capricorn One. Elliot Gould, James Brolin & Hal Holbrook. Directed by Peter Hyams. 1978. Warners. 127 min. Sound. 16mm Color. *Rental:* Modern Sound, Swank Motion & Williams Films. *Rental:* Swank Motion, Videotape version.

Captain America. Dick Purcell & Lorna Gray. Directed by John English & Elmer Clifton. 1944. Republic. 235 min. Sound. 16mm B&W. *Rental:* Ivy Films.

Captain Apache. Lee Van Cleef & Carroll Baker. Directed by Alexander Singer. 1971. Italy. 94 min. Sound. 16mm Color. dubbed. *Rental:* Arcus Film, Films Inc, Video Comm & Westcoast Films. *Rental:* Budget Films, Anamorphic version.

Captain Blood. Errol Flynn & Olivia De Havilland. Directed by Michael Curtiz. 1935. Warners. 99 min. Sound. 16mm B&W. *Rental:* MGM United.

Captain Boycott. Stewart Granger & Cecil Parker. Directed by Frank Launder. 1947. Britain. 92 min. Sound. 16mm B&W. *Rental:* Budget Films.

Captain Caution. Victor Mature & Leo Carillo. Directed by Richard Wallace. 1940. United Artists. 85 min. Sound. 16mm B&W. *Rental:* Budget Films.

Captain Eddie. Fred MacMurray & Lynn Bari. Directed by Lloyd Bacon. 1945. Fox. 107 min. Sound. 16mm B&W. *Rental:* Video Comm Westcoast Films.

Captain Fly-by-Night. Johnny Walker. Directed by William K. Howard. 1922. FBO. 60 min. Silent. 8mm B&W. *Rental:* Mogulls Films.

Captain from Castile, The. Tyrone Power & Jean Peters. Directed by Henry King. Fox. 140 min. Sound. 16mm Color. *Rental:* Films Inc.

Captain from Koepenick, The. Trans. Title: Hauptmann Von Koepenick. Heinz Ruhmann. Directed by Helmut Kautner. Ger. 1957. Germany. 93 min. Sound. 16mm Color. subtitles. *Rental:* Budget Films, Films Inc, Ivy Films, Kit Parker, Video Comm & Wholesome Film Ctr. *Rental:* Ivy Films, Dubbed B&W version. *Rental:* Video Comm, Videotape version.

Captain from Kopenick. Orig. Title: Hauptmann von Kopenick, Der. Max Adalbert. Directed by Richard Oswald. 1931. 90 min. 16mm *Rental:* A Twyman Pres.

Captain from Toledo, The. Stephen Forsyth. Directed by Eugenio Martin. 1966. Germany-Italy-Spain. 96 min. Sound. 16mm Color. dubbed. *Rental:* Westcoast Films.

Captain Fury. Brian Aherne & Victor McLaglen. Directed by Hal Roach. 1939. United Artists. 94 min. Sound. 16mm B&W. *Rental:* Budget Films, Modern Sound & Newman Film Lib.

Captain Hates the Sea, The. John Gilbert & Victor McLaglen. Directed by Lewis Milestone. 1934. Columbia. 92 min. Sound. 16mm B&W. *Rental:* Kit Parker.

Captain Horatio Hornblower. Gregory Peck & Virginia Mayo. Directed by Raoul Walsh. 1951. Warners. 117 min. Sound. 16mm Color. *Rental:* Charard Motion Pics, Films Inc, Inst Cinema, Twyman Films & Westcoast Films.

Captain Hurricane. James Barton & Gene Lockhart. Directed by John Robertson. 1935. RKO. 72 min. Sound. 16mm *Rental:* RKO General Pics.

Captain James Cook. Directed by John Irvin. 1977. Britain. (Cast unlisted). 49 min. Sound. 16mm Color. *Rental:* Time-Life Multimedia. *Sale:* Time-Life Multimedia. *Sale:* Time-Life Multimedia, Videotape version.

Captain January. Shirley Temple & Guy Kibbee. Directed by David Butler. 1936. Fox. 75 min. Sound. 16mm B&W. *Rental:* Films Inc.

Captain January. Baby Peggy. Directed by Edward Cline. 1924. Principal. 60 min. Silent. 16mm B&W. *Rental:* Em Gee Film Lib.

Captain John Smith & Pocahontas. Orig. Title: Burning Arrows. Anthony Dexter & Jody Lawrence. Directed by Lew Landers. 1953. United Artists. 76 min. Sound. 16mm Color. *Rental:* Charard Motion Pics, Inst Cinema & MGM United.

Captain Kidd. Charles Laughton & Randolph Scott. Directed by Rowland V. Lee. 1945. United Artists. 89 min. Sound. 16mm B&W. *Rental:* Alba House, Budget Films, Classic Film Mus, Em Gee Film Lib, Film Classics, Mogulls Films, Newman Film Lib, Roas Films, SD AV Ctr & Westcoast Films. *Sale:* Cinema Concepts. *Sale:* Cinema ConceptsTamarelles French Film, Videotape version.

Captain Korda. 1971. Czechoslovakia. (Cast unlisted). 48 min. Sound. 16mm Color. dubbed. *Rental:* Films Inc. *Sale:* Films Inc.

Captain Kronos: Vampire Hunter. Horst Janson. Directed by Brian Clemens. 1974. Germany. 91 min. Sound. 16mm Color. dubbed. *Rental:* Films Inc.

Captain Lightfoot. Rock Hudson & Barbara Rush. Directed by Douglas Sirk. 1955. Universal. 92 min. Sound. 16mm Color. *Rental:* Swank Motion.

Captain Mephisto & the Transformation Machine. Richard Bailey & Linda Stirling. Directed by Spencer G. Bennett, Wallace Grissell & Yakima Canutt. 1945. Republic. 100 min. Sound. 16mm B&W. *Rental:* Ivy Films. *Sale:* Rep Pic Film.

Captain Moonlight *see* D'ye Ken John Peel.

Captain Nemo & the Underwater City. Robert Ryan & Chuck Connors. Directed by James Hill. 1970. MGM. (Anamorphic). 106 min. Sound. 16mm Color. *Rental:* MGM United.

Captain Newman, M. D. Gregory Peck & Tony Curtis. Directed by David Miller. 1964. Universal. 126 min. Sound. 16mm Color. *Rental:* Swank Motion.

Captain Scarlett. Richard Greene. Directed by Thomas Carr. 1953. United Artists. 75 min. Sound. 16mm Color. dubbed. *Rental:* Ivy Films. *Sale:* Rep Pic Film.

Captain Sinbad. Guy Williams & Pedro Armendariz. Directed by Byron Haskin. 1963. MGM. 85 min. Sound. 16mm Color. *Rental:* MGM United.

Captain Sirocco *see* Pirates of Capri.

Captain Swagger. Rod La Rocque & Sue Carol. Directed by Cecil B. DeMille. 1928. Pathe. 60 min. Silent. 16mm B&W. *Rental:* Film Classics. *Sale:* Film Classics. *Rental:* Film Classics. *Sale:* Film Classics, Silent 8mm version. *Rental:* Film Classics, Videotape version.

Captain Thunder. Fay Wray & Victor Varconi. Directed by Alan Crosland. 1931. Warners. 62 min. Sound. 16mm B&W. *Rental:* MGM United.

Captain Tugboat Annie. Jane Darwell & Edgar Kennedy. Directed by Phil Rosen. 1945. Republic. 70 min. Sound. 16mm B&W. *Rental:* Ivy Films.

Captains Courageous. Spencer Tracy & Freddie Bartholomew. Directed by Victor Fleming. 1937. MGM. 116 min. Sound. 16mm B&W. *Rental:* MGM United. *Lease:* MGM United. *Rental:* MGM United, Videotape version.

Captain's Kid, The. Sybil Jason, Guy Kibbee & May Robson. Directed by Nick Grinde. 1936. Warners. 72 min. Sound. 16mm B&W. *Rental:* MGM United.

Captains of the Clouds. James Cagney & Dennis Morgan. Directed by Michael Curtiz. 1942. Warners. 113 min. Sound. 16mm B&W. *Rental:* MGM United. *Rental:* MGM United, Color version.

Captain's Paradise, The. Sir Alec Guinness & Celia Johnson. Directed by Anthony Kimmins. 1953. United Artists. 76 min. Sound. 16mm B&W. *Rental:* Cine Craft, Twyman Films & Wholesome Film Ctr.

Captive City. John Forsythe & Joan Camden. Directed by Robert Wise. 1952. United Artists. 90 min. Sound. 16mm B&W. *Rental:* MGM United & Newman Film Lib.

Captive Girl. Johnny Weissmuller & Buster Crabbe. Directed by William Berke. 1950. Columbia. 73 min. Sound. 16mm B&W. *Rental:* Bosco Films.

Captive Heart, The. Sir Michael Redgrave & Mervyn Johns. Directed by Basil Dearden. 1947. Britain. 87 min. Sound. 16mm B&W. *Rental:* Janus Films.

Captive of Billy the Kid. Allan Lane. Directed by Fred C. Brannon. 1951. Republic. 54 min. Sound. 16mm B&W. *Rental:* Ivy Films. *Sale:* Rep Pic Film.

Captive Wild Woman. Acquanetta & John Carradine. Directed by Edward Dmytryk. 1943. Universal. 60 min. Sound. 16mm B&W. *Rental:* Swank Motion.

Captive's Island. Akira Nitta & Rentaro Mikuni. Directed by Masahiro Shinoda. 1966. Japan. 87 min. Sound. 16mm Color. *Rental:* Films Inc.

Captives of Care. 1981. 48 min. Sound. 16mm Color. *Rental:* U Mich Media.

Capture That Capsule! Richard Miller. Directed by Will Zens. 1961. Riviera. 75 min. Sound. 16mm B&W. *Rental:* Ivy Films.

Captured. Leslie Howard & Douglas Fairbanks Jr. Directed by Roy Del Ruth. 1933. Warners. 72 min. Sound. 16mm B&W. *Rental:* MGM United.

Car, The. James Brolin & Kathleen Lloyd. Directed by Eliot Silverstein. 1977. Universal. 98 min. Sound. 16mm Color. *Sale:* Swank Motion.

Car Wash. Richard Pryor & George Carlin. Directed by Michael Schultz. 1976. Universal. 97 min. Sound. 16mm Color. *Rental:* Swank Motion.

Caraba, La. Trans. Title: Young Girl. Span. 1953. Mexico. (Cast unlisted). 85 min. Sound. 16mm B&W. *Rental:* Film Classics.

Carabiniers, Les. Marino Mase. Directed by Jean-Luc Godard. Fr. 1963. France. 75 min. Sound. 16mm B&W. subtitles. *Rental:* French Am Cul & New Yorker Films. *Rental:* French Am Cul, Videotape version.

Caravan Trail. Eddie Dean. Directed by Robert Tansey. 1946. PRC. 57 min. Sound. 16mm B&W. *Sale:* Classics Assoc NY.

Caravans. Anthony Quinn & Jennifer O'Neill. Directed by James Fargo. 1978. Universal. 123 min. Sound. 16mm Color. *Rental:* Williams Films. *Rental:* Williams Films, Anamorphic version.

Caravans West see Wagon Wheels.

Carbine Williams. James Stewart & Wendell Corey. Directed by Richard Thorpe. 1952. MGM. 92 min. Sound. 16mm B&W. *Rental:* MGM United.

Carbon Copy. Charles Aznavour & Robert Hossein. Directed by Sergio Gobbi. 1972. France. 92 min. Sound. 16mm Color. dubbed. *Rental:* Budget Films.

Carcinoma of the Lung. 1980. 60 min. videotape *Sale:* Natl AV Ctr.

Cardboard Cavalier, The. Sid Field & Margaret Lockwood. Directed by Walter Forde. 1949. Britain. 97 min. Sound. 16mm B&W. *Rental:* Cinema Five.

Cardigan's Last Case see State's Attorney.

Cardinal, The. June Duprez & Eric Portman. Directed by Sinclair Hill. 1936. Britain. 76 min. Sound. 16mm B&W. *Rental:* Ivy Films. *Sale:* Rep Pic Film.

Cardinal, The. Tom Tryon & Romy Schneider. Directed by Otto Preminger. 1963. Columbia. 175 min. Sound. 16mm Color. *Rental:* Alba House, Bosco Films, Budget Films, Cine Craft, Charard Motiion Pics, Corinth Films, Film Ctr DC, Films Inc, Natl Film Video, Roas Films, Twyman Films, Welling Motion Pictures, Wholesome Film Ctr & Williams Films. *Rental:* Corinth Films, Anamorphic version.

Career. Dean Martin & Shirley MacLaine. Directed by Joseph Anthony. 1959. Paramount. 105 min. Sound. 16mm B&W. *Rental:* Films Inc.

Carefree. Fred Astaire & Ginger Rogers. Directed by Mark Sandrich. 1938. RKO. 83 min. Sound. 16mm B&W. *Rental:* Films Inc.

Careful, Soft Shoulders. James Ellison & Virginia Bruce. Directed by Oliver Garrett. 1942. Fox. 69 min. Sound. 16mm B&W. *Rental:* Films Inc.

Careless see Senelita.

Careless Years. Dean Stockwell. Directed by Arthur Hiller. 1957. Warners. 70 min. Sound. 16mm B&W. *Rental:* MGM United.

Caressed. Robert Howay. Directed by Laurence L. Kent. 1965. Canada. 81 min. Sound. 16mm B&W. *Rental:* Charard Motion Pics.

Caretaker, The. Donald Pleasence & Alan Bates. Directed by Clive Donner. 1963. Britain. 105 min. Sound. 16mm B&W. *Rental:* A Cantor. *Sale:* A Cantor.

Carey Treatment, The. Orig. Title: Emergency Ward. James Coburn & Jennifer O'Neill. Directed by Blake Edwards. 1972. MGM. 100 min. Sound. 16mm Color. *Rental:* MGM United.

Caribbean. John Payne & Arlene Dahl. Directed by Edward Ludwig. 1952. Paramount. 98 min. Sound. 16mm B&W. *Rental:* Video Comm & Willoughby Peer.

Caribbean Mystery, The. James Dunn & Sheila Ryan. Directed by Robert Webb. 1945. Fox. 65 min. Sound. 16mm B&W. *Rental:* Films Inc.

Cariboo Trail. Randolph Scott & Bill Williams. Directed by Edwin L. Marin. 1950. Fox. 81 min. Sound. 16mm B&W. *Rental:* Cine Craft, Lewis Film & Film Ctr DC. *Rental:* Budget Films, Color version. *Sale:* Cinema Concepts, Super 8 sound version.

Caring for Your Newborn. Benjamin Spock. 111 min. Sound. Videotape Color. *Sale:* Vidamerica.

Carl Sandburg at Gettysburg. 1961. CBS. (Documentary). 50 min. Sound. 16mm B&W. *Sale:* Carousel Films.

Carlton-Browne of the F. O. see Man in a Cocked Hat.

Carmen. Viviane Romance & Jean Marais. Directed by Christian-Jaque. Fr. 1943. France-Italy. 100 min. Sound. 16mm B&W. subtitles. *Rental:* A Twyman Pres, Film Classics, Modern Sound & Twyman Films.

Carmen. Antonio Gades & Laura Del Sol. Directed by Carlos Saura. Span. 1983. Orion. 95 min. Sound. 16mm Color. subtitles Eng. *Rental:* Films Inc.

Carmen Jones. Harry Belafonte & Dorothy Dandridge. Directed by Otto Preminger. 1954. Fox. (Anamorphic). 107 min. Sound. 16mm Color. *Rental:* Films Inc & Twyman Films. *Sale:* Blackhawk Films, Golden Tapes, Magnetic Video & Video Lib, Videotape version.

Carnal Knowledge. Jack Nicholson & Ann-Margret. Directed by Mike Nichols. 1971. Embassy. 96 min. Sound. 16mm Color. *Rental:* Films Inc.

Carnegie Hall. Walter Damrosch & Bruno Walter. Directed by Edgar G. Ulmer. 1947. United Artists. 134 min. Sound. 16mm B&W. *Rental:* Films Inc & Inst Cinema.

Carnival. Jimmy Durante & Sally Eilers. Directed by Walter Lang. 1935. Columbia. 80 min. Sound. 16mm B&W. *Lease:* Time-Life Multimedia.

Carnival Boat. Ginger Rogers & Bill Boyd. Directed by Leigh Jason. 1932. RKO. 80 min. Sound. 16mm *Rental:* RKO General Pics.

Carnival in Costa Rica. Dick Haymes & Vera-Ellen. Directed by Gregory Ratoff. 1947. Fox. 95 min. Sound. 16mm Color. *Rental:* Films Inc.

Carnival in Flanders. Trans. Title: Kermesse Heroique, La. Francoise Rosay & Louis Jouvet. Directed by Jacques Feyder. Fr. 1936. France. 95 min. Sound. 16mm B&W. subtitles. *Rental:* Budget Films, Corinth Films, Em Gee Film Lib, Iowa Films & Kit Parker. *Sale:* Cinema Concepts, Festival Films, Glenn Photo & Reel Images. *Lease:* Corinth Films. *Sale:* Festival Films & Tamarelles French Film, Videotape version.

Carnival in Moscow. Igor Llynsky. Directed by Eldar Ryazanov. 1956. Russia. Sound. 16mm Color. dubbed. *Rental:* Corinth Films.

Carnival of Crime. Jean-Pierre Aumont. Directed by George M. Cahan. 1964. Crown. 83 min. Sound. 16mm B&W. dubbed. *Rental:* Video Comm. *Lease:* Video Comm. *Rental:* Video Comm, *Lease:* Video Comm, Videotape version.

Carnival of Pretense. Marlena Franca. Directed by Dan Dunkelberger. 1966. Ken Anderson. 60 min. Sound. 16mm B&W. *Rental:* G Herne.

Carnival of Souls. Candace Hilligoss. Directed by Herk Harvey. 1962. Herts-Lion. 75 min. Sound. 16mm B&W. *Rental:* Willoughby Peer.

Carnival Under the Sea. 1965. New Caledonia. (Documentary). 70 min. Sound. 16mm Color. narrated Eng. *Rental:* U Cal Media.

Carnivals. Directed by Martyn Burke. 1975. Britain. (Documentary). 90 min. Sound. 16mm Color. *Rental:* B Raymond. *Sale:* B Raymond.

Carnivore. 1979. PBS. (Documentary). 59 min. Videotape Color. *Rental:* PBS Video. *Sale:* PBS Video.

Carny. Gary Busey & Jodie Foster. Directed by Robert Kaylor. 1980. United Artists. 107 min. Sound. 16mm Color. *Rental:* Swank Motion.

Carol & Dr. Fischer. 1967. Grove. (Documentary). 49 min. Sound. 16mm B&W. *Rental:* BYU Media.

Carol for Another Christmas, A. Peter Fonda, Eva Marie Saint & Peter Sellers. 1964. Xerox. 90 min. Sound. 16mm B&W. *Rental:* U Mich Media. *Sale:* Xerox Films.

Carolina Blues. Ann Miller. Directed by Leigh Jason. 1944. Columbia. 80 min. Sound. 16mm B&W. *Rental:* Welling Motion Pictures.

Carolina Cannonball. Judy Canova & Andy Clyde. Directed by Charles Lamont. 1955. Republic. 70 min. Sound. 16mm B&W. *Rental:* Ivy Films. *Sale:* Rep Pic Film.

Carolina Moon. Gene Autry. Directed by Frank McDonald. 1940. Republic. 54 min. Sound. 16mm B&W. *Rental:* Ivy Films.

Caroline Cherie. Maria Dea & Paul Bernard. Directed by Richard Pottier. Fr. 1954. France. 115 min. Sound. 16mm B&W. subtitles. *Rental:* Film Classics. *Rental:* Film Classics, Videotape version.

Carousel. Gordon MacRae & Shirley Jones. Directed by Henry King. 1956. Fox. 128 min. Sound. 16mm Color. *Rental:* Films Inc & Williams Films. *Rental:* Films Inc, Anamorphic color version.

Carpetbaggers, The. George Peppard & Carroll Baker. Directed by Edward Dmytryk. 1964. Paramount. (Anamorphic). 150 min. Sound. 16mm Color. *Rental:* Films Inc.

Carriage to Vienna. Iva Janzurova & Jaromir Hanslik. Directed by Karel Kachyna. 1966. 79 min. Sound. 16mm Color. *Rental:* Films Inc.

Carrie. Sir Laurence Olivier & Jennifer Jones. Directed by William Wyler. 1952. Paramount. 118 min. Sound. 16mm B&W. *Rental:* Films Inc.

Carrie. Sissy Spacek & John Travolta. Directed by Brian De Palma. 1976. United Artists. 98 min. Sound. 16mm Color. *Rental:* MGM United. *Rental:* MGM United, Videotape version.

Carrington, V.C. *see* Court Martial.

Carry On, Admiral. David Tomlinson & Peggy Cummins. Directed by Val Guest. 1956. Britain. 81 min. Sound. 16mm B&W. *Rental:* Video Comm. *Rental:* Video Comm, Videotape version.

Carry On, Constable. Sidney James & Kenneth Williams. Directed by Peter Rogers. 1960. Britain. 86 min. Sound. 16mm B&W. *Rental:* Mogulls Films.

Carry On, Doctor. Frankie Howerd & Sidney James. Directed by Gerald Thomas. 1967. Britain. 95 min. Sound. 16mm Color. *Rental:* Budget Films & Welling Motion Pictures.

Carry On, Emmannuelle. Kenneth Williams & Jean Sims. Directed by Gerald Thomas. 1978. Britain. 90 min. Sound. 16mm Color. *Rental:* Williams Films.

Carry On, Henry VIII. Kenneth Williams & Charles Hawtrey. Directed by Gerald Thomas. 1971. Britain. 90 min. Sound. 16mm Color. *Rental:* Swank Motion.

Carry On, Nurse. Kenneth Connor & Kenneth Williams. Directed by Gerald Thomas. 1960. Britain. 88 min. Sound. 16mm B&W. *Rental:* Charard Motion Pics.

Carry On, Regardless. Sidney James & Kenneth Connor. Directed by Peter Rogers. 1961. Britain. 93 min. Sound. 16mm B&W. *Rental:* Modern Sound.

Carry On Screaming *see* Screaming.

Carry On, Sergeant. Directed by Bruce Bairnsfather. 1928. Canada. (Cast unlisted). 98 min. Silent. 16mm B&W. *Rental:* Museum Mod Art. *Lease:* Museum Mod Art.

Carry On, Sergeant. William Hartnell & Shirley Eaton. Directed by Gerald Thomas. 1959. Britain. 88 min. Sound. 16mm B&W. *Rental:* Modern Sound.

Carry On, Spying. Kenneth Williams & Barbara Windor. Directed by Peter Rogers. 1964. Britain. 87 min. Sound. 16mm B&W. *Rental:* Modern Sound.

Carry On, Teacher. Ted Ray & Kenneth Connor. Directed by Peter Rogers. 1959. Britain. 86 min. Sound. 16mm B&W. *Rental:* Modern Sound.

Carry On, Cowboy *see* Rumpo Kid.

Cars That Ate Paris. Melissa Jaffa. Directed by Peter Weir. 1976. New Line Cinema. 90 min. Sound. 16mm Color. *Rental:* New Line Cinema.

Carson City Cyclone. Don Barry. Directed by Howard Bretherton. 1943. Republic. 55 min. Sound. 16mm B&W. *Rental:* Ivy Films.

Carson City Kid. Roy Rogers. Directed by Joseph Kane. 1940. Republic. 54 min. Sound. 16mm B&W. *Rental:* Ivy Films. *Sale:* Rep Pic Film.

Carson City Raiders. Allan Lane. Directed by Yakima Canutt. 1947. Republic. 60 min. Sound. 16mm B&W. *Rental:* Ivy Films. *Sale:* Rep Pic Film & Nostalgia Merchant.

Carter & Country. 1979. WNET. (Documentary). 58 min. Sound. Videotape Color. *Rental:* WNET Media. *Sale:* WNET Media.

Carve Her Name with Pride. Virginia McKenna & Paul Scofield. Directed by Lewis Gilbert. 1958. Britain. 116 min. Sound. 16mm B&W. *Rental:* Kit Parker, Learning Corp Am & Twyman Films. *Sale:* Learning Corp Am.

Cary & the Bishop's Wife *see* Bishop's Wife.

Caryl of the Mountains. Orig. Title: Get That Girl. Rin-Tin-Tin Jr. & Francis X. Bushman. Directed by Sam Newfield. 1936. Reliable. 60 min. Sound. 16mm B&W. *Rental:* Mogulls Films.

Casa, La *see* Hunt.

Casa Colorada, La. Trans. Title: Red House, The. Pedro Armendariz. Directed by Miguel Morayta. 1950. Mexico. 89 min. Sound. 16mm B&W. *Rental:* Trans-World Films.

Casa de Mujeres. Dolores Del Rio & Fernando Soler. Directed by Julian Soler. Span. Mexico. 103 min. Sound. 16mm Color. *Rental:* Westcoast Films.

Casa Manana. Robert Clarke & Virginia Wells. Directed by Jean Yarbrough. 1951. Monogram. 73 min. Sound. 16mm B&W. *Rental:* Hurlock Cine.

Casablanca. Humphrey Bogart, Ingrid Bergman & Claude Rains. Directed by Michael Curtiz. 1942. Warners. 102 min. Sound. 16mm B&W. *Rental:* MGM United. *Rental:* MGM United, Videotape version.

Casals Master Class. 1961. NET. (Documentary). 59 min. Sound. 16mm B&W. *Rental:* Indiana AV Ctr. *Sale:* Indiana AV Ctr.

Casamiento en Buenos Aires. Span. 1950. Mexico. (Cast unlisted). 90 min. Sound. 16mm B&W. *Rental:* Film Classics.

Casanova *see* Fellini's Casanova.

Casanova Brown. Gary Cooper & Teresa Wright. Directed by Sam Wood. 1944. United Artists. 99 min. Sound. 16mm B&W. *Rental:* Film Classics, MGM United, Roas Films & Welling Motion Pictures.

Casanova in Burlesque. Joe E. Brown & June Havoc. Directed by Leslie Goodwins. 1944. Republic. 74 min. Sound. 16mm B&W. *Rental:* Ivy Films. *Sale:* Rep Pic Film.

Casanova 'Seventy. Virna Lisi & Michele Mercier. Directed by Mario Monicelli. Ital. 1965. Embassy. 113 min. Sound. 16mm Color. subtitles Eng. *Rental:* Films Inc.

Casanova's Big Night. Bob Hope & Joan Fontaine. Directed by Norman Z. McLeod. 1954. Paramount. 86 min. Sound. 16mm B&W. *Rental:* Films Inc.

Casbah. Tony Martin, Yvonne De Carlo & Peter Lorre. Directed by John Berry. 1948. Universal. 92 min. Sound. 16mm B&W. *Rental:* Budget Films, Cine Craft & Ivy Films. *Sale:* Rep Pic Film.

Case for a Young Hangman, A. Directed by Pavel Juracek. Czech. 1973. Czechoslovakia. (Cast unlisted). 98 min. Sound. 16mm B&W. subtitles. *Rental:* Films Inc.

Case History of a Rumor, The. 1964. CBS. (Documentary). 52 min. Sound. 16mm B&W. *Rental:* ADL, BYU Media, Mass Media, Syracuse U Film, U Col Media Ctr & U of IL Film. *Sale:* Carousel Films.

Case of Amnesia, A see Home at Seven.

Case of Barbara Parsons, The. 1979. Canada. (Documentary). 52 min. Sound. 16mm Color. *Rental:* U Cal Media & Natl Film CN.

Case of Mrs. Pembrooke, The see Two Against the World.

Case of the Bermuda Triangle, The. 1976. Britain. 52 min. Sound. 16mm Color. *Rental:* Kent St U Film, U of IL Film & U Mich Media. *Sale:* Films Inc. *Rental:* U Cal Media, Films Inc & U of IL Film, *Sale:* Films Inc, Videotape version.

Case of the Black Cat, The. Ricardo Cortez & June Travis. Directed by William McGann. 1936. Warners. 66 min. Sound. 16mm B&W. *Rental:* MGM United.

Case of the Black Parrot, The. William Lundigan & Eddie Foy Jr. Directed by Noel Smith. 1941. Warners. 60 min. Sound. 16mm B&W. *Rental:* MGM United.

Case of the Guardian Angel, The. Hugh Latimer. 1956. Britain. 70 min. Sound. 16mm B&W. *Rental:* Mogulls Films.

Case of the Lucky Legs, The. Warren William & Allen Jenkins. Directed by Archie Mayo. 1935. Warners. 77 min. Sound. 16mm B&W. *Rental:* MGM United.

Case of the Missing Blonde, The see Lady in the Morgue.

Case of the Missing Brides, The see Corpse Vanishes.

Case of the Missing Heiress, The. Valentine Dyall. 1949. Britain. 90 min. Sound. 16mm B&W. *Rental:* Mogulls Films.

Case of the Red Monkey, The. Orig. Title: Little Red Monkey. Richard Conte & Rona Anderson. Directed by Ken Hughes. 1955. Allied Artists. 73 min. Sound. 16mm B&W. *Rental:* Hurlock Cine.

Case of the Stuttering Bishop, The. Ann Dvorak & Donald Woods. Directed by William Clemens. 1937. Warners. 70 min. Sound. 16mm B&W. *Rental:* MGM United.

Case of the U. F. O.'s. 1983. Nova. (Documentary). 57 min. Sound. 16mm Color. *Rental:* U Cal Media.

Casey at the Bat. Wallace Beery. Directed by Monte Brice. 1927. Paramount. 60 min. Silent. 16mm B&W. *Rental:* Films Inc.

Casey's Shadow. Walter Matthau & Alexis Smith. Directed by Martin Ritt. 1977. Columbia. 117 min. Sound. 16mm Color. *Rental:* Arcus Film, Budget Films, Films Inc, Modern sound, Newman Film Lib, Swank Motion, Twyman Films, Westcoast Films, Wholesome Film Ctr & Williams Films.

Cash. Orig. Title: For Love or Money. Robert Donat & Wendy Barrie. Directed by Zoltan Korda. 1933. Britain. 65 min. Sound. 16mm Color. *Rental:* Budget Films & Classic Film Mus. *Sale:* Classic Film Mus.

Cash on Demand. Peter Cushing. Directed by Michael Carreras. 1961. Columbia. 66 min. Sound. 16mm B&W. *Lease:* Time-Life Multimedia.

Cashing In on the Ocean. 1979. 58 min. Sound. Videotape *Rental:* PBS Video. *Sale:* PBS Video.

Casino de Paree see Go Into Your Dance.

Casino de Paris. Lina Renaud. HBO. 75 min. Videotape Color. *Rental:* Films Inc.

Casino Murder Case, The. Paul Lukas & Allison Skipworth. Directed by Edwin L. Marin. 1935. MGM. 85 min. Sound. 16mm B&W. *Rental:* Films Inc & MGM United.

Casino Royale. Peter Sellers & David Niven. Directed by John Huston, Ken Hughes & Val Guest. 1967. Columbia. 130 min. Sound. 16mm Color. *Rental:* Arcus Film, Bosco Films, Buchan Pic, Budget Films, Cine Craft, Charard Motion Pics, Films Inc, Inst Cinema, Kit Parker, Modern Sound, Natl Film Video, Roas Films, Swank Motion, Twyman Films, Video Comm, Welling Motion Pictures, Westcoast Films, Wholesome Film Ctr, Williams Films & Willoughby Peer. *Rental:* Kit Parker & Twyman Films,

Casque d'Or. Orig. Title: Golden Marie. Simone Signoret. Directed by Jacques Becker. Fr. 1952. France. 94 min. Sound. 16mm B&W. subtitles. *Rental:* Janus Films. *Sale:* Reel Images. *Sale:* Tamarelles French Film, Videotape version.

Cass. (Cast unlisted). Videotape *Sale:* Vidamerica.

Cass Timberlane. Lana Turner & Spencer Tracy. Directed by George Sidney. 1947. MGM. 119 min. Sound. 16mm B&W. *Rental:* MGM United.

Cassandra Cat. Orig. Title: When the Cat Comes. Vlastimil Brodsky. Directed by Vojtech Jasny. Czech. 1963. Czechoslovakia. 87 min. Sound. 16mm Color. dubbed. *Rental:* Budget Films, Macmillan Films & Modern Sound. *Lease:* Macmillan Films.

Cassandra Crossing, The. Sophia Loren, Richard Harris & Martin Sheen. Directed by George Pan Cosmatos. 1977. Embassy. 125 min. Sound. 16mm Color. *Rental:* Films Inc.

Casse, Le see Burglars.

Cassidy of Bar Twenty. William Boyd. Directed by Lesley Selander. 1938. Paramount. 54 min. Sound. 16mm B&W. *Lease:* Cinema Concepts. *Rental:* Budget Films.

Cast a Dark Shadow. Dirk Bogarde & Margaret Lockwood. Directed by Lewis Gilbert. 1957. Britain. 84 min. Sound. 16mm B&W. *Rental:* Budget Films, Charard Motion Pics, Ivy Films & Video Comm. *Lease:* Video Comm. *Rental:* Video Comm, *Lease:* Video Comm, Videotape version.

Cast a Giant Shadow. Kirk Douglas & Senta Berger. Directed by Melville Shavelson. 1966. United Artists. 139 min. Sound. 16mm Color. *Rental:* Budget Films, MGM United, Welling Motion Pictures & Westcoast Films.

Cast a Long Shadow. Audie Murphy & Terry Moore. Directed by Thomas Carr. 1959. United Artists. 82 min. Sound. 16mm Color. *Rental:* MGM United.

Castaway, The see Cheaters.

Castillos en el Aire. Christina Telles & Pilar Arcos. Directed by Jaime Salvador. Span. 1950. Spain. 80 min. Sound. 16mm B&W. *Rental:* Film Classics.

Castle, The. Maximillian Schell & Cordula Trantow. Directed by Rudolph Noelte. Ger. 1968. Germany. 90 min. Sound. 16mm Color. subtitles Eng. *Rental:* Budget Films & Kino Intl. *Sale:* Kino Intl. *Lease:* Kino Intl.

Castle in the Desert. Orig. Title: Charlie Chan in Castle in the Desert. Sidney Toler & Arleen Whalen. Directed by Harry Lachman. 1942. Fox. 62 min. Sound. 16mm B&W. *Rental:* Swank Motion.

Castle Keep. Burt Lancaster & Peter Falk. Directed by Sydney Pollack. 1969. Columbia. 119 min. Sound. 16mm Color. *Rental:* Arcus Film, Budget Films, Cine Craft, Bosco Films, Films Inc, Inst Cinema, Modern Sound, Swank Motion, Film Ctr DC, Westcoast Films, Welling Motion Pictures & Wholesome Film Ctr.

Castle of Blood. Barbara Steele. Directed by Anthony Dawson. 1964. Britain. 85 min. Sound. 16mm B&W. *Rental:* Willoughby Peer.

Castle of Doom *see* Vampyr.

Castle of Evil. Scott Brady & Virginia Mayo. Directed by Francis D. Lyon. 1966. World Entertainment. 81 min. Sound. 16mm Color. *Rental:* Ivy Films. *Sale:* Rep Pic Film.

Castle of Fu Manchu, The. Christopher Lee & Richard Greene. Directed by Jess Franco. 1970. Britain. 87 min. Sound. 16mm Color. . *Sale:* Glenn Photo, Super 8 sound version. *Sale:* Video Lib, Videotape version.

Castle of Purity. Claudio Brook & Rita Moreno. Directed by Arturo Ripstein. Span. 1972. Mexico. 108 min. Sound. 16mm Color. subtitles. *Rental:* New Yorker Films.

Castle on the Hudson. Orig. Title: Years Without Days. John Garfield & Ann Sherdan. Directed by Anatole Litvak. 1940. Warners. 77 min. Sound. 16mm B&W. *Rental:* MGM United.

Castles of Clay. Directed by Alan Root. 1978. Benchmark. (Documentary). 55 min. Sound. 16mm Color. *Rental:* Benchmark Films, Iowa Films, U Cal Media, U Mich Media & Viewfinders. *Sale:* Benchmark Films. *Sale:* Benchmark Films, 8mm version available version.

Castro Connection, The. 1980. NBC. (Documentary). 77 min. Videotape Color. *Rental:* Films Inc. *Sale:* Films Inc.

Castro, Cuba & Communism. 1961. Britain. (Documentary). 60 min. Sound. 16mm B&W. *Rental:* Budget Films.

Cat, The. Peggy Ann Garner & Barry Coe. Directed by Ellis Kadison. 1966. Embassy. 87 min. Sound. 16mm B&W. *Rental:* Films Inc.

Cat, The *see* Chat.

Cat & Mouse. Lars Brandt & Peter Brandt. Directed by Hansjurgen Pohland. Ger. 1966. Germany. 100 min. Sound. 16mm B&W. subtitles. *Rental:* Grove.

Cat & Mouse. Michele Morgan & Jean-Pierre Aumont. Directed by Claude Lelouch. 1975. Quartet. 110 min. Sound. 16mm Color. subtitles. *Rental:* Films Inc. *Sale:* Festival Films. *Sale:* Festival Films, Videotape version.

Cat & the Canary, The. Laura La Plante & Creighton Hale. Directed by Paul Leni. 1927. Universal. 78 min. Silent. 16mm B&W. *Rental:* A Twyman Pres, Budget Films, Em Gee Film Lib, Films Inc, Ivy Films, Kerr Film, Kit Parker, Museum Mod Art, Video Comm, Westcoast Films & Willoughby Peer. *Sale:* Natl Cinema, Glenn Photo & Video Comm. *Sale:* Natl Cinema, Sound 16mm tinted restored version. *Rental:* Ivy Films, *Sale:* Glenn Photo, Super 8 silent version. *Sale:* Glenn Photo, Silent 8mm version. *Rental:* Video Comm, *Lease:* Video Comm, Videotape version.

Cat & the Fiddle, The. Ramon Navarro & Jeanette MacDonald. Directed by William K. Howard. 1934. MGM. 90 min. Sound. 16mm B&W. *Rental:* MGM United.

Cat Ballou. Jane Fonda, Lee Marvin & Michael Callan. Directed by Eliot Silverstein. 1965. Columbia. 96 min. Sound. 16mm Color. *Rental:* Arcus Film, Bosco Films, Buchan Pic, Budget Films, Cinema Craft, Film Ctr DC, Film Pres, Films Inc, Images Film, Inst Cinema, Ivy Films, Kit Parker, Modern Sound, Natl Film Video, Newman Film Lib, Roas Films, Swank Motion, Twyman Films, U of IL Film, Video Comm, Welling Motion Pictures, Williams Films & Wholesome Film Ctr. *Rental:* Swank Motion, Videotape version.

Cat Creeps, The. Noah Beery, Lois Collier & Paul Kelly. Directed by Erle C. Kenton. 1946. Universal. 70 min. Sound. 16mm B&W. *Rental:* Swank Motion.

Cat from Outer Space, The. Ken Berry, Sandy Duncan & McLean Stevenson. Directed by Norman Tokar. 1978. Disney. 103 min. Sound. 16mm Color. *Rental:* Bosco Films, Buchan Pic, Disney Prod, Elliot Film Co, Film Ctr DC, Film Pres, Films Inc, MGM United, Modern Sound, Roas Films, Swank Motion, Twyman Films, U of IL Film, Welling Motion Pictures, Westcoast Films & Williams Films.

Cat Girl, The. Barbara Shelly & Kay Callard. Directed by Alfred Shaughnessey. 1958. Britain. 70 min. Sound. 16mm B&W. *Rental:* Films Inc & Westcoast Films.

Cat on a Hot Tin Roof. Elizabeth Taylor & Paul Newman. Directed by Richard Brooks. 1958. MGM. 108 min. Sound. 16mm Color. *Rental:* MGM United. *Rental:* MGM United, Videotape version.

Cat O'Nine Tails, The. Karl Malden, James Franciscus & Catherine Spaak. Directed by Dario Argento. 1971. National General. (Anamorphic). 112 min. Sound. 16mm Color. *Rental:* Twyman Films.

Cat People, The. Simone Simon & Kent Smith. Directed by Jacques Tourneur. 1942. RKO. 73 min. Sound. 16mm B&W. *Rental:* Films Inc.

Cat People, The. Nastassia Kinski, Malcolm McDowell & John Heard. Directed by Paul Schrader. 118 min. Sound. 16mm Color. *Rental:* Swank Motion. *Rental:* Swank Motion, Videotape version.

Cat, Two Women, & One Man, A. Hisaya Morishige & Chieko Naniwa. Directed by Shiro Toyoda. 1956. Toho. 106 min. Sound. 16mm B&W. *Rental:* Films Inc.

Cat Women of the Moon. Sonny Tufts & Marie Windsor. Directed by Arthur Hilton. 1954. United Artists. 65 min. Sound. 16mm B&W. *Rental:* Budget Films, Ivy Films & Video Comm. *Sale:* Festival Films. *Rental:* Video Comm, *Sale:* Festival Films, Videotape version.

Catarina de Inglaterra. Orig. Title: Catherine of England. Maruchi Fresno. Directed by Arturo Ruiz-Castillo. Span. 1953. Spain. 98 min. Sound. 16mm B&W. subtitles. *Rental:* Film Classics.

Catch Thirty-Six Twenty-Four Thirty-Six. 1983. Britain. (Documentary). 50 min. Sound. Videotape Color. *Sale:* Films Inc.

Catch Twenty-Two. Alan Arkin, Richard Benjamin & Art Garfunkel. Directed by Mike Nichols. 1970. Paramount. (Anamorphic). 121 min. Sound. 16mm Color. *Rental:* Films Inc.

Catered Affair, The. Orig. Title: Wedding Breakfast. Bette Davis & Ernest Borgnine. Directed by Richard Brooks. 1956. MGM. 92 min. Sound. 16mm B&W. *Rental:* MGM United. *Rental:* MGM United, Videotape version.

Catherine. Directed by Jean Renoir & Albert Dieudonne. 1925. 80 min. Sound. 16mm B&W. *Sale:* Natl Cinema & Learning Corp Am.

Catherine & Co. (Cast unlisted). Videotape *Sale:* Vidamerica.

Catherine Howard. Keith Michell. 1976. Britain. 90 min. Videotape Color. *Rental:* Films Inc. *Sale:* Films Inc.

Catherine of Aragon. 1976. Britain. (Documentary). 90 min. Videotape Color. *Rental:* Films Inc. *Sale:* Films Inc.

Catherine of England *see* Catarina de Inglaterra.

Catherine of Russia. Hildegarde Neff & Sergio Fantoni. 1962. Germany-Italy. 105 min. Sound. 16mm Color. dubbed. *Rental:* Ivy Films.

Catherine Parr. 1976. Britain. (Documentary). 90 min. Videotape Color. *Rental:* Films Inc. *Sale:* Films Inc.

Catherine the Great. Elizabeth Bergner & Douglas Fairbanks Jr. Directed by Paul Czinner. 1934. Britain. 93 min. Sound. 16mm B&W. *Rental:* Budget Films, Classic Film Mus, Films Inc, Ivy Films, Kit Parker, Mogulls Films & Welling Motion Pictures. *Sale:* Blackhawk Films, Classic Film Mus, Cinema Concepts, Natl Cinema & Reel Images. *Sale:* Cinema Concepts, Golden Tapes & Tamarelles French Film, Videotape version.

Cathode Colors Them Human. 1966. NET. (Documentary). 60 min. Sound. 16mm B&W. *Rental:* Indianna AV Ctr. *Lease:* Indiana AV Ctr.

Catholicism: Rome, Leeds & the Desert. 1978. Britain. (Documentary). 52 min. Sound. 16mm Color. *Rental:* U Cal Media.

Catholics, The. Trevor Howard & Martin Sheen. Directed by Jack Gold. 1974. CBS. 74 min. Sound. 16mm Color. *Rental:* Budget Films, Modern Sound, Syracuse U Film, Twyman Films & Wholesome Film Ctr. *Sale:* Carousel Films.

Cathy Come Home. 1969. Britain. (Cast unlisted). 78 min. Sound. 16mm B&W. *Rental:* Time-Life Multimedia. *Sale:* Time-Life Multimedia.

Catlow. Yul Brynner & Richard Crenna. Directed by Sam Wanamaker. 1971. MGM. 101 min. Sound. 16mm Color. *Rental:* MGM United.

Catman of Paris. Gerald Mohr & Carl Esmond. Directed by Lesley Selander. 1940. Republic. 65 min. Sound. 16mm B&W. *Rental:* Ivy Films. *Sale:* Rep Pic Film.

Cats, The. Eva Dahlbeck & Gio Petre. Directed by Henning Carlsen. Swed. 1964. Sweden. 93 min. Sound. 16mm B&W. subtitles Eng. *Rental:* Films Inc.

Catskill Comedians. Verve. (Performance). 82 min. Videotape Color. *Rental:* Films Inc.

Catspaw. William Shatner & Leonard Nimoy. Directed by Joseph Pevney. 1967. Star Trek. 50 min. Sound. 16mm Color. *Rental:* Roas Films & Westcoast Films. *Sale:* Reel Images.

Cattle Annie & Little Britches. Burt Lancaster, John Savage & Rod Steiger. Directed by Lamont Johnson. 95 min. Sound. 16mm Color. *Rental:* Swank Motion.

Cattle Drive. Joel McCrea & Dean Stockwell. Directed by Kurt Neumann. 1951. Universal. 77 min. Sound. 16mm Color. *Rental:* Swank Motion.

Cattle Empire. Joel McCrea & Gloria Talbott. Directed by Charles Marquis Warren. 1958. Fox. (Anamorphic). 83 min. Sound. 16mm Color. *Rental:* Films Inc.

Cattle King. Robert Taylor & Joan Caulfield. Directed by Tay Garnett. 1963. MGM. 88 min. Sound. 16mm Color. *Rental:* MGM United.

Cattle Queen of Montana. Barbara Stanwyck & Ronald Reagan. Directed by Allan Dwan. 1954. RKO. 88 min. Sound. 16mm Color. *Rental:* Films Inc. *Sale:* Cinema Concepts, Super 8 sound version.

Caudillo: The History of the Spanish Civil War. Directed by Basilio Martin Patino. 1980. Films for the Humanities. (Documentary). 111 min. Sound. 16mm Color. subtitles. *Rental:* Films Human. *Sale:* Films Human.

Caught. James Mason & Robert Ryan. Directed by Max Ophuls. 1949. MGM. 88 min. Sound. 16mm B&W. *Rental:* Budget Films, Ivy Films & Kit Parker. *Sale:* Rep Pic Film.

Caught in the Act *see* Boss Foreman.

Caught in the Draft. Bob Hope & Dorothy Lamour. Directed by David Miller. 1941. Paramount. 82 min. Sound. 16mm B&W. *Rental:* Swank Motion.

Caught Plastered. Bert Wheeler & Robert Woolsey. Directed by William A. Seiter. 1932. RKO. 68 min. Sound. 16mm *Rental:* RKO General Pics.

Caught Short. Marie Dressler & Polly Moran. Directed by Charles Reisner. 1930. MGM. 80 min. Sound. 16mm B&W. *Rental:* MGM United.

Cause for Alarm. Loretta Young & Barry Sullivan. Directed by Tay Garnett. 1951. MGM. 73 min. Sound. 16mm B&W. *Rental:* MGM United.

Cavalcade. Diana Wynard & Clive Brook. Directed by Frank Lloyd. 1933. Fox. 115 min. Sound. 16mm B&W. *Rental:* Films Inc.

Cavalcade des Heures. Orig. Title: Love Around the Clock. Fernandel & Charles Trenet. Directed by Yvan Noe. Fr. 1950. France. 95 min. Sound. 16mm B&W. subtitles. *Rental:* Film Classics.

Cavalcade of the West. Hoot Gibson. 1936. Diversion. 62 min. Sound. 16mm B&W. *Sale:* Morcraft Films. *Sale:* Video Comm, Videotape version.

Cavaleur, Le. Orig. Title: Practice Makes Perfect. Jean Rochefort & Nicole Garcia. Directed by Philippe De Broca. 1980. France. 102 min. Sound. Videotape Color. *Sale:* Tamarelles French Films.

Cavalleria Rusticana. Mario Del Monaco & Richard Torigi. 1952. Italy. 52 min. Sound. 16mm B&W. narrated Eng. *Rental:* Budget Films & Video Comm. *Rental:* Video Comm, Videotape version.

Cavalry. Bob Steele. Directed by Robert N. Bradbury. 1936. Republic. 60 min. Sound. 16mm B&W. *Rental:* Ivy Films & Mogulls Films.

Cavalry Command. John Agar & Richard Arlen. Directed by Eddie Romero. 1965. Parade. 82 min. Sound. 16mm Color. *Rental:* Ivy Films.

Cavalry Scout. Rod Cameron & Audrey Long. Directed by Lesley Selander. 1951. Monogram. 76 min. Sound. 16mm Color. *Rental:* Budget Films & Hurlock Cine.

Cave of Outlaws. MacDonald Carey & Alexis Smith. Directed by William Castle. 1951. Universal. 75 min. Sound. 16mm Color. *Rental:* Swank Motion.

Cave of the Living Dead. Erika Remberg & Carl Mohner. Directed by Akos Von Rathony. 1965. Germany-Yugoslavia. 87 min. Sound. 16mm B&W. dubbed. *Rental:* Modern Sound.

Cave-In, The *see* Draegerman Courage.

Caveman, The. Ringo Starr & Barbara Bach. Directed by Carl Gottlieb. 1981. United Artists. 92 min. Sound. 16mm Color. *Rental:* MGM United. *Rental:* MGM United, Videotape version.

Cavern, The. John Saxon & Brian Aherne. Directed by Edgar G. Ulmer. 1968. Fox. 98 min. Sound. 16mm B&W. *Rental:* Films Inc & MGM United.

CBW: The Secrets of Secrecy. 1969. NBC. (Documentary). 47 min. Sound. 16mm Color. *Rental:* Films Inc, U of IL Film & U Mich Media. *Sale:* Films Inc. *Sale:* Films Inc, Videotape version.

Ce Soir Ou Jamais. Anna Karina & Francoise Dorleac. Directed by Michel Deville. Fr. 1961. France. 90 min. Sound. 16mm B&W. subtitles. *Rental:* French Am Cul.

Ceddo. Directed by Ousmane Sembene. 1977. Senegal. (Cast unlisted). 120 min. Sound. 16mm Color. subtitles. *Rental:* New Yorker Films.

Celebrated Jumping Frog, The *see* Best Man Wins.

Celebration & Succession. Directed by Munroe Scott. 1971. Canada. (Documentary). 58 min. Sound. 16mm Color. *Rental:* Natl Film CN. *Sale:* Natl Film CN.

Celebration at Big Sur. Directed by Baird Bryant & Johanna Demetrakis. 1971. Fox. (Documentary). 82 min. Sound. 16mm Color. *Rental:* Films Inc.

Celeste. Eva Mattes & Jurgen Arndt. Directed by Percy Adlon. 1982. 107 min. Sound. 16mm Color. *Rental:* New Yorker Films.

Celia. Hy Hazell & Bruce Lester. Directed by Francis Searle. 1949. Britain. 68 min. Sound. 16mm B&W. *Rental:* Mogulls Films.

Celibataires, Les. Fernand Ledoux & Andre Luguet. France. 99 min. Sound. 16mm B&W. *Rental:* French Am Cul.

Celine & Julie Go Boating. Dominique Labourier & Juliet Berto. Directed by Jacques Rivette. 1974. France. 192 min. Sound. 16mm Color. subtitles. *Rental:* New Cinema & New Yorker Films.

Cell, The: A Functioning Structure. 1972. CRM. (Documentary). 61 min. Sound. 16mm Color. *Rental:* BYU Media.

Celtic Trilogy, A. Siobhan McKenna. Directed by Kathleen Dowdey. First Run. 96 min. Sound. 16mm Color. *Rental:* First Run.

Cenas Da Luta De Classa Em Portugal *see* Scenes from the Class Struggle in Portugal.

Cenerentola, La. Italy. (Opera). 95 min. Sound. 16mm B&W. narrated Eng. *Rental:* Corinth Films.

Centennial Summer. Jeanne Crain, Cornel Wilde & Linda Darnell. Directed by Otto Preminger. 1946. Fox. 102 min. Sound. 16mm B&W. *Rental:* Films Inc.

Centerfold. Videotape *Rental:* Video Comm.

Central Airport. Richard Barthelmess & Sally Eilers. Directed by William A. Wellman. 1933. Warners. 75 min. Sound. 16mm B&W. *Rental:* MGM United.

Central American Peace Concert, The. Directed by Jan Kees De Roy. 1983. 55 min. 16mm Color. *Rental:* Icarus Films.

Central Park. Joan Blondell & Wallace Ford. Directed by John Adolfi. 1932. Warners. 61 min. Sound. 16mm B&W. *Rental:* MGM United.

Central Region, The *see* Region Centrale.

Ceremony, The. Kenzo Kawarzaki. Directed by Nagisa Oshima. Jap. 1971. Japan. (Anamorhpic). 122 min. Sound. 16mm Color. subtitles. *Rental:* New Yorker Films.

Cermony, The. Laurence Harvey & Sarah Miles. Directed by Laurence Harvey. 1963. United Artists. 105 min. Sound. 16mm B&W. *Rental:* MGM United.

Cerro Pelado. Span. 1966. Cuba. (Documentary). 60 min. Sound. 16mm B&W. subtitles. *Rental:* CA Newsreel & Tricontinental Film. *Sale:* Tricontinental Film.

Certain Amount of Violence, A. 1975. Britain. (Documentary). 52 min. Sound. 16mm Color. *Rental:* U of IL Film, Videotape version.

Certain Smile, A. Rossano Brazzi & Joan Fontaine. Directed by Jean Negulesco. 1958. Fox. (Anamorphic). 106 min. Sound. 16mm Color. *Rental:* Films Inc.

Certain Tradition of Quality, A: 1945-1955. Directed by Armand Panigel. Fr. France. (Documentary). 70 min. Sound. 16mm B&W. subtitles. *Rental:* French Am Cul.

Cervantes. Orig. Title: Young Rebel-Cervantes. Horst Buchholz, Gina Lollobrigida & Jose Ferrer. Directed by Vincent Sherman. 1968. Commonwealth. 128 min. Sound. 16mm Color. *Rental:* Films Inc, Inst Cinema, Ivy Films, Roas Films, Video Comm & Welling Motion Pictures. *Rental:* Video Comm & Willoughby Peer, Anamorphic color version.

Cesar. Orig. Title: Pagnol Trilogy. Raimu & Pierre Fresnay. Directed by Marcel Pagnol. Fr. 1936. France. 121 min. Sound. 16mm B&W. subtitles. *Rental:* Budget Films, Corinth Films, Em Gee Film Lib & Kit Parker. *Sale:* Cinema Concepts, Natl Cinema & Reel Images. *Sale:* Tamarelles French Film, Videotape version.

Cesar & Rosalie. Yves Montand, Romy Schneider & Sami Frey. Directed by Claude Sautet. Fr. 1973. France. 110 min. Sound. 16mm Color. subtitles. *Rental:* Cinema Five. *Lease:* Cinema Five.

Cesar's Bark Canoe. 1972. Canada. 58 min. Sound. 16mm Color. *Rental:* Educ Dev Ctr. *Sale:* Educ Dev Ctr.

Chac. Trans. Title: God of Rain. Pablo Canche Balam. Directed by Rolando Klein. Mayan. 1975. Mexico. 95 min. Sound. 16mm Color. subtitles. *Rental:* A Twyman Pres & New Cinema.

Chacal de Nahuel Toro, El. Orig. Title: Jackal of Nahuel Toro, The. Directed by Miguel Littin. Span. 1969. Chile. (Documentary). 90 min. Sound. 16mm B&W. subtitles. *Rental:* New Yorker Films & Unifilm. *Sale:* Unifilm.

Chachaji: My Poor Relation. Directed by Ved Mehta. 1978. Ved Mehta. (Documentary). 58 min. Sound. 16mm Color. *Rental:* U Cal Media & Inst Cinema. *Sale:* Inst Cinema.

Chaco Legacy, The. 1979. Odyssey. (Documentary). 59 min. 16mm Color. *Rental:* Iowa Films & PBS Video. *Sale:* PBS Video.

Chaika *see* Sea Gull.

Chain Gang Women. Michael Stearns & Barbara Mills. Directed by Lee Frost & Wes Bishop. 1972. Crown. 85 min. Sound. 16mm Color. *Rental:* Video Comm. *Lease:* Video Comm. *Rental:* Video Comm, *Lease:* Video Comm, Videotape version.

Chain Lightning. Humphrey Bogart & Eleanor Parker. Directed by Stuart Heisler. 1950. Warners. 94 min. Sound. 16mm B&W. *Rental:* MGM United.

Chain of Evidence. Bill Elliott & Claudia Barrett. Directed by Paul Landres. 1957. Allied Artists. 64 min. Sound. 16mm B&W. *Rental:* Hurlock Cine.

Chained. Joan Crawford & Clark Gable. Directed by Clarence Brown. 1934. MGM. 74 min. Sound. 16mm B&W. *Rental:* MGM United.

Chained for Life. Hilton Twins. 1941. 75 min. Sound. 16mm B&W. *Rental:* Budget Films & Kit Parker.

Chair, The. 1965. Time-Life. (Documentary). 54 min. Sound. 16mm B&W. *Lease:* Direct Cinema.

Chairman, The. Gregory Peck & Anne Heywood. Directed by J. Lee Thompson. 1969. Fox. (Anamorphic). 104 min. Sound. 16mm Color. *Rental:* Films Inc.

Chairman of the Board. Directed by Jean Bruce & Edmund Reid. 1973. Canada. (Documentary). 63 min. Sound. 16mm Color. *Rental:* Natl Film Lib & Natl film CN. *Sale:* Natl Film CN.

Chalk Garden, The. Deborah Kerr & Hayley Mills. Directed by Ronald Neame. 1964. Universal. 106 min. Sound. 16mm Color. *Rental:* Swank Motion.

Chalk Talk: Alcohol & Alcoholism. 1973. Navy. (Lecture). 66 min. Sound. 16mm Color. *Rental:* Iowa Films, Natl AV Ctr & U Cal Media.

Challenge, The *see* It Takes a Thief.

Challenge, The. Luis Trenker & Robert Douglas. Directed by Milton Rosmer. 1938. Britain. 90 min. Sound. 1938 B&W. *Rental:* Budget Films & Mogulls Films.

Challenge, The. Directed by Joseph Roland. Salesians. (Cast unlisted). 75 min. Sound. 16mm B&W. *Rental:* Bosco Films.

Challenge, The. Scott Glenn & Toshiro Mifune. Directed by John Frankenheimer. 1982. Embassy. 106 min. Sound. 16mm Color. *Rental:* Films Inc.

Challenge, The: A Tribute to Modern Art. Directed by Herbert Kline. 1975. New Line Cinema. (Documentary). 104 min. Sound. 16mm Color. *Rental:* New Line Cinema.

Challenge for Robin Hood, A *see* Legend of Robin Hood.

Challenge for Robin Hood, A. Barrie Ingham & James Hayter. Directed by C. M. Pennington-Richards. 1968. Britain. 85 min. Sound. 16mm Color. *Rental:* Films Inc.

Challenge in the Classroom: Methods of R. L. Moore. 1966. 54 min. Sound. 16mm Color. *Rental:* Utah Media.

Challenge of the Frontier *see* Man of the Forest.

Challenge of the Gladiator. Peter Lupus & Gloria Milland. Directed by Domenico Paolella. 1964. Italy. 89 min. Sound. 16mm B&W. dubbed. *Rental:* Video Comm.

Challenge to Lassie, A. Edmund Gwenn & Donald Crisp. Directed by Richard Thorpe. 1949. MGM. 76 min. Sound. 16mm Color. *Rental:* MGM United.

Chamade, La. Catherine Deneuve & Michel Piccoli. Directed by Alain Cavalier. Fr. 1969. France. 102 min. Sound. 16mm Color. subtitles. *Rental:* MGM United.

Chamber of Horrors. Lilli Palmer & Leslie Banks. Directed by Norman Lee. 1940. Britain. 89 min. Sound. 16mm B&W. *Rental:* Budget Films, Classic Film Mus, Films Inc, Video Comm & Westcoast Films. *Sale:* Classic Film Mus. *Rental:* Budget Films, 80 mins. version.

Chamber of Horrors. Patrick O'Neal & Wilfred Hyde-White. Directed by Hy Averback. 1966. Warners. 99 min. Sound. 16mm Color. *Rental:* Inst Cinema, Mogulls Films, #Swank Motion, Twyman Films, Video Commm & Westcoast Films.

Chambre, La. Michel Auclair & Genevieve Page. Fr. France. 74 min. Sound. 16mm B&W. *Rental:* French Am Cul.

Champ, The. Wallace Beery & Jackie Cooper. Directed by King Vidor. 1931. MGM. 86 min. Sound. 16mm B&W. *Rental:* MGM United.

Champ, The. Jon Voight & Faye Dunaway. Directed by Franco Zeffirelli. 1979. MGM. 122 min. Sound. 16mm Color. *Rental:* MGM United. *Rental:* MGM United, Videotape version.

Champ for a Day. Audrey Totter & Alex Nichol. Directed by Irving Shulman. 1951. Republic. 90 min. Sound. 16mm B&W. *Rental:* Ivy Films. *Sale:* Natl Telefilm.

Champagne. Betty Balfour & Gordon Harker. Directed by Alfred Hitchcock. 1928. Britain. 87 min. Silent. 16mm B&W. *Rental:* Janus Films.

Champagne for Caesar. Ronald Colman & Celeste Holm. Directed by Richard Whorf. 1950. United Artists. 115 min. Sound. 16mm B&W. *Rental:* Budget Films, Film Ctr DC, Inst Cinema, Video Comm, Westcoast Films & Wholesome Film Ctr. *Lease:* Video Comm. *Rental:* Video Comm, Videotape version.

Champagne Waltz, The. Gladys Swarthout & Fred MacMurray. Directed by Edward Sutherland. 1937. Paramount. 85 min. Sound. 16mm B&W. *Rental:* Swank Motion.

Champion. Kirk Douglas & Arthur Kennedy. Directed by Mark Robson. 1949. United Artists. 99 min. Sound. 16mm B&W. *Rental:* Budget Films, Film Ctr DC, Ivy Films, Kit Parker, Rep Pic Film, Film Ctr DC, Video Comm, Wholesome Film Ctr & Willoughby Peer. *Sale:* Rep Pic Film. *Rental:* Video Comm, *Lease:* Video Comm, Videotape version.

Champion of Death. Sonny Chiba. Directed by Kazuhiko Yamaguchi. 1976. Hong Kong. 83 min. Sound. 16mm Color. *Rental:* MGM United.

Champion Skier's Class: Austrian Wedeln Technique & Parallel Swinging. 1967. Austria. (Documentary). 55 min. Sound. 16mm B&W. narrated Eng. *Rental:* U Cal Media.

Champions, The. 1978. Canada. (Documentary). 120 min. Sound. 16mm Color. *Rental:* Natl Film CN.

Champs Elysees. Sacha Guitry. Directed by Sacha Guitry. Fr. 1939. France. 105 min. Sound. 16mm B&W. subtitles. *Rental:* Film Classics.

Chan Is Missing. Moy Wood & Marc Hayashi. Directed by Wayne Wang. 1982. 80 min. Sound. 16mm Color. *Rental:* New Yorker Films.

Chance at Heaven, A. Ginger Rogers & Joel McCrea. Directed by Merian C. Cooper. 1934. RKO. 70 min. Sound. 16mm *Rental:* RKO General Pics.

Chance Meeting. Hardy Kruger & Micheline Presle. Directed by Joseph Losey. 1960. Paramount. 85 min. Sound. 16mm B&W. *Rental:* Films Inc.

Chance of a Night Time. Ralph Lynn. Directed by Herbert Wilcox. 1931. 16mm *Rental:* A Twyman Pres.

Chances. Douglas Fairbanks Jr. & Rose Hobart. Directed by Allan Dwan. 1931. Warners. 72 min. Sound. 16mm B&W. *Rental:* MGM United.

Chandler. Warren Oates & Leslie Caron. Directed by Paul Magwood. 1972. MGM. 88 min. Sound. 16mm Color. *Rental:* MGM United.

Chandu on the Magic Island. Bela Lugosi. Directed by Ray Taylor. 1940. United Artists. 65 min. Sound. 16mm B&W. *Rental:* Budget Films. *Sale:* Cinema Concepts & Natl Cinema. *Sale:* Reel Images, Videotape version.

Chandu the Magician. Edmund Lowe & Bela Lugosi. Directed by Marcel Varnel & William Cameron Menzies. 1932. Fox. 74 min. Sound. 16mm B&W. *Rental:* Films Inc.

Change of Habit. Elvis Presley & Mary Tyler Moore. Directed by William Graham. 1969. Universal. 105 min. Sound. 16mm Color. *Rental:* Williams Films.

Change of Heart. Susan Hayward & John Carroll. Directed by Albert S. Rogell. 1943. Republic. 67 min. Sound. 16mm B&W. *Rental:* Ivy Films. *Sale:* Rep Pic Film.

Change of Life. 1981. Britain. (Documentary). 50 min. Sound. 16mm Color. *Rental:* Films Inc & Syracuse U Film. *Sale:* Films Inc. *Sale:* Films Inc, Videotape version.

Change of Seasons, A. Shirley MacLaine & Bo Derek. Directed by Richard Lang. 1980. Fox. 102 min. Sound. 16mm Color. *Rental:* Williams Films. *Rental:* Williams Films, Videotape version.

Changeling, The. George C. Scott & Trish Van Devere. Directed by Peter Medak. 1980. 113 min. Sound. 16mm Color. *Rental:* Swank Motion.

Changes After Death. 1978. 46 min. Sound. 16mm B&W. *Rental:* Natl AV Ctr.

Changing. 1979. 65 min. 16mm Color. *Sale:* Aust Info Serv. *Rental:* Aust Info Serv.

Changing Voice. 1960. IFB. 45 min. Sound. 16mm B&W. *Rental:* Syracuse U Film.

Chant of Jimmie Blacksmith, The. Tommy Lewis. Directed by Fred Schepisi. 1978. Australia. (Anamorphic). 108 min. Sound. 16mm Color. *Rental:* New Yorker Films.

Chapayev. Boris Babotchkin & Boris Blinov. Directed by Georgy Vassiliev & Sergei Vassiliev. Rus. 1934. Russia. 100 min. Sound. 16mm B&W. subtitles. *Rental:* Corinth Films.

Chapeau De Paille D'Italie see Italian Straw Hat.

Chaplin Revue, The. Charles Chaplin. Directed by Charles Chaplin. 1959. First National. (Musical score only). 119 min. Sound. 16mm B&W. *Rental:* Films Inc & Learning Corp Am. *Sale:* Blackhawk Films & Magnetic Video, Videotape version.

Chaplinesque-My Life & Hard Times see Eternal Tramp.

Chaplin's Art of Comedy. 1969. Allied Artists. (Anthology). 82 min. Videotape B&W. *Sale:* Blackhawk Films.

Chaplin's Essanay Films. 1915. Essanay. (Anthology). 82 min. Silent. 16mm B&W. *Rental:* Museum Mod Art.

Chaplin's Keystone Films. 1914. Keystone. (Anthology). 73 min. Sound. 16mm B&W. *Rental:* Museum Mod Art.

Chaplin's Mutual Period, 1916-1917. 52 min. Sound. 16mm Color. *Rental:* Media Guild.

Chapter Three. Brian. 60 min. Videotape Color. *Sale:* Astro Video.

Chapter Two. James Caan & Marsha Mason. Directed by Robert Moore. 1979. Columbia. 124 min. Sound. 16mm Color. *Rental:* Arcus Film, Budget Films, Swank Motion, Welling Motion Pictures, Westcoast Films & Wholesome Film Ctr. *Rental:* Swank Motion, Videotape version.

Charade. Cary Grant & Audrey Hepburn. Directed by Stanley Donen. 1963. Universal. 113 min. Sound. 16mm Color. *Rental:* Swank Motion.

Charge of the Lancers, The. Paulette Goddard & Jean-Pierre Aumont. Directed by William Castle. 1954. Columbia. 74 min. Sound. 16mm Color. *Rental:* Maljack. *Lease:* Maljack. *Lease:* Maljack, Videotape version.

Charge of the Light Brigade, The. Errol Flynn & Olivia De Havilland. Directed by Michael Curtiz. 1936. Warners. 115 min. Sound. 16mm B&W. *Rental:* MGM United.

Charge of the Light Brigade, The. Vanessa Redgrave, David Hemmings, Sir John Gielgud. Directed by Tony Richardson. 1968. United Artists. (Anamorphic). 128 min. Sound. 16mm Color. *Rental:* MGM United.

Chariots of Fire. Ben Cross, Ian Charleson & Ian Holm. Directed by Hugh Hudson. 1985. The Ladd Company. 124 min. Sound. 16mm Color. *Rental:* Swank Motion. *Rental:* Swank Motion, Videotape version.

Chariots of the Gods? Directed by Harold Reinl. 1974. Landsburg. (Documentary). 98 min. Sound. Videotape Color. *Sale:* Video Corp.

Charles-Dead or Alive. François Simon. Directed by Alain Tanner. Fr. 1969. Switzerland. 93 min. Sound. 16mm B&W. subtitles. *Rental:* New Yorker Films.

Charles Dickens Show, The. Victor Spinetti. 1973. Britain. 52 min. Sound. 16mm Color. *Rental:* Inst Film, Syracuse U Film, U Mich Media & Utah Media. *Sale:* Inst Film.

Charles Doughty: Arabia 1877. Directed by David McCallum. 1977. Britain. (Cast unlisted). 49 min. Sound. 16mm Color. *Rental:* Time-Life Multimedia. *Sale:* Time-Life Multimedia. *Sale:* Time-Life Multimedia, Videotape version.

Charles Evans Hughes. Kent Smith. Directed by Robert Butler. (Profiles in Courage Ser.). 1965. Saudek. 50 min. Sound. 16mm B&W. *Rental:* IQ Film & Syracuse U Film. *Sale:* IQ Film. *Sale:* IQ film, Spanish dubbed version.

Charles Francis Adams II: Industrialist. 1976. WNET. (Cast unlisted). 59 min. Sound. 16mm Color. *Rental:* U of IL Film, Indiana Av Ctr & Iowa Films. *Sale:* Films Inc, Videotape version.

Charles Francis Adams: Minister to Great Britain. 1976. WNET. (Cast unlisted). 59 min. Sound. 16mm Color. *Rental:* U of IL Film & Iowa Films. *Sale:* Films Inc, Videotape version.

Charles I. 1980. Britain. (Documentary). 60 min. Sound. 16mm Color. *Rental:* Films Inc. *Sale:* Films Inc. *Sale:* Films Inc, Videotape version.

Charley & the Angel. Fred MacMurray, Harry Morgan, Cloris Leachman & Kurt Russell. Directed by Vincent McEveety. 1973. Disney. 93 min. Sound. 16mm Color. *Rental:* Bosco Films, Cine Craft, Disney Prod, Elliot Film Co, Film Ctr DC, Films Inc, Modern Sound, Newman Film Lib, Roas Films, Twyman Films, U of IL Film, Welling Motion Pictures, Westcoast Films & Williams Films.

Charley Moon. Max Byraves & Dennis Price. Directed by Guy Hamilton. 1955. Britain. 92 min. Sound. 16mm B&W. *Rental:* Charard Motion Pics.

Charley One-Eye. Richard Roundtree & Roy Thinnes. Directed by Don Chaffey. 1973. Paramount. 107 min. Sound. 16mm Color. *Rental:* Films Inc.

Charley's Aunt. Sydney Chaplin & Alec B. Francis. Directed by Scott Sidney. 1925. PDC. 85 min. Silent. Super 8 B&W. *Rental:* Ivy Films. *Sale:* Blackhawk Films. *Sale:* Blackhawk Films, Silent 8mm version.

Charley's Aunt. Jack Benny & Kay Francis. Directed by Archie Mayo. 1941. Fox. 81 min. Sound. 16mm B&W. *Rental:* Arcus Film.

Charlie Chan at Monte Carlo. Warner Oland & Keye Luke. Directed by Eugene Forde. 1937. Fox. 71 min. Sound. 16mm B&W. *Rental:* Films Inc.

Charlie Chan at the Olympics. Warner Oland & Keye Luke. Directed by Bruce Humberstone. 1937. Fox. 71 min. Sound. 16mm B&W. *Rental:* Films Inc.

Charlie Chan at the Race Track. Warner Oland & Keye Luke. Directed by Bruce Humberstone. 1936. Fox. 70 min. Sound. 16mm B&W. *Rental:* Films Inc.

Charlie Chan at Treasure Island. Sidney Toler & Arleen Whalen. Directed by Norman Foster. 1939. Fox. 75 min. Sound. 16mm B&W. *Rental:* Films Inc & Swank Motion.

Charlie Chan in Castle in the Desert *see* Castle in the Desert.

Charlie Chan in Honolulu. Sidney Toler & Phyllis Brooks. Directed by Bruce Humberstone. 1938. Fox. 65 min. Sound. 16mm B&W. *Rental:* Films Inc.

Charlie Chan in London. Warner Oland & Ray Milland. Directed by Eugene Forde. 1934. Fox. 80 min. Sound. 16mm B&W. *Rental:* Films Inc & Swank Motion.

Charlie Chan in Panama. Sidney Toler. Directed by Norman Foster. 1940. Fox. 65 min. Sound. 16mm B&W. *Rental:* Films Inc.

Charlie Chan in Paris. Warner Oland & Mary Brian. Directed by Lewis Seiler. 1935. Fox. 71 min. Sound. 16mm B&W. *Rental:* Films Inc.

Charlie Chan in Shanghai. Watner Oland. Directed by James Tinling. 1935. Fox. 70 min. Sound. 16mm B&W. *Rental:* Films Inc & Swank Motion.

Charlie Chan in the Secret Service. Sidney Toler & Mantan Moreland. Directed by Phil Rosen. 1944. Monogram. 68 min. Sound. 16mm B&W. *Rental:* MGM United & Mogulls Films.

Charlie Chan on Broadway. Warner Oland & Keye Luke. Directed by Eugene Forde. 1937. Fox. 68 min. Sound. 16mm B&W. *Rental:* Films Inc.

Charlie Chan's Murder Cruise. Sidney Toler. Directed by Eugene Forde. 1940. Fox. 65 min. Sound. 16mm B&W. *Rental:* Films Inc.

Charlie Chan's Secret. Warner Oland & Henrietta Crosman. Directed by Gordon Wiles. 1935. Fox. 71 min. Sound. 16mm B&W. *Rental:* Films Inc.

Charlie Chaplin Carnival. Directed by Charles Chaplin. 1916. United Artists. 80 min. Sound. 16mm B&W. *Rental:* Budget Films.

Charlie Chaplin Cavalcade. Charlie Chaplin & Edna Purviance. Directed by Charles Chaplin. 1916. 80 min. Sound. 16mm *Rental:* Budget Films.

Charlie Chaplin Festival. Charlie Chaplin & Edna Purviance. Directed by Charles Chaplin. 1917. 80 min. Sound. 16mm *Rental:* Budget Films.

Charlie Is My Darling. Directed by Peter Whitehead. 1965. Britain. (Concert). 50 min. Sound. 16mm B&W. *Rental:* Budget Films, Ivy Films & Video Comm. *Rental:* Video Comm, Videotape version.

Charlotte's Web. Directed by Charles A. Nichols & Iwao Takamoto. 1973. Paramount. (Animated). 94 min. Sound. 16mm Color. *Rental:* Films Inc.

Charly. Cliff Robertson & Claire Bloom. Directed by Ralph Nelson. 1968. ABC. 103 min. Sound. 16mm Color. *Rental:* Films Inc. *Rental:* Films Inc, Anamorphic color version. *Sale:* ABC Film Lib, Super 8 sound version.

Charm of La Boheme, The. Jan Kiepura & Marta Eggerth. Directed by Geza Von Bolvary. Ger. 1936. Germany. 80 min. Sound. 16mm B&W. subtitles. *Rental:* Budget Films. *Sale:* Natl Cinema.

Charmed Particles: Adventure of the Exquisite Corpse. Directed by Andrew Noren. 1978. Noren. 78 min. Sound. 16mm B&W. *Rental:* Museum Mod Art.

Charro! Elvis Presley & Ina Balin. Directed by Charles Marquis Warren. 1969. National General. 98 min. Sound. 16mm Color. *Rental:* Williams Films & Swank Motion.

Charter Pilot. Lloyd Nolan & Lynn Bari. Directed by Eugene Forde. 1940. Fox. 70 min. Sound. 16mm B&W. *Rental:* Films Inc.

Chartero, El. Span. 1950. Mexico. (Cast unlisted). 90 min. Sound. 16mm B&W. *Rental:* Film Classics.

Chartreuse de Parme, La. Gerard Philipe. Directed by Christian-Jaque. 1947. France. 180 min. Sound. 16mm B&W. *Rental:* French Am Cul. *Rental:* French Am Cul, Videotape version.

Charulata. Orig. Title: Lonely Wife. Soumitra Chatterjec. Directed by Satyajit Ray. Hindi. 1965. India. 115 min. Sound. 16mm B&W. subtitles. *Rental:* Trans-World Films.

Chase, The. Marlon Brando, Jane Fonda & Robert Redford. Directed by Arthur Penn. 1966. Columbia. 135 min. Sound. 16mm Color. *Rental:* Arcus Film, Budget Films, Cine Craft, Charard Motion Pics, Corinth Films, Films Inc, Williams Films, Inst Cinema, Ivy Films, Kit Parker, Modern Sound, Newman Film Lib, Natl Film Video, Roas Films, Twyman Films, Video Comm, Westcoast Films, Welling Motion Pictures & Wholesome Film Ctr. *Rental:* Corinth Films, Images Film & Kit Parker, Anamorphic version.

Chase, The. Robert Cummings & Michele Morgan. Directed by Arthur Ripley. 1946. United Artists. 81 min. Sound. 16mm B&W. *Rental:* Mogulls Films & Budget Films.

Chaser, The. Harry Langdon. Directed by Harry Langdon. 1928. First National. 84 min. Silent. 16mm B&W. *Rental:* A Twyman Pres & Twyman Films.

Chaser, The. Dennis O'Keefe & Ann Moriss. Directed by Edwin L. Marin. 1938. MGM. 75 min. Sound. 16mm B&W. *Rental:* MGM United.

Chasing Rainbows. Bessie Love & Charles King. Directed by Charles Reisner. 1930. MGM. (Color sequences). 110 min. Sound. 16mm *Rental:* MGM United.

Chasing Trouble. Frankie Darro & Mantan Moreland. Directed by Howard Bretherton. 1940. Monogram. 64 min. Sound. 16mm B&W. *Rental:* Hurlock Cine.

Chasing Yesterday. Anne Shirley & Helen Westley. Directed by George Nicholls Jr. 1935. RKO. 77 min. Sound. 16mm *Rental:* RKO General Pics.

Chat, Le. Orig. Title: Cat, The. Simone Signoret & Jean Gabin. Directed by Pierre Granier Defere. Fr. 1975. France. 88 min. Sound. Videotape Color. subtitles. *Rental:* J Green Pics. *Sale:* Tamarelles French Film.

Chateaubriand. Fr. France. (Cast unlisted). 60 min. Sound. 16mm B&W. *Rental:* French Am Cul.

Chato's Land. Charles Bronson & Jack Palance. Directed by Michael Winner. 1972. United Artists. 100 min. Sound. 16mm Color. *Rental:* MGM United & Westcoast Films.

Chatterbox. Joe E. Brown & Judy Canova. Directed by Joseph Santley. 1942. Republic. 77 min. Sound. 16mm B&W. *Rental:* Ivy Films.

Chatterbox. Lucille Ball & Anne Shirley. Directed by George Nicholls Jr. 1936. RKO. 68 min. Sound. 16mm *Rental:* RKO General Pics.

Che! Omar Sharif & Jack Palance. Directed by Richard Fleischer. 1969. Fox. 96 min. Sound. 16mm Color. *Rental:* Films Inc.

Cheap Detective, The. Peter Falk, Ann-Margret & Sid Caesar. Directed by Robert Moore. 1978. Columbia. 92 min. Sound. 16mm Color. *Rental:* Arcus Film, Budget Films, Cine Craft, Images Film, Kit Parker, Modern Sound, Newman Film Lib, Swank Motion, Twyman Films, Welling Motion Pictures, Westcoast Films, Wholesome Film Ctr & Williams Films. *Rental:* Swank Motion, Videotape version.

Cheaper by the Dozen. Clifton Webb & Jeanne Crain. Directed by Walter Lang. 1950. Fox. 85 min. Sound. 16mm B&W. *Rental:* Films Inc, Twyman Films & Williams Films.

Cheat, The. Sessue Hayakawa & Fanny Ward. Directed by Cecil B. DeMille. 1915. Paramount. 55 min. Silent. 16mm B&W. *Rental:* Em Gee Film Lib. *Sale:* Reel Images. *Sale:* Reel Images, Super 8 silent version. *Sale:* Cinema Concepts, Silent 8mm version.

Cheat, The. Tallulah Bankhead & Irving Pichel. Directed by George Abbott. 1931. Paramount. 69 min. Sound. 16mm B&W. *Rental:* Swank Motion.

Cheaters, The. Orig. Title: Castaway, The. Joseph Schildkraut & Billie Burke. Directed by Joseph Kane. 1945. Republic. 87 min. Sound. 16mm B&W. *Rental:* Ivy Films.

Check & Double Check. Amos & Andy. Directed by Melville Brown. 1930. RKO. 84 min. Sound. 16mm B&W. *Rental:* Budget Films, Classic Film Mus, Em Gee Film Lib, Kit Parker, Video Comm & Westcoast Films. *Sale:* Natl Cinema. *Rental:* Ivy Films, Cinema Concepts & Ivy Films, Super 8 sound version. *Rental:* Video Comm, Videotape version. *Rental:* Classic Film Mus, 73 mins. version.

Check Your Guns. Eddie Dean. Directed by Ray Taylor. 1948. Eagle Lion. 55 min. Sound. 16mm B&W. *Sale:* Classics Assoc NY.

Checkered Flag or Crash. Joe Don Baker. Directed by Alan Gibson. 1977. Universal. 93 min. Sound. 16mm Color. *Rental:* Swank Motion.

Checkmate *see* Desert Horseman.

Cheech & Chong Perform. (Concert). 50 min. Videotape Color. *Sale:* Cinema Concepts.

Cheech & Chong's Next Movie. Cheech Marin & Thomas Chong. Directed by Thomas Chong. 99 min. 16mm Color. *Rental:* Swank Motion. *Rental:* Swank Motion, Videotape version.

Cheech & Chong's Things Are Tough All Over. Cheech Marin & Tommy Chong. Directed by Thomas K. Avildsen. 1982. Columbia. 87 min. Sound. 16mm Color. *Rental:* Swank Motion. *Rental:* Swank Motion, Videotape version.

Cheering Section, The. Rhonda Foxx & Tom Leindecker. Directed by Harry E. Kerwin. 1977. Dimension. 84 min. Sound. 16mm Color. *Sale:* Salz Ent.

Cheers for Miss Bishop. Martha Scott & William Gargan. Directed by Tay Garnett. 1940. United Artists. 74 min. Sound. 16mm B&W. *Rental:* Alba House, Budget Films, Classic Film Mus, Film Classics, Films Inc, Ivy Films, Mogulls Films, Rep Pic Film, Video Comm & Wholesome Film Ctr. *Sale:* Rep Pic Film. *Rental:* Video Comm, *Sale:* Tamarelles French Film, Videotape version. *Rental:* Classic Film Mus, 94 mins. version.

Cheever Short Stories. Edward Herrman, Sigourney Weaver, Eileen Heckart & Rachel Roberts. Directed by Jeff Bleckner & Jack Hofsiss. 1979. WNET. 120 min. Sound. 16mm Color. *Sale:* Films Inc. *Rental:* Films Inc, *Sale:* Films Inc, Videotape version.

Chekhov's Uncle Vanya in Perspective. 1975. Films for the Humanities. (Documentary). 48 min. Sound. 16mm B&W. *Rental:* Films Human. *Sale:* Films Human. *Sale:* Films Human, *Sale:* Films Human, Color version.

Cheloveks Kinosapparotom *see* Man with the Movie Camera.

Cherokee Flash, The. Sunset Carson. Directed by Thomas Carr. 1945. Republic. 54 min. Sound. 16mm B&W. *Rental:* Ivy Films. *Sale:* Rep Pic Film.

Cherokee Strip, The. Orig. Title: Fighting Marshal. Dick Foran & Jane Bryan. Directed by Noel Smith. 1937. Warners. 55 min. Sound. 16mm B&W. *Rental:* MGM United.

Cherokee Uprising. Whip Wilson. Directed by Lewis D. Collins. 1950. Monogram. 55 min. Sound. 16mm B&W. *Rental:* Budget Films.

Cherry, Harry & Raquel. Larissa Ely. Directed by Russ Meyer. 1969. Eve. 71 min. Sound. 16mm Color. *Rental:* Corinth Films. *Sale:* Cinema Concepts, Videotape version.

Cheryl Surrenders. 60 min. Videotape Color. *Sale:* Videx Home Lib.

Chess Players, The. Richard Attenborough & Sanjeev Kumar. Directed by Satyajit Ray. Hindi. 1978. India. 135 min. Sound. 16mm Color. subtitles. *Rental:* Janus Films.

Chester Ronning Story, The: China Mission. Directed by Tom Radford. 1980. National Film Board of Canada. 57 min. 16mm Color. *Rental:* Natl Film CN. *Sale:* Natl Film CN.

Chesty Anderson: U. S. Navy. Shari Eubank. Directed by Ed Forsyth. 1975. Coast Industries. 88 min. Sound. 16mm Color. *Rental:* Films Inc.

Cheyenne. Orig. Title: Wyoming Kid, The. Dennis Morgan & Jane Wyman. Directed by Raoul Walsh. 1947. Warners. 100 min. Sound. 16mm B&W. *Rental:* MGM United.

Cheyenne Autumn. James Stewart & Richard Widmark. Directed by John Ford. 1964. Warners. 160 min. Sound. 16mm Color. *Rental:* Buchan Pic, Charard Motion Pics, Williams Films, Films Inc, Modern Sound, Swank Motion & Twyman Films.

Cheyenne Kid. Jack Randall. Directed by Raymond K. Johnson. 1940. Monogram. 55 min. Sound. 16mm B&W. *Rental:* Hurlock Cine. *Sale:* Cinema Concepts.

Cheyenne Kid, The. Tom Keene & Mary Mason. Directed by Jacques Jaccard. 1933. RKO. 54 min. Sound. 16mm *Rental:* RKO General Pics.

Cheyenne Rides Again. Tom Tyler. Directed by Robert Hill. 1938. Victory. 60 min. Sound. 16mm B&W. *Rental:* Mogulls Films. *Sale:* Cinema Concepts, Natl Cinema & Rep Pic Film.

Cheyenne Social Club, The. James Stewart, Henry Fonda & Shirley Jones. 1970. National General. 103 min. Sound. 16mm Color. *Rental:* Swank Motion & Williams Films.

Cheyenne Takes Over. Lash LaRue. Directed by Ray Taylor. 1947. Eagle Lion. 58 min. Sound. 16mm B&W. *Sale:* Classics Assoc NY.

Cheyenne Wildcat. Bill Elliott. Directed by Lesley Selander. 1944. Republic. 53 min. Sound. 16mm B&W. *Rental:* Ivy Films.

Chicago Confidential. Brian Keith, Beverly Garland & Dick Foran. Directed by Sidney Salkow. 1957. United Artists. 74 min. Sound. 16mm B&W. *Rental:* MGM United.

Chicago Conspiracy Trial, The. Directed by Christopher Burstoll. 1968. (Cast unlisted). 150 min. Sound. 16mm B&W. *Rental:* Budget Films.

Chicago Deadline. Alan Ladd & Donna Reed. Directed by Lewis Allen. 1949. Paramount. 87 min. Sound. 16mm B&W. *Rental:* Swank Motion.

Chicago Kid, The. Otto Kruger & Tom Powers. Directed by Frank McDonald. 1957. Republic. 96 min. Sound. 16mm B&W. *Rental:* Ivy Films.

Chicago Maternity Center Story, The. 1977. Kartemquin. (Documentary). 60 min. Sound. 16mm B&W. *Rental:* Unifilm. *Sale:* Unifilm.

Chicago Picasso, The. 1967. NET. (Documentary). 60 min. Sound. 16mm Color. *Rental:* Indiana AV Ctr. *Sale:* Indiana AV Ctr.

Chicken Chronicles, The. Phil Silvers & Steven Guttenberg. Directed by Francis Simon. 1977. Embassy. 94 min. Sound. Videotape Color. *Sale:* Films Inc.

Chicken Every Sunday. Dan Dailey & Celeste Holm. Directed by George Seaton. 1948. Fox. 94 min. Sound. 16mm B&W. *Rental:* Films Inc.

Chicken Ranch. 1983. Britain. (Documentary). 84 min. Sound. 16mm Color. *Rental:* First Run.

Chico, the Misunderstood Coyote. 1961. Disney. (Documentary). 48 min. Sound. 16mm Color. *Rental:* Buchan Pic, Cine Craft, Cousino Visual Ed, Film Ctr DC, Films Inc, Disney Prod, Modern Sound, Newman Film Lib, Roas Films & Twyman Films.

Chief, The. Ed Wynn & William Boyd. Directed by Charles Reisner. 1933. MGM. 67 min. Sound. 16mm B&W. *Rental:* MGM United.

Chief Crazy Horse. Orig. Title: Valley of Fury. Victor Mature & John Lund. Directed by George Sherman. 1955. Universal. 86 min. Sound. 16mm Color. *Rental:* Williams Films.

Chief Justice John Marshall *see* John Marshall.

Chienne, La. Michel Simon & Janie Mareze. Directed by Jean Renoir. Fr. 1931. 100 min. Sound. 16mm B&W. subtitles Eng. *Rental:* Films Inc.

Chikamatsu Monogatari. Trans. Title: Legend of the Grand Scrollmaker. Kazuo Hasegewa. Directed by Kenji Mizoguchi. Jap. 1955. Japan. 100 min. Sound. 16mm B&W. subtitles. *Rental:* New Line Cinema.

Child, The. 1971. 48 min. Sound. 16mm Color. *Rental:* Utah Media.

Child, The. Rosalie Cole, Frank Janson & Richard Hanners. 65 min. Sound. 16mm Color. *Rental:* BF Video.

Child Abuse & Neglect, a Basic View. 1977. 55 min. Sound. Videotape Color. *Rental:* Iowa Films.

Child Bride, The. 1938. 60 min. Sound. 16mm B&W. *Sale:* Morcraft Films.

Child Development. 1979. 53 min. Sound. Videotape Color. *Rental:* Iowa Films.

Child for Tony, A. Xerox. (Cast unlisted). 60 min. Sound. 16mm B&W. *Sale:* Xerox Films.

Child Is Born, A. Nanette Fabray & Jeffrey Lynn. Directed by Lloyd Bacon. 1940. Warners. 79 min. Sound. 16mm B&W. *Rental:* MGM United.

Child is Waiting, A. Burt Lancaster & Judy Garland. Directed by John Cassavetes. 1963. United Artists. 104 min. Sound. 16mm B&W. *Rental:* MGM United, Westcoast Films & Welling Motion Pictures.

Child of Divorce, A. Regis Toomey & Sharyn Moffett. Directed by Richard Fleischer. 1947. RKO. 62 min. Sound. 16mm *Rental:* RKO General Pics.

Child of Glass, A. Nina Foch, Anthony Zerbe, Biff McGuire & Steve Shaw. Directed by John Erman. 1978. Disney. 94 min. Sound. 16mm Color. *Rental:* Bosco Films, Elliot Film Co, Films Inc, MGM United, Modern Sound, Roas Films, Welling Motion Pictures, Westcoast Films & Williams Films.

Child of Manhattan, A. Nancy Carroll, John Boles & Buck Jones. Directed by Edward Buzzell. 1933. Columbia. 73 min. Sound. 16mm B&W. *Rental:* Kit Parker.

Child of the Future, A. 1965. Canada. (Documentary). 59 min. Sound. 16mm B&W. *Rental:* Natl Film CN, U Col Media Ctr, U Nev AV Ctr & U Mich Media. *Sale:* McGraw-Hill Films & Natl Film CN.

Child of the Paris Streets, A. Mae Marsh. Directed by Lloyd Ingraham. 1916. Fine Arts Triangle. 46 min. Silent. 16mm B&W. *Rental:* Em Gee Film Lib. *Sale:* Cinema Concepts.

Child of the Regiment *see* Daughter of the Regiment.

Child Series, The. 5 pts. Directed by Robert Humble. 1976. Canada. 138 min. Sound. 16mm Color. *Rental:* McGraw-Hill Films. *Sale:* McGraw-Hill Films. *Sale:* McGraw-Hill Films, Videotape version.

Child Under a Leaf. Dyan Cannon & Donald Pilon. Directed by George Bloomfield. 1974. Canada. 88 min. Sound. 16mm Color. *Rental:* Budget Films.

Childbirth, & Problems of Child Patients. 1974. US Government. (Documentary). 59 min. Sound. 16mm Color. *Sale:* Natl AV Ctr.

Childhood of Maxim Gorky, The. Alexei Lyarsky. Directed by Mark Donskoi. Rus. 1938. Russia. 100 min. Sound. 16mm B&W. *Rental:* Corinth Films. *Lease:* Corinth Films.

Childhood Sexual Abuse: Four Case Studies. 1977. Motorola. (Documentary). 50 min. Sound. 16mm Color. *Rental:* Iowa Films & MTI Tele. *Sale:* MTI Tele. *Sale:* MTI Tele, Videotape version.

Childhood: The Enchanted Years. 1971. MGM. (Documentary). 52 min. Sound. 16mm Color. *Rental:* Films Inc, Syracuse U Film, U of IL Film, U Mich Media & Utah Media. *Sale:* Films Inc. *Sale:* Films Inc, Videotape version.

Children. 1971. Family of Man. (Documentary). 50 min. Sound. 16mm Color. *Rental:* Films Inc. *Sale:* Films Inc. *Sale:* Films Inc, Videotape version.

Children, The. Directed by Terrence Davies. 1974. Britain. (Documentary). 46 min. Sound. 16mm B&W. *Rental:* Museum Mod Art.

Children, The. Martin Shakar & Gill Rogers. 89 min. Sound. Videotape *Rental:* WW Enter.

Children & Sports. (Documentary). 58 min. Sound. 16mm Color. *Rental:* Pyramid Film. *Sale:* Pyramid Film.

Children Galore. Eddie Byrne & June Thorburn. Directed by Terence Fisher. 1954. Britain. 60 min. Sound. 16mm B&W. *Rental:* Cinema Five.

Children in the Balance: The Tragedy of Biafra. 1969. NET. 60 min. Sound. 16mm B&W. *Rental:* Indiana AV Ctr. *Sale:* Indiana AV Ctr.

Children in the Holocaust. 1982. Phoenix. (Documentary). 70 min. Sound. 16mm Color. *Rental:* Phoenix Films. *Sale:* Phoenix Films. *Sale:* Phoenix Films, Videotape version.

Children in the Hospital. 1966. 44 min. Sound. 16mm Color. *Rental:* Utah Media.

Children in the House. Norma Talmadge, Eugene Pallette & Walter Long. 1916. Fine Arts-Triangle. 50 min. Sound. 16mm B&W. *Rental:* Film Classics.

Children of China, The. 1979. PBS. (Documentary). 59 min. Sound. Videotape Color. *Rental:* PBS Video. *Sale:* PBS Video.

Children of Marx & Coca-Cola *see* Masculine-Feminine.

Children of Our Time. 1974. Canada. (Documentary). 52 min. Sound. 16mm Color. *Rental:* U Mich Media.

Children of Paradise. Jean-Louis Barrault & Arletty. Directed by Marcel Carne. Fr. 1946. France. 188 min. Sound. 16mm B&W. subtitles. *Rental:* Films Inc.

Children of Pleasure. Lawrence Gray & Helen Johnson. Directed by Harry Beaumont. 1930. MGM. 61 min. Sound. 16mm B&W. *Rental:* MGM United.

Children of Rage. Simon Ward & Cyril Cusack. Directed by Arthur Allan Seidelman. 1975. Britain. 106 min. Sound. 16mm Color. *Rental:* Films Inc, Welling Motion Pictures & Westcoast Films.

Children of Revolution. 1965. NET. (Documentary). 60 min. Sound. 16mm B&W. *Rental:* Indiana AV Ctr. *Lease:* Indiana AV Ctr.

Children of the Corn. John Franklin & Peter Horton. Directed by Fritz Kiersch. 1985. Warners. 93 min. Sound. 16mm Color. *Rental:* Swank Motion. *Rental:* Swank Motion, Videotape version.

Children of the Damned. Alan Badel & Ian Hendry. Directed by Anton M. Leader. 1964. Britain. 90 min. Sound. 16mm B&W. *Rental:* MGM United.

Children of the Golden West. 1975. 59 min. Sound. S8mm Color. *Rental:* Canyon Cinema.

Children of the River. Directed by Jean Rouch. 1952. (Documentary). 77 min. 16mm Color. *Rental:* A Twyman Pres.

Children of the Wild. Joan Valerie. 70 min. Sound. 16mm B&W. *Rental:* Alba House.

Children of Theater Street, The. Directed by Robert Dornhelm & Earle Mack. 1977. Russia. (Documentary). 90 min. Sound. 16mm Color. narrated Eng. *Rental:* Corinth Films. *Lease:* Corinth Films.

Children on Trial. 1946. Britain. (Documentary). 61 min. Sound. 16mm B&W. *Rental:* U of IL Film.

Children Shouldn't Play with Dead Things! Alan Ormsby. Directed by Benjamin Clark. 1972. Benjamin Clark. 80 min. Sound. 16mm Color. *Rental:* Ivy Films & Maljack Productions.

Children's Hour, The. Audrey Hepburn & Shirley MacLaine. Directed by William Wyler. 1962. United Artists. 107 min. Sound. 16mm B&W. *Rental:* MGM United & Westcoast Films.

Children's Key Concert. 1979. PBS. (Concert). 58 min. Sound. Videotape Color. *Rental:* PBS Video. *Sale:* PBS Video.

Child's Play. James Mason & Robert Preston. Directed by Sidney Lumet. 1972. Paramount. 100 min. Sound. 16mm Color. *Rental:* Films Inc.

Chile, I Don't Take Your Name in Vain. 1984. 55 min. 16mm Color. *Rental:* Icarus Films. *Sale:* Icarus Films, Videotape version.

Chile with Poems & Guns. Span. 1973. Lucha. (Documentary, color sequences). 55 min. Sound. 16mm Color. subtitles. *Rental:* Unifilm. *Sale:* Unifilm.

Chill to the Bones, A. 1981. CTW. (Cast unlisted). 60 min. Sound. Videotape Color. *Rental:* PBS Video. *Sale:* PBS Video.

Chillysmith Farm. 1981. 55 min. Sound. 16mm Color. *Rental:* U Mich Media.

Chimes at Midnight. Orig. Title: Falstaff. Orson Welles, Jeanne Moreau, Margaret Rutherford, Sir John Gielgud. Directed by Orson Welles. 1967. Peppercorn-Wormser. 119 min. Sound. 16mm B&W. *Rental:* A Cantor. *Sale:* A Cantor.

China. 1971. Britain. (Documentary). 50 min. Sound. 16mm Color. *Rental:* Time-Life Multimedia. *Sale:* Time-Life Multimedia. *Sale:* Time-Life Multimedia, Spanish language version. *Rental:* Time-Life Multimedia, *Sale:* Time-Life Multimedia, Videotape version.

China. Alan Ladd & Loretta Young. Directed by John Farrow. 1943. Paramount. 79 min. Sound. 16mm B&W. *Rental:* Swank Motion.

China: A Class by Itself. Directed by Darold Murray. 1979. NBC. (Documentary). 52 min. Sound. 16mm Color. *Rental:* Films Inc & Syracuse U Film. *Sale:* Films Inc. *Sale:* Films Inc, Videotape version.

China: A Revolution Revisited. 1971. Metromedia. (Documentary). 82 min. Sound. 16mm B&W. *Rental:* Films Inc, Syracuse U Film & Wholesome Film Ctr. *Sale:* Films Inc.

China: Century of Revolution. 3 pts. 1968. Films Inc. (Documentary). 80 min. Sound. 16mm B&W. *Rental:* Films Inc. *Sale:* Films Inc.

China Clipper. Pat O'Brien & Marie Wilson. Directed by Ray Enright. 1936. Warners. 89 min. Sound. 16mm B&W. *Rental:* MGM United.

China Doll. Victor Mature & Stuart Whitman. Directed by Frank Borzage. 1958. United Artists. 88 min. Sound. 16mm B&W. *Rental:* MGM United.

China Express. Trans. Title: Goluboi Ekspress. Directed by Ilya Trauberg, Sun Bo-Yang, Chou Hsi-fan & Chang Kai. 1929. Russia. (Cast unlisted). 90 min. Silent. 16mm B&W. *Rental:* Museum Mod Art. *Rental:* Museum Mod Art, Russian titled version.

China Gate. Gene Barry & Angie Dickinson. Directed by Samuel Fuller. 1957. Fox. (Anamorphic). 97 min. Sound. 16mm B&W. *Rental:* Ivy Films, Westcoast Films & Kit Parker. *Lease:* Rep Pic Film.

China Girl. Gene Tierney & George Montgomery. Directed by Henry Hathaway. 1942. Fox. 95 min. Sound. 16mm B&W. *Rental:* Films Inc.

China Is Near. Elda Tattloli. Directed by Marco Bellocchio. Ital. 1968. Italy. 108 min. Sound. 16mm B&W. subtitles. *Rental:* Corinth Films & Swank Motion.

China Mission: The Chester Ronning Story. 1980. 57 min. Sound. 16mm Color. *Rental:* U Cal Media.

China Passage. Anita Colby & Vinton Hayworth. Directed by Edward Killy. 1937. RKO. 65 min. Sound. 16mm *Rental:* RKO General Pics.

China: Revolution Revisited. 1973. 79 min. Sound. 16mm B&W. *Rental:* Utah Media.

China: Roots of Madness. 1967. Wolper. (Documentary). 83 min. Sound. 16mm B&W. *Rental:* Films Inc. *Sale:* Films Inc. *Sale:* Films Inc, Videotape version.

China Seas. Jean Harlow & Clark Gable. Directed by Tay Garnett. 1935. MGM. 89 min. Sound. 16mm B&W. *Rental:* MGM United.

China Sky. Randolph Scott & Ruth Warrick. Directed by Ray Enright. 1945. RKO. 78 min. Sound. 16mm B&W. *Rental:* Films Inc.

China Syndrome, The. Jane Fonda, Michael Douglas & Jack Lemmon. Directed by James Bridges. 1979. Columbia. 122 min. Sound. 16mm Color. *Rental:* Arcus Film, Budget Films, Williams Films, Images Film, Kit Parker, Swank Motion, Welling Motion Pictures & Wholesome Film Ctr. *Rental:* Swank Motion & Direct Cinema, Videotape version.

China Today: A People's Dynasty. 1975. Canada. (Documentary). 52 min. Sound. 16mm Color. *Rental:* B Raymond. *Sale:* B Raymond.

China Venture. Edmond O'Brien & Barry Sullivan. Directed by Don Siegel. 1953. Columbia. 90 min. Sound. 16mm B&W. *Rental:* Bosco Films & Kit Parker.

China's Little Devils. Paul Kelly & Harry Carey. Directed by Monta Bell. 1945. Monogram. 75 min. Sound. 16mm B&W. *Rental:* Hurlock Cine.

Chinatown. Jack Nicholson & Faye Dunaway. Directed by Roman Polanski. 1974. Paramount. (Anamorphic). 130 min. Sound. 16mm Color. *Rental:* Films Inc. *Sale:* Cinema Concepts, Super 8 sound version.

Chinatown. 1976. Downtown Community TV Center. (Documentary). 60 min. Videotape Color. *Rental:* Electro Art. *Lease:* Electro Art.

Chinatown: Immigrants in America. 1977. WNET. 60 min. Sound. 16mm Color. *Rental:* CA Newsreel. *Sale:* CA Newsreel.

Chinatown Kid, The. Alexander Fu Sheng & Sun Chien. 115 min. Sound. 16mm *Rental:* WW Enter. *Rental:* WW Enter, Videotape version.

Chinatown Nights. Wallace Beery & Florence Vidor. Directed by William A. Wellman. 1929. Paramount. 83 min. Sound. 16mm B&W. *Rental:* Swank Motion.

Chinese Affair, The. 58 min. Sound. Videotape *Rental:* PBS Video. *Sale:* PBS Video.

Chinese Cat, The. Sidney Toler & Joan Woodbury. Directed by Phil Rosen. 1944. Monogram. 70 min. Sound. 16mm B&W. *Rental:* MGM United & Mogulls Films.

Chinese Connection, The. Bruce Lee. Directed by Lo Wei. 1973. National General. 107 min. Sound. 16mm Color. *Rental:* Swank Motion.

Chinese Folktales. 1984. China. (Animated anthology). 100 min. Sound. 16mm Color. *Rental:* Distribution Sixteen. *Sale:* Distriubtion Sixteen. *Rental:* Distribution Sixteen, *Sale:* Distribution Sixteen, Videotape, color version.

Chinese Godfather, The. (Cast unlisted). 105 min. Videotape Color. dubbed. *Sale:* Cinema Concepts.

Chinese Ring, The. Roland Winters. Directed by William Beaudine. 1947. Monogram. 60 min. Sound. 16mm B&W. *Rental:* Hurlock Cine.

Chinese Roulette. Margit Carstensen & Anna Karina. Directed by Rainer Werner Fassbinder. Ger. 1976. Germany. 86 min. Sound. 16mm Color. subtitles. *Rental:* New Cinema & New Yorker Films.

Chinese Way, The. 1979. 58 min. Sound. Videotape *Rental:* PBS Video. *Sale:* PBS Video.

Chino. Charles Bronson & Jill Ireland. Directed by John Sturges. 1976. Intercontinental. 98 min. Sound. 16mm Color. *Rental:* Films Inc.

Chinoise, La. Jean-Pierre Leaud. Directed by Jean-Luc Godard. Fr. 1967. France. 95 min. Sound. 16mm Color. subtitles. *Rental:* New Cinema & New Yorker Films.

Chisum. John Wayne & Forrest Tucker. Directed by Andrew V. McLaglen. 1960. Warners. 111 min. Sound. 16mm Color. *Rental:* Arcus Film.

Chitty Chitty, Bang Bang. Dick Van Dyke & Sally Ann Howes. Directed by Ken Hughes. 1968. United Artists. 142 min. Sound. 16mm Color. *Rental:* Buchan Pic, MGM United, Modern Sound, Roas Films, Westcoast Films, Wholesome Film Ctr & Williams Films. *Rental:* MGM United, Videotape version.

Chloe in the Afternoon. Bernard Verley. Directed by Eric Rohmer. Fr. 1972. France. 95 min. Sound. 16mm Color. subtitles. *Rental:* Corinth Films & Swank Motion.

Chocolate Eclair, Le. Lise Thouin & Colin Fox. Directed by Jean-Claude Lord. Fr. 1978. Canada. 105 min. Sound. 16mm Color. subtitles. *Rental:* Natl Film CN. *Sale:* Natl Film CN.

Chocolate Soldier, The. Nelson Eddy & Rise Stevens. Directed by Roy Del Ruth. 1941. MGM. 125 min. Sound. 16mm B&W. *Rental:* MGM United.

Choirboys, The. Charles Durning, Louis Gossett Jr., Perry King & Don Stroud. Directed by Robert Aldrich. 1978. Universal. 120 min. Sound. 16mm Color. *Rental:* Swank Motion.

Cholesterol, Diet & Heart Disease. 1980. US Government. (Documentary). 60 min. Videotape Color. *Sale:* Natl AV Ctr.

C.H.O.M.P.S. Wesley Eure & Valerie Bertinelli. Directed by Don Chaffey. 1979. American International. 89 min. Sound. 16mm Color. *Rental:* Williams Films, Swank Motion & Welling Motion Pictures.

Chopper, The. 1983. Britain. (Documentary). 55 min. Sound. Videotape Color. *Sale:* Films Inc.

Choppers, The. Arch Hall Jr. Directed by Leigh Jason. 1965. Fairway. 66 min. Sound. 16mm Color. *Rental:* Ivy Films.

Chorus & Principals on Stage Please. Directed by Oliver Howes. 1976. Australia. (Documentary). 61 min. Sound. 16mm Color. *Rental:* MGM United.

Chosen Child, The. 1963. NBC. (Documentary). 54 min. Sound. 16mm B&W. *Rental:* McGraw-Hill Films & Syracuse U Film. *Sale:* McGraw-Hill Films.

Chosen People, The. 1977. Britain. (Documentary). 52 min. Sound. 16mm Color. *Rental:* U of IL Film, Iowa Films & U Mich Media.

Chosen Survivors. Jackie Cooper & Richard Jaeckel. Directed by Sutton Rody. 1974. Columbia. 99 min. Sound. 16mm Color. *Rental:* Arcus Film, Cine Craft, Film Ctr DC, Films Inc, Modern Sound, Swank Motion & Westcoast Films.

Christ in Concrete. Orig. Title: Give Us This Day. Sam Wanamaker & Lea Padovani. Directed by Edward Dmytryk. 1949. Britain. 116 min. Sound. 16mm B&W. *Rental:* Films Inc.

Christ Is Born. Directed by John Secondari. 1969. CBS. (Documentary). 54 min. Sound. 16mm Color. *Rental:* Budget Films, Learning Corp Am, Modern Sound, NYU Film Lib & Syracuse U Film. *Sale:* Learning Corp Am.

Christ of the Rooftops, The. 1970. 70 min. Sound. 16mm B&W. *Rental:* Canyon Cinema.

Christ the King. 1935. (Cast unlisted). 82 min. Sound. 16mm B&W. *Rental:* Willoughby Peer.

Christian Licorice Store, The. Beau Bridges & Maud Adams. Directed by James Frawley. 1971. National General. 90 min. Sound. 16mm Color. *Rental:* Swank Motion.

Christian the Lion. Bill Travers & Virginia McKenna. Directed by Bill Travers. 1974. Scotia. 89 min. Sound. 16mm Color. *Rental:* Films Inc.

Christianity. 1960. NET. (Documentary). 90 min. Sound. 16mm B&W. *Rental:* Syracuse U Film.

Christians at War. 1972. Britain. (Documentary). 50 min. Sound. 16mm Color. *Rental:* Films Inc. *Sale:* Films Inc.

Christine. Keith Gordon & John Stockwell. Directed by John Carpenter. 1983. Columbia. 110 min. Sound. 16mm Color. *Rental:* Swank Motion. *Sale:* Tamarelles French Film, *Rental:* Swank Motion, Videotape version.

Christine Jorgensen Story, The. John Hansen. Directed by Irving Rapper. 1970. United Artists. 90 min. Sound. 16mm Color. *Rental:* MGM United.

Christmas Carol, A. Reginald Owen & Terry Kilburn. Directed by Edwin L. Marin. 1938. MGM. 69 min. Sound. 16mm B&W. *Rental:* MGM United.

Christmas Carol, A. Alastair Sim, Mervyn Johns & Hermione Baddeley. Directed by Brian Desmond-Hurst. 1951. Britain. 86 min. Sound. 16mm B&W. *Rental:* Budget Films, Films Inc, Ivy Films, Maljack & Video Comm. *Lease:* Video Comm. *Rental:* Video Comm, *Lease:* Video Comm, Videotape version.

Christmas Carol, A. Basil Rathbone & Fredric March. Directed by Ralph Levy. 1956. CBS. 54 min. Sound. 16mm B&W. *Rental:* Budget Films, Films Inc, G Herne, Kit Parker, Lewis Film, Roas Films, U Mich Media & Video Comm. *Sale:* Carousel Films.

Christmas Carol, A. 1970. Australia. (Animated). 60 min. Sound. 16mm Color. *Rental:* Budget Films, Inst Cinema & Modern Sound. *Lease:* Inst Cinema.

Christmas Carol with Mr. Magoo, A. Orig. Title: Magoo's Christmas Carol. 1965. UPA. (Animated). 60 min. Sound. 16mm Color. *Rental:* Budget Films, Film Ctr DC, Films Inc, Macmillan Films, Roas Films, Welling Motion Pictures & Westcoast Films. *Sale:* Films Inc.

Christmas Eve. George Raft & Joan Blondell. Directed by Edwin L. Marin. 1947. United Artists. 90 min. Sound. 16mm B&W. *Rental:* Ivy Films, Mogulls Films, Rep Pic Film & Video Comm. *Sale:* Rep Pic Film.

Christmas in Connecticut. Orig. Title: Indiscretion. Barbara Stanwyck & Dennis Morgan. Directed by Peter Godfrey. 1945. Warners. 104 min. Sound. 16mm B&W. *Rental:* MGM United.

Christmas in July. Dick Powell & Ellen Drew. Directed by Preston Sturges. 1940. Paramount. 67 min. Sound. 16mm B&W. *Rental:* Williams Films.

Christmas Kid, The. Jeffrey Hunter & Louis Hayward. Directed by Sidney Pink. 1967. Spain. 87 min. Sound. 16mm Color. dubbed. *Rental:* Westcoast Films.

Christmas Lilies of the Field. Billy Dee Williams & Maria Schell. Directed by Ralph Nelson. 1979. Osmond. 96 min. Sound. 16mm Color. *Rental:* Maljack & Natl Film Video.

Christmas Martian, The. Trans. Title: Martien De Noel. Directed by Bernard Gosselin. 1971. Canada. (Cast unlisted). 65 min. Sound. 16mm Color. *Sale:* Xerox Films.

Christmas Story, A. Melinda Dillon & Darren McGavin. Directed by Bob Clark. 1983. MGM-UA. 95 min. Sound. 16mm Color. *Rental:* MGM United. *Rental:* MGM United, Videotape version.

Christmas Tree, The. William Burleigh. Directed by James B. Clark. 1962. Britain. 57 min. Sound. 16mm B&W. *Sale:* Lucerne Films.

Christmas Tree, The. William Holden & Virna Lisi. Directed by Terence Young. 1969. Continental. 110 min. Sound. 16mm Color. *Rental:* Budget Films.

Christo: Ten Works in Progress. Directed by Ray Witlin. 1979. Blackwood. (Documentary). 52 min. Sound. 16mm Color. *Rental:* Blackwood Films. *Sale:* Blackwood Films.

Christopher Columbus. Fredric March & Florence Eldridge. Directed by David MacDonald. 1949. Britain. 100 min. Sound. 16mm Color. *Rental:* Budget Films, Films Inc, U of IL Film, Kit Parker, Learning Corp Am & Twyman Films. *Sale:* Learning Corp Am. *Rental:* Budget Films, 108 mins. version.

Christopher Columbus. Directed by Lawrence Gordon Clark. 1977. Britain. (Cast unlisted). 52 min. Sound. 16mm Color. *Rental:* Time-Life Multimedia. *Sale:* Time-Life Multimedia.

Christopher Isherwood: Over There on a Visit. 1977. (Documentary). 42 min. Sound. 16mm Color. *Rental:* A Cantor. *Sale:* A Cantor.

Christopher Strong. Katharine Hepburn, Colin Clive & Billie Burke. Directed by Dorothy Arzner. 1933. RKO. 77 min. Sound. 16mm B&W. *Rental:* Films Inc. *Lease:* Films Inc.

Christus, The. 1917. Italy. 100 min. Silent. 16mm B&W. *Rental:* Budget Films.

Chrome & Hot Leather. William Smith. Directed by Lee Frost. 1971. American International. 95 min. Sound. 16mm Color. *Rental:* Swank Motion.

Chronicle of a Summer: Paris 1960. Directed by Jean Rouch & Edgar Morin. Fr. 1961. France. (Documentary). 90 min. Sound. 16mm B&W. subtitles. *Rental:* Corinth Films. *Lease:* Corinth Films.

Chronicle of Anna Magdalena Bach, The. Gustav Leonhardt & Christiane Lang. Directed by Jean-Marie Straub. Ger. 1967. Germany. 93 min. Sound. 16mm B&W. subtitles. *Rental:* New Yorker Films.

Chronicle of Gray House, The. Paul Hartmann & Lil Dagover. Directed by Arthur Von Gerlach. Ger. 1925. Germany. 100 min. Silent. 16mm B&W. *Rental:* Film Classics & Museum Mod Art. *Rental:* Film Classics, *Sale:* Film Classics, Silent 8mm version.

Chronicles of the Dead: 1969-70. 85 min. Sound. 16mm Color. *Rental:* Canyon Cinema.

Chu Chu & the Philly Flash. Alan Arkin & Carol Burnett. Directed by David Lowell Rich. 1981. Fox. 100 min. Sound. 16mm Color. *Rental:* Films Inc.

Chubasco. Richard Egan & Susan Strasburg. Directed by Allen H. Miner. 1968. Warners. 100 min. Sound. 16mm Color. *Rental:* Cine Craft & Charard Motion Pic.

Chuka. Rod Taylor & John Mills. Directed by Gordon Douglas. 1967. Paramount. 105 min. Sound. 16mm Color. *Rental:* Films Inc.

Chulas Fronteras. Directed by Les Blank. 1975. Brazos. (Documentary). 58 min. Sound. 16mm Color. *Rental:* Brazos Films, Canyon Cinema, Unifilm & U Mich Media. *Sale:* Brazos Films & Unifilm.

Chump at Oxford, A. Stan Laurel & Oliver Hardy. Directed by Alfred Goulding. 1940. United Artists. 64 min. Sound. 16mm B&W. *Rental:* Kit Parker, Newman Film Lib, Roas Films & Welling Motion Pictures. *Sale:* Blackhawk Films. *Sale:* Blackhawk Films, Super 8 sound version. *Rental:* Budget Films, Cine Craft, Em Gee Film Lib, Film Ctr DC, Inst Cinema, Modern Sound, Mogulls Films, Swank Motion, Westcoast Films, Wholesome Film Ctr & Willoughby Peer, *Sale:* Blackhawk Films, 45 min. version. *Rental:* Williams Films, 17 min. version. *Rental:* Welling Motion Pictures, 75 mins. version. *Rental:* Williams Films, 81 min. version.

Chuquiago. Directed by Antonio Eguino. Span. 1977. Bolivia. (Documentary). 87 min. Sound. 16mm Color. subtitles Eng. *Rental:* New Yorker Films & Unifilm. *Sale:* Unifilm.

Church Mouse, The. Ian Hunter & Laura La Plante. Directed by Monty Banks. 1935. Warners. 75 min. Sound. 16mm B&W. *Rental:* MGM United.

Church of the Russians, The. 2 pts. CC Films. 60 min. Sound. Videotape Color. *Rental:* Natl Churches Christ.

Churchill the Man. Directed by Peter Lambert. 1972. Lambert. (Documentary). 53 min. Sound. 16mm Color. *Rental:* Pyramid Film & Syracuse U Film. *Sale:* Pyramid Film. *Rental:* Pyramid Film, *Sale:* Pyramid Film, Videotape version.

Churchill, Man of the Century *see* Man of the Century.

Churchmouse & the Mayflower *see* Mouse on the Mayflower.

Chute de la Maison Usher, La *see* Fall of the House of Usher.

Ciao, Federico. Directed by Gideon Bachman. 1971. New Line Cinema. (Documentary). 55 min. Sound. 16mm Color. *Rental:* U Cal Media, New Line Cinema, Syracuse U Film & Films Inc. *Sale:* New Line Cinema.

CIA's Secret Army, The. 1977. CBS. (Documentary). 90 min. Sound. 16mm Color. *Rental:* U Mich Media & Syracuse U Film. *Sale:* Carousel Films.

Cid, El. Charlton Heston & Sophia Loren. Directed by Anthony Mann. 1961. Allied Artists. 181 min. Sound. 16mm Color. *Rental:* Arcus Film, Budget Films, Cine Craft, Films Inc, Inst Cinema, Modern Sound, Swank Motion, Twyman Films, Video Comm, Westcoast Films & Wholesome Film Ctr. *Sale:* Tamarelles French Film, Videotape version.

Cigarette Girl. Leslie Brooks & Ludwig Donath. Directed by Gunther Fritsch. 1947. Columbia. 67 min. Sound. 16mm B&W. *Rental:* Kit Parker.

Cigarette Girl of Mosselprom, The. Yulia Solntseva. Directed by Yuri Zhelyabuzhsky. 1924. Russia. (Musical score only). 85 min. Sound. 16mm B&W. *Rental:* Film Images. *Sale:* Film Images.

Cimarron. Irene Dunne & Richard Dix. Directed by Wesley Ruggles. 1931. RKO. 124 min. Sound. 16mm B&W. *Rental:* MGM United.

Cimarron. Glenn Ford & Maria Schell. Directed by Anthony Mann. 1960. MGM. 140 min. Sound. 16mm Color. *Rental:* MGM United. *Rental:* MGM United,

Cimarron Kid, The. Audie Murphy & Yvette Dugay. Directed by Budd Boetticher. 1951. Universal. 84 min. Sound. 16mm Color. *Rental:* Swank Motion.

Cincinnati Kid, The. Steve McQueen & Edward G. Robinson. Directed by Norman Jewison. 1966. MGM. 113 min. Sound. 16mm Color. *Rental:* MGM United.

Cinco de la Tarde. Francisco Rabal & German Cobos. Directed by Juan Bardem. 1962. Mexico. Sound. 16mm B&W. dubbed. *Rental:* MGM United.

Cinco Vidas. Trans. Title: Five Lives. Directed by Jose Luis Ruiz. Span. 1972. Educational Media. (Documentary). 52 min. Sound. 16mm Color. subtitles. *Sale:* Educ Media CA & U Mich Media.

Cinderella. Yanina Zheimo & A. Knovsky. Directed by N. Kosheverova. Rus. 1947. Russia. 81 min. Sound. 16mm B&W. subtitles. *Rental:* Corinth Films, Films Inc & Macmillan Films. *Lease:* Macmillan Films.

Cinderella. 1966. Childhood. (Cast unlisted). 72 min. Sound. 16mm Color. narrated Eng. *Rental:* Cine Craft, Charard Motion Pics, Welling Motion Pictures & Willoughby Peer.

Cinderella. Directed by Clyde Geronimi, Wilfred Jackson & Hamilton Luske. 1949. Disney. 74 min. Sound. 16mm Color. *Rental:* Swank Motion.

Cinderella Jones. Joan Leslie & Robert Alda. Directed by Busby Berkeley. 1946. Warners. 88 min. Sound. 16mm B&W. *Rental:* MGM United.

Cinderella Liberty. James Caan & Marsha Mason. Directed by Mark Rydell. 1973. Fox. (Anamorphic). 120 min. Sound. 16mm Color. *Rental:* Films Inc.

Cinderfella. Jerry Lewis. Directed by Frank Tashlin. 1960. Paramount. 91 min. Sound. 16mm Color. *Rental:* Films Inc & Westcoast Films.

Cindy & Donna. Debbie Osborne. Directed by Robert Anderson. 1971. Crown. 84 min. Sound. 16mm Color. *Rental:* Video Comm. *Lease:* Video Comm. *Rental:* Video Comm, *Lease:* Video Comm, Videotape version.

Cinema: Dead or Alive?. Directed by Urs Graf, Mathias Knauer & Hans Sturm. 1977. Switzerland. (Documentary). 105 min. Sound. 16mm Color. subtitles. *Rental:* New Cinema.

Cinema du Diable. Fr. France. (Anthology). 80 min. Sound. 16mm B&W. *Rental:* French Am Cul. *Rental:* French Am Cul, Videotape version.

Cinquante Ans ou la Vie d'un Skieur. Directed by Marcel Ichac. 1972. France. (Documentary, color sequences). 49 min. Sound. 16mm B&W. dubbed. *Rental:* French Am Cul.

Circle, The: An Approach to Drug Addiction. 1966. Canada. (Documentary). 58 min. Sound. 16mm B&W. *Rental:* NYU Film Lib, U Cal Media & U Mich Media. *Sale:* McGraw-Hill Films & Natl Film CN.

Circle in the Fire. Directed by Victor Nunez. 1976. Perspective. (Cast unlisted). 50 min. Sound. 16mm Color. *Rental:* Syracuse U Film. *Sale:* Perspect Film. *Sale:* Perspect Film, Videocassette version.

Circle of Danger. Ray Milland & Marjorie Fielding. Directed by Jacques Tourneur. 1951. Britain. 90 min. Sound. 16mm B&W. *Rental:* Mogulls Films.

Circle of Deceit. Bruno Ganz & Hanna Schygulla. 1981. France-Germany. 108 min. Sound. 16mm Color. *Rental:* MGM United. *Rental:* MGM United, Videotape version.

Circle of Deception. Bradford Dillman & Suzy Parker. Directed by Jack Lee. 1961. Fox. (Anamorphic). 100 min. Sound. 16mm B&W. *Rental:* Willoughby Peer.

Circle of Iron. David Carradine & Jeff Cooper. Directed by Richard Moore. 1979. Embassy. 102 min. Sound. 16mm Color. *Rental:* Films Inc.

Circle of Love. Jane Fonda & Claude Giraud. Directed by Roger Vadim. 1965. France. 104 min. Sound. 16mm Color. dubbed. *Rental:* Budget Films.

Circle of Two. Richard Burton & Tatum O'Neal. 1981. 99 min. Sound. 16mm *Rental:* WW Enter & World Northal. *Rental:* WW Enter, Videotape version.

Circumstantial Evidence. Michael O'Shea & Lloyd Nolan. Directed by John Larkin. 1945. Fox. 67 min. Sound. 16mm B&W. *Rental:* Films Inc.

Circus, The. Charles Chaplin. Directed by Charles Chaplin. 1928. United Artists. (Musical score only). 72 min. Sound. 16mm B&W. *Rental:* Films Inc. *Lease:* Glenn Photo, Super 8 sound version.

Circus. 1962. NBC. (Documentary). 51 min. Sound. 16mm Color. *Rental:* Films Inc. *Sale:* Films Inc. *Sale:* Films Inc, Videotape version.

Circus Clown. Joe E. Brown & William Demarest. Directed by Ray Enright. 1934. Warners. 68 min. Sound. 16mm B&W. *Rental:* MGM United.

Circus Friends. Carole White. Directed by Gerald Thomas. 1958. Britain. 63 min. Sound. 16mm B&W. *Sale:* Lucerne Films.

Circus Girl. June Travis & Robert Livingston. Directed by John H. Auer. 1937. Republic. 54 min. Sound. 16mm B&W. *Rental:* Ivy Films. *Sale:* Rep Pic Film.

Circus of Blood *see* Berserk!.

Circus of Fear. Christopher Lee & Leo Genn. Directed by John Moxey. 1966. American International. 91 min. Sound. 16mm Color. *Rental:* Bosco Films, Video Comm, Westcoast Films & Willoughby Peer.

Circus of Horrors. Anton Diffring & Erika Remberg. Directed by Sidney Hayers. 1960. Britain. 89 min. Sound. 16mm Color. *Rental:* Corinth Films & Budget Films.

Circus Queen Murder, The. Adolphe Menjou & Greta Nissen. Directed by Roy William Neill. 1933. Columbia. 70 min. Sound. 16mm B&W. *Rental:* Kit Parker.

Circus Town. 1971. NBC. (Documentary). 48 min. Sound. 16mm Color. *Rental:* Films Inc, Syracuse U Film, Utah Media, Twyman Films & U Mich Media. *Sale:* Films Inc.

Circus World. John Wayne & Rita Hayworth. Directed by Henry Hathaway. 1964. Paramount. 135 min. Sound. 16mm Color. *Rental:* Films Inc.

Cisco Kid in Old New Mexico, The. Gilbert Roland. 1945. Monogram. 60 min. Sound. Videotape B&W. *Sale:* Video Comm.

Cisco Kid Returns, The. Duncan Renaldo. Directed by J. P. McCarthy. 1945. Monogram. 65 min. Sound. 16mm B&W. *Rental:* Budget Films. *Sale:* Video Comm, Videotape version.

Cisco Pike. Kris Kristofferson & Gene Hackman. Directed by B. W. L. Norton. 1971. Columbia. 94 min. Sound. 16mm Color. *Rental:* Budget Films, Cine Craft, Films Inc, Inst Cinema, Kerr Film, Kit Parker, Modern Sound, Video Comm, Welling Motion Pictures, Westcoast Films & Willoughby Peer.

Citadel, The. Robert Donat, Rex Harrison & Rosalind Russell. Directed by King Vidor. 1938. MGM. 110 min. Sound. 16mm B&W. *Rental:* MGM United.

Citadel of Crime. Robert Armstrong & Linda Hayes. Directed by George Sherman. 1941. Republic. 54 min. Sound. 16mm B&W. *Rental:* Ivy Films. *Sale:* Rep Pic Film.

Cite de l'Indicible Peur, La. Bourvil & Jean-Louis Barrault. Directed by Jean-Pierre Mocky. Fr. 1964. France. 80 min. Sound. 16mm B&W. subtitles. *Rental:* French Am Cul.

Cities. 50 min. Sound. 16mm Color. *Rental:* Learning Corp Am.

Cities: A City Is to Live in. 1968. CBS. (Documentary). 54 min. Sound. 16mm Color. *Rental:* Syracuse U Film. *Sale:* Phoenix Films. *Sale:* Phoenix Films, Color version.

Cities & the Poor. 1966. NET. (Documentary). 2 reels 120 min. Sound. 16mm B&W. *Rental:* Indiana AV Ctr, Syracuse U Film & U Cal Media. *Sale:* Indiana Av Ctr.

Cities: Dilemma in Black & White. 1968. CBS. (Documentary). 54 min. Sound. 16mm Color. *Rental:* Syracuse U Film. *Sale:* Phoenix Films. *Sale:* Phoenix Films, Color version.

Cities for People. 1976. EMC. (Documentary). 49 min. Sound. 16mm Color. *Rental:* U Cal Media. *Sale:* U Cal Media.

Cities Have No Limits. 1969. NBC. (Documentary). 53 min. Sound. 16mm Color. *Rental:* Films Inc & Utah Media. *Sale:* Films Inc. *Sale:* Films Inc, Videotape version.

Cities: To Build a Future. 1968. CBS. (Documentary). 54 min. Sound. 16mm Color. *Rental:* Syracuse U Film. *Sale:* Phoenix Films. *Sale:* Phoenix Films, Color version.

Cities, The: Uncle Sam Can You Spare a Dime. 1979. PBS. (Documentary). 59 min. Sound. Videotape Color. *Rental:* PBS Video. *Sale:* PBS Video.

Cities, Crime in the Streets *see* Crime in the Streets.

Cities, The Rise of New Towns *see* Rise of New Towns.

Citizen Kane. Orson Welles & Joseph Cotten. Directed by Orson Welles. 1941. RKO. 119 min. Sound. B&W. *Rental:* Films Inc. *Sale:* Cinema Concepts, Videotape version.

Citizen: The Political Life of Allard K. Lowenstein. Directed by Julie Thompson. Cinema Guild. (Documentary). 72 min. Sound. 16mm Color. *Rental:* Cinema Guild. *Sale:* Cinema Guild. *Sale:* Cinema Guild, Videotape version.

Citizens Band. Orig. Title: Handle with Care. Paul LeMat, Candy Clark & Marcia Rodd. Directed by Jonathan Demme. 1977. Paramount. 98 min. Sound. 16mm Color. *Rental:* Films Inc.

City, The. Directed by Ralph Steiner & Willard Van Dyke. 1939. 45 min. Sound. 16mm Color. *Sale:* Festival Films & Pyramid Film. *Sale:* Festival Films, Videotape version.

City Across the River, The. Stephen McNally & Thelma Ritter. Directed by Maxwell Shane. 1949. Universal. 90 min. Sound. 16mm B&W. *Rental:* Swank Motion.

City After Midnight. Phyllis Kirk & Dan O'Herlihy. Directed by Compton Bennett. 1959. RKO. 84 min. Sound. 16mm B&W. *Rental:* Ivy Films. *Sale:* Rep Pic Film.

City & the Self, The. 1973. Milgrim-From. (Documentary). 52 min. Sound. 16mm Color. *Rental:* BYU Media & Films Inc. *Sale:* Films Inc. *Rental:* Films Inc, *Sale:* Films Inc, Videotape version.

City at Chandigarh, The. Directed by Alain Tanner. 1966. France. (Documentary). 51 min. Sound. 16mm Color. dubbed. *Rental:* New Yorker Films.

City at Dawn, A: Saigon After Liberation. 1976. South Vietnam. (Documentary, Anamorphic). 60 min. Sound. 16mm Color. *Rental:* CA Newsreel. *Sale:* CA Newsreel.

City Beneath the Sea, The. Robert Ryan & Anthony Quinn. Directed by Budd Boetticher. 1953. Universal. 87 min. Sound. 16mm B&W. *Rental:* Swank Motion.

City Centers & Pedestrians. 1975. Canada. (Documentary). 57 min. Sound. 16mm Color. *Rental:* Natl Film CN. *Sale:* Natl Film CN.

City for Conquest. James Cagney & Ann Sheridan. Directed by Anatole Litvak. 1940. Warners. 106 min. Sound. 16mm B&W. *Rental:* MGM United.

City Girl. Phyllis Brooks & Ricardo Cortez. Directed by F. W. Murnau. 1929. Fox. 89 min. Sound. 16mm B&W. *Rental:* Films Inc.

City Is to Live In, A. 54 min. Sound. 16mm Color. *Rental:* Budget Films.

City Jungle, The *see* Young Philadelphians.

City Lights. Charlie Chaplin. Directed by Charles Chaplin. 1931. United Artists. (Musical score only). 81 min. Sound. 16mm B&W. *Rental:* Films Inc. *Sale:* Cinema Concepts, Super 8 sound version.

City Limits. Frank Craven & Sally Blane. Directed by Jean Yarbrough. 1940. Monogram. 67 min. Sound. 16mm B&W. *Rental:* Hurlock Cine.

City of Bad Men. Jeanne Crain & Dale Robertson. Directed by Harmon Jones. 1953. Fox. 82 min. Sound. 16mm Color. *Rental:* Films Inc.

City of Coral. 1983. Nova. (Documentary). 57 min. Sound. 16mm Color. *Rental:* U Cal Media.

City of Missing Girls. John Archer & Gale Storm. Directed by Elmer Clifton. 1941. Select Attractions. 73 min. Sound. 16mm B&W. *Rental:* Ivy Films. *Sale:* Rep Pic Film.

City of Shadows. Victor McLaglen & Buddy Baer. Directed by William Witney. 1955. Republic. 70 min. Sound. 16mm B&W. *Rental:* Ivy Films. *Sale:* Rep Pic Film.

City of the Big Shoulders. (Destination America Ser.). 1976. Media Guild. (Documentary). 52 min. Sound. 16mm Color. *Rental:* Media Guild. *Sale:* Media Guild. *Sale:* Media Guild, Videotape version.

City of the Dead. Christopher Lee. Directed by John Moxey. 1962. 75 min. 16mm *Rental:* A Twyman Pres.

City of Women. Marcello Mastroianni. Directed by Federico Fellini. Ital. 1979. 138 min. Sound. 16mm Color. subtitles Eng. *Rental:* New Yorker Films.

City on Fire. Barry Newman & Susan Clark. Directed by Alvin Rakoff. 1979. Embassy. 101 min. Sound. 16mm Color. *Rental:* Films Inc.

City on the Edge of Forever, The. William Shatner & Leonard Nimoy. Directed by Joseph Pevney. 1967. Star Trek. 50 min. Sound. 16mm Color. *Rental:* Em Gee Film Lib, U of IL Film & Westcoast Films.

City Streets. Gary Cooper & Sylvia Sidney. Directed by Rouben Mamoulian. 1931. Paramount. 86 min. Sound. 16mm B&W. *Rental:* Swank Motion.

City That Never Sleeps, The. Gig Young & Edward Arnold. Directed by John H. Auer. 1953. Republic. 90 min. Sound. 16mm B&W. *Rental:* Ivy Films. *Sale:* Rep Pic Film.

City That Waits to Die, The. 1970. Britain. (Documentary). 57 min. Sound. 16mm Color. *Rental:* Films Inc, Iowa Films, OK AV Ctr, SD AV Ctr, Syracuse U Film & U Mich Media. *Sale:* Films Inc. *Sale:* Films Inc, Videotape version.

City Under the Sea *see* War Gods of the Deep.

City Without Men. Linda Darnell. Directed by Sidney Salkow. 1943. Columbia. 70 min. Sound. 16mm B&W. *Rental:* Film Classics. *Sale:* Natl Cinema.

Ciudad de los Ninos. Arturo de Cordova & Marga Lopez. Directed by Gilberto Martinez Solares. Mexico. 103 min. Sound. 16mm B&W. *Rental:* Trans-World Films.

Civil Disorder: The Kerner Report. 3 pts. 1967. NET. (Documentary). 80 min. Sound. 16mm B&W. *Rental:* Indiana AV Ctr & U of IL Film. *Sale:* Indiana Av Ctr.

Civil Rights Movement, The. 5 pts. 1967. NBC. (Documentary). 109 min. Sound. 16mm B&W. *Rental:* Ency Brit Ed. *Sale:* Ency Brit Ed.

Civilization. Howard Hickman, Enid Markey & Herschel Mayall. Directed by Raymond B. West & Irvin Willat. 1916. Ince. 100 min. Silent. 16mm B&W. *Rental:* Budget Films, Em Gee Film Lib, Films Inc & Museum Mod Art. *Sale:* Glenn Photo & Reel Images. *Rental:* Ivy Films, *Sale:* Glenn Photo, Super 8 silent version.

Civilization: Hero As Artist. 1970. 55 min. Sound. 16mm Color. *Rental:* Utah Media.

Civilization: Protest & Communocation. 1970. 55 min. Sound. 16mm Color. *Rental:* Utah Media.

Claes Oldenburg. 1975. Blackwood. (Documentary). 52 min. Sound. 16mm Color. *Rental:* Blackwood Films. *Sale:* Blackwood Films.

Clair de Femme: Womanlight. Romy Schneider & Yves Montand. Directed by Costa-Gavras. Fr. 1979. France. 103 min. Sound. 16mm Color. subtitles. *Rental:* Ivy Films.

Claire's Knee. Jean-Claude Brialy & Beatrice Romand. Directed by Eric Rohmer. Fr. 1971. France. 105 min. Sound. 16mm Color. subtitles. *Rental:* Swank Motion. *Rental:* Swank Motion, Dubbed version.

Clairvoyant, The. Orig. Title: Evil Mind, The. Claude Rains & Fay Wray. Directed by Maurice Elvey. 1935. Britain. 80 min. Sound. 16mm B&W. *Rental:* Budget Films & Video Comm. *Sale:* Classic Film Mus & Reel Images. *Rental:* Video Comm, Videotape version.

Clairvoyant, The *see* Evil Mind.

Clambake. Elvis Presley & Will Hutchins. Directed by Arthur H. Nadel. 1967. United Artists. 90 min. Sound. 16mm Color. *Rental:* MGM United.

Clancy Street Boys. East Side Kids. Directed by William Beaudine. 1943. Monogram. 67 min. Sound. 16mm B&W. *Rental:* Budget Films, Ivy Films & Video Comm. *Rental:* Video Comm, Videotape version.

Clarence & Angel. 75 min. Sound. 16mm Color. *Rental:* Texture Film.

Clarence Darrow. Henry Fonda. 1979. Sunrise. 120 min. Sound. 16mm Color. *Rental:* Williams Films.

Clarence, the Cross-Eyed Lion. Marshall Thompson & Betsy Drake. Directed by Andrew Marton. 1965. MGM. 98 min. Sound. 16mm B&W. *Rental:* MGM United.

Clash by Night. Barbara Stanwyck, Paul Douglas & Marilyn Monroe. Directed by Fritz Lang. 1952. RKO. 114 min. Sound. 16mm B&W. *Rental:* Films Inc. *Rental:* Welling Motion Pictures & Westcoast Films, Videotape version, 105 mins. version.

Clash of the Titans, The. Sir Laurence Olivier, Claire Bloom & Maggie Smith. Directed by Desmond Davis. 1981. 118 min. Sound. 16mm Color. *Rental:* MGM United. *Rental:* MGM United, Videotape version.

Clash of the Wolves, The. Rin-Tin-Tin. Directed by Noel Smith. 1925. Warners. 60 min. Silent. 16mm B&W. *Rental:* Budget Films, Em Gee Film Lib & Kit Parker. *Sale:* Glenn Photo & Reel Images. *Sale:* Glenn Photo, Super 8 silent version.

Class. Jacqueline Bisset & Rob Lowe. Directed by Lewis John Carlino. 1983. Orion. 98 min. Sound. 16mm Color. *Rental:* Films Inc.

Class & the Classroom. 1977. Edupac. (Documentary). 50 min. Sound. 16mm Color. *Rental:* Edupac. *Sale:* Edupac.

Class of ... 1965. Wolper. (Documentary). 50 min. Sound. 16mm B&W. *Rental:* Films Inc. *Sale:* Films Inc. *Sale:* Films Inc, Videotape version.

Class of Fifty Eight. 1968. CBS. (Documentary). 52 min. Sound. 16mm B&W. *Rental:* Macmillan Films. *Sale:* Macmillan Films.

Class Relations. Directed by Jean-Marie Straub. Ger. 1983. 126 min. Sound. 16mm B&W. subtitles Eng. *Rental:* New Yorker Films.

Classe Operaia Va in Paradiso, La *see* Working Class Goes to Heaven.

Classical Art Under the Occupation & the Liberation. Directed by Armand Panigel. Fr. France. (Documentary). 75 min. Sound. 16mm B&W. subtitles. *Rental:* French Am Cul.

Classified Caper, The. 60 min. Videotape Color. *Sale:* Vydio Philms.

Claudel. Directed by Daniel Castelle. Fr. France. (Cast unlisted). 75 min. Sound. 16mm Color. *Rental:* French Am Cul, Black & White version.

Claudia. Dorothy McGuire & Robert Young. Directed by Edmund Goulding. 1943. Fox. 91 min. Sound. 16mm B&W. *Rental:* Films Inc.

Claudia & David. Dorothy McGuire & Robert Young. Directed by Walter Lang. 1946. Fox. 78 min. Sound. 16mm B&W. *Rental:* Films Inc.

Claudine. James Earl Jones & Diahann Carroll. Directed by John Berry. 1974. Universal. 92 min. Sound. 16mm Color. *Rental:* Films Inc.

Claw, The. Norman Kerry & Claire Windsor. Directed by Sidney Olcott. 1927. Universal. 55 min. Silent. 16mm B&W. *Rental:* Em Gee Film Lib. *Sale:* Glenn Photo. *Sale:* Glenn Photo,

Claw Monsters, The. Phyllis Coates & Myron Healey. Directed by Franklin Adreon. 1954. Republic. 100 min. Sound. 16mm B&W. . *Sale:* Rep Pic Film.

Clay Pigeon. Bill Williams & Barbara Hale. Directed by Richard Fleischer. 1949. RKO. 63 min. Sound. 16mm B&W. *Rental:* Films Inc.

Clear All Wires. James Gleason & Lee Tracy. Directed by George Hill. 1933. MGM. 79 min. Sound. 16mm B&W. *Rental:* MGM United.

Clearing the Range. Hoot Gibson. Directed by Otto Brower. 1931. Capital. 60 min. Sound. 16mm B&W. *Sale:* Cinema Concepts & Natl Cinema. *Sale:* Video Comm, Videotape version.

Cleo from Five to Seven. Corinne Marchand & Antonie Bourseiller. Directed by Agnes Varda. Fr. 1961. France. (Color sequences). 90 min. Sound. 16mm B&W. subtitles. *Rental:* New Yorker Films.

Cleopatra. Helen Gardner. Directed by Charles L. Gaskill. 1912. Helen Gardner. 58 min. Silent. 16mm B&W. *Rental:* A Twyman Pres & Twyman Films.

Cleopatra. Elizabeth Taylor, Richard Burton & Rex Harrison. Directed by Joseph L. Mankiewicz. 1963. Fox. (Anamorphic). 186 min. Sound. 16mm Color. *Rental:* Williams Films, Films Inc & Twyman Films.

Cleopatra. Claudette Colbert & Warren William. Directed by Cecil B. DeMille. 1934. 102 min. Sound. 16mm B&W. *Rental:* Swank Motion.

Cleopatra Jones. Tamara Dobson & Shelley Winters. Directed by Jack Starrett. 1973. Warners. 89 min. Sound. 16mm Color. *Rental:* Swank Motion, Twyman Films & Williams Films.

Cleopatra Jones & the Casino of Gold. Tamara Dobson. Directed by Charles Bail. 1974. Warners. 96 min. Sound. 16mm Color. *Rental:* Modern Sound, Swank Motion & Twyman Films.

Clickety-Clack *see* Dodes'Ka-Den.

Clifton Chenier. Phoenix. (Documentary). 58 min. Sound. 16mm Color. *Rental:* Phoenix Films. *Sale:* Phoenix Films. *Sale:* Phoenix Films, Videotape version.

Climax, The. Ugo Tognazzi & Gigi Billista. Directed by Pietro Germi. 1967. Italy. 97 min. Sound. 16mm B&W. subtitles. *Rental:* MGM United.

Climax, The. Boris Karloff & Susanna Foster. Directed by George Waggner. 1944. Universal. 86 min. Sound. 16mm Color. *Rental:* Swank Motion.

Climb, The. Jim Vaughan & Cindy Vaughan. 1976. Gospel. 55 min. Sound. 16mm Color. *Rental:* Gospel Films.

Climb a Tall Mountain. 45 min. Sound. 16mm Color. *Rental:* Gospel Films.

Climb to Glory. 2 pts. 1963. Army. (Documentary). 58 min. Sound. 16mm B&W. *Rental:* Natl AV Ctr.

Clinton & the Law. 1958. CBS. (Documentary). 60 min. Sound. 16mm B&W. *Rental:* U Nev AV Ctr. *Sale:* Carousel Films.

Clipped Wings. Lloyd Hughes & Rosalind Keith. Directed by Stuart Paton. 1937. Treo. 60 min. Sound. 16mm B&W. *Rental:* Mogulls Films.

Clive of India. Ronald Colman & Loretta Young. Directed by Richard Boleslawski. 1935. Fox. 90 min. Sound. 16mm B&W. *Rental:* Films Inc.

Cloak & Dagger. Gary Cooper & Lilli Palmer. Directed by Fritz Lang. 1947. Warners. 106 min. Sound. 16mm B&W. *Rental:* Corinth Films. *Lease:* Corinth Films.

Cloak, The: Shinel. Sergei Gerasimov. Directed by Grigori Kozintsev & Leonid Trauberg. 1926. Russia. 51 min. Silent. 16mm B&W. *Rental:* Corinth Films & Museum Mod Art.

Clock, The. Judy Garland & Robert Walker. Directed by Vincente Minnelli. 1945. MGM. 90 min. Sound. 16mm B&W. *Rental:* MGM United.

Clockmaker, The. Philippe Noiret. Directed by Bertrand Tavernier. Fr. 1976. France. 90 min. Sound. 16mm Color. subtitles. *Rental:* J Green Pics. *Sale:* Tamarelles French Film, Videotape version.

Clockwork Orange, A. Malcolm MacDowell. Directed by Stanley Kubrick. 1971. Warners. 137 min. Sound. 16mm Color. *Rental:* Swank Motion. *Rental:* Swank Motion, Videotape version.

Clodhopper, The. Charles Ray. 1917. Triangle. 55 min. Silent. 16mm B&W. *Rental:* Em Gee Film Lib. *Sale:* Blackhawk Films, Super 8 silent version.

Clones. Michael Greene. Directed by Paul Hunt. 1973. Filmmakers International. 90 min. Sound. 16mm Color. *Sale:* Morcraft Films. *Sale:* Glenn Photo, Super 8 sound version.

Cloportes. Lino Ventura & Charles Aznavour. Directed by Pierre Granier-Deferre. Fr. 1966. Fox. (Anamorphic). 102 min. Sound. 16mm B&W. subtitles. *Rental:* Films Inc.

Close Call for Boston Blackie, A. Chester Morris & Lynn Merrick. Directed by Lew Landers. 1946. Columbia. 70 min. Sound. 16mm B&W. *Rental:* Kit Parker.

Close Call for Ellery Queen, A. William Gargan & Margaret Lindsay. Directed by James Hogan. 1942. Columbia. 70 min. Sound. 16mm B&W. *Rental:* Budget Films & Mogulls Films.

Close Encounters of the Third Kind. Richard Dreyfuss & Teri Garr. Directed by Steven Spielberg. 1977. Columbia. 135 min. Sound. 16mm Color. *Rental:* Swank Motion. *Rental:* Swank Motion, Anamorphic version. *Rental:* Swank Motion, Videotape version.

Close Harmony *see* Cowboy Canteen.

Close-Up in Time, A. Directed by Agnes DeMille. 1977. DeMille. (Dance). 60 min. Sound. 16mm Color. *Rental:* Em Gee Film Lib.

Closed Vision. 1954. France. (Experimental). 70 min. Sound. 16mm B&W. dubbed. *Rental:* A Twyman Pres & Twyman Films.

Closely Watched Trains. Vaclav Neckar & Jitka Bendova. Directed by Jiri Menzel. Czech. 1966. Czechoslovakia. 89 min. Sound. 16mm B&W. subtitles. *Rental:* Films Inc. *Sale:* Tamarelles French Film, Videotape version.

Closing the Gap. 1979. PBS. (Documentary). 60 min. Videotape Color. *Rental:* PBS Video. *Sale:* PBS Video.

Clouded Yellow, The. Jean Simmons & Trevor Howard. Directed by Ralph Thomas. 1951. Britain. 85 min. Sound. 16mm B&W. *Rental:* Budget Films, Video Comm & Wholesome Film Ctr. *Rental:* Video Comm, Videotape version.

Clouds of Doubt. 1979. 58 min. Sound. 16mm Color. *Rental:* U Mich Media.

Clouds Over Israel. Yiftach Spector & Ehud Banai. Directed by Ivan Lengyel. Hebrew & Arabic. 1962. 85 min. Sound. 16mm B&W. subtitles. *Rental:* Films Inc.

Clown, The. Red Skelton & Jane Greer. Directed by Robert Z. Leonard. 1953. MGM. 82 min. Sound. 16mm B&W. *Rental:* MGM United. *Rental:* MGM United, Videotape version.

Clown & the Kids in Outer Space, The *see* Rocket to Nowhere.

Clown & the Kid, The. John Lupton. Directed by Edward L. Cahn. 1961. United Artists. 65 min. Sound. 16mm B&W. *Rental:* MGM United.

Clown & the Kids, The. Emmett Kelly. Directed by Mende Brown. 1968. Childhood. 70 min. Sound. 16mm Color. *Rental:* Welling Motion Pictures & Westcoast Films.

Clowns, The. Directed by Federico Fellini. 1971. Italy. (Documentary). 90 min. Sound. 16mm Color. *Rental:* Films Inc.

Club de Femmes. Danielle Darrieux & Betty Stockfield. Directed by Jacques Deval. Fr. 1936. France. 90 min. Sound. 16mm B&W. subtitles. *Rental:* Budget Films & Em Gee Film Lib. *Sale:* Festival Films. *Sale:* Festival Films, Videotape version.

Club Havana. Tom Neal & Margaret Lindsay. Directed by Edgar G. Ulmer. 1946. Republic. 62 min. Sound. 16mm B&W. *Sale:* Classics Assoc NY.

Club of Rome, The. 1969. Canada. (Documentary). 57 min. Sound. 16mm Color. *Rental:* CBC. *Sale:* CBC.

Clue of the Missing Ape, The. Orig. Title: Gibraltar Adventure. George Cole. Directed by James Hill. 1965. Britain. 58 min. Sound. 16mm B&W. *Sale:* Lucerne Films.

Cluny Brown. Jennifer Jones & Charles Boyer. Directed by Ernst Lubitsch. 1946. Fox. 100 min. Sound. 16mm B&W. *Rental:* Films Inc.

C'mon, Let's Live a Little. Bobby Vee & Eddie Hodges. Directed by David Butler. 1966. Paramount. 85 min. Sound. 16mm Color. *Rental:* Films Inc.

Coach, The. Cathy Lee Crosby. Directed by Bud Townsend. 1978. Crown. 100 min. Sound. 16mm Color. *Rental:* Films Inc & Swank Motion.

Coaches. 1976. Canada. (Documentary). 57 min. Sound. 16mm Color. *Rental:* U Cal Media & Natl Film CN. *Sale:* Natl Film CN.

Coal Miner's Daughter, The. Sissy Spacek & Tommy Lee Jones. Directed by Michael Apted. 1980. Universal. 125 min. Sound. 16mm Color. *Rental:* Swank Motion. *Rental:* Swank Motion, Videotape version.

Coast Guard. Randolph Scott & Ralph Bellamy. Directed by Edward Ludwig. 1939. Columbia. 72 min. Sound. 16mm B&W. *Rental:* Kit Parker.

Coast of Skeletons. Richard Todd. Directed by Robert Lynn. 1965. 91 min. 16mm Color. *Rental:* A Twyman Pres.

Coast Patrol. Fay Wray & Kenneth McDonald. Directed by Irving J. Barsky. 1925. Barsky. 55 min. Silent. 16mm B&W. *Rental:* Mogulls Films. *Sale:* Morcraft Films.

Coast to Coast. Robert Blake & Dyan Cannon. Directed by Joseph Sergent. 1980. Paramount. 94 min. Sound. 16mm Color. *Rental:* Films Inc.

Coastal Command. Directed by J. B. Holmes. 1942. Britain. (Documentary). 65 min. Sound. 16mm B&W. *Rental:* Film Images. *Sale:* Film Images.

Cobalt Blues. 1983. Nova. (Documentary). 57 min. Sound. 16mm Color. *Rental:* U Cal Media.

Cobra. Rudolph Valentino. Directed by Joseph Henabery. 1925. Paramount. (Musical score only). 70 min. Sound. 16mm B&W. *Rental:* Budget Films & Em Gee Film Lib. *Rental:* Films Inc, Silent version.

Cobra Strikes, The. Richard Fraser & Sheila Ryan. Directed by Charles Reisner. 1948. Eagle Lion. 62 min. Sound. 16mm B&W. *Sale:* Classics Assoc NY.

Cobra Woman. Maria Montez & Sabu. Directed by Robert Siodmak. 1944. Universal. 90 min. Sound. 16mm Color. *Rental:* Swank Motion.

Cobweb, The. Lauren Bacall & Richard Widmark. Directed by Vincente Minnelli. 1955. MGM. 124 min. Sound. 16mm Color. *Rental:* MGM United.

Cocaine Fiends, The. Lois January. Directed by William A. O'Connor. 1938. New Line Cinema. 75 min. Sound. 16mm B&W. *Rental:* Budget Films & New Line Cinema. *Sale:* Cinema Concepts, Videotape version.

Cockeyed Cavaliers, The. Bert Wheeler, Robert Woolsey & Dorothy Lee. Directed by Mark Sandrich. 1934. RKO. 70 min. Sound. Super 8 B&W. *Sale:* Blackhawk Films.

Cockeyed Cowboys of Calico County, The. Orig. Title: Woman for Charlie, A. Dan Blocker & Mickey Rooney. Directed by Anton M. Leader. 1969. Universal. 98 min. Sound. 16mm Color. *Rental:* Williams Films.

Cockeyed Miracle, The. Orig. Title: Mister Griggs Returns. Frank Morgan & Keenan Wynn. Directed by S. Sylvan Simon. 1946. MGM. 81 min. Sound. 16mm B&W. *Rental:* MGM United.

Cockeyed World, The. Edmund Lowe & Victor McLaglen. Directed by Raoul Walsh. 1929. Fox. 120 min. Sound. 16mm B&W. *Rental:* Films Inc.

Cockfighter, The. Warren Oates & Laurie Bird. Directed by Monte Hellman. 1974. New World. 84 min. Sound. 16mm Color. *Rental:* Films Inc. *Sale:* Tamarelles French Film, Videotape version.

Cockleshell Heroes. Trevor Howard & Jose Ferrer. Directed by Jose Ferrer. 1956. Britain. 97 min. Sound. 16mm Color. *Rental:* Inst Cinema & Modern Sound.

Cocktail Hour, The. Bebe Daniels & Randolph Scott. Directed by Victor Schertzinger. 1933. Columbia. 80 min. Sound. 16mm B&W. *Rental:* Kit Parker.

Cocktail Molotov. Directed by Diane Kurys. Fr. 1980. 100 min. Sound. 16mm Color. subtitles Eng. *Rental:* New Yorker Films.

Cocoanuts. Marx Brothers. Directed by Joseph Santley. 1929. Paramount. 96 min. Sound. 16mm B&W. *Rental:* Swank Motion.

Code Name, Jaguar. Ray Danton & Pascale Petit. Directed by Maurice Labro. 1966. RKO. 111 min. Sound. 16mm Color. dubbed. *Rental:* Video Comm.

Code Name-Morituri *see* Morituri (The Saboteur).

Code Name, Operation Crossbow see Operation Crossbow.

Code of Honor. Mahlon Hamilton. 1930. Syndicate. 60 min. Sound. 16mm B&W. *Rental:* Mogulls Films.

Code of the Fearless. Fred Scott. Directed by Raymond K. Johnson. 1939. Spectrum. 56 min. Sound. 16mm B&W. *Rental:* Budget Films.

Code of the Lawless. Orig. Title: Mysterious Stranger, The. Kirby Grant. Directed by Wallace Fox. 1945. Universal. 70 min. Sound. 16mm B&W. *Rental:* Westcoast Films.

Code of the Outlaw. Tom Tyler & Bob Steele. Directed by John English. 1941. 58 min. Sound. 16mm B&W. *Rental:* Ivy Films. *Sale:* Rep Pic Film.

Code of the Plains. Buster Crabbe. 1947. Eagle Lion. 57 min. Sound. 16mm B&W. *Rental:* Budget Films & Video Comm.

Code of the Prairie. Sunset Carson. Directed by Spencer G. Bennett. 1944. Republic. 56 min. Sound. 16mm B&W. *Rental:* Ivy Films. *Sale:* Rep Pic Film.

Code of the Rangers. Tim McCoy. Directed by Sam Newfield. 1938. Monogram. 55 min. Sound. 16mm B&W. *Rental:* Hurlock Cine.

Code of the Redmen see King of the Stallions.

Code of the Secret Service. Ronald Reagan. Directed by Noel Smith. 1939. Warners. 58 min. Sound. 16mm B&W. *Rental:* MGM United.

Code of the Silver Sage. Allan Lane. Directed by Fred C. Brannon. 1949. Republic. 60 min. Sound. 16mm B&W. *Rental:* Ivy Films. *Sale:* Rep Pic Film.

Code Seven, Victim Five. Lex Barker & Ronald Fraser. Directed by Robert Lynn. 1965. Britain. 88 min. Sound. 16mm B&W. *Lease:* Time-Life Multimedia. *Rental:* A Twyman Pres, 87 min. color 16 version.

Code Six Forty-Five. Clayton Moore & Ramsay Ames. Directed by Fred C. Brannon & Yakima Canutt. 1948. Republic. 100 min. Sound. 16mm B&W. *Rental:* Ivy Films. *Sale:* Rep Pic Film.

Code Two. Ralph Meeker & Sally Forrest. Directed by Fred M. Wilcox. 1953. MGM. 69 min. Sound. 16mm B&W. *Rental:* MGM United.

Codine. Francoise Brion. Directed by Henri Colpi. Romanian. 1963. Rumania. 90 min. Sound. 16mm Color. subtitles. *Rental:* Swank Motion & Twyman Films.

Cody. Tony Becker & Terry Evans. 86 min. Sound. 16mm Color. *Rental:* Williams Films.

Coeur Simple, Un. France. (Cast unlisted). 45 min. Sound. 16mm B&W. *Rental:* French Am Cul.

Coffy. Pam Grier. Directed by Jack Hill. 1973. American International. 91 min. Sound. 16mm Color. *Rental:* Swank Motion & Williams Films.

Cohens & Kellys in Hollywood, The. George Sidney & Charles Murray. Directed by John Francis Dillon. 1932. Universal. 78 min. Sound. 16mm B&W. *Rental:* Swank Motion.

Cohens & Kellys in Trouble, The. George Sidney & Charles Murray. Directed by George Stevens. 1933. Universal. 80 min. Sound. 16mm B&W. *Rental:* Swank Motion.

Cold Anger. France. (Cast unlisted). 100 min. Sound. 16mm B&W. dubbed. *Rental:* Bosco Films.

Cold Sweat. Trans. Title: De La Part Des Copains. Charles Bronson, Liv Ullmann & James Mason. Directed by Terence Young. 1970. MGM. 94 min. Sound. 16mm Color. *Rental:* Films Inc, Welling Motion Pictures & Westcoast Films.

Cold Turkey. Dick Van Dyke & Bob Newhart. Directed by Norman Lear. 1971. United Artists. 102 min. Sound. 16mm Color. *Rental:* MGM United.

Cold Wind in August. Lola Albright & Scott Marlowe. Directed by Alexander Singer. 1961. United Artists. 78 min. Sound. 16mm B&W. *Rental:* MGM United.

Cole Younger, Gunfighter. Frank Lovejoy & Abby Dalton. Directed by R. G. Springsteen. 1958. Allied Artists. 78 min. Sound. 16mm Color. *Rental:* Hurlock Cine.

Coleman Report, The: Equality of Educational Opportunity. 1967. Anti-Defamation League. 55 min. Sound. 16mm B&W. *Rental:* ADL. *Sale:* ADL.

Coleridge: The Fountain & the Cave. Directed by Bayley Silleck. 1974. Britain. (Documentary). 57 min. Sound. 16mm Color. *Rental:* Pyramid Film. *Sale:* Pyramid Film. *Rental:* Pyramid Film, *Sale:* Pyramid Film, Videotape version.

Collector, The. Terence Stamp & Samantha Eggar. Directed by William Wyler. 1965. Columbia. 119 min. Sound. 16mm Color. *Rental:* Arcus Film, Bosco Films, Budget Films, Films Inc, Inst Cinema, Images Film, Kit Parker, Natl Film Video, Swank Motion, Twyman Films, U of IL Film, Westcoast Films & Wholesome Film Ctr. *Rental:* Swank Motion, Videotape version.

Colleen. Ruby Keeler & Dick Powell. Directed by Alfred E. Green. 1936. Warners. 89 min. Sound. 16mm B&W. *Rental:* MGM United.

College. Buster Keaton & Ann Cornwall. Directed by James W. Horne. 1927. United Artists. (Musical score only). 75 min. Sound. 16mm B&W. *Rental:* A Twyman Pres, Films Inc & Kit Parker. *Sale:* Blackhawk Films & Cinema Concepts. *Rental:* Budget Films, Classic Film Mus, Em Gee Film Lib, Kit Parker, Modern Sound, Swank Motion, Twyman Films & Westcoast Films, *Sale:* Blackhawk Films, Silent 16mm version. *Rental:* Killiam Collect & New Cinema, Tinted version. *Sale:* Blackhawk Films, Super 8 sound version. *Rental:* Ivy Films, *Sale:* Blackhawk Films & Cinema Concepts, Super 8 silent version. *Sale:* Blackhawk Films, Videotape tinted version. *Sale:* Tamarelles French Film, Videotape version. *Sale:* Festival Films, 70 min. 16mm sound version.

College, The. 1963. Vernon Zimmerman. (Documentary). 55 min. Sound. 16mm B&W. *Rental:* Canyon Cinema & Utah Media. *Rental:* Utah Media, 67 mins. version.

College Can Be Killing. 1978. WTTW. (Documentary). 60 min. Sound. 16mm Color. *Rental:* U of IL Film, Utah Media & Iowa Films, Videotape version.

College Coach. Orig. Title: Football Coach. Dick Powell, Pat O'Brien & Ann Dvorak. Directed by William A. Wellman. 1933. Warners. 75 min. Sound. 16mm B&W. *Rental:* MGM United.

College Confidential. Steve Allen & Jayne Meadows. Directed by Albert Zugsmith. 1960. Universal. 91 min. Sound. 16mm B&W. *Rental:* Swank Motion.

College Days see Ziz, Boom, Bah.

College Girl Murders. Joachim Fuchsberger. 1968. Germany. 90 min. Sound. Super 8 Color. dubbed. *Rental:* Ivy Films. *Sale:* Ivy Films.

College Holiday. Jack Benny, George Burns & Gracie Allen. Directed by Frank Tuttle. 1936. Paramount. 88 min. Sound. 16mm B&W. *Rental:* Swank Motion.

College Racehorse see Silks & Saddles.

College Rhythm. Jack Oakie & Joe Penner. Directed by Norman Taurog. 1934. Paramount. 86 min. Sound. 16mm B&W. *Rental:* Swank Motion.

College Swing. George Burns & Gracie Allen. Directed by Raoul Walsh. 1936. Paramount. 86 min. Sound. 16mm B&W. *Rental:* Swank Motion.

Collegiate. Joe Penner & Jack Oakie. Directed by Ralph Murphy. 1936. Paramount. 84 min. Sound. 16mm B&W. *Rental:* Swank Motion.

Colombia Connection, The. Directed by Gustavo Nieto-Roa. 1979. Columbia. (Cast unlisted). 100 min. Sound. 16mm Color. subtitles. *Rental:* Liberty Co.

Colonel Blood. Frank Cellier. Directed by W. P. Lipscomb. 1936. Britain. 70 min. Sound. 16mm B&W. *Rental:* Film Classics.

Colonel Culpepper's Flying Circus. 1981. Britain. (Documentary). 50 min. Sound. 16mm Color. *Rental:* Films Inc. *Sale:* Films Inc. *Sale:* Films Inc, Videotape version.

Colonel Durand, Le. Paul Meurisse. Fr. 1948. France. 110 min. Sound. 16mm B&W. *Rental:* French Am Cul. *Rental:* French Am Cul, Videotape version.

Colonel Effingham's Raid. Charles Coburn & Joan Bennett. Directed by Irving Pichel. 1945. Fox. 70 min. Sound. 16mm B&W. *Rental:* Classic Film Mus & Films Inc.

Colonial Idea, The. 1976. Britain. (Documentary). 60 min. Sound. 16mm Color. *Rental:* Films Inc, Syracuse U Film & U of IL Film. *Sale:* Films Inc. *Sale:* Films Inc, Videotape version.

Colonial Naturalist, The. 1964. Colonial Williamsburg. (Documentary). 55 min. Sound. 16mm Color. *Rental:* Colonial. *Sale:* Colonial.

Color Me Blood Red. Don Joseph & Candi Conder. Directed by Herschell G. Lewis. 1965. Boxoffice Spectaculars. 74 min. Sound. 16mm Color. *Rental:* Films Inc.

Color Me Dead. Tom Tryon & Carolyn Jones. Directed by Eddie Davis. 1970. Goldsworthy. 97 min. Sound. 16mm Color. *Rental:* Ivy Films, Rep Pic Film, Welling Motion Pictures & Willoughby Peer. *Lease:* Rep Pic Film.

Color of Friendship, The. 1979. ABC. (Cast unlisted). 47 min. Sound. 16mm Color. *Rental:* Learning Corp Am. *Sale:* Learning Corp Am. *Sale:* Learning Corp Am, Videotape version.

Color Us Black. 1968. NET. (Documentary). 60 min. Sound. 16mm B&W. *Rental:* Indiana AV Ctr. *Sale:* Indiana AV Ctr.

Colorado. Roy Rogers. Directed by Joseph Kane. 1940. Republic. 54 min. Sound. 16mm B&W. *Rental:* Ivy Films. *Sale:* Cinema Concepts & Rep Pic Film.

Colorado Ambush. Johnny Mack Brown. Directed by Lewis D. Collins. 1951. Monogram. 51 min. Sound. 16mm B&W. *Rental:* Hurlock Cine.

Colorado Kid. Bob Steele. Directed by Sam Newfield. 1937. Republic. 60 min. Sound. 16mm B&W. *Rental:* Ivy Films, Mogulls Films & Film Ctr DC.

Colorado Pioneers. Bill Elliott. Directed by R. G. Springsteen. 1945. Republic. 54 min. Sound. 16mm B&W. *Rental:* Ivy Films & Rep Pic Film. *Lease:* Rep Pic Film.

Colorado Pioneers, The *see* Ten Who Dared.

Colorado Serenade. Eddie Dean & Roscoe Ates. Directed by Robert Tansey. 1946. PRC. 68 min. Sound. 16mm Color. *Sale:* Classics Assoc NY.

Colorado Sundown. Rex Allen. Directed by William Witney. 1951. Republic. 67 min. Sound. 16mm B&W. *Rental:* Ivy Films. *Sale:* Rep Pic Film.

Colorado Sunset. Gene Autry. Directed by George Sherman. 1939. Republic. 54 min. Sound. 16mm B&W. *Rental:* Ivy Films.

Colorado Territory. Joel McCrea & Virginia Mayo. Directed by Raoul Walsh. 1949. Warners. 94 min. Sound. 16mm B&W. *Rental:* MGM United.

Colors of Battle. Directed by Jerzy Passendorfer. 1965. Poland. 100 min. Sound. 16mm B&W. subtitles. *Rental:* Polish People.

Colossus of New York. John Baragrey & Mala Powers. Directed by Eugene Lourie. 1958. Paramount. 70 min. Sound. 16mm B&W. *Rental:* Films Inc.

Colossus of Rhodes. Rory Calhoun & Lea Massari. Directed by Sergio Leone. 1961. Italy. 128 min. Sound. 16mm Color. dubbed. *Rental:* MGM United. *Rental:* MGM United, Anamorphic color version.

Colossus: The Forbin Project. Orig. Title: Day the World Changed Hands, The. Eric Braedon & Susan Clark. Directed by Joseph Sergent. 1970. Universal. 100 min. Sound. 16mm Color. *Rental:* Films Inc, Swank Motion & Williams Films.

Colt Comrades. William Boyd. Directed by Lesley Selander. 1943. United Artists. 67 min. Sound. 16mm B&W. *Lease:* Cinema Concepts. *Sale:* Cinema Concepts, Super 8 sound version. *Sale:* Cinema Concepts, Videotape version.

Columbia Revolt, The. 1969. Tricontinental. (Documentary). 50 min. Sound. 16mm B&W. *Rental:* Kit Parker, CA Newsreel & Tricontinental Film.

Coma. Genevieve Bujold, Michael Douglas & Richard Widmark. Directed by Michael Crichton. 1978. 112 min. Sound. 16mm Color. *Rental:* MGM United. *Rental:* MGM United, Videotape version.

Comanche Station. Randolph Scott & Nancy Gates. Directed by Budd Boetticher. 1960. Columbia. 74 min. Sound. 16mm Color. *Rental:* Bosco Films, Corinth Films, Films Inc, Inst Cinema, Kerr Film, Modern Sound, Roas Films, Welling Motion Pictures, Westcoast Films & Wholesome Film Ctr. *Rental:* Corinth Films & Kit Parker, Anamorphic version.

Comancheros, The. John Wayne & Stuart Whitman. Directed by Michael Curtiz. 1961. Fox. 107 min. Sound. 16mm Color. *Rental:* Films Inc, Twyman Films & Williams Films. *Rental:* Films Inc, Anamorphic version.

Combat America. 1944. US Government. (Documentary). 63 min. Sound. 16mm Color. *Rental:* SD AV Ctr.

Combat Squad. John Ireland & Lon McCallister. Directed by Cy Roth. 1953. Columbia. 72 min. Sound. 16mm B&W. *Rental:* Film Ctr DC & Inst Cinema.

Combative Measures-Judo. 1951. US Government. (Documentary). 120 min. Sound. 16mm B&W. *Sale:* Natl AV ctr.

Come & Get It. Joel McCrea, Edward Arnold & Frances Farmer. Directed by Howard Hawks. 1936. Goldwyn. 99 min. Sound. 16mm B&W. *Rental:* Films Inc.

Come Back, Africa. Directed by Lionel Rogosin. 1960. Rogosin. (Native Cast). 90 min. Sound. 16mm B&W. *Rental:* Inst Cinema. *Sale:* Inst Cinema.

Come Back Baby. John Terry Riebling & Barbara Teitelbaum. Directed by David Greene. 1968. David Allen Greene. 100 min. Sound. 16mm B&W. *Rental:* Canyon Cinema.

Come Back, Charleston Blue. Godfrey Cambridge & Raymond St. Jacques. Directed by Mark Warren. 1972. Warners. 101 min. Sound. 16mm Color. *Rental:* Film Ctr DC, Inst Cinema, Modern Sound, Twyman Films & Williams Films.

Come Back Little Sheba. Shirley Booth & Burt Lancaster. Directed by Daniel Mann. 1952. Paramount. 99 min. Sound. 16mm B&W. *Rental:* Films Inc.

Come Back to Me *see* Doll Face.

Come Back to the Five & Dime, Jimmy Dean, Jimmy Dean. Sandy Dennis & Cher. Directed by Robert Altman. 1982. Viacom. 109 min. Sound. 16mm Color. *Rental:* Films inc.

Come Blow Your Horn. Frank Sinatra & Lee J. Cobb. Directed by Bud Yorkin. 1963. Paramount. 112 min. Sound. 16mm Color. *Rental:* Films Inc. *Rental:* Films Inc, Anamorphic color version.

Come Fill the Cup. James Cagney & Gig Young. Directed by Gordon Douglas. 1951. Warners. 113 min. Sound. 16mm B&W. *Rental:* Swank Motion & Twyman Films.

Come Fly with Me. Hugh O'Brien & Karl Malden. Directed by Henry Levin. 1963. MGM. 109 min. Sound. 16mm Color. *Rental:* MGM United. *Rental:* MGM United, Anamorphic color version.

Come Next Spring. Ann Sheridan, Steve Cochran & Walter Brennan. Directed by R. G. Springsteen. 1955. Republic. 92 min. Sound. 16mm Color. *Rental:* Budget Films. *Sale:* Rep Pic Film.

Come On, The. Anne Baxter & Sterling Hayden. Directed by Russell Birdwell. 1956. Allied Artists. 83 min. Sound. 16mm B&W. *Rental:* Ivy Films. *Sale:* Rep Pic Film.

Come On, Cowboys. Robert Livingston. Directed by Joseph Kane. 1937. Republic. 55 min. Sound. 16mm B&W. *Rental:* Ivy Films. *Sale:* Rep Pic Film.

Come On Danger. Tom Keene & Julie Haydon. Directed by Robert Hill. 1932. RKO. 54 min. Sound. 16mm *Rental:* RKO General Pics.

Come On, Danger. Tim Holt & Ray Whitley. Directed by Bert Gilroy. 1942. RKO. 58 min. Sound. 16mm *Rental:* RKO General Pics.

Come On, Leathernecks. Leon Ames & Edward Brophy. Directed by James Cruze. 1938. Republic. 65 min. Sound. 16mm B&W. *Rental:* Ivy Films.

Come On, Rangers. Roy Rogers. Directed by Joseph Kane. 1938. Republic. 54 min. Sound. 16mm B&W. *Rental:* Ivy Films. *Sale:* Rep Pic Film.

Come On, Tarzan. Ken Maynard. Directed by Alan James. 1933. World Wide. 60 min. Sound. 16mm B&W. *Sale:* Cinema Concepts.

Come Out, Come Out, Whoever You Are. 1969. NET. (Documentary). 59 min. Sound. 16mm B&W. *Rental:* Indiana AV Ctr & U Cal Media. *Sale:* Indiana AV Ctr.

Come September. Rock Hudson & Gina Lollobrigida. Directed by Robert Mulligan. 1961. Universal. 112 min. Sound. 16mm Color. *Rental:* Swank Motion.

Come to the Fairs. 58 min. Sound. Videotape *Rental:* PBS Video. *Sale:* PBS Video.

Come to the Stable. Loretta Young & Celeste Holm. Directed by Henry Koster. 1949. Fox. 94 min. Sound. 16mm B&W. *Rental:* Films Inc.

Come Up Smiling *see* Sing Me a Love Song.

Comeback, The. Jack Jones & David Doyle. Directed by Peter Walker. 1978. Britain. 100 min. Sound. 16mm Color. *Rental:* Swank Motion.

Comedian, The. Mickey Rooney. 1957. CBS. (Kinescope). 80 min. Sound. 16mm B&W. *Rental:* Bosco Films.

Comedians, The. Elizabeth Taylor & Richard Burton. Directed by Peter Glenville. 1967. MGM. 160 min. Sound. 16mm Color. *Rental:* MGM United. *Rental:* MGM United, Anamorphic color version.

Comedy Man, The. Kenneth Moore, Cecil Parker & Dennis Price. Directed by Alvin Rakoff. 1966. Britain. 82 min. Sound. 16mm B&W. *Rental:* Budget Films.

Comedy of Errors, A. 1984. 109 min. Sound. Videotape Color. *Rental:* Iowa Films.

Comedy of Terrors, A. Vincent Price, Boris Karloff & Peter Lorre. Directed by Jacques Tourneur. 1963. American International. 88 min. Sound. 16mm Color. *Rental:* Cine Craft, Charard Motion Pics, Images Film, Inst Cinema, Newman Film Lib, Twyman Films, Video Comm, Welling Motion Pictures, Westcoast Films, Wholesome Film Ctr, Williams Films & Willoughby Peer. *Rental:* Images Film, Anamorphic version.

Comes a Horseman. Jane Fonda & James Caan. Directed by Alan J. Pakula. 1978. United Artists. 118 min. Sound. 16mm Color. *Rental:* MGM United. *Rental:* MGM United, Anamorphic version. *Rental:* MGM United, Videotape version.

Comet Over Broadway. Kay Francis & Ian Hunter. Directed by Busby Berkeley. 1938. Warners. 72 min. Sound. 16mm B&W. *Rental:* MGM United.

Comic, The. Dick Van Dyke, Mickey Rooney & Steve Allen. Directed by Carl Reiner. 1969. Columbia. 94 min. Sound. 16mm Color. *Rental:* Arcus Film, Budget Films, Cine Craft, Charard Motion Pics, Films Inc, Inst Cinema, Kerr Film, Modern Sound, Newman Film Lib, Westcoast Films, Welling Motion Pictures, Wholesome Film Ctr & Willoughby Peer.

Comin' Round the Mountain. Gene Autry. Directed by Mack V. Wright. 1936. Republic. 54 min. Sound. 16mm B&W. *Rental:* Ivy Films.

Comin' Round the Mountain. Bud Abbott & Lou Costello. Directed by Charles Lamont. 1951. Universal. 77 min. Sound. 16mm B&W. *Rental:* Williams Films.

Coming Apart. Rip Torn & Sally Kirkland. Directed by Milton Moses Ginsberg. 1970. Kaleidoscope. 110 min. Sound. 16mm B&W. *Rental:* New Line Cinema. *Sale:* New Line Cinema.

Coming Attractions. Frances Francine. Directed by Beverly Conrad. 1977. Beverly Conrad. 77 min. Sound. 16mm Color. *Rental:* Canyon Cinema.

Coming Home. 1973. Canada. (Documentary). 85 min. Sound. 16mm Color. *Rental:* U Cal Media & Natl Film CN. *Sale:* Natl Film CN.

Coming Home. Jane Fonda, Jon Voight & Bruce Dern. Directed by Hal Ashby. 1978. United Artists. 127 min. Sound. 16mm Color. *Rental:* MGM United. *Rental:* MGM United, Videotape version.

Coming of Amos, The. Rod LaRocque, Jetta Goudal & Noah Beery. Directed by Paul Sloane. 1925. PDC. 60 min. Silent. 16mm B&W. *Rental:* Em Gee Film LIG. *Sale:* Cinema Concepts, Silent 8mm version.

Command Decision. Clark Gable & Walter Pidgeon. Directed by Sam Wood. 1948. MGM. 111 min. Sound. 16mm B&W. *Rental:* MGM United.

Command Performance. Arthur Tracy & Lilli Palmer. Directed by Sinclair Hill. 1937. Britain. 81 min. Sound. 16mm B&W. *Rental:* Ivy Films. *Sale:* Classics Assoc NY.

Committe, The. Committe Troupe. Directed by Del Jack. 1968. Commonwealth. 105 min. Sound. 16mm Color. *Rental:* Budget Films, Cine Craft, Ivy Films, Roas Films, Video Comm, Wholesome Film Ctr & Willoughby Peer.

Common Behavioral Problems. 1979. 61 min. Sound. Videotape Color. *Rental:* Iowa Films.

Common Man, The *see* Dupont Lajoie.

Common Tongue, The. 1976. Britain. (Documentary). 57 min. Sound. 16mm Color. *Rental:* U of IL Film & Utah Media.

Common Touch, The. Greta Gynt & Geoffrey Hibbert. Directed by John Baxter. 1947. Britain. 101 min. Sound. 16mm B&W. *Rental:* Ivy Films. *Sale:* Rep Pic Film.

Communist Conspiracy, The. Wolper. (Documentary). 55 min. Sound. 16mm B&W. *Rental:* Films Inc. *Sale:* Films Inc.

Community, The. 1965. NET. (Documentary). 60 min. Sound. 16mm B&W. *Rental:* Educ Media CA, Indiana AV Ctr, Mass Media, SD AV Ctr & Syracuse U Film. *Sale:* Indiana AV Ctr.

Community Called Earth, A. 1979. PBS. (Documentary). 59 min. Videotape Color. *Rental:* PBS Video. *Sale:* PBS Video.

Companeras & Companeros. Directed by Barbara Stone, David C. Stone & Adolfas Mekas. 1970. Monument. (Documentary). 80 min. Sound. 16mm Color. *Rental:* Canyon Cinema.

Company Limited. Baru Chanda. Directed by Satyajit Ray. Bengali. 1971. Bengal. 112 min. Sound. 16mm B&W. subtitles Eng. *Rental:* Films Inc.

Company of Killers. Van Johnson & Ray Milland. Directed by Jerry Thorpe. 1969. Universal. 87 min. Sound. 16mm Color. *Rental:* Swank Motion.

Company She Keeps, The. Lizabeth Scott & Dennis O'Keefe. Directed by John Cromwell. 1950. RKO. 83 min. Sound. 16mm B&W. *Rental:* Films Inc.

Comparisons-Suburban Living *see* Suburban Living.

Competition, The. Milos Forman & Jiri Suchy. Directed by Milos Forman. Czech. 1963. 84 min. Sound. 16mm B&W. subtitles. *Rental:* Films Inc.

Competition, The. Richard Dreyfuss, Amy Irving & Lee Remick. Directed by Joel Oliansky. 129 min. Sound. 16mm Color. *Rental:* Swank Motion. *Rental:* Swank Motion, Videotape version.

Complete History & Physical Examination, The. 1975. 65 min. Sound. 16mm *Rental:* Natl AV Ctr.

Compulsion. Orson Welles & Dean Stockwell. Directed by Richard Fleischer. 1959. Fox. 103 min. Sound. 16mm B&W. *Rental:* Films Inc & Twyman Films. *Rental:* Films Inc, Anamorphic B&W version.

Compulsive Communicators, The. 1980. Britain. (Documentary). 58 min. Sound. Videotape Color. *Rental:* Films Inc. *Sale:* Films Inc.

Computadora Jugadora, La. Kurt Russell & Cesar Romero. Directed by Robert Butler. 1969. Spain. 91 min. Sound. 16mm Color. dubbed. *Rental:* Twyman Films.

Computer Wore Tennis Shoes, The. Kurt Russell, Cesar Romero & Joe Flynn. Directed by Robert Butler. 1970. Disney. 91 min. Sound. 16mm Color. *Rental:* Bosco Films, Buchan Pic, Cine Craft, Disney Prod, Elliot Film Co, Film Ctr DC, MGM United, Modern Sound, Newman Film Lib, Roas Films, Swank Motion, Twyman Films, U of IL Film, Williams Films, Welling Motion Pictures, Westcoast Films & Williams Films.

Computers, Spies & Private Lives. 1982. Nova. (Documentary). 57 min. Sound. Videotape Color. *Rental:* Iowa Films & U Cal Media.

Comrade X. Hedy Lamarr. Directed by King Vidor. 1940. MGM. 90 min. Sound. 16mm B&W. *Rental:* MGM United.

Comradeship *see* Kameradschaft.

Con Artists, The. Anthony Quinn. 86 min. Sound. Videotape Color. *Sale:* Vidamerica.

Con los Mujeres Cubanas. Trans. Title: With the Cuban Women. Directed by Octavio Cartazor. Span. 1975. Cuba. (Documentary). 60 min. Sound. 16mm Color. *Rental:* Unifilm. *Sale:* Unifilm.

Conan the Barbarian. Arnold Schwarzenegger, Earl James Jones & Sandahl Bergman. Directed by John Milius. 115 min. Sound. 16mm Color. *Rental:* Swank Motion. *Rental:* Swank Motion, Videotape version.

Concealment *see* Secret Bride.

Concert for Bangladesh. Directed by Saul Swimmer. 1972. Fox. (Documentary). 100 min. 16mm Color. *Rental:* Films Inc.

Concert for Kampuchea. 1980. Britain. (Concert). 71 min. Sound. 16mm Color. *Rental:* Cinema Five.

Concert of Stars. Galina Ulanova. Directed by Vasil Lapoknysh. 1952. Russia. 86 min. Sound. 16mm B&W. *Rental:* Corinth Films.

Concerto *see* I've Always Loved You.

Concerto for Orchestra: The Music of Bela Bartok. 1972. CBS. (Documentary). 49 min. Sound. 16mm B&W. *Rental:* Phoenix Films & Syracuse U Film. *Sale:* Phoenix Films. *Sale:* Phoenix Films, Videotape version.

Concorde, The. Orig. Title: Airport '79. Alain Delon, Susan Blakely & Robert Wagner. Directed by David Lowell Rich. 1979. 123 min. Sound. 16mm Color. *Rental:* Swank Motion.

Concrete Jungle *see* Criminal.

Condemned. Orig. Title: Condemned to Devil's Island. Ronald Colman & Ann Harding. Directed by Wesley Ruggles. 1929. Goldwyn. 86 min. Sound. 16mm B&W. *Rental:* Films Inc.

Condemned of Altona, The. Sophia Loren & Maximillian Schell. Directed by Vittorio De Sica. 1963. Fox. 114 min. Sound. 16mm B&W. *Rental:* Films Inc.

Condemned to Devil's Island *see* Condemned.

Condemned Women. Louis Hayward & Anne Shirley. Directed by John Cromwell. 1938. RKO. 77 min. Sound. 16mm *Rental:* RKO General Pics.

Condor, The. Trans. Title: Condor, El. Jim Brown & Lee Van Cleef. Directed by John Guillermin. 1970. Italy. 102 min. Sound. 16mm Color. dubbed. *Rental:* Films Inc, Swank Motion & Williams Films.

Condor, El *see* Condor.

Condorman. Michael Crawford, Oliver Reed & Barbara Carrera. 90 min. Sound. 16mm Color. *Rental:* Bosco Films, Elliot Film Co, Films Inc, Welling Motion Pictures, Westcoast Films & Williams Films.

Conduct Unbecoming. Michael York & Stacy Keach. Directed by Michael Anderson. 1975. Britain. 107 min. Sound. 16mm Color. *Rental:* Hurlock Cine.

Coney Island. Betty Grable & George Montgomery. Directed by Walter Lang. 1943. Fox. 96 min. Sound. 16mm Color. *Rental:* Films Inc.

Confess, Dr. Corda! Hardy Kruger & Elisabeth Mueller. Directed by Josef Von Baky. Ger. 1958. Germany. 101 min. Sound. 16mm B&W. *Rental:* Films Inc.

Confession, The. Henry B. Walthall. Directed by Sidney Franklin. 1919. Fox. (Musical score only). 75 min. Sound. 16mm B&W. *Sale:* E Finney & Griggs Movie. *Rental:* Kerr Film, *Sale:* E Finney, Silent 16mm version.

Confession. Kay Francis & Basil Rathbone. Directed by Joe May. 1937. Warners. 90 min. Sound. 16mm B&W. *Rental:* MGM United.

Confession, The. Yves Montand & Simone Signoret. Directed by Costa-Gavras. Fr. 1970. France-Italy. 138 min. Sound. 16mm Color. subtitles. *Rental:* Films Inc.

Confession, The. Directed by Nobuhiko Ohbayashi. Japan. 75 min. Sound. 16mm Color. *Rental:* Canyon Cinema.

Confessional, The. Anthony Sharp, Stephanie Beacham & Susan Penhaligon. Directed by Alvin Rakoff. 1976. Cinemation. 92 min. Sound. 16mm Color. *Rental:* Films Inc.

Confessions of a Nazi Spy. Edward G. Robinson & Francis Lederer. Directed by Anatole Litvak. 1937. Warners. 102 min. Sound. 16mm B&W. *Rental:* MGM United.

Confessions of a Police Captain. Martin Balsam & Franco Nero. Directed by Damiano Damiani. 1972. Italy. 104 min. Sound. 16mm Color. dubbed. *Rental:* Films Inc.

Confessions of a Window Cleaner. Robin Askwith. Directed by Val Guest. 1974. Britain. 90 min. Sound. 16mm Color. *Rental:* Swank Motion & Welling Motion Pictures.

Confessions of an Opium Eater. Orig. Title: Evils of Chinatown. Vincent Price & Linda Ho. Directed by Albert Zugsmith. 1962. Allied Artists. 85 min. Sound. 16mm B&W. *Rental:* Hurlock Cine.

Confessions of Boston Blackie. Chester Morris & Harriet Hillard. Directed by Edward Dmytryk. 1941. Columbia. 60 min. Sound. 16mm B&W. *Rental:* Kit Parker.

Confessions of Felix Krull. Trans. Title: Bekenntnisse der Hockstaplers. Horst Buchholtz & Lilo Pulver. Directed by Kurt Hoffman. 1958. Germany. 107 min. Sound. 16mm B&W. dubbed. *Rental:* Budget Films, Ivy Films, Kit Parker & Video Comm. *Rental:* Video Comm, Videotape version.

Confidence. Ildiko Bansagi & Peter Andorai. Directed by Istvan Szabo. 1979. Hungary. 104 min. Sound. 16mm Color. *Rental:* New Yorker Films.

Confidential Agent. Charles Boyer & Lauren Bacall. Directed by Herman Shumlin. 1945. Warners. 122 min. Sound. 16mm B&W. *Rental:* MGM United.

Confidential Report *see* Mr. Arkadin.

Confidentially Connie. Janet Leigh & Van Johnson. Directed by Edward Buzzell. 1953. MGM. 72 min. Sound. 16mm B&W. *Rental:* MGM United.

Confirm or Deny. Don Ameche & Joan Bennett. Directed by Archie Mayo. 1941. Fox. 73 min. Sound. 16mm B&W. *Rental:* Films Inc.

Conflagration *see* Enjo.

Conflict Management. 1983. Embassy. (Documentary). 57 min. Sound. 16mm Color. *Rental:* Films Inc. *Sale:* Films Inc. *Sale:* Films Inc, Videotape version.

Conformist, The. Jean-Louis Trintignant & Stefanie Sandrelli. Directed by Bernardo Bertolucci. Fr. 1970. France-Italy. 116 min. Sound. 16mm Color. subtitles. *Rental:* Films Inc.

Conformity. 1963. WCAU. (Documentary, kinescope). 49 min. Sound. 16mm B&W. *Rental:* Mass Media. *Sale:* Carousel Films.

Confrontation, The. Orig. Title: Konfrontation. 1969. NBC. (Documentary). 81 min. Sound. 16mm Color. *Rental:* Films Inc, Iowa Films & U Mich Media. *Sale:* Films Inc. *Sale:* Films Inc, Videotape version.

Confrontation, The. Peter Ballag. Directed by Rolf Lyssy. 1975. Switzerland. 115 min. Sound. 16mm B&W. *Rental:* New Cinema.

Confrontation: Creation Evolution. 4 pts. 1982. Am. Assoc. for Adv. of Science. (Lecture). 179 min. Videotape Color. *Sale:* U Cal Media.

Confronted. 1966. NET. (Documentary). 60 min. Sound. 16mm B&W. *Rental:* Indiana AV Ctr. *Sale:* Indiana AV Ctr.

Confronting Catastrophe: Lessons for the Nuclear Age. 1983. 58 min. Sound. 16mm Color. *Rental:* U Mich Media.

Conga Swing *see* Blondie Goes Latin.

Congo Maisie. Ann Sothern & John Carroll. Directed by H. C. Potter. 1940. MGM. 70 min. Sound. 16mm B&W. *Rental:* MGM United.

Congolaise *see* Wild Rapture.

Congorilla. Directed by Martin Johnson. 1934. Fox. (Documentary). 70 min. Sound. 16mm B&W. *Rental:* Charard Motion Pics.

Connecticut Yankee in King Arthur's Court, A. Bing Crosby & Rhonda Fleming. Directed by Tay Garnett. 1949. Paramount. 107 min. Sound. 16mm Color. *Rental:* Films Inc.

Connecticut Yankee in King Arthur's Court, A. 1970. Australia. (Animated). 84 min. Sound. 16mm Color. *Rental:* Buchan Pic, Budget Films, Inst Cinema, Modern Sound, Roas Films, Swank Motion & Westcoast Films. *Lease:* Inst Cinema.

Connection, The. William Redfield & Gary Goodrow. Directed by Shirley Clarke. 1961. Films Around the World. 102 min. Sound. 16mm B&W. *Rental:* New Yorker Films.

Connemara Family, A. 1982. Britain. (Documentary). 55 min. Sound. Videotape Color. *Sale:* Films Inc.

Conquered Dream, The. 1973. Canada. (Documentary). 51 min. Sound. 16mm Color. *Rental:* Centron Films & Natl Film CN. *Sale:* Centron Films & Natl Film CN. *Rental:* Natl Film CN, *Sale:* Natl Film CN, Videotape version.

Conquering Power, The. Rudolph Valentino. Directed by Rex Ingram. 1921. MGM. 75 min. Silent. 16mm B&W. *Rental:* MGM United.

Conqueror Worm, The. Orig. Title: Witchfinder General. Vincent Price & Ian Ogilvy. Directed by Michael Reeves. 1968. American International. 87 min. Sound. 16mm Color. *Rental:* Films Inc, Cine Craft, Ivy Films, Roas Films, Video Comm, Film Ctr DC, Welling Motion Pictures, Westcoast Films, Wholesome Film Ctr & Willoughby Peer.

Conquest. Orig. Title: Maria Walewska. Greta Garbo & Charles Boyer. Directed by Clarence Brown. 1937. MGM. 65 min. Sound. 16mm B&W. *Rental:* MGM United.

Conquest of Cheyenne. Bill Elliott. Directed by R. G. Springsteen. 1946. Republic. 54 min. Sound. 16mm B&W. *Rental:* Ivy Films.

Conquest of Cochise. John Hodiak & Robert Stack. Directed by William Castle. 1953. Columbia. 70 min. Sound. 16mm Color. *Rental:* Cine Craft, Charard Motion Pics, Inst Cinema, Welling Motion Pictures & Westcoast Films.

Conquest of Mycene. Gordon Scott. Directed by Giorgio Ferroni. 1965. Italy. 102 min. Sound. 16mm Color. dubbed. *Rental:* Budget Films & Modern Sound.

Conquest of Space. Ross Martin & Eric Fleming. Directed by Byron Haskin. 1955. Paramount. 80 min. Sound. 16mm Color. *Rental:* Films Inc.

Conquest of the Planet of the Apes. Roddy MacDowall & Don Murray. Directed by J. Lee Thompson. 1972. Fox. 87 min. Sound. 16mm Color. *Rental:* Films Inc.

Conquest of the Waters, The. 1980. Britain. (Documentary). 58 min. Videotape Color. *Rental:* Films Inc. *Sale:* Films Inc.

Conrack. Jon Voight & Hume Cronyn. Directed by Martin Ritt. 1974. Fox. 106 min. Sound. 16mm Color. *Rental:* Films Inc, Twyman Films & Williams Films. *Rental:* Films Inc, Anamorphic color version.

Conscience of America 1776-1976, The. 1975. ABC. (Interview). 60 min. Sound. 16mm Color. *Rental:* Natl Churches Christ.

Consequence, The. Jurgen Prochnow. Directed by Wolfgang Peterson. 1979. Germany. 100 min. Sound. 16mm B&W. subtitles. *Rental:* Cinema Five.

Consequences of Behavior, The. 1976. 50 min. Sound. 16mm Color. *Rental:* Iowa Films.

Consolation Marriage. Irene Dunne & Pat O'Brien. Directed by Paul Sloane. 1932. RKO. 81 min. Sound. 16mm *Rental:* RKO General Pics.

Conspiracy. Bessie Love & Ned Sparks. Directed by Christy Cabanne. 1930. RKO. 75 min. Sound. 16mm B&W. *Rental:* Em Gee Film Lib. *Sale:* Glenn Photo.

Conspiracy. Allan Lane & Linda Hayes. Directed by Lew Landers. 1930. RKO. 59 min. Sound. 16mm *Rental:* RKO General Pics.

Conspiracy of Hearts. Lilli Palmer & Sylvia Syms. Directed by Ralph Thomas. 1960. Britain. 113 min. Sound. 16mm B&W. *Rental:* Bosco Films, Budget Films, Film Pres, Films Inc, Kit Parker, Learning Corp Am, Modern Sound, Roas Films, Twyman Films & U of IL Film. *Lease:* Learning Corp Am. *Sale:* Learning Corp Am, *Rental:* Learning Corp Am, Videotape version.

Conspiracy of the Borgias. Frank Latimore & Constance Smith. 1965. Italy. 93 min. Sound. 16mm Color. dubbed. *Rental:* Westcoast Films.

Conspiration Malet, La. Jacques Fabri. Directed by Jean-Pierre Decourt. Fr. 1975. France. 52 min. Sound. 16mm Color. subtitles. *Rental:* French Am Cul. *Rental:* French Am Cul, Videotape version.

Conspirator, The. Robert Taylor & Elizabeth Taylor. Directed by Victor Saville. 1950. MGM. 88 min. Sound. 16mm B&W. *Rental:* MGM United.

Constant Factor, The. Tadeusz Bradecki. Directed by Krzysztof Zanussi. Pol. 1980. Poland. Sound. 16mm Color. subtitles. *Rental:* New Yorker Films.

Constant Husband, The. Rex Harrison & Kay Kendall. Directed by Sidney Gilliat. 1954. Britain. 114 min. Sound. 16mm Color. *Rental:* Charard Motion Pics.

Constantine & the Cross. Cornel Wilde & Belinda Lee. Directed by Lionello De Felice. 1962. Italy. 114 min. Sound. 16mm Color. dubbed. *Rental:* Films Inc, Westcoast Films & Willoughby Peer.

Contemporary Views of Human Nature. 1977. Miami-Dade. (Documentary). 60 min. Videotape Color. *Rental:* Films Inc. *Sale:* Films Inc.

Contempt. Trans. Title: Mepris, Le. Brigitte Bardot & Jack Palance. Directed by Jean-Luc Godard. Fr. 1964. France. 103 min. Sound. Videotape Color. subtitles. *Sale:* Films Inc & Tamarelles French Films.

Continental Divide. John Belushi & Blair Brown. Directed by Michael Apted. 103 min. Sound. 16mm Color. *Rental:* Swank Motion. *Rental:* Swank Motion, Videotape version.

Continuing Creation. CC Films. 60 min. Sound. 16mm Color. *Rental:* Natl Council Of The Churches of Christ.

Continuum: Special Theory of Relativity. 1981. 45 min. Sound. 16mm Color. *Rental:* Media Guild, Cinema Guild & U Mich Media.

Contract, The. Orig. Title: Katz and Carasso. Yehuda Barkan. Directed by Menahem Golan. 1974. Israel. 86 min. Sound. 16mm Color. dubbed. *Rental:* Budget Films & Films Inc.

Contract, The. Directed by Krzysztof Zanussi. Pol. 1980. 114 min. 16mm Color. subtitles. *Rental:* New Yorker Films.

Control & Therapy of Genetic Disease. 1980. 45 min. Sound. 16mm *Rental:* Natl AV Ctr.

Controlling Interest: The World of the Multinational Corporation. 1978. California Newsreel. 45 min. Sound. 16mm Color. *Rental:* CA Newsreel & U Mich Media.

Conversation, The. Gene Hackman. Directed by Francis Ford Coppola. 1974. Paramount. 113 min. Sound. 16mm Color. *Rental:* Films Inc.

Conversation Piece. Trans. Title: Gruppo di Famiglia in un Interno. Burt Lancaster, Silvana Mangano, Helmut Berger & Dominique Sanda. Directed by Luchino Visconti. 1976. Italy. 122 min. Sound. 16mm Color. dubbed. *Rental:* New Line Cinema.

Conversation with Helmut Schmidt, A. 1973. WNET. (Interview). 60 min. Sound. 16mm Color. *Rental:* WNET Media. *Sale:* WNET Media. *Sale:* WNET Media, Videotape version.

Conversation with Henry Kissinger, A. 1973. WNET. (Interview). 60 min. Sound. 16mm Color. *Rental:* WNET Media, Videotape version.

Conversation with Huw Wheldon, A. 1973. WNET. (Interview). 60 min. Sound. 16mm Color. *Rental:* WNET Media. *Sale:* WNET Media. *Sale:* WNET Media, Videotape version.

Conversation with Ingrid Bergman, A. 1969. NET. (Documentary). 59 min. Sound. 16mm B&W. *Rental:* Indiana AV Ctr. *Sale:* Indiana AV Ctr.

Conversation with Robert McNamara, A. 1973. WNET. (Interview). 60 min. Sound. 16mm Color. . *Sale:* WNET Media, Videotape version.

Conversation with Willard Van Dyke, A. Directed by Amalie R. Rothschild. 59 min. Sound. 16mm Color. *Rental:* Cinema Guild.

Conversion from Military to Civilian Economy. 1983. 55 min. Sound. 16mm Color. *Rental:* U Mich Media.

Convict Ninety Nine. Will Hay & Moore Marriott. Directed by Marcel Varnel. 1938. Britain. 87 min. Sound. 16mm B&W. *Rental:* Cinema Five.

Convict Stage. Harry Lauter & Donald Barry. Directed by Lesley Selander. 1965. Fox. 71 min. Sound. 16mm B&W. *Rental:* Films Inc.

Convicted. Glenn Ford & Broderick Crawford. Directed by Henry Levin. 1950. Columbia. 91 min. Sound. 16mm B&W. *Rental:* Maljack. *Lease:* Maljack. *Lease:* Maljack, Videotape version.

Convicted Woman. Frieda Incescot & Rochelle Hudson. Directed by Edward Dmytryk. 1940. Columbia. 66 min. Sound. 16mm B&W. *Rental:* Kit Parker.

Convoy. Kris Kristofferson & Ali McGraw. Directed by Sam Peckinpah. 1978. United Artists. (Anamorphic). 111 min. Sound. 16mm Color. *Rental:* MGM United.

Coogan's Bluff. Clint Eastwood & Susan Clark. Directed by Don Siegel. 1968. Universal. 94 min. Sound. 16mm Color. *Rental:* Swank Motion.

Cooking Up Trouble *see* Three of a Kind.

Cooking Up Trouble. Billy Gilbert & Shemp Howard. Directed by D. Ross Lederman. 1945. United Artists. 60 min. Sound. 16mm B&W. *Rental:* Budget Films.

Cool & the Crazy, The. Scott Marlowe & Gigi Perreau. Directed by William Witney. 1958. American International. 78 min. Sound. 16mm B&W. *Rental:* Westcoast Films.

Cool Breeze. Raymond St. Jacques & Thalmus Rasulala. Directed by Barry Pollack. 1972. MGM. 101 min. Sound. 16mm Color. *Rental:* MGM United.

Cool Hand Luke. Paul Newman & George Kennedy. Directed by Stuart Rosenberg. 1967. Warners. 129 min. Sound. 16mm Color. *Rental:* Arcus Film.

Cool World, The. Directed by Shirley Clarke. 1964. Shirley Clarke. 104 min. Sound. 16mm B&W. *Rental:* Zipporah Films. *Lease:* Zipporah Films. *Sale:* Zipporah Films. *Rental:* Zipporah Films, Videotape version.

Cooley High. Glynn Turman. Directed by Michael Schultz. 1975. American International. 107 min. Sound. 16mm Color. *Rental:* Swank Motion, Welling Motion Pictures & Wholesome Film Ctr.

Coonskin. Directed by Ralph Bakshi. 1974. Bryanston. (Animated). 82 min. Sound. 16mm Color. *Rental:* Swank Motion.

Cop in Blue Jeans, The. Jack Palance & Thomas Milian. 92 min. Sound. 16mm *Rental:* WW Enter. *Rental:* WW Enter, Videotape version.

Cop Out. James Mason & Geraldine Chaplin. Directed by Pierre Rouve. 1968. ABC. 104 min. Sound. 16mm Color. *Rental:* Films Inc.

Copacabana. Groucho Marx & Carmen Miranda. Directed by Alfred E. Green. 1947. United Artists. 80 min. Sound. B&W. *Rental:* Ivy Films. *Rental:* Ivy Films, *Sale:* Cinema Concepts & Ivy Films, Super 8 sound version. *Sale:* Video Tape Network, Videotape version.

Copland Celebration, A. 1971. CBS. (Documentary). 47 min. Sound. 16mm B&W. *Rental:* Syracuse U Film. *Sale:* Phoenix Films. *Sale:* Phoenix Films, Videotape version.

Copper Canyon. Ray Milland & Hedy Lamarr. Directed by John Farrow. 1950. Paramount. 82 min. Sound. 16mm Color. *Rental:* Films Inc.

Copper Sky. Jeff Morrow & Coleen Gray. Directed by Charles Marquis Warren. 1957. Fox. (Anamorphic). 75 min. Sound. 16mm B&W. *Rental:* Ivy Films. *Sale:* Rep Pic Film.

Cops & Robbers. Cliff Gorman & Joseph Bologna. Directed by Aram Avakian. 1973. 87 min. 16mm Color. *Rental:* MGM United.

Corajo Del Pueblo, El *see* Courage of the People.

Coral Jungle, The. 1970. Metromedia. 52 min. Sound. 16mm Color. *Rental:* Churchill Films. *Sale:* Churchill Films. *Rental:* Churchill Films, Videotape version.

Corbeau, Le. Pierre Fresnay & Pierre Larquey. Directed by Henri-Georges Clouzot. Fr. 1943. France. 92 min. Sound. 16mm B&W. subtitles Eng. *Rental:* Cinema Concepts, Films Inc, Westcoast Films & Kit Parker. *Sale:* Festival Films & Reel Images. *Sale:* Festival Films, Videotape version.

Corbusier, Le. 1970. 46 min. Sound. 16mm Color. *Rental:* U Mich Media & Utah Media.

Core Skills for Field Instructor One. 1983. McGill. 90 min. Sound. 16mm B&W. *Rental:* Syracuse U Film.

Core Skills for Field Instructor Two. 1983. McGill. 68 min. Sound. 16mm B&W. *Rental:* Films Inc.

Coriolanus. Alan Howard & Irene Worth. 1983. 120 min. Sound. Videotape Color. *Rental:* Iowa Films.

Corky. Robert Blake & Charlotte Rampling. Directed by Leonard Horn. 1972. MGM. (Anamorphic). 88 min. Sound. 16mm Color. *Rental:* MGM United.

Corn is Green, The. Bette Davis & John Dall. Directed by Irving Rapper. 1945. Warners. 118 min. Sound. 16mm B&W. *Rental:* MGM United.

Cornbread, Earl & Me. Moses Gunn & Rosalind Cash. Directed by Joe Manduke. 1976. American International. 95 min. Sound. 16mm Color. *Rental:* Swank Motion, Welling Motion Pictures, Wholesome Film Ctr & Williams Films.

Cornered. Dick Powell & Walter Slezak. Directed by Edward Dmytryk. 1945. RKO. 102 min. Sound. 16mm B&W. *Rental:* Films Inc.

Corn's a Poppin'. Jerry Wallace. 70 min. Sound. 16mm B&W. *Sale:* Morcraft Films. *Sale:* Morcraft Films, Super 8 sound version.

Coronary Artery Disease: Newer Dimensions. 1968. US Government. (Documentary). 81 min. Sound. 16mm B&W. *Sale:* Natl AV Ctr.

Coroner Creek. Randolph Scott & Marguerite Chapman. Directed by Ray Enright. 1968. Columbia. 90 min. Sound. 16mm Color. *Rental:* Roas Films & Welling Motion Pictures.

Corporation, The. 1973. CBS. (Documentary). 53 min. Sound. 16mm B&W. *Rental:* Budget Films, Syracuse U Film & Iowa Films. *Sale:* Carousel Films. *Rental:* U Mich Media, *Sale:* Carousel Films, Color version.

Corpse Came C. O. D., The George Brent & Joan Blondell. Directed by Henry Levin. 1947. Columbia. 87 min. Sound. 16mm B&W. *Rental:* Films Inc.

Corpse Grinders, The. Sean Kennedy & Monika Kelly. Directed by Ted V. Mikels. 1971. Gemini. 80 min. Sound. 16mm Color. *Rental:* Budget Films, Films Inc, Ivy Films, Modern Sound, Roas Films, Video Comm & Westcoast Films.

Corpse Vanishes, The. Orig. Title: Case of the Missing Brides, The. Bela Lugosi & Luana Walters. Directed by Wallace Fox. 1942. Monogram. 64 min. Sound. Videotape B&W. *Sale:* Films Inc & Vidamerica. *Sale:* Classic Film Mus.

Corpus Christi Bandits. Allan Lane. Directed by Wallace Grissell. 1948. Republic. 55 min. Sound. 16mm B&W. *Rental:* Ivy Films. *Sale:* Rep Pic Film.

Correction Please. Directed by Noel Burch. 1979. Britain. (Anthology, color sequence). 52 min. Sound. 16mm B&W. *Rental:* Museum Mod Art. *Sale:* Museum Mod Art.

Correctional Process, The. 1966. Canada. (Documentary). 52 min. Sound. 16mm B&W. *Rental:* U of IL Film.

Corregidor. Elissa Landi. Directed by William Nigh. 1943. PRC. 70 min. Sound. 16mm B&W. *Rental:* Mogulls Films.

Corridor of Mirrors. Eric Portman & Barbara Mullen. Directed by Terence Young. 1949. Britain. 110 min. Sound. 16mm B&W. *Rental:* Mogulls Films.

Corridors of Blood. Boris Karloff & Christopher Lee. Directed by Robert Day. 1963. Britain. 86 min. Sound. 16mm B&W. *Rental:* Budget Films, Modern Sound, Roas Films & Video Comm. *Sale:* Reel Images, Super 8 sound version. *Sale:* Video Lib, Videotape version.

Corridors of Time. 1982. Films Inc. (Documentary). 60 min. Sound. 16mm Color. *Rental:* Films Inc. *Sale:* Films Inc. *Sale:* Films Inc, Videotape version.

Corrupt City, The. 1977. Edupac. (Documentary). 50 min. Sound. 16mm Color. *Rental:* Edupac. *Sale:* Edupac.

Corruption. Peter Cushing & Sue Lloyd. Directed by Robert Hartford-Davis. 1968. Columbia. 91 min. Sound. 16mm Color. *Rental:* Cine Craft, Films Inc, Inst Cinema, Kerr Film, Modern Sound, Roas Films, Welling Motion Pictures & Westcoast Films.

Corruption of the Damned. Mary Flannagan. Directed by George Kuchar. 1965. George Kuchar. 55 min. Sound. 16mm B&W. *Rental:* Canyon Cinema.

Corsair. Chester Morris & Frank McHugh. Directed by Roland West. 1931. United Artists. 78 min. Sound. 16mm B&W. *Rental:* A Twyman Pres, Classic Film Mus, Em Gee Film Lib & Film Classics. *Sale:* Cinema Concepts, Natl Cinema & Reel Images.

Corsican Brothers, The. Douglas Fairbanks Jr. & Ruth Warrick. Directed by Gregory Ratoff. 111 min. Sound. 16mm B&W. *Rental:* Budget Films.

Cortez & the Legend. 1968. ABC. (Documentary). 52 min. Sound. 16mm Color. *Rental:* BYU Media, Iowa Films, McGraw-Hill Films, Syracuse U Film, U Cal Media & U of IL Film. *Sale:* McGraw-Hill Films. *Rental:* McGraw-Hill Films, *Sale:* McGraw-Hill Films, Spanish version.

Cortile Cascino. Directed by Michael Roemer & Robert M. Young. 1961. 46 min. Sound. 16mm B&W. *Rental:* Museum Mod Art.

Corvette Summer. Mark Hamill & Annie Potts. Directed by Matthew Robbins. 1978. MGM. 110 min. Sound. 16mm Color. *Rental:* MGM United.

Cosi Come Sei *see* Stay the Way You Are.

Cosmopolis: Big City 2000 A. D.. 1968. ABC. (Documentary). 52 min. Sound. 16mm Color. *Rental:* McGraw-Hill Films, U Mich Media & Syracuse U Film. *Sale:* McGraw-Hill Films.

Cossacks Beyond the Danube. Ivan Patorzhinsky. Directed by Vasil Lapoknysh. Rus. 1954. Russia. 97 min. Sound. 16mm B&W. subtitles. *Rental:* Corinth Films.

Cossacks of the Kuban. Mariana Ladinina. Directed by Ivan Pyriev. Rus. 1949. 105 min. Sound. 16mm B&W. subtitles. *Rental:* Corinth Films.

Cottage on Dartmoor, A. Norah Baring & Uno Henning. Directed by Anthony Asquith. 1930. Britain. 75 min. Silent. 16mm B&W. *Rental:* Museum Mod Art.

Cotter. Don Murray, Carol Lynley & Rip Torn. 1972. Gold Key. 94 min. Sound. 16mm Color. *Rental:* Budget Films, Video Comm & Westcoast Films. *Sale:* Video Comm. *Rental:* Video Comm, Videotape version.

Cotton Comes to Harlem. Calvin Lockhart, Raymond St. Jacques & Godfrey Cambridge. Directed by Ossie Davis. 1970. United Artists. 90 min. Sound. 16mm Color. *Rental:* MGM United.

Cottontail. 1953. Calif. Dept. of Fish & Game. (Documentary). 50 min. Sound. 16mm Color. *Rental:* U Mich Media.

Cougar Country. 1970. American National. (Documentary). 100 min. Sound. 16mm Color. *Rental:* Budget Films, Modern Sound, Roas Films, Video Comm & Westcoast Films. *Lease:* Video Comm. *Rental:* Video Comm, *Lease:* Video Comm, Videotape version.

Counselor at Crime. Martin Balsam & Tomas Milian. Directed by Alberto De Martino. 1976. Italy. (Anamorphic). 99 min. Sound. 16mm Color. dubbed. *Rental:* J Green Pics.

Counselor at Law. John Barrymore & Bebe Daniels. Directed by William Wyler. 1933. Universal. 82 min. Sound. 16mm B&W. *Rental:* Swank Motion.

Count Down Under. 1966. NET. (Documentary). 59 min. Sound. 16mm B&W. *Rental:* Indiana AV Ctr. *Sale:* Indiana AV Ctr.

Count Dracula. Christopher Lee & Herbert Lom. Directed by Jess Franco. 1972. Britain. 98 min. Sound. 16mm Color. *Rental:* Budget Films, Ivy Films, Rep Pic Film, Video Comm, Welling Motion Pictures & Westcoast Films. *Lease:* Rep Pic Film.

Count Five & Die. Jeffrey Hunter & Nigel Patrick. Directed by Victor Vicas. 1958. Britain. (Anamorphic). 92 min. Sound. 16mm B&W. *Rental:* Willoughby Peer.

Count of Monte Cristo, The. James O'Neill. Directed by Edwin S. Porter. 1912. Famous Players. 65 min. Silent. 16mm B&W. *Sale:* Morcraft Films.

Count of Monte Cristo, The. Richard Chamberlain & Tony Curtis. Directed by David Greene. 1974. ITC. 90 min. Sound. 16mm Color. *Rental:* Swank Motion.

Count of Monte Cristo, The. Robert Donat & Elissa Landi. Directed by Roland V. Lee. 119 min. Sound. 16mm B&W. *Rental:* Budget Films.

Count the Hours. Orig. Title: Every Minute Counts. Teresa Wright, MacDonald Carey & Adele Mara. Directed by Don Siegel. 1953. RKO. 74 min. Sound. 16mm B&W. *Rental:* Films Inc. *Sale:* Films Inc.

Count Three & Pray. Van Heflin & Joanne Woodward. Directed by George Sherman. 1955. Columbia. 102 min. Sound. 16mm B&W. *Rental:* Inst Cinema & Modern Sound. *Rental:* Charard Motion Pics & Film Ctr DC, Color version.

Count Yorga, Vampire. Robert Quarry & Roger Perry. Directed by Bob Kelljan. 1971. American International. 91 min. Sound. 16mm Color. *Rental:* Films Inc, Ivy Films, Video Comm, Westcoast Films, Wholesome Film Ctr & Arcus Film.

Count Your Blessings. Deborah Kerr & Rosanno Brazzi. Directed by Jean Negulesco. 1959. MGM. 102 min. Sound. 16mm Color. *Rental:* MGM United. *Rental:* MGM United, Anamorphic color version.

Countdown. 1978. Connections. (Documentary). 53 min. Sound. 16mm Color. *Rental:* Iowa Films, Kent St U Film, U Cal Media, U Mich Media & U of IL Film.

Countdown at Kusini. Ruby Dee, Ossie Davis & Greg Morris. Directed by Ossie Davis. 1976. Columbia. 99 min. Sound. 16mm Color. *Rental:* Budget Films, Cine Craft, Swank Motion & Westcoast Films.

Countdown to Danger. 1974. Germany. (Cast unlisted). 45 min. Sound. 16mm Color. *Rental:* Janus Films. *Sale:* Lucerne Films & Sterling Ed Film.

Countdown to Doomsday. George Arridson. 1967. 90 min. Sound. 16mm Color. dubbed. *Rental:* Westcoast Films.

Counter Espionage. Warren William & Eric Blore. Directed by Edward Dmytryk. 1942. 72 min. Sound. 16mm B&W. *Rental:* Kit Parker.

Counterfeit Killer, The. Jack Lord & Shirley Knight. Directed by Joseph Leytes. 1968. Universal. 95 min. Sound. 16mm Color. *Rental:* Swank Motion.

Counterfeit Traitor, The. William Holden & Lilli Palmer. Directed by George Seaton. 1962. Paramount. 147 min. Sound. 16mm Color. *Rental:* Films Inc.

Counterfeiters of Paris, The. Jean Gabin & Bernard Blier. Directed by Gilles Grangier. 1963. MGM. 80 min. Sound. 16mm B&W. dubbed. *Rental:* MGM United.

Counterplot. Forrest Tucker. Directed by Kurt Neumann. 1959. United Artists. 77 min. Sound. 16mm B&W. *Rental:* MGM United.

Counterpoint. Charlton Heston & Maximilian Schell. Directed by Ralph Nelson. 1968. Universal. 105 min. Sound. 16mm Color. *Rental:* Swank Motion.

Counterspy vs. Scotland Yard. Willard Parker & Audrey Long. Directed by Seymour Friedman. 1950. Columbia. 90 min. Sound. 16mm B&W. *Rental:* Inst Cinema.

Countess Dracula. Ingrid Pitt & Nigel Green. Directed by Peter Sasdy. 1972. Fox. 94 min. Sound. 16mm Color. *Rental:* Films Inc.

Countess from Hong Kong, A. Marlon Brando & Sophia Loren. Directed by Charles Chaplin. 1967. Universal. 108 min. Sound. 16mm Color. *Rental:* Williams Films & Swank Motion.

Countess of Monte Cristo. Sonja Henie & Olga San Juan. Directed by Frederick De Cordova. 1948. Universal. 90 min. Sound. 16mm B&W. *Rental:* Budget Films, Charard Motion Pics, Inst Cinema & Ivy Films. *Sale:* Rep Pic Film.

Country Fair. Eddie Foy Jr. & William Demarest. Directed by Frank McDonald. 1941. Republic. 74 min. Sound. 16mm B&W. *Rental:* Ivy Films.

Country Fair, The. Helen Jerome Eddy & David Butler. Directed by Maurice Tourneur. 1920. Paramount. 55 min. Silent. 16mm B&W. *Rental:* Em Gee Film Lib. *Sale:* Morcraft Films. *Sale:* Morcraft Films, Super 8 sound version. *Sale:* Morcraft Films, Videotape version.

Country Fair. Rory Calhoun & Jane Nigh. Directed by William Beaudine. 1950. Monogram. 76 min. Sound. 16mm Color. *Rental:* Inst Cinema & Ivy Films. *Lease:* Rep Pic Film.

Country Gentlemen. Olsen & Johnson. Directed by Ralph Staub. 1936. Republic. 54 min. Sound. 16mm B&W. *Rental:* Budget Films & Ivy Films. *Sale:* Rep Pic Film & Reel Images.

Country Girl, The. Bing Crosby, Grace Kelly & William Holden. Directed by George Seaton. 1954. Paramount. 104 min. Sound. 16mm B&W. *Rental:* Films Inc.

Country Music Holiday. Zsa Zsa Gabor & Ferlin Husky. Directed by Alvin Ganzer. 1958. Paramount. 81 min. Sound. 16mm B&W. *Rental:* Films Inc.

Coup de Grace. Margarethe Von Trotta. Directed by Volker Schlondorff. Ger. 1977. Germany. 95 min. Sound. 16mm B&W. subtitles. *Rental:* Cinema Five.

Coup de Tete: Hothead. Patrick Dewaere & Jean Bouise. Directed by Jean-Jacques Annaud. Fr. 1979. France. 88 min. Sound. 16mm Color. subtitles. *Rental:* Films Inc & New Cinema.

Coup de Torchon. Phillippe Noiret & Stephane Audran. Directed by Bertrand Tavernier. Fr. 1982. QFI. 128 min. Sound. 16mm Color. subtitles Eng. *Rental:* Films Inc.

Coup Pour Coup *see* Blow for Blow.

Couples. 1975. Penn State. (Documentary). 50 min. Sound. 16mm B&W. *Rental:* Penn St AV Serv. *Sale:* Penn St AV Serv.

Courage of Black Beauty. Johnny Crawford & Mimi Gibson. Directed by Harold Schuster. 1957. Fox. 78 min. Sound. 16mm Color. *Rental:* Films Inc.

Courage Of Kavik. Ronny Cox, John Ireland & Linda Soresen. Arcus Film. 90 min. 16mm Color. *Rental:* Arcus Film.

Courage of Lassie. Elizabeth Taylor & Frank Morgan. Directed by Fred M. Wilcox. 1946. MGM. 92 min. Sound. 16mm Color. *Rental:* MGM United.

Courage of the People. Trans. Title: Corajo Del Pueblo, El. Federico Vallejo & Felicidad Coca. Directed by Jorge Sanjines. Span. 1968. Bolivia-Italy. 95 min. Sound. 16mm Color. subtitles. *Rental:* Cinema Guild. *Sale:* Cinema Guild.

Courageous Avenger. Johnny Mack Brown. 1935. Supreme. 55 min. Sound. 16mm B&W. *Sale:* Cinema Concepts.

Courageous Cat. Videotape *Sale:* Vidamerica.

Courageous Dr. Christian. Jean Hersholt. Directed by Bernard Vorhaus. 1940. RKO. 67 min. Sound. 16mm B&W. *Rental:* Ivy Films, Rep Pic Film, Welling Motion Pictures & Budget Films. *Lease:* Rep Pic Film.

Courageous Mr. Penn. Orig. Title: Penn of Pennsylvania. Clifford Evans & Deborah Kerr. Directed by Lance Comfort. 1942. Britain. 79 min. Sound. 16mm B&W. *Rental:* Budget Films, Film Classics, Films Inc, Ivy Films & Mogulls Films. *Sale:* Rep Pic Film & Reel Images.

Court Jester, The. Danny Kaye & Glynis Johns. Directed by Norman Panama & Melvin Frank. 1956. Paramount. 101 min. Sound. 16mm Color. *Rental:* Films Inc.

Court Martial. Orig. Title: Carrington, V.C. David Niven & Margaret Leighton. Directed by Anthony Asquith. 1955. Britain. 100 min. Sound. 16mm B&W. *Rental:* Mogulls Films.

Court Martial of Billy Mitchell, The. Orig. Title: One Man Mutiny. Gary Cooper. Directed by Otto Preminger. 1955. Warners. 100 min. Sound. 16mm Color. *Rental:* B Raymond. *Rental:* Corinth Films, Anamorphic version.

Courtin' Trouble. Jimmy Wakely. Directed by Ford Beebe. 1948. Monogram. 55 min. Sound. 16mm B&W. *Rental:* Hurlock Cine.

Courtship & Marriage. 1961. Canada. (Documentary). 60 min. Sound. 16mm B&W. *Rental:* Syracuse U Film. *Sale:* McGraw-Hill Films.

Courtship of Eddie's Father, The. Glenn Ford & Shirley Jones. Directed by Vincente Minnelli. 1963. MGM. 117 min. Sound. 16mm Color. *Rental:* MGM United. *Rental:* MGM United, Anamorphic color version.

Cousin Angelica. Directed by Carlos Saura. Span. 1974. Spain. 90 min. Sound. 16mm Color. subtitles. *Rental:* New Yorker Films.

Cousin, Cousine. Marie-Christine Barrault & Victor Lanoux. Directed by Jean-Charles Tacchella. Fr. 1975. France. 95 min. Sound. 16mm Color. *Rental:* Cinema Five & World Northal.

Cousine Bette. France. (Cast unlisted). 121 min. Sound. 16mm B&W. *Rental:* French Am Cul.

Cousteau Odyssey: Calypso's Search for Atlantis. 1977. Cousteau Society. (Documentary). 50 min. Sound. 16mm Color. *Rental:* U of IL Film.

Couturier de Ces Dames, Le: Fernandel, the Dressmaker. Fernandel. Directed by Jean Boyer. 1956. France. 95 min. Sound. 16mm B&W. subtitles. *Rental:* Em Gee Film Lib, Festival Films & Kit Parker. *Sale:* Natl Cinema. *Sale:* Festival Films, Tamarelles French Film, Videotape version.

Cover Girl. Rita Hayworth, Gene Kelly & Phil Silvers. Directed by Charles Vidor. 1944. Columbia. 107 min. Sound. 16mm Color. *Rental:* Arcus Film, Bosco Films, Buchan Film, Budget Films, Films Inc, Images Film, Kit Parker, Modern Sound, Natl Film Serv, Natl Film Video, Swank Motion, Twyman Films, U of IL Film, Welling Motion Pictures, Westcoast Films & Wholesome Film Ctr, B&W videotape version.

Covered Trailer, The. Jackie Gleason & Mary Beth Hughes. Directed by Gus Meins. 1939. Republic. 54 min. Sound. 16mm B&W. *Rental:* Ivy Films. *Sale:* Rep Pic Film.

Covered Wagon, The. Ernest Torrance & Lois Wilson. Directed by James Cruze. 1923. Paramount. (Musical score only). 98 min. 16mm B&W. *Rental:* Films Inc. *Rental:* Films Inc, Museum Mod Art & Mogulls Films, Silent 16mm version. *Rental:* Cinema Concepts, Super 8 silent version.

Covered Wagon Days. Robert Livingston. Directed by George Sherman. 1940. Republic. 54 min. Sound. 16mm B&W. *Rental:* Ivy Films. *Sale:* Rep Pic Film.

Covered Wagon Raid. Allan Lane. Directed by R. G. Springsteen. 1950. Republic. 60 min. Sound. 16mm B&W. *Rental:* Ivy Films. *Sale:* Rep Pic Film.

Covered Wagon Trails. Jack Randall. Directed by Raymond K. Johnson. 1940. Monogram. 55 min. Sound. 16mm B&W. *Rental:* Hurlock Cine.

Cow, The. Ezat Entezami & Ali Nasirian. Directed by Daryush Mehjui. Persian. 1968. 101 min. Sound. 16mm B&W. *Rental:* Films Inc..

Cow & I, The. Fernandel & Rene Havard. Directed by Henri Verneuil. Fr. 1959. France. 120 min. Sound. 16mm B&W. subtitles Eng. *Rental:* Films Inc.

Cow Country. Edmond O'Brien & Helen Wescott. Directed by Lesley Selander. 1953. Monogram. 82 min. Sound. 16mm B&W. *Rental:* Hurlock Cine.

Coward, The. Charles Ray & Frank Keenan. Directed by Reginald Barker. 1915. Triangle. 74 min. Silent. 16mm B&W. *Rental:* Em Gee Film Lib.

Cowboy. Orig. Title: American Cowboy, The. Jack Lennon & Glenn Ford. Directed by Delmer Daves. 1958. Columbia. 92 min. Sound. 16mm Color. *Rental:* Arcus Film, Bosco Films, Buchan Film, Budget Films, Cine Craft, Charard Motion Pics, Kit Parker, Modern Sound, Roas Films, Twyman Films, Video Comm & Welling Motion Pictures.

Cowboy. 1972. Time-Life. (Documentary). 54 min. Sound. 16mm Color. *Rental:* Films Inc & U Cal Media. *Sale:* Films Inc.

Cowboy & the Blonde, The. Mary Beth Hughes & George Montgomery. Directed by Ray McCarey. 1941. Fox. 68 min. Sound. 16mm B&W. *Rental:* Films Inc.

Cowboy & the Lady, The. Gary Cooper & Merle Oberon. Directed by H. C. Potter. 1938. Goldwyn. 91 min. Sound. 16mm B&W. *Rental:* Films Inc.

Cowboy & the Prizefighter, The. Jim Bannon. Directed by Lewis D. Collins. 1950. Eagle Lion. 59 min. Sound. 16mm Color. *Rental:* Budget Films.

Cowboy & the Senorita, The. Roy Rogers. Directed by Joseph Kane & Dale Evans. 1944. Republic. 54 min. Sound. 16mm B&W. *Rental:* Budget Films & Ivy Films. *Sale:* Rep Pic Film. *Rental:* Budget Films, 60 mins. version.

Cowboy Canteen. Orig. Title: Close Harmony. Jane Frazee & Red River Dave. Directed by Lew Landers. 1944. Columbia. 72 min. Sound. 16mm B&W. *Rental:* Inst Cinema.

Cowboy Cavalier. Jimmy Wakely. Directed by Derwin Abrahams. 1948. Monogram. 55 min. Sound. 16mm B&W. *Rental:* Hurlock Cine.

Cowboy Commandos. The Range Busters. Directed by S. Roy Luby. 1944. Monogram. 60 min. Sound. 16mm B&W. *Rental:* Modern Sound. *Sale:* Morcraft Films. *Sale:* Morcraft Films, Super 8 sound version. *Sale:* Mocraft Films, Videotape version.

Cowboy Counsellor. Hoot Gibson. Directed by George Melford. 1933. Allied. 60 min. Sound. Videotape B&W. *Sale:* Video Comm.

Cowboy from Brooklyn, The. Dick Powell & Pat O'Brien. Directed by Lloyd Bacon. 1938. Warners. 80 min. Sound. 16mm B&W. *Rental:* MGM United.

Cowboy Millionaire. George O'Brien. Directed by Edward Cline. 1935. Fox. 70 min. Sound. 16mm B&W. *Sale:* Morcraft Films.

Cowboy Musketeer. Tom Tyler. Directed by Robert De Lacy. 1925. FBO. 55 min. Silent. 16mm B&W. .

Cowboy Quarterback, The. Bert Wheeler & Marie Wilson. Directed by Noel Smith. 1939. Warners. 56 min. Sound. 16mm B&W. *Rental:* MGM United.

Cowboy Serenade. Gene Autry. Directed by William Morgan. 1942. Republic. 54 min. Sound. 16mm B&W. *Rental:* Ivy Films.

Cowboys, The. John Wayne & Bruce Dern. Directed by Mark Rydell. 1971. 128 min. Sound. Videotape Color. *Sale:* Tamarelles French Films.

Cowboys & the Indians, The. Gene Autry. Directed by John English. 1949. Columbia. 70 min. Sound. 16mm B&W. *Rental:* Roas Films.

Cowboys from Texas. Robert Livingston. Directed by George Sherman. 1939. Republic. 54 min. Sound. 16mm B&W. *Rental:* Ivy Films. *Sale:* Rep Pic Film.

Cowtown. Gene Autry. Directed by John English. 1950. Columbia. 72 min. Sound. 16mm B&W. *Rental:* Inst Cinema.

Coyote Trail. Tom Tyler. 1935. Commodore. 60 min. Sound. 16mm B&W. *Rental:* Mogulls Films. *Sale:* Reel Images. *Sale:* Reel Images, Super 8 sound version.

Crab Nebula, The. 1971. Britain. 50 min. Sound. 16mm Color. *Rental:* Films Inc, Kent St U Film, U Cal Media, U Mich Media & Utah Media. *Sale:* Films Inc. *Rental:* Films Inc, *Sale:* Films Inc, Videotape version. *Rental:* Utah Media, 58 mins. version.

Crack in the Mirror. Orson Welles & Juliette Greco. Directed by Richard Fleischer. 1960. Fox. (Anamorphic). 97 min. Sound. 16mm B&W. *Rental:* Films Inc.

Crack in the World. Dana Andrews & Janette Scott. Directed by Andrew Marton. 1965. Paramount. 96 min. Sound. 16mm Color. *Rental:* Films Inc.

Crack-Up. Pat O'Brien & Claire Trevor. Directed by Irving Reis. 1946. RKO. 93 min. Sound. 16mm B&W. *Rental:* Films Inc & RKO General.

Cracked Nuts. Bert Wheeler & Robert Woolsey. Directed by Edward Cline. 1931. RKO. 64 min. Sound. 16mm B&W. *Rental:* Films Inc.

Cracked Nuts. Stu Erwin & Una Merkel. Directed by Edward Cline. 1941. Universal. 62 min. Sound. 16mm B&W. *Rental:* Mogulls Films, Newman Film Lib & Film Ctr DC.

Crackerjack, The. Johnny Hines. Directed by Charles Hines. 1925. East Coast. 60 min. Silent. 16mm B&W. *Rental:* E Finney. *Sale:* E Finney, Silent 8mm version.

Crackers. Donald Sutherland & Jack Warden. Directed by Louis Malle. 1984. Universal. 92 min. Sound. 16mm Color. *Rental:* Swank Motion.

Cracking the Stone-Age Code. 1974. Britain. (Documentary). 52 min. Sound. 16mm Color. *Rental:* Films Inc, U Cal Media & U Mich Media. *Sale:* Films Inc. *Rental:* Films Inc, *Sale:* Films Inc, Videotape version.

Cracking Up. Philip Proctor. Directed by Rowby Goren & Chuck Staley. 1977. American International. 74 min. Sound. 16mm Color. *Rental:* Welling Motion Pictures.

Cradle of Courage. William S. Hart & Tom Santschi. Directed by Lambert Hillyer. 1920. Paramount. 74 min. Silent. 16mm B&W. *Rental:* Budget Films, Em Gee Film Lib & Museum Mod Art. *Sale:* Glenn Photo. *Sale:* Glenn Photo, Super 8 silent version.

Craft of History, The. Directed by George Robertson. 1972. Canada. (Documentary). 58 min. Sound. 16mm Color. *Rental:* Natl Film CN. *Sale:* Natl Film CN.

Craig's Wife. Rosalind Russell & John Boles. Directed by Dorothy Arzner. 1936. Columbia. 75 min. Sound. 16mm B&W. *Rental:* Budget Films, Kit Parker, Swank Motion, Twyman Films, Westcoast Films & Welling Motion Pictures.

Crainquebille. Orig. Title: Bill. Maurice De Feraudy. Directed by Jacques Feyder. 1923. France. 49 min. Silent. 16mm B&W. *Rental:* Budget Films, Em Gee Film Lib, Film Classics & Film Images. *Sale:* Film Classics. *Rental:* Film Classics, Videotape version.

Cranes Are Flying, The. Alexi Batalow & Tania Samoilova. Directed by Mikhail Kalatozov. Rus. 1957. Russia. 94 min. Sound. 16mm B&W. subtitles. *Rental:* Corinth Films & Films Inc. *Lease:* Corinth Films.

Crash, The. Helen Vinson, Ruth Chatterton & George Brent. Directed by William Dieterle. 1932. Warners. 58 min. Sound. 16mm B&W. *Rental:* MGM United.

Crash Dive. Tyrone Power & Anne Baxter. Directed by Archie Mayo. 1943. Fox. 105 min. Sound. 16mm Color. *Rental:* Films Inc.

Crash Landing. Gary Merrill & Roger Smith. Directed by Fred F. Sears. 1958. Columbia. 77 min. Sound. 16mm B&W. *Rental:* Inst Cinema.

Crash of Silence see Mandy.

Crashin' Through Danger. Guinn Williams & Sally Blane. Directed by Sam Newfield. 1938. Excelsior. 55 min. Sound. 16mm B&W. *Rental:* Ivy Films. *Sale:* Rep Pic Film.

Crashing Hollywood. Jack Carson & Lee Tracy. Directed by Lew Landers. 1938. RKO. 61 min. Sound. 16mm *Rental:* RKO General Pics.

Crashout. William Bendix & Gene Evans. Directed by Lewis R. Foster. 1955. Filmakers. 82 min. Sound. 16mm B&W. *Rental:* Ivy Films. *Sale:* Rep Pic Film.

Crater Lake Monster, The. Richard Garrison & Richard Cardella. Directed by William R. Stromberg. 1977. Crown. 85 min. Sound. 16mm Color. *Rental:* Films Inc.

Crawling Eye, The. Orig. Title: Trollenberg Terror, The. Forrest Tucker & Janet Munro. Directed by Quentin Lawrence. 1957. Britain. 85 min. Sound. 16mm B&W. *Rental:* Budget Films, Ivy Films, Modern Sound, Roas Films, Swank Motion & Video Comm.

Crawling Hand, The *see* Strike Me Deadly.

Crazies, The. Lane Carroll, Harold W. Jones & W. G. McMillan. Directed by George A. Romero. 1973. Cinema Five. 99 min. Sound. 16mm Color. *Rental:* Cinema Five.

Crazy for Love. Trans. Title: Trou Normand, Le. Brigitte Bardot & Bourvil. Directed by Jean Boyer. Fr. 1952. France. 87 min. Sound. 16mm B&W. subtitles. *Rental:* Budget Films. *Sale:* Natl Cinema. *Sale:* Tamarelles French Film, Videotape version.

Crazy House. Olsen & Johnson. Directed by Edward Cline. 1943. Universal. 80 min. Sound. 16mm B&W. *Rental:* Swank Motion.

Crazy Joe. Peter Boyle & Paula Prentiss. Directed by Carlo Lizzani. 1974. Columbia. 100 min. Sound. 16mm Color. *Rental:* Ivy Films, Kerr Film, Swank Motion & Welling Motion Pictures.

Crazy Mama. Cloris Leachman & Stuart Whitman. Directed by Jonathan Demme. 1975. New World. 82 min. Sound. 16mm Color. *Rental:* Films Inc.

Crazy Quilt. Tom Rosqui & Ina Mela. Directed by John Korty. 1966. Farallen. 80 min. Sound. 16mm B&W. *Rental:* Budget Films & Kino Intl. *Sale:* Kino Intl. *Lease:* Kino Intl.

Crazy Ray, The. Trans. Title: Paris Qui Dort. Henri Rollan & Albert Prejan. Directed by Rene Clair. 1923. France. 62 min. Silent. 16mm B&W. *Rental:* Budget Films, Em Gee Film Lib, Kit Parker & Museum Mod Art. *Sale:* Blackhawk Films, Cinema Concepts, Festival Films, Glenn Photo & Reel Images. *Rental:* Ivy Films, *Sale:* Glenn Photo, Super 8 silent version. *Sale:* Festival Films, Videotape version.

Crazy World of Julius Vrooder, The. Trans. Title: Vrooder's Hooch. Timothy Bottoms & Barbara Seagull. Directed by Arthur Hiller. 1974. Fox. 101 min. Sound. 16mm Color. *Rental:* Films Inc.

Crazy World of Laurel & Hardy. Stan Laurel & Oliver Hardy. Directed by Hal Roach. 1968. 83 min. Silent. 16mm B&W. *Rental:* A Twyman Pres.

Cream: The Farewell Concert. Directed by Tony Palmer. 1969. Richard Price. (Documentary). 88 min. Sound. 16mm Color. *Rental:* Budget Films, Films Inc, Ivy Films, Kit Parker, Maljack & Video Comm. *Sale:* Reel Images. *Sale:* Maljack, Reel Images & Video Comm, Videotape version.

Created Equal. 1980. Penn. (Documentary). 60 min. Sound. Videotape Color. *Rental:* Iowa Films. *Sale:* Ency Brit Ed. *Sale:* Ency Brit Ed, 2 pt. 16mm version version. *Sale:* Ency Brit Ed, 2 pt. videotape version version.

Creation of the Humanoids. Don Megowan & Frances McCann. Directed by Wesley Barry. 1962. Emerson. 75 min. Sound. 16mm B&W. *Rental:* Willoughby Peer.

Creation vs Evolution: Battle in the Classroom. 1982. 58 min. Sound. Videotape *Rental:* PBS Video. *Sale:* PBS Video.

Creature from the Black Lagoon, The. Richard Carlson & Julie Adams. Directed by Jack Arnold. 1954. Universal. 79 min. Sound. 16mm B&W. *Rental:* Swank Motion. *Rental:* Swank Motion, 3-D version.

Creature from the Haunted Sea. Anthony Carbone. Directed by Roger Corman. 1957. Allied Artists. 72 min. Sound. 16mm B&W. *Rental:* Budget Films & Kit Parker. *Sale:* Reel Images.

Creature Walks Among Us, The. Jeff Morrow & Rex Reason. Directed by John Sherwood. 1956. Universal. 78 min. Sound. 16mm B&W. *Rental:* Swank Motion.

Creature With the Atom Brain, The. Richard Denning. Directed by Edward L. Cahn. 1955. Columbia. 70 min. Sound. 16mm B&W. *Lease:* Time-Life Multimedia.

Creature's Revenge, The. Grant Williams & Kent Taylor. 1971. Hemisphere. 90 min. Sound. 16mm Color. *Sale:* Morcraft Films. *Sale:* Morcraft Films, Super 8 sound version.

Creatures the World Forgot. Julie Ege. Directed by Don Chaffey. 1971. Columbia. 95 min. Sound. 16mm Color. *Rental:* Cine Craft, Films Inc, Kerr Film, Modern Sound, Welling Motion Pictures, Westcoast Films & Willoughby Peer.

Cree Hunters of Mistassini. Directed by Boyce Richardson & Tony Ianzelo. 1975. Canada. (Documentary). 57 min. Sound. 16mm Color. *Rental:* U Cal Media, Iowa Films, Natl Film CN, SD AV Ctr & U Mich Media. *Sale:* Natl Film CN. *Sale:* Natl Film CN, *Rental:* Natl Film CN, Videotape version.

Cree of Painted Hills, The. Canada. (Documentary). 57 min. Sound. 16mm Color. *Rental:* CBC. *Sale:* CBC.

Creeping Flesh, The. Peter Cushing & Christopher Lee. Directed by Freddie Francis. 1973. Britain. 92 min. Sound. 16mm Color. *Rental:* Arcus Film, Bosco Films, Buchan Film, Budget Films, Cine Craft, Film Ctr DC, Film Pres, Ivy Films, Modern Sound, Roas Films, Swank Motion, Welling Motion Pictures & Westcoast Films.

Creeping Terror. Vic Savage & Shannon O'Neill. 1964. Gold Key. 81 min. Sound. 16mm B&W. *Rental:* Budget Films, Films Inc, Ivy Films & Video Comm. *Lease:* Video Comm. *Rental:* Video Comm, *Lease:* Video Comm, Videotape version. *Rental:* Budget Films, 75 mins. version.

Creepshow. Adrienne Barbeau, Hal Holbrook & E. G. Marshall. Directed by George A. Romero. 120 min. Sound. 16mm Color. *Rental:* Swank Motion. *Rental:* Swank Motion, Videotape version.

Crest of the Wave. Gene Kelly & John Justin. Directed by John Boulting & Roy Boulting. 1954. MGM. 90 min. Sound. 16mm B&W. *Rental:* MGM United.

Crete & Mycenae. 1972. Museum Without Walls. (Documentary). 54 min. Sound. 16mm Color. *Rental:* U Mich Media.

Cria! Geraldine Chaplin & Ana Torrent. Directed by Carlos Saura. Span. 1977. Spain. 115 min. Sound. 16mm Color. subtitles. *Rental:* Cinema Five & World Northal.

Cricket on the Hearth, The. Josef Swickard & Virginia Brown Faire. Directed by Lorimer Johnson. 1923. Selznick. 90 min. Silent. 16mm B&W. *Rental:* Films Inc. *Sale:* Blackhawk Films & Films Inc. *Rental:* Ivy Films, *Sale:* Blackhawk Films, Super 8 silent version.

Cricket on the Hearth. 1968. UPA. (Animated). 57 min. Sound. 16mm Color. *Rental:* Budget Films, Cine Craft, Film Ctr DC, Inst Cinema, Kerr Film, Modern Sound, Film Ctr DC, Welling Motion Pictures, Westcoast Films & Willoughby Peer.

Cries & Whispers. Harriet Anderson, Ingrid Thulin & Liv Ullmann. Directed by Ingmar Bergman. 1972. Sweden. 95 min. Sound. 16mm Color. *Rental:* Films Inc.

Crime & Insanity. 1983. NBC. (Documentary). 52 min. Videotape Color. *Sale:* Films Inc.

Crime & Passion. Omar Sharif & Karen Black. Directed by Ivan Passer. 1976. American International. 92 min. Sound. 16mm Color. *Rental:* Swank Motion.

Crime & Punishment. Peter Lorre, Edward Arnold & Marion Marsh. Directed by Josef Von Sternberg. 1935. Columbia. 90 min. Sound. 16mm B&W. *Rental:* Bosco Films, Budget Films, Films Inc, Images Film, Kit Parker, Modern Sound, Natl Film Video, Swank Motion, Twyman Films, Welling Motion Pictures, Westcoast Films & Wholesome Film Ctr.

Crime & Punishment. Innokenty Smoktunovsky. Directed by Lev Kulidjanov. Rus. 1970. Russia. (Anamorphic). 220 min. Sound. 16mm B&W. subtitles. *Rental:* Corinth Films.

Crime & Punishment. Pierre Blanchar & Harry Baur. Directed by Pierre Chenal. Fr. 1935. 103 min. Sound. 16mm B&W. subtitles Eng. *Rental:* Films Inc.

Crime & Punishment U. S. A. George Hamilton & Mary Murphy. Directed by Denis Sanders. 1959. Allied Artists. 96 min. Sound. 16mm B&W. *Rental:* Hurlock Cine.

Crime by Night. Jane Wyman & Eleanor Parker. Directed by William Clemens. 1944. Warners. 72 min. Sound. 16mm B&W. *Rental:* MGM United.

Crime Does Not Pay. 1945. United Artists. (Documentary). 45 min. Sound. 16mm B&W. *Rental:* Budget Films.

Crime in the Clouds see Fly-Away Baby.

Crime in the Streets. Orig. Title: Cities, Crime in the Streets. 1966. NET. (Documentary). 60 min. Sound. 16mm B&W. *Rental:* Indiana AV Ctr. *Sale:* Indiana AV Ctr.

Crime in the Streets. Sal Mineo & John Cassavetes. Directed by Don Siegel. 1956. Allied Artists. 91 min. Sound. 16mm B&W. *Rental:* Hurlock Cine.

Crime, Inc. Tom Neal & Martha Tilton. Directed by Lew Landers. 1945. PRC. 76 min. Sound. 16mm B&W. *Rental:* Ivy Films & Mogulls Films. *Sale:* Classics Assoc NY.

Crime Ne Paie Pas, Le see And Suddenly It's Murder.

Crime of Dr. Crespi, The. Erich Von Stroheim. Directed by John H. Auer. 1935. Republic. 63 min. Sound. 16mm B&W. *Rental:* Budget Films & Em Gee Film Lib. *Sale:* Cinema Concepts.

Crime of Monsieur Lange, The. Rene Lefevre. 1935. France. 90 min. Sound. 16mm B&W. subtitles. *Rental:* Films Inc.

Crime of Our Courts. 1974. Westinghouse. (Documentary). 50 min. Sound. 16mm Color. *Rental:* Edupac & NYU Film Lib. *Sale:* Edupac.

Crime of Passion. Barbara Stanwyck, Sterling Hayden & Fay Wray. Directed by Gerd Oswald. 1957. United Artists. 84 min. Sound. 16mm B&W. *Rental:* MGM United.

Crime of the Century. Stephanie Batchelor. Directed by Philip Ford. 1946. Republic. 56 min. Sound. 16mm B&W. *Rental:* Ivy Films.

Crime of the Century, The see Walk East on Beacon.

Crime Patrol, The. Ray Walker & Hooper Atchley. Directed by Eugene Cummings. 1936. Empire. 65 min. Sound. 16mm B&W. *Rental:* Modern Sound.

Crime Ring. Allan Lane & Frances Mercer. Directed by Leslie Goodwins. 1938. RKO. 70 min. Sound. 16mm *Rental:* RKO General Pics.

Crime School. Humphrey Bogart & Gale Page. Directed by Lewis Seiler. 1938. Warners. 86 min. Sound. 16mm B&W. *Rental:* MGM United.

Crime to Fit the Punishment, A. 1982. 46 min. Sound. 16mm Color. *Rental:* First Run.

Crime Without Passion. Claude Rains & Margo. Directed by Ben Hecht & Charles MacArthur. 1934. Paramount. 72 min. Sound. 16mm B&W. *Rental:* Swank Motion.

Crimen see Gentle Art of Murder.

Crimen de Pepe Conde, La. Miguel Ligero. Directed by Rigoberto Lopez. Mexico. Sound. 16mm B&W. *Rental:* Film Classics.

Crimes at the Dark House. Tod Slaughter. Directed by George King. 1940. Britain. 61 min. Sound. 16mm B&W. *Rental:* Budget Films.

Crimes of Dr. Mabuse, The. Orig. Title: Testament of Dr. Mabuse, The. Rudolph Klein-Rogge. Directed by Fritz Lang. 1932. Germany. 80 min. Sound. 16mm B&W. dubbed. *Rental:* Budget Films, Classic Film Mus, Em Gee Film Lib, Janus Films & Kit Parker. *Sale:* Classic Film Mus, Cinema Concepts, Festival Films & Natl Cinema.

Crimes of Steven Hawke. Tod Slaughter. Directed by George King. 1936. Britain. 65 min. Sound. 16mm B&W. *Rental:* Budget Films.

Criminal, The. Orig. Title: Concrete Jungle, The. Stanley Baker & Sam Wanamaker. Directed by Joseph Losey. 1960. Britain. 97 min. Sound. 16mm B&W. *Rental:* Corinth Films.

Criminal Affair, A. Ann-Margret & Rossano Brazzi. 1971. Italy. 95 min. Sound. 16mm Color. dubbed. *Rental:* Video Comm. *Lease:* Video Comm. *Rental:* Video Comm, Videotape version.

Criminal Code, The. Walter Huston. Directed by Howard Hawks. 1931. Columbia. 98 min. Sound. 16mm B&W. *Rental:* Films Inc, Swank Motion & Wholesome Film Ctr.

Criminal Conversation. Directed by Kieran Hickey. 1978. Ireland. (Cast unlisted). 48 min. Sound. 16mm Color. *Rental:* Liberty Co.

Criminal Court. Tom Conway & Martha O'Driscoll. Directed by Robert Wise. 1946. RKO. 59 min. Sound. 16mm B&W. *Rental:* Films Inc.

Criminal Justice Test, The. 1975. 60 min. Sound. Videotape *Rental:* PBS Video. *Sale:* PBS Video.

Criminal Lawyer. Lee Tracy & Margot Grahame. Directed by Christy Cabanne. 1937. RKO. 72 min. Sound. 16mm *Rental:* RKO General Pics.

Criminal Life of Archibaldo de la Cruz, The. Ernesto Alonso & Miroslava. Directed by Luis Bunuel. 1955. 91 min. Sound. 16mm B&W. *Rental:* Films Inc.

Crimson Cult, The. Boris Karloff & Christopher Lee. Directed by Vernon Sewell. 1970. American International. 87 min. Sound. 16mm Color. *Rental:* Budget Films, Film Ctr DC, Ivy Films & Video Comm.

Crimson Ghost, The. Charles Quigley & Linda Stirling. Directed by William Witney. 1946. Republic. 163 min. Sound. 16mm B&W. *Rental:* Ivy Films.

Crimson Kimono, The. Glenn Corbett & James Shigeta. Directed by Samuel Fuller. 1959. Columbia. 82 min. Sound. 16mm B&W. *Rental:* Kit Parker.

Crimson Romance, A. Erich Von Stroheim. Directed by David Howard. 1934. Mascot. 80 min. Sound. 16mm B&W. *Sale:* Cinema Concepts, Classic Film Mus & Reel Images.

Crisis. Cary Grant & Jose Ferrer. Directed by Richard Brooks. 1950. MGM. 96 min. Sound. 16mm B&W. *Rental:* MGM United.

Crisis: Behind a Presidential Commitment. 1963. 58 min. Sound. Color. *Rental:* Direct Cinema. *Sale:* Direct Cinema. *Sale:* Direct Cinema, Videotape version.

Crisis in the Presidency. 1971. 51 min. Sound. 16mm Color. *Rental:* Utah Media.

Crisis of Presidential Succession, The. 1964. CBS. (Documentary). 49 min. Sound. 16mm B&W. *Sale:* Carousel Films & U Mich Media.

Criss Cross. Burt Lancaster & Yvonne De Carlo. Directed by Robert Siodmak. 1948. Universal. 87 min. Sound. 16mm B&W. *Rental:* Swank Motion.

Critical Care Nursing. 1980. 96 min. videotape *Sale:* Natl AV Ctr.

Crocodile. 1975. Australia. (Documentary). 51 min. Sound. 16mm Color. *Rental:* Aust Info Serv. *Sale:* Aust Info Serv.

Cromwell. Richard Harris, Sir Alec Guinness & Robert Morley. Directed by Ken Hughes. 1970. Columbia. 139 min. Sound. 16mm Color. *Rental:* Arcus Film, Bosco Films, Budget Films, Cine Craft, Films Inc, Images Film, Inst Cinema, Ivy Films, Kit Parker, Modern Sound, Natl Film Video, Roas Films, Swank Motion, Twyman Films, Video Comm, Welling Motion Pictures, Westcoast Films, Wholesome Film Ctr, Williams Films & Willoughby Peer.

Crook, The. Trans. Title: Voyou, Le. Jean-Louis Trintignant & Charles Denner. Directed by Claude Lelouch. Fr. 1971. France. 120 min. Sound. 16mm Color. subtitles. *Rental:* MGM United.

Crooked Beak of Heaven. 1975. Britain. (Documentary). 52 min. Sound. 16mm Color. *Rental:* Iowa Films, U Cal Media, U of IL Film & U Mich Media.

Crooked Circle, The. ZaSu Pitts & James Gleason. Directed by Bruce Humberstone. 1932. World Wide. 84 min. Sound. 16mm B&W. *Rental:* Lewis Film.

Crooked Circle, The. Fay Spain & John Smith. Directed by Joseph Kane. 1957. Republic. 72 min. Sound. 16mm B&W. *Rental:* Ivy Films. *Sale:* Rep Pic Film.

Crooked River. James Ellison & Russell Hayden. Directed by Thomas Carr. 1950. 58 min. Sound. 16mm *Rental:* Budget Films.

Crooked Road, The. Irene Hervey & Paul Fix. Directed by Phil Rosen. 1940. Republic. 54 min. Sound. 16mm B&W. *Rental:* Ivy Films. *Sale:* Rep Pic Film.

Crooks Anonymous. Leslie Phillips & Stanley Baxter. Directed by Ken Annakin. 1962. Britain. 88 min. Sound. 16mm B&W. *Rental:* Modern Sound.

Crooner, The. Ken Murray & Ann Dvorak. Directed by Lloyd Bacon. 1932. Warners. 68 min. Sound. 16mm B&W. *Rental:* MGM United.

Cross Channel. Wayne Morris. Directed by R. G. Springsteen. 1955. Republic. 60 min. Sound. 16mm B&W. *Rental:* Ivy Films. *Sale:* Rep Pic Film.

Cross Country Romance. Gene Raymond & Wendy Barrie. Directed by Merian C. Cooper. 1940. RKO. 68 min. Sound. 16mm *Rental:* RKO General Pics.

Cross Creek. Mary Steenburgen, Rip Torn & Peter Coyote. Directed by Martin Ritt. 1985. Universal. 127 min. Sound. 16mm Color. *Rental:* Swank Motion. *Sale:* Tamarelles French Film, *Rental:* Swank Motion, Videotape version.

Examination Debate: A
on & Critique. 1968. 48 min.
m B&W. *Rental:* Iowa Films.

Cross Fire El Salvador. 58 min. Sound. Videotape *Rental:* PBS Video. *Sale:* PBS Video.

Cross of Iron, The. James Coburn & Maximillan Schell. Directed by Sam Peckinpah. 1977. Embassy. 120 min. Sound. 16mm Color. *Rental:* Films Inc.

Cross of Lorraine, The. Jean-Pierre Aumont & Gene Kelly. Directed by Tay Garnett. 1978. MGM. 90 min. Sound. 16mm B&W. *Rental:* MGM United.

Crossbar. Kate Reid & John Ireland. Directed by John Trent. 1978. Canada. 78 min. Sound. 16mm Color. *Rental:* Natl Film CN & Roas Films. *Sale:* Natl Film CN.

Crossed Signals. Helen Holmes & Henry Victor. Directed by J. P. McGowan. 1926. Rayart. 50 min. Silent. 16mm B&W. *Rental:* Mogulls Films.

Crossed Swords. Mark Lester & Raquel Welch. Directed by Richard Fleischer. 1978. Warners. 121 min. Sound. 16mm Color. *Rental:* Modern Sound, Twyman Films & Williams Films. *Rental:* Twyman Films, Anamorphic version.

Crossfire. Robert Mitchum & Robert Young. Directed by Edward Dmytryk. 1947. RKO. 86 min. 16mm B&W. *Rental:* Films Inc & RKO General Pics.

Crossing of the Rhine, The *see* Passage Du Rhin.

Crossroads. William Powell & Hedy Lamarr. Directed by Jack Conway. 1942. MGM. 84 min. Sound. 16mm B&W. *Rental:* MGM United.

Crossroads Africa. 1961. CBS. (Documentary). 54 min. Sound. 16mm B&W. *Rental:* McGraw-Hill Films. *Sale:* McGraw-Hill Films.

Crossroads of Civilization: Descent of the Hordes. 1980. (Documentary). 60 min. Sound. 16mm Color. *Rental:* Syracuse U Film.

Crossroads-South Africa. Directed by Jonathan Wacks. 1980. California Newsreel. (Documentary). 50 min. Sound. 16mm Color. *Rental:* CA Newsreel.

Crosswinds. John Payne & Rhonda Fleming. Directed by Lewis R. Foster. 1951. Paramount. 94 min. Sound. 16mm B&W. *Rental:* Video Comm.

Crow Dog. Directed by David Baxter & Mike Cuesta. 1979. Unifilm. (Documentary). 57 min. Sound. 16mm Color. *Rental:* Cinema Guild. *Sale:* Cinema Guild.

Crow Hollow. Donald Houston & Natasha Parry. Directed by Michael McCarthy. 1952. Britain. 69 min. Sound. 16mm B&W. *Rental:* Budget Films & Video Comm.

Crowd, The. James Murray. Directed by King Vidor. 1928. MGM. 93 min. Sound. 16mm B&W. *Rental:* MGM United.

Crowd Roars, The. James Cagney & Joan Blondell. Directed by Howard Hawks. 1932. Warners. 85 min. Sound. 16mm B&W. *Rental:* MGM United.

Crowded Idol, The. 1962. Hearst. (Documentary). 50 min. Sound. 16mm Color. *Sale:* King Features.

Crowded Sky, The. Dana Andrews & Rhonda Fleming. Directed by Joseph Pevney. 1960. Warners. 103 min. Sound. 16mm Color. *Rental:* Cine Craft, Films Inc & Video Comm.

Crown & Crisis. 1962. Hearst. (Documentary). 50 min. Sound. 16mm B&W. *Sale:* King Features.

Crown of Thorns. 1917. Italy. (Cast unlisted, music & sound effects only). 70 min. Sound. 16mm B&W. *Rental:* Film Classics & Film Ctr DC.

Crowning Touch, The. Greta Gynt. Directed by David Eady. 1957. 67 min. 16mm *Rental:* A Twyman Pres.

Crucified Lovers, The. Kazuo Hasegewa & Kyrko Kogawa. Directed by Kenji Mizoguchi. 1959. Japan. 90 min. Sound. 16mm *Rental:* New Line Cinema.

Cruel Sea, The. Jack Hawkins & Donald Sinden. Directed by Charles Frend. 1953. Britain. 121 min. Sound. 16mm B&W. *Rental:* Budget Films, U of IL Film, Kit Parker, Learning Corp Am & Twyman Films. *Lease:* Learning Corp Am. *Lease:* Learning Corp Am, *Rental:* Learning Corp Am, Videotape version.

Cruel Story of Youth, The. Directed by Nagisa Oshima. Jap. 1960. 96 min. Sound. 16mm Color. subtitles Eng. *Rental:* New Yorker Films.

Cruel Tower, The. John Erickson & Mari Blanchard. Directed by Lew Landers. 1956. Allied Artists. 80 min. Sound. 16mm B&W. *Rental:* Ivy Films. *Sale:* Rep Pic Film.

Crueles, Las *see* Exquisite Cadaver.

Cruisin' Down the River. Dick Haymes & Audrey Totter. Directed by Richard Quine. 1953. Columbia. 81 min. Sound. 16mm Color. *Rental:* Bosco Films, Inst Cinema, Film Ctr DC & Welling Motion Pictures.

Cruising. Al Pacino, Paul Sorvino & Karen Allen. Directed by William Friedkin. 1980. United Artists. 102 min. Sound. 16mm Color. *Rental:* MGM United & Swank Motion. *Rental:* Swank Motion, Videotape version.

Crusades, The. Loretta Young & Henry Wilcoxen. Directed by Cecil B. DeMille. 1935. Paramount. 127 min. Sound. 16mm B&W. *Rental:* Swank Motion.

Cry Danger. Dick Powell & Rhonda Fleming. Directed by Robert Parrish. 1951. RKO. 79 min. Sound. 16mm B&W. *Rental:* Ivy Films. *Sale:* Rep Pic Film.

Cry for Happy. Glenn Ford & Donald O'Connor. Directed by George Marshall. 1961. Columbus. 110 min. Sound. 16mm Color. *Rental:* Inst Cinema, REP Pic Film & Welling Motion Pictures.

Cry from the Streets, A. Max Bygraves & Barbara Murray. Directed by Lewis Gilbert. 1958. Britain. 100 min. Sound. 16mm B&W. *Rental:* Inst Cinema.

Cry Havoc! Margaret Sullivan & Ann Sothern. Directed by Richard Thorpe. 1944. MGM. 97 min. Sound. 16mm B&W. *Rental:* MGM United.

Cry Help. 1970. NBC. (Documentary). 82 min. Sound. 16mm Color. *Rental:* Films Inc, Iowa Films, U Cal Media & Utah Media. *Sale:* Films Inc. *Sale:* Films Inc, Videotape version.

Cry in the Night. Edmond O'Brien, Natalie Wood & Raymond Burr. Directed by Frank Tuttle. 1956. Warners. 76 min. Sound. 16mm B&W. *Rental:* Budget Films & Video Comm. *Lease:* Video Comm. *Rental:* Video Comm, Videotape version.

Cry of Nukumanu. 1971. Australia. (Documentary). 52 min. Sound. 16mm Color. *Rental:* Films Inc. *Sale:* Films Inc. *Sale:* Films Inc, Videotape version.

Cry of the Banshee. Vincent Price, Essy Persson & Hugh Griffith. Directed by Gordon Hessler. 1970. American International. 87 min. Sound. 16mm Color. *Rental:* Arcus Film, Ivy Films, Video Comm & Westcoast Films.

Cry of the City. Victor Mature, Richard Conte & Shelley Winters. Directed by Robert Siodmak. 1948. Fox. 95 min. Sound. 16mm B&W. *Rental:* Films Inc.

Cry of the Hunted. Vittorio Gassman & Barry Sullivan. Directed by Joseph Lewis. 1953. MGM. 80 min. Sound. 16mm B&W. *Rental:* MGM United.

Cry of the Penguins. John Hurt & Hayley Mills. Directed by Al Viola. 1975. Cinema Shares. 90 min. Sound. 16mm Color. *Rental:* Budget Films, Films Inc, Roas Films & Westcoast Films.

Cry of the People. Juan J. Torres & Hugo Baner. Directed by Humberto Rios. Span. 1972. Argentina. 65 min. Sound. 16mm Color. subtitles. *Rental:* Unifilm. *Sale:* Unifilm.

Cry of the Werewolf. Nina Foch. Directed by Henry Levin. 1944. Columbia. 63 min. Sound. 16mm B&W. *Rental:* Modern Sound.

Cry of the Wild. Directed by Bill Mason. 1972. Canada. (Documentary). 87 min. Sound. 16mm Color. *Rental:* Budget Films, Films Inc, Kit Parker, Maljack, Films Inc, Video Comm, Westcoast Films & Wholesome Film Ctr. *Lease:* Natl Film CN. *Rental:* Video Comm, *Lease:* Video Comm, Videotape version.

Cry Terror! James Mason & Rod Steiger. Directed by Andrew Stone. 1958. MGM. 96 min. Sound. 16mm B&W. *Rental:* MGM United.

Cry the Beloved Country. Orig. Title: African Fury. Canada Lee & Sidney Poitier. Directed by Zoltan Korda. 1951. United Artists. 96 min. Sound. 16mm Color. *Rental:* Budget Films, Corinth Films, Films Inc & Wholesome Film Ctr.

Cry Tough. John Saxon & Linda Cristal. Directed by Paul Stanley. 1959. United Artists. 83 min. Sound. 16mm B&W. *Rental:* MGM United.

Cry Uncle! Allen Garfield & Madeleine Le Roux. Directed by John G. Avildsen. 1971. 87 min. Sound. 16mm Color. *Rental:* Films Inc. *Rental:* Enter Video, Videotape version.

Cry Vengeance. Mark Stevens & Martha Hyer. Directed by Mark Stevens. 1954. Allied Artists. 83 min. Sound. 16mm B&W. *Rental:* Ivy Films. *Sale:* Rep Pic Film.

Cry Wolf. Errol Flynn & Barbara Stanwyck. Directed by Peter Godfrey. 1947. Warners. 84 min. Sound. 16mm B&W. *Rental:* MGM United.

Cry Wolf. 1974. Britain. (Cast unlisted). 45 min. Sound. 16mm Color. *Rental:* Janus Films. *Sale:* Lucerne Films & Sterling Ed Film.

Crystal Ball, The. Paulette Goddard & Ray Milland. Directed by Elliott Nugent. 1943. United Artists. 81 min. Sound. 16mm B&W. *Rental:* Films Inc, Learning Corp Am, Mogulls Films & U of IL Film. *Sale:* Learning Corp Am.

Cuarto en la Frontera. 1950. Mexico. (Cast unlisted). 90 min. Sound. 16mm B&W. *Rental:* Film Classics.

Cuba. Sean Connery & Brooke Adams. Directed by Richard Lester. 1979. United Artists. 122 min. Sound. 16mm Color. *Rental:* MGM United.

Cuba: Art & Revolution. 46 min. Sound. 16mm Color. *Rental:* U Cal Media.

Cuba: Bay of Pigs. (Documentary). 55 min. Sound. 16mm Color. *Rental:* Wholesome Film Ctr.

Cuba: The Castro Generation. 1977. ABC. (Documentary). 53 min. Sound. 16mm Color. *Rental:* Iowa Films, McGraw-Hill Films, U Cal Media & U of Il Film. *Sale:* McGraw-Hill Films. *Sale:* McGraw-Hill Films, Videotape version.

Cuba: The Missile Crisis. 1965. NBC. (Documentary). 52 min. Sound. 16mm B&W. *Rental:* McGraw-Hill Films & Syracuse U Film. *Sale:* McGraw-Hill Films.

Cuba: The People. 1976. WNET. (Documentary). 85 min. Sound. 16mm Color. *Rental:* CA Newsreel. *Sale:* CA Newsreel.

Cuba Va! Directed by Felix Greene. 1970. Britain. (Documentary). 76 min. Sound. 16mm Color. *Rental:* Icarus Films.

Cuban Fireball. Estelita Rodriquez & Warren Douglas. Directed by William Beaudine. 1950. Republic. 78 min. Sound. 16mm B&W. *Rental:* Ivy Films. *Sale:* Rep Pic Film.

Cuban Love Song. Lupe Velez & Jimmy Durante. Directed by W. S. Van Dyke. 1931. MGM. 86 min. Sound. 16mm B&W. *Rental:* MGM United.

Cubana en Espana. Blanquita Amaro. Directed by Bayou Heurrero. Span. 1953. Spain. 78 min. Sound. 16mm B&W. subtitles. *Rental:* Film Classics.

Cube, The. 1969. NBC. (Documentary). 56 min. Sound. 16mm B&W. *Rental:* Films Inc, Iowa Films & Syracuse U Film. *Sale:* Films Inc. *Sale:* Films Inc, Videotape version.

Cubist Epoch, The. 1972. Museum Without Walls. (Documentary). 53 min. Sound. 16mm Color. *Rental:* U Mich Media.

Cubitos de Hielo. 1950. Mexico. (Cast unlisted). 90 min. Sound. 16mm B&W. *Rental:* Film Classics.

Cuckoos, The. Bert Wheeler & Robert Woolsey. Directed by Paul Sloane. 1930. RKO. 102 min. Sound. 16mm B&W. *Rental:* Films Inc.

Cujo. Dee Wallace & Danny Pintauro. Directed by Lewis Teague. 1983. Warners. 91 min. Sound. 16mm Color. *Rental:* Swank Motion. *Rental:* Swank Motion, Videotape version.

Cul-de-Sac. Donald Pleasance & Lionel Stander. Directed by Roman Polanski. 1966. Britain. 107 min. Sound. 16mm B&W. *Rental:* Em Gee Film Lib & Films Inc. *Sale:* Tamarelles French Film, Videotape version.

Culloden *see* Battle of Culloden.

Culpepper Cattle Company, The. Gary Grimes & Luke Askew. Directed by Dick Richards. 1972. Fox. 92 min. Sound. 16mm B&W. *Rental:* Films Inc, Twyman Films, Westcoast Films & Williams Films.

Cult of the Cobra, The. Richard Long & Faith Domergue. Directed by Francis D. Lyon. 1955. Universal. 80 min. Sound. 16mm B&W. *Sale:* Swank Motion.

Culture As Nature. 1979. Britain. (Documentary). 52 min. Sound. 16mm Color. *Rental:* Time-Life Multimedia & U Cal Media. *Sale:* Time-Life Multimedia. *Sale:* Time-Life Multimedia, Videotape version.

Culture Explosion, The. 1966. NET. (Documentary). 60 min. Sound. 16mm B&W. *Rental:* Indiana AV Ctr. *Lease:* Indiana AV Ctr.

Cultures Clashing. 1977. Penn State. (Documentary). 59 min. Videotape Color. *Rental:* Penn St AV Serv. *Sale:* Penn St AV Serv.

Cuore see Heart & Soul.

Cupboard Was Bare. Fernandel. 1957. 82 min. 16mm *Rental:* A Twyman Pres.

Curious Cat, The. 1980. Britain. (Documentary). 50 min. Sound. 16mm Color. *Rental:* Films Inc. *Sale:* Films Inc. *Rental:* Films Inc, *Sale:* Films Inc, Videotape version.

Curley. Larry Olsen & Frances Rafferty. Directed by Bernard Carr. 1947. United Artists. 54 min. Sound. 16mm B&W. *Rental:* Alba House, Budget Films, Cine Craft, Newman Film Lib, Roas Films & Film Ctr DC.

Curly Top. Shirley Temple & John Boles. Directed by Irving Cummings. 1935. Fox. 75 min. Sound. 16mm B&W. *Rental:* Films Inc.

Curse of Adam, The. 1977. WNET. (Documentary). 60 min. Videotape Color. *Rental:* WNET Media. *Sale:* WNET Media.

Curse of Bigfoot, The. William Simonsen. 1972. Gold Key. 87 min. Sound. 16mm Color. *Rental:* Films Inc, Video Comm & Westcoast Films. *Lease:* Video Comm. *Rental:* Video Comm, *Lease:* Video Comm, Videotape version.

Curse of Drink, The. Harry Morey & Miriam Battista. Directed by Harry Hoyt. 1922. Apollo. 60 min. Silent. 16mm B&W. *Rental:* Mogulls Films.

Curse of Nostradamus, The. Gorman Robles & Julio Aleman. Directed by Frederico Curiel. 1960. Mexico. 77 min. Sound. 16mm *Rental:* Budget Films.

Curse of Simba see Curse of the Voodoo.

Curse of the Aztec Mummy, The. Trans. Title: Maldicion de la Monia Azteca, La. Ramon Gay & Rosita Arenas. Directed by Rafael Portillo. 1957. Mexico. 65 min. Sound. 16mm dubbed Spanish. *Rental:* Budget Films.

Curse of the Cat People. Simone Simon & Kent Smith. Directed by Robert Wise. 1944. RKO. 70 min. Sound. 16mm B&W. *Rental:* Films Inc. *Lease:* Films Inc. *Rental:* RKO General Pics, 60 min. version.

Curse of the Crying Woman, The. Trans. Title: Maldicion De la Llorona, La. Rosita Arenas & Abel Salazar. Directed by Rafael Baledon. 1961. Mexico. 74 min. Sound. 16mm *Rental:* Budget Films.

Curse of the Demon. Orig. Title: Night of the Demon. Dana Andrews & Peggy Cummins. Directed by Jacques Tourneur. 1957. Britain. 95 min. Sound. 16mm B&W. *Rental:* Corinth Films.

Curse of the Fly. Brian Donlevy. Directed by Don Sharp. 1965. Fox. 86 min. Sound. 16mm B&W. *Rental:* Films Inc.

Curse of the Living Corpse, The. Helen Warren. Directed by Del Tenney. 1964. Fox. 84 min. Sound. 16mm B&W. *Rental:* Films Inc.

Curse of the Mummy's Tomb. Terence Morgan & Ronald Howard. Directed by Michael Carreras. 1965. Columbia. 86 min. Sound. 16mm B&W. *Rental:* Arcus Film, Budget Films, Inst Cinema, Ivy Films, Modern Sound, Welling Motion Pictures, Westcoast Films & Williams Films.

Curse of the Pink Panther. Ted Wass & David Niven. Directed by Blake Edwards. 1983. MGM. 99 min. Sound. 16mm Color. *Rental:* MGM United. *Rental:* MGM United, Videotape version.

Curse of the Undead. Eric Fleming & Michael Pate. Directed by Edward Dein. 1959. Universal. 79 min. Sound. 16mm B&W. *Rental:* Swank Motion.

Curse of the Voodoo. Orig. Title: Curse of Simba. Bryant Haliday & Dennis Price. Directed by Lindsay Shonteff. 1965. Allied Artists. 77 min. Sound. 16mm B&W. *Rental:* Films Inc & Modern Sound. *Sale:* Video Lib, Videotape version.

Curse of the Werewolf. Clifford Evans & Oliver Reed. Directed by Terence Fisher. 1961. Britain. 91 min. Sound. 16mm Color. *Rental:* Swank Motion.

Curtain Call. Barbara Reed & John Archer. Directed by Frank Woodruff. 1940. RKO. 63 min. Sound. 16mm *Rental:* RKO General Pics.

Curtain Call at Cactus Creek. Donald O'Connor & Gale Storm. Directed by Charles Lamont. 1950. Universal. 86 min. Sound. 16mm Color. *Rental:* Swank Motion.

Curtain Up. Robert Morley & Margaret Rutherford. Directed by Ralph Smart. 1952. Britain. 82 min. Sound. 16mm B&W. *Rental:* Kit Parker, Learning Corp Am, Twyman Films & U of IL Film. *Sale:* Learning Corp Am.

Curtains. John Vernon & Samantha Eggar. Directed by Jonathan Stryker. 1983. Simcom. 90 min. Sound. 16mm Color. *Rental:* Swank Motion. *Rental:* Swank Motion, Videotape version.

Cushing Webb. 52 min. Sound. 16mm *Rental:* OK AV Ctr.

Custer of the West. Robert Shaw & Mary Ure. Directed by Robert Siodmak. 1968. ABC. 141 min. Sound. 16mm Color. *Rental:* Films Inc.

Custer's Last Stand. Rex Lease & Ruth Mix. Directed by Elmer Clifton. 1936. Stage & Screen. 80 min. Sound. 16mm B&W. *Rental:* Budget Films.

Custodio De Senoras. Jorge Porcel, Graciela Alfano & Javier Portal. Spain. 100 min. Sound. Videotape Color. *Sale:* Tamarelles French Films.

Customs Agent. William Eythe & Marjorie Reynolds. Directed by Seymour Friedman. 1950. Columbia. 90 min. Sound. 16mm B&W. *Rental:* Inst Cinema.

Cutter & Bone see Cutter's Way.

Cutter's Way. Orig. Title: Cutter & Bone. John Heard & Jeff Bridges. Directed by Ivan Passer. 1981. United Artists. 105 min. Sound. 16mm Color. *Rental:* MGM United. *Rental:* MGM United, Videotape version.

Cyborg Two Thousand Eighty-Seven. Michael Rennie & Wendell Corey. Directed by Franklin Adreon. 1966. Britain. 90 min. Sound. 16mm Color. *Rental:* Budget Films, Films Inc, Ivy Films & Westcoast Films.

Cycle Savages. Bruce Dern & Chris Robinson. Directed by Bill Brame. 1970. Trans American. 82 min. Sound. 16mm Color. *Rental:* Video Comm.

Cycles South. Don Marshall & Bobby Garcia. Directed by Don Marshall. 1971. Dal Arts. 91 min. Sound. 16mm Color. *Rental:* Williams Films.

Cyclone. Helen Mirren, Richard Johnson & Claire Bloom. 1982. 173 min. Sound. Videotape Color. *Rental:* Iowa Films.

Cyclone Cavalier. Reed Howes. Directed by Albert S. Rogell. 1925. Rayart. 55 min. Silent. 16mm B&W. *Rental:* Em Gee Film Lib. *Sale:* E Finney & Glenn Photo. *Sale:* Glenn Photo, Super 8 silent version.

Cyclone Kid, The. Don Barry. Directed by George Sherman. 1942. Republic. 56 min. Sound. 16mm B&W. *Sale:* Rep Pic Film.

Cyclone of the Saddle . Rex Lease & Bobby Nelson. Directed by Elmer Clifton. 1935. 54 min. Sound. 16mm *Rental:* Budget Films.

Cyclone on Horseback. Tim Holt & Marjorie Reynolds. Directed by Bert Gilroy. 1941. RKO. 60 min. Sound. 16mm *Rental:* General Pics.

Cyclotrode X. Charles Quigley & Linda Stirling. Directed by William Witney & Fred C. Brannon. 1946. Republic. 100 min. Sound. 16mm B&W. *Rental:* Ivy Films. *Sale:* Rep Pic Film.

Cymbeline. 1982. 173 min. Sound. Videotape Color. *Rental:* Iowa Films.

Cynara. Ronald Colman & Kay Francis. Directed by King Vidor. 1932. Goldwyn. 78 min. Sound. 16mm B&W. *Rental:* Films Inc.

Cynthia. Orig. Title: Rich, Full Life, The. Elizabeth Taylor & George Murphy. Directed by Robert Z. Leonard. 1947. MGM. 97 min. Sound. 16mm B&W. *Rental:* MGM United.

Cynthia's Secret see Dark Delusion.

Cyprus: Anatomy of a Crisis. Directed by Elais Kulukundis. 1979. Cinema V. (Documentary). 52 min. Sound. 16mm Color. *Rental:* Cinema Five.

Cyrano de Bergerac. Jose Ferrer, Mala Powers & William Prince. Directed by Michael Gordon. 1950. United Artists. 112 min. Sound. 16mm B&W. *Rental:* Arcus Film, Budget Films, Corinth Films, Films Inc, Images Film, Ivy Films, Kit Parker, Roas Films, Twyman Films & Westcoast Films. *Sale:* Cinema Concepts, Festival Films, Images Film, Reel Images & Arcus Film. *Lease:* Corinth Films. *Sale:* Festival Films & Images Film, Videotape version. *Sale:* Reel Images, Super 8 sound version.

Czarina see Royal Scandal.

D. C. Cab. Adam Baldwin, Irene Cara & Mr. T. Directed by Joel Schumacher. 1983. Universal. 104 min. Sound. 16mm Color. *Rental:* Swank Motion. *Rental:* Swank Motion, Videotape version.

D-Day. 1967. Wolper. (Documentary). 50 min. Sound. 16mm B&W. *Rental:* Films Inc, Wholesome Film Ctr & U Mich Media. *Sale:* FIlms Inc.

D-Day on Mars. Dennis Moore & Linda Stirling. Directed by Spencer G. Bennett & Fred C. Brannon. 1945. Republic. 100 min. Sound. 16mm B&W. *Rental:* Ivy Films. *Sale:* Rep Pic Film.

D-Day, The Sixth of June. Robert Taylor & Richard Todd. Directed by Henry Koster. 1956. Fox. 106 min. Sound. 16mm Color. *Rental:* Films Inc.

D. I. Jack Webb & Virginia Gregg. Directed by Jack Webb. 1957. Warners. 106 min. Sound. 16mm B&W. *Rental:* Swank Motion.

D. N. A. Story, The. 1978. McGraw Hill. (Documentary). 48 min. Sound. 16mm Color. *Rental:* U of IL Film & McGraw-Hill Films. *Sale:* McGraw-Hill Films.

D. O. A. Edmond O'Brien. Directed by Rudolph Mate. 1949. United Artists. 83 min. Sound. 16mm B&W. *Rental:* Budget Films, Classic Film Mus, Em Gee Film Lib, Ivy Films, Kit Parker, Video Comm, Westcoast Films, Wholesome Film Ctr & Willoughby Peer. *Lease:* Video Comm. *Sale:* Festival Films & Natl Cinema. *Rental:* Ivy Films & Video Comm, *Lease:* Video Comm, *Sale:* Festival Films, Videotape version.

D. O. A. Sex Pistols. Directed by Lech Kowalski. 1981. USA. 99 min. Sound. 16mm Color. *Rental:* Corinth Films.

D. W. Griffith: An American Genius. 1970. Killiam. (Anthology). 60 min. Sound. 16mm B&W. *Rental:* U of IL Film & Killiam Collect. *Sale:* Killiam Collect. *Sale:* Ivy Films, Videotape version.

D-Z Normandy: Employment of Troop Carrier Forces. 1944. US Government. (Documentary). 95 min. Sound. 16mm B&W. *Sale:* Natl AV Ctr.

Daddies. Mae Marsh & Claude Gillingwater. Directed by William A. Seiter. 1924. Warner Brothers. 50 min. Silent. 16mm B&W. *Rental:* Willoughby Peer.

Daddy Long Legs. Janet Gaynor & Warner Baxter. Directed by Alfred Santell. 1931. Fox. 73 min. Sound. 16mm B&W. *Rental:* Films Inc.

Daddy Long Legs. Fred Astaire & Leslie Caron. Directed by Jean Negulesco. 1955. Fox. (Anamorphic). 126 min. Sound. 16mm Color. *Rental:* Williams Films & Films Inc.

Daddy's Gone A-Hunting. Carol White & Paul Burke. Directed by Mark Robson. 1969. Fox. 108 min. Sound. 16mm Color. *Rental:* Swank Motion & Twyman Films.

Dadi's Family. 58 min. Sound. Videotape *Rental:* PBS Video. *Sale:* PBS Video.

Dagger of the Mind. William Shatner & Leonard Nimoy. Directed by Vincent McEveety. 1966. Star Trek. 50 min. Sound. 16mm Color. *Sale:* Reel Images.

Daguerreotypes. Directed by Agnes Varda. 1975. France. (Documentary). 74 min. Sound. 16mm Color. *Rental:* Films Inc & Texture Film. *Sale:* Texture Film.

Dahana-Arania see Middleman.

Daisies. Directed by Vera Chytilova. Czech. 1966. Czechoslovakia. 74 min. Sound. 16mm Color. *Rental:* Films Inc.

Daisy Goes Hollywood see Hollywood & Vine.

Daisy Kenyon. Joan Crawford & Dana Andrews. Directed by Otto Preminger. 1947. Fox. 99 min. Sound. 16mm B&W. *Rental:* Films Inc.

Daisy Miller. Cybill Shepherd & Barry Brown. Directed by Peter Bogdanovich. 1974. Paramount. 91 min. Sound. 16mm Color. *Rental:* Films Inc.

Daisy: The Story of a Face Lift. 58 min. Sound. Videotape *Rental:* PBS Video. *Sale:* PBS Video.

Daitozoku see Lost World of Sinbad.

Dakota. John Wayne & Vera Ralston. Directed by Joseph Kane. 1945. Republic. 81 min. Sound. Videotape B&W. *Rental:* Ivy Films. *Sale:* Rep Pic Film & Tamarelles French Film.

Dakota Incident. Linda Darnell & Dale Robertson. Directed by Lewis R. Foster. 1956. Republic. 88 min. Sound. 16mm Color. *Rental:* Ivy Films. *Sale:* Rep Pic Film.

Dakota Kid, The. Michael Chapin & Eilene Janssen. Directed by Philip Ford. 1951. Republic. 60 min. Sound. 16mm B&W. *Sale:* Rep pic Film.

Dakota Lil. George Montgomery & Marie Windsor. Directed by Lesley Selander. 1950. Fox. 88 min. Sound. 16mm B&W. *Rental:* Charard Motion Pics & Wholesome Film Ctr.

Dallas. Gary Cooper & Ruth Roman. Directed by Stuart Heisler. 1950. Warners. 94 min. Sound. 16mm Color. *Rental:* Swank Motion.

Dalton Gang, The. Orig. Title: Outlaw Gang. Don Barry & Robert Lowery. Directed by Ford Beebe. 1949. Lippert. 59 min. Sound. 16mm B&W. *Rental:* Film Ctr DC, Mogulls Films & Westcoast Films.

Dalyokaya Nevesta see Under Sunny Skies.

Dama S Sobachkoy see Lady With a Dog.

111

Damage Control: The Chemistry of Fire. 1943. US Government. (Documentary). 50 min. Sound. 16mm B&W. *Sale:* Natl AV Ctr.

Damaged Lives. Directed by Edgar G. Ulmer. 1933. Weldon. (Cast unlisted). 50 min. Sound. 16mm B&W. *Sale:* MGM United.

Dame Edith Evans: I Caught Acting Like the Measles. Directed by Bryan Forbes. 1977. Britain. 56 min. Sound. 16mm Color. *Rental:* A Cantor. *Sale:* A Cantor.

Dames. Dick Powell & Ruby Keeler. Directed by Ray Enright. 1934. Warners. 92 min. Sound. 16mm B&W. *Rental:* MGM United.

Damien: Omen II. William Holden & Lee Grant. Directed by Don Taylor. 1978. Fox. 110 min. Sound. 16mm Color. *Rental:* Films Inc, Twyman Films & Williams Films. *Rental:* Williams Films, VIdeotape version.

Damn the Defiant! Orig. Title: H. M. S. Defiant. Sir Alec Guinness & Dirk Bogarde. Directed by Lewis Gilbert. 1962. Britain. 101 min. Sound. 16mm B&W. *Rental:* Bosco Films, Buchan Film, Cine Craft, Modern Sound, Natl Films Serv, Roas Films, Welling Motion Pictures & Westcoast Films, Color version.

Damn Yankees. Orig. Title: Whatever Lola Wants. Tab Hunter & Gwen Verdon. Directed by George Abbott & Stanley Donen. 1958. Warners. 110 min. Sound. 16mm Color. *Rental:* Films Inc, Swank Motion, Twyman Films & Williams Films. *Sale:* Tamarelles French Film, Videotape version.

Damnation Alley. Jan-Michael Vincent & George Peppard. Directed by Jack Smight. 1977. Fox. 91 min. Sound. 16mm Color. *Rental:* Films Inc & Williams Films.

Damned, The. Dirk Bogarde & Ingrid Thulin. Directed by Luchino Visconti. 1970. Britain. 155 min. Sound. 16mm Color. *Rental:* Films Inc, Swank Motion & Twyman Films.

Damon & Pythias. Guy Williams & Don Burnett. Directed by Curtis Bernhardt. 1962. Italy. 99 min. Sound. 16mm Color. dubbed. *Rental:* MGM United.

Damsel in Distress, A. Fred Astaire, George Burns & Gracie Allen. Directed by George Stevens. 1937. RKO. 101 min. Sound. 16mm B&W. *Rental:* Films Inc.

Dance: Africa. 1969. 60 min. Sound. Videotape *Rental:* PBS Video. *Sale:* PBS Video.

Dance, Charlie, Dance. Stuart Erwin & Glenda Farrell. Directed by Frank McDonald. 1937. Warners. 64 min. Sound. 16mm B&W. *Rental:* MGM United.

Dance, Fools, Dance. Joan Crawford & Clark Gable. Directed by Harry Beaumont. 1931. MGM. 82 min. Sound. 16mm B&W. *Rental:* MGM United.

Dance, Girl, Dance. Maureen O'Hara & Lucille Ball. Directed by Dorothy Arzner. 1940. RKO. 89 min. Sound. 16mm B&W. *Rental:* Films Inc.

Dance Hall. Cesar Romero & Carole Landis. Directed by Irving Pichel. 1941. Fox. 74 min. Sound. 16mm B&W. *Rental:* Films Inc.

Dance Hall. Olive Borden & Arthur Lake. Directed by Melville Brown. 1929. RKO. Sound. 16mm *Rental:* RKO General Pics.

Dance Little Lady. Terence Morgan & Mai Zetterling. Directed by Val Guest. 1955. Britain. 87 min. Sound. 16mm Color. *Rental:* Video Comm. *Rental:* Video Comm, Videotape version.

Dance of the Vampires *see* Fearless Vampire Killers.

Dance Theater of Harlem. 1976. WNET. (Dance). 58 min. Sound. 16mm Color. *Rental:* Indiana AV Ctr & WNET Media. *Sale:* WNET Media. *Rental:* Indiana AV Ctr, *Sale:* Indiana AV Ctr, Videotape version.

Dance With Me, Henry. Bud Abbott, Lou Costello & Gigi Perreau. Directed by Charles Barton. 1956. United Artists. 79 min. Sound. 16mm B&W. *Rental:* MGM United.

Dancers & Musicians of the Burmese National Theater, The. 1975. Asia Society. (Ballet). 60 min. Sound. Videotape Color. *Rental:* Asia Soc. *Sale:* Asia Soc.

Dancers in the Dark. Miriam Hopkins & Jack Oakie. Directed by David Burton. 1932. Paramount. 76 min. Sound. 16mm B&W. *Rental:* Swank Motion.

Dancer's Peril. Alice Brady. Directed by Travers Vale. 1917. Peerless-World. 60 min. Silent. 16mm B&W. *Sale:* E Finney. *Sale:* E Finney, Silent 8mm version.

Dancin' Fool. Wallace Reid, Bebe Daniels & Raymond Hatton. Directed by Sam Wood. 1920. Paramount. 50 min. Silent. 16mm B&W. *Rental:* Museum Mod Art.

Dancing Coed. Lana Turner & Artie Shaw. Directed by S. Sylvan Simon. 1939. MGM. 84 min. Sound. 16mm B&W. *Rental:* MGM United.

Dancing Feet. Ben Lyon & Eddie Nugent. Directed by Joseph Santley. 1936. Republic. 54 min. Sound. 16mm B&W. *Rental:* Ivy Films. *Sale:* Rep pic Film.

Dancing Fool, The *see* Harold Teen.

Dancing in the Dark. William Powell & Mark Stevens. Directed by Irving Reis. 1949. Fox. 92 min. Sound. 16mm B&W. *Rental:* Films Inc.

Dancing Lady. Joan Crawford & Clark Gable. Directed by Robert Z. Leonard. 1933. MGM. 82 min. Sound. 16mm B&W. *Rental:* MGM United.

Dancing Masters, The. Stan Laurel & Oliver Hardy. Directed by Mal St. Clair. 1943. Fox. 63 min. Sound. 16mm B&W. *Rental:* Buchan Pic, Films Inc, Inst Cinema & Willoughby Peer.

Dancing Mothers. Clara Bow & Alice Joyce. Directed by Herbert Brenon. 1926. Paramount. 70 min. Silent. 16mm B&W. *Rental:* Budget Films, Classic Film Mus & Em Gee Film Lib. *Sale:* Glenn Photo. *Rental:* Ivy Films, Super 8 silent version. *Sale:* Festival Films, 50 min. 16mm silent version.

Dancing Pirate, The. Charles Collins & Frank Morgan. Directed by Lloyd Corrigan. 1936. RKO. 80 min. Sound. 16mm B&W. *Rental:* Ivy Films & Mogulls Films. *Sale:* Classics Assoc NY,

Dancing Sweeties. Grant Withers & Sue Carol. Directed by Ray Enright. 1930. Warners. 62 min. Sound. 16mm B&W. *Rental:* MGM United.

Dandy in Aspic, A. Laurence Harvey, Tom Courtenay & Mia Farrow. Directed by Anthony Mann. 1968. Columbia. 107 min. Sound. 16mm Color. *Rental:* Charard Motion Pics, Modern Sound, Welling Motion Pictures, Wholesome Film Ctr & Willoughby Peer.

Dandy, the All-American Girl *see* Sweet Revenge.

Danger Ahead. James Newill. Directed by Ralph Staub. 1940. Monogram. 60 min. Sound. 16mm B&W. *Rental:* Mogulls Films.

Danger: Diabolik. John Philip Law & Terry-Thomas. Directed by Mario Bava. 1968. Paramount. 102 min. Sound. 16mm Color. *Rental:* Films Inc.

Danger Grows Wild *see* Poppy is Also a Flower.

Danger in Sports: Paying the Price. 1974. ABC. (Documentary). 56 min. Sound. 16mm Color. *Rental:* Films Inc.

Danger Lights. Robert Armstrong & Jean Arthur. Directed by George B. Seitz. 1930. RKO. 70 min. Sound. 16mm B&W. *Sale:* Cinema Concepts, Classic Film Mus, Natl Cinema & Reel Images. *Sale:* Blackhawk Films, Super 8 sound version. *Sale:* Blackhawk Films, Videotape version.

Danger on Dartmoor. 1981. Britain. (Cast unlisted). 57 min. Sound. 16mm Color. *Sale:* Lucerne Films.

Danger on the Air. Donald Woods & Nan Grey. Directed by Otis Garrett. 1938. Universal. 60 min. Sound. 16mm B&W. *Rental:* Mogulls Films.

Danger Patrol. John Beal & Harry Carey. Directed by Lew Landers. 1938. RKO. 60 min. Sound. 16mm *Rental:* RKO General Pics.

Danger Point. 1974. Britain. (Cast unlisted). 45 min. Sound. 16mm Color. *Rental:* Janus Films. *Sale:* Lucerne Films & Sterling Ed Film.

Danger! Radioactive Waste. 1977. NBC. (Documentary). 50 min. Sound. 16mm Color. *Rental:* Films Inc, Iowa Films & U Mich Media. *Sale:* Films Inc. *Sale:* Films Inc, Videotape version.

Danger Rides the Range *see* Three Texas Steers.

Danger Route. Richard Johnson & Carol Lynley. Directed by Seth Holt. 1968. United Artists. 91 min. Sound. 16mm Color. *Rental:* MGM United.

Danger Trails. Guinn Williams. Directed by Robert Hill. 1935. First Division. 60 min. Sound. 16mm B&W. *Rental:* Mogulls Films.

Danger, Women at Work. Patsy Kelly & Mary Brian. Directed by Sam Newfield. 1943. PRC. 60 min. Sound. 16mm B&W. *Rental:* Mogulls Films.

Dangerous. Bette Davis & Franchot Tone. Directed by Alfred E. Green. 1935. Warners. 78 min. Sound. 16mm B&W. *Rental:* MGM United.

Dangerous Age *see* Wild Boys of the Road.

Dangerous Blondes. Evelyn Keyes & Anita Louise. Directed by Charles Barton. 1943. Columbia. 80 min. Sound. 16mm B&W. *Rental:* Kit Parker.

Dangerous Cargo. Erich Von Stroheim. Directed by Jack Watling. 1954. Britain. 70 min. Sound. 16mm B&W. *Rental:* Mogulls Films.

Dangerous Charter. Chris Warfield & Sally Fraser. Directed by Robert Gottschalk. 1962. Britain. 76 min. Sound. 16mm Color. *Rental:* Video Comm & Welling Motion Pictures. *Rental:* Video Comm, Videotape version.

Dangerous Corner. Melvyn Douglas & Conrad Nagel. Directed by Phil Rosen. 1935. RKO. 67 min. Sound. 16mm *Rental:* RKO General Pics.

Dangerous Crossing. Jeanne Crain & Michael Rennie. Directed by Joseph Newman. 1953. Fox. 75 min. Sound. 16mm B&W. *Rental:* Films Inc.

Dangerous Curves. Clara Bow & Richard Arlen. Directed by Lothar Mendes. 1929. Paramount. 79 min. Sound. 16mm B&W. *Rental:* Swank Motion.

Dangerous Decades. 1968. Canada. (Documentary). 58 min. Sound. 16mm B&W. *Rental:* Natl Film CN. *Sale:* Natl Film CN.

Dangerous Holiday. Jack La Rue. Directed by Nicholas Barrows. 1937. Republic. 54 min. Sound. 16mm B&W. *Rental:* Ivy Films. *Sale:* Rep pic Film.

Dangerous Hours. Claire Dubrey. Directed by Fred Niblo. 1920. Paramount. 80 min. Silent. 16mm B&W. *Rental:* Em Gee Film Lib. *Sale:* Blackhawk Films & Griggs Movie. *Rental:* Ivy Films, *Sale:* Blackhawk Films, Super 8 silent version. *Sale:* Cinema Concepts, Silent 8mm version.

Dangerous Intruder. Charles Arnt & Veda Ann Borg. Directed by Vernon Keays. 1945. PRC. 60 min. Sound. 16mm B&W. *Sale:* Classics Assoc NY.

Dangerous Journey. Directed by Armand Denis & Leila Roosevelt. 1944. Fox. 73 min. Sound. 16mm B&W. *Rental:* Films Inc.

Dangerous Maid. Constance Talmadge. Directed by Victor Heerman. 1923. 16mm *Rental:* A Twyman Pres.

Dangerous Mission. Victor Mature & Piper Laurie. Directed by Louis King. 1954. RKO. 74 min. Sound. 16mm Color. *Rental:* Films Inc.

Dangerous Money. Sidney Toler. Directed by Terry Morse. 1946. Monogram. Sound. 16mm B&W. *Rental:* Hurlock Cine.

Dangerous Moonlight. Anton Walbrook & Sally Grey. Directed by Brian Desmond-Hurst. 1942. RKO. 79 min. Sound. 16mm *Rental:* RKO General Pics.

Dangerous Number. Robert Young & Ann Sothern. Directed by Richard Thorpe. 1937. MGM. 71 min. Sound. 16mm B&W. *Rental:* MGM United.

Dangerous Partners. James Craig & Signe Hasso. Directed by Edward L. Cahn. 1945. MGM. 74 min. Sound. 16mm B&W. *Rental:* MGM United.

Dangerous Profession. George Raft & Pat O'Brien. Directed by Ted Tetzlaff. 1949. RKO. 79 min. Sound. 16mm B&W. *Rental:* Films Inc.

Dangerous Secrets. Paul Lukas. Directed by Edmond Greville. 1938. Grand National. 60 min. Sound. 16mm B&W. *Rental:* Mogulls Films.

Dangerous Traffic. Francis X Bushman Jr. & Mildred Harris. Directed by Bennett Cohn. 1926. Goodwill. 60 min. Silent. 16mm B&W. *Rental:* Mogulls Films. *Rental:* Mogulls Films, Silent 8mm version.

Dangerous Venture. William Boyd. Directed by George Archainbaud. 1947. United Artists. 59 min. Sound. 16mm B&W. *Sale:* Cinema Concepts.

Dangerous When Wet. Esther Williams & Fernando Lamas. Directed by Charles Walters. 1953. MGM. 95 min. Sound. 16mm Color. *Rental:* MGM United.

Dangerously They Live. John Garfield & Nancy Coleman. Directed by Robert Florey. 1942. Warners. 77 min. Sound. 16mm B&W. *Rental:* MGM United.

Daniel. Timothy Hutton & Edward Asner. Directed by Sidney Lumet. 1983. Paramount. 129 min. Sound. 16mm Color. *Rental:* Films inc. *Sale:* Tamarelles French Film, Videotape version.

Daniel & Nebuchadnezzar. 1979. Lucerne. 51 min. Sound. 16mm Color. *Sale:* Lucerne Films & Syracuse U Film. *Rental:* Budget Films. *Sale:* Lucerne Films, Videotape version.

Daniel Boone. George O'Brien. Directed by David Howard. 1936. RKO. 80 min. Sound. 16mm B&W. *Rental:* Alba House, Budget Films, Classic Film Mus, Film Classics & Mogulls Films. *Sale:* Morcraft Films, Super 8 sound version.

Daniel Boone Through the Wilderness. Bob Steele & Roy Stewart. Directed by Robert N. Bradbury & Frank S. Mattison. 1926. Sunset. 60 min. Silent. 16mm B&W. *Rental:* Film Classics. *Sale:* Film Classics. *Sale:* Film Classics, Silent 8mm version.

Daniel Boone, Trailblazer. Bruce Bennett & Lon Chaney Jr. Directed by Albert C. Gannaway & Ismael Rodriguez. 1956. Republic. 76 min. Sound. 16mm B&W. *Rental:* Welling Motion Pictures.

Daniel Henri Kahnweiler. 1966. NET. (Documentary). 59 min. Sound. 16mm B&W. *Rental:* Indiana AV Ctr. *Sale:* Indiana AV Ctr.

Daniel in the Lion's Den. David Birney & Sherry Jackson. Directed by James L. Conway. 1979. NBC. 40 min. Sound. 16mm Color. *Rental:* Roas Films. *Sale:* Lucerne Films.

Daniel Webster. Martin Gabel. Directed by Robert Gist. (Profiles in Courage Ser.). 1978. Saudek. 50 min. Sound. 16mm B&W. *Rental:* BYU Media, IQ Film, Syracuse U Film & U Mich Media. *Sale:* IQ Film. *Sale:* IQ Film, Spanish dubbed version.

Danish Energy. Directed by Per Mannstaedt. 1980. Green Mountain Post. (Documentary). 47 min. Sound. 16mm Color. *Rental:* Green Mt.

Danny. Rebecca Page & Janet Zarish. Directed by Gene Feldman. 1980. Tanner National. 90 min. Sound. 16mm Color. *Rental:* U Cal Media & Wombat Productions. *Sale:* Wombat Productions, Videotape version.

Danny & Nicky. 1969. Canada. (Documentary). 56 min. Sound. 16mm Color. *Rental:* Films Inc, Natl Films CN & U Mich Media. *Sale:* Films Inc & Natl Film CN. *Sale:* Films Inc, *Rental:* Natl Film CN, Videotape version.

Danny Boy. Orig. Title: Adventures of Danny Boy, The. Buzzy Henry & Ralph Lewis. Directed by Terry Morse. 1946. PRC. 70 min. Sound. 16mm B&W. *Rental:* Budget Films & Inst Cinema.

Dante's Inferno. 1911. Italy. (Cast Unlisted). 50 min. Silent. 16mm B&W. *Rental:* Twyman Films.

Dante's Inferno. Spencer Tracy & Claire Trevor. Directed by Harry Lachman. 1935. Fox. 88 min. Sound. 16mm B&W. *Rental:* Films Inc.

Dante's Inferno. Directed by Ken Russell. 1968. Britain. 90 min. Sound. 16mm B&W. *Rental:* Films Inc. *Sale:* Films Inc. *Rental:* Films Inc, *Sale:* Films Inc, Videotape version.

Dante's Inferno: The Life of Dante Gabriel Rossetti. Oliver Reed. Directed by Ken Russell. 1969. 90 min. Sound. 16mm *Rental:* Budget Films.

Danton. Directed by Andrzej Wajda. 1983. France-Poland. 136 min. Sound. 16mm Color. subtitles. *Rental:* Swank Motion. *Sale:* Tamarelles French Film, Videotape version.

Darby O'Gill & the Little People. Sean Connery & Janet Munro. Directed by Robert Stevenson. 1959. Disney. 90 min. Sound. 16mm Color. *Rental:* Bosco Films, Buchan Pic, Cine Craft, Disney Prod, Elliot Film Co, Films Inc, Film Ctr DC, MGM United, Modern Sound, Newman Film Lib, Roas Films, Swank Motion, Twyman Films, Welling Motion Pictures, Westcoast Films & Williams Films. *Rental:* Williams Films, Videotape version.

Daredevil, The. George Montgomery & Terry Moore. 1971. Gold Key. 91 min. Sound. 16mm Color. *Rental:* Video Comm. *Lease:* Video Comm. *Rental:* Video Comm, *Lease:* Video Comm, Videotape version.

Daredevil Drivers. Dick Purcell & Beverly Roberts. Directed by B. Reeves Eason. 1938. Warners. 59 min. Sound. 16mm B&W. *Rental:* MGM United.

Daredevils of the Clouds. Robert Livingston & Ray Teal. Directed by George Blair. 1948. Republic. 60 min. Sound. 16mm B&W. *Rental:* Ivy Films. *Sale:* Rep Pic Film.

Daring Caballero, The. Duncan Renaldo. Directed by Wallace Fox. 1949. United Artists. 60 min. Sound. Videotape B&W. *Sale:* Video Comm.

Daring Deeds. Billy Sullivan. Directed by Duke Worne. 1927. Rayart. 60 min. Silent. 16mm B&W. *Rental:* Mogulls Films.

Daring Dobermans, The. Joan Caulfield & Tim Considine. Directed by Byron Chudnow. 1973. Dimension. 90 min. Sound. 16mm Color. *Rental:* Buchan Pic, Cine Craft, Film Ctr DC, Swank Motion, Twyman Films & Williams Films.

Daring Game, The. Lloyd Bridges & Joan Blackman. Directed by Laslo Benedek. 1968. Paramount. 100 min. Sound. 16mm Color. *Rental:* Ivy Films & Welling Motion Pictures. *Lease:* Rep Pic Film.

Daring Young Man, The. Joe E. Brown. Directed by Frank R. Strayer. 1942. Columbia. 73 min. Sound. 16mm B&W. *Rental:* Films Inc, Inst Cinema & Welling Motion Pictures.

Dark Alibi. Sidney Toler & Mantan Moreland. Directed by Phil Karlson. 1945. Monogram. 61 min. Sound. 16mm B&W. *Rental:* Hurlock Cine.

Dark Angel. Merle Oberon & Fredric March. Directed by Sidney Franklin. 1935. Goldwyn. 106 min. Sound. 16mm B&W. *Rental:* Films Inc.

Dark Circle. Marlene Batley, Richard McHugh & Raye Fleming. Directed by Chris Beaver & Judy Irving. 1982. 82 min. Sound. 16mmq Color. *Rental:* New Yorker Films.

Dark City. Charlton Heston & Lisbeth Scott. Directed by William Dieterle. 1950. Paramount. 88 min. Sound. 16mm B&W. *Rental:* Films Inc.

Dark Command. John Wayne & Claire Trevor. Directed by Raoul Walsh. 1940. Republic. 92 min. Sound. 16mm B&W. *Rental:* Budget Films & Ivy Films. *Lease:* Films Inc & Rep Pic Film. *Sale:* Tamarelles French Film, Videotape version.

Dark Corner. Lucille Ball & Clifton Webb. Directed by Henry Hathaway. 1946. Fox. 99 min. Sound. 16mm B&W. *Rental:* Films Inc.

Dark Crystal, The. Directed by Jim Henson & Frank Oz. 1985. Universal. (Animation). 94 min. Sound. 16mm Color. *Rental:* Swank Motion.

Dark Delusion. Orig. Title: Cynthia's Secret. Lionel Barrymore & James Craig. Directed by Willis Goldbeck. 1947. MGM. 90 min. Sound. 16mm B&W. *Rental:* MGM United.

Dark End of the Street, The. Directed by Jan Egleson. First Run. (Cast unlisted). 90 min. Sound. 16mm Color. *Rental:* First Run.

Dark Eyes of London *see* Human Monster.

Dark Hazard. Edward G. Robinson & Glenda Farrell. Directed by Alfred E. Green. 1934. Warners. 74 min. Sound. 16mm B&W. *Rental:* MGM United.

Dark Horse, The. Bette Davis & Warren William. Directed by Alfred E. Green. 1932. Warners. 75 min. Sound. 16mm B&W. *Rental:* MGM United.

Dark Interval. Zena Marshall. Directed by Charles Saunders. 1944. Britain. 58 min. Sound. 16mm B&W. *Rental:* Film Classics & Liberty Co.

Dark Intruder. Leslie Nielsen & Judi Meredith. Directed by Harvey Hart. 1965. Universal. 59 min. Sound. 16mm B&W. *Rental:* Swank Motion.

Dark Journey. Conrad Veidt & Vivien Leigh. Directed by Victor Saville. 1937. Britain. 77 min. Sound. 16mm B&W. *Rental:* A Twyman Pres, Budget Films, Classic Film Mus & Em Gee Film Lib. *Sale:* Glenn Photo & Festival Films. *Sale:* Festival Films & Tamarelles French Film, Videotape version.

Dark Mirror. Olivia De Havilland & Lew Ayres. Directed by Robert Siodmak. 1946. Universal. 85 min. Sound. 16mm B&W. *Rental:* Budget Films, Ivy Films & Kit Parker. *Lease:* Rep Pic Film.

Dark Mountain. Robert Lowery & Ellen Drew. Directed by William Berke. 1944. Paramount. 66 min. Sound. 16mm B&W. *Sale:* Morcraft Films. *Rental:* Budget Films. *Sale:* Morcraft Films, Super 8 sound version.

Dark of the Sun. Rod Taylor & Jim Brown. Directed by Jack Cardiff. 1968. MGM. 100 min. Sound. 16mm Color. *Rental:* MGM United.

Dark Page, The *see* Scandal Sheet.

Dark Passage. Humphrey Bogart & Lauren Bacall. Directed by Delmer Daves. 1947. Warners. 106 min. Sound. 16mm B&W. *Rental:* MGM United.

Dark Past, The. William Holden & Nina Foch. Directed by Rudolph Mate. 1949. Columbia. 75 min. Sound. B&W. *Rental:* Inst Cinema & Kit Parker.

Dark Place, The. Christopher Lee & Joan Collins. Directed by Don Sharp. 1974. Britain. 69 min. Sound. 16mm Color. *Rental:* Swank Motion.

Dark Sands *see* Jericho.

Dark Star. Dan O'Bannon. Directed by John Carpenter. 1974. Bryanston. 91 min. Sound. 16mm Color. *Rental:* Modern Sound, Swank Motion, Westcoast Films & Wholesome Film Ctr.

Dark Victory. Bette Davis & George Brent. Directed by Edmund Goulding. 1939. Warner. 106 min. Sound. 16mm B&W. *Rental:* MGM United.

Dark Waters. Merle Oberon, Franchot Tone & Thomas Mitchell. Directed by Andre De Toth. 1944. United Artists. 90 min. Sound. 16mm B&W. *Sale:* Classics Assoc NY.

Darkening Trail, The. William S. Hart. Directed by William S. Hart. 1915. New York. 62 min. Silent. 16mm B&W. *Rental:* Em Gee Film Lib. *Sale:* Blackhawk Films. *Rental:* Ivy Films, Super 8 silent version.

Darling. Julie Christie, Dirk Bogarde & Laurence Harvey. Directed by John Schlesinger. 1965. Embassy. 122 min. Sound. 16mm B&W. *Rental:* Films Inc.

Darling Lili. Julie Andrews & Rock Hudson. Directed by Blake Edwards. 1970. Paramount. 136 min. Sound. 16mm Color. *Rental:* Films Inc. *Rental:* Films Inc, Anamorphic color version.

D'Artagnan. Orrin Johnson, Dorothy Dalton & Louise Glaum. Directed by Thomas H. Ince. 1916. Fine Art-Triangle. 65 min. Silent. 16mm B&W. *Rental:* Em Gee Film Lib. *Sale:* Blackhawk Films & Morcraft Films. *Rental:* Ivy Films, Super 8 silent version.

Darwin Adventure, The. Nicholas Clay. Directed by Jack Couffer. 1972. Fox. 91 min. Sound. 16mm Color. *Rental:* Films Inc.

Darwin's Bulldog. 1971. Britain. (Documentary). 50 min. Sound. 16mm Color. *Rental:* Films Inc & U Mich Media. *Sale:* Films Inc. *Rental:* Films Inc, *Sale:* Films Inc, Videotape version.

Date with Destiny, A *see* Return of October.

Date with Judy, A. Wallace Beery & Jane Powell. Directed by Richard Thorpe. 1948. MGM. 113 min. Sound. 16mm Color. *Rental:* MGM United.

Date with the Falcon, A. George Sanders & Wendy Barrie. Directed by Irving Reis. 1941. RKO. 63 min. Sound. 16mm B&W. *Rental:* Films Inc. *Lease:* Films Inc.

Daughter, The. Orig. Title: I, A Woman (Part III). Inger Sundh & Tom Scott. Directed by Mac Ahlberg. 1970. Sweden. 81 min. Sound. 16mm Color. *Rental:* Films Inc.

Daughter of Deceit, The. Fernando Soler & Alicia Caro. Directed by Luis Bunuel. 1951. 80 min. Sound. 16mm B&W. *Rental:* Films Inc.

Daughter of Dr. Jekyll. Gloria Talbott & John Agar. Directed by Edgar G. Ulmer. 1957. Monogram. 74 min. Sound. 16mm B&W. *Rental:* Hurlock Cine.

Daughter of Mata Hari. Orig. Title: Mata Hari's Daughter. Ludmilla Tcherina & Frank Latimore. Directed by Renzo Merusi. 1955. Italy. 104 min. Sound. 16mm Color. dubbed. *Rental:* Films Inc.

Daughter of Shanghai. Anna May Wong & Charles Bickford. Directed by Robert Florey. 1937. Paramount. 63 min. Sound. 16mm B&W. *Rental:* Swank Motion.

Daughter of the Jungle. Lois Hall & Sheldon Leonard. Directed by George Blair. 1948. Republic. 71 min. Sound. 16mm B&W. *Rental:* Ivy Films. *Sale:* Rep Pic Film.

Daughter of the Regiment. Orig. Title: Child of the Regiment. Anny Ondra. Ger. 1936. Germany. 67 min. Sound. 16mm B&W. subtitles. *Rental:* Film Classics.

Daughter of the Sioux, A. Neva Gerber & Ben Wilson. Directed by Ben Wilson. 1925. Davis. 55 min. Silent. 16mm B&W. *Rental:* Williams Films.

Daughter of the Sioux. Doug McClure. 60 min. Sound. 16mm B&W. *Rental:* Westcoast Films.

Daughter of the Tong. Evelyn Brent & Grant Withers. Directed by Raymond K. Johnson. 1939. Times. 60 min. Sound. 16mm B&W. *Sale:* Reel Images. *Sale:* Reel Images, Super 8 sound version.

Daughter of the West. Martha Vickers & Philip Reed. Directed by Harold Daniels. 1949. Film Classics. 85 min. Sound. 16mm B&W. *Rental:* Mogulls Films & Wectcoast Films. *Rental:* Westcoast Films, 60 mins version.

Daughter of Two Worlds. Norma Talmadge. Directed by James Young. 1920. 16mm *Rental:* A Twyman Pres.

Daughters Courageous. John Garfield & Claude Rains. Directed by Michael Curtiz. 1939. Warners. 107 min. Sound. 16mm B&W. *Rental:* MGM United.

Daughters Daughters! Shai K. Ophir & Michal Bat Adam. Directed by Moshe Mizrahi. Hebrew. 1975. Israel. 88 min. Sound. 16mm Color. subtitles. *Rental:* Films Inc.

Daughters of Eve. Anny Ondra. Ger. Germany. 70 min. Silent. 16mm B&W. *Rental:* Em Gee Film Lib. *Sale:* Glenn Photo.

Dave Brubeck. 1978. Britain. (Documentary). 52 min. Sound. 16mm Color. *Rental:* Budget Films, Films Inc, U Cal Media & U of IL Film. *Sale:* Films Inc. *Rental:* Films Inc, *Sale:* Films Inc, Videotape version.

Davey Jones' Locker. 1973. Britain. (Cast Unlisted). 60 min. Sound. 16mm Color. *Sale:* Lucerne Films.

David. 1965. Time-Life. (Documentary). 54 min. Sound. 16mm B&W. *Rental:* U Cal Media. *Lease:* Direct Cinema.

David. Directed by Peter Lilienthal. 1979. West Germany. 106 min. Sound. 16mm Color. *Rental:* Kino Intl. *Lease:* Kino Intl.

David & Bathsheba. Gregory Peck & Susan Hayward. Directed by Henry King. 1951. Fox. 116 min. Sound. 16mm Color. *Rental:* Films Inc.

David & Goliath. Orson Welles & Elennora Rossi Drago. Directed by Richard Pottier & Ferdinando Baldi. Ital. 1961. Italy. 95 min. Sound. 16mm Color. *Rental:* Bosco Films, Films Inc & Willoughby Peer. *Rental:* Willoughby Peer, Anamorphic color version.

David & Goliath. Ted Cassidy & Hugh O'Brian. Directed by James L. Conway. 1979. NBC. 104 min. Sound. 16mm Color. *Sale:* Lucerne Films.

David & Lisa. Keir Dullea & Janet Margolin. Directed by Frank Perry. 1962. Continental. 94 min. Sound. 16mm B&W. *Rental:* Budget Films, Films Inc, U Cal Media & Wholesome Film Ctr. *Sale:* Festival Films. *Sale:* Festival Films, Videotape version.

David Copperfield. W. C. Fields & Freddie Bartholomew. Directed by George Cukor. 1935. MGM. 133 min. Sound. 16mm B&W. *Rental:* MGM United. *Rental:* MGM United, Videotape version.

David Harding, Counterspy. Willard Parker & Audrey Long. Directed by Ray Nazarro. 1950. Columbia. 71 min. Sound. 16mm B&W. *Rental:* Inst Cinema.

David Harum. Harold Lockwood, May Allison & Jack Pickford. 1915. Mutual. 55 min. Silent. 16mm B&W. *Rental:* Film Classics. *Sale:* Film Classics. *Sale:* Film Classics, Silent 8mm version. *Rental:* Film Classics, Videotape version.

David Harum. Will Rogers & Louise Dresser. Directed by James Cruze. 1934. Fox. 82 min. Sound. 16mm B&W. *Rental:* Films Inc.

David Holzman's Diary. Directed by Jim McBride. 1968. Paradigm. (Documentary). 78 min. Sound. 16mm B&W. *Rental:* Direct Cinema & Films Inc. *Lease:* Direct Cinema.

David Lean: A Self-Portrait. 1971. Pyramid. (Documentary). 60 min. Sound. 16mm Color. *Rental:* Budget Films, Pyramid Film, Syracuse U Film, Twyman Films, U Cal Media, U of IL Film & U Mich Media. *Sale:* Pyramid Film. *Rental:* Pyramid Film, *Sale:* Pyramid Film, Videotape version.

David Smith: Steel into Sculpture. 1983. 58 min. Sound. Color. *Rental:* Direct Cinema Ltd. *Sale:* Direct Cinema. *Rental:* Direct Cinema Ltd, Videotape version.

David, the Outlaw *see* Story of David.

Davy Crockett - King of the Wild Frontier. Fess Parker & Buddy Ebsen. Directed by Norman Foster. 1955. Disney. 93 min. Sound. 16mm Color. *Rental:* Bosco Films, Buchan Pic, Cine Craft, Cousino Visual Ed, Disney Prod, Elliot Film Co, Film Ctr DC, Film Pres, Films Inc, MGM United, Modern Sound, Newman Film Lib, Roas Films, Swank Motion, Twyman Films, U of IL Film, Welling Motion Pictures, Westcoast Films & Williams Films. *Rental:* Williams Films, Videotape version.

Davy Crockett & the River Pirates. Fess Parker & Buddy Ebsen. Directed by Norman Foster. 1955. Disney. 81 min. Sound. 16mm Color. *Rental:* Buchan Pic, Cine Craft, Cousino Visual Ed, Disney Prod, Film Ctr DC, Film Pres, Films Inc, MGM United, Newman Film Lib, Roas Films, Twyman Films & Williams Films. *Rental:* Williams Films, Videotape version.

Davy Crockett, Indian Scout. Orig. Title: Indian Scout. George Montgomery & Ellen Drew. Directed by Lew Landers. 1950. United Artists. 71 min. Sound. 16mm B&W. *Rental:* Alba House, Cine Craft, Films Inc, Inst Cinema, MGM United & Roas Films.

Davy Is Entitled. 1978. 58 min. Sound. 16mm Color. *Rental:* U Mich Media.

Dawn Express. Anne Nagel. Directed by Al Herman. 1942. PRC. 66 min. Sound. 16mm B&W. *Rental:* Budget Films.

Dawn of America. 1954. Spain. (Cast unlisted). 60 min. Sound. 16mm B&W. dubbed. *Rental:* Roas Films.

Dawn of the Dead. David Emge, Ken Foree, Gaylen Ross & Scott Reiniger. Directed by George A. Romero. 1979. Laurel. 140 min. Sound. 16mm Color. *Rental:* Cinema Five.

Dawn of the Solar Age. 1977. Nova. (Documentary). 58 min. Sound. 16mm Color. *Rental:* U Cal Media.

Dawn on the Great Divide. Buck Jones. Directed by Howard Bretherton. 1942. Monogram. 57 min. Sound. 16mm B&W. *Rental:* Budget Films, Em Gee Film Lib & Video Comm. *Sale:* Cinema Concepts. *Rental:* Ivy Films, *Sale:* Ivy Films, Super 8 sound version. *Rental:* Video Comm, *Sale:* Video Comm, Videotape version.

Dawn Patrol. Errol Flynn & David Niven. Directed by Edmund Goulding. 1938. Warners. 103 min. Sound. 16mm B&W. *Rental:* MGM United.

Dawn Patrol. Orig. Title: Flight Commander. Richard Barthelmess & Douglas Fairbanks Jr. Directed by Howard Hawks. 1930. Warners. 82 min. Sound. 16mm B&W. *Rental:* MGM United.

Dawn Rider. John Wayne. Directed by Robert N. Bradbury. 1935. Monogram. 59 min. Sound. 16mm B&W. *Rental:* Ivy Films. *Sale:* Classics Assoc NY & Rep Pic Film.

Dawn to Dawn. Orig. Title: Black Dawn. Julie Haydon. Directed by Joseph Berne. 1934. 50 min. 16mm *Rental:* A Twyman Pres.

Dax's Case. 1984. American. (Cast unlisted). 55 min. Sound. 16mm Color. *Rental:* Concern Dying. *Sale:* Concern Dying. *Rental:* Concern Dying, *Sale:* Concern Dying, Videotape version.

Day After Tomorrow, The *see* Strange Holiday.

Day After Trinity, The: J. Robert Oppenheimer & the Atomic Bomb. Directed by Jon Else. 1980. Pyramid. (Documentary). 90 min. Sound. 16mm Color. *Rental:* Pyramid Film, Syracuse U Film, U Mich Media & U of IL Film. *Sale:* Pyramid Film. *Rental:* Pyramid Film, *Sale:* Pyramid Film, Videotape version.

Day at the Races, A. Marx Brothers & Maureen O'Sullivan. Directed by Sam Wood. 1937. MGM. 109 min. Sound. 16mm B&W. *Rental:* MGM United. *Rental:* MGM United, Videotape version.

Day for Night. Francois Truffaut & Jacqueline Bisset. Directed by Francois Truffaut. Fr. 1973. Warners. 116 min. Sound. 16mm Color. subtitles. *Rental:* Swank Motion.

Day in the Death of Joe Egg, A. Alan Bates & Janet Suzman. Directed by Peter Medak. 1972. Columbia. 100 min. Sound. 16mm Color. *Rental:* Corinth Films & Swank Motion.

Day Mars Invaded Earth, The. Kent Taylor & Marie Windsor. Directed by Maury Dexter. 1963. Fox. 70 min. Sound. 16mm B&W. *Rental:* Films Inc.

Day of Empires Has Arrived, The. 1975. Britain. (Documentary). 52 min. Sound. 16mm Color. *Rental:* U of IL Film.

Day of Reckoning, The. Madge Evans, Una Merkel & Richard Dix. Directed by Charles Brabin. 1933. MGM. 70 min. Sound. 16mm B&W. *Rental:* MGM United.

Day of the Animals, The. Christopher George & Leslie Nielsen. Directed by William Girdler. 1977. Film Ventures. 97 min. Sound. 16mm Color. *Rental:* Modern Sound.

Day of the Dolphins, The. George C. Scott & Trish Van Devere. Directed by Mike Nichols. 1973. Embassy. (Anamorphic). 104 min. Sound. 16mm Color. *Rental:* Films Inc.

Day of the Evil Gun. Glenn Ford & Arthur Kennedy. Directed by Jerry Thorpe. 1968. MGM. 95 min. Sound. 16mm Color. *Rental:* MGM United. *Rental:* MGM United, Anamorphic color version.

Day of the Jackal, The. Edward Fox & Alan Badel. Directed by Fred Zinnemann. 1973. Universal. 144 min. Sound. 16mm Color. *Rental:* Swank Motion.

Day of the Locust, The. Donald Sutherland & Karen Black. Directed by John Schlesinger. 1975. Paramount. 144 min. Sound. 16mm Color. *Rental:* Films Inc.

Day of the Outlaw, The. Robert Ryan & Burl Ives. Directed by Andre De Toth. 1959. United Artists. 90 min. Sound. 16mm B&W. *Rental:* MGM United.

Day of the Triffids, The. Howard Keel & Janette Scott. Directed by Steve Sekely. 1963. Allied Artists. 94 min. Sound. 16mm Color. *Rental:* Hurlock Cine. *Sale:* Cinema Concepts, Videotape version.

Day of the Wolves, The. Richard Egan & Martha Hyer. Directed by Ferde Grofe Jr. 1971. Gold Key. 95 min. Sound. 16mm Color. *Rental:* Budget Films, Video Comm & Westcoast Films.

Day of Triumph. Lee J. Cobb & Joanne Dru. Directed by Irving Pichel & John Coyle. 1954. Century. 120 min. Sound. 16mm Color. *Rental:* Ivy Films & Modern Sound.

Day of Wrath. Trans. Title: Vreden's Dag. Thorkild Roose. Directed by Carl Th. Dreyer. Danish. 1943. Denmark. 98 min. Sound. 16mm B&W. subtitles. *Rental:* Budget Films, Corinth Films, Films Inc, Images Film & Kit Parker. *Sale:* Cinema Concepts, Images Film, Natl Cinema & Reel Images. *Lease:* Corinth Films. *Sale:* Images Film & Tamarelles French Film, Videotape version. *Sale:* Festival Films, 110 min. 16mm version. *Sale:* Festival Films, 110 min. Videotape version.

Day The Bookies Wept, The. Betty Grable & Joe Penner. Directed by Leslie Goodwins. 1940. RKO. 64 min. Sound. 16mm *Rental:* RKO General Pics.

Day the Earth Caught Fire, The. Janet Munro & Leo McKern. Directed by Val Guest. 1962. Britain. 91 min. Sound. 16mm B&W. *Rental:* A Twyman Pres, Films Inc, Ivy Films, Twyman Films, Video Comm & Budget Films.

Day the Earth Froze, The. Marvin Miller. Directed by Gregg Sebelious. 1964. American International. 67 min. Sound. 16mm B&W. *Rental:* Films Inc.

Day the Earth Stood Still, The. Michael Rennie & Patricia Neal. Directed by Robert Wise. 1951. Fox. 92 min. Sound. 16mm B&W. *Rental:* Films Inc. *Sale:* Blackhawk Films, Cinema Concepts, Golden Tapes, Magnetic Video & Video Lib, Videotape version.

Day the Fish Came Out, The. Tom Courtenay & Candice Bergen. Directed by Michael Cacoyannis. 1967. Fox. 109 min. Sound. 16mm Color. *Rental:* Films Inc.

Day the Hot Line Got Hot, The. Charles Boyer & Robert Taylor. Directed by Etienne Perier. 1969. Commonwealth. 99 min. Sound. 16mm Color. *Rental:* Budget Films, Ivy Films & Rep Pic Film. *Sale:* Rep Pic Film.

Day the Leaves Clapped Hands, The. 1972. NBC. 59 min. Sound. 16mm Color. *Rental:* Natl Churches Christ & Roas Films. *Sale:* Natl Churches Christ.

Day the Sky Exploded, The. Paul Hubschmid. Directed by Paolo Heusch. 1960. Italy. 80 min. Sound. 16mm B&W. dubbed. *Rental:* Ivy Films.

Day the World Changed Hands, The *see* Colossus.

Day the World Ended, The. Richard Denning & Adele Jergens. Directed by Roger Corman. 1956. American Releasing. 79 min. Sound. 16mm B&W. *Rental:* Films Inc.

Day They Changed the Alphabet, The. 1973. WBBM. (Documentary). 52 min. Sound. 16mm B&W. *Sale:* Carousel Films. *Sale:* Carousel Films, Color version.

Day They Robbed the Bank of England, The. Aldo Ray & Peter O'Toole. Directed by John Guillermin. 1960. Britain. 85 min. Sound. 16mm B&W. *Rental:* MGM United.

Day-Time Wife. Tyrone Power & Linda Darnell. Directed by Gregory Ratoff. 1939. Fox. 72 min. Sound. 16mm B&W. *Rental:* Films Inc.

Day with Bill Cosby, A. 1971. NBC. (Documentary). 48 min. Sound. 16mm Color. *Rental:* Films Inc. *Sale:* Films Inc. *Sale:* Film Inc, Videotape version.

Day with Darlene, A. 1976. Penn State. (Experimental). 59 min. Videotape B&W. *Rental:* Penn St AV Serv.

Day Without Sunshine, A. Directed by Robert Thurber. 1976. WPBT. (Documentary). 60 min. Sound. 16mm Color. *Rental:* CA Newsreel, CC Films, Natl Churches Christ & U Mich Media. *Rental:* CC Films & Natl Churches Christ, *Sale:* CC Films & Natl Churches Christ, Videotape version.

Daybreak *see* Jour Se Leve.

Daybreak. Ramon Navarro & Karen Morley. Directed by Jacques Feyder. 1931. MGM. 75 min. Sound. 16mm B&W. *Rental:* MGM United.

Daybreak. Eric Portman & Ann Todd. Directed by Compton Bennett. 1949. Britain. 81 min. Sound. 16mm B&W. *Rental:* Films Inc.

Daybreakers, The: The Sacketts. Glenn Ford & Tom Selleck. Directed by Robert Totten. 1980. CBS. 105 min. Sound. 16mm Color. *Rental:* Twyman Films & Westcoast Films.

Daydream. Kanako Michi. Directed by Tetsuji Takechi. Jap. 1975. Japan. (Anamorphic). 90 min. Sound. 16mm Color. subtitles. *Rental:* J Green Pics.

Daydreamer, The. Paul O'Keefe, Jack Gilford & Ray Bolger. Directed by Jules Bass. 1967. Embassy. (Animated). 101 min. Sound. 16mm Color. *Rental:* Films Inc.

Daydreamer, The. Pierre Richard & Bernard Blier. Directed by Pierre Richard. Fr. 1975. France. 90 min. Sound. 16mm Color. subtitles. *Rental:* Graphic Curr. *Sale:* Tamarelles French Film, Videotape version.

Days & Nights in the Forest. Trans. Title: Aranyer Din Ratri. Soumitra Chatterjee. Directed by Satyajit Ray. Hindi. 1970. India. 120 min. Sound. 16mm B&W. subtitles. *Rental:* Corinth Films & Cinema Guild. *Lease:* Corinth Films.

Days Are Numbered, The. Salva Randome. 1958. Italy. 101 min. Sound. 16mm B&W. dubbed. *Rental:* MGM United.

Days of Adventure: Dreams of Gold. 1975. Productions Unlimited. (Documentary). 52 min. Sound. 16mm Color. *Rental:* Westcoast Films.

Days of Buffalo Bill. Sunset Carson. Directed by Thomas Carr. 1946. Republic. 54 min. Sound. 16mm B&W. *Rental:* Ivy Films.

Days of Glory. Gregory Peck & Tamara Toumanova. Directed by Jacques Tourneur. 1944. RKO. 86 min. Sound. 16mm B&W. *Rental:* RKO General Pics.

Days of Heaven. Richard Gere & Brooke Adams. Directed by Terrence Malick. 1978. Paramount. 110 min. Sound. 16mm Color. *Rental:* Films Inc.

Days of Jesse James. Roy Rogers. Directed by Joseph Kane. 1939. Republic. 54 min. Sound. 16mm B&W. *Rental:* Ivy Films. *Sale:* Cinema Concepts & Rep Pic Film.

Days of Old Cheyenne. Don Barry. Directed by Elmer Clifton. 1943. Republic. 55 min. Sound. 16mm B&W. *Rental:* Ivy Films. *Sale:* Rep Pic Film & Nostalgia Merchant.

Days of Our Years. Directed by Denise Tual & Roland Tual. Fr. 1951. France. (Documentary). 81 min. Sound. 16mm B&W. subtitles. *Rental:* Kit Parker. *Sale:* Kit Parker.

Days of Thrills & Laughter. 1961. Fox. (Anthology). 93 min. Sound. 16mm B&W. *Rental:* Budget Films, Charard Motion Pics, Films Inc, Kit Parker, Modern Sound, Roas Films, Twyman Films, Video Comm, Viewfinders, Welling Motion Pictures, Wholesome Film Ctr & Willoughby Peer. *Lease:* Carousel Films. *Rental:* Ivy Films, *Sale:* Ivy Films, Super 8 sound version, Sound 8mm version.

Days of Water. Idalia Anreus. Directed by Manuel Octavio Gomez. Span. 1971. Cuba. 110 min. Sound. 16mm Color. subtitles. *Rental:* Tricontinental Film.

Days the World Went Mad, The. 1965. Britain. (Documentary). 52 min. Sound. 16mm B&W. *Rental:* Time-Life Multimedia. *Sale:* Time-Life Multimedia. *Rental:* Time-Life Multimedia, *Sale:* Time-Life Multimedia, Videotape version.

Dayton's Devils. Rory Calhoun & Lainie Kazan. Directed by Jack Shea. 1968. Commonealth United. 107 min. Sound. 16mm Color. *Rental:* Ivy Films, Kerr Film, Rep Pic Film, Video Comm, Welling Motion Pictures & Willoughby Peer. *Lease:* Rep Pic Film.

De America Soy Hijo: Y a Ella Me Debo. Trans. Title: I Am the Son of America. Directed by Santiago Alvarez. 1975. Cuba. 188 min. Sound. 16mm B&W. *Rental:* Unifilm. *Sale:* Unifilm.

De Hombre a Hombre. Enrique Muno. Directed by Hugo Fregonese. Span. 1950. Mexico. 92 min. Sound. 16mm B&W. subtitles. *Rental:* Film Classics.

De Kooning on De Kooning. 1982. 58 min. Sound. Color. *Rental:* Direct Cinema. *Sale:* Direct Cinema. *Rental:* Direct Cinema, Videotape version.

De La Part Des Copains *see* Cold Sweat.

De Lorean. 1979-81. 53 min. Sound. 16mm Color. *Rental:* Pennebaker.

De Sade. Kier Dullea & John Huston. Directed by Cy Endfield. 1969. American International. 113 min. Sound. 16mm Color. *Rental:* Budget Films, Films Inc & Video Comm.

Dead Are Alive, The. Alex Cord, Samantha Eggar & John Marley. Directed by Armando Crispino. 1972. National General. 98 min. Sound. 16mm Color. *Rental:* Swank Motion.

Dead Birds. Directed by Robert Gardner. 1963. Phoenix. (Documentary). 83 min. Sound. 16mm Color. *Rental:* Budget Films, BYU Media, Images Film, Iowa Films, McGraw-Hill Films, Phoenix Films, Syracuse U Film, U Cal Media & U Mich Media. *Sale:* McGraw-Hill Films & Phoenix Films.

Dead Don't Dream, The. William Boyd. Directed by George Archainbaud. 1948. United Artists. 62 min. Sound. 16mm B&W. *Sale:* Cinema Concepts.

Dead End. Joel McCrea & Humphrey Bogart. Directed by William Wyler. 1937. United Artists. 92 min. Sound. 16mm B&W. *Rental:* Films Inc & Wholesome Film Ctr.

Dead Eyes of London. Dieter Borsche. Directed by Alfred Vohrer. 1965. Germany. 108 min. Sound. 16mm B&W. dubbed. *Rental:* Films Inc.

Dead Heat see Savage Season.

Dead Heat on a Merry-Go-Round. James Coburn & Camilla Sparv. Directed by Bernard Girard. 1966. Columbia. 104 min. Sound. 16mm Color. *Rental:* Arcus Film, Buchan Pic, Cine Craft, Charard Motion Pics, Films Inc, Inst Cinema, Modern Sound, Welling Motion Pictures, Westcoast Films & Wholesome Film Ctr.

Dead Man's Gulch. Don Barry. Directed by John English. 1943. Republic. 55 min. Sound. 16mm B&W. *Rental:* Ivy Films. *Sale:* Rep Pic Film.

Dead Man's Trail. Johnny Mack Brown. Directed by Lewis D. Collins. 1952. Monogram. 54 min. Sound. 16mm B&W. *Rental:* Hurlock Cine.

Dead Men Don't Wear Plaid. Steve Martin & Rachel Ward. Directed by Carl Reiner. Universal. 89 min. Sound. 16mm B&W. *Rental:* Swank Motion. *Rental:* Swank Motion, Videotape version.

Dead Men Tell. Sidney Toler. Directed by Harry Lachman. 1941. Fox. 65 min. Sound. 16mm B&W. *Rental:* Films Inc.

Dead Men Walk. George Zucco & Mary Carlisle. Directed by Sam Newfield. 1944. PRC. 65 min. Sound. 16mm B&W. *Sale:* Classic Film Mus. *Rental:* Budget Films.

Dead of Night. Michael Redgrave & Mervyn Johns. Directed by Alberto Cavalcanti. 1945. Great Britain. 98 min. Sound. 16mm B&W. *Rental:* Budget Films.

Dead or Alive. Tex Ritter & Dave O'Brien. Directed by Elmer Clifton. 1944. PRC. 56 min. Sound. 16mm B&W. *Rental:* Budget Films & Ivy Films. *Sale:* Classics Assoc NY & Rep Pic Film.

Dead Pigeon on Beethoven Street. Glenn Corbett. Directed by Samuel Fuller. 1973. Germany. 102 min. Sound. 16mm Color. dubbed. *Rental:* Films Inc & Westcoast Films.

Dead Reckoning. Humphrey Bogart & Lisabeth Scott. Directed by John Cromwell. 1947. Columbia. 100 min. Sound. 16mm B&W. *Rental:* Bosco Films, Budget Films, Films Inc, Kit Parker, Modern Sound, U of IL Film, Welling Motion Pictures, Westcoast Films & Willoughby Films.

Dead Ringer. Bette Davis & Peter Lawford. Directed by Paul Henried. 1964. Warners. 116 min. Sound. 16mm B&W. *Rental:* Films Inc, Swank Motion & Twyman Films.

Dead Run. Peter Lawford & Ira Furstenburg. Directed by Christian-Jaque. 1969. Universal. 98 min. Sound. 16mm Color. *Rental:* Swank Motion.

Dead Sea Lives, The. 1980. Britain. (Documentary). 57 min. Sound. 16mm Color. *Rental:* Time-Life Multimedia. *Sale:* Time-Life Multimedia. *Sale:* Time-Life Multimedia, Videotape version.

Dead Zone, The. Christopher Walken & Martin Sheen. Directed by David Cronenberg. 1983. Paramount. 104 min. Sound. 16mm Color. *Rental:* Films Inc. *Sale:* Tamarelles French Film, Videotape version.

Deadfall. Michael Caine & Eric Portman. Directed by Bryan Forbes. 1968. Fox. 120 min. Sound. 16mm Color. *Rental:* Films Inc.

Deadlier Than the Male. Richard Johnson & Elke Sommer. Directed by Ralph Thomas. 1967. Britain. 98 min. Sound. 16mm Color. *Rental:* Swank Motion.

Deadline. Sunset Carson. 1948. Astor. 60 min. Sound. 16mm B&W. *Sale:* Natl Cinema.

Deadline at Dawn. Susan Hayward & Paul Lukas. Directed by Harold Clurman. 1946. RKO. 82 min. Sound. 16mm B&W. *Rental:* Films Inc. *Lease:* Films Inc.

Deadline U.S.A. Humphrey Bogart & Kim Hunter. Directed by Richard Brooks. 1952. Fox. 87 min. Sound. 16mm B&W. *Rental:* Films Inc.

Deadlock. Cecile Chevreau & John Slater. Directed by Ronald Haines. 1943. Britain. 58 min. Sound. 16mm B&W. *Rental:* Ivy Films. *Sale:* Classics Assoc NY.

Deadly Affair, The. James Mason, Simone Signoret & Maximilian Schell. Directed by Sidney Lumet. 1967. Britain. 107 min. Sound. 16mm Color. *Rental:* Bosco Films, Budget Films, Cine Craft, Charard Motion Pics, Films Inc, Images Film, Inst Cinema, Modern Sound, Video Comm, Welling Motion Pictures, Westcoast Films & Wholesome Film Ctr.

Deadly Bees, The. Suzanna Leigh & Frank Finlay. Directed by Freddie Francis. 1966. Paramount. 84 min. Sound. 16mm Color. *Rental:* Films Inc.

Deadly China Doll. Angela Mao. Directed by Huang Feng. 1973. China. (Anamorphic). 94 min. Sound. 16mm Color. dubbed. *Rental:* MGM United.

Deadly Duo. Craig Hill & Marcia Henderson. Directed by Reginald Le Borg. 1962. United Artists. 69 min. Sound. 16mm B&W. *Rental:* MGM United.

Deadly Eyes. Sam Groom & Sara Botsford. Directed by Robert Clouse. 1983. Warners. 87 min. Sound. 16mm Color. *Rental:* Swank Motion. *Rental:* Swank Motion, Videotape version.

Deadly Fathoms. Directed by M. Harris. 1973. Harris. (Documentary). 93 min. Sound. 16mm Color. *Rental:* Films Inc, Kit Parker, Maljack, Video Comm & Budget Films. *Lease:* Video Comm. *Rental:* Video Comm, *Lease:* Video Comm, Videotape version.

Deadly Force. Wings Hauser & Joyce Ingalls. Directed by Paul Aaron. 1983. Embassy. 96 min. Sound. 16mm Color. *Rental:* Films Inc.

Deadly Hero. Don Murray & Diahann Williams. Directed by Ivan Nagy. 1976. Embassy. 102 min. Sound. 16mm Color. *Rental:* Films Inc.

Deadly Honeymoon. Dack Rambo & Pat Hingle. 1973. MGM. 87 min. Sound. 16mm Color. *Rental:* MGM United.

Deadly Hunt, The. Tony Franciosa & Peter Lawford. Directed by John Newland. 1971. Embassy. 74 min. Sound. 16mm Color. *Rental:* Video Comm.

Deadly Mantis, The. Craig Stevens. Directed by Nathan Juran. 1957. Universal. 98 min. Sound. 16mm B&W. *Rental:* Swank Motion.

Deadly Mantis. David Chiang & Huang Hsing Liu. 101 min. Sound. 16mm *Rental:* WW Enter. *Rental:* WW Enter, Videotape version.

Deadly Ray from Mars see Mars Attacks the World.

Deadly Strike, The. Bruce Li. 92 min. Sound. 16mm Color. *Rental:* BF Video.

Deadly Trackers, The. Richard Harris & Rod Taylor. Directed by Barry Shear. 1973. Warners. 105 min. Sound. 16mm Color. *Rental:* Film Ctr DC.

Deadly Trap, The. Frank Langella & Faye Dunaway. Directed by Rene Clement. 1972. France. 93 min. Sound. 16mm Color. *Rental:* Budget Films & Swank Motion.

Deadly Winds of War, The. 1980. 55 min. Sound. 16mm Color. *Rental:* Utah Media.

Deadwood Seventy Six. Arch Hall Jr. Directed by James Landis. 1965. Rushmore. (Anamorphic). 100 min. Sound. 16mm Color. *Rental:* Ivy Films.

Deaf Smith & Johnny Ears. Anthony Quinn & Franco Nero. Directed by Paolo Cavara. 1973. MGM. 91 min. Sound. 16mm Color. *Rental:* MGM United.

Deal, The. Directed by John Schott & E. J. Vaughn. 1978. (Documentary). 95 min. Sound. 16mm Color. *Rental:* Museum Mod Art. *Lease:* Museum Mod Art.

Deal of the Century. Chevy Chase & Sigourney Weaver. Directed by William Friedkin. 1983. Universal. 98 min. Sound. 16mm Color. *Rental:* Swank Motion. *Sale:* Tamarelles French Film, *Rental:* Swank Motion, Videotape version.

Dealing: Or the Berkeley-to-Boston Forty Brick Lost-Bag Blues. Robert F. Lyons & Barbara Hershey. Directed by Paul Williams. 1972. Warners. 88 min. Sound. 16mm Color. *Rental:* Swank Motion & Twyman Films. *Rental:* Swank Motion, Anamorphic color version.

Dean Martin & Jerry Lewis: Television Party for Muscular Dystrophy. 1950. 105 min. Sound. 16mm *Rental:* Budget Films.

Dear Brat. Mona Freeman & Billy De Wolfe. Directed by William A. Seiter. 1951. Paramount. 82 min. Sound. 16mm B&W. *Rental:* Films Inc.

Dear Brigitte. James Stewart & Glynis Johns. Directed by Henry Koster. 1965. Fox. 100 min. Sound. 16mm Color. *Rental:* Films Inc, Anamorphic version.

Dear Dead Delilah. Agnes Morehead & Will Geer. Directed by John Farris. 1975. Southern Star. 87 min. Videotape Color. *Sale:* Cinema Concepts & Video Lib.

Dear Irene. Mette Knudsen. Directed by Braad Thomsen. Danish. 1970. Denmark. 100 min. Sound. 16mm B&W. subtitles. *Rental:* Film Images.

Dear John. Jarl Kulle. Directed by Lars Magnus Lindgren. Swed. 1966. Sweden. 115 min. Sound. 16mm B&W. subtitles Eng. *Rental:* Films Inc.

Dear Ruth. William Holden & Joan Caulfield. Directed by William D. Russell. 1947. Paramount. 95 min. Sound. 16mm B&W. *Rental:* Swank Motion.

Dear Wife. William Holden & Joan Caulfield. Directed by Richard Haydn. 1949. Paramount. 88 min. Sound. 16mm B&W. *Rental:* Films Inc.

Deardevils! Verve. 52 min. Videotape Color. *Rental:* Films Inc.

Death. 1971. Family of Man. (Documentary). 50 min. Sound. 16mm Color. *Rental:* Films Inc. *Sale:* Films Inc. *Rental:* Films Inc, *Sale:* Films Inc, Videotape version.

Death Be Not Proud. Robby Benson & Arthur Hill. Directed by Donald Wrye. 1974. CBS. 81 min. Sound. 16mm Color. *Rental:* Budget Films, Kent St U Film, Kit Parker, Learning Corp Am, Twyman Films, U of IL Film & Westcoast Films. *Sale:* Mass Media. *Lease:* Learning Corp Am. *Rental:* Learning Corp Am, *Lease:* Learning Corp Am, Videotape version.

Death by Hanging. Directed by Nagisa Oshima. Jap. 1968. 114 min. Sound. 16mm B&W. subtitles Eng. *Rental:* New Yorker Films.

Death by Someone's Choice. 50 min. Sound. 16mm Color. *Rental:* Gospel Films.

Death Dimension. Jim Kelly, George Lazenby & Harold Odd Job Sakata. 87 min. Sound. 16mm Color. *Rental:* BF Video.

Death Dream. 88 min. Sound. Videotape Color. *Rental:* Maljack.

Death Drums of New Guinea. (Documentary). Sound. 16mm B&W. *Rental:* Film Classics. *Rental:* Film Classics. *Rental:* Film Classics, Videotape version.

Death Games. Lou Brown & David Clendinning. Directed by Mike Williams & Frank Gardiner. 78 min. Sound. Videotape Color. *Sale:* Vidamerica.

Death Goddess, The. 1971. Japan. (Opera). 60 min. Sound. 16mm B&W. *Sale:* Japan Society. *Sale:* Japan Society, Videotape version.

Death Hunt. Charles Bronson & Lee Marvin. Directed by Peter Hunt. 1981. Fox. 97 min. Sound. 16mm Color. *Rental:* Films Inc.

Death in Small Doses. Peter Graves & Chuck Connors. Directed by Joseph Newman. 1957. Allied Artists. 79 min. Sound. 16mm B&W. *Rental:* Hurlock Cine.

Death in the Air *see* Pilot X.

Death in the Garden. Simone Signoret & Michel Piccoli. Directed by Luis Bunuel. 1956. Fox. 97 min. Sound. 16mm Color. *Rental:* Films Inc.

Death in the Morning. 1978. Connections. (Documentary). 53 min. Sound. 16mm Color. *Rental:* Iowa Films, Kent St U Film, U Cal Media, U of IL Film & U Mich Media, Videotape version.

Death in Venice. Dirk Bogarde & Sylvana Mangano. Directed by Luchino Visconti. 1971. Warners. 130 min. Sound. 16mm Color. *Rental:* Swank Motion. *Rental:* Swank Motion, Videotape version.

Death is a Number. Terence Alexander. Directed by Robert Henryson. 1951. Britain. 50 min. Sound. 16mm B&W. *Rental:* Film Classics.

Death Journey. Fred Williamson & Bernard Kuby. Directed by Fred Williamson. 1976. Coast Industries. 86 min. Sound. 16mm Color. *Rental:* Films Inc. *Rental:* Films Inc, Anamorphic version.

Death Kiss, The. Bela Lugosi & David Manners. Directed by Edwin L. Marin. 1933. World Wide. 75 min. Sound. 16mm B&W. *Rental:* Budget Films & Films Inc. *Sale:* Classic Film Mus & Cinema Concepts. *Rental:* Ivy Films, *Sale:* Ivy Films, Super 8 sound version.

Death Machines. Michael Chong & Ron Marchini. Directed by Paul Kyriazi. 1976. Crown. 90 min. Sound. 16mm Color. *Rental:* Films Inc.

Death of a Bureaucrat, The. Directed by Tomas Gutierrez Alea. Span. 1966. 87 min. Sound. 16mm B&W. subtitles Eng. *Rental:* New Yorker Films.

Death of a Cyclist, The. Orig. Title: Age of Infidelity. Lucia Bose. Directed by Juan Bardem. Span. 1958. Spain. 86 min. Sound. 16mm B&W. subtitles. *Rental:* Films Inc & Janus Films.

Death of a Disease, The. 1976. Nova. (Documentary). 58 min. Sound. 16mm Color. *Rental:* Time-Life Multimedia. *Sale:* Time-Life Multimedia. *Rental:* Time-Life Multimedia, *Sale:* Time-Life Multimedia, Videotape version.

Death of a Friend. Gianni Garko & Spiros Focas. Directed by Franco Rossi. Ital. 1960. Italy. 95 min. Sound. 16mm B&W. subtitles Eng. *Rental:* Films Inc.

Death of a Gunfighter, The. Richard Widmark & Lena Horne. Directed by Allen Smithee. 1969. Universal. 97 min. Sound. 16mm Color. *Rental:* Swank Motion.

Death of a Legend, The. 1971. Canada. (Documentary). 51 min. Sound. 16mm Color. *Rental:* Iowa Films & Natl Film CN. *Sale:* Natl Film CN. *Rental:* Natl Film CN, *Sale:* Natl Film CN, Videotape version.

Death of a Princess. 1980. 118 min. Sound. Videotape *Rental:* PBS Video. *Sale:* PBS Video.

Death of a Scoundrel, The. George Sanders & Zsa Zsa Gabor. Directed by Charles Martin. 1956. RKO. 119 min. Sound. 16mm B&W. *Rental:* Budget Films, Kit Parker, Video Comm & Westcoast Films. *Lease:* Video Comm. *Rental:* Video Comm, *Lease:* Video Comm, Videotape version.

Death of Alex Litsky, The. 1969. 52 min. Sound. 16mm Color. *Rental:* Canyon Cinema.

Death of Richie, The. Ben Gazzara, Robby Benson & Eileen Brennan. Directed by Paul Wendkos. 1976. Learning Corp. 97 min. Sound. 16mm Color. *Rental:* U of IL Film, Kit Parker, Learning Corp Am, Twyman Films & Budget Films. *Lease:* Learning Corp Am. *Rental:* Learning Corp Am, *Lease:* Learning Corp Am, Videotape version.

Death of Socrates, The. 1967. Britain. (Cast unlisted). 45 min. Sound. 16mm B&W. *Rental:* U Mich Media. *Sale:* Time-Life Multimedia.

Death of Stalin, The. 1963. NBC. (Documentary). 54 min. Sound. 16mm B&W. *Rental:* BYU Media, McGraw-Hill Films & Syracuse U Film. *Sale:* McGraw-Hill Films.

Death of the Ape Man, The. Rudolf Hrusinsky & Jana Stepankova. Directed by Jaroslav Balik. 1962. 72 min. Sound. 16mm B&W. *Rental:* Films Inc.

Death on the Diamond. Robert Young & Madge Evans. Directed by Edward Sedgwick. 1934. MGM. 72 min. Sound. 16mm B&W. *Rental:* MGM United.

Death on the Highway. 1965. NET. (Documentary). 60 min. Sound. 16mm B&W. *Rental:* BYU Media & Syracuse U Film.

Death on the Nile. Bette Davis, Angela Lansbury, Peter Ustinov & Mia Farrow. Directed by John Guillermin. 1978. Paramount. 140 min. Sound. 16mm Color. *Rental:* Films Inc.

Death on the Set. Henry Kendall & Jeanne Stuart. Directed by Leslie Hiscott. 1936. Britain. 72 min. Sound. 16mm B&W. *Rental:* Film Classics.

Death Penalty, The. 1967. New World. (Documentary). 60 min. Sound. 16mm B&W. *Rental:* Time-Life Multimedia. *Sale:* Time-Life Multimedia.

Death Race Two Thousand. David Carradine. Directed by Roger Corman. 1975. New World. 78 min. Sound. 16mm Color. *Rental:* Films Inc.

Death Riders. Crown. (Documentary). 88 min. Sound. 16mm Color. *Rental:* Films Inc.

Death Rides a Horse. Lee Van Cleef & John Philip Law. Directed by Giulio Petroni. 1969. Italy. 115 min. Sound. 16mm Color. dubbed. *Rental:* MGM United.

Death Rides the Range. Ken Maynard. Directed by Sam Newfield. 1940. Colony. 57 min. Sound. 16mm B&W. *Sale:* Morcraft Films. *Sale:* Video Comm, Videotape version.

Death Row. 1971. Britain. (Documentary). 49 min. Sound. 16mm Color. *Rental:* Time-Life Multimedia. *Sale:* Time-Life Multimedia.

Death Ship. George Kennedy & Richard Crenna. Directed by Alvin Rakoff. 1980. Embassy. 91 min. Sound. 16mm Color. *Rental:* Films Inc.

Death Sport. David Carradine & Claudia Jennings. Directed by Henry Suso & Allan Arkush. 1978. New World. 83 min. Sound. 16mm Color. *Rental:* Films Inc.

Death Takes a Holiday. Fredric March & Evelyn Venable. Directed by Mitchell Leisen. 1935. 84 min. Sound. 16mm B&W. *Rental:* Swank Motion.

Death Valley. Paul LeMat, Catherine Hicks & Peter Billingsley. Directed by Dick Richards. 90 min. Sound. 16mm Color. *Rental:* Swank Motion. *Rental:* Swank Motion, Videotape version.

Death Valley Gunfighter. Allan Lane. Directed by R. G. Springsteen. 1949. Republic. 60 min. Sound. 16mm B&W. *Rental:* Ivy Films. *Sale:* Rep Pic Film & Nostalgia Merchant.

Death Valley Manhunt. Bill Elliott. Directed by John English. 1943. Republic. 55 min. Sound. 16mm B&W. *Rental:* Ivy Films. *Sale:* Rep Pic Film & Nostalgia Merchant.

Death Valley Outlaws. Don Barry. Directed by George Sherman. 1941. Republic. 54 min. Sound. 16mm B&W. *Rental:* Ivy Films. *Sale:* Rep Pic Film.

Death Watch. Romy Schneider & Harvey Keitel. Directed by Bertrand Tavernier. 1982. QFI. 110 min. Sound. 16mm Color. *Rental:* Films Inc.

Death Wish. Charles Bronson, Jill Ireland & Vincent Gardenia. Directed by Michael Winner. 1974. 93 min. Sound. 16mm Color. *Rental:* Films Inc & Swank Motion.

Deathmaster. Robert Quarry & Bill Ewing. Directed by Ray Danton. 1972. American International. 88 min. Sound. 16mm Color. *Rental:* Swank Motion.

Deathstyles. Directed by Richard Myers. 1972. American Film Institute. (Experimental). 50 min. Sound. 16mm Color. *Rental:* Time-Life Multimedia & Canyon Cinema. *Sale:* Time-Life Multimedia.

Deathtrap. Michael Caine & Christopher Reeve. Directed by Sidney Lumet. 1982. Warners. 115 min. Sound. 16mm Color. *Rental:* Swank Motion. *Rental:* Swank Motion, Videotape version.

Debate: Is School Desegregation Working?. 1979. PBS. (Documentary). 59 min. Videotape Color. *Rental:* PBS Video. *Sale:* PBS Video.

Decade of Decision. Directed by Dirk Ross. 1961. World Wide. (Documentary). 65 min. Sound. 16mm B&W. *Rental:* Roas Films.

Decameron, The. Franco Citti. Directed by Pier Paolo Pasolini. Ital. 1972. Italy. 111 min. Sound. 16mm Color. subtitles. *Rental:* MGM United.

Decameron Nights. Louis Jourdan & Joan Fontaine. Directed by Hugo Fregonese. 1953. Britain. 85 min. Sound. 16mm Color. *Rental:* Liberty Co.

Deceased, The. Directed by Leon Hirszman. Port. 1965. Brazil. (Cast unlisted). 110 min. Sound. 16mm B&W. subtitles. *Rental:* New Yorker Films.

Deceived Two. Mel White. 45 min. Sound. 16mm Color. *Rental:* Gospel Films.

Deceiver, The. 1973. Ken Anderson. (Cast unlisted). 70 min. Sound. 16mm Color. *Rental:* G Herne & Roas Films.

December. Jacques Godin. Directed by Jean-Paul Fugere. Fr. 1978. Canada. 90 min. Sound. 16mm Color. subtitles. *Rental:* Natl Film CN. *Sale:* Natl Film CN.

December Seventh: Day of Infamy. 1963. Wolper. (Documentary). 50 min. Sound. 16mm B&W. *Rental:* BYU Media, Films Inc, Utah Media & Wholesome Film Ctr. *Sale:* Films Inc. *Sale:* Films Inc, Videotape version.

December Seventh: The Attack on Pearl Harbor. 1963. Wolper. (Documentary). 55 min. Sound. 16mm B&W. *Rental:* Films Inc. *Sale:* Films Inc.

Deception. Bette Davis & Claude Rains. Directed by Irving Rapper. 1946. Warners. 112 min. Sound. 16mm B&W. *Rental:* MGM United.

Decision Against Time. Orig. Title: Man in the Sky. Jack Hawkins & Elizabeth Sellers. Directed by Charles Crichton. 1957. Britain. 87 min. Sound. 16mm B&W. *Rental:* MGM United.

Decision at Sundown. Randolph Scott & John Carroll. Directed by Budd Boetticher. 1957. Columbia. 77 min. Sound. 16mm B&W. *Rental:* Budget Films & Kit Parker. *Rental:* Budget Films, 81 mins. version.

Decision Before Dawn. Oskar Werner & Richard Basehart. Directed by Anatole Litvak. 1952. Fox. 120 min. Sound. 16mm B&W. *Rental:* Films Inc.

Decision Making & Management Process in Family Practice. 1979. 55 min. videotape *Sale:* Natl AV Ctr.

Decision of Christopher Blake, The. Alexis Smith & Robert Douglas. Directed by Peter Godfrey. 1948. Warners. 75 min. Sound. 16mm B&W. *Rental:* MGM United.

Decision to Drop the Bomb, The. 1965. NBC. (Documentary). 81 min. Sound. 16mm B&W. *Rental:* Films Inc & Syracuse U Film. *Sale:* Film Inc. *Sale:* Films Inc, Videotape version.

Decision to Win, The. 1981. 75 min. 16mm Color. *Rental:* Icarus Films. *Sale:* Icarus Films, Videotape version.

Decks Ran Red, The. James Mason & Dorothy Dandridge. Directed by Andrew Stone. 1958. MGM. 84 min. Sound. 16mm B&W. *Rental:* MGM United.

Decline & Fall of a Bird Watcher. Robin Philips & Genevieve Page. Directed by John Krish. 1969. Fox. 113 min. Sound. 16mm Color. *Rental:* Films Inc.

Decline of Western Civilization, The. 1981. Nulmage. (Documentary, color sequences). 100 min. Sound. 16mm *Rental:* Corinth Films.

Decoy. Edward Norris & Jean Gilles. Directed by Jack Bernhard. 1946. Monogram. 76 min. Sound. 16mm B&W. *Rental:* Hurlock Cine.

Decoy. Orig. Title: Mystery Submarine. 1961. 16mm *Rental:* A Twyman Pres.

Deeds of Daring. George Larkin. 50 min. Silent. 8mm B&W. *Sale:* E Finney.

Deep, The. Robert Shaw, Jacqueline Bisset & Nick Nolte. Directed by Peter Yates. 1977. Columbia. 123 min. Sound. 16mm Color. *Rental:* Arcus Film, Bosco Films, Budget Films, Cine Craft, Films Inc, Modern Sound, Newman Film Lib, Swank Motion, Twyman Films, Welling Motion Pictures, Westcoast Films, Wholesome Film Ctr, Williams Films & Images Film. *Rental:* Images Film, Anamorphic version. *Rental:* Swank Motion, Videotape version.

Deep Blue Sea. Vivien Leigh & Kenneth More. Directed by Anatole Litvak. 1955. Fox. 99 min. Sound. 16mm Color. *Rental:* Films Inc.

Deep Cold War, The. 1980. Britain. (Documentary). 50 min. Sound. 16mm Color. *Rental:* Films Inc & U Mich Media. *Sale:* Films Inc. *Rental:* Films Inc, *Sale:* Films Inc, Videotape version.

Deep End. John Moulder-Brown, Jane Asher & Diana Dors. Directed by Jerzy Skolimowski. 1971. Britain. 88 min. Sound. 16mm Color. *Rental:* Films Inc.

Deep Hearts. 53 min. Sound. 16mm Color. *Rental:* Phoenix Films. *Sale:* Phoenix Films. *Sale:* Phoenix Films, Videotape version.

Deep in My Heart. Jose Ferrer & Merle Oberon. Directed by Stanley Donen. 1954. MGM. 132 min. Sound. 16mm Color. *Rental:* MGM United.

Deep Red. David Hemmings & Daria Nicolodi. Directed by Dario Argento. 1975. Italy. 98 min. Sound. 16mm Color. *Rental:* Films Inc.

Deep Sea Diving: The Diving Dress. 1944. US Government. (Documentary). 48 min. Sound. 16mm B&W. *Sale:* Natl AV Ctr.

Deep Six, The. Alan Ladd, William Bendix & Keenan Wynn. Directed by Rudolph Mate. 1958. Warners. 108 min. Sound. 16mm Color. *Rental:* Budget Films, Video Comm & Westcoast Films. *Lease:* Video Comm. *Rental:* Video Comm, *Lease:* Video Comm, Videotape version.

Deep Thrust. Angela Mao. Directed by Huang Feng. 1973. American International. 88 min. Sound. 16mm Color. dubbed. *Rental:* Swank Motion.

Deep Valley. Ida Lupino & Dane Clark. Directed by Jean Negulesco. 1947. Warners. 104 min. Sound. 16mm B&W. *Rental:* MGM UNited.

Deep Waters. Dana Andrews & Jean Peters. Directed by Henry King. 1948. Fox. 86 min. Sound. 16mm B&W. *Rental:* Films Inc.

Deer Hunter, The. Robert DeNiro, Meryl Streep & John Savage. Directed by Michael Cimino. 183 min. Sound. 16mm Color. *Rental:* Swank Motion. *Rental:* Swank Motion, Videotape version.

Deerslayer, The. Directed by Arthur Wellin. 1923. Selznick. (Cast unlisted). 60 min. Silent. 16mm B&W. *Rental:* Film Classics & Mogulls Films. *Sale:* Film Classics. *Sale:* Film Classics, Silent 8mm version.

Deerslayer, The. Lex Barker & Rita Moreno. Directed by Kurt Neumann. 1957. Fox. 78 min. Sound. 16mm Color. *Rental:* #Charard Motion Pics, Ivy Films, Roas Films, Westcoast Films & Welling Motion Pictures. *Lease:* Rep Pic Film.

Deerslayer, The. Steve Forrest. Directed by Dick Friedenberg. 1979. Viacom. 104 min. Sound. 16mm Color. *Rental:* Budget Films, Williams Films, Film Pres & Modern Sound. *Sale:* Lucerne Films. *Sale:* Lucerne Films & Williams Films, Videotape version. *Rental:* Budget Films, 98 mins. version.

Defector, The. Trans. Title: Espion, L'. Montgomery Clift & Hardy Kruger. Directed by Raoul Levy. 1966. Warners. 106 min. Sound. 16mm Color. *Rental:* Charard Motion Pics, Welling Motion Pictures & Willoughby Peer.

Defenders of the Law. Catherine Dale Owen. Directed by Joseph Levering. 1931. Syndicate. 65 min. Sound. 16mm B&W. *Rental:* Mogulls Films.

Defense & Domestic Needs: Contest for Tomorrow. 1969. Public Broadcasting. (Documentary). 77 min. Sound. 16mm B&W. *Rental:* U Cal Media, Color version.

Defense Rests, The. Jack Holt & Jean Arthur. Directed by Lambert Hillyer. 1934. Columbia. 70 min. Sound. 16mm B&W. *Rental:* Kit Parker.

Defiant Ones, The. Tony Curtis & Sidney Poitier. Directed by Stanley Kramer. 1958. United Artists. 97 min. Sound. 16mm B&W. *Rental:* Budget Films, Films Inc, MGM United & Welling Motion Pictures.

Deflections of Love. Japan. (Cast unlisted). 90 min. Sound. 16mm B&W. *Sale:* Japan Society.

Delhi Way, The. Directed by James Ivory. 1966. India. (Documentary). 45 min. Sound. 16mm Color. *Rental:* Film Images, Iowa Films, U Mich Media & Utah Media. *Sale:* Film Images. *Rental:* Utah Media, 1964 version.

Delicate Balance, A. Katharine Hepburn & Paul Scofield. Directed by Tony Richardson. 1973. AFT. 132 min. Sound. 16mm Color. *Rental:* Films Inc.

Delicate Delinquent, The. Jerry Lewis. Directed by Don McGuire. 1957. Paramount. 101 min. Sound. 16mm B&W. *Rental:* Films Inc.

Delicious. Janet Gaynor & Charles Farrell. Directed by David Butler. 1931. Fox. 106 min. Sound. 16mm B&W. *Rental:* Films Inc.

Delightful Rogue, The. Rod LaRocque & Bebe Daniels. Directed by Leslie Pierce. 1930. RKO. 73 min. Sound. 16mm *Rental:* RKO General Pics.

Delightfully Dangerous. Jane Powell & Ralph Bellamy. Directed by Arthur Lubin. 1945. United Artists. 90 min. Sound. 16mm B&W. *Rental:* Budget Films.

Delinquents, The. Sacha Distel & Bernadette Lafont. Directed by Rene Jolivet. 1960. France. 96 min. Sound. 16mm B&W. dubbed. *Rental:* Films Inc, Macmillan Films & Video Comm. *Sale:* Macmillan Films.

Deliver Us from Evil: Joey. Lloyd Bridges, Dina Merrill & Pat Hingle. Directed by Robert McCahon. 1975. Dimenison. 104 min. Sound. 16mm Color. *Sale:* Salz Ent.

Delta Blues Singer: James Sonny Ford Thomas. 1970. 45 min. Sound. 16mm B&W. *Rental:* Films Inc.

Deluge, The. Lew Ayres & Rita Gam. Directed by James L. Conway. 1979. NBC. 50 min. Sound. 16mm Color. *Rental:* Budget Films, Modern Sound & Roas Films. *Sale:* Lucerne Films. *Sale:* Lucerne Films, Videotape version.

Deluge, The. Stephen Elliott & Barry Williams. Directed by Jack Hively. 1970. 50 min. Sound. 16mm Color. *Rental:* Budget Films.

Deluge & Noah's Ark, The. 1980. Lucerne. 50 min. Sound. 16mm Color. *Rental:* Films Inc & Syracuse U Film.

Delusions of Grandeur. Yves Montand & Louis De Funes. Directed by Gerard Oury. Fr. 1975. France. 85 min. Sound. 16mm Color. subtitles. *Rental:* J Green Pics. *Sale:* Tamarelles French Film, Videotape version.

Deluxe Annie. Norma Talmadge. Directed by Roland West. 1918. 16mm *Rental:* A Twyman Pres.

Dementia. Adrienne Barrett. Directed by John Parker. 1955. Van Wolf. 55 min. Sound. 16mm B&W. *Rental:* A Twyman Pres & Twyman Films.

Dementia Thirteen. Orig. Title: Haunted & the Hunted, The. Patrick McGee & William Campbell. Directed by Francis Ford Coppola. 1963. Britain. 81 min. Sound. 16mm B&W. *Rental:* Budget Films, Em Gee Film Lib, Films Inc, Ivy Films & Natl Film Video Comm. *Sale:* Natl Cinema & Reel Images. *Sale:* Tamarelles French Film & Video Comm, Videotape version. *Sale:* Reel Images, Super 8 sound version.

Demetrius & the Gladiators. Victor Mature & Susan Hayward. Directed by Delmer Daves. 1954. Fox. 101 min. Sound. 16mm Color. *Rental:* Films Inc. *Rental:* Films Inc, Anamorphic color version.

Demeure Mysterieuse, La. George Descrieres. Directed by Jean-Pierre Desagnat. 1971. France. 53 min. Sound. 16mm Color. *Rental:* French Am Cul.

Demi Paradise. Sir Laurence Olivier, Penelope Ward & Felix Aylmer. 1945. Brtain. 114 min. Sound. 16mm B&W. *Rental:* Budget Films & Janus Films. *Sale:* Morcraft Films, Super 8 Sound version.

Democracy & Dissent. 2 pts. 1977. Macmillan. (Documentary). 112 min. Sound. 16mm Color. *Rental:* Syracuse U Film.

Democracy in America: A Conversation with Henry Steele Commager. 1979. WNET. (Documentary). 58 min. Videotape Color. *Rental:* WNET Media. *Sale:* WNET Media.

Democracy, Leadership & Commitment. 1976. Britain. (Documentary). 60 min. Sound. 16mm Color. *Rental:* Film Inc, Syracuse U Film, U Cal Media & U of IL Film. *Sale:* Films Inc. *Sale:* Films Inc, Videotape version.

Democrat & the Dictator, The. 58 min. Sound. Videotape *Rental:* PBS Video. *Sale:* PBS Video.

Demon, The. Cameron Mitchell & Jennifer Holmes. Directed by Percival Rubens. 1981. 94 min. Sound. 16mm Color. *Rental:* Budget Films.

Demon Barber of Fleet Street, The. Tod Slaughter & Eve Lister. Directed by George King. 1939. Britain. 68 min. Sound. 16mm B&W. *Rental:* Budget Films.

Demon for Trouble. Bob Steele. Directed by Robert Hill. 1934. Steiner. 61 min. Sound. 16mm B&W. *Rental:* Budget Films.

Demon Planet, The see Planet of the Vampires.

Demon Pond. Directed by Masahiro Shinoda. Jap. 1980. 123 min. Sound. 16mm Color. subtitles Eng. *Rental:* New Yorker Films.

Demon Seed. Julie Christie & Fritz Weaver. Directed by Donald Cammell. 1977. MGM. (Anamorphic). 95 min. Sound. 16mm Color. *Rental:* MGM United.

Demons. Directed by Toshio Matsumoto. Jap. 1972. Japan. (Cast unlisted). 135 min. Sound. 16mm B&W. subtitles. *Rental:* Film Images.

Demons of the Mind. Patrick Magee & Michael Hordern. Directed by Peter Sykes. 1971. Britain. 89 min. Sound. 16mm Color. *Rental:* Corinth Films.

Denise: The Tragedy of Child Abuse. 1980. ABC. (Documentary). 58 min. Sound. 16mm Color. *Sale:* MTI Tele. *Sale:* MTI Tele. *Sale:* MTI Tele, Videotape version.

Dentist in the Chair. Kenneth Connor & Peggy Cummins. Directed by C. M. Pennington-Richards. 1961. Britain. 88 min. Sound. 16mm B&W. *Rental:* Inst Cinema.

Dentist on the Job see Get On With It.

Denver & the Rio Grande, The. Edmond O'Brien & Sterling Hayden. Directed by Byron Haskin. 1952. Paramount. 89 min. Sound. 16mm Color. *Rental:* Films Inc.

Denver Kid, The. Allan Lane. Directed by Philip Ford. 1948. Republic. 60 min. Sound. 16mm B&W. *Rental:* Ivy Films. *Sale:* Rep Pic Film.

Deported. Jeff Chandler & Marta Toren. Directed by Robert Siodmak. 1950. Universal. 80 min. Sound. 16mm B&W. *Rental:* Swank Motion.

Depression: The Shadowed Valley. 1975. PBS. (Documentary). 59 min. Sound. 16mm Color. *Rental:* Indiana AV Ctr, Iowa Films, Syracuse U Film & U Cal Media. *Sale:* Indiana AV Ctr.

Deputy, The see Diputado.

Deputy Drummer. Lupino Lane. Directed by Henry W. George. 1935. Britain. 75 min. Sound. 16mm B&W. *Rental:* Mogulls Films.

Deputy Marshal. Jon Hall & Frances Langford. Directed by William Berke. 1950. Lippert. 75 min. Sound. 16mm B&W. *Rental:* Budget Films.

Der Bajazzo see Pagliacci.

Der Spieler. Renee Adoree & Alan Hale. Directed by Tay Garnett. 1929. Pathe. 60 min. Silent. 16mm B&W. *Rental:* Budget Films, Em Gee Film Lib & Films Inc.

Deranged. Roberts Blossom. Directed by Jeff Gillen & Alan Ormsby. 1974. American International. 82 min. Sound. 16mm Color. *Rental:* Swank Motion.

Derby. Charlie O'Connell & Joan Weston. Directed by Robert Kaylor. 1971. Cinerama. 91 min. Sound. 16mm Color. *Rental:* Swank Motion.

Dermatology in General Medicine. 1980. 55 min. videotape *Sale:* Natl AV Ctr.

Dernieres Vacances, Les. Odile Versois & Pierre Dux. Directed by Roger Leenhardt. Fr. 1947. France. 95 min. Sound. 16mm B&W. subtitles. *Rental:* Freanch Am Cul.

Dersu Uzala. Directed by Akira Kurosawa. Jap. 1975. Japan-Russia. (Cast unlisted). 137 min. Sound. 16mm Color. subtitles. *Rental:* Films Inc.

Descendants, The: Nehru. Directed by Serge Friendman. 1972. United Artists. 55 min. Sound. 16mm Color. *Rental:* Budget Films.

Descendants of Graham Bell, The. Directed by Victor Vicas. 1972. AIF. (Documentary). 60 min. Sound. 16mm B&W. *Sale:* Americas Films. *Sale:* Americas Films, Color version. *Sale:* Americas Films, Spanish version.

Descendants, The: Tolstoy. 55 min. Sound. 16mm *Rental:* Budget Films.

Desde el Abismo. Thelma Biral, Alberto Argibay & Olga Zubarry. Spain. 115 min. Sound. Videotape Color. *Sale:* Tamarelles French Films.

Desert, The. Directed by Hugh Raggett. 1974. Britain. (Documentary). 60 min. Sound. 16mm Color. *Rental:* U Cal Media.

Desert Attack *see* Ice Cold in Alex.

Desert Bandit, The. Don Barry. Directed by George Sherman. 1941. Republic. 54 min. Sound. 16mm B&W. *Rental:* Ivy Films. *Sale:* Rep Pic Film.

Desert Fox, The. James Mason, Sir Cedric Hardwicke. Directed by Henry Hathaway. 1951. Fox. 91 min. Sound. 16mm B&W. *Rental:* Films Inc.

Desert Furlough. Orig. Title: Furlough in the Desert. Giovanna Ralli. 1958. Italy. 99 min. Sound. 16mm B&W. dubbed. *Rental:* Films Inc.

Desert Fury. Wendell Corey & Lizabeth Scott. Directed by Lewis Allen. 1947. Paramount. 96 min. Sound. 16mm Color. *Rental:* Swank Motion.

Desert Gold. Buster Crabbe. Directed by James Hogan. 1936. Paramount. 60 min. Sound. 16mm B&W. *Sale:* Cinema Concepts & Reel Images. *Rental:* Budget Films.

Desert Guns. Conway Tearle. Directed by Charles Hutchinson. 1934. Beaumont. 60 min. Sound. 16mm B&W. *Rental:* Budget Films, Mogulls Films & Video Comm. *Sale:* Video Comm, Videotape version.

Desert Hawk, The. Yvonne De Carlo & Rock Hudson. Directed by Frederick De Cordova. 1950. Universal. 77 min. Sound. 16mm Color. *Rental:* Swank Motion.

Desert Hell. Brian Keith & Barbara Hale. Directed by Robert Stabler. 1958. Fox. (Anamorphic). 82 min. Sound. 16mm B&W. *Rental:* Willoughby Peer.

Desert Horseman, The. Orig. Title: Checkmate. Charles Starrett. Directed by Ray Nazarro. 1946. Columbia. 56 min. Sound. 16mm B&W. *Rental:* Inst Cinema.

Desert Legion. Alan Ladd & Richard Conte. Directed by Joseph Pevney. 1953. Universal. 86 min. Sound. 16mm B&W. *Rental:* Swank Motion.

Desert, The: North Africa-1940-1943. (World at War Ser.). : Pt. 8.). 1973. Media Guild. (Documentary). 52 min. Sound. 16mm Color. *Rental:* Media Guild. *Sale:* Media Guild. *Sale:* Media Guild, Videotape version.

Desert of Lost Men. Allan Lane. Directed by Harry Keller. 1951. Republic. 54 min. Sound. 16mm B&W. *Rental:* Ivy Films. *Sale:* Rep Pic Film.

Desert of the Tartars, The. Dino Buzzati & Jacques Perrin. Directed by Valerio Zurlini. 1976. Italy. 140 min. Sound. Videotape Color. *Sale:* Tamarelles French Films.

Desert Passage. Tim Holt & Joan Dixon. Directed by Lesley Selander. 1952. RKO. 61 min. Sound. 16mm *Rental:* RKO General Pics.

Desert Patrol. Bob Steele. Directed by Sam Newfield. 1938. Republic. 56 min. Sound. 16mm B&W. *Rental:* Ivy Films & Mogulls Films.

Desert People. 1966. Australia. (Documentary). 51 min. Sound. 16mm B&W. *Rental:* Aust Info Serv, U Cal Media, McGraw-Hill Films, U Mich Media & Syracuse U Film. *Sale:* McGraw-Hill Films.

Desert Pursuit. Wayne Morris & Virginia Grey. Directed by George Blair. 1952. Monogram. 71 min. Sound. 16mm B&W. *Rental:* Hurlock Cine.

Desert Rats. Richard Burton & James Mason. Directed by Robert Wise. 1953. Fox. 88 min. Sound. 16mm B&W. *Rental:* Films Inc.

Desert Trail. John Wayne. Directed by Lewis D. Collins. 1938. Monogram. 61 min. Sound. 16mm B&W. *Rental:* Budget Films, Ivy Films & Mogulls Films. *Sale:* Classics Assoc NY & Rep Pic Film. *Rental:* Ivy Films, *Sale:* Ivy Films, Super 8 sound version. *Sale:* Video Comm, Videotape version.

Desert Victory. Directed by David MacDonald. 1943. Great Britain. 65 min. Sound. 16mm B&W. *Rental:* Budget Films.

Desert Warrior, The. Ricardo Montalban & Gino Cervi. Directed by Fernando Cerchio. 1960. Italy. 87 min. Sound. 16mm B&W. dubbed. *Rental:* Welling Motion Pictures.

Desert Whales. 1970. Churchill Films. (Documentary). 52 min. Sound. 16mm Color. *Rental:* Churchill Films. *Rental:* Churchill Films, Videotape version.

Desert Wooing, The. Jack Holt. Directed by J. G. Hawks. 1916. Paramount. 55 min. Silent. 16mm B&W. *Rental:* Mogulls Films.

Deserter, The. Charles Ray. Directed by Scott Sidney. 1916. Paramount. 59 min. Silent. 16mm B&W. *Rental:* Museum Mod Art.

Deserter, The. Bekim Fehmiu & Richard Crenna. Directed by Burt Kennedy. 1971. Paramount. 99 min. Sound. 16mm B&W. *Rental:* Films Inc.

Deserter, The. Directed by Vsevolod I. Pudovkin. 1933. Russia. (Cast unlisted). 120 min. Sound. 16mm B&W. *Rental:* Museum Mod Art.

Desert's Edge. 1978. 58 min. Sound. Videotape *Rental:* PBS Video. *Sale:* PBS Video.

Design for Living. Gary Cooper, Miriam Hopkins & Fredric March. Directed by Ernst Lubitsch. 1933. 95 min. Sound. 16mm B&W. *Rental:* Swank Motion.

Designing Woman. Gregory Peck & Lauren Bacall. Directed by Vincente Minnelli. 1957. MGM. 117 min. Sound. 16mm Color. *Rental:* MGM United. *Rental:* MGM United, Anamorphic color version. *Rental:* MGM United, Videotape version.

Desirable. George Brent & Jean Muir. Directed by Archie Mayo. 1934. Warners. 68 min. Sound. 16mm B&W. *Rental:* MGM United.

Desirable Lady. Orig. Title: Foolish Girls. Jan Wiley & Paul Warren. Directed by Donald Brodie. 1945. Belmont. 96 min. Sound. 16mm B&W. *Rental:* Film Ctr DC.

Desire. Marlene Dietrich & Gary Cooper. Directed by Frank Borzage. 1936. Paramount. 96 min. Sound. 16mm B&W. *Rental:* Museum Mod Art & Swank Motion.

Desire. Directed by Dominique Delouche. Fr. 1979. France. (Cast unlisted). 90 min. Sound. 16mm B&W. subtitles. *Rental:* Liberty Co.

Desire in the Dust. Raymond Burr & Joan Bennett. Directed by William Claxton. 1960. Fox. 102 min. Sound. 16mm B&W. *Rental:* Films Inc.

Desire Me. Greer Garson & Robert Mitchum. Directed by Arthur Hornblow Jr. 1947. MGM. 91 min. Sound. 16mm B&W. *Rental:* MGM United.

Desire Under the Elms. Sophia Loren, Burl Ives & Anthony Perkins. Directed by Delbert Mann. 1958. Paramount. 111 min. Sound. 16mm B&W. *Rental:* Films Inc.

Desiree. Marlon Brando & Jean Simmons. Directed by Henry Koster. 1954. Fox. 110 min. Sound. 16mm Color. *Rental:* Films Inc.

Desk for Billie, A. 1956. National Education Association. (Documentary). 60 min. Sound. 16mm B&W. *Rental:* U of IL Film & OK AV Ctr.

Desk Set, The. Spencer Tracy & Katharine Hepburn. Directed by Walter Lang. 1957. Fox. (Anamorphic). 104 min. Sound. 16mm Color. *Rental:* Williams Films & Films Inc.

Desordre a Vingt Ans, Le *see* Disorder & Afterwards.

Despair. Dirk Bogarde & Andrea Ferreol. Directed by Rainer Werner Fassbinder. Ger. 1978. Germany. 120 min. Sound. 16mm Color. subtitles. *Rental:* New Line Cinema.

Despair. Directed by Luchino Visconti. 1969. 150 min. Sound. Videotape Color. *Sale:* Festival Films.

Despegue a las Diez y Ocho *see* Takeoff at Eighteen Hundred.

Desperado, The. Wayne Morris & Beverly Garland. Directed by Thomas Carr. 1954. Allied Artists. 81 min. Sound. 16mm B&W. *Rental:* Hurlock Cine.

Desperadoes, The. Randolph Scott & Glenn Ford. Directed by Charles Vidor. 1943. Columbia. 90 min. Sound. 16mm B&W. *Rental:* Films Inc, Westcoast Films & Welling Motion Pictures.

Desperadoes, The. Vince Edwards & Jack Palance. Directed by George Maharis. 1969. Columbia. 90 min. Sound. 16mm Color. *Rental:* Arcus Film, Cine Craft, Charard Motion Pictures & Inst Cinema.

Desperadoes Are in Town, The. Rex Reason & Kathy Nolan. Directed by Kurt Neumann. 1956. Fox. 78 min. Sound. 16mm B&W. *Rental:* Willoughby Peer. *Sale:* Rep Pic Film.

Desperadoes of Dodge City, The. Allan Lane. Directed by Philip Ford. 1948. Republic. 60 min. Sound. 16mm B&W. *Rental:* Ivy Films. *Sale:* Rep Pic Film & Nostalgia Merchant.

Desperadoes Outpost. Allan Lane. Directed by Philip Ford. 1952. Republic. 54 min. Sound. 16mm B&W. *Rental:* Ivy Films. *Sale:* Rep Pic Film.

Desperate. Steve Brodie & Audrey Long. Directed by Anthony Mann. 1947. RKO. 71 min. Sound. 16mm B&W. *Rental:* Films Inc.

Desperate Adventure. Orig. Title: It Happened in Paris. Ramon Navarro & Marion Marsh. Directed by John H. Auer. 1938. Republic. 54 min. Sound. 16mm B&W. *Rental:* Ivy Films.

Desperate Chance. Bob Reeves. Directed by J. P. McGowan. 1926. Rayart. 55 min. Silent. 16mm B&W. *Rental:* Mogulls Films.

Desperate Characters. Shirley MacLaine & Kenneth Mars. Directed by Frank D. Gilroy. 1971. Paramount. 88 min. Sound. 16mm Color. *Rental:* Films Inc.

Desperate Hours, The. Humphrey Bogart & Fredric March. Directed by William Wyler. 1955. Paramount. 112 min. Sound. 16mm B&W. *Rental:* Films Inc.

Desperate Journey. Errol Flynn & Ronald Reagan. Directed by Raoul Walsh. 1942. Paramount. 109 min. Sound. 16mm B&W. *Rental:* MGM United.

Desperate Living. Liz Renay & Mink Stole. Directed by John Waters. New Line Cinema. 90 min. Sound. 16mm Color. *Rental:* New Line Cinema.

Desperate Moment. Dirk Bogarde & Mai Zetterling. Directed by Compton Bennett. 1953. Britain. 88 min. Sound. 16mm B&W. *Rental:* Budget Films.

Desperate Ones. Maximilian Schell & Raf Vallone. Directed by Alexander Ramati. 1968. Commonwealth. 104 min. Sound. 16mm Color. *Rental:* Ivy Films.

Desperate Search. Howard Keel & Jane Greer. Directed by Joseph Lewis. 1952. MGM. 71 min. Sound. 16mm B&W. *Rental:* MGM United.

Desperate Siege *see* Rawhide.

Destination America Series. 9 pts. 1975. Britain. (Documentary). 416 min. Sound. 16mm Color. *Rental:* B Raymond. *Sale:* B Raymond. *Sale:* Media Guild, Videotape version.

Destination Big House. Robert Rockwell & Dorothy Patrick. Directed by George Blair. 1950. Republic. 60 min. Sound. 16mm B&W. *Rental:* Ivy Films. *Sale:* Rep Pic Film.

Destination: Easter Island. 1974. Explo Mundo. (Documentary). 52 min. Sound. 16mm Color. *Rental:* B Raymond. *Sale:* B Raymond.

Destination Gobi. Richard Widmark & Don Taylor. Directed by Robert Wise. 1953. Fox. 89 min. Sound. 16mm Color. *Rental:* Films Inc.

Destination Inner Space. Scott Brady & Sheree North. Directed by Francis D. Lyon. 1966. Magna. 83 min. Sound. 16mm Color. *Rental:* Budget Films, Films Inc, Ivy Films, Video Comm & Westcoast Films.

Destination Moon. Warner Anderson & John Archer. Directed by Irving Pichel. 1950. Eagle Lion. 91 min. Sound. 16mm Color. *Rental:* Budget Films, Charard Motion Pics, Ivy Films, Video Comm & Welling Motion Pictures. *Lease:* Video Comm.

Destination Murder. Joyce Mackenzie & Hurd Hatfield. Directed by Edward L. Cahn. 1950. RKO. 72 min. Sound. 16mm B&W. *Rental:* Films Inc.

Destination North Pole. 1968. CBS. (Documentary). 54 min. Sound. 16mm B&W. *Sale:* Phoenix Films. *Sale:* Phoenix Films, Color version.

Destination Saturn. Buster Crabbe & Constance Moore. Directed by Ford Beebe & Saul A. Goodkind. 1939. Universal. 90 min. Sound. B&W. *Rental:* Budget Films, Ivy Films & Video Comm. *Sale:* Cinema Concepts & Natl Cinema. *Sale:* Cinema Concepts, Videotape version.

Destination Sixty Thousand. Preston Foster & Colleen Gray. Directed by George Waggner. 1957. Allied Artists. 65 min. Sound. 16mm B&W. *Rental:* Hurlock Cine.

Destination Tokyo. Cary Grant & John Garfield. Directed by Delmer Daves. 1944. Warners. 135 min. Sound. 16mm B&W. *Rental:* MGM United.

Destiny. Trans. Title: Mude Tod, Der. Lil Dagover. Directed by Fritz Lang. 1921. Germany. (Musical score only). 122 min. Sound. 16mm B&W. *Rental:* Films Inc & Kit Parker. *Sale:* Cinema Concepts, Glenn Photo, Natl Cinema & Reel Images. *Rental:* Budget Films, Classic Film Mus, Em Gee Film Lib, Images Film, Ivy Films, Janus Films, Museum Mod Art & Video Comm, *Sale:* Glenn Photo, Natl Cinema & Images Film, Silent 16mm version. *Sale:* Reel Images, Super 8 sound version. *Rental:* Ivy Films, *Sale:* Glenn Photo, Super 8 silent version. *Rental:* Video Comm, *Sale:* Images Film, Videotape version. *Sale:* Festival Films, 82 min. version. *Sale:* Festival Films, 82 min. Videotape version.

Destiny's Toy. Louise Huff. Directed by John B. O'Brien. 1916. Paramount. 45 min. Silent. 16mm B&W. *Sale:* E Finney.

Destroy All Monsters! Akira Kubo. Directed by Inoshiro Honda. 1969. Japan. 88 min. Sound. 16mm Color. dubbed. *Rental:* Welling Motion Pictures.

Destroy, She Said. Catherine Sellers & Nicole Hiss. Directed by Marguerite Duras. Fr. 1969. France. 100 min. Sound. 16mm B&W. subtitles. *Rental:* Grove. *Sale:* Grove.

Destroyer. Edward G. Robinson & Glenn Ford. Directed by William A. Seiter. 1943. 99 min. Sound. 16mm *Rental:* Budget Films.

Destroyers. Lu Feng, Lo Meng & Sun Chien. 105 min. Sound. 16mm *Rental:* WW Enter. *Rental:* WW Enter, Videotape version.

Destructors, The. Richard Egan & Patricia Owens. Directed by Francis D. Lyon. 1967. United. 97 min. Sound. 16mm Color. *Rental:* Films Inc, Ivy Films & Video Comm.

Destry. Audie Murphy & Thomas Mitchell. Directed by George Marshall. 1954. Universal. 95 min. Sound. 16mm Color. *Rental:* Swank Motion.

Destry Rides Again. Tom Mix & ZaSu Pitts. Directed by Ben Stoloff. 1932. Universal. 55 min. Sound. 16mm B&W. *Rental:* Williams Films.

Destry Rides Again. Marlene Dietrich & James Stewart. Directed by George Marshall. 1939. Universal. 82 min. Sound. 16mm B&W. *Rental:* Swank Motion, 94 min. version.

Detective, The. Sir Alec Guinness & Joan Greenwood. Directed by Robert Hamer. 1954. Britain. 91 min. Sound. 16mm B&W. *Rental:* Alba House, Arcus Film, Bosco Films, Budget Films, Cine Craft, Films Inc, Kit Parker, Modern Sound, Newman Films & Twyman Films.

Detective, The. Frank Sinatra & Lee Remick. Directed by Gordon Douglas. 1968. Fox. 114 min. Sound. 16mm Color. *Rental:* Films Inc & Twyman Films. *Rental:* Films Inc, Anamorphic color version. *Sale:* Blackhawk Films, Cinema Concepts, Golden Tapes, Magnetic Video & Video Lib, Videotape version.

Detective Kitty O'Day. Jean Parker & Peter Cookson. Directed by William Beaudine. 1944. Monogram. 63 min. Sound. 16mm B&W. *Rental:* MGM United.

Detective Story. Kirk Douglas & Eleanor Parker. Directed by William Wyler. 1951. Paramount. 103 min. Sound. 16mm B&W. *Rental:* Films Inc.

Determining Force, A. 1975. ABC. (Documentary). 60 min. Sound. 16mm Color. *Rental:* Natl Churches Christ.

Detour. Tom Neal & Ann Savage. Directed by Edgar G. Ulmer. 1946. PRC. 69 min. Sound. 16mm B&W. *Rental:* Budget Films, Classic Film Mus, Em Gee Film Lib, Ivy Films, Kit Parker, Mogulls Films, Video Comm & Welling Motion Pictures. *Sale:* Classics Assoc NY, Festival Films, Glenn Photo, Natl Cinema, Rep Pic Film & Reel Images. *Rental:* Video Comm, *Sale:* Festival Films, Videotape version.

Detroit Connection, The. 1977. Edupac. (Documentary). 50 min. Sound. 16mm Color. *Rental:* Edupac. *Sale:* Edupac.

Detroit Model, The. Directed by Alan Levin. 1980. California Newsreel. (Documentary). 45 min. Sound. 16mm Color. *Rental:* CA Newsreel.

Deus E O Biabo Na Terra Do Sol *see* Black God, White Devil.

Deux Voix. John Heuer. 1967. Rosalind Stevenson. 80 min. Sound. 16mm B&W. *Rental:* Canyon Cinema.

Devi. Soumitra Chatterjee. Directed by Satyajit Ray. Hindi. 1960. India. 99 min. Sound. 16mm B&W. subtitles. *Rental:* Budget Films, Em Gee Film Lib, Films Inc & Kit Parker. *Sale:* Festival Films. *Sale:* Festival Films, Videotape version.

Devil & Daniel Webster, The. Orig. Title: All that Money can Buy. James Craig, Simone Simon & Walter Huston. Directed by William Dieterle. 1941. RKO. 109 min. Sound. 16mm B&W. *Rental:* Janus Films & Films Inc.

Devil & Max Devlin, The. Elliot Gould & Bill Cosby. Directed by Steven Hilliard Stern. 1981. Disney. 96 min. Sound. 16mm Color. *Rental:* MGM United & Swank Motion.

Devil & Miss Jones, The. Jean Arthur & Robert Cummings. Directed by Sam Wood. 1941. RKO. 97 min. Sound. 16mm B&W. *Rental:* Films Inc. *Rental:* Video Comm, *Sale:* Tamarelles French Film, Videotape version.

Devil & the Deep, The. Tallulah Bankhead, Cary Grant & Gary Cooper. Directed by Marion Gering. 1932. Paramount. 78 min. Sound. 16mm B&W. *Rental:* Swank Motion.

Devil at Four O'Clock, The. Spencer Tracy & Frank Sinatra. Directed by Mervyn LeRoy. 1961. Columbia. 126 min. Sound. 16mm Color. *Rental:* Alba House, Bosco Films, Buchan Pic, Cine Craft, Charard Motion Pics, Film Ctr DC, Films Inc, Modern Sound, Natl Film Video, Roas Films, Twyman Films, Welling Motion Pictures, Westcoast Films & Budget Films.

Devil at My Heels, The. Sami Frey & Francoise Hardy. Directed by Jean-Daniel Pollet. 1966. France. 88 min. Sound. 16mm Color. dubbed. *Rental:* Films Inc.

Devil at Your Heels, The. Directed by Robert Fortier. 1981. 102 min. Sound. 16mm Color. *Rental:* National Film.

Devil Bat, The. Orig. Title: Killer Bats. Bela Lugosi & Dave O'Brien. Directed by Jean Yarbrough. 1942. PRC. 70 min. Sound. 16mm B&W. *Rental:* Budget Films, Classic Film Mus, Ivy Films, Video Comm & Westcoast Films. *Sale:* Classic Film Mus & Cinema Concepts. *Rental:* Video Comm, Videotape version.

Devil Bat's Daughter, The. Rosemary La Planche. Directed by Frank Wisbar. 1946. PRC. 66 min. Sound. 16mm B&W. *Sale:* Classics Assoc NY.

Devil by the Tail, The. Yves Montand & Maria Schell. Directed by Philippe De Broca. 1969. United Artists. 93 min. Sound. 16mm Color. dubbed. *Rental:* MGM United.

Devil Checks Up, The. Alan Mowbray & Majorie Woodworth. Directed by Gordon Douglas. 1942. 45 min. Sound. 16mm B&W. *Rental:* Wholesome Film Ctr.

Devil Commands, The. Boris Karloff & Anne Revere. Directed by Edward Dmytryk. 1941. Columbia. 70 min. Sound. 16mm B&W. *Rental:* Bosco Films & Kit Parker.

Devil Dogs of the Air. James Cagney & Pat O'Brien. Directed by Lloyd Bacon. 1935. Warners. 86 min. Sound. 16mm B&W. *Rental:* MGM United.

Devil Doll, The. Lionel Barrymore & Maureen O'Sullivan. Directed by Tod Browning. 1936. MGM. 79 min. Sound. 16mm B&W. *Rental:* MGM United.

Devil Doll, The. William Syvester & Bryant Halliday. Directed by Lindsay Shonteff. 1963. Britain. 80 min. Sound. 16mm B&W. *Rental:* Budget Films, Maljack, Modern Sound & Willoughby Film Ctr. *Sale:* Reel Images, Sound 8mm version. *Sale:* Cinema Concepts & Video Lib, Videotape version.

Devil Girl from Mars, The. Hazel Court & Hugh McDermott. Directed by David McDonald. 1955. DCA. 82 min. Sound. 16mm B&W. *Rental:* Wade Williams.

Devil in the House of Exorcism, The. Elke Sommer & Telly Savalas. 90 min. Sound. Videotape Color. *Rental:* Maljack Productions.

Devil Is a Sissy, The. Orig. Title: Devil Takes the Count. Mickey Rooney, Freddie Bartholomew & Jackie Cooper. Directed by W. S. Van Dyke II. 1936. MGM. 92 min. Sound. 16mm B&W. *Rental:* MGM United.

Devil Is a Woman, The. Marlene Dietrich & Cesar Romero. Directed by Josef Von Sternberg. 1935. Paramount. 82 min. Sound. 16mm B&W. *Rental:* Museum Mod Art & Swank Motion.

Devil Makes Three, The. Gene Kelly & Pier Angeli. Directed by Andrew Marton. 1952. MGM. 90 min. Sound. 16mm B&W. *Rental:* MGM United.

Devil May Care. Ramon Navarro & Marion Harris. Directed by Sidney Franklin. 1929. MGM. 75 min. Sound. 16mm B&W. *Rental:* MGM United.

Devil of the Desert Against the Sons of Hercules *see* Devil of the Desert vs. Son of Hercules.

Devil of the Desert vs. Son of Hercules. Orig. Title: Devil of the Desert Against the Sons of Hercules. Kirk Morris. 1964. Italy. 85 min. Sound. 16mm Color. dubbed. *Rental:* Films Inc.

Devil on Horseback. Fred Keating. Directed by Crane Wilbur. 1936. Grand National. 60 min. Sound. 16mm B&W. *Rental:* Mogulls Films.

Devil on Wheels *see* Indianapolis Speedway.

Devil on Wheels. Darryl Hickman & Noreen Nash. Directed by Crane Wilbur. 1947. PRC. 67 min. Sound. 16mm B&W. *Rental:* Cine Craft & Ivy Films. *Sale:* Classics Assoc NY & Rep Pic Film.

Devil Pays Off, The. Osa Massen & William Wright. Directed by John H. Auer. 1941. Republic. 54 min. Sound. 16mm B&W. *Rental:* Ivy Films. *Sale:* Rep Pic Film.

Devil Riders, The. Buster Crabbe. Directed by Sam Newfield. 1943. PRC. 59 min. Sound. 16mm B&W. *Rental:* Mogulls Films.

Devil Rides Out, The *see* Devil's Bride.

Devil Strikes at Night, The. Mario Adorf & Claus Holm. Directed by Robert Siodmak. 1958. Germany. 97 min. Sound. 16mm B&W. *Rental:* Films Inc.

Devil Takes the Count *see* Devil Is a Sissy.

Devil Thumbs A Ride, The. Lawrence Tierney & Glenn Vernon. Directed by Felix Feist. 1947. RKO. 63 min. Sound. 16mm *Rental:* RKO General Pics.

Devil to Pay, The. Ronald Colman & Loretta Young. Directed by George Fitzmaurice. 1930. Goldwyn. 72 min. Sound. 16mm B&W. *Rental:* Films Inc.

Devil's Envoys *see* Visiteurs du Soir.

Devil's Men, The *see* Land of the Minotaur.

Devil's Weed, The *see* Marihuana.

Devils, The. Oliver Reed & Vanessa Redgrave. Directed by Ken Russell. 1971. Warners. 108 min. Sound. 16mm Color. *Rental:* Swank Motion. *Rental:* Swank Motion, Videotape version.

Devil's Angels, The. John Cassavetes & Beverly Adams. Directed by Daniel Haller. 1967. American International. 83 min. Sound. 16mm Color. *Rental:* Westcoast Films & Wholesome Film Ctr.

Devil's Bride, The. Orig. Title: Devil Rides Out, The. Christopher Lee. Directed by Terence Fisher. 1968. Fox. 95 min. Sound. 16mm Color. *Rental:* Films Inc.

Devil's Brigade, The. William Holden & Cliff Robertson. Directed by Andrew V. McLaglen. 1968. United Artists. (Anamorphic). 130 min. Sound. 16mm Color. *Rental:* MGM United.

Devil's Brother, The. Trans. Title: Fra Diavolo. Stan Laurel & Oliver Hardy. Directed by Hal Roach. 1936. MGM. 90 min. Sound. 16mm B&W. *Rental:* MGM United.

Devil's Canyon, The. Virginia Mayo & Dale Robertson. Directed by Alfred M. Werker. 1953. RKO. 92 min. Sound. 16mm Color. *Rental:* Films Inc.

Devil's Cavaliers, The. Frank Latimore & Emma Danieli. 1958. Italy. 82 min. Sound. 16mm Color. dubbed. *Rental:* Films Inc.

Devil's Circus, The. Norma Shearer & Charles Emmett. Directed by Benjamin Christiansen. 1926. MGM. 75 min. Silent. 16mm B&W. *Rental:* Films Inc.

Devil's Daffodil. Christopher Lee. Directed by Akos Rathony. 1961. 77 min. 16mm *Rental:* A Twyman Pres.

Devil's Daughter, The. Nina Mae McKinney & Arthur Leonard. 1933. 61 min. Sound. 16mm B&W. *Rental:* Budget Films & Em Gee Film Lib.

Devil's Disciple, The. Sir Laurence Oliver & Burt Lancaster. Directed by Guy Hamilton. 1959. United Artists. 82 min. Sound. 16mm B&W. *Rental:* MGM United.

Devil's Doorway, The. Robert Taylor & Louis Calhern. Directed by Anthony Mann. 1950. MGM. 85 min. Sound. 16mm B&W. *Rental:* MGM United.

Devil's Eight, The. Fabian & Christopher George. Directed by Burt Topper. 1969. American International. 97 min. Sound. 16mm Color. *Rental:* Films Inc & Westcoast Films.

Devil's Eye, The. Jarl Kulle & Bibi Anderson. Directed by Ingmar Bergman. Swed. 1960. Sweden. 90 min. Sound. 16mm B&W. subtitles. *Rental:* Films Inc, Janus Films & New Cinema. *Sale:* Tamarelles French Film, Videotape version.

Devil's Hand, The. Robert Alda & Linda Christian. Directed by William J. Hole Jr. 1962. Crown. 71 min. Sound. 16mm B&W. *Rental:* Budget Films & Video Comm. *Lease:* Video Comm. *Rental:* Video Comm, *Lease:* Video Comm, Videotape version.

Devil's Harbor, The. Richard Arlen & Greta Gynt. Directed by Montgomery Tully. 1954. Fox. 71 min. Sound. 16mm B&W. *Rental:* Films Inc.

Devil's Island. Pauline Frederick & John Miljan. Directed by Frank O'Connor. 1926. Chadwick. 72 min. Silent. 16mm B&W. *Rental:* Mogulls Films.

Devil's Island. Boris Karloff & James Stevenson. Directed by William Clemens. 1939. Warners. 63 min. Sound. 16mm B&W. *Rental:* MGM United.

Devil's Island. Directed by Walter Heynowski & Gerhard Scheumann. Vietnamese. 1975. Vietnam. (Documentary). 65 min. Sound. 16mm Color. subtitles. *Rental:* Unifilm. *Sale:* Unifilm.

Devil's Messenger, The. Lon Chaney Jr. & Karen Kadler. Directed by Herbert L. Strock. 1962. Herts-Lion. 75 min. Sound. 16mm B&W. *Sale:* Rep Pic Film & Classics Assoc NY.

Devil's Mistress, The. Jean Stapleton & Robert Gregory. Directed by Orville Wanzer. 1965. Emerson. 66 min. Sound. 16mm B&W. *Rental:* Films Inc.

Devils of Darkness. William Sylvester. Directed by Lance Comfort. 1965. Fox. 88 min. Sound. 16mm B&W. *Rental:* Films Inc.

Devil's Own, The. Joan Fontaine & Kay Walsh. Directed by Cyril Frankel. 1967. Fox. 90 min. 16mm *Rental:* Films Inc.

Devil's Party, The. Victor McLaglen, William Gargan & Paul Kelly. Directed by Ray McCarey. 1938. 65 min. 16mm *Rental:* Budget Films & Classic Film Mus.

Devil's Playground, The. William Boyd. Directed by George Archainbaud. 1946. United Artists. 65 min. Sound. 16mm B&W. *Sale:* Cinema Concepts.

Devil's Rain, The. Ernest Borgnine, Ida Lupino & Eddie Albert. Directed by Robert Fuest. 1975. Bryanston. 85 min. 16mm. *Rental:* Swank Motion.

Devil's Saddle Legion. Dick Foran & Anne Nagel. Directed by Bobby Connolly. 1937. Warners. 52 min. Sound. 16mm B&W. *Rental:* MGM United.

Devils Three: The Karate Killers. Lee Merrie & Johnny Wilson. Directed by Bobby A. Suarez. 1974. Arista. 90 min. 16mm. dubbed. *Rental:* Films Inc.

Devil's Wanton, The. Orig. Title: Fangelse. Doris Svedlund. Directed by Ingmar Bergman. Swed. 1949. Sweden. 72 min. 16mm B&W. subtitles. *Rental:* Kit Parker & Budget Films. *Sale:* Cinema Concepts & Reel Images. *Sale:* Tamarelles French Film, Videotape version.

Devil's Wedding Night. Mark Damon. Directed by Paul Solday. 1973. Dimension. 85 min. Sound. 16mm *Rental:* Films Inc.

Devil's Wheel, The. Directed by Grigori Kozintsev & Leonid Trauberg. 1926. 60 min. Silent. 16mm B&W. subtitles Eng. *Rental:* Films Inc.

Devoir, Le. 2 pts. Directed by Tony Ianzelo & George Robertson. 1972. Canada. (Documentary). 55 min. Sound. 16mm Color. *Rental:* Natl Film CN. *Sale:* Natl Film CN.

Devotion. Ann Harding & Leslie Howard. Directed by Robert Milton. 1931. RKO. 84 min. Sound. 16mm B&W. *Rental:* Films Inc.

Devotion. Ida Lupino, Olivia De Havilland & Arthur Kennedy. Directed by Curtis Bernhardt. 1946. Warners. 107 min. Sound. 16mm B&W. *Rental:* MGM United.

Devotion of a Boy. Gordon Jones & June Travis. 75 min. Sound. 16mm B&W. *Rental:* Alba House.

Dew Lines. 1957. U. S. Government. (Documentary). 56 min. Sound. 16mm Color. *Sale:* Natl AV Ctr.

Diable Boiteux, Le. Sacha Guitry & Lana Maconi. Directed by Sacha Guitry. 1948. France. 120 min. Sound. 16mm B&W. *Rental:* French Am Cul.

Diablo Rides, El. Bob Steele. Directed by Ira S. Webb. 1939. Metropolitan. 60 min. Sound. 16mm B&W. *Sale:* Morcraft Films.

Diabolic Wedding. Margaret O'Brien. 1974. Dimension. 85 min. Sound. 16mm Color. *Sale:* Salz Ent.

Diabolique. Simone Signoret & Vera Clouzot. Directed by Henri-Georges Clouzot. 1955. France. 92 min. Sound. 16mm B&W. *Rental:* Budget Films, Corinth Films, Em Gee Film Lib, Films Inc, U of IL Film, Images Film, Ivy Films, Kit Parker, Roas Films, Twyman Films, Video Comm & Westcoast Films. *Sale:* Cinema Concepts, Festival Films, Images Film, Natl Cinema & Reel Images. *Lease:* Corinth Films. *Sale:* Reel Images, Super 8 sound version. *Sale:* Cinema Concept, Festival Films, Images Film & Tamarelles French Film, Videotape version.

Diagnosis & Management of the Solitary Thyroid Nodule. 1980. 58 min. Sound. videotape *Sale:* Natl AV Ctr.

Dial a Deadly Number. Patrick Macnee & Diana Rigg. 1965. Britain. 55 min. Videotape B&W. *Sale:* Reel Images.

Dial Eleven Nineteen. Orig. Title: Violent Hour, The. Marshall Thompson & Leon Ames. Directed by Gerald Mayer. 1950. MGM. 75 min. Sound. 16mm B&W. *Rental:* MGM United.

Dial M for Murder. Ray Milland & Grace Kelly. Directed by Alfred Hitchcock. 1954. 105 min. Sound. 16mm Color. *Sale:* Festival Films. *Sale:* Festival Films, Videotape version.

Dial Red "O". Bill Elliott & Helene Stanley. Directed by Daniel B. Ullman. 1955. Allied Artists. 63 min. Sound. 16mm B&W. *Rental:* Hurlock Cine.

Dialogo Con Che: Che is Alive. Directed by Jose Rodriguez-Soltero. Span. 1968. Cuba. 60 min. Sound. 16mm B&W. .

Dialogue. Anita Semjen. Directed by Janos Hersko. Hungarian. 1964. Hungary. 130 min. Sound. 16mm B&W. subtitles. *Rental:* Icarus Films.

Dialogue for a Decade. 1962. Encyclopedia Britannica. (Documentary). 49 min. Sound. 16mm B&W. *Rental:* U Cal Media.

Dialogue on Biofeedback. 1974. US Government. (Documentary). 48 min. Sound. 16mm Color. *Sale:* Natl AV Ctr.

Dialogue with Malcolm Boyd. 1967. NET. (Documentary). 60 min. Sound. 16mm B&W. *Rental:* Mass Media.

Dialogues: Dr. Jean Piaget. 2 pts. 1970. CCM. (Documentary). 80 min. Sound. 16mm Color. *Rental:* U Cal Media.

Dialogues: Dr. Carl Rogers *see* Discussion with Dr. Carl Rogers.

Diamond, The *see* Diamond Wizard.

Diamond Country: Run Like a Thief. Brian Donlevy & Kieron Moore. Directed by Paul Landres. 1966. Britain. 98 min. Sound. 16mm Color. *Rental:* Films Inc, Ivy Films & Willoughby Peer.

Diamond Earrings *see* Earrings of Madame de ....

Diamond Head. Charles Heston & Yvette Mimieux. Directed by Guy Green. 1962. Columbia. 107 min. Sound. 16mm Color. *Rental:* Arcus Film, Cine Craft, Charard Motion Pics, Film Ctr DC, Films Inc, Modern Sound & Welling Motion Pictures.

Diamond Jim. Edward Arnold & Jean Arthur. Directed by Edward Sutherland. 1935. Universal. 93 min. Sound. 16mm B&W. *Rental:* Swank Motion.

Diamond Queen, The. Arlene Dahl & Fernando Lamas. Directed by John Brahm. 1953. Warners. 80 min. Sound. 16mm Color. *Rental:* Films Inc.

Diamond Trail. Rex Bell. Directed by Harry Fraser. 1933. Monogram. 60 min. Sound. 16mm B&W. *Rental:* Mogulls Films.

Diamond Wizard, The. Orig. Title: Diamond, The. Dennis O'Keefe & Margaret Sheridan. Directed by Montgomery Tully. 1954. United Artists. 83 min. Sound. 16mm B&W. *Rental:* A Twyman Pres & MGM United.

Diamonds. Robert Shaw & Richard Roundtree. Directed by Menahem Golan. 1975. Embassy. 108 min. Sound. 16mm Color. *Rental:* Films Inc.

Diamonds & Crime *see* Hi Diddle Diddle.

Diamonds Are Forever. Sean Connery & Jill St. John. Directed by Guy Hamilton. 1971. United Artists. 119 min. Sound. 16mm Color. *Rental:* MGM United. *Rental:* MGM United, Videotape version.

Diamonds of the Night. Antonin Kumbera. Directed by Jan Nemec. 1964. Czechoslovakia. 70 min. Sound. 16mm B&W. *Rental:* Icarus Films.

Diane. Lana Turner & Pedro Armandariz. Directed by David Miller. 1956. MGM. 110 min. Sound. 16mm Color. *Rental:* MGM United.

Diaries, Notes & Sketches. Orig. Title: Walden. Directed by Jonas Mekas. 1969. Jonas Mekas. (Experimental). 160 min. Sound. 16mm Color. *Rental:* Canyon Cinema.

Diario de Mi Madre, El. Marga Lopez. Directed by Roberto Rodriguez. 1958. Mexico. 103 min. Sound. 16mm B&W. *Rental:* Trans-World Films.

Diary of a Chambermaid. Paulette Goddard. Directed by Jean Renoir. 1946. United Artists. 76 min. Sound. 16mm B&W. *Rental:* Budget Films & Ivy Films. *Sale:* Rep Pic Film.

Diary of a Chambermaid. Jeanne Moreau & Michel Piccoli. Directed by Luis Bunuel. Fr. 1965. France. 97 min. Sound. 16mm B&W. subtitles. *Rental:* Films Inc.

Diary of a Country Priest. Nicole Maurey & Claudia Laydu. Directed by Robert Bresson. Fr. 1951. France. 95 min. Sound. 16mm B&W. subtitles. *Rental:* Films Inc. *Sale:* Festival Films & Reel Images. *Sale:* Festival Films & Tamarelles French Film, Videotape version.

Diary of a High School Bride. Anita Sands & Ronald Foster. Directed by Burt Topper. 1959. American International. 73 min. Sound. 16mm B&W. *Rental:* Video Comm.

Diary of a Lost Girl. Trans. Title: Tagenbuch Einer Verlorenin, Das. Louise Brooks & Fritz Rasp. Directed by G. W. Pabst. 1929. Germany. (Musical score only). 100 min. Sound. 16mm B&W. *Rental:* A Twyman Pres, Kino Intl & Twyman Films. *Lease:* Kino Intl. *Rental:* A Twyman Pres, Silent version.

Diary of a Lover. Directed by Sohrab Shahid Sales. Ger. 1977. Germany. (Cast unlisted). 92 min. Sound. 16mm Color. subtitles. *Rental:* Liberty Co.

Diary of a Mad Housewife. Richard Benjamin & Carrie Snodgress. Directed by Frank Perry. 1970. Universal. 100 min. Sound. 16mm Color. *Rental:* Swank Motion.

Diary of a Rape, The. 1976. Group One. 75 min. Sound. 16mm Color. *Rental:* Twyman Films.

Diary of a Schizophrenic Girl. Ghislaine D'Orsay. Directed by Nelo Risi. Ital. 1968. Italy. 108 min. Sound. 16mm Color. subtitles. *Rental:* Hurlock Cine.

Diary of a Shinjuku Thief. Tadanori Yokoo & Rie Yokoyama. Directed by Nagisa Oshima. Jap. 1970. Japan. 94 min. Sound. 16mm B&W. subtitles. *Rental:* New Yorker Films.

Diary of a Student Revolution. 1969. NET. (Documentary). 59 min. Sound. 16mm B&W. *Rental:* Indiana AV Ctr. *Sale:* Indiana AV Ctr.

Diary of a Telephone Operator. Claudia Cardinale & John Philip Law. 1972. G. G.. 90 min. Sound. 16mm Color. dubbed. *Rental:* Video Comm.

Diary of Anne Frank, The. Millie Perkins, Joseph Schildkraut & Shelley Winters. Directed by George Stevens. 1959. Fox. 170 min. Sound. 16mm B&W. *Rental:* Films Inc. *Rental:* Films Inc, Anamorphic B&W version.

Dias Calientes, Los. Isabel Sarli & Mario Pasano. Directed by Armando Bo. Span. Mexico. 98 min. Sound. 16mm B&W. subtitles. *Rental:* Williams Films.

Dick Barton Strikes Back. Bruce Walker. Directed by Godfrey Grayson. 1948. Britain. 70 min. Sound. 16mm B&W. *Rental:* Mogulls Films.

Dick Tracy. Ralph Byrd & Kay Hughes. Directed by Ray Taylor & Alan James. 1937. Republic. 100 min. Sound. 16mm B&W. *Rental:* Budget Films. *Sale:* Cinema Concepts.

Dick Tracy, Detective. Ralph Byrd. Directed by William Berke. 1945. RKO. 62 min. Sound. 16mm B&W. *Rental:* Budget Films, Modern Sound & Video Comm. *Rental:* Video Comm, *Lease:* Video Comm, Videotape version.

Dick Tracy Meets Gruesome. Orig. Title: Dick Tracy's Amazing Adventure. Ralph Byrd. 1947. RKO. 65 min. Sound. 16mm B&W. *Rental:* Films Inc. *Sale:* Cinema Concepts, Natl Cinema & Video Comm.

Dick Tracy vs. Crime Inc. Ralph Byrd & Jan Wiley. Directed by William Witney & John English. 1942. Republic. 100 min. Sound. 16mm B&W. *Rental:* Budget Films.

Dick Tracy vs. Cueball. Morgan Conway & Anne Jeffreys. Directed by Gordon Douglas. 1946. RKO. 62 min. Sound. 16mm B&W. *Rental:* Films Inc. *Rental:* Video Comm, *Lease:* Video Comm, Videotape version.

Dick Tracy's Amazing Adventure *see* Dick Tracy Meets Gruesome.

Dick Tracy's Dilemma. Orig. Title: Mark of the Claw. Ralph Byrd. Directed by John Rawlins. 1947. RKO. 60 min. Sound. 16mm B&W. *Rental:* Films Inc. *Rental:* Video Comm, *Lease:* Video Comm, Videotape version.

Dick Turpin. Tom Mix. Directed by John G. Blystone. 1925. Fox. 73 min. Silent. 16mm B&W. *Rental:* Em Gee Film Lib & Killiam Collect.

Dick Turpin's Ride *see* Lady & the Bandit.

Dickens Chronicle, A. 1963. CBS. (Documentary). 54 min. Sound. 16mm B&W. *Rental:* U of IL Film, McGraw-Hill Films & U Mich Media. *Sale:* McGraw-Hill Films.

Did You Hear the One About the Traveling Saleslady? Phyllis Diller. Directed by Don Weis. 1968. Universal. 97 min. Sound. 16mm Color. *Rental:* Williams Films.

Die, Die My Darling. Orig. Title: Fanatic. Tallulah Bankhead & Stephanie Powers. Directed by Silvio Narizzano. 1965. Columbia. 97 min. Sound. 16mm Color. *Rental:* Arcus Film, Budget Films, Charard Motion, Modern Sound & Welling Motion Pictures. *Rental:* Budget Films, 105 mins. version.

Die Is Cast, The. Trans. Title: Jeux Sonts Faits, Les. Micheline Presle. Directed by Jean Delannoy. 1947. France. 105 min. Sound. 16mm B&W. *Rental:* Trans-World Films. *Lease:* Trans-World Films.

Die Laughing. Robby Benson & Linda Grovenor. Directed by Jeff Werner. 1980. Orion. 108 min. Sound. 16mm Color. *Rental:* Films Inc.

Die, Monster, Die. Orig. Title: Monster of Terror. Boris Karloff & Nick Adams. Directed by Daniel Haller. 1965. American International. 80 min. Sound. 16mm Color. *Rental:* Budget Films, Ivy Films, Roas Films, Video Comm, Westcoast Films & Wholesome Film Ctr.

Die Tausand Augen des Dr. Mabuse *see* Thousand Eyes of Dr. Mabuse.

Dietrich Bonhoeffer: Memories & Perspectives. 1981. Cinema Guild. 90 min. Sound. 16mm B&W. *Rental:* Cinema Guild & U Mich Media. *Rental:* Cinema Guild.

Diez Anos. 1950. Mexico. (Cast unlisted). 90 min. Sound. 16mm B&W. *Rental:* Film Classics.

Difference Between, The. 1966. NET. (Documentary). 60 min. Sound. 16mm B&W. *Rental:* Indiana AV Ctr. *Sale:* Indiana AV Ctr.

Different Sons. 1970. Bowling Green. (Documentary). 52 min. Sound. 16mm Color. *Rental:* New Yorker Films.

Different Story, A. Perry King & Meg Foster. Directed by Paul Aaron. 1978. Embassy. 107 min. Sound. 16mm Color. *Rental:* Films Inc.

Digby, the Biggest Dog In the World. Jim Dale. Directed by Joseph McGrath. 1973. Cinerama. 88 min. Sound. 16mm Color. *Rental:* Buchan Pic, Budget Films, Film Pres, Modern Sound, Swank Motion, Welling Motion Pictures, Westcoast Films & Wholesome Film Ctr.

Dilemma In Black & White. 54 min. Sound. 16mm Color. *Rental:* Budget Films.

Dillinger. Lawrence Tierney & Edmund Lowe. Directed by Max Nosseck. 1945. Monogram. 70 min. Sound. 16mm B&W. *Rental:* Hurlock Cine.

Dillinger. Warren Oates, Ben Johnson & Cloris Leachman. Directed by John Milius. 1972. American International. 106 min. Sound. 16mm Color. *Rental:* Swank Motion & Westcoast Films.

Dime With a Halo. Barbara Luna. Directed by Boris Sagal. 1963. MGM. 94 min. Sound. 16mm B&W. *Rental:* MGM United.

Dimension Five. Jeffrey Hunter & France Nuyen. Directed by Franklin Adreon. 1966. Emerson. 91 min. Sound. 16mm Color. *Rental:* Budget Films, Films Inc, Ivy Films, Film Ctr DC & Westcoast Films.

Dimensions of Black. 1979. PBS. (Documentary). 59 min. Videotape Color. *Rental:* PBS Video. *Sale:* PBS Video.

Dimenstoogia. Three Stooges. 1953. Columbia. (Anthology, 3-D special glasses required). 96 min. Sound. 16mm B&W. *Rental:* Kit Parker.

Dimka. Alyosha Zagorsky. Directed by Ilya Frez. Rus. 1963. 79 min. Sound. 16mm B&W. subtitles. *Rental:* Corinth Films.

Dimples. Shirley Temple. Directed by William A. Seiter. 1936. Fox. 78 min. Sound. 16mm B&W. *Rental:* Films Inc.

Dineh the People: Portrait of the Navajo. 1976. Western World. (Documentary). 77 min. Sound. 16mm Color. *Rental:* Films Inc.

Diner. Steve Guttenberg, Daniel Stern & Mickey Rourke. Directed by Barry Levinson. 1982. 110 min. Sound. 16mm *Rental:* MGM United. *Rental:* MGM United, Videotape version.

Ding Dong Williams. Orig. Title: Melody Maker. Glenn Vernon & Anne Jeffreys. Directed by William Berke. 1946. RKO. 62 min. Sound. 16mm B&W. *Rental:* Films Inc.

Dingaka. Stanley Baker & Juliet Prowse. Directed by Jamie Uys. 1965. Embassy. 96 min. Sound. 16mm Color. *Rental:* Films Inc.

Dinner at Eight. Wallace Beery & John Barrymore. Directed by George Cukor. 1933. MGM. 113 min. Sound. 16mm B&W. *Rental:* MGM United. *Rental:* MGM United, Videotape version.

Dinner at the Ritz. David Niven & Annabella. Directed by Harold Schuster. 1937. Fox. 77 min. Sound. 16mm B&W. *Sale:* Cinema Concepts, Classic Film Mus & Reel Images. *Rental:* A Twyman Pres & Kit Parker. *Sale:* Cinema Concepts & Tamarelles French Film, Videotape version.

Dino. Sal Mineo & Brian Keith. Directed by Thomas Carr. 1957. Allied Artists. 96 min. Sound. 16mm B&W. *Rental:* Ivy Films. *Sale:* Rep Pic Film.

Dinosaur Hunters, The. 1971. Britain. (Documentary). 50 min. Sound. 16mm Color. *Rental:* Time-Life Multimedia. *Sale:* Time-Life Multimedia. *Rental:* Time-Life Multimedia, *Sale:* Time-Life Multimedia, Videotape version. *Rental:* Time-Life Multimedia, *Sale:* Time-Life Multimedia, Spanish language version.

Dinosaurus! Ward Ramsey. Directed by Irvin Yeaworth Jr. 1960. Universal. 85 min. Sound. 16mm Color. *Rental:* Budget Films, Charard Motion Pics, Films Inc, Ivy Films & Video Comm. *Rental:* Budget Films, Anamorphic color version.

Dionne Quintuplets, The. Directed by Donald Brittain. 1978. Canada. (Documentary). 88 min. Sound. 16mm Color. *Rental:* Natl Film CN. *Sale:* Natl Film CN. *Sale:* Natl Film CN, *Rental:* Natl Film CN, Videotape version.

Diplomaniacs. Bert Wheeler & Robert Woolsey. Directed by Merian C. Cooper & William A. Seiter. 1933. RKO. 63 min. Sound. 16mm *Rental:* Films Inc. *Rental:* RKO General Pics, 76 mins. version.

Diplomatic Courier. Tyrone Power, Patricia Neal & Hildegarde Neff. Directed by Henry Hathaway. 1952. Fox. 98 min. Sound. 16mm B&W. *Rental:* Films Inc.

Diputado, El. Orig. Title: Deputy, The. Jose Sacristan & Angel Pardo. Directed by Eloy De la Iglesia. Span. 1978. Spain. 111 min. Sound. Videotape Color. subtitles Eng. *Sale:* Tamarelles French Films.

Direct Action. Directed by Steven Doran. 1980. Green Mountain Post. (Documentary). 54 min. Sound. 16mm Color. *Rental:* Green Mt. *Sale:* Green Mt.

Directed by John Ford. Directed by Peter Bogdanovich. 1972. American Film Institute. (Documentary). 92 min. Sound. 16mm Color. *Rental:* Films Inc, U of IL Film & Texture Film. *Sale:* Texture Film. *Rental:* U of IL Film, 100 mins. version.

Direction: Berlin. Directed by Jerzy Passendorfer. Pol. 1946. Poland. (Documentary). 100 min. Sound. 16mm B&W. subtitles. *Rental:* Polish People.

Direction'78: Morality of Television. 1979. PBS. (Documentary). 59 min. Videotape Color. *Rental:* PBS Video. *Sale:* PBS Video.

Dirigible. Ralph Graves & Fay Wray. Directed by Frank Capra. 1931. Columbia. 93 min. Sound. 16mm B&W. *Rental:* Bosco Films & Budget Films.

Dirkie. Jamie Hayes & Sue Berman. 88 min. Sound. 16mm Color. *Rental:* Welling Motion Pictures.

Dirt Gang, The. Paul Carr. Directed by Jerry Jameson. 1972. American International. 89 min. Sound. 16mm Color. *Rental:* Swank Motion.

Dirty Dingus Magee. Frank Sinatra, George Kennedy & Anne Jackson. Directed by Burt Kennedy. 1971. MGM. 91 min. Sound. 16mm Color. *Rental:* MGM United.

Dirty Dozen, The. Lee Marvin, Ernest Borgnine & Jim Brown. Directed by Robert Aldrich. 1967. MGM. 149 min. Sound. 16mm Color. *Rental:* MGM United. *Rental:* MGM United, Videotape version.

Dirty Duck. Directed by Charles Swenson. 1976. New World. (Animated). 90 min. Sound. 16mm Color. *Rental:* Films Inc.

Dirty Game, The. Henry Fonda & Robert Ryan. Directed by Terence Young, Christian-Jaque & Carlo Lizzani. 1966. American Interntional. 120 min. Sound. 16mm B&W. *Rental:* Films Inc & Ivy Films.

Dirty Gertie from Harlem, U.S.A. Gertie LaRue. Directed by Spencer Williams. 1946. 60 min. Sound. 16mm B&W. *Rental:* Budget Films & Em Gee Film Lib. *Sale:* Morcraft Films. *Sale:* Morcraft Films, Super 8 sound version.

Dirty Hands. Pierre Brasseur & Daniel Gelin. Directed by Ferand Rivers. Fr. 1952. France. 100 min. Sound. 16mm B&W. subtitles. *Rental:* Trans-World Films.

Dirty Hands. Rod Steiger & Romy Schneider. Directed by Claude Chabrol. 1977. France. 120 min. Sound. 16mm *Rental:* New Line Cinema.

Dirty Harry. Clint Eastwood. Directed by Don Siegel. 1972. Warners. 103 min. Sound. 16mm Color. *Rental:* Cine Craft, Film Ctr DC, Films Inc, Inst Cinema, Modern Sound, Swank Motion, Twyman Films & Williams Films. *Rental:* Twyman Films, Anamorphic color version. *Rental:* Swank Motion, Videotape version.

Dirty Heroes, The. Frederick Stafford, Daniele Bianchi & Curt Jurgens. Directed by Alberto De Martino. 1967. Italy. 105 min. Sound. 16mm Color. dubbed. *Rental:* Budget Films, Films Inc, Video Comm & Willoughby Peer.

Dirty Ho. Wong Yu Lo Lieh. 103 min. Sound. 16mm *Rental:* WW Enter. *Rental:* WW Enter, Videotape version.

Dirty Knights' Work. John Mills & David Birney. Directed by Kevin Connor. 1976. Gamma III. 88 min. Sound. 16mm Color. *Rental:* Swank Motion.

Dirty Little Billy. Michael J. Pollard & Lee Purcell. Directed by Stan Dragoti. 1972. Columbia. 100 min. Sound. 16mm Color. *Rental:* Budget Films, Kit Parker & Swank Motion.

Dirty Mary, Crazy Larry. Peter Fonda & Susan George. Directed by John Hough. 1974. Fox. 93 min. Sound. 16mm Color. *Rental:* Films Inc, Twyman Films, Welling Motion Pictures & Williams Films. *Rental:* Williams Films, Videotape version.

Dirty, Mean & Nasty. Orig. Title: Down & Dirty. Nino Manfredi. Directed by Ettore Scola. Ital. 1975. Italy. 120 min. Sound. 16mm Color. subtitles. *Rental:* New Line Cinema.

Dirty Money. Trans. Title: Flic, Un. Catherine Deneuve & Richard Crenna. Directed by Jean-Pierre Melville. 1972. France. 92 min. Sound. 16mm Color. dubbed. *Rental:* Hurlock Cine.

Dirty O'Neal: The Love Life of a Cop. Morgan Paul. Directed by Howard Freen & Lewis Teague. 1974. American International. 89 min. Sound. 16mm Color. *Rental:* Swank Motion.

Dirty Tricks. Elliott Gould & Kate Jackson. Directed by Alvin Rakoff. 1981. Embassy. 93 min. Sound. 16mm Color. *Rental:* Films Inc.

Disabled Women's Theater Project, The. 1982. Women Make Movies. (Documentary). 60 min. videotape Color. *Rental:* Women Movies. *Sale:* Women Movies.

Disappearance, The. Lassie. 1955. Wrather. 124 min. Sound. 16mm B&W. *Rental:* Films Inc.

Disappearance, The. John Hurt, Christopher Plummer & Donald Sutherland. 96 min. Sound. 16mm *Rental:* WW Enter. *Rental:* WW Enter, Videotape version.

Disappearance of Aimee, The. Bette Davis & Faye Dunaway. Directed by Anthony Harvey. 1976. NBC. 103 min. Sound. 16mm Color. *Rental:* Modern Sound, Learning Corp Am & Wholesome Film Ctr. *Lease:* Learning Corp Am.

Disc Jockey. Ginny Sims & Tom Drake. Directed by Will Jason. 1951. Allied Artists. 77 min. Sound. 16mm B&W. *Rental:* Hurlock Cine, Inst Cinema & Film Ctr DC.

Disc Jockey. Jim Stafford & Judy Jordan. Directed by Lee Frost. 1979. USA. 95 min. Sound. 16mm Color. *Rental:* Budget Films & Welling Motion Pictures.

Disc Jockey Jamboree *see* Jamboree.

Disciple, The. Williams S. Hart, Dorothy Dalton & Robert McKim. Directed by William S. Hart. 1915. Ince. 60 min. Sound. 16mm B&W. *Rental:* Em Gee Film Lib & Film Images. *Sale:* Blackhawk Films. *Sale:* Blackhawk Films, Silent 8mm version.

Discovering the Art of Korea: 5000 Years of Korean Art. Directed by Paula Lee Haller. 1980. Films for the Humanities. (Documentary). 58 min. Sound. 16mm Color. *Rental:* Films Human & U of IL Film. *Sale:* Films Human. *Sale:* Films Human, Videotape version.

Discovery. 1948. Film Classics. (Documentary). 85 min. Sound. 16mm B&W. *Rental:* Cine Craft & SD AV Ctr.

Discovery of America, The. Directed by Jaime Barrios. 1969. Jaime Barrios. 86 min. Sound. 16mm Color. *Rental:* Canyon Cinema.

Discreet Charm of the Bourgeoisie, The. Fernando Rey & Delphine Seyrig. Directed by Luis Bunuel. Fr. 1972. France. 100 min. Sound. 16mm Color. subtitles. *Rental:* Films Inc & New Cinema.

Discussion with Dr. Carl Rogers, A. Orig. Title: Dialogues: Dr. Carl Rogers. 2 pts. 1970. Macmillan. (Documentary). 110 min. Sound. 16mm Color. *Rental:* Macmillan Films. *Sale:* Macmillan Films.

Discussion with Dr. Gordon Allport, A. 2 pts. 1973. Macmillan. (Documentary). 100 min. Sound. 16mm B&W. *Rental:* Syracuse U Film.

Discussion with Dr. Henry Murray, A. 2 pts. 1973. Macmillan. (Documentary). 74 min. Sound. 16mm B&W. *Rental:* Macmillan Films. *Sale:* Macmillan Films.

Disembodied, The. Paul Burke & Allison Hayes. Directed by Walter Grauman. 1957. Allied Artists. 65 min. Sound. 16mm B&W. *Rental:* Hurlock Cine.

Dishonored. Marlene Dietrich & Victor McLaglen. Directed by Josef Von Sternberg. 1931. Paramount. 94 min. Sound. 16mm B&W. *Rental:* Swank Motion.

Dishonored Lady. Hedy Lamarr & Dennis O'Keefe. Directed by Robert Stevenson. 1947. United Artists. 83 min. Sound. 16mm B&W. *Rental:* Budget Films.

Disney's Best 1931-1948. (Anthology). 48 min. Sound. 16mm Color. *Rental:* Festival Films.

Disobedient. Orig. Titlc: Intimate Relations & Parents Terribles, Les. Harold Warrender. Directed by Charles Frank. 1956. Britain. 85 min. Sound. 16mm B&W. *Rental:* Budget Films, Ivy Films & Video Comm.

Disorder & Afterwards. Trans. Title: Desordre a Vingt Ans, Le. Directed by Armand Panigel. Fr. 1967. France. (Documentary). 85 min. Sound. 16mm B&W. subtitles. *Rental:* French Am Cul. *Rental:* French Am Cul, Videotape version.

Disorderly Orderly, The. Jerry Lewis. Directed by Frank Tashlin. 1964. Paramount. 101 min. Sound. 16mm B&W. *Rental:* Films Inc.

Disparus de Saint Agil, Les. Erich Von Stroheim & Michel Simon. Directed by Christian-Jaque. Fr. 1938. France. 100 min. Sound. 16mm B&W. subtitles. *Rental:* French Am Cul.

Dispatch from Reuters, A. Edward G. Robinson & Eddie Albert. Directed by William Dieterle. 1940. Warners. 90 min. Sound. 16mm B&W. *Rental:* MGM United.

Dispersed, The. 1964. NET. (Documentary). 60 min. Sound. 16mm B&W. *Rental:* BYU Media & Syracuse U Film. *Lease:* Syracuse U Film.

Dispersion Theory Approach to Nucleon Nuclear Scattering. 1961. US Government. (Documentary). 54 min. Sound. 16mm Color. *Sale:* Natl AV Ctr.

Displaced Person, The. Irene Worth & John Houseman. 1977. Learning in Focus. 57 min. Sound. 16mm Color. *Rental:* U of IL Film, Iowa Films, Kent St U Film, SD AV Ctr, Syracuse U Film, U Mich Media & Utah Media. *Sale:* Perspect Film. *Sale:* Perspect Film, Videocassette version.

Dispute, The. 2 pts. 1950. Britain. (Documentary). 50 min. Sound. 16mm B&W. *Rental:* Time-Life Multimedia. *Sale:* Time-Life Multimedia.

Disraeli. George Arliss & Joan Bennett. Directed by Alfred E. Green. 1929. Warners. 89 min. Sound. 16mm B&W. *Rental:* MGM United.

Dissent of the Governed: The Duffey Campaign in 1970. 1972. United Church Board. (Documentary). 58 min. Sound. 16mm Color. *Sale:* Natl Churches Christ.

Distant Drums. Gary Cooper & Mari Alden. Directed by Raoul Walsh. 1951. Warners. 101 min. Sound. 16mm Color. *Rental:* Corinth Films. *Lease:* Corinth Films.

Distant Thunder. Soumitra Chatterjee. Directed by Satyajit Ray. Hindi. 1973. India. 100 min. Sound. 16mm Color. subtitles. *Rental:* Cinema Five.

Distant Voices. 1978. Connection. (Documentary). 53 min. Sound. 16mm Color. *Rental:* U Cal Media, U of IL Film, Iowa Films, Kent St U Film & U Mich Media, Videotape version.

Distant War, Sept. 1939 - May 1940. Directed by Hugh Raggett. (World at War). : Pt. 2.). 1973. Media Guild. 52 min. Sound. 16mm Color. *Rental:* Media Guild & U Cal Media. *Sale:* Media Guild. *Sale:* Media Guild, Videotape version.

Distinguished Leaders in Nursing: Lucile P. Leone. 1977. US Government. (Documentary). 50 min. Sound. 16mm B&W. *Sale:* Natl AV Ctr.

Diva. Frederic Andrei & Roland Bertin. Directed by Jean-Jacques Beineix. 1982. 123 min. Sound. 16mm *Rental:* MGM United. *Rental:* MGM United, Videotape version.

Dive Bomber. Errol Flynn, Fred MacMurray & Alexis Smith. Directed by Michael Curtiz. 1941. Warners. 137 min. Sound. 16mm Color. *Rental:* MGM United.

Dive to the Edge of Creation, The. 1980. 59 min. Sound. 16mm Color. *Rental:* Natl Geog. *Sale:* Natl Geog. *Sale:* Natl Geog, Videotape version.

Divide & Conquer. Directed by Frank Capra. 1943. War Department. (Documentary). 58 min. Sound. 16mm B&W. *Rental:* Iowa Films, Maljack Productions, Natl AV Ctr, Trans-World Films & Budget Films. *Sale:* Natl AV Ctr.

Divided Heart, The. Cornell Borchers & Yvonne Mitchell. Directed by Charles Crichton. 1955. Britain. 89 min. Sound. 16mm B&W. *Rental:* Janus Films.

Dividing Line, The *see* Lawless.

Divine Emma, The. Bozidara Turronovova & George Kukura. Directed by Jiri Krejcik. Czech. 1983. 107 min. 16mm Color. subtitles. *Rental:* MGM United.

Divine Madness. Bette Midler. Directed by Michael Ritchie. 94 min. Sound. 16mm Color. *Rental:* Swank Motion. *Rental:* Swank Motion, Videotape version.

Divine Nymph. Laura Antonelli, Marcello Mastroianni & Terence Stamp. 90 min. Sound. Videotape Color. *Rental:* Maljack.

Divorce. Kay Francis & Bruce Cabot. Directed by William Nigh. 1945. Monogram. 80 min. Sound. 16mm B&W. *Rental:* MGM United & Mogulls Films.

Divorce, American Style. Dick Van Dyke & Debbie Reynolds. Directed by Bud Yorkin. 1967. Columbia. 109 min. Sound. 16mm Color. *Rental:* Arcus Film, Cine Craft, Film Ctr DC, Films Inc, Inst Cinema, Kerr Film, Modern Sound, Roas Films, Welling Motion Pictures, Westcoast Films & Wholesome Film Ctr.

Divorce Among Friends. Natalie Morehead & Lew Cody. Directed by Roy Del Ruth. 1931. Warners. 67 min. Sound. 16mm B&W. *Rental:* MGM United.

Divorce: For Better or for Worse. 1976. ABC. (Documentary). 49 min. Sound. 16mm Color. *Rental:* Iowa Films, McGraw-Hill Films & Syracuse U Film. *Sale:* McGraw-Hill Films. *Rental:* McGraw-Hill Films & U Cal Media, *Sale:* McGraw-Hill Films, Videotape version.

Divorce: For Better or Worst. 1977. 49 min. Sound. 16mm Color. *Rental:* Utah Media.

Divorce in the Family. Jackie Cooper & Lois Wilson. Directed by Charles Reisner. 1932. MGM. 83 min. Sound. 16mm B&W. *Rental:* MGM United.

Divorce of Lady X, The. Merle Oberon, Sir Laurence Olivier. Directed by Tim Whelan. 1938. Britain. 91 min. Sound. 16mm B&W. *Rental:* Budget Films & Mogulls Films.

Dixiana. Bert Wheeler & Robert Woolsey. Directed by Luther Reed. 1931. RKO. 99 min. Sound. 16mm *Rental:* RKO General Pics.

Dixie. Bing Crosby, Dorothy Lamour & Billy De Wolfe. Directed by Anthony Mann. 1943. Paramount. 90 min. Sound. 16mm Color. *Rental:* Swank Motion.

Dixie Dugan. James Ellison & Charlotte Greenwood. Directed by Otto Brower. 1943. Fox. 67 min. Sound. 16mm B&W. *Rental:* Films Inc.

Dixie Dynamite. Warren Oates & Christopher George. Directed by Lee Frost. 1976. Dimension. 90 min. Sound. 16mm Color. *Rental:* Welling Motion Pictures & Williams Films. *Sale:* Salz Ent. *Rental:* Welling Motion Pictures, 79 min. version.

Dixie Jamboree. Frances Langford & Guy Kibbee. Directed by Christy Cabanne. 1944. PRC. 80 min. Sound. 16mm B&W. *Rental:* Ivy Films, Mogulls Films & SD AV Ctr. *Sale:* Classics Assoc NY & Rep Pic Film.

Django Shoots First. Glenn Saxon. Directed by Alberto De Martino. 1966. Spain. 88 min. Sound. 16mm Color. dubbed. *Rental:* Budget Films & Video Comm.

Djibo: Zarma of Nigeria. 1982. Films Inc. 52 min. Sound. 16mm Color. *Rental:* Syracuse U Film.

DNA Story, The. 45 min. Sound. 16mm Color. *Rental:* Media Guild.

Do I Have to Kill My Child? Jacki Weaver. Directed by Donald Crombie. 1976. Australia. 52 min. Sound. 16mm Color. *Rental:* Aust Info Serv. *Sale:* Aust Info Serv.

Do I Look Like I Want to Die? 1979. PBS. (Documentary). 59 min. Videotape Color. . *Sale:* PBS Video.

Do-It-Yourself Messiah. 1980. PBS. (Documentary). 59 min. Sound. 16mm Color. *Rental:* PBS Video.

Do Not Disturb. Doris Day & Rod Taylor. Directed by Ralph Levy. 1965. Fox. 102 min. Sound. 16mm Color. *Rental:* Films Inc. *Rental:* Films Inc, Anamorphic color version.

Do Not Fold, Staple, Spindle or Multilate. Orig. Title: Labor Relations: Do Not Fold, Staple, Spindle or Multilate. Ed Begley. 1966. Canada. 50 min. Sound. 16mm B&W. *Rental:* Natl Film CN, U of IL Film & U Mich Media. *Sale:* Natl Film CN. *Rental:* Natl Film CN, *Sale:* Natl Film CN, Videotape version.

Do Not Go Gentle *see* Old Age.

Do We Really Need the Rockies? 1980. WGBH. (Documentary). 57 min. Sound. 16mm Color. *Rental:* Time-Life Multimedia. *Sale:* Time-Life Multimedia. *Sale:* Time-Life Multimedia, Videotape version.

Do You Keep a Lion at Home? Josef Filip. Directed by Pavel Hobl. 1964. Czechoslovakia. (Color sequences). 81 min. Sound. 16mm dubbed. *Rental:* Budget Films, Films Inc, Macmillan Films & Modern Sound. *Sale:* Macmillan Films.

Do You Love Me? Maureen O'Hara & Dick Haymes. Directed by Gregory Ratoff. 1946. Fox. 91 min. Sound. 16mm Color. *Rental:* Films Inc.

Do You Think a Job is the Answer? 1969. PBS. (Documentary). 68 min. Sound. 16mm B&W. *Rental:* Indiana AV Ctr. *Sale:* Indiana AV Ctr.

Doberman Gang, The. Julie Parrish. Directed by Byron Chudnow. 1972. Dimension. 90 min. Sound. 16mm Color. *Rental:* Arcus Film, Bosco Films, Budget Films, Film Pres, Films Inc, Kerr Film, Video Comm, Welling Motion Pictures, Westcoast Films & Williams Films.

Doc. Stacy Keach & Faye Dunaway. Directed by Frank Perry. 1971. United Artists. 96 min. Sound. 16mm Color. *Rental:* MGM United.

Doc Savage: The Man of Bronze. Ron Ely. Directed by Michael Anderson. 1970. Warners. 100 min. Sound. 16mm Color. *Rental:* Buchan Pic, Cine Craft, Films Inc, Modern Sound, Twyman Films, Welling Motion Pictures & Williams Films.

Docks of New Orleans. Roland Winters. Directed by Derwin Abrahams. 1948. Monogram. 70 min. Sound. 16mm B&W. *Rental:* Hurlock Cine.

Docks of New York. George Bancroft & Betty Compson. Directed by Josef Von Sternberg. 1928. Paramount. 60 min. Sound. 16mm B&W. *Rental:* Films Inc.

Docks of New York. Bowery Boys. Directed by Wallace Fox. 1945. Monogram. 63 min. Sound. 16mm B&W. *Rental:* Modern Sound.

Doctor & the Girl, The. Glenn Ford & Charles Coburn. Directed by Curtis Bernhardt. 1949. MGM. 98 min. Sound. 16mm B&W. *Rental:* Films Inc.

Doctor & the Playgirl, The. Mark O'Daniels & Rocky Graziano. Directed by William Martin. 1965. Emerson. 80 min. Sound. 16mm B&W. *Rental:* Films Inc.

Doctor at Large. Dirk Bogarde & Muriel Pavlow. Directed by Ralph Thomas. 1957. Britain. 98 min. Sound. 16mm Color. *Rental:* Budget Films & Learning Corp Am. *Sale:* Learning Corp Am. *Rental:* Vidamerica, Videotape version.

Doctor at Sea. Dirk Borgade & Brigette Bardot. Directed by Ralph Thomas. 1956. Britain. 92 min. Sound. Videotape Color. *Rental:* Learning Corp Am & Vidamerica. *Sale:* Learning Corp Am.

Doctor Beware *see* Teresa Venerdi.

Dr. Black, Mr. Hyde. Bernie Casey & Rosalind Cash. Directed by William Crain. 1975. Dimension. 87 min. Sound. 16mm Color. *Rental:* Williams Films. *Sale:* Salz Ent.

Dr. Blood's Coffin. Hazel Court & Kieron Moore. Directed by Sidney J. Furie. 1961. United Artists. 92 min. Sound. 16mm B&W. *Rental:* MGM United.

Dr. Bull. Will Rogers & Marion Nixon. Directed by John Ford. 1933. Fox. 76 min. Sound. 16mm B&W. *Rental:* Films Inc.

Doctor Christian Meets the Women. Jean Hersholt. Directed by William McGann. 1940. RKO. 70 min. Sound. 16mm B&W. *Rental:* Budget Films, Ivy Films, Mogulls Films & Rep Pic Film. *Lease:* Rep Pic Film.

Dr. Coppelius. Directed by Ted Kneeland. 1970. Germany. (Ballet). 94 min. Sound. 16mm Color. *Rental:* Budget Films, Video Comm & Westcoast Films.

Dr. Cyclops. Albert Dekker. Directed by Ernest B. Schoedsack. 1940. Paramount. 76 min. Sound. 16mm Color. *Rental:* Williams Films.

Doctor Detroit. Dan Aykroyd & Howard Hesseman. Directed by Michael Pressman. 1982. Universal. 89 min. Sound. 16mm Color. *Rental:* Swank Motion. *Rental:* Swank Motion, Videotape version.

Doctor Dolittle. Rex Harrison & Anthony Newley. Directed by Richard Fleischer. 1967. Fox. (Anamorphic). 152 min. Sound. 16mm Color. *Rental:* Films Inc, Twyman Films, Twyman Films, Welling Motion Pictures, Westcoast Films & Williams Films. *Sale:* Blackhawk Films, Cinema Concepts, Golden Tapes, Magnetic Video, Video Lib & Williams Films, Videotape version.

Dr. Dragstedt. 1973. U. S. Government. (Documentary). 60 min. Sound. 16mm B&W. *Sale:* Natl AV Ctr.

Dr. Duane Gish. 1982. American Association for the Advancement of Science Symposium. 55 min. Color. *Rental:* U Cal Media.

Dr. Ehrlich's Magic Bullet. Orig. Title: Story of Dr. Ehrlich's Magic Bullet, The. Edward G. Robinson & Ruth Gordon. Directed by William Dieterle. 1940. Warners. 103 min. Sound. 16mm B&W. *Rental:* MGM United.

Dr. Einstein Before Lunch. Orig. Title: Einstein Before Lunch. 1975. Graphic Curriculum. (Documentary). 58 min. Sound. 16mm Color. *Rental:* Graphic Curr. *Sale:* Graphic Curr.

Dr. Erich Fromm. 2 pts. 1968. Macmillan. (Documentary). 110 min. Sound. 16mm B&W. *Rental:* U Cal Media.

Dr. Erik Erikson. 1967. 55 min. Sound. 16mm B&W. *Rental:* Iowa Films.

Dr. Faustus. Richard Burton & Elizabeth Taylor. Directed by Richard Burton & Nevill Coghill. 1968. Columbia. 93 min. Sound. 16mm Color. *Rental:* Budget Films, Cine Craft, Films Inc, Kit Parker, Modern Sound, Natl Film Video, Swank Motion, Welling Motion Pictures & Westcoast Films.

Dr. Frank Thwaites. 1967. 49 min. Sound. 16mm Color. *Rental:* U Cal Media.

Dr. Gillespie's Criminal Case. Lionel Barrymore, Donna Reed & Van Johnson. Directed by Willis Goldbeck. 1943. MGM. 89 min. Sound. 16mm B&W. *Rental:* MGM United.

Dr. Goldfoot & the Bikini Machine. Vincent Price & Frankie Avalon. Directed by Norman Taurog. 1965. American International. 90 min. Sound. 16mm Color. *Rental:* Westcoast Films.

Dr. Hastings. 1973. US Government. (Documentary). 60 min. Sound. 16mm B&W. *Sale:* Natl AV Ctr.

Dr. Hawaii. 45 min. Sound. 16mm Color. *Rental:* Canyon Cinema.

Dr. Huggins. 1973. US Government. (Documentary). 60 min. Sound. 16mm B&W. *Sale:* Natl AV Ctr.

Doctor, I Want. 58 min. Sound. Videotape *Rental:* PBS Video. *Sale:* PBS Video.

Doctor in Distress. Dirk Bogarde. Directed by Ralph Thomas. 1963. Britain. 112 min. Sound. 16mm Color. *Rental:* Vidamerica.

Doctor in Love. Michael Craig & James Robertson Justice. Directed by Ralph Thomas. 1962. Britain. 97 min. Sound. 16mm Color. *Rental:* Budget Films.

Doctor Jack. Harold Lloyd & Mildred Davis. Directed by Fred Newmeyer. 1922. Pathe. (Music track only). 55 min. Sound. 16mm B&W. *Rental:* Films Inc, Images Film, Janus Films & Kino Intl.

Doctor Jekyll & Mr. Hyde. John Barrymore & Martha Mansfield. Directed by John Robertson. 1920. Paramount. 69 min. Silent. 16mm B&W. *Rental:* Film Classics, Films Inc & Mogulls Films. *Sale:* Festival Films & Film Classics. *Rental:* Killiam Collect & New Cinema, Sound 16mm & tinted, musical score only version. *Rental:* Ivy Films & Swank Motion, *Sale:* Blackhawk Films, Super 8 sound version. *Rental:* Video Comm, *Sale:* Blackhawk Films & Festival Films, Videotape version. *Sale:* Film Classics, Silent 8mm version.

Dr. Jekyll & Mr. Hyde. Fredric March & Miriam Hopkins. Directed by Rouben Mamoulian. 1932. Paramount. 85 min. Sound. 16mm B&W. *Rental:* MGM United. *Rental:* MGM United, Videotape version.

Dr. Jekyll & Mr. Hyde. Spencer Tracy, Ingrid Bergman & Lana Turner. Directed by Victor Fleming. 1941. MGM. 113 min. Sound. 16mm B&W. *Rental:* MGM United.

Dr. Jekyll & Sister Hyde. Ralph Bates & Martine Beswick. Directed by Roy Ward Baker. 1972. Britain. 95 min. Sound. 16mm Color. *Rental:* Swank Motion.

Dr. Jekyll & the Werewolf. Orig. Title: Dr. Jekyll & the Wolfman. Paul Naschy. Directed by Leon Klimovsky. 1975. 91 min. Sound. 16mm Color. *Rental:* Films Inc.

Dr. Kildare Goes Home. Lew Ayres & Lionel Barrymore. Directed by Harold S. Bucquet. 1940. MGM. 79 min. Sound. 16mm B&W. *Rental:* MGM United.

Dr. Kildare's Strange Case. Lew Ayres, Lionel Barrymore & Laraine Day. Directed by Harold S. Bucquet. 1940. MGM. 76 min. Sound. 16mm B&W. *Rental:* Budget Films & MGM United.

Dr. Kildare's Wedding Day. Lew Ayres & Laraine Day. Directed by Harold S. Bucquet. 1941. MGM. 83 min. Sound. 16mm B&W. *Rental:* MGM United.

Dr. Leakey & the Dawn of Man. 1966. National Geographic. (Documentary). 50 min. Sound. 16mm Color. *Rental:* Films Inc, Syracuse U Film, U Mich Media & Wholesome Film Ctr. *Sale:* Films Inc.

Dr. Mabuse, King of Crime. Rudolf Klein-Rogge. Directed by Fritz Lang. 1922. Germany. 93 min. Silent. 16mm B&W. *Rental:* Em Gee Film Lib, Films Inc & Janus Films. *Sale:* Glenn Photo & Reel Images.

Dr. Mabuse, the Gambler. 2 pts. Rudolph Klein-Rogge. Directed by Fritz Lang. 1922. Germany. 225 min. Silent. 16mm B&W. *Rental:* Films Inc & Janus Films. *Sale:* Reel Images. *Sale:* Tamarelles French Film, Videotape version.

Dr. McDermott. 1973. US Government. (Documentary). 60 min. Sound. 16mm B&W. *Sale:* Natl AV Ctr.

Dr. Martin Luther King Jr: An Amazing Grace. 1978. Mcgraw-Hill. (Documentary, color sequences). 62 min. Sound. 16mm *Rental:* U Cal Media, La Inst Res Ctr, McGraw-Hill Films & Utah Media. *Sale:* McGraw-Hill Films.

Dr. Minx. Edy Williams & Randy Boone. Directed by Hikmet Avedis. 1976. Dimension. 94 min. Sound. 16mm Color. *Sale:* Salz Ent.

Doctor Monica. Kay Francis & Warren William. Directed by William Keighley. 1934. Warners. 53 min. Sound. 16mm B&W. *Rental:* MGM United.

Dr. No. Sean Connery & Ursula Andress. Directed by Terence Young. 1962. United Artists. 111 min. Sound. 16mm Color. *Rental:* MGM United. *Rental:* MGM United, Videotape version.

Dr. Norman Bethune. Gerald Tannebaum. 1964. Cinema Guild. 117 min. Sound. 16mm Color. subtitles. *Rental:* Cinema Guild.

Doctor of Doom. Trans. Title: Luchadoras Contra el Medico Asesino, Las. Lorena Velazque & Elizabeth Campbell. Directed by Rene Cardona. Span. 1962. Mexico. 77 min. Sound. 16mm dubbed. *Rental:* Budget Films.

Dr. Orloff's Monster. Jose Rufio. Directed by John Frank. 1967. American International. 85 min. Sound. 16mm B&W. *Rental:* Films Inc.

Doctor Petronius, Seducer of Women. 1974. (Sepia). 55 min. Sound. 16mm Color. *Rental:* Canyon Cinema.

Dr. Phibes Rises Again. Vincent Price & Robert Quarry. Directed by Robert Fuest. 1972. Fox. 89 min. Sound. 16mm Color. *Rental:* Swank Motion, Welling Motion Pictures & Wholesome Film Ctr.

Doctor Renault's Secret. J. Carroll Naish & George Zucco. Directed by Harry Lachman. 1942. Fox. 58 min. Sound. 16mm B&W. *Rental:* Films Inc.

Dr. Rhythm. Bing Crosby & Beatrice Lillie. Directed by Frank Tuttle. 1938. Paramount. 81 min. Sound. 16mm B&W. *Rental:* Swank Motion.

Dr. Robert Gentry: Part Four. 1982. American Association for Advancement of Science Symposium. 50 min. Color. *Rental:* UCSB.

Dr. Robert Koch. Emil Jannings. Ger. 1929. Germany. 115 min. Sound. 16mm B&W. subtitles. *Rental:* Trans-World Films. *Rental:* Trans-World Films, Unsubtitled version.

Dr. Satan's Robot. Eduardo Ciannelli & Robert Wilcox. Directed by William Witney & John English. 1940. Republic. 100 min. Sound. 16mm B&W. *Rental:* Ivy Films. *Sale:* Rep Pic Film.

Dr. Schweitzer. Pierre Fresnay & Marie Winter. Directed by Andre Haguet. 1952. France. 92 min. Sound. 16mm B&W. dubbed. *Rental:* Films Inc, Budget Films & Ivy Films.

Dr. Socrates. Paul Muni & Ann Dvorak. Directed by William Dieterle. 1935. Warners. 70 min. Sound. 16mm B&W. *Rental:* MGM United.

Dr. Spock: An American Institution. 48 min. Sound. 16mm Color. *Rental:* Phoenix Films. *Sale:* Phoenix Films. *Sale:* Phoenix Films, Videotape version.

Dr. Strangelove: How I Learned to Stop Worrying & Love the Bomb. Orig. Title: Two Hours to Doom. Peter Sellers & George C. Scott. Directed by Stanley Kubrick. 1964. Columbia. 93 min. Sound. B&W. *Rental:* Swank Motion. *Sale:* Cinema Concepts, *Rental:* Swank Motion, Videotape version.

Dr. Syn. George Arliss & Margaret Lockwood. Directed by Roy William Neill. 1937. Britain. 80 min. Sound. 16mm B&W. *Rental:* Budget Films, Classic Film Mus & Classic Film Mus. *Sale:* Classic Film Mus. *Sale:* Tamarelles French Film, Videotape version.

Dr. Syn: Alias the Scarecrow. Patrick McGoohan & George Cole. Directed by James Neilson. 1964. Disney. 98 min. Sound. 16mm Color. *Rental:* Buchan Pic, Cine Craft, Cousino Visual Ed, Disney Prod, Films Inc, U of IL Film, Newman Film Lib, Film Ctr Dc & Twyman Films.

Doctor Takes a Wife, The. Loretta Young & Ray Milland. Directed by Alexander Hall. 1940. Columbia. 88 min. Sound. 16mm B&W. *Rental:* Inst Cinema & Roas Films.

Dr. Tarr's Torture Dungeon. 1972. Mexico. (Cast unlisted). 88 min. Sound. 16mm Color. dubbed. *Rental:* Twyman Films.

Dr. Teen Dilemma. 60 min. Videotape Color. *Sale:* Videx Home Lib.

Dr. Terror's House of Horrors. Peter Cushing & Christopher Lee. Directed by Freddie Francis. 1965. Paramount. 98 min. Sound. 16mm B&W. *Rental:* Budget Films, Cine Craft, Ivy Films, Modern Sound & Video Comm. *Lease:* Rep Pic Film.

Dr. Wangensteen. 1973. US Government. (Documentary). 60 min. Sound. 16mm B&W. *Sale:* Natl AV Ctr.

Dr. William Thwaites: Part Three. 1982. American Association for the Symposium. 49 min. Color. *Rental:* U Cal Media.

Dr. Wood. 1973. US Government. (Documentary). 60 min. Sound. 16mm B&W. *Sale:* Natl AV Ctr.

Doctor X. Lee Tracy & Lionel Atwill. Directed by Michael Curtiz. 1932. Warners. 77 min. Sound. 16mm B&W. *Rental:* MGM United.

Doctor, You've Got to Be Kidding. Sandra Dee & George Hamilton. Directed by Peter Tewksbury. 1967. MGM. 94 min. Sound. 16mm Color. *Rental:* MGM United. *Rental:* MGM United, Anamorphic color version.

Doctor Zhivago. Julie Christie, Omar Sharif, Rod Steiger, Sir Alec Guinness. Directed by David Lean. 1965. MGM. 194 min. Sound. 16mm Color. *Rental:* MGM United. *Rental:* MGM United, Videotape version.

Doctor's Dilemma, The. Leslie Caron, Dirk Bogarde & Alastair Sim. Directed by Anthony Asquith. 1958. Britain. 98 min. Sound. 16mm B&W. *Rental:* MGM United. *Rental:* MGM United, Color version.

Doctors Don't Tell. John Beal & Edward Norris. Directed by Jacques Tourneur. 1941. Republic. 54 min. Sound. 16mm B&W. *Rental:* Ivy Films. *Sale:* Rep Pic Film.

Doctors of Nigeria, The. 1980. WGBH. (Documentary). 57 min. Sound. 16mm Color. *Rental:* Time-Life Multimedia. *Sale:* Time-Life Multimeda. *Sale:* Time-Life Multimedia, Videotape version.

Doctors' Wives. Dyan Cannon & Richard Crenna. Directed by George Schaefer. 1971. Columbia. 95 min. Sound. 16mm Color. *Rental:* Budget Films, Cine Craft, Films Inc, Kerr Film, Modern Sound, Welling Motion Pictures & Wholesome Film Ctr.

Documentary! 1978. Texture. (Anthology). 135 min. Sound. 16mm B&W. *Rental:* Texture Film. *Sale:* Texture Film. *Sale:* Texture Film, Videotape version.

Dodes'Ka-Den. Trans. Title: Clickety-Clack. Yoshitaka Zushi. Directed by Akira Kurosawa. Jap. 1972. Japan. 140 min. Sound. 16mm Color. subtitles. *Rental:* Films Inc & Janus Films.

Dodge City. Errol Flynn & Olivia De Havilland. Directed by Michael Curtiz. 1939. Warners. 104 min. Sound. 16mm Color. *Rental:* MGM United.

Dodsworth. Walter Huston & Ruth Chatterton. Directed by William Wyler. 1936. Goldwyn. 101 min. Sound. 16mm B&W. *Rental:* Films Inc, Macmillan Films & Syracuse U Film. *Lease:* Macmillan Films.

Dofar: Guerilla War on the Arabian Gulf. 1977. Syria. (Documentary). 58 min. Sound. 16mm Color. *Rental:* Inst Cinema. *Sale:* Inst Cinema.

Dog & the Diamonds, The. Kathleen Harrison & George Coulouris. Directed by Ralph Thomas. 1953. Britain. 55 min. Sound. 16mm B&W. *Sale:* Lucerne Films.

Dog Day Afternoon. Al Pacino & John Cazale. Directed by Sidney Lumet. 1975. Warners. 129 min. Sound. 16mm Color. *Rental:* Swank Motion, Twyman Films & Williams Films. *Rental:* Swank Motion, Videotape version.

Dog of Flanders, A. Frankie Thomas & O. P. Heggie. Directed by Edward Sloman. 1935. RKO. 72 min. Sound. 16mm B&W. *Rental:* Films Inc. *Rental:* Westcoast Films, 97 mins. version.

Dog of Flanders, A. David Ladd & Donald Crisp. Directed by James B. Clark. 1959. United Artists. 97 min. Sound. 16mm Color. *Rental:* Budget Films.

Dog Star Man. Directed by Stan Brakhage. 1964. Stan Brakhage. (Experimental). 74 min. Silent. 16mm Color. *Rental:* Canyon Cinema & Museum Mod Art.

Dogan, The. France. (Documentary). 50 min. Sound. 16mm Color. *Rental:* Inst Cinema. *Sale:* Inst Cinema.

Doggie & Three. Directed by A. Kosnar. 1955. Czechoslovakia. (Cast unlisted). 51 min. Sound. 16mm Color. dubbed. *Rental:* Films Inc & Westcoast Films. *Sale:* Films Inc.

Dogs. David McCallum. Directed by Burt Brinckerhoff. 1976. Mar Vista. 90 min. Sound. 16mm Color. *Rental:* Twyman Films.

Dog's Best Friend, A. Bill Williams & Marcia Henderson. Directed by Edward L. Cahn. 1959. United Artists. 84 min. Sound. 16mm Color. *Rental:* MGM United.

Dogs of War, The. Christopher Walken & Tom Berenger. Directed by John Irvin. 1981. United Artists. 102 min. Sound. 16mm Color. *Rental:* MGM United. *Rental:* MGM United, Videotape version.

Dogs to the Rescue. Dorine Dron. Directed by Paul Fritzemeth. 1972. Bulgaria-Canada. 84 min. Sound. 16mm Color. *Sale:* Xerox Films.

Doktor Glas. Orig. Title: Dr. Glas. Per Oscarsson. Directed by Mai Zetterling. Danish. 1969. Denmark. 83 min. Sound. 16mm B&W. subtitles. *Rental:* Films Inc.

Dolce Vita, La. Marcello Mastroianni, Anita Ekberg & Anouk Aimee. Directed by Federico Fellini. Ital. 1961. Italy. 180 min. Sound. Videotape B&W. subtitles. *Rental:* Films Inc, Ivy Films, Rep Pic Film & Twyman Films. *Sale:* Rep Pic Film & Tamarelles French Film.

Dolci Signore, Le *see* Anyone Can Play.

Dolemite. Ray Rudy Moore. Directed by D'Urville Martin. 1975. Dimension. 88 min. Sound. 16mm Color. *Sale:* Saltz Ent.

Doll, The. Per Oscarsson. Directed by Arne Mattsson. Swed. 1962. Sweden. 94 min. Sound. 16mm B&W. subtitles. *Rental:* Budget Films & Kit Parker. *Sale:* Festival Films.

Doll Face. Orig. Title: Come Back to Me. Vivian Blaine & Dennis O'Keefe. Directed by Lewis Seiler. 1945. Columbia. 80 min. Sound. 16mm B&W. *Rental:* Budget Films, Films Inc & Natl Film Video. *Sale:* Festival Films. *Sale:* Festival Films, Videotape version.

Dollars. Goldie Hawn & Warren Beatty. Directed by Richard Brooks. 1971. Columbia. 119 min. Sound. 16mm Color. *Rental:* Arcus Film, Bosco Films, Budget Films, Cine Craft, Film Ctr DC, Inst Cinema, Ivy Films, Modern Sound, Swank Motion, Welling Motion Pictures, Wholesome Film Ctr & Williams Films.

Dollars for a Fast Gun *see* One Hundred Thousand Dollars for Lassiter.

Doll's House, A. 2 pts. Directed by John Barnes. 1967. Encyclopaedia Britannica. (Cast unlisted). 61 min. Sound. 16mm Color. *Rental:* U of IL Film, Syracuse U Film & Ency Brit Ed. *Sale:* Ency Brit Ed. *Sale:* Ency Brit Ed, Videotape version.

Doll's House, A. Jane Fonda. Directed by Joseph Losey. 1972. CBS. 108 min. Sound. 16mm Color. *Rental:* Budget Films, Films Inc, Inst Cinema, Images Film, Kent St U Film, Kit Parker, Learning Corp Am, Modern Sound, Swank Motion, Syracuse U Film, Twyman Films, U Cal Media, U of IL Film, Welling Motion Pictures, Westcoast Films & Wholesome Film Ctr. *Lease:* Learning Corp Am. *Sale:* Tamarelles French Film, Videotape version.

Doll's House, A. Claire Bloom, Sir Ralph Richardson. Directed by Patrick Garland. 1973. Britain. 95 min. Sound. 16mm Color. *Rental:* Films Inc.

Dolly Sisters, The. Betty Grable & June Haver. Directed by Irving Cummings. 1945. Fox. 114 min. Sound. 16mm Color. *Rental:* Williams Films & Films Inc.

Dolphin. Verve. (Documentary). 58 min. Videotape Color. *Rental:* Films Inc.

Dombey & Son. Norman McKinnel. Directed by Maurice Elvey. 1917. Britain. 50 min. Silent. 16mm B&W. *Rental:* Film Classics. *Sale:* Film Classics. *Rental:* Film Classics, *Sale:* Film Classics, Silent 8mm version.

Domino Principle, The. Gene Hackman, Candice Bergen & Richard Widmark. Directed by Stanley Kramer. 1977. Embassy. 100 min. Sound. 16mm Color. *Rental:* Films Inc.

Don Amigo. Duncan Renaldo. Directed by Wallace Fox. 1950. United Artists. 65 min. Sound. Videotape B&W. *Sale:* Video Comm.

Don Bosco. Orig. Title: Life Story of St. John Bosco. Directed by Geoffredo Alessandrini. 1936. Italy. (Cast unlisted). 75 min. Sound. 16mm B&W. *Rental:* Bosco Films.

Don Daredevil Rides Again. Ken Curtis & Aline Towne. Directed by Fred C. Brannon. 1951. Republic. 163 min. Sound. 16mm B&W. *Rental:* Ivy Films.

Don Giovanni. Ruggero Raimondi & Edda Moser. Directed by Joseph Losey. Ital. 1979. France-Italy. 185 min. Sound. 16mm Color. subtitles. *Rental:* New Yorker Films.

Don Juan. John Barrymore & Mary Astor. Directed by Alan Crosland. 1926. Warners. (Music & sound effects only). 111 min. Sound. 16mm B&W. *Rental:* MGM United. *Rental:* Killiam Collect, Sound 16mm condensed, music & narration only version. *Rental:* MGM United, Silent 16mm version.

Don Juan. Cesare Danova & Josef Neinrad. 1956. Austria. 85 min. Sound. 16mm Color. dubbed. *Rental:* Films Inc.

Don Juan in Hell: Bernard Shaw. APA. (Cast unlisted). 54 min. Sound. 16mm B&W. *Rental:* Modern Mass. *Sale:* Modern Sound.

Don Juan Quilligan. William Bendix & Joan Blondell. Directed by Frank Tuttle. 1945. Fox. 75 min. Sound. 16mm B&W. *Rental:* Films Inc.

Don Juan: The History of the Motion Picture. Directed by Alan Crosland. 50 min. Sound. 16mm B&W. *Rental:* U of IL Film.

Don Messer: His Land & His Music. 1971. Canada. (Documentary). 70 min. Sound. 16mm Color. *Rental:* Natl Film CN. *Sale:* Natl Film CN.

Don Pedro: La Vida de un Pueblo. Span. 1976. Puerto Rico. (Documentary). 50 min. Sound. 16mm Color. subtitles. *Rental:* CA Newsreel. *Sale:* CA Newsreel.

Don Q, Son of Zorro. Douglas Fairbanks & Mary Astor. Directed by Donald Crisp. 1925. Elton Corp. 113 min. Silent. 16mm B&W. *Rental:* A Twyman Pres, Budget Films, Em Gee Film Lib, Kit Parker, Museum Mod Art & Twyman Films. *Sale:* Blackhawk Films & Glenn Photo. *Sale:* Blackhawk Films, Sound 16mm version. *Rental:* Ivy Films, *Sale:* Blackhawk Films, Super 8 sound version. *Sale:* Blackhawk Films & Glenn Photo, Super 8 silent version.

Don Quixote. Fyodor Chaliapin. Directed by G. W. Pabst. Fr. 1932. France. 85 min. Sound. 16mm B&W. subtitles. *Rental:* Classic Film Mus.

Don Quixote. Nikolai Cherkassov. Directed by Grigori Kozintsev. Rus. 1957. Russia. 110 min. Sound. 16mm Color. subtitles. *Rental:* Corinth Films.

Don Quixote. Sir Directed by Robert Helpmann. 1973. Australia. (Dance). 109 min. Sound. 16mm Color. *Rental:* W Reade Sixteen.

Don Quixote de la Mancha. Rafael Rivelles. Directed by Rafael Gil. Span. 1948. Spain. 143 min. Sound. 16mm B&W. subtitles. *Rental:* Films Inc.

Don Quixote with Mr. Magoo. 1965. UPA. (Animated). 50 min. Sound. 16mm Color. *Rental:* Films Inc & Welling Motion Pictures. *Sale:* Films Inc. *Rental:* Twyman Films, Spanish Language version.

Don Ricardo Returns. Isabelita. Directed by Terry Morse. 1946. PRC. 63 min. Sound. 16mm B&W. *Sale:* Classics Assoc NY.

Don't Pull Your Punches see Kid Comes Back.

Dona Barbara. Maria Felix. Directed by Fernando De Fuentes. Span. 1943. Mexico. 137 min. Sound. 16mm B&W. subtitles. *Rental:* Trans-World Films.

Dona Flor & Her Two Husbands. Sonia Braga & Jose Wiker. Directed by Bruno Barreto. 1977. Brazil. 106 min. Sound. 16mm Color. subtitles. *Rental:* New Yorker Films.

Dona Perfecta. Dolores Del Rio. Directed by Alejandro Galindo. 1949. Mexico. 114 min. Sound. 16mm B&W. *Rental:* Trans-World Films.

Dondi. David Janssen & Patti Page. Directed by Albert Zugsmith. 1961. Allied Artists. 100 min. Sound. 16mm B&W. *Rental:* Hurlock Cine.

Done: The First Transcontinental Railway. 1979. PBS. (Documentary). 58 min. Videotape B&W. *Rental:* PBS Video. *Sale:* PBS Video.

Donkey Skin. Trans. Title: Peau D'Ane. Catherine Deneuve. Directed by Jacques Demy. Fr. 1974. France. 90 min. Sound. 16mm Color. subtitles. *Rental:* Films Inc & Janus Films.

Donner Pass. Robert Fuller, Michael Callan & Andrew Prine. Directed by James L. Conway. 1979. NBC. 99 min. Sound. 16mm Color. *Rental:* Williams Films & Westcoast Films. *Sale:* Lucerne Films. *Sale:* Lucerne Films & Williams Films, *Sale:* Tamarelles French Film, Videotape version.

Donovan Affair, The. Jack Holt. Directed by Frank Capra. 1929. Columbia. 72 min. Sound. 16mm B&W. *Rental:* Kit Parker.

Donovan's Brain. Lew Ayres & Gene Evans. Directed by Felix Feist. 1953. United Artists. 81 min. Sound. 16mm B&W. *Rental:* MGM United & Westcoast Films.

Donovan's Reef. John Wayne & Lee Marvin. Directed by John Ford. 1963. Paramount. 112 min. Sound. 16mm Color. *Rental:* Films Inc.

Don's Party. Ray Barrett & Clare Binney. Directed by Bruce Beresford. 1976. Australia. 90 min. Sound. 16mm Color. *Rental:* Vidamerica. *Sale:* Tamarelles French Film & Vidamerica, Videotape version.

Don't Bet on Blondes. Warren William & Errol Flynn. Directed by Robert Florey. 1935. Warners. 60 min. Sound. 16mm B&W. *Rental:* MGM United.

Don't Bother to Knock. Richard Widmark, Marilyn Monroe & Anne Bancroft. Directed by Roy Baker. 1952. Fox. 76 min. Sound. 16mm B&W. *Rental:* Films Inc.

Don't Count the Candles. 1968. CBS. (Documentary). 54 min. Sound. 16mm B&W. *Sale:* Phoenix Films. *Sale:* Phoenix Films, Color version.

Don't Drink the Water. Jackie Gleason & Estelle Parsons. Directed by Howard Morris. 1969. Embassy. 98 min. Sound. 16mm Color. *Rental:* Films Inc.

Don't Fence Me In. Roy Rogers. Directed by John English. 1945. Republic. 54 min. Sound. 16mm B&W. *Rental:* Ivy Films, Rep Pic Film & Nostalgia Merchant.

Don't Gamble with Strangers. Kane Richmond & Bernadine Hayes. Directed by William Beaudine. 1940. Monogram. 68 min. Sound. 16mm B&W. *Rental:* Hurlock Cine.

Don't Get Personal. Hugh Herbert & Robert Paige. Directed by Charles Lamont. 1942. Universal. 60 min. Sound. 16mm B&W. *Rental:* Mogulls Films & Film Ctr DC.

Don't Give Up the Ship. Jerry Lewis & Dina Merrill. Directed by Norman Taurog. 1959. Paramount. 85 min. Sound. 16mm B&W. *Rental:* Budget Films, Williams Films, Newman Films & Wholesome Film Ctr. *Rental:* Williams Films, Super 8 sound version, Videotape version.

Don't Go Near the Water. Glenn Ford & Gia Scala. Directed by Charles Walters. 1957. MGM. 102 min. Sound. 16mm Color. *Rental:* MGM United.

Don't Just Stand There. Robert Wagner & Mary Tyler Moore. Directed by Ron Winston. 1968. Universal. 99 min. Sound. 16mm Color. *Rental:* Swank Motion.

Don't Knock the Rock. Alan Dale & Alan Freed. Directed by Fred F. Sears. 1956. Columbia. 84 min. Sound. 16mm B&W. *Rental:* Budget Films, Corinth Films, Kit Parker, Swank Motion & Westcoast Films.

Don't Knock the Twist. Chubby Checker. Directed by Oscar Rudolph. 1962. Columbia. 87 min. Sound. 16mm B&W. *Rental:* Budget Films & Ivy Films.

Don't Look Back. Bob Dylan. 1965. Bob Dylan. 90 min. Sound. 16mm B&W. *Rental:* Pennebaker. *Sale:* Pennebaker.

Don't Look in the Basement. Anne Macadams. Directed by S. F. Brownrigg. 1973. Hallmark. 95 min. Sound. 16mm Color. *Rental:* Ivy Films & Maljack.

Don't Look Now. Donald Sutherland & Julie Christie. Directed by Nicolas Roeg. 1973. Paramount. 110 min. Sound. 16mm Color. *Rental:* Films Inc.

Don't Lose Your Head. Sidney James & Jim Dale. Directed by Gerald Thomas. 1966. Britain. 90 min. Sound. 16mm B&W. *Rental:* Cinema Five.

Don't Make Waves. Tony Curtis & Claudia Cardinale. Directed by Alexander Mackendrick. 1966. MGM. 97 min. Sound. 16mm Color. *Rental:* MGM United. *Rental:* MGM United, Anamorphic color version.

Don't Raise the Bridge, Lower the River. Jerry Lewis & Terry-Thomas. Directed by Jerry Paris. 1968. Columbia. 99 min. Sound. 16mm Color. *Rental:* Arcus Film, Buchan Pic, Budget Films, Cine Craft, Williams Films, Film Pres, Inst Cinema, Modern Sound, Newman Films, Roas Films, Swank Motion, Film Ctr DC, Twyman Films, Westcoast Films, Welling Motion Pictures & Wholesome Film Ctr.

Don't Take It to Heart. Richard Greene & Patricia Medina. Directed by Jeffrey Dell. 1945. Britain. 89 min. Sound. 16mm B&W. *Rental:* Budget Films.

Don't Tell the Wife. Lucille Ball & Guy Kibbee. Directed by Christy Cabanne. 1937. RKO. 62 min. Sound. 16mm B&W. *Rental:* RKO General Pics.

Don't Trust Your Husband. Orig. Title: Innocent Affair, An. Madeleine Carroll & Fred MacMurray. Directed by Lloyd Bacon. 1948. United Artists. 85 min. Sound. 16mm B&W. *Rental:* Budget Films.

Don't Turn 'Em Loose. Betty Grable & Bruce Cabot. Directed by Ben Stoloff. 1936. RKO. 65 min. Sound. 16mm *Rental:* RKO General Pics.

Don't Turn the Other Cheek. Trans. Title: Viva la Muerte. Eli Wallach, Lynn Redgrave & Franco Nero. Directed by Duccio Tessari. 1973. MGM. (Anamorphic). 96 min. Sound. 16mm Color. *Rental:* Budget Films & Films Inc.

Don't Turn the Other Cheek. Anouk Ferjac. Directed by Fernando Arrabel. 1974. International Amusement. 90 min. Sound. 16mm Color. subtitles. *Rental:* New Line Cinema.

Doolins of Oklahoma, The. Randolph Scott & George Macready. Directed by Gordon Douglas. 1949. Columbia. 90 min. Sound. 16mm B&W. *Lease:* Time-Life Multimedia.

Doomed at Sundown. Bob Steele. Directed by Sam Newfield. 1937. Republic. 60 min. Sound. 16mm B&W. *Rental:* Ivy Films & Mogulls Films.

Doomed Caravan. William Boyd. Directed by Lesley Selander. 1941. Paramount. 54 min. Sound. 16mm B&W. *Lease:* Cinema Concepts.

Doomed to Die. Orig. Title: Mystery of the Wentworth Castle, The. Boris Karloff & Marjorie Reynolds. Directed by William Nigh. 1940. Monogram. 67 min. Sound. 16mm B&W. *Rental:* Budget Films & MGM United. *Sale:* Reel Images. *Sale:* Reel Images, Super 8 sound version.

Doomsday. Florence Vidor & Gary Cooper. Directed by Rowland V. Lee. 1928. Paramount. 60 min. Silent. 16mm B&W. *Rental:* Films Inc.

Doomsday Flight, The. Van Johnson & Jack Lord. Directed by William Graham. 1966. Universal. 100 min. Sound. 16mm Color. *Rental:* Swank Motion.

Doomsday Voyage. Joseph Cotten. Directed by John Vidette. 1971. Futurama. 88 min. Sound. 16mm Color. *Rental:* Budget Films & Video Comm.

Doomwatch. George Sanders, Ian Bannen & Simon Oates. Directed by Peter Sasdy. 1976. Embassy. 63 min. Sound. 16mm Color. *Rental:* Budget Films, Inst Cinema & Roas Films.

Doorway to Hell, The. Orig. Title: Handful of Clouds, A. Lew Ayres & James Cagney. Directed by Archie Mayo. 1930. Warners. 78 min. Sound. 16mm B&W. *Rental:* MGM United.

Dope. Directed by Sheldon Rochlin. New Line Cinema. (Cast unlisted). 90 min. 16mm Color. *Rental:* New Line Cinema.

Doppelganger *see* Journey to the Far Side of the Sun.

Dorian Gray *see* Secret of Dorian Gray.

Dorian Gray *see* Picture of Dorian Gray.

Dorothea Lange. Directed by Richard Moore. 1965. Richard Moore. (Documentary). 60 min. Sound. 16mm B&W. *Rental:* Museum Mod Art.

Dos Corazones y un Tango. Andres Falgas. Directed by Mario Del Rio. Span. Mexico. Sound. 16mm B&W. *Rental:* Film Classics.

Dos Noches. Conchita Montenegro. Directed by Fanchon Royer. Span. Spain. Sound. 16mm B&W. *Rental:* Film Classics.

Dossier Fifty-One. Roger Planchon & Francoise Lugagne. Directed by Michel Deville. Fr. 1978. France. 108 min. Sound. 16mm Color. subtitles. *Rental:* New Yorker Films.

Dostigayev & Others. Nina Olkhina. Directed by Y. Muzykant & Natalya Rashevskaya. 1959. Russia. 99 min. Sound. 16mm B&W. *Rental:* Corinth Films.

Dostoevsky Eighteen Twenty-One to Eighteen Eighty-One. 1975. Learning Corp. (Documentary). 54 min. Sound. 16mm Color. *Rental:* Budget Films, U of IL Film, Learning Corp Am, Syracuse U Film & Utah Media. *Sale:* Learning Corp Am. *Rental:* Learning Corp Am, *Sale:* Learning Corp Am, Videotape version.

Dot and the Bunny. 1982. Australia. 79 min. Sound. Videotape Color. *Sale:* Tamarelles French Films.

Dot, Dot, Dot. Directed by Edgardo Cozarinsky. Span. 1971. Argentina. (Documentary). 93 min. Sound. 16mm B&W. subtitles. *Rental:* New Yorker Films.

Double Bunk. Ian Carmichael & Janette Scott. Directed by C. M. Pennington-Richards. 1961. Britain. 92 min. Sound. 16mm B&W. *Rental:* Video Comm.

Double Confession. Derek Farr & Peter Lorre. Directed by Ken Annakin. 1950. Britain. 85 min. Sound. 16mm B&W. *Rental:* Charard Motion Pics.

Double Cross *see* Roses Are Red.

Double Crossbones. Donald O'Connor. Directed by Charles Barton. 1950. Universal. 73 min. Sound. 16mm Color. *Rental:* Swank Motion.

Double Danger. Preston Foster & Paul Guilfoyle. Directed by Lew Landers. 1938. RKO. 62 min. Sound. 16mm *Rental:* RKO General Pics.

Double Day, The. 1974. Tricontinental. (Documentary). 56 min. Sound. 16mm Color. *Rental:* Cinema Guild, U Mich Media & Unifilm. *Sale:* Cinema Guild & Unifilm. *Rental:* Unifilm, *Sale:* Unifilm, Spanish language version.

Double Deal. Richard Denning & Marie Windsor. Directed by Abby Berlin. 1950. RKO. 65 min. Sound. 16mm B&W. *Rental:* Films Inc.

Double Dynamite. Frank Sinatra & Jane Russell. Directed by Irving Cummings Jr. 1951. RKO. 80 min. Sound. 16mm B&W. *Rental:* Films Inc.

Double Exposure. John Bentley & Rona Anderson. Directed by John Gilling. 1954. Britain. 75 min. Sound. 16mm B&W. *Rental:* Bosco Films.

Double Exposure. Michael Callan & Joanna Pettet. Directed by Byron Hillman. 1983. Crown. 95 min. Sound. 16mm Color. *Rental:* Swank Motion.

Double Exposure of Holly. 1941. Republic. 77 min. Videotape Color. *Rental:* Quality X Video.

Double Identity. Orig. Title: Hurricane Smith. Ray Middleton & Jane Wyatt. Directed by Bernard Vorhaus. 1941. Republic. 68 min. Sound. 16mm B&W. *Rental:* Ivy Films.

Double Identity *see* River's End.

Double Indemnity. Fred MacMurray, Barbara Stanwyck & Edward G. Robinson. Directed by Billy Wilder. 1944. Paramount. 112 min. Sound. 16mm B&W. *Rental:* Swank Motion & Williams Films.

Double Jeopardy. Rod Cameron & Gale Robbins. Directed by R. G. Springsteen. 1955. Republic. 70 min. Sound. 16mm B&W. *Rental:* Ivy Films. *Sale:* Rep Pic Film.

Double Life, A. Ronald Colman, Signe Hasso & Shelley Winters. Directed by George Cukor. 1947. Universal. 103 min. Sound. 16mm B&W. *Rental:* Budget Films, Charard Motion Pics, Ivy Films & Kit Parker. *Lease:* Rep Pic Film.

Double McGuffin, The. Ernest Borgnine & George Kennedy. Directed by Joe Camp. 1979. Sunrise. 89 min. Sound. 16mm Color. *Rental:* Modern Sound, Swank Motion, Twyman Films & Williams Films.

Double Man, The. Yul Brynner & Lloyd Nolan. Directed by Franklin Schaffner. 1968. Warners. 105 min. Sound. 16mm Color. *Rental:* Charard Motion Pics, Inst Cinema, Video Comm, Welling Motion Pictures & Willoughby Peer.

Double Stop. Jeremiah Sullivan. Directed by Gerald Seth Sindell. 1968. World Entertainment. 95 min. Sound. 16mm B&W. *Rental:* Ivy Films.

Double Suicide. Kichiemon Nakamura & Shima Iwashita. Directed by Masahiro Shinoda. Jap. 1969. Japan. 142 min. Sound. 16mm B&W. subtitles. *Rental:* Films Inc.

Double Take. Reg Varney & Norman Rossington. Directed by Harry Booth. Britain. 85 min. Sound. 16mm B&W. *Rental:* Cinema Five.

Double Trouble. Harry Langdon & Charlie Rogers. Directed by William West. 1941. Monogram. 62 min. Sound. 16mm B&W. *Rental:* Hurlock Cine.

Double Trouble. Elvis Presley. Directed by Norman Taurog. 1967. MGM. 90 min. Sound. 16mm Color. *Rental:* MGM United. *Rental:* MGM United, Anamorphic color version.

Double Wedding. William Powell & Myrna Loy. Directed by Richard Thorpe. 1937. MGM. 87 min. Sound. 16mm B&W. *Rental:* MGM United.

Doubting Thomas. Will Rogers & Billie Burke. Directed by David Butler. 1935. Fox. 73 min. Sound. 16mm B&W. *Rental:* Films Inc.

Doughboys, The. Orig. Title: Forward March. Cliff Edwards & Buster Keaton. Directed by Edward Sedgwick. 1930. MGM. 65 min. Sound. 16mm B&W. *Rental:* MGM United.

Doughgirls, The. Ann Sheridan & Jane Wyman. Directed by James V. Kern. 1944. Warners. 102 min. Sound. 16mm B&W. *Rental:* MGM United.

Douglas MacArthur. 1976. Britain. (Documentary). 62 min. Sound. 16mm Color. *Rental:* Time-Life Multimedia. *Sale:* Time-Life Multimedia. *Rental:* Time-Life Multimedia, *Sale:* Time-Life Multimedia, Videotape version.

Dove, The. Joseph Bottoms & Deborah Raffin. Directed by Charles Jarrott. 1974. Paramount. 105 min. Sound. 16mm Color. *Rental:* Films Inc. *Rental:* Budget Films, Abridged version.

Dove, The. Norma Talmadge. Directed by Roland West. 1927. 16mm *Rental:* A Twyman Pres.

Down & Dirty *see* Dirty, Mean & Nasty.

Down Among the Sheltering Palms. William Lundigan & Jane Greer. Directed by Edmund Goulding. 1953. Fox. 87 min. Sound. 16mm Color. *Rental:* Films Inc.

Down Argentine Way. Betty Grable, Don Ameche & Carmen Miranda. Directed by Irving Cummings. 1940. Fox. 88 min. Sound. 16mm Color. *Rental:* Films Inc.

Down Dakota Way. Roy Rogers. Directed by William Witney. 1949. Republic. 67 min. Sound. 16mm B&W. *Rental:* Ivy Films. *Sale:* Rep Pic Film.

Down For The Count: An Inside Look At Boxing. 1984. Churchill Films and KCOP-TV. 46 min. Sound. 16mm Color. *Rental:* Churchill Films. *Rental:* Churchill Films, Videotape version.

Down in Arkansas. Ralph Byrd. Directed by Nick Grinde. 1938. Republic. 72 min. Sound. 16mm B&W. *Rental:* Ivy Films. *Sale:* Rep Pic Film.

Down in San Diego. Bonita Granville & Leo Gorcey. Directed by Robert B. Sinclair. 1941. MGM. 70 min. Sound. 16mm B&W. *Rental:* MGM United.

Down Laredo Way. Rex Allen. Directed by William Witney. 1953. Republic. 54 min. Sound. 16mm B&W. *Rental:* Ivy Films. *Sale:* Rep Pic Film.

Down Memory Lane. Directed by Phil Karlson. 1949. Eagle Lion. (Anthology). 72 min. Sound. 16mm B&W. *Rental:* A Twyman Pres & Westcoast Films.

Down Mexico Way. Gene Autry. Directed by Joseph Santley. 1941. Republic. 54 min. Sound. 16mm B&W. *Rental:* Ivy Films.

Down Missouri Way. John Carradine & Martha O'Driscoll. Directed by Joseph Berne. 1946. PRC. 75 min. Sound. 16mm B&W. *Sale:* Classics Assoc NY.

Down on the Farm. Jed Prouty & Spring Byington. Directed by Mal St. Clair. 1938. Fox. 61 min. Sound. 16mm B&W. *Rental:* Films Inc.

Down on the Farm. 1969. NBC. (Documentary). 50 min. Sound. 16mm Color. *Rental:* Films Inc. *Sale:* Films Inc. *Sale:* Films Inc, Videotape version.

Down Texas Way. Buck Jones & Tim McCoy. Directed by Howard Bretherton. 1942. Monogram. 57 min. Sound. 16mm B&W. *Rental:* Hurlock Cine.

Down the Corner. Directed by Joe Comerford. 1977. Britain. (Documentary). 53 min. Sound. 16mm Color. *Rental:* Museum Mod Art. *Lease:* Museum Mod Art.

Down the Stretch. Mickey Rooney & Patricia Ellis. Directed by William Clemens. 1936. Warners. 66 min. Sound. 16mm B&W. *Rental:* MGM United.

Down the Wyoming Trail. Tex Ritter. Directed by Al Herman. 1939. Monogram. 55 min. Sound. 16mm B&W. *Rental:* Hurlock Cine.

Down Three Dark Streets. Broderick Crawford & Ruth Roman. Directed by Arnold Laven. 1954. United Artists. 85 min. Sound. 16mm B&W. *Rental:* Cine Craft.

Down to Earth. Douglas Fairbanks & Eileen Percy. Directed by John Emerson. 1917. Artcraft. 75 min. Silent. 16mm B&W. *Rental:* A Twyman Pres & Twyman Films, Super 8 silent version.

Down to Earth. Rita Hayworth. Directed by Alexander Hall. 1947. Columbia. 102 min. Sound. 16mm Color. *Rental:* Arcus Film, Bosco Films, Budget Films, Kit Parker, Modern Sound, Natl Film Video, Swank Motion, Twyman Films & Welling Motion Pictures.

Down to the Sea. Ann Rutherford & Russell Hardie. Directed by Lewis D. Collins. 1936. Republic. 54 min. Sound. 16mm B&W. *Rental:* Ivy Films. *Sale:* Rep Pic Film.

Down to the Sea in Ships. Clara Bow. Directed by Elmer Clifton. 1923. Hodgkinson. (Musical score only). 83 min. Sound. 16mm B&W. *Rental:* Killiam Collect. *Sale:* Blackhawk Films, Super 8 sound version. *Sale:* Blackhawk Films, Super 8 silent version.

Down to the Sea in Ships. Richard Widmark & Lionel Barrymore. Directed by Henry Hathaway. 1949. Fox. 120 min. Sound. 16mm B&W. *Rental:* Films Inc & Twyman Films.

Down to the Sea in Ships. 1969. NBC. (Documentary). 55 min. Sound. 16mm Color. *Rental:* Films Inc. *Sale:* Films Inc. *Sale:* Films Inc, Videotape version.

Down to Their Last Yacht. Sidney Blackmer & Mary Boland. Directed by Pandro S. Berman. 1934. RKO. 64 min. Sound. 16mm *Rental:* RKO General Pics.

Downhill Fever. 1982. 55 min. Sound. Videotape *Rental:* PBS Video. *Sale:* PBS Video.

Downhill Racer. Robert Redford & Gene Hackman. Directed by Michael Ritchie. 1969. Paramount. 102 min. Sound. 16mm Color. *Rental:* Films Inc.

Downstairs. John Gilbert & Virginia Bruce. Directed by Monta Bell. 1932. MGM. 84 min. Sound. 16mm B&W. *Rental:* MGM United.

Dozens, The. Directed by Randall Conrad & Christine Dall. First Run. (Documentary). 80 min. Sound. 16mm Color. *Rental:* First Run.

Dr. Glas *see* Doktor Glas.

Dr. Hastings *see* Leaders in American Medicine.

Dr. Huggins *see* Leaders in American Medicine.

Dr. Mabuse, Der Spieler *see* Fatal Passion of Dr. Mabuse.

Dracula. Bela Lugosi. Directed by Tod Browning. 1931. Universal. 75 min. Sound. 16mm B&W. *Rental:* Festival Films & Swank Motion. *Rental:* Swank Motion, Videotape version.

Dracula. Frank Langella, Sir Laurence Olivier & Donald Pleasence. Directed by John Badham. 109 min. Sound. 16mm Color. *Rental:* Swank Motion. *Rental:* Swank Motion, Videotape version.

Dracula A.D. 1972. Christopher Lee. Directed by Alan Gibson. 1972. Warners. 95 min. Sound. 16mm Color. *Rental:* Swank Motion, Twyman Films & Williams Films.

Dracula Has Risen from the Grave. Christopher Lee & Rupert Davies. Directed by Freddie Francis. 1969. Britain. 92 min. Sound. 16mm Color. *Rental:* Buchan Pic, Film Ctr DC, Films Inc, Inst Cinema, Ivy Films, Modern Sound, Swank Motion, Film Ctr DC, Twyman Films, Video Comm, Welling Motion Pictures & Willoughby Peer.

Dracula, Prince of Darkness. Christopher Lee & Barbara Shelley. Directed by Terence Young. 1966. Britain. 90 min. Sound. 16mm Color. *Rental:* Films Inc. *Rental:* Films Inc, Anamorphic color version.

Dracula Saga, The. Tina Sainz. Directed by Leon Klimovsky. 1973. Spain. 91 min. Sound. 16mm Color. *Rental:* Budget Films.

Dracula's Daughter. Gloria Holden. Directed by Lambert Hillyer. 1936. Universal. 75 min. Sound. 16mm B&W. *Rental:* Williams Films.

Dracula's Dog. Jose Ferrer & Michael Pataki. Directed by Albert Band. 1978. Crown. 90 min. Sound. 16mm Color. *Rental:* Films Inc.

Dracula's Great Love. Trans. Title: El Gran Amor Del Conde Dracula. Paul Naschy. Directed by J. Aguirre. 1972. Spain. 85 min. Sound. 16mm Color. dubbed. *Rental:* Films Inc.

Draegerman Courage. Orig. Title: Cave-In, The. Barton MacLane & Henry O'Neill. Directed by Louis King. 1937. Warners. 58 min. Sound. 16mm B&W. *Rental:* MGM United.

Dragnet. Mary Brian & Henry Wilcoxen. Directed by Leslie Goodwins. 1947. Screen Guild. 71 min. Sound. 16mm B&W. *Rental:* Ivy Films & Mogulls Films.

Dragnet for Diabetes. 1975. Britain. (Documentary). 50 min. Sound. 16mm Color. *Rental:* Films Inc. *Sale:* Films Inc. *Sale:* Films Inc, Videotape version.

Dragon Lady. Tom Keena & Anna Ling. Directed by Joel M. Reed. 1975. Hong Kong. 88 min. Sound. 16mm Color. dubbed. *Rental:* J Green Pics.

Dragon Murder Case, The. Warren William & Margaret Lindsay. Directed by Bruce Humberstone. 1934. Warners. 67 min. Sound. 16mm B&W. *Rental:* MGM United.

Dragon Seed. Katharine Hepburn & Walter Huston. Directed by Jack Conway & Harold S. Bucquet. 1944. MGM. 148 min. Sound. 16mm B&W. *Rental:* MGM United.

Dragons of Galapagos. 1978. Churchill Films. 52 min. Sound. 16mm Color. *Rental:* Churchill Films. *Rental:* Churchill Films, Videotape version.

Dragons of Paradise. 1979. PBS. (Documentary). 59 min. Videotape Color. *Rental:* PBS Video. *Sale:* PBS Video.

Dragonslayer. Peter MacNicol & Caitlin Clarke. Directed by Matthew Robbins. 1981. Paramount. 110 min. Sound. 16mm B&W. *Rental:* Films Inc.

Dragonwyck. Gene Tierney, Vincent Price & Walter Huston. Directed by Joseph L. Mankiewicz. 1946. Fox. 103 min. Sound. 16mm B&W. *Rental:* Films Inc.

Dragoon Wells Massacre. Barry Sullivan & Dennis O'Keefe. Directed by Harold Schuster. 1957. Allied Artists. 88 min. Sound. 16mm Color. *Rental:* Ivy Films. *Lease:* Rep Pic Film.

Drake Case, The. Directed by Edward Laemmle. 1929. Universal. (Cast unlisted). 60 min. Silent. 16mm B&W. *Rental:* Mogulls Films. *Sale:* Film Classics. *Rental:* Film Classics, *Sale:* Film Classics, Silent 8mm version.

Drake the Pirate. Matheson Lang & Athene Seyler. Directed by Arthur Woods. 1938. Britain. 70 min. Sound. 16mm B&W. *Rental:* Film Classics.

Drama of Jealousy & Other Things, A. Marcello Mastroianni & Monica Vitti. Directed by Ettore Scola. 1971. Italy. 106 min. Sound. 16mm Color. dubbed. *Rental:* Swank Motion & Twyman Films.

Dramatic School. Luise Rainer & Paulette Goddard. Directed by Robert B. Sinclair. 1938. MGM. 80 min. Sound. 16mm B&W. *Rental:* MGM United.

Draughtsman's Contract, The. Anthony Higgins, Janet Suzman & Anne Louise. Directed by Peter Greenaway. 1983. 107 min. Sound. 16mm *Rental:* MGM United. *Rental:* MGM United, Videotape version.

Dream Is What You Wake Up From, A. Directed by Larry Bullard. 1978. Third World Newsreel. (Documentary). 50 min. Sound. 16mm Color. *Rental:* CA Newsreel. *Sale:* CA Newsreel.

Dream Life, The. Lilianne Lemaitre & Auger Veronique. Directed by Mireille Dansereau. 1972. Canada. 90 min. Sound. 16mm *Rental:* New Line Cinema.

Dream Never Dies, The. 1980. 53 min. Sound. Videotape *Rental:* PBS Video. *Sale:* PBS Video.

Dream of a Cossack, The. Sergei Bondarchuk. Directed by Yuli Raizman. Rus. 1950. 108 min. Sound. 16mm B&W. subtitles. *Rental:* Corinth Films.

Dream of Kings, A. Anthony Quinn & Irene Papas. Directed by Anthony Mann. 1969. National General. 108 min. Sound. 16mm Color. *Rental:* Swank Motion.

Dream of Passion, A. Melina Mercouri & Ellen Burstyn. Directed by Jules Dassin. 1978. Embassy. 110 min. Sound. 16mm Color. *Rental:* Films Inc.

Dream on Monkey Mountain, The. 1969. NBC. (Native cast). 53 min. Sound. 16mm Color. *Rental:* Films Inc & U Mich Media. *Sale:* Films Inc. *Sale:* Films Inc, Videotape version.

Dream Street. Carol Dempster & Ralph Graves. Directed by D. W. Griffith. 1921. United Artists. 102 min. Silent. 16mm B&W. *Rental:* A Twyman Pres, Budget Films & Twyman Films. *Sale:* Cinema Concepts, Natl Cinema & Reel Images.

Dream Wife. Cary Grant & Deborah Kerr. Directed by Sidney Sheldon. 1953. MGM. 99 min. Sound. 16mm B&W. *Rental:* MGM United.

Dreamboat. Clifton Webb & Ginger Rogers. Directed by Claude Binyon. 1952. Fox. 83 min. Sound. 16mm B&W. *Rental:* Films Inc.

Dreamer, The. Tuvia Tavi. Directed by Dan Wolman. Hebrew. 1974. Israel. 87 min. Sound. 16mm Color. subtitles. *Rental:* Budget Films, Films Inc, Welling Motion Pictures & Williams Films. *Rental:* Films Inc, Dubbed version.

Dreamer, The. Tim Matheson & Susan Blakely. Directed by Noel Nosseck. 1979. Fox. 90 min. Sound. 16mm Color. *Rental:* Films Inc.

Dreamers & Dissenters. 1963. Hearst. (Documentary). 50 min. Sound. 16mm B&W. *Sale:* King Features.

Dreaming Lips. Elizabeth Bergner & Raymond Massey. Directed by Paul Czinner. 1937. 70 min. 16mm *Rental:* A Twyman Pres.

Dreaming Out Loud. Lum & Abner, Frances Langford, Frank Craven & Phil Harris. Directed by Harold Young. 1940. RKO. 71 min. Sound. 16mm B&W. *Rental:* Budget Films & Em Gee Film Lib.

Dreamland: A History of Early Canadian Movies. 1976. Canada. (Documentary). 86 min. Sound. 16mm B&W. *Rental:* Natl Film CN. *Sale:* Natl Film CN.

Dreams. Eva Dahlbeck & Gunnar Bjornstrand. Directed by Ingmar Bergman. 1955. Sweden. 86 min. Sound. 16mm B&W. *Rental:* Janus Films & New Cinema.

Dreams & Nightmares. Directed by Abe Osheroff & Larry Klingman. 1974. New Yorker. 60 min. Sound. 16mm Color. *Rental:* New Yorker Films.

Dreams of Love. Annie Ducaux. Fr. 1954. France. 104 min. Sound. 16mm B&W. subtitles. *Rental:* Film Classics. *Rental:* Film Classics, Videotape version.

Dreams That Money Can Buy. Directed by Hans Richter. 1947. Richter. (Experimental). 80 min. Sound. 16mm Color. *Rental:* Museum Mod Art. *Sale:* Museum Mod Art.

Dreamspeaker. Ian Tracey & George Clutesi. Directed by Claude Jutra. 1976. Filmakers Library. 75 min. Sound. 16mm Color. *Rental:* Film Makers & U Mich Media. *Sale:* Film Makers.

Dreigroschenoper, Die *see* Threepenny Opera.

Dress Parade. William Boyd & Bessie Love. Directed by Donald Crisp. 1927. Pathe. 80 min. Silent. 16mm B&W. *Rental:* Film Classics. *Sale:* Film Classics.

Dressed to Kill. Lloyd Nolan & Mary Beth Hughes. Directed by Eugene Forde. 1941. Fox. 72 min. Sound. 16mm B&W. *Rental:* Willoughby Peer & Films Inc.

Dressed to Kill. Basil Rathbone. Directed by Roy William Neill. 1946. Universal. 72 min. Sound. 16mm B&W. *Rental:* Budget Films, Em Gee Film Lib, Learning Corp Am, Natl Film Video, RKO General Pics, Roas Films, Video Comm & Reel Images. *Sale:* Cinema Concepts, Festival Films, Glenn Photo & Learning Corp Am. *Sale:* Glenn Photo, Super 8 sound version. *Sale:* Cinema Concepts, Festival Films, Reel Images & Tamarelles French Film, Videotape version. *Sale:* Reel Images, Super 8 sound version.

Dressed to Kill. Michael Caine, Angie Dickinson & Nancy Allen. Directed by Brian De Palma. 105 min. Sound. 16mm Color. *Rental:* Swank Motion.

Dresser, The. Albert Finney & Tom Courtenay. Directed by Peter Yates. 1983. Columbia. 118 min. Sound. 16mm Color. *Rental:* Swank Motion.

Drift Fence. Tom Keene & Buster Crabbe. Directed by Otho Lovering. 1936. Paramount. 56 min. Sound. 16mm B&W. *Rental:* Budget Films.

Driftin' River. Eddie Dean. Directed by Robert Tansey. 1946. PRC. 57 min. Sound. 16mm B&W. *Sale:* Classics Assoc NY.

Drifting Along. Johnny Mack Brown. Directed by Derwin Abrahams. 1946. Monogram. 65 min. Sound. 16mm B&W. *Rental:* Hurlock Cine.

Drifting of the Continents. 1970. Britain. (Documentary). 50 min. Sound. 16mm Color. *Rental:* Films Inc, Iowa Films, Syracuse U Film & U Mich Media. *Sale:* Films Inc. *Rental:* Films Inc, *Sale:* Films Inc, Videotape version.

Driftwood. Natalie Wood & Walter Brennan. Directed by Allan Dwan. 1947. Republic. 90 min. Sound. 16mm B&W. *Rental:* Ivy Films. *Sale:* Rep Pic Film.

Drink, Drank, Drunk. 1974. WQED. (Documentary). 59 min. Sound. 16mm Color. *Rental:* U Cal Media, Indiana AV Ctr & PBS Video. *Sale:* Indiana AV Ctr.

Drinking American, The. 1968. NET. (Documentary). 60 min. Sound. 16mm B&W. *Rental:* Indiana AV Ctr. *Sale:* Indiana AV Ctr.

Drive a Crooked Road. Mickey Rooney & Dianne Foster. Directed by Richard Quine. 1954. Columbia. 82 min. Sound. 16mm B&W. *Rental:* Inst Cinema & Film Ctr DC.

Drive for Power, The. (Ascent of Man Ser.). 1974. Britain. (Documentary). 52 min. Sound. 16mm Color. *Rental:* Iowa Films, U Cal Media, U Mich Media & Utah Media, Videotape version.

Drive, He Said! William Tepper, Karen Black & Bruce Dern. Directed by Jack Nicholson. 1971. CBS. 90 min. Sound. 16mm Color. *Rental:* Films Inc.

Drive-In. Lisa Lamole & Glenn Morshower. Directed by Rod Amateau. 1976. Columbia. 96 min. Sound. 16mm B&W. *Rental:* Cine Craft, Films Inc, Modern Sound, Swank Motion, Twyman Films, Welling Motion Pictures, Westcoast Films & Williams Films.

Driver, The. Ryan O'Neal & Bruce Dern. Directed by Walter Hill. 1978. Fox. 91 min. Sound. 16mm Color. *Rental:* Films Inc.

Drole de Drame *see* Bizarre, Bizarre.

Drole de Paroissien, Un. Bourvil. Directed by Jean-Pierre Mocky. Fr. France. 82 min. Sound. 16mm B&W. subtitles. *Rental:* French Am Cul.

Drop Kick. Richard Barthelmess & Hedda Hopper. Directed by Millard Webb. 1927. First National. 60 min. Silent. 16mm B&W. *Rental:* Film Classics. *Sale:* Film Classics. *Sale:* Film Classics, Silent 8mm version.

Drought. 1979. PBS. (Documentary). 59 min. Videotape Color. *Rental:* PBS Video. *Sale:* PBS Video.

Drowning Pool, The. Paul Newman & Joanne Woodward. Directed by Stuart Rosenberg. 1975. Warners. 108 min. Sound. 16mm Color. *Rental:* Films Inc, Swank Motion, Twyman Films & Williams Films.

Drugs in the Tenderloin. 1967. NET. (Documentary). 52 min. Sound. 16mm B&W. *Rental:* U Cal Media & U of IL Film.

Drugstore, The. Directed by Joris Ivens & Marceline Loridan. 1973. China. (Documentary). 81 min. Sound. 16mm Color. *Rental:* Cinema Arts & Inst Cinema.

Drugstore Romance. Helen Sugere & Nicolas Silberg. Directed by Paul Vecchiali. Fr. 1979. France. 126 min. Sound. 16mm subtitles. *Rental:* Cinema Five.

Drum. Warren Oates & Ken Norton. Directed by Steve Carver. 1976. United Artists. 102 min. Sound. 16mm Color. *Rental:* MGM United.

Drum Taps. Ken Maynard. Directed by J. P. McGowan. 1933. World Wide. 60 min. Sound. 16mm B&W. *Sale:* Cinema Concepts, Natl Cinema & Reel Images. *Sale:* Video Comm, Videotape version.

Drumbeat. Alan Ladd & Charles Bronson. Directed by Delmer Daves. 1954. Warner. 107 min. Sound. 16mm Color. *Rental:* Budget Films, Natl Film Video, Video Comm & Westcoast Films. *Lease:* Video Comm. *Rental:* Video Comm, *Sale:* Video Comm, Videotape version.

Drums. Sabu & Raymond Massey. Directed by Zoltan Korda. 1938. United Artists. 96 min. Sound. 16mm Color. *Rental:* Films Inc, Inst Cinema & Mogulls Films.

Drums Across the River. Audie Murphy, Walter Brennan & Nathan Juran. 1954. Universal. 78 min. Sound. 16mm Color. *Rental:* Swank Motion.

Drums Along the Mohawk. Henry Fonda & Claudette Colbert. Directed by John Ford. 1939. Fox. 105 min. Sound. 16mm Color. *Rental:* Films Inc.

Drums Begin to Roll, The. 1975. Britain. (Documentary). 52 min. Sound. 16mm Color. *Rental:* U of IL Film.

Drums in the Deep South. James Craig & Guy Madison. Directed by William Cameron Menzies. 1951. RKO. 78 min. Sound. 16mm Color. *Rental:* Films Inc.

Drums of Africa. Mariette Hartley & Lloyd Bochner. Directed by James B. Clark. 1963. MGM. 87 min. Sound. 16mm Color. *Rental:* MGM United.

Drums of Destiny. Tom Keene. Directed by Ray Taylor. 1937. Crescent. 60 min. Sound. 16mm B&W. *Rental:* Mogulls Films.

Drums of Destiny. Directed by George Michael. 1962. NTA. (Documentary). 80 min. Sound. 16mm Color. *Rental:* Welling Motion Pictures & Willoughby Peer.

Drunkard, The *see* Villain Still Pursued Her.

Drunken Angel, The. Toshiro Mifune & Takashi Shimura. Directed by Akira Kurosawa. Jap. 1948. Toho. 102 min. Sound. 16mm B&W. subtitles Eng. *Rental:* Films Inc. *Sale:* Festival Films, Videotape version.

Dry Weather Chronicle. 1980. ABC. (Documentary). 70 min. Sound. 16mm Color. *Rental:* Films Inc. *Sale:* Films Inc. *Sale:* Films Inc, Videotape version.

Drylanders. 1963. Canada. (Documentary). 70 min. Sound. 16mm B&W. *Rental:* Natl Film CN. *Sale:* Natl Film CN.

Du Bist Die Welt Fur Mich *see* Richard Tauber Story.

Du Cote de Memphis. 1979. Center for Southern Folklore. (Documentary). 58 min. Sound. 16mm Color. *Rental:* Ctr South Folklore. *Sale:* Ctr South Filklore.

Du Guesclin. Fernand Gravey. Directed by Bernard De Latour. Fr. 1948. France. 100 min. Sound. 16mm B&W. subtitles. *Rental:* French Am Cul.

Du Rififi Chez les Hommes *see* Rififi.

Dual Alibi. Herbert Lom. Directed by Alfred Travers. 1947. Britain. 80 min. Sound. 16mm B&W. *Rental:* Ivy Films. *Sale:* Rep Pic Film.

Dubarry. Orig. Title: Dubarry-Woman of Passion. Norma Talmadge & Conrad Nagel. Directed by Sam Taylor. 1930. United Artists. Sound. 16mm B&W. *Rental:* Film Classics. *Rental:* Film Classics, Videotape version.

Dubarry-Woman of Passion *see* Dubarry.

Duchess & the Dirtwater Fox, The. Goldie Hawn & George Segal. Directed by Melvin Frank. 1976. Fox. 105 min. Sound. 16mm Color. *Rental:* Films Inc, Welling Motion Pictures & Williams Films. *Rental:* Williams Films, Videotape version.

Duchess of Buffalo. Constance Talmadge. Directed by Sidney A. Franklin. 1926. 16mm *Rental:* A Twyman Pres.

Duchess of Idaho, The. Esther Williams & Van Johnson. Directed by Robert Z. Leonard. 1950. MGM. 98 min. Sound. 16mm Color. *Rental:* MGM United.

Duchess of Malfi, The. 1976. Britain. (Cast unlisted). 123 min. Videotape Color. *Rental:* Time-Life Multimedia. *Sale:* Time-Life Multimedia.

Duck Soup. Marx Brothers. Directed by Leo McCarey. 1933. Paramount. 70 min. Sound. 16mm B&W. *Rental:* Museum Mod Art & Swank Motion. *Rental:* Swank Motion, Videotape version.

Duck, You Sucker! Orig. Title: Fistful of Dynamite, A. Rod Steiger & James Coburn. Directed by Sergio Leone. 1972. United Artists. 138 min. Sound. 16mm Color. *Rental:* MGM United.

Dude Bandit. Hoot Gibson. Directed by George Melford. 1933. Allied. 67 min. Sound. 16mm B&W. *Rental:* Roas Films. *Sale:* Cinema Concepts & Natl Cinema, Super 8 sound version. *Sale:* Video Comm, Videotape version.

Dude Cowboy. Tim Holt & Ray Whitley. Directed by David Howard. 1942. RKO. 59 min. Sound. 16mm *Rental:* RKO General Pics.

Dude Goes West, The. Eddie Albert & Gale Storm. Directed by Kurt Neumann. 1948. Allied Artists. 90 min. Sound. 16mm B&W. *Rental:* Budget Films, Cine Craft, Hurlock Cine & Film Ctr DC.

Dude Ranger, The. George O'Brien. Directed by Edward Cline. 1934. Fox. 60 min. Sound. 16mm B&W. *Rental:* Mogulls Films.

Duel. Dennis Weaver, Lucille Benson & Eddie Firestone. Directed by Steven Spielberg. 1971. Universal. 74 min. Sound. 16mm Color. *Rental:* Swank Motion. *Rental:* Swank Motion, Videotape version.

Duel, The. Lyudmila Shagalova. Directed by Tatiana Berezantseva & Lev Rudnik. 1962. Russia. 82 min. Sound. 16mm B&W. *Rental:* Corinth Films.

Duel at Apache Wells. Jim Davis & Ben Cooper. Directed by Joseph Kane. 1956. Republic. 72 min. Sound. 16mm B&W. *Rental:* Ivy Films. *Sale:* Rep Pic Film.

Duel at Diablo. James Garner & Sidney Poitier. Directed by Ralph Nelson. 1966. United Artists. 103 min. Sound. 16mm Color. *Rental:* MGM United.

Duel at Silver Creek. Audie Murphy & Stephen McNally. Directed by Don Siegel. 1952. Universal. 77 min. Sound. 16mm Color. *Rental:* Swank Motion.

Duel at the Rio Grande. Sean Flynn. Directed by Mario Caiano. 1964. Spain. 93 min. Sound. 16mm Color. dubbed. *Rental:* Modern sound.

Duel in the Sun. Gregory Peck & Jennifer Jones. Directed by King Vidor. 1947. Selznick. 135 min. Sound. 16mm Color. *Rental:* Cine Craft, Films Inc, Syracuse U Film, Twyman Films, Video Comm, Wholesome Film Ctr & Willoughby Peer. *Sale:* ABC Film Lib.

Duel in the Wind. 1970. Time-Life. (Documentary). 70 min. Sound. 16mm Color. *Rental:* Budget Films.

Duel of the Iron Fist. David Chiang & Chuen Yuan. 1973. Hong Kong. 95 min. Sound. 16mm Color. dubbed. *Rental:* Budget Films, Films Inc, Video Comm, Welling Motion Pictures & Westcoast Films.

Duel of the Titans. Steve Reeves & Gordon Scott. Directed by Sergio Corbucci. 1963. Paramount. 90 min. Sound. 16mm Color. *Rental:* Films Inc.

Duel on the Mississippi. Lex Barker & Patricia Medina. Directed by William Castle. 1955. Columbia. 72 min. Sound. 16mm Color. *Rental:* Film Ctr DC.

Duellists, The. Keith Carradine, Harvey Keitel & Albert Finney. Directed by Ridley Scott. 1977. Paramount. 101 min. Sound. 16mm Color. *Rental:* Films Inc.

Duet for Cannibals. Adriana Asti. Directed by Susan Sontag. Swed. 1969. Sweden. 105 min. Sound. 16mm B&W. subtitles. *Rental:* Grove. *Sale:* Grove.

Duffy. James Coburn & Susannah York. Directed by Robert Parrish. 1968. Columbia. 101 min. Sound. 16mm Color. *Rental:* Arcus Film, Budget Films, Cine Craft, Inst Cinema, Films Inc, Kerr Film, Modern Sound, Welling Motion Pictures, Westcoast Films & Wholesome Film Ctr.

Duke Comes Back, The. Orig. Title: Call of the Ring, The. Allan Lane & Heather Angel. Directed by Irving Pichel. 1937. Republic. 54 min. Sound. 16mm B&W. *Rental:* Ivy Films. *Sale:* Rep Pic Film.

Duke is Tops, The: Bronze Venus. Lena Horne & Ralph Cooper. Directed by William Nolte. 1938. 80 min. Sound. 16mm *Rental:* Budget Films.

Duke of Chicago, The. Tom Brown & Audrey Long. Directed by George Blair. 1948. Republic. 61 min. Sound. 16mm B&W. *Rental:* Ivy Films.

Duke of West Point, The. Richard Carlson & Joan Fontaine. Directed by Alfred E. Green. 1938. United Artists. 109 min. Sound. 16mm B&W. *Sale:* Budget Films.

Dulcy *see* Not So Dumb.

Dumas, Fils. France. (Cast unlisted). 60 min. Sound. 16mm B&W. *Rental:* French Am Cul.

Dumas Malone: Journey with Mr. Jefferson. 1983. 54 min. Sound. Videotape *Sale:* Natl AV Ctr.

Dumas, Pere. France. (Cast unlisted). 60 min. Sound. 16mm B&W. *Rental:* French Am Cul. *Rental:* French Am Cul, Videotape version.

Dumbo. Directed by Ben Sharpsteen. 1941. Disney. (Animated). 70 min. Sound. 16mm Color. *Rental:* Bosco Films, Elliot Film Co, Films Inc, MGM United, Modern Sound, Roas Films, Swank Motion, Twyman Films, Welling Motion Pictures & Westcoast Films. *Rental:* Williams Films, 63 min. version. *Rental:* Williams Films & Swank Motion, Videotape version.

Dummy Talks, The. Jack Warner & Claude Hulbert. Directed by Oswald Mitchell. 1943. Britain. 68 min. Sound. 16mm B&W. *Rental:* Ivy Films. *Sale:* Rep Pic Film.

Dummy Trouble. Harry Langdon & Betty Blythe. Directed by William Beaudine. 1941. PRC. 75 min. Sound. 16mm B&W. *Rental:* Budget Films.

Duncan's World. Larry Tobian. 1977. Duncan's World Prod. 93 min. Sound. 16mm Color. *Rental:* Best Film, Video Corp & Williams Films.

Dunderklumpen. Directed by Per Ahlin. 1979. 85 min. Sound. 16mm Color. *Rental:* Films Inc & Williams Films.

Dungeon Of Terror. 65 min. Sound. 16mm Color. *Rental:* BF Video.

Dunkirk. John Mills & Richard Attenborough. Directed by Leslie Norman. 1958. Britain. 135 min. Sound. 16mm B&W. *Rental:* MGM United.

Dunwich Horror, The. Sandra Dee, Dean Stockwell & Ed Begley. Directed by Daniel Haller. 1970. American International/Filmways. 90 min. Sound. 16mm Color. *Rental:* Video Comm, Westcoast Films, Welling Motion Pictures & Wholesome Film Ctr.

Dupont Lajoie. Trans. Title: Common Man, The. Jean Carnet & Pierre Tornade. Directed by Yves Boisset. Fr. 1975. France. 95 min. Sound. 16mm Color. subtitles. *Rental:* New Line Cinema.

Durango Kid, The. Charles Starrett. Directed by Lambert Hillyer. 1940. Columbia. 60 min. Sound. 16mm B&W. *Rental:* Modern Sound, Wholesome Film Ctr & Williams Films.

Durango Valley Raiders. Bob Steele. Directed by Sam Newfield. 1938. Republic. 60 min. Sound. 16mm B&W. *Rental:* Ivy Films & Mogulls Films. *Sale:* Rep Pic Film.

Dust Be My Destiny. John Garfield & Priscilla Lane. Directed by Robert Rossen. 1939. Warners. 88 min. Sound. 16mm B&W. *Rental:* MGM United.

Dusty & Sweets McGee. Billy Gray. Directed by Floyd Mutrux. 1971. Warners. 88 min. Sound. 16mm Color. *Rental:* Swank Motion.

Dusty Bates. Anthony Newley. Directed by Darrell Catling. 1947. Britain. 110 min. Sound. 16mm B&W. *Rental:* Roas Films.

Dusty Ermine. Ronald Squire & Jane Baxter. Directed by Bernard Vorhaus. 1941. Britain. 85 min. Sound. 16mm B&W. *Rental:* Ivy Films.

Dutchman. Shirley Knight & Al Freeman Jr. Directed by Anthony Harvey. 1957. Britain. 55 min. Sound. 16mm B&W. *Rental:* Kit Parker.

Duty Bound. 1975. ABC. (Documentary). 60 min. Sound. 16mm Color. *Rental:* Natl Churches Christ.

Dwight D. Eisenhower. 1976. Britain. (Documentary). 62 min. Sound. 16mm Color. *Rental:* Time-Life Multimedia. *Sale:* Time-Life Multimedia. *Rental:* Time-Life Multimedia, *Sale:* Time-Life Multimedia, Videotape version.

Dybbuk, The. Directed by Michael Waszynsky. Pol. 1938. Poland. (Cast unlisted). 125 min. Sound. 16mm B&W. subtitles. *Rental:* Classic Film Mus.

Dybbuk, The. David Opatoshu. Directed by Ilan Eldad. 1970. Israel. 95 min. Sound. 16mm Color. *Rental:* Films Inc.

D'ye Ken John Peel. Orig. Title: Captain Moonlight. John Patrick & Stanley Hollway. Directed by Henry Edwards. 1942. Britain. 56 min. Sound. 16mm B&W. *Rental:* Ivy Films.

Dying. Michael Roemer. 1976. WGBH. (Documentary). 97 min. Sound. 16mm Color. *Rental:* U Mich Media. *Rental:* PBS Video, *Sale:* PBS Video, Videotape version.

Dynamite. Conrad Nagel & Kay Johnson. Directed by Cecil B. DeMille. 1929. Pathe. 127 min. Sound. 16mm B&W. *Rental:* MGM United.

Dynamite Canyon. Tom Keene. Directed by Robert Tansey. 1941. Monogram. 60 min. Sound. 16mm B&W. *Rental:* Mogulls Films.

Dynamite Chicken. Joan Baez & Richard Pryor. Directed by Ernest Pintoff. 1970. EYR. 85 min. Videotape Color. *Sale:* Cinema Concepts & Video Lib.

Dynamite Dan. Kenneth MacDonald & Boris Karloff. Directed by Bruce Mitchell. 1924. Sunset. 45 min. Silent. 16mm B&W. *Sale:* Film Classics.

Dynamite Pass. Tim Holt & Lynn Roberts. Directed by Lew Landers. 1950. RKO. 61 min. Sound. 16mm *Rental:* RKO General Pics.

Dynamite Ranch. Ken Maynard. Directed by Forrest Sheldon. 1932. World Wide. 60 min. Sound. 16mm B&W. *Rental:* Budget Films. *Sale:* Video Comm, Videotape version.

Dynamo, The. Bruce Li. 81 min. Sound. 16mm *Rental:* WW Enter. *Rental:* WW Enter, Videotape version.

Dynasty *see* James A. Michener's Dynasty.

Dynasty of Blood. David Chiang & Ti Lung. 103 min. Sound. 16mm *Rental:* WW Enter. *Rental:* WW Enter, Videotape version.

Dysplastic Nevi & Hereditary Melanoma. 1981. 58 min. Sound. Videotape *Sale:* Natl AV Ctr.

Each Dawn I Die. James Cagney & George Raft. Directed by William Keighley. 1939. Warners. 84 min. Sound. 16mm B&W. *Rental:* MGM United.

Eadie Was a Lady. Ann Miller & Joe Besser. Directed by Arthur Dreifuss. 1944. Columbia. 70 min. Sound. 16mm B&W. *Rental:* Kit Parker.

Eadweard Muybridge, Zoopraxographer. Directed by Thom Anderson. 1975. New Yorker. (Documentary, sepia). 60 min. Sound. 16mm *Rental:* New Yorker Films.

Eagle, The. Rudolph Valentino & Vilma Banky. Directed by Clarence Brown. 1925. United Artists. (Music & sound effects only). 77 min. Sound. 16mm B&W. *Rental:* A Twyman Pres, Budget Films, Classic Film Mus, Charard Motion Pics, Em Gee Film Lib, Kerr Film, Killiam Collect, Kit Parker, Swank Motion, Video Comm, Westcoast Films, Wholesome Film Ctr & Willoughby Peer. *Sale:* Festival Films, Morcraft Films & Natl Cinema. *Rental:* Killiam Collect, Tinted version. *Rental:* Twyman Films & Video Comm, *Sale:* Glenn Photo, Silent 16mm version. *Rental:* Ivy Films, *Sale:* Glenn Photo, Super 8 silent version. *Rental:* Golden Tapes, Ivy Films & Video Comm, *Sale:* Festival Films, Videotape version.

Eagle & the Hawk, The. Fredric March & Cary Grant. Directed by Stuart Walker. 1933. Paramount. 68 min. Sound. 16mm Color. *Rental:* Swank Motion.

Eagle Has Landed, The. Michael Caine, Bertil Taube & Donald Sutherland. Directed by John Sturges. 1977. Britain. 123 min. Sound. 16mm Color. *Rental:* Arcus Film, Bosco Films, Budget Films, Films Inc, Modern Sound, Swank Motion, Twyman Films, Westcoast Films & Williams Films. *Rental:* Swank Motion, Videotape version.

Eagle in a Cage. Sir John Gielgud, Sir Ralph Richardson. Directed by Fielder Cook. 1972. Britain. 100 min. Sound. 16mm Color. *Rental:* Bosco Films, Budget Films & Swank Motion.

Eagle of the Sea. John Gilbert. Directed by Frank Lloyd. 1926. Paramount. 75 min. Silent. 16mm B&W. *Rental:* Film Classics. *Sale:* Film Classics. *Sale:* Film Classics, Silent 8mm version.

Eagles Attack at Dawn, The. Rick Jason & Peter Brown. Directed by Menahem Golan. 1970. Israel. 98 min. Sound. 16mm Color. *Rental:* Modern Sound & Video Comm.

Eagle's Brood, The. William Boyd. Directed by Howard Bretherton. 1935. Paramount. 66 min. Sound. 16mm B&W. *Rental:* Films Inc.

Eagles of the Fleet *see* Flat Top.

Eagle's Wing. Martin Sheen & Sam Waterston. Directed by Anthony Harvey. 1979. Britain. 104 min. Sound. 16mm Color. *Rental:* Twyman Films.

Eagleville: You're Not Alone. 1971. WPVI. (Documentary). 52 min. Sound. 16mm Color. *Rental:* U Cal Media.

Eames Celebration, An: Several Worlds of Charles & Ray Eames. 1975. NET. (Documentary). 90 min. Sound. 16mm Color. *Rental:* Indiana AV Ctr, U Cal Media & U Mich Media. *Sale:* Indiana AV Ctr. *Sale:* Indiana AV Ctr, Videotape version.

Earl Carroll's Sketchbook. Constance Moore & Bill Goodwin. Directed by Albert S. Rogell. 1946. Republic. 90 min. Sound. 16mm B&W. *Rental:* Ivy Films. *Sale:* Rep Pic Film.

Earl Carroll's Vanities. Dennis O'Keefe & Constance Moore. Directed by Joseph Santley. 1945. Republic. 91 min. Sound. 16mm B&W. *Rental:* Ivy Films. *Sale:* Rep Pic Film.

Earl of Chicago, The. Robert Montgomery & Edward Arnold. Directed by Richard Thorpe. 1940. MGM. 87 min. Sound. 16mm B&W. *Rental:* MGM United.

Earl of Puddlestone, The. James Gleason. Directed by Gus Meins. 1940. Republic. 54 min. Sound. 16mm B&W. *Rental:* Ivy Films.

Early Bird, The. Norman Wisdom & Edward Chapman. Directed by Robert Asher. 1965. Britain. 97 min. Sound. 16mm B&W. *Rental:* Cinema Five.

Early Returns: The Press & Presidential Politics. 1977. Wayne Ewing. (Documentary). 59 min. Sound. 16mm Color. *Rental:* W Ewing Films. *Sale:* W Ewing Films.

Early Spring. Chishu Ryu. Directed by Yasujiro Ozu. Jap. 1956. Japan. 144 min. Sound. 16mm B&W. subtitles. *Rental:* New Cinema & New Yorker Films.

Early Warning. 86 min. Sound. 16mm Color. *Rental:* Gospel Films.

Early Works. Milja Vujanovic. Directed by Zelimir Zilnik. Serbo-Croatian. 1969. Yugoslavia. 87 min. Sound. 16mm B&W. subtitles. *Rental:* Grove.

Earrings of Madame de ..., The Orig. Title: Diamond Earrings. Danielle Darrieux & Charles Boyer. Directed by Max Ophuls. Fr. 1953. France. 105 min. Sound. 16mm B&W. subtitles. *Rental:* Corinth Films, Images Film & Ivy Films. *Sale:* Festival Films & Reel Images. *Lease:* Corinth Films & Images Film. *Sale:* Festival Films, Videotape version.

Earth. Trans. Title: Zemlya. Directed by Alexander Dovzhenko. 1930. Russia. (Cast unlisted). 54 min. Silent. 16mm B&W. *Rental:* Budget Films, Corinth Films, Em Gee Film Lib, Images Film, Kit Parker, U Cal Media & Westcoast Films. *Sale:* Glenn Photo, Natl Cinema & Reel Images. *Rental:* Film Images, *Sale:* Film Images, Sound 16mm version. *Sale:* Festival Films, Images Film & Tamarelles French Film, Videotape version.

Earth. 1930. 88 min. Sound. 16mm B&W. *Rental:* Utah Media.

Earth Dies Screaming, The. Willard Parker & Virginia Field. Directed by Terence Fisher. 1964. Fox. 62 min. Sound. 16mm B&W. *Rental:* Films Inc.

Earth People, The. 1976. Phoenix. (Documentary). 54 min. Sound. 16mm Color. *Rental:* Phoenix Films. *Sale:* Phoenix Films. *Sale:* Phoenix Films, Videotape version.

Earth Sings, The *see* Zem Spieva.

Earth vs. the Flying Saucers, The. Hugh Marlowe & Joan Taylor. Directed by Fred F. Sears. 1956. Columbia. 83 min. Sound. 16mm B&W. *Rental:* Budget Films, Cine Craft, Charard Motion Pics, Film Ctr DC, Films Inc, Inst Cinema, Ivy Films, Kit Parker, Modern Sound, Natl Film Video, Twyman Films, Video Comm, Westcoast Films & Williams Films.

Earthquake. Charles Heston & Ava Gardner. Directed by Mark Robson. 1974. Universal. 129 min. Sound. 16mm Color. *Rental:* Swank Motion.

Earthspace. 1977. US Government. (Documentary). 48 min. Sound. 16mm Color. *Sale:* Natl AV Ctr.

Earthwatch from Nairobi: A Visit with Maurice Strong & Joy Adamson. 1973. WNET. (Interview). 60 min. Sound. 16mm Color. *Rental:* WNET Media. *Sale:* WNET Media. *Rental:* WNET Media, Videotape version.

Earthworm Tractors. Orig. Title: Natural Born Salesman. A. Joe E. Brown. Directed by Ray Enright. 1936. Warners. 69 min. Sound. 16mm B&W. *Rental:* MGM United.

Easiest Way, The. Constance Bennett & Robert Montgomery. Directed by Jack Conway. 1931. MGM. 75 min. Sound. 16mm B&W. *Rental:* MGM United.

East Africa: Ends & Beginnings. 1974. PBS. (Documentary). 48 min. Sound. 16mm B&W. *Rental:* Indiana AV Ctr. *Sale:* Indiana AV Ctr.

East Germany: Land Beyond the Wall. 1961. CBS. (Documentary). 53 min. Sound. 16mm B&W. *Rental:* Syracuse U Film, U of IL Film & U Mich Media. *Sale:* Carousel Films.

East Is East. Florence Turner & Edith Evans. Directed by Henry Edwards. 1916. Mutual. 60 min. Silent. 16mm B&W. *Sale:* Blackhawk Films.

East Is Red, The. 1965. 130 min. Sound. 16mm Color. *Rental:* Asia Film Library.

East Is West. Lew Ayres & Edward G. Robinson. Directed by Monta Bell. 1930. Universal. 74 min. Sound. 16mm B&W. *Rental:* Swank Motion.

East Lynne. William Russell & Alan Hale. 1915. Fox. 50 min. Silent. 16mm B&W. *Rental:* Film Classics. *Sale:* Film Classics. *Rental:* Film Classics, *Sale:* Film Classics, Silent 8mm version.

East Meets West. George Arliss. Directed by Herbert Mason. 1930. Britain. 80 min. Sound. 16mm B&W. *Rental:* Janus Films & Mogulls Films.

East of Borneo. Rose Hobart & Charles Bickford. Directed by George Melford. 1931. Universal. 102 min. Sound. 16mm B&W. *Rental:* Budget Films.

East of Eden. James Dean & Dennis Harris. Directed by Elia Kazan. 1969. Warners. 115 min. Sound. 16mm Color. *Sale:* Festival Films. *Sale:* Festival Films, Videotape version.

East of Kilimanjaro. Orig. Title: Big Search, The. Marshall Thompson. Directed by Arnold Belgard & Edoardo Capolino. 1956. Parade. (Anamorphic). 75 min. Sound. 16mm Color. *Rental:* Ivy Films.

East of Shanghai *see* Rich & Strange.

East of Sumatra. Jeff Chandler & Marilyn Maxwell. Directed by Budd Boetticher. 1953. Universal. 82 min. Sound. 16mm Color. *Rental:* Swank Motion.

East of the River. John Garfield & Brenda Marshall. Directed by Alfred E. Green. 1940. Warners. 73 min. Sound. 16mm B&W. *Rental:* MGM United.

East One Hundred & Third Street. Directed by Chris Menges. 1980. Inst. for Study of Human Issues. (Documentary). Sound. 16mm Color. *Rental:* Human Issues.

East Side Kids, The. Bowery Boys. Directed by Robert Hill. 1940. Monogram. 64 min. Sound. Videotape B&W. *Sale:* Kerr Film, Mogulls Films & Vidamerica. *Sale:* Reel Images, Super 8 sound version. *Sale:* Cinema Concepts, Videotape version.

East Side, West Side. Barbara Stanwyck & James Mason. Directed by Mervyn LeRoy. 1950. MGM. 106 min. Sound. 16mm B&W. *Rental:* Films Inc & MGM United.

Easter Parade. Fred Astaire & Judy Garland. Directed by Charles Walters. 1948. MGM. 103 min. Sound. 16mm Color. *Rental:* Films Inc & MGM United. *Sale:* Tamarelles French Film, Videotape version.

Easy Alice. Quality X. 75 min. Videotape Color. *Sale:* Quality X Video.

Easy Go. Orig. Title: Free & Easy. Buster Keaton. Directed by Edward Sedgwick. 1930. MGM. 73 min. Sound. 16mm B&W. *Rental:* Films Inc & MGM United.

Easy Living. Jean Arthur & Ray Milland. Directed by Mitchell Leisen. 1937. Paramount. 88 min. Sound. 16mm B&W. *Rental:* Museum Mod Art.

Easy Living. Victor Mature & Lucille Ball. Directed by Jacques Tourneur. 1949. RKO. 77 min. Sound. 16mm B&W. *Rental:* Films Inc.

Easy Money. Rodney Dangerfield & Joe Pesci. Directed by James Signorelli. 1983. Orion. 100 min. Sound. 16mm Color. *Rental:* Films Inc.

Easy Riches. George Carney. Directed by Maclean Rogers. 1938. Britain. 67 min. Sound. 16mm B&W. *Rental:* Mogulls Films.

Easy Rider. Peter Fonda, Dennis Hopper & Jack Nicholson. Directed by Dennis Hopper. 1969. Columbia. 95 min. Sound. 16mm Color. *Rental:* Films Inc, Swank Motion & Wholesome Film Ctr. *Rental:* Swank Motion, Videotape version.

Easy To Love. Adolphe Menjou & Mary Astor. Directed by William Keighley. 1934. Warners. 61 min. Sound. 16mm B&W. *Rental:* MGM United.

Easy To Love. Esther Williams & Van Johnson. Directed by Charles Walters. 1953. MGM. 95 min. Sound. 16mm Color. *Rental:* Films Inc & MGM United.

Easy Virtue. Isabel Jeans. Directed by Alfred Hitchcock. 1927. Britain. 75 min. Sound. 16mm B&W. *Rental:* Budget Films, Classic Film Mus, Em Gee Film Lib, Films Inc, Images Film & Kit Parker. *Sale:* Classic Film Mus, Cinema Concepts, Glenn Photo, Images Film, Morcraft Films & Reel Images. *Rental:* Images Film & Ivy Films, *Sale:* Glenn Photo, Super 8 silent version. *Sale:* Images Film & Tamarelles French Film, Videotape version. *Sale:* Festival Films, 62 min. 16mm version. *Sale:* Festival Films, 62 min. Videotape version.

Eat, Drink & Be Merry. 1978. Britain. (Documentary). 53 min. Sound. 16mm Color. *Rental:* Iowa Films, Kent St U Film, U Cal Media, U of IL Film & U Mich Media.

Eat My Dust. Ron Howard & Warren Kemmerling. Directed by Charles B. Griffith. 1976. New World. 90 min. Sound. 16mm Color. *Rental:* Films Inc.

Eating Raoul. Mary Woronov & Paul Bartel. Directed by Paul Bartel. 1982. QFI-Fox. 87 min. Sound. 16mm Color. *Rental:* Films Inc.

Eavesdropper, The. Stathis Giallelis & Janet Margolin. Directed by Leopoldo Torre-Nilsson. 1966. Argentina. 90 min. Sound. 16mm B&W. *Rental:* Kit Parker.

Ebb Tide. Ray Milland & Frances Farmer. Directed by James Hogan. 1937. Paramount. 92 min. Sound. 16mm Color. *Rental:* Swank Motion.

Ebony, Ivory & Jade. Rosanne Katon & Colleen Camp. Directed by Cirio H. Santiago. 1975. Dimension. 80 min. Sound. 16mm Color. *Sale:* Select Ent.

Ecce Bombo. Nanni Moretti. Directed by Nanni Moretti. Ital. 1978. Italy. 100 min. Sound. 16mm Color. subtitles. *Rental:* Films Inc.

Echharpe de Sole Rouge, L'. George Descrieres. Directed by Jean-Pierre Desagnat. 1971. France. 55 min. Sound. 16mm Color. *Rental:* French Am Cul.

Echo, The *see* Sounds from the Mountains.

Echoes. (Cast unlisted). 90 min. Sound. Videotape Color. *Sale:* Vidamerica.

Echoes of a Summer. Jodie Foster & Richard Harris. Directed by Don Taylor. 1976. Cine Arts. 99 min. Sound. 16mm Color. *Rental:* Swank Motion.

Echoes of Silence. Directed by Peter Emmanuel Goldman. 1965. Peter Emmanuel Goldman. (Experimental). 75 min. Sound. 16mm B&W. *Rental:* Canyon Cinema.

Eclipse. Monica Vitti & Alain Delon. Directed by Michelangelo Antonioni. Ital. 1962. Italy. 123 min. 16mm B&W. subtitles. *Rental:* Museum Mod Art & Wholesome Film Ctr. *Sale:* Natl Cinema.

Ecstasy. Hedy Lamarr. Directed by Gustav Machaty. Czech. 1933. Czechoslovakia. 82 min. Sound. 16mm B&W. subtitles. *Rental:* Budget Films, Classic Film Mus, Em Gee Film Lib, Images Film, Ivy Films & Video Comm. *Sale:* Cinema Concepts, Natl Cinema & Reel Images. *Rental:* Ivy Films, *Sale:* Ivy Films & Reel Images, Super 8 sound version. *Sale:* Morcraft Films, Super 8 silent version. *Sale:* Tamarelles French Film, Videotape version.

Eddie. 1965. Time-Life. (Documentary). 54 min. Sound. 16mm B&W. *Lease:* Direct Cinema.

Eddie & the Cruisers. Tom Berenger & Michael Pare. Directed by Martin Davidson. 1983. Embassy. 92 min. Sound. 16mm Color. *Rental:* Films Inc.

Eddie Cantor: The Colgate Comedy Hour. 1950. 55 min. Sound. 16mm B&W. *Rental:* Budget Films. *Rental:* Festival Films, Videotape version.

Eddie Macon's Run. Kirk Douglas & John Schneider. Directed by Jeff Kanew. 1982. Universal. 95 min. Sound. 16mm Color. *Rental:* Swank Motion. *Rental:* Swank Motion, Videotape version.

Eddy Duchin Story, The. Tyrone Power & Kim Novak. Directed by George Sidney. 1956. Columbia. 123 min. Sound. 16mm Color. *Rental:* Arcus Film, Bosco Films, Budget Films, Cine Craft, Charard Motion Pics, Film Ctr DC, Films Inc, Kit Parker, Modern Sound, Roas Films, Twyman Films, Welling Motion Pictures, Westcoast Films & Wholesome Film Ctr.

Edgar Allan Poe Special, The. (Anthology). 56 min. Sound. 16mm Color. *Rental:* Macmillan Films, Syracuse U Film, Westcoast Films & Wholesome Film Ctr. *Lease:* Macmillan Films.

Edge, The. Jack Rader. Directed by Robert Kramer. 1967. Newsreel. 105 min. Sound. 16mm B&W. *Rental:* New Cinema.

Edge, The. Directed by Roger Brown & Barry Corbet. 1978. Crystal. (Documentary). 96 min. Sound. 16mm Color. *Rental:* Crystal. *Sale:* Crystal.

Edge of Abundance, The. Orig. Title: America-Edge of Abundance. 1965. NET. (Documentary). 60 min. Sound. 16mm B&W. *Rental:* Indiana AV Ctr & Syracuse U Film. *Sale:* Indiana AV Ctr. *Sale:* Indiana AV Ctr, Videotape version.

Edge of Darkness, The. Errol Flynn & Ann Sheridan. Directed by Lewis Milestone. 1943. Warners. 124 min. Sound. 16mm B&W. *Rental:* MGM United.

Edge of Divorce, The. Valerie Hobson & Philip Friend. Directed by Daniel Birt. 1954. Britain. 90 min. Sound. 16mm B&W. *Rental:* Liberty Co.

Edge of Doom, The. Orig. Title: Stronger Than Fear. Dana Andrews & Farley Granger. Directed by Mark Robson. 1950. Goldwyn. 97 min. Sound. 16mm B&W. *Rental:* Films Inc.

Edge of Eternity, The. Cornel Wilde & Victoria Shaw. Directed by Don Siegel. 1959. Columbia. (Anamorphic). 80 min. Sound. 16mm Color. *Rental:* Films Inc, Kit Parker & Welling Motion Pictures.

Edge of Forever, The. 1980. Cosmos. (Documentary). 60 min. Sound. 16mm Color. *Rental:* Films Inc. *Sale:* Films Inc. *Rental:* Films Inc, *Sale:* Films Inc, Videotape version.

Edge of Survival, The. 1982. Wharton. 58 min. Sound. 16mm Color. *Rental:* U Cal Media.

Edge of the City, The. Orig. Title: Man is Ten Feet Tall, A. John Cassavetes & Sidney Poitier. Directed by Martin Ritt. 1957. MGM. 85 min. Sound. 16mm B&W. *Rental:* MGM United.

Edge of the World, The. Niall MacGinnis & Finlay Currie. Directed by Michael Powell. 1937. Britain. 80 min. Sound. 16mm B&W. *Rental:* A Twyman Pres & Twyman Films.

Edinburgh. 1977. Britain. (Documentary). 49 min. Sound. 16mm Color. *Rental:* Films Inc. *Sale:* Films Inc. *Rental:* Films Inc, *Sale:* Films Inc, Videotape version.

Edison the Man. Spencer Tracy & Rita Johnson. Directed by Clarence Brown. 1940. MGM. 107 min. Sound. 16mm B&W. *Rental:* MGM United.

Edmund G. Ross. Bradford Dillman. Directed by Gerald Mayer. (Profiles in Courage Ser.). 1965. Saudek. 50 min. Sound. 16mm B&W. *Rental:* IQ Film, Syracuse U Film & U Mich Media. *Sale:* IQ Film.

Edo Festival Music & Pantomime. 1975. Asia Society. (Ballet). 55 min. Videotape Color. *Rental:* Asia Soc. *Sale:* Asia Soc.

Eduardo the Healer. Directed by Richard Cowan. 1978. Serious Business. (Documentary). 55 min. Sound. 16mm Color. *Rental:* U Cal Media & U Mich Media.

Eduardo, Uruguayo. 1983. 45 min. 16mm Color. *Rental:* Icarus Films. *Sale:* Icarus Films, Videotape version.

Educating Rita. Michael Caine & Julie Walters. Directed by Lewis Gilbert. 1983. Britain. 114 min. Sound. 16mm Color. *Rental:* Swank Motion. *Sale:* Tamarelles French Film, *Rental:* Swank Motion, Videotape version.

Education & the Mexican-American. 1969. University of California. (Documentary). 57 min. Sound. 16mm B&W. *Rental:* U Cal Media & Utah Media.

Education of George Waruhiu, The. 1964. CBS. (Documentary). 54 min. Sound. 16mm B&W. *Rental:* CBC Inc.

Educational Gamimg. 1970. University of California. (Documentary, Kinescope). 59 min. Sound. 16mm B&W. *Rental:* U Cal Media. *Sale:* U Cal Media.

Edvard Munch. Directed by Clifford B. West. Norwegian. 1967. Norway. (Documentary). 70 min. Sound. 16mm Color. *Rental:* Film Images & New Cinema. *Sale:* Film Images.

Edvard Munch. Geir Westby. Directed by Peter Watkins. Norwegian. 1976. Norway. 167 min. Sound. 16mm Color. subtitles. narrated Eng. *Rental:* New Yorker Films.

Edward, My Son. Spencer Tracy & Deborah Kerr. Directed by George Cukor. 1949. MGM. 112 min. Sound. 16mm B&W. *Rental:* MGM United.

Edward S. Curtis, the Shadow *see* Shadow Catcher.

Edward the Second. 1976. Britain. (Cast unlisted). 128 min. Videotape Color. *Rental:* Films Inc. *Sale:* Films Inc.

Edward VII & the House of Windsor. 1980. Britain. (Documentary). 60 min. Sound. 16mm Color. *Rental:* Films Inc. *Sale:* Films Inc. *Rental:* Films Inc, *Sale:* Films Inc, Videotape version.

Eegah. Richard Kiel. Directed by Nicholas Merriwether. 1962. Fairway. 93 min. Sound. 16mm Color. *Rental:* Ivy Films & Video Comm.

Effect of Gamma Rays on Man-in-the-Moon Marigolds, The. Joanne Woodward. Directed by Paul Newman. 1972. Fox. 100 min. Sound. 16mm Color. *Rental:* Films Inc & Twyman Films.

Effi Briest. Hanna Schygulla. Directed by Rainer Werner Fassbinder. Ger. 1974. Germany. 167 min. Sound. 16mm Color. subtitles. narrated Eng. *Rental:* New Cinema & New Yorker Films.

Efficiency Edgar's Courtship. Taylor Holmes, Rod La Rocque & Virginia Valli. Directed by Lawrence Windom. 1917. Essanay. 50 min. Silent. 16mm B&W. *Rental:* Film Classics. *Sale:* Film Classics.

Egypt: Quest for Eternity. 59 min. Sound. 16mm Color. *Rental:* Natl Geog. *Sale:* Natl Geog. *Sale:* Natl Geog, Videotape version.

Egyptian, The. Victor Mature & Jean Simmons. Directed by Michael Curtiz. 1954. Fox. 140 min. Sound. 16mm Color. *Rental:* Films Inc & Twyman Films. *Rental:* Films Inc, Anamorphic color version.

Eiger Sanction, The. Clint Eastwood. Directed by Clint Eastwood. 1975. Universal. 125 min. Sound. 16mm Color. *Rental:* Swank Motion & Twyman Films. *Rental:* Twyman Films, Anamorphic version. *Rental:* Swank Motion, Videotape version.

Eight & a Half. Marcello Mastroianni, Claudia Cardinale & Anouk Aimee. Directed by Federico Fellini. Ital. 1963. Italy. 135 min. Sound. 16mm B&W. subtitles. *Rental:* Syracuse U Film. *Lease:* Corinth Films.

Eight Minutes to Midnight: A Portrait of Dr. Helen Caldicott. Directed by Mary Benjamin. 1981. Direct Cinema. (Documentary). 60 min. Sound. 16mm Color. *Rental:* Direct Cinema. *Sale:* Direct Cinema. *Sale:* Direct Cinema, Videotape version.

Eight Times Eight. Directed by Hans Richter, Jean Cocteau & Willem De Vogel. 1957. Richter. (Experimental). 80 min. Sound. 16mm Color. *Rental:* Museum Mod Art. *Sale:* Museum Mod Art.

Eighteen. 1976. Gospel. (Cast unlisted). 52 min. Sound. 16mm Color. *Rental:* Gospel Films & Roas Films. *Rental:* Gospel Films, Videotape version.

Eighteen Corridors of Time. 1983. Britain. 60 min. Sound. 16mm Color. *Rental:* Films Inc. *Sale:* Films Inc. *Sale:* Films Inc, Videotape version.

Eighteen Ninety-Eight. 1964. ABC. (Documentary). 54 min. Sound. 16mm Color. *Rental:* BYU Media, McGraw-Hill Films, OK AV Ctr, Syracuse U Film, U of IL Film & U Mich Media.

Eighteen Sixty. Trans. Title: Mille Di Garibaldi, I. Aida Belia. Directed by Alessandro Blasetti. Ital. 1933. Italy. 73 min. Sound. 16mm B&W. subtitles. *Rental:* Museum Mod Art.

Eighteen-Twelve: Napoleon in Moscow. A. Dukki. Directed by Vladimir Petrov. 1943. Russia. 95 min. Sound. 16mm B&W. *Rental:* Corinth Films.

Eighty Million Women Want *see* Eighty Million Women Want What?.

Eighty Million Women Want What? Orig. Title: Eighty Million Women Want. 1912. Cosmos. (Documentary). 50 min. Silent. 16mm B&W. *Rental:* Film Classics & Kit Parker. *Sale:* Film Classics. *Rental:* Film Classics, Videotape version.

Eine Nacht in Venedig. Trans. Title: A Night in Venice. Johann Strauss, Anni Rosar & Marianne Schonauer. Ger. 1950. Austria. 90 min. Sound. Videotape Color. subtitles. *Sale:* Tamarelles French Film.

Einstein. 1980. Nova. (Documentary). 58 min. Sound. 16mm Color. *Rental:* Films Inc. *Sale:* Films Inc. *Rental:* Films Inc, *Sale:* Films Inc, Videotape version.

Einstein Before Lunch *see* Dr. Einstein Before Lunch.

Einstein's Universe. 1979. BBC-WGBH. (Documentary). 120 min. Sound. 16mm Color. *Rental:* Corinth Films. *Lease:* Corinth Films. *Rental:* Corinth Films, *Lease:* Corinth Films, Videotape version.

Eisenstein *see* Sergei Eisenstein.

Eisenstein's Mexican Film: Episodes for Study. Directed by Jay Leyda. 1955. Museum of Modern Art. (Documentary). 230 min. Silent. 16mm B&W. *Rental:* Museum Mod Art. *Sale:* Museum Mod Art.

Ejecutivo Muy Mono, El. Kurt Russell & Joe Flynn. Directed by Robert Butler. 1971. Disney. 96 min. Sound. 16mm Color. dubbed. *Rental:* Twyman Films.

El Alamein. Scott Brady & Rita Moreno. Directed by Fred F. Sears. 1953. Columbia. 67 min. Sound. 16mm B&W. *Rental:* Cine Craft, Film Ctr DC & Modern Sound.

El Dorado. John Wayne & Robert Mitchum. Directed by Howard Hawks. 1967. Paramount. 126 min. Sound. 16mm Color. *Rental:* Films Inc.

El Gran Amor Del Conde Dracula *see* Dracula's Great Love.

El Greco. Mel Ferrer & Rosanna Schiaffino. Directed by Luciano Salce. 1968. Fox. 95 min. Sound. 16mm Color. *Rental:* Films Inc.

El Paso. John Payne, Gail Russell & Sterling Hayden. Directed by Lewis R. Foster. 1949. Paramount. 101 min. Sound. 16mm B&W. *Rental:* Willoughby Peer.

El Paso Kid. Sunset Carson. Directed by Thomas Carr. 1946. Republic. 54 min. Sound. 16mm B&W. *Rental:* Ivy Films. *Sale:* Rep Pic Film.

El Paso Stampede. Allan Lane. Directed by Harry Keller. 1953. Republic. 50 min. Sound. 16mm B&W. *Rental:* Ivy Films. *Sale:* Rep Pic Film. *Sale:* Video Comm, Videotape version.

El Salvador *see* El Salvador, Another Vienam.

El Salvador: Another Vietnam. Directed by Glenn Silber, Tete Vasconcellos & Deborah Shaffer. 1980. Catalyst Media. (Documentary). 50 min. Sound. 16mm Color. *Rental:* Icarus Films & U Mich Media. *Rental:* U Cal Media, *Sale:* Icarus Films, Videotape version.

El Salvador: The People Will Win. Directed by Diego De la Texera. El Salvador. (Documentary). 80 min. Sound. 16mm Color. *Rental:* Cinema Guild. *Sale:* Cinema Guild.

El Viaje Fantastico en Globo *see* Fantastic Balloon Voyage.

Elders, The. 1979. KDIN. (Documentary). 59 min. Videotape Color. *Rental:* Iowa Films & PBS Video. *Sale:* PBS Video.

Eldridge Cleaver Story, The. Eldridge Cleaver. 1977. Gospel. 50 min. Sound. 16mm Color. *Rental:* Roas Films.

Eleanor & Franklin, the Early Years. Jane Alexander & Edward Herrmann. Directed by Daniel Petrie. 1976. Talent Associates. 103 min. Sound. 16mm Color. *Rental:* Budget Films & U of IL Film.

Eleanor & Franklin, the Rise to Leadership. Jane Alexander & Edward Herrmann. Directed by Daniel Petrie. 1975. Talent Associates. 103 min. Sound. 16mm Color. *Rental:* Budget Films & U of IL Film, Videotape version.

Eleanor & Franklin, the White House Years. Edward Herrmann & Jane Alexander. Directed by Daniel Petrie. 1976. Talent Associates. 140 min. Sound. 16mm Color. *Rental:* Time-Life Multimedia. *Sale:* Time-Life Multimedia. *Sale:* Time-Life Multimedia, Videotape version.

Eleanor Roosevelt Story, The. Directed by Richard Kaplan. 1965. Landau. (Documentary). 90 min. Sound. 16mm B&W. *Rental:* Films Inc & Ivy Films. *Sale:* Texture Film.

Election, The. 1981. CTW. (Documentary). 60 min. Sound. 16mm Color. *Rental:* Indiana AV Ctr. *Sale:* Indiana AV Ctr.

Election, The: Patronage or Paradise. 1979. PBS. (Documentary). 59 min. Videotape Color. *Rental:* PBS Video. *Sale:* PBS Video.

Electra. Irene Papas. Directed by Michael Cacoyannis. Gr. 1963. Greece. 110 min. Sound. 16mm B&W. subtitles. *Rental:* MGM United.

Electra Glide in Blue. Robert Blake & Jeannine Riley. Directed by James William Guercio. 1973. United Artists. 113 min. Sound. 16mm Color. *Rental:* MGM United.

Electric Company, The: Number 1. 1971. Children's TV Workshop. (Television Program). 60 min. Sound. 16mm Color. *Rental:* Childrens Work. *Lease:* Childrens Work.

Electric Company, The: Number 35. 1971. Children's TV Workshop. (Television program). 60 min. Sound. 16mm Color. *Rental:* Childrens Work. *Lease:* Childrens Work.

Electric Company, The: Number 43. 1971. Children's TV Workshop. (Television program). 60 min. Sound. 16mm Color. *Rental:* Childrens Work. *Lease:* Childrens Work.

Electric Company, The: Number 53. 1971. Children's TV Workshop. (Television program). 60 min. Sound. 16mm Color. *Rental:* Childrens Work.

Electric Eskimo, The. 1980. Britain. (Cast unlisted). 58 min. Sound. 16mm Color. *Sale:* Lucerne Films.

Electric Family, The: How to Deal with Media Overload. Mel White. 45 min. Sound. 16mm Color. *Rental:* Gospel Films.

Electric Grandmother, The. Maureen Stapleton. 1982. NBC. 49 min. Sound. 16mm Color. *Rental:* Learning Corp Am. *Sale:* Learning Corp Am. *Rental:* Learning Corp Am, *Sale:* Learning Corp Am, Videotape version.

Electric Horseman, The. Robert Redford & Jane Fonda. Directed by Sydney Pollack. 1979. Universal. 120 min. Sound. 16mm Color. *Rental:* Swank Motion. *Rental:* Swank Motion, Anamorphic version, Videotape version.

Element Three. Directed by Jacques Giraldeau. 1965. Canada. (Documentary). 46 min. Sound. 16mm Color. *Rental:* Intl Film, Intl Film & Syracuse U Film. *Sale:* Intl Film.

Elements of Survival: Food. Canada. (Documentary). 57 min. Sound. 16mm Color. *Rental:* CBC. *Sale:* CBC.

Elements of Survival: Population.
Canada. (Documentary). 57 min. Sound.
16mm Color. *Rental:* CBC. *Sale:* CBC.

Elephant Boy. Sabu. Directed by Robert
Flaherty & Zoltan Korda. 1937. United
Artists. 80 min. Sound. 16mm B&W.
Rental: Films Inc, Inst Cinema & Roas
Films. *Sale:* Cinema Concepts.

Elephant Called Slowly, An. Bill Travers
& Virginia McKenna. Directed by James
Hill. 1970. Britain. 91 min. Sound. 16mm
Color. *Rental:* Budget Films, Films Inc,
Modern Sound, Twyman Films &
Willoughby Peer.

Elephant Man, The. Anthony Hopkins,
John Hurt & Anne Bancroft. Directed by
David Lynch. 1980. Paramount. 125 min.
Sound. 16mm B&W. *Rental:* Films Inc.

Elephant Stampede, The see Bomba &
the Elephant Stampede.

Elephant Walk. Elizabeth Taylor & Dana
Andrews. Directed by William Dieterle.
1954. Paramount. 103 min. Sound. 16mm
Color. *Rental:* Films Inc.

Elephants Never Forget see Zenobia.

Eleven Harrowhouse. Charles Grodin &
Candice Bergen. Directed by Aram
Avakian. 1974. Fox. (Anamorphic). 95
min. Sound. 16mm Color. *Rental:* Films
Inc.

Eleven Men & a Girl see Maybe It's
Love.

Eleven P. M. Richard D. Maurice.
Directed by Richard D. Maurice. 1926.
Maurice. (Musical score only). 55 min.
Sound. 16mm B&W. *Rental:* Standard
Film. *Sale:* Reel Images. *Sale:* Natl
Cinema, Silent 16mm version.

Eleven Powers, The. Directed by Larry
Gartenstein. 1980. Filmakers Library
Australian. (Documentary). 48 min.
Sound. 16mm Color. *Rental:* Film
Makers. *Sale:* Film Makers.

**Eleventh International Tournee of
Animation.** Orig. Title: International
Tournee of Animation. 1976. Film
Wright. (Anthology). 100 min. Sound.
16mm Color. *Rental:* Film Wright.

Elie Wiesel's Jerusalem. 1977. Learning
Corp. (Documentary). 50 min. Sound.
16mm Color. *Rental:* Kent ST U Film &
Learning Corp Am. *Sale:* Learning Corp
Am.

Elisa, My Life. Geraldine Chaplin &
Fernando Rey. Directed by Carlos Saura.
Span. 1977. Janus. 125 min. Sound.
16mm Color. subtitles. *Rental:* Films Inc.

Elizabeth & Essex see Private Lives of
Elizabeth & Essex.

Elizabeth of Ladymead. Anna Neagle.
Directed by Herbert Wilcox. 1949.
Britain. 97 min. Sound. 16mm Color.
Rental: Budget Films & Charard Motion
Pics.

Elizabeth R. 6 pts. Glenda Jackson. 1976.
Britain. 540 min. Sound. 16mm Color.
Rental: Films Inc. *Sale:* Films Inc. *Sale:*
Films Inc, *Sale:* Films Inc, Videotape
version.

Ella Cinders. Colleen Moore. Directed by
Alfred E. Green. 1926. First National. 70
min. Silent. 16mm B&W. *Rental:* Em
Gee Film Lib, Kerr Film & Westcoast
Films. *Sale:* Cinema Concepts, Griggs
Movie & Natl Cinema, Silent 8mm
version. *Sale:* Festival Films, 50 min.
16mm version. *Sale:* Festival Films, 50
min. Videotape version.

Ellen see Second Woman.

Ellery Queen, Master Detective. Ralph
Bellamy, Margaret Lindsay & Charlie
Grapewin. Directed by Kurt Neumann.
1940. Columbia. 69 min. Sound. 16mm
B&W. *Rental:* Kit Parker.

Ellery Queen's Penthouse Mystery.
Ralph Bellamy & Anna May Wong.
Directed by James Hogan. 1941.
Columbia. 70 min. Sound. 16mm B&W.
Rental: Kit Parker.

Elliot Carter at Buffalo. 45 min. Sound.
16mm Color. *Rental:* Pennebaker
Associates Inc. *Sale:* Pennebaker.

Ellis Island. Donald Cook & Jack
LaRue. Directed by Phil Rosen. 1936.
Chesterfield. 75 min. Sound. 16mm
B&W. *Rental:* Film Ctr DC.

Elmer. 76 min. Sound. 16mm Color.
Rental: Williams Films.

Elmer Gantry. Burt Lancaster & Jean
Simmons. Directed by Richard Brooks.
1960. United Artists. 146 min. Sound.
16mm Color. *Rental:* MGM United.

Elmer the Great. Joe E. Brown. Directed
by Mervyn LeRoy. 1933. Warners. 74
min. Sound. 16mm B&W. *Rental:* MGM
United.

Elopement. Clifton Webb & Anne
Francis. Directed by Henry Koster. 1951.
Fox. 81 min. Sound. 16mm B&W.
Rental: Films Inc.

Elusive Corporal, The. Jean-Pierre Cassel
& Claude Brasseur. Directed by Jean
Renoir. 1962. France. 108 min. Sound.
16mm B&W. *Rental:* Films Inc.

Elvira Madigan. Pia Dagermark &
Thommy Berggren. Directed by Bo
Widerberg. 1967. Sweden. 90 min. Sound.
16mm Color. dubbed. *Rental:* Films Inc
& Swank Motion.

Elvis. Directed by Steve Binder. 1965.
United Artists. 55 min. Sound. 16mm
Color. *Rental:* Budget Films.

Elvis Concert in Hawaii. 1973. (Concert).
59 min. Sound. 16mm Color. *Rental:*
Westcoast Films.

Elvis in Concert 1968-1972. 1978. 91
min. Sound. Videotape Color. *Sale:* Reel
Images.

Elvis on Tour. Directed by Pierre Adidge
& Robert Abel. 1972. MGM.
(Documentary). 93 min. Sound. 16mm
Color. *Rental:* MGM United. *Rental:*
MGM United, Anamorphic version.
Rental: MGM United, Videotape version.

Elvis-That's the Way It Is. Orig. Title:
That's the Way It Is. Directed by Denis
Sanders. 1970. MGM. (Documentary). 97
min. Sound. 16mm Color. *Rental:* MGM
United. *Rental:* MGM United,
Anamorphic version.

Embezzled Heaven. Annie Rosar & Hans
Holt. Directed by Ernst Marischka. 1959.
Germany. 91 min. Sound. 16mm Color.
dubbed. *Rental:* Films Inc.

Embraceable You. Dane Clark &
Geraldine Brooks. Directed by Felix
Jacoves. 1948. Warners. 80 min. Sound.
16mm B&W. *Rental:* MGM United.

Embracers, The. Directed by Gary
Graver. 1968. Gary Graver.
(Experimental). 62 min. Sound. 16mm
B&W. *Rental:* Canyon Cinema.

Embryo. Rock Hudson & Diane Ladd.
Directed by Ralph Nelson. 1976. Cine
Artists. 103 min. Sound. 16mm Color.
Rental: Swank Motion.

Emerald Cities. 1981. 85 min. Sound.
16mm Color. *Rental:* Canyon Cinema.

Emerald of Artatama. Rory Calhoun &
James Philbrook. 1967. Italy. 86 min.
Sound. 16mm Color. dubbed. *Rental:*
Films Inc & Westcoast Films.

Emergency Call. Betty Furness & Bill
Boyd. Directed by Merian C. Cooper.
1933. RKO. 60 min. Sound. 16mm
Rental: RKO General Pics.

Emergency Ward see Carey Treatment.

Emergency Wedding. Larry Parks &
Barbara Hale. Directed by Edward
Buzzell. 1950. Columbia. 78 min. Sound.
16mm B&W. *Lease:* Time-Life
Multimedia.

Emigrants, The. Max Von Sydow & Liv
Ullmann. Directed by Jan Troell. 1972.
Warners. 151 min. Sound. 16mm Color.
Rental: Swank Motion & Williams Films.

Emil & the Detectives. George Hayes &
John Williams. Directed by Milton
Rosmer. 1935. Britain. 80 min. Sound.
16mm B&W. *Rental:* Alba House & Film
Classics.

Emil und Die Detektive. Fritz Rasp. Directed by Gerhard Lamprecht. 1931. Germany. 77 min. Sound. 16mm B&W. *Rental:* Trans-World Films.

Emilienne. (Cast unlisted). Videotape *Sale:* Vidamerica.

Emilienne & Nicole. Betty Mars & Pierre Oudry. Directed by Guy Casaril. Fr. 1975. France. 95 min. Sound. 16mm Color. subtitles. *Rental:* J Green Pics.

Emilio & His Magical Bull. 1978. Nassour. (Cast unlisted). 90 min. Sound. 16mm Color. *Rental:* Williams Films. *Sale:* Salz Ent. *Sale:* Salz Ent, Super 8 sound version. *Sale:* Salz Ent, Videotape version.

Emitai. Orig. Title: Lord of the Sky. Robert Fontaine. Directed by Ousmane Sembene. Senegalese. 1972. Senegal. 101 min. Sound. 16mm Color. subtitles. *Rental:* New Yorker Films.

Emlyn Williams As Charles Dickens. Emlyn Williams. 1977. 120 min. Sound. 16mm Color. *Rental:* A Cantor. *Sale:* A Cantor.

Emma. Marie Dressler & Myrna Loy. Directed by Clarence Brown. 1932. MGM. 72 min. Sound. 16mm B&W. *Rental:* MGM United.

Emmanuelle. Sylvia Kristel, Alain Cuny & Marika Green. Directed by Just Jaeckin. 1976. 92 min. Sound. 16mm Color. dubbed Eng. *Rental:* Swank Motion. *Rental:* Swank Motion, Videotape version.

Emmanuelle II: The Joys of a Woman. Sylvia Kristel. Directed by Francis Giacobetti. 1976. Paramount. 90 min. Sound. 16mm Color. dubbed. *Rental:* Films Inc.

Emmanuelle in America. (Cast unlisted). Videotape *Sale:* Vidamerica.

Emmanuelle in Bangkok. (Cast unlisted). Videotape *Sale:* Vidamerica.

Emmanuelle the Queen. (Cast unlisted). Videotape *Sale:* Vidamerica.

Emotional Dilemma. Orig. Title: America's Crises: The Emotional Dilemma. 1966. NET. (Documentary). 60 min. Sound. 16mm B&W. *Rental:* Indiana AV Ctr, Mass Media & SD AV Ctr. *Sale:* Indiana AV Ctr.

Emperor Jones. Paul Robeson & Fredi Washington. Directed by Dudley Murphy. 1933. Britain. 72 min. Sound. 16mm B&W. *Rental:* A Twyman Pres, Budget Films, Classic Film Mus, Em Gee Film Lib, Films Inc, Images Film, Inst Cinema, Janus Films & Phoenix Films. *Sale:* Festival Films, Film Images, Images Film, Phoenix Films & Reel Images. *Sale:* Festival Films, Images Film & Tamarelles French Film, Videotape version.

Emperor of the North. Lee Marvin & Ernest Borgnine. Directed by Robert Aldrich. 1973. Fox. 120 min. Sound. 16mm Color. *Rental:* Films Inc, Twyman Films, Welling Motion Pictures, Westcoast Films & Williams Films.

Emperor Waltz, The. Bing Crosby & Joan Fontaine. Directed by Billy Wilder. 1948. Paramount. 106 min. Sound. 16mm Color. *Rental:* Swank Motion.

Emperor's Nightingale. Directed by Jiri Trnka. 1951. Czechoslovakia. (Animated). 60 min. Sound. 16mm B&W. narrated Eng. *Rental:* Charard Motion Pics, Em Gee Film Lib & Macmillan Films. *Lease:* Macmillan Films. *Rental:* Films Inc & Syracuse U Film, Color version.

Empire City. Directed by Michael Blackwood. 89 min. 16mm *Rental:* Blackwood. *Sale:* Blackwood.

Empire of Passion, The. Kazuko Yoshiyuki. Directed by Nagisa Oshima. Jap. 1978. Japan. 106 min. Sound. 16mm Color. subtitles. *Rental:* Kit Parker.

Empire of the Ants, The. Joan Collins, Robert Lansing & Albert Salmi. 98 min. Sound. 16mm Color. *Rental:* Welling Motion Pictures.

Empire of the Sun. Enrico Paca. Directed by Enrico Gras. 1956. Peru. 90 min. Sound. 16mm Color. narrated Eng. *Rental:* Films Inc & Macmillan Films. *Lease:* Macmillan Films.

Employee's Entrance. Loretta Young & Warren William. Directed by Roy Del Ruth. 1933. Warners. 75 min. Sound. 16mm B&W. *Rental:* MGM United.

Employing the Disadvantaged. 1968. 45 min. Sound. 16mm Color. *Rental:* U Mich Media.

Empty Canvas, The. Bette Davis & Catherine Spaak. Directed by Damiano Damiani. 1964. Embassy. 118 min. Sound. 16mm B&W. *Rental:* Films Inc.

Empty Cradle, The. Mary Alden & Harry Morey. Directed by Burton King. 1923. Truart. 60 min. Silent. 16mm B&W. *Rental:* Mogulls Films.

Empty Frame, The. 1976. Gould. (Documentary). 53 min. Sound. 16mm Color. *Rental:* Lucerne Films. *Sale:* Lucerne Films. *Sale:* Lucerne Films, Videotape version.

Empty Holsters. Dick Foran & Patricia Walthall. Directed by B. Reeves Eason. 1937. Warners. 62 min. Sound. 16mm B&W. *Rental:* MGM United.

Empty Quarter. 1969. ITT. (Documentary). 48 min. Sound. 16mm Color. *Rental:* Films Inc. *Sale:* Films Inc.

Empty Space, The. 1970. Seven Valley. (Documentary). 60 min. Sound. 16mm Color. *Rental:* Green Mt. *Sale:* Green Mt.

En Natt. Bjorn Berglund. Directed by Gustav Molander. Swed. 1931. Sweden. 80 min. Sound. 16mm B&W. *Rental:* Museum Mod Art.

Enchanted April, The. Frank Morgan & Anne Harding. Directed by Harry Beaumont. 1935. RKO. 66 min. Sound. 16mm *Rental:* RKO General Pics.

Enchanted Cottage, The. Robert Young & Dorothy McGuire. Directed by John Cromwell. 1945. RKO. 92 min. Sound. 16mm B&W. *Rental:* Films Inc. *Rental:* RKO General Pics, 78 min. version.

Enchanted Forest, The. Brenda Joyce & Harry Davenport. Directed by Lew Landers. 1945. PRC. 78 min. Sound. 16mm Color. *Sale:* Classics Assoc NY, B&W version.

Enchanted Island. Jane Powell & Dana Andrews. Directed by Allan Dwan. 1958. Warners. 87 min. Sound. 16mm Color. *Rental:* Budget Films & Video Comm. *Lease:* Video Comm. *Rental:* Video Comm, *Lease:* Video Comm, Videotape version.

Enchanted Loom, The. 1974. Media Guild. (Documentary). 52 min. Sound. 16mm Color. *Rental:* Media Guild. *Sale:* Media Guild. *Sale:* Media Guild, Videotape version.

Enchantment. David Niven & Teresa Wright. Directed by Irving Reis. 1948. Goldwyn. 101 min. Sound. 16mm B&W. *Rental:* Films Inc.

Encounter, The. Japan. (Cast unlisted). 75 min. 16mm B&W. *Sale:* Japan Society. *Sale:* Japan Society, Videotape version.

Encounter on Urban Environment. 1971. Canada. (Documentary). 108 min. Sound. 16mm B&W. *Rental:* Natl Film CN. *Sale:* Natl Film CN.

Encounter with Disaster, An. 1979. Lucerne. (Documentary). 95 min. Sound. 16mm Color. *Rental:* Modern Sound & Budget Films. *Sale:* Lucerne Films. *Sale:* Lucerne Films, Videotape version.

Encounter with Saul Alinsky, An. 2 pts. 1969. Canada. (Documentary). 60 min. Sound. 16mm B&W. *Sale:* Natl Film CN.

Encyclopaedia Galactica. 1980. Cosmos. 60 min. Sound. 16mm Color. *Rental:* Films Inc. *Sale:* Films Inc. *Rental:* Films Inc, *Sale:* Films Inc, Videotape version.

End, The. Burt Reynolds & Dom Deluise. Directed by Burt Reynolds. 1978. United Artists. 100 min. Sound. 16mm Color. *Rental:* MGM United.

End of a Priest, The. Vlastimil Brodsky. Directed by Evald Schorm. Czech. 1969. Czechoslovakia. 82 min. Sound. 16mm B&W. subtitles. *Rental:* Grove & New Cinema.

End of an Era, The. Directed by Munroe Scott. 1971. Canada. (Documentary). 58 min. sound. 16mm Color. *Rental:* Natl Film CN. *Sale:* Natl Film CN.

End of August at the Hotel Ozone, The. Directed by Jan Schmidt & Ondrej Jariabek. Czech. 1967. Czechoslovakia. (Cast unlisted). 87 min. Sound. 16mm B&W. subtitles. *Rental:* New Cinema & New Line Cinema.

End of Modernity, The. 1979. Britain. (Documentary). 52 min. Sound. 16mm Color. *Rental:* Films Inc. *Sale:* Films Inc. *Sale:* Films Inc, Videotape version.

End of St. Petersburg, The. Trans. Title: Konyets Sankt Peterburga. Vera Baranovskaya. Directed by Vsevolod I. Pudovkin. Rus. 1927. Russia. 95 min. Silent. 16mm B&W. *Rental:* Budget Films, Corinth Films, Em Gee Film Lib, Film Images, Iowa Films, Kit Parker, Museum Mod Art, Twyman Films, U Cal Media, Westcoast Films & Images Film. *Sale:* Blackhawk Films & Glenn Photo. *Sale:* Blackhawk Films & Twyman Films, Sound 16mm version. *Sale:* Blackhawk Films, Super 8 Sound version. *Rental:* Ivy Films, *Sale:* Blackhawk Films & Glenn Photo, Super 8 Silent version.

End of Summer, The. Orig. Title: Autumn of the Kohayagawa Family, The. Ganjiro Nakamura. Directed by Yasujiro Ozu. Jap. 1961. Japan. 103 min. Sound. 16mm Color. subtitles. *Rental:* New Cinema & New Yorker Films.

End of the Affair, The. Deborah Kerr, Van Johnson & John Mills. Directed by Edward Dmytryk. 1955. Columbia. 106 min. Sound. 16mm B&W. *Rental:* Kit Parker.

End of the Game, The. Jon Voight & Jacqueline Bisset. Directed by Maximillian Schell. 1976. Fox. 106 min. Sound. 16mm Color. *Rental:* Films Inc & Williams Films.

End of the Ho Chi Minh Trail, The. 1979. PBS. (Documentary). 89 min. Videotape Color. *Rental:* PBS Video. *Sale:* PBS Video.

End of the Rainbow *see* Northwest Outpost.

End of the Rainbow, The. 1979. 58 min. Sound. Videotape *Rental:* PBS Video. *Sale:* PBS Video. *Sale:* PBS Video, 16mm version.

End of the Road, The. Edward Norris & John Abbott. Directed by George Blair. 1944. Republic. 51 min. Sound. 16mm B&W. *Rental:* Ivy Films. *Sale:* Rep Pic Film.

End of the Road. Stacy Keach, James Earl Jones & James Coco. Directed by Aram Avakian. 1970. Allied Artists. 110 min. Sound. 16mm Color. *Rental:* Hurlock Cine.

End of the Trail, The. Tim McCoy & Laura Walters. Directed by D. Ross Lederman. 1932. Columbia. 60 min. Sound. 16mm B&W. *Rental:* Swank Motion.

End of the Trail, The. 1966. NBC. (Documentary). 54 min. Sound. 16mm B&W. *Rental:* BYU Media, McGraw-Hill Films, SD AV Ctr, Syracuse U Film, U of IL Film & U Mich Media. *Sale:* McGraw-Hill Films.

End of the World, The. Christopher Lee, Sue Lyon & Macdonald Carey. Directed by John Hayes. 1977. Irwin Yablans. 92 min. Sound. 16mm Color. *Rental:* Films Inc.

End of the World in Our Usual Bed in a Night Full of Rain, The *see* Night Full of Rain.

Endangered Species. Robert Urich & Jobeth Williams. Directed by Alan Rudolph. 1982. MGM. 97 min. Sound. 16mm Color. *Rental:* MGM United. *Rental:* MGM United, Videotape version.

Endless Love. Brooke Shields, Martin Hewitt & Don Murray. Directed by Franco Zeffirelli. 115 min. Sound. 16mm Color. *Rental:* Swank Motion. *Rental:* Swank Motion, Videotape version.

Endless Sea, The. (Documentary). 76 min. Sound. 16mm Color. *Rental:* Films Inc.

Endless Summer, The. Mike Hynson & Robert August. (Documentary). 91 min. Sound. 16mm Color. *Rental:* Bosco Films.

Enemy, The. 1973. Ken Anderson. (Cast unlisted). 70 min. Sound. 16mm B&W. *Rental:* G Herne.

Enemy Agent *see* British Intelligence.

Enemy Agents Meet Ellery Queen. William Gargan & Margaret Lindsay. Directed by James Hogan. 1942. 64 min. Sound. 16mm *Rental:* Budget Films.

Enemy Below, The. Robert Mitchum & Curt Jurgens. Directed by Dick Powell. 1957. Fox. 98 min. Sound. 16mm Color. *Rental:* Films Inc. *Rental:* Films Inc, Anamorphic color version.

Enemy of the Law, The. Tex Ritter. Directed by Harry Fraser. 1945. PRC. 60 min. Sound. 16mm B&W. *Rental:* Ivy Films & Mogulls Films. *Sale:* Classics Assoc NY & Rep Pic Film.

Enemy of the People, An. Steve McQueen & Charles Durning. Directed by George Schaefer. 1977. Warners. 107 min. Sound. 16mm Color. *Rental:* Films Inc, Swank Motion, Twyman Films & Williams Films.

Enemy of Women, The. Claudia Drake & Paul Andor. Directed by Alfred Zeisler. 1944. 88 min. Sound. 16mm B&W. *Rental:* Budget Films.

Enemy Within, The *see* Red Menace.

Energy Crisis, The: The Nuclear Alternative. 1973. Xerox. (Documentary). 52 min. Sound. 16mm Color. *Rental:* U Cal Media & Xerox Films. *Sale:* Xerox Films.

Energy Crunch, The: The Best Way Out. 1979. CBS. (Documentary). 51 min. Sound. 16mm Color. *Sale:* Carousel Films & U Mich Media. *Rental:* Iowa Films. *Sale:* Carousel Films, Videotape version.

Energy Game, The. 1973. WNET. (Documentary). 58 min. Sound. 16mm Color. *Rental:* WNET Media. *Sale:* WNET Media. *Sale:* WNET Media, Videotape version.

Energy: The Fact... The Fears... The Future. 1978. CBS. (Documentary). 55 min. Sound. 16mm Color. *Rental:* La Inst Res Ctr & Phoenix Films. *Sale:* Phoenix Films. *Sale:* Phoenix Films, Videotape version.

Energy War, The. 3 pts. Directed by D. A. Pennebaker. 1978. Pennebaker. (Documentary). 300 min. Sound. 16mm Color. dubbed. *Rental:* Pennebaker. *Sale:* Pennebaker. *Rental:* Pennebaker, *Sale:* Pennebaker, Videotape version.

Enfant Dans la Foule, L'. Jean-Francois Cimino & Annie Kovacs. Directed by Gerard Blain. Fr. 1975. France. 85 min. Sound. 16mm Color. subtitles. *Rental:* French Am Cul.

Enfants Gates, Les *see* Spoiled Children.

Enfants Terribles, Les. Nicole Stephane & Edouard Dermithe. Directed by Jean-Pierre Melville. Fr. 1949. France. 90 min. Sound. 16mm B&W. subtitles. *Rental:* Cinema Five.

Enforcer, The. Orig. Title: Murder, Inc. Humphrey Bogart & Zero Mostel. Directed by Bretaigne Windust. 1950. Warners. 87 min. Sound. 16mm B&W. *Rental:* Corinth Films. *Lease:* Corinth Films.

Enforcer, The. Clint Eastwood & Tyne Daly. Directed by James Fargo. 1976. Warners. 88 min. Sound. 16mm Color. *Rental:* Modern Sound, Swank Motion, Twyman Films & Williams Films. *Rental:* Swank Motion, Videotape version.

England Made Me. Michael York & Hildegarde Neil. Directed by Peter Duffell. 1974. Britain. 100 min. Sound. 16mm Color. *Rental:* Films Inc.

England: Puritan vs. Cavalier. 1973. Britain. (Documentary). 54 min. Sound. 16mm B&W. *Rental:* Modern Mass. *Sale:* Modern Mass.

English, D-Day & the Holocaust, The: With Hardship Their Garment. 1976. Britain. (Documentary). 52 min. Sound. 16mm Color. *Rental:* Time-Life Multimedia. *Sale:* Time-Life Multimedia. *Rental:* Time-Life Multimedia. *Sale:* Time-Life Multimedia, Videotape version.

Enigma. Martin Sheen & Brigitte Fossey. Directed by Jeannot Szwarc. 1983. Embassy. 101 min. Sound. 16mm Color. *Rental:* Films Inc.

Enigma of Kaspar Hauser, The *see* Every Man for Himself & God Against All.

Enigmas of Easter Island. 1974. Explo Mundo. (Documentary). 52 min. Sound. 16mm Color. *Rental:* B Raymond. *Sale:* B Raymond.

Enjo. Orig. Title: Conflagration. Raizo Ichikawa. Directed by Kon Ichikawa. Jap. 1958. Japan. 96 min. Sound. 16mm B&W. subtitles. *Rental:* New Yorker Films.

Enough Rope. Gert Frobe & Marina Vlady. Directed by Claude Autant-Lara. 1965. 104 min. Sound. 16mm B&W. dubbed. *Rental:* Films Inc.

Entebbe, Operation Thunderbolt *see* Operation Thunderbolt.

Enter Laughing. Jose Ferrer, Shelley Winters & Elaine May. Directed by Carl Reiner. 1967. Columbia. 112 min. Sound. 16mm Color. *Rental:* Arcus Film, Budget Films, Films Inc, Ivy Films, Modern Sound, Video Comm & Welling Motion Pictures.

Enter Madame. Cary Grant & Elissa Landi. Directed by Elliott Nugent. 1935. Paramount. 83 min. Sound. 16mm Color. *Rental:* Swank Motion.

Enter the Devil. Irene Kelly & Josh Bryant. 86 min. Sound. 16mm Color. *Rental:* Ivy Films. *Rental:* Video Comm, Videotape version.

Enter the Ninja. Franco Nero, Susan George & Christopher George. Directed by Menahem Golan. 1981. Cannon. 108 min. Sound. 16mm Color. *Rental:* Swank Motion.

Enter with Caution: The Atomic Age. 1968. CBS. (Documentary). 52 min. Sound. 16mm B&W. *Rental:* Macmillan Films. *Sale:* Macmillan Films.

Enterprise. 1966. Wolper. (Documentary). 50 min. Sound. 16mm B&W. *Rental:* Films Inc. *Sale:* Films Inc. *Sale:* Films Inc, Videotape version.

Enterprise of England, The. Glenda Jackson. 1976. Britain. 90 min. Videotape Color. *Rental:* Films Inc. *Sale:* Films Inc.

Entertainer, The. Laurence Olivier & Joan Plowright. Directed by Tony Richardson. 1960. 97 min. Sound. 16mm *Rental:* Budget Films.

Entertaining Mr. Sloane. Beryl Reid, Harry Andrews & Peter McEnery. Directed by Douglas Hickox. 1970. Britain. 94 min. Sound. 16mm Color. *Rental:* Budget Films.

Enthusiasm. Orig. Title: Symphony of the Don Basin. Directed by Dziga Vertov. 1931. Russia. (Cast unlisted). 60 min. Sound. 16mm B&W. *Rental:* Budget Films, Images Film, Kit Parker & Museum Mod Art. *Sale:* Festival Films, Images Film & Natl Cinema. *Sale:* Festival Films, Videotape version.

Entity, The. Barbara Hershey & Ron Silver. Directed by Sidney J. Furie. 1983. Fox. 115 min. Sound. 16mm Color. *Rental:* Films Inc.

Entre Nous. Miou Miou & Isabelle Huppert. Directed by Diane Kurys. Fr. 1984. 110 min. 16mm Color. subtitles. *Rental:* MGM United.

Environment. 1973. Sterling. (Documentary). 56 min. Sound. 16mm Color. *Sale:* Sterling Ed Film.

E.P: The Estate Planner. 58 min. Sound. Videotape *Rental:* PBS Video. *Sale:* PBS Video.

Epic of Flight, The. 1966. Wolper. (Documentary). 50 min. Sound. 16mm B&W. *Rental:* Films Inc. *Sale:* Films Inc. *Sale:* Films Inc, Videotape version.

Epic That Never Was, The. Orig. Title: I, Claudius. Charles Laughton & Merle Oberon. Directed by Bill Duncalf. 1968. Britain. 80 min. Sound. 16mm B&W. *Rental:* Budget Films, Inst Cinema, Images Film, Kit Parker & Twyman Films. *Sale:* Cinema Concepts, Festival Films, Images Film, Natl Cinema, Reel Images & Twyman Films. *Sale:* Festival Films, Images Film & Tamarelles French Film, Videotape version.

Epidemic: America Fights Back. Gannett Broadcast Group. 51 min. Sound. 16mm Color. *Rental:* MTI Telep.

Epitaph for an Age. 1981. Cantor. (Documentary). 60 min. Sound. 16mm Color. *Rental:* A Cantor. *Sale:* A Cantor.

Equal Justice Under Law: United States vs. Aaron Burr. 1977. US Government. (Documentary, color sequences). 76 min. Sound. 16mm *Rental:* U of IL Film, Natl AV Ctr, Syracuse U Film & Utah Media. *Sale:* Natl AV Ctr.

Equality. 1976. 59 min. Sound. Videotape *Rental:* PBS Video. *Sale:* PBS Video.

Equinox. Edward Connell & Barbara Hewitt. Directed by Jack Woods. 1972. Harris. 82 min. Sound. 16mm Color. *Rental:* Budget Films, Films Inc, Ivy Films, Video Comm & Westcoast Films.

Equinox Flower. Shin Saburi. Directed by Yasujiro Ozu. Jap. 1958. Japan. 118 min. Sound. 16mm Color. subtitles. *Rental:* New Cinema & New Yorker Films.

Equus. Richard Burton & Peter Firth. Directed by Sidney Lumet. 1977. United Artists. 138 min. Sound. 16mm Color. *Rental:* MGM United.

Era Notte a Roma. Leo Genn & Giovanni Ralli. Directed by Roberto Rossellini. 1960. 145 min. Sound. 16mm B&W. *Rental:* Films Inc.

ERA: The War Between Women. 1979. ABC. (Documentary). 55 min. Sound. 16mm Color. *Rental:* MTI Tele. *Sale:* MTI Tele. *Sale:* MTI Tele, Videotape version.

Eraserhead. John Nance & Charlotte Stewart. Directed by David Lynch. 1977. AFI. 90 min. Sound. 16mm B&W. *Rental:* Corinth Films. *Sale:* Festival Films. *Sale:* Festival Films, Videotape version.

Erendira. Irene Papas & Claudia Ohana. Directed by Ruy Guerra. 1983. 103 min. Sound. 16mm Color. *Rental:* New Yorker Films.

Eric Hoffer: Passionate State of Mind. 1967. CBS. (Documentary). 53 min. Sound. 16mm Color. *Rental:* Mass Media, Syracuse U Film & U Mich Media. *Sale:* Carousel Films.

Eric Hoffer: The Crowded Life. 1977. 89 min. Sound. Videotape *Rental:* PBS Video. *Sale:* PBS Video.

Erik the Conqueror. Cameron Mitchell. Directed by Mario Bava. 1963. Italy. 83 min. Sound. 16mm Color. dubbed. *Rental:* Charard Motion Pics, Films Inc, Kerr Film, Westcoast Films & Wholesome Film Ctr.

Ernie Game, The. 1973. Canada. (Cast unlisted). 89 min. Sound. 16mm Color. *Rental:* Natl Film CN. *Sale:* Natl Film CN.

Erotic Dreams. Directed by Nicholas Ray. 85 min. Sound. 16mm Color. *Rental:* New Line Cinema.

Erotic Signal. 1978. 50 min. Sound. 16mm Color. *Rental:* Canyon Cinema.

Errand Boy, The. Jerry Lewis. Directed by Jerry Lewis. 1962. Paramount. 92 min. Sound. 16mm B&W. *Rental:* Films Inc.

Erwin Rommel. 1976. Britain. (Documentary). 54 min. Sound. 16mm Color. *Rental:* Time-Life Multimedia. *Sale:* Time-Life Multimedia. *Rental:* Time-Life Multimedia, *Sale:* Time-LIfe Multimedia, Videotape version.

Escapade. Anthony Bushell. Directed by Richard Thorpe. 1932. Invincible. 70 min. Sound. 16mm B&W. *Rental:* Ivy Films.

Escapade. John Mills & Alastair Sim. Directed by Philip Leacock. 1955. Britain. 87 min. Sound. 16mm B&W. *Rental:* Charard Motion Pics & Video Comm.

Escapade in Japan. Cameron Mitchell & Teresa Wright. Directed by Arthur Lubin. 1957. RKO. 93 min. Sound. 16mm Color. *Rental:* Films Inc. *Rental:* Video Comm, *Lease:* Video Comm, Videotape version.

Escape. Norma Shearer & Robert Taylor. Directed by Mervyn LeRoy. 1940. MGM. 104 min. Sound. 16mm B&W. *Rental:* MGM United.

Escape. Rex Harrison & Peggy Cummins. Directed by Joseph L. Mankiewicz. 1948. Fox. 78 min. Sound. 16mm B&W. *Rental:* Films Inc.

Escape by Night. Ward Bond & Dean Jagger. Directed by Hamilton McFadden. 1937. Republic. 67 min. Sound. 16mm B&W. *Rental:* Ivy Films. *Sale:* Rep Pic Film.

Escape by Night. Terrence Longdon & Jennifer Jayne. Directed by Montgomery Tully. 1964. Britain. 75 min. Sound. 16mm B&W. *Rental:* Hurlock Cine.

Escape from Alcatraz. Clint Eastwood & Patrick McGoohan. Directed by Don Siegel. 1978. Paramount. 112 min. Sound. 16mm Color. *Rental:* Films Inc.

Escape from Crime. Richard Travis & Julie Bishop. Directed by D. Ross Lederman. 1942. Warners. 51 min. Sound. 16mm B&W. *Rental:* MGM United.

Escape from East Berlin. Don Murray & Christine Kaufmann. Directed by Robert Siodmak. 1962. MGM. 96 min. Sound. 16mm B&W. *Rental:* MGM United.

Escape from Fort Bravo. William Holden & Eleanor Parker. Directed by John Sturges. 1953. MGM. 98 min. Sound. 16mm B&W. *Rental:* MGM United. *Rental:* MGM United, Color version.

Escape from Hell Island. Orig. Title: Man in the Water. Mark Stevens & Linda Scott. Directed by Mark Stevens. 1964. Crown. 80 min. Sound. 16mm B&W. *Rental:* Video Comm & Welling Motion Pictures. *Lease:* Video Comm. *Rental:* Video Comm, Videotape version.

Escape from Iran. Gordon Pinsent & Tisa Chang. Directed by Chris Wiggins. 100 min. Sound. 16mm Color. *Rental:* Williams Films.

Escape from Madness. Rosemary Clooney. 1978. NBC. (Documentary). 52 min. Sound. 16mm Color. *Rental:* Films Inc & Syracuse U Film. *Sale:* Films Inc. *Rental:* Films Inc, *Sale:* Films Inc, Videotape version.

Escape from New York. Kurt Russell & Lee Van Cleef. Directed by John Carpenter. 1981. Embassy. 95 min. Sound. 16mm Color. *Rental:* Films Inc.

Escape from Red Rock. Brian Donlevy. Directed by Edward Bernds. 1958. Fox. 75 min. Sound. 16mm B&W. *Rental:* Ivy Films & Westcoast Films. *Sale:* Rep Pic Film.

Escape from the Planet of the Apes. Kim Hunter & Roddy McDowell. Directed by Don Taylor. 1971. Fox. 97 min. Sound. 16mm Color. *Rental:* Films Inc, Twyman Films, Welling Motion Pictures, Westcoast Films & Williams Films.

Escape If You Can *see* Saint Benny the Dip.

Escape in the Desert. Helmut Dantine & Philip Dorn. Directed by Edward A. Blatt. 1945. Warners. 81 min. Sound. 16mm B&W. *Rental:* MGM United.

Escape in the Fog. Otto Kruger & Nina Foch. Directed by Budd Boetticher. 1945. Columbia. 60 min. Sound. 16mm B&W. *Rental:* Bosco Films & Kit Parker.

Escape Me Never. Errol Flynn & Ida Lupino. Directed by Peter Godfrey. 1947. Warners. 104 min. Sound. 16mm B&W. *Rental:* MGM United.

Escape to Athena. Telly Savalas, David Niven & Sonny Bono. Directed by George Pan Cosmatos. 1980. AFD. 102 min. Sound. 16mm Color. *Rental:* Swank Motion.

Escape to Burma. Barbara Stanwyck & Robert Ryan. Directed by Allan Dwan. 1955. RKO. 87 min. Sound. Super 8 Color. *Sale:* Cinema Concepts.

Escape to Happiness *see* Intermezzo.

Escape to Paradise. Bobby Breen & Kent Taylor. Directed by Erle C. Kenton. 1939. RKO. 75 min. Sound. 16mm B&W. *Rental:* Alba House & Classic Film Mus. *Sale:* Cinema Concepts & Reel Images.

Escape to the Sun. John Bentley. Directed by George Breakston Jr. 1957. Britain. 64 min. Sound. 16mm B&W. *Rental:* Budget Films & Ivy Films. *Sale:* Rep Pic Film.

Escape to Witch Mountain. Eddie Albert & Ray Milland. Directed by John Hough. 1975. Disney. 97 min. Sound. 16mm Color. *Rental:* Bosco Films, Buchan Pic, Disney Prod, Elliot Film Co, Film Ctr DC, Films Inc, MGM United, Modern Sound, Roas Films, Swank Motion, Twyman Films, Welling Motion Pictures, Westcoast Films & Williams Films.

Eshet Ha'Gibor *see* Hero's Wife.

Eskimo. Orig. Title: Mala the Magnificent. Directed by W. S. Van Dyke. 1933. MGM. (Native cast). 117 min. Sound. 16mm B&W. *Rental:* MGM United.

Eskimo: Fight for Life. 1973. CBS. (Documentary). 51 min. Sound. 16mm Color. *Rental:* Educ Dev Ctr & U Mich Media.

Eskimo Summer. 1974. Britain. (Documentary). 52 min. Sound. 16mm Color. *Rental:* Educ Dev Ctr. *Sale:* Educ Dev Ctr.

Eskimo Winter. 1974. Britain. (Documentary). 52 min. Sound. 16mm Color. *Rental:* Educ Dev Ctr. *Sale:* Educ Dev Ctr.

Espion, L' *see* Defector.

Espionage Agent. Joel McCrea & Brenda Marshall. Directed by Lloyd Bacon. 1939. Warners. 83 min. Sound. 16mm B&W. *Rental:* MGM United.

Essay on English, An. 1968. CBS. (Documentary). 54 min. Sound. 16mm B&W. *Rental:* Phoenix Films. *Sale:* Phoenix Films. *Rental:* Phoenix Films, *Sale:* Phoenix Films, Color version.

Essay on Watergate, An. 1973. PBS. (Documentary). 59 min. Sound. 16mm Color. *Rental:* Syracuse U Films & U Cal Media. *Rental:* Indiana AV Ctr, Videotape version.

Essay on William Blake, An. 1971. NET. (Documentary). 52 min. Sound. 16mm Color. *Rental:* U Cal Media & Indiana AV Ctr. *Sale:* Indiana Av Ctr.

Essence of Being Human, The. 1977. Miami-Dade. (Documentary). 60 min. Sound. Videotape Color. *Rental:* Films Inc. *Sale:* Films Inc.

Essene. Directed by Frederick Wiseman. 1972. Zipporah. (Documentary). 89 min. Sound. 16mm B&W. *Rental:* Zipporah Films.

Essential Nehru. 1964. NET. (Documentary). 59 min. Sound. 16mm B&W. *Rental:* Indiana AV Ctr. *Sale:* Indiana AV Ctr.

Essential to Patient Care. 1980. 60 min. Sound. Videotape Color. *Rental:* Natl Av Ctr.

Essie. 1982. 55 min. Sound. 16mm Color. *Rental:* U Mich Media.

Esther & the King. Joan Collins & Richard Egan. Directed by Raoul Walsh. 1960. Fox. 109 min. Sound. 16mm Color. *Rental:* Films Inc.

Etait une Fois le Cap Horn, Il. Directed by Alain Colas. France. (Documentary). 75 min. Sound. 16mm Color. *Rental:* French Am Cul. *Rental:* French Am Cul, Videotape version.

Eternal Flame. Norma Talmadge & Adolphe Menjou. Directed by Frank Lloyd. 1922. 16mm *Rental:* A Twyman Pres.

Eternal Frontier, The. 1979. PBS. (Documentary). 58 min. Sound. Videotape Color. *Rental:* PBS Video. *Sale:* PBS Video.

Eternal Mask, The. Peter Peterson. Directed by Werner Hochbaum. Ger. 1934. Austria-Switzerland. 74 min. Sound. 16mm B&W. subtitles. *Rental:* Janus Films.

Eternal Return, The. Jean Marais & Madeleine Sologne. Directed by Jean Delannoy. Fr. 1943. France. 100 min. Sound. 16mm B&W. subtitles. *Rental:* Janus Films.

Eternal Sea, The. Sterling Hayden & Alexis Smith. Directed by John H. Auer. 1955. Republic. 103 min. Sound. 16mm B&W. *Rental:* Ivy Films. *Lease:* Rep Pic Film.

Eternal Tramp, The. Orig. Title: Chaplinesque-My Life & Hard Times. 1967. Harry Hurwitz. (Documentary). 55 min. Sound. 16mm B&W. *Rental:* Films Inc, Syracuse U Film, Video Comm & Willoughby Peer.

Eternal Waltz, The. Bernhard Wicki & Hilde Krahl. Directed by Paul Verhoeven. 1959. Germany. 97 min. Sound. 16mm Color. dubbed. *Rental:* Films Inc.

Eternally Yours. Loretta Young & David Niven. Directed by Tay Garnett. 1939. United Artists. 95 min. Sound. 16mm B&W. *Rental:* Budget Films, Classic Film Mus, Film Classics, Films Inc, Learning Corp Am, Mogulls Films & Welling Motion Pictures. *Sale:* Cinema Concepts, Festival Films & Learning Corp Am. *Sale:* Cinema Concepts, Super 8 sound version. *Sale:* Festival Films, Videotape version.

Ethiopia: Empire on the Mountain. 1965. Sterling. (Documentary). 60 min. Sound. 16mm Color. *Sale:* Sterling Ed Film.

Ethiopia: Hidden Empire. 1970. National Geographic. (Documentary). 51 min. Sound. 16mm Color. *Rental:* BYU Media, Films Inc, SD AV Ctr, Syracuse U Film, U Mich Media & Wholesome Film Ctr. *Sale:* Films Inc.

Ethiopia: The Lion & the Cross. 1963. CBS. (Documentary). 52 min. Sound. 16mm B&W. *Rental:* Macmillan Films. *Sale:* Macmillan Films.

Etoiles Du Midi, Les. Directed by Marcel Ichac. Fr. France. (Documentary). 79 min. Sound. 16mm Color. *Rental:* French Am Cul.

Etosha: Place of Dry Water. 59 min. Sound. 16mm Color. *Rental:* Natl Geog. *Sale:* Natl Geog. *Rental:* Natl Geog, Videotape version.

Eugene Onegin. Ariadna Shengelava. Directed by Roman Tikhomirov. Rus. 1958. Russia. 106 min. Sound. 16mm Color. subtitles. *Rental:* Corinth Films. *Lease:* Corinth Films. *Lease:* Corinth Films, *Rental:* Corinth Films, Videotape version.

Europe: The Mighty Continent. 13 pts. 1976. Britain. (Documentary). 686 min. Sound. 16mm Color. *Rental:* Time-Life Multimedia. *Sale:* Time-Life Multimedia. *Rental:* Time-Life Multimedia, *Sale:* Time-Life Multimedia, Videotape version.

European Experience, The. 1966. NET. (Documentary). 60 min. Sound. 16mm B&W. *Rental:* BYU Media & Indiana AV Ctr. *Sale:* Indiana AV Ctr.

European Idea, The. 1975. Britain. (Documentary). 52 min. Sound. 16mm Color. *Rental:* U of IL Film, Videotape version.

Europeans, The. Lee Remick, Lisa Eichhorn & Robin Ellis. Directed by James Ivory. 1979. Britain. 90 min. Sound. 16mm Color. *Rental:* Films Inc & New Yorker Films.

Eva... Was Everything But Legal. Solveig Anderson. Directed by Torgny Wickman. Sweden. 93 min. Sound. 16mm Color. dubbed. *Rental:* Swank Motion.

Eve. Robert Walker, Fred Clark & Celeste Yarnall. Directed by Jeremy Summers. 1968. Britain. 97 min. Sound. 16mm Color. *Rental:* Ivy Films, Rep Pic Film & Video Comm. *Lease:* Rep Pic Film.

Eve & the Handyman. Eve Meyer. Directed by Russ Meyer. 1960. Padram. 65 min. Sound. 16mm B&W. *Rental:* Corinth Films.

Eve Knew Her Apples. Ann Miller. Directed by Will Jason. 1945. Columbia. 60 min. Sound. 16mm B&W. *Lease:* Time-Life Multimedia.

Eve of St. Mark, The. Anne Baxter & William Eythe. Directed by John M. Stahl. 1944. Fox. 96 min. Sound. 16mm B&W. *Rental:* Films Inc.

Eve Wants to Sleep. Barbara Lass. Directed by Tadeusz Chmielewski. Pol. 1958. Poland. 98 min. Sound. 16mm B&W. subtitles Eng. *Rental:* Films Inc.

Evel Knievel. George Hamilton & Sue Lyon. Directed by Marvin J. Chomsky. 1971. Fanfare. 90 min. Sound. 16mm Color. *Rental:* Arcus Film, Budget Films, Films Inc, Kerr Film, Maljack, Roas Films, Video Comm, Welling Motion Pictures, Westcoast Films, Wholesome Film Ctr & Willoughby Peer. *Rental:* Ivy Films, *Sale:* Cinema Concepts & Ivy Films, Super 8 sound version.

Evelyn Prentice. William Powell & Myrna Loy. Directed by William K. Howard. 1934. MGM. 80 min. Sound. 16mm B&W. *Rental:* MGM United.

Even Dwarfs Started Small. Directed by Werner Herzog. 1971. New Line. (Cast unlisted). 96 min. Sound. 16mm B&W. *Rental:* New Cinema & New Line Cinema. *Sale:* New Line Cinema.

Evening with Bullwinkle & His Friends, An. 1977. Jay Ward. (Animated, anthology). 90 min. Sound. 16mm Color. *Rental:* Williams Films. *Sale:* Salz Ent.

Evening with Lou Rawls, An. Verve. 52 min. Videotape Color. *Rental:* Films Inc.

Evening With the Royal Ballet, An. Dame Margot Fonteyn. Rudolph Nureyev. Directed by Anthony Asquith & Anthony Havelock-Allan. 1964. Britain. 94 min. Sound. 16mm Color. *Rental:* Corinth Films & Films Inc.

Eventful Journey *see* Hitch-Hike Lady.

Ever in My Heart. Barbara Stanwyck & Ralph Bellamy. Directed by Archie Mayo. 1933. Warners. 68 min. Sound. 16mm B&W. *Rental:* MGM United.

Ever Since Eve. Marion Davies & Robert Montgomery. Directed by Lloyd Bacon. 1937. Warners. 79 min. Sound. 16mm B&W. *Rental:* MGM United.

Ever Since Venus. Glenda Farrell & Alan Mowbray. Directed by Arthur Dreifuss. 1944. Columbia. 80 min. Sound. 16mm B&W. *Rental:* Films Inc & Mogulls Films.

Everglades, The. 1970. NBC. (Documentary). 51 min. Sound. 16mm Color. *Rental:* Films Inc. *Sale:* Films Inc.

Evergreen. Jessie Matthews & Sonnie Hale. Directed by Victor Saville. 1934. Britain. 90 min. Sound. 16mm B&W. *Rental:* Budget Films, Films Inc, Em Gee Film Lib, Janus Films, Kit Parker, Newman Film Lib & Video Comm. *Sale:* Glenn Photo & Reel Images. *Sale:* Glenn Photo, *Rental:* Video Comm, Super 8 sound version. *Sale:* Tamarelles French Film, Videotape version.

Every Bastard a King. Pier Angeli & William Berger. Directed by Uri Zohar. 1970. Israel. 93 min. Sound. 16mm Color. dubbed. *Rental:* Budget Films, Kino Intl & W Reade Sixteen. *Sale:* Kino Intl.

Every Day's a Holiday. Mae West & Edmund Lowe. Directed by Edward Sutherland. 1938. Paramount. 79 min. Sound. 16mm Color. *Rental:* Swank Motion.

Every Girl Should Be Married. Cary Grant & Betsy Drake. Directed by Don Hartman. 1948. RKO. 84 min. Sound. 16mm B&W. *Rental:* Films Inc.

Every Little Crook & Nanny. Victor Mature & Lynn Redgrave. Directed by Cy Howard. 1972. MGM. 92 min. Sound. 16mm Color. *Rental:* MGM United.

Every Man for Himself. Isabelle Huppert & Jacques Dutronc. Directed by Jean-Luc Godard. Fr. 1980. France. 87 min. Sound. 16mm Color. subtitles. *Rental:* New Yorker Films.

Every Man for Himself & God Against All. Orig. Title: Enigma of Kaspar Hauser, The. S. Bruno. Directed by Werner Herzog. Ger. 1975. Germany. 110 min. Sound. 16mm Color. subtitles. *Rental:* New Cinema.

Every Minute Counts see Count the Hours.

Every Two Seconds. 1983. MTI. (Documentary). 54 min. Sound. 16mm Color. *Sale:* MTI Tele.

Every Which Way But Loose. Clint Eastwood, Sondra Locke & Geoffrey Lewis. Directed by Buddy Van Horn. Warners. 114 min. Sound. 16mm Color. *Rental:* Swank Motion & Williams Films. *Rental:* Swank Motion, Videotape version.

Everybody Does It. Paul Douglas & Linda Darnell. Directed by Edmund Goulding. 1949. Fox. 100 min. Sound. 16mm B&W. *Rental:* Films Inc.

Everybody Rides the Carousel. Directed by John Hubley & Faith Hubley. 1975. Hubley. (Animated). 72 min. Sound. 16mm Color. *Rental:* Iowa Films, Mass Media, Pyramid Film, Syracuse U Film, U Cal Media & U Mich Media. *Sale:* Pyramid Film. *Rental:* Pyramid Film, *Sale:* Pyramid Film, Videotape version.

Everybody's Baby. Jed Prouty & Spring Byington. Directed by Mal St. Clair. 1939. Fox. 75 min. Sound. 16mm B&W. *Rental:* Films Inc.

Everybody's Dancing. James Ellison & Spade Cooley. Directed by Will Jason. 1950. Lippert. 65 min. Sound. 16mm B&W. *Rental:* Film Ctr DC & Mogulls Films.

Everybody's Doing It. Preston Foster & Cecil Kellaway. Directed by Christy Cabanne. 1938. RKO. 67 min. Sound. 16mm *Rental:* RKO General Pics.

Everybody's Hobby. Irene Rich & Henry O'Neal. Directed by William McGann. 1939. Warners. 54 min. Sound. 16mm B&W. *Rental:* MGM United.

Everybody's Wedeln. 1960. International Film Bureau. (Documentary). 49 min. Sound. 16mm Color. *Rental:* Syracuse U Film. *Sale:* Intl Films.

Everyone's a Negotiator. 1980. Films Inc. (Lecture). 70 min. Sound. 16mm Color. *Rental:* Films Inc. *Sale:* Films Inc. *Sale:* Films Inc, Videotape version.

Everything But the Truth. Maureen O'Hara & Tim Hovey. Directed by Jerry Hopper. 1956. Universal. 86 min. Sound. 16mm Color. *Rental:* Swank Motion.

Everything for Sale. Directed by Andrzej Wajda. Pol. 1969. Poland. (Cast unlisted). 98 min. Sound. 16mm Color. subtitles. *Rental:* New Yorker Films.

Everything Happens at Night. Sonja Henie & Ray Milland. Directed by Irving Cummings. 1939. Fox. 77 min. Sound. 16mm B&W. *Rental:* Films Inc.

Everything I Have Is Yours. Marge Champion & Gower Champion. Directed by Robert Z. Leonard. 1952. MGM. 92 min. Sound. 16mm Color. *Rental:* MGM United.

Everything You Always Wanted to Know About Sex But Were Afraid to Ask. Woody Allen, John Carradine & Gene Wilder. Directed by Woody Allen. 1972. United Artists. 88 min. Sound. 16mm Color. *Rental:* MGM United. *Rental:* MGM United, Videotape version.

Everything's Ducky. Mickey Rooney & Buddy Hackett. Directed by Don Taylor. 1961. Columbia. 80 min. Sound. 16mm B&W. *Rental:* Buchan Pic, Cine Craft, Film Ctr DC, Films Inc, Modern Sound, Roas Films & Welling Motion Pictures. *Rental:* Welling Motion Pictures, 90 mins. version.

Everything's Rosie. Anita Louise & John Darrow. Directed by Clyde Bruckman. 1931. RKO. 76 min. Sound. 16mm *Rental:* RKO General Pics.

Evictors, The. Michael Parks & Jessica Harper. Directed by Charles B. Pierce. 1979. 92 min. Sound. 16mm Color. *Rental:* Swank Motion.

Evidentiary Problems & Trial Techniques. Army. (Documentary). 67 min. Sound. 16mm B&W. *Rental:* Natl AV Ctr.

Evil, The. Richard Crenna & Joanna Pettet. Directed by Gus Trikonis. 1978. New World. 89 min. Sound. 16mm Color. *Rental:* Films Inc.

Evil Brain from Outer Space, The. Ken Utsui. Directed by Chogi Akaska. 1959. Japan. 83 min. Sound. 16mm B&W. dubbed. *Rental:* Films Inc.

Evil Eye, The. John Saxon & Valentina Cortese. Directed by Mario Bava. 1964. Italy. 93 min. Sound. 16mm Color. dubbed. *Rental:* Video Comm.

Evil Mind, The see Clairvoyant.

Evil Mind, The. Orig. Title: Clairvoyant, The. Claude Rains & Ray Wray. Directed by Maurice Elvey. 1935. Great Britain. 72 min. Sound. 16mm B&W. *Rental:* Budget Films.

Evil of Frankenstein, The. Peter Cushing & Peter Woodthorpe. Directed by Freddie Francis. 1964. Britain. 86 min. Sound. 16mm Color. *Rental:* Twyman Films & Williams Films.

Evil Under the Sun. Peter Ustinov, Maggie Smith & Roddy McDowall. Directed by Guy Hamilton. 117 min. Sound. 16mm Color. *Rental:* Swank Motion.

Evils of Chinatown see Confessions of an Opium Eater.

Evolution. Directed by Max Fleischer. 1923. Fleischer. (Animated, tinted). 65 min. Silent. 16mm *Rental:* Budget Films. *Sale:* Glenn Photo. *Sale:* Glenn Photo, B&W version. *Sale:* Glenn Photo, Super 8 silent tinted version. *Sale:* Glenn Photo, Super 8 silent B&W version.

Ex-Lady. Bette Davis & Gene Raymond. Directed by Robert Florey. 1933. Warners. 70 min. Sound. 16mm B&W. *Rental:* MGM United.

Ex-Mrs. Bradford, The. William Powell & Jean Arthur. Directed by Stephen Roberts. 1936. RKO. 81 min. Sound. 16mm *Rental:* RKO General Pics.

Examination: Patient with Arthritis. 1978. 54 min. Sound. Videotape *Sale:* Natl AV Ctr.

Excalibur. Nigel Terry & Nicol Williamson. Directed by John Boorman. 1981. Orion. Sound. 16mm Color. *Rental:* Films Inc.

Exceptional Child, The. 1964. Britain. (Documentary). 51 min. Sound. 16mm B&W. *Rental:* Time-Life Multimedia. *Sale:* Time-Life Multimedia.

Exclusive Story. Franchot Tone & Madge Evans. Directed by George B. Seitz. 1936. MGM. 75 min. Sound. 16mm B&W. *Rental:* MGM United.

Excuse Me, America. 46 min. Sound. 16mm Color. *Rental:* Budget Films & Phoenix Films.

Excuse My Dust. Orig. Title: Mister Belden's Amazing Gasmobile. Red Skelton & Sally Forrest. Directed by Roy Rowland. 1951. MGM. 82 min. Sound. 16mm Color. *Rental:* MGM United.

Excuse My Dust. Wallace Reid & Ann Little. Directed by Sam Wood. 1920. Paramount. 68 min. Silent. 16mm B&W. *Rental:* Museum Mod Art.

Executioner, The. George Peppard & Joan Collins. Directed by Sam Wanamaker. 1970. Britain. 107 min. Sound. 16mm Color. *Rental:* Cine Craft, Inst Cinema, Films Inc, Kerr Film, Modern Sound, Swank Motion, Video Comm & Wholesome Film Ctr. *Rental:* Video Comm, Videotape version.

Executive Action. Burt Lancaster, Robert Ryan & Will Geer. Directed by David Miller. 1973. National General. 110 min. Sound. 16mm Color. *Rental:* Swank Motion. *Rental:* Swank Motion, Videotape version.

Executive Suite. Fredric March, William Holden & Barbara Stanwyck. Directed by Robert Wise. 1954. MGM. 104 min. Sound. 16mm B&W. *Rental:* MGM United. *Rental:* MGM United, Videotape version.

Exhibition, The. Directed by Jean-Francois Davy. Fr. 1975. France. (Documentary). 118 min. Sound. 16mm Color. subtitles. *Rental:* Corinth Films.

Exile, The. Douglas Fairbanks Jr. & Maria Montez. Directed by Max Ophuls. 1947. Universal. 95 min. Sound. 16mm B&W. *Rental:* Swank Motion.

Exiled to Shanghai. Wallace Ford & June Taylor. Directed by Nick Grinde. 1937. Republic. 54 min. Sound. 16mm B&W. *Rental:* Ivy Films. *Sale:* Rep Pic Film.

Exiles, The. Directed by Kent Mackenzie. 1963. Kent Mackenzie. (Documentary). 72 min. Sound. 16mm B&W. *Rental:* BYU Media, U Cal Media, Syracuse U Film & Utah Media. *Sale:* U Cal Media. *Sale:* U Cal Media, Videotape version.

Exit Smiling. Beatrice Lillie & Jack Pickford. Directed by Sam Taylor. 1926. MGM. 75 min. Silent. 16mm B&W. *Rental:* MGM United.

Exit the Dragon, Enter the Tiger. Bruce Li. Directed by Lee Tse Nam. 1976. Dimension. 84 min. Sound. 16mm Color. *Rental:* Budget Films, Modern Sound, Welling Motion Pictures, Westcoast Films & Williams Films. *Sale:* Salz Ent.

Exodus. Paul Newman & Eva Marie Saint. Directed by Otto Preminger. 1960. United Artists. 207 min. Sound. 16mm Color. *Rental:* MGM United. *Rental:* MGM United, Videotape version.

Exorcist, The. Ellen Burstyn & Linda Blair. Directed by William Friedkin. 1974. Warners. 121 min. Sound. 16mm Color. *Rental:* Swank Motion. *Rental:* Swank Motion, Videotape version.

Exorcist II, The: The Heretic. Richard Burton & Linda Blair. Directed by John Boorman. 1977. Warners. 117 min. Sound. 16mm Color. *Rental:* Swank Motion, Twyman Films & Williams Films. *Rental:* Swank Motion, Videotape version.

Expensive Husbands. Patric Knowles & Beverly Roberts. Directed by Bobby Connolly. 1937. Warners. 62 min. Sound. 16mm B&W. *Rental:* MGM United.

Expensive Women. Dolores Costello & Warren William. Directed by Hobart Henley. 1931. Warners. 63 min. Sound. 16mm B&W. *Rental:* MGM United.

Experiment Alcatraz. John Howard & Joan Dixon. Directed by Edward L. Cahn. 1950. RKO. 90 min. Sound. 16mm B&W. *Rental:* Films Inc.

Experiment in Evil *see* Testament of Dr. Cordelier.

Experiment in Terror. Orig. Title: Grip of Fear. Lee Remick & Glenn Ford. Directed by Blake Edwards. 1962. Columbia. 123 min. Sound. 16mm B&W. *Rental:* Bosco Films, Budget Films, Cine Craft, Charard Motion Pics, Film Ctr DC, Films Inc, Images Film, Modern Sound, Roas Films, Welling Motion Pictures & Wholesome Film Ctr.

Experiment Perilous. Hedy Lamarr & George Brent. Directed by Jacques Tourneur. 1944. RKO. 90 min. Sound. 16mm B&W. *Rental:* Films Inc.

Experiments in Film: Women. Directed by Jodie Lowe. New Line Cinema. (Anthology). 85 min. Sound. 16mm Color. *Rental:* New Line Cinema.

Expert, The. Chic Sale & Lois Wilson. Directed by Archie Mayo. 1932. Warners. 69 min. Sound. 16mm B&W. *Rental:* MGM United.

Expertos en Pinchazos. Alberto Olmedo, Jorge Porcel & Moria Casan. Span. Spain. 100 min. Sound. Videotape Color. *Sale:* Tamarelles French Films.

Exploring the Spectrum. 1963. 46 min. Sound. 16mm Color. *Rental:* Utah Media.

Explosion. Don Stroud & Gordon Thomson. Directed by Jules Bricken. 1971. Canada. 96 min. Sound. 16mm Color. *Rental:* Swank Motion.

Explosions in the Mind: Strokes. 1980. Britain. (Documentary). 50 min. Sound. 16mm Color. *Rental:* Films Inc. *Sale:* Films Inc. *Rental:* Films Inc, *Sale:* Films Inc, Videotape version.

Exposed. Adrian Booth & Robert Armstrong. Directed by George Blair. 1947. Republic. 59 min. Sound. 16mm B&W. *Rental:* Ivy Films. *Sale:* Rep Pic Film.

Exposed. Nastassja Kinski & Rudolph Nureyev. Directed by James Toback. 1983. MGM-UA. 99 min. Sound. 16mm Color. *Rental:* MGM United. *Rental:* MGM United, Videotape version.

Exposure. Catherine Schell. Directed by Kieran Hickey. 1980. Ireland. 61 min. Sound. 16mm Color. *Rental:* Liberty Co.

Expresso Bongo. Laurence Harvey & Sylvia Sims. Directed by Val Guest. 1960. 108 min. 16mm *Rental:* A Twyman Pres.

Exquisite Cadaver, The. Trans. Title: Crueles, Las. Capucine. Directed by Vincente Aranda. 1971. Spain. 94 min. Sound. 16mm Color. dubbed. *Rental:* Video Comm. *Rental:* Video Comm. *Lease:* Video Comm, Videotape version.

Exterminating Angel, The. Silvia Pinal. Directed by Luis Bunuel. 1962. Mexico. 90 min. Sound. 16mm B&W. subtitles. *Sale:* Films Inc & Reel Images. *Rental:* Budget Films.

Exterminator, The *see* Inheritor.

Exterminator, The. Robert Ginty & Christopher George. Directed by James Glickenhaus. 1980. Embassy. 101 min. Sound. 16mm Color. *Rental:* Films Inc.

Extinction: The Last Tasmanian. Tasmania. (Documentary). 60 min. Sound. 16mm Color. *Rental:* U Cal Media, McGraw-Hill Films & Syracuse U Film. *Sale:* McGraw-Hill Films.

Extra Girl, The. Mabel Normand. Directed by Richard Jones. 1923. Associated Exhibitors. (Tinted, musical score only). 69 min. Sound. 16mm *Rental:* Killiam Collect. *Rental:* Em Gee Film Lib, Modern Sound & Willoughby Peer, *Sale:* Blackhawk Films, Silent 16mm B&W version. *Rental:* Ivy Films, *Sale:* Blackhawk Films, Super 8 silent version. *Sale:* Blackhawk Films, Silent 8mm version.

Extraordinary Adventures of Mr. West in the Land of the Bolsheviks, The. Porfiri Podobed. Directed by Lev Kuleshov. Rus. 1924. Russia. 90 min. Silent. 16mm B&W. subtitles. *Rental:* Films Inc & Museum Mod Art. *Rental:* Museum Mod Art, Russian titled version.

Extraordinary Seaman, The. David Niven & Faye Dunaway. Directed by John Frankenheimer. 1969. MGM. 80 min. Sound. 16mm Color. *Rental:* MGM United.

Eye & Ears of the Medical World, The. 1968. US Government. (Documentary). 90 min. Sound. 16mm B&W. *Sale:* Natl AV Ctr.

Eye for an Eye, An. Orig. Title: Eyes of the Sahara. Robert Lansing & Pat Wayne. Directed by Michael Moore. 1966. Embassy. 92 min. Sound. 16mm Color. *Rental:* Films Inc.

Eye Hears & the Ear Sees, The. 1969. Britain. (Documentary). 58 min. Sound. 16mm Color. *Rental:* Budget Films, Intl Film, U Mich Media, Natl Film CN, Syracuse U Film, Twyman Films & Utah Media. *Sale:* Natl Film CN, Intl Film & Learning Corp Am.

Eye of the Cat. Eleanor Parker & Michael Sarrazin. Directed by David Lowell Rich. 1969. Universal. 110 min. Sound. 16mm Color. *Rental:* Swank Motion.

Eye of The Devil, The. Orig. Title: Thirteen. Deborah Kerr & David Niven. Directed by J. Lee Thompson. 1966. MGM. 92 min. Sound. 16mm B&W. *Rental:* MGM United.

Eye of the Needle, The. Donald Sutherland & Kate Nelligan. Directed by Richard Marquand. 1981. Canada. 118 min. Sound. 16mm Color. *Rental:* MGM United. *Rental:* MGM United, Videotape version.

Eye on the Media: Business & the Press. 1982. CBS. (Documentary). 49 min. Videotape *Rental:* U Mich Media. *Sale:* Carousel Films & Syracuse U Film.

Eye Witness. Robert Montgomery & Leslie Banks. Directed by Robert Montgomery. 1950. Britain. 93 min. Sound. 16mm B&W. *Rental:* Budget Films.

Eyes in the Night. Edward Arnold, Ann Harding & Donna Reed. Directed by Fred Zinnemann. 1942. MGM. 80 min. Sound. 16mm B&W. *Rental:* MGM United.

Eyes of a Stranger, The. Lauren Tewes, Jennifer Jason Leigh & John Di Santi. Warners. 85 min. Sound. 16mm Color. *Rental:* Swank Motion & Williams Films. *Rental:* Swank Motion, Videotape version.

Eyes of Annie Jones, The. Richard Conte & Joyce Carey. Directed by Reginald Le Borg. 1964. Fox. 73 min. Sound. 16mm B&W. *Rental:* Films Inc.

Eyes of Hell, The. Orig. Title: Mask, The. Directed by Julian Roffman & Jim Moran. 1961. Canada. (Cast unlisted, 3D glasses required). 82 min. Sound. 16mm Color. *Rental:* New Line Cinema. *Sale:* New Line Cinema.

Eyes of Julia Deep, The. Mary Miles Minter & Alan Forrest. Directed by Lloyd Ingraham. 1918. American. 45 min. Silent. 16mm B&W. *Rental:* Budget Films, Film Images & Video Comm. *Sale:* Blackhawk Films. *Rental:* Ivy Films, *Sale:* Blackhawk Films, Super 8 silent version.

Eyes of Laura Mars, The. Faye Dunaway & Tommy Lee Jones. Directed by Irwin Kershner. 1978. Columbia. 103 min. Sound. 16mm Color. *Rental:* Budget Films, Films Inc, Swank Motion, Westcoast Films, Wholesome Film Ctr & Williams Films. *Rental:* Swank Motion, Videotape version.

Eyes of Texas, The. Roy Rogers. Directed by William Witney. 1948. Republic. 70 min. Sound. 16mm B&W. *Rental:* Ivy Films. *Sale:* Natl Cinema, Rep Pic Film & Nostalgia Merchant.

Eyes of the Sahara see Eye for an Eye.

Eyes of the Skies see Mission Over Korea.

Eyes of the Underworld, The. Richard Dix & Lon Chaney Jr. Directed by Roy William Neill. 1943. Universal. 60 min. Sound. 16mm B&W. *Rental:* Mogulls Films.

Eyes of Youth, The. Clara Kimball Young. 1919. Equity. 65 min. Silent. 16mm B&W. *Rental:* Em Gee Film Lib & Willoughby Peer.

Eyes Right. Francis X. Bushman Jr. Directed by Louis Chaudet. 1926. Goodwill. 55 min. Silent. 16mm B&W. *Rental:* Mogulls Films.

Eyes, the Mouth, The. Lou Castel & Angela Molina. Directed by Marco Bellocchio. 1985. Columbia. 100 min. Sound. 16mm Color. *Rental:* Swank Motion.

Eyes Without a Face. Pierre Brasseur & Alida Valli. Directed by Georges Franju. Fr. 1960. France. 88 min. Sound. 16mm B&W. subtitles. *Rental:* Films Inc.

Eyewitness. Donald Sinden & Muriel Pavlow. Directed by Muriel Box. 1956. Britain. 82 min. Sound. 16mm B&W. *Rental:* Cinema Five.

Eyewitness. William Hurt & Sigourney Weaver. Directed by Peter Yates. 1981. Fox. 102 min. Sound. 16mm Color. *Rental:* Films Inc.

F for Fake. Directed by Orson Welles. 1973. France. (Documentary). 85 min. Sound. 16mm Color. *Rental:* New Line Cinema & Specialty Films.

F. Scott Fitzgerald in Hollywood. Tuesday Weld & Jason Miller. Directed by Anthony Page. 1976. Titus. 109 min. Sound. 16mm Color. *Rental:* Budget Films. *Sale:* Lucerne Films. *Sale:* Lucerne Films & Time-Life Multimedia, *Rental:* Time-Life Multimedia, Videotape version. *Rental:* Budget Films, 99 mins. version.

F.P.I. *see* Flying Platform Number 1.

Fabian. Hans Peter Hallwachs & Hermann Lause. Ger. 1980. 116 min. 16mm Color. subtitles. *Rental:* MGM United. *Rental:* MGM United, Videotape version.

Fabiani Affair, The. Charles Aznavour & Raymond Pellegrin. Directed by A. Versini. 1962. France. 95 min. Sound. 16mm B&W. dubbed. *Rental:* Films Inc.

Fabiola. Directed by Enrico Guazzoni. 1920. Italy. (Cast unlisted). 60 min. Silent. 16mm B&W. *Rental:* Willoughby Peer.

Fabiola. Michele Morgan, Michel Simon & Gino Cervi. Directed by Alessandro Blasetti. 1948. Italy. 96 min. Sound. 16mm B&W. dubbed. *Rental:* Budget Films.

Fabulous Baron Munchausen, The. Milos Kopecky. Directed by Karel Zeman. Czech. 1961. Czechoslovakia. (Tinted). 87 min. Sound. 16mm subtitles. *Rental:* Films Inc.

Fabulous Country, The. 1972. NBC. (Documentary). 52 min. Sound. 16mm Color. *Rental:* Films Inc, Iowa Films, U Mich Media & Utah Media. *Sale:* Films inc.

Fabulous Dorseys, The. Tommy Dorsey, Jimmy Dorsey & Janet Blair. Directed by Alfred E. Green. 1947. United Artists. 91 min. Sound. 16mm B&W. *Rental:* Budget Films, Charard Motion Pics, Classic Film Mus, Em Gee Film Lib, Ivy Films, Mogulls Films, Newman Film Lib & Video Comm. *Sale:* Festival Films, Glenn Photo & Rep Pic Film. *Sale:* Glenn Photo, Super 8 sound version. *Rental:* Video Comm, *Sale:* Festival Films, Videotape version.

Fabulous Fred Astaire, The. Fred Astaire. 1958. NBC. 71 min. Videotape B&W. *Sale:* Reel Images.

Fabulous Senorita, The. Rita Moreno & Robert Clarke. Directed by R. G. Springsteen. 1951. Republic. 80 min. Sound. 16mm B&W. *Rental:* Ivy Films. *Sale:* Rep Pic Film.

Fabulous Texan, The. John Carroll & Andy Devine. Directed by Edward Ludwig. 1947. Republic. 96 min. Sound. 16mm B&W. *Rental:* Ivy Films. *Sale:* Rep Pic Film.

Fabulous World of Jules Verne, The. Louis Tock. Directed by Karel Zeman. 1958. Czechoslovakia. 83 min. Sound. 16mm Color. dubbed. *Rental:* Budget Films & Ivy Films.

Face at the Window. Tod Slaughter. Directed by George King. 1939. Britain. 65 min. Sound. 16mm B&W. *Rental:* Budget Films & Film Classics.

Face Behind the Mask, The. Peter Lorre & Evelyn Keyes. Directed by Robert Florey. 1941. Columbia. 70 min. Sound. 16mm B&W. *Rental:* Budget Films & Cine Craft.

Face in the Crowd, A. Andy Griffith, Patricia Neal & Walter Matthau. Directed by Elia Kazan. 1957. Warners. 127 min. Sound. 16mm B&W. *Rental:* Castle Hill, Films Inc & Schoenfeld.

Face in the Fog, A. June Clyde & Lloyd Hughes. Directed by Robert Hill. 1935. Victory. 60 min. Sound. 16mm B&W. *Rental:* Mogulls Films.

Face in the Night. Vincent Ball. Directed by Lance Comfort. 1957. 75 min. 16mm *Rental:* A Twyman Pres.

Face in the Rain, The. Rory Calhoun & Niall McGinnis. Directed by Irwin Kershner. 1963. Italy. 90 min. Sound. 16mm B&W. dubbed. *Rental:* Films Inc.

Face of a Fugitive, The. Fred MacMurray & Alan Baxter. Directed by Paul Wendkos. 1959. Columbia. 81 min. Sound. 16mm Color. *Rental:* Modern Sound.

Face of Crime, The. 1968. CBS. (Documentary). 52 min. Sound. 16mm B&W. *Rental:* Macmillan Films. *Sale:* Macmillan Films.

Face of Famine, The. 1982. Britain. (Documentary). 75 min. Sound. 16mm Color. *Rental:* Films Inc. *Sale:* Films Inc. *Sale:* Films Inc, Videotape version.

Face of Fear *see* Peeping Tom.

Face of Fire. Cameron Mitchell & James Whitmore. Directed by Albert Band. 1959. Allied Artists. 80 min. Sound. 16mm B&W. *Rental:* Hurlock Cine.

Face of Fu Manchu, The. Christopher Lee & Nigel Green. Directed by Don Sharp. 1965. Britain. 96 min. Sound. 16mm Color. *Rental:* Charard Motion Pics, Films Inc, Inst Cinema & Willoughby Peer. *Rental:* Willoughby Peer, Anamorphic color version.

Face of Man, The. Directed by Eugene S. Jones. 1968. Commonwealth. (Documentary). 72 min. Sound. 16mm B&W. *Rental:* Kerr Film.

Face of Marble, The. John Carradine. Directed by William Beaudine. 1946. Monogram. 72 min. Sound. 16mm B&W. *Rental:* MGM United.

Face of Red China, The. 1958. CBS. (Documentary). 54 min. Sound. 16mm B&W. *Rental:* BYU Media, U Mich Media & Syracuse U Film. *Sale:* McGraw-Hill Films.

Face of Terror *see* Profile of Terror.

Face of War, The. Directed by Tore Sjoberg. 1964. Sweden. (Documentary). 105 min. Sound. 16mm B&W. narrated Eng. *Rental:* Budget Films & Video Comm.

Face of War, The. Directed by Eugene S. Jones. 1968. Commonwealth. (Documentary). 72 min. Sound. 16mm B&W. *Rental:* Ivy Films, Kit Parker, Video Comm & Westcoast Films. *Lease:* Video Comm.

Face on the Barroom Floor, The. Bramwell Fletcher & Walter Miller. 1932. Invincible. 70 min. Sound. 16mm B&W. *Sale:* Morcraft Films.

Face to Face. 2 pts. James Mason & Robert Preston. Directed by John Brahm & Bretaigne Windust. 1951. RKO. 90 min. Sound. 16mm B&W. *Rental:* Kit Parker.

Face to Face. Liv Ullmann, Gunnar Bjornstrand & Erland Josephson. Directed by Ingmar Bergman. Swed. 1976. Sweden. 136 min. Sound. 16mm Color. subtitles. *Rental:* Films Inc.

Faces. John Marley, Gena Rowlands & Lynn Carlin. Directed by John Cassavetes. 1968. Continental. 130 min. Sound. 16mm B&W. *Rental:* U Cal Media.

Faces in the Fog. Paul Kelly & John Litel. Directed by John English. 1944. Republic. 71 min. Sound. 16mm B&W. *Rental:* Ivy Films.

Faces of a Wing, The. 1975. Penn State. (Documentary). 58 min. Sound. 16mm B&W. *Rental:* Penn St AV Serv. *Sale:* Penn St AV Serv. *Rental:* Penn St AV Serv, *Sale:* Penn St Av Serv, Videotape version.

Faces of Death. 105 min. Sound. Videotape Color. *Rental:* Maljack.

Facing Up to the Bomb. Directed by Gerald Polikoff. 1982. NBC. (Documentary). 52 min. Sound. 16mm Color. *Rental:* Films Inc, Syracuse U Film & U Mich Media. *Sale:* Films Inc.

Factory, The. Directed by Arthur Barron & Evelyn Barron. 1972. Barron. (Documentary). 56 min. Sound. 16mm B&W. *Rental:* U Cal Media & U Mich Media.

Fahrenheit Four Fifty-One. Julie Christie & Oskar Werner. Directed by Francois Truffaut. 1966. Universal. 112 min. Sound. 16mm Color. *Rental:* Films Inc & Swank Motion.

Fail-Safe. Henry Fonda & Walter Matthau. Directed by Sidney Lumet. 1964. Columbia. 111 min. Sound. 16mm B&W. *Rental:* Arcus Film, Bosco Films, Budget Films, Cine Craft, Films Inc, Images Film, Ivy Films, Kerr Film, Kit Parker, Modern Sound, Natl Film Video, Newman Film Lib, Roas Films, Swank Motion, Twyman Films, U of IL Film, Video Comm, Westcoast Films, Wholesome Film Ctr, Williams Films & Willoughby Peer. *Rental:* Swank Motion, Videotape version.

Failing to Learn: Learning to Fail. 1977. NBC. (Documentary). 52 min. Sound. 16mm Color. *Rental:* Films Inc, Syracuse U Film & U Mich Media. *Sale:* Films Inc. *Sale:* Films Inc, Videotape version.

Fair Wind to Java. Fred MacMurray & Victor McLaglen. Directed by Joseph Kane. 1953. Republic. 92 min. Sound. 16mm B&W. *Rental:* Films Inc & Ivy Films. *Lease:* Rep Pic Film.

Faith in Numbers. 1978. Britain. (Documentary). 53 min. Sound. 16mm Color. *Rental:* Iowa Films, Kent St U Film, U Cal Media, U of IL Film & U Mich Media. *Sale:* Time-Life Multimedia, Videotape version.

Faithful in My Fashion. Tom Drake & Donna Reed. Directed by Sidney Salkow. 1946. MGM. 81 min. Sound. 16mm B&W. *Rental:* MGM United.

Fake, The. Dennis O'Keefe. Directed by Godfrey Grayson. 1951. 80 min. 16mm *Rental:* A Twyman Pres.

Faking of the President 1974, The. Marshall Efron. Directed by Jeanne Abel & Alan Abel. 1974. Specer Production. 80 min. Sound. 16mm Color. *Rental:* Ivy Films. *Rental:* Ivy Films, Super 8 sound version. *Rental:* Ivy Films, Videotape version.

Falasha: Exile of the Black Jews. Directed by Simcha Jacobovici. 1984. 80 min. Sound. 16mm Color. *Rental:* New Yorker Films.

Falcon & the Co-Eds, The. Tom Conway & Rita Corday. Directed by William Clemens. 1944. RKO. 68 min. Sound. 16mm *Rental:* Films Inc. *Lease:* Films Inc.

Falcon in Danger, The. Tom Conway. Directed by William Clemens. 1943. RKO. 70 min. Sound. 16mm B&W. *Rental:* Films Inc. *Lease:* Films Inc.

Falcon in Hollywood, The. Tom Conway. Directed by Gordon Douglas. 1944. RKO. 70 min. Sound. 16mm B&W. *Rental:* Films Inc. *Lease:* Films Inc.

Falcon in Mexico, The. Tom Conway. Directed by William Berke. 1944. RKO. 70 min. Sound. 16mm B&W. *Rental:* Films Inc. *Lease:* Films Inc.

Falcon in San Francisco, The. Tom Conway. Directed by Joseph Lewis. 1945. RKO. 70 min. Sound. 16mm B&W. *Rental:* Films Inc. *Lease:* Films Inc.

Falcon Out West, The. Tom Conway. Directed by William Clemens. 1944. RKO. 70 min. Sound. 16mm B&W. *Rental:* Films Inc. *Lease:* Films Inc.

Falcon Strikes Back, The. Tom Conway & Harriet Hilliard. Directed by Edward Dmytryk. 1943. RKO. 65 min. Sound. 16mm *Rental:* Films Inc.

Falcon Takes Over, The. Tom Conway. Directed by Irving Reis. 1942. RKO. 70 min. Sound. 16mm B&W. *Rental:* Films Inc. *Lease:* Films Inc.

Falcon's Adventure, The. Tom Conway. Directed by William Berke. 1946. RKO. 70 min. Sound. 16mm B&W. *Rental:* Films Inc. *Lease:* Films Inc.

Falcon's Alibi, The. Tom Conway. Directed by Ray McCarey. 1946. RKO. 70 min. Sound. 16mm B&W. *Rental:* Films Inc. *Lease:* Films Inc.

Falcon's Brother, The. George Sanders & Tom Conway. Directed by Stanley Logan. 1942. RKO. 63 min. Sound. 16mm B&W. *Rental:* Films Inc. *Lease:* Films Inc.

Fall, The. Elsa Daniel. Directed by Leopoldo Torre-Nilsson. Span. 1959. Argentina. 90 min. Sound. 16mm B&W. subtitles. *Rental:* A Twyman Pres & Twyman Films.

Fall Guy. Robert Armstrong & Clifford Penn. Directed by Reginald Le Borg. 1947. Monogram. 63 min. Sound. 16mm B&W. *Rental:* Hurlock Cine.

Fall Guy. Ed Dugan & Fabian Dean. 1962. Fairway. 62 min. Sound. 16mm B&W. *Rental:* Ivy Films.

Fall Guy, The. Ned Sparks & Jack Mulhall. Directed by Leslie Pierce. 1930. RKO. 70 min. Sound. 16mm *Rental:* RKO General Pics.

Fall In. William Tracy & Joe Sawyer. Directed by Kurt Neumann. 1942. Hal Roach. 50 min. Sound. 16mm B&W. *Rental:* Mogulls Films.

Fall of Babylon, The. Constance Talmadge & Elmo Lincoln. Directed by D. W. Griffith. 1919. Griffith. 65 min. Silent. 16mm B&W. *Rental:* A Twyman Pres & Twyman Films.

Fall of Berlin, The. Directed by Yuli Raizman. 1945. Russia. (Documentary). 66 min. Sound. 16mm B&W. narrated Eng. *Rental:* Corinth Films.

Fall of the House of Usher. Vincent Price & Mark Damon. Directed by Roger Corman. 1960. American International. 85 min. Sound. 16mm Color. *Rental:* Arcus Film, Budget Films, Charard Motion Pics, Cine Craft, Film Ctr DC, Ivy Films, Twyman Films, Video Comm, Welling Motion Pictures, Wholesome Film Ctr & Willoughby Peer. *Rental:* Willoughby Peer, Anamorphic color version.

Fall of the House of Usher, The. Martin Landau. Directed by James L. Conway. 1979. Viacom. 97 min. Sound. 16mm Color. *Sale:* Lucerne Films. *Rental:* Williams Films. *Rental:* Williams Films, Videotape version.

Fall of the House of Usher, The. Trans. Title: Chute de la Maison Usher, La. Jean Debucourt & Marguerite Gance. Directed by Jean Epstein. 1928. France. 62 min. Silent. 16mm B&W. *Rental:* A Twyman Pres, Em Gee Film Lib, Museum Mod Art & Twyman Films. *Sale:* Glenn Photo, Natl Cinema & Reel Images. *Rental:* Kit Parker, French titled version. *Sale:* Glenn Photo, Super 8 silent version. *Sale:* Tamarelles French Film, Videotape version.

Fall of the House of Usher, The. Kay Tendeter & Irving Steen. Directed by Ivan Barnett. 1952. Britain. 75 min. Sound. 16mm B&W. *Sale:* Cinema Concepts.

Fall of the House of Usher, The. 1979. American. (Cast unlisted). 98 min. Sound. 16mm Color. *Rental:* Budget Films, Modern Sound & Westcoast Films. *Sale:* Lucerne Films. *Sale:* Lucerne Films, Videotape version. *Sale:* Lucerne Films, 48 min. version.

Fall of the Roman Empire, The. Sophia Loren, Stephen Boyd & Sir Alec Guinness. Directed by Anthony Mann. 1964. Paramount. 180 min. Sound. 16mm Color. *Rental:* Films Inc. *Rental:* Budget Films, 149 mins. version. *Sale:* Tamarelles French Film, Videotape version.

Fall of the Romanov Dynasty, The. Directed by Esther Shub. 1927. Russia. (Documentary). 101 min. Silent. 16mm B&W. *Rental:* Museum Mod Art. *Rental:* Museum Mod Art, Russian titled version.

Fall X-701 *see* Frozen Alive.

Fallacies of Hope, The. (Civilization Ser.). 1968. Britain. (Documentary). 60 min. Sound. 16mm Color. *Rental:* Films Inc, OK AV Ctr, Syracuse U Film, U Cal Media & Utah Media. *Sale:* Films Inc. *Sale:* Films Inc, Videotape version.

Fallen Angel. Alice Faye, Dana Andrews & Linda Darnell. Directed by Otto Preminger. 1945. Fox. 120 min. Sound. 16mm B&W. *Rental:* Films Inc.

Fallen Angel, The. Dana Hill, Melinda Dillon & Richard Mazur. 96 min. Sound. 16mm Color. *Rental:* Welling Motion Pictures.

Fallen Idol, The. Sir Ralph Richardson, Michele Morgan & Sonia Dresdel. Directed by Sir Carol Reed. 1949. Britain. 92 min. Sound. 16mm B&W. *Rental:* Budget Films, Em Gee Film Lib, Films Inc, Images Film, Kit Parker & Wholesome Film Ctr. *Sale:* Cinema Concepts, Festival Films & Reel Images. *Sale:* Festival Films & Tamarelles French Film, Videotape version.

Fallen Sparrow. John Garfield & Maureen O'Hara. Directed by Richard Wallace. 1943. RKO. 93 min. Sound. 16mm B&W. *Rental:* Films Inc.

Falling Man, The. Henry Silva & Keenan Wynn. 1968. NTA. 88 min. Sound. 16mm B&W. *Rental:* Ivy Films. *Lease:* Rep Pic Film.

Falls, The. Directed by Peter Greenaway. 1980. Great Britain. (Experimental). 185 min. Sound. 16mm Color. *Rental:* Museum Mod Art.

False Colors. William Boyd. Directed by George Archainbaud. 1943. United Artists. 60 min. Sound. 16mm B&W. *Rental:* Budget Films.

False Faces *see* Scalpel.

False Faces. Veda Ann Borg. Directed by George Sherman. 1943. Republic. 54 min. Sound. 16mm B&W. *Rental:* Ivy Films. *Sale:* Rep Pic Film.

False Paradise. William Boyd. Directed by George Archainbaud. 1948. United Artists. 60 min. Sound. 16mm B&W. *Sale:* Cinema Concepts.

Falstaff *see* Chimes at Midnight.

Fame. Anne Meara & Irene Cara. Directed by Alan Parker. 1981. MGM. 134 min. Sound. 16mm Color. *Rental:* MGM United. *Rental:* MGM United, Videotape version.

Fame Is the Spur. Michael Redgrave & Rosamund John. Directed by Roy Boulting. 1948. Britain. 116 min. Sound. 16mm B&W. *Rental:* Liberty Co.

Familiar Places. 1981. EMC. (Documentary). 53 min. Sound. 16mm Color. *Rental:* U Cal Media. *Sale:* U Cal Media.

Family, The. Charles Bronson & Telly Savalas. Directed by Sergio Sollima. 1973. Italy. 94 min. Sound. 16mm Color. *Rental:* Films Inc, Maljack & Video Comm. *Rental:* Video Comm, Videotape version.

Family Affair, A. Lionel Barrymore & Mickey Rooney. Directed by George B. Seitz. 1937. MGM. 69 min. Sound. 16mm B&W. *Rental:* MGM United.

Family Assessment. 49 min. Sound. 16mm Color. *Rental:* U Mich Media.

Family Business. Milton Berle. 1983. MTI. 90 min. Sound. 16mm Color. *Sale:* MTI Tele. *Rental:* Iowa Films. *Sale:* MTI Tele, Videotape version.

Family Dynamics. 1979. 90 min. Sound. Videotape *Sale:* Natl AV Ctr.

Family Honeymoon. Claudette Colbert & Fred MacMurray. Directed by Claude Binyon. 1948. Universal. 78 min. Sound. 16mm B&W. *Rental:* Swank Motion.

Family Jewels, The. Jerry Lewis. Directed by Jerry Lewis. 1965. Paramount. 100 min. Sound. 16mm Color. *Rental:* Films Inc.

Family Life. Jan Kreczmar. Directed by Krzysztof Zanussi. Pol. 1971. Poland. 98 min. Sound. 16mm Color. subtitles. *Rental:* Films Inc.

Family Life. Directed by Kenneth Loach. 1972. Britain. (Documentary). 108 min. Sound. 16mm Color. *Rental:* Cinema Five.

Family of Man, The. 7 pts. 1971. Britain. (Documentary). 350 min. Sound. 16mm Color. *Rental:* Films Inc & Kent St U Film. *Sale:* Films Inc. *Sale:* Films Inc, Videotape version.

Family of Strangers. Danny Aiello & Maria Tucci. Directed by Robert Fuest. 1980. ABC. 47 min. Sound. 16mm Color. *Rental:* Learning Corp Am & Roas Films. *Sale:* Learning Corp Am. *Sale:* Learning Corp Am, Videotape version.

Family Plot. Karen Black, Bruce Dern & Barbara Harris. Directed by Alfred Hitchcock. 1976. Universal. 120 min. Sound. 16mm Color. *Rental:* Swank Motion. *Rental:* Swank Motion, Videotape version.

Family Way, The. Hayley Mills, John Mills & Hywel Bennett. Directed by John Boulting & Roy Boulting. 1967. Britain. 115 min. Sound. 16mm Color. *Rental:* Inst Cinema & Video Comm.

Famous Ferguson Case, The. Joan Blondell & Leslie Fenton. Directed by Lloyd Bacon. 1932. Warners. 74 min. Sound. 16mm B&W. *Rental:* MGM United.

Fan, The. Lauren Bacall & Michael Biehn. Directed by Edward Bianchi. 1981. Paramount. 95 min. Sound. 16mm Color. *Rental:* Films Inc.

Fanatic *see* Die, Die My Darling.

Fancy Pants. Bob Hope & Lucille Ball. Directed by George Marshall. 1950. Paramount. 92 min. Sound. 16mm Color. *Rental:* Films Inc.

Fang & Claw. Orig. Title: Frank's Buck's Fang & Claw. Directed by Frank Buck. 1935. RKO. (Documentary). 74 min. Sound. 16mm B&W. *Rental:* Films Inc.

Fangelse *see* Devil's Wanton.

Fangs of Fate. William Patton. Directed by Horace B. Carpenter. 1925. Chesterfield. 60 min. Silent. 8mm B&W. *Sale:* Morcraft Films.

Fangs of the Arctic. Kirby Grant & Warren Douglas. Directed by Rex Bailey. 1953. Monogram. 63 min. Sound. 16mm B&W. *Rental:* Hurlock Cine.

Fangs of the Wild. Martin Spellman & Dennis Moore. 1940. Metropolitan. 60 min. Sound. 16mm B&W. *Rental:* Alba House.

Fanny. Orig. Title: Pagnol Trilogy. Raimu & Pierre Fresnay. Directed by Marc Allegret. Fr. 1932. France. 120 min. Sound. 16mm B&W. subtitles. *Rental:* Budget Films, Corinth Films & Kit Parker. *Sale:* Cinema Concepts, Natl Cinema & Reel Images. *Sale:* Tamarelles French Film, Videotape version.

Fanny. Leslie Caron & Charles Boyer. Directed by Joshua Logan. 1961. Warners. 133 min. Sound. 16mm Color. *Rental:* Films Inc, Swank Motion, Twyman Films & Williams Films.

Fanny & Alexander. Pernilla Allwin & Bertil Guve. Directed by Ingmar Bergman. Swed. 1983. Embassy. 190 min. Sound. 16mm Color. subtitles Eng. *Rental:* Films Inc.

Fanny Foley Herself. Edna May Oliver & Rochelle Hudson. Directed by Melville Brown. 1931. RKO. Sound. 16mm *Rental:* RKO General Pics.

Fanny Hill. Diana Kjaer. Directed by Mac Ahlberg. 1972. Sweden. 92 min. Sound. 16mm Color. dubbed. *Rental:* Swank Motion.

Fantasma de Barbanegra, El. Peter Ustinov & Dean Jones. Directed by Robert Stevenson. 1968. Disney. 107 min. Sound. 16mm Color. dubbed. *Rental:* Twyman Films.

Fantastic Animation Festival, The. 1977. Crest. (Anthology). 100 min. Videotape Color. *Rental:* Films Inc, New Cinema & Wholesome Film Ctr. *Sale:* Cinema Concepts.

Fantastic Balloon Voyage, The. Trans. Title: El Viaje Fantastico en Globo. Hugo Stiglitz & Jeff Cooper. Directed by Rene Cardona. 1976. Mexico. 86 min. Sound. 16mm Color. dubbed. *Sale:* Salz Ent.

Fantastic Night, The. Trans. Title: Nuit Fantastique, La. Micheline Presle & Fernand Gravet. Directed by Marcel L'Herbier. Fr. 1952. France. 81 min. Sound. 16mm B&W. subtitles. *Rental:* Film Classics.

Fantastic Planet, The. Directed by Rene Laloux. 1973. France. (Animated). 72 min. Sound. 16mm Color. *Rental:* Budget Films, Films Inc, Inst Cinema, Ivy Films & Westcoast Films. *Sale:* Cinema Concepts, Natl Cinema & Reel Images. *Sale:* Tamarelles French Film, Videotape version. *Sale:* Festival Films, 68 min. 16mm version. *Sale:* Festival Films, 68 min. Videotape version.

Fantastic Plastic Machine, The. 1970. Crown. (Documentary). 90 min. Sound. 16mm Color. *Rental:* Films Inc & Budget Films.

Fantastic Variations: Don Quixote. 1969. CBS. (Documentary). 54 min. Sound. 16mm Color. *Rental:* McGraw-Hill Films. *Sale:* McGraw-Hill Films.

Fantastic Voyage, The. Stephen Boyd & Arthur Kennedy. Directed by Richard Fleischer. 1966. Fox. 105 min. Sound. 16mm Color. *Rental:* Films Inc, Twyman Films & Williams Films. *Rental:* Films Inc, Anamorphic color version. *Rental:* Williams Films, Videotape version.

Fantomas. Rene Navarre. Directed by Louis Feuillade. 1913. France. 64 min. Silent. 16mm B&W. *Rental:* Museum Mod Art.

Fantomas: Juve vs. Fantomas. 2 pts. Directed by Louis Feuillade & Rene Navarre. 1913. France. (Cast unlisted). 40 min. Silent. 16mm B&W. *Rental:* Em Gee Film Lib, Kit Parker, Museum Mod Art & Tamarelles French Film. *Sale:* Glenn Photo & Tamarelles French Film. *Rental:* Tamarelles French Film, Videotape version.

Far Country, The. James Stewart & Ruth Roman. Directed by Anthony Mann. 1955. Universal. 97 min. Sound. 16mm Color. *Rental:* Williams Films.

Far From the Madding Crowd. Julie Christie, Peter Finch & Alan Bates. Directed by John Schlesinger. 1967. MGM. (Anamorphic). 192 min. Sound. 16mm Color. *Rental:* MGM United. *Rental:* MGM United, Videotape version.

Far Frontier, The. Roy Rogers. Directed by William Witney. 1948. Republic. 54 min. Sound. 16mm B&W. *Rental:* Ivy Films. *Sale:* Cinema Concepts & Rep Pic Film.

Far Horizons, The. Fred MacMurray & Charles Heston. Directed by Rudolph Mate. 1955. Paramount. 108 min. Sound. 16mm B&W. *Rental:* Budget Films, Film Ctr DC, Video Comm & Willoughby Peer.

Far Out, Star Route. 1971. 64 min. Sound. 16mm Color. *Rental:* Canyon Cinema.

Farewell Again. Orig. Title: Troopship. Flora Robson, Leslie Banks & Robert Newton. Directed by Tim Whelan. 1938. 16mm *Rental:* A Twyman Pres.

Farewell Arabia. 1967. NET. (Documentary). 52 min. Sound. 16mm B&W. *Rental:* Indiana AV Ctr. *Sale:* Indiana AV Ctr.

Farewell Concert of Cream. (Concert). 84 min. Videotape Color. *Sale:* Cinema Concepts.

Farewell, Doves. Alexei Lokhtov. Directed by Yakov Segel. Rus. 1960. Russia. 94 min. Sound. 16mm B&W. subtitles. *Rental:* Corinth Films.

Farewell, My Lovely. Robert Mitchum & Charlotte Rampling. Directed by Dick Richards. 1975. Embassy. 97 min. Sound. 16mm Color. *Rental:* Films Inc.

Farewell to Arms, A. Helen Hayes, Gary Cooper & Mary Phillips. Directed by Frank Borzage. 1933. Paramount. 78 min. Sound. 16mm B&W. *Rental:* Budget Films, Classic Film Mus, Em Gee Film Lib, Images Film, Ivy Films, Kit Parker, Maljack, Natl Film Video, Video Comm, Westcoast Films & Wholesome Film Ctr. *Sale:* Cinema Concepts, Classic Film Mus, Festival Films, Glenn Photo, Images Film, Natl Cinema & Reel Images. *Rental:* Ivy Films, *Sale:* Cinema Concepts & Ivy Films, Super 8 sound version. *Sale:* Festival Films, Tamarelles French Film & Images Film, Videotape version.

Farewell to Arms, A. Rock Hudson & Jennifer Jones. Directed by Charles Vidor. 1957. Fox. (Anamorphic). 151 min. Sound. 16mm Color. *Rental:* Films Inc & Twyman Films.

Farewell to Cinderella. Ann Phicon & Arthur Rees. Directed by Maclean Rogers. 1937. Britain. 80 min. Sound. 16mm B&W. *Rental:* Mogulls Films.

Farewell to Yesterday. 1950. Fox. (Documentary). 90 min. Sound. 16mm B&W. *Rental:* Willoughby Peer.

Fargo. Bill Elliott & Myron Healey. Directed by Lewis D. Collins. 1952. Monogram. 69 min. Sound. 16mm B&W. *Rental:* Hurlock Cine.

Fargo Express. Ken Maynard. Directed by Alan James. 1932. World Wide. 60 min. Sound. 16mm B&W. *Sale:* Video Comm. *Sale:* Video Comm, Videotape version.

Fargo Kid, The. Tim Holt & Ray Whitley. Directed by Bert Gilroy. 1941. RKO. 63 min. Sound. 16mm *Rental:* RKO General Pics.

Farm Diary. Peter Orlovsky & Allen Ginsberg. Directed by Gordon Ball. 1970. Gordon Ball. 64 min. Silent. 8mm Color. *Rental:* Canyon Cinema.

Farm Song. Directed by John Nathan. 1978. PBS. (Documentary). 58 min. Sound. 16mm Color. *Rental:* Iowa Films & Japan Society. *Sale:* Japan Society.

Farmacia de Guardio. 1950. Mexico. (Documentary). 90 min. Sound. 16mm B&W. *Rental:* Film Classics.

Farmer, The. Gary Conway. Directed by David Bertatsky. 1977. Columbia. 98 min. Sound. 16mm Color. *Rental:* Swank Motion & Westcoast Films.

Farmer in the Dell. Lucille Ball. Directed by Ben Holmes. 1936. RKO. 67 min. Sound. 16mm *Rental:* RKO General Pics.

Farmer Takes a Wife, The. Betty Grable & Dale Robertson. Directed by Henry Levin. 1953. Fox. 81 min. Sound. 16mm B&W. *Rental:* Films Inc. *Rental:* Films Inc, Color version.

Farmer's Daughter, The. Loretta Young & Joseph Cotten. Directed by H. C. Potter. 1947. RKO. 100 min. Sound. 16mm B&W. *Rental:* Films Inc.

Farmer's Daughter, The. Martha Raye & Charles Ruggles. Directed by Lewis R. Foster. 1940. Paramount. 61 min. Sound. 16mm B&W. *Rental:* Swank Motion.

Farmer's Wife, The. Jameson Thomas & Lillian Hall-Davies. Directed by Alfred Hitchcock. 1928. Britain. 97 min. Sound. 16mm B&W. *Rental:* Films Inc & Janus Films. *Rental:* Janus Films, Silent version. *Rental:* Janus Films, 67 mins. version.

Farming Is Farming: The Small Farm in America. 1976. 45 min. Sound. 16mm Color. *Rental:* U Mich Media.

Farming of Fish, The. Directed by Paul MacLeod. 1977. Canada. (Documentary). 58 min. Sound. 16mm Color. *Rental:* Natl Film CN. *Sale:* Natl Film CN. *Sale:* Natl Film CN, Videotape version.

Farrakhan the Minister. 1973. WNET. (Documentary). 58 min. Sound. 16mm Color. *Rental:* WNET Media, Videotape version.

Farrebique. Directed by Georges Rouquier. Fr. 1948. (Documentary). 100 min. Sound. 16mm B&W. subtitles. *Rental:* New Yorker Films.

Farthest Frontier, The. 1967. CBS. (Documentary). 47 min. Sound. 16mm B&W. *Rental:* U of IL Film. *Sale:* Carousel Films.

Fascination see Love in the Afternoon.

Fascista. (Documentary). 120 min. Sound. 16mm B&W. *Rental:* Films Inc.

Fashions of Nineteen Thirty Four. Bette Davis & William Powell. Directed by William Dieterle. 1934. Warners. 78 min. Sound. 16mm B&W. *Rental:* MGM United. *Sale:* Reel Images, Videotape version.

Fast & Furious. Franchot Tone & Ann Sothern. Directed by Busby Berkeley. 1939. MGM. 73 min. Sound. 16mm B&W. *Rental:* MGM United.

Fast & Loose. Carole Lombard & Miriam Hopkins. Directed by Fred Newmeyer. 1930. Paramount. 70 min. Sound. 16mm B&W. *Rental:* Swank Motion.

Fast & Loose. Robert Montgomery & Rosalind Russell. Directed by Edwin L. Marin. 1939. MGM. 79 min. Sound. 16mm B&W. *Rental:* MGM United.

Fast & Sexy. Gina Lollobrigida & Vittorio De Sica. Directed by Reginald Denham. 1960. Italy. 98 min. Sound. 16mm B&W. *Rental:* Kit Parker.

Fast & the Furious, The. John Ireland, Dorothy Malone & Iris Adrian. Directed by Edward Sampson & John Ireland. 1954. American International. 74 min. Sound. 16mm B&W. *Rental:* Films Inc & Westcoast Films.

Fast Break. Gabriel Kaplan & Michael Warren. Directed by Jack Smight. 1979. Columbia. 107 min. Sound. 16mm Color. *Rental:* Arcus Film, Budget Films, Swank Motion, Welling Motion Pictures & Williams Films. *Rental:* Swank Motion, Videotape version.

Fast Charlie... The Moonbeam Rider. David Carradine & Brenda Vaccaro. Directed by Steve Carver. 1979. Universal. 99 min. Sound. 16mm Color. *Rental:* Williams Films.

Fast Company. Howard Keel & Polly Bergen. Directed by John Sturges. 1953. MGM. 68 min. Sound. 16mm B&W. *Rental:* MGM United.

Fast Company. Melvyn Douglas, Louis Calhern & Florence Rice. Directed by Edward Buzzell. 1938. MGM. 75 min. Sound. 16mm B&W. *Rental:* MGM United.

Fast Lady, The. James Robertson Justice & Julie Christie. Directed by Ken Annakin. 1963. Britain. 95 min. Sound. 16mm Color. *Rental:* Cousino Visual Ed.

Fast Life. William Haines & Madge Evans. Directed by Harry Pollard. 1932. MGM. 88 min. Sound. 16mm B&W. *Rental:* MGM United.

Fast on the Draw see Sudden Death.

Fast Times at Ridgemont High. Sean Penn & Jennifer Jason Leigh. Directed by Amy Heckerling. 1985. Universal. 92 min. Sound. 16mm Color. *Rental:* Swank Motion. *Rental:* Swank Motion, Videotape version.

Fast Way Nowhere. 1966. Gospel. (Documentary). 63 min. Sound. 16mm Color. *Rental:* Roas Films.

Fasten Your Seatbelts: A Report on Airline Safety. 1968. NET. (Documentary). 60 min. Sound. 16mm B&W. *Rental:* Indiana AV Ctr. *Sale:* Indiana Av Ctr.

Faster, Pussycat, Kill, Kill! Lori Williams. Directed by Russ Meyer. 1966. Meyer. 71 min. Sound. 16mm B&W. *Rental:* Corinth Films. *Sale:* Cinema Concepts & Video Lib, Videotape version.

Fastest Guitar Alive. Roy Orbison & Sammy Jackson. Directed by Michael Moore. 1967. MGM. 85 min. Sound. 16mm Color. *Rental:* MGM United.

Fastest Gun Alive. Glenn Ford & Jeanne Crain. Directed by Russell Rouse. 1956. MGM. 91 min. Sound. 16mm B&W. *Rental:* MGM United.

Fat American, The. 1962. CBS. (Documentary). 51 min. Sound. 16mm B&W. *Rental:* U Mich Media & Syracuse U Film. *Sale:* Carousel Films.

Fat Black Pussy Cat, The. 1965. 90 min. Sound. 16mm B&W. *Rental:* Ivy Films.

Fat City. Stacy Keach, Jeff Bridges & Susan Tyrell. Directed by John Huston. 1972. Columbia. 96 min. Sound. 16mm Color. *Rental:* Arcus Film, Budget Films, Films Inc, Images Film, Ivy Films, Kit Parker, Modern Sound, Natl Film Video, Swank Motion, Twyman Films, Welling Motion Pictures, Westcoast Films & Wholesome Film Ctr. *Rental:* Twyman Films, Anamorphic version.

Fat in the Fire. 1981. Britain. (Documentary). 50 min. Sound. 16mm Color. *Rental:* U Cal Media, Films Inc & Syracuse U Film. *Sale:* Films Inc. *Rental:* Films Inc, *Sale:* Films Inc, Videotape version.

Fat Spy, The. Phyllis Diller & Jack E. Leonard. Directed by Joseph Cates. 1966. Magna. 93 min. Sound. 16mm Color. *Rental:* Films Inc.

Fata Morgana. Directed by Werner Herzog. 1971. New Line. (Experimental). 78 min. Sound. 16mm Color. *Rental:* New Line Cinema. *Sale:* New Line Cinema.

Fatal Competition, The. 1976. Britain. (Documentary). 60 min. Sound. 16mm Color. *Rental:* Films Inc, Syracuse U Film, U Cal Media & U of IL Film. *Sale:* Films Inc. *Rental:* Films Inc, *Sale:* Films Inc, Videotape version.

Fatal Hour, The. Orig. Title: Mister Wong at Headquarters. Boris Karloff. Directed by William Nigh. 1940. Monogram. 68 min. Sound. 16mm B&W. *Rental:* MGM United.

Fatal Passion of Dr. Mabuse, The. Orig. Title: Dr. Mabuse, Der Spieler. Rudolph Klein-Rogge. Directed by Fritz Lang. 1922. Germany. 100 min. Silent. 16mm B&W. *Rental:* Budget Films, Classic Film Mus, Em Gee Film Lib, Kit Parker & Museum Mod Art. *Sale:* Glenn Photo. *Rental:* Ivy Films, *Sale:* Glenn Photo, Super 8 silent version. *Sale:* Tamarelles French Film, Videotape version.

Fatal Witness. Evelyn Ankers & Richard Fraser. Directed by Lesley Selander. 1945. Republic. 59 min. Sound. 16mm B&W. *Rental:* Ivy Films.

Fate Is the Hunter. Glenn Ford & Rod Taylor. Directed by Ralph Nelson. 1964. Fox. 106 min. Sound. 16mm B&W. *Rental:* Films Inc. *Rental:* Films Inc, Anamorphic B&W version.

Fate of a Man. Sergei Bondarchuk. Directed by Sergei Bondarchuk. Rus. 1959. Russia. 101 min. Sound. 16mm B&W. subtitles. *Rental:* Corinth Films.

Fate of Gum Hui & Un Hui, The. Korean. 1976. Korea. (Anamorphic, cast unlisted). 100 min. Sound. 16mm Color. subtitles. *Rental:* CA Newsreel. *Sale:* CA Newsreel.

Father. Andras Balint & Miklos Gabor. Directed by Istvan Szabo. Hungarian. 1968. Hungary. 95 min. Sound. 16mm B&W. subtitles. *Rental:* Budget Films. *Lease:* W Reade Sixteen.

Father, The. Musseref Tezcan & Kuzey Vargin. Directed by Yilmaz Guney. Turkish. 1973. Turkey. 95 min. Sound. 16mm Color. subtitles Eng. *Rental:* Films Inc.

Father Brown, Detective. Walter Connolly & Gertrude Michael. Directed by Edward Sedgwick. 1935. Paramount. 67 min. Sound. 16mm B&W. *Rental:* Swank Motion & Film Ctr DC.

Father Came Too. James Robertson Justice & Leslie Phillips. Directed by Peter Graham Scott. 1963. Britain. 93 min. Sound. 16mm B&W. *Rental:* Cousino Visual Ed.

Father Christopher's Prayer. 1950. Italy. (Cast unlisted). 90 min. Sound. 16mm B&W. subtitles. *Rental:* G Herne & Willoughby Peer. *Rental:* Bosco Films, 80 min. version.

Father Dear Father. Patrick Cargill & Natasha Pyne. Directed by William G. Stewart. Britain. 85 min. Sound. 16mm B&W. *Rental:* Cinema Five.

Father Goose. Cary Grant & Leslie Carson. Directed by Ralph Nelson. 1964. Universal. 115 min. Sound. 16mm Color. *Rental:* Budget Films, Films Inc, Ivy Films, Modern Sound, Video Comm, Welling Motion Pictures & Westcoast Films. *Lease:* Rep Pic Film.

Father Is a Bachelor. William Holden & Coleen Gray. Directed by Norman Foster. 1950. Columbia. 90 min. Sound. 16mm B&W. *Rental:* Arcus Film, Buchan Pic, Cine Craft, Charard Motion Pics, Film Ctr DC, Films Inc, Modern Sound, Newman Film Lib, Welling Motion Pictures & Westcoast Films.

Father Is a Prince. Grant Mitchell & Nana Bryant. Directed by Noel Smith. 1940. Warners. 57 min. Sound. 16mm B&W. *Rental:* MGM United.

Father of a Soldier. Sergo Zakariadze. Directed by Rezo Chkeidze. Rus. 1965. Russia. 83 min. Sound. 16mm B&W. subtitles. *Rental:* Corinth Films.

Father of the Bride. Spencer Tracy & Elizabeth Taylor. Directed by Vincente Minnelli. 1950. MGM. 92 min. Sound. 16mm B&W. *Rental:* MGM United. *Rental:* MGM United, Videotape version.

Father Sergius. Trans. Title: Otets Sergii. Sergei Bondarchuk. Directed by Igor Talankin. Rus. 1979. Russia. 99 min. Sound. 16mm Color. subtitles. *Rental:* Corinth Films.

Father Sergius: Otets Sergei. Ivan Moshukin. Directed by Yakov Protazanov. 1918. Russia. 84 min. Silent. 16mm B&W. *Rental:* Corinth Films & Museum Mod Art.

Father Steps Out. Bruce Seton & Dinah Sheridan. Directed by Maclean Rogers. 1937. Britain. 62 min. Sound. 16mm B&W. *Rental:* Alba House. *Sale:* Rep Pic Film.

Father Takes a Walk *see* Mr. Cohen Takes a Walk.

Father Takes a Wife. Gloria Swanson & Adolphe Menjou. Directed by Jack Hively. 1942. RKO. 79 min. Sound. 16mm *Rental:* RKO General Pics.

Father Takes the Air. Raymond Walburn & Walter Catlett. Directed by Frank McDonald. 1951. Monogram. 61 min. Sound. 16mm B&W. *Rental:* Hurlock Cine & Inst Cinema.

Father Was a Fullback. Fred MacMurray & Maureen O'Hara. Directed by John M. Stahl. 1949. Fox. 84 min. Sound. 16mm B&W. *Rental:* Films Inc.

Fathers & Sons: Mothers & Daughters. 2 pts. 1969. CBS. (Documentary). 57 min. Sound. 16mm B&W. *Sale:* Carousel Films.

Father's Dilemma. Aldo Fabrizi & Gaby Morlay. Directed by Alessandro Blasetti. 1950. 84 min. Sound. 16mm B&W. *Rental:* Films Inc.

Father's Little Dividend. Spencer Tracy, Elizabeth Taylor & Joan Bennett. Directed by Vincente Minnelli. 1951. MGM. 82 min. Sound. 16mm B&W. *Rental:* MGM United. *Sale:* Festival Films & Natl Cinema. *Sale:* Festival Films, Videotape version.

Father's Son. John Litel & Frieda Inescort. 1941. Warners. 57 min. Sound. 16mm B&W. *Rental:* MGM United.

Fathom. Raquel Welch & Tony Franciosa. Directed by Leslie Martinson. 1967. Fox. (Anamorphic). 99 min. Sound. 16mm Color. *Rental:* Films Inc.

Fatso. Dom Deluise & Anne Bancroft. Directed by Anne Bancroft. 1980. Fox. 94 min. Sound. 16mm Color. *Rental:* Films Inc.

Faust. Emil Jannings, Yvette Guilbert & William Dieterle. Directed by F. W. Murnau. 1926. Germany. 95 min. Silent. 16mm B&W. *Rental:* A Twyman Pres, Budget Films, Classic Film Mus, Em Gee Film Lib, Films Inc, Inst Cinema, Images Film & Kit Parker. *Sale:* Glenn Photo & Reel Images. *Sale:* Glenn Photo, Super 8 silent version.

Faust. Gustav Grundgens. Directed by Peter Gorski. 1960. Germany. 134 min. Sound. 16mm Color. *Rental:* Trans-World Films.

Faute de L'abbe Mouret, La. Francis Huster & Margo Lion. Directed by Georges Franju. Fr. 1970. France. 94 min. Sound. 16mm Color. subtitles. *Rental:* Images Film.

Favorita, La. Sophia Loren. 1954. Italy. 85 min. Sound. 16mm B&W. narrated Eng. *Rental:* Corinth Films.

Fayette Story, The. 1970. Warren Schloat. (Documentary). 53 min. Sound. 16mm Color. *Rental:* U Mich Media & NYU Film Lib.

F.B.I. Girl. Audrey Totter & George Brent. Directed by William Berke. 1952. Lippert. 74 min. Sound. 16mm B&W. *Rental:* Mogulls Films.

F.B.I. Ninety-Nine. Orig. Title: Federal Operator. Marten Lamont & Helen Talbot. Directed by Spencer G. Bennett & Wallace Grissell. 1945. Republic. 100 min. Sound. 16mm B&W. *Rental:* Ivy Films. *Sale:* Rep Pic Film.

F.B.I. Story, The. James Stewart & Vera Miles. Directed by Mervyn LeRoy. 1959. Warners. 149 min. Sound. 16mm Color. *Rental:* Charard Motion Pics, Films Inc, Inst Cinema, Twyman Films & Video Comm.

FDR. 1963. Wolper. (Documentary). 52 min. Sound. 16mm B&W. *Rental:* McGraw-Hill Films, Syracuse U Film, U of IL Film & U Mich Media. *Sale:* McGraw-Hill Films.

F.D.R: That Man in the White House. Robert Vaughn. Directed by Gerald Krell. 1978. Sunrise. 104 min. Sound. 16mm Color. *Rental:* Twyman Films.

Fear. Peter Cookson & Warren William. Directed by Alfred Zeisler. 1946. Monogram. 70 min. Sound. 16mm B&W. *Rental:* Mogulls Films.

Fear. Ljuba Tadic. Directed by Matjaz Klopcic. 1975. Yugoslavia. 102 min. Sound. 16mm Color. dubbed. *Sale:* Salz Ent.

Fear. Ingrid Bergman & Mathias Wiedman. Directed by Roberto Rossellini. 1954. 84 min. Sound. 16mm B&W. *Rental:* Films Inc. *Rental:* Films Inc, English language version.

Fear & Present Danger. 1981. CBS. (Documentary). 55 min. Videotape Color. *Rental:* Indiana AV Ctr. *Sale:* Indiana AV Ctr.

Fear Chamber. Boris Karloff & Carlos East. Directed by Jack Hill. 1969. Mexico. 85 min. Sound. 16mm Color. dubbed. *Rental:* Modern Sound.

Fear in the Night. Judy Geeson. Directed by Jimmy Sangster. 1971. Britain. 94 min. Sound. 16mm Color. *Rental:* Corinth Films.

Fear is the Key. Barry Newman & Suzy Kendall. Directed by Michael Tuchner. 1973. Paramount. 105 min. Sound. 16mm Color. *Rental:* Films Inc.

Fear No Evil. Stefan Arngrim & Elizabeth Hoffman. Directed by Frank LaLoggia. 1981. Embassy. 99 min. Sound. 16mm Color. *Rental:* Films Inc.

Fear Strikes Out. Tony Perkins & Karl Malden. Directed by Robert Mulligan. 1957. Paramount. 100 min. Sound. 16mm B&W. *Rental:* Films Inc.

Fear That Binds Us, The. 52 min. Sound. 16mm Color. *Rental:* New Front. *Sale:* New Front. *Rental:* New Front, *Sale:* New Front, Videotape version.

Fearless Fagin. Janet Leigh & Carleton Carpenter. Directed by Stanley Donen. 1952. MGM. 78 min. Sound. 16mm B&W. *Rental:* MGM United.

Fearless Fighters, The. Chang Ching. Directed by Wu Min Hsiung. 1973. Hong Kong. 90 min. Sound. 16mm Color. *Rental:* Budget Films. *Sale:* Cinema Concepts, Super 8 sound version. *Sale:* Cinema Concepts, Videotape version.

Fearless Frank. Jon Voight & Monique Van Vooren. Directed by Philip Kaufman. 1969. American International. 79 min. Sound. 16mm Color. *Rental:* Video Comm.

Fearless Vampire Killers, The. Orig. Title: Dance of the Vampires. Roman Polanski & Sharon Tate. Directed by Roman Polanski. 1967. MGM. 98 min. Sound. 16mm Color. *Rental:* MGM United.

Fearmakers, The. Dana Andrews & Dick Foran. Directed by Jacques Tourneur. 1958. United Artists. 84 min. Sound. 16mm B&W. *Rental:* MGM United.

Feathered Serpent, The. Roland Winters. Directed by William Beaudine. 1948. Monogram. 61 min. Sound. 16mm B&W. *Rental:* Hurlock Cine.

Federal Agent. William Boyd & Irene Ware. Directed by Sam Newfield. 1936. Winchester. 60 min. Sound. 16mm B&W. *Rental:* Ivy Films & Wholesome Film Ctr.

Federal Budget: Inflow & Outflow. 2 pts. 1963. (Documentary). 58 min. Sound. 16mm B&W. *Rental:* U Cal Media.

Federal Bullets. Milburn Stone & Terry Walker. Directed by Carl Brown. 1940. Monogram. 61 min. Sound. 16mm B&W. *Rental:* Hurlock Cine.

Federal Manhunt. Orig. Title: Flight from Justice. Robert Livingston. Directed by Nick Grinde. 1938. Republic. 54 min. Sound. 16mm B&W. *Rental:* Ivy Films.

Federal Operator *see* F.B.I. Ninety-Nine.

Fedora. William Holden, Marthe Keller & Henry Fonda. Directed by Billy Wilder. 1979. United Artists. 114 min. Sound. 16mm Color. *Rental:* MGM United.

Feel My Pulse. Bebe Daniels. Directed by Gregory La Cava. 1928. Paramount. 60 min. Silent. 16mm B&W. *Rental:* Films Inc. *Sale:* Festival Films. *Sale:* Festival Films, Videotape version.

Feet First. Harold Lloyd. Directed by Clyde Bruckman. 1930. Paramount. (Silent with music track). 85 min. Sound. 16mm B&W. *Rental:* Budget Films, Images Film, Janus Films, Kino Intl & Kit Parker.

Feliz Ano Amor Mio. Arturo De Cordova. Directed by Tulio Demichelli. Mexico. 86 min. Sound. 16mm B&W. *Rental:* Trans-World Films.

Fellini: A Director's Notebook. Directed by Federico Fellini. 1970. NBC. (Documentary). 53 min. Sound. 16mm Color. *Rental:* U Cal Media, Films Inc, Images Film, Kent St U Film & Twyman Films. *Sale:* Texture Film. *Sale:* Texture Film, Videotape version.

Fellini Satyricon. Martin Potter & Hiram Keller. Directed by Federico Fellini. Ital. 1970. Italy. (Cinemascope only). 129 min. Sound. 16mm Color. subtitles. *Rental:* MGM United.

Fellini's Casanova. Orig. Title: Casanova. Donald Sutherland & Tina Aumont. Directed by Federico Fellini. Ital. 1977. Italy. 158 min. Sound. 16mm Color. dubbed. *Rental:* Williams Films & Swank Motion.

Fellini's Roma. Stefano Majore & Peter Gonzales. Directed by Federico Fellini. Ital. 1972. Italy. 117 min. Sound. 16mm Color. subtitles. *Rental:* MGM United.

Female. George Brent & Ruth Chatterton. Directed by Michael Curtiz. 1933. Warners. 60 min. Sound. 16mm B&W. *Rental:* MGM United.

Female Fugitive. Evelyn Venable & Craig Reynolds. Directed by William Nigh. 1940. Monogram. 56 min. Sound. 16mm B&W. *Rental:* Hurlock Cine.

Female Genital Examination: Humanistic Approach. 1981. 45 min. Sound. Videotape *Sale:* Natl AV Ctr.

Female Line, The. Directed by Robin Hardy. 1980. Corinth. (Documentary). 58 min. Sound. 16mm Color. *Rental:* Corinth Films. *Sale:* Corinth Films.

Female Rebellion, The. 1963. Hearst. (Documentary). 50 min. Sound. 16mm B&W. *Sale:* King Features.

Female Trap, The *see* Name of the Game Is Kill.

Female Trouble. Divine & Mink Stole. Directed by John Waters. 1975. New Line. 95 min. Sound. 16mm Color. *Rental:* New Line Cinema.

Females at Play. 1952. France. (Cast unlisted). 77 min. Sound. 16mm B&W. *Rental:* Film Classics.

Femme Douce, La. Trans. Title: Gentle Creature, A. Dominique Sanda. Directed by Robert Bresson. Fr. 1969. France. 87 min. Sound. 16mm Color. subtitles. *Rental:* New Yorker Films.

Femme Du Boulanger, La *see* Baker's Wife.

Femme en Bleu, La. Trans. Title: Woman in Blue, The. Michel Piccoli, Lea Massari & Simone Simon. Directed by Michel Deville. 1972. France. 90 min. Sound. 16mm Color. *Rental:* French Am Cul.

Femme Est Une Femme, Une *see* Woman is a Woman.

Femme Infidele, La. Trans. Title: Unfaithful Wife, The. Stephane Audran & Maurice Ronet. Directed by Claude Chabrol. Fr. 1968. France. 97 min. Sound. 16mm B&W. subtitles. *Rental:* Hurlock Cine.

Femmes Fatales. Orig. Title: Calmos. Jean Rochefort & Jean-Pierre Marielle. Directed by Bertrand Blier. Fr. 1976. France. (Anamorphic). 85 min. Sound. 16mm Color. subtitles. *Rental:* New Line Cinema.

Femmes Savantes, Les. Renee Devilliers. Directed by Jean Meyer. Fr. 1965. France. 100 min. Sound. 16mm B&W. subtitles. *Rental:* Films Inc.

Femomenil. Directed by Don Walls. Don Walls. (Experimental) 50 min. Sound. 16mm B&W. *Rental:* Film Ctr DC.

Fern, the Red Deer. Candid Prior & Craig McFarland. 55 min. 16mm Color. *Rental:* Arcus Film. *Sale:* Lucerne Films. *Sale:* Lucerne Films, 48 min. Videotape version.

Festival in Adelaide. 1962. Austrralia. (Documentary). 55 min. Sound. 16mm Color. *Rental:* Aust Info Serv.

Festival of Bards. 1973. 55 min. Sound. 16mm Color. *Rental:* Canyon Cinema.

Festival of Folk Heroes. 1969. Disney. (Animated). 89 min. Sound. 16mm Color. *Rental:* Cine Craft, Williams Films, Bosco Films, Disney Prod, Elliot Film Co, Films Inc, Film Pres, U of IL Film, MGM United, Modern Sound, Newman Film Lib, Roas Films, Swank Motion, Film Ctr DC, Twyman Films, Westcoast Films & Welling Motion Pictures.

Festival of the Dance. Directed by Ted Steeg. 1973. Dance Film Archive. (Dance). 60 min. Sound. 16mm Color. *Rental:* Dance Film Archive.

Feud Maker, The. Bob Steele. Directed by Sam Newfield. 1938. Republic. 60 min. Sound. 16mm B&W. *Rental:* Ivy Films & Mogulls Films.

Feud of the Range. Bob Steele. Directed by Harry S. Webb. 1939. Webb. 55 min. Sound. 16mm B&W. *Sale:* Morcraft Films.

Feud of the West. Orig. Title: Vengeance of Gregory Walters, The. Hoot Gibson. Directed by Harry Fraser. 1937. Grand National. 60 min. Sound. 16mm B&W. *Rental:* Budget Films & Video Comm. *Rental:* Video Comm, *Sale:* Video Comm, Videotape version.

Feudin' Rhythm. Eddy Arnold & Gloria Henry. Directed by Edward Bernds. 1949. Columbia. 66 min. Sound. 16mm B&W. *Rental:* Budget Films.

Fever Heat. Nick Adams & Norman Alden. Directed by Russell S. Doughten Jr. 1968. Paramount. 105 min. Sound. 16mm Color. *Rental:* Films Inc.

Fever Mounts in El Pao. Gerard Philipe. Directed by Luis Bunuel. 1960. Sound. 16mm Color. *Sale:* Reel Images.

Few Bullets More, A. Peter Lee Lawrence & Gloria Milland. Directed by Julio Buchs. 1968. Italy. (Anamorphic). 98 min. Sound. 16mm Color. dubbed. *Rental:* Kerr Film.

Fiances, Les. Trans. Title: Fidanzati, I. Carlo Cabrini. Directed by Ermanno Olmi. Ital. 1963. Italy. 76 min. Sound. 16mm B&W. subtitles Eng. *Rental:* Films Inc & Janus Films.

Fiasco in Milan. Vittorio Gassman & Claudia Cardinale. Directed by Nanni Loy. Ital. 1963. Italy. 104 min. Sound. 16mm B&W. subtitles. *Rental:* Swank Motion.

Fidanzati, I *see* Fiances.

Fiddler on the Roof. Topol & Molly Picon. Directed by Norman Jewison. 1971. United Artists. 179 min. Sound. 16mm Color. *Rental:* MGM United. *Rental:* MGM United, Anamorphic color version, R#MGM United version.

Fidelio. Claude Nollier & Richard Holm. Directed by Walter Felsenstein. Ger. 1955. Germany. 90 min. Sound. 16mm B&W. subtitles Eng. *Rental:* Corinth Films & Films Inc.

Fidelio: A Celebration of Life. 1969. CBS. (Documentary). 54 min. Sound. 16mm B&W. *Rental:* McGraw-Hill Films. *Sale:* McGraw-Hill Films.

Fields of Endless Day. Directed by Terence Macartney-Filgate. 1978. Canada. (Documentary). 59 min. Sound. 16mm Color. *Rental:* Natl Film CN. *Sale:* Natl Film CN.

Fields of the Senses, The. 3 pts. Directed by Graham Coleman & David Lascelles. 50 min. 16mm Color. *Rental:* U Cal Media. *Sale:* U Cal Media. *Sale:* U Cal Media, *Rental:* U Cal Media, Videotape version.

Fiend Without a Face, The. Marshall Thompson & Terence Kilburn. Directed by Arthur Crabtree. 1958. MGM. 75 min. Sound. 16mm B&W. *Rental:* Budget Films, Modern Sound, Roas Films, Liberty Co & Video Comm. *Sale:* Reel Images, Super 8 sound version.

Fiendish Plot of Dr. Fu Manchu, The. Peter Sellers & Helen Mirren. Directed by Piers Haggard. 1980. Orion. 108 min. Sound. 16mm Color. *Rental:* Films Inc.

Fiercest Heart, The. Stuart Whitman & Juliet Prowse. Directed by George Sherman. 1961. Fox. 91 min. Sound. 16mm Color. *Rental:* Inst Cinema. *Rental:* Film Ctr DC & Willoughby Peer, Anamorphic color version.

Fiesta. Trans. Title: Gaiety. Ann Ayars & Armida. Directed by LeRoy Prinz. 1942. United Artists. 44 min. Sound. 16mm B&W. *Rental:* Budget Films. *Sale:* Morcraft Films. *Sale:* Natl Cinema, Color version.

Fiesta. Esther Williams & Ricardo Montalban. Directed by Richard Thorpe. 1947. MGM. 104 min. Sound. 16mm B&W. *Rental:* MGM United. *Rental:* MGM United, Color version.

Fievre. Isabel Sarli & Armando Bo. Directed by Armando Bo. Mexico. 92 min. Sound. 16mm Color. *Rental:* Budget Films.

Fifteen Maiden Lane. Claire Trevor & Cesar Romero. Directed by Allan Dwan. 1936. Fox. 65 min. Sound. 16mm B&W. *Rental:* Films Inc.

Fifth Avenue Girl. Ginger Rogers. Directed by Gregory La Cava. 1939. RKO. 83 min. Sound. 16mm B&W. *Rental:* Films Inc.

Fifth Chair, The see It's in the Bag.

Fifth Chair, The see Twelve Chairs.

Fifth Floor, The. Bo Hopkins, Julie Adams & Mel Ferrer. Directed by Howard Avedis. 1980. Film Ventures. 90 min. Sound. 16mm Color. *Rental:* Twyman Films.

Fifth Frontier, The. Directed by Pastor Vega. Span. 1975. Cuba. (Documentary). 90 min. Sound. 16mm B&W. subtitles. *Rental:* Tricontinental Film.

Fifth Horseman Is Fear, The. Miroslav Machacek & Olga Scheinpflugova. Directed by Zbynek Brynych. Czech. 1966. Czechoslovakia. 100 min. Sound. 16mm B&W. subtitles Eng. *Rental:* Films Inc.

Fifth Musketeer, The. Beau Bridges & Sylvia Kristel. Directed by Ken Annakin. 1977. Columbia. 103 min. Sound. 16mm Color. *Rental:* Arcus Film, Bosco Films, Cine Craft, Modern Sound, Swank Motion, Twyman Films & Williams Films. *Sale:* Tamarelles French Film, Videotape version.

Fifth Season, The. Martin Dreyer, Louise Roux & Barry Trengove. 97 min. Sound. 16mm Color. *Rental:* Welling Motion Pictures.

Fifty-Fifty Chance, A. 58 min. Sound. Videotape *Rental:* PBS Video. *Sale:* PBS Video.

Fifty-First Volcano, The. 1971. Britain. (Documentary). 51 min. Sound. 16mm Color. *Rental:* Time-Life Multimedia. *Sale:* Time-Life Multimedia.

Fifty-Five Days to Peking. David Niven, Ava Gardner & Charlton Heston. Directed by Nicholas Ray. 1963. Allied Artists. 154 min. Sound. 16mm Color. *Rental:* Budget Films, Cine Craft, Films Inc, Film Ctr DC, Twyman Films, Video Comm, Westcoast Films, Welling Motion Pictures & Wholesome Film Ctr. *Sale:* Tamarelles French Film, Videotape version.

Fifty Million Frenchmen. Olsen & Johnson. Directed by Lloyd Bacon. 1931. Warners. 68 min. Sound. 16mm B&W. *Rental:* MGM United.

Fifty Second Street. Kenny Baker & ZaSu Pitts. Directed by Harold Young. 1937. United Artists. 85 min. Sound. 16mm B&W. *Rental:* Films Inc & Learning Corp Am. *Sale:* Learning Corp Am.

Fifty Thousand Dollars Reward. Ken Maynard & Esther Ralston. 1924. Elfelt. 55 min. Silent. 16mm B&W. *Rental:* Em Gee Film Lib & Iowa Films. *Sale:* Blackhawk Films. *Rental:* Modern Sound, *Sale:* Blackhawk Films, Sound 16mm version. *Sale:* Blackhawk Films, Super 8 sound version. *Rental:* Ivy Films, *Sale:* Blackhawk Films, Super 8 silent version.

Fifty-Two Miles to Terror see Hot Rods to Hell.

Fig Leaves. George O'Brien & Olive Borden. Directed by Howard Hawks. 1926. Fox. (Color sequences). 109 min. Silent. 16mm B&W. *Rental:* Films Inc.

Figaro see Barber of Seville.

Fight for Life. Directed by Pare Lorentz. 1940. Pare Lorentz. (Documentary). 70 min. Sound. 16mm B&W. *Rental:* Iowa Films, Kit Parker, Natl AV Ctr & Viewfinders. *Sale:* Natl AV Ctr.

Fight for Peace, The. 1938. Warwick. (Documentary). 70 min. Sound. 16mm B&W. *Rental:* Buchan Pic & Film Classics. *Rental:* Film Classics, Videotape version.

Fight for Your Lady. Ida Lupino & Jack Oakie. Directed by Ben Stoloff. 1938. RKO. 67 min. Sound. 16mm *Rental:* RKO General Pics.

Fight to Be Male, The. 1981. Britain. (Documentary). 50 min. Sound. 16mm Color. *Rental:* Films Inc, Iowa Films, Syracuse U Film, U Cal Media & U Mich Media. *Sale:* Films Inc. *Rental:* Films Inc, *Sale:* Films Inc, Videotape version.

Fighter, The. Richard Conte & Lee J. Cobb. Directed by Herbert Kline. 1952. United Artists. 78 min. Sound. 16mm B&W. *Rental:* Budget Films & Modern Sound.

Fighter Attack. Sterling Hayden. Directed by Lesley Selander. 1953. Allied Artists. 80 min. Sound. 16mm Color. *Rental:* Ivy Films. *Lease:* Rep Pic Film.

Fighter Squadron. Edmond O'Brien & Robert Stack. Directed by Raoul Walsh. 1948. Warners. 96 min. Sound. 16mm B&W. *Rental:* MGM United.

Fightin' Thru. Orig. Title: California in 1878. Ken Maynard. Directed by William Nigh. 1930. Tiffany. 60 min. Sound. 16mm B&W. *Sale:* Cinema Concepts. *Sale:* Video Comm, Videotape version.

Fighting Back. Tom Skerritt & Patti LuPone. Directed by Lewis Teague. 1982. Paramount. 98 min. Sound. 16mm Color. *Rental:* Films Inc.

Fighting Bill Carson. Buster Crabbe. Directed by Sam Newfield. 1945. PRC. 56 min. Sound. 16mm B&W. *Sale:* Classics Assoc NY.

Fighting Chance. Rod Cameron & Julie London. Directed by William Witney. 1955. Republic. 70 min. Sound. 16mm B&W. *Rental:* Ivy Films. *Sale:* Rep Pic Film.

Fighting Coast Guard. Brian Donlevy & Forrest Tucker. Directed by Joseph Kane. 1951. Republic. 89 min. Sound. 16mm B&W. *Rental:* Ivy Films. *Sale:* Rep Pic Film.

Fighting Coward. Mary Astor. Directed by James Cruze. 1924. Paramount. 50 min. Silent. 16mm B&W. *Rental:* Film Classics. *Sale:* Film Classics & E Finney. *Sale:* Film Classics, Silent 8mm version.

Fighting Coward. Ray Walker & Joan Woodbury. Directed by Dan Milner. 1935. Victory. 60 min. Sound. 16mm B&W. *Rental:* Mogulls Films.

Fighting Doctor, The see Hangman's Wharf.

Fighting Eagle, The. Phyllis Haver & Rod La Rocque. Directed by Donald Crisp. 1927. Pathe. 65 min. Silent. 16mm B&W. *Rental:* Em Gee Film Lib & Film Classics. *Sale:* Em Gee Film Lib, Film Classics & Glenn Photo. *Sale:* Glenn Photo, Super 8 silent version.

Fighting Father Dunne. Pat O'Brien & Darryl Hickman. Directed by Ted Tetzlaff. 1948. RKO. 93 min. Sound. 16mm B&W. *Rental:* Films Inc.

Fighting Frontier. Tim Holt. Directed by Lambert Hillyer. 1943. RKO. 57 min. Sound. 16mm B&W. *Rental:* Films Inc.

Fighting Fury. Orig. Title: Outlaw's Highway. Kazan & The Wonder Dog. Directed by Robert Hill. 1938. Britain. 60 min. Sound. 16mm B&W. *Rental:* Mogulls Films.

Fighting Gringo. George O'Brien & Dick Lane. Directed by Bert Gilroy. 1939. RKO. 59 min. Sound. 16mm *Rental:* RKO General Pics.

Fighting Hero. Tom Tyler. Directed by Harry S. Webb. 1934. Steiner. 60 min. Sound. 16mm B&W. *Rental:* Mogulls Films.

Fighting Kentuckian, The. John Wayne & Oliver Hardy. Directed by George Waggner. 1949. Republic. 103 min. Sound. 16mm B&W. *Rental:* Budget Films & Ivy Films. *Sale:* Rep Pic Film & Tamarelles French Film.

Fighting Lady, The. Directed by Edward Steichen. 1944. Fox. (Documentary). 61 min. Sound. 16mm Color. *Rental:* Budget Films.

Fighting Lawman, The. Wayne Morris & Virginia Grey. Directed by Thomas Carr. 1952. Allied Artists. 71 min. Sound. 16mm B&W. *Rental:* Hurlock Cine.

Fighting Mad. James Newill. Directed by Sam Newfield. 1939. Monogram. 60 min. Sound. 16mm B&W. *Rental:* Mogulls Films & Rep Pic Film.

Fighting Mad. Peter Fonda & Lynn Lowry. Directed by Jonathan Demme. 1976. Fox. 88 min. Sound. 16mm Color. *Rental:* Films Inc.

Fighting Man of the Plains. Randolph Scott & Dale Robertson. Directed by Edwin L. Marin. 1949. Fox. 90 min. Sound. 16mm B&W. *Rental:* Budget Films, Cine Craft & Newman Film Lib. *Sale:* Cinema Concepts, Super 8 sound version.

Fighting Marshal *see* Cherokee Strip.

Fighting Musketeers. Gerard Baray & Mylene Demongeot. 1963. France. 95 min. Sound. 16mm Color. dubbed. *Rental:* Welling Motion Pictures.

Fighting Mustang. Sunset Carson. Directed by Oliver Drake. 1948. Astor. 60 min. Sound. 16mm B&W. *Rental:* Budget Films.

Fighting Odds. Hoot Gibson. 1917. Goldwyn. 55 min. Silent. 16mm B&W. *Sale:* E Finney.

Fighting Parson, The. Hoot Gibson. Directed by Harry Fraser. 1932. Allied. 60 min. Videotape B&W. *Sale:* Video Comm.

Fighting Phantom *see* Mysterious Rider.

Fighting Redhead. Jim Bannon. Directed by Lewis D. Collins. 1949. Eagle Lion. 55 min. Sound. 16mm Color. *Rental:* Mogulls Film.

Fighting Renegade, The. Tim McCoy. Directed by Sam Newfield. 1939. Victory. 60 min. Sound. 16mm B&W. *Rental:* Budget Films.

Fighting Rookie, The. Jack LaRue. Directed by Spencer G. Bennett. 1934. Mayfair. 67 min. Sound. 16mm B&W. *Rental:* Modern Sound.

Fighting Seabees. John Wayne & Susan Hayward. Directed by Edward Ludwig. 1944. Republic. 100 min. Sound. B&W. *Rental:* Budget Films & Ivy Films. *Lease:* Rep Pic Film. *Sale:* Cinema Concepts, Videotape version.

Fighting Seventh, The *see* Little Big Horn.

Fighting Sixty-Ninth. James Cagney & Pat O'Brien. Directed by William Keighley. 1940. Warners. 90 min. Sound. 16mm B&W. *Rental:* MGM United.

Fighting Stallion. Yakima Canutt. Directed by Ben Wilson. 1926. Goodwill. 62 min. Silent. 16mm B&W. *Rental:* Film Classics. *Sale:* Film Classics.

Fighting Stallion. Bill Edwards. Directed by Robert Tansey. 1950. Eagle Lion. 65 min. Sound. 16mm B&W. *Rental:* Alba House, Budget Films, Mogulls Films & Westcoast Films.

Fighting Texan, The. Kermit Maynard. Directed by Charles Abbott. 1937. Ambassador. 60 min. Sound. 16mm B&W. *Rental:* Budget Films, Modern Sound & Mogulls Films.

Fighting Throughbreds. Ralph Byrd & Mary Carlisle. Directed by Sidney Salkow. 1939. Republic. 54 min. Sound. 16mm B&W. *Sale:* Rep Pic Film.

Fighting to Live. Reb Russell. Directed by Edward F. Clime. 1935. Ambassador. 60 min. Sound. 16mm B&W. *Rental:* Mogulls Films.

Fighting Vigilantes. Lash LaRue. Directed by Ray Taylor. Eagle Lion. 61 min. Sound. 16mm B&W. *Sale:* Classics Assoc NY.

Fighting Westerner. Orig. Title: Rocky Mountain Mystery. Randolph Scott, Ann Sheridan & Chic Sale. Directed by Charles Barton. 1936. Paramount. 70 min. Sound. 16mm B&W. *Rental:* Budget Films & Mogulls Films.

File of the Golden Goose, The. Yul Brynner & Edward Woodward. Directed by Sam Wanamaker. 1969. United Artists. 105 min. Sound. 16mm Color. *Rental:* MGM United.

File on Thelma Jordan, The. Barbara Stanwyck & Wendell Corey. Directed by Robert Siodmak. 1949. Paramount. 100 min. Sound. 16mm B&W. *Rental:* Films Inc.

File One Thirteen. Lew Cody. Directed by Chester M. Franklin. 1932. Hollywood. 70 min. Sound. 16mm B&W. *Rental:* Mogulls Films.

Fille de L'Eau, La. Trans. Title: Whirlpool of Life, The. Catherine Hessling. Directed by Jean Renoir. 1924. France. 85 min. Silent. 16mm B&W. *Rental:* Em Gee Film Lib & Images Film. *Sale:* Reel Images.

Fille Des Fusil, Une *see* To Be a Crook.

Fille Du Puisatier, La *see* Well-Digger's Daughter.

Fillmore. Directed by Richard T. Heffron. 1971. Fox. (Anamorphic) (Documentary). 105 min. Sound. 16mm Color. *Rental:* Films Inc.

Film "Firsts". 1960. Killiam. (Documentary). 55 min. Sound. 16mm B&W. *Rental:* BYU Media & Killiam Collect. *Sale:* Blackhawk Films, Videotape version.

Film for Max, A. 1971. Canada. (Documentary). 75 min. Sound. 16mm Color. *Rental:* Natl Film CN. *Sale:* Natl Film CN.

Film Portrait. Jerome Hill. 80 min. Sound. 16mm Color. *Rental:* Filmmakers Coop.

Films of Georges Melies. 1964. KQED. (Anthology). 60 min. Sound. 16mm B&W. *Rental:* Indiana AV Ctr. *Sale:* Indiana AV Ctr.

Final Conflict, The. Sam Neill, Rossano Brazzi & Don Gordon. Fox. 100 min. Sound. 16mm Color. *Rental:* Williams Films.

Final Countdown, The. Kirk Douglas & Martin Sheen. Directed by Don Taylor. 1980. United Artists. 103 min. Sound. 16mm Color. *Rental:* MGM United. *Rental:* MGM United, Videotape version.

Final Edition, The. Pat O'Brien & Mae Clarke. Directed by Howard Higgin. 1932. Columbia. 70 min. Sound. 16mm B&W. *Rental:* Kit Parker.

Final Exam, The. Cecile Bagdadi. Directed by Jimmy Huston. 1982. Embassy. 90 min. Sound. 16mm Color. *Rental:* Films Inc.

Final Frontier, The. 1978. Time-Life. (Documentary). 58 min. Sound. 16mm Color. *Rental:* U of IL Film & Utah Media.

Final Option, The. Judy Davis & Richard Widmark. Directed by Ian Sharp. 1983. 124 min. Sound. 16mm *Rental:* MGM United. *Rental:* MGM United, Videotape version.

Final, Proud Days of Elsie Wurster, The. 1975. Penn State. (Documentary). 58 min. Sound. 16mm B&W. *Rental:* Penn St AV Serv. *Sale:* Penn St AV Serv. *Sale:* Penn St AV Serv, Videotape version.

Final Solution, The: Auschwitz. 208 min. Sound. Videotape Color. *Rental:* Media Guild. *Sale:* Media Guild.

Finally Got the News. 1972. Tricontinental. (Documentary, color sequences). 55 min. Sound. 16mm B&W. *Rental:* Cinema Guild. *Sale:* Cinema Guild.

Fincho. Patrick Akponu. Directed by Sam Zebba. 1958. Africa. 75 min. Sound. 16mm Color. *Rental:* A Twyman Pres, Films Inc & Twyman Films.

Find a Place to Die. Jeffrey Hunter & Pascale Petit. Directed by Anthony Ascott. 1968. GG Productions. 89 min. Sound. 16mm Color. *Rental:* Budget Films & Video Comm. *Rental:* Video Comm, Videotape version.

Find the Blackmailer. Faye Emerson & Jerome Cowan. Directed by D. Ross Lederman. 1943. Warners. 55 min. Sound. 16mm B&W. *Rental:* MGM United.

Finders Keepers. Michael O'Keefe, David Wayne & Beverly D'Angelo. Directed by Richard Lester. 1985. Warners. 96 min. Sound. 16mm Color. *Rental:* Swank Motion.

Finders Keepers, Lovers Weepers. Anne Chapman. Directed by Russ Meyer. 1968. Eve. 71 min. Sound. 16mm Color. *Rental:* Corinth Films. *Sale:* Cinema Concepts & Video Lib, Videotape version.

Findings: A Film About Reinhold Marxhausen. 1979. PBS. (Documentary). 57 min. Videotape Color. *Rental:* PBS Video. *Sale:* PBS Video.

Fine Madness, A. Sean Connery & Joanne Woodward. Directed by Irwin Kershner. 1966. Warners. 112 min. Sound. 16mm Color. *Rental:* Cine Craft, Inst Cinema, Films Inc, Swank Motion & Video Comm.

Fine Manners. Gloria Swanson. Directed by Richard Rosson. 1926. Paramount. 70 min. Silent. 16mm B&W. *Rental:* Films Inc.

Fine Pair, A. Rock Hudson & Claudia Cardinale. Directed by Francesco Maselli. 1969. National General. 89 min. Sound. 16mm Color. *Rental:* Swank Motion.

Fine Structure & Pattern of Living Things. 1961. US Government. (Documentary). 59 min. Sound. 16mm B&W. *Rental:* Natl AV Ctr. *Sale:* Natl AV Ctr.

Finest Hours, The. Directed by Peter Baylis. 1964. Columbia. (Documentary). 116 min. Sound. 16mm Color. *Rental:* Films Inc & Macmillan Films. *Sale:* Macmillan Films.

Finger Man, The. Frank Lovejoy & Forrest Tucker. Directed by Harold Schuster. 1955. Allied Artists. 82 min. Sound. 16mm B&W. *Rental:* Ivy Films. *Sale:* Rep Pic Film.

Finger of Guilt, The. Orig. Title: Intimate Stranger. Richard Basehart & Constance Cummings. Directed by Alec Snowden. 1956. RKO. 84 min. Sound. 16mm B&W. *Rental:* Budget Films, Kit Parker & Video Comm. *Lease:* Video Comm. *Rental:* Video Comm, *Lease:* Video Comm, Videotape version.

Finger of Justice, The. Directed by Crane Wilbur. 1919. Arrow. (Cast Unlisted). 16mm B&W. *Rental:* Em Gee Film Lib.

Finger Points, The. Fay Wray & Richard Barthelmess. Directed by John Francis Dillon. 1931. Warners. 88 min. Sound. 16mm B&W. *Rental:* MGM United.

Fingerprints Don't Lie. Richard Travis & Sheila Ryan. Directed by Sam Newfield. 1951. Lippert. 72 min. Sound. 16mm B&W. *Rental:* Inst Cinema & Mogulls Films.

Fingers. Harvey Keitel & Tisa Farrow. Directed by James Toback. 1978. Brut. 90 min. Videotape Color. *Sale:* Cinema Concepts.

Finian's Rainbow. Fred Astaire & Petula Clark. Directed by Francis Ford Coppola. 1968. Warners. 160 min. Sound. 16mm Color. *Rental:* Charard Motion Pics, Williams Films, Films Inc, Inst Cinema, Willoughby Peer, Newman Film Lib, Swank Motion, Twyman Films & Video Comm. *Sale:* Natl Cinema. *Sale:* Tamarelles French Film, Videotape version.

Finis. 54 min. Sound. 16mm Color. *Rental:* Ency Brit Ed & Iowa Films. *Sale:* Ency Brit Ed. *Sale:* Ency Brit Ed, Videotape version.

Finishing School. Ginger Rogers & Bruce Cabot. Directed by Merian C. Cooper. 1934. RKO. 73 min. Sound. 16mm *Rental:* RKO General Pics.

Finnegan's Wake. Martin J. Kelly & Jane Reilley. Directed by Mary Ellen Bute. 1965. Evergreen. 97 min. Sound. 16mm B&W. *Rental:* C Starr & U Cal Media. *Sale:* C Starr. *Sale:* C Starr, Videotape version.

Fire! 1968. North Vietnam. (Cast unlisted). Sound. 16mm B&W. subtitles. *Rental:* CA Newsreel.

Fire! Pamela Hill. 1974. ABC. (Documentary). 54 min. Sound. 16mm Color. *Rental:* Phoenix Films, Syracuse U Film & U of IL Film. *Sale:* Phoenix Films. *Sale:* Phoenix Films, Videotape version.

Fire & Ice. Directed by Ralph Bakshi. 1983. Fox. 81 min. Sound. 16mm Color. *Rental:* Films Inc.

Fire Down Below. Rita Hayworth, Robert Mitchum & Jack Lemmon. Directed by Robert Parrish. 1957. Columbia. 116 min. Sound. 16mm Color. *Rental:* Budget Films, Cine Craft, Liberty Co & Welling Motion Pictures. *Rental:* Kit Parker, Anamorphic version.

Fire: High Rise & Bldg Codes. 1974. Phoenix. 54 min. Sound. 16mm Color. *Rental:* Syracuse U Film. *Sale:* Phoenix Films.

Fire in the Sky. 45 min. Sound. 16mm Color. *Rental:* Gospel Films.

Fire in the Water. 1980. McGraw-Hill. (Documentary). 48 min. Sound. 16mm Color. *Rental:* Iowa Films, McGraw-Hill Films, Syracuse U Film & U Cal Media. *Sale:* McGraw-Hill Films. *Sale:* McGraw-Hill Films, Videotape version.

Fire Maidens of Outer Space. Anthony Dexter. Directed by Cy Roth. 1956. Britain. 68 min. Sound. 16mm B&W. *Rental:* Ivy Films & Rep Pic Film. *Lease:* Rep Pic Film.

Fire Monsters Against the Son of Hercules. Reg Lewis. Directed by Guido Malatesta. 1963. Italy. 83 min. Sound. 16mm Color. dubbed. *Rental:* Films Inc.

Fire Next Door, The. 1977. CBS. (Documentary). 52 min. Sound. 16mm Color. *Rental:* Syracuse U Films, U Cal Media & U Mich Media. *Sale:* Carousel Films.

Fire on the Water. 1982. HILR. 56 min. Sound. 16mm Color. *Rental:* U Cal Media.

Fire Over Africa. Maureen O'Hara & MacDonald Carey. Directed by Richard Sale. 1954. Columbia. 84 min. Sound. 16mm Color. *Rental:* Inst Cinema & Film Ctr DC.

Fire Over England. Sir Laurence Olivier & Vivien Leigh. Directed by William K. Howard. 1937. Britain. 81 min. Sound. 16mm B&W. *Rental:* A Twyman Pres, Budget Films, Classic Film Mus, Janus Films & Kit Parker. *Sale:* Cinema Concepts, Festival Films & Reel Images. *Sale:* Festival Films & Tamarelles French Film, Videotape version.

Fire Sale. Alan Arkin & Rob Reiner. Directed by Alan Arkin. 1977. Fox. 88 min. Sound. 16mm Color. *Rental:* Films Inc.

Fire Trap. 1977. Edupac. (Documentary). 50 min. Sound. 16mm Color. *Rental:* EDUPAC. *Sale:* EDUPAC.

Fire Within, The. Maurice Ronet & Lena Skerla. Directed by Louis Malle. Fr. 1964. France. 108 min. Sound. 16mm B&W. subtitles. *Rental:* New Yorker Films.

Fireball, The. Mickey Rooney, Marilyn Monroe & Pat O'Brien. Directed by Tay Garnett. 1950. Fox. 84 min. Sound. 16mm B&W. *Rental:* Budget Films.

Fireball Five Hundred. Frankie Avalon & Annette Funicello. Directed by William Asher. 1966. American International. 92 min. Sound. 16mm Color. *Rental:* Westcoast Films.

Firebell in the Night, A. 1972. Britain. (Documentary). 52 min. Sound. 16mm Color. *Rental:* Films Inc, Kent St U Film, OK Av Ctr, Syracuse U Film & Utah Media. *Sale:* Films Inc. *Rental:* Films Inc, *Sale:* Films Inc, Videotape version.

Firebird, The. Ricardo Cortez & Lionel Atwill. Directed by William Dieterle. 1934. Warners. 74 min. Sound. 16mm B&W. *Rental:* MGM United.

Firebrands of Arizona. Sunset Carson. Directed by Lesley Selander. 1944. Republic. 55 min. Sound. 16mm B&W. *Rental:* Ivy Films. *Sale:* Rep Pic Film.

Firecracker. Jillian Kessner & Darby Hinton. Directed by Cirio H. Santiago. 1981. New World. 82 min. Sound. 16mm Color. *Rental:* Films Inc.

Firefly, The. Jeanette MacDonald & Allan Jones. Directed by Robert Z. Leonard. 1937. MGM. 131 min. Sound. 16mm B&W. *Rental:* MGM United.

Fireman, Save My Child. Joe E. Brown & Guy Kibbee. Directed by Lloyd Bacon. 1932. Warners. 67 min. Sound. 16mm B&W. *Rental:* MGM United.

Fireman's Ball, The. Vaclav Stockel. Directed by Milos Forman. Czech. 1968. Czechoslovakia. 73 min. Sound. 16mm Color. subtitles. *Rental:* Cinema Five. *Lease:* Cinema Five.

Fires of Youth. Jeanne Eagles & Frederick Warde. Directed by Rupert Julian. 1917. Pathe. 45 min. Silent. 16mm B&W. *Rental:* Film Classics. *Sale:* Film Classics. *Rental:* Film Classics, *Sale:* Film Classics, Silent 8mm version. *Rental:* Film Classics, Videotape version.

Fires on the Plain. Orig. Title: Nobi. Eiji Funakoshi. Directed by Kon Ichikawa. Jap. 1959. Japan. 105 min. Sound. 16mm B&W. subtitles. *Rental:* Budget Films, Em Gee Film Lib, Films Inc, Kit Parker & New Cinema. *Sale:* Festival Films & Natl Cinema. *Sale:* Festival Films, Videotape version.

Fires Were Started. Directed by Humphrey Jennings. 1943. Britain. (Documentary). 62 min. Sound. 16mm B&W. *Rental:* Images Film. *Sale:* Images Film.

Firesign Funnies. Firesign Theater. New Line Cinema. 92 min. Sound. 16mm Color. *Rental:* New Line Cinema.

Firestarter. David Keith, Drew Barrymore & George C. Scott. Directed by Mark L. Lester. 1985. Universal. 115 min. Sound. 16mm Color. *Rental:* Swank Motion.

First Age of the French Cinema 1895-1914, The. Directed by Armand Panigel. Fr. France. (Documentary). 75 min. Sound. 16mm B&W. subtitles. *Rental:* French Am Cul.

First Americans, The. 1969. NBC. (Documentary). 53 min. Sound. 16mm Color. *Rental:* BYU Media, Films Inc, Iowa Films, Syracuse U Film, U Cal Media & U of IL Film. *Sale:* Films Inc, Videotape version.

First & Essential Freedom, The. 1974. Xerox. (Documentary). 52 min. Sound. 16mm Color. *Rental:* Xerox Films & Utah Media. *Sale:* Xerox Films.

First Annual Zany Awards, The. Verve. (Performance). 60 min. Videotape Color. *Rental:* Films Inc.

First Blood. Sylvester Stallone & Richard Crenna. Directed by Ted Kotcheff. 1985. Carolco. 94 min. Sound. 16mm Color. *Rental:* Swank Motion. *Rental:* Swank Motion, Videotape version.

First Casualty, The. 1974. Britain. (Documentary). 60 min. Sound. 16mm Color. *Rental:* U of IL Film & Media Guild. *Sale:* Media Guild. *Sale:* Media Guild, Videotape version.

First Charge of the Machete, The. Idalia Anreus & Eslina Nunez. Directed by Manuel Octavio Gomez. Span. 1972. Mexico. 84 min. Sound. 16mm B&W. subtitles. *Rental:* Tricontinental Film.

First Circle, The. Gunther Malzacher. Directed by Aleksander Ford. 1973. Paramount. 97 min. Sound. 16mm Color. subtitles. *Rental:* Films Inc.

First Classics of the French Talkies, The. Directed by Armand Panigel. France. (Documentary). 80 min. Sound. 16mm B&W. subtitles. *Rental:* French Am Cul.

First Comes Courage. Merle Oberon & Brian Aherne. Directed by Dorothy Arzner. 1943. Columbia. 86 min. Sound. 16mm B&W. *Rental:* Kit Parker.

First Contact. 1983. FL. 54 min. Sound. 16mm Color. *Rental:* U Cal Media.

First Deadly Sin, The. Frank Sinatra, Faye Dunaway & Brenda Vaccaro. Directed by Brian Hutton. 1980. Filmways. 112 min. Sound. 16mm Color. *Rental:* Williams Films.

First Erotic Film Festival, The: Erotic Film Festival No. 1. New Line Cinema. (Anthology). 110 min. Sound. 16mm Color. *Rental:* New Line Cinema.

First Family, The. Gilda Radner, Bob Newhart & Madeline Kahn. Directed by Buck Henry. 1980. Warners. 103 min. Sound. 16mm Color. *Rental:* Swank Motion & Williams Films. *Rental:* Swank Motion, Videotape version.

First Flickers, The. 1960. Killiam. (Documentary). 55 min. Sound. 16mm B&W. *Rental:* Twyman Films.

First Freedom, The. 1977. WNET. (Documentary). 60 min. Videotape Color. *Rental:* WNET Media. *Sale:* WNET Media.

First Freedom, The: The Moscow Trial. Arthur Hill & Peter Vaughan. 1967. Britain. 90 min. Sound. 16mm B&W. *Rental:* Time-Life Multimedia. *Sale:* Time-Life Multimedia.

First Hundred Years, The. Robert Montgomery & Virginia Bruce. Directed by Richard Thorpe. 1938. MGM. 73 min. Sound. 16mm B&W. *Rental:* MGM United.

First Jay Ward Cartoon Festival, The. 1977. Jay Ward. (Animated, anthology). 90 min. Sound. 16mm Color. *Lease:* Cinema Concepts. *Lease:* Cinema Concepts, Videotape version.

First Lady of the World, The. 1962. Hearst. (Documentary). 50 min. Sound. 16mm B&W. *Sale:* King Features.

First Legion, The. Charles Boyer & Walter Hampden. Directed by Douglas Sirk. 1951. United Artists. 85 min. Sound. 16mm B&W. *Rental:* Bosco Films, Budget Films & Mogulls Films.

First Look. Directed by Kavery Dutta. 1983. Cuba. (Documentary). 60 min. Sound. 16mm Color. *Rental:* Icarus Films. *Sale:* Icarus Films. *Sale:* Icarus Films, Videotape version.

First Love. John Moulder-Brown & Dominique Sanda. Directed by Maximillian Schell. 1970. Warners. 90 min. Sound. 16mm Color. dubbed. *Rental:* Films Inc.

First Love. William Katt & Susan Dey. Directed by Joan Darling. 1977. Paramount. 92 min. Sound. 16mm Color. *Rental:* Films Inc.

First Man Into Space. Marshall Thompson & Marla Landi. Directed by Robert Day. 1959. MGM. 76 min. Sound. 16mm B&W. *Rental:* Ivy Films, MGM United & Video Comm. *Sale:* Cinema Concepts, Super 8 sound version.

First Men in the Moon. Edward Judd & Martha Hyer. Directed by Nathan Juran. 1964. Columbia. 103 min. Sound. 16mm Color. *Rental:* Arcus Film, Bosco Films, Buchan Pic, Budget Films, Cine Craft, Film Ctr DC, Films Inc, Kit Parker, Modern Sound, Natl Film Video, Roas Films, Twyman Films, Video Comm, Welling Motion Pictures, Westcoast Films & Williams Films. *Rental:* Kit Parker, Anamorphic version.

First Nudie Musical, The. Stephen Nathan & Cindy Williams. Directed by Mark Haggard & Bruce Kimmel. 1976. Haggard-Kimmel. 100 min. Sound. 16mm Color. *Rental:* World Northal. *Sale:* Cinema Concepts, Videotape version.

First Rice, The. Directed by Walter Heynowski & Gerhard Scheumann. Vietnamese. 1977. Vietnam. (Documentary). 57 min. Sound. 16mm Color. subtitles. *Rental:* Unifilm. *Sale:* Unifilm.

First Signs of Washoe, The. 1976. Nova. (Documentary). 59 min. Sound. 16mm Color. *Rental:* Iowa Films, Kent St U Film, Syracuse U Film, U Cal Media, U of IL Film & U Mich Media.

First Spaceship on Venus, The. Yoko Tani. Directed by Kurt Maetzig. 1962. Crown International. (Anamorphic). 80 min. Sound. 16mm Color. dubbed. *Rental:* Budget Films, Films Inc, Ivy Films, Video Comm, Welling Motion Pictures, Westcoast Films & Willoughby Peer. *Lease:* Video Comm. *Rental:* Video Comm, *Lease:* Video Comm, Videotape version.

First Swallow, The. David Dodo Adashidze. Directed by Nana Mchedlidze. Rus. 1976. Russia. (Anamorphic). 88 min. Sound. 16mm Color. subtitles. *Rental:* Corinth Films.

First Ten Months of Life, The. 2 pts. 1967. CBS. (Documentary). 54 min. Sound. 16mm Color. *Rental:* McGraw-Hill Films. *Sale:* McGraw-Hill Films.

First Texan, The. Joel McCrea & Felicia Farr. Directed by Byron Haskin. 1956. Allied Artists. 54 min. Sound. 16mm B&W. *Rental:* Hurlock Cine.

First Three Georges, The. 1980. Royal Heritage. (Documentary). 60 min. Sound. 16mm Color. *Rental:* Films Inc. *Sale:* Films Inc. *Sale:* Films Inc, *Sale:* Films Inc, Videotape version.

First Time, The. Robert Cummings & Barbara Hale. Directed by Frank Tashlin. 1952. Columbia. 89 min. Sound. 16mm B&W. *Rental:* Inst Cinema.

First Time, The. Jacqueline Bisset & Wes Stern. Directed by James Neilson. 1969. United Artists. 90 min. Sound. 16mm Color. *Rental:* MGM United.

First Time, The. Alain Cohen & Charles Denner. Directed by Claude Berri. Fr. 1978. France. 85 min. Sound. 16mm Color. subtitles. *Rental:* Films Inc.

First Traveling Saleslady, The. Ginger Rogers & Carol Channing. Directed by Arthur Lubin. 1956. RKO. 92 min. Sound. 16mm Color. *Rental:* Budget Films, Video Comm & Westcoast Films. *Lease:* Video Comm. *Rental:* Video Comm, *Lease:* Video Comm, Videotape version.

First World War, The. 1934. Film Classic Exchange. (Documentary). 78 min. Sound. 16mm B&W. *Sale:* Films Inc. *Rental:* Film Classics. *Rental:* Film Classics, Videotape version.

First Yank into Tokyo, The. Tom Neal & Barbara Hale. Directed by Gordon Douglas. 1946. RKO. 72 min. Sound. 16mm *Rental:* RKO General Pics.

Fish Hawk. Will Sampson & Don Francks. Modern. 93 min. Sound. 16mm Color. *Rental:* Modern Sound.

Fish That Saved Pittsburgh, The. Jonathan Winters, Flip Wilson & Stockard Channing. Directed by Gilbert Moses. 1979. United Artists. 104 min. Sound. 16mm Color. *Rental:* MGM United & Swank Motion.

Fishing at the Stone Weir. 1964. MLA. (Documentary). 58 min. Sound. 16mm Color. *Rental:* U Cal Media.

Fishing, U. S. A. Directed by Vernon Gadabout Gaddis. 1971. United. (Documentary). 105 min. Sound. 16mm Color. *Rental:* Budget Films & Video Comm. *Lease:* Video Comm.

Fishing Village, The. Directed by Joris Ivens & Marceline Loridan. 1973. China. (Documentary). 102 min. Sound. 16mm Color. *Rental:* Cinema Arts & Inst Cinema.

F.I.S.T. Sylvester Stallone & Rod Steiger. Directed by Norman Jewison. 1978. United Artists. 145 min. Sound. 16mm Color. *Rental:* MGM United. *Rental:* MGM United, Videotape version.

Fist of Fear, Touch of Death. Bruce Lee & Fred Williamson. Directed by Matthew Mallinson. 1981. Aquarius. 90 min. Sound. 16mm Color. *Rental:* Films Inc.

Fist of Fury. Directed by Lo Wei. 1972. Pagoda. 103 min. Sound. 16mm Color. *Rental:* Swank Motion.

Fist. Right of Freedom *see* Fox & His Friends.

Fistful of Dollars, A. Clint Eastwood & Marianne Koch. Directed by Sergio Leone. 1966. Italy. 96 min. Sound. 16mm Color. dubbed. *Rental:* MGM United. *Rental:* MGM United, Videotape version.

Fistful of Dynamite, A *see* Duck, You Sucker!.

Fists in the Pockets. Orig. Title: I Pugni Om Tasca. Lou Castel & Paola Pitagora. Directed by Marco Bellocchio. Ital. 1966. Italy. 95 min. Sound. 16mm B&W. subtitles. *Rental:* Janus Films.

Fists of the Double K. Henry Yue Young. 1973. Cannon. 90 min. Sound. 16mm Color. *Rental:* Swank Motion.

Fists of the White Lotus. Liu Chia Hui & Lo Lieh. 94 min. Sound. 16mm *Rental:* WW Enter. *Rental:* WW Enter, Videotape version.

Fit for a King. Joe E. Brown & Leo Carillo. Directed by Edward Sedgwick. 1937. RKO. 73 min. Sound. 16mm B&W. *Rental:* Alba House, Mogulls Films & Welling Motion Pictures.

Fit to Be Untied. 1975. 105 min. Sound. 16mm B&W. *Rental:* Canyon Cinema.

Fitzcarraldo. Klaus Kinski & Claudia Cardinale. Directed by Werner Herzog. 1982. New World. 157 min. Sound. 16mm Color. *Rental:* Films Inc.

Fitzwilly. Dick Van Dyke & Dame Edith Evans. Directed by Delbert Mann. 1967. United Artists. 102 min. Sound. 16mm Color. *Rental:* MGM United.

Five. Susan Douglas & William Phipps. Directed by Arch Oboler. 1951. Columbia. 93 min. Sound. 16mm B&W. *Rental:* Kit Parker.

Five Against the House. Guy Madison, Kim Novak & William Conrad. Directed by Phil Karlson. 1955. Columbia. 84 min. Sound. 16mm B&W. *Rental:* Kit Parker.

Five & Ten. Leslie Howard & Irene Rich. Directed by Robert Z. Leonard. 1931. MGM. 89 min. Sound. 16mm B&W. *Rental:* MGM United.

Five Artists Billbobbillbillbob. 1971. 70 min. Sound. 16mm Color. *Rental:* Canyon Cinema.

Five Billion People. Directed by Nicole Duchene & Claude Lortie. Les Films sur Place. (Documentary). 351 min. Sound. 16mm Color. *Rental:* Cinema Guild. *Sale:* Cinema Guild.

Five Branded Women. Van Heflin & Silvana Mangano. Directed by Martin Ritt. 1960. Paramount. 100 min. Sound. 16mm B&W. *Rental:* Films Inc.

Five Came Back. Lucille Ball & Chester Morris. Directed by John Farrow. 1939. RKO. 75 min. Sound. 16mm B&W. *Rental:* RKO General Pics.

Five Card Stud. Dean Martin & Robert Mitchum. Directed by Henry Hathaway. 1968. Paramount. 103 min. Sound. 16mm Color. *Rental:* Films Inc.

Five-Day Lover. Jean-Pierre Cassel & Micheline Presle. Directed by Philippe De Broca. Fr. 1961. France. 86 min. Sound. 16mm B&W. subtitles. *Rental:* Swank Motion.

Five Days from Home. George Peppard & Neville Brand. Directed by George Peppard. 1979. Universal. 109 min. Sound. 16mm Color. *Rental:* Williams Films.

Five Days One Summer. Sean Connery, Betsy Brantley & Lambert Wilson. Directed by Fred Zinnemann. 1982. 110 min. Sound. 16mm Color. *Rental:* Swank Motion. *Rental:* Swank Motion, Videotape version.

Five Deadly Venoms. Sun Chien & Kue Chue. 102 min. Sound. 16mm *Rental:* Corinth Films & WW Enter. *Rental:* WW Enter, Videotape version.

Five Easy Pieces. Jack Nicholson, Karen Black & Sally Struthers. Directed by Bob Rafelson. 1970. BBS. 97 min. Sound. 16mm Color. *Rental:* Films Inc, Museum Mod Art & Swank Motion.

Five Faces of Tokyo, The. USDS. (Documentary). 55 min. Sound. 16mm B&W. *Rental:* U Mich Media.

Five Filosophical Fables. Directed by Donald Richie. 1967. Japan. (Experimental). 97 min. Sound. 16mm B&W. *Rental:* Museum Mod Art.

Five Finger Exercise. Rosalind Russell & Jack Hawkins. Directed by Daniel Mann. 1962. Columbia. 109 min. Sound. 16mm B&W. *Rental:* Budget Films, Films Inc & Kerr Film.

Five Fingers. James Mason & Danielle Darrieux. Directed by Joseph L. Mankiewicz. 1952. Fox. 108 min. Sound. 16mm B&W. *Rental:* Films Inc.

Five Fingers of Death. Wang Ping. Directed by Cheng Chang Ho. 1973. Warners. 104 min. Sound. 16mm Color. dubbed. *Rental:* Films Inc, Twyman Films & Williams Films.

Five Forty-Eight, The. Laurence Luckinbill & Mary Beth Hurt. Directed by James Ivory. 1979. Films Inc. 60 min. Sound. 16mm Color. *Rental:* Films Inc. *Sale:* Films Inc. *Sale:* Films Inc, Videotape version.

Five Gates to Hell. Patricia Owens & Dolores Michaels. Directed by James Clavel. 1959. Fox. 98 min. Sound. 16mm B&W. *Rental:* Films Inc.

Five Golden Dragons. Robert Cummings & Brian Donlevy. Directed by Jeremy Summers. 1967. Britain. 93 min. Sound. 16mm Color. *Rental:* Ivy Films, Rep Pic Film & Video Comm. *Sale:* Rep Pic Film.

Five Golden Hours. Cyd Charisse & George Sanders. Directed by Mario Zampi. 1961. Columbia. 90 min. Sound. 16mm B&W. *Rental:* Films Inc, Inst Cinema & Welling Motion Pictures.

Five Guns to Tombstone. James Brown. Directed by Edward L. Cahn. 1961. United Artists. 71 min. Sound. 16mm B&W. *Rental:* MGM United.

Five Guns West. John Lund & Dorothy Malone. Directed by Roger Corman. 1955. American International. 79 min. Sound. 16mm Color. *Rental:* Westcoast Films.

Five Hundred Million Years Beneath the Sea. 1976. Metromedia. (Documentary). 52 min. Sound. 16mm Color. *Rental:* Churchill Films. *Rental:* Churchill Films, Videotape version.

Five Little Peppers & How They Grew. Edith Fellows. Directed by Charles Barton. 1939. Columbia. 60 min. Sound. 16mm B&W. *Rental:* Buchan Pic, Cine Craft, Inst Cinema & Modern Sound.

Five Little Peppers at Home. Edith Fellows. Directed by Charles Barton. 1940. Columbia. 65 min. Sound. 16mm B&W. *Rental:* Cine Craft & Inst Cinema.

Five Little Peppers in Trouble. Edith Fellows. Directed by Charles Barton. 1940. Columbia. 65 min. Sound. 16mm B&W. *Rental:* Charard Motion Pics & Inst Cinema.

Five Lives *see* Cinco Vidas.

Five-Man Army. Peter Graves & James Daly. Directed by Don Taylor. 1970. MGM. 105 min. Sound. 16mm Color. *Rental:* MGM United.

Five Miles to Midnight. Sophia Loren & Anthony Perkins. Directed by Anatole Litvak. 1963. United Artists. 107 min. Sound. 16mm B&W. *Rental:* MGM United.

Five Million Years to Earth. Orig. Title: Quatermass & the Pit. James Donald & Andrew Keir. Directed by Roy Baker. 1968. Fox. 96 min. Sound. 16mm Color. *Rental:* Films Inc & Twyman Films.

Five Minutes to Midnight. 1976. World Focus. (Documentary). 89 min. Sound. 16mm Color. *Rental:* Films Inc. *Sale:* Films Inc. *Sale:* Films Inc, Videotape version.

Five on the Black Hand Side. Leonard Jackson & Virginia Capers. Directed by Oscar Williams. 1973. United Artists. 96 min. Sound. 16mm Color. *Rental:* Films Inc & MGM United.

Five Pennies, The. Danny Kaye & Barbara Bel Geddes. Directed by Melville Shavelson. 1959. Paramount. 117 min. Sound. 16mm Color. *Rental:* Films Inc.

Five Star Final. Edward G. Robinson & Douglas Fairbanks Jr. Directed by Mervyn Leroy. 1931. Warners. 89 min. Sound. 16mm B&W. *Rental:* MGM United.

Five Steps to Danger. Sterling Hayden & Ruth Roman. Directed by Henry S. Kesler. 1957. United Artists. 80 min. Sound. 16mm B&W. *Rental:* MGM United.

Five Thousand Fingers of Dr. T, The. Hans Conried & Peter Lind Hayes. Directed by Roy Rowland. 1953. Columbia. 88 min. Sound. 16mm Color. *Rental:* Buchan Pic, Budget Films, Cine Craft, Bosco Films, Film Pres, Films Inc, Inst Cinema, U of IL Film, Kit Parker, Modern Sound, Newman Film Lib, Natl Film Video, Twyman Films, Westcoast Films, Welling Motion Pictures & Wholesome Film Ctr.

Five Weeks in a Balloon. Red Buttons & Barbara Eden. Directed by Irwin Allen. 1962. Fox. 101 min. Sound. 16mm Color. *Rental:* Films Inc. *Rental:* Films Inc, Anamorphic color version.

Fixed Bayonets. Richard Basehart & Gene Evans. Directed by Samuel Fuller. 1951. Fox. 92 min. Sound. 16mm B&W. *Rental:* Films Inc.

Fixer, The. Alan Bates & Dirk Bogarde. Directed by John Frankenheimer. 1968. MGM. 132 min. Sound. 16mm Color. *Rental:* MGM United. *Rental:* Films Inc, Anamorphic color version. *Rental:* MGM United, Videotape version.

Fixer Dugan. Lee Tracy & Virginia Weidler. Directed by Lew Landers. 1939. RKO. 68 min. Sound. 16mm *Rental:* RKO General Pics.

Flame, The. Vera Ralston & John Carroll. Directed by John H. Auer. 1947. Republic. 97 min. Sound. 16mm B&W. *Rental:* Ivy Films. *Sale:* Rep Pic Film.

Flame, The. Arne Ragneborn & Catrin Westlund. Directed by Arne Ragneborn. 1957. Sweden. 74 min. Sound. 16mm B&W. subtitles. *Rental:* A Twyman Pres & Twyman Films.

Flame & the Fire, The. Directed by Pierre-Dominique Gaisseau. 1966. Continental. (Documentary). 80 min. Sound. 16mm Color. *Rental:* Budget Films & Kino Intl. *Sale:* Kino Intl. *Lease:* Kino Intl.

Flame of Araby. Maureen O'Hara & Jeff Chandler. Directed by Charles Lamont. 1951. Universal. 77 min. Sound. 16mm Color. *Rental:* Swank Motion.

Flame of Stamboul, The. Richard Denning. Directed by Ray Nazarro. 1951. Columbia. 90 min. Sound. 16mm B&W. *Rental:* Inst Cinema.

Flame of the Barbary Coast. John Wayne & Ann Dvorak. Directed by Joseph Kane. 1945. Republic. 91 min. Sound. Videotape B&W. *Rental:* Ivy Films. *Lease:* Rep Pic Film. *Rental:* Tamarelles French Film.

Flame of the Islands. Yvonne De Carlo & James Arness. Directed by Edward Ludwig. 1955. Republic. 90 min. Sound. 16mm Color. *Rental:* Ivy Films. *Sale:* Rep Pic Film.

Flame of the West. Johnny Mack Brown. Directed by Lambert Hillyer. 1945. Monogram. 55 min. Sound. 16mm B&W. *Rental:* Hurlock Cine.

Flame of Youth. Ray MacDonald & Barbara Fuller. Directed by R. G. Springsteen. 1949. Republic. 60 min. Sound. 16mm B&W. *Rental:* Ivy Films. *Sale:* Rep Pic Film.

Flame Over India. Orig. Title: Northwest Frontier. Lauren Bacall & Kenneth More. Directed by J. Lee Thompson. 1960. Britain. 129 min. Sound. 16mm Color. *Rental:* Budget Films, Learning Corp Am & Arcus Film. *Sale:* Learning Corp Am.

Flame Within, The. Ann Harding & Herbert Marshall. Directed by Edmund Goulding. 1935. MGM. 73 min. Sound. 16mm B&W. *Rental:* MGM United.

Flamenco. Pilar Lopez & Maria Luz. Directed by Edgar Neville. Span. 1954. Spain. 79 min. Sound. 16mm Color. subtitles Eng. *Rental:* Films Inc.

Flames on the Volga. Misha Merkulov. Directed by Grigori Roshal. Rus. 1955. Russia. 110 min. Sound. 16mm B&W. subtitles. *Rental:* Corinth Films.

Flaming Bullets. Tex Ritter & Dave O'Brien. Directed by Harry Fraser. 1945. PRC. 59 min. Sound. 16mm B&W. *Sale:* Classics Assoc NY.

Flaming City. Directed by Dick Higgins. 1963. Dick Higgins. (Experimental). 135 min. Sound. 16mm Color. *Rental:* Canyon Cinema.

Flaming Feather. Sterling Hayden & Forrest Tucker. Directed by Ray Enright. 1951. Paramount. 78 min. Sound. 16mm Color. *Rental:* Films Inc.

Flaming Frontier. Bruce Bennett & Jim Davis. Directed by Sam Newfield. 1958. Fox. (Anamorphic). 70 min. Sound. 16mm B&W. *Rental:* Willoughby Peer.

Flaming Fury. Roy Roberts. Directed by George Blair. 1949. Republic. 60 min. Sound. 16mm B&W. *Rental:* Ivy Films. *Sale:* Rep Pic Film.

Flaming Gold. Pat O'Brien & Bill Boyd. Directed by Ralph Ince. 1933. RKO. 52 min. Sound. 16mm *Rental:* RKO General Pics.

Flaming Lead. Ken Maynard. 1939. Saland. 57 min. Sound. 16mm B&W. *Sale:* Cinema Concepts & Reel Images, Videotape version.

Flaming Star. Elvis Presley. Directed by Don Siegel. 1960. Fox. (Anamorphic). 101 min. Sound. 16mm Color. *Rental:* Films Inc.

Flaming Torch, The see Bob Mathias Story.

Flaming Urge, The. Cathy Downs & Harold Lloyd Jr. Directed by Harold Ericson. 1953. Republic. 67 min. Sound. 16mm B&W. *Rental:* Ivy Films.

Flamingo Road. Joan Crawford & Zachary Scott. Directed by Michael Curtiz. 1949. Warners. 96 min. Sound. 16mm B&W. *Rental:* MGM United.

Flannagan Boy, The. Orig. Title: Bad Blonde. Barbara Payton. Directed by Reginald Le Borg. 1953. Lippert. 72 min. Sound. 16mm B&W. *Rental:* Inst Cinema.

Flannelfoot. Ronald Howard. Directed by Maclean Rogers. 1953. Britain. 60 min. Sound. 16mm B&W. *Rental:* Inst Cinema.

Flap. Orig. Title: Nobody Loves Flapping Eagle. Anthony Quinn, Claude Akins & Shelley Winters. Directed by Sir Carol Reed. 1971. Warners. 105 min. Sound. 16mm Color. *Rental:* Films Inc & Inst Cinema.

Flare Up. Raquel Welch & James Stacy. Directed by James Neilson. 1969. MGM. 97 min. Sound. 16mm Color. *Rental:* MGM United.

Flash Gordon. Sam Jones, Melody Anderson & Max Von Sydow. Directed by Mike Hodges. 113 min. Sound. 16mm Color. *Rental:* Swank Motion. *Rental:* Swank Motion, Videotape version.

Flash Gordon Conquers the Universe. Orig. Title: Space Soldiers Conquer the Universe. Buster Crabbe. 1940. Universal. 80 min. Sound. 16mm B&W. *Rental:* Film Pres, Ivy Films, Newman Film Lib & Roas Films. *Sale:* Cinema Concepts. *Sale:* Cinema Concepts, Videotape version.

Flash, the Sheepdog. 1982. Britain. (Cast unlisted). 43 min. Sound. 16mm Color. *Rental:* Janus Films. *Sale:* Lucerne Films.

Flash, the Teenage Otter. 1961. Disney. (Documentary). 48 min. Sound. 16mm Color. *Rental:* Buchan Pic, Cine Craft, Cousino Visual Ed, Disney Prod, Film Ctr DC, Films Inc, Iowa Films, Kent St U Films, Modern Sound, Roas Films, Swank Motion & Twyman Films.

Flashdance. Jennifer Beals & Michael Nouri. Directed by Adrian Lyne. 1983. Paramount. 96 min. Sound. 16mm Color. *Rental:* Films Inc.

Flashing Steeds. Orig. Title: Lighting Steeds. Bill Patton. Directed by Horace B. Carpenter. 1925. Chesterfield. 60 min. Silent. 16mm B&W. *Sale:* Blackhawk Films. *Sale:* Blackhawk Films, Super 8 silent version.

Flashpoint. 1973. Australia. (Cast unlisted). 56 min. Sound. 16mm Color. *Rental:* Aust Info Serv. *Sale:* Aust Info Serv.

Flat Top. Orig. Title: Eagles of the Fleet. Sterling Hayden & Richard Carlson. Directed by Lesley Selander. 1952. Allied Artists. 77 min. Sound. 16mm Color. *Rental:* Ivy Films. *Lease:* Rep Pic Film.

Flatfoot. Bud Spencer & Raymond Pellegrin. Directed by Stefano Vanzina. Ital. 1975. Italy. 100 min. Sound. 16mm Color. subtitles. *Rental:* Modern Sound.

Flaubert. France. (Cast unlisted). 60 min. Sound. 16mm B&W. *Rental:* French Am Cul.

Flavor of Green Tea Over Rice, The. Trans. Title: Ochazuke No Aji. Shin Saburi. Directed by Yasujiro Ozu. Jap. 1953. Japan. 115 min. Sound. 16mm B&W. subtitles. *Rental:* New Cinema & New Yorker Films.

Flaxy Martin. Virginia Mayo & Zachary Scott. Directed by Richard Bare. 1949. Warners. 86 min. Sound. 16mm B&W. *Rental:* MGM United.

Flea in Her Ear, A. Rex Harrison & Rosemary Harris. Directed by Jacques Charon. 1968. Fox. 95 min. Sound. 16mm Color. *Rental:* Films Inc. *Rental:* Films Inc, Anamorphic color version.

Flesh. Wallace Beery & Karen Morley. Directed by John Ford. 1932. MGM. 95 min. Sound. 16mm B&W. *Rental:* MGM United.

Flesh & Blood. Lon Chaney, Noah Beery & Jack Mulhall. Directed by Irving Cummings. 1922. Cummings. 65 min. Silent. 16mm B&W. *Rental:* Budget Films & Em Gee Film Lib. *Sale:* Natl Cinema.

Flesh & the Devil. Greta Garbo & John Gilbert. Directed by Clarence Brown. 1927. MGM. 92 min. Silent. 16mm B&W. *Rental:* MGM United.

Flesh Eaters, The. Martin Kosleck & Rita Morley. Directed by Jack Curtis. 1967. Vulcan. 87 min. Sound. 16mm B&W. *Rental:* Films Inc.

Flesh Gordon. Jason Williams. Directed by Howard Ziehm & Michael Benveniste. 1974. Mammoth. 70 min. Sound. 16mm Color. *Rental:* Ivy Films. *Sale:* Cinema Concepts, Videotape version.

Flic, Un see Dirty Money.

Fliegende Klassenzimmer, Das. Trans. Title: Flying Classroom. Paul Dahlke. Directed by Kurt Hoffman. Ger. 1954. Germany. 90 min. Sound. 16mm B&W. subtitles. *Rental:* Syracuse U Film & Trans-World Films.

Flight. Jack Holt & Ralph Graves. Directed by Frank Capra. 1929. Columbia. 116 min. Sound. 16mm B&W. *Rental:* Kit Parker.

Flight. Efrian Ramirez & Louis Bispo. 1961. San Francisco Films. 81 min. Sound. 16mm B&W. *Rental:* Kit Parker.

Flight Angels. Jane Wyman & Dennis Morgan. Directed by Lewis Seiler. 1940. Warners. 74 min. Sound. 16mm B&W. *Rental:* MGM United.

Flight at Midnight. Jean Parker & Robert Armstrong. Directed by Sidney Salkow. 1939. Republic. 54 min. Sound. 16mm B&W. *Rental:* Ivy Films. *Sale:* Rep Pic Film.

Flight Commander *see* Dawn Patrol.

Flight for Freedom. Rosalind Russell & Fred MacMurray. Directed by Lothar Mendes. 1943. RKO. 101 min. Sound. 16mm B&W. *Rental:* Films Inc.

Flight for Glory. Dagoberto Rodriguez. 1962. Mexico. 84 min. Sound. 16mm Color. *Rental:* Ivy Films.

Flight from Ashiya. Richard Widmark & Yul Brynner. Directed by Michael Anderson. 1964. United Artists. 100 min. Sound. 16mm Color. *Rental:* MGM United.

Flight from Destiny. Orig. Title: Invitation to a Murder. Thomas Mitchell & Jeffrey Lynn. Directed by Vincent Sherman. 1941. Warners. 74 min. Sound. 16mm B&W. *Rental:* MGM United.

Flight from Glory. Van Heflin & Chester Morris. Directed by Lew Landers. 1937. RKO. 67 min. Sound. 16mm *Rental:* RKO General Pics.

Flight from Hollywood. 1963. CBS. (Documentary). 60 min. Sound. 16mm B&W. *Sale:* CBS Inc.

Flight from Justice *see* Federal Manhunt.

Flight from Singapore. Patrick Allen. Directed by Dudley Birch. 1965. Commonwealth. 80 min. Sound. 16mm B&W. *Rental:* Ivy Films.

Flight Lieutenant. Glenn Ford & Pat O'Brien. Directed by Sidney Salkow. 1942. Columbia. 90 min. Sound. 16mm B&W. *Lease:* Time-Life Multimedia.

Flight Nurse. Joan Leslie & Forrest Tucker. Directed by Allan Dwan. 1953. Republic. 88 min. Sound. 16mm B&W. *Rental:* Ivy Films. *Sale:* Rep Pic Film.

Flight of the Cougar, The. Lassie & Merry Anders. Wrather. 75 min. Sound. 16mm Color. *Rental:* Modern Sound.

Flight of the Doves, The. Ron Moody, Jack Wild & Dorothy McGuire. Directed by Ralph Nelson. 1970. Columbia. 101 min. Sound. 16mm Color. *Rental:* Alba House, Arcus Film, Bosco Films, Buchan Pic, Budget Films, Cine Craft, Film Ctr DC, Films Inc, Inst Cinema, Modern Sound, Newman Film Lib, Roas Films, Swank Motion, Twyman Films, Video Comm, Welling Motion Pictures, Westcoast Films, Wholesome Film Ctr, Williams Films & Willoughby Peer.

Flight of the Lost Balloon, The. Marshall Thompson & Mala Powers. Directed by Bernard Woolner. 1961. Woolner. 91 min. Sound. 16mm Color. *Rental:* Budget Films, Ivy Films, Video Comm & Westcoast Films.

Flight of the Penguins, The. 1976. Metromedia. (Documentary). 52 min. Sound. 16mm Color. *Rental:* Churchill Films. *Rental:* Churchhill Films, Videotape version.

Flight of the Phoenix, The. James Stewart & Richard Attenborough. Directed by Robert Aldrich. 1966. Fox. 147 min. Sound. 16mm Color. *Rental:* Films Inc & Twyman Films.

Flight of the White Heron, The. Orig. Title: Royal Tour of Queen Elizabeth & Philip, The. 1954. Britain. (Anamorphic) (Documentary). 52 min. Sound. 16mm Color. *Rental:* Films Inc.

Flight of the Whooping Crane, The. 59 min. Sound. 16mm Color. *Rental:* Natl Geog. *Sale:* Natl Geog. *Sale:* Natl Geog, Videotape version.

Flight That Disappeared, The. Craig Hill & Paula Raymond. Directed by Reginald Le Borg. 1961. United Artists. 72 min. Sound. 16mm B&W. *Rental:* MGM United.

Flight to Fury. Dewey Martin & Fay Spain. Directed by Monte Hellman. 1964. Mexico. 80 min. Sound. 16mm B&W. *Rental:* Ivy Films.

Flight to Hong Kong. Rory Calhoun & Barbara Rush. Directed by Joseph Newman. 1956. United Artists. 88 min. Sound. 16mm B&W. *Rental:* MGM United.

Flight to Mars. Marguerite Chapman & Cameron Mitchell. Directed by Lesley Selander. 1951. Monogram. 72 min. Sound. 16mm Color. *Rental:* Wade Williams. *Sale:* Rep Pic Film.

Flight to Nowhere. Alan Curtis & Evelyn Ankers. Directed by William Rowland. 1948. Screen Guild. 77 min. Sound. 16mm B&W. *Rental:* Charard Motion Pics, Inst Cinema & Mogulls Films.

Flight to Tangier. Joan Fontaine & Jack Palance. Directed by Charles Marquis Warren. 1953. Paramount. 90 min. Sound. 16mm Color. *Rental:* Films Inc.

Flim-Flam Man. George C. Scott & Michael Sarrazin. Directed by Irwin Kershner. 1967. Fox. (Anamorphic). 104 min. Sound. 16mm Color. *Rental:* Films Inc, Twyman Films, Welling Motion Pictures, Westcoast Films & Williams Films.

Flip Side. 1970. Gospel. (Cast unlisted). 51 min. Sound. 16mm Color. *Rental:* Roas Films.

Flipchicks. 60 min. Videotape Color. *Sale:* Videx Home Lib.

Flipper. Chuck Connors & Luke Halpin. Directed by James B. Clark. 1963. MGM. 90 min. Sound. 16mm Color. *Rental:* MGM United.

Flipper & the Elephant. Brian Kelly, Luke Halpin & Tommy Norden. 70 min. Sound. 16mm Color. *Rental:* Williams Films.

Flipper & the Odyssey. Brian Kelly, Luke Halpin & Tommy Norden. 70 min. Sound. 16mm Color. *Rental:* Williams Films.

Flipper's New Adventure. Luke Halpin & Pamela Franklin. Directed by Leon Benson. 1964. MGM. 103 min. Sound. 16mm Color. *Rental:* MGM United.

Flirtation Walk. Dick Powell & Ruby Keeler. Directed by Frank Borzage. 1934. Warners. 97 min. Sound. 16mm B&W. *Rental:* MGM United.

Flirting Widow, The. Basil Rathbone & Leila Hyams. Directed by William A. Seiter. 1930. Warners. 74 min. Sound. 16mm B&W. *Rental:* MGM United.

Flirting with Danger. Robert Armstrong & Edgar Kennedy. Directed by Vin Moore. 1934. Monogram. 70 min. Sound. 16mm B&W. *Rental:* Mogulls Films.

Flirting with Fate. Douglas Fairbanks. Directed by Christy Cabanne. 1916. Fine Arts-Triangle. 55 min. Silent. 16mm B&W. *Rental:* Budget Films & Em Gee Film Lib. *Sale:* Blackhawk Films, E Finney & Morcraft Films. *Rental:* Ivy Films, *Sale:* Blackhawk Films, Super 8 silent version.

Flirting with Fate. Joe E. Brown. Directed by Frank McDonald. 1938. MGM. 70 min. Sound. 16mm B&W. *Rental:* Alba House, Film Ctr DC, Ivy Films & Welling Motion Pictures.

Float Like a Butterfly, Sting Like a Bee. Directed by William Klein. 1969. Grove. (Documentary). 94 min. Sound. 16mm B&W. *Rental:* Grove. *Sale:* Grove.

Floating Cloud. Hideko Takamine. Directed by Mikio Naruse. Jap. 1955. Japan. 123 min. Sound. 16mm B&W. subtitles. *Rental:* Corinth Films.

Floating Dutchman, The. Dermot Walsh & Sidney Tafler. Directed by Vernon Sewell. 1953. Britain. 82 min. Sound. 16mm B&W. *Rental:* Video Comm.

Floating Weeds. Orig. Title: Ukigusa. Ganjiro Nakamura & Haruko Sugimura. Directed by Yasujiro Ozu. Jap. 1959. Japan. 128 min. Sound. 16mm Color. subtitles. *Rental:* Budget Films, Films Inc, Janus & Kit Parker.

Floorshow. 1978. 90 min. Sound. 16mm B&W. *Rental:* Canyon Cinema.

Flora: Scenes from a Leadership Convention. Directed by Peter Raymont. 1977. Canada. (Documentary). 59 min. Sound. 16mm Color. *Rental:* Natl Film CN. *Sale:* Natl Film CN.

Floradora Girl. Trans. Title: Gay Nineties, The. Marion Davies & Ilka Chase. Directed by Harry Beaumont. 1930. MGM. 80 min. Sound. 16mm B&W. *Rental:* MGM United.

Florentine Dagger, The. Donald Woods & Margaret Lindsay. Directed by Robert Florey. 1935. Warners. 69 min. Sound. 16mm B&W. *Rental:* MGM United.

Florian. Robert Young & Helen Gilbert. Directed by Edwin L. Marin. 1940. MGM. 93 min. Sound. 16mm B&W. *Rental:* MGM United.

Flower Drum Song, The. Nancy Kwan & James Shigeta. Directed by Henry Koster. 1961. Universal. 131 min. Sound. 16mm Color. *Rental:* Williams Films.

Flower Out of Place, A. Linda Ronstadt & Johnny Cash. 50 min. Videotape Color. *Sale:* Cinema Concepts.

Flower Thief, The. Taylor Mead. Directed by Ron Rice. 1961. Ron Rice. 70 min. Sound. 16mm B&W. *Rental:* Canyon Cinema.

Flowering of Harmony, The. 1980. Canada. (Documentary). 57 min. Sound. 16mm Color. *Rental:* Time-Life Multimedia. *Sale:* Time-Life Multimedia. *Sale:* Time-Life Multimedia, Videotape version.

Flowers of Nice, The *see* Blumen Aus Nizza.

Flowers on a One-Way Street. 1969. Canada. (Documentary). 60 min. Sound. 16mm B&W. *Rental:* U Cal Media, Films Inc, Syracuse U Film & U Mich Media. *Sale:* Films Inc. *Sale:* Films Inc, Videotape version.

Flowing Gold. John Garfield & Pat O'Brien. Directed by Alfred E. Green. 1940. Warners. 82 min. Sound. 16mm B&W. *Rental:* MGM United.

Fluffy. Tony Randall & Shirley Jones. Directed by Earl Bellamy. 1965. Universal. 92 min. Sound. 16mm Color. *Rental:* Swank Motion.

Flute & the Arrow, The. Ginju & Riga. Directed by Arne Sucksdorff. 1958. Janus. 78 min. Sound. 16mm Color. *Rental:* Janus Films.

Fly, The. Vincent Price & Patricia Owens. Directed by Kurt Neumann. 1958. Fox. 95 min. Sound. 16mm Color. *Rental:* Charard Motion Pics, Films Inc, Twyman Films, Video Comm, Williams Films & Willoughby Peer. *Rental:* Films Inc, Anamorphic color version.

Fly-Away Baby. Orig. Title: Crime in the Clouds. Glenda Farrell & Barton Maclane. Directed by Frank McDonald. 1937. Warners. 60 min. Sound. 16mm B&W. *Rental:* MGM United.

Flying Carpet, The. Orig. Title: Old Khottabych. Nikolai Volkov. Directed by G. Kazansky. 1956. 85 min. Sound. 16mm B&W. *Rental:* Corinth Films.

Flying Classroom *see* Fliegende Klassenzimmer.

Flying Deuces. Stan Laurel & Oliver Hardy. Directed by Edward Sutherland. 1939. RKO. 70 min. Sound. B&W. *Rental:* Arcus Film, Budget Films, Classic Film Mus, Charard Motion Pics, Em Gee Film Lib, Film Ctr DC, Ivy Films, Newman Film Lib, Roas Films, Swank Motion, Syracuse U Film, Video Comm, Westcoast Films, Wholesome Film Ctr, Williams Films & Willoughby Peer. *Sale:* Classic Film Mus, Cinema Concepts, Festival Films, Morcraft Films, Natl Cinema, Reel Images & Video Comm. *Rental:* Ivy Films, *Sale:* Festival Films, Ivy Films, Morcraft Films & Tamarelles French Film, Videotape version.

Flying Devils. Ralph Bellamy & Bruce Cabot. Directed by Merian C. Cooper. 1933. RKO. 62 min. Sound. 16mm *Rental:* RKO General Pics.

Flying Down to Rio. Fred Astaire & Ginger Rogers. Directed by Thornton Freeland. 1933. RKO. 100 min. Sound. 16mm B&W. *Rental:* Films Inc. *Lease:* Films Inc. *Rental:* RKO General Pics, 89 min. version.

Flying Dutchman, The. Anna Prucnal & Fred Duren. Directed by Joachim Herz. Ger. 1964. Germany. 100 min. Sound. 16mm B&W. subtitles Eng. *Rental:* Films Inc.

Flying Eye, The. Julia Lockwood & Harcourt Williams. Directed by William Hammond. 1955. Britain. 54 min. Sound. 16mm B&W. *Sale:* Lucerne Films.

Flying Fontaines, The. Michael Callan & Joan Evans. Directed by George Sherman. 1959. Columbia. 84 min. Sound. 16mm Color. *Rental:* Cine Craft, Charard Motion Pics, Film Ctr DC, Films Inc & Welling Motion Pictures.

Flying Fool, The. William Boyd & Marie Prevost. Directed by Lewis Seiler. 1929. Pathe. 75 min. Sound. 16mm B&W. *Rental:* Em Gee Film Lib. *Sale:* Cinema Concepts, Natl Cinema & Reel Images.

Flying Fortress, The. Richard Greene. Directed by William Forde. 1942. Warners. 68 min. Sound. 16mm B&W. *Rental:* MGM United.

Flying Irishman, The. Douglas Corrigan & Paul Kelly. Directed by Leigh Jason. 1939. RKO. 72 min. Sound. 16mm B&W. *Rental:* Films Inc.

Flying Lariats. Wally Wales. Directed by Alvin J. Neitz. Sound. 16mm B&W. *Sale:* Morcraft Films.

Flying Leathernecks. John Wayne & Robert Ryan. Directed by Nicholas Ray. 1951. RKO. 102 min. Sound. Videotape Color. *Sale:* Films Inc.

Flying Matchmaker, The. Mike Burstein. Directed by Israel Baker. 1970. Israel. 104 min. Sound. 16mm Color. *Rental:* Films Inc.

Flying Missile. Glenn Ford & Viveca Lindfors. Directed by Henry Levin. 1950. Columbia. 90 min. Sound. 16mm B&W. *Rental:* Films Inc & Inst Cinema.

Flying Platform: Number 1. Orig. Title: F.P.I. Leslie Fenton, Conrad Veidt & Jill Esmond. 1932. Britain. 77 min. Sound. 16mm B&W. *Rental:* Janus Films.

Flying Serpent, The. George Zucco & Ralph Lewis. Directed by Sherman Scott. 1946. PRC. 60 min. Sound. 16mm B&W.

Flying Tigers, The. John Wayne & John Carroll. Directed by David Miller. 1942. Republic. 101 min. Sound. 16mm B&W. *Rental:* Budget Films & Ivy Films. *Lease:* Rep Pic Film. *Sale:* Nostalgia Merchant, Super 8 sound version. *Sale:* Tamarelles French Film, Videotape version.

Flying Wild. East Side Kids. Directed by William West. 1941. Monogram. 63 min. Sound. 16mm B&W. *Rental:* Budget Films.

FM. Michael Brandon, Eileen Brennan & Alex Karras. Directed by John A. Alonzo. 1978. Universal. 104 min. Sound. 16mm Color. *Rental:* Swank Motion.

Focus on Nineteen-Ten & Nineteen-Nineteen. 58 min. Sound. 16mm Color. *Rental:* MTI Teleprograms Inc.

Focus on the Fifties. 1983. ABC. (Documentary). 58 min. Sound. 16mm Color. *Rental:* MTI Tele. *Sale:* MTI Tele.

Focus on the Forties. 1980. ABC. (Documentary). 58 min. Sound. 16mm Color. *Rental:* U of IL Film. *Sale:* MTI Tele, Videotape version.

Focus on the Thirties. 1981. ABC. (Documentary). 58 min. Sound. 16mm Color. *Rental:* MTI Tele.

Focus on the Twenties. 1981. ABC. (Documentary). 58 min. Sound. 16mm Color. *Rental:* MTI Tele.

Focus on 1960-1964: The Kennedy Years. 1983. ABC. (Documentary). 58 min. Sound. 16mm Color. *Rental:* MTI Tele. *Sale:* MTI Tele.

Focus on 1965-1969: The Angry Years. 1983. ABC. (Documentary). 58 min. Sound. 16mm Color. *Rental:* MTI Tele. *Sale:* MTI Tele.

Fog, The. Adrienne Barbeau, Janet Leigh & Jamie Lee Curtis. Directed by John Carpenter. 1980. Embassy. 91 min. Sound. 16mm Color. *Rental:* Films Inc. *Rental:* Films Inc, Anamorphic version.

Fog Island. Lionel Atwill & George Zucco. Directed by Terry Morse. 1945. PRC. 75 min. Sound. 16mm B&W. *Rental:* Ivy Films, Mogulls Films & Westcoast Films. *Sale:* Classics Assoc NY, Morcraft Films & Rep Pic Film. *Sale:* Morcraft Films, Super 8 sound version. *Sale:* Morcraft Films, Videotape version.

Fog Over Frisco. Bette Davis & Donald Woods. Directed by William Dieterle. 1934. Warners. 68 min. Sound. 16mm B&W. *Rental:* MGM United.

Folies Bergere. Orig. Title: Man from the Folies Bergere, The. Maurice Chevalier & Ann Sothern. Directed by Roy Del Ruth. 1935. United Artists. 84 min. Sound. 16mm B&W. *Rental:* Films Inc.

Folk Music in the Concert Hall. 1964. CBS. (Documentary). 53 min. Sound. 16mm B&W. *Rental:* U of IL Film, McGraw-Hill Films. *Sale:* McGraw-Hill Films.

Folk Way, The. 1979. PBS. (Documentary). 59 min. Videotape Color. *Rental:* PBS Video. *Sale:* PBS Video.

Folks, The. Directed by Jimmie Mannas. 1970. Grove. (Documentary). 55 min. Sound. 16mm B&W. *Rental:* Grove. *Sale:* Grove.

Follow Me. Directed by Gene McCabe. 1969. Cinerama. (Documentary). 93 min. Sound. 16mm Color. *Rental:* Swank Motion.

Follow Me, Boys. Fred MacMurray, Lillian Gish & Vera Miles. Directed by Norman Tokar. 1966. Disney. 128 min. Sound. 16mm Color. *Rental:* Buchan Pic, Cine Craft, Disney Prod, Elliot Film Co, Film Ctr DC, Film Pres, Films Inc, MGM United, Modern Sound, Newman Film Lib, Swank Motion, Twyman Films, U of IL Film & Williams Films.

Follow Me Quietly. William Lundigan & Dorothy Patrick. Directed by Richard Fleischer. 1950. RKO. 59 min. Sound. 16mm *Rental:* RKO General Pics.

Follow That Camel. (Cast unlisted). Videotape *Sale:* Vidamerica.

Follow That Dream. Elvis Presley & Arthur O'Connell. Directed by Gordon Douglas. 1962. United Artists. 109 min. Sound. 16mm Color. *Rental:* MGM United.

Follow the Boys. Paula Prentiss & Jim Hutton. Directed by Richard Thorpe. 1963. MGM. 95 min. Sound. 16mm Color. *Rental:* Bosco Films, MGM United, Welling Motion Pictures & Westcoast Films. *Rental:* MGM United, Anamorphic version. *Rental:* Welling Motion Pictures, 128 mins. version.

Follow the Fleet. Fred Astaire & Ginger Rogers. Directed by Mark Sandrich. 1936. RKO. 110 min. Sound. 16mm B&W. *Rental:* Films Inc.

Follow the Hunter. Onslow Stevens. Directed by William Claxton. 1954. Lippert. 70 min. Sound. 16mm B&W. *Rental:* Budget Films, Film Ctr DC & Willoughby Peer.

Follow the Leader. Bowery Boys. Directed by William Beaudine. 1944. Monogram. 63 min. Sound. 16mm B&W. *Rental:* Ivy Films & Modern Sound.

Follow the North Star. 1975. ABC. (Cast unlisted). 47 min. Sound. 16mm Color. *Rental:* Time-Life Multimedia & U Mich Media. *Sale:* Time-Life Multimedia. *Rental:* Time-Life Multimedia, *Sale:* Time-Life Multimedia, Videotape version.

Follow the Sun. Glenn Ford & Anne Baxter. Directed by Sidney Lanfield. 1951. Fox. 93 min. Sound. 16mm B&W. *Rental:* Films Inc.

Follow Your Heart. Marian Talley & Michael Bartlett. Directed by Aubrey Scotto. 1936. Republic. 80 min. Sound. 16mm B&W. *Rental:* Ivy Films. *Sale:* Rep Pic Film.

Folly on the Hill. Directed by Vincent Tovell. 1972. Canada. (Documentary). 57 min. Sound. 16mm Color. *Rental:* Natl Film CN. *Sale:* Natl Film CN.

Food Crisis. 1966. NET. (Documentary). 60 min. Sound. 16mm B&W. *Rental:* Indiana AV Ctr. *Sale:* Indiana AV Ctr.

Food, Fads & Misinformation. 1976. US Government. (Lecture). 68 min. Videotape Color. *Sale:* Natl AV Ctr.

Food for All. 1975. ABC. (Documentary). 60 min. Sound. 16mm Color. *Rental:* Natl Churches Christ.

Food for Special Dietary Uses. 1976. US Government. (Lecture). 73 min. Videotape Color. *Sale:* Natl AV Ctr.

Food: Green Grow the Profits. 1974. ABC. (Documentary). 56 min. Sound. 16mm Color. *Rental:* Films Inc. *Sale:* Films Inc.

Food of the Gods, The. Marjoe Gortner & Ida Lupino. Directed by Bert I. Gordon. 1976. American International. 89 min. Sound. 16mm Color. *Rental:* Swank Motion & Welling Motion Picture.

Food Sense. 1976. Penn State. (Documentary). 59 min. Videotape Color. *Rental:* Penn St AV Serv. *Sale:* Penn St AV Ctr.

Food Show, The. 1980. Consumer Reports. (Documentary). 47 min. Sound. 16mm Color. *Sale:* Films Inc. *Sale:* Films Inc, Videotape version.

Fool Killer, The. Anthony Perkins & Arnold Moss. Directed by Servando Gonzales. 1965. Landau. 98 min. Sound. 16mm B&W. *Rental:* Ivy Films & Rep Pic Film. *Lease:* Rep Pic Film.

Fool There Was, A. Theda Bara. Directed by Frank Powell. 1914. Fox. 82 min. Silent. 16mm B&W. *Rental:* Budget Films, Em Gee Film Lib & Museum Mod Art. *Sale:* Glenn Photo. *Sale:* Glenn Photo, Super 8 silent version.

Foolin' Around. Gary Busey & Annette O'Toole. Directed by Richard T. Heffron. 1980. USA. 101 min. Sound. 16mm Color. *Rental:* Budget Films & Welling Motion Pictures.

Foolish Girls *see* Desirable Lady.

Foolish Wives. Erich Von Stroheim & Mae Busch. Directed by Erich Von Stroheim. 1921. Universal. 88 min. Silent. 16mm B&W. *Rental:* A Twyman Pres, Budget Films, Em Gee Film Lib, Films Inc, Iowa Films, Ivy Films, Kerr Film, Museum Mod Art, Swank Motion, Utah Media, Video Comm, Welling Motion Pictures & Willoughby Peer. *Sale:* Cinema Concepts, E Finney, Griggs Movie & Reel Images. *Rental:* Kit Parker & Twyman Films, *Sale:* Blackhawk Films & See-Art Films, Sound 16mm version. *Rental:* Ivy Films, *Sale:* Blackhawk Films, Super 8 silent version. *Sale:* Tamarelles French Film & Video Comm, Videotape version. *Rental:* Utah Media, 80 min. version. *Sale:* Festival Films, *Rental:* Kit Parker, 81 min. version. *Rental:* Images Film & Kit Parker, 107 min., Music Score version.

Fools. Jason Robards & Katherine Ross. Directed by Tom Gries. 1970. Cinerama. 93 min. Sound. 16mm Color. *Rental:* Swank Motion.

Fools for Scandal. Carole Lombard & Ralph Bellamy. Directed by Mervyn LeRoy. 1938. Warners. 81 min. Sound. 16mm B&W. *Rental:* MGM United.

Fool's Gold. William Boyd. Directed by George Archainbaud. 1946. United Artists. 64 min. Sound. 16mm B&W. *Sale:* Cinema Concepts.

Fool's Parade. James Stewart, George Kennedy & Anne Baxter. Directed by Andrew V. McLaglen. 1971. Columbia. 98 min. Sound. 16mm Color. *Rental:* Cine Craft, Films Inc, Kerr Film, Images Film, Roas Films, Welling Motion Pictures, Westcoast Films, Wholesome Film Ctr & Willoughby Peer.

Football Coach *see* College Coach.

Football Follies: Super Bowl V. 48 min. Sound. Videotape Color. *Sale:* Vidamerica.

Footlight Fever. Elyse Knox & Alan Mowbray. Directed by Irving Reis. 1941. RKO. 69 min. Sound. 16mm *Rental:* RKO General Pics.

Footlight Glamour. Penny Singleton & Arthur Lake. Directed by Frank R. Strayer. 1944. Columbia. 75 min. Sound. 16mm B&W. *Rental:* Video Comm. *Lease:* King Features.

Footlight Parade. James Cagney & Joan Blondell. Directed by Lloyd Bacon. 1933. Warners. 104 min. Sound. 16mm B&W. *Rental:* MGM United.

Footlight Serenade. Betty Grable, John Payne & Victor Mature. Directed by Gregory Ratoff. 1942. Fox. 80 min. Sound. 16mm B&W. *Rental:* Films Inc.

Footlight Varieties. Red Buttons & Jack Paar. Directed by Hal Yates. 1951. RKO. (Anthology). 61 min. Sound. 16mm *Rental:* Films Inc.

Footloose Heiress. Ann Sheridan & Craig Reynolds. Directed by William Clemens. 1937. Warners. 59 min. Sound. 16mm B&W. *Rental:* MGM United.

Footnotes on the Atomic Age. 1970. 52 min. Sound. 16mm Color. *Rental:* U Mich Media.

Footprint of the Buddha, The. 1977. Britain. (Documentary). 52 min. Sound. 16mm Color. *Rental:* Iowa Films, U of Il Film & U Mich Media.

Footsteps in the Dark. Errol Flynn & Brenda Marshall. Directed by Lloyd Bacon. 1941. Warners. 96 min. Sound. 16mm B&W. *Rental:* MGM United.

Footsteps in the Fog. Stewart Granger & Jean Simmons. Directed by Arthur Lubin. 1958. Columbia. 90 min. Sound. 16mm B&W. *Rental:* Charard Motion Pics, Films Inc, Inst Cinema & Modern Sound.

Footsteps in the Night. Bill Elliott & Don Haggerty. Directed by Jean Yarbrough. 1957. Allied Artists. 61 min. Sound. 16mm B&W. *Rental:* Hurlock Cine.

Footsteps of Youth. Orig. Title: In His Steps. Eric Linden & Cecelia Parker. Directed by Karl Brown. 1936. Grand National. 80 min. Sound. 16mm B&W. *Rental:* Film Classics & Mogulls Films.

Footsteps on the Moon. 1967. Seven Arts. (Documentary). 60 min. Sound. 16mm Color. *Rental:* Video Comm. *Lease:* Video Comm. *Rental:* Video Comm, Videotape version.

For a Few Dollars More. Clint Eastwood & Lee Van Cleef. Directed by Sergio Leone. 1967. Italy. 130 min. Sound. 16mm Color. dubbed. *Rental:* MGM United.

For Beauty's Sake. Ned Sparks & Marjorie Weaver. Directed by Shepard Traube. 1941. Fox. 62 min. Sound. 16mm B&W. *Rental:* Films Inc.

For Boys Only Is for Girls, Too. Xerox. (Cast unlisted). 61 min. Sound. 16mm Color. *Sale:* Xerox Films.

For Export Only: Pesticides & Pills. 2 pts. 1981. 56 min. 16mm Color. *Rental:* Icarus Films. *Sale:* Icarus Films. *Rental:* Icarus Films, *Sale:* Icarus Films, Videotape version.

For Heaven's Sake. Harold Lloyd. Directed by Sam Taylor. 1926. Paramount. (Music & sound effects only). 60 min. Sound. 16mm B&W. *Rental:* Budget Films, Films Inc & Kino Intl. *Sale:* Films Inc. *Sale:* Blackhawk Films, Super 8 sound version. *Sale:* Blackhawk Films, Super 8 silent version.

For Heaven's Sake. Joan Bennett, Clifton Webb & Robert Cummings. Directed by George Seaton. 1950. Fox. 92 min. Sound. 16mm B&W. *Rental:* Films Inc.

For King & Country. Directed by Munroe Scott. 1973. Canada. (Documentary). 57 min. Sound. 16mm Color. *Rental:* Natl Film CN. *Sale:* Natl Film CN.

For Love of Ivy. Sidney Poitier & Abbey Lincoln. Directed by Daniel Mann. 1969. ABC. 102 min. Sound. 16mm Color. *Rental:* Films Inc. *Sale:* ABC Film Lib, Super 8 sound version.

For Love or Money *see* Cash.

For Love or Money. Kirk Douglas & Mitzi Gaynor. Directed by Michael Gordon. 1963. Universal. 108 min. Sound. 16mm Color. *Rental:* Swank Motion.

For Me & My Gal. Judy Garland, George Murphy & Gene Kelly. Directed by Busby Berkeley. 1942. MGM. 109 min. Sound. 16mm B&W. *Rental:* MGM United. *Rental:* MGM United, Videotape version.

For Men Only *see* Tall Lie.

For Pete's Sake. Barbra Streisand & Estelle Parsons. Directed by Peter Yates. 1974. Columbia. 90 min. Sound. 16mm Color. *Rental:* Arcus Film, Bosco Films, Buchan Pic, Budget Films, Cine Craft, Film Ctr DC, Films Inc, Inst Cinema, Ivy Films, Modern Sound, Newman Film Lib, Roas Films, Swank Motion, Twyman Films, Welling Motion Pictures, Westcoast Films, Wholesome Film Ctr & Williams Films.

For Singles Only. John Saxon, Lana Wood & Milton Berle. Directed by Arthur Dreifuss. 1968. Columbia/USA. 91 min. Sound. 16mm Color. *Rental:* Budget Films, Charard Motion Pics & Welling Motion Pictures.

For the Child's Own Good. 1980. NBC. (Documentary). 46 min. Sound. 16mm Color. *Rental:* Films Inc. *Sale:* Films Inc. *Sale:* Films Inc, Videotape version.

For the First Time. Mario Lanza & Zsa Zsa Gabor. Directed by Rudolph Mate. 1959. MGM. 97 min. Sound. 16mm Color. *Rental:* MGM United. *Rental:* MGM United, Anamorphic color version.

For the Good of All. 58 min. Sound. Videotape *Rental:* PBS Video. *Sale:* PBS Video.

For the Love of Benji. Benji, Patsy Garrett & Ed Nelson. Directed by Joe Camp. 1977. Mulberry Square. 85 min. Sound. 16mm Color. *Rental:* Films Inc, Modern Sound, Swank Motion, Twyman Films & Williams Films.

For the Love of Dance. Directed by John N. Smith. 1981. 57 min. Sound. 16mm Color. *Rental:* Natl Film CN & U Cal Media.

For the Love of Fred. Ritts Puppets. 1971. NBC. 48 min. Sound. 16mm Color. *Rental:* Films Inc & Twyman Films. *Sale:* Films Inc.

For the Love of Mary. Deanna Durbin & Edmond O'Brien. Directed by Frederick De Cordova. 1948. Universal. 92 min. Sound. 16mm B&W. *Rental:* Swank Motion.

For the Love of Mike. Richard Basehart & Rex Allen. Directed by George Sherman. 1960. Fox. 84 min. Sound. 16mm Color. *Rental:* Films Inc & Willoughby Peer.

For the Love of Rusty. Ted Donaldson. Directed by John Sturges. 1947. Columbia. 69 min. Sound. 16mm B&W. *Rental:* Cine Craft, Inst Cinema & Roas Films.

For Those Who Think Young. James Darren & Pamela Tiffin. Directed by Leslie Martinson. 1964. United Artists. (Anamorphic). 96 min. Sound. 16mm Color. *Rental:* MGM United.

For Whom the Bell Tolls. Ingrid Bergman & Gary Cooper. Directed by Sam Wood. 1943. Paramount. 132 min. Sound. 16mm Color. *Rental:* Twyman Films.

For Your Eyes Only. Roger Moore & Topol. Directed by John Glen. 1981. MGM-UA. 127 min. Sound. 16mm Color. *Rental:* MGM United. *Rental:* MGM United, Videotape version.

Forbidden. Barbara Stanwyck & Adolphe Menjou. Directed by Frank Capra. 1932. Columbia. 87 min. Sound. 16mm B&W. *Rental:* Kit Parker.

Forbidden Alliance. Norma Shearer, Fredric March & Charles Laughton. Directed by Sidney Franklin. 1934. MGM. 111 min. Sound. 16mm B&W. *Rental:* MGM United.

Forbidden Area. Charlton Heston, Charles Bickford & Vincent Price. Directed by Tab Hunter. 1957. CBS. 99 min. Sound. 16mm B&W. *Rental:* Bosco Films.

Forbidden City. Thomas Meighan & Norma Talmadge. Directed by Sidney Franklin. 1918. Select. 60 min. Silent. 16mm B&W. *Rental:* Em Gee Film Lib. *Sale:* Cinema Concepts & Em Gee Film Lib. *Sale:* Tamarelles French Film, Videotape version.

Forbidden Desire. Trevor Howard. Directed by Henri Verneuil. France. Sound. 16mm B&W. dubbed. *Rental:* Em Gee Film Lib.

Forbidden Fruit. Fernandel & Francoise Arnall. Directed by Henri Verneuil. 1959. France. 97 min. Sound. 16mm B&W. dubbed. *Rental:* Charard Motion Pics.

Forbidden Games. Brigitte Fossey & Georges Poujouly. Directed by Rene Clement. Fr. 1952. France. 90 min. Sound. 16mm B&W. subtitles. *Rental:* Films Inc & New Cinema.

Forbidden Heaven. Charles Farrell & Charlotte Henry. Directed by Reginald Barker. 1936. Republic. 70 min. Sound. 16mm B&W. *Rental:* Ivy Films. *Sale:* Rep Pic Film.

Forbidden Jungle. Don Harvey & Forrest Taylor. Directed by Robert Tansey. 1950. Eagle Lion. 67 min. Sound. 16mm B&W. *Rental:* Budget Films.

Forbidden Music. Trans. Title: Musica Proibita. Richard Tauber & Jimmy Durante. Directed by Walter Forde. 1938. Britain. 80 min. Sound. 16mm B&W. *Rental:* Budget Films, Em Gee Film Lib & Mogulls Films. *Sale:* Cinema Concepts & Natl Cinema.

Forbidden Music. Tito Gobbi & Maria Mercader. Ital. 1942. Italy. 85 min. Sound. 16mm B&W. subtitles. *Rental:* Mogulls Films.

Forbidden Planet. Walter Pidgeon & Anne Francis. Directed by Fred M. Wilcox. 1956. MGM. 98 min. Sound. 16mm Color. *Rental:* MGM United. *Rental:* MGM United, Anamorphic color version. *Rental:* MGM United, Videotape version.

Forbidden Street. Maureen O'Hara & Dana Andrews. Directed by Jean Negulesco. 1949. RKO. 91 min. Sound. 16mm B&W. *Rental:* Films Inc.

Forbidden Trails. Buck Jones & Tim McCoy. Directed by Robert N. Bradbury. 1941. Monogram. 55 min. Sound. 16mm B&W. *Rental:* Hurlock Cine. *Sale:* Cinema Concepts & Reel Images. *Sale:* Video Comm, Videotape version.

Force of Destiny see Forza del Destino.

Force of One, A. Chuck Norris & Jennifer O'Neill. Directed by Paul Aaron. 1979. American Cinema. 90 min. Sound. 16mm Color. *Rental:* Modern Sound, Twyman Films, Westcoast Films & Wholesome Film Ctr.

Force on Thunder Mountain. Christopher Cain. 1977. 93 min. Sound. 16mm Color. *Rental:* Westcoast Films.

Force Ten from Navarone. Robert Shaw, Harrison Ford & Edward Fox. Directed by Guy Hamilton. 1979. American International. 118 min. Sound. 16mm Color. *Rental:* Swank Motion, Welling Motion Pictures & Williams Films.

Forced Landing. Esther Ralston & Sidney Blackmer. Directed by Melville Brown. 1935. Republic. 63 min. Sound. 16mm B&W. *Rental:* Ivy Films.

Forced Vengeance. Chuck Norris, Mary Louise Weller & Bob Minor. Directed by James Fargo. 1982. 103 min. Sound. 16mm Color. *Rental:* MGM United. *Rental:* MGM United, Videotape version.

Foreign Affair, A. Jean Arthur, Marlene Dietrich & John Lund. Directed by Billy Wilder. 1948. Paramount. 116 min. Sound. 16mm B&W. *Rental:* Swank Motion.

Foreman Went to France, The. Robert Morley & Constance Cummings. Directed by Charles Frend. 1941. Britain. 85 min. Sound. 16mm B&W. *Rental:* Janus Films.

Forensic Autopsy. 1978. 56 min. Sound. Videotape Color. *Rental:* Budget Films.

Forensic Identification. 1978. 56 min. Sound. Videotape Color. *Sale:* Natl AV Ctr.

Forever Amber. Linda Darnell & Cornel Wilde. Directed by Otto Preminger. 1947. Fox. 138 min. Sound. 16mm Color. *Rental:* Films Inc.

Forever & a Day. Ida Lupino & Ray Milland. Directed by Rene Clair, Edmund Goulding, Frank Lloyd, Victor Saville, Robert Stevenson & Herbert Wilcox. 1943. RKO. 105 min. Sound. 16mm B&W. *Rental:* A Twyman Pres & Janus Films.

Forever Beethoven. 1967. CBS. (Documentary). 53 min. Sound. 16mm Color. *Sale:* McGraw-Hill Films.

Forever Darling. Lucille Ball & Desi Arnaz. Directed by Alexander Hall. 1956. MGM. 91 min. Sound. 16mm Color. *Rental:* MGM United.

Forever Female. Ginger Rogers & William Holden. Directed by Irving Rapper. 1953. Paramount. 93 min. Sound. 16mm B&W. *Rental:* Films Inc.

Forever in Love see Pride of the Marines.

Forever Young. Directed by Robin Lehman. 1981. Learning Corp. (Documentary). 58 min. Sound. 16mm Color. *Rental:* Cal Media, Iowa Films & Learning Corp Am. *Sale:* Learning Corp Am.

Forever Young, Forever Free. Jose Ferrer & Karen Valentine. Directed by Ashley Lazarus. 1976. Universal. 85 min. Sound. 16mm Color. *Rental:* Swank Motion.

Forever Yours. Gale Storm & Conrad Nagel. Directed by William Nigh. 1944. Monogram. 84 min. Sound. 16mm B&W. *Rental:* Hurlock Cine.

Forged Passport. Paul Kelly & Lyle Talbot. Directed by John H. Auer. 1923. Republic. 54 min. Sound. 16mm B&W. *Rental:* Ivy Films. *Sale:* Rep Pic Film.

Forgery see Southside One.

Forgive & Forget. Estelle Taylor. Directed by Howard Mitchell. 1923. CBC. 60 min. Silent. 16mm B&W. *Rental:* Em Gee Film Lib.

Forgotten Girls. Donald Woods. Directed by Phil Rosen. 1940. Republic. 54 min. Sound. 16mm B&W. *Rental:* Ivy Films.

Forgotten Village. Directed by Herbert Kline. 1941. USA. (Documentary). 68 min. Sound. 16mm B&W. *Rental:* Budget Films, Em Gee Film Lib, Films Inc, Kit Parker, Macmillan Films & Museum Mod Art. *Sale:* Cinema Concepts & Reel Images.

Forgotten Women. Elyse Knox & Edward Norris. Directed by William Beaudine. 1949. Monogram. 65 min. Sound. 16mm B&W. *Rental:* Hurlock Cine.

Forlorn River. Buster Crabbe, June Martel & Monte Blue. Directed by Charles Barton. 1936. Paramount. 60 min. Sound. 16mm B&W. *Rental:* Budget Films & Lewis Film.

Form! Riflemen, Form! 1975. Britain. (Documentary). 52 min. Sound. 16mm Color. *Rental:* U of IL Film.

Formula, The. George C. Scott, Marlon Brando & Marthe Keller. Directed by John G. Avildsen. 1980. 117 min. Sound. 16mm Color. *Rental:* MGM United. *Rental:* MGM United, Videotape version.

Formula C-12-Beirut. Frederick Stafford & Genevieve Cluny. 1966. France. 93 min. Sound. 16mm Color. dubbed. *Rental:* Westcoast Films.

Forsaking All Others. Joan Crawford & Clark Gable. Directed by W. S. Van Dyke II. 1935. MGM. 84 min. Sound. 16mm B&W. *Rental:* MGM United.

Forsyte Saga, The *see* That Forsyte Woman.

Fort Algiers. Yvonne De Carlo & Raymond Burr. Directed by Lesley Selander. 1953. United Artists. 78 min. Sound. 16mm B&W. *Rental:* Westcoast Films.

Fort Apache. John Wayne & Henry Fonda. Directed by John Ford. 1948. RKO. 127 min. Sound. Videotape B&W. *Sale:* Films Inc.

Fort Apache, the Bronx. Paul Newman & Edward Asner. Directed by Daniel Petrie. 1981. United Artists. 124 min. Sound. 16mm Color. *Rental:* MGM United.

Fort Bowie. Ben Johnson & Kent Taylor. Directed by Howard Koch. 1958. United Artists. 80 min. Sound. 16mm B&W. *Rental:* MGM United.

Fort Courageous. Donald Barry. Directed by Lesley Selander. 1965. Fox. 72 min. Sound. 16mm B&W. *Rental:* Films Inc.

Fort Dodge Stampede. Allan Lane. Directed by Harry Keller. 1951. Republic. 60 min. Sound. 16mm B&W. *Rental:* Ivy Films. *Sale:* Rep Pic Film & Nostalgia Merchant.

Fort Good Hope. Directed by Ron Orieux. 1977. Canada. (Documentary). 48 min. Sound. 16mm Color. *Rental:* Natl Film CN. *Sale:* Natl Film CN. *Sale:* Natl Film CN, Videotape version.

Fort Massacre. Joel McCrea & Forrest Tucker. Directed by Joseph Newman. 1958. United Artists. (Anamorphic). 80 min. Sound. 16mm Color. *Rental:* MGM United.

Fort Osage. Rod Cameron & Jane Nigh. Directed by Lesley Selander. 1952. Monogram. 70 min. Sound. 16mm Color. *Rental:* Hurlock Cine.

Fort Ti. George Montgomery. Directed by William Castle. 1953. Warners. 78 min. Sound. 16mm Color. *Rental:* Cine Craft, Film Ctr DC & Modern Sound.

Fort Utah. John Ireland & Virginia Mayo. Directed by Lesley Selander. 1967. Paramount. 83 min. Sound. 16mm Color. *Rental:* Films Inc.

Fort Vengeance. James Craig & Rita Moreno. Directed by Lesley Selander. 1953. Allied Artists. 75 min. Sound. 16mm Color. *Rental:* Hurlock Cine.

Fort Yuma. James Davis. Directed by Edward L. Cahn. 1955. United Artists. 78 min. Sound. 16mm Color. *Rental:* MGM United.

Fortini-Cani. Directed by Jean-Marie Straub & Daniele Huillet. Ital. 1977. Italy. (Cast unlisted). 86 min. Sound. 16mm Color. subtitles. *Rental:* New Yorker Films.

Fortune, The. Jack Nicholson, Warren Beatty & Stockard Channing. Directed by Mike Nichols. 1975. Columbia. 95 min. Sound. 16mm Color. *Rental:* Arcus Film, Budget Films, Corinth Films, Williams Films, Films Inc, Inst Cinema, Ivy Films, Kit Parker, Modern Sound, Newman Film Lib, Natl Film Video, Swank Motion, Syracuse U Film, Twyman Films, U of IL Film, Welling Motion Pictures, Westcoast Films & Wholesome Film Ctr. *Rental:* Corinth Films, Images Film, Kit Parker & Twyman Films, Anamorphic version.

Fortune & Men's Eyes. Wendell Burton & Micheal Greer. Directed by Harvey Hart. 1971. MGM. 102 min. Sound. 16mm Color. *Rental:* MGM United.

Fortune Cookie, The. Jack Lemmon & Walter Matthau. Directed by Billy Wilder. 1966. United Artists. 125 min. Sound. 16mm B&W. *Rental:* MGM United. *Rental:* MGM United, Videotape version.

Fortune Hunter, The *see* Outcast.

Fortune's Fool. Emil Jannings. Directed by Reinhold Schunzel. 1921. Germany. 60 min. Silent. 16mm B&W. *Sale:* Reel Images.

Fortunes of Captain Blood. Louis Hayward & Patricia Medina. Directed by Gordon Douglas. 1950. Columbia. 91 min. Sound. 16mm B&W. *Rental:* Newman Film Lib & Roas Films.

Forty Carats. Liv Ullman, Edward Albert & Gene Kelly. Directed by Milton Katselas. 1973. Columbia. 110 min. Sound. 16mm Color. *Rental:* Arcus Film, Bosco Films, Budget Films, Film Ctr DC, Films Inc, Kerr Film, Modern Sound, Natl Film Video, Roas Films, Swank Motion, Twyman, Welling Motion Pictures & Westcoast Films.

Forty-Eight Hrs. Nick Nolte & Eddie Murphy. Directed by Walter Hill. 1982. Paramount. 97 min. Sound. 16mm Color. *Rental:* Films Inc.

Forty-First, The. Trans. Title: Sorok Pervyi. Izolda Iizvitskaya. Directed by Grigori Chukrai. 1956. Russia. 100 min. Sound. 16mm Color. *Rental:* Corinth Films.

Forty Guns. Barbara Stanwyck & Barry Sullivan. Directed by Samuel Fuller. 1957. Fox. (Anamorphic). 85 min. Sound. 16mm B&W. *Rental:* Films Inc.

Forty Guns to Apache Pass. Audie Murphy & Kenneth Tobey. Directed by William Witney. 1967. Admiral. 95 min. Sound. 16mm Color. *Rental:* Films Inc.

Forty Little Mothers. Eddie Cantor. Directed by Busby Berkeley. 1940. MGM. 90 min. Sound. 16mm B&W. *Rental:* MGM United.

Forty-Nine-Seventeen. Joseph Girard. Directed by Ruth Baldwin. 1917. Universal. 60 min. Silent. 16mm B&W. *Rental:* Kit Parker. *Sale:* Kit Parker.

Forty-Niners, The. Bill Elliott & Virginia Gray. Directed by Thomas Carr. 1954. Allied Artists. 71 min. Sound. 16mm B&W. *Rental:* Hurlock Cine.

Forty-Ninth Man, The. John Ireland & Richard Denning. Directed by Fred F. Sears. 1953. Columbia. 73 min. Sound. 16mm B&W. *Rental:* Inst Cinema.

Forty Ninth Parallel: The Invaders. Sir Laurence Olivier & Leslie Howard. 122 min. Sound. Videotape B&W. *Sale:* Vidamerica.

Forty Pounds of Trouble. Tony Curtis & Phil Silvers. Directed by Norman Jewison. 1962. Universal. 105 min. Sound. 16mm Color. *Rental:* Williams Films.

Forty Second Street. Dick Powell & Ruby Keeler. Directed by Lloyd Bacon. 1933. Warners. 89 min. Sound. 16mm B&W. *Rental:* MGM United.

Forty-Seventh Ronin, The. Chojuro Kawarasaki & Kanemon Nakamura. Directed by Kenji Mizoguchi. Jap. 1941. Japan. 111 min. Sound. 16mm B&W. subtitles Eng. *Rental:* Films Inc.

Forty Thieves. William Boyd. Directed by Lesley Selander. 1944. United Artists. 56 min. Sound. 16mm B&W. *Lease:* Cinema Concepts. *Rental:* Budget Films. *Lease:* Cinema Concepts, Super 8 sound version. *Lease:* Cinema Concepts, Videotape version.

Forty Three: The Petty Story. Darren McGavin & Richard Petty. Directed by Edward J. Lakso. 1974. Victory Lane. 80 min. Sound. 16mm Color. *Rental:* Budget Films & Westcoast Films.

Forward March *see* Doughboys.

Forward Together. Directed by Nicole Duchene & Claude Lortie. 1977. Canada. (Documentary). 58 min. Sound. 16mm Color. *Rental:* Cine Info, Lat Amer Film & Unifilm. *Sale:* Unifilm. *Rental:* Cine Info & Lat Amer Film, French Language version.

Forza del Destino, La. Trans. Title: Force of Destiny. Tito Gobbi. Directed by Carmine Gallone. 1953. Italy. 100 min. Sound. 16mm B&W. narrated Eng. *Rental:* Trans-World Films.

Foto: Sven Nykvist. 1974. Sweden. (Documentary). 52 min. Sound. 16mm Color. *Rental:* Films Inc.

Foul Play. Goldie Hawn & Chevy Chase. Directed by Colin Higgins. 1978. Paramount. 116 min. Sound. 16mm Color. *Rental:* Films Inc.

Found Alive. Barbara Bedford. Directed by Charles Hutchinson. 1933. Ideal. 60 min. Sound. 16mm B&W. *Rental:* Em Gee Film Lib, Ivy Films & Mogulls Films. *Sale:* Cinema Concepts.

Foundation Belong to the Incas, The. Directed by David Bilcock. 1978. Institutional Cinema. (Documentary). 52 min. Sound. 16mm Color. *Sale:* Inst Cinema.

Foundation of Love, The. Eddie Arent. Directed by Ernest Hoffbauer. 1968. Germany. 83 min. Sound. 16mm Color. dubbed. *Rental:* Video Comm. *Lease:* Video Comm. *Rental:* Video Comm, *Lease:* Video Comm, Videotape version.

Fountainhead, The. Gary Cooper & Patricia Neal. Directed by King Vidor. 1949. Warners. 112 min. Sound. 16mm B&W. *Rental:* MGM United.

Four Children. 1978. Young People's Specials. (Documentary). 50 min. Sound. 16mm Color. *Sale:* Young People Media.

Four Clowns. Stan Laurel & Oliver Hardy. Directed by Charley Chase. 1970. Fox. 97 min. Sound. 16mm B&W. *Rental:* Films Inc & Twyman Films.

Four Corners, The. 1982. Bullfrog. (Documentary). 59 min. Sound. 16mm Color. *Sale:* Bullfrog Films. *Rental:* Bullfrog Films. *Sale:* Bullfrog Films, Videotape version.

Four-D Man, The. Robert Lansing. Directed by Irvin Yeaworth Jr. 1959. Universal. 85 min. Sound. 16mm B&W. *Rental:* Budget Films, Charard Motion Pics & Films Inc.

Four-D Special Agents. 1982. 60 min. Color. *Sale:* Lucerne Films.

Four Daughters. John Garfield & Claude Rains. Directed by Michael Curtiz. 1938. Warners. 90 min. Sound. 16mm B&W. *Rental:* MGM United.

Four Days in November. Directed by Mel Stuart. 1964. United Artists. (Documentary). 100 min. Sound. 16mm B&W. *Rental:* MGM United.

Four Days' Leave. Cornel Wilde & Simone Signoret. Directed by Leopold Lindtberg. 1950. Film Classics. 98 min. Sound. 16mm B&W. *Rental:* Budget Films & Mogulls Films.

Four Days of Naples. Trans. Title: Quatro Giornate Di Napoli, Le. Jean Sorel & Regina Bianchi. Directed by Nanni Loy. Ital. 1963. Italy. 124 min. Sound. 16mm B&W. subtitles. *Rental:* MGM United.

Four Desperate Men. Aldo Ray & Heather Sears. Directed by Harry Watt. 1960. Australia. 104 min. Sound. 16mm B&W. *Rental:* Williams Films.

Four Faces West. Joel McCrea & Frances Dee. Directed by Alfred E. Green. 1948. United Artists. 90 min. Sound. 16mm B&W. *Rental:* Ivy Films, Kit Parker & Willoughby Peer. *Sale:* Rep Pic Film.

Four Families. 1961. Canada. (Documentary). 60 min. Sound. 16mm B&W. *Rental:* BYU Media, McGraw-Hill Films, Natl Film CN, SD AV Ctr, Syracuse U Film & U Cal Media. *Sale:* Mcgraw-Hill Films & Natl Film CN.

Four Feathers. Sir Ralph Richardson & June Duprez. Directed by Zoltan Korda. 1939. Britain. 115 min. Sound. 16mm B&W. *Rental:* Charard Motion Pics, Films Inc, Inst Cinema, Mogulls Films & Swank Motion. *Rental:* Buchan Pic & Films Inc, Color version.

Four Flies on Gray Velvet. Michael Brandon & Mimsy Farmer. Directed by Dario Argento. 1972. Italy. 101 min. Sound. 16mm Color. *Rental:* Films Inc.

Four for Texas. Frank Sinatra & Dean Martin. Directed by Robert Aldrich. 1963. Warners. 124 min. Sound. 16mm Color. *Rental:* Charard Motion Pics, Films Inc, Inst Cinema, Video Comm & Willoughby Peer.

Four Friends. Craig Wasson & Jodi Thelen. Directed by Arthur Penn. 1981. Filmways. 115 min. Sound. 16mm Color. *Rental:* Swank Motion & Wholesome Film Ctr.

Four from the Infantry *see* Westfront Nineteen Eighteen.

Four Girls in White. Florence Rice & Ann Rutherford. Directed by S. Sylvan Simon. 1939. MGM. 73 min. Sound. 16mm B&W. *Rental:* MGM United.

Four Guns to the Border. George Nader & Rory Calhoun. Directed by Richard Carlson. 1954. Universal. 83 min. Sound. 16mm Color. *Rental:* Swank Motion.

Four Horseman of the Apocalypse. Rudolph Valentino. Directed by Rex Ingram. 1921. MGM. 120 min. Silent. 16mm B&W. *Rental:* Films Inc.

Four Horseman of the Apocalypse. Glenn Ford & Ingrid Thulin. Directed by Vincente Minnelli. 1962. MGM. 142 min. Sound. 16mm Color. *Rental:* MGM United. *Rental:* MGM United, Anamorphic color version.

Four Hundred Blows. Jean-Pierre Leaud. Directed by Francois Truffaut. Fr. 1959. France. 98 min. Sound. 16mm B&W. subtitles. *Rental:* Janus Films & New Cinema.

Four Jacks & a Jill. Ray Bolger & Desi Arnaz. Directed by Jack Hively. 1941. RKO. 68 min. Sound. 16mm B&W. *Rental:* Films Inc.

Four Jills in a Jeep. Kay Francis, Carole Landis & Martha Raye. Directed by William A. Seiter. 1944. Fox. 89 min. Sound. 16mm B&W. *Rental:* Films Inc.

Four Journeys into Mystic Time. Directed by Shirley Clarke. 1978. Museum of Modern Art. (Anthology). 58 min. Sound. 16mm Color. *Rental:* Museum Mod Art.

Four More Years. 1972. TVTV. (Documentary). 60 min. Videotape B&W. *Rental:* Electro Art. *Lease:* Electro Art.

Four Mothers. Eddie Albert & Claude Rains. Directed by William Keighley. 1941. Warners. 86 min. Sound. 16mm B&W. *Rental:* MGM United.

Four Musketeers, The. Michael York & Raquel Welch. Directed by Richard Lester. 1975. Fox. 105 min. Sound. 16mm Color. *Rental:* Films Inc. *Sale:* Tamarelles French Film, Videotape version.

Four Nights of a Dreamer. Isabelle Weingarten. Directed by Robert Bresson. Fr. 1971. France. 83 min. Sound. 16mm Color. subtitles. *Rental:* New Yorker Films.

Four Ninety-Eight Third Avenue. Directed by Klaus Wildenham. 1968. Cunningham. (Dance). 120 min. Sound. 16mm B&W. *Rental:* M Cunningham.

Four Ninety-One. Lars Lind. Directed by Vilgot Sjoman. Swed. 1964. Sweden. 110 min. Sound. 16mm B&W. subtitles. *Rental:* Janus Films & New Cinema.

Four Poster, The. Rex Harrison & Lilli Palmer. Directed by Irving Reis. 1952. Columbia. 103 min. Sound. 16mm B&W. *Rental:* Films Inc.

Four Religions. 1961. Canada. (Documentary). 60 min. Sound. 16mm B&W. *Rental:* BYU Media, Natl Film CN & Syracuse U Film. *Sale:* McGraw-Hill Films & Natl Film CN.

Four Rode Out. Sue Lyon, Pernell Roberts & Leslie Nielsen. Directed by John Peyser. 1969. Sagitarius. 99 min. Sound. 16mm Color. dubbed. *Rental:* Willoughby Peer.

Four Seasons, The. Alan Alda, Carol Burnett & Sandy Dennis. Directed by Alan Alda. Universal. 107 min. Sound. 16mm Color. *Rental:* Swank Motion. *Rental:* Swank Motion, Videotape version.

Four Skulls of Jonathan Drake, The. Eduard Franz & Henry Daniell. Directed by Edward L. Cahn. 1959. United Artists. 70 min. Sound. 16mm B&W. *Rental:* MGM United & Westcoast Films.

Four Sons. Margaret Mann & James Hall. Directed by John Ford. 1928. Fox. (Musical score only). 100 min. Sound. 16mm B&W. *Rental:* Killiam Collect.

Four Students. 4 pts. Directed by John Baehrend. 1967. Indiana University. (Documentary). 88 min. Sound. 16mm B&W. *Rental:* Indiana AV Ctr. *Sale:* Indiana AV Ctr.

Four Teachers. 1961. Canada. (Documentary). 60 min. Sound. 16mm B&W. *Rental:* U Cal Media.

Four Ways Out. Gina Lollobrigida. Directed by Pietro Germi. 1954. Italy. 77 min. Sound. 16mm B&W. dubbed. *Rental:* Willoughby Peer.

Four Wives. Claude Rains & Eddie Albert. Directed by Michael Curtiz. 1939. Warners. 99 min. Sound. 16mm B&W. *Rental:* MGM United.

Four Women in Black. Helen Hayes & Ralph Meeker. 1957. CBS. (Kinescope). 75 min. Sound. 16mm B&W. *Rental:* Bosco Films.

Four's a Crowd. Errol Flynn & Rosalind Russell. Directed by Michael Curtiz. 1938. Warners. 91 min. Sound. 16mm B&W. *Rental:* Films Inc & MGM United.

Fourteen Americans: Directions of the 1970s. Directed by Michael Blackwood. 16mm *Rental:* Blackwood. *Sale:* Blackwood.

Fourteen Hours. Paul Douglas & Richard Basehart. Directed by Henry Hathaway. 1951. Fox. 91 min. Sound. 16mm B&W. *Rental:* Films Inc.

Fourteen Ninty-Two: Saga of Western Man. 1964. ABC. (Documentary). 54 min. Sound. 16mm Color. *Rental:* BYU Media, McGraw-Hill Films, OK AV Ctr & U of IL Film. *Sale:* McGraw-Hill Films. *Rental:* McGraw-Hill Films & Syracuse U Film, *Sale:* McGraw-Hill Films, videotape version.

Fourth Annual Young Comedians Show, The. 1979. Verve. (Performance). 88 min. Videotape Color. *Rental:* Films Inc.

Fourth for Marriage, A. Tommy Holden. 1964. Fairway. 80 min. Sound. 16mm Color. *Rental:* Ivy Films.

Fox, The. Sandy Dennis, Kier Dullea & Anne Heywood. Directed by Mark Rydell. 1968. Warners. 110 min. Sound. 16mm Color. *Rental:* Swank Motion.

Fox & His Friends, The. Orig. Title: Fist Right of Freedom. Rainer Werner Fassbinder. Directed by Rainer Werner Fassbinder. Ger. 1975. Germany. 123 min. Sound. 16mm Color. subtitles. *Rental:* New Yorker Films.

Fox & the Hound, The. 1981. Disney. (Animated). 83 min. Sound. 16mm Color. *Rental:* Swank Motion.

Foxes. Jodie Foster & Sally Kellerman. Directed by Adrian Lyne. 1980. United Artists. 106 min. Sound. 16mm Color. *Rental:* MGM United.

Foxhole in Cairo. James Robertson Justice. Directed by John Moxey. 1961. Paramount. 79 min. Sound. 16mm B&W. *Rental:* Films Inc.

Foxy Brown. Pam Grier & Peter Brown. Directed by Jack Hill. 1974. American International. 94 min. Sound. 16mm B&W. *Rental:* Swank Motion.

Fra Diavolo see Devil's Brother.

Fragile Mind, The. 1977. Best. (Documentary). 52 min. Sound. 16mm Color. *Rental:* Best Films & U of IL Film. *Sale:* Best Films.

Fragment of an Empire. Fyodor Nikitin. Directed by Friedrich Ermler. 1929. Russia. 103 min. Silent. 16mm B&W. *Rental:* Corinth Films & Museum Mod Art.

Fragment of Fear. David Hemmings & Gayle Hunnicut. Directed by Richard C. Sarafian. 1971. Britain. 94 min. Sound. 16mm Color. *Rental:* Arcus Film, Budget Films, Cine Craft, Kerr Film, Roas Films, Swank Motion, Welling Motion Pictures, Westcoast Films, Willoughby Peer & U of CAL Media.

Fragrance of Wild Flowers, The. Ljuba Tadic & Sonja Divac. Directed by Srdjan Karanovic. 1978. Yugoslavia. 110 min. Sound. 16mm Color. subtitles. *Rental:* New Yorker Films.

Framed. Glenn Ford, Barry Sullivan & Janis Carter. Directed by Harold Schuster. 1947. Columbia. 81 min. Sound. 16mm B&W. *Rental:* Kit Parker.

Framed. Gabriel Dell, John Marley & Brock Peters. Directed by Phil Karlson. 1975. Paramount. 106 min. Sound. 16mm Color. *Rental:* Films Inc.

Framed. Evelyn Brent & Regis Toomey. Directed by George Archainbaud. 1930. RKO. Sound. 16mm *Rental:* RKO General Pics.

France: Conquest to Liberation. 1964. Wolper. (Documentary). 50 min. Sound. 16mm B&W. *Rental:* Films Inc. *Sale:* Films Inc. *Sale:* Films Inc, Videotape version.

France Falls: May-June 1940. Directed by Hugh Raggett. (World at War Ser.). : Pt. 3.). 1973. Media Guild. (Documentary). 52 min. Sound. 16mm Color. *Rental:* Media Guild & U Cal Media. *Sale:* Media Guild. *Sale:* Media Guild, Videotape version.

France: The Faces of Love. Claude Dauphin. Modern. 54 min. Sound. 16mm B&W. *Rental:* Modern Mass. *Sale:* Modern Mass.

Frances. Jessica Lange, Sam Shepard & Kim Stanley. Directed by Graeme Clifford. 1982. Universal. 140 min. Sound. 16mm Color. *Rental:* Swank Motion.

Frances Flaherty: Hidden & Seeking. Directed by Peter Werner. 1971. Peter Werner. (Documentary). 58 min. Sound. 16mm B&W. *Rental:* U Mich Media.

Francesca, Baby. Directed by Larry Elikann. 1977. Disney. (Cast unlisted). 47 min. Sound. 16mm Color. *Rental:* Disney Prod, Iowa Films, U of IL Film & U Mich Media. *Sale:* Disney Prod.

Francis Covers the Big Town. Donald O'Connor. Directed by Arthur Lubin. 1953. Universal. 86 min. Sound. 16mm B&W. *Rental:* Swank Motion.

Francis Goes to the Races. Donald O'Connor. Directed by Arthur Lubin. 1951. Universal. 88 min. Sound. 16mm B&W. *Rental:* Swank Motion.

Francis Goes to West Point. Donald O'Connor. Directed by Arthur Lubin. 1952. Universal. 98 min. Sound. 16mm B&W. *Rental:* Swank Motion.

Francis in the Haunted House. Mickey Rooney. Directed by Charles Lamont. 1956. Universal. 80 min. Sound. 16mm B&W. *Rental:* Swank Motion.

Francis in the Navy. Donald O'Connor. Directed by Arthur Lubin. 1955. Universal. 80 min. Sound. 16mm B&W. *Rental:* Williams Films.

Francis Joins the Wacs. Donald O'Connor. Directed by Arthur Lubin. 1954. Universal. 94 min. Sound. 16mm B&W. *Rental:* Swank Motion.

Francis of Assisi. Bradford Dillman & Stuart Whitman. Directed by Michael Curtiz. 1961. Fox. 105 min. Sound. 16mm Color. *Rental:* Bosco Films, Films Inc & Williams Films. *Sale:* Films Inc, Anamorphic color version.

Francis (The Talking Mule). Donald O'Connor. Directed by Arthur Lubin. 1949. Universal. 90 min. Sound. 16mm B&W. *Rental:* Williams Films.

Francisco Pizarro. Directed by Fred Burnley. 1977. Britain. (Cast unlisted). 52 min. Sound. 16mm Color. *Rental:* Time-Life Multimedia. *Sale:* Time-Life Multimedia.

Franco Spain. 1963. CBS. (Documentary). 52 min. Sound. 16mm B&W. *Rental:* Macmillan Films. *Sale:* Macmillan Films.

Francois Villon. Renee Foure. Directed by Andre Zwobada. Fr. 1948. France. 95 min. Sound. 16mm B&W. subtitles. *Rental:* Film Classics.

Frank Buck's Jungle Cavalcade see Jungle Cavalcade.

Frank Buck's Jungle Cavalcade. Directed by Clyde Elliott & Armand Denis. 1941. RKO. 79 min. Sound. 16mm B&W. *Rental:* Films Inc.

Frank Capra. 1978. American Film Institute. 55 min. Videotape Color. *Sale:* Am Film Inst.

Frank Sinatra in Concert in Japan. 1974. Japan. (Concert). 52 min. Videotape Color. *Sale:* Reel Images.

Frank Sinatra Story, The. (Anthology). 59 min. Videotape B&W. *Sale:* Reel Images.

Frank Terpil: Confessions of a Dangerous Man. 1981. 118 min. Sound. Videotape *Rental:* PBS Video. *Sale:* PBS Video.

Frank's Buck's Fang & Claw see Fang & Claw.

Frankenstein. Boris Karloff & Mae Clarke. Directed by James Whale. 1931. Universal. 71 min. Sound. 16mm B&W. *Rental:* Swank Motion & Twyman Films. *Rental:* Swank Motion, Videotape version.

Frankenstein & the Monster from Hell. Peter Cushing. Directed by Terence Fisher. 1974. Britain. 93 min. Sound. 16mm Color. *Rental:* Films Inc.

Frankenstein Conquers the World. Nick Adams. Directed by Inoshiro Honda. 1966. Japan. 92 min. Sound. 16mm Color. dubbed. *Rental:* Buchan Pic, Budget Films, Ivy Films & Video Comm.

Frankenstein Created Woman. Peter Cushing & Susan Denberg. Directed by Terence Fisher. 1966. Britain. 92 min. Sound. 16mm Color. *Rental:* Films Inc.

Frankenstein Meets the Space Monster. Marilyn Hanold. Directed by Robert Gaffney. 1965. Allied Artists. 78 min. Sound. 16mm B&W. *Rental:* Charard Motion Pics & Films Inc.

Frankenstein Meets the Wolf Man. Lon Chaney Jr. & Bela Lugosi. Directed by Roy William Neill. 1943. Universal. 73 min. Sound. 16mm B&W. *Rental:* Swank Motion.

Frankenstein Must Be Destroyed. Peter Cushing & Veronica Carlson. Directed by Terence Fisher. 1970. Warners. 97 min. Sound. 16mm Color. *Rental:* Film Ctr DC, Films Inc, Newman Film Lib, Twyman Films, Video Comm & Willoughby Peer.

Frankenstein-Nineteen Seventy. Boris Karloff & Donald Barry. Directed by Howard Koch. 1958. Allied Artists. 83 min. Sound. 16mm B&W. *Rental:* Hurlock Cine.

Frankenstein '80. 90 min. Sound. Videotape Color. *Rental:* Maljack.

Frankenstein's Castle of Freaks. Rossano Brazzi, Micheal Dunn & Edmund Purdom. 90 min. Sound. Videotape Color. *Sale:* Best Film & Vidamerica.

Frankenstein's Daughter. John Ashley & Sandra Knight. Directed by Richard Cunha. 1958. Astor. 85 min. Sound. 16mm B&W. *Rental:* Ivy Films, Rep Pic Film, Roas Films & Video Comm. *Lease:* Rep Pic Film. *Sale:* Cinema Concepts, Super 8 Sound version. *Rental:* Video Comm, Videotape version.

Frankie & Johnny. Helen Morgan & Chester Morris. Directed by Chester Erskine. 1935. Republic. 70 min. Sound. 16mm B&W. *Rental:* Budget Films & Kerr Film. *Sale:* Natl Cinema.

Frankie & Johnny. Elvis Presley. Directed by Frederick De Cordova. 1966. United Artists. 87 min. Sound. 16mm Color. *Rental:* MGM United.

Frantic. Trans. Title: Ascenseur Pour l'Echaufaud. Jeanne Moreau & Maurice Ronet. Directed by Louis Malle. Fr. 1958. France. 90 min. Sound. 16mm B&W. *Rental:* Budget Films, Em Gee Film Lib & New Yorker Films. *Sale:* Festival Films, Reel Images & New Cinema. *Sale:* Festival Films & Tamarelles French Film, Videotape version.

Franz Boas 1858-1942. 1979. Odyssey. (Documentary). 59 min. Videotape Color. *Rental:* PBS Video. *Sale:* PBS Video.

Fraternally Yours see Sons of the Desert.

Fraternity Row. Peter Fox & Scott Newman. Directed by Thomas J. Tobin. 1977. Paramount. 99 min. Sound. 16mm Color. *Rental:* Films Inc.

Frau Im Mond, Die see Woman in the Moon.

Fraulein. Mel Ferrer & Dana Wynter. Directed by Henry Koster. 1958. Fox. (Anamorphic). 98 min. Sound. 16mm Color. *Rental:* Films Inc.

Fraulein Doktor. Orig. Title: Betrayed, The. Suzy Kendall & Kenneth More. Directed by Alberto Lattuada. 1968. Yugoslavia. 102 min. Sound. 16mm Color. dubbed. *Rental:* Films Inc.

Fraulein Von Barnhelm, Das. Kathe Gold & Ewald Balser. Directed by Hans Schweikart. 1940. Germany. 92 min. Sound. 16mm B&W. *Rental:* Trans-World Films. *Rental:* Trans-World Films, Subtitled version.

Freaks. Olga Baclanova. Directed by Tod Browning. 1932. MGM. 69 min. Sound. 16mm B&W. *Rental:* MGM United. *Rental:* MGM United, Videotape version.

Freaky Friday. Jodie Foster, Barbara Harris & John Astin. Directed by Gary Nelson. 1976. Disney. 95 min. Sound. 16mm Color. *Rental:* Bosco Films, Disney Prod, Elliot Film Co, Film Ctr DC, Films Inc, MGM United, Modern Sound, Roas Films, Swank Motion, Twyman Films, Welling Motion Pictures, Westcoast Films & Williams Films.

Freckles. Martin West. Directed by Andrew V. McLaglen. 1960. Fox. 84 min. Sound. 16mm Color. *Rental:* Films Inc. *Rental:* Willoughby Peer, Anamorphic color version.

Freckles Comes Home. Johnny Downs, Gale Storm & Mantan Moreland. Directed by Jean Yarbrough. 1942. Monogram. 63 min. Sound. 16mm B&W. *Rental:* Budget Films.

Freddie Steps Out. Freddie Stewart & Frankie Darro. Directed by Arthur Dreifuss. 1946. Monogram. 75 min. Sound. 16mm B&W. *Rental:* Hurlock Cine.

Frederick Douglass. Robert Hooks. Directed by Sherman Marks. (Profiles in Courage Ser.). 1965. Saudek. 50 min. Sound. 16mm B&W. *Rental:* IQ Films, Syracuse U Film, U Cal Media & U Mich Media. *Sale:* IQ Films. *Rental:* IQ Films, *Sale:* IQ Films, Spanish dubbed version.

Free & Easy see Easy Go.

Free & Easy. Robert Cummings & Ruth Hussey. Directed by George Sidney. 1940. MGM. 56 min. Sound. 16mm B&W. *Rental:* MGM United.

Free, Blonde & Twenty-One. Lynn Bari & Mary Beth Hughes. Directed by Ricardo Cortez. 1940. Fox. 67 min. Sound. 16mm B&W. *Rental:* Willoughby Peer.

Free Forever. Anthony Zedi. 56 min. Sound. 16mm Color. *Rental:* Gospel Films.

Free Paper Come. 1977. Britain. (Cast unlisted). 53 min. Sound. 16mm Color. *Rental:* U of IL Film & U Mich Media. *Sale:* Time-Life Multimedia. *Rental:* Time-Life Multimedia, Videotape version.

Free People in Guinea-Bissau. Directed by Axel Lohman & Rudi Spee. Port. 1970. Portugal. (Documentary). 50 min. Sound. 16mm B&W. subtitles. *Rental:* Unifilm. *Sale:* Unifilm.

Free Show Tonight. 1983. 59 min. Color. *Rental:* Educ Media CA.

Free Soul, A. Norma Shearer & Lionel Barrymore. Directed by Clarence Brown. 1931. MGM. 91 min. Sound. 16mm B&W. *Rental:* MGM United.

Free to Love. Clara Bow. Directed by Frank O'Connor. 1925. Paramount. 60 min. Silent. 16mm B&W. *Rental:* Budget Films, Em Gee Film Lib, Film Classics & Kit Parker. *Sale:* Morcraft Films. *Sale:* Festival Films, 50 min. version.

Free Voice of Labor: The Jewish Anarchists. 55 min. Sound. 16mm Color. *Rental:* Westcoast Films.

Free Woman, A. Orig. Title: Strohfeuer. Margarethe Von Trotta. Directed by Volker Schlondorff. Ger. 1972. German. 100 min. Sound. 16mm Color. subtitles. *Rental:* New Yorker Films.

Freebie & the Bean. James Caan & Alan Arkin. Directed by Richard Rush. 1974. Warners. 113 min. Sound. 16mm Color. *Rental:* Swank Motion, Twyman Films & Williams Films.

Freedom. (Cast unlisted). Videotape *Sale:* Vidamerica.

Freedom: Then, Now, & Tomorrow. 1976. Penn State. (Documentary). 55 min. Videotape Color. *Rental:* Penn St AV Serv. *Sale:* Penn St AV Serv.

Freedom to Love. Directed by Phyllis Kronhausen & Eberhard Kronhausen. 1970. Grove. (Documentary). 90 min. Sound. 16mm Color. *Rental:* Grove.

Freedom's Finest Hour. 1967. McGraw-Hill. (Documentary). 54 min. Sound. 16mm Color. *Rental:* McGraw-Hill Films, U of IL Film & U Nev AV Ctr. *Sale:* McGraw-Hill Films.

Freighters of Destiny. Tom Keene. Directed by Fred Allen. 1931. RKO. 60 min. Sound. 16mm B&W. *Rental:* Mogulls Films.

French Blue. Brigitte Maier. Directed by Falcon Stuart. 1974. Netherlands. 70 min. Sound. 16mm Color. dubbed. *Rental:* New Line Cinema.

French Cigarettes see Gauloises Bleues.

French Connection, The. Gene Hackman & Fernando Rey. Directed by William Friedkin. 1971. Fox. 104 min. Sound. 16mm Color. *Rental:* Films Inc, Twyman Films & Williams Films. *Rental:* Williams Films, Videotape version.

French Connection II, The. Gene Hackman & Fernando Rey. Directed by John Frankenheimer. 1975. Fox. 118 min. Sound. 16mm Color. *Rental:* Films Inc, Twyman Films & Williams Films.

French Detective, The. Lino Ventura & Patrick Dewaere. Directed by Pierre Granier-Deferre. 1979. France. 93 min. Sound. 16mm Color. dubbed. *Rental:* Films Inc.

French Key, The. Richard Arlen & Albert Dekker. Directed by Walter Colmes. 1946. Republic. 64 min. Sound. 16mm B&W. *Sale:* Classics Assoc NY.

French Leave. Jackie Cooper & Jackie Coogan. Directed by Frank McDonald. 1948. Monogram. 64 min. Sound. 16mm B&W. *Rental:* Hurlock Cine.

French Lieutenant's Woman, The. Meryl Streep & Jeremy Irons. Directed by Karel Reisz. 1981. United Artists. 124 min. Sound. 16mm Color. *Rental:* MGM United. *Rental:* MGM United, Videotape version.

French Line, The. Jane Russell & Gilbert Roland. Directed by Lloyd Bacon. 1954. RKO. 102 min. Sound. 16mm Color. *Rental:* Films Inc.

French Nineteenth Century Painters. 1966. NET. (Documentary). 59 min. Sound. 16mm B&W. *Rental:* Indiana AV Ctr. *Sale:* Indiana AV Ctr.

French Postcards. Marie-France Pisier & Jean Rochefort. Directed by Willard Huyck. 1979. Paramount. 94 min. Sound. 16mm Color. *Rental:* Films Inc.

French Provincial. Jeanne Moreau. Directed by Andre Techine. Fr. 1975. France. 95 min. Sound. 16mm Color. subtitles. *Rental:* New Cinema & New Yorker Films.

French Quarter, The. Bruce Davison & Virginia Mayo. Directed by Dennis Kane. 1978. Crown. 101 min. Sound. 16mm Color. *Rental:* Films Inc.

Frenchmen Go Wild. 1957. 16mm *Rental:* A Twyman Pres.

Frenzy. Jon Finch & Anna Massey. Directed by Alfred Hitchcock. 1972. Universal. 116 min. Sound. 16mm Color. *Rental:* Swank Motion. *Rental:* Swank Motion, Videotape version.

Freshman, The. Harold Lloyd. Directed by Fred Newmeyer & Sam Taylor. 1925. Pathe. (Music & sound effects only). 75 min. Sound. 16mm B&W. *Rental:* Budget Films, Images Film, Janus Films, Kino Intl & Kit Parker. *Rental:* Budget Films, Silent version.

Freshman Love. Orig. Title: Rhythm on the River. Frank McHugh & Patricia Ellis. Directed by William McGann. 1936. Warners. 67 min. Sound. 16mm B&W. *Rental:* MGM United.

Freud. Orig. Title: Secret Passion, The. Montgomery Clift & Susannah York. Directed by John Huston. 1962. Universal. 140 min. Sound. 16mm B&W. *Rental:* Williams Films.

Freudlose Gasse, Die see Joyless Street.

Friday Foster. Pam Grier & Yaphet Kotto. Directed by Arthur Marks. 1975. American International. 89 min. Sound. 16mm Color. *Rental:* Swank Motion.

Friday the Thirteenth. Betsy Palmer & Harry Crosby. Directed by Sean Cunningham. 1980. Paramount. 89 min. Sound. 16mm Color. *Rental:* Films Inc.

Friday the Thirteenth: Part II. Amy Steel & John Furey. Directed by Steve Miner. 1981. Paramount. 87 min. Sound. 16mm Color. *Rental:* Films Inc.

Friday the Thirteenth: Part III. Dana Kimmell & Paul Kratka. Directed by Steve Miner. 1982. Paramount. 95 min. Sound. 16mm Color. *Rental:* Films Inc.

Fried Shoes, Cooked Diamonds. Allen Ginsberg & William Burroughs. 1980. Centre. 55 min. Sound. 16mm Color. *Rental:* Centre Co. *Sale:* Centre Co. *Sale:* Centre Co, Videotape version.

Friedemann Bach. Gustaf Grundgens & Eugen Klopfer. Directed by Traugott Muller. 1941. Germany. 100 min. Sound. 16mm B&W. *Rental:* Trans-World Films. *Rental:* Trans-World Films, Subtitled version.

Friedrich Schiller. Orig. Title: Triumph of a Genius. Directed by Herbert Maisch. 1936. Germany. (Cast unlisted). 95 min. Sound. 16mm B&W. *Rental:* Trans World Films.

Friend of the Family, A. Jean Marais & Danielle Darrieux. Directed by Robert Thomas. Fr. 1965. France. 95 min. Sound. 16mm B&W. subtitles. *Rental:* Films Inc.

Friend or Foe? 1982. Britain. (Cast unlisted). 70 min. Sound. 16mm B&W. *Rental:* Lucerne Films. *Sale:* Lucerne Films.

Friendly Fifties & the Sinister Sixties, The. 1968. Canada. (Documentary). 58 min. Sound. 16mm B&W. *Rental:* Natl Film CN. *Sale:* Natl Film CN.

Friendly Persuasion. Gary Cooper, Tony Perkins & Dorothy McGuire. Directed by William Wyler. 1956. Allied Artists. 140 min. Sound. 16mm Color. *Rental:* Hurlock Cine.

Friends. Sean Bury. Directed by Lewis Gilbert. 1971. Paramount. 102 min. Sound. 16mm Color. *Rental:* Films Inc.

Friends & Lovers. Sir Laurence Olivier, Erich Von Stroheim & Adolphe Menjou. Directed by Victor Schertzinger. 1931. RKO. 68 min. Sound. 16mm B&W. *Rental:* Films Inc.

Friends of Eddie Coyle, The. Robert Mitchum & Peter Boyle. Directed by Peter Yates. 1973. Paramount. 100 min. Sound. 16mm Color. *Rental:* Films Inc.

Friends of Mr. Sweeney, The. Charles Ruggles & Ann Dvorak. Directed by Edward Ludwig. 1934. Warners. 68 min. Sound. 16mm B&W. *Rental:* MGM United.

Friendship Seven. 1962. NASA. (Documentary). 58 min. Sound. 16mm Color. *Rental:* Natl AV Ctr.

Fright. Susan George & Ian Bannen. Directed by Peter Collinson. 1972. Britain. 87 min. Sound. 16mm Color. *Rental:* Hurlock Cine.

Frightened City, The. Sean Connery & Herbert Lom. Directed by John Lemont. 1962. Britain. 97 min. Sound. 16mm B&W. *Rental:* Bosco Films.

Frisco Jenny. Ruth Chatterton & Donald Cook. Directed by William A. Wellman. 1933. Warners. 73 min. Sound. 16mm B&W. *Rental:* MGM United.

Frisco Kid, The. James Cagney & Margaret Lindsay. Directed by Lloyd Bacon. 1935. Warners. 77 min. Sound. 16mm B&W. *Rental:* MGM United.

Frisco Kid, The. Gene Wilder & Harrison Ford. Directed by Robert Aldrich. 1980. Warners. 122 min. Sound. 16mm Color. *Rental:* Swank Motion. *Rental:* Swank Motion, Videotape version.

Frisco Tornado. Allan Lane. Directed by R. G. Springsteen. 1950. Republic. 61 min. Sound. 16mm B&W. *Rental:* Ivy Films. *Sale:* Rep Pic Film.

Frisco Waterfront. Ben Lyon & Rod La Rocque. Directed by Arthur Lubin. 1935. Republic. 54 min. Sound. 16mm B&W. *Rental:* Ivy Films.

Fritz the Cat. Directed by Ralph Bakshi. 1972. Cinemation. (Animated). 78 min. Sound. 16mm Color. *Rental:* Images Film & Welling Motion Pictures.

Frog, The. Gordon Harker & Jack Hawkins. Directed by Herbert Wilcox. 1937. 16mm *Rental:* A Twyman Pres.

Frogmen, The. Richard Widmark & Dana Andrews. Directed by Lloyd Bacon. 1951. Fox. 96 min. Sound. 16mm B&W. *Rental:* Films Inc.

Frogs, The. Ray Milland. Directed by George McCowan. 1972. American International. 91 min. Sound. 16mm Color. *Rental:* Swank Motion.

From Beyond the Grave. Peter Cushing & Margaret Leighton. Directed by Kevin Connor. 1976. Britain. 96 min. Sound. 16mm Color. *Rental:* Film Ctr DC & Films Inc.

From China with Death. 1974. United International. (Cast unlisted). 109 min. Sound. 16mm. Color. dubbed. *Rental:* Films Inc.

From Cradle to Classroom. 1968. CBS. (Documentary). 50 min. Sound. 16mm Color. *Rental:* McGraw-Hill Films. *Sale:* McGraw-Hill Films.

From Cradle to Grave. 1980. Penn. (Documentary). 60 min. Videotape Color. *Rental:* #Iowa Films. *Sale:* Ency Brit Ed. *Sale:* Ency Brit Ed, 2 pt. 16mm version version.

From Dada to Surrealism: Forty Years of Experiment. Directed by Hans Richter. 1961. Contemporary. (Color sequences-Documentary). 60 min. Sound. 16mm B&W. *Rental:* Museum Mod Art & Syracuse U Film. *Sale:* Museum Mod Art.

From Earth to Moon. (Animated). 55 min. Sound. 16mm Color. *Rental:* Westcoast Films.

From Headquarters. George Brent & Margaret Lindsay. Directed by William Dieterle. 1933. Warners. 63 min. Sound. 16mm B&W. *Rental:* MGM United.

From Hell to Borneo. George Montgomery & Torin Thatcher. Directed by George Montgomery. 1964. Philippines. 96 min. Sound. 16mm Color. *Rental:* Video Comm. *Lease:* Video Comm. *Rental:* Video Comm, *Lease:* Video Comm, Videotape version.

From Hell to Texas. Don Murray & Diane Varsi. Directed by Henry Hathaway. 1958. Fox. (Anamorphic). 99 min. Sound. 16mm Color. *Rental:* Films Inc.

From Here to Eternity. Montgomery Clift, Burt Lancaster & Deborah Kerr. Directed by Fred Zinnemann. 1953. Columbia. 118 min. Sound. 16mm B&W. *Rental:* Arcus Film, Bosco Films, Budget Films, Cine Craft, Charard Motion Pics, Films Ctr DC, Film Pres, Films Inc, Images Film, Ivy Films, Kerr Film, Kit Parker, Modern Sound, Natl Film Video, Roas Films, Twyman Films, U of IL Film, Video Comm, Welling Motion Pictures, Wholesome Film Ctr, Williams Films & Willoughby Peer.

From King to Congress. 1975. Quaker Oats. (Documentary). 50 min. Sound. 16mm Color. *Rental:* Modern Talking.

From Mao to Mozart: Issac Stern in China. Directed by Murray Lerner. 1979. United Artists. (Documentary). 90 min. Sound. 16mm Color. *Rental:* MGM United.

From Munich to the Funny War. Directed by Armand Panigel. Fr. France. (Documentary). 70 min. Sound. 16mm B&W. subtitles. *Rental:* French Am Cul.

From Noon Till Three. Charles Bronson & Jill Ireland. Directed by Frank D. Gilroy. 1976. United Artists. 99 min. Sound. 16mm Color. *Rental:* MGM United.

From Russia with... Bruno Gerussi. 1977. Canada. (Documentary). 52 min. Sound. 16mm Color. *Rental:* U of IL Film.

From Russia with Love. Sean Connery & Robert Shaw. Directed by Terence Young. 1963. United Artists. 118 min. Sound. 16mm Color. *Rental:* MGM United. *Rental:* MGM United, Videotape version.

From Sentences to Paragraphs. 1956. NET. (Documentary). 60 min. Sound. 16mm B&W. *Rental:* BYU Media.

From Spikes to Spindles: A History of the Chinese in New York. Directed by Christine Choy. 1976. Third World Newsreel. (Documentary). 50 min. Sound. 16mm Color. *Rental:* CA Newsreel. *Sale:* CA Newsreel. *Rental:* CA Newsreel, *Sale:* CA Newsreel, Cantonese Language version.

From the Ashes: Nicaragua Today. 1981. 60 min. Sound. 16mm Color. *Rental:* U Mich Media & Cinema Guild.

From the Cloud to the Resistance. Directed by Jean-Marie Straub & Daniele Huillet. Ger. 1979. Germany. (Cast unlisted). 105 min. Sound. 16mm Color. subtitles. *Rental:* New Yorker Films.

From the Earth to the Moon. Joseph Cotten & George Sanders. Directed by Byron Haskin. 1958. Warners. 100 min. Sound. 16mm Color. *Rental:* Budget Films, Ivy Films, Maljack, Modern Sound, Natl Film Video, Video Comm & Wholesome Film Ctr. *Lease:* Video Comm. *Rental:* Video Comm, *Sale:* Video Comm, Videotape version.

From the Life of the Marionettes. Robert Atzorn & Christine Buchegger. Directed by Ingmar Bergman. 1980. Germany. 104 min. Sound. 16mm Color. subtitles. *Rental:* Swank Motion.

From the Manger to the Cross. Directed by Sidney Olcott. 1913. Kalem. (Cast unlisted-Musical score only). 60 min. Sound. 16mm B&W. *Rental:* Film Classics. *Sale:* Film Classics. *Rental:* Film Classics, *Sale:* Film Classics, Silent 8mm version. *Rental:* Film Classics, Videotape version.

From the Mixed-up Files of Mrs. Basil E. Frankweiler *see* Hideaways.

From the Ocean to the Sky. Directed by Michael Dillon. 1979. Films Inc. (Documentary). 50 min. Sound. 16mm Color. *Rental:* Films Inc, Syracuse U Film & Utah Media. *Sale:* Films Inc. *Rental:* Films Inc, *Sale:* Films Inc, Videotape version.

From the Terrace. Paul Newman & Joanne Woodward. Directed by Mark Robson. 1960. Fox. (Anamorphic). 144 min. Sound. 16mm Color. *Rental:* Films Inc.

From This Day Forward. Joan Fontaine & Mark Stevens. Directed by John Berry. 1946. RKO. 95 min. Sound. 16mm B&W. *Rental:* RKO General Pics.

From Yellowstone to Tomorrow. 1972. NBC. (Documentary). 51 min. Sound. 16mm Color. *Rental:* Films Inc & U of IL Film. *Sale:* Films Inc. *Sale:* Films Inc, Videotape version.

Front, The. Woody Allen & Zero Mostel. Directed by Martin Ritt. 1976. Columbia. 94 min. Sound. 16mm Color. *Rental:* Arcus Film, Bosco Films, Budget Films, Cine Craft, Films Inc, Images Film, Kit Parker, Modern Sound, Swank Motion, Twyman Films, Welling Motion Pictures, Westcoast Films, Wholesome Film Ctr & Williams Films. *Rental:* Swank Motion, Videotape version.

Front Line: A New Look at the Vietnam War. Directed by David Bradbury. 1981. Filmmakers. (Documentary). 55 min. Sound. 16mm Color. *Rental:* Film Makers. *Sale:* Film Makers. *Sale:* Film Makers, Videotape version.

Front Page, The. Pat O'Brien & Adolphe Menjou. Directed by Lewis Milestone. 1931. United Artists. 103 min. Sound. 16mm B&W. *Rental:* Budget Films, Classic Film Mus, Em Gee Film Lib, Images Film & Kit Parker. *Sale:* Classic Film Mus, Cinema Concepts, Festival Films, Images Film & Reel Images. *Sale:* Festival Films, Images Film & Tamarelles French Film, Videotape version.

Front Page, The. Jack Lemmon & Walter Matthau. Directed by Billy Wilder. 1975. Universal. 105 min. Sound. 16mm Color. *Rental:* Swank Motion. *Rental:* Swank Motion, Anamorphic Color version.

Front Page Woman. Bette Davis & George Brent. Directed by Michael Curtiz. 1935. Warners. 82 min. Sound. 16mm B&W. *Rental:* MGM United.

Frontier, The. Directed by Roman Wionczek. 1947. Poland. (Documentary). 50 min. Sound. 16mm B&W. narrated Eng. *Rental:* Polish People.

Frontier Crusader. Tim McCoy. Directed by Peter Stewart. 1940. PRC. 64 min. Sound. 16mm B&W. *Sale:* Natl Cinema.

Frontier Feud. Jimmy Wakely. Directed by Lambert Hillyer. 1945. Monogram. 54 min. Sound. 16mm B&W. *Rental:* Hurlock Cine.

Frontier Fighters. Buster Crabbe. Directed by Sam Newfield. 1944. 59 min. Sound. 16mm B&W. *Rental:* Video Comm.

Frontier Fugitives. Tex Ritter & Dave O'Brien. Directed by Harry Fraser. 1945. PRC. 58 min. Sound. 16mm B&W. *Sale:* Classics Assoc NY.

Frontier Gal. Yvonne De Carlo & Rod Cameron. Directed by Charles Lamont. 1945. Universal. 115 min. Sound. 16mm Color. *Rental:* Swank Motion.

Frontier Gambler. John Bromfield & Coleen Gray. Directed by Sam Newfield. 1956. Associated. 75 min. Sound. 16mm B&W. *Rental:* Ivy Films. *Sale:* Rep Pic Film.

Frontier Gun. John Agar & Barton MacLane. Directed by Paul Landres. 1958. Fox. (Anamorphic). 70 min. Sound. 16mm B&W. *Rental:* Willoughby Peer.

Frontier Hellcat. Elke Sommer & Stewart Granger. Directed by Alfred Vohrer. 1966. Germany. 98 min. Sound. 16mm Color. dubbed. *Lease:* Time-Life Multimedia.

Frontier Horizon. John Wayne & Jennifer Jones. Directed by George Sherman. 1938. Republic. 55 min. Sound. 16mm B&W. *Rental:* Ivy Films. *Sale:* Rep Pic Film.

Frontier Investigator. Allen Lane. Directed by Fred C. Brannon. 1949. Republic. 60 min. Sound. 16mm B&W. *Rental:* Ivy Films. *Sale:* Rep Pic Film.

Frontier Justice. Hoot Gibson. Directed by Robert McGowan. 1935. First Division. 60 min. Videotape B&W. *Sale:* Video Comm.

Frontier Marshal. Randolph Scott & Nancy Kelly. Directed by Allan Dwan. 1939. Fox. 71 min. Sound. 16mm B&W. *Rental:* Films Inc.

Frontier Outlaws. Buster Crabbe. Directed by Sam Newfield. 1944. PRC. 60 min. Sound. 16mm B&W. *Rental:* Film Ctr DC. *Sale:* Natl Cinema.

Frontier Pony Express. Roy Rogers. Directed by Joseph Kane. 1939. Republic. 54 min. Sound. 16mm B&W. *Rental:* Budget Films & Ivy Films. *Sale:* Rep Pic Film.

Frontier Rangers. Keith Larsen & Buddy Ebsen. Directed by Jacques Tourneur. 1959. MGM. 86 min. Sound. 16mm Color. *Rental:* MGM United.

Frontier Scout. George Houston & Mantan Moreland. Directed by Sam Newfield. 1938. Grand National. 60 min. Sound. 16mm B&W. *Sale:* Morcraft Films.

Frontier Scout *see* Quincannon, Frontier Scout.

Frontier Uprising. James Davis. Directed by Edward L. Cahn. 1961. United Artists. 68 min. Sound. 16mm B&W. *Rental:* MGM United.

Frontier Vengeance. Don Barry. Directed by Nate Watt. 1940. Republic. 54 min. Sound. 16mm B&W. *Rental:* Ivy Films. *Sale:* Rep Pic Film.

Frontier Wolf. Piero Lulli & Maria Frau. 1950. Italy. 82 min. Sound. 16mm B&W. dubbed. *Rental:* Films Inc.

Frontiers of Forty-Nine. Bill Elliott. Directed by Joseph Levering. 1939. Columbia. 60 min. Sound. 16mm B&W. *Rental:* Mogulls Films & Newman Film Lib.

Frontiers of the Mind. 1966. Wolper. (Documentary). 50 min. Sound. 16mm B&W. *Rental:* Films Inc. *Sale:* Films Inc. *Sale:* Films Inc, Videotape version.

Frontiersman, The. William Boyd. Directed by Lesley Selander. 1938. Paramount. 60 min. Sound. 16mm B&W. *Lease:* Cinema Concepts.

Frontline. Directed by David Bradbury. 1978. Australia. (Documentary). 55 min. Sound. 16mm Color. *Rental:* Film Makers. *Sale:* Film Makers.

Frou Frou *see* Toy Wife.

Frozen Alive. Orig. Title: Fall X-701. Mark Stevens & Marianne Koch. Directed by Bernard Knowles. 1964. Germany. 80 min. Sound. 16mm B&W. dubbed. *Rental:* Budget Films & Ivy Films.

Frozen Dead, The. Dana Andrews & Anna Polk. Directed by Herbert J. Leder. 1967. Britain. 95 min. Sound. 16mm B&W. *Rental:* Buchan Pic, Cine Craft & Films Inc.

Frozen Ghost, The. Lon Chaney Jr. & Evelyn Ankers. Directed by Harold Young. 1945. Universal. 61 min. Sound. 16mm B&W. *Rental:* Swank Motion.

Frozen World, The. (Civilization Ser.). 1970. Britain. (Documentary). 50 min. Sound. 16mm Color. *Rental:* Educ Media CA, Films Inc, OK AV Ctr & Syracuse U Film. *Sale:* Films Inc. *Sale:* Films Inc, Videotape version.

Fruhling Auf Dem Eis. Von Nico Dostal, Eva Pawlik & Herta Mayen. 1951. Austria. 90 min. Sound. Videotape Color. *Sale:* Tamarelles French Film.

Fruit of Paradise, The. Directed by Vera Chytilova. Czech. 1971. Czechoslovakia. (Cast unlisted). 98 min. Sound. 16mm Color. subtitles. *Rental:* Images Film.

Fruits of Summer. Edwige Feulliere & Etchika Choureau. Directed by Raymond Bernard. 1954. France. 90 min. Sound. 16mm B&W. dubbed. *Rental:* Ivy Films.

Frustrated Campus, The. 1967. NET. (Documentary). 47 min. Sound. 16mm B&W. *Rental:* U of IL Film, Indiana AV Ctr & La Inst Res Ctr. *Sale:* Indiana AV Ctr.

F.T.A. Jane Fonda & Donald Sutherland. Directed by Francine Parker. 1972. Gold Key. 94 min. Sound. 16mm Color. *Rental:* Films Inc & Video Comm. *Rental:* Video Comm, Videotape version.

Fucking City, The. 1981. 88 min. Sound. 16mm B&W. *Rental:* Canyon Cinema.

Fugitive, The. Henry Fonda & Dolores Del Rio. Directed by John Ford. 1947. RKO. 99 min. Sound. 16mm B&W. *Rental:* Films Inc.

Fugitive from Justice, A. Roger Pryor. Directed by Terry Morse. 1940. Warners. 53 min. Sound. 16mm B&W. *Rental:* MGM United.

Fugitive from Sonora, The. Don Barry. Directed by Howard Bretherton. 1943. Republic. 55 min. Sound. 16mm B&W. *Rental:* Ivy Films. *Sale:* Rep Pic Film.

Fugitive in the Sky. Warren Hull & John Litel. Directed by Nick Grinde. 1937. Warners. 58 min. Sound. 16mm B&W. *Rental:* MGM United.

Fugitive Kind, The. Marlon Brando & Anna Magnani. Directed by Sidney Lumet. 1960. United Artists. 120 min. Sound. 16mm B&W. *Rental:* MGM United.

Fugitive Lovers, The. Robert Montgomery & Madge Evans. Directed by Richard Boleslawski. 1934. MGM. 84 min. Sound. 16mm B&W. *Rental:* MGM United.

Fugitive Valley. Range Busters. Directed by S. Roy Luby. 1941. Monogram. 61 min. Sound. 16mm B&W. *Rental:* Budget Films & Films Inc. *Sale:* Cinema Concepts.

Fugitives for a Night. Frank Albertson & Eleanor Lynn. Directed by Leslie Goodwins. 1939. RKO. 63 min. Sound. 16mm *Rental:* RKO General Pics.

Full Confession. Victor MacLaglen & Barry Fitzgerald. Directed by John Farrow. 1940. RKO. 73 min. Sound. 16mm *Rental:* RKO General Pics.

Full House see O. Henry's Full House.

Full Life, A. Koshiro Harada & Ineko Arima. Directed by Susumi Hani. Jap. 1962. Japan. (Anamorphic). 108 min. Sound. 16mm B&W. subtitles. *Rental:* New Yorker Films.

Full Moon Lunch. 1976. Japan. (Documentary). 57 min. Sound. 16mm Color. narrated Eng. *Rental:* U of IL Film, Iowa Films & Japan Society. *Sale:* Japan Society. *Sale:* Japan Society, Videotape version.

Full of Life. Judy Holliday & Richard Conte. Directed by Richard Quine. 1957. Columbia. 91 min. Sound. 16mm B&W. *Rental:* Arcus Film, Budget Films, Film Ctr DC, Films Inc, Inst Cinema, Kit Parker & Welling Motion Pictures.

Fuller Brush Girl, The. Lucille Ball & Eddie Albert. Directed by Lloyd Bacon. 1950. Columbia. 85 min. Sound. 16mm B&W. *Rental:* Bosco Films, Cine Craft, Films Inc, Inst Cinema, Modern Sound, Roas Films, Welling Motion Pictures & Westcoast Films.

Fuller Brush Man, The. Orig. Title: That Mad Mr. Jones. Red Skelton & Janet Blair. Directed by S. Sylvan Simon. 1948. Columbia. 93 min. Sound. 16mm B&W. *Rental:* Arcus Film, Bosco Films, Budget Films, Buchan Pic, Cine Craft Films, Film Pres, Inst Cinema, Modern Sound, Welling Motion Pictures & Westcoast Films.

Fun & Fancy Free. 1947. Disney. (Animated). 73 min. Sound. 16mm Color. *Rental:* Bosco Films, Buchan Pic, Cine Craft, Cousino Visual Ed, Disney Prod, Elliot Film Co, Film Ctr DC, Film Pres, Films Inc, MGM United, Modern Sound, Newman Film Lib, Roas Films, Swank Motion, Twyman Films, U of IL Film, Welling Motion Pictures, Westcoast Films & Williams Films.

Fun House, The. Elizabeth Berridge, Cooper Huckabee & Sylvia Miles. Directed by Tobe Hooper. 1981. Universal. 96 min. Sound. 16mm Color. *Rental:* Swank Motion. *Rental:* Swank Motion, Videotape version.

Fun in Acapulco. Elvis Presley & Ursula Andress. Directed by Richard Thorpe. 1963. Paramount. 97 min. Sound. Color. *Rental:* Films Inc. *Sale:* Blackhawk Films, Cinema Concepts & Williams Films, Videotape version.

Fun with Dick & Jane. Jane Fonda & George Segal. Directed by Ted Kotcheff. 1977. Columbia. 95 min. Sound. 16mm Color. *Rental:* Arcus Film, Budget Films, Films Inc, Modern Sound, Swank Motion, Twyman Films, Westcoast Films, Wholesome Film Ctr & Williams Films. *Rental:* Swank Motion, Videotape version.

Funabenkei. 1970. 60 min. Sound. Videotape Color. *Rental:* Iowa Films.

Functional Anatomy of the Hypothalamus & Pituitary. 1980. 46 min. Sound. Videotape Color. *Rental:* Natl AV Ctr.

Fundamentals of Radioactivity, The. 1952. Atomic Energy Commission. (Documentary). 59 min. Sound. 16mm B&W. *Rental:* Natl AV Ctr.

Fundi: The Story of Ella Baker. Directed by Joanne Grant. 1980. New Day. (Documentary). 63 min. Sound. 16mm Color. *Rental:* New Day Films. *Sale:* New Day Films. *Sale:* New Day Films, Videotape version.

Funeral in Berlin. Michael Caine & Oscar Homolka. Directed by Guy Hamilton. 1966. Paramount. (Anamorphic). 102 min. Sound. 16mm Color. *Rental:* Films Inc.

Funny Car Summer. Jim Dunn. Directed by Ron Philips. 1974. Ambassador. 88 min. Sound. 16mm Color. *Rental:* Westcoast Films.

Funny Face see Bright Lights.

Funny Face. Fred Astaire & Audrey Hepburn. Directed by Stanley Donen. 1957. Paramount. 103 min. Sound. 16mm Color. *Rental:* Films Inc.

Funny Girl. Barbra Streisand, Omar Sharif & Walter Pidgeon. Directed by William Wyler. 1968. Columbia. 155 min. Sound. 16mm Color. *Rental:* Arcus Film, Bosco Films, Budget Films, Cine Craft, Films Inc, Images Film, Modern Sound, Newman Film Lib, Swank Motion, Twyman Films, Welling Motion Pictures, Westcoast Films & Wholesome Film Ctr. *Rental:* Images Film & Swank Motion, Anamorphic version. *Rental:* Swank Motion, Videotape version.

Funny Lady. Barbra Streisand & James Caan. Directed by Herbert Ross. 1975. Columbia. 136 min. Sound. 16mm Color. *Rental:* Arcus Film, Budget Films, Cine Craft, Films Inc, Modern Sound, Newman Film, Film Lib, Swank Motion, Twyman Films, Welling Motion Pictures, Westcoast Films, Wholesome Film Ctr & Williams Films. *Rental:* Twyman Films, Anamorphic version. *Rental:* Swank Motion, Videotape version.

Funny Thing Happened on the Way to the Garbage Dump, A. 1974. Time-Life. (Documentary). 50 min. Sound. 16mm B&W. *Rental:* Time-Life Multimedia. *Sale:* Time-Life Multimedia.

Funny Thing Happened on the Way to the Forum, A. Zero Mostel & Phil Silvers. Directed by Richard Lester. 1966. United Artists. 97 min. Sound. 16mm Color. *Rental:* MGM United. *Rental:* MGM United, Videotape version.

Funnyman. Peter Bonerz. Directed by John Korty. 1967. John Korty. (Color Sequences). 98 min. Sound. 16mm B&W. *Rental:* New Yorker Films.

Furia. Isa Pola & Rosanno Brazzi. Directed by Geoffredo Alessandrini. 1948. Italy. 90 min. Sound. 16mm B&W. dubbed. *Rental:* Ivy Films.

Furies, The. Barbara Stanwyck & Walter Huston. Directed by Anthony Mann. 1950. Paramount. 109 min. Sound. 16mm B&W. *Rental:* Films Inc.

Furious Encounter. Rodolfo De Anda. 1962. Mexico. 84 min. Sound. 16mm Color. dubbed. *Rental:* Ivy Films.

Furlough in the Desert *see* Desert Furlough.

Further Perils of Laurel & Hardy, The. 1967. Fox. (Anthology). 99 min. Sound. 16mm B&W. *Rental:* Films Inc.

Furtivos. Trans. Title: Poachers. Lola Gaos & Alicia Sanchez. Directed by Jose Luis Borau. Span. 1975. Spain. 88 min. Sound. 16mm Color. subtitles. *Rental:* New Yorker Films.

Fury. Spencer Tracy & Sylvia Sidney. Directed by Fritz Lang. 1936. MGM. 94 min. Sound. 16mm B&W. *Rental:* Films Inc & MGM United.

Fury, The. Kirk Douglas & John Cassavetes. Directed by Brian De Palma. 1978. Fox. 118 min. Sound. 16mm Color. *Rental:* Williams Films.

Fury at Furnace Creek. Victor Mature & Coleen Gray. Directed by Bruce Humberstone. 1948. Fox. 88 min. Sound. 16mm B&W. *Rental:* Films Inc.

Fury at Gunsight Pass. David Brian & Neville Brand. Directed by Fred F. Sears. 1956. Columbia. 68 min. Sound. 16mm B&W. *Rental:* Inst Cinema.

Fury at Showdown. Nick Adams & John Derek. Directed by Gerd Oswald. 1957. United Artists. 75 min. Sound. 16mm B&W. *Rental:* MGM United.

Fury at Smuggler's Bay. Peter Cushing & John Fraser. Directed by John Gilling. 1963. Embassy. 92 min. Sound. 16mm B&W. *Rental:* Films Inc.

Fury in Paradise. Peter Thompson. Directed by George Bruce. 1954. Mexico. 77 min. Sound. 16mm Color. dubbed. *Rental:* Ivy Films. *Sale:* Rep Pic Film.

Fury of Hercules. Orig. Title: Fury of Samson. Brad Harris & Alan Steel. Directed by Gianfranco Parolini. 1961. Italy. 100 min. Sound. 16mm Color. dubbed. *Rental:* Welling Motion Pictures.

Fury of Samson *see* Fury of Hercules.

Fury of the Congo. Johnny Weissmuller & Sherry Moreland. Directed by William Berke. 1951. Columbia. 69 min. Sound. 16mm B&W. *Rental:* Inst Cinema & Newman Film Lib.

Fury of the Orinoco. South America. (Documentary). 50 min. Sound. 16mm Color. *Rental:* Inst Cinema. *Sale:* Inst Cinema.

Fury of the Sabers. Lex Barker & Gustavo Rojo. 1964. Balcazar. 90 min. Sound. 16mm Color. *Rental:* Westcoast Films.

Fury River. Keith Larsen & Buddy Ebsen. Directed by Jacques Tourneur. 1959. MGM. 75 min. Sound. 16mm Color. *Rental:* MGM United.

Fury Unleashed *see* Hot Rod Gang.

Fusion: The Energy Promise. 1976. Britain. (Documentary). 56 min. Sound. 16mm Color. *Rental:* U of IL Film. *Sale:* PBS Video. *Rental:* PBS Video, Videotape version.

Future & the Negro, The. 1965. NET. (Documentary). 75 min. Sound. 16mm B&W. *Rental:* Indiana AV Ctr. *Sale:* Indiana AV Ctr.

Future Shock. Orson Welles. Directed by Orson Welles. 1972. Metromedia. 42 min. Sound. 16mm Color. *Rental:* OK AV Ctr, Utah Media & Wholesome Film Ctr.

Future That Was, The. (Shock of the New Ser.). 1980. Time-Life. (Documentary). 52 min. Sound. 16mm Color. *Rental:* U Cal Media.

Futureworld. Blythe Danner, Yul Brynner & Peter Fonda. Directed by Richard T. Heffron. 1976. American International. 104 min. Sound. 16mm Color. *Rental:* Swank Motion, Welling Motion Pictures, Wholesome Film Ctr & Williams Films.

Futz. Seth Allen. Directed by Tom O'Horgan. 1969. Landau. 92 min. Sound. 16mm Color. *Rental:* Films Inc, Ivy Films & Rep Pic Film. *Lease:* Rep Pic Film.

Fuzz. Burt Reynolds & Raquel Welch. Directed by Richard A. Colla. 1972. United Artists. (Anamorphic). 93 min. Sound. 16mm Color. *Rental:* Budget Films, MGM United, Welling Motion Pictures & Westcoast Films.

Fuzzy Pink Nightgown. Jane Russell & Keenan Wynn. Directed by Norman Taurog. 1957. United Artists. 87 min. Sound. 16mm B&W. *Rental:* MGM United.

Fuzzy Settles Down. Buster Crabbe & Al St. John. Directed by Sam Newfield. 1944. PRC. 62 min. Videotape B&W. *Sale:* Video Comm.

FX-Eighteen Super Spy. Richard Wyler. Directed by Riccardo Freda. 1965. Italy. 95 min. Sound. 16mm Color. dubbed. *Rental:* Video Comm.

Fyre. Lynn Theel & Allen Goorwitz. Directed by Richard Grand. Compass. 82 min. Sound. 16mm Color. *Rental:* Films Inc.

G. I. Blues. Elvis Presley & Juliet Prowse. Directed by Norman Taurog. 1960. Paramount. 104 min. Sound. Color. *Rental:* Films Inc. *Sale:* Blackhawk Films, Cinema Concepts & Williams Films, Videotape version.

G. I. Honeymoon. Gale Storm & Peter Cookson. Directed by Phil Karlson. 1945. Monogram. 70 min. Sound. 16mm B&W. *Rental:* Mogulls Films.

G. I. Joe. 1963. Hearst. (Documentary). 50 min. Sound. 16mm B&W. *Sale:* King Features.

G. I. Joe *see* Story of G. I. Joe.

G. I. War Brides. Anna Lee & Robert Armstrong. Directed by George Blair. 1946. Republic. 69 min. Sound. 16mm B&W. *Rental:* Ivy Films.

G-Man's Wife *see* Public Enemy's Wife.

G-Men. James Cagney & Lloyd Nolan. Directed by William Keighley. 1935. Warners. 85 min. Sound. 16mm B&W. *Rental:* MGM United.

G-Men Never Forget. Clayton Moore & Roy Barcroft. Directed by Fred C. Brannon. 1948. Republic. 163 min. Sound. 16mm B&W. *Rental:* Ivy Films.

G-Men vs. the Black Dragon. Rod Cameron. Directed by William Witney. 1943. Republic. 224 min. Sound. 16mm B&W. *Rental:* Ivy Films.

Gable & Lombard. James Brolin & Jill Clayburgh. Directed by Sidney J. Furie. 1976. Universal. 131 min. Sound. 16mm Color. *Rental:* Swank Motion.

Gabriel Over the White House. Walter Huston & Karen Morley. Directed by Gregory La Cava. 1933. MGM. 87 min. Sound. 16mm B&W. *Rental:* MGM United.

Gabriela. Sonia Braga & Marcello Mastroianni. Directed by Bruno Barreto. Port. 1984. 102 min. 16mm Color. subtitles. *Rental:* MGM United.

Gaby. Leslie Caron & John Kerr. Directed by Curtis Bernhardt. 1956. MGM. 97 min. Sound. 16mm Color. *Rental:* MGM United.

Gadfly, The. Trans. Title: Poprigunya. Oleg Strizhenov. Directed by A. Feinzimmer. Rus. 1955. Russia. 94 min. Sound. 16mm B&W. subtitles. *Rental:* Corinth Films.

Gai Savoir, Le. Jean-Pierre Leaud & Juliette Bertho. Directed by Jean-Luc Godard. Fr. 1970. France. 91 min. Sound. 16mm Color. subtitles. *Rental:* Images Film & Twyman Films. *Sale:* Images Film & Twyman Films. *Sale:* Images Film, Videotape version.

Gaiety *see* Fiesta.

Gaijin. Kyoto Tsukamoto & Antonio Fagundes. Directed by Tizuka Yamasaki. Jap. & Port. 1979. 105 min. Sound. 16mm Color. subtitles. *Rental:* New Yorker Films.

Gaily, Gaily. Beau Bridges & Melina Mercouri. Directed by Norman Jewison. 1970. United Artists. 106 min. Sound. 16mm Color. *Rental:* MGM United.

Gal Young Un. Directed by Victor Nunez. 1980. First Run. (Cast unlisted). 105 min. Sound. 16mm Color. *Rental:* First Run.

Galaxina. Dorothy Stratten, Avery Schreiber & David James Hinton. Directed by William Sachs. 96 min. Sound. 16mm Color. *Rental:* Swank Motion.

Galaxy Criminals, The *see* Wild, Wild Planet.

Galaxy of Terror. Edward Albert & Erin Moran. Directed by Bruce Clark. 1981. New World. 83 min. Sound. 16mm Color. *Rental:* Films Inc.

Gale Is Dead. 1970. Britain. (Documentary). 51 min. Sound. 16mm Color. *Rental:* Films Inc. *Sale:* Films Inc. *Sale:* Films Inc, Videotape version.

Galia. Mireille Darc & Venantino Venantini. Directed by Georges Lautner. Fr. 1966. France. Sound. 16mm B&W. subtitles. *Rental:* Films Inc.

Galileo. Cyril Cusack. Directed by Liliana Cavani. 1971. Italy. 98 min. Sound. 16mm Color. dubbed. *Rental:* Swank Motion.

Galileo. Topol. Directed by Joseph Losey. 1973. AFT. 155 min. Sound. 16mm Color. *Rental:* Films Inc.

Galileo Seven, The. William Shatner & Leonard Nimoy. Directed by Robert Gist. 1967. Star Trek. 50 min. Sound. 16mm Color. *Rental:* Westcoast Films.

Gallant Defender. Charles Starrett. Directed by David Selman. 1935. Columbia. 60 min. Sound. 16mm B&W. *Rental:* Williams Films.

Gallant Hours. James Cagney & Dennis Weaver. Directed by Robert Montgomery. 1960. United Artists. 115 min. Sound. 16mm B&W. *Rental:* MGM United.

Gallant Journey. Glenn Ford & Janet Blair. Directed by William A. Wellman. 1946. Columbia. 86 min. Sound. 16mm B&W. *Rental:* Bosco Films & Kit Parker.

Gallant Legion, The. Joseph Schildkraut & Adrian Booth. Directed by Joseph Kane. 1948. Republic. 88 min. Sound. 16mm B&W. *Rental:* Ivy Films. *Sale:* Rep Pic Film & Nostalgia Merchant.

Gallant Prince, The. 1938. Germany. (Cast unlisted). 79 min. Sound. 16mm B&W. dubbed. *Rental:* Film Classics.

Gallant Sons. Jackie Cooper & Leo Gorcey. Directed by George B. Seitz. 1940. MGM. 76 min. Sound. 16mm B&W. *Rental:* MGM United.

Gallipoli. Directed by Peter Weir. 1981. Australia. 110 min. Sound. 16mm Color. *Rental:* Festival Films. *Rental:* Festival Films, Videotape version.

Galloping Dynamite. Kermit Maynard. Directed by Harry Fraser. 1937. Ambassador-Conn. 58 min. Sound. 16mm B&W. *Rental:* Modern Sound. *Sale:* Cinema Concepts & Natl Cinema.

Gals, Inc. Grace McDonald & Leon Errol. Directed by Leslie Goodwins. 1943. Universal. 60 min. Sound. 16mm B&W. *Rental:* Mogulls Films & Film Ctr DC.

Gambit. Shirley MacLaine & Michael Caine. Directed by Ronald Neame. 1966. Universal. 109 min. Sound. 16mm Color. *Rental:* Swank Motion.

Gambler, The. James Caan. Directed by Karel Reisz. 1974. Paramount. 111 min. Sound. 16mm Color. *Rental:* Films Inc.

Gambler, The. Nikolai Burliayev. Directed by Alexei Batalov. Rus. 1978. Russia. 95 min. Sound. 16mm Color. subtitles. *Rental:* Corinth Films.

Gambler from Natchez, The. Dale Robertson & Debra Paget. Directed by Henry Levin. 1954. Fox. 83 min. Sound. 16mm Color. *Rental:* Films Inc.

Gambler, The: Kenny Rogers As the Gambler. Kenny Rogers & Bruce Boxleitner. Directed by Dick Lowry. 1980. Viacom. 94 min. Sound. 16mm Color. *Rental:* Williams Films.

Gambler Wore a Gun, The. James Davis & Merry Anders. Directed by Edward L. Cahn. 1961. United Artists. 66 min. Sound. 16mm B&W. *Rental:* MGM United.

Gamblers, The. Don Gordon & Suzy Kendall. Directed by Ron Winston. 1969. UMC. 93 min. Sound. 16mm Color. *Rental:* Swank Motion.

Gambling. 1980. NBC. (Documentary). 78 min. Videotape Color. *Rental:* Films Inc. *Sale:* Films Inc.

Gambling House. Victor Mature & Terry Moore. Directed by Ted Tetzlaff. 1950. RKO. 80 min. Sound. 16mm B&W. *Rental:* Films Inc.

Gambling Lady. Barbara Stanwyck & Joel McCrea. Directed by Archie Mayo. 1934. Warners. 66 min. Sound. 16mm B&W. *Rental:* MGM United.

Gambling on the High Seas. Jane Wyman & Gilbert Roland. Directed by George Amy. 1940. Warners. 56 min. Sound. 16mm B&W. *Rental:* MGM United.

Gambling Terror. Johnny Mack Brown. Directed by Sam Newfield. 1937. Republic. 60 min. Sound. 16mm B&W. *Rental:* Mogulls Films. *Sale:* Reel Images.

Gambling with Souls. Directed by Elmer Clifton. 1936. Jay Dee Kay. (Exploitation). 75 min. Sound. 16mm B&W. *Sale:* Morcraft Films.

Game Is Over, The. Jane Fonda & Peter McEnery. Directed by Roger Vadim. Fr. 1967. France. 96 min. Sound. 16mm Color. subtitles. *Rental:* Swank Motion & Twyman Films.

Game of Death *see* Bruce Lee's Game of Death.

Game of Death, The. John Loder & Edgar Barrier. Directed by Norman Houston. 1946. RKO. 72 min. Sound. 16mm B&W. *Rental:* Ivy Films & Swank Motion. *Sale:* Rep Pic Film.

Games. Simone Signoret, James Caan & Katharine Ross. Directed by Curtis Harrington. 1967. Universal. 100 min. Sound. 16mm Color. *Rental:* Swank Motion. *Rental:* Swank Motion, Anamorphic version.

Games, The. Michael Crawford & Ryan O'Neal. Directed by Michael Winner. 1970. Fox. 95 min. Sound. 16mm Color. *Rental:* Films Inc. *Rental:* Films Inc, Anamorphic color version.

Games of Desire. Ingrid Thulin. Directed by Hans Albin & Peter Bernis. 1967. Germany. 92 min. Sound. 16mm B&W. dubbed. *Rental:* Budget Films & Video Comm.

Games of the XXI Olympiad, The. Directed by Jean-Claude Labreque. 1976. Canada. (Documentary). 119 min. Sound. 16mm Color. *Rental:* Films Inc & Modern Sound. *Sale:* Films Inc.

Games of the XXI Olympiad *see* Montreal Olympiad.

Gandhi. Ben Kingsley, Candice Bergen, Sir John Gielgud. Directed by Sir Richard Attenborough. 1985. Columbia. 188 min. Sound. 16mm Color. *Rental:* Swank Motion. *Sale:* Festival Films. *Sale:* Festival Films, *Rental:* Swank Motion, Videotape version.

Gandhi's India. 1970. Britain. (Documentary). 58 min. Sound. 16mm B&W. *Rental:* U Cal Media & Indiana AV Ctr. *Sale:* Indiana AV Ctr.

Gang, The. Ralph Reeder & Gina Malo. Directed by Alfred Goulding. 1937. Britain. 55 min. Sound. 16mm B&W. *Rental:* Film Classics & Mogulls Films.

Gang Busters *see* Arizona Gang Busters.

Gang Made Good, The *see* Tuxedo Junction.

Gang That Couldn't Shoot Straight, The. Jerry Orbach & Jo Van Fleet. Directed by James Goldstone. 1971. MGM. 96 min. Sound. 16mm Color. *Rental:* MGM United.

Gang War. Kent Taylor & Charles Bronson. Directed by Gene Fowler Jr. 1958. Fox. 74 min. Sound. 16mm B&W. *Rental:* Films Inc.

Gang War *see* Odd Man Out.

Ganga Zumba. Antonio Pitanga. Directed by Carlos Diegues. Port. 1963. Brazil. 99 min. Sound. 16mm B&W. subtitles. *Rental:* New Yorker Films.

Gangbusters. Myron Healey. Directed by Bill Karn. 1955. RKO. 78 min. Sound. 16mm B&W. *Rental:* Budget Films, Video Comm & Westcoast Films. *Lease:* Video Comm. *Rental:* Video Comm, *Lease:* Video Comm, Videotape version.

Gang's All Here, The. Alice Faye & Carmen Miranda. Directed by Busby Berkeley. 1943. Fox. 103 min. Sound. 16mm Color. *Rental:* Films Inc.

Gangs of Chicago. Lloyd Nolan & Barton MacLane. Directed by Arthur Lubin. 1940. Republic. 54 min. Sound. 16mm B&W. *Rental:* Ivy Films.

Gangs of New York. Charles Bickford & Ann Dvorak. Directed by James Cruze. 1938. Republic. 54 min. Sound. 16mm B&W. *Rental:* Ivy Films. *Sale:* Rep Pic Film.

Gangs of Sonora. Robert Livingston & Bob Steele. Directed by John English. 1941. Republic. 56 min. Sound. 16mm B&W. *Rental:* Ivy Films. *Sale:* Rep Pic Film & Nostalgia Merchant.

Gangs of the City. Orig. Title: Public Enemies. Wendy Barrie & Russell Hicks. Directed by Albert S. Rogell. 1941. Republic. 54 min. Sound. 16mm B&W. *Rental:* Ivy Films.

Gangs of the Waterfront. Robert Armstrong. Directed by George Blair. 1945. Republic. 55 min. Sound. 16mm B&W. *Rental:* Ivy Films.

Gangster, The. Barry Sullivan & John Ireland. Directed by Gordon Wiles. 1947. Allied Artists. 84 min. Sound. 16mm B&W. *Rental:* Hurlock Cine.

Gangster Story, The. Walter Matthau & Carol Grace. Directed by Walter Matthau. 1959. RCIP. 70 min. Sound. 16mm B&W. *Rental:* Ivy Films. *Sale:* Rep Pic Film.

Gangster We Made, The *see* Vicious Years.

Gangster's Boy. Jackie Cooper & Robert Warwick. Directed by William Nigh. 1938. Monogram. 80 min. Sound. 16mm B&W. *Rental:* Budget Films.

Gangster's Den. Buster Crabbe. Directed by Sam Newfield. 1945. PRC. 55 min. Sound. 16mm B&W. *Rental:* Ivy Films. *Sale:* Classics Assoc NY & Rep Pic Film.

Gangsters of the Frontier. Tex Ritter & Dave O'Brien. Directed by Elmer Clifton. 1944. PRC. 56 min. Sound. 16mm B&W. *Rental:* Ivy Films, Mogulls Films, Welling Motion Pictures & Westcoast Films. *Sale:* Classics Assoc NY.

Gangway. Jessie Matthews, Nat Pendleton & Alastair Sim. Directed by Sonnie Hale. 1937. Britain. 88 min. Sound. 16mm B&W. *Rental:* Budget Films.

Gangway for Tomorrow. Robert Ryan & John Carradine. Directed by John H. Auer. 1944. RKO. 69 min. Sound. 16mm *Rental:* RKO General Pics.

Garden Murder Case, The. Edmund Lowe & Virginia Bruce. Directed by Edwin L. Marin. 1936. MGM. 62 min. Sound. 16mm B&W. *Rental:* MGM United.

Garden of Allah, The. Marlene Dietrich & Charles Boyer. Directed by Richard Boleslawski. 1936. United Artists. 80 min. Sound. 16mm B&W. *Rental:* Em Gee Film Lib & Films Inc.

Garden of Beauty, The. Florence Carrol & Marion Game. Directed by Eric Lipman. 1976. France. 92 min. Sound. 16mm Color. subtitles. *Rental:* World Northal.

Garden of Eden, The. Corrine Griffith & Charles Ray. Directed by Lewis Milestone. 1928. United Artists. 85 min. Silent. 16mm B&W. *Rental:* Em Gee Film Lib, Kerr Film & Kit Parker. *Sale:* Cinema Concepts, Em Gee Film Lib, Griggs Movie & Natl Cinema. *Sale:* Tamarelles French Film, Videotape version.

Garden of Eden, The. Mickey Knox & Jamie O'Hara. Directed by Max Nosseck. 1957. Excelsior. 90 min. Sound. 16mm Color. *Rental:* Ivy Films.

Garden of Evil, The. Gary Cooper & Susan Hayward. Directed by Henry Hathaway. 1954. Fox. 100 min. Sound. 16mm Color. *Rental:* Films Inc.

Garden of the Finzi-Continis, The. Dominique Sanda & Helmut Berger. Directed by Vittorio De Sica. 1970. Italy. 103 min. Sound. 16mm Color. subtitles. *Rental:* Cinema Five & Festival Films. *Lease:* Cinema Five.

Garden of the Moon, The. John Payne & Pat O'Brien. Directed by Busby Berkeley. 1938. Warners. 94 min. Sound. 16mm B&W. *Rental:* MGM United.

Garibaldi. Directed by Roberto Rossellini. 1960. Italy. (Cast unlisted). 90 min. Sound. 16mm Color. *Rental:* Liberty Co.

Garlic Is As Good As Ten Mothers. Directed by Les Blank. 1980. 51 min. Sound. 16mm Color. *Rental:* Canyon Cinema.

Garment Jungle, The. Lee J. Cobb & Kerwin Mathews. Directed by Vincent Sherman. 1957. Columbia. 88 min. Sound. 16mm B&W. *Rental:* Films Inc & Inst Cinema.

Gas. Susan Anspach & Donald Sutherland. Directed by Les Rose. 1981. Paramount. 100 min. Sound. 16mm Color. *Rental:* Films Inc.

Gas House Kids, The. Robert Lowery & Billy Halop. Directed by Sam Newfield. 1946. PRC. 68 min. Sound. 16mm B&W. *Sale:* Classics Assoc NY.

Gas House Kids Go West, The. Carl Switzer & Chili Williams. Directed by Edward L. Cahn. 1947. PRC. 62 min. Sound. 16mm B&W. *Sale:* Classics Assoc NY.

Gas House Kids in Hollywood. Carl Switzer & Tommy Bond. Directed by William Beaudine. 1947. Eagle Lion. 63 min. Sound. 16mm B&W. *Sale:* Classics Assoc NY.

Gas Pump Girls, The. Kirsten Baker. Directed by Joel Bender. 1979. Cannon. 90 min. Sound. 16mm Color. *Rental:* Swank Motion.

Gas-S-S-S. Robert Corff & Elaine Giftos. Directed by Roger Corman. 1970. American International. 79 min. Sound. 16mm Color. *Rental:* Films Inc, Welling Motion Pictures & Wholesome Film Ctr.

Gaslight. Orig. Title: Angel Street. Ingrid Bergman & Charles Boyer. Directed by George Cukor. 1944. MGM. 114 min. Sound. 16mm B&W. *Rental:* MGM United.

Gaslight Follies. Rudolph Valentino & William S. Hart. 1955. Embassy. (Anthology, music & sound effects only). 110 min. Sound. 16mm B&W. *Rental:* Films Inc.

Gasparone. Carl Millokers, Karl Paryla & Wolfgang Heinz. Ger. 1952. Austria. 90 min. Sound. Videotape Color. subtitles. *Sale:* Tamarelles French Films.

Gate of Hell: Jigokuman. Machiko Kyo. Directed by Teinosuke Kinugasa. Jap. 1954. Japan. 86 min. Sound. 16mm Color. subtitles. *Rental:* Films Inc, Janus Films & New Cinema.

Gatemouth Brown. Phoenix. (Documentary). 58 min. Sound. 16mm Color. *Rental:* Phoenix Films. *Sale:* Phoenix Films. *Sale:* Phoenix Films, Videotape version.

Gates of Heaven. Floyd McClure & Florence Rasmussen. Directed by Errol Morris. 1978. New Yorker. 85 min. Sound. 16mm Color. *Rental:* New Yorker Films.

Gates of Paris, The. Pierre Brasseur & Georges Brassens. Directed by Rene Clair. Fr. 1957. France. 95 min. Sound. 16mm B&W. subtitles. *Rental:* Films Inc.

Gateways to the Mind. 1962. 58 min. Sound. 16mm Color. *Rental:* Utah Media.

Gathering of Eagles, A. Rock Hudson & Rod Taylor. Directed by Delbert Mann. 1963. Universal. 116 min. Sound. 16mm Color. *Rental:* Williams Films.

Gathering of One, A. 1976. ABC. (Cast unlisted). 60 min. Sound. 16mm Color. *Rental:* Natl Churches Christ. *Sale:* Natl Churches Christ.

Gathering Storm, The. Richard Burton & Virginia McKenna. Directed by Herbert Wise. 1974. 75 min. Sound. 16mm Color. *Rental:* Films Inc.

Gatling Gun, The. Guy Stockwell & Woody Strode. Directed by Robert Gordon. 1971. Gold Key. 93 min. Sound. 16mm Color. *Rental:* Video Comm.

Gatopardo, Il *see* Leopard.

Gator. Burt Reynolds, Jack Weston & Jerry Reed. Directed by Burt Reynolds. 1976. United Artists. 116 min. Sound. 16mm Color. *Rental:* Budget Films, MGM United, Welling Motion Pictures & Westcoast Films.

Gaucho. 1978. ABC. (Cast unlisted). 47 min. Sound. 16mm Color. *Rental:* Time-Life Multimedia. *Sale:* Time-Life Multimedia. *Sale:* Time-Life Multimedia, Videotape version.

Gaucho, The. Douglas Fairbanks & Lupe Velez. Directed by F. Richard Jones. 1928. United Artists. 105 min. Sound. 16mm B&W. *Rental:* A Twyman Pres & Museum Mod Art. *Rental:* A Twyman Pres, 132 min. silent version.

Gaucho Serenade. Gene Autry. Directed by Frank McDonald. 1940. Republic. 70 min. Sound. 16mm B&W. *Rental:* Film Ctr DC.

Gauchos of Eldorado. Tom Tyler, Bob Steele & Lois Collier. Directed by Lester Orlebeck. 1941. Republic. 56 min. Sound. 16mm B&W. *Sale:* Rep Pic Film & Nostalgia Merchant.

Gauguin in Tahiti: The Search for Paradise. 1967. CBS. (Documentary). 54 min. Sound. 16mm Color. *Rental:* McGraw-Hill Films. *Sale:* McGraw-Hill Films.

Gauloises Bleues, Les. Trans. Title: French Cigarettes. Annie Giradot & Bruno Cremer. Directed by Michel Cournot. Fr. 1969. France. 93 min. Sound. 16mm Color. subtitles. *Rental:* MGM United.

Gauntlet, The. Clint Eastwood & Sondra Locke. Directed by Clint Eastwood. 1977. Warners. 113 min. Sound. 16mm Color. *Rental:* Modern Sound, Swank Motion, Twyman Films & Williams Films. *Rental:* Swank Motion, Videotape version.

Gay Amigo, The. Duncan Renaldo & Leo Carillo. Directed by Wallace Fox. 1949. United Artists. 60 min. Sound. 16mm B&W. *Rental:* Budget Films.

Gay Blades *see* Tournament Tempo.

Gay Bride, The. Carole Lombard & Chester Morris. Directed by Jack Conway. 1934. MGM. 81 min. Sound. 16mm B&W. *Rental:* MGM United.

Gay Cavalier, The. Gilbert Roland. Directed by William Nigh. 1946. Monogram. 70 min. Sound. 16mm B&W. *Rental:* Westcoast Films. *Sale:* Video Comm, Videotape version.

Gay Deceivers, The. Kevin Coughlin, Larry Casey & Michael Greer. Directed by Bruce Kessler. 1969. Fanfare. 91 min. Sound. 16mm Color. *Rental:* Budget Films.

Gay Desperado, The. Nino Martini & Ida Lupino. Directed by Rouben Mamoulian. 1936. United Artists. 95 min. Sound. 16mm B&W. *Rental:* Em Gee Film Lib.

Gay Diplomat, The. Ilka Chase & Rita La Roy. Directed by Pandro S. Berman. 1931. RKO. 67 min. Sound. 16mm *Rental:* RKO General Pics.

Gay Divorcee, The. Fred Astaire & Ginger Rogers. Directed by Mark Sandrich. 1934. RKO. 108 min. Sound. 16mm B&W. *Rental:* Films Inc.

Gay Falcon, The. George Sanders. Directed by Irving Reis. 1941. RKO. 66 min. Sound. 16mm B&W. *Rental:* Films Inc. *Lease:* Films Inc.

Gay Nineties, The *see* Floradora Girl.

Gay Purr-ee. 1962. Warners. 86 min. Sound. 16mm Color. *Rental:* Arcus Film.

Gay Ranchero, The. Roy Rogers. Directed by William Witney. 1948. Republic. 54 min. Sound. 16mm B&W. *Rental:* Ivy Films. *Sale:* Rep Pic Film & Nostalgia Merchant.

Gay Senorita, The. Jinx Falkenburg & Steve Cochran. Directed by Arthur Dreifuss. 1945. Columbia. 70 min. Sound. 16mm B&W. *Rental:* Kit Parker.

Gay Sisters, The. Barbara Stanwyck & George Brent. Directed by Irving Rapper. 1942. Warners. 110 min. Sound. 16mm B&W. *Rental:* MGM United.

Gay U. S. A. Directed by Arthur J. Bressan. 1977. Artists United for Gay Rights. (Documentary). 78 min. Sound. 16mm Color. *Rental:* Kit Parker, Videotape version.

Gay Vagabond, The. Roscoe Karns & Ruth Donnelly. Directed by William Morgan. 1941. Republic. 54 min. Sound. 16mm B&W. *Rental:* Ivy Films. *Sale:* Rep Pic Film.

Gazebo, The. Glenn Ford & Debbie Reynolds. Directed by George Marshall. 1959. MGM. 102 min. Sound. 16mm B&W. *Rental:* MGM United. *Rental:* MGM United, Anamorphic B&W version. *Rental:* MGM United, Videotape version.

Geburt der Nation, Die. Directed by Klaus Wyborny. 1973. Germany. (Experimental,color sequences). 70 min. Sound. 16mm B&W. *Lease:* Museum Mod Art. *Sale:* Museum Mod Art. *Rental:* Museum Mod Art.

Geisha, A. Michiyo Kogure. Directed by Kenji Mizoguchi. Jap. 1953. Japan. 87 min. Sound. 16mm B&W. subtitles. *Rental:* New Yorker Films.

Geisha Boy. Jerry Lewis & Sessue Hayakawa. Directed by Frank Tashlin. 1958. Paramount. 98 min. Sound. 16mm Color. *Rental:* Films Inc.

Geisha Girl *see* Oriental Evil.

Gene Engineers, The. 1977. Nova. (Documentary). 57 min. Sound. 16mm Color. *Rental:* Iowa Films, Kent St U Films, Syracuse U Film & U of IL Film. *Rental:* U Cal Media & U Mich Media, Videotape version.

Gene Krupa Story, The. Sal Mineo & Susan Kohner. Directed by Don Weis. 1960. Columbia. 101 min. Sound. 16mm B&W. *Rental:* Arcus Film, Film Ctr DC, Inst Cinema & Welling Motion Pictures.

General, The. Buster Keaton & Marian Mack. Directed by Buster Keaton. 1926. United Artists. (Musical score only). 79 min. Silent. 16mm B&W. *Rental:* A Twyman Pres, Creative Film, Film Pres, Films Inc, Inst Cinema, Kit Parker, Modern Sound, Natl Film Video, Newman Film Lib, Roas Films, Video Tape Network & Westcoast Films. *Sale:* Festival Films & See-Art Films. *Sale:* Blackhawk Films, Abridged tinted videotape version. *Rental:* Killiam Collect & New Cinema, Sound tinted 16mm, musical score only version. *Rental:* Budget Films, Charard Motion Pics, Classic Film Mus, Em Gee Film Lib, Films Images, Films Inc, Ivy Films, Kerr Film, Kit Parker, Museum Mod Art, Standard Film, Swank Motion, Twyman Films, U Cal Media, Welling Motion Pictures, Wholesome Film Ctr, Williams Films & Willoughby Peer, *Sale:* Blackhawk Films, Cinema Concepts, E Finney, Glenn Photo, Morcraft Films & Museum Mod Art, Silent 16mm version. *Rental:* Ivy Films, *Sale:* Blackhawk Films, Griggs Movie & Glenn Photo, Super 8 silent version. *Rental:* Video Comm, *Sale:* Festival Films & Tamarelles French Film, Videotape version. *Sale:* Blackhawk Films, Ivy Films & Reel Images, 90 min. version. *Rental:* Bosco Films, Ivy Films & Westcoast Films, 50 min. version.

General, The. 1966. Wolper. (Documentary). 50 min. Sound. 16mm B&W. *Rental:* Films Inc. *Sale:* Films Inc.

General Concepts of Analytic Epidemiology. 1978. 55 min. Sound. Videotape Color. *Sale:* Natl AV Ctr.

General Concepts of Descriptive Epidemiology. 1978. 48 min. Sound. Videotape Color. *Sale:* Natl AV Ctr.

General Court-Martial. Army. (Documentary). 73 min. Sound. 16mm B&W. *Rental:* Natl AV Ctr.

General Custer at Little Big Horn *see* With Custer at Little Big Horn.

General Della Rovere. Vittorio De Sica & Hannes Messemer. Directed by Roberto Rossellini. Ital. 1960. Italy. 139 min. Sound. 16mm B&W. subtitles. *Rental:* Budget Films, Films Inc, Images Film & New Cinema. *Sale:* Festival Films. *Sale:* Festival Films, Videotape version.

General, The: Douglas MacArthur. 1962. Hearst. (Documentary). 50 min. Sound. 16mm B&W. *Sale:* King Features.

General Line, The: Old & New. Marfa Lapkina. Directed by Sergei Eisenstein & Grigori Alexandrov. Rus. 1929. Russia. 76 min. Silent. 16mm B&W. *Rental:* Budget Films, Corinth Films, Em Gee Film Lib, Glenn Photo & Kit Parker. *Sale:* Festival Films. *Sale:* Glenn Photo & Festival Films, Super 8 silent version, Videotape version.

General Spanky. Spanky McFarland & Little Rascals. Directed by Fred Newmeyer & Gordon Douglas. 1936. RKO. 75 min. Sound. 16mm B&W. *Rental:* Budget Films & MGM United.

Generation, A. Trans. Title: Wajda Trilogy. Tadeusz Lomnicki. Directed by Andrzej Wajda. Pol. 1955. Poland. 85 min. Sound. 16mm B&W. subtitles. *Rental:* Films Inc.

Generation. David Janssen & Kim Darby. Directed by George Schaefer. 1969. Embassy. 104 min. Sound. 16mm Color. *Rental:* Films Inc.

Generation on the Wind. 1980. Windmill Movie Company. 58 min. Sound. 16mm Color. *Rental:* Churchill Films. *Rental:* Churchill Films, Videotape version.

Generation Upon Generation. (Ascent of Man Ser.). 1974. Britain. (Documentary). 52 min. Sound. 16mm Color. *Rental:* Iowa Films, U Cal Media, U Mich Media & Utah Media. *Rental:* U Cal Media, Iowa Films, U Mich Media & Utah Media, Videotape version.

Generations. 1981. CTW. (Cast unlisted). 120 min. Sound. Videotape Color. *Rental:* PBS Video. *Sale:* PBS Video.

Generations of Resistance. Directed by Peter Davis. 1980. United Nations. (Documentary). 52 min. Sound. 16mm Color. *Rental:* CA Newsreel & U Mich Media. *Sale:* CA Newsreel.

Generator Factory, The. Directed by Joris Ivens & Marceline Loridan. 1973. China. (Documentary). 129 min. Sound. 16mm Color. *Rental:* Cinema Arts.

Genesis. Phil Collins & Bill Brutford. Directed by Tony Maylam. 1981. Miramax. 48 min. Sound. 16mm Color. *Rental:* Films Inc.

Genetic Chance, The. 1976. Britain. (Documentary). 60 min. Sound. 16mm Color. *Rental:* U Mich Media.

Genetic Defects: The Broken Code. 1975. PBS. (Documentary). 90 min. Sound. 16mm Color. *Rental:* Indiana AV Ctr & U Cal Media. *Sale:* Indiana AV Ctr.

Genetic Screening: The Ultimate Preventive Medicine?. 58 min. Sound. Videotape *Rental:* PBS Video. *Sale:* PBS Video.

Genetics. 1961. US Government. (Documentary). 53 min. Sound. 16mm Color. *Rental:* SD AV Ctr. *Sale:* Natl AV Ctr.

Genetics: A Question of Morality. 1975. WNET. (Documentary). 58 min. Sound. 16mm Color. *Rental:* B Raymond & WNET Media. *Sale:* B Raymond. *Sale:* WNET Media, Videotape version.

Genetics & Recombinant DNA. 1980. US Government. (Documentary). 60 min. Videotape Color. *Sale:* Natl AV Ctr.

Geneva Event, The. 1983. Media Guild. (Documentary). 60 min. Sound. 16mm Color. *Rental:* Media Guild. *Sale:* Media Guild. *Sale:* Media Guild, Videotape version.

Genevieve. John Gregson & Kay Kendall. Directed by Henry Cornelius. 1953. Britain. 86 min. Sound. 16mm Color. *Rental:* Arcus Film, Budget Films, Films Inc, Kit Parker, Learning Corp Am, Modern Sound, Roas Films, Twyman Films, U of IL Film & Westcoast Films. *Sale:* Learning Corp Am.

Genghis Khan. Manuel Conde. Directed by Manuel Conde. 1953. Philippine Islands. 90 min. Sound. 16mm B&W. *Rental:* Film Classics.

Genghis Khan. Omar Shariff & Stephen Boyd. Directed by Henry Levin. 1965. USA. 124 min. Sound. 16mm Color. *Rental:* Budget Films.

Genius at Work. Alan Carney & Wally Brown. Directed by Leslie Goodwins. 1946. RKO. 61 min. Sound. 16mm B&W. *Rental:* Films Inc.

Genocide. Directed by Arnold Schwartzman. 1982. MGM-UA. (Documentary). 82 min. Sound. 16mm Color. *Rental:* MGM United. *Rental:* MGM United, Videotape version.

Genocide 1941-1945. Directed by Hugh Raggett. (World at War Ser.). : Pt. 20.). 1973. Media Guild. (Documentary). 52 min. Sound. 16mm Color. *Rental:* Alden Films & Media Guild. *Sale:* Media Guild. *Sale:* Media Guild, Videotape version.

Gentle Art of Murder, The. Orig. Title: Crimen. Danielle Darrieux & Richard Todd. Directed by Gerard Oury. Fr. 1962. France. 82 min. Sound. 16mm B&W. dubbed. *Rental:* Films Inc.

Gentle Creature, A *see* Femme Douce.

Gentle Giant. Dennis Weaver & Vera Miles. Directed by James Neilson. 1967. Paramount. 93 min. Sound. 16mm Color. *Rental:* Cine Craft, Ivy Films, Modern Sound, Welling Motion Pictures, Westcoast Films & Williams Films. *Lease:* Rep Pic Film. *Rental:* Ivy Films, *Sale:* Ivy Films, Super 8 Sound version.

Gentle Sergeant, The *see* Three Stripes in the Sun.

Gentle Way to Die, A. Edwin Newman & Dr. Saunders. CC Films. 60 min. Sound. 16mm Color. *Rental:* National Council of the Churches Of Christ.

Gentleman at Heart, A. Cesar Romero & Milton Berle. Directed by Ray McCarey. 1942. Fox. 66 min. Sound. 16mm B&W. *Rental:* Films Inc.

Gentleman Bandit, The. Ralph Waite. 1981. CBS. 96 min. Sound. 16mm Color. *Rental:* Learning Corp Am & Modern Sound. *Lease:* Learning Corp Am.

Gentleman for a Day *see* Union Depot.

Gentleman from Louisiana, The. Eddie Quillan & Charlotte Henry. Directed by Irving Pichel. 1936. Republic. 54 min. Sound. 16mm B&W. *Rental:* Ivy Films. *Sale:* Rep Pic Film.

Gentleman from Texas, The. Johnny Mack Brown. Directed by Lambert Hillyer. 1946. Monogram. 60 min. Sound. 16mm B&W. *Rental:* Hurlock Cine, Lewis Film & Mogulls Films.

Gentleman Jim. Errol Flynn & Alexis Smith. Directed by Raoul Walsh. 1942. Warners. 105 min. Sound. 16mm B&W. *Rental:* MGM United.

Gentleman Joe Palooka. Joe Kirkwood & Leon Errol. Directed by Cy Endfield. 1946. Monogram. 72 min. Sound. 16mm B&W. *Rental:* Film Ctr DC & Newman Film Lib.

Gentleman Misbehaves, The. Robert Stanton. Directed by George Sherman. 1946. Columbia. 75 min. Sound. 16mm B&W. *Rental:* Inst Cinema.

Gentleman Tramp, The. Directed by Richard Patterson. 1973. RBC. (Documentary, color sequences). 78 min. Sound. 16mm B&W. *Rental:* Films Inc & U Mich Media.

Gentleman's Agreement. Gregory Peck & Dorothy McGuire. Directed by Elia Kazan. 1947. Fox. 118 min. Sound. 16mm B&W. *Rental:* Films Inc.

Gentlemen Are Born. Franchot Tone & Ann Dvorak. Directed by Alfred E. Green. 1934. Warners. 74 min. Sound. 16mm B&W. *Rental:* MGM United.

Gentlemen Marry Brunettes. Jeanne Crain & Jane Russell. Directed by Richard Sale. 1955. United Artists. 97 min. Sound. 16mm Color. *Rental:* MGM United.

Gentlemen Prefer Blondes. Marilyn Monroe & Jane Russell. Directed by Howard Hawks. 1953. Fox. 91 min. Sound. 16mm Color. *Rental:* Films Inc.

Gentlemen with Guns. Buster Crabbe. Directed by Sam Newfield. 1945. PRC. 51 min. Sound. 16mm B&W. *Sale:* Classics Assoc NY.

Gentlemen's Fate. John Gilbert & Leila Hyams. Directed by Mervyn LeRoy. 1931. MGM. 90 min. Sound. 16mm B&W. *Rental:* MGM United.

Genuine. Fern Andra. Directed by Robert Wiene. 1920. 16mm *Rental:* A Twyman Pres.

Georg. Lynn Averill. Directed by Stanton Kaye. 1964. Stanton Kaye. 55 min. Sound. 16mm B&W. *Rental:* Canyon Cinema.

George. Marshall Thompson. Directed by Wallace C. Bennett. 1972. Capital. 87 min. Sound. 16mm Color. *Rental:* Bosco Films, Buchan Pic, Budget Films, Film Pres, Newman Film Lib, Roas Films, Twyman Films, Video Comm & Westcoast Films. *Rental:* Video Comm, Videotape version.

George Crumb: Voice of the Whale. Directed by Robert Mugge. 1978. Direct Cinema. (Documentary). 54 min. Sound. 16mm Color. *Rental:* Direct Cinema. *Lease:* Direct Cinema.

George IV. 1980. Royal Heritage. (Documentary). 60 min. Sound. 16mm Color. *Rental:* Films Inc. *Sale:* Films Inc. *Rental:* Films Inc, *Sale:* Films Inc, Videotape version.

George Kennan: A Critical Voice. 58 min. 16mm *Rental:* Blackwood. *Sale:* Blackwood.

George Kennan Discusses Soviet Objectives. 1954. Department of Defense. (Lecture). 58 min. Sound. 16mm B&W. *Rental:* U of IL Film.

George Kuchar: The Comedy of the Underground (1982). 66 min. Sound. 16mm Color. *Rental:* Canyon Cinema.

George Mason. Laurence Naismith. Directed by Joseph Anthony. (Profiles in Courage Ser.). 1965. Saudek. 50 min. Sound. 16mm B&W. *Rental:* Syracuse U Film, U of IL Film & U Mich Media. *Sale:* IQ Films. *Rental:* IQ Films, *Sale:* IQ Films, Spanish dubbed version.

George Meany: Reflections. 1979. (Documentary). 52 min. Sound. 16mm Color. *Rental:* Natl AV Ctr.

George Plimpton's New York. 1978. Learning Corp. (Documentary). 50 min. Sound. 16mm Color. *Rental:* Kent St U Film & Learning Corp Am. *Sale:* Learning Corp Am.

George Raft Story. Ray Danton & Jayne Mansfield. Directed by Joseph Newman. 1961. Allied Artists. 105 min. Sound. 16mm B&W. *Rental:* Hurlock Cine.

George Segal. Directed by Ray Witlin. 1979. Blackwood. (Documentary). 58 min. Sound. 16mm Color. *Rental:* Blackwood Films. *Sale:* Blackwood Films.

George W. Norris. Tom Bosley. Directed by Stuart Rosenberg. (Profiles in Courage Ser.). 1965. Saudek. 50 min. Sound. 16mm B&W. *Rental:* Syracuse U Film & U of IL Film. *Sale:* IQ Films. *Rental:* IQ Films, *Sale:* IQ Films, Spanish dubbed version.

George Washington Slept Here. Jack Benny & Ann Sheridan. Directed by William Keighley. 1942. Warners. 93 min. Sound. 16mm B&W. *Rental:* MGM United.

George White's Scandals. Joan Davis & Jack Haley. Directed by Felix Feist & Ernst Matray. 1945. RKO. 95 min. Sound. 16mm B&W. *Rental:* Films Inc.

Georges of New York City, The. Directed by Arthur Barron. 1976. Group W. (Documentary). 59 min. Sound. 16mm Color. *Rental:* Iowa Films, Syracuse U Film, U Cal Media & U Mich Media. *Sale:* Carousel Films. *Sale:* Carousel Films, Videotape version.

Georgi Zhukov. 1976. Britain. (Documentary). 51 min. Sound. 16mm Color. *Rental:* Time-Life Multimedia. *Sale:* Time-Life Multimedia. *Rental:* Time-Life Multimedia, *Sale:* Time-Life Multimedia, Videotape version.

Georgia, Georgia. Diana Sands. Directed by Stig Bjorkman. 1972. Cinerama. 91 min. Sound. 16mm Color. *Rental:* Swank Motion.

Georgia O'Keeffe, a Celebration. Directed by Perry Miller Adato. 1977. PBS. (Documentary). 58 min. Sound. 16mm Color. *Rental:* Films Inc, Iowa Film, U Cal Media, U of IL Media, U Mich Media & Utah Media. *Sale:* Films Inc. *Sale:* Films Inc, Videotape version.

Georgy Girl. James Mason, Lynn Redgrave & Alan Bates. Directed by Silvio Narizzano. 1966. Britain. 100 min. Sound. 16mm B&W. *Rental:* Arcus Film, Cine Craft, Charard Motion Pics, Film Ctr DC, Films Inc, Inst Cinem, Kit Parker, Modern Sound, Natl Film Video, Newman Film Lib, Roas Films, Swank Motion, Twyman Films, Welling Motion Pictures, Wholesome Film Ctr & Willoughby.

Gerald Holt. 1968. NET. (Documentary). 60 min. Sound. 16mm B&W. *Rental:* Indiana AV Ctr. *Sale:* Indiana AV Ctr.

Geraldine. John Carroll & Mala Powers. Directed by R. G. Springsteen. 1953. Republic. 90 min. Sound. 16mm B&W. *Rental:* Ivy Films. *Sale:* Rep Pic Film.

Germans, The. 1967. CBS. (Documentary). 52 min. Sound. 16mm B&W. *Sale:* Phoenix Films & Utah Media. *Rental:* Syracuse U Film & U of IL Film, *Sale:* Phoenix Films, Color version. *Sale:* Phoenix Films, Videotape version.

Germany After the Fall. 1969. NET. (Documentary). 58 min. Sound. 16mm B&W. *Rental:* Indiana AV Ctr. *Sale:* Indiana AV Ctr.

Germany & Its Shadow. 1967. NET. (Documentary). 60 min. Sound. 16mm B&W. *Rental:* Indiana AV Ctr. *Sale:* Indiana AV Ctr.

Germany Awake! Directed by Erwin Leiser. Ger. 1968. Germany. (Documentary). 90 min. Sound. 16mm B&W. subtitles. *Rental:* Museum Mod Art. *Sale:* Museum Mod Art.

Germany-Dada. 1968. Museum Without Walls. (Documentary). 55 min. Sound. 16mm Color. *Rental:* U Mich Media.

Germany in Autumn. Directed by Heinrich Boll, Rainer Werner Fassbinder, Alexander Kluge & Volker Schlondorff. Ger. 1977. Germany. (Experimental). 116 min. Sound. 16mm Color. subtitles. *Rental:* New Cinema & New Line Cinema.

Germany Pale Mother. Directed by Helma Sanders Brahms. Ger. 1980. 123 min. Sound. 16mm Color. subtitles Eng. *Rental:* New Yorker Films.

Germany Since Hitler: Adenauer Sums Up. 1965. 65 min. Sound. 16mm B&W. *Rental:* Iowa Films.

Germany, Year Zero. Edmund Moeschke & Franz Kruger. Directed by Roberto Rossellini. Ger. 1947. Germany. 75 min. Sound. 16mm B&W. subtitles. *Rental:* Films Inc.

Geronimo! Chuck Connors & Ross Martin. Directed by Arnold Laven. 1962. United Artists. 101 min. Sound. 16mm Color. *Rental:* MGM United.

Geronimo! Preston Foster & Ellen Drew. Directed by Paul Sloane. 1939. Paramount. 90 min. Sound. 16mm B&W. *Rental:* Swank Motion.

Gerontological Nursing. 1980. 60 min. Sound. Videotape Color. *Sale:* Natl AV Ctr.

Gertrud. Nina Pens Rode & Bendt Rothe. Directed by Carl Th. Dreyer. Danish. 1964. Denmark. 116 min. Sound. 16mm B&W. subtitles. *Rental:* Budget Films, Corinth Films, Inst Cinema, Images Film & Kit Parker. *Sale:* Festival Films, Images Film & Natl Cinema. *Sale:* Festival Films & Tamarelles French Films, Videotape version.

Gertrude Stein: When This You See, Remember Me. Directed by Perry Miller Adato. 1971. NET. (Documentary). 90 min. Sound. 16mm Color. *Rental:* Corinth Films, McGraw-Hill Films, Syracuse U Film, U Cal Media, U of IL Film & U Mich Media. *Lease:* Corinth Films & McGraw-Hill Films.

Gervaise. Maria Schell & Francoise Perier. Directed by Rene Clement. Fr. 1957. France. 116 min. Sound. 16mm B&W. subtitles. *Rental:* Budget Films & Kit Parker. *Sale:* Festival Films, Natl Cinema & Reel Images. *Sale:* Festival Films & Tamarelles French Film, Videotape version.

Get Carter! Michael Caine & Britt Ekland. Directed by Mike Hodges. 1971. MGM. 110 min. Sound. 16mm Color. *Rental:* MGM United.

Get Crazy. Malcolm McDowell & Allen Goorwitz. Directed by Allan Arkush. 1983. Embassy. 92 min. Sound. 16mm B&W. *Rental:* Films Inc.

Get Down & Boogie. Trina Parks & Roger E. Mosley. Directed by William Witney. 1972. New World. 90 min. Sound. 16mm Color. *Rental:* Films Inc.

Get Happy. Blackhawk. (Anthology). 59 min. Videotape B&W. *Sale:* Blackhawk Films.

Get On With It. Orig. Title: Dentist on the Job. Bob Monkhouse & Kenneth Connor. Directed by C. M. Pennington-Richards. 1961. Britain. 88 min. Sound. 16mm B&W. *Rental:* Modern Sound.

Get Out Your Handkerchiefs. Gerard Depardieu & Patrick Dewaere. Directed by Bertrand Blier. Fr. 1978. Belgium-France. 95 min. Sound. 16mm Color. subtitles. *Rental:* New Line Cinema.

Get That Girl see Caryl of the Mountains.

Get That Venus. Jean Arthur & Ernest Truex. 1933. 70 min. Sound. 16mm B&W. *Rental:* Mogulls Films.

Get to Know Your Rabbit. Tom Smothers. Directed by Brian De Palma. 1972. Warners. 92 min. Sound. 16mm Color. *Rental:* Films Inc, Swank Motion & Twyman Films.

Get Yourself a College Girl. Mary Ann Mobley & Nancy Sinatra. Directed by Sidney Miller. 1964. MGM. 86 min. Sound. 16mm Color. *Rental:* MGM United.

Getaway, The. Steve McQueen & Ali McGraw. Directed by Sam Peckinpah. 1972. Warners. 122 min. Sound. 16mm Color. *Rental:* Films Inc, Swank Motion, Twyman Films & Williams Films.

Getaway, The. Robert Sterling & Donna Reed. Directed by Edward Buzzell. 1941. MGM. 89 min. Sound. 16mm B&W. *Rental:* MGM United.

Getting Married. Directed by Charles Braverman. 1976. Braverman. (Documentary). 26 min. Sound. 16mm Color. *Rental:* Pyramid Film. *Sale:* Pyramid Film. *Rental:* Pyramid Film, *Sale:* Pyramid Film, Videotape version.

Getting of Wisdom, The. Susannah Fowle & Barry Humphries. Directed by Bruce Beresford. 1977. Australia. 100 min. Sound. 16mm Color. *Rental:* Ivy Films.

Getting Straight. Elliott Gould & Candice Bergen. Directed by Richard Rush. 1970. Columbia. 124 min. Sound. 16mm Color. *Rental:* Inst Cinema, Ivy Films, Swank Motion, Welling Motion Pictures & Westcoast Films.

Ghost & Mr. Chicken, The. Don Knotts & Joan Staley. Directed by Alan Rafkin. 1966. Universal. 90 min. Sound. 16mm Color. *Rental:* Swank Motion.

Ghost & Mrs. Muir, The. Rex Harrison & Gene Tierney. Directed by Joseph L. Mankiewicz. 1947. Fox. 104 min. Sound. 16mm B&W. *Rental:* Films Inc, Twyman Films & Williams Films.

Ghost & the Guest, The. James Dunn & Florence Rice. Directed by William Nigh. 1943. PRC. 70 min. Sound. 16mm B&W. *Rental:* Mogulls Films & Newman Film Lib.

Ghost Breakers, The. Bob Hope & Paulette Goddard. Directed by George Marshall. 1940. Paramount. 85 min. Sound. 16mm B&W. *Rental:* Williams Films.

Ghost Catchers, The. Olsen & Johnson. Directed by Edward Cline. 1943. Universal. 68 min. Sound. 16mm B&W. *Rental:* Swank Motion.

Ghost City, The. Bill Cody. Directed by Harry Fraser. 1932. Monogram. 60 min. Sound. 16mm B&W. *Rental:* MGM United.

Ghost Comes Home, The. Frank Morgan & Billie Burke. Directed by William Thiele. 1940. MGM. 79 min. Sound. 16mm B&W. *Rental:* MGM United.

Ghost Diver, The. James Craig & Audrey Totter. Directed by Richard Einfeld & Merrill J. White. 1957. Fox. (Anamorphic). 76 min. Sound. 16mm B&W. *Rental:* Ivy Films.

Ghost Goes West, The. Robert Donat & Jean Parker. Directed by Rene Clair. 1936. United Artists. 85 min. Sound. 16mm B&W. *Rental:* Films Inc, Ivy Films & Mogulls Films.

Ghost Goes Wild, The. Anne Gwynne & Edward Everett Horton. Directed by George Blair. 1947. RKO. 66 min. Sound. 16mm B&W. *Rental:* Ivy Films.

Ghost Guns. Johnny Mack Brown. Directed by Lambert Hillyer. 1945. Monogram. 55 min. Sound. 16mm B&W. *Rental:* Hurlock Cine.

Ghost in the Invisible Bikini, The. Deborah Walley & Tommy Kirk. Directed by Don Weis. 1966. American International. 82 min. Sound. 16mm Color. *Rental:* Westcoast Films.

Ghost of a Chance, A. 1973. Britain. (Cast unlisted). 60 min. Sound. 16mm Color. *Sale:* Lucerne Films.

Ghost of Dragstrip Hollow, The. Jody Fair. Directed by William J. Hole. 1959. American International. 55 min. Sound. 16mm B&W. *Rental:* Budget Films.

Ghost of Frankenstein, The. Lon Chaney Jr. & Ralph Bellamy. Directed by Erle C. Kenton. 1942. Universal. 67 min. Sound. 16mm B&W. *Rental:* Swank Motion.

Ghost of Hidden Valley. Buster Crabbe. Directed by Sam Newfield. 1946. PRC. 56 min. Sound. 16mm B&W. *Sale:* Classics Assoc NY.

Ghost of Horror Castle, The. Christopher Lee & Senta Berger. Germany. 90 min. Sound. 16mm Color. *Rental:* Bosco Films.

Ghost of the China Seas, The. David Brian & Jonathan Haze. Directed by Fred F. Sears. 1958. Columbia. 90 min. Sound. 16mm B&W. *Rental:* Inst Cinema.

Ghost of Thomas Kempe, The. Directed by Robert Chenault. 1979. ABC. (Cast unlisted). 48 min. Sound. 16mm Color. *Rental:* MTI Tele. *Sale:* MTI Tele. *Sale:* MTI Tele, Videotape version.

Ghost of Zorro, The. Clayton Moore & Pamela Blake. Directed by Fred C. Brannon. 1959. Republic. 163 min. Sound. 16mm B&W. *Rental:* Ivy Films. *Sale:* Rep Pic Film.

Ghost Patrol. Tim McCoy. Directed by Sam Newfield. 1936. Puritan. 60 min. Videotape B&W. *Sale:* Video Comm.

Ghost Rider. Johnny Mack Brown. Directed by Wallace Fox. 1943. Monogram. 56 min. Sound. 16mm B&W. *Rental:* Hurlock Cine.

Ghost Riders of the West. Robert Kent & Peggy Stewart. Directed by Spencer G. Bennett. 1946. Republic. 163 min. Sound. 16mm B&W. *Rental:* Ivy Films.

Ghost Ship. Richard Dix. Directed by Mark Robson. 1943. RKO. 69 min. Sound. 16mm B&W. *Rental:* Films Inc.

Ghost Sonata, The. 1978. Films Inc. (Documentary). 60 min. Videotape Color. *Rental:* Films Inc. *Sale:* Films Inc.

Ghost Story. Fred Astaire, Melvyn Douglas & Douglas Jr. Fairbanks. Directed by John Irvin. 1981. Universal. 110 min. Sound. 16mm Color. *Rental:* Swank Motion. *Rental:* Swank Motion, Videotape version.

Ghost That Never Returns, The. Maxim Strauch. Directed by Abram Room. 1929. Russia. 75 min. Silent. 16mm B&W. *Rental:* Corinth Films & Film Images. *Sale:* Film Images.

Ghost Town *see* Lone Rider in Ghost Town.

Ghost Town Gold. Robert Livingston. Directed by Joseph Kane. 1937. Republic. 54 min. Sound. 16mm B&W. *Rental:* Ivy Films. *Sale:* Rep Pic Film.

Ghost Town Law. Buck Jones & Tim McCoy. Directed by Howard Bretherton. 1942. Monogram. 55 min. Sound. 16mm B&W. *Rental:* Hurlock Cine. *Sale:* Cinema Concepts & Reel Images.

Ghost Town Renegades. Lash La Rue. Directed by Ray Taylor. 1947. PRC. 58 min. Sound. 16mm B&W. *Sale:* Classics Assoc NY.

Ghost Town Riders. Bob Baker. Directed by George Waggner. 1936. Universal. 60 min. Sound. 16mm B&W. *Rental:* Mogulls Films.

Ghost Valley. Tom Keene & Merna Kennedy. Directed by Fred Allen. 1932. RKO. 54 min. Sound. 16mm B&W. *Rental:* RKO General Pics.

Ghost Valley Raiders. Don Barry & Lona Andre. Directed by George Sherman. 1940. Republic. 54 min. Sound. 16mm B&W. *Rental:* Ivy Films. *Sale:* Rep Pic Film & Nostalgia Merchant.

Ghostbusters. Bill Murray & Dan Aykroyd. Directed by Harold Reitman. 1985. Columbia. 103 min. Sound. 16mm Color. *Rental:* Swank Motion.

Ghostkeeper. Riva Spier, Murray Ord & George Collins. 87 min. Sound. 16mm Color. *Rental:* Williams Films.

Ghosts. Henry B. Walthall & Mary Alden. Directed by George Nicholls. 1915. Griffith. 60 min. Silent. 8mm B&W. *Sale:* Griggs Movie.

Ghosts-Italian Style. Sophia Loren & Vittorio Gassman. Directed by Renato Castellani. 1969. Italy. 92 min. Sound. 16mm Color. dubbed. *Rental:* MGM United.

Ghosts of Berkeley Square, The. Robert Morley & Felix Aylmer. Directed by Vernon Sewell. 1947. Britain. 61 min. Sound. 16mm B&W. *Rental:* Ivy Films. *Sale:* Rep Pic Film.

Ghosts of Cape Horn. 1981. ABC. (Documentary). 58 min. Sound. 16mm Color. *Rental:* Iowa Films, MTI Tele & Syracuse U Film. *Sale:* MTI Tele.

Ghosts of Yesterday. Norma Talmadge. Directed by Charles Miller. 1918. 16mm *Rental:* A Twyman Pres.

Ghosts on the Loose: Ghosts in the Night. Bela Lugosi & Bowery Boys. Directed by William Beaudine. 1943. Monogram. 68 min. Sound. 16mm B&W. *Rental:* Budget Films, Classic Film Mus, Ivy Films, Modern Sound, Newman Film Lib, Video Comm, Westcoast Films & Wholesome Film Ctr. *Sale:* Classic Film Mus, Cinema Concepts, Festival Films & Natl Cinema. *Rental:* Video Comm, *Sale:* Festival Films & Tamarelles French Film, Videotape version.

Ghoul, The. Boris Karloff, Sir Cedric Hardwicke, Sir Ralph Richardson. Directed by Hayes T. Hunter. 1933. Britain. 90 min. Sound. 16mm B&W. *Rental:* Classic Film Mus & Janus Films.

Giant Behemoth, The. Gene Evans & Andre Morrell. Directed by Eugene Lourie. 1959. Allied Artists. 83 min. Sound. 16mm B&W. *Rental:* Hurlock Cine.

Giant from the Unknown, The. Bob Steele & Joline Brand. Directed by Richard Cunha. 1957. Astor. 80 min. Sound. 16mm B&W. *Rental:* Ivy Films & Video Comm.

Giant of Marathon, The. Steve Reeves. Directed by Jacques Tourneur. 1960. Italy. 90 min. Sound. 16mm Color. dubbed. *Rental:* Films Inc. *Rental:* Films Inc, Anamorphic version.

Giant of Metropolis, The. Gordon Mitchell. Directed by Umberto Scarpelli. 1963. Italy. 92 min. Sound. 16mm Color. dubbed. *Rental:* Willoughby Peer.

Giants & the Common Men. 1969. NBC. (Documentary). 53 min. Sound. 16mm Color. *Rental:* Films Inc. *Sale:* Films Inc. *Sale:* Films Inc, Videotape version.

Giants of Rome. Richard Harrison & Ettore Manni. 1963. Italy. 100 min. Super 8 sound Color. *Rental:* Ivy Films. *Sale:* Ivy Films.

Gibraltar Adventure *see* Clue of the Missing Ape.

Gide. Fr. France. (Cast unlisted). 60 min. Sound. 16mm B&W. *Rental:* French Am Cul.

Gideon of Scotland Yard: Gideon's Day. Jack Hawkins & Anna Massey. Directed by John Ford. 1959. Britain. 100 min. Sound. 16mm Color. *Rental:* Corinth Films & Kit Parker. *Rental:* Westcoast Films, . B&W version. *Rental:* Bosco Films, 91 mins. version.

Gidget. Sandra Dee & Cliff Robertson. Directed by Paul Wendkos. 1959. Columbia. 96 min. Sound. 16mm Color. *Rental:* Bosco Films, Budget Films, Cine Craft, Films Inc, Inst Cinema, Modern Sound, Welling Motion Pictures & Westcoast Films.

Gidget Goes Hawaiian. Deborah Walley & Michael Callan. Directed by Paul Wendkos. 1961. Columbia. 102 min. Sound. 16mm Color. *Rental:* Budget Films, Cine Craft, Bosco Films, Modern Sound, Westcoast Films & Welling Motion Pictures.

Gidget Goes to Rome. Cindy Carol & James Darren. Directed by Paul Wendkos. 1963. Columbia. 103 min. Sound. 16mm Color. *Rental:* Budget Films, Cine Craft, Films Inc, Modern Sound, Newman Film Lib, Roas Films, Westcoast Films & Welling Motion Picturees.

Gift for Heidi, A. Douglas Fowley & Van Dyke Parks. Directed by George Templeton. 1962. RKO. 71 min. Sound. 16mm Color. *Rental:* Films Inc.

Gift of Choice, The. 1967. NET. (Documentary). 60 min. Sound. 16mm B&W. *Rental:* BYU Media.

Gift of Love, The. Marie Osmond & Timothy Bottoms. Directed by Don Chaffey. 1978. Osmond. 96 min. Sound. 16mm Color. *Lease:* Natl Film Video.

Gifted Hands. 1976. Penn State. (Documentary). 59 min. Videotape Color. *Rental:* Penn St AV Serv. *Sale:* Penn St AV Serv.

Gigantis, the Fire Monster. Hiroshi Koizumi. Directed by Hugo Grimaldi. 1959. Japan. 78 min. Sound. 16mm B&W. dubbed. *Rental:* Budget Films & Willoughby Peer.

Gigi. Leslie Caron & Louis Jourdan. Directed by Vincente Minnelli. 1958. MGM. 116 min. Sound. 16mm Color. *Rental:* MGM United. *Rental:* MGM United, Anamorphic color version. *Rental:* MGM United, Videotape version.

Gigot. Jackie Gleason & Diana Gardner. Directed by Gene Kelly. 1962. Fox. 104 min. Sound. 16mm Color. *Rental:* Films Inc.

Gilda. Rita Hayworth, Glenn Ford & Steven Geray. Directed by Charles Vidor. 1946. Columbia. 110 min. Sound. 16mm B&W. *Rental:* Budget Films, Cine Craft, Films Inc, Images Film, Kit Parker, Natl Film Video, Swank Motion, Welling Motion Pictures, Westcoast Films & Wholesome Film Ctr. *Rental:* Swank Motion, Videotape version.

Gilda Live! Gilda Radner & Guido Sarducci. Warners. (Performance). 95 min. Sound. 16mm Color. *Rental:* Swank Motion & Williams Films. *Rental:* Swank Motion, Videotape version.

Gildersleeve on Broadway. Harold Peary & Billie Burke. Directed by Gordon Douglas. 1943. RKO. 62 min. Sound. 16mm B&W. *Rental:* RKO General Pics.

Gildersleeve's Bad Day. Harold Peary & Nancy Gates. Directed by Gordon Douglas. 1943. RKO. 62 min. Sound. 16mm B&W. *Rental:* Films Inc.

Gildersleeve's Ghost. Harold Peary & Marion Martin. Directed by Gordon Douglas. 1944. RKO. 64 min. Sound. 16mm B&W. *Rental:* RKO General Pics.

Gimmie Shelter. Directed by David Maysles, Albert Maysles & Charlotte Zwerin. 1970. Cinema V. (Documentary). 91 min. Sound. 16mm Color. *Rental:* Cinema Five & New Cinema. *Lease:* Cinema Five.

Ginger. Frank Albertson & Barbara Reed. Directed by Oliver Drake. 1946. Monogram. 69 min. Sound. 16mm B&W. *Rental:* Charard Motion Pics, Film Ctr DC, Lewis Film, Modern Sound, Newman Film Lib & Wholesome Film Ctr.

Ginger in the Morning. Sissy Spacek & Monte Markham. Directed by Gordon Wiles. 1973. Adrian Weiss. 90 min. Sound. 16mm Color. *Rental:* Budget Films & Video Comm.

Giotto & the Pre-Renaissance. 1969. 47 min. Sound. 16mm Color. *Rental:* U Mich Media.

Gipsies, The. Directed by Victor Vicas. 1972. AIF. (Documentary). 60 min. Sound. 16mm B&W. *Sale:* Americas Films. *Sale:* Americas Films, Spanish version.

Girl, a Guy & a Gob, A. Orig. Title: Navy Steps Out, The. George Murphy & Lucille Ball. Directed by Richard Wallace. 1941. RKO. 91 min. Sound. 16mm B&W. *Rental:* Films Inc.

Girl & the General, The. Rod Steiger & Virna Lisi. Directed by Pasquale Festa Campanile. 1967. MGM. 103 min. Sound. 16mm Color. *Rental:* MGM United.

Girl Can't Help It, The. Tom Ewell & Jayne Mansfield. Directed by Frank Tashlin. 1956. Fox. (Anamorphic). 96 min. Sound. 16mm Color. *Rental:* Films Inc & Williams Films.

Girl Crazy. Mickey Rooney & Judy Garland. Directed by Norman Taurog. 1943. MGM. 99 min. Sound. 16mm B&W. *Rental:* MGM United.

Girl from Alaska, The. Ray Middleton & Jean Parker. Directed by Nick Grinde. 1942. Republic. 54 min. Sound. 16mm B&W. *Rental:* Ivy Films. *Sale:* Rep Pic Film.

Girl from Chicago, The. Directed by Oscar Micheaux. 1936. Micheaux. (All-black cast). 69 min. Sound. 16mm B&W. *Rental:* Standard Film.

Girl from God's Country, The. Jane Wyatt & Charles Bickford. Directed by Sidney Salkow. 1940. Republic. 54 min. Sound. 16mm B&W. *Rental:* Ivy Films. *Sale:* Rep Pic Film.

Girl from Havana, The. Dennis O'Keefe & Victor Jory. Directed by Lew Landers. 1940. Republic. 54 min. Sound. 16mm B&W. *Rental:* Ivy Films. *Sale:* Rep Pic Film.

Girl from Jones Beach, The. Ronald Reagan & Virginia Mayo. Directed by Peter Godfrey. 1949. Warners. 78 min. Sound. 16mm B&W. *Rental:* MGM United.

Girl from Mandalay, The. Conrad Nagel & Donald Cook. Directed by Howard Bretherton. 1936. Republic. 54 min. Sound. 16mm B&W. *Rental:* Ivy Films. *Sale:* Rep Pic Film.

Girl from Manhattan, The. Dorothy Lamour & Charles Laughton. Directed by Alfred E. Green. 1948. United Artists. 81 min. Sound. 16mm B&W. *Rental:* Ivy Films. *Sale:* Rep Pic Film.

Girl from Mexico, The. Lupe Velez & Leon Errol. Directed by Leslie Goodwins. 1939. RKO. 71 min. Sound. 16mm *Rental:* RKO General Pics.

Girl from Missouri, The. Jean Harlow, Franchot Tone & Lewis Stone. Directed by Jack Conway. 1934. MGM. 75 min. Sound. 16mm B&W. *Rental:* MGM United.

Girl from Monterey, The. Armida & Edgar Kennedy. Directed by Wallace Fox. 1943. PRC. 60 min. Sound. 16mm B&W. *Rental:* Mogulls Films.

Girl from Petrovka, The. Goldie Hawn & Hal Holbrook. Directed by Robert Ellis Miller. 1974. Universal. 104 min. Sound. 16mm Color. *Rental:* Swank Motion.

Girl-Getters, The. Oliver Reed & Barbara Ferris. Directed by Michael Winner. 1964. Britain. 93 min. Sound. 16mm B&W. *Rental:* Films Inc & Ivy Films.

Girl Happy. Elvis Presley. Directed by Boris Sagal. 1965. MGM. 96 min. Sound. 16mm Color. *Rental:* MGM United.

Girl Hunters, The. Mickey Spillane & Lloyd Nolan. Directed by Roy Rowland. 1963. Britain. 103 min. Sound. 16mm B&W. *Rental:* Budget Films, Modern Sound & Video Comm. *Rental:* Willoughby Peer, *Sale:* Morcraft Films, Anamorphic. *Sale:* Morcraft Films, Super 8 sound version.

Girl in Black Stockings, The. Lex Barker & Anne Bancroft. Directed by Howard Koch. 1957. United Artists. 75 min. Sound. 16mm B&W. *Rental:* MGM United.

Girl in Every Port, A. Victor McLaglen & Louise Brooks. Directed by Howard Hawks. 1928. Fox. (Musical score only). 62 min. Sound. 16mm B&W. *Rental:* Killiam Collect.

Girl in Every Port, A. Groucho Marx, William Bendix & Marie Wilson. Directed by Chester Erskine. 1952. RKO. 86 min. Sound. 16mm B&W. *Rental:* Films Inc. *Lease:* Films Inc. *Sale:* Blackhawk Films, Videotape version.

Girl in Room Seventeen, The *see* Vice Squad.

Girl in Room Thirteen, The. Brian Donlevy. Directed by Richard Cunha. 1961. Brazil. 79 min. Sound. 16mm B&W. dubbed. *Rental:* Ivy Films & Video Comm.

Girl in the Pullman, The. Marie Prevost & Franklin Pangborn. Directed by Cecil B. DeMille. 1927. Pathe. 65 min. Silent. 16mm B&W. *Rental:* Em Gee Film Lib. *Sale:* Glenn Photo & Natl Cinema. *Sale:* Glenn Photo, Super 8 silent version.

Girl in the Red Velvet Swing, The. Ray Milland & Joan Collins. Directed by Richard Fleischer. 1955. Fox. 109 min. Sound. 16mm Color. *Rental:* Films Inc.

Girl in White, The. June Allyson & Arthur Kennedy. Directed by John Sturges. 1952. MGM. 93 min. Sound. 16mm B&W. *Rental:* MGM United. *Rental:* MGM United, Videotape version.

Girl Missing. Glenda Farrell & Ben Lyon. Directed by Robert Florey. 1933. Warners. 69 min. Sound. 16mm B&W. *Rental:* MGM United.

Girl Most Likely, The. Jane Powell & Cliff Robertson. Directed by Mitchell Leisen. 1957. Universal. 98 min. Sound. 16mm Color. *Rental:* Arcus Film, Budget Films, Video Comm, Welling Motion Pictures & Westcoast Films. *Lease:* Video Com, Videotape version.

Girl Named Tamiko, A. Laurence Harvey & France Nuyen. Directed by John Sturges. 1962. Paramount. 110 min. Sound. 16mm Color. *Rental:* Films Inc.

Girl Next Door, The. Dan Dailey & June Haver. Directed by Richard Sale. 1953. Fox. 92 min. Sound. 16mm B&W. *Rental:* Films Inc.

Girl of the Golden West, The. Jeanette MacDonald & Nelson Eddy. Directed by Robert Z. Leonard. 1938. MGM. 120 min. Sound. 16mm B&W. *Rental:* MGM United.

Girl of the Port. Sally O'Neill & Mitchell Lewis. Directed by Bert Glennon. 1930. RKO. 69 min. Sound. 16mm *Rental:* RKO General Pics.

Girl on the Third Floor, The. Marina Vlady & Peter Van Eyck. Directed by Pierre Gaspard-Huit. 1954. Ellis. 103 min. Sound. 16mm B&W. dubbed. *Rental:* Ivy Films.

Girl Rush, The. Wally Brown & Alan Carney. Directed by Gordon Douglas. 1944. RKO. 65 min. Sound. 16mm B&W. *Rental:* Films Inc.

Girl Rush, The. Rosalind Russell & Fernando Lamas. Directed by Robert Pirosh. 1955. Paramount. 85 min. Sound. 16mm Color. *Rental:* RKO General Pics.

Girl Said No, The. Marie Dressler & Polly Moran. Directed by Sam Wood. 1930. MGM. 93 min. Sound. 16mm B&W. *Rental:* MGM United.

Girl Shy. Harold Lloyd. Directed by Fred Newmeyer & Sam Taylor. 1924. Pathe. (Music & sound effects only). 65 min. Sound. 16mm B&W. *Rental:* Budget Films, Images Film, Janus Film, Kino Intl & Kit Parker. *Sale:* Blackhawk Films, Super 8 sound version. *Sale:* Blackhawk Films, Super 8 silent version, Videotape version. *Rental:* Budget Films, Silent version.

Girl Trouble. Don Ameche & Joan Bennett. Directed by Harold Schuster. 1942. Fox. 82 min. Sound. 16mm B&W. *Rental:* Films Inc.

Girl Was Young, The *see* Young & Innocent.

Girl Who Dared, The. Veda Ann Borg. Directed by Howard Bretherton. 1944. Republic. 54 min. Sound. 16mm B&W. *Rental:* Ivy Films. *Sale:* Rep Pic Film.

Girl Who Had Everything, The. Elizabeth Taylor & Fernando Lamas. Directed by Richard Thorpe. 1953. MGM. 69 min. Sound. 16mm B&W. *Rental:* MGM United. *Rental:* MGM United, Videotape version.

Girl Who Knew Too Much, The. Adam West & Nancy Kwan. Directed by Francis D. Lyon. 1968. Commonwealth United. 98 min. Sound. 16mm Color. *Rental:* Ivy Films.

Girl Who Stayed at Home, The. Clarine Seymour. Directed by D. W. Griffith. 1919. Art-craft. 75 min. Silent. 16mm B&W. *Rental:* Museum Mod Art. *Lease:* Museum Mod Art.

Girl with a Suitcase, The. Claudia Cardinale & Jacques Perrin. Directed by Valerio Zurlini. Ital. 1961. Italy. 101 min. Sound. 16mm B&W. subtitles Eng. *Rental:* Films Inc. *Rental:* Ivy Films, Dubbed version.

Girl with Red Hair, The. Renee Soutendijk & Peter Tuinman. Directed by Ben Verbong. Dutch. 1981. The Netherlands. 116 min. 16mm Color. subtitles. *Rental:* MGM United.

Girl with the Green Eyes, The. Rita Tushingham & Lynn Redgrave. Directed by Desmond Davis. 1964. Britain. 91 min. Sound. 16mm Color. *Rental:* MGM United.

Girl with the Hatbox, The. Anna Sten. Directed by Boris Barnet. Rus. 1927. Russia. (Musical score only). 67 min. Sound. 16mm B&W. *Rental:* Film Images. *Sale:* Film Images.

Girlfriends. Melanie Mayron & Anita Skinner. Directed by Claudia Weill. 1978. Warners. 88 min. Sound. 16mm Color. *Rental:* Swank Motion. *Rental:* Swank Motion, Videotape version.

Girls, Les. Gene Kelly & Mitzi Gaynor. Directed by George Cukor. 1957. MGM. 117 min. Sound. 16mm Color. *Rental:* MGM United. *Rental:* MGM United, Anamorphic Color version.

Girls, The. Directed by Sumitra Peries. 1977. Sri Lanka. (Cast unlisted). 103 min. Sound. 16mm B&W. *Rental:* Liberty Co.

Girls, The. Harriet Anderson, Bibi Andersson & Gunnel Lindblom. Directed by Mai Zetterling. Swed. 1971. Sweden. 100 min. Sound. 16mm B&W. *Rental:* New Cinema & New Line Cinema. *Sale:* New Line Cinema.

Girls About Town. Kay Francis & Joel McCrea. Directed by George Cukor. 1931. Paramount. 82 min. Sound. 16mm B&W. *Rental:* Swank Motion.

Girl's Dormitory. Herbert Marshall & Ruth Chatterton. Directed by Irving Cummings. 1936. Fox. 66 min. Sound. 16mm B&W. *Rental:* Films Inc.

Girl's Folly, A. Doris Kenyon & Robert Warwick. Directed by Maurice Tourneur. 1917. Peerless-Brady-World. 60 min. Silent. 16mm B&W. *Rental:* Em Gee Film Lib. *Sale:* Cinema Concepts.

Girls, Girls, Girls. Elvis Presley & Stella Stevens. Directed by Norman Taurog. 1962. Paramount. 106 min. Sound. 16mm Color. *Rental:* Ivy Films, Modern Sound, Video Comm & Williams Films. *Rental:* Ivy Films, *Sale:* Cinema Concepts & Ivy Films, Super 8 sound version. *Rental:* Williams Films, Videotape version.

Girls in Action *see* Operation Dames.

Girls in Chains. Arline Judge. Directed by Edgar G. Ulmer. 1943. PRC. 70 min. Sound. 16mm B&W. *Rental:* Budget Films, Ivy Films, Video Comm & Westcoast Films. *Sale:* Natl Cinema. *Rental:* Video Comm, Videotape version.

Girls in Prison. Richard Denning & Adele Jergens. Directed by Edward L. Cahn. 1956. American International. 87 min. Sound. 16mm B&W. *Rental:* Westcoast Films.

Girls in the Night. Harvey Lembeck & Joyce Holden. Directed by Jack Arnold. 1953. Universal. 83 min. Sound. 16mm B&W. *Rental:* Swank Motion.

Girls Never Tell see Her First Romance.

Girls of Pleasure Island, The. Leo Genn & Don Taylor. Directed by Alvin Ganzer & F. Hugh Herbert. 1953. Paramount. 95 min. Sound. 16mm Color. *Rental:* Films Inc.

Girls of the Big House. Lynne Roberts & Adele Mara. Directed by George Archainbaud. 1946. Republic. 71 min. Sound. 16mm B&W. *Rental:* Ivy Films. *Sale:* Rep Pic Film.

Girls of the Road. Ann Dvorak, Lola Lane & Helen Mack. Directed by Nick Grinde. 1940. Columbia. 61 min. Sound. 16mm B&W. *Rental:* Kit Parker.

Girls on Probation. Ronald Reagan & Jane Bryan. Directed by William McGann. 1938. Warners. 63 min. Sound. 16mm B&W. *Rental:* MGM United.

Girls on the Beach. Martin West. Directed by William Witney. 1965. Paramount. 80 min. Sound. 16mm Color. *Rental:* Films Inc.

Girl's School. Anne Shirley & Ralph Bellamy. Directed by John Brahm. 1938. Columbia. 80 min. Sound. 16mm B&W. *Rental:* Kit Parker.

Girls Under Twenty-One. Rochelle Hudson & Paul Kelly. Directed by Max Nosseck. 1940. Columbia. 64 min. Sound. 16mm B&W. *Rental:* Budget Films.

Giselle. 1950. NBC. (Ballet, kinescope). 56 min. Sound. 16mm B&W. *Rental:* Em Gee Film Lib.

Giselle. Directed by Enrique Pineda Barnet. 1964. Cuba. (Ballet). 90 min. Sound. 16mm B&W. *Rental:* Tricontinental Film & Unifilm. *Sale:* Unifilm.

Git! Jack Chaplain. Directed by Ellis Kadison. 1965. Embassy. 92 min. Sound. 16mm Color. *Rental:* Films Inc.

Git Along Little Dogies. Gene Autry. Directed by Joseph Kane. 1937. Republic. 54 min. Sound. 16mm B&W. *Rental:* Budget Films & Ivy Films. *Sale:* Morcraft Films & Reel Images. *Sale:* Morcraft Films & Reel Images, Super 8 sound version.

Give a Girl a Break. Debbie Reynolds, Marge Champion & Gower Champion. Directed by Stanley Donen. 1953. MGM. 82 min. Sound. 16mm Color. *Rental:* Films Inc & MGM United.

Give Earth a Chance. 1974. Edupac. (Documentary). 50 min. Sound. 16mm Color. *Rental:* Edupac & NYU Film Lib. *Sale:* Edupac.

Give Her the Moon. Philippe Noiret & Bert Convy. Directed by Philippe De Broca. Fr. 1970. France. 92 min. Sound. 16mm Color. subtitles. *Rental:* MGM United.

Give Me the Stars. Will Fyffe & Leni Lynn. Directed by Maclean Rogers. 1944. Britain. 95 min. Sound. 16mm B&W. *Rental:* Ivy Films. *Sale:* Rep Pic Film.

Give Me Your Heart. Kay Francis & George Brent. Directed by Archie Mayo. 1936. Warners. 88 min. Sound. 16mm B&W. *Rental:* MGM United.

Give My Regards to Broadway. Dan Dailey & Charles Winninger. Directed by Lloyd Bacon. 1948. Fox. 98 min. Sound. 16mm B&W. *Rental:* Films Inc.

Give Us the Children. 1970. NBC. (Documentary). 56 min. Sound. 16mm Color. *Rental:* Films Inc. *Sale:* Films Inc. *Sale:* Films Inc, Videotape version.

Give Us This Day see Christ in Concrete.

Give Us Wings. Wallace Ford, Victor Jory & Dead End Kids. Directed by Charles Lamont. 1940. Universal. 62 min. Sound. 16mm B&W. *Rental:* Mogulls Films.

Givers, Takers, & Other Kinds of Lovers. Josh McDowell. 50 min. Sound. 16mm Color. *Rental:* Gospel Films.

Giving Birth: Four Portraits. 1976. WNET. (Documentary). 60 min. Videotape B&W. *Rental:* Electro Art, Iowa Films & U Mich Media. *Lease:* Electro Art.

Gizmo. Directed by Howard Smith. New Line Cinema. (Documentary). 79 min. Sound. 16mm Color. *Rental:* New Line Cinema.

Gladiator, The. Joe E. Brown & June Travis. Directed by Albert D'Agostino. 1938. Columbia. 72 min. Sound. 16mm B&W. *Rental:* Alba House, Budget Films, Films Inc, Ivy Films, Roas Films & Welling Motion Pictures. *Rental:* Budget Films, 82 mins. version.

Gladiators, The. Directed by Peter Watkins. Swed. 1969. Sweden. (Documentary). 102 min. Sound. 16mm Color. *Rental:* New Cinema & New Line Cinema.

Gladiators Seven. Richard Harrison. Directed by Pedro Lazaga. Ital. 1964. Italy. (Anamorphic). 93 min. Sound. 16mm Color. dubbed. *Rental:* MGM United.

Gladys Knight & the Pips, with Ray Charles. Verve. (Concert). 75 min. Videotape Color. *Rental:* Films Inc.

Glamour. Paul Lukas & Constance Cummings. Directed by William Wyler. 1934. Paramount. 75 min. Sound. 16mm B&W. *Rental:* Swank Motion.

Glass Alibi, The. Paul Kelly & Anne Gwynne. Directed by W. Lee Wilder. 1946. Republic. 70 min. Sound. 16mm B&W. *Sale:* Classics Assoc NY.

Glass Bottom Boat, The. Doris Day & Rod Taylor. Directed by Frank Tashlin. 1966. MGM. 110 min. Sound. 16mm Color. *Rental:* MGM United. *Rental:* MGM United, Anamorphic color version. *Rental:* MGM United, Videotape version.

Glass House, The see Truman Capote's "The Glass House".

Glass Houses. Jennifer O'Neill. Directed by Alexander Singer. 1972. Columbia. 90 min. Sound. 16mm Color. *Rental:* Films Inc, Swank Motion, Twyman Films & U Mich Media.

Glass Menagerie, The. Gertrude Lawrence & Jane Wyman. Directed by Irving Rapper. 1950. Warners. 107 min. Sound. 16mm B&W. *Rental:* Films Inc & Williams Films.

Glass Mountain, The: Legend of Glass Mountain. Tito Gobbi & Valentina Cortese. Directed by Henry Cass. 1950. Britain. 94 min. Sound. 16mm B&W. *Rental:* Inst Cinema & Willoughby Peer.

Glass Slipper, The. Leslie Caron & Michael Wilding. Directed by Charles Walters. 1955. MGM. 94 min. Sound. 16mm Color. *Rental:* MGM United.

Glass Wall, The. Gloria Grahame & Vittorio Gassman. Directed by Maxwell Shane. 1953. Columbia. 78 min. Sound. 16mm B&W. *Rental:* Kit Parker.

Gleiwitz Case, The. Hannjo Hasee & Herwart Grosse. Directed by Gerhard Klein. Ger. 1961. Germany. 66 min. Sound. 16mm B&W. subtitles. *Rental:* Films Inc.

Glen or Glenda? see I Changed My Sex.

Glenn & Randa. Directed by Jim McBride. 1971. UMC. (Cast unlisted). 94 min. Sound. 16mm Color. *Rental:* Swank Motion.

Glenn Gould: Off the Record & on the Record. Directed by Wolf Koenig & Roman Kroitor. 1959. Canada. (Documentary). 60 min. Sound. 16mm B&W. *Rental:* Museum Mod Art.

Glenn Miller Story, The. James Stewart & June Allyson. Directed by Anthony Mann. 1954. Universal. 116 min. Sound. 16mm Color. *Rental:* Williams Films.

Glitterball, The. Ben Buckton & Keith Jayne. Directed by Harley Cockliss. 1979. Britain. 57 min. Sound. 16mm Color. *Rental:* Lucerne Films. *Sale:* Lucerne Films.

Global Affair, A. Bob Hope & Lilo Pulver. Directed by Jack Arnold. 1964. MGM. 84 min. Sound. 16mm B&W. *Rental:* MGM United.

Gloria. Gena Rowlands & John Adams. Directed by John Cassavetes. 1980. Columbia. 121 min. Sound. 16mm Color. *Rental:* Arcus Film, Budget Films, Films Inc, Kit Parker, Swank Motion, Welling Motion Pictures, Westcoast Films, Wholesome Film Ctr & Williams Films. *Rental:* Swank Motion, Videotape version.

Glorifying the American Girl. Eddie Cantor & Helen Morgan. Directed by Millard Webb. 1929. Paramount. 87 min. Sound. 16mm B&W. *Rental:* Budget Films, Classic Film Mus, Em Gee Film Lib, Kit Parker, Roas Films, Swank Motion & Video Comm. *Sale:* Glenn Photo, Festival Films & Reel Images. *Rental:* Video Comm, *Sale:* Festival Films, Videotape version.

Glorious System of Things, A. 1983. Colonial Williamsburg. (Documentary). 59 min. Sound. 16mm Color. *Rental:* Colonial. *Sale:* Lucerne Films. *Sale:* Colonial. *Sale:* Colonial, Videotape version.

Glory. Margaret O'Brien & Walter Brennan. Directed by David Butler. 1956. RKO. 100 min. Sound. 16mm Color. *Rental:* Budget Films, Modern Sound, Video Comm & Welling Motion Pictures. *Lease:* Video Comm. *Rental:* Video Comm, *Lease:* Video Comm, Videotape version.

Glory Alley. Leslie Caron & Ralph Meeker. Directed by Raoul Walsh. 1952. MGM. 79 min. Sound. 16mm B&W. *Rental:* MGM United.

Glory Brigade. Victor Mature & Alexander Scourby. Directed by Robert Webb. 1953. Fox. 82 min. Sound. 16mm B&W. *Rental:* Films Inc.

Glory Guys, The. Tom Tryon & Senta Berger. Directed by Arnold Laven. 1965. United Artists. 112 min. Sound. 16mm Color. *Rental:* MGM United.

Glory of Europe Nineteen Hundred: The Hey-Day Fever. 1976. Britain. (Documentary). 52 min. Sound. 16mm Color. *Rental:* Time-Life Multimedia. *Sale:* Time-Life Multimedia. *Rental:* Time-Life Multimedia, *Sale:* Time-Life Multimedia, Videotape version.

Glory of the Garden, The. 1983. Rothschild-Cassatt. (Documentary). 53 min. Sound. 16mm Color. *Rental:* Films Inc. *Sale:* Films Inc. *Sale:* Films Inc, Videotape version.

Glory of Their Times, The. 1970. Macmillan. (Documentary). 50 min. Sound. 16mm B&W. *Rental:* Macmillan Films. *Sale:* Macmillan Films.

Glory Stompers, The. Dennis Hopper & Jody McCrea. Directed by Anthony Lanza. 1967. American International. 90 min. Sound. 16mm Color. *Rental:* Willoughby Peer.

Glory Trail, The. Tom Keene. Directed by Lynn Shores. 1936. Crescent. 70 min. Sound. 16mm B&W. *Rental:* Mogulls Films.

Glove, The. John Saxon & Roosevelt Grier. Directed by Ross Hagen. 1980. Producers Distributing. 93 min. Sound. 16mm Color. *Rental:* Twyman Films.

Gnome-Mobile, The. Walter Brennan & Richard Deacon. Directed by Robert Stevenson. 1967. Disney. 84 min. Sound. 16mm Color. *Rental:* Disney Prod & Films Inc.

Gnomes. 48 min. Sound. 16mm Color. *Rental:* Pyramid Film. *Sale:* Pyramid Film.

Gnomo-Movil, El. Walter Brennan & Robert Stevenson. 1967. Disney. 90 min. Sound. 16mm Color. dubbed Span. *Rental:* Twyman Films.

Go, & I'll Be with You. 1979. Penn State. (Documentary). 58 min. Sound. 16mm Color. *Rental:* Penn St AV Serv. *Sale:* Penn St AV Serv. *Sale:* Penn St AV Serv, *Sale:* Penn St AV Serv, Videotape version.

Go Ask Alice. Andy Griffith & Julie Adams. Directed by John Korty. 1973. Metromedia. 74 min. Sound. 16mm Color. *Rental:* Swank Motion, Twyman Films, Westcoast Films & Wholesome Film Ctr.

Go-Between, The. Julie Christie, Alan Bates & Margaret Leighton. Directed by Joseph Losey. 1971. Columbia. 116 min. Sound. 16mm Color. *Rental:* Arcus Film, Budget Films, Films Inc, Images Film, Ivy Films, Kit Parker, Natl Film Video, Swank Motion, Twyman Films, Welling Motion Pictures, Westcoast Films & Wholesome Film Ctr.

Go Chase Yourself. Lucille Ball & Jack Carson. Directed by Edward Cline. 1938. RKO. 70 min. Sound. 16mm B&W. *Rental:* RKO General Pics.

Go Down Death. Directed by Spencer Williams. 1941. (All-black cast). 63 min. Sound. 16mm B&W. *Rental:* Budget Films. *Sale:* Glenn Photo & Natl Cinema.

Go for Broke! Van Johnson. Directed by Robert Pirosh. 1951. MGM. 92 min. Sound. 16mm B&W. *Rental:* MGM United.

Go for It. 1977. Pyramid. (Documentary). 90 min. Sound. 16mm Color. *Rental:* Pyramid Film. *Sale:* Pyramid Film. *Rental:* Pyramid Film, *Sale:* Pyramid Film, Videotape version.

Go Get 'Em Haines. William Boyd. Directed by Sam Newfield. 1936. Republic. 65 min. Sound. 16mm B&W. *Rental:* Film Classics.

Go Getter, The. George Brent & Anita Louise. Directed by Busby Berkeley. 1937. Warners. 92 min. Sound. 16mm B&W. *Rental:* MGM United.

Go-Getter, The. Hank McCune & Beverly Garland. 1955. Pacific Coast. 92 min. Sound. 16mm B&W. *Rental:* Ivy Films.

Go Go Go World. Directed by Renato Mavi & Anthony Dawson. Ital. 1960. Italy. 90 min. Sound. 16mm Color. *Rental:* Budget Films.

Go Into Your Dance. Orig. Title: Casino De Paree. Al Jolson & Ruby Keeler. Directed by Archie Mayo. 1935. Warners. 89 min. Sound. 16mm B&W. *Rental:* MGM United.

Go, Johnny, Go. Allan Freed. Directed by Paul Landres. 1958. Valiant. 75 min. Sound. 16mm B&W. *Rental:* Ivy Films.

Go Kart Go. Denis Waterman. Directed by Jan Darnley-Smith. 1964. Britain. 55 min. Sound. 16mm B&W. *Sale:* Lucerne Films.

Go, Man, Go. Dane Clark & Harlem Globetrotters. Directed by James Wong Howe. 1954. United Artists. 82 min. Sound. 16mm B&W. *Rental:* Cine Craft & Charard Motion Pics.

Go Naked in the World. Gina Lollobrigida & Anthony Franciosa. Directed by Ranald MacDougall. 1961. MGM. (Anamorphic). 103 min. Sound. 16mm Color. *Rental:* MGM United.

Go Play in the Nuclear Park. 1972. Britain. (Documentary). 52 min. Sound. 16mm Color. *Rental:* Time-Life Multimedia. *Sale:* Time-Life Multimedia.

Go Tell the Spartans. Burt Lancaster & Marc Singer. Directed by Ted Post. 1978. Embassy. 114 min. Sound. 16mm Color. *Rental:* Films Inc.

Go West. Buster Keaton & Kathleen Myers. Directed by Buster Keaton. 1925. Metro. (Musical score only). 93 min. Sound. 16mm B&W. *Rental:* Twyman Films. *Rental:* A Twyman Pres & Twyman Films, Silent 16mm version.

Go West. Marx Brothers & Diana Lewis. Directed by Edward Buzzell. 1940. MGM. 80 min. Sound. 16mm B&W. *Rental:* MGM United. *Rental:* MGM United, Videotape version.

Go West, Young Lady. Ann Miller & Glenn Ford. Directed by Frank R. Strayer. 1941. Columbia. 70 min. Sound. 16mm B&W. *Lease:* Time-Life Multimedia.

Go West, Young Man. (Destination America Ser.). 1976. Media Guild. (Documentary). 52 min. Sound. 16mm Color. *Rental:* Media Guild. *Sale:* Media Guild. *Sale:* Media Guild, Videotape version.

Goal! Directed by Abidene Dino & Ross Devenish. 1966. Britain. (Documentary). 107 min. Sound. 16mm Color. *Rental:* Buchan Pic, Inst Cinema, Modern Sound, Twyman Films, Westcoast Films, Wholesome Film Ctr, Williams Films & Willoughby Peer.

Goal to Go. Directed by Bob O'Donnell. Gospel. (Cast unlisted). 60 min. Sound. 16mm B&W. *Rental:* Roas Films.

Goalie's Anxiety at the Penalty Kick, The. Arthur Brauss. Directed by Wim Wenders. Ger. 1972. Germany. 101 min. Sound. 16mm Color. subtitles. *Rental:* Liberty Co.

Goalkeeper Also Lives on Our Street, The. Czech. 1978. Czechoslovakia. (Cast unlisted). 51 min. Sound. 16mm Color. dubbed. *Rental:* Films Inc. *Sale:* Films Inc.

Goat Horn, The. Katia Paskaleva & Anton Gortchev. Directed by Metodi Andonov. Bulgarian. 1972. 100 min. Sound. 16mm B&W. subtitles. *Rental:* Films Inc.

Gobineau. France. (Cast unlisted). 60 min. Sound. 16mm B&W. *Rental:* French Am Cul. *Rental:* French Am Cul, Videotape version.

Gobs & Gals. George Bernard. Directed by R. G. Springsteen. 1951. Republic. 86 min. Sound. 16mm B&W. *Rental:* Ivy Films. *Sale:* Rep Pic Film.

God Forgives, I Don't. Terrence Hill & Bud Spencer. Directed by Giuseppe Collizzi. Ital. 1969. Italy. 101 min. Sound. 16mm Color. dubbed. *Rental:* Westcoast Films.

God Is My Co-Pilot. Dennis Morgan & Dane Clark. Directed by Robert Florey. 1945. Warners. 89 min. Sound. 16mm B&W. *Rental:* MGM United.

God Is My Partner. Walter Brennan & John Hoyt. Directed by William Claxton. 1957. Fox. (Anamorphic). 80 min. Sound. 16mm B&W. *Rental:* Budget Films, Ivy Films, Rep Pic Film & Westcoast Films. *Lease:* Rep Pic Film.

God of Rain see Chac.

God Owns My Business. (Cast unlisted). 50 min. Sound. 16mm Color. *Rental:* G Herne.

God Told Me To. Tony Lo Bianco & Sandy Dennis. Directed by Larry Cohen. 1976. New World. 87 min. Sound. 16mm Color. *Rental:* Films Inc.

God Under the Skin. Directed by Folco Quilici. Italy. (Documentary). Sound. 16mm B&W. *Rental:* MGM United.

Godchildren, The. Lindsey Hillard. Directed by Robert E. Pearson. 1973. American International. 90 min. Sound. 16mm Color. *Rental:* Swank Motion.

Goddess, The. Kim Stanley & Lloyd Bridges. Directed by John Cromwell. 1958. Columbia. 105 min. Sound. 16mm B&W. *Rental:* Budget Films, Films Inc & Kit Parker.

Godelureaux, Les. Jean-Claude Brialy & Bernadette Lafont. Directed by Claude Chabrol. Fr. 1960. France. 99 min. Sound. 16mm B&W. subtitles. *Rental:* New Line Cinema.

Godfather, The. Marlon Brando, Al Pacino & James Caan. Directed by Francis Ford Coppola. 1972. Paramount. 175 min. Sound. Color. *Rental:* Films Inc. *Sale:* Cinema Concepts, Videotape version.

Godfather II, The. Al Pacino, Robert Duvall & Robert De Niro. Directed by Francis Ford Coppola. 1975. Paramount. 200 min. Sound. Color. *Rental:* Films Inc. *Sale:* Cinema Concepts, Videotape version.

Gods & the Dead, The. Othon Bastos. Directed by Ruy Guerra. Port. 1971. Brazil. 97 min. Sound. 16mm Color. subtitles. *Rental:* New Yorker Films.

God's Country & the Woman. Orig. Title: Avenging Stranger, The. George Brent & Beverly Roberts. Directed by William Keighley. 1936. Warners. 80 min. Sound. 16mm B&W. *Rental:* MGM United.

God's Gift to Women. Frank Fay, Laura La Plante & Joan Blondell. Directed by Michael Curtiz. 1931. Warners. 71 min. Sound. 16mm B&W. *Rental:* MGM United.

God's Gun. Lee Van Cleef, Richard Boone & Jack Palance. Directed by Frank Kramer. 1978. Irwin Yablans. 90 min. Sound. 16mm Color. *Rental:* Swank Motion.

God's Little Acre. Robert Ryan, Tina Louise & Michael Landon. Directed by Anthony Mann. 1958. United Artists. 118 min. Sound. 16mm B&W. *Rental:* Budget Films & Kit Parker. *Sale:* Cinema Concepts. *Sale:* Cinema Concepts, Videotape version.

Gods of the Plague. Hanna Schuygulla. Directed by Rainer Werner Fassbinder. Ger. 1969. Germany. 90 min. Sound. 16mm B&W. subtitles. *Rental:* New Yorker Films.

God's Stepchildren. Alice B. Russell & Jacqueline Lewis. Directed by Oscar Micheaux. 1938. 65 min. Sound. 16mm. *Rental:* Budget Films.

God's War. Claude Laydn. Directed by Rafael Gil. 1963. 87 min. Sound. 16mm B&W. subtitles. *Rental:* Films Inc. *Rental:* Films Inc, English language version.

Godsend, The. Cyd Hayman, Malcolm Stoddard & Angela Pleasence. Directed by Gabrielle Braumont. 93 min. Sound. 16mm Color. *Rental:* Swank Motion. *Rental:* Swank Motion, Videotape version.

Godspell. Victor Garber. Directed by David Greene. 1973. Columbia. 103 min. Sound. 16mm Color. *Rental:* Swank Motion.

Godzilla on Monster Island. Anguirus, Godzilla, Gigan & Hirosh Ishikawa. Directed by Jun Fukuda. 1977. Japan. 89 min. Sound. 16mm Color. dubbed. *Rental:* Films Inc, Modern Sound & Roas Films.

Godzilla vs. Megalon. Yukata Hayashi. Directed by Jun Fukuda. 1976. Japan. 90 min. Sound. 16mm Color. dubbed. *Rental:* Budget Films, Modern Sound, Roas Films, Westcoast Films & Wholesome Film Ctr.

Godzilla vs the Bionic Monster. Akihiko Hirata. Directed by Jun Fukuda. 1974. Japan. 84 min. Sound. 16mm Color. dubbed. *Rental:* Films Inc.

Godzilla vs the Cosmic Monster. Akihiko Hirata. Directed by Jun Fukuda. 1978. Japan. 84 min. Sound. 16mm Color. dubbed. *Rental:* Budget Films & Modern Sound.

Godzilla vs the Sea Monster. Akira Takarada & Kumi Mizuno. Directed by Jun Fukuda. 1966. Japan. 86 min. Sound. 16mm Color. dubbed. *Rental:* Budget Films.

Godzilla vs the Smog Monster. Akira Yamauchi. Directed by Yoshimitu Banno. 1972. Japan. 85 min. Sound. 16mm Color. dubbed. *Rental:* Welling Motion Pics & Williams Films.

Godzilla vs the Thing. Yuriko Hosi. Directed by Inoshiro Honda. 1964. Japan. 90 min. Sound. 16mm Color. dubbed. *Rental:* Westcoast Films & Wholesome Film Ctr.

Godzilla's Revenge. Kenji Sahara. Directed by Inoshiro Honda. 1969. Japan. 92 min. Sound. 16mm Color. dubbed. *Rental:* Budget Films, Films Inc, Westcoast Films & Willoughby Peer.

Gog. Richard Egan & Herbert Marshall. Directed by Herbert L. Strock. 1954. United Artists. 85 min. Sound. 16mm Color. *Rental:* MGM United.

Goin' Coconuts. Donny Osmond & Marie Osmond. Directed by Howard Morris. 1978. Osmond. 110 min. Sound. 16mm Color. *Rental:* Swank Motion. *Lease:* Natl Film Video.

Goin' Down the Road. Doug McGrath, Paul Bradley & Jane Eastwood. Directed by Donald Shebib. 1972. Canada. 87 min. Sound. 16mm Color. *Rental:* Films Inc, Janus Films & New Cinema.

Goin' South. Jack Nicholson & Mary Steenburgen. Directed by Jack Nicholson. 1978. Paramount. 108 min. Sound. 16mm Color. *Rental:* Films Inc.

Goin' to Town. Lum & Abner. Directed by Leslie Goodwins. 1944. RKO. 69 min. Sound. 16mm B&W. *Rental:* Em Gee Film Lib. *Sale:* Glenn Photo.

Goin' to Town. Mae West & Paul Cavanaugh. Directed by Alexander Hall. 1935. Paramount. 74 min. Sound. 16mm B&W. *Rental:* Swank Motion.

Going Ape. Tony Danza & Danny DeVito. Directed by Jeremy Joe Kronsberg. 1981. Paramount. 89 min. Sound. 16mm Color. *Rental:* Films Inc.

Going Back: A Return to Vietnam. 1984. 52 min. Sound. 16mm Color. *Rental:* Bullfrog Films. *Sale:* Bullfrog Films. *Sale:* Bullfrog Films, Videotape version.

Going Berserk. John Candy & Joe Flaherty. Directed by David Steinberg. 1983. Universal. 85 min. Sound. 16mm Color. *Rental:* Swank Motion. *Rental:* Swank Motion, Videotape version.

Going Highbrow. Guy Kibbee & ZaSu Pitts. Directed by Robert Florey. 1935. Warners. 67 min. Sound. 16mm B&W. *Rental:* MGM United.

Going Hollywood. Marion Davies & Bing Crosby. Directed by Raoul Walsh. 1933. MGM. 80 min. Sound. 16mm B&W. *Rental:* MGM United.

Going Home. Robert Mitchum & Jan-Michael Vincent. Directed by Herbert B. Leonard. 1971. MGM. (Anamorphic). 97 min. Sound. 16mm Color. *Rental:* MGM United.

Going in Style. George Burns, Art Carney & Lee Strasberg. Directed by Martin Brest. 1979. Warners. 96 min. Sound. 16mm Color. *Rental:* Swank Motion. *Rental:* Swank Motion, Videotape version.

Going My Way. Bing Crosby & Barry Fitzgerald. Directed by Leo McCarey. 1944. Paramount. 126 min. Sound. 16mm B&W. *Rental:* Williams Films.

Going Past Go: An Essay on Sexism. 1979. PBS. (Documentary). 59 min. Videotape Color. *Rental:* PBS Video. *Sale:* PBS Video.

Going Places. Dick Powell & Anita Louise. Directed by Ray Enright. 1939. Warners. 84 min. Sound. 16mm B&W. *Rental:* MGM United.

Going Places. Jeanne Moreau. Directed by Bertrand Blier. Fr. 1974. France. 112 min. Sound. 16mm Color. subtitles. *Rental:* Cinema Five. *Lease:* Cinema Five.

Going the Distance. 1979. Canada. (Documentary). 90 min. Sound. 16mm Color. *Rental:* Museum Mod Art & Natl Film CN. *Sale:* Natl Film CN. *Rental:* Natl Film CN, *Sale:* Natl Film CN, Videotape version.

Going Wild. Joe E. Brown & Walter Pidgeon. Directed by William A. Seiter. 1931. Warners. 68 min. Sound. 16mm B&W. *Rental:* MGM United.

Gold. Robert Moore & Susannah York. Directed by Peter Hunt. 1975. Allied Artists. 120 min. Sound. 16mm Color. *Rental:* Hurlock Cine.

Gold! 1978. National Geographic. (Documentary). 59 min. Sound. 16mm Color. *Rental:* Natl Geog. *Sale:* Natl Geog. *Sale:* Natl Geog, Videotape version.

Gold Diggers in Paris. Rudy Vallee & Rosemary Lane. Directed by Ray Enright. 1938. Warners. 97 min. Sound. 16mm B&W. *Rental:* MGM United.

Gold Diggers of Nineteen-Thirty-Five. Dick Powell & Gloria Stuart. Directed by Busby Berkeley. 1935. Warners. 90 min. Sound. 16mm B&W. *Rental:* MGM United.

Gold Diggers of Nineteen-Thirty-Seven. Dick Powell & Joan Blondell. Directed by Lloyd Bacon. 1937. Warners. 101 min. Sound. 16mm B&W. *Rental:* MGM United.

Gold Diggers of Nineteen-Thirty-Three. Joan Blondell & Ginger Rogers. Directed by Mervyn LeRoy. 1933. Warners. 98 min. Sound. 16mm B&W. *Rental:* Iowa Films & MGM United.

Gold Dust Gertie. Winnie Lightner, Olsen & Johnson. Directed by Lloyd Bacon. 1931. Warners. 66 min. Sound. 16mm B&W. *Rental:* MGM United.

Gold Fever. Ralph Morgan & John Calvert. Directed by Leslie Goodwins. 1952. Monogram. 63 min. Sound. 16mm B&W. *Rental:* Hurlock Cine.

Gold for the Caesars. Jeffrey Hunter & Ron Randell. Directed by Andre De Toth. 1964. MGM. 86 min. Sound. 16mm Color. *Rental:* MGM United.

Gold Mine in the Sky. Gene Autry. Directed by Joseph Kane. 1938. Republic. 54 min. Sound. 16mm B&W. *Rental:* Ivy Films.

Gold of Naples, The. Trans. Title: Oro Di Napoli. Vittorio De Sica & Sophia Loren. Directed by Vittorio De Sica. Ital. 1955. Italy. 107 min. Sound. 16mm B&W. subtitles. *Rental:* Ivy Films, Kit Parker & Video Comm. *Rental:* Video Comm, Videotape version.

Gold of Rome, The. Anna Maria Ferrero & Gerard Blain. Directed by Carlo Lizzani. Ital. 1961. Italy. 102 min. Sound. 16mm B&W. subtitles Eng. *Rental:* Films Inc.

Gold of the Amazon Women, The. Bo Svenson & Anita Ekberg. Directed by Mark L. Lester. 1979. NBC. 98 min. Sound. 16mm Color. *Rental:* Films Inc.

Gold Raiders, The. Three Stooges. Directed by Edward Bernds. 1951. United Artists. 56 min. Sound. 16mm B&W. *Rental:* Budget Films, Inst Cinema, Swank Motion & Willoughby Peer.

Gold Rush, The. Charlie Chaplin & Mack Swain. Directed by Charles Chaplin. 1925. United Artists. (Musical score only). 81 min. Sound. 16mm B&W. *Rental:* Em Gee Film Lib, Films Inc, Film Pres, Inst Cinema, Images Film, Janus Films, Kit Parker, Maljack, Newman Film Lib, Roas Films, Syracuse U Film, Twyman Films, Utah Media, Video Comm, Welling Motion Pictures & Wholesome Film Ctr. *Sale:* Cinema Concepts, Images Film, See-Art Films & Select Film. *Rental:* Budget Films, Charard Motion Pics, Classic Film Mus, Creative Film, Em Gee Film Lib, Films Images, Films Inc, Ivy Films, Maljack, Natl Film Video, Swank Motion, U Cal Media, Video Comm, Welling Motion Pictures, Westcoast Films & Willoughby Peer, *Sale:* Cinema Concepts, E Finney & Natl Cinema, Silent 16mm version. *Rental:* Killiam Collect, Sound Tinted 16mm version. *Sale:* Glenn Photo & Reel Images, Super 8 sound version. *Sale:* Blackhawk Films, Cinema Concepts, Golden Tapes, Ivy Films, Maljack, Tamarelles French Film, Video Comm, Video Home Lib & Images Film, Videotape version. *Sale:* Cinema Concepts, Tinted videotape version. *Rental:* Ivy Films, 100 min. version.

Gold Rush Maisie. Ann Sothern & Lee Bowman. Directed by Edwin L. Marin. 1940. MGM. 82 min. Sound. 16mm B&W. *Rental:* MGM United.

Gold Rush 'Sixty-Eight, The. Charles Chaplin & Mack Swain. Directed by Charles Chaplin. 1968. Spectra. (Musical score only). 60 min. Sound. 16mm B&W. narrated Eng. *Rental:* BYU Media, Standard Film & Swank Motion.

Gold: Supreme Possession. 1979. Nat Geog Soc. 60 min. Sound. 16mm Color. *Rental:* Syracuse U Film.

Golda Meir. Britain. (Documentary). 55 min. Sound. 16mm Color. *Rental:* Alden Films & U Mich Media.

Goldbergs, The see Molly.

Golden Age of Comedy, The. 1957. Youngson. (Anthology). 86 min. Sound. 16mm B&W. *Rental:* Budget Films, U Cal Media, Charard Motion Pics, Williams Films, Em Gee Film Lib, Films Inc, Film Pres, Images Film, Ivy Films, Kerr Film, Kit Parker, Lewis Film, Modern Sound, Natl AV Ctr, Newman Film Lib, Pyramid Film, Roas Films, Swank Motion, Syracuse U Film, Welling Motion Pictures, Wholesome Film Ctr, Viewfinders, Film Ctr DC, Westcoast Films, Trans-World Films, Willoughby Peer & Twyman Films. *Lease:* Carousel Films. *Sale:* Cinema Concepts & Vidamerica, Videotape version.

Golden Age of Greece, The. 1964. CBS. (Documentary). 52 min. Sound. 16mm B&W. *Rental:* U of IL Films. *Sale:* Carousel Films.

Golden Age of Second Avenue, The. Molly Picon & Herschel Bernardi. Directed by Morton Silverstein. 1968. Cantor. 80 min. Sound. 16mm Color. *Rental:* A Cantor. *Sale:* A Cantor.

Golden Age of the Silent Film, The: 1915-1928. Directed by Armand Panigel. Fr. France. (Documentary). 90 min. Sound. 16mm B&W. subtitles. *Rental:* French Am Cul.

Golden Arrow, The. Tab Hunter & Rossana Podesta. Directed by Antonio Margheriti. 1964. Italy. 91 min. Sound. 16mm Color. *Rental:* MGM United.

Golden Blade, The. Rock Hudson & Piper Laurie. Directed by Nathan Juran. 1953. Universal. 80 min. Sound. 16mm Color. *Rental:* Twyman Films.

Golden Boy. William Holden & Barbara Stanwyck. Directed by Rouben Mamoulian. 1938. Columbia. 108 min. Sound. 16mm B&W. *Rental:* Bosco Films, Budget Films, Films Inc, Film Ctr DC, Kit Parker, Modern Sound, Welling Motion Pictures, Westcoast Films & Williams Films.

Golden Breed, The. 1968. Dale Davis. (Documentary). 90 min. Sound. 16mm Color. *Rental:* Budget Films.

Golden Calf, The. 1968. King Screen. (Documentary). 51 min. Sound. 16mm B&W. *Rental:* McGraw-Hill Films. *Sale:* MacGraw-Hill Films.

Golden Coach, The. Anna Magnani & Galina Ulanova. Directed by Jean Renoir. Ital. 1953. Italy. 100 min. Sound. 16mm Color. subtitles. *Rental:* Corinth Films. *Lease:* Corinth Films.

Golden Dawn, The. Vivienne Segal & Noah Beery. Directed by Ray Enright. 1930. Warners. 82 min. Sound. 16mm B&W. *Rental:* MGM United.

Golden Demon, The. Jun Negami & Fujiko Yamamoto. Directed by Koji Shima. Jap. 1956. Japan. 95 min. Sound. 16mm Color. subtitles Eng. *Rental:* Films Inc & Janus Films.

Golden Disc, The *see* In-Between Age.

Golden Earrings. Ray Milland & Marlene Dietrich. Directed by Mitchell Leisen. 1947. Paramount. 95 min. Sound. 16mm B&W. *Rental:* Swank Motion.

Golden Eye, The. Ronald Winters. Directed by William Beaudine. 1948. Monogram. 69 min. Sound. 16mm B&W. *Rental:* Hurlock Cine.

Golden Fleecing, The. Lew Ayres & Rita Johnson. Directed by Leslie Fenton. 1940. MGM. 68 min. Sound. 16mm B&W. *Rental:* MGM United.

Golden Girl, The. Mitzi Gaynor & Dale Robertson. Directed by Lloyd Bacon. 1951. Fox. 107 min. Sound. 16mm Color. *Rental:* Films Inc.

Golden Gloves, The. Richard Denning & Robert Ryan. Directed by Edward Dmytryk. 1940. Paramount. 69 min. Sound. 16mm B&W. *Rental:* Swank Motion.

Golden Gloves Story, The. James Dunn & Dewey Martin. Directed by Felix Feist. 1950. Eagle Lion. 90 min. Sound. 16mm B&W. *Rental:* Budget Films, Ivy Films, Mogulls Films & Westcoast Films. *Sale:* Rep Pic Film.

Golden Goose, The. 1965. K. Gordon Murray. (Cast unlisted). 72 min. Sound. 16mm Color. *Rental:* Charard Motion Pics & Westcoast Films.

Golden Hands of Kurigal, The. Kirk Alyn & Rosemary La Planche. Directed by Fred C. Brannon. 1949. Republic. 100 min. Sound. 16mm B&W. *Rental:* Ivy Films. *Sale:* Rep Pic Film.

Golden Hawk, The. Rhonda Fleming & Sterling Hayden. Directed by Sidney Salkow. 1952. Columbia. 83 min. Sound. 16mm Color. *Rental:* Modern Sound.

Golden Honeymoon, The. 1980. Perspective. (Cast unlisted). 53 min. Sound. 16mm Color. *Rental:* Iowa Films, Kent St U Film, Syracuse U Film & U Mich Media. *Sale:* Perspect Film. *Sale:* Perspect Film, Videocassette version.

Golden Idol, The. Johnny Sheffield. Directed by Ford Beebe. 1954. Allied Artists. 71 min. Sound. 16mm B&W. *Rental:* Hurlock Cine.

Golden Isthmus, The. 1967. Britain. (Documentary). 52 min. Sound. 16mm Color. *Rental:* U of IL Film.

Golden Madonna, The. Phyllis Calvert & Michael Rennie. Directed by Ladislao Vajda. 1949. Britain. 88 min. Sound. 16mm B&W. *Rental:* A Twyman Pres & Modern Sound.

Golden Marie *see* Casque d'Or.

Golden Needles. Joe Don Baker & Elizabeth Ashley. Directed by Robert Clouse. 1974. American International. 95 min. Sound. 16mm Color. *Rental:* Swank Motion.

Golden Ring, The. 1967. Britain. (Documentary). 91 min. Sound. 16mm B&W. *Rental:* Time-Life Multimedia. *Sale:* Time-Life Multimedia.

Golden Salamander, The. Trevor Howard & Anouk Aimee. Directed by Ronald Neame. 1951. Britain. 96 min. Sound. 16mm B&W. *Rental:* Budget Films.

Golden Stallion, The. Roy Rogers. Directed by William Witney. 1949. Republic. 67 min. Sound. 16mm B&W. *Rental:* Ivy Films & Modern Sound. *Sale:* Rep Pic Film & Nostalgia Merchant. *Sale:* Nostalgia Merchant, Color version.

Golden Tales & Legends. 48 min. Sound. Videotape Color. *Rental:* Maljack.

Golden Trail, The *see* Riders of the Whistling Skull.

Golden Trail, The. Tex Ritter. Directed by Al Herman. 1940. Monogram. 55 min. Sound. 16mm B&W. *Rental:* Hurlock Cine.

Golden Twenties, The. 1950. RKO. (Documentary). 68 min. Sound. 16mm B&W. *Rental:* Films Inc.

Golden Voyage of Sinbad, The. John Phillip Law. Directed by Gordon Hessler. 1974. Columbia. 105 min. Sound. 16mm Color. *Rental:* Arcus Film, Budget Films, Buchan Pic, Cine Craft, Williams Films, Bosco Films, Films Inc, Film Press, Inst Cinema, Ivy Films, Kerr Film, Kit Parker, Modern Sound, Newman FilmLib, Natl Film Video, Roas Films, Swank Motion, Film Ctr DC, Twyman Films, Westcoast Films, Welling Motion Pictures & Wholesome Film Ctr. *Lease:* Macmillan Films.

Goldengirl. Susan Anton & James Coburn. Directed by Joseph Sargent. 1979. Embassy. 105 min. Sound. 16mm Color. *Rental:* Films Inc.

Goldfinger. Sean Connery & Gert Frobe. Directed by Guy Hamilton. 1964. United Artists. 112 min. Sound. 16mm Color. *Rental:* MGM United. *Rental:* MGM United, Videotape version.

Goldfish, The. Constance Talmadge. Directed by Jerome Storm. 1924. 16mm *Rental:* A Twyman Pres.

Goldie Gets Along. Lili Damita & Charles Morton. Directed by Mal St. Clair. 1933. RKO. 68 min. Sound. 16mm *Rental:* RKO General Pics.

Goldsnake. Stanley Kent. Directed by Ferdinando Baldi. 1966. Italy. (Anamorphic). 104 min. Sound. 16mm Color. dubbed. *Rental:* Westcoast Films.

Goldstein. Severn Darden & Jack Burns. Directed by Philip Kaufman. 1965. 85 min. Sound. 16mm B&W. *Rental:* Films Inc.

Golem, The. Paul Wegener & Albert Steinruck. Directed by Paul Wegener & Carl Boese. Ger. 1920. Germany. 70 min. Silent. 16mm B&W. *Rental:* A Twyman Pres, Budget Films, Films Inc, Em Gee Film Lib, Film Images, Ivy Films, Janùs Films, Kerr Film, Kit Parker, Museum Mod Art, Video Comm, Westcoast Films, Wholesome Film Ctr, Willoughby Peer & Images Film. *Sale:* Cinema Concepts, Festival Films, Griggs Movie, Film Images & Reel Images. *Sale:* Images Film & Reel Images, *Rental:* Kit Parker, 16mm with musical score version. *Rental:* Video Comm, *Sale:* Festival Films & Images Film, Videotape version.

Golem, The. Orig. Title: Legend of Prague. Harry Baur. Directed by Julien Duvivier. 1936. 83 min. 16mm *Rental:* A Twyman Pres.

Golfo, El. Shirley Jones. Directed by Vicente Escriva. Span. Mexico. 92 min. Sound. 16mm Color. *Rental:* Westcoast Films.

Golgotha. Jean Gabin & Harry Baur. Directed by Julien Duvivier. Fr. 1937. France. 97 min. Sound. 16mm B&W. dubbed. *Rental:* Films Inc.

Goliath & the Barbarians. Steve Reeves & Chelo Alonson. Directed by Carlo Campogalliani. 1960. 86 min. Sound. 16mm Color. *Rental:* Budget Films.

Goliath & the Dragon. Mark Forest & Broderick Crawford. Directed by Vittorio Cottafavi. 1960. Italy. 90 min. Sound. 16mm Color. dubbed. *Rental:* Charard Motion Pics, Welling Motion Pictures, Westcoast Films & Willoughby Peer. *Rental:* Willoughby Peer, Anamorphic color version.

Goliath & the Vampires. Gordon Scott. Directed by Giacomo Gentilomo. 1964. Italy. 93 min. Sound. 16mm Color. dubbed. *Rental:* Westcoast Films & Wholesome Film Ctr.

Goluboi Ekspress see China Express.

Gondoliers, The. 1974. Britain. (Operetta). 52 min. Sound. 16mm Color. *Rental:* B Raymond. *Sale:* B Raymond. *Sale:* B Raymond, Videotape version.

Gone in Sixty Seconds. H. B. Halicki. Directed by H. B. Halicki. 1975. Halicki International. 97 min. Sound. 16mm Color. *Rental:* Films Inc.

Gone With the Wave. (Documentary). 80 min. Sound. 16mm Color. *Rental:* Budget Films.

Gone With the Wind. Clark Gable, Vivien Leigh, Leslie Howard & Olivia De Havilland. Directed by Victor Fleming. 1939. MGM. 222 min. Sound. 16mm Color. *Rental:* MGM United.

Good Day for a Hanging, A. Fred MacMurray & Robert Vaughan. Directed by Nathan Juran. 1958. Columbia. 85 min. Sound. 16mm Color. *Rental:* Arcus Film, Modern Sound & Welling Motion Pictures.

Good Die Young, The. Laurence Harvey & Richard Basehart. Directed by Lewis Gilbert. 1955. United Artists. 100 min. Sound. 16mm B&W. *Rental:* MGM United.

Good Dissonance Like a Man, A. John Bottoms & Richard Ramos. Directed by Theodor Timreck. 1976. Ives. 60 min. Sound. 16mm Color. *Rental:* U of IL Film.

Good Earth, The. Paul Muni & Luise Rainer. Directed by Sidney Franklin. 1937. MGM. 138 min. Sound. 16mm B&W. *Rental:* MGM United. *Rental:* MGM United, Videotape version.

Good Fairy, The. Margaret Sullavan. Directed by William Wyler. 1935. Universal. 100 min. Sound. 16mm B&W. *Rental:* Swank Motion.

Good Fight, The. Directed by Noel Buckner, Mary Dore & Sam Sills. 1983. First Run. (Documentary). 98 min. Sound. 16mm Color. *Rental:* First Run. *Rental:* First Run, Videotape version.

Good Girls Go to Paris. Joan Blondell & Melvyn Douglas. Directed by Alexander Hall. 1939. Columbia. 80 min. Sound. 16mm B&W. *Rental:* Kit Parker.

Good Guys & the Bad Guys, The. Robert Mitchum & George Kennedy. Directed by Burt Kennedy. 1969. Warners. 91 min. Sound. 16mm Color. *Rental:* Films Inc, Video Comm, Welling Motion Pictures, Westcoast Films, Williams Films & Willoughby Peer.

Good Humor Man, The. Jack Carson & Lola Albright. Directed by Lloyd Bacon. 1950. Columbia. 82 min. Sound. 16mm B&W. *Rental:* Films Inc, Modern Sound, Newman Film Lib, Welling Motion Pictures & Westcoast Films.

Good Luck, Mr. Robinson: Managing Stress. 1979. ABC. (Documentary). 50 min. Sound. 16mm Color. *Rental:* MTI Tele. *Sale:* MTI Tele. *Sale:* MTI Tele, Videotape version.

Good Mornin' Blues. 1979. PBS. (Documentary). 59 min. Videotape Color. *Rental:* PBS Video. *Sale:* PBS Video.

Good Morning, Boys: Where There's a Will. Will Hay. Directed by Marcel Varnel. 1937. Britain. 78 min. Sound. 16mm B&W. *Rental:* Cinema Five.

Good Morning, Miss Dove. Jennifer Jones & Robert Stack. Directed by Henry Koster. 1955. Fox. 108 min. Sound. 16mm Color. *Rental:* Films Inc. *Rental:* Films Inc, Anamorphic color version.

Good Morning, Doctor see You Belong to Me.

Good News. June Allyson & Peter Lawford. Directed by Charles Walters. 1947. MGM. 92 min. Sound. 16mm Color. *Rental:* MGM United.

Good News: Hip Hip Happy. Bessie Love & Cliff Edwards. Directed by Nick Grinde. 1930. MGM. 85 min. Sound. 16mm B&W. *Rental:* MGM United.

Good Night, Sweetheart. Robert Livingston & Henry Hull. Directed by Joseph Santley. 1944. Republic. 67 min. Sound. 16mm B&W. *Rental:* Ivy Films.

Good Old Soak, The. Wallace Beery. Directed by Walter J. Ruben. 1937. MGM. 80 min. Sound. 16mm B&W. *Rental:* MGM United.

Good Sam. Gary Cooper & Ann Sheridan. Directed by Leo McCarey. 1948. RKO. 78 min. Sound. 16mm B&W. *Rental:* Ivy Films, Mogulls Films & Rep Pic Film. *Lease:* Rep Pic Film.

Good Soldier Schweik, The. Heinz Ruhmann & Ernst Stankowski. Directed by Axel Von Ambesser. 1960. 98 min. Sound. 16mm B&W. *Rental:* Films Inc.

Good, the Bad & the Ugly, The. Clint Eastwood & Eli Wallach. Directed by Sergio Leone. 1967. Italy. 161 min. Sound. 16mm Color. dubbed. *Rental:* MGM United. *Rental:* MGM United, Videotape version.

Good Times. Sonny & Cher. Directed by William Friedkin. 1967. Columbia. 91 min. Sound. 16mm Color. *Rental:* Williams Films.

Good Times, Wonderful Times. Directed by Lionel Rogosin. 1965. Columbia. (Documentary). 70 min. Sound. 16mm B&W. *Rental:* Icarus Films. *Sale:* Icarus Films.

Goodbye Again. Joan Blondell & Warren William. Directed by Michael Curtiz. 1933. Warners. 66 min. Sound. 16mm B&W. *Rental:* MGM United.

Goodbye Again. Ingrid Bergman, Anthony Perkins & Yves Montand. Directed by Anatole Litvak. 1961. United Artists. 120 min. Sound. 16mm B&W. *Rental:* MGM United.

Goodbye, Bruce Lee: His Last Game of Death. Bruce Lee & Kareem Abdul Jabbar. 1977. Aquarius. 82 min. Sound. 16mm Color. *Rental:* Films Inc.

Goodbye Charlie. Tony Curtis & Debbie Reynolds. Directed by Vincente Minnelli. 1964. Fox. (Anamorphic). 117 min. Sound. 16mm Color. *Rental:* Films Inc.

Goodbye Columbus. Richard Benjamin & Ali McGraw. Directed by Larry Peerce. 1969. Paramount. 105 min. Sound. 16mm Color. *Rental:* Films Inc.

Goodbye Emmanuelle. Sylvia Kristel & Umberto Orsini. Directed by Francois Leterrier. 1981. Miramax. 108 min. Sound. 16mm B&W. dubbed. *Rental:* Films Inc.

Goodbye Girl, The. Richard Dreyfuss & Marsha Mason. Directed by Herbert Ross. 1977. Warners. 110 min. Sound. 16mm Color. *Rental:* Swank Motion.

Goodbye Gutenberg. 1981. WNET. 90 min. Sound. 16mm Color. *Rental:* U Mich Media.

Goodbye in the Mirror. Rosa Fradell & Franco Volpino. Directed by Storm De Hirsch. Ital. 1964. Italy. 80 min. Sound. 16mm B&W. subtitles. *Rental:* Canyon Cinema.

Goodbye Louisiana. 1983. Nova. (Documentary). 57 min. Sound. 16mm Color. *Rental:* U Cal Media. *Sale:* U Cal Media.

Goodbye Love. Charles Ruggles & Sidney Blackmer. Directed by Bruce Humberstone. 1934. RKO. 68 min. Sound. 16mm B&W. *Rental:* Ivy Films.

Goodbye, Mr. Chips. Robert Donat & Greer Garson. Directed by Sam Wood. 1939. MGM. 114 min. Sound. 16mm B&W. *Rental:* MGM United. *Rental:* MGM United, Videotape version.

Goodbye, Mr. Chips. Peter O'Toole & Petula Clark. Directed by Herbert Ross. 1969. MGM. (Anamorphic). 130 min. Sound. 16mm Color. *Rental:* MGM United.

Goodbye, My Fancy. Joan Crawford & Robert Young. Directed by Vincent Sherman. 1951. Warners. 107 min. Sound. 16mm B&W. *Rental:* Swank Motion.

Goodbye Old Man. Directed by David MacDougall. 1975. Australia. (Documentary). 70 min. Sound. 16mm Color. *Rental:* U Cal Media. *Sale:* U Cal Media, Videotape version.

Goona Goona. 1932. First Division. (Documentary, music & sound effects only). 80 min. Sound. 16mm B&W. *Sale:* Morcraft Films.

Goose & the Gander, The. Kay Francis & George Brent. Directed by Alfred E. Green. 1935. Warners. 65 min. Sound. 16mm B&W. *Rental:* MGM United.

Goose Step see Hell's Devils.

Goose Woman, The. Louise Dresser. Directed by Clarence Brown. 1925. Universal. 80 min. Silent. 16mm B&W. *Rental:* Em Gee Film Lib. *Rental:* Em GEE Film Lib, Silent 8mm version.

Gordon's War. Paul Winfield. Directed by Ossie Davis. 1973. Fox. 90 min. Sound. 16mm Color. *Rental:* Films Inc.

Goreme. Institutional Cinema. (Documentary). 52 min. Sound. 16mm Color. *Rental:* Inst Cinema. *Sale:* Inst Cinema.

Gorgeous Hussey, The. Joan Crawford & Robert Taylor. Directed by Clarence Brown. 1936. MGM. 105 min. Sound. 16mm B&W. *Rental:* MGM United.

Gorgo. Bill Travers & William Sylvester. Directed by Eugene Lourie. 1961. Britain. 78 min. Sound. 16mm Color. *Rental:* Films Inc & Roas Films. *Sale:* Natl Cinema. *Rental:* Films Inc & Roas Films, Videotape version.

Gorgon, The. Peter Cushing & Christopher Lee. Directed by Terence Fisher. 1965. Britain. 83 min. Sound. 16mm Color. *Rental:* Budget Films, Film Ctr DC, Inst Cinema, Modern Sound & Welling Motion Pictures. *Rental:* Budget Films, 88 mins. version.

Gorilla, The. Ritz Brothers & Anita Louise. Directed by Allan Dwan. 1940. Fox. 63 min. Sound. 16mm B&W. *Rental:* Budget Films, Kit Parker & Natl Film Video. *Sale:* Cinema Concepts. *Sale:* Blackhawk Films & Reel Images, Super 8 sound version. *Sale:* Festival Films, 66 min. 16mm version. *Sale:* Festival Films, 66 min. Videotape version.

Gorilla, The. Lars-Henrik Ottoson. Swed. Sweden. 80 min. Sound. 16mm Color. *Rental:* Video Comm.

Gorilla, The. 59 min. Sound. 16mm Color. *Rental:* Natl Geog. *Sale:* Natl Geog. *Sale:* Natl Geog, Videotape version.

Gorilla At Large. Cameron Mitchell & Anne Bancroft. Directed by Harmon Jones. 1954. Fox. 84 min. Sound. 16mm Color. *Rental:* Films Inc.

Gorky Park. William Hurt & Joanna Pacula. Directed by Michael Apted. 1983. Orion. 140 min. Sound. Videotape Color. *Sale:* Tamarelles French Films.

Goshawk. Institutional Cinema. (Cast unlisted). 52 min. Sound. 16mm Color. *Rental:* Inst Cinema. *Sale:* Inst Cinema.

Gospel, The. James Cleveland & Walter Hawkins. Directed by David Leivick. 1982. Pacific Film Enterprises. 92 min. Sound. 16mm Color. *Rental:* Gospel Films.

Gospel According to St. Matthew, The. Enrique Irazoque. Directed by Pier Paolo Pasolini. 1965. Italy. 136 min. Sound. 16mm B&W. dubbed Eng. *Rental:* Budget Films, Corinth Films, Films Inc, Images Film, Kit Parker, Macmillan Films, Syracuse U Film & Utah Media. *Sale:* Festival Films, Natl Cinema, Natl Film Video & Reel Images. *Lease:* Images Film, Macmillan Films & Corinth Films. *Sale:* Festival Films & Natl Film Video, Videotape version. *Rental:* Museum Mod Art, *Sale:* Films Inc, Subtitled version. *Rental:* Utah Media, 106 mins. version.

Gossamer Albatross: Flight of Imagination. 1979. Britain. (Documentary). 51 min. Sound. 16mm Color. *Rental:* U of IL Film. *Sale:* Perspect Film. *Sale:* Perspect Film, Videotape version.

Gosta Berling's Saga see Story of Gosta Berling.

Goto L'Ile d'Amour. Pierre Brasseur. Directed by Walerian Borowczyk. Fr. 1968. France. 92 min. Sound. 16mm Color. subtitles. *Rental:* French Am Cul.

Goulaleuse, La. Lys Gauty. Fr. 1940. France. 89 min. Sound. 16mm B&W. subtitles. *Rental:* Film Classics.

Goupi-Main's Rouges, Les. Fernand Ledoux. Directed by Jacques Becker. Fr. 1943. France. 95 min. Sound. 16mm B&W. subtitles. *Rental:* French Am Cul.

Government Agents vs. Phantom Legion. Walter Reed. Directed by Fred C. Brannon. 1951. Republic. 163 min. Sound. 16mm B&W. *Rental:* Ivy Films.

Government as It Is: The Executive Branch. 58 min. Sound. 16mm Color. *Rental:* Pyramid Film. *Sale:* Pyramid Film. *Rental:* Pyramid Film, *Sale:* Pyramid Film, Videotape version.

Government as It Is: The Judicial Branch. 58 min. Sound. 16mm Color. *Rental:* Pyramid Film. *Sale:* Pyramid Film. *Rental:* Pyramid Film, *Sale:* Pyramid Film, Videotape version.

Government as It Is: The Legislative Branch. 58 min. Sound. 16mm Color. *Rental:* Pyramid Film. *Sale:* Pyramid Film. *Sale:* Pyramid Film, *Rental:* Pyramid Film, Videotape version.

Government Girl. Olivia De Havilland, Sonny Tufts & Agnes Moorehead. Directed by Dudley Nichols. 1943. RKO. 93 min. Sound. 16mm B&W. *Rental:* Films Inc.

Governor, The. Directed by Stan Brakhage. 1977. Brakhage. (Experimental). 60 min. Silent. 16mm Color. *Rental:* Canyon Cinema & Museum Mod Art. *Lease:* Museum Mod Art.

Governor John M. Slaton *see* John M. Slaton.

Goya. 1972. Museum Without Walls. (Documentary). 54 min. Sound. 16mm Color. *Rental:* U Mich Media.

Goya: His Life & Art. Directed by Jesus Fernandez Santos. 1980. Spain. (Documentary). 50 min. Sound. 16mm Color. *Rental:* Films Human. *Sale:* Films Human. *Sale:* Films Human, Videotape version.

Gracie Allen Murder Case, The. Gracie Allen & Warren William. Directed by Alfred E. Green. 1939. Paramount. 75 min. Sound. 16mm B&W. *Rental:* Swank Motion.

Graduate, The. Dustin Hoffman & Anne Bancroft. Directed by Mike Nichols. 1967. Avco Embassy. 115 min. Sound. 16mm Color. *Rental:* Budget Films, Cine Craft, Films Inc, Inst Cinema, Roas Films, Swank Motion, Twyman Films, Video Comm, Welling Motion Pictures & Wholesome Films.

Grain De Sable, Le: Circular Triangle. Pierre Brasseur, Paul Hubschmid & Lilli Palmer. Directed by Pierre Kast. Fr. 1964. France. 102 min. Sound. Videotape B&W. subtitles. *Sale:* Tamarelles French Film.

Grain in the Stone. 1974. Britain. (Documentary). 52 min. Sound. 16mm Color. *Rental:* U Cal Media, Iowa Films & U Mich Media.

Grammar. 1957. NET. (Documentary). 60 min. Sound. 16mm B&W. *Rental:* BYU Media.

Gramophone Man, The. Warren Pincus & Jack Smith. Directed by David Devensky. 1973. Devensky. 86 min. Sound. 16mm Color. *Rental:* Canyon Cinema.

Gran Espectaculo, El. Lola Flores & Lalo Gonzalez. Directed by Miguel Zacarias. 1960. Mexico. 80 min. Sound. 16mm B&W. *Rental:* Trans-World Films.

Grand Amour, Un. Pierre Etaix. Directed by Pierre Etaix. Fr. 1968. France. 90 min. Sound. 16mm B&W. subtitles. *Rental:* Trans-World Films.

Grand Amour de Beethoven *see* Beethoven.

Grand Canyon. Mary Beth Hughes & Richard Arlen. Directed by Paul Landres. 1949. Screen Guild. 75 min. Sound. 16mm B&W. *Rental:* Westcoast Films.

Grand Canyon Trail. Roy Rogers. Directed by William Witney. 1948. Republic. 54 min. Sound. 16mm B&W. *Rental:* Ivy Films. *Sale:* Rep Pic Film & Nostalgia Merchant.

Grand Concert, The. Maria Masakova & Galina Ulanova. Directed by Vera Stroyeva. Rus. 1951. Russia. 102 min. Sound. 16mm Color. *Rental:* Corinth Films.

Grand Duchess & the Waiter, The. Florence Vidor & Adolphe Menjou. Directed by Mal St. Clair. 1926. Paramount. 75 min. Silent. 8mm B&W. *Sale:* Cinema Concepts.

Grand Duel, The. Lee Van Cleef & Peter O'Brien. Directed by Giancarlo Santi. 1976. Cinema Shares. 92 min. Sound. 16mm Color. dubbed. *Rental:* Budget Films, Films Inc & Westcoast Films.

Grand Hotel. John Barrymore, Greta Garbo, Joan Crawford & Wallace Beery. Directed by Edmund Goulding. 1932. MGM. 113 min. Sound. 16mm B&W. *Rental:* MGM United. *Rental:* MGM United, Videotape version.

Grand Illusion. Erich Von Stroheim, Jean Gabin & Pierre Fresnay. Directed by Jean Renoir. Fr. 1938. France. 111 min. Sound. 16mm B&W. subtitles. *Rental:* Budget Films, Corinth Films, Films Inc, Images Film, Iowa Film, Ivy Films, Janus Films, La Inst Res Ctr, Wholesome Film Ctr & Westcoast Films. *Sale:* Classic Film Mus, Cinema Concepts, Festival Films, Glenn Photo, Images Film, Reel Images & Utah Media. *Sale:* Glenn Photo, *Lease:* Corinth Films, Super 8 sound version. *Sale:* Cinema Concepts, Festival Films, Ivy Films, Tamarelles French Film, Video Lib, Video Comm & Images Film, Videotape version.

Grand Illusions, The: 1939-1941. Directed by Armand Panigel. Fr. France. (Documentary). 70 min. Sound. 16mm B&W. subtitles. *Rental:* French Am Cul.

Grand Jury. 1978. Direct Cinema. (Documentary). 59 min. Sound. 16mm Color. *Rental:* Direct Cinema. *Lease:* Direct Cinema.

Grand Jury. Fred Stone & Louise Latimer. Directed by Albert S. Rogell. 1936. RKO. 61 min. Sound. 16mm B&W. *Rental:* RKO General Pics.

Grand Jury, The: An Institution Under Fire. 55 min. Sound. 16mm Color. *Rental:* Cinema Guild.

Grand Ocean, The. Directed by Jean Pierre & Daniel Millet. Fr. France. (Documentary). 95 min. Sound. 16mm Color. subtitles. *Rental:* French Am Cul. *Rental:* French Am Cul, Videotape version.

Grand Old Girl. Fred MacMurray & Alan Hale. Directed by John Robertson. 1935. RKO. 72 min. Sound. 16mm B&W. *Rental:* RKO General Pics.

Grand Ole Opry. Roy Acuff & Lois Ranson. Directed by Frank McDonald. 1940. Republic. 67 min. Sound. 16mm B&W. *Rental:* Ivy Films. *Sale:* Rep Pic Film.

Grand Olympics, The: Rome-1960. Directed by Romolo Marcellini. 1961. 120 min. Sound. 16mm Color. *Rental:* Films Inc.

Grand Prix. James Garner, Eva Marie Saint & Toshiro Mifune. Directed by John Frankenheimer. 1966. MGM. (Anamorphic). 175 min. Sound. 16mm Color. *Rental:* MGM United.

Grand Remue-Menage, Le. Ginette Bergeron. Directed by Sylvie Groulx & Francine Allaire. Fr. 1978. Canada. 70 min. Sound. 16mm Color. subtitles. *Rental:* Natl Film CN. *Sale:* Natl Film CN.

Grand Slam. Paul Lukas & Loretta Young. Directed by William Dieterle. 1933. Warners. 67 min. Sound. 16mm B&W. *Rental:* MGM United.

Grand Slam. Edward G. Robinson & Janet Leigh. Directed by Guiliano Montaldo. 1968. Paramount. 120 min. Sound. 16mm Color. *Rental:* Films Inc.

Grand Theft Auto. Nancy Morgan. Directed by Ron Howard. 1977. New World. 89 min. Sound. 16mm Color. *Rental:* Films Inc.

Grande Bourgeoise, La. Giancarlo Giannini & Catherine Deneuve. Directed by Mauro Bolognini. Ital. 1977. Italy. Sound. 16mm Color. subtitles. *Rental:* New Line Cinema.

Grande Breteche, La. Directed by Claude Barma. Fr. 1960. France. (Cast unlisted). 64 min. Sound. 16mm B&W. subtitles. *Rental:* French Am Cul.

Grande Cidade, El. Trans. Title: Big City. Leonardo Vilar & Anecy Rocha. Directed by Carlos Diegues. Port. 1966. Brazil. 80 min. Sound. 16mm B&W. subtitles. *Rental:* Hurlock Cine.

Grande de Coca Cola, El. 1973. Verve. (Cast unlisted). 55 min. Videotape Color. *Rental:* Films Inc.

Grande Illusion, La. Directed by Jean Renoir. Fr. 1937. 111 min. Sound. 16mm B&W. subtitles. *Rental:* Iowa Films.

Grandeur & Obedience. (Civilization Ser.). 1968. Britain. (Documentary). 60 min. Sound. 16mm Color. *Rental:* Films Inc, OK AV Ctr, Syracuse U Film, U Cal Media & Utah Media. *Sale:* Films Inc. *Sale:* Films Inc, Videotape version.

Grandma's Boy. Harold Lloyd. Directed by Fred Newmeyer. 1922. Associated Exhibitors. (Music & sound effects only). 60 min. Sound. 16mm B&W. *Rental:* Films Inc, Images Film, Janus Films & Kino Intl. *Sale:* Films Inc. *Sale:* Blackhawk Films, Super 8 sound version. *Sale:* Blackhawk Films, Super 8 silent version.

Grandpa Chillie-Challa. Xerox. (Cast unlisted). 80 min. Sound. 16mm Color. *Sale:* Xerox Films.

Grandpa Goes to Town. Harry Davenport & Maxie Rosenbloom. Directed by Gus Meins. 1940. Republic. 54 min. Sound. 16mm B&W. *Rental:* Ivy Films & Rep Pic Film. *Lease:* Rep Pic Film.

Granny Get Your Gun. May Robson & Harry Davenport. Directed by George Amy. 1940. Warners. 56 min. Sound. 16mm B&W. *Rental:* MGM United.

Grape Dealer's Daughter, The. Directed by Walter Gutman. 1968. Walter Gutman. 72 min. Sound. 16mm Color. *Rental:* Canyon Cinema.

Grapes of Wrath, The. Henry Fonda & Jane Darwell. Directed by John Ford. 1940. Fox. 115 min. Sound. 16mm B&W. *Rental:* Films Inc & Ivy Films. *Sale:* Blackhawk Films, Golden Tapes, Magnetic Video & Video Lib, Videotape version.

Grass. Directed by Merian C. Cooper & Ernest B. Schoedsack. 1925. Paramount. (Documentary). 86 min. Silent. 16mm B&W. *Rental:* Film Classics, Mogulls Films, Museum Mod Art, U Cal Media, U Mich Media & Utah Media. *Sale:* Museum Mod Art. *Sale:* Film Classics, Silent 8mm version. *Rental:* U Mich Media, 66 min. version. *Rental:* Film Classics, Videotape version. *Rental:* Utah Media, 66 mins. version.

Grass Is Greener, The. Cary Grant & Deborah Kerr. Directed by Stanley Donen. 1960. Universal. 105 min. Sound. 16mm Color. *Rental:* Ivy Films, Video Comm & Welling Motion Pictures. *Sale:* Rep Pic Film. *Sale:* Tamarelles French Film, Videotape version.

Grass Roots. Directed by Luciano Martinengo & Thomas Wahlberg. 1975. Phoenix. (Documentary). 54 min. Sound. 16mm Color. *Rental:* Budget Films, Phoenix Films & Syracuse U Film. *Sale:* Phoenix Films. *Sale:* Phoenix Films, Videotape version.

Grasshopper, The. Jacqueline Bisset & Jim Brown. Directed by Jerry Paris. 1970. Fox. 95 min. Sound. 16mm Color. *Rental:* Swank Motion.

Grasshopper, The. Sergei Bondarchuk. Directed by Samson Samsonov. Rus. 1955. Russia. 90 min. Sound. 16mm B&W. subtitles. *Rental:* Corinth Films.

Grateful Dead Concert Film, The. (Concert). Sound. 16mm Color. *Rental:* Films Inc.

Grateful Dead: Live at Radio City Music Hall. Directed by Len Dell'Amico. 1980. 118 min. Sound. 16mm Color. *Rental:* Films Inc.

Grateful Peasantry, A. 1977. Britain. (Cast unlisted). 56 min. Sound. 16mm Color. *Rental:* U of IL Film & U Mich Media.

Graustark. Norma Talmadge. Directed by Dimitri Buchowetzki. 1925. 16mm *Rental:* A Twyman Pres.

Grave Robbers from Outer Space *see* Plan Nine from Outer Space.

Gravy Train, The: The Dion Brothers. Stacy Keach, Frederic Forrest & Margot Kidder. Directed by Jack Starrett. 1974. Columbia. 94 min. Sound. 16mm Color. *Rental:* Budget Films, Modern Sound, Swank Motion, Twyman Films & Welling Motion Pictures.

Gray Lady Down. Charlton Heston & David Carradine. Directed by David Greene. 1978. Universal. 111 min. Sound. 16mm Color. *Rental:* Williams Films. *Rental:* Swank Motion, Anamorphic version.

Grayeagle. Ben Johnson & Iron Eyes Cody. Directed by Charles B. Pierce. 1978. American International. 104 min. Sound. 16mm Color. *Rental:* Swank Motion & Welling Motion Pictures.

Grease. John Travolta, Olivia Newton-John & Stockard Channing. Directed by Randal Kleiser. 1978. Paramount. (Anamorphic). 110 min. Sound. 16mm Color. *Rental:* Films Inc.

Grease Two. Maxwell Caulfield & Michelle Pfeiffer. Directed by Patricia Birch. 1982. Paramount. 114 min. Sound. 16mm Color. *Rental:* Films Inc.

Greaseband. 1979. PBS. (Concert). 59 min. Videotape Color. *Rental:* PBS Video. *Sale:* PBS Video.

Greased Lightning. Richard Pryor, Beau Bridges & Pam Grier. Directed by Michael Schultz. 1977. Warners. 96 min. Sound. 16mm Color. *Rental:* Films Inc, Modern Sound, Swank Motion & Williams Films. *Rental:* Swank Motion, Videotape version.

Greaser's Palace. Allan Arbus. Directed by Robert Downey. 1972. Herald. 91 min. Sound. 16mm Color. *Rental:* Castle Hill & Cinema Five.

Great Adventure, The. Anders Norberg. Directed by Arne Sucksdorff. Swed. 1955. Sweden. (Documentary). 75 min. Sound. 16mm B&W. narrated Eng. *Rental:* Budget Films, Films Inc, Syracuse U Film & Willoughby Peer.

Great Alligator, The. 89 min. Sound. Videotape Color. *Rental:* Maljack.

Great American Broadcast, The. Alice Faye & Jack Oakie. Directed by Archie Mayo. 1941. Fox. 92 min. Sound. 16mm B&W. *Rental:* Films Inc & Willoughby Peer.

Great American Cowboy, The. Larry Mahan. Directed by Keith Merrill. 1975. Doty-Dayton. 90 min. Sound. 16mm Color. *Rental:* Swank Motion.

Great American Cowboy, The. 1980. Disney. (Documentary). 48 min. Sound. 16mm Color. *Rental:* Disney Prod & U of IL Film.

Great American Funeral, The. 1964. CBS. (Documentary). 54 min. Sound. 16mm B&W. *Rental:* Mass Media & Syracuse U Film. *Sale:* McGraw-Hill Films.

Great American Novel, The. 1968. CBS. (Documentary). 54 min. Sound. 16mm B&W. *Rental:* Phoenix Films. *Sale:* Phoenix Films. *Rental:* Phoenix Films, *Sale:* Phoenix Films, Color version.

Great American Pastime, The. Tom Ewell & Anne Francis. Directed by Herman Hoffman. 1956. MGM. 89 min. Sound. 16mm B&W. *Rental:* MGM United.

Great Barrier Reef, The. 1970. NBC. (Documentary). 53 min. Sound. 16mm Color. *Rental:* Films Inc, Syracuse U Film & Twyman Films. *Sale:* Films Inc. *Sale:* Films Inc, Videotape version.

Great Battle of the Volga, The. Directed by Maria Slavinskaya. Rus. 1945. Russia. (Documentary). 75 min. Sound. 16mm B&W. narrated Eng. *Rental:* Kit Parker.

Great Brain, The. Jimmy Osmond & James Jarnigan. Directed by Sidney Levin. 1978. Osmond. 96 min. Sound. 16mm Color. *Rental:* Swank Motion. *Lease:* Natl Film Video.

Great Caruso, The. Mario Lanza & Ann Blyth. Directed by Richard Thorpe. 1951. MGM. 109 min. Sound. 16mm B&W. *Rental:* MGM United. *Rental:* MGM United, Color version. *Rental:* MGM United, Videotape version.

Great Chase, The. 1963. Continental. (Anthology). 84 min. Sound. 16mm B&W. *Rental:* Budget Films, Films Inc, Texture Film, Video Comm & Wholesome Film Ctr. *Sale:* Texture Film. *Rental:* Budget Films, 77 mins. version. *Sale:* Texture Film, Videotape version.

Great Chicago Conspiracy Circus, The. Directed by Kenny Feltham. 1972. New Line. (Experimental). 93 min. Sound. 16mm Color. *Rental:* New Line Cinema. *Sale:* New Line Cinema.

Great Cleanup, The. 1976. US Government. (Documentary). 53 min. Sound. 16mm Color. *Rental:* Natl AV Ctr & Natl Film CN. *Sale:* Natl AV Ctr & Natl Film CN. *Sale:* Natl AV Ctr, Videotape version.

Great Commandment, The. John Beal & Albert Dekker. 1939. Fox. 82 min. Sound. 16mm B&W. *Rental:* Lewis Film.

Great Conservation Principles. 1964. Britain. (Documentary, kinescope). 56 min. Sound. 16mm B&W. *Rental:* U Cal Media.

Great Conversation, The. 1963. ABC. (Documentary). 54 min. Sound. 16mm B&W. *Rental:* McGraw-Hill Films. *Sale:* McGraw-Hill Films.

Great Dan Patch. Dennis O'Keefe & Gail Russell. Directed by Joseph Newman. 1949. United Artists. 94 min. Sound. 16mm B&W. *Rental:* Budget Films & Roas Films.

Great Day, The. Eric Portman & Flora Robson. Directed by Lance Comfort. 1947. RKO. 94 min. Sound. 16mm *Rental:* RKO General Pics.

Great Day in the Morning. Robert Stack & Ruth Roman. Directed by Jacques Tourneur. 1956. RKO. 92 min. Sound. 16mm Color. *Rental:* Budget Films, Modern Sound, Video Comm & Westcoast Films. *Lease:* Video Comm. *Rental:* Video Comm, *Lease:* Video Comm, Videotape version.

Great Depression, The: A Human Diary. 1972. Hoelscher. (Documentary). 52 min. Sound. 16mm B&W. *Rental:* Mass Media. *Sale:* Mass Media.

Great Diamond Robbery, The. Red Skelton & Cara Williams. Directed by Robert Z. Leonard. 1953. MGM. 69 min. Sound. 16mm B&W. *Rental:* MGM United.

Great Dictator, The. Charles Chaplin, Jack Oakie & Paulette Goddard. Directed by Charles Chaplin. 1940. United Artists. 128 min. Sound. B&W. *Rental:* Films Inc. *Sale:* Cinema Concepts, Videotape version.

Great Director, The. 1966. Britain. (Documentary). 52 min. Sound. 16mm B&W. *Rental:* Killiam Collect. *Sale:* Killiam Collect.

Great Divide, The. Ian Keith, Myrna Loy & Dorothy Mackaill. Directed by Reginald Barker. 1930. Warners. 73 min. Sound. 16mm B&W. *Rental:* MGM United.

Great Dollar Robbery, The. 1971. ABC. (Documentary). 52 min. Sound. 16mm B&W. *Rental:* Syracuse U Film. *Sale:* McGraw-Hill Films.

Great Ecstasy of the Sculptor Steiner, The. Directed by Werner Herzog. Ger. 1975. Germany. (Documentary). 45 min. Sound. 16mm Color. subtitles. *Rental:* New Cinema & New Yorker Films.

Great Escape, The. Steve McQueen & James Garner. Directed by John Sturges. 1963. United Artists. 172 min. Sound. 16mm Color. *Rental:* MGM United. *Rental:* MGM United, Videotape version.

Great Expectations. John Mills, Valerie Hobson & Jean Simmons. Directed by David Lean. 1947. Britain. 115 min. Sound. 16mm B&W. *Rental:* Budget Films, Williams Films, Films Inc, Inst Cinema, U of IL Film, Images Film, Kit Parker, Learning Corp Am, Modern Sound, Roas Films, Twyman Films, Westcoast Films, Welling Motion Pictures & Wholesome Film Ctr. *Lease:* Learning Corp Am. *Rental:* Learning Corp Am, *Lease:* Learning Corp Am, Videotape version.

Great Expectations. James Mason & Michael York. Directed by Joseph Hardy. 1974. ITC. 90 min. Sound. 16mm Color. *Rental:* Swank Motion.

Great Expectations. Henry Hull & Jane Wyatt. Directed by Stuart Walker. 1934. Universal. 101 min. Sound. 16mm B&W. *Rental:* Swank Motion.

Great Flamarion, The. Erich Von Stroheim & Dan Duryea. Directed by Anthony Mann. 1945. Republic. 78 min. Sound. 16mm B&W. *Rental:* Ivy Films. *Sale:* Classics Assoc NY.

Great Gabbo, The. Erich Von Stroheim & Betty Compson. Directed by James Cruze. 1929. World Wide. 90 min. Sound. B&W. *Rental:* A Twyman Pres, Budget Films, Classic Film Mus, Em Gee Film Lib, Films Inc, Kit Parker, Maljack, Twyman Films & Video Comm. *Sale:* Morcraft Films & Reel Images. *Sale:* Reel Images & Tamarelles French Film, Videotape version. *Sale:* Festival Films, 100 min. 16mm version.

Great Garrick, The. Brian Aherne & Olivia De Havilland. Directed by James Whale. 1937. Warners. 82 min. Sound. 16mm B&W. *Rental:* MGM United.

Great Gatsby, The. Robert Redford & Mia Farrow. Directed by Jack Clayton. 1974. Paramount. 146 min. Sound. 16mm Color. *Rental:* Films Inc. *Rental:* Budget Films, La Inst Res Ctr & Modern Sound, Abridged 61 min. version.

Great Gatsby, The. Alan Ladd, Betty Field & Macdonald Carey. Directed by Elliott Nugent. 93 min. Sound. 16mm B&W. *Rental:* Swank Motion.

Great Georgia Bank Hoax, The: Shenanigans. Richard Basehart, Ned Beatty & Michael Murphy. Directed by Joseph Jacoby. 1977. Warners. 87 min. Sound. 16mm Color. *Rental:* Swank Motion & Williams Films.

Great Gildersleeve, The. Harold Peary & Nancy Gates. Directed by Gordon Douglas. 1942. RKO. 62 min. Sound. 16mm B&W. *Rental:* Films Inc & RKO General Pics.

Great Glinka, The. Boris Chirkov. Directed by Lev Arnshtam. Rus. 1947. 103 min. Sound. 16mm B&W. subtitles. *Rental:* Corinth Films.

Great Gundown, The. Robert Padilla & Milila St. Duval. Directed by Paul Hunt. 98 min. Sound. Videotape Color. *Sale:* Vidamerica.

Great Guns. Stan Laurel, Oliver Hardy & Sheila Ryan. Directed by Monty Banks. 1941. Fox. 74 min. Sound. 16mm B&W. *Rental:* Films Inc.

Great Guy: Pluck of the Irish. James Cagney & Mae Clarke. Directed by John G. Blystone. 1936. Grand National. 73 min. Sound. 16mm B&W. *Rental:* Alba House, Budget Films, Classic Film Mus, Em Gee Film Lib, Film Classics, Maljack, Mogulls Films & Video Comm. *Sale:* Cinema Concepts, Morcraft Films, Natl Cinema, Reel Images & Video Comm. *Sale:* Reel Images, *Rental:* Maljack & Video Comm, Super 8 sound version. *Rental:* Film Classics, Videotape version.

Great Holiday Massacre, The. 1960. CBS. (Documentary). 54 min. Sound. 16mm B&W. *Rental:* Syracuse U Film. *Sale:* Carousel Films.

Great Hospital Mystery, The. Jane Darwell & Sig Rumann. Directed by James Tinling. 1937. Fox. 81 min. Sound. 16mm B&W. *Rental:* Films Inc.

Great Hotel Murder, The. Edmund Lowe & Victor McLaglen. Directed by Eugene Forde. 1935. Fox. 70 min. Sound. 16mm B&W. *Rental:* Films Inc.

Great Imposter, The. Tony Curtis & Edmond O'Brien. Directed by Robert Mulligan. 1960. Universal. 112 min. Sound. 16mm B&W. *Rental:* Swank Motion.

Great Jesse James Raid, The. Willard Parker & Wallace Ford. Directed by Reginald Le Borg. 1954. Lippert. 70 min. Sound. 16mm B&W. *Rental:* Budget Films, Cine Craft, Mogulls Films & Westcoast Films.

Great John L., The Greg McClure & Linda Darnell. Directed by Frank Tuttle. 1945. United Artists. 98 min. Sound. 16mm B&W. *Rental:* Budget Films, Cine Craft & Mogulls Films.

Great K & A Train Robbery, The. Tom Mix. Directed by Lewis Seiler. 1926. Fox. (Musical score only). 53 min. Sound. 16mm B&W. *Rental:* Killiam Collect. *Sale:* Blackhawk Films. *Rental:* Em Gee Film Lib, Silent 16mm version. *Sale:* Blackhawk Films, Super 8 sound version. *Sale:* Blackhawk Films, Super 8 silent version.

Great Label Mystery, The. 1965. NET. (Documentary). 60 min. Sound. 16mm B&W. *Rental:* Indiana AV Ctr & Syracuse U Film. *Sale:* Indiana AV Ctr.

Great Lie, The. Bette Davis, George Brent & Mary Astor. Directed by Edmund Goulding. 1941. Warners. 107 min. Sound. 16mm B&W. *Rental:* MGM United.

Great Locomotive Chase, The. Fess Parker, Jeffrey Hunter & John Lupton. Directed by Francis D. Lyon. 1956. Disney. 90 min. Sound. 16mm Color. *Rental:* Bosco Films, Buchan Pic, Cine Craft, Cousino Visual Ed, Elliot Film Co, Film Ctr DC, Films Inc, #Film Pres, Modern Sound, MGM United, Newman Film Lib, Roas Films, Swank Motion, Twyman Films, U of IL Film, Welling Motion Pictures, Westcoast Films & Williams Films. *Rental:* Films Inc, Anamorphic color version.

Great Lover, The. Adolphe Menjou & Irene Dunne. Directed by Harry Beaumont. 1931. MGM. 71 min. Sound. 16mm B&W. *Rental:* MGM United.

Great McGinty, The. Brian Donlevy & Akim Tamiroff. Directed by Preston Sturges. 1940. Paramount. 83 min. Sound. 16mm B&W. *Rental:* Swank Motion.

Great Madcap, The. Fernando Soler & Rosario Granados. Directed by Luis Bunuel. Span. 1949. 90 min. Sound. 16mm B&W. subtitles. *Rental:* Films Inc.

Great Man Votes, The. John Barrymore & Virginia Weidler. Directed by Garson Kanin. 1939. RKO. 70 min. Sound. 16mm B&W. *Rental:* Films Inc.

Great Manhunt, The. Lino Ventura & Lea Massari. Directed by Sidney Gilliat. 1970. France. 118 min. Sound. 16mm Color. dubbed. *Rental:* Swank Motion.

Great Meadow, The. Johnny Mack Brown & Anita Louise. Directed by Charles Brabin. 1931. MGM. 80 min. Sound. 16mm B&W. *Rental:* MGM United.

Great Mike, The. Stuart Erwin & Robert Henry. Directed by Wallace Fox. 1944. PRC. 73 min. Sound. 16mm B&W. *Rental:* Alba House, Budget Films, Ivy Films, Mogulls Films & Welling Motion Pictures. *Sale:* Classics Assoc NY & Rep Pic Film.

Great Missouri Raid, The. Wendell Corey & Macdonald Carey. Directed by Gordon Douglas. 1951. Paramount. 83 min. Sound. 16mm B&W. *Rental:* Films Inc.

Great Mr. Nobody, The. Eddie Albert & Joan Leslie. Directed by Ben Stoloff. 1941. Warners. 71 min. Sound. 16mm B&W. *Rental:* MGM United.

Great Mojave Desert, The. 1971. National Geographic. (Documentary). 52 min. Sound. 16mm Color. *Rental:* Films Inc, Iowa Films, SD AV Ctr, Syracuse U Film, U Mich Media & Wholesome Film Ctr. *Sale:* Films Inc.

Great Moment, The. Joel McCrea & Betty Field. Directed by Preston Sturges. 1944. Paramount. 83 min. Sound. 16mm B&W. *Rental:* Swank Motion.

Great Movie Stunts: Raiders of the Lost Ark. Harrison Ford. Directed by Robert Guenette. 1981. 52 min. Sound. 16mm Color. *Rental:* Films Inc & U of IL Film. *Rental:* U of IL Film, 48 mins. version.

Great Northfield Minnesota Raid, The. Cliff Robertson, Robert Duvall & Luke Askew. Directed by Philip Kaufman. 1972. Universal. 91 min. Sound. 16mm Color. *Rental:* Williams Films.

Great O'Malley, The. Pat O'Brien & Ann Sheridan. Directed by William Dieterle. 1937. Warners. 71 min. Sound. 16mm B&W. *Rental:* United Artists Sixteen & MGM United.

Great Pony Raid, The. 1973. Britain. (Cast unlisted). 60 min. Sound. 16mm Color. *Sale:* Lucerne Films.

Great Profile, The. John Barrymore & Mary Beth Hughes. Directed by Walter Lang. 1940. Fox. 71 min. Sound. 16mm B&W. *Rental:* Films Inc & Willoughby Peer.

Great Radio Comedians, The. 1973. PBS. (Documentary). 88 min. Sound. 16mm Color. *Rental:* McGraw-Hill Films, U Mich Media & Roas Films. *Sale:* McGraw-Hill Films.

Great Railway Journeys of the World. 7 pts. 1981. Britain. (Documentary). 400 min. Sound. 16mm Color. *Rental:* Films Inc. *Sale:* Films Inc. *Sale:* Films Inc, Videotape version.

Great Rupert, The. Jimmy Durante & Terry Moore. Directed by Irving Pichel. 1950. Eagle Lion. 86 min. Sound. 16mm B&W. *Rental:* Budget Films, Cine Craft, Ivy Films & Video Comm.

Great Santini, The. Robert Duvall & Blythe Danner. Directed by Lewis John Carlino. 1980. Orion. 118 min. Sound. 16mm Color. *Rental:* Films Inc.

Great Schnozzola, The *see* Palooka.

Great Scout & Cathouse Thursday, The. Lee Marvin & Oliver Reed. Directed by Don Taylor. 1976. American International. 102 min. Sound. 16mm Color. *Rental:* Swank Motion & Welling Motion Pictures.

Great Sinner, The. Gregory Peck & Ava Gardner. Directed by Robert Siodmak. 1949. MGM. 110 min. Sound. 16mm B&W. *Rental:* MGM United. *Rental:* MGM United, Videotape version.

Great Sioux Massacre, The. Joseph Cotten & Darren McGavin. Directed by Sidney Salkow. 1965. Columbia. 91 min. Sound. 16mm Color. *Rental:* Inst Cinema & Modern Sound.

Great Sioux Uprising, The. Jeff Chandler. Directed by Lloyd Bacon. 1953. Universal. 80 min. Sound. 16mm Color. *Rental:* Swank Motion.

Great Smokey Roadblock, The. Henry Fonda & Eileen Brennan. Directed by John Leone. 1978. Dimension. 90 min. Sound. 16mm Color. *Rental:* Westcoast Films.

Great Spy Chase, The. Lino Ventura & Bernard Blier. Directed by Georges Lautner. 1966. France. 84 min. Sound. 16mm B&W. dubbed. *Rental:* Westcoast Films.

Great Stagecoach Robbery, The. Bill Elliott & Bobby Blake. Directed by Lesley Selander. 1945. Republic. 54 min. Sound. 16mm B&W. *Rental:* Ivy Films.

Great Stone Face, The. Buster Keaton. 1968. Rohauer. 110 min. Sound. 16mm B&W. *Rental:* A Twyman Pres, Budget Films, Films Inc, Kit Parker, Twyman Films & Westcoast Films. *Sale:* Natl Cinema. *Sale:* Blackhawk Films & Video Lib, Videotape version.

Great Texas Dynamite Chase, The. Claudia Jennings & Jocelyn Jones. Directed by Michael Pressman. 1976. New World. 90 min. Sound. 16mm Color. *Rental:* Films Inc.

Great Thaw, The. 1968. Britain. (Documentary). 60 min. Sound. 16mm Color. *Rental:* Films Inc, OK AV Ctr, Syracuse U Film & U Cal Media. *Sale:* Films Inc. *Sale:* Films Inc, Videotape version.

Great Train Robbery, The. Milburn Stone & Claire Carleton. Directed by Joseph Kane. 1941. Republic. 54 min. Sound. 16mm B&W. *Rental:* Ivy Films. *Sale:* Rep Pic Film.

Great Train Robbery, The. Sean Connery & Donald Sutherland. Directed by Michael Crichton. 1979. United Artists. 111 min. Sound. 16mm Color. *Rental:* MGM United. *Rental:* MGM United, Videotape version.

Great Train Robbery. Horst Tappert. Directed by Egon Monk. 1966. 16mm *Rental:* A Twyman Pres.

Great Trolley Strike, The. 1981. CTW. (Cast unlisted). 60 min. Sound. 16mm Color. *Rental:* Indiana AV Ctr. *Sale:* Indiana AV Ctr.

Great Van Robbery, The. Denis Shaw & Kay Callard. Directed by Max Varnel. 1963. Britain. 73 min. Sound. 16mm B&W. *Rental:* MGM United.

Great Victor Herbert, The. Mary Martin & Allan Jones. Directed by Andrew Stone. 1939. Paramount. 91 min. Sound. 16mm B&W. *Rental:* Swank Motion.

Great Violin Mystery, The. 1982. Time-Life. (Documentary). 57 min. Sound. 16mm Color. *Rental:* Iowa Films.

Great Waldo Pepper, The. Robert Redford. Directed by George Roy Hill. 1975. Universal. 107 min. Sound. 16mm Color. *Rental:* Swank Motion. *Rental:* Twyman Films, Anamorphic version.

Great Wall, The. Shintaro Katsu. 1963. Japan. 104 min. Sound. 16mm Color. dubbed. *Rental:* Westcoast Films.

Great Wallendas, The. 1980. Daniel Wilson. 90 min. Sound. 16mm Color. *Rental:* Daniel Wilson. *Rental:* Daniel Wilson, Videotape version.

Great Waltz, The. Luise Rainer & Fernand Gravet. Directed by Julien Duvivier. 1938. MGM. 103 min. Sound. 16mm B&W. *Rental:* MGM United.

Great Waltz, The. Horst Buchholz & Mary Costa. Directed by Andrew Stone. 1972. MGM. (Anamorphic). 135 min. Sound. 16mm Color. *Rental:* MGM United.

Great War, The. Blackhawk. (Documentary). 52 min. Sound. Super 8 B&W. *Sale:* Blackhawk Films & U Mich Media.

Great War, The: This Generation Has No Future. 1976. Britain. (Documentary). 52 min. Sound. 16mm Color. *Rental:* Time-Life Multimedia & Utah Media. *Sale:* Time-Life Multimedia. *Rental:* Time-Life Multimedia, *Sale:* Time-Life Multimedia, Videotape version.

Great War, 1914-1918, The. 1966. NBC. (Documentary). 52 min. Sound. 16mm B&W. *Rental:* La Inst Res Ctr, McGraw-Hill Films, Syracuse U Film, U Cal Media & U Mich Media. *Sale:* McGraw-Hill Films.

Great Whales, The. 59 min. Sound. 16mm Color. *Rental:* Natl Geog. *Sale:* Natl Geog. *Sale:* Natl Geog, Videotape version.

Great White Bird, The. Directed by Mike McKennirey. 1976. Canada. (Documentary). 51 min. Sound. 16mm Color. *Rental:* Natl AV Ctr, Natl Film CN & U Mich Media. *Sale:* Natl Film CN. *Sale:* Natl AV Ctr, Videotape version.

Great White Hope, The. James Earl Jones, Jane Alexander & Chester Morris. Directed by Martin Ritt. 1970. Fox. (Anamorphic). 103 min. Sound. 16mm Color. *Rental:* Films Inc & Twyman Films.

Great White Trail, The. Doris Kenyon. Directed by Leopold Wharton. 1917. Wharton. 60 min. Silent. 16mm B&W. *Rental:* Em Gee Film Lib. *Sale:* Morcraft Films. *Sale:* Morcraft Films, Silent 8mm version.

Great Ziegfeld, The. William Powell & Myrna Loy. Directed by Robert Z. Leonard. 1936. MGM. 176 min. Sound. 16mm B&W. *Rental:* MGM United. *Rental:* MGM United, Videotape version.

Great Zoos of the World: San Diego. Films Inc. (Documentary). 60 min. Sound. 16mm Color. *Sale:* Films Inc. *Sale:* Films Inc, Videotape version.

Greatest, The. Muhammad Ali & Ernest Borgnine. Directed by Tom Gries. 1977. Columbia. 103 min. Sound. 16mm Color. *Rental:* Arcus Film, Bosco Films, Budget Films, Films Inc, Modern Sound, Swank Motion, Twyman Films, Welling Motion Pictures, Westcoast Films & Williams Films.

Greatest Adventure, The: The History of Space. 1981. ABC. (Documentary). 51 min. Sound. 16mm Color. *Rental:* MTI Tele. *Sale:* MTI Tele.

Greatest Battle, The. Henry Fonda & Stacy Keach. 1980. Time-Life. 92 min. Sound. Videotape Color. *Rental:* Time-Life Multimedia. *Sale:* Time-Life Multimedia.

Greatest Man in the World, The. 1980. Perspective. (Cast unlisted). 52 min. Sound. 16mm Color. *Rental:* Iowa Films, Kent St U Film, Syracuse U Film & U Mich Media. *Sale:* Perspect Film. *Sale:* Perspect Sale, Videocassette version.

Greatest Show on Earth, The. Betty Hutton & Charlton Heston. Directed by Cecil B. DeMille. 1952. Paramount. 153 min. Sound. 16mm Color. *Rental:* Films Inc.

Greatest Story Ever Told, The. Max Von Sydow & Charlton Heston. Directed by George Stevens. 1965. United Artists. (Anamorphic). 141 min. Sound. 16mm Color. *Rental:* MGM United.

Greatest Story Never Told, The. Jeff Williams. 46 min. Sound. 16mm Color. *Rental:* Gospel Films.

Greece: The Inner World. Katina Paxinou. Modern. 54 min. Sound. 16mm B&W. *Rental:* Modern Mass. *Sale:* Modern Mass.

Greed. Gibson Gowland, ZaSu Pitts & Jean Hersholt. Directed by Erich Von Stroheim. 1923. MGM. 150 min. Silent. 16mm B&W. *Rental:* Films Inc & MGM United. *Rental:* MGM United, 109 mins. version.

Greed in the Sun. Jean-Paul Belmondo & Lino Ventura. Directed by Henri Verneuil. 1965. France. (Anamorphic). 112 min. Sound. 16mm Color. dubbed. *Rental:* Films Inc.

Greek Myths. 2 pts. 1971. Encyclopaedia Britannica. (Documentary). 54 min. Sound. 16mm Color. *Rental:* Ency Brit Ed. *Sale:* Ency Brit Ed. *Sale:* Ency Brit Ed, Videotape version.

Greek Street. Sari Maritza & Martin Lewis. Directed by Sinclair Hill. 1930. 51 min. Sound. 16mm B&W. *Sale:* Morcraft Films. *Sale:* Morcraft Films, Super 8 sound version. *Sale:* Morcraft Films, Videotape version.

Greek Temple, The. 1972. Museum Without Walls. (Documentary). 54 min. Sound. 16mm Color. *Rental:* U Mich Media.

Greek Tycoon, The. Anthony Quinn & Jacqueline Bisset. Directed by J. Lee Thompson. 1978. Universal. 106 min. Sound. 16mm Color. *Rental:* Williams Films.

Greeks Had a Word for Them, The: Three Broadway Girls. Joan Blondell, Ina Claire & Madge Evans. Directed by Lowell Sherman. 1932. United Artists. 60 min. Sound. 16mm B&W. *Rental:* Budget Films, Classic Film Mus, Mogulls Films & Video Comm. *Sale:* Cinema Concepts & Reel Images. *Sale:* Cinema Concepts, Videotape version.

Green Berets, The. John Wayne & David Janssen. Directed by John Wayne & Ray Kellogg. 1968. Warners. 141 min. Sound. 16mm Color. *Rental:* Charard Motion Pics, Films Inc, Inst Cinema, Swank Motion & Video Comm, 110 min. version.

Green Buddha, The. Wayne Morris & Mary Germaine. Directed by John Lamont. 1955. Republic. 62 min. Sound. 16mm B&W. *Rental:* Ivy Films. *Sale:* Rep Pic film.

Green Cockatoo. Robert Newton & John Mills. Directed by William Cameron Menzies. 1940. 64 min. 16mm *Rental:* A Twyman Pres.

Green Dolphin Street. Lana Turner, Van Heflin & Donna Reed. Directed by Victor Saville. 1947. MGM. 141 min. Sound. 16mm B&W. *Rental:* MGM United.

Green Fingers. Robert Beatty & Carol Raye. Directed by John Harlow. 1948. Republic. 82 min. Sound. 16mm B&W. *Rental:* Ivy Films. *Sale:* Rep Pic Film.

Green Fire. Stewart Granger & Grace Kelly. Directed by Andrew Marton. 1954. MGM. 100 min. Sound. 16mm Color. *Rental:* MGM United. *Rental:* MGM United, Anamorphic color version.

Green for Danger. Trevor Howard, Alastair Sim & Sally Gray. Directed by Sidney Gilliat. 1947. Britain. 95 min. Sound. 16mm B&W. *Rental:* Budget Films, Images Film, Kit Parker, Learning Corp Am & U of IL Film. *Lease:* Learning Corp Am.

Green Glove, The. Glenn Ford & Geraldine Brooks. Directed by Rudolph Mate. 1952. United Artists. 88 min. Sound. 16mm B&W. *Rental:* MGM United.

Green Goddess, The. George Arliss & H. B. Warner. Directed by Alfred E. Green. 1930. Warners. 74 min. Sound. 16mm B&W. *Rental:* MGM United.

Green Grass of Wyoming, The. Peggy Cummins & Lloyd Nolan. Directed by Louis King. 1948. Fox. 89 min. Sound. 16mm Color. *Rental:* Films Inc.

Green Helmet, The. Bill Travers & Ed Begley. Directed by Michael Forlong. 1961. Britain. 88 min. Sound. 16mm B&W. *Rental:* MGM United.

Green Light, The. Errol Flynn & Anita Louise. Directed by Frank Borzage. 1937. Warners. 85 min. Sound. 16mm B&W. *Rental:* MGM United.

Green Machine, The. 1978. Nova. (Documentary). 49 min. Sound. 16mm Color. *Rental:* U Cal Media, U of IL Film, Kent St U Film, U Mich Media & Syracuse U Film.

Green Mansions. Audrey Hepburn & Anthony Perkins. Directed by Mel Ferrer. 1959. MGM. 101 min. Sound. 16mm Color. *Rental:* MGM United. *Rental:* MGM United, Anamorphic color version.

Green Pastures, The. Rex Ingram & Eddie Anderson. Directed by Marc Connelly & William Keighley. 1936. Warners. 93 min. Sound. 16mm B&W. *Rental:* MGM United.

Green Promise, The. Marguerite Chapman & Walter Brennan. Directed by William D. Russell. 1949. RKO. 102 min. Sound. 16mm B&W. *Rental:* Budget Films.

Green Room, The. Francois Truffaut & Nathalie Baye. Directed by Francois Truffaut. Fr. 1978. New World. 94 min. Sound. 16mm Color. subtitles Eng. *Rental:* Films Inc.

Green Sea Turtle. 1970. Metromedia. (Documentary). 52 min. Sound. 16mm Color. *Rental:* Churchill Films. *Sale:* Churchill Films, Videotape version.

Green Slime, The: Battle Beyond the Stars. Robert Horton & Richard Jaeckel. Directed by Kinji Fukasaku. Jap. 1969. Japan. (Anamorphic). 85 min. Sound. 16mm Color. dubbed. *Rental:* Films Inc & MGM United.

Green Tree, The. 75 min. Sound. 16mm B&W. *Rental:* Bosco Films.

Green Wall, The. Julio Aleman. Directed by Armando Robles Godoy. 1982. Films Inc. (Documentary). 110 min. Sound. 16mm Color. *Lease:* Films Inc. *Sale:* Films Inc, Videotape version.

Green Years, The. Charles Coburn & Tom Drake. Directed by Victor Saville. 1946. MGM. 128 min. Sound. 16mm B&W. *Rental:* MGM United.

Greenaway Program, The. Directed by Peter Greenaway. 1976. Britain. (Anthology). 85 min. Sound. 16mm Color. *Rental:* Museum Mod Art. *Lease:* Museum Mod Art.

Greenbergs of California, The. Directed by Mark Obenhaus. 1976. Group W. (Documentary). 59 min. Sound. 16mm Color. *Rental:* Iowa Films, Syracuse U Film, U Cal Media & U Mich Media. *Sale:* Carousel Films. *Sale:* Carousel Films, Videotape version.

Greengage Summer *see* Loss of Innocence.

Greetings. Jonathan Warden & Robert De Niro. Directed by Brian De Palma. 1968. 88 min. Sound. 16mm Color. *Rental:* Films Inc.

Grenada: The Future Coming Toward Us. Directed by Carmen Ashhurst, John Douglas & Samori Marksman. 1983. Caribbean Resource Inst.. (Documentary). 55 min. Sound. 16mm Color. *Rental:* Cinema Guild. *Sale:* Cinema Guild. *Sale:* Cinema Guild, Videotape version.

Grenfell of Labrador: The Great Adventure. Directed by Terence Macartney-Filgate. 1977. Canada. (Documentary). 57 min. Sound. 16mm Color. *Rental:* Natl Film CN. *Sale:* Natl Film CN. *Sale:* Natl Film CN, Videotape version.

Grenoble. Jean-Claude Killy. Directed by Claude Lelouch & Francois Reichenbach. 1969. France. 95 min. Sound. 16mm Color. *Rental:* Budget Films, Films Inc, Welling Motion Pictures & Willoughby Peer.

Grenoble-La Villeneuve: The City Conceived Anew. 1975. Canada. (Documentary). 57 min. Sound. 16mm Color. *Rental:* Natl Film CN. *Sale:* Natl Film CN.

Greta, the Misfit Greyhound. Directed by Larry Lansburg. 1963. Disney. (Documentary). 46 min. Sound. 16mm Color. *Rental:* Buchan Pic, Cine Craft, Cousino Visual Ed, Disney Prod, Film Ctr DC, Films Inc, Modern Sound, Newman Film Lib, Roas Films & Twyman Films.

Grey Fox, The. Richard Farnsworth. Directed by Phillip Borsos. 1983. MGM-UA. 92 min. Sound. 16mm Color. *Rental:* MGM United. *Rental:* MGM United, Videotape version.

Grey Gardens. Directed by Albert Maysles & David Maysles. 1976. Maysles. (Documentary). 94 min. Sound. 16mm Color. *Rental:* Maysles Films. *Sale:* Maysles Films.

Grey Owl. Directed by Nancy Ryley. 1972. Canada. (Documentary). 57 min. Sound. 16mm Color. *Rental:* Natl Film CN. *Sale:* Natl Film CN.

Grey Vulture. Ken Maynard. Directed by Forrest Sheldon. 1926. Davis. 50 min. Silent. 8mm B&W. *Rental:* Film Classics. *Sale:* Film Classics.

Greyfriar's Bobby. Donald Crisp & Laurence Naismith. Directed by Don Chaffey. 1961. Disney. 91 min. Sound. 16mm Color. *Rental:* Buchan Pic, Cine Craft, Cousino Visual Ed, Disney Prod, Film Ctr DC, Films Inc, Newman Film Lib & U of IL Film.

Greystoke, the Legend of Tarzan. Christopher Lambert, Sir Ralph Richardson. Directed by Hugh Hudson. 1985. Warners. 130 min. Sound. 16mm Color. *Rental:* Swank Motion.

Gribouille *see* Heart of Paris.

Gridiron Flash, The. Eddie Quillan & Betty Furness. Directed by Pandro S. Berman. 1935. RKO. 64 min. Sound. 16mm *Rental:* RKO General Pic.

Grief. 52 min. Sound. 16mm Color. *Rental:* Media Guild. *Sale:* Media Guild. *Sale:* Media Guild, Videotape version.

Grierson. Directed by Roger Blais. 1973. Canada. (Documentary). 58 min. Sound. 16mm Color. *Rental:* U Cal Media & Museum Mod Art. *Sale:* Museum Mod Art & Natl Film CN. *Rental:* Natl Film CN, Videotape version.

Griffin & Phoenix. Jill Clayburgh & Peter Falk. Directed by Daryl Duke. 1976. ABC. 96 min. Sound. 16mm Color. *Rental:* U of IL Film, Videotape version.

Griffith: Actor, Director, Supervisor. 1979. Museum of Modern Art. (Anthology). 60 min. Silent. 16mm B&W. *Rental:* Museum Mod Art. *Lease:* Museum Mod Art.

Griffith's Westerns: 1911. 1979. Museum of Modern Art. (Anthology). 60 min. Silent. 16mm B&W. *Rental:* Museum Mod Art. *Lease:* Museum Mod Art.

Grimace. Directed by Gudmundur Ferro. Gudmundur Ferro. (Experimental). 45 min. Sound. 16mm B&W. *Rental:* Canyon Cinema.

Grip of Fear *see* Experiment in Terror.

Grissly's Millions. Paul Kelly & Adele Mara. Directed by John English. 1944. Republic. 54 min. Sound. 16mm B&W. *Rental:* Ivy Films. *Sale:* Rep Pic Film.

Grissom Gang, The. Kim Darby & Scott Wilson. Directed by Robert Aldrich. 1971. Cinerama. 127 min. Sound. 16mm Color. *Rental:* Films Inc.

Grito de la Muerte, El *see* Living Coffin.

Grizzly! 1967. National Geographic. (Documentary). 52 min. Sound. 16mm Color. *Rental:* Films Inc, Syracuse U Film, U Cal Media, U Mich Media & Natl Geog. *Sale:* Films Inc & Natl Geog. *Sale:* Natl Geog, Videotape version.

Grizzly! Christopher George & Richard Jaeckel. Directed by William Girdler. 1977. Film Ventures. 96 min. Sound. 16mm Color. *Rental:* Westcoast Films & Wholesome Film Ctr.

Grizzly & the Treasure, The. 1974. Gold Key. (Documentary). 98 min. Sound. 16mm Color. *Rental:* Budget Films & Video Comm. *Lease:* Video Comm. *Rental:* Video Comm, *Lease:* Video Comm, Videotape version.

Groove Tube, The. Ken Shapiro & Chevy Chase. Directed by Ken Shapiro. 1974. Shapiro. 73 min. Sound. 16mm Color. *Rental:* Films Inc. *Sale:* Cinema Concepts & Films Inc, Videotape version.

Groovie Goolies. Filmation. (Animated). 66 min. Sound. 16mm Color. *Rental:* Williams Films.

Grosse Spiel, Das. 1938. Germany. (Cast unlisted). 88 min. Sound. 16mm B&W. *Rental:* Film Classics.

Ground Zero. 50 min. Sound. 16mm Color. *Rental:* U Mich Media.

Grounds for Marriage. Van Johnson & Kathryn Grayson. Directed by Robert Z. Leonard. 1950. MGM. 91 min. Sound. 16mm B&W. *Rental:* MGM United.

Groundstar Conspiracy, The. George Peppard & Michael Sarrazin. Directed by Lamont Johnson. 1972. Universal. 96 min. Sound. 16mm Color. *Rental:* Williams Films.

Group, The. Candice Bergen & Elizabeth Hartman. Directed by Sidney Lumet. 1966. United Artists. 150 min. Sound. 16mm Color. *Rental:* MGM United.

Group Therapy: Children in Conflict. 1968. 60 min. Sound. 16mm B&W. *Rental:* Utah Media.

Groupies. Joe Cocker. Directed by Ron Dorfman & Peter Nevard. 1972. New Line. 88 min. Sound. 16mm Color. *Rental:* New Line Cinema. *Sale:* New Line Cinema, Videotape version.

Grover Cleveland. Carroll O'Connor. Directed by Lamont Johnson. (Profiles in Courage Ser.). 1965. Saudek. 50 min. Sound. 16mm B&W. *Rental:* Syracuse U Film, U Mich Media & U of IL Film. *Sale:* IQ Films. *Rental:* IQ Films, *Sale:* IQ Films, Spanish dubbed version.

Growing Up Female: As Six Become One. Directed by Julia Reichert & James Klein. 1970. New Day. (Documentary). 60 min. Sound. 16mm B&W. *Rental:* Iowa Films, U Mich Media, New Day Films & Tricontinental Film. *Sale:* New Day Films.

Growing Up Together: Four Teen Mothers & Their Babies. 1974. Children's Home Society. (Documentary). 55 min. Sound. 16mm Color. *Rental:* U Mich Media. *Rental:* U Mich Media, Videotape version.

Growth of the Soil. Directed by Gunnar Sommerfeldt. 1920. Norway. (Cast unlisted). 77 min. Silent. 16mm B&W. *Rental:* Budget Films & Em Gee Film Lib.

Grumpy. Cyril Maude & Phillips Holmes. Directed by George Cukor. 1930. Paramount. 74 min. Sound. 16mm B&W. *Rental:* Swank Motion.

Gruppo di Famiglia in un Interno *see* Conversation Piece.

Guadalcanal Diary. Preston Foster & Lloyd Nolan. Directed by Lewis Seiler. 1943. Fox. 93 min. Sound. 16mm B&W. *Rental:* Films Inc.

Guadalcanal: Island of Death. 1970. NBC. (Documentary). 53 min. Sound. 16mm Color. *Rental:* Films Inc. *Sale:* Films Inc, Videotape version.

Guadalcanal Odyssey. 1974. Gold Key. (Documentary). 90 min. Sound. 16mm Color. *Rental:* Video Comm. *Lease:* Video Comm. *Rental:* Video Comm, *Lease:* Video Comm, Videotape version.

Guadalcanal Requiem. Directed by Nam June Paik. 1977. WNET. (Concert). 50 min. Videotape Color. *Rental:* Electro Art. *Lease:* Electro Art.

Guale. Directed by Albert Scardino & Marjorie Morris Scardino. 1977. Southern Chroniclers. (Documentary). 59 min. Sound. 16mm Color. *Rental:* Southern Chroniclers. *Sale:* Southern Chroniclers. *Sale:* Southern Chroniclers, Videotape version.

Guambianos. 1979. 55 min. 16mm Color. *Rental:* Icarus Films. *Sale:* Icarus Films, Videotape version.

Guardsman, The. Alfred Lunt & Lynn Fontanne. Directed by Sidney Franklin. 1931. MGM. 83 min. Sound. 16mm B&W. *Rental:* MGM United.

Guerilla. 1961. CBS. (Documentary). 52 min. Sound. 16mm B&W. *Rental:* Macmillan Films. *Sale:* Macmillan Films.

Guerillas in Pink Lace. George Montgomery & Joan Shawlee. 1964. Gold Key. 89 min. Sound. 16mm B&W. *Rental:* Video Comm. *Lease:* Video Comm. *Rental:* Video Comm, *Sale:* Video Comm, Videotape version.

Guerillas on the Plains. Chinese. 1955. China. 90 min. Sound. 16mm B&W. *Rental:* Asian Film Lib.

Guernica. Mariangelo Melato. Directed by Fernando Arrabal. Span. 1973. Spain. 110 min. Sound. 16mm Color. subtitles. *Rental:* New Line Cinema.

Guerre Est Finie, La. Trans. Title: War Is Over, The. Yves Montand & Ingrid Thulin. Directed by Alain Resnais. Fr. 1966. France. 121 min. Sound. 16mm B&W. subtitles. *Sale:* Reel Images. *Rental:* Films Inc, English language version.

Guess What Happened to Count Dracula? Des Roberts & Claudia Barron. Directed by Laurence Merrick. 1970. 80 min. Sound. 16mm Color. *Rental:* Budget Films.

Guess Who's Coming to Dinner? Spencer Tracy, Katharine Hepburn & Sidney Poitier. Directed by Stanley Kramer. 1967. Columbia. 108 min. Sound. 16mm Color. *Rental:* Arcus Film, Bosco Films, Buchan Pic, Budget Films, Charard Motion Pics, Cine Craft, Film Ctr DC, Films Inc, Inst Cinema, Kit Parker, Modern Sound, Natl Film Video, Roas Films, Swank Motion, Twyman Films, U of IL Film, Video Comm, Welling Motion Pictures, Westcoast Films, Wholesome Film Ctr, Williams Films & Willoughby Peer.

Guess Who's Pregnant? 1977. WTTW. (Documentary). 60 min. Sound. Videotape Color. *Rental:* U Cal Media, U of IL Film & PBS Video. *Sale:* PBS Video.

Guess Who's Pregnant: An Update. 1980. PBS. (Documentary). 69 min. Videotape Color. *Rental:* PBS Video. *Sale:* PBS Video.

Guest, The. Athol Fugard. Directed by Ross Devenish. 1978. South Africa. 120 min. Sound. 16mm Color. subtitles. *Rental:* Liberty Co.

Guest in the House. Anne Baxter &
Ralph Bellamy. Directed by John Brahm.
1944. United Artists. 122 min. Sound.
16mm B&W. *Rental:* Budget Films.

Guest Wife. Claudette Colbert & Don
Ameche. Directed by Sam Wood. 1945.
United Artists. 90 min. Sound. 16mm
B&W. *Rental:* Ivy Films. *Sale:* Rep Pic
Film.

Gui Dao *see* On the Way, Some Chinese
Women Told Us.

Gui Dao *see* On the Way, a Station on
the Yangzi.

Gui Dao *see* On the Way, Round Trip to
Beijing.

**Gui Dao-on the Way, a Station on the
Yangzi.** 1980. 59 min. Sound. 16mm
Color. *Rental:* U Cal Media.

Guide for the Married Man, A. Walter
Matthau & Robert Morse. Directed by
Gene Kelly. 1967. Fox. (Anamorphic). 91
min. Sound. 16mm Color. *Rental:* Films
Inc.

Guilt of Janet Ames, The. Rosalind
Russell & Melvyn Douglas. Directed by
Henry Levin. 1947. Columbia. 80 min.
Sound. 16mm B&W. *Rental:* Bosco Films
& Kit Parker.

Guilt: The Psychic Censor. 1975. PBS.
(Documentary). 59 min. Sound. 16mm
Color. *Rental:* Indiana AV Ctr, Iowa
Films & U Cal Media. *Sale:* Indiana AV
Ctr.

Guilty. Donald Wolfit. Directed by
Edmond Greville. 1956. 93 min. 16mm
Rental: A Twyman Pres.

Guilty by Reason of Race. 1972. NBC.
(Documentary). 53 min. Sound. 16mm
Color. *Rental:* Films Inc, Iowa Films,
Syracuse U Film, U Mich Media & Utah
Media. *Sale:* Films Inc. *Sale:* Films Inc,
Videotape version.

Guilty Generation, The. Robert Young &
Constance Cummings. Directed by
Rowland V. Lee. 1931. Columbia. Sound.
16mm B&W. *Rental:* Kit Parker.

Guilty Hands. Lionel Barrymore, Madge
Evans & Kay Francis. Directed by W. S.
Van Dyke II. 1931. MGM. 69 min.
Sound. 16mm B&W. *Rental:* MGM
United.

Guilty Madonnas. 52 min. videotape
Sale: McGraw-Hill Films & Syracuse U
Film.

Gulliver's Travels. Richard Harris,
Norman Shelley & Murray Melvin.
Directed by Peter Hunt. 1980. Britain-
Belgium. 84 min. Sound. 16mm Color.
Rental: Budget Films, Modern Sound,
Roas Films, U of IL Film & Westcoast
Films. *Sale:* Lucerne Films. *Sale:* Lucerne
Films, Videotape version.

Gulliver's Travels. Directed by Dave
Fleischer. 1939. (Animated). 77 min.
Sound. 16mm Color. *Rental:* Classic Film
Mus. *Sale:* Festival Films. *Sale:* Festival
Films & Tamarelles French Film,
Videotape version.

Gumball Rally, The. Michael Sarrazin,
Raul Julia & Susan Flannery. Directed by
Charles Bail. 1976. Warners. 107 min.
Sound. 16mm Color. *Rental:* Swank
Motion, Twyman Films & Williams
Films.

Gumbymania. 1983. Art Clokey. 90 min.
Sound. 16mm Color. *Rental:* Creative
Film.

Gumshoe. Albert Finney & Billie
Whitelaw. Directed by Stephen Frears.
1972. Columbia. 85 min. Sound. 16mm
Color. *Rental:* Budget Films, Corinth
Films & Swank Motion.

Gun, The *see* Os Fuzis.

Gun Battle at Monterey. Sterling Hayden
& Lee Van Cleef. Directed by Carl K.
Hittleman. 1957. Republic. 74 min.
Sound. 16mm B&W. *Rental:* Ivy Films.
Sale: Rep Pic Film.

Gun Crazy: Deadly Is the Female. Peggy
Cummins & John Dall. Directed by
Joseph Lewis. 1950. United Artists. 87
min. Sound. 16mm B&W. *Rental:*
Hurlock Cine.

Gun Fury. Rock Hudson & Donna Reed.
Directed by Raoul Walsh. 1953.
Columbia. 83 min. Sound. 16mm Color.
Rental: Inst Cinema & Modern Sound.

Gun Glory. Stewart Granger & Rhonda
Fleming. Directed by Roy Rowland.
1957. MGM. 88 min. Sound. 16mm
Color. *Rental:* MGM United. *Rental:*
MGM United, Anamorphic version.

Gun Hawk. Rory Calhoun & Rod
Cameron. Directed by Edward Ludwig.
1963. Allied Artists. 92 min. Sound.
16mm Color. *Rental:* Hurlock Cine.

Gun Law. George O'Brien & Rita
Oehman. Directed by Bert Gilroy. 1938.
RKO. 61 min. Sound. 16mm *Rental:*
RKO General Pics.

Gun Law Justice. Jimmy Wakely.
Directed by Lambert Hillyer. 1949.
Monogram. 55 min. Sound. 16mm B&W.
Rental: Hurlock Cine.

Gun Lords of Stirrup Basin. Bob Steele.
Directed by Sam Newfield. 1937.
Republic. 60 min. Sound. 16mm B&W.
Rental: Ivy Films.

Gun Packer. Jack Randall. Directed by
Wallace Fox. 1938. Monogram. 55 min.
Sound. 16mm B&W. *Rental:* Hurlock
Cine.

Gun, The: Pro & Con. 1976. ABC.
(Documentary). 51 min. Sound. 16mm
Color. *Rental:* McGraw-Hill Films & U
Cal Media. *Sale:* McGraw-Hill Films.
Sale: McGraw-Hill Films, Videotape
version.

Gun Ranger. Bob Steele. Directed by
Robert N. Bradbury. 1937. Republic. 60
min. Sound. 16mm B&W. *Rental:* Ivy
Films.

Gun Riders, The. Jim Davis & Scott
Brady. 1969. Allied Artists. 85 min.
Videotape Color. *Rental:* Blackhawk
Films.

Gun Runner. Jimmy Wakely & Mae
Clarke. Directed by Lambert Hillyer.
1949. Monogram. 60 min. Sound. 16mm
B&W. *Rental:* Hurlock Cine.

Gun Smoke. Johnny Mack Brown.
Directed by Howard Bretherton. 1945.
Monogram. 55 min. Sound. 16mm B&W.
Rental: Hurlock Cine & Mogulls Films.

Gun Smugglers. Tim Holt & Richard
Martin. Directed by Frank MacDonald.
1948. RKO. 62 min. Sound. 16mm B&W.
Rental: Films Inc.

Gun Street. James Brown & Jean Willes.
Directed by Edward L. Cahn. 1961.
United Artists. 67 min. Sound. 16mm
B&W. *Rental:* MGM United.

Gun That Won the West, The. Dennis
Morgan & Paula Raymond. Directed by
William Castle. 1955. Columbia. 72 min.
Sound. 16mm Color. *Rental:* Modern
Sound.

Gun, The Pro & Con. 1976. ABC.
(Documentary). 51 min. Sound. 16mm
Color. *Rental:* McGraw-Hill Films & U
Cal Media. *Sale:* McGraw-Hill Films.
Sale: McGraw-Hill Films, Videotape
version.

Gun Trouble. Tim McCoy. 60 min.
Sound. 16mm B&W. *Rental:* Mogulls
Films.

Guna Reels, The. 45 min. Sound. 16mm
B&W. *Rental:* Canyon Cinema.

Gunfight, A. Kirk Douglas, Johnny Cash,
Raf Vallone & Jane Alexander. Directed
by Lamont Johnson. 1971. Paramount. 90
min. Sound. 16mm Color. *Rental:* Films
Inc.

Gunfight at Casa Grande. Jorge Mistral
& Alex Nicol. 1970. MGM. 92 min.
Sound. 16mm Color. *Rental:* Films Inc.

Gunfight at Commanche Creek. Audie
Murphy. Directed by Frank McDonald.
1963. Allied Artists. 90 min. Sound.
16mm B&W. *Rental:* Hurlock Cine.

Gunfight at Dodge City, The. Joel
McCrea & Julie Adams. Directed by
Joseph Newman. 1959. United Artists. 80
min. Sound. 16mm Color. *Rental:* MGM
United.

Gunfight at Red Sands. Richard Harrison. 1965. Italy. 97 min. Sound. 16mm Color. dubbed. *Rental:* Westcoast Films.

Gunfight at the O. K. Corral, The. Burt Lancaster & Kirk Douglas. Directed by John Sturges. 1957. Paramount. 122 min. Sound. Color. *Rental:* Films Inc. *Sale:* Cinema Concepts & Nostalgia Merchant, Videotape version.

Gunfight in Abilene. Bobby Darin & Leslie Nielsen. Directed by William Hale. 1967. Universal. 86 min. Sound. 16mm Color. *Rental:* Swank Motion. *Sale:* Swank Motion, Anamorphic version.

Gunfight, USA. 58 min. Sound. Videotape *Rental:* PBS Video. *Sale:* PBS Video.

Gunfighter, The. Gregory Peck & Millard Mitchell. Directed by Henry King. 1950. Fox. 85 min. Sound. 16mm B&W. *Rental:* Films Inc.

Gunfighters of Abilene. Buster Crabbe & Barton MacLane. Directed by Edward L. Cahn. 1960. United Artists. 67 min. Sound. 16mm B&W. *Rental:* MGM United.

Gunfire. Rex Bell. Directed by Harry Fraser. 1935. First Division. 60 min. Sound. 16mm B&W. *Rental:* Mogulls Films.

Gunfire. Don Barry & Robert Lowery. Directed by William Berke. 1950. Lippert. 60 min. Sound. 16mm B&W. *Rental:* Budget Films & Mogulls Films.

Gunfire at Indian Gap. Anthony George & Barry Kelley. Directed by Joseph Kane. 1957. Republic. 70 min. Sound. 16mm B&W. *Rental:* Ivy Films. *Sale:* Rep Pic Film.

Gung Ho! Randolph Scott & Alan Curtis. Directed by Ray Enright. 1943. Universal. 88 min. Sound. 16mm B&W. *Rental:* Budget Films & Classic Film Mus. *Sale:* Cinema Concepts & Festival Films. *Sale:* Cinema Concepts, Festival Films & Tamarelles French Film, Videotape version.

Gunga Din. Cary Grant & Douglas Fairbanks Jr. Directed by George Stevens. 1939. RKO. 129 min. Sound. Videotape B&W. *Rental:* Films Inc, RKO General Pics & VidAmerica. *Lease:* Films Inc.

Gunman, The. Whip Wilson. Directed by Lewis D. Collins. 1952. Monogram. 52 min. Sound. 16mm B&W. *Rental:* Hurlock Cine.

Gunman from Bodie, The. Buck Jones & Tim McCoy. Directed by Spencer G. Bennett. 1941. Monogram. 55 min. Sound. 16mm B&W. *Rental:* Hurlock Cine & Em Gee Film Lib. *Sale:* Cinema Concepts, Glenn Photo & Natl Cinema. *Sale:* Em Gee Film Lib & Video Comm, Videotape version.

Gunman of Abilene. Allan Lane. Directed by Fred C. Brannon. 1949. Republic. 60 min. Sound. 16mm B&W. *Rental:* Ivy Films. *Sale:* Rep Pic Film & Nostalgia Merchant.

Gunman's Walk. Van Heflin & Tab Hunter. Directed by Phil Karlson. 1958. Columbia. 97 min. Sound. 16mm Color. *Rental:* Kit Parker.

Gunn. Craig Stevens & Laura Devon. Directed by Blake Edwards. 1967. Paramount. 94 min. Sound. 16mm Color. *Rental:* Films Inc.

Gunners & Guns: Racketeers Roundup. Black King. Directed by Jerry Callahan. 1935. Beaumont. 60 min. Sound. 16mm B&W. *Rental:* Budget Films & Video Comm. *Sale:* Video Comm, Videotape version.

Gunning for Vengeance. Charles Starrett. Directed by Ray Nazarro. 1946. Columbia. 60 min. Sound. 16mm B&W. *Rental:* Westcoast Films.

Gunplay. Tim Holt & Joan Dixon. Directed by Lesley Selander. 1951. RKO. 61 min. Sound. 16mm *Rental:* RKO General Pics.

Gunpoint. Audie Murphy & Joan Staley. Directed by Earl Bellamy. 1966. Universal. 86 min. Sound. 16mm Color. *Rental:* Swank Motion.

Guns & Guitars. Gene Autry. Directed by Joseph Kane. 1936. Republic. 54 min. Sound. 16mm B&W. *Rental:* Ivy Films.

Guns at Batasi. Richard Attenborough & Jack Hawkins. Directed by John Guillermin. 1964. Britain. 103 min. Sound. 16mm B&W. *Rental:* Films Inc.

Guns Don't Argue. Myron Healey & Lyle Talbot. Directed by Bill Karn & Richard C. Kahn. 1958. Visual Drama. 92 min. Sound. 16mm B&W. *Rental:* Video Comm. *Lease:* Video Comm. *Rental:* Video Comm, *Lease:* Video Comm, Videotape version.

Guns for Diablo. Charles Bronson & Susan Oliver. 1964. MGM. 79 min. Sound. 16mm B&W. *Rental:* MGM United.

Guns for San Sebastian. Anthony Quinn & Anjanette Comer. Directed by Henri Verneuil. 1968. MGM. (Anamorphic). 150 min. Sound. 16mm Color. *Rental:* MGM United.

Guns in the Afternoon see Ride the High Country.

Guns in the Dark. Johnny Mack Brown. Directed by Sam Newfield. 1937. Republic. 60 min. Sound. 16mm B&W. *Rental:* Ivy Films. *Sale:* Rep Pic Film.

Guns of August. Directed by Nathan Kroll. 1965. Universal. (Documentary). 99 min. Sound. 16mm B&W. *Rental:* Swank Motion & Twyman Films.

Guns of Autumn, The. 1974. CBS. (Documentary). 77 min. Sound. 16mm Color. *Rental:* Budget Films, U Cal Media, Iowa Films & U Mich Media. *Sale:* Carousel Films.

Guns of Darkness. David Niven & Leslie Caron. Directed by Anthony Asquith. 1962. Warners. 95 min. Sound. 16mm B&W. *Rental:* Swank Motion.

Guns of Fort Petticoat. Audie Murphy & Kathryn Grant. Directed by George Marshall. 1957. Columbia. 82 min. Sound. 16mm Color. *Rental:* Modern Sound & Film Ctr DC.

Guns of Hate. Tim Holt & Nan Leslie. Directed by Lesley Selander. 1948. RKO. 62 min. Sound. 16mm B&W. *Rental:* Films Inc.

Guns of Navarone, The. Gregory Peck, David Niven & Anthony Quinn. Directed by J. Lee Thompson. 1961. Columbia. (Anamorphic). 155 min. Sound. 16mm Color. *Rental:* Arcus Film, Bosco Films, Buchan Pic, Budget Films, Charard Motion Pics, Cine Craft, Film Ctr DC, Films Inc, Film Pres, Images Film, Ivy Films, Kit Parker, Modern Sound, Newman Film Lib, Natl Film Video, Roas Films, Swank Motion, Twyman Films, U of IL Film, Video Comm, Welling Motion Pictures, Westcoast Films, Wholesome Film Ctr, Williams Films & Willouhby Peer. *Rental:* Kit Parker, Anamorphic version.

Guns of the Pecos. Dick Foran. Directed by Noel Smith. 1937. Warners. 56 min. Sound. 16mm B&W. *Rental:* MGM United.

Guns of the Timberland. Alan Ladd & Jeanne Crain. Directed by Robert Webb. 1960. Warners. 94 min. Sound. 16mm Color. *Rental:* Budget Films, Films Inc, Video Comm & Westcoast Films. *Lease:* Video Comm. *Rental:* Video Comm, *Lease:* Video Comm, Videotape version.

Guns of the Trees. Directed by Jonas Mekas. Jonas Mekas. (Experimental). 75 min. Sound. 16mm B&W. *Rental:* Canyon Cinema.

Guns, Sin & Bathtub Gin. Pamela Sue Martin & Robert Conrad. Directed by Lewis Teague. 1979. New World. 93 min. Sound. 16mm Color. *Rental:* Films Inc.

Gunsight Ridge. Joel McCrea & Mark Stevens. Directed by Francis D. Lyon. 1957. United Artists. 85 min. Sound. 16mm B&W. *Rental:* MGM United.

Gunslinger. John Ireland & Beverly Garland. Directed by Roger Corman. 1956. American Releasing. 77 min. Sound. 16mm B&W. *Rental:* Westcoast Films.

Gunslingers. Whip Wilson. Directed by Wallace Fox. 1950. Monogram. 55 min. Sound. 16mm B&W. *Rental:* Hurlock Cine.

Gunsmith of Williamsburg, The. 1983. Colonial Williamsburg. (Documentary). 59 min. Sound. 16mm Color. *Rental:* Colonial. *Sale:* Colonial. *Sale:* Colonial, Videotape version.

Gunsmoke. Audie Murphy & Susan Cabot. Directed by Nathan Juran. 1953. Universal. 79 min. Sound. 16mm Color. *Rental:* Swank Motion.

Gunsmoke in Tucson. Mark Stevens & Forrest Tucker. Directed by Thomas Carr. 1958. Allied Artists. 80 min. Sound. 16mm Color. *Rental:* Hurlock Cine.

Gunsmoke Mesa. Tex Ritter. Directed by Harry Fraser. 1944. PRC. 60 min. Sound. 16mm B&W. *Rental:* Film Ctr DC. *Sale:* Natl Cinema.

Gunsmoke Ranch. Robert Livingston. Directed by Joseph Kane. 1937. Republic. 54 min. Sound. 16mm B&W. *Rental:* Ivy Films. *Sale:* Rep Pic Film.

Gunsmoke Trail. Jack Randall. Directed by Sam Newfield. 1938. Monogram. 55 min. Sound. 16mm B&W. *Rental:* Hurlock Cine.

Guru, The. Michael York & Rita Tushingham. Directed by James Ivory. 1969. Fox. 112 min. Sound. 16mm Color. *Rental:* Films Inc.

Gus. Edward Asner, Don Knotts & Tim Conway. Directed by Vincent McEveety. 1976. Disney. 96 min. Sound. 16mm Color. *Rental:* Bosco Films, Buchan Pic, Elliot Film Co, Film Ctr DC, Films Inc, Film Pres, MGM United, Modern Sound, Newman Film Lib, Roas Films, Swank Motion, Twyman Films, U of IL Film, Welling Motion Pictures, Westcoast Films & Williams Films.

Guy, a Gal, & a Pal, A. Ross Hunter & Lynn Merrick. Directed by Budd Boetticher. 1945. Columbia. 63 min. Sound. 16mm B&W. *Rental:* Kit Parker.

Guy Could Change, A. Bobby Blake & Gerald Mohr. Directed by William K. Howard. 1945. Republic. 65 min. Sound. 16mm B&W. *Rental:* Ivy Films. *Sale:* Rep Pic Film.

Guy Named Joe, A. Irene Dunne & Spencer Tracy. Directed by Victor Fleming. 1943. MGM. 120 min. Sound. 16mm B&W. *Rental:* MGM United.

Guy Who Came Back, The. Paul Douglas & Joan Bennett. Directed by Joseph Newman. 1951. Fox. 91 min. Sound. 16mm B&W. *Rental:* Films Inc.

Guyana, Cult of the Damned. Stuart Whitman. Directed by Rene Cardona Jr. 1980. Universal. 90 min. Sound. 16mm Color. *Rental:* Swank Motion.

Guys & Dolls. Marlon Brando, Frank Sinatra & Jean Simmons. 1955. Goldwyn. 149 min. Sound. 16mm Color. *Rental:* Films Inc, Ivy Films, Twyman Films & Video Comm.

Gypsy. Rosalind Russell & Natalie Wood. Directed by Mervyn Leroy. 1962. Warners. 149 min. Sound. 16mm Color. *Rental:* Arcus Film. *Sale:* Tamarelles French Film, Videotape version.

Gypsy Blood. Pola Negri. Directed by Ernst Lubitsch. 1921. First National. 75 min. Silent. 16mm B&W. *Rental:* Em Gee Film Lib & Film Classics. *Sale:* Cinema Concepts & Film Classics. *Rental:* Film Classics, Sound 16mm musical score only version. *Rental:* Ivy Films, Super 8 silent version. *Sale:* Film Classics, Silent 8mm version. *Rental:* Film Classics, Videotape version.

Gypsy Camp Vanishes into the Blue, The. Grigory Grigoriou & Svetlana Toma. Directed by Emil Lotianu. Rus. 1976. Russia. 102 min. Sound. 16mm Color. subtitles. *Rental:* Films Inc.

Gypsy Colt. Donna Corcoran & Ward Bond. Directed by Andrew Marton. 1954. MGM. 72 min. Sound. 16mm Color. *Rental:* MGM United.

Gypsy Fury. Viveca Lindfors. Directed by Christian-Jaque. 1951. Monogram. 63 min. Sound. 16mm B&W. *Rental:* Hurlock Cine.

Gypsy Moths, The. Burt Lancaster & Deborah Kerr. Directed by John Frankenheimer. 1969. MGM. 110 min. Sound. 16mm Color. *Rental:* MGM United.

Gypsy Romance, A. Shannon Day & Thur Fairfax. 1926. Prime. 60 min. Silent. 16mm B&W. *Sale:* Morcraft Films.

H. B. O. Magic Show, The. Dick Cavett. HBO. 86 min. Videotape Color. *Rental:* Films Inc.

H. B. O. Puppet Show, The. Bil Baird Puppets & Rita Moreno. HBO. 50 min. Videotape Color. *Rental:* Films Inc.

H. M. Pulham, Esquire. Robert Young & Hedy Lamarr. Directed by King Vidor. 1941. MGM. 120 min. Sound. 16mm B&W. *Rental:* MGM United.

H. M. S. Pinafore. 1974. Britain. (Operetta). 52 min. Sound. 16mm Color. *Rental:* B Raymond. *Sale:* B Raymond. *Sale:* B Raymond, Videotape version.

H-Man, The. Yumi Shirakawa. Directed by Inoshiro Honda. 1959. Japan. 79 min. Sound. 16mm Color. dubbed. *Rental:* Modern Sound.

H. S. T: Days of Decision. 1963. Hearst. (Documentary). 50 min. Sound. 16mm B&W. *Sale:* King Features.

H. G. Wells' New Invisible Man see New Invisible Man.

H. M. S. Defiant see Damn the Defiant!.

Hadaka No Shima see Island.

Hail Hero. Michael Douglas & Arthur Kennedy. Directed by David Miller. 1969. National General. 97 min. Sound. 16mm Color. *Rental:* Swank Motion.

Hail the Conquering Hero. Eddie Bracken & Ella Raines. Directed by Preston Sturges. 1944. Paramount. 100 min. Sound. 16mm B&W. *Rental:* Williams Films.

Hail to the Chief. Richard B. Shull & Dan Resin. Directed by Fred Levinson. 1973. Townshend. 85 min. Sound. 16mm Color. *Rental:* Films Inc.

Hair. Treat Williams & John Savage. Directed by Milos Forman. 1979. United Artists. 121 min. Sound. 16mm Color. *Rental:* MGM United. *Rental:* MGM United, Videotape version.

Hajj Malik, El: El Shabazz Malcolm X. 1979. McGraw Hill. (Documentary). 58 min. Sound. 16mm B&W. *Rental:* Kent St U Film, La Inst Res Ctr, McGraw-Hill Films, U Cal Media & U Mich Media. *Sale:* McGraw-Hill Films.

Hakuta Den see Panda & the Magic Serpent.

Half a Hero. Red Skelton & Jean Hagen. Directed by Don Weis. 1953. MGM. 71 min. Sound. 16mm B&W. *Rental:* MGM United.

Half a Sixpence. Tommy Steele. Directed by George Sidney. 1967. Paramount. 148 min. Sound. 16mm Color. *Rental:* Films Inc.

Half Angel. Joseph Cotten & Loretta Young. Directed by Richard Sale. 1951. Fox. 77 min. Sound. 16mm B&W. *Rental:* Films Inc.

Half-Breed, The. Robert Young & Jack Buetel. Directed by Stuart Gilmore. 1952. RKO. 81 min. Sound. 16mm Color. *Rental:* Films Inc & RKO General Pics.

Half Marriage. Olive Borden & Ken Murray. Directed by William Gowen. 1934. RKO. Sound. 16mm *Rental:* RKO General Pics.

Half-Naked Truth, The. Lupe Velez, Lee Tracy & Frank Morgan. Directed by Gregory La Cava. 1933. RKO. 77 min. Sound. 16mm B&W. *Rental:* RKO General Pics.

Half Shot at Sunrise. Bert Wheeler & Robert Woolsey. Directed by Paul Sloane. 1930. RKO. 100 min. Sound. 16mm B&W. *Rental:* Classic Film Mus, Em Gee Film Lib & Kit Parker. *Sale:* Cinema Concepts & Festival Films. *Sale:* Festival Films, Videotape version.

Halfway House. Francoise Rosay & Mervyn Johns. Directed by Basil Dearden. 1944. Britain. 94 min. Sound. 16mm B&W. *Rental:* Janus Films.

Halfway to Shanghai. Kent Taylor & Irene Hervey. Directed by John Rawlins. 1943. Universal. 62 min. Sound. 16mm B&W. *Rental:* Mogulls Films.

Hall of Kings: Westminster Abbey. 1967. ABC. (Documentary). 53 min. Sound. 16mm Color. *Rental:* McGraw-Hill Films, Syracuse U Film, U Mich Media & U of IL Film. *Sale:* McGraw-Hill Films.

Hallelujah. Daniel L. Haynes & Nina Mae McKinney. Directed by King Vidor. 1929. MGM. 107 min. Sound. 16mm B&W. *Rental:* MGM United.

Hallelujah, I'm a Bum. Al Jolson & Madge Evans. Directed by Lewis Milestone. 1932. United Artists. 83 min. Sound. 16mm *Rental:* A Twyman Pres & Budget Films.

Hallelujah the Hills. Directed by Adolfas Mekas. 1963. Mekas. (Experimental). 82 min. Sound. 16mm B&W. *Rental:* Canyon Cinema & Museum Mod Art.

Hallelujah Trail, The. Burt Lancaster & Lee Remick. Directed by John Sturges. 1965. United Artists. 145 min. Sound. 16mm Color. *Rental:* MGM United.

Halliday Brand, The. Joseph Cotten & Viveca Lindfors. Directed by Joseph Lewis. 1957. United Artists. 77 min. Sound. 16mm B&W. *Rental:* MGM United.

Halloween. Donald Pleasence & Jamie Lee Curtis. Directed by John Carpenter. 1978. Compass. 93 min. Sound. 16mm Color. *Rental:* Films Inc.

Halloween II. Jamie Lee Curtis & Donald Pleasence. Directed by Richard Rosenthal. 1981. Universal. 92 min. Sound. 16mm Color. *Rental:* Swank Motion. *Rental:* Swank Motion, Videotape version.

Halloween III: Season of the Witch. Tom Atkins, Stacey Nelkin & Dan O'Herlihy. Directed by Tommy Lee Wallace. 1982. Universal. 96 min. Sound. 16mm Color. *Rental:* Swank Motion. *Rental:* Swank Motion, Videotape version.

Halls of Anger, The. Calvin Lockhart & Janet MacLachlan. Directed by Paul Bogart. 1970. United Artists. 100 min. Sound. 16mm Color. *Rental:* MGM United.

Halls of Montezuma, The. Richard Widmark & Robert Wagner. Directed by Lewis Milestone. 1950. Fox. 113 min. Sound. 16mm B&W. *Rental:* Films Inc.

Hallucination Generation, The. George Montgomery & Danny Stone. Directed by Edward Mann. 1970. American International. (Color sequences). 90 min. Sound. 16mm B&W. *Rental:* Ivy Films.

Hamilton Fish. Henry Jones. Directed by Harvey Hart. 1965. Saudek. 50 min. Sound. 16mm B&W. *Rental:* U of IL Film. *Sale:* IQ Films. *Rental:* IQ Films, *Sale:* IQ Films, Spanish Dubbed version.

Hamlet. Sir Laurence Olivier & Jean Simmons. Directed by Sir Laurence Olivier. 1948. Britain. 152 min. Sound. 16mm B&W. *Rental:* Arcus Film, Budget Films, Films Inc, Images Film, Kit Parker, Learning Corp Am, Roas Films, Swank Motion, Syracuse U Film, Twyman Films, U Cal Media, U of IL Films, Welling Motion Pictures & Wholesome Film Ctr. *Lease:* Learning Corp Am. *Lease:* Learning Corp Am, Videotape version.

Hamlet. 4 pts. 1959. Encyclopaedia Britannica. (Cast unlisted). 120 min. Sound. 16mm Color. *Rental:* Ency Brit Ed. *Sale:* Ency Brit Ed. *Sale:* Ency Brit Ed, Videotape version.

Hamlet. Maxmilian Schell. Directed by Edward Dmytryk & Franz Peter Wirth. 1964. Germany. 127 min. Sound. 16mm B&W. dubbed. *Rental:* Cine Craft, Films Inc, Macmillan Films, Syracuse U Film, Video Comm & Westcoast Films. *Lease:* Macmillan Films.

Hamlet. Nicol Williamson & Marianne Faithfull. Directed by Tony Richardson. 1969. Britain. 114 min. Sound. 16mm Color. *Rental:* Budget Films, Films Inc, Images Film, Kent St U Film, Kit Parker, Learning Corp Am, Mass Media, Modern Sound, Roas Films, Swank Motion, Syracuse U Film & Wholesome Film Ctr. *Lease:* Learning Corp Am. *Lease:* Learning Corp Am, Videotape version.

Hamlet. Derek Jacobi. 1979. Britain. 150 min. Videotape Color. *Rental:* Iowa Films & Time-Life Multimedia. *Sale:* Time-Life Multimedia.

Hamlet. Richard Chamberlain, Sir Michael Redgrave. Directed by Peter Wood. 1970. 104 min. Sound. 16mm Color. *Rental:* Films Inc.

Hamlet. Innokenty Smoktunovsky. Directed by Grigori Kozintsev. 1964. Russia. 149 min. Sound. 16mm B&W. subtitles. *Rental:* Corinth Films.

Hammer. Fred Williamson & Bernie Hamilton. Directed by Bruce Clark. 1972. United Artists. 91 min. Sound. 16mm Color. *Rental:* Films Inc & MGM United.

Hammerhead. Vince Edwards & Diana Dors. Directed by David Miller. 1968. Columbia. 99 min. Sound. 16mm Color. *Rental:* Welling Motion Pictures & Westcoast Films.

Hammersmith Is Out. Elizabeth Taylor & Richard Burton. Directed by Peter Ustinov. 1973. Cinerama. 108 min. Sound. 16mm Color. *Rental:* Swank Motion.

Hammond Mystery, The *see* Undying Monster.

Hamnstad *see* Port of Call.

Hand, The. Michael Caine & Andrea Marcovicci. Directed by Oliver Stone. 1981. Orion. 108 min. Sound. 16mm Color. *Rental:* Films Inc.

Hand in Hand. John Gregson & Dame Sybil Thorndike. Directed by Philip Leacock. 1961. Britain. 83 min. Sound. 16mm B&W. *Rental:* Alba House, Arcus Film, Budget Films, Cine Craft, Film Ctr DC, Films Inc, Modern Sound, Roas Films, Welling Motion Pictures & Willoughby Peer. *Rental:* Bosco Films, 75 min version.

Hand-Me-Down Kid, The. 1982. ABC. (Cast unlisted). 47 min. Sound. 16mm Color. *Sale:* Learning Corp Am. *Sale:* Learning Corp Am, *Rental:* Learning Corp Am, Videotape version.

Hand of Death, The. John Agar & Paula Raymond. Directed by Gene Nelson. 1962. Fox. (Anamorphic). 60 min. Sound. 16mm B&W. *Rental:* Films Inc.

Handcuffs. Trans. Title: Lisice. Fabijan Sovagovic. Directed by Krsto Papic. Serbo-Croatian. 1970. Yugoslavia. 90 min. Sound. 16mm B&W. subtitles. *Rental:* Films Inc.

Handford's Point. Lassie. 1960. Wrather. 78 min. Sound. 16mm Color. *Rental:* Films Inc, Kerr Film, Modern Sound & Budget Films.

Handful of Clouds, A *see* Doorway to Hell.

Handle with Care *see* Citizens Band.

Handle with Care. Dean Jones & Thomas Mitchell. Directed by David Friedkin. 1958. MGM. 82 min. Sound. 16mm B&W. *Rental:* MGM United.

Handling Grievances. 1983. 59 min. Sound. 16mm Color. *Rental:* Natl AV Ctr. *Sale:* Natl AV Ctr.

Handmaidens of God, The. Directed by Diane Letourneau. 1979. Canada. (Documentary). 90 min. Sound. 16mm Color. subtitles. *Rental:* Liberty Co.

Hands Across the Border. Roy Rogers. Directed by Joseph Kane. 1943. Republic. 54 min. Sound. 16mm B&W. *Rental:* Budget Films & Ivy Films. *Sale:* Rep Pic Film.

Hands Across the Table. Carole Lombard & Fred MacMurray. Directed by Mitchell Leisen. 1935. Paramount. 81 min. Sound. 16mm B&W. *Rental:* Swank Motion.

Hands of Orlac, The. Trans. Title: Orlacs Hande. Conrad Veidt & Fritz Kortner. Directed by Robert Wiene. 1924. Germany. (Musical score only). 65 min. Sound. 16mm B&W. *Rental:* A Twyman Pres & Twyman Films.

Hands of Orlac. Christopher Lee. Directed by Edmond Greville. 1961. 95 min. 16mm *Rental:* A Twyman Pres.

Hands of the Ripper, The. Eric Porter. Directed by Peter Sasdy. 1972. Britain. 85 min. Sound. 16mm Color. *Rental:* Swank Motion.

Hands Up! Raymond Griffith. Directed by Clarence Badger. 1926. Paramount. 65 min. Silent. 16mm B&W. *Rental:* Em Gee Film Lib & Museum Mod Art. *Rental:* Film Classics, *Sale:* Film Classics, Silent 8mm version.

Hanford's Point. Tony Dow & Jan Michael Vincent. Directed by Jack Hively. 1969. 72 min. Sound. 16mm Color. *Rental:* Budget Films.

Hang 'Em High. Clint Eastwood & Inger Stevens. Directed by Ted Post. 1968. United Artists. 114 min. Sound. 16mm Color. *Rental:* Budget Films, MGM United, Westcoast Films & Wholesome Film Ctr.

Hang Your Hat on the Wind. Angel Tompkins. 1970. Disney. 46 min. Sound. 16mm Color. *Rental:* Buchan Pic, Cine Craft, Disney Prod, Films Ctr DC, Films Inc, Kent St U Film, Modern Sound, Roas Films & Twyman Films.

Hangman, The. Robert Taylor & Tina Louise. Directed by Michael Curtiz. 1959. Paramount. 86 min. Sound. 16mm B&W. *Rental:* Films Inc.

Hangman's House. Victor McLaglen & Hobart Bosworth. Directed by John Ford. 1928. Fox. 72 min. Silent. 16mm B&W. *Rental:* Killiam Collect.

Hangman's Knot. Randolph Scott & Donna Reed. Directed by Roy Huggins. 1952. Columbia. 81 min. Sound. 16mm Color. *Rental:* Inst Cinema & Welling Motion Pictures.

Hangman's Wharf. Orig. Title: Fighting Doctor, The. John Witty. Directed by Cecil H. Williamson. 1950. Britain. 67 min. Sound. 16mm B&W. *Rental:* Mogulls Films.

Hangmen Also Die. Brian Donlevy & Walter Brennan. Directed by Fritz Lang. 1943. United Artists. 131 min. Sound. 16mm B&W. *Rental:* Budget Films & Willoughby Peer.

Hangover Square. Laird Creegar & Linda Darnell. Directed by John Brahm. 1945. Fox. 77 min. Sound. 16mm B&W. *Rental:* Films Inc, Ivy Films & Twyman Films.

Hanky Panky. Gene Wilder & Gilda Radner. Directed by Sidney Poitier. 1982. Columbia. 110 min. Sound. 16mm Color. *Rental:* Swank Motion. *Rental:* Swank Motion, Videotape version.

Hanna K. Jill Clayburgh, Jean Yanne & Gabriel Byrne. Directed by Costa-Gavras. 1985. Universal. 111 min. Sound. 16mm Color. *Rental:* Swank Motion. *Sale:* Tamarelles French Film, *Rental:* Swank Motion, Videotape version.

Hannibal. Victor Mature & Rita Gam. Directed by Edgar G. Ulmer. 1960. Italy. 103 min. Sound. 16mm Color. dubbed. *Rental:* Films Inc & Willoughby Peer.

Hannibal Brooks. Oliver Reed & Michael J. Pollard. Directed by Michael Winner. 1969. United Artists. 101 min. Sound. 16mm Color. *Rental:* MGM United.

Hannie Caulder. Raquel Welch & Robert Culp. Directed by Burt Kennedy. 1972. Paramount. 85 min. Sound. 16mm Color. *Rental:* Films Inc.

Hanover Street. Harrison Ford & Lesley-Anne Down. Directed by Peter Hyams. 1979. Columbia. 109 min. Sound. 16mm Color. *Rental:* Budget Films, Modern Sound, Swank Motion & Williams Films. *Rental:* Bosco Films, 100 version.

Hans Bethe. Directed by Michael Blackwood. 58 min. 16mm *Rental:* Blackwood. *Sale:* Blackwood.

Hans Christian Andersen. Danny Kaye, Farley Granger & Jeanmaire. Directed by Charles Vidor. 1952. Goldwyn. 112 min. Sound. 16mm Color. *Rental:* Arcus Film.

Hans Richter: Artist & Filmmaker. Directed by Erwin Lesser. 1979. International Film Bureau. (Documentary). 46 min. Sound. 16mm Color. *Rental:* Intl Film. *Sale:* Intl Film. *Sale:* Intl Film, Videotape version.

Hans Richter: Artist & Filmmaker. 1978. 46 min. Sound. 16mm Color. *Rental:* Utah Media.

Hansel & Gretel. Directed by John Paul. 1954. Meyerberg. (Animated puppets). 75 min. Sound. 16mm Color. *Rental:* Budget Films, Films Inc, Modern Sound, Film Ctr DC & Welling Motion Pictures.

Hansel & Gretel. Jurgen Miksch. Directed by Walter Janssen. 1965. Childhood. 52 min. Sound. 16mm Color. dubbed. *Rental:* Cine Craft, Westcoast Films & Willoughby Peer.

Hansel & Gretel. 1979. PBS. (Opera). 59 min. Sound. Videotape Color. *Rental:* PBS Video. *Sale:* PBS Video.

Happening, The. Anthony Quinn, Michael Parks & Faye Dunaway. Directed by Eliot Silverstein. 1967. Columbia. 92 min. Sound. 16mm Color. *Rental:* Budget Films, Charard Motion Pics, Cine Craft, Films Inc, Modern Sound, Video Comm, Welling Motion Pictures & Wholesome Film Ctr.

Happily Ever after *see* More Than a Miracle.

Happiness. Piotr Zinoviev. Directed by Alexander Medvedkin. Rus. 1934. Russia. (Musical score only). 74 min. Sound. 16mm B&W. *Rental:* New Cinema & New Yorker Films.

Happiness Ahead. Dick Powell & Josephine Hutchinson. Directed by Mervyn LeRoy. 1934. Warners. 86 min. Sound. 16mm B&W. *Rental:* MGM United.

Happy Birthday, Gemini. Alan Rosenberg, Rita Moreno & Madeline Kahn. Directed by Richard Benner. 1980. United Artists. 112 min. Sound. 16mm Color. *Rental:* MGM United.

Happy Birthday to Me. Glen Ford. Directed by J. Lee Thompson. 1981. Canada. 108 min. Sound. 16mm Color. *Rental:* Swank Motion. *Rental:* Swank Motion, Videotape version.

Happy Birthday, Wanda June. Rod Steiger & Susannah York. Directed by Mark Robson. 1971. Columbia. 105 min. Sound. 16mm Color. *Rental:* Arcus Film, Films Inc, Inst Cinema, Ivy Films, Kit Parker, Natl Film Video, Swank Motion, Twyman Films, Welling Motion Pictures & Westcoast Films.

Happy Ending, The. Jean Simmons & John Forsythe. Directed by Richard Brooks. 1970. United Artists. (Anamorphic). 110 min. Sound. 16mm Color. *Rental:* MGM United.

Happy Family, The *see* Merry Frinks.

Happy Go Lucky. Phil Regan. Directed by Curtis Bernhardt. 1936. Republic. 54 min. Sound. 16mm B&W. *Rental:* Ivy Films. *Sale:* Rep Pic Film.

Happy Hooker, The. Lynn Redgrave & Lovelady Powell. Directed by Nicholas Sgarro. 1975. Cannon. 96 min. Sound. 16mm Color. *Rental:* Swank Motion.

Happy Hooker Goes Hollywood, The. Martine Beswick & Chris Lemmon. Directed by Alan Roberts. 1980. Cannon. 85 min. Sound. 16mm Color. *Rental:* Swank Motion.

Happy Hooker Goes to Washington, The. Joey Heatherton & George Hamilton. Directed by William A. Levey. 1977. Cannon. 89 min. Sound. 16mm Color. *Rental:* Swank Motion.

Happy Land. Don Ameche & Frances Dee. Directed by Irving Pichel. 1943. Fox. 75 min. Sound. 16mm B&W. *Rental:* Films Inc.

Happy Landing. Orig. Title: Air Patrol. Jacqueline Wells & Ray Walker. Directed by Robert N. Bradbury. 1934. Monogram. 70 min. Sound. 16mm B&W. *Rental:* Mogulls Films.

Happy Landing. Sonja Henie & Don Ameche. Directed by Roy Del Ruth. 1938. Fox. 102 min. Sound. 16mm B&W. *Rental:* Films Inc.

Happy New Year *see* Happy New Year Caper.

Happy New Year Caper, The. Orig. Title: Happy New Year. Lino Ventura & Charles Gerard. Directed by Claude Lelouch. Fr. 1973. France. 112 min. Sound. 16mm Color. subtitles. *Rental:* Swank Motion.

Happy Road, The. Gene Kelly, Sir Michael Redgrave. Directed by Gene Kelly. 1957. MGM. 100 min. Sound. 16mm B&W. *Rental:* MGM United.

Happy Thieves, The. Rex Harrison & Rita Hayworth. Directed by George Marshall. 1962. United Artists. 88 min. Sound. 16mm B&W. *Rental:* MGM United.

Happy Time, The. Charles Boyer & Louis Jourdan. Directed by Richard Fleischer. 1952. Columbia. 94 min. Sound. 16mm B&W. *Rental:* Budget Films, Cine Craft, Inst Cinema, Newman Film Lib & Film Ctr DC.

Happy Years, The. Dean Stockwell & Darryl Hickman. Directed by William A. Wellman. 1950. MGM. 110 min. Sound. 16mm Color. *Rental:* MGM United.

Hapsburgs, The. Directed by Victor Vicas. 1972. AIF. (Documentary). 60 min. Sound. 16mm B&W. *Sale:* Americas Films. *Sale:* Americas Films, Spanish version.

Harakiri. Tatsuya Nakadai & Shima Iwashita. Directed by Masaki Kobayashi. 1962. Shochiku. 135 min. Sound. 16mm B&W. *Rental:* Films Inc.

Harbor Lights. Kent Taylor & Miriam Colon. Directed by Maury Dexter. 1963. Fox. 68 min. Sound. 16mm B&W. *Rental:* Films Inc.

Harbor of Missing Men. Richard Denning & Steven Geray. Directed by R. G. Springsteen. 1949. Republic. 60 min. Sound. 16mm B&W. *Rental:* Ivy Films.

Hard Chargers, The. 1970. Time-Life. (Documentary). 52 min. Sound. 16mm Color. *Rental:* Films Inc. *Sale:* Films Inc. *Rental:* Films Inc, *Sale:* Films Inc, Videotape version.

Hard Choices. 1981. 360 min. Sound. Videotape *Rental:* PBS Video. *Sale:* PBS Video.

Hard Contract. James Coburn & Lee Remick. Directed by S. Lee Pogostin. 1969. Fox. 106 min. Sound. 16mm Color. *Rental:* Films Inc.

Hard Day's Night. The Beatles. Directed by Richard Lester. 1964. Britain. 90 min. Sound. 16mm B&W. *Rental:* MGM United.

Hard, Fast & Beautiful. Claire Trevor & Sally Forrest. Directed by Ida Lupino. 1951. Filmmakers. 76 min. Sound. 16mm B&W. *Rental:* Ivy Films. *Sale:* Rep Pic Film.

Hard Hombre. Hoot Gibson. Directed by Otto Brower. 1931. Allied. 64 min. Sound. 16mm B&W. *Rental:* Budget Films. *Sale:* Morcraft Films. *Sale:* Video Comm, Videotape version.

Hard Man. Guy Madison. Directed by George Sherman. 1957. Columbia. 80 min. Sound. 16mm Color. *Lease:* Time-Life Multimedia.

Hard Ride, The. Robert Fuller. Directed by Burt Topper. 1971. American International. 90 min. Sound. 16mm Color. *Rental:* Swank Motion.

Hard Rider. Directed by Josef Reeve. 1972. Canada. (Documentary). 58 min. Sound. 16mm Color. *Rental:* Films Inc, Macmillan Films, Films Inc, Syracuse U Film & Welling Motion Pictures. *Sale:* Macmillan Films & Natl Film CN.

Hard Times. Charles Bronson & James Coburn. Directed by Walter Hill & Tony Richardson. 1975. Columbia. 97 min. Sound. 16mm Color. *Rental:* Budget Films, Films Inc, Modern Sound, Swank Motion, Twyman Films, Welling Motion Pictures, Westcoast Films, Wholesome Film Ctr & Williams Films. *Rental:* Images Film & Kit Parker, Anamorphic version.

Hard Times. 1977. WNET. (Cast unlisted). 232 min. Videotape Color. *Rental:* WNET Media. *Sale:* WNET Media.

Hard Times in the Country. 1970. NET. (Documentary). 58 min. Sound. 16mm Color. *Rental:* Indiana AV Ctr & U Mich Media. *Sale:* Indiana AV Ctr & New Time Films.

Hard to Get. Dick Powell & Olivia De Havilland. Directed by Ray Enright. 1938. Warners. 80 min. Sound. 16mm B&W. *Rental:* MGM United.

Hard to Handle. James Cagney & Mary Brian. Directed by Mervyn LeRoy. 1933. Warners. 81 min. Sound. 16mm B&W. *Rental:* MGM United.

Hard to Hold. Rick Springfield, Janet Eilber & Patti Hansen. Directed by Larry Peerce. 1985. Universal. 93 min. Sound. 16mm Color. *Rental:* Swank Motion. *Rental:* Swank Motion, Videotape version.

Hard Way, The. Ida Lupino, Dennis Morgan & Joan Leslie. Directed by Vincent Sherman. 1943. Warners. 91 min. Sound. 16mm B&W. *Rental:* MGM United.

Hard Way, The. 1965. NET. (Documentary). 60 min. Sound. 16mm B&W. *Rental:* BYU Media, Indiana AV Ctr, SD AV Ctr, Syracuse U Film & U of IL Film. *Sale:* Indiana AV Ctr.

Hardbodies. Grant Cramer & Teal Roberts. Directed by Mark Griffiths. 1985. Columbia. 88 min. Sound. 16mm Color. *Rental:* Swank Motion.

Harder They Come, The. Jimmy Cliff. Directed by Perry Henzel. 1973. New World. 100 min. Sound. 16mm Color. subtitles. *Rental:* Films Inc.

Harder They Fall, The. Humphrey Bogart & Rod Steiger. Directed by Mark Robson. 1956. Columbia. 110 min. Sound. 16mm B&W. *Rental:* Bosco Films, Budget Films, Cine Craft, Films Inc, Kit Parker, Modern Sound, Swank Motion, Twyman Films, U of IL Film, Welling Motion Pictures, Westcoast Films & Wholesome Film Ctr.

Hardly Working. Jerry Lewis & Susan Oliver. Directed by Jerry Lewis. 1981. Fox. 91 min. Sound. 16mm Color. *Rental:* Films Inc.

Hardrock Harrigan. George O'Brien & Irene Hervey. Directed by David Howard. 1935. Fox. 70 min. Sound. 16mm B&W. *Rental:* Lewis Film & Mogulls Films.

Hardys Ride High, The. Mickey Rooney & Lewis Stone. Directed by George B. Seitz. 1938. MGM. 81 min. Sound. 16mm B&W. *Rental:* MGM United.

Hare Census, The. Isaac Fintsi & Todor Koev. Directed by Eduard Zahariev. 1973. 103 min. Sound. 16mm Color. subtitles. *Rental:* Films Inc.

Harem Girl. Joan Davis. Directed by Edward Bernds. 1952. Columbia. 70 min. Sound. 16mm B&W. *Rental:* Maljack. *Lease:* Maljack. *Lease:* Maljack, Videotape version.

211

Harlan Country, U. S. A. Directed by Barbara Kopple. 1976. Cinema V. (Documentary). 103 min. Sound. 16mm Color. *Rental:* Cinema Five & New Cinema.

Harlem Globetrotters, The. Thomas Gomez & Dorothy Dandridge. Directed by Phil Brown. 1951. Columbia. 80 min. Sound. 16mm B&W. *Rental:* Arcus Film, Budget Films, Buchan Pic, Budget Films, Charard Motion Pics, Cine Craft, Film Ctr DC, Films Inc, Modern Sound, Natl Film Video Comm, Roas Films, Twyman Films, Welling Motion Pictures, Westcoast Films, Wholesome Film Ctr & Williams Films.

Harlem Hot Shot *see* Black King.

Harlem Rides the Range. Herb Jeffries & Spencer Williams. Directed by Sam Newfield. 1939. Hollywood. 50 min. Sound. 16mm B&W. *Rental:* Budget Films. *Sale:* Cinema Concepts & Reel Images.

Harlem Temper, The. CBS. (Documentary). 54 min. Sound. 16mm B&W. *Rental:* CBS Inc.

Harlow. Carroll Baker & Red Buttons. Directed by Gordon Douglas. 1965. Paramount. (Anamorphic). 125 min. Sound. 16mm Color. *Rental:* Films Inc.

Harmon of Michigan. Tom Harmon & Anita Louise. Directed by Charles Barton. 1941. Columbia. 66 min. Sound. 16mm B&W. *Rental:* Budget Films, Inst Cinema & Film Ctr DC.

Harmony Inn *see* Home in San Antone.

Harmony Lane. Douglas Montgomery & Evelyn Venable. Directed by Joseph Santley. 1935. Mascot. 89 min. Sound. 16mm B&W. *Rental:* Alba House, Classic Film Mus & Newman Film Lib. *Sale:* Morcraft Films.

Harmony of the Worlds, The. 1980. Cosmos. (Documentary). 60 min. Sound. 16mm Color. *Rental:* Films Inc. *Sale:* Films Inc. *Rental:* Films Inc, *Sale:* Films Inc, Videotape version.

Harmony Trail *see* White Stallion.

Harold & Maude. Ruth Gordon, Bud Cort & Vivian Pickles. Directed by Hal Ashby. 1972. Paramount. 91 min. Sound. 16mm Color. *Rental:* Films Inc.

Harold Lloyd's World of Comedy. 1980. Time-Life. (Anthology). 89 min. Sound. 16mm B&W. *Rental:* Budget Films, Kent St U Film & OK AV Ctr.

Harold Teen. Orig. Title: Dancing Fool, The. Arthur Lake & Mary Brian. Directed by Mervyn LeRoy. 1928. Warners. 84 min. Silent. 16mm B&W. *Rental:* MGM United.

Harold Teen. Hal LeRoy & Rochelle Hudson. Directed by Murray Roth. 1934. Warners. 66 min. Sound. 16mm B&W. *Rental:* MGM United.

Harp of Burma *see* Burmese Harp.

Harper. Paul Newman & Lauren Bacall. Directed by Jack Smight. 1966. Warners. 121 min. Sound. 16mm Color. *Rental:* Arcus Film.

Harper Valley P. T. A. Barbara Eden & Ronny Cox. Directed by Richard Bennett. 1978. April Fools. 102 min. Sound. 16mm Color. *Rental:* Swank Motion.

Harpsichord Building in America. 1976. Colonial Williamsburg. (Documentary). 49 min. Sound. 16mm Color. *Rental:* U of IL Film.

Harrad Experiment, The. James Whitmore, Tippi Hedren & Don Johnson. Directed by Ted Post. 1974. Cinerama. 95 min. Sound. 16mm Color. *Rental:* Images Film, Swank Motion & Welling Motion Pictures.

Harrad Summer, The. Richard Doran & Bill Dana. Directed by Steven Hilliard Stern. 1975. Cinerama. 103 min. Sound. 16mm Color. *Rental:* Swank Motion.

Harriet Craig. Joan Crawford & Wendell Corey. Directed by Vincent Sherman. 1950. Columbia. 94 min. Sound. 16mm B&W. *Rental:* Cine Craft, Kit Parker & Westcoast Films.

Harriet Tubman & the Underground Railroad. 1964. CBS. (Documentary). 54 min. Sound. 16mm B&W. *Rental:* Budget Films, McGraw-Hill Films, Syracuse U Film, U Cal Media, U Mich Media & Utah Media. *Sale:* McGraw-Hill Films.

Harrigan's Kid. William Gargan & Frank Craven. Directed by Charles Reisner. 1943. MGM. 80 min. Sound. 16mm B&W. *Rental:* MGM United.

Harry & Tonto. Art Carney & Ellen Burstyn. Directed by Paul Mazursky. 1974. Fox. 115 min. Sound. 16mm Color. *Rental:* Films Inc & Twyman Films.

Harry & Walter Go to New York. James Caan, Elliott Gould & Diane Keaton. Directed by Mark Rydell. 1976. Columbia. 120 min. Sound. 16mm Color. *Rental:* Arcus Film, Budget Films, Films Inc, Modern Sound, Swank Motion, Twyman Films, Welling Motion Pictures, Westcoast Films, WholesomeFilm Ctr & Williams Films.

Harry Black & the Tiger. Stewart Granger & Barbara Rush. Directed by Hugo Fregonese. 1958. Fox. 117 min. Sound. 16mm Color. *Rental:* Films Inc.

Harry Chapin: The Book of Chapin. 1980. Verve. (Concert). 58 min. Videotape Color. *Rental:* Films Inc.

Harry in Your Pocket. James Coburn, Michael Sarrazin & Walter Pidgeon. Directed by Bruce Geller. 1973. United Artists. 103 min. Sound. 16mm Color. *Rental:* MGM United.

Harry S. Truman. 1964. McGraw-Hill. (Documentary). 52 min. Sound. 16mm B&W. *Rental:* McGraw-Hill Films. *Sale:* McGraw-Hill Films.

Harry Tracy. Bruce Dern & Helen Shaver. Directed by William Graham. 1982. QFI. 111 min. Sound. 16mm Color. *Rental:* Films Inc.

Harum Scarum. Elvis Presley. Directed by Gene Nelson. 1965. MGM. 95 min. Sound. 16mm Color. *Rental:* Films Inc & MGM United.

Harvard, Here I Come. Maxie Rosenbloom & Arline Judge. Directed by Lew Landers. 1941. Columbia. 70 min. Sound. 16mm B&W. *Rental:* Kit Parker.

Harvest. Orig. Title: Regain. Fernandel. Directed by Marcel Pagnol. Fr. 1937. France. 105 min. Sound. 16mm B&W. subtitles. *Rental:* Budget Films, Corinth Films & Kit Parker. *Rental:* Budget Films, 128 mins. version.

Harvest. 1979. WNET. (Documentary). 58 min. Videotape Color. *Rental:* WNET Media. *Sale:* WNET Media.

Harvest *see* Return of Vassili Bortnikov.

Harvest of Seasons. (Ascent of Man Ser.). 1974. Britain. (Documentary). 52 min. Sound. 16mm Color. *Rental:* U Cal Media, Iowa Films, U Mich Media & Utah Media.

Harvest of Shame. 1960. CBS. (Documentary). 54 min. Sound. 16mm B&W. *Rental:* U Cal Media, U of IL Film, Iowa Films, U Mich Media, Mass Media, Syracuse U Film & Utah Media. *Sale:* McGraw-Hill Films. *Rental:* McGraw-Hill Films, *Sale:* McGraw-Hill Films, videotape version.

Harvest, Three Thousand Years. Harege-Weyn Tafere. Directed by Haile Gerima. African Dialects. 1975. Ethiopia. 150 min. Sound. 16mm B&W. subtitles. *Rental:* Unifilm. *Sale:* Unifilm.

Harvey Girls, The. Judy Garland, John Hodiak & Angela Lansbury. Directed by George Sidney. 1946. MGM. 104 min. Sound. 16mm Color. *Rental:* Films Inc & MGM United.

Harvey Middleman, Fireman. Eugene Troobnick & Hermione Gingold. Directed by Ernest Pintoff. 1965. Columbia. 75 min. Sound. 16mm Color. *Rental:* Charard Motion Pics, Films Inc & Welling Motion Pictures.

Has Anybody Here Seen Canada? Directed by John Kramer. 1978. Canada. (Documentary). 85 min. Sound. 16mm Color. *Rental:* Natl Film CN. *Sale:* Natl Film CN.

Hasta el Viento Tiene Miedo. Marga Lopez. Directed by Carlos Enrique Taboada. Span. Mexico. 88 min. Sound. 16mm Color. subtitles. *Rental:* Westcoast Films.

Hat, Coat & Glove. Ricardo Cortez & John Beal. Directed by Worthington Miner. 1934. RKO. 70 min. Sound. 16mm B&W. *Rental:* Films Inc. *Lease:* Films Inc.

Hatari! John Wayne & Red Buttons. Directed by Howard Hawks. 1962. Paramount. 158 min. Sound. 16mm Color. *Rental:* Films Inc.

Hatbox Mystery, The. Tom Neal & Pamela Blake. Directed by Lambert Hillyer. 1947. Screen Guild. 60 min. Sound. 16mm B&W. *Rental:* Mogulls Films.

Hatchet for the Honeymoon, A. Stephen Forsyth. 1971. GG Productions. 89 min. Sound. 16mm Color. *Rental:* Budget Films & Video Comm.

Hatchet Man, The. Edward G. Robinson & Loretta Young. Directed by William A. Wellman. 1932. Warners. 74 min. Sound. 16mm B&W. *Rental:* MGM United.

Hate That Hate Produced, The. 1959. (Documentary). 58 min. Sound. 16mm B&W. *Rental:* Syracuse U Film.

Hatful of Rain, A. Don Murray & Eva Marie Saint. Directed by Fred Zinnemann. 1957. Fox. 107 min. Sound. 16mm B&W. *Rental:* Films Inc & Twyman Films. *Rental:* Films Inc, Anamorphic B&W version.

Haunted & the Hunted, The *see* Dementia Thirteen.

Haunted Castle, The. Trans. Title: Schloss Vogelod. Olga Tschechowa. Directed by F. W. Murnau. 1921. German. 55 min. Silent. 16mm B&W. *Rental:* Budget Films, Em Gee Film Lib, Films Inc & Kit Parker. *Sale:* Cinema Concepts & Reel Images. *Rental:* Ivy Films, *Rental:* Reel Images, Super 8 Silent version, Silent 8mm version.

Haunted Gold. John Wayne. Directed by Mack V. Wright. 1932. Warners. 58 min. Sound. 16mm B&W. *Rental:* MGM United.

Haunted Harbor. Kane Richmond & Kay Aldridge. Directed by Ronald Davidson. 1944. Republic. 210 min. Sound. 16mm B&W. *Rental:* Ivy Films.

Haunted Honeymoon. Robert Montgomery & Constance Cummings. Directed by Arthur Woods. 1940. MGM. 83 min. Sound. 16mm B&W. *Rental:* MGM United.

Haunted Mansion Mystery, The. 1983. ABC. (Cast unlisted). 50 min. Sound. 16mm Color. *Rental:* MTI Tele & Syracuse U Film. *Sale:* MTI Tele.

Haunted Mine. Johnny Mack Brown. Directed by Derwin Abrahams. 1946. Monogram. 60 min. Sound. 16mm B&W. *Rental:* Mogulls Films.

Haunted Palace, The. Vincent Price & Debra Paget. Directed by Roger Corman. 1963. American International. 96 min. Sound. 16mm Color. *Rental:* Arcus Film, Budget Films, Charard Motion Pics, Cine Craft, Film Ctr DC, Inst Cinema, Ivy Films, Newman Film Lib, Video Comm, Welling Motion Pictures, Westcoast Films, Wholesome Film Ctr & Willoughby Peer.

Haunted Strangler, The. Boris Karloff & Jean Kent. Directed by Robert Day. 1958. Britain. 80 min. Sound. B&W. *Rental:* Budget Films, Ivy Films, Modern Sound, Roas Films & Video Comm. *Sale:* Reel Images, *Sale:* Video Lib, Videotape version.

Haunted West, The. 1973. National Geographic. (Documentary). 52 min. Sound. 16mm Color. *Rental:* Natl Geog. *Sale:* Natl Geog. *Sale:* Natl Geog, Videotape version.

Haunting, The. Julie Harris & Claire Bloom. Directed by Robert Wise. 1963. MGM. (Anamorphic). 112 min. Sound. 16mm B&W. *Rental:* MGM United. *Rental:* MGM United, Videotape version.

Hauptmann Von Koepenick *see* Captain from Koepenick.

Hauptmann von Kopenick, Der *see* Captain from Kopenick.

Havana Rose. Estelita Rodriguez & Bill Williams. Directed by William Beaudine. 1951. Republic. 77 min. Sound. 16mm B&W. *Rental:* Ivy Films. *Sale:* Rep Pic Film.

Havana Widows. Joan Blondell & Glenda Farrell. Directed by Ray Enright. 1933. Warners. 62 min. Sound. 16mm B&W. *Rental:* MGM United.

Have a Heart. Jean Parker & James Dunn. Directed by David Butler. 1934. MGM. 82 min. Sound. 16mm B&W. *Rental:* MGM United.

Have I Ever Lied to You Before? Directed by John Spotton. 1977. Canada. (Documentary). 57 min. Sound. 16mm Color. *Rental:* Natl Film CN. *Sale:* Natl Film CN. *Sale:* Natl Film CN, Videotape version.

Have Rocket, Will Travel. The Three Stooges. Directed by David Lowell Rich. 1959. Columbia. 76 min. Sound. 16mm B&W. *Rental:* Arcus Film, Buchan Pic, Budget Films, Cine Craft, Charard Motion Pics, Film Ctr DC, Films Inc, Modern Sound, Natl Film Video, Roas Films, Swank Motion, Welling Motion Pictures & Westcoast Films.

Having Wonderful Crime. Pat O'Brien, George Murphy & Carol Landis. Directed by Edward Sutherland. 1945. RKO. 70 min. Sound. 16mm B&W. *Rental:* Films Inc. *Lease:* Films Inc.

Having Wonderful Time. Ginger Rogers, Douglas Fairbanks & Lucille Ball. Directed by Alfred Santell. 1938. RKO. 69 min. Sound. 16mm B&W. *Rental:* Films Inc & RKO General Pics.

Hawaii. Julie Andrews & Max Von Sydow. Directed by George Roy Hill. 1966. United Artists. 161 min. Sound. 16mm Color. *Rental:* MGM United & Twyman Films. *Rental:* MGM United, Anamorphic version. *Rental:* MGM United, Videotape version.

Hawaii Calls. Bobby Breen & Ned Sparks. Directed by Edward Cline. 1938. RKO. 75 min. Sound. 16mm B&W. *Rental:* Alba House.

Hawaii Revisited. Directed by Julian Krainin. 1977. Reader's Digest. (Documentary). 58 min. Sound. 16mm Color. *Rental:* Budget Films & Pyramid Film. *Sale:* Pyramid Film. *Rental:* Pyramid Film, *Sale:* Pyramid Film, Videotape version.

Hawaiians, The. Charlton Heston & Geraldine Chaplin. Directed by Tom Gries. 1970. United Artists. 134 min. Sound. 16mm Color. *Rental:* MGM United, Welling Motion Pictures, Westcoast Films & Wholesome Film Ctr.

Hawk of Castille, The. German Cobos & Maria Luz Real. 1964. Spain. 87 min. Sound. 16mm Color. dubbed. *Rental:* Westcoast Films.

Hawk of Powder River, The. Eddie Dean. Directed by Ray Taylor. 1948. Eagle Lion. 60 min. Sound. 16mm B&W. *Sale:* Classics Assoc NY.

Hawk of the Hills, The. Walter Miller & Allene Ray. Directed by Spencer G. Bennett. 1927. Pathe. 60 min. Silent. 8mm B&W. *Sale:* Griggs Movie. *Rental:* Ivy Films, Super 8 silent version.

Hawk of the Wilderness. Bruce Bennett & Mala. Directed by William Witney. 1938. Republic. 216 min. Sound. 16mm B&W. *Rental:* Ivy Films.

Hawks & the Sparrows, The. Toto & Ninetto Diavoli. Directed by Pier Paolo Pasolini. Ital. 1965. Italy. 91 min. Sound. 16mm B&W. subtitles Eng. *Rental:* Films Inc.

Hawmps. James Hampton, Christopher Connelly & Slim Pickens. Directed by Joe Camp. 1976. Mulberry Square. 120 min. Sound. 16mm Color. *Rental:* Films Inc, Modern Sound, Swank Motion, Twyman Films & Williams Films.

Haxan *see* Witchcraft Through the Ages.

He Couldn't Say No. Jane Wyman & Frank McHugh. Directed by Lewis Seiler. 1938. Warners. 57 min. Sound. 16mm B&W. *Rental:* MGM United.

He Found a Star. Vic Oliver & Sarah Churchill. Directed by John Paddy Carstairs. 1941. Britain. 88 min. Sound. 16mm B&W. *Rental:* Mogulls Films.

He Hired the Boss. Stuart Erwin & Vivian Blaine. Directed by Thomas Loring. 1943. Fox. 73 min. Sound. 16mm B&W. *Rental:* Films Inc.

He Is My Brother. Keenan Wynn & Bobby Sherman. Directed by Edward Dmytryk. 1974. CFA. 90 min. Sound. 16mm Color. *Rental:* Budget Films.

He Knew Women. Lowell Sherman & Alice Joyce. Directed by F. Hugh Herbert. 1930. RKO. 70 min. Sound. 16mm *Rental:* RKO General Pics.

He Knows You're Alone. Don Scardino, Caitlin O'Heaney & Elizabeth Kemp. Directed by Armond Mastroianni. 1980. MGM. 94 min. Sound. 16mm Color. *Rental:* MGM United. *Rental:* MGM United, Videotape version.

He Laughed Last. Frankie Laine, Lucy Marlow & Anthony Dexter. Directed by Blake Edwards. 1956. Columbia. 90 min. Sound. 16mm Color. *Rental:* Kit Parker.

He Loved an Actress. Orig. Title: Mad About Money. Lupe Velez & Ben Lyon. Directed by Melville Brown. 1938. Grand National. 78 min. Sound. 16mm B&W. *Rental:* Video Comm.

He Makes Me Feel Like Dancin'. Directed by Emile Ardolino. 1984. Emile Ardolino. 51 min. Sound. Color. *Rental:* Direct Cinema. *Sale:* Direct Cinema. *Sale:* Direct Cinema, Videotape version.

He Married His Wife. Joel McCrea & Nancy Kelly. Directed by Roy Del Ruth. 1940. Fox. 83 min. Sound. 16mm B&W. *Rental:* Films Inc.

He Ran All the Way. John Garfield & Shelley Winters. Directed by John Berry. 1951. United Artists. 77 min. Sound. 16mm B&W. *Rental:* MGM United.

He Shall Touch Thy Mouth. 1980. 77 min. Sound. 16mm Color. *Sale:* Natl AV Ctr.

He Walked by Night. Richard Basehart & Scott Brady. Directed by Alfred M. Werker. 1948. Eagle Lion. 80 min. Sound. 16mm B&W. *Rental:* Budget Films & Classic Film Mus. *Sale:* Morcraft Films. *Sale:* Morcraft Films, Super 8 sound version. *Sale:* Tamarelles French Film, Videotape version.

He Was Her Man. James Cagney & Joan Blondell. Directed by Lloyd Bacon. 1934. Warners. 70 min. Sound. 16mm B&W. *Rental:* MGM United.

He Who Gets Slapped. Lon Chaney & Norma Shearer. Directed by Victor Seastrom. 1924. MGM. 75 min. Silent. 16mm B&W. *Rental:* Films Inc & MGM United.

He Who Rides a Tiger. Tom Bell & Judi Dench. Directed by Charles Crichton. 1966. Britain. 103 min. Sound. 16mm B&W. *Rental:* Films Inc.

He Wooed Her. Jack Holt. 60 min. Silent. 8mm B&W. *Rental:* Mogulls Films.

Head. The Monkees. Directed by Bob Rafelson. 1968. Columbia. 86 min. Sound. 16mm Color. *Rental:* Films Inc.

Head of the Family. Trans. Title: Padre Di Famiglia, Il. Leslie Caron & Nino Manfredi. Directed by Nanni Loy. 1968. Italy. 105 min. Sound. 16mm Color. dubbed. *Rental:* Ivy Films & Video Comm.

Head Over Heels. John Heard, Mary Beth Hurt & Gloria Grahame. Directed by Joan Micklin Silver. 1979. United Artists. 99 min. Sound. 16mm Color. *Rental:* MGM United.

Headhunters of the Amazon. Directed by Paul Lambert. 1968. American International. (Documentary). 76 min. Sound. 16mm Color. *Rental:* Film Classics.

Headin' for Broadway. Rex Smith. Directed by Joseph Brooks. 1980. Fox. 93 min. Sound. 16mm Color. *Rental:* Films Inc.

Headin' for God's Country. William Lundigan & Virginia Dale. Directed by William Morgan. 1942. Republic. 78 min. Sound. 16mm B&W. *Rental:* Ivy Films.

Headin' for the Rio Grande. Tex Ritter. Directed by Robert N. Bradbury. 1936. Grand National. 60 min. Sound. 16mm B&W. *Rental:* Mogulls Films. *Sale:* Cinema Concepts, Super 8 sound version.

Heading for Heaven. Stuart Erwin & Glenda Farrell. Directed by Lewis D. Collins. 1947. Eagle Lion. 71 min. Sound. 16mm B&W. *Rental:* Inst Cinema.

Headless Ghost, The. Richard Lyon. Directed by Peter Graham Scott. 1959. American International. 63 min. Sound. 16mm B&W. *Rental:* Films Inc.

Headless Horseman, The. Orig. Title: Legend of Sleepy Hollow. Will Rogers. Directed by Edward Venturini. 1922. Hodkinson. (Musical score only). 50 min. Sound. 16mm B&W. *Rental:* Em Gee Film Lib, Film Classics & Mogulls Films. *Sale:* Glenn Photo. *Rental:* Budget Films & Film Classics, *Sale:* Blackhawk Films, Glenn Photo & Film Classics, Silent 16mm version. *Rental:* Ivy Films, *Sale:* Blackhawk Films & Glenn Photo, Super 8 Silent version. *Rental:* Film Classics, Videotape version.

Headline Hunters. Rod Cameron & Ben Cooper. Directed by William Witney. 1955. Republic. 70 min. Sound. 16mm B&W. *Rental:* Ivy Films. *Sale:* Rep Pic Film.

Headline Hunters. Leonard Brockwell. Directed by Jonathan Ingrams. 1968. Britain. 60 min. Sound. 16mm Color. *Sale:* Lucerne Films.

Headline Shooter. Ralph Bellamy & Betty Furness. Directed by Merian C. Cooper. 1938. RKO. 61 min. Sound. 16mm *Rental:* RKO General Pics.

Heads & Tails. 1979. Body in Question. (Documentary). 60 min. Videotape Color. *Rental:* Films Inc & Syracuse U Film. *Sale:* Films Inc.

Heads I Win, Tails You Lose. 1982. Britain. (Documentary). 50 min. Sound. Videtape Color. *Sale:* Films Inc.

Headstart in Mississippi. 1967. NET. (Documentary). 60 min. Sound. 16mm B&W. *Rental:* U Cal Media.

Healer, The. Ralph Bellamy & Mickey Rooney. Directed by Reginald Barker. 1935. Monogram. 80 min. Sound. 16mm B&W. *Rental:* Mogulls Films.

Healing. Directed by Pierre Lasry. 1977. Canada. (Documentary). 57 min. Sound. 16mm Color. *Rental:* Film Makers, Iowa Films & Natl Film CN. *Sale:* Natl Film CN. *Sale:* Film Maker & Natl Film CN, Videotape version.

Health. Glenda Jackson & James Garner. Directed by Robert Altman. 1980. Fox. 96 min. Sound. 16mm Color. *Rental:* Films Inc.

Health Care: Your Money or Your Life!. Directed by Jon Alpert. 1977. Downtown Community TV. (Documentary). 60 min. Sound. Videotape Color. *Sale:* Electro Art.

Hear Me Good. Hal March & Merry Anders. Directed by Don McGuire. 1957. Paramount. 80 min. Sound. 16mm B&W. *Rental:* Films Inc.

Hear Us O Lord. 1968. Public Broadcasting Laboratory. (Documentary). 51 min. Sound. 16mm B&W. *Rental:* Indiana AV Ctr. *Sale:* Indiana AV Ctr. *Rental:* Indiana AV Ctr, *Sale:* Indiana AV Ctr, Color version.

Hearse, The. Trish Van Devere & Joseph Cotten. Directed by George Bowers. 1980. Mark Tenser. 100 min. Sound. 16mm Color. *Rental:* Swank Motion.

Heart & Soul. Orig. Title: Cuore. Vittorio De Sica. Directed by Guilio Coletti. Ital. 1950. Italy. 91 min. Sound. 16mm B&W. subtitles. *Rental:* Budget Films.

Heart Attack. 1974. NBC. (Documentary). 52 min. Sound. 16mm Color. *Rental:* Films Inc & Syracuse U Film. *Sale:* Films Inc. *Sale:* Films Inc, Videotape version.

Heart Attacks. 1980. US Government. (Documentary). 60 min. Videotape Color. *Sale:* Natl AV Ctr.

Heart Beat. Nick Nolte & Sissy Spacek. Directed by John Byrum. 1979. Orion. 109 min. Sound. 16mm Color. *Rental:* Films Inc.

Heart Is a Lonely Hunter, The. Alan Arkin & Sondra Locke. Directed by Robert Ellis Miller. 1968. Warners. 124 min. Sound. 16mm Color. *Rental:* Arcus Film.

Heart Like a Wheel, A. Bonnie Bedalia & Beau Bridges. Directed by Jonathan Kaplan. 1983. Fox. 110 min. Sound. 16mm Color. *Rental:* Films Inc. *Sale:* Tamarelles French Film, Videotape version.

Heart of a Hero. Robert Warwick & Gail Kane. Directed by Emile Chautard. 1916. Peerless-World. 72 min. Silent. 16mm B&W. *Rental:* Mogulls Films.

Heart of a Nation. Michele Morgan, Raimu, Louis Jouvet & Julien Duvivier. 1943. France. 90 min. Sound. 16mm B&W. dubbed. *Rental:* Budget Films. *Sale:* Reel Images.

Heart of Arizona, The. William Boyd. Directed by Lesley Selander. 1938. Paramount. 60 min. Sound. 16mm B&W. *Lease:* Cinema Concepts.

Heart of Glass, The. Josef Bierbichler. Directed by Werner Herzog. Ger. 1976. Germany. 93 min. Sound. 16mm Color. subtitles. *Rental:* New Yorker Films.

Heart of Humanity, The. Dorothy Phillips & Erich Von Stroheim. Directed by Alan Holubar. 1919. Universal. 68 min. Silent. 16mm B&W. *Rental:* Em Gee Film Lib & Film Images. *Sale:* Glenn Photo. *Sale:* Glenn Photo, Super 8 silent version.

Heart of New York, The. Smith & Dale & Donald Cook. Directed by Mervyn LeRoy. 1932. Warners. 74 min. Sound. 16mm B&W. *Rental:* MGM United.

Heart of Paris, The. Trans. Title: Gribouille. Raimu & Michele Morgan. Directed by Marc Allegret. Fr. 1944. France. 82 min. Sound. 16mm B&W. subtitles. *Rental:* Film Classics.

Heart of Texas Ryan, The. Tom Mix. Directed by E. A. Martin. 1917. Selig. 65 min. Silent. 16mm B&W. *Rental:* Budget Films, Em Gee Film Lib, Kit Parker, Mogulls Films, OK AV Ctr, Swank Motion, Video Comm & Wholesome Film Ctr. *Sale:* Morcraft Films & Natl Cinema. *Sale:* Cinema Concepts, Silent 8mm version. *Rental:* Video Comm, Videotape version. *Rental:* Westcoast Films, 45 mins version.

Heart of the Dragon, The. 12 pts. 1983. Time-Life. (Documentary). 684 min. Sound. 16mm Color. *Rental:* Time-Life Multimedia. *Sale:* Time-Life Multimedia. *Sale:* Time-Life Multimedia, Videotape version.

Heart of the Golden West, The. Roy Rogers. Directed by Joseph Kane. 1942. Republic. 54 min. Sound. 16mm B&W. *Rental:* Ivy Films. *Sale:* Rep Pic Film & Reel Images.

Heart of the Matter, The. Trevor Howard & Maria Schell. Directed by George More O'Ferrall. 1954. Britain. 104 min. Sound. 16mm B&W. *Rental:* Budget Films.

Heart of the Matter, The. 1979. Body in Question. (Documentary). 60 min. Silent. Videotape Color. *Rental:* Films Inc & Syracuse U Film. *Sale:* Films Inc.

Heart of the North, The. Dick Foran & Gloria Dickson. Directed by Lewis Seiler. 1938. Warners. 85 min. Sound. 16mm Color. *Rental:* MGM United.

Heart of the Rio Grande, The. Gene Autry. Directed by William Morgan. 1942. Republic. 54 min. Sound. 16mm B&W. *Rental:* Ivy Films.

Heart of the Rockies, The. Robert Livingston. Directed by Joseph Kane. 1937. Republic. 54 min. Sound. 16mm B&W. *Rental:* Ivy Films. *Sale:* Rep Pic Film.

Heart of the Rockies, The. Roy Rogers. Directed by William Witney. 1951. Republic. 67 min. Sound. 16mm B&W. *Rental:* Ivy Films. *Sale:* Rep Pic Film.

Heart of the West, The. William Boyd. Directed by Howard Bretherton & James Hayes. 1936. Paramount. 54 min. Sound. 16mm B&W. *Lease:* Cinema Concepts. *Rental:* Budget Films. *Rental:* Budget Films, 60 mins. version.

Heart of Wetona, The. Norma Talmadge. Directed by Sidney Franklin. 1918. Select. 60 min. Silent. 16mm B&W. *Rental:* Budget Films & Em Gee Film Lib.

Heart to Heart. Directed by Pascal Thomas. Fr. 1978. 110 min. Sound. 16mm Color. subtitles. *Rental:* New Yorker Films.

Heartaches. Sheila Ryan, Edward Norris & Chill Wills. Directed by Basil Wrangell. 1947. PRC. 70 min. Sound. 16mm B&W. *Rental:* Ivy Films & Mogulls Films. *Sale:* Classics Assoc NY & Rep Pic Film.

Heartbeat. Ginger Rogers & Jean-Pierre Aumont. Directed by Sam Wood. 1946. RKO. 102 min. Sound. 16mm B&W. *Rental:* Ivy Films & Mogulls Films.

Heartbreak Kid, The. Charles Grodin, Jeannie Berlin & Cybill Shepherd. Directed by Elaine May. 1972. Fox. 104 min. Sound. 16mm Color. *Rental:* Films Inc.

Heartland. Rip Torn & Conchata Ferrell. Directed by Richard Pearce. 1981. Wilderness Women. 95 min. Sound. 16mm Color. *Rental:* Westcoast Films.

Heartmakers, The. 1969. NET. (Documentary). 59 min. Sound. 16mm Color. *Rental:* Indiana AV Ctr. *Sale:* Indiana AV Ctr. *Sale:* Indiana AV Ctr, Videotape version.

Hearts & Minds. Directed by Peter Davis. 1974. BBS. (Documentary). 112 min. Sound. 16mm Color. *Rental:* Films Inc & U Mich Media.

Heart's Desire. Richard Tauber. 1937. Germany. 90 min. Sound. 16mm B&W. *Sale:* Cinema Concepts & Natl Cinema.

Hearts Divided. Marion Davies & Dick Powell. Directed by Frank Borzage. 1936. Warners. 76 min. Sound. 16mm B&W. *Rental:* MGM United.

Heart's Haven. Lenore Ulric. Directed by Benjamin B. Hampton. 1922. Hodkinson. 50 min. Silent. 16mm B&W. *Rental:* Willoughby Peer.

Hearts in Bondage. James Dunn & Mae Clarke. Directed by Lew Ayres. 1936. Republic. 54 min. Sound. 16mm B&W. *Rental:* Ivy Films. *Sale:* Rep Pic Film.

Hearts of Humanity. Jackie Searle & Jean Hersholt. 1932. Majestic. 70 min. Sound. 16mm B&W. *Rental:* Mogulls Films. *Rental:* Ivy Films, *Sale:* Blackhawk Films, Super 8 silent version.

Hearts of the West. Orig. Title: Hollywood Cowboy. Alan Arkin & Jeff Bridges. Directed by Howard Zieff. 1975. MGM. 102 min. Sound. 16mm Color. *Rental:* Films Inc & MGM United.

Hearts of the World. Lillian Gish & Robert Harron. Directed by D. W. Griffith. 1918. D.W. Griffith Corp. 136 min. Silent. 16mm B&W. *Rental:* Budget Films, Em Gee Film Lib, Kit Parker, Museum Mod Art & Twyman Films. *Sale:* Blackhawk Films, Cinema Concepts, Glenn Photo & Reel Images. *Rental:* Kit Parker, *Sale:* Glenn Photo, 80 min, part tinted version. *Rental:* Killiam Collect, Sound 16mm tinted 122 min, musical score only version. *Rental:* Ivy Films, *Sale:* Blackhawk Films & Glenn Photo, Super 8 silent version. *Sale:* Glenn Photo, Super 8 silent tinted version. *Sale:* Glenn Photo, Silent 8mm tinted version. *Sale:* Blackhawk Films, Cinema Concepts & Glenn Photo, Silent 8mm version. *Sale:* A Twyman Pres & Festival Films, 80 min. version.

Heat & Dust. Julie Christie & Shashi Kapoor. Directed by James Ivory. 1985. Universal. 130 min. Sound. 16mm Color. *Rental:* Swank Motion. *Sale:* Tamarelles French Film, Videotape version.

Heat Lightning. Ann Dvorak & Preston Foster. Directed by Mervyn LeRoy. 1934. Warners. 63 min. Sound. 16mm B&W. *Rental:* MGM United.

Heat of Desire: Plein Sud. Patrick Dewaere, Clio Goldsmith & Jeanne Moreau. Directed by Luc Beraud. 1985. Columbia. 90 min. Sound. 16mm Color. subtitles. *Rental:* Swank Motion.

Heat Treatment of Aluminum. 1945. NAC. (Documentary). 51 min. Sound. 16mm B&W. *Rental:* BYU Media.

Heat's On, The. Mae West. Directed by Gregory Ratoff. 1943. Columbia. 79 min. Sound. 16mm B&W. *Rental:* Budget Films, Cine Craft, Films Inc, Roas Films, Swank Motion, Twyman Films, Welling Motion Pictures & Westcoast Films.

Heaven. 45 min. Sound. 16mm Color. *Rental:* Mass Media Ministries.

Heaven & Earth Magic Feature. Directed by Harry Smith. 1968. Harry Smith. (Experimental). 70 min. Sound. 16mm B&W. *Rental:* Canyon Cinema.

Heaven & Hell. 1980. Cosmos. (Documentary). 60 min. Sound. 16mm Color. *Rental:* Films Inc. *Sale:* Films Inc. *Rental:* Films Inc, *Sale:* Films Inc, Videotape version.

Heaven Can Wait. Warren Beatty & Julie Christie. Directed by Warren Beatty & Buck Henry. 1978. Paramount. 101 min. Sound. 16mm Color. *Rental:* Films Inc.

Heaven Is 'Round the Corner. Will Fyffe & Leni Lynn. Directed by Maclean Rogers. 1945. Britain. 99 min. Sound. 16mm B&W. *Rental:* Ivy Films. *Sale:* Rep Pic Film.

Heaven Knows, Mr. Allison. Deborah Kerr & Robert Mitchum. Directed by John Huston. 1957. Fox. 107 min. Sound. 16mm Color. *Rental:* Films Inc. *Rental:* Films Inc, Anamorphic color version.

Heaven on Earth. Barbara Florian. Directed by Robert Spafford. 1960. Italy. 84 min. Sound. 16mm Color. dubbed. *Rental:* Films Inc.

Heaven Only Knows. Robert Cummings & Marjorie Reynolds. Directed by Albert S. Rogell. 1947. United Artists. 95 min. Sound. 16mm B&W. *Rental:* Newman Film Lib.

Heaven with a Barbed Wire Fence. Jean Rogers & Glenn Ford. Directed by Ricardo Cortez. 1939. Fox. 62 min. Sound. 16mm B&W. *Rental:* Films Inc.

Heaven with a Gun. Glenn Ford & Carolyn Jones. Directed by Lee Katzin. 1969. MGM. 101 min. Sound. 16mm Color. *Rental:* MGM United. *Rental:* MGM United, Anamorphic color version.

Heavenly Body, The. Hedy Lamarr & William Powell. Directed by Alexander Hall. 1944. MGM. 95 min. Sound. 16mm B&W. *Rental:* MGM United.

Heavenly Days. Fibber McGee & Molly. Directed by Howard Estabrook. 1944. RKO. 72 min. Sound. 16mm B&W. *Rental:* Films Inc.

Heavens Above. Peter Sellers & Cecil Parker. Directed by John Boulting. 1963. Britain. 105 min. Sound. 16mm B&W. *Rental:* Corinth Films.

Heaven's Gate. Kris Kristofferson & Isabelle Huppert. Directed by Michael Cimino. 1981. United Artists. 147 min. Sound. 16mm Color. *Rental:* MGM United.

Heavy Metal. Directed by Gerald Potterton. 92 min. Sound. 16mm Color. *Rental:* Swank Motion.

Heavy Traffic. Directed by Ralph Bakshi. 1973. American International. (Animated). 76 min. Sound. 16mm Color. *Rental:* Images Film.

Heavy Traffic. Joseph Kaufman & Beverly Hope Atkinson. 77 min. Sound. 16mm Color. *Rental:* Welling Motion Pictures.

Hecklers, The. 1975. Canada. (Documentary). 59 min. Sound. 16mm Color. *Rental:* U Cal Media.

Hedda. Glenda Jackson & Timothy West. Directed by Trevor Nunn. 1976. Gamma III. 98 min. Sound. 16mm Color. *Rental:* Swank Motion.

Hedda Gabler. Janet Suzman. 1976. Britain. 114 min. Videotape Color. *Rental:* Films Inc. *Sale:* Films Inc.

Hedda Gabler: The Theater of Social Problems. Darlene Johnson. Directed by Philip Hedley. 1976. Britain. 58 min. Sound. 16mm Color. *Rental:* Films Human & U Mich Media. *Sale:* Films Human. *Sale:* Films Human, Videotape version.

Heidi. Shirley Temple & Jean Hersholt. Directed by Allan Dwan. 1937. Fox. 90 min. Sound. 16mm B&W. *Rental:* Williams Films. *Rental:* Williams Films, Videotape version.

Heidi. Elsbeth Sigmund & Heinrich Gretler. Directed by Luigi Comencini. 1953. Switzerland. 98 min. Sound. 16mm B&W. dubbed. *Rental:* Budget Films, Cine Craft, Films Inc, Inst Cinema, Macmillan Films & Syracuse U Film. *Lease:* Macmillan Films.

Heidi. Eva Maria Singhammer. Directed by Werner Jacobs. 1968. Warners. 95 min. Sound. 16mm Color. dubbed. *Rental:* Arcus Film, Charard Motion Pics, Films Inc, Inst Cinema, Modern Sound, Welling Motion Pictures & Williams Films. *Rental:* Williams Films, Videotape version.

Heidi & Peter. Elsbeth Sigmund & Heinrich Gretler. Directed by Franz Schnyder. 1955. Switzerland. 89 min. Sound. 16mm Color. dubbed. *Rental:* Budget Films, Films Inc, Macmillan Films & Syracuse U Film. *Lease:* Macmillan Films.

Heidi's Song. Lorne Greene & Margery Gray. Directed by Richard Taylor. 1982. Paramount. 94 min. Sound. 16mm Color. *Rental:* Films Inc.

Heights of Danger. Sebastian Cabot & Basil Appleby. Directed by Peter Bradford. 1953. Britain. 60 min. Sound. 16mm B&W. *Rental:* Lucerne Films.

Heimkehr *see* Homecoming.

Heiress, The. Olivia De Havilland, Montgomery Clift, Sir Ralph Richardson. Directed by William Wyler. 1949. Paramount. 115 min. Sound. 16mm B&W. *Rental:* Williams Films.

Heirs, The. Sergio & Cardozo. Directed by Carlos Diegues. Port. 1969. Brazil. 110 min. Sound. 16mm Color. subtitles. *Rental:* New Yorker Films.

Held in Trust. Guy Vernet & Dorothy Shaw. Directed by Cecil H. Williamson. 1949. Britain. 58 min. Sound. 16mm B&W. *Rental:* Mogulls Films.

Helden *see* Arms & the Man.

Helen Frankenthaler - Toward a New Climate: The Originals, Women in Art Series. Directed by Perry Miller Adato. 1977. WNET. (Documentary). 30 min. Sound. 16mm Color. *Rental:* Films Inc.

Helen Hayes: Portrait of an American Actress. 1973. Phoenix. (Documentary). 90 min. Sound. 16mm Color. *Rental:* Budget Films, Phoenix Films, Syracuse U Film & U of IL Film. *Sale:* Phoenix Films. *Sale:* Phoenix Films, Videotape version.

Helen Keller in Her Story. Directed by Nancy Hamilton. 1955. Phoenix Films. (Documentary). 48 min. Sound. 16mm B&W. *Rental:* Budget Films, Mass Media, Phoenix Films, Syracuse U Films & U Mich Media. *Sale:* McGraw-Hill Films.

Helen Morgan Story, The. Polly Bergen. 1957. CBS. (Kinescope). 90 min. Sound. 16mm B&W. *Rental:* Bosco Films.

Helen of Troy *see* Lion of Thebes.

Helen of Troy. Rossana Podesta, Jacques Sernas, Sir Cedric Hardwicke. Directed by Robert Wise. 1955. Warners. 118 min. Sound. 16mm Color. *Rental:* Twyman Films.

Helga. Ruth Gassman. Directed by Erich F. Bender. 1968. Sweden. 87 min. Sound. 16mm Color. dubbed. *Rental:* Video Comm.

Helicopter Canada. Directed by Eugene Boyko. 1966. Canada. (Documentary). 51 min. Sound. 16mm Color. *Rental:* Natl Film CN. *Sale:* Natl Film CN.

Helicopter Spies. Robert Vaughan & David McCallum. Directed by Boris Sagal. 1967. MGM. 93 min. Sound. 16mm Color. *Rental:* MGM United.

Hell. 45 min. Sound. 16mm Color. *Rental:* Mass Media.

Hell & High Water. Richard Widmark & Bella Darvi. Directed by Samuel Fuller. 1954. Fox. 103 min. Sound. 16mm Color. *Rental:* Films Inc.

Hell Below. Robert Montgomery & Madge Evans. Directed by Jack Conway. 1933. MGM. 105 min. Sound. 16mm B&W. *Rental:* MGM United.

Hell Below Zero. Alan Ladd & Joan Tetzel. Directed by Mark Robson. 1954. Columbia. 91 min. Sound. 16mm Color. *Rental:* Buchan Pic, Cine Craft, Films Inc & Welling Motion Pictures.

Hell Boats. James Franciscus. Directed by Paul Wendkos. 1970. United Artists. 95 min. Sound. 16mm Color. *Rental:* MGM United.

Hell Divers. Wallace Beery & Clark Gable. Directed by George Hill. 1931. MGM. 113 min. Sound. 16mm B&W. *Rental:* MGM United.

Hell-Fire Austin. Ken Maynard. Directed by Forrest Sheldon. 1932. Tiffany. 70 min. Sound. 16mm B&W. *Sale:* Natl Cinema.

Hell Harbor. Jean Hersholt & Lupc Velez. Directed by Henry King. 1930. United Artists. 80 min. Sound. 16mm B&W. *Sale:* Mogulls Films.

Hell Hounds of Alaska. Doug McClure. 1976. Dimension. 92 min. Sound. 16mm Color. *Rental:* Modern Sound & Welling Motion Pictures. *Sale:* Salz Ent.

Hell in the Pacific. Lee Marvin & Toshiro Mifune. Directed by John Boorman. 1968. ABC. 103 min. Sound. 16mm Color. *Rental:* Films Inc. *Rental:* Films Inc, Anamorphic color version.

Hell is for Heroes. Steve McQueen & Bobby Darin. Directed by Don Siegel. 1962. Paramount. 90 min. Sound. 16mm B&W. *Rental:* Films Inc.

Hell of Manitoba *see* Place Called Glory.

Hell on Devil's Island. Helmut Dantine. Directed by Christian Nyby. 1957. Republic. 76 min. Sound. 16mm B&W. *Rental:* Ivy Films.

Hell on Frisco Bay. Alan Ladd & Edward G. Robinson. Directed by Frank Tuttle. 1956. Warners. 98 min. Sound. 16mm Color. *Rental:* Budget Films, Films Inc, Video Comm & Westcoast Films. *Lease:* Video Comm. *Rental:* Video Comm, *Lease:* Video Comm, Videotape version.

Hell on Wheels. Marty Robbins & John Ashley. Directed by Will Zens. 1967. Crown. 96 min. Sound. 16mm Color. *Rental:* Video Comm. *Lease:* Video Comm. *Rental:* Video Comm, *Lease:* Video Comm, Videotape version.

Hell Ship Mutiny. Peter Lorre & John Carradine. Directed by Lee Sholem & Elmo Williams. 1958. Republic. 66 min. Sound. 16mm B&W. *Rental:* Ivy Films.

Hell Squad. Wally Campo. Directed by Burt Topper. 1958. American International. 64 min. Sound. 16mm B&W. *Rental:* Williams Films.

Hell to Eternity. Jeffrey Hunter & David Janssen. Directed by Phil Karlson. 1960. Allied Artists. 132 min. Sound. 16mm B&W. *Rental:* Hurlock Cine.

Hell Town. Orig. Title: Heritage of the Plains. John Wayne. Directed by Charles Barton. 1937. Paramount. 55 min. Sound. 16mm B&W. *Rental:* Budget Films. *Sale:* Cinema Concepts & Natl Cinema.

Hell Up in Harlem. Fred Williamson & Gloria Hendry. Directed by Larry Cohen. 1973. American International. 96 min. Sound. 16mm Color. *Rental:* Swank Motion.

Hell with Heroes, The. Rod Taylor & Claudia Cardinale. Directed by Joseph Sargent. 1968. Universal. 95 min. Sound. 16mm Color. *Rental:* Swank Motion.

Hellbenders, The. Joseph Cotten & Norma Bengell. Directed by Sergio Corbucci. 1967. Embassy. 92 min. Sound. 16mm Color. dubbed. *Rental:* Films Inc.

Hellcats, The. Ross Hagen & Lee Duffy. Directed by Robert F. Slatzer. 1968. Crown. 90 min. Sound. 16mm Color. *Rental:* Video Comm. *Lease:* Video Comm. *Rental:* Video Comm, *Lease:* Video Comm, Videotape version.

Hellcats of the Navy. Ronald Reagan & Nancy Davis. Directed by Nathan Juran. 1957. Columbia. 82 min. Sound. 16mm B&W. *Rental:* Budget Films, Film Ctr DC, Inst Cinema, Modern Sound, Swank Motion, Welling Motion Pictures & Westcoast Films.

Helldorado. Roy Rogers. Directed by William Witney. 1946. Republic. 54 min. Sound. 16mm B&W. *Rental:* Ivy Films. *Sale:* Rep Pic Film & Reel Images.

Heller in Pink Tights. Sophia Loren & Anthony Quinn. Directed by George Cukor. 1960. Paramount. 100 min. Sound. 16mm Color. *Rental:* Films Inc.

Hellfighters. John Wayne, Jim Hutton & Katharine Ross. Directed by Andrew V. McLaglen. 1969. Universal. 121 min. Sound. 16mm Color. *Rental:* Williams Films.

Hellfire. Forrest Tucker & Jim Davis. Directed by R. G. Springsteen. 1949. Republic. 90 min. Sound. 16mm B&W. *Rental:* Ivy Films. *Sale:* Rep Pic Film & Nostalgia Merchant.

Hellgate. Sterling Hayden & Joan Leslie. Directed by Charles Marquis Warren. 1953. Lippert. 87 min. Sound. 16mm B&W. *Rental:* Budget Films & Mogulls Films.

Hellhounds of the Plains. Yakima Canutt. 1928. Prairie. 60 min. Silent. 16mm B&W. *Rental:* Film Classics. *Sale:* Film Classics. *Rental:* Film Classics, *Sale:* Film Classics, Silent 8mm version.

Hellions, The. Richard Todd. Directed by Ken Annakin. 1962. Columbia. 87 min. Sound. 16mm Color. *Lease:* Time-Life Multimedia.

Hello Annapolis. Orig. Title: Personal Honor. Tom Brown & Jean Parker. Directed by Charles Barton. 1942. Columbia. 62 min. Sound. 16mm B&W. *Rental:* Inst Cinema.

Hello, Dolly! Barbra Streisand & Walter Matthau. Directed by Gene Kelly. 1969. Fox. 148 min. Sound. 16mm Color. *Rental:* Films Inc & Williams Films. *Rental:* Films Inc, 118 mins. version.

Hello Down There. Tony Randall & Janet Leigh. Directed by Jack Arnold. 1969. Paramount. 98 min. Sound. 16mm Color. *Rental:* Films Inc.

Hello, Frisco, Hello. Alice Faye & John Payne. Directed by Bruce Humberstone. 1943. Fox. 90 min. Sound. 16mm B&W. *Rental:* Films Inc.

Hello, Sister. Orig. Title: Walking Down Broadway. ZaSu Pitts & James Dunn. Directed by Alan Crosland & Erich Von Stroheim. 1933. Fox. 62 min. Sound. 16mm B&W. *Rental:* Films Inc.

Hell's Angels. Ben Lyon, James Hall & Jean Harlow. Directed by James Whale. 1930. United Artists. 90 min. Sound. 16mm B&W. *Rental:* Swank Motion. *Sale:* Morcraft Films, Super 8 sound version. *Sale:* Morcraft Films, Videotape version.

Hell's Angels on Wheels. Adam Roarke & Jack Nicholson. Directed by Richard Rush. 1967. Fanfare. 95 min. Sound. 16mm Color. *Rental:* Films Inc, Westcoast Films & Wholesome Film Ctr. *Rental:* Ivy Films, *Sale:* Ivy Films, Super 8 sound version.

Hell's Angels 'Sixty Nine. Tom Stern & Jeremy Slate. Directed by Lee Madden. 1969. American International. 97 min. Sound. 16mm Color. *Rental:* Budget Films & Films Inc.

Hell's Belles. Jeremy Slate & Adam Roarke. Directed by Maury Dexter. 1969. American International. 95 min. Sound. 16mm Color. *Rental:* Films Inc.

Hell's Brigade. Jack Palance & John Douglas. 99 min. Sound. Videotape Color. *Rental:* Maljack.

Hell's Crossroads. Stephen McNally & Peggie Castle. Directed by Franklin Adreon. 1956. Republic. 76 min. Sound. 16mm Color. *Rental:* Ivy Films. *Sale:* Rep Pic Film.

Hell's Devils. Orig. Title: Goose Step. Alan Ladd & Steffi Duna. Directed by Sherman Scott. 1939. Producers. 60 min. Sound. 16mm B&W. *Rental:* Mogulls Films. *Rental:* Bosco Films, 84 mins. version.

Hell's Five Hours. Stephen McNally & Colleen Gray. Directed by Jack L. Copeland. 1958. Allied Artists. 75 min. Sound. 16mm B&W. *Rental:* Ivy Films. *Sale:* Rep Pic Film.

Hell's Half Acre. Wendell Corey & Evelyn Keyes. Directed by John H. Auer. 1954. Republic. 91 min. Sound. 16mm B&W. *Rental:* Ivy Films. *Sale:* Rep Pic Film.

Hell's Highway. Richard Dix, Rochelle Hudson & Tom Brown. Directed by Rowland Brown. 1932. RKO. 80 min. Sound. 16mm B&W. *Rental:* Films Inc.

Hell's Hinges. William S. Hart. Directed by Thomas H. Ince. 1916. Triangle. 55 min. Silent. 16mm B&W. *Rental:* Budget Films, Em Gee Film Lib, Film Images, Films Inc, Mogulls Films & Westcoast Films. *Sale:* E Finney. *Rental:* Killiam Collect, Sound 16mm condensed, musical & narration only version. *Rental:* Ivy Films, Super 8 silent version. *Sale:* Cinema Concepts & Select Film, Silent 8mm version.

Hell's House. Bette Davis & Pat O'Brien. Directed by Howard Higgin. 1932. Zeidman. 80 min. Sound. 16mm B&W. *Rental:* Budget Films & Classic Film Mus. *Sale:* Morcraft Films & Reel Images. *Sale:* Reel Images, Super 8 sound version.

Hell's Island. John Payne & Mary Murphy. Directed by Phil Karlson. 1955. Paramount. 84 min. Sound. 16mm B&W. *Rental:* Films Inc.

Hell's Kitchen. Ronald Reagan & Margaret Lindsay. Directed by Lewis Seiler & E. A. Dupont. 1939. Warners. 81 min. Sound. 16mm B&W. *Rental:* MGM United.

Hell's Outpost. Rod Cameron & John Russell. Directed by Joseph Kane. 1954. Republic. 90 min. Sound. 16mm B&W. *Rental:* Ivy Films. *Sale:* Rep Pic Film.

Hellstrom Chronicles, The. Directed by Walon Green. 1971. Cinema V. (Documentary). 90 min. Sound. 16mm Color. *Rental:* Cinema Five. *Lease:* Cinema Five.

Helter Skelter Murders. Charles Manson & Debbie Duff. Directed by Frank Howard. 1970. Auric. (Color sequences). Sound. 16mm B&W. *Rental:* Iowa Films & Wade Williams.

Hemingway. 1965. NBC. (Documentary). 54 min. Sound. 16mm B&W. *Rental:* McGraw-Hill Films, Syracuse U Film & U Cal Media. *Sale:* McGraw-Hill Films.

Hemingway's Adventures of a Young Man. Orig. Title: Adventures of A Young Man. Richard Beymer & Diane Baker. Directed by Martin Ritt. 1962. Fox. 145 min. Sound. 16mm Color. *Rental:* Films Inc & Twyman Films. *Rental:* Films Inc, Anamorphic color version.

Hemo, the Magnificent. 1957. Bell Telephone. (Animated). 60 min. Sound. 16mm Color. *Rental:* Utah Media.

Hendrix at Berkeley. Jimi Hendrix. 1968. New Line. 64 min. Sound. 16mm Color. *Rental:* New Cinema & New Line Cinema.

Hennessy. Rod Steiger & Lee Remick. Directed by Don Sharp. 1975. American International. 103 min. Sound. 16mm Color. *Rental:* Swank Motion.

Henpecked see Blondie in Society.

Henry Adams: Historian. 1976. WNET. (Documentary). 59 min. Sound. Videotape Color. *Rental:* Indiana AV Ctr, Iowa Films & U of IL Film. *Sale:* Films Inc,

Henry Ford's America. 1977. Canada. (Documentary). 56 min. Sound. 16mm Color. *Rental:* U Cal Media, U Mich Media & U of IL Film.

Henry Goes to Arizona. Frank Morgan & Guy Kibbee. Directed by Edwin L. Marin. 1939. MGM. 66 min. Sound. 16mm B&W. *Rental:* MGM United.

Henry IV, Part One. Jon Finch & Anthony Quayle. 1979. Britain. 147 min. Videotape Color. *Rental:* Iowa Films.

Henry IV, Part Two. Jon Finch & Anthony Quayle. 1979. Britain. 151 min. Videotape Color. *Rental:* Iowa Films.

Henry Miller Odyssey, The. Directed by Robert Snyder. 1969. Robert Snyder. (Documentary). 110 min. Sound. 16mm Color. *Rental:* A Cantor. *Sale:* A Cantor.

Henry Morton Stanley. Directed by Fred Burnley. 1977. Britain. (Cast unlisted). 49 min. Sound. 16mm Color. *Rental:* Time-Life Multimedia. *Sale:* Time-Life Multimedia. *Sale:* Time-Life Multimedia, Videotape version.

Henry Phipps Goes Skiing. Directed by Bruce Cronin. 1976. Cronin. (Cast unlisted). 52 min. Sound. 16mm Color. *Rental:* Films Inc, Texture Film & U of IL Film. *Sale:* Texture Film. *Sale:* Texture Film, Videotape version.

Henry V. Sir Laurence Olivier & Robert Newton. Directed by Sir Laurence Olivier. 1945. Britain. 137 min. Sound. 16mm Color. *Rental:* Budget Films, Films Inc, Images Film, Kit Parker, Learning Corp Am, MGM United, Modern Sound, Roas Films, Twyman Films, U Cal Media, U of IL Film, Welling Motion Pictures, Westcoast Films, Wholesome Film Ctr & Williams Films. *Lease:* Learning Corp Am. *Lease:* Learning Corp Am, Videotape version.

Henry V. David Gwillim & Rod Edwards. 1979. Britain. 163 min. Sound. Videotape Color. *Rental:* Iowa Films & Time-Life Multimedia. *Sale:* Time-Life Multimedia.

Henry VI: Part One. Peter Benson & Trevor Peacock. 1982. 186 min. Sound. Videotape Color. *Rental:* Iowa Films.

Henry VI: Part Three. Peter Benson & Bernard Hill. 1979. 200 min. Sound. Videotape Color. *Rental:* Iowa Films.

Henry VI: Part Two. Peter Benson & Julia Foster. 1982. 212 min. Sound. Videotape Color. *Rental:* Iowa Films.

Henry VIII. Claire Bloom & John Stride. 1979. Britain. 165 min. Videotape Color. *Rental:* Iowa Films & Time-Life Multimedia. *Sale:* Time-Life Multimedia.

Henry VIII & His Six Wives. Keith Michell & Donald Pleasance. Directed by Waris Hussein. 1973. Britain. 125 min. Sound. 16mm Color. *Lease:* Lucerne Films.

Hephaestus Plague, The *see* Bug.

Her & She & Him. 1970. France. 90 min. Videotape-color *Sale:* Video Lib.

Her Bridal Night. Brigitte Bardot & Louis Jourdan. Directed by Pierre Gaspard-Huit. France. (Color sequences). 90 min. Sound. 16mm B&W. *Rental:* Video Comm & Ivy Films. *Rental:* Video Comm, Videotape version.

Her Favorite Patient. Orig. Title: Bedside Manner. John Carroll & Ruth Hussey. Directed by Andrew Stone. 1945. United Artists. 75 min. Sound. 16mm B&W. *Rental:* Budget Films, Ivy Films, Mogulls Films & Rep Pic Film. *Lease:* Rep Pic Film.

Her First Romance *see* Right Man.

Her First Romance. Orig. Title: Girls Never Tell. Margaret O'Brien. Directed by Seymour Friedman. 1951. Columbia. 73 min. Sound. 16mm B&W. *Rental:* Buchan Pic, Film Ctr DC & Inst Cinema.

Her Husband's Affairs. Lucille Ball & Franchot Tone. Directed by S. Sylvan Simon. 1947. Columbia. 86 min. Sound. 16mm B&W. *Rental:* Bosco Films & Kit Parker.

Her Husband's Secretary. Warren Hull & Beverly Roberts. Directed by Frank McDonald. 1937. Warners. 61 min. Sound. 16mm B&W. *Rental:* MGM United.

Her Kind of Man. Dane Clark & Janis Paige. Directed by Frederick De Cordova. 1946. Warners. 78 min. Sound. 16mm B&W. *Rental:* MGM United.

Her Lucky Night. Noah Beery Jr. & Martha O'Driscoll. Directed by Edward Lilley. 1945. Universal. 63 min. Sound. 16mm B&W. *Rental:* Mogulls Films.

Her Majesty Love. Marilyn Miller & W. C. Fields. Directed by William Dieterle. 1931. Warners. 76 min. Sound. 16mm B&W. *Rental:* MGM United.

Her Primitive Man. Louise Allbritton & Robert Benchley. Directed by Charles Lamont. 1944. Universal. 81 min. Sound. 16mm B&W. *Rental:* Film Ctr DC, Inst Cinema & Mogulls Films.

Her Private Affair. Ann Harding & John Loder. Directed by Paul L. Stein. 1929. Pathe. 77 min. Sound. 16mm B&W. *Rental:* Film Classics.

Her Sister From Paris. Constance Talmadge & Ronald Colman. Directed by Sidney A. Franklin. 1925. 16mm *Rental:* A Twyman Pres.

Her Sister's Secret. Nancy Coleman & Margaret Lindsay. Directed by Edgar G. Ulmer. 1946. PRC. 85 min. Sound. 16mm B&W. *Sale:* Classics Assoc NY.

Her Three Bachelors. Jerry Demonde. 1954. Britain. 75 min. Sound. 16mm B&W. *Rental:* Inst Cinema.

Her Twelve Men. Greer Garson & Robert Ryan. Directed by Robert Z. Leonard. 1954. MGM. 90 min. Sound. 16mm Color. *Rental:* MGM United.

Her Wanton Destiny *see* Shifting Sands.

Herbert Hoover. 1958. Encyclopaedia Britannica. (Documentary). 55 min. Sound. 16mm B&W. *Rental:* U Mich Media.

Herbie Goes to Monte Carlo. Dean Jones, Don Knotts & Julie Sommars. Directed by Vincent McEveety. 1977. Disney. 105 min. Sound. 16mm Color. *Rental:* Bosco Films, Elliot Film Co, Roas Films, Welling Motion Pictures, Westcoast Films & Williams Films.

Herbie Rides Again. Helen Hayes, Ken Berry & Stefanie Powers. Directed by Robert Stevenson. 1974. Disney. 88 min. Sound. 16mm Color. *Rental:* Bosco Films, Elliot Film Co, MGM United, Roas Films, Welling Motion Pictures, Westcoast Films & Williams Films.

Hercules. Steve Reeves. Directed by Pietro Francisci. 1959. Italy. 107 min. Sound. 16mm Color. dubbed. *Rental:* Films Inc, Newman Film Lib, Video Comm, Welling Motion Pictures & Wholesome Film Ctr.

Hercules & the Black Pirates. Alan Steele. 1960. Italy. 91 min. Sound. 16mm Color. dubbed. *Rental:* Willoughby Peer.

Hercules & the Captive Women. Fay Spain & Reg Park. Directed by Vittorio Cottafavi. 1961. Italy. 94 min. Sound. 16mm Color. dubbed. *Rental:* Budget Films & Video Comm.

Hercules Goes Bananas. Trans. Title: Hercules in New York. Arnold Stang & Arnold Schwartzenegger. Directed by Arthur Allan Seidelman. 1969. RAF-Filmpartners. 90 min. 16mm Color. *Rental:* Kit Parker.

Hercules in New York *see* Hercules Goes Bananas.

Hercules in the Haunted World. Christopher Lee & Reg Park. Directed by Mario Bava. 1961. Woolner. 83 min. Sound. 16mm Color. dubbed. *Rental:* Budget Films, Video Comm & Westcoast Films.

Hercules, Samson & Ulysses. Kirk Morris. Directed by Pietro Francisci. 1965. Italy. 85 min. Sound. 16mm Color. dubbed. *Rental:* MGM United.

Hercules Unchained. Steve Reeves & Sylvia Koscina. Directed by Pietro Francisci. 1960. Italy. 101 min. Sound. 16mm Color. dubbed. *Rental:* Films Inc, Newman Film Lib, Video Comm & Westcoast Films.

Hercules vs. the Hydra. Orig. Title: Loves of Hercules, The. Jayne Mansfield & Mickey Hargitay. 1964. Italy. 94 min. Sound. 16mm Color. dubbed. *Rental:* Budget Films & Modern Sound.

Hercules vs. the Sons of the Sun. Mark Forrest. Directed by Osvaldo Civirani. 1963. Italy. 90 min. 16mm Color. dubbed. *Rental:* Ivy Films & Modern Sound. *Rental:* Ivy Films, *Sale:* Ivy Films, Super 8 sound version.

Hercules vs.the Giant Warriors *see* Triumph of Hercules.

Here Are Ladies. Siobhan McKenna. Directed by John Quested. 1972. Cantor. 58 min. Sound. 16mm Color. *Rental:* A Cantor. *Sale:* A Cantor.

Here Come the Coeds. Bud Abbott & Lou Costello. Directed by Jean Yarbrough. 1945. Universal. 87 min. Sound. 16mm B&W. *Rental:* Swank Motion.

Here Come the Girls. Bob Hope & Arlene Dahl. Directed by Claude Binyon. 1953. Paramount. 78 min. Sound. 16mm Color. *Rental:* Films Inc.

Here Come the Jets. Steve Brodie & Lyn Thomas. Directed by Gene Fowler Jr. 1959. Fox. (Anamorphic). 71 min. Sound. 16mm B&W. *Rental:* Willoughby Peer.

Here Come the Nelsons. Ozzie Nelson & Harriet Nelson. Directed by Frederick De Cordova. 1952. Universal. 76 min. Sound. 16mm B&W. *Rental:* Swank Motion.

Here Come the Tigers. Richard Lincoln. Directed by Sean Cunningham. 1978. American International. 90 min. Sound. 16mm Color. *Rental:* Swank Motion & Welling Motion Pictures.

Here Comes Carter. Orig. Title: Voice of Scandal, The. Glenda Farrell & Graig Reynolds. Directed by William Clemens. 1936. Warners. 60 min. Sound. 16mm B&W. *Rental:* MGM United.

Here Comes Cookie. George Burns & Gracie Allen. Directed by Norman Z. McLeod. 1935. Paramount. 66 min. Sound. 16mm B&W. *Rental:* Swank Motion.

Here Comes Elmer. Al Pearce & Gloria Stuart. Directed by Joseph Santley. 1943. Republic. 74 min. Sound. 16mm B&W. *Rental:* Ivy Films.

Here Comes Every Body. Directed by John Whitmore. 1974. Vision Quest. (Documentary). 96 min. Sound. 16mm Color. *Rental:* Films Inc.

Here Comes Happiness. Edward Norris & Mildred Coles. Directed by Noel Smith. 1941. Warners. 58 min. Sound. 16mm B&W. *Rental:* MGM United.

Here Comes Mr. Jordan. Robert Montgomery & Claude Rains. Directed by Alexander Hall. 1941. Columbia. 93 min. Sound. 16mm B&W. *Rental:* Arcus Film, Budget Films, Cine Craft, Charard Motion Pictures, Images Film, Ivy Films, Kit Parker, Modern Sound, Natl Film Video, Swank Motion, Twyman Films, U of IL Film, Welling Motion Pictures, Westcoast Films, Wholesome Film Ctr & Williams Films. *Rental:* Swank Motion, Videotape version.

Here Comes the Band. Ted Healy & Virginia Bruce. Directed by Paul Sloane. 1936. MGM. 87 min. Sound. 16mm B&W. *Rental:* MGM United.

Here Comes the Groom. Bing Crosby & Jane Wyman. Directed by Frank Capra. 1951. Paramount. 116 min. Sound. 16mm B&W. *Rental:* Films Inc.

Here Comes the Navy. James Cagney & Pat O'Brien. Directed by Lloyd Bacon. 1934. Warners. 86 min. Sound. 16mm B&W. *Rental:* MGM United.

Here Comes Trouble. William Tracy & Joe Sawyer. Directed by Fred Guiol. 1948. United Artists. 71 min. Sound. 16mm B&W. *Rental:* Inst Cinema & Newman Film Lib.

Here He Comes. Earle Douglas. Directed by Francis Corby. 1927. Sierra. 55 min. Silent. 16mm B&W. *Rental:* Mogulls Films.

Here I Am a Stanger. Richard Greene & Richard Dix. Directed by Roy Del Ruth. 1939. Fox. 84 min. Sound. 16mm B&W. *Rental:* Films Inc.

Here Is Germany. 1945. 52 min. Sound. 16mm Color. *Rental:* Natl AV Ctr. *Sale:* Natl AV Ctr.

Here It Is: Burlesque. Ann Corio. HBO. 88 min. Videotape Color. *Rental:* Films Inc.

Here We Go Again. Fibber McGee and Molly & Edgar Bergen. Directed by Allan Dwan. 1942. RKO. 76 min. Sound. 16mm B&W. *Rental:* Films Inc.

Here We Go Again *see* Pride of the Bowery.

Here We Go Round the Mulberry Bush. Barry Evans & Judy Geeson. Directed by Clive Donner. 1968. Britain. 114 min. Sound. 16mm Color. *Rental:* MGM United.

Here's Looking at You, Kid. 1983. Nova. 57 min. Sound. 16mm Color. *Rental:* U Cal Media.

Heritage of Slavery. 1968. CBS. (Documentary). 55 min. Sound. 16mm B&W. *Rental:* Iowa Films, NYU Film Lib, Phoenix Films, U Cal Media, U Mich Media & Utah Media. *Sale:* Phoenix Films. *Sale:* Phoenix Films, Videotape version.

Heritage of the Desert. Donald Woods & Evelyn Venable. Directed by Lesley Selander. 1939. Paramount. 70 min. Sound. 16mm B&W. *Rental:* Budget Films.

Heritage of the Plains *see* Hell Town.

Heritage of the West *see* When the West Was Young.

Hero, The. Richard Harris & Romy Schneider. Directed by Richard Harris. 1972. Embassy. 97 min. Sound. 16mm Color. *Rental:* Films Inc.

Hero, The *see* Nayak.

Hero Ain't Nothin' But a Sandwich, A. Cicely Tyson & Paul Winfield. Directed by Ralph Nelson. 1977. New World. 105 min. Sound. 16mm Color. *Rental:* Films Inc.

Hero As Artist, The. 1968. Britain. (Documentary). 60 min. Sound. 16mm Color. *Rental:* U Cal Media, Films Inc, OK AV Ctr, Syracuse U Film & Utah Media. *Sale:* Films Inc. *Sale:* Films Inc, Videotape version.

Hero At Large. John Ritter & Anne Archer. Directed by Martin Davidson. 1980. MGM. 99 min. Sound. 16mm Color. *Rental:* MGM United.

Hero for a Night. Patsy Ruth Miller & Glenn Tryon. Directed by Harry Hoyt. 1927. Universal. 60 min. Silent. 16mm B&W. *Rental:* Mogulls Films.

Hero of Our Time, A. Alfonso Gil. Directed by J. Ferrater-Mora. 1969. J. Ferrater-Mora. 67 min. Sound. 16mm B&W. *Rental:* Canyon Cinema.

Hero of Pine Ridge, The *see* Yodelin' Kid from Pine Ridge.

Hero of the Revolution. 1975. HB. (Animated). 64 min. Sound. 16mm Color. *Rental:* Williams Films.

Hero Prince, The. Orig. Title: Legend of Harap Alb, The. Xerox. (Cast Unlisted). 78 min. Sound. 16mm Color. *Sale:* Xerox Films.

Heroes. Directed by Rick Becker. 1974. Becker. (Experimental). 90 min. Sound. 16mm Color. *Rental:* Vision Quest. *Sale:* Vision Quest.

Heroes. Henry Winkler & Sally Field. Directed by Jeremy Paul Kagan. 1977. Universal. 113 min. Sound. 16mm Color. *Rental:* Swank Motion.

Heroes Die Young. Erika Peters. Directed by Gerald S. Shepard. 1960. Allied Artists. 76 min. Sound. 16mm B&W. *Rental:* Hurlock Cine.

Heroes for Sale. Loretta Young & Richard Barthelmess. Directed by William A. Wellman. 1933. Warners. 73 min. Sound. 16mm B&W. *Rental:* MGM United.

Heroes of Shipka. S. Papov. Directed by Sergei Vassiliev. Rus. 1955. Russia. 90 min. Sound. 16mm B&W. subtitles. *Rental:* Corinth Films.

Heroes of Telemark. Kirk Douglas, Sir Michael Redgrave. Directed by Anthony Mann. 1965. Columbia. 131 min. Sound. 16mm Color. *Rental:* Bosco Films, Budget Films, Cine Craft, Charard Motion Pics, Film Ctr DC, Films Inc, Roas Films, Westcoast Films & Wholesome Film Ctr. *Rental:* Kit Parker, Anamorphic version.

Heroes of the Alamo. Lane Chandler & Earl Hodgins. Directed by Harry Fraser. 1938. Columbia. 75 min. Sound. 16mm B&W. *Rental:* Alba House.

Heroes of the Hills. Robert Livingston. Directed by George Sherman. 1938. Republic. 54 min. Sound. 16mm B&W. *Rental:* Ivy Films. *Sale:* Rep Pic Film.

Heroes of the Range. Ken Maynard. Directed by Spencer G. Bennett. 1936. Columbia. 51 min. Sound. 16mm B&W. *Rental:* Willoughby Peer.

Heroes of the Saddle. Robert Livingston. Directed by William Witney. 1940. Republic. 54 min. Sound. 16mm B&W. *Rental:* Ivy Films. *Sale:* Rep Pic Film & Nostalgia Merchant.

Heroic Beginnings. Directed by George Robertson. 1973. Canada. (Documentary). 57 min. Sound. 16mm Color. *Rental:* Natl Film CN. *Sale:* Natl Film CN.

Heroic Materialism. (Civilization Ser.). 1968. Britain. (Documentary). 60 min. Sound. 16mm Color. *Rental:* Films Inc, OK AV Ctr, Syracuse U Film, U Cal Media & Utah Media. *Sale:* Films Inc. *Sale:* Films Inc, Videotape version.

Hero's Island. James Mason & Neville Brand. Directed by Leslie Stevens. 1962. United Artists. 94 min. Sound. 16mm Color. *Rental:* MGM United.

Hero's Wife. Trans. Title: Eshet Ha'Gibor. Gidon Shemer & Batya Lancet. Directed by Peter Frye. Hebrew. 1963. Israel. 90 min. Sound. 16mm B&W. subtitles. *Rental:* Budget Films, Ivy Films, Kit Parker & Video Comm.

Herowork. Rod Browning. 1978. NBS. 90 min. Sound. 16mm Color. *Sale:* Salz Ent. *Sale:* Salz Ent, Super 8 sound version. *Sale:* Salz Ent, Videotape version.

He's a Cockeyed Wonder. Mickey Rooney & Terry Moore. Directed by Peter Godfrey. 1950. Columbia. 86 min. Sound. 16mm B&W. *Rental:* Cine Craft & Welling Motion Pictures.

Hester Street. Carol Kane. Directed by Joan Micklin Silver. 1975. Midwest. 90 min. Sound. 16mm Color. *Rental:* Cinema Five.

Hewitt's Just Different. Directed by Larry Elikann. 1977. Daniel Wilson. (Cast unlisted). 47 min. Sound. 16mm Color. *Rental:* D Wilson, Kent St U Film & U Mich Media.

Hex. Keith Carradine & Scott Glenn. Directed by Leo Garen. 1973. Fox. 92 min. Sound. 16mm Color. *Rental:* Films Inc.

Hey, Abbott! Directed by Jim Gates. 1980. CBS. (Anthology). 80 min. Sound. Videotape Color. *Sale:* Twyman Films, Vidamerica & Welling Motion Pictures. *Rental:* Welling Motion Pictures, 70 min. version.

Hey Boy! Hey Girl! Louis Prima & Keely Smith. Directed by David Lowell Rich. 1959. Columbia. 81 min. Sound. 16mm B&W. *Rental:* Cine Craft, Inst Cinema, Modern Sound & Welling Motion Pictures.

Hey-Day Fever. 1975. Britain. (Documentary). 52 min. Sound. 16mm Color. *Rental:* U of IL Film.

Hey, Let's Twist. Joey Dee. Directed by Greg Garrison. 1961. Paramount. 80 min. Sound. 16mm B&W. *Rental:* Films Inc.

Hey, Rookie. Ann Miller & Larry Parks. Directed by Charles Barton. 1944. Columbia. 80 min. Sound. 16mm B&W. *Rental:* Kit Parker.

Hey There, It's Yogi Bear. Directed by William Hanna & Joseph Barbera. 1964. Columbia. (Animated). 88 min. Sound. 16mm Color. *Rental:* Arcus Film, Buchan Pic, Budget Films, Cine Craft, Charard Motion Pics, Film Ctr DC, Films Inc, Inst Cinema, Kerr Film, Modern Sound, Newman Film Lib, Roas Films, Twyman Films, Welling Motion Pictures, Westcoast Films, Wholesome Film Ctr, Williams Films & Willoughby Peer.

Hey! What About Us? 1967. NET. (Documentary). 57 min. Sound. 16mm B&W. *Rental:* Indiana AV Ctr.

Hi Diddle Diddle. Orig. Title: Diamonds & Crime. Adolphe Menjou, Martha Scott & Dennis O'Keefe. Directed by Andrew Stone. 1943. United Artists. 80 min. Sound. 16mm B&W. *Rental:* Budget Films & Mogulls Films.

Hi Gaucho. John Carroll & Steffi Duna. Directed by Thomas Atkins. 1936. RKO. 49 min. Sound. 16mm *Rental:* RKO General Pics.

Hi, Good Lookin'. Ozzie Nelson & Harriet Hilliard. Directed by Edward Lilley. 1944. Universal. 60 min. Sound. 16mm B&W. *Rental:* Mogulls Films.

Hi, I'm Ann. Ann Kiemel. 55 min. Sound. 16mm Color. *Rental:* Gospel Films.

Hi-Jacked. Jim Davis. Directed by Sam Newfield. 1950. Lippert. 70 min. Sound. 16mm B&W. *Rental:* Mogulls Films.

Hi Mom! Robert De Niro. Directed by Brian De Palma. 1970. Sigma III. 87 min. Sound. 16mm Color. *Rental:* Films Inc.

Hi, Neighbor! John Archer & Jean Parker. Directed by Charles Lamont. 1942. Republic. 72 min. Sound. 16mm B&W. *Rental:* Ivy Films.

Hi, Nellie! Paul Muni & Glenda Farrell. Directed by Mervyn LeRoy. 1934. Warners. 79 min. Sound. 16mm B&W. *Rental:* MGM United.

Hiawatha. Vincent Edwards & Yvette Dugay. Directed by Kurt Neumann. 1952. Allied Artists. 80 min. Sound. 16mm B&W. *Rental:* Hurlock Cine.

Hickey & Boggs. Bill Cosby & Robert Culp. Directed by Robert Culp. 1972. United Artists. 111 min. Sound. 16mm Color. *Rental:* Films Inc & MGM United.

Hidden Aces. Charles Hutchison. Directed by Bernard B. Ray. 1926. Pathe. 75 min. Silent. 16mm B&W. *Sale:* Blackhawk Films. *Rental:* Ivy Films, *Sale:* Blackhawk Films, Super 8 silent version. *Sale:* Blackhawk Films, Silent 8mm version.

Hidden Crime see Scattergood Pulls the Strings.

Hidden Enemy. Warren Hull & Kay Linaker. Directed by Howard Bretherton. 1940. Monogram. 60 min. Sound. 16mm B&W. *Rental:* Mogulls Films.

Hidden Eye, The. Edward Arnold & Frances Rafferty. Directed by Richard Whorf. 1945. MGM. 69 min. Sound. 16mm B&W. *Rental:* MGM United.

Hidden Fear. John Payne & Conrad Nagel. Directed by Andre De Toth. 1957. United Artists. 83 min. Sound. 16mm B&W. *Rental:* MGM United.

Hidden Fortress, The. Toshiro Mifune. Directed by Akira Kurosawa. Jap. 1958. Japan. 126 min. Sound. 16mm B&W. subtitles. *Rental:* Film Images.

Hidden Gold. William Boyd. Directed by Lesley Selander. 1940. Paramount. 54 min. Sound. 16mm B&W. *Lease:* Cinema Concepts. *Sale:* Natl Cinema. *Sale:* Video Comm, Videotpae version.

Hidden Guns. Bruce Bennett & Angie Dickinson. Directed by Albert C. Gannaway. 1956. Republic. 66 min. Sound. 16mm B&W. *Rental:* Ivy Films & Westcoast Films.

Hidden Hand, The. Craig Stevens & Elizabeth Frazer. Directed by Ben Stoloff. 1942. Warners. 67 min. Sound. 16mm B&W. *Rental:* MGM United.

Hidden Homicide. Griffith Jones & Charles Farrell. Directed by Tony Young. 1959. Republic. 70 min. Sound. 16mm B&W. *Rental:* Ivy Films. *Sale:* Rep Pic Film.

Hidden River. Maria Felix & Carlos Lopez. Directed by Emilio Fernandez. Span. 1947. Mexico. 100 min. 16mm B&W. subtitles. *Rental:* Trans-World Films & Twyman Films. *Rental:* Trans-World Films & Twyman Films, Subtitled version.

Hidden Room, The. Robert Newton & Sally Gray. Directed by Edward Dmytryk. 1950. Britain. 98 min. Sound. 16mm B&W. *Rental:* Modern Sound & Video Comm.

Hidden Structure. (Ascent of Man Ser.). 1974. Britain. (Documentary). 52 min. Sound. 16mm Color. *Rental:* U Cal Media, Iowa Films, U Mich Media & Utah Media.

Hidden Universe, The: The Brain. 1977. McGraw-Hill. (Documentary). 48 min. Sound. 16mm Color. *Rental:* Iowa Films, La Inst Res Ctr, McGraw-Hill Films, Syracuse U Film, U Cal Media, U Mich Media, U of IL Film & Utah Media. *Sale:* McGraw-Hill Films. *Sale:* McGraw-Hill Films, Videotape version.

Hidden Valley. Bob Steele. Directed by Robert N. Bradbury. 1932. Monogram. 60 min. Sound. 16mm B&W. *Rental:* Mogulls Films.

Hidden Valley Outlaws. Bill Elliott. Directed by Howard Bretherton. 1944. Republic. 56 min. Sound. 16mm B&W. *Rental:* Ivy Films. *Sale:* Rep Pic Film & Nostalgia Merchant.

Hidden World, The. 1966. National Geographic. 51 min. 16mm Color. *Rental:* Natl Geog, Syracuse U Film & Wholesome Film Ctr. *Sale:* Natl Geog. *Sale:* Natl Geog, Videotape version.

Hide in Plain Sight. James Caan & Jill Eikenberry. Directed by James Caan. 1980. MGM. 92 min. Sound. 16mm Color. *Rental:* MGM United. *Rental:* MGM United, Anamorphic version. *Rental:* MGM United, Videotape version.

Hide Out. 1981. 83 min. Sound. 16mm Color. *Rental:* Utah Media.

Hideaway. Fred Stone & Marjorie Lord. Directed by Richard Rosson. 1937. RKO. 58 min. Sound. 16mm B&W. *Rental:* RKO General Pics.

Hideaways, The. Orig. Title: From the Mixed-up Files of Mrs. Basil E. Frankweiler. Ingrid Bergman & Sally Prager. Directed by Fielder Cook. 1973. Westfall. 87 min. Sound. 16mm Color. *Rental:* Films Inc, Macmillan Films, Modern Sound, Roas Films & Westcoast Films. *Lease:* Macmillan Films.

Hideout. Lloyd Bridges & Ray Collins. Directed by Philip Ford. 1948. Republic. 65 min. Sound. 16mm B&W. *Rental:* Ivy Films. *Sale:* Rep Pic Film.

Hideout. Robert Montgomery & Edward Arnold. Directed by W. S. Van Dyke II. 1934. MGM. 83 min. Sound. 16mm B&W. *Rental:* MGM United.

Higgins Family, The. James Gleason & Harry Davenport. Directed by Gus Meins. 1938. Republic. 54 min. Sound. 16mm B&W. *Rental:* Ivy Films. *Sale:* Rep Pic Film.

High & Happy. Eddie Albert & Bill Goodwin. Directed by Frank McDonald. 1947. Republic. 90 min. Sound. 16mm B&W. *Rental:* Ivy Films. *Sale:* Rep Pic Film.

High & Low. Toshiro Mifune. Directed by Akira Kurosawa. 1962. Japan. 143 min. Sound. 16mm B&W. *Rental:* Budget Films & Films Inc.

High Anxiety. Mel Brooks, Madeline Kahn & Cloris Leachman. Directed by Mel Brooks. 1977. Fox. 94 min. Sound. 16mm Color. *Rental:* Williams Films. *Rental:* Williams Films, Videotape version.

High Ballin'. Peter Fonda & Jerry Reed. Directed by Peter Carter. 1978. American International. 100 min. Sound. 16mm Color. *Rental:* Swank Motion.

High Command. Lionel Atwill & James Mason. Directed by Thorold Dickinson. 1938. Britain. 75 min. Sound. 16mm B&W. *Rental:* Liberty Co.

High Commissioner, The. Rod Taylor & Christopher Plummer. Directed by Ralph Thomas. 1968. ABC. 101 min. Sound. 16mm Color. *Rental:* Films Inc.

High Conquest. Anna Lee & Gilbert Roland. Directed by Irving Allen. 1947. Monogram. 79 min. Sound. 16mm B&W. *Rental:* Cine Craft, Hurlock Cine, Mogulls Films, Film Ctr DC & Westcoast Films.

High Cost of Loving, The. Jose Ferrer & Gena Rowlands. Directed by Jose Ferrer. 1958. MGM. 87 min. Sound. 16mm B&W. *Rental:* MGM United. *Rental:* MGM United, Anamorphic B&W version. *Rental:* MGM United, Videotape version.

High Gear. Orig. Title: Big Thrill, The. Joan Marsh & Theodore Von Eltz. Directed by George Stevens. 1933. Goldsmith. 70 min. Sound. 16mm B&W. *Rental:* Mogulls Films.

High Grass Circus. Directed by Torben Schioler & Tony Ianzelo. 1976. Canada. (Documentary). 57 min. Sound. 16mm Color. *Rental:* Natl Film CN. *Sale:* Natl Film CN. *Sale:* Natl Film CN, Videotape version.

High Hell. John Derek & Elaine Stewart. Directed by Burt Balaban. 1958. Paramount. 87 min. Sound. 16mm B&W. *Rental:* Films Inc.

High Lonesome. John Drew Barrymore & Chill Wills. Directed by Alan Le May. 1950. Eagle Lion. 81 min. Sound. 16mm B&W. *Rental:* Budget Films, Ivy Films & Mogulls Films.

High Noon. Gary Cooper & Grace Kelly. Directed by Fred Zinnemann. 1952. United Artists. 85 min. Sound. 16mm B&W. *Rental:* Arcus Film, Budget Films, Cine Craft, Films Inc, Inst Cinema, Images Film, Ivy Films, Kit Parker, Modern Sound, Twyman Films, Welling Motion Pictures, Westcoast Films, Wholesome Film Ctr & Williams Films. *Lease:* Rep Pic Film. *Sale:* Blackhawk Films, Cinema Concepts & Ivy Films, Videotape version.

High Plains Drifter. Clint Eastwood. Directed by Clint Eastwood. 1973. Universal. 105 min. Sound. 16mm Color. *Rental:* Swank Motion. *Rental:* Swank Motion, Anamorphic color version. *Rental:* Swank Motion, Videotape version.

High-Powered Rifle, The. Willard Parker & Allison Hayes. Directed by Maury Dexter. 1960. Fox. 62 min. Sound. 16mm B&W. *Rental:* Willoughby Peer.

High Pressure. William Powell & Evelyn Brent. Directed by Mervyn LeRoy. 1932. Warners. 74 min. Sound. 16mm B&W. *Rental:* MGM United.

High Rise Donkey. 1981. Britain. (Cast unlisted). 57 min. Sound. 16mm Color. *Sale:* Lucerne Films.

High Road to China. Tom Selleck & Bess Armstrong. Directed by Brian Hutton. 1983. Warners. 120 min. Sound. 16mm Color. *Rental:* Swank Motion. *Rental:* Swank Motion, Videotape version.

High School. Jane Withers. Directed by George Nicholls Jr. 1940. Fox. 74 min. Sound. 16mm B&W. *Rental:* Films Inc.

High School. Directed by Frederick Wiseman. 1968. Frederick Wiseman. (Documentary). 75 min. Sound. 16mm B&W. *Rental:* Zipporah Films. *Lease:* Zipporah Films, Videotape version.

High School Confidential. Orig. Title: Young Killers, The. Russ Tamblyn & Mamie Van Doren. Directed by Jack Arnold. 1958. MGM. 85 min. Sound. 16mm B&W. *Rental:* Budget Films, Ivy Films & Rep Pic Film. *Sale:* Rep Pic Film.

High School Girl. Directed by Crane Wilbur. 1935. Bryan Foy. (Exploitation). 60 min. Sound. 16mm B&W. *Sale:* Reel Images.

High School Hero. Freddie Stewart & June Preisser. Directed by Arthur Dreifuss. 1946. Monogram. 69 min. Sound. 16mm B&W. *Rental:* Hurlock Cine & Film Ctr DC.

High Sierra. Humphrey Bogart & Ida Lupino. Directed by Raoul Walsh. 1941. Warners. 100 min. Sound. 16mm B&W. *Rental:* MGM United.

High Society. Bing Crosby, Grace Kelly & Frank Sinatra. Directed by Charles Walters. 1956. MGM. 107 min. Sound. 16mm Color. *Rental:* MGM United. *Rental:* MGM United, Videotape version.

High Stakes. Jack Carson & Lupe Velez. Directed by Edward Cline. 1938. RKO. 70 min. Sound. 16mm *Rental:* RKO General Pics.

High Tide. Lee Tracy & Don Castle. Directed by John Reinhardt. 1947. 70 min. Sound. 16mm B&W. *Rental:* Mogulls Films.

High Time. Bing Crosby & Tuesday Weld. Directed by Blake Edwards. 1960. Fox. 103 min. Sound. 16mm Color. *Rental:* Films Inc. *Rental:* Films Inc, Anamorphic color version.

High Voltage. William Boyd & Carole Lombard. Directed by Howard Higgin. 1929. Pathe. 60 min. Sound. 16mm B&W. *Sale:* Cinema Concepts, Classic Film Mus & Reel Images.

High Wall, The. Robert Taylor & Audrey Totter. Directed by Curtis Bernhardt. 1948. MGM. 99 min. Sound. 16mm B&W. *Rental:* MGM United.

High, Wide & Handsome. Irene Dunne & Randolph Scott. Directed by Rouben Mamoulian. 1937. Paramount. 104 min. Sound. 16mm B&W. *Rental:* Swank Motion.

High, Wild & Free. Directed by Gordon Eastman. 1968. American International. (Documentary). 105 min. Sound. 16mm Color. *Rental:* Budget Films & Films Inc.

High Wind in Jamaica. Anthony Quinn & Lila Kedrova. Directed by Alexander Mackendrick. 1965. Fox. 104 min. Sound. 16mm Color. *Rental:* Films Inc. *Rental:* Films Inc, Anamorphic version.

Higher & Higher. Frank Sinatra & Michele Morgan. Directed by Tim Whelan. 1943. RKO. 88 min. Sound. 16mm B&W. *Rental:* Film Inc & RKO General Pics.

Higher Education: Who Needs It?. 1972. CBS. (Documentary). 51 min. Sound. 16mm B&W. *Rental:* U Mich Media & Syracuse U Film. *Sale:* Carousel Films.

Higher Form of Killing: Gas Warfare. 1981. Britain. (Documentary). 50 min. Videotape Color. *Rental:* Films Inc. *Sale:* Films Inc.

Higher We Fly, The. John Denver. 1980. Stouffer. 50 min. Sound. 16mm Color. *Rental:* Stouffer Ent. *Sale:* Stouffer Ent.

Highway Dragnet. Richard Conte & Joan Bennett. Directed by Nathan Juran. 1954. Allied Artists. 71 min. Sound. 16mm B&W. *Rental:* Ivy Films. *Sale:* Rep Pic Film.

Highway Soil Engineering. 1950. US Government. (Documentary). 110 min. Sound. 16mm Color. *Sale:* Natl AV Ctr.

Highway Thirteen. Robert Lowery & Pamela Blake. Directed by William Berke. 1948. Screen Guild. 58 min. Sound. 16mm B&W. *Rental:* Mogulls Films, Film Ctr DC & Westcoast Films.

Highway West. Arthur Kennedy & Brenda Marshall. Directed by William McGann. 1941. Warners. 63 min. Sound. 16mm B&W. *Rental:* MGM United.

Highwayman, The. Philip Friend & Wanda Hendrix. Directed by Lesley Selander. 1951. Allied Artists. 84 min. Sound. 16mm Color. *Rental:* Ivy Films. *Sale:* Rep Pic Film.

Highways by Night. Richard Carlson & Jane Randolph. Directed by Peter Godfrey. 1942. RKO. 63 min. Sound. 16mm B&W. *Rental:* Films Inc.

Hilary. 1980. 90 min. Sound. Videotape B&W. *Rental:* Iowa Films.

Hilda Crane. Jean Simmons & Guy Madison. Directed by Philip Dunne. 1956. Fox. (Anamorphic). 87 min. Sound. 16mm Color. *Rental:* Films Inc.

Hildur & the Magician. 1969. 70 min. Sound. 16mm B&W. *Rental:* Canyon Cinema.

Hill, The. Sean Connery & Harry Andrews. Directed by Sidney Lumet. 1965. MGM. 122 min. Sound. 16mm B&W. *Rental:* MGM United.

Hill Twenty-Four Doesn't Answer. Michael Wager & Edward Mulhare. Directed by Thorold Dickinson. 1955. Israel. 90 min. Sound. 16mm B&W. *Rental:* Films Inc.

Hillbillies in a Haunted House. Molly Bee & Joi Lansing. Directed by Jean Yarbrough. 1970. Woolner. 88 min. Sound. 16mm Color. *Rental:* Budget Films, Ivy Films & Video Comm.

Hills Have Eyes, The. Susan Lanier & Robert Houston. Directed by Wes Craven. 1977. New Line Cinema. 81 min. Sound. 16mm Color. *Rental:* New Line Cinema.

Hills of Home. Orig. Title: Master of Lassie. Edmund Gwenn & Janet Leigh. Directed by Fred M. Wilcox. 1948. MGM. 94 min. Sound. 16mm Color. *Rental:* MGM United.

Hills of Ireland. Directed by Harry Dugan. 1951. Ireland. (Documentary). 60 min. Sound. 16mm Color. *Rental:* Films Inc.

Hills of Kentucky. Rin Tin Tin. Directed by Howard Bretherton. 1927. Warner Brothers. 50 min. Silent. 16mm B&W. *Rental:* Film Classics. *Sale:* Film Classics. *Rental:* Film Classics, *Sale:* Film Classics, Silent 8mm version.

Hills of Oklahoma. Rex Allen. Directed by R. G. Springsteen. 1950. Republic. 67 min. Sound. 16mm B&W. *Rental:* Ivy Films. *Sale:* Rep Pic Film.

Hills of Old Wyoming. William Boyd. Directed by Nate Watt. 1937. Paramount. 60 min. Sound. 16mm B&W. *Lease:* Cinema Concepts. *Sale:* Morcraft Films, Super 8 sound version.

Hilter's Secret Weapon. 1976. 58 min. Sound. Videotape *Rental:* PBS Video. *Sale:* PBS Video.

Hindenberg, The. George C. Scott & Anne Bancroft. Directed by Robert Wise. 1975. Universal. 125 min. Sound. 16mm Color. *Rental:* Swank Motion & Williams Films.

Hinduism. 3 pts. 1956. Indiana University. 90 min. Sound. 16mm B&W. *Rental:* Indiana AV Ctr & Syracuse U Film. *Sale:* Indiana AV Ctr.

Hinduism: 330 Million Gods. 1978. Britain. (Documentary). 52 min. Sound. 16mm Color. *Rental:* U Cal Media.

Hippie Temptation, The. 1968. CBS. (Documentary). 51 min. Sound. 16mm Color. *Rental:* U of IL Film, Iowa Films, Kit Parker, McGraw-Hill Films, U Mich Media & U Nev AV Ctr. *Sale:* McGraw-Hill Films.

Hips Hips Hooray. Bert Wheeler & Robert Woolsey. Directed by Mark Sandrich. 1934. RKO. 68 min. Sound. Super 8 B&W. *Rental:* Blackhawk Films & RKO General Pics. *Sale:* Blackhawk Films, Videotape version.

Hired Gun, The. Rory Calhoun & Anne Francis. Directed by Ray Nazarro. 1957. MGM. 64 min. Sound. 16mm B&W. *Rental:* MGM United. *Rental:* MGM United, Anamorphic B&W version.

Hired Hand, The. Peter Fonda & Warren Oates. Directed by Peter Fonda. 1971. Universal. 93 min. Sound. 16mm Color. *Rental:* Swank Motion & Twyman Films.

Hired Killer, The. Robert Webber & Franco Nero. Directed by Frank Shannon. 1967. Paramount. 94 min. Sound. 16mm Color. *Rental:* Films Inc.

Hireling, The. Robert Shaw, Sarah Miles & Peter Egan. Directed by Alan Bridges. 1973. Britain. 108 min. Sound. 16mm Color. *Rental:* Budget Films, Films Inc, Images Film, Kit Parker, Swank Motion & Welling Motion Pictures.

Hiroshima & Nagasaki: The Harvest of Nuclear War. 1982. Japan Foundation. (Documentary). 46 min. Sound. 16mm Color. *Rental:* U Cal Media.

Hiroshima, Mon Amour. Emmanuelle Riva & Eiji Okada. Directed by Alain Resnais. Fr. 1959. France. 88 min. Sound. 16mm B&W. subtitles. *Rental:* Budget Films, Films Inc, Images Film, Kit Parker, Natl Cinema, Natl Film Video, Reel Images & Utah Media. *Sale:* Festival Films. *Sale:* Festival Films & Tamarelles French Film, Videotape version.

His Brother's Ghost. Buster Crabbe. Directed by Sam Newfield. 1946. PRC. 56 min. Sound. 16mm B&W. *Rental:* Ivy Films, Mogulls Films, Rep Pic Film & Westcoast Films. *Sale:* Cinema Concepts, Classics Assoc NY, Natl Cinema & Rep Pic Film.

His Brother's Wife. Robert Taylor & Barbara Stanwyck. Directed by W. S. Van Dyke II. 1936. MGM. 90 min. Sound. 16mm B&W. *Rental:* MGM United.

His Butler's Sister. Deanna Durbin & Pat O'Brien. Directed by Frank Borzage. 1943. Universal. 87 min. Sound. 16mm B&W. *Rental:* Swank Motion.

His Destiny. Directed by Neal Hart. 1928. Canada. (Cast unlisted). 72 min. Silent. 16mm B&W. *Rental:* Museum Mod Art. *Lease:* Museum Mod Art.

His Family Tree. James Barton & Maureen Delaney. Directed by Charles Vidor. 1936. RKO. 68 min. Sound. 16mm *Rental:* RKO General Pics.

His Girl Friday. Cary Grant & Rosalind Russell. Directed by Howard Hawks. 1940. Columbia. 92 min. Sound. Videotape B&W. *Sale:* Tamarelles French Film.

His Greatest Gamble. Richard Dix & Dorothy Wilson. Directed by Pandro S. Berman. 1934. RKO. 70 min. 16mm *Rental:* RKO General Pics.

His Kind of Woman. Robert Mitchum & Jane Russell. Directed by John Farrow. 1951. RKO. 120 min. Sound. 16mm B&W. *Rental:* Films Inc.

His Lordship Goes to Press. June Clyde & Hugh Winters. Directed by Maclean Rogers. 1938. Britain. 67 min. Sound. 16mm B&W. *Rental:* Ivy Films.

His Lordship Regrets. Claude Hulbert. Directed by Maclean Rogers. 1938. Britain. 65 min. Sound. 16mm B&W. *Rental:* Ivy Films. *Sale:* Classics Assoc NY & Rep Pic Film.

His Majesty O'Keefe. Burt Lancaster & Joan Rice. Directed by Byron Haskin. 1953. Warners. 88 min. Sound. 16mm Color. *Rental:* Films Inc, Swank Motion, Twyman Films & Williams Films.

His Majesty, the American. Douglas Fairbanks & Marjorie Daw. Directed by Joseph Henabery. 1919. Douglas Fairbanks Pictures. 114 min. Silent. 16mm B&W. *Rental:* A Twyman Pres & Museum Mod Art.

His Majesty, the Scarecrow of Oz. Orig. Title: New Wizard of Oz, The. Frank Moore & Mildred Harris. Directed by L. Frank Baum. 1914. Oz. 50 min. Silent. 16mm B&W. *Rental:* Em Gee Film Lib. *Sale:* Cinema Concepts & Glenn Photo. *Rental:* Ivy Films, *Sale:* Glenn Photo, Super 8 silent version. *Sale:* Glenn Photo, Silent 8mm version.

His Picture in the Papers. Douglas Fairbanks. Directed by John Emerson. 1916. Fine Arts-Triangle. 60 min. Silent. 16mm B&W. *Rental:* Em Gee Film Lib & Film Images. *Sale:* Blackhawk Films. *Rental:* Ivy Films, *Sale:* Blackhawk Films, Super 8 silent version. *Sale:* Blackhawk Films, Silent 8mm version.

His Private Secretary. John Wayne. Directed by Philip H. Whitman. 1933. Showman's. 60 min. Sound. 16mm B&W. *Rental:* Video Comm. *Rental:* Video Comm, Videotape version.

His Worship, Mr. Montreal. Directed by Donald Brittain, M. Canell & Albert Duncan. 1976. Canada. (Documentary). 58 min. Sound. 16mm Color. *Rental:* Natl Film CN. *Sale:* Natl Film CN. *Sale:* Natl Film CN, Videotape version.

Historia de una Escalera. Span. 1950. Mexico. (Cast unlisted). 90 min. Sound. 16mm B&W. subtitles. *Rental:* Film Classics.

Historical Relics Unearthed in New China. 1976. China. (Documentary). 60 min. Sound. 16mm Color. *Rental:* Grove. *Sale:* Grove.

History & Culture. 1964. Canada. (Documentary). 56 min. Sound. 16mm B&W. *Rental:* OK AV Ctr. *Sale:* McGraw-Hill Films.

History Is Made at Night. Charles Boyer & Jean Arthur. Directed by Frank Borzage. 1937. United Artists. 97 min. Sound. 16mm B&W. *Rental:* Buchan Pic, Budget Films, Inst Cinema, Kit Parker, Learning Corp Am, Mogulls Films, Twyman Films & U of IL Film. *Sale:* Glenn Photo & Learning Corp Am. *Lease:* Films Inc. *Sale:* Glenn Photo, Super 8 sound version.

History Lessons. Gottfried Bold. Directed by Jean-Marie Straub. Ger. 1973. Germany. 85 min. Sound. 16mm Color. subtitles. *Rental:* New Yorker Films.

History of Mr. Polly, The. John Mills & Sally Ann Howes. Directed by Anthony Pelissier. 1949. Britain. 96 min. Sound. 16mm B&W. *Rental:* Budget Films & Kit Parker.

History of the Blue Movie, A. 1972. Thunderbird. (Anthology, color sequences). 120 min. Sound. 16mm B&W. *Sale:* Morcraft Films. *Sale:* Morcraft Films, Super 8 sound version. *Sale:* Morcraft Films, Videotape version.

History of the Korean War, The. 1958. Navy. (Documentary). 58 min. Sound. 16mm B&W. *Rental:* Natl AV Ctr.

History of the Negro in America, The. 3 pts. 1965. Niagara. (Documentary). 68 min. Sound. 16mm B&W. *Rental:* McGraw-Hill Films & Syracuse U Film. *Sale:* McGraw-Hill Films.

History of the U. S. Navy, The: Born of the Sea. 1977. 54 min. Sound. 16mm Color. *Rental:* OK AV Ctr.

History of the World, The: Part 1. Mel Brooks & Dom DeLuise. Directed by Mel Brooks. 1981. United Artists. 93 min. Sound. 16mm Color. *Rental:* MGM United.

History of U. S. Foreign Relations, A: A Series (4 pts.). 1972. US Government. (Documentary). 119 min. Sound. 16mm Color. *Sale:* Natl AV Ctr. *Rental:* Natl AV Ctr.

Hit! Billy Dee Williams & Richard Pryor. Directed by Sidney J. Furie. 1973. Paramount. (Anamorphic). 134 min. Sound. 16mm Color. *Rental:* Films Inc.

Hit & Run. Hugo Haas, Cleo Moore & Vincent Edwards. Directed by Hugo Haas. 1957. United Artists. 85 min. Sound. 16mm B&W. *Rental:* MGM United.

Hit & Run. Hoot Gibson. Directed by Edward Sedgwick. 1924. Universal. 45 min. Silent. 16mm B&W. *Rental:* Film Classics. *Sale:* Film Classics. *Rental:* Film Classics, *Sale:* Film Classics, Silent 8mm version.

Hit Man, The. Bernie Casey & Pamela Grier. Directed by George Armitage. 1972. MGM. 90 min. Sound. 16mm Color. *Rental:* Films Inc & MGM United.

Hit Man, The: Il Sicario. Belinda Lee & Alberto Lupo. Directed by Damiano Damiani. 1961. Italy. 100 min. 16mm B&W. dubbed. *Rental:* Cimena Guild.

Hit the Deck. Jane Powell & Tony Martin. Directed by Roy Rowland. 1955. MGM. 112 min. Sound. 16mm Color. *Rental:* MGM United. *Rental:* MGM United, Anamorphic color version.

Hit the Hay. Judy Canova. Directed by Del Lord. 1945. Columbia. 70 min. Sound. 16mm B&W. *Rental:* Kit Parker.

Hit the Ice. Bud Abbott & Lou Costello. Directed by Charles Lamont. 1943. Universal. 80 min. Sound. 16mm B&W. *Rental:* Swank Motion.

Hit the Road. Barton McLane & Gladys George. Directed by Joe May. 1941. Universal. 61 min. Sound. 16mm B&W. *Rental:* Mogulls Films & Swank Motion.

Hit the Saddle. Robert Livingston. Directed by Mack V. Wright. 1937. Republic. 54 min. Sound. 16mm B&W. *Rental:* Ivy Films. *Sale:* Rep Pic Film.

Hitch-Hike Lady. Orig. Title: Eventful Journey. Arthur Treacher & James Ellison. Directed by Aubrey Scotto. 1936. Republic. 54 min. Sound. 16mm B&W. *Rental:* Ivy Films. *Sale:* Rep Pic Film.

Hitch-Hike to Happiness. Brad Taylor & William Frawley. Directed by Joseph Santley. 1945. Republic. 74 min. Sound. 16mm B&W. *Rental:* Ivy Films. *Sale:* Rep Pic Film.

Hitch-Hike to Hell. Russell Johnson, Robert Robert & John Harmon. 88 min. Sound. 16mm Color. *Rental:* BF Video.

Hitch: Portrait of a Black Leader. Al Fann. Directed by Irving Jacoby. 1972. Mental Health Film Board. 90 min. Sound. 16mm Color. *Rental:* Intl Film, Syracuse U Film, Twyman Films & U Cal Media. *Sale:* Intl Film.

Hitler. Richard Basehart. Directed by Stuart Heisler. 1962. Allied Artists. 103 min. Sound. 16mm B&W. *Rental:* Hurlock Cine.

Hitler. 2 Pts. 1968. McGraw-Hill. (Documentary). 52 min. Sound. 16mm B&W. *Rental:* McGraw-Hill Films, OK AV Ctr, SD AV Ctr, Syracuse U Film & U Cal Media. *Sale:* McGraw-Hill Films.

Hitler, Dead or Alive. Ward Bond & Dorothy Tree. Directed by Nick Grinde. 1943. Judell. 64 min. Sound. 16mm B&W. *Rental:* Ivy Films & Mogulls Films. *Sale:* Classics Assoc NY & Rep Pic Film.

Hitler: The Last Ten Days. Sir Alec Guinness & Simon Ward. Directed by Ennio De Concini. 1973. Paramount. 106 min. Sound. 16mm Color. *Rental:* Films Inc.

Hitlerjunge Quex. Heinrich George. Directed by Hans Steinhoff. Ger. 1933. Germany. 102 min. Sound. 16mm B&W. subtitles. *Rental:* Museum Mod Art.

Hitler's Children. Tim Holt & Bonita Granville. Directed by Edward Dmytryk. 1943. RKO. 83 min. Sound. 16mm B&W. *Rental:* Films Inc.

Hitler's Executioners. Orig. Title: Nuremberg Trial, The. 1958. Germany. (Documentary). 78 min. Sound. 16mm B&W. narrated Eng. *Rental:* Films Inc.

Hitler's Germany. 1974. Media Guild. (Documentary). 156 min. Sound. 16mm Color. *Sale:* Media Guild.

Hitler's Henchmen. 60 min. Sound. Videotape B&W. *Rental:* Maljack.

Hitler's Madman. Patricia Morrison & John Carradine. Directed by Douglas Sirk. 1943. MGM. 84 min. Sound. 16mm B&W. *Rental:* MGM United.

Hittin' the Trail. Tex Ritter. Directed by Robert N. Bradbury. 1961. Grand National. 100 min. Sound. 16mm B&W. *Sale:* Cinema Concepts, Natl Cinema & Reel Images.

Hitting a New High. Lily Pons & Jack Oakie. Directed by Raoul Walsh. 1938. RKO. 85 min. Sound. 16mm *Rental:* RKO General Pics.

Hizzoner the Mayor. 1963. Hearst. (Documentary). 50 min. Sound. 16mm B&W. *Rental:* King Features.

Hobbit, The. Directed by Arthur Rankin & Jules Bass. 1977. Rankin-Bass. 78 min. Sound. 16mm Color. *Rental:* Budget Films, Films Inc, Roas Films & Xerox Films. *Sale:* Xerox Films.

Hobson's Choice. Charles Laughton & John Mills. Directed by David Lean. 1954. Britain. 107 min. Sound. 16mm B&W. *Rental:* Janus Films.

Hocus Pocus, It's Magic. Dick Cavett. HBO. 83 min. Videotape Color. *Rental:* Films Inc.

Hog Wild. Michael Biehn & Patti D'Urbanville. Directed by Les Rose. 1980. Embassy. 97 min. Sound. 16mm Color. *Rental:* Films Inc.

Hohenzollerns, The. Directed by Victor Vicas. 1972. AIF. (Documentary). 60 min. Sound. 16mm B&W. *Sale:* Americas Films. *Sale:* Americas Films, Color version. *Sale:* Americas Films, Spanish version.

Hold Back the Dawn. Charles Boyer & Olivia De Havilland. Directed by Mitchell Leisen. 1941. Paramount. 115 min. Sound. 16mm B&W. *Rental:* Swank Motion.

Hold Back the Night. John Payne & Mona Freeman. Directed by Allan Dwan. 1956. Republic. 80 min. Sound. 16mm B&W. *Rental:* Ivy Films. *Sale:* Rep Pic Film.

Hold 'em Jail. Betty Grable & Bert Wheeler. Directed by Norman Taurog. 1933. RKO. 75 min. Sound. 16mm *Rental:* RKO General Pics.

Hold On. Peter Noone. Directed by Arthur Lubin. 1966. MGM. 85 min. Sound. 16mm Color. *Rental:* MGM United.

Hold That Co-ed. John Barrymore & George Murphy. Directed by George Marshall. 1938. Fox. 80 min. Sound. 16mm Color. *Rental:* Films Inc.

Hold That Ghost. Bud Abbott & Lou Costello. Directed by Arthur Lubin. 1941. Universal. 80 min. Sound. 16mm B&W. *Rental:* Williams Films.

Hold That Line. Bowery Boys. Directed by William Beaudine. 1952. Monogram. 64 min. Sound. 16mm B&W. *Rental:* Film Ctr DC & Modern Sound.

Hold That Woman. James Dunn & Frances Gifford. Directed by Sherman Scott. 1940. PRC. 70 min. Sound. 16mm B&W. *Rental:* Budget Films.

Hold Your Man. Jean Harlow & Clark Gable. Directed by Sam Wood. 1933. MGM. 89 min. Sound. 16mm B&W. *Rental:* MGM United.

Holding. 1973. Robert Francis Logan. (Documentary, color sequences). 50 min. Sound. 16mm B&W. *Rental:* Threshold Films. *Sale:* Threshold Films.

Holes, The. Philippe Noiret. 1975. France. 90 min. Videotape Color. dubbed. *Sale:* Cinema Concepts.

Holiday. Ann Harding & Mary Astor. Directed by Edward H. Griffith. 1930. Columbia. 90 min. Sound. 16mm B&W. *Rental:* Kit Parker.

Holiday. Katharine Hepburn & Cary Grant. Directed by George Cukor. 1938. Columbia. 93 min. Sound. 16mm B&W. *Rental:* Arcus Film, Bosco Films, Budget Films, Cine Craft, Films Inc, Images Film, Ivy Films, Kit Parker, Modern Sound, Natl Film Video, Swank Motion, Twyman Films, Welling Motion Pictures, Westcoast Films & Wholesome Film Ctr. *Sale:* Cinema Concepts, Super 8 sound version.

Holiday Affair. Robert Mitchum & Janet Leigh. Directed by Don Hartman. 1949. RKO. 87 min. Sound. 16mm B&W. *Rental:* Films Inc.

Holiday for Lovers. Clifton Webb & Jane Wyman. Directed by Henry Levin. 1959. Fox. (Anamorphic). 103 min. Sound. 16mm Color. *Rental:* Films Inc.

Holiday for Sinners. Gig Young & Janice Rule. Directed by Gerald Mayer. 1952. MGM. 72 min. Sound. 16mm B&W. *Rental:* Films Inc & MGM United.

Holiday in Havana. Desi Arnaz, Mary Hatcher & Ann Doran. Directed by Jean Yarbrough. 1949. Columbia. 73 min. Sound. 16mm B&W. *Rental:* Kit Parker.

Holiday Rhythm. Mary Beth Hughes & David Street. Directed by Jack Scholl. 1950. Lippert. 60 min. Sound. 16mm B&W. *Rental:* Mogulls Films.

Holidays: Hollow Days. 1973. NPACT. 59 min. Sound. 16mm B&W. *Rental:* U Cal Media.

Holland Against the Sea. 1970. National Geographic. 51 min. Sound. 16mm Color. *Rental:* Iowa Films, Natl Geog, Syracuse U Film & Wholesome Film Ctr. *Sale:* Natl Geog. *Sale:* Natl Geog, Videotape version.

Hollow, The. Directed by George T. Nierenberg. 1975. Nierenberg. (Documentary). 64 min. Sound. 16mm Color. *Rental:* Phoenix Films. *Sale:* Phoenix Films. *Sale:* Phoenix Films, Videotape version.

Hollow Triumph: The Scar. Paul Henreid & Joan Bennett. Directed by Steve Sekely. 1948. Eagle Lion. 86 min. Sound. 16mm *Rental:* Budget Films.

Hollywood & Vine. Orig. Title: Daisy Goes Hollywood. James Ellison & Wanda McKay. Directed by Alexis Thurn-Taxis. 1945. PRC. 60 min. Sound. 16mm B&W. *Rental:* Ivy Films & Mogulls Films. *Sale:* Classics Assoc NY.

Hollywood Boulevard. Candace Rialson & Mary Woronov. Directed by Allan Arkush & Joe Dante. 1976. New World. 83 min. Sound. 16mm Color. *Rental:* Films Inc.

Hollywood Canteen. Bette Davis & Jack Carson. Directed by Delmer Daves. 1944. Warners. 123 min. Sound. 16mm B&W. *Rental:* MGM United.

Hollywood Cavalcade. Alice Faye & Don Ameche. Directed by Irving Cummings. 1939. Fox. 96 min. Sound. 16mm Color. *Rental:* Films Inc.

Hollywood Cowboy *see* Hearts of the West.

Hollywood Cowboy *see* Wings Over Wyoming.

Hollywood Hoodlum *see* Hollywood Mystery.

Hollywood Hotel. Dick Powell, Lola Lane & Rosemary Lane. Directed by Busby Berkeley. 1937. Warners. 109 min. Sound. 16mm B&W. *Rental:* MGM United.

Hollywood Knights, The. Tony Danza. Directed by Floyd Mutrux. 1980. Columbia. 95 min. Sound. 16mm Color. *Rental:* Swank Motion. *Rental:* Swank Motion, Videotape version.

Hollywood Memory Book. Film Classic Exchange. (Anthology, musical score only). 57 min. Sound. 16mm B&W. narrated. *Rental:* Film Classics. *Rental:* Film Classics, Videotape version.

Hollywood, My Home Town. Directed by Ken Murray. 1950. 55 min. Sound. 16mm *Rental:* Budget Films.

Hollywood Mystery. Orig. Title: Hollywood Hoodlum. June Clyde & Frank Albertson. 1934. Regal. 76 min. Sound. 16mm B&W. *Rental:* Mogulls Films & Video Comm.

Hollywood on Trial. Directed by David Helpern Jr. 1977. PBS. (Documentary, color squences). 100 min. Sound. 16mm B&W Color. *Rental:* Corinth Films & Images Film. *Rental:* Corinth Films, Videotape version.

Hollywood or Bust. Dean Martin & Jerry Lewis. Directed by Frank Tashlin. 1956. Paramount. 95 min. Sound. 16mm Color. *Rental:* Films Inc.

Hollywood Out-Takes & Rare Footage. 1983. USA. 83 min. Sound. 16mm B&W. *Rental:* Kino Intl. *Lease:* Kino Intl.

Hollywood Party. Jimmy Durante, Lupe Velez, Stan Laurel & Oliver Hardy. Directed by Allan Dwan. 1934. MGM. 70 min. 16mm B&W. *Rental:* MGM United.

Hollywood Revue of 1929. Marion Davies, John Gilbert & Norma Shearer. Directed by Charles Reisner. 1929. MGM. (Color sequences). 113 min. Sound. 16mm B&W. *Rental:* MGM United.

Hollywood Stadium Mystery, The. Neil Hamilton & Lynn Roberts. Directed by David Howard. 1938. Republic. 54 min. Sound. 16mm B&W. *Rental:* Ivy Films. *Sale:* Rep Pic Film.

Hollywood: The Dream Factory. 1972. Ronox. (Documentary). 52 min. Sound. 16mm Color. *Rental:* Kent St U Film, MGM United, Syracuse U Film & Texture Film. *Sale:* Films Inc & Texture Film, Videotape version.

Hollywood: The Golden Years. 1964. Wolper. (Documentary). 55 min. Sound. 16mm B&W. *Rental:* Budget Films, Kit Parker & Westcoast Films.

Hollywood: The Selznick Years. 1970. Selznick. (Documentary). 53 min. Sound. 16mm Color. *Rental:* Films Inc, Kent St U Film & Texture Film. *Sale:* Texture Film.

Hollywood Varieties. Robert Alda & Peggy Stewart. Directed by Paul Landres. 1950. Lippert. 60 min. Sound. 16mm B&W. *Rental:* Mogulls Films.

Hollywood Without Makeup. 1965. Filmaster. (Documentary). 52 min. Sound. 16mm Color. *Rental:* Budget Films. *Sale:* Cinema Concepts.

Hollywood: You Must Remember This. 1972. NET. (Documentary). 80 min. Sound. 16mm B&W. *Rental:* MGM United.

Hollywood's Musical Moods. Directed by Christian Blackwood. 1973. Blackwood. (Documentary). 52 min. Sound. 16mm Color. *Rental:* Blackwood Films. *Sale:* Blackwood Films.

Holocaust, The. Directed by Dick Moder. 1968. 52 min. Sound. 16mm Color. *Rental:* Budget Films.

Holocaust: The Final Solution. Pt. 3. Michael Moriarty & Rosemary Harris. Directed by Marvin J. Chomsky. 1978. Titus. 94 min. Sound. 16mm Color. *Rental:* Films Inc, Learning Corp Am, Modern Sound, Twyman Films, U of IL Film, Welling Motion Pictures & Westcoast Films. *Lease:* Learning Corp Am. *Lease:* Learning Corp Am, Videotape version.

Holocaust: The Gathering Darkness. Pt. 1. Michael Moriarty & Rosemary Harris. Directed by Marvin J. Chomsky. 1978. Titus. 144 min. Sound. 16mm Color. *Rental:* Films Inc, Learning Corp Am, Modern Sound, Twyman Films, U of IL Film, Welling Motion Pictures & Westcoast Films. *Lease:* Learning Corp Am. *Lease:* Learning Corp Am, Videotape version.

Holocaust: The Road to Babi Yar. Pt. 2. Michael Moriarty & Rosemary Harris. Directed by Marvin J. Chomsky. 1978. Titus. 99 min. Sound. 16mm Color. *Rental:* Films Inc, Learning Corp Am, Modern Sound, Twyman Films, U of IL Film, Westcoast Films & Welling Motion Pictures. *Lease:* Learning Corp Am. *Lease:* Learning Corp Am, Videotape version.

Holocaust: The Saving Remnant. Pt. 4. Michael Moriarty & Rosemary Harris. Directed by Marvin J. Chomsky. 1978. Titus. 116 min. Sound. 16mm Color. *Rental:* Films Inc, Learning Corp Am, Modern Sound, Twyman Films, U of IL Film, Welling Motion Pictures & Westcoast Films. *Lease:* Learning Corp Am. *Lease:* Learning Corp Am, Videotape version.

Holy Father. 1982. Britain. 50 min. Sound. 16mm Color. *Rental:* U Cal Media.

Holy Ghost People. 1967. Peter Adair. (Documentary). 53 min. Sound. 16mm B&W. *Rental:* Iowa Films, McGraw-Hill Films, NYU Film Lib, Syracuse U Film, U Cal Media & U Mich Media. *Sale:* McGraw-Hill Films.

Holy Land, The. 1977. CC Film. (Documentary). 60 min. Sound. 16mm Color. *Sale:* Natl Churches Christ.

Holy Matrimony. Monty Woolley & Gracie Fields. Directed by John M. Stahl. 1943. Fox. 65 min. Sound. 16mm B&W. *Rental:* Films Inc.

Holy Outlaw, The. Directed by Lee Lockwood & Don Lenzer. 1970. NET. (Documentary). 59 min. Sound. 16mm B&W. *Rental:* New Yorker Films.

Holy Year, The. Directed by Anthony Muto. 1950. 42 min. Sound. 16mm B&W. *Rental:* Films Inc.

Homage a Debussy. 1962. France. (Dance). 65 min. Sound. 16mm B&W. *Rental:* French Am Cul.

Homage to a Great Man. Britain. (Documentary). 49 min. Sound. 16mm B&W. *Rental:* Time-Life Multimedia. *Sale:* Time-Life Multimedia.

Homage to Chagall. Directed by Harry Rasky. 1977. Canada. (Documentary). 90 min. Sound. 16mm Color. *Rental:* Kino Intl. *Lease:* Kino Intl.

Homage to Verdi. Sherrill Milnes. 1975. Auteur. 52 min. Sound. 16mm Color. *Rental:* Auteur Films. *Sale:* Auteur Films.

Hombre. Paul Newman & Fredric March. Directed by Martin Ritt. 1967. Fox. 111 min. Sound. 16mm Color. *Rental:* Films Inc. *Rental:* Films Inc, Anamorphic color version.

Hombre de las Sorpresas, El. Span. 1950. Mexico. (Cast unlisted). 90 min. Sound. 16mm B&W. *Rental:* Film Classics.

Hombre del Alazan, El. Fernando Casanova & Martha Mizares. Span. 1959. Mexico. 98 min. Sound. 16mm B&W. *Rental:* Trans-World Films.

Home at Seven. Orig. Title: Case of Amnesia, A. Sir Ralph Richardson & Margaret Leighton. Directed by Sir Ralph Richardson. 1953. Britain. 85 min. Sound. 16mm B&W. *Rental:* Budget Films & Inst Cinema.

Home Country, USA. 1969. NBC. (Documentary). 53 min. Sound. 16mm Color. *Rental:* Films Inc. *Sale:* Film Inc. *Sale:* Films Inc, Videotape version.

Home Fires: Britain 1940-1941. Directed by Hugh Raggett. (World at War Ser.). : Pt. 15.). 1973. Media Guild. (Documentary). 52 min. Sound. 16mm Color. *Rental:* Media Guild. *Sale:* Media Guild. *Sale:* Media Guild, Videotape version.

Home for Life. Directed by Gerald Tamaner & Gordon Quinn. 1966. Drexel Home. (Documentary). 86 min. Sound. 16mm B&W. *Rental:* Films Inc & Northwest Film Lib. *Sale:* Films Inc. *Rental:* Films Inc, *Sale:* Films Inc, Condensed 58 min version. *Sale:* Films Inc, Videotape version.

Home from the Hill. Robert Mitchum, Eleanor Parker & George Peppard. Directed by Vincente Minnelli. 1960. MGM. 150 min. Sound. 16mm Color. *Rental:* MGM United. *Rental:* MGM United, Anamorphic version.

Home in Indiana. Jeanne Crain & June Haver. Directed by Henry Hathaway. 1944. Fox. 103 min. Sound. 16mm Color. *Rental:* Films Inc.

Home in Oklahoma. Roy Rogers. Directed by William Witney. 1946. Republic. 54 min. Sound. 16mm B&W. *Rental:* Ivy Films. *Sale:* Rep Pic Film, Reel Images & Nostalgia Merchant.

Home in San Antone. Orig. Title: Harmony Inn. Roy Acuff & Jacqueline Thomas. Directed by Ray Nazarro. 1949. Columbia. 62 min. Sound. 16mm B&W. *Rental:* Budget Films.

Home in Wyoming. Gene Autry. Directed by William Witney. 1942. Republic. 54 min. Sound. 16mm B&W. *Rental:* Ivy Films.

Home is the Hero. Arthur Kennedy. Directed by Fielder Cook. 1959. 83 min. 16mm *Rental:* A Twyman Pres.

Home Movies. Nancy Allen, Kirk Douglas & Vincent Gardenia. Directed by Brian De Palma. 1980. United Artists. 90 min. Sound. 16mm Color. *Rental:* MGM United.

Home of the Brave. Lloyd Bridges & Frank Lovejoy. Directed by Mark Robson. 1949. United Artists. 88 min. Sound. 16mm B&W. *Rental:* Budget Films, Charard Motion Pics, Film Classics, Film Ctr DC, Films Inc, Ivy Films, Kit Parker, Film Ctr DC, Video Comm, Westcoast Films, Wholesome Film Ctr & Willoughby Peer. *Sale:* Natl Film Serv.

Home on the Prairie. Gene Autry. Directed by William Morgan. 1939. Republic. 54 min. Sound. 16mm B&W. *Rental:* Ivy Films.

Home on the Range. Monte Hale. Directed by Jack Townley. 1946. Republic. 55 min. Sound. 16mm B&W. *Rental:* Ivy Films. *Sale:* Rep Pic Film. *Sale:* Nostalgia Merchant, Color version.

Home Run for Love, A. 1978. ABC. (Cast unlisted). 47 min. Sound. 16mm Color. *Rental:* Time-Life Multimedia. *Sale:* Time-Life Multimedia. *Sale:* Time-Life Multimedia, Videotape version.

Home Stretch, The. Douglas MacLean & Margaret Livingston. Directed by Jack Nelson. 1921. Paramount. (Musical score only). 55 min. Sound. 16mm B&W. *Sale:* Blackhawk Films. *Rental:* Ivy Films, *Sale:* Blackhawk Films, Super 8 silent version. *Sale:* Blackhawk Films, Silent 8mm version.

Home Sweet Home. Lillian Gish, Dorothy Gish, Henry B. Walthall & Mae Marsh. Directed by D. W. Griffith. 1914. Mutual. 64 min. Silent. 16mm B&W. *Rental:* Museum Mod Art. *Sale:* Glenn Photo & Reel Images. *Sale:* Glenn Photo & Reel Images, Super 8 silent version.

Home Sweet Homicide. Peggy Ann Garner & Randolph Scott. Directed by Lloyd Bacon. 1946. Fox. 90 min. Sound. 16mm B&W. *Rental:* Films Inc.

Home to Stay. Henry Fonda. Directed by Delbert Mann. 1978. ABC. 47 min. Sound. 16mm Color. *Rental:* Kent St U Film, U Mich Media & U of IL Film.

Homebodies. Frances Fuller & Peter Brocco. Directed by Larry Yust. 1974. Embassy. 96 min. Sound. 16mm Color. *Rental:* Films Inc.

Homeboys. Directed by Christine Burrill, David Davis & Bill Yahraus. 1978. Unifilm. (Documentary). 60 min. Sound. 16mm Color. *Rental:* Cinema Guild. *Sale:* Cinema Guild.

Homecoming. Trans. Title: Heimkehr. Lars Hanson & Dita Parlo. Directed by Joe May. 1928. Germany. 74 min. Silent. 16mm B&W. *Rental:* Film Images & Kit Parker. *Sale:* Cinema Concepts & Reel Images. *Sale:* Tamarelles French Film, Videotape version.

Homecoming. Cyril Cusack & Michael Jayston. Directed by Peter Hall. 1973. AFT. 111 min. Sound. 16mm Color. *Rental:* Films Inc.

Homer Comes Home. Charles Ray & Priscilla Bonner. Directed by Jerome Storm. 1920. Paramount. 60 min. Silent. 16mm B&W. *Sale:* Blackhawk Films. *Rental:* Ivy Films, *Sale:* Blackhawk Films, Super 8 silent version. *Sale:* Blackhawk Films, Silent 8mm version.

Homer's Odyssey. 1912. Italy. (Cast unlisted). 50 min. Silent. 16mm B&W. *Rental:* Film Classics. *Sale:* Film Classics. *Sale:* Film Classics, Silent 8mm version. *Rental:* Film Classics, Videotape version.

Homesteaders, The. William Elliott & Robert Lowery. Directed by Lewis D. Collins. 1953. Allied Artists. 62 min. Sound. 16mm B&W. *Rental:* Hurlock Cine.

Homesteaders of Paradise Valley. Allan Lane & Robert Blake. Directed by R. G. Springsteen. 1947. Republic. 54 min. Sound. 16mm B&W. *Rental:* Ivy Films & Rep Pic Film. *Sale:* Cinema Concepts, Rep Pic Film & Reel Images.

Homicidal. Jean Arless & Glenn Corbett. Directed by William Castle. 1961. Columbia. 87 min. Sound. 16mm B&W. *Rental:* Bosco Films, Charard Motion Pics, Modern Sound & Williams Films.

Homicide. Robert Douglas & Robert Alda. Directed by Felix Jacoves. 1949. Warners. 77 min. Sound. 16mm B&W. *Rental:* MGM United.

Homicide for Three. Orig. Title: Interrupted Honeymoon, An. Audrey Long & Warren Douglas. Directed by George Blair. 1948. Republic. 60 min. Sound. 16mm B&W. *Rental:* Ivy Films. *Sale:* Rep Pic Film.

Hommage to Nicanor Parra. 44 min. Sound. 16mm Color. *Rental:* Filmmakers Coop.

Homme Au Chapeau Noir, L'. George Descrieres. Directed by Jean-Pierre Desagnat. Fr. 1971. France. 55 min. Sound. 16mm Color. subtitles. *Rental:* French Am Cul.

Homme de Trop, Un *see* Shock Troops.

Homme Qui Dort, Un. Jacques Spiesser. Directed by George Perec & Bernard Queysanne. France. 75 min. Sound. 16mm B&W. *Rental:* French Am Cul.

Homme Sans Visage, L' *see* Man Without a Face.

Homo Varsoviensis. Directed by Roman Wionczek. Pol. 1960. Poland. (Documentary). 48 min. Sound. 16mm B&W. narrated Eng. *Rental:* Polish People.

Homosexuality in Men & Women. 1966. NET. (Documentary). 60 min. Sound. 16mm B&W. *Rental:* U Cal Media.

Homosexuals, The. 1967. CBS. (Documentary). 48 min. Sound. 16mm B&W. *Rental:* Iowa Films & Mass Media. *Sale:* Carousel Films.

Honey. Nancy Carroll & Lillian Roth. Directed by Wesley Ruggles. 1930. Paramount. 75 min. Sound. 16mm B&W. *Rental:* Swank Motion.

Honey Pot, The. Orig. Title: It Comes Up Murder. Rex Harrison & Susan Hayward. Directed by Joseph L. Mankiewicz. 1967. United Artists. 131 min. Sound. 16mm Color. *Rental:* MGM United.

Honeychile. Judy Canova & Eddie Foy Jr. Directed by R. G. Springsteen. 1951. Republic. 89 min. Sound. 16mm Color. *Rental:* Ivy Films. *Sale:* Rep Pic Film.

Honeymoon. Orig. Title: Two Men & a Girl. Shirley Temple & Franchot Tone. Directed by William Keighley. 1947. RKO. 74 min. Sound. 16mm B&W. *Rental:* Films Inc.

Honeymoon Ahead. Allan Jones & Grace McDonald. Directed by Reginald Le Borg. 1945. Universal. 70 min. Sound. 16mm B&W. *Rental:* Mogulls Films.

Honeymoon Hotel. Robert Goulet & Robert Morse. Directed by Henry Levin. 1964. MGM. (Anamorphic). 89 min. Sound. 16mm Color. *Rental:* Films Inc & MGM United.

Honeymoon Killers, The. Tony Lo Bianco & Shirley Stoller. Directed by Leonard Kastle. 1970. Cinerama. 107 min. Sound. 16mm B&W. *Rental:* A Cantor. *Sale:* A Cantor.

Honeymoon Lodge. Ozzie Nelson & Harriet Hilliard. Directed by Edward Lilley. 1943. Universal. 60 min. Sound. 16mm B&W. *Rental:* Film Ctr DC & Mogulls Films.

Honeymoon Machine, The. Steve McQueen & Jim Hutton. Directed by Richard Thorpe. 1961. MGM. 87 min. Sound. 16mm Color. *Rental:* Films Inc & MGM United. *Rental:* Films Inc, Anamorphic color version.

Honeysuckle Rose. Willie Nelson, Dyan Cannon & Amy Irving. Directed by Jerry Schatzberg. 1980. Warners. 119 min. Sound. 16mm Color. *Rental:* Swank Motion. *Rental:* Swank Motion, Videotape version.

Hong Kong. Ronald Reagan & Rhonda Fleming. Directed by Lewis R. Foster. 1951. Paramount. 91 min. Sound. 16mm B&W. *Rental:* Budget Films, Video Comm & Willoughby Peer.

Hong Kong: A Family Portrait. 1978. National Geographic. (Documentary). 59 min. Sound. 16mm Color. *Rental:* Natl Geog. *Sale:* Natl Geog. *Sale:* Natl Geog, Videotape version.

Hong Kong Affair. Jack Kelly & May Wynn. Directed by Paul Heard. 1958. Allied Artists. 73 min. Sound. 16mm B&W. *Rental:* Hurlock Cine.

Hong Kong Cat, The. Cheung Nick. Directed by Kong Hung. 1973. Hong Kong. 90 min. Sound. 16mm Color. dubbed. *Rental:* Swank Motion.

Honkers, The. James Coburn & Lois Nettleton. Directed by Steve Ihnat. 1972. United Artists. 103 min. Sound. 16mm Color. *Rental:* MGM United.

Honky Tonk. Lana Turner & Clark Gable. Directed by Jack Conway. 1941. MGM. 105 min. Sound. 16mm B&W. *Rental:* MGM United.

Honky Tonk Freeway. William Devane & Beverly D'Angelo. Directed by John Schlesinger. 1981. Universal. 107 min. Sound. 16mm Color. *Rental:* Swank Motion.

Honkytonk Man. Clint Eastwood, Kyle Eastwood & John McIntire. Directed by Clint Eastwood. 122 min. Sound. 16mm Color. *Rental:* Swank Motion. *Rental:* Swank Motion, Videotape version.

Honolulu Lu. Lupe Velez & Leo Carillo. Directed by Charles Barton. 1941. Columbia. 72 min. Sound. 16mm B&W. *Rental:* Films Inc.

Honor on the Range. Ken Maynard & Fred Kohler. Directed by Alan James. 1934. Universal. 61 min. Sound. 16mm B&W. *Rental:* Swank Motion.

Honorable Sam Houston, The. Charles Aidman, Lynn Carlin & Robert Stack. Directed by Richard T. Heffron. 1974. Daniel Wilson. 53 min. Sound. 16mm Color. *Rental:* Films Inc, Syracuse U Film & U of IL Film. *Sale:* Films Inc.

Hooded Terror, The. Tod Slaughter. Directed by George King. 1938. Britain. 70 min. Sound. 16mm B&W. *Rental:* Budget Films.

Hoodlum Empire, The. Brian Donlevy & Claire Trevor. Directed by Bob Considine. 1951. Republic. 98 min. Sound. 16mm B&W. *Rental:* Ivy Films. *Sale:* Rep Pic Film.

Hoodlum Priest, The. Don Murray & Keir Dullea. Directed by Irwin Kershner. 1961. United Artists. 101 min. Sound. 16mm B&W. *Rental:* MGM United.

Hoodlum Saint, The. William Powell & Esther Williams. Directed by Norman Taurog. 1946. MGM. 91 min. Sound. 16mm B&W. *Rental:* MGM United.

Hoodlum Soldier, The. Shintaro Katsu & Takahiro Tamura. Directed by Yasuzo Masumura. Jap. 1965. Japan. 103 min. Sound. 16mm B&W. subtitles. *Rental:* Films Inc.

Hoodoo Ann. Mae Marsh & Robert Harron. 1916. Fine Arts-Triangle. 65 min. Silent. 16mm B&W. *Rental:* Em Gee Film Lib. *Sale:* Blackhawk Films & Cinema Five. *Rental:* Ivy Films, *Sale:* Blackhawk Films, Super 8 silent version. *Sale:* Blackhawk Films, Silent 8mm version.

Hook, The. Kirk Douglas & Robert Walker. Directed by George Seaton. 1963. MGM. (Anamorphic). 98 min. Sound. 16mm B&W. *Rental:* MGM United.

Hook, Line & Sinker. Bert Wheeler & Robert Woolsey. Directed by Edward Cline. 1930. RKO. 71 min. Sound. 16mm B&W. *Rental:* Films Inc.

Hook, Line & Sinker. Jerry Lewis, Anne Francis & Peter Lawford. Directed by George Marshall. 1969. Columbia. 91 min. Sound. 16mm Color. *Rental:* Arcus Film, Buchan Pic, Budget Films, Films Inc, Film Pres, Kerr Film, Modern Sound, Natl Film Video, Swank Motion, Twyman Films, Video Comm, Williams Films, Welling Motion Pictures & Westcoast Films.

Hooper. Burt Reynolds & Jan-Michael Vincent. Directed by Hal Needham. 1978. Warners. 97 min. Sound. 16mm Color. *Rental:* Williams Films & Swank Motion. *Rental:* Swank Motion, Videotape version.

Hooray for Love. Ann Sothern & Gene Raymond. Directed by Walter Lang. 1935. RKO. 72 min. Sound. 16mm *Rental:* RKO General Pics.

Hoosier Schoolboy. Orig. Title: Yesterday's Hero. Mickey Rooney & Anne Nagel. Directed by William Nigh. 1937. Monogram. 62 min. Sound. 16mm B&W. *Rental:* Mogulls Films.

Hoosier Schoolmaster, The. Henry Hull & Frank Dane. Directed by Oliver L. Sellers. 1924. PDC. 50 min. Silent. 8mm B&W. *Rental:* Em Gee Film Lib, Film Classics & Mogulls Films.

Hoosier Schoolmaster, The. Norman Foster & Charlotte Henry. Directed by Lewis D. Collins. 1935. Monogram. 76 min. Sound. 16mm B&W. *Rental:* Film Classics & Mogulls Films.

Hootenanny Hoot. Peter Breck & Ruta Lee. Directed by Gene Nelson. 1963. MGM. 91 min. Sound. 16mm B&W. *Rental:* MGM United.

Hopalong Cassidy Enters. William Boyd. Directed by Howard Bretherton. 1938. Paramount. 60 min. Sound. 16mm B&W. *Lease:* Cinema Concepts. *Sale:* Video Comm, Videotape version.

Hopalong Cassidy Returns. William Boyd & Gabby Hayes. Directed by Nate Watt. 1936. Paramount. 54 min. Sound. 16mm B&W. *Lease:* Cinema Concepts.

Hopalong Rides Again. William Boyd. Directed by Lesley Selander. 1937. Paramount. 60 min. Sound. 16mm B&W. *Rental:* Budget Films & Em Gee Film Lib. *Sale:* Video Comm, Videotape version.

Hope of Mankind, The. 1975. Britain. (Documentary). 52 min. Sound. 16mm Color. *Rental:* U of IL Film.

Hoppity Goes to Town. Orig. Title: Mister Bug Goes to Town. Directed by Dave Fleischer. 1941. Paramount. (Animated). 78 min. Sound. 16mm Color. *Rental:* Buchan Pic, Budget Films, Charard Motion Pics, Inst Cinema, Ivy Films, Kit Parker, Modern Sound, Newman Film Lib, Film Ctr DC, Welling Motion Pictures & Westcoast Films. *Sale:* Cinema Concepts & Rep Pic Film. *Sale:* Ivy Films, Super 8 sound color version. *Sale:* Cinema Concepts, Videotape version.

Hoppy Serves a Writ. William Boyd. Directed by George Archainbaud. 1943. United Artists. 68 min. Sound. 16mm B&W. *Lease:* Cinema Concepts. *Sale:* Cinema Concepts, Super 8 sound version. *Sale:* Cinema Concepts, Videotape version.

Hoppy's Holiday. William Boyd. Directed by George Archainbaud. 1947. United Artists. 69 min. Sound. 16mm B&W. *Sale:* Cinema Concepts.

Hopscotch. Walter Matthau & Glenda Jackson. Directed by Ronald Neame. 1980. Embassy. 102 min. Sound. 16mm Color. *Rental:* Films Inc.

Hora e Vez de Augusto Matraga *see* Hour & Time of Augusto Matraga.

Horace Takes Over. Orig. Title: One Thrilling Night. John Beal & Wanda McKay. Directed by William Beaudine. 1942. Monogram. 75 min. Sound. 16mm B&W. *Rental:* Mogulls Films.

Horizons. Directed by Larry Gottheim. 1973. Gottheim. (Experimental). 75 min. Silent. 16mm Color. *Rental:* Canyon Cinema.

Horizons of the Sea. 1972. Gold Key. (Documentary). 94 min. Sound. 16mm Color. *Rental:* Budget Films, Films Inc, Maljack & Video Comm.

Horizons West. Robert Ryan & Julie Adams. Directed by Budd Boetticher. 1952. Universal. 81 min. Sound. 16mm Color. *Rental:* Swank Motion.

Horizontal Lieutenant, The. Jim Hutton & Paula Prentiss. Directed by Richard Thorpe. 1962. MGM. (Anamorphic). 90 min. Sound. 16mm Color. *Rental:* MGM United.

Horn Blows at Midnight, The. Jack Benny & Alexis Smith. Directed by Raoul Walsh. 1945. Warners. 80 min. Sound. 16mm B&W. *Rental:* MGM United.

Hornet's Nest, The. Rock Hudson & Sylva Koscina. Directed by Phil Karlson. 1970. United Artists. 110 min. Sound. 16mm Color. *Rental:* MGM United.

Horrible Conspiracies. Glenda Jackson. 1976. Britain. 90 min. Sound. 16mm Color. *Rental:* Films Inc. *Sale:* Films Inc. *Rental:* Films Inc, *Sale:* Films Inc, Videotape version.

Horrible Dr. Hitchcock, The. Barbara Steele & Robert Fleming. Directed by Riccardo Freda. 1962. Italy. 84 min. Sound. 16mm Color. dubbed. *Rental:* Ivy Films. *Sale:* Rep Pic Film.

Horror Castle. Rossana Podesta & Christopher Lee. Directed by Anthony Dawson. 1965. Italy. 83 min. Sound. Super 8 Color. dubbed. *Rental:* Ivy Films. *Sale:* Ivy Films.

Horror Compilation: No. One. 70 min. Sound. 16mm *Rental:* Budget Films.

Horror Compilation: No. Two. 70 min. Sound. 16mm *Rental:* Budget Films.

Horror Express. Telly Savalas, Christopher Lee & Peter Cushing. Directed by Gene Martin. 1973. International. 95 min. Sound. Color. *Rental:* Budget Films. *Sale:* Cinema Concepts & Glenn Photo, Videotape version.

Horror Garden. Jack Palance, Burgess Meredith & Peter Cushing. Directed by Freddie Francis. 1968. Britain. 93 min. Sound. 16mm Color. *Rental:* Williams Films.

Horror Hospital. Michael Gough & Dennis Price. Directed by Anthony Balch. 1976. Britain. 91 min. Sound. 16mm Color. *Rental:* Budget Films & Modern Sound.

Horror Hotel. Christopher Lee. Directed by John Moxey. 1962. Britain. 80 min. Sound. 16mm B&W. *Sale:* Reel Images & Classics Assoc NY.

Horror House. Frankie Avalon & Jill Haworth. Directed by Michael Armstrong. 1970. American International. 79 min. Sound. 16mm Color. *Rental:* Arcus Film, Budget Films & Westcoast Films.

Horror Island. Andy Devine & Leo Carillo. Directed by George Waggner. 1941. Universal. 60 min. Sound. 16mm B&W. *Rental:* Swank Motion.

Horror of It All, The. Pat Boone & Erica Rogers. Directed by Terence Fisher. 1964. Britain. 76 min. Sound. 16mm B&W. *Rental:* Films Inc.

Horror of Party Beach, The. John Scott. Directed by Del Tenney. 1964. Fox. 82 min. Sound. 16mm B&W. *Rental:* Films Inc.

Horror on Snape Island, The. Bryant Halliday & Jill Haworth. Directed by Jim O'Connolly. 1972. Britain. 86 min. Sound. 16mm Color. *Rental:* Budget Films, Films Inc, Video Comm, Welling Motion Pictures & Westcoast Films.

Horrors of the Black Museum. Michael Gough & Shirley Ann Field. Directed by Arthur Crabtree. 1959. American International. 94 min. Sound. 16mm B&W. *Rental:* Budget Films, Films Inc, Video Comm & Westcoast Films.

Horse Called Jester, A. 1981. Britain. (Cast unlisted). 55 min. Sound. 16mm Color. *Sale:* Lucerne Films.

Horse Feathers. Marx Brothers. Directed by Norman Z. McLeod. 1932. Paramount. 69 min. Sound. 16mm B&W. *Rental:* Swank Motion.

Horse in the Gray Flannel Suit, The. Dean Jones & Diane Baker. Directed by Norman Tokar. 1968. Disney. 113 min. Sound. 16mm Color. *Rental:* Buchan Pic, Cine Craft, Disney Prod, Elliot Film Co, Film Ctr DC, Films Inc, Film Pres, Modern Sound, Newman Film Lib, Roas Films, Swank Motion, Twyman Films & U of IL Film.

Horse Soldiers, The. John Wayne & William Holden. Directed by John Ford. 1959. United Artists. 119 min. Sound. 16mm Color. *Rental:* MGM United.

Horse That Played Center Field, The. Directed by Rudy Larriva & Manuel Perez. 1979. ABC. (Animated). 48 min. Sound. 16mm Color. *Rental:* MTI Tele. *Sale:* MTI Tele. *Sale:* MTI Tele, Videotape version.

Horse with the Flying Tail, The. 1963. Disney. (Documentary). 47 min. Sound. 16mm Color. *Rental:* Cine Craft, Disney Prod, Film Ctr DC, Films Inc, Films Pres, Kent St U Film, Modern Sound, Roas Films & Twyman Films.

Horseman Pass By. Directed by Malcom Brown. 1966. Britain. (Documentary). 59 min. Sound. 16mm B&W. *Rental:* Time-Life Multimedia. *Sale:* Time-Life Multimedia.

Horsemen, The. Omar Sharif & Jack Palance. Directed by John Frankenheimer. 1971. Columbia. 109 min. Sound. 16mm Color. *Rental:* Arcus Film, Budget Films, Inst Cinema, Kerr Film, Modern Sound, Roas Films, Welling Motion Pictures, Westcoast Films, Wholesome Film Ctr & Willoughby Peer. *Rental:* Kit Parker, Anamorphic version.

Horse's Mouth, The. Sir Alec Guinness & Kay Walsh. Directed by Ronald Neame. 1958. United Artists. 96 min. Sound. 16mm Color. *Rental:* Janus Films & New Cinema.

Horses Without Man. 1981. Britain. (Documentary). 50 min. Sound. 16mm Color. *Rental:* Films Inc. *Sale:* Films Inc. *Rental:* Films Inc, *Sale:* Films Inc, Videotape version.

Hospital. Directed by Frederick Wiseman. 1970. Frederick Wiseman. (Documentary). 84 min. Sound. 16mm B&W. *Rental:* Zipporah Films. *Lease:* Zipporah Films.

Hospital, The. George C. Scott & Diana Rigg. Directed by Arthur Hiller. 1972. United Artists. 103 min. Sound. 16mm Color. *Rental:* Budget Films, MGM United, Welling Motion Pictures, Westcoast Films & Wholesome Film Ctr.

Hostage, The. Harry Dean Stanton & John Carradine. Directed by Russell S. Doughten Jr. 1966. Heartland. 82 min. Sound. 16mm Color. *Rental:* Video Comm. *Rental:* Video Comm, *Sale:* Video Comm, Videotape version. *Rental:* Swank Motion.

Hostages, The. 1981. Britain. (Cast unlisted). 60 min. Sound. 16mm Color. *Sale:* Lucerne Films.

Hostages. Luise Rainer & Arturo De Cordova. Directed by Frank Tuttle. 1943. Paramount. 87 min. Sound. 16mm B&W. *Rental:* Swank Motion.

Hostile Guns. George Montgomery & Yvonne De Carlo. Directed by R. G. Springsteen. 1967. Paramount. 91 min. Sound. 16mm Color. *Rental:* Films Inc.

Hot Blood. Jane Russell & Cornell Wilde. Directed by Nicholas Ray. 1956. Columbia. 85 min. Sound. 16mm B&W. *Rental:* Cine Craft & Westcoast Films. *Rental:* Kit Parker, Anamorphic version.

Hot-Blooded Dinosaurs. 1977. Nova. (Documentary). 52 min. Sound. 16mm Color. *Rental:* Syracuse U Film, U Cal Media & U of IL Film. *Rental:* U of IL Film, Videotape version.

Hot Cars. John Bromfield & Joi Lansing. Directed by Donald McDougall. 1956. United Artists. 60 min. Sound. 16mm B&W. *Rental:* MGM United.

Hot Dog. David Naughton & Patrick Houser. Directed by Peter Markle. 1983. MGM-UA. 96 min. Sound. 16mm Color. *Rental:* MGM United. *Rental:* MGM United, Videotape version.

Hot Heiress, The. Ona Munson & Walter Pidgeon. Directed by Ben Lyon & Vincent Sherman. 1931. Warners. 80 min. Sound. 16mm B&W. *Rental:* MGM United.

Hot Lead. Tim Holt & Joan Dixon. Directed by Stuart Gilmore. 1951. RKO. 60 min. Sound. 16mm B&W. *Rental:* RKO General Pics.

Hot Lead & Cold Feet. Jim Dale, Don Knotts & Karen Valentine. Directed by Robert Butler. 1978. Disney. 90 min. Sound. 16mm Color. *Rental:* Bosco Films, Buchan Pic, Disney Prod, Elliot Film Co, Film Ctr DC, Films Inc, Film Pres, MGM United, Modern Sound, Roas Films, Swank Motion, U of IL Film, Welling Motion Pictures & Westcoast Films.

Hot Millions. Peters Ustinov & Maggie Smith. Directed by Eric Till. 1968. MGM United. 105 min. Sound. 16mm Color. *Rental:* MGM United.

Hot Money. Ross Alexander & Beverly Roberts. Directed by William McGann. 1936. Warners. 68 min. Sound. 16mm B&W. *Rental:* MGM United.

Hot News. Stanley Clements & Gloria Henry. Directed by Edward Bernds. 1953. Monogram. 60 min. Sound. 16mm B&W. *Rental:* Hurlock Cine.

Hot Pepper. Edmund Lowe & Lupe Velez. Directed by John G. Blystone. 1933. Fox. 76 min. Sound. 16mm B&W. *Rental:* Films Inc.

Hot Pepper. Directed by Les Blank. 1973. Flower. (Documentary). 54 min. Sound. 16mm Color. *Rental:* Canyon Cinema & Flower Films. *Sale:* Flower Films.

Hot Potato. Jim Kelly. Directed by Oscar Williams. 1976. Warners. 87 min. Sound. 16mm Color. *Rental:* Twyman Films, Swank Motion & Williams Films.

Hot Rhythm. Robert Lowery & Dona Drake. Directed by William Beaudine. 1944. Monogram. 70 min. Sound. 16mm B&W. *Rental:* Mogulls Films.

Hot Rock, The. Robert Redford & George Segal. Directed by Peter Yates. 1972. Fox. 101 min. Sound. 16mm Color. *Rental:* Films Inc. *Rental:* Films Inc, Anamorphic color version.

Hot Rod. James Lydon & Art Baker. Directed by Lewis D. Collins. 1950. Monogram. 61 min. Sound. 16mm B&W. *Rental:* Hurlock Cine & Lewis Film.

Hot Rod Gang. Orig. Title: Fury Unleashed. John Ashley. Directed by Lew Landers. 1958. American International. 72 min. Sound. 16mm B&W. *Rental:* Westcoast Films.

Hot Rods to Hell. Orig. Title: Fifty-Two Miles to Terror. Dana Andrews & Jeanne Crain. Directed by John Brahm. 1967. MGM. 92 min. Sound. 16mm Color. *Rental:* MGM United.

Hot Saturday. Cary Grant & Nancy Carroll. Directed by William A. Seiter. 1932. Paramount. 74 min. Sound. 16mm B&W. *Rental:* Swank Motion.

Hot Spell. Shirley Booth & Anthony Quinn. Directed by Daniel Mann. 1958. Paramount. 86 min. Sound. 16mm B&W. *Rental:* Films Inc.

Hot Stuff. Dom DeLuise & Suzanne Pleshette. Directed by Dom DeLuise. 1979. Columbia. 103 min. Sound. 16mm Color. *Rental:* Arcus Film, Budget Films, Modern Sound, Swank Motion, Welling Motion Pictures & Williams Films.

Hot Summer Night. Leslie Nielson & Colleen Miller. Directed by David Friedkin. 1957. MGM. 86 min. Sound. 16mm B&W. *Rental:* MGM United.

Hot to Handle. 1966. Britain. (Documentary). 60 min. Sound. 16mm B&W. *Rental:* Time-Life Multimedia. *Sale:* Films Inc & Time-Life Multimedia.

Hot Water. Harold Lloyd & Jobyna Ralston. Directed by Sam Taylor. 1924. Pathe. (Musical Score Only). 81 min. Silent. 16mm B&W. *Rental:* Budget Films, Kino Intl & U of Mich Media. *Rental:* Budget Films, Silent version.

Hot World, The. 1977. Penn State. (Documentary). 59 min. Sound. 16mm Color. *Rental:* Penn St AV Serv. *Sale:* Penn St AV Serv. *Rental:* Penn St AV Serv, *Sale:* Penn St AV Serv, Videotape version.

Hotel Berlin. Helmut Dantine & Raymond Massey. Directed by Peter Godfrey. 1945. Warners. 98 min. Sound. 16mm B&W. *Rental:* MGM United.

Hotel-Chateau. Fr. 1971. Canada. (Cast unlisted). 59 min. Sound. 16mm B&W. *Rental:* Natl Film CN. *Sale:* Natl Film CN.

Hotel Imperial. Pola Negri. Directed by Mauritz Stiller. 1927. Paramount. 78 min. Silent. 16mm B&W. *Rental:* Films Inc. *Rental:* Hurlock Cine, Super 8 silent version.

Hotel Imperial. Isa Miranda & Ray Milland. Directed by Robert Florey. 1939. Paramount. 80 min. Sound. 16mm B&W. *Rental:* Swank Motion.

Hotel Paradiso. Sir Alec Guinness & Gina Lollobrigida. Directed by Peter Glenville. 1966. MGM. 100 min. Sound. 16mm Color. *Rental:* MGM United.

Hotel Reserve. James Mason & Lucie Mannheim. Directed by Victor Hamberg. 1943. RKO. 89 min. Sound. 16mm B&W. *Rental:* RKO General Pics.

Hotel Sahara. Peter Ustinov & Yvonne De Carlo. Directed by Ken Annakin. 1951. 87 min. 16mm *Rental:* A Twyman Pres.

Houdini. Tony Curtis & Janet Leigh. Directed by George Marshall. 1953. Paramount. 106 min. Sound. 16mm Color. *Rental:* Films Inc.

Hound-Dog Man, The. Stuart Whitman & Carol Lynley. Directed by Don Siegel. 1959. Fox. (Anamorphic). 87 min. Sound. 16mm Color. *Rental:* Films Inc.

Hound of the Baskervilles, The. Basil Rathbone & Nigel Bruce. Directed by Sidney Lanfield. 1939. Fox. 80 min. Sound. 16mm B&W. *Rental:* Budget Films, Films Inc, Inst Cinema, Images Film, Kit Parker, Learning Corp Am, Modern Sound, Roas Films, Twyman Films, U of IL Film, Westcoast Films, Wholesome Film Ctr & Williams Films. *Sale:* Learning Corp Am.

Hound of the Baskervilles, The. Peter Cushing & Christopher Lee. Directed by Terence Fisher. 1959. Britain. 84 min. Sound. 16mm Color. *Rental:* Budget Films, MGM United, Welling Motion Pictures & Westcoast Films. *Rental:* MGM United, Videotape version.

Hound of the Baskervilles, The. Dudley Moore & Peter Cook. Directed by Paul Morrissey. 1980. Britain. (Anamorphic). 87 min. Sound. 16mm Color. *Rental:* Ivy Films.

Hound That Thought He Was a Raccoon, The. Directed by Tom McGowan. 1964. Disney. (Documentary). 47 min. Sound. 16mm Color. *Rental:* Buchan Pic, BYU Media, Cine Craft, Disney Prod, Film Ctr DC, Films Inc, Iowa Films, Kent St U Film, Modern Sound, Roas Films, Syracuse U Film, Twyman Films & U Mich Media.

Hour & Time of Augusto Matraga, The. Trans. Title: Hora e Vez de Augusto Matraga. Leonardo Vilar & Jofre Soares. Directed by Roberto Santos. Port. 1966. Brazil. 110 min. Sound. 16mm B&W. subtitles. *Rental:* Hurlock Cine.

Hour Before the Dawn, The. Franchot Tone & Veronica Lake. Directed by Frank Tuttle. 1944. Paramount. 75 min. Sound. 16mm B&W. *Rental:* Swank Motion.

Hour of Decision, The. Hazel Court & Jeff Morrow. Directed by C. M. Pennington-Richards. 1955. Britain. 74 min. Sound. 16mm B&W. *Rental:* Ivy Films, Rep Pic Film & Video Comm. *Lease:* Rep Pic Film. *Rental:* Video Comm, Videotape version.

Hour of Liberation Has Struck, The. Directed by Heiny Srour. 1974. France-Lebanon. (Documentary). 62 min. Sound. 16mm Color. *Rental:* Tricontinental Film.

Hour of the Furnaces. Span. 1970. Argentina. (Documentary). 260 min. Sound. 16mm Color. subtitles. *Rental:* New Yorker Films & Unifilm. *Sale:* Unifilm.

Hour of the Gun. James Garner & Jason Robards Jr. Directed by John Sturges. 1967. United Artists. 100 min. Sound. 16mm Color. *Rental:* MGM United.

Hour of the Wolf. Liv Ullmann & Max Von Sydow. Directed by Ingmar Bergman. Swed. 1968. Sweden. 88 min. Sound. 16mm B&W. subtitles. *Rental:* MGM United.

Hour of Thirteen, The. Peter Lawford & Dawn Adams. Directed by Harold French. 1952. MGM. 79 min. Sound. 16mm B&W. *Rental:* MGM United.

House Across the Bay, The. Joan Bennett, George Raft & Walter Pidgeon. Directed by Archie Mayo. 1940. United Artists. 92 min. Sound. 16mm B&W. *Rental:* Budget Films, Learning Corp Am, Mogulls Films & Roas Films. *Sale:* Learning Corp Am. *Sale:* Tamarelles French Film, Videotape version.

House Across the Street, The. Wayne Morris & Janis Paige. Directed by Richard Bare. 1949. Warners. 70 min. Sound. 16mm B&W. *Rental:* MGM United.

House by the River, The. Louis Hayward & Jane Wyatt. Directed by Fritz Lang. 1950. Republic. 88 min. Sound. 16mm B&W. *Sale:* Festival Films.

House Calls. Walter Matthau & Glenda Jackson. Directed by Howard Zieff. 1978. Universal. 98 min. Sound. 16mm Color. *Rental:* Swank Motion. *Rental:* Swank Motion, Videotape version.

House Divided, A. Walter Huston & Kent Douglas. Directed by William Wyler. 1932. Universal. 70 min. Sound. 16mm B&W. *Rental:* Swank Motion.

House Divided, A: The Lincoln-Douglas Debates. John Anderson. 1970. House Divided Co. 52 min. Sound. 16mm Color. *Rental:* Films Inc. *Sale:* Films Inc. *Rental:* Films Inc, *Sale:* Films Inc, Videotape version.

House is Not a Home, A. Shelley Winters & Robert Taylor. Directed by Russell Rouse. 1964. Embassy. 95 min. Sound. 16mm B&W. *Rental:* Films Inc.

House Made of Dawn, A. John Saxon. Directed by Richardson Morse. New Line Cinema. 85 min. Sound. 16mm Color. *Rental:* New Line Cinema.

House of a Thousand Candles, The. Phillips Holmes & Mischa Auer. Directed by Arthur Lubin. 1936. Republic. 54 min. Sound. 16mm B&W. *Rental:* Ivy Films. *Sale:* Rep Pic Film.

House of Bamboo, The. Robert Ryan & Robert Stack. Directed by Samuel Fuller. 1955. Fox. (Anamorphic). 102 min. Sound. 16mm Color. *Rental:* Films Inc.

House of Cards, The. George Peppard & Inger Stevens. Directed by John Guillermin. 1969. Universal. 105 min. Sound. 16mm Color. *Rental:* Swank Motion.

House of Dark Shadows. Jonathan Frid & Joan Bennett. Directed by Dan Curtis. 1970. MGM. 96 min. Sound. 16mm Color. *Rental:* MGM United.

House of Doom, The *see* Black Cat.

House of Dracula, The. Lon Chaney Jr. & John Carradine. Directed by Erle C. Kenton. 1945. Universal. 67 min. Sound. 16mm B&W. *Rental:* Twyman Films.

House of Exorcism, The. Telly Savalas & Elke Sommer. Directed by Mickey Lion. 1979. Scotia-Barber. 91 min. Sound. 16mm Color. dubbed. *Rental:* Films Inc.

House of Fear, The. Basil Rathbone. Directed by Roy William Neill. 1945. Universal. 69 min. Sound. 16mm B&W. *Rental:* Learning Corp Am, Mogulls Films, RKO General Pics & Video Comm. *Sale:* Learning Corp Am. *Sale:* Cinema Concepts, Super 8 sound version.

House of Frankenstein, The. Boris Karloff & Carroll J. Naish. Directed by Erle C. Kenton. 1944. Universal. 71 min. Sound. 16mm B&W. *Rental:* Williams Films.

House of Horrors, The. Bill Goodwin & Robert Lowery. Directed by Jean Yarbrough. 1946. Universal. 66 min. Sound. 16mm B&W. *Rental:* Swank Motion.

House of Kittens. 1975. 60 min. Sound. Videotape Color. *Rental:* Iowa Films.

House of Kitties. Jap. Japan. (Cast unlisted). 60 min. Sound. 16mm B&W. *Sale:* Japan Society.

House of Lords, The. Britain. (Documentary). 64 min. Sound. 16mm Color. *Rental:* Arcus Film.

House of Numbers. Jack Palance & Barbara Lang. Directed by Russell Rouse. 1957. MGM. (Anamorphic). 92 min. Sound. 16mm B&W. *Rental:* MGM United.

231

House of Rothschild, The. George Arliss & Loretta Young. Directed by Alfred M. Werker. 1934. United Artists. 88 min. Sound. 16mm B&W. *Rental:* Films Inc.

House of Secrets, The. Leslie Fenton & Muriel Evans. Directed by Roland Reed. 1936. Britain. 70 min. Sound. 16mm B&W. *Rental:* Bosco Films & Video Comm.

House of Seven Corpses, The. Faith Domergue & John Ireland. Directed by Paul Harrison. 1973. International Amusements. 90 min. Sound. 16mm Color. *Rental:* Budget Films, Films Inc & Roas Films.

House of Strangers. Edward G. Robinson & Susan Hayward. Directed by Joseph L. Mankiewicz. 1949. Fox. 101 min. Sound. 16mm B&W. *Rental:* Films Inc.

House of the Damned. Ronald Foster & Merry Anders. Directed by Maury Dexter. 1963. Fox. 60 min. Sound. 16mm B&W. *Rental:* Films Inc.

House of the Seven Gables, The. George Sanders, Vincent Price & Margaret Lindsay. Directed by Joe May. 1940. Universal. 66 min. Sound. 16mm B&W. *Rental:* Swank Motion.

House of the Seven Hawks, The. Robert Taylor & Linda Christian. Directed by Richard Thorpe. 1959. MGM. 91 min. Sound. 16mm B&W. *Rental:* MGM United.

House on Chelouche St., The Gila Almagor & Shai K. Ophir. Directed by Moshe Mizrahi. Hebrew. 1973. Israel. 115 min. Sound. 16mm Color. subtitles. *Rental:* Film Classics & Films Inc.

House on Fifty Sixth Street, The. Kay Francis & Ricardo Cortez. Directed by Robert Florey. 1933. Warners. 68 min. Sound. 16mm B&W. *Rental:* MGM United.

House on Haunted Hill, The. Vincent Price & Carol Ohmart. Directed by William Castle. 1959. Allied Artists. 75 min. Sound. 16mm B&W. *Rental:* Hurlock Cine.

House on Ninety-Second Street, The. Lloyd Nolan & Signe Hasso. Directed by Henry Hathaway. 1945. Fox. 89 min. Sound. 16mm B&W. *Rental:* Films Inc.

House on Telegraph Hill, The. Richard Basehart & Valentina Cortesa. Directed by Robert Wise. 1951. Fox. 93 min. Sound. 16mm B&W. *Rental:* Films Inc.

House on the Beach, The. 1965. NET. (Documentary). 60 min. Sound. 16mm B&W. *Rental:* Indiana AV Ctr. *Lease:* Indiana AV Ctr.

House on the Sand, The. Sandra Evans. 1964. Emerson. 90 min. Sound. 16mm B&W. *Rental:* Films Inc.

House Opening, The. Directed by David MacDougall & Judith MacDougall. 1975. 45 min. Sound. 16mm Color. *Rental:* U Cal Media. *Sale:* U Cal Media.

House That Dripped Blood, The. Christopher Lee & Peter Cushing. Directed by Peter Duffell. 1971. Cinerama. 101 min. Sound. 16mm Color. *Rental:* Modern Sound & Swank Motion.

House That I Live In, The. Directed by Lev Kulidjanov & Yakov Segel. Rus. 1957. Russia. 98 min. Sound. 16mm B&W. *Rental:* Corinth Films.

House Where Evil Dwells, The. Edward Albert, Susan George & Doug McClure. Directed by Kevin Connor. 1982. 88 min. Sound. 16mm Color. *Rental:* MGM United. *Rental:* MGM United, Videotape version.

Houseboat. Cary Grant & Sophia Loren. Directed by Melville Shavelson. 1958. Paramount. 110 min. Sound. 16mm Color. *Rental:* Films Inc.

Householder, The. Shashi Kapoor. Directed by James Ivory. 1963. India. 100 min. Sound. 16mm B&W. subtitles. *Rental:* Corinth Films, New Cinema & New Yorker Films.

Housekeeper's Daughter, The. Joan Bennett & Adolphe Menjou. Directed by Hal Roach. 1939. United Artists. 80 min. Sound. 16mm B&W. *Rental:* Budget Films & Mogulls Films.

Housemaster, The. Jimmy Hanley & Rene Ray. Directed by Herbert Brenon. 1939. Britain. 95 min. Sound. 16mm B&W. *Rental:* Janus Films.

Housewife. Bette Davis & George Brent. Directed by Alfred E. Green. 1934. Warners. 69 min. Sound. 16mm B&W. *Rental:* MGM United.

Housing. 1973. Sterling. 56 min. Sound. 16mm Color. *Sale:* Sterling Ed Film.

How Are the Mighty Fallen. 1975. Britain. (Documentary). 52 min. Sound. 16mm Color. *Rental:* U of IL Film.

How Do I Love Thee? Jackie Gleason & Shelley Winters. Directed by Michael Gordon. 1970. ABC. 110 min. Sound. 16mm Color. *Rental:* Films Inc.

How Do You Feel? (Body in Question Series). 1979. (Documentary). 60 min. Sound. Videotape Color. *Rental:* Films Inc & Syracuse U Film. *Sale:* Films Inc.

How Do You Like the World? 1979. PBS. (Documentary). 58 min. Videotape Color. *Rental:* PBS Video. *Sale:* PBS Video.

How Doooo You Do? Bert Gordon. Directed by Ralph Murphy. 1945. PRC. 80 min. Sound. 16mm B&W. *Sale:* Classics Assoc NY.

How Green Was My Valley. Walter Pidgeon, Maureen O'Hara & Donald Crisp. Directed by John Ford. 1941. Fox. 118 min. Sound. 16mm B&W. *Rental:* Films Inc, Twyman Films & Williams Films. *Sale:* Blackhawk Films, Magnetic Video & Video Lib, Videotape version.

How I Won the War. Michael Crawford & John Lennon. Directed by Richard Lester. 1967. Britain. 111 min. Sound. 16mm Color. *Rental:* MGM United.

How Life Begins. Directed by Gene Feldman. 1968. Minnesota Mining. (Documentary). 46 min. Sound. 16mm Color. *Rental:* McGraw-Hill Films, Syracuse U Film & U Nev AV Ctr. *Sale:* McGraw-Hill Films.

How Much Do You Smell? 1981. Britain. (Documentary). 50 min. Sound. 16mm Color. *Rental:* Films Inc. *Sale:* Films Inc. *Rental:* Films Inc, *Sale:* Films Inc, Videotape version.

How Much Is Enough: Decision Making in the Nuclear Age. 1982. Documerica. (Documentary). 60 min. Sound. 16mm Color. *Rental:* U Cal Media & U Mich Media.

How Musical Are You? 1966. CBS. (Documentary). 53 min. Sound. 16mm Color. *Rental:* McGraw-Hill Films. *Sale:* McGraw-Hill Films.

How Sweet It Is! James Garner & Debbie Reynolds. Directed by Jerry Paris. 1969. National General. (Anamorphic). 99 min. Sound. 16mm Color. *Rental:* Films Inc & Swank Motion.

How Tasty Was My Little Frenchman. Arduino Colassanti. Directed by Nelson Pereira dos Santos. Port. 1971. Brazil. 80 min. Sound. 16mm Color. subtitles. *Rental:* New Yorker Films.

How the Myth Was Made. Directed by James Brown & George Stoney. 1978. Stoney. (Documentary). 59 min. Sound. 16mm Color. *Rental:* Films Inc, Texture Film & Viewfinders. *Sale:* Texture Film. *Sale:* Texture Film, Videotape version.

How the West Was Won. Spencer Tracy & Carroll Baker. Directed by John Ford, George Marshall & Henry Hathaway. 1962. MGM. 155 min. Sound. 16mm Color. *Rental:* MGM United. *Rental:* MGM United, Anamorphic version.

How They Filmed the "Grand Prix". 1968. Britain. (Documentary). 45 min. Sound. 16mm Color. *Rental:* Time-Life Multimedia. *Sale:* Time-Life Multimedia.

How to Be a Good Lover. Jeff Rutledge. Josh McDowell. 45 min. Sound. 16mm Color. *Rental:* Gospel Films.

How to Be a Homosexual. 1980. (Documentary). 60 min. Sound. 16mm Color. *Rental:* Canyon Cinema.

How to Be a Jewish Son. Susskind. (Interview). 60 min. Videotape Color. *Sale:* Time-Life Multimedia.

How to Be Very, Very Popular. Betty Grable & Sheree North. Directed by Nunnally Johnson. 1955. Fox. 89 min. Sound. 16mm Color. *Rental:* Films Inc.

How to Beat the High Cost of Living. Susan Saint James & Jane Curtin. Directed by Robert Sheerer. 1980. Filmways. 110 min. Sound. 16mm Color. *Rental:* Swank Motion.

How to Cure Inflation. 1980. Penn. (Documentary). 60 min. Sound. 16mm Color. *Rental:* Iowa Films. *Sale:* Ency Brit Ed. *Rental:* Iowa Films, *Sale:* Ency Brit Ed, Videotape version. *Sale:* Ency Brit Ed, 2 pt. 16mm version version.

How to Frame a Figg. Don Knotts & Joe Flynn. Directed by Alan Rafkin. 1971. Universal. 103 min. Sound. 16mm Color. *Rental:* Swank Motion.

How to Get a Job. Directed by Wayne Ewing. 1979. WNET. (Documentary). 58 min. Sound. 16mm Color. *Rental:* Films Inc. *Sale:* Films Inc. *Rental:* Films Inc, *Sale:* Films Inc, Videotape version.

How to Make a Monster. Robert H. Harris & Gary Conway. Directed by Herbert L. Strock. 1958. American International. 74 min. Sound. 16mm B&W. *Rental:* Films Inc & Westcoast Films.

How to Make a Woman. Directed by Alvin Feiring. 1972. Polymorph. (Documentary). 58 min. Sound. 16mm Color. *Rental:* U Cal Media.

How to Marry a Millionaire. Betty Grable, Marilyn Monroe & Lauren Bacall. Directed by Jean Negulesco. 1953. Fox. 96 min. Sound. 16mm Color. *Rental:* Films Inc. *Rental:* Films Inc, Anamorphic color version. *Sale:* Blackhawk Films, Golden Tapes, Magnetic Video & Video Lib, Videotape version.

How to Murder a Rich Uncle. Charles Coburn, Wendy Hiller & Nigel Patrick. Directed by Nigel Patrick. 1958. Columbia. 80 min. Sound. 16mm Color. *Rental:* Bosco Films & Kit Parker.

How to Murder Your Wife. Jack Lemmon, Virna Lisi & Terry-Thomas. Directed by Richard Quine. 1965. United Artists. 118 min. Sound. 1mm Color. *Rental:* MGM United.

How to Save a Marriage & Ruin Your Life. Dean Martin & Stella Stevens. Directed by Fielder Cook. 1968. Columbia. 102 min. Sound. 16mm Color. *Rental:* Cine Craft, Films Inc, Inst Cinema, Kerr Film, Modern Sound, Welling Motion Pictures & Wholesome Film Ctr.

How to Say No to a Rapist & Survive. Directed by David Hoffman. 1975. Learning Corp. Lecture 55 min. Sound. 16mm Color. *Rental:* Budget Films, Learning Corp Am, Syracuse U Film & Twyman Films. *Sale:* Learning Corp Am. *Rental:* Learning Corp Am, *Sale:* Learning Corp Am, Videotape version.

How to Stay Free. 1983. Penn. (Documentary). 60 min. Sound. 16mm Color. *Sale:* Ency Brit Ed. *Sale:* Ency Brit Ed, Videotape version.

How to Steal a Million. Audrey Hepburn & Peter O'Toole. Directed by William Wyler. 1966. Fox. 127 min. Sound. 16mm Color. *Rental:* Films Inc. *Rental:* Films Inc, Anamorphic color version.

How to Steal the World. Robert Vaughan & David McCallum. 1968. MGM. 89 min. Sound. 16mm Color. *Rental:* MGM United.

How to Stuff a Wild Bikini. Annette Funicello & Mickey Rooney. Directed by William Asher. 1965. American International. 93 min. Sound. 16mm Color. *Rental:* Twyman Films.

How to Succeed in Business Without Really Trying. Robert Morse & Rudy Vallee. Directed by David Swift. 1967. United Artists. 119 min. Sound. 16mm Color. *Rental:* Arcus Film, Budget Films, MGM United, Twyman Films, Welling Motion Pictures, Westcoast Films & Wholesome Film Ctr.

How We Got the Vote. 1976. Gould. (Documentary). 53 min. Sound. 16mm Color. *Rental:* Budget Films & U Mich Media. *Sale:* Lucerne Films. *Sale:* Videotape, Videotape version.

How Yakong Moved the Mountains. 12 pts. 1975. France. (Documentary). 721 min. Sound. 16mm Color. narrated Eng. *Rental:* Museum Mod Art. *Sale:* Museum Mod Art.

Howard E. Mitchell. 1967. NET. (Documentary). 59 min. Sound. 16mm B&W. *Rental:* Indiana AV Ctr. *Sale:* Indiana AV Ctr.

Howards of Virginia. Orig. Title: Tree of Liberty, The. Cary Grant & Martha Scott. Directed by Frank Lloyd. 1940. Columbia. 117 min. Sound. 16mm B&W. *Rental:* Arcus Film, Buchan Pic, Films Inc, Inst Cinema, Modern Sound, Roas Films, Twyman Films, Welling Motion Pictures & Westcoast Films.

Howling, The. Dee Wallace & Patrick Macnee. Directed by Joe Dante. 1981. Embassy. 91 min. Sound. 16mm Color. *Rental:* Films Inc.

Hubert Humphrey: New Man on Campus. 1969. NET. (Documentary). 59 min. Sound. 16mm B&W. *Rental:* Indiana AV Ctr. *Sale:* Indiana AV Ctr.

Huckleberry Finn. Jackie Coogan & Mitzi Green. Directed by Norman Taurog. 1931. Paramount. 71 min. 16mm B&W. *Rental:* Williams Films.

Huckleberry Finn. 3 pts. 1965. Encyclopaedia Britannica. Cast unlisted 78 min. Sound. 16mm Color. *Rental:* OK AV Ctr & Ency Brit Ed. *Sale:* Ency Brit Ed, Videotape version.

Huckleberry Finn. Jeff East. Directed by J. Lee Thompson. 1974. United Artists. 117 min. Sound. 16mm Color. *Rental:* Arcus Film, Buchan Pic, MGM United, Modern Sound, Roas Films, Westcoast Films, Wholesome Film Ctr & Williams Films.

Huckleberry Finn. Ron Howard, Donny Most & Antonio Fargas. Directed by Robert Totten. 1975. ABC. 74 min. Sound. 16mm Color. *Rental:* U of IL Film. *Sale:* ABC Learn. *Sale:* ABC Learn, Videotape version.

Hucksters, The. Clark Gable & Deborah Kerr. Directed by Jack Conway. 1947. MGM. 97 min. Sound. 16mm B&W. *Rental:* MGM United.

Hud. Paul Newman, Patricia Neal & Melvyn Douglas. Directed by Martin Ritt. 1963. Paramount. (Anamorphic). 112 min. Sound. 16mm B&W. *Rental:* Films Inc.

Huddle, The. Ramon Navarro & Una Merkel. Directed by Sam Wood. 1932. MGM. 104 min. Sound. 16mm B&W. *Rental:* MGM United.

Hudson's Bay. Paul Muni & Laird Creegar. Directed by Irving Pichel. 1941. Fox. 94 min. Sound. 16mm B&W. *Rental:* Films Inc.

Hue & Cry. Alastair Sim & Jack Warner. Directed by Charles Crichton. 1947. Britain. 85 min. Sound. 16mm B&W. *Rental:* Cine Craft.

Huelga. 1968. King Screen. (Documentary). 50 min. Sound. 16mm Color. *Rental:* CA Newsreel. *Sale:* McGraw-Hill Films.

Huggetts Abroad, The. Jack Warner & Petula Clark. Directed by Ken Annakin. Britain. 87 min. Sound. 16mm B&W. *Rental:* Cinema Five.

Hugo & Josefin. Marie Ohman & Fredrik Becklen. Directed by Kjell Grede. 1970. Sweden. 82 min. Sound. 16mm Color. dubbed. *Rental:* Inst Cinema & Welling Motion Pictures.

Hugs & Kisses. Agneta Ekmanner & Hakan Serner. Directed by Jonas Cornell. Swed. 1967. Embassy. 93 min. Sound. 16mm B&W. subtitles. *Rental:* Films Inc.

Huit Coups de l'Horloge, Les. George Descrieres. Directed by Jean-Pierre Desagnat. Fr. 1971. France. 53 min. Sound. 16mm Color. *Rental:* French Am Cul.

Hullabaloo Over Georgie & Bonnie's Pictures, The. Dame Peggy Ashcroft & Jane Booker. Directed by James Ivory. 1978. India. 85 min. Sound. 16mm Color. subtitles. *Rental:* Corinth Films.

Human Beast, The see Bete Humaine.

Human Comedy, The. Mickey Rooney & Van Johnson. Directed by Clarence Brown. 1943. MGM. 120 min. Sound. 16mm B&W. *Rental:* MGM United.

Human Desire, The. Anita Stewart & Conway Tearle. Directed by Wilfrid North. 1920. First National. 75 min. Silent. 16mm B&W. *Sale:* Blackhawk Films. *Sale:* Blackhawk Films, Super 8 silent version. *Sale:* Blackhawk Films, Silent 8mm version.

Human Desire. Glenn Ford & Gloria Grahame. Directed by Fritz Lang. 1954. Columbia. 90 min. Sound. 16mm B&W. *Rental:* Corinth Films.

Human Duplicators, The. George Nader & Barbara Nichols. Directed by Hugo Grimaldi. 1965. Woolner. 82 min. Sound. 16mm Color. *Rental:* Budget Films, Video Comm & Willoughby Peer.

Human Experiments. (Cast unlisted). 82 min. Sound. Videotape Color. *Sale:* Vidamerica.

Human Experiments: The Price of Knowledge. PBS. 58 min. Sound. Videotape *Rental:* PBS Video. *Sale:* PBS Video.

Human Factor, The. Nicol Williamson, Sir Richard Attenborough. Directed by Otto Preminger. 1979. MGM. 115 min. Sound. 16mm Color. *Rental:* MGM United.

Human Gorilla, The see Behind Locked Doors.

Human Jungle, The. Jan Sterling & Gary Merrill. Directed by Joseph Newman. 1954. Allied Artists. 82 min. Sound. 16mm B&W. *Rental:* Ivy Films. *Sale:* Rep Pic Film.

Human Monster, The. Orig. Title: Dark Eyes of London. Bela Lugosi. Directed by Walter Summers. 1940. Monogram. 76 min. Sound. 16mm B&W. *Rental:* Budget Films, Charard Motion Pics, Classic Film Mus, Em Gee Film Lib, Films Inc, Janus Films, Kit Parker, Video Comm & Wholesome Film Ctr. *Sale:* Cinema Concepts, Classic Film Mus & Natl Cinema. *Rental:* Video Comm, Videotape version.

Human Rights, Fundamental Freedoms. 1975. Britain. (Documentary). 52 min. Sound. 16mm Color. *Rental:* U of IL Film.

Human, Too Human. Directed by Louis Malle. 1972. France. (Documentary). 60 min. Sound. 16mm Color. *Rental:* New Yorker Films.

Human Voice, The see Amore.

Humanoids from the Deep. Doug McClure & Ann Turkel. Directed by Barbara Peeters. 1980. New World. 82 min. Sound. 16mm Color. *Rental:* Films Inc.

Humongous. Janet Julian & David Wallace. Directed by Paul Lynch. 1982. Embassy. 93 min. Sound. 16mm Color. *Rental:* Films Inc.

Humor in Music. 1959. CBS. (Documentary). 59 min. Sound. 16mm B&W. *Rental:* McGraw-Hill Films, Syracuse U Film & U of IL Film. *Sale:* McGraw-Hill Films.

Humoresque. Joan Crawford & John Garfield. Directed by Jean Negulesco. 1946. Warners. 125 min. Sound. 16mm B&W. *Rental:* MGM United.

Hunchback of Notre Dame, The. Lon Chaney & Patsy Ruth Miller. Directed by Wallace Worsley. 1923. Universal. 90 min. Sound. 16mm B&W. *Rental:* A Twyman Pres, Budget Films, Film Classics & Maljack. *Sale:* Blackhawk Films & See-Art Films. *Rental:* Killiam Collect & New Cinema, Tinted version. *Rental:* Classic Film Mus, Em Gee Film Lib, Film Images, Films Inc, Ivy Films, Kerr Film, Kit Parker, Maljack, Mogulls Films, Roas Films, Swank Motion, Twyman Films, U Cal Media, Video Comm, Welling Motion Pictures, Westcoast Films, Wholesome Film Ctr & Willoughby Peer, *Sale:* Blackhawk Films, Glenn Photo & Natl Cinema, Silent 16mm version. *Sale:* Blackhawk Films & Nostalgia Merchant, Super 8 sound version. *Rental:* Ivy Films, *Sale:* Blackhawk Films & Glenn Photo, Super 8 silent version.

Hunchback of Notre Dame, The. Charles Laughton & Maureen O'Hara. Directed by William Dieterle. 1939. RKO. 115 min. Sound. 16mm B&W. *Rental:* Films Inc. *Rental:* RKO General Pics, 117 min. version.

Hunchback of Notre Dame, The. Anthony Quinn & Gina Lollobrigida. Directed by Jean Delannoy. 1956. Allied Artists. 104 min. Sound. 16mm Color. *Rental:* Films Inc & Newman Films.

Hunchback of Notre Dame, The. Anthony Hopkins, Derek Jacobi & Lesley Anne Down. 1982. CBS. 102 min. Sound. 16mm Color. *Rental:* Budget Films, Welling Motion Pictures & Williams Films.

Hunchback of Paris, The see King's Avenger.

Hunchback of Soho, The. Gunther Stoll. Directed by Alfred Vohrer. 1967. Germany. 87 min. Sound. 16mm Color. dubbed. *Rental:* Budget Films.

Hundred Years War, The. 2 pts. Directed by Ilan Ziv. 1983. 120 min. 16mm Color. *Rental:* Icarus Films. *Sale:* Icarus Films. *Sale:* Icarus Films, Videotape version.

Hunger, The. Catherine Deneuve & David Bowie. Directed by Tony Scott. 1983. MGM-UA. 98 min. Sound. 16mm Color. *Rental:* MGM United. *Rental:* MGM United, Videotape version.

Hunger in America. 1968. CBS. (Documentary). 54 min. Sound. 16mm B&W. *Rental:* Budget Films, BYU Media, Film Ctr DC, Iowa Films, Newman Film Lib, Roas Films, Syracuse U Film, Twyman Films, U Cal Media & U Mich Media. *Sale:* Carousel Films. *Rental:* Kit Parker, *Sale:* Carousel Films, Color version.

Hungry Giants, The: World Hunger. 1963. Hearst. (Documentary). 50 min. Sound. 16mm B&W. *Sale:* King Features.

Hungry I Reunion, The. Directed by Thomas A. Cohen. 1981. Cinema Ventures. (Performance). 93 min. Sound. 16mm Color. *Rental:* Kit Parker.

Hunt, The. Trans. Title: Casa, La. Alfredo Mayo. Directed by Carlos Saura. Span. 1967. Spain. 93 min. Sound. 16mm B&W. subtitles. *Rental:* Twyman Films & Westcoast Films.

Hunt the Man Down. Gig Young & Lynn Roberts. Directed by George Archainbaud. 1950. RKO. 68 min. Sound. 16mm B&W. *Rental:* Films Inc.

Hunted, The. Preston Foster & Belita. Directed by Jack Bernhard. 1948. Monogram. 67 min. Sound. 16mm B&W. *Rental:* Hurlock Cine.

Hunted, The. Dirk Bograde & Jon Whiteley. Directed by Charles Crichton. 1952. Britain. 79 min. Sound. 16mm B&W. *Rental:* Budget Films.

Hunted in Holland. Sean Scully. Directed by Derek Williams. 1966. Britain. 61 min. Sound. 16mm Color. *Rental:* Films Inc & Wholesome Film Ctr.

Hunter, The. Steve McQueen & Eli Wallach. Directed by Buzz Kulik. 1980. Paramount. 97 min. Sound. 16mm Color. *Rental:* Films Inc.

Hunters, The. Robert Mitchum & Richard Egan. Directed by Dick Powell. 1958. Fox. 108 min. Sound. 16mm Color. *Rental:* Films Inc.

Hunters Are the Hunted, The. Trans. Title: Jagdszene Aus Niederbayern. Martin Sperr & Angelika Winkler. Directed by Peter Fleischmann. Ger. 1967. Germany. 90 min. Sound. 16mm B&W. subtitles. *Rental:* Film Images. *Sale:* Film Images.

Hunters of the Deep. 1955. DCA. (Documentary). 64 min. Sound. 16mm Color. *Rental:* Modern Sound & Video Comm.

Hunters of the Kalahari Desert, The. Directed by John Marshall. 1958. Film Study Center. 73 min. Sound. 16mm B&W. *Rental:* BYU Media, Iowa Films, Syracuse U Film, Texture Film, U Mich Media & U of IL Film. *Sale:* Texture Film. *Rental:* U Cal Media, Em Gee Film Lib, Films Inc & Texture Film, *Sale:* Texture Film, Color version. *Sale:* Texture Film, Videotape version.

Hunters of the Wild. 1974. Gold Key. (Documentary). 94 min. Sound. 16mm Color. *Rental:* Films Inc, Vidoe Comm & Westcoast Films. *Lease:* Video Comm. *Rental:* Video Comm, *Lease:* Video Comm, Videotape version.

Hunting Accident, The. Oleg Yankovsky. Directed by Emil Lotianu. Rus. 1978. Russia. 107 min. Sound. 16mm Color. subtitles. *Rental:* Corinth Films.

Hunting Flies. Directed by Andrzej Wajda. Pol. 1969. Poland. 108 min. Sound. 16mm Color. *Rental:* Films Inc.

Hunting Party, The. Oliver Reed & Candice Bergen. Directed by Don Medford. 1971. United Artists. 108 min. Sound. 16mm Color. *Rental:* MGM United & Westcoast Films.

Hunza. Directed by Renee Taylor. 1973. Renee Taylor. (Documentary). 50 min. Sound. 16mm Color. *Rental:* Morcraft Films. *Sale:* Morcraft Films.

Hurricane. Dorothy Lamour & Jon Hall. Directed by John Ford & Stuart Heisler. 1937. Goldwyn. 108 min. Sound. 16mm B&W. *Rental:* Samuel Goldwin & Video Comm.

Hurricane. Jason Robards, Mia Farrow & Max Von Sydow. Directed by Jan Troell. 1979. Paramount. 131 min. Sound. 16mm Color. *Rental:* Films Inc.

Hurricane at Pilgrim Hill. Virginia Grey & David Bruce. Directed by Richard Bare. 1953. Howco. 60 min. Sound. 16mm B&W. *Rental:* Budget Films.

Hurricane Smith. John Ireland & Yvonne De Carlo. Directed by Jerry Hopper. 1952. Paramount. 90 min. Sound. 16mm B&W. *Rental:* Films Inc.

Hurricane Smith see Double Identity.

Hurry, Charlie, Hurry. Leon Errol. Directed by Charles E. Roberts. 1941. RKO. 65 min. 16mm B&W. *Rental:* Films Inc.

Hurry Sundown. Michael Caine & Jane Fonda. Directed by Otto Preminger. 1967. Paramount. 146 min. Sound. 16mm Color. *Rental:* Films Inc.

Hurry Tomorrow. Directed by Richard Cohen & Kevin Rafferty. 1975. Tricontinental. (Documentary). 80 min. Sound. 16mm B&W. *Rental:* U of IL Film, U Mich Media & Unifilm. *Sale:* Unifilm.

Husbands. Ben Gazzara, Peter Falk & John Cassavetes. Directed by John Cassavetes. 1972. Columbia. 138 min. Sound. 16mm Color. *Rental:* Corinth Films, Swank Motion & Twyman Films.

Hush...Hush, Sweet Charlotte. Bette Davis & Olivia De Havilland. Directed by Robert Aldrich. 1965. Fox. 133 min. Sound. 16mm B&W. *Rental:* Films Inc & Twyman Films.

Hussy, The. Helen Mirren & John Shea. 95 min. Sound. 16mm *Rental:* WW Enter. *Rental:* WW Enter, Videotape version.

Hustle. Burt Reynolds & Catherine Deneuve. Directed by Robert Aldrich. 1975. Paramount. 120 min. Sound. 16mm Color. *Rental:* Films Inc.

Hustler, The. Paul Newman, George C. Scott & Piper Laurie. Directed by Robert Rossen. 1961. Fox. (Anamorphic). 135 min. Sound. 16mm B&W. *Rental:* Films Inc.

Hustler Squad. John Ericson & Karen Ericson. Directed by Cesar Gallardo. 1978. Crown. 98 min. Sound. 16mm Color. *Rental:* Films Inc.

Hyde Park Corner. Gordon Harker. Directed by Sinclair Hill. 1941. Britain. 85 min. Sound. 16mm B&W. *Rental:* Ivy Films & Rep Pic Film. *Lease:* Rep Pic Film.

Hypnosis. 4 pts. 1982. Britain. (Documentary). 210 min. Videotape Color. *Sale:* Films Inc.

Hypnosis & Healing. 1983. Britain. (Documentary). 55 min. Videotape Color. *Rental:* U Cal Media.

Hypnosis: Can Your Mind Control Pain?. 1983. Britain. (Documentary). 53 min. Videotape Color. *Rental:* U Cal Media.

Hypnosis: Can Your Mind Control Your Body?. 1983. Britain. (Documentary). 49 min. Videotape Color. *Rental:* U Cal Media.

Hypnosis on Trial. 1983. Britain. (Documentary). 53 min. Videotape Color. *Rental:* U Cal Media.

Hypnotic Eye, The. Jacqucs Bergerac & Merry Anders. Directed by George Blair. 1960. Allied Artists. 79 min. Sound. 16mm B&W. *Rental:* Hurlock Cine.

Hypnotized. Moran & Mack, Charlie Murray & Hattie McDaniel. Directed by Mack Sennett. 1932. World Wide. 58 min. Sound. 16mm B&W. *Sale:* Natl Cinema.

Hysteria. Robert Webber & Maurice Denham. Directed by Freddie Francis. 1965. MGM. 86 min. Sound. 16mm B&W. *Rental:* MGM United.

I, a Woman: Part II. Gio Petre & Lars Lunde. Directed by Mac Ahlberg. 1970. Sweden. 81 min. Sound. 16mm Color. dubbed. *Rental:* Films Inc.

I Accuse. Jose Ferrer & Viveca Lindfors. Directed by Jose Ferrer. 1958. MGM. (Anamorphic). 99 min. Sound. 16mm B&W. *Rental:* MGM United.

I Accuse My Parents. Mary Beth Hughes. Directed by Sam Newfield. 1944. PRC. 70 min. Sound. 16mm B&W. *Rental:* Ivy Films & Mogulls Films. *Sale:* Classics Assoc NY.

I Aim at the Stars. Curt Jurgens & Victoria Shaw. Directed by J. Lee Thompson. 1960. Columbia. 107 min. Sound. 16mm B&W. *Rental:* Cine Craft, Films Inc & Welling Motion Pictures.

I Ain't Playin' No More. 1971. EDC. (Documentary). 61 min. Sound. 16mm B&W. *Rental:* Educ Dev Ctr. *Sale:* Educ Dev Ctr.

I Am a Camera. Julie Harris, Laurence Harvey & Shelley Winters. Directed by Henry Cornelius. 1955. Britain. 98 min. Sound. 16mm B&W. *Rental:* Budget Films, Ivy Films, Kit Parker & Video Comm. *Rental:* Video Comm, Videotape version.

I Am a Criminal. John Carroll. Directed by William Nigh. 1940. Monogram. 73 min. Sound. 16mm B&W. *Rental:* Hurlock Cine.

I Am a Dancer. Rudolf Nureyev & Pierre Jourdain. 1976. Britain. 93 min. Sound. 16mm Color. *Rental:* Jer Pictures. *Sale:* Jer Pictures.

I Am a Fugitive from a Chain Gang. Paul Muni & Glenda Farrell. Directed by Mervyn LeRoy. 1932. Warners. 90 min. Sound. 16mm B&W. *Rental:* Iowa Films & MGM United.

I Am a Groupie. Esme Johns. Directed by Derek Ford. 1970. 78 min. Sound. 16mm Color. *Rental:* Films Inc.

I Am a Soldier. 1966. ABC. (Documentary). 51 min. Sound. 16mm Color. *Rental:* McGraw-Hill Films & Syracuse U Film. *Sale:* McGraw-Hill Films.

I Am a Thief. Ricardo Cortez & Mary Astor. Directed by Robert Florey. 1935. Warners. 64 min. Sound. 16mm B&W. *Rental:* MGM United.

I Am an Old Tree. Directed by Michael Rubbo. 1975. Canada. (Documentary). 51 min. Sound. 16mm Color. *Rental:* Natl Film CN. *Sale:* Natl Film CN.

I Am Curious: Blue. Lena Nyman & Peter Lindgren. Directed by Vilgot Sjoman. Swed. 1970. Sweden. 110 min. Sound. 16mm B&W. subtitles. *Rental:* Grove. *Sale:* Grove.

I Am Curious: Yellow. Lena Nyman. Directed by Vilgot Sjoman. Swed. 1969. Sweden. 110 min. Sound. 16mm B&W. subtitles. *Rental:* Grove. *Sale:* Grove.

I Am My Films: A Portrait of Werner Herzog. Directed by Erwin Keusch & Christian Weisenborn. Ger. 1978. Germany. (Documentary). 96 min. Sound. 16mm Color. subtitles. *Rental:* New Yorker Films.

I Am the Cheese. Robert MacNaughton. 1983. Almi. Sound. 16mm Color. *Rental:* Cinema Five.

I Am the Son of America *see* De America Soy Hijo.

I Am Truly Sorry. Directed by Walter Heynowski & Gerhard Scheumann. Span. 1977. Vietnam. (Documentary). 53 min. Sound. 16mm Color. subtitles. *Rental:* Unifilm.

I Beheld His Glory. Trans. Title: Yo Contemple Su Gloria. Directed by John Coyle. 1953. Cathedral. (Cast unlisted). 55 min. Sound. 16mm B&W. *Rental:* G Herne.

I Can Get It for You Wholesale. Susan Hayward & Dan Dailey. Directed by Michael Gordon. 1951. Fox. 91 min. Sound. 16mm B&W. *Rental:* Films Inc.

I Changed My Sex. Orig. Title: Glen or Glenda? Lyle Talbot. Directed by Edward D. Wood Jr. 1953. 75 min. Sound. 16mm B&W. *Rental:* Budget Films, Em Gee Film Lib, Ivy Films & Liberty Co. *Sale:* Morcraft Films.

I, Claudius. 13 pts. Derek Jacobi, Sian Phillips & John Hurt. Directed by Herbert Wise. 1977. London. 780 min. Sound. 16mm Color. *Rental:* Budget Films, Films Inc & Syracuse U Film. *Sale:* Films Inc. *Sale:* Films Inc, Videotape version.

I Compagni *see* Organizer.

I Confess. Montgomery Clift & Anne Baxter. Directed by Alfred Hitchcock. 1953. Warners. 95 min. Sound. 16mm B&W. *Rental:* Films Inc, Swank Motion & Twyman Films.

I Conquer the Sea. Dennis Morgan & Steffi Duna. Directed by Victor Halperin. 1936. Academy. 70 min. Sound. 16mm B&W. *Rental:* Mogulls Films.

I Could Go on Singing. Judy Garland & Dirk Bogarde. Directed by Ronald Neame. 1963. United Artists. 99 min. Sound. 16mm Color. *Rental:* Budget Films, MGM United & Westcoast Films.

I Cover Big Town *see* I Cover the Underworld.

I Cover the Underworld. Orig. Title: I Cover Big Town. Philip Reed & Hillary Brooke. Directed by William C. Thomas. 1947. Paramount. 69 min. Sound. 16mm B&W. *Rental:* Ivy Films. *Sale:* Rep Pic Film.

I Cover the Waterfront. Claudette Colbert & Ben Lyon. Directed by James Cruze. 1933. United Artists. 70 min. Sound. 16mm B&W. *Rental:* Budget Films, Classic Film Mus, Kit Parker & Mogulls Films. *Sale:* Classic Film Mus, Festival Films & Natl Cinema. *Sale:* Festival Films, Videotape version.

I Deal in Danger. Robert Goulet & Donald Harron. Directed by Walter Grauman. 1966. Fox. 89 min. Sound. 16mm Color. *Rental:* Films Inc.

I Don't Care Girl, The. Mitzi Gaynor & David Wayne. Directed by Lloyd Bacon. 1953. Fox. 77 min. Sound. 16mm Color. *Rental:* Films Inc.

I Don't Know Why. 1979. PBS. (Documentary). 58 min. Videotape Color. *Rental:* PBS Video. *Sale:* PBS Video.

I Dood It. Orig. Title: By Hook or by Crook. Red Skelton & Lena Horne. Directed by Vincente Minnelli. 1943. MGM. 102 min. Sound. 16mm B&W. *Rental:* MGM United.

I Dream of Jeannie. Ray Middleton & Lynn Bari. Directed by Allan Dwan. 1952. Republic. 90 min. Sound. 16mm B&W. *Rental:* Ivy Films. *Sale:* Rep Pic Film.

I Dream Too Much. Lily Pons & Henry Fonda. Directed by John Cromwell. 1935. RKO. 95 min. Sound. 16mm B&W. *Rental:* Films Inc.

I Escaped from Devil's Island. James Brown & Christopher George. Directed by William Witney. 1973. United Artists. 87 min. Sound. 16mm Color. *Rental:* MGM United.

I Escaped from the Gestapo *see* No Escape.

I. F. Stone's Weekly. Directed by Jerry Bruck Jr. 1973. I. F. Stone Project. (Documentary). 60 min. Sound. 16mm B&W. *Rental:* Open Circle. *Sale:* Open Circle.

I Found Stella Parish. Kay Francis & Paul Lukas. Directed by Mervyn LeRoy. 1935. Warners. 85 min. Sound. 16mm B&W. *Rental:* MGM United.

I Got a Name *see* Last American Hero.

I Hate to Lose. Directed by Michael Rubbo. 1977. Canada. (Documentary). 57 min. Sound. 16mm Color. *Rental:* Natl Film CN. *Sale:* Natl Film CN. *Sale:* Natl Film CN, Videotape version.

I Heard the Owl Call My Name. Tom Courtenay & Dean Jagger. 1973. CBS. 78 min. Sound. 16mm Color. *Rental:* Budget Films, Films Inc, Kent St U Film, Kit Parker, Learning Corp Am, Mass Media, Modern Sound, Syracuse U Film, Twyman Films, U Cal Media, U Mich Media, U of IL Film, Welling Motion Pictures, Westcoast Films & Wholesome Film Ctr. *Lease:* Learning Corp Am. *Rental:* Learning Corp Am, *Lease:* Learning Corp Am, Videotape version.

I, Jane Doe. Ruth Hussey & Gene Lockhart. Directed by John H. Auer. 1948. Republic. 85 min. Sound. 16mm B&W. *Rental:* Ivy Films. *Sale:* Rep Pic Film.

I Killed That Man. Ricardo Cortez & Joan Woodbury. Directed by Phil Rosen. 1941. Monogram. 71 min. Sound. 16mm B&W. *Rental:* Hurlock Cine.

I Know Where I'm Going. Wendy Hiller & Roger Livesey. Directed by Michael Powell & Emeric Pressburger. 1947. Britain. 99 min. Sound. 16mm B&W. *Rental:* Budget Films, Kit Parker, Learning Corp Am, Twyman Films & U of IL Film. *Sale:* Learning Corp Am. *Rental:* Images Film, 90 mins. version.

I Know Why the Caged Bird Sings. 1978. 96 min. Sound. 16mm Color. *Rental:* Learning Corp Am. *Lease:* Learning Corp Am. *Rental:* Learning Corp Am, *Lease:* Learning Corp Am, Videotape version.

I, Leonardo da Vinci. 1965. ABC. (Documentary). 54 min. Sound. 16mm Color. *Rental:* Iowa Films & McGraw-Hill Films. *Sale:* McGraw-Hill Films. *Sale:* McGraw-Hill Films, Syracuse U Film, U of IL Film & U Nev AV Ctr, videotape version.

I Like Your Nerve. Douglas Fairbanks Jr. & Loretta Young. Directed by William McGann. 1931. Warners. 62 min. Sound. 16mm B&W. *Rental:* MGM United.

I Live for Love. Dolores Del Rio. Directed by Busby Berkeley. 1935. Warners. 64 min. Sound. 16mm B&W. *Rental:* MGM United.

I Live in Fear. Toshiro Mifune & Eiko Miyoshi. Directed by Akira Kurosawa. Jap. 1955. Japan. 105 min. Sound. 16mm B&W. subtitles. *Rental:* Films Inc.

I Live in Grosvenor Square *see* Yank in London.

I Live My Life. Joan Crawford & Brian Aherne. Directed by W. S. Van Dyke II. 1935. MGM. 99 min. Sound. 16mm B&W. *Rental:* MGM United.

I Love a Bandleader. Phil Harris. Directed by Del Lord. 1945. Columbia. 70 min. Sound. 16mm B&W. *Lease:* Time-Life Multimedia.

I Love Melvin. Debbie Reynolds & Donald O'Connor. Directed by Don Weis. 1953. MGM. 79 min. Sound. 16mm Color. *Rental:* MGM United.

I Love My Wife. Elliot Gould & Brenda Vaccaro. Directed by Mel Stuart. 1971. Universal. 95 min. Sound. 16mm Color. *Rental:* Swank Motion.

I Love You. Sonia Braga & Paulo Cesar. Directed by Arnaldo Jabor. Port. 1981. Atlantic. 96 min. Sound. 16mm Color. subtitles. *Rental:* Films Inc.

I Love You Again. William Powell & Myrna Loy. Directed by W. S. Van Dyke. 1940. MGM. 99 min. Sound. 16mm B&W. *Rental:* MGM United.

I Love You, Alice B. Toklas. Peter Sellers & Jo Van Fleet. Directed by Hy Averback. 1968. Warners. 93 min. Sound. 16mm Color. *Rental:* Charard Motion Pics, Cine Craft, Films Inc, Inst Cinema, Swank Motion, Twyman Films, Video Comm, Welling Motion Pictures, Westcoast Films & Willoughby Peer.

I Love You, Goodbye. Hope Lange & Earl Holliman. Directed by Sam O'Steen. 1973. CBS. 74 min. Sound. 16mm Color. *Rental:* Budget Films, Kent St U Film, Learning Corp Am, Modern Sound, Syracuse U Film, Twyman Films, U Cal Media, U of IL Film, Westcoast Films & Wholesome Film Ctr. *Sale:* Learning Corp Am.

I Love You, Rosa. Michal Bat-Adam. Directed by Moshe Mizrahi. Hebrew. 1972. Israel. 84 min. Sound. 16mm Color. subtitles. *Rental:* Films Inc & Ivy Films.

I Loved a Woman. Edward G. Robinson & Kay Francis. Directed by Alfred E. Green. 1933. Warners. 91 min. Sound. 16mm B&W. *Rental:* MGM United.

I Married a Doctor. Pat O'Brien & Josephine Hutchinson. Directed by Archie Mayo. 1936. Warners. 87 min. Sound. 16mm B&W. *Rental:* MGM United.

I Married a Heathen. 1974. 55 min. Sound. 16mm B&W. *Rental:* Canyon Cinema.

I Married a Monster from Outer Space. Tom Tryon & Gloria Talbot. Directed by Gene Fowler Jr. 1958. Paramount. 78 min. Sound. 16mm B&W. *Rental:* Films Inc.

I Married a Spy. Neil Hamilton & Brigitte Horney. Directed by Edmond Greville. 1938. Britain. 60 min. Sound. 16mm B&W. *Rental:* Mogulls Films.

I Married a Woman. George Gobel & Diana Dors. Directed by Hal Kanter. 1958. RKO. 84 min. Sound. 16mm B&W. *Rental:* Budget Films & Video Comm. *Rental:* Video Comm, Videotape version.

I Married Adventure. 1940. Columbia. (Documentary). 70 min. Sound. 16mm B&W. *Rental:* Mogulls Films.

I Married an Angel. Jeanette MacDonald & Nelson Eddy. Directed by W. S. Van Dyke. 1942. MGM. 84 min. Sound. 16mm B&W. *Rental:* MGM United.

I Met a Murderer. James Mason. Directed by Roy Kellino. 1939. Britain. 70 min. Sound. 16mm B&W. *Rental:* Ivy Films.

I Met Him in Paris. Claudette Colbert & Melvyn Douglas. Directed by Wesley Ruggles. 1937. Paramount. 86 min. Sound. 16mm B&W. *Rental:* Swank Motion.

I Met My Love Again. Joan Bennett & Henry Fonda. Directed by Arthur Ripley. 1938. United Artists. 80 min. Sound. 16mm B&W. *Rental:* Learning Corp Am. *Sale:* Learning Corp Am.

I, Mobster. Steve Cochran & Lita Milan. Directed by Roger Corman. 1958. Fox. (Anamorphic). 80 min. Sound. 16mm B&W. *Rental:* Films Inc.

I Never Promised You a Rose Garden. Kathleen Quinlan, Bibi Andersson & Sylvia Sidney. Directed by Anthony Page. 1977. New World. 94 min. Sound. 16mm Color. *Rental:* Films Inc.

I Never Sang for My Father. Melvyn Douglas & Gene Hackman. Directed by Gilbert Cates. 1970. Columbia. 90 min. Sound. 16mm Color. *Rental:* Arcus Film, Bosco Films, Budget Films, Cine Craft, Films Inc, Inst Cinema, Kit Parker, Modern Sound, Newman Film Lib, Roas Films, Swank Motion, Twyman Films, Video Comm, Welling Motion Pictures, Westcoast Films, Wholesome Film Ctr, Williams Films & Willoughby Peer.

I Ought to Be in Pictures. Walter Matthau & Ann-Margret. Directed by Herbert Ross. 1982. Fox. 108 min. Sound. 16mm Color. *Rental:* Films Inc.

I Owe It All to the Songs I Sing. 1979. Carnation. (Documentary). 58 min. Sound. 16mm Color. *Rental:* Modern Talking.

I Passed for White. James Franciscus & Sonya Wilde. Directed by Fred M. Wilcox. 1960. Allied Artists. 92 min. Sound. 16mm B&W. *Rental:* Hurlock Cine.

I Promise to Pay. Chester Morris & Leo Carillo. Directed by D. Ross Lederman. 1937. Columbia. 69 min. Sound. 16mm B&W. *Rental:* Kit Parker.

I Pugni Om Tasca *see* Fists in the Pockets.

I. Q. Myth, The. 1975. CBS. (Documentary). 51 min. Sound. 16mm Color. *Rental:* Budget Films, Iowa Films, Syracuse U Film, U Cal Media & U Mich Media. *Sale:* Carousel Films.

I Remember Harlem. 4 pts. Directed by William Miles. 1980. Films for the Humanities. (Documentary). 232 min. Sound. 16mm Color. *Rental:* Films Human & U of IL Film. *Sale:* Films Human. *Sale:* Films Human, Videotape version.

I Remember, I Remember. 1970. Films Inc. (Documentary). 58 min. Sound. 16mm Color. *Rental:* Films Inc. *Sale:* Films Inc. *Sale:* Films Inc, Videotape version.

I Remember Mama. Irene Dunne & Barbara Bel Geddes. Directed by George Stevens. 1948. RKO. 134 min. Sound. 16mm B&W. *Rental:* Films Inc. *Rental:* RKO General Pics, 119 min. version.

I Ring Doorbells. Robert Shayne & Anne Gwynne. Directed by Frank R. Strayer. 1945. PRC. 67 min. Sound. 16mm B&W. *Sale:* Classics Assoc NY.

I Sailed to Tahiti with an All-Girl Crew. Gardner McKay & Fred Clark. Directed by Richard Bare. 1968. World Entertainment. 95 min. Sound. 16mm Color. *Rental:* Ivy Films. *Sale:* Rep Pic Film.

I Saw What You Did. Joan Crawford & John Ireland. Directed by William Castle. 1965. Universal. 83 min. Sound. 16mm B&W. *Rental:* Swank Motion.

I Sell Anything. Pat O'Brien & Ann Dvorak. Directed by Robert Florey. 1934. Warners. 70 min. Sound. 16mm B&W. *Rental:* MGM United.

I Sent a Letter to My Love. Simone Signoret & Jean Rochefort. Directed by Moshe Mizrahi. Fr. 1981. France. 102 min. Sound. 16mm Color. subtitles Eng. *Rental:* Films Inc.

I Shall Moulder Before I Shall Be Taken. S. Allen Counter Jr. Directed by David L. Evans. 1977. Surinam. (Documentary). 58 min. Sound. 16mm Color. *Rental:* Educ Media CA. *Sale:* Educ Media CA. *Sale:* Educ Media CA, Videotape version.

I Shot Jesse James. Preston Foster & John Ireland. Directed by Samuel Fuller. 1949. Screen Guild. 83 min. Sound. 16mm B&W. *Rental:* Budget Films, Inst Cinema, Kit Parker & Westcoast Films.

I Stand Accused. Robert Cummings & Lyle Talbot. Directed by John H. Auer. 1938. Republic. 54 min. Sound. 16mm B&W. *Rental:* Ivy Films. *Sale:* Rep Pic Film.

I Stand Condemned. Orig. Title: Moscow Nights. Sir Laurence Olivier & Harry Baur. Directed by Anthony Asquith. 1936. Britain. 74 min. Sound. 16mm B&W. *Rental:* Classic Film Mus & Em Gee Film Lib. *Sale:* Cinema Concepts & Glenn Photo.

I Take This Woman. Hedy Lamarr & Spencer Tracy. Directed by W. S. Van Dyke. 1940. MGM. 97 min. Sound. 16mm B&W. *Rental:* MGM United.

I Thank a Fool. Susan Hayward & Peter Finch. Directed by Robert Stevens. 1962. MGM. (Anamorphic). 100 min. Sound. 16mm Color. *Rental:* MGM United.

I, the Jury. Biff Elliott & Preston Foster. Directed by Harry Essex. 1953. United Artists. 87 min. Sound. 16mm B&W. *Rental:* Films Inc.

I, the Jury. Armand Assante & Barbara Carrera. Directed by Richard T. Heffron. 1982. Fox. 109 min. Sound. 16mm Color. *Rental:* Films Inc.

I Wake Up Screaming. Betty Grable. Directed by Bruce Humberstone. 1941. Fox. 82 min. 16mm B&W. *Rental:* Films Inc.

I Walk Alone. Burt Lancaster & Lizabeth Scott. Directed by Byron Haskin. 1947. Paramount. 98 min. Sound. 16mm B&W. *Rental:* Films Inc.

I Walk the Line. Gregory Peck & Tuesday Weld. Directed by John Frankenheimer. 1970. Columbia. 93 min. Sound. 16mm Color. *Rental:* Budget Films, Cine Craft, Film Ctr DC, Films Inc, Inst Cinema, Modern Sound, Newman Film Lib, Welling Motion Pictures & Westcoast Films.

I Walked with a Zombie. Tom Conway & Frances Dee. Directed by Jacques Tourneur. 1943. RKO. 68 min. Sound. 16mm B&W. *Rental:* Films Inc.

I Wanna Hold Your Hand. Nancy Allen & Susan Kendall Newman. Directed by Robert Zemeckis. 1978. Universal. 99 min. Sound. 16mm Color. *Rental:* Swank Motion.

I Want It All Now! 1978. NBC. (Documentary). 51 min. Sound. 16mm Color. *Rental:* Films Inc & Syracuse U Film. *Sale:* Films Inc. *Sale:* Films Inc & Utah Media, Videotape version.

I Want to Live! Susan Hayward. Directed by Robert Wise. 1958. MGM United. 120 min. Sound. 16mm B&W. *Rental:* MGM United.

I Want What I Want. Anne Heywood & Harry Andrews. Directed by John Dexter. 1972. Cinerama. 91 min. Sound. 16mm Color. *Rental:* Swank Motion.

I Want You. Dana Andrews & Dorothy McGuire. Directed by Mark Robson. 1951. Goldwyn. 101 min. Sound. 16mm B&W. *Rental:* Films Inc.

I Wanted Wings. Ray Milland & William Holden. Directed by Mitchell Leisen. 1941. Paramount. 135 min. Sound. 16mm B&W. *Rental:* Swank Motion.

I Was a Communist see Woman on Pier Thirteen.

I Was a Convict. Barton MacLane & Beverly Roberts. Directed by Aubrey Scotto. 1939. Republic. 65 min. Sound. 16mm B&W. *Rental:* Ivy Films.

I Was a Criminal see Passport to Heaven.

I Was a Male War Bride. Orig. Title: You Can't Sleep Here. Cary Grant & Ann Sheridan. Directed by Howard Hawks. 1949. Fox. 105 min. Sound. 16mm B&W. *Rental:* Films Inc.

I Was a Teenage Frankenstein. Orig. Title: Teenage Frankenstein. Whit Bissell, Phyllis Coates & Gary Conway. Directed by Herbert L. Strock. 1957. American International. 72 min. Sound. 16mm B&W. *Rental:* Films Inc, Ivy Films, Video Comm & Westcoast Films.

I Was a Teenage Werewolf. Michael Landon & Yvonne Lime. Directed by Gene Fowler. 1957. American International. 76 min. Sound. 16mm B&W. *Rental:* Budget Films, Ivy Films, Video Comm & Westcoast Films.

I Was an Adventuress. Vera Zorina & Richard Greene. Directed by Gregory Ratoff. 1940. Fox. 90 min. Sound. 16mm B&W. *Rental:* Films Inc.

I Was an American Spy. Ann Dvorak & Gene Evans. Directed by Lesley Selander. 1951. Allied Artists. 85 min. Sound. 16mm B&W. *Rental:* Hurlock Cine & Inst Cinema.

I Was Born at Home. 1979. PBS. (Documentary). 59 min. Videotape Color. *Rental:* PBS Video. *Sale:* PBS Video.

I Was Born, But... Tatsuo Saito. Directed by Yasujiro Ozu. Jap. 1932. Japan. 89 min. Silent. 16mm B&W. *Rental:* New Cinema & New Yorker Films.

I Was Framed. Michael Ames & Julie Bishop. Directed by D. Ross Lederman. 1942. Warners. 61 min. Sound. 16mm B&W. *Rental:* MGM United.

I Was Monty's Double. John Mills & Cecil Parker. Directed by John Guillermin. 1959. Britain. 100 min. Sound. 16mm B&W. *Rental:* Janus Films.

I Will Fight No More Forever. Ned Romero & Linda Redfern. 1974. Wolper. 106 min. Sound. 16mm Color. *Rental:* Films Inc, Macmillan Films, Modern Sound, Syracuse U Film & Texture Film. *Sale:* Texture Film.

I Wonder Who's Killing Her Now. Bob Dishy, Joanna Barnes & Bill Dana. Directed by Steven Hilliard Stern. 1975. Cinema Arts. 87 min. Sound. Super 8 Color. *Rental:* Budget Films.

I Wonder Who's Kissing Her Now. June Haver & Mark Stevens. Directed by Lloyd Bacon. 1947. Fox. 104 min. Sound. 16mm B&W. *Rental:* Films Inc.

I Wonder Who's Kissing Her Now. 1979. PBS. (Concert). 57 min. Videotape Color. *Rental:* PBS Video. *Sale:* PBS Video.

I Wouldn't Be in Your Shoes. Don Castle & Bill Kennedy. Directed by William Nigh. 1948. Monogram. 76 min. Sound. 16mm B&W. *Rental:* Hurlock Cine & Mogulls Films.

I, A Woman see Daughter.

I, Claudius see Epic That Never Was.

Ibanez' Torrent see Torrent.

Icarus' Children. 1978. 58 min. Sound. Videotape *Rental:* PBS Video. *Sale:* PBS Video.

Ice. 1970. New Cinema. (Documentary). 132 min. Sound. 16mm B&W. *Rental:* New Cinema.

Ice. Alain Delon. 123 min. Sound. 16mm *Rental:* WW Enter. *Rental:* WW Enter, Videotape version.

Ice Capades see Rhythm Hits the Ice.

Ice Castles. Robby Benson, Colleen Dewhurst & Lynn-Holly Johnson. Directed by Donald Wrye. 1979. Columbia. 113 min. Sound. 16mm Color. *Rental:* Arcus Film, Budget Films, Swank Motion, Welling Motion Pictures, Wholesome Film Ctr & Williams Films. *Rental:* Swank Motion, Videotape version.

Ice Cold in Alex. Orig. Title: Desert Attack. John Mills & Sylvia Sims. Directed by J. Lee Thompson. 1960. Britain. 76 min. Sound. 16mm B&W. *Rental:* Ivy Films & Janus Films.

Ice Flood. Viola Dana. Directed by George B. Seitz. 1926. Universal. 70 min. Silent. 16mm B&W. *Rental:* Mogulls Films.

Ice Follies of 1939. Joan Crawford, Lew Ayres & James Stewart. Directed by Reinhold Schunzel. 1939. MGM. (Color sequence). 82 min. Sound. 16mm B&W. *Rental:* MGM United.

Ice Palace. Richard Burton & Robert Ryan. Directed by Vincent Sherman. 1960. Warners. 143 min. Sound. 16mm Color. *Rental:* Swank Motion, Twyman Films & Williams Films.

Ice Pirates, The. Robert Urich & Mary Crosby. Directed by Stewart Raffil. 1984. MGM-UA. 95 min. Sound. 16mm Color. *Rental:* MGM United. *Rental:* MGM United, Videotape version.

Ice Station Zebra. Rock Hudson, Jim Brown & Patric McGoohan. Directed by John Sturges. 1968. MGM. 152 min. Sound. 16mm Color. *Rental:* MGM United. *Rental:* MGM United, Anamorphic color version.

Iceland. Orig. Title: Katina. Sonja Henie & John Payne. Directed by Bruce Humberstone. 1942. Fox. 79 min. Sound. 16mm B&W. *Rental:* Welling Motion Pictures & Willoughby Peer.

Iceman. Timothy Hutton & Lindsay Crouse. Directed by Fred Schepisi. 1985. Universal. 101 min. Sound. 16mm Color. *Rental:* Swank Motion. *Rental:* Swank Motion, Videotape version.

Iceman Cometh, The. Fredric March & Lee Marvin. Directed by John Frankenheimer. 1972. AFT. 239 min. Sound. 16mm Color. *Rental:* Films Inc.

Ichabod & Mr. Toad. 1949. Disney. (Animated). 68 min. Sound. 16mm Color. *Rental:* Bosco Films, Buchan Pic, Cine Craft, Cousino Visual Ed, Elliot Film Co, Film Ctr DC, Films Inc, Film Pres, MGM United, Modern Sound, Newman Film Lib, Roas Films, Swank Motion, Twyman Films, U of IL Film, Welling Motion Pictures, Westcoast Films & Williams Films.

Icy Breasts. Alain Delon, Mireille Darc & Claude Brasseur. Directed by Georges Lautner. Fr. 1975. France. 105 min. Sound. 16mm Color. subtitles. *Rental:* J Green Pics. *Sale:* Tamarelles French Film, Videotape version.

I'd Climb the Highest Mountain. Susan Hayward & William Lundigan. Directed by Henry King. 1951. Fox. 88 min. Sound. 16mm B&W. *Rental:* Films Inc. *Rental:* Films Inc, Color version.

I'd Give My Life. Tom Brown & Frances Drake. Directed by Edwin L. Marin. 1936. Paramount. 70 min. Sound. 16mm B&W. *Rental:* Mogulls Films.

I'd Rather Be a Blind Man. 1972. University of California. 60 min. Sound. 16mm Color. *Rental:* U Cal Media. *Sale:* U Cal Media.

I'd Rather Be Rich. Sandra Dee & Robert Goulet. Directed by Jack Smight. 1964. Universal. 96 min. Sound. 16mm Color. *Rental:* Swank Motion & Twyman Films.

Idaho. Roy Rogers. Directed by Joseph Kane. 1943. Republic. 54 min. Sound. 16mm B&W. *Rental:* Ivy Films. *Sale:* Rep Pic Film.

Idaho Kid, The. Rex Bell. Directed by Robert Hill. 1936. Colony. 60 min. Sound. 16mm B&W. *Sale:* Cinema Concepts.

Idea of Freedom, The. Directed by Michael Chanan. 1972. Oxford. 60 min. Sound. 16mm Color. *Rental:* New Yorker Films.

Identification Marks: None. Jerzy Skolimowski & Elizbieta Czywska. Directed by Jerzy Skolimowski. Pol. 1964. Poland. 74 min. Sound. 16mm B&W. *Rental:* New Yorker Films.

Identity Parade see Lineup.

Identity Unknown. Richard Arlen & Lola Lane. Directed by Walter Colmes. 1945. Republic. 63 min. Sound. 16mm B&W. *Rental:* Mogulls Films. *Sale:* Classics Assoc NY.

Idi Amin Dada. Directed by Barbet Schroeder. 1976. France. (Documentary). 90 min. Sound. 16mm Color. narrated Eng. *Rental:* Cinema Five & New Cinema.

Idiot, The. Gerard Philippe & Edwige Feuillere. Directed by George Lampin. Fr. 1946. France. 95 min. Sound. 16mm B&W. subtitles. *Rental:* Macmillan Films. *Lease:* Macmillan Films.

Idiot, The. Toshiro Mifune. Directed by Akira Kurosawa. Jap. 1951. Japan. 166 min. Sound. 16mm B&W. subtitles. *Rental:* New Yorker Films.

Idiot, The. Yuri Yakolev. Directed by Ivan Pyriev. Rus. 1958. Russia. 122 min. Sound. 16mm B&W. subtitles. *Rental:* Corinth Films.

Idiot's Delight. Clark Gable & Norma Shearer. Directed by Clarence Brown. 1939. MGM. 100 min. Sound. 16mm B&W. *Rental:* MGM United.

Idle Rich, The. Conrad Nagel & Bessie Love. Directed by William DeMille. 1929. MGM. 81 min. Sound. 16mm B&W. *Rental:* MGM United.

Idol, The. Yves Montand. 1956. France. 90 min. Sound. 16mm B&W. dubbed. *Rental:* Ivy Films.

Idol, The. Jennifer Jones & Michael Parks. Directed by Daniel Petrie. 1966. Embassy. 107 min. Sound. 16mm B&W. *Rental:* Films Inc.

Idol Dancer, The. Richard Barthelmess & Clarine Seymour. Directed by D. W. Griffith. 1920. First National. 113 min. Silent. 16mm B&W. *Rental:* Budget Films, Em Gee Film Lib & Kit Parker. *Sale:* Glenn Photo & Reel Images. *Sale:* Glenn Photo & Reel Images, Super 8 silent version. *Sale:* Glenn Photo, Silent 8mm version.

Idol of Paris. Michael Rennie. Directed by Leslie Arliss. 1948. 16mm *Rental:* A Twyman Pres.

Idolmaker, The. Ray Sharkey & Tovah Feldshuh. Directed by Taylor Hackford. 1980. United Artists. 119 min. Sound. 16mm Color. *Rental:* MGM United. *Rental:* MGM United, Videotape version.

Idols in the Dust see Saturday's Hero.

Idols of the Ring. Charard. (Documentary). 105 min. Sound. 16mm B&W. *Rental:* Charard Motion Pics.

If... Malcolm McDowell & David Wood. Directed by Lindsay Anderson. 1969. Paramount. 111 min. Sound. 16mm Color. *Rental:* Films Inc.

If a Man Answers. Sandra Dee & Bobby Darin. Directed by Henry Levin. 1962. Universal. 102 min. Sound. 16mm Color. *Rental:* Swank Motion.

If Elected. 1972. Wayne Ewing. (Documentary). 55 min. Sound. 16mm Color. *Rental:* U Mich Media & W Ewing Films. *Sale:* W Ewing Films.

If He Hollers, Let Him Go. Barbara McNair, Dana Wynter & Raymond St. Jacques. Directed by Charles Martin. 1968. Cinerama. 111 min. Sound. 16mm Color. *Rental:* Swank Motion.

If I Ever See You Again. Joseph Brooks & Shelley Hack. Directed by Joseph Brooks. 1978. Columbia. 105 min. Sound. 16mm Color. *Rental:* Swank Motion.

If I Had a Gun. Marian Bernat & Josef Graf. Directed by Stefan Uher. Slovak. 1971. 90 min. Sound. 16mm B&W. subtitles. *Rental:* Films Inc.

If I Had a Million. Directed by Ernst Lubitsch & Norman Taurog. 1932. Paramount. (Anthology). 73 min. Sound. 16mm B&W. *Rental:* Swank Motion.

If I Had My Way. Bing Crosby & Gloria Jean. Directed by David Butler. 1940. Universal. 94 min. Sound. 16mm B&W. *Rental:* Swank Motion.

If I Were Free. Irene Dunne & Clive Brook. Directed by Merian C. Cooper. 1934. RKO. 66 min. Sound. 16mm *Rental:* RKO General Pics.

If I Were King. Ronald Colman & Ellen Drew. Directed by Frank Lloyd. 1938. Paramount. 101 min. Sound. 16mm Color. *Rental:* Swank Motion.

If I Were King. William Farnum. Directed by J. Gordon Edwards. 1920. 16mm *Rental:* A Twyman Pres.

If I'm Lost, How Come I Found You? Moosie Drier, Ron Soble & Irene Tedrow. Directed by Arthur Lubin. 1978. ABC. 48 min. Sound. 16mm Color. *Rental:* MTI Tele. *Sale:* MTI Tele. *Sale:* MTI Tele, Videotape version.

If I'm Lucky. Vivian Blaine & Perry Como. Directed by Lewis Seiler. 1946. Fox. 79 min. Sound. 16mm B&W. *Rental:* Films Inc.

If It's Tuesday, This Must Be Belgium. Suzanne Pleshette & Ian McShane. Directed by Mel Stuart. 1969. United Artists. 98 min. Sound. 16mm Color. *Rental:* Arcus Film, MGM United, Welling Motion Pictures & Westcoast Films.

If Japan Can, Why Can't We? 1980. NBC News. (Documentary). 80 min. Sound. 16mm Color. *Rental:* Films Inc, OK AV Ctr, Roas Films, Syracuse U Film & U Mich Media. *Sale:* Films Inc. *Sale:* Films Inc, Videotape version.

If There Weren't Any Blacks You'd Have to Invent Them. Directed by Charles Jarrott. 1969. Britain. (Cast unlisted). 58 min. Sound. 16mm B&W. *Rental:* Mass Media & Westcoast Films. *Sale:* Mass Media.

If We Only Had Love. 55 min. Sound. 16mm Color. *Rental:* Alden Films.

If You Could Only Cook. Jean Arthur & Herbert Marshall. Directed by William A. Seiter. 1935. Columbia. 70 min. Sound. 16mm B&W. *Rental:* Modern Sound & Welling Motion Pictures.

If You Could See What I Hear. Marc Singer & H. R. Thomas. Directed by Eric Till. 1982. Canada. 103 min. Sound. 16mm Color. *Rental:* Swank Motion. *Rental:* Swank Motion, Videotape version.

If You Don't Come in Sunday, Don't Come in Monday. 1975. Manpower. (Documentary). 60 min. Sound. 16mm Color. *Rental:* Iowa Films & U Mich Media.

If You Feel Like Singing see Summer Stock.

If You Knew Susie. Eddie Cantor & Joan Davis. Directed by Gordon Douglas. 1948. RKO. 90 min. Sound. 16mm B&W. *Rental:* Films Inc. *Sale:* Blackhawk Films, Videotape version.

If You Loved Me. 1978. Operation Cork. (Cast unlisted). 54 min. Sound. 16mm Color. *Rental:* Modern Talking.

Ike. 1963. Hearst. (Documentary). 50 min. Sound. 16mm B&W. *Sale:* King Features.

Ikiru. Orig. Title: To Live. Takashi Shimura. Directed by Akira Kurosawa. Jap. 1952. Japan. 140 min. Sound. Videotape B&W. *Rental:* Films Inc.

Il Faut Tuer Birgitt Hass see Birgitt Hass Must Be Killed.

I'll Be Seeing You. Ginger Rogers & Joseph Cotten. Directed by William Dieterle. 1945. United Artists. 88 min. Sound. 16mm B&W. *Rental:* Films Inc.

I'll Cry Tomorrow. Susan Hayward & Jo Van Fleet. Directed by Daniel Mann. 1955. MGM. 117 min. Sound. 16mm B&W. *Rental:* MGM United.

I'll Get By. Dennis Day & Victor Mature. Directed by Richard Sale. 1950. Fox. 83 min. Sound. 16mm B&W. *Rental:* Films Inc. *Rental:* Films Inc, Color version.

I'll Get You. George Raft & Sally Gray. Directed by Seymour Friedman. 1953. Lippert. 79 min. Sound. 16mm B&W. *Rental:* Alba House & Budget Films.

I'll Give a Million. Warner Baxter & Marjorie Weaver. Directed by Walter Lang. 1938. Fox. 75 min. Sound. 16mm B&W. *Rental:* Films Inc.

I'll Love You Always. Nancy Carroll & George Murphy. Directed by Leo Bulgakov. 1935. Columbia. 75 min. Sound. 16mm B&W. *Rental:* Kit Parker.

Ill Met by Moonlight. Dirk Bogarde & Marius Goring. Directed by Michael Powell. 1958. 92 min. Sound. 16mm B&W. *Rental:* Budget Films, Kit Parker & U of IL Film.

I'll Name the Murderer. Ralph Forbes & Marion Shilling. Directed by Raymond K. Johnson. 1936. Puritan. 70 min. Sound. 16mm B&W. *Rental:* Mogulls Films.

I'll Never Cry! Trans. Title: Watashi Wa Nakanai. Masako Izumi & Kazuo Kitamura. Directed by Kenji Yoshida. Jap. 1966. Japan. 91 min. Sound. 16mm B&W. subtitles. *Rental:* Transworld Films & Twyman Films.

I'll Never Forget What's 'Is Name. Orson Welles & Oliver Reed. Directed by Michael Winner. 1967. Britain. 99 min. Sound. 16mm Color. *Rental:* Swank Motion.

I'll Reach for a Star. Frances Langford & Phil Regan. Directed by Gus Meins. 1936. Republic. 83 min. Sound. 16mm B&W. *Rental:* Ivy Films.

I'll Sell My Life. Michael Whalen & Rose Hobart. Directed by Elmer Clifton. 1941. Select Attractions. 71 min. Sound. 16mm B&W. *Rental:* Ivy Films & Mogulls Films. *Sale:* Rep Pic Film.

I'll Take Romance. Grace Moore & Melvyn Douglas. Directed by Edward H. Griffith. 1937. Columbia. 85 min. Sound. 16mm B&W. *Rental:* Bosco Films & Kit Parker.

I'll Take Sweden. Bob Hope & Tuesday Weld. Directed by Frederick De Cordova. 1965. United Artists. 96 min. Sound. 16mm Color. *Rental:* MGM United.

I'll Turn to You. Terry Randall. Directed by Geoffrey Faithfull. 1946. Britain. 96 min. Sound. 16mm B&W. *Rental:* Mogulls Films.

I'll Wait for You. Robert Sterling & Marsha Hunt. Directed by Robert B. Sinclair. 1941. MGM. 73 min. Sound. 16mm B&W. *Rental:* MGM United.

Illegal. Margot Grahame & Isobel Elsom. Directed by William McGann. 1932. Warners. 72 min. Sound. 16mm B&W. *Rental:* MGM United.

Illegals, The. Directed by Meyer Levin. 1947. Israel. (Documentary). 56 min. Sound. 16mm B&W. narrated Eng. *Rental:* Alden Films & Films Inc.

Illicit. Barbara Stanwyck & Joan Blondell. Directed by Archie Mayo. 1931. Warners. 81 min. Sound. 16mm B&W. *Rental:* MGM United.

Illicit Interlude see Summer Interlude.

Illusion Travels by Streetcar, The. Lilia Prado & Carlos Navarro. Directed by Luis Bunuel. 1953. 90 min. Sound. 16mm B&W. *Rental:* Films Inc.

Illusions of a Lady. Directed by Jonas Middleton. 70 min. Sound. 16mm Color. *Rental:* New Line Cinema.

Illusions Two. Threshold. (Anthology). 100 min. Sound. 16mm Color. *Rental:* Threshold Films.

Illustrated Man, The. Rod Steiger & Claire Bloom. Directed by Jack Smight. 1969. Warners. 103 min. Sound. 16mm Color. *Rental:* Films Inc, Inst Cinema, Ivy Films, Video Comm, Welling Motion Pictures & Willoughby Peer. *Rental:* Twyman Film, Anamorphic version.

Ilya Mourmoretz see Sword & the Dragon.

I'm a Stranger Here Myself. Directed by David Helpern Jr. 1974. Victor. (Documentary). 61 min. Sound. 16mm Color. *Rental:* Films Inc & Texture Film. *Sale:* Texture Film.

I'm All Right, Jack. Peter Sellers & Ian Carmichael. Directed by John Boulting. 1960. Britain. 104 min. Sound. 16mm B&W. *Rental:* Corinth Films.

I'm Dancing As Fast As I Can. Jill Clayburgh & Nicol Williamson. Directed by Jack Hofsiss. 1982. Paramount. 57 min. Sound. 16mm Color. *Rental:* Films Inc.

I'm Dependent, You're Addicted. 1972. Britain. (Documentary). 51 min. Sound. 16mm Color. *Rental:* Films Inc. *Sale:* Films Inc. *Rental:* Films Inc, *Sale:* Films Inc, Videotape version.

I'm from Arkansas. Slim Summerville. Directed by Lew Landers. 1944. PRC. 60 min. Sound. 16mm B&W. *Rental:* Ivy Films. *Sale:* Classics Assoc NY & Rep Pic Film.

I'm from the City. Joe Penner & Kay Sutton. Directed by Ben Holmes. 1938. RKO. 66 min. Sound. 16mm *Rental:* RKO General Pics.

I'm Going to Tamper with Your Beliefs a Little. Directed by Michael Chanan. 1972. Oxford U.. (Interview). 60 min. Sound. 16mm Color. *Rental:* New Yorker Films.

I'm No Angel. Mae West & Cary Grant. Directed by Wesley Ruggles. 1933. Paramount. 88 min. Sound. 16mm B&W. *Rental:* Williams Films.

I'm Still Alive. Kent Taylor & Linda Hayes. Directed by Irving Reis. 1941. RKO. 72 min. Sound. 16mm *Rental:* RKO General Pics.

Image Before My Eyes. Directed by Josh Waletzky. 1980. Yivo. (Documentary). 90 min. Sound. 16mm Color. *Rental:* Cinema Five.

Image, Flesh & Voice. Directed by Ed Emschwiller. 1969. Ed Emschwiller. (Ballet). 77 min. Sound. 16mm B&W. *Rental:* Canyon Cinema.

Image Makers, The. 58 min. Sound. Videotape *Rental:* PBS Video. *Sale:* PBS Video.

Images. Susannah York. Directed by Robert Altman. 1972. Columbia. 101 min. Sound. 16mm Color. *Rental:* Corinth Films, Swank Motion & Twyman Films. *Rental:* Twyman Films, Anamorphic version. *Rental:* Swank Motion, Videotape version.

Imaginary Voyage, The see Voyage Imaginaire.

Imagination & the Rise of the Popular Front. Directed by Armand Panigel. France. (Documentary). 70 min. Sound. 16mm B&W. subtitles. *Rental:* French Am Cul.

Imaginero. Directed by Jorge Preloran & Robert Gardner. 1971. Argentina. (Documentary). 52 min. Sound. 16mm Color. *Rental:* Phoenix Films, Syracuse U Film, U Cal Media & U of IL Film. *Sale:* Phoenix Films. *Sale:* Phoenix Films, Videotape version.

Imitation General, The. Glenn Ford & Dean Jones. Directed by George Marshall. 1958. MGM. 88 min. Sound. 16mm B&W. *Rental:* MGM United. *Rental:* MGM United, Anamorphic version.

Imitation of Life. Claudette Colbert & Warren William. Directed by John M. Stahl. 1934. Universal. 109 min. Sound. 16mm B&W. *Rental:* Williams Films.

Immaculate Emperor, The: Hirohito. 1971. Britain. 52 min. Sound. 16mm Color. *Rental:* Films Inc. *Sale:* Films Inc. *Rental:* Films Inc, *Sale:* Films Inc, Spanish language version. *Rental:* Films Inc, *Sale:* Films Inc, Videotape version.

Immoral Mr. Teas, The. Directed by Russ Meyer. 1959. Padram. (Cast unlisted). 61 min. Sound. 16mm Color. *Rental:* Corinth Films. *Sale:* Cinema Concepts & Video Lib, Videotape version.

Immoral Tales. Paloma Picasso. Directed by Walerian Borowczyk. 1976. New Line Cinema. 90 min. Sound. 16mm Color. subtitles. *Rental:* New Line Cinema.

Immortal Batallion, The. David Niven & Stanley Holloway. Sir Directed by Sir Carol Reed. 1944. Britain. 91 min. Sound. 16mm *Rental:* Budget Films.

Immortal Saint, The. Maria Falconetti. Directed by Carl Th. Dreyer. 1928. France. 60 min. Silent. 16mm B&W. dubbed. *Rental:* Budget Films.

Immortal Sergeant, The. Henry Fonda & Maureen O'Hara. Directed by John M. Stahl. 1943. Fox. 91 min. Sound. 16mm B&W. *Rental:* Films Inc.

Immortelle, L'. Francoise Brion. Directed by Alain Robbe-Grillet. Fr. 1963. France. 95 min. Sound. 16mm B&W. subtitles. *Rental:* Grove.

Immunity. 1980. US Government. (Documentary). 60 min. Videotape Color. *Sale:* Natl AV Ctr.

Impact. Brian Donlevy & Ella Raines. Directed by Arthur Lubin. 1949. United Artists. 83 min. Sound. 16mm B&W. *Rental:* Budget Films & Video Comm. *Lease:* Video Comm. *Rental:* Video Comm, *Lease:* Video Comm, Videotape version.

Impatient Maiden, The. Lew Ayers & Mae Clarke. Directed by James Whale. 1932. Universal. 90 min. Sound. 16mm B&W. *Rental:* Swank Motion.

Impeachment of Andrew Johnson, The. 1979. PBS. (Cast unlisted). 60 min. Videotape Color. *Rental:* PBS Video. *Sale:* PBS Video.

Imperial City, The. 1980. 45 min. Sound. 16mm Color. *Rental:* A Cantor. *Sale:* A Cantor.

Implacable Three, The. Geoffrey Horne. Directed by J. R. Marchent. 1966. Italy. 90 min. Sound. 16mm Color. dubbed. *Rental:* Video Comm.

Importance of Being Earnest, The. Sir Michael Redgrave & Joan Greenwood. Directed by Anthony Asquith. 1952. Britain. 95 min. Sound. 16mm Color. *Rental:* Films Inc.

Impossible Years, The. David Niven & Lola Albright. Directed by Michael Gordon. 1968. MGM. 92 min. Sound. 16mm Color. *Rental:* MGM United. *Rental:* MGM United, Anamorphic color version.

Imposter, The. Jean Gabin & Richard Whorf. Directed by Julien Duvivier. 1944. Universal. 95 min. Sound. 16mm B&W. *Rental:* Swank Motion.

Imposters, The. Directed by Mark Rappaport. 1980. First Run. (Cast unlisted). 110 min. Sound. 16mm Color. *Rental:* First Run.

Impressionists, The. 1971. 42 min. Sound. 16mm Color. *Rental:* U Mich Media.

Impressions of a City: Shanghai. Directed by Joris Ivens & Marceline Loridan. 1973. China. 60 min. Sound. 16mm B&W. *Rental:* Icarus Films. *Rental:* Icarus Films, Color version.

Improper Channels. Alan Arkin & Mariette Hartley. Directed by Eric Till. 1981. Canada. 92 min. Sound. 16mm Color. *Rental:* Swank Motion.

Improper Conduct. Reinaldo Arenas, Susan Sontag & Armando Valladares. Span. & Fr. 1984. 115 min. Sound. 16mm Color. subtitles. *Rental:* New Yorker Films.

Improvised Drama. 1969. Time-Life. (Documentary). 60 min. Sound. 16mm B&W. *Rental:* BYU Media.

In a Class All by Himself. 1974. NBC. (Documentary). 50 min. Sound. 16mm Color. *Rental:* Films Inc & Iowa Films. *Sale:* Films Inc & Utah Media. *Sale:* Films Inc, Videotape version.

In a Far Country. 1982. EBE. (Documentary). 54 min. Sound. 16mm Color. *Sale:* Ency Brit Ed. *Rental:* Iowa Films & Ency Brit Ed. *Sale:* Ency Brit Ed, Videotape version.

In a Lonely Place. Humphrey Bogart & Gloria Grahame. Directed by Nicholas Ray. 1950. Columbia. 94 min. Sound. 16mm B&W. *Rental:* Bosco Films, Budget Films, Cine Craft, Films Inc, Images Film, Kit Parker, Roas Films, Swank Motion, Twyman Films, Welling Motion Pictures, Westcoast Films & Wholesome Film Ctr.

In a Woman, a Family. Directed by Joris Ivens & Marceline Loridan. 1973. China. (Documentary). 108 min. Sound. 16mm Color. *Rental:* Cinema Arts.

In a Year of Thirteen Moons. Elvira Weishaupt. Directed by Rainer Werner Fassbinder. Ger. 1979. Germany. 129 min. Sound. 16mm Color. subtitles. *Rental:* New Cinema & New Yorker Films.

In Again, Out Again. Douglas Fairbanks & Arlene Pretty. Directed by John Emerson. 1917. Artcraft. 80 min. Silent. 16mm B&W. *Rental:* A Twyman Pres & Twyman Films.

In-Between Age. Orig. Title: Golden Disc, The. Lee Patterson & Mary Steele. Directed by Don Sharp. 1958. Allied Artists. 78 min. Sound. 16mm B&W. *Rental:* Hurlock Cine.

In Caliente. Dolores Del Rio & Pat O'Brien. Directed by Lloyd Bacon. 1935. Warners. 84 min. Sound. 16mm B&W. *Rental:* MGM United.

In Celebration. Alan Bates & Brian Cox. Directed by Lindsay Anderson. 1973. AFT. 131 min. Sound. 16mm Color. *Rental:* Films Inc.

In Cold Blood. Robert Blake & Scott Wilson. Directed by Richard Brooks. 1967. Columbia. 134 min. Sound. 16mm B&W. *Rental:* Arcus Film, Budget Films, Cine Craft, Films Inc, Inst Cinema, Modern Sound, Natl Film Video, Swank Motion, Twyman Films, U of IL Film, Welling Motion Pictures, Westcoast Films, Wholesome Film Ctr & Williams Films. *Rental:* Images Film, Kit Parker & Swank Motion, Anamorphic, B&W version. *Rental:* Budget Films, 113 mins. version. *Rental:* Swank Motion, Videotape version.

In Dark Places: Remembering the Holocaust. Directed by Gina Blumenfeld. 1978. Phoenix. (Documentary). 58 min. Sound. 16mm Color. *Rental:* Iowa Films & Phoenix Films. *Sale:* Phoenix Films. *Sale:* Phoenix Films, Videotape version.

In Defense of Rome. 3 pts. 1964. CBS. (Documentary). 54 min. Sound. 16mm B&W. *Rental:* McGraw-Hill Films & Syracuse U Film. *Sale:* McGraw-Hill Films.

In Enemy Country. Anthony Franciosa & Anjanette Comer. Directed by Harry Keller. 1968. Universal. 107 min. Sound. 16mm Color. *Rental:* Swank Motion.

In Fast Company. Bowery Boys. Directed by Del Lord. 1946. Monogram. 65 min. Sound. 16mm B&W. *Rental:* Buchan Pic & Modern Sound.

In for Treatment: The Patient Is Always the Last to Know. Helmut Woudenberg & Frank Groothof. Directed by Marja Kok & Erik Van Zuylen. 1982. Netherlands. 92 min. Sound. Videotape Color. subtitles. *Sale:* IFEX.

In Gay Madrid. Ramon Navarro & Dorothy Jordan. Directed by Robert Z. Leonard. 1930. MGM. 85 min. Sound. 16mm B&W. *Rental:* MGM United.

In God We Trust. 1974. Ken Anderson. (Cast unlisted). 60 min. Sound. 16mm Color. *Rental:* G Herne & Roas Films.

In God We Trust. Marty Feldman, Peter Boyle & Richard Pryor. Directed by Marty Feldman. 1980. Universal. 97 min. Sound. 16mm Color. *Rental:* Swank Motion.

In Harm's Way. John Wayne & Patricia Neal. Directed by Otto Preminger. 1965. Paramount. (Anamorphic). 165 min. Sound. 16mm B&W. *Rental:* Films Inc.

In Heaven There Is No Beer. Directed by Les Blank. 1984. Les Blank. (Dance). 50 min. Sound. 16mm Color. *Rental:* Flower Films. *Sale:* Flower Films.

In His Steps. Cheryl Lee Morrison. Directed by Ken Anderson. 1963. Ken Anderson. 70 min. Sound. 16mm B&W. *Rental:* G Herne & Roas Films.

In His Steps *see* Footsteps of Youth.

In Justice *see* Road Gang.

In-Laws, The. Peter Falk & Alan Arkin. Directed by Arthur Hiller. 1979. Warners. 103 min. Sound. 16mm Color. *Rental:* Swank Motion. *Rental:* Swank Motion, Videotape version.

In Like Flint. James Coburn & Lee J. Cobb. Directed by Gordon Douglas. 1967. Fox. (Anamorphic). 114 min. Sound. 16mm Color. *Rental:* Films Inc.

In Love & War. Robert Wagner & Dana Wynter. Directed by Philip Dunne. 1958. Fox. 111 min. Sound. 16mm Color. *Rental:* Films Inc.

In Macarthur Park. Adam Silver & Anita Noble. Directed by Bruce R. Schwartz. 1977. New Line Cinema. 70 min. Sound. 16mm Color. *Rental:* New Line Cinema.

In Memory of the Land & People. Directed by Robert Gates. 1979. Green Mountain Post. 50 min. Sound. 16mm Color. *Rental:* Green Mt. *Sale:* Green Mt.

In Name Only. Carole Lombard, Cary Grant & Kay Francis. Directed by John Cromwell. 1939. RKO. 94 min. Sound. 16mm B&W. *Rental:* Films Inc.

In Old Amarillo. Roy Rogers. Directed by William Witney. 1951. Republic. 67 min. Sound. 16mm B&W. *Rental:* Ivy Films. *Sale:* Rep Pic Film.

In Old Caliente. Roy Rogers. Directed by William Witney. 1951. Republic. 67 min. Sound. 16mm B&W. *Rental:* Ivy Films. *Sale:* Cine Concepts & Rep Pic Film. *Sale:* Video Comm, Videotape version.

In Old California. John Wayne & Albert Dekker. Directed by William McGann. 1942. Republic. 89 min. Sound. 16mm B&W. *Rental:* Ivy Films. *Lease:* Rep Pic Film.

In Old Cheyenne. Rex Lease. Directed by Stuart Payton. 1931. World Wide. 60 min. Sound. 16mm B&W. *Rental:* Budget Films. *Sale:* Reel Images, Super 8 sound version.

In Old Cheyenne. Roy Rogers. Directed by Joseph Kane. 1941. Republic. 60 min. Sound. 16mm B&W. *Rental:* Budget Films, Ivy Films & Westcoast Films. *Sale:* Rep Pic Film & Reel Images.

In Old Chicago. Tyrone Power, Alice Faye & Don Ameche. Directed by Henry King. 1938. Fox. 111 min. Sound. 16mm B&W. *Rental:* Films Inc.

In Old Colorado. William Boyd. Directed by Howard Bretherton. 1941. Paramount. 65 min. Sound. 16mm B&W. *Lease:* Cinema Concepts.

In Old Kentucky. Will Rogers & Dorothy Wilson. Directed by George Marshall. 1935. Fox. 84 min. Sound. 16mm B&W. *Rental:* Films Inc.

In Old Mexico. William Boyd. Directed by Edward Venturini. 1938. Paramount. 54 min. Sound. 16mm B&W. *Sale:* Cinema Concepts.

In Old Missouri. Alan Ladd & June Storey. Directed by Frank McDonald. 1940. Republic. 71 min. Sound. 16mm B&W. *Rental:* Ivy Films.

In Old Monterey. Gene Autry. Directed by Joseph Kane. 1939. Republic. 54 min. Sound. 16mm B&W. *Rental:* Ivy Films.

In Old Oklahoma *see* War of the Wildcats.

In Old Sacramento. Constance Moore & Jack La Rue. Directed by Joseph Kane. 1946. Republic. 89 min. Sound. 16mm B&W. *Rental:* Ivy Films. *Sale:* Rep Pic Film.

In Old Santa Fe. Ken Maynard & Gene Autry. Directed by David Howard. 1934. Mascot. 50 min. Sound. 16mm B&W. *Rental:* OK AV Ctr. *Sale:* Cinema Concepts & Natl Cinema. *Rental:* Ivy Films, Super 8 sound version. *Sale:* Video Comm, Videotape version.

In Old Vienna. Heinz Roettinger. 1956. Republic. 69 min. Sound. 16mm B&W. dubbed. *Rental:* Ivy Films. *Sale:* Rep Pic Film.

In Our Hands. 1983. Almi. (Documentary). Sound. 16mm Color. *Rental:* Cinema Five.

In Our Own Backyard: The First Love Canal. 1982. 59 min. Videotape *Rental:* Bullfrog Films. *Sale:* Bullfrog Films.

In Our Time. Ida Lupino & Paul Henreid. Directed by Vincent Sherman. 1944. Warners. 110 min. Sound. 16mm B&W. *Rental:* MGM United.

In Our Water. Directed by Meg Switzgable. 1981. New Day. (Documentary). 60 min. Sound. 16mm Color. *Rental:* New Day Films. *Sale:* New Day Films. *Sale:* New Day Films, Videotape version.

In Person. Ginger Rogers & George Brent. Directed by William A. Seiter. 1935. RKO. 87 min. Sound. 16mm B&W. *Rental:* Films Inc.

In Praise of Folly. 1966. France. (Ballet). 52 min. Sound. 16mm Color. *Rental:* Macmillian Films. *Sale:* Macmillian Films.

In Praise of Older Women. Tom Berenger & Karen Black. Directed by George Kaczender. 1978. Canada. 105 min. Sound. 16mm Color. *Rental:* Films Inc.

In Rosie's Room *see* Rosie the Riveter.

In Saigon: Some May Live. Joseph Cotten & Martha Hyer. Directed by Vernon Sewell. 1966. RKO. 100 min. Sound. 16mm Color. *Rental:* Budget Films & Video Comm.

In Search of a Past. 1968. CBS. (Documentary). 55 min. Sound. 16mm B&W. *Rental:* Budget Films, U Mich Media & NYU Film Lib. *Sale:* Phoenix Films. *Sale:* Phoenix Films, Videotape version.

In Search of a Sinner. Constance Talmadge. Directed by David Kirkland. 1920. 16mm *Rental:* A Twyman Pres.

In Search of Ancient Astronauts. 1972. Xerox. (Documentary). 52 min. Sound. 16mm Color. *Rental:* Budget Films, LA Inst Res Ctr, Natl Film Video, Syracuse U Film, U of IL Film, U Mich Media & Williams Films.

In Search of Ancient Mysteries. 1973. Xerox. (Documentary). 52 min. Sound. 16mm Color. *Rental:* Budget Films, Kent St U Film, LA Inst Res Ctr, Syracuse U Film & U of IL Film.

In Search of Gregory. Julie Christie & Michael Sarrazin. Directed by Peter Wood. 1970. Universal. 107 min. Sound. 16mm Color. *Rental:* Swank Motion.

In Search of Hart Crane. Orig. Title: Poetry: In Search of Hart Crane. 1966. NET. (Documentary). 90 min. Sound. 16mm B&W. *Rental:* Indiana AV Ctr. *Sale:* Indiana AV Ctr.

In Search of Historic Jesus. John Rubinstein, John Anderson, Nehemiah Persoff & Royal Dano. Directed by Henning Schellerup. 1979. Sunn. 90 min. Sound. 16mm Color. *Rental:* Modern Sound. *Sale:* Lucerne Films. *Sale:* Lucerne Films, Videotape version.

In Search of Man. 1966. Wolper. (Documentary). 50 min. Sound. 16mm B&W. *Rental:* Films Inc. *Sale:* Films Inc. *Sale:* Films Inc, Videotape version.

In Search of Noah's Ark. Directed by James L. Conway. 1979. Sunn. (Documentary). 100 min. Sound. 16mm Color. *Rental:* Welling Motion Pictures & Williams Films. *Sale:* Lucerne Films. *Sale:* Lucerne Films, *Rental:* Williams Films, Videotape version.

In Search of the Bowhead Whale. 1974. Canada. (Documentary). 50 min. Sound. 16mm Color. *Rental:* U Cal Media.

In Search of the Lost World. 1971. MGM. (Documentary). 52 min. Sound. 16mm Color. *Rental:* Films Inc, Syracuse U Film, U Cal Media, U of IL Film & Wholesome Film Ctr. *Sale:* Films Inc. *Sale:* Films Inc, Videotape version.

In Spring One Plants Alone. Directed by Vincent Ward. 1980. New Zealand. (Documentary). 45 min. Sound. 16mm Color. *Rental:* Liberty Co.

In the Bag. 90 min. Sound. 16mm B&W. *Rental:* Bosco Films.

In the Beginning. Georgina Spelvin & Gloria Grant. Directed by Wakefield Poole. 1974. Poole. 85 min. Sound. 16mm Color. *Rental:* J Green Pics.

In the Beginning. Directed by Colin Clark. 1975. Britain. 60 min. Sound. 16mm Color. *Rental:* Budget Films & Pyramid Film. *Sale:* Pyramid Film. *Sale:* Pyramid Film, *Rental:* Pyramid Film, Super 8 sound version. *Sale:* Pyramid Film, *Rental:* Pyramid Film, Videotape version.

In the Circus Arena. 1952. Russia. (Documentary). 65 min. Sound. 16mm Color. *Rental:* Films Inc.

In the Company of Men. Directed by William Greaves. 1969. Newsweek. (Documentary). 52 min. Sound. 16mm Color. *Rental:* U Cal Media & U Mich Media. *Sale:* McGraw-Hill Films.

In the Cool of the Day. Jane Fonda & Peter Finch. Directed by Robert Stevens. 1963. MGM. (Anamorphic). 89 min. Sound. 16mm Color. *Rental:* Films Inc & MGM United.

In the Country. William Devane. Directed by Robert Kramer. 1966. Robert Kramer. 65 min. Sound. 16mm B&W. *Rental:* New Cinema.

In the Event Anyone Disappears. 1973. Monument. (Documentary). 50 min. Sound. 16mm B&W. *Rental:* Tricontinental Film. *Sale:* Tricontinental Film.

In the Event of a Catastrope. 1978. 58 min. Sound. Videotape *Rental:* PBS Video. *Sale:* PBS Video.

In the Forest. Directed by Phillip Mulloy. 1978. Britain. 80 min. Sound. 16mm B&W. *Rental:* Museum Mod Art. *Lease:* Museum Mod Art.

In the Good Old Summertime. Judy Garland & Van Johnson. Directed by Robert Z. Leonard. 1949. MGM. 103 min. Sound. 16mm Color. *Rental:* MGM United.

In the Heat of the Night. Rod Steiger & Sidney Poitier. Directed by Norman Jewison. 1967. United Artists. 109 min. Sound. 16mm Color. *Rental:* MGM United.

In the King of Prussia. Martin Sheen. 1983. Sound. 16mm *Rental:* Bullfrog Films. *Sale:* Bullfrog Films.

In the Land of the War Canoes. 1973. University of Washington. (Documentary). 47 min. Sound. 16mm Color. *Rental:* U Cal Media.

In the Meantime, Darling. Jeanne Crain. Directed by Otto Preminger. 1944. Fox. 72 min. Sound. 16mm B&W. *Rental:* Films Inc.

In the Money. Bowery Boys. Directed by William Beaudine. 1958. Allied Artists. 61 min. Sound. 16mm B&W. *Rental:* Budget Films.

In the Name of Allah. 1970. Britain. (Documentary). 76 min. Sound. 16mm B&W. *Rental:* Indiana AV Ctr. *Sale:* Indiana AV Ctr.

In the Name of the Father. Lou Castel. Directed by Marco Bellocchio. Ital. 1971. Italy. 115 min. Sound. 16mm Color. subtitles. *Rental:* New Yorker Films.

In the National Interest. 1963. US Government. (Documentary). 60 min. Sound. 16mm Color. *Sale:* Natl AV Ctr.

In the Rapture. 1976. Indiana U.. (Concert). 60 min. Sound. 16mm Color. *Rental:* Indiana AV Ctr. *Sale:* Indiana AV Ctr.

In the Realm of the Senses. Tatsuya Fuji & Eiko Matsuda. Directed by Nagisa Oshima. Jap. 1977. Japan. 115 min. Sound. 16mm Color. subtitles. *Rental:* Cinema Five.

In the Steel Net of Dr. Mabuse *see* Return of Dr. Mabuse.

In the Studio. Fifth Dimension. 60 min. Videotape Color. *Sale:* Cinema Concepts.

In the Wake of a Stranger. Shirley Eaton. Directed by David Eady. 1958. 65 min. 16mm *Rental:* A Twyman Pres.

In the Year of the Pig. Directed by Emile De Antonio. 1969. Emile De Antonio. (Documentary). 101 min. Sound. 16mm B&W. *Rental:* New Cinema & New Yorker Films.

In This Corner. Scott Brady. Directed by Charles Reisner. 1948. Eagle Lion. 60 min. Sound. 16mm B&W. *Sale:* Classics Assoc NY.

In This House of Brede. Diana Rigg. Directed by George Schaefer. 1975. Tomorrow Entertainment. 105 min. Sound. 16mm Color. *Rental:* Budget Films, Kent St U Film, Kit Parker, Learning Corp Am, Mass Media & Syracuse U Film. *Sale:* Learning Corp Am.

In This Our Life. Bette Davis & Olivia De Havilland. Directed by John Huston. 1942. Warners. 96 min. Sound. 16mm B&W. *Rental:* MGM United.

In Which We Serve. Noel Coward & John Mills. Directed by Noel Coward & David Lean. 1942. Britain. 114 min. Sound. 16mm B&W. *Rental:* Budget Films, Images Film, Kit Parker, Learning Corp, Twyman Films & U of IL Film.

In White Collar America. 1974. NBC. (Documentary). 52 min. Sound. 16mm Color. *Rental:* Films Inc, U Cal Media & U Mich Media. *Sale:* Films Inc. *Sale:* Films Inc, Videotape version.

Inaugural Evening at Ford's Theatre, The. 1968. CBS. (Documentary). 54 min. Sound. 16mm B&W. *Rental:* Phoenix Films. *Sale:* Phoenix Films. *Rental:* Phoenix Films, *Sale:* Phoenix Films, Color version.

Inaugural Souvenir. 1976. Gould. (Documentary). 56 min. Sound. 16mm Color. *Rental:* Lucerne Films. *Sale:* Lucerne Films. *Sale:* Lucerne Films, Videotape version.

Incas, The. 1979. PBS. (Documentary). 59 min. Sound. Videotape Color. *Rental:* PBS Video & U Mich Media. *Sale:* PBS Video.

Incident. Warren Douglas & Jane Frazee. Directed by William Beaudine. 1949. Monogram. 68 min. Sound. 16mm B&W. *Rental:* Cinema Concepts & Hurlock Cine.

Incident, The. Martin Sheen & Thelma Ritter. Directed by Larry Peerce. 1967. Fox. 106 min. Sound. 16mm B&W. *Rental:* Films Inc.

Incident at Brown's Ferry: Nuke Fire. 1977. Nova. (Documentary). 58 min. Sound. 16mm Color. *Rental:* Syracuse U Film & U of IL Film.

Incident at Phantom Hill. Robert Fuller & Dan Duryea. Directed by Earl Bellamy. 1966. Universal. 88 min. Sound. 16mm Color. *Rental:* Swank Motion.

Incident in an Alley. Chris Warfield. Directed by Edward L. Cahn. 1962. United Artists. 83 min. Sound. 16mm B&W. *Rental:* MGM United.

Incident on Wilson Street. 1964. NBC. (Documentary). 51 min. Sound. 16mm B&W. *Rental:* U Mich Media. *Sale:* McGraw-Hill Films.

Including Me. 1976. CAPAC. (Documentary). 59 min. Sound. 16mm Color. *Rental:* Films Inc & U of IL Film. *Sale:* Films Inc, *Rental:* Indiana AV Ctr, *Sale:* Films Inc & Indiana AV Ctr, Videotape version.

Inconceivable Commerce, An. 1970. 60 min. Sound. 16mm Color. *Rental:* U Mich Media.

Incredible Book Escape, The. 1980. Churchill Films. 45 min. Sound. 16mm Color. *Rental:* Churchill Films. *Rental:* Churchill Films, Videotape version.

Incredible Bread Machine Film, The. 1976. World. (Documentary). 55 min. Sound. 16mm Color. *Rental:* Roas Films & U Cal Media.

Incredible Flight of the Snow Goose, The. 1972. NBC. (Documentary). 60 min. Sound. 16mm Color. *Rental:* Syracuse U Film.

Incredible, Indelible, Magical Mystery Tour. 1973. DePatie-Freleng. (Animated). 47 min. Sound. 16mm Color. *Rental:* Films Inc. *Sale:* Films Inc.

Incredible Journey, The. Directed by Fletcher Markle. 1963. Disney. (Animal cast). 80 min. Sound. 16mm Color. *Rental:* Bosco Films, Buchan Pic, Cine Craft, Disney Prod, Elliot Film Co, FilmS Inc, MGM United, Newman Film Lib, Roas Films, Swank Motion, Twyman Films, Welling Motion Pictures, Westcoast Films & Williams Films.

Incredible Journey of Dr. Meg Laurel, The. Lindsay Wagner, Jane Wyman & Dorothy McGuire. 141 min. Sound. 16mm Color. *Rental:* Welling Motion Pictures.

Incredible Melting Man, The. Burr De Benning & Myron Healey. Directed by William Sachs. 1978. American International. 86 min. Sound. 16mm Color. *Rental:* Swank Motion.

Incredible Mr. Limpet, The. Orig. Title: Be Careful How You Wish. Don Knotts. Directed by Arthur Lubin. 1964. Warners. 102 min. Sound. 16mm B&W. *Rental:* Buchan Pic, Charard Motion Pics, Film Ctr DC, Films Inc, Modern Sound, Swank Motion, Twyman Films, Welling Motion Pictures, Williams Films & Willoughby Peer. *Rental:* Williams Films, Color version.

Incredible Paris Incident, The. Roger Brown & Dick Palmer. 1968. France. 98 min. Sound. 16mm Color. dubbed. *Rental:* Video Comm.

Incredible Rocky Mountain Race, The. Christopher Connelly & Forrest Tucker. Directed by James L. Conway. 1979. Viacom. 102 min. Sound. 16mm Color. *Rental:* Budget Films, Modern Sound, Welling Motion Pictures & Williams Films. *Sale:* Lucerne Films. *Sale:* Lucerne Films, *Rental:* Williams Films, Videotape version.

Incredible Sarah, The. Glenda Jackson, Daniel Massey & Yvonne Mitchell. Directed by Richard Fleischer. 1976. Britain. 105 min. Sound. 16mm Color. *Rental:* Films Inc.

Incredible Shrinking Man, The. Grant Williams & Randy Stewart. Directed by Jack Arnold. 1957. Universal. 94 min. Sound. 16mm B&W. *Rental:* Swank Motion.

Incredible Shrinking Woman, The. Lily Tomlin & Charles Grodin. Directed by Joel Schumacher. 1981. Universal. 88 min. Sound. 16mm Color. *Rental:* Swank Motion. *Rental:* Swank Motion, Videotape version.

Incredible Two-Headed Transplant, The. Bruce Dern & Pat Priest. Directed by Anthony Lanza. 1971. American International. 88 min. Sound. 16mm Color. *Rental:* Video Comm.

Independence Day. Mel Rosier. Directed by Bobby Roth. 1976. Western World. 87 min. Sound. 16mm Color. *Rental:* Unifilm. *Sale:* Unifilm.

Independence Day. Kathleen Quinlan, David Keith & Frances Sternhagen. Directed by Robert Mandel. 110 min. Sound. 16mm Color. *Rental:* Swank Motion.

Indestructible Man, The. Lon Chaney Jr. & Casey Adams. Directed by Jack Pollexfen. 1956. Allied Artists. 70 min. Sound. 16mm B&W. *Rental:* Cinema Concepts & Hurlock Cine.

India: Haunting Passage. 1973. India. (Documentary). 54 min. Sound. 16mm B&W. *Rental:* Modern Mass. *Sale:* Modern Mass.

India: Machinery of Hope. 1979. 58 min. Sound. 16mm *Rental:* PBS Video. *Sale:* PBS Video. *Sale:* PBS Video, Videotape version.

India! My India! 1967. India. (Documentary). 104 min. Sound. 16mm B&W. *Rental:* McGraw-Hill Films. *Sale:* McGraw-Hill Films.

India Trip, The. 1971. Canada. (Documentary). 50 min. Sound. 16mm Color. *Rental:* Natl Film CN. *Sale:* Natl Film CN.

India: Writings on the Sand. 1965. NET. (Documentary). 60 min. Sound. 16mm B&W. *Rental:* BYU Media. *Rental:* BYU Media, Color version.

Indian Agent. Tim Holt & Richard Martin. Directed by Lesley Selander. 1948. RKO. 65 min. Sound. 16mm B&W. *Rental:* Budget Films.

Indian America. 1969. Creative Cine-Tel. (Documentary). 48 min. Sound. 16mm Color. *Rental:* Budget Films, BYU Media & Westcoast Films. *Sale:* Sterling Ed Film.

Indian Paint. Johnny Crawford & Jay Silverheels. Directed by Norman Foster. 1963. Eagle-American. 76 min. Sound. 16mm Color. *Rental:* Cine Craft, Charard Motion Pics, Film Ctr DC, Films Inc, Inst Cinema, Modern Sound, Welling Motion Pictures, Westcoast Films & Willoughby Peer. *Rental:* Video Comm, Videotape version. *Rental:* Bosco Films, 91 min. version.

Indian Rights, Indian Law. Directed by Joseph Consentino & Sandra Consentino. 1978. Ford Foundation. (Documentary). 60 min. Sound. 16mm Color. *Rental:* Films Inc. *Sale:* Films Inc. *Sale:* Films Inc, Videotape version.

Indian Scout *see* Davy Crockett, Indian Scout.

Indian Summer *see* Judge Steps Out.

Indian Uprising. George Montgomery & Audrey Long. Directed by Ray Nazarro. 1952. Columbia. 75 min. Sound. 16mm Color. *Rental:* Buchan Pic, Cine Craft, Films Inc & Newman Film Lib.

Indianapolis Speedway. Orig. Title: Devil on Wheels. Ann Sheridan & Pat O'Brien. Directed by Lloyd Bacon. 1939. Warners. 82 min. Sound. 16mm B&W. *Rental:* MGM United.

Indians Are Still Far Away, The. Christine Pascal & Isabelle Huppert. Directed by Patricia Moraz. 1977. New Line Cinema. 90 min. Sound. 16mm Color. *Rental:* New Line Cinema.

Indians of Northern Tribes, The. Directed by Victor Vicas. 1972. AIF. (Documentary). 60 min. Sound. 16mm B&W. *Sale:* Americas Films. *Sale:* Americas Films, Spanish version.

Indira Gandhi of India. 1972. Britain. (Documentary). 60 min. Sound. 16mm Color. *Rental:* Time-Life Multimedia. *Sale:* Time-Life Multimedia. *Rental:* Time-Life Multimedia, *Sale:* Time-Life Multimedia, Spanish-Language version. *Rental:* Time-Life Multimedia, *Sale:* Time-Life Multimedia, Videotape version.

Indiscreet. Gloria Swanson & Ben Lyon. Directed by Leo McCarey. 1931. United Artists. 80 min. Sound. 16mm B&W. *Rental:* Budget Films, Classic Film Mus & Film Classics. *Sale:* Classic Film Mus & Festival Films.

Indiscreet. Cary Grant & Ingrid Bergman. Directed by Stanley Donen. 1958. Warners. 100 min. Sound. 16mm Color. *Rental:* Arcus Film, Budget Films, Ivy Films, Video Comm & Welling Motion Pictures. *Lease:* Rep Pic Film. *Rental:* Ivy Films, *Sale:* Ivy Films, Super 8 sound version.

Indiscretion *see* Christmas in Connecticut.

Indiscretion of an American Wife. Jennifer Jones & Montgomery Clift. Directed by Vittorio De Sica. 1954. Columbia. 63 min. Sound. 16mm B&W. *Rental:* Budget Films & Films Inc.

Individual, The. 1965. NET. (Documentary). 60 min. Sound. 16mm B&W. *Rental:* BYU Media & Mass Media.

Indomitable Teddy Roosevelt, The. 1983. Churchill Films. 93 min. Sound. 16mm Color. *Rental:* Churchill Films. *Rental:* Churchill Films, Videotape version.

Industrial Applications of Radioisotopes. 1960. Atomic Energy Commission. (Documentary). 57 min. Sound. 16mm Color. *Rental:* Natl AV Ctr.

Infamous Crimes *see* Philo Vance Returns.

Infection Control. 1981. 87 min. Sound. Videotape Color. *Sale:* Natl AV Ctr.

Infernal Triangle, The. Directed by Gary Vaughan. 1974. Australia. (Documentary). 53 min. Sound. 16mm Color. *Rental:* Odeon Films. *Sale:* Odeon Films.

Inferno. Robert Ryan & Rhonda Fleming. Directed by Roy Baker. 1935. RKO. 107 min. Sound. 16mm Color. *Rental:* Films Inc.

Inferno of First Love *see* Namami.

Infinite Tenderness. Jose Guerra & Jean Christophe. Directed by Pierre Jallaud. 1972. France. (No dialog). 93 min. Sound. 16mm B&W. *Rental:* MGM United.

Infinite Variety of Music, The. Directed by William Graham. 1967. Saudek. (Documentary, kinescope). 60 min. Sound. 16mm B&W. *Rental:* IQ Films & U of IL Film. *Sale:* IQ Films.

Inflation. 1975. Phoenix. (Documentary). 54 min. Sound. 16mm Color. *Rental:* Phoenix Films. *Sale:* Phoenix Films. *Sale:* Phoenix Films, Videotape version.

Inflation: ABC Closeup. 1976. Phoenix. 54 min. Sound. 16mm Color. *Rental:* Syracuse U Film.

Inflation: The Fire That Won't Go Out. 1980. ABC/MTI. 45 min. Sound. 16mm Color. *Rental:* Syracuse U Film.

Influential Americans. 1960. CBS. (Documentary). 52 min. Sound. 16mm B&W. *Rental:* U Cal Media. *Sale:* Carousel Films.

Information Society, The. 58 min. Sound. Videotape *Rental:* PBS Video. *Sale:* PBS Video.

Informer, The. Victor McLaglen & Margot Grahame. Directed by John Ford. 1935. RKO. 91 min. Sound. 16mm B&W. *Rental:* Films Inc. *Lease:* Films Inc.

Inga. Marie Liljedahl. Directed by Joseph W. Sarno. 1968. Sweden. 81 min. Sound. 16mm B&W. dubbed. *Rental:* Swank Motion.

Ingmar Bergman. 1973. Sweden. (Documentary). 50 min. Sound. 16mm Color. *Rental:* Films Inc, Kent St U Film, U Cal Media & U Mich Media. *Sale:* Films Inc & Texture Film.

Ingrid. Directed by Gene Feldman. 1984. Wombat. (Documentary). 70 min. Sound. 16mm Color. *Rental:* Wombat Productions. *Sale:* Wombat Productions.

Inherit the Wind. Spencer Tracy & Fredric March. Directed by Stanley Kramer. 1960. United Artists. 127 min. Sound. 16mm B&W. *Rental:* MGM United.

Inheritance, The. Directed by Harold Mayer. 1964. Harold Mayer. (Documentary). 60 min. Sound. 16mm B&W. *Rental:* Budget Films, Iowa Films, Roas Films, Syracuse U Film, U Cal Media, U of IL Film & U Mich Media.

Inheritance, The. Dominique Sanda & Anthony Quinn. Directed by Mauro Bolognini. 1976. Durham. 95 min. Sound. 16mm Color. dubbed. *Rental:* Modern Sound & Vidamerica.

Inheritor, The. Orig. Title: Exterminator, The. Jean-Paul Belmondo. Directed by Philippe Labro. 1973. France. 111 min. Sound. 16mm Color. dubbed. *Rental:* Budget Films & Films Inc.

Inmate Training. 1969. Canada. (Documentary). 58 min. Sound. 16mm B&W. *Rental:* Intl Film. *Sale:* Intl Film.

Inn of the Sixth Happiness. Ingrid Bergman, Robert Donat & Curt Jurgen. Directed by Mark Robson. 1958. Fox. 158 min. Sound. 16mm Color. *Rental:* Films Inc & Twyman Films. *Rental:* Films Inc, Anamorphic version.

Inner Circle. Adele Mara & Warren Douglas. Directed by Philip Ford. 1946. Republic. 57 min. Sound. 16mm B&W. *Rental:* Ivy Films.

Innocence Unprotected. Dragoljub Aleksic. Directed by Dusan Makavejev. 1970. Yugoslavia. 75 min. Sound. 16mm B&W. subtitles. *Rental:* New Yorker Films.

Innocent, The. Giancarlo Giannini & Laura Antonelli. Directed by Luchino Visconti. Ital. 1979. Italy. 115 min. Sound. 16mm Color. subtitles. *Rental:* Films Inc.

Innocent Affair, An *see* Don't Trust Your Husband.

Innocent Bystanders. Stanley Baker & Dana Andrews. Directed by Peter Collinson. 1972. Paramount. 111 min. Sound. 16mm Color. *Rental:* Films Inc.

Innocent Sorcerers. Tadeusz Lomnicki. Directed by Andrzej Wajda. Pol. 1961. Poland. 85 min. Sound. 16mm B&W. subtitles. *Rental:* Janus Films.

Innocent Years, The: 1901-1914. 1965. NBC. (Documentary). 54 min. Sound. 16mm B&W. *Rental:* BYU Media, La Inst Res Ctr, McGraw-Hill Films, U Cal Media, U of IL Film U Mich Media & Utah Media. *Sale:* McGraw-Hill Films.

Innocents, The. Deborah Kerr, Sir Michael Redgrave. Directed by Jack Clayton. 1961. Fox. 99 min. Sound. 16mm B&W. *Rental:* Films Inc.

Innocents in Paris, The. Alastair Sim & Margaret Rutherford. Directed by Gordon Parry. 1955. Britain. 103 min. Sound. 16mm B&W. *Rental:* Liberty Co.

Inquiry Film, The. Directed by Jesse Nishihata. 1977. Canada. (Documentary). 90 min. Sound. 16mm Color. *Sale:* CFC.

Insect Alternative. 1978. Britain. (Documentary). 57 min. Sound. 16mm Color. *Rental:* Kent St U Film & U of Mich Media.

Inserts. Richard Dreyfuss. Directed by John Byrum. 1976. United Artists. 117 min. Sound. 16mm Color. *Rental:* MGM United.

Inside a Girl's Dormitory. Jean Marais & Francoise Arnoul. Directed by Henri Decoin. 1956. France. 102 min. Sound. 16mm B&W. dubbed. *Rental:* Ivy Films.

Inside Moves. John Savage & Diana Scarwid. Directed by Richard Donner. 1980. AFD. 113 min. Sound. 16mm Color. *Rental:* Swank Motion.

Inside North Vietnam. Directed by Felix Greene. 1968. Felix Greene. (Documentary). 85 min. Sound. 16mm Color. *Rental:* Icarus Films.

Inside Out. 1970. Jack Robertson. (Documentary). 56 min. Sound. 16mm Color. *Rental:* NYU Film Lib & U Mich Media.

Inside Out. Telly Savalas & James Mason. Directed by Peter Duffell. 1975. Britain-Germany. 97 min. Sound. 16mm Color. *Rental:* Swank Motion.

Inside Red China. 1967. CBS. (Documentary). 51 min. Sound. 16mm B&W. *Rental:* U of IL Film. *Sale:* Carousel Films. *Rental:* Syracuse U Film & U Cal Media, *Sale:* Carousel Films, Color version.

Inside Russia. Rus. 1941. Russia. (Documentary). 70 min. Sound. 16mm B&W. narrated Eng. *Rental:* Film Classics.

Inside Story, The. William Lundigan & Marsha Hunt. Directed by Allan Dwan. 1948. Republic. 87 min. Sound. 16mm B&W. *Rental:* Ivy Films. *Sale:* Rep Pic Film.

Inside Straight. David Brian & Arlene Dahl. Directed by Gerald Meyer. 1951. MGM. 87 min. Sound. 16mm B&W. *Rental:* MGM United.

Inside the Cell. 2 pts. 1949. US Government. (Documentary). 90 min. Sound. 16mm Color. *Sale:* Natl AV Ctr.

Inside the Cuckoo's Nest. 1977. PBS. (Documentary). 78 min. Videotape Color. *Rental:* PBS Video. *Sale:* PBS Video.

Inside the Foreign Office. 1968. NET. (Documentary). 52 min. Sound. 16mm B&W. *Rental:* Indiana AV Ctr. *Lease:* Indiana AV Ctr.

Inside the Golden Gate. 1977. Nova. (Documentary). 59 min. Sound. 16mm Color. *Rental:* Kent St U Film, U Cal Media, U of IL Film & U Mich Media, Videotape version.

Inside the Law. Wallace Ford & Luana Walters. Directed by Hamilton MacFadden. 1942. PRC. 60 min. Sound. 16mm B&W. *Rental:* Mogulls Films.

Inside the Mafia. Cameron Mitchell & Robert Strauss. Directed by Edward L. Cahn. 1959. United Artists. 72 min. Sound. 16mm B&W. *Rental:* MGM United.

Inside the Reich: Germany 1940-1944. Directed by Hugh Raggett. (World at War Ser.). : Pt. 16.). 1973. Media Guild. (Documentary). 52 min. Sound. 16mm Color. *Rental:* Media Guild & U Cal Media. *Sale:* Media Guild. *Sale:* Media Guild, Videotape version.

Inside the Shark. 1977. Nova. (Documentary). 50 min. Sound. 16mm Color. *Rental:* OK AV Ctr, #U Cal Media & U of IL Film.

Inspection & Palpitation of the Anterior Chest, The. 1966. US Government. (Documentary). 52 min. Sound. 16mm B&W. *Sale:* Natl AV Ctr.

Inspector Clouseau. Alan Arkin & Frank Finlay. Directed by Bud Yorkin. 1968. United Artists. 94 min. Sound. 16mm Color. *Rental:* Budget Films, MGM United, Welling Motion Pictures, Westcoast Films & Wholesome Film Ctr.

Inspector General, The. Danny Kaye & Walter Slezak. Directed by Henry Koster. 1949. Warners. 102 min. Sound. 16mm Color. *Rental:* Arcus Film, Budget Films, Classic Film Mus, Film Pres, MGM United, Westcoast Films & Wholesome Film Ctr. *Sale:* Cinema Concepts & Festival Films. *Sale:* Festival Films, Videotape version.

Inspector General, The. Orig. Title: Revizor. Directed by Vladimir Petrov. Rus. 1954. Russia. 128 min. Sound. 16mm B&W. *Rental:* Corinth Films.

Inspector Maigret. Orig. Title: Maigret Sets a Trap. Jean Gabin & Annie Giradot. Directed by Jean Delannoy. 1958. France. 110 min. Sound. 16mm B&W. dubbed. *Rental:* Westcoast Films.

Inspiration. Greta Garbo & Robert Montgomery. Directed by Clarence Brown. 1931. MGM. 74 min. Sound. 16mm B&W. *Rental:* MGM United.

Instant Coffee. Rita Tushingham. Directed by Gian Luigi Polidoro. Italy. 91 min. Sound. 16mm Color. dubbed. *Rental:* Films Inc.

Instinct for Survival. 1975. (Documentary). 92 min. Sound. 16mm Color. *Rental:* Films Inc & Video Comm. *Lease:* Video Comm.

Instructional Television at Pennsylvania State University. 1970. US Government. (Documentary). 60 min. Sound. 16mm B&W. *Sale:* Natl AV Ctr.

Instructors of Death. Hui Ying Hung & Mai Te Lo. 110 min. Sound. 16mm *Rental:* WW Enter. *Rental:* WW Enter, Videotape version.

Insurance Investigator. Richard Denning & Hillary Brooke. Directed by George Blair. 1951. Republic. 91 min. Sound. 16mm B&W. *Rental:* Ivy Films. *Sale:* Rep Pic Film.

Intelligence Testing of Tom. 1961. US. 52 min. Sound. 16mm Color. *Rental:* Syracuse U Film.

Intent to Kill. Richard Todd & Betsy Drake. Directed by Jack Cardiff. 1958. Fox. 91 min. Sound. 16mm B&W. *Rental:* Films Inc.

Intercat Sixty-Nine. 1969. Intercat Festival. (Anthology, color sequences). 96 min. Sound. 16mm Color. *Rental:* Canyon Cinema.

Interferon. 1982. 60 min. Sound. Videotape Color. *Sale:* Natl AV Ctr.

Interiors. Diane Keaton, Geraldine Page & Maureen Stapleton. Directed by Woody Allen. 1978. United Artists. 93 min. Sound. 16mm Color. *Rental:* MGM United.

Interlude. Oskar Werner & Barbara Ferris. Directed by Kevin Billington. 1968. Columbia. 113 min. Sound. 16mm Color. *Rental:* Budget Films, Cine Craft, Charard Motion Pics, Films Inc, Swank Motion, Twyman Film, Video Comm, Welling Motion Pictures & Wholesome Film Ctr.

Intermezzo: A Love Story. Orig. Title: Escape to Happiness. Leslie Howard & Ingrid Bergman. Directed by Gregory Ratoff. 1939. United Artists. 73 min. Sound. 16mm B&W. *Rental:* Films Inc, Twyman Films & Wholesome Film Ctr. *Sale:* ABC Film Lib, Super 8 sound version.

International Animation Festival. 70 min. Sound. 16mm Color. *Rental:* Films Inc.

International Crime. Rod La Rocque & Valerie Hobson. Directed by Charles Lamont. 1938. Grand National. 87 min. Sound. 16mm B&W. *Rental:* Wholesome Film Ctr.

International House. W. C. Fields & Rudy Vallee. Directed by Edward Sutherland. 1933. Paramount. 72 min. Sound. 16mm B&W. *Rental:* Swank Motion & Williams Films.

International Lady. George Brent, Ilona Massey & Basil Rathbone. Directed by Tim Whelan. 1941. United Artists. 102 min. Sound. 16mm B&W. *Lease:* Mogulls Films.

International Tournee of Animation *see* Tenth International Tournee of Animation.

International Tournee of Animation *see* Twelfth International Tournee of Animation.

International Tournee of Animation *see* Eleventh International Tournee of Animation.

International Velvet. Tatum O'Neal & Nanette Newman. Directed by Bryan Forbes. 1978. MGM. 126 min. Sound. 16mm Color. *Rental:* MGM United.

Internecine Project, The. James Coburn & Lee Grant. Directed by Ken Hughes. 1974. Allied Artists. 89 min. Sound. 16mm Color. *Rental:* Cinema Concepts.

Internes Can't Take Money. Barbara Stanwyck & Joel McCrea. Directed by Alfred Santell. 1937. Paramount. 77 min. Sound. 16mm B&W. *Rental:* Swank Motion.

Interns, The. Cliff Robertson & Michael Callan. Directed by David Swift. 1962. Columbia. 120 min. Sound. 16mm B&W. *Rental:* Cine Craft, Films Inc, Modern Sound & Welling Motion Pictures.

Interrupted Honeymoon, An *see* Homicide for Three.

Interrupted Melody. Eleanor Parker & Glenn Ford. Directed by Curtis Bernhardt. 1955. MGM. 106 min. Sound. 16mm Color. *Rental:* MGM United. *Rental:* MGM United, Anamorphic version.

Interval, The. Merle Oberon & Robert Wolders. Directed by Daniel Mann. 1973. Mexico. 84 min. Sound. 16mm Color. *Rental:* Films Inc.

Interview with Dr. B. F. Skinner, An. 1964. Macmillan. 50 min. Sound. 16mm B&W. *Rental:* Iowa Films & Syracuse U Film.

Interview with Dr. Erich Fromm, An. 2 pts. 1973. Macmillan. 110 min. Sound. 16mm B&W. *Rental:* Macmillan Films & Syracuse U Film. *Sale:* Macmillan Films.

Interview with Dr. Hinckley, An. 1970. 54 min. Sound. 16mm B&W. *Rental:* Utah Media.

Interviewing. 1975. 90 min. Sound. 16mm B&W. *Rental:* U Mich Media.

Interviews, The. PBS. 58 min. Sound. Videotape *Rental:* PBS Video. *Sale:* PBS Video.

Intimate Lighting. Vera Kresdalova & Zdenek Bezusek. Directed by Ivan Passer. Czech. 1965. Czechoslovakia. 72 min. Sound. 16mm B&W. subtitles Eng. *Rental:* Films Inc.

Intimate Moments. Alexandra Stewart & Dirke Altevogt. Directed by Francois E. Mimet. 1982. Embassy. 99 min. Sound. 16mm Color. *Rental:* Films Inc.

Intimate Playmates. Entertainment. 78 min. Videotape Color. *Sale:* Enter Video.

Intimate Relations. 1983. Britain. (Documentary). 50 min. Sound. 16mm Color. *Rental:* Films Inc. *Sale:* Films Inc. *Sale:* Films Inc, Videotape version.

Intimate Relations & Parents Terribles, Les *see* Disobedient.

Intimate Stranger *see* Finger of Guilt.

Into the Blue. Michael Wilding & Constance Cummings. Directed by Herbert Wilcox. 1951. Britain. 85 min. Sound. 16mm B&W. *Rental:* Liberty Co.

Intoccabili, Gli *see* Machine Gun McCain.

Intolerance. Lillian Gish, Mae Marsh, Robert Harron & Erich Von Stroheim. Directed by D. W. Griffith. 1916. Griffith. 170 min. Silent. 16mm B&W. *Rental:* Budget Films, Classic Film Mus, Em Gee Film Lib, Film Images, Images Film, Iowa Films, Ivy Films, Kerr Film, Kit Parker, Museum Mod Art, Video Comm, Wholesome Film Ctr & Willoughby Peer. *Sale:* Cinema Concepts, Film Images, Griggs Movie, Glenn Photo, Images Film, Morcraft Films, Natl Cinema & Reel Images. *Rental:* Film Images, Films Inc, Killiam Collect, Kit Parker, Museum Mod Art & Twyman Films, *Sale:* Cinema Concepts, Film Images, Glenn Photo & Museum Mod Art, Silent tinted 16mm version. *Rental:* Images Film, Inst Cinema & Twyman Films, *Sale:* Blackhawk Films, Sound 16mm, musical score only version. *Rental:* Ivy Films, *Sale:* Blackhawk Films, Super 8 silent version. *Rental:* Ivy Films & Video Comm, *Sale:* Festival Films & Images Film, Videotape version. *Rental:* Westcoast Films, 45 mins. version. *Rental:* Utah Media, 121 mins. version. *Sale:* Festival Films, 124 min. version.

Intrepide, L'. Louis Velle, Claudine Auger & Juliet Mills. Directed by Jean Girault. Fr. 1975. France. 90 min. Sound. 16mm Color. subtitles. *Rental:* French Am Cul.

Intrigue. George Raft & June Havoc. Directed by Edwin L. Marin. 1947. United Artists. 90 min. Sound. 16mm B&W. *Rental:* Ivy Films. *Sale:* Rep Pic Film.

Introducing Managers to Organizational Development. 1976. EMC. (Documentary). 55 min. Sound. 16mm B&W. *Rental:* U Cal Media. *Sale:* U Cal Media, Videotape version.

Introduction to Analog Computers. 1963. Argonne National Laboratory. (Documentary). 120 min. Sound. 16mm Color. *Rental:* Natl AV Ctr.

Introduction to Chile. Directed by Miguel Tores. 1972. Chile. (Documentary). 60 min. Sound. 16mm B&W. subtitles. *Rental:* Unifilm. *Sale:* Unifilm.

Introduction to Super Conductivity, An. 1966. 48 min. Sound. 16mm B&W. *Rental:* U Mich Media.

Intruder in the Dust. Juano Hernandez & Claude Jarman. Directed by Clarence Brown. 1949. MGM. 87 min. Sound. 16mm B&W. *Rental:* MGM United. *Rental:* MGM United, Videotape version.

Invader, The *see* Old Spanish Custom.

Invaders from Mars. Helen Carter & Arthur Franz. Directed by William Cameron Menzies. 1953. 78 min. Sound. 16mm Color. *Rental:* Budget Films.

Invaders from Space. 1964. Teleworld. 83 min. Sound. Super 8 Color. dubbed. *Rental:* Ivy Films. *Sale:* Ivy Films.

Invasion. Edward Judd & Yoko Tani. Directed by Alan Bridges. 1965. American International. 80 min. Sound. 16mm B&W. *Rental:* Films Inc & Mogulls Films.

Invasion of the Astros, The. Orig. Title: Monster Zero. Nick Adams. 1966. Japan. 75 min. Sound. 16mm Color. dubbed. *Rental:* Buchan Pic, Budget Films, Westcoast Films & Williams Films.

Invasion of the Bee Girls, The. William Smith & Anitra Ford. Directed by Denis Sanders. 1973. Dimension. 85 min. Sound. 16mm Color. *Rental:* Budget Films.

Invasion of the Body Snatchers, The. Kevin McCarthy & Dana Wynter. Directed by Don Siegel. 1956. Allied Artists. 80 min. Sound. B&W. *Rental:* Buchan Pic, Budget Films, Cinema Concepts, Films Inc, Inst Cinema, Images Film, Ivy Films, Kit Parker, Twyman Films, Westcoast Films & Wholesome Film Ctr. *Lease:* Rep Pic Film. *Rental:* Kit Parker, Anamorphic version. *Sale:* Cinema Concepts, Ivy Films & Reel Images, Videotape version.

Invasion of the Body Snatchers, The. Donald Sutherland, Brooke Adams & Leonard Nimoy. Directed by Philip Kaufman. 1978. United Artists. 114 min. Sound. 16mm Color. *Rental:* MGM United.

Invasion of the Hell Creatures, The *see* Invasion of the Saucer Men.

Invasion of the Land, The. 1980. Britain. (Documentary). 58 min. Videotape Color. *Rental:* Films Inc. *Sale:* Films Inc.

Invasion of the Saucer Men, The. Orig. Title: Invasion of the Hell Creatures, The. Steve Terrell & Frank Gorshin. Directed by Edward L. Cahn. 1957. American International. 69 min. Sound. 16mm B&W. *Rental:* Films Inc.

Invasion of the Star Creatures, The. Bob Ball. Directed by Bernard De Voto. 1963. Italy. 79 min. Sound. 16mm Color. dubbed. *Rental:* Films Inc.

Invasion of the Virions, The. 1981. Britain. (Documentary). 50 min. Sound. 16mm Color. *Rental:* Films Inc, Syracuse U Film & U Cal Media. *Sale:* Films Inc. *Rental:* Films Inc, *Sale:* Films Inc, Videotape version.

Invasion Quartet. Bill Travers & Spike Milligan. Directed by Jay Lewis. 1961. Britain. 87 min. Sound. 16mm B&W. *Rental:* MGM United.

Invasion, U.S.A. Gerald Mohr & Peggie Castle. Directed by Alfred E. Green. 1952. Columbia. 74 min. Sound. 16mm B&W. *Rental:* Willoughby Peer.

Investigation of a Citizen Above Suspicion. Gian-Maria Volonte & Florinda Bolkan. Directed by Elio Petri. 1971. Italy. 114 min. Sound. 16mm Color. subtitles. *Rental:* Corinth Films, Swank Motion & Twyman Films.

Invincible Gladiator, The *see* Invincible Swordsman.

Invincible One. Alexander Fu Sheng & Chi-Kuan Chun. 113 min. Sound. 16mm *Rental:* WW Enter. *Rental:* WW Enter, Videotape version.

Invincible Swordsman, The. Orig. Title: Invincible Gladiator, The. Jean Marais & Elsa Martinelli. Directed by Antonio Momplet. 1963. Italy. 105 min. Sound. 16mm Color. dubbed. *Rental:* Bosco Films & Westcoast Films.

Invisible Agent, The. Ilona Massey & Jon Hall. Directed by Edwin L. Marin. 1942. Universal. 84 min. Sound. 16mm B&W. *Rental:* Swank Motion.

Invisible Boy. Richard Eyer & Philip Abbott. Directed by Herman Hoffman. 1957. MGM. 99 min. Sound. 16mm B&W. *Rental:* MGM United.

Invisible Creature, The. Tony Wright. Directed by Montgomery Tully. 1960. American International. 70 min. Sound. 16mm B&W. dubbed. *Rental:* Films Inc.

Invisible Enemy, The. Alan Marshall & Tala Birell. Directed by John H. Auer. 1938. Republic. 54 min. Sound. 16mm B&W. *Rental:* Ivy Films & Rep Pic Film. *Sale:* Rep Pic Film.

Invisible Flame, The. 57 min. Sound. 16mm Color. *Rental:* OK AV Ctr.

Invisible Ghost, The. Bela Lugosi & Polly Ann Young. Directed by Joseph Lewis. 1941. Monogram. 65 min. Sound. 16mm B&W. *Rental:* Budget Films, Ivy Films & Video Comm. *Sale:* Video Comm. *Rental:* Ivy Films, *Sale:* Ivy Films, Super 8 sound version. *Rental:* Video Comm, *Lease:* Video Comm, Videotape version.

Invisible Informer, The. Adele Mara & Linda Sterling. Directed by Philip Ford. 1964. Republic. 53 min. Sound. 16mm B&W. *Rental:* Inst Cinema & Ivy Films.

Invisible Invaders, The. John Agar & John Carradine. Directed by Edward L. Cahn. 1959. United Artists. 67 min. Sound. 16mm B&W. *Rental:* MGM United.

Invisible Killer, The. Grace Bradley & Roland Drew. Directed by Sherman Scott. 1940. PRC. 70 min. Sound. 16mm B&W. *Rental:* Mogulls Films & Video Comm. *Rental:* Video Comm, Videotape version.

Invisible Man, The. Claude Rains. Directed by James Whale. 1933. Universal. 74 min. Sound. 16mm B&W. *Rental:* Swank Motion & Williams Films.

Invisible Man Returns, The. Sir Cedric Hardwicke & Vincent Price. Directed by Joe May. 1940. Universal. 81 min. Sound. 16mm B&W. *Rental:* Swank Motion.

Invisible Man's Revenge, The. Jon Hall & Evelyn Ankers. Directed by Ford Beebe. 1944. Universal. 78 min. Sound. 16mm B&W. *Rental:* Swank Motion.

Invisible Menace, The. Boris Karloff & Marie Wilson. Directed by John Farrow. 1938. Warners. 55 min. Sound. 16mm B&W. *Rental:* MGM United.

Invisible Ray, The. Boris Karloff & Bela Lugosi. Directed by Lambert Hillyer. 1936. Universal. 89 min. Sound. 16mm B&W. *Rental:* Swank Motion.

Invisible Stripes. Humphrey Bogart & William Holden. Directed by Lloyd Bacon. 1939. Warners. 82 min. Sound. 16mm B&W. *Rental:* MGM United.

Invisible Woman, The. Virginia Bruce & John Barrymore. Directed by Edward Sutherland. 1940. Universal. 75 min. Sound. 16mm B&W. *Rental:* Swank Motion.

Invitation. Van Johnson & Dorothy McGuire. Directed by Gottfried Reinhardt. 1952. MGM. 84 min. Sound. 16mm B&W. *Rental:* MGM United.

Invitation, The. Jean-Luc Bideau & Francois Simon. Directed by Claude Goretta. Fr. 1973. France. 100 min. Sound. 16mm Color. subtitles Eng. *Rental:* Films Inc & Janus Films.

Invitation Au Voyage. Laurent Malet. Directed by Peter Del Monte. 1983. France. 93 min. Sound. 16mm Color. subtitles. *Rental:* Swank Motion.

Invitation to a Gunfighter. Yul Brynner & George Segal. Directed by Richard Wilson. 1964. United Artists. 92 min. Sound. 16mm Color. *Rental:* MGM United.

Invitation to a Murder *see* Flight from Destiny.

Invitation to Happiness. Irene Dunne & Fred MacMurray. Directed by Wesley Ruggles. 1939. Paramount. 99 min. Sound. 16mm B&W. *Rental:* Swank Motion.

Iolanthe. 1974. Britain. (Operetta). 52 min. Sound. 16mm Color. *Rental:* B Raymond. *Sale:* B Raymond. *Sale:* B Raymond, Videotape version.

Ipcress File, The. Michael Caine & Nigel Green. Directed by Sidney J. Furie. 1965. Universal. 107 min. Sound. 16mm Color. *Rental:* Films Inc, Swank Motion , Video Comm & Twyman Films. *Rental:* Twyman Films, Anamorphic version.

Iphigenia. Irene Papas. Directed by Michael Cacoyannis. Gr. 1977. Greece. 130 min. Sound. 16mm Color. subtitles. *Rental:* Cinema Five & New Cinema.

Iracema. Directed by Jorge Bodanzky. 90 min. Sound. 16mm Color. *Rental:* Cinema Guild.

Iran, Religion & World Conflict. 1979. PBS. 59 min. Videotape Color. *Rental:* PBS Video. *Sale:* PBS Video.

Ireland: Behind the Wire. 1974. Great Britian. (Documentary). 110 min. Sound. 16mm B&W. *Rental:* Museum Mod Art.

Ireland: Making of a Republic. 1972. Britain. (Documentary). 52 min. Sound. 16mm B&W. *Rental:* Time-Life Multimedia. *Sale:* Time-Life Multimedia.

Ireland: The Tear & the Smile. 1961. CBS. (Documentary). 52 min. Sound. 16mm B&W. *Rental:* Macmillan Films. *Sale:* Macmillan Films.

Irene. Anna Neagle & Ray Milland. Directed by Herbert Wilcox. 1940. RKO. 101 min. Sound. 16mm B&W. *Rental:* Films Inc.

Irish Eyes Are Smiling. Orig. Title: When Irish Eyes Are Smiling. Dick Haymes & June Haver. Directed by Gregory Ratoff. 1944. Fox. 90 min. Sound. 16mm Color. *Rental:* Budget Films.

Irish Luck. Frankie Darro & Mantan Moreland. Directed by Howard Bretherton. 1940. Monogram. 58 min. Sound. 16mm B&W. *Rental:* Cinema Concepts.

Irish Tapes, The. Directed by John Reilly & Stefan Moore. 1974. Reilly-Moore. (Documentary). 60 min. Sound. Videotape B&W. *Rental:* Electro Art. *Lease:* Electro Art.

Irish Whiskey Rebellion, The. Richard Mulligan & Anne Meara. Directed by J. C. Works. 1972. GSF. 93 min. Sound. 16mm Color. *Rental:* Swank Motion.

Irma la Douce. Jack Lemmon & Shirley MacLaine. Directed by Billy Wilder. 1963. United Artists. 142 min. Sound. 16mm Color. *Rental:* MGM United. *Rental:* MGM United, Videotape version.

Iron Curtain. Dana Andrews & Gene Tierney. Directed by William A. Wellman. 1948. Fox. 87 min. Sound. 16mm B&W. *Rental:* Films Inc.

Iron Duke, The. George Arliss. Directed by Victor Saville. 1934. Britain. 85 min. Sound. 16mm B&W. *Rental:* Alba House & Kit Parker.

Iron Glove, The. Robert Stack & Ursula Thiess. Directed by William Castle. 1954. Columbia. 77 min. Sound. 16mm Color. *Rental:* Inst Cinema.

Iron Horse, The. George O'Brien & Madge Bellamy. Directed by John Ford. 1924. Fox. 110 min. Silent. 16mm B&W. *Rental:* Museum Mod Art. *Rental:* Killiam Collect, Sound 16mm version. *Sale:* Blackhawk Films, Super 8 sound version. *Sale:* Blackhawk Films, Super 8 silent version.

Iron Maiden, The. Orig. Title: Swingin' Maiden, The. Michael Craig & Anne Helm. Directed by Gerald Thomas. 1962. Britain. 81 min. Sound. 16mm Color. *Rental:* Buchan Pic, Cine Craft, Roas Films & Westcoast Films.

Iron Major, The. Pat O'Brien & Ruth Warrick. Directed by Ray Enright. 1943. RKO. 85 min. Sound. 16mm B&W. *Rental:* Films Inc.

Iron Man, The. Jeff Chandler & Evelyn Keyes. Directed by Joseph Pevney. 1951. Universal. 82 min. Sound. 16mm B&W. *Rental:* Swank Motion.

Iron Man, The. Lew Ayres & Jean Harlow. Directed by Tod Browning. 1931. Universal. 73 min. Sound. 16mm B&W. *Rental:* Swank Motion.

Iron Mask, The. Douglas Fairbanks & Belle Bennett. Directed by Allan Dwan. 1929. United Artists. (Musical score only). 98 min. Sound. 16mm B&W. *Rental:* A Twyman Pres, Buchan Pic, Budget Films, Em Gee Film Lib & Twyman Films. *Sale:* Cinema Concepts & Morcraft Films. *Rental:* Killiam Collect, Silent tinted 16mm version. *Rental:* Em Gee Film Lib, Kit Parker, Museum Mod Art & Video Comm, *Sale:* Cine Concepts & Glenn Photo,

Iron Master, The. Reginald Denny & Lila Lee. Directed by Chester M. Franklin. 1933. Allied. 70 min. Sound. 16mm B&W. *Rental:* Mogulls Films.

Iron Mountain Trail. Rex Allen. Directed by William Witney. 1953. Republic. 54 min. Sound. 16mm B&W. *Rental:* Ivy Films. *Sale:* Rep Pic Film & Nostalgia Merchant.

Iron Petticoat, The. Bob Hope & Katharine Hepburn. Directed by Ralph Thomas. 1956. MGM. 96 min. Sound. 16mm Color. *Rental:* MGM United.

Iron Road, The *see* Buckskin Frontier.

Iron Sheriff, The. Sterling Hayden & Constance Ford. Directed by Sidney Salkow. 1957. United Artists. 73 min. Sound. 16mm B&W. *Rental:* MGM United.

Iroquois Trail, The. Orig. Title: Tomahawk Trail, The. George Montgomery & Brenda Marshall. Directed by Phil Karlson. 1950. United Artists. 86 min. Sound. 16mm B&W. *Rental:* Budget Films, Film Ctr DC, Films Inc, MGM United, Roas Films, Welling Motion Pictures & Westcoast Films.

Irresistible Force, The. 1983. Britain. (Documentary). 50 min. Videotape Color. *Sale:* Films Inc.

Is Anyone Out There Learning? 1978. CBS. (Documentary). 3 Reels 144 min. Sound. 16mm Color. *Rental:* Carousel Films, Iowa Films & Syracuse U Film. *Sale:* Carousel Films. *Sale:* Carousel Films, Videotape version.

Is It Walandwe. Directed by Barry Feinberg. 1980. Britain. (Documentary). 51 min. Sound. 16mm Color. *Rental:* Liberty Co.

Is My Face Red. Robert Armstrong & Arline Judge. Directed by William A. Seiter. 1943. RKO. 66 min. Sound. 16mm *Rental:* RKO General Pics.

Is Paris Burning? Orson Wells & Leslie Caron. Directed by Rene Clement. 1966. Paramount. (Anamorphic). 138 min. Sound. 16mm B&W. dubbed. *Rental:* Films Inc.

Is There an Adolescent in the House? Dr. Kevin Leman. 45 min. Sound. 16mm Color. *Rental:* Gospel Films.

Is There Sex After Death? Buck Henry, Robert Downey & Holly Woodlawn. Directed by Jeanne Abel & Alan Abel. 1971. Oppidan. 78 min. Sound. 16mm Color. *Rental:* New Line Cinema. *Sale:* New Line Cinema.

Isaac Stern. 1966. Nathan Kroll. (Documentary). 59 min. Sound. 16mm B&W. *Rental:* Indiana AV Ctr. *Sale:* Indiana AV Ctr.

Isabel. Genevieve Bujold. Directed by Paul Almond. 1968. Canada. 108 min. Sound. 16mm Color. *Rental:* Films Inc.

Isadora. Orig. Title: Loves of Isadora. Vanessa Redgrave & Jason Robards. Directed by Karel Reisz. 1969. Universal. 131 min. Sound. 16mm Color. *Rental:* Swank Motion & Twyman Films.

Isadora Duncan, the Biggest Dancer in the World. Vivian Pickles. Directed by Ken Russell. 1966. Britain. 63 min. Sound. 16mm B&W. *Rental:* Dance Film Archive, Images Film & Kit Parker. *Sale:* Festival Films, Images Film, Reel Images & Tamarelles French Films. *Sale:* Festival Films, Videotape version.

Isis. Filmation. (Cast unlisted). 66 min. Sound. 16mm Color. *Rental:* Williams Films.

Islam. 1967. KETC. (Documentary). 60 min. Sound. 16mm B&W. *Rental:* BYU Films, Indiana AV Ctr & Syracuse U Film. *Sale:* Indiana AV Ctr.

Islam: There Is No God but God. 1978. Britain. (Documentary). 52 min. Sound. 16mm Color. *Rental:* U Cal Media.

Island, The. Trans. Title: Hadaka No Shima. Nobuko Otowa. Directed by Kaneto Shindo. 1961. Japan. 96 min. Sound. 16mm B&W. *Rental:* Budget Films, Em Gee Film Lib, Films Inc, Ivy Films & Kit Parker. *Sale:* Cine Concepts, Festival Films & Reel Images. *Sale:* Tamarelles French Film & Festival Films, Videotape version.

Island, The. Michael Caine & David Warner. Directed by Michael Ritchie. 1980. Britain. 114 min. Sound. 16mm Color. *Rental:* Swank Motion.

Island Called Ellis, The. 1967. NBC. (Documentary). 53 min. Sound. 16mm Color. *Rental:* McGraw-Hill Films, Syracuse U Film, U of IL Film & Utah Media. *Sale:* McGraw-Hill Films.

Island Captives. Eddie Nugent. 1937. Principal. 60 min. Sound. 16mm B&W. *Rental:* Mogulls Films.

Island in the Sun. Harry Belafonte & Joan Fontaine. Directed by Robert Rossen. 1957. Fox. 119 min. Sound. 16mm Color. *Rental:* Films Inc.

Island Monster. Boris Karloff. Directed by Roberto Montero. 1958. Italy. 87 min. Sound. 16mm B&W. dubbed. *Rental:* Films Inc.

Island of Dr. Moreau, The. Burt Lancaster & Michael York. Directed by Don Taylor. 1977. American International. 104 min. Sound. 16mm Color. *Rental:* Wholesome Film Ctr.

Island of Doomed Men, The. Peter Lorre & Rochelle Hudson. Directed by Charles Barton. 1940. Columbia. 70 min. Sound. 16mm B&W. *Rental:* Cine Concepts.

Island of Lost Souls, The. Charles Laughton & Bela Lugosi. Directed by Erle C. Kenton. 1933. Paramount. 74 min. Sound. 16mm B&W. *Rental:* Swank Motion & Williams Films.

Island of Lost Women, The. Jeff Richards & Venetia Stevenson. Directed by Frank Tuttle. 1959. Warners. 67 min. Sound. 16mm B&W. *Rental:* Budget Films & Video Comm. *Lease:* Video Comm.

Island of Monte Cristo *see* Sword of Venus.

Island of Terror, The. Peter Cushing & Edward Judd. Directed by Terence Fisher. 1966. Britain. 87 min. Sound. 16mm Color. *Rental:* Swank Motion.

Island of the Blue Dolphins, The. Celia Kay & Larry Domasin. Directed by James B. Clark. 1964. Universal. 101 min. Sound. 16mm Color. *Rental:* Williams Films.

Island of the Burning Doomed, The. Orig. Title: Night of the Big Heat. Christopher Lee & Peter Cushing. Directed by Terence Fisher. 1970. Britain. 94 min. Sound. 16mm Color. *Rental:* Budget Films, Video Comm & Westcoast Films.

Island of the Lost. Richard Greene & Luke Halpin. 1968. MGM. 92 min. Sound. 16mm Color. *Rental:* Welling Motion Pictures. *Lease:* Rep Pic Film. *Rental:* Video Comm, *Lease:* Video Comm, Videotape version.

Island of the Moon: Madagascar. 1979. 60 min. Sound. 16mm Color. *Rental:* U Mich Media.

Island of the Red Prawns, The. Directed by William R. Geddes. 1980. U. of California. (Documentary). 52 min. Sound. 16mm Color. *Rental:* U Cal Media. *Sale:* U Cal Media. *Sale:* U Cal Media, Videotape version.

Island Princess. Orig. Title: Isola. Marcello Mastroianni & Silvana Pampanini. Directed by Paolo Moffa. 1955. Italy. 98 min. Sound. 16mm Color. dubbed. *Rental:* Films Inc & Willoughby Peer.

Island Rescue. Orig. Title: Appointment with Venus. David Niven & Glynis Johns. Directed by Ralph Thomas. 1952. Britain. 87 min. Sound. 16mm B&W. *Rental:* Budget Films.

Islands in the Stream. George C. Scott & David Hemmings. Directed by Franklin Schaffner. 1977. Paramount. 105 min. Sound. 16mm Color. *Rental:* Films Inc & Twyman Films. *Rental:* Films Inc, Anamorphic version.

Islands of Bliss, The. Directed by Arthur Kahane. 1913. 50 min. Silent. 16mm B&W. *Rental:* Films Inc.

Isle of Fury. Humphrey Bogart & Donald Woods. Directed by Frank McDonald. 1936. Warners. 60 min. Sound. 16mm B&W. *Rental:* MGM United.

Isle of Missing Men. John Howard & Helen Gilbert. Directed by Richard Oswald. 1942. Monogram. 67 min. Sound. 16mm B&W. *Rental:* Budget Films.

Isle of the Dead. Boris Karloff & Ellen Drew. Directed by Mark Robson. 1945. RKO. 72 min. Sound. 16mm B&W. *Rental:* Films Inc. *Lease:* Films Inc.

Isn't Life Wonderful? Carol Dempster & Neil Hamilton. Directed by D. W. Griffith. 1924. 135 min. Silent. 16mm B&W. *Rental:* A Twyman Pres, Budget Films, Em Gee Film Lib, Museum Mod Art & Twyman Films. *Sale:* Glenn Photo & Reel Images, Super 8 silent version.

Isola *see* Island Princess.

Isoroku Yamamoto. 1976. Britain. (Documentary). 62 min. Sound. 16mm Color. *Rental:* Time-Life Multimedia. *Sale:* Time-Life Multimedia. *Rental:* Time-Life Multimedia, *Sale:* Time-Life Multimedia, Videotape version.

Israel: Search for Faith. 1977. Readers Digest. (Documentary). 58 min. Sound. 16mm Color. *Rental:* Budget Films, Pyramid Film & Roas Films. *Sale:* Pyramid Film. *Rental:* Pyramid Film, *Sale:* Pyramid Film, Videotape version.

Israel: The Right to Be. Alden. (Documentary). 52 min. Sound. 16mm Color. *Rental:* ADL.

Israel: The 20th Century Miracle. 1974. Israel. (Documentary). 55 min. Sound. 16mm Color. *Rental:* Alden Films.

Israelis, The. 1974. 45 min. Sound. 16mm Color. *Rental:* Budget Films.

Istanbul. Errol Flynn. Directed by Joseph Pevney. 1957. Universal. 84 min. Sound. 16mm Color. *Rental:* Swank Motion.

It. Clara Bow & Antonio Moreno. Directed by Clarence Badger. 1927. Paramount. (Musical score only). 72 min. Sound. 16mm B&W. *Rental:* Killiam Collect. *Sale:* Blackhawk Films. *Sale:* Blackhawk Films, Super 8 sound version. *Sale:* Blackhawk Films, Super 8 silent version.

It Came from Beneath the Sea. Kenneth Tobey. Directed by Robert Gordon. 1955. Columbia. 80 min. Sound. 16mm B&W. *Rental:* Bosco Films, Budget Films, Cine Craft, Film Ctr DC, Films Inc, Ivy Films, Modern Sound, Twyman Films, Video Comm, Wholesome Films Ctr & Williams Films.

It Came from Hollywood. Dan Aykroyd & John Candy. Directed by Malcolm Leo & Andrew Solt. 1982. Paramount. 80 min. Sound. 16mm Color. *Rental:* Films Inc.

It Came from Outer Space. Richard Carlson & Barbara Rush. Directed by Jack Arnold. 1953. Universal. 80 min. Sound. 16mm B&W. *Rental:* Swank Motion. *Rental:* Swank Motion, Three-D version.

It Comes Up Murder see Honey Pot.

It Conquered the World. Peter Graves & Beverly Garland. Directed by Roger Corman. 1956. American International. 71 min. Sound. 16mm B&W. *Rental:* Budget Films, Films Inc, Ivy Films, Video Comm & Westcoast Films.

It Could Happen to You. Alan Baxter & Andrea Leeds. Directed by Phil Rosen. 1937. 54 min. Sound. 16mm B&W. *Rental:* Ivy Films. *Sale:* Rep Pic Film.

It Couldn't Be Done. 1970. NBC. (Documentary). 53 min. Sound. 16mm Color. *Rental:* Films Inc, Iowa Films & Twyman Films. *Sale:* Films Inc. *Sale:* Films Inc, Videotape version.

It Grows on Trees. Irene Dunne & Dean Jagger. Directed by Arthur Lubin. 1952. Universal. 84 min. Sound. 16mm B&W. *Rental:* Swank Motion.

It Had to Be You. Ginger Rogers & Cornel Wilde. Directed by Don Hartman & Rudolph Mate. 1947. Columbia. 98 min. Sound. 16mm B&W. *Rental:* Bosco Films & Welling Motion Pics.

It Had to Happen. George Raft & Rosalind Russell. Directed by Roy Del Ruth. 1936. Fox. 79 min. Sound. 16mm B&W. *Rental:* Films Inc.

It Happened at the World's Fair. Elvis Presley. Directed by Norman Taurog. 1963. MGM. 105 min. Sound. 16mm Color. *Rental:* MGM United.

It Happened Here. Pauline Murray & Sebastian Shaw. Directed by Kevin Brownlow & Andrew Mollo. 1966. Britain. 95 min. Sound. 16mm B&W. *Rental:* MGM United.

It Happened in Athens. Jayne Mansfield & Trax Colton. Directed by Andrew Marton. 1962. Fox. 92 min. Sound. 16mm Color. *Rental:* Films Inc. *Rental:* Films Inc, Anamorphic color version.

It Happened in Brooklyn. Frank Sinatra & Kathryn Grayson. Directed by Richard Whorf. 1947. MGM. 103 min. Sound. 16mm B&W. *Rental:* MGM United.

It Happened in Flatbush. Lloyd Nolan. Directed by Ray McCarey. 1942. Fox. 80 min. Sound. 16mm B&W. *Rental:* Films Inc.

It Happened in Hualfin. Directed by Raymundo Gleyzer. 1970. Pictura. 50 min. Sound. 16mm Color. *Rental:* Cinema Guild. *Sale:* Cinema Guild.

It Happened In New Orleans see Rainbow on the River.

It Happened in Paris see Desperate Adventure.

It Happened in the Park. Anna Ferrero. Directed by Gianni Franciolini. 1956. France-Italy. 95 min. Sound. 16mm B&W. dubbed. *Rental:* Ivy Films.

It Happened on Fifth Avenue. Don DeFore & Victor Moore. Directed by Roy Del Ruth. 1947. Allied Artists. 115 min. Sound. 16mm B&W. *Rental:* Cine Craft, Film Ctr DC & Hurlock Cine.

It Happened One Night. Clark Gable, Claudette Colbert & Alan Hale. Directed by Frank Capra. 1934. Columbia. 105 min. Sound. 16mm B&W. *Rental:* Arcus Film, Budget Films, Images Film, Kit Parker, Modern Sound, Swank Motion, Welling Motion Pictures, Wholesome Film Ctr & Williams Films.

It Happened One Summer see State Fair.

It Happened Out West. Orig. Title: Man from the Big City, The. Paul Kelly & Judith Allen. Directed by Howard Bretherton. 1937. Fox. 70 min. Sound. 16mm B&W. *Rental:* Mogulls Films.

It Happened to Jane. Doris Day & Jack Lemmon. Directed by Richard Quine. 1959. Columbia. 98 min. Sound. 16mm Color. *Rental:* Arcus Film, Buchan Pic, Budget Films, Cine Craft, Charard Motion Pics, Film Ctr DC, Films Inc, Modern Sound, Newman Film Lib, Roas Films, Twyman Films & Welling Motion Pictures.

It Happened Tomorrow. Dick Powell & Linda Darnell. Directed by Rene Clair. 1944. United Artists. 84 min. Sound. 16mm B&W. *Rental:* A Twyman Pres, Budget Films & Mogulls Films.

It Happens Every Spring. Ray Milland & Jean Peters. Directed by Lloyd Bacon. 1949. Fox. 87 min. Sound. 16mm B&W. *Rental:* Films Inc & Williams Films.

It Happens Every Thursday. Loretta Young & John Forsythe. Directed by Joseph Pevney. 1953. Universal. 80 min. Sound. 16mm B&W. *Rental:* Swank Motion.

It Lives Again. Frederic Forrest & Kathleen Lloyd. Directed by Larry Cohen. 1978. Warners. 91 min. Sound. 16mm Color. *Rental:* Swank Motion & Williams Films.

It Should Happen to You. Judy Holliday & Jack Lemmon. Directed by George Cukor. 1954. Columbia. 87 min. Sound. 16mm B&W. *Rental:* Arcus Film, Bosco Films, Films Inc, Inst Cinema, Images Film, Kit Parker, Swank Motion & Welling Motion Pictures. *Sale:* Tamarelles French Film, Videotape version.

It Shouldn't Happen to a Dog. Carole Landis & Allyn Joslyn. Directed by Herbert I. Leeds. 1946. Fox. 75 min. Sound. 16mm B&W. *Rental:* Films Inc.

It Started in Naples. Clark Gable & Sophia Loren. Directed by Melville Shavelson. 1960. Paramount. 100 min. Sound. 16mm Color. *Rental:* Films Inc.

It Started with a Kiss. Glenn Ford & Debbie Reynolds. Directed by George Marshall. 1959. MGM. (Anamorphic). 104 min. Sound. 16mm Color. *Rental:* MGM United.

It Started with Eve. Deanna Durbin & Charles Laughton. Directed by Henry Koster. 1941. Universal. 90 min. Sound. 16mm B&W. *Rental:* Swank Motion.

It Takes a Thief. Orig. Title: Challenge, The. Jayne Mansfield & Anthony Quayle. Directed by John Gilling. 1959. Britain. 90 min. Sound. 16mm B&W. *Rental:* Films Inc.

It Takes All Kinds. Vera Miles & Robert Lansing. Directed by Eddie Davis. 1968. Commonwealth United. 97 min. Sound. 16mm Color. *Rental:* Ivy Films, Rep Pic Film, Video Comm & Willoughby Peer. *Lease:* Rep Pic Film.

It: The Terror from Beyond Space. Marshall Thompson & Kim Spalding. Directed by Edward L. Cahn. 1958. United Artists. 68 min. Sound. 16mm B&W. *Rental:* MGM United.

It Won't Rub Off, Baby see Sweet Love Bitter.

It's Magic see Romance on the High Seas.

Italian, The. George Beban & Clara Williams. Directed by Reginald Barker. 1915. New York. 78 min. Silent. 16mm B&W. *Rental:* Em Gee Film Lib. *Sale:* Glenn Photo.

Italian Job, The. Michael Caine & Noel Coward. Directed by Peter Collinson. 1969. Paramount. (Anamorphic). 100 min. Sound. 16mm Color. *Rental:* Films Inc.

Italian Straw Hat, The. Trans. Title: Chapeau De Paille D'Italie. Alice Tissot & Albert Prejean. Directed by Rene Clair. 1927. France. (Music & sound effects). 76 min. Sound. 16mm B&W. *Rental:* Budget Films, Films Inc, Em Gee Film Lib, Images Film, Iowa Films, Museum Mod Art & U Cal Media. *Sale:* Cinema Concepts, Images Film & Reel Images. *Sale:* Cinema Concepts, Festival Films, Glenn Photo, Kit Parker, Museum Mod Art & Select Film, Silent 16mm version. *Rental:* Ivy Films, Super 8 silent version. *Sale:* Images Film & Tamarelles French Film, Videotape version, Videotape version.

Italianamerican. Directed by Martin Scorsese. 1975. Ruben-Attias. (Documentary). 45 min. Sound. 16mm Color. *Rental:* Museum Mod Art.

Italiano Brava Gente. Arthur Kennedy & Peter Falk. Directed by Giuseppe De Santis. Ger. Ital. & Rus. 1963. Embassy. 156 min. Sound. 16mm B&W. subtitles Eng. *Rental:* Films Inc.

Italy, Chain Reaction. 1979. 58 min. Sound. Videotape *Rental:* PBS Video. *Sale:* PBS Video.

It's a Big Country. Ethel Barrymore & Keefe Brasselle. Directed by Richard Thorpe, John Sturges, Charles Vidor, Don Weis, Clarence Brown, William A. Wellman & Don Hartman. 1951. MGM. 88 min. Sound. 16mm B&W. *Rental:* MGM United.

It's a Bikini World. Deborah Walley & Tommy Kirk. Directed by Stephanie Rothman. 1967. Trans American. 86 min. Sound. 16mm Color. *Rental:* Films Inc.

It's a Dog's Life. Orig. Title: Almost Human. Edmund Gwenn & Jeff Richards. Directed by Herman Hoffman. 1955. MGM. 88 min. Sound. 16mm Color. *Rental:* MGM United.

It's a Gift. W. C. Fields & Baby LeRoy. Directed by Norman Z. McLeod. 1934. Paramount. 71 min. Sound. 16mm B&W. *Rental:* Williams Films.

It's a Great Feeling. Doris Day & Jack Carson. Directed by David Butler. 1949. Warners. 85 min. Sound. 16mm B&W. *Rental:* MGM United.

It's a Great Life. Penny Singleton & Arthur Lake. Directed by Frank R. Strayer. 1943. Columbia. 75 min. Sound. 16mm B&W. *Rental:* Films Inc & Video Comm. *Lease:* King Features.

It's a Great Life. Vivian Duncan & Rosetta Duncan. Directed by Sam Wood. 1929. MGM. (Color sequences). 110 min. Sound. 16mm *Rental:* MGM United.

It's a Joke, Son. Kenny Delmar. Directed by Ben Stoloff. 1947. Eagle Lion. 63 min. Sound. 16mm B&W. *Rental:* Ivy Films. *Sale:* Classics Assoc NY, Morcraft Films & Rep Pic Film. *Sale:* Morcraft Films, Super 8 sound version.

It's a Living. 1979. PBS. (Documentary). 58 min. Videotape Color. *Rental:* PBS Video. *Sale:* PBS Video.

It's a Lovely Day Tomorrow: Burma 1942-1944. Directed by Hugh Raggett. (World at War). : Pt. 14). 1973. Media Guild. (Documentary). 52 min. Sound. 16mm Color. *Rental:* Media Guild & U of Cal Media. *Sale:* Media Guild. *Sale:* Media Guild, Videotape version.

It's a Mad, Mad, Mad, Mad World. Spencer Tracy & Milton Berle. Directed by Stanley Kramer. 1963. United Artists. 192 min. Sound. 16mm Color. *Rental:* MGM United. *Rental:* MGM United, 154 min. version, Videotape version.

It's a Mile from Here to Glory. Steve Shaw & David Haskell. Directed by Richard Bennett. 1978. Time-Life. 47 min. Sound. 16mm Color. *Rental:* Time-Life Multimedia. *Sale:* Time-Life Multimedia. *Rental:* Time-Life Multimedia, *Sale:* Time-Life Multimedia, Videotape version.

It's a Pleasure. Sonja Henie & Michael O'Shea. Directed by William A. Seiter. 1945. RKO. 90 min. Sound. 16mm B&W. *Rental:* Roas Films & Wholesome Film Ctr.

It's a Small World. Paul Dale & Lorraine Miller. Directed by William Castle. 1950. Eagle Lion. 74 min. Sound. 16mm B&W. *Rental:* Budget Films & Mogulls Films.

It's a Wise Child. Marion Davies. Directed by Robert Z. Leonard. 1931. MGM. 90 min. Sound. 16mm B&W. *Rental:* MGM United.

It's a Wonderful Life. James Stewart & Donna Reed. Directed by Frank Capra. 1946. RKO. 120 min. Sound. 16mm B&W. *Rental:* Films Inc. *Sale:* Cinema Concepts, Glenn Photo, Reel Images & Images Film. *Lease:* Rep Pic Film. *Sale:* Glenn Photo & Reel Images, Super 8 sound version. *Sale:* Blackhawk Films, Cinema Concepts & Tamarelles French Film, Videotape version. *Rental:* Swank Motion, 129 min. version. *Sale:* Festival Films, 130 min. 16mm version. *Sale:* Festival Films, 130 min. Videotape version.

It's a Wonderful World. Claudette Colbert & James Stewart. Directed by W. S. Van Dyke. 1939. MGM. 86 min. Sound. 16mm B&W. *Rental:* MGM United.

It's Alive. Sharon Farrell. Directed by Larry Cohen. 1975. Warners. 91 min. Sound. 16mm Color. *Rental:* Modern Sound, Twyman Films & Williams Films.

It's Always Fair Weather. Gene Kelly & Cyd Charisse. Directed by Gene Kelly & Stanley Donen. 1955. MGM. 101 min. Sound. 16mm Color. *Rental:* MGM United. *Rental:* MGM United, Anamorphic version.

It's in the Air. George Formby & Polly Ward. Directed by Anthony Kimmins. 1938. Britain. 87 min. Sound. 16mm B&W. *Rental:* Janus Films.

It's in the Air. Jack Benny & Una Merkel. Directed by Charles Reisner. 1935. MGM. 82 min. Sound. 16mm B&W. *Rental:* MGM United.

It's in the Bag. Orig. Title: Fifth Chair, The. Jack Benny & Fred Allen. Directed by Richard Wallace. 1945. United Artists. 70 min. Sound. 16mm B&W. *Rental:* Budget Films & Ivy Films. *Sale:* Rep Pic Film.

It's Love Again. Jessie Matthews & Robert Young. Directed by Victor Saville. 1935. Britain. 83 min. Sound. 16mm B&W. *Rental:* Budget Films & Kit Parker. *Sale:* Glenn Photo.

It's Love I'm After. Bette Davis & Leslie Howard. Directed by Archie Mayo. 1937. Warners. 90 min. Sound. 16mm B&W. *Rental:* MGM United.

It's My Turn. Michael Douglas, Charles Grodin & Jill Clayburgh. Directed by Claudia Weill. 1980. Columbia. 91 min. Sound. 16mm Color. *Rental:* Swank Motion. *Rental:* Swank Motion, Videotape version.

It's Never Too Late to Mend. Orig. Title: Never Too Late to Mend. Tod Slaughter. Directed by David MacDonald. 1936. Britain. 67 min. Sound. 16mm B&W. *Rental:* Budget Films.

It's No Crush, I'm in Love. 1982. ABC. (Cast unlisted). 46 min. Sound. 16mm Color. *Sale:* Learning Corp Am. *Sale:* Learning Corp Am. *Rental:* Learning Corp Am, Videotape version.

It's Only Money. Jerry Lewis. Directed by Frank Tashlin. 1962. Paramount. 84 min. Sound. 16mm B&W. *Rental:* Films Inc.

It's Raining in Santiago. Bill Anderson & Jean-Louis Trintignant. Directed by Helvio Soto. Fr. 1974. France. 84 min. Sound. 16mm Color. subtitles. *Rental:* New Line Cinema & Specialty Films.

It's Showtime. Orig. Title: Wonderful World of Those Cuckoo Crazy Animals, The. Fred Weintraub. Directed by Paul Heller. 1976. United Artists. (Anthology). 87 min. Sound. 16mm Color. *Rental:* MGM United, Welling Motion Pictures, Westcoast Films & Wholesome Film Ctr.

It's That Man Again. Tommy Handley & Jack Train. Directed by Walter Forde. 1943. Britain. 84 min. Sound. 16mm B&W. *Rental:* Cinema Five.

It's Tough to Be Famous. Douglas Fairbanks Jr. & Mary Brian. Directed by Alfred E. Green. 1932. Warners. 79 min. Sound. 16mm B&W. *Rental:* MGM United.

It's Tough to Make It in This League. 1977. Lucerne. (Documentary). 55 min. Sound. 16mm Color. *Rental:* Budget Films. *Sale:* Lucerne Films. *Sale:* Lucerne Films, Videotape version.

It's Trad Dad. Orig. Title: Ring-A-Ding Rhythm. Chubby Checker. Directed by Richard Lester. 1962. Britain. 78 min. Sound. 16mm B&W. *Rental:* Kit Parker.

Ivan Pavlov. Alexander Borisov & Nikolai Cherkassov. Directed by Grigori Roshal. Rus. 1950. Russia. 91 min. Sound. 16mm B&W. subtitles. *Rental:* Corinth Films.

Ivan the Terrible. Rus. 1977. Russia. (Anamorphic, dance). 91 min. 16mm Color. *Rental:* Corinth Films & Utah Media.

Ivan the Terrible: Part One. Nikolai Cherkassov. Directed by Sergei Eisenstein. Rus. 1944. Russia. 96 min. Sound. 16mm B&W. subtitles. . *Sale:* Classic Film Mus, Cinema Concepts, Festival Films, Images Film, Morcraft Films & Reel Images. *Lease:* Corinth Films. *Sale:* Festival Films & Morcraft Films, Super 8 sound version. *Sale:* Cinema Concepts, Silent 8mm version. *Sale:* Cinema Concepts & Tamarelles French Film, Videotape version.

Ivan the Terrible: Part Two. Nikolai Cherkassov. Directed by Sergei Eisenstein. Rus. 1946. Russia. (Color sequence). 90 min. Sound. 16mm B&W. subtitles. *Rental:* Budget Films, Classic Film Mus, Corinth Films, Em Gee Film Lib, Films Inc, Images Film, Iowa Films, Janus Films, Kit Parker, Natl Film Video Comm, U Cal Media & Westcoast Films. *Sale:* Classic Film Mus, Cine Concepts, Festival Films, Images Film & Reel Images. *Sale:* Morcraft Films, *Lease:* Corinth Films, Super 8 version. *Sale:* Morcraft Films, Silent 8mm version. *Sale:* Cinema Concepts, Festival Films, Tamarelles French Film, Video Comm & Images Film, Videotape version.

Ivanhoe. Robert Taylor & Elizabeth Taylor. Directed by Richard Thorpe. 1952. MGM. 106 min. Sound. 16mm Color. *Rental:* MGM United & Roas Films. *Rental:* MGM United, Videotape version.

Ivanhoe. Australia. (Animated). 55 min. Sound. 16mm Color. *Rental:* Budget Films, Modern Sound, Westcoast Films, Wholesome Film Ctr & Williams Films. *Rental:* Budget Films, 60 mins. version.

Ivanhoe. James Mason, Michael Hordern & Olivia Hussey. Columbia. 142 min. Sound. 16mm Color. *Rental:* Budget Films, Welling Motion Pictures & Williams Films.

Ivanhoe Donaldson. Directed by Harold Becker & Warren Forma. 1964. 57 min. Sound. 16mm B&W. *Rental:* Films Inc.

I've Always Loved You. Orig. Title: Concerto. Philip Dorn & Catherine McLeod. Directed by Frank Borzage. 1946. Republic. 117 min. Sound. 16mm Color. *Rental:* Ivy Films & Rep Pic Film. *Lease:* Rep Pic Film.

I've Got Your Number. Joan Blondell & Glenda Farrell. Directed by Ray Enright. 1934. Warners. 68 min. Sound. 16mm B&W. *Rental:* MGM United.

Ivy. Joan Fontaine & Patric Knowles. Directed by Sam Wood. 1947. Universal. 99 min. Sound. 16mm B&W. *Rental:* Swank Motion.

Izu Dancer, The. Jap. 1974. 90 min. Sound. 16mm Color. *Rental:* Iowa Films.

J. A. Martin, Photographer. Directed by Jean Beaudin. 1977. Canada. (Cast unlisted). 101 min. Sound. 16mm Color. *Rental:* New Cimena & Natl Film CN. *Sale:* Natl Film CN. *Sale:* Natl Film CN, Videotape version.

J. D.'s Revenge. Glynn Turman & Louis Gossett. Directed by Arthur Marks. 1976. American International. 95 min. Sound. 16mm Color. *Rental:* Swank Motion.

J. T. Kevin Hooks. Directed by Robert Young. 1969. CBS. 51 min. Sound. 16mm B&W. *Rental:* Budget Films, Iowa Films, Roas Films, Twyman Films & U Mich Media. *Sale:* Carousel Films. *Rental:* Pyramid Film, *Sale:* Carousel Films, Color version.

J. W. Coop. Cliff Robertson & Geraldine Page. Directed by Cliff Robertson. 1972. Columbia. 112 min. Sound. 16mm *Rental:* Arcus Film, Budget Films, Images Film, Inst Cinema, Kit Parker, Modern Sound, Newman Film Lib, Welling Motion Pictures, Westcoast Films, Wholesome Film Ctr & Williams Films.

Jabberwocky. Michael Palin. Directed by Terry Gilliam. 1977. Britain. 100 min. Sound. 16mm Color. *Rental:* Cinema Five.

Jablonski. 1973. Canada. (Documentary). 50 min. Sound. 16mm Color. *Rental:* Natl Film Video. *Sale:* Natl Film Video.

Jacare. Frank Buck. Directed by Charles E. Ford. 1942. United Artists. 64 min. Sound. 16mm B&W. *Rental:* Inst Cinema.

J'Accuse. Victor Francen. Directed by Abel Gance. Fr. 1937. France. 125 min. Sound. 16mm B&W. subtitles. *Rental:* Images Film.

Jack & the Beanstalk. The Fox Kids. Directed by Sidney Franklin & Chester M. Franklin. 1917. Fox. 60 min. Silent. 16mm B&W. *Rental:* Mogulls Films.

Jack & the Beanstalk. Bud Abbott & Lou Costello. Directed by Jean Yarbrough. 1952. Warners. 76 min. Sound. 16mm B&W. *Rental:* Alba House, Budget Films, Cine Concepts, Charard Motion Pictures, Film Ctr DC, Films Inc, Lewis Film, Maljack, Modern Sound, Natl Film Video, Newman Film Lib, Roas Films, Video Comm, Welling Motion Pictures, Westcoast Films, Wholesome Film Ctr & Williams Films. *Sale:* Cinema Concepts. *Rental:* Video Corp & Video Comm, Videotape version.

Jack & the Beanstalk. 1976. Germany. (Animated). 92 min. Sound. 16mm Color. dubbed. *Rental:* Arcus Film, Cine Concepts, Film Ctr DC, Newman Film CN, Swank Motion, Twyman Film, Welling Motion Pictures, Westcoast Films & Williams Films.

Jack & the Witch. Directed by Taiji Yabushita. 1967. Japan. (Animated). 80 min. Sound. 16mm Color. dubbed. *Rental:* Budget Films & Welling Motion Pictures.

Jack Bush. Directed by Murray Battle. 1979. Canada. (Documentary). 57 min. Sound. 16mm Color. *Rental:* Natl Film CN. *Sale:* Natl Film CN.

Jack Frost. Natasha Sedykh. Directed by Alexander Row. 1966. Russia. 69 min. Sound. 16mm Color. *Rental:* Films Inc.

Jack Johnson. Directed by William Cayton. 1970. Big Fights. (Documentary). 90 min. Sound. 16mm B&W. *Rental:* Cine Craft, Film Ctr DC, Films Inc, Macmillan Films & U Cal Media. *Lease:* Macmillan Films.

Jack Knife Man, The. Florence Vidor. Directed by King Vidor. 1920. First National. 60 min. Silent. 16mm B&W. *Rental:* Budget Films, Classic Film Mus, Em Gee Film Lib, Film Classics, Kerr Film & Willoughby Peer. *Sale:* Classic Film Mus, Cinema Concepts, Film Classics, Griggs Movie, Natl Cinema & Reel Images. *Sale:* Cine Concepts & Film Classics, Silent 8mm version. *Rental:* Film Classics, *Sale:* Tamarelles French Film, Videotape version.

Jack London. Susan Hayward & Michael O'Shea. Directed by Alfred Santell. 1943. United Artists. 93 min. Sound. 16mm B&W. *Rental:* Alba House, Buchan Pic, Budget Films, Classic Film Mus, Film Ctr DC, Films Inc, Learning Corp Am, Mogulls Films, Twyman Films, U of IL Film, Westcoast Films & Willoughby Peer. *Sale:* Learning Corp Am. *Sale:* Mogulls Films, Videotape version.

Jack London's Tales of Adventure. Orig. Title: Life of Jack London, The. 1954. Learning Corp. (Anthology). 90 min. Sound. 16mm B&W. *Rental:* Budget Films, Learning Corp Am & Roas Films. *Sale:* Learning Corp Am.

Jack of Diamonds. Nigel Patrick. Directed by Vernon Sewell. 1950. Britain. 70 min. Sound. 16mm B&W. *Rental:* Mogulls Films.

Jack of Diamonds. George Hamilton & Joseph Cotten. Directed by Don Taylor. 1967. MGM. 108 min. Sound. 16mm Color. *Rental:* MGM United.

Jack Slade. Mark Stevens & Dorothy Malone. Directed by Harold Schuster. 1953. Allied Artists. 90 min. Sound. 16mm B&W. *Rental:* Ivy Films. *Sale:* Rep Pic Film.

Jack, the Giant Killer. Kerwin Matthews & Anna Lee. Directed by Nathan Juran. 1962. United Artists. (Anamorphic). 94 min. Sound. 16mm Color. *Rental:* MGM United.

Jackal of Nahuel Toro, The *see* Chacal de Nahuel Toro.

Jackass Mail. Wallace Beery & Marjorie Main. Directed by Norman Z. McLeod. 1942. MGM. 80 min. Sound. 16mm B&W. *Rental:* MGM United.

Jackie Robinson Story, The. Jackie Robinson & Ruby Dee. Directed by Alfred E. Green. 1950. Eagle Lion. 76 min. Sound. 16mm B&W. *Rental:* Budget Films, Films Inc & Mogulls Films.

Jackpot, The. James Stewart & Barbara Hale. Directed by Walter Lang. 1950. Fox. 85 min. Sound. 16mm B&W. *Rental:* Films Inc.

Jackson County Jail. Yvette Mimieux & Tommy Lee Jones. Directed by Michael Miller. 1976. CBS. 85 min. Sound. 16mm Color. *Rental:* Films Inc.

Jackson Pollack: Portrait. 1984. 54 min. Sound. Color. *Rental:* Direct Cinema. *Sale:* Direct Cinema. *Rental:* Direct Cinema, Videotape version.

Jacob the Liar. Vlastimil Brodsky. Directed by Frank Beyer. Ger. 1974. E. Germany. 95 min. Sound. 16mm Color. subtitles. *Rental:* Films Inc.

Jacob Two-Two Meets the Hooded Fang. Stephen Rosenberg & Alex Karras. 90 min. Sound. 16mm Color. *Rental:* Williams Films.

Jacob's Challenge. 1979. Lucerne. (Cast unlisted). 52 min. Sound. 16mm Color. *Sale:* Lucerne Films. *Sale:* Lucerne Films, Videotape version.

Jacqueline Susann's Once Is Not Enough. Orig. Title: Once Is Not Enough. Kirk Douglas, Alexis Smith & Brenda Vaccaro. 1975. Paramount. 120 min. Sound. 16mm Color. *Rental:* Films Inc.

Jacques Brel is Alive & Well & Living in Paris. Elly Stone & Mort Shuman. Directed by Denis Heroux & Guy Green. 1973. AFT. 98 min. Sound. 16mm Color. *Rental:* Films Inc.

Jacques le Fataliste. Madeleine Renaud. Fr. France. 67 min. Sound. 16mm B&W. *Rental:* French Am Cul.

Jacques Lipchitz. Directed by Bruce Bassett. 1978. Institutional Cinema. (Documentary). 52 min. Sound. 16mm Color. *Sale:* Inst Cinema.

Jade Mask, The. Sidney Toler. Directed by Phil Rosen. 1945. Monogram. 66 min. Sound. 16mm B&W. *Rental:* MGM United & Mogulls Films.

Jagdszene Aus Niederbayern *see* Hunters Are the Hunted.

Jaguar. Sabu & Barton MacLane. Directed by George Blair. 1956. Republic. 70 min. Sound. 16mm B&W. *Rental:* Ivy Films. *Sale:* Rep Pic Film.

Jaguar. Directed by Jean Rouch. Fr. 1971. France. (Documentary). 93 min. Sound. 16mm Color. *Rental:* U Cal Media.

Jaguar Lives. Christopher Lee & Barbara Bach. Directed by Ernest Pintoff. 1979. 90 min. Sound. 16mm Color. *Rental:* Swank Motion.

Jail, The. Directed by Michael Anderson, Saul Landau, Paul Jacobs & Bill Yahraus. 1972. Delator. 81 min. Sound. 16mm B&W. *Rental:* Cinema Five.

Jail Bait. Eva Mattes & Hary Baer. Directed by Rainer Werner Fassbinder. Ger. 1972. Germany. 99 min. Sound. 16mm Color. subtitles. *Rental:* New Yorker Films.

Jail for Women, A. 1977. Penn State. (Documentary). 57 min. Sound. 16mm B&W. *Rental:* Penn St AV Serv. *Sale:* Penn St AV Serv. *Rental:* Penn St AV Serv, *Sale:* Penn St AV Serv, Videotape version.

Jailbirds *see* Pardon Us.

Jailbreak. June Travis & Barton MacLane. Directed by Nick Grinde. 1936. Warners. 60 min. Sound. 16mm B&W. *Rental:* MGM United.

Jailhouse Rock. Elvis Presley & Judy Tyler. Directed by Richard Thorpe. 1957. MGM. 96 min. Sound. 16mm Color. *Rental:* MGM United. *Rental:* MGM United, Anamorphic color version, Videotape version.

Jalna. Peggy Wood & Ian Hunter. Directed by John Cromwell. 1935. RKO. 78 min. Sound. 16mm B&W. *Rental:* RKO General Pics.

Jam Session. Ann Miller & Louis Armstrong. Directed by Charles Barton. 1944. Columbia. 80 min. Sound. 16mm B&W. *Rental:* Kit Parker.

Jamaica Inn. Charles Laughton & Maureen O'Hara. Directed by Alfred Hitchcock. 1939. Paramount. 98 min. Sound. 16mm B&W. *Rental:* A Twyman Pres & Films Inc, Videotape version.

Jamaica Run. Ray Milland & Arlene Dahl. Directed by Lewis R. Foster. 1953. Paramount. 92 min. Sound. 16mm B&W. *Rental:* Budget Films, Video Comm & Willoughby Peer.

Jamaica: The Other Caribbean. 1976. PBS. (Documentary). 60 min. Sound. 16mm Color. *Rental:* WNET Media. *Sale:* WNET Media. *Sale:* WNET Media, Videotape version.

Jamboree. Orig. Title: Disc Jockey Jamboree. George Byron & Paul Harvey. Directed by Joseph Santley. 1944. Republic. 71 min. Sound. 16mm B&W. *Rental:* Ivy Films.

James A. Michener's Dynasty. Orig. Title: Dynasty. Sarah Miles & Stacy Keach. Directed by Lee Philips. 1976. Paradine. 105 min. Sound. 16mm Color. *Rental:* Lucerne Films. *Sale:* Lucerne Films. *Sale:* Lucerne Films, Videotape version.

James Bay Special Report. 1979. Canada. (Documentary). 56 min. Sound. 16mm Color. *Rental:* Natl Film CN. *Sale:* Natl Film CN.

James Brothers, The *see* True Story of Jesse James.

James Earl Jones. Orig. Title: No Easy Walk to Freedom. 1979. WNET. (Documentary). 58 min. Videotape Color. *Rental:* WNET Media. *Sale:* WNET Media.

James Joyce's Ulysses *see* Ulysses.

James Michener's World. 130 min. Sound. 16mm Color. *Rental:* Pyramid Film. *Sale:* Pyramid Film. *Rental:* Pyramid Film, *Sale:* Pyramid Film, Spanish version.

James Whitney Retrospective, A. Directed by James Whitney. 1977. Whitney. (Anthology, sound & silent). 76 min. 16mm Color. *Rental:* Creative Film.

Jamilya. Natalia Arinbasarova. Directed by Irina Poplavskaya. Rus. 1970. Russia. (Color sequences). 78 min. Sound. 16mm B&W. subtitles. *Rental:* Corinth Films. *Lease:* Corinth Films.

Jan Kadar. 1978. American Film Institute. (Lecture). 55 min. Sound. Color. *Sale:* Am Film Inst.

Jane Eyre. Virginia Bruce & Colin Clive. Directed by Christy Cabanne. 1934. Monogram. 70 min. Sound. 16mm B&W. *Rental:* Hurlock Cine.

Jane Eyre. Joan Fontaine & Orson Welles. Directed by Robert Stevenson. 1944. Fox. 96 min. Sound. 16mm B&W. *Rental:* Films Inc & La Inst Res Ctr.

Jane Eyre. George C. Scott, Susannah York & Jack Hawkins. 1970. Britain. 108 min. Sound. 16mm Color. *Rental:* Arcus Film, Bosco Films, Budget Films, Films Inc, Ivy Films, Kit Parker, Roas Films, Video Comm, Westcoast Films, Wholesome Film Ctr & Willoughby Peer.

Jane Fonda. 1965. Time-Life. (Documentary). 54 min. Sound. 16mm B&W. *Lease:* Direct Cinema.

Jane Is Jane Forever. 1978. Germany. (Cast unlisted). 90 min. Sound. 16mm Color. subtitles. *Rental:* New Line Cinema.

Jane Seymour. Keith Michell. 1976. Britain. 90 min. Color. *Rental:* Films Inc. *Sale:* Films Inc, Videotape version.

Janie. Joyce Reynolds & Robert Hutton. Directed by Michael Curtiz. 1944. Warners. 102 min. Sound. 16mm B&W. *Rental:* MGM United.

Janie Gets Married. Joan Leslie & Robert Hutton. Directed by Vincent Sherman. 1946. Warners. 91 min. Sound. 16mm B&W. *Rental:* MGM United.

Janis: The Way She Was. Directed by Howard Alk & Seaton Findlay. 1975. Universal. (Documentary). 96 min. Sound. 16mm Color. *Rental:* Swank Motion.

January Seventeen, Nineteen Seventy-Seven. 1981. CTW. (Cast unlisted). 60 min. Sound. 16mm Color. *Sale:* PBS Video. *Sale:* PBS Video. *Rental:* PBS Video, Videotape version.

Japan. Directed by Hugh Raggett. 1974. Britain. (Documentary). 60 min. Sound. 16mm Color. *Rental:* U Cal Media.

Japan. 1974. Japan Foundation. (Documentary). 80 min. Sound. 16mm Color. *Rental:* U Cal Media.

Japan: A New Dawn Over Asia. 1965. Wolper. (Documentary). 50 min. Sound. 16mm B&W. *Rental:* BYU Media, Films Inc & Wholesome Film Ctr. *Sale:* Films Inc. *Sale:* Films Inc, Videotape version.

Japan: Answer in the Orient. 1966. NET. (Documentary). 60 min. Sound. 16mm B&W. *Rental:* BYU Media. *Rental:* U Cal Media, Color version.

Japan: The Changing Tradition. 16 pts. 1979. 406 min. Sound. Videotape Color. *Rental:* Iowa Films.

Japan: The/Frozen Moment. Sessue Hayakawa. 1973. Modern. 54 min. Sound. 16mm B&W. *Rental:* Modern Mass. *Sale:* Modern Mass.

Japan: The Living Tradition. 7 pts. 1978. 420 min. Sound. Videotape Color. *Rental:* Iowa Films.

Japan: 1941-1945. (World at War). : Pt. 22.). 1973. Media Guild. (Documentary). 52 min. Sound. 16mm Color. *Rental:* Media Guild. *Sale:* Media Guild. *Sale:* Media Guild, Videotape version.

Japanese, The. 1968. CBS. (Documentary). 52 min. Sound. 16mm Color. *Rental:* BYU Media, Iowa Films, Syracyse U Film, U Cal Media & U Mich Media. *Sale:* Carousel Films.

Japan's Changing Face. 1960. CBS. (Documentary). 52 min. Sound. 16mm B&W. *Rental:* Macmillan Films. *Sale:* Macmillan Films.

Jari. Directed by Jorge Bodanzky. 60 min. Sound. 16mm Color. *Rental:* Cinema Guild.

Jason & the Argonauts. Todd Armstrong & Nancy Kovack. Directed by Don Chaffey. 1963. Italy. 104 min. Sound. 16mm Color. *Rental:* Arcus Film, Bosco Films, Budget Films, Cine Craft, Film Ctr DC, Films Pres, Films Inc, Kerr Film, Kit Parker, Modern Sound, Natl Film Video, Newman Film Lib, Roas Films, Syracuse U Film, Twyman Films, U of IL Film, Video Comm, Welling Motion Pictures, Westcoast Films, Wholesome Film Ctr & Williams Films.

Jason of Star Command. Filmation. (Cast unlisted). 66 min. Sound. 16mm Color. *Rental:* Williams Films.

Jassy. Margaret Lockwood & Patricia Roe. Directed by Bernard Knowles. 1948. Britain. 96 min. Sound. 16mm Color. *Rental:* Kit Parker.

Jaws. Roy Scheider, Richard Dreyfuss & Robert Shaw. Directed by Steven Spielberg. 1975. Universal. 124 min. Sound. 16mm Color. *Rental:* Swank Motion. *Rental:* Swank Motion, Videotape version.

Jaws II. Roy Scheider, Lorraine Gray & Murray Hamilton. Directed by Jeannot Szwarc. Universal. 120 min. Sound. 16mm Color. *Rental:* Swank Motion. *Rental:* Swank Motion, Videotape version.

Jaws III. Dennis Quaid & Bess Armstrong. Directed by Joe Alves. 1983. Universal. 97 min. Sound. 16mm Color. *Rental:* Swank Motion. *Rental:* Swank Motion, Anamorphic version. *Rental:* Swank Motion, Videotape version.

Jayhawkers, The. Jeff Chandler & Fess Parker. Directed by Melvin Frank. 1959. Paramount. 100 min. Sound. 16mm Color. *Rental:* Films Inc.

Jazz Age, The: 1919-1929. Directed by Henry Solomon. 1955. NBC. (Documentary). 52 min. Sound. 16mm B&W. *Rental:* Budget Films, BYU Media, Iowa Films, Kit Parker, La Inst Res Ctr, McGraw-Hill Films, Syracuse U Film, U Cal Media & U Mich Media. *Sale:* McGraw-Hill Films.

Jazz Ball. 1957. NTA. (Anthology). 60 min. Sound. 16mm B&W. *Rental:* Budget Films & Ivy Films. *Sale:* Reel Images. *Sale:* Golden Tapes, Videotape version.

Jazz Heaven. John Mack Brown & Sally O'Neil. Directed by Melville Brown. 1930. RKO. 71 min. Sound. 16mm B&W. *Rental:* RKO General Pics.

Jazz in Exile. 1982. 58 min. Sound. 16mm Color. *Sale:* Festival Films. *Sale:* Festival Films, Videotape version.

Jazz in the Concert Hall. 1964. CBS. (Documentary). 54 min. Sound. 16mm B&W. *Rental:* Syracuse U Film & U of IL Film. *Sale:* McGraw-Hill Films.

Jazz Is My Religion. Directed by John Jeremy. 1972. John Jeremy. (Documentary). 50 min. Sound. 16mm B&W. *Rental:* Icarus Films.

Jazz Mad. Jean Hersolt & Joan Crawford. Directed by Harmon Wright. 1928. Universal. 93 min. Silent. 16mm B&W. *Rental:* Em Gee Film Lib.

Jazz on a Summer's Day. Directed by Bert Stern. 1960. Raven. (Performance). 85 min. Sound. 16mm Color. *Rental:* New Yorker Films.

Jazz Singer, The. Al Jolson. Directed by Alan Crosland. 1928. Warners. 89 min. Sound. 16mm B&W. *Rental:* MGM United.

Jazz Singer, The. Neil Diamond, Sir Laurence Olivier. Directed by Richard Fleischer. 1980. AFD. 115 min. Sound. 16mm Color. *Rental:* Swank Motion.

Jazz: The Intimate Art. 1968. Drew Associates. (Documentary). 55 min. Sound. 16mm Color. *Rental:* Direct Cinema. *Sale:* Direct Cinema. *Sale:* Direct Cinema, Videotape version.

Jealousy. Nancy Carroll & George Murphy. Directed by Roy William Neill. 1934. Columbia. 70 min. Sound. 16mm B&W. *Rental:* Kit Parker.

Jean Carignan, Violoneux. Directed by Bernard Gosselin. 1975. Canada. (Documentary). 88 min. Sound. 16mm Color. *Rental:* Museum Mod Art.

Jeanne Dielman: Twenty Three Quai Du Commerce, Ten Eighty Bruxelles. Directed by Chantal Akerman. Fr. 1975. 198 min. Sound. 16mm Color. subtitles Eng. *Rental:* New Yorker Films.

Jeanne Eagles. Kim Novak & Jeff Chandler. Directed by George Sidney. 1957. Columbia. 109 min. Sound. 16mm B&W. *Rental:* Welling Motion Pictures.

Jeannie. Michael Redgrave & Barbara Mullen. Directed by Harold French. 1943. 90 min. 16mm *Rental:* A Twyman Pres.

Jedediah Smith. 1977. Britain. (Cast unlisted). 52 min. Sound. 16mm Color. *Rental:* Time-Life Multimedia. *Sale:* Time-Life Multimedia. *Rental:* Time-Life Multimeida, *Sale:* Time-Life Multimedia, Videotape version.

Jeepers Creepers. Orig. Title: Money Isn't Everything. Weaver Brothers & Elviry. Directed by Frank McDonald. 1939. Republic. 67 min. Sound. 16mm B&W. *Rental:* Ivy Films.

Jeff Gordon, Special Agent. Eddie Constance. Directed by Guy LaFranc. 1963. France. 90 min. Sound. 16mm B&W. dubbed. *Rental:* Films Inc.

Jekyll & Hyde: Together Again. Mark Blankfield & Bess Armstrong. Directed by Jerry Belson. 1982. Paramount. 88 min. Sound. 16mm Color. *Rental:* Films Inc.

Jennie Gerhardt. Sylvia Sidney & Donald Cook. Directed by Marion Gering. 1933. Paramount. 85 min. Sound. 16mm B&W. *Rental:* Swank Motion.

Jennifer. Howard Duff & Ida Lupino. Directed by Joel Newton. 1953. Allied Artists. 73 min. Sound. 16mm B&W. *Rental:* Ivy Films. *Sale:* Rep Pic Film.

Jennifer. Lisa Pelikan & Bert Convy. Directed by Brice Mack. 1978. American International. 90 min. Sound. 16mm Color. *Rental:* Swank Motion.

Jennifer on My Mind. Michael Brandon & Tippy Walker. Directed by Noel Black. 1971. United Artists. 90 min. Sound. 16mm Color. *Rental:* MGM United.

Jenny. Marlo Thomas & Alan Alda. Directed by George Bloomfield. 1970. ABC. 88 min. Sound. 16mm Color. *Rental:* Films Inc.

Jeopardy. Barbara Stanwyck & Barry Sullivan. Directed by John Sturges. 1953. MGM. 69 min. Sound. 16mm B&W. *Rental:* MGM United. *Sale:* Reel Images.

Jeremy. Robby Benson & Glynis O'Connor. Directed by Arthur Barron. 1973. United Artist. 90 min. Sound. 16mm Color. *Rental:* MGM United.

Jericho. Orig. Title: Dark Sands. Paul Robeson, Henry Wilcoxon & Wallace Ford. Directed by Thornton Freeland. 1937. Britain. 75 min. Sound. 16mm B&W. *Rental:* A Twyman Pres & Budget Films. *Sale:* Festival Films. *Sale:* Festival Films, Videotape version.

Jericho Mile, The. Peter Strauss & Richard Lawson. Directed by Michael Mann. 1979. ABC. 96 min. Sound. 16mm Color. *Rental:* U of IL Film. *Sale:* ABC Learn. *Sale:* ABC Learn, Videotape version.

Jerk, The. Steve Martin & Bernadette Peters. Directed by Carl Reiner. 1980. Universal. 94 min. Sound. 16mm Color. *Rental:* Swank Motion. *Rental:* Swank Motion, Videotape version.

Jerusalem File, The. Bruce Davidson & Donald Pleasance. Directed by John Flynn. 1972. MGM. 95 min. Sound. 16mm Color. *Rental:* MGM United.

Jerusalem Lives. 1977. Alden. (Documentary). 52 min. Sound. 16mm Color. *Rental:* Alden Films & Modern Talking.

Jerusalem Peace. Directed by Mark Benjamin. 1977. Phoenix. (Documentary). 57 min. Sound. 16mm Color. *Rental:* Phoenix Films & Syracuse U Film. *Sale:* Phoenix Films. *Sale:* Phoenix Films, Videotape version.

Jesse James. Tyrone Power & Henry Fonda. Directed by Henry King. 1939. Fox. 105 min. Sound. 16mm B&W. *Rental:* Charard Motion Pics, Films Inc & Willoughby Peer. *Rental:* Twyman Films, Video Comm & Willoughby Peer. *Rental:* Video Comm & Willoughby Peer, Color version.

Jesse James at Bay. Roy Rogers. Directed by Joseph Kane. 1941. Republic. 54 min. Sound. 16mm B&W. *Rental:* Budget Films, Em Gee Film Lib & Ivy Films. *Sale:* Rep Pic Film. *Sale:* Video Comm, Videotape version.

Jesse James Meets Frankenstein's Daughter. John Lupton & Jim Davis. Directed by William Beaudine. 1966. Embassy. 82 min. Sound. 16mm Color. *Rental:* Films Inc.

Jesse Owens Returns to Berlin. 1969. CBS. (Documentary). 51 min. Sound. 16mm B&W. *Rental:* McGraw-Hill Films & U Mich Media. *Sale:* McGraw-Hill Films.

Jesus Christ, Superstar. Ted Neely. Directed by Norman Jewison. 1973. Universal. (Anamorphic). 108 min. 16mm Color. *Rental:* Swank Motion. *Rental:* Swank Motion & Twyman Films, *Rental:* Swank Motion, Videotape version.

Jesus of Nazareth. Robert Powell & Anne Bancroft. Directed by Franco Zeffirelli. 1976. 376 min. Sound. Videotape Color. *Sale:* Tamarelles French Film.

Jesus Trip, The. 1972. Britain. (Documentary). 50 min. Sound. 16mm Color. *Rental:* Time-Life Multimedia. *Sale:* Time-Life Multimedia.

Jet Attack. John Agar & Audrey Totter. Directed by Edward L. Cahn. 1958. American International. 68 min. Sound. 16mm Color. *Rental:* Westcoast Films.

Jet Job. Stanley Clements & Elena Verdugo. Directed by William Beaudine. 1952. Monogram. 63 min. Sound. 16mm B&W. *Rental:* Hurlock Cine.

Jet Pilot. John Wayne & Janet Leigh. Directed by Josef Von Sternberg. 1957. RKO. 112 min. Sound. 16mm Color. *Rental:* Swank Motion.

Jet Propelled. 1966. Britain. (Documentary). 52 min. Sound. 16mm B&W. *Rental:* Time-Life Multimedia. *Sale:* Time-Life Multimedia.

Jetstorm. Stanley Baker & Richard Attenborough. Directed by Cy Endfield. 1962. 16mm *Rental:* A Twyman Pres.

Jeunes Filles de Paris. Fr. 1935. France. (Cast unlisted). 87 min. Sound. 16mm B&W. subtitles. *Rental:* Film Classics.

Jeux Sonts Faits, Les *see* Die Is Cast.

Jew in the Middle Ages, The: The Evolution of a Stereotype. Anti-Defamation League. (Lecture). 60 min. Sound. 16mm B&W. *Rental:* ADL. *Sale:* ADL.

Jew Suss. Conrad Veidt & Benita Hume. Directed by Lothar Mendes. 1934. Britain. 109 min. Sound. 16mm B&W. *Rental:* Janus Films.

Jewel in the Crown, A. Directed by Brian Nolan. 1973. Canada. (Documentary). 58 min. Sound. 16mm Color. *Rental:* Natl Film CN. *Sale:* Natl Film CN.

Jewel Robbery. William Powell & Kay Francis. Directed by William Dieterle. 1932. Warners. 68 min. Sound. 16mm B&W. *Rental:* MGM United.

Jewels from the Coral Sea. 1974. Explo Mundo. (Documentary). 52 min. Sound. 16mm Color. *Rental:* B Raymond. *Sale:* B Raymond.

Jewish Legends & Tales. Anti-Defamation League. (Lecture). 60 min. Sound. 16mm B&W. *Rental:* ADL. *Sale:* ADL.

Jewish Stereotype in Literature, The. Anti-Defamation League. (Lecture). 60 min. Sound. 16mm B&W. *Rental:* ADL. *Sale:* ADL.

Jews of Lodz, The. Poland-Sweden. (Documentary). 55 min. Sound. 16mm Color. *Rental:* Cinema Guild. *Sale:* Cinema Guild. *Sale:* Cinema Guild, Videotape version.

Jezebel. Bette Davis, Henry Fonda & Fay Bainter. Directed by William Wyler. 1938. Warners. 104 min. Sound. 16mm B&W. *Rental:* MGM United.

JFK: A History of Our Times. 1967. CCM. 50 min. Sound. 16mm B&W. *Rental:* Syracuse U Film.

JFK: Focus on 1960-1964 Kennedy Years. 1983. ABC. 58 min. Sound. 16mm Color. *Rental:* Films Inc.

Jigsaw. Franchot Tone & Jean Wallace. Directed by Fletcher Markle. 1949. Artists. 70 min. Sound. 16mm B&W. *Rental:* Mogulls Film.

Jigsaw. Bradford Dillman & Hope Lange. Directed by James Goldstone. 1968. Universal. 97 min. Sound. 16mm Color. *Rental:* Swank Motion.

Jigsaw. Jack Warner. Directed by Val Guest. 1959. 16mm *Rental:* A Twyman Pres.

Jilting of Granny Weatherall, The. 1980. Perspective. (Cast unlisted). 57 min. Sound. 16mm Color. *Rental:* Iowa Films, Kent St U Film, Syracuse U Film & U Mich Media. *Sale:* Perspect Film. *Sale:* Perspect Film, Videocassette version.

Jim Fixx on Running. 1966. Embassy. (Documentary). 58 min. Sound. 16mm Color. *Rental:* Films Inc.

Jim Hanvey, Detective. Tom Brown. Directed by Phil Rosen. 1938. Republic. 54 min. Sound. 16mm B&W. *Rental:* Ivy Films. *Sale:* Rep Pic Film.

Jim Stirling's Architecture. 1973. Britain. (Documentary). 50 min. Sound. 16mm Color. *Rental:* Films Inc. *Sale:* Films Inc. *Sale:* Films Inc, Videotape version.

Jim the Man. Scott Beach. Directed by Max Katz. 1967. Max Katz. 77 min. 16mm Color. *Rental:* Canyon Cinema.

Jim, the Penman. Mark Dignan & Beatrice Kane. Directed by Frank Chisnell. 1947. Britain. 55 min. Sound. 16mm B&W. *Rental:* Mogulls Films.

Jim Thorpe, All American. Orig. Title: Man of Bronze, The. Burt Lancaster & Charles Brickford. Directed by Michael Curtiz. 1951. Warners. 107 min. Sound. 16mm B&W. *Rental:* Films Inc, Inst Cinema, Modern Sound, Twyman Films & Williams Films.

Jimi Plays Berkeley. Directed by Peter Pilafian. 1973. New Line Cinema. (Concert). 102 min. Sound. 16mm Color. *Rental:* New Line Cinema, Swank Motion & Westcoast Films. *Sale:* New Line Cinema.

Jimmy the Gent. James Cagney & Bette Davis. Directed by Michael Curtiz. 1934. Warners. 67 min. Sound. 16mm B&W. *Rental:* MGM United.

Jitterbugs. Stan Laurel & Oliver Hardy. Directed by Mal St. Clair. 1943. Fox. 80 min. Sound. 16mm B&W. *Rental:* Films Inc.

Jive. Elsie Downey. Directed by Robert Downey. 1978. New Line Cinema. 82 min. Sound. 16mm Color. *Rental:* New Line Cinema.

Jive Junction. Orig. Title: Swing High. Dickie Moore & Tina Thayer. Directed by Edgar G. Ulmer. 1943. PRC. 70 min. Sound. 16mm B&W. *Rental:* Mogulls Films.

Jivin' in Be Bop. Dizzy Gillespie. Directed by Spencer Williams. 1948. 62 min. Sound. 16mm B&W. narrated. *Rental:* Budget Films & Em Gee Film Lib.

Joan of Arc. Ingrid Bergman & Jose Ferrer. Directed by Victor Fleming. 1948. RKO. 145 min. Sound. 16mm Color. *Rental:* Films Inc. *Rental:* Video Comm, *Lease:* Video Comm, Videotape version.

Joan of Ozark. Orig. Title: Queen of Spies. Judy Canova & Jerome Cowan. Directed by Joseph Santley. 1942. Republic. 82 min. Sound. 16mm B&W. *Rental:* Ivy Films.

Joan of Paris. Michele Morgan. Directed by Robert Stevenson. 1942. RKO. 91 min. Sound. 16mm B&W. *Rental:* Films Inc.

Joan of the Angels. Lucyna Winnicka. Directed by Jerzy Kawalerowicz. 1961. Poland. 101 min. Sound. 16mm B&W. subtitles. *Rental:* Films Inc.

Joanna. Genevieve Waite. Directed by Michael Sarne. 1968. Fox. 107 min. Sound. 16mm Color. *Rental:* Films Inc.

Job Discrimination: Doing Something About It. 1977. Indiana University. (Documentary). 59 min. Sound. 16mm Color. *Rental:* Indiana AV Ctr, Iowa Films, Syracuse U Films, U of IL Film & U Mich Media. *Sale:* Indiana AV Ctr. *Sale:* Indiana AV Ctr, Videotape version.

Joe. Peter Boyle & Dennis Patrick. Directed by John G. Avildsen. 1970. Cannon. 107 min. Sound. 16mm Color. *Rental:* Films Inc, Inst Cinema, Swank Motion & Welling Motion Pictures. *Rental:* Swank Motion, Videotape version.

Joe & Maxi. Directed by Maxi Cohen & Joel Gold. First Run. (Documentary). 80 min. Sound. 16mm Color. *Rental:* First Run. *Lease:* First Run.

Joe Cocker-Mad Dogs & Englishman *see* Mad Dogs & Englishmen.

Joe Hill. Thommy Berggren. Directed by Bo Widerberg. 1971. Sweden. 114 min. Sound. 16mm Color. *Rental:* Films Inc.

Joe Kidd. Clint Eastwood & Robert Duvall. Directed by John Sturges. 1972. Universal. 88 min. Sound. 16mm Color. *Rental:* Swank Motion. *Rental:* Swank Motion, Vidoetape version.

Joe Louis Story, The. Coley Wallace & Paul Stewart. Directed by Robert Gordon. 1972. United Artist. 87 min. Sound. 16mm B&W. *Rental:* Budget Films, Films Inc, MacMillan Films, Twyman Films & Westcoast Films.

Joe Macbeth. Paul Douglas & Ruth Roman. Directed by Ken Hughes. 1955. Columbia. 91 min. Sound. 16mm B&W. *Rental:* Kit Parker.

Joe Palooka. Jimmy Durante & Stuart Erwin. Directed by Ben Stoloff. 1934. 86 min. Sound. 16mm Color. *Rental:* Classic Film Mus.

Joe Palooka, Champ. Joe Kirkwood & Leon Errol. Directed by Reginald Le Borg. 1946. Monogram. 70 min. Sound. 16mm B&W. *Rental:* Budget Films.

Joe Palooka in the Big Fight *see* Big Fight.

Joe Palooka Meets Humphrey. Joe Kirkwood & Leon Errol. Directed by Jean Yarbrough. 1950. Monogram. 65 min. Sound. 16mm B&W. *Rental:* Budget Films.

Joe Panther. Brian Keith & Ricardo Montalban. Directed by Paul Krasny. 1977. Artist Creation. 110 min. Sound. 16mm Color. *Rental:* Modern Sound, Swank Motion & Westcoast Films.

Joe Smith, American. Robert Young & Marsha Hunt. Directed by Richard Thorpe. 1942. MGM. 62 min. Sound. 16mm B&W. *Rental:* MGM United.

Joe the Busy Body. Louis De Funes, Claude Gensac & Bernard Blier. Directed by Jean Girault. 1971. France. 85 min. Sound. 16mm Color. dubbed. *Rental:* MGM United.

Joe's Bed-Stuy Barbershop: We Cut Heads. Directed by Spike Lee. 1982. First Run. (Documentary). 60 min. Sound. 16mm Color. *Rental:* First Run. *Lease:* First Run.

Joeur D'Echec, Le. Conrad Veidt & Francoise Rosay. Directed by Jean Dreville. Fr. 1942. France. 94 min. Sound. 16mm B&W. subtitles. *Rental:* Film Classics.

Joey. Carla Pinza. Directed by Luis San Andres. 1975. Institutional Cinema. 54 min. Sound. 16mm Color. *Rental:* Budget Films, Inst Cinema. *Sale:* Inst Cinema.

Joey. 1977. Nova. (Documentary). 70 min. Sound. 16mm Color. *Rental:* Films Inc & U Mich Media. *Sale:* Films Inc. *Rental:* Films Inc, *Sale:* Films Inc, Videotape version.

Joey: The Autobiography of Joey Deacon. 1978. Time-Life. (Documentary). 73 min. Sound. 16mm Color. *Rental:* U of IL Film.

Jog's Trot. Directed by John Papadopoulos. 1978. Australia. (Cast unlisted). 60 min. Sound. 16mm Color. *Rental:* Museum Mod Art. *Sale:* Museum Mod Art.

John. 1977. 60 min. Sound. Videotape B&W. *Rental:* Iowa Films.

John Adams. David McCallum. Directed by Robert Stevens. (Profiles in Courage Ser.). 1965. Saudek. 50 min. Sound. 16mm B&W. *Rental:* BYU Media, OK AV Ctr, Syracuse U Film, U of IL Film & U Mich Media. *Sale:* IQ Film. *Rental:* IQ Film, *Sale:* IQ Film, Spanish dubbed version.

John Adams: Diplomat. 1976. WNET. (Cast unlisted). 59 min. Sound. 16mm Color. *Sale:* Films Inc. *Rental:* Indiana AV Ctr & Iowa Films, Videotape version.

John Adams: Lawyer. 1976. WNET. (Cast unlisted). 59 min. Sound. 16mm Color. *Rental:* Indiana AV Ctr, Iowa Films & U of IL Film. *Sale:* Films Inc, Videotape version.

John Adams: Minister to Great Britain. 1976. WNET. (Cast unlisted). 59 min. Sound. 16mm Color. *Rental:* Iowa Films & U of IL Film. *Sale:* Films Inc, Videotape version.

John Adams: President. 1976. WNET. (Cast unlisted). 59 min. Sound. 16mm Color. *Rental:* Iowa Films, Syracuse U Film & U of IL Film. *Sale:* Films Inc, Videotape version.

John Adams: Revolutionary. 1976. WNET. (Cast unlisted). 59 min. Sound. 16mm Color. *Rental:* Indiana AV Ctr, Iowa Films & U of IL Film. *Sale:* Films Inc, Videotape version.

John Adams: Vice President. 1976. WNET. (Cast unlisted). 59 min. Sound. 16mm Color. *Rental:* Indiana AV Ctr, Iowa Films & U of IL Film. *Sale:* Films Inc, Videotape version.

John & Mary. Dustin Hoffman & Mia Farrow. Directed by Peter Yates. 1969. Fox. 92 min. Sound. 16mm Color. *Rental:* Films Inc.

John Callaway Interviews Leo Buscaglia. 1982. 58 min. Sound. Videotape Color. *Rental:* PBS Video. *Sale:* PBS Video.

John Doe, Dynamite *see* Meet John Doe.

John F. Kennedy: Years of Lightning, Day of Drums. 1964. 88 min. Sound. 16mm Color. *Rental:* Natl AV Ctr. *Sale:* Natl AV Ctr.

John Fitzgerald Kennedy: A History of Our Times. 1967. Fleetwood. (Documentary). 50 min. Sound. 16mm B&W. *Rental:* Budget Films, Films Inc, MacMillan Films & Syracuse U Film. *Lease:* MacMillan Films. *Sale:* Films Inc, Videotape version.

John Goldfarb, Please Come Home. Shirley MacLaine & Richard Crenna. Directed by J. Lee Thompson. 1964. Fox. 96 min. Sound. 16mm Color. *Rental:* Films Inc.

John Keats: His Life & Death. 1973. EBE. (Documentary). 55 min. Sound. 16mm Color. *Rental:* Ency Brit Ed, LA Inst Res Ctr & U Mich Media. *Sale:* Ency Brit Ed. *Sale:* Ency Brit Ed, Videotape version.

John Loves Mary. Ronald Reagan & Patricia Neal. Directed by David Butler. 1949. Warners. 98 min. Sound. 16mm B&W. *Rental:* MGM United.

John M. Slaton. Orig. Title: Governor John M. Slaton. Walter Matthau. Directed by Robert Gist. 1955. Saudek. 50 min. Sound. 16mm B&W. *Rental:* U of IL Film. *Sale:* IQ Film. *Rental:* IQ Film, *Sale:* IQ Film, Spanish dubbed version.

John Marshall. Orig. Title: Chief Justice John Marshall. Gary Merrill. Directed by Joseph Anthony. (Profiles in Courage Ser.). 1965. Saudek. 50 min. Sound. 16mm B&W. *Rental:* BYU Media, Iowa Films, Syracuse U Film, U of IL Film & U Mich Media. *Sale:* IQ Film. *Rental:* IQ Film, *Sale:* IQ Film, Spanish dubbed version.

John of the Fair. John Charlesworth. Directed by Michael McCarthy. 1952. Britain. 62 min. Sound. 16mm B&W. *Sale:* Sterling Ed Film.

John Paul Jones. Robert Stack & Charles Coburn. Directed by John Farrow. 1959. Warners. 126 min. Sound. 16mm Color. *Rental:* Buchan Pic, Cine Craft, Films Inc, Modern Sound, Twyman Films, Williams Films & Willoughby Peer.

John Peter Altgeld. Burgess Meredith. Directed by Daniel Petrie. (Profiles in Courage Ser.). 1965. Saudek. 50 min. Sound. 16mm B&W. *Rental:* Syracuse U Film & U of IL Film. *Sale:* IQ Film. *Rental:* IQ Film, *Sale:* IQ Film, Spanish dubbed version.

John Quincy Adams. Douglas Campbell. Directed by Michael Ritchie. (Profiles in Courage Ser.). 1965. Saudek. 50 min. Sound. 16mm B&W. *Rental:* Syracuse U Film, U of IL Film & U Mich Media. *Sale:* IQ Film. *Rental:* IQ Film, *Sale:* IQ Film, Spanish dubbed version.

John Quincy Adams: Congressman. 1976. WNET. (Cast unlisted). 59 min. Sound. 16mm Color. *Rental:* U of IL Film & Indiana AV Ctr. *Sale:* Films Inc, Videotape version.

John Quincy Adams: Diplomat. 1976. WNET. (Cast unlisted). 59 min. Sound. 16mm Color. *Rental:* Indiana AV Ctr & U of IL Film. *Sale:* Films Inc, Videotape version.

John Quincy Adams: President. 1976. WNET. (Cast unlisted). 59 min. Sound. 16mm Color. *Rental:* Indiana AV Ctr & U of IL Film. *Sale:* Films Inc, Videotape version.

John Quincy Adams: Secretary of State. 1976. WNET. (Cast unlisted). 59 min. Sound. 16mm Color. *Rental:* Indiana AV Ctr, Iowa Films & U of IL Film. *Sale:* Films Inc, Videotape version.

Johnny Allegro. George Raft & Nina Foch. Directed by Ted Tetzlaff. 1949. Columbia. 81 min. Sound. 16mm B&W. *Rental:* Charard Motion Pics & Inst Cinema.

Johnny Angel. George Raft & Claire Trevor. Directed by Edwin L. Marin. 1945. RKO. 79 min. Sound. 16mm B&W. *Rental:* Films Inc. *Lease:* Films Inc.

Johnny Apollo. Tyrone Power & Dorothy Lamour. Directed by Henry Hathaway. 1940. Fox. 93 min. Sound. 16mm B&W. *Rental:* Films Inc.

Johnny Belinda. Jane Wyman, Lew Ayers & Charles Brickford. Directed by Jean Negulesco. 1948. Warners. 103 min. Sound. 16mm B&W. *Rental:* MGM United.

Johnny Cash. Directed by Robert Elfstrom. 1970. Continental. (Documentary). 94 min. Sound. 16mm Color. *Rental:* Budget Films & Westcoast Films.

Johnny Come Lately. James Cagney. Directed by William K. Howard. 1943. United Artists. 97 min. Sound. 16mm B&W. *Rental:* Corinth Films.

Johnny Comes Flying Home. Richard Crane & Faye Marlow. Directed by Ben Stoloff. 1946. Fox. 65 min. Sound. 16mm B&W. *Rental:* Films Inc.

Johnny Dark. Tony Curtis & Piper Laurie. Directed by George Sherman. 1954. Universal. 85 min. Sound. 16mm Color. *Rental:* Swank Motion.

Johnny Doughboy. Jane Withers & Henry Wilcoxen. Directed by John H. Auer. 1942. Republic. 64 min. Sound. 16mm B&W. *Rental:* Ivy Films.

Johnny Eager. Robert Taylor, Lana Turner & Van Heflin. Directed by Mervyn LeRoy. 1941. MGM. 110 min. Sound. 16mm B&W. *Rental:* MGM United.

Johnny Got His Gun. Timothy Bottoms & Diane Varsi. Directed by Dalton Trumbo. 1971. Cinemation. 112 min. Sound. 16mm B&W. *Rental:* Films Inc.

Johnny Guitar. Joan Crawford & Sterling Hayden. Directed by Nicholas Ray. 1954. Republic. 110 min. Sound. 16mm Color. *Rental:* Budget Films, Images Film, Ivy Films, Kit Parker, Welling Motion Pictures, Westcoast Films & Wholesome Film Ctr. *Sale:* Rep Pic Film. *Sale:* Tamarelles French Film, Videotape version.

Johnny Holiday. Orig. Title: Boys' Prison. William Bendix & Stanley Clements. Directed by Willis Goldbeck. 1949. United Artists. 92 min. Sound. 16mm B&W. *Rental:* Alba House, Bosco Films, Budget Films, Cine Craft, Film Ctr DC, Ivy Films, Roas Film, Video Comm, Wholesome Film Ctr & Willoughby Peer. *Rental:* Video Comm, Videotape version.

Johnny Lionheart *see* Johnny the Giant Killer.

Johnny North *see* Killers.

Johnny O'Clock. Dick Powell & Evelyn Keyes. Directed by Robert Rossen. 1947. Columbia. 93 min. Sound. 16mm B&W. *Rental:* Bosco Films, Budget Films & Inst Cinema.

Johnny Reno. Dana Andrews & Jane Russell. Directed by R. G. Springsteen. 1966. Paramount. Sound. 16mm Color. *Rental:* Films Inc.

Johnny Rocco. Richard Eyer & Stephen McNally. Directed by Paul Landres. 1958. Allied Artists. 83 min. Sound. 16mm B&W. *Rental:* Ivy Films. *Sale:* Rep Pic Film.

Johnny Shiloh. Brian Keith & Eddie Hodges. Directed by James Neilson. 1963. Disney. 90 min. Sound. 16mm Color. *Rental:* Buchan Pic, Cine Craft, Cousino Visual Ed, Disney Prod, Film Ctr DC, Film Pres, Films Inc, Newman Film, Lib, Swank Motion, Twyman Films & U of IL Film.

Johnny the Giant Killer. Orig. Title: Johnny Lionheart. 1954. France. (Animated). 60 min. Sound. 16mm B&W. narrated Eng. *Rental:* Cine Craft, Films Inc & Newman Film Lib.

Johnny Tough. Dion Gossett & Christopher Towns. Directed by Horace Jackson. 1976. Dimension. 90 min. Sound. 16mm Color. *Rental:* Williams Films. *Sale:* Salz Ent.

Johnny Tremain. Dick York, Luana Patten & Hal Stalmaster. Directed by Robert Stevenson. 1957. Disney. 80 min. Sound. 16mm Color. *Rental:* Bosco Films, Buchan Pic, Cine Craft, Cousino Visual Ed, Elliot Film Co, Film Ctr DC, Film Pres, Films Inc, MGM United, Modern Sound, Roas Films, Swank Motion, Twyman Films, U of IL Film, Welling Motion Pictures, Westcoast Films & Williams Films. *Rental:* U of IL Film, Two Part version.

Johnny, We Hardly Knew Ye. Paul Rudd. Directed by Gilbert Cates. 1977. NBC. 92 min. Sound. 16mm Color. *Rental:* Time-Life Multimedia. *Sale:* Time-Life Multimedia. *Sale:* Time-Life Multimedia, Videotape version.

Johnstown Monster, The. Simon Tully. Directed by Olaf Polley. 1971. Britain. 45 min. Sound. 16mm Color. *Rental:* Janus Films. *Sale:* Janus Films.

Join the Marines. Paul Kelly & Reginald Denny. Directed by Ralph Staub. 1937. Republic. 71 min. Sound. 16mm B&W. *Rental:* Ivy Films.

Joke, The. Josef Somr. Directed by Jaromil Jires. Czech. 1969. Czechoslovakia. 80 min. Sound. 16mm B&W. subtitles. *Rental:* Grove & New Cinema.

Jokers, The. Michael Crawford & Oliver Reed. Directed by Michael Winner. 1964. Britain. 94 min. Sound. 16mm Color. *Rental:* Swank Motion.

Jokes My Folks Never Told Me. 1977. New World. (Cast Unlisted). 85 min. Sound. 16mm Color. *Rental:* Films Inc.

Joli Mai, Le. Directed by Chris Marker. Fr. 1962. France. (Documentary). 124 min. Sound. 16mm B&W. subtitles. *Rental:* New Cinema.

Jolly Bad Fellow, A. Leo McKern. Directed by Robert Hamer. 1964. 16mm *Rental:* A Twyman Pres.

Jolson Sings Again. Larry Parks & Barbara Hale. Directed by Henry Levin. 1949. Columbia. 96 min. Sound. 16mm Color. *Rental:* Arcus Film, Budget Films, Films Inc, Modern Sound & Welling Motion Pictures.

Jolson Story, The. Larry Parks & Evelyn Keyes. Directed by Alfred E. Green. 1946. Columbia. 128 min. Sound. 16mm Color. *Rental:* Arcus Film, Buchan Pic, Budget Films, Cine CRaft, Film Ctr DC, Films Inc, Kit Parker, Modern Sound, Natl Film Video, Roas Films, Twyman Films, U of IL Film, Welling Motion Pictures, Westcoast Films, Wholesome Film Ctr & Willoughby Peer.

Jom: The Story of a People. Directed by Ababacar Samb. Wolof. 1982. 80 min. Sound. 16mm Color. *Rental:* New Yorker Films.

Jonah Who Will Be Twenty-Five in the Year Two Thousand. Jean-Luc Bideau & Miou Miou. Directed by Alain Tanner. 1976. Switzerland. 110 min. Sound. 16mm Color. subtitles. *Rental:* New Cinema & New Yorker Films.

Jonas. Robert Graf. Directed by Ottomar Domnick. 1957. 81 min. Sound. 16mm B&W. narrated Eng. *Rental:* Films Inc.

Jonathan Livingston Seagull. Directed by Hall Bartlett. 1973. Paramount. (Documentary). 114 min. Sound. 16mm Color. *Rental:* Films Inc.

Jory. John Marley & Robby Benson. Directed by Jorge Fons. 1972. Embassy. 96 min. Sound. 16mm Color. *Rental:* Films Inc.

Joseph & His Brethren. Geoffrey Horne & Robert Morley. Directed by Irving Rapper. 1962. Britain. 103 min. Sound. 16mm Color. *Rental:* Bosco Films, Budget Films, Charard Motion Pic, Film Ctr DC, Ivy Films, Roas Films, Video Comm & Willoughby Peer. *Lease:* Video Comm. *Rental:* Video Comm, *Lease:* Video Comm, Videotape version. *Rental:* Willoughby Peer, Anamorphic Color version.

Joseph Andrews. Ann-Margret & Peter Firth. Directed by Tony Richardson. 1977. Paramount. 103 min. Sound. 16mm Color. *Rental:* Films Inc.

Joseph in Eygpt. Sam Bottoms & Barry Nelson. Directed by James L. Conway. 1979. NBC. 52 min. Sound. 16mm Color. *Rental:* Budget Films & Roas Films. *Sale:* Lucerne Films. *Sale:* Lucerne Films, Videotape version.

Josepha. Miou-Miou & Claude Brasseur. Fr. 1983. France. 140 min. Sound. 16mm Color. subtitles. *Rental:* Swank Motion.

Josephine & Men. Glynis Johns & Donald Sinden. Directed by Roy Boulting. 1955. Britain. 97 min. Sound. 16mm Color. *Rental:* Charard Motion Pics.

Josette. Simone Simon & Don Ameche. Directed by Allan Dwan. 1938. Fox. 73 min. Sound. 16mm B&W. *Rental:* Films Inc.

Joshua at Jericho. Robert Culp & William Daniels. Directed by James L. Conway. 1979. NBC. 61 min. Sound. 16mm Color. *Sale:* Budget Films, Lucerne Films & Syracuse U Film. *Sale:* Lucerne Films, Videotape version.

Jour de Fete. Trans. Title: The Big Day. Jacques Tati & Guy Decomble. Directed by Jacques Tati. Fr. 1948. 74 min. Sound. 16mm B&W. subtitles. *Rental:* Films Inc.

Jour Se Leve, Le. Trans. Title: Daybreak. Jean Gabin. Directed by Marcel Carne. Fr. 1939. France. 85 min. Sound. 16mm B&W. subtitles. *Rental:* Budget Films, Em Gee Film Lib, Images Film, Iowa Films, Westcoast Films & Utah Media. *Sale:* Glenn Photo, Images Film & Reel Images. *Sale:* Festival Films, 92 min. version. *Sale:* Festival Films & Tamarelles French Film, 92 min. Videotape version.

Journal d'un Fou, Le. Directed by Roger Coggio. Fr. France. (Cast Unlisted). 105 min. Sound. 16mm B&W. subtitles. *Rental:* French AM Cul. *Rental:* French AM Cul, Videotape version.

Journal of a Crime. Adolphe Menjou & Ruth Chatterton. Directed by William Keighley. 1934. Warners. 65 min. Sound. 16mm B&W. *Rental:* MGM United.

Journalism: Mirror, Mirror on the World. 1967. NET. (Documentary). 52 min. Sound. 16mm B&W. *Rental:* BYU Media, Indiana AV Ctr, Iowa Films, U Cal Media & U Mich Media. *Sale:* Indiana AV Ctr.

Journals of Lewis & Clark. 1966. NBC. (Documentary). 53 min. Sound. 16mm B&W. *Sale:* Ency Brit Ed. *Sale:* Ency Brit Ed, Color version.

Journey, The. Yul Brynner & Deborah Kerr. Directed by Anatole Litvak. 1959. MGM. 122 min. Sound. 16mm Color. *Rental:* MGM United.

Journey for Margaret. Margaret O'Brien & Robert Young. Directed by W. S. Van Dyke. 1942. MGM. 81 min. Sound. 16mm B&W. *Rental:* MGM United.

Journey Into Fear. Orson Welles & Joseph Cotton. Directed by Norman Foster. 1942. RKO. 71 min. Sound. 16mm B&W. *Rental:* Films Inc.

Journey Into Fear. Sam Waterson, Zero Mostel & Shelley Winters. Directed by Daniel Mann. 1974. Canada. 98 min. Sound. 16mm Color. *Rental:* Bosco Films, Budget Films & Films Inc.

Journey Into Light. Sterling Hayden & Viveca Lindfors. Directed by Stuart Heisler. 1951. Fox. 87 min. Sound. 16mm B&W. *Rental:* Films Inc.

Journey Into Self. 1968. 47 min. Sound. 16mm B&W. *Rental:* U Mich Media.

Journey Into Summer. 1970. Fox. (Documentary). 87 min. Sound. 16mm Color. *Rental:* Cinema Guild, NYU Film Lib & Syracuse U Film. *Rental:* Cinema Guild, 51 mins. version.

Journey Into the Beyond. Directed by Rolf Olsen. 1977. BIP. (Documentary). 90 min. Sound. Videotape Color. *Sale:* Cinema Concepts. *Sale:* Cinema Concepts & Video Lib, Videotape version.

Journey of Lyndon Johnson, The. 1974. NBC. (Documentary). 51 min. Sound. 16mm Color. *Rental:* Films Inc, Syracuse U Film & U of IL Film. *Sale:* Films Inc, Videotape version.

Journey of Robert F. Kennedy, The. Directed by Mel Stuart. 1968. Wolper. (Documentary). 73 min. Sound. 16mm B&W. *Rental:* Budget Films, Films Inc, Swank Motion & Wholesome Film Ctr.

Journey Through Rosebud. Robert Forster & Kristoffer Tabori. Directed by Tom Gries. 1972. GSF. 93 min. Sound. 16mm Color. *Rental:* Swank Motion.

Journey Through the Past. Directed by Neil Young. 1974. Marvin. (Concert). 78 min. Sound. 16mm Color. *Rental:* New Line Cinema.

Journey to Russia. 58 min. Sound. Videotape *Rental:* PBS Video. *Sale:* PBS Video.

Journey to Shiloh. James Caan & Michael Sarrazin. Directed by William Hale. 1968. Universal. 92 min. Sound. 16mm Color. *Rental:* Williams Films.

Journey to the Beginning of Time. James Lucas & Victor Betral. Directed by Karel Zeman. 1960. Czechoslovakia. 87 min. Sound. 16mm Color. dubbed. *Rental:* Films Inc.

Journey to the Center of Earth. Directed by Leif Gram. 1970. Australia. (Animated). 50 min. Sound. 16mm Color. *Rental:* Budget Films, Westcoast Films & Wholesome Film Ctr.

Journey to the Center of the Earth. James Mason & Arlene Dahl. Directed by Henry Levin. 1959. Fox. 123 min. Sound. 16mm Color. *Rental:* Films Inc & Roas Films. *Rental:* Films Inc, Anamorphic color version.

Journey to the Center of Time. Scott Brady & Gigi Perreau. Directed by David L. Hewitt. 1967. Western International. 85 min. Sound. 16mm Color. *Rental:* Budget Films, Ivy Films & Video Comm.

Journey to the Far Side of the Sun. Orig. Title: Doppelganger. Ian Hendry & Roy Thinnes. Directed by Robert Parrish. 1969. Universal. 99 min. Sound. 16mm Color. *Rental:* Williams Films.

Journey to the High Arctic. 1971. National Geographic. (Documentary). 52 min. Sound. 16mm Color. *Rental:* Iowa Films, Natl Geog, Syracuse U Film, U Mich Media & Wholesome Film Ctr. *Sale:* Natl Geog. *Sale:* Natl Geog, Videotape version.

Journey to the Outer Limits. 1974. National Geographic. (Documentary). 52 min. Sound. 16mm Color. *Sale:* Natl Geog & Syracuse U Film. *Rental:* Natl Geog. *Sale:* Natl Geog, Videotape version.

Journey to the Seventh Planet. John Agar & Greta Thyssen. Directed by Sidney Pink. 1962. American International. 80 min. Sound. 16mm Color. *Rental:* Budget Films, Films Inc & Westcoast Films.

Journey with Mr. Jefferson, A. 1983. 54 min. Sound. Videotape *Rental:* Natl AV Ctr.

Journey Without Arrival: A Personal Point of View from Northrop Frye. Directed by Vincent Tovell. 1975. Canada. (Documentary). 57 min. Sound. 16mm Color. *Rental:* Natl Film CN. *Sale:* Natl Film CN.

Journeys from Berlin. Directed by Yvonne Rainer. 1980. Britain. (Experimental). 125 min. Sound. 16mm Color. *Rental:* Museum Mod Art.

Journeys in Space & Time. 1980. Cosoms. (Documentary). 60 min. Sound. 16mm Color. *Rental:* Films Inc. *Sale:* Films Inc. *Rental:* Films Inc, *Sale:* Films Inc, Videotape version.

Joy. 1977. Mature. 75 min. Sound. Videotape Color. *Sale:* Quality X Video.

Joy in the Morning. Richard Chamberlain & Yvette Mimieux. Directed by Alex Segal. 1965. MGM. 103 min. Sound. 16mm Color. *Rental:* MGM United. *Rental:* MGM United, Videotape version.

Joy of Bach, The. Brian Blessed. Directed by Paul Lammen. 1980. 58 min. Sound. 16mm Color. *Rental:* Lutheran Film.

Joy of Living, The. Irene Dunne & Douglas Fairbanks Jr. Directed by Tay Garnett. 1938. RKO. 90 min. Sound. 16mm B&W. *Rental:* Films Inc.

Joy Ride. Rad Fulton, Ann Doran & Regis Toomey. Directed by Edward Bernds. 1958. Allied Artists. 60 min. Sound. 16mm B&W. *Rental:* Swank Motion.

Joy Unspeakable. 1981. Indiana Unversity. (Documentary). 59 min. Sound. Videotape Color. *Rental:* Indiana AV Ctr. *Sale:* Indiana AV Ctr.

Joyless Street, The. Orig. Title: Street of Sorrow. Trans. Title: Freudlose Gasse, Die. Greta Garbo, Asta Nielsen & Werner Krauss. Directed by G. W. Pabst. 1925. Germany. 126 min. Silent. 16mm B&W. *Rental:* Budget Films, Em Gee Film Lib, Films Inc, Images Film, Kit Parker, Museum Mod Art & Utah Media. *Sale:* Festival Films, Glenn Photo, Images Film & Reel Images. *Rental:* Ivy Films, Super 8 silent version. *Rental:* A Twyman Pres & Utah Media, 79 mins. version. *Sale:* Festival Films & Images Film, Videotape version.

Joyous Sound, The. Lassie & Larry Pennell. Wrather. 72 min. Sound. 16mm Color. *Rental:* Modern Sound.

Joyride. Desi Arnaz Jr. & Robert Carradine. Directed by Joseph Ruben. 1977. American International. 91 min. Sound. 16mm Color. *Rental:* Swank Motion.

Juarez. Paul Muni, Bette Davis & Brian Aherne. Directed by William Dieterle. 1939. Warners. 132 min. Sound. 16mm B&W. *Rental:* MGM United.

Jubal. Glenn Ford & Ernest Borgnine. Directed by Delmer Daves. 1956. Columbia. 101 min. Sound. 16mm Color. *Rental:* Budget Films, Charard Motion Pics, Film Ctr DC, Modern Sound & Welling Motion Pictures. *Rental:* Kit Parker, Anamorphic version.

Jubilee. Jenny Runacre. Directed by Derek Jarman. 1978. Megalovision. 103 min. Sound. 16mm Color. *Rental:* Cinema Five.

Jubilee Trail. Vera Ralston & Forrest Tucker. Directed by Joseph Kane. 1953. Republic. 103 min. Sound. 16mm Color. *Rental:* Ivy Films. *Lease:* Rep Pic Film.

Judaism. 1967. KETC. (Documentary). 60 min. Sound. 16mm B&W. *Rental:* Indiana AV Ctr & Syracuse U Film. *Sale:* Indiana AV Ctr.

Judaism: The Chosen People. 1978. Britain. (Documentary). 52 min. Sound. 16mm Color. *Rental:* U Cal Media.

Judex. Michel Vitold & Channing Pollack. Directed by Georges Franju. Fr. 1963. France-Italy. 103 min. Sound. 16mm B&W. subtitles. *Rental:* Budget Films, Em Gee Film Lib, Images Film & Kit Parker. *Sale:* Natl Cinema & Reel Images. *Sale:* Tamarelles French Film, Videotape version.

Judge & the Assassin, The. Philippe Noiret & Isabelle Huppert. Directed by Bertrand Tavernier. Fr. 1976. France. (Anamorphic). 123 min. Sound. 16mm Color. subtitles. *Rental:* Corinth Films.

Judge Hardy's Children. Mickey Rooney & Lewis Stone. Directed by George B. Seitz. 1938. MGM. 77 min. Sound. 16mm B&W. *Rental:* MGM United.

Judge Horton & the Scottsboro Boys. Arthur Hill, Lewis J. Stadlen & Vera Miles. Directed by Fielder Cook. 1976. Tomorrow Entertainment. 98 min. Sound. 16mm Color. *Rental:* Budget Films, Kit Parker, Learning Corp Am, Roas Films, Westcoast Films & Wholesome Film Ctr. *Lease:* Learning Corp Am. *Rental:* Learning Corp Am, *Lease:* Learning Corp Am, Videotape version.

Judge Priest. Will Rogers & Anita Louise. Directed by John Ford. 1934. Fox. 80 min. Sound. 16mm B&W. *Rental:* Budget Films, Classic Film Mus, Em Gee Film Lib, Films Inc, OK AV Ctr, Video Comm & Kit Parker. *Sale:* Festival Films, Morcraft Films & Reel Images. *Sale:* Reel Images, Super 8 version. *Sale:* Festival Films & Tamarelles French Film, Videotape version.

Judge Steps Out, The. Orig. Title: Indian Summer. Ann Sothern & Alexander Knox. Directed by Boris Ingster. 1949. RKO. 91 min. Sound. 16mm B&W. *Rental:* Films Inc.

Judgement at Nuremberg. Spencer Tracy & Maximilian Schell. Directed by Stanley Kramer. 1961. United Artists. 186 min. Sound. 16mm B&W. *Rental:* MGM United.

Judgment of Solomon, The. John Carradine & John Saxon. Directed by James L. Conway. 1979. NBC. 33 min. Sound. 16mm Color. *Rental:* Budget Films. *Sale:* Budget Films & Lucerne Films. *Rental:* Budget Films, 58 min. version.

Judith. Sophia Loren & Peter Finch. Directed by Daniel Mann. 1966. Paramount. 109 min. Sound. 16mm Color. *Rental:* Films Inc.

Judith & Holofernes *see* Judith of Bethulia.

Judith of Bethulia. Orig. Title: Judith & Holofernes. Blanche Sweet, Henry B. Walthall, Mae Marsh & Lillian Gish. Directed by D. W. Griffith. 1914. Biograph. 68 min. Silent. 16mm B&W. *Rental:* A Twyman Pres, Budget Films, Classic Film Mus, Creative Film, Em Gee Film Lib, Film Images, Kit Parker & Museum Mod Art. *Lease:* Museum Mod Art. *Sale:* Blackhawk Films, Glenn Photo, Morcraft Films, Natl Cinema & Reel Images. *Rental:* Killiam Collect, Tinted Sound version. *Rental:* Ivy Films, *Sale:* Blackhawk Films & Glenn Photo, Super 8 Silent version.

Judy & Her Guests. 1963. CBS. (Anthology). 52 min. Videotape B&W. *Sale:* Reel Images.

Judy & Liza Live at the London Palladium. 1964. Britain. (Concert). 57 min. Videotape B&W. *Sale:* Reel Images.

Judy Collins & Leonard Cohen. 1980. Verve. (Concert). 58 min. Videotape Color. *Rental:* Films Inc.

Judy Garland Sings. 1957. CBS. (Concert, kinescope). 75 min. Sound. 16mm B&W. *Rental:* Bosco Films & Ivy Films.

Judy Goes to Town *see* Puddin' Head.

Judy! Judy! Judy! (Anthology, color sequences). 61 min. Videotape B&W. *Sale:* Reel Images.

Juggernaut. Orig. Title: Terror on the Britannia. Richard Harris & Omar Sharif. Directed by Richard Lester. 1974. United Artists. 110 min. Sound. 16mm Color. *Rental:* Budget Films, Roas Film, Westcoast Films & Wholesome Film Ctr.

Juggler, The. Kirk Douglas & Milly Vitale. Directed by Edward Dmytryk. 1953. Columbia. 88 min. Sound. 16mm B&W. *Rental:* Charard Motion Pics & Films Inc.

Jugoslav Folk Dances. 1948. Dennis Boxwell. (Documentary). 55 min. Sound. 16mm Color. *Rental:* U Cal Media.

Juilliard. Directed by Christian Blackwood. 1977. Blackwood. (Documentary). 52 min. Sound. 16mm Color. *Rental:* Blackwood Films. *Sale:* Blackwood Films.

Juke Box Rhythm. Jo Morrow & Jack Jones. Directed by Arthur Dreifuss. 1959. Columbia. 81 min. Sound. 16mm B&W. *Rental:* Modern Sound.

Juke Girl. Ann Sheridan & Ronald Reagan. Directed by Curtis Bernhardt. 1942. Warners. 90 min. Sound. 16mm B&W. *Rental:* MGM United.

Jules & Jim. Jeanne Moreau & Oskar Werner. Directed by Francois Truffaut. Fr. 1961. France. 104 min. Sound. 16mm B&W. subtitles. *Rental:* Films Inc & New Cinema.

Jules Verne's Rocket to the Moon *see* Those Fantastic Flying Fools.

Julia. Jane Fonda, Vanessa Redgrave & Jason Robards. Directed by Fred Zinnemann. 1977. Fox. 117 min. Sound. 16mm Color. *Rental:* Films Inc.

Julia Misbehaves. Greer Garson & Walter Pidgeon. Directed by Jack Conway. 1948. MGM. 100 min. Sound. 16mm B&W. *Rental:* MGM United.

Julie. Doris Day & Louis Jourdan. Directed by Andrew Stone. 1956. MGM. 97 min. Sound. 16mm B&W. *Rental:* MGM United.

Julie the Redhead. Daniel Gelin & Pascale Petit. Directed by Claude Boissol. Fr. 1963. France. 96 min. Sound. 16mm B&W. *Rental:* Films Inc.

Juliet of the Spirits. Giulietta Massina & Sandra Milo. Directed by Federico Fellini. Ital. 1965. Italy. 137 min. Sound. 16mm Color. subtitles. *Rental:* Films Inc & Kino Intl.

Julius Caesar. Antonio Novelli. 1914. Italy. 50 min. Silent. 16mm B&W. *Rental:* Budget Films. *Sale:* Morcraft Films.

Julius Caesar. Marlon Brando & James Mason. Directed by Joseph L. Mankiewicz. 1953. MGM. 121 min. Sound. 16mm B&W. *Rental:* MGM United. *Rental:* MGM United, Videotape version.

Julius Caesar. Charlton Heston, Jason Robards & Richard Johnson. Directed by Stuart Berge. 1969. Commonwealth United. 117 min. Sound. 16mm Color. *Rental:* Budget Films, Films Inc, Ivy Films, Modern Sound, Rep Pic Film, Twyman Films, Video Comm, Westcoast Films & Wholesome Film Ctr. *Lease:* Rep Pic Film & Video Comm. *Rental:* Video Comm, Anamorphic color version. *Rental:* Ivy Films, *Sale:* Ivy Films, Super 8 sound version.

Julius Caesar. 4 pts. Britain. (Cast unlisted). 120 min. Sound. 16mm B&W. *Rental:* Time-Life Multimedia. *Sale:* Time-Life Multimedia.

Julius Caesar. Richard Pasco & Keith Michell. 1979. Britain. 161 min. Videotape Color. *Rental:* Iowa Films.

Julius Caesar. Charlton Heston & David Bradley. Directed by David Bradley. 1950. David Bradley. 90 min. Sound. 16mm B&W. *Rental:* Trans-World Films. *Lease:* Macmillan Films.

Jumbo *see* Billy Rose's Jumbo.

Jump for Glory. Orig. Title: When Thief Meets Thief. Douglas Fairbanks Jr. & Valerie Hobson. Directed by Raoul Walsh. 1937. Britain. 89 min. Sound. 16mm B&W. *Rental:* Kit Parker.

Jumping Jacks. Dean Martin & Jerry Lewis. Directed by Norman Taurog. 1952. Paramount. 96 min. Sound. 16mm B&W. *Rental:* Films Inc.

June Bride. Bette Davis & Robert Montgomery. Directed by Bretaigne Windust. 1948. Warners. 97 min. Sound. 16mm B&W. *Rental:* MGM United.

Jungle. 55 min. Color. *Rental:* EMC.

Jungle Book, The. Sabu & Joseph Calleia. Directed by Alexander Korda. 1942. United Artists. 115 min. Sound. 16mm Color. *Rental:* Arcus Film, Bosco Films, Buchan Pic, Budget Films, Classic Film Mus, Charard Motion Pics, Elliot Film Co, Em Gee Film Lib, Inst Cinema, Images Film, Kit Parker, Maljack, Mogulls Film, Natl Film Video, Newman Film Lib, Roas Films, Video Comm, Welling Motion Pictures, Wholesome Film Ctr & Williams Films. *Sale:* Cinema Concepts, Glenn Photo, Images Film, Morcraft Films & Reel Images. *Rental:* Ivy Films, *Sale:* Cinema Concepts, Glenn Photo & Ivy Films, Super 8 version. *Rental:* Tamarelles French Film & Video Comm, *Lease:* Video Comm, *Sale:* Video Lib, Videotape version. *Rental:* Westcoast Films, 78 mins. version.

Jungle Book, The. Directed by Wolfgang Reitherman. 1967. Disney. (Animated). 86 min. Sound. 16mm Color. *Rental:* Disney Prod, Film Inc, MGM United, Modern Sound, Swank Motion & Williams Films.

Jungle Cavalcade. Orig. Title: Frank Buck's Jungle Cavalcade. 1941. RKO. (Documentary). 79 min. Sound. 16mm B&W. *Rental:* Films Inc.

Jungle Fighters. Orig. Title: Long & the Short & the Tall, The. Laurence Harvey & Richard Todd. Directed by Leslie Norman. 1961. Britain. 84 min. Sound. 16mm B&W. *Rental:* Films Inc.

Jungle Freaks see Macunaima.

Jungle Gold. Allan Lane & Linda Stirling. Directed by Wallace Grissell. 1966. Republic. 100 min. Sound. 16mm B&W. *Rental:* Ivy Films. *Sale:* Rep Pic Film.

Jungle Jim. Johnny Weissmuller. Directed by William Berke. 1949. Columbia. 88 min. Sound. 16mm B&W. *Rental:* Bosco Films, Films Inc, Inst Cinema, Newman Film Lib & Westcoast Films.

Jungle Jim & the Killer Ape see Killer Ape.

Jungle Jim & the Moon Men see Jungle Moon Men.

Jungle Jim in the Forbidden Land. Johnny Weissmuller. Directed by Lew Landers. 1952. Columbia. 65 min. Sound. 16mm B&W. *Rental:* Bosco Films, Charard Motion Pics & Inst Cinema.

Jungle Jim on Pygmy Island see Pygmy Island.

Jungle Man. Buster Crabbe & Sheila Darcy. Directed by Harry Fraser. 1941. PRC. 64 min. Sound. 16mm B&W. *Sale:* Natl Cinema.

Jungle Manhunt. Johnny Weissmuller & Sheila Ryan. Directed by Lew Landers. 1951. Columbia. 66 min. Sound. 16mm B&W. *Rental:* Films Inc, Inst Cinema, Newman Film Lib & Threshold Films.

Jungle Moon Men. Orig. Title: Jungle Jim & the Moon Men. Johnny Weissmuller. Directed by Charles S. Gould. 1955. Columbia. 70 min. Sound. 16mm B&W. *Rental:* Bosco Films & Buchan Pic.

Jungle Princess, The. Orig. Title: Lost City. Juanita Hansen & George Chesbro. 1920. Warners. 45 min. Silent. 16mm B&W. *Rental:* Mogulls Films. *Sale:* Blackhawk Films. *Sale:* Blackhawk Films, Super 8 Silent version.

Jungle Stampede. Directed by George Breakston. 1950. Republic. (Documentary). 60 min. Sound. 16mm B&W. *Rental:* Ivy Films. *Sale:* Rep Pic Film.

Junior Bonner. Steve McQueen, Robert Preston & Ida Lupino. Directed by Sam Peckinpah. 1972. ABC. 100 min. Sound. 16mm Color. *Rental:* Films Inc. *Sale:* ABC Film Lib, Super 8 Sound version.

Junior Miss. Peggy Ann Garner & Allyn Joslyn. Directed by George Seaton. 1945. Fox. 96 min. Sound. 16mm B&W. *Rental:* Films Inc.

Junior Prom. Freddie Stewart & June Preisser. Directed by Arthur Dreifuss. 1945. Monogram. 69 min. Sound. 16mm B&W. *Rental:* Hurlock Cine.

Junket Eighty Nine. 1973. Britian. (Cast unlisted). 60 min. Sound. 16mm Color. *Sale:* Lucerne Films.

Juno & the Paycock. Sara Allgood. Directed by Alfred Hitchcock. 1930. Britain. 85 min. Sound. 16mm B&W. *Rental:* Classic Film Mus.

Jupiter's Darling. Esther Williams & Howard Keel. Directed by George Sidney. 1955. MGM. 96 min. Sound. 16mm Color. *Rental:* MGM United. *Rental:* MGM United, Anamorphic color version.

Jupiter's Thigh. Annie Girardot & Philippe Noiret. Directed by Philippe De Broca. Fr. 1981. QFI. 96 min. Sound. 16mm Color. *Rental:* Films Inc.

Jury of One, A. Sophia Loren & Jean Gabin. Directed by Andre Cayatte. 1975. Embassy. 90 min. Sound. Videotape Color. *Sale:* Cinema Concepts.

Jury's Secret, The. Kent Taylor & Fay Wray. Directed by Edward Sloman. 1938. Universal. 60 min. Sound. 16mm B&W. *Rental:* Film Ctr DC & Mogulls Films.

Jusqu'Au Coeur. Robert Charlebois & Claudine Monfette. Fr. 1974. Canada. 93 min. Sound. 16mm Color. subtitles. *Rental:* Natl Film CN. *Sale:* Natl Film CN.

Just a Gigolo. David Bowie & Marlene Dietrich. Directed by David Hemmings. 1978. United Artist. 98 min. Sound. 16mm Color. *Rental:* MGM United.

Just Another Missing Kid. 1983. (Cast Unlisted). 90 min. Sound. 16mm Color. *Rental:* Pyramid Film. *Sale:* Pyramid Film.

Just Around the Corner. Shirley Temple, Joan Davis & Bert Lahr. Directed by Irving Cummings. 1938. Fox. 70 min. Sound. 16mm B&W. *Rental:* Films Inc.

Just Around the Corner. 1976. Gould. (Documentary). 53 min. Sound. 16mm Color. *Rental:* Lucerne Films. *Sale:* Lucerne Films. *Sale:* Lucerne Films, Videotape version.

Just Because You're Grown Up. Xerox. (Cast unlisted). 78 min. Sound. 16mm B&W. *Sale:* Xerox Films.

Just Before Nightfall. Stephane Audran & Francois Perier. Directed by Claude Chabrol. Fr. 1973. France. 107 min. Sound. 16mm Color. subtitles. *Rental:* Corinth Films.

Just For You. Bing Crosby & Jane Wyman. Directed by Elliott Nugent. 1952. Paramount. 104 min. Sound. 16mm Color. *Rental:* Films Inc.

Just Hold My Hand: Dying of Cancer. 1979. ABC. (Documentary). 48 min. Sound. 16mm Color. *Rental:* MTI Tele. *Sale:* MTI Tele. *Sale:* MTI Tele, Videotape version.

Just Imagine. El Brendel & Maureen O'Sullivan. Directed by David Butler. 1930. Fox. 110 min. Sound. 16mm B&W. *Rental:* Films Inc.

Just Last Summer. 1976. Gospel. (Cast unlisted). 50 min. Sound. 16mm Color. *Rental:* Gospel Films.

Just Like at Home. Zsuzsa Czinkoczy & Jan Nowicki. Directed by Marta Meszaros. Hungarian. 1978. Hungary. 108 min. Sound. 16mm Color. subtitles. *Rental:* New Cinema.

Just My Luck. Ray Charles. Directed by Russell Ray Heinz. 1936. Corona. 65 min. Sound. 16mm B&W. *Rental:* Film Classics.

Just Off Broadway. Ann Christy & Don Keith. Directed by Edmund Mortimer. 1929. Chesterfield. 75 min. Silent. 16mm B&W. *Rental:* Mogulls Films.

Just Off Broadway. Lloyd Nolan & Phil Silvers. Directed by Herbert I. Leeds. 1942. Fox. 66 min. Sound. 16mm B&W. *Rental:* Films Inc.

Just Out of Reach. (Cast unlisted). Videotape *Sale:* Vidamerica.

Just Pals. Buck Jones & George E. Stone. Directed by John Ford. 1920. Fox. 50 min. Silent. 16mm B&W. *Rental:* Films Inc.

Just Tell Me What You Want. Ali MacGraw & Alan King. Directed by Sidney Lumet. 1980. Warners. 135 min. Sound. 16mm Color. *Rental:* Swank Motion & Williams Films.

Just This Once. Janet Leigh & Peter Lawford. Directed by Don Weis. 1952. MGM. 91 min. Sound. 16mm B&W. *Rental:* MGM United.

Just Tony. Tom Mix. Directed by Lynn Reynolds. 1922. Fox. (Musical Score Only). 58 min. Sound. 16mm B&W. *Rental:* Killiam Collect. *Sale:* Blackhawk Films & Reel Images. *Sale:* Blackhawk Films & Reel Images, Silent 16mm version.

Just You & Me, Kid. George Burns & Brooke Shields. Directed by Leonard Stern. 1979. Columbia. 96 min. Sound. 16mm Color. *Rental:* Arcus Film, Modern Sound, Swank Motion, Welling Motion Pictures, Wholesome Film Ctr & Williams Films.

Justice? 1971. NET. (Documentary). 59 min. Sound. 16mm B&W. *Rental:* Indiana AV Ctr. *Sale:* Indiana AV Ctr.

Justice & the Poor. 1966. NET. (Documentary). 60 min. Sound. 16mm B&W. *Rental:* U Cal Media & Indiana AV Ctr. *Sale:* Indiana AV Ctr.

Justice on Trial. 1976. ABC. (Documentary). 49 min. Sound. 16mm Color. *Rental:* Iowa Films, McGraw-Hill Films, Syracuse U Film, U Cal Media & U of IL Film. *Sale:* McGraw-Hill Films. *Sale:* McGraw-Hill Films, Videotape version.

Justice Rides Again. Tom Mix. Universal. 55 min. Sound. 16mm B&W. *Rental:* Em Gee Film Lib. *Sale:* Cinema Concepts & Natl Cinema.

Justice Takes a Holiday. H. B. Warner & Robert Fraser. Directed by Spencer G. Bennett. 1933. Mayfair. 70 min. Sound. 16mm B&W. *Rental:* Mogulls Films.

Justine. Anouk Aimee & Dirk Bogarde. Directed by George Cukor. 1969. Fox. 115 min. Sound. 16mm Color. *Rental:* Films Inc.

Jutro Meksyk. Trans. Title: Tomorrow Mexico. Directed by Aleksander Scibor-Rylski. Poland. (Documentary). 100 min. Sound. 16mm B&W. *Rental:* Polish People.

Juvenile Court. Bette Davis & Pat O'Brien. Directed by D. Ross Lederman. 1938. Columbia. 60 min. Sound. 16mm B&W. *Rental:* Mogulls Films.

Juvenile Court. Directed by Frederick Wiseman. 1973. Zipporah. (Documentary). 144 min. Sound. 16mm B&W. *Rental:* U Mich Media & Zipporah Films.

Juvenile Jungle, The. Corey Allen & Rebecca Welles. Directed by William Witney. 1958. Republic. 72 min. Sound. 16mm B&W. *Rental:* Ivy Films. *Sale:* Rep Pic Film.

Juvenile Liasion. Directed by Nick Broomfield & Joan Churchill. 1976. Churchill. (Documentary). 97 min. Sound. 16mm Color. *Rental:* Charard Motion Pics & Churchill Films. *Sale:* Charard Motion Pics & Churchill Films.

Kaddish. Directed by Steve Brand. 1983. First Run. (Documentary). Sound. 16mm Color. *Rental:* First Run.

Kagemusha. Tatsuya Nakadai & Tsutomu Yamazaki. Directed by Akira Kurosawa. Jap. 1980. Fox. 159 min. Sound. 16mm Color. subtitles. *Rental:* Films Inc.

Kagi *see* Odd Obsession.

Kaleidoscope. Warren Beatty & Susannah York. Directed by Jack Smight. 1966. Warners. 103 min. Sound. 16mm Color. *Rental:* Charard Motion Pics, Films Inc, Inst Cinema & Willoughby Peer.

Kambur. Fatima Girik. Directed by Atif Yilmaz. Turkish. 1974. 93 min. Sound. 16mm Color. subtitles. *Rental:* Films Inc.

Kameradschaft. Orig. Title: Comradeship. Alexander Granach. Directed by G. W. Pabst. Ger. 1931. Germany. 78 min. Sound. 16mm B&W. subtitles. *Rental:* Budget Films, Em Gee Film Lib, Festival Films, Films Inc, Janus Films & Kit Parker. *Sale:* Reel Images, Festival Films & Natl Cinema. *Sale:* Festival Films & Tamarelles French Film, Videotape version.

Kamikaze. Directed by Perry Wolff. 1961. France. (Documentary). 87 min. Sound. 16mm B&W. *Rental:* Budget Films. *Sale:* Festival Films.

Kamouraska. Genevieve Bujold & Richard Jordon. Directed by Claude Jutra. 1975. Canada. 119 min. Sound. 16mm *Rental:* New Line Cinema.

Kanal. Trans. Title: Wajda Trilogy. Teresa Izewsk. Directed by Andrzej Wajda. Pol. 1956. Poland. 96 min. Sound. 16mm B&W. subtitles. *Rental:* Films Inc.

Kaname & Yokichi. Japan. (Cast unlisted). 60 min. Sound. 16mm B&W. narrated Eng. *Sale:* Japan Society. *Sale:* Japan Society, Videotape version.

Kanchenjungha. Karuna Bannerjee. Directed by Satyajit Ray. Bengali. 1962. 102 min. Sound. 16mm Color. subtitles Eng. *Rental:* Films Inc.

Kansan, The. Richard Dix & Jane Wyatt. Directed by George Archainbaud. 1943. United Artists. 82 min. 16mm B&W. *Rental:* Budget Films, Classic Film Mus, Em Gee Film Lib, Films Inc, Learning Corp Am & Mogulls Films. *Sale:* Learning Corp Am.

Kansas City Bomber, The. Raquel Welch & Kevin McCarthy. Directed by Jerrold Freedman. 1972. United Artists. 100 min. Sound. 16mm Color. *Rental:* MGM United.

Kansas City Confidential. Orig. Title: Secret Four, The. John Payne, Preston Foster & Lee Van Cleef. Directed by Phil Karlson. 1953. United Artists. 98 min. Sound. 16mm B&W. *Rental:* MGM United.

Kansas City Kitty. Joan Davis. Directed by Del Lord. 1944. Columbia. 70 min. Sound. 16mm B&W. *Rental:* Welling Motion Pictures.

Kansas City Princess, The. Joan Blondell & Glenda Farrell. Directed by William Keighley. 1934. Warners. 64 min. Sound. 16mm B&W. *Rental:* MGM United.

Kansas Cyclone. Don Barry. Directed by George Sherman. 1941. Republic. 54 min. Sound. 16mm B&W. *Rental:* Ivy Films.

Kansas Pacific. Sterling Hayden & Eve Miller. Directed by Ray Nazarro. 1953. Allied Artists. 73 min. Sound. 16mm Color. *Rental:* Hurlock Cine.

Kansas Territory. Bill Elliott & Pamela Blake. Directed by Lewis D. Collins. 1952. Monogram. 68 min. Sound. 16mm B&W. *Rental:* Hurlock Cine.

Kansas Terrors, The. Robert Livingston. Directed by George Sherman. 1939. Republic. 54 min. Sound. 16mm B&W. *Rental:* Ivy Films. *Sale:* Rep Pic Film & Nostalgia Merchant.

Kapo. Susan Strasberg & Emmanuelle Riva. Directed by Gillo Pontecorvo. 1960. 116 min. Sound. 16mm B&W. subtitles. *Rental:* Films Inc. *Rental:* Films Inc, Dubbed version.

Karamazov. Orig. Title: Morder Dimitri Karamazov, Der. Fritz Kortner. Directed by Fedor Ozep. Ger. 1931. 95 min. 16mm subtitles. *Rental:* A Twyman Pres.

Karate Kid, The. Ralph Macchio & Elisabeth Shue. Directed by John G. Avildsen. 1985. Columbia. 118 min. Sound. 16mm Color. *Rental:* Swank Motion.

Karate Killer, The. Directed by Barry Shear. 1967. United International. (Cast unlisted). 96 min. Sound. 16mm Color. dubbed. *Rental:* Films Inc.

Karen Kain: Ballerina. 1977. Canada. (Documentary). 54 min. Sound. 16mm Color. *Rental:* U of IL Film.

Karl Marx: The Massive Dissent. 1976. Britain. (Documentary). 66 min. Sound. 16mm Color. *Rental:* Films Inc, Syracuse U Film, U Cal Media & U of IL Film. *Sale:* Films Inc. *Sale:* Films Inc, Videotape version.

Karol Lir *see* King Lear.

Kaseli. Shin Saburi. Directed by Masaki Kobayashi. Jap. 1974. Japan. 213 min. Sound. 16mm Color. subtitles. *Rental:* New Yorker Films.

Kashima Paradise. 1973. Japan. (Documentary). 110 min. Sound. 16mm B&W. *Rental:* U Mich Media & Unifilm. *Sale:* Unifilm.

Kashmiri Run. Pernell Roberts. Directed by John Peyser. 1969. Sagitarius. 105 min. Sound. 16mm Color. dubbed. *Rental:* Willoughby Peer.

Kathleen. Shirley Temple & Herbert Marshall. Directed by Harold S. Bucquet. 1941. MGM. 85 min. Sound. 16mm B&W. *Rental:* MGM United.

Kathy-O. Dan Duryea & Jan Sterling. Directed by Jack Sher. 1958. Universal. 99 min. Sound. 16mm Color. *Rental:* Swank Motion.

Katia & the Emperor. Orig. Title: Magnificent Sinner, The. Curt Jurgens & Romy Schneider. Directed by Robert Siodmak. 1963. France. 91 min. Sound. 16mm Color. dubbed. *Rental:* Inst Cinema.

Katina *see* Iceland.

Katz and Carasso *see* Contract.

Katzelmacher. Lilith Ungerer. Directed by Rainer Werner Fassbinder. Ger. 1969. Germany. 88 min. Sound. 16mm B&W. subtitles. *Rental:* New Yorker Films.

Kavik the Wolf Dog. Ronny Cox & John Ireland. Directed by Peter Carter. 90 min. Sound. 16mm Color. *Rental:* Westcoast Films.

Kazablan. Yehoram Gaon. Directed by Menahem Golan. Hebrew. 1974. Israel. 95 min. Sound. 16mm Color. subtitles. *Rental:* MGM United.

Kazan. Joe Sawyer & Stephen Dunne. Directed by Will Jason. 1949. Columbia. 65 min. Sound. 16mm B&W. *Rental:* Cine Craft.

Kean. Ivan Mousjoukine. Directed by Herbert Brenon. 1922. France. 123 min. Silent. 16mm B&W. *Rental:* Em Gee Film Lib.

Kean. Kenneth Griffith. Directed by David Munro. 1975. Cantor. 90 min. Sound. 16mm Color. *Rental:* A Cantor. *Sale:* A Cantor.

Keaton & Kovacs Anthology. 60 min. Sound. 16mm Color. *Rental:* Festival Films. *Rental:* Festival Films, Videotape version.

Keep, The. Scott Glenn & Alberta Watson. Directed by Michael Mann. 1983. Paramount. 96 min. Sound. 16mm Color. *Rental:* Films Inc.

Keep 'em Flying. Bud Abbott & Lou Costello. Directed by Arthur Lubin. 1941. Universal. 81 min. Sound. 16mm B&W. *Rental:* Williams Films.

Keep 'em Rolling. Walter Huston & Frances Dee. Directed by Merian C. Cooper. 1934. RKO. 69 min. Sound. 16mm B&W. *Rental:* RKO General Pics.

Keep It Cool *see* Let's Rock.

Keep on Rockin'. Directed by D. A. Pennebaker. 1973. Leacock. (Documentary). 90 min. Sound. 16mm Color. *Rental:* Pennebaker. *Sale:* Pennebaker.

Keep Rollin'. Gene Autry. Directed by Frank McDonald. 1940. Republic. 54 min. Sound. 16mm B&W. *Rental:* Ivy Films. *Sale:* Cinema Concepts & Natl Cinema.

Keep the Wheels Rolling. 1977. Penn State. (Documentary). 59 min. Sound. 16mm Color. *Rental:* Penn St AV Serv. *Sale:* Penn St AV Srev. *Rental:* Penn St AV Serv, *Sale:* Penn St AV Srev, Videotape version.

Keep Your Powder Dry. Lana Turner & Laraine Day. Directed by Edward Buzzell. 1945. MGM. 93 min. Sound. 16mm B&W. *Rental:* MGM United.

Keeper of the Bees. Neil Hamilton & Betty Furness. Directed by Christy Cabanne. 1935. Monogram. 80 min. Sound. 16mm B&W. *Rental:* Mogulls Films.

Keeper of the Bees. Michael Duane & Jane Darwell. Directed by John Sturges. 1947. Columbia. 68 min. Sound. 16mm B&W. *Rental:* Bosco Films.

Keeper of the Flame. Katharine Hepburn & Spencer Tracy. Directed by George Cukor. 1942. MGM. 100 min. Sound. 16mm B&W. *Rental:* MGM United.

Keeping Company. Frank Morgan & Irene Rich. Directed by S. Sylvan Simon. 1940. MGM. 80 min. Sound. 16mm B&W. *Rental:* MGM United.

Kekec. France Prestenick. Directed by Joze Gale. 1955. Czechoslovakia. 90 min. Sound. 16mm B&W. narrated Eng. *Rental:* Inst Cinema.

Kelek. Directed by Werner Nekes. 1968. Germany. (Experimental). 59 min. Silent. 16mm B&W. *Rental:* Canyon Cinema.

Kelly & Me. Van Johnson & Piper Laurie. Directed by Robert Z. Leonard. 1957. Universal. 86 min. Sound. 16mm Color. *Rental:* Williams Films.

Kelly the Second. Patsy Kelly & Charlie Chase. Directed by Gus Meins. 1936. MGM. 70 min. Sound. 16mm B&W. *Rental:* Budget Films, Mogulls Films & Willoughby Peer.

Kelly's Heroes. Clint Eastwood & Telly Savalas. Directed by Brian Hutton. 1970. MGM. 145 min. Sound. 16mm Color. *Rental:* MGM United. *Rental:* MGM United, Anamorphic version.

Kennedys Don't Cry. 1977. Document Associates. (Documentary). 100 min. Sound. 16mm B&W. *Rental:* Cinema Guild & Maljack. *Sale:* Cinema Guild.

Kennedys of Albuquerque, The. Directed by William Jersey. 1976. Group W. (Documentary). 59 min. Sound. 16mm Color. *Rental:* Iowa Films, U Cal Media & U Mich Media. *Sale:* Carousel Films. *Sale:* Carousel Films, Videotape version.

Kennel Murder Case, The. William Powell & Mary Astor. Directed by Michael Curtiz. 1933. Warners. 73 min. Sound. 16mm B&W. *Rental:* Budget Films, Classic Film Mus, Em Gee Film Lib, Kit Parker & MGM United. *Sale:* Festival Films. *Sale:* Festival Films, Videotape version.

Kenner. Jim Brown. Directed by Steve Sekely. 1969. MGM. 87 min. Sound. 16mm Color. *Rental:* MGM United.

Kentuckian, The. Burt Lancaster, Diana Lynn & Walter Matthau. Directed by Burt Lancaster. 1955. United Artists. 104 min. Sound. 16mm Color. *Rental:* MGM United.

Kentucky. Loretta Young, Richard Greene & Walter Brennan. Directed by David Butler. 1938. Fox. 96 min. Sound. 16mm B&W. *Rental:* Films Inc.

Kentucky Blue Streak, The. Eddie Nugent & Patricia Scott. Directed by Raymond K. Johnson. 1935. Puritan. 70 min. Sound. 16mm B&W. *Rental:* Mogulls Films.

Kentucky Fried Movie, The. Donald Sutherland, Bill Bixby & Henry Gibson. Directed by John Landis. 1977. United Film. 84 min. Sound. 16mm Color. *Rental:* Films Inc.

Kentucky Jubilee. Jerry Colonna & Jean Porter. Directed by Ron Ormond. 1951. Lippert. 70 min. Sound. 16mm B&W. *Rental:* Mogulls Film.

Kentucky Kernels. Bert Wheeler & Robert Woolsey. Directed by George Stevens. 1934. RKO. 70 min. Sound. 16mm B&W. *Rental:* Films Inc.

Kentucky: Kith & Kin. Directed by Christian Blackwood. 1977. Blackwood. (Documentary). 52 min. Sound. 16mm Color. *Rental:* Blackwood Films. *Sale:* Blackwood Films.

Kenyatta. 1974. NBC. (Documentary). 51 min. Sound. 16mm Color. *Rental:* Films Inc & U Mich Media. *Sale:* Films Inc. *Sale:* Films Inc, Videotape version.

Keoma. Franco Nero, William Berger & Woody Strode. 81 min. Sound. 16mm Color. *Rental:* Welling Motion Pictures.

Kept Husbands. Joel McCrea & Dorothy Mackaill. Directed by Lloyd Bacon. 1931. RKO. 76 min. Sound. 16mm B&W. *Rental:* Films Inc.

Kermesse Heroique, La *see* Carnival in Flanders.

Kes. David Bradley. Directed by Kenneth Loach. 1970. United Artists. 109 min. Sound. 16mm Color. *Rental:* MGM United.

Kettles in the Ozarks, The. Marjorie Main & Arthur Hunnicutt. Directed by Charles Lamont. 1956. Universal. 81 min. Sound. 16mm B&W. *Rental:* Swank Motion.

Kettles on Old MacDonald's Farm, The. Marjorie Main & Parker Fennally. Directed by Virgil Vogel. 1957. Universal. 80 min. Sound. 16mm B&W. *Rental:* Swank Motion.

Kevin Can Wait. Jim Peterson John Schmidt. 51 min. Sound. 16mm Color. *Rental:* Gospel Films.

Key, The. William Powell & Colin Clive. Directed by Michael Curtiz. 1934. Warners. 72 min. Sound. 16mm B&W. *Rental:* MGM United.

Key, The. William Holden, Sophia Loren & Trevor Howard. Directed by Sir Carol Reed. 1958. Columbia. 113 min. Sound. 16mm B&W. *Rental:* Charard Motion Pics, Corinth Films & Welling Motion Pictures. *Rental:* Corinth Films & Kit Parker, Anamorphic version. *Rental:* Bosco Films, 133 mins version.

Key Largo. Humphrey Bogart, Edward G. Robinson & Lauren Bacall. Directed by John Huston. 1948. Warner. 101 min. Sound. 16mm B&W. *Rental:* MGM United.

Key to the City. Clark Gable & Loretta Young. Directed by George Sidney. 1950. MGM. 101 min. Sound. 16mm B&W. *Rental:* MGM United. *Rental:* MGM United, Videotape version.

Key to the Universe. 1977. Britain. (Documentary). 120 min. Sound. Videotape Color. *Sale:* Films Inc.

Key Witness. Jeff Hunter & Pat Crowley. Directed by Phil Karlson. 1960. MGM. 82 min. Sound. 16mm B&W. *Rental:* MGM United.

Keyhole, The. Kay Francis & George Brent. Directed by Michael Curtiz. 1933. Warners. 69 min. Sound. 16mm B&W. *Rental:* MGM United.

Keys of Paradise, The. 1979. Time-Life. (Documentary). 57 min. Sound. 16mm Color. *Rental:* Iowa Films, OK AV Ctr, Syracuse U Film & U of IL Film.

Keys of the Kingdom. Gregory Peck & Thomas Mitchell. Directed by John M. Stahl. 1944. Fox. 137 min. Sound. 16mm B&W. *Rental:* Films Inc.

Khartoum. Charlton Heston, Sir Laurence Olivier. Directed by Basil Dearden. 1966. United Artists. 128 min. Sound. 16mm Color. *Rental:* MGM United, Westcoast Films & Wholesome Film Ctr.

Khruschev & Berlin. 1962. NBC. (Documentary). 54 min. Sound. 16mm B&W. *Rental:* Syracuse U Film. *Sale:* McGraw-Hill Films.

Khruschev in Exile. 1968. NBC. (Documentary). 54 min. Sound. 16mm Color. *Rental:* McGraw-Hill Films. *Sale:* McGraw-Hill Films.

Khyber Patrol. Richard Egan & Raymond Burr. Directed by Seymour Friedman. 1954. United Artists. 72 min. Sound. 16mm Color. *Rental:* Budget Films & MGM United.

Kid, The. Charles Chaplin & Jackie Coogan. Directed by Charles Chaplin. 1921. First National. 55 min. Sound. 16mm B&W. *Rental:* Films Inc. *Sale:* Cinema Concepts. *Sale:* Blackhawk Films & Magnetic Video, Videotape version.

Kid Blue. Dennis Hopper, Warren Oates, Peter Boyle & Ben Johnson. Directed by James Frawley. 1973. Fox. 100 min. Sound. 16mm Color. *Rental:* Films Inc.

Kid Boots. Eddie Cantor & Clara Bow. Directed by Frank Tuttle. 1926. Paramount. 85 min. Silent. 16mm B&W. *Rental:* Films Inc.

Kid Brother, The. Harold Lloyd. Directed by Ted Wilde. 1927. Paramount. (Music & sound effects only). 84 min. 16mm B&W. *Rental:* Budget Films, Images Film, Janus Films, Kino Intl & Kit Parker. *Sale:* Blackhawk Films, Super 8 sound version. *Sale:* Blackhawk Films, Super 8 silent version. *Rental:* Budget Films, Silent version.

Kid Comes Back, The. Orig. Title: Don't Pull Your Punches. Wayne Morris & Barton MacLane. Directed by B. Reeves Eason. 1938. Warners. 61 min. Sound. 16mm B&W. *Rental:* MGM United.

Kid Dynamite. Bowery Boys. Directed by Wallace Fox. 1943. Monogram. 70 min. Sound. 16mm B&W. *Rental:* Budget Films, Ivy Films & Video Comm. *Sale:* Cinema Concepts. *Rental:* Video Comm, Videotape version.

Kid for Two Farthings, A. Orig. Title: Lucky Kid. Celia Johnson & Diana Dors. Directed by Sir Carol Reed. 1956. Britain. 91 min. Sound. 16mm Color. *Rental:* Films Inc & Janus Films.

Kid from Canada, The. Christopher Braden. Directed by Kay Mander. 1957. Britain. 57 min. Sound. 16mm B&W. *Sale:* Lucerne Films.

Kid from Cleveland, The. George Brent & Lynn Bari. Directed by Herbert Kline. 1949. Republic. 92 min. Sound. 16mm B&W. *Rental:* Ivy Films. *Sale:* Rep Pic Film.

Kid from Gower Gulch, The. Spade Cooley. Directed by Oliver Drake. 1950. Monogram. 57 min. Sound. 16mm B&W. *Rental:* Budget Films.

Kid from Kansas, The. Dick Foran & Leo Carillo. Directed by William Nigh. 1941. Universal. 60 min. Sound. 16mm B&W. *Rental:* Mogulls Films.

Kid from Kokomo, The. Wayne Morris & Pat O'Brien. Directed by Lewis Seiler. 1939. Warners. 92 min. Sound. 16mm B&W. *Rental:* MGM United.

Kid from Left Field, The. Dan Dailey & Anne Bancroft. Directed by Harmon Jones. 1953. Fox. 87 min. Sound. 16mm B&W. *Rental:* Films Inc.

Kid from Santa Fe, The. Jack Randall. Directed by Raymond K. Johnson. 1940. Monogram. 50 min. Sound. 16mm B&W. *Rental:* Hurlock Cine.

Kid from Texas, The. Dennis O'Keefe, Florence Rice & Buddy Ebsen. Directed by S. Sylvan Simon. 1939. MGM. 71 min. Sound. 16mm B&W. *Rental:* MGM United.

Kid from Texas, The. Audie Murphy & Gail Storm. Directed by Kurt Neumann. 1950. Universal. 78 min. Sound. 16mm Color. *Rental:* Swank Motion.

Kid Galahad. Orig. Title: Battling Bellhop, The. Edward G Robinson & Humphrey Bogart. Directed by Michael Curtiz. 1936. Warners. 101 min. Sound. 16mm B&W. *Rental:* MGM United.

Kid Galahad. Elvis Presley & Lola Albright. Directed by Phil Karlson. 1962. United Artists. 95 min. Sound. 16mm Color. *Rental:* MGM United.

Kid Monk Baroni. Orig. Title: Young Paul Baroni. Richard Rober & Bruce Cabot. Directed by Harold Schuster. 1952. Realart. 80 min. Sound. 16mm B&W. *Rental:* Budget Films.

Kid Nightingale. John Payne & Jane Wyman. Directed by George Amy. 1939. Warners. 57 min. Sound. 16mm B&W. *Rental:* MGM United.

Kid Ranger. Bob Steele. Directed by Robert N. Bradbury. 1936. Supreme. 60 min. Sound. 16mm B&W. *Rental:* Budget Films. *Sale:* Morcarft Films.

Kid Rodelo. Janet Leigh & Don Murray. Directed by Richard Carlson. 1966. Paramount. 91 min. Sound. 16mm B&W. *Rental:* Films Inc.

Kid Sentiment. Francois Guy. Directed by Jacques Godbout. 1968. Canada. 88 min. Sound. 16mm B&W. *Rental:* Natl Film CN. *Sale:* Natl Film CN.

Kid Sister. Judy Clark & Roger Pryor. Directed by Sam Newfield. 1945. PRC. 56 min. Sound. 16mm B&W. *Rental:* Ivy Films. *Sale:* Classics Assoc NY & Rep Pic Film.

Kid Thomas & the Preservation Hall Jazz Band. Phoenix. (Performance). 58 min. Sound. 16mm Color. *Rental:* Phoenix Films. *Sale:* Phoenix Films.

Kid Vengeance. Lee Van Cleef & Jim Brown. Directed by Joe Manduke. 1977. 94 min. Sound. 16mm Color. *Rental:* Swank Motion.

Kidnapped. Warner Baxter. Directed by Alfred M. Werker. 1938. Fox. 90 min. Sound. 16mm B&W. *Rental:* Films Inc.

Kidnapped. Roddy McDowell & Sue England. Directed by William Beaudine. 1948. Monogram. 81 min. Sound. 16mm B&W. *Rental:* Hurlock Cine.

Kidnapped. Peter Finch & James MacArthur. Directed by Robert Stevenson. 1960. Disney. 94 min. Sound. 16mm Color. *Rental:* Buchan Pic, Cine Craft, Cousino Visual Ed, Disney Prod, Film Ctr DC, Films Inc, MGM United, Swank Motion, U of IL Film, Welling Motion Pictures & Westcoast Films.

Kidnapped. Michael Caine, Trevor Howard, Jack Hawkins & Donald Pleasance. Directed by Delbert Mann. 1971. American International. 100 min. Sound. 16mm Color. *Rental:* Arcus Film, Video Comm, Wholesome Film Ctr & Williams Films.

Kidnapped. 1972. Australia. (Animated). 50 min. Sound. 16mm Color. *Rental:* Budget Films, Inst Cinema, Modern Sound, Westcoast Films & Wholesome Film Ctr. *Sale:* Inst Cinema.

Kidnapped see Social Error.

Kidnapped Coed. Jack Canon & Leslie Ann Rivers. 76 min. Sound. 16mm Color. *Rental:* BF Video.

Kids Are Alright, The. The Who. Directed by Jeff Stein. 1979. New World. 106 min. Sound. 16mm Color. *Rental:* Film Inc.

Kids Are People Too! 1972. Macmillan. (Documentary). 48 min. Sound. 16mm Color. *Rental:* BYU Media.

Kid's Last Ride, The. Range Busters. Directed by S. Roy Luby. 1941. Monogram. 60 min. Sound. 16mm B&W. *Rental:* Films Inc. *Sale:* Reel Images. *Sale:* Reel Images, Super 8 Sound version.

Kierkegaard. Directed by Julian Cairol. Cairol. (Experimental). 75 min. Sound. 16mm Color. *Rental:* Caynon Cinema.

Kierkegaard. 1979. Canada. (Documentary). 57 min. Sound. 16mm Color. *Rental:* Kent St U Film.

Kifaru: The Black Rhinoceros. 1970. MGM. (Documentary). 52 min. Sound. 16mm Color. *Rental:* Films Inc, Syracuse U Film & Wholesome Film Ctr. *Sale:* Films Inc. *Sale:* Films Inc, Videotape version.

Kiki. Norma Talmadge & Ronald Colman. Directed by Clarence Brown. 1926. 16mm *Rental:* A Twyman Pres.

Kill! Tatsuya Nakadai & Etsushi Takahashi. Directed by Kihachi Okamoto. Jap. 1968. Toho. 115 min. Sound. 16mm B&W. subtitles Eng. *Rental:* Films Inc.

Kill Castro! Stuart Whitman & Caren Kaye. 1980. 90 min. Sound. Videotape Color. *Sale:* Tamarelles French Film.

Kill, Kill, Kill! Stephen Boyd & Jean Seberg. Directed by Romain Gary. 1973. Cinerama. 121 min. Sound. 16mm Color. *Rental:* Swank Motion.

Kill or Be Killed. Lawerence Tierney & George Coulouris. Directed by Max Nosseck. 1950. Eagel Lion. 67 min. Sound. 16mm B&W. *Rental:* Ivy Films. *Sale:* Rep Pic Film.

Kill or Cure. Terry-Thomas & Eric Sykes. Directed by George Pollock. 1962. Britain. 88 min. Sound. 16mm B&W. *Rental:* MGM United.

Kill the Umpire. William Bendix & Una Merkel. Directed by Lloyd Bacon. 1950. Columbia. 78 min. Sound. 16mm B&W. *Rental:* Buchan Pic, Cine Craft, Films Inc, Modern Sound, Roas Films & Welling Motion Pictures. *Rental:* Welling Motion Pictures & Westcoast Films, 90 mins version.

Killed the Family & Went to the Movies. Directed by Julio Bressane. Port. 1970. Brazil. (Cast unlisted). 80 min. Sound. 16mm B&W. subtitles. *Rental:* New Yorker Films.

Killer Ape. Orig. Title: Jungle Jim & the Killer Ape. Johnny Weissmuller. Directed by Spencer G. Bennett. 1953. Columbia. 68 min. Sound. 16mm B&W. *Rental:* Bosco Films.

Killer Army. Lu Feng, Sun Chien & Kuo Chue. 94 min. Sound. 16mm *Rental:* WW Enter. *Rental:* WW Enter, Videotape version.

Killer at Large. Robert Lowery & Anabel Shaw. Directed by William Beaudine. 1947. PRC. 63 min. Sound. 16mm B&W.

Killer Bats see Devil Bat.

Killer Dill. Stuart Erwin & Anne Gwynne. Directed by Lewis D. Collins. 1947. Screen Guild. 74 min. Sound. 16mm B&W. *Rental:* Budget Films & Mogulls Films.

Killer Diller. Butterfly McQueen & Moms Mabley. Directed by Josh Binney. 1948. All American. 80 min. Sound. 16mm B&W. *Rental:* Budget Films, Em Gee Film Lib & Video Comm. *Sale:* Cinema Concepts & Glenn Photo. *Rental:* Em Gee Film Lib & Video Comm, Videotape version.

Killer Elite, The. James Caan, Robert Duvall & Gig Young. Directed by Sam Peckinpah. 1975. United Artists. 130 min. Sound. 16mm Color. *Rental:* Budget Films, MGM United, Welling Motion Pictures & Westcoast Films.

Killer Fish. Lee Majors, Karen Black & James Franciscus. Directed by Anthony Dawson. 1979. AFD. 101 min. Sound. 16mm Color. *Rental:* Swank Motion.

Killer in the Village. 1983. Britain. (Documentary). 56 min. Sound. 16mm Color. *Rental:* Films Inc. *Sale:* Films Inc. *Sale:* Films Inc, Videotape version.

Killer Is Loose, A. Joseph Cotton & Wendell Corey. Directed by Budd Boetticher. 1956. United Artists. 73 min. Sound. 16mm B&W. *Rental:* MGM United.

Killer Leopard. John Sheffield & Beverly Garland. Directed by Budd Boetticher. 1954. Allied Artists. 70 min. Sound. 16mm B&W. *Rental:* Hurlock Cine.

Killer McCoy. Mickey Rooney & Brian Donlevy. Directed by Roy Rowland. 1947. MGM. 103 min. Sound. 16mm B&W. *Rental:* MGM United.

Killer of Killers *see* Mechanic.

Killer Shark. Roddy McDowell. Directed by Budd Boetticher. 1950. Monogram. 78 min. Sound. 16mm B&W. *Rental:* Hurlock Cine.

Killers, The. Orig. Title: Johnny North. Burt Lancaster & Ava Gardner. Directed by Robert Siodmak. 1946. Universal. 102 min. Sound. 16mm B&W. *Rental:* Swank Motion & Williams Films.

Killers, The. Lee Marvin & Angie Dickinson. Directed by Don Siegel. 1964. Universal. 95 min. Sound. 16mm Color. *Rental:* Swank Motion & Twyman Films. *Rental:* Swank Motion, Videotape version.

Killer's Kiss. Jamie Smith & Irene Kane. Directed by Stanley Kubrick. 1955. United Artists. 67 min. Sound. 16mm B&W. *Rental:* MGM United.

Killers of Kilimanjaro. Robert Taylor & Anthony Newley. Directed by Richard Thorpe. 1960. Columbia. 91 min. Sound. 16mm Color. *Rental:* Cine Craft, Modern Sound & Welling Motion Pictures.

Killers Three. Robert Walker, Diane Varsi & Dick Clark. Directed by Bruce Kessler. 1968. American International. 97 min. Sound. 16mm Color. *Rental:* Cine Craft & Video Comm.

Killing, The. Sterling Hayden & Coleen Gray. Directed by Stanley Kubrick. 1956. United Artists. 83 min. Sound. 16mm B&W. *Rental:* MGM United.

Killing Ground, The. 1979. ABC. (Documentary). 50 min. Sound. 16mm Color. *Rental:* Syracuse U Film, U of IL Film & U Mich Media. *Sale:* MTI Tele, Videotape version.

Killing Machine, The. Sonny Chiba. 1974. Japan. 89 min. Sound. 16mm Color. dubbed. *Rental:* Budget Films, Films Inc, Modern Sound & Westcoast Films.

Killing of Angel Street, The. Liz Alexander & John Hargreaves. Directed by Donald Crombie. 100 min. Sound. Videotape Color. *Sale:* Vidamerica.

Killing of President Kennedy, The: New Revelations Twenty Years Later. 80 min. Sound. Videotape Color. *Sale:* Vidamerica.

Killing of Sister George, The. Beryl Reid & Susannah York. Directed by Robert Aldrich. 1968. ABC. 138 min. Sound. 16mm Color. *Rental:* Films Inc. *Sale:* ABC Film Lib, Super 8 Sound version.

Kilroy Was Here. Jackie Cooper & Jackie Coogan. Directed by Phil Karlson. 1947. Monogram. 70 min. Sound. 16mm B&W. *Rental:* Cine Craft, Mogulls Films & Hurlock Cine.

Kim. Errol Flynn & Dean Stockwell. Directed by Victor Saville. 1950. MGM. 113 min. Sound. 16mm B&W. *Rental:* MGM United. *Rental:* MGM United, Color version.

Kimberly Jim. Jim Reeves. Directed by Emil Nofal. 1965. Embassy. 82 min. Sound. 16mm Color. *Rental:* Films Inc.

Kind Hearts & Coronets. Orig. Title: Noblesse Oblige. Sir Alec Guinness & Dennis Price. Directed by Robert Hamer. 1950. Britain. 106 min. Sound. 16mm B&W. *Rental:* Films Inc.

Kind Lady. Ethel Barrymore & Maurice Evans. Directed by John Sturges. 1951. MGM. 78 min. Sound. 16mm B&W. *Rental:* MGM United.

Kind Lady: House of Menace. Aline MacMahon & Basil Rathbone. Directed by George B. Seitz. 1935. MGM. 78 min. Sound. 16mm B&W. *Rental:* MGM United.

Kind of Loving, A. Alan Bates & June Ritchie. Directed by John Schlesinger. 1962. Britain. 112 min. Sound. 16mm B&W. *Rental:* Corinth Films.

Kinesics. 1964. Penn State. (Documentary). 73 min. Sound. 16mm B&W. *Rental:* Penn St AV Serv. *Sale:* Penn St AV Serv.

King: A Filmed Record, Montgomery to Memphis. Directed by Richard Kaplan. 1969. Landau. (Documentary). 103 min. Sound. 16mm B&W. *Rental:* Film Images, Films Inc & Texture Film. *Sale:* Film Images & Texture Film. *Rental:* Film Images, *Sale:* Film Images, 81 mins. version. *Sale:* Texture Film & Video Tape Network, Videotape version.

King & Country. Tom Courtenay & Dirk Bogarde. Directed by Joseph Losey. 1964. Britain. 86 min. Sound. 16mm B&W. *Rental:* Films Inc & Ivy Films.

King & Four Queens, The. Clark Gable & Eleanor Parker. Directed by Raoul Walsh. 1957. United Artists. 86 min. Sound. 16mm Color. *Rental:* Films Inc, MGM United, Welling Motion Pictures, Westcoast Films & Wholesome Film Ctr.

King & I, The. Deborah Kerr & Yul Brynner. Directed by Walter Lang. 1956. Fox. 133 min. Sound. 16mm Color. *Rental:* Films Inc. *Rental:* Films Inc, Anamorphic color version.

King & the Chorus Girl, The. Fernand Gravet, Jane Wyman & Joan Blondell. Directed by Mervyn LeRoy. 1937. Warners. 94 min. Sound. 16mm B&W. *Rental:* MGM United.

King Arthur & the Siege of the Saxons *see* Siege of the Saxons.

King Coal. 1962. Hearst. (Documentary). 50 min. Sound. 16mm B&W. *Sale:* King Features.

King Creole. Elvis Presley & Walter Matthau. Directed by Michael Curtiz. 1958. Paramount. 115 min. Sound. 16mm B&W. *Rental:* Films Inc. *Rental:* Ivy Films, *Sale:* Cinema Concepts, Super 8 Sound version. *Rental:* Williams Films, Videotape version.

King Gun. Guy Stockwell & Robert Fuller. 1970. Universal Enterainment. 97 min. Sound. 16mm Color. *Rental:* Video Comm & Westcoast Films. *Lease:* Video Comm.

King in New York, A. Charles Chaplin & Dawn Addams. Directed by Charles Chaplin. 1957. United Artists. 116 min. Sound. 16mm B&W. *Rental:* Films Inc. *Lease:* Cinema Concepts & Glenn Photo, Super 8 sound version.

King in Shadow, A. Horst Buchholz & O. W. Fischer. Directed by Harald Braun. Ger. 1959. 78 min. Sound. 16mm B&W. subtitles. *Rental:* Films Inc. *Rental:* Films Inc, English language version.

King Kong. Bruce Cabot & Fay Wray. Directed by Walter Daniels. 1933. RKO. 111 min. Sound. 16mm B&W. *Rental:* Films Inc, Janus Films, New Cinema & RKO General Pics. *Sale:* Blackhawk Films, Cinema Concepts & Festival Films.

King Kong. Jeff Bridges, Charles Grodin & Jessica Lange. Directed by John Guillermin. 1977. Paramount. (Anamorphic). 133 min. Sound. 16mm Color. *Rental:* Films Inc.

King Kong: A Family Portrait. 59 min. Sound. 16mm Color. *Rental:* Natl Geog. *Sale:* Natl Geog. *Sale:* Natl Geog, Video version.

King Kong Escapes. Rhodes Reason & Linda Miller. Directed by Inoshiro Honda. 1968. Japan. 96 min. Sound. 16mm Color. dubbed. *Rental:* Williams Films. *Rental:* Williams Films, Anamorphic Color version.

King Kong vs. Godzilla. Michael Keith. Directed by Inoshiro Honda & Thomas Montgomery. 1963. Japan. 90 min. Sound. 16mm Color. dubbed. *Rental:* Twyman Films & Williams Films.

King Lear. Trans. Title: Karol Lir. Yuri Jarvet. Directed by Grigori Kozintsev. Rus. 1971. Russia. (Anamorphic). 140 min. Sound. 16mm B&W. subtitles. *Rental:* Corinth Films.

King Lear. Frederick Warde. 1917. Britain. 50 min. Silent. 16mm B&W. *Rental:* Budget Films & Film Classics. *Sale:* Film Classics. *Rental:* Film Classics, *Sale:* Film Classics, Silent 8mm version. *Rental:* Film Classics, Videotape version.

King Lear. Paul Scofield & Irene Worth. Directed by Peter Brook. 1971. Britain. 134 min. Sound. 16mm B&W. *Rental:* Films Inc & MacMillan Films. *Lease:* MacMillan Films.

King Lear. Michael Hordern, John Shrapnel & Brenda Bletyn. 1982. 184 min. Sound. Videotape Color. *Rental:* Iowa Films.

King, Murray. Murray King. Directed by David Hoffman. 1969. Amram. 86 min. Sound. 16mm Color. *Rental:* Twyman Films & Ivy Films. *Sale:* Twyman Films & Ivy Films.

King of Africa *see* One Step to Hell.

King of Canada. Directed by Munroe Scott. 1973. Canada. (Documentary). 57 min. Sound. 16mm Color. *Rental:* Natl Film CN. *Sale:* Natl Film CN.

King of Hearts. Alan Bates & Pierre Brasseur. Directed by Philippe De Broca. Fr. 1967. France. 101 min. Sound. 16mm Color. subtitles. *Rental:* MGM United. *Rental:* MGM United, Videotape version.

King of Hockey. Orig. Title: King of the Ice Rink. Dick Purcell & Wayne Morris. Directed by Noel Smith. 1936. Warners. 55 min. Sound. 16mm B&W. *Rental:* MGM United.

King of Jazz. Directed by John Murray Anderson. 1930. Universal. 85 min. Sound. Videotape Color. *Sale:* Festival Films.

King of Kings. H. B. Warner & Ernest Torrence. Directed by Cecil B. Demille. 1927. Pathe. (Music & sound effects only). 115 min. Silent. 16mm B&W. *Rental:* Bosco Films, Budget Films, BYU Media, Cine Craft, Em Gee Film Lib, Film Ctr DC, Films Inc, Ivy Films, Kerr Film, Kit Parker, Lewis Film, Modern Sound, Newman Film Lib, Roas Films, Video Comm, Twyman Films, Welling Motion Pictures, Wholesome Film Ctr & Willoughby Peer. *Rental:* Films Inc, Silent version. *Rental:* Kit Parker, Part Color version.

King of Kings. Jeffrey Hunter & Siobhan McKenna. Directed by Nicholas Ray. 1961. MGM. 163 min. Sound. 16mm Color. *Rental:* MGM United. *Rental:* MGM United, Anamorphic color version. *Rental:* MGM United, *Sale:* Tamarelles French Film, Videotape version.

King of Marvin Gardens, The. Jack Nicholson, Bruce Dern & Ellen Burstyn. Directed by Bob Rafelson. 1972. BBS. 103 min. Sound. 16mm Color. *Rental:* Films Inc & Swank Motion.

King of Paris, The. Cedric Hardwicke & Ralph Richardson. Directed by Jack Raymond. 1934. 16mm *Rental:* A Twyman Pres.

King of the Bandits. Gilbert Roland. Directed by Christy Cabanne. 1947. Monogram. 67 min. Videotape B&W. *Sale:* Video Comm.

King of the Cowboys. Roy Rogers. Directed by Joseph Kane. 1943. Republic. 54 min. Sound. 16mm B&W. *Rental:* Budget Films & IvyFilms. *Sale:* Cinema Concepts, Natl Cinema, Rep Pic Film & Nostalgia Merchant.

King of the Gamblers. Janet Martin. Directed by George Blair. 1948. Republic. 60 min. Sound. 16mm B&W. *Rental:* Ivy Films. *Sale:* Rep Pic Film.

King of the Grizzlies. 1970. Disney. (Documentary). 93 min. Sound. 16mm Color. *Rental:* Buchan Pic, Cine Craft, Film Ct DC, Films Inc & Swank Motion.

King of the Gypsies. Eric Roberts & Shelley Winters. Directed by Frank Pierson. 1978. Paramount. 112 min. Sound. 16mm Color. *Rental:* Films Inc.

King of the Hill. Directed by William Canning & Donald Brittain. 1974. Canada. (Documentary). 57 min. Sound. 16mm Color. *Rental:* New Cimena.

King of the Ice Rink *see* King of Hockey.

King of the Jungle. Buster Crabbe & Frances Dee. Directed by Bruce Humberstone & Max Marcin. 1933. Paramount. 75 min. Sound. 16mm B&W. *Rental:* Swank Motion.

King of the Khyber Rifles. Tyrone Power & Terry Moore. Directed by Henry King. 1953. Fox. 99 min. Sound. 16mm Color. *Rental:* Films Inc.

King of the Lumberjacks. John Payne & Gloria Dickson. Directed by William Clemens. 1940. Warners. 58 min. Sound. 16mm B&W. *Rental:* MGM United.

King of the Mountain. Harry Hamlin & Joseph Bottoms. Directed by Noel Nosseck. 1981. Universal. 90 min. Sound. 16mm Color. *Rental:* Swank Motion.

King of the Newsboys. Lew Ayres & Helen Mack. Directed by Bernard Vorhaus. 1938. Republic. 69 min. Sound. 16mm B&W. *Rental:* Ivy Films.

King of the Pecos. John Wayne. Directed by Joseph Kane. 1936. Republic. 56 min. Sound. 16mm B&W. *Rental:* Ivy Films. *Sale:* Rep Pic Film.

King of the Roaring Twenties. David Janssen & Diane Foster. Directed by Joseph Newman. 1961. Allied Artists. 106 min. Sound. 16mm B&W. *Rental:* Hurlock Cine.

King of the Rocketmen *see* Lost Planet Airmen.

King of the Rodeo. Hoot Gibson. Directed by Henry Macrae. 1929. Universal. 60 min. Sound. 16mm B&W. *Sale:* Film Classics.

King of the Stallions. Orig. Title: Code of the Redmen. Chief Thundercloud. Directed by Edward Finney. 1942. Monogram. 59 min. Sound. 16mm B&W. *Rental:* Willoughby Peer.

King of the Texas Rangers. Neil Hamilton. Directed by William Witney. 1941. Republic. 217 min. Sound. 16mm B&W. *Rental:* Ivy Films.

King of the Underwater World. 1975. (Documentary). 88 min. Sound. 16mm Color. *Rental:* Budget Films & Video Comm.

King of the Underworld. Humphrey Bogart & Kay Francis. Directed by Lewis Seiler. 1939. Warners. 60 min. Sound. 16mm B&W. *Rental:* MGM United.

King of the Vikings. Antonio Vilar. Directed by Luis Lucia. 1964. Spain. 81 min. Sound. 16mm Color. dubbed. *Rental:* Westcoast Films.

King of the Wild Horses. Orig. Title: Rex, King of the Wild Horses. Rex the Devil Horse. Directed by Fred W. Jackman. 1924. Pathe. 45 min. Silent. 8mm B&W. *Rental:* Film Classics. *Sale:* Film Classics.

King of the Wild Horses. Preston Foster & Gail Patrick. Directed by George Archainbaud. 1947. Columbia. 78 min. Sound. 16mm B&W. *Rental:* Westcoast Films.

King of the Wild Stallions. George Montgomery & Diane Brewster. Directed by R. G. Springsteen. 1959. Allied Artists. 75 min. Sound. 16mm Color. *Rental:* Hurlock Cine.

King of the Zombies. Dick Purcell & Joan Woodbury. Directed by Jean Yarbrough. 1941. Monogram. 67 min. Sound. 16mm B&W. *Sale:* Natl Cinema.

King or Chaos. Directed by Brian Nolan. 1973. Canada. (Documentary). 57 min. Sound. 16mm Color. *Rental:* Natl Film CN. *Sale:* Natl Film CN.

King Rat. George Segal, Tom Courtenay & James Fox. Directed by Bryan Forbes. 1965. Columbia. 133 min. Sound. 16mm B&W. *Rental:* Bosco Films, Budget Films, Cine Craft, Films Inc, Ivy Films, Kit Parker, Modern Sound, Swank Motion, Twyman Films, U of IL Film, Welling Motion Pictures, Westcoast Films & Wholesome Film Ctr.

King Solomon's Mines. Sir Cedric Hardwicke & Anna Lee. Directed by Robert Stevenson. 1937. Britain. 80 min. Sound. 16mm B&W. *Rental:* Classic Film Mus, Films Inc & Janus Films.

King Solomon's Mines. Stewart Granger & Deborah Kerr. Directed by Compton Bennett & Andrew Marton. 1950. MGM. 102 min. Sound. 16mm B&W. *Rental:* MGM United. *Rental:* MGM United, Color version. *Rental:* MGM United, Videotape version.

King Steps Out, The. Grace Moore & Franchot Tone. Directed by Josef Von Sternberg. 1936. Columbia. 86 min. Sound. 16mm B&W. *Rental:* Kit Parker.

Kingdom in the Clouds. Xerox. (Cast Unlisted). 88 min. Sound. 16mm Color. *Sale:* Xerox Films.

Kingdom of Bronze. 1975. Britain. (Documentary). 52 min. Sound. 16mm Color. *Rental:* Iowa Films, U Cal Media, U of IL Film & U Mich Media.

Kingdom of the Crooked Mirrors, The. Olga Yukina & Tanya Yukina. Directed by Alexander Row. 1962. Russia. 80 min. Sound. 16mm Color. dubbed. *Rental:* Films Inc & MacMillan Films. *Sale:* MacMillan Films.

Kingfisher Caper, The. Hayley Mills & David McCallum. Directed by Dirk DeVilliers. 1975. South Africa. 90 min. Sound. 16mm Color. *Rental:* Films Inc.

King's Avenger, The. Orig. Title: Hunchback of Paris, The. Jean Marais & Sabina Steelman. 1961. Medallion. 107 min. Sound. 16mm Color. dubbed. *Rental:* Westcoast Films.

King's Cup, The. Dorothy Bouchier. Directed by Brian Desmond-Hurst. 1933. 16mm *Rental:* A Twyman Pres.

Kings Go Forth. Frank Sinatra, Tony Curtis & Natalie Wood. Directed by Delmer Daves. 1958. United Artists. 109 min. Sound. 16mm B&W. *Rental:* MGM United.

Kings of the Hill. Jason Sommers. Directed by Michael Dmytryk. 1976. Lone Star. 91 min. Sound. 16mm Color. *Rental:* Swank Motion.

Kings of the Sun. Yul Brynner & George Chakiris. Directed by J. Lee Thompson. 1963. United Artists. 108 min. Sound. 16mm Color. *Rental:* MGM United & Westcoast Films.

King's Revolution. 1966. Net. (Documentary). 54 min. Sound. 16mm B&W. *Rental:* Indiana AV Ctr. *Sale:* Indiana AV Ctr.

King's Row. Ann Sheridan, Robert Cummings & Betty Field. Directed by Sam Wood. 1941. Warners. 137 min. Sound. 16mm B&W. *Rental:* MGM United.

King's Story, A. Directed by Harry Booth. 1967. Britain. (Documentary). 100 min. Sound. 16mm Color. *Rental:* Budget Films & Kit Parker.

King's Thief, The. Ann Blyth & David Niven. Directed by Robert Z. Leonard. 1955. MGM. 79 min. Sound. 16mm Color. *Rental:* MGM United. *Rental:* MGM United, Anamorphic color version.

King's Vacation, The. George Arliss & Dick Powell. Directed by John Adolfi. 1933. Warners. 62 min. Sound. 16mm B&W. *Rental:* MGM United.

Kino-Eye. 1924. 77 min. Silent. 16mm B&W. subtitles Eng. *Rental:* Films Inc.

Kipperbang. John Albasiny & Abigail Crittenden. Directed by Michael Apted. 1984. 85 min. 16mm Color. *Rental:* MGM United.

Kipps. John Mills & Phyllis Calvert. Directed by Sir Carol Reed. 1941. Britain. 82 min. Sound. 16mm B&W. *Rental:* Budget Films, Classic Film Mus, Em Gee Film Lib, Films Inc, Kit Parker & Video Comm. *Sale:* Festival Films, Glenn Photo, Natl Cinema & Reel Images. *Rental:* Video Comm, *Sale:* Festival Films, Videotape version.

Kirlian Witness, The. Nancy Snyder & Ted Leplat. Directed by Jonathan Sarno. 1978. Sarno. 87 min. Sound. 16mm Color. *Rental:* Corinth Films.

Kismet. Otis Skinner. Directed by Louis Gasnier. 1920. Robertson/Cole. 70 min. Silent. 16mm B&W. *Rental:* Em Gee Film Lib & Film Classics. *Sale:* Film Classics. *Sale:* Film Classics, Silent 8mm version.

Kismet. Ronald Colman & Marlene Dietrich. Directed by William Dieterle. 1944. MGM. 100 min. Sound. 16mm Color. *Rental:* MGM United.

Kismet. Howard Keel & Ann Blyth. Directed by Vincente Minnelli. 1955. MGM. 113 min. Sound. 16mm Color. *Rental:* MGM United. *Rental:* MGM United, Anamorphic version. *Rental:* MGM United, Videotape version.

Kiss, The. Greta Garbo, Conrad Nagel & Lew Ayres. Directed by Jacques Feyder. 1929. MGM. 61 min. Silent. 16mm B&W. *Rental:* MGM United.

Kiss & Kill. Orig. Title: Against All Odds. Christopher Lee & Richard Greene. Directed by Jess Franco. 1969. Britain. 92 min. Sound. 16mm Color. *Rental:* Budget Films, Charard Motion Pics, Films Inc, Ivy Films, Video Comm & Westcoast Films. *Lease:* Video Comm.

Kiss Before Dying, A. Robert Wagner & Joanne Woodward. Directed by Gerd Oswald. 1956. United Artists. (Anamorphic). 94 min. Sound. 16mm Color. *Rental:* MGM United.

Kiss Before the Mirror, A. Paul Lukas & Nancy Carroll. Directed by James Whale. 1933. Universal. 66 min. Sound. 16mm B&W. *Rental:* Swank Motion.

Kiss Kiss, Kill Kill. Tony Kendall & Maria Perschy. Directed by Gianfranco Parolini. 1966. Italy. 86 min. Sound. 16mm Color. dubbed. *Rental:* Kerr Film & Westcoast Films.

Kiss Me Again. Walter Pidgeon & Bernice Claire. Directed by William A. Seiter. 1931. Warners. 74 min. Sound. 16mm B&W. *Rental:* MGM United.

Kiss Me Deadly. Ralph Meeker & Albert Dekker. Directed by Robert Aldrich. 1955. United Artists. 105 min. Sound. 16mm B&W. *Rental:* MGM United.

Kiss Me Goodbye. Sally Field & James Caan. Directed by Robert Mulligan. 1982. Fox. 95 min. Sound. 16mm Color. *Rental:* Films Inc.

Kiss Me, Kate. Howard Keel & Kathryn Grayson. Directed by George Sidney. 1953. MGM. 109 min. Sound. 16mm Color. *Rental:* MGM United.

Kiss Me, Petruchio. Meryl Streep & Raul Julia. 1982. NY Shakespeare Festival. 58 min. Sound. 16mm Color. *Rental:* Films Inc. *Sale:* Films Inc. *Sale:* Films Inc, Videotape version.

Kiss Me, Stupid. Dean Martin & Kim Novak. Directed by Billy Wilder. 1964. United Artists. 124 min. Sound. 16mm B&W. *Rental:* MGM United.

Kiss of Death, The. Victor Mature & Richard Widmark. Directed by Henry Hathaway. 1947. Fox. 99 min. Sound. 16mm B&W. *Rental:* Films Inc & MGM United.

Kiss of Fire, The. Jack Palance & Barbara Rush. Directed by Joseph Newman. 1955. Universal. 87 min. Sound. 16mm Color. *Rental:* Swank Motion.

Kiss of the Tarantula. 89 min. Sound. Videotape Color. *Rental:* Maljack.

Kiss of the Vampire. Clifford Evans & Noel Willman. Directed by Don Sharp. 1963. Britain. 88 min. Sound. 16mm Color. *Rental:* Swank Motion.

Kiss the Blood Off My Hands. Burt Lancaster & Joan Fontaine. Directed by Norman Foster. 1948. Universal. 84 min. Sound. 16mm B&W. *Rental:* Swank Motion.

Kiss the Girls & Make Them Die. Michael Conners & Dorothy Provine. Directed by Henry Levin. 1967. Columbia. 101 min. Sound. 16mm Color. *Rental:* Welling Motion Pictures.

Kiss the Other Sheik. Marcello Mastroianni & Pamela Tiffin. Directed by Luciano Salce. 1968. France-Italy. 86 min. Sound. 16mm Color. dubbed. *Rental:* MGM United.

Kiss Them for Me. Cary Grant & Suzy Parker. Directed by Stanley Donen. 1957. Fox. 103 min. Sound. 16mm Color. *Rental:* Films Inc.

Kiss Tomorrow Goodbye. James Cagney & Barbara Payton. Directed by Gordon Douglas. 1950. Warners. 102 min. Sound. 16mm B&W. *Rental:* Corinth Films. *Lease:* Corinth Films.

Kisses for Breakfast. Dennis Morgan & Jane Wyatt. Directed by Lewis Seiler. 1941. Warners. 82 min. Sound. 16mm B&W. *Rental:* MGM United.

Kisses for My President. Polly Bergen & Fred MacMurray. Directed by Curtis Bernhardt. 1964. Warners. 113 min. 16mm B&W. *Rental:* Arcus Film.

Kissin' Cousins. Elvis Presley & Arthur O'Connell. Directed by Gene Nelson. 1964. MGM. 96 min. Sound. 16mm B&W. *Rental:* MGM United.

Kissing Bandit, The. Frank Sinatra & Kathryn Grayson. Directed by Laslo Benedek. 1948. MGM. 100 min. Sound. 16mm B&W. *Rental:* MGM United. *Rental:* MGM United, Color version.

Kit Carson. Jon Hall & Dana Andrews. Directed by George B. Seitz. 1940. United Artists. 105 min. Sound. 16mm B&W. *Rental:* Budget Films, Newman Film Lib, Westcoast Films & Willoughby Peer.

Kitten With a Whip. Ann-Margret & John Forsythe. Directed by Douglas Heyes. 1964. Universal. 83 min. Sound. 16mm B&W. *Rental:* Swank Motion.

Kitty. Paulette Goddard & Ray Milland. Directed by Mitchell Leisen. 1945. Paramount. 104 min. Sound. 16mm B&W. *Rental:* Swank Motion.

Kitty Foyle. Ginger Rogers & Dennis Morgan. Directed by Sam Wood. 1941. RKO. 107 min. Sound. Videotape B&W. *Sale:* Films Inc. *Sale:* Blackhawk Films & Video Corp, Videotape version.

Kitty Hawk to Paris. 1969. CBS. (Documentary). 54 min. Sound. 16mm Color. *Rental:* Learning Corp Am, Syracuse U Film & U Mich Media. *Sale:* Learning Corp Am. *Rental:* Learning Corp Am, *Lease:* Learning Corp Am, Videotape version.

Kitty: Return to Auschwitz. 1970. (Documentary). 54 min. Sound. 16mm Color. *Rental:* U Mich Media.

Klansman, The. Richard Burton & Lee Marvin. Directed by Terence Young. 1974. Paramount. 112 min. Sound. 16mm Color. *Rental:* Films Inc.

Kliou, the Killer. 1937. DuWorld. (Documentary). 60 min. Sound. 16mm B&W. *Rental:* Mogulls Films.

Klondike Annie. Mae West & Victor McLaglen. Directed by Raoul Walsh. 1936. Paramount. 83 min. Sound. 16mm B&W. *Rental:* Williams Films.

Klondike Fever. Rod Steiger & Angie Dickinson. Directed by Peter Carter. 1980. World Entertainment. 110 min. Sound. 16mm Color. *Rental:* Twyman Films.

Klondike Fury. Edmund Lowe & Ralph Morgan. Directed by William K. Howard. 1942. Monogram. 62 min. Sound. 16mm B&W. *Rental:* Hurlock Cine.

Klondike Kate. Ann Savage & Tom Neal. Directed by William Castle. 1943. Columbia. 64 min. Sound. 16mm B&W. *Rental:* Kit Parker.

Klute. Jane Fonda & Donald Sutherland. Directed by Alan J. Pakula. 1971. Warners. 114 min. Sound. 16mm Color. *Rental:* Arcus Film, Cine Craft, Film Ctr DC, Films Inc, Inst Cinema, Swank Motion, Twyman Films, Welling Motion Pictures & Williams Films. *Rental:* Swank Motion, Videotape version.

Knack, The: And How to Get It. Rita Tushingham & Michael Crawford. Directed by Richard Lester. 1965. United Artists. 84 min. Sound. 16mm B&W. *Rental:* MGM United.

Knickerbocker Holiday. Nelson Eddy & Constance Dowling. Directed by Harry Joe Brown. 1944. United Artists. 85 min. Sound. 16mm B&W. *Rental:* Film Classics & Mogulls Films. *Rental:* Film Classics, Videotape version.

Knife in the Head. Bruno Ganz & Angela Winkler. Directed by Reinhard Hauff. Ger. 1978. Germany. 108 min. Sound. 16mm Color. subtitles. *Rental:* New Cinema & New Yorker Films.

Knife in the Water. Leon Niemczyk & Jolanta Umecka. Directed by Roman Polanski. Pol. 1962. Poland. 95 min. Sound. 16mm B&W. subtitles. *Rental:* Budget Films, Em Gee Film Lib, Films Inc, Inst Cinema, Images Film, Kit Parker, Roas Film & Liberty Co. *Sale:* Festival Films, Reel Images & Images Film. *Sale:* Tamarelles French Film, Festival Films & Images Film, Videotape version.

Knight Without Armor. Robert Donat & Marlene Dietrich. Directed by Jacques Feyder. 1937. United Artists. 105 min. Sound. 16mm B&W. *Rental:* Films Inc, Inst Cinema & Mogulls Films.

Knights of the Black Cross, The. Urszula Modrzynska & Grazyna Staniszewska. Directed by Aleksander Ford. 1962. Poland. 175 min. Sound. 16mm Color. dubbed. *Rental:* Amerpol Ent.

Knights of the Range. Russell Hayden & Victor Jory. Directed by Lesley Selander. 1940. Paramount. 60 min. Sound. 16mm B&W. *Rental:* Budget Films & SD AV Ctr.

Knights of the Round Table. Robert Taylor & Ava Gardner. Directed by Richard Thorpe. 1953. MGM. 106 min. Sound. 16mm Color. *Rental:* MGM United. *Rental:* MGM United, Anamorphic color version.

Knives of the Avenger. Cameron Mitchell. Directed by Mario Bava. 1967. Italy. 86 min. Sound. 16mm Color. dubbed. *Rental:* Ivy Films.

Knock on Any Door. Humphrey Bogart & John Derek. Directed by Nicholas Ray. 1949. Columbia. 99 min. Sound. 16mm B&W. *Rental:* Bosco Films, Budget Films, Cine Craft, Film Inc, Inst Cinema, Kit Parker, Roas Films, Swank Motion, Twyman Films, Welling Motion Pictures, Westcoast Films & Williams Films.

Knock on Wood. Danny Kaye & Mai Zetterling. Directed by Norman Panama & Melvin Frank. 1954. Paramount. 103 min. Sound. 16mm Color. *Rental:* Films Inc.

Knockout, The. Arthur Kennedy, Anthony Quinn & Cornel Wilde. Directed by William Clemens. 1941. Warners. 103 min. Sound. 16mm Color. *Rental:* MGM United.

Knockout, The. Joe Kirkwood Jr. & Leon Errol. Directed by Reginald Le Borg. 1947. Monogram. 70 min. Sound. 16mm B&W. *Rental:* Mogulls Films.

Knots. Actors Company. Directed by David Munro. 1975. Cinegate. 62 min. Sound. 16mm Color. *Rental:* A Cantor, Films Inc & New Cinema. *Sale:* A Cantor.

Know Your Enemy: Japan. 1945. U S Government. (Documentary). 63 min. Sound. 16mm B&W. *Rental:* Iowa Films & Kit Parker. *Sale:* Natl AV Ctr. *Sale:* Natl AV Ctr, *Rental:* Natl AV Ctr, Videotape version.

Knowing to Learn. 1966. Canada. (Documentary). 59 min. Sound. 16mm B&W. *Rental:* Films Inc. *Sale:* Films Inc. *Sale:* Films Inc, Videotape version.

Knowledge or Certainty. (Ascent of Man Ser.). 1974. Britain. (Documentary). 52 min. Sound. 16mm Color. *Rental:* Iowa Films, U Cal Media, U Mich Media & Utah Media.

Known & the Unknown, The. 1980. Canada. (Documentary). 57 min. Sound. 16mm Color. *Rental:* Budget Films & Iowa Films.

Knute Rockne: All American. Orig. Title: American Hero, An. Pat O'Brien & Donald Crisp. Directed by Lloyd Bacon. 1940. Warners. 98 min. Sound. 16mm B&W. *Rental:* MGM United.

Kodak Ghost Poems. Directed by Andrew Noren. 1970. Andrew Noren. (Experimental). 50 min. Silent. 16mm Color. *Rental:* Canyon Cinema.

Koko: A Talking Gorilla. Directed by Barbet Schroeder. 1978. New Yorker. (Documentary). 85 min. Sound. 16mm Color. dubbed. *Rental:* New Yorker Films.

Komodianten. Kathe Dorsch & Henny Porten. Directed by G. W. Pabst. Ger. 1941. Germany. 111 min. Sound. 16mm B&W. subtitles. *Rental:* Trans-World Films. *Rental:* Trans-World Films, Subtitled version.

Kon-Tiki. Directed by Thor Heyerdahl. 1951. RKO. (Documentary). 75 min. Sound. 16mm B&W. *Rental:* Kit Parker & Syracuse U Film. *Sale:* Janus Films.

Konfrontation *see* Confrontation.

Konga. Michael Gough & Margo Johns. Directed by John Lemont. 1961. Britain. 94 min. Sound. 16mm Color. *Rental:* Budget Films, Cine Craft, Twyman Films, Welling Motion Pictures, Westcoast Films & Willoughby Peer.

Kongi's Harvest. Directed by Ossie Davis. 1973. New Cinema. (Cast Unlisted). 94 min. Sound. 16mm Color. *Rental:* New Line Cinema.

Kongo. Walter Huston, Lupe Velez & Virginia Bruce. Directed by Will Cowan. 1932. MGM. 85 min. Sound. 16mm B&W. *Rental:* MGM United.

Konyets Sankt Peterburga *see* End of St. Petersburg.

Kook's Tour. Three Stooges. 1969. Normandy. 60 min. Sound. Super 8 Color. *Sale:* Cinema Concepts.

Korea: Battleground for Liberty. 1961. US Government. (Documentary). 48 min. Sound. 16mm Color. *Sale:* Natl AV Ctr.

Korea: Thirty-Eighth Parallel. 1965. Wolper. (Documentary). 50 min. Sound. 16mm B&W. *Rental:* Films Inc. *Sale:* Films Inc. *Sale:* Films Inc, Videotape version.

Korkarlen *see* Phantom Chariot.

Kosciuszko: An American Portrait. 1976. Reader's Digest. (Documentary). 58 min. Sound. 16mm Color. *Rental:* Pyramid Film. *Sale:* Pyramid Film. *Rental:* Pyramid Film, *Sale:* Pyramid Film, Videotape version.

Kotch. Walter Matthau & Deborah Winters. Directed by Jack Lemmon. 1971. Cinerama. 114 min. Sound. 16mm Color. *Rental:* Films Inc.

Koumiko Mystery, The. Directed by Chris Marker. Fr. 1965. France. (Experimental). 47 min. Sound. 16mm Color. subtitles. *Rental:* New Yorker Films.

Kowloon Assignment, The. Sonny Chiba. 96 min. Sound. 16mm Color. *Rental:* WW Enter. *Rental:* WW Enter, Videotape version.

Krakatit. Florence Marly & Karel Hoger. Directed by Otakar Vavra. Czech. 1951. Czechoslovakia. 97 min. Sound. 16mm B&W. subtitles Eng. *Rental:* Films Inc.

Krakatoa, East of Java. Maximillian Schell & Diane Baker. Directed by Bernard Kowalski. 1969. ABC. 126 min. Sound. 16mm Color. *Rental:* Films Inc. *Rental:* Films Inc, Anamorphic Color version.

Kramer vs. Kramer. Dustin Hoffman, Meryl Streep & Justin Henry. Directed by Robert Benton. 1979. Columbia. 104 min. Sound. 16mm Color. *Rental:* Arcus Film, Budget Films, Images Film, Kit Parker, Swank Motion, Welling Motion Pictures, Wholesome Film Ctr & Williams Films. *Rental:* Swank Motion, Videotape version.

Kremlin, The. 1963. NBC. (Documentary). 54 min. Sound. 16mm Color. *Rental:* McGraw-Hill Films, Syracuse U Film, U of IL Film & U Mich Media. *Sale:* McGraw-Hill Films.

Kremlin Letter, The. Bibi Anderson & Richard Boone. Directed by John Huston. 1970. Fox. 113 min. Sound. 16mm Color. *Rental:* Films Inc.

Kriemhilde's Revenge. Orig. Title: Nibelungen, Die. Paul Richter. Directed by Fritz Lang. 1924. Germany. 90 min. Silent. 16mm B&W. *Rental:* Budget Films, Classic Film Mus, Em Gee Film Lib, Film Images, Images Film, Kit Parker & Museum Mod Art. *Sale:* Blackhawk Films, Cinema Concepts & Film Images. *Rental:* Iowa Film & Kit Parker, Sound 16mm version. *Rental:* Ivy Films, *Sale:* Blackhawk Films, Super 8 Silent version. *Sale:* Tamarelles French Film, Videotape version.

Kristina Talking Pictures. Directed by Yvonne Rainer. 1976. Museum of Modern Art. (Documentary). 92 min. Sound. 16mm Color. *Rental:* Museum Mod Art.

Kronos. Jeff Morrow & Barbara Lawrence. Directed by Kurt Neumann. 1957. Fox. (Anamorphic). 78 min. Sound. 16mm B&W. *Rental:* Wade Williams. *Sale:* Rep Pic Film.

Krull. Ken Marshall & Lysette Anthony. Directed by Peter Yates. 1983. Columbia. 117 min. Sound. 16mm Color. *Rental:* Swank Motion. *Rental:* Swank Motion, Videotape version.

Ku Klux Klan: The Invisible Empire. 1966. CBS. (Documentary). 47 min. Sound. 16mm B&W. *Rental:* Budget Films, Mass Media, Syracuse U Film, U Cal Media, U of IL Film & U Mich Media. *Sale:* Carousel Films.

Kuhle Wampe. Ernst Busch & Hertha Thiele. Directed by Slatan Dudow. Ger. 1932. Germany. 70 min. Sound. 16mm B&W. subtitles. *Rental:* Films Inc.

Kung Fu Gold. Tze Lam. 1974. Mallard. 90 min. Sound. 16mm Color. *Rental:* Budget Films, Films Inc, Modern Sound & Westcoast Films.

Kung Fu Instructor. Ti Ling & Wang Yu. 105 min. Sound. 16mm *Rental:* WW Enter. *Rental:* WW Enter, Videotape version.

Kung Fu of Eight Drunkards. 95 min. Sound. 16mm Color. *Rental:* BF Video.

Kung Fu: The Invisible Fist. 1974. United International. (Cast unlisted). 93 min. Sound. 16mm Color. dubbed. *Rental:* Films Inc.

Kuroneko. Nobuko Otowa. Directed by Kaneto Shindo. Jap. 1968. Japan. (Anamorphic). 160 min. Sound. 16mm B&W. subtitles. *Rental:* Corinth Films. *Lease:* Corinth Films.

Kurt Vonnegut Jr: Deadeye Dick. 1982. Britain. (Documentary). 60 min. Sound. 16mm Color. *Sale:* Wombat Productions. *Sale:* Wombat Productions, Videotape version.

Kwaidan. Directed by Masaki Kobayashi. Jap. 1965. Japan. (Anthology). 160 min. Sound. 16mm Color. subtitles. *Rental:* Budget Films & Films Inc.

Kwegu, The. 1982. Britain. (Documentary). 52 min. Videotape Color. *Rental:* Film Makers. *Sale:* Film Makers.

L-Shaped Room, The. Leslie Caron, Tom Bell & Anthony Booth. Directed by Bryan Forbes. 1963. Columbia. 124 min. Sound. 16mm B&W. *Rental:* Corinth Films, Images Film & Swank Motion.

La Brava: Prison and Beyond. Rel. 1974. (Documentary). 54 min. 16mm Color. *Rental:* U Cal Media. *Sale:* U Cal Media. *Sale:* U Cal Media, Videotape version.

L.A: Making It in Los Angeles. 1979. Caroline & Frank Mouris. 58 min. Sound. Color. *Rental:* Direct Cinema. *Sale:* Direct Cinema, Videotape version.

La Monia Azteca Contra la Roboto Humano *see* Robot vs. the Aztec Mummy.

La Piege *see* Any Man's Woman.

Labiche. France. (Cast unlisted). 60 min. Sound. 16mm B&W. *Rental:* French Am Cul. *Rental:* French Am Cul, Videotape version.

Labor in the Promised Land. Directed by Tom Spain. 1982. NBC. 52 min. Videotape Color. *Rental:* Films Inc. *Sale:* Films Inc.

Labor More Than Once. Directed by Liz Mersky. 1983. Women Make Movies. (Documentary). 52 min. Videotape Color. *Rental:* Women Movies. *Sale:* Women Movies.

Labor Relations: Do Not Fold, Staple, Spindle or Multilate *see* Do Not Fold, Staple, Spindle or Multilate.

Lac du Dames, La. Simone Simon. Directed by Marc Allegret. Fr. 1934. France. 90 min. Sound. Videotape B&W. subtitles. *Sale:* Tamarelles French Film.

Lacemaker, The. Isabelle Huppert. Directed by Claude Goretta. Fr. 1977. Switzerland. 108 min. Sound. 16mm Color. subtitles. *Rental:* New Cinema & New Yorker Films.

Lacombe, Lucien. Pierre Blaise. Directed by Louis Malle. Fr. 1974. France. 141 min. Sound. 16mm Color. subtitles. *Rental:* Films Inc.

Ladder of Creation. (Ascent of Man Ser.). 1974. Britain. (Documentary). 52 min. Sound. 16mm Color. *Rental:* Iowa Films, U Cal Media, U Mich Media & Utah Media.

Ladies & Gentlemen: The Rolling Stones. Directed by Rollin Binzer. 1973. Dragon Aire. (Documentary). 88 min. Sound. 16mm Color. *Rental:* Twyman Films.

Ladies at Ease. James Gardener & Pauline Garon. Directed by Jerome Storm. 1927. First Division. 60 min. Silent. 16mm B&W. *Rental:* Mogulls Films.

Ladies' Day. Lupe Velez & Eddie Albert. Directed by Leslie Goodwins. 1943. RKO. 62 min. Sound. 16mm B&W. *Rental:* Films Inc.

Ladies in Distress. Robert Livingston. Directed by Gus Meins. 1938. Republic. 54 min. Sound. 16mm B&W. *Rental:* Ivy Films. *Sale:* Rep Pic Film.

Ladies in Retirement. Ida Lupino & Louis Haywood. Directed by Charles Vidor. 1941. Columbia. 93 min. Sound. 16mm B&W. *Rental:* Kit Parker.

Ladies in Washington. Trudy Marshall & Ronald Graham. Directed by Louis King. 1944. Fox. 61 min. Sound. 16mm B&W. *Rental:* Films Inc.

Ladies' Man, The. Jerry Lewis & Helen Traubel. Directed by Jerry Lewis. 1961. Paramount. 96 min. Sound. 16mm Color. *Rental:* Films Inc.

Ladies Must Live. Wayne Morris & Priscilla Lane. Directed by Noel Smith. 1940. Warners. 58 min. Sound. 16mm B&W. *Rental:* MGM United.

Ladies of Leisure. Barbara Stanwyck & Lowell Sherman. Directed by Frank Capra. 1930. Columbia. 98 min. Sound. 16mm B&W. *Rental:* Kit Parker.

Ladies of the Chorus. Adele Jergens & Marilyn Monroe. Directed by Phil Karlson. 1949. Columbia. 61 min. Sound. 16mm B&W. *Rental:* Bosco Films & Kit Parker.

Ladies of the Jury. Ken Murray & Edna May Oliver. Directed by Lowell Sherman. 1932. RKO. 64 min. Sound. 16mm *Rental:* RKO General Pics.

Ladies They Talk About. Barbara Stanwyck & Lillian Roth. Directed by William Keighley. 1933. Warners. 69 min. Sound. 16mm B&W. *Rental:* MGM United.

Lady, The. Norma Talmadge. Directed by Frank Borzage. 1925. 16mm *Rental:* A Twyman Pres.

Lady & the Corpse, The *see* Lady in the Car with Glasses & a Gun.

Lady & the Bandit, The. Orig. Title: Dick Turpin's Ride. Louis Hayward & Patricia Medina. Directed by Ralph Murphy. 1951. Columbia. 79 min. Sound. 16mm B&W. *Rental:* Arcus Film, Film Ctr DC & Inst Cinema.

Lady & the Mob, The. Fay Bainter & Ida Lupino. Directed by Ben Stoloff. 1939. Columbia. 70 min. Sound. 16mm B&W. *Rental:* Kit Parker.

Lady & the Monster, The. Orig. Title: Tiger Man. Erich Von Stroheim & Richard Arlen. Directed by George Sherman. 1944. Republic. 86 min. Sound. 16mm B&W. *Rental:* Ivy Films. *Sale:* Rep Pic Film.

Lady at Midnight, A. Frances Rafferty & Richard Denning. Directed by Sherman Scott. 1948. Republic. 62 min. Sound. 16mm B&W. *Rental:* Ivy Films & Mogulls Films. *Sale:* Rep Pic Film.

Lady Be Good. Ann Sothern & Robert Young. Directed by Norman Z. McLeod. 1941. MGM. 111 min. Sound. 16mm B&W. *Rental:* MGM United.

Lady, Behave. Sally Eilers & Neil Hamilton. Directed by Lloyd Corrigan. 1937. Republic. 54 min. Sound. 16mm B&W. *Rental:* Ivy Films. *Sale:* Rep Pic Film.

Lady by Choice, A. Carole Lombard & May Robson. Directed by David Burton. 1934. Columbia. 80 min. Sound. 16mm B&W. *Rental:* Bosco Films & Kit Parker.

Lady Chaser, The. Robert Lowery & Ann Savage. Directed by Sam Newfield. 1945. PRC. 60 min. Sound. 16mm B&W. *Sale:* Classics Assoc NY.

Lady Chatterley's Lover. Trans. Title: Amant de Lady Chatterley, L'. Danielle Darrieux & Leo Genn. Directed by Marc Allegret. Fr. 1955. France. 98 min. Sound. 16mm B&W. subtitles. *Rental:* Budget Films, Em Gee Film Lib & Kit Parker. *Sale:* Festival Films & Tamarelles French Film, Videotape version.

Lady Chatterley's Lover. Sylvia Kristel, Shane Briant & Nicholas Clay. Directed by Just Jaeckin. 1982. Cannon. 107 min. Sound. 16mm Color. *Rental:* Swank Motion.

Lady Cocoa. Orig. Title: Pop Goes the Weasel. Lola Falana & Gene Washington. Directed by Matt Cimber. 1975. Dimension. 93 min. Sound. 16mm Color. *Rental:* Budget Films.

Lady Confesses, A. Mary Beth Hughes & Hugh Beaumont. Directed by Sam Newfield. 1945. PRC. 66 min. Sound. 16mm B&W. *Rental:* Budget Films, Ivy Films & Mogulls Films. *Sale:* Classics Assoc NY & Rep Pic Film.

Lady Consents, A. Herbert Marshall & Ann Harding. Directed by Stephen Roberts. 1936. RKO. 76 min. Sound. 16mm *Rental:* RKO General Pics.

Lady Eve, The. Henry Fonda & Barbara Stanwyck. Directed by Preston Sturges. 1941. Paramount. 97 min. Sound. 16mm B&W. *Rental:* Williams Films.

Lady for a Night. John Wayne & Joan Blondell. Directed by Leigh Jason. 1942. Republic. 88 min. Sound. 16mm B&W. *Rental:* Ivy Films. *Lease:* Rep Pic Film.

Lady Frankenstein. Joseph Cotten & Sarah Bay. Directed by Mel Welles. 1972. New World. 85 min. Sound. 16mm Color. *Rental:* Films Inc.

Lady from Lisbon, The. Jane Carr & Francis L. Sullivan. Directed by Leslie Hiscott. 1943. Britain. 78 min. Sound. 16mm B&W. *Rental:* Ivy Films. *Sale:* Rep Pic Film.

Lady from Louisiana, The. John Wayne & Ona Munson. Directed by John Wayne. 1942. Republic. 84 min. Sound. 16mm B&W. *Rental:* Ivy Films. *Lease:* Rep Pic Film.

Lady from Shanghai, The. Rita Hayworth & Orson Welles. Directed by Orson Welles. 1948. Columbia. 87 min. Sound. 16mm B&W. *Rental:* Bosco Films, Budget Films, Cine Craft, Films Inc, Images Film, Inst Cinema, Kit Parker, Natl Film Video, Swank Motion, Twyman Films, U of IL Film, Welling Motion Pictures, Wholesome Film Ctr & Williams Films.

Lady Gambles, The. Barbara Stanwyck & Robert Preston. Directed by Michael Gordon. 1949. Universal. 99 min. Sound. 16mm B&W. *Rental:* Swank Motion.

Lady Gangster. Faye Emerson, Julie Bishop & Jackie Gleason. Directed by Florian Roberts. 1942. Warners. 62 min. Sound. 16mm B&W. *Rental:* MGM United.

Lady Godiva. Maureen O'Hara & George Nader. Directed by Arthur Lubin. 1955. Universal. 89 min. Sound. 16mm Color. *Rental:* Swank Motion.

Lady Hamilton *see* That Hamilton Woman.

Lady Ice. Donald Sutherland & Jennifer O'Neill. Directed by Tom Gries. 1973. National General. 93 min. Sound. 16mm Color. *Rental:* Swank Motion.

Lady in a Cage. Olivia De Havilland & Ann Sothern. Directed by Walter Grauman. 1964. Paramount. 93 min. Sound. 16mm B&W. *Rental:* Films Inc.

Lady in a Jam. Irene Dunne & Patric Knowles. Directed by Gregory La Cava. 1942. Universal. 78 min. Sound. 16mm B&W. *Rental:* Swank Motion.

Lady in Cement. Frank Sinatra & Raquel Welch. Directed by Gordon Douglas. 1968. Fox. 94 min. Sound. 16mm Color. *Rental:* Films Inc. *Rental:* Films Inc, Anamorphic Color version.

Lady in Question, The. Rita Hayworth & Brian Aherne. Directed by Charles Vidor. 1940. Columbia. 90 min. Sound. 16mm B&W. *Lease:* Time-Life Multimedia.

Lady in the Car with Glasses & a Gun, The. Orig. Title: Lady & the Corpse, The. Samantha Eggar & Oliver Reed. Directed by Anatole Litvak. 1971. Columbia. 105 min. Sound. 16mm Color. *Rental:* Arcus Film, Inst Cinema, Modern Sound & Wholesome Film Ctr.

Lady in the Dark. Ginger Rogers & Ray Milland. Directed by Mitchell Leisen. 1944. Paramount. 100 min. Sound. 16mm Color. *Rental:* Swank Motion.

Lady in the Death House. Jean Parker & Lionel Atwill. Directed by Steve Sekely. 1944. PRC. 60 min. Sound. 16mm B&W. *Rental:* Mogulls Films.

Lady in the Lake, The. Robert Montgomery & Audrey Totter. Directed by Robert Montgomery. 1946. MGM. 103 min. Sound. 16mm B&W. *Rental:* MGM United.

Lady in the Morgue, The. Orig. Title: Case of the Missing Blonde, The. Preston Foster & Patricia Ellis. Directed by Otis Garrett. 1938. Universal. 60 min. Sound. 16mm B&W. *Rental:* Mogulls Films.

Lady Is Willing, The. Leslie Howard & Binnie Barnes. Directed by Gilbert Miller. 1934. Columbia. 74 min. Sound. 16mm B&W. *Rental:* Kit Parker.

Lady Is Willing, The. Marlene Dietrich & Fred MacMurray. Directed by Mitchell Leisen. 1942. Columbia. 91 min. Sound. 16mm B&W. *Rental:* Bosco Films & Kit Parker.

Lady Killer. James Cagney, Margaret Lindsay & Mae Clark. Directed by Roy Del Ruth. 1933. Warners. 76 min. Sound. 16mm B&W. *Rental:* MGM United.

Lady Kung Fu. Angela Mao. Directed by Huang Feng. 1973. National General. 104 min. Sound. 16mm Color. dubbed. *Rental:* Swank Motion.

Lady L. Sophia Loren & Paul Newman. Directed by Peter Ustinov. 1966. MGM. 107 min. Sound. 16mm Color. *Rental:* MGM United. *Rental:* MGM United, Anamorphic version.

Lady, Let's Dance. Belita & James Ellison. Directed by Frank Woodruff. 1944. Monogram. 60 min. Sound. 16mm B&W. *Rental:* Budget Films, Hurlock Cine.

Lady Liberty. Trans. Title: Mortadella, La. Sophia Loren & William Devane. Directed by Mario Monicelli. 1972. Italy. 95 min. Sound. 16mm Color. dubbed. *Rental:* MGM United.

Lady Luck. Barbara Hale & Robert Young. Directed by Edwin L. Marin. 1949. RKO. 97 min. Sound. 16mm B&W. *Rental:* Films Inc.

Lady Named Baybie, A. Directed by Martha Sandlin. 1980. Direct Cinema. (Documentary). 60 min. Sound. 16mm B&W. *Sale:* Direct Cinema. *Rental:* Direct Cinema. *Sale:* Direct Cinema, Videotape version.

Lady of Burlesque. Orig. Title: Strip Tease Murders, The. Barbara Stanwyck. Directed by William A. Wellman. 1943. United Artists. 91 min. Sound. B&W. *Rental:* Budget Films, Classic Film Mus, Em Gee Films, Kit Parker & Video Comm. *Sale:* Cinema Concepts. *Rental:* Video Comm, *Sale:* Cinema Concepts, Reel Images & Tamarelles French Film, Videotape version.

Lady of Monza. Anne Heywood. Directed by Eriprando Visconti. 1971. Italy. 97 min. Sound. 16mm Color. dubbed. *Rental:* Swank Motion.

Lady of Scandal. Ruth Chatterton & Basil Rathbone. Directed by Sidney Franklin. 1930. MGM. 80 min. Sound. 16mm B&W. *Rental:* MGM United.

Lady of Secrets. Ruth Chatterton & Otto Kruger. Directed by Marion Gering. 1936. Columbia. 70 min. Sound. 16mm B&W. *Rental:* Kit Parker.

Lady of the Boulevards *see* Nana.

Lady of the Lake. Benita Hume & Percy Marmont. Directed by James A. Fitzpatrick. 1930. Britain. (Music and Sound Effects Only). 50 min. Sound. 16mm B&W. *Rental:* Em Gee Film Lib, Film Classics & Mogulls Films. *Sale:* Cinema Concepts. *Rental:* Film Classics, Videotape version.

Lady on a Train. Deanna Durbin & Ralph Bellamy. Directed by Charles David. 1945. Universal. 93 min. Sound. 16mm B&W. *Rental:* Swank Motion.

Lady on the Bus. Sonia Braga & Nuno Leal Maia. Directed by Neville D'Almeida. 1982. Atlantic. 99 min. Sound. 16mm Color. *Rental:* Films Inc. *Sale:* Tamarelles French Film, Videotape version.

Lady Pays Off, The. Linda Darnell & Stephen McNally. Directed by Douglas Sirk. 1951. Universal. 80 min. Sound. 16mm B&W. *Rental:* Swank Motion.

Lady Possessed, A. June Havoc & James Mason. Directed by William Spier. 1952. Republic. 87 min. Sound. 16mm B&W. *Rental:* Ivy Films. *Sale:* Rep Pic Film.

Lady Refuses, The. Betty Compson & John Darrow. Directed by George Archainbaud. 1931. RKO. 72 min. Sound. 16mm B&W. *Sale:* Morcraft Films. *Sale:* Morcraft Films, Super 8 Sound version.

Lady Reporter *see* Bulldog Edition.

Lady Says No, The. David Niven & Joan Caulfield. Directed by Frank Ross. 1951. United Artists. 80 min. Sound. 16mm B&W. *Rental:* Ivy Films. *Sale:* Rep Pic Film.

Lady Scarface. Dennis O'Keefe & Judith Anderson. Directed by Frank Woodruff. 1942. RKO. 66 min. Sound. 16mm B&W. *Rental:* RKO General Pics.

Lady Sings the Blues. Diana Ross & Billy Dee Williams. Directed by Sidney J. Furie. 1972. Paramount. 144 min. Sound. 16mm Color. *Rental:* Films Inc.

Lady Takes a Chance, The. Jean Arthur & John Wayne. Directed by William A. Seiter. 1943. RKO. 86 min. Sound. Videotape B&W. *Sale:* Cinema Concepts, Tamarelles French Film & Video Lib. *Sale:* Vidamerica.

Lady Takes a Flyer, The. Lana Turner & Jeff Chandler. Directed by Jack Arnold. 1958. Universal. 95 min. Sound. 16mm Color. *Rental:* Swank Motion. *Rental:* Swank Motion, Anamorphic version.

Lady Takes a Sailor, The. Jane Wyman & Dennis Morgan. Directed by Michael Curtiz. 1949. Warners. 99 min. Sound. 16mm B&W. *Rental:* MGM United.

Lady Vanishes, The. Sir Michael Redgrave & Margaret Lockwood. Directed by Alfred Hitchcock. 1938. Britain. 101 min. Sound. B&W. *Rental:* Arcus Film, Budget Films, Em Gee Film Lib, Films Inc, Images Film, Ivy Films, Kit Parker, Newman Film Lib, OK AV Ctr, Roas Films, U of IL Film, Video Comm, Welling Motion Pictures & Wholesome Film Ctr. *Sale:* Cinema Concepts, Images Film, Natl Cinema & Reel Images. *Sale:* Cinema Concepts, Images Film, Tamarelles French Film, Video Lib & Video Comm, Videotape version.

Lady Wants Mink, The. Ruth Hussey & Dennis O'Keefe. Directed by William A. Seiter. 1953. Republic. 92 min. Sound. 16mm B&W. *Rental:* Ivy Films. *Sale:* Rep Pic Film.

Lady Windermere's Fan. Ronald Colman, Irene Rich & Bert Lytell. Directed by Ernst Lubitsch. 1925. Warners. 85 min. Silent. 16mm B&W. *Rental:* A Twyman Pres, Budget Films, Em Gee Film Lib, Film Classics, Images Film, Museum Mod Art, Twyman Films & Willoughby Peer. *Lease:* Museum Mod Art. *Sale:* Glenn Photo & Images Film. *Sale:* Select Film, Super 8 silent version. *Sale:* Images Film, Videotape version.

Lady With a Dog, The. Trans. Title: Dama S Sobachkoy. Iya Savvina & Alexei Batalov. Directed by Josef Heifitz. Rus. 1960. Russia. 86 min. Sound. 16mm B&W. subtitles. *Rental:* Corinth Films.

Lady With a Lamp. Anna Neagle & Michael Wilding. Directed by Herbert Wilcox. 1952. Britain. 110 min. Sound. 16mm B&W. *Rental:* Films Inc.

Lady With a Past. Constance Bennett & Ben Lyon. Directed by Edward H. Griffith. 1932. RKO. 80 min. Sound. 16mm *Rental:* RKO General Pics.

Lady With Red Hair, The. Miriam Hopkins & Claude Rains. Directed by Curtis Bernhardt. 1940. Warners. 81 min. Sound. 16mm B&W. *Rental:* MGM United.

Lady Without Camelias, The. Lucia Bose & Gino Cervi. Directed by Michelangelo Antonioni. Ital. 1953. Italy. 106 min. Sound. 16mm B&W. subtitles. *Rental:* Cimena Guild.

Lady Without Passport, A. Hedy Lamarr & John Hodiak. Directed by Joseph Lewis. 1950. MGM. 72 min. Sound. 16mm B&W. *Rental:* MGM United.

Ladybird. Betty Compson & Hank Mann. Directed by Walter Lang. 1927. Chadwick. 84 min. Silent. 16mm B&W. *Rental:* Mogulls Films.

Ladybug, Ladybug. Estelle Parsons & Jane Connell. Directed by Frank Perry. 1963. United Artists. 81 min. Sound. 16mm B&W. *Rental:* MGM United.

Ladykillers, The. Sir Alec Guinness, Katie Johnson & Peter Sellers. Directed by Alexander Mackendrick. 1955. Britain. 97 min. Sound. 16mm Color. *Rental:* Budget Films, Films Inc, Images Film, Kit Parker, Learning Corp Am, Roas Film, Twyman Films, Westcoast Films & Wholesome Film Ctr. *Lease:* Learning Corp Am.

Lady's Morals, A. Grace Moore & Wallace Beery. Directed by Sidney Franklin. 1930. MGM. 87 min. Sound. 16mm B&W. *Rental:* MGM United.

Lafayette: The Story of a Friendship. Directed by Victor Vicas. 1972. AIF. (Documentary). 60 min. Sound. 16mm B&W. *Sale:* Americas Films. *Sale:* Americas Films, Color version. *Sale:* Americas Films, Spanish version.

Lake Placid Serenade. Vera Ralston & Eugene Pallette. Directed by Steve Sekely. 1944. Republic. 85 min. Sound. 16mm B&W. *Rental:* Ivy Films. *Sale:* Rep Pic Film.

Lake Titicaca. 1977. Metromedia. (Documentary). 54 min. Sound. 16mm Color. *Rental:* Churchill Films. *Sale:* Churchill Films.

Lamb, The. Douglas Fairbanks & Seena Owen. Directed by Christy Cabanne. 1915. Arts/Triangle. 70 min. Silent. 16mm B&W. *Rental:* A Twyman Pres & Twyman Films.

Lament of Arthur O'Leary, The. Directed by Bob Quinn. 1975. Cinagael. (Documentary). 60 min. Sound. 16mm Color. *Rental:* CA Newsreel. *Sale:* CA NewsReel.

L'Amour Fou. Bulle Ogier. Directed by Jacques Rivette. Fr. 1968. France. 252 min. Sound. 16mm B&W. subtitles. *Rental:* New Cinema.

Lancelot & Guinevere *see* Sword of Lancelot.

Lancelot of the Lake. Luc Simon. Directed by Robert Bresson. Fr. 1974. France. 83 min. Sound. 16mm Color. subtitles. *Rental:* Films Inc & New Yorker Films.

Lancer Spy. Dolores Del Rio & George Sanders. Directed by Gregory Ratoff. 1937. Fox. 84 min. Sound. 16mm B&W. *Rental:* Films Inc.

Land, The. 1971. NBC. (Documentary). 54 min. Sound. 16mm Color. *Rental:* McGraw-Hill Films. *Sale:* McGraw-Hill Films.

Land, The. Directed by Robert Flaherty. 1942. US Film Service. (Documentary). 51 min. Sound. 16mm B&W. *Rental:* Images Film & Museum Mod Art. *Sale:* Images Film.

Land, The: American Farmer. 1962. MCG-H. 54 min. Sound. 16mm B&W. *Rental:* Syracuse U Film.

Land & the People, The. 1976. Britain. (Documentary). 60 min. Sound. 16mm Color. *Rental:* Films Inc, Syracuse U Film, U Cal Media & U of IL Film. *Sale:* Films Inc. *Sale:* Films Inc, Videotape version.

Land Beyond the Law. Dick Foran & Wayne Morris. Directed by B. Reeves Eason. 1937. Warners. 58 min. Sound. 16mm B&W. *Rental:* MGM United.

Land of Fear, Land of Courage. Edwin Newman. CC Films. 60 min. Sound. Videotape Color. *Rental:* Natl Churches Christ.

Land of Hunted Men. John King & David Sharpe. Directed by S. Roy Luby. 1943. Monogram. 100 min. Sound. 16mm B&W. *Rental:* Budget Films, Film Ctr DC & Modern Sound.

Land of Liberty. 5 pts. 1939. Teaching Films Custodians. (Anthology, color sequences). 100 min. Sound. 16mm B&W. *Rental:* Indiana AV Ctr & SD AV Ctr. *Sale:* SD AV Ctr.

Land of Missing Men. Bob Steele. Directed by J. P. McCarthy. 1930. Tiffany. 60 min. Sound. 16mm B&W. *Rental:* Film Classics & Mogulls Films. *Sale:* Film Classics, Silent 8mm version.

Land of Silence & Darkness. Directed by Werner Herzog. Ger. 1971. Germany. (Documentary). 90 min. Sound. 16mm Color. subtitles. *Rental:* New Yorker Films.

Land of Sleeping Mountains, The. 1982. Films Inc. (Documentary). 60 min. Sound. 16mm Color. *Rental:* Films Inc. *Sale:* Films Inc. *Sale:* Films Inc, Videotape version.

Land of the Disappearing Buddha. 1977. Britain. (Documentary). 52 min. Sound. 16mm Color. *Rental:* Iowa Films, U of IL Film & U Mich Media.

Land of the Fighting Men. Jack Randall. Directed by Alan James. 1938. Monogram. 53 min. Sound. 16mm B&W. *Rental:* Hurlock Cine.

Land of the Minotaur. Orig. Title: Devil's Men, The. Peter Cushing & Donald Pleasance. Directed by Costa Carajiannis. 1977. Britain. 88 min. Sound. 16mm Color. *Rental:* Films Inc.

Land of the Open Range. Tim Holt & Ray Whitley. Directed by Edward Killy. 1942. RKO. 60 min. Sound. 16mm *Rental:* RKO General Pics.

Land of the Outlaws. Johnny Mack Brown. Directed by Lambert Hillyer. 1944. Monogram. 55 min. Sound. 16mm Color. *Rental:* Hurlock Cine.

Land of the Pharaohs. Jack Hawkins & Joan Collins. Directed by Howard Hawks. 1955. Warners. 105 min. Sound. 16mm Color. *Rental:* Films Inc & Video Comm.

Land of the Six Guns. Jack Randall. Directed by Raymond K. Johnson. 1940. Monogram. 54 min. Sound. 16mm B&W. *Rental:* Hurlock Cine.

Land of the Sleeping Mountains, The. 1983. Britain. (Documentary). 60 min. Sound. 16mm Color. *Rental:* Films Inc. *Sale:* Films Inc. *Sale:* Films Inc, Videotape version.

Land Raiders. Telly Savalas, George Maharis & Arlene Dahl. Directed by Nathan Juran. 1970. Columbia. 100 min. Sound. 16mm Color. *Rental:* Film Ctr DC, Films Inc & Modern Sound.

Land That Time Forgot, The. Doug McClure & John McEnery. Directed by Kevin Conner. 1974. American International. 90 min. Sound. 16mm Color. *Rental:* Swank Motion & Welling Motion Pictures.

Land Unknown, A. Jock Mahoney & William Reynolds. Directed by Virgil Vogel. 1957. Universal. 78 min. Sound. 16mm B&W. *Rental:* Swank Motion.

Land Where the Blues Began, The. Phoenix. (Documentary). 58 min. Sound. 16mm Color. *Rental:* Phoenix Films & Syracuse U Film. *Sale:* Phoenix Films. *Sale:* Phoenix Films, Videotape version.

Landlord, The. Beau Bridges & Lee Grant. Directed by Hal Ashby. 1970. United Artists. 110 min. Sound. 16mm Color. *Rental:* MGM United.

Landscape After Battle. Daniel Olbrychski. Directed by Andrzej Wajda. Pol. 1970. Poland. 110 min. Sound. 16mm Color. subtitles. *Rental:* New Yorker Films.

Landscape of Pleasure, The. 1979. Britain. (Documentary). 52 min. Sound. 16mm Color. *Rental:* Time-Life Multimedia & U of Cal Media. *Sale:* Time-Life Multimedia. *Sale:* Time-Life Multimedia, Videotape version.

Language & Creativity. Directed by Michael Chanan. 1972. Oxford U. (Interview). 60 min. Sound. 16mm Color. *Rental:* New Yorker Films.

Language of Listening, The. Dr. Kevin Leman. 45 min. Sound. 16mm Color. *Rental:* Gospel Films.

Language of the Silent Cinema, The. Directed by Vladimir Petric. 1973. Museum Modern Art. (Anthology). 190 min. Silent. 16mm B&W. *Rental:* Museum Mod Art. *Lease:* Museum Mod Art.

Laramie Trail, The. Robert Livingston. Directed by John English. 1944. Republic. 54 min. Sound. 16mm B&W. *Rental:* Ivy Films. *Sale:* Rep Pic Film.

Larceny in Her Heart. Hugh Beaumont & Cheryl Walker. Directed by Sam Newfield. 1946. PRC. 68 min. Sound. 16mm B&W. *Sale:* Classics Assoc NY.

Larceny Lane *see* Blond Crazy.

Larceny on the Air. Robert Livingston & Grace Bradley. Directed by Irving Pichel. 1937. Republic. 54 min. Sound. 16mm B&W. *Rental:* Ivy Films. *Sale:* Rep Pic Film.

Laredo *see* Three Guns for Texas.

Larry. Frederic Forrest & Tyne Daly. Directed by William Graham. 1974. CBS. 78 min. Sound. 16mm Color. *Rental:* Budget Films, Films Inc, Kent ST U Film, Kit Parker, Learning Corp Am, Mass Media, Syracuse U Film, Twyman Films, U of IL Film, U Mich Media & Wholesome Film Ctr. *Lease:* Learning Corp Am. *Rental:* Learning Corp Am, *Lease:* Learning Corp Am, Videotape version.

Larsen, Wolf of the Seven Seas. Chuck Connors. 1975. Germany. 90 min. Sound. 16mm Color. dubbed. *Rental:* Films Inc & Westcoast Films.

Las Vegas Hillbillies. Jane Mansfield & Mamie Van Doren. Directed by Arthur C. Pierce. 1966. Woolner. 90 min. Sound. 16mm Color. *Rental:* Budget Films, Welling Motion Pictures & Willoughby Peer.

Las Vegas Lady. Stella Stevens & Stuart Whitman. Directed by Noel Nosseck. 1975. Crown. 90 min. Sound. 16mm Color. *Rental:* Films Inc.

Las Vegas Nights. Constance Moore & Phil Regan. Directed by Ralph Murphy. 1941. Paramount. 89 min. Sound. 16mm B&W. *Rental:* Swank Motion.

Las Vegas Story, The. Jane Russell & Victor Mature. Directed by Robert Stevenson. 1952. RKO. 88 min. Sound. 16mm B&W. *Rental:* Films Inc.

Laserblast. Roddy McDowall & Kim Milford. Directed by Michael Rae. 1978. Yablans. 85 min. Sound. 16mm Color. *Rental:* Films Inc & Budget Films.

Lash, The. Richard Barthelmess & Mary Astor. Directed by Frank Lloyd. 1930. Warners. 75 min. Sound. 16mm B&W. *Rental:* MGM United.

Lash of the Law, The. Bill Bailey. 1925. Goodwill. 55 min. Silent. 16mm B&W. *Sale:* Morcraft Films. *Sale:* Morcraft Films, Super 8 Silent version.

Lassie & the Flight of the Cougar. Robert Bray & Merry Anders. 1955. Wrather. 80 min. Sound. 16mm Color. *Rental:* Williams Films.

Lassie & the Fugitive. Lassie. 1955. Wrather. 52 min. Sound. 16mm B&W. *Rental:* Budget Films & Films Inc.

Lassie & the Wayfarers. Jon Provost. 1955. Wrather. 76 min. Sound. 16mm B&W. *Rental:* Modern Sound.

Lassie Come Home. Roddy McDowall & Elizabeth Taylor. Directed by Fred Taylor. 1943. MGM. 90 min. Sound. 16mm Color. *Rental:* MGM United.

Lassie from Lancashire, The. Marjorie Brown. Directed by John Paddy Carstairs. 1949. Britain. 67 min. Sound. 16mm B&W. *Rental:* Ivy Films.

Lassie's Adventures in the Goldrush *see* Painted Hills.

Lassie's Gift of Love. Lassie. 1955. Wrather. 52 min. Sound. 16mm B&W. *Rental:* Budget Films, Films Inc & Modern Sound.

Lassie's Great Adventure. Jon Provost & June Lockhart. Directed by William Beaudine. 1963. Fox. 73 min. Sound. 16mm Color. *Rental:* Buchan Pic, Budget Films, Films Inc, Ivy Films, Kerr Film, Modern Sound, Natl Film Video, Roas Films, Twyman Films, Welling Motion Pictures, Westcoast Films, Wholesome Film Ctr & Williams Films.

Lassiter. Tom Selleck & Jane Seymour. Directed by Roger Young. 1985. Warners. 100 min. Sound. 16mm Color. *Rental:* Swank Motion.

Last American Hero, The. Orig. Title: I Got a Name. Jeff Bridges & Geraldine Fitzgerald. Directed by Lamont Johnson. 1973. Fox. 95 min. Sound. 16mm Color. *Rental:* Films Inc.

Last American Virgin, The. Lawrence Monoson & Diane Franklin. Directed by Boaz Davidson. 1982. Cannon. 90 min. Sound. 16mm Color. *Rental:* Swank Motion. *Rental:* Swank Motion, Videotape version.

Last Angry Man, The. Paul Muni & David Wayne. Directed by Daniel Mann. 1959. Columbia. 100 min. Sound. 16mm B&W. *Rental:* Arcus Film, Budget Films, Cine Craft, Charard Motion Pics, Films Inc, Images Film, Kit Parker, Modern Sound, Roas Film, Twyman Film, Welling Motion Pictures, Westcoast Films & Wholesome Film Ctr.

Last Bandit, The. Forrest Tucker & Jack Holt. Directed by Joseph Kane. 1949. Republic. 80 min. Sound. 16mm Color. *Rental:* Ivy Films. *Sale:* Rep Pic Film & Nostalgia Merchant.

Last Banzai, The. 1962. Hearst. (Documentary). 50 min. Sound. 16mm B&W. *Sale:* King Features.

Last Cause, The. Directed by Alex Cramer & Stephen F. Franklin. 1976. Grove. (Documentary,Color Sequences). 165 min. Sound. 16mm B&W. *Rental:* Grove. *Sale:* Grove.

Last Challenge, The. Glenn Ford & Angie Dickinson. Directed by Richard Thorpe. 1967. MGM. 102 min. Sound. 16mm Color. *Rental:* MGM United. *Rental:* MGM United, Anamorphic version.

Last Chance. Michael Rennie, Daniella Bianchi & Tab Hunter. Directed by Mino Rosati. 1968. NTA. 95 min. Sound. 16mm Color. *Rental:* Ivy Films. *Sale:* Rep Pic Film.

Last Chance, The. John Hoy & Ray Reagan. Directed by Leopold Lindtberg. Fr. 1945. Switzerland. 105 min. Sound. 16mm B&W. subtitles. *Rental:* Kit Parker.

Last Command, The. Emil Jannings. Directed by Josef Von Sternberg. 1928. Paramount. 90 min. Silent. 16mm B&W. *Rental:* Films Inc.

Last Command, The. Sterling Hayden & Ernest Borgnine. Directed by Frank Lloyd. 1955. Republic. 110 min. Sound. 16mm B&W. *Rental:* Ivy Films. *Lease:* Rep Pic Film. *Sale:* Blackhawk Films & Cinema Concepts, Videotape version.

Last Crooked Mile, The. Don Barry & Ann Savage. Directed by Philip Ford. 1947. Republic. 71 min. Sound. 16mm B&W. *Rental:* Ivy Films. *Sale:* Rep Pic Film.

Last Day of the War, The. Trans. Title: Ultimo Dia de la Guerra, El. George Maharis & Maria Perschy. Directed by Juan Bardem. 1970. MGM. 90 min. Sound. 16mm Color. *Rental:* Willoughby Peer.

Last Days of John Dillinger, The. 1974. NBC. (Documentary, tinted). 52 min. Sound. 16mm *Rental:* Films Inc, Syracuse U Film & U Mich Media. *Sale:* Films Inc.

Last Days of Living, The. Directed by Malca Gillson. 1980. 57 min. Sound. 16mm Color. *Rental:* U Cal Media & Natl Film CN. *Sale:* Natl Film CN. *Sale:* Natl Film CN, *Rental:* Natl Film CN, Videotape version.

Last Days of Man on Earth, The. Jon Finch & Jenny Runacre. Directed by Robert Fuest. 1974. New World. 89 min. Sound. 16mm Color. *Rental:* Films Inc.

Last Days of Pompeii. 1914. Italy. (Cast unlisted, Music & sound effects only). 65 min. Sound. 16mm B&W. *Rental:* Budget Films & Film Classics. *Sale:* Film Classics. *Rental:* Film Classics, Videotape version.

Last Days of Pompeii, The. Preston Foster & Basil Rathbone. Directed by Ernest B. Schoedsack. 1935. RKO. 101 min. Sound. 16mm B&W. *Rental:* Films Inc.

Last Detail, The. Jack Nicholson & Randy Quaid. Directed by Hal Ashby. 1973. Columbia. 105 min. Sound. 16mm Color. *Rental:* Arcus Film, Budget Films, Films Inc, Inst Cinema, Images Film, Kit Parker, Newman Film Lib, Swank Motion, Twyman Films, Westcoast Films & Wholesome Film Ctr.

Last Embrace, The. Roy Scheider, Janet Margolin & Christoper Walken. Directed by Jonathan Demme. 1979. United Artists. 102 min. Sound. 16mm Color. *Rental:* MGM United.

Last Escape, The. Stuart Whitman. Directed by Walter Grauman. 1970. United Artists. 110 min. Sound. 16mm Color. *Rental:* MGM United.

Last Flight, The. Richard Barthelmess & Johnny Mack Brown. Directed by William Dieterle. 1931. Warners. 77 min. Sound. 16mm B&W. *Rental:* MGM United.

Last Flight of Noah's Ark, The. Elliot Gould & Genevieve Bujold. Directed by Charles Jarrott. 1980. Disney. 97 min. Sound. 16mm Color. *Rental:* MGM United, Swank Motion & Williams Films.

Last Frontier, The. Victor Mature & Robert Preston. Directed by Anthony Mann. 1955. Columbia. 98 min. Sound. 16mm Color. *Rental:* Arcus Film, Corinth Films, Modern Sound & Video Comm. *Rental:* Corinth Films, Anamorphic version.

Last Frontier Uprising, The. Monte Hale. Directed by Lesley Selander. 1947. Republic. 67 min. Sound. 16mm B&W. *Rental:* Ivy Films. *Sale:* Rep Pic Film.

Last Gangster, The. Edward G. Robinson & James Stewart. Directed by Edward Ludwig. 1939. MGM. 81 min. Sound. 16mm B&W. *Rental:* MGM United.

Last Giraffe, The. Susan Anspach & Simon Ward. Directed by Jack Couffer. 1979. Westfall. 106 min. Sound. 16mm Color. *Rental:* Films Inc & Modern Sound.

Last Grave at Dimbaza, The. 1974. South Africa. (Documentary). 57 min. Sound. 16mm Color. *Rental:* U Cal Media, U Mich Media, Unifilm & CA Newsreel. *Sale:* Natl Churches Christ, CA Newsreel & Unifilm.

Last Great Race, The. 1979. Northrim-Ruddy. (Documentary). 50 min. Sound. 16mm Color. *Rental:* Films Inc. *Sale:* Films Inc. *Sale:* Films Inc, Videotape version.

Last Guerilla, The. Trans. Title: Partisani. Rod Taylor & Adam West. Directed by Stole Jankovic. 1974. Yugoslavia. 118 min. Sound. 16mm Color. dubbed. *Rental:* Budget Films.

Last Hard Men, The. Charlton Heston & James Coburn. Directed by Andrew V. McLaglen. 1976. Fox. (Anamorphic). 103 min. Sound. 16mm Color. *Rental:* Films Inc & Williams Films.

Last Holiday, The. Sir Alec Guinness & Kay Walsh. Directed by Henry Cass. 1950. Britain. 88 min. Sound. 16mm B&W. *Rental:* Budget Films, Films Inc, Images Film, Kit Parker, Learning Corp Am, Twyman Films & U of IL Film. *Lease:* Learning Corp Am. *Rental:* Learning Corp Am, *Lease:* Learning Corp Am, Videotape version.

Last House on the Left, The. David Hess. Directed by Wes Craven. 1973. American International. 91 min. Sound. 16mm Color. *Rental:* Swank Motion.

Last Hunt, The. Robert Taylor & Stewart Granger. Directed by Richard Brooks. 1956. MGM. 103 min. Sound. 16mm Color. *Rental:* MGM United. *Rental:* MGM United, Videotape version.

Last Hunter, The. David Warbek & Tisa Farrow. 97 min. Sound. 16mm *Rental:* WW Enter. *Rental:* WW Enter, Videotape version.

Last Hurrah, The. Spencer Tracy & Jeffrey Hunter. Directed by John Ford. 1958. Columbia. 124 min. Sound. 16mm B&W. *Rental:* Arcus Films, Bosco Films, Buchan Pic, Budget Films, Cine Craft, Charard Motion Pics, Corinth Films, Films Inc, Images Film, Kit Parker, Natl Film Video, Roas Films, Swank Motion, Twyman Films, U of IL Films, Welling Motion Pictures, Westcoast Films, Wholesome Film Ctr & Williams Films. *Rental:* Swank Motion, Videotape version.

Last Laugh, The. Trans. Title: Letzte Mann, Der. Emil Jannings. Directed by F. W. Murnau. 1924. Germany. (Silent with music track). 107 min. Sound. B&W. *Rental:* Creative Film, Em Gee Film Lib, Film Images, Films Inc, Images Film, Kino Intl & Wholesome Film Ctr. *Sale:* Film Images, Images Film & Reel Images. *Rental:* Budget Films, Em Gee Film Lib, Janus Films, Kit Parker, Museum Mod Art, SD AV Ctr, U Cal Media, Wholesome Film Ctr & Willoughby Peer, *Sale:* Cinema Concepts, Festival Films, Griggs Movie, Morcraft Films, Natl Cinema & Reel Images, 75 min. 16mm version. *Rental:* Ivy Films, Super 8 silent version. *Sale:* Cinema Concepts & Images Film, Videotape version. *Sale:* Festival Films, 75 min. Videotape version.

Last Man on Earth, The. Vincent Price & Emma Danieli. Directed by Sidney Salkow. 1964. American International. 86 min. 16mm. *Rental:* Budget Films, Ivy Films, Roas Films, Welling Motion Pictures, Westcoast Films & Willoughby Peer.

Last Man on Earth. Jon Finch. Directed by Robert Fuest. Rel. 1974. New World. 78 min. Sound. 16mm. *Rental:* Films Inc.

Last Married Couple in America, The. George Segal & Natalie Wood. Directed by Gilbert Cates. 1980. Universal. 103 min. 16mm. *Rental:* Swank Motion.

Last Metro, The. Catherine Deneuve & Gerard Depardieu. Directed by Francois Truffaut. Fr. 1980. France. 133 min. 16mm. subtitles. *Rental:*   MGM United.

Last Mile, The. Orig. Title: All the World Wondered. Preston Foster & George E. Stone. Directed by Sam Bischoff. 1932. World Wide. 70 min. Sound. 16mm B&W. *Rental:* Budget Films, Classic Film Mus, Em Gee Film Lib & Video Comm. *Sale:* Am Mut Bio, Glenn Photo & Reel Images. *Sale:* Glenn Photo, Super 8 sound version. *Rental:* Video Comm, Videotape version.

Last Mile, The. Mickey Rooney & Don Barry. Directed by Howard Koch. 1959. United Artists. 81 min. Sound. 16mm B&W. *Rental:* MGM United.

Last Movie, The. Dennis Hopper, Julie Adams & Rod Cameron. Directed by Dennis Hopper. 1972. Universal. 95 min. Sound. 16mm Color. *Rental:* Swank Motion.

Last Musketeer, The. Dawn Addams & Georges Marchal. Directed by Fernando Cerchio. 1954. France. 95 min. Sound. 16mm B&W. dubbed. *Rental:* Ivy Films. *Sale:* Rep Pic Film.

Last Nazi, The: Albert Speer. Directed by Brian Nolan. 1976. Learning Corp. (Documentary). 72 min. Sound. 16mm Color. *Rental:* Budget Films, Iowa Films, Kent ST U Film, Learning Corp Am, Syracuse U Film & U of IL Film. *Sale:* Learning Corp Am.

Last of Mrs. Cheyney, The. Norma Shearer & Basil Rathbone. Directed by Sidney Franklin. 1929. MGM. 94 min. Sound. 16mm B&W. *Rental:* MGM United.

Last of Mrs. Cheyney, The. Joan Crawford & William Powell. Directed by Richard Boleslawski. 1937. MGM. 117 min. Sound. 16mm B&W. *Rental:* MGM United.

Last of Sheila, The. Richard Benjamin & Dyan Cannon. Directed by Herbert Ross. 1973. Warners. 120 min. Sound. 16mm Color. *Rental:* Film Ctr DC, Films Inc & Inst Cinema.

Last of the Badmen, The. George Montgomery & James Best. Directed by Paul Landres. 1957. Allied Artists. 79 min. Sound. 16mm Color. *Rental:* Ivy Films. *Sale:* Rep Pic Film.

Last of the Blue Devils, The. Directed by Bruce Ricker. 1980. Direct Cinema. (Documentary). 90 min. Sound. 16mm Color. *Rental:* Direct Cinema. *Sale:* Direct Cinema.

Last of the Buccaneers, The. Paul Henreid, Karin Booth & Jack Oakie. Directed by Lew Landers. 1950. Columbia. 79 min. Sound. 16mm Color. *Rental:* Maljack. *Lease:* Maljack. *Lease:* Maljack, Videotape version.

Last of the Cavalry, The *see* Army Girl.

Last of the Comanches, The. Broderick Crawford & Barbara Hale. Directed by Andre De Toth. 1953. Columbia. 85 min. Sound. 16mm Color. *Rental:* Bosco Films, Buchan Pic, Budget Films & Film Ctr DC.

Last of the Cuiva, The. Directed by Brian Moser. 1978. Britain. (Documentary). 65 min. Sound. 16mm Color. *Rental:* U Mich Media.

Last of the Desperados, The. James Craig & Jim Davis. Directed by Sam Newfield. 1955. Associated. 75 min. Sound. 16mm B&W. *Rental:* Ivy Films. *Sale:* Rep Pic Film.

Last of the Duanes, The. George O'Brien & Lucille Brown. Directed by Alfred M. Werker. 1930. Fox. 66 min. Sound. 16mm B&W. *Rental:* Films Inc.

Last of the Mobile Hot-Shots, The. James Coburn, Lynn Redgrave & Robert Hooks. Directed by Sidney Lumet. 1970. Warners. 108 min. Sound. 16mm Color. *Rental:* Swank Motion.

Last of the Mohicans, The. Wallace Beery & Barbara Bedford. Directed by Maurice Tourneur. 1920. Associated Producers. 50 min. Silent. 16mm B&W. *Rental:* Film Classics. *Sale:* Film Classics. *Sale:* Film Classics, Silent 8mm version. *Rental:* Film Classics, Videotape version.

Last of the Mohicans, The. Steve Forrest & Andrew Prine. Directed by James L. Conway. 1979. Viacom. 99 min. Sound. 16mm Color. *Rental:* Budget Films, Film Pres, Modern Sound, Westcoast Films & Williams Films. *Sale:* Lucerne Films. *Sale:* Lucerne Films, Videotape version.

Last of the Pagans, The. Ray Mala & Lotus Long. Directed by Richard Thorpe. 1935. MGM. 72 min. Sound. 16mm B&W. *Rental:* MGM United.

Last of the Red Hot Lovers, The. Alan Arkin, Paula Prentiss & Sally Kellerman. Directed by Arthur Hiller. 1972. Paramount. 98 min. Sound. 16mm Color. *Rental:* Films Inc.

Last of the Secret Agents?, The Marty Allen & Steve Rossi. Directed by Norman Abbott. 1966. Paramount. 90 min. Sound. 16mm Color. *Rental:* Films Inc.

Last of the Ski Bums, The. Directed by Dick Barrymore. 1969. UMC. (Documentary). 86 min. Sound. 16mm Color. *Rental:* Swank Motion & Twyman Films.

Last of the Vikings, The. Cameron Mitchell & Edmund Purdom. Directed by Giacomo Gentilomo. 1962. Italy. 102 min. Sound. 16mm Color. dubbed. *Rental:* Film Ctr DC.

Last of the Wild Horses, The. James Ellison & Mary Beth Hughes. Directed by Robert L. Lippert. 1949. Screen Guild. 82 min. Sound. 16mm B&W. *Rental:* Budget Films, Film Ctr DC, Lewis Films & Westcoast Films.

Last Outlaw, The. Gary Cooper. Directed by Arthur Rosson. 1927. Paramount. 70 min. Silent. 16mm B&W. *Sale:* Blackhawk Films.

Last Outlaw, The. Harry Carey, Hoot Gibson & Henry B. Walthall. Directed by Christy Cabanne. 1936. RKO. 72 min. Sound. 16mm B&W. *Rental:* Learning Corp Am, Modern Sound & Budget Films. *Sale:* Glenn Photo & Learning Corp Am.

Last Outpost, The. Ronald Reagan & Rhonda Fleming. Directed by Lewis R. Foster. 1951. Paramount. 89 min. Sound. 16mm B&W. *Rental:* Video Comm & Willoughby Peer.

Last Performance, The. Orig. Title: Magician, The. Conrad Veidt & Mary Philbin. Directed by Paul Fejos. 1927. Universal. 70 min. Silent. 16mm B&W. *Rental:* Em Gee Film Lib.

Last Picture Show, The. Timothy Bottoms, Jeff Bridges, Ben Johnson & Cloris Leachman. Directed by Peter Bogdanovich. 1971. BBS. 118 min. Sound. 16mm B&W. *Rental:* Films Inc & Swank Motion.

Last Posse, The. Broderick Crawford & John Derek. Directed by Alfred M. Werker. 1953. Columbia. 73 min. Sound. 16mm B&W. *Rental:* Inst Cinema & Modern Sound.

Last Rebel, The. Joe Namath & Woody Strode. Directed by Denys McCoy. 1971. Columbia. 88 min. Sound. 16mm Color. *Rental:* Cine Craft, Westcoast Films & Williams Films, videotape version.

Last Remake of Beau Geste, The. Marty Feldman, Ann-Margret & Michael York. Directed by Marty Feldman. 1977. Universal. 85 min. Sound. 16mm Color. *Rental:* Swank Motion.

Last Resort, The. Directed by Daniel Keller. 1976. Green Mountain Post. (Documentary). 60 min. Sound. 16mm Color. *Rental:* Green MT & U Mich Media. *Sale:* Green MT. *Rental:* Green MT, *Sale:* Green MT, Videotape version.

Last Rhino, The. David Ellis & Tim Samuels. Directed by Henry Geddes. 1965. Britain. 55 min. Sound. 16mm Color. *Rental:* Films Inc & Wholesome Film Ctr.

Last Ride, The. Richard Travis & Eleanor Parker. Directed by D. Ross Lederman. 1944. Warners. 56 min. Sound. 16mm B&W. *Rental:* MGM United.

Last Roman, The. Orson Welles & Laurence Harvey. Directed by Robert Siodmak. 1969. Allied Artists. 92 min. Sound. 16mm Color. *Sale:* Blackhawk Films.

Last Run, The. George C. Scott & Tony Musante. Directed by Richard Fleischer. 1971. MGM. 99 min. Sound. 16mm Color. *Rental:* MGM United.

Last Safari, The. Kaz Garas & Stewart Granger. Directed by Henry Hathaway. 1967. Paramount. 114 min. Sound. 16mm Color. *Rental:* Films Inc.

Last Shot You Hear, The. Hugh Marlowe. Directed by Gordon Hessler. 1969. Fox. 91 min. Sound. 16mm B&W. *Rental:* Films Inc.

Last Stagecoach West, The. Jim Davis & Mary Castle. Directed by Joseph Kane. 1957. Republic. 70 min. Sound. 16mm B&W. *Rental:* Ivy Films. *Sale:* Rep Pic Film.

Last Stand in Eden, The. 1978. National Geographic. (Documentary). 59 min. Sound. 16mm Color. *Rental:* Natl Geog & U Mich Media. *Sale:* Natl Geog. *Sale:* Natl Geog, Videotape version.

Last Starfighter, The. Robert Preston, Lance Guest & Dan O'Herlihy. Directed by Nick Castle. 1985. Universal. 100 min. Sound. 16mm Color. *Rental:* Swank Motion.

Last Summer. Barbara Hershey & Cathy Burns. Directed by Frank Perry. 1969. Allied Artists. 97 min. Sound. 16mm Color. *Rental:* Hurlock Cine.

Last Summer, The. Grigor Vachkov & Bogdan Spasov. Directed by Christo Christov. Bulgarian. 1974. 90 min. Sound. 16mm Color. subtitles. *Rental:* Films Inc.

Last Summer Won't Happen. 60 min. Sound. 16mm Color. *Rental:* Westcoast Films.

Last Sunset, The. Rock Hudson & Kirk Douglas. Directed by Robert Aldrich. 1961. Universal. 112 min. Sound. 16mm Color. *Rental:* Swank Motion.

Last Supper, The. Directed by Tomas Gutierrez Alea. Span. 1977. Cuba. (Cast Unlisted). 110 min. Sound. 16mm Color. subtitles. *Rental:* New Cinema & New Yorker Films. *Sale:* Unifilm. *Rental:* New Cinema, French subtitled version.

Last Tango in Paris, The. Marlon Brando. Directed by Bernardo Bertolucci. 1973. United Artists. 125 min. Sound. 16mm Color. *Rental:* MGM United. *Rental:* MGM United, Videotape version.

Last Ten Days, The. Oskar Werner & Albin Skoda. Directed by G. W. Pabst. Ger. 1955. Columbia. 108 min. Sound. 16mm B&W. subtitles. *Rental:* Films Inc.

Last Three, The. Orig. Title: That Nazty Nuisance. Robert Watson & Johnny Arthur. Directed by Glenn Tryon. 1943. United Artists. 44 min. Sound. 16mm B&W. *Rental:* Budget Films.

Last Time I Saw Archie, The. Robert Mitchum & Jack Webb. Directed by Jack Webb. 1961. United Artists. 98 min. Sound. 16mm B&W. *Rental:* MGM United.

Last Time I Saw Paris, The. Elizabeth Taylor & Van Johnson. Directed by Richard Brooks. 1954. MGM. 116 min. Sound. 16mm Color. *Rental:* MGM United.

Last to Know, The. Directed by Bonnie Friedman. 1980. New Day. (Documentary). 55 min. Sound. 16mm Color. *Rental:* New Day Films. *Sale:* New Day Films. *Sale:* New Day Films, Videotape version.

Last Tomahawk, The. Anthony Steffens & Karin Dor. 1966. Italy. 90 min. Sound. 16mm Color. dubbed. *Rental:* Westcoast Films.

Last Trail, The. Tom Mix & Carmelita Geraghty. Directed by Lewis Seiler. 1927. Fox. 58 min. Silent. 16mm B&W. *Rental:* Killiam Collect.

Last Train, The. Romy Schneider & Jean-Louis Trintignant. Directed by Pierre Granier-Deferre. 1973. Italy. 90 min. Sound. 16mm Color. dubbed. *Rental:* Budget Films.

Last Train from Bombay, The. Jon Hall. Directed by Fred F. Sears. 1952. Columbia. 72 min. Sound. 16mm B&W. *Rental:* Inst Cinema.

Last Train from Gun Hill, The. Kirk Douglas & Anthony Quinn. Directed by John Sturges. 1959. Paramount. 98 min. Sound. Color. *Rental:* Films Inc. *Sale:* Blackhawk Films & Cinema Concepts, Videotape version.

Last Tribes of Mindanao, The. 1972. National Geographic. (Documentary). 52 min. Sound. 16mm Color. *Rental:* Iowa Films, Natl Geog, Syracuse U Film, U Mich Media & Wholesome Film Ctr. *Sale:* Natl Geog. *Sale:* Natl Geog, Videotape version.

Last Tycoon, The. Robert De Niro, Robert Mitchum & Tony Curtis. Directed by Elia Kazan. 1976. Paramount. 122 min. Sound. 16mm Color. *Rental:* Films Inc.

Last Unicorn, The. Directed by Jules Bass & Arthur Rankin. 1982. AFD. (Animated). 88 min. Sound. 16mm Color. *Rental:* Swank Motion.

Last Valley, The. Michael Caine & Omar Sharif. Directed by James Clavel. 1971. ABC. 126 min. Sound. 16mm Color. *Rental:* Films Inc. *Sale:* ABC Film Lib, Super 8 sound version.

Last Vikings, The. 1972. National Geographic. (Documentary). 52 min. Sound. 16mm Color. *Rental:* Natl Geog, Syracuse U Film, U Mich Media & Wholesome Film Ctr. *Sale:* Natl Geog. *Sale:* Natl Geog, Videotape version.

Last Voyage, The. Robert Stack & Dorothy Malone. Directed by Andrew Stone. 1960. MGM. 91 min. Sound. 16mm Color. *Rental:* MGM United.

Last Wagon, The. Richard Widmark & Felicia Farr. Directed by Delmer Daves. 1956. Fox. 98 min. Sound. 16mm Color. *Rental:* Films Inc. *Rental:* Films Inc, Anamorphic version.

Last Waltz, The. Directed by Martin Scorsese. 1978. United Artists. (Concert). 106 min. Sound. 16mm Color. *Rental:* MGM United. *Rental:* MGM United, Videotape version.

Last Warning, The. Laura La Plante & Montagu Love. Directed by Paul Leni. 1929. Universal. 89 min. Sound. 16mm B&W. *Rental:* Swank Motion.

Last Wave, The. Richard Chamberlain & Olivia Hammett. Directed by Peter Weir. 1978. Australia. 106 min. Sound. 16mm Color. *Rental:* Budget Films, Cinema Five, Corinth Films & Ivy Films. *Rental:* Cinema Five & WW Enter, Videotape version.

Last Woman, The. Gerard Depardieu & Ornella Muti. Directed by Marco Ferreri. Fr. 1976. France. 111 min. Sound. 16mm Color. subtitles. *Rental:* Corinth Films.

Last Woman on Earth, The. Anthony Carbone. Directed by Roger Corman. 1957. Allied Artists. 72 min. Sound. 16mm Color. *Rental:* Hurlock Cine.

Last Words, The. 1979. Penn State. (Documentary). 58 min. Sound. 16mm Color. *Rental:* Penn St AV Serv. *Sale:* Penn St AV Serv. *Rental:* Penn St AV Serv, *Sale:* Penn St AV Serv, Videotape version.

Last Year at Marienbad. Trans. Title: Annee Derniere a Marienbad, L'. Delphine Seyrig. Directed by Alain Resnais. Fr. 1962. France. 93 min. Sound. 16mm B&W. subtitles. *Rental:* Budget Films, Corinth Films, Images Film, Macmillan Films, Syracuse U Film & Wholesome Film Ctr. *Sale:* Cinema Concepts, Festival Films, Natl Cinema, Reel Images & Images Film. *Lease:* Macmillan Films & Corinth Films. *Sale:* Tamarelles French Film, Festival Films & Images Film, Videotape version.

Late Autumn. Trans. Title: Akibiyori. Chishu Ryu. Directed by Yasujiro Ozu. Jap. 1960. Japan. 127 min. Sound. 16mm B&W. subtitles. *Rental:* New Cinema & New Yorker Films.

Late George Apley, The. Ronald Colman & Edna Best. Directed by Joseph L. Mankiewicz. 1947. Fox. 90 min. Sound. 16mm B&W. *Rental:* Films Inc.

Late Great Me, Story of a Teenage Alcoholic, The. 1980. Daniel Wilson. 71 min. Sound. 16mm Color. *Rental:* Daniel Wilson. *Rental:* Daniel Wilson, Videotape version.

Late Great Planet Earth, The. Directed by Robert Amram. 1979. Pacific International. (Documentary). 90 min. Sound. 16mm Color. *Rental:* Twyman Films.

Late Matthew Pascal, The. Lois Moran & Ivan Mozhukhin. Directed by Marcel L'Herbier. Fr. 1926. France. 159 min. Silent. 16mm B&W. *Rental:* Museum Mod Art.

Late Show, The. Lily Tomlin & Art Carney. Directed by Robert Benton. 1977. Warners. 94 min. Sound. 16mm Color. *Rental:* Films Inc, Swank Motion, Twyman Films & Williams Films.

Late Spring. Chishu Ryu. Directed by Yasujiro Ozu. Jap. 1949. Japan. 107 min. Sound. 16mm B&W. subtitles. *Rental:* New Cinema & New Yorker Films.

Latin America. 1964. Canada. (Documentary). 59 min. Sound. 16mm B&W. *Rental:* McGraw-Hill Films. *Sale:* McGraw-Hill Films.

Latin Lovers. Lana Turner & Ricardo Montalban. Directed by Mervyn LeRoy. 1953. MGM. 104 min. Sound. 16mm Color. *Rental:* MGM United.

Latitude Zero. Joseph Cotten & Cesar Romero. Directed by Inoshiro Honda. 1970. Japan. 99 min. Sound. 16mm Color. *Rental:* Swank Motion.

Laugh & Get Rich. Edna May Oliver & Dorothy Lee. Directed by Gregory La Cava. 1931. RKO. 72 min. Sound. 16mm *Rental:* RKO General Pics.

Laughing Anne. Margaret Lockwood & Wendell Corey. Directed by Herbert Wilcox. 1954. Britain. 91 min. Sound. 16mm B&W. *Rental:* Ivy Films.

Laughing at Danger. Richard Talmadge. Directed by James W. Horne. 1924. FBO. 60 min. Silent. Super 8 B&W. *Rental:* Ivy Films. *Sale:* Cinema Concepts.

Laughing at Danger. Frankie Darro & Mantan Moreland. Directed by Howard Bretherton. 1940. Monogram. 62 min. Sound. 16mm B&W. *Rental:* Hurlock Cine.

Laughing Irish Eyes. Phil Regan & Raymond Hatton. Directed by Joseph Santley. 1936. Republic. 54 min. Sound. 16mm B&W. *Rental:* Alba House & Ivy Films. *Sale:* Rep Pic Film.

Laughing Lady, The. Francis L. Sullivan & Felix Aylmer. Directed by Paul L. Stein. 1947. Britain. 92 min. Sound. 16mm Color. *Rental:* Ivy Films. *Sale:* Rep Pic Film.

Laughing Policeman, The. Walter Matthau & Bruce Dern. Directed by Stuart Rosenberg. 1974. Fox. 111 min. Sound. 16mm Color. *Rental:* Films Inc.

Laughing Till It Hurts. Charlie Chaplin. Directed by Nathan Segaloff. 1969. Wholesome. 70 min. Sound. 16mm B&W. *Rental:* Wholesome Film Ctr.

Laughter. Nancy Carroll & Fredric March. Directed by Harry D'Arrast. 1930. Paramount. 79 min. Sound. 16mm B&W. *Rental:* Swank Motion.

Laughter in Paradise. Alastair Sim & Audrey Hepburn. Directed by Mario Zampi. 1951. Britain. 95 min. Sound. 16mm B&W. *Rental:* Films Inc & Janus Films.

Laughter in the Dark. Nicol Williamson & Anna Karina. Directed by Tony Richardson. 1969. Britain. 104 min. Sound. 16mm Color. *Rental:* MGM United.

Laughter Thru Tears. Yiddish Art Theatre. Directed by G. Gricher. Yiddish. 1933. 82 min. Sound. 16mm B&W. subtitles. *Rental:* Films Inc.

Laura. Gene Tierney, Dana Andrews & Clifton Webb. Directed by Otto Preminger. 1944. Fox. 88 min. Sound. 16mm B&W. *Rental:* Films Inc. *Sale:* Festival Films, Videotape version.

Laurel & Hardy's Laughing Twenties. 1965. MGM. (Antholgy). 91 min. Sound. 16mm B&W. *Rental:* MGM United.

Lavender Hill Mob, The. Sir Alec Guinness & Stanley Holloway. Directed by Charles Crichton. 1951. Britain. 80 min. Sound. 16mm B&W. *Rental:* Budget Films, Films Inc, Images Film, Kit Parker, Learning Corp Am, Roas Films, Syracuse U Film, Twyman Films, U of IL Film, Westcoast Films & Wholesome Film Ctr. *Sale:* Learning Corp Am.

Law & Order *see* Billy the Kid's Law & Order.

Law & Disorder. Sir Michael Redgrave & Robert Morley. Directed by Henry Cornelius & Charles Crichton. 1958. Britain. 76 min. Sound. 16mm B&W. *Rental:* Cine Craft & Welling Motion Pictures.

Law & Disorder. Carroll O'Connor & Ernest Borgnine. Directed by Ivan Passer. 1974. Columbia. 99 min. Sound. 16mm Color. *Rental:* Arcus Film, Swank Motion, Westcoast Films & Williams Films.

Law & Jake Wade, The. Robert Taylor & Richard Widmark. Directed by John Sturges. 1958. MGM. 88 min. Sound. 16mm Color. *Rental:* MGM United. *Rental:* MGM United, Anamorphic version.

Law & Lawless. Jack Hoxie. Directed by Armand Schaefer. 1932. Majestic. 60 min. Sound. 16mm B&W. *Rental:* Mogulls Films.

Law & Order. Directed by Frederick Wiseman. 1969. Frederick Wiseman. (Documentary). 81 min. Sound. 16mm B&W. *Rental:* U Mich Media & Zipporah Films. *Lease:* Zipporah Films.

Law & Order. Walter Huston & Harry Carey. Directed by Edward L. Cahn. 1932. Universal. 70 min. Sound. 16mm B&W. *Rental:* Swank Motion.

Law & Order. Ronald Reagan & Dorothy Malone. Directed by Nathan Juran. 1953. Universal. 80 min. Sound. 16mm Color. *Rental:* Swank Motion.

Law & the Lady, The. Greer Garson & Michael Wilding. Directed by Edwin Knopf. 1951. MGM. 90 min. Sound. 16mm B&W. *Rental:* MGM United.

Law & the Prophets, The. 1967. NBC. (Documentary). 51 min. Sound. 16mm Color. *Rental:* McGraw-Hill Films & Syracuse U Film. *Sale:* McGraw-Hill Films.

Law in Her Hands, The. Margaret Lindsay & Glenda Farrell. Directed by William Clemens. 1936. Warners. 58 min. Sound. 16mm B&W. *Rental:* MGM United.

Law Men. Johnny Mack Brown. Directed by Lambert Hillyer. 1944. Monogram. 55 min. Sound. 16mm B&W. *Rental:* Hurlock Cine.

Law of Compensation. Norma Talmadge & Chester Barnett. Directed by Julius Steger & Joseph A. Golden. 1917. 16mm *Rental:* A Twyman Pres.

Law of Gravitation, The. 1969. Britain. (Documentary, kinescope). 55 min. Sound. 16mm B&W. *Rental:* U Cal Media.

Law of the Badlands. Tim Holt & Joan Dixon. Directed by Lesley Selander. 1951. RKO. 60 min. Sound. 16mm *Rental:* RKO General Pics.

Law of the Golden West. Monte Hale. Directed by Philip Ford. 1949. Republic. 59 min. Sound. 16mm B&W. *Rental:* Ivy Films. *Sale:* Rep Pic Film & Nostalgia Merchant.

Law of the Lash. Lash LaRue. Directed by Ray Taylor. 1947. PRC. 54 min. Sound. 16mm B&W. *Rental:* Ivy Films. *Sale:* Classics Assoc NY, Rep Pic Film & Nostalgia Merchant.

Law of the Lawless. Dale Robertson & Yvonne De Carlo. Directed by William Claxton. 1964. Paramount. (Anamorphic). 87 min. Sound. 16mm Color. *Rental:* Films Inc.

Law of the North. Bill Cody. Directed by Harry Fraser. 1932. Monogram. 60 min. Sound. 16mm B&W. *Rental:* Mogulls Film.

Law of the Pampas. William Boyd. Directed by Nate Watt. 1939. Paramount. 60 min. Sound. 16mm B&W. *Rental:* Mogulls Films.

Law of the Panhandle. Johnny Mack Brown. Directed by Lewis D. Collins. 1950. Monogram. 55 min. Sound. 16mm B&W. *Rental:* Cinema Concepts.

Law of the Range. Johnny Mack Brown. Directed by Ray Taylor. 1941. Universal. 60 min. Sound. 16mm B&W. *Rental:* Willoughby Peer.

Law of the Rio Grande. Bob Custer. Directed by Bennett Cohn & Forrest Sheldon. 1931. Syndicate. 57 min. Sound. 16mm B&W. *Sale:* Natl Cinema.

Law of the Saddle. Bob Livingston. Directed by Melville De Loy. 1944. PRC. 60 min. Sound. 16mm B&W. *Sale:* Natl Cinema.

Law of the Sea. Ralph Ince & Sally Blane. Directed by Otto Brower. 1932. Monogram. 70 min. Sound. 16mm B&W. *Rental:* Mogulls Films.

Law of the Timber. Marjorie Reynolds & Monte Blue. Directed by Bernard B. Ray. 1941. PRC. 70 min. Sound. 16mm B&W. *Rental:* Mogulls Films.

Law of the Tropics. Constance Bennett & Jeffery Lynn. Directed by Ray Enright. 1941. Warners. 76 min. Sound. 16mm B&W. *Rental:* MGM United.

Law of the Underworld. Chester Morris, Anne Shirley & Walter Abel. Directed by Lew Landers. 1938. RKO. 60 min. Sound. 16mm B&W. *Rental:* Films Inc. *Lease:* Films Inc.

Law of the Valley. Johnny Mack Brown. Directed by Howard Bretherton. 1945. Monogram. 55 min. Sound. 16mm B&W. *Rental:* Hurlock Cine.

Law of the Wolf. Dennis Moore & Rin-Tin-Tin Jr. Directed by Raymond K. Johnson. 1942. Metropolitan. 55 min. Sound. 16mm B&W. *Rental:* Westcoast Films.

Law Rides, The. Bob Steele. Directed by Robert N. Bradbury. 1936. Monogram. 60 min. Sound. 16mm B&W. *Rental:* Budget Films.

Law Rides Again, The. Hoot Gibson & Betty Miles. Directed by Alan James. 1943. 58 min. Sound. 16mm *Rental:* Budget Films.

Law vs. Billy the Kid, The. Scott Brady & Betta St. John. Directed by William Castle. 1954. Columbia. 73 min. Sound. 16mm Color. *Rental:* Modern Sound.

Law West of Tombstone, The. Ward Bond & Harry Carey. Directed by Glenn Tryon. 1939. RKO. 73 min. Sound. 16mm *Rental:* RKO General Pics.

Lawbreakers, The. Jack Warden, Ken Lynch & Vera Miles. Directed by Joseph Newman. 1961. MGM. 80 min. Sound. 16mm B&W. *Rental:* MGM United.

Lawful Larceny. Bebe Daniels. Directed by Lowell Sherman. 1930. RKO. 70 min. Sound. 16mm B&W. *Rental:* Films Inc. *Lease:* Films Inc.

Lawless, The. Orig. Title: Dividing Line, The. McDonald Carey & Gail Russell. Directed by Joseph Losey. 1950. Paramount. 83 min. Sound. 16mm B&W. *Rental:* Film Ctr DC & Willoughby Peer.

Lawless Breed, The. Rock Hudson & Julia Adams. Directed by Raoul Walsh. 1952. Universal. 83 min. Sound. 16mm Color. *Rental:* Swank Motion.

Lawless Code, The. Johnny Wakely. Directed by Oliver Drake. 1949. Monogram. 55 min. Sound. 16mm B&W. *Rental:* Hurlock Cine.

Lawless Cowboys, The. Whip Wilson. Directed by Lewis D. Collins. 1951. Monogram. 58 min. Sound. 16mm B&W. *Rental:* Hurlock Cine.

Lawless Eighties, The. Buster Crabbe. Directed by Joseph Kane. 1957. Republic. 70 min. Sound. 16mm B&W. *Rental:* Ivy Films. *Sale:* Rep Pic Film.

Lawless Frontier, The. John Wayne. Directed by Robert N. Bradbury. 1935. Monogram. 58 min. Sound. 16mm B&W. *Rental:* Ivy Films, Mogulls Films & Willoughby Peer. *Sale:* Cinema Concepts, Classics Assoc NY & Rep Pic Film.

Lawless Land, The. Johnny Mack Brown. Directed by Sam Newfield. 1936. Republic. 60 min. Sound. 16mm B&W. *Rental:* Ivy Films.

Lawless Nineties, The. John Wayne & Ann Rutherford. Directed by Joseph Kane. 1936. Republic. 56 min. Sound. 16mm B&W. *Rental:* Ivy Films.

Lawless Range. John Wayne. Directed by Robert N. Bradbury. 1935. Republic. 56 min. Sound. 16mm B&W. *Rental:* Budget Films & Ivy Films. *Sale:* Rep Pic Film.

Lawless Rider. Johnny Carpenter. Directed by Yakima Canutt. 1954. United Artists. 65 min. Sound. 16mm B&W. *Rental:* Westcoast Films.

Lawless Street, A. Randolph Scott & Angela Lansbury. Directed by Joseph Lewis. 1955. Columbia. 78 min. Sound. 16mm Color. *Rental:* Kit Parker.

Lawless Valley. George O'Brien. Directed by David Howard. 1938. RKO. 59 min. Sound. 16mm B&W. *Rental:* Films Inc.

Lawman. Burt Lancaster, Robert Ryan & Lee J. Cobb. Directed by Michael Winner. 1971. United Artists. 99 min. Sound. 16mm Color. *Rental:* MGM United & Westcoast Films.

Lawman Is Born, A. Johnny Mack Brown. Directed by Albert Gray. 1937. Republic. 60 min. Sound. 16mm B&W. *Rental:* Ivy Films & Mogulls Films. *Sale:* Cinema Concepts, Natl Cinema & Reel Images.

Lawrence of Arabia. Peter O'Toole & Jose Ferrer. Directed by David Lean. 1962. Columbia. 200 min. Sound. 16mm Color. *Rental:* Arcus Film, Buchan Pic, Budget Films, Cine Craft, Corinth Films, Films Inc, Inst Cinema, Ivy Films, Kit Parker, Modern Sound, Natl Film Video, Newman Film Lib, Swank Motion, Syracuse U Film, Twyman Films, U of IL Film, Welling Motion Pictures, Westcoast Films, Wholesome Film Ctr & Images Film. *Rental:* Corinth Films, Images Films, Kit Parker, Swank Motion, Twyman Films & Williams Films, Anamorphic version. *Rental:* Swank Motion, Videotape version.

Law's Lash, The. Klondike & Robert Ellis. Directed by Noel Smith. 1928. Pathe. 60 min. Silent. 16mm B&W. *Sale:* Blackhawk Films. *Rental:* Ivy Films, *Sale:* Blackhawk Films, Super 8 Silent version. *Sale:* Blackhawk Films, Silent 8mm version.

Lawyer, The. Barry Newman. Directed by Sidney J. Furie. 1969. Paramount. 117 min. Sound. 16mm Color. *Rental:* Films Inc.

Lawyer, The. 1968. (Color sequences). 45 min. Sound. 16mm Color. *Rental:* Canyon Cinema.

Lawyer Man. William Powell & Joan Blondell. Directed by William Dieterle. 1932. Warners. 68 min. Sound. 16mm B&W. *Rental:* MGM United.

Lawyers, The. 1967. Britain. (Documentary). 87 min. Sound. 16mm B&W. *Rental:* U Mich Media.

Laxdale Hall *see* Scotch on the Rocks.

Lay My Burden Down. Directed by Jack Willis. 1966. NET. (Documentary). 60 min. Sound. 16mm B&W. *Rental:* Budget Films, Indiana AVCtr, New Time Films & U Cal Media. *Sale:* Indiana AV Ctr & New Time Films.

Lay That Rifle Down. Robert Lowery. Directed by Charles Lamont. 1955. Republic. 71 min. Sound. 16mm B&W. *Rental:* Ivy Films. *Sale:* Rep Pic Film.

Lazarillo. Marco Paoletti & Juan Jose Menendez. Directed by Cesar Ardavin. Span. 1959. Spain. 100 min. Sound. 16mm B&W. subtitles. *Rental:* Films Inc.

Lazy Bones. Buck Jones & Zasu Pitts. Directed by Frank Borzage. 1925. Fox. 79 min. Silent. 16mm B&W. *Rental:* Killiam Collect.

Lazy River. Robert Young & Jean Parker. Directed by George B. Seitz. 1934. MGM. 77 min. Sound. 16mm B&W. *Rental:* MGM United.

L'Chaim-To Life. Directed by Harold Mayer. 1973. Mayer. (Documentary). 82 min. Sound. 16mm B&W. *Rental:* Alden Films & Welling Motion Pictures.

Le Mans. Steve McQueen. Directed by Lee Katzin. 1971. National General. 106 min. Sound. 16mm Color. *Rental:* Inst Cinema, Swank Motion, Twyman Films & Williams Films.

Leadbelly. Roger E. Mosley & Madge Sinclair. Directed by Gordon Parks. 1976. Paramount. 126 min. Sound. 16mm Color. *Rental:* Films Inc.

Leaders in American Medicine: Albert Band Hastings. Orig. Title: Dr. Hastings. 1973. US Government. (Documentary). 60 min. Sound. 16mm B&W. *Sale:* Natl AV Ctr.

Leaders in American Medicine: Cecil J. Watson, MD. 1974. US Government. (Documentary). 58 min. Sound. 16mm B&W. *Sale:* Natl AV Ctr.

Leaders in American Medicine: Charles Higgins, MD. Orig. Title: Dr. Huggins. 1973. US Government. (Documentary). 60 min. Sound. 16mm B&W. *Sale:* Natl AV Ctr.

Leaders in American Medicine: Emile Holman MD. 1974. US Government. (Documentary). 51 min. Sound. 16mm B&W. *Sale:* Natl AV Ctr.

Leaders in American Medicine: George L. Engle MD. 1974. US Government. (Documentary). Sound. 16mm B&W. *Sale:* Natl AV Ctr.

Leaders in American Medicine: George W. Corner MD. 1974. US Government. (Documentary). 57 min. Sound. 16mm B&W. *Sale:* Natl AV Ctr.

Leaders in American Medicine: Grace A. Goldsmith MD. 1974. US Government. (Documentary). 58 min. Sound. 16mm B&W. *Sale:* Natl AV Ctr.

Leaders in American Medicine: Helen B. Tausig MD. 1973. US Government. (Documentary). 50 min. Sound. 16mm B&W. *Sale:* Natl AV Ctr.

Leaders in American Medicine: Howard C. Taylor Jr. MD. 1974. US Government. (Documentary). 57 min. Sound. 16mm B&W. *Sale:* Natl AV Ctr.

Leaders in American Medicine: Jacques Genest MD. 1974. US Government. (Documentary). 51 min. Sound. 16mm B&W. *Sale:* Natl AV Ctr.

Leaders in American Medicine: Joseph T. Wearn MD. 1973. US Government. (Documentary). 48 min. Sound. 16mm B&W. *Sale:* Natl AV Ctr.

Leaders in American Medicine: Karl F. Meyer MD. 1974. US Government. (Documentary). 59 min. Sound. 16mm B&W. *Sale:* Natl AV Ctr.

Leaders in American Medicine: L. T. Coggeshall MD. 1975. US Government. (Documentary). 55 min. Sound. 16mm B&W. *Sale:* Natl AV Ctr.

Leaders in American Medicine: Leo G. Rigler MD. 1973. US Government. (Documentary). 60 min. Sound. 16mm B&W. *Sale:* Natl AV Ctr.

Leaders in American Medicine: Lester R. Dragstedt MD. 1973. US Government. (Documentary). 60 min. Sound. 16mm B&W. *Sale:* Natl AV Ctr.

Leaders in American Medicine: Martin M. Cummings MD. 1973. US Gonernment. (Documentary). 51 min. Sound. 16mm B&W. *Sale:* Natl AV Ctr.

Leaders in American Medicine: Matthew Walker MD. 1974. US Government. (Documentary). 56 min. Sound. 16mm B&W. *Sale:* Natl AV Ctr.

Leaders in American Medicine: Maxwell M. Wintrobe MD. 1974. US Government. (Documentary). 57 min. Sound. 16mm B&W. *Sale:* Natl AV Ctr.

Leaders in American Medicine: Owen H. Wangensteen MD. 1973. US Government. (Documentary). 60 min. Sound. 16mm B&W. *Sale:* Natl AV Ctr.

Leaders in American Medicine: Shields Warren MD. 1973. US Government. (Documentary). 61 min. Sound. 16mm B&W. *Sale:* Natl AV Ctr.

Leaders in American Medicine: T. R. Harrison MD. 1975. US Government. (Documentary). 55 min. Sound. 16mm B&W. *Sale:* Natl AV Ctr.

Leaders in American Medicine: W. Barry Wood Jr. MD. 1973. US Government. (Documentary). 60 min. Sound. 16mm B&W. *Sale:* Natl AV Ctr.

Leaders in American Medicine: W. Montague Cobb MD. 1976. US Government. (Documentary). 58 min. Sound. 16mm B&W. *Sale:* Natl AV Ctr.

Leaders in American Medicine: Walsh McDermott MD. 1973. US Government. (Documentary). 60 min. Sound. 16mm B&W. *Sale:* Natl AV Ctr.

Leading Discussions: Whole Class. 1976. Indiana University. (Lecture). 49 min. Videotape Color. *Sale:* Indiana AV Ctr.

Leadville Gunslinger. Allan Lane. Directed by Harry Keller. 1951. Republic. 54 min. Sound. 16mm B&W. *Rental:* Ivy Films. *Sale:* Rep Pic Film & Nostalgia Merchant.

League of Frightened Men, The. Walter Connolly & Lionel Stander. Directed by Alfred E. Green. 1936. Columbia. Sound. 16mm B&W. *Rental:* Kit Parker.

League of Gentlemen, The. Jack Hawkins & Nigel Patrick. Directed by Basil Dearden. 1961. Britain. 114 min. Sound. 16mm B&W. *Rental:* Janus Films & Films Inc.

League of Nations, The: The Hope of Mankind. 1976. Britain. (Documentary). 52 min. Sound. 16mm Color. *Rental:* Time-Life Multimedia. *Sale:* Time-Life Multimedia. *Rental:* Time-Life Multimedia, *Sale:* Time-Life Multimedia, Videotape version.

Learning to Love. Constance Talmadge. Directed by Sidney A. Franklin. 1925. 16mm *Rental:* A Twyman Pres.

Lease of Life. Robert Donat & Kay Walsh. Directed by Charles Frend. 1955. Britain. 93 min. Sound. 16mm Color. *Rental:* Janus Films.

Leather Boys, The. Rita Tushingham & Colin Campbell. Directed by Sidney J. Furie. 1963. 103 min. Sound. Videotape B&W. *Sale:* Films Inc & Vidamerica.

Leather Burners, The. William Boyd. Directed by Joseph Henabery. 1943. United Artists. 68 min. Sound. 16mm B&W. *Lease:* Cinema Concepts. *Rental:* Budget Films. *Sale:* Cinema Concepts, Super 8 Sound version. *Sale:* Cinema Concepts, Videotape version.

Leather Pushers, The. Richard Arlen & Andy Devine. Directed by John Rawlins. 1940. Universal. 60 min. Sound. 16mm B&W. *Rental:* Film Ctr DC, Mogulls Films & Newman Film Lib.

Leather Saint, The. John Derek & Paul Douglas. Directed by Alvin Ganzer. 1956. Paramount. 86 min. Sound. 16mm B&W. *Rental:* Films Inc.

Leatherneck, The. William Boyd. Directed by Howard Higgin. 1929. Pathe. 65 min. Silent. 16mm B&W. *Sale:* Griggs Movie. *Sale:* Film Classics & Griggs Movie, Silent 8mm version.

Leathernecks Have Landed, The. Orig. Title: Marines Have Landed, The. Lew Ayers & J. Carroll Naish. Directed by Howard Bretherton. 1936. Republic. 71 min. Sound. 16mm B&W. *Rental:* Ivy Films. *Sale:* Rep Pic Film.

Leave Her to Heaven. Gene Tierney, Jeanne Crain & Cornel Wilde. Directed by John M. Stahl. 1945. Fox. 110 min. Sound. 16mm B&W. *Rental:* Films Inc.

Leave It to Blondie. Penny Singleton & Arthur Lake. Directed by Abby Berlin. 1945. Columbia. 75 min. Sound. 16mm B&W. *Rental:* Video Comm. *Lease:* King Features.

Leave It to the Marines. Sid Melton. Directed by Sam Newfield. 1951. Lippert. 66 min. Sound. 16mm B&W. *Rental:* Alba House, Film Ctr DC & Rep Pic Film.

Leavenworth Case, The. Donald Cook & Norman Foster. Directed by Lewis D. Collins. 1936. Republic. 54 min. Sound. 16mm B&W. *Rental:* Ivy Films. *Sale:* Rep Pic Film.

Leaves from Satan's Book. Directed by Carl Th. Dreyer. 1919. 120 min. Silent. 16mm B&W. subtitles Eng. *Rental:* Films Inc.

Leaving Home Blues. 1970. NBC. (Documentary). 53 min. Sound. 16mm Color. *Rental:* Films Inc, U Mich Media, NYU Film Lib & Syracuse U Film. *Sale:* Films Inc, Videotape version.

Leda. Madeleine Robinson & Jean-Paul Belmondo. Directed by Claude Chabrol. Fr. 1960. France. 101 min. Sound. 16mm Color. subtitles. *Rental:* Films Inc.

Lee Kuan Yew of Singapore. 1972. Britain. (Documentary). 50 min. Sound. 16mm Color. *Rental:* Time-Life Multimedia. *Sale:* Time-Life Multimedia.

Leech Woman, The. Coleen Gray & Phillip Terry. Directed by Edward Dein. 1960. Universal. 77 min. Sound. 16mm B&W. *Rental:* Swank Motion.

Left Brain, Right Brain. 1980. Canada. 56 min. Sound. 16mm Color. *Rental:* Film Makers, Iowa Films & Syracuse U Film. *Sale:* Film Makers.

Left Hand of God, The. Humphrey Bogart & Gene Tierney. Directed by Edward Dmytryk. 1955. Fox. (Anamorphic). 102 min. Sound. 16mm Color. *Rental:* Films Inc.

Left-Handed Woman, The. Directed by Peter Handke. Ger. 1978. Germany. (Cast unlisted). 119 min. Sound. 16mm Color. subtitles. *Rental:* New Yorker Films.

Legacy, The. Katharine Ross & Sam Elliott. Directed by Richard Marquand. 1979. Britain. 100 min. Sound. 16mm Color. *Rental:* Swank Motion.

Legacy. Joan Hotchkiss. Directed by Karen Arthur. 1976. Karen Arthur. 94 min. Sound. 16mm Color. *Rental:* Direct Cinema.

Legacy of Blood. John Carradine & Merry Anders. Directed by Carl Monson. 1971. 92 min. Sound. 16mm Color. *Rental:* Budget Films, Bosco Films, Ivy Films, Video Comm, Westcoast Films, Welling Motion Pictures & Willoughby Peer.

Legacy of Genius: The Story of Thomas Alva Edison. 1979. PBS. (Documentary). 59 min. Videotape Color. *Rental:* PBS Video. *Sale:* PBS Video.

Legacy of L.S.B. Leakey, The. 1977. National Geographic. (Documentary). 59 min. Sound. 16mm Color. *Sale:* Natl Geog. *Rental:* Natl Geog. *Sale:* Natl Geog, Videotape version.

Legacy of Rome. 1968. ABC. (Documentary). 55 min. Sound. 16mm Color. *Rental:* Iowa Films, McGraw-Hill Films & Syracuse U Film. *Sale:* McGraw-Hill Films.

Legend of a Gunfighter. Ron Randell & Judith Dornys. Directed by Ralph Olsen. 1966. Germany. 95 min. Sound. 16mm Color. *Rental:* Video Comm.

Legend of Amaluk, The. 1974. Alaska. (Documentary). 103 min. Sound. 16mm Color. *Rental:* Films Inc & Video Comm. *Lease:* Video Comm. *Rental:* Films Inc, Videotape version.

Legend of Cougar Canyon. 1974. Gold Key. (Documentary). 98 min. Sound. 16mm Color. *Rental:* Video Comm. *Lease:* Video Comm. *Rental:* Video Comm, *Lease:* Video Comm, Videotape version.

Legend of Frenchie King, The. Brigitte Bardot & Guy Casaril. Directed by Christian-Jaque. 1971. France. 97 min. Sound. 16mm Color. dubbed. *Rental:* Williams Films.

Legend of Harap Alb, The see Hero Prince.

Legend of Hell House, The. Pamela Franklin & Roddy McDowall. Directed by John Hough. 1973. Fox. 94 min. Sound. 16mm Color. *Rental:* Films Inc & Twyman Films.

Legend of Lake Titicaca, The. 1977. Metromedia. (Documentary). 52 min. Sound. 16mm Color. *Rental:* Churchill Films. *Rental:* Churchill Films, Videotape version.

Legend of Lobo, The. Directed by James Algar. 1962. Disney. (Documentary). 68 min. Sound. 16mm Color. *Rental:* Buchan Pics, Budget Films, Cine Craft, Cousino Visual Ed, Disney Prod, Films Inc, U of IL Film, Modern Sound, Newman Film Lib, Roas Films, Film Ctr DC & Twyman Films.

Legend of Lylah Claire. Kim Novak & Peter Finch. Directed by Robert Aldrich. 1968. MGM. 130 min. Sound. 16mm Color. *Rental:* MGM United.

Legend of Nigger Charlie, The. Fred Williamson. Directed by Martin Goldman. 1972. Paramount. 115 min. Sound. 16mm Color. *Rental:* Films Inc.

Legend of Prague see Golem.

Legend of Robin Hood, The. Orig. Title: Challenge for Robin Hood, A. Barrie Ingham. Directed by C. M. Pennington-Richards. 1968. Britain. 85 min. Sound. 16mm Color. *Rental:* Buchan Pic, Films Inc & Wholesome Film Ctr.

Legend of Rudolph Valentino, The. 1965. Janus. (Documentary). 71 min. Sound. 16mm B&W. *Rental:* Texture Film. *Sale:* Texture Film. *Sale:* Texture Film, Videotape version.

Legend of Sleepy Hollow. Jeff Goldblum & Paul Sand. Directed by Henning Schellerup. 1980. Viacom. 99 min. Sound. 16mm Color. *Rental:* Williams Films. *Sale:* Lucerne Films.

Legend of Sleepy Hollow, The. 1979. Lucerne. (Cast unlisted). 99 min. Sound. 16mm Color. *Sale:* Modern Sound & Film Pres. *Sale:* Lucerne Films, Videotape version.

Legend of Sleepy Hollow see Headless Horseman.

Legend of Sleepy Hollow, The. Jeff Goldblum, Dick Butkus & Meg Foster. 97 min. Sound. 16mm Color. *Rental:* Budget Films & Williams Films.

Legend of Soupspoon, The. 1972. Dan-Glenn. (Documentary). 46 min. Sound. 16mm Color. *Rental:* Films Inc.

Legend of the Grand Scrollmaker *see* Chikamatsu Monogatari.

Legend of the Lone Ranger, The. Clayton Moore & Jay Silverheels. 1958. Wrather. 75 min. Sound. 16mm B&W. *Rental:* Budget Films, Williams Films, Films Inc, Ivy Films, Kit Parker, Roas Films, Swank Motion & Westcoast Films.

Legend of the Lone Ranger, The. Klinton Spilsbury, Michael Horse & Jason Robards. Directed by William Fraker. 1981. 98 min. Sound. 16mm Color. *Rental:* Swank Motion. *Rental:* Swank Motion, Videotape version.

Legend of the Lost. John Wayne & Sophia Loren. Directed by Henry Hathaway. 1957. United Artists. (Anamorphic). 109 min. Sound. 16mm Color. *Rental:* MGM United.

Legend of the Northwest, The. Rand Brooks & Fritz Feld. 1962. GG Communications. 83 min. Sound. 16mm Color. *Rental:* Films Inc & Williams Films.

Legend of Tom Dooley, The. Michael Landon & Jo Morrow. Directed by Ted Post. 1959. Columbia. 79 min. Sound. 16mm B&W. *Rental:* Films Inc & Inst Cinema.

Legend of Valentino, The. 1960. Killiam. 60 min. Sound. 16mm B&W. *Rental:* Budget Films & Kent St U Film. *Sale:* Tamarelles French Film, Videotape version.

Legendary Champions, The. Directed by Harry Chaplin. 1960. Big Fights. (Documentary). 99 min. Sound. 16mm B&W. *Rental:* Films Inc, Macmillan Films, Syracuse U Film, Film Ctr DC & Westcoast Films. *Lease:* Macmillan Films.

Legendary West, The. 1976. Gould. (Documentary). 53 min. Sound. 16mm Color. *Rental:* Budget Films & Modern Sound. *Sale:* Lucerne Films. *Sale:* Lucerne Films, Videotape version.

Legion Etrangere, La. Canada. (Documentary). 56 min. Sound. 16mm Color. dubbed. *Rental:* CBS Inc. *Sale:* CBS Inc.

Legion of Missing Men. Ralph Forbes & Ben Alexander. Directed by Hamilton MacFadden. 1937. Monogram. 60 min. Sound. 16mm B&W. *Rental:* Mogulls Films.

Legion of the Doomed. Bill Williams & Kurt Krueger. Directed by Thor Brooks. 1958. Allied Artists. 75 min. Sound. 16mm B&W. *Rental:* Ivy Films. *Sale:* Rep Pic Film.

Legion of the Lawless. George O'Brien & Virginia Vale. Directed by Bert Gilroy. 1940. RKO. 59 min. Sound. 16mm B&W. *Rental:* RKO General Pics.

Legions of the Nile. Linda Cristal & George Marchal. Directed by Vittorio Cottafavi. 1960. Italy. 91 min. Sound. 16mm Color. dubbed. *Rental:* Films Inc.

Legislative Branch. 58 min. Sound. 16mm Color. *Rental:* Pyramid Film.

Legless Veteran, The. 60 min. Sound. 16mm B&W. *Rental:* New Front. *Sale:* New Front. *Rental:* New Front, *Sale:* New Front, Videotape version.

Legong: Dance of the Virgins. Directed by Henri De La Falaise. 1935. Du-World. (Documentary). 60 min. Sound. 16mm B&W. *Rental:* Mogulls Films.

Leili & Mejnun. Directed by Tatiana Berezantseva & Gafar Valamat-Zade. 1960. Russia. (Dance). 79 min. Sound. 16mm Color. narrated Eng. *Rental:* Corinth Films.

Lemon Drop Kid, The. Bob Hope & Marilyn Maxwell. Directed by Sidney Lanfield. 1951. Paramount. 91 min. Sound. 16mm B&W. *Rental:* Films Inc.

Lena Rivers. Charlotte Henry & James Kirkwood. Directed by Phil Rosen. 1932. Tiffany. 70 min. Sound. 16mm B&W. *Rental:* Mogulls Films.

Lenin & the Great Ungluing. 1976. Britain. (Documentary). 60 min. Sound. 16mm Color. *Rental:* U Cal Media, Films Inc, U of IL Film & Syracuse U Film. *Sale:* Films Inc. *Sale:* Films Inc, Videotape version.

Lenin in October. Trans. Title: Lenin V Oktyabre. Boris Shchukin & S. Goldstab. Directed by Mikhail Romm. Rus. 1937. Russia. 101 min. Sound. 16mm B&W. subtitles. *Rental:* Corinth Films.

Lenin V Oktyabre *see* Lenin in October.

Lenin v Polshe *see* Portrait of Lenin.

Leningrad. 1967. NBC. (Documentary). 54 min. Sound. 16mm Color. *Rental:* U of IL Film & McGraw-Hill Films. *Sale:* McGraw-Hill Films.

Lenny. Dustin Hoffman & Valerie Perrine. Directed by Bob Fosse. 1974. United Artists. 111 min. Sound. 16mm B&W. *Rental:* MGM United. *Rental:* MGM United, Videotape version.

Lenny Bruce. 1967. Filmmakers. (Documentary). 60 min. Sound. 16mm B&W. *Rental:* Budget Films. *Sale:* Reel Images, Videotape version.

Lenny Bruce Without Tears. Directed by Fred Baker. 1971. National Talent Service. (Documentary). 100 min. Sound. 16mm B&W. *Rental:* Video Tape Network.

Lenz. Alexandre Rockwell. 95 min. Sound. 16mm B&W. *Rental:* Starr Cecile.

Leo Buscaglia. 1983. PBS. 60 min. Sound. 16mm *Rental:* Syracuse U Film.

Leo the Last. Marcello Mastroianni & Billie Whitelaw. Directed by John Boorman. 1970. United Artists. 100 min. Sound. 16mm Color. *Rental:* MGM United.

Leonard Bernstein & the New York Philharmonic in Berlin. Directed by William Graham. 1967. Saudek. (Documentary, kinescope). 60 min. Sound. 16mm B&W. *Rental:* U of IL Film. *Sale:* IQ Film.

Leonard Bernstein & the New York Philharmonic in Moscow. Directed by Richard Leacock. 1967. Saudek. (Documentary). 60 min. Sound. 16mm B&W. *Rental:* U of IL Film. *Sale:* IQ Film.

Leonardo Da Vinci: Man of Mystery. 1952. Italy. (Documentary, color sequences). 68 min. Sound. 16mm B&W. narrated Eng. *Rental:* Inst Cinema.

Leonardo Da Vinci: Tell Me if Anything Ever Was Done. 1968. Britain. (Documentary). 50 min. Sound. 16mm Color. *Rental:* Time-Life Multimedia. *Sale:* Time-Life Multimedia.

Leonardo: To Know How to See. 1972. US Government. (Documentary). 60 min. Sound. 16mm Color. *Sale:* Natl AV Ctr.

Leonor. Liv Ullmann. Directed by Juan Bunuel. 1975. New Line Cinema. 90 min. Sound. 16mm Color. subtitles. *Rental:* New Line Cinema.

Leopard, The. Trans. Title: Gatopardo, Il. Burt Lancaster, Alain Delon & Claudia Cardinale. Directed by Luchino Visconti. 1963. Italy. 161 min. Sound. 16mm Color. dubbed. *Rental:* Films Inc. *Rental:* Films Inc, Anamorphic color version.

Leopard Man, The. Dennis O'Keefe & Margo. Directed by Jacques Tourneur. 1943. RKO. 59 min. Sound. 16mm B&W. *Rental:* Films Inc & RKO General Pics.

Leopard Woman, The. Louise Glaum & House Peters. Directed by Wesley Ruggles. 1920. Associated Producers. 60 min. Silent. 16mm B&W. *Rental:* Em Gee Film Lib. *Sale:* Blackhawk Films, Em Gee Film Lib & Glenn Photo. *Rental:* Ivy Films, Super 8 Silent version. *Sale:* Em Gee Film Lib, Silent 8mm version.

Lepke. Tony Curtis. Directed by Menahem Golan. 1975. Warners. 110 min. Sound. 16mm Color. *Rental:* Swank Motion.

Les Animaux *see* Animals.

Lesson, The. Fred Gwynne. Directed by Glenn Jordan. 1967. Grove. 67 min. Sound. 16mm B&W. *Rental:* Grove. *Sale:* Grove.

Lesson in Life, A. V. Kalinina & Ivan Pereverzev. Directed by Yuli Raizman. Rus. 1955. Russia. 110 min. Sound. 16mm B&W. *Rental:* Corinth Films.

Lesson in Love, A. Eva Dahlbeck. Directed by Ingmar Bergman. Swed. 1954. Sweden. 95 min. Sound. 16mm B&W. subtitles. *Rental:* Films Inc, Janus Films & New Cinema.

Lessons in Love. Constance Talmadge. Directed by Chet Withey. 1921. 16mm *Rental:* A Twyman Pres.

Let Freedom Ring. Nelson Eddy & Virginia Bruce. Directed by Jack Conway. 1939. MGM. 100 min. Sound. 16mm B&W. *Rental:* MGM United.

Let It Be. The Beatles. Directed by Michael Lindsay-Hogg. 1970. United Artists. 80 min. Sound. 16mm Color. *Rental:* MGM United. *Rental:* MGM United, Videotape version.

Let Joy Reign Supreme. Trans. Title: Que la Fete Commence. Philippe Noiret & Christine Pascal. Directed by Bertrand Tavernier. Fr. 1975. France. 119 min. Sound. 16mm Color. subtitles. *Rental:* New Line Cinema & Specialty Films.

Let My People Go. 1969. Metromedia. (Documentary). 82 min. Sound. 16mm B&W. *Rental:* Alden Films, Films Inc, U Mich Media, Syracuse U Film & Wholesome Film Ctr. *Sale:* Films Inc. *Sale:* Films Inc, Videotape version.

Let No Man Write My Epitaph. Burl Ives & Shelley Winters. Directed by Philip Leacock. 1960. Columbia. 106 min. Sound. 16mm B&W. *Rental:* Budget Films, Cine Craft, Kit Parker & Welling Motion Pictures.

Let the Church Say Amen. 1972. Chamba. (Documentary). 78 min. Sound. 16mm Color. *Sale:* Natl Churches Christ.

Let the Good Times Roll. Directed by Sidney Levin. 1973. Columbia. (Documentary). 99 min. Sound. 16mm Color. *Rental:* Budget Films, Corinth Films, Williams Films, U of IL Film, Modern Sound, Newman Film Lib, Natl Film Video, Swank Motion, Film Ctr DC, Twyman Films, Westcoast Films & Welling Motion Pictures. *Rental:* Kit Parker, Anamorphic version.

Let There Be Light. Directed by John Huston. 1946. US Government. (Documentary). 59 min. Sound. 16mm B&W. *Rental:* Budget Films, Em Gee Film Lib, IFEX, Images Film, Kino Intl, Kit Prker, Modern Mod Art, Natl AV Ctr & Natl Cinema. *Sale:* Festival Films, Kino Intl, Natl AV Ctr & Images Film. *Lease:* Kino Intl. *Sale:* Festival Films, Natl AV Ctr & IFEX, Videotape version.

Let Us Be Gay. Norma Shearer, Marie Dressler & Rod La Rocque. Directed by Robert Z. Leonard. 1930. MGM. 79 min. Sound. 16mm B&W. *Rental:* MGM United.

Let Us Live. Henry Fonda & Maureen O'Sullivan. Directed by John Brahm. 1939. Columbia. 75 min. Sound. 16mm B&W. *Lease:* Time-Life Multimedia.

Let Us Teach Guessing. Modern Learning Aids. (Documentary). 61 min. Sound. 16mm Color. *Rental:* OK AV Ctr.

Let's Fall in Love *see* Slightly French.

L'Etoile du Nord. Simone Signoret & Phillipe Noiret. Directed by Pierre Granier-Deferre. Fr. 1982. 120 min. 16mm Color. subtitles. *Rental:* MGM United.

Let's Be Happy. Tony Martin & Vera-Ellen. Directed by Henry Levin. 1957. Britain. 93 min. Sound. 16mm Color. *Rental:* Hurlock Cine.

Let's Dance. Betty Hutton, Fred Astaire & Roland Young. Directed by Norman Z. McLeod. 1950. Paramount. 111 min. Sound. 16mm Color. *Rental:* Films Inc.

Let's Do It! Greg Bradford & Britt Helfer. Directed by Bert I. Gordon. 85 min. 16mm Color. *Rental:* BF Video.

Let's Do It Again. Jane Wyman, Ray Milland & Aldo Ray. Directed by Alexander Hall. 1953. Columbia. 95 min. Sound. 16mm Color. *Rental:* Maljack. *Lease:* Maljack. *Lease:* Maljack, Videotape version.

Let's Do It Again. Sidney Poitier & Bill Cosby. Directed by Sidney Poitier. 1975. Warners. 112 min. Sound. 16mm Color. *Rental:* Williams Films & Swank Motion. *Rental:* Swank Motion, Videotape version.

Let's Fall in Love. Ann Sothern & Edmund Lowe. Directed by David Burton. 1934. Columbia. 70 min. Sound. 16mm B&W. *Rental:* Kit Parker.

Let's Get Tough. East Side kids. Directed by Wallace Fox. 1942. Monogram. 62 min. Sound. Videotape B&W. *Sale:* Budget Films, Roas Films & VidAmerica. *Sale:* Classic Film Mus & Morcraft Films. *Sale:* Cinema Concepts & Reel Images, Super 8 Sound version. *Sale:* CInema Concepts, Videotape version.

Let's Go. Richard Talmadge. Directed by William K. Howard. 1923. Truart. 50 min. Silent. 16mm B&W. *Rental:* Em Gee Film Lib. *Sale:* Glenn Photo.

Let's Go Native. Jack Oakie & Jeanette MacDonald. Directed by Leo McCarey. 1930. Paramount. 75 min. Sound. 16mm B&W. *Rental:* Swank Motion.

Let's Go Navy. The Bowery Boys. Directed by William Beaudine. 1951. Monogram. 68 min. Sound. 16mm B&W. *Rental:* Budget Films, Modern Sound & Roas Films.

Let's Have Fun. Margaret Lindsay & John Beal. Directed by Charles Barton. 1943. Columbia. 63 min. Sound. 16mm B&W. *Rental:* Inst Cinema.

Let's Kill Uncle. Nigel Green & Mary Badham. Directed by William Castle. 1966. Universal. 92 min. Sound. 16mm Color. *Rental:* Swank Motion.

Let's Live a Little. Hedy Lamarr & Robert Cummings. Directed by Richard Wallace. 1948. Eagle Lion. 85 min. Sound. 16mm B&W. *Rental:* Ivy Films. *Sale:* Rep Pic Film.

Let's Live Tonight. Lillian Harvey & Tullio Carminati. Directed by Victor Schertzinger. 1935. Columbia. Sound. 16mm B&W. *Rental:* Kit Parker.

Let's Make It Legal. Claudette Colbert & MacDonald Carey. Directed by Richard Sale. 1951. Fox. 77 min. Sound. 16mm B&W. *Rental:* Films Inc.

Let's Make Love. Marilyn Monroe & Yves Montand. Directed by George Cukor. 1960. Fox. 118 min. Sound. 16mm Color. *Rental:* Films Inc.

Let's Make Music. Bob Crosby & Jean Rogers. Directed by Leslie Goodwins. 1941. RKO. 85 min. Sound. 16mm B&W. *Rental:* Films Inc.

Let's Play Hospital. US Government. (Documentary). 53 min. Sound. 16mm Color. *Sale:* Natl AV Ctr.

Let's Rock. Orig. Title: Keep It Cool. Julius LaRosa & Paul Anka. Directed by Harry Foster. 1958. Columbia. 79 min. Sound. 16mm B&W. *Rental:* Modern Sound.

Let's Scare Jessica to Death. Zohra Lampert. Directed by John Hancock. 1971. Paramount. 89 min. Sound. 16mm Color. *Rental:* Films Inc.

Let's Sing Again. Bobby Breen. Directed by Kurt Neumann. 1936. RKO. 74 min. Sound. 16mm B&W. *Rental:* Budget Films & Film Classics.

Let's Spend the Night Together. Mick Jagger & Keith Richards. Directed by Hal Ashby. 1982. Embassy. Sound. 16mm Color. *Rental:* Films Inc.

Let's Talk About Men. Nino Manfredi & Luciana Palluzzi. Directed by Lina Wertmuller. 1965. Italy. 93 min. Sound. 16mm B&W. *Rental:* Hurlock Cine.

Let's Try Again. Diana Wynard & Clive Brook. Directed by Worthington Miner. 1934. RKO. 67 min. Sound. 16mm B&W. *Rental:* RKO General Pics.

Letter, The. Bette Davis & Herbert Marshall. Directed by William Wyler. 1940. Warners. 97 min. Sound. 16mm B&W. *Rental:* MGM United.

Letter for Evie, A. Marsha Hunt & John Carroll. Directed by Jules Dassin. 1946. MGM. 89 min. Sound. 16mm B&W. *Rental:* MGM United.

Letter from an Unknown Woman, A. Joan Fontaine & Louis Jourdan. Directed by Max Ophuls. 1948. Universial. 80 min. Sound. 16mm B&W. *Rental:* Budget Films, Charard Films, Images Film & Kit Parker. *Sale:* Rep Pic Film.

Letter from Morazan, A. 1982. 55 min. 16mm Color. *Rental:* Icarus Films. *Sale:* Icarus Films, Videotape version.

Letter from Siberia, A. Directed by Chris Marker. Fr. 1957. Fox. (Documentary). 60 min. Sound. 16mm Color. subtitles. *Rental:* New Yorker Films.

Letter of Introduction. Adolphe Menjou & Andrea Leeds. Directed by John M. Stahl. 1938. Universial. 104 min. Sound. 16mm B&W. *Rental:* Budget Films & Classic Film Mus. *Sale:* Cinema Concepts.

Letter That Was Never Sent, The. Tatyana Samoilova & Innokenty Smoktunovsky. Directed by Mikhail Kalatozov. Rus. 1959. Russia. 98 min. Sound. 16mm B&W. subtitles. *Rental:* Corinth Films.

Letter to Jane, A. Directed by Jean-Luc Godard & Jean-Paul Gorin. Fr. 1972. France. (Experimental). 55 min. Sound. 16mm B&W. subtitles. *Rental:* New Cinema & New Yorker Films.

Letter to Three Wives, A. Jeanne Crain, Linda Darnell & Ann Sothern. Directed by Joseph L. Mankiewicz. 1948. Fox. 103 min. Sound. 16mm B&W. *Rental:* Williams Films & Films Inc, videotape version.

Letters from My Windmill. Henri Vilbert. Directed by Marcel Pagnol. Fr. 1954. France. 116 min. Sound. 16mm B&W. subtitles. *Rental:* Budget Films, Corinth Films & Kit Parker. *Rental:* Budget Films, 134 mins. version.

Letzte Mann, Der *see* Last Laugh.

Level of Business Activity: Knowns & Unknowns. 1963. Indiana University. (Lecture). 58 min. Sound. 16mm B&W. *Rental:* U Cal Media.

Lewis Mumford on the City. 1963. Canada. (Documentary). 50 min. Sound. 16mm B&W. *Rental:* Kit Parker & Natl FilmCN. *Sale:* Natl Film CN.

Lewis Mumford: Toward Human Architecture. Directed by Ray Hubbard. 1979. Corinth. (Documentary). 90 min. Sound. 16mm Color. *Rental:* Corinth Films. *Lease:* Corinth Films. *Lease:* Corinth Films, Videotape version.

Liaisons Dangereuses, Les. Gerard Philipe & Jeanne Moreau. Directed by Roger Vadim. Fr. 1961. France. 106 min. Sound. 16mm B&W. *Rental:* Films Inc.

Lianna. Linda Griffiths. Directed by John Sayles. 1983. MGM-UA. 110 min. Sound. 16mm Color. *Rental:* MGM United. *Rental:* MGM United, Videotape version.

Liar's Moon. Matt Dillon & Cindy Fisher. Directed by David Fisher. 1982. Crown. 106 min. Sound. 16mm Color. *Rental:* Swank Motion.

Libel. Olivia DeHavilland & Dirk Bogarde. Directed by Anthony Asquith. 1959. MGM. 100 min. Sound. 16mm B&W. *Rental:* MGM United.

Libeled Lady. Jean Harlow, Myrna Loy & William Powell. Directed by Jack Conway. 1936. MGM. 98 min. Sound. 16mm B&W. *Rental:* MGM United.

Liberation of L.B. Jones, The. Lee J. Cobb & Roscoe Lee Browne. Directed by William Wyler. 1970. Columbia. 102 min. Sound. 16mm Color. *Rental:* Budget Films & Kit Parker.

Liberte Une. Maurice Ronet & Corinne Marchand. Directed by Yves Ciampi. Fr. 1962. France. 87 min. Sound. 16mm B&W. subtitles. *Rental:* French Am Cul.

Libertine, The. Catherine Spaak & Jean-Louis Trintignant. Directed by Pasquale Festa Campanile. 1969. Italy. 90 min. Sound. Videotape Color. subtitles. *Sale:* Video Lab.

Librarians Communicate. 1977. 51 min. Sound. Videotape Color. *Sale:* Natl AV Ctr.

Library of Congress, The. Directed by Ann Turner. 1979. Britain. (Documentary). 90 min. Sound. 16mm Color. *Rental:* Films Inc. *Sale:* Films Inc. *Rental:* Films Inc, *Sale:* Films Inc, Videotape version.

Libro de Piedra, El. Marga Lopez & Joaquin Cordero. Directed by Carlos Enrique Taboada. Mexico. 99 min. Sound. 16mm Color. subtitles. *Rental:* Westcoast Films.

Licensed to Kill *see* Second Best Secret Agent in the Whole Wide World.

Liciguena Dijo Si. 1950. Mexico. (Cast unlisted). 90 min. Sound. 16mm B&W. subtitles. *Rental:* Film Classics.

Lickerish Quartet, The. Sylvana Venturelli. Directed by Radley Metzger. 1970. Audubon. 90 min. Videotape Color. *Sale:* Video Lib.

Lie Detector, The *see* Truth About Murder.

Liebalala. Orig. Title: Sweetheart. Directed by Margaret Carson Hubbard. 1935. University of California. (Documentary). 58 min. Sound. 16mm B&W. *Rental:* U Cal Media. *Sale:* U Cal Media.

Liebe Der Jeanne Ney, Das *see* Love of Jeanne Ney.

Liebelei. Wolfgang Liebeneiner & Magda Schneider. Directed by Max Ophuls. Ger. 1932. Germany. 88 min. Sound. 16mm B&W. subtitles. *Rental:* Corinth Films & Images Film. *Sale:* Images Film. *Sale:* Images Film, Videotape version.

Lies My Father Told Me. Yossi Yadin. Directed by Jan Kadar. Yiddish. 1975. Columbia. 102 min. Sound. 16mm Color. subtitles. *Rental:* Arcus Film, Budget Films, Williams Films, Films Inc, Ivy Films, Kit Parker, Modern Sound, Natl Film Video, Swank Motion, Twyman Films, Westcoast Films, Welling Motion Pictures & Wholesome Film Ctr.

Lieutenant Wore Skirts, The. Tom Ewell & Sheree North. Directed by Frank Tashlin. 1956. Fox. 99 min. Sound. 16mm Color. *Rental:* Films Inc.

Life & Adventures of Nicholas Nickleby, The. 1981. Britian. 350 min. Sound. Videotape Color. *Sale:* Tamarelles French Film.

Life & Assassination of the Kingfish, The. Edward Asner & Nicholas Pryor. Directed by Robert Collins. 1977. NBC. 97 min. Sound. 16mm Color. *Rental:* Kit Parker, Learning Corp Am, Modern Sound, Roas Films, Wholesome Film Ctr & Budget Films. *Lease:* Learning Corp Am. *Rental:* Learning Corp Am, *Lease:* Learning Corp Am, Videotape version.

Life & Death of Colonel Blimp. (Cast unlisted). Videotape *Rental:* Vidamerica.

Life & Times of Bertrand Russell, The. 1964. Britain. (Documentary). 50 min. Sound. 16mm B&W. *Rental:* Time-Life Multimedia. *Sale:* Time-Life Multimedia.

Life & Times of Colonel Blimp, The. Roger Livesey. Directed by Michael Powell & Emeric Pressburger. 1943. Britian. (Cast unlisted). 163 min. Sound. 16mm *Rental:* Vidamerica.

Life & Times of Grizzly Adams, The. 1975. Sunn. (Documentary). 93 min. Sound. 16mm Color. *Rental:* Arcus Film, Budget Films, Cine Craft, Films Inc, Maljack, Natl Fil Video, Roas Films, Video Comm, Westcoast Films, Welling Motion Pictures & Wholesome Film Ctr. *Lease:* Video Comm. *Rental:* Video Comm, *Lease:* Video Comm, Videotape version.

Life & Times of John Huston, Esquire, The. 1966. NET. (Documentary). 60 min. Sound. 16mm B&W. *Rental:* Indiana AV Ctr.

Life & Times of Judge Roy Bean, The. Paul Newman & Ava Gardner. Directed by John Huston. 1973. National General. 120 min. Sound. 16mm Color. *Rental:* Williams Films, Films Inc, Modern Sound, Swank Motion & Twyman Films.

Life & Times of Rosie the Riveter, The. Directed by Connie Field. 1978. First Run. (Documentary, color sequences). 65 min. Sound. 16mm B&W. *Rental:* Direct Cinema & U Mich Media. *Sale:* Direct Cinema. *Sale:* Direct Cinema, Videotape version.

Life at Stake, A. Angela Lansbury & Keith Andes. Directed by Jiri Weiss. 1956. Czechoslovakia. 78 min. Sound. 16mm B&W. dubbed. *Rental:* Budget Films.

Life at the Top. Laurence Harvey & Jean Simmons. Directed by Ted Kotcheff. 1965. Britain. 117 min. Sound. 16mm B&W. *Rental:* Budget Films, Charard Motion Pictures, Films Inc & Modern Sound.

Life Begins. Loretta Young & Eric Linden. Directed by Elliott Nugent & James Flood. 1932. Warners. 72 min. Sound. 16mm B&W. *Rental:* MGM United.

Life Begins. 1967. Gesell. (Documentary). 58 min. Sound. 16mm B&W. *Rental:* SD AV Ctr. *Sale:* Ency Brit Ed.

Life Begins at Eight Thirty. Orig. Title: Light of Heart, The. Monte Woolley & Ida Lupino. Directed by Irving Pichel. 1942. Fox. 85 min. Sound. 16mm B&W. *Rental:* Films Inc.

Life Begins for Andy Hardy. Mickey Rooney & Judy Garland. Directed by George B. Seitz. 1941. MGM. 103 min. Sound. 16mm B&W. *Rental:* MGM United.

Life Begins in College. Ritz Brothers & Joan Davis. Directed by William A. Seiter. 1937. Fox. 94 min. Sound. 16mm B&W. *Rental:* Films Inc.

Life, Death & the American Woman. 1977. Best. (Documentary). 54 min. Sound. 16mm Color. *Rental:* Best Films & U of IL Film. *Sale:* Best Films.

Life for Ruth: Walk in the Shadow. Patrick McGoohan & Michael Craig. Directed by Basil Dearden. 1962. Britain. 91 min. Sound. 16mm B&W. *Rental:* Cinema Five.

Life Goes On *see* Vie Continue.

Life Goes to the Movies. 5 pts. 1977. Fox. (Anthology). 153 min. Sound. 16mm Color. *Rental:* Budget Films, U of IL Films, Images Film, Kit Parker & U Mich Media. *Rental:* Films Inc, Videotape version.

Life in the Balance, A. Ricardo Montalban & Anne Bancroft. Directed by Harry Horner. 1955. Fox. 74 min. Sound. 16mm B&W. *Rental:* Films Inc.

Life in the Jomon Period. 1976. Japan Foundation. (Documentary). 47 min. Sound. 16mm Color. *Rental:* U Cal Media.

Life in the Thirties. 1965. NBC. (Documentary). 52 min. Sound. 16mm B&W. *Rental:* Budget Films, BYU Media, U Cal Media, U of IL Film, Iowa Films, Kit Parker, La Inst Res Ctr, McGraw-Hill Films, U Mich Media & Syracuse U Film. *Sale:* McGraw-Hill Films.

Life, Love & Death. Caroline Cellier. Directed by Claude Lelouch. Fr. 1969. France. 115 min. Sound. 16mm Color. subtitles. *Rental:* MGM United.

Life of Anton Bruckner, The. 1974. West Germany. 135 min. Sound. 16mm Color. narrated Eng. *Rental:* Corinth Films. *Lease:* Corinth Films. *Rental:* Corinth Films, Videotape version.

Life of Donizetti, The. Italy. (Cast unlisted). 90 min. Sound. 16mm B&W. dubbed. *Rental:* Corinth Films.

Life of Emile Zola, The. Paul Muni & Joseph Schildkraut. Directed by William Dieterle. 1937. Warners. 118 min. Sound. 16mm B&W. *Rental:* MGM United.

Life of Her Own, A. Lana Turner & Ray Milland. Directed by George Cukor. 1950. MGM. 108 min. Sound. 16mm B&W. *Rental:* MGM United.

Life of Jack London, The *see* Jack London's Tales of Adventure.

Life of Jesus Christ, The. Threshold. (Cast unlisted). 90 min. Sound. 16mm Color. *Rental:* Budget Films & Threshold Films. *Sale:* Threshold Films.

Life of Jimmy Dolan, The. Douglas Fairbanks Jr., Loretta Young & Mickey Rooney. Directed by Archie Mayo. 1933. Warners. 89 min. Sound. 16mm B&W. *Rental:* MGM United.

Life of Moses, The. Directed by J. Stuart Blackton. 1910. Vitagraph. (Cast unlisted). 70 min. Silent. 16mm B&W. *Rental:* Museum Mod Art. *Lease:* Museum Mod Art.

Life of Mozart, The. Directed by Hans Conrad Fischer. 1967. West Germany. 148 min. Sound. 16mm B&W. narrated Eng. *Rental:* Corinth Films. *Lease:* Corinth Films. *Rental:* Corinth Films, Videotape version.

Life of O-Haru, The. Toshiro Mifune & Kinuyo Tanaka. Directed by Kenji Mizoguchi. Jap. 1952. Japan. 133 min. Sound. 16mm B&W. subtitles. *Rental:* New Yorker Films.

Life of Robert Burns, The. Andrew Cruikshank. Directed by James A. Fitzpatrick. 1937. Britain. 74 min. Sound. 16mm B&W. *Rental:* Film Classics. *Rental:* Film Classics, Videotape version.

Life of St. Benedict, The. (Cast unlisted). 85 min. Sound. 16mm B&W. *Rental:* Alba House.

Life of the Beaver, The. 1974. Survival Anglia. (Documentary). 50 min. Sound. 16mm Color. *Rental:* Syracuse U Film.

Life of the Party, The. Charles Butterworth & Winnie Lightner. Directed by Roy Del Ruth. 1930. Warners. 78 min. Sound. 16mm B&W. *Rental:* MGM United.

Life of the Party, The. Ann Miller & Gene Raymond. Directed by William A. Seiter. 1938. RKO. 77 min. Sound. 16mm *Rental:* RKO General Pics.

Life of Verdi, The. Italy. (Cast unlisted). 90 min. Sound. 16mm Color. dubbed. *Rental:* Corinth Films.

Life of Vergie Winters, The. Betty Furness & Ben Alexander. Directed by Pandro S. Berman. 1934. RKO. 82 min. Sound. 16mm B&W. *Rental:* RKO General Pics.

Life on the Mississippi. David Knell & Robert Lansing. Directed by Peter Hunt. 1980. WNET. 120 min. Sound. 16mm Color. *Rental:* Films Inc. *Sale:* Films Inc. *Rental:* Films Inc, *Sale:* Films Inc, Videotape version.

Life: Patent Pending. 1982. Nova. (Documentary). 57 min. Sound. 16mm Color. *Rental:* U Cal Media.

Life Story of Baal, The. Directed by Edward Bennett. 1978. Britain. (Documentary). 58 min. Sound. 16mm Color. *Rental:* Museum Mod Art.

Life Story of St. John Bosco *see* Don Bosco.

Life Upside Down. Charles Denner. Directed by Alain Jessua. Fr. 1964. France. 93 min. Sound. 16mm B&W. subtitles. *Rental:* Ivy Films.

Life with Blondie. Penny Singleton & Arthur Lake. Directed by Abby Berlin. 1946. Columbia. 75 min. Sound. 16mm B&W. *Lease:* King Features.

Life with Father. William Powell & Irene Dunne. Directed by Michael Curtiz. 1947. Warners. 118 min. Sound. 16mm Color. *Rental:* Arcus Film, Budget Films, Natl Film Video, Roas Films, Twyman Films, Video Comm, Westcoast Films & Welling Motion Pictures. *Sale:* Cinema Concepts & Reel Images. *Sale:* Reel Images, Super 8 sound version. *Rental:* Video Comm, *Sale:* Blackhawk Films & Video Lab, Videotape version.

Life Worth Living, A. 1982. Britain. (Cast unlisted). 52 min. Sound. 16mm Color. *Rental:* Concern Dying. *Sale:* Concern Dying. *Rental:* Concern Dying, *Sale:* Concern Dying, Videotape version.

Lifeboat. Tallulah Bankhead & John Hodiak. Directed by Alfred Hitchcock. 1943. Fox. 97 min. Sound. 16mm B&W. *Rental:* Films Inc.

Lifeguard. Sam Elliott, Parker Stevenson & Kathleen Quinlan. Directed by Daniel Petrie. 1976. Paramount. 96 min. Sound. 16mm Color. *Rental:* Films Inc.

Light at the Edge of the World, The. Kirk Douglas & Yul Brynner. Directed by Kevin Billington. 1971. National General. (Anamorphic). 121 min. Sound. 16mm Color. *Rental:* Swank Motion.

Light Fantastick, The. Directed by Rupert Glover & Michel Patenaude. 1974. Canada. (Anthology, color sequences). 58 min. Sound. 16mm B&W. *Rental:* Images Film, U Cal Media, U Mich Media, Iowa Films & Natl Film CN.

Light in the Dark *see* Light of Faith.

Light in the Forest. James MacArthur, Fess Parker & Wendell Corey. Directed by Herschel Daugherty. 1958. Disney. 93 min. Sound. 16mm Color. *Rental:* Buchan Pic, Cine Craft, Cousino Visual Ed, Williams Films, Bosco Films, Disney Prod, Elliot Film Co, Films Inc, Fllm Pres, U of IL Films, MGM United, Modern Sound, Newman Film Lib, Roas Films, Swank Motion, Film Ctr DC, Twyman Films, Westcoast Films & Welling Motion Pictures.

Light in the Piazza, A. Olivia De Havilland & Rossano Brazzi. Directed by Guy Green. 1962. MGM. 105 min. Sound. 16mm Color. *Rental:* MGM United. *Rental:* MGM United, Anamorphic version.

Light of Experience, The. (Civilization Ser.). 1968. Britain. (Documentary). 60 min. Sound. 16mm Color. *Rental:* U Cal Media, Films Inc, OK AV Ctr & Utah Media. *Sale:* Films Inc. *Sale:* Films Inc, Videotape version.

Light of Faith, The. Orig. Title: Light in the Dark. Lon Chaney & Hope Hampton. Directed by Elmo Lincoln. 1924. First National. 45 min. Silent. 16mm B&W. *Rental:* Budget Films, Em Gee Film Lib, Film Classics & Willoughby Peer. *Sale:* Film Classics, Tinted 16mm version. *Sale:* Phoenix Films, Videotape version, Silent Tinted version.

Light of Heart, The *see* Life Begins at Eight Thirty.

Light That Failed, The. Ronald Colman & Ida Lupino. Directed by William A. Wellman. 1939. Paramount. 97 min. Sound. 16mm B&W. *Rental:* Swank Motion.

Light Touch, The. Stewart Granger & Pier Angeli. Directed by Richard Brooks. 1951. MGM. 93 min. Sound. 16mm B&W. *Rental:* MGM United.

Light Years Away. Directed by Alain Tanner. Fr. 1980. France. 105 min. Sound. 16mm Color. subtitles. *Rental:* New Yorker Films.

Lighthouse. June Lang & Don Castle. Directed by Frank Wisbar. 1946. PRC. 62 min. Sound. 16mm B&W. *Rental:* Ivy Films & Mogulls Films. *Sale:* Classics Assoc NY & Rep Pic Film.

Lighting Steeds *see* Flashing Steeds.

Lightnin' Bill Carson. Tim McCoy. Directed by Sam Newfield. 1936. Puritan. 60 min. Sound. 16mm B&W. *Sale:* Natl Cinema.

Lightnin' Crandall. Bob Steele. Directed by Sam Newfield. 1937. Republic. 60 min. Sound. 16mm B&W. *Rental:* Ivy Films.

Lightnin' in the Forest. Lynn Roberts & Warren Douglas. Directed by George Blair. 1948. Republic. 58 min. Sound. 16mm B&W. *Rental:* Ivy Films. *Sale:* Rep Pic Film.

Lightning Bolt. Orig. Title: Operation Goldman. Anthony Eisley. Directed by Anthony Dawson. 1967. Italy-Spain. (Anamorphic). 90 min. Sound. 16mm Color. dubbed. *Rental:* Willoughby Peer.

Lightning Raiders. Buster Crabbe. Directed by Sam Newfield. 1945. PRC. 61 min. Sound. 16mm B&W. *Sale:* Classics Assoc NY.

Lightning Slinger. Michael Callan, Rosemary DeCamp & Adam Arkin. Sunn. 50 min. Sound. 16mm Color. *Rental:* Williams Films, videotape version.

Lightning Strikes Twice. Ben Lyon & Pert Kelton. Directed by Ben Holmes. 1935. RKO. 66 min. Sound. 16mm B&W. *Rental:* RKO General Pics.

Lightning Strikes West. Ken Maynard. Directed by Harry Fraser. 1940. Colony. 57 min. Videotape B&W. *Sale:* Video Comm.

Lightning Swords of Death. Orig. Title: Sword of Vengeance III. Tom Wakayama. Directed by Kenji Misumi. 1974. Japan. 83 min. Sound. 16mm Color. dubbed. *Rental:* Budget Films, Cine Craft, Williams Films, Modern Sound, Natl Film Video, Swank Motion, Film Ctr DC, Twyman Films, Westcoast Films & Welling Motion Pictures.

Lights, Action, Africa. 55 min. Sound. 16mm Color. *Rental:* Benchmark Films, Iowa Films & Syracuse U Film. *Sale:* Benchmark Films. *Sale:* Benchmark Films, 8 mm version avail. version.

Lights of New York, The. Helene Costello & Cullen Landis. Directed by Bryan Foy. 1928. Warners. 56 min. Sound. 16mm B&W. *Rental:* Museum Mod Art.

Lights of Old Santa Fe, The. Roy Rogers. Directed by Frank McDonald. 1944. Republic. 54 min. Sound. 16mm B&W. *Rental:* Ivy Films. *Sale:* Cinema Concepts & Rep Pic Film.

Like a Mighty Army. Dean White & Grandon Rhodes. Directed by John Coyle. 1971. Cathedral. 50 min. Sound. 16mm B&W. *Rental:* Gospel Films & G Herne.

Like the Wind. 1979. PBS. (Documentary). 59 min. Videotape Color. *Rental:* PBS Video. *Sale:* PBS Video.

Likely Story, A. Bill William & Barbara Hale. Directed by H. C. Potter. 1947. RKO. 88 min. Sound. 16mm B&W. *Rental:* RKO General Pics.

Li'l Abner. Orig. Title: Little Abner. Granville Owen & Martha O'Driscoll. Directed by Albert S. Rogell. 1940. RKO. 78 min. Sound. 16mm B&W. *Rental:* Alba House, Budget Films, Classic Film Mus, Em Gee Film Lib, Mogulls Films & Film Ctr DC. *Sale:* Classic Film Mus.

Li'l Abner. Peter Palmer & Leslie Parrish. Directed by Melvin Frank. 1959. Paramount. 114 min. Sound. 16mm Color. *Rental:* Films Inc.

Li'l Scratch. Directed by Larry Jones. 1973. Gold Key. (Documentary). 93 min. Sound. 16mm Color. *Rental:* Films Inc, Video Comm & Westcoast Films. *Lease:* Video Comm.

Lila-Love Under the Midnight Sun *see* Make Way for Lila.

Lilacs in the Spring. Errol Flynn & Anna Neagle. Directed by Herbert Wilcox. 1954. 16mm *Rental:* A Twyman Pres.

Lileya. Directed by Vachtang Vronsky & Vasil Lapoknysh. 1960. Russia. 88 min. Sound. 16mm Color. narrated Eng. *Rental:* Corinth Films.

Lili. Leslie Caron & Mel Ferrer. Directed by Charles Walters. 1953. MGM. 81 min. Sound. 16mm Color. *Rental:* MGM United. *Rental:* MGM United, Videotape version.

Lili Marleen. Giancarlo Giannini, Hanna Schygulla & Mel Ferrer. Directed by Rainer Werner Fassbinder. 1981. 121 min. Sound. 16mm Color. *Rental:* MGM United.

Lilith. Jean Seberg & Warren Beatty. Directed by Robert Rossen. 1964. Columbia. 114 min. Sound. 16mm B&W. *Rental:* Budget Films, Cine Craft, Charard Motion Pics, Corinth Films, Kit Parker, Modern Sound, Swank Motion, Welling Motion Pictures & Wholesome Film Ctr.

Lillian Russell. Alice Faye & Don Ameche. Directed by Irving Cummings. 1940. Fox. 127 min. Sound. 16mm B&W. *Rental:* Films Inc.

Lilies of the Field. Sidney Poitier & Lilia Skala. Directed by Ralph Nelson. 1963. United Artists. 97 min. Sound. 16mm B&W. *Rental:* Budget Films, MGM United, Roas Films, Twyman Films, Westcoast Films & Wholesome Film Ctr.

Lilly Turner. Ruth Chatterton & George Brent. Directed by William A. Wellman. 1933. Warners. 65 min. Sound. 16mm B&W. *Rental:* MGM United.

Limbo. Kate Jackson. Directed by Mark Robson. 1972. Universal. 112 min. Sound. 16mm Color. *Rental:* Swank Motion.

Limelight. Charles Chaplin, Claire Bloom & Buster Keaton. Directed by Charles Chaplin. 1952. United Artists. 145 min. Sound. 16mm B&W. *Rental:* Films Inc. *Sale:* Festival Films, Videotape version.

Limelight. Anna Neagle. 1935. 16mm *Rental:* A Twyman Pres.

Limits to Growth, The. 1974. Britain. (Documentary). 60 min. Sound. 16mm Color. *Rental:* U Cal Media, U of IL Film & U Mich Media.

Limping Man, The. Lloyd Bridges & Moira Lister. Directed by Charles De Latour. 1953. Lippert. 69 min. Sound. 16mm B&W. *Rental:* Budget Films.

Lincoln Conspiracy, The. Bradford Dillman, John Anderson, Whit Bissell & John Dehner. Directed by James L. Conway. 1979. Sunn. 91 min. Videotape Color. *Sale:* Modern Sound, Twyman Films, VidAmerica & Williams Films. *Sale:* Lucerne Films. *Sale:* Lucerne Films, Videotape version.

Lincoln: Trial by Fire. 1974. NBC. (Documentary). 52 min. Sound. 16mm Color. *Rental:* Films Inc, U Mich Media, Syracuse U Film & Utah Media. *Sale:* Films Inc.

Linda Be Good. Elyse Knox & Marie Wilson. Directed by Frank McDonald. 1947. Eagle-Lion. 68 min. Sound. 16mm B&W. *Rental:* Charard Motion Pics.

Line of Apogee. Charles Braun. Directed by Lloyd Williams. Lloyd Williams. (Color Sequences). 60 min. Sound. 16mm B&W. *Rental:* Canyon Cinema.

Line of Demarcation. Jean Seberg & Maurice Ronet. Directed by Claude Chabrol. Fr. 1966. France. 112 min. Sound. 16mm B&W. subtitles. *Rental:* Films Inc.

Lineup, The. Orig. Title: Identity Parade. Eli Wallach & Robert Keith. Directed by Don Siegel. 1958. Columbia. 86 min. Sound. 16mm B&W. *Rental:* Budget Films, Charard Motion Pics, Inst Cinema, Kit Parker & Fi lm Ctr DC.

Ling Speech Program. 5 pts. 1982. McGill. 250 min. Sound. 16mm *Rental:* Syracuse U film.

Linus Pauling: Crusading Scientist. Directed by Robert Richter. 1978. Corinth. (Documentary). 58 min. Sound. 16mm Color. *Rental:* Corinth Films. *Lease:* Corinth Films. *Rental:* Corinth Films, Videotape version.

Lion, The. William Holden & Trevor Howard. Directed by Jack Cardiff. 1962. Fox. 96 min. Sound. 16mm Color. *Rental:* Films Inc. *Rental:* Films Inc, Anamorphic version.

Lion & the Eagle, The. 2 pts. 1966. NET. (Documentary). 60 min. Sound. 16mm B&W. *Rental:* Indiana AV Ctr. *Lease:* Indiana AV Ctr.

Lion & the Horse, The. Steve Cochran & Ray Teal. Directed by Louis King. 1952. Warners. 83 min. Sound. 16mm Color. *Rental:* Buchan Pics, Films Inc, Inst Cinema, Twyman Films & Welling Motion Pictures.

Lion Has Seven Heads, The. Jean-Pierre Leaud. Directed by Glauber Rocha. 1970. Brazil/Congo. 97 min. Sound. 16mm Color. subtitles. *Rental:* New Yorker Films. *Sale:* New Yorker Films.

Lion Has Wings, The. Directed by Michael Powell, Brian Desmond-Hurst & Adrian Brunel. 1940. Britain. (Documentary). 76 min. Sound. 16mm B&W. *Rental:* Inst Cinema & Mogulls Films.

Lion Hunters, The. Directed by Jean Rouch. 1969. France. (Documentary). 68 min. Sound. 16mm Color. *Rental:* U Cal Film, Film Ctr DC & Films Inc.

Lion Hunters, The. Johnny Sheffield & Morris Ankrum. Directed by Ford Beebe. 1951. 80 min. Sound. 16mm B&W. *Rental:* Budget Films.

Lion in Winter, The. Katharine Hepburn & Peter O'Toole. Directed by Anthony Harvey. 1968. Embassy. 132 min. Sound. 16mm Color. *Rental:* Films Inc.

Lion Man, The. Steve Arkin, Barbara Lake & Charles Garrett. Stephen Sloane. 91 min. Sound. 16mm Color. *Rental:* Best Film & Video Corp..

Lion of Judah, The. 1972. Britain. (Documentary). 50 min. Sound. 16mm Color. *Rental:* Time-Life Multimedia. *Sale:* Time-Life Multimedia. *Sale:* Time-Life Multimedia, Videotape version. *Sale:* Time-Life Multimedia, Spanish Language version.

Lion of the Desert. Anthony Quinn & Oliver Reed. Directed by Moustapha Akkad. 146 min. 16mm Color. *Rental:* Westcoast Films.

Lion of Thebes, The. Orig. Title: Helen of Troy. Mark Forrest & Yvonne Furneaux. 1964. Italy. 87 min. Sound. 16mm Color. dubbed. *Rental:* Budget Films & Modern Sound.

Lion Who Thought He Was People, The. Bill Travers & Virginia McKenna. Directed by Bill Travers & James Hill. 1975. Britain. 89 min. Sound. 16mm Color. *Rental:* Films Inc.

Lionheart. James Forlong. Directed by Michael Forlong. 1968. Britain. 45 min. Sound. 16mm Color. *Rental:* Janus Films. *Sale:* Lucerne Films & Sterling Ed Film.

Lion's Cub, The. Glenda Jackson. 1976. Britain. 90 min. Sound. 16mm Color. *Rental:* Films Inc. *Sale:* Films Inc. *Rental:* Films Inc, *Sale:* Films Inc, Videotape version.

Lions for Breakfast. Jim Henshaw. 1977. Goldstone. 80 min. Sound. 16mm Color. *Rental:* Westcoast Films.

Lion's Love. Viva, Jerome Ragni & James Rado. Directed by Agnes Varda. 1969. EYR. 110 min. Sound. 16mm Color. *Rental:* New Cinema & Twyman Films. *Sale:* Twyman Films.

Lion's Roar, The. 50 min. 16mm *Rental:* Centre Co. *Sale:* Centre Co. *Sale:* Centre Co, Videotape version avail. version.

Lipid Storage Disease: Past, Present, & Future. 1978. 60 min. Sound. videotape Color. *Sale:* Natl AV Ctr.

Lipstick. Margaux Hemingway, Chris Sarandon, Perry King & Anne Bancroft. Directed by Lamont Johnson. 1976. Paramount. 89 min. Sound. 16mm Color. *Rental:* Films Inc.

Lipstick. Pietro Germi & Giorgia Moll. Directed by Damiano Damiani. 1959. Italy. 90 min. Sound. 16mm Color. dubbed. *Rental:* Cinema Guild.

Liquid Sky. Anne Carlisle. Directed by Slava Tsukerman. 1982. Z Films. 118 min. Sound. 16mm Color. *Rental:* New Yorker Films.

Liquidator, The. Rod Taylor & Jill St. John. Directed by Jack Cardiff. 1966. MGM. 105 min. Sound. 16mm Color. *Rental:* MGM United. *Rental:* MGM United, Anamorphic version.

Lisa. Dolores Hart & Stephen Boyd. Directed by Philip Dunne. 1962. Fox. 112 min. Sound. 16mm Color. *Rental:* Films Inc. *Rental:* Films Inc, Anamorphic version.

Lisa & the Devil. Elke Sommer & Telly Savalas. Directed by Mario Bava. 1973. Allied Artists. 97 min. Sound. 16mm Color. *Rental:* Hurlock Cine.

Lisbon. Ray Milland, Maureen O'Hara & Claude Rains. Directed by Ray Milland. 1956. Republic. (Anamorphic). 90 min. Sound. 16mm Color. *Rental:* Ivy Films. *Lease:* Rep Pic Film.

Lisbon Story, The. David Farrar. Directed by Paul L. Stein. 1947. Britain. 98 min. Sound. 16mm B&W. *Rental:* Ivy Films.

Lisice *see* Handcuffs.

Lissy. Sonja Sutter & Horst Drinda. Directed by Konrad Wolf. Ger. 1957. Germany. 88 min. Sound. 16mm B&W. subtitles. *Rental:* Films Inc.

List of Adrian Messenger, The. George C. Scott & Dana Wynter. Directed by John Huston. 1963. Universal. 98 min. Sound. 16mm B&W. *Rental:* Swank Motion.

Listen, Darling. Judy Garland & Walter Pidgeon. Directed by Edwin L. Marin. 1938. MGM. 70 min. Sound. 16mm B&W. *Rental:* MGM United.

Listen, Let's Make Love. Pierre Clementi & Claudine Auger. Directed by Vittorio Caprioli. Ital. 1969. Italy. 91 min. Sound. 16mm Color. subtitles. *Rental:* MGM United.

Listen Listen Listen. 1975. Canada. (Documentary). 83 min. Sound. 16mm Color. *Rental:* U Cal Media.

Lisztomania. Roger Daltrey & Ringo Starr. Directed by Ken Russell. 1975. Warners. 106 min. Sound. 16mm Color. *Rental:* Films Inc, Swank Motion & Twyman Films.

Little Abner *see* Li'l Abner.

Little Angel, The. Maria Gracia. Directed by K. Gordon Murray. 1960. Spain. 90 min. Sound. 16mm Color. narrated Eng. *Rental:* Charard Motion Pics.

Little Annie Rooney. Mary Pickford & William Haines. Directed by William Beaudine. 1925. Pickford. 97 min. Silent. 16mm B&W. *Rental:* Killiam Collect. *Sale:* Blackhawk Films, Videotape version.

Little Bear Keepers, The. Czechoslovakia. (Cast unlisted). 51 min. Sound. 16mm Color. dubbed. *Rental:* Films Inc & Westcoast Films. *Sale:* Films Inc.

Little Big Horn. Orig. Title: Fighting Seventh, The. Lloyd Bridges & John Ireland. Directed by Charles Marquis Warren. 1951. Lippert. 85 min. Sound. 16mm B&W. *Rental:* Budget Films, Roas Films, Westcoast Films & Welling Motion Pictures.

Little Big Man. Dustin Hoffman & Chief Dan George. Directed by Arthur Penn. 1971. National General. 150 min. Sound. 16mm Color. *Rental:* Swank Motion. *Rental:* Swank Motion, 139 min. version.

Little Big Shot. Sybil Jason & Glenda Farrell. Directed by Michael Curtiz. 1935. Warners. 74 min. Sound. 16mm B&W. *Rental:* MGM United.

Little Boy. Willie Jaramillo & Steve Baer. Directed by Danny Lyon. 1977. (Documentary). 54 min. Sound. 16mm Color. *Rental:* Museum Mod Art. *Lease:* Museum Mod Art.

Little Boy Blue & Pancho. Directed by K. Gordon Murray. 1963. K. Gordon Murray. (Cast unlisted). 86 min. Sound. 16mm Color. dubbed. *Rental:* Westcoast Films.

Little Boy Lost. Bing Crosby & Claude Dauphin. Directed by George Seaton. 1953. Paramount. 95 min. Sound. 16mm B&W. *Rental:* Films Inc.

Little Caesar. Edward G. Robinson & Glenda Farrell. Directed by Mervyn LeRoy. 1930. Warners. 80 min. Sound. 16mm B&W. *Rental:* MGM United.

Little Church Around the Corner, The. Claire Windsor & Hobart Bosworth. Directed by William A. Seiter. 1923. Warners. 70 min. Silent. 16mm B&W. *Rental:* Mogulls Films, Silent 8mm version.

Little Cigars, The. Angel Tompkins & Billy Curtis. Directed by Chris Christenberry. 1974. American International. 92 min. Sound. 16mm Color. *Rental:* Swank Motion.

Little Colonel, The. Shirley Temple. Directed by David Butler. 1935. Fox. (Color sequences). 80 min. Sound. 16mm B&W. *Rental:* Films Inc.

Little Damozel, The. Anna Neagle. Directed by Herbert Wilcox. 1933. 16mm *Rental:* A Twyman Pres.

Little Dark Angels. Trans. Title: Angelitos Negros. Pedro Infante. Directed by Ismael Rodriguez. Span. 1950. Mexico. 95 min. Sound. 16mm B&W. subtitles. *Rental:* Trans-World Films.

Little Darlings. Tatum O'Neal & Kristy McNichol. Directed by Ronald F. Maxwell. 1980. Paramount. 92 min. Sound. 16mm Color. *Rental:* Films Inc.

Little Dog Lost. 1970. Disney. (Documentaty). 48 min. Sound. 16mm Color. *Rental:* Cine Craft, Roas Films, Film Ctr DC & Twyman Films.

Little Duchess, The. Directed by Harley Knowles. 1917. Powers. (Cast unlisted). 60 min. Silent. 16mm B&W. *Rental:* Mogulls Film. *Sale:* E Finney.

Little Egypt. Rhonda Fleming & Mark Stevens. Directed by Frederick De Cordova. 1951. Universal. 82 min. Sound. 16mm Color. *Rental:* Swank Motion.

Little Fauss & Big Halsy. Robert Redford & Michael J. Pollard. Directed by Sidney J. Furie. 1971. Paramount. 97 min. Sound. 16mm Color. *Rental:* Films Inc.

Little Fellow from Gambo, A. 1971. Canada. (Documentaty). 57 min. Sound. 16mm Color. *Rental:* Natl Film CN. *Sale:* Natl Film CN.

Little Foxes, The. Bette Davis & Herbert Marshall. Directed by William Wyler. 1941. Goldwyn. 116 min. Sound. 16mm B&W. *Rental:* Films Inc.

Little Fugitive, The. Richie Andrusco. Directed by Ray Ashley. 1953. Burstyn. 75 min. Sound. 16mm B&W. *Rental:* Budget Films, Rep Pic Film, Newman Film Lib & Film Ctr DC.

Little Giant, The. Orig. Title: On the Carpet. Edward G. Robinson & Mary Astor. Directed by Roy Del Ruth. 1933. Warners. 75 min. Sound. 16mm B&W. *Rental:* MGM United.

Little Girl Who Lives Down the Lane, The. Jodie Foster & Martin Sheen. Directed by Nicolas Gessner. 1977. American International. 94 min. Sound. 16mm Color. *Rental:* Swank Motion.

Little Hobo, The *see* Littlest Hobo.

Little Humpbacked Horse, The. 1961. Russia. (Ballet). 85 min. Sound. 16mm Color. narrated Eng. *Rental:* Corinth Films.

Little Hut, The. Ava Gardner, Stewart Granger & David Niven. Directed by Mark Robson. 1957. MGM. 91 min. Sound. 16mm Color. *Rental:* MGM United.

Little Injustices: Laura Nader Looks at the Law. 1981. PBS. (Documentary). 60 min. Sound. Videotape Color. *Rental:* Iowa Films & PBS Video. *Sale:* PBS Video.

Little Jungle Boy, The. Malay. (Native cast). 85 min. Sound. 16mm Color. *Rental:* Films Inc.

Little Kidnappers, The. Duncan MacRae & Adrienne Corri. Directed by Philip Leacock. 1954. Britain. 93 min. Sound. 16mm B&W. *Rental:* Janus Films & Films Inc.

Little Laura & Big John. Karen Black & Fabian Forte. Directed by Luke Moberly & Bob Woodburn. 1975. American International. 82 min. Sound. 16mm Color. *Rental:* Budget Films, Films Inc & Video Comm. *Lease:* Video Comm. *Rental:* Video Comm, *Lease:* Video Comm, Videotape version.

Little League Moochie. Kevin Corcoran & Jim Brown. 1962. Disney. 96 min. Sound. 16mm B&W. *Rental:* Buchan Pic, Cine Craft, Cousino Visual Ed, Williams Films, Films Inc, Film Pres, U of IL Film, Modern Sound, Newman Film Lib, Roas Films, Film Ctr DC, Welling Motion Pictures & Westcoast Films.

Little Lord Fauntleroy. Freddie Barthlomew & Dolores Costello. Directed by John Cromwell. 1936. United Artists. 102 min. Sound. 16mm B&W. *Rental:* Alba House, Budget Films, Classic Film Mus, Films Inc, Film Classics, Macmillan Films, Mogulls Films, Syracuse U Film, Video Comm, Welling Motion Pictures & Wholesome Film Ctr. *Lease:* Macmillan Films. *Sale:* ABC Film Lib, Super 8 sound version. *Rental:* Video Comm, Videotape version.

Little Man, What Now? Margaret Sullavan & Douglas Montgomery. Directed by Frank Borzage. 1934. Universal. 91 min. Sound. 16mm B&W. *Rental:* Swank Motion.

Little Match Girl, The *see* Petite Marchand d'Allumettes.

Little Men. Dickie Moore & Junior Durkin. Directed by Phil Rosen. 1934. Mascot. 80 min. Sound. 16mm B&W. *Rental:* Budget Films & Film Classics.

Little Men. Kay Francis & Jack Oakie. Directed by Norman Z. McLeod. 1940. RKO. 75 min. Sound. 16mm B&W. *Rental:* Alba House, Budget Films, Classic Film Mus, Ivy Films, Mogulls Films, Liberty Co, Video Comm & Wholesome Film Ctr. *Rental:* Video Comm, Videotape version.

Little Mermaid, The. 1979. G. G. Communications. (Animated). 71 min. Sound. 16mm Color. *Rental:* Williams Films, Films Inc & Modern Sound.

Little Minister, The. Katharine Hepburn & John Beal. Directed by Richard Wallace. 1934. RKO. 104 min. Sound. 16mm B&W. *Rental:* Films Inc. *Lease:* Films Inc.

Little Miss Broadway. Shirley Temple & Jimmy Durante. Directed by Irving Cummings. 1938. Fox. 70 min. Sound. 16mm B&W. *Rental:* Films Inc.

Little Miss Marker. Adolphe Menjou & Shirley Temple. Directed by Alexander Hall. 1934. Paramount. 80 min. Sound. 16mm B&W. *Rental:* Swank Motion.

Little Miss Marker. Walter Matthau & Julie Andrews. Directed by Walter Bernstein. 1980. Universal. 103 min. Sound. 16mm Color. *Rental:* Swank Motion.

Little Miss Thoroughbred. Ann Sherdian & John Litel. Directed by John Farrow. 1938. Warners. 63 min. Sound. 16mm B&W. *Rental:* MGM United.

Little Mister Jim. Butch Jenkins. Directed by Fred Zinnemann. 1946. MGM. 61 min. Sound. 16mm B&W. *Rental:* MGM United.

Little Murders. Elliot Gould & Donald Sutherland. Directed by Alan Arkin. 1971. Fox. 110 min. Sound. 16mm Color. *Rental:* Films Inc, Twyman Films, Westcoast Films, Welling Motion Pictures & Williams Films.

Little Nellie Kelly. Judy Garland & George Murphy. Directed by Norman Taurog. 1940. MGM. 98 min. Sound. 16mm B&W. *Rental:* MGM United.

Little Night Music, A. Elizabeth Taylor, Diana Rigg & Len Cariou. Directed by Harold Prince. 1978. New World. 124 min. Sound. 16mm Color. *Rental:* Films Inc.

Little Norse Prince, The. Directed by Isao Takahata. Japan. (Animated). 82 min. Sound. 16mm Color. dubbed. *Rental:* Budget Films, Kerr Film, Westcoast Films & Welling Motion Pictures.

Little Nuns, The. Catherine Spaak & Sylva Koscina. Directed by Luciano Salce. 1965. Italy. 101 min. Sound. 16mm B&W. *Rental:* Films Inc.

Little Old New York. Alice Faye & Brenda Joyce. Directed by Henry King. 1940. Fox. 100 min. Sound. 16mm B&W. *Rental:* Films Inc.

Little Orphan Annie. Colleen Moore & Tom Santschi. Directed by Colin Campbell. 1919. Pioneer. 55 min. Silent. 16mm B&W. *Rental:* Film Classics & Mogulls Films. *Sale:* Classic Film Mus & Film Classics. *Rental:* Film Classics, *Sale:* FIlm Classics, Silent 8mm version.

Little Orphan Annie. Mitzi Green, Edgar Kennedy & May Robson. Directed by John Robertson. 1932. RKO. 60 min. Sound. 16mm B&W. *Rental:* RKO General Pics. *Sale:* Blackhawk Films, Super 8 Sound version. *Sale:* Blackhawk Films, Videotape version.

Little Prince, The. Steven Warner & Richard Kiley. Directed by Stanley Donen. 1974. Paramount. 88 min. Sound. 16mm Color. *Rental:* Films Inc.

Little Prince & the Eight-Headed Dragon, The. 1978. Japan. (Animated). 85 min. Sound. 16mm Color. *Rental:* Cine Craft, Williams Films, Bosco Films, Modern Sound, Film Ctr DC, Twyman Films, Westcoast Films & Welling Motion Pictures.

Little Princess, The. Shirley Temple & Richard Greene. Directed by Walter Lang. 1939. Fox. 93 min. Sound. 16mm Color. *Rental:* Budget Films, Classic Film Mus, Em Gee FilmLib, Kit Parker, Newman Film Lib, Roas Films, Video Comm & Welling Motion Pictures. *Sale:* Classic Film Mus, Cinema Concepts, Natl Cinema & Reel Images. *Rental:* Video Comm, *Sale:* Morcraft Films, Sound B&W 16mm version. *Sale:* Morcraft Films, Super 8 sound B&W version. *Sale:* Reel Images, Super 8 sound color version. *Sale:* Tamarelles French Film, Videotape version.

Little Red Monkey *see* Case of the Red Monkey.

Little Red Riding Hood. Baby Peggy. Directed by Alfred Goulding. 1925. Selznick. 60 min. Silent. 8mm B&W. *Sale:* Film Classics.

Little Red Riding Hood. Maria Gracia. Directed by Roberto Rodriguez. 1960. Mexico. 87 min. Sound. 16mm Color. dubbed. *Rental:* Westcoast Films.

Little Red Schoolhouse, The. Frank Coughlan & Ann Doran. Directed by Charles Lamont. 1936. Chesterfield. 75 min. Sound. 16mm B&W. *Rental:* Alba House.

Little Romance, A. Sir Laurence Olivier, Diane Lane & Broderick Crawford. Directed by George Roy Hill. 1979. Orion. 108 min. Sound. 16mm Color. *Rental:* Films Inc. *Rental:* Films Inc, Anamorphic version.

Little Savage, The. Pedro Armendariz. Directed by Byron Haskin. 1959. Mexico. 72 min. Sound. 16mm B&W. dubbed. *Rental:* Films Inc.

Little Sex, A. Tim Matheson & Kate Capshaw. Directed by Bruce Paltrow. 1982. Universal. 94 min. Sound. 16mm Color. *Rental:* Swank Motion. *Rental:* Swank Motion, Videotape version.

Little Shepherd of Kingdom Come, The. Jimmie Rodgers & Chill Wills. Directed by Andrew V. McLaglen. 1961. Fox. 108 min. Sound. 16mm Color. *Rental:* Charard Motion Pics, Films Inc & Video Comm. *Rental:* Willoughby Peer, Anamorphic version.

Little Shop of Horrors, The. Jonathan Haze. Directed by Roger Corman. 1960. Allied Artists. 73 min. Sound. 16mm B&W. *Rental:* Budget Films, Hurlock Cine, Film Pres, Ivy Films, Kit Parker, Maljack & Video Comm. *Sale:* Reel Images. *Rental:* Maljack & Video Comm, *Sale:* Reel Images, Videotape version.

Little Theatre of Jean Renoir, The *see* Petit Theatre de Jean Renoir.

Little Tough Guys, The. Helen Parrish & Billy Halop. Directed by Harold Young. 1938. Universal. 63 min. Sound. 16mm B&W. *Rental:* Budget Films & Swank Motion. *Sale:* Cinema Concepts. *Rental:* Classic Film Mus, 84 min. version.

Little Tough Guys in Society, The. Mischa Auer & Edward Everett Horton. Directed by Erle C. Kenton. 1939. Universal. 63 min. Sound. 16mm B&W. *Rental:* Swank Motion.

Little Women. Katharine Hepburn & Joan Bennett. Directed by George Cukor. 1933. RKO. 115 min. Sound. 16mm B&W. *Rental:* Films Inc. *Rental:* MGM United, Videotape version.

Little Women. Elizabeth Taylor, June Allyson & Margaret O'Brien. Directed by Mervyn LeRoy. 1949. MGM. 122 min. Sound. 16mm B&W. *Rental:* MGM United. *Rental:* MGM United, Color version.

Little World of Don Camillo, The. Fernandel & Gino Cervi. Directed by Julien Duvivier. 1953. France-Italy. 100 min. Sound. 16mm B&W. dubbed. *Rental:* Inst Cinema.

Littlest Hobo, THe. Orig. Title: Little Hobo, The. Buddy Hart & Wendy Stuart. Directed by Charles R. Rondeau. 1958. Allied Artists. 77 min. Sound. 16mm B&W. *Rental:* Hurlock Cine.

Littlest Horse Thieves, The. Alastair Sim & Peter Barkworth. Directed by Charles Jarrott. 1976. Disney. 104 min. Sound. 16mm Color. *Rental:* Cine Craft, Williams Films, Bosco Films, Disney Prod, Elliot Film Co, Films Inc, MGM United, Modern Sound, Newman Film Lib, Roas Films, Swank Motion, Twyman Films, Westcoast Films & Welling Motion Pictures.

Littlest Outlaw, The. Joseph Calleia & Pedro Armendariz. Directed by Roberto Gavaldon. 1955. Disney. 75 min. Sound. 16mm Color. *Rental:* Buchan Pic, Cine Craft, Cousino Visual Ed, Disney Prod, Films Inc, Film Pres, U of IL Film, Modern Sound, Newman Film Lib, Swank Motion & Film Ctr DC.

Littlest Rebel, The. Shirley Temple & John Boles. Directed by David Butler. 1935. Fox. 70 min. Sound. 16mm B&W. *Rental:* Films Inc.

Littlest Warrior, The. 1962. Japan. (Animated). 70 min. Sound. 16mm Color. dubbed. *Rental:* Budget Films, Cine Craft, Charard Films, Films Inc, Kerr Film, Film Ctr DC, Twyman Films, Video Comm, Westcoast Films, Welling Motion Pictures & Willoughby Peer.

Lit...Ze Bawdy Bed, Le. Alice Sapritch. Directed by Jacques Lem. Fr. 1975. France. 82 min. Sound. 16mm Color. subtitles. *Rental:* J Green Pics. *Rental:* J Green Pics, Dubbed version.

Live a Little, Love a Little. Elvis Presley. Directed by Norman Taurog. 1968. MGM. 90 min. Sound. 16mm Color. *Rental:* MGM United.

Live a Little, Steal a Lot. Robert Conrad & Don Stroud. Directed by Marvin J. Chomsky. 1974. American International. 101 min. Sound. 16mm Color. *Rental:* Swank Motion.

Live & Let Die. Roger Moore & Yaphet Kotto. Directed by Guy Hamilton. 1973. United Artists. 125 min. Sound. 16mm Color. *Rental:* MGM United. *Rental:* MGM United, Videotape version.

Live for Life. Yves Montand & Candice Bergen. Directed by Claude Lelouch. Fr. 1968. France. 130 min. Sound. 16mm Color. subtitles. *Rental:* Films Inc & MGM United.

Live, Love & Learn. Robert Montgomery & Rosalind Russell. Directed by George Fitzmaurice. 1937. MGM. 78 min. Sound. 16mm B&W. *Rental:* MGM United.

Live Wire, The. Richard Talmadge. Directed by Charles Hines. 1925. First National. 60 min. Silent. 16mm B&W. *Rental:* Em Gee Film Lib & Mogulls Films. *Sale:* E Finney.

Lively Art of Picture Books, The. 1964. Weston Woods. (Documentary). 56 min. Sound. 16mm Color. *Rental:* BYU Media, Iowa Films, U Mich Media & Syracuse U Film. *Sale:* Weston Woods Studios.

Lively Set, The. James Darren & Pamela Tiffin. Directed by Jack Arnold. 1965. Universal. 95 min. Sound. 16mm Color. *Rental:* Cousino Visual Ed & Swank Motion.

Lives of a Bengal Lancer, The. Gary Cooper & Franchot Tone. Directed by Henry Hathaway. 1935. Paramount. 108 min. Sound. 16mm B&W. *Rental:* Museum Mod Art & Swank Motion.

Lives of the Stars, The. 1980. Cosmos. (Documentary). 60 min. Sound. 16mm Color. *Rental:* Films Inc. *Sale:* Films Inc. *Rental:* Films Inc, *Sale:* Films Inc, Videotape version.

Living Anatomy of the Cat, The. 1979. McGill Univ. 72 min. Sound. 16mm Color. *Rental:* Syracuse U Film.

Living Arctic, The. Canada. (Documentary). 56 min. Sound. 16mm Color. *Rental:* CBC Films. *Sale:* CBC Films.

Living Coffin, The. Trans. Title: Grito de la Muerte, El. Gaston Santo & Maria Duval. Directed by Fernando Mendez. 1958. Mexico. 72 min. Sound. 16mm *Rental:* Budget Films.

Living Dangerously. Otto Kruger. Directed by Herbert Brenon. 1936. Britain. 70 min. Sound. 16mm B&W. *Rental:* Mogulls Films.

Living Dead, The. Sir Gerald Du Maurier. Directed by Thomas Bentley. 1934. Britain. 70 min. Sound. 16mm B&W. *Rental:* Classic Film Mus.

Living Desert, The. Directed by James Algar. 1953. Disney. (Documentary). 70 min. Sound. 16mm Color. *Rental:* Buchan Pic, Cine Craft, Cousino Visual Ed, Williams Films, Bosco Films, Disney Prod, Elliot Film Co, Films Inc, Film Pres, U of IL Film, MGM United, Modern Sound, Newman Film Lib, Roas Films, Swank Motion, Film Ctr DC, Twyman Films, Westcoast Films & Welling Motion Pictures.

Living Desert of Libya, The. 1974. Explo Mundo. (Documentary). 52 min. Sound. 16mm Color. *Rental:* B Raymond. *Sale:* B Raymond.

Living Free. Susan Hampshire & Nigel Davenport. Directed by Jack Couffer. 1972. Columbia. 91 min. Sound. 16mm Color. *Rental:* Arcus Film, Buchan Pic, Cine Craft, Williams Films, Film Pres, Inst Cinema, Modern Sound, Roas Films, Swank Motion, Twyman Films, Westcoast Films, Welling Motion Pictures & Budget Films.

Living Ghost, The. Orig. Title: Walking Nightmare. James Dunn & Joan Woodbury. Directed by William Beaudine. 1942. PRC. 70 min. Sound. 16mm B&W. *Rental:* Mogulls Films.

Living Head, The. Trans. Title: Cabeza Viviente, La. Ana Luisa Peluffo & Mauricio Garces. Directed by Chano Urueta. 1959. Mexico. 75 min. Sound. 16mm dubbed. *Rental:* Budget Films.

Living History: Eccles Interviews. 1971. 52 min. Sound. 16mm B&W. *Rental:* Utah Media.

Living in a Big Way. Gene Kelly & Marie McDonald. Directed by Gregory La Cava. 1947. MGM. 103 min. Sound. 16mm B&W. *Rental:* MGM United.

Living in Fear. Directed by Christian Blackwood. 1977. Blackwood. (Documentary). 52 min. Sound. 16mm Color. *Rental:* Blackwood Films. *Sale:* Blackwood Films.

Living It Up. Dean Martin & Jerry Lewis. Directed by Norman Taurog. 1954. Paramount. 94 min. Sound. 16mm Color. *Rental:* Films Inc.

Living Life Fully with Leo Buscaglia. 1982. 58 min. Sound. Videotape *Rental:* PBS Video. *Sale:* PBS Video.

Living Machine, The. 1961. Canada. (Documentary). 59 min. Sound. 16mm B&W. *Rental:* U Mich Media.

Living Machines, The. 1980. Britain. (Documentary). 50 min. Sound. 16mm Color. *Rental:* Films Inc & U of IL Films. *Sale:* Films Inc. *Sale:* Films Inc, Videotape version.

Living North. Directed by Stig Wessley. 1956. Finland. (Documentary). 75 min. Sound. 16mm B&W. *Rental:* Films Inc.

Living on Velvet. George Brent & Kay Francis. Directed by Frank Borzage. 1935. Warners. 80 min. Sound. 16mm B&W. *Rental:* MGM United.

Living Sands of Namib, The. 59 min. Sound. 16mm Color. *Rental:* Natl Geog. *Rental:* Natl Geog, Videotape version.

Living Sea, The. 1972. Britain. (Documentary). 50 min. Sound. 16mm Color. *Rental:* Time-Life Multimedia. *Sale:* Time-Life Multimedia. *Rental:* Time-Life Multimedia, *Sale:* Time-Life Multimedia, Videotape version.

Living Treasures of Japan, The. 59 min. Sound. 16mm Color. *Rental:* Natl Geog. *Rental:* Natl Geog, Videotape version.

Lizzie. Eleanor Parker & Richard Boone. Directed by Hugo Haas. 1957. MGM. 81 min. Sound. 16mm B&W. *Rental:* MGM United.

Llanito. Directed by Danny Lyon. 1971. Museum of Modern Art. (Documentary). 51 min. Sound. 16mm B&W. *Rental:* Museum Mod Art. *Lease:* Museum Mod Art.

Lloyd Reynolds. 1968. NET. (Documentary). 60 min. Sound. 16mm B&W. *Rental:* Indiana AV Ctr. *Sale:* Indiana AV Ctr.

Lloyds of London. Tyrone Power & Madeleine Carroll. Directed by Henry King. 1936. Fox. 115 min. Sound. 16mm B&W. *Rental:* Films Inc.

Lo Que Cuesta Vivar. 1950. Mexico. (Cast unlisted). 90 min. Sound. 16mm B&W. subtitles. *Rental:* Film Classics.

Loaded Pistols. Gene Autry. Directed by John English. 1948. Columbia. 80 min. Sound. 16mm B&W. *Sale:* Natl Cinema. *Sale:* Cinema Concepts. *Sale:* Reel Images, Super 8 sound version.

Local Bad Man, The. Hoot Gibson. Directed by Otto Brower. 1932. Allied. 60 min. Videotape B&W. *Rental:* Budget Films. *Sale:* Video Comm.

Local Boy Makes Good. Joe E. Brown & Dixie Lee. Directed by Mervyn LeRoy. 1931. Warners. 68 min. Sound. 16mm B&W. *Rental:* MGM United.

Local Color. Directed by Mark Rappaport. 1978. First Run. (Cast unlisted). 116 min. Sound. 16mm B&W. *Rental:* New Line Cinema & First Run. *Lease:* First Run.

Local Hero. Burt Lancaster & Peter Riegert. Directed by Bill Forsyth. 1983. Warners. 111 min. Sound. 16mm Color. *Rental:* Swank Motion. *Rental:* Swank Motion, Videotape version.

Lock Up Your Daughters. Christopher Plummer & Susannah York. Directed by Peter Coe. 1969. Britain. 108 min. Sound. 16mm Color. *Rental:* Welling Motion Pictures.

Lock Your Doors see Ape Man.

Locket, The. Laraine Day & Brian Aherne. Directed by John Brahm. 1946. RKO. 86 min. Sound. 16mm B&W. *Rental:* Films Inc.

Lodger, The. Ivor Novello. Directed by Alfred Hitchcock. 1926. Britain. 87 min. Silent. 16mm B&W. *Rental:* Budget Films, Classic Film Mus, Em Gee Film Lib, Films Inc, Images Film, Ivy Films, Kit Parker, Museum Mod Art & Video Comm. *Sale:* Cinema Concepts, Natl Cinema, Reel Images & Images Film. *Rental:* Ivy Films, Super 8 silent version. *Sale:* Tamarelles French Film & Images Film, *Rental:* Video Comm, Videotape version. *Rental:* Westcoast Films, *Sale:* Festival Films, 66 mins. version. *Sale:* Festival Films, 66 min. Videotape version.

Lodger, The. Merle Oberon & Laird Cregar. Directed by John Brahm. 1944. Fox. 84 min. Sound. 16mm B&W. *Rental:* Films Inc & Twyman Films.

Lodger, The. Orig. Title: The Phantom Fiend. Jack Hawkins. Directed by Maurice Elvey. 1932. 85 min. Sound. 16mm B&W. *Rental:* A Twyman Pres.

Logan's Run. Michael York, Jenny Agutter & Richard Jordan. Directed by Michael Anderson. 1976. 118 min. Sound. 16mm Color. *Rental:* MGM United. *Rental:* MGM United, Videotape version.

Logic Lane. Directed by Michael Chanan. 1972. Oxford. (Interview). 60 min. Sound. 16mm Color. *Rental:* New Yorker Films.

Lola. Charles Bronson & Susan George. 1971. American International. 80 min. Sound. 16mm Color. *Rental:* Swank Motion.

Lola. Barbara Sukowa & Armin Mueller-Stahl. Directed by Rainer Werner Fassbinder. Ger. 1982. 114 min. 16mm Color. subtitles. *Rental:* MGM United. *Rental:* MGM United, Videotape version.

Lola la Piconera. Juanita Reina. Directed by Luis Lucia. Span. 1953. Spain. 89 min. Sound. 16mm B&W. subtitles. *Rental:* Film Classics.

Lola Montes. Peter Ustinov & Martine Carol. Directed by Max Ophuls. Fr. 1955. France. 110 min. Sound. 16mm Color. subtitles. *Rental:* Films Inc.

Lolita. Peter Sellers, James Mason & Shelley Winters. Directed by Stanley Kubrick. 1962. MGM. 152 min. Sound. 16mm B&W. *Rental:* MGM United. *Rental:* MGM United, Videotape version.

Lolly Madonna XXX. Rod Steiger & Robert Ryan. Directed by Richard C. Sarafian. 1973. MGM. 95 min. Sound. 16mm Color. *Rental:* MGM United.

London Blackout Murders. John Abbott & Mary McLeod. Directed by George Sherman. 1942. Republic. 54 min. Sound. 16mm B&W. *Rental:* Ivy Films. *Sale:* Rep Pic Film.

London by Night. George Murphy & Leo G. Carroll. Directed by William Thiele. 1937. MGM. 69 min. Sound. 16mm B&W. *Rental:* MGM United.

London-Capital City. 1963. NET. (Documentary). 120 min. Sound. 16mm B&W. *Rental:* Indiana AV Ctr. *Sale:* Indiana AV Ctr.

London Connection, The see Omega Connection.

London Melody. Anna Neagle & Tullio Carminati. Directed by Herbert Wilcox. 1936. Britain. 74 min. Sound. 16mm B&W. *Rental:* A Twyman Pres & Ivy Films. *Sale:* Rep Pic Film.

London: The Making of a City. 2 pts. 1936. Britain. (Documentary). 104 min. Sound. 16mm Color. *Rental:* B Raymond. *Sale:* B Raymond.

Lone Avenger, The. Ken Maynard. Directed by Alan James. 1933. World Wide. 60 min. Sound. 16mm B&W. *Rental:* Budget Films & Video Comm. *Sale:* Reel Images. *Sale:* Reel Images, Super 8 Sound version. *Rental:* Video Comm, *Sale:* Video Comm, Videotape version.

Lone Bandit, The. Lane Chandler. Directed by J. P. McGowan. 1934. Empire. 60 min. Sound. 16mm B&W. *Rental:* Budget Films & Video Comm. *Sale:* Video Comm, Videotape version.

Lone Ranger, The. Clayton Moore & Jay Silverheels. Directed by Stuart Heisler. 1956. Warners. 86 min. Sound. 16mm Color. *Rental:* Budget Films, Williams Films, Ivy Films, Kerr Film, Modern Sound, Natl Film Video, Roas Films, Video Comm, Westcoast Films, Wholesome Film Ctr & Willoughby Peer. *Sale:* Nostalgia Merchant.

Lone Ranger & the Lost City of Gold, The. Orig. Title: Lost City of Gold, The. Clayton Moore & Jay Silverheels. Directed by Lesley Selander. 1958. United Artists. 80 min. Sound. 16mm Color. *Rental:* Budget Films, Williams Films, Films Inc, Ivy Films, Modern Sound, Natl Film Video, Roas Film, Video Comm, Westcoast Films & Wholesome Film Ctr. *Sale:* Nostalgia Merchant.

Lone Ranger Rides Again, The. Clayton Moore. 1955. Wrather. 70 min. Sound. 16mm Color. *Rental:* Westcoast Films. *Sale:* Nostalgia Merchant.

Lone Rider Ambushed, The. George Houston. Directed by Sam Newfield. 1941. PRC. 67 min. Sound. 16mm B&W. *Sale:* Natl Cinema.

Lone Rider & the Bandit, The. George Houston. Directed by Sam Newfield. 1942. PRC. 56 min. Sound. 16mm B&W. *Sale:* Natl Cinema.

Lone Rider Crosses the Rio, The. George Houston. Directed by Sam Newfield. 1941. PRC. 64 min. Sound. 16mm B&W. *Sale:* Natl Cinema.

Lone Rider in Cheyenne, The. George Houston. Directed by Sam Newfield. 1942. PRC. 60 min. Sound. 16mm B&W. *Rental:* Mogulls Films.

Lone Rider in Ghost Town, The. Orig. Title: Ghost Town. George Houston. Directed by Sam Newfield. 1941. PRC. 64 min. Sound. 16mm B&W. *Rental:* Mogulls Films. *Sale:* Cinema Concepts.

Lone Star. Clark Gable & Ava Gardner. Directed by Vincent Sherman. 1952. MGM. 95 min. Sound. 16mm B&W. *Rental:* MGM United.

Lone Star Raiders. Robert Livingston & Bob Steele. Directed by George Sherman. 1940. Republic. 54 min. Sound. 16mm B&W. *Rental:* Ivy Films. *Sale:* Rep Pic Film.

Lone Texan. Willard Parker. Directed by Paul Landres. 1959. Fox. 70 min. Sound. 16mm B&W. *Rental:* Films Inc.

Lone Texas Ranger. Bill Elliott. Directed by Spencer G. Bennett. 1945. Republic. 54 min. Sound. 16mm B&W. *Rental:* Ivy Films.

Lone Troubador, The see Two-Gun Troubador.

Lone Wolf, The. Britain. (Cast unlisted). 45 min. Sound. 16mm Color. *Rental:* Ivy Films.

Lone Wolf McQuade. Chuck Norris & David Carradine. Directed by Steve Carver. 1983. Orion. 105 min. Sound. 16mm Color. *Rental:* Films Inc.

Lone Wolf Returns, The. Melvyn Douglas & Gail Patrick. Directed by Roy William Neill. 1936. Columbia. 69 min. Sound. 16mm B&W. *Rental:* Films Inc.

Lone Wolf Spy Hunt, The. Warren William, Ida Lupino & Rita Hayworth. Directed by Peter Godfrey. 1939. Columbia. 80 min. Sound. 16mm B&W. *Rental:* Kit Parker.

Lone Wolf Strikes, The. Warren William & Joan Perry. Directed by Sidney Salkow. 1940. 67 min. Sound. 16mm *Rental:* Budget Films.

Loneliness of the Long Distance Runner, The. Tom Courtenay, Sir Michael Redgrave. Directed by Tony Richardson. 1962. Britain. 103 min. Sound. 16mm B&W. *Rental:* Budget Films, Films Inc, Twyman Films & Wholesome Film Ctr.

Loneliness of the Long Distance Singer, The: The Yves Montand Story. Yves Montand. Directed by Chris Marker. Fr. 1974. France. 60 min. Sound. 16mm Color. subtitles. *Rental:* Icarus Films. *Sale:* Icarus Films. *Rental:* French Am Cul, Videotape version.

Lonely Are the Brave. Kirk Douglas & Gena Rowlands. Directed by David Miller. 1962. Universal. 107 min. Sound. 16mm B&W. *Rental:* Swank Motion.

Lonely Dorymen, The. 1967. National Geographic. (Documentary). 51 min. Sound. 16mm Color. *Rental:* U Mich Media, Natl Geog & Wholesome Film Ctr. *Sale:* Natl Geog. *Sale:* Natl Geog, Videotape version.

Lonely Guy, The. Steve Martin & Charles Grodin. Directed by Arthur Hiller. 1984. Universal. 93 min. Sound. 16mm Color. *Rental:* Swank Motion. *Rental:* Swank Motion, Videotape version.

Lonely Hearts. Wendy Hughes & Norman Kaye. Directed by Paul Cox. 1982. Australia. 95 min. Sound. Videotape Color. *Sale:* Tamarelles French Films.

Lonely Hearts Bandits. Robert Rockwell & Dorothy Patrick. Directed by George Blair. 1950. Republic. 60 min. Sound. 16mm B&W. *Rental:* Ivy Films. *Sale:* Rep Pic Film.

Lonely Lady, The. Pia Zadora & Lloyd Bochner. Directed by Peter Sasdy. 1983. Universal. 92 min. Sound. 16mm Color. *Rental:* Swank Motion.

Lonely Man. Anthony Perkins & Jack Palance. Directed by Henry Levin. 1957. Paramount. 87 min. Sound. 16mm B&W. *Rental:* Films Inc.

Lonely Night. Marian Seldes. 1954. Mental Health Film Board. 62 min. Sound. 16mm B&W. *Rental:* Syracuse U Film.

Lonely Trail, The. John Wayne. Directed by Joseph Kane. 1936. Republic. 56 min. Sound. 16mm B&W. *Rental:* Ivy Films. *Sale:* Rep Pic Film.

Lonely Wife see Charulata.

Lonely Wives. Edward E. Horton & Esther Ralston. Directed by Russell Mack. 1932. RKO. 90 min. Sound. 16mm *Rental:* RKO General Pics.

Lonelyhearts. Montgomery Clift & Robert Ryan. Directed by Vincent J. Donahue. 1958. United Artists. 102 min. Sound. 16mm B&W. *Rental:* MGM United.

Lonesome Trail. Yakima Canutt & Art Mix. Directed by Bruce Mitchell. 1930. Syndicate. 57 min. Sound. 16mm B&W. *Sale:* Natl Cinema.

Lonesome Trail. Jimmy Wakely. Directed by Oliver Drake. 1945. Monogram. 55 min. Sound. 16mm B&W. *Rental:* Hurlock Cine.

Lonesome Trail. John Agar & Wayne Morris. Directed by Richard Bartlett. 1955. Lippert. 73 min. Sound. 16mm B&W. *Rental:* Budget Films, Welling Motion Pictures & Willoughby Peer.

Long & the Short & the Tall, The see Jungle Fighters.

Long Ago Tomorrow. Nanette Newman & Malcolm McDowell. Directed by Bryan Forbes. 1971. Britain. 110 min. Sound. 16mm Color. *Rental:* Cinema Five.

Long Canyon. Directed by Don Cambou. 1979. Fremontia. (Documentary). 59 min. 16mm *Rental:* Fremontia. *Sale:* Fremontia.

Long Chain, The. 1978. Britain. (Documentary). 53 min. Sound. 16mm Color. *Rental:* U Cal Media, U of IL Film, Iowa Films, Kent St U Film & U Mich Media, Videotape version.

Long Childhood, The. (Ascent of Man Ser.). 1974. Britain. (Documentary). 52 min. 16mm *Rental:* U Cal Media. Iowa Films, U Mich Media & Utah Media.

Long Childhood of Timmy, The. 1967. ABC. (Documentary). 53 min. Sound. 16mm B&W. *Rental:* Iowa Films, McGraw-Hill Films & U Nev AV Ctr. *Sale:* McGraw-Hill Films.

Long Dark Hall, The. Rex Harrison & Lilli Palmer. Directed by Anthony Bushell. 1951. Britain. 86 min. Sound. 16mm B&W. *Rental:* Budget Films.

Long Day's Dying, A. David Hemmings Directed by Peter Collinson. 1968. Paramount. 93 min. 16mm *Rental:* Films Inc.

Long Day's Journey into Night. Katharine Hepburn, Sir Ralph Richardson. Directed by Sidney Lumet. 1962. Embassy. 136 min. 16mm B&W. *Rental:* Arcus Films, Budget Films, Cine Craft, Charard Motion Pics, Bosco Films, Film Ctr DC. Films Inc, Films Human, Inst Cinema, Ivy Films, Kit Parker, Twyman Films, U of IL Film, Video Comm, Westcoast Films, Welling Motion Pictures, Wholesome Film Ctr & Willoughby Peer. *Sale:* Films Human, Abridged 54 min & Videotape version.

Long Duel, The. Yul Brynner Directed by Ken Annakin. 1967. Paramount. 115 min. 16mm. *Rental:* Films Inc.

Long Good Friday, The. Bob Hoskins & Helen Mirren. Directed by John Mackenzie. 1982. Embassy. 114 min. Sound. 16mm Color. *Rental:* Films Inc.

Long Goodbye, The. Elliott Gould & Sterling Hayden. Directed by Robert Altman. 1973. United Artists. (Anamorphic). 112 min. Sound. 16mm Color. *Rental:* MGM United.

Long Gray Line, The. Tyrone Power & Maureen O'Hara. Directed by John Ford. 1955. Columbia. 138 min. Sound. 16mm Color. *Rental:* Arcus Film, Buchan Pic, Budget Films, Cine Craft, Corinth Films, Bosco Films, Films Inc, Images Film, Modern Sound, Film Ctr DC, Westcoast Films, Welling Motion Pictures & Wholesome Film Ctr. *Rental:* Corinth Films, Images Film & Kit Parker, Anamorphic version.

Long Haul, The. Victor Mature Directed by Ken Hughes. 1957. Britain. 88 min. 16mm B&W. *Rental:* Kit Parker.

Long, Hot Summer, The. Orson Welles, Paul Newman & Joanne Woodward. Directed by Martin Ritt. 1958. Fox. (Anamorphic). 115 min. Sound. 16mm Color. *Rental:* Williams Films, Films Inc & Twyman Films, videotape version.

Long John Silver Returns to Treasure Island. Robert Newton. Directed by Byron Haskin. 1955. Australia. 109 min. Sound. 16mm Color. *Rental:* Arcus Film, Budget Films, Video Comm, Westcoast Films & Willoughby Peer.

Long Lane's Turning, A. Henry B. Walthall & Mary Charleson. Directed by Louis Chaudet. 1919. Exclusive. 55 min. Silent. 16mm B&W. *Sale:* Griggs Movie.

Long Live the Republic see Viva la Republica.

Long, Long Trailer, The. Lucille Ball & Desi Arnaz. Directed by Vincente Minnelli. 1954. MGM. 95 min. Sound. 16mm Color. *Rental:* MGM United.

Long Lost Father, The. John Barrymore & Donald Cook. Directed by Merian C. Cooper. 1934. RKO. 63 min. Sound. 16mm *Rental:* RKO General Pics.

Long Night, The. Henry Fonda & Ann Dvorak. Directed by Anatole Litvak. 1947. RKO. 101 min. Sound. 16mm B&W. *Rental:* Budget Films.

Long Pants. Harry Langdon. Directed by Frank Capra. 1927. First National. 60 min. Sound. 16mm B&W. *Rental:* A Twyman Pres & Twyman Films.

Long Riders, The. Stacy Keach & David Carradine. Directed by Walter Hill. 1980. United Artists. 100 min. Sound. 16mm Color. *Rental:* MGM United.

Long Ships, The. Richard Widmark & Sidney Poitier. Directed by Jack Cardiff. 1964. Columbia. 125 min. Sound. 16mm Color. *Rental:* Arcus Film, Budget Films, Films Inc, Film Ctr DC & Twyman Films.

Long Valley, The: A Study of Bereavement. 1976. Britain. (Documentary). 59 min. Sound. 16mm Color. *Rental:* Films Inc, U of IL Film & U Mich Media. *Sale:* Films Inc. *Rental:* U Cal Media & Films Inc, *Sale:* Films Inc, Videotape version.

Long Voyage Home, The. John Wayne & Thomas Mitchell. Directed by John Ford. 1940. United Artists. 105 min. Sound. 16mm B&W. *Rental:* Budget Films.

Long Wait, The. Anthony Quinn & James Coburn. Directed by Victor Saville. 1954. United Artists. 93 min. Sound. 16mm B&W. *Rental:* Films Inc.

Long Walk, The. 1973. KQED. (Documentary). 60 min. Sound. 16mm Color. *Rental:* Film Wright. *Sale:* Film Wright.

Long Walk of Fred Young, The. 1979. 58 min. Sound. Videotape *Rental:* PBS Video. *Sale:* PBS Video, 16mm version.

Longest Day, The. John Wayne & Richard Burton. Directed by Ken Annakin, Andrew Marton & Bernhard Wicki. 1962. Fox. (Anamorphic). 180 min. Sound. 16mm B&W. *Rental:* Films Inc & Twyman Films.

Longest Hunt, The see Around the World Under the Sea.

Longest Night, The. Robert Young & Florence Rice. Directed by Errol Taggart. 1936. MGM. 51 min. Sound. 16mm B&W. *Rental:* MGM United.

Longest Yard, The. Orig. Title: Mean Machine, The. Burt Reynolds & Eddie Albert. Directed by Robert Aldrich. 1974. Paramount. 123 min. Sound. 16mm Color. *Rental:* Films Inc. *Sale:* Cinema Concepts, Super 8 sound version.

Longhorn, The. Bill Elliott & Phyllis Coates. Directed by Lewis D. Collins. 1952. Monogram. 70 min. Sound. 16mm B&W. *Rental:* Hurlock Cine.

Longs, The: A Louisiana Dynasty. 1966. Wolper. (Documentary). 50 min. Sound. 16mm B&W. *Rental:* Films Inc. *Sale:* Films Inc. *Sale:* Films Inc, Videotape version.

Look at Liv, A. Directed by Richard Kaplan. 1977. Macmillan. (Documentary). 67 min. Sound. 16mm Color. *Rental:* U of IL Film, Texture Film & Films Inc. *Sale:* Texture Film. *Sale:* Texture Film, Videotape version.

Look for the Silver Lining. June Haver & Ray Bolger. Directed by David Butler. 1949. Warners. 105 min. Sound. 16mm B&W. *Rental:* MGM United.

Look Homeward Lassie. Lassie. 1955. Wrather. 78 min. Sound. 16mm B&W. *Rental:* Budget Films, Films Inc & Modern Sound.

Look in any Window. Paul Anka, Jack Cassidy & Ruth Roman. Directed by William Alland. 1961. Allied Artists. 87 min. Sound. 16mm B&W. *Rental:* Hurlock Cine.

Look of a Lithographer, The. 1968. Films Inc. (Documentary). 55 min. Sound. 16mm B&W. *Rental:* Films Inc.

Look Out, Sister. Louis Jordan & Tympany Five. 1946. Astor. 67 min. Sound. 16mm B&W. *Rental:* Budget Films.

Look Who's Laughing. Edgar Bergen. Directed by Allan Dwan. 1941. RKO. 79 min. Sound. 16mm B&W. *Rental:* Films Inc.

Looker. Albert Finney & James Coburn. Directed by Michael Crichton. 1982. Ladd Co.. 94 min. Sound. 16mm Color. *Rental:* Williams Films & Swank Motion. *Rental:* Swank Motion, Videotape version.

Looking at Leaders, A. 1981. CBS. 29 min. Sound. 16mm Color. *Rental:* U Mich Media.

Looking for Love. Connie Francis & Jim Hutton. Directed by Don Weis. 1964. MGM. 83 min. Sound. 16mm Color. *Rental:* MGM United.

Looking for Mao. 58 min. Sound. Videotape *Rental:* PBS Video. *Sale:* PBS Video.

Looking for Mr. Goodbar. Diane Keaton, Tuesday Weld & William Atherton. Directed by Richard Brooks. 1977. Paramount. 136 min. Sound. 16mm Color. *Rental:* Films Inc.

Looking Forward. Lewis Stone & Lionel Barrymore. Directed by Clarence Brown. 1933. MGM. 83 min. Sound. 16mm B&W. *Rental:* MGM United.

Looking Glass War, The. Christopher Jones & Pia Degermark. Directed by Frank Pierson. 1969. Britian. 107 min. Sound. Videotape Color. *Sale:* Tamarelles French Films.

Looney, Looney, Looney Bugs Bunny Movie, The. 1981. Warners. (Animated). 90 min. Sound. 16mm Color. *Rental:* Williams Films & Swank Motion.

Loonies on Broadway *see* Zombies on Broadway.

Loophole. Barry Sullivan & Dorothy Malone. Directed by Harold Schuster. 1954. Allied Artists. 80 min. Sound. 16mm B&W. *Rental:* Hurlock Cine.

Loose Ankles. Douglas Fairbanks Jr. & Loretta Young. Directed by Ted Wilde. 1930. Warners. 78 min. Sound. 16mm B&W. *Rental:* MGM United.

Loose Ends. Chris Mulkey. Directed by David Burton Morris & Victoria Wozniak. 1975. Twyman. 108 min. Sound. 16mm B&W. *Rental:* A Twyman Pres, New Cinema & Twyman Films. *Sale:* Twyman Films.

Loose Shoes. Bill Murray & Howard Hesseman. Directed by Ira Miller. 1980. Atlantic. 75 min. Sound. 16mm Color. *Rental:* Ivy Films.

Lorang's Way. Directed by David MacDougall & Judith MacDougall. 1979. Extension Media Center. (Documentary). 69 min. Sound. 16mm Color. *Rental:* U Cal Media. *Sale:* U Cal Media. *Sale:* U Cal Media, Videotape version.

Lord Byng, Canada Welcomes You. Directed by Brian Nolan. 1973. Canada. (Documentary). 58 min. Sound. 16mm Color. *Rental:* Natl Film CN. *Sale:* Natl Film CN.

Lord Byron of Broadway. Cliff Edwards. Directed by Harry Beaumont. 1930. MGM. 78 min. Sound. 16mm B&W. *Rental:* MGM United.

Lord Jim. Peter O'Toole. Directed by Richard Brooks. 1965. Columbia. 154 min. Sound. 16mm Color. *Rental:* Alba House, Arcus Film, Budget Films, Cine Craft, Charard Motion Pics, Corinth Films, Williams Films, Bosco Films, Films Inc, U of IL Film, Images Film, Kerr Film, Kit Parker, Modern Sound, Natl Film Video, Roas Films, Swank Motion, Syracuse U Film, Twyman Films, Video Comm, Westcoast Films, Welling Motion Pictures & Wholesome Film Ctr. *Rental:* Corinth Films, Images Film & Kit Parker, Anamorphic version. *Rental:* Swank Motion, Videotape version.

Lord Love a Duck. Roddy McDowall & Tuesday Weld. Directed by George Axelrod. 1966. United Artists. 109 min. Sound. 16mm B&W. *Rental:* MGM United.

Lord of the Flies. James Aubrey & Tom Chapin. Directed by Peter Glenville. 1963. Britain. 90 min. Sound. 16mm B&W. *Rental:* Budget Films, U Cal Media, Films Inc, Inst Cinema, Macmillan Films, Roas Films, Twyman Films, Welling Motion Pictures & Wholesome Film Ctr. *Lease:* Macmillan Films.

Lord of the Jungle. John Sheffield. Directed by Ford Beebe. 1955. Allied Artists. 77 min. Sound. 16mm B&W. *Rental:* Hurlock Cine.

Lord of the Rings. Directed by Ralph Bakshi. 1978. United Artists. (Animated). 131 min. Sound. 16mm Color. *Rental:* MGM United.

Lord of the Sky *see* Emitai.

Lord of the Universe, The. 1974. WNET. (Documentary, color sequences). 60 min. Videotape B&W. *Sale:* Electro Art.

Lord Thing. 2 pts. Viewfinders. (Tinted, documentary). 54 min. Sound. 16mm Color. *Rental:* Viewfinders.

Lords of Discipline, The. David Keith & Robert Prosky. Directed by Franc Roddam. 1983. Paramount. 103 min. Sound. 16mm Color. *Rental:* Films Inc.

Lords of Flatbush, The. Perry King, Henry Winkler & Sylvester Stallone. Directed by Stephen F. Verona. 1974. Columbia. 86 min. Sound. 16mm Color. *Rental:* Arcus Film, Buchan Pic, Budget Films, Cine Craft, Williams Films, Bosco Films, Films Inc, Ivy Films, Modern Sound, Newman Film Lib, Natl Film Video, Swank Motion, Twyman Films, Westcoast Films, Welling Motion Pictures & Wholesome Film Ctr.

Lords of the Air. 1980. Britain. (Documentary). 58 min. Sound. Videotape Color. *Rental:* Films Inc. *Sale:* Films Inc.

Loren MacIver. Directed by Maryette Charlton. 1967. Maryette Charlton. (Documentary). 46 min. Sound. 16mm Color. *Rental:* Film Images. *Sale:* Film Images.

Lorna Doone. Madge Bellamy & John Bowers. Directed by Maurice Tourneur. 1923. First National. 60 min. Silent. 16mm B&W. *Rental:* Budget Films, Em Gee Film Lib & Film Classics. *Sale:* E Finney, Silent 8mm version.

Lorna Doone. Margaret Lockwood & John Loder. Directed by Basil Dean. 1934. Britain. 89 min. Sound. 16mm B&W. *Rental:* Janus Films.

Lorna Doone. Barbara Hale & Richard Greene. Directed by Phil Karlson. 1951. Columbia. 84 min. Sound. 16mm B&W. *Rental:* Bosco Films & Inst Cinema. *Rental:* Buchan Pic, Williams Films, Modern Sound, Twyman Films, Westcoast Films & Welling Motion Pictures, *Rental:* Arcus Film, Color version.

Losers, The. Bernie Hamilton & Adam Roarke. Directed by Jack Starrett. 1968. Fanfare. 96 min. Sound. 16mm Color. *Rental:* Budget Films & Westcoast Films.

Losin' It. Tom Cruise & Jackie Earle Haley. Directed by Curtis Hanson. 1983. Embassy. 98 min. Sound. 16mm Color. *Rental:* Films Inc.

Losing Just the Same. 1966. NET. (Documentary). 60 min. Sound. 16mm B&W. *Rental:* Indiana AV Ctr. *Sale:* Indiana AV Ctr.

Loss & Grieving: You & Your Patient. 1980. 115 min. Sound. Videotape Color. *Sale:* Natl AV Ctr.

Loss of Innocence, A. Orig. Title: Greengage Summer. Kenneth More, Danielle Darrieux & Susannah York. Directed by Lewis Gilbert. 1961. Britain. 90 min. Sound. 16mm Color. *Rental:* Films Inc, Inst Cinema, Welling Motion Pictures & Wholesome Film Ctr.

Lost. Sandra Dee, Don Stewart & Ken Curtis. Sound. 16mm Color. *Rental:* Williams Films.

Lost & Found. George Segal & Glenda Jackson. Directed by Melvin Frank. 1979. Columbia. 112 min. Sound. 16mm Color. *Rental:* Budget Films, Cine Craft, Modern Sound & Swank Motion.

Lost Angel, The. Margaret O'Brien & James Craig. Directed by Roy Rowland. 1943. MGM. 90 min. Sound. 16mm B&W. *Rental:* MGM United.

Lost Boundaries. Mel Ferrer & Beatrice Pearson. Directed by Alfred M. Werker. 1949. De Rochemont. 97 min. Sound. 16mm B&W. *Rental:* Swank Motion & Twyman Films.

Lost Canyon. William Boyd. Directed by Lesley Selander. 1942. United Artists. 54 min. Sound. 16mm B&W. *Lease:* Cinema Concepts.

Lost City *see* Jungle Princess.

Lost City, The. Kane Richmond & Claudia Dell. Directed by Harry Revier. 1935. Krellberg. 70 min. Sound. 16mm B&W. *Rental:* Budget Films. *Sale:* Morcraft Films. *Rental:* Ivy Films, Super 8 Sound version.

Lost City of Altantis, The. American National. (Documentary). 93 min. Sound. 16mm Color. *Rental:* Westcoast Films.

Lost City of Gold, The *see* Lone Ranger & the Lost City of Gold.

Lost Command, The. Anthony Quinn & Alain Delon. Directed by Mark Robson. 1966. Columbia. 129 min. Sound. 16mm Color. *Rental:* Arcus Film, Budget Films, Cine Craft, Charard Motion PicsBosco Films, Films Inc, Modern Sound, Roas Film & Westcoast Films. *Rental:* Budget Films, 99 mins. version.

Lost Continent, The. Cesar Romero & Hillary Brooke. Directed by Sam Newfield. 1951. Lippert. 86 min. Sound. 16mm B&W. *Rental:* Budget Films, Lewis Film & Mogulls Films.

Lost Continent, The. Eric Porter & Hildegard Neff. Directed by Michael Carreras. 1968. Fox. 89 min. Sound. 16mm Color. *Rental:* Films Inc.

Lost Expedition, The. 1920. Germany. (Cast unlisted). 50 min. Silent. 16mm B&W. *Rental:* Film Classics. *Sale:* Film Classics, Silent 8mm version.

Lost Express, The. Helen Holmes & Henry Barrows. Directed by J. P. McGowan. 1926. Rayart. 50 min. Silent. 16mm B&W. *Rental:* Budget Films, Em Gee Film Lib & Mogulls Films. *Rental:* Ivy Films, *Sale:* Blackhawk Films, Super 8 silent version.

Lost Flight, The. Anne Francis. Directed by Lloyd Bridges & Paul Donnelly. 1969. Universal. 101 min. Sound. 16mm Color. *Rental:* Williams Films.

Lost Heiress, The *see* Wife's Relations.

Lost History, A. Lynn Redgrave. CC Films. 60 min. Sound. Videotape Color. *Rental:* Natl Council Of The Churches of Christ.

Lost Honeymoon. Franchot Tone & Tom Conway. Directed by Leigh Jason. 1947. Eagle Lion. 69 min. Sound. 16mm B&W. *Rental:* Mogulls Films.

Lost Honor of Katharina Blum, The. Angela Winkler. Directed by Volker Schlondorff & Margarethe Von Trotta. Ger. 1975. Germany. 102 min. Sound. 16mm Color. subtitles. *Rental:* Films Inc.

Lost Horizon. Ronald Colman & Jane Wyatt. Directed by Frank Capra. 1937. Columbia. 120 min. Sound. 16mm B&W. *Rental:* Arcus Film, Budget Films, Cine Craft, Williams Films, Bosco Films, Films Inc, Inst Cinema, U of IL Film, Images Film, Ivy Films, Kit Parker, Modern Sound, Newman Film Lib, Natl Film Video, Roas Films, Swank Motion, Twyman Films, Westcoast Films, Welling Motion Pictures & Wholesome Film Ctr.

Lost Horizon. Peter Finch & Liv Ullman. Directed by Charles Jarrott. 1973. Columbia. 134 min. Sound. 16mm Color. *Rental:* Arcus Film, Budget Films, Williams Films, Films Inc, Modern Sound, Swank Motion, Westcoast Films & Welling Motion Picture Wholesome Film Ctr. *Rental:* Swank Motion, Anamorphic version.

Lost in a Harem. Bud Abbott & Lou Costello. Directed by Charles Reisner. 1944. MGM. 89 min. Sound. 16mm B&W. *Rental:* MGM United.

Lost in Alaska. Bud Abbott & Lou Costello. Directed by Jean Yarbrough. 1952. Universal. 76 min. Sound. 16mm B&W. *Rental:* Swank Motion.

Lost in Pajamas. Xerox. (Cast unlisted). 72 min. Sound. 16mm B&W. *Sale:* Xerox Films.

Lost in the Stars. Brock Peters. Directed by Daniel Mann. 1973. AFT. 114 min. Sound. 16mm Color. *Rental:* Films Inc.

Lost in the Stratosphere. William Cagney & Eddie Nugent. Directed by Melville Brown. 1934. Monogram. 70 min. Sound. 16mm B&W. *Rental:* Mogulls Films.

Lost in the Wild. Brett Maxworthy & Spike Milligan. 1980. Columbia. 84 min. Sound. 16mm Color. *Rental:* Arcus Film, Cine Craft, Williams Films, Bosco Films, Moderm Sound, Twyman Films, Westcoast Films.

Lost Island of Kioga, The. Bruce Bennett. Directed by William Witney. 1966. Republic. 100 min. Sound. 16mm B&W. *Rental:* Ivy Films. *Sale:* Rep Pic Film.

Lost Jungle, The. Clyde Beatty, Mickey Rooney & Cecilia Parker. Directed by Armand Schaefer & David Howard. 1934. Mascot. 75 min. Sound. 16mm B&W. *Rental:* Budget Films & Kerr Film. *Sale:* Morcraft Films.

Lost Lady, The *see* Safe in Hell.

Lost Lagoon, The. Jeffrey Lyon & Peter Donat. Directed by John Rawlins. 1958. United Artists. 79 min. Sound. 16mm B&W. *Rental:* MGM United.

Lost Man, The. Sidney Poitier & Joanna Shimkus. Directed by Robert Alan Aurthur. 1969. Universal. 110 min. Sound. 16mm Color. *Rental:* Williams Films & Swank Motion.

Lost Missile, The. Robert Loggia. Directed by Lester W. Berke. 1958. United Artists. 70 min. Sound. 16mm B&W. *Rental:* MGM United.

Lost Moment, The. Susan Hayward & Robert Cummings. Directed by Martin Gabel. 1947. Universal. 91 min. Sound. 16mm B&W. *Rental:* Budget Films, Charard Motion Pics, Ivy Films & Kit Parker. *Sale:* Rep Pic Film.

Lost Patrol, The. Boris Karloff & Victor McLaglen. Directed by John Ford. 1934. RKO. 74 min. Sound. 16mm B&W. *Rental:* Films Inc. *Lease:* Films Inc. *Sale:* Blackhawk Films, Super 8 sound version. *Sale:* Blackhawk Films, Videotape version.

Lost Pharaoh, The *see* Search for Akhenaten.

Lost Planet Airmen. Orig. Title: King of the Rocketmen. Don Haggerty & Mae Clarke. Directed by Fred C. Brannon. 1951. Republic. 65 min. Sound. 16mm B&W. *Rental:* Ivy Films. *Sale:* Cinema Concepts & Rep Pic Film.

Lost Souls. Virna Lisi. Italy. Sound. 16mm B&W. dubbed. *Rental:* Ivy Films & Mogulls Films.

Lost Squadron. Richard Dix & Mary Astor. Directed by George Archainbaud. 1932. RKO. 79 min. Sound. 16mm B&W. *Rental:* Films Inc. *Lease:* Films Inc.

Lost Trail. Johnny Mack Brown. Directed by Lambert Hillyer. 1945. Monogram. 53 min. Sound. 16mm B&W. *Rental:* Hurlock Cine.

Lost Tribe. Johnny Weissmuller. Directed by William Berke. 1949. Columbia. 90 min. Sound. 16mm B&W. *Rental:* Inst Cinema & Roas Films.

Lost Weekend, The. Ray Milland & Jane Wyman. Directed by Billy Wilder. 1945. Paramount. 101 min. Sound. 16mm B&W. *Rental:* Swank Motion & Williams Films.

Lost World, The. Wallace Beery, Lewis Stone & Bessie Love. Directed by Harry Hoyt. 1925. First National. 62 min. Silent. 16mm B&W. *Rental:* Budget Films, Em Gee Film Lib, Films Inc, Ivy Films, Kerr Film, Kit Parker, Mogulls Films, Film Images, Swank Motion, Video Comm, Westcoast Films, Wholesome Film Ctr & Willoughy Peer. *Sale:* Cinema Concepts, Natl Cinema & Video Comm. *Rental:* Ivy Films, *Rental:* Ivy Films & Video Comm, *Sale:* Tamarelles French Film, *Lease:* Video Comm, Videotape version. *Sale:* Festival Films, 50 mins. 16mm version. *Sale:* Festival Films, 50 min. Videotape version. *Rental:* Kit Parker, music only version.

Lost World, The. Michael Rennie & Jill St. John. Directed by Irwin Allen. 1960. Fox. (Anamorphic). 98 min. Sound. 16mm Color. *Rental:* Films Inc.

Lost World of Sinbad, The. Trans. Title: Daitozoku. Toshiro Mifune. Directed by Senkichi Taniguchi. 1965. Japan. 90 min. Sound. 16mm Color. dubbed. *Rental:* Budget Films, Welling Motion Pictures & Westcoast Films.

Lottery Bride, The. Jeanette MacDonald & Joe E. Brown. Directed by Paul L. Stein. 1930. United Artists. 80 min. Sound. 16mm B&W. *Rental:* A Twyman Pres, Em Gee Film Lib, Film Classics & Mogulls Films. *Sale:* Blackhawk Films. *Sale:* Blackhawk Films, Super 8 Sound version.

Lottery Lover, The. Lew Ayres & Pat Patterson. Directed by William Thiele. 1935. Fox. 82 min. Sound. 16mm B&W. *Rental:* Films Inc.

Lotus for Miss Quon, A. Lang Jeffries & Werner Peters. 1967. Italy. 82 min. Sound. 16mm Color. dubbed. *Rental:* Westcoast Films.

Loudspeaker, The. Orig. Title: Radio Star, The. Charles Grapewin & Ray Walker. Directed by Joseph Santley. 1934. Monogram. 80 min. Sound. 16mm B&W. *Rental:* Mogulls Films.

Louisa. Spring Byington & Charles Coburn. Directed by Alexander Hall. 1950. Universal. 90 min. Sound. 16mm B&W. *Rental:* Swank Motion.

Louisiana. Jimmy Davis & Margaret Lindsay. Directed by Phil Karlson. 1947. Monogram. 90 min. Sound. 16mm B&W. *Rental:* Hurlock Cine.

Louisiana Diary. 1964. NET. (Documentary). 60 min. Sound. 16mm B&W. *Rental:* Indiana AV Ctr. *Sale:* Indiana AV Ctr.

Louisiana Hayride. Judy Canova. Directed by Charles Barton. 1944. Columbia. 70 min. Sound. 16mm B&W. *Lease:* Time-Life Multimedia.

Louisiana Purchase. Bob Hope & Vera Zorina. Directed by Irving Cummings. 1941. Paramount. 98 min. Sound. 16mm Color. *Rental:* Swank Motion.

Louisiana Story. Directed by Robert Flaherty. 1948. Lopert. (Documentary). 77 min. Sound. 16mm B&W. *Rental:* Budget Films, U Cal Media, Films Inc, Kit Parker, U Mich Media, Syracuse U Film, Texture Film & Viewfinders. *Sale:* Texture Film. *Sale:* Blackhawk Films, Super 8 sound version. *Rental:* Kit Parker, Music only version.

Louisiana Story Study Film. 1962. Flaherty. (Documentary). 128 min. Sound. 16mm B&W. *Rental:* Museum Mod Art.

Louisiana Territory. Val Winter. Directed by Harry W. Smith. 1953. RKO. 65 min. Sound. 16mm Color. *Rental:* Films Inc.

Loulou. Gerard Depardieu & Isabelle Huppert. Directed by Maurice Pialat. Fr. 1980. France. 110 min. Sound. 16mm Color. subtitles. *Rental:* New Yorker Films.

Louvre, The. 1966. 45 min. Sound. 16mm Color. *Rental:* Iowa Films & U Mich Media.

Lovable Cheat, The. Charles Ruggles, Peggy Ann Garner & Buster Keaton. Directed by Richard Oswald. 1949. Film Classics. 80 min. Sound. 16mm B&W. *Rental:* Budget Films, Mogulls Films & Film Ctr DC.

Love. Greta Garbo & John Gilbert. Directed by Edmund Goulding. 1927. MGM. 80 min. Silent. 16mm B&W. *Rental:* MGM United.

Love a la Carte. Simone Signoret & Marcello Mastroianni. Directed by Antonio Pietrangeli. Ital. 1960. Italy. 91 min. Sound. 16mm B&W. subtitles. *Rental:* Films Inc.

Love Affair. Humphrey Bogart & Dorothy Mackaill. Directed by Thornton Freeland. 1932. Columbia. 70 min. Sound. 16mm B&W. *Rental:* Kit Parker.

Love Affair. Irene Dunne & Charles Boyer. Directed by Leo McCarey. 1939. RKO. 89 min. Sound. 16mm B&W. *Rental:* Films Inc.

Love Affair: Or the Case of the Missing Switchboard Operator. Eva Ras & Slobodan Aligrudic. Directed by Dusan Makavejev. Serbo-Croatian. 1967. Yugoslavia. 70 min. Sound. 16mm B&W. subtitles. *Rental:* Films Inc.

Love Among the Millionaires. Clara Bow & Stuart Erwin. Directed by Frank Tuttle. 1930. Paramount. 81 min. Sound. 16mm B&W. *Rental:* Swank Motion.

Love & Anarchy. Giancarlo Giannini. Directed by Lina Wertmuller. Ital. 1974. Italy. 108 min. Sound. 16mm Color. subtitles. *Rental:* Cinema Five. *Lease:* Cinema Five.

Love & Bullets. Charles Bronson & Rod Steiger. Directed by Stuart Rosenberg. 1979. Britain. 103 min. Sound. 16mm Color. *Rental:* Swank Motion.

Love & Death. Woody Allen & Diane Keaton. Directed by Woody Allen. 1975. United Artists. 89 min. Sound. 16mm Color. *Rental:* MGM United. *Rental:* MGM United, Videotape version.

Love & Faith. Toshiro Mifune & Takashi Shimura. Directed by Kei Kumai. Jap. 1978. Japan. 154 min. Sound. Videotape Color. subtitles. *Sale:* Tamarelles French Films.

Love & Hisses. Walter Winchell & Ben Bernie. Directed by Sidney Lanfield. 1938. Fox. 84 min. Sound. 16mm B&W. *Rental:* Films Inc.

Love & Kisses. Rick Nelson & Jack Kelly. Directed by Ozzie Nelson. 1965. Universal. 87 min. Sound. 16mm Color. *Rental:* Swank Motion.

Love & Learn. Jack Carson & Janis Paige. Directed by Frederick De Cordova. 1947. Warners. 83 min. Sound. 16mm B&W. *Rental:* MGM United.

Love & Loneliness. 1979. PBS. (Documentary). 59 min. Videotape Color. *Rental:* PBS Video. *Sale:* PBS Video.

Love & Pain & the Whole Damn Thing. Maggie Smith & Timothy Bottoms. Directed by Alan J. Pakula. 1973. Columbia. 110 min. Sound. 16mm Color. *Rental:* Corinth Films & Swank Motion.

Love & the Frenchwoman. Jean-Paul Belmondo & Annie Girardot. Directed by Rene Clair. Fr. 1961. France. 143 min. Sound. 16mm B&W. subtitles. *Rental:* Ivy Films.

Love Around the Clock *see* Cavalcade des Heures.

Love at First Bite. George Hamilton, Susan St. James & Richard Benjamin. Directed by Stan Dragoti. 1978. American International. 93 min. Sound. 16mm Color. *Rental:* Images Film, Swank Motion, Wholesome Film Ctr & Williams Films.

Love Before Breakfast. Carole Lombard & Preston Foster. Directed by Walter Lang. 1936. Paramount. 70 min. Sound. 16mm B&W. *Rental:* Swank Motion.

Love Begins at Twenty. Hugh Herbert & Patricia Ellis. Directed by Frank McDonald. 1936. Warners. 58 min. Sound. 16mm B&W. *Rental:* MGM United.

Love Bug, The. Dean Jones, Buddy Hackett & Michele Lee. Directed by Robert Stevenson. 1969. Disney. 109 min. Sound. 16mm Color. *Rental:* Buchan Pic, Williams Films, Bosco Films, DisneyProd, Elliot Film Co, Films Inc, MGM United, Modern Sound, Roas Films, Swank Motion, Film Ctr DC & Twyman Films, videotape version.

Love Child. Amy Madigan & Beau Bridges. Directed by Larry Peerce. 1983. Ladd Co.. 97 min. Sound. 16mm Color. *Rental:* Swank Motion. *Rental:* Swank Motion, Videotape version.

Love Class with Leo Buscaglia, A. 1981. 46 min. Sound. Videotape *Rental:* PBS Video. *Sale:* PBS Video.

Love Comes Along. Bebe Daniels & Ned Sparks. Directed by Rupert Julian. 1930. RKO. 78 min. Sound. 16mm B&W. *Rental:* RKO General Pics.

Love Crazy. William Powell & Myrna Loy. Directed by Jack Conway. 1941. MGM. 99 min. Sound. 16mm B&W. *Rental:* MGM United.

Love 'Em & Leave 'Em. Evelyn Brent & Louise Brooks. Directed by Frank Tuttle. 1926. Paramount. 70 min. Silent. 16mm B&W. *Rental:* Films Inc.

Love Everlasting. Lyda Borelli & Mario Bonnard. Directed by Mario Caserini. 1913. Italy. 70 min. Silent. 16mm B&W. *Rental:* Museum Mod Art.

Love Finds Andy Hardy. Mickey Rooney & Lewis Stone. Directed by George B. Seitz. 1938. MGM. 90 min. Sound. 16mm B&W. *Rental:* MGM United.

Love from a Stranger. Ann Harding & Basil Rathbone. Directed by Rowland V. Lee. 1937. Britain. 82 min. Sound. 16mm B&W. *Rental:* Classic Film Mus.

Love from a Stranger. John Hodiak & Sylvia Sidney. Directed by Richard Whorf. 1947. Eagle Lion. 81 min. Sound. 16mm B&W. *Sale:* Classics Assoc NY. *Rental:* A Twyman Pres.

Love God?, The Don Knotts & Anne Francis. Directed by Nat Hiken. 1969. Universal. 101 min. Sound. 16mm Color. *Sale:* Swank Motion.

Love Goddesses, The. 1963. Continental. (Color sequences) (Anthology). 87 min. Sound. 16mm B&W. *Rental:* New Cinema, Films Inc & Texture Film. *Sale:* Texture Film. *Sale:* Texture Film, Videotape version.

Love Happy. Marx Brothers & Ilona Massey. Directed by David Miller. 1949. United Artists. 91 min. Sound. B&W. *Rental:* Budget Films, Ivy Films, Modern Sound, Westcoast Films & Welling Motion Pictures. *Lease:* Rep Pic Film. *Rental:* Ivy Films, *Sale:* Cinema Concepts, Ivy Films & Reel Images, Videotape version. *Sale:* Video Tape Network,

Love Has Many Faces. Lana Turner & Cliff Roberson. Directed by Tony Richardson. 1965. Columbia. 105 min. Sound. 16mm Color. *Lease:* Time-Life Multimedia.

Love, Honor & Goodbye. Virginia Bruce & Victor McLaglen. Directed by Albert S. Rogell. 1945. Republic. 87 min. Sound. 16mm B&W. *Rental:* Ivy Films. *Sale:* Rep Pic Film.

Love in a Goldfish Bowl. Fabian Forte & Tommy Sands. Directed by Jack Sher. 1961. Paramount. 88 min. Sound. 16mm Color. *Rental:* Films Inc.

Love in the Afternoon. Orig. Title: Fascination. Audrey Hepburn, Gary Cooper & Maurice Chevalier. Directed by Billy Wilder. 1957. Allied Artists. 126 min. Sound. 16mm B&W. *Rental:* Hurlock Cine.

Love in the City. Directed by Federico Fellini, Cesare Zavattini, Dino Risi, Alberto Lattuada, Michelangelo Antonioni & Francesco Maselli. 1953. Italy. (Anthology). 86 min. Sound. 16mm B&W. *Rental:* Budget Films & Liberty Co. *Sale:* Festival Films. *Sale:* Festival Films, Videotape version.

Love in the Rough. Dorothy Jordan & Robert Montgomery. Directed by Charles Reisner. 1930. MGM. 85 min. Sound. 16mm B&W. *Rental:* MGM United.

Love Is a Ball. Glenn Ford & Hope Lange. Directed by David Swift. 1963. United Artists. 111 min. Sound. 16mm Color. *Rental:* MGM United.

Love Is a Funny Thing. Jean-Paul Belmondo & Annie Giradot. Directed by Claude Lelouch. 1970. United Artists. 110 min. Sound. 16mm Color. dubbed. *Rental:* MGM United.

Love Is a Headache. Franchot Tone & Gladys George. Directed by Richard Thorpe. 1938. MGM. 73 min. Sound. 16mm B&W. *Rental:* MGM United.

Love is a Many Splendored Thing. William Holden & Jennifer Jones. Directed by Henry King. 1955. Fox. (Anamorphic). 102 min. Sound. 16mm Color. *Rental:* Films Inc.

Love Is a Racket. Douglas Fairbanks Jr. & Ann Dvorak. Directed by William A. Wellman. 1932. Warners. 72 min. Sound. 16mm B&W. *Rental:* MGM United.

Love Is Better Than Ever. Larry Parks & Elizabeth Taylor. Directed by Stanley Donen. 1952. MGM. 80 min. Sound. 16mm B&W. *Rental:* MGM United.

Love Is on the Air. Orig. Title: Radio Murder Mystery, The. Ronald Reagan & June Travis. Directed by Nick Grinde. 1937. Warners. 61 min. Sound. 16mm B&W. *Rental:* MGM United.

Love Island. Eva Gabor & Paul Valentine. Directed by Bud Pollard. 1953. Astor. 66 min. Sound. 16mm B&W. *Rental:* Budget Films & Video Comm. *Rental:* Video Comm, Videotape version.

Love Laughs at Andy Hardy. Mickey Rooney & Lewis Stone. Directed by Willis Goldbeck. 1947. MGM. 93 min. Sound. 16mm B&W. *Rental:* Budget Films, Classic Film Mus & MGM United.

Love Letters. Jennifer Jones & Joseph Cotten. Directed by William Dieterle. 1945. Paramount. 101 min. Sound. 16mm B&W. *Rental:* Swank Motion.

Love Machine, The. John Philip Law, Robert Ryan & Jackie Cooper. Directed by Jack Haley Jr. 1971. Columbia. 108 min. Sound. 16mm Color. *Rental:* Cine Craft, Films Inc, Kerr Film, Modern Sound, Welling Motion Pictures & Willoughby Peer.

Love Me Forever. Grace Moore & Leo Carillo. 1935. Columbia. 100 min. Sound. 16mm B&W. *Rental:* Bosco Films & Kit Parker.

Love Me or Leave Me. Doris Day & James Cagney. Directed by Charles Vidor. 1955. MGM. 112 min. Sound. 16mm Color. *Rental:* MGM United. *Rental:* MGM United, Anamorphic version. *Rental:* MGM United, Videotape version.

Love Me Tender. Elvis Presley. Directed by Robert Webb. 1956. Fox. 89 min. Sound. 16mm B&W. *Rental:* Films Inc.

Love Me Tonight. Maurice Chevalier & Jeanette MacDonald. Directed by Rouben Mamoulian. 1932. Paramount. 96 min. Sound. 16mm B&W. *Rental:* Williams Films.

Love Nest. William Lundigan & June Haver. Directed by Joseph Newman. 1951. Fox. 84 min. Sound. 16mm B&W. *Rental:* Films Inc.

Love Never Dies. Madge Bellamy & Lloyd Hughes. Directed by King Vidor. 1921. First National. (Tinted). 75 min. Silent. 16mm B&W. *Rental:* Budget Films, Classic Film Museum & Em Gee Film Lib. *Sale:* Classic Film Mus, Reel Images & Glenn Photo. *Rental:* Ivy Films, *Sale:* Glenn Photo & Reel Images, Super 8 silent B&W version. *Sale:* Glenn Photo, Super 8 silent tinted version.

Love of a Clown. Tito Gobbi & Gina Lollobrigida. Directed by Alfredo H. Manzi. Ital. 1950. Italy. 68 min. Sound. 16mm B&W. subtitles. *Rental:* Budget Films & Ivy Films.

Love of Jeanne Ney, The. Trans. Title: Liebe Der Jeanne Ney, Das. Ilja Ehrenburg & Brigitte Helm. Directed by G. W. Pabst. 1927. Germany. 139 min. Silent. 16mm B&W. *Rental:* A Twyman Pres, Budget Films, Em Gee Film Lib, Kit Parker, Museum Mod Art & Images Film. *Sale:* Glenn Photo, Images Film & Reel Images.

Love of Life. Orig. Title: Artur Rubinstein Love of Life. Directed by Francois Reichenbach & S. G. Patris. Fr. 1968. France. (Documentary). 91 min. Sound. 16mm Color. subtitles. *Rental:* New Cinema & New Yorker Films.

Love on a Bet. Gene Raymond & Wendy Barrie. Directed by Leigh Jason. 1936. RKO. 77 min. Sound. 16mm *Rental:* RKO General Pics.

Love on the Riviera. Marcello Mastroianni & Michele Morgan. Directed by Gianni Franciolini. 1964. Italy. 88 min. Sound. 16mm Color. dubbed. *Rental:* Budget Films.

Love on the Run. Joan Crawford & Clark Gable. Directed by W. S. Van Dyke. 1936. MGM. 80 min. Sound. 16mm B&W. *Rental:* MGM United.

Love on the Run. Jean-Paul Leaud & Marie-France Pisier. Directed by Francois Truffaut. Fr. 1979. France. 95 min. Sound. 16mm Color. subtitles. *Rental:* Films Inc.

Love Parade, The. Maurice Chevalier & Jeanette MacDonald. Directed by Ernst Lubitsch. 1929. Paramount. 107 min. Sound. 16mm B&W. *Rental:* Museum Mod Art & Swank Motion.

Love Storm, The. Fay Compton. Directed by E. A. Dupont. 1931. Britain. 60 min. Sound. 16mm B&W. *Rental:* Em Gee Film Lib & Film Classics.

Love Story. Ryan O'Neal, Ali McGraw & Ray Milland. Directed by Arthur Hiller. 1970. Paramount. 99 min. Sound. 16mm Color. *Rental:* Films Inc.

Love That Brute. Paul Douglas & Jean Peters. Directed by Alexander Hall. 1950. Fox. 86 min. Sound. 16mm B&W. *Rental:* Films Inc.

Love: The Ultimate Affirmation. 1979. 58 min. Sound. Videotape *Rental:* PBS Video. *Sale:* PBS Video.

Love Those Trains. 59 min. Sound. 16mm Color. *Rental:* Natl Geog. *Rental:* Natl Geog, Videotape version.

Love: What Is Essential Is Invisible to the Eye. 1974. 90 min. Sound. 16mm Color. *Rental:* U Mich Media.

Love with the Proper Stranger. Natalie Wood & Steve McQueen. Directed by Robert Mulligan. 1963. Paramount. 100 min. Sound. 16mm B&W. *Rental:* Films Inc.

Loved One, The. Rod Steiger & Robert Morse. Directed by Tony Richardson. 1965. MGM. 116 min. Sound. 16mm B&W. *Rental:* MGM United. *Rental:* MGM United, Videotape version.

Lovejoy's Nuclear War. 1975. Green Mountain Post. (Documentary). 58 min. Sound. 16mm Color. *Rental:* Bullfrog Films, U Cal Media, U Mich Media, Serious Bus, Tricontinental Film & Green Mt. *Sale:* Bullfrog Films, Green Mt & Serious Bus. *Sale:* Bullfrog Films & Green Mt, *Sale:* Green Mt, Videotape version.

Lovely to Look At. Howard Keel, Kathryn Grayson & Red Skelton. Directed by Mervyn LeRoy. 1952. 102 min. Sound. 16mm Color. *Rental:* MGM United.

Lovely Way to Die, A. Kirk Douglas & Eli Wallach. Directed by David Lowell Rich. 1968. Universal. 104 min. Sound. 16mm Color. *Rental:* Swank Motion.

Lover Come Back. Rock Hudson & Doris Day. Directed by Delbert Mann. 1961. Universal. 107 min. Sound. 16mm Color. *Rental:* Williams Films.

Lovers, The. Trans. Title: Amants, Les. Jeanne Moreau & Alain Cuny. Directed by Louis Malle. Fr. 1958. France. (Anamorphic). 90 min. Sound. 16mm B&W. subtitles. *Rental:* New Cinema & New Yorker Films.

Lovers & Lollipops. Lori March & Gerald O'Loughlin. Directed by Morris Engel. 1956. Engel. 83 min. Sound. 16mm B&W. *Rental:* Films Inc.

Lovers & Other Strangers. Gig Young & Anne Jackson. Directed by Cy Howard. 1970. ABC. 106 min. Sound. 16mm Color. *Rental:* Films Inc. *Sale:* ABC Film Lib, Super 8 sound version.

Lovers Beyond the Tomb *see* Nightmare Castle.

Lovers Courageous. Robert Montgomery & Madge Evans. Directed by Robert Z. Leonard. 1932. MGM. 78 min. Sound. 16mm B&W. *Rental:* MGM United.

Loves & Times of Scaramouche, The. Michael Sarrazin & Ursula Andress. Directed by Enzo G. Castellari. 1976. Embassy. 92 min. Sound. 16mm Color. *Sale:* Films Inc.

Loves of a Blonde, The. Hana Brejchova. Directed by Milos Forman. Czech. 1965. Czechoslovakia. 88 min. Sound. 16mm B&W. subtitles. *Rental:* Films Inc.

Loves of Carmen, The. Rita Hayworth & Glenn Ford. Directed by Charles Vidor. 1948. Columbia. 98 min. Sound. 16mm Color. *Rental:* Cine Craft, Kit Parker & Swank Motion.

Loves of Edgar Allan Poe, The. Shepherd Strudwick. Directed by Harry Lachman. 1942. Fox. 67 min. Sound. 16mm B&W. *Rental:* Films Inc.

Loves of Hercules, The *see* Hercules vs. the Hydra.

Loves of Isadora *see* Isadora.

Loves of Salammbo, The. Jacques Sernas & Edmund Purdom. Directed by Sergio Grieco. 1962. Italy. 72 min. Sound. 16mm Color. dubbed. *Rental:* Films Inc.

Lovesick. Dudley Moore & Elizabeth McGovern. Directed by Marshall Brickman. 1983. Ladd Co.. 96 min. Sound. 16mm Color. *Rental:* Swank Motion. *Rental:* Swank Motion, Videotape version.

Lovey: A Circle of Children. Jane Alexander. Directed by Jud Taylor. 1978. Time-Life. 92 min. Sound. 16mm Color. *Rental:* Time-Life Multimedia. *Sale:* Time-Life Multimedia.

Lovin' Molly. Anthony Perkins & Beau Bridges. Directed by Sidney Lumet. 1974. Columbia. 105 min. Sound. 16mm Color. *Rental:* Budget Films & Kit Parker.

Loving. George Segal & Eva Marie Saint. Directed by Irwin Kershner. 1970. Columbia. 89 min. Sound. 16mm Color. *Rental:* Budget Films, Cine Craft, Swank Motion & Welling Motion Pictures.

Loving Couples. Harriett Anderson & Gunnel Lindblom. Directed by Mai Zetterling. Swed. 1966. Sweden. 113 min. Sound. 16mm B&W. subtitles. *Rental:* Films Inc.

Loving Daughter. 60 min. Videotape Color. *Sale:* Videx Home Lib.

Loving Memory. Tony Scott. 1969. Britain. 53 min. Sound. 16mm B&W. *Rental:* Museum Mod Art.

Loving the Ladies. Richard Dix & Lois Wilson. Directed by Melville Brown. 1930. RKO. 68 min. Sound. 16mm *Rental:* RKO General Pics.

Lower Depths, The: Underground. Trans. Title: Bas Fonds, Les. Jean Gabin & Louis Jouvet. Directed by Jean Renoir. Fr. 1936. France. 91 min. Sound. 16mm B&W. subtitles. *Rental:* Budget Films, Em Gee Film Lib, Films Inc, Iowa Films & Kit Parker. *Sale:* Festival Films Glenn Photo & Reel Images.

Lower Than the Angels. (Ascent of Man Ser.). 1974. Britain. (Documentary). 52 min. Sound. Videotape Color. *Rental:* Iowa Films, U Cal Media, U Mich Media & Utah Media.

Loyal Heart, The. Percy Marmont. Directed by Oswald Mitchell. 1945. Britain. 69 min. Sound. 16mm B&W. *Rental:* Ivy Films. *Sale:* Rep Pic Film.

Loyola. Directed by Jose Diaz Morales. 1952. Simplex. (Cast unlisted). 90 min. Sound. 16mm B&W. *Rental:* Alba House & Films Inc.

LSD: Lettvin vs. Leary. 1967. NET. (Documentary). 51 min. Sound. 16mm B&W. *Rental:* Indiana AV Ctr. *Sale:* Indiana AV Ctr.

LSD: The Spring Grove Experiment. 1966. CBS. (Documentary). 54 min. Sound. 16mm B&W. *Rental:* U of IL Film, McGraw-Hill Films & U Mich Media. *Sale:* McGraw-Hill Films.

Lt. Robin Crusoe, U.S.N. Dick Van Dyke, Nancy Kwan & Akim Tamiroff. Directed by Byron Paul. 1966. Disney. 114 min. Sound. 16mm Color. *Rental:* Bosco Films, Buchan Pic, Disney Prod, Elliot Film Co, Film Pres, Film Ctr DC, Films Inc, MGM United, Modern Sound, Newman Film Lib, Roas Films, Swank Motion, Twyman Films, U of IL Film, Welling Motion Pictures & Williams Films.

Luchadoras Contra el Medico Asesino, Las *see* Doctor of Doom.

Luchadoras Contra la Momia, Las *see* Wrestling Women vs. the Aztec Mummy.

Lucia. Raquel Revuelta & Eslinda Nunez. Directed by Humberto Solas. Span. 1972. Cuba. 160 min. Sound. 16mm B&W. subtitles. *Rental:* New Yorker Films & Unifilm. *Sale:* Unifilm.

Lucia Di Lammermoor. Directed by Piero Ballerini. 1947. Italy. (Opera). 100 min. Sound. 16mm B&W. *Rental:* Corinth Films & Willoughby Peer.

Luck. Johnny Hines. 1923. Burr. 60 min. Silent. 16mm B&W. *Sale:* E Finney.

Luck of Ginger Coffey, The. Robert Shaw & Mary Ure. Directed by Irwin Kershner. 1964. Canada. 100 min. Sound. 16mm B&W. *Rental:* Budget Films & Kino Intl. *Sale:* Kino Intl.

Luck of Roaring Camp, The. Joan Woodbury & Owen Davis Jr. Directed by Irvin Willat. 1937. Monogram. 60 min. Sound. 16mm B&W. *Rental:* Film Classics, MGM United & Mogulls Films.

Luck of the Irish, The. Tyrone Power & Anne Baxter. Directed by Henry Koster. 1948. Fox. 99 min. Sound. 16mm B&W. *Rental:* Films Inc.

Lucky *see* Boy, a Girl & a Dog.

Lucky Boots. Guinn Williams. 55 min. Sound. 16mm B&W. *Sale:* Cinema Concepts & Reel Images.

Lucky Devil. Richard Dix. Directed by Frank Tuttle. 1925. Paramount. 50 min. Silent. 16mm B&W. *Rental:* Film Classics.

Lucky Devils. Betty Furness & Bill Boyd. Directed by Ralph Ince. 1933. RKO. 60 min. Sound. 16mm B&W. *Rental:* RKO General Pics.

Lucky Girl. Gene Gerrard & Molly Lamont. Directed by Gene Gerrard & Frank Miller. 1932. Britain. 70 min. Sound. 16mm B&W. *Rental:* Film Classics.

Lucky Jim. Ian Carmichael & Terry-Thomas. Directed by John Boulting. 1958. Britain. 95 min. Sound. 16mm B&W. *Rental:* Roas Films.

Lucky Jordan. Alan Ladd & Helen Walker. Directed by Frank Tuttle. 1942. Paramount. 83 min. Sound. 16mm B&W. *Rental:* Swank Motion.

Lucky Kid *see* Kid for Two Farthings.

Lucky Lady, The. Greta Nissen & Lionel Barrymore. Directed by Raoul Walsh. 1926. Paramount. 70 min. Silent. 16mm B&W. *Rental:* Films Inc.

Lucky Lady. Burt Reynolds, Liza Minnelli & Gene Hackman. Directed by Stanley Donen. 1975. Fox. 117 min. Sound. 16mm Color. *Rental:* Films Inc, Twyman Films, Welling Motion Pictures & Williams Films.

Lucky Luciano. Rod Steiger & Gian-Maria Volante. Directed by Francesco Rosi. 1973. Italy. 108 min. Sound. Videotape Color. dubbed. *Sale:* Films Inc.

Lucky Nick Cain. George Raft & Coleen Gray. Directed by Joseph Newman. 1951. Fox. 87 min. Sound. 16mm B&W. *Rental:* Films Inc.

Lucky Night. Myrna Loy & Robert Taylor. Directed by Norman Taurog. 1939. MGM. 82 min. Sound. 16mm B&W. *Rental:* MGM United.

Lucky Partners. Ginger Rogers & Ronald Colman. Directed by Lewis Milestone. 1940. RKO. 102 min. Sound. 16mm B&W. *Rental:* Films Inc.

Lucky Stiff, The. Dorothy Lamour & Brian Donlevy. Directed by Lewis R. Foster. 1949. United Artists. 99 min. Sound. 16mm B&W. *Rental:* Ivy Films. *Sale:* Rep Pic Film.

Lucky Terror. Hoot Gibson. Directed by Alan James. 1936. Grand National. 61 min. Sound. 16mm B&W. *Rental:* Budget Films & Video Comm. *Sale:* Reel Images. *Sale:* Reel Images, Super 8 Sound version. *Rental:* Video Comm, *Sale:* Video Comm, Videotape version.

Lucky Texan. John Wayne. Directed by Robert N. Bradbury. 1934. Monogram. 61 min. Sound. 16mm B&W. *Rental:* Budget Films, Ivy Films & Mogulls Films. *Sale:* Classics Assoc NY & Rep Pic Film. *Sale:* Video Comm, Videotape version.

Lucrece Borgia. Edwige Feuillere. Directed by Abel Gance. Fr. 1935. France. 90 min. Sound. 16mm B&W. subtitles. *Rental:* Images Film. *Lease:* Images Film.

Lucy Gallant. Jane Wyman & Charlton Heston. Directed by Robert Parrish. 1955. Paramount. 104 min. Sound. 16mm B&W. *Rental:* Video Comm.

Lucy in Disguise. 1982. 58 min. Sound. 16mm Color. *Rental:* Utah Media.

Ludwig. Helmut Berger, Trevor Howard & Romy Schneider. Directed by Luchino Visconti. 1973. MGM. (Anamorphic). 136 min. Sound. 16mm Color. *Rental:* MGM United.

Ludwig Van Beethoven. Directed by Hans Conrad Fischer. Ger. 1970. West Germany. 112 min. Sound. 16mm Color. narrated Eng. *Rental:* Corinth Films. *Lease:* Corinth Films.

Luigi Pirandello: Six Characters in Search of an Author-The Theater of the Absurd. 1976. Film for the Humanities. (Documentary). 55 min. Sound. 16mm Color. *Rental:* Films Human & U of IL Film. *Sale:* Films Human.

Luke Was There. Scott Baio. 1980. Learning Corp.. 47 min. Sound. 16mm Color. *Rental:* Learning Corp Am. *Sale:* Learning Corp Am. *Sale:* Learning Corp Am, Videotape version.

Lulu Belle. Dorothy Lamour & George Montgomery. Directed by Leslie Fenton. 1948. Columbia. 87 min. Sound. 16mm B&W. *Rental:* Ivy Films & Maljack. *Sale:* Rep Pic Film. *Lease:* Maljack. *Lease:* Maljack, Videotape version.

Lulu in Berlin. Directed by Richard Leacock & Susan Wohl. 1984. USA. (Documentary). 50 min. Sound. 16mm B&W. *Rental:* Kino Intl. *Lease:* Kino Intl.

Lumberjack. William Boyd. Directed by Lesley Selander. 1944. United Artists. 54 min. Sound. 16mm B&W. *Sale:* Cinema Concepts.

Lumiere. Jeanne Moreau & Lucia Bose. Directed by Jeanne Moreau. Fr. 1976. France. 95 min. Sound. 16mm Color. subtitles. *Rental:* Films Inc.

Lumiere d'Ete. Madeleine Renaud, Pierre Brasseur & Madeleine Robinson. Directed by Jean Gremillon. Fr. 1943. France. 90 min. Sound. 16mm B&W. subtitles. *Rental:* French Am Cul.

Lumiere Years, The. 1974. France. (Documentary). 93 min. Sound. 16mm B&W. *Rental:* Films Inc, Syracuse U Film & U Cal Media. *Sale:* Films Inc.

Luminous Procuress. The Cockettes. Directed by Steven Arnold. 1973. New Line. 87 min. Sound. 16mm Color. *Rental:* New Line Cinema. *Sale:* New Line Cinema.

Lummox. Winifred Westover. Directed by Herbert Brenon. 1930. 16mm *Rental:* A Twyman Pres.

Luna. Jill Clayburgh & Matthew Barry. Directed by Bernardo Bertolucci. 1979. Fox. 145 min. Sound. 16mm Color. *Rental:* Films Inc & Twyman Films.

Lupe. Directed by Jose Rodriguez-Soltero. 1966. Rodriguez-Soltero. (Documentary). 50 min. Sound. 16mm Color. *Rental:* Canyon Cinema.

Lupinek Case, The. 1978. Czechoslovakia. (Cast unlisted). 51 min. Sound. 16mm Color. dubbed. *Rental:* Films Inc. *Sale:* Films Inc.

Lupo. Yuda Barkan. Directed by Menahem Golan. Hebrew. 1978. Israel. 51 min. Sound. 16mm Color. *Rental:* Films Inc.

Lure of the Islands. Margie Hart & Gail Storm. Directed by Jean Yarbrough. 1942. Monogram. 60 min. Sound. 16mm B&W. *Rental:* Mogulls Films.

Lure of the Range. Dick Hatton. 50 min. Silent. 16mm B&W. *Sale:* Select Film.

Lure of the Swamp. Marshall Thompson & William Parker. Directed by Hubert Cornfield. 1957. Fox. (Anamorphic). 75 min. Sound. 16mm B&W. *Rental:* Ivy Films. *Sale:* Rep Pic Film.

Lure of the Wilderness. Jean Peters & Jeffrey Hunter. Directed by Jean Negulesco. 1952. Fox. 92 min. Sound. 16mm Color. *Rental:* Films Inc.

Lust for Ecstasy. 1963. 45 min. Sound. 8mm Color. *Rental:* Canyon Cinema.

Lust for Gold. Ida Lupino & Glenn Ford. Directed by S. Sylvan Simon. 1949. Columbia. 90 min. Sound. 16mm B&W. *Rental:* Kit Parker.

Lust for Life. Kirk Douglas & Anthony Quinn. Directed by Vincente Minnelli. 1956. MGM. 122 min. Sound. 16mm Color. *Rental:* MGM United. *Rental:* MGM United, Anamorphic version.

Lusty Men. Robert Mitchum & Susan Hayward. Directed by Nicholas Ray. 1952. RKO. 122 min. Sound. 16mm B&W. *Rental:* Films Inc. *Rental:* Video Comm, *Lease:* Video Comm, Videotape version.

Luther. Stacy Keach. Directed by Guy Green. 1973. AFT. 112 min. Sound. 16mm Color. *Rental:* Films Inc.

Luv. Jack Lemmon, Peter Falk & Elaine May. Directed by Clive Donner. 1967. Columbia. 95 min. Sound. 16mm Color. *Rental:* Budget Films, Cine Craft, Charard Motion Pics, Film Ctr DC, Films Inc, Inst Cinema, Modern Sound, Welling Motion Pictures, Westcoast Films & Wholesome Film Ctr.

Luxury Liner. George Brent & Jane Powell. Directed by Richard Whorf. 1948. MGM. 99 min. Sound. 16mm B&W. *Rental:* MGM United.

Lydia. Merle Oberon, Joseph Cotton & Edna May Oliver. Directed by Julien Duvivier. 1941. United Artists. 98 min. Sound. 16mm B&W. *Rental:* Films Inc.

Lying Lips. Edna Mae Harris & Earl Jones. Directed by Oscar Micheaux. 1933. Micheaux. 60 min. Sound. 16mm B&W. *Rental:* Budget Films.

Lys Blancs, Les. Jacques Fabri. Directed by Jean-Pierre Decourt. Fr. 1975. France. 52 min. Sound. 16mm Color. subtitles. *Rental:* French AV Cul. *Rental:* French AV Cul, Videotape version.

Lysenko Affair, The. 1979. PBS. (Documentary). 60 min. Videotape Color. *Rental:* PBS Video. *Sale:* PBS Video.

M. Peter Lorre. Directed by Fritz Lang. Ger. 1931. Germany. 103 min. Sound. 16mm B&W. subtitles. *Rental:* Budget Films, U Cal Media, Classic Film Mus, Corinth Films, Films Inc, Images Film, Ivy Films, Janus Films, Kit Parker, Twyman Films, Video Comm, Westcoast Films, Wholesome Film Ctr & Willoughby Peer. *Sale:* Cinema Concepts, Griggs Movie, Images Film, Natl Cinema & Reel Images. *Lease:* Corinth Films. *Rental:* Ivy Films, *Sale:* Ivy Films, Super 8 sound version. *Sale:* Cinema Concepts, Ivy Films, Tamarelles French Film, Video Lib & Images Film, Videotape version. *Sale:* Festival Films, *Rental:* A Twyman Pres, 95 min. 16mm version. *Rental:* Kit Parker, *Sale:* Festival Films, 95 min. Videotape version, Limited subtitles 521 version.

Ma & Pa Kettle. Marjorie Main & Percy Kilbride. Directed by Charles Lamont. 1949. Universal. 72 min. Sound. 16mm B&W. *Rental:* Williams Films.

Ma & Pa Kettle at the Fair. Marjorie Main & Percy Kilbride. Directed by Charles Barton. 1952. Universal. 80 min. Sound. 16mm B&W. *Rental:* Williams Films.

Ma & Pa Kettle at Waikiki. Marjorie Main & Percy Kilbride. Directed by Lee Sholem. 1955. Universal. 79 min. Sound. 16mm B&W. *Rental:* Williams Films.

Ma & Pa Kettle Back on the Farm. Marjorie Main & Percy Kilbride. Directed by Edward Sedgwick. 1951. Universal. 80 min. Sound. 16mm B&W. *Rental:* Swank Motion.

Ma & Pa Kettle Go to Paris *see* Ma & Pa Kettle on Vacation.

Ma & Pa Kettle Go to Town. Marjorie Main & Percy Kilbride. Directed by Charles Lamont. 1950. Universal. 82 min. Sound. 16mm B&W. *Rental:* Williams Films.

Ma & Pa Kettle on Vacation. Orig. Title: Ma & Pa Kettle Go to Paris. Marjorie Main & Percy Kilbride. Directed by Charles Lamont. 1953. Universal. 74 min. Sound. 16mm B&W. *Rental:* Williams Films.

Macabre. William Prince & Jim Backus. Directed by William Castle. 1958. Allied Artists. 73 min. Sound. 16mm B&W. *Rental:* Hurlock Cine.

Macao. Jane Russell & Robert Mitchum. Directed by Josef Von Sternberg. 1952. RKO. 81 min. Sound. 16mm B&W. *Rental:* Films Inc.

MacArthur. Gregory Peck & Ed Flanders. Directed by Joseph Sargent. 1977. Universal. 130 min. Sound. 16mm Color. *Rental:* Swank Motion.

Macbeth. Orson Welles & Jeanette Nolan. Directed by Orson Welles. 1948. Republic. 85 min. Sound. 16mm B&W. *Rental:* Budget Films, Charard Motion Pics, Film Classics, Film Ctr DC, Films Inc, Images Film, Ivy Films, Kit Parker, Macmillan Films, Museum Mod Art, Modern Sound, Roas Films, Syracuse U Film, Twyman Films, Welling Motion Pictures, Westcoast Films & Wholesome Film Ctr. *Sale:* Macmillan Films. *Lease:* Rep Pic Film.

Macbeth. Maurice Evans & Judith Anderson. Directed by George Schaefer. 1961. Britain. 107 min. Sound. 16mm Color. *Rental:* Cine Craft, Iowa Films & Macmillan Films. *Sale:* Macmillan Films.

Macbeth. 3 pts. 1964. Encyclopaedia Britannica. (Cast unlisted). 89 min. Sound. 16mm Color. *Rental:* Ency Brit Ed. *Sale:* Ency Brit Ed. *Sale:* Ency Brit Ed, Videotape version.

Macbeth. Jon Finch & Francesca Annis. Directed by Roman Polanski. 1972. Columbia. 120 min. Sound. 16mm Color. *Rental:* Swank Motion. *Rental:* Swank Motion, Anamorphic version, 140 version.

Macbeth. 1977. Miami-Dade. (Cast unlisted). 60 min. Videotape Color. *Sale:* Films Inc.

Macbeth. 1982. 147 min. Sound. Videotape Color. *Rental:* Iowa Films.

McCabe & Mrs. Miller. Warren Beatty & Julie Christie. Directed by Robert Altman. 1971. Warners. 120 min. Sound. 16mm Color. *Rental:* Swank Motion. *Rental:* Swank Motion, Anamorphic version.

McClintock! John Wayne & Maureen O'Hara. Directed by Andrew V. McLaglen. 1963. United Artists. 126 min. Sound. 16mm Color. *Rental:* MGM United.

McCullochs, The. Forrest Tucker, Max Baer & Julie Adams. Directed by Max Baer. 1975. American International. 93 min. Sound. 16mm Color. *Rental:* Budget Films.

McGuerins from Brooklyn, The. William Bendix & Joe Sawyer. Directed by Kurt Neumann. 1942. Hal Roach. 64 min. Sound. 16mm B&W. *Rental:* Budget Films & Mogulls Films.

McGuire Go Home! Dirk Bogarde & Susan Strasberg. Directed by Ralph Thomas. 1965. Britain. 114 min. Sound. 16mm Color. *Rental:* Liberty Co.

McHale's Navy. Ernest Borgnine & Joe Flynn. Directed by Edward J. Montagne. 1964. Universal. 93 min. Sound. 16mm Color. *Rental:* Williams Films.

McHale's Navy Joins the Air Force. Tim Conway & Joe Flynn. Directed by Edward J. Montagne. 1965. Universal. 90 min. Sound. 16mm Color. *Rental:* Williams Films.

Machine Gun Kelly. Charles Bronson. 1968. American International. 84 min. Sound. 16mm B&W. *Rental:* Budget Films, Cine Craft, Film Ctr DC, Westcoast Films & Willoughby Peer.

Machine Gun McCain. Trans. Title: Intoccabili, Gli. John Cassavetes & Gena Rowlands. Directed by Guiliano Montaldo. 1969. Columbia. 94 min. Sound. 16mm Color. *Rental:* Cine Craft, Films Inc, Inst Cinema, Kerr Film, Film Ctr DC, Westcoast Films, Welling Motion Pictures & Wholesome Film Ctr.

Macho Callahan. David Janssen & Jean Seberg. Directed by Bernard Kowalski. 1970. Embassy. 100 min. Sound. 16mm Color. *Rental:* Films Inc.

Mack, The. Max Julien & Don Gordon. Directed by Michael Campus. 1973. Cinerama. 110 min. Sound. 16mm Color. *Rental:* Swank Motion.

Mack Sennett Program, A. 1916. Keystone. (Anthology). 76 min. Silent. 16mm B&W. *Rental:* Museum Mod Art.

Mackenna's Gold. Gregory Peck & Omar Sharif. Directed by J. Lee Thompson. 1969. Columbia. 128 min. Sound. 16mm Color. *Rental:* Buchan Pic, Budget Films, Cine Craft, Charard Motion Pics, Williams Films, Bosco Films, Films Inc, Inst Cinema, Kerr Film, Modern Sound, Natl Film Video, Roas Films, Swank Motion, Twyman Films, Video Comm, Westcoast Films & Welling Motion Pictures.

Mackintosh & T.J. Roy Rogers & Joan Hackett. Directed by Marvin J. Chomsky. 1975. Penland. 96 min. Sound. 16mm Color. *Rental:* Films Inc, Modern Sound & Westcoast Films.

Mackintosh Man, The. Paul Newman. Directed by John Huston. 1973. Warners. 99 min. Sound. 16mm Color. *Rental:* Films Inc, Swank Motion & Williams Films.

M'Liss. John Beal & Anne Shirley. Directed by George Nicholls. 1936. RKO. 66 min. Sound. 16mm B&W. *Rental:* RKO General Pics.

McMasters, The. Burl Ives, Brock Peters & David Carradine. Directed by Alf Kjellin. 1970. Chevron. 90 min. Sound. 16mm Color. *Rental:* Budget Films, Films Inc, Video Comm & Westcoast Films.

Macon County Line. Max Baer & Alan Vint. Directed by Richard Compton. 1974. American International. 90 min. Sound. 16mm Color. *Rental:* Swank Motion.

McQ. John Wayne. Directed by John Sturges. 1974. Warners. 111 min. Sound. 16mm Color. *Rental:* Cine Craft, Films, Inst Cinema, Modern Sound, Twyman Films & Williams Films.

Macunaima. Orig. Title: Jungle Freaks. Directed by Joaquin Pedro De Andrade. 1971. New Line Cinema. (Documentary). 95 min. Sound. 16mm Color. *Rental:* New Line Cinema.

McVicar. Roger Daltrey, Adam Faith & Cheryl Campbell. Directed by Tom Clegg. 1980. Britain. 91 min. Sound. 16mm Color. *Rental:* Swank Motion. *Sale:* Tamarelles French Films, Videotape version.

Mad About Money *see* He Loved an Actress.

Mad About Music. Deanna Durbin & Herbert Marshall. Directed by Norman Taurog. 1938. Universal. 98 min. Sound. 16mm B&W. *Rental:* Swank Motion.

Mad Adventures of "Rabbi" Jacob, The. Louis De Funes. Directed by Gerard Oury. Fr. 1974. France. 96 min. Sound. 16mm Color. subtitles. *Rental:* Films Inc & Twyman Films.

Mad at the World. Frank Lovejoy & Keefe Brasselle. Directed by Harry Essex. 1955. Filmakers. 91 min. Sound. 16mm B&W. *Rental:* Ivy Films. *Sale:* Rep Pic Film.

Mad Bomber, The. Vince Edwards & Chuck Connors. Directed by Bert I. Gordon. 1972. Gordon. 91 min. Sound. 16mm Color. *Rental:* Budget Films.

Mad Butcher, The. Victor Buono, Brad Harris & Karen Field. 81 min. Sound. 16mm Color. *Rental:* BF Video.

Mad Doctor of Market Street, The. Lionel Atwill & Una Merkel. Directed by Joseph Lewis. 1942. Universal. 61 min. Sound. 16mm B&W. *Rental:* Swank Motion.

Mad Dog Morgan. Dennis Hopper, David Culpilil & Frank Thring. Directed by Philippe Mora. 1976. Australia. 95 min. Sound. 16mm Color. *Rental:* Films Inc, Welling Motion Pictures & Westcoast Films.

Mad Dogs & Englishmen. Orig. Title: Joe Cocker-Mad Dogs & Englishman. Directed by Pierre Adidge. 1971. MGM. (Documentary, Anamorphic). 114 min. Sound. 16mm Color. *Rental:* Films Inc.

Mad Driver, The. 1981. 58 min. Sound. 16mm Color. *Rental:* Canyon Cinema.

Mad Genius, The. John Barrymore & Boris Karloff. Directed by Michael Curtiz. 1931. Warners. 81 min. Sound. 16mm B&W. *Rental:* MGM United.

Mad Ghoul, The. David Bruce & Evelyn Ankers. Directed by James Hogan. 1943. Universal. 65 min. Sound. 16mm B&W. *Rental:* Swank Motion.

Mad Holiday. Edmund Lowe & Elissa Landi. Directed by George B. Seitz. 1936. MGM. 71 min. Sound. 16mm B&W. *Rental:* MGM United.

Mad Love. Peter Lorre & Frances Drake. Directed by Karl Freund. 1935. MGM. 70 min. Sound. 16mm B&W. *Rental:* MGM United.

Mad Magician, The. Vincent Price & Eva Gabor. Directed by John Brahm. 1954. Columbia. (Special glasses required). 72 min. Sound. 16mm B&W. *Rental:* Bosco Films, Charard Motion Pics, Modern Sound & Roas Films. *Rental:* Kit Parker, Three-D version.

Mad Max. Mel Gibson, Joanne Samuel & Hugh Keays Byre. Directed by George Miller. 1980. Australia. 93 min. Sound. 16mm Color. *Rental:* Images Film & Swank Motion.

Mad Miss Manton, The. Barbara Stanwyck & Henry Fonda. Directed by Leigh Jason. 1938. RKO. 80 min. Sound. 16mm B&W. *Rental:* Films Inc.

Mad Monster, The. George Zucco, Johnny Downs & Anne Nagel. Directed by Sam Newfield. 1942. PRC. 78 min. Sound. 16mm B&W. *Rental:* Bosco Films & Films Inc.

Mad Monster Party, The. 1967. Embassy. (Animated). 92 min. Sound. 16mm Color. *Rental:* Films Inc.

Mad River: Hard Times in Humboldt County. 1982. (Documentary). 60 min. Sound. 16mm Color. *Rental:* U Mich Media.

Mad Room, The. Shelley Winters & Stella Stevens. Directed by Bernard Girard. 1969. Columbia. 91 min. Sound. 16mm Color. *Rental:* Budget Films, Cine Craft, Charard Motion Pics, Film Ctr DC, Films Inc, Inst Cinema, Ivy Films, Modern Sound, Roas Films, Swank Motion, Video Comm, Welling Motion Pictures, Westcoast Films & Wholesome Film Ctr.

Mad Wednesday. Orig. Title: Sin of Harold Diddlebock, The. Harold Lloyd. Directed by Preston Sturges. 1947. United Artists. 90 min. Sound. 16mm B&W. *Rental:* Budget Films, Em Gee Film Lib, Swank Motion & Video Comm. *Sale:* Glenn Photo.

Mad Whirl, The. Jack Mulhall & May McAvoy. Directed by William A. Seiter. 1924. Universal. 75 min. Silent. 16mm B&W. *Rental:* Em Gee Film Lib. *Sale:* Griggs Movie.

Madam Satan. Lillian Roth & Roland Young. Directed by Cecil B. DeMille. 1930. MGM. 105 min. Sound. 16mm B&W. *Rental:* Films Inc & MGM United.

Madam Spy. Constance Bennett & John Litel. Directed by Roy William Neill. 1942. Universal. 60 min. Sound. 16mm B&W. *Rental:* Mogulls Films.

Madame Bovary. Jennifer Jones & James Mason. Directed by Vincente Minnelli. 1949. MGM. 106 min. Sound. 16mm B&W. *Rental:* MGM United. *Rental:* MGM United, Videotape version.

Madame Bovary. Valentine Tessier & Pierre Renoir. Directed by Jean Renoir. Fr. 1934. France. 117 min. Sound. 16mm B&W. subtitles. *Rental:* Films Inc.

Madame Butterfly. Sylvia Sidney & Cary Grant. Directed by Marion Gering. 1932. Paramount. 86 min. Sound. 16mm B&W. *Rental:* Swank Motion.

Madame Curie. Greer Garson & Walter Pidgeon. Directed by Mervyn LeRoy. 1943. MGM. 124 min. Sound. 16mm B&W. *Rental:* MGM United.

Madame Dery. Directed by Gyula Maar. Hungarian. 1976. Hungary. (Cast unlisted). 102 min. Sound. 16mm Color. subtitles. *Rental:* Liberty Co.

Madame Du Barry. Dolores Del Rio & Reginald Owen. Directed by William Dieterle. 1934. Warners. 77 min. Sound. 16mm B&W. *Rental:* MGM United.

Madame Pimpernel see Paris Underground.

Madame Rosa. Simone Signoret. Directed by Moshe Mizrahi. Fr. 1977. France. 110 min. Sound. 16mm Color. subtitles. *Rental:* New Cinema & New Line Cinema. *Sale:* Cinema Concepts, Videotape version.

Madame Sin. Bette Davis & Robert Wagner. Directed by David Greene. 1972. Britain. 75 min. Sound. 16mm Color. *Rental:* Swank Motion.

Madame X. Lana Turner, Keir Dullea & John Forsythe. Directed by David Lowell Rich. 1966. Universal. 100 min. Sound. 16mm Color. *Rental:* MGM United & Swank Motion.

Madarrpa Funeral at Gurka'wuy. 1979. Aboriginals. 87 min. 16mm Color. *Sale:* Aust Info Serv. *Rental:* Aust Info Serv.

Made for Each Other. Carole Lombard & James Stewart. Directed by John Cromwell. 1939. United Artists. 97 min. Sound. 16mm B&W. *Rental:* Alba House, Budget Films, Classic Film Mus, Em Gee Film Lib, Films Inc, Images Film, Mogulls Films & Wholesome Film Ctr. *Sale:* Classic Film Mus, Cinema Concepts, Festival Films & Reel Images. *Sale:* Reel Images, Super 8 sound version. *Sale:* Cinema Concepts, Festival Films & Tamarelles French Film, Videotape version.

Made for Each Other. Renee Taylor & Joseph Bologna. Directed by Robert B. Bean. 1972. Fox. 103 min. Sound. 16mm Color. *Rental:* Films Inc.

Made in Britain. (Destination America Ser.). 1976. Media Guild. (Documentary). 52 min. Sound. 16mm Color. *Rental:* Media Guild. *Sale:* Media Guild. *Sale:* Media Guild, Videotape version.

Made in Heaven. (Cast unlisted). Sound. Videotape *Sale:* Vidamerica.

Made in Italy. Anna Magnani & Virna Lisi. Directed by Nanni Loy. 1967. France-Italy. 101 min. Sound. 16mm Color. dubbed. *Rental:* Kit Parker.

Made in Japan. 1970. Britain. (Documentary). 52 min. Sound. 16mm B&W. *Rental:* Time-Life Multimedia. *Sale:* Time-Life Multimedia.

Made in Paris. Ann-Margret & Louis Jourdan. Directed by Boris Sagal. 1966. MGM. 101 min. Sound. 16mm Color. *Rental:* MGM United.

Made in the U. S. A. Directed by Jean-Luc Godard. 1966. France. (Anamorphic). 85 min. Sound. Color. *Rental:* Kino Intl. *Lease:* Kino Intl.

Made on Broadway. Robert Montgomery & Madge Evans. Directed by Harry Beaumont. 1933. MGM. 70 min. Sound. 16mm B&W. *Rental:* MGM United.

Madeleine. Ann Todd. Directed by David Lean. 1950. Britain. 101 min. Sound. 16mm B&W. *Rental:* Budget Films, Kit Parker, Learning Corp Am, Twyman Films & U of IL Film. *Sale:* Learning Corp Am.

Mademoiselle. Jeanne Moreau & Ettore Manni. Directed by Tony Richardson. Fr. 1966. France. 103 min. Sound. 16mm B&W. subtitles. *Rental:* MGM United.

Mademoiselle Fifi. Simone Simon & Kurt Kreuger. Directed by Robert Wise. 1944. RKO. 69 min. Sound. 16mm B&W. *Rental:* Films Inc.

Madhouse. Vincent Price & Peter Cushing. Directed by Jim Clark. 1974. American International. 89 min. Sound. 16mm Color. *Rental:* Swank Motion.

Madigan. Richard Widmark & Henry Fonda. Directed by Don Siegel. 1968. Universal. 101 min. Sound. 16mm Color. *Rental:* Swank Motion.

Madigan's Million. Dustin Hoffman, Elsa Martinelli & Cesar Romero. Directed by Stanley Prager. 1967. Spain. 92 min. Sound. 16mm Color. dubbed. *Rental:* Films Inc & Welling Motion Pictures.

Madison Avenue. Dana Andrews & Eleanor Parker. Directed by Bruce Humberstone. 1962. Fox. 94 min. Sound. 16mm B&W. *Rental:* Films Inc. *Rental:* Films Inc, Anamorphic version.

Madman of Mandoras see They Saved Hitler's Brain.

Madness & Medicine. 1976. ABC. (Documentary). 49 min. Sound. 16mm Color. *Rental:* Iowa Films, La Inst Res Ctr, McGraw-Hill Films, U Cal Media & U of IL Film. *Sale:* McGraw-Hill Films. *Sale:* McGraw-Hill Films, Videotape version.

Madness of the Heart. Margaret Lockwood. Directed by Charles Bennett. 1949. Britain. 105 min. Sound. 16mm B&W. *Rental:* Cinema Five.

Mado. Michel Piccoli, Ottavia Piccolo & Romy Schneider. Directed by Claude Sautet. Fr. 1977. France. 130 min. Sound. 16mm Color. subtitles. *Rental:* J Green Pics. *Rental:* J Green Pics, Dubbed version. *Sale:* Tamarelles French Film, Videotape version.

Madonna of the Desert. Lynn Roberts & Don Castle. Directed by George Blair. 1945. Republic. 60 min. Sound. 16mm B&W. *Rental:* Ivy Films. *Sale:* Rep Pic Film.

Madonna of the Seven Moons. Phyllis Calvert. Directed by Arthur Crabtree. 1946. Britain. 100 min. Sound. 16mm B&W. *Rental:* Budget Films.

Madonna of the Streets. Evelyn Brent & Robert Ames. Directed by John Robertson. 1930. Columbia. 80 min. Sound. 16mm B&W. *Rental:* Kit Parker.

Madonna's Secret, The. Gail Patrick & Ann Rutherford. Directed by William Thiele. 1946. Republic. 79 min. Sound. 16mm B&W. *Rental:* Ivy Films. *Sale:* Rep Pic Film.

Madron. Richard Boone & Leslie Caron. Directed by Jerry Hopper. 1970. Four Star Excelsior. 93 min. Sound. 16mm Color. *Rental:* Budget Films, Films Inc, Kerr Film, Video Comm, Welling Motion Pictures & Westcoast Films.

Maedchen in Uniform. Dorothea Wieck. Directed by Carl Froelich. Ger. 1932. Germany. 89 min. Sound. 16mm B&W. subtitles. *Rental:* Films Inc & Janus Films.

Mafia Girls. Cindy Stevens. Directed by Ed Ross. 1969. Stage Four. 74 min. Sound. 16mm Color. *Rental:* Video Comm.

Mafioso. Alberto Sordi & Norma Bengell. Directed by Alberto Lattuada. Ital. 1964. Italy. 100 min. Sound. 16mm B&W. subtitles. *Rental:* Films Inc.

Mag Wheels. Shelley Horner & John McLaughlin. Directed by Bethel Buckalew. 1978. Peter Perry. 90 min. Sound. 16mm Color. *Rental:* Swank Motion.

Magic. Anthony Hopkins & Ann Margret. Directed by Sir Richard Attenborough. 1978. Fox. 106 min. Sound. 16mm Color. *Rental:* Films Inc.

Magic Adventures of Sinbad, the Sailor *see* Sinbad the Sailor.

Magic Bow, The. Stewart Granger & Phyllis Calvert. Directed by Bernard Knowles. 1947. Britain. 105 min. Sound. 16mm B&W. *Rental:* Budget Films.

Magic Box, The. Robert Donat & Leo Genn. Directed by John Boulting & Roy Boulting. 1954. Britain. 98 min. Sound. 16mm Color. *Rental:* Budget Films & Corinth Films.

Magic Boy, The. 1961. Japan. (Anamorphic, animated). 75 min. Sound. 16mm Color. dubbed. *Rental:* MGM United.

Magic Carpet, The. Lucille Ball & John Agar. Directed by Lew Landers. 1951. Columbia. 84 min. *Rental:* Bosco Films.

Magic Christian, The. Peter Sellers & Ringo Starr. Directed by Joseph McGrath. 1969. Commonwealth United. 95 min. Sound. 16mm Color. *Rental:* Budget Films, Film Ctr DC, Films Inc, Ivy Films, Rep Pic Film, Video Comm, Welling Motion Pictures & Westcoast Films. *Lease:* Rep Pic Film. *Sale:* Morcraft Films, Videotape version.

Magic Circle, The. Directed by Carol Myers. 1973. Canada. (Documentary). 58 min. Sound. 16mm Color. *Rental:* Natl Film CN. *Sale:* Natl Film CN.

Magic Cloak of Oz, The. Directed by L. Frank Baum. 1914. Oz. (Cast unlisted). 45 min. Silent. 16mm B&W. *Rental:* Em Gee Film Lib.

Magic Fire. Alan Badel, Yvonne De Carlo & Rita Gam. Directed by William Dieterle. 1956. Republic. 95 min. Sound. 16mm Color. *Rental:* Ivy Films. *Sale:* Rep Pic Film.

Magic Flute, The. Directed by Ingmar Bergman. Swed. 1975. Sweden. (Opera). 134 min. Sound. 16mm Color. subtitles. *Rental:* Films Inc.

Magic Fountain, The. Sir Cedric Hardwicke & Hans Conried. 1961. Classic World. 78 min. Sound. 16mm Color. *Rental:* Film Ctr DC, Films Inc, Newman Film Lib & Wholesome Film Ctr.

Magic Garden, The. Orig. Title: Pennywhistle Blues. Tommy Ramokgopa. Directed by Donald Swanson. 1952. South Africa. 63 min. Sound. 16mm B&W. *Rental:* Budget Films. *Sale:* Reel Images. *Sale:* Reel Images, Super 8 sound version.

Magic Garden of Stanley Sweetheart, The. Don Johnson & Michael Greer. Directed by Leonard Horn. 1970. MGM. 117 min. Sound. 16mm Color. *Rental:* MGM United.

Magic Horse, The. Directed by I. Vano. 1946. Russia. (Animated). 57 min. Sound. 16mm Color. dubbed. *Rental:* Films Inc, Macmillan Films & Newman Film Lib. *Sale:* Macmillan Films.

Magic in the Hills. 1972. Britain. (Documentary). 52 min. Sound. 16mm Color. *Rental:* Time-Life Multimedia. *Sale:* Time-Life Multimedia.

Magic of Dance, The: The Reflections of Margot Fonteyn. 6 pts. 1979. Britain. (Dance). 360 min. Sound. 16mm Color. *Rental:* Budget Films & Dance Film Archive.

Magic of Lassie, The. James Stewart, Alice Faye, Mickey Rooney & Lassie. Directed by Don Chaffey. 1978. International Picture Show. 100 min. Sound. 16mm Color. *Rental:* Modern Sound, Swank Motion, Twyman Film & Williams Films.

Magic of the Kite. Xerox. (Cast unlisted). 74 min. Sound. 16mm Color. *Sale:* Xerox Films.

Magic Sword, The. Basil Rathbone & Estelle Winwood. Directed by Bert I. Gordon. 1962. United Artists. 80 min. Sound. 16mm Color. *Rental:* Arcus Film, MGM United, Modern Sound, Roas Films, Westcoast Films, Wholesome Film Ctr & Williams Films. *Sale:* Cinema Concepts.

Magic Town. James Stewart & Jane Wyman. Directed by William A. Wellman. 1947. RKO. 100 min. Sound. 16mm B&W. *Rental:* Films Inc. *Lease:* Rep Pic Film.

Magic Way of Going, A: The Thoroughbred. 1982. Wombat. (Documentary). 50 min. Sound. 16mm Color. *Sale:* Wombat Produtions. *Sale:* Wombat Productions, Videotape version.

Magic Witch, The. (Cast unlisted). 80 min. Sound. 16mm Color. *Rental:* Films Inc.

Magic World of Topo Gigio. Directed by Luca De Rico. 1965. Italy. (Animated). 75 min. Sound. 16mm Color. dubbed. *Rental:* Arcus Film, Buchan Pic, Cine Craft, Films Inc, Modern Sound, Newman Film Lib, Roas Films, Twyman Films, Welling Motion Pictures, Westcoast Films & Wholesome Film.

Magical Mystery Tour, The. Beatles. Directed by Dennis O'Dell. 1967. Britain. 52 min. Sound. 16mm Color. *Rental:* Budget Films, U of IL Film, New Line Cinema & Video Comm. *Sale:* Cinema Concepts & Glenn Photo. *Rental:* Ivy Films, Super 8 sound version.

Magical Mystery Trip Through Little Red's Head, A. 1974. ABC. (Animated). 47 min. Sound. 16mm Color. *Rental:* Films Inc. *Sale:* Films Inc.

Magician, The *see* Last Performance.

Magician, The. Alice Terry & Paul Wegener. Directed by Rex Ingram. 1926. MGM. 90 min. Silent. 16mm B&W. *Rental:* MGM United.

Magician, The. Max Von Sydow & Ingrid Thulin. Directed by Ingmar Bergman. Swed. 1959. Sweden. 102 min. Sound. 16mm B&W. subtitles. *Rental:* Budget Films, Janus Films, Images Film & New Cinema. *Sale:* Festival Films & Images Film. *Rental:* Festival Films & Tamarelles French Film, Videotape version.

Magnet, The. Kay Walsh. Directed by Charles Frend. 1950. Britain. 79 min. Sound. 16mm B&W. *Rental:* Em Gee Film Lib.

Magnet Earth, The. 1982. Britain. (Documentary). 50 min. Sound. 16mm Color. *Rental:* Films Inc. *Sale:* Films Inc. *Sale:* Films Inc, Videotape version.

Magnificent Adventure, The. 1957. Cathedral. (Cast unlisted). 80 min. Sound. 16mm B&W. *Rental:* Roas Films.

Magnificent Ambersons, The. Joseph Cotten & Anne Baxter. Directed by Orson Welles. 1942. RKO. 88 min. Sound. 16mm B&W. *Rental:* Films Inc. *Sale:* Cinema Concepts & Festival Films, Videotape version.

Magnificent Doll, The. Ginger Rogers & David Niven. Directed by Frank Borzage. 1946. Universal. 95 min. Sound. 16mm B&W. *Rental:* Inst Cinema & Ivy Films. *Sale:* Rep Pic Film.

Magnificent Dope, The. Henry Fonda & Lynn Bari. Directed by Walter Lang. 1942. Fox. 84 min. Sound. 16mm B&W. *Rental:* Films Inc.

Magnificent Gift, The. Canada. (Documentary). 56 min. Sound. 16mm Color. *Rental:* CBC Film. *Sale:* CBC Film.

Magnificent Matador, The. Anthony Quinn & Maureen O'Hara. Directed by Budd Boetticher. 1955. Fox. 94 min. Sound. 16mm Color. *Rental:* Budget Films, Charard Motion Pics, Ivy Films & Willoughby Peer.

Magnificent Men in Their Flying Machines *see* Those Magnificent Men in Their Flying Machines.

Magnificent Obsession. Irene Dunne & Robert Taylor. Directed by John M. Stahl. 1935. Universal. 130 min. Sound. 16mm B&W. *Rental:* Williams Films.

Magnificent Obsession. Rock Hudson & Jane Wyman. Directed by Douglas Sirk. 1954. Universal. 108 min. Sound. 16mm Color. *Rental:* Williams Films.

Magnificent Rebel, The. Carl Boehm. Directed by Georg Tressler. 1961. Disney. 92 min. Sound. 16mm Color. *Rental:* Buchan Pic, Cine Craft, Cousino Visual Ed, Film Ctr DC, Film Pres, Films Inc, Newman Film Lib, Swank Motion & U of IL Film.

Magnificent Rogue, The. Lynn Roberts & Gerald Mohr. Directed by Albert S. Rogell. 1947. Republic. 74 min. Sound. 16mm B&W. *Rental:* Ivy Films. *Sale:* Rep Pic Film.

Magnificent Roughnecks, The. Jack Carson & Mickey Rooney. Directed by Sherman Rose. 1956. Allied Artists. 78 min. Sound. 16mm B&W. *Rental:* Ivy Films. *Sale:* Rep Pic Film.

Magnificent Seven, The. Toshiro Mifune. Directed by Akira Kurosawa. Jap. 1954. Japan. 141 min. Sound. 16mm B&W. subtitles. *Rental:* Budget Films & Films Inc. *Sale:* Cinema Concepts.

Magnificent Seven, The. Yul Brynner, Steve McQueen & James Coburn. Directed by John Sturges. 1960. 127 min. Sound. 16mm Color. *Rental:* MGM United. *Rental:* MGM United, Videotape version.

Magnificent Seven Ride!, The Lee Van Cleef & Michael Callan. Directed by George McGowan. 1972. United Artists. 100 min. Sound. 16mm Color. *Rental:* MGM United.

Magnificent Sinner, The *see* Katia & the Emperor.

Magnificent Yankee, The. Orig. Title: Man with Thirty Sons, The. Louis Calhern & Ann Harding. Directed by John Sturges. 1950. MGM. 88 min. Sound. 16mm B&W. *Rental:* MGM United. *Rental:* MGM United, Videotape version.

Magnifique, Le. Jean-Paul Belmondo. Directed by Philippe De Broca. Fr. 1974. France. 93 min. Sound. 16mm Color. subtitles. *Rental:* Specialty Films. *Sale:* Cinema Concepts & Video Lib, Videotape version.

Magnum Force. Clint Eastwood. Directed by Ted Post. 1973. Warners. 123 min. Sound. 16mm Color. *Rental:* Williams Films, Modern Sound, Swank Motion & Twyman Films. *Rental:* Swank Motion, Videotpae version.

Magoo at Sea. Orig. Title: Mister Magoo at Sea. 1964. UPA. (Animated anthology). 112 min. Sound. 16mm Color. *Rental:* Budget Films, Films Inc, Kerr Film, Macmillan Films & Westcoast Films. *Sale:* Macmillan Films.

Magoo in Sherwood Forest. Orig. Title: Robin Hood with Mr.Magoo. 1964. UPA. (Animated). 82 min. Sound. 16mm Color. *Rental:* Budget Films, Cine Craft, Films Inc, Kerr Film, Macmillan Films, Natl Film, Serv, New Film Lib, Twyman Films, Welling Motion Pictures, Westcoast Films & OK AV Ctr. *Sale:* Macmillan Films.

Magoo in the King's Service. Orig. Title: Mister Magoo in the King's Service. 1964. UPA. (Animated, Anthology). 92 min. Sound. 16mm Color. *Rental:* Films Inc & Westcoast Films.

Magoo's Christmas Carol *see* Christmas Carol with Mr. Magoo.

Magus, The. Anthony Quinn, Michael Caine & Candice Bergen. Directed by Guy Green. 1969. Fox. (Anamorphic). 116 min. Sound. 16mm Color. *Rental:* Films Inc.

Mahanagar. Anil Chatterji & Madhabie Mukherjee. Directed by Satyajit Ray. Bengali. 1964. India. 122 min. Sound. 16mm B&W. subtitles. *Rental:* Films Inc.

Mahatma: The Great Soul. 1963. Hearst. (Documentary). 50 min. Sound. 16mm B&W. *Rental:* Films Inc. *Sale:* King Features.

Mahler. Robert Powell & Georgina Hale. Directed by Ken Russell. 1974. Britain. 115 min. Sound. 16mm Color. *Rental:* New Line Cinema & Specialty Films.

Mahogany. Diana Ross & Tony Perkins. Directed by Berry Gordy. 1975. Paramount. (Anamorphic). 105 min. Sound. 16mm Color. *Rental:* Films Inc.

Mai Zetterling's Stockholm. 1977. Learning Corp. (Documentary). 50 min. Sound. 16mm Color. *Rental:* Kent St U Film & Learning Corp Am. *Sale:* Learning Corp Am.

Maid, The. Directed by Tomotaka Tazaka. Japan. (Cast unlisted). Sound. 16mm B&W. subtitles. *Sale:* Cinema Concepts.

Maid of Salem. Claudette Colbert & Fred MacMurray. Directed by Frank Lloyd. 1937. Paramount. 86 min. Sound. 16mm B&W. *Rental:* Swank Motion.

Maids, The. Glenda Jackson & Susannah York. Directed by Christopher Miles. 1973. AFT. 95 min. Sound. 16mm Color. *Rental:* Films Inc.

Maid's Night Out. Joan Fontaine & Hedda Hopper. Directed by Ben Holmes. 1938. RKO. 65 min. Sound. 16mm *Rental:* RKO General Pics.

Maidstone. Rip Torn & Joy Bang. Directed by Norman Mailer. 1971. New Line. 110 min. Sound. 16mm Color. *Rental:* New Line Cinema. *Sale:* New Line Cinema.

Maigret Sets a Trap *see* Inspector Maigret.

Mail Order Bride. Buddy Ebsen & Keir Dullea. Directed by Burt Kennedy. 1964. MGM. 85 min. Sound. 16mm Color. *Rental:* MGM United. *Rental:* MGM United, Anamorphic version.

Main Attraction, The. Pat Boone & Nancy Kwan. Directed by Daniel Petrie. 1963. MGM. 90 min. Sound. 16mm Color. *Rental:* MGM United.

Main Event, The. Barbra Streisand & Ryan O'Neal. Directed by Howard Zieff. 1979. Warners. 112 min. Sound. 16mm Color. *Rental:* Swank Motion & Williams Films. *Rental:* Swank Motion, Videotape version.

Main Street Kid, The. Al Pearce & Janet Martin. Directed by R. G. Springsteen. 1948. Republic. 64 min. Sound. 16mm B&W. *Rental:* Ivy Films. *Sale:* Rep Pic Film.

Main Street Lawyer. Edward Ellis & Anita Lewis. Directed by Dudley Murphy. 1939. Republic. 54 min. Sound. 16mm B&W. *Sale:* Rep Pic Film.

Main Street to Broadway. Tallulah Bankhead & Ethel Barrymore. Directed by Tay Garnett. 1953. MGM. 102 min. Sound. 16mm B&W. *Rental:* Video Comm.

Maison Des Bois, La. 7 pts. Fernand Gravey. Directed by Maurice Pialat. France. 392 min. Sound. 16mm Color. *Rental:* French Am Cul.

Maison Des Femmes, La *see* Caged Women.

Maitre de Santiago, Le. Directed by Jacques-Gerard Cornu. Fr. France. (Cast unlisted). 60 min. Sound. 16mm B&W. subtitles. *Rental:* French Am Cul.

Maitre d'Ecole, Le. Jacques Fabri. Directed by Jean-Pierre Decourt. Fr. 1975. France. 52 min. Sound. 16mm Color. subtitles. *Rental:* French Am Cul. *Rental:* French Am Cul, Videotape version.

Maja Del Capote, La. 1950. Mexico. (Cast unlisted). 90 min. Sound. 16mm B&W. *Rental:* Film Classics.

Majestic Clockwork. (Ascent of Man Ser.). 1974. Britain. (Documentary). 52 min. Sound. 16mm Color. *Rental:* U Cal Media, Iowa Films, U Mich Media, Utah Media & Time-Life Multimedia. *Sale:* Time-Life Multimedia. *Rental:* Time-Life Multimedia, *Sale:* Time-Life Multimedia, Videotape version.

Major & the Minor, The. Ginger Rogers & Ray Milland. Directed by Billy Wilder. 1942. Paramount. 100 min. Sound. 16mm B&W. *Rental:* Williams Films.

Major Barbara. Wendy Hiller & Rex Harrison. Directed by Gabriel Pascal. 1941. Britain. 115 min. Sound. 16mm B&W. *Rental:* Films Inc, Learning Corp Am, New Cinema & U of IL Film. *Lease:* Learning Corp Am.

Major Dundee. Charlton Heston & Richard Harris. Directed by Sam Peckinpah. 1965. Columbia. 134 min. Sound. 16mm Color. *Rental:* Arcus Film, Buchan Pics, Budget Films, Cine Craft, Corinth Films, Film Ctr DC, Ivy Films, Kerr Film, Kit Parker, Modern Sound, Natl Film Video, Video Comm, Welling Motion Pictures, Westcoast Films & Wholesome Film Ctr. *Rental:* Corinth Films & Kit Parker, Anamorphic version. *Sale:* Tamarelles French Film, Videotape version.

Make a Mighty Reach. 1964. Teacher Education. (Documentary). 46 min. Sound. 16mm Color. *Rental:* OK AV Ctr.

Make a Wish. Bobby Breen. Directed by Kurt Neumann. 1937. RKO. 80 min. Sound. 16mm B&W. *Rental:* Budget Films, Classic Film Mus & Roas Film. *Sale:* Natl Cinema. *Sale:* Morcraft Films, Super 8 sound version. *Sale:* Morcraft Films, Videotape version.

Make-Believe Marriage, The. Lonny Price & Janina Matthews. Directed by Robert Fuest. 1979. Learning Corp. 50 min. Sound. 16mm Color. *Rental:* Iowa Films & Learning Corp Am. *Sale:* Learning Corp Am.

Make Haste to Live. Dorothy McGuire & Stephen McNally. Directed by William A. Seiter. 1954. Republic. 90 min. Sound. 16mm B&W. *Rental:* Ivy Films. *Sale:* Rep Pic Film.

Make Like a Thief. Richard Long. Directed by Richard Long & Palmer Thompson. 1967. Emerson. 80 min. Sound. 16mm Color. *Rental:* Films Inc.

Make Mine a Double. Brian Rix & Cecil Parker. Directed by Darcy Conyers. 1962. Britain. 86 min. Sound. 16mm B&W. *Rental:* Ivy Films & Welling Motion Pictures.

Make Mine Laughs. Ray Bolger & Anne Shirley. Directed by Richard Fleischer. 1949. RKO. 64 min. Sound. 16mm B&W. *Rental:* Films Inc.

Make Mine Mink. Terry-Thomas & Hattie Jacques. Directed by Robert Asher. 1960. Britain. 95 min. Sound. 16mm B&W. *Rental:* Budget Films. *Rental:* Vidamerica, Videotape version.

Make Mine Music. 1946. Disney. (Animated). 75 min. Sound. 16mm Color. *Rental:* Bosco Films, Buchan Pic, Cine Craft, Cousino Visual Ed, Disney Prod, Elliot Film Co, Film Ctr DC, Film Pres, Films Inc, MGM United, Modern Sound, Roas Films, Swank Motion, Twyman Films, U of IL Film, Welling Motion Pictures, Westcoast Films & Williams Films.

Make Way for a Lady. Herbert Marshall & Anne Shirley. Directed by David Burton. 1937. RKO. 65 min. Sound. 16mm B&W. *Rental:* RKO General Pics.

Make Way for Lila. Orig. Title: Lila-Love under the Midnight Sun. Erika Remberg. Directed by Rolf Hosberg. 1965. Finland. 90 min. Sound. 16mm Color. dubbed. *Rental:* Budget Films, Ivy Films, Video Comm, Welling Motion Pictures & Willoughby Peer.

Make Way for Tomorrow. Fay Bainter & Victor Moore. Directed by Leo McCarey. 1937. Paramount. 91 min. Sound. 16mm B&W. *Rental:* Museum Mod Art & Swank Motion.

Making a Natural History Film. Orig. Title: Making of a Natural History Film, The. 1974. Britain. (Documentary). 52 min. Sound. 16mm Color. *Rental:* Images Film & Syracuse U Film. *Rental:* U Mich Media, Videotape version.

Making It. Kristoffer Tabori & Joyce Van Patten. Directed by John Erman. 1971. Fox. 97 min. Sound. 16mm Color. *Rental:* Films Inc.

Making Love. Michael Ontkean & Kate Jackson. Directed by Arthur Hiller. 1982. Fox. 109 min. Sound. 16mm Color. *Rental:* Films Inc.

Making of A Clinician, The. 2 pts. 1977. 86 min. Sound. 16mm B&W. *Sale:* Natl AV Ctr.

Making of a King, The *see* Alte und der Junge Konig.

Making of "Butch Cassidy & the Sundance Kid", The. Directed by Robert Crawford. 1969. EYR. (Documentary). 52 min. Sound. 16mm Color. *Rental:* Budget Films, Films Inc, Images Film, Kent St U Film, Modern Sound, New Cinema, Swank Motion, Twyman Films, U Cal Media, U Mich Media & Willoughby Peer. *Sale:* Images Film.

Making Of Gandhi, The. Ben Kingsley. Directed by Sir Richard Attenborough. 1984. 51 min. Sound. Color. *Rental:* Direct Cinema. *Sale:* Direct Cinema. *Sale:* Direct Cinema, Videotape version.

Making of Nineteen Hundred, The. Directed by Bernardo Bertolucci. Ital. 1975. Italy. (Documentary). 70 min. Sound. 16mm Color. subtitles. *Rental:* Liberty Co.

Making of Raiders of the Lost Ark, The. Directed by Phillp Schuman. 1982. Howard Kazanjian. 58 min. Sound. Color. *Rental:* Direct Cinema. *Sale:* Direct Cinema. *Sale:* Direct Cinema, Videotape version.

Making of "Silent Running", The. 1973. Barbee. (Documentary). 52 min. Sound. 16mm Color. *Rental:* Films Inc, Images Film & Syracuse U Film. *Sale:* Films Inc.

Making of "Star Wars", The. Directed by Robert Guenette. 1978. Films Inc. (Documentary). 52 min. Sound. 16mm Color. *Rental:* Films Inc, U of IL Film & Syracuse U Film. *Sale:* Films Inc. *Rental:* Films Inc, *Sale:* Cinema Concepts, Videotape version.

Making of the English Landscape, The. 1972. Britain. (Documentary). 52 min. Sound. 16mm B&W. *Rental:* Syracuse U Film.

Making of the President, The: Nineteen Seventy-Two. 1973. Time/Life. (Documentary). 90 min. Sound. 16mm Color. *Rental:* Iowa Films, Time-Life Multimedia & Utah Media. *Sale:* Time-Life Multimedia. *Rental:* Time-Life Multimedia, *Sale:* Time-Life Multimedia, Videotape version.

Making of the President, The: Nineteen Sixty Eight. 1969. Metromedia. (Documentary). 82 min. Sound. 16mm B&W. *Rental:* BYU Media, Films Inc, Iowa Films, U Mich Media & Syracuse U Film. *Sale:* Films Inc. *Sale:* Films Inc, Videotape version.

Making of the President, The: Nineteen Sixty Four. 1964. Xerox. (Documentary). 81 min. Sound. 16mm B&W. *Rental:* Films Inc, Iowa Films, Syracuse U Film & U Mich Media. *Sale:* Films Inc. *Sale:* Films Inc, Videotape version.

Making Up for Lost Time. 1978. Britain. (Documentary). 53 min. Sound. 16mm Color. *Rental:* U of IL Film.

Mal Vie, La: Algerian Migrants. 1980. 58 min. Sound. Videotape *Rental:* PBS Video. *Sale:* PBS Video.

Mala the Magnificent *see* Eskimo.

Malady of Health Care, The. 1980. WGBH. (Documentary). 57 min. Sound. 16mm Color. *Rental:* U Mich Media & Time-Life Multimedia. *Sale:* Time-Life Multimedia. *Sale:* Time-Life Multimedia, Videotape version.

Malaya. Spencer Tracy & James Stewart. Directed by Richard Thorpe. 1949. MGM. 95 min. Sound. 16mm B&W. *Rental:* MGM United.

Malcolm X. 1972. Warners. (Documentary). 92 min. Sound. 16mm Color. *Rental:* Swank Motion.

Maldicion De la Llorona, La *see* Curse of the Crying Woman.

Maldicion de la Monia Azteca, La *see* Curse of the Aztec Mummy.

Male & Female. Gloria Swanson. Directed by Cecil B. DeMille. 1919. Paramount. 133 min. Silent. 16mm B&W. *Rental:* Museum Mod Art.

Male Animal, The. Henry Fonda & Olivia De Havilland. Directed by Wolfgang Reinhardt. 1942. Warners. 101 min. Sound. 16mm B&W. *Rental:* MGM United.

Male Menopause: The Pause that Perplexes. 1979. PBS. (Documentary). 59 min. Videotape Color. *Rental:* PBS Video. *Sale:* PBS Video.

Male of the Century. Claude Berri & Juliet Berto. Directed by Claude Berri. Fr. 1976. France. 95 min. Sound. 16mm Color. subtitles. *Rental:* J Green Pics. *Sale:* Tamarelles French Film, Videotape version.

Malibu Beach. Kim Lankford. Directed by Robert J. Rosenthal. 1978. Crown. 94 min. Sound. 16mm Color. *Rental:* Films Inc & Swank Motion.

Malibu High. Jill Lansing. Directed by Irvin Berwick. 1979. Crown. 92 min. Sound. 16mm Color. *Rental:* Films Inc.

Malicious: Malizia. Laura Antonelli & Turi Ferro. Directed by Salvatore Samperi. Ital. 1974. Italy. 98 min. Sound. 16mm Color. dubbed. *Rental:* Films Inc.

Malizia *see* **Malicious**

Malou. Ingrid Caven & Grischa Huber. Directed by Jeanine Meerapfel. Ger. 1983. Germany. Sound. 16mm Color. subtitles. *Rental:* Films Inc.

Malta Story, The. Sir Alec Guinness & Jack Hawkins. Directed by Brian Desmond-Hurst. 1954. Britain. 103 min. Sound. 16mm B&W. *Rental:* Budget Films, Learning Corp Am & U of IL Film. *Sale:* Learning Corp Am.

Maltese Bippy, The. Dan Rowan & Dick Martin. Directed by Norman Panama. 1969. MGM. 92 min. Sound. 16mm Color. *Rental:* MGM United.

Maltese Falcon, The. Bebe Daniels & Ricardo Cortez. Directed by Roy Del Ruth. 1931. Warners. 80 min. Sound. 16mm B&W. *Rental:* MGM United.

Maltese Falcon, The. Humphrey Bogart & Mary Astor. Directed by John Huston. 1941. Warners. 100 min. Sound. 16mm B&W. *Rental:* MGM United.

Mama Loves Papa. Lawrence Tierney & Leon Errol. Directed by Ben Stoloff. 1946. RKO. 60 min. Sound. 16mm B&W. *Rental:* RKO General Pics.

Mama Runs Wild. William Henry & Lynne Roberts. Directed by Ralph Staub. 1939. Republic. 54 min. Sound. 16mm B&W. *Rental:* Ivy Films. *Sale:* Rep Pic Film.

Mama Steps Out. Betty Furness & Guy Kibbee. Directed by George B. Seitz. 1937. MGM. 65 min. Sound. 16mm B&W. *Rental:* MGM United.

Mama's Affair. Constance Talmadge. Directed by Victor Fleming. 1921. 16mm *Rental:* A Twyman Pres.

Mammy. Al Jolson & Louise Dresser. Directed by Michael Curtiz. 1930. Warners. 84 min. Sound. 16mm B&W. *Rental:* MGM United.

Man, The. James Earl Jones & Martin Balsam. Directed by Joseph Sergent. 1972. Paramount. 93 min. Sound. 16mm Color. *Rental:* Films Inc.

Man & His Mate *see* One Million B. C..

Man, a Woman & a Bank, A. Donald Sutherland & Brooke Adams. Directed by Noel Black. 1979. Embassy. 100 min. Sound. 16mm Color. *Rental:* Films Inc.

Man about Town *see* Silence est d'Or.

Man About Town. Jack Benny & Dorothy Lamour. Directed by Mark Sandrich. 1939. Paramount. 85 min. Sound. 16mm B&W. *Rental:* Swank Motion.

Man Alive. Pat O'Brien & Ellen Drew. Directed by Ray Enright. 1946. RKO. 70 min. Sound. 16mm B&W. *Rental:* RKO General Pics.

Man Alone, A. Ray Milland & Ward Bond. Directed by Ray Milland. 1966. Republic. 102 min. Sound. 16mm Color. *Rental:* Ivy Films. *Sale:* Rep Pic Film. *Sale:* Tamarelles French Film, Videotape version.

Man & a Woman, A. Anouk Aimee & Jean-Louis Trintignant. Directed by Claude Lelouch. Fr. 1966. France. 102 min. Sound. 16mm Color. subtitles. *Rental:* MGM United. *Rental:* MGM United, *Sale:* Blackhawk Films, Videotape version.

Man & Boy. Bill Cosby & Gloria Foster. Directed by E. W. Swackhamer. 1972. Levitt-Pickman. 98 min. Sound. 16mm Color. *Lease:* Lucerne Films.

Man & His World: The Animated Vision of Bruno Bozzetto. Directed by Bruno Bozzetto. 1977. Italy. (Animated, anthology). 79 min. Sound. 16mm Color. *Rental:* Distribution Sixteen.

Man & the Atom. 1965. NET. (Documentary). 59 min. Sound. 16mm Color. *Rental:* Natl AV Ctr. *Sale:* Natl AV Ctr.

Man & the Legend, The. 1962. Hearst. (Documentary). 50 min. Sound. 16mm B&W. *Sale:* King Features.

Man at Large: Poet Robert Bly. 1979. WNET. (Documentary). 58 min. Videotape Color. *Rental:* WNET Media. *Sale:* WNET Media.

Man Bait. George Brent & Marguerite Chapman. Directed by Terence Fisher. 1952. Lippert. 80 min. Sound. 16mm B&W. *Rental:* Mogulls Films.

Man Behind the Mask, The. 1982. Britain. (Documentary). 50 min. Sound. 16mm Color. *Sale:* Films Inc.

Man Betrayed, A. Eddie Nugent & Kay Hughes. Directed by John H. Auer. 1936. Republic. 54 min. Sound. 16mm B&W. *Rental:* Ivy Films. *Sale:* Rep Pic Film.

Man Between, The. James Mason & Claire Bloom. Directed by Sir Carol Reed. 1953. Britain. 98 min. Sound. 16mm B&W. *Rental:* Budget Films.

Man Blong Custom. 1975. Britain. (Documentary). 52 min. Sound. 16mm Color. *Rental:* Iowa Films, U Cal Media & U of IL Film.

Man Called Adam, A. Sammy Davis Jr. Directed by Leo Penn. 1966. Embassy. 99 min. Sound. 16mm B&W. *Rental:* Films Inc.

Man Called Dagger, A. Terry Moore & Jan Murray. Directed by Richard Rush. 1967. MGM. 82 min. Sound. 16mm Color. *Rental:* MGM United.

Man Called Flintstone, A. 1966. Columbia. (Animated). 87 min. Sound. 16mm Color. *Rental:* Arcus Film, Budget Films, Cine Craft, Charard Motion Pics, Film Ctr DC, Film Pres, Films Inc, Kerr Film, Modern Sound, Newman Film Lib, Roas Films, Twyman Films, U of IL Film, Welling Motion Pictures, Westcoast Films, Wholesome Film Ctr, Williams Films & Willoughby Peer.

Man Called Horse, A. Richard Harris, Dame Judith Anderson. Directed by Eliot Silverstein. 1970. Cinema Center. 114 min. Sound. 16mm Color. *Rental:* Swank Motion.

Man Called Peter, A. Richard Todd & Jean Peters. Directed by Henry Koster. 1955. Fox. 119 min. Sound. 16mm Color. *Rental:* Films Inc & Twyman Films. *Rental:* Films Inc, Anamorphic color version.

Man Called Sledge, A. James Garner & Dennis Weaver. Directed by Vic Morrow. 1971. Columbia. 90 min. Sound. 16mm Color. *Rental:* Cine Craft, Films Inc, Kerr Film, Modern Sound, Welling Motion Pictures, Westcoast Films, Wholesome Film Ctr & Willoughby Peer.

Man Called Tiger, A. Jimmy Wang Yu. 97 min. Sound. 16mm *Rental:* WW Enter. *Rental:* WW Enter, Videotape version.

Man Could Get Killed, A. James Garner & Melina Mercouri. Directed by Ronald Neame. 1966. Universal. 99 min. Sound. 16mm Color. *Rental:* Swank Motion.

Man-Eater of Kumaon. Wendell Corey & Sabu. Directed by Byron Haskin. 1948. Universal. 80 min. Sound. 16mm B&W. *Rental:* Ivy Films. *Sale:* Rep Pic Film.

Man Escaped, A. Francois Leterrier. Directed by Robert Bresson. Fr. 1956. France. 102 min. Sound. 16mm B&W. subtitles. *Rental:* New Yorker Films.

Man for All Seasons, A. Paul Scofield & Wendy Hiller. Directed by Fred Zinnemann. 1966. Columbia. 120 min. Sound. 16mm Color. *Rental:* Swank Motion. *Rental:* Swank Motion, Videotape version.

Man Friday. Peter O'Toole & Richard Roundtree. Directed by Jack Gold. 1976. Embassy. 109 min. Sound. 16mm Color. *Rental:* Films Inc.

Man from Beyond, The. Harry Houdini & Nita Naldi. Directed by Burton King. 1922. Houdini. 50 min. Silent. 16mm B&W. *Rental:* Budget Films, Em Gee Film Lib & Film Classics. *Sale:* Morcraft Films. *Sale:* Reel Images, Sound 16mm, musical score only version. *Sale:* Reel Images, Super 8 sound version. *Rental:* Film Classics, Videotape version.

Man from Black Hills, The. Johnny Mack Brown. Directed by Thomas Carr. 1952. Monogram. 58 min. Sound. 16mm B&W. *Rental:* Hurlock Cine.

Man from Button Willow, The. Howard Keel & Edgar Buchanan. (Animated). 83 min. Sound. 16mm Color. *Rental:* Bosco Films.

Man from Cairo, The. George Raft & Gianna Maria Canale. Directed by Edorardo Anton. 1954. Lippert. 81 min. Sound. 16mm B&W. *Rental:* Budget Films.

Man from Cheyenne, The. Roy Rogers. Directed by Joseph Kane. 1942. Republic. 54 min. Sound. 16mm B&W. *Rental:* Budget Films & Ivy Films. *Sale:* Morcraft Films, Rep Pic Film & Reel Images. *Sale:* Morcraft Films, Super 8 sound version.

Man from Colorado, The. Glenn Ford, William Holden & Ellen Drew. 1948. Columbia. 99 min. Sound. 16mm Color. *Rental:* Kit Parker.

Man from Dakota, The. Wallace Beery & Dolores Del Rio. Directed by Leslie Fenton. 1940. MGM. 75 min. Sound. 16mm B&W. *Rental:* MGM United.

Man from Del Rio, The. Anthony Quinn & Katy Jurado. Directed by Harry Horner. 1956. United Artists. 82 min. Sound. 16mm B&W. *Rental:* MGM United.

Man from Frisco, The. Michael O'Shea & Anne Shirley. Directed by Robert Florey. 1944. Republic. 80 min. Sound. 16mm B&W. *Rental:* Ivy Films. *Sale:* Rep Pic Film.

Man from God's Country, The. George Montgomery & Randy Stuart. Directed by Paul Landres. 1958. Allied Artists. 70 min. Sound. 16mm Color. *Rental:* Hurlock Cine.

Man from Hell's Edges, The. Bob Steele. Directed by Robert N. Bradbury. 1933. World Wide. 60 min. Super 8 sound B&W. *Sale:* Cinema Concepts.

Man from Laramie, The. James Stewart & Donald Crisp. Directed by Anthony Mann. 1955. Columbia. 104 min. Sound. 16mm Color. *Rental:* Arcus Film, Bosco Films, Buchan Pic, Budget Films, Cine Craft, Corinth Films, Film Ctr DC, Films Inc, Kit Parker, Modern Sound, Natl Film Video, U of IL Film, Welling Motion Pictures, Westcoast Films & Williams Films. *Rental:* Corinth Films, Anamorphic version, Videotape version.

Man from Maisinicu, The. Sergio Corrieri. Directed by Manuel Perez. Span. 1973. Cuba. 124 min. Sound. 16mm B&W. subtitles. *Rental:* New Cinema & Unifilm. *Sale:* Unifilm. *Sale:* New Cinema, French Subtitled version.

Man from Monterey, The. John Wayne & Ruth Hall. Directed by Mack V. Wright. 1933. Warners. 57 min. Sound. 16mm B&W. *Rental:* MGM United.

Man from Music Mountain, The. Gene Autry. Directed by Joseph Kane. 1938. Republic. 54 min. Sound. 16mm B&W. *Rental:* Budget Films & Ivy Films. *Sale:* Cinema Concepts & Natl Cinema. *Sale:* Morcraft Films, Super 8 sound version. *Sale:* Em Gee Film Lib & Video Comm, Videotape version.

Man from Nowhere, The. Giuliano Gemma & Corinne Marchand. Directed by Michael Wolf. Italy. (Anamorphic). 107 min. Sound. 16mm Color. dubbed. *Rental:* Budget Films & Video Comm.

Man from Nowhere, The. 1978. Britain. (Cast unlisted). 60 min. Sound. 16mm Color. *Sale:* Lucerne Films.

Man from Oklahoma, The. Roy Rogers. Directed by Frank McDonald. 1945. Republic. 54 min. Sound. 16mm B&W. *Rental:* Ivy Films. *Sale:* Rep Pic Film.

Man from Oliver Street, The. 1962. Hearst. (Documentary). 50 min. Sound. 16mm B&W. *Sale:* King Features.

Man from Painted Post, The. Douglas Fairbanks. Directed by Joseph Henabery. 1917. Artcraft. 50 min. Silent. 16mm B&W. *Rental:* Em Gee Film Lib.

Man from Rainbow Valley, The. Monte Hale. Directed by R. G. Springsteen. 1946. Republic. 56 min. Sound. 16mm B&W. *Rental:* Ivy Films. *Sale:* Rep Pic Film.

Man from Snowy River, The. Kirk Douglas & Tom Burlinson. Directed by George Miller. 1982. Fox. 105 min. Sound. 16mm Color. *Rental:* Films Inc.

Man from Sonora, The. Johnny Mack Brown. Directed by Lewis D. Collins. 1951. Monogram. 104 min. Sound. 16mm B&W. *Rental:* Hurlock Cine.

Man from Texas, The. Tex Ritter. Directed by Al Herman. 1939. Monogram. 60 min. Sound. 16mm B&W. *Sale:* Cinema Concepts.

Man from Texas, The. James Craig & Lynn Bari. Directed by Leigh Jason. 1947. Eagle Lion. 71 min. Sound. 16mm B&W. *Rental:* Budget Films.

Man from the Alamo, The. Glenn Ford & Julie Adams. Directed by Budd Boetticher. 1953. Universal. 79 min. Sound. 16mm Color. *Rental:* Swank Motion.

Man from the Big City, The *see* It Happened Out West.

Man from the Diners' Club, The. Danny Kaye. Directed by Frank Tashlin. 1963. Columbia. 96 min. Sound. 16mm B&W. *Rental:* Buchan Pic, Budget Films, Charard Motion Pics, Film Ctr DC, Films Inc, Modern Sound, Roas Films, Welling Motion Pictures, Westcoast Films & Wholesome Film Ctr.

Man from the Folies Bergere, The *see* Folies Bergere.

Man from the Rio Grande, The. Don Barry. Directed by Howard Bretherton. 1943. Republic. 55 min. Sound. 16mm B&W. *Rental:* Ivy Films. *Sale:* Rep Pic Film & Nostalgia Merchant.

Man from the Tumbleweeds, The. Bill Elliott. Directed by Joseph Lewis. 1940. Columbia. 90 min. Sound. 16mm B&W. *Rental:* Newman Film Lib.

Man from Thunder River, The. Bill Elliott. Directed by John English. 1943. Republic. 55 min. Sound. 16mm B&W. *Rental:* Ivy Films. *Sale:* Rep Pic Film & Nostalgia Merchant.

Man from Utah, The. John Wayne. Directed by Robert N. Bradbury. 1934. Monogram. 59 min. Sound. 16mm B&W. *Rental:* Budget Films & Ivy Films. *Sale:* Classics Assoc NY, Morcraft Films & Rep Pic Film. *Sale:* Video Comm, Videotape version.

Man Hunt. Walter Pidgeon & Joan Bennett. Directed by Fritz Lang. 1941. Fox. 95 min. Sound. 16mm B&W. *Rental:* Films Inc.

Man Hunt. Junior Durkin & Charlotte Henry. Directed by Irving Cummings. 1933. RKO. 68 min. Sound. 16mm *Rental:* RKO General Pics.

Man Hunters, The. 1970. MGM. (Documentary). 52 min. Sound. 16mm Color. *Rental:* Films Inc, Syracuse U Film, U Cal Media & Wholesome Film Ctr. *Sale:* Films Inc. *Sale:* Films Inc, Videotape version.

Man I Killed, The *see* Broken Lullaby.

Man I Love, The. Ida Lupino & Robert Alda. Directed by Raoul Walsh. 1946. Warners. 90 min. Sound. 16mm B&W. *Rental:* MGM United.

Man in a Cocked Hat, The. Orig. Title: Carlton-Browne of the F. O. Peter Sellers & Terry-Thomas. Directed by Jeffrey Dell & Roy Boulting. 1960. Britain. 88 min. Sound. 16mm B&W. *Rental:* Budget Films, Kit Parker & Video Comm. *Lease:* Video Comm. *Rental:* Video Comm, Videotape version.

Man in Grey, The. James Mason & Stewart Granger. Directed by Leslie Arliss. 1943. Britain. 90 min. Sound. Videotape B&W. *Rental:* Video Comm.

Man in Outer Space. Milos Kopecky. Directed by Oldrich Lipsky. 1966. MGM. 85 min. Sound. 16mm Color. dubbed. *Rental:* Films Inc.

Man in Possession, The *see* Personal Property.

Man in Space. 1959. Wolper. (Documentary). 50 min. Sound. 16mm B&W. *Rental:* Films Inc. *Sale:* Films Inc.

Man in the Attic, The. Jack Palance & Constance Smith. Directed by Hugo Fregonese. 1953. Fox. 82 min. Sound. 16mm B&W. *Rental:* Films Inc.

Man in the Dark, The. Edmond O'Brien & Audrey Totter. Directed by Lew Landers. 1953. Columbia. 80 min. Sound. 16mm B&W. *Rental:* Bosco Films.

Man in the Glass Booth, The. Maximillian Schell. Directed by Arthur Hiller. 1973. AFT. 117 min. Sound. 16mm Color. *Rental:* Films Inc.

Man in the Gray Flannel Suit, The. Gregory Peck, Jennifer Jones & Fredric March. Directed by Nunnally Johnson. 1956. Fox. 152 min. Sound. 16mm Color. *Rental:* Films Inc. *Rental:* Films Inc, Anamorphic version.

Man in the Iron Mask, The. Louis Hayward & Joan Bennett. Directed by James Whale. 1939. United Artists. 110 min. Sound. 16mm B&W. *Rental:* Budget Films, Kit Parker, Mogulls Films & Video Comm. *Rental:* Video Comm, Videotape version.

Man in the Iron Mask, The. Richard Chamberlain & Louis Jourdan. Directed by Mike Newell. 1978. Independent Television. 103 min. Sound. 16mm Color. *Rental:* Swank Motion.

Man in the Middle, The. Robert Mitchum & France Nuyen. Directed by Guy Hamilton. 1964. Fox. 94 min. Sound. 16mm B&W. *Rental:* Films Inc.

Man in the Middle, The: The State Legislator. 1962. NBC. (Documentary). 54 min. Sound. 16mm B&W. *Rental:* McGraw-Hill Films, SD AV Ctr, Syracuse U Film & Utah Media. *Sale:* McGraw-Hill Films.

Man in the Moon, The. Kenneth Moore & Shirley Ann Field. Directed by Basil Dearden. 1960. Britain. 90 min. Sound. 16mm B&W. *Rental:* Cinema Five.

Man in the Net, The. Alan Ladd & Carolyn Jones. Directed by Michael Curtiz. 1959. United Artists. 97 min. Sound. 16mm B&W. *Rental:* MGM United.

Man in the Raincoat, The. Fernandel & John McIver. Directed by Julien Duvivier. Fr. 1958. France. 97 min. Sound. 16mm B&W. subtitles. *Rental:* Films Inc.

Man in the Road, The. Donald Wolfit & Ella Raines. Directed by Lance Comfort. 1956. 84 min. 16mm *Rental:* A Twyman Pres.

Man in the Saddle, The. Orig. Title: Outcast, The. Randolph Scott & Ellen Drew. Directed by Andre De Toth. 1951. Columbia. 87 min. Sound. 16mm Color. *Rental:* Bosco Films, Cine Craft, Inst Cinema, Newman Film Lib & Video Comm.

Man in the Shadow, The. Orson Welles & Jeff Chandler. Directed by Jack Arnold. 1957. Universal. 80 min. Sound. 16mm B&W. *Rental:* Swank Motion.

Man in the Sky *see* Decision Against Time.

Man in the Trunk, The. Raymond Walburn & Lynne Roberts. Directed by Mal St. Clair. 1942. Fox. 71 min. Sound. 16mm B&W. *Rental:* Films Inc.

Man in the Water *see* Escape from Hell Island.

Man in the White Suit, The. Sir Alec Guinness & Joan Greenwood. Directed by Alexander Mackendrick. 1951. Britain. 85 min. Sound. 16mm Color. *Rental:* Budget Films, Films Inc, Images Film, Kit Parker, Learning Corp Am, Roas Films, Twyman Films, U of IL Film & Wholesome Film Ctr. *Lease:* Learning Corp Am. *Rental:* Learning Corp Am, *Lease:* Learning Corp Am, Videotape version.

Man in the Wilderness. Richard Harris. Directed by Richard C. Sarafian. 1972. Warners. 105 min. Sound. 16mm Color. *Rental:* Buchan Pic, Films Inc, Inst Cinema, Swank Motion, Twyman Films & Williams Films.

Man Inside, The. Jack Palance & Anita Ekberg. Directed by John Gilling. 1958. Britain. 89 min. Sound. 16mm B&W. *Rental:* Kit Parker.

Man is Armed, The. Dane Clark & William Tallman. Directed by Franklin Adreon. 1956. Republic. 74 min. Sound. 16mm B&W. *Rental:* Ivy Films. *Sale:* Rep Pic Film.

Man is Ten Feet Tall, A *see* Edge of the City.

Man Killer *see* Private Detective 62.

Man Mad *see* No Place to Land.

Man-Made Monster, The. Lon Chaney Jr. & Lionel Atwill. Directed by George Waggner. 1941. Universal. 59 min. Sound. 16mm B&W. *Rental:* Swank Motion.

Man Named John, A. Orig. Title: And There Came a Man. Rod Steiger & Adelfo Celi. Directed by Ermanno Olmi. 1965. Italy. 94 min. Sound. 16mm Color. *Rental:* Films Inc.

Man Named Lombardi, A. 1977. Lucerne. (Documentary). 53 min. Sound. 16mm Color. *Rental:* Budget Films, Roas Films & Syracuse U Film. *Sale:* Lucerne Films. *Sale:* Lucerne Films, Videotape version.

Man of a Thousand Faces, The. James Cagney & Dorothy Malone. Directed by Joseph Pevney. 1957. Universal. 122 min. Sound. 16mm B&W. *Rental:* Williams Films.

Man of Aran. Directed by Robert Flaherty. 1934. Britain. (Documentary). 77 min. Sound. 16mm B&W. *Rental:* Budget Films, Em Gee Film Lib, Films Inc, Kit Parker, U Mich Media, Syracuse U Film, Texture Film & Viewfinder. *Sale:* Films Inc & Texture Film.

Man of Bronze, The *see* Jim Thorpe, All American.

Man of Conquest. Richard Dix & Joan Fontaine. Directed by George Nicholls Jr. 1939. Republic. 99 min. Sound. 16mm B&W. *Rental:* Ivy Films. *Sale:* Rep Pic Film.

Man of Iron. Barton MacLane & Mary Astor. Directed by William McGann. 1935. Warners. 61 min. Sound. 16mm B&W. *Rental:* MGM United.

Man of Iron. Jerzy Radziwilowicz & Ksystyna Janda. Directed by Andrzej Wajda. Pol. 1981. 140 min. 16mm Color. subtitles. *Rental:* MGM United.

Man of La Mancha. Peter O'Toole & Sophia Loren. Directed by Arthur Hiller. 1972. United Artists. 130 min. Sound. 16mm Color. *Rental:* MGM United & Welling Motion Pictures. *Rental:* MGM United, Videotape version.

Man of Marble. Krystyna Janda & Jerzy Radziwilowicz. Directed by Andrzej Wajda. Pol. 1977. 160 min. Sound. 16mm Color. subtitles Eng. *Rental:* New Yorker Films.

Man of Steel. 1967. Ken Anderson. (Cast unlisted). 83 min. Sound. 16mm Color. *Rental:* G Herne.

Man of the Century. Orig. Title: Churchill, Man of the Century. 1957. CBS. (Documentary). 54 min. Sound. 16mm B&W. *Rental:* McGraw-Hill Films, U Mich Media & OK AV Ctr. *Sale:* McGraw-Hill Films & Utah Media.

Man of the East. Terence Hill & Harry Carey. Directed by E. B. Clucher. 1974. United Artists. 123 min. Sound. 16mm Color. dubbed. *Rental:* MGM United.

Man of the Forest. Orig. Title: Challenge of the Frontier. Randolph Scott & Harry Carey. Directed by Henry Hathaway. 1933. Paramount. 64 min. Sound. 16mm B&W. *Sale:* Natl Cinema, Super 8 sound version.

Man of the Frontier. Gene Autry. Directed by B. Reeves Eason. 1936. Republic. 54 min. Sound. 16mm B&W. *Rental:* Budget Films & Ivy Films. *Sale:* Video Comm, Videotape version.

Man of the Moment, The. Norman Wisdom & Lane Morris. Directed by John Paddy Carstairs. 1955. Britain. 101 min. Sound. 16mm B&W. *Rental:* Cinema Five.

Man of the People, The. Joseph Calleia, Florence Rice & Thomas Mitchell. Directed by Edwin L. Marin. 1937. MGM. 81 min. Sound. 16mm B&W. *Rental:* MGM United.

Man of the Serengeti. 1971. National Geographic. (Documentary). 52 min. Sound. 16mm Color. *Rental:* Natl Geog, Syracuse U Film, U Mich Media & Wholesome Film Ctr. *Sale:* Natl Geog. *Sale:* Natl Geog, Videotape version.

Man of the West. Gary Cooper & Julie London. Directed by Anthony Mann. 1958. United Artists. 100 min. Sound. 16mm Color. *Rental:* MGM United.

Man of the World. William Powell & Carole Lombard. Directed by Richard Wallace. 1931. Paramount. 73 min. Sound. 16mm B&W. *Rental:* Swank Motion.

Man of the Year. Lando Buzzanca. Directed by Marco Vicario. 1973. Universal. 90 min. Sound. 16mm Color. dubbed. *Rental:* Swank Motion.

Man of Two Worlds. Francis Lederer & Elissa Landi. Directed by Merian C. Cooper. 1934. RKO. 96 min. Sound. 16mm B&W. *Rental:* RKO General Pics.

Man on a String. Ernest Borgnine & Kerwin Matthews. Directed by Andre De Toth. 1960. Columbia. 92 min. Sound. 16mm B&W. *Rental:* Cine Craft, Film Ctr DC, Films Inc & Wholesome Film Ctr.

Man on a Swing. Cliff Robertson & Joel Grey. Directed by Frank Perry. 1974. Paramount. 109 min. Sound. 16mm Color. *Rental:* Films Inc.

Man on a Tightrope. Fredric March & Gloria Grahame. Directed by Elia Kazan. 1953. Fox. 105 min. Sound. 16mm B&W. *Rental:* Films Inc & Twyman Films.

Man on America's Conscience, The *see* Tennessee Johnson.

Man on Fire. Bing Crosby & Inger Stevens. Directed by Ranald MacDougall. 1957. MGM. 96 min. Sound. 16mm B&W. *Rental:* MGM United.

Man on the Box, The. Sydney Chaplin & Alice Calhoun. Directed by Charles Reisner. 1925. Warners. 90 min. Silent. 16mm B&W. *Rental:* Em Gee Film Lib & Mogulls Films. *Sale:* Glenn Photo. *Sale:* Glenn Photo, Super 8 silent version.

Man on the Eiffel Tower, The. Charles Laughton & Franchot Tone. Directed by Burgess Meredith. 1949. RKO. 85 min. Sound. 16mm Color. *Rental:* Arcus Film & Wholesome Film Ctr. *Sale:* Cinema Concepts & Natl Cinema. *Rental:* Ivy Films, *Sale:* Ivy Films, Super 8 sound version. *Sale:* Tamarelles French Film, Videotape version.

Man on the Flying Trapeze, The. W. C. Fields & Mary Brian. Directed by Clyde Bruckman. 1935. Paramount. 68 min. Sound. 16mm B&W. *Rental:* Swank Motion.

Man on the Roof, The. Carl Gustaf Lindstedt. Directed by Bo Widerberg. Swed. 1977. Sweden. 110 min. Sound. 16mm Color. subtitles. *Rental:* Cinema Five & New Cinema.

Man or Gun. MacDonald Carey & James Craig. Directed by Albert C. Gannaway. 1958. Republic. 81 min. Sound. 16mm B&W. *Rental:* Ivy Films. *Sale:* Rep Pic Film.

Man Outside, The. Directed by Joseph Marzano. 1965. Joseph Marzano. (Experimental). 100 min. Sound. 16mm B&W. *Rental:* Canyon Cinema.

Man-Proof. Walter Pidgeon & Myrna Loy. Directed by Richard Thorpe. 1938. MGM. 75 min. Sound. 16mm B&W. *Rental:* MGM United.

Man That Corrupted Hadleyburg, The. 1980. Perpective. (Cast unlisted). 46 min. Sound. 16mm Color. *Rental:* Kent St U Film. *Sale:* Perspect Film.

Man, the Esthetic Being Man. 1977. Miami-Dade. (Documentary). 60 min. Videotape Color. *Sale:* Films Inc.

Man: The Measure of All Things. 1968. Britain. (Documentary). 60 min. Sound. 16mm Color. *Rental:* Films Inc & U Cal Media. *Sale:* Films Inc. *Sale:* Films Inc, Videotape version.

Man: The Polluter. 1972. Canada/Yugoslavia. (Animated). 54 min. Sound. 16mm Color. *Rental:* U Cal Media.

Man They Could Not Hang, The. Boris Karloff & Roger Pryor. Directed by Nick Grinde. 1939. Columbia. 70 min. Sound. 16mm B&W. *Rental:* Bosco Films & Kit Parker.

Man to Man. Philips Holmes & Grant Mitchell. Directed by Allan Dwan. 1931. Warners. 69 min. Sound. 16mm B&W. *Rental:* MGM United.

Man Trap, The. William Shatner & Leonard Nimoy. Directed by Marc Daniels. 1966. Star Trek. 50 min. Sound. 16mm Color. *Rental:* Westcoast Films. *Sale:* Reel Images. *Sale:* Reel Images, Super 8 sound version.

Man Wanted. Kay Francis & Guy Kibbee. Directed by William Dieterle. 1932. Warners. 63 min. Sound. 16mm B&W. *Rental:* MGM United.

Man Whirl. 1924. Silent. 16mm B&W. *Sale:* Cinema Concepts.

Man Who Came to Dinner, The. Monty Woolley, Ann Sheridan & Bette Davis. Directed by William Keighley. 1942. Warners. 121 min. Sound. 16mm B&W. *Rental:* MGM United.

Man Who Can't Stop, The. 1974. Australia-Canada. (Documentary). 58 min. Sound. 16mm Color. *Rental:* Aust Info Serv. *Sale:* Aust Info Serv.

Man Who Changed His Mind, The *see* Man Who Lived Again.

Man Who Could Work Miracles, The. Roland Young & Joan Gardner. Directed by Lothar Mendes. 1937. Britain. 82 min. Sound. 16mm B&W. *Rental:* Charard Motion Pics, Films Inc, Inst Cinema & Mogulls Films.

Man Who Cried Wolf, The. Tom Browm & Lewis Stone. Directed by Lewis R. Foster. 1937. Universal. 66 min. Sound. 16mm B&W. *Rental:* Swank Motion.

Man Who Dances: Edward Villella. Edward Villella & Patricia McBride. 1980. Robert Drew. (Documentary). 54 min. Sound. Color. *Rental:* Direct Cinema. *Sale:* Direct Cinema. *Sale:* Direct Cinema, Videotape version.

Man Who Dared, The. Charles Grapewin & Henry O'Neill. Directed by Crane Wilbur. 1939. Warners. 60 min. Sound. 16mm B&W. *Rental:* MGM United.

Man Who Dared, The. George Macready & Leslie Brooks. Directed by John Sturges. 1946. Columbia. 70 min. Sound. 16mm B&W. *Rental:* Kit Parker.

Man Who Died Twice, The. Rod Cameron & Mike Mazurki. Directed by Joseph Kane. 1958. Republic. 70 min. Sound. 16mm B&W. *Rental:* Ivy Films. *Sale:* Rep Pic Film.

Man Who Fell to Earth, The. David Bowie & Candy Clark. Directed by Nicolas Roeg. 1976. Cinema V. 118 min. Sound. 16mm Color. *Rental:* Cinema Five. *Rental:* Cinema Five, Anamorphic, 138 min. version.

Man Who Found Himself, The. Joan Fontaine & Joan Beal. Directed by Lew Landers. 1937. RKO. 67 min. Sound. 16mm B&W. *Rental:* RKO General Pics.

Man Who Had His Hair Cut Short, The. Directed by Andre Delvaux. 16mm 94 min. Sound. B&W. *Rental:* Trans-World Films.

Man Who Had Power Over Women, The. Rod Taylor & Carol White. Directed by John Krish. 1970. Embassy. 89 min. Sound. 16mm Color. *Rental:* Films Inc.

Man Who Knew Too Much, The. Leslie Banks, Edna Best & Peter Lorre. Directed by Alfred Hitchcock. 1935. Britain. 90 min. Sound. 16mm B&W. *Rental:* Budget Films, Em Gee Film Lib, Films Inc, Inst Cinema, Images Film, Ivy Films, Janus Films, Kit Parker, Maljack, Modern Sound, Swank Motion, Video Comm, Westcoast Films & Wholesome Film Ctr. *Sale:* Festival Films, Images Film, Natl Cinema & Reel Images. *Sale:* Blackhawk Films, Cinema Concepts, Festival Films, Maljack, Tamarelles French Film, Video Comm & Images Film, Videotape version.

Man Who Knew Too Much, The. James Stewart & Doris Day. Directed by Alfred Hitchcock. 1956. Universal. 120 min. Sound. 16mm Color. *Rental:* Swank Motion.

Man Who Laughed: l'Homme Qui Rit. 1966. France. (Cast unlisted). 101 min. Sound. 16mm Color. *Rental:* MGM United.

Man Who Laughs, The. Conrad Veidt & Mary Philbin. Directed by Paul Leni. 1928. Universal. (Musical score only). 124 min. Sound. 16mm B&W. *Rental:* Swank Motion.

Man Who Left His Will on Film, The. Trans. Title: Tokyo Senso Sengo Hiwa. Kazuo Goto. Directed by Nagisa Oshima. Jap. 1970. Japan. 93 min. Sound. 16mm B&W. subtitles. *Rental:* New Yorker Films.

Man Who Lies, The. Jean-Louis Trintignant. Directed by Alain Robbe-Grillet. Czech. 1969. Czechoslovakia-France. 95 min. Sound. 16mm B&W. subtitles. *Rental:* Grove.

Man Who Lived Again, The. Orig. Title: Man Who Changed His Mind, The. Boris Karloff, Anna Lee & John Loder. Directed by Robert Stevenson. 1936. Britain. 66 min. Sound. 16mm B&W. *Rental:* Mogulls Films.

Man Who Lost Himself, The. Brian Aherne & Kay Francis. Directed by Edward Ludwig. 1941. Universal. 63 min. Sound. 16mm B&W. *Rental:* Mogulls Films.

Man Who Loved Bears, The. 1976. Stouffer. (Documentary). 50 min. Sound. 16mm Color. *Rental:* Iowa Films & Stouffer Ent. *Sale:* Stouffer Ent. *Sale:* Stouffer Ent, Videotape version.

Man Who Loved Cat Dancing, The. Burt Reynolds & Sarah Miles. Directed by Richard C. Sarafian. 1973. MGM. (Anamorphic). 114 min. Sound. 16mm Color. *Rental:* MGM United.

Man Who Loved Redheads, The. Moira Shearer & John Justin. Directed by Harold French. 1955. Britain. 89 min. Sound. 16mm B&W. *Rental:* Film Classics.

Man Who Loved Women, The. Charles Denner, Brigitte Fossey & Leslie Caron. Directed by Francois Truffaut. Fr. 1977. France. 119 min. Sound. 16mm Color. subtitles. *Rental:* Cinema Five & New Cinema. *Sale:* Tamarelles French Film, Videotape version.

Man Who Loved Women, The. Burt Reynolds & Julie Andrews. Directed by Blake Edwards. 1983. Columbia. 110 min. Sound. 16mm Color. *Rental:* Swank Motion. *Rental:* Swank Motion, Videotape version.

Man Who Murdered Himself, The *see* Scar.

Man Who Never Was, The. Clifton Webb & Stephen Boyd. Directed by Ronald Neame. 1956. Warners. 104 min. Sound. 16mm Color. *Rental:* Films Inc. *Rental:* Films Inc, Anamorphic version.

Man Who Played God, The. George Arliss & Bette Davis. Directed by John Adolfi. 1932. Warners. 83 min. Sound. 16mm B&W. *Rental:* MGM United.

Man Who Reclaimed His Head, The. Claude Rains & Lionel Atwill. Directed by Edward Ludwig. 1934. Universal. 80 min. Sound. 16mm B&W. *Rental:* Swank Motion.

Man Who Saw Tomorrow, The. Directed by Robert Guenette. 1981. Warners. (Documentary). 88 min. Sound. 16mm Color. *Rental:* Swank Motion.

Man Who Shot Liberty Valance, The. James Stewart & John Wayne. Directed by John Ford. 1962. Paramount. 122 min. Sound. 16mm B&W. *Rental:* Films Inc.

Man Who Shot the Pope, The. 1982. NBC. (Documentary). 52 min. Sound. 16mm Color. *Sale:* Films Inc.

Man Who Skied Down Everest, The. 1975. Canada. (Documentary, Anamorphic). 80 min. Sound. 16mm Color. *Rental:* Specialty Films.

Man Who Talked Too Much, The. George Brent, Brenda Marshall & Virginia Bruce. Directed by Vincent Sherman. 1940. Warners. 75 min. Sound. 16mm B&W. *Rental:* MGM United.

Man Who Turned to Stone, The. Victor Jory & Ann Doran. Directed by Leslie Kardos. 1957. Columbia. 80 min. Sound. 16mm B&W. *Rental:* Kit Parker.

Man Who Understood Women, The. Henry Fonda & Leslie Caron. Directed by Nunnally Johnson. 1959. Fox. 105 min. Sound. 16mm Color. *Rental:* Films Inc & Willoughby Peer.

Man Who Wagged His Tail, The. Orig. Title: Angel Passes over Brooklyn, An. Peter Ustinov. Directed by Ladislao Vajda. 1961. Spain. 91 min. Sound. 16mm B&W. dubbed. *Rental:* Films Inc.

Man Who Walked Alone, The. David O'Brien & Kay Aldridge. Directed by Christy Cabanne. 1945. PRC. 63 min. Sound. 16mm B&W. *Rental:* Budget Films, Inst Cinema, Ivy Films & Mogulls Film. *Sale:* Classics Assoc NY & Rep Pic Film.

Man Who Walked Through the Wall, The. Heinz Ruhmann & Nicole Courcel. Directed by Ladislao Vajda. Ger. 1964. Germany. 99 min. Sound. 16mm B&W. subtitles. *Rental:* Films Inc.

Man Who Was Sherlock Holmes, The. Orig. Title: Mann der Sherlock Holmes War, Der. Hans Albers. Directed by Karl Hartl. 1937. 95 min. 16mm *Rental:* A Twyman Pres.

Man Who Wasn't There, The. Steve Guttenberg & Lisa Langlois. Directed by Bruce Malmuth. 1983. Paramount. 111 min. Sound. 16mm Color. *Rental:* Films Inc.

Man Who Would Be King, The. Sean Connery & Michael Caine. Directed by John Huston. 1975. Allied Artists. 129 min. Sound. 16mm Color. *Rental:* Hurlock Cine. *Sale:* Tamarelles French Film, Videotape version.

Man Who Wouldn't Die, The. Lloyd Nolan & Marjorie Weaver. Directed by Herbert I. Leeds. 1942. Fox. 90 min. Sound. 16mm B&W. *Rental:* Films Inc.

Man with a Cloak, The. Joseph Cotten & Barbara Stanwyck. Directed by Fletcher Markle. 1951. MGM. 81 min. Sound. 16mm B&W. *Rental:* MGM United.

Man with a Gun, The. Lee Patterson & Rona Anderson. Directed by Montgomery Tully. 1958. Britain. 65 min. Sound. 16mm B&W. *Rental:* Video Comm.

Man with a Millon, The. Gregory Peck & A. E. Matthews. Directed by Ronald Neame. 1954. United Artists. 90 min. Sound. 16mm Color. *Rental:* MGM United & Twyman Films.

Man with a Steel Whip, The. Richard Simmons. Directed by Franklin Adreon. 1954. Republic. 163 min. Sound. 16mm B&W. *Rental:* Ivy Films.

Man with Bogart's Face, The. Robert Sacchi & Franco Nero. Directed by Robert Day. 1980. Fox. 106 min. Sound. 16mm Color. *Rental:* Films Inc.

Man with Icy Eyes, The. Keenan Wynn & Victor Buono. 1970. Gold Key. 90 min. Sound. 16mm Color. dubbed. *Rental:* Video Comm. *Lease:* Video Comm. *Rental:* Video Comm, *Lease:* Video Comm, Videotape version.

Man with Nine Lives, The. Orig. Title: Behind the Door. Boris Karloff. Directed by Nick Grinde. 1940. Columbia. 73 min. Sound. 16mm B&W. *Rental:* Budget Films, Inst Cinema & Roas Films.

Man with the Balloons, The. Marcello Mastroianni & Catherine Spaak. Directed by Marco Ferreri. Ital. 1968. Italy. 85 min. Sound. 16mm Color. subtitles Eng. *Rental:* Films Inc.

Man with the Golden Arm, The. Frank Sinatra, Kim Novak & Eleanor Parker. Directed by Otto Preminger. 1955. United Artists. 119 min. Sound. 16mm B&W. *Rental:* Films Inc & Wholesome Film Ctr.

Man with the Golden Gun, The. Roger Moore & Christopher Lee. Directed by Guy Hamilton. 1974. United Artists. 123 min. Sound. 16mm Color. *Rental:* MGM United. *Rental:* MGM United, Videotape version.

Man with the Movie Camera, The. Trans. Title: Cheloveks Kinosapparotom. Directed by Dziga Vertov. 1929. Russia. (Documentary). 89 min. Silent. 16mm B&W. *Rental:* Budget Films, Corinth Films, Em Gee Film Lib, Inst Cinema, Images Film, Ivy Films, Museum Mod Art, U Cal Media, U Mich Media, Utah Media, Video Comm & Westcoast Films. *Sale:* Glenn Photo, Images Film & Reel Images. *Rental:* Ivy Films, *Sale:* Glenn Photo, Reel Images & Images Film, Super 8 silent version. *Rental:* Video Comm, Videotape version. *Rental:* Kit Parker, *Sale:* Festival Films, 69 min. version. *Sale:* Festival Films, 69 min. Videotape version.

Man with the Synthetic Brain, The. John Carradine & Tommy Kirk. 1969. Independent International. 85 min. Videotape Color. *Sale:* Blackhawk Films.

Man with Thirty Sons, The see Magnificent Yankee.

Man with Two Brains, The. Steve Martin & Kathleen Turner. Directed by Carl Reiner. 1983. Warners. 90 min. Sound. 16mm Color. *Rental:* Swank Motion. *Rental:* Swank Motion, Videotape version.

Man with Two Faces, The. Edward G. Robinson & Mary Astor. Directed by Archie Mayo. 1934. Warners. 75 min. Sound. 16mm B&W. *Rental:* MGM United.

Man with Two Faces, The. Tab Hunter & Zena Walker. 1964. Britain. 80 min. Sound. 16mm B&W. *Rental:* Films Inc & Ivy Films.

Man Without a Conscience, The see Tomorrow We Live.

Man Without a Country, The. Florence LaBadie & A. P. Herbert. Directed by Ernest C. Warde. 1917. Thanhouser. 60 min. Silent. 16mm B&W. *Rental:* Film Classics. *Sale:* Film Classics. *Rental:* Film Classics, Videotape version.

Man Without a Face, The. Trans. Title: Homme Sans Visage, L'. Directed by Georges Franju. Fr. 1974. France. (Cast unlisted). 105 min. Sound. 16mm B&W. subtitles. *Rental:* New Line Cinema. *Sale:* New Line Cinema.

Man Without a Star, The. Kirk Douglas & Jeanne Crain. Directed by King Vidor. 1955. Universal. 89 min. Sound. 16mm Color. *Rental:* Swank Motion.

Man, Woman & Child. Martin Sheen & Blythe Danner. Directed by Dick Richards. 1983. Paramount. 100 min. Sound. 16mm Color. *Rental:* Films Inc.

Man You Loved to Hate, The. Directed by Patrick Montgomery. 1979. Killiam. (Documentary). 90 min. Sound. 16mm Color. *Rental:* Corinth Films. *Lease:* Corinth Films.

Man, a Horse & a Pistol, A see Stranger Returns.

Managing Organizational Reality. Films Inc. (Lecture). 90 min. Videotape Color. *Rental:* Films Inc. *Sale:* Films Inc.

Manchu Eagle Murder Caper Mystery, The. Gabriel Dell & Will Geer. Directed by Dean Hargrove. 1975. United Artists. 82 min. Sound. 16mm Color. *Rental:* MGM United.

Mandabi. Mamadou Guye. Directed by Ousmane Sembene. Fr. 1968. France-Senegal. 90 min. Sound. 16mm Color. subtitles. *Rental:* New Yorker Films.

Mandalay. Ricardo Cortez & Kay Francis. Directed by Michael Curtiz. 1934. Warners. 65 min. Sound. 16mm B&W. *Rental:* MGM United.

Mandarin Mystery, The. Eddie Quillan & Kay Hughes. Directed by Ralph Staub. 1936. Republic. 54 min. Sound. 16mm B&W. *Rental:* Ivy Films. *Sale:* Rep Pic Film.

Mandarin Revolution, The. 1976. Britain. (Documentary). 60 min. Sound. 16mm Color. *Rental:* Films Inc, Syracuse U Film, U Cal Media & U of IL Film. *Sale:* Films Inc. *Sale:* Films Inc, Videotape version.

Mandate to Assist, A. 1974. Malaysia. (Documentary). 50 min. Sound. 16mm Color. *Rental:* Malaysia Emb.

Mandingo. James Mason & Perry King. Directed by Richard Fleischer. 1975. Paramount. 143 min. Sound. 16mm Color. *Rental:* Films Inc.

Mandragola, La: The Mandrake. 97 min. Sound. 16mm B&W. *Rental:* Trans-World Films.

Mandy. Orig. Title: Crash of Silence. Phyllis Calvert & Jack Hawkins. Directed by Alexander Mackendrick. 1953. Britain. 93 min. Sound. 16mm B&W. *Rental:* Budget Films, Films Inc, Janus Films, Learning Corp Am, Roas Films & U of IL Film. *Sale:* Learning Corp Am.

Mango Tree, The. (Cast unlisted). Sound. Videotape Color. *Sale:* Vidamerica.

Manhandled. Gloria Swanson, Tom Moore & Frank Morgan. Directed by Allan Dwan. 1924. Paramount. 75 min. Silent. 16mm B&W. *Rental:* A Twyman Pres & Em Gee Film Lib. *Sale:* Cinema Concepts & Select Film, Silent 8mm version.

Manhandled. Dorothy Lamour & Dan Duryea. Directed by Lewis R. Foster. 1949. Paramount. 97 min. Sound. 16mm B&W. *Rental:* Video Comm & Willoughby Peer.

Manhattan. Woody Allen, Diane Keaton, Meryl Streep & Mariel Hemingway. Directed by Woody Allen. 1979. United Artists. 96 min. Sound. 16mm B&W. *Rental:* MGM United. *Rental:* MGM United, Anamorphic version. *Rental:* MGM United, Videotape version.

Manhattan Heartbeat. Virginia Gilmore & Joan Davis. Directed by David Burton. 1940. Fox. 71 min. Sound. 16mm B&W. *Rental:* Films Inc.

Manhattan Melodrama. Clark Gable, William Powell & Myrna Loy. Directed by W. S. Van Dyke. 1934. MGM. 93 min. Sound. 16mm B&W. *Rental:* MGM United.

Manhattan Merry-Go-Round. Orig. Title: Manhattan Music Box. Phil Regan & Leo Carillo. Directed by Charles Reisner. 1937. Republic. 89 min. Sound. 16mm B&W. *Rental:* Budget Films, Em Gee Film Lib & Ivy Films. *Sale:* Festival FilmsRep Pic Film & Reel Images. *Sale:* Festival Films & Video Comm, Videotape version.

Manhattan Music Box *see* Manhattan Merry-Go-Round.

Manhattan Parade. Winnie Lightner & Charles Butterworth. Directed by Lloyd Bacon. 1932. Warners. 77 min. Sound. 16mm B&W. *Rental:* MGM United.

Manhunt in the African Jungle. Rod Cameron. Directed by Spencer G. Bennett. 1954. Republic. 250 min. Sound. 16mm B&W. *Rental:* Ivy Films.

Manhunt of Mystery Island. Richard Bailey. Directed by Spencer G. Bennett. 1945. Republic. 221 min. Sound. 16mm B&W. *Rental:* Ivy Films.

Mania for Melody. Orig. Title: Melody Girl. Johnny Downs & Ruth Terry. Directed by Lew Landers. 1940. Republic. 71 min. Sound. 16mm B&W. *Rental:* Ivy Films.

Maniac. Directed by Dwain Esper. 1934. Dwain Esper. (Exploitation). 52 min. Sound. 16mm B&W. *Rental:* Budget Films. *Sale:* Festival Films & Morcraft Films. *Rental:* Kino Intl, *Sale:* Festival Films, 67 min. version, Videotape version.

Maniac. Kerwin Mathews & Nadia Gray. Directed by Michael Carreras. 1963. Britain. 87 min. Sound. 16mm Color. *Rental:* Modern Sound.

Manifestations of Shiva. 1980. Asia Society. (Documentary). 61 min. Sound. 16mm Color. *Rental:* Asia Soc. *Sale:* Asia Soc.

Manila Calling. Lloyd Nolan & Carole Landis. Directed by Herbert I. Leeds. 1942. Fox. 81 min. Sound. 16mm B&W. *Rental:* Films Inc.

Manipulator, The. Stephen Boyd & Silva Koscina. Directed by Fred Wilson. 1972. Atlantic. 85 min. Sound. 16mm Color. *Rental:* Video Comm. *Lease:* Video Comm. *Rental:* Video Comm, *Sale:* Video Comm, Videotape version.

Manitou, The. Tony Curtis & Michael Ansara. Directed by William Girdler. 1978. Embassy. 104 min. Sound. 16mm Color. *Rental:* Films Inc.

Mann der Sherlock Holmes War, Der *see* Man Who Was Sherlock Holmes.

Mannequin. Joan Crawford & Spencer Tracy. Directed by Frank Borzage. 1938. MGM. 95 min. Sound. 16mm B&W. *Rental:* MGM United.

Manners & Morals of High Capitalism, The. 1976. Britain. (Documentary). 60 min. Sound. 16mm Color. *Rental:* Films Inc, Syracuse U Film, U Cal Media & U of IL Film. *Sale:* Films Inc. *Sale:* Films Inc, Videotape version.

Manoeuvre. Directed by Frederick Wiseman. 1979. Zipporah. (Documentary). 115 min. Sound. 16mm B&W. *Rental:* Zipporah Films. *Lease:* Zipporah Films, Videotape version.

Manos a la Obra: The Story of Operation Bootstrap. Directed by Pedro A. Rivera & Susan Zeid. Puerto Rico. (Documentary). 59 min. Sound. 16mm Color. narrated Eng. *Rental:* Cinema Guild. *Sale:* Cinema Guild. *Sale:* Cinema Guild, Videotape version.

Manos: The Hands of Fate. Tom Neyman & John Reynolds. Directed by Hal Warren. 1966. Emerson. 92 min. Sound. 16mm Color. *Rental:* Films Inc.

Manpower. Edward G. Robinson, Marlene Dietrich & George Raft. Directed by Raoul Walsh. 1941. Warners. 103 min. Sound. 16mm B&W. *Rental:* MGM United.

Man's Ability to Search & Reason. 1969. Great Plains. (Documentary). 60 min. Sound. 16mm B&W. *Rental:* Great Plains. *Sale:* Great Plains.

Man's Best Friend. Lightning the Wonder Dog. 1935. Krellberg. 60 min. Sound. 16mm B&W. *Rental:* Mogulls Films.

Man's Castle, A. Spencer Tracy & Loretta Young. Directed by Frank Borzage. 1933. Columbia. 75 min. Sound. 16mm B&W. *Rental:* Bosco Films, Budget Films, Cine Craft, Kit Parker, Swank Motion & Welling Motion Pictures.

Man's Country. Jack Randall. Directed by Robert Tansey. 1938. Monogram. 55 min. Sound. 16mm B&W. *Rental:* Hurlock Cine.

Man's Land, A. Tex Ritter. Directed by Phil Rosen. 1932. Allied. 60 min. Sound. 16mm B&W. *Rental:* Video Comm. *Rental:* Video Comm, Videotape version.

Man's Thumb on Nature's Balance. 1970. NBC. (Documentary). 51 min. Sound. 16mm Color. *Rental:* Films Inc. *Sale:* Films Inc.

Manslaughter. Leatrice Joy & Thomas Meighan. Directed by Cecil B. DeMille. 1922. Paramount. 100 min. Silent. 16mm B&W. *Rental:* Films Inc.

Manson. Directed by Robert Hendrickson. 1972. RBC. (Documentary). 83 min. Sound. 16mm Color. *Rental:* Films Inc.

Mantegna. 1970. NET. (Documentary). 59 min. Sound. 16mm B&W. *Rental:* Indiana AV Ctr. *Sale:* Indiana AV Ctr.

Manthan. Directed by Shyam Benegal. 1976. India. (Cast unlisted). 130 min. Sound. 16mm Color. subtitles. *Rental:* Liberty Co.

Mantis in Lace. Zooey Hall. 79 min. Sound. 16mm Color. *Rental:* BF Video.

Mantrap, The. Henry Stephenson & Lloyd Corrigan. Directed by George Sherman. 1943. Republic. 58 min. Sound. 16mm B&W. *Rental:* Ivy Films.

Mantrap, The. Jeffrey Hunter, David Janssen & Stella Stevens. Directed by Edmond O'Brien. 1961. Paramount. 93 min. Sound. 16mm B&W. *Rental:* Films Inc.

Manwatcher, The. 1980. Britain. (Documentary). 50 min. Videotape Color. *Rental:* Films Inc & Syracuse U Film. *Sale:* Films Inc.

Manxman, The. Carl Brisson & Anny Ondra. Directed by Alfred Hitchcock. 1929. Britain. 85 min. Sound. Super 8 B&W. *Rental:* Budget Films, Films Inc, Janus Films & Kit Parker. *Sale:* Reel Images. *Rental:* Films Inc, 90 mins. version.

Many Adventures of Winnie the Pooh, The. Directed by Wolfgang Reitherman. 1977. Disney. (Animated). 89 min. Sound. 16mm Color. *Rental:* Bosco Films, Disney Prod, Elliot Film Co, Films Inc, MGM United, Modern Sound, Roas Films, Swank Motion, Twyman Films, Welling Motion Pictures & Williams Films, videotape version.

Many Different Gifts. 1974. Mass Media. (Documentary). 50 min. Sound. 16mm Color. *Rental:* Museum Mod Art.

Many Faces of Argonne, The. 1963. Atomic Energy Commission. (Documentary). 60 min. Sound. 16mm Color. *Rental:* Natl AV Ctr. *Sale:* Natl AV Ctr.

Many Happy Returns. George Burns & Gracie Allen. Directed by Norman Z. McLeod. 1934. Paramount. 66 min. Sound. 16mm B&W. *Rental:* Swank Motion.

Many Rivers to Cross. Robert Taylor & Eleanor Parker. Directed by Roy Rowland. 1955. MGM. 92 min. Sound. 16mm Color. *Rental:* MGM United. *Rental:* MGM United, Anamorphic version.

Mao: Long March to Power. 1976. 60 min. Sound. Videotape Color. *Rental:* Iowa Films.

Mao's China. Directed by Dejan Kosanovic. 1972. Yugoslavia. (Documentary). 77 min. Sound. 16mm Color. narrated Eng. *Rental:* Film Ctr DC, Films Inc, Macmillan Films & Syracuse U Film.

Mara Maru. Errol Flynn & Raymond Burr. Directed by Gordon Douglas. 1952. Warners. 98 min. Sound. 16mm B&W. *Rental:* Swank Motion.

Mara of the Wilderness. Adam West & Linda Saunders. Directed by Frank McDonald. 1965. Allied Artists. 90 min. Sound. 16mm Color. *Rental:* Hurlock Cine.

Maracaibo. Cornel Wilde & Jean Wallace. Directed by Cornel Wilde. 1958. Paramount. 88 min. Sound. 16mm Color. *Rental:* Films Inc.

Maragoli. Directed by Sandra Nichols. 1977. Kenya. (Documentary). 58 min. Sound. 16mm Color. *Rental:* U Cal Media. *Sale:* U Cal Media. *Rental:* U Cal Media, *Sale:* U Cal Media, Videotape version.

Marat-Sade. Orig. Title: Persecution & Assassination of Jean-Paul Marat as Performed by the Inmates of the Asylum of Charenton Under the Direction of the Marquis de Sade, The. Patrick Magee & Glenda Jackson. Directed by Peter Brook. 1967. Britain. 115 min. Sound. 16mm Color. *Rental:* MGM United.

Marathon Man. Dustin Hoffman, Sir Laurence Olivier & Roy Scheider. Directed by John Schlesinger. 1976. Paramount. 125 min. Sound. Color. *Rental:* Films Inc. *Sale:* Cinema Concepts, Viedotape version.

Marathon: The Story of the Young Drug Users. 1969. ABC. (Documentary). 51 min. Sound. 16mm B&W. *Rental:* Films Inc. *Sale:* Films Inc.

Marauders, The. William Boyd. Directed by George Archainbaud. 1947. United Artists. 64 min. Sound. 16mm B&W. *Sale:* Cinema Concepts.

Marauders, The. Dan Duryea & Jeff Richards. Directed by Gerald Mayer. 1955. MGM. 81 min. Sound. 16mm Color. *Rental:* MGM United.

Marcados, Los. Antonio Aguila. Directed by Alberta Mariscal. Mexico. 90 min. Sound. 16mm Color. subtitles. *Rental:* Westcoast Films.

Marcelino: Pan y Vino. Orig. Title: Miracle of Marcelino. Pablito Calvo. Directed by Ladislao Vajda. 1955. Spain. Videotape B&W. dubbed. *Sale:* Cinema Concepts & Tamarelles French Film.

March of the Wooden Soldiers, The. Orig. Title: Babes in Toyland. Stan Laurel & Oliver Hardy. Directed by Gus Meins. 1934. Hal Roach. 76 min. Sound. 16mm B&W. *Rental:* Films Inc & Welling Motion Pictures. *Rental:* Welling Motion Pictures & Westcoast Films, 85 mins. version.

March Or Die. Gene Hackman, Terence Hill, Catherine Deneuve & Max Von Sydow. Directed by Dick Richards. 1977. Columbia. 106 min. Sound. 16mm Color. *Rental:* Arcus Film, Budget Films, Films Inc, Modern Sound, Swank Motion, Welling Motion Pictures, Westcoast Films & Williams Films.

Marching Along *see* Stars & Stripes Forever.

Marco. Desi Arnaz Jr., Jack Weston & Zero Mostel. Directed by Seymour Robbie. 1974. Cinerama. 109 min. Sound. 16mm Color. *Rental:* Swank Motion.

Marco. Directed by Gerald Tamaner & Gordon Quinn. 1971. Images Film. (Documentary). 83 min. Sound. 16mm B&W. *Rental:* Images Film. *Sale:* Images Film.

Marco Polo. Rory Calhoun & Yoko Tani. Directed by Hugo Fregonese. 1962. American International. 98 min. Sound. 16mm Color. dubbed. *Rental:* Buchan Pic, Budget Films, Cine Craft, Charard Motion Pics, Westcoast Films, Welling Motion Pictures & Willoughby Peer. *Rental:* Willoughby Peer, Anamorphic color version.

Marco Polo. 1970. Australia. (Animated). 55 min. Sound. 16mm Color. *Rental:* Budget Films, Inst Cinema, Modern Sound, Roas Films, Twyman Films & Wholesome Film Ctr.

Marco Polo Jr. Directed by Eric Porter. 1974. Solo Cup. (Animated). 85 min. Sound. 16mm Color. *Rental:* Arcus Film & Kerr Film.

Marco the Magnificent. Horst Buchholz & Anthony Quinn. Directed by Denys De la Patelliere. 1966. Yugoslavia. 100 min. Sound. 16mm Color. dubbed. *Rental:* Cine Craft, Films Inc, Video Comm, Westcoast Films & Willoughby Peer.

Mardi Gras. Pat Boone & Tommy Sands. Directed by Edmund Goulding. 1958. Fox. (Anamorphic). 107 min. Sound. 16mm Color. *Rental:* Films Inc.

Mare's Tail, The. Directed by David Larcher. 1969. Britain. (Cast unlisted). 150 min. Sound. 16mm Color. *Rental:* Canyon Cinema.

Margaret Laurence: The First Lady of Manawaka. Directed by Robert Duncan. 1978. Canada. (Documentary). 53 min. Sound. 16mm Color. *Rental:* Natl Film CN. *Sale:* Natl Film CN.

Margaret Mead: Taking Notes. 1981. PBS. (Documentary). 60 min. Sound. Videotape Color. *Rental:* Natl AV Ctr, Iowa Films & PBS Video.

Margaret Mead's New Guinea Journal. 1968. NET. (Documentary). 90 min. Sound. 16mm B&W. *Rental:* U Mich Media. *Rental:* BYU Media, U Cal Media & Indiana AV Ctr, Color version.

Margie. Jeanne Crain & Glenn Langan. Directed by Henry King. 1946. Fox. 94 min. Sound. 16mm Color. *Rental:* Films Inc, Twyman Films & Willoughby Peer.

Margin, The. Mario Benvenuti & Valeria Vidal. Directed by Ouzualdo R. Daneias. Port. 1969. Brazil. 66 min. Sound. 16mm B&W. subtitles. *Rental:* Films Inc.

Margin for Error. Joan Bennett & Milton Berle. Directed by Otto Preminger. 1943. Fox. 74 min. Sound. 16mm B&W. *Rental:* Films Inc.

Margins of the Land. 55 min. Color. *Rental:* Educ Media CA.

Margo. Levana Finkelstein. Directed by Menahem Golan. Hebrew. 1971. Israel. 96 min. Sound. 16mm B&W. subtitles. *Rental:* Films Inc.

Margot Fonteyn. 1975. Britain. (Documentary). 53 min. Sound. 16mm Color. *Rental:* U of IL Film.

Maria Marten *see* Murder in the Red Barn.

Maria Walewska *see* Conquest.

Marianne. Marion Davies & Oscar Shaw. Directed by Robert Z. Leonard. 1929. MGM. 112 min. Sound. 16mm B&W. *Rental:* MGM United.

Marianne & Juliane. Jutta Lampe, Barbara Sukowa & Rudiger Vogler. Directed by Margarethe Von Trotta. Ger. 1981. Germany. 105 min. Sound. 16mm Color. subtitles. *Rental:* New Yorker Films.

Marie Antoinette. Norma Shearer & Tyrone Power. Directed by W. S. Van Dyke. 1938. MGM. 160 min. Sound. 16mm B&W. *Rental:* MGM United.

Marie-Louise. Josiane. Directed by Leopold Lindtberg. Fr. 1945. France. 90 min. Sound. 16mm B&W. subtitles. *Rental:* Mogulls Films.

Marihuana, L. S. D. & the Mind: A Dilemma for Medicine & Society. 1968. US Government. (Documentary). 90 min. Sound. 16mm B&W. *Sale:* Natl AV Ctr.

Marihuana: Weed with Roots in Hell. Orig. Title: Devil's Weed, The. Harley Wood. Directed by Dwain Esper. 1936. Esper. 62 min. Sound. 16mm B&W. *Rental:* Budget Films, Ivy Films, Kit Parker, Maljack, Video Comm & Westcoast Films. *Sale:* Glenn Photo, Natl Cinema & Video Comm. *Rental:* Maljack & Video Comm, Videotape version.

Marijuana. 1968. CBS. (Documentary). 52 min. Sound. 16mm B&W. *Rental:* U Mich Media & Twyman Films. *Sale:* Carousel Films.

Mariken. Ronnie Montagne. Directed by Jos Stelling. Dutch. 1975. Holland. 90 min. Sound. 16mm Color. subtitles. *Rental:* J Green Pics.

Marilyn. 1963. Fox. (Anamorphic) (Documentary). 83 min. Sound. 16mm Color. *Rental:* Films Inc.

Marine Raiders. Pat O'Brien & Robert Ryan. Directed by Harold Schuster. 1943. RKO. 90 min. Sound. 16mm B&W. *Rental:* Films Inc.

Marineros Sin Brujala. Robert Morse & Phil Silvers. Directed by Norman Tokar. 1970. Disney. 100 min. Sound. 16mm Color. dubbed Span. *Rental:* Twyman Films.

Mariners of the Sky. William Gargan. 1936. Republic. 68 min. Sound. 16mm B&W. *Rental:* Ivy Films.

Marines Fly High, The. Lucille Ball & Richard Dix. Directed by George Nicholls. 1944. RKO. 68 min. Sound. 16mm *Rental:* RKO General Pics.

Marines Have Landed, The *see* Leathernecks Have Landed.

Marines, Let's Go. Tom Tryon & David Hedison. Directed by Raoul Walsh. 1961. Fox. (Anamorphic). 104 min. Sound. 16mm B&W. *Rental:* Willoughby Peer.

Marius. Orig. Title: Pagnol Trilogy. Raimu & Pierre Fresnay. Directed by Alexander Korda. Fr. 1931. France. 125 min. Sound. 16mm B&W. subtitles. *Rental:* Budget Films, Corinth Films & Kit Parker. *Sale:* Cinema Concepts, Natl Cinema & Reel Images. *Sale:* Tamarelles French Film, Videotape version.

Marjoe. Marjoe Gortner. Directed by Howard Smith & Sarah Kernochan. 1972. Cinema V. 88 min. Sound. 16mm Color. *Rental:* Cinema Five. *Lease:* Cinema Five.

Marjorie Morningstar. Natalie Wood & Gene Kelly. Directed by Irving Rapper. 1958. Warners. 123 min. Sound. 16mm Color. *Rental:* Corinth Films. *Lease:* Corinth Films.

Mark, The. Stuart Whitman, Rod Steiger & Maria Schell. Directed by Guy Green. 1961. Britain. (Anamorphic). 127 min. Sound. 16mm B&W. *Rental:* Budget Films & Kino Intl. *Sale:* Kino Intl. *Lease:* Kino Intl.

Mark of the Apache *see* Tomahawk Trail.

Mark of the Claw *see* Dick Tracy's Dilemma.

Mark of the Devil, The: Part II. Anton Diffring. Directed by Adrian Hoven. 1974. American International. 90 min. Sound. 16mm Color. *Rental:* Swank Motion.

Mark of the Gorilla, The. Johnny Weissmuller. Directed by William Berke. 1950. Columbia. 70 min. Sound. 16mm B&W. *Rental:* Bosco Films, Inst Cinema & Roas Films.

Mark of the Hawk, The. Sidney Poitier & Eartha Kitt. Directed by Michael Audley. 1958. Universal. 85 min. Sound. 16mm Color. *Rental:* Swank Motion.

Mark of the Vampire, The. Lionel Barrymore & Bela Lugosi. Directed by Tod Browning. 1935. MGM. 61 min. Sound. 16mm B&W. *Rental:* MGM United.

Mark of the Whistler, The. Richard Dix & Janis Carter. Directed by William Castle. 1944. 61 min. Sound. 16mm B&W. *Rental:* Budget Films.

Mark of Zorro, The. Douglas Fairbanks & Marguerite De La Motte. Directed by Fred Niblo. 1920. United Artists. (Musical score only). 90 min. Silent. 16mm *Rental:* A Twyman Pres, Wholesome Film Ctr, Willoughby Peer, Budget Films, Classic Film Mus, Em Gee Film, Ivy Films, Kit Parker, Museum Mod Art, Modern Sound, Swank Motion, Video Comm & Westcoast Films. *Sale:* Blackhawk Films, Festival Films, Reel Images, Cinema Concepts, E Finney & Glenn Photo. *Rental:* Killiam Collect & New Cinema, *Sale:* Blackhawk Films, Cinema Concepts, E Finney & Glenn Photo, Tinted sound version. *Sale:* Blackhawk Films & Reel Images, Super 8 sound version. *Rental:* Ivy Films, *Sale:* Blackhawk Films & Glenn Photo, 136 min. version. *Rental:* Video Comm & Kit Parker, *Sale:* Blackhawk Films, 77 mins version. *Sale:* Festival Films, Videotape version.

Mark of Zorro, The. Tyrone Power & Linda Darnell. Directed by Rouben Mamoulian. 1940. Fox. 92 min. Sound. 16mm B&W. *Rental:* Films Inc.

Mark Twain: Beneath the Laughter. Dan O'Herlihy. Directed by Marsha Jeffer & Larry Yust. 1979. Pyramid. 58 min. Sound. 16mm Color. *Rental:* Pyramid Film. *Sale:* Pyramid Film. *Sale:* Pyramid Film, *Rental:* Pyramid Film, Videotape version.

Mark Twain's America. 1960. NBC. (Documentary). 54 min. Sound. 16mm B&W. *Rental:* U Cal Media, La Inst Res Ctr, McGraw-Hill Films, Syracuse U Film & Utah Media. *Sale:* McGraw-Hill Films. *Rental:* Utah Media, Color version.

Marked for Failure. 1965. NET. (Documentary). 60 min. Sound. 16mm B&W. *Rental:* BYU Media, U of IL Film, U Mich Media & Indiana AV Ctr. *Sale:* Indiana AV Ctr.

Marked for Murder. Tex Ritter. Directed by Elmer Clifton. 1945. PRC. 56 min. Sound. 16mm B&W. *Rental:* Ivy Films. *Sale:* Classics Assoc NY & Rep Pic Film.

Marked Trails. Hoot Gibson & Pat Steele. Directed by J. P. McCarthy. 1944. Monogram. 59 min. Sound. 16mm B&W. *Rental:* Hurlock Cine.

Marked Woman. Bette Davis & Humphrey Bogart. Directed by Lloyd Bacon. 1937. Warners. 95 min. Sound. 16mm B&W. *Rental:* MGM United.

Marksman, The. Wayne Morris & Elena Verdugo. Directed by Lewis D. Collins. 1953. Allied Artists. 60 min. Sound. 16mm B&W. *Rental:* Hurlock Cine.

Marlowe. James Garner & Gayle Hunnicutt. Directed by Paul Bogart. 1969. MGM. 97 min. Sound. 16mm Color. *Rental:* MGM United.

Marnie. Tippi Hedren & Sean Connery. Directed by Alfred Hitchcock. 1964. Universal. 110 min. Sound. 16mm Color. *Rental:* Films Inc & Swank Motion.

Maroc Seven. Cyd Charisse & Gene Barry. Directed by Gerry O'Hara. 1967. Paramount. (Anamorphic). 92 min. Sound. 16mm Color. *Rental:* Films Inc.

Marooned. Gregory Peck, Richard Crenna, David Janssen & Gene Hackman. Directed by John Sturges. 1969. Columbia. 134 min. Sound. 16mm Color. *Rental:* Arcus Film, Buchan Pic, Budget Films, Cine Craft, Charard Motion Pics, Film Ctr DC, Films Inc, Inst Cinema, Ivy Films, Modern Sound, Natl Film Video, Newman Film Lib, Roas Films, Swank Motion, Twyman Films, Video Comm, Welling Motion Pictures, Westcoast Films, Wholesome Film Ctr, Williams Films & Willoughby Peer.

Marquise of O, The. Edith Clever & Bruno Ganz. Directed by Eric Rohmer. Fr. 1976. France. 102 min. Sound. 16mm Color. subtitles. *Rental:* New Line Cinema.

Marriage Circle, The. Florence Vidor, Monte Blue & Adolphe Menjou. Directed by Ernst Lubitsch. 1924. Warners. 118 min. Silent. 16mm B&W. *Rental:* Budget Films, Films Inc, Kit Parker, Museum Mod Art. *Sale:* Em Gee Film Lib, Glenn Photo & Reel Images. *Sale:* Glenn Photo & Reel Images, Super 8 silent version. *Sale:* Festival Films, 85 min. 16mm version.

Marriage Game, The. Glenda Jackson. 1976. Britain. 90 min. Sound. 16mm Color. *Rental:* Films Inc. *Sale:* Films Inc. *Rental:* Films Inc, *Sale:* Films Inc, Videotape version.

Marriage-Go-Round, The. Susan Haywood & James Mason. Directed by Walter Lang. 1960. Fox. 98 min. Sound. 16mm Color. *Rental:* Charard Motion Pics & Inst Cinema. *Rental:* Select Film & Willoughby Peer, Anamorphic version.

Marriage-Italian Style. Sophia Loren & Marcello Mastroianni. Directed by Vittorio De Sica. Ital. 1964. Italy. 102 min. Sound. 16mm Color. subtitles. *Rental:* Films Inc. *Rental:* Films Inc, English language version.

Marriage of a Young Stockbroker, The. Richard Benjamin & Joanna Shimkus. Directed by Lawrence Turman. 1971. Fox. 95 min. Sound. 16mm Color. *Rental:* Films Inc. *Sale:* Blackhawk Films, Golden Tapes, Magnetic Video & Video Lib, Videotape version.

Marriage of Figaro, The. George Descrieres. Directed by Jean Meyer. Fr. 1958. France. 105 min. Sound. 16mm Color. subtitles. *Rental:* Budget Films & Films Inc.

Marriage of Maria Braun, The. Hanna Schygulla & Ivan Desny. Directed by Rainer Werner Fassbinder. Ger. 1978. Germany. 120 min. Sound. 16mm Color. subtitles. *Rental:* New Yorker Films.

Married? Constance Bennett & Owen Moore. Directed by George Terwilliger. 1925. Janus. 65 min. Silent. 8mm B&W. *Rental:* Em Gee Film Lib. *Sale:* Glenn Photo. *Sale:* Glenn Photo, Super 8 silent version. *Sale:* Glenn Photo, Silent 16mm Part Tinted version.

Married & In Love. Patric Knowles & Alan Marshall. Directed by John Farrow. 1940. RKO. 59 min. Sound. 16mm *Rental:* RKO General Pics.

Married Before Breakfast. Robert Young & Florence Rice. Directed by Edwin L. Marin. 1937. MGM. 71 min. Sound. 16mm B&W. *Rental:* MGM United.

Married Couple, A. Billy Edwards & Antoinette Edwards. Directed by Allan King. 1970. Janus. Sound. 16mm Color. *Rental:* Films Inc.

Married Life. 1971. Family of Man. (Documentary). 50 min. Sound. 16mm Color. *Rental:* Films Inc. *Sale:* Films Inc. *Rental:* Films Inc, *Sale:* Films Inc, Videotape version.

Married Too Young. Harold Lloyd Jr. & Jana Lund. Directed by George Moscov. 1961. 75 min. Sound. 16mm B&W. *Rental:* Budget Films.

Married Woman, A. Macha Meril. Directed by Jean-Luc Godard. Fr. 1965. France. 94 min. Sound. 16mm Color. subtitles. *Rental:* Corinth Films, Kit Parker, Swank Motion & Twyman Films. *Sale:* Festival Films & Reel Images. *Sale:* Festival Films & Tamarelles French Film, Videotape version.

Marry Me! Marry Me! Trans. Title: Mazel Tov. Claude Berri & Elizabeth Wiener. Directed by Claude Berri. Fr. 1969. France. 87 min. Sound. 16mm Color. subtitles. *Rental:* Hurlock Cine.

Marry the Girl. Frank McHugh & Mary Boland. Directed by William McGann. 1937. Warners. 68 min. Sound. 16mm B&W. *Rental:* MGM United.

Marrying Kind, The. Judy Holliday & Aldo Ray. Directed by George Cukor. 1952. Columbia. 93 min. Sound. 16mm B&W. *Rental:* Budget Films, Films Inc, Inst Cinema, Kit Parker & Welling Motion Pictures.

Mars Attacks the World. Orig. Title: Deadly Ray from Mars. Buster Crabbe. Directed by Frederick Stephani. 1938. Universal. 70 min. Sound. 16mm B&W. *Rental:* Em Gee Film Lib, Ivy Films, Video Comm, Westcoast Films & Wholesome Film Ctr. *Sale:* Cinema Concepts & Reel Images. *Rental:* Ivy Films, *Sale:* Ivy Films & Reel Images, Super 8 sound version. *Rental:* Cinema Concepts, Golden Tapes, Video Lib & Video Tape Network, Videotape version.

Marseillaise, La. Pierre Renoir & Louis Jouvet. Directed by Jean Renoir. Fr. 1937. France. 131 min. Sound. 16mm B&W. subtitles. *Rental:* Budget Films, Corinth Films, Images Film & Kit Parker. *Sale:* Images Film. *Lease:* Corinth Films. *Sale:* Images Film, Videotape version.

Marshal of Amarillo, The. Allan Lane. Directed by Philip Ford. 1948. Republic. 60 min. Sound. 16mm B&W. *Rental:* Ivy Films. *Sale:* Rep Pic Film.

Marshal of Cedar Rock, The. Allan Lane. Directed by Harry Keller. 1952. Republic. 54 min. Sound. 16mm B&W. *Rental:* Ivy Films. *Sale:* Rep Pic Film.

Marshal of Cripple Creek, The. Allan Lane. Directed by R. G. Springsteen. 1947. Republic. 54 min. Sound. 16mm B&W. *Rental:* Ivy Films.

Marshal of Laredo, The. Bill Elliott. Directed by R. G. Springsteen. 1945. Republic. 54 min. Sound. 16mm B&W. *Rental:* Ivy Films.

Marshal of Mesa City, The. George O'Brien. Directed by David Howard. 1940. RKO. 60 min. Sound. 16mm B&W. *Sale:* Natl Cinema.

Marshal of Reno, The. Bill Elliott. Directed by Wallace Grissell. 1944. Republic. 54 min. Sound. 16mm B&W. *Rental:* Ivy Films.

Marshal, Texas. 90 min. Sound. Videotape *Rental:* PBS Video. *Sale:* PBS Video.

Marshmallow Moon *see* **Aaron Slick from Punkin'Creek.**

Marta. Marisa Mell & Stephen Boyd. Directed by Jose Antonio Nieves Conde. 1971. Atlantida. 90 min. Sound. 16mm Color. *Rental:* Video Comm.

Martha Clarke Light & Dark. Directed by Joyce Chopra & Martha Clarke. 1981. Phoenix. (Dance). 54 min. Sound. 16mm Color. *Rental:* Budget Films & Phoenix Films. *Sale:* Phoenix Films. *Sale:* Phoenix Films, Videotape version.

Martha Graham Dance Company, The. Directed by Merrill Brockway. 1977. WNET. (Ballet). 90 min. Sound. 16mm Color. *Rental:* Indiana AV Ctr, U Cal Media & U of IL Film. *Sale:* Indiana AV Ctr.

Martien De Noel *see* Christmas Martian.

Martin. John Amplas. Directed by George A. Romero. 1977. Laurel. 95 min. Sound. 16mm Color. *Rental:* Cinema Five.

Martin Luther. Niall McGinnis. Directed by Irving Pichel. 1953. DeRochemont. 103 min. Sound. 16mm B&W. *Rental:* Budget Films, BYU Media, Films Inc, G Herne, Lutheran Film, Modern Sound, Roas Films & Willoughby Peer. *Sale:* Lutheran Film.

Martin Luther: His Life & Times. 1924. Lutheran. (Musical score only, Cast unlisted). 101 min. Videotape B&W. *Sale:* Reel Images.

Martin Luther King: The Man & the March. 1967. NET. (Documentary). 83 min. Sound. 16mm B&W. *Rental:* U Cal Media & Indiana AV Ctr. *Sale:* Indiana AV Ctr.

Martin Mull. 1980. Verve. (Performance). 56 min. Videotape Color. *Rental:* Films Inc.

Martin the Soldier. Robert Hirsch & Marlene Jobert. Directed by Michel Deville. Fr. 1966. France. 90 min. Sound. 16mm Color. subtitles. *Rental:* Films Inc.

Marty. Ernest Borgnine & Betsy Blair. Directed by Delbert Mann. 1955. United Artists. 91 min. Sound. 16mm B&W. *Rental:* MGM United.

Martyr, The. Francis Ford. 1924. United. 50 min. Silent. 8mm B&W. *Sale:* Film Classics.

Martyr, The. Leo Genn. Directed by Aleksander Ford. 1976. Germany-Israel. 90 min. Sound. 16mm Color. dubbed. *Rental:* J Green Pics.

Martyrs of Love. Directed by Jan Nemec. Czech. 1967. Czechoslovakia. (Anthology). 73 min. Sound. 16mm B&W. subtitles. *Rental:* New Cinema & New Line Cinema.

Martyrs of the Alamo, The. Sam DeGrasse & Walter Long. Directed by Christy Cabanne. 1915. Triangle/Fine Arts. 74 min. Silent. 16mm B&W. *Rental:* Museum Mod Art. *Lease:* Museum Mod Art.

Marvelous Visit, The. Trans. Title: Merveilleuse Visite, La. Gilles Kohler. Directed by Marcel Carne. Fr. 1975. France-Italy. 102 min. Sound. 16mm Color. subtitles. *Rental:* Twyman Films. *Rental:* Twyman Films, Videotape version.

Mary Burns, Fugitive. Sylvia Sidney & Melvyn Douglas. Directed by William K. Howard. 1935. Paramount. 84 min. Sound. 16mm B&W. *Rental:* Swank Motion.

Mary Jane Grows Up: Marijuana in the Seventies. 1975. NBC. (Documentary). 52 min. Sound. 16mm Color. *Rental:* Films Inc & Syracuse U Film. *Sale:* Films Inc. *Rental:* Films Inc, *Sale:* Films Inc, Videotape version.

Mary Jane's Pa. Orig. Title: Wanderlust. Guy Kibbee & Tom Brown. Directed by William Keighley. 1935. Warners. 71 min. Sound. 16mm B&W. *Rental:* MGM United.

Mary Kingsley. 1977. Britain. (Cast unlisted). 49 min. Sound. 16mm Color. *Rental:* Kent St U Film & U of IL Film, Videotape version.

Mary of Scotland. Katharine Hepburn & Fredric March. Directed by John Ford. 1936. RKO. 121 min. Sound. 16mm B&W. *Rental:* Films Inc.

Mary Poppins. Julie Andrews & Dick Van Dyke. Directed by Robert Stevenson. 1964. Disney. 140 min. Sound. 16mm Color. *Rental:* Disney Prod, Roas Films, Swank Motion, Film Ctr DC & Twyman Films.

Mary, Queen of Scots. Vanessa Redgrave & Glenda Jackson. Directed by Charles Jarrott. 1971. Universal. 128 min. Sound. 16mm Color. *Rental:* Swank Motion. *Rental:* Swank Motion, Anamorphic version.

Mary S. McDowell. Rosemary Harris. Directed by Jose Quintero. (Profiles in Courage Ser.). 1965. Saudek. 50 min. Sound. 16mm B&W. *Rental:* IQ Film, Syracuse U Film & U Mich Media. *Sale:* IQ Film. *Sale:* IQ Film, Spanish Dubbed version.

Mary Stevens, M. D. Kay Francis & Lyle Talbot. Directed by Lloyd Bacon. 1933. Warners. 72 min. Sound. 16mm B&W. *Rental:* MGM United.

Mary Tudor. Ellen Richter. 1923. World. 60 min. Silent. 8mm B&W. *Sale:* Film Classics.

Maryjane. Fabian Forte & Diane McBain. Directed by Maury Dexter. 1968. American International. 94 min. Sound. 16mm Color. *Rental:* Budget Films.

Maryland. John Payne & Walter Brennan. Directed by Henry King. 1940. Fox. 91 min. Sound. 16mm Color. *Rental:* Films Inc.

Masai Manhood. Directed by Chris Curling. 1978. Britain. (Documentary). 53 min. Sound. 16mm Color. *Rental:* Human Issues. *Sale:* Human Issues.

Masai Women. Directed by Chris Curling. 1978. Britain. (Documentary). 52 min. Sound. 16mm Color. *Rental:* Human Issues. *Sale:* Human Issues.

Masculine-Feminine. Orig. Title: Children of Marx & Coca-Cola. Jean-Pierre Leaud & Chantal Goya. Directed by Jean-Luc Godard. Fr. 1966. France. 103 min. Sound. 16mm B&W. subtitles. *Rental:* Corinth Films, Natl Cinema & Swank Motion. *Sale:* Festival Films & Reel Images. *Rental:* Festival Films, Videotape version.

MASH. Elliott Gould & Donald Sutherland. Directed by Robert Altman. 1970. Fox. (Anamorphic). 116 min. Sound. 16mm Color. *Rental:* Films Inc. *Sale:* Blackhawk Films, Cinema Concepts, Golden Tapes, Magnetic Video & Video Lib, Videotape version.

Mashenka. Valentina Karayeva. Directed by Yuli Raizman. Rus. 1942. Russia. 67 min. Sound. 16mm B&W. subtitles. *Rental:* Corinth Films.

Mask, The *see* Eyes of Hell.

Mask of Dijon, The. Erich Von Stroheim. Directed by Lew Landers. 1946. PRC. 73 min. Sound. 16mm B&W. *Sale:* Classics Assoc NY.

Mask of Dimitrios, The. Zachary Scott & Faye Emerson. Directed by Jean Negulesco. 1944. Warners. 95 min. Sound. 16mm B&W. *Rental:* MGM United.

Mask of Fu Manchu, The. Boris Karloff & Myrna Loy. Directed by Charles Brabin. 1932. MGM. 70 min. Sound. 16mm B&W. *Rental:* MGM United.

Mask of the Avenger, The. John Derek & Anthony Quinn. Directed by Phil Karlson. 1952. Columbia. 83 min. Sound. 16mm Color. *Rental:* Budget Films.

Mask of the Musketeers, The. Gordon Scott & Jose Greco. 1960. Italy. 101 min. Sound. 16mm B&W. dubbed. *Rental:* Westcoast Films.

Masked Avengers, The. Chiang Sheng & Cho Ku. Hong Kong. 92 min. 16mm *Rental:* WW Enter. *Rental:* WW Enter, Videotape version.

Masked Dance, The. Directed by Adrian Cowell. 1976. Britain. (Documentary). 52 min. Sound. 16mm Color. *Rental:* Human Issues. *Sale:* Human Issues.

Masked Raiders, The. Tim Holt. Directed by Lesley Selander. 1949. RKO. 60 min. Sound. 16mm B&W. *Rental:* Films Inc.

Maslow & Self-Actualization. 1968. Psychological. (Lecture). 60 min. Sound. 16mm Color. *Rental:* U Mich Media.

Masque of the Red Death, The. Vincent Price & Hazel Court. Directed by Roger Corman. 1964. American International. 89 min. Sound. 16mm Color. *Rental:* Arcus Film, Cine Craft, Films Inc, Images Film, Inst Cinema, Ivy Films, Twyman Films, Video Comm, Welling Motion Pictures, Westcoast Films, Wholesome Film Ctr & Willoughby Peer. *Rental:* Images Film, Anamorphic color version.

Masquerade. Clayton Moore. 1960. Wrather. 75 min. Sound. 16mm Color. *Rental:* Video Comm.

Masquerade. Cliff Robertson & Marisa Mell. Directed by Basil Dearden. 1965. United Artists. 101 min. Sound. 16mm Color. *Rental:* MGM United.

Masquerader, The. Ronald Colman & Elissa Landi. Directed by Richard Wallace. 1933. Goldwyn. 77 min. Sound. 16mm B&W. *Rental:* Films Inc.

Mass of Atoms, A. 1966. Atomic Energy Commission. (Documentary). 47 min. Sound. 16mm B&W. *Rental:* Syracuse U Film.

Massacre. Richard Barthelmess & Ann Dvorak. Directed by Alan Crosland. 1934. Warners. 70 min. Sound. 16mm B&W. *Rental:* MGM United.

Massacre at Sand Creek. John Derek. 1956. CBS. (Kinescope). 80 min. Sound. 16mm B&W. *Rental:* Bosco Films.

Massacre Canyon. Phil Carey & Audrey Totter. Directed by Fred F. Sears. 1954. Columbia. 66 min. Sound. 16mm Color. *Rental:* Inst Cinema.

Massacre in Rome. Richard Burton & Marcello Mastroianni. Directed by George Pan Cosmatos. 1973. National General. 103 min. Sound. 16mm Color. *Rental:* Swank Motion.

Massacre River. Guy Madison & Rory Calhoun. Directed by John Rawlins. 1949. Allied Artists. 75 min. Sound. 16mm B&W. *Rental:* Hurlock Cine.

Master Controlled. Ken Anderson. (Cast unlisted). 62 min. Sound. 16mm Color. *Rental:* Roas Films.

Master Killer. Liu Chia Hui & Wang Yu. Hong Kong. 116 min. Sound. 16mm *Rental:* WW Enter & Corinth Films. *Rental:* WW Enter & Corinth Films, Videotape version.

Master of Ballantrae, The. Errol Flynn & Beatrice Campbell. Directed by William Keighley. 1953. Warners. 89 min. Sound. 16mm Color. *Rental:* Films Inc, Swank Motion & Twyman Films.

Master of Disaster, The. 110 min. Sound. 16mm *Rental:* WW Enter. *Rental:* WW Enter, Videotape version.

Master of Lassie *see* Hills of Home.

Master of the House. Orig. Title: Thou Shalt Honor Thy Wife. Johanna Meyer & Astrid Holm. Directed by Carl Th. Dreyer. 1925. Denmark. 126 min. Silent. 16mm B&W. *Rental:* Budget Films, Em Gee Film Lib, Films Inc & Kit Parker. *Sale:* Glenn Photo & Reel Images. *Sale:* Reel Images, Videotape version. *Rental:* Films Inc, subtitled version. *Rental:* Films Inc, 70 min. version.

Master of the World. Vincent Price & Charles Bronson. Directed by William Witney. 1961. American International. 94 min. Sound. 16mm Color. *Rental:* Cine Craft, Charard Motion Pics, Ivy Films, Twyman Films, Video Comm, Welling Motion Pictures, Westcoast Films & Willoughby Peer.

Master Plan, The. Norman Wooland. Directed by Hugh Baker. 1957. 78 min. 16mm *Rental:* A Twyman Pres.

Master Race, The. George Coulouris & Stanley Ridges. Directed by Herbert Biberman. 1944. RKO. 96 min. Sound. 16mm B&W. *Rental:* Films Inc.

Master Spy. Stephen Murray & June Thornburn. Directed by Montgomery Tully. 1964. Britain. 71 min. Sound. 16mm B&W. *Rental:* Hurlock Cine.

Mastermind. Zero Mostel & Bradford Dillman. 1969. Goldstone. 92 min. Sound. 16mm Color. *Rental:* Films Inc, Welling Motion Pictures & Westcoast Films.

Masters of Modern Sculpture: Beyond Cubism. Directed by Ray Witlin. 1979. Blackwood. (Documentary). 58 min. Sound. 16mm Color. *Rental:* Blackwood Films. *Sale:* Blackwood Films.

Masters of Modern Sculpture: The New World. Directed by Ray Witlin. 1979. Blackwood. (Documentary). 58 min. Sound. 16mm Color. *Rental:* Blackwood Films. *Sale:* Blackwood Films.

Masters of Modern Sculpture: The Pioneers. Directed by Ray Witlin. 1979. Blackwood. (Documentary). 58 min. Sound. 16mm Color. *Rental:* Blackwood Films. *Sale:* Blackwood Films.

Masters of the Congo Jungle. Directed by Heinz Sielmann & Henry Brandt. 1959. Fox. (Documentary, anamorphic). 88 min. Sound. 16mm Color. *Rental:* Budget Films, Phoenix Films & Willoughby Peer. *Sale:* Phoenix Films. *Sale:* Phoenix Films, Videotape version.

Masterson of Kansas. George Montgomery. Directed by William Castle. 1954. Columbia. 73 min. Sound. 16mm Color. *Rental:* Film Ctr DC, Inst Cinema, Modern Sound & Roas Films.

Mastery of Space, The. 1962. NASA. (Documentary). 58 min. Sound. 16mm Color. *Rental:* OK AV Ctr & U Mich Media. *Sale:* Natl AV Ctr.

Mata Hari. Greta Garbo & Ramon Novarro. Directed by George Fitzmaurice. 1932. MGM. 90 min. Sound. 16mm B&W. *Rental:* MGM United.

Mata Hari's Daughter *see* Daughter of Mata Hari.

Matador. 1970. Britain. (Documentary). 52 min. Sound. 16mm B&W. *Rental:* Time-Life Multimedia. *Sale:* Time-Life Multimedia. *Sale:* Time-Life Multimedia, Spanish Language version, Videotape version.

Match King, The. William Warren & Lili Damita. Directed by William Keighley. 1932. Warners. 80 min. Sound. 16mm B&W. *Rental:* MGM United.

Matchless. Patrick O'Neal & Donald Pleasance. Directed by Alberto Lattuada. 1967. United Artists. 103 min. Sound. 16mm Color. *Rental:* MGM United.

Matchless. Directed by John Papadopoulos. 1974. Australia. 54 min. Sound. 16mm B&W. *Rental:* Museum Mod Art. *Lease:* Museum Mod Art.

Matchmaker, The. Shirley Booth & Anthony Perkins. Directed by Joseph Anthony. 1958. Paramount. 101 min. Sound. 16mm B&W. *Rental:* Films Inc.

Materialakitonsfilme. 1970. 47 min. Sound. 16mm Color. *Rental:* Filmmakers Coop.

Maternelle, La. Madeleine Renaud. Directed by Jean Benoit-Levy. Fr. 1933. France. 83 min. Sound. 16mm B&W. subtitles. *Rental:* Museum Mod Art.

Mathematical Induction. 1965. 62 min. Sound. 16mm Color. *Rental:* Iowa Films.

Matilda. Elliot Gould & Robert Mitchum. Directed by Daniel Mann. 1978. American International. 103 min. Sound. 16mm Color. *Rental:* Swank Motion & Welling Motion Pictures.

Matinee Idol. Buster Collier Jr. Directed by Frank Capra. 1928. Columbia. 60 min. Silent. 16mm B&W. *Rental:* Kit Parker.

Mating, Dating, & Waiting. Dr. Kevin Leman. 45 min. Sound. 16mm Color. *Rental:* Gospel Films.

Mating Game, The. Debbie Reynolds & Tony Randall. Directed by George Marshall. 1959. MGM. 97 min. Sound. 16mm Color. *Rental:* MGM United. *Rental:* MGM United, Anamorphic version.

Mating Season, The. Gene Tierney, John Lund & Thelma Ritter. Directed by Mitchell Leisen. 1951. Paramount. 101 min. Sound. 16mm B&W. *Rental:* Films Inc.

Matrimaniac, The. Douglas Fairbanks & Constance Talmadge. Directed by John Emerson. 1916. Fine Arts/Triangle. 45 min. Silent. 16mm B&W. *Rental:* Em Gee Film Lib & Images Film. *Sale:* Blackhawk Films. *Rental:* Ivy Films, *Sale:* Blackhawk Films, Super 8 silent version. *Sale:* Blackhawk Films, Silent 8mm version.

Matrimonial Bed, The. Orig. Title: Matrimonial Problem, A. Frank Fay & Lilyan Tashman. Directed by Michael Curtiz. 1930. Warners. 98 min. Sound. 16mm B&W. *Rental:* MGM United.

Matrimonial Problem, A *see* Matrimonial Bed.

Matter of Fat, A. 1971. Canada. (Documentary). 99 min. Sound. 16mm Color. *Rental:* U Cal Media.

Matter of Indifference, A. Directed by Leonardo Dacchille. 1974. Phoenix. (Documentary). 45 min. Sound. 16mm B&W. *Rental:* Budget Films, Phoenix Films & Syracuse U Film.

Matter of Innocence, A. Hayley Mills & Trevor Howard. Directed by Guy Green. 1968. Britain. 102 min. Sound. 16mm Color. *Rental:* Swank Motion.

Matter of Insurance, A. 1977. Britain. (Cast unlisted). 52 min. Sound. 16mm Color. *Rental:* U of IL Film & U Mich Media, Videotape version.

Matter of Life, A. Trans. Title: Question De la Vie. Fr. 1974. Canada. (Documentary). 66 min. Sound. 16mm B&W. subtitles. *Rental:* Natl Film CN. *Sale:* Natl Film CN.

Matter of Life & Death, A *see* Stairway to Heaven.

Matter of Resistance, A. Trans. Title: Vie de Chateau, La. Catherine Deneuve & Philippe Noiret. Directed by Jean-Paul Rappeneau. Fr. 1967. France. 92 min. Sound. 16mm B&W. subtitles. *Rental:* New Yorker Films.

Matter of Time, A. 1969. NET. (Documentary). 53 min. Sound. 16mm B&W. *Rental:* Indiana AV Ctr. *Lease:* Indiana AV Ctr.

Matter of Time, A. Liza Minnelli, Ingrid Bergman & Charles Boyer. Directed by Vincente Minnelli. 1976. American International. 97 min. Sound. 16mm Color. *Rental:* Swank Motion.

Mau Mau. 1973. Anthony/David. (Documentary). 51 min. Sound. 16mm Color. *Rental:* Films Inc & U Mich Media. *Sale:* Films Inc. *Sale:* Films Inc, Videotape version.

Maurie. Bernie Casey & Bo Svenson. Directed by Daniel Mann. 1973. National General. 110 min. Sound. 16mm Color. *Rental:* Swank Motion. *Rental:* Swank Motion, Anamorphic version.

Mauro the Gypsy. Britain. (Cast unlisted). 43 min. Sound. 16mm Color. *Rental:* Janus Films. *Sale:* Lucerne Films.

Mauvaises Frequentations, Les *see* Bad Company.

Maverick, The. Bill Elliott & Myron Healey. Directed by Thomas Carr. 1953. Monogram. 71 min. Sound. 16mm B&W. *Rental:* Hurlock Cine.

Maverick Queen, The. Barbara Stanwyck & Barry Sullivan. Directed by Joseph Kane. 1955. Republic. 90 min. Sound. 16mm Color. *Rental:* Ivy Films. *Sale:* Tamarelles French Film, Videotape version.

Max Havelaar. Peter Faber & Sacha Bulthuis. Directed by Fons Rademakers. Dutch. 1978. Holland. 165 min. Sound. 16mm Color. subtitles. *Rental:* New Line Cinema.

Max Linder: Comic Genius. (Anthology). Sound. 16mm B&W. *Rental:* Ivy Films.

Maxime. Charles Boyer & Michelle Morgan. Directed by Henri Verneuil. 1958. France. 93 min. Sound. 16mm B&W. dubbed. *Rental:* Ivy Films.

Maximka. Tola Bovykin. Directed by V. Braun. Rus. 1955. Russia. 75 min. Sound. 16mm B&W. subtitles. *Rental:* Corinth Films.

Maximum Dating. Josh McDowell. 45 min. Sound. 16mm Color. *Rental:* Gospel Films.

May Night. N. Losenko. Directed by Alexander Row. Rus. 1953. Russia. 58 min. Sound. 16mm B&W. subtitles. *Rental:* Corinth Films.

Maya. Clint Walker & Jay North. Directed by John Berry. 1966. MGM. 91 min. Sound. 16mm Color. *Rental:* MGM United.

Maya Lords of the Jungle. 1981. PBS. (Documentary). 60 min. Sound. Videotape Color. *Rental:* Iowa Films & PBS Video.

Maybe It's Love. Orig. Title: Eleven Men & a Girl. Gloria Stuart & Ross Alexander. Directed by William McGann. 1930. Warners. 65 min. Sound. 16mm B&W. *Rental:* MGM United.

Mayday! Mayday! 1983. ABC. (Cast unlisted). 50 min. Sound. 16mm Color. *Rental:* MTI Tele. *Sale:* MTI Tele.

Mayerling. Charles Boyer & Danielle Darrieux. Directed by Anatole Litvak. Fr. 1937. France. 90 min. Sound. 16mm B&W. subtitles. *Rental:* Budget Films, Em Gee Film Lib & Kit Parker. *Sale:* Reel Images, Glenn Photo & Natl Cinema. *Sale:* Glenn Photo, Super 8 sound version. *Sale:* Em Gee Film Lib & Tamarelles French Film, Videotape version.

Mayerling. Omar Sharif, Catherine Deneuve & Ava Gardner. Directed by Terence Young. 1969. MGM. (Anamorphic). 138 min. Sound. 16mm Color. *Rental:* MGM United.

Mayhem on a Sunday Afternoon. 1965. Wolper. (Documentary). 50 min. Sound. 16mm B&W. *Rental:* Films Inc. *Sale:* Films Inc. *Sale:* Films Inc, Videotape version.

Mayor of Forty-Fourth Street. George Murphy & Anne Shirley. Directed by Alfred E. Green. 1942. RKO. 86 min. Sound. 16mm *Rental:* RKO General Pics.

Mayor of Hell, The. James Cagney & Madge Evans. Directed by Archie Mayo. 1933. Warners. 90 min. Sound. 16mm B&W. *Rental:* MGM United.

Mayor's Nest, The *see* Return of Daniel Boone.

Maytime. Jeanette MacDonald & Nelson Eddy. Directed by Robert Z. Leonard. 1937. MGM. 113 min. Sound. 16mm B&W. *Rental:* MGM United.

Maze, The. Richard Carlson & Veronica Hurst. Directed by William Cameron Menzies. 1953. Allied Artists. 81 min. Sound. 16mm B&W. *Rental:* Ivy Films. *Lease:* Rep Pic Film.

Mazel Tov *see* Marry Me! Marry Me!.

McDonald of the Canadian Mounties *see* Pony Soldier.

Me & Dad's New Wife. 1976. Daniel Wilson. 47 min. Sound. Color. *Rental:* Daniel Wilson. *Rental:* Daniel Wilson, Video version.

Me & My Gal. Orig. Title: Pier Thirteen. Spencer Tracy & Joan Bennett. Directed by Raoul Walsh. 1932. Fox. 79 min. Sound. 16mm B&W. *Rental:* Films Inc.

Me & the Colonel. Danny Kaye & Curt Jurgens. Directed by Peter Glenville. 1958. Columbia. 109 min. Sound. 16mm B&W. *Rental:* Bosco Films, Buchan Pic, Budget Films, Cine Craft, Charard Motion Pics, Films Inc, Modern Sound & Welling Motion Pictures.

Meadow, The. Directed by Vittorio Taviani & Paolo Taviani. Ital. 1979. 120 min. Sound. 16mm Color. subtitles. *Rental:* New Yorker Films.

Mean Dog Blues. George Kennedy & Kay Lenz. Directed by Mel Stuart. 1978. American International. 108 min. Sound. 16mm Color. *Rental:* Swank Motion.

Mean Johnny Barrows. Fred Williamson, Roddy McDowall & Luther Adler. Directed by Fred Williamson. 1976. Atlas. 85 min. Sound. 16mm Color. *Rental:* Films Inc.

Mean Machine, The *see* Longest Yard.

Mean Streets. Harvey Keitel. Directed by Martin Scorsese. 1973. Warners. 112 min. Sound. 16mm Color. *Rental:* Swank Motion. *Rental:* Swank Motion, Videotape version.

Meanest Gal in Town, The. James Gleason & ZaSu Pitts. Directed by Merian C. Cooper. 1934. RKO. 67 min. Sound. 16mm *Rental:* RKO General Pics.

Meanest Man in the World, The. Jack Benny & Priscilla Lane. Directed by Sidney Lanfield. 1943. Fox. 57 min. Sound. 16mm B&W. *Rental:* Willoughby Peer.

Meanwhile, Back at the Ranch. Directed by Richard Patterson. 1977. Curtco. (Anthology). 105 min. Sound. 16mm Color. *Rental:* Twyman Films.

Measure for Measure. Kate Nelligan & Tom Pigott-Scott. 1979. Britain. 145 min. Sound. Videotape Color. *Rental:* Iowa Films.

Meat. Directed by Frederick Wiseman. 1976. Zipporah. (Documentary). 113 min. Sound. 16mm B&W. *Rental:* Zipporah Films.

Meatballs. Bill Murray & Kate Lynch. Directed by Ivan Reitman. 1979. Paramount. 94 min. Sound. 16mm Color. *Rental:* Films Inc.

Mechanic, The. Orig. Title: Killer of Killers. Charles Bronson & Jan-Michael Vincent. Directed by Michael Winner. 1972. United Artists. 100 min. Sound. 16mm Color. *Rental:* Budget Films, MGM United, Welling Motion Pictures & Westcoast Films.

Mechanical Paradise, The. (Shock of the New Ser.). 1979. Britain. (Documentary). 52 min. Sound. 16mm Color. *Rental:* U Cal Media, Videotape version.

Mechanics of the Brain. Trans. Title: Mekhanika Golovnovo Mozga. Directed by Vsevolod I. Pudovkin. Rus. 1926. Russia. (Documentary). 64 min. Silent. 16mm B&W. *Rental:* Corinth Films.

Medal for Benny, A. Dorothy Lamour & Arturo De Cordova. Directed by Irving Pichel. 1945. Paramount. 77 min. Sound. 16mm B&W. *Rental:* Swank Motion.

Medal for the General, A. Godfrey Tearle. Directed by Maurice Elvey. 1945. Britain. 80 min. Sound. 16mm B&W. *Rental:* Ivy Films. *Sale:* Rep Pic Film.

Medal of Honor, The. 1960. 60 min. Sound. 16mm *Rental:* Budget Films.

Medal of Honor Rag, The. Hector Elizondo. 1983. Chopra. 54 min. Sound. Videotape Color. *Rental:* Films Inc. *Sale:* Films Inc.

Medea. Maria Callas. Directed by Pier Paolo Pasolini. 1971. Italy. 110 min. Sound. 16mm Color. *Rental:* New Cinema & New Line Cinema.

Medecin Malgre Lui, Le. Jean-Pierre Darras & Rosy Varte. France. 90 min. Sound. 16mm B&W. *Rental:* French Am Cul.

Media & Message. 1977. Films Inc. (Documentary). 60 min. Videotape Color. *Rental:* Films Inc. *Sale:* Films Inc.

Media in the Classroom. 1976. Indiana University. (Lecture). 48 min. Videotape Color. *Sale:* Indiana AV Ctr.

Medical & Surgical Management of Angina Pectoris, The. 1980. 58 min. Sound. Videotape Color. *Sale:* Natl AV Ctr.

Medical Emergencies. 2 pts. 1974. US Government. (Documentary). 106 min. Sound. 16mm Color. *Sale:* Natl AV Ctr.

Medical Genetics. Directed by Gene Starbucker. 1960. National Foundation. (Documentary). 60 min. Sound. 16mm Color. *Rental:* OK AV Ctr.

Medicine & Money. 1977. ABC. (Documentary). 48 min. Sound. 16mm Color. *Rental:* McGraw-Hill Films & Syracuse U Film. *Sale:* McGraw-Hill Films. *Sale:* McGraw-Hill Films, Videotape version.

Medicine Ball Caravan. Directed by Francois Reichenbach. 1971. Warners. (Documentary). 89 min. Sound. 16mm Color. *Rental:* Swank Motion.

Medicine in America. 3 pts. 1978. Films Inc. (Documentary). 180 min. Videotape Color. *Rental:* Films Inc. *Sale:* Films Inc.

Medicine Man, The. Jack Benny & Betty Bronson. Directed by Scott Pembroke. 1930. Tiffany. 57 min. Sound. 16mm B&W. *Sale:* Budget Films, Classic Film Mus, Cinema Concepts & Natl Cinema.

Medicine Men of Africa. 1967. NET. (Documentary). 60 min. Sound. 16mm B&W. *Rental:* Indiana AV Ctr. *Lease:* Indiana AV Ctr.

Medieval Kings, The. 1980. Royal Heritage. (Documentary). 60 min. Sound. 16mm Color. *Rental:* Films Inc. *Sale:* Films Inc. *Rental:* Films Inc, *Sale:* Films Inc, Videotape version.

Medio Million Por una Mujer. Span. 1950. Mexico. (Cast unlisted). 90 min. Sound. 16mm B&W. *Rental:* Film Classics.

Mediterranean Holiday. Directed by Herman Leitner & Rudolph Nussgruber. 1964. Continental. (Documentary). 128 min. Sound. 16mm Color. *Rental:* Budget Films.

Mediterranean Prospect. 1979. 58 min. Sound. Videotape *Rental:* PBS Video. *Sale:* PBS Video.

Medium, The. Marie Powers & Anna Maria Alberghetti. Directed by Gian-Carlo Menotti. 1951. Italy. 85 min. Sound. 16mm B&W. *Rental:* A Cantor. *Sale:* A Cantor.

Medium Cool. Robert Forster. Directed by Haskell Wexler. 1969. Paramount. 110 min. Sound. 16mm Color. *Rental:* Films Inc.

Medusa Touch, The. Richard Burton, Lee Remick & Lino Ventura. Directed by Jack Gold. 1978. Warners. 110 min. Sound. 16mm Color. *Rental:* Williams Films, Modern Sound, Swank Motion & Twyman Films.

Medusa vs. the Son of Hercules, The. Orig. Title: Perseus the Invincible. Richard Harrison. 1962. Italy. 90 min. Sound. 16mm Color. dubbed. *Rental:* Modern Sound.

Meet Boston Blackie. Chester Morris & Rochelle Hudson. Directed by Robert Florey. 1941. Columbia. 61 min. Sound. 16mm B&W. *Rental:* Kit Parker.

Meet Comrade Student. 1963. ABC. (Documentary). 54 min. Sound. 16mm B&W. *Rental:* McGraw-Hill Films, U of IL Film & Utah Media. *Sale:* McGraw-Hill Films.

Meet Dr. Christian. Jean Hersholt & Bernard Vorhaus. 1939. RKO. 70 min. Sound. 16mm B&W. *Rental:* Budget Films, Ivy Films, Mogulls Films & Rep Pic Film. *Lease:* Rep Pic Film.

Meet George Washington. 1969. NBC. (Documentary). 53 min. Sound. 16mm Color. *Rental:* Films Inc & Utah Media. *Sale:* Films Inc.

Meet John Doe. Orig. Title: John Doe, Dynamite. Barbara Stanwyck & Gary Cooper. Directed by Frank Capra. 1941. Warners. 134 min. Sound. 16mm B&W. *Rental:* Alba House, Buchan Pic, Budget Films, Classic Film Mus, Em Gee Film Lib, Film Classics, Film Ctr DC, Films Inc, Inst Cinema, Images Film, Ivy Films, Kit Parker, Natl Film Video, Video Comm & Wholesome Film Ctr. *Sale:* Classic Film Mus, Cinema Concepts, Festival Films, Glenn Photo, Images Film & Reel Images. *Rental:* Ivy Films, *Sale:* Glenn Photo, Ivy Films & Reel Images, Super 8 version. *Sale:* Cinema Cincepts, Festival Films, Ivy Films, Tamarelles French Film, Video Comm & Images Film, Videotape version.

Meet Marcel Marceau. Marcel Marceau. 1965. France. 56 min. Sound. 16mm B&W. *Sale:* Reel Images. *Sale:* Reel Images, Videotape version.

Meet Me After the Show. Betty Grable & Rory Calhoun. Directed by Richard Sale. 1951. Fox. 86 min. Sound. 16mm Color. *Rental:* Films Inc.

Meet Me at Dawn. William Eythe. Directed by Marcel Hellman. 1948. 16mm *Rental:* A Twyman Pres.

Meet Me at the Fair. Dan Dailey & Diana Lynn. Directed by Douglas Sirk. 1952. Universal. 87 min. Sound. 16mm Color. *Rental:* Swank Motion.

Meet Me in Las Vegas. Dan Dailey & Cyd Charisse. Directed by Roy Rowland. 1956. MGM. 112 min. Sound. 16mm Color. *Rental:* MGM United.

Meet Me in St. Louis. Judy Garland & Margaret O'Brien. Directed by Vincente Minnelli. 1944. MGM. 113 min. Sound. 16mm Color. *Rental:* MGM United. *Rental:* MGM United, Color version. *Rental:* MGM United, Videotape version.

Meet Me Tonight. Orig. Title: Tonight at Eight Thirty. Valerie Hobson & Stanley Holloway. Directed by Anthony Pelissier. 1952. Britain. 85 min. Sound. 16mm Color. *Rental:* Learning Corp Am. *Sale:* Learning Corp Am.

Meet Nero Wolfe. Edward Arnold, Rita Hayworth & Lionel Stander. Directed by Herbert Biberman. 1936. Columbia. 70 min. Sound. 16mm B&W. *Rental:* Kit Parker.

Meet Simon Cherry. John Bailey & Zena Marshall. Directed by Godfrey Grayson. 1950. Britain. 70 min. Sound. 16mm B&W. *Rental:* Mogulls Films.

Meet the Baron. Jimmy Durante & Jack Pearl. Directed by Walter Lang. 1933. MGM. 68 min. Sound. 16mm B&W. *Rental:* MGM United.

Meet the Boy Friend. Carol Hughes & David Carlyle. Directed by Ralph Staub. 1937. Republic. 54 min. Sound. 16mm B&W. *Rental:* Ivy Films. *Sale:* Rep Pic Film.

Meet the Mayor. Frank Fay. 1932. Times. 75 min. Sound. 16mm B&W. *Sale:* Cinema Concepts & Natl Cinema.

Meet the Missus. Roscoe Karns & Ruth Donnelly. Directed by Mal St. Clair. 1940. Republic. 54 min. Sound. 16mm B&W. *Rental:* Ivy Films. *Sale:* Rep Pic Film.

Meet the Missus. Anne Shirley & Victor Moore. Directed by Joseph Santley. 1937. RKO. 60 min. Sound. 16mm B&W. *Rental:* RKO General Pics.

Meet the Navy. Jackie Hunter & Eddie Gray. Directed by Alfred Travers. 1946. Britain. 81 min. Sound. 16mm B&W. *Rental:* Ivy Films. *Sale:* Rep Pic Film.

Meet the People. Lucille Ball & Dick Powell. Directed by Charles Reisner. 1944. MGM. 100 min. Sound. 16mm B&W. *Rental:* MGM United.

Meet the Wife. Laura LaPlante, Lew Cody & Joan Marsh. Directed by Al Christie. 1931. Columbia. 80 min. Sound. 16mm B&W. *Rental:* Modern Sound.

Meet the Wildcat. Margaret Lindsay & Ralph Bellamy. Directed by Arthur Lubin. 1940. Universal. 60 min. Sound. 16mm B&W. *Rental:* Mogulls Films.

Meeting at Midnight. Orig. Title: Black Magic. Sidney Toler & Mantan Moreland. Directed by Phil Rosen. 1944. Monogram. 65 min. Sound. 16mm B&W. *Rental:* Budget Films, Classic Film Mus, Em Gee Film Lib & Roas Films. *Sale:* Classic Film Mus & Cinema Concepts. *Rental:* Ivy Films, *Sale:* Ivy Films, Super 8 sound version, Sound 8mm version.

Meeting in Salzburg. Curt Jurgens & Nadia Gray. Directed by Max Friedmann. 1965. Germany. 100 min. Sound. 16mm B&W. dubbed. *Rental:* Video Comm.

Meeting of the Minds. 13 pts. Steve Allen. 1977. KCET. 754 min. Videotape Color. *Sale:* Films Inc.

Meetings with Remarkable Men. Terence Stamp & Dragan Maksimovic. Directed by Peter Brook. 1979. Britain. 110 min. Sound. 16mm Color. *Rental:* Corinth Films. *Lease:* Corinth Films.

Megaforce. Barry Bostwick & Michael Beck. Directed by Hal Needham. 1982. Fox. 99 min. Sound. 16mm Color. *Rental:* Films Inc.

Mein Kampf. Trans. Title: Blodiga Tiden, Das. Directed by Erwin Leiser. 1961. Germany-Sweden. (Documentary). 117 min. Sound. 16mm B&W. narrated Eng. *Rental:* Budget Films, Film Ctr DC, Kit Parker, Twyman Films & Wholesome Film Ctr. *Sale:* Festival Films, 121 min. version. *Sale:* Festival Films, 121 min. Videotape version.

Mekhanika Golovnovo Mozga see Mechanics of the Brain.

Melba. Robert Morley & Patrice Munsel. Directed by Lewis Milestone. 1953. Horizon. 115 min. Sound. 16mm Color. *Rental:* Ivy Films.

Melinda. Vonetta McGee & Calvin Lockhart. Directed by Hugh A. Robertson. 1972. MGM. 109 min. Sound. 16mm Color. *Rental:* MGM United.

Melody. Orig. Title: S.W.A.L.K. & To Love Somebody. Mark Lester & Jack Wild. Directed by Waris Hussein. 1971. Britain. 103 min. Sound. 16mm Color. *Rental:* Budget Films, Bosco Films, Films Inc, Twyman Films, Video Comm, Welling Motion Pictures, Westcoast Films & Willoughby Peer.

Melody & Moonlight. Johnny Downs & Mary Lee. Directed by Joseph Santley. 1940. Republic. 54 min. Sound. 16mm B&W. *Rental:* Ivy Films.

Melody Cruise. Phil Harris & Charles Ruggles. Directed by Mark Sandrich. 1933. RKO. 75 min. Sound. 16mm *Rental:* RKO General Pics.

Melody for Three. Jean Hersholt. Directed by Erle C. Kenton. 1941. RKO. 70 min. Sound. 16mm B&W. *Rental:* Alba House, Budget Films & Welling Motion Pictures.

Melody for Two. James Melton & Patricia Ellis. Directed by Louis King. 1937. Warners. 60 min. Sound. 16mm B&W. *Rental:* MGM United.

Melody Girl see Mania for Melody.

Melody Lane. Leon Errol & Robert Paige. Directed by Charles Lamont. 1941. Universal. 61 min. Sound. 16mm B&W. *Rental:* Mogulls Films.

Melody Lingers On, The. Josephine Hutchinson & George Houston. Directed by David Burton. 1935. United Artists. 85 min. Sound. 16mm B&W. *Rental:* Alba House.

Melody Maker see Ding Dong Williams.

Melody Master & New Wine see Schubert, the Melody Master.

Melody of the Plains. Fred Scott. Directed by Irvin Willat. 1937. Spectrum. 60 min. Sound. 16mm B&W. *Rental:* Mogulls Films.

Melody Parade. Mary Beth Hughes & Irene Ryan. Directed by Arthur Dreifuss. 1943. Monogram. 70 min. Sound. 16mm B&W. *Rental:* Mogulls Films.

Melody Ranch. Gene Autry, Jimmy Durante & Ann Miller. Directed by Joseph Santley. 1940. Republic. 53 min. Sound. 16mm B&W. *Rental:* Ivy Films & Modern Sound. *Sale:* Blackhawk Films, Super 8 sound version.

Melody Time. 1948. Disney. (Animated). 75 min. Sound. 16mm Color. *Rental:* Bosco Films, Buchan Pic, Cine Craft, Cousino Visual Ed, Elliot Film Co, Film Ctr DC, Film Pres, Films Inc, MGM United, Modern Sound, Newman Film Lib, Roas Films, Twyman Films, U of IL Film, Welling Motion Pictures & Williams Films.

Melody Trail. Gene Autry. Directed by Joseph Kane. 1935. Republic. 54 min. Sound. 16mm B&W. *Rental:* Ivy Films & Modern Sound. *Sale:* Blackhawk Films, Super 8 sound version.

Melvin & Howard. Jason Robards, Paul Le Mat & Mary Steenbergen. Directed by Jonathan Demme. 1980. Universal. 95 min. Sound. 16mm Color. *Rental:* Swank Motion. *Rental:* Swank Motion, Videotape version.

Member of the Wedding, A. Julie Harris & Ethel Waters. Directed by Fred Zinnemann. 1952. Columbia. 91 min. Sound. 16mm B&W. *Rental:* Buchan Pic, Films Inc & Kit Parker.

Memoirs of a French Whore. Miou Miou & Maria Schneider. Directed by Daniel Duval. Fr. 1981. 16mm Color. subtitles. *Rental:* MGM United. *Rental:* MGM United, Videotape version.

Memoirs of a Movie Palace. Directed by Christian Blackwood. 45 min. 16mm *Rental:* Blackwood. *Sale:* Blackwood.

Memorabilia. 1981. 60 min. Sound. 16mm B&W. *Rental:* Canyon Cinema.

Memorandum. 1966. Canada. (Documentary). 58 min. Sound. 16mm B&W. *Rental:* ADL, Images Film, Kit Parker, Natl Film CN, U Mich Media & Syracuse U Film. *Sale:* Natl Film CN. *Sale:* Natl Film CN, *Rental:* Natl Film CN, Videotape version.

Memorias de un Mexicano. Span. 1971. Mexico. 90 min. Sound. 16mm B&W. subtitles. *Rental:* Iowa Films.

Memories & Conversation. Directed by Hans Schaal. 1978. Serious Business. (Documentary). 90 min. Sound. 16mm B&W. *Rental:* Serious Bus. *Sale:* Serious Bus.

Memories from Eden. 1977. 57 min. Sound. 16mm Color. *Rental:* U Mich Media.

Memories of Berlin: Twlight of the Weimar Culture. 1976. Canada. (Documentary). 72 min. Sound. 16mm B&W. *Rental:* A Cantor & U Mich Media. *Sale:* A Cantor.

Memories of Underdevelopment. Sergio Corrieri. Directed by Tomas Gutierrez Alea. Span. 1962. Cuba. 104 min. Sound. 16mm B&W. subtitles. *Rental:* Unifilm. *Sale:* Unifilm. *Rental:* New Yorker Films, 97 mins. version.

Memory Fixing. 1983. Embassy. (Documentary). 67 min. Sound. 16mm Color. *Rental:* Films Inc. *Sale:* Films Inc. *Sale:* Films Inc, Videotape version.

Memory of Justice, The. Directed by Marcel Ophuls. 1976. Paramount. (Documentary, Color sequences). 278 min. Sound. 16mm B&W. *Rental:* Films Inc.

Memphis Belle, The. 1944. U. S. Government. (Documentary). 43 min. Sound. 16mm Color. *Rental:* Budget Films, Intl Film Exchange, Images Film, Iowa Films, Kit Parker & Natl AV Ctr. *Sale:* Cinema Concepts, Images Film, Natl AV Ctr & Reel Images. *Sale:* Natl AV Ctr, Videotape version.

Men, The. Marlon Brando & Teresa Wright. Directed by Fred Zinnemann. 1950. United Artists. 85 min. Sound. 16mm B&W. *Rental:* Budget Films, Charard Motion Pics, Inst Cinema, Ivy Films, Kit Parker & Welling Motion Pictures. *Lease:* Rep Pic Film.

Men Against the Sky. Kent Taylor & Richard Dix. Directed by Leslie Goodwins. 1941. RKO. 75 min. Sound. 16mm B&W. *Rental:* RKO General Pics.

Men Are Not Gods. Rex Harrison & Miriam Hopkins. Directed by Walter Reisch. 1937. Britain. 82 min. Sound. 16mm B&W. *Rental:* Film Classics, Films Inc, Ivy Films & Mogulls Films.

Men Are Such Fools. Leo Carrillo & Vivienne Osborne. Directed by William Nigh. 1933. RKO. 62 min. Sound. 16mm B&W. *Rental:* Ivy Films. *Sale:* Rep Pic Film.

Men Are Such Fools. Humphrey Bogart & Wayne Morris. Directed by Busby Berkeley. 1938. Warners. 69 min. Sound. 16mm B&W. *Rental:* MGM United.

Men Call It Love. Adolphe Menjou & Hedda Hopper. Directed by Edgar Selwyn. 1931. MGM. 71 min. Sound. 16mm B&W. *Rental:* MGM United.

Men for Others. 1965. NET. (Documentary). 60 min. Sound. 16mm B&W. *Rental:* Mass Media.

Men from the Boys, The. 1967. Army. (Documentary). 51 min. Sound. 16mm Color. *Rental:* Modern Talking.

Men in Black. 1966. NET. (Documentary). 60 min. Sound. 16mm B&W. *Rental:* Indiana AV Ctr. *Sale:* Indiana AV Ctr.

Men in Cages. 1967. CBS. (Documentary). 52 min. Sound. 16mm B&W. *Rental:* BYU Media, Mass Media, Iowa Films & Syracuse U Film. *Sale:* Carousel Films.

Men in Exile. Dick Purcell & June Travis. Directed by John Farrow. 1937. Warners. 58 min. Sound. 16mm B&W. *Rental:* MGM United.

Men in Her Life, The. Loretta Young & Conrad Veidt. Directed by Gregory Ratoff. 1941. Columbia. 90 min. Sound. 16mm B&W. *Rental:* Kit Parker.

Men in War. Robert Ryan & Aldo Ray. Directed by Anthony Mann. 1957. United Artists. 102 min. Sound. 16mm B&W. *Rental:* Budget Films & Kit Parker.

Men in White. Clark Gable & Myrna Loy. Directed by Richard Boleslawski. 1934. MGM. 75 min. Sound. 16mm B&W. *Rental:* MGM United.

Men Must Fight. Diana Wynyard & Lewis Stone. Directed by Edgar Selwyn. 1933. MGM. 72 min. Sound. 16mm B&W. *Rental:* MGM United.

Men of America. Bill Boyd & Dorothy Wilson. Directed by Ralph Ince. 1933. RKO. 75 min. Sound. 16mm B&W. *Rental:* RKO General Pics.

Men of Boys Town. Spencer Tracy & Mickey Rooney. Directed by Norman Taurog. 1941. MGM. 106 min. Sound. 16mm B&W. *Rental:* MGM United.

Men of Bronze. Directed by William Miles. 1977. Killiam/Miles. (Documentary). 58 min. Sound. 16mm Color. *Rental:* Films Inc, Iowa Films, Syracuse U Film & U of IL Film. *Sale:* Films Inc. *Sale:* Films Inc, Videotape version.

Men of Chance. Mary Astor & Ricardo Cortez. Directed by Pandro S. Berman. 1932. RKO. 63 min. Sound. 16mm *Rental:* RKO General Pics.

Men of Serengeti. 1972. 51 min. Sound. 16mm Color. *Rental:* Iowa Films.

Men of Sherwood Forest. Don Taylor & Eileen Moore. Directed by Val Guest. 1954. Astor. 77 min. Sound. 16mm Color. *Rental:* Budget Films.

Men of Steel *see* Bill Cracks Down.

Men of the Fighting Lady. Van Johnson & Walter Pidgeon. Directed by Andrew Marton. 1954. MGM. 79 min. Sound. 16mm Color. *Rental:* MGM United.

Men of the North. Gilbert Roland & Hal Roach. 1930. MGM. 61 min. Sound. 16mm B&W. *Rental:* MGM United.

Men of the Sea *see* Midshipman Easy.

Men of the Tall Ships. 1978. Drew Associates. (Documentary). 56 min. Sound. 16mm Color. *Rental:* Direct Cinema. *Sale:* Direct Cinema. *Sale:* Direct Cinema, Videotape version.

Men of the Timberland. Richard Arlen & Andy Devine. Directed by Charles S. Gould. 1941. Universal. 60 min. Sound. 16mm B&W. *Rental:* Mogulls Films.

Men Under Siege: Life with the Modern Woman. 1979. ABC. (Documentary). 50 min. Sound. 16mm Color. *Sale:* MTI Tele. *Sale:* MTI Tele, Videotape version.

Men Who Made Movies, The: Howard Hawks. Directed by Richard Schickel. 1973. Museum of Modern Art. (Documentary). 58 min. Sound. 16mm Color. *Rental:* Museum Mod Art. *Lease:* Museum Mod Art.

Men Who Made the Movies, The: Frank Capra. Directed by Richard Schickel. 1973. Museum of Modern Art. (Documentary). 80 min. Sound. 16mm Color. *Rental:* Museum Mod Art. *Lease:* Museum Mod Art.

Men Who Made the Movies, The: George Cukor. Directed by Richard Schickel. 1973. Museum of Modern Art. (Documentary). 58 min. Sound. 16mm Color. *Rental:* Museum Mod Art. *Lease:* Museum Mod Art.

Men Who Made the Movies, The: King Vidor. Directed by Richard Schickel. 1973. Museun of Modern Art. (Documentary). 58 min. Sound. 16mm Color. *Rental:* Museum Mod Art. *Lease:* Museum Mod Art.

Men Who Made the Movies, The: Raoul Walsh. Directed by Richard Schickel. 1973. Museum of Modern Art. (Documentary). 88 min. Sound. 16mm Color. *Rental:* Museum Mod Art. *Lease:* Museum Mod Art.

Men Who Made the Movies, The: Sir Alfred Hitchcock. Directed by Richard Schickel. 1973. Museum of Modern Art. (Documentary). 58 min. Sound. 16mm Color. *Rental:* Museum Mod Art. *Lease:* Museum Mod Art.

Men Who Made the Movies, The: Vincente Minnelli. Directed by Richard Schickel. 1973. Museum of Modern Art. (Documentary). 58 min. Sound. 16mm Color. *Rental:* Museum Mod Art. *Lease:* Museum Mod Art.

Men Who Made the Movies, The: William A. Wellman. Directed by Richard Schickel. 1973. Museum of Modern Art. (Documentary). 58 min. Sound. 16mm Color. *Rental:* Museum Mod Art. *Lease:* Museum Mod Art.

Men Who Tread on the Tiger's Tail. Orig. Title: They Who Tread on the Tiger's Tail. Hanshiro Iwai. Directed by Akira Kurosawa. Jap. 1945. Japan. 60 min. Sound. 16mm B&W. subtitles. *Sale:* Reel Images. *Rental:* Kit Parker & Natl Cinema. *Sale:* Tamarelles French Film, Videotape version.

Men With Wings. Fred MacMurray & Ray Milland. Directed by William A. Wellman. 1938. Paramount. 106 min. Sound. 16mm Color. *Rental:* Swank Motion.

Men, Women & Money. Ethel Clayton. Directed by George Melford. 1919. 16mm *Rental:* A Twyman Pres.

Menace, The. Bette Davis & H. B. Warner. Directed by Roy Chanslor. 1932. Columbia. 70 min. Sound. 16mm B&W. *Rental:* Kit Parker.

Menagerie, The. William Shatner, Leonard Nimoy & Jeffrey Hunter. Directed by Marc Daniels & Robert Butler. 1966. Star Trek. 105 min. Sound. 16mm Color. *Rental:* Roas Films & Westcoast Films.

Mendi, The. Canada. (Documentary). 57 min. Sound. 16mm Color. *Rental:* CBC. *Sale:* CBC.

Menino De Engenho *see* Plantation Boy.

Mental Illness. 1954. 56 min. Sound. 16mm Color. *Rental:* Iowa Films.

Mental Retardation. 1967. 64 min. Sound. 16mm Color. *Rental:* Iowa Films.

Mephisto Waltz. Alan Alda & Jacqueline Bisset. Directed by Paul Wendkos. 1971. Fox. 108 min. Sound. 16mm Color. *Rental:* Films inc.

Mepris, Le *see* Contempt.

Merce Cunningham. 1979. (Documentary). 60 min. Sound. 16mm Color. *Rental:* M Cunningham. *Sale:* M Cunningham. *Sale:* M Cunningham, Videotape version.

Merce Cunningham & Co. 1976. WNET. (Documentary). 58 min. Videotape Color. *Rental:* WNET Media. *Sale:* WNET Media.

Merce Cunningham & Co. Louise Burns. Directed by Benoit Jacquot. 1982. 45 min. Sound. 16mm Color. *Rental:* M Cunningham. *Sale:* M Cunningham, Videotape version.

Mercenary, The. Jack Palance & Tony Musante. Directed by Sergio Corbucci. 1970. United Artists. (Anamorphic). 105 min. Sound. 16mm Color. dubbed. *Rental:* MGM United.

Mercenary Game, The. Directed by Jean-Claude Burger. 60 min. Sound. 16mm Color. *Rental:* Cinema Guild.

Merchant of Four Seasons, The. Irma Hermann. Directed by Rainer Werner Fassbinder. Ger. 1972. Germany. 88 min. Sound. 16mm Color. subtitles. *Rental:* New Yorker Films.

Merchant of Venice, The. Gemma Jones & Warren Mitchell. 1980. Britain. 157 min. Videotape Color. *Rental:* Time-Life Multimedia. *Sale:* Time-Life Multimedia.

Mercy Island. Ray Middleton & Otto Kruger. Directed by William Morgan. 1941. Republic. 73 min. Sound. 16mm B&W. *Rental:* Ivy Films.

Mermoz. Robert Hugues-Lambert. Directed by Louis Cuny. France. 90 min. Sound. 16mm B&W. *Rental:* French Am Cul. *Rental:* French Am Cul, Videotape version.

Merriest Pranksters, The. Blackhawk. (Anthology). 57 min. Videotape B&W. *Sale:* Blackhawk Films.

Merrily We Roll Along. 1970. Xerox. (Documentary). 51 min. Sound. 16mm Color. *Rental:* NYU Film Lib, Syracuse U Film & U Cal Media. *Sale:* Xerox Films.

Merry Andrew. Danny Kaye. Directed by Michael Kidd. 1958. MGM. 103 min. Sound. 16mm Color. *Rental:* MGM United. *Rental:* MGM United, Anamorphic version.

Merry Christmas, Mr. Lawrence. David Bowie & Tom Conti. Directed by Nagisa Oshima. 1983. Universal. 124 min. Sound. 16mm Color. *Rental:* Swank Motion. *Rental:* Swank Motion, *Sale:* Tamarelles French Film, Videotape version.

Merry Frinks, The. Orig. Title: Happy Family, The. Guy Kibbee & Aline MacMahon. Directed by Alfred E. Green. 1934. Warners. 68 min. Sound. 16mm B&W. *Rental:* MGM United.

Merry Go Around. 45 min. Sound. 16mm Color. *Rental:* Natl AV Ctr.

Merry-Go-Round. Norman Kerry. Directed by Erich Von Stroheim. 1923. Universal. 96 min. Silent. 16mm B&W. *Rental:* A Twyman Pres, Creative Film & Film Images.

Merry-Go-Round. Maria Schneider, Helmut Berger & Senta Berger. Directed by Otto Schenk. Ger. 1976. Germany. 90 min. Sound. 16mm Color. subtitles. *Rental:* New Line Cinema.

Merry-Go-Round of 1938. Bert Lahr & Billy House. Directed by Irving Cummings. 1937. Universal. 87 min. Sound. 16mm B&W. *Rental:* Swank Motion.

Merry Widow, The. Mae Murray. Directed by Erich Von Stroheim. 1925. MGM. 105 min. Silent. 16mm B&W. *Rental:* MGM United.

Merry Widow, The. Fernando Lamas & Lana Turner. Directed by Curtis Bernhardt. 1952. MGM. 105 min. Sound. 16mm Color. *Rental:* MGM United.

Merry Widow, The: The Lady Dances. Maurice Chevalier, Jeanette MacDonald & Una Merkel. Directed by Ernst Lubitsch. 1934. 99 min. Sound. 16mm B&W. *Rental:* MGM United.

Merry Wives of Reno, The. Margaret Lindsay & Glenda Farrell. Directed by Bruce Humberstone. 1934. Warners. 64 min. Sound. 16mm B&W. *Rental:* MGM United.

Merry Wives of Windsor, The. Norman Foster, Colete Boky & Mildred Miller. Directed by Georg Tressler. 1965. Austria. 97 min. Sound. 16mm Color. *Rental:* Corinth Films. *Lease:* Macmillan Films.

Merry Wives of Windsor, The. Richard Griffiths, Ben Kingsley & Judy David. 1982. Britain. 167 min. Sound. 16mm Color. *Rental:* Iowa Films.

Merry World of Leopold Z, The. 1966. Canada. (Documentary). 68 min. Sound. 16mm B&W. *Sale:* Natl Film CN.

Merton. 1984. First Run. (Documentary). 57 min. Sound. 16mm Color. *Rental:* First Run. *Lease:* First Run. *Lease:* First Run, Videotape version.

Merveilleuse Visite, La *see* Marvelous Visit.

Mesa of Lost Women, The. Jackie Coogan & Allan Nixon. Directed by Herbert Tevos & Ron Ormond. 1952. Lippert. 75 min. Sound. 16mm B&W. *Rental:* Budget Films.

Message from Space, A. Vic Morrow & Sonny Chiba. Directed by Kinji Fukasaku. 1978. Japan. 106 min. Sound. 16mm Color. dubbed. *Rental:* MGM United.

Message in the Rocks, A. 1980. Britain. (Documentary). 57 min. Sound. 16mm Color. *Rental:* Time-Life Multimedia. *Sale:* Time-Life Multimedia. *Sale:* Time-Life Multimedia, Videotape version.

Message to Garcia, A. John Boles, Barbara Stanwyck & Wallace Beery. Directed by George Marshall. 1936. Fox. 110 min. Sound. 16mm B&W. *Rental:* Films Inc.

Metalstorm: The Desctruction of Jared-Syn. Jeffrey Byron & Mike Preston. Directed by Charles Band. 1983. Universal. 84 min. Sound. 16mm Color. *Rental:* Swank Motion. *Rental:* Swank Motion, Videotape version.

Metamedia. Directed by Jud Yalcut. 1966. Yalcut. (Anthology). 50 min. Silent. 16mm Color. *Rental:* Films Inc.

Metempsycho *see* Tomb of Torture.

Meteor. Sean Connery & Natalie Wood. Directed by Ronald Neame. 1979. American International. 104 min. Sound. 16mm Color. *Rental:* Williams Films & Welling Motion Pictures.

Metropolis. Gustav Frohlich, Brigitte Helm & Algred Abel. Directed by Fritz Lang. 1926. Germany. (Musical score only). 96 min. 16mm B&W. *Rental:* Budget Films, Creative Film, Em Gee Film Lib, Films Inc, Images Film, Ivy Films, Janus Films, Kino Intl, Kit Parker, Maljack, Natl Film Video, Roas Film, Swank Motion, Video Comm, Westcoast Films, Wholesome Film Ctr, Williams Films & Willoughby Peer. *Sale:* Cinema Concepts, E Finney, Festival Films, Film Images, Images Film, Natl Cinema & Reel Images. *Rental:* Maljack, Video Comm & Wholesome Film Ctr, *Sale:* Reel Images, Sound 16mm version, Super 8 sound version. *Rental:* Ivy Films, *Sale:* Reel Images, Super 8 Silent version. *Sale:* Cinema Concepts, Festival Films, Ivy Films, Maljack & Video Comm, Videotape version.

Metropolis, The. 1976. Britain. (Documentary). 60 min. Sound. 16mm Color. *Rental:* Films Inc, Syracuse U Film, U Cal Media & U of IL Film. *Sale:* Films Inc. *Sale:* Films Inc, Videotape version.

Metropolitan. Laurence Tibbett & Virginia Bruce. Directed by Richard Boleslawski. 1935. Fox. 81 min. Sound. 16mm B&W. *Rental:* Films Inc.

Mexicali Kid, The. Jack Randall. Directed by Wallace Fox. 1938. Monogram. 55 min. Sound. 16mm B&W. *Rental:* Hurlock Cine.

Mexicali Rose. Gene Autry. Directed by George Sherman. 1939. Republic. 54 min. Sound. 16mm B&W. *Rental:* Kit Parker.

Mexican-Americans: Viva la Raza!. 1971. CBS. (Documentary). 54 min. Sound. 16mm B&W. *Rental:* McGraw-Hill Films & U Mich Media. *Sale:* McGraw-Hill Films.

Mexican Hayride. Bud Abbott & Lou Costello. Directed by Charles Barton. 1948. Universal. 70 min. Sound. 16mm B&W. *Rental:* Swank Motion.

Mexican Manhunt. George Brent & Hillary Brooke. Directed by Rex Bailey. 1953. Monogram. 71 min. Sound. 16mm B&W. *Rental:* Hurlock Cine.

Mexican Spitfire. Lupe Velez & Donald Woods. Directed by Leslie Goodwins. 1940. RKO. 67 min. Sound. 16mm B&W. *Rental:* RKO General Pics.

Mexican Spitfire at Sea. Lupe Velez & Donald Woods. Directed by Leslie Goodwins. 1942. RKO. 72 min. Sound. 16mm B&W. *Rental:* RKO General Pics.

Mexican Spitfire Out West. Lupe Velez & Errol Leon. Directed by Leslie Goodwins. 1941. RKO. 76 min. Sound. 16mm B&W. *Rental:* RKO General Pics.

Mexican Spitfire Sees a Ghost. Lupe Velez & Leon Errol. Directed by Leslie Goodwins. 1942. RKO. 69 min. Sound. 16mm B&W. *Rental:* RKO General Pics.

Mexican Spitfire's Baby. Lupe Velez & Leon Errol. Directed by Leslie Goodwins. 1942. RKO. 70 min. Sound. 16mm B&W. *Rental:* RKO General Pics.

Mexican Spitfire's Blessed Event. Lupe Velez & Leon Errol. Directed by Leslie Goodwins. 1943. RKO. 63 min. Sound. B&W. *Rental:* RKO General Pics.

Mexican Spitfire's Elephant. Lupe Velez & Leon Errol. Directed by Leslie Goodwins. 1943. RKO. 64 min. Sound. 16mm B&W. *Rental:* RKO General Pics.

Mexicana. Constance Moore & Leo Carillo. Directed by Alfred Santell. 1945. Republic. 83 min. Sound. 16mm B&W. *Rental:* Ivy Films & Rep Pic Film.

Mexico: The Frozen Revolution. Directed by Raymundo Gleyzer. 1970. Argentina. (Documentary). 60 min. 16mm Color. *Rental:* Cinema Guild & U Mich Media. *Sale:* Cinema Guild.

MGM Cartoon Magic: Rel. 1930-40. 53 min. Sound. 16mm Color. *Rental:* Festival Films.

MGM Story, The. 1951. MGM. (Anthology). 50 min. Sound. 16mm B&W. *Sale:* MGM United. *Sale:* Morcraft Films, Super 8 silent version. *Sale:* Morcraft Films, Videotape version.

MGM's Big Parade of Comedy. Orig. Title: Big Parade of Comedy. 1964. MGM. (Anthology). 109 min. Sound. 16mm B&W. *Rental:* MGM United.

Mi Amigo el Fantasma. Peter Ustinov & Dean Jones. Directed by Robert Stevenson. 1968. Disney. 107 min. Sound. 16mm Color. dubbed Span. *Rental:* Twyman Films.

Mi Cerebro Es Electronico. Kurt Russell & Cesar Romero. Directed by Robert Butler. 1969. Disney. 91 min. Sound. 16mm Color. dubbed Span. *Rental:* Twyman Films.

Miami Story, The. Barry Sullivan & Luther Adler. Directed by Fred F. Sears. 1954. Columbia. 75 min. Sound. 16mm B&W. *Rental:* Films Inc & Inst Cinema.

Miao Year. 1970. Thailand. (Documentary). 62 min. Sound. 16mm Color. *Rental:* Iowa Films & U Cal Media.

Michael Kohlhaas. David Warner & Anna Karina. Directed by Volker Schlondorff. 1968. Britain-Germany. 95 min. Sound. 16mm Color. *Rental:* Corinth Films.

Michael O'Halloran. Scotty Beckett & Allene Roberts. Directed by John Rawlins. 1948. Monogram. 79 min. Sound. 16mm B&W. *Rental:* Ivy Films. *Sale:* Rep Pic Film.

Michael Shayne, Private Detective. Lloyd Nolan & Marjorie Weaver. Directed by Eugene Forde. 1940. Fox. 90 min. Sound. 16mm B&W. *Rental:* Films Inc.

Michaelangelo Antonioni. 1966. Canada. (Documentary). 60 min. Sound. 16mm B&W. *Rental:* Natl Film CN.

Michaelangelo: The Last Giant. 1966. NBC. (Documentary). 67 min. Sound. 16mm Color. *Rental:* BYU Media, McGraw-Hill Films, Syracuse U Film & U of IL Film. *Sale:* McGraw-Hill Film.

Michel's Mixed-Up Musical Bird. DePatie-Freleng. (Animated). 47 min. Sound. 16mm Color. *Rental:* Films Inc.

Mickey. Mabel Normand. Directed by F. Richard Jones. 1918. Western. 102 min. Silent. 16mm B&W. *Rental:* Budget Films, Em Gee Film Lib & Museum Mod Art. *Sale:* Morcraft Films.

Mickey. Lois Butler & Bill Goodwin. Directed by Ralph Murphy. 1948. Eagle Lion. 87 min. Sound. 16mm B&W. *Rental:* Budget Films & Inst Cinema.

Mickey & the Beanstalk. 1947. 73 min. Sound. 16mm Color. *Sale:* Festival Films. *Sale:* Festival Films, Videotape version.

Mickey One. Warren Beatty & Hurd Hatfield. Directed by Arthur Penn. 1965. Columbia. 93 min. Sound. 16mm B&W. *Rental:* Arcus Film, Budget Films, Images Film, Ivy Films, Kit Parker, Modern Sound, Video Comm, Welling Motion Pictures, Westcoast Films & Wholesome Film Ctr.

Mickey the Great. Directed by J. A. Duffy. (Anthology). 51 min. Sound. 16mm B&W. *Rental:* Budget Films & Video Comm. *Sale:* Cinema Concepts, Morcraft Films, Natl Cinema & Reel Images. *Rental:* Video Comm, Videotape version.

Mickey the Kid. Bruce Cabot & Ralph Byrd. Directed by Arthur Lubin. 1939. Republic. 54 min. Sound. 16mm B&W. *Rental:* Ivy Films. *Sale:* Rep Pic Film.

Midchannel. Clara Kimball Young. Directed by Harry Garson. 1920. Equity. 60 min. Silent. 16mm B&W. *Sale:* Morcraft Films.

Midas Run. Richard Crenna & Anne Heywood. Directed by Alf Kjellin. 1969. ABC. 104 min. Sound. 16mm Color. *Rental:* Films Inc.

Midday Sun. Orig. Title: Miracle of Bali. 1971. Xerox. 52 min. Sound. 16mm Color. *Rental:* U Cal Media & Syracuse U Film. *Sale:* Xerox Films.

Middle East, The: The Search for Peace. 1973. WNET. (Documentary). 60 min. Sound. 16mm Color. *Rental:* WNET Media. *Sale:* WNET Media, Videotape version.

Middle of the Night. Fredric March & Kim Novak. Directed by Delbert Mann. 1959. Columbia. 118 min. Sound. 16mm B&W. *Rental:* Films Inc, Modern Sound & Welling Motion Pictures.

Middle of the World, The. Olimpia Carlisi & Philippe Leotard. Directed by Alain Tanner. Fr. 1975. France. 115 min. Sound. 16mm Color. subtitles. *Rental:* New Yorker Films.

Middleman, The. Trans. Title: Dahana-Arania. Upal Dutt. Directed by Satyajit Ray. Hindi. 1977. India. 115 min. Sound. 16mm B&W. subtitles. *Rental:* Liberty Co.

Middletown Second Time Around. 1982. 60 min. Sound. 16mm Color. *Rental:* Iowa Films.

Middletown: The Campaign. 1982. 90 min. Sound. 16mm Color. *Rental:* Iowa Films.

Midnight see Call It Murder.

Midnight. John Barrymore & Claudette Colbert. Directed by Mitchell Leisen. 1939. Paramount. 94 min. Sound. 16mm B&W. *Rental:* Swank Motion.

Midnight at Madame Tussaud's. Orig. Title: Midnight in the Wax Museum. Lucille Lisle & Bernard Miles. Directed by George Pearson. 1936. Britain. 67 min. Sound. 16mm B&W. *Sale:* Blackhawk Films & Budget Films. *Sale:* Blackhawk Films, Super 8 sound version.

Midnight Blue Follies of 1975. 1975. Screw. (Anthology). 50 min. Sound. 16mm Color. *Rental:* Video Comm. *Sale:* Ivy Films, Videotape version.

Midnight Blue Follies of 1976. 1976. Screw. (Anthology). 50 min. Videotape Color. *Rental:* Video Comm. *Sale:* Ivy Films, Videotape version.

Midnight Court. Ann Dvorak & John Litel. Directed by Frank McDonald. 1937. Warners. 63 min. Sound. 16mm B&W. *Rental:* MGM United.

Midnight Cowboy. Dustin Hoffman & Jon Voight. Directed by John Schlesinger. 1969. United Artists. 111 min. Sound. 16mm Color. *Rental:* MGM United. *Rental:* MGM United, Videotape version.

Midnight Express. Brad Davis, Randy Quaid & John Hurt. Directed by Alan Parker. 1978. Columbia. 120 min. Sound. 16mm Color. *Rental:* Swank Motion. *Rental:* Swank Motion, Videotape version.

Midnight Faces. Francis X. Bushman Jr. Directed by Bennett Cohn. 1926. Goodwill. 60 min. Silent. 16mm B&W. *Rental:* Willoughby Peer.

Midnight Girl. Lila Lee & Bela Lugosi. Directed by Wilfred Noy. 1925. Chadwick. 60 min. Silent. 16mm B&W. *Rental:* Em Gee Film Lib & Willoughby Peer. *Sale:* Morcraft Films, Silent 16mm tinted version.

Midnight in the Wax Museum see Midnight at Madame Tussaud's.

Midnight Lace. Doris Day & Rex Harrison. Directed by David Miller. 1960. Universal. 108 min. Sound. 16mm Color. *Rental:* Swank Motion.

Midnight Man, The. Burt Lancaster & Susan Clark. Directed by Roland Kibbee & Burt Lancaster. 1974. Universal. 119 min. Sound. 16mm Color. *Rental:* Swank Motion.

Midnight Mary. Loretta Young, Franchot Tone & Ricardo Cortez. Directed by William A. Wellman. 1933. MGM. 76 min. Sound. 16mm B&W. *Rental:* MGM United.

Midnight Melody see Murder in the Music Hall.

Midnight Message. Mary Carr. Directed by Paul Hurst. 1926. Goodwill. 45 min. Silent. 16mm B&W. *Rental:* Mogulls Films, Silent 8mm version.

Midnight Movie. 1976. Twyman. (Anthology). 114 min. Sound. 16mm Color. *Rental:* Twyman Films.

Midnight Mystery. Betty Compson & Lowell Sherman. Directed by George B. Seitz. 1930. RKO. 72 min. Sound. 16mm B&W. *Rental:* RKO General Pics.

Midshipman Easy. Orig. Title: Men of the Sea. Roger Livesey & Margaret Lockwood. Directed by Sir Carol Reed. 1940. Britain. 70 min. Sound. 16mm B&W. *Rental:* Janus Films & Mogull Films.

Midshipman Jack. Betty Furness & Bruce Cabot. Directed by Merian C. Cooper. 1934. RKO. 65 min. Sound. 16mm B&W. *Rental:* RKO General Pics.

Midsummer Night's Dream, A. David Warner, Diana Rigg, Paul Rogers & Bill Travers. Directed by Peter Hall. 1968. Britain. 124 min. Sound. 16mm Color. *Rental:* Films Inc, Museum Mod Art & Syracuse U Film. *Lease:* Macmillan Films.

Midsummer Night's Dream, A. 1980. NY City Ballet. (Dance). 60 min. Sound. 16mm Color. *Rental:* Corinth Films.

Midsummer Night's Dream, A. Helen Mirren & Peter McEnery. 1981. Time-Life. 108 min. Videotape Color. *Rental:* Iowa Films.

Midsummer Night's Dream, A. James Cagney, Dick Powell & Olivia De Havilland. Directed by Max Reinhardt & William Dieterle. 1935. Warners. 117 min. Sound. 16mm B&W. *Rental:* MGM United.

Midway. Charlton Heston, Henry Fonda & James Coburn. Directed by Jack Smight. 1976. Universal. 132 min. Sound. 16mm Color. *Rental:* Swank Motion.

Mighty Barnum, The. Wallace Beery & Adolphe Menjou. Directed by Walter Lang. 1934. United Artists. 86 min. Sound. 16mm B&W. *Rental:* Ivy Films.

Mighty Crusaders, The. Sylva Koscina & Rick Battaglia. Directed by Carlo Bragaglia. 1961. Italy. 100 min. Sound. 16mm Color. dubbed. *Rental:* Inst Cinema & Ivy Films.

Mighty Gorgo, The. Scott Brady & Kent Taylor. Directed by David L. Hewitt. 1969. Western International. 86 min. Sound. 16mm Color. *Rental:* Video Comm.

Mighty Joe Young. Terry Moore & Robert Armstrong. Directed by Ernest B. Schoedsack. 1949. RKO. 103 min. Sound. 16mm B&W. *Rental:* Films Inc. *Rental:* RKO General Pics, 94 min. version.

Mighty McGurk, The. Wallace Beery. Directed by John A. Waters. 1946. MGM. 85 min. Sound. 16mm B&W. *Rental:* MGM United.

Migrant, The. 1970. NBC. (Documentary). 53 min. Sound. 16mm B&W. *Rental:* Films Inc, Iowa Films, Syracuse U Film, Twyman Films, U Cal Media, U of IL Film & U Mich Media. *Sale:* Films Inc. *Sale:* Films Inc, Videotape version.

Migrants, The: 1981. 1980. NBC. (Documentary). 52 min. Sound. 16mm Color. *Rental:* Films Inc & Syracuse U Film. *Sale:* Films Inc. *Rental:* Films Inc, *Sale:* Films Inc, Videotape version.

Mikado, The. Directed by Stuart Burge. 1967. Warners. (Opera). 125 min. Sound. 16mm Color. *Rental:* Films Inc & Swank Motion.

Mikado, The. 1974. Britain. (Operetta). 52 min. Sound. 16mm Color. *Rental:* B Raymond. *Sale:* B Raymond. *Rental:* B Raymond, *Sale:* B Raymond, Videotape version.

Milady. Jacques Dufilho. Directed by Francois Leterrier. Fr. France. 82 min. Sound. 16mm Color. subtitles. *Rental:* French Am Cul.

Mildred Pierce. Joan Crawford & Jack Carson. Directed by Michael Curtiz. 1945. Warners. 111 min. Sound. 16mm B&W. *Rental:* MGM United.

Miles of Smiles. Years of Struggle. 1982. Benchmark. (Documentary). 59 min. Sound. 16mm Color. *Rental:* Benchmark Films, Syracuse U Film & U Cal Media. *Sale:* Benchmark Films. *Sale:* Benchmark Films, 8mm version avail. version.

Miles to Go. Directed by Hilary Maddux & Deborah Boldt. 1983. (Documentary). 55 min. Sound. 16mm Color. *Rental:* Film Makers. *Sale:* Film Makers.

Miles to Go Before I Sleep. Martin Balsam & Mackenzie Phillips. Directed by Fielder Cook. 1974. CBS. 81 min. Sound. 16mm Color. *Rental:* Kent St U Film, Learning Corp Am, Museum Mod Art, Roas Films, Syracuse U Film, Twyman Films, U of IL Film & U Mich Media. *Lease:* Learning Corp Am. *Rental:* Learning Corp Am, *Lease:* Learning Corp Am, Videotape version.

Military Academy. Stanley Clements. Directed by D. Ross Lederman. 1950. Columbia. 64 min. Sound. 16mm B&W. *Rental:* Buchan Pic, Inst Cinema & Newman Film Lib.

Military-Industrial Firm, The. 1983. 55 min. Sound. 16mm Color. *Rental:* U Mich Media.

Military Justice. 1954. US Government. (Documentary). 94 min. Sound. 16mm B&W. *Sale:* Natl AV Ctr.

Military Police see Off Limits.

Milkman, The. Donald O'Connor & Jimmy Durante. Directed by Charles Barton. 1950. Universal. 90 min. Sound. 16mm B&W. *Rental:* Swank Motion.

Milky Way, The. Trans. Title: Voie Lactee, La. Paul Frankeur & Laurent Terzieff. Directed by Luis Bunuel. 1969. France. 102 min. Sound. 16mm Color. dubbed. *Rental:* Swank Motion.

Milky Way, The. Harold Lloyd, Adolphe Menjou & Helen Mack. Directed by Leo McCarey. 1936. USA. 89 min. Sound. 16mm B&W. *Rental:* Budget Films & Images Film. *Sale:* Festival Films, Natl Cinema & Images Film. *Sale:* Festival Films, Videotape version.

Mill of Stone Women, The. Pierre Brice & Scilla Gabel. Directed by Giorgio Ferroni. 1963. France-Italy. 94 min. Sound. 16mm B&W. dubbed. *Rental:* Ivy Films.

Mill on the Floss, The. Mignon Anderson. 1915. Mutual. 50 min. Silent. 16mm B&W. *Rental:* Film Classics. *Sale:* Film Classics. *Rental:* Film Classics, *Sale:* Film Classics, Silent 8mm version.

Mill on the Floss, The. James Mason & Geraldine Fitzgerald. Directed by Tim Whelan. 1939. Britain. 80 min. Sound. 16mm B&W. *Rental:* Budget Films & Classic Film Mus. *Sale:* Morcraft Films.

Mille Di Garibaldi, I see Eighteen Sixty.

Millhouse: A White Comedy. Directed by Emile De Antonio. 1971. National Talent Service. (Documentary). 100 min. Sound. 16mm B&W. *Rental:* New Cinema & New Yorker Films. *Rental:* New Cinema, 93 mins. version.

Millie. Joan Blondell & Anita Louise. Directed by John Francis Dillon. 1931. RKO. 85 min. Sound. 16mm B&W. *Rental:* RKO General Pics.

Million, Le. Rene Lefevre & Anabella. Directed by Rene Clair. Fr. 1931. France. 80 min. Sound. 16mm B&W. subtitles Eng. *Rental:* Corinth Films, Images Film, Museum Mod Art, Westcoast Films, Video Comm & Kit Parker. *Lease:* Corinth Films. *Sale:* Cinema Concepts, Festival Films, Glenn Photo, Reel Images & Images Film. *Sale:* Cinema Concepts, Video Comm & Images Film, *Sale:* Tamarelles French Film, Videotape version. *Rental:* Films Inc, 190 min. version. *Rental:* Iowa Films, 85 min. version.

Million Dollar Baby. Arline Judge & Ray Walker. Directed by Joseph Santley. 1934. Monogram. 69 min. Sound. 16mm B&W. *Rental:* Mogulls Films.

Million Dollar Baby. Ronald Reagan & May Robson. Directed by Curtis Bernhardt. 1941. Warners. 100 min. Sound. 16mm B&W. *Rental:* MGM United.

Million Dollar Dixie Deliverance, The. Brock Peters, Kip Niven & Kyle Richards. Directed by Russ Mayberry. 1978. Disney. 95 min. Sound. 16mm Color. *Rental:* Bosco Films, Disney Prod, Elliot Film Co, Films Inc, MGM United, Modern Sound, Roas Films, Welling Motion Pictures, Westcoast Films & Williams Films.

Million Dollar Duck, The. Dean Jones, Sandy Duncan & Joe Flynn. Directed by Vincent McEveety. 1971. Disney. 92 min. Sound. 16mm Color. *Rental:* Bosco Films, Buchan Pic, Disney Prod, Elliot Film Co, Film Ctr DC, Film Pres, Films Inc, MGM United, Modern Sound, Newman Film Lib, Roas Films, Twyman Films, U of IL Film, Welling Motion Pictures, Westcoast Films & Williams Films.

Million Dollar Kid, The. Bowery Boys. Directed by Wallace Fox. 1944. Monogram. 77 min. Sound. 16mm B&W. *Rental:* Budget Films & Ivy Films. *Sale:* Cinema Concepts & Morcraft Films. *Sale:* Morcraft Films, Super 8 sound version.

Million Dollar Legs. W. C. Fields & Jack Oakie. Directed by Edward Cline. 1932. Paramount. 66 min. Sound. 16mm B&W. *Rental:* Museum Mod Art & Swank Motion.

Million Dollar Mermaid, The. Orig. Title: One-Piece Bathing Suit, The. Esther Williams & Victor Mature. Directed by Mervyn LeRoy. 1952. MGM. 115 min. Sound. 16mm Color. *Rental:* MGM United.

Million Dollar Mystery, The. James Kirkwood & Lila Lee. Directed by Charles Hunt. 1927. Rayart. 65 min. Silent. 16mm B&W. *Rental:* Willoughby Peer.

Million Dollar Pursuit, The. Penny Edwards & Grant Withers. Directed by R. G. Springsteen. 1951. Republic. 60 min. Sound. 16mm B&W. *Rental:* Ivy Films.

Million Dollar Weekend. Gene Raymond & Francis Lederer. Directed by Gene Raymond. 1948. Eagle Lion. 73 min. Sound. 16mm B&W. *Rental:* Mogulls Films.

Millionaire, The. George Arliss & James Cagney. Directed by John Adolfi. 1931. Warners. 80 min. Sound. 16mm B&W. *Rental:* MGM United.

Millionaire Playboy. Joe Penner & Linda Hayes. Directed by Leslie Goodwins. 1940. RKO. 64 min. Sound. 16mm *Rental:* RKO General Pics.

Millionaires in Prison. Lee Tracy & Linda Hayes. Directed by Ray MacCarey. 1940. RKO. 64 min. Sound. 16mm B&W. *Rental:* RKO General Pics.

Millionairess, The. Sophia Loren, Peter Sellers & Alastair Sim. Directed by Anthony Asquith. 1961. Fox. 90 min. Sound. 16mm Color. *Rental:* Williams Films & Films Inc.

Millionarios! Por una Pata. Dean Jones & Sandy Duncan. Directed by Vincent McEveety. 1971. Disney. 92 min. Sound. 16mm Color. dubbed Span. *Rental:* Twyman Films.

Millions. Gordon Harker. Directed by Herbert Wilcox. 1936. 16mm *Rental:* A Twyman Pres.

Milton Berle Show. Rel. 1956. 60 min. Sound. 16mm Color. *Rental:* Festival Films. *Rental:* Festival Films, Videotape version.

Mimi. Gertrude Lawrence & Douglas Fairbanks Jr. Directed by Paul L. Stein. 1935. Britain. 64 min. Sound. 16mm B&W. *Rental:* Budget Films, Em Gee Film Lib, Janus Films & Video Comm. *Sale:* Natl Cinema. *Rental:* Video Comm, Videotape version. *Sale:* Festival Films, 55 min. 16mm version.

Min & Bill. Marie Dressler & Wallace Beery. Directed by George Hill. 1930. MGM. 65 min. Sound. 16mm B&W. *Rental:* MGM United.

Mind at Large: Adler on Aristotle. 1979. WNET. (Documentary). 58 min. Videotape *Rental:* WNET Media. *Sale:* WNET Media.

Mind Benders, The. Dirk Bogarde & Mary Ure. Directed by Basil Dearden. 1963. American International. 98 min. 16mm B&W. *Rental:* Corinth Films.

Mind Machines, The. 1978. Nova. (Documentary). 59 min. Sound. 16mm Color. *Rental:* Iowa Films, U Cal Media & U of IL Film, Videotape version.

Mind of Man, The. 1971. NET. (Documentary). 119 min. Sound. 16mm Color. *Rental:* Indiana AV Ctr & U Mich Media. *Sale:* Indiana AV Ctr. *Sale:* Indiana AV Ctr, Videotape version.

Mind of Mr. Soames, The. Terence Stamp. Directed by Alan Cooke. 1970. Columbia. 94 min. 16mm *Rental:* Budget Films, Cine Craft, Films Inc, Inst Cinema, Modern Sound, Roas Films, Video Comm, Welling Motion Pictures, Westcoast Films, Wholesome Film Ctr & Willoughby Peer.

Mind Over Body. 1972. Britain. (Documentary). 49 min. Sound. 16mm Color. *Rental:* U Mich Media.

Mind Reader, The. Warren William & Constance Cummings. Directed by Roy Del Ruth. 1933. Warners. 70 min. Sound. 16mm B&W. *Rental:* MGM United.

Mind Snatchers, The. Christopher Walken & Joss Ackland. Directed by Bernard Girard. 1973. Cinerama. 94 min. Sound. 16mm Color. *Rental:* Swank Motion.

Mind's Eye, The. 1981. Britain. (Documentary). 50 min. Sound. 16mm Color. *Rental:* Films Inc. *Sale:* Films Inc. *Rental:* Films Inc, *Sale:* Films Inc, Videotape version.

Mine & the Minotaur, The. 1981. Britain. (Cast unlisted). 59 min. Sound. 16mm Color. *Sale:* Lucerne Films.

Mine Own Executioner. Burgess Meredith & Dulcie Gray. Directed by Anthony Kimmins. 1948. Britain. 103 min. Sound. 16mm B&W. *Rental:* Budget Films & Kit Parker.

Mine with the Iron Door, The. Richard Arlen & Cecilia Parker. Directed by David Howard. 1936. Columbia. 70 min. Sound. 16mm B&W. *Rental:* Mogulls Films.

Mingus. Directed by Thomas Reichman. 1967. Inlet. (Documentary). 60 min. Sound. 16mm B&W. *Rental:* Icarus Films. *Sale:* Icarus Films.

Minimata. Directed by Noriaki Tsuchimoto. Jap. 1973. Japan. (Documentary). 105 min. Sound. 16mm B&W. subtitles. *Rental:* Odeon Films. *Sale:* Odeon Films. *Rental:* Odeon Films, *Sale:* Odeon Films, 60 Mins. version.

Ministry of Fear. Ray Milland & Marjorie Reynolds. Directed by Fritz Lang. 1944. Paramount. 86 min. Sound. 16mm B&W. *Rental:* Williams Films.

Minnesota Clay. 1966. Italy. 89 min. Sound. 16mm Color. dubbed. *Rental:* Westcoast Films.

Minnie & Moscowitz. Gena Rowlands & Seymour Cassel. Directed by John Cassavetes. 1972. Universal. 114 min. Sound. 16mm Color. *Rental:* Swank Motion.

Minnie the Moocher & Many Many More. 1984. First Run. (Documentary). 55 min. Sound. 16mm Color. *Rental:* First Run. *Lease:* First Run.

Minor Oral Surgery Technics in Dentistry. 1974. 135 min. Sound. Videotape Color. *Sale:* Natl AV Ctr.

Minotaur, The. Trans. Title: Warlords of Crete. Bob Mathias & Rosanna Schiaffino. Directed by Mario Bonnard. 1961. Italy. (Anamorphic). 95 min. Sound. 16mm Color. dubbed. *Rental:* MGM United.

Minstrel Man, The. Orig. Title: Minstrel Melodies. Benny Fields & Gladys George. Directed by Joseph Lewis. 1944. PRC. 80 min. Sound. 16mm B&W. *Rental:* Mogulls Films.

Minstrel Melodies see Minstrel Man.

Minute to Pray, a Second to Die, A. Alex Cord & Arthur Kennedy. Directed by Franco Giraldi. 1968. ABC. 97 min. Sound. 16mm Color. dubbed. *Rental:* Films Inc.

Miracle, The. 1928. Conquest. (Cast unlisted). 60 min. Silent. 16mm B&W. *Rental:* Film Classics. *Sale:* Film Classics. *Rental:* Film Classics, Videotape version.

Miracle, The. Lassie & Skip Homeier. Wrather. 90 min. Sound. 16mm Color. *Rental:* Modern Sound & Roas Films.

Miracle Goes On, The. 1977. Gospel. (Documentary). 75 min. Sound. 16mm Color. *Rental:* Gospel Films.

Miracle in Milan. Paolo Stoppa. Directed by Vittorio De Sica. Ital. 1951. Italy. 95 min. Sound. 16mm B&W. subtitles. *Rental:* Janus Films.

Miracle in the Sand, The: Three Godfathers. Lewis Stone, Walter Brennan & Chester Morris. Directed by Richard Boleslawski. 1936. MGM. 82 min. Sound. 16mm B&W. *Rental:* MGM United.

Miracle Kid, The. Tom Neal & Carol Hughes. Directed by William Beaudine. 1941. PRC. 60 min. Sound. 16mm B&W. *Rental:* Budget Films.

Miracle of Bali *see* Midday Sun.

Miracle of Dr. Petrov, The. Trans. Title: Vo Imya Zhizni. Victor Kokriakov & Nikolai Cherkassov. Directed by Alexander Zharki. Rus. 1947. Russia. 99 min. Sound. 16mm B&W. subtitles. *Rental:* Corinth Films.

Miracle of Faith, The. Jean-Pierre Aumont. Fr. France. 80 min. Sound. 16mm B&W. subtitles. *Rental:* Alba House.

Miracle of Fatima, The. Orig. Title: Miracle of Our Lady of Fatima. Gilbert Roland. Directed by John Brahm. 1952. Warners. 102 min. Sound. 16mm Color. *Rental:* Bosco Films, Cine Craft, Modern Sound & Twyman Films.

Miracle of Lake Placid, The. 1980. ABC. (Documentary). 90 min. Sound. 16mm Color. *Sale:* ABC Learn. *Sale:* ABC Learn, Videotape version.

Miracle of Life, The. 1983. Nova. (Documentary). 57 min. Sound. 16mm Color. *Rental:* U Cal Media.

Miracle of Marcelino *see* Marcelino. Pan y vino.

Miracle of Morgan's Creek, The. Betty Hutton & Eddie Bracken. Directed by Preston Sturges. 1944. Paramount. 99 min. 16mm B&W. *Rental:* Films Inc.

Miracle of Our Lady of Fatima *see* Miracle of Fatima.

Miracle of St. Therese, The. Directed by George Bernier. 1959. Ellis. (Cast unlisted). 90 min. Sound. 16mm B&W. dubbed. *Rental:* Films Inc & Ivy Films.

Miracle of Taxila, The. 1947. James F. Robinson. 49 min. Sound. 16mm Color. *Rental:* Mass Media.

Miracle of the Bells, The. Frank Sinatra & Fred MacMurray. Directed by Irving Pichel. 1948. RKO. 120 min. Sound. 16mm B&W. *Rental:* Ivy Films. *Lease:* Rep Pic Film.

Miracle of the Hills, The. Rex Reason & Nan Leslie. Directed by Paul Landres. 1959. Fox. (Anamorphic). 73 min. Sound. 16mm B&W. *Rental:* Westcoast Films & Willoughby Peer.

Miracle of the White Stallions, The. Robert Taylor, Lilli Palmer & Eddie Albert. Directed by Arthur Hiller. 1963. Disney. 115 min. Sound. 16mm Color. *Rental:* Bosco Films, Buchan Pic, Cine Craft, Cousino Visual Ed, Disney Prod, Elliot Film Co, Film Ctr DC, Film Pres, Films Inc, Modern Sound, Newman Film Lib, Roas Films, Swank Motion, Twyman Films, U of IL Film, Welling Motion Pictures, Westcoast Films & Williams Films.

Miracle of the White Suit, The. Miguelito Gil. Directed by Rafael Gil. 1960. Italy. 94 min. Sound. 16mm B&W. *Rental:* Film Ctr DC, Films Inc & Ivy Films.

Miracle on Main Street, The. Walter Abel & Margo. Directed by Steve Sekely. 1940. Columbia. 78 min. Sound. 16mm B&W. *Rental:* Film Classics & Modern Sound. *Sale:* Blackhawk Films, Super 8 sound version.

Miracle on Thirty-Fourth Street, The. Orig. Title: Big Heart, The. Maureen O'Hara, John Payne & Edmund Gwenn. Directed by George Seaton. 1947. Fox. 96 min. Sound. 16mm B&W. *Rental:* Films Inc.

Miracle Woman, The. Barbara Stanwyck & David Manners. Directed by Frank Capra. 1931. Columbia. 87 min. Sound. 16mm B&W. *Rental:* Kit Parker.

Miracle Worker, The. Anne Bancroft, Patty Duke & Victor Jory. Directed by Arthur Penn. 1962. 107 min. Sound. 16mm B&W. *Rental:* MGM United.

Miracles for Sale. Robert Young & Florence Rice. Directed by Tod Browning. 1939. MGM. 71 min. Sound. 16mm B&W. *Rental:* MGM United.

Mirage. Gregory Peck & Daine Baker. Directed by Edward Dmytryk. 1965. Universal. 109 min. Sound. 16mm B&W. *Rental:* Swank Motion.

Miri. William Shatner, Leonard Nimoy & Kim Darby. Directed by Vincent McEveety. Star Trek. 52 min. Sound. 16mm Color. *Rental:* Em Gee Film Lib, Roas Films, U of IL Film & Westcoast Films. *Sale:* Morcraft Films.

Mirror Crack'd, The. Elizabeth Taylor, Rock Hudson & Angela Lansbury. Directed by Guy Hamilton. 1980. AFD. 105 min. Sound. 16mm Color. *Rental:* Swank Motion.

Mirror of America, The. 1969. NBC. (Documentary). 53 min. Sound. 16mm Color. *Rental:* Films Inc. *Sale:* Films Inc. *Sale:* Films Inc, Videotape version.

Mirror Phase, The. Directed by Carola Klein. 1978. Britain. (Experimental). 47 min. Sound. 16mm Color. *Rental:* Museum Mod Art.

Misadventures of Buster Keaton, The. 1955. (Anthology). 70 min. Sound. 16mm B&W. *Rental:* Budget Films.

Misadventures of Merlin Jones, The. Tommy Kirk & Leon Ames. Directed by Robert Stevenson. 1964. Disney. 91 min. Sound. 16mm Color. *Rental:* Bosco Films, Buchan Pic, Cine Craft, Cousino Visual Ed, Disney Prod, Film Ctr DC, Film Pres, Films Inc, MGM United, Modern Sound, Newman Film Lib, Swank Motion, Twyman Films & U of IL Film.

Misanthrope, Le. Jacques Dumesnil. Directed by Bernard Dheran. France. 55 min. Sound. 16mm B&W. *Rental:* French Am Cul.

Misanthrope, The. Edward Petherbridge. 1976. Britain. 52 min. Sound. 16mm Color. *Rental:* Films Human. *Sale:* Films Human. *Sale:* Films Human, Videotape version.

Mischief. Paul Fraser. Directed by Ian Shand. 1969. Britain. 57 min. Sound. 16mm Color. *Sale:* Arcus Film & Lucerne Films.

Miserables, Les. Michael Rennie & Robert Newton. Directed by Lewis Milestone. 1952. Fox. 104 min. Sound. 16mm B&W. *Rental:* Films Inc & Twyman Films.

Miserables, Les. Richard Jordan & Anthony Perkins. Directed by Glenn Jordan. 1978. Independent Television Corp. 103 min. Sound. 16mm Color. *Rental:* Swank Motion.

Miserables, Les. 1946. 45 min. Sound. 16mm B&W. *Rental:* U Mich Media.

Miserables, Les. Fredric March & Charles Laughton. Directed by Richard Boleslawski. 1935. Fox. 120 min. Sound. 16mm B&W. *Rental:* Films Inc.

Misfit, The. 1965. Gospel. (Documentary). 63 min. Sound. 16mm Color. *Rental:* Roas Films.

Misfits, The. Clark Gable, Marilyn Monroe & Montgomery Clift. Directed by John Huston. 1961. United Artists. 124 min. Sound. 16mm B&W. *Rental:* MGM United. *Rental:* MGM United, Videotape version.

Mislabeled & Unlabeled Deaths: 4 Parts. 1978. Sound. Videotape Color. *Sale:* Natl AV Ctr.

Miss Annie Rooney. Shirley Temple & William Gargan. Directed by Edwin L. Marin. 1942. United Artists. 90 min. Sound. 16mm B&W. *Rental:* Alba House & Charard Motion Pic.

Miss Bluebeard. Bebe Daniels & Raymond Griffith. Directed by Frank Tuttle. 1925. Paramount. 60 min. Silent. 8mm B&W. *Sale:* Select Film.

Miss Goodall & the Baboons of Gombe. 1974. Metromedia. (Documentary). 52 min. Sound. 16mm Color. *Rental:* Films Inc & U Mich Media. *Sale:* Films Inc. *Sale:* Films Inc, Videotape version.

Miss Goodall & the Hyena Story. 1974. Metromedia. (Documentary). 52 min. Sound. 16mm Color. *Rental:* Films Inc & Syracuse U Film. *Sale:* Films Inc. *Sale:* Films Inc, Videotape version.

Miss Goodall & the Lions of Serengeti. Directed by Hugo Van Lawick. 1976. Metromedia. (Documentary). 52 min. Sound. 16mm Color. *Rental:* Syracuse U Film. *Sale:* Films Inc. *Sale:* Films Inc, Videotape version.

Miss Goodall & the Wild Chimpanzees. 1967. National Geographic. (Documentary). 52 min. Sound. 16mm Color. *Rental:* BYU Media, Films Inc, Natl Geog, Syracuse U Film, U of IL Film, U Mich Media & Wholesome Film Ctr. *Sale:* Films Inc & Natl Geog. *Sale:* Natl Geog, Videotape version.

Miss Goodall & the Wild Dogs of Africa. Orig. Title: Wild Dogs of Africa, The. 1972. Metromedia. (Documentary). 52 min. Sound. 16mm Color. *Rental:* Films Inc & U Mich Media. *Sale:* Films Inc. *Sale:* Films Inc, Videotape version.

Miss Grant Takes Richmond. Lucille Ball & William Holden. Directed by Lloyd Bacon. 1949. Columbia. 87 min. Sound. 16mm B&W. *Rental:* Arcus Film, Bosco Films, Budget Films, Films Inc, Modern Sound & Welling Motion Pictures.

Miss Julie. Anita Bjork & Ulf Palme. Directed by Alf Sjoberg. Swed. 1950. Sweden. 90 min. Sound. 16mm B&W. subtitles. *Rental:* Janus Films & New Cinema.

Miss Julie. Patrick Stewart & Lisa Harrow. 1977. Miami-Dade. 60 min. Videotape Color. *Sale:* Films Inc.

Miss Lulu Bett. Lois Wilson, Milton Sills & Theodore Roberts. Directed by William DeMille. 1921. Paramount. 99 min. Silent. 16mm B&W. *Rental:* Em Gee Film Lib & Museum Mod Art.

Miss Pacific Fleet. Joan Blondell & Glenda Farrell. Directed by Ray Enright. 1935. Warners. 76 min. Sound. 16mm B&W. *Rental:* MGM United.

Miss Pinkerton. Joan Blondell & George Brent. Directed by Lloyd Bacon. 1932. Warners. 66 min. Sound. 16mm B&W. *Rental:* MGM United.

Miss Polly. ZaSu Pitts & Slim Summerville. Directed by Fred Guiol. 1941. Hal Roach. 50 min. Sound. 16mm B&W. *Rental:* Roas Films.

Miss Sadie Thompson. Rita Hayworth, Jose Ferrer & Aldo Ray. Directed by Curtis Bernhardt. 1953. Columbia. 91 min. Sound. 16mm Color. *Rental:* Cine Craft, Films Inc, Kit Parker, Welling Motion Pictures & Williams Films.

Miss Tatlock's Millions. Wanda Hendrix & John Lund. Directed by Richard Haydn. 1948. Paramount. 101 min. Sound. 16mm B&W. *Rental:* Swank Motion.

Missile Base at Taniak. Bill Henry & Susan Morrow. Directed by Franklin Adreon. 1953. Republic. 100 min. Sound. 16mm B&W. *Rental:* Ivy Films. *Sale:* Rep Pic Film.

Missile Monster. Walter Reed & Lois Collier. Directed by Fred C. Brannon. 1958. Republic. 75 min. Sound. 16mm B&W. *Rental:* Ivy Films. *Sale:* Rep Pic Film.

Missile to the Moon. Richard Travis & Cathy Downs. Directed by Richard Cunha. 1958. Astor. 80 min. Sound. 16mm B&W. *Lease:* Budget Films, Ivy Films, Roas Films & Video Comm. *Rental:* Video Comm, Videotape version.

Missiles of October, The. Martin Sheen & Ralph Bellamy. 1974. CBS. 156 min. Sound. 16mm Color. *Rental:* Budget Films, Films Inc, Kent St U Film, Kit Parker, Maljack, Modern Sound, Roas Films, Syracuse U Film, Twyman Films, U of IL Film, U Mich Media, Welling Motion Pictures & Wholesome Film Ctr. *Rental:* Learning Corp Am, *Lease:* Learning Corp Am, Videotape version.

Missing. Jack Lemmon, Sissy Spacek & John Shea. Directed by Costa-Gavras. 1985. Universal. 122 min. Sound. 16mm Color. *Rental:* Swank Motion. *Rental:* Swank Motion, Videotape version.

Missing Corpse, The. J. Edward Bromberg. Directed by Al Herman. 1945. PRC. 70 min. Sound. 16mm B&W. *Rental:* Mogulls Films. *Sale:* Rep Pic Film & Classics Assoc NY.

Missing Girls. Roger Pryor & Muriel Evans. Directed by Phil Rosen. 1937. Chesterfield. 70 min. Sound. 16mm B&W. *Rental:* Modern Sound.

Missing Juror, The. George Macready & Janis Carter. Directed by Budd Boetticher. 1944. Columbia. 71 min. Sound. 16mm B&W. *Rental:* Kit Parker.

Missing Link, The. 1972. Britain. (Documentary). 52 min. Sound. 16mm Color. *Rental:* Time-Life Multimedia. *Sale:* Time-Life Multimedia. *Rental:* Time-Life Multimedia, *Sale:* Time-Life Multimedia, Spanish language version. *Sale:* Time-Life Multimedia, Videotape version.

Missing Witness. John Litel & Dick Purcell. Directed by William Clemens. 1937. Warners. 61 min. Sound. 16mm B&W. *Rental:* MGM United.

Missing Woman. Penny Edwards & James Millican. Directed by Philip Ford. 1951. Republic. 60 min. Sound. 16mm B&W. *Rental:* Ivy Films. *Sale:* Rep Pic Film.

Mission Batangas. Dennis Weaver & Vera Miles. Directed by Keith Larsen. 1968. Diba. 100 min. Sound. 16mm B&W. *Rental:* Welling Motion Pictures & Westcoast Films.

Mission in Morocco. Lex Barker & Fernando Rey. Directed by Anthony Squire. 1959. Britain. 71 min. Sound. 16mm B&W. *Rental:* Corinth Films & Film Ctr DC. *Lease:* Corinth Films.

Mission: Mind Control. 1979. ABC. (Documentary). 52 min. Sound. 16mm Color. *Rental:* MTI Tele & Syracuse U Film. *Sale:* MTI Tele. *Sale:* MTI Tele, Videotape version.

Mission of Danger. Keith Larsen & Taing Elg. Directed by George Waggner. 1959. MGM. 83 min. Sound. 16mm Color. *Rental:* MGM United.

Mission of Fear. 1973. Canada. (Documentary). 80 min. Sound. 16mm B&W. *Rental:* U Cal Media.

Mission Over Korea. Orig. Title: Eyes of the Skies. John Hodiak & John Derek. Directed by Fred F. Sears. 1953. Columbia. 86 min. Sound. 16mm B&W. *Rental:* Inst Cinema & Modern Sound.

Mission Stardust. Essy Persson & Lang Jeffries. Directed by Primo Zeglio. 1968. Times. 95 min. Sound. 16mm Color. dubbed. *Rental:* Films Inc.

Mission to Mars. Darren McGavin & Nick Adams. Directed by Nicholas Webster. 1967. Sagittarius. 91 min. Sound. 16mm Color. *Rental:* Westcoast Films, Wholesome Film Ctr & Willoughby Peer.

Mission to Moscow. Walter Huston & Ann Harding. Directed by Michael Curtiz. 1943. Warners. 124 min. Sound. 16mm B&W. *Rental:* MGM United.

Missionary, The. Michael Palin, Maggie Smith & Trevor Howard. Directed by Richard Loncraine. 1982. Columbia. 86 min. Sound. 16mm Color. *Rental:* Swank Motion.

Mississippi. Bing Crosby & W. C. Fields. Directed by Edward Sutherland. 1935. Paramount. 64 min. Sound. 16mm B&W. *Rental:* Swank Motion.

Mississippi Gambler. Tyrone Power & Piper Laurie. Directed by Rudolph Mate. 1953. Universal. 98 min. Sound. 16mm Color. *Rental:* Swank Motion.

Mississippi Mermaid. Jean-Paul Belmondo & Catherine Deneuve. Directed by Francois Truffaut. Fr. 1970. France. (Anamorphic). 110 min. Sound. 16mm Color. subtitles. *Rental:* MGM United.

Mississippi Rhythm. Joan Davis. Directed by Derwin Abrahams. 1949. Monogram. 68 min. Sound. 16mm B&W. *Rental:* Hurlock Cine.

Mississippi Summer. Directed by Bill Byers. 1972. (Cast unlisted). 88 min. Sound. 16mm Color. *Rental:* New Line Cinema.

Missouri Breaks, The. Marlon Brando & Jack Nicholson. Directed by Arthur Penn. 1976. United Artists. 85 min. Sound. 16mm Color. *Rental:* Budget Films, Films Inc, MGM United, Roas Films, Westcoast Films & Wholesome Film Ctr. *Rental:* MGM United, 126 min. version. *Rental:* MGM United, Videotape version.

Missouri Outlaw, The. Don Barry. Directed by Edwin L. Marin. 1941. Republic. 85 min. Sound. 16mm B&W. *Rental:* Ivy Films.

Missouri Traveler, The. Lee Marvin & Brandon De Wilde. Directed by Jerry Hopper. 1958. Whitney. 103 min. Sound. 16mm Color. *Rental:* Alba House, Swank Motion & Film Ctr DC.

Missourians, The. Monte Hale. Directed by George Blair. 1950. Republic. 60 min. Sound. 16mm B&W. *Rental:* Ivy Films. *Sale:* Rep Pic Film & Nostalgia Merchant.

Mr. Ace. George Raft & Sylvia Sidney. Directed by Edwin L. Marin. 1946. United Artists. 90 min. Sound. 16mm B&W. *Sale:* Classics Assoc NY.

Mr. Adler & the Opera. 1983. EBE. (Documentary). 59 min. Sound. 16mm Color. *Sale:* Ency Brit Ed & Syracuse U Film. *Rental:* Ency Brit Ed. *Sale:* Ency Brit Ed, Videotape version.

Mr. & Mrs. Smith. Carole Lombard & Robert Montgomery. Directed by Alfred Hitchcock. 1941. RKO. 95 min. Sound. 16mm B&W. *Rental:* Films Inc.

Mr. Arkadin. Orig. Title: Confidential Report. Orson Welles, Sir Michael Redgrave. Directed by Orson Welles. 1955. Britain. 99 min. Sound. 16mm B&W. *Rental:* Budget Films, Corinth Films & Images Film. *Sale:* Corinth Films & Festival Films. *Lease:* Corinth Films. *Sale:* Festival Films, Videotape version.

Mr. Aspin & the Pentagon. 1977. Wayne Ewing. (Documentary). 55 min. Sound. 16mm Color. *Rental:* W Ewing Films. *Sale:* W Ewing Films.

Mister Belden's Amazing Gasmobile see Excuse My Dust.

Mr. Belvedere Goes to College. Clifton Webb & Shirley Temple. Directed by Elliott Nugent. 1949. Fox. 84 min. Sound. 16mm B&W. *Rental:* Films Inc, Welling Motion Pictures & Willoughby Peer.

Mr. Belvedere Rings the Bell. Orig. Title: Belvedere Rings the Bell. Clifton Webb & Zero Mostel. Directed by Henry Koster. 1951. Fox. 87 min. Sound. 16mm B&W. *Rental:* Films Inc.

Mr. Billion. Terrence Hill & Valerie Perrine. Directed by Jonathan Kaplan. 1977. Fox. 93 min. Sound. 16mm Color. *Rental:* Williams Films & Twyman Films.

Mr. Blandings Builds His Dream House. Cary Grant, Myrna Loy & Melvyn Douglas. Directed by H. C. Potter. 1948. RKO. 94 min. Sound. 16mm B&W. *Rental:* Films Inc.

Mr. Boggs Steps Out. Stuart Erwin & Toby Wing. Directed by Gordon Wiles. 1938. Grand National. 61 min. Sound. 16mm B&W. *Rental:* Film Classics & Mogulls Films.

Mister Buddwing. Orig. Title: Woman Without a Face. James Garner & Suzanne Pleshette. Directed by Delbert Mann. 1966. MGM. 100 min. Sound. 16mm B&W. *Rental:* MGM United.

Mister Bug Goes to Town see Hoppity Goes to Town.

Mister Celebrity see Turf Boy.

Mr. Chump. Johnnie Davis, Lola Lane & Penny Singleton. Directed by William Clemens. 1938. Warners. 60 min. Sound. 16mm B&W. *Rental:* MGM United.

Mister Cinderella see Movie Struck.

Mr. Cohen Takes a Walk. Orig. Title: Father Takes a Walk. Paul Graetz. Directed by William Beaudine. 1936. Warners. 81 min. Sound. 16mm B&W. *Rental:* MGM United.

Mister Cory. Tony Curtis & Charles Bickford. Directed by Blake Edwards. 1957. Universal. 92 min. Sound. 16mm Color. *Rental:* Swank Motion.

Mr. Deeds Goes to Town. Gary Cooper & Jean Arthur. Directed by Frank Capra. 1936. Columbia. 118 min. Sound. 16mm B&W. *Rental:* Arcus Film, Bosco Films, Budget Films, Cine Craft, Film Ctr DC, Films Inc, Images Film, Ivy Films, Kit Parker, Modern Sound, Natl Film Video, Roas Films, Swank Motion, Twyman Films, U of IL Film, Video Comm, Welling Motion Pictures, Wholesome Film Ctr, Williams Films & Willoughby Peer.

Mr. Dickens of London. 1967. ABC. (Documentary). 52 min. Sound. 16mm Color. *Rental:* McGraw-Hill Films. *Sale:* McGraw-Hill Films.

Mr. Dodd Takes the Air. Kenny Baker & Jane Wyman. Directed by Alfred E. Green. 1937. Warners. 90 min. Sound. 16mm B&W. *Rental:* MGM United.

Mr. Doodle Kicks Off. Jack Carson & Ben Alexander. Directed by Leslie Goodwins. 1939. RKO. 76 min. Sound. 16mm B&W. *Rental:* RKO General Pics.

Mister Eight Hundred & Eighty. Burt Lancaster & Edmund Gwenn. Directed by Edmund Goulding. 1950. Fox. 90 min. Sound. 16mm B&W. *Rental:* Films Inc.

Mr. Emmanuel. Felix Aylmer & Greta Gynt. Directed by Harold French. 1945. Britain. 90 min. Sound. 16mm B&W. *Rental:* Budget Films, Films Inc, Kit Parker & Learning Corp Am. *Sale:* Learning Corp Am.

Mr. Europe & the Common Market. 1962. CBS. (Documentary). 51 min. Sound. 16mm B&W. *Rental:* U of IL Film. *Sale:* Carousel Films.

Mister Freedom. Donald Pleasance & Delphine Seyrig. Directed by William Klein. 1968. France. 95 min. Sound. 16mm Color. dubbed. *Rental:* Grove.

Mister Griggs Returns see Cockeyed Miracle.

Mr. Hex. Bowery Boys. Directed by William Beaudine. 1946. Monogram. 63 min. Sound. 16mm B&W. *Rental:* Modern Sound & Film Ctr DC.

Mr. Hobbs Takes a Vacation. James Stewart & Maureen O'Hara. Directed by Henry Koster. 1962. Fox. 116 min. Sound. 16mm Color. *Rental:* Williams Films, Films Inc & Twyman Films. *Rental:* Films Inc, Anamorphic version.

Mr. Horatio Knibbles. 1973. Britain. (Cast unlisted). 60 min. Sound. 16mm Color. *Sale:* Lucerne Films.

Mr. Hulot's Holiday. Trans. Title: Vacances de Monsieur Hulot, Les. Jacques Tati. Directed by Jacques Tati. 1954. France. 85 min. Sound. 16mm B&W. dubbed. *Rental:* Budget Films, Corinth Films, Em Gee Film Lib, Images Film, Ivy Films, Natl Film Video, Liberty Co & Wholesome Film Ctr. *Sale:* Images Film, Glenn Photo, Natl Cinema & Reel Images. *Sale:* Em Gee Film Lib, Tamarelles French Film & Images Film, Videotape version. *Sale:* Festival Films, 92 min. Videotape version, Super 8 sound version. *Sale:* Reel Images,

Mr. Imperium. Ezio Pinza & Lana Turner. Directed by Don Hartman. 1951. MGM. 87 min. Sound. 16mm Color. *Rental:* MGM United.

Mr. Justice Douglas. 1972. Carousel. (Documentary). 52 min. Sound. 16mm B&W. *Rental:* U Cal Media, Iowa Films, U Mich Media & Syracuse U Film. *Sale:* Carousel Films.

Mister Kingstreet's War. John Saxon. Directed by Percival Rubens. 1973. Gold Key. 95 min. Sound. 16mm Color. dubbed. *Rental:* Budget Films & Video Comm. *Rental:* Video Comm, *Lease:* Video Comm, Videotape version.

Mr. Klein. Alain Delon & Jeanne Moreau. Directed by Joseph Losey. 1977. Quartet. 122 min. Sound. 16mm Color. subtitles. *Rental:* Films Inc.

Mr. Lucky. Cary Grant & Laraine Day. Directed by H. C. Potter. 1943. RKO. 100 min. Sound. 16mm B&W. *Rental:* Films Inc.

Mr. Ludwig's Tropical Dreamland. 1980. 57 min. Sound. 16mm Color. *Rental:* U Mich Media.

Mister Magoo at Sea see Magoo at Sea.

Mr. Magoo in One Thousand & One Arabian Nights. Orig. Title: Mr. Magoo's Arabian Nights. Directed by Jack Kenney. 1959. Columbia. (Animated). 76 min. Sound. 16mm Color. *Rental:* Arcus Film, Bosco Films, Buchan Pic, Budget Films, Cine Craft, Charard Motion Pics, Film Ctr DC, Film Pres, Films Inc, Modern Sound, Newman Film Lib, Roas Films, Welling Motion Pictures, Westcoast Films, Wholesome Film Ctr & Williams Films.

Mister Magoo in the King's Service see Magoo in the King's Service.

Mr. Magoo: Man of Mystery. 1964. UPA. (Animated, anthology). 96 min. Sound. 16mm Color. *Rental:* Budget Films, Film Ctr DC, Kerr Films & Westcoast Films.

Mr. Magoo's Arabian Nights see Mr. Magoo in One Thousand & One Arabian Nights.

Mr. Magoo's Christmas. Directed by Abe Levitow. 1967. UPA. (Animated Anthology). 52 min. Sound. 16mm Color. *Rental:* Budget Films.

Mr. Magoo's Favorite Heroes. 1964. UPA. (Animated, anthology). 96 min. Sound. 16mm Color. *Rental:* Budget Films, Films Inc, Modern Sound & Westcoast Films.

Mister Magoo's Snow White see Snow White with Mr. Magoo.

Mr. Magoo's Storybook. 1964. UPA. (Animated, Anthology). 113 min. Sound. 16mm Color. *Rental:* Westcoast Films.

Mr. Magoo's Three Musketeers. 1965. UPA. (Animated). 50 min. Sound. 16mm Color. *Rental:* Films Inc, Syracuse U Film, Welling Motion Pictures & Westcoast Films. *Sale:* Macmillan Films.

Mister Magoo's Treasure Island see Treasure Island.

Mr. Majestyk. Charles Bronson. Directed by Richard Fleischer. 1974. United Artists. 104 min. Sound. 16mm Color. *Rental:* Budget Films, MGM United, Westcoast Films & Welling Motion Pictures.

Mr. Mom. Michael Keaton & Teri Garr. Directed by Stan Dragoti. 1983. Fox. 95 min. Sound. 16mm Color. *Rental:* Films Inc.

Mister Moses. Robert Mitchum & Carroll Baker. Directed by Ronald Neame. 1965. United Artists. 113 min. Sound. 16mm Color. *Rental:* MGM United.

Mr. Moto Takes a Vacation. Peter Lorre. Directed by Norman Foster. 1939. Fox. 90 min. Sound. 16mm B&W. *Rental:* Films Inc.

Mr. Moto's Last Warning. Peter Lorre & Ricardo Cortez. Directed by Norman Foster. 1939. Fox. 71 min. Sound. 16mm B&W. *Rental:* Budget Films & Classic Film Mus. *Sale:* Festival Films, Film Classics & Reel Images. *Sale:* Reel Images, Super 8 sound version. *Sale:* Festival Films, Videotape version.

Mr. Muggs Steps Out. Bowery Boys. Directed by William Beaudine. 1943. Monogram. 63 min. Sound. 16mm B&W. *Rental:* Modern Sound.

Mr. Music. Bing Crosby & Nancy Olson. Directed by Richard Haydn. 1950. Paramount. 113 min. Sound. 16mm B&W. *Rental:* Films Inc.

Mr. Peabody & the Mermaid. William Powell & Ann Blyth. Directed by Irving Pichel. 1948. Universal. 89 min. Sound. 16mm B&W. *Rental:* Budget Films & Ivy Films. *Sale:* Rep Pic Film. *Sale:* Tamarelles French Film, Videotape version.

Mr. Perrin & Mr. Traill. Marius Goring & David Farrar. Directed by Lawrence Huntington. 1948. Britain. 90 min. Sound. 16mm B&W. *Rental:* Budget Films.

Mr. President, Mr. President. 58 min. Sound. Videotape Color. *Rental:* PBS Video. *Sale:* PBS Video.

Mr. Quilp. Orig. Title: Old Curiosity Shop, Ye. Anthony Newley & David Hemmings. Directed by Michael Tuchner. 1975. Embassy. 118 min. Sound. 16mm Color. *Rental:* Swank Motion. *Sale:* Blackhawk Films.

Mr. Reeder in Room Thirteen. Orig. Title: Mystery of Room 13. Gibb McLaughlin & Sara Seeger. Directed by Norman Lee. 1938. Britain. 66 min. Sound. 16mm B&W. *Rental:* Ivy Films & Mogulls Films. *Sale:* Rep Pic Film.

Mr. Ricco. Dean Martin. Directed by Paul Bogart. 1975. MGM. (Anamorphic). 98 min. Sound. 16mm Color. *Rental:* MGM United.

Mister Roberts. Henry Fonda, James Cagney & Jack Lemmon. 1955. Warners. 123 min. Sound. 16mm Color. *Rental:* Arcus Films Inc, Charard Motions Pics, Williams Films, Swank Motion, Film DC, Trans-World Films, Twyman Films, Westcoast Films & Welling Motion Pictures.

Mr. Robinson Crusoe. Douglas Fairbanks. Directed by Edward Sutherland. 1932. United Artists. (Music & Sound Effects Only). 70 min. Sound. 16mm B&W. *Rental:* Budget Films, Classic Film Mus, Em Gee Film Lib, Kerr Film, Museum Mod Art & Willoughby Peer. *Sale:* Blackhawk Films, Classic Film Museum, Cinema Concepts, E Finney, Griggs Movie & Natl Cinema. *Rental:* Killiam Collect, Tinted version. *Rental:* Ivy Films, *Sale:* Blackhawk Films & Ivy Films, Super 8 sound version. *Sale:* Blackhawk Films, Super 8 silent version. *Sale:* Blackhawk Films, Silent 8mm version.

Mister Rock & Roll. Alan Freed. Directed by Charles Dubin. 1957. Paramount. 86 min. Sound. 16mm B&W. *Rental:* Films Inc.

Mister Rogers Talks with Parents About Competition. 58 min. Sound. Videotape Color. *Rental:* PBS Videotape. *Sale:* PBS Video.

Mister Rogers Talks with Parents About Divorce. 58 min. Sound. Videotape Color. *Rental:* PBS Video. *Sale:* PBS Video.

Mr. Rooney Goes to Work. 1978. CBS. (Documentary). 53 min. Sound. 16mm Color. *Rental:* La Inst Res Ctr, Phoenix Films & U of IL Film. *Sale:* Phoenix Films. *Sale:* Phoenix Films, Videotape version.

Mr. Rossi Looks for Happiness. Directed by Bruno Bozzetto. 1977. Italy. (Animated). 75 min. Sound. 16mm Color. dubbed. *Rental:* Distribution Sixteen.

Mr. Sardonicus. Ronald Lewis & Oscar Homolka. Directed by William Castle. 1961. Columbia. 89 min. Sound. 16mm B&W. *Rental:* Williams Films, Inst Cinema & Modern Sound.

Mister Scoutmaster. Clifton Webb & Edmund Gwenn. Directed by Henry Levin. 1953. Fox. 87 min. Sound. 16mm B&W. *Rental:* Films Inc.

Mr. Skeffington. Bette Davis & Claude Rains. Directed by Vincent Sherman. 1944. Warners. 127 min. Sound. 16mm B&W. *Rental:* MGM United.

Mr. Smith Goes to Washington. James Stewart & Jean Arthur. Directed by Frank Capra. 1939. Columbia. 95 min. Sound. 16mm B&W. *Rental:* Budget Films, Cine Craft, Film Ctr DC, Films Inc, Inst Cinema, Images Film, Kit Parker, Modern Sound, Mogulls Films, Natl Film Video, Roas Films, Swank Motion, Twyman Films, U of IL Film, Video Comm, Welling Motion Pictures, Wholesome Film Ctr & Willoughby Peer. *Rental:* Bosco Films, 130 mins version. *Rental:* Swank Motion, Videotape version.

Mr. Soft Touch. Glenn Ford & Evelyn Keyes. Directed by Henry Levin & Gordon Douglas. 1949. Columbia. 93 min. Sound. 16mm B&W. *Rental:* Maljack. *Lease:* Maljack. *Lease:* Maljack, Videotape version.

Mr. Speaker: A Portrait of Tip O'Neill. Directed by Nancy Porter. 1978. WGBH. (Documentary). 58 min. Sound. 16mm Color. *Rental:* Films Inc. *Sale:* Films inc. *Sale:* Films Inc, Videotape version.

Mr. Superinvisible. Dean Jones & Gastone Moschin. Directed by Anthony Dawson. 1973. 90 min. Sound. 16mm Color. *Rental:* Films Inc, Roas Films & Welling Motion Pictures.

Mr. Symbol Man. Orig. Title: Symbol Man, The. 1975. Canada. (Documentary). 49 min. Sound. 16mm Color. *Rental:* Benchmark Films, U Cal Media & Natl Film CN, 8mm version avail. version.

Mr. Too Little. Rossano Brazzi & Carmine Caridi. Directed by Stuart McGowan. Italy. 90 min. Sound. 16mm Color. dubbed. *Rental:* Williams Films.

Mr. Universe. Bert Lahr & Jack Carson. Directed by Joseph Lerner. 1951. Eagle Lion. 79 min. Sound. 16mm B&W. *Rental:* Budget Films.

Mister V *see* Pimpernell Smith.

Mr. Walkie Talkie. William Tracy & Joe Sawyer. Directed by Fred Guiol. 1952. Lippert. 65 min. Sound. 16mm B&W. *Rental:* Budget Films & Film Ctr DC.

Mr. Winkle Goes to War. Orig. Title: Arms & the Woman. Edward G. Robinson & Ruth Warrick. Directed by Alfred E. Green. 1944. Columbia. 80 min. Sound. 16mm B&W. *Rental:* Cine Craft & Welling Motion Pictures.

Mr. Wise Guy. East Side Kids. Directed by William Nigh. 1941. Monogram. 60 min. Sound. 16mm B&W. *Rental:* Budget Films & Mogulls Films.

Mister Wong at Headquarters *see* Fatal Hour.

Mr. Wong, Detective. Boris Karloff. Directed by William Nigh. 1938. Monogram. 60 min. Sound. 16mm B&W. *Rental:* Budget Films, Mogulls Films & MGM United. *Sale:* Natl Cinema.

Mr. Wong in Chinatown. Boris Karloff & Grant Withers. Directed by William Nigh. 1939. Monogram. 70 min. Sound. 16mm B&W. *Rental:* MGM United.

Mr. Wu. Lon Chaney. Directed by William Nigh. 1927. MGM. 90 min. Silent. 16mm B&W. *Rental:* MGM United.

Mistress, The. Hideko Takamine & Hiroshi Akutagawa. Directed by Shiro Toyoda. Jap. 1953. Japan. 106 min. Sound. 16mm B&W. subtitles. *Rental:* Films Inc.

Mistress of the Mountains, The. Vivi Gioli. Ital. 1953. Italy. 90 min. Sound. 16mm B&W. subtitles. *Rental:* Film Classics. *Rental:* Film Classics, Videotape version.

Mistress Pamela. Anna Quayle. Directed by Jim O'Connolly. 1973. Fanfare. 91 min. Sound. 16mm Color. *Rental:* Budget Films & Films Inc.

Misty. David Ladd & Arthur O'Connell. Directed by James B. Clark. 1961. Fox. 92 min. Sound. 16mm Color. *Rental:* Budget Films, Films Inc & Westcoast Films.

Misty Wharf *see* Port of Shadows.

Misunderstanding China. 1972. CBS. (Documentary). 52 min. Sound. 16mm Color. *Rental:* U Mich Media & Utah Media.

Mitchell. Joe Don Baker & Martin Balsam. Directed by Andrew V. McLaglen. 1975. Allied Artists. 96 min. Sound. 16mm Color. *Rental:* Hurlock Cine.

Mix Me a Person. Anne Baxter & Donald Sinden. Directed by Leslie Norman. 1961. Britain. 108 min. Sound. 16mm B&W. *Rental:* Ivy Films.

Mixed Company. Barbara Harris & Joseph Bologna. Directed by Melville Shavelson. 1974. United Artists. 109 min. Sound. 16mm Color. *Rental:* MGM United.

Moana. Directed by Robert Flaherty. 1926. Paramount. (Documentary). 85 min. Silent. 16mm B&W. *Rental:* Films Inc.

Mob, The. Broderick Crawford & Richard Kiley. Directed by Robert Parrish. 1951. Columbia. 87 min. Sound. 16mm B&W. *Rental:* Kit Parker.

Mob Town. Dead End Kids. Directed by William Nigh. 1941. Universal. 60 min. Sound. 16mm B&W. *Rental:* Swank Motion.

Moby Dick. John Barrymore & Joan Bennett. Directed by Lloyd Bacon. 1930. Warners. 77 min. Sound. 16mm B&W. *Rental:* MGM United.

Moby Dick. Gregory Peck & Richard Basehart. Directed by John Huston. 1956. United Artists. 116 min. Sound. 16mm Color. *Rental:* MGM United. *Sale:* Tamarelles French Film, Videotape version.

Moby Dick. (Animated). 55 min. Sound. 16mm Color. *Rental:* Budget Films, Modern Sound, Roas Films, Westcoast Films & Williams Films.

Moby Dick. Directed by Zoran Tanzic. 1971. Australia. (Animated). 60 min. Sound. 16mm Color. *Rental:* Wholesome Film Ctr.

Mock Trial, A: "In Re Roger Ackroyd". 1980. (Cast unlisted). 140 min. Videotape Color. *Rental:* Concern Dying. *Sale:* Concern Dying.

Mock Turtle Soup. 1976. Image Union. (Experimental). 60 min. Videotape Color. *Rental:* Electro Art. *Lease:* Electro Art.

Mockery. Lon Chaney. Directed by Benjamin Christiansen. 1927. MGM. 75 min. Silent. 16mm B&W. *Rental:* Films Inc.

Model, The. Directed by Frederick Wiseman. 1980. Zipporah. (Documentary). 129 min. Sound. 16mm B&W. *Rental:* Zipporah Films. *Lease:* Zipporah Films. *Rental:* Zipporah Films, Videotape version.

Model & the Marriage Broker, The. Jeanne Crain, Thelma Ritter & Zero Mostel. Directed by George Cukor. 1951. Fox. 103 min. Sound. 16mm B&W. *Rental:* Films Inc.

Model Shop, The. Anouk Aimee & Gary Lockwood. Directed by Jacques Demy. 1969. Columbia. 96 min. Sound. 16mm Color. *Rental:* Films Inc, Modern Sound & Welling Motion Pictures.

Moderato Cantabile. Jeanne Moreau & Jean-Paul Belmondo. Directed by Peter Brook. Fr. 1960. France. 93 min. Sound. 16mm B&W. subtitles. *Rental:* Swank Motion.

Modern Corporation, A. 2 pts. 1963. Indiana University. (Lecture). 58 min. Sound. 16mm B&W. *Rental:* U Cal Media.

Modern Hero, A. Richard Barthelmess & Jean Muir. Directed by G. W. Pabst. 1934. Warners. 70 min. Sound. 16mm B&W. *Rental:* MGM United.

Modern Miracle, The *see* Story of Alexander Graham Bell.

Modern Musketeer, A. Douglas Fairbanks. Directed by Allan Dwan. 1918. Artcraft. 65 min. Silent. 16mm B&W. *Rental:* Em Gee Film Lib. *Sale:* Glenn Photo. *Sale:* Glenn Photo, Super 8 silent version.

Modern Problems. Chevy Chase. Directed by Ken Shapiro. Fox. 93 min. Sound. 16mm Color. *Rental:* Williams Films.

Modern Romance, A. Albert Brooks & Kathryn Harold. Directed by Albert Brooks. 1981. Columbia. 93 min. Sound. 16mm Color. *Rental:* Swank Motion. *Rental:* Swank Motion, Videotape version.

Modern Times. Charles Chaplin & Paulette Goddard. Directed by Charles Chaplin. 1936. United Artists. 89 min. Sound. B&W. *Rental:* Films Inc. *Lease:* Cinema Concepts & Glenn Photo, Videotape version.

Modern Women: The Uneasy Life. 1967. NET. (Documentary). 60 min. Sound. 16mm B&W. *Rental:* Indiana AV Ctr, Mass Media & U Mich Media. *Sale:* Indiana AV Ctr.

Modern X-Ray Tubes: Part 1. 1982. 50 min. Sound. Videotape Color. *Sale:* Natl AV Ctr.

Modesty Blaise. Monica Vitti & Terence Stamp. Directed by Joseph Losey. 1966. Fox. 119 min. Sound. 16mm Color. *Rental:* Films Inc.

Module One: Change. 58 min. Sound. Videotape Color. *Rental:* PBS Video. *Sale:* PBS Video.

Mogambo. Clark Gable, Ava Gardner & Grace Kelly. Directed by John Ford. 1953. MGM. 116 min. Sound. 16mm Color. *Rental:* MGM United. *Rental:* MGM United, Videotape version.

Mohammad, Messenger of God. Anthony Quinn & Irene Papas. Directed by Moustapha Akkad. 1977. Filmco International. 180 min. Sound. 16mm Color. *Rental:* Films Inc & Twyman Films.

Mohawk. Scott Brady & Rita Gam. Directed by Kurt Neumann. 1956. Fox. 80 min. Sound. 16mm Color. *Rental:* Charard Motion Pics, Westcoast Films & Willoughby Peer.

Mojave Firebrand. Bill Elliott. Directed by Spencer G. Bennett. 1944. Republic. 55 min. Sound. 16mm B&W. *Rental:* Ivy Films. *Sale:* Rep Pic Film.

Mokey. Bobby Blake & Donna Reed. Directed by Wells Root. 1942. MGM. 88 min. Sound. 16mm B&W. *Rental:* MGM United.

Mokil. 1974. Special Purpose. (Documentary). 61 min. Sound. 16mm Color. *Rental:* U Cal Media & U Mich Media.

Molders of Troy. 1980. PBS. (Documentary). 59 min. Sound. 16mm Color. *Rental:* PBS Video.

Mole People, The. John Agar. Directed by Virgil Vogel. 1956. Universal. 78 min. Sound. 16mm B&W. *Rental:* Swank Motion.

Moliere. France. (Cast unlisted). 60 min. Sound. 16mm B&W. *Rental:* French Am Cul.

Moliere: The Misanthrope-the Comedy of Manners. Cyril Ritchard. 1975. Films for the Humanities. 49 min. Sound. 16mm Color. *Rental:* Films Human & U of IL Film. *Sale:* Films Human.

Molly. Orig. Title: Goldbergs, The. Gertrude Berg & Edward Franz. Directed by Walter Hart. 1950. Paramount. 75 min. Sound. 16mm B&W. *Rental:* Films Inc.

Molly & Me. Gracie Fields & Monty Woolley. Directed by Lewis Seiler. 1945. Fox. 75 min. Sound. 16mm B&W. *Rental:* Films Inc.

Molly Maguires, The. Sean Connery & Richard Harris. Directed by Martin Ritt. 1970. Paramount. (Anamorphic). 123 min. Sound. 16mm Color. *Rental:* Films Inc.

Mollycoddle, The. Douglas Fairbanks & Wallace Beery. Directed by Victor Fleming. 1920. United Artists. 94 min. Silent. 16mm B&W. *Rental:* A Twyman Pres & Museum Mod Art.

Mom & Dad Can't Hear Me. Rosanna Arquette. Directed by Daniel Wilson. 1978. Time-Life. 47 min. Sound. 16mm Color. *Rental:* D Wilson, U of IL Film & U Mich Media.

Mom, I Want to Come Home Now. Directed by Fleming Fuller. 1980. Corinth. 60 min. Sound. 16mm Color. *Rental:* Corinth Films.

Moment by Moment. John Travolta & Lily Tomlin. Directed by Jane Wagner. 1978. Universal. 103 min. Sound. 16mm Color. *Rental:* Williams Films.

Moment in Time, A. 1976. Gould. (Documentary). 53 min. Sound. 16mm Color. *Rental:* Budget Films. *Sale:* Lucerne Films. *Rental:* Lucerne Films, Videotape version.

Moment of Truth, The. Miguel Mateo & Pedro Basauri. Directed by Francesco Rosi. Span. 1965. Sound. 16mm Color. subtitles Eng. *Rental:* Films Inc.

Moment to Moment. Jean Seberg & Honor Blackman. Directed by Mervyn LeRoy. 1966. Universal. 108 min. Sound. 16mm Color. *Rental:* Swank Motion.

Moments. Keith Michell. Britain. 105 min. Sound. 16mm Color. *Rental:* Video Comm.

Mommie Dearest. Faye Dunaway & Diana Scarwid. Directed by Frank Perry. 1981. Paramount. 129 min. Sound. 16mm Color. *Rental:* Films Inc.

Mon Oncle. Trans. Title: My Uncle. Jacques Tati, Jeanne-Pierre Zola & Alain Becourt. Directed by Jacques Tati. 1958. France. 108 min. Sound. 16mm Color. dubbed. *Rental:* Budget Films & Images Film. *Sale:* Festival Films & Natl Cinema. *Sale:* Festival Films, Videotape version.

Momugi Pass. Shinobu Otake & Mieko Harada. Directed by Satsuyo Yamaoto. Rel. 1979. Japan. 154 min. Sound. Color. *Sale:* Tamarelles French Film, Videotape version.

Mon Oncle D'Amerique. Gerard Depardieu & Nicole Garcia. Directed by Alain Resnais. Fr. 1981. New World. 123 min. Sound. 16mm Color. subtitles. *Rental:* Films Inc.

Moncada Program, The. Directed by Octavio Cortazar. Span. 1974. Cuba. (Documentary). 51 min. Sound. 16mm B&W. subtitles. *Rental:* Cinema Guild. *Sale:* Cinema Guild.

Monde Sans Soleil, Le *see* World Without Sun.

Mondo Cane. Directed by Gualtierro Jacopetti. 1963. Italy. (Documentary). 105 min. Sound. 16mm Color. narrated Eng. *Rental:* Films Inc.

Mondo Nudo. Directed by Bill Dunn, Anthony Kay & Tom Taylor. 1979. Canada. (Documentary). 86 min. Sound. 16mm Color. *Rental:* Natl Film CN. *Sale:* Natl Film CN.

Mondo Pazzo. Directed by Mario Maffei & Giorgio Cecchini. 1965. Italy. (Documentary). 94 min. Sound. 16mm Color. narrated Eng. *Rental:* Films Inc.

Mondo Trasho. Divine. Directed by John Waters. 1969. New Line Cinema. 87 min. Sound. 16mm B&W. *Rental:* New Line Cinema.

Mondragon Experiment, The. 1981. Britain. (Documentary). 50 min. Sound. 16mm Color. *Rental:* Films Inc & U Mich Media. *Sale:* Films Inc. *Rental:* Films Inc, *Sale:* Films Inc, Videotape version.

Money & the Woman. Jeffrey Lynn & Brenda Marshall. Directed by William K. Howard. 1940. Warners. 67 min. Sound. 16mm B&W. *Rental:* MGM United.

Money Isn't Everything *see* Jeepers Creepers.

Money Jungle, The. John Ericson & Lola Albright. Directed by Francis D. Lyon. 1968. United Pictures. 95 min. Sound. 16mm Color. *Rental:* Ivy Films, Rep Pic Film & Video Comm. *Lease:* Rep Pic Film.

Money Madness. Directed by Michael Mason. 92 min. Sound. 16mm Color. *Rental:* New Line Cinema.

Money Talks. Directed by Allen Funt. 1972. United Artists. (Documentary). 81 min. Sound. 16mm Color. *Rental:* MGM United.

Money to Burn. James Gleason. Directed by Gus Meins. 1940. Republic. 60 min. Sound. 16mm B&W. *Rental:* Ivy Films. *Sale:* Rep Pic Film.

Money Trap, The. Glenn Ford & Elke Sommer. Directed by Burt Kennedy. 1966. MGM. 92 min. Sound. 16mm B&W. *Rental:* MGM United.

Moneylenders, The. 58 min. Sound. Videotape *Rental:* PBS Video. *Sale:* PBS Video.

Moneywatchers, The. 3 pts. 1979. PBS. (Documentary). 177 min. Videotape Color. *Rental:* PBS Video. *Sale:* PBS Video.

Monika. Harriet Anderson. Directed by Ingmar Bergman. Swed. 1952. Sweden. 82 min. Sound. 16mm B&W. subtitles. *Rental:* Janus Films & New Cinema.

Monitors, The. Susan Oliver & Keenan Wynn. Directed by Jack Shea. 1968. Commonwealth. 105 min. Sound. 16mm Color. *Rental:* Films Inc, Ivy Films, Video Comm & Welling Motion Pictures.

Monkey Business. Marx Brothers. Directed by Norman Z. McLeod. 1931. Paramount. 77 min. Sound. 16mm B&W. *Rental:* Museum Mod Art & Swank Motion.

Monkey Business. Cary Grant, Ginger Rogers & Marilyn Monroe. Directed by Howard Hawks. 1952. Fox. 97 min. Sound. 16mm B&W. *Rental:* Films Inc.

Monkey Business. 1960. Gospel. (Cast unlisted). 49 min. Sound. 16mm Color. *Rental:* Roas Films.

Monkey Hustle, The. Yaphet Kotto & Rosalind Cash. Directed by Arthur Marks. 1976. American International. 90 min. Sound. 16mm Color. *Rental:* Swank Motion & Welling Motion Pictures.

Monkey in Winter, The. Jean Gabin & Jean-Paul Belmondo. Directed by Henri Verneuil. Fr. 1963. France. 104 min. Sound. 16mm B&W. subtitles. *Rental:* MGM United.

Monkey on My Back. Cameron Mitchell & Jack Albertson. Directed by Andre De Toth. 1957. United Artists. 94 min. Sound. 16mm B&W. *Rental:* MGM United.

Monkeys, Apes & Man. 1972. National Geographic. (Documentary). 52 min. Sound. 16mm Color. *Rental:* Iowa Films, Natl Geog, Syracuse U Film, U Mich Media & Wholesome Film Ctr. *Sale:* Natl Geog. *Sale:* Natl Geog, Videotape version.

Monkeys Go Home! Maurice Chevalier, Dean Jones & Yvette Mimieux. Directed by Andrew V. McLaglen. 1967. Disney. 101 min. Sound. 16mm Color. *Rental:* Buchan Pic, Cine Craft, Williams Films, Bosco Films, Disney Prod, Elliot Film Co, Films Inc, Film Pres, U of IL Film, MGM United, Modern Sound, Newman Film Lib, Roas Films, Swank Motion, Film Ctr DC, Twyman Films, Westcoast Films & Welling Motion Pictures.

Monkey's Uncle, The. Tommy Kirk, Leon Ames & Annette Funicello. Directed by Robert Stevenson. 1965. Disney. 87 min. Sound. 16mm Color. *Rental:* Bosco Films, Buchan Pics, Cine Craft, Cousino Visual Ed, Disney Prod, Elliot Film Co, Film Ctr DC, Film Pres, Film Inc, MGM United, Modern Sound, Newman Film Lib, Roas Films, Swank Motion, Twyman Films, U of IL Film, Welling Motion Pictures, Westcoast Films & Williams Films.

Monolith Monsters, The. Grant Williams & Lola Albright. Directed by John Sherwood. 1957. Universal. 77 min. Sound. 16mm B&W. *Rental:* Swank Motion.

Monsieur Beaucaire. Rudolph Valentino, Bebe Daniels & Lois Wilson. Directed by Sidney Olcott. 1924. Paramount. 106 min. Silent. 16mm B&W. *Rental:* Museum Mod Art.

Monsieur Beaucaire. Bob Hope & Joan Caulfield. Directed by George Marshall. 1946. Paramount. 93 min. Sound. 16mm B&W. *Rental:* Swank Motion.

Monsieur Verdoux. Charles Chaplin & Martha Raye. Directed by Charles Chaplin. 1947. United Artists. 123 min. Sound. 16mm B&W. *Rental:* Films Inc.

Monsieur Vincent. Pierre Fresnay. Directed by Maurice Cloche. Fr. 1947. France. 112 min. Sound. 16mm B&W. subtitles. *Rental:* Films IncRoas Films & Tamarelles French Film. *Lease:* Macmillan Films. *Sale:* Tamarelles French Film, Videotape version.

Monsignor. Christopher Reeve & Genevieve Bujold. Directed by Frank Perry. 1982. Fox. 122 min. Sound. 16mm Color. *Rental:* Films Inc.

Monster, The. Lon Chaney. Directed by Roland West. 1925. MGM. 80 min. Silent. 16mm B&W. *Rental:* Films Inc.

Monster a Go-Go. June Travis. Directed by Herschell G. Lewis. 1965. B.I.L.. 70 min. Sound. 16mm B&W. *Rental:* Video Comm.

Monster Demolisher, The. German Robels & Julio Aleman. Directed by Frederico Curiel. 1960. Mexico. 75 min. Sound. 16mm dubbed. *Rental:* Budget Films.

Monster from Green Hell, The. Jim Davis & Barbara Turner. Directed by Kenneth G. Crane. 1957. Hal Roach. 71 min. Sound. 16mm B&W. *Rental:* Budget Films, Video Comm & Willoughby Peer. *Sale:* Cinema Concepts. *Sale:* Reel Images & Video Comm, Videotape version.

Monster from Mars *see* Robot Monster.

Monster from the Ocean Floor, The. Stuart Wade. Directed by Wyatt Ardung. 1954. Lippert. 60 min. Sound. 16mm B&W. *Rental:* Budget Films.

Monster from the Prehistoric Planet, The. Tamio Kawaji. Directed by Harayasu Noguchi. 1967. Japan. 90 min. Sound. 16mm Color. dubbed. *Rental:* Films Inc.

Monster from the Surf, The. Jon Hall. Directed by Jon Hall. 1963. American International. 75 min. Sound. 16mm B&W. *Rental:* Films Inc.

Monster Maker, The. J. Carrol Naish & Ralph Morgan. Directed by Sam Newfield. 1944. PRC. 65 min. Sound. 16mm B&W. *Rental:* Budget Films, Films Inc, Video Comm & Westcoast Films. *Sale:* Classic Film Mus. *Rental:* Video Comm, Videotape version.

Monster of Highgate Pond, The. Rachel Clay & Michael Wade. Directed by Alberto Cavalcanti. 1970. Britain. 60 min. Sound. 16mm B&W. *Rental:* Films Inc & Wholesome Film Ctr. *Sale:* Lucerne Films.

Monster of Terror *see* Die, Monster, Die.

Monster on the Campus. Arthur Franz & Johanna Moore. Directed by Jack Arnold. 1958. Universal. 76 min. Sound. 16mm B&W. *Rental:* Swank Motion.

Monster That Challenged the World, The. Tim Holt & Hans Conried. Directed by Arnold Laven. 1957. United Artists. 83 min. Sound. 16mm B&W. *Rental:* MGM United.

Monster Walks, The. Mischa Auer & Vera Reynolds. 1932. Mayfair. 60 min. Sound. 16mm B&W. *Rental:* Budget Films, Em Gee Film Lib, Mogulls Films & Roas Films. *Sale:* Blackhawk Films. *Sale:* Blackhawk Films, Super 8 Sound version.

Monster Zero *see* Invasion of the Astros.

Monsters: Mysteries or Myths?. 1976. Wolper. (Documentary). 49 min. Sound. 16mm Color. *Rental:* Films Inc & Syracuse U Film. *Sale:* Films Inc. *Sale:* Films Inc, Videotape version.

Monstrosity *see* Atomic Brain.

Montana. Errol Flynn & Alexis Smith. Directed by Ray Enright. 1950. Warners. 76 min. Sound. 16mm Color. *Rental:* Swank Motion & Twyman Films.

Montana Belle. Jane Russell & George Brent. Directed by Allan Dwan. 1952. RKO. 81 min. Sound. 16mm Color. *Rental:* Films Inc.

Montana Desperado. Johnny Mack Brown. Directed by Wallace Fox. 1951. Monogram. 51 min. Sound. 16mm B&W. *Rental:* Hurlock Cine.

Montana Incident. Whip Wilson. Directed by Lewis D. Collins. 1952. Monogram. 54 min. Sound. 16mm B&W. *Rental:* Hurlock Cine.

Monte Carlo. Jeanette MacDonald & Jack Buchanan. Directed by Ernst Lubitsch. 1930. Paramount. 95 min. Sound. 16mm B&W. *Rental:* Swank Motion.

Monte Carlo Nights. Mary Brian & John Darrow. Directed by William Nigh. 1934. Monogram. 70 min. Sound. 16mm B&W. *Rental:* Mogulls Films.

Monte Carlo Story, The. Marlene Dietrich & Vittorio De Sica. Directed by Samuel Taylor. 1957. United Artists. 99 min. Sound. 16mm Color. *Rental:* MGM United.

Montenegro. Susan Anspach & Erland Josephson. Directed by Dusan Makavejev. 1981. Atalantic. 97 min. Sound. 16mm Color. dubbed. *Rental:* Films Inc.

Monterey Pop. Directed by D. A. Pennebaker. 1968. Pennebaker. (Documentary). 80 min. Sound. 16mm Color. *Rental:* Pennebaker & New Cinema. *Sale:* Pennebaker.

Montreal Main. Steven Lack & Alan Moyle. Directed by Frank Vitale. 1974. Canada. 86 min. Sound. 16mm Color. *Rental:* New Cinema.

Montreal Olympiad, The. Orig. Title: Games of the XXI Olympiad. Fr. 1976. ABC. (Documentary). 80 min. Sound. 16mm Color. subtitles. *Rental:* Buchan Pic & Budget Films. *Rental:* Welling Motion Pictures, Videotape version.

Montreal: The Neighborhood Revived. 1975. Canada. (Documentary). 57 min. Sound. 16mm Color. *Rental:* Natl Film Ctr. *Sale:* Natl Film Ctr.

Monty Python & the Holy Grail. Graham Chapman. Directed by Terry Gilliam & Terry Jones. 1975. Britain. 90 min. Sound. 16mm Color. *Rental:* Cinema Five. *Lease:* Cinema Five.

Monty Python Live at the Bowl. Graham Chapman, John Cleese & Terry Gilliam. Directed by Terry Hughes. 77 min. Sound. 16mm Color. *Rental:* Swank Motion. *Rental:* Swank Motion, Videotape version.

Monty Python Meets Beyond the Fringe. Dudley Moore & Eleanor Bron. Directed by Roger Graef. 85 min. Sound. 16mm Color. *Rental:* New Line Cinema.

Monty Python's Life of Brian. Graham Chapman & John Cleese. Directed by Terry Jones. 1979. Warners. 91 min. Sound. 16mm Color. *Rental:* Swank Motion. *Rental:* Swank Motion, Videotape version.

Monty Python's Meaning of Life. Graham Chapman & John Cleese. Directed by Terry Jones. 1983. Universal. 103 min. Sound. 16mm Color. *Rental:* Swank Motion.

Moon & Sixpence, The. George Sanders & Herbert Marshall. Directed by Albert Lewin. 1943. United Artists. 85 min. Sound. 16mm B&W. *Rental:* Film Classics, Ivy Films, Film Ctr DC & Wholesome Film Ctr.

Moon in the Gutter, The. Gerard Depardieu & Nastassia Kinski. Directed by Jean-Jacques Beineix. 1983. France. 126 min. Sound. 16mm Color. subtitles. *Rental:* Swank Motion. *Rental:* Swank Motion, *Sale:* Tamarelles French Film, Videotape version.

Moon Is Blue, The. William Holden, Maggie McNamara & David Niven. Directed by Otto Preminger. 1953. United Artists. 90 min. Sound. 16mm B&W. *Rental:* Films Inc & Wholesome Film Ctr.

Moon Is Down, The. Sir Cedric Hardwicke & Lee J. Cobb. Directed by Irving Pichel. 1943. Fox. 90 min. Sound. 16mm B&W. *Rental:* Films Inc & Twyman Films.

Moon Over Harlem. Bud Harris & Cora Green. Directed by Edgar G. Ulmer. 1939. 75 min. Sound. 16mm *Rental:* Budget Films.

Moon Over Her Shoulder. Lynn Bari & Dan Dailey. Directed by Alfred M. Werker. 1941. Fox. 68 min. Sound. 16mm B&W. *Rental:* Films Inc.

Moon Over Las Vegas. David Bruce & Anne Gwynne. Directed by Jean Yarbrough. 1944. Universal. 69 min. Sound. 16mm B&W. *Rental:* Film Ctr DC, Film Classics & Mogulls Films.

Moon Over Montana. Jimmy Wakely. Directed by Oliver Drake. 1946. Monogram. 54 min. Sound. 16mm B&W. *Rental:* Hurlock Cine.

Moon Over the Alley. Directed by Joseph Despins. 1975. Britain. (Cast unlisted). 104 min. Sound. 16mm B&W. *Rental:* New Cinema.

Moon Zero Two. James Olson & Adrienne Corri. Directed by Roy Ward Baker. 1969. Warners. 100 min. Sound. 16mm Color. *Rental:* Films Inc & Welling Motion Pictures.

Moonchild. 1982. Pyramid. (Documentary). 49 min. Sound. 16mm Color. *Rental:* Pyramid Film & U Cal Media. *Sale:* Pyramid Film.

Mooney vs. Fowle. 1965. Time-Life. (Documentary). 54 min. Sound. 16mm B&W. *Lease:* Direct Cinema.

Moonfleet. Stewart Granger & George Sanders. Directed by Fritz Lang. 1955. MGM. 89 min. Sound. 16mm Color. *Rental:* MGM United.

Moonlight in Havana. Allan Jones & Jane Frazee. Directed by Anthony Mann. 1942. Universal. 70 min. Sound. 16mm B&W. *Rental:* Swank Motion.

Moonlight in Hawaii. Johnny Downs, Leon Errol & Mischa Auer. Directed by Charles Lamont. 1941. Universal. 60 min. Sound. 16mm B&W. *Rental:* Mogulls Films & Film Ctr DC.

Moonlight Masquerade. Dennis O'Keefe & Paul Harvey. Directed by John H. Auer. 1942. Republic. 68 min. Sound. 16mm B&W. *Rental:* Ivy Films.

Moonlight Murder. Chester Morris & Madge Evans. Directed by Edwin L. Marin. 1936. MGM. 67 min. Sound. 16mm B&W. *Rental:* MGM United.

Moonlight on the Prairie. Dick Foran. Directed by D. Ross Lederman. 1935. Warners. 63 min. Sound. 16mm B&W. *Rental:* MGM United.

Moonlight on the Range. Fred Scott. Directed by Sam Newfield. 1935. Spectrum. 60 min. Sound. 16mm B&W. *Rental:* Mogulls Films.

Moonlight Sonata. Charles Farrell & Ignace Jan Paderewski. Directed by Lothar Mendes. 1938. Britain. 81 min. Sound. 16mm B&W. *Rental:* A Twyman Pres & Inst Cinema.

Moonlighting. Jeremy Irons & Eugene Lipinski. Directed by Jerzy Skolimowski. 1981. Universal. 97 min. Sound. 16mm Color. *Rental:* Swank Motion.

Moonraker, The. Roger Moore, Lois Chiles & Richard Kiel. Directed by Lewis Gilbert. 1979. United Artists. 126 min. Sound. 16mm Color. *Rental:* MGM United. *Rental:* MGM United, Videotape version.

Moonrise. Dane Clark & Gail Russell. Directed by Frank Borzage. 1948. Republic. 90 min. Sound. 16mm B&W. *Rental:* Ivy Films. *Sale:* Rep Pic Film.

Moonrunners, The. James Mitchum & Arthur Hunnicut. Directed by Guy Waldron. 1975. United Artists. 102 min. Sound. 16mm Color. *Rental:* MGM United.

Moon's Our Home, The. Margaret Sullavan & Henry Fonda. Directed by William A. Seiter. 1936. Paramount. 76 min. Sound. 16mm B&W. *Rental:* Swank Motion.

Moonshine County Express. John Saxon & Susan Howard. Directed by Gus Trikonis. 1977. New World. 84 min. Sound. 16mm Color. *Rental:* Films Inc.

Moonshine War, The. Richard Widmark & Patrick McGoohan. Directed by Richard Quine. 1970. MGM. 100 min. Sound. 16mm Color. *Rental:* MGM United.

Moonspinners, The. Hayley Mills & Eli Wallach. Directed by James Neilson. 1964. Disney. 118 min. Sound. 16mm Color. *Rental:* Buchan Pic, Cine Craft, Cousino Visual Ed, Film Ctr DC, Film Pres, Films Inc, Roas Films, Swank Motion, U of IL Film & Williams Films.

Moonstone, The. David Manners. Directed by Reginald Barker. 1934. Britain. 70 min. Sound. 16mm B&W. *Rental:* Mogulls Films.

Moontide. Jean Gabin & Ida Lupino. Directed by Archie Mayo. 1942. Fox. 94 min. Sound. 16mm B&W. *Rental:* Films Inc.

Moontrap, The. Trans. Title: Pour la Suite du Monde. Directed by Michel Brault, Marcel Carriere & Pierre Perrault. 1963. Canada. (Documentary). 84 min. Sound. 16mm B&W. narrated Eng. *Rental:* Museum Mod Art & U Cal Media.

Moonwalk, The. Directed by Francis Thompson. 1979. NASA. (Documentary). 95 min. Sound. 16mm Color. *Rental:* Learning Corp Am. *Sale:* Learning Corp Am. *Rental:* Learning Corp Am, *Sale:* Learning Corp Am, Videotape version.

Moonwalk One. Directed by Theo Kamecke. 1973. Walter Reade. (Documentary). 94 min. Sound. 16mm Color. *Rental:* Budget Films.

Moppet & the Rest Diver, The. 1970. Japan. (Cast unlisted). 50 min. Sound. 16mm B&W. *Sale:* Japan Society.

Morder Dimitri Karamazov, Der *see* Karamazov.

More. Mimsy Farmer. Directed by Barbet Schroeder. 1969. Cinema V. 110 min. Sound. 16mm Color. *Rental:* Cinema Five.

More Abundant Life, A. 1972. Britain. (Documentary). 52 min. Sound. 16mm Color. *Rental:* Kent St U Film & Utah Media.

More American Graffiti. Candy Clark & Ron Howard. Directed by B. W. L. Norton. 1979. Universal. 111 min. Sound. 16mm Color. *Rental:* Swank Motion.

More Dead Than Alive. Clint Walker & Vincent Price. Directed by Robert Sparr. 1969. United Artists. 101 min. Sound. 16mm Color. *Rental:* MGM United.

More Music from Aspen. 1979. PBS. (Concert). 59 min. Videotape Color. *Rental:* PBS Video. *Sale:* PBS Video.

More Nuclear Power Stations. 1976. Denmark. (Documentary). 55 min. Sound. 16mm Color. *Rental:* Green Mt & U Mich Media. *Sale:* Green Mt.

More Than a Champion: The Gospel in Real Life. Heinz Fussle. 56 min. Sound. 16mm Color. *Rental:* Gospel Films.

More Than a Miracle. Orig. Title: Happily Ever after. Sophia Loren & Omar Sharif. Directed by Francesco Rosi. 1967. MGM. (Anamorphic). 105 min. Sound. 16mm Color. *Rental:* MGM United.

More Than a Place to Die. 1975. Penn State. (Documentary). 59 min. Sound. 16mm B&W. *Rental:* Penn St AV Serv. *Sale:* Penn St AV Serv. *Rental:* Penn St AV Serv, *Sale:* Penn St AV Serv, Videotape version.

More Than a Place to Die. 1977. 59 min. Sound. 16mm Color. *Rental:* Iowa Films.

More Than a School. 1974. Robertson. (Documentary). 55 min. Sound. 16mm Color. *Rental:* Films Inc. *Sale:* Films Inc. *Sale:* Films Inc, Videotape version.

More Than a Secretary. Jean Arthur & George Brent. Directed by Alfred E. Green. 1936. Columbia. 80 min. Sound. 16mm B&W. *Lease:* Time-Life Multimedia.

More Than Bows & Arrows. 1978. 56 min. Sound. 16mm Color. *Rental:* U Mich Media.

More Than Magic. Clayton Moore. 1960. Wrather. 75 min. Sound. 16mm Color. *Rental:* Video Comm.

More the Merrier, The. Jean Arthur, Charles Coburn & Joel McCrea. Directed by George Stevens. 1943. Columbia. 104 min. Sound. 16mm B&W. *Rental:* Corinth Films & Swank Motion.

Morgan! David Warner & Vanessa Redgrave. Directed by Karel Reisz. 1966. Britain. 97 min. Sound. 16mm B&W. *Rental:* Swank Motion.

Morgan the Pirate. Steve Reeves. Directed by Andre De Toth. 1961. Italy. 93 min. Sound. 16mm Color. dubbed. *Rental:* Films Inc & Westcoast Films. *Sale:* Blackhawk Films, Super 8 sound version.

Morituri (The Saboteur). Orig. Title: Code Name-Morituri. Marlon Brando & Yul Brynner. Directed by Bernhard Wicki. 1965. Fox. 123 min. Sound. 16mm B&W. *Rental:* Films Inc.

Morning. Directed by Hugh Raggett. 1974. Britain. (Documentary). 60 min. Sound. 16mm Color. *Rental:* U Cal Media.

Morning Glory. Katharine Hepburn, Douglas Fairbanks Jr. & Adolphe Menjou. Directed by Lowell Sherman. 1933. RKO. 70 min. Sound. 16mm B&W. *Rental:* Films Inc. *Lease:* Films Inc.

Morning: 1944. (World at War Ser.). : Pt. 17.). 1973. Media Guild. (Documentary). 52 min. Sound. 16mm Color. *Rental:* Media Guild. *Sale:* Media Guild. *Sale:* Media Guild, Videotape version.

Moro Witch Doctor. Jock Mahoney & Margia Dean. Directed by Eddie Romero. 1964. Fox. 61 min. Sound. 16mm B&W. *Rental:* Films Inc.

Morocco. Marlene Dietrich & Gary Cooper. Directed by Josef Von Sternberg. 1930. Paramount. 97 min. Sound. 16mm B&W. *Rental:* Williams Films.

Mortadella, La *see* Lady Liberty.

Mortal Combat. Chan Kuan Tai. Hong Kong. 106 min. Sound. 16mm *Rental:* WW Enter. *Rental:* WW Enter, Videotape version.

Mortal Storm, The. Margaret Sullavan & James Stewart. Directed by Frank Borzage. 1940. MGM. 100 min. Sound. 16mm B&W. *Rental:* MGM United.

Moryak iz Komety *see* Sailor from the Comet.

Moscow Does Not Believe in Tears. Vera Alentova & Alexei Batalov. Directed by Vladimir Menshov. 1980. Russia. 148 min. Sound. Videotape Color. *Sale:* Tamarelles French Films.

Moscow Nights *see* I Stand Condemned.

Moscow on the Hudson. Robin Williams, Maria Conchita Alonso & Cleavent Derricks. Directed by Paul Mazursky. 1985. Columbia. 107 min. Sound. 16mm Color. *Rental:* Swank Motion.

Moses. Julie Adams, Robert Alda & Anne Francis. Directed by James L. Conway. 1979. NBC. 63 min. Sound. 16mm Color. *Rental:* Budget Films & Modern Sound. *Sale:* Lucerne Films. *Sale:* Lucerne Films, Videotape version.

Moses & Aaron. Directed by Jean-Marie Straub & Daniele Huillet. Ger. 1975. Germany. (Opera). 105 min. Sound. 16mm Color. subtitles. *Rental:* New Yorker Films.

Moses Coady. Directed by Kent Martin. 1976. Canada. (Documentary). 58 min. Sound. 16mm Color. *Rental:* Bullfrog Films. *Sale:* Bullfrog Films. *Sale:* Bullfrog Films, Videotape version.

Mosquito Squadron. David McCallum. Directed by Boris Sagal. 1969. United Artists. 90 min. Sound. 16mm Color. *Rental:* MGM United.

Moss Rose. Peggy Cummings & Victor Mature. Directed by Gregory Ratoff. 1947. Fox. 82 min. Sound. 16mm B&W. *Rental:* Films Inc.

Most Beautiful Age, The. Jan Stockl. Directed by Jaroslav Papousek. Czech. 1969. Czechoslovakia. 80 min. Sound. 16mm B&W. subtitles. *Rental:* Grove.

Most Dangerous Game, A. Joel McCrea & Fay Wray. Directed by Ernest B. Schoedsack & Irving Pichel. 1932. RKO. 65 min. Sound. 16mm B&W. *Rental:* Budget Films, Classic Film Mus, Em Gee Film Lib, Janus Films, Kit Parker, New Cinema, Video Comm & Williams Films. *Sale:* Cinema Concepts & Glenn Photo. *Sale:* Tamarelles French Film, Videotape version.

Most Precious Thing in Life, The. Jean Arthur & Donald Cook. Directed by Lambert Hillyer. 1934. Columbia. 70 min. Sound. 16mm B&W. *Rental:* Kit Parker.

Most Wanted Man, The. Fernandel & Zsa Zsa Gabor. 1953. France. 85 min. Sound. 16mm B&W. subtitles. *Rental:* Films Inc.

Most Wonderful Moment, The. Marcello Mastroianni & Giovanna Ralli. Directed by Luciano Emmer. 1955. Italy. 94 min. Sound. 16mm B&W. dubbed. *Rental:* Ivy Films.

Motel Hell. Rory Calhoun. Directed by Kevin Connor. 1980. United Artists. 102 min. Sound. 16mm Color. *Rental:* MGM United.

Moth, The. Norma Talmadge. Directed by Edward Jose. 1917. 16mm *Rental:* A Twyman Pres.

Mother. Orig. Title: Nineteen Hundred & Five. Vera Baranovskaya. Directed by Vsevolod I. Pudovkin. 1926. Russia. 104 min. Silent. 16mm B&W. *Rental:* Budget Films, Corinth Films, Em Gee Film Lib, Images Film, Kit Parker, Museum Mod Art, Tamarelles French Film, U Cal Media, Utah Media & Westcoast Films. *Sale:* Cinema Concepts, Glenn Photo, Images Film, Morcraft Films & Reel Images. *Rental:* Ivy Films, Super 8 Silent version. *Sale:* Images Film & Tamarelles French Film, Videotape version. *Rental:* Westcoast Films, 87 mins. version.

Mother. Jap. 1971. Japan. (Cast unlisted). 56 min. Sound. 16mm B&W. *Sale:* Japan Society. *Sale:* Japan Society, Color version. *Sale:* Japan Society, Videotape version. *Sale:* Japan Society, Subtitled version.

Mother & the Law, The. Lillian Gish & Robert Harron. Directed by D. W. Griffith. 1919. Biograph. 104 min. Silent. 16mm B&W. *Rental:* A Twyman Pres, Museum Mod Art & Twyman Films. *Sale:* Blackhawk Films. *Rental:* Ivy Films, *Sale:* Blackhawk Films, Super 8 silent version.

Mother & the Whore, The. Bernadette Lafont & Jean-Pierre Leaud. Directed by Jean Eustache. Fr. 1974. France. 210 min. Sound. 16mm Color. subtitles. *Rental:* New Yorker Films.

Mother Cabrini. 1942. (Documentary). 81 min. Sound. 16mm B&W. *Rental:* Film Classics.

Mother Carey's Chickens. Fay Bainter, Anne Shirley & Ruby Keeler. Directed by Rowland V. Lee. 1938. RKO. 82 min. Sound. 16mm B&W. *Rental:* Films Inc.

Mother Didn't Tell Me. Dorothy McQuire & William Lundigan. Directed by Claude Binyon. 1950. Fox. 88 min. Sound. 16mm B&W. *Rental:* Films Inc.

Mother Elizabeth Seton. 1961. (Documentary). 53 min. Sound. 16mm B&W. *Rental:* Roas Films.

Mother Goose a Go-Go. Tommy Kirk & Anne Helm. Directed by Jack Harris. 1966. Tonlyn. 90 min. Sound. 16mm Color. *Rental:* Films Inc.

Mother Is a Freshman. Orig. Title: Mother Knows Best. Loretta Young & Van Johnson. Directed by Lloyd Bacon. 1949. Fox. 80 min. Sound. 16mm B&W. *Rental:* Films Inc. *Rental:* Films Inc, Color version.

Mother, Jugs & Speed. Raquel Welch, Bill Cosby & Harvey Keitel. Directed by Peter Yates. 1976. Fox. 98 min. Sound. 16mm Color. *Rental:* Films Inc, Twyman Films, Welling Motion Pictures & Williams Films.

Mother Knows Best *see* Mother Is a Freshman.

Mother Kusters Goes to Heaven. Brigitte Mira. Directed by Rainer Werner Fassbinder. Ger. 1975. Germany. 91 min. Sound. 16mm Color. subtitles. *Rental:* New Cinema & New Yorker Films.

Mother Lode. Charlton Heston & Nick Mancuso. Directed by Charlton Heston. 1982. MGM-UA. 101 min. Sound. 16mm Color. *Rental:* MGM United.

Mother of Many Children. Directed by Alanis Obomsawin. 1977. 57 min. 16mm Color. *Rental:* Natl Film CN & U Cal Media.

Mother of the Kennedys: A Portrait of Rose Fitzgerald Kennedy. 1973. Mass Media. (Documentary). 47 min. Sound. 16mm Color. *Rental:* Mass Media. *Sale:* Mass Media.

Mother Teresa of Calcutta. 1971. Britain. (Documentary). 51 min. Sound. 16mm Color. *Rental:* Films Inc. *Sale:* Films Inc.

Mother-to-Be. 1974. Canada. (Documentary). 76 min. Sound. 16mm B&W. *Rental:* Natl Film CN.

Mother Wore Tights. Betty Grable & Dan Dailey. Directed by Walter Lang. 1947. Fox. 107 min. Sound. 16mm Color. *Rental:* Films Inc.

Mother-Sir *see* Navy Wife.

Mothers Cry. Dorothy Peterson & Evalyn Knapp. Directed by Hobart Henley. 1930. Warners. 75 min. Sound. 16mm B&W. *Rental:* MGM United.

Mothers of Eve. Anny Ondra. 1925. Germany. 75 min. Silent. 16mm B&W. *Sale:* Natl Cinema.

Mothra. Franky Sakai. Directed by Inoshiro Honda. 1962. Japan. 101 min. Sound. 16mm Color. dubbed. *Rental:* Bosco Films, Budget Films, Cine Craft, Film Ctr DC, Films Inc, Inst Cinema, Ivy Films, Kit Parker, Modern Sound, Natl Film Video, Roas Films, Video Comm, Welling Motion Pictures & Westcoast Films.

Motion Picture History of the Korean War, A. 1958. US Government. (Documentary). 58 min. Sound. 16mm B&W. *Sale:* Natl AV Ctr. *Rental:* Natl AV Ctr.

Motor Patrol. Don Castle & Reed Hadley. Directed by Sam Newfield. 1950. Lippert. 67 min. Sound. 16mm B&W. *Rental:* Inst Cinema.

Motorcycle Gang. John Ashley. Directed by Edward L. Cahn. 1957. American International. 78 min. Sound. 16mm B&W. *Rental:* Films Inc & Westcoast Films.

Mouchette. Nadine Nortier & Marie Cardinal. Directed by Robert Bresson. Fr. 1966. France. 80 min. Sound. 16mm B&W. subtitles. *Rental:* New Line Cinema. *Sale:* New Line Cinema.

Moulin Rouge. Eve Gray. Directed by E. A. Dupont. 1928. Britain. 112 min. Silent. 16mm B&W. *Rental:* Budget Films, Em Gee Film Lib, Janus Films & Kit Parker. *Sale:* Glenn Photo & Reel Images.

Moulin Rouge. Jose Ferrer & Zsa Zsa Gabor. Directed by John Huston. 1952. United Artists. 119 min. Sound. 16mm Color. *Rental:* MGM United.

Mountain, The. Spencer Tracy & Claire Trevor. Directed by Edward Dmytryk. 1956. Paramount. 105 min. Sound. 16mm Color. *Rental:* Films Inc.

Mountain Justice. George Brent & Josephine Hutchinson. Directed by Michael Curtiz. 1937. Warners. 82 min. Sound. 16mm B&W. *Rental:* MGM United.

Mountain Lady. Skyline Productions. 59 min. Sound. 16mm Color. *Rental:* Gospel Films.

Mountain Man. Denver Pyle & Ken Berry. Directed by Daniel O'Malley. 1979. Viacom. 98 min. Sound. 16mm Color. *Rental:* Modern Sound & Williams Films. *Sale:* Lucerne Films. *Sale:* Lucerne Films, Videotape version.

Mountain Men, The. Charlton Heston & Brian Keith. Directed by Richard Lang. 1980. Columbia. 102 min. Sound. 16mm Color. *Rental:* Arcus Film, Swank Motion & Westcoast Films.

Mountain Moonlight. Orig. Title: Moving in Society. John Archer & George Chandler. Directed by Nick Grinde. 1942. Republic. 68 min. Sound. 16mm B&W. *Rental:* Ivy Films.

Mountain People. Directed by Cinda Firestone. 1978. Cinema V. (Documentary). 52 min. Sound. 16mm Color. *Rental:* Cinema Five.

Mountain Rhythm. Gene Autry. Directed by B. Reeves Eason. 1939. Republic. 54 min. Sound. 16mm B&W. *Rental:* Ivy Films.

Mountain Rhythm. Lynne Merrick. Directed by Frank McDonald. 1942. Republic. 70 min. Sound. 16mm B&W. *Rental:* Ivy Films.

Mountain Road, The. James Stewart & Glenn Corbett. Directed by Daniel Mann. 1960. Columbia. 102 min. Sound. 16mm B&W. *Rental:* Budget Films, Cine Craft, Film Ctr DC, Films Inc & Modern Sound.

Mounting Millions. 1966. NET. (Documentary). 60 min. Sound. 16mm B&W. *Rental:* Indiana AV Ctr. *Sale:* Indiana AV Ctr.

Mourir a Tue-Tete. Julie Vincent & Germain Houde. Directed by Anne-Claire Poirier. 1978. Canada. 96 min. Sound. 16mm Color. subtitles. *Rental:* Natl Film CN. *Sale:* Natl Film CN.

Mourir D' Aimer *see* To Die of Love.

Mourning Becomes Electra. Rosalind Russell & Sir Michael Redgrave. Directed by Dudley Nichols. 1947. RKO. 175 min. Sound. 16mm B&W. *Rental:* A Twyman Pres & Films Inc. *Lease:* Films Inc.

Mourning for Mangatopi. 1977. Australia. (Documentary). 56 min. Sound. 16mm Color. *Rental:* U Cal Media. *Sale:* U Cal Media. *Sale:* U Cal Media, Videotape version.

Mouse & His Child, The. Cloris Leachman & Sally Kellerman. Directed by Fred Wolf. 1978. 83 min. Sound. 16mm Color. *Rental:* Films Inc.

Mouse on the Mayflower, The. Orig. Title: Churchmouse & the Mayflower. 1967. UPA. (Animated). 57 min. Sound. 16mm Color. *Rental:* Arcus Film, Cine Craft, Film Ctr DC, Films Inc, Inst Cinema, Kerr Film, Modern Mass, Welling Motion Pictures & Westcoast Films. *Sale:* Macmillan Films.

Mouse on the Moon, The. Terry-Thomas & Margaret Rutherford. Directed by Richard Lester. 1963. United Artists. 82 min. Sound. 16mm Color. *Rental:* MGM United.

Mouse That Roared, The. Peter Sellers. Directed by Jack Arnold. 1959. Britain. 83 min. Sound. 16mm Color. *Rental:* Arcus Film, Bosco Films, Buchan Pic, Budget Films, Cine Craft, Charard Motion Pics, Film Ctr DC, Film Pres, Film Inc, Images Film, Inst Cinema, Ivy Films, Kit Parker, Modern Sound, Newman Film Lib, Roas Films, Swank Motion, Twyman Films, U of IL Film, Video Comm, Welling Motion Pictures, Westcoast Films, Wholesome Film Ctr & Williams Films. *Sale:* Natl Film Video. *Rental:* Swank Motion, Videotape version.

Mouthpiece, The. Warren William & Sydney Fox. Directed by James Flood. 1932. Warners. 86 min. Sound. 16mm B&W. *Rental:* MGM United.

Mouton a Cinq Pattes, Le *see* Sheep Has Five Legs.

Move. Elliott Gould & Paula Prentiss. Directed by Stuart Rosenberg. 1971. Fox. (Anamorphic). 90 min. Sound. 16mm Color. *Rental:* Films Inc.

Move Over, Darling. Doris Day & James Garner. Directed by Michael Gordon. 1963. Fox. (Anamorphic). 103 min. Sound. 16mm Color. *Rental:* Films Inc.

Movie Crazy Years, The. 1972. NET. (Documentary). 90 min. Sound. 16mm B&W. *Rental:* MGM United.

Movie, Movie. George C. Scott & Trish Van Devere. Directed by Stanley Donen. 1979. Warners. (Color sequences). 105 min. Sound. 16mm B&W. *Rental:* Modern Sound, Swank Motion, Twyman Films & Williams Films.

Movie Star's Daughter, A. Frank Converse & Trini Alvarado. Directed by Robert Fuest. 1979. Learning Corp. of America. 46 min. Sound. 16mm Color. *Rental:* Learning Corp Am. *Sale:* Learning Corp Am. *Sale:* Learning Corp Am, Videotape version.

Movie Stills. 1977. 45 min. Sound. 16mm B&W. *Rental:* Canyon Cinema.

Movie Struck. Orig. Title: Mister Cinderella. Stan Laurel, Oliver Hardy, Jack Haley & Patsy Kelly. Directed by Edward Sedgwick. 1937. Hal Roach. 80 min. Sound. 16mm B&W. *Rental:* Em Gee Film Lib, MGM United & Video Comm. *Rental:* Ivy Films, *Sale:* Ivy Films & Reel Images, Super 8 sound version.

Movin' On. 1973. Harold Mayer. (Documentary, color sequences). 53 min. Sound. 16mm B&W. *Rental:* Syracuse U Film & U Cal Media. *Sale:* McGraw-Hill Films.

Moving Children. 1977. 79 min. Sound. 16mm Color. *Rental:* Iowa Films.

Moving in Society *see* Mountain Moonlight.

Moving On. 1975. Australia. (Documentary). 58 min. Sound. 16mm Color. *Rental:* Aust Info Serv. *Sale:* Aust Info Serv.

Moving On: The Hunger For Land in Zimbabwe. Directed by Peter Entell & Bruce Robbins. 1982. Peter Entell. (Documentary). 52 min. Sound. 16mm Color. *Rental:* CA Newsreel, U Cal Media & Syracuse U Film. *Sale:* CAl Newsreel,

Moving Picture Boys in the Great War, The. 1975. Blackhawk. (Documentary). 51 min. Sound. 16mm Color. *Rental:* Em Gee Film Lib, Iowa Films, Modern Sound & U Mich Media. *Sale:* Blackhawk Films. *Sale:* Blackhawk Films, Super 8 sound version. *Sale:* Blackhawk Films, Videotape version.

Moving Still. 1980. Britain. (Documentary). 57 min. Sound. 16mm Color. *Rental:* Iowa Films.

Mozambique. Steve Cochran. Directed by Robert Lynn. 1965. 96 min. Sound. 16mm Color. *Rental:* A Twyman Pres.

Mozart Story, The. Winnie Markus. Directed by Frank Wisbar. 1948. Germany. 83 min. Sound. 16mm B&W. dubbed. *Rental:* Lewis Film & New Cinema.

Mrs. Brown, You've Got a Lovely Daughter. Peter Noone. Directed by Saul Swimmer. 1968. MGM. 110 min. Sound. 16mm Color. *Rental:* MGM United. *Rental:* MGM United, Anamorphic version.

Mrs. Fitzherbert. Peter Graves. Directed by Montgomery Tully. 1950. Britain. 82 min. Sound. 16mm B&W. *Rental:* Ivy Films. *Sale:* Rep Pic Film.

Mrs. Ghandi's India. 1976. (Documentary). 55 min. Sound. 16mm Color. *Rental:* Films Inc.

Mrs. Mike. Dick Powell & Evelyn Keyes. Directed by Louis King. 1949. United Artists. 99 min. Sound. 16mm B&W. *Rental:* Ivy Films. *Sale:* Rep Pic Film.

Mrs. Miniver. Greer Garson, Walter Pidgeon & Teresa Wright. Directed by William Wyler. 1942. MGM. 135 min. Sound. 16mm B&W. *Rental:* MGM United.

Mrs. O'Malley & Mr. Malone. Marjorie Main & James Whitmore. Directed by Norman Taurog. 1950. MGM. 69 min. Sound. 16mm B&W. *Rental:* MGM United.

Mrs. Parkington. Greer Carson & Walter Pidgeon. Directed by Tay Garnett. 1944. MGM. 124 min. Sound. 16mm B&W. *Rental:* MGM United.

Mrs. Pollifax: Spy. Rosalind Russell & Darren McGavin. Directed by Leslie Martinson. 1971. United Artists. 110 min. Sound. 16mm Color. *Rental:* MGM United.

Mrs. Warren's Profession. 1976. Britain. (Cast unlisted). 115 min. Videotape Color. *Rental:* Films Inc. *Sale:* Films Inc.

Mrs. Wiggs of the Cabbage Patch. Fay Bainter & Hugh Herbert. Directed by Ralph Murphy. 1942. Paramount. 80 min. Sound. 16mm B&W. *Rental:* Swank Motion.

Mrs. Wiggs of the Cabbage Patch. W. C. Fields & Pauline Lord. Directed by Norman Taurog. 1934. Paramount. 80 min. Sound. 16mm B&W. *Rental:* Swank Motion.

Muchachos Que Estudian. Span. 1950. Mexico. (Cast unlisted). 90 min. Sound. 16mm B&W. *Rental:* Film Classics.

Muchachos Se Divierten, Los. Span. 1950. Mexico. (Cast unlisted). 90 min. Sound. 16mm B&W. *Rental:* Film Classics.

Mud & Water Man, The. 1973. Britain. (Documentary). 50 min. Sound. 16mm Color. *Rental:* Films Inc & U Mich Media. *Sale:* Films Inc. *Sale:* Films Inc, Videotape version.

Mud Honey. Hal Hopper. Directed by Russ Meyer. 1965. Eve. 92 min. Sound. 16mm B&W. *Rental:* Corinth Films.

Muddy River. Nobutake Asahara, Takahiro Tamura & Yumiko Fujita. Directed by Kohei Oguri. Jap. 1981. Japan. 105 min. Sound. 16mm B&W. subtitles. *Rental:* New Yorker Films.

Muddy Waters. Ken Mitsuta & Akiko Tamura. Directed by Tadashi Imai. Jap. 1953. Japan. 104 min. Sound. 16mm B&W. subtitles. *Rental:* Films Inc.

Mude Tod, Der *see* Destiny.

Mudlark, The. Irene Dunne, Sir Alec Guinness. Directed by Jean Negulesco. 1950. Britain. 99 min. Sound. 16mm B&W. *Rental:* Films Inc.

Muerte Civil. Span. 1950. Mexico. (Cast unlisted). 90 min. Sound. 16mm B&W. *Rental:* Film Classics.

Muerte de Che Guevara, El. Francisco Rabal & John Ireland. Directed by Paolo Heusch. 1968. Italy. 98 min. Sound. 16mm Color. *Rental:* Films Inc & Ivy Films. *Sale:* Tamarelles French Film, Videotape version.

Muerto, El. Thelma Biral, Juan Jose Camero & Francisco Rabal. Span. Spain. 105 min. Sound. Videotape Color. *Sale:* Tamarelles French Films.

Mug Town. Grace McDonald & Edward Norris. Directed by Ray Taylor. 1942. Universal. 60 min. Sound. 16mm B&W. *Rental:* Swank Motion.

Muggers, The. Kent Smith & James Franciscus. Directed by William Berke. 1958. United Artists. 74 min. Sound. 16mm B&W. *Rental:* MGM United.

Muhammad Ali - Skill, Brains & Guts. 1975. Macmillan. (Documentary). 90 min. Sound. 16mm Color. *Rental:* Films Inc.

Muhymatsu *see* Rikisha Man.

Mujer Del Zapatero, La. Isabel Sarli & Pepe Arias. Directed by Armando Bo. Span. Mexico. 100 min. Sound. 16mm B&W. subtitles. *Rental:* Westcoast Films.

Mule Train. Gene Autry. Directed by John English. 1950. Columbia. 63 min. Sound. 16mm B&W. *Rental:* Inst Cinema.

Multi-Disciplinary Study, A. 1971. 45 min. 16mm Color. *Rental:* Natl AV Ctr.

Multiple Maniacs. David Lochary & Mary Vivian Pearce. Directed by John Waters. 1970. John Waters. 94 min. Sound. 16mm B&W. *Rental:* New Line Cinema.

Multiply: And Subdue the Earth. 1969. PBL. (Documentary). 67 min. Sound. 16mm B&W. *Rental:* Indiana AV Ctr & U Mich Media. *Rental:* Indiana AV Ctr & U Cal Media, Color version, Videotape version.

Mummy, The. Boris Karloff. Directed by Karl Freund. 1932. Universal. 72 min. Sound. 16mm B&W. *Rental:* Films InC, Swank Motion & Twyman Films.

Mummy, The. Peter Cushing & Christopher Lee. Directed by Terence Fisher. 1959. Universal. 88 min. Sound. 16mm Color. *Rental:* Films Inc, Modern Sound, Swank Motion & Twyman Films.

Mummy's Boys. Bert Wheeler & Robert Woolsey. Directed by Fred Guiol. 1937. RKO. 68 min. Sound. 16mm *Rental:* RKO General Pics.

Mummy's Curse, The. Lon Chaney Jr. & Martin Kosleck. Directed by Leslie Goodwins. 1944. Universal. 62 min. Sound. 16mm B&W. *Rental:* Swank Motion.

Mummy's Ghost, The. Lon Chaney Jr. & George Zucco. Directed by Reginald Le Borg. 1944. Universal. 61 min. Sound. 16mm B&W. *Rental:* Swank Motion.

Mummy's Hand, The. Dick Foran & Peggy Moran. Directed by Christy Cabanne. 1940. Universal. 72 min. Sound. 16mm B&W. *Rental:* Film Ctr DC & Swank Motion.

Mummy's Shroud, The. Andre Morell & John Philips. Directed by John Gilling. 1967. Fox. 91 min. Sound. 16mm Color. *Rental:* Films Inc.

Mummy's Tomb, The. Dick Foran & Lon Chaney Jr. Directed by Harold Young. 1942. Universal. 67 min. Sound. 16mm B&W. *Rental:* Swank Motion.

Mumu. Afanasi Kochetkov. Directed by Anatoli Bobrovsky & Yevgeni Teterin. Rus. 1960. Russia. 71 min. Sound. 16mm B&W. subtitles. *Rental:* Corinth Films.

Mundo de los Vampiros, El *see* World of the Vampires.

Munster Go Home. Fred Gwynne & Yvonne De Carlo. Directed by Earl Bellamy. 1966. Universal. 96 min. Sound. 16mm Color. *Rental:* Swank Motion.

Muppet Movie, The. Jim Henson & Frank Oz. Directed by James Frawley. 1979. AFD. 98 min. Sound. 16mm Color. *Rental:* Swank Motion.

Muralla Invisible, La. Michael Gwynne. Directed by Stuart Rosenberg. 1961. DeRochemont. 107 min. Sound. 16mm B&W. dubbed Span. *Rental:* Lutheran Film. *Sale:* Lutheran Film.

Murder. Herbert Marshall. Directed by Alfred Hitchcock. 1930. Britain. 102 min. Sound. 16mm B&W. *Rental:* Budget Films, Em Gee Film Lib, Films Inc, Inst Cinema, Images Film, Ivy Films, Janus Films, Kit Parker, Westcoast Films & Wholesome Film Ctr. *Sale:* Cinema Concepts, Natl Cinema, Reel Images & Images Film. *Rental:* Ivy Films, *Sale:* Ivy Films & Images Film, Super 8 sound version. *Sale:* Cinema Concepts, Festival Films & Tamarelles French Film, Videotape version.

Murder Ahoy. Margaret Rutherford & Lionel Jeffries. Directed by George Pollock. 1964. Britain. 93 min. Sound. 16mm B&W. *Rental:* MGM United.

Murder Among Friends. Marjorie Weaver & John Hubbard. Directed by Ray McCarey. 1941. Fox. 68 min. Sound. 16mm B&W. *Rental:* Willoughby Peer.

Murder at Malibu Beach see Trap.

Murder at Midnight. Aileen Pringle & Alice White. Directed by Frank R. Strayer. 1931. Tiffany. 60 min. Sound. 16mm B&W. *Sale:* Morcraft Films.

Murder at the Baskervilles see Silver Blaze.

Murder at the Burlesque see Murder at the Windmill.

Murder at the Gallop. Margaret Rutherford & Robert Morley. Directed by George Pollock. 1963. Britain. 81 min. Sound. 16mm B&W. *Rental:* MGM United.

Murder at the Vanities. Carl Brisson & Kitty Carlisle. Directed by Mitchell Leisen. 1934. Paramount. 89 min. Sound. 16mm B&W. *Rental:* Swank Motion.

Murder at the Windmill. Orig. Title: Murder at the Burlesque. Garry Marsh. Directed by Val Guest. 1949. Britain. 70 min. Sound. 16mm B&W. *Rental:* Bosco Films & Charard Motion Pics.

Murder by an Aristocrat. Lyle Talbot & Marguerite Churchill. Directed by Frank McDonald. 1936. Warners. 60 min. Sound. 16mm B&W. *Rental:* MGM United.

Murder by Contract. Vincent Edwards & Herschel Bernardi. Directed by Irving Lerner. 1958. Columbia. 81 min. Sound. 16mm B&W. *Rental:* Kit Parker.

Murder by Death. Truman Capote, Peter Falk, Peter Sellers, Sir Alec Guinness. Directed by Robert Moore. 1976. Columbia. 94 min. Sound. 16mm Color. *Rental:* Arcus Film, Budget Films, Film, Images Film, Kit Parker, Swank Motion, Welling Motion Pictures, Westcoast Films & Williams Films. *Rental:* Swank Motion, Videotape version.

Murder by Decree. Christopher Plummer & James Mason. Directed by Bob Clark. 1979. Embassy. 121 min. Sound. 16mm Color. *Rental:* Films Inc.

Murder by Rope. Wilfred Hyde-White. Directed by George Pearson. 1936. Britain. 64 min. Sound. 16mm B&W. *Rental:* Film Classics.

Murder by Television. Bela Lugosi & George Meeker. 1935. Cameo. 60 min. Sound. 16mm B&W. *Rental:* Budget Films & Mogulls Films.

Murder Clinic, The. William Berger & Francoise Prevost. Directed by Michael Hamilton. 1966. France & Italy. 87 min. Sound. 16mm Color. dubbed. *Rental:* Video Comm. *Rental:* Video Comm, Videotape version.

Murder Game, The. Ken Scott & Marla Landi. Directed by Sidney Salkow. 1968. Britain. 75 min. Sound. 16mm B&W. *Rental:* Films Inc.

Murder, He Says. Fred MacMurray & Helen Walker. Directed by George Marshall. 1945. Paramount. 91 min. Sound. 16mm B&W. *Rental:* Swank Motion.

Murder in Greenwich Village. Richard Arlen & Fay Wray. Directed by Albert S. Rogell. 1937. Columbia. 70 min. Sound. 16mm B&W. *Rental:* Kit Parker.

Murder in Reverse. William Hartnell & Dinah Sheridan. Directed by Montgomery Tully. 1945. Republic. 78 min. Sound. 16mm B&W. *Rental:* Ivy Films.

Murder in the Air. Ronald Reagan & John Litel. Directed by Lewis Seiler. 1940. Warners. 55 min. Sound. 16mm B&W. *Rental:* MGM United.

Murder in the Blue Room. Donald Cook & Anne Gwynne. Directed by Leslie Goodwins. 1944. Universal. 60 min. Sound. 16mm B&W. *Rental:* Mogulls Films & Film Ctr DC.

Murder in the Cathedral. Leo McKern & Niall MacGinnis. Directed by George Hoellering. 1952. Britain. 140 min. Sound. 16mm B&W. *Rental:* Films Inc.

Murder in the Clouds. Lyle Talbot & Ann Dvorak. Directed by D. Ross Lederman. 1934. Warners. 61 min. Sound. 16mm B&W. *Rental:* MGM United.

Murder in the Doll House. Yusaka Matsuda & Hiroko Shino. Directed by Susumu Kodama. Jap. 1979. Japan. 92 min. Sound. Videotape Color. subtitles. *Sale:* Tamarelles French Films.

Murder in the Fleet. Robert Taylor & Jean Parker. Directed by Edward Sedgwick. 1935. MGM. 71 min. Sound. 16mm B&W. *Rental:* MGM United.

Murder in the Footlights. Orig. Title: Trojan Brothers, The. David Farrar. Directed by Maclean Rogers. 1946. Britain. 85 min. Sound. 16mm B&W. *Rental:* Ivy Films.

Murder in the Music Hall. Orig. Title: Midnight Melody. Vera Ralston & William Marshall. Directed by John English. 1946. Republic. 89 min. Sound. 16mm B&W. *Rental:* Ivy Films.

Murder in the Private Car. Charles Ruggles & Una Merkel. Directed by Harry Beaumont. 1934. MGM. 52 min. Sound. 16mm B&W. *Rental:* MGM United.

Murder in the Red Barn. Orig. Title: Maria Marten. Tod Slaughter & Eric Portman. Directed by George King. 1935. Britain. 65 min. Sound. 16mm B&W. *Rental:* Budget Films.

Murder, Inc. Stuart Whitman & Peter Falk. Directed by Burt Balaban. 1960. Fox. 103 min. Sound. 16mm B&W. *Rental:* Mogulls Films. *Rental:* Willoughby Peer, Anamorphic B&W version.

Murder Is My Business. Hugh Beaumont & Cheryl Walker. Directed by Sam Newfield. 1946. PRC. 63 min. Sound. 16mm B&W. *Sale:* Classics Assoc NY.

Murder Man, The. Spencer Tracy, James Stewart & Virginia Bruce. Directed by Tim Whelan. 1935. MGM. 71 min. Sound. 16mm B&W. *Rental:* MGM United.

Murder Most Foul, A. Margaret Rutherford & Stringer Davis. Directed by George Pollock. 1964. Britain. 90 min. Sound. 16mm B&W. *Rental:* MGM United.

Murder, My Sweet. Dick Powell & Claire Trevor. Directed by Edward Dmytryk. 1944. RKO. 95 min. Sound. 16mm B&W. *Rental:* Films Inc. *Lease:* Films Inc.

Murder, My Sweet. Dick Powell & Claire Trevor. Directed by Edward Dmytryk. 1945. RKO. 95 min. Sound. 16mm *Rental:* RKO General Pics.

Murder of Dr. Harrigan, The. Ricardo Cortez & Mary Astor. Directed by Frank McDonald. 1936. Warners. 67 min. Sound. 16mm B&W. *Rental:* MGM United.

Murder of Fred Hampton, The. 1971. National Talent Service. (Documentary). 88 min. Sound. 16mm B&W. *Rental:* Tricontinental Film & Video Tape Network. *Rental:* Video Tape Network, Videotape version.

Murder on a Honeymoon. Edna May Oliver & James Gleason. Directed by Lloyd Corrigan. 1935. RKO. 73 min. Sound. 16mm B&W. *Rental:* RKO General Pics.

Murder on Diamond Row. Orig. Title: Squeaker, The. Edmund Lowe, Robert Newton & Alastair Sim. Directed by William K. Howard. 1937. Britain. 77 min. Sound. 16mm B&W. *Rental:* Mogulls Films.

Murder on Lennox Avenue. Mamie Smith & Alec Lovejoy. 60 min. Sound. 16mm B&W. *Rental:* Budget Films & Em Gee Film Lib.

Murder on the Blackboard. Regis Toomey & Bruce Cabot. Directed by Pandro S. Berman. 1934. RKO. 71 min. Sound. 16mm B&W. *Rental:* RKO General Pics.

Murder on the Bridal Path. Helen Broderick & James Gleason. Directed by William Sistrom. 1936. RKO. 66 min. Sound. 16mm B&W. *Rental:* RKO General Pics.

Murder on the Campus. Charles Starrett & Shirley Grey. Directed by Richard Thorpe. 1932. Chesterfield. 70 min. Sound. 16mm B&W. *Rental:* Budget Films.

Murder on the Orient Express. Albert Finney, Ingrid Bergman & Lauren Bacall. Directed by Sidney Lumet. 1974. Paramount. 128 min. Sound. 16mm Color. *Rental:* Films Inc.

Murder on the Waterfront. Warren Douglas & John Loder. Directed by B. Reeves Eason. 1943. Warners. 49 min. Sound. 16mm B&W. *Rental:* MGM United.

Murder One. Directed by Tex Fuller. 1978. Benchmark. 50 min. Sound. 16mm Color. *Rental:* Benchmark Films, Best Films, U of Il Film & Utah Media. *Sale:* Benchmark Films & Best Films.

Murder Over New York. Sidney Toler. Directed by Harry Lachman. 1940. Fox. 65 min. Sound. 16mm B&W. *Rental:* Films Inc.

Murder She Said. Margaret Rutherford & Arthur Kennedy. Directed by George Pollock. 1962. Britain. 87 min. Sound. 16mm B&W. *Rental:* MGM United.

Murder With Music. Bob Howard. Directed by George P. Quigley. 1945. Century. 60 min. Sound. 16mm B&W. *Rental:* Budget Films. *Sale:* Morcraft Films.

Murder Without Tears. Craig Stevens & Joyce Holden. Directed by William Beaudine. 1953. Allied Artists. 64 min. Sound. 16mm B&W. *Rental:* Ivy Films. *Sale:* Rep Pic Film.

Murder, Inc. *see* Enforcer.

Murderer Stalks, A. John Gardner. 1953. Britain. 72 min. Sound. 16mm B&W. *Rental:* Film Classics.

Murderers Are Among Us. Hildgegard Knef & Ernst Wilhelm. Directed by Wolfgang Staudte. Ger. 1946. 84 min. Sound. 16mm B&W. subtitles Eng. *Rental:* Films Inc.

Murderers' Row. Dean Martin & Karl Malden. Directed by Henry Levin. 1966. Columbia. 108 min. Sound. 16mm Color. *Rental:* Cine Craft, Film Ctr DC, Films Inc, Inst Cinema, Modern Sound, Roas Films, Video Comm, Welling Motion Pictures, Westcoast Films & Wholesome Film Ctr.

Murders in the Rue Morgue. Jason Robards. Directed by Gordon Hessler. 1971. American International. 87 min. Sound. 16mm Color. *Rental:* Arcus Film, Buchan Pic, Swank Motion & Wholesome Film Ctr.

Murders in the Rue Morgue, The. Bela Lugosi & Sidney Fox. Directed by Robert Florey. 1932. Universal. 75 min. Sound. 16mm B&W. *Rental:* Swank Motion & Welling Motion Pictures.

Murders in the Zoo. Charles Ruggles & Lionel Atwill. Directed by Edward Sutherland. 1933. Paramount. 64 min. Sound. 16mm B&W. *Rental:* Swank Motion.

Muria, The. 1982. Britain. (Documentary). 55 min. Sound. 16mm Color. *Rental:* Films Inc. *Sale:* Films Inc. *Sale:* Films Inc, Videotape version.

Muriel. Delphine Seyrig. Directed by Alain Resnais. Fr. 1963. France. 120 min. Sound. 16mm Color. subtitles. *Rental:* Corinth Films & Images Film. *Lease:* Corinth Films.

Murmur of the Heart. Lea Massari & Benoit Ferreaux. Directed by Louis Malle. Fr. 1971. France. 110 min. Sound. 16mm Color. subtitles. *Rental:* Kino Intl. *Sale:* Kino Intl.

Murphy's War. Peter O'Toole & Sian Phillips. Directed by Peter Yates. 1971. Paramount. (Anamorphic). 106 min. Sound. 16mm Color. *Rental:* Films Inc.

Mursi, The. 1974. Ethiopia. (Documentary). 53 min. Sound. 16mm Color. *Rental:* Human Issues. *Sale:* Human Issues.

Murudruni. 1962. Lamport. (Documentary). 60 min. Sound. 16mm Color. *Rental:* U Cal Media.

Musashi Miyamoto *see* Samurai.

Muscle Beach Party. Frankie Avalon & Annette Funicello. Directed by William Asher. 1964. American International. 96 min. Sound. 16mm Color. *Rental:* Cine Craft, Roas Films, Welling Motion Pictures, Westcoast Films & Williams Films. *Rental:* Budget Films, Anamorphic version.

Muscles & Flowers. Directed by Walter Gutman. 1969. Walter Gutman. (Experimental). 90 min. Sound. 16mm Color. *Rental:* Canyon Cinema.

Museum & the Fury, The. Directed by Leo Hurwitz. 1956. Poland. (Documentary). 60 min. Sound. 16mm B&W. *Rental:* Museum Mod Art.

Music. 1969. NBC. (Documentary). 53 min. Sound. 16mm Color. *Rental:* Films Inc, Syracuse U Film, Twyman Films, U Cal Media & U Mich Media. *Sale:* Films Inc. *Sale:* Films Inc, Videotape version.

Music. 1969. 50 min. Sound. 16mm Color. *Rental:* Iowa Films.

Music & People of the Northeast. Directed by Taia Quaresma. 1978. Brazil. (Documentary). 60 min. Sound. 16mm Color. narrated Eng. *Rental:* Lat Amer Film.

Music Box Kid, The. Ron Foster & Luana Patten. Directed by Edward L. Cahn. 1960. United Artists. 75 min. Sound. 16mm B&W. *Rental:* MGM United.

Music Child. Directed by David Parry. Rel. 1976. Benhaven. (Documentary). 47 min. Sound. 16mm Color. *Rental:* Benchmark Films, U Cal Media & U of IL Film.

Music for Madame. Joan Fontaine & Jack Carson. Directed by John G. Blystone. 1938. RKO. 81 min. Sound. 16mm *Rental:* RKO General Pics.

Music for Millions. Margaret O'Brien & June Allyson. Directed by Henry Koster. 1944. MGM. 117 min. Sound. 16mm B&W. *Rental:* MGM United.

Music from Aspen. 1979. PBS. (Concert). 59 min. Videotape Color. *Rental:* PBS Video. *Sale:* PBS Video.

Music I Morker *see* Night Is My Future.

Music in Manhattan. Anne Shirley & Dennis Day. Directed by John H. Auer. 1943. RKO. 80 min. Sound. 16mm B&W. *Rental:* Films Inc.

Music in My Heart. Tony Martin & Rita Hayworth. Directed by Joseph Santley. 1940. Columbia. 80 min. Sound. 16mm B&W. *Rental:* Films Inc, Newman Film Lib & Welling Motion Pictures.

Music is Magic. Bebe Daniels & Alice Faye. Directed by George Marshall. 1935. Fox. 65 min. Sound. 16mm B&W. *Rental:* Films Inc.

Music Lovers, The. Richard Chamberlain & Glenda Jackson. Directed by Ken Russell. 1971. United Artists. 122 min. Sound. 16mm Color. *Rental:* MGM United.

Music Makers of the Blue Ridge, The. 1967. NET. (Documentary). 48 min. Sound. 16mm B&W. *Rental:* Indiana AV Ctr. *Sale:* Indiana AV Ctr. *Sale:* Indiana AV Ctr, Videotape version.

Music Man. Freddie Stewart. Directed by Will Jason. 1948. Monogram. 66 min. Sound. 16mm B&W. *Rental:* Hurlock Cine.

Music Man, The. Robert Preston & Shirley Jones. Directed by Morton Da Costa. 1962. 151 min. Sound. 16mm Color. *Rental:* Cine Craft, Charard Motion Pics, Inst Cinema, Swank Motion, Trans-World Films, Video Comm & Willoughby Peer.

Music of Man: The Sound or Unsound. 1981. Time-Life. (Documentary). 57 min. Videotape Color. *Rental:* Iowa Films.

Music of the Spheres. (Ascent of Man Ser.). 1974. Britain. (Documentary). 52 min. Sound. 16mm Color. *Rental:* Iowa Films, U Cal Media, U Mich Media & Utah Media.

Music on the River. 1962. NET. (Documentary). 54 min. Sound. 16mm B&W. *Rental:* Indiana AV Ctr. *Sale:* Indiana AV Ctr.

Music Room, The. Chhabi Biswas & Padma Devi. Directed by Satyajit Ray. Bengali. 1959. India. 95 min. Sound. 16mm B&W. subtitles. *Rental:* Films Inc.

Musica En la Noche. Martha Victoria. Mexico. 85 min. Sound. 16mm B&W. *Rental:* Trans-World Films.

Musica Proibita *see* Forbidden Music.

Musical Compliation. 88 min. Sound. 16mm Color. *Rental:* Budget Films.

Musical Holdouts. Directed by John Cohen. 1975. Phoenix. (Documentary). 51 min. Sound. 16mm Color. *Rental:* Budget Films, Phoenix Films & U of IL Film. *Sale:* Phoenix Films. *Sale:* Phoenix Films, Videotape version.

Musical Instrument Maker, The: Spinet Making in Colonial America. 1981. Colonial Williamsburg. (Documentary). 53 min. Sound. 16mm Color. *Rental:* Colonial. *Sale:* Colonial.

Muss 'em Up. Preston Foster & Ward Bond. Directed by Pandro S. Berman. 1936. RKO. 68 min. Sound. 16mm *Rental:* RKO General Pics.

Mustang Country. Joel McCrea. Directed by John Champion. 1976. Universal. 79 min. Sound. 16mm Color. *Rental:* Twyman Films.

Mutations. Donald Pleasence & Tom Baker. Directed by Jack Cardiff. 1973. Britain. 96 min. Sound. 16mm Color. *Rental:* Modern Sound, Swank Motion, Welling Motion Pictures & Westcoast Films.

Muthers, The. Jeanne Bell. Directed by Cirio H. Santiago. 1976. Dimension. 83 min. Sound. 16mm Color. *Rental:* Williams Films. *Sale:* Salz Ent.

Mutiny. Mark Stevens & Patric Knowles. Directed by Edward Dmytryk. 1952. United Artists. 77 min. Sound. 16mm Color. *Rental:* Films Inc.

Mutiny at Fort Sharp. Broderick Crawford. 1965. Italy. 91 min. Sound. 16mm Color. dubbed. *Rental:* Video Comm.

Mutiny in Outer Space. William Leslie & Dolores Faith. Directed by Hugo Grimaldi. 1965. Woolner. 82 min. Sound. 16mm B&W. *Rental:* Willoughby Peer.

Mutiny in the South Seas. John Hansen & Horst Frank. 1966. Germany. 83 min. Sound. 16mm Color. dubbed. *Rental:* Westcoast Films.

Mutiny on the Bounty. Clark Gable & Charles Laughton. Directed by Frank Lloyd. 1935. MGM. 132 min. Sound. 16mm B&W. *Rental:* MGM United. *Sale:* MGM United. *Sale:* Films Inc, Abridged 72 min. version.

Mutiny on the Bounty. Marlon Brando & Trevor Howard. Directed by Lewis Milestone. 1962. MGM. (Anamorphic). 179 min. Sound. 16mm Color. *Rental:* MGM United. *Rental:* MGM United, Videotape version.

Mutiny on the Elsinore. Paul Lukas. Directed by Roy Lockwood. 1939. Regal. 80 min. Sound. 16mm B&W. *Rental:* Film Classics, Learning Corp Am & Mogulls Films. *Sale:* Learning Corp Am.

Mutt & Jeff & Bugoff. (Animated). 76 min. Sound. 16mm Color. *Rental:* Films Inc & Westcoast Films.

My Ain Folk. 1975. Britain. (Documentary). 55 min. Sound. 16mm B&W. *Rental:* Films Inc & Museum Mod Art. *Sale:* Films Inc. *Sale:* Films Inc, Videotape version.

My Apprenticeship. Alexei Lyarsky & Varvara Massalitinova. Directed by Mark Donskoi. Rus. 1939. Russia. 101 min. Sound. 16mm B&W. subtitles. *Rental:* Corinth Films.

My Beloved. Alexei Batalov & Inna Makarova. Directed by Josef Heifitz. Rus. 1958. Russia. 105 min. Sound. 16mm B&W. subtitles. *Rental:* Corinth Films.

My Best Friend. Heintje. Germany. 93 min. Sound. 16mm Color. dubbed. *Rental:* Budget Films, Modern Sound & Roas Films.

My Best Gal. Jane Withers & Jimmy Lydon. Directed by Anthony Mann. 1941. Republic. 67 min. Sound. 16mm B&W. *Rental:* Ivy Films.

My Bill. Kay Francis & Bonita Granville. Directed by John Farrow. 1938. Warners. 64 min. Sound. 16mm B&W. *Rental:* MGM United.

My Bloody Valentine. Paul Kelman & Lori Hallier. Directed by George Mihalka. 1981. Paramount. 91 min. Sound. 16mm Color. *Rental:* Films Inc.

My Blue Heaven. Betty Grable & Dan Dailey. Directed by Henry Koster. 1950. Fox. 96 min. Sound. 16mm B&W. *Rental:* Films Inc. *Rental:* Films Inc, Color version.

My Bodyguard. Chris Makepeace & Adam Baldwin. Directed by Tony Bill. 1980. Fox. 96 min. Sound. 16mm Color. *Rental:* Films Inc.

My Boy. Jackie Coogan. Directed by Victor Heerman & Albert Austin. 1922. First National. 60 min. Silent. 8mm B&W. *Rental:* Film Classics. *Sale:* Cinema Concepts & Film Classics.

My Boys Are Good Boys. Ralph Meeker & Ida Lupino. Directed by Bethel Buckalew. 1978. 90 min. Sound. 16mm Color. *Rental:* Swank Motion.

My Brilliant Career. Judy Davis. Directed by Gillian Armstrong. 1980. Australia. 101 min. Sound. 16mm Color. *Rental:* Cinema Five.

My Brother Talks to Horses. Butch Jenkins & Peter Lawford. Directed by Fred Zinnemann. 1946. MGM. 93 min. Sound. 16mm B&W. *Rental:* MGM United.

My Buddy. Don Barry & Lynne Roberts. Directed by Steve Sekely. 1944. Republic. 71 min. Sound. 16mm B&W. *Rental:* Ivy Films.

My Childhood. 2 Pts. 1967. Metromedia. (Documentary). 51 min. Sound. 16mm B&W. *Rental:* Benchmark Films, Films Inc, Iowa Films, SD AV Ctr, Syracuse U Film & U Mich Media. *Sale:* Benchmark Films & Films Inc. *Sale:* Films Inc, Videotape version. *Sale:* Benchmark Films, 8mm version avail. version.

My Childhood. Stephen Archibald, Jean-Taylor Smith & Hughie Restorick. Directed by Bill Douglas. 1972. Britain. 48 min. Sound. 16mm B&W. *Rental:* Museum Mod Art.

My Cousin Rachel. Olivia De Havilland & Richard Burton. Directed by Henry Koster. 1952. Fox. 98 min. Sound. 16mm B&W. *Rental:* Films Inc.

My Darling Clementine. Henry Fonda, Victor Mature & Linda Darnell. Directed by John Ford. 1946. Fox. 97 min. Sound. 16mm B&W. *Rental:* Films Inc.

My Dear Miss Aldrich. Edna May Oliver & Maureen O'Sullivan. Directed by George B. Seitz. 1937. MGM. 73 min. Sound. 16mm B&W. *Rental:* MGM United.

My Dear Secretary. Laraine Day & Kirk Douglas. Directed by Charles Martin. 1948. United Artists. 94 min. Sound. 16mm B&W. *Rental:* Video Comm. *Lease:* Video Comm. *Rental:* Video Comm, Videotape version.

My Dinner with Andre. Wallace Shawn. Directed by Louis Malle. 1981. New Yorker. 110 min. Sound. 16mm Color. *Rental:* New Yorker Films.

My Dog Buddy. Ken Curtis. Directed by Ray Kellogg. 1960. Columbia. 77 min. Sound. 16mm B&W. *Rental:* Cine Craft, Modern Sound & Film Ctr DC. *Rental:* Westcoast Films, 90 mins. version.

My Dog Rusty. Ted Donaldson & John Litel. Directed by Lew Landers. 1948. Columbia. 70 min. Sound. 16mm B&W. *Rental:* Charard Motion Pics, Films Inc & Inst Cinema.

My Dog Shep. William Farnum & Tom Neal. Directed by Ford Beebe. 1948. Screen Guild. 88 min. Sound. 16mm B&W. *Rental:* Alba House, Film Classics, Mogulls Films, #Film Ctr DC, Welling Motion Pictures & Westcoast Films.

My Dream Is Yours. Doris Day & Jack Carson. Directed by Michael Curtiz. 1949. Warners. 101 min. Sound. Color. *Rental:* MGM United.

My Fair Lady. Rex Harrison, Audrey Hepburn & Stanley Holloway. Directed by George Cukor. 1964. Warners. 170 min. Sound. 16mm Color. *Rental:* Swank Motion. *Rental:* Swank Motion, Anamorphic color version. *Rental:* Swank Motion, Videotape version.

My Father's House. Ronnie Cohen & Irene Broza. Directed by Herbert Kline. 1946. 56 min. Sound. 16mm B&W. *Rental:* Films Inc.

My Favorite Blonde. Bob Hope & Madeline Carroll. Directed by Sidney Lanfield. 1942. Paramount. 77 min. Sound. 16mm B&W. *Rental:* Swank Motion.

My Favorite Brunette. Bob Hope & Dorothy Lamour. Directed by Elliott Nugent. 1947. Paramount. 88 min. Sound. 16mm B&W. *Rental:* Films Inc. *Sale:* Festival Films & Natl Cinema. *Rental:* Maljack & Video Comm, *Sale:* Festival Films & Tamarelles French Film, Videotape version.

My Favorite Spy. Jane Wyman & Kay Kayser. Directed by Tay Garnett. 1942. RKO. 86 min. Sound. 16mm B&W. *Rental:* Films Inc.

My Favorite Spy. Bob Hope & Hedy Lamarr. Directed by Norman Z. McLeod. 1951. Paramount. 93 min. Sound. 16mm B&W. *Rental:* Films Inc.

My Favorite Wife. Irene Dunne, Cary Grant, Randolph Scott & Gail Patrick. Directed by Garson Kanin. 1940. RKO. 88 min. Sound. 16mm B&W. *Rental:* Films Inc. *Lease:* Films Inc.

My Favorite Year. Peter O'Toole, Jessica Harper & Mark Linn Baker. Directed by Richard Benjamin. 1982. 93 min. Sound. 16mm Color. *Rental:* MGM United. *Rental:* MGM United, Videotape version.

My Foolish Heart. Susan Hayward & Dana Andrews. Directed by Mark Robson. 1949. Goldwyn. 98 min. Sound. 16mm B&W. *Rental:* Films Inc.

My Forbidden Past. Robert Mitchum & Ava Gardner. Directed by Robert Stevenson. 1951. RKO. 81 min. Sound. 16mm B&W. *Rental:* Films Inc. *Sale:* Tamarelles French Film, Videotape version.

My Four Years in Germany. Louis Dean. Directed by William Nigh. 1918. Warners. (Musical Score Only). 70 min. Sound. 16mm B&W. *Rental:* Budget Films & Em Gee Film Lib. *Sale:* Glenn Photo. *Sale:* Cinema Concepts & Glenn Photo, Super 8 silent version. *Sale:* Cinema Concepts, Silent 8mm version.

My Friend Flicka. Roddy McDowall, Preston Foster & Rita Johnson. Directed by Harold Schuster. 1943. Fox. 90 min. Sound. 16mm Color. *Rental:* Films Inc, Twyman Films & Williams Films.

My Friends. Ugo Tognazzi & Philippe Noiret. Directed by Mario Monicelli. Ital. 1976. Italy. 110 min. Sound. 16mm Color. subtitles. *Rental:* Hurlock Cine.

My Gal Sal. Rita Hayworth & Victor Mature. Directed by Irving Cummings. 1942. Fox. 103 min. Sound. 16mm Color. *Rental:* Films inc.

My Geisha. Shirley MacLaine & Yves Montand. Directed by Jack Cardiff. 1962. Anamorphic. 120 min. Sound. 16mm Color. *Rental:* Films Inc.

My Girl Tisa. Lilli Palmer & Akim Tamiroff. Directed by Elliott Nugent. 1948. Warners. 95 min. Sound. 16mm B&W. *Rental:* Corinth Films. *Lease:* Corinth Films.

My Gun Is Quick. Robert Bray & Whitney Blake. Directed by George White & Phil Victor. 1957. United Artists. 88 min. Sound. 16mm B&W. *Rental:* MGM United.

My Hands Are the Tools of My Soul. Directed by Arthur Barron. 1977. Barron. (Documentary). 54 min. Sound. 16mm Color. *Rental:* Texture Film, U of IL Film & U Mich Media. *Sale:* Texture Film. *Sale:* Texture Film, Videotape version.

My Heart Flies. Chinese. 1979. Taiwan. 60 min. Sound. 16mm Color. subtitles. *Rental:* Iowa Films.

My Hero *see* Southern Yankee.

My Husband, His Mistress & I. Bibi Andersson. Directed by Sergio Gobbi. 1975. France. 95 min. Sound. 16mm Color. dubbed. *Rental:* J Green Pics.

My Lady of Whims. Clara Bow. Directed by Dallas M. Fitzgerald. 1926. Arrow. 55 min. Silent. 8mm B&W. *Sale:* Cinema Concepts.

My Life to Live. Trans. Title: Vivre Sa Vie. Anna Karina. Directed by Jean-Luc Godard. Fr. 1962. France. 82 min. Sound. 16mm B&W. subtitles. *Rental:* Corinth Films, Images Film & New Yorker Films. *Sale:* Reel Images & Images Film.

My Little Chickadee. W. C. Fields & Mae West. Directed by Edward Cline. 1940. Universal. 92 min. Sound. 16mm B&W. *Rental:* Swank Motion. *Rental:* Swank Motion, Videotape version.

My Love Came Back. Olivia De Havilland, Jeffrey Lynn & Eddie Albert. Directed by Curtis Bernhardt. 1940. Warners. 81 min. Sound. 16mm B&W. *Rental:* MGM United.

My Love for Yours. Fred MacMurray, Madeleine Carroll & Allan Jones. Directed by Edward H. Griffith. 1939. Paramount. 95 min. Sound. 16mm B&W. *Sale:* Reel Images. *Sale:* Morcraft Films & Reel Images, Super 8 sound version.

My Love Has Been Burning. Kinuyo Tanaka. Directed by Kenji Mizoguchi. Jap. 1949. Japan. 84 min. Sound. 16mm B&W. subtitles. *Rental:* New Yorker Films.

My Love, My Enemy. Jason Robards & Hardy Kruger. 1977. Burbank International. 92 min. Videotape Color. *Sale:* Cinema Concepts. *Sale:* Cinema Concepts & Video Lib, Videotape version.

My Lover, My Son. Romy Schneider & Donald Houston. Directed by John Newland. 1970. MGM. 99 min. Sound. 16mm Color. *Rental:* MGM United.

My Man & I. Shelley Winters & Ricardo Montalban. Directed by William A. Wellman. 1952. MGM. 99 min. Sound. 16mm B&W. *Rental:* MGM United.

My Man Godfrey. William Powell, Carole Lombard & Alice Brady. Directed by Gregory La Cava. 1936. Universal. 90 min. Sound. 16mm B&W. *Rental:* Arcus Film, Budget Films, Classic Film Mus, Em Gee Film Lib, Films Inc, Inst Cinema, Images Film, Kit Parker, Maljack, Natl Film Video, Newman Film Lib, Swank Motion, Welling Motion Pictures, Westcoast Films & Wholesome Film Ctr. *Sale:* Classic Film Mus, Cinema Concepts, Glenn Photo, Morcraft Films, Reel Images & Images Film. *Rental:* Ivy Films, *Sale:* Blackhawk Films, Cinema Concepts, Glenn Photo, Ivy Films & Morcraft Films, Super 8 sound version. *Sale:* Tamarelles French Film & Images Film, Videotape version.

My Man Godfrey. June Allyson & David Niven. Directed by Henry Koster. 1957. Universal. 92 min. Sound. 16mm Color. *Rental:* Swank Motion & Utah Media. *Sale:* Festival Films. *Rental:* Utah Media, B&W version. *Sale:* Festival Films, Videotape version.

My Mom's Having a Baby. 1977. Depatie. (Cast unlisted). 47 min. Sound. 16mm Color. *Rental:* U Mich Media.

My Mother Was Never a Kid. Directed by Robert Fuest. 1981. ABC. (Cast unlisted). 46 min. Sound. 16mm Color. *Rental:* Learning Corp Am. *Sale:* Learning Corp Am.

My Name Is Barbra. Barbra Streisand. 1965. CB. 57 min. Videotape B&W. *Sale:* Reel Images.

My Name Is Children. 1966. Net. (Documentary). 60 min. Sound. 16mm B&W. *Rental:* Indiana AV Ctr, Iowa Films, Mass Media & SD AV Ctr.

My Name Is Ivan. Kolya Bursalev. Directed by Andrei Tarkovsky. 1962. Russia. 84 min. Sound. 16mm B&W. subtitles. *Rental:* Corinth Films.

My Name is Julia Ross. Nina Foch & Dame May Whitty. Directed by Joseph Lewis. 1945. Columbia. 65 min. Sound. 16mm B&W. *Rental:* Corinth Films & Films Inc.

My Name Is Nobody. Henry Fonda & Terence Hill. Directed by Tonino Valerii. 1974. Italy. 115 min. Sound. 16mm Color. dubbed. *Rental:* Films, Swank Motion, Twyman Films & Williams Films. *Rental:* Williams Films, Anamorphic version.

My Old Dutch. May McAvoy. Directed by Lawrence Trimble. 1926. Universal. 90 min. Silent. 16mm B&W. *Rental:* Em Gee Film Lib.

My Old Man's Place: Glory Boy. Arthur Kennedy & William Devane. Directed by Edwin Sherin. 1972. Cinerama. 93 min. Sound. 16mm Color. *Rental:* Swank Motion.

My Outlaw Brother. Mickey Rooney & Robert Preston. Directed by Elliott Nugent. 1951. United Artists. 82 min. Sound. 16mm B&W. *Rental:* Budget Films.

My Pal Gus. Richard Widmark & Joanne Dru. Directed by Robert Parrish. 1952. Fox. 83 min. Sound. 16mm B&W. *Rental:* Films Inc.

My Pal Trigger. Roy Rogers. Directed by Frank McDonald. 1946. Republic. 60 min. Sound. 16mm B&W. *Rental:* Ivy Films & Roas Films. *Sale:* Cinema Concepts & Rep Pic Film. *Sale:* Video Comm, Videotape version.

My Pal Wolf. Sharyn Moffett & Jill Esmond. Directed by Alfred M. Werker. 1944. RKO. 76 min. Sound. 16mm B&W. *Rental:* Films Inc.

My Past. Bebe Daniels & Ben Lyon. Directed by Roy Del Ruth. 1931. Warners. 72 min. Sound. 16mm B&W. *Rental:* MGM United.

My Reputation. Barbara Stanwyck, George Brent & Eve Arden. Directed by Curtis Bernhardt. 1946. Warners. 96 min. Sound. 16mm B&W. *Rental:* MGM United.

My Side of the Mountain. Ted Eccles & Theodore Bikel. Directed by James B. Clark. 1969. Paramount. (Anamorphic). 100 min. Sound. 16mm Color. *Rental:* Films Inc.

My Sin. Tallulah Bankhead & Fredric March. Directed by George Abbott. 1931. Paramount. 79 min. Sound. 16mm B&W. *Rental:* Swank Motion.

My Sister Eileen. Rosalind Russell & Janet Blair. Directed by Alexander Hall. 1942. Columbia. 96 min. Sound. 16mm B&W. *Rental:* Kit Parker.

My Sister Eileen. Janet Leigh, Jack Lemmon & Betty Garrett. Directed by Richard Quine. 1955. Columbia. 108 min. Sound. 16mm Color. *Rental:* Arcus Film, Budget Films, Film Ctr DC, Films Inc, Kit Parker, Roas Films, Twyman Films & Welling Motion Pictures. *Rental:* Bosco Films & Kit Parker, Anamorphic version.

My Six Convicts. Gilbert Roland & John Beal. Directed by Hugo Fregonese. 1952. Columbia. 104 min. Sound. 16mm B&W. *Rental:* Cine Craft, Films Inc, Inst Cinema & Modern Sound.

My Six Loves. Debbie Reynolds & Cliff Robertson. Directed by Gower Champion. 1963. Paramount. 101 min. Sound. 16mm Color. *Rental:* Films Inc.

My Son John. Helen Hayes & Robert Walker. Directed by Leo McCarey. 1952. Paramount. 122 min. Sound. 16mm B&W. *Rental:* Films Inc.

My Son, My Son. 1974. Ken Anderson. (Cast unlisted). 80 min. Sound. 16mm Color. *Rental:* G Herne.

My Son, the Hero. Pedro Armendariz. Directed by Duccio Tessari. 1963. Italy. 119 min. Sound. 16mm Color. dubbed. *Rental:* MGM United.

My Son, the Vampire. Orig. Title: Old Mother Riley Meets the Vampire. Bela Lugosi & Dora Bryan. Directed by John Gilling. 1946. Britain. 72 min. Sound. 16mm B&W. *Rental:* Films Inc.

My Song Goes Round the World. Josef Schmidt. Directed by Richard Oswald. 1934. Germany. 90 min. Sound. 16mm B&W. *Sale:* Cinema Concepts & Natl Cinema.

My Survival As an Aboriginal. Directed by Essie Coffey. 1980. Australia. (Documentary). Sound. 16mm Color. *Rental:* Icarus Films. *Sale:* Icarus Films. *Sale:* Icarus Films, Videotape version.

My Sweet Charlie. Patty Duke & Al Freeman Jr. Directed by Lamont Johnson. 1970. Universal. 97 min. Sound. 16mm Color. *Rental:* Cine Craft & Swank Motion.

My Tutor. Caren Kaye & Matt Lattanzi. Directed by George Bowers. 1983. Crown. 97 min. Sound. 16mm Color. *Rental:* Swank Motion.

My Uncle *see* Mon Oncle.

My Uncle. 110 min. Sound. 16mm Color. *Sale:* Natl Cinema.

My Uncle Antoine. Jean Duceppe. Directed by Claude Jutra. Fr. 1972. Canada. 110 min. Sound. 16mm Color. subtitles. *Rental:* Films Inc, Janus Films & Natl Film CN. *Sale:* Natl Film CN.

My Universities. Nicolai Valbert. Directed by Mark Donskoi. 1940. Russia. 101 min. Sound. 16mm B&W. *Rental:* Corinth Films.

My Way Home. Stephen Archibald, Joseph Blatchley & Paul Kermack. Directed by Bill Douglas. 1978. Britain. 80 min. Sound. 16mm B&W. *Rental:* Films Inc & Museum Mod Art.

My Wife's Best Friend. Anne Baxter & MacDonald Carey. Directed by Richard Sale. 1952. Fox. 87 min. Sound. 16mm B&W. *Rental:* Films Inc.

MAIN INDEX   MYSTERY

My Wife's Relatives. James Gleason & Harry Davenport. Directed by Gus Meins. 1939. Republic. 54 min. Sound. 16mm B&W. *Rental:* Ivy Films. *Sale:* Rep Pic Film.

My Wild Irish Rose. Dennis Morgan & Arlene Dahl. Directed by David Butler. 1947. Warners. 101 min. Sound. 16mm Color. *Rental:* MGM United.

My Woman. Helen Twelvetrees & Victor Jory. Directed by Victor Schertzinger. 1933. Columbia. 71 min. Sound. 16mm B&W. *Rental:* Kit Parker.

Myra Breckenridge. Mae West & Raquel Welch. Directed by Michael Sarne. 1970. Fox. (Anamorphic). 94 min. Sound. 16mm Color. *Rental:* Films Inc & Twyman Films.

Mysteres De Paris, Les. Jacques Dacqumine. Directed by Andre Hunebelle. 1962. France. 139 min. Sound. 16mm B&W. *Rental:* French Am Cul.

Mysterians, The. Kenji Sahara. Directed by Inoshiro Honda. 1954. Japan. 85 min. Sound. 16mm Color. dubbed. *Rental:* Budget Films, Films Inc, Ivy Films & Video Comm. *Lease:* Video Comm. *Rental:* Video Comm, *Lease:* Video Comm, Videotape version.

Mysteries of Outer Space. Directed by Wheeler Dixon. 1979. Gold Key. (Documentary). 96 min. Sound. 16mm Color. *Rental:* Gold Key.

Mysteries of the Bible. Directed by Wheeler Dixon. 1979. Gold Key. (Documentary). 96 min. Sound. 16mm Color. *Rental:* Gold Key.

Mysteries of the Great Pyramid. Directed by William Kronick. 1977. Wolper. (Documentary). 52 min. Sound. 16mm Color. *Rental:* U Cal Media, Films Inc, U of IL Film, U Mich Media & Syracuse U Film. *Sale:* Films Inc.

Mysteries of the Hidden Reefs, The. 1978. Metromedia. (Documentary). 52 min. Sound. 16mm Color. *Rental:* Churchill Films. *Rental:* Churchill Films, Videotape version.

Mysteries of the Mind, The. 59 min. Sound. 16mm Color. *Rental:* National Geographic Society. *Rental:* National Geographic Society, Video version.

Mysterious Bee, The. 1981. Phil Simon. (Documentary). 50 min. Sound. 16mm Color. *Rental:* U Cal Media, Films Inc & Syracuse U Film. *Sale:* Films Inc. *Rental:* Films Inc, *Sale:* Films Inc, Videotape version.

Mysterious Deep, The. 1968. CBS. (Documentary). 52 min. Sound. 16mm B&W. *Rental:* Macmillan Films. *Sale:* Macmillan Films.

Mysterious Desperado, The. Tim Holt & Richard Martin. Directed by Lesley Selander. 1950. RKO. 61 min. Sound. 16mm *Rental:* RKO General Pics.

Mysterious Discovery, The. V. Grachov. Directed by B. Bureyev. Rus. 1956. Russia. 73 min. Sound. 16mm B&W. subtitles. *Rental:* Corinth Films.

Mysterious Doctor, The. Eleanor Parker & John Loder. Directed by Ben Stoloff. 1943. Warners. 57 min. Sound. 16mm B&W. *Rental:* MGM United.

Mysterious Doctor Satan. Edward Ciannelli & Robert Wilcox. Directed by William Witney. 1940. Republic. 269 min. Sound. 16mm B&W. *Rental:* Ivy Films.

Mysterious Giants, The. Sunn. (Documentary). 90 min. Sound. 16mm Color. *Rental:* Williams Films, videotape version.

Mysterious Intruder, The. Richard Dix & Barton MacLane. Directed by William Castle. 1946. Columbia. 62 min. Sound. 16mm B&W. *Rental:* Kit Parker.

Mysterious Island, The. Lionel Barrymore. Directed by Lucien Hubbard. 1929. MGM. 94 min. Sound. 16mm B&W. *Rental:* MGM United.

Mysterious Island, The. Michael Craig & Joan Greenwood. Directed by Cy Endfield. 1962. Columbia. 101 min. Sound. 16mm Color. *Rental:* Bosco Films, Buchan Pic, Budget Films, Cine Craft, Charard Motion Pics, Film Ctr DC, Film Pres, Films Inc, Kerr Film, Kit Parker, Modern Sound, Natl Film Video, Newman Film Lib, Twyman Films, U of IL Film, Video Comm, Welling Motion Pictures, Westcoast Films, Wholesome Film Ctr & Williams Films.

Mysterious Island, The. Directed by Leif Gram. 1972. Australia. 60 min. Sound. 16mm Color. *Rental:* Budget Films & Wholesome Film Ctr.

Mysterious Lady, The. Greta Garbo. Directed by Fred Niblo. 1928. MGM. 90 min. Silent. 16mm B&W. *Rental:* MGM United.

Mysterious Miss X. Chick Chandler & Mary Hart. Directed by Gus Meins. 1939. Republic. 65 min. Sound. 16mm B&W. *Rental:* Ivy Films.

Mysterious Mr. Eliot, The. 1973. Britain. (Documentary). 62 min. Sound. 16mm Color. *Rental:* McGraw-Hill Films, Syracuse U Film & U Mich Media. *Sale:* McGraw-Hill Films.

Mysterious Mr. Valentine, The. William Henry & Linda Stirling. Directed by Philip Ford. 1946. Republic. 56 min. Sound. 16mm B&W. *Rental:* Ivy Films.

Mysterious Mr. Wong, The. Bela Lugosi & Wallace Ford. Directed by William Nigh. 1935. Monogram. 56 min. Sound. 16mm B&W. *Rental:* Budget Films, Classic Film Mus, Em Gee Film Lib, MGM United, Video Comm, Westcoast Films & Wholesome Film Ctr. *Sale:* Classic Film Mus & Natl Cinema. *Rental:* Ivy Films, *Sale:* Ivy Films, Super 8 sound version.

Mysterious Monsters, The. Directed by Richard Guenette. 1979. Viacom. (Documentary). 92 min. Sound. 16mm Color. *Sale:* Lucerne Films. *Sale:* Lucerne Films, Videotape version.

Mysterious Rider, The. Orig. Title: Fighting Phantom. Russell Hayden & Sidney Toler. Directed by Lesley Selander. 1938. Paramount. 68 min. Sound. 16mm B&W. *Rental:* Budget Films.

Mysterious Stranger, The see Code of the Lawless.

Mystery Broadcast. Frank Albertson & Paul Harvey. Directed by George Sherman. 1943. Republic. 54 min. Sound. 16mm B&W. *Rental:* Ivy Films. *Sale:* Rep Pic Film.

Mystery House. Ann Sheridan & Dick Purcell. Directed by Noel Smith. 1938. Warners. 57 min. Sound. 16mm B&W. *Rental:* MGM United.

Mystery in Mexico. William Lundigan & Ricardo Cortez. Directed by Robert Wise. 1948. RKO. 66 min. Sound. 16mm B&W. *Rental:* Films Inc.

Mystery Junction. Sidney Tafler. Directed by Michael McCarthy. 1951. Britain. 68 min. Sound. 16mm B&W. *Rental:* Video Comm.

Mystery Man. William Boyd. Directed by George Archainbaud. 1944. United Artists. 54 min. Sound. 16mm B&W. *Sale:* Cinema Concepts.

Mystery Mansion. Dallas McKennon, Greg Wynne & Randi Brown. Directed by David E. Jackson. 96 min. Sound. 16mm Color. *Rental:* Swank Motion.

Mystery of Animal Behavior. 1969. National Geographic. (Documentary). 51 min. Sound. 16mm Color. *Rental:* Iowa Films, La Inst Res Ctr, Natl Geog, Syracuse U Film, U Mich Media & Wholesome Film Ctr. *Sale:* Natl Geog. *Sale:* Natl Geog, Videotape version.

Mystery of Diamond Island, The see Rip Roaring Riley.

Mystery of Edwin Drood, The. Claude Rains & Heather Angel. Directed by Stuart Walker. 1935. Universal. 87 min. Sound. 16mm B&W. *Rental:* Swank Motion.

345

Mystery of Marie Roget, The. Maria Montez & John Litel. Directed by Phil Rosen. 1942. Universal. 91 min. Sound. 16mm B&W. *Rental:* Swank Motion.

Mystery of Mr. Wong, The. Boris Karloff & Grant Withers. Directed by William Nigh. 1939. Monogram. 67 min. Sound. 16mm B&W. *Rental:* MGM United & Mogulls Films.

Mystery of Mr. X, The. Robert Montgomery & Lewis Stone. Directed by Edgar Selwyn. 1934. MGM. 85 min. Sound. 16mm B&W. *Rental:* MGM United.

Mystery of Nefertiti, The. 1939. Monogram. (Documentary). 67 min. Sound. 16mm Color. *Rental:* Indiana AV Ctr. *Sale:* Indiana AV Ctr. *Rental:* Indiana AV Ctr, *Sale:* Indiana AV Ctr, Videotape version.

Mystery of Room 13 *see* Mr. Reeder in Room Thirteen.

Mystery of Stonehenge, The. 1965. CBS. (Documentary). 57 min. Sound. 16mm Color. *Rental:* Iowa Films, McGraw-Hill Films, Syracuse U Film, U Cal Media, U of IL Film, U Mich Media & Utah Media. *Sale:* McGraw-Hill Films.

Mystery of the Anasazi, The. 1976. Nova. (Documentary). 59 min. Sound. 16mm Color. *Rental:* Syracuse U Film, U of IL Film & U Mich Media. *Rental:* PBS Video, *Sale:* PBS Video, Videotape version.

Mystery of the Black Jungle *see* Black Devils of Kali.

Mystery of the Himalayas. Japan. (Cast unlisted). 79 min. Sound. 16mm Color. *Rental:* Films Inc.

Mystery of the Hooded Horseman. Tex Ritter. Directed by Ray Taylor. 1937. Grand National. 60 min. Sound. 16mm B&W. *Rental:* Budget Films.

Mystery of the Mary Celeste, The *see* Phantom Ship.

Mystery of the Maya, The. 1973. WNET. (Documentary). 60 min. Sound. 16mm Color. *Rental:* U Cal Media & WNET Media. *Sale:* WNET Media. *Sale:* WNET Media, Videotape version.

Mystery of the Wax Museum. Vincent Price, Diana Rigg & Jack Hendry. Directed by Michael Curtiz. 1973. 104 min. Sound. 16mm Color. *Rental:* MGM United.

Mystery of the Wentworth Castle, The *see* Doomed to Die.

Mystery of the White Room, The. Bruce Cabot & Helen Mack. Directed by Otis Garrett. 1939. Paramount. 58 min. Sound. 16mm B&W. *Rental:* Swank Motion.

Mystery of Thug Island, The. Guy Madison. Directed by Luigi Capuano. 1966. Italy. 96 min. Sound. 16mm Color. dubbed. *Lease:* Time-Life Multimedia.

Mystery on Bird Island, The. Mavis Sage & Vernon Morris. Directed by John Haggarty. 1955. Britain. 57 min. Sound. 16mm B&W. *Sale:* Lucerne Films.

Mystery Plane. John Trent & Milburn Stone. Directed by George Waggner. 1939. Monogram. 60 min. Sound. 16mm B&W. *Rental:* Budget Films. *Sale:* Morcraft Films. *Sale:* Morcarft Films, Super 8 sound version.

Mystery Range. Tom Tyler. Directed by Bernard B. Ray. 1934. Steiner. 52 min. Sound. 16mm B&W. *Rental:* Film Classics. *Sale:* Morcraft Films.

Mystery Street. Ricardo Montalban & Sally Forrest. Directed by John Sturges. 1950. MGM. 93 min. Sound. 16mm B&W. *Rental:* MGM United.

Mystery Submarine *see* Decoy.

Myths & Identity. 1977. Miami-Dade. (Documentary). 60 min. Videotape Color. *Sale:* Films Inc.

Myths & Moundbuilders. 58 min. Sound. Videotape Color. *Rental:* PBS Video. *Sale:* PBS Video.

Mzima: Portrait of a Spring. Directed by Alan Root & Joan Root. 1972. Root. (Documentary). 53 min. Sound. 16mm Color. *Rental:* McGraw-Hill Films, Syracuse U Film, U Cal Media & U Mich Media. *Sale:* McGraw-Hill Films.

Nabonga. Orig. Title: White Gorilla, The. Julie London & Buster Crabbe. Directed by Sam Newfield. 1942. PRC. 75 min. Sound. 16mm B&W. *Rental:* Budget Films & Video Comm.

Nada. Orig. Title: Nada Gang, The. Fabio Testi & Mariangela Melato. Directed by Claude Chabrol. Fr. 1974. France. 91 min. Sound. 16mm Color. subtitles. *Rental:* New Line Cinema.

Nada Gang, The *see* Nada.

Nagaya Shinshiroku *see* Record of a Tenement Gentleman.

N'ai: The Story of a Kung Woman. 1980. 59 min. Sound. 16mm Color. *Rental:* U Mich Media.

Naim & Jabar. 1974. Fieldstaff. (Documentary). 50 min. Sound. 16mm Color. *Rental:* U Cal Media.

Naissance Du Cinema, La. 1947. France. (Documentary). 45 min. Sound. 16mm B&W. *Rental:* French Am Cul. *Rental:* French Am Cul, Videotape version.

Naked Alibi. Sterling Hayden & Gloria Grahame. Directed by Jerry Hopper. 1954. Universal. 86 min. Sound. 16mm B&W. *Rental:* Swank Motion.

Naked & the Dead, The. Cliff Robertson, Raymond Massey & Aldo Ray. Directed by Raoul Walsh. 1958. RKO. 131 min. Sound. 16mm Color. *Rental:* Budget Films, Maljack, Natl Film Video, Video Comm & Wholesome Film Ctr. *Lease:* Video Comm. *Rental:* Kit Parker, 168 min. version. *Rental:* Video Comm, Videotape version.

Naked Ape, The. Johnny Crawford & Victoria Principal. Directed by Donald Driver. 1973. Universal. 85 min. Sound. 16mm Color. *Rental:* Swank Motion.

Naked Brigade, The. Shirley Eaton & Ken Scott. Directed by Maury Dexter. 1965. Britain. 100 min. Sound. 16mm B&W. *Rental:* Cine Craft.

Naked City. Barry Fitzgerald & Howard Duff. Directed by Jules Dassin. 1948. Universal. 96 min. Sound. 16mm B&W. *Rental:* Ivy Films.

Naked Civil Servant, The. John Hurt. Directed by Jack Gold. 1975. Britain. 80 min. Sound. 16mm Color. *Rental:* U of IL Film, Media Guild & Natl Film CN. *Sale:* Media Guild & Natl Film CN. *Sale:* Media Guild, Videotape version.

Naked Dawn, The. Arthur Kennedy. Directed by Edgar G. Ulmer. 1955. Universal. 82 min. Sound. 16mm Color. *Rental:* Swank Motion.

Naked Earth, The. Juliette Greco & Richard Todd. Directed by Vincent Sherman. 1958. Fox. 96 min. Sound. 16mm B&W. *Rental:* Films Inc.

Naked Edge, The. Gary Cooper & Deborah Kerr. Directed by Michael Anderson. 1961. United Artists. 100 min. Sound. 16mm B&W. *Rental:* MGM United.

Naked Evil, The. Anthony Ainley. Directed by Stanley Goulder. 1966. Britain. 86 min. Sound. 16mm Color. *Rental:* A Twyman Pres, Budget Films, Modern Sound & Video Comm.

Naked Eye, The. Directed by Louis Clyde Stoumen. 1957. Film Representations. (Documentary, color sequences). 70 min. Sound. 16mm B&W. *Rental:* Images Film & Syracuse U Film.

Naked Gun, The. Willard Parker & Mara Corday. Directed by Edward Dew. 1956. Associated. 69 min. Sound. 16mm B&W. *Rental:* Ivy Films. *Sale:* Rep Pic Film.

Naked Hills, The. David Wayne & Keenan Wynn. Directed by Josef Shaftel. 1956. Allied Artists. 73 min. Sound. 16mm Color. *Rental:* Hurlock Cine.

Naked in the Sun. James Craig & Lita Baron. Directed by John Hugh. 1957. Allied Artists. 82 min. Sound. 16mm Color. *Rental:* Ivy Films. *Sale:* Rep Pic Film.

Naked Jungle, The. Charlton Heston & Eleanor Parker. Directed by Byron Haskin. 1954. Paramount. 95 min. Sound. 16mm Color. *Rental:* Films Inc.

Naked Kiss, The. Constance Towers & Anthony Eisley. Directed by Samuel Fuller. 1964. Allied Artists. 90 min. Sound. 16mm B&W. *Rental:* Hurlock Cine.

Naked Maja, The. Ava Gardner & Anthony Franciosa. Directed by Henry Koster. 1959. United Artists. 111 min. Sound. 16mm Color. *Rental:* MGM United.

Naked Night, The. Harriet Andersson & Ake Gronberg. Directed by Ingmar Bergman. Swed. 1953. Sweden. 95 min. Sound. 16mm B&W. subtitles. *Rental:* Janus Films & New Cinema.

Naked Prey, The. Cornel Wilde. Directed by Cornel Wilde. 1966. Paramount. 94 min. Sound. 16mm Color. *Rental:* Films Inc.

Naked Runner, The. Frank Sinatra & Nadia Gray. Directed by Sidney J. Furie. 1967. Warners. 103 min. Sound. 16mm Color. *Rental:* Arcus Film, Films Inc, Video Comm & Willoughby Peer.

Naked Spur, The. James Stewart & Janet Leigh. Directed by Anthony Mann. 1953. MGM. 91 min. Sound. 16mm B&W. *Rental:* MGM United.

Naked Under Leather. Marianne Faithfull & Alain Delon. Directed by Jack Cardiff. 1968. Warners. 91 min. Sound. 16mm Color. *Rental:* Swank Motion.

Namami: First Love. Orig. Title: Inferno of First Love. Akio Takahashi. Directed by Susumi Hani. Jap. 1970. Japan. 108 min. Sound. 16mm B&W. subtitles. *Rental:* Budget Films, Ivy Films, Kit Parker & Video Comm.

Name for Evil, A. Robert Culp & Samantha Eggar. Directed by Bernard Girard. 1973. Cinerama. 97 min. Sound. 16mm Color. *Rental:* Swank Motion.

Name of the Game Is Kill, The. Orig. Title: Female Trap, The. Jack Lord & Susan Strasberg. Directed by Gunnar Hellstrom. 1968. Fanfare. 81 min. Sound. 16mm Color. *Rental:* Budget Films & Video Comm.

Naming the Parts. (Body in Question Series). 1979. (Documentary). 60 min. Videotape Color. *Rental:* Films Inc & Syracuse U Film. *Sale:* Films Inc.

Namu, the Killer Whale. Orig. Title: Wonderful Tale of Namu. Robert Lansing & Lee Meriwether. Directed by Laslo Benedek. 1966. United Artists. 89 min. Sound. 16mm Color. *Rental:* Arcus Film, MGM United, Westcoast Films, Wholesome Film Ctr & Williams Films.

Nana. Orig. Title: Lady of the Boulevards. Anna Sten. Directed by Dorothy Arzner. 1934. Goldwyn. 87 min. Sound. 16mm B&W. *Rental:* Films Inc.

Nana, Mom & Me. Directed by Amalie R. Rothschild. 1974. Rothschild. (Documentary). 47 min. Sound. 16mm Color. *Rental:* New Day Films. *Sale:* New Day Films.

Nancy Goes to Rio. Ann Sothern & Jane Powell. Directed by Robert Z. Leonard. 1950. MGM. 99 min. Sound. 16mm Color. *Rental:* MGM United.

Nancy Steele Is Missing. Victor McLaglen & Walter Connolly. Directed by George Marshall. 1937. Fox. 85 min. Sound. 16mm B&W. *Rental:* Films Inc.

Nanny, The. Bette Davis & Jill Bennett. Directed by Seth Holt. 1965. Britain. 93 min. Sound. 16mm B&W. *Rental:* Films Inc.

Nanook of the North. Directed by Robert Flaherty. 1922. Paramount. (Documentary, Silent with music track). 100 min. Sound. 16mm B&W. narrated Eng. *Rental:* Budget Films, Film Ctr DC, Em Gee Film Lib, Films Inc, Images Film, Ivy Films, Kino Intl, Kit Parker, Natl Film Video, Syracuse U Film, Texture Film, U Cal Media, U of IL Film, U Mich Media, U Nev AV Ctr, Utah Media, Viewfinders & Willoughby Peer. *Sale:* Cinema Concepts. *Rental:* Museum Mod Art & Texture Film, *Sale:* Texture Film, Restored 64 min. version. *Rental:* Utah Media, 50 mins. version. *Rental:* Ivy Films, *Sale:* Blackhawk Films, Super 8 silent version.

Nao Capitana, La. Jorge Mistral. Directed by Florian Rey. Spain. Sound. 16mm B&W. subtitles. *Rental:* Film Classics.

Napoleon. Albert Dieudionne. Directed by Abel Gance. 1926. France. 75 min. Silent. 16mm B&W. *Rental:* Em Gee Film Lib & Ivy Films. *Rental:* Images Film, *Lease:* Images Film, Tinted & toned, 240 Min. version.

Napoleon. Yves Montand, Jean Marais, Maria Schell & Orson Welles. 1956. France. 120 min. Sound. 16mm Color. dubbed. *Sale:* Cinema Concepts.

Napoleon & Samantha. Michael Douglas, Will Geer & Johnny Whitaker. Directed by Bernard McEveety. 1972. Disney. 91 min. Sound. 16mm Color. *Rental:* Bosco Films, Buchan Pic, Cine Craft, Elliot Film Co, Film Ctr DC, Film Pres, Film Inc, MGM United, Modern Sound, Newman Film Lib, Roas Films, Swank Motion, U of IL Film, Welling Motion Pictures, Westcoast Films & Williams Films.

Napoleon Conquers America. Directed by Jim Painten & Mary Bell. 1982. USA. (Documentary). 52 min. Sound. 16mm Color. *Rental:* Images Film.

Napoleon II, l'Aiglon. Jean Marais & Bernard Verley. 1964. France. 105 min. Sound. 16mm Color. dubbed. *Rental:* Films Inc.

Narco Men, The. Trans. Title: Persecucion Hasta Valencia. Tom Tryon & Richard Deacon. Directed by Julio Coll. 1967. NMF. (Anamorphic). 95 min. Sound. 16mm Color. dubbed. *Rental:* Kerr Film.

Narrow Corner, The. Douglas Fairbanks Jr. & Ralph Bellamy. Directed by Alfred E. Green. 1933. Warners. 71 min. Sound. 16mm B&W. *Rental:* MGM United.

Narrow Margin, The. Charles McGraw & Marie Windsor. Directed by Richard Fleischer. 1952. RKO. 70 min. Sound. 16mm B&W. *Rental:* Films Inc.

Narrow Trail, The. William S. Hart. Directed by William S. Hart. 1917. Paramount. 55 min. Silent. 16mm B&W. *Rental:* Budget Films. *Sale:* Blackhawk Films. *Rental:* Ivy Films, Super 8 silent version.

Nashville. Ronee Blakely, Henry Gibson & Lily Tomlin. Directed by Robert Altman. 1975. Paramount. (Anamorphic). 159 min. Sound. 16mm Color. *Rental:* Films Inc.

Nashville Girl. Monica Gayle & Glenn Corbett. Directed by Gus Trikonis. 1976. New World. 90 min. Sound. 16mm Color. *Rental:* Films Inc.

Nashville Sound, The. Earl Scruggs, Porter Wagoner & Dolly Parton. 1976. Nashville. 87 min. Sound. 16mm Color. *Rental:* Films Inc.

Nasty Habits. Glenda Jackson, Geraldine Page & Sandy Dennis. Directed by Michael Lindsay-Hogg. 1976. Brut. 96 min. Sound. 16mm Color. *Rental:* Films Inc.

Nasty Rabbit, The see Spies a-Go-Go.

Nate & Hayes. Tommy Lee Jones & Michael O'Keefe. Directed by Ferdinand Fairfax. 1983. Paramount. 98 min. Sound. 16mm Color. *Rental:* Films Inc. *Sale:* Tamarelles French Film, Videotape version.

Nate for Hate. Alain Delon & Maurice Biraud. 1962. France. 118 min. Sound. 16mm B&W. dubbed. *Rental:* MGM United.

Nathalie Granger. Lucia Bose & Jeanne Moreau. Directed by Marguerite Duras. Fr. 1972. France. 85 min. Sound. 16mm B&W. subtitles. *Rental:* French Am Cul & Liberty Co. *Rental:* French Am Cul, Videotape version.

Nation of Immigrants, A. (Destination America Ser.). 1969. Metromedia. (Documentary). 52 min. Sound. 16mm B&W. *Rental:* Films Inc, Media Guild & Wholesome Film Ctr. *Sale:* Films Inc & Media Guild. *Sale:* Films Inc & Media Guild, Videotape version.

National Citizenship Test, The. 1966. CBS. (Documentary). 51 min. Sound. 16mm B&W. *Rental:* McGraw-Hill Films, U Mich Media. *Sale:* McGraw-Hill Films.

National Driver's Test, The. 1967. CBS. (Documentary). 48 min. Sound. 16mm B&W. *Rental:* McGraw-Hill Films, Syracuse U Film & U Mich Media. *Sale:* McGraw-Hill Films.

National Gallery of Art, The. 1967. NBC. (Documentary). 49 min. Sound. 16mm Color. *Rental:* U of IL Film & U Mich Media. *Sale:* McGraw-Hill Films.

National Health, The. Lynn Redgrave, Colin Blakely, Jim Dale & Eleanor Bron. Directed by Jack Gold. 1975. Britain. 100 min. Sound. 16mm Color. *Rental:* Corinth Films & Films Inc.

National Health Test. 1967. CBS. (Documentary). 87 min. Sound. 16mm B&W. *Rental:* U of IL Film & McGraw-Hill Films. *Sale:* McGraw-Hill Films.

National Lampoon Goes to the Movies, The. Robby Benson & Richard Widmark. Directed by Robert Giraldi & Henry Jaglom. 1981. United Artists. 93 min. Sound. 16mm Color. *Rental:* MGM United.

National Lampoon's Animal House. John Belushi & Tim Matheson. Directed by John Landis. 1978. Universal. 109 min. Sound. 16mm Color. *Rental:* Swank Motion. *Rental:* Swank Motion, Videotape version.

National Lampoon's Class Reunion. Gerrit Graham & Fred McCarren. Directed by Michael Miller. 1982. Fox. 85 min. Sound. 16mm B&W. *Rental:* Films Inc.

National Lampoon's Vacation. Chevy Chase & Beverly D'Angelo. Directed by Harold Ramis. 1983. Warners. 98 min. Sound. 16mm Color. *Rental:* Swank Motion. *Rental:* Swank Motion, Videotape version.

National Nuclear Debate, The. 1979. PBS. (Documentary). 120 min. Videotape Color. *Rental:* PBS Video. *Sale:* PBS Video.

National Parks: Playground or Paradise? 59 min. Sound. 16mm Color. *Rental:* Natl Geog. *Sale:* Natl Geog. *Sale:* Natl Geog, Videotape version.

National Pro-Am Raquetball. 1979. PBS. (Documentary). 59 min. Videotape Color. *Rental:* PBS Video. *Sale:* PBS Video.

National Smoking Test, The. 1968. CBS. (Documentary). 51 min. Sound. 16mm B&W. *Rental:* Phoenix Films. *Sale:* Phoenix Films. *Rental:* Phoenix Films, *Sale:* Phoenix Films, Color version.

National Velvet. Mickey Rooney & Elizabeth Taylor. Directed by Clarence Brown. 1944. MGM. 123 min. Sound. 16mm Color. *Rental:* MGM United.

Nationtime, Gary. Directed by William Greaves. 1973. William Greaves. (Documentary). 90 min. Sound. 16mm Color. *Rental:* W Greaves. *Sale:* W Greaves. *Sale:* W Greaves, Videotape version.

Native American Odyssey, A. Directed by Jerry Aronson. 1978. Phoenix. (Documentary). 52 min. Sound. 16mm Color. *Rental:* Phoenix Films. *Sale:* Phoenix Films.

Native Land. Directed by Leo Hurwitz & Paul Strand. 1942. Frontier. (Documentary). 85 min. Sound. 16mm B&W. *Rental:* Film Images.

Native Medicine. (Body in Question Series). 1979. (Documentary). 60 min. Videotape Color. *Rental:* Films Inc & Syracuse U Film. *Sale:* Films Inc.

Native Son. Richard Wright, Jean Wallace & Nicholas Joy. Directed by Pierre Chenal. 1950. Classic. 91 min. Sound. 16mm B&W. *Rental:* Films Inc.

Natural Born Salesman, A *see* Earthworm Tractors.

Natural Enemies. Hal Holbrook & Louise Fletcher. Directed by Jeff Kanew. 1979. Cinema V. 100 min. Sound. 16mm Color. *Rental:* Cinema Five.

Natural History of Our World, The: The Time of Man. 50 min. Sound. 16mm Color. *Rental:* Phoenix Films. *Sale:* Phoenix Films. *Sale:* Phoenix Films, Videotape version.

Nature of Human Color Change, the Genetic, Hormonal, Neoplastic. 1968. US Government. (Documentary). 90 min. Sound. 16mm B&W. *Sale:* Natl AV Ctr. *Rental:* PBS Video. *Rental:* PBS Video, 58 mins. version.

Naughty Arlette *see* Romantic Age.

Naughty But Nice. Ann Sheridan, Dick Powell & Ronald Reagan. Directed by Ray Enright. 1939. Warners. 90 min. Sound. 16mm B&W. *Rental:* MGM United.

Naughty Flirt, The. Myrna Loy & Alice White. Directed by Edward Cline. 1931. Warners. 57 min. Sound. 16mm B&W. *Rental:* MGM United.

Naughty Marietta. Jeanette MacDonald & Nelson Eddy. Directed by W. S. Van Dyke. 1935. MGM. 80 min. Sound. 16mm B&W. *Rental:* MGM United. *Rental:* MGM United, *Sale:* Tamarelles French Film, Videotape version.

Naughty Nineties, The. Bud Abbott & Lou Costello. Directed by Jean Yarbrough. 1945. Universal. 75 min. Sound. 16mm B&W. *Rental:* Williams Films.

Navaho. 1967. KETC. (Documentary). 58 min. Sound. 16mm B&W. *Rental:* Indiana AV Ctr. *Sale:* Indiana AV Ctr.

Navajo. Directed by Norman Foster. 1952. Lippert. (Native cast). 71 min. Sound. 16mm B&W. *Rental:* Budget Films & Twyman Films.

Navajo. 1970. 58 min. Sound. 16mm B&W. *Rental:* Iowa Films.

Navajo Joe. Burt Reynolds. Directed by Sergio Corbucci. 1967. United Artists. (Anamorphic). 89 min. Sound. 16mm Color. dubbed. *Rental:* MGM United.

Navajo Kid, The. Bob Steele. Directed by Harry Fraser. 1945. PRC. 59 min. Sound. 16mm B&W. *Sale:* Classics Assoc NY.

Navajo: The Last Red Indians. 1972. Britain. (Documentary). 52 min. Sound. 16mm Color. *Rental:* U Cal Media.

Navajo Trail, The. Johnny Mack Brown. Directed by Howard Bretherton. 1945. Monogram. 58 min. Sound. 16mm B&W. *Rental:* Hurlock Cine.

Navajo Trail Raiders. Allan Lane. Directed by R. G. Springsteen. 1949. Republic. 60 min. Sound. 16mm B&W. *Rental:* Ivy Films. *Sale:* Rep Pic Film.

Navajo Way, The. 1975. Films Inc. (Documentary). 52 min. Sound. 16mm Color. *Rental:* Films Inc. *Sale:* Films Inc. *Sale:* Films Inc, Videotape version.

Navajos Film Themselves, The. 1966. Museum of Modern Art. (Anthology). 150 min. Silent. 16mm B&W. *Rental:* Museum Mod Art. *Lease:* Museum Mod Art.

Navigator, The. Buster Keaton & Kathryn McGuire. Directed by Donald Crisp & Buster Keaton. 1924. Metro. (Musical score only). 62 min. Sound. 16mm B&W. *Rental:* Films Inc. *Rental:* A Twyman Pres & Twyman Films, Silent 16mm version.

Navy Blue & Gold. Robert Young & James Stewart. Directed by Sam Wood. 1937. MGM. 94 min. Sound. 16mm B&W. *Rental:* MGM United.

Navy Blues. Dick Purcell & Mary Brian. Directed by Ralph Staub. 1937. Republic. 68 min. Sound. 16mm B&W. *Rental:* Ivy Films. *Sale:* Rep Pic Film.

Navy Blues. William Haines & Anita Page. Directed by Clarence Brown. 1930. MGM. 76 min. Sound. 16mm B&W. *Rental:* MGM United.

Navy Bound. Tom Neal. Directed by Paul Landres. 1951. Monogram. 61 min. Sound. 16mm B&W. *Rental:* Hurlock Cine & Inst Cinema.

Navy Comes Through, The. Pat O'Brien, Desi Arnaz & Jackie Cooper. Directed by Islin Auster. 1943. RKO. 81 min. Sound. 16mm B&W. *Rental:* RKO General Pics.

Navy Lark, The. Cecil Parker. Directed by Gordon Parry. 1959. 16mm *Rental:* A Twyman Pres.

Navy Steps Out, The *see* Girl, a Guy & a Gob.

Navy Wife. Orig. Title: Mother-Sir. Joan Bennett & Gary Merrill. Directed by Edward Bernds. 1956. Allied Artists. 83 min. Sound. 16mm B&W. *Rental:* Ivy Films. *Sale:* Rep Pic Film.

Nayak. Orig. Title: Hero, The. Uttam Kumar, Sharmila & Tagore. Directed by Satyajit Ray. Hindi. 1966. India. 120 min. Sound. 16mm B&W. subtitles. *Rental:* Trans-World Films.

Nazarin. Francisco Rabal & Marga Lopez. Directed by Luis Bunuel. Span. 1958. 92 min. Sound. 16mm B&W. subtitles. *Rental:* Films Inc.

Nazi Agent. Conrad Veidt & Ann Ayars. Directed by Jules Dassin. 1942. MGM. 84 min. Sound. 16mm B&W. *Rental:* MGM United.

Nazi Cinema: Deutschland Erwache. Directed by Erwin Leiser. Germany. (Anthology). 85 min. Sound. 16mm B&W. narrated. subtitles. *Rental:* Kit Parker.

Nazi Concentration Camps. 1945. US Government. (Documentary). 59 min. Sound. 16mm B&W. *Rental:* Natl AV Ctr & U Mich Media. *Sale:* Natl AV Ctr. *Sale:* Natl AV Ctr, Videotape version.

Nazis Strike, The. Directed by Frank Capra & Anatole Litvak. 1942. War Department. 41 min. Sound. 16mm B&W. *Rental:* Budget Films, Images Films, Kit Parker, Maljack, Museum Mod Art, OK AV Ctr & Twyman Films. *Sale:* Cinema Concepts & Reel Images. *Sale:* Natl AV Ctr, Videotape version.

Nea. Sami Frey & Micheline Presle. Directed by Nelly Kaplan. Fr. 1977. France. 101 min. Sound. 16mm Color. subtitles. *Rental:* Cinema Five.

Near & Far Away. Lilga Kovanko & Robert Farrant. Directed by Marianne Ahrne. Swed. 1978. Sweden. (Cast unlisted). 98 min. Sound. 16mm Color. subtitles. *Rental:* Cinema Five & New Cinema.

Near Trails End. Bob Steele. Directed by William Fox. 1931. Tiffany. 60 min. Sound. 16mm B&W. *Rental:* Mogulls Films.

Nearly a Nasty Accident. Shirley Eaton. Directed by Don Chaffey. 1959. 16mm *Rental:* A Twyman Pres.

Neath Brooklyn Bridge. East Side Kids. Directed by Wallace Fox. 1942. Monogram. 61 min. Sound. 16mm B&W. *Rental:* Budget Films.

Neath the Arizona Skies. John Wayne. Directed by Harry Fraser. 1931. Tiffany. 59 min. Sound. 16mm B&W. *Rental:* Ivy Films & Mogulls Films. *Sale:* Classics Assoc NY & Rep Pic Film.

Nebo Zowet *see* Battle Beyond the Sun.

Necromancy. Orson Welles & Pamela Franklin. Directed by Bert I. Gordon. 1972. Cinerama. 82 min. Sound. 16mm Color. *Rental:* Swank Motion.

Ned Kelly. Mick Jagger. Directed by Tony Richardson. 1970. United Artists. 103 min. Sound. 16mm Color. *Rental:* MGM United.

Nefertiti, Queen of the Nile *see* Queen of the Nile.

Negatives. Peter McEnery, Diane Cilento & Glenda Jackson. Directed by Peter Medak. 1968. Britain. 90 min. Sound. 16mm Color. *Rental:* Budget Films & Kino Intl. *Sale:* Kino Intl. *Lease:* Kino Intl.

Negro & the American Promise, The. 1963. NET. (Documentary). 60 min. Sound. 16mm B&W. *Rental:* Indiana AV Ctr, Mass Media, Syracuse U Film & U Cal Media.

Negro Soldier, The. Directed by Stuart Heisler. 1944. Sound. 16mm B&W. *Rental:* Budget Films & Images Film.

Negus, The. Directed by Victor Vicas. 1972. AIF. (Documentary). 60 min. Sound. 16mm B&W. *Sale:* Americas Films. *Sale:* Americas Films, Color version. *Sale:* Americas Films, Spanish version.

Nehru. 1965. Time/Life. (Documentary). 54 min. Sound. 16mm B&W. *Lease:* Direct Cinema. *Rental:* Budget Films.

Nehru Family, The. Directed by Victor Vicas. 1965. AIF. (Documentary). 60 min. Sound. 16mm B&W. *Sale:* Americas Films. *Sale:* Americas Films, Color version. *Sale:* Americas Films, Spanish version.

Neighbors. John Belushi & Dan Aykroyd. Directed by John G. Avildsen. 1981. Columbia. 94 min. Sound. 16mm Color. *Rental:* Swank Motion. *Rental:* Swank Motion, Videotape version.

Neither the Sea Nor the Sand. Directed by Fred Burnley. 1973. International Amusement. 110 min. Sound. 16mm Color. *Rental:* Films Inc.

Nell Gwyn. Anna Neagle & Cedric Hardwicke. Directed by Herbert Wilcox. 1934. 16mm *Rental:* A Twyman Pres.

Nellie Bly. Orig. Title: Amazing Nellie Bly, The. Linda Purl & Gene Barry. Directed by Henning Schellerup. 1979. Viacom. 97 min. Sound. 16mm Color. *Rental:* Williams Films. *Sale:* Lucerne Films.

Nelson Affair, The. Peter Finch & Glenda Jackson. Directed by James Cellan Jones. 1973. Britain. 118 min. Sound. 16mm Color. *Rental:* Swank Motion.

Nemesis: Germany, Feb.-May 1945. Directed by Hugh Raggett. (World at War Ser.). : Pt. 21.). 1973. Media Guild. (Documentary). 52 min. Sound. 16mm Color. *Rental:* Media Guild & U Cal Media. *Sale:* Media Guild. *Sale:* Media Guild, Videotape version.

Neptune Factor, The. Ben Gazzara, Yvette Mimieux & Walter Pidgeon. Directed by Daniel Petrie. 1973. Fox. (Anamorphic). 98 min. Sound. 16mm Color. *Rental:* Films Inc.

Neptune's Daughter. Esther Williams & Red Skelton. Directed by Edward Buzzell. 1949. MGM. 93 min. Sound. 16mm Color. *Rental:* MGM United.

Nest, The. Hector Alterio & Ana Torrent. Directed by Jaime de Arminan. Span. 1980. QFI. 105 min. Sound. 16mm Color. subtitles. *Rental:* Films Inc.

Nest of Gentry. Irina Kupchenko. Directed by Andrei Konchalovsky. Rus. 1969. Russia. 116 min. Sound. 16mm Color. subtitles. *Rental:* Corinth Films. *Rental:* Corinth Films, Videotape version.

Nestsilik Eskimo, Yesterday, Tomorrow, The. Directed by Gilles Blais. 1971. Canada. (Documentary). 58 min. Sound. 16mm Color. *Rental:* U Cal Media, Educ Dev Ctr, Natl Film CN, U Mich Media. *Sale:* Educ Dev Ctr.

Network. Faye Dunaway, William Holden & Peter Finch. Directed by Sidney Lumet. 1976. United Artists. 120 min. Sound. 16mm Color. *Rental:* MGM United. *Rental:* MGM United, Videotape version.

Neuroanatomy Demonstrations. 10 pts. 1972. 472 min. Sound. Videotape Color. *Sale:* Natl AV Ctr.

Nevada. Gary Cooper. Directed by John A. Waters. 1927. Paramount. 75 min. Silent. 16mm B&W. *Rental:* Em Gee Film Lib.

Nevada Badmen. Whip Wilson. Directed by Lewis D. Collins. 1951. Monogram. 58 min. Sound. 16mm B&W. *Rental:* Hurlock Cine.

Nevada Buckaroo. Bob Steeele. Directed by J. P. McCarthy. 1931. Tiffany. 60 min. Sound. 16mm B&W. *Rental:* Mogulls Films.

Nevada City. Roy Rogers. Directed by Joseph Kane. 1941. Republic. 54 min. Sound. 16mm B&W. *Rental:* Ivy Films. *Sale:* Rep Pic Film. *Sale:* Blackhawk Films, Super 8 sound version.

Nevada Smith. Steve McQueen & Brian Keith. Directed by Henry Hathaway. 1966. Paramount. 135 min. Sound. 16mm Color. *Rental:* Films Inc.

Nevadan, The. Randolph Scott & Forrest Tucker. Directed by Gordon Douglas. 1950. Columbia. 81 min. Sound. 16mm B&W. *Lease:* Time-Life Multimedia.

Neveim Street. Directed by Amnon Rubenstein. Israel. (Documentary). 58 min. Sound. 16mm Color. *Rental:* Icarus Films. *Sale:* Icarus Films.

Never a Backward Step. 1966. Canada. (Documentary). 57 min. Sound. 16mm B&W. *Rental:* U Mich Media.

Never a Dull Moment. Irene Dunne & Fred MacMurray. Directed by George Marshall. 1950. Universal. 89 min. Sound. 16mm B&W. *Rental:* Films Inc.

Never Cry Wolf. Charles Martin Smith & Brian Dennehy. 1984. Disney. 105 min. Sound. 16mm Color. *Rental:* Bosco Films, Elliot Film Co, Roas Films, Swank Motion, Welling Motion Pictures, Westcoast Films & Williams Films.

Never Fear *see* Young Lovers.

Never Give a Sucker an Even Break. Orig. Title: What a Man. W. C. Fields. Directed by Edward Cline. 1941. Universal. 63 min. Sound. 16mm B&W. *Rental:* Films Inc & Swank Motion.

Never Let Go. Peter Sellers & Richard Todd. Directed by John Guillermin. 1963. Britain. 90 min. Sound. 16mm B&W. *Rental:* Budget Films.

Never Let Me Go. Clark Gable & Gene Tierney. Directed by Delmer Daves. 1953. MGM. 93 min. Sound. 16mm B&W. *Rental:* Films Inc & MGM United.

Never Love a Stranger. John Barrymore Jr. & Steve McQueen. Directed by Robert Stevens. 1958. Allied Artists. 91 min. Sound. 16mm B&W. *Rental:* Ivy Films. *Lease:* Rep Pic Film.

Never Mind the Quality: Feel the Width. John Bluthal & Joe Lynch. 1973. MGM. 95 min. Sound. 16mm Color. *Rental:* MGM United.

Never Never Princess, The. 1967. Childhood. (Cast unlisted). 69 min. Sound. 16mm Color. dubbed. *Rental:* Films Inc.

Never Put It in Writing. Pat Boone. Directed by Andrew Stone. 1964. Allied Artists. 93 min. Sound. 16mm B&W. *Rental:* Hurlock Cine.

Never Say Die. Bob Hope & Martha Raye. Directed by Elliott Nugent. 1939. Paramount. 80 min. Sound. 16mm B&W. *Rental:* Swank Motion.

Never Say Goodbye. Errol Flynn & Eleanor Parker. Directed by James V. Kern. 1946. Warners. 97 min. Sound. 16mm B&W. *Rental:* MGM United.

Never Say Goodbye. Rock Hudson & Cornell Borchers. Directed by Jerry Hopper. 1956. Universal. 96 min. Sound. 16mm Color. *Rental:* Swank Motion.

Never Say Never Again. Sean Connery & Max Von Sydow. Directed by Irwin Kershner. 1983. Warners. 130 min. Sound. 16mm Color. *Rental:* Swank Motion. *Rental:* Swank Motion, Videotape version.

Never So Few. Frank Sinatra & Gina Lollobrigida. Directed by John Sturges. 1959. MGM. 126 min. Sound. 16mm Color. *Rental:* MGM United.

Never Steal Anything Small. James Cagney, Cara Williams & Shirley Jones. Directed by Charles Lederer. 1959. Universal. 126 min. Sound. 16mm Color. *Rental:* Swank Motion.

Never Take No for an Answer. Dennis O'Dea. Directed by Maurice Cloche. 1952. Britain. 82 min. Sound. 16mm B&W. *Rental:* Roas Films.

Never the Twain Shall Meet. Leslie Howard & Conchita Montenegro. Directed by W. S. Van Dyke. 1931. MGM. 89 min. Sound. 16mm B&W. *Rental:* MGM United.

Never Too Late. 1975. Penn State. (Documentary). 58 min. Sound. 16mm Color. *Rental:* Penn St AV Serv. *Sale:* Penn St AV Serv. *Rental:* Penn St AV Serv, *Sale:* Penn St AV Serv, Videotape version.

Never Too Late to Mend *see* It's Never Too Late to Mend.

Never Trust Anyone Under Sixty. 1971. US Government. (Documentary). 60 min. Sound. 16mm Color. *Rental:* Natl AV Ctr.

Never Wave at a W. A. C. Orig. Title: Private Wore Skirts, The. Rosalind Russell & Paul Douglas. Directed by Norman Z. McLeod. 1952. RKO. 87 min. Sound. 16mm B&W. *Rental:* Video Comm.

Never Weaken. Harold Lloyd. Directed by Sam Taylor. 1921. Pathe. (Silent with music track). 78 min. 16mm B&W. *Rental:* Budget Films, Kino Intl & Kit Parker.

Neverending Story, The. Noah Hathaway, Barret Olivier & Tami Stronach. Directed by Wolfgang Peterson. 1985. Warners. 94 min. Sound. 16mm Color. *Rental:* Swank Motion.

New Actors for the Classics. Stacy Keach & David Schram. Directed by Kirk Browning. 1972. Cantor. 80 min. Sound. 16mm B&W. *Rental:* A Cantor. *Sale:* A Cantor.

New Adventures of Tarzan, The. Bruce Bennett. Directed by Edward Kull. 1935. Burroughs-Tarzan. 75 min. Sound. 16mm B&W. *Sale:* Cinema Concepts.

New Alchemy, The: A Rediscovery of Promise. 1984. 58 min. Sound. 16mm Color. *Rental:* Bullfrog Films. *Sale:* Bullfrog Films. *Rental:* Bullfrog Films, *Sale:* Bullfrog Films, Videotape version.

New American Cinema, The. 1976. Grove. (Anthology, color sequences). 88 min. Sound. 16mm B&W. *Rental:* Grove.

New American Revolution of 1963, The. Directed by Chet Hagan. 1963. NBC. (Documentary). 55 min. Sound. 16mm B&W. *Rental:* Kit Parker.

New Centurions, The. George C. Scott & Stacy Keach. Directed by Richard Fleischer. 1972. Columbia. 103 min. Sound. 16mm Color. *Rental:* Arcus Film, Cine Craft, Films Inc, Images Film, Kit Parker, Modern Sound, Natl Film Video, Swank Motion, Twyman Films, Welling Motion Pictures, Westcoast Films & Williams Films.

New Cinema Animation Festival, The. 1972. Janus. (Animated anthology, color sequences). 108 min. Sound. 16mm B&W. *Rental:* Films Inc & Janus Films.

New Clown White, The. Martin Harbury. 51 min. Sound. Color. *Sale:* MTI Tele. *Sale:* MTI Tele, Videotape version.

New Deal for Artists, A. Directed by Wieland Schulz-Keil. 1979. USA. (Documentary, color sequences). 92 min. Sound. 16mm *Rental:* Corinth Films. *Lease:* Corinth Films.

New England & New France. 1968. Canada. (Documentary). 58 min. Sound. 16mm B&W. *Rental:* U Cal Media.

New Equation: Annexation & Reciprocity. 1968. Canada. (Documentary). 58 min. Sound. 16mm B&W. *Rental:* U Cal Media.

New Faces. Paul Lynde, Eartha Kitt & Robert Clary. Directed by Harry Horner. 1954. Fox. (Anamorphic). 98 min. Sound. 16mm Color. *Rental:* Films Inc & Willoughby Peer.

New Faces of Africa. 1978. Britain. (Documentary). 53 min. Sound. 16mm B&W. *Rental:* U of IL Film.

New Faces of 1937. Milton Berle & Anne Miller. Directed by Leigh Jason. 1937. RKO. 100 min. Sound. 16mm B&W. *Rental:* RKO General Pics.

New Frontier, The. John Wayne & Jennifer Jones. Directed by Carl Pierson. 1935. Republic. 55 min. Sound. 16mm B&W. *Rental:* Ivy Films. *Sale:* Rep Pic Film.

New Germany, A: 1933-1934. Directed by Hugh Raggett. (World at War). : Pt. 1.). 1973. Media Guild. (Documentary). 52 min. Sound. 16mm Color. *Rental:* Media Guild & U Cal Media. *Sale:* Media Guild. *Sale:* Media Guild, Videotape version.

New Gold for Alaska. 1974. Canada. (Documentary). 50 min. Sound. 16mm Color. *Rental:* U Cal Media.

New Healers, The. 1977. 58 min. Sound. Videotape *Rental:* PBS Video. *Sale:* PBS Video.

New Indians, The. 59 min. Sound. 16mm Color. *Rental:* Natl Geog. *Rental:* Natl Geog, Videotape version.

New Interns, The. Michael Callan & Dean Jones. Directed by John Rich. 1964. Columbia. 123 min. Sound. 16mm B&W. *Rental:* Arcus Film & Modern Sound.

New Invisible Man, The. Orig. Title: H. G. Wells' New Invisible Man. Arturo De Cordova. 1962. Mexico. 87 min. Sound. 16mm B&W. dubbed. *Rental:* Newman Film Lib & Video Comm. *Lease:* Video Comm.

New Italian, The. 1963. NET. (Documentary). 55 min. Sound. 16mm B&W. *Rental:* Indiana AV Ctr. *Sale:* Indiana AV Ctr.

New Jobs for Natural Gas. 1970. EMC. (Documentary). 59 min. Sound. 16mm B&W. *Rental:* U Cal Media. *Sale:* U Cal Media.

New Kind of Love, A. Paul Newman & Joanne Woodward. Directed by Melville Shavelson. 1963. Paramount. 110 min. Sound. 16mm B&W. *Rental:* Films Inc.

New Klan, The. Directed by Eleanor Bingham & Leslie Shatz. 1978. Corinth. (Documentary). 58 min. Sound. 16mm Color. *Rental:* Corinth Films. *Lease:* Corinth Films. *Rental:* Corinth Films, *Lease:* Corinth Films, Videotape version.

New Land, The. Max Von Sydow & Liv Ullmann. Directed by Jan Troell. 1970. Sweden. 161 min. Sound. 16mm Color. *Rental:* Swank Motion, Twyman Films & Williams Films.

New Leaf, A. Elaine May & Walter Matthau. Directed by Elaine May. 1971. Paramount. 102 min. Sound. 16mm Color. *Rental:* Films Inc.

New Left, The. CBS. (Documentary). 52 min. Sound. 16mm B&W. *Rental:* OK AV Ctr. *Sale:* CBS Inc.

New Look at the Retarded Child, A. 1976. 60 min. Sound. 16mm Color. *Rental:* Iowa Films.

New Mexico. Lew Ayres, Andy Devine & Marilyn Maxwell. Directed by Irving Reis. 1951. United Artists. 76 min. Sound. 16mm B&W. *Rental:* Budget Films & Westcoast Films.

New Moon, The. Orig. Title: Parisian Belle. Grace Moore & Lawrence Tibbett. Directed by Jack Conway. 1930. MGM. 77 min. Sound. 16mm B&W. *Rental:* MGM United.

New Moon, The. Jeanette MacDonald & Nelson Eddy. Directed by Robert Z. Leonard. 1940. MGM. 105 min. Sound. 16mm B&W. *Rental:* MGM United.

New Morals for Old. Myrna Loy & Robert Young. Directed by Charles Brabin. 1932. MGM. 77 min. Sound. 16mm B&W. *Rental:* MGM United.

New Opium Route, The. Directed by Catherine Lamour & Marianne Lamour. 1973. Icarus. (Documentary). 54 min. Sound. 16mm Color. *Rental:* Icarus Films. *Sale:* Icarus Films.

New Orleans. Arturo De Cordova, Louis Armstrong & Billie Holliday. Directed by Arthur Lubin. 1947. United Artists. 89 min. Sound. 16mm B&W. *Rental:* Willoughby Peer.

New Orleans After Dark. Stacy Harris. Directed by John Sledge. 1958. Allied Artists. 75 min. Sound. 16mm B&W. *Rental:* Ivy Films. *Sale:* Rep Pic Film.

New Orleans Uncensored. Arthur Franz & Beverly Garland. Directed by William Castle. 1955. Columbia. 76 min. Sound. 16mm B&W. *Rental:* Kit Parker.

New Reality, A. 1965. Denmark. (Documentary). 49 min. Sound. 16mm Color. *Rental:* Intl Film & Syracuse U Film. *Sale:* Intl Film.

New Russia, The. Directed by Theodore Holcomb. 1977. Holcomb. (Documentary). 52 min. Sound. 16mm Color. *Sale:* T Holcomb & Syracuse U Film.

New School, The *see* Nueva Escuela.

New South, The. 1970. NET. (Documentary). 58 min. Sound. 16mm B&W. *Rental:* Indiana AV Ctr. *Sale:* Indiana AV Ctr.

New Teacher, The. Chic Sale. Directed by Joseph Franz. 1922. Fox. 50 min. Silent. 16mm B&W. *Rental:* Mogulls Films. *Rental:* Film Classics, *Sale:* Film Classics, Silent 8mm version.

New Times, The. 1979. PBS. (Cast unlisted). 59 min. Videotape Color. *Rental:* PBS Video. *Sale:* PBS Video, Sound 16mm version.

New Voices for Man. 1980. Canada. (Documentary). 57 min. Sound. 16mm Color. *Rental:* Budget Films & Time-Life Multimedia. *Sale:* Time-Life Multimedia. *Sale:* Time-Life Multimedia, Videotape version.

New Wizard of Oz, The *see* His Majesty, the Scarecrow of Oz.

New World, The. Directed by Ray Witlin. 1977. Blackwood. (Documentary). 58 min. Sound. 16mm Color. *Rental:* Blackwood Films. *Lease:* Blackwood Films.

New World-Hard Choices. 1976. NBC. (Documentary). 60 min. Sound. Color. *Sale:* Films Inc.

New Worlds. 55 min. Color. *Rental:* U Cal Media.

New York City: The Most. 1968. New York Times. (Documentary). 51 min. Sound. 16mm Color. *Rental:* Modern Talking.

New York City Too Far from Tampa Blues. 1979. Daniel Wilson. 47 min. Sound. Videotape Color. *Rental:* Daniel Wilson.

New York Festival of Women's Films. 1976. New Line Cinema. (Anthology). 103 min. Sound. 16mm Color. *Rental:* New Line Cinema.

New York, New York. Liza Minnelli & Robert De Niro. Directed by Martin Scorsese. 1977. United Artists. 163 min. Sound. 16mm Color. *Rental:* MGM United.

New York Nights. Norma Talmadge & Gilbert Roland. Directed by Lewis Milestone. 1930. United Artists. 69 min. Sound. 16mm B&W. *Rental:* Film Classics.

New York School, The. 1975. Blackwood. (Documentary). 55 min. Sound. 16mm Color. *Rental:* Blackwood Films. *Sale:* Blackwood Films.

New York Town. Fred MacMurray & Mary Martin. Directed by Charles Vidor. 1941. Paramount. 94 min. Sound. 16mm B&W. *Rental:* Swank Motion.

New York: Twin Park's Project T.V. Channel 13. 1975. Canada. (Documentary). 57 min. Sound. 16mm Color. *Rental:* U Cal Media.

Newcomers, The: 1832. 1979. Canada. (Cast unlisted). 58 min. Sound. 16mm Color. *Rental:* Natl Film CN.

Newcomers, The: 1840. 1979. Canada. (Cast unlisted). 58 min. Sound. 16mm Color. *Rental:* Natl Film CN.

Newcomers: 1911. 1979. Canada. (Cast unlisted). 58 min. Sound. 16mm Color. *Rental:* Natl Film CN.

Newcomers, The: 1927. 1979. Canada. (Cast unlisted). 58 min. Sound. 16mm Color. *Rental:* Natl Film Video.

Newcomers, The: 1978. 1979. Canada. (Cast unlisted). 58 min. Sound. 16mm Color. *Rental:* Natl Film CN.

Newman's Law. George Peppard. Directed by Richard T. Heffron. 1974. Universal. 98 min. Sound. 16mm Color. *Rental:* Swank Motion.

Newport Jazz Festival: 1962. 1962. (Concert). 50 min. Sound. 16mm B&W. *Sale:* Festival Films, Glenn Photo & Reel Images. *Sale:* Festival Films, Videotape version.

Newsboy's Home. Jackie Cooper & Edmund Lowe. Directed by Harold Young. 1939. Universal. 80 min. Sound. 16mm B&W. *Rental:* Swank Motion.

Newsfront. Bill Hunter & Wendy Hughes. Directed by Phillip Noyce. 1978. Australia. 110 min. Sound. 16mm Color. *Rental:* New Yorker Films.

Newsreel of Dreams, A. 3 pts. Directed by Stan Vanderbeek. 1976. Vanderbeek. (Experimental). 90 min. Sound. Videotape Color. *Rental:* Electro Art. *Lease:* Electro Art.

Next Man, The. Sean Connery & Cornelia Sharpe. Directed by Richard C. Sarafian. 1976. Allied Artists. 108 min. Sound. 16mm Color. *Rental:* Hurlock Cine.

Next of Kin, The. Directed by Thorold Dickinson. 1942. Britain. (Documentary). 90 min. Sound. 16mm B&W. *Rental:* Film Images. *Sale:* Film Images.

Next Stop, Greenwich Village. Lenny Baker & Shelley Winters. Directed by Paul Mazursky. 1976. Fox. 111 min. Sound. 16mm Color. *Rental:* Films Inc.

Next Time I Marry. Lucille Ball & Lee Bowman. Directed by Garson Kanin. 1939. RKO. 75 min. Sound. 16mm *Rental:* RKO General Pics.

Next Time We Love. Margaret Sullavan & James Stewart. Directed by Edward H. Griffith. 1936. Universal. 87 min. Sound. 16mm B&W. *Rental:* Swank Motion.

Next Voice You Hear, The. James Whitmore & Nancy Davis. Directed by William A. Wellman. 1950. MGM. 83 min. Sound. 16mm B&W. *Rental:* MGM United.

NFL SymFunny, The: Super Bowl II. 48 min. Sound. Videotape Color. *Sale:* Vidamerica.

Nguba Connection, The. 1978. 58 min. Sound. Videotape *Rental:* PBS Video. *Sale:* PBS Video.

Niagara. Marilyn Monroe & Joseph Cotten. Directed by Henry Hathaway. 1953. Fox. 89 min. Sound. 16mm Color. *Rental:* Films Inc.

Niagara for Sale. Directed by William Canning. 1975. Canada. (Documentary). 51 min. Sound. 16mm Color. *Rental:* Natl Film CN. *Sale:* Natl Film CN.

Nibelungen, Die see Kriemhilde's Revenge.

Nicaragua: Free Homeland or Death. Directed by Victor Vega & Antonio Yglesias. Span. 1978. Nicaragua. (Documentary). 75 min. Sound. 16mm Color. subtitles. *Rental:* Cinema Guild. *Sale:* Cinema Guild.

Nicaragua: Report from the Front. Directed by Deborah Shaffer. 1983. (Documentary). 73 min. Sound. 16mm Color. *Rental:* First Run.

Nice Dreams. Richard Marin, Thomas Chong & Stacy Keach. Directed by Thomas Chong. Sound. 16mm Color. *Rental:* Swank Motion.

Nice Girl Like Me, A. Barbara Ferris & Dame Gladys Cooper. Directed by Desmond Davis. 1969. Embassy. 91 min. Sound. 16mm Color. *Rental:* Films Inc.

Nice Little Bank That Should Be Robbed, A. Tom Ewell & Mickey Rooney. Directed by Henry Levin. 1958. Fox. 88 min. Sound. 16mm B&W. *Rental:* Charard Motion Pics & Films Inc. *Rental:* Westcoast Films, *Sale:* Willoughby Peer, Anamorphic B&W version.

Nicholas & Alexandra. Michael Jayston & Janet Suzman. Directed by Franklin Schaffner. 1971. Columbia. 170 min. Sound. 16mm Color. *Rental:* Arcus Film, Budget Films, Films Inc, Modern Sound, Natl Film Video, Swank Motion, Welling Motion Pictures, Wholesome Films Ctr & Williams Films. *Rental:* Swank Motion, Videotape version.

Nicholas & Alexandra: Trilogy. 1976. LCA. 80 min. Sound. 16mm Color. *Rental:* Syracuse U Film.

Nicholas Nickleby. Sir Cedric Hardwicke & Dame Sybil Thorndyke. Directed by Alberto Cavalcanti. 1947. Britain. 109 min. Sound. 16mm B&W. *Rental:* Budget Films, Films Inc, Images Film, Kit Parker, Learning Corp Am, Modern Sound, Twyman Films & U of IL Film. *Sale:* Learning Corp Am.

Nick Carter, Master Detective. Walter Pidgeon & Rita Johnson. Directed by Jacques Tourneur. 1939. MGM. 60 min. Sound. 16mm B&W. *Rental:* MGM United.

Nickel Ride, The. Jason Miller & Linda Hayes. Directed by Robert Mulligan. 1975. Fox. 99 min. Sound. 16mm Color. *Rental:* Films Inc.

Nickelodeon. Ryan O'Neal & Burt Reynolds. Directed by Peter Bogdanovich. 1976. Columbia. 121 min. Sound. 16mm Color. *Rental:* Bosco Films, Budget Films, Cine Craft, Films Inc, Images Film, Modern Sound, Newman Film Lib, Swank Motion, Twyman Films, Welling Motion Pictures, Westcoast Films, Wholesome Film Ctr & Williams Films.

Niebelungen see Siegfried.

Niebelungen, Der. Paul Richter & Margarete Schon. Directed by Fritz Lang. 1924. Ufa. 195 min. Silent. 16mm B&W. *Rental:* Kit Parker. *Rental:* Kit Parker, Music version version.

Nigeria: Culture in Transition. 1973. Nigeria. (Documentary). 54 min. Sound. 16mm B&W. *Rental:* Modern Mass. *Sale:* Modern Mass.

Nigeria: Giant in Africa. Directed by Ronald Dick. 1960. Canada. (Documentary). 59 min. Sound. 16mm B&W. *Rental:* McGraw-Hill Films. *Sale:* McGraw-Hill Films.

Night, The see Notte La

Night. 1971. Xerox. (Documentary). 51 min. Sound. 16mm Color. *Rental:* U Cal Media. *Sale:* Xerox Films.

Night After Night. George Raft & Mae West. Directed by Archie Mayo. 1932. Paramount. 70 min. Sound. 16mm B&W. *Rental:* Swank Motion.

Night Ambush. Marius Goring & Cyril Cusack. Directed by Michael Powell & Emeric Pressburger. 1957. Britain. 104 min. Sound. 16mm B&W. *Rental:* Budget Films, Learning Corp Am & U of IL Film. *Sale:* Learning Corp Am.

Night & Day. Cary Grant & Alexis Smith. Directed by Michael Curtiz. 1946. Warners. 128 min. Sound. 16mm Color. *Rental:* MGM United.

Night & the City. Richard Widmark & Gene Tierney. Directed by Jules Dassin. 1950. Fox. 95 min. Sound. 16mm B&W. *Rental:* Films Inc.

Night at the Opera, A. Marx Brothers. Directed by Sam Wood. 1935. MGM. 90 min. Sound. 16mm B&W. *Rental:* MGM United. *Rental:* MGM United, Videotape version.

Night at the Ritz, A. William Gargan & Patricia Ellis. Directed by William McGann. 1935. Warners. 62 min. Sound. 16mm B&W. *Rental:* MGM United.

Night Before the Divorce, The. Lynn Bari & Mary Beth Hughes. Directed by Robert Siodmak. 1942. Fox. 67 min. Sound. 16mm B&W. *Rental:* Films Inc.

Night Caller, The. Jean-Paul Belmondo & Charles Denner. Directed by Henri Verneuil. Fr. 1975. France. 91 min. Sound. 16mm Color. subtitles. *Rental:* Budget Films, Swank Motion, Westcoast Films & Williams Films.

Night Club, The. Raymond Griffith. Directed by Frank Urson & Paul Iribe. 1925. Paramount. 60 min. Silent. 16mm B&W. *Rental:* Em Gee Film Lib & Film Classics. *Sale:* Film Classics.

Night Club Lady. Adolphe Menjou & Mayo Methot. Directed by Irving Cummings. 1932. Columbia. 70 min. Sound. 16mm B&W. *Rental:* Kit Parker.

Night Court. Walter Huston & Lewis Stone. Directed by W. S. Van Dyke. 1932. MGM. 96 min. Sound. 16mm B&W. *Rental:* MGM United.

Night Creatures. Peter Cushing & Oliver Reed. Directed by Peter Graham Scott. 1962. Britain. 81 min. Sound. 16mm Color. *Rental:* Swank Motion.

Night Crossing. John Hurt & Jane Alexander. Directed by Delbert Mann. 1981. Disney. 106 min. Sound. 16mm Color. *Rental:* Bosco Films, Elliot Film Co, Films Inc, MGM United, Roas Films, Swank Motion, Welling Motion Pictures, Westcoast Films & Williams Films, Videotape version.

Night Cry. Rin-Tin-Tin. Directed by Herman C. Raymaker. 1926. Warner Brothers. 55 min. Silent. 16mm B&W. *Rental:* Em Gee Film Lib. *Sale:* Glenn Photo. *Sale:* Glenn Photo, Super 8 silent version. *Rental:* Budget Films, 85 mins. version.

Night Digger. Patricia Neal & Pamela Brown. Directed by Alastair Reid. 1971. MGM. 110 min. Sound. 16mm Color. *Rental:* MGM United.

Night Drum. Renarto Mikuni & Ineko Arlma. Directed by Tadashi Imai. Jap. 1958. Japan. 95 min. Sound. 16mm B&W. subtitles. *Rental:* Films Inc.

Night Editor. Janis Carter & William Gargan. Directed by Henry Levin. 1946. Columbia. 58 min. Sound. 16mm B&W. *Rental:* Kit Parker.

Night Encounter. Marina Vlady & Robert Hossein. Directed by Robert Hossein. Fr. 1959. France. 80 min. Sound. 16mm B&W. subtitles. *Rental:* Films Inc. *Rental:* Films Inc, English language version.

Night Ferry. 1979. Britain. (Cast unlisted). 62 min. Sound. 16mm Color. *Sale:* Lucerne Films. *Rental:* Lucerne Films.

Night Fighters, The. Robert Mitchum & Anne Heywood. Directed by Tay Garnett. 1960. United Artists. 88 min. Sound. 16mm B&W. *Rental:* MGM United.

Night Flight to Berlin. Directed by Stephen Collins. 1970. 50 min. 16mm *Rental:* A Twyman Pres.

Night for Crime, A. Glenda Farrell & Lyle Talbot. Directed by Alexis Thurn-Taxis. 1942. PRC. 70 min. Sound. 16mm B&W. *Rental:* Mogulls Films.

Night Full of Rain, A. Orig. Title: End of the World in Our Usual Bed in a Night Full of Rain, The. Giancarlo Giannini & Candice Bergen. Directed by Lina Wertmuller. Ital. 1978. Italy. 104 min. Sound. 16mm Color. subtitles. *Rental:* Films Inc, Swank Motion & Twyman Films.

Night Games. Cindy Pickett & Barry Primus. Directed by Roger Vadim. 1980. Embassy. 100 min. Sound. 16mm Color. *Rental:* Films Inc.

Night Has a Thousand Eyes, The. Edward G. Robinson & Gail Russell. Directed by John Farrow. 1948. Paramount. 80 min. Sound. 16mm B&W. *Rental:* Swank Motion.

Night Hawk, The. Robert Livingston. Directed by Sidney Salkow. 1938. Republic. 54 min. Sound. 16mm B&W. *Rental:* Ivy Films.

Night Hawks. Ken Robertson. 1978. Britain. 113 min. Sound. 16mm Color. *Rental:* Swank Motion.

Night Hawks. Sylvester Stallone & Billy Dee Williams. Directed by Bruce Malmuth. 1981. Universal. 99 min. Sound. 16mm Color. *Rental:* Swank Motion. *Rental:* Swank Motion, Videotape version.

Night Holds Terror, The. Jack Kelly & John Cassavetes. Directed by Andrew Stone. 1954. Columbia. 86 min. Sound. 16mm B&W. *Rental:* Kit Parker.

Night in a Harem, A. Dale Robertson. 1968. NTA. 16mm Color. *Rental:* Ivy Films.

Night in Casablanca, A. Marx Brothers. Directed by Archie Mayo. 1946. United Artists. 84 min. Sound. B&W. *Rental:* Ivy Films. *Rental:* Ivy Films, *Sale:* Cinema Concepts & Ivy Films, Videotape version.

Night in Havana, A *see* Big Boodle.

Night in Heaven, A. Christopher Atkins & Lesley Ann Warren. Directed by John G. Avildsen. 1983. Fox. 88 min. Sound. 16mm Color. *Rental:* Films Inc.

Night in Paradise, A. Merle Oberon & Turhan Bey. Directed by Arthur Lubin. 1946. Universal. 84 min. Sound. 16mm Color. *Rental:* Films Inc.

Night in Venice, A *see* Eine Nacht in Venedig.

Night Into Morning. Ray Milland & John Hodiak. Directed by Fletcher Markle. 1951. MGM. 86 min. Sound. 16mm B&W. *Rental:* MGM United.

Night is Ending, The *see* Paris After Dark.

Night Is My Future. Orig. Title: Music I Morker. Mai Zetterling. Directed by Ingmar Bergman. Swed. 1947. Sweden. 87 min. Sound. 16mm B&W. subtitles. *Rental:* Budget Films, Kit Parker & Westcoast Films. *Sale:* Cinema Concepts & Reel Images. *Sale:* Tamarelles French Film, Videotape version.

Night is Young, The. Ramon Navarro & Evelyn Laye. Directed by Dudley Murphy. 1935. MGM. 78 min. Sound. 16mm B&W. *Rental:* Films Inc & MGM United.

Night Key, The. Boris Karloff. Directed by Lloyd Corrigan. 1937. Universal. 67 min. Sound. 16mm Color. *Rental:* Swank Motion.

Night Monster, The. Irene Hervey & Bela Lugosi. Directed by Ford Beebe. 1942. Universal. 73 min. Sound. 16mm B&W. *Rental:* Swank Motion.

Night Moves. Gene Hackman & Susan Clark. Directed by Arthur Penn. 1975. Warners. 100 min. Sound. 16mm Color. *Rental:* Swank Motion, Twyman Films & Williams Films.

Night Must Fall. Robert Montgomery & Dame May Whitty. Directed by Richard Thorpe. 1937. MGM. 116 min. Sound. 16mm B&W. *Rental:* MGM United.

Night Must Fall. Albert Finney & Mona Washbourne. Directed by Karel Reisz. 1964. MGM. 105 min. Sound. 16mm B&W. *Rental:* MGM United.

Night My Number Came Up, The. Sir Michael Redgrave & Sheila Sim. Directed by Leslie Norman. 1955. Britain. 94 min. Sound. 16mm B&W. *Rental:* Janus Films.

Night Nurse. Barbara Stanwyck & Clark Gable. Directed by William A. Wellman. 1931. Warners. 73 min. Sound. 16mm B&W. *Rental:* MGM United.

Night of Adventure, A. Tom Conway & Audrey Long. Directed by Gordon Douglas. 1944. RKO. 65 min. Sound. 16mm B&W. *Rental:* Films Inc. *Lease:* Films Inc.

Night of Chills & Horror, A. 90 min. Sound. 16mm B&W. *Rental:* Williams Films.

Night of Counting the Years, The. Ahmad Marei. Directed by Shadi Abdelsalam. Arabic. 1975. Egypt. 100 min. Sound. 16mm Color. subtitles. *Rental:* Icarus Films & New Yorker Films.

Night of Dark Shadows. David Selby & Grayson Hall. Directed by Dan Curtis. 1971. MGM. 96 min. Sound. 16mm Color. *Rental:* MGM United.

Night of Romance. Constance Talmadge & Ronald Colman. Directed by Sidney Franklin. 1924. 16mm *Rental:* A Twyman Pres.

Night of Terror. Bela Lugosi & Wallace Ford. Directed by Ben Stoloff. 1933. Columbia. 61 min. Sound. 16mm B&W. *Rental:* Buchan Pic & Welling Motion Pictures.

Night of the Big Heat *see* Island of the Burning Doomed.

Night of the Blood Beast. Michael Emmet. Directed by Bernard Kowalski. 1958. American International. 63 min. Sound. 16mm B&W. *Rental:* Films Inc.

Night of the Blood Monster. Christopher Lee, Maria Schell & Leo Genn. Directed by Jess Franco. 1972. Britain. 82 min. Sound. 16mm Color. *Rental:* Swank Motion.

Night of the Bloody Apes. 84 min. Sound. Videotape Color. *Rental:* Maljack.

Night of the Cobra Woman. Joy Bang & Marlene Clark. Directed by Andrew Meyer. 1972. New World. 77 min. Sound. 16mm Color. *Rental:* Films Inc.

Night of the Demon *see* Curse of the Demon.

Night of the Eagle *see* Burn, Witch, Burn.

Night of the Following Day. Marlon Brando, Richard Boone & Rita Moreno. Directed by Hubert Cornfield. 1969. Universal. 93 min. Sound. 16mm Color. *Rental:* Swank Motion & Twyman Films.

Night of the Generals. Peter O'Toole, Omar Sharif & Tom Courtenay. Directed by Anatole Litvak. 1967. Britain. 148 min. Sound. 16mm Color. *Rental:* Budget Films, Bosco Films & Westcoast Films.

Night of the Ghouls. Rel. 1961. 65 min. Sound. 16mm Color. *Sale:* Festival Films. *Sale:* Festival Films, Videotape version.

Night of the Grizzly. Clint Walker & Martha Hyer. Directed by Joseph Pevney. 1966. Paramount. 100 min. Sound. 16mm Color. *Rental:* Films Inc. *Rental:* Films Inc, Anamorphic version.

Night of the Hummingbird, The. 1983. Britain. (Documentary). 60 min. Sound. 16mm. *Rental:* Films Inc. *Sale:* Films Inc. *Sale:* Films Inc, Videotape version.

Night of the Hunter. Robert Mitchum & Shelley Winters. Directed by Charles Laughton. 1955. United Artists. 91 min. 16mm B&W. *Rental:* MGM United.

Night of the Iguana. Richard Burton, Deborah Kerr & Ava Gardner. Directed by John Huston. 1964. MGM. 125 min. Sound. 16mm B&W. *Rental:* MGM United. *Rental:* MGM United, Videotape version.

Night of the Juggler. James Brolin & Cliff Gorman. Directed by Robert Butler. 1980. Columbia. 101 min. Sound. 16mm *Rental:* Swank Motion & Williams Films.

Night of the Lepus. Rory Calhoun, Stuart Whitman & Janet Leigh. Directed by William Claxton. 1972. MGM. 88 min. Sound. 16mm Color. *Rental:* MGM United.

Night of the Living Dead. Judith O'Dea. Directed by George A. Romero. 1968. Continental. 90 min. Sound. 16mm B&W. *Rental:* Budget Films, Cinema Five, Williams Films, Em Gee Film Lib, Films Inc, Images Film, Inst Cinema, Ivy Films, Kit Parker, Maljack, Natl Cinema, Natl Film Video, Roas Films, Twyman Films, Utah Media, Video Comm, Westcoast Films & Wholesome Film Ctr. *Sale:* Cinema Concepts, Festival Films & Reel Images. *Sale:* Reel Images, Super 8 sound version. *Rental:* Cinema Concepts, Maljack & Video Comm, *Sale:* Festival Films, Videotape version.

Night of the Quarter Moon. Julie London & John Drew Barrymore. Directed by Hugo Haas. 1959. MGM. 96 min. Sound. 16mm B&W. *Rental:* Budget Films & Rep Pic Film. *Lease:* Rep Pic Film.

Night of the Shooting Stars, The. Omero Antonutti. Directed by Paolo Taviani & Vittorio Taviani. Ital. 1983. Italy. 106 min. Sound. 16mm Color. subtitles. *Rental:* MGM United. *Rental:* MGM United, *Sale:* Tamarelles French Film, Videotape version.

Night of the Squid, The. 1976. Metromedia. (Documentary). 52 min. Sound. 16mm Color. *Rental:* Churchill Films. *Rental:* Churchill Films, Videotape version.

Night Parade, The. Hugh Trevor & Ann Pennington. Directed by Mal St. Clair. 1930. RKO. 74 min. Sound. 16mm B&W. *Rental:* RKO General Pics.

Night Patrol. Richard Talmadge. Directed by Noel Smith. 1926. FBO. 50 min. Silent. 16mm B&W. *Sale:* Blackhawk Films. *Rental:* Ivy Films, *Sale:* Blackhawk Films, Super 8 silent version.

Night People. Gregory Peck & Broderick Crawford. Directed by Nunnally Johnson. 1954. Fox. 93 min. Sound. 16mm Color. *Rental:* Films Inc.

Night Raiders. Whip Wilson. Directed by Howard Bretherton. 1952. Monogram. 52 min. Sound. 16mm B&W. *Rental:* Hurlock Cine.

Night Riders, The. John Wayne. Directed by George Sherman. 1939. Republic. 60 min. Sound. 16mm B&W. *Rental:* Ivy Films. *Sale:* Nostalgia Merchant.

Night Riders. Gaston Santos. 1963. Mexico. 77 min. Sound. 16mm B&W. dubbed. *Rental:* Ivy Films. *Sale:* Rep Pic Film.

Night Riders of Montana. Allan Lane. Directed by Fred C. Brannon. 1950. Republic. 60 min. Sound. 16mm B&W. *Rental:* Ivy Films. *Sale:* Rep Pic Film.

Night Shift. Henry Winkler, Michael Keaton & Shelley Long. Directed by Ron Howard. 1985. Warners. 105 min. Sound. 16mm Color. *Rental:* Swank Motion. *Rental:* Swank Motion, Videotape version.

Night Song. Dana Andrews & Merle Oberon. Directed by John Cromwell. 1947. RKO. 102 min. Sound. 16mm B&W. *Rental:* Films Inc.

Night Spot. Jack Carson & Allan Lane. Directed by Christy Cabanne. 1938. RKO. 60 min. Sound. 16mm B&W. *Rental:* RKO General Pics.

Night the Lights Went Out in Georgia, The. Kristy McNichol & Dennis Quaid. Directed by Ronald F. Maxwell. 1981. Embassy. 110 min. Sound. 16mm Color. *Rental:* Films Inc.

Night the World Exploded, The. Kathryn Grant & William Leslie. Directed by Fred F. Sears. 1957. Columbia. 54 min. Sound. 16mm B&W. *Rental:* Inst Cinema, Modern Sound, Roas Films & Westcoast Films.

Night They Killed Rasputin, The *see* Rasputin.

Night They Raided Minsky's, The. Jason Robards, Norman Wisdom & Bert Lahr. Directed by William Friedkin. 1968. United Artists. 100 min. Sound. 16mm Color. *Rental:* MGM United.

Night Tide. Dennis Hopper & Linda Lawson. Directed by Curtis Harrington. 1963. American International. 82 min. Sound. 16mm B&W. *Rental:* Budget Films & Films Inc. *Sale:* Reel Images.

Night Time in Nevada. Roy Rogers. Directed by William Witney. 1948. Republic. 54 min. Sound. 16mm B&W. *Rental:* Ivy Films. *Sale:* Rep Pic Film & Nostalgia Merchant.

Night to Remember, A. Loretta Young & Brian Aherne. Directed by Richard Wallace. 1942. Columbia. 90 min. Sound. 16mm B&W. *Rental:* Kit Parker.

Night to Remember, A. Kenneth More. Directed by Roy Baker. 1958. Britain. 123 min. Sound. 16mm B&W. *Rental:* Arcus Film, Budget Films, Films Inc, U of IL Film, Images Film, Kit Parker, Learning Corp Am, Modern Sound, Roas Films, Twyman Films, Welling Motion Pictures & Wholesome Film Ctr. *Lease:* Learning Corp Am.

Night Train to Memphis. Roy Acuff & Adele Mara. Directed by Lesley Selander. 1946. Republic. 67 min. Sound. 16mm B&W. *Rental:* Ivy Films & Rep Pic Film. *Lease:* Rep Pic Film.

Night Train to Paris. Leslie Nielsen. Directed by Robert Douglas. 1964. Fox. 65 min. Sound. 16mm B&W. *Rental:* Films Inc.

Night Unto Night. Ronald Reagan & Viveca Lindfors. Directed by Don Siegel. 1949. Warners. 85 min. Sound. 16mm B&W. *Rental:* MGM United.

Night Visitor, The. Max Von Sydow, Liv Ullmann & Per Oscarsson. Directed by Laslo Benedek. 1970. UMC. 106 min. Sound. 16mm Color. *Rental:* Budget Films, Cine Craft, Film Ctr DC, Films Inc & Kerr Film.

Night Visitors *see* Visiteurs du Soir.

Night Voices, Day Voices: Thirty-Five Years After the Final Solution. 51 min. Sound. 16mm Color. *Rental:* Alden Films.

Night Waitress. Don Marney & Gordon Jones. Directed by Lew Landers. 1937. RKO. 57 min. Sound. 16mm *Rental:* RKO General Pics.

Night Walker, The. Barbara Stanwyck & Robert Taylor. Directed by William Castle. 1965. Universal. 86 min. Sound. 16mm B&W. *Rental:* Swank Motion.

Night Watch. Elizabeth Taylor & Laurence Harvey. Directed by Brian Hutton. 1973. Embassy. 97 min. Sound. 16mm Color. *Rental:* Swank Motion.

Night Without Sleep. Linda Darnell & Gary Merrill. Directed by Roy Baker. 1952. Fox. 77 min. Sound. 16mm B&W. *Rental:* Films Inc.

Nightbeat. Jack Mulhall & Patsy Ruth Miller. 1931. Action. 61 min. Sound. 16mm B&W. *Rental:* Ivy Films.

Nightcomers, The. Marlon Brando & Stephanie Beacham. Directed by Michael Winner. 1972. Britain. 95 min. Sound. 16mm Color. *Rental:* Budget Films, Films Inc & Video Comm.

Nightfall. Aldo Ray, Brian Keith & Anne Bancroft. Directed by Jacques Tourneur. 1957. Columbia. 90 min. Sound. 16mm B&W. *Rental:* Inst Cinema, Film Ctr DC, Kit Parker, Welling Motion Pictures & Westcoast Films.

Nightkill. Jaclyn Smith & Mike Connors. Directed by Ted Post. 1980. Embassy. 97 min. Sound. 16mm Color. *Rental:* Films Inc.

Nightmare. Edward G. Robinson & Kevin McCarthy. Directed by Maxwell Shane. 1956. United Artists. 89 min. Sound. 16mm B&W. *Rental:* MGM United.

Nightmare Alley. Tyrone Power & Joan Blondell. Directed by Edmund Goulding. 1947. Fox. 111 min. Sound. 16mm B&W. *Rental:* Films Inc & Ivy Films.

Nightmare Castle. Orig. Title: Lovers Beyond the Tomb. Barbara Steele & Paul Miller. Directed by Allan Grunewald. 1966. Italy. 84 min. Sound. 16mm B&W. dubbed. *Rental:* Budget Films & Hurlock Cine.

Nightmare for the Bold. 1959. US Government. (Documentary). 53 min. Sound. 16mm B&W. *Sale:* Natl AV Ctr.

Nightmare in Red. 1955. NBC. (Documentary). 54 min. Sound. 16mm B&W. *Rental:* McGraw-Hill Films, Syracuse U Film, U Cal Media, U of IL Film & U Mich Media. *Sale:* McGraw-Hill Films.

Nightmare in Red China. 1958. (Cast unlisted). 70 min. Sound. 16mm B&W. *Sale:* Morcraft Films.

Nightmare in the Sun. John Derek, Aldo Ray & Ursula Andress. Directed by Marc Lawrence. 1965. Zodiac. 81 min. Sound. 16mm Color. *Rental:* Willoughby Peer.

Nightmare in Wax. Cameron Mitchell & Scott Brady. Directed by Bud Townsend. 1969. Crown. 95 min. Sound. 16mm Color. *Rental:* Films Inc & Ivy Films. *Rental:* Video Comm. *Rental:* Video Comm, Videotape version.

Nightmares. Christina Raines & Emilio Estevez. Directed by Joseph Sargent. 1983. Universal. 99 min. Sound. 16mm Color. *Rental:* Swank Motion. *Rental:* Swank Motion, Videotape version.

Night's Darkness, a Day's Sail. Britain. (Documentary). 49 min. Sound. 16mm Color. *Rental:* U Cal Media.

Nights of Cabiria, The. Giulietta Masina & Francois Perier. Directed by Federico Fellini. Ital. 1957. Italy. 110 min. Sound. 16mm B&W. subtitles. *Rental:* Films Inc.

Nightwing. Nick Mancuso, Kathryn Harrold & David Warner. Directed by Arthur Hiller. 1979. Columbia. 105 min. Sound. 16mm Color. *Rental:* Cine Craft, Modern Sound, Swank Motion, Westcoast Films, Wholesome Film Ctr & Williams Films. *Rental:* Swank Motion, Videotape version.

Nine Days a Queen *see* Tudor Rose.

Nine Days of One Year. Alexei Batalov. Directed by Mikhail Romm. 1962. Russia. 108 min. Sound. 16mm B&W. dubbed. *Rental:* Corinth Films.

Nine Girls. Ann Harding, Evelyn Keyes & Nina Foch. 1944. Columbia. 78 min. Sound. 16mm B&W. *Rental:* Kit Parker.

Nine Hours to Rama. Horst Buchholz & Jose Ferrer. Directed by Mark Robson. 1963. Fox. (Anamorphic). 125 min. Sound. 16mm Color. *Rental:* Films Inc.

Nine Lives Are Not Enough. Ronald Reagan & Joan Perry. Directed by Edward Sutherland. 1941. Warners. 63 min. Sound. 16mm B&W. *Rental:* MGM United.

Nine Lives of Fritz the Cat, The. 1974. American International. (Animated). 76 min. Sound. 16mm Color. *Rental:* Swank Motion & Welling Motion Pictures.

Nine Months. Directed by Marta Meszaros. Hungarian. 1977. Hungary. (Cast unlisted). 93 min. Sound. 16mm Color. subtitles. *Rental:* New Cinema & New Yorker Films.

Nine to Five. Jane Fonda & Lily Tomlin. Directed by Colin Higgins. 1980. Fox. 110 min. Sound. 16mm Color. *Rental:* Films Inc.

Nineteen-Eighteen. Rufina Nifontova. Directed by Grigori Roshal. Rus. 1958. Russia. 120 min. Sound. 16mm B&W. subtitles. *Rental:* Corinth Films.

Nineteen Eighty Eight: The Remake. 1978. 97 min. Sound. 16mm B&W. *Rental:* Canyon Cinema.

Nineteen Eighty-Five. 1969. Metromedia. (Documentary). 56 min. Sound. 16mm B&W. *Rental:* Films Inc & U Cal Media. *Sale:* Films Inc.

Nineteen Eighty-Four. Edmond O'Brien & Jan Sterling. Directed by Michael Anderson. 1956. Columbia. 91 min. Sound. 16mm B&W. *Rental:* Charard Motion Pics.

Nineteen Forty One. Dan Aykroyd & John Belushi. Directed by Steven Spielberg. 1979. Universal-Columbia. 120 min. Sound. 16mm Color. *Rental:* Swank Motion. *Rental:* Swank Motion, Videotape version.

Nineteen-Hundred. Robert De Niro, Gerard Depardieu, Donald Sutherland & Burt Lancaster. Directed by Bernardo Bertolucci. 1977. Paramount. 243 min. Sound. 16mm Color. *Rental:* Films Inc.

Nineteen Hundred & Five *see* Mother.

Nineteen Seventy-Two Olympics: Munich. 1972. Clayton-Jacobs. (Documentary). 112 min. Sound. 16mm Color. *Rental:* Films Inc.

Nineteen Sixty-Eight: A Look for New Meanings. 1978. CBS. (Documentary). 110 min. Sound. 16mm Color. *Rental:* Films Human. *Sale:* Films Human.

Nineteen Sixty-Four. 2 Pts. 1964. ABC. (Documentary). 54 min. Sound. 16mm Color. *Rental:* U of IL Film, McGraw-Hill Films, U Mich Media, OK AV Ctr, Syracuse U Film & Utah Media. *Sale:* McGraw-Hill Films.

Nineteen Sixty-Two Newport Jazz Festival. 1962. (Documentary). Sound. 16mm Color. *Sale:* Reel Images.

Ninety Degrees in the Shade. Trans. Title: Tricetjedna Vestinu. James Booth & Ann Todd. Directed by Jiri Weiss. 1966. Britain. 75 min. Sound. 16mm B&W. *Rental:* Budget Films, Ivy Films, Kit Parker & Video Comm.

Ninety Degrees South. Directed by Herbert G. Ponting. 1933. Britain. (Documentary). 72 min. Sound. 16mm B&W. *Rental:* Museum Mod Art.

Ninety-Nine & Forty-Four One-Hundred Percent Dead. Orig. Title: Call Harry Crown. Richard Harris & Edmond O'Brien. Directed by John Frankenheimer. 1974. Fox. 98 min. Sound. 16mm Color. *Rental:* Films Inc.

Ninety-Nine Days to Survival. 1972. Smithsonian. (Documentary). 52 min. Sound. 16mm Color. *Rental:* Budget Films, Pyramid Film & Syracuse U Film. *Sale:* Pyramid Film. *Rental:* Pyramid Film, *Sale:* Pyramid Film, Videotape version.

Ninety-Nine River Street. John Payne & Evelyn Keyes. Directed by Phil Karlson. 1953. United Artists. 83 min. Sound. 16mm B&W. *Rental:* MGM United.

Ninety-Nine Women. Maria Schell & Herbert Lom. Directed by Jess Franco. 1969. Commonwealth. 90 min. Sound. 16mm Color. *Rental:* Budget Films, Ivy Films & Video Comm.

Ninety-Third Congress, The: Restoring the Balance. 1979. PBS. (Documentary). 60 min. Videotape Color. *Rental:* PBS Video. *Sale:* PBS Video.

Ninety-Two in the Shade. Peter Fonda & Warren Oates. Directed by Thomas McGuane. 1975. United Artists. 93 min. Sound. 16mm Color. *Rental:* MGM United.

Ninos Abandonados, Los. Trans. Title: Abandoned Children, The. Directed by Danny Lyon. 1974. Serious Business. (Documentary). 63 min. Sound. 16mm Color. subtitles. *Rental:* Museum Mod Art & Serious Bus. *Sale:* Serious Bus. *Rental:* Serious Bus, *Sale:* Serious Bus, Spanish Language version.

Ninotchka. Greta Garbo & Melvyn Douglas. Directed by Ernst Lubitsch. 1939. MGM. 110 min. Sound. 16mm B&W. *Rental:* MGM United. *Rental:* MGM United, Videotape version.

Nitwits, The. Betty Grable & Gordon Jones. Directed by George Stevens. 1935. RKO. 81 min. Sound. 16mm *Rental:* RKO General Pics.

Nixon-Frost Interview, The. 1977. Swank. (Interview). Sound. 16mm Color. *Rental:* Swank Motion.

N'Jangaan. Mame N'Diaye. Directed by Mahama Johnson Traore. 1974. Senegal. 80 min. Sound. 16mm Color. subtitles. *Rental:* New Yorker Films.

Nju. Elisabeth Bergner & Emil Jannings. Directed by Paul Czinner. 1924. 16mm *Rental:* A Twyman Pres.

No Blade of Grass. Nigel Davenport & Jean Wallace. Directed by Cornel Wilde. 1971. MGM. 93 min. Sound. 16mm Color. *Rental:* Films Inc & MGM United. *Rental:* Films Inc, Anamorphic color version.

No Deposit, No Return. David Niven & Darren McGavin. Directed by Norman Tokar. 1976. Disney. 112 min. Sound. 16mm Color. *Rental:* Bosco Films, Elliot Film Co, Film Ctr DC, Films Inc, MGM United, Modern Sound, Roas Films, Swank Motion, Welling Motion Pictures, Westcoast Films & Williams Films.

No Down Payment. Joanne Woodward & Tony Randall. Directed by Martin Ritt. 1957. Fox. 105 min. Sound. 16mm B&W. *Rental:* Films Inc. *Rental:* Films Inc, Anamorphic version.

No Drums, No Bugles. Martin Sheen. Directed by Clyde Ware. 1972. Cinerama. 85 min. Sound. 16mm Color. *Rental:* Swank Motion.

No Easy Walk to Freedom *see* James Earl Jones.

No Escape. Orig. Title: I Escaped from the Gestapo. Dean Jagger & John Carradine. Directed by Charles Bennett. 1943. Monogram. 75 min. Sound. 16mm B&W. *Rental:* Hurlock Cine.

No Expectations. 1971. Canada. (Documentary). 57 min. Sound. 16mm Color. *Rental:* U Cal Media. *Sale:* Natl Churches Christ.

No Funny Business. Gertrude Lawrence & Laurence Olivier. Directed by John Stafford & Victor Hanbury. 1933. 16mm *Rental:* A Twyman Pres.

No Greater Love. Tatsuya Nakadai. Directed by Masaki Kobayashi. Jap. 1959. Japan. 208 min. Sound. 16mm B&W. subtitles. *Rental:* Films Inc.

No Hiding Place. George C. Scott & Ruby Dee. 1964. Talent Associates. 51 min. Sound. 16mm B&W. *Rental:* Mass Media, Modern Sound & U Mich Media. *Sale:* Carousel Films.

No Hiding Place. 1968. Net. (Documentary). 59 min. Sound. 16mm B&W. *Rental:* Indiana AV Ctr. *Sale:* Indiana AV Ctr.

No Highway in the Sky. James Stewart & Marlene Dietrich. Directed by Henry Koster. 1951. Fox. 98 min. Sound. 16mm B&W. *Rental:* Films Inc.

No Joy in Heaven. Directed by Munroe Scott. 1971. Canada. (Documentary). 58 min. Sound. 16mm Color. *Rental:* Natl Film CN. *Sale:* Natl Film CN.

No Kidding *see* Beware of Children.

No Leave, No Love. Van Johnson & Keenan Wynn. Directed by Charles Martin. 1946. MGM. 119 min. Sound. 16mm B&W. *Rental:* MGM United.

No Man is an Island. Marshall Thompson & Jeffrey Hunter. Directed by Richard Goldstone & John Monks. 1962. Universal. 114 min. Sound. 16mm Color. *Rental:* Swank Motion.

No Man of Her Own. Clark Gable & Carole Lombard. Directed by Wesley Ruggles. 1932. Paramount. 85 min. Sound. 16mm B&W. *Rental:* Swank Motion.

No Man's Land. Russ Harvey & Kim Lee. Directed by Russ Harvey. 1964. Cinema Video. 72 min. Sound. 16mm B&W. dubbed. *Rental:* Ivy Films.

No Man's Law. Oliver Hardy & Rex King of the Wild Horses. Directed by Del Andrews. 1925. FBO. 60 min. Silent. 16mm B&W. *Rental:* Willoughby Peer.

No Man's Range. Johnny Mack Brown. Directed by Robert N. Bradbury. 1935. Supreme. 60 min. Sound. 16mm B&W. *Sale:* Morcraft Films.

No Man's Woman. Marie Windsor & John Archer. Directed by Franklin Adreon. 1955. Republic. 70 min. Sound. 16mm B&W. *Rental:* Ivy Films. *Sale:* Rep Pic Film.

No Maps on My Taps. Sandman Sims, Bunny Briggs & Chuck Green. Directed by George T. Nierenberg. 1979. Direct Cinema. 58 min. Sound. 16mm Color. *Rental:* Direct Cinema. *Lease:* Direct Cinema. *Rental:* Direct Cinema, Videotape version.

No Minor Vices. Lilli Palmer & Louis Jourdan. Directed by Lewis Milestone. 1948. MGM. 96 min. Sound. 16mm B&W. *Rental:* Ivy Films. *Sale:* Rep Pic Film.

No More Excuses. Robert Downey & Allen Abel. Directed by Robert Downey. 1968. Phantasma. 60 min. Sound. 16mm B&W. *Rental:* Grove.

No More Hibakusha. Directed by Martin Duckworth. 1984. Icarus. 55 min. 16mm Color. *Rental:* Icarus Films. *Sale:* Icarus Films. *Rental:* Icarus Films, *Sale:* Icarus Films, Videotape version.

No More Ladies. Joan Crawford & Robert Montgomery. Directed by Edward H. Griffith. 1935. MGM. 82 min. Sound. 16mm B&W. *Rental:* MGM United.

No More Mountains: The Story of the Hmong. 1981. 58 min. Sound. Videotape Color. *Rental:* PBS Video. *Sale:* PBS Video.

No More Orchids. Carole Lombard & Lyle Talbot. Directed by Walter Lang. 1932. Columbia. 70 min. Sound. 16mm B&W. *Rental:* Kit Parker.

No More Vietnams....But. 1979. NBC. (Documentary). 103 min. Videotape Color. *Rental:* Films Inc. *Sale:* Films Inc.

No Need to Hide. Art Linkletter. 1976. Gospel. 55 min. Sound. 16mm Color. *Rental:* Gospel Films & Roas Films.

No Nukes. Directed by Julian Schlossberg. 1980. Paramount. (Concert). 103 min. Sound. 16mm Color. *Rental:* Swank Motion.

No One Man. Carole Lombard & Ricardo Cortez. Directed by Lloyd Corrigan. 1932. Paramount. 76 min. Sound. 16mm B&W. *Rental:* Swank Motion.

No Other Love. Julie Kavner & Richard Thomas. 1980. DePatie-Freling. 58 min. Sound. 16mm Color. *Rental:* Time-Life Multimedia. *Sale:* Time-Life Multimedia.

No Other Woman. Irene Dunne & Charles Bickford. Directed by Walter J. Ruben. 1933. RKO. 58 min. Sound. 16mm B&W. *Rental:* Mogulls Films.

No Parking. Gordon Harker. Directed by Jack Raymond. 1938. 16mm *Rental:* A Twyman Pres.

No Place Like Home. 1981. WNET. (Documentary). 60 min. Videotape *Rental:* Films Inc. *Sale:* Films Inc.

No Place Like Homicide. Orig. Title: What a Carve-up. Kenneth Connor & Sidney James. Directed by Patrick Jackson. 1961. Britain. 87 min. Sound. 16mm B&W. *Rental:* Films Inc.

No Place to Go. Dennis Morgan & Gloria Dickson. Directed by Terry Morse. 1939. Warners. 57 min. Sound. 16mm B&W. *Rental:* MGM United.

No Place to Land. Orig. Title: Man Mad. John Ireland & Mari Blanchard. Directed by Albert C. Gannaway. 1958. Republic. 78 min. Sound. 16mm B&W. *Rental:* Ivy Films. *Sale:* Rep Pic Film.

No Problem. Miou Miou. 1976. France. 94 min. Videotape Color. dubbed. *Sale:* Cinema Concepts. *Sale:* Cinema Concepts & Video Lib, Videotape version.

No Questions Asked. Barry Sullivan & Arlene Dahl. Directed by Harold Kress. 1951. MGM. 81 min. Sound. 16mm B&W. *Rental:* MGM United.

No Regrets for Our Youth. 1946. Japan. (Cast unlisted). 111 min. Sound. 16mm B&W. subtitles. *Rental:* Corinth Films.

No Road Back. Sean Connery & Skip Homeier. Directed by Montgomery Tully. 1957. Britain. 83 min. Sound. 16mm B&W. *Rental:* A Twyman Pres & Ivy Films.

No Room at the Inn. Freda Jackson. Directed by Daniel Birt. 1950. Britain. 63 min. Sound. 16mm B&W. *Rental:* Ivy Films. *Sale:* Rep Pic Film.

No Room for the Groom. Tony Curtis & Piper Laurie. Directed by Douglas Sirk. 1952. Universal. 82 min. Sound. 16mm B&W. *Rental:* Swank Motion.

No Room to Run. Richard Benjamin, Paula Prentiss & Barry Sullivan. Directed by Robert Michael Lewis. 1978. Sunrise. 97 min. Sound. 16mm Color. *Rental:* Modern Sound & Twyman Films.

No Sad Songs For Me. Margaret Sullavan & Wendell Corey. Directed by Rudolph Mate. 1950. Columbia. 89 min. Sound. 16mm B&W. *Rental:* Kit Parker.

No Time for Breakfast. Annie Girardot & Jean-Pierre Cassel. Directed by Jean-Louis Bertucelli. 1976. Daniel Bourla. 100 min. Sound. 16mm Color. *Rental:* Films Inc.

No Time for Comedy. James Stewart & Rosalind Russell. Directed by William Keighley. 1940. Warners. 93 min. Sound. 16mm B&W. *Rental:* MGM United.

No Time for Flowers. Viveca Lindfors. Directed by Don Siegel. 1952. RKO. 82 min. Sound. 16mm B&W. *Rental:* Film Classics.

No Vietnamese Ever Called Me Nigger. Directed by David Loeb Weiss. 1968. Paradigm. (Documentary). 65 min. Sound. 16mm B&W. *Sale:* Cinema Guild.

No Way Out. Sidney Poitier, Richard Widmark & Linda Darnell. Directed by Joseph L. Mankiewicz. 1950. Fox. 106 min. Sound. 16mm B&W. *Rental:* Films Inc.

No Way to Treat a Lady. Rod Steiger, George Segal & Lee Remick. Directed by Jack Smight. 1968. Paramount. 108 min. Sound. 16mm Color. *Rental:* Films Inc.

Noah's Ark. Dolores Costello & George O'Brien. Directed by Michael Curtiz. 1929. Warners. (Music & Sound effects only). 75 min. Sound. 16mm B&W. *Rental:* MGM United.

Nob Hill. George Raft & Vivian Blaine. Directed by Henry Hathaway. 1945. Fox. 95 min. Sound. 16mm Color. *Rental:* Films Inc & Willoughby Peer.

Nobi *see* Fires on the Plain.

Noblesse Oblige *see* Kind Hearts & Coronets.

Nobody Ever Died of Old Age. 1974. Henry St. Settlement. (Documentary). 58 min. Sound. 16mm Color. *Rental:* Films Inc, Iowa Films, Syracuse U Film & U of IL Film. *Sale:* Films Inc.

Nobody Lives Forever. John Garfield & Faye Emerson. Directed by Jean Negulesco. 1946. Warners. 100 min. Sound. 16mm B&W. *Rental:* MGM United.

Nobody Loves Flapping Eagle *see* Flap.

Nobody Waved Goodbye. Peter Kastner & Julie Biggs. Directed by Don Owen. 1964. Canada. 80 min. Sound. 16mm B&W. *Rental:* Charard Motion Pics, Films Inc, Macmillan Films, Syracuse U Film & U Cal Media. *Lease:* Macmillan Films.

Nobody's Baby. Directed by Gus Meins. 1937. MGM. (Cast unlisted). 70 min. Sound. 16mm B&W. *Rental:* MGM United.

Nobody's Darling. Mary Lee, Louis Calhern & Gladys George. Directed by Anthony Mann. 1943. Republic. 71 min. Sound. 16mm B&W. *Rental:* Ivy Films.

Nobody's Perfect. Gabe Kaplan & Susan Clark. Directed by Peter Bonerz. 1981. Columbia. 103 min. Sound. 16mm Color. *Rental:* Swank Motion.

Nobody's Perfect. Doug McClure & Nancy Kwan. Directed by Alan Rafkin. 1968. Universal. 103 min. Sound. 16mm Color. *Rental:* Swank Motion.

Noche Del Halcon, La. Andrea Garcia. Directed by Rogelio A. Gonzalez. Mexico. 90 min. Sound. 16mm Color. subtitles. *Rental:* Westcoast Films.

Nocturne. George Raft & Lynn Bari. Directed by Edwin L. Marin. 1946. RKO. 87 min. Sound. 16mm B&W. *Rental:* Films Inc.

Noel Coward & Mary Martin Live in '55. Mary Martin, Sir Noel Coward. 1955. CBS. 80 min. Videotape B&W. *Sale:* Reel Images.

Noise Invasion, The. 1972. Britain. (Documentary). 52 min. Sound. 16mm Color. *Rental:* Time-Life Multimedia. *Sale:* Time-Life Multimedia. *Rental:* Time-Life Multimedia, *Sale:* Time-Life Multimedia, Spanish language version. *Rental:* Time-Life Multimedia, *Sale:* Time-Life Multimedia, Videotape version.

Nomads of the North. Lewis Stone & Lon Chaney. Directed by David Hartford. 1920. First National. 50 min. Silent. 16mm B&W. *Rental:* Em Gee Film Lib, Film Classics, Mogulls Films & Willoughby Peer. *Sale:* Blackhawk Films & Film Classics. *Sale:* Blackhawk Films, Super 8 silent version.

Nomugi Pass. Shinobu Otake & Mieko Harada. Directed by Satsuyo Yamaoto. 1979. Japan. 154 min. Sound. Videotape Color. subtitles. *Sale:* Tamarelles French Film.

Non-Stop New York. Anna Lee & John Loder. Directed by Robert Stevenson. 1937. Britain. 72 min. Sound. 16mm B&W. *Rental:* Janus Films.

None But the Brave. Frank Sinatra & Clint Walker. Directed by Frank Sinatra. 1965. Warners. 105 min. Sound. 16mm Color. *Rental:* Cine Craft, Films Inc, Video Comm & Willoughby Peer.

None But the Lonely Heart. Cary Grant & Ethel Barrymore. Directed by Clifford Odets. 1944. RKO. 115 min. Sound. 16mm B&W. *Rental:* Films Inc.

None of My Business. 1968. NET. (Documentary). 50 min. Sound. 16mm Color. *Rental:* Indiana AV Ctr. *Sale:* Indiana AV Ctr.

None Shall Escape. Alexander Knox & Marsha Hunt. Directed by Andre De Toth. 1943. Columbia. 85 min. Sound. 16mm B&W. *Rental:* Kit Parker.

Nooks & Crannies. 1979. PBS. (Concert). 59 min. Videotape Color. *Rental:* PBS Video. *Sale:* PBS Video.

Noon Sunday. Mark Lenard & Keye Luke. 104 min. Sound. 16mm Color. *Rental:* Video Comm.

Noose for a Gunman, A. Jim Davis & Barton MacLane. Directed by Edward L. Cahn. 1960. United Artists. 69 min. Sound. 16mm B&W. *Rental:* MGM United.

Noose Hangs High, The. Bud Abbott & Lou Costello. Directed by Charles Barton. 1948. Eagle Lion. 77 min. Sound. 16mm B&W. *Rental:* Budget Films, Cine Craft, Roas Films & Video Comm. *Rental:* Video Comm, Videotape version.

Nora Prentiss. Ann Sheridan & Robert Alda. Directed by Vincent Sherman. 1947. Warners. 116 min. Sound. 16mm B&W. *Rental:* MGM United.

Norm Crosby. Verve. (Performance). 52 min. Videotape Color. *Rental:* Films Inc.

Norma Rae. Sally Field & Ron Liebman. Directed by Martin Ritt. 1979. Fox. 120 min. Sound. 16mm Color. *Rental:* Films Inc. *Rental:* Films Inc, Anamorphic version.

Normal Face, A: The Wonders of Plastic Surgery. 1983. Nova. (Documentary). 57 min. Sound. 16mm Color. *Rental:* U Cal Media.

Norman Conquest. Orig. Title: Park Plaza 605. Tom Conway & Eva Bartok. Directed by Bernard Knowles. 1953. Lippert. 79 min. Sound. 16mm B&W. *Rental:* Budget Films.

Norman Jacobson. 1967. NET. (Documentary). 59 min. Sound. 16mm B&W. *Rental:* Indiana AV Ctr. *Sale:* Indiana AV Ctr.

Norman Jewison, Film-Maker. 1973. Canada. (Documentary). 50 min. Sound. 16mm Color. *Rental:* Natl Film CN. *Sale:* Natl Film CN.

Norman Loves Rose. Carol Kane & Tony Owen. Directed by Henry Safran. 1983. MGM-UA. 98 min. Sound. 16mm Color. *Rental:* MGM United. *Rental:* MGM United, Videotape version.

Normande. Carole Laure & Reynald Bouchard. Directed by Gilles Carle. Fr. 1975. France. 93 min. Sound. 16mm Color. subtitles. *Rental:* Films Inc.

Norseman, The. Lee Majors & Cornel Wilde. Directed by Charles B. Pierce. 1978. American International. 90 min. Sound. 16mm Color. *Rental:* Swank Motion.

Norstad of NATO: War & Peace?. 1962. CBS. (Documentary). 52 min. Sound. 16mm B&W. *Rental:* Macmillan Films. *Sale:* Macmillan Films.

North American Indian, The. Directed by Ross Devenish. 1974. McGraw-Hill. (Documentary). 67 min. Sound. 16mm Color. *Rental:* McGraw-Hill Films. *Sale:* McGraw-Hill Films.

North Avenue Irregulars, The. Edward Herrmann & Susan Clark. Directed by Bruce Bilson. 1979. Disney. 99 min. Sound. 16mm Color. *Rental:* Bosco Films, Disney Prod, Elliot Film Co, Film Pres, Films Inc, MGM United, Roas Films, Swank Motion Twyman Films, Welling Motion Pictures, Westcoast Films & Williams Films.

North by Northwest. Cary Grant, Eva Marie Saint & James Mason. Directed by Alfred Hitchcock. 1959. MGM. 136 min. Sound. 16mm Color. *Rental:* MGM United. *Rental:* MGM United, Videotape version.

North China Commune. Directed by Boyce Richardson. 1979. 80 min. 16mm Color. *Rental:* National Film & U Cal Media.

North China Factory. Directed by Tony Ianzelo. 1980. 56 min. 16mm Color. *Rental:* National Film & U Cal Media.

North Country. Directed by Ron Hayes. 1972. American National. (Documentary). 105 min. Sound. 16mm Color. *Rental:* Budget Films, Films Inc, Video Comm & Westcoast Films. *Lease:* Video Comm. *Rental:* Video Comm, *Lease:* Video Comm, Videotape version.

North Dallas Forty. Nick Nolte, Mac Davis & Charles Durning. Directed by Ted Kotcheff. 1979. Paramount. 117 min. Sound. 16mm Color. *Rental:* Films Inc.

North of the Great Divide. Roy Rogers. Directed by William Witney. 1950. Republic. 67 min. Sound. 16mm Color. *Rental:* Ivy Films. *Sale:* Rep Pic Film & Nostalgia Merchant.

North of the Rio Grande. William Boyd. Directed by Nate Watt. 1937. Paramount. 60 min. Sound. 16mm B&W. *Lease:* Cinema Concepts.

North Star, The. Orig. Title: Armored Attack. Dana Andrews, Walter Huston & Jane Withers. Directed by Lewis Milestone. 1943. Goldwyn. 102 min. Sound. 16mm B&W. *Rental:* Budget Films, Classic Film Mus, Films Inc, Ivy Films, Kit Parker & Mogulls Films. *Sale:* Cinema Concepts, Festival Films & Rep Pic Film, Videotape version.

North to Alaska. John Wayne & Stewart Granger. Directed by Henry Hathaway. 1960. Fox. 122 min. Sound. 16mm Color. *Rental:* Films Inc. *Rental:* Films Inc, Anamorphic version.

North to the Klondike. Broderick Crawford & Lon Chaney Jr. Directed by Erle C. Kenton. 1942. Universal. 70 min. Sound. 16mm B&W. *Rental:* Mogulls Films & Film Ctr DC.

North With the Spring. 1970. Xerox. (Documentary). 52 min. Sound. 16mm Color. *Rental:* Cinema Guild, NYU FIlm Lib & Syracuse U FIlm. *Sale:* Xerox Films.

Northern Forests. 55 min. Color. *Rental:* EMC.

Northern Lights. Directed by John Hanson & Rob Nilsson. 1979. (Cast unlisted). 93 min. Sound. 16mm B&W. *Rental:* Films Inc, First Run & New Front.

Northern Patrol. Kirby Grant & Marian Carr. Directed by Rex Bailey. 1953. Allied Artists. 63 min. Sound. 16mm B&W. *Rental:* Hurlock Cine.

Northwest Frontier *see* Flame Over India.

Northwest Mounted Police. Gary Cooper & Madeline Carroll. Directed by Cecil B. DeMille. 1940. Paramount. 126 min. Sound. 16mm Color. *Rental:* Swank Motion.

Northwest Outpost. Orig. Title: End of the Rainbow. Joseph Schildkraut, Ilona Massey & Nelson Eddy. Directed by Allan Dwan. 1947. Republic. 91 min. Sound. 16mm B&W. *Rental:* Ivy Films. *Sale:* Rep Pic Film.

Northwest Passage. Spencer Tracy & Robert Young. Directed by King Vidor. 1940. MGM. 126 min. Sound. 16mm Color. *Rental:* MGM United.

Northwest Rangers. James Craig & William Lundigan. Directed by Joseph Newman. 1943. MGM. 65 min. Sound. 16mm B&W. *Rental:* MGM United.

Northwest Stampede. James Craig, Joan Leslie & Jack Oakie. Directed by Albert S. Rogell. 1948. Eagle Lion. 76 min. Sound. 16mm Color. *Rental:* Ivy Films & Lewis Film. *Sale:* Rep Pic Film.

Northwest Territory. Kirby Grant. Directed by Frank McDonald. 1951. Monogram. 61 min. Sound. 16mm B&W. *Rental:* Hurlock Cine, Modern Sound & Westcoast Films.

Northwest Trail. John Litel, Bob Steele & Joan Woodbury. Directed by Derwin Abrahams. 1946. Screen Guild. 61 min. Sound. 16mm Color. *Rental:* Budget Films.

Norway at War. 1943. Norway. (Documentary). 70 min. Sound. 16mm B&W. narrated Eng. *Rental:* Film Classics.

Norwood. Glen Campbell & Kim Darby. Directed by Jack Haley Jr. 1970. Paramount. 96 min. Sound. 16mm Color. *Rental:* Films Inc.

Nosey Dobson. 1979. Britain. (Cast unlisted). 61 min. Sound. 16mm Color. *Sale:* Lucerne Films. *Rental:* Lucerne Films.

Nosferatu. Orig. Title: Original Dracula, The. Max Schreck. Directed by F. W. Murnau. 1922. Germany. (Musical score). 88 min. Sound. 16mm B&W. *Rental:* Budget Films, Creative Film, Em Gee Film Lib, Films Inc, Images Film, Inst Cinema, Iowa Films, Ivy Films, Janus Films, Kino Intl, Kit Parker, Museum Mod Art, Natl Film Video, Swank Motion, Utah Media, Video Comm, Willoughby Peer & Wholesome Film Ctr. *Sale:* Blackhawk Films, Cinema Concepts, Glenn Photo, Morcraft Films, Natl Cinema, Images Film & Reel Images. *Sale:* Reel Images, Super 8 sound version. *Sale:* Blackhawk Films, Glenn Photo & Morcraft Films, Super 8 silent version. *Rental:* Em Gee Film Lib, Ivy Films & Video Comm, *Sale:* Blackhawk Films, Morcraft Films, Reel Images & Images Film, Videotape version. *Rental:* Utah Media, 52 min. version. *Rental:* Westcoast Films, 45 mins. version.

Nosferatu the Vampire. Klaus Kinski & Isabelle Adjani. Directed by Werner Herzog. Ger. 1979. Germany. 63 min. Sound. 16mm Color. subtitles. *Rental:* Films Inc & Twyman Films. *Sale:* Festival Films. *Sale:* Festival Films, Videotape version.

Not a Love Story: A Film About Pornography. Directed by Bonnie Sherr Klein. 1981. Canada. 68 min. Sound. 16mm Color. *Rental:* National Film & U Cal Media.

Not a Pretty Picture. Directed by Martha Coolidge. 1976. Films Inc. (Documentary). 82 min. Sound. 16mm Color. *Rental:* Films Inc & U Mich Media. *Sale:* Films Inc.

Not Above Suspicion. Clayton Moore. 1960. Wrather. 75 min. Sound. 16mm Color. *Rental:* Video Comm.

Not As a Stranger. Robert Mitchum & Olivia De Havilland. Directed by Stanley Kramer. 1955. United Artists. 136 min. Sound. 16mm B&W. *Rental:* MGM United.

Not for Sale. Dixie Lee & Clayton Frye. Directed by E. K. Fox. 1924. Reputable. 60 min. Silent. 16mm B&W. *Rental:* Mogulls Films.

Not Guilty. Richard Dix. Directed by Sidney A. Franklin. 1921. 16mm *Rental:* A Twyman Pres.

Not Me. Allen Savage. 1971. (Documentary). 51 min. Sound. 16mm B&W. *Rental:* Syracuse U Film & U Mich Media.

Not Now, Darling. Leslie Philips & Julie Ege. Directed by Ray Cooney & David Croft. 1972. 97 min. Sound. 16mm Color. *Rental:* Budget Films.

Not on Your Life. Trans. Title: Verdugo, El. Nino Manfredi. Directed by Luis G. Berlanga. Span. 1964. Italy-Spain. 90 min. Sound. 16mm B&W. subtitles. *Rental:* Janus Films.

Not Reconciled. Henning Harmssen & Ulrich Hopmann. Directed by Jean-Marie Straub. Ger. 1965. Germany. 51 min. Sound. 16mm B&W. subtitles. *Rental:* New Yorker Films.

Not So Dumb. Orig. Title: Dulcy. Marion Davies & Elliot Nugent. Directed by King Vidor. 1929. MGM. 76 min. Sound. 16mm B&W. *Rental:* MGM United.

Not So Long Ago - 1945-1950. 1965. NBC. (Documentary). 54 min. Sound. 16mm B&W. *Rental:* Budget Films, Iowa Films, LA Inst Res Ctr, McGraw-Hill Films, Syracuse U Film, U Cal Media, U of IL Film, U Mich Media & Utah Media. *Sale:* McGraw-Hill Films.

Not the Giant...Nor the Dwarf. 1971. NBC. (Documentary). 57 min. Sound. 16mm Color. *Rental:* Films Inc. *Sale:* Films Inc. *Sale:* Films Inc, Videotape version.

Not the Same Old Story. 1983. DBA. (Documentary). 58 min. Sound. 16mm Color. *Rental:* Films Inc. *Sale:* Films Inc. *Sale:* Films Inc, Videotape version.

Notes for a Film About Donna & Gail. 1966. Canada. (Documentary). 49 min. Sound. 16mm B&W. *Rental:* McGraw-Hill Films. *Sale:* McGraw-Hill Films.

Notes for an African Orestes. Orig. Title: Africane Orestes. Directed by Pier Paolo Pasolini. Ital. 1970. Italy. (Documentary). 75 min. Sound. 16mm B&W. dubbed. *Rental:* Cinema Guild.

Notes for Jerome. Directed by Jonas Mekas. 1978. Mekas. (Experimental). 46 min. Sound. 16mm Color. *Rental:* Museum Mod Art.

Notes of a Biology Watcher: Lewis Thomas. 1982. 57 min. Sound. 16mm Color. *Rental:* U Mich Media.

Notes on a Community Hospital. 1976. Penn State. 58 min. Sound. 16mm B&W. *Rental:* Penn St AV Serv. *Sale:* Penn St AV Serv. *Rental:* Penn St AV Serv, *Sale:* Penn St AV Serv, Videotape version.

Nothing But a Man. Ivan Dixon & Abbey Lincoln. Directed by Michael Roemer. 1963. Cinema V. 92 min. Sound. 16mm B&W. *Rental:* Films Inc, Macmillan Films, Syracuse U Film & U Cal Media. *Lease:* Macmillan Films.

Nothing But the Best. Alan Bates & Millicent Martin. Directed by Clive Donner. 1964. Britain. 98 min. Sound. 16mm Color. *Rental:* Cine Craft, Images Film, Modern Sound & Welling Motion Pictures.

Nothing But Trouble. Stan Laurel & Oliver Hardy. Directed by Sam Taylor. 1944. MGM-UA. 69 min. Sound. 16mm B&W. *Rental:* MGM United.

Nothing by Chance. Directed by William H. Barnett. 1977. Barnett. (Documentary). 93 min. Sound. 16mm Color. *Rental:* Corinth Films. *Lease:* Corinth Films.

Nothing Lasts Forever. Zach Galligan & Lauren Tom. Directed by Tom Schiller. 1983. United Artists. Sound. 16mm Color. *Rental:* MGM United. *Rental:* MGM United, Videotape version.

Nothing Personal. Donald Sutherland & Suzanne Somers. Directed by George Bloomfield. 1980. Canada. 97 min. Sound. 16mm Color. *Rental:* Swank Motion.

Nothing Sacred. Carole Lombard & Fredric March. Directed by William A. Wellman. 1937. United Artists. 85 min. Sound. 16mm B&W. *Rental:* Budget Films, Mogulls Films, Roas Films & Video Comm. *Sale:* Cinema Concepts. *Rental:* Em Gee Film Lib, Ivy Films, Kit Parker, Maljack, Video Comm, Wholesome Film Ctr & Images Film, *Sale:* Cinema Concepts, Natl Cinema & Reel Images, Color version. *Rental:* Red Fox Ent & Reel Images, Super 8 sound version. *Sale:* Cinema Concepts, Maljack, Video Comm & Tamarelles French Film, Videotape version. *Sale:* Festival Films, 67 min. 16mm version. *Sale:* Festival Films, 67 min. Videotape version.

Notorious. Cary Grant & Ingrid Bergman. Directed by Alfred Hitchcock. 1946. 101 min. Sound. Videotape B&W. *Sale:* Festival Films, Videotape version.

Notorious Affair, The. Basil Rathbone & Kay Francis. Directed by Lloyd Bacon. 1930. Warners. 67 min. Sound. 16mm B&W. *Rental:* MGM United.

Notorious Landlady, The. Kim Novak & Jack Lemmon. Directed by Richard Quine. 1962. Columbia. 123 min. Sound. 16mm B&W. *Rental:* Buchan Pic, Cine Craft, Films Inc, Modern Sound, Welling Motion Pictures, Westcoast Films & Wholesome Film Ctr.

Notorious Mr. Monks, The. Luana Anders & Lyle Talbot. Directed by Joseph Kane. 1958. Republic. 70 min. Sound. 16mm B&W. *Rental:* Ivy Films. *Sale:* Rep Pic Film.

Notte, La. Orig. Title: Night, The. Marcello Mastroianni & Jeanne Moreau. Directed by Michelangelo Antonioni. Ital. 1961. Italy. 120 min. Sound. 16mm B&W. subtitles. *Rental:* Corinth Films.

Notte Brava, La: Lusty Night in Rome. Rosanna Schiaffino & Elsa Martinelli. Directed by Mauro Bolognini. 1959. Italy. 96 min. Sound. 16mm B&W. dubbed. *Rental:* Cinema Guild.

Now...After All These Years. Directed by Harold Luders & Pavel Schnabel. 1972. Cantor. (Documentary). 60 min. Sound. 16mm Color. *Rental:* A Cantor. *Sale:* A Cantor.

Now Is Forever. 1972. (Documentary). 53 min. Sound. 16mm Color. *Rental:* U Cal Media.

Now Or Never. 1978. 81 min. Sound. 16mm B&W. *Rental:* Canyon Cinema.

Now That the Buffalo's Gone. 1969. Media Guild. (Documentary). 75 min. Sound. 16mm Color. *Rental:* Media Guild. *Sale:* Media Guild. *Sale:* Media Guild, Videotape version.

Now the Chips Are Down. 1979. Britain. (Documentary). 50 min. Sound. 16mm Color. *Rental:* Films Inc & Syracuse U Film. *Sale:* Films Inc & U Mich Media. *Rental:* Films Inc, *Sale:* Films Inc, Videotape version.

Now, Voyager. Bette Davis, Claude Rains & Paul Henried. Directed by Irving Rapper. 1942. Warners. 117 min. Sound. 16mm B&W. *Rental:* MGM United.

Now You See Him, Now You Don't. Kurt Russell, Cesar Romero & Joe Flynn. Directed by Robert Butler. 1972. Disney. 88 min. Sound. 16mm Color. *Rental:* Bosco Films, Buchan Pic, Disney Prod, Elliot Film Co, Film Ctr DC, Film Pres, Film Inc, MGM United, Modern Sound, Newman Film Lib, Roas Films, Swank Motion, Twyman Films, U of IL Film, Welling Motion Pictures, Westcoast Films & Williams Films.

Now You're Talking. 46 min. 16mm B&W. *Sale:* Aust Info Serv.

Nowhere to Go. George Nader & Bernard Lee. Directed by Seth Holt. 1959. MGM. 87 min. Sound. 16mm B&W. *Rental:* MGM United.

Nuclear Battlefield, The. 1981. 50 min. Sound. 16mm Color. *Rental:* U Mich Media.

Nuclear Dilemma, The. Films Inc. (Documentary). 50 min. Sound. 16mm Color. *Sale:* Films Inc. *Sale:* Films Inc, Videotape version.

Nuclear Nightmare, The. 1983. US Government. (Documentary). 50 min. Sound. 16mm Color. *Rental:* Natl AV Ctr. *Sale:* Natl AV Crt. *Sale:* Natl AV Ctr, Videotape version.

Nuclear Nightmares. Directed by Nigel Calder. 1980. Britain. (Documentary). 90 min. Sound. 16mm Color. *Rental:* Corinth Films. *Lease:* Corinth Films. *Rental:* Corinth Films, *Lease:* Corinth Films, Videotape version.

Nuclear Power: Pro & Con. 1979. ABC. (Documentary). 50 min. Sound. 16mm Color. *Rental:* Iowa Films, McGraw-Hill Films & U Cal Media. *Sale:* McGraw-Hill Films. *Sale:* McGraw-Hill Films, Videotape version.

Nuclear Strategy for Beginners. 1983. 52 min. Sound. 16mm Color. *Rental:* U Mich Media.

Nuclear War: The Incurable Disease. 1982. Physicians for the Prevention of War. (Documentary). 60 min. Videotape Color. *Sale:* Films Inc.

Nuer, The. Directed by Robert Gardner & Hilary Harris. 1970. Peabody Museum. (Documentary). 75 min. Sound. 16mm Color. *Rental:* McGraw-Hill Films, NYU Film Lib, Syracuse U Film, U Cal Media, U Mich Media & Utah Media. *Sale:* McGraw-Hill Films.

Nueva Escuela, La. Orig. Title: New School, The. Directed by Jorge Fraga. 1975. Cuba. (Documentary). 88 min. Sound. 16mm Color. *Rental:* Cinema Guild & Doc Assocs. *Sale:* Cinema Guild & Doc Assocs.

Nuguria: Enchanted Lagoon. South Pacific. (Documentary). 50 min. Sound. 16mm Color. *Rental:* Inst Cinema. *Sale:* Inst Cinema.

Nuisance, The. Frank Morgan & Madge Evans. Directed by Jack Conway. 1933. MGM. 85 min. Sound. 16mm B&W. *Rental:* MGM United.

Nuit De Varennes, La. Directed by Ettore Scola. Fr. 1983. France. (Cast unlisted). 150 min. Sound. 16mm Color. subtitles. *Rental:* Swank Motion.

Nuit Fantastique, La see Fantastic Night.

Number One. Charlton Heston & Jessica Walter. Directed by Tom Gries. 1969. United Artists. 105 min. Sound. 16mm Color. *Rental:* MGM United.

Number Seventeen. Barry Jones. Directed by Alfred Hitchcock. 1932. Britain. 63 min. Sound. 16mm B&W. *Rental:* Budget Films, Classic Film Mus, Em Gee Film Lib, Films Inc, Images Film, Janus Films & Kit Parker. *Sale:* Classic Film Mus, Festival Films, Reel Images & Natl Cinema, Super 8 sound version. *Sale:* Festival Films, Videotape version.

Numbered Men. Conrad Nagel & Ralph Ince. Directed by Mervyn LeRoy. 1930. Warners. 68 min. Sound. 16mm B&W. *Rental:* MGM United.

Nun, The. Anna Karina & Liselotte Pulver. Directed by Jacques Rivette. Fr. 1965. France. 140 min. Sound. 16mm Color. subtitles. *Rental:* Films Inc.

Nun at the Crossroads, A. Rosanna Shiaffino & John Richardson. Directed by Julio Buchs. 1970. Italy-Spain. 100 min. Sound. 16mm Color. *Rental:* Swank Motion.

Nunca es Tarde: It's Never Too Late. Angela Molina & Jose Luis Gomez. Directed by Jaime De Arminan. Span. 1977. Spain. 110 min. Sound. 16mm Color. subtitles. *Rental:* Films Inc.

Nunzio. David Proval & Tovah Feldshuh. Directed by Paul Williams. 1978. Universal. 92 min. Sound. 16mm Color. *Rental:* Swank Motion.

Nuremberg. 1948. Army. (Documentary). 75 min. Sound. 16mm B&W. *Rental:* U Mich Media, Museum Mod Art & Natl AV Ctr. *Sale:* Natl AV Ctr, Videotape version.

Nuremberg Trial, The *see* Hitler's Executioners.

Nuremberg Trials, The. Directed by Pare Lorentz. 1946. Russia. (Documentary). 90 min. Sound. 16mm B&W. narrated Eng. *Rental:* Budget Films & Images Film. *Sale:* Reel Images & Images Film. *Sale:* Images Film, Videotape version.

Nureyev's Don Quixote. 4 pts. Rudolf Nureyev. Directed by Sir Robert Helpmann. 1973. Continental. (Dance). 60 min. Sound. 16mm Color. *Sale:* Sterling Ed Film.

Nurse Edith Cavell. Anna Neagle & George Sanders. Directed by Herbert Wilcox. 1939. RKO. 98 min. Sound. 16mm B&W. *Rental:* Budget Films, Classic Film Mus, Em Gee Film Lib, Kit Parker & Video Comm. *Sale:* Glenn Photo. *Rental:* Video Comm, Videotape version.

Nurse, Where Are You? 1982. CBS. (Documentary). 49 min. Videotape Color. *Sale:* Carousel Films & Syracuse U Film.

Nurse's Role in Acute Psychiatric Emergencies, The. 2 Pts. 1980. 120 min. Sound. Videotape Color. *Sale:* Natl AV Ctr.

Nurses' Secret, The. Lee Patrick & Regis Toomey. Directed by Noel Smith. 1941. Warners. 65 min. Sound. 16mm B&W. *Rental:* MGM United.

Nursing Career Development. 1981. 45 min. Sound. Videotape Color. *Rental:* Natl AV Ctr.

Nut, The. Douglas Fairbanks & Barbara La Marr. Directed by Theodore Reed. 1921. United Artists. 85 min. Silent. 16mm B&W. *Rental:* A Twyman Pres, Budget Films, Em Gee Film Lib & Museum Mod Art.

Nutcracker, The. 1966. Warner-Seven Arts. (Ballet). 55 min. Sound. 16mm Color. *Rental:* Films Inc, Swank Motion & Twyman Films.

Nutcracker Fantasy, The. Directed by Takeo Nakamura. 1981. Japan. (Animated). 85 min. Sound. 16mm Color. dubbed. *Rental:* Modern Sound & Budget Films.

Nutrition: The Chemistry of Life. 1961. US Government. (Documentary). 58 min. Sound. 16mm B&W. *Sale:* SD AV Ctr.

Nuts to You. Directed by Mal Sharpe. 1975. Sharpe. (Anthology). 85 min. Sound. 16mm Color. *Rental:* Films Inc.

Nutty, Naughty Chateau. Monica Vitti & Curt Jurgens. Directed by Roger Vadim. Fr. 1963. France. 102 min. Sound. 16mm Color. subtitles. *Rental:* MGM United.

Nutty Professor, The. Jerry Lewis. Directed by Jerry Lewis. 1963. Paramount. 107 min. Sound. 16mm Color. *Rental:* Films Inc. *Sale:* Tamarelles French Film, Videotape version.

Nyoka & the Lost Secrets of Hippocrates. Kay Aldridge & Clayton Moore. Directed by William Witney. 1942. Republic. 100 min. Sound. 16mm B&W. *Rental:* Ivy Films. *Sale:* Rep Pic Film & Nostalgia Merchant.

O. H. M. S. John Mills & Wallace Ford. Directed by Raoul Walsh. 1937. Britain. 91 min. Sound. 16mm B&W. *Rental:* Classic Film Mus.

O. Henry's Full House. Orig. Title: Full House. Directed by Henry Koster, Henry Hathaway, Henry King, Howard Hawks & Jean Negulesco. 1952. Fox. (Anthology). 117 min. Sound. 16mm B&W. *Rental:* Films Inc, Twyman Films & Williams Films.

O Lucky Man. Malcolm MacDowell. Directed by Lindsay Anderson. 1973. Warners. 165 min. Sound. 16mm Color. *Rental:* Swank Motion.

O. S. S. Alan Ladd & Geraldine Fitzgerald. Directed by Irving Pichel. 1946. Paramount. 107 min. Sound. 16mm B&W. *Rental:* Swank Motion.

O. S. S. One-Hundred-Seventeen: Mission for a Killer. Frederick Stafford & Mylene Demongeot. Directed by Andre Hunebelle. 1966. Embassy. 115 min. Sound. 16mm Color. dubbed. *Rental:* Films Inc.

O Youth & Beauty. Michael Murphy & Kathryn Walker. Directed by Jeff Bleckner. 1979. Films Inc. 60 min. Sound. 16mm Color. *Rental:* Films Inc. *Sale:* Films Inc. *Sale:* Films Inc, Videotape version.

Oahe: A Question of Values. 1975. Cottonwood. (Documentary). 55 min. Sound. 16mm Color. *Rental:* SD AV Ctr.

Oath of Vengeance. Buster Crabbe. Directed by Sam Newfield. 1944. PRC. 57 min. Sound. 16mm B&W. *Rental:* Budget Films, Ivy Films, Mogulls Films & Welling Motion Pictures. *Sale:* Classics Assoc NY & Natl Cinema.

Obedience. 1965. 45 min. Sound. 16mm B&W. *Rental:* Iowa Films & U Mich Media.

Obesity & Energy Metabolism. 1980. US Government. (Documentary). 60 min. Videotape Color. *Sale:* Natl AV Ctr.

Objective Burma! Errol Flynn & George Tobias. Directed by Raoul Walsh. 1945. Warners. 141 min. Sound. 16mm B&W. *Rental:* MGM United.

Objective: Five Hundred Million. Bruno Cremer & Marisa Mell. 1966. Italy. 110 min. Sound. 16mm B&W. dubbed. *Rental:* Films Inc.

Obliging Young Lady. Edmond O'Brien & Eve Arden. Directed by Richard Wallace. 1942. RKO. 80 min. Sound. 16mm *Rental:* RKO General Pics.

Oblong Box, The. Vincent Price & Christopher Lee. Directed by Gordon Hessler. 1969. American International. 95 min. Sound. 16mm Color. *Rental:* Buchan Pic, Films Pres, Ivy Films, Video Comm, Westcoast Films & Wholesome Film Ctr.

Observing Teaching. 1976. Indiana U.. (Lecture). 50 min. Videotape Color. *Sale:* Indiana AV Ctr.

Obsession. Cliff Robertson & Genevieve Bujold. Directed by Brian De Palma. 1976. Columbia. 98 min. Sound. 16mm Color. *Rental:* Arcus Films, Budget Films, Films Inc, Images Film, Kit Parker, Modern Sound, Swank Motion, Twyman Films, Westcoast Films, Wholesome Film Ctr & Williams Films. *Rental:* Kit Parker, Twyman Films & Images Film, Anamorphic version.

Occult, The. 1976. Gospel. (Documentary). 52 min. Sound. 16mm Color. *Rental:* Budget Films, Gospel Films & Syracuse U Film.

Occupation. Directed by Hugh Raggett. 1974. Britain. (Documentary). 60 min. Sound. 16mm Color. *Rental:* U Cal Media.

Occupation: Holland 1940-1944. (World at War). : Pt. 18.). 1973. Media Guild. (Documentary). 52 min. Sound. 16mm Color. *Rental:* Media Guild. *Sale:* Media Guild. *Sale:* Media Guild, Videotape version.

Oceans. 55 min. Color. *Rental:* EMC.

Ochazuke No Aji *see* Flavor of Green Tea Over Rice.

Octagon, The. Chuck Norris & Lee Van Cleef. Directed by Eric Karson. 1980. American Cinema. 103 min. Sound. 16mm Color. *Rental:* Modern Sound, Twyman Films, Westcoast Films & Wholesome Film Ctr.

October *see* Ten Days That Shook the World.

October. 1980. 106 min. Silent. 16mm B&W. *Rental:* Iowa Films.

October Man, The. John Mills & Kay Walsh. Directed by Roy Baker. 1947. Britain. 89 min. Sound. 16mm B&W. *Rental:* Learning Corp Am, Twyman Films & U of IL Film. *Sale:* Learning Corp Am.

Octopus, Octopus. 1977. Metromedia. (Documentary). 52 min. Sound. 16mm Color. *Rental:* Churchill Films. *Rental:* Churchill Films, Videotape version.

Octopussy. Roger Moore, Maud Adams & Louis Jourdan. Directed by John Glen. 1983. United Artists. 128 min. Sound. 16mm Color. *Rental:* MGM United. *Rental:* MGM United, *Sale:* Tamarelles French Film, Videotape version.

Odd Couple, The. Jack Lemmon & Walter Matthau. Directed by Gene Saks. 1968. Paramount. (Anamorphic). 106 min. Sound. 16mm Color. *Rental:* Films Inc.

Odd Man Out. Orig. Title: Gang War. James Mason & Robert Newton. Directed by Sir Carol Reed. 1947. Britain. 117 min. Sound. 16mm B&W. *Rental:* Budget Films, Films Inc, Images Film, Janus Films, Kit Parker, Learning Corp Am, Twyman Films & U of IL Film. *Sale:* Learning Corp Am.

Odd Obsession. Orig. Title: Kagi. Machiko Kyo. Directed by Kon Ichikawa. Jap. 1959. Japan. 107 min. Sound. 16mm B&W. subtitles. *Rental:* Films Inc.

Odds Against Tomorrow. Harry Belafonte & Robert Ryan. Directed by Robert Wise. 1959. MGM. 95 min. Sound. 16mm B&W. *Rental:* MGM United.

Ode to Billy Joe. Robby Benson & Glynnis O'Connor. Directed by Max Baer. 1976. Warners. 106 min. Sound. 16mm Color. *Rental:* Films Inc, Swank Motion, Twyman Films & Williams Films.

Odessa File, The. Jon Voight & Maximillian Schell. Directed by Ronald Neame. 1974. Columbia. 128 min. Sound. 16mm Color. *Rental:* Arcus Film, Bosco Films, Buchan Pic, Budget Films, Films Inc, Images Film, Ivy Films, Modern Sound, Natl Film Video, Swank Motion, Twyman Films, Welling Motion Pictures, Westcoast Films, Wholesome Film Ctr, Williams Films. *Rental:* Twyman Films, Anamorphic version.

Odongo. Macdonald Carey & Rhonda Fleming. Directed by John Gilling. 1956. Columbia. 90 min. Sound. 16mm Color. *Rental:* Kit Parker.

Odyssey, The. 3 pts. 1966. Encyclopaedia Britannica. (Cast unlisted). 83 min. Sound. 16mm Color. *Rental:* OK AV Ctr. *Sale:* Ency Brit Ed. *Sale:* Ency Brit Ed, 195 min. version. *Sale:* Ency Brit Ed, Videotape version.

Oedipus Rex. Douglas Campbell. Directed by Sir Tyrone Guthrie. 1957. Canada. 88 min. Sound. 16mm Color. *Rental:* Corinth Films. *Lease:* Corinth Films.

Oedipus Rex. 3 pts. 1959. Encyclopaedia Britannica. (Cast unlisted). 90 min. Sound. 16mm Color. *Rental:* SD AV Ctr. *Sale:* Ency Brit Ed. *Rental:* Ency Brit Ed, 120 min. version. *Sale:* Ency Brit Ed, Videotape version.

Oedipus the King. Christopher Plummer & Orson Welles. Directed by Philip Saville. 1968. Britain. 97 min. Sound. 16mm Color. *Rental:* Swank Motion.

Oedipus Tyrannus. 1977. Miami-Dade. (Cast unlisted). 60 min. Videotape Color. *Sale:* Films Inc.

Oeros: The Shape of Survival. 1980. Films Inc. (Documentary). 50 min. Sound. 16mm Color. *Sale:* Films Inc.

Of Human Bondage. Bette Davis & Leslie Howard. Directed by John Cromwell. 1934. RKO. 83 min. Sound. 16mm B&W. *Rental:* Films Inc. *Rental:* Ivy Films, *Sale:* Ivy Films, Super 8 sound version. *Sale:* Cinema Concepts, Ivy Films, Tamarelles French Film, Video Comm & Images Film, Videotape version.

Of Human Bondage. Kim Novak & Laurence Harvey. Directed by Ken Hughes. 1964. Britain. 99 min. Sound. 16mm B&W. *Rental:* MGM United. *Rental:* MGM United, Videotape version.

Of Human Hearts. Walter Huston & James Stewart. Directed by Clarence Brown. 1938. MGM. 100 min. Sound. 16mm B&W. *Rental:* MGM United.

Of Love & Desire. Merle Oberon & Curt Jurgens. Directed by Richard Rush. 1963. Fox. 93 min. Sound. 16mm Color. *Rental:* Films Inc.

Of Mice & Men. Burgess Meredith, Betty Field & Lon Chaney Jr. Directed by Lewis Milestone. 1939. Hal Roach. 105 min. Sound. 16mm B&W. *Rental:* Corinth Films & Ivy Films. *Lease:* Corinth Films.

Of Mules & Men. 1979. PBS. (Documentary). 51 min. Videotape Color. *Rental:* PBS Video. *Sale:* PBS Video.

Of Race & Blood. 1979. PBS. (Documentary). 89 min. Videotape Color. *Rental:* PBS Video. *Sale:* PBS Video.

Of Stars & Men. Directed by John Hubley & Faith Hubley. 1961. Britain. (Animated). 63 min. Sound. 16mm Color. *Rental:* Images Film, Museum Mod Art & Texture Film. *Sale:* Images Film, Museum Mod Art & Texture Film.

Of Those Who Are Lost. Directed by Eric Durschmied. Cyprus. (Documentary). 50 min. Sound. 16mm Color. *Rental:* Inst Cinema. *Sale:* Inst Cinema.

Of Unknown Origin. Peter Weller, Jennifer Dale & Lawrence Dane. Directed by George Pan Cosmatos. 89 min. Sound. 16mm Color. *Rental:* Swank Motion. *Rental:* Swank Motion, Videotape version.

Off Limits. Orig. Title: Military Police. Bob Hope & Mickey Rooney. Directed by George Marshall. 1953. Paramount. 89 min. Sound. 16mm B&W. *Rental:* Films Inc.

Off on a Comet. 1980. France. (Animated). 55 min. Sound. 16mm Color. *Rental:* Modern Sound & Westcoast Films.

Off the Record. Pat O'Brien & Joan Blondell. Directed by James Flood. 1939. Warners. 71 min. Sound. 16mm B&W. *Rental:* MGM United.

Offence, The. Sean Connery & Trevor Howard. Directed by Sidney Lumet. 1973. United Artists. 112 min. Sound. 16mm Color. *Rental:* MGM United.

Office Wife, The. Lewis Stone & Joan Blondell. Directed by Lloyd Bacon. 1930. Warners. 59 min. Sound. 16mm B&W. *Rental:* MGM United.

Officer & a Gentleman, An. Richard Gere, Debra Winger & Louis Gossett Jr. Directed by Taylor Hackford. Paramount. 126 min. Sound. 16mm Color. *Rental:* Films Inc & Williams Films.

Officier de Police Sans Importance, Un. Robert Hossein & Raymond Pellegrin. Directed by Jean Larriage. Fr. France. 70 min. Sound. 16mm Color. subtitles. *Rental:* French Am Cul.

Oh! Calcutta! Videotape *Sale:* Vidamerica.

Oh, Dad, Poor Dad, Mama's Hung You in the Closet & I'm Feeling So Sad. Rosalind Russell, Robert Morse & Barbara Harris. Directed by Richard Quine. 1967. Paramount. 86 min. Sound. 16mm Color. *Rental:* Films Inc.

Oh, God! George Burns & John Denver. Directed by Carl Reiner. 1977. Warners. 104 min. Sound. 16mm Color. *Rental:* Swank Motion. *Rental:* Swank Motion, Videotape version.

Oh, God! Book II. George Burns & Suzanne Pleshette. Directed by Carl Reiner. Warners. 94 min. Sound. 16mm Color. *Rental:* Swank Motion & Williams Films. *Rental:* Swank Motion, Videotape version.

Oh, Heavenly Dog. Chevy Chase, Jane Seymour & Benji. Directed by Joe Camp. 1980. Fox. 103 min. Sound. 16mm Color. *Rental:* Films Inc & Williams Films.

Oh Men! Oh Women! Dan Dailey & Ginger Rogers. Directed by Nunnally Johnson. 1957. Fox. (Anamorphic). 89 min. Sound. 16mm Color. *Rental:* Films Inc.

Oh, Mr. Porter. Will Hay. Directed by Marcel Varnel. 1933. Britain. 85 min. Sound. 16mm B&W. *Rental:* Janus Films.

Oh, My Darling Clementine. Lorna Gray & Irene Ryan. Directed by Frank McDonald. 1943. Republic. 69 min. Sound. 16mm B&W. *Rental:* Ivy Films. *Sale:* Rep Pic Film.

Oh, Sailor Behave. Charles King, Olsen & Johnson. Directed by Archie Mayo. 1930. Warners. 68 min. Sound. 16mm B&W. *Rental:* MGM United.

Oh, Susanna. Rod Cameron & Forrest Tucker. Directed by Joseph Kane. 1950. Republic. 90 min. Sound. 16mm B&W. *Rental:* Budget Films & Ivy Films. *Sale:* Cinema Concepts & Rep Pic Film.

Oh! What a Lovely War. Sir Laurence Olivier & Sir Ralph Richardson. Directed by Sir Richard Attenborough. 1969. Paramount. (Anamorphic). 139 min. Sound. 16mm Color. *Rental:* Films Inc.

Oh, What a Night. Edmund Lowe & Marjorie Rambeau. Directed by William Beaudine. 1944. Monogram. 60 min. Sound. 16mm B&W. *Rental:* Mogulls Films.

Oh Yeah? James Gleason & ZaSu Pitts. Directed by Tay Garnett. 1930. Pathe. 85 min. Sound. 16mm B&W. *Rental:* Film Classics. *Rental:* Films Classics, Videotape version.

Oh, You Beautiful Doll. Mark Stevens & June Haver. Directed by John M. Stahl. 1949. Fox. 94 min. Sound. 16mm B&W. *Rental:* Films Inc. *Rental:* Films Inc, Color version.

Oh! for a Man *see* Will Success Spoil Rock Hunter?.

Ohayo. Koji Shidara & Masahiko Shimazu. Jap. 1959. Japan. 93 min. Sound. 16mm Color. subtitles. *Rental:* Films Inc.

Oil. Stuart Whitman & Ray Milland. 1978. 95 min. Sound. 16mm Color. *Rental:* Westcoast Films.

Oil for the Lamps of China. Pat O'Brien & Josephine Hutchinson. Directed by Mervyn LeRoy. 1935. Warners. 98 min. Sound. 16mm B&W. *Rental:* MGM United.

Oil from the Deep Ocean. 1970. EMC. (Documentary). 59 min. Sound. 16mm B&W. *Rental:* U Cal Media. *Sale:* U Cal Media.

Oil Raider, The. Buster Crabbe & Gloria Shea. Directed by Spencer G. Bennett. 1934. Mayfair. 65 min. Sound. 16mm B&W. *Rental:* Modern Sound. *Sale:* Glenn Photo.

Oil Weapon, The. 1975. CTV. (Documentary). 50 min. Sound. 16mm Color. *Rental:* Films Inc, Syracuse U Film & U of IL Film. *Sale:* Films Inc. *Sale:* Films Inc, Videotape version.

Oilfields, The. Directed by Joris Ivens & Marceline Loridan. 1973. China. (Documentary). 87 min. Sound. 16mm Color. *Rental:* Cinema Arts.

Okay America. Lew Ayres & Maureen O'Sullivan. Directed by Tay Garnett. 1932. Universal. 80 min. Sound. 16mm B&W. *Rental:* Swank Motion.

Okinawa. Pat O'Brien & Cameron Mitchell. Directed by Leigh Jason. 1952. Columbia. 67 min. Sound. 16mm Color. *Rental:* Film Ctr DC.

Oklahoma! Gordon MacRae, Gloria Grahame & Gene Nelson. Directed by Fred Zinnemann. 1955. Magna. 148 min. Sound. 16mm Color. *Rental:* Bosco Films & Welling Motion Pictures.

Oklahoma Annie. Judy Canova & Allen Jenkins. Directed by R. G. Springsteen. 1952. Republic. 90 min. Sound. 16mm Color. *Rental:* Ivy Films. *Sale:* Rep Pic Film.

Oklahoma Badlands. Allan Lane. Directed by Yakima Canutt. 1948. Republic. 59 min. Sound. 16mm B&W. *Rental:* Ivy Films. *Sale:* Rep Pic Film & Nostalgia Merchant.

Oklahoma Blues. Jimmy Wakely. Directed by Lambert Hillyer. 1948. Monogram. 55 min. Sound. 16mm B&W. *Rental:* Hurlock Cine.

Oklahoma Crude. George C. Scott, Faye Dunaway & John Mills. Directed by Stanley Kramer. 1973. Columbia. 112 min. Sound. 16mm Color. *Rental:* Arcus Film, Buchan Pic, Budget Films, Films Inc, Modern Sound, Roas Films, Swank Motion, Welling Motion Pictures, Westcoast Films, Wholesome Film Ctr & Williams Films. *Rental:* Swank Motion, Anamorphic version.

Oklahoma Cyclone. Bob Steele. Directed by J. P. McCarthy. 1930. Tiffany. 60 min. Sound. 16mm B&W. *Sale:* Cinema Concepts.

Oklahoma Hard Times. 4 pts. Oklahoma State. (Documentary). 116 min. Sound. 16mm Color. *Rental:* OK AV Ctr.

Oklahoma Justice. Johnny Mack Brown. Directed by Lewis D. Collins. 1951. Monogram. 55 min. Sound. 16mm B&W. *Rental:* Hurlock Cine.

Oklahoma Kid. Humphrey Bogart & James Cagney. Directed by Lloyd Bacon. 1939. Warners. 80 min. Sound. 16mm B&W. *Rental:* MGM United.

Oklahoma Renegades. Robert Livingston. Directed by Nate Watt. 1940. Republic. 54 min. Sound. 16mm B&W. *Rental:* Ivy Films.

Oklahoma Territory. Bill Williams & Gloria Talbott. 1960. United Artists. 67 min. Sound. 16mm B&W. *Rental:* MGM United.

Oklahoma Terror. Jack Randall. Directed by Spencer G. Bennett. 1939. Monogram. 55 min. Sound. 16mm B&W. *Rental:* Hurlock Cine.

Oklahoma Woman, The. Peggie Castle & Richard Denning. Directed by Roger Corman. 1956. American International. 72 min. Sound. 16mm B&W. *Rental:* Films Inc & Westcoast Films.

Oklahoman, The. Joel McCrea & Barbara Hale. Directed by Francis D. Lyon. 1957. Allied Artists. 80 min. Sound. 16mm Color. *Rental:* Hurlock Cine.

Olaf Wieghorst: Painter of the American West. (Documentary). 52 min. Sound. 16mm Color. *Rental:* Modern Sound.

Old Acquaintance. Bette Davis, Miriam Hopkins & Gig Young. Directed by Vincent Sherman. 1943. Warners. 110 min. Sound. 16mm B&W. *Rental:* MGM United.

Old African Blasphemer, The. 1977. Britain. (Documentary). 55 min. Sound. 16mm Color. *Rental:* U of IL Film & U Mich Media, Videotape version.

Old Age. Orig. Title: Do Not Go Gentle. 2 pts. 1978. ABC. (Documentary). 104 min. Sound. 16mm Color. *Rental:* MTI Tele. *Sale:* MTI Tele. *Sale:* MTI Tele, Videotape version.

Old Age: Out of Sight, Out of Mind.
1966. NET. (Documentary). 60 min.
Sound. 16mm B&W. *Rental:* Indiana AV
Ctr & Syracuse U Film. *Sale:* Indiana AV
Ctr.

Old Age: The Wasted Years. 1966. NET.
(Documentary). 60 min. Sound. 16mm
B&W. *Rental:* Indiana AV Ctr &
Syracuse U Film. *Sale:* Indiana AV Ctr.

Old Barn Dance, The. Gene Autry.
Directed by Joseph Kane. 1938. Republic.
54 min. Sound. 16mm B&W. *Rental:* Ivy
Films. *Sale:* Cinema Concepts. *Sale:*
Video Comm, Videotape version.

Old Boyfriends. Talia Shire & Keith
Carradine. Directed by Joan Tewksbury.
1979. Embassy. 103 min. Sound. 16mm
Color. *Rental:* Films Inc.

Old Corral, The *see* Song of the Gringo.

Old Corral, The. Orig. Title: Texas
Serenade. Gene Autry. Directed by
Joseph Kane. 1937. Republic. 60 min.
Sound. 16mm B&W. *Rental:* Budget
Films. *Sale:* Cinema Concepts & Natl
Cinema.

Old Country, The. Directed by Jean-
Pierre Lefebvre. Fr. 1978. Canada. (Cast
unlisted). 113 min. Sound. 16mm Color.
subtitles. *Rental:* Liberty Co.

Old Curiosity Shop, Ye *see* Mr. Quilp.

Old Curiosity Shop, The. Anthony
Newley & David Hemmings. 1972.
Britain. 114 min. Videotape Color. *Sale:*
Blackhawk Films.

Old Dark House, The. Melvyn Douglas
& Boris Karloff. Directed by James
Whale. 1932. Universal. 75 min. Sound.
16mm B&W. *Rental:* A Twyman Pres &
Twyman Films.

Old Dark House, The. Tom Poston,
Robert Morley & Joyce Grenfell.
Directed by William Castle. 1963.
Columbia. 86 min. Sound. 16mm B&W.
Rental: Buchan Pic, Budget Films, Film
Ctr DC, Film Pres, Films Inc, Modern
Sound, Roas Films, Twyman Films &
Westcoast Films.

Old Dracula. David Niven & Teresa
Graves. Directed by Clive Donner. 1976.
American International. 89 min. Sound.
16mm Color. *Rental:* Swank Motion &
Welling Motion Pictures.

Old English. George Arliss & Doris
Lloyd. Directed by Alfred E. Green.
1930. Warners. 87 min. Sound. 16mm
B&W. *Rental:* MGM United.

Old Fashioned Girl, An. Gloria Jean &
James Lydon. Directed by Arthur
Dreifuss. 1948. Eagle Lion. 80 min.
Sound. 16mm B&W. *Rental:* Charard
Motion Pics & Ivy Films.

Old Fashioned Way, The. W. C. Fields.
Directed by William Beaudine. 1934.
Paramount. 74 min. Sound. 16mm B&W.
Rental: Williams Films.

Old-Fashioned Woman, An. Directed by
Martha Coolidge. 1974. Coolidge.
(Documentary). 49 min. Sound. 16mm
Color. *Rental:* Films Inc, Syracuse U
Film & U of IL Film. *Sale:* Films Inc.

Old Frontier, The. Monte Hale. Directed
by Philip Ford. 1950. Republic. 60 min.
Sound. 16mm B&W. *Rental:* Ivy Films.
Sale: Rep Pic Film.

Old Glory, The *see* Benito Cereno.

Old Greatheart *see* Way Back Home.

Old Homestead, The. Dick Purcell &
Anne Jeffreys. Directed by Frank
McDonald. 1942. Republic. 67 min.
Sound. 16mm B&W. *Rental:* Ivy Films.

Old House, Passing, The. 1967. 45 min.
Sound. 16mm B&W. *Rental:* Canyon
Cinema.

Old Hutch. Wallace Beery & Eric
Linden. Directed by Walter J. Ruben.
1936. MGM. 80 min. Sound. 16mm
B&W. *Rental:* MGM United.

Old Ironsides. George Bancroft. Directed
by James Cruze. 1926. Paramount. 80
min. Silent. 16mm B&W. *Rental:* Films
Inc.

Old Khottabych *see* Flying Carpet.

Old Los Angeles. John Carroll &
Catherine McLeod. Directed by Joseph
Kane. 1948. Republic. 87 min. Sound.
16mm B&W. *Rental:* Ivy Films. *Sale:*
Rep Pic Film & Nostalgia Merchant.

Old Louisiana: Treason. Tom Keene &
Rita Hayworth. Directed by Irvin Willat.
1937. Crescent. 68 min. Sound. 16mm
B&W. *Rental:* Film Classics.

Old Maid, The. Bette Davis, Miriam
Hopkins & George Brent. Directed by
Edmund Goulding. 1939. Warners. 95
min. Sound. 16mm B&W. *Rental:* MGM
United.

Old Man & the Sea, The. Spencer Tracy.
Directed by John Sturges. 1959. Warners.
86 min. Sound. 16mm Color. *Rental:* Inst
Cinema, Modern Sound, Twyman Films,
Westcoast Films & Williams Films.

Old Man Rhythm. Betty Grable &
Johnny Mercer. Directed by Edward
Ludwig. 1935. RKO. 75 min. Sound.
16mm B&W. *Rental:* RKO General Pics.

Old Mother Riley at Home. Kitty
McShane. Directed by Oswald Mitchell.
1946. Britain. 74 min. Sound. 16mm
B&W. *Rental:* Ivy Films & Rep Pic Film.
Sale: Rep Pic Film.

Old Mother Riley, Detective. Kitty
McShane. Directed by Lance Comfort.
1947. Britain. 58 min. Sound. 16mm
B&W. *Rental:* Ivy Films & Rep Pic Film.
Sale: Rep Pic Film.

Old Mother Riley in Business. Kitty
McShane. Directed by John Baxter. 1946.
Britain. 71 min. Sound. 16mm B&W.
Rental: Ivy Films.

Old Mother Riley in Society. Kitty
McShane. Directed by John Baxter. 1947.
Britain. 79 min. Sound. 16mm B&W.
Rental: Ivy Films & Rep Pic Film. *Sale:*
Rep Pic Film.

Old Mother Riley Joins Up. Kitty
McShane. Directed by Maclean Rogers.
1945. Britain. 73 min. Sound. 16mm
B&W. *Rental:* Ivy Films.

Old Mother Riley Meets the Vampire *see*
My Son, the Vampire.

Old Mother Riley Overseas. Kitty
McShane. Directed by Oswald Mitchell.
1947. Britain. 80 min. Sound. 16mm
B&W. *Rental:* Ivy Films.

Old Mother Riley's Circus. Kitty
McShane. Directed by Thomas Bentley.
1945. Britain. 75 min. Sound. 16mm
B&W. *Rental:* Ivy Films & Rep Pic Film.
Sale: Rep Pic Film.

Old Mother Riley's Ghosts. Kitty
McShane. Directed by Wallace Orton.
1948. Britain. 78 min. Sound. 16mm
B&W. *Rental:* Ivy Films & Rep Pic Film.
Sale: Rep Pic Film.

Old Myths, New Realities. 1975. Penn
State. (Documentary). 58 min. Sound.
16mm Color. *Rental:* Penn St AV Serv.
Sale: Penn St AV Serv. *Rental:* Penn St
AV Serv, *Sale:* Penn St AV Serv,
Videotape version.

Old Oklahoma Plains. Rex Allen.
Directed by William Witney. 1952.
Republic. 60 min. Sound. 16mm B&W.
Rental: Ivy Films. *Sale:* Rep Pic Film.

Old Overland Trail. Rex Allen. Directed
by William Witney. 1952. Republic. 60
min. Sound. 16mm B&W. *Rental:* Ivy
Films. *Sale:* Rep Pic Film.

Old San Francisco. Dolores Costello &
Warner Oland. Directed by Alan
Crosland. 1927. Warners. 88 min. Silent.
16mm B&W. *Rental:* MGM United.

Old Spanish Custom, An. Orig. Title:
Invader, The. Buster Keaton & Lupita
Tovar. Directed by Adrian Brunel. 1936.
Hofberg. 60 min. Sound. 16mm B&W.
Rental: Mogulls Films.

Old Swimmin' Hole, The. Charles Ray.
Directed by Joseph De Grasse. 1921.
First National. 85 min. Silent. 16mm
B&W. *Rental:* Em Gee Film Lib.

Old Swimming Hole, The. Jackie Moran & Marcia Mae Jones. Directed by Robert McGowan. 1940. Monogram. 90 min. Sound. 16mm B&W. *Sale:* Cinema Concepts & Natl Cinema.

Old Treasures from New China. 1977. EMC. (Documentary). 55 min. Sound. 16mm Color. *Rental:* Iowa Films & U Cal Media. *Sale:* U Cal Media. *Sale:* U Cal Media, Videotape version.

Old World, New World. (Destination America Ser.). 1975. Media Guild. (Documentary). 52 min. Sound. 16mm Color. *Rental:* Media Guild. *Sale:* Media Guild. *Sale:* Media Guild, Videotape version.

Old Yeller. Fess Parker, Chuck Connors & Dorothy McGuire. Disney. 83 min. Sound. 16mm Color. *Rental:* Bosco Films, Elliot Film Co, Roas Films, Welling Motion Pictures, Westcoast Films & Williams Films, videotape version.

Oldest Profession, The. Jean Moreau & Michele Mercier. Directed by Mauro Bolognini. 1967. France. 97 min. Sound. 16mm Color. dubbed. *Rental:* Films Inc.

Olga: Gymnast. 1975. Carousel. 48 min. Sound. 16mm Color. *Rental:* Syracuse U Film.

Oliver! Ron Moody & Shanni Wallis. Directed by Sir Carol Reed. 1968. Columbia. 153 min. Sound. 16mm Color. *Rental:* Arcus Film, Bosco Films, Buchan Pic, Cine Craft, Film Ctr DC, Film Pres, Films Inc, Inst Cinema, Images Film, Kit Parker, Modern Sound, Nat Film Lib, Natl Film Video, Newman Film Lib, Roas Films, Swank Motion, U of IL Film, Welling Motion Pictures, Wholesome Film Ctr & Williams Films. *Rental:* Images Film, Kit Parker, Swank Motion & Twyman Films, Anamorphic version. *Rental:* Swank Motion, Videotape version.

Oliver Twist. Dickie Moore. Directed by William J. Cowen. 1933. Monogram. 77 min. Sound. 16mm B&W. *Rental:* Alba House, Classic Film Mus, Em Gee Film Lib & Film Classics. *Sale:* Cinema Concepts & Reel Images. *Sale:* Tamarelles French Film, Videotape version.

Oliver Twist. Sir Alec Guinness, Robert Newton & Kay Walsh. Directed by David Lean. 1948. Britain. 116 min. Sound. 16mm B&W. *Rental:* Films Inc.

Oliver Twist. Jackie Coogan & Lon Chaney. Directed by Frank Lloyd. 1922. First National. (Musical score only). 76 min. Silent. 16mm B&W. *Rental:* Iowa Films, Kit Parker & Twyman Films. *Rental:* Budget Films & Ivy Films, *Sale:* Blackhawk Films, Super 8 silent version.

Oliver's Story. Ryan O'Neal, Candice Bergen & Ray Milland. Directed by John Korty. 1978. Paramount. 90 min. Sound. 16mm Color. *Rental:* Films Inc.

Olly Olly Oxen Free. Katharine Hepburn & Kevin McKenzie. Directed by Richard A. Colla. 1979. 88 min. Sound. 16mm Color. *Rental:* Welling Motion Pictures.

Olvidados, Los *see* Young & the Damned.

Olympiad: Part One. Directed by Leni Riefenstahl. 1938. Germany. (Documentary). 115 min. Sound. 16mm B&W. subtitles. *Rental:* A Twyman Pres, Budget Films, Corinth Films, Em Gee Film Lib, Images Film, Janus Films, Kit Parker, Phoenix Films, Syracuse U Film, U Cal Media, U of IL Film & Wholesome Film Ctr. *Sale:* Phoenix Films, Images Film & Reel Images. *Lease:* Corinth Films. *Rental:* Films Inc, Eng. Narrated version.

Olympiad: Part Two. Directed by Leni Riefenstahl. 1938. Germany. (Documentary). 97 min. Sound. 16mm B&W. *Rental:* A Twyman Pres, Budget Films, Corinth Films, Em Gee Film Lib, Images Film, Janus Films, Kit Parker, Phoenix Films, Syracuse U Film, U Cal Media, U of IL Film & Wholesome Film Ctr. *Sale:* Phoenix Films, Images Film & Reel Images. *Lease:* Corinth Films. *Rental:* Films Inc, Eng. Narrated version.

Olympics in Mexico, The. Directed by Alberto Isaac. 1968. Mexico. (Documentary). 112 min. Sound. 16mm Color. *Rental:* Budget Films, Cine Craft, Kerr Film, Films Ctr DC, Films Inc, Twyman Films, Welling Motion Pictures & Westcoast Films.

Olympics Nineteen-Seven-Two: Munich. 1972. Germany. (Documentary). 112 min. Sound. 16mm Color. *Rental:* Welling Motion Pictures.

Omaha Trail, The. James Craig, Chill Wills & Donald Meek. Directed by Edward Buzzell. 1942. MGM. 62 min. Sound. 16mm B&W. *Rental:* MGM United.

O'Malley of the Mounted. George O'Brien & Irene Ware. Directed by David Howard. 1936. Fox. 70 min. Sound. 16mm B&W. *Rental:* Lewis Film.

Omar Khayyam. Cornel Wilde & Michael Rennie. Directed by William Dieterle. 1957. Paramount. 101 min. Sound. 16mm Color. *Rental:* Films Inc.

Omega Connection, The. Orig. Title: London Connection, The. Jeffrey Byron & Roy Kinnear. 1979. Disney. 93 min. Sound. 16mm Color. *Rental:* Disney Prod & MGM United.

Omen, The. Gregory Peck & Lee Remick. Directed by Richard Donner. 1976. Fox. 111 min. Sound. 16mm Color. *Rental:* Films Inc, Twyman Films & Williams Films, videotape version.

Omoo, Omoo, the Shark God. Ron Randell. Directed by Don Leonard. 1949. Screen Guild. 60 min. Sound. 16mm B&W. *Rental:* Em Gee Film Lib & Mogulls Films.

On a Clear Day You Can See Forever. Barbara Streisand & Yves Montand. Directed by Vincente Minnelli. 1970. Paramount. (Anamorphic). 129 min. Sound. 16mm Color. *Rental:* Films Inc. *Sale:* Tamarelles French Film, Videotape version.

On a Clear Day You Could See Boston. (Destination America Ser.). 1975. Media Guild. (Documentary). 52 min. Sound. 16mm Color. *Rental:* Media Guild. *Sale:* Media Guild. *Sale:* Media Guild, Videotape version.

On a Paving Stone Mounted. Directed by Thaddeus O'Sullivan. 1978. Ireland. (Documentary). 96 min. Sound. 16mm B&W. *Rental:* Museum Mod Art.

On Again - Off Again. Bert Wheeler & Robert Woolsey. Directed by Edward Cline. 1937. RKO. 68 min. Sound. 16mm B&W. *Rental:* RKO General Pics.

On an Island with You. Esther Williams & Peter Lawford. Directed by Richard Thorpe. 1948. MGM. 107 min. Sound. 16mm Color. *Rental:* MGM United.

On Any Sunday. Directed by Bruce Brown. 1971. Cinema V. (Documentary). 89 min. Sound. 16mm Color. *Rental:* Cinema Five & New Cinema. *Lease:* Cinema Five.

On Approval. Beatrice Lillie & Clive Brook. Directed by Clive Brook. 1944. Britain. 80 min. Sound. 16mm B&W. *Rental:* Budget Films, Em Gee Film Lib & Kit Parker. *Sale:* Cinema Concepts, Festival Films, Natl Cinema & Reel Images. *Sale:* Festival Films & Tamarelles French Film, Videotape version.

On Being an Effective Parent. 1973. 45 min. Sound. 16mm Color. *Rental:* Iowa Films.

On Borrowed Time. Lionel Barrymore, Sir Cedric Hardwicke. Directed by Harold S. Bucquet. 1939. MGM. 100 min. Sound. 16mm B&W. *Rental:* MGM United.

On Borrowed Time: Living with Heart Disease. 1980. ABC. (Documentary). 50 min. Sound. 16mm Color. *Rental:* MTI Tele. *Sale:* MTI Tele. *Sale:* MTI Tele, Videotape version.

On C'Est Trompe d'Histoire d'Amour. Directed by Jean-Louis Bertucelli. Fr. 1974. France. (Cast unlisted). 94 min. Sound. 16mm Color. subtitles. *Rental:* French Am Cul.

On Dangerous Ground. Ida Lupino & Robert Ryan. Directed by Nicholas Ray. 1951. RKO. 82 min. Sound. 16mm B&W. *Rental:* Films Inc.

On Death & Dying. Directed by Martin Haode. 1974. NBC. (Documentary). 58 min. Sound. 16mm Color. *Rental:* Films Inc, PBS Video & U Cal Media. *Sale:* Films Inc. *Sale:* Films Inc, Videotape version.

On Giant's Shoulders. Terry Wiles, Brian Pringle & Judi Dench. Directed by Anthony Simmons. 1979. Britain. 91 min. Sound. 16mm Color. *Rental:* Films Inc. *Sale:* Films Inc. *Sale:* Films Inc, Videotape version.

On Golden Pond. Katharine Hepburn, Henry Fonda & Jane Fonda. Directed by Mark Rydell. 1985. Universal. 109 min. Sound. 16mm Color. *Rental:* Swank Motion.

On Her Majesty's Secret Service. George Lazenby & Diana Rigg. Directed by Peter Hunt. 1969. United Artists. 140 min. Sound. 16mm Color. *Rental:* MGM United. *Rental:* MGM United, Videotape version.

On L'Appelle France. Directed by Serge Leroy. Fr. 1967. France. (Documentary). 75 min. Sound. 16mm Color. *Rental:* French Am Cul. *Rental:* French Am Cul, Videotape version.

On Ne Badine Pas Avec L'Amour. Jean Desailly & Fernand Ledoux. Directed by Jean Desailly. Fr. 1955. France. 89 min. Sound. 16mm Color. *Rental:* French Am Cul.

On Ne Saurait Penser a Tout. Jacques Charon. Fr. France. 45 min. Sound. 16mm B&W. *Rental:* French Am Cul.

On Our Land. Directed by Antonia Caccia. 1981. 55 min. 16mm Color. *Rental:* Icarus Films. *Sale:* Icarus Films. *Sale:* Icarus Films, Videotape version.

On Our Way. U. S. A. 1939-1942. Directed by Hugh Raggett. (World at War Ser.). : Pt. 7.). 1973. Media Guild. (Documentary). 52 min. Sound. 16mm Color. *Rental:* Media Guild. *Sale:* Media Guild & U Cal Media. *Sale:* Media Guild, Videotape version.

On Reversing the Arms Race. 1983. 55 min. Sound. 16mm Color. *Rental:* U Mich Media.

On Snow White. 1978. Czechoslovakia. (Cast unlisted). 51 min. Color. dubbed. *Rental:* Films Inc. *Sale:* Films Inc.

On the Avenue. Dick Powell & Alice Faye. Directed by Roy Del Ruth. 1937. Fox. 90 min. Sound. 16mm B&W. *Rental:* Films Inc & Willoughby Peer.

On the Battlefield. Charles Koen & Bob Williams. Directed by Peter Biskind. 1972. Tricontinental. 82 min. Sound. 16mm B&W. *Rental:* Cinema Guild. *Sale:* Cinema Guild.

On the Beach. Gregory Peck & Ava Gardner. Directed by Stanley Kramer. 1959. United Artists. 133 min. Sound. 16mm B&W. *Rental:* Budget Films, MGM United, Westcoast Films & Wholesome Film Ctr. *Rental:* MGM United, Videotape version.

On the Bowery. Directed by Lionel Rogosin. 1952. Rogosin. (Documentary). 65 min. Sound. 16mm B&W. *Rental:* Icarus Films. *Sale:* Icarus Films.

On the Carpet *see* Little Giant.

On the Cowboy Trail. 1981. PBS. (Documentary). 60 min. Sound. Videotape Color. *Rental:* Iowa Films.

On the Double. Danny Kaye & Dana Wynter. Directed by Melville Shavelson. 1961. Paramount. 92 min. Sound. 16mm Color. *Rental:* Films Inc.

On the Great White Trail *see* Renfrew on the Great White Trail.

On the Isle of Samoa. Jon Hall & Susan Cabot. Directed by William Berke. 1950. Columbia. 65 min. Sound. 16mm B&W. *Rental:* Roas Films.

On the Line. Directed by Barbara Margolis. 1976. Margolis. (Documentary). 50 min. Sound. 16mm Color. *Rental:* Cine Info, Cinema Guild & Lat Amer Film.

On the Loose. Joan Evans & Melvyn Douglas. Directed by Charles Lederer. 1951. RKO. 76 min. Sound. 16mm B&W. *Rental:* Ivy Films. *Sale:* Rep Pic Film.

On the Night Stage. William S. Hart. Directed by Thomas H. Ince. 1915. Ince. 60 min. Silent. 16mm B&W. *Rental:* Budget Films, Em Gee Film Lib, Images Film & Kit Parker. *Sale:* Blackhawk Films. *Sale:* Blackhawk Films & Morcraft Films, Super 8 silent version.

On the Old Spanish Trail. Roy Rogers. Directed by William Witney. 1947. Republic. 54 min. Sound. 16mm B&W. *Rental:* Ivy Films. *Sale:* Natl Cinema, Rep Pic Film & Nostalgia Merchant. *Sale:* Video Comm, Videotape version.

On the Right Track. Gary Coleman & Maureen Stapleton. Directed by Lee Philips. 1981. Fox. 98 min. Sound. 16mm Color. *Rental:* Films Inc.

On the Riviera. Danny Kaye & Gene Tierney. Directed by Walter Lang. 1951. Fox. 90 min. Sound. 16mm Color. *Rental:* Films Inc.

On the Road with Duke Ellington. 1967. Drew Associates. (Documentary). 58 min. Sound. 16mm Color. *Rental:* Direct Cinema. *Sale:* Direct Cinema. *Sale:* Direct Cinema, Videotape version.

On the Run. Dennis Conoley. Directed by Patrick Jackson. 1969. Britain. 67 min. Sound. 16mm Color. *Sale:* Lucerne Films.

On the Spot. Frankie Darro & Mantan Moreland. Directed by Howard Bretherton. 1940. Monogram. 62 min. Sound. 16mm B&W. *Rental:* Hurlock Cine.

On the Sunny Side. Roddy McDowall & Jane Darwell. Directed by Harold Schuster. 1942. Fox. 69 min. Sound. 16mm B&W. *Rental:* Films Inc & Willoughby Peer.

On the Sunny Side of the Street *see* Sunny Side of the Street.

On the Threshold of Space. Guy Madison & Virginia Leith. Directed by Robert Webb. 1956. Fox. (Anamorphic). 96 min. Sound. 16mm Color. *Rental:* Films Inc.

On the Town. Gene Kelly, Frank Sinatra & Betty Garrett. Directed by Gene Kelly & Stanley Donen. 1949. MGM. 98 min. Sound. 16mm Color. *Rental:* MGM United. *Rental:* MGM United, Videotape version.

On the Waterfront. Marlon Brando, Rod Steiger & Eva Marie Saint. Directed by Elia Kazan. 1954. Columbia. 108 min. Sound. 16mm B&W. *Rental:* Arcus Film, Bosco Films, Budget Films, Cine Craft, Film Ctr DC, Films Inc, Images Film, Inst Cinema, Ivy Films, Kerr Film, Kit Parker, Natl Film Video, Roas Films, Swank Motion, Syracuse U Film, Twyman Films, U of IL Film, Video Comm, Welling Motion Pictures, Westcoast Films, Wholesome Films Ctr, Williams Films & Willoughby Peer.

On the Way, a Station on the Yangzi. Trans. Title: Gui Dao. Directed by Georges Dufaux. 1980. 59 min. 16mm Color. *Rental:* National Film & U Cal Media.

On the Way, Round Trip to Beijing. Trans. Title: Gui Dao. Directed by Georges Dufaux. 1980. 59 min. 16mm Color. *Rental:* National Film & U Cal Media.

On the Way, Some Chinese Women Told Us. Trans. Title: Gui Dao. Directed by Georges Dufaux. 1980. 80 min. 16mm Color. *Rental:* National Film & U Cal Media.

On Thin Ice *see* Big Freeze.

On Trial. Margaret Lindsay & John Litel. Directed by Terry Morse. 1939. Warners. 61 min. Sound. 16mm B&W. *Rental:* MGM United.

On Trial: Criminal Justice. 1977. Edupac. (Documentary). 75 min. Sound. 16mm Color. *Rental:* Edupac. *Sale:* Edupac.

On With the Show. Joe E. Brown, Ethel Waters & Arthur Lake. Directed by Alan Crosland. 1929. Warners. 108 min. Sound. 16mm B&W. *Rental:* MGM United.

On Your Toes. Reginald Denny. Directed by Fred Newmeyer. 1927. Universal. 60 min. Silent. 16mm B&W. *Rental:* Mogulls Films.

On Your Toes. Vera Zorina & Eddie Albert. Directed by Ray Enright. 1939. Warners. 94 min. Sound. 16mm B&W. *Rental:* MGM United.

Once a Doctor. Donald Woods & Gordon Oliver. Directed by William Clemens. 1937. Warners. 58 min. Sound. 16mm B&W. *Rental:* MGM United.

Once a Thief. Alain Delon & Ann-Margret. Directed by Ralph Nelson. 1965. United Artists. 107 min. Sound. 16mm B&W. *Rental:* Films Inc & MGM United.

Once Before I Die. Directed by Alvin Yudkoff. 1970. 52 min. Sound. 16mm *Rental:* Budget Films.

Once in a Blue Moon. Jimmy Savo. Directed by Ben Hecht & Charles MacArthur. 1936. Paramount. 66 min. Sound. 16mm B&W. *Rental:* Swank Motion.

Once in a Million Years. 1982. Britain. (Documentary). 50 min. Sound. 16mm Color. *Rental:* Films Inc & Syracuse U Film. *Sale:* Films Inc. *Sale:* Films Inc, Videotape version.

Once in Paris. Wayne Rogers & Gayle Hunnicutt. Directed by Frank D. Gilroy. 1978. L & M. 100 min. Sound. 16mm Color. *Rental:* Films Inc.

Once Is Not Enough *see* Jacqueline Susann's Once Is Not Enough.

Once More, With Feeling. Yul Brynner & Kay Kendall. Directed by Stanley Donen. 1960. Columbia. 92 min. Sound. 16mm Color. *Rental:* Cine Craft, Film Ctr DC, Films Inc, Kit Parker & Welling Motion Pictures.

Once There Was a Girl. Nina Ivanova. Directed by Victor Eisimont. Rus. 1945. Russia. 71 min. Sound. 16mm B&W. subtitles. *Rental:* Corinth Films.

Once Upon a Dream. Googie Withers & Griffith Jones. Directed by Ralph Thomas. 1949. Britain. 99 min. Sound. 16mm B&W. *Rental:* Cinema Five.

Once Upon a Honeymoon. Ginger Rogers & Cary Grant. Directed by Leo McCarey. 1942. RKO. 128 min. Sound. 16mm B&W. *Rental:* Films Inc.

Once Upon a Horse. Dan Rowan & Dick Martin. Directed by Hal Kanter. 1958. Universal. 85 min. Sound. 16mm B&W. *Rental:* Swank Motion.

Once Upon a Sunday. Pavle Mincic. Czechoslovakia. 80 min. Sound. 16mm B&W. dubbed. subtitles. *Rental:* Inst Cinema.

Once Upon a Time. Cary Grant & Janet Blair. Directed by Alexander Hall. 1944. Columbia. 90 min. Sound. 16mm B&W. *Rental:* Budget Films, Newman Film Lib & Welling Motion Pictures.

Once Upon a Time. Directed by Rolf Kauka. 1976. Germany-Italy. (Animated). 83 min. Sound. 16mm Color. subtitles. *Rental:* Films Inc & Williams Films.

Once Upon a Time, & Now. 1982. 59 min. Sound. Videotape *Rental:* PBS Video. *Sale:* PBS Video.

Once Upon a Time in America. Robert DeNiro & Elizabeth McGovern. 1985. Warners. 150 min. Sound. 16mm Color. *Rental:* Swank Motion.

Once Upon a Time in the West. Henry Fonda, Claudia Cardinale & Jason Robards. Directed by Sergio Leone. 1969. Italy. (Anamorphic). 165 min. Sound. 16mm Color. dubbed. *Rental:* Films Inc. *Sale:* Cinema Concepts, Super 8 sound version.

Once You Kiss a Stranger. Carol Lynley & Paul Burke. Directed by Robert Sparr. 1969. Warners. 106 min. Sound. 16mm Color. *Rental:* Kerr Film & Swank Motion.

One & One. Ingrid Thulin & Erland Josephson. Directed by Erland Josephson. 1977. Sweden. 90 min. Sound. 16mm Color. subtitles. *Rental:* New Cinema & New Line Cinema.

One & Only, The. Henry Winkler & Kim Darby. Directed by Carl Reiner. 1978. Paramount. 98 min. Sound. 16mm Color. *Rental:* Films Inc.

One & Only Genuine Original Family Band, The. Walter Brennan, Buddy Ebsen & John Davidson. Directed by Michael O'Herlihy. 1968. Disney. 110 min. Sound. 16mm Color. *Rental:* Bosco Films, Cine Craft, Elliot Film Co, Film Ctr DC, Films Inc, MGM United, Modern Sound, Roas Films, Swank Motion, Twyman Films, U of IL Film, Welling Motion Pictures, Westcoast Films & Williams Films.

One Body Too Many. Jack Haley & Bela Lugosi. Directed by Frank McDonald. 1945. Paramount. 75 min. Sound. 16mm B&W. *Rental:* Budget Films & Willoughby Peer.

One Crowded Night. Gale Storm & Anne Revere. Directed by Irving Reis. 1940. RKO. 68 min. Sound. 16mm B&W. *Rental:* RKO General Pics.

One Dark Night. Meg Tilly, David Mason Daniels & Adam West. Directed by Tom McLaughlin. 1983. Comworld. 92 min. Sound. 16mm Color. *Rental:* Swank Motion.

One Day at Teton Marsh. 1964. Disney. (Documentary). 47 min. Sound. 16mm Color. *Rental:* Buchan Pic, Cousino Visual Ed, Films Inc, Iowa Films, Modern Sound, Roas Films, Syracuse U Film, U of IL Film & U Mich Media.

One Day in the Life of Ivan Denisovich. Tom Courtenay. Directed by Casper Wrede. 1971. Cinerama. 100 min. Sound. 16mm Color. *Rental:* Swank Motion, Welling Motion Pictures, Wholesome Film Ctr & Williams Films.

One Exciting Week. Jerome Cowan & Arlene Harris. Directed by William Beaudine. 1946. Republic. 69 min. Sound. 16mm B&W. *Rental:* Ivy Films.

One-Eyed Jacks. Marlon Brando & Karl Malden. Directed by Marlon Brando. 1961. Paramount. 141 min. Sound. 16mm Color. *Rental:* Films Inc.

One-Eyed Soldiers, The. Dale Robertson & Luciana Paluzzi. Directed by Jean Christophe. 1966. United Screen Arts. 92 min. Sound. 16mm Color. dubbed. *Rental:* Ivy Films.

One Fine Day. Directed by Ermanno Olmi. Ital. Italy. (Cast unlisted). Sound. 16mm B&W. subtitles. *Rental:* Janus Films.

One Flew over the Cuckoo's Nest. Jack Nicholson & Louise Fletcher. Directed by Milos Forman. 1976. United Artists. 134 min. Sound. 16mm Color. *Rental:* MGM United.

One Foot in Heaven. Fredric March & Martha Scott. Directed by Irving Rapper. 1941. Warners. 118 min. Sound. 16mm B&W. *Rental:* MGM United.

One Foot in Hell. Alan Ladd & Don Murray. Directed by James B. Clark. 1960. Fox. 90 min. Sound. 16mm Color. *Rental:* Films Inc. *Rental:* Films Inc, Anamorphic color version.

One for All *see* President's Mystery.

One Frightened Night. Mary Carlisle & Charles Grapewin. Directed by Christy Cabanne. 1935. Mascot. 70 min. Sound. 16mm B&W. *Rental:* Classic Film Mus & Reel Images. *Sale:* Cinema Concepts.

One from the Heart. Frederic Forrest & Teri Garr. Directed by Francis Ford Coppola. 1982. Columbia. 97 min. Sound. 16mm Color. *Rental:* Swank Motion. *Rental:* Swank Motion, Videotape version.

One Girl's Confession. Cleo Moore & Hugo Haas. Directed by Hugo Haas. 1953. Columbia. 74 min. Sound. 16mm B&W. *Rental:* Kit Parker.

One Good Turn. Norman Wisdom & Joan Rice. Directed by John Paddy Carstairs. 1954. Britain. 90 min. Sound. 16mm B&W. *Rental:* Cinema Five.

One Heavenly Night. John Boles & Evelyn Laye. Directed by George Fitzmaurice. 1930. Goldwyn. 80 min. Sound. 16mm B&W. *Rental:* Films Inc.

One Hour to Zero. 1980. Britain. (Cast unlisted). 56 min. Sound. 16mm Color. *Sale:* Lucerne Films. *Rental:* Lucerne Films.

One Hour With You. Maurice Chevalier & Jeanette MacDonald. Directed by George Cukor & Ernst Lubitsch. 1932. Paramount. 84 min. Sound. 16mm B&W. *Rental:* Swank Motion.

One Hundred & Twenty Days of Sodom *see* Salo.

One-Hundred & Fifty Lire Escape, The. 1965. CBS. (Documentary). 54 min. Sound. 16mm B&W. *Sale:* CBS Inc.

One Hundred & One Dalmatians. Directed by Wolfgang Reitherman. 1961. Disney. (Animated). 80 min. Sound. 16mm Color. *Rental:* Disney Prod, Films Inc, MGM United, Twyman Films & U of IL Film.

One Hundred Men & a Girl. Deanna Durbin & Leopold Stokowski. Directed by Henry Koster. 1937. Universal. 87 min. Sound. 16mm B&W. *Rental:* Swank Motion.

One-Hundred Percent Sound & Songs. Directed by Armand Panigel. Fr. France. (Documentary). 70 min. Sound. 16mm B&W. subtitles. *Rental:* French Am Cul.

One Hundred Rifles. Jim Brown & Raquel Welch. Directed by Tom Gries. 1969. Fox. 110 min. Sound. 16mm Color. *Rental:* Films Inc.

One Hundred Thousand Dollars for Lassiter. Orig. Title: Dollars for a Fast Gun. Robert Hundar & Pamela Tudor. Directed by J. R. Marchent. 1966. Italy-Spain. 91 min. Sound. 16mm B&W. dubbed. *Rental:* Ivy Films.

One in Every Hundred. 1966. NET. (Documentary). 60 min. Sound. 16mm B&W. *Rental:* Indiana AV Ctr. *Lease:* Indiana AV Ctr.

One Is a Lonely Number. Trish Van Devere, Melvyn Douglas & Janet Leigh. Directed by Mel Stuart. 1972. MGM. 97 min. Sound. 16mm Color. *Rental:* MGM United.

One Last Fling. Zachary Scott & Alexis Smith. Directed by Peter Godfrey. 1949. Warners. 89 min. Sound. 16mm B&W. *Rental:* MGM United.

One Little Indian. James Garner, Vera Miles & Jodie Foster. Directed by Bernard McEveety. 1973. Disney. 90 min. Sound. 16mm Color. *Rental:* Bosco Films, Cine Craft, Disney Prod, Elliot Film Co, Film Ctr DC, Films Inc, MGM United, Modern Sound, Newman Film Lib, Roas Films, Swank Motion, Twyman Films, U of IL Film, Welling Motion Pictures, Westcoast Films & Williams Films.

One-Man. Directed by Robin Spry. 1977. 87 min. Sound. 16mm Color. *Rental:* Natl Film CN & U Cal Media.

One-Man Jury. Jack Palance & Christopher Mitchum. Directed by Charles Martin. 1978. Cal-Am. 104 min. Sound. 16mm Color. *Rental:* Films Inc.

One Man Mutiny *see* Court Martial of Billy Mitchell.

One-Man Show. Peter Kubelka. 48 min. Sound. 16mm Color. *Rental:* Canyon Cinema.

One Man's Fight for Life. 1983. DBA Communications. (Documentary). 56 min. Sound. 16mm Color. *Rental:* Films Inc. *Sale:* Films Inc. *Sale:* Films Inc, Videotape version.

One Man's Law. Don Barry. Directed by George Sherman. 1940. Republic. 64 min. Sound. 16mm B&W. *Rental:* Ivy Films. *Sale:* Rep Pic Film.

One Man's Property. 1977. Britain. (Cast unlisted). 56 min. Sound. 16mm Color. *Rental:* U of IL Film & U Mich Media, Videotape version.

One Man's War. Directed by Edgardo Cozarinsky. Fr. 1981. France. 105 min. Sound. 16mm B&W. subtitles. *Rental:* New Yorker Films.

One Man's Way. Don Murray & Diana Hyland. Directed by Denis Sanders. 1964. United Artists. 105 min. Sound. 16mm B&W. *Rental:* MGM United.

One Mask Too Many. Clayton Moore & Jay Silverheels. 1956. Wrather. 75 min. Videotape B&W. *Sale:* Blackhawk Films.

One Million B. C. Orig. Title: Man & His Mate. Victor Mature & Carole Landis. Directed by Hal Roach & Hal Roach Jr. 1940. Hal Roach. 82 min. Sound. 16mm B&W. *Rental:* Budget Films, Film Ctr DC, Modern Sound, Twyman Films & Willoughby Peer. *Lease:* Lucerne Films.

One Million Years B. C. Raquel Welch & John Richardson. Directed by Don Chaffey. 1966. Britain. 91 min. Sound. 16mm Color. *Rental:* Films Inc.

One Minute Before Death. Wanda Hendrix & Barry Coe. 1976. Dimension. 87 min. Sound. 16mm Color. *Sale:* Salz Ent.

One-Minute Manager. 1983. CBS. (Documentary). 50 min. Videotape Color. *Sale:* Films Inc.

One Minute to Zero. Robert Mitchum & Ann Blyth. Directed by Tay Garnett. 1952. RKO. 105 min. Sound. 16mm B&W. *Rental:* Films Inc.

One More River. Diana Wynyard & Colin Clive. Directed by James Whale. 1934. Universal. 88 min. Sound. 16mm B&W. *Rental:* Swank Motion.

One More Time. Peter Lawford & Sammy Davis Jr. Directed by Jerry Lewis. 1970. United Artists. 90 min. Sound. 16mm Color. *Rental:* MGM-United.

One More Tomorrow. Ann Sheridan & Dennis Morgan. Directed by Peter Godfrey. 1946. Warners. 89 min. Sound. 16mm B&W. *Rental:* MGM United.

One More Train to Rob. George Peppard & Diana Muldaur. Directed by Andrew V. McLaglen. 1971. Universal. 108 min. Sound. 16mm Color. *Rental:* Swank Motion.

One Mysterious Night. William Wright & Janis Carter. Directed by Budd Boetticher. 1944. Columbia. 70 min. Sound. 16mm B&W. *Rental:* Kit Parker.

One Nation, Indivisible. 1956. Saudek. (Documentary, Kinescope). 60 min. Sound. 16mm B&W. *Rental:* U of IL Film. *Sale:* IQ Films.

One New York Night. Franchot Tone, Una Merkel & Conrad Nagel. Directed by Jack Conway. 1935. MGM. 71 min. Sound. 16mm B&W. *Rental:* MGM United.

One Night at Susie's. Billie Dove & Douglas Fairbanks Jr. Directed by John Francis Dillon. 1930. Warners. 85 min. Sound. 16mm B&W. *Rental:* MGM United.

One Night of Love. Grace Moore. Directed by Victor Schertzinger. 1934. Columbia. 82 min. Sound. 16mm B&W. *Rental:* Budget Films & Kit Parker.

One of a Kind. Diane Baker. Directed by Harry Winer. 1978. Phoenix. 58 min. Sound. 16mm Color. *Rental:* Phoenix Films & Viewfinders. *Sale:* Phoenix Films. *Sale:* Phoenix Films, Videotape version.

One of Our Aircraft Is Missing. Eric Portman & Godfrey Tearle. Directed by Michael Powell. 1942. Britain. 106 min. Sound. 16mm B&W. *Rental:* Budget Films & Ivy Films. *Sale:* Rep Pic Film.

One of Our Dinosaurs is Missing. Helen Hayes & Peter Ustinov. Directed by Robert Stevenson. 1975. Disney. 94 min. Sound. 16mm Color. *Rental:* Disney Prod, Films Inc & Twyman Films.

One of Our Own. 1981. Canada. (Documentary). 55 min. Sound. 16mm Color. *Rental:* Film Makers. *Sale:* Film Makers.

One of Our Spies Is Missing. Robert Vaughan & David McCallum. Directed by E. Darrell Hallenbeck. 1967. MGM. 100 min. Sound. 16mm Color. *Rental:* MGM United.

One of the Bravest. Ralph Lewis & Edward Hearne. Directed by Frank O'Connor. 1925. Gotham. 72 min. Silent. 16mm B&W. *Rental:* Mogulls Films.

One of the Missing. Talmadge Armstrong. Directed by Julius D. Feigelson. 1971. Julius D. Feigelson. 56 min. Sound. 16mm Color. *Rental:* Films Inc & Video Comm. *Lease:* Video Comm.

One on One. Robby Benson & Annette O'Toole. Directed by Lamont Johnson. 1977. Warners. 98 min. Sound. 16mm Color. *Rental:* Swank Motion. *Rental:* Swank Motion, Videotape version.

One on Top of the Other. Marsa Mell & Jean Sorel. Directed by Lucio Fulci. 1973. France. 104 min. Sound. 16mm Color. dubbed. *Rental:* Video Comm.

One Plus One *see* Sympathy for the Devil.

One PM. Eldridge Cleaver, Jefferson Airplane & Rip Torn. Directed by Jean-Luc Godard & D. A. Pennebaker. 1968. 95 min. Sound. 16mm Color. *Rental:* Pennebaker. *Sale:* Pennebaker.

One Potato, Two Potato. Barbara Barrie & Bernie Hamilton. Directed by Larry Peerce. 1964. Cinema V. 92 min. Sound. 16mm B&W. *Rental:* Corinth Films.

One Rainy Afternoon. Francis Lederer & Ida Lupino. Directed by Rowland V. Lee. 1936. United Artists. 80 min. Sound. 16mm B&W. *Rental:* Budget Films & Classic Film Mus. *Sale:* Reel Images.

One Romantic Night *see* Swan.

One Romantic Night. Lillian Gish. Directed by Paul L. Stein. 1930. 74 min. Sound. 16mm B&W. *Rental:* A Twyman Pres.

One Sings, the Other Doesn't. Valerie Mairesse & Therese Liotard. Directed by Agnes Varda. Fr. 1977. France. 105 min. Sound. 16mm Color. subtitles. *Rental:* Cinema Five & New Cinema.

One Sixth of the World. Directed by Dziga Vertov. 1926. Russia. 60 min. Silent. 16mm B&W. subtitles. *Rental:* Films Inc.

One Small Step. 1978. Time-Life. (Documentary). 59 min. Sound. 16mm Color. *Rental:* U of IL Film, Videotape version.

One Small Step For Man. 60 min. Sound. Videotape Color. *Rental:* Maljack.

One Spy Too Many. Robert Vaughan & David McCallum. Directed by Joseph Sargent. 1966. MGM. 101 min. Sound. 16mm Color. *Rental:* MGM United.

One Step Away. Directed by David Neuman & Ed Pincus. 1968. (Documentary). 54 min. Sound. 16mm Color. *Rental:* Museum Mod Art.

One Step to Eternity. Danielle Darrieux & Corrine Calvet. Directed by Henri Decoin. 1954. France. 96 min. Sound. 16mm B&W. dubbed. *Rental:* Ivy Films.

One Step to Hell. Orig. Title: King of Africa. Ty Hardin & Rossano Brazzi. Directed by Sandy Howard. 1968. Italy. 90 min. Sound. 16mm Color. dubbed. *Rental:* Ivy Films. *Lease:* Rep Pic Film.

One Summer of Happiness. Edvin Adolphson & Ulla Jacobsson. Directed by Arne Mattsson. Swed. 1951. Sweden. 92 min. Sound. 16mm B&W. subtitles. *Rental:* Films Inc.

One Sunday Afternoon. Dennis Morgan & Janis Paige. Directed by Raoul Walsh. 1949. Warners. 90 min. Sound. 16mm B&W. *Rental:* MGM United.

One That Got Away, The. Hardy Kruger. Directed by Roy Baker. 1957. Britain. 111 min. Sound. 16mm B&W. *Rental:* Learning Corp Am & U of IL Film. *Sale:* Learning Corp Am.

One Third of a Nation. Sylvia Sidney & Leif Erickson. Directed by Dudley Murphy. 1939. Paramount. 80 min. Sound. 16mm B&W. *Rental:* Ivy Films & Mogulls Films. *Sale:* Rep Pic Film.

One Thousand & One Nights *see* Scheherazade.

One Thousand & One Danish Delights. EVR. 80 min. Videotape Color. *Sale:* Enter Video.

One Thousand Dollars a Minute. Edgar Kennedy & Edward Brophy. Directed by Aubrey Scotto. 1935. Republic. 54 min. Sound. 16mm B&W. *Rental:* Ivy Films. *Sale:* Rep Pic Film.

One Thousand Dollars Reward. Guinn Williams. 60 min. Silent. 16mm B&W. *Rental:* Mogulls Films.

One Thousand Dozen, The. 55 min. Sound. 16mm Color. *Rental:* Ency Brit Ed & Iowa Films. *Sale:* Ency Brit Ed. *Sale:* Ency Brit Ed, Videotape version.

One Thousand Plane Raid, The. Christopher George & J. D. Cannon. Directed by Boris Sagal. 1969. United Artists. 94 min. Sound. 16mm Color. *Rental:* MGM United.

One Thrilling Night *see* Horace Takes Over.

One Touch of Venus. Ava Gardner & Dick Haymes. Directed by William A. Seiter. 1948. Universal. 81 min. Sound. 16mm B&W. *Rental:* Budget Films & Ivy Films. *Lease:* Rep Pic Film.

One-Trick Pony. Paul Simon, Blair Brown & Rip Torn. Directed by Robert M. Young. 1980. 98 min. Sound. 16mm Color. *Rental:* Swank Motion. *Rental:* Swank Motion, Videotape version.

One Two Three. James Cagney & Horst Buchholz. Directed by Billy Wilder. 1961. United Artists. 108 min. Sound. 16mm B&W. *Rental:* MGM United.

One Voice in the Cosmic Fugue. 1980. Cosmos. (Documentary). 60 min. Sound. 16mm Color. *Rental:* Films Inc. *Sale:* Films Inc. *Rental:* Films Inc, *Sale:* Films Inc, Videotape version.

One Way or Another. Mario Balmaseda. Directed by Sara Gomez. Span. 1974. Cuba. 78 min. Sound. 16mm B&W. subtitles. *Rental:* Cinema Guild & New Yorker Films. *Sale:* Cinema Guild.

One-Way Passage. William Powell & Kay Francis. Directed by Tay Garnett. 1932. Warners. 69 min. Sound. 16mm B&W. *Rental:* MGM United.

One-Way Pendulum. Eric Sykes & George Cole. Directed by Peter Yates. 1965. Britain. 84 min. Sound. 16mm B&W. *Rental:* MGM United.

One-Way Street. James Mason & Marta Toren. Directed by Hugo Fregonese. 1950. Universal. 79 min. Sound. 16mm B&W. *Rental:* Swank Motion.

One Way to Love. Willard Parker & Marguerite Chapman. Directed by Ray Enright. 1946. Columbia. 65 min. Sound. 16mm B&W. *Rental:* Inst Cinema.

One Way to Quit. 1974. Films Inc. (Documentary). 52 min. Sound. 16mm Color. *Rental:* Films Inc.

One Wild Moment. Jean-Pierre Marielle & Victor Lannoux. Directed by Claude Berri. Fr. 1978. France. 88 min. Sound. 16mm Color. subtitles. *Rental:* Films Inc.

One Wild Oat. Stanley Holloway & Joan Rice. Directed by Charles Saunders. 1951. Britain. 78 min. Sound. 16mm B&W. *Rental:* Mogulls Films.

One Wish Too Many. Anthony Richmond. Directed by John Durst. 1963. Britain. 55 min. Sound. 16mm B&W. *Rental:* Films Inc & Wholesome Film Ctr.

One-Piece Bathing Suit, The see Million Dollar Mermaid.

Onibaba. Nobuko Otowa. Directed by Kaneto Shindo. Jap. 1964. Japan. (Anamorphic). 104 min. Sound. 16mm B&W. subtitles. *Rental:* Corinth Films. *Lease:* Corinth Films.

Onion Field, The. John Savage & James Woods. Directed by Harold Becker. 1979. Embassy. 126 min. Sound. 16mm Color. *Rental:* Films Inc.

Only a Woman. Maria Schell & Paul Christian. Directed by Alfred Weidenmann. 1962. Germany. 86 min. Sound. 16mm Color. dubbed. *Rental:* Ivy Films.

Only Angels Have Wings. Cary Grant & Jean Arthur. Directed by Howard Hawks. 1939. Columbia. 120 min. Sound. 16mm B&W. *Rental:* Budget Films, Films Inc, Images Film, Kit Parker, Modern Sound, Swank Motion, Twyman Films, U of IL Film, Welling Motion Pictures, Westcoast Films & Wholesome Film Ctr.

Only Game in Town, The. Elizabeth Taylor & Warren Beatty. Directed by George Stevens. 1970. Fox. 113 min. Sound. 16mm Color. *Rental:* Films Inc.

Only God Can Stop Me. (Cast unlisted). 90 min. Sound. 16mm B&W. *Rental:* Alba House.

Only Once in a Lifetime. Miguel Robelo & Estrellita Lenore Lopez. Directed by Alexander Grattan. Span. 1979. Sierra Madre. 97 min. Sound. 16mm Color. subtitles. *Rental:* Budget Films & Westcoast Films.

Only One New York. 1964. Embassy. (Documentary). 75 min. Sound. 16mm B&W. *Rental:* Films Inc.

Only Son, The. Choko Iida & Shinichi Mimore. Directed by Yasujiro Ozu. Jap. 1936. Japan. 82 min. Sound. 16mm B&W. subtitles. *Rental:* Films Inc.

Only the Cool. Lilli Palmer & Stephane Audran. Directed by Jean Delannoy. 1972. France. 103 min. Sound. 16mm Color. *Rental:* Budget Films.

Only the Valiant. Gregory Peck & Ward Bond. Directed by Gordon Douglas. 1950. Warners. 105 min. Sound. 16mm B&W. *Rental:* Corinth Films. *Lease:* Corinth Films.

Only Then Regale My Eyes. 1979. PBS. (Documentary). 59 min. Videotape Color. *Rental:* PBS Video. *Sale:* PBS Video.

Only Two Can Play. Peter Sellers & Mai Zetterling. Directed by Sidney Gilliat. 1962. Britain. 106 min. Sound. 16mm B&W. *Rental:* Cine Craft, Films Inc, Images Film, Kit Parker, Swank Motion, Twyman Films & Wholesome Film Ctr.

Only Way, The. Directed by Benjamin Christiansen. Denmark. (Cast unlisted). 86 min. Sound. 16mm Color. dubbed. *Rental:* Swank Motion.

Only When I Larf. Sir Richard Attenborough & David Hemmings. Directed by Basil Dearden. 1968. Paramount. 104 min. Sound. 16mm Color. *Rental:* Films Inc.

Only When I Laugh. Marsha Mason, Kristy McNichol & David Dukes. Directed by Glenn Jordan. 1981. Columbia. 120 min. Sound. 16mm Color. *Rental:* Swank Motion. *Rental:* Swank Motion, Videotape version.

Only Woman, The. Norma Talmadge. Directed by Sidney Olcott. 1924. 16mm *Rental:* A Twyman Pres.

Only Yesterday. Margaret Sullavan & John Boles. Directed by John M. Stahl. 1933. Universal. 105 min. Sound. 16mm B&W. *Rental:* Swank Motion.

Only You Can Put Your Best Foot Forward. 1978. US Government. (Documentary). 51 min. Videotape Color. *Sale:* Natl AV Ctr.

Open City. Trans. Title: Roma, Citta Aperta. Anna Magnani & Aldo Fabrizi. Directed by Roberto Rossellini. Ital. 1945. Italy. 103 min. Sound. 16mm B&W. subtitles. *Rental:* Budget Films, Corinth Films, Em Gee Film Lib, Films Inc, Images Film, Iowa Films, Kit Parker, Mogulls Films, Natl Film Video, Liberty Co, U Cal Media, Utah Media, Video Comm & Westcoast Films. *Sale:* Cinema Concepts, Festival Films, Glenn Photo, Images Film & Reel Images. *Lease:* Corinth Films. *Sale:* Cinema Concepts, Festival Films, Ivy Films, Tamarelles French Film, Video Comm & Images Film, Videotape version.

Open Secret. John Ireland & Jane Randolph. Directed by John Reinhardt. 1948. Eagle Lion. 80 min. Sound. 16mm B&W. *Rental:* Mogulls Films.

Open Theater Presents the Serpent, The. Directed by Joseph Chaikin. 1972. Open Theater. (Cast unlisted). 80 min. Sound. 16mm B&W. subtitles. *Rental:* Natl Film CN. *Sale:* Natl Film CN.

Opening in Moscow. 45 min. Sound. 16mm Color. *Rental:* Pennebaker. *Sale:* Pennebaker.

Operation Annihilate. William Shatner & Leonard Nimoy. Directed by Herschel Daugherty. 1967. Star Trek. 52 min. Sound. 16mm Color. *Rental:* Kit Parker.

Operation Barbarossa. Peter Blatty. 1970. Peter Blatty. (Documentary). 50 min. Sound. 16mm Color. *Rental:* Kit Parker.

Operation Bikini. Tab Hunter & Frankie Avalon. Directed by Anthony Carras. 1963. American International. 83 min. Sound. 16mm B&W. *Rental:* Films Inc & Westcoast Films.

Operation Bottleneck. Ron Foster & Miiko Taka. Directed by Edward L. Cahn. 1961. United Artists. 78 min. Sound. 16mm B&W. *Rental:* MGM United.

Operation C. I. A. Burt Reynolds & Danielle Aubry. Directed by Christian Nyby. 1965. Allied Artists. 90 min. Sound. 16mm B&W. *Rental:* Hurlock Cine.

Operation Camel. Nora Hayden. Directed by Sven Methling. 1961. American International. 71 min. Sound. 16mm B&W. dubbed. *Rental:* Westcoast Films.

Operation Cross Eagles. Richard Conte & Rory Calhoun. Directed by Richard Conte. 1969. Continental. 90 min. Sound. 16mm Color. *Rental:* Budget Films & Westcoast Films.

Operation Crossbow. Orig. Title: Code Name, Operation Crossbow. Sophia Loren & George Peppard. Directed by Michael Anderson. 1965. MGM. 114 min. Sound. 16mm Color. *Rental:* MGM United. *Rental:* MGM United, Anamorphic version.

Operation Dames. Orig. Title: Girls in Action. Eve Meyer & Don Devlin. Directed by Louis Clyde Stoumen. 1959. American International. 74 min. Sound. 16mm B&W. *Rental:* Westcoast Films.

Operation Daybreak. Timothy Bottoms & Anton Diffring. Directed by Lewis Gilbert. 1976. Warners. 106 min. Sound. 16mm Color. *Rental:* Swank Motion.

Operation Eichmann. Werner Klemperer & Ruta Lee. Directed by R. G. Springsteen. 1961. United Artists. 94 min. Sound. 16mm B&W. *Rental:* Hurlock Cine.

Operation Goldman see Lightning Bolt.

Operation Haylift. Bill Williams & Ann Rutherford. Directed by William Berke. 1950. Lippert. 75 min. Sound. 16mm B&W. *Rental:* Film Ctr DC.

Operation Kid Brother. Neil Connery & Bernard Lee. Directed by Alberto De Martino. 1967. United Artists. 104 min. Sound. 16mm Color. dubbed. *Rental:* MGM United.

Operation Lovebirds. Essy Persson & Morten Greenwald. Directed by Erik Balling. 1968. Denmark. 102 min. Sound. 16mm Color. dubbed. *Rental:* Video Comm & Ivy Films. *Rental:* Video Comm, Videotape version.

Operation Mad Ball. Jack Lemmon & Ernie Kovacs. Directed by Richard Quine. 1957. Columbia. 105 min. Sound. 16mm B&W. *Rental:* Buchan Pic, Budget Films, Cine Craft, Film Ctr DC, Films Inc, Inst Cinema, Modern Sound, Roas Films, Welling Motion Pictures & Westcoast Films.

Operation Mermaid *see* Bay of St. Michel.

Operation Moonlight. Orig. Title: Whiskey & Sofa. Maria Schell. 1961. Germany. 87 min. Sound. 16mm Color. dubbed. *Rental:* Ivy Films.

Operation Pacific. John Wayne & Patricia Neal. Directed by George Waggner. 1951. Warners. 91 min. Sound. 16mm B&W. *Rental:* Swank Motion.

Operation Petticoat. Cary Grant & Tony Curtis. Directed by Blake Edwards. 1959. Universal. 120 min. Sound. 16mm Color. *Rental:* Budget Films, Cine Craft, Ivy Films, Modern Sound, Video Comm, Welling Motion Pictures & Wholesome Film Ctr. *Lease:* Rep Pic Film.

Operation Snafu. Sean Connery, Stanley Holloway & Alan King. Directed by Cyril Frankel. 1964. Britain. 84 min. Sound. 16mm B&W. *Rental:* Budget Films.

Operation Snatch. Terry-Thomas & George Sanders. Directed by Robert Day. 1962. Britain. 83 min. Sound. 16mm B&W. *Sale:* Morcraft Films. *Sale:* Morcraft Films, Super 8 sound version.

Operation Thunderbolt. Orig. Title: Entebbe, Operation Thunderbolt. Assaf Dayan & Yehoram Gaon. Directed by Menahem Golan. 1977. Israel. 133 min. Sound. 16mm Color. dubbed. *Rental:* Films Inc & Modern Sound. *Sale:* Tamarelles French Film, Videotape version.

Ophelia. Andre Jocelyn & Alida Valli. Directed by Claude Chabrol. Fr. 1962. France. 105 min. Sound. 16mm B&W. subtitles. *Rental:* New Line Cinema.

Opium: The Politicians. Directed by Adrian Cowell. 1978. Britain. (Documentary). 58 min. Sound. 16mm Color. *Rental:* Human Issues. *Sale:* Human Issues.

Opium: The White Powder Opera. Directed by Adrian Cowell. 1978. Britain. (Documentary). 58 min. Sound. 16mm Color. *Rental:* Human Issues. *Sale:* Human Issues.

Opium War, The. Directed by Lin Tse-Hsu. 1959. China. 90 min. Sound. 16mm B&W. *Rental:* Films Inc.

Opium Warlords, The. Directed by Adrian Cowell. 1978. Britain. (Documentary). 75 min. Sound. 16mm Color. *Rental:* Human Issues. *Sale:* Human Issues.

Opposite Sex, The. June Allyson, Joan Collins & Ann Sheridan. Directed by David Miller. 1956. MGM. 116 min. Sound. 16mm Color. *Rental:* MGM United. *Rental:* MGM United, Anamorphic version.

Optimists, The. Peter Sellers. Directed by Anthony Simmons. 1973. Paramount. 110 min. Sound. 16mm Color. *Rental:* Films Inc.

Orca, the Killer Whale. Richard Harris & Charlotte Rampling. Directed by Michael Anderson. 1977. Paramount. (Anamorphic). 92 min. Sound. 16mm Color. *Rental:* Films Inc.

Orchestra Conductor, The. Sir John Gielgud. Directed by Andrzej Wajda. 1980. Poland. 101 min. Sound. 16mm Color. *Rental:* New Yorker Films.

Orchestra Rehearsal, The. Balduin Bass. Directed by Federico Fellini. Ital. 1979. Italy. 50 min. Sound. 16mm Color. subtitles. *Rental:* New Cinema & New Yorker Films.

Orchestra Rehearsal. Directed by Federico Fellini. Ital. 1979. 72 min. Sound. 16mm Color. subtitles Eng. *Rental:* New Yorker Films.

Orchestra Wives. George Montgomery & Ann Rutherford. Directed by Archie Mayo. 1942. Fox. 98 min. Sound. 16mm B&W. *Rental:* Films Inc.

Orchids & Ermine. Colleen Moore, Jack Mulhall & Mickey Rooney. Directed by Alfred Santell. 1927. First National. 50 min. Silent. 16mm B&W. *Rental:* Budget Films. *Sale:* Film Classics, Silent 8mm version.

Orders to Kill. Paul Massie, Eddie Albert & Lillian Gish. Directed by Anthony Asquith. 1958. Britain. 111 min. Sound. 16mm B&W. *Rental:* Budget Films.

Ordet. Orig. Title: Word, The. Henrik Malberg. Directed by Carl Th. Dreyer. Danish. 1954. Denmark. 126 min. Sound. 16mm B&W. subtitles. *Rental:* Budget Films, Kit Parker, Corinth Films, Images Film & Utah Media. *Sale:* Reel Images, Festival Films, Natl Cinema & Images Film. *Lease:* Corinth Films. *Sale:* Tamarelles French Film, Festival Films & Images Film, Videotape version.

Ordinary People. Mary Tyler Moore, Donald Sutherland & Timothy Hutton. Directed by Robert Redford. 1980. Paramount. 125 min. Sound. 16mm Color. *Rental:* Films Inc. *Sale:* Tamarelles French Film, Videotape version.

Ordres, Les. Directed by Michel Brault. 1974. Canada. (Documentary). 107 min. Sound. 16mm B&W. *Rental:* New Cinema.

Oregon Passage. John Ericson & Lola Albright. Directed by Paul Landres. 1957. Allied Artists. 82 min. Sound. 16mm Color. *Rental:* Hurlock Cine.

Oregon Trail, The. Sunset Carson. Directed by Thomas Carr. 1945. Republic. 54 min. Sound. 16mm B&W. *Rental:* Ivy Films. *Sale:* Rep Pic Film.

Oregon Trail, The. Fred MacMurray & William Bishop. Directed by Gene Fowler Jr. 1959. Fox. 82 min. Sound. 16mm Color. *Rental:* Films Inc. *Rental:* Films Inc, Anamorphic version.

Oregon Trail Scouts. Allan Lane. Directed by R. G. Springsteen. 1947. Republic. 54 min. Sound. 16mm B&W. *Rental:* Ivy Films.

Organism & the Environment. 1961. US Government. (Documentary). 57 min. Sound. 16mm B&W. *Sale:* SD AV Ctr.

Organization, The. Sidney Poitier & Barbara McNair. Directed by Don Medford. 1971. United Artists. 107 min. Sound. 16mm Color. *Rental:* MGM United.

Organizer, The. Trans. Title: I Compagni. Marcello Mastroianni & Annie Giradot. Directed by Mario Monicelli. 1964. ITA. 126 min. Sound. 16mm B&W. subtitles. *Rental:* Budget Films & Images Film. *Sale:* Images Film, Videotape version.

Oriental Evil. Orig. Title: Geisha Girl. Martha Hyer & William Andrews. Directed by George Breakston. 1952. Realart. 67 min. Sound. 16mm B&W. *Rental:* Mogulls Films.

Original Dracula, The *see* Nosferatu.

Orlacs Hande *see* Hands of Orlac.

Oro Di Napoli *see* Gold of Naples.

Orphan, The. Peggy Feury & JoAnna Miles. 80 min. Sound. 16mm B&W. *Rental:* WW Enter. *Rental:* WW Enter, Videotape version.

Orphan Boy of Vienna, The. Orig. Title: Singende Jugend. Vienna Boys Choir. Directed by Max Neufeld. Ger. 1937. Austria. 85 min. Sound. 16mm B&W. subtitles. *Rental:* Trans-World Films.

Orphans, The. Youzas Budraitis & Alyosha Tcherstov. Directed by Nikolai Gubenko. Rus. Russia. Sound. Videotape Color. subtitles. *Sale:* Tamarelles French Film.

Orphans of the North. Directed by Norman Dawn. 1940. Monogram. (Cast unlisted). 60 min. Sound. 16mm B&W. *Rental:* Mogulls Films.

Orphans of the Storm. Dorothy Gish & Lillian Gish. Directed by D. W. Griffith. 1922. United Artists. (Tinted, Musical score only). 176 min. Sound. 16mm *Rental:* Films Inc, Killiam Collect, New Cinema, Twyman Films & U of IL Film. *Rental:* A Twyman Pres & Ivy Films, Silent 16mm B&W version. *Sale:* Blackhawk Films, Super 8 sound B&W version. *Sale:* Blackhawk Films, Super 8 silent B&W version. *Sale:* Blackhawk Films, Videota version. *Rental:* U of IL Film, 52 min. version.

Orphans of the Street. Robert Livingston & Ralph Morgan. Directed by John H. Auer. 1938. Republic. 64 min. Sound. 16mm B&W. *Rental:* Ivy Films.

Orphee *see* Orpheus.

Orpheus. Orig. Title: Orphee. Jean Marais & Maria Casares. Directed by Jean Cocteau. Fr. 1949. France. 94 min. Sound. 16mm B&W. subtitles. *Rental:* Budget Films, Corinth Films, Em Gee Film Lib, Films Inc, Images Film, Janus Films, Iowa Films, Kit Parker & Liberty Co. *Sale:* Cinema Concepts, Festival Films, Natl Cinema, Reel Images & Images Film. *Lease:* Corinth Films. *Sale:* Tamarelles French Film, Fesitval Films & Images Film, Videotape version.

Orthodox Christianity: The Rumanian Solution. 1978. Britain. (Documentary). 52 min. Sound. 16mm Color. *Rental:* U Cal Media.

Os Fuzis. Trans. Title: Gun, The. Atila Iorio. Directed by Ruy Guerra. Port. 1963. Brazil. 109 min. Sound. 16mm B&W. subtitles. *Rental:* New Yorker Films.

Osaka Elegy. Isuzu Yamada & Kensaku Hara. Directed by Kenji Mizoguchi. Jap. 1966. Embassy. 71 min. Sound. 16mm B&W. subtitles. *Rental:* Films Inc.

Oscar, The. Stephen Boyd. Directed by Lamont Johnson. 1966. Embassy. 119 min. Sound. 16mm B&W. *Rental:* Films Inc.

Oscar W. Underwood. Sidney Blackmer. Directed by Lamont Johnson. (Profiles in Courage Ser.). 1965. Saudek. 50 min. Sound. 16mm B&W. *Rental:* U of IL Film & U Mich Media. *Sale:* IQ Film. *Rental:* IQ Film, *Sale:* IQ Film, Spanish dubbed version.

Oscar Wilde. Robert Morley, Sir Ralph Richardson. Directed by Gregory Ratoff. 1960. Britain. 96 min. Sound. 16mm B&W. *Rental:* Films Inc, Swank Motion & Twyman Films.

O'Shaughnessy's Boy. Wallace Beery & Jackie Cooper. Directed by Richard Boleslawski. 1935. MGM. 88 min. Sound. 16mm B&W. *Rental:* MGM United.

Oskar Fischinger: Absolute Filmartist. 1976. 75 min. Sound. 16mm B&W. *Rental:* Creative Film Society.

Osterman Weekend, The. Burt Lancaster & Rutger Hauer. Directed by Sam Peckinpah. 1983. Fox. 102 min. Sound. 16mm Color. *Rental:* Films Inc. *Sale:* Tamarelles French Film, Videotape version.

Otets Sergii *see* Father Sergius.

Othello. Emil Jannings & Werner Krauss. Directed by Dimitri Buchowetzski. 1922. Germany. 61 min. Silent. 16mm B&W. *Rental:* A Twyman Pres, Budget Films, Em Gee Film Lib, Films Inc & Kit Parker. *Sale:* Glenn Photo & Reel Images. *Sale:* Morcraft Films, Super 8 sound version. *Sale:* Glenn Photo & Reel Images, Super 8 silent version. *Rental:* Kit Parker, 81 min. version.

Othello. Orson Welles. Directed by Orson Welles. 1952. United Artists. 92 min. Sound. 16mm B&W. *Rental:* Corinth Films.

Othello. Sir Laurence Olivier & Maggie Smith. Directed by Stuart Burge. 1965. Britain. 166 min. Sound. 16mm Color. *Rental:* Swank Motion & Twyman Films.

Othello. Sergei Bondarchuk. Directed by Sergei Yutkevich. 1955. Russia. 105 min. Sound. 16mm Color. dubbed. *Rental:* Corinth Films.

Othello. Anthony Hopkins, Bob Hoskins & Penelope Wilton. 1981. 208 min. Sound. Videotape Color. *Rental:* Iowa Films.

Other, The. Uta Hagen & Diana Maldaur. Directed by Robert Mulligan. 1972. Fox. 102 min. Sound. 16mm Color. *Rental:* Films Inc.

Other Face of Dixie, The. 1962. CBS. (Documentary). 54 min. Sound. 16mm B&W. *Sale:* Carousel Films.

Other Francisco, The. Miguel Benavides & Ramon Veloz. Directed by Sergio Giral. Span. 1975. Cuba. 100 min. Sound. 16mm B&W. subtitles. *Rental:* Cinema Guild. *Sale:* Cinema Guild.

Other Guy, The. 1970. Blues. (Documentary). 60 min. Sound. 16mm Color. *Rental:* U Cal Media.

Other Half of the Sky, The: A China Memoir. Directed by Claudia Weill. 1947. New Day. (Documentary). 74 min. Sound. 16mm Color. *Rental:* New Day Films.

Other Love, The. Barbara Stanwyck, David Niven & Richard Conte. Directed by Andre De Toth. 1947. United Artists. 86 min. Sound. 16mm B&W. *Sale:* Rep Pic Film.

Other Men's Women. James Cagney & Joan Blondell. Directed by William A. Wellman. 1931. Warners. 70 min. Sound. 16mm B&W. *Rental:* MGM United.

Other People's Garbage. 1979. Odyssey. (Documentary). 59 min. Videotape Color. *Rental:* PBS Video. *Sale:* PBS Video.

Other Side, The. Trans. Title: Otro Lado, El. Directed by Danny Lyon. 1979. Museum of Modern Art. (Documentary). 60 min. Sound. 16mm Color. *Rental:* Museum Mod Art. *Lease:* Museum Mod Art.

Other Side of Midnight, The. John Beck & Marie-France Pisier. Directed by Charles Jarrott. 1977. Fox. 165 min. Sound. 16mm Color. *Rental:* Films Inc.

Other Side of Paradise, The. 1967. NET. (Documentary). 55 min. Sound. 16mm B&W. *Rental:* Indiana AV Ctr. *Sale:* Indiana AV Ctr.

Other Side of the Mountain, The. Marilyn Hassett & Beau Bridges. Directed by Larry Peerce. 1975. Universal. 103 min. Sound. 16mm Color. *Rental:* Swank Motion.

Other Side of the Mountain, The: Part 2. Marilyn Hassett & Timothy Bottoms. Directed by Larry Peerce. 1978. Universal. 97 min. Sound. 16mm Color. *Rental:* Swank Motion.

Other Way, The. 1975. Britain. (Documentary). 50 min. Sound. 16mm Color. *Rental:* Films Inc. *Sale:* Films Inc. *Rental:* Films Inc, *Sale:* Films Inc, Videotape version.

Other Woman, The. Cleo Moore & Hugo Haas. Directed by Hugo Haas. 1954. Fox. 81 min. Sound. 16mm B&W. *Rental:* Willoughby Peer.

Other World of Winston Churchill, The. Directed by Louis Clyde Stoumen. 1966. Britain. (Documentary). 50 min. Sound. 16mm Color. *Rental:* Films Inc & Macmillan Films. *Sale:* Macmillan Films.

Others, The. 1979. PBS. (Documentary). 59 min. Videotape Color. *Rental:* PBS Video. *Sale:* PBS Video.

Othon. Adriano Apra & Ennio Lauricella. Directed by Jean-Marie Straub. Ital. 1969. Germany-Italy. 83 min. Sound. 16mm Color. subtitles. *Rental:* New Yorker Films.

Otley. Tom Courtenay & Romy Schneider. Directed by Dick Clement. 1969. Columbia. 90 min. Sound. 16mm Color. *Rental:* Films Inc.

Otro Lado, El *see* Other Side.

Otto. 1975. Indiana U. (Documentary). 132 min. Sound. 16mm Color. *Rental:* Indiana AV Ctr. *Sale:* Indiana AV Ctr.

Otto: Zoo Gorilla. Directed by Dugan Rosalini. (Documentary). 58 min. Sound. 16mm Color. *Rental:* Films Inc & Syracuse U Film. *Sale:* Films Inc. *Sale:* Films Inc, Videotape version.

Our Betters. Constance Bennett. Directed by George Cukor. 1933. RKO. 75 min. Sound. 16mm B&W. *Rental:* Films Inc.

Our Blushing Brides. Joan Crawford & Hedda Hopper. Directed by Harry Beaumont. 1930. MGM. 101 min. Sound. 16mm B&W. *Rental:* MGM United.

Our Changing World: Two Views. 1976. PBS. (Documentary). 60 min. Sound. 16mm Color. *Rental:* WNET Media. *Rental:* WNET Media, Videotape version.

Our Daily Bread. Karen Morley & Tom Keene. Directed by King Vidor. 1934. United Artists. (Color Introduction). 71 min. Sound. 16mm B&W. *Rental:* Budget Films, Classic Film Mus, Em Gee Film Lib, Films Inc, Janus Films, Images Film, Iowa Films, Kit Parker, Museum Mod Art, Video Comm & Wholesome Film Ctr. *Sale:* Cinema Concepts, Festival Films, Images Film & Reel Images. *Sale:* Blackhawk Films, Super 8 sound version. *Sale:* Cinema Concepts, Festival Films, Tamarelles French Film & Video Comm, Videotape version.

Our Dancing Daughters. Joan Crawford. Directed by Harry Beaumont. 1928. MGM. 90 min. Silent. 16mm B&W. *Rental:* MGM United.

Our Election Day Illusions: The Beat Majority. 1960. CBS. (Documentary). 54 min. Sound. 16mm B&W. *Rental:* Syracuse U Film. *Sale:* Carousel Films.

Our Endangered Wildlife. 1967. NBC. (Documentary). 51 min. Sound. 16mm Color. *Rental:* Iowa Films, McGraw-Hill Films & U of IL Film. *Sale:* McGraw-Hill Films.

Our Fighting Navy *see* Torpedoed.

Our Fighting Navy. H. B. Warner. Directed by Norman Walker. 1937. Sound. 16mm B&W. *Rental:* A Twyman Pres.

Our Friend, the Atom. 1957. Disney. (Documentary). 48 min. Sound. 16mm Color. *Rental:* Buchan Pic, Cousino Visual Ed, Films Inc, SD AV Ctr, Syracuse U Film, U of IL Film & U Mich Media.

Our Hearts Were Growing up. Gail Russell & Diana Lynn. Directed by William D. Russell. 1946. Paramount. 83 min. Sound. 16mm B&W. *Rental:* Swank Motion.

Our Hearts Were Young & Gay. Gail Russell & Diana Lynn. Directed by Lewis Allen. 1944. Paramount. 81 min. Sound. 16mm B&W. *Rental:* Swank Motion.

Our Hispanic Heritage. 1977. Merco International. (Documentary). 62 min. Sound. 16mm Color. Narrated Orson Wells. *Rental:* Merco Intl. *Sale:* Merco, *Rental:* Merco Intl, Spanish version.

Our Hospitality. Buster Keaton & Natalie Talmadge. Directed by Buster Keaton & John G. Blystone. 1923. Metro. (Musical score only). 72 min. Sound. 16mm B&W. *Rental:* Films Inc. *Rental:* A Twyman Pres & Twyman Films, Silent 16mm B&W version.

Our Invisible Government. Orig. Title: Regulators, The. 1982. USA. 50 min. Sound. 16mm Color. narrated Eng. *Rental:* Budget Films & Iowa Films.

Our Lady of Fatima. 1962. France. (Documentary). 60 min. Sound. 16mm B&W. narrated Eng. *Rental:* Roas Films.

Our Land Is Our Life. Directed by Tony Ianzelo & Boyce Richardson. 1974. Canada. (Documentary). 58 min. Sound. 16mm Color. *Rental:* Natl Film CN & U Mich Media. *Sale:* Natl Film CN.

Our Largest Minority: The Disabled. Edwin Newman. CC Films. (Documentary). 60 min. Sound. 16mm Color. *Rental:* Natl Churches Christ. *Rental:* Natl Churches Christ, Videotape version.

Our Little Girl. Shirley Temple & Joel McCrea. Directed by John Robertson. 1935. Fox. 63 min. Sound. 16mm B&W. *Rental:* Films Inc.

Our Man Flint. James Coburn & Lee J. Cobb. Directed by Daniel Mann. 1966. Fox. 107 min. Sound. 16mm Color. *Rental:* Films Inc. *Rental:* Films Inc, Anamorphic version.

Our Man from Marrakesh. George Hamilton & Claudine Auger. Directed by Jacques Deray. 1967. Allied Artists. 90 min. Sound. 16mm Color. *Rental:* Hurlock Cine.

Our Man in Havana. Sir Alec Guinness & Maureen O'Hara. Directed by Sir Carol Reed. 1960. Columbia. 112 min. Sound. 16mm B&W. *Rental:* Budget Films, Corinth Films, Film Ctr DC, Inst Cinema, Kit Parker, Modern Sound, Twyman Films & Welling Motion Pictures. *Rental:* Corinth Films & Kit Parker, Anamorphic version.

Our Man in Hong Kong. 1961. NBC. (Documentary). 54 min. Sound. 16mm B&W. *Rental:* McGraw-Hill Films. *Sale:* McGraw-Hill Films.

Our Mr. Sun. 1956. Bell Telephone. (Animated). 60 min. Sound. 16mm Color. *Rental:* Utah Media.

Our Mother's House. Dirk Bogarde & Pamela Franklin. Directed by Jack Clayton. 1967. MGM. 105 min. Sound. 16mm Color. *Rental:* MGM United.

Our Relations. Stan Laurel & Oliver Hardy. Directed by Harry Lachman. 1936. MGM. 70 min. Sound. 16mm B&W. *Rental:* Budget Films, Em Gee Film Lib, Film Pres, Films Inc, Film Images, Kit Parker, Modern Sound, Roas Films, Swank Motion, Twyman Films, Welling Motion Pictures, Westcoast Films & Willoughby Peer. *Sale:* Blackhawk Films. *Rental:* Welling Motion Pictures, 85 mins. version.

Our Russian Front. 1942. Harry Rathner. (Documentary). 60 min. Sound. 16mm B&W. *Rental:* Film Classics. *Rental:* Film Classics, Videotape version.

Our Time. Pamela Sue Martin. Directed by Peter Hyams. 1974. Warners. 91 min. Sound. 16mm Color. *Rental:* Swank Motion.

Our Town. William Holden & Martha Scott. Directed by Sam Wood. 1940. United Artists. 86 min. Sound. 16mm B&W. *Rental:* Budget Films, Classic Film Mus, Corinth Films, Em Gee Film Lib, Films Inc, Images Film, Ivy Films, Kit Parker, Maljack, Mogulls Films, Newman Film Lib, Phoenix Films, Roas Films, Twyman Films, Video Comm, Welling Motion Pictures & Wholesome Film Ctr. *Sale:* Cinema Concepts, Festival Films, Glenn Photo, Images Film, Phoenix Films & Reel Images, Super 8 sound version. *Sale:* Cinema Concepts, Festival Films, Images Film, Maljack, Phoenix Films & Video Comm, Videotape version.

Our Town. Hal Holbrook, Robby Benson & Sada Thompson. Directed by George Schaefer. 1977. Saul Jaffe. 120 min. Sound. 16mm Color. *Rental:* Modern Sound.

Our Town. 2 pts. 1959. Encyclopaedia Britannica. 60 min. Sound. 16mm Color. *Rental:* Ency Brit Ed. *Sale:* Ency Brit Ed.

Our Very Own. Ann Blyth & Farley Granger. Directed by David Miller. 1950. Goldwyn. 93 min. Sound. 16mm B&W. *Rental:* Films Inc.

Our Vines Have Tender Grapes. Edward G. Robinson & Margaret O'Brien. Directed by Roy Rowland. 1945. MGM. 105 min. Sound. 16mm B&W. *Rental:* MGM United.

Our Winning Season. Scott Jacoby & Dennis Quaid. Directed by Joseph Reuben. 1978. American International. 92 min. Sound. 16mm Color. *Rental:* Swank Motion.

Out California Way. Monte Hale. Directed by Lesley Selander. 1946. Republic. 67 min. Sound. 16mm B&W. *Rental:* Ivy Films, Modern Sound & Rep Pic Film. *Sale:* Nostalgia Merchant. *Sale:* Nostalgia Merchant, Color version.

Out of the Blue. George Brent & Virginia Mayo. Directed by Leigh Jason. 1947. Eagle Lion. 87 min. Sound. 16mm B&W. *Sale:* Classics Assoc NY.

Out of the Darkness *see* Teenage Caveman.

Out of the Darkness. 1956. Natl. Assoc. for Mental Health. (Documentary). 55 min. Sound. 16mm B&W. *Rental:* Syracuse U Film. *Sale:* McGraw-Hill Films.

Out of the Darkness. Donald Pleasence, Nancy Kwan & Ross Hagen. 98 min. Sound. 16mm Color. *Rental:* Welling Motion Pictures.

Out of the Depths. Jim Bannon & Ross Hunter. Directed by D. Ross Lederman. 1945. Columbia. 61 min. Sound. 16mm B&W. *Lease:* Time-Life Multimedia.

Out of the Fog. John Garfield & Ida Lupino. Directed by Anatole Litvak. 1941. Warners. 86 min. Sound. 16mm B&W. *Rental:* MGM United.

Out of the Limelight: Home in the Rain. 1981. 49 min. Sound. 16mm Color. *Rental:* Utah Media.

Out of the Night *see* Strange Illusion.

Out of the Past. Orig. Title: Build My Gallows High. Robert Mitchum & Jane Greer. Directed by Jacques Tourneur. 1947. RKO. 97 min. Sound. 16mm B&W. *Rental:* Films Inc.

Out of the Storm. James Lydon & Marc Lawrence. Directed by R. G. Springsteen. 1948. Republic. 61 min. Sound. 16mm B&W. *Rental:* Ivy Films. *Sale:* Rep Pic Film.

Out of Thin Air. 1979. PBS. (Documentary). 59 min. Videotape Color. *Rental:* PBS Video. *Sale:* PBS Video.

Out of This World. 1954. Carroll. (Documentary). 90 min. Sound. 16mm Color. *Rental:* Films Inc.

Out of This World. Directed by Wheeler Dixon. 1979. Gold Key. (Documentary). 96 min. Sound. 16mm Color. *Rental:* Gold Key.

Out-of-Towners, The. Jack Lemmon & Sandy Dennis. Directed by Arthur Hiller. 1970. Paramount. 97 min. Sound. 16mm Color. *Rental:* Films Inc. *Sale:* Tamarelles French Film, Videotape version.

Out There. Skyline Productions. 55 min. Sound. 16mm Color. *Rental:* Gospel Films.

Out There, a Lone Island. Directed by Humphrey W. Leynse. 1972. Korea. (Documentary). 67 min. Sound. 16mm B&W. *Rental:* U Cal Media.

Out West with the Hardys. Mickey Rooney & Lewis Stone. Directed by George B. Seitz. 1938. MGM. 84 min. Sound. 16mm B&W. *Rental:* MGM United.

Out West with the Peppers. Edith Fellows & Dorothy Peterson. Directed by Charles Barton. 1940. Columbia. 62 min. Sound. 16mm B&W. *Rental:* Modern Sound.

Outcast, The *see* Man in the Saddle.

Outcast, The. Orig. Title: Fortune Hunter, The. John Derek & Joan Evans. Directed by William Witney. 1954. Republic. 90 min. Sound. 16mm Color. *Rental:* Ivy Films. *Sale:* Rep Pic Film.

Outcast Lady. Constance Bennett & Herbert Marshall. Directed by Robert Z. Leonard. 1934. MGM. 79 min. Sound. 16mm B&W. *Rental:* MGM United.

Outcast of the Islands. Trevor Howard, Sir Ralph Richardson. Directed by Sir Carol Reed. 1952. United Artists. 92 min. Sound. 16mm B&W. *Rental:* Budget Films, Films Inc, Inst Cinema & Wholesome Film Ctr.

Outcast of the Trail. Monte Hale. Directed by Philip Ford. 1949. Republic. 60 min. Sound. 16mm B&W. *Rental:* Ivy Films. *Sale:* Rep Pic Film & Nostalgia Merchant.

Outcasts of Poker Flat, The. Dale Robertson & Anne Baxter. Directed by Joseph Newman. 1952. Fox. 81 min. Sound. 16mm B&W. *Rental:* Films Inc & Willoughby Peer.

Outcasts Of Poker Flat, The. Van Heflin & Preston Foster. Directed by Christy Cabanne. 1937. RKO. 68 min. Sound. 16mm *Rental:* RKO General Pics.

Outer Fringe, The: Politics. 51 min. Sound. 16mm B&W. *Rental:* Utah Media.

Outer Gate, The. Ralph Morgan. Directed by Raymond Cannon. 1940. Monogram. 64 min. Sound. 16mm B&W. *Rental:* Hurlock Cine.

Outer Space Connection, The. 1974. Landsburg. (Documentary). 95 min. Sound. 16mm Color. *Rental:* Budget Films, Films Inc, Video Comm & Westcoast Films. *Lease:* Video Comm. *Rental:* Video Comm, *Lease:* Video Comm, Videotape version.

Outfit, The. Robert Duvall & Karen Black. Directed by John Flynn. 1974. MGM. 103 min. Sound. 16mm Color. *Rental:* MGM United.

Outland. Sean Connery & Peter Boyle. Directed by Peter Hyams. 1981. Warners. 109 min. Sound. 16mm Color. *Rental:* Swank Motion. *Rental:* Swank Motion, Videotape version.

Outlaw, The. Jane Russell & Jack Beutel. Directed by Howard Hughes. 1943. United Artists. 115 min. Sound. 16mm B&W. *Rental:* Budget Films, Classic Film Mus, Em Gee Film Lib & Swank Motion. *Sale:* Reel Images. *Rental:* Ivy Films, *Sale:* Cinema Concepts & Ivy Films, Super 8 sound version. *Rental:* Swank Motion, Videotape version.

Outlaw & His Wife, The. Victor Seastrom. Directed by Victor Seastrom. 1918. Sweden. 130 min. Silent. 16mm B&W. *Rental:* Museum Mod Art.

Outlaw Blues. Peter Fonda & Susan St. James. Directed by Richard T. Heffron. 1977. Warners. 102 min. Sound. 16mm Color. *Rental:* Swank Motion & Twyman Films.

Outlaw Brand, The. Jimmy Wakely. Directed by Lambert Hillyer. 1948. Monogram. 55 min. Sound. 16mm B&W. *Rental:* Hurlock Cine.

Outlaw Breaker, The. Yakima Canutt. 1926. 55 min. Silent. 16mm B&W. *Sale:* E Finney.

Outlaw Express. Bob Baker. Directed by George Waggner. 1937. Universal. 57 min. Sound. 16mm B&W. *Sale:* Cinema Concepts & Reel Images.

Outlaw Gang *see* Dalton Gang.

Outlaw Gold. Johnny Mack Brown. Directed by Wallace Fox. 1950. Monogram. 55 min. Sound. 16mm B&W. *Rental:* Hurlock Cine.

Outlaw Josey Wales, The. Clint Eastwood & Chief Dan George. Directed by Clint Eastwood. 1976. Warners. 135 min. Sound. 16mm Color. *Rental:* Swank Motion & Williams Films. *Rental:* Swank Motion, Videotape version.

Outlaw of Red River, The. George Montgomery. 1966. Spain. 85 min. Sound. 16mm Color. dubbed. *Rental:* Ivy Films.

Outlaw Roundup. James Newill & Dave O'Brien. Directed by Harry Fraser. 1944. PRC. 56 min. Sound. 16mm B&W. *Sale:* Natl Cinema.

Outlaw Stallion. Phil Carey & Dorothy Patrick. Directed by Fred F. Sears. 1954. Columbia. 64 min. Sound. 16mm Color. *Rental:* Arcus Film, Buchan Pic & Modern Sound.

Outlaw Tamer, The. Lane Chandler. Directed by J. P. McGowan. 1934. Empire. 56 min. Videotape B&W. *Sale:* Video Comm.

Outlaw Trail, The. Hoot Gibson & Bob Steele. Directed by Robert Tansey. 1944. Monogram. 53 min. Sound. 16mm B&W. *Rental:* Budget Films.

Outlaw Women. Richard Rober & Marie Windsor. Directed by Ron Ormond. 1952. Lippert. 76 min. Sound. 16mm B&W. *Rental:* Budget Films.

Outlaw's Highway see Fighting Fury.

Outlaws is Coming, The. Three Stooges. Directed by Norman Maurer. 1965. Columbia. 90 min. Sound. 16mm B&W. *Rental:* Buchan Pic, Budget Films, Cine Craft, Film Ctr DC, Film Pres, Films Inc, Inst Cinema, Modern Sound, Roas Films, Twyman Films, Welling Motion Pictures, Westcoast Films, Wholesome Film Ctr & Williams Films.

Outlaws of Pine Ridge. Don Barry. Directed by William Witney. 1943. Republic. 56 min. Sound. 16mm B&W. *Rental:* Ivy Films. *Sale:* Rep Pic Film.

Outlaws of Santa Fe. Don Barry. Directed by Howard Bretherton. 1944. Republic. 56 min. Sound. 16mm B&W. *Rental:* Ivy Films. *Sale:* Rep Pic Film.

Outlaws of Sonora. Robert Livingston. Directed by George Sherman. 1938. Republic. 55 min. Sound. 16mm B&W. *Rental:* Ivy Films. *Sale:* Rep Pic Film.

Outlaws of Stampede Pass. Johnny Mack Brown. Directed by Wallace Fox. 1943. Monogram. 55 min. Sound. 16mm B&W. *Rental:* Hurlock Cine.

Outlaws of Texas. Whip Wilson. Directed by Thomas Carr. 1950. Monogram. 55 min. Sound. 16mm B&W. *Rental:* Hurlock Cine.

Outlaws of the Cherokee Trail. Tom Tyler. Directed by Lester Orlebeck. 1941. Republic. 56 min. Sound. 16mm B&W. *Rental:* Ivy Films. *Sale:* Rep Pic Film.

Outlaws of the Desert. William Boyd. Directed by Howard Bretherton. 1941. Paramount. 54 min. Sound. 16mm B&W. *Lease:* Cinema Concepts.

Outlaws of the Panhandle. Charles Starrett. Directed by Sam Nelson. 1941. Columbia. 60 min. Sound. 16mm B&W. *Rental:* Westcoast Films.

Outlaws of the Plains. Buster Crabbe. Directed by Sam Newfield. 1946. PRC. 56 min. Sound. 16mm B&W. *Sale:* Classics Assoc NY.

Outlaws of the West see Call the Mesquiteers.

Outlaw's Son, The. Dane Clark, Lori Nelson & Ellen Drew. Directed by Lesley Selander. 1957. United Artists. 87 min. Sound. 16mm B&W. *Rental:* MGM United.

Outrage. Mala Powers & Tod Andrews. Directed by Ida Lupino. 1950. RKO. 75 min. Sound. 16mm B&W. *Rental:* MGM United. *Sale:* Rep Pic Film.

Outrage, The. Paul Newman, Claire Bloom & Laurence Harvey. Directed by Martin Ritt. 1964. MGM. (Anamorphic). 97 min. Sound. 16mm B&W. *Rental:* Films Inc.

Outrageous. Craig Russell & Hollis McLaren. Directed by Richard Benner. 1977. Canada. 100 min. Sound. 16mm Color. *Rental:* Cinema Five & New Cinema.

Outriders, The. Joel McCrea & Arlene Dahl. Directed by Roy Rowland. 1950. MGM. 94 min. Sound. 16mm Color. *Rental:* MGM United.

Outside of Paradise. Penny Singleton & Bert Gordon. Directed by John H. Auer. 1938. Republic. 54 min. Sound. 16mm B&W. *Rental:* Ivy Films. *Sale:* Rep Pic Film.

Outside the Law. Lon Chaney & Priscilla Dean. Directed by Tod Browning. 1921. Universal. (Musical score only). 77 min. Sound. 16mm B&W. *Rental:* Modern Sound. *Sale:* Blackhawk Films. *Sale:* Blackhawk Films, Super 8 sound version. *Sale:* Blackhawk Films, Super 8 silent version. *Sale:* Blackhawk Films, Videotape version.

Outside the Law. Ray Danton & Leigh Snowden. Directed by Jack Arnold. 1956. Universal. 80 min. Sound. 16mm B&W. *Rental:* Swank Motion.

Outside the Wall. Richard Basehart & Marilyn Maxwell. Directed by Crane Wilbur. 1950. Universal. 80 min. Sound. 16mm B&W. *Rental:* Swank Motion.

Outsider, The. George Sanders & Mary Maguire. Directed by Paul L. Stein. 1940. Alliance. 78 min. Sound. 16mm B&W. *Rental:* Film Classics & Mogulls Films.

Outsider, The. Tony Curtis & James Franciscus. Directed by Delbert Mann. 1961. Universal. 108 min. Sound. 16mm B&W. *Rental:* Swank Motion.

Outsiders, The. C. Thomas Howell & Matt Dillon. Directed by Francis Ford Coppola. 1983. Warners. 91 min. Sound. 16mm Color. *Rental:* Swank Motion.

Outskirts of Hope, The. Directed by David Davis. 1982. New Day. (Documentary). 54 min. Sound. 16mm Color. *Rental:* New Day Films. *Sale:* New Day Films. *Sale:* New Day Films, Videotape version.

Outward Bound. Leslie Howard & Douglas Fairbanks Jr. Directed by Robert Milton. 1930. Warners. 83 min. Sound. 16mm B&W. *Rental:* MGM United.

Oval Portrait, The. Wanda Hendrix & Barry Coe. Directed by Gisele Mackenzie. 1976. Dimension. 89 min. Sound. 16mm Color. *Sale:* Salz Ent & Welling Motion Pictures.

Over-Exposed. Cleo Moore & Richard Crenna. Directed by Lewis Seiler. 1956. Columbia. 80 min. Sound. 16mm B&W. *Rental:* Kit Parker.

Over My Dead Body. Milton Berle & Mary Beth Hughes. Directed by Mal St. Clair. 1942. Fox. 67 min. Sound. 16mm B&W. *Rental:* Films Inc.

Over the Border. Johnny Mack Brown. Directed by Wallace Fox. 1950. Monogram. 55 min. Sound. 16mm B&W. *Rental:* Hurlock Cine.

Over the Edge. Micheal Kramer & Matt Dillon. Directed by Jonathan Kaplan. 1979. Orion. 95 min. Sound. 16mm Color. *Rental:* Films Inc.

Over the Goal. June Travis & William Hopper. Directed by Noel Smith. 1937. Warners. 63 min. Sound. 16mm B&W. *Rental:* MGM United.

Over the Moon. Rex Harrison & Merle Oberon. Directed by Thornton Freeland. 1940. United Artists. 78 min. Sound. 16mm B&W. *Rental:* Ivy Films.

Over the Rainbow. 1952. Russia. 70 min. Sound. 16mm B&W. dubbed. *Rental:* Alba House.

Over the Wall. Dick Foran & Ward Bond. Directed by Frank McDonald. 1938. Warners. 66 min. Sound. 16mm B&W. *Rental:* MGM United.

Over There: 1914-1918. Directed by Jean Aurel. 1963. France. (Documentary). 90 min. Sound. 16mm B&W. narrated Eng. *Rental:* Budget Films & U Cal Media.

Overcoat, The. Roland Bykov. Directed by Alexei Batalov. Rus. 1959. Russia. 73 min. Sound. 16mm B&W. subtitles. *Rental:* Budget Films & Corinth Films. *Lease:* Corinth Films.

Overland Mail. Jack Randall. Directed by Robert Hill. 1939. Monogram. 55 min. Sound. 16mm B&W. *Rental:* Hurlock Cine.

Overland Mail Robbery. Bill Elliott. Directed by John English. 1943. Republic. 56 min. Sound. 16mm B&W. *Rental:* Ivy Films. *Sale:* Rep Pic Film & Nostalgia Merchant.

Overland Riders. Buster Crabbe. Directed by Sam Newfield. 1946. PRC. 54 min. Sound. 16mm B&W. *Sale:* Classics Assoc NY.

Overland Stage Raiders. John Wayne. Directed by George Sherman. 1938. Republic. 54 min. Sound. 16mm B&W. *Rental:* Ivy Films. *Sale:* Rep Pic Film & Nostalgia Merchant.

Overland Telegraph. Tim Holt & Richard Martin. Directed by Lesley Selander. 1952. RKO. 60 min. Sound. 16mm *Rental:* RKO General Pics.

Overland Trail *see* Trail Riders.

Overlanders, The. Chips Rafferty & Daphne Campbell. Directed by Harry Watt. 1946. Australia. 91 min. Sound. 16mm B&W. *Rental:* Budget Films.

Overlord, The. Directed by Stuart Cooper. 1975. Corinth. (Documentary). 85 min. Sound. 16mm B&W. *Rental:* Corinth Films.

Owl & the Pussycat, The. Barbra Streisand & George Segal. Directed by Herbert Ross. 1970. Columbia. 97 min. Sound. 16mm Color. *Rental:* Cine Craft, Films Inc, Images Film, Modern Sound, Natl Film Video, Newman Film Lib, Roas Films, Swank Motion, Twyman Films, Welling Motion Pictures, Westcoast Films, Wholesome Film Ctr & Williams Films. *Rental:* Swank Motion & Twyman Films, Anamorphic version.

Ox-Bow Incident, The. Henry Fonda & Dana Andrews. Directed by William A. Wellman. 1943. Fox. 75 min. Sound. 16mm B&W. *Rental:* Films Inc.

P-Four-W: Prison for Women. Directed by Janis Cole & Holly Dale. 1982. First Run. (Documentary). 80 min. Sound. 16mm Color. *Rental:* First Run. *Lease:* First Run.

P. J. George Peppard & Raymond Burr. Directed by John Guillermin. 1968. Universal. 109 min. Sound. 16mm Color. *Rental:* Swank Motion.

P. J. & the President's Son. Lance Kerwin. 1977. Time-Life. 47 min. Sound. 16mm Color. *Rental:* D Wilson, Kent St U Film & U of IL Film.

P. O. W. 1961. CBS. (Documentary). 52 min. Sound. 16mm B&W. *Rental:* Macmillan Films. *Sale:* Macmillan Films.

Pablo Picasso: The Legacy of a Genius. Directed by Michael Blackwood. 89 min. Sound. 16mm Color. *Rental:* Blackwood. *Sale:* Blackwood.

Pace That Kills, The. Thelma Daniels & Owen Gorin. Directed by Norton S. Parker. 1928. Willis Kent. 66 min. Silent. 16mm B&W. *Rental:* Budget Films & Em Gee Film Lib. *Sale:* Glenn Photo. *Sale:* Glenn Photo, Super 8 silent version.

Pace That Thrills, The. Bill Williams & Carla Balenda. Directed by Leon Barsha. 1952. RKO. 63 min. Sound. 16mm B&W. *Rental:* Films Inc.

Pacific: Feb. 1942 - July 1945. Directed by Hugh Raggett. (World at War Ser.). : Pt. 23.). 1973. Media Guild. (Documentary). 52 min. Sound. 16mm Color. *Rental:* Media Guild & U Cal Media. *Sale:* Media Guild. *Sale:* Media Guild, Videotape version.

Pacific Liner. Victor MacLaglen & Barry Fitzgerald. Directed by Lew Landers. 1939. RKO. 59 min. Sound. 16mm *Rental:* RKO General Pics.

Pacific Rendezvous. Lee Bowman, Blanche Yurka & Mona Maris. Directed by George Sidney. 1942. MGM. 76 min. Sound. 16mm B&W. *Rental:* MGM United.

Pack, The. Joe Don Baker & Hope Alexander-Willis. Directed by Robert Clouse. 1977. Warners. 99 min. Sound. 16mm Color. *Rental:* Swank Motion & Williams Films.

Pack Up Your Troubles. Orig. Title: We're in the Army Now. Jane Withers & Ritz Brothers. Directed by Bruce Humberstone. 1939. Fox. 75 min. Sound. 16mm B&W. *Rental:* Willoughby Peer.

Pack Up Your Troubles. Stan Laurel & Oliver Hardy. Directed by George Marshall. 1931. Hal Roach. 60 min. Sound. 16mm B&W. *Rental:* Budget Films, Em Gee Film Lib, Films Inc, Kit Parker, Modern Sound, Roas Films, Twyman Films, Video Comm, Welling Motion Pictures, Wholesome Film Ctr, Williams Films & Willoughby Peer. *Sale:* Blackhawk Films. *Sale:* Blackhawk Films, Super 8 sound version.

Paco. Jose Ferrer & Allen Garfield. Directed by Robert Vincent. 1975. 87 min. Sound. 16mm Color. *Rental:* Budget Films, Bosco Films, Films Inc, Roas Films & Westcoast Films. *Sale:* Salz Ent.

Pad, The: And How to Use It. Brian Bedford & James Farrentino. Directed by Brian Hutton. 1966. Universal. 86 min. Sound. 16mm Color. *Rental:* Swank Motion.

Paddy. Des Cave & Milo O'Shea. Directed by Daniel Haller. 1969. Allied Artists. 97 min. Sound. 16mm Color. *Rental:* Hurlock Cine.

Padre Di Famiglia, Il *see* Head of the Family.

Padre e a Moca, O *see* Priest & the Girl.

Padre Padrone. Omero Antonutti. Directed by Paolo Taviani & Paolo Taviani. Ital. 1977. Italy. 114 min. Sound. 16mm Color. subtitles. *Rental:* Cinema Five & New Cinema.

Pagan Love Song. Esther Williams & Howard Keel. Directed by Robert Alton. 1950. MGM. 76 min. Sound. 16mm B&W. *Rental:* MGM United. *Rental:* Films Inc, Color version.

Paganini Strikes Again. 1974. Britain. (Cast unlisted). 45 min. Sound. 16mm Color. *Rental:* Janus Films. *Sale:* Lucerne Films & Sterling Ed Film.

Page of Madness. Nasao Inoue & Yoshie Nakagawa. Directed by Teinosuke Kinugasa. 1926. Japan. 60 min. Sound. 16mm *Rental:* New Line Cinema.

Pagliacci. Trans. Title: Der Bajazzo. Richard Tauber & Steffi Duna. Directed by Karl Grune. 1938. Germany. 92 min. Sound. 16mm B&W. *Rental:* Corinth Films. *Sale:* Cinema Concepts & Natl Cinema.

Pagliacci. Italy. (Opera). 78 min. Sound. 16mm Color. *Rental:* Willoughby Peer.

Pagliacci. 1975. Britain. (Opera). 61 min. Sound. 16mm Color. *Rental:* Centron Films. *Sale:* Centron Films.

Pagnol Trilogy *see* Cesar.

Pagnol Trilogy *see* Fanny.

Pagnol Trilogy *see* Marius.

Paid. Joan Crawford. Directed by Sam Wood. 1930. MGM. 80 min. Sound. 16mm B&W. *Rental:* MGM United.

Paid to Dance. Rita Hayworth & Jacqueline Wells. Directed by C. C. Coleman Jr. 1937. Columbia. 60 min. Sound. 16mm B&W. *Rental:* Kit Parker.

Pain in the A..., A. Lino Ventura & Jacques Brel. Directed by Edouard Molinaro. Fr. 1975. France. 90 min. Sound. 16mm Color. subtitles. *Rental:* Films Inc.

Pain! Where Does It Hurt Most? 1972. NBC. (Documentary). 51 min. Sound. 16mm Color. *Rental:* Films Inc, Iowa Films & U Mich Media. *Sale:* Films Inc. *Rental:* Films Inc, Videotape version.

Paint Your Wagon. Clint Eastwood & Lee Marvin. Directed by Joshua Logan. 1969. Paramount. 159 min. Sound. 16mm Color. *Rental:* Films Inc.

Painted Desert, The. Clark Gable & William Boyd. Directed by Howard Higgin. 1931. RKO. 83 min. Sound. 16mm B&W. *Rental:* Films Inc. *Sale:* Tamarelles French Film, Videotape version.

Painted Desert, The. William Boyd & George O'Brien. Directed by Bert Gilroy. 1938. RKO. 59 min. Sound. 16mm *Rental:* RKO General Pics.

Painted Hills, The. Orig. Title: Lassie's Adventures in the Goldrush. Paul Kelly & Ann Doran. Directed by Harold Kress. 1951. MGM. 68 min. Sound. 16mm Color. *Rental:* Ivy Films & MGM United.

Painted Stallion, The. Ray Corrigan. Directed by Alan James. 1937. Republic. 215 min. Sound. 16mm B&W. *Rental:* Ivy Films.

Painted Trail, The. Tom Keene. Directed by Robert Hill. 1938. Monogram. 55 min. Sound. 16mm B&W. *Rental:* Hurlock Cine.

Painted Veil, The. Greta Garbo, Herbert Marshall & George Brent. Directed by Richard Boleslawski. 1934. MGM. 83 min. Sound. 16mm B&W. *Rental:* MGM United.

Painters of the 1980s. Directed by Michael Blackwood. 1984. 58 min. Sound. 16mm Color. *Rental:* Blackwood. *Sale:* Blackwood.

Painters Painting. Directed by Emile De Antonio. 1972. De Antonio. (Documentary, color sequences). 116 min. Sound. 16mm B&W. *Rental:* New Cinema & New Yorker Films.

Painting by Numbers. 1982. Britain. (Documentary). 60 min. Sound. 16mm Color. *Rental:* Films Inc, U Cal Media & U Mich Media. *Sale:* Films Inc. *Sale:* Films Inc, Videotape version.

Paintings: The Permanent Collection of the Art Institute of Chicago. 1979. PBS. (Documentary). 58 min. Videotape Color. *Rental:* PBS Video. *Sale:* PBS Video.

Pair of Briefs, A. Michael Craig & Mary Peach. Directed by Ralph Thomas. 1962. Britain. 90 min. Sound. 16mm B&W. *Rental:* Cinema Five.

Paisan. Carmella Salzo & Gar Moore. Directed by Roberto Rossellini. Ital. 1946. Italy. 115 min. Sound. 16mm B&W. subtitles. *Rental:* Budget Films, Em Gee Film Lib, Films Inc, Images Film, Kit Parker, U Cal Media & Utah Media. *Sale:* Cinema Concepts, Reel Images & Images Film. *Sale:* Reel Images, Tamarelles French Film & Images Film, Videotape version.

Pajama Party. Tommy Kirk & Annette Funicello. Directed by Don Weis. 1964. American International. 85 min. Sound. 16mm Color. *Rental:* Welling Motion Pictures.

Pajaros Sin Nido. Span. 1950. Mexico. (Cast unlisted). 90 min. Sound. 16mm B&W. *Rental:* Film Classics.

Pal Joey. Frank Sinatra, Rita Hayworth & Kim Novak. Directed by George Sidney. 1957. Columbia. 111 min. Sound. 16mm Color. *Rental:* Arcus Film, Bosco Films, Budget Films, Cine Craft, Charard Motion Pics, Films Inc, Kit Parker, Modern Sound, Natl Film Video, Roas Films, U of IL Film, Westcoast Films, Welling Motion Pictures, Wholesome Film Ctr & Willoughby Peer.

Paleface, The. Bob Hope & Jane Russell. Directed by Norman Z. McLeod. 1948. Paramount. 91 min. Sound. 16mm Color. *Rental:* Arcus Film & Williams Films.

Palestine: Abdication. 1978. Media Guild. (Documentary). 86 min. Sound. 16mm Color. *Rental:* Media Guild. *Sale:* Media Guild. *Sale:* Media Guild, Videotape version.

Palestine: Promises. 1978. Media Guild. (Documentary). 72 min. Sound. 16mm Color. *Rental:* Media Guild. *Sale:* Media Guild. *Sale:* Media Guild, Videotape version.

Palestine: Rebellion. 1978. Media Guild. (Documentary). 86 min. Sound. 16mm Color. *Rental:* Media Guild. *Sale:* Media Guild. *Sale:* Media Guild, Videotape version.

Palestinian People Do Have Rights, The. 1979. United Artists. (Documentary). 48 min. Sound. 16mm Color. *Rental:* Icarus Films, Inst Cinema & U Cal Media. *Sale:* Inst Cinema & Icarus Films. *Sale:* Icarus Films, Videotape version.

Palladio: Architect & His Influence in America. 47 min. Sound. 16mm Color. *Rental:* Utah Media.

Palm Beach Story, The. Claudette Colbert & Joel McCrea. Directed by Preston Sturges. 1942. Paramount. 88 min. Sound. 16mm B&W. *Rental:* Swank Motion.

Palomino, The. Jerome Courtland & Beverly Tyler. Directed by Ray Nazarro. 1950. Columbia. 73 min. Sound. 16mm Color. *Rental:* Williams Films.

Palooka. Orig. Title: Great Schnozzola, The. Jimmy Durante & Stuart Erwin. Directed by Ben Stoloff. 1934. Edward Small. 86 min. Sound. 16mm B&W. *Rental:* Budget Films, Mogulls Films, Video Comm & Wholesome Film Ctr. *Sale:* Cinema Concepts & Reel Images. *Sale:* Reel Images, Super 8 sound version. *Rental:* Video Comm, Videotape version.

Pals of the Golden West. Roy Rogers. Directed by William Witney. 1951. Republic. 68 min. Sound. 16mm B&W. *Rental:* Ivy Films. *Sale:* Rep Pic Film.

Pals of the Pecos. Robert Livingston & Bob Steele. Directed by Lester Orlebeck. 1941. Republic. 56 min. Sound. 16mm B&W. *Rental:* Ivy Films. *Sale:* Rep Pic Film.

Pals of the Saddle. John Wayne. Directed by George Sherman. 1938. Republic. 54 min. Sound. 16mm B&W. *Rental:* Ivy Films. *Sale:* Rep Pic Film & Nostalgia Merchant.

Pals of the Silver Sage. Tex Ritter. Directed by Al Herman. 1940. Monogram. 55 min. Sound. 16mm B&W. *Rental:* Hurlock Cine.

Pan-Americana. Phillip Terry & Audrey Long. Directed by John H. Auer. 1945. RKO. 84 min. Sound. 16mm B&W. *Rental:* Films Inc & RKO General Pics.

Panama: Danger Zone. 1961. NBC. (Documentary). 54 min. Sound. 16mm B&W. *Rental:* McGraw-Hill Films. *Sale:* McGraw-Hill Films.

Panama Flo. Charles Bickford & Robert Armstrong. Directed by Ralph Murphy. 1932. RKO. 70 min. Sound. 16mm B&W. *Rental:* RKO General Pics.

Panama Lady. Lucille Ball & Allan Lane. Directed by Jack Hively. 1939. RKO. 65 min. Sound. Videotape B&W. *Sale:* RKO General Pics & Vidamerica.

Panama Sal. Elena Verdugo. Directed by William Witney. 1957. Republic. 70 min. Sound. 16mm B&W. *Rental:* Ivy Films. *Sale:* Rep Pic Film.

Panama: The Fifth Frontier. Directed by Pastor Vega. Span. 1975. Cuba. (Documentary). 78 min. Sound. 16mm B&W. subtitles. *Rental:* Cinema Guild. *Sale:* Cinema Guild.

Panamint's Bad Man. Smith Ballew & Noah Beery Jr. Directed by Ray Taylor. 1938. Fox. 60 min. Sound. 16mm B&W. *Rental:* Mogulls Films.

Panare, The: Scenes from the Frontier. 1982. Britain. (Documentary). 60 min. Sound. 16mm Color. *Rental:* Films Inc. *Sale:* Films Inc. *Sale:* Films Inc, Videotape version.

Pancho Villa. Telly Savalas & Clint Walker. Directed by Gene Martin. 1971. Spain. 92 min. Sound. 16mm Color. *Rental:* Budget Films & Westcoast Films.

Panda & the Magic Serpent. Trans. Title: Hakuta Den. 1961. Japan. (Animated). 76 min. Sound. 16mm Color. narrated Eng. *Rental:* Budget Films, Cine Craft, Charard Motion Pics, Film Ctr DC, Films Inc, Video Comm, Westcoast Films, Welling Motion Pictures, Wholesome Film Ctr & Willoughby Peer.

Pandora & the Flying Dutchman. James Mason & Ava Gardner. Directed by Albert Lewin. 1951. 122 min. 16mm *Rental:* A Twyman Pres. *Rental:* A Twyman Pres, 103 min. British version.

Pandora's Box. Louise Brooks. Directed by G. W. Pabst. 1928. Germany. 110 min. Silent. 16mm B&W. *Rental:* Films Inc & Janus Films. *Rental:* New Cinema, Musical score only version.

Panhandle Trail, The. Buster Crabbe. Directed by Sam Newfield. 1947. Eagle Lion. 57 min. Sound. 16mm B&W. *Rental:* Video Comm. *Sale:* Video Comm, Videotape version.

Panic see Panique.

Panic Button. Jayne Mansfield & Michael Connors. Directed by George Sherman. 1964. Gordon. 90 min. Sound. 16mm B&W. *Rental:* Films Inc.

Panic in Needle Park, The. Al Pacino & Kitty Winn. Directed by Jerry Schatzberg. 1971. Fox. 110 min. Sound. 16mm Color. *Rental:* Films Inc.

Panic in the City. Howard Duff, Linda Cristal & Stephen McNally. Directed by Eddie Davis. 1968. United. 96 min. Sound. 16mm Color. *Rental:* Charard Motion Pics, Ivy Films & Video Comm.

Panic in the Streets. Richard Widmark & Barbara Bel Geedes. Directed by Elia Kazan. 1950. Fox. 96 min. Sound. 16mm B&W. *Rental:* Films Inc.

Panic in Year Zero. Ray Milland & Jean Hagen. Directed by Ray Milland. 1962. American International. 92 min. Sound. 16mm B&W. *Rental:* Films Inc & Video Comm.

Panic on the Air. Lew Ayres & Florence Rice. Directed by D. Ross Lederman. 1936. Columbia. 56 min. Sound. 16mm B&W. *Rental:* Kit Parker.

Panique. Orig. Title: Panic. Michel Simon & Viviane Romance. Directed by Julien Duvivier. Fr. 1946. France. 82 min. Sound. 16mm B&W. subtitles. *Rental:* Budget Films, Em Gee Film Lib, Images Film, Kit Parker & Westcoast Films. *Sale:* Cinema Concepts, Natl Cinema, Reel Images & Images Film. *Sale:* Reel Images, Super 8 sound version. *Sale:* Reel Images, Tamarelles French Film & Images Film, Videotape version.

Panther Girl of the Kongo. Phyllis Coates & Myron Healey. Directed by Franklin Adreon. 1954. Republic. 163 min. Sound. 16mm B&W. *Rental:* Ivy Films.

Panther Island *see* Bomba on Panther Island.

Panther's Claw, The. Sidney Blackmer & Rick Vallin. Directed by William Beaudine. 1942. PRC. 70 min. Sound. 16mm B&W. *Rental:* Mogulls Films & Video Comm.

Papa's Delicate Condition. Jackie Gleason & Glynis Johns. Directed by George Marshall. 1963. Paramount. 98 min. Sound. 16mm Color. *Rental:* Films Inc.

Paper Chase, The. Timothy Bottoms & John Houseman. Directed by James Bridges. 1973. Fox. 112 min. Sound. 16mm Color. *Rental:* Films Inc. *Rental:* Films Inc, Anamorphic version.

Paper Lion, The. Alan Alda & Alex Karras. Directed by Alex March. 1969. United Artists. 107 min. Sound. 16mm Color. *Rental:* Buchan Pic, MGM United, Modern Sound, Roas Films, Westcoast Films, Wholesome Film Ctr & Williams Films.

Paper Moon. Ryan O'Neal & Tatum O'Neal. Directed by Peter Bogdanovich. 1973. Paramount. 102 min. Sound. 16mm B&W. *Rental:* Films Inc.

Paper Prison: Your Government Records. 1974. ABC. (Documentary). 56 min. Sound. 16mm Color. *Rental:* Films Inc.

Paper Tiger, The. David Niven, Toshiro Mifune & Hardy Kruger. Directed by Ken Annakin. 1974. Fox. 101 min. Sound. 16mm Color. *Rental:* Films Inc.

Paper Wheat. Directed by Albert Kish. 1979. Canada. (Documentary). 58 min. Sound. 16mm Color. *Rental:* Natl Film CN. *Sale:* Natl Film CN.

Paperback Hero. Keir Dullea & Elizabeth Ashley. Directed by Peter Pearson. 1975. Sunrise. 87 min. Sound. 16mm Color. *Rental:* New Cinema & Twyman Films.

Papillon. Steve McQueen & Dustin Hoffman. Directed by Franklin Schaffner. 1973. Allied Artists. 120 min. Sound. 16mm Color. *Rental:* Hurlock Cine.

Paracelsus. Werner Krauss & Mathias Wiemann. Directed by G. W. Pabst. 1943. Germany. 105 min. Sound. 16mm B&W. *Rental:* Trans-World Films. *Rental:* Trans-World Films, Subtitled version.

Parachute Battalion. Robert Preston & Nancy Kelly. Directed by Leslie Goodwins. 1941. RKO. 75 min. Sound. 16mm B&W. *Rental:* Films Inc.

Parachute Jumper. Douglas Fairbanks Jr. & Bette Davis. Directed by Alfred E. Green. 1933. Warners. 72 min. Sound. 16mm B&W. *Rental:* MGM United.

Parades. David Doyle. Directed by Robert Siegel. 1972. Cinerama. 95 min. Sound. 16mm Color. *Rental:* Swank Motion.

Paradine Case, The. Gregory Peck, Charles Laughton & Alida Valli. Directed by Alfred Hitchcock. 1947. Selznick. 115 min. Sound. 16mm B&W. *Rental:* Films Inc, Trans-World Films & Twyman Films. *Sale:* ABC Film Lib, Super 8 sound version.

Paradis Perdu. Fernand Gravey & Micheline Presle. Directed by Abel Gance. Fr. 1939. France. 95 min. B&W. subtitles. *Rental:* French Am Cul.

Paradise Alley. Sylvester Stallone & Kevin Conway. Directed by Sylvester Stallone. 1978. Universal. 108 min. Sound. 16mm Color. *Rental:* Swank Motion.

Paradise Canyon. John Wayne. Directed by Carl Pierson. 1935. Monogram. 59 min. Sound. 16mm B&W. *Rental:* Budget Films, Ivy Films & Mogulls Films. *Sale:* Classics Assoc NY & Rep Pic Film.

Paradise Express. Grant Withers. Directed by Joseph Kane. 1937. Republic. 54 min. Sound. 16mm B&W. *Rental:* Ivy Films. *Sale:* Rep Pic Film.

Paradise for Three. Robert Young, Frank Morgan & Florence Rice. Directed by Edward Buzzell. 1938. MGM. 78 min. Sound. 16mm B&W. *Rental:* MGM United.

Paradise: Hawaiian Style. Elvis Presley & James Shigeta. Directed by Michael Moore. 1966. Paramount. 91 min. Sound. 16mm Color. *Rental:* Modern Sound, Video Comm & Williams Films. *Rental:* Ivy Films, *Sale:* Blackhawk Films & Video Comm, Super 8 sound version, videotape version.

Paradise in Harlem. Mamie Smith & Frank Wilson. Directed by Joseph Seiden. 1939. 85 min. Sound. 16mm B&W. *Rental:* Budget Films & Em Gee Film Lib. *Sale:* Glenn Photo & Natl Cinema.

Paradise Island. Kenneth Harlan & Marceline Day. Directed by Bert Glennon. 1930. Tiffany. 80 min. Sound. 16mm B&W. *Rental:* Mogulls Films.

Paradise Now. Directed by Sheldon Rochlin. 1972. New Line. (Cast unlisted). 95 min. Sound. 16mm Color. *Rental:* New Line Cinema. *Sale:* New Line Cinema.

Paradise Restored. 1967. Britain. (Cast unlisted). 90 min. Videotape Color. *Rental:* Films Inc. *Sale:* Films Inc.

Paradox on Seventy Second Street: People Watching. 1983. WNET. 60 min. Sound. 16mm Color. *Rental:* Films Inc & Syracuse U Film.

Parallax View, The. Warren Beatty & Hume Cronyn. Directed by Alan J. Pakula. 1974. Paramount. 101 min. Sound. 16mm Color. *Rental:* Films Inc.

Paralyzed Face, The. 1980. 60 min. Sound. Videotape Color. *Sale:* Natl AV Ctr.

Paramount on Parade. Maurice Chavelier & Clara Bow. Directed by Ernst Lubitsch. 1930. Paramount. 77 min. Sound. 16mm B&W. *Rental:* Swank Motion.

Paranoia. Carroll Baker & Lou Castel. Directed by Salvatore Alibiso. 1969. Italy. 91 min. Sound. 16mm Color. *Rental:* Charard Motion Pics, Ivy Films & Rep Pic Film. *Lease:* Rep Pic Film.

Paranoiac. Janette Scott & Oliver Reed. Directed by Freddie Francis. 1963. Britain. 80 min. Sound. 16mm B&W. *Rental:* Swank Motion.

Parasite. Robert Glaudini & Dennie Moore. Directed by Norman Taurog. 1956. Embassy. 86 min. Sound. 16mm Color. *Rental:* Films Inc.

Paratroop Command. Jack Hogan. Directed by William Witney. 1958. American International. 71 min. Sound. 16mm B&W. *Rental:* Williams Films.

Paratroop Command. Jack Hogan & Jimmy Murphy. Directed by William Witney. 71 min. Sound. 16mm B&W. *Rental:* Westcoast Films.

Paratroopers. Directed by Yehuda Ne'eman. 1980. (Anamorphic 16mm). 95 min. 16mm Color. *Rental:* Icarus Films. *Sale:* Icarus Films.

Pardners. Jerry Lewis & Dean Martin. Directed by Norman Taurog. 1956. Paramount. 88 min. Sound. 16mm Color. *Rental:* Films Inc.

Pardon, The. Pedro Armendariz & Aurora Bautista. Directed by Jose Juis & Saenz De Heredia. 1962. Mexico. 90 min. Sound. 16mm B&W. *Rental:* MGM United.

Pardon Mon Affaire. Jean Rochefort & Claude Brasseur. Directed by Yves Robert. Fr. 1977. France. 102 min. Sound. 16mm Color. subtitles. *Rental:* Films Inc. *Sale:* Tamarelles French Film, Videotape version.

Pardon My Past. Fred MacMurray & Marguerite Chapman. Directed by Leslie Fenton. 1945. Columbia. 98 min. Sound. 16mm B&W. *Rental:* Inst Cinema.

Pardon My Sarong. Lou Abbott, Bud Costello & Virginia Bruce. Directed by Erle C. Kenton. 1942. Universal. 84 min. Sound. 16mm B&W. *Rental:* Roas Films.

Pardon My Stripes. Edgar Kennedy & Sheila Ryan. Directed by John H. Auer. 1942. Republic. 64 min. Sound. 16mm B&W. *Rental:* Ivy Films.

Pardon Us. Orig. Title: Jailbirds. Stan Laurel & Oliver Hardy. Directed by James Parrott. 1931. Hal Roach. 50 min. Sound. 16mm B&W. *Rental:* Alba House, Budget Films, Em Gee Film Lib, Inst Cinema, Iowa Films, Kit Parker, Mogulls Films, Modern Sound, Roas Films, Swank Motion, Twyman Films, Welling Motion Pictures, Wholesome Film Ctr, Willoughby Peer & Williams Films. *Sale:* Blackhawk Films. *Sale:* Blackhawk Films, Super 8 sound version.

Parent, The. 1967. KETC. (Documentary). 58 min. Sound. 16mm B&W. *Rental:* Indiana AV Ctr.

Parent Trap, The. Hayley Mills, Maureen O'Hara & Brian Keith. Directed by David Swift. 1961. Disney. 129 min. Sound. 16mm Color. *Rental:* Disney Prod, Films Inc & Twyman Films.

Parents, The. Orig. Title: America's Crises: The Parent. 1964. NET. (Documentary). 60 min. Sound. 16mm B&W. *Rental:* Indiana AV Ctr, Mass Media, SD AV Ctr & U of IL Film. *Sale:* Indiana AV Ctr.

Parents Terribles, Les. Jean Marais & Josette Day. Directed by Jean Cocteau. 1949. France. 86 min. Sound. Videotape B&W. subtitles. *Rental:* Video Comm.

Paris After Dark. Orig. Title: Night is Ending, The. George Sanders & Philip Dorn. Directed by Leonide Moguy. 1943. Fox. 85 min. Sound. 16mm B&W. *Rental:* Films Inc.

Paris Air Show: 1969. 2 pts. 1969. Interface. (Documentary). 60 min. Sound. 16mm Color. *Rental:* U Cal Media. *Sale:* U Cal Media.

Paris Belongs to Us. Betty Schneider. Directed by Jacques Rivette. Fr. 1958. France. 124 min. Sound. 16mm B&W. subtitles. *Rental:* Films Inc & Janus Films.

Paris Blues. Paul Newman & Joanne Woodward. Directed by Martin Ritt. 1961. United Artists. 98 min. Sound. 16mm B&W. *Rental:* MGM United & Welling Motion Pictures.

Paris Incident. Gerard Gervais. Directed by Henri Decoin. Fr. 1952. France. 96 min. Sound. 16mm B&W. subtitles. *Rental:* Film Classics.

Paris Interlude. Robert Young & Una Merkel. Directed by Edwin L. Marin. 1934. MGM. 73 min. Sound. 16mm B&W. *Rental:* MGM United.

Paris Model. Marilyn Maxwell & Paulette Goddard. Directed by Alfred E. Green. 1953. Columbia. 81 min. Sound. 16mm B&W. *Rental:* Kit Parker.

Paris Nineteen Hundred. 1950. France. (Documentary). 76 min. Sound. 16mm B&W. *Rental:* Budget Films, Films Inc, Kit Parker, Macmillan Films & U Mich Media. *Sale:* Festival Films & Macmillan Films. *Sale:* Festival Films, Videotape version.

Paris Pick-up. Robert Hossein & Lea Massari. Directed by Marcel Bluwal. Fr. 1963. France. 90 min. Sound. 16mm B&W. dubbed. *Rental:* Films Inc.

Paris Qui Dort *see* Crazy Ray.

Paris Underground. Orig. Title: Madame Pimpernel. Gracie Fields & Constance Bennett. Directed by Gregory Ratoff. 1945. United Artists. 97 min. Sound. 16mm B&W. *Rental:* Budget Films.

Paris When It Sizzles. Audrey Hepburn & William Holden. Directed by Richard Quine. 1964. Paramount. 110 min. Sound. 16mm Color. *Rental:* Films Inc.

Parisian Belle *see* New Moon.

Parisian Romance. Gilbert Roland. 1932. 77 min. Sound. 16mm Color. *Rental:* Classic Film Mus.

Park Avenue Logger. Orig. Title: Tall Timber. George O'Brien & Marjorie Reynolds. Directed by David Howard. 1937. RKO. 67 min. Sound. 16mm B&W. *Rental:* Film Classics & Mogulls Films.

Park Plaza 605 *see* Norman Conquest.

Park Row. Gene Evans & Mary Welch. Directed by Samuel Fuller. 1952. United Artists. 83 min. Sound. 16mm B&W. *Rental:* MGM United.

Parlor, Bedroom & Bath. Buster Keaton & Charlotte Greenwood. Directed by Edward Sedgwick. 1931. MGM. 73 min. Sound. 16mm B&W. *Rental:* Budget Films, Kit Parker & MGM United. *Sale:* Festival Films. *Sale:* Cinema Concepts & Morcaft Films, Super 8 sound version. *Sale:* Festival Films, Videotape version.

Parnell. Clark Gable & Myrna Loy. Directed by John M. Stahl. 1937. MGM. 120 min. Sound. 16mm B&W. *Rental:* MGM United.

Parole. 1979. PBS. (Documentary). 59 min. Videotape Color. *Rental:* PBS Video. *Sale:* PBS Video.

Parole Game, The. 1982. CBS. (Documentary). 48 min. Sound. 16mm Color. *Rental:* MTI Tele. *Sale:* MTI Tele.

Parole Inc. Turhan Bey & Micheal O'Shea. Directed by Alfred Zeisler. 1949. Eagle Lion. 80 min. Sound. 16mm B&W. *Rental:* Charard Motion Pics & Mogulls Films.

Paroled To Die. Bob Steele. Directed by Sam Newfield. 1937. Republic. 60 min. Sound. 16mm B&W. *Rental:* Ivy Films & Mogulls Films. *Sale:* Rep Pic Film.

Parsifal. 1983. France-Germany. (Cast unlisted). Sound. 16mm Color. subtitles. *Rental:* Swank Motion.

Parson of Panamint, The. Charles Ruggles & Ellen Drew. Directed by William McGann. 1941. Paramount. 84 min. Sound. 16mm B&W. *Rental:* Swank Motion.

Part of the Family, A. Directed by Paul Ronder. 1971. Summer Morning. (Documentary). 75 min. Sound. 16mm Color. *Rental:* Museum Mod Art. *Sale:* Museum Mod Art.

Part-Time Wife. Anton Rodgers. Directed by Max Varnel. 1961. 16mm *Rental:* A Twyman Pres.

Partie de Plaisir, Une *see* Piece of Pleasure.

Parting of the Ways, The. 1980. Canada. (Documentary). 57 min. Sound. 16mm Color. *Rental:* Budget Films.

Partisani *see* Last Guerilla.

Partition, The. 1982. Media Guild. (Documentary). 54 min. Sound. 16mm Color. *Rental:* Media Guild. *Sale:* Media Guild. *Sale:* Media Guild, Videotape version.

Partizan, The. Adam West & Rod Taylor. 106 min. Sound. 16mm Color. *Rental:* Modern Sound.

Partner, The. Pierre Clementi & Stefania Sandrelli. Directed by Bernardo Bertolucci. Ital. 1968. Italy. (Anamorphic). 107 min. Sound. 16mm Color. subtitles. *Rental:* New Yorker Films.

Partners. Ryan O'Neal & John Hurt. Directed by James Burrows. 1982. Paramount. 90 min. Sound. 16mm Color. *Rental:* Films Inc.

Partners. Tom Keene & Nancy Drexel. Directed by Fred Allen. 1932. RKO. 58 min. Sound. 16mm B&W. *Rental:* RKO General Pics.

Partners of the Plains. William Boyd. Directed by Lesley Selander. 1937. Paramount. 60 min. Sound. 16mm B&W. *Lease:* Cinema Concepts.

Partners of the Sunset. Jimmy Wakely. Directed by Lambert Hillyer. 1948. Monogram. 55 min. Sound. 16mm B&W. *Rental:* Hurlock Cine.

Partners of the Trail. Johnny Mack Brown. Directed by Lambert Hillyer. 1944. Monogram. 55 min. Sound. 16mm B&W. *Rental:* Hurlock Cine.

Party, The. Peter Sellers & Claudine Longet. Directed by Blake Edwards. 1968. United Artists. 99 min. Sound. 16mm Color. *Rental:* MGM United.

Party Crashers, The. Mark Damon & Connie Stevens. Directed by Bernard Girard. 1958. Paramount. 78 min. Sound. 16mm B&W. *Rental:* Films Inc.

Party Girl. Douglas Fairbanks Jr. Directed by Victor Halperin. 1933. Victory. 70 min. Sound. 16mm B&W. *Sale:* Morcraft Films. *Sale:* Morcraft Films, Videotape version. *Sale:* Morcraft Films, Super 8 sound version.

Party Girl. Robert Taylor & Cyd Charisse. Directed by Nicholas Ray. 1958. MGM. 99 min. Sound. 16mm Color. *Rental:* MGM United. *Rental:* MGM United, Anamorphic version.

Party's Over, The. Stuart Erwin & Ann Sothern. Directed by Walter Lang. 1933. Columbia. 68 min. Sound. 16mm B&W. *Rental:* Kit Parker.

Pascal. France. (Cast unlisted). 60 min. Sound. 16mm B&W. *Rental:* French Am Cul.

Pascal. 1979. Canada. (Documentary). 57 min. Sound. 16mm Color. *Rental:* Kent St U Film.

Pasciaks of Chicago, The. Directed by Mark Obenhaus. 1976. Group W. 59 min. Sound. 16mm Color. *Rental:* Iowa Films, Syracuse U Film & U Mich Media. *Sale:* Carousel Films. *Sale:* Carousel Films, Videotape version.

Pasqualino, Seven Beauties *see* Seven Beauties.

Passage Du Rhin, La. Orig. Title: Crossing of the Rhine, The. Charles Aznavour & Nicole Courcel. Directed by Andre Cayatte. Fr. 1960. France. 105 min. Sound. 16mm B&W. subtitles. *Rental:* French Am Cul.

Passage from Hong Kong. Lucille Fairbanks & Paul Cavanaugh. Directed by D. Ross Lederman. 1941. Warners. 61 min. Sound. 16mm B&W. *Rental:* MGM United.

Passage to Marseille. Humphrey Bogart & Claude Rains. Directed by Michael Curtiz. 1944. Warners. 110 min. Sound. 16mm B&W. *Rental:* MGM United.

Passage West. John Payne & Dennis O'Keefe. Directed by Lewis R. Foster. 1951. Paramount. 81 min. Sound. 16mm B&W. *Rental:* Video Comm.

Passage West: A Dream of Freedom. 1977. Canada. (Documentary). 53 min. Sound. 16mm Color. *Rental:* Natl Film CN. *Sale:* Natl Film CN. *Sale:* Natl Film CN, Videotape version.

Passage West: The Awakening. 1977. Canada. (Documentary). 54 min. Sound. 16mm Color. *Rental:* Natl Film CN. *Sale:* Natl Film CN. *Sale:* Natl Film CN, Videotape version.

Passaic Textile Strike. 1926. International Workers Aid. (Documentary). 70 min. Silent. 16mm B&W. *Rental:* Museum Mod Art. *Sale:* Museum Mod Art.

Passenger, The. Jack Nicholson & Maria Schneider. Directed by Michelangelo Antonioni. 1975. United Artists. 119 min. Sound. 16mm Color. *Rental:* MGM United. *Rental:* MGM United, VIdeotape version.

Passenger, The. Aleksandra Slaska & Anna Ciepielewska. Directed by Andrzej Munk. Pol. 1963. Poland. 60 min. Sound. 16mm Color. subtitles. *Rental:* Films Inc.

Passengers. Directed by Annie Tresgot. Fr. 1971. France. (Documentary). 90 min. Sound. 16mm B&W. subtitles. *Rental:* Tricontinental Film.

Passing Fancy. Takeshi Sakamoto & Tokkankozo. Directed by Yasujiro Ozu. 1933. Japan. 103 min. Silent. 16mm B&W. subtitles. *Rental:* Films Inc.

Passing of the Third Floor Back. Sir John Forbes Robertson. Directed by Raymond B. West. 1918. First National. 45 min. Silent. 16mm B&W. *Rental:* Film Classics. *Sale:* Film Classics. *Rental:* Film Classics, Silent 8mm version.

Passing the Message. 1981. 47 min. 16mm Color. *Rental:* Icarus Films. *Sale:* Icarus Films.

Passion. Pola Negri, Emil Jannings & Harry Liedtke. Directed by Ernst Lubitsch. 1919. Germany. 124 min. Silent. 16mm B&W. *Rental:* Budget Films, Em Gee Films Lib, Kit Parker & Museum Mod Art. *Sale:* Em Gee Film Lib & Reel Images. *Rental:* Ivy Films, *Sale:* Reel Images, Super 8 silent version.

Passion. Isabelle Huppert & Hanna Schygulla. Directed by Jean-Luc Godard. Fr. 1983. France. 87 min. Sound. 16mm Color. subtitles. *Rental:* MGM United. *Rental:* MGM United, Videotape version.

Passion Flower. Norma Talmadge. Directed by Herbert Brenon. 1921. 16mm *Rental:* A Twyman Pres.

Passion for Life. Bernard Blier & Juliette Faber. Directed by Jean-Paul Le Chanois. Fr. 1948. France. 85 min. Sound. 16mm B&W. subtitles. *Rental:* Films Inc, Iowa Films, Macmillan Films, Museum Mod Art & Syracuse U Film. *Lease:* Macmillan Films.

Passion in Hot Hollows, The. Lola Valentine. Directed by Joseph W. Sarno. 1969. Cinetex. 80 min. Sound. 16mm B&W. *Sale:* Morcraft Films. *Sale:* Morcraft Films, Super 8 sound version.

Passion of Anna, The. Max Von Sydow & Liv Ullman. Directed by Ingmar Bergman. 1970. Sweden. 99 min. Sound. 16mm Color. subtitles. *Rental:* MGM United.

Passion of Joan of Arc, The. Maria Falconetti. Directed by Carl Th. Dreyer. 1928. France. (Musical score only). 119 min. Sound. 16mm B&W. *Rental:* Films Inc, Images Film & U Cal Media. *Sale:* Film Classics. *Rental:* Em Gee Film Lib, Film Classics, Kit Parker & Museum Mod Art, *Sale:* Cinema Concepts, Glenn Photo & Reel Images, Silent 16mm version. *Sale:* Morcraft Films, Tinted 16mm version. *Rental:* Ivy Films, *Sale:* Glenn Photo & Reel Images, Super 8 silent version. *Rental:* Film Classics & Video Comm, *Sale:* Tamarelles French Film, Videotape version. *Sale:* Festival Films & Images Film, 82 min. Videotape version. *Sale:* Festival Films, 82 min. version.

Passion Play, The. Directed by Felix Alland. 1914. Pathe. (Cast unlisted). 120 min. Silent. 16mm B&W. *Sale:* Natl Cinema. *Rental:* Wholesome Film Ctr, Silent with musical track, 80 min. version.

Passionate Industry, The. 1975. Australia. (Documentary). 59 min. Sound. 16mm B&W. *Rental:* Aust Info Serv. *Sale:* Aust Info Serv.

Passionate Plumber, The. Buster Keaton & Jimmy Durante. Directed by Edward Sedgwick. 1932. MGM. 75 min. Sound. 16mm B&W. *Rental:* MGM United.

Passionate Thief, The. Ben Gazzara. Directed by Mario Monicelli. 1962. Italy. 105 min. Sound. 16mm B&W. dubbed. *Rental:* Films Inc.

Passkey to Danger. Kane Richmond & Gerald Mohr. Directed by Lesley Selander. 1936. Republic. 58 min. Sound. 16mm B&W. *Rental:* Ivy Films.

Passover Plot, The. Harry Andrews. Directed by Michael Campus. 1976. 108 min. Sound. 16mm Color. *Rental:* Films Inc.

Passport Husband. Stuart Erwin & Douglas Fowley. Directed by James Tinling. 1938. Fox. 88 min. Sound. 16mm B&W. *Rental:* Films Inc.

Passport to China. Richard Basehart & Lisa Gastoni. Directed by Michael Carreras. 1961. Columbia. 75 min. Sound. 16mm B&W. *Rental:* Natl Film Serv.

Passport to Destiny. Elsa Lanchester & Lloyd Corrigan. Directed by Ray MacCarey. 1944. RKO. 64 min. Sound. 16mm B&W. *Rental:* RKO General Pics.

Passport to Heaven. Orig. Title: I Was a Criminal. Albert Basserman & Eric Blore. 1945. Film Classics. 73 min. Sound. 16mm B&W. *Rental:* Ivy Films. *Sale:* Classics Assoc NY & Rep Pic Film.

Passport to Pimlico. Margaret Rutherford & Stanley Holloway. Directed by Henry Cornelius. 1949. Britain. 81 min. Sound. 16mm B&W. *Rental:* Budget Films, Films Inc, Janus Films & Kit Parker.

Passport to Suez. Warren William, Eric Blore & Ann Savage. Directed by Andre De Toth. 1943. Columbia. 72 min. Sound. 16mm B&W. *Rental:* Kit Parker.

Passport to Treason. Rod Cameron, Lois Maxwell & Clifford Evans. Directed by Robert Baker. 1955. Commonwealth. 71 min. Sound. 16mm B&W. *Rental:* Ivy Films. *Rental:* Video Comm. *Rental:* Video Comm, Videotape version.

Password Is Courage, The. Dirk Bogarde & Maria Pershy. Directed by Andrew Stone. 1963. Britain. 116 min. Sound. 16mm B&W. *Rental:* MGM United.

Password: Kill Agent Gordon. Roger Browne. Directed by Terence Hathaway. 1965. American International. 93 min. Sound. 16mm Color. dubbed. *Rental:* Video Comm.

Pat & Mike. Spencer Tracy & Katharine Hepburn. Directed by George Cukor. 1952. MGM. 95 min. Sound. 16mm B&W. *Rental:* MGM United. *Rental:* MGM United, Videotape version.

Pat Garrett & Billy the Kid. James Coburn & Kris Kristofferson. Directed by Sam Peckinpah. 1973. MGM. 106 min. Sound. 16mm Color. *Rental:* MGM United. *Rental:* MGM United, Anamorphic version. *Sale:* Tamarelles French Film, Videotape version.

Patch of Blue, A. Sidney Poitier, Shelley Winters & Elizabeth Hartman. Directed by Guy Green. 1965. MGM. 105 min. Sound. 16mm B&W. *Rental:* MGM United. *Rental:* MGM United, Anamorphic version.

Patchwork. 1977. France. (Anthology, animated). 67 min. Sound. 16mm Color. *Rental:* Cinema Guild.

Patchwork Girl of Oz, The. Pierre Couderc. Directed by L. Frank Baum. 1914. Paramount. 55 min. Silent. 16mm B&W. *Rental:* Em Gee Film Lib. *Sale:* Glenn Photo. *Sale:* Glenn Photo, Super 8 silent version.

Patent Leather Kid, The. Richard Barthelmess & Molly O'Day. Directed by Alfred Santell. 1927. First National. 120 min. Silent. 16mm B&W. *Rental:* MGM United.

Patent Pending. 1976. Gould. (Documentary). 53 min. Sound. 16mm Color. *Rental:* Budget Films & U of IL Film. *Sale:* Lucerne Films. *Sale:* Lucerne Films, Videotape version.

Paternity. Burt Reynolds & Beverly D'Angelo. Directed by David Steinberg. 1981. Paramount. 94 min. Sound. 16mm Color. *Rental:* Films Inc.

Pather Panchali. Kanu Bannerjee. Directed by Satyajit Ray. Hindi. 1955. India. 112 min. Sound. 16mm B&W. subtitles. *Sale:* Films Inc. *Rental:* Budget Films.

Pathfinder, The. George Montgomery & Helena Carter. Directed by Sidney Salkow. 1954. Columbia. 78 min. Sound. 16mm Color. *Rental:* Arcus Film, Buchan Pic, Budget Films, Charard Motion Pics, Inst Cinema, Modern Sound, Welling Motion Pictures & Williams Films.

Pathfinders from the Stars. 1973. 48 min. Sound. 16mm Color. *Sale:* Natl AV Ctr.

Paths of Glory. Kirk Douglas & Ralph Meeker. Directed by Stanley Kubrick. 1957. United Artists. 87 min. Sound. 16mm B&W. *Rental:* MGM United.

Patient in Room Eighteen, The. Ann Sheridan & Patric Knowles. Directed by Crane Wilbur. 1938. Warners. 60 min. Sound. 16mm B&W. *Rental:* MGM United.

Patio Andaluz. 1950. Mexico. (Cast unlisted). 90 min. Sound. 16mm B&W. *Rental:* Film Classics.

Patrick. Susan Penhaligon, Sir Robert Helpmann. Directed by Richard Franklin. 1978. Vanguard. 96 min. Sound. 16mm Color. *Rental:* Twyman Films, Westcoast Films & Wholesome Film Ctr.

Patriot, The. Harry Baur. Fr. 1938. France. 93 min. Sound. 16mm B&W. subtitles. *Rental:* Film Classics.

Patriot Game, The. Directed by Arthur MacCaig. 1980. Icarus. (Documentary). 93 min. Sound. 16mm Color. *Rental:* Inst Cinema.

Patrunla Chiflada, La. Span. 1950. Mexico. (Cast unlisted). 90 min. Sound. 16mm B&W. *Rental:* Film Classics.

Patsy, The. Marion Davies & Marie Dressler. Directed by King Vidor. 1928. MGM. 75 min. Silent. 16mm B&W. *Rental:* MGM United.

Patsy, The. Jerry Lewis & Ina Balin. Directed by Jerry Lewis. 1964. Paramount. 101 min. Sound. 16mm Color. *Rental:* Films Inc.

Pattern for Murder. George Mathers & Julie Roding. 1964. Britain. 84 min. Sound. 16mm B&W. *Rental:* Films Inc.

Patton: A Salute to a Rebel. George C. Scott & Karl Malden. Directed by Franklin Schaffner. 1970. Fox. (Anamorphic). 171 min. Sound. 16mm Color. *Rental:* Films Inc & Williams Films. *Sale:* Festival Films. *Sale:* Festival Films, Videotape version.

Paul & Michelle. Keir Dullea. Directed by Lewis Gilbert. 1974. Paramount. 103 min. Sound. 16mm Color. *Rental:* Films Inc.

Paul Carlson Story, The. 1965. Gospel. (Cast unlisted). 53 min. Sound. 16mm Color. *Rental:* Gospel Films.

Paul L. Tillich. 1967. NET. (Documentary). 87 min. Sound. 16mm B&W. *Rental:* Indiana AV Ctr. *Sale:* Indiana AV Ctr.

Paul McCartney & Wings Rock Show. 1980. Minamax. (Concert). 100 min. Sound. 16mm Color. *Rental:* Films Inc.

Paul Robeson: The Tallest Tree in Our Forest. Directed by Gil Noble. 1977 Phoenix. (Documentary). 90 min. Sound. 16mm Color. *Rental:* Budget Films, Phoenix Films & U Cal Media. *Sale:* Phoenix Films. *Sale:* Phoenix Films, Videotape version.

Paul Robeson: Tribute to an Artist. James Earl Jones. 1979. Sunrise. 120 min. Sound. 16mm Color. *Rental:* Films Inc & Twyman Films.

Paul Taylor. 1980. WNET. (Dance). 60 min. Sound. 16mm Color. *Rental:* Films Inc. *Sale:* Films Inc, Videotape version.

Paul Taylor Dance Co. 1976. WNET. (Documentary). 58 min. Sound. Videotape Color. *Rental:* WNET Media. *Sale:* WNET Media.

Paula. Loretta Young & Kent Smith. Directed by Rudolph Mate. 1952. Columbia. 80 min. Sound. 16mm B&W. *Rental:* Bosco Films & Kit Parker.

Pauline at the Beach. Amanda Langlet & Arielle Dombasle. Directed by Eric Rohmer. Fr. 1983. Orion. 94 min. Sound. 16mm Color. subtitles. *Rental:* Films Inc.

Paul's Case. 1980. Perspective. (Cast unlisted). 55 min. Sound. 16mm Color. *Rental:* Iowa Film, Kent St U Film, Syracuse U Film & U Mich Media. *Sale:* Perspect Film. *Sale:* Perspect Film, Videocassette version.

Pavarotti at Juilliard. 168 min. Sound. 16mm Color. *Rental:* Phoenix Films. *Sale:* Phoenix Films. *Sale:* Phoenix Films, Videotape version.

Paw see Boy of Two Worlds.

Pawnbroker, The. Rod Steiger & Geraldine Fitzgerald. Directed by Sidney Lumet. 1964. Landau. 114 min. Sound. 16mm B&W. *Rental:* Budget Films, Films Inc, Ivy Films, Rep Pic Film, Twyman Films & Welling Motion Pictures. *Lease:* Rep Pic Film.

Pawnee. George Montgomery & Lola Albright. Directed by George Waggner. 1957. Republic. 80 min. Sound. 16mm B&W. *Rental:* Ivy Films. *Sale:* Rep Pic Film.

Pay-Off, The. (Documentary). 60 min. Videotape Color. *Sale:* Videx Home Lib. *Rental:* MGM United.

Pay-Off, The. Orig. Title: Payoff. Lowell Sherman & Marian Dixon. Directed by Lowell Sherman. 1931. RKO. 70 min. Sound. 16mm *Rental:* RKO General Pics.

Pay or Die. Ernest Borgnine & Zohra Lampert. Directed by Richard Wilson. 1960. Allied Artists. 111 min. Sound. 16mm B&W. *Rental:* Hurlock Cine.

Payday. Rip Torn & Ahna Capri. Directed by Daryl Duke. 1974. Cinerama. 103 min. Sound. 16mm Color. *Rental:* Swank Motion.

Payment Deferred. Charles Laughton & Ray Milland. Directed by Lothar Mendes. 1932. MGM. 82 min. Sound. 16mm B&W. *Rental:* MGM United.

Payoff, The. Lee Tracy & Tom Brown. Directed by Arthur Dreifuss. 1942. PRC. 70 min. Sound. 16mm B&W. *Rental:* Mogulls Films.

Payoff see Pay-Off.

Payroll. Michael Craig & Billie Whitelaw. Directed by Sidney Hayers. 1961. Britain. 94 min. Sound. 16mm B&W. *Rental:* Bosco Films.

Pays Sans Etoiles. Jany Holt, Pierre Brasseur & Gerard Philippe. Directed by George Lacombe. Fr. France. 100 min. Sound. 16mm B&W. subtitles. *Rental:* French Am Cul.

Pays Sans Son Sens, Un see Wake Up, Mes Bons Amis.

Peace, Order & Prosperity. Directed by Carol Myers. 1973. Canada. (Documentary). 58 min. Sound. 16mm Color. *Rental:* Natl Film CN. *Sale:* Natl Film CN.

Peace to Him Who Enters. Directed by Alexander Alov & Vladimir Naumov. Rus. 1963. Russia. 88 min. Sound. 16mm B&W. subtitles. *Rental:* Corinth Films.

Peaceful Detonator, The. Japan. (Cast unlisted). 70 min. Sound. 16mm B&W. subtitles. *Sale:* Japan Society. *Sale:* Japan Society, Videotape version.

Peaceful Use of Nuclear Explosives, The. 1971. Britain. (Lecture). 56 min. 16mm B&W. *Rental:* Time-Life Multimedia. *Sale:* Time-Life Multimedia.

Peacemaker, The. James Mitchell & Jess Barker. Directed by Ted Post. 1956. United Artists. 83 min. Sound. 16mm B&W. *Rental:* Ivy Films & Rep Pic Film. *Lease:* Rep Pic Film.

Peach O'Reno. Bert Wheeler & Robert Woolsey. Directed by William A. Seiter. 1932. RKO. 70 min. Sound. 16mm B&W. *Rental:* RKO General Pics.

Peach Thief, The. Nevena Kokanova & Rade Markovich. Directed by Vulo Radev. 1954. Bulgaria. 84 min. Sound. 16mm B&W. subtitles. *Rental:* Films Inc.

Peacock Fan, The. Dorothy Dwan & Lucien Prival. Directed by Phil Rosen. 1929. Chesterfield. 60 min. Silent. 16mm B&W. *Rental:* Budget Films, Mogulls Films & Willoughby Peer.

Peanuts to the Presidency. Directed by Charles Braverman. 1977. Braverman. (Animated). 75 min. Sound. 16mm Color. *Rental:* Budget Films & Pyramid Film. *Sale:* Pyramid Film. *Rental:* Pyramid Film, *Sale:* Pyramid Film, Videotape version.

Pearl, The. Trans. Title: Perla, La. Pedro Armendariz & Maria Elena Marques. Directed by Emilio Fernandez. 1948. Mexico. 77 min. Sound. 16mm B&W. dubbed. *Rental:* Budget Films, Films Inc, Macmillan Films & Syracuse U Film. *Lease:* Macmillan Films.

Pearl in the Crown, The. Directed by Kazimierz Kutz. Pol. 1971. Poland. 121 min. Sound. 16mm Color. subtitles. *Rental:* Films Inc.

Pearl of Death, The. Basil Rathbone. Directed by Roy William Neill. 1944. Universal. 69 min. Sound. 16mm B&W. *Rental:* Learning Corp Am & Video Comm. *Sale:* Learning Corp Am. *Sale:* Cinema Concepts, Super 8 sound version.

Pearl of Paradise, The. Margarita Fischer. Directed by Harry Pollard. 1916. Mutual. 60 min. Silent. 8mm B&W. *Sale:* Blackhawk Films.

Pearls of the Crown. Harry Baur. Directed by Sacha Guitry. Fr. 1937. France. 121 min. Sound. 16mm B&W. subtitles. *Rental:* Films Inc.

Peary's Race for the North Pole. 1974. NBC. (Documentary, tinted). 52 min. Sound. 16mm *Rental:* Films Inc & U Mich Media. *Sale:* Films Inc.

Peasants, The. Emilia Krakowska & Ignacy Gogolewski. Directed by Jan Rybkowski. Pol. 1975. Poland. 180 min. Sound. 16mm Color. subtitles. *Rental:* Amerpol Ent.

Peasants of the Second Fortress, The. Directed by Shinsuke Ogawa. Jap. 1971. Japan. (Documentary). 143 min. Sound. 16mm B&W. subtitles. *Rental:* Cinema Guild. *Sale:* Cinema Guild.

Peau D'Ane see Donkey Skin.

Peau Douce, La see Soft Skin.

Pecado Por Mes, Un. 1950. Mexico. (Cast unlisted). 90 min. Sound. 16mm B&W. *Rental:* Film Classics.

Peck's Bad Boy. Jackie Coogan. Directed by Sam Wood. 1921. First National. (Musical score only). 55 min. Sound. 16mm B&W. *Rental:* Killiam Collect. *Sale:* Blackhawk Films. *Rental:* Em Gee Film Lib, *Sale:* Blackhawk Films, Silent 16mm version. *Rental:* Killiam Collect, Silent 16mm tinted version. *Sale:* Blackhawk Films, Super 8 sound version. *Rental:* Ivy Films, *Sale:* Blackhawk Films, Super 8 silent version.

Peck's Bad Boy. Jackie Cooper & Thomas Meighan. Directed by Edward Cline. 1934. Fox. 80 min. Sound. 16mm B&W. *Rental:* Mogulls Films.

Peck's Bad Boy with the Circus. Tommy Kelly & Ann Gillis. Directed by Edward Cline. 1938. RKO. 75 min. Sound. 16mm B&W. *Rental:* Alba House, Budget Films, Charard Motion Pic, Inst Cinema, Mogulls Films & Wholesome Film Ctr.

Pecos Clean Up. Robert Woods & Erno Crisa. Italy. 88 min. Sound. 16mm Color. dubbed. *Rental:* Video Comm. *Rental:* Video Comm, Videotape version.

Pecos Kid, The. Fred Kohler Jr. 1935. Commodore. 60 min. Sound. 16mm B&W. *Rental:* Mogulls Films.

Pedagogical Poem, A. V. Yemelianov. Directed by A. Maslyukov & M. Mayevskaya. Rus. 1955. Russia. 108 min. Sound. 16mm B&W. subtitles. *Rental:* Corinth Films.

Pediatric Examination, The: Examination of the Preschool Child. 1981. 45 min. Sound. 16mm Color. *Rental:* Iowa Films.

Pediatric Examination, The: Examination of the School Age Child. 1981. 45 min. Sound. 16mm Color. *Rental:* Iowa Films.

Peeper, The. Natalie Wood & Michael Caine. Directed by Peter Hyams. 1975. Fox. (Anamorphic). 87 min. Sound. 16mm Color. *Rental:* Films Inc.

Peeping Tom. Orig. Title: Face of Fear. Moira Shearer, Anna Massey & Karl Boehm. Directed by Michael Powell. 1960. Britain. 85 min. Sound. 16mm B&W. *Rental:* Corinth Films.

Peer Gynt. Charlton Heston. Directed by David Bradley. 1941. Independent. (Musical score only). 85 min. Sound. 16mm B&W. *Rental:* Films Inc.

Peer Gynt. 1977. Miami-Dade. (Cast unlisted). 60 min. Videotape Color. *Sale:* Film Inc.

Peg O' My Heart. Marion Davies & Onslow Stevens. Directed by Robert Z. Leonard. 1933. MGM. 86 min. Sound. 16mm B&W. *Rental:* MGM United.

Peg of Old Drury. Anna Neagle, Cedric Hardwicke & Jack Hawkins. Directed by Herbert Wilcox. 1948. 16mm *Rental:* A Twyman Pres.

Penalty, The. Lon Chaney. Directed by Wallace Worsley. 1920. MGM. 75 min. Silent. 16mm B&W. *Rental:* MGM United.

Pendulum. George Peppard & Jean Seberg. Directed by George Schaefer. 1969. Columbia. 105 min. Sound. 16mm Color. *Rental:* Cine Craft, Films Inc, Film Ctr DC, Inst Cinema, Kerr Film, Roas Films, Swank Motion, Video Comm, Westcoast Films & Wholesome Film Ctr.

Penelope. Natalie Wood & Dick Shawn. Directed by Arthur Hiller. 1966. MGM. 125 min. Sound. 16mm Color. *Rental:* MGM United. *Rental:* MGM United, Anamorphic version.

Penguin Pool Murder, The. Edna Mae Oliver, Edgar Kennedy & James Gleason. Directed by George Archainbaud. 1932. RKO. 75 min. Sound. 16mm B&W. *Rental:* RKO General Pics.

Penitentiary II. Leon Isaac Kennedy, Glynn Turman & Mr. T. Directed by Jamaa Fanaka. 1982. 109 min. Sound. 16mm Color. *Rental:* MGM United. *Rental:* MGM United, Videotape version.

Penn of Pennsylvania see Courageous Mr. Penn.

Pennies from Heaven. Bing Crosby & Madge Evans. Directed by Norman Z. McLeod. 1936. Columbia. 81 min. Sound. 16mm B&W. *Rental:* Arcus Film, Budget Films, Film Ctr DC, Kit Parker, Natl Film Video, U of IL Film, Westcoast Films & Wholesome Film Ctr.

Pennies from Heaven. Steve Martin, Bernadette Peters & Jessica Harper. Directed by Herbert Ross. 1981. MGM. 108 min. Sound. 16mm Color. *Rental:* MGM United. *Rental:* MGM United, Videotape version.

Penny Serenade. Cary Grant & Irene Dunne. Directed by George Stevens. 1941. Columbia. 124 min. Sound. 16mm B&W. *Rental:* Budget Films, Classic Film Mus, Em Gee Film Lib, Ivy Films, Kit Parker & Video Comm. *Lease:* Rep Pic Film. *Sale:* Festival Films. *Sale:* Festival Films, Videotape version.

Pennywhistle Blues see Magic Garden.

Penrod & His Twin Brother. Frank Craven & Spring Byington. Directed by William McGann. 1938. Warners. 63 min. Sound. 16mm B&W. *Rental:* MGM United.

Penrod & Sam. Billy Mauch & Frank Craven. Directed by William McGann. 1937. Warners. 64 min. Sound. 16mm B&W. *Rental:* MGM United.

Pentagon Papers & the American, The. 1972. American Documentary. (Documentary). 54 min. Sound. 16mm B&W. *Rental:* Films Inc.

Penthouse. Myrna Loy & Warner Baxter. Directed by W. S. Van Dyke. 1933. MGM. 90 min. Sound. 16mm B&W. *Rental:* MGM United.

People Against O'Hara, The. Spencer Tracy & Pat O'Brien. Directed by John Sturges. 1951. MGM. 103 min. Sound. 16mm B&W. *Rental:* MGM United.

People Chosen: Who Is a Jew?. Directed by Herbert Krosney. 1974. Canada. (Documentary). 57 min. Sound. 16mm Color. *Rental:* Alden Films, Budget Films, Iowa Films, Phoenix Films & U of IL Film. *Sale:* Phoenix Films. *Sale:* Phoenix Films, Videotape version.

People Next Door, The. Lloyd Bridges & Kim Hunter. Directed by David Greene. 1968. CBS. 79 min. Sound. 16mm B&W. *Rental:* NYU Film Lib, Roas Films, Syracuse U Film & Video Comm. *Sale:* Phoenix Films. *Sale:* Phoenix Films, Videotape version.

People Next Door, The. Eli Wallach, Julie Harris & Hal Holbrook. Directed by David Greene. 1970. Embassy. 93 min. Sound. 16mm Color. *Rental:* Films Inc.

People of Nes Ammim, The. 1979. WNET. (Documentary). 58 min. Videotape Color. *Rental:* Alden Films & WNET Media. *Sale:* Alden Films & WNET Media.

People of People's China. 1974. Xerox. (Documentary). 52 min. Sound. 16mm Color. *Rental:* U Cal Media. *Sale:* Xerox Films.

People of the Seal. 2 pts. 1973. CBS. (Documentary). 104 min. Sound. 16mm Color. *Rental:* Educ Dev Ctr. *Sale:* Educ Dev Ctr.

People of the Wind. Directed by Anthony Howarth. 1976. Elizabeth E. Rogers. (Documentary). 108 min. Sound. 16mm Color. narrated Eng. *Rental:* Cinema Guild. *Sale:* Cinema Guild.

People on Sunday. Directed by Billy Wilder & Robert Siodmak. 1929. 70 min. 16mm *Rental:* A Twyman Pres.

People That Time Forgot, The. Patrick Wayne & Doug McClure. Directed by Kevin Connor. 1977. American International. 90 min. Sound. 16mm Color. *Rental:* Swank Motion & Welling Motion Pictures.

People vs. Dr. Kildare, The. Lew Ayres, Lionel Barrymore & Laraine Day. 1941. MGM. 78 min. Sound. 16mm B&W. *Rental:* MGM United.

People vs. Inez Garcia, The. 1979. PBS. (Cast unlisted). 88 min. Videotape Color. *Rental:* PBS Video. *Sale:* PBS Video.

People Will Talk. Cary Grant & Jeanne Crain. Directed by Joseph L. Mankiewicz. 1951. Fox. 110 min. Sound. 16mm B&W. *Rental:* Films Inc.

Pepe. Cantinflas & Dan Dailey. Directed by George Sidney. 1960. Columbia. 157 min. Sound. 16mm Color. *Rental:* Arcus Film, Buchan Pic, Budget Films, Cine Craft, Charard Motion Pics, Films Inc, Film Ctr DC, Modern Sound, Roas Films, Twyman Films, Welling Motion Pictures & Westcoast Films.

Pepe le Moko. Jean Gabin. Directed by Julien Duvivier. Fr. 1937. France. 95 min. Sound. 16mm B&W. subtitles. *Rental:* Budget Films, Images Film, Kit Parker, Westcoast Films & Utah Media. *Sale:* Cinema Concepts, Festival Films, Images Film & Reel Images. *Sale:* Cinema Concepts, Festival Films & Tmarelles French Film, Videotape version.

Pepe's Family. 1978. Mintz. (Documentary). 45 min. Sound. 16mm Color. *Rental:* Indiana AV Ctr. *Sale:* Indiana AV Ctr. *Sale:* Indiana AV Ctr, Videotape version.

Peppermint Soda. Eleanore Klarwein. Directed by Diane Kurys. Fr. 1978. France. 97 min. Sound. 16mm Color. subtitles. *Rental:* New Cinema & New Yorker Films.

Peptic Ulcer. 1980. US Government. (Documentary). 60 min. Videotape Color. *Sale:* Natl AV Ctr.

Perceval. Fabrice Luchini & Andre Dussolier. Directed by Eric Rohmer. Fr. 1978. France. 140 min. Sound. 16mm Color. subtitles. *Rental:* New Yorker Films.

Perch of the Devil. Pat O'Malley & Mae Busch. Directed by King Baggott. 1927. Universal. 80 min. Silent. 16mm B&W. *Rental:* Mogulls Films.

Percy. Hywel Bennett & Denholm Elliot. Directed by Ralph Thomas. 1971. MGM. 103 min. Sound. 16mm Color. *Rental:* MGM United.

Perfect Alibi, The *see* Alibi.

Perfect Clown, The. Larry Semon, Oliver Hardy & Dorothy Dwan. Directed by Fred Newmeyer. 1925. Chadwick. 50 min. Silent. 16mm B&W. *Rental:* Budget Films, Em Gee Film Lib & Ivy Films. *Sale:* Blackhawk Films. *Rental:* Ivy Films, Super 8 sound version. *Sale:* Blackhawk Films, Silent 8mm version.

Perfect Couple, A. Paul Dooley & Marta Heflin. Directed by Robert Altman. 1979. Fox. 110 min. Sound. 16mm Color. *Rental:* Films Inc.

Perfect Friday. Ursula Andress, Stanley Baker & David Warner. Directed by Peter Hall. 1970. Chevron. 94 min. Sound. 16mm Color. *Rental:* Budget Films & Video Comm.

Perfect Furlough, The. Tony Curtis & Janet Leigh. Directed by Blake Edwards. 1958. Universal. 93 min. Sound. 16mm Color. *Rental:* Swank Motion.

Perfect Gentleman, The. Frank Morgan & Heather Angel. Directed by Tim Whelan. 1935. MGM. 73 min. Sound. 16mm B&W. *Rental:* MGM United.

Perfect Marriage, The. Loretta Young & David Niven. Directed by Lewis Allen. 1946. Paramount. 88 min. Sound. 16mm B&W. *Rental:* Swank Motion.

Perfect President, The: A Man for His Times. 1976. Post-Newsweek. (Documentary). 51 min. Sound. 16mm Color. *Rental:* U of IL Film. *Sale:* Lucerne Films. *Sale:* Lucerne Films, Videotape version.

Perfect Specimen, The. Errol Flynn, Joan Blondell & May Robson. Directed by Michael Curtiz. 1937. Warners. 97 min. Sound. 16mm B&W. *Rental:* MGM United.

Perfect Weekend, The *see* St. Louis Kid.

Performance. Mick Jagger & Rolling Stones. Directed by Donald Cammell & Nicolas Roeg. 1970. Britain. 110 min. Sound. 16mm Color. *Rental:* Films Inc, Swank Motion & Twyman Films. *Rental:* Swank Motion, Videotape version.

Performed Word, The. 58 min. Sound. 16mm Color. *Rental:* Ctr South Folklore. *Sale:* Ctr South Folklore. *Sale:* Ctr South Folklore, Videotape version.

Performer, The. Directed by Donald Ginsberg. 1959. Canada. (Documentary). 57 min. Sound. 16mm B&W. *Rental:* Natl Film CN. *Sale:* Natl Film CN.

Pergaud. France. (Cast unlisted). 60 min. Sound. 16mm B&W. *Rental:* French Am Cul. *Rental:* French Am Cul, Videotape version.

Pericles. Mike Gwilym & Amanda Redman. 1984. 120 min. Sound. 16mm Color. *Rental:* Iowa Films.

Perilous Journey, A. David Brian & Scott Brady. Directed by R. G. Springsteen. 1952. Republic. 90 min. Sound. 16mm B&W. *Rental:* Ivy Films. *Sale:* Rep Pic Film.

Perilous Waters. Don Castle & Audrey Long. Directed by Jack Bernhard. 1948. Monogram. 70 min. Sound. 16mm B&W. *Rental:* Mogulls Films.

Perils from the Planet Mongo. Buster Crabbe & Jean Rogers. Directed by Ford Beebe & Robert Hill. 1939. Universal. 85 min. Sound. 16mm B&W. *Rental:* Ivy Films & Video Comm.

Perils of Paris, The. Orig. Title: Terror. Pearl White & Robert Lee. Directed by Edward Jose. France. 50 min. Silent. 16mm Color. *Rental:* Budget Films.

Perils of Pauline, The. Betty Hutton & John Lund. Directed by George Marshall. 1947. Paramount. 112 min. Sound. 16mm Color. *Rental:* Films Inc. *Sale:* Reel Images, Videotape version. *Sale:* Festival Films, 96 min. 16mm version. *Sale:* Festival Films, 96 min. Videotape version, Super 8 sound version. *Sale:* Reel Images,

Perils of Pauline, The. Pat Boone & Pamela Austin. Directed by Herbert B. Leonard & Joshua Shelley. 1967. Universal. 107 min. Sound. 16mm Color. *Rental:* Williams Films.

Perils of the Darkest Jungle. Orig. Title: Tiger Woman, The. Allan Lane & Linda Stirling. Directed by Wallace Grissell. 1951. Republic. 201 min. Sound. 16mm B&W. *Rental:* Ivy Films.

Perils of the Rails. Helen Holmes & Edward Hearn. Directed by J. P. McGowan. 1926. Anchor. 50 min. Silent. 16mm B&W. *Rental:* Mogulls Films.

Period of Adjustment. Jane Fonda & Jim Hutton. Directed by George Roy Hill. 1962. MGM. 112 min. Sound. 16mm B&W. *Rental:* MGM United.

Periodontal Surgery. 1970. 180 min. Sound. Videotape Color. *Sale:* Natl AV Ctr.

Perishable Goods. 1979. (Documentary). 60 min. Videotape Color. *Rental:* Films Inc & Syracuse U Film. *Sale:* Films Inc.

Perla, La *see* Pearl.

Permanent War Economy, The. 1983. 55 min. Sound. 16mm Color. *Rental:* U Mich Media.

Permission to Kill. Dirk Bogarde & Ava Gardner. Directed by Cyril Frankel. 1975. Embassy. 96 min. Sound. 16mm Color. *Rental:* Swank Motion.

Persecucion Hasta Valencia *see* Narco Men.

Persecution & Assassination of Jean-Paul Marat as Performed by the Inmates of the Asylum of Charendon Under the Direction of the Marquis de Sade, The see Marat-Sade.

Perseus the Invincible see Medusa vs. the Son of Hercules.

Persistence of Memory, The. 1980. Cosmos. (Documentary). 60 min. Sound. 16mm Color. *Rental:* Films Inc. *Sale:* Films Inc. *Rental:* Films Inc, *Sale:* Films Inc, Videotape version.

Persistent & Finagling. 1973. Canada. (Documentary). 57 min. Sound. 16mm B&W. *Rental:* Natl Film CN. *Sale:* Natl Film CN.

Persona. Bibi Anderson & Liv Ullmann. Directed by Ingmar Bergman. Swed. 1967. Sweden. 81 min. Sound. 16mm B&W. subtitles. *Rental:* Budget Films, Corinth Films, Films Inc, Em Gee Films Lib, Images Film, Ivy Films, MGM United, U of IL Film & Utah Media. *Sale:* Cinema Concepts, Festival Films, Reel Images & Images Film. *Sale:* Tamarelles French Film & Images Film, Videotape version.

Persona Honorada Se Necesita. 1950. Mexico. (Cast unlisted). 90 min. Sound. 16mm B&W. *Rental:* Film Classics.

Personal Best. Mariel Hemingway & Scott Glenn. Directed by Robert Towne. 1982. Warners. 122 min. Sound. 16mm Color. *Rental:* Swank Motion. *Rental:* Swank Motion, Videotape version.

Personal Encounter. 1951. US Government. (Documentary). 60 min. Sound. 16mm B&W. *Sale:* Natl AV Ctr.

Personal Honor see Hello Annapolis.

Personal Maid's Secret. Margaret Lindsay & Warren Hull. Directed by Arthur G. Collins. 1935. Warners. 58 min. Sound. 16mm B&W. *Rental:* MGM United.

Personal Power. Films Inc. (Lecture). 90 min. Videotape Color. *Rental:* Films Inc. *Sale:* Films Inc.

Personal Property. Orig. Title: Man in Possession, The. Jean Harlow & Robert Taylor. Directed by W. S. Van Dyke. 1937. MGM. 84 min. Sound. 16mm B&W. *Rental:* MGM United.

Personal Secretary. William Gargan & Joy Hodges. Directed by Otis Garrett. 1938. Universal. 60 min. Sound. 16mm B&W. *Rental:* Film Ctr DC & Mogulls Films.

Personality Kid, The. Pat O'Brien & Glenda Farrell. Directed by Alan Crosland. 1934. Warners. 68 min. Sound. 16mm B&W. *Rental:* MGM United.

Persuasive Negotiating. 1980. Films Inc. 60 min. Sound. 16mm Color. *Rental:* Films Inc. *Sale:* S & Films Inc. *Rental:* Films Inc, *Sale:* Films Inc, Videotape version.

Pete & Johnny. 1965. Time-Life. (Documentary). 54 min. Sound. 16mm B&W. *Rental:* Time-Life Multimedia. *Sale:* Time-Life Multimedia.

Pete Kelly's Blues. Jack Webb, Janet Leigh & Peggy Lee. 1955. Warners. 95 min. Sound. 16mm Color. *Rental:* Films Inc & Swank Motion.

Pete 'n' Tillie. Carol Burnett & Walter Matthau. Directed by Martin Ritt. 1972. Universal. 100 min. Sound. 16mm Color. *Rental:* Williams Films.

Pete Seeger: A Song & a Stone. Directed by Robert Elfstrom. 1972. Elfstrom. (Documentary). 85 min. Sound. 16mm Color. *Rental:* Films Inc.

Peter Ibbetson. Gary Cooper & Ann Harding. Directed by Henry Hathaway. 1935. Paramount. 88 min. Sound. 16mm B&W. *Rental:* Swank Motion.

Peter Lind Hayes Show, The. Peter Lind Hayes, Mary Healy & Jack Whiting. TV. 51 min. Videotape B&W. *Sale:* Reel Images.

Peter-No-Tail. Directed by Jan Gissberg & Stig Lasseby. 1982. Atlantic. (Animated). 90 min. Sound. 16mm Color. *Rental:* MGM United.

Peter Pan. Directed by Wolfgang Reitherman. 1953. Disney. (Animated). 77 min. Sound. 16mm Color. *Rental:* Bosco Films, Disney Prod, Films Inc, MGM United, Modern Sound, Swank Motion, Westcoast Films, Welling Motion Pictures & Williams Films.

Peter Pan. Mary Martin & Cyril Ritchard. 1955. NBC. 120 min. Videotape Color. *Sale:* Reel Images.

Peter Rabbit & the Tales of Beatrix Potter. Royal Ballet & Julie Wood. Directed by Reginald Mills. 1971. Britain. (Ballet). 98 min. Sound. 16mm Color. *Rental:* Films Inc.

Peter the First. Nikolai Simonov & Claude Cherkassov. Directed by Vladimir Petrov. Rus. 1938. Russia. 104 min. Sound. B&W. subtitles. *Rental:* Corinth Films.

Peter the Great: Part Two. Dmitry Zolotukhin. Directed by Sergei Gerassimov. Rus. 1981. Russia. 136 min. Sound. 16mm Color. subtitles. *Rental:* Corinth Films. *Rental:* Corinth Films, Videotape version.

Peter Ustinov's Leningrad. 1978. Learning Corp.. (Documentary). 50 min. Sound. 16mm Color. *Rental:* Kent St U Film & Learning Corp Am. *Sale:* Learning Corp Am.

Pete's Dragon. Helen Reddy, Mickey Rooney & Red Buttons. Directed by Don Chaffey. 1977. Disney. 135 min. Sound. 16mm Color. *Rental:* Buchan Pic & MGM United.

Petit Marcel, Le. Jacques Spiesser & Isabelle Huppert. Directed by Jacques Fansten. Fr. 1976. France. 120 min. Sound. 16mm Color. subtitles. *Rental:* French Am Cul.

Petit Matelot, Le. Jacques Fabri. Directed by Jean-Pierre Decourt. Fr. 1975. France. 52 min. Sound. 16mm Color. subtitles. *Rental:* French Am Cul. *Rental:* French Am Cul, Videotape version.

Petit Theatre de Jean Renoir, Le. Trans. Title: Little Theatre of Jean Renoir, The. Jeanne Moreau. Directed by Jean Renoir. 1974. France. (Anthology). 100 min. Sound. 16mm Color. *Rental:* Budget Films, Films Inc, Kit Parker, Phoenix Films, Viewfinders, Texture Film & U Mich Media. *Sale:* Phoenix Films & Texture Film. *Sale:* Phoenix Films, Texture Film & Tamarelles French Film, Videotape version.

Petite Marchand d'Allumettes, La. Trans. Title: Little Match Girl, The. Catherine Hessling. Directed by Jean Renoir. 1928. France. 45 min. Silent. 16mm B&W. *Rental:* Em Gee Film Lib & Museum Mod Art. *Sale:* Cinema Concepts & Reel Images.

Petria's Wreath. Directed by Srdjan Karanovic. Serbo-Croatian. 1980. 100 min. Sound. 16mm Color. subtitles. *Rental:* New Yorker Films.

Petrified Forest, The. Leslie Howard, Bette Davis & Humphrey Bogart. Directed by Archie Mayo. 1936. Warners. 83 min. Sound. 16mm B&W. *Rental:* MGM United.

Petticoat Larceny. Ruth Warrick & Paul Guilfoyle. Directed by Ben Holmes. 1943. RKO. 61 min. Sound. 16mm B&W. *Rental:* RKO General Pics.

Petticoat Politics. James Gleason & Polly Moran. Directed by Erle C. Kenton. 1941. Republic. 71 min. Sound. 16mm B&W. *Rental:* Ivy Films.

Petty Girl. Robert Cummings & Joan Caulfield. Directed by Henry Levin. 1950. Columbia. 87 min. Sound. 16mm Color. *Rental:* Kit Parker.

Peyton Place. Lana Turner & Lloyd Nolan. Directed by Mark Robson. 1957. Fox. (Anamorphic). 165 min. Sound. 16mm Color. *Rental:* Films Inc.

Phaedra. Melina Mercouri & Anthony Perkins. Directed by Jules Dassin. 1962. Greece. 115 min. Sound. 16mm B&W. *Rental:* MGM United.

Phans of Jersey City, The. 1979. Films Inc. (Documentary). 49 min. Sound. 16mm Color. *Rental:* Films Inc. *Sale:* Films Inc. *Sale:* Films Inc, Videotape version.

Phantasm. Michael Baldwin & Bill Thornbury. Directed by Don Coscarelli. 1979. Embassy. 96 min. Sound. 16mm Color. *Rental:* Films Inc.

Phantom. Alfred Abel. Directed by F. W. Murnau. 1922. 16mm *Rental:* A Twyman Pres.

Phantom Baron, The. Jean Cocteau. Directed by Serge De Poligny. Fr. 1944. France. 105 min. Sound. 16mm B&W. subtitles. *Rental:* A Twyman Pres & Film Classics.

Phantom Chariot, The. Trans. Title: Korkarlen. Victor Seastrom & Astrid Holm. Directed by Victor Seastrom. 1921. Sweden. 92 min. Silent. 16mm B&W. *Rental:* Budget Films, Em Gee Film Lib, Films Inc, Kit Parker & Museum Mod Art. *Sale:* Glenn Photo & Reel Images. *Sale:* Glenn Photo & Reel Images, Super 8 Silent version. *Sale:* Festival Films, 62 min. version.

Phantom Cowboy, The. Don Barry. Directed by George Sherman. 1941. Republic. 56 min. Sound. 16mm B&W. *Rental:* Ivy Films. *Sale:* Rep Pic Film.

Phantom Creeps, The. Bela Lugosi & Regis Toomey. Directed by Ford Beebe. 1939. Universal. 65 min. Sound. 16mm B&W. *Rental:* Budget Films, Classic Film Mus, Kerr Film & Video Comm. *Rental:* Classic Film Mus, 12 episodes version.

Phantom Express, The. J. Farrell McDonald & Sally Blane. Directed by Emory Johnson. 1932. Majestic. 60 min. Sound. 16mm B&W. *Rental:* Em Gee Film Lib. *Sale:* Morcraft Films. *Sale:* Morcraft Films, Super 8 sound version.

Phantom Fiend, The. Ivor Novello & Jack Hawkins. Directed by Maurice Elvey. 1935. Britain. 70 min. Sound. 16mm B&W. *Rental:* Budget Films.

Phantom Flyer, The. Al Wilson. Directed by Bruce Mitchell. 1928. Universal. 45 min. Silent. 16mm B&W. *Sale:* Cinema Concepts & Griggs Movie.

Phantom from Ten Thousand Leagues, The. Kent Taylor, Cathy Downs & Michael Whelan. Directed by Dan Milner. 1956. American Releasing. 80 min. Sound. 16mm Color. *Rental:* Swank Motion.

Phantom in the House, The. Ricardo Cortez & Henry B. Walthall. Directed by Phil Rosen. 1929. Continental. 70 min. Sound. 16mm B&W. *Rental:* Mogulls Films.

Phantom India. 7 pts. Directed by Louis Malle. 1967-68. France-India. (Documentary). 364 min. Sound. 16mm Color. narrated Eng. *Rental:* New Yorker Films.

Phantom Killer, The. Dick Purcell & Joan Woodbury. Directed by William Beaudine. 1942. Monogram. 60 min. Sound. 16mm B&W. *Rental:* Mogulls Films.

Phantom Lady. Ella Raines & Franchot Tone. Directed by Robert Siodmak. 1944. Universal. 87 min. Sound. 16mm B&W. *Rental:* Swank Motion.

Phantom of Chinatown, The. Keye Luke & Lotus Long. Directed by Phil Rosen. 1940. Monogram. 61 min. Sound. 16mm B&W. *Rental:* MGM United.

Phantom Of Crestwood, The. Ricardo Cortez & Anita Louise. Directed by Walter J. Ruben. 1933. RKO. 77 min. Sound. 16mm B&W. *Rental:* RKO General Pics.

Phantom of Forty Second Street, The. Alan Mowbray. Directed by Al Herman. 1945. PRC. 60 min. Sound. 16mm B&W. *Rental:* Film Classics, Ivy Films & Mogulls Films. *Sale:* Classics Assoc NY & Rep Pic Film.

Phantom of Liberte, The. Jean-Claude Brialy & Adolfo Celi. Directed by Luis Bunuel. Fr. 1974. France. 104 min. Sound. 16mm Color. subtitles Eng. *Rental:* Films Inc.

Phantom of Paris, The. John Gilbert & Lewis Stone. Directed by John Robertson. 1931. MGM. 73 min. Sound. 16mm B&W. *Rental:* MGM United.

Phantom of the Desert, The. Jack Perrin. Directed by Harry S. Webb. 1930. Syndicate. 57 min. Sound. 16mm B&W. *Sale:* Natl Cinema.

Phantom of the Opera, The. Lon Chaney & Mary Philbin. Directed by Rupert Julian. 1925. Universal. (Musical Score Only). 79 min. Sound. 16mm B&W. *Rental:* A Twyman Pres, Creative Film, Films Inc, Iowa Films, Video Comm, Welling Motion Pictures, Wholesome Film Ctr & Willoughby Peer. *Sale:* Festival Films, Natl Film Video, Natl Cinema, See-Art Films, Sterling Ed Film & Video Comm. *Rental:* Budget Films, Charard Motion Pics, Film Images, Films Inc, Ivy Films, Kerr Film, Kit Parker, Mogulls Films, Roas Films, Swank Motion, Twyman Films, Video Comm, Westcoast Films & Wholesome Film Ctr, *Sale:* Blackhawk Films, Cinema Concepts, Natl Cinema & Video Comm, Silent 16mm version. *Rental:* Bosco Films & Twyman Films, *Sale:* Blackhawk Films, Silent 16mm with color sequences version. *Rental:* Em Gee Film Lib, Silent 16mm tinted version. *Rental:* Killiam Collect & New Cinema, Sound 16mm tinted version, Super 8 sound version. *Sale:* Blackhawk Films, Super 8 silent version. *Sale:* Blackhawk Films, Super 8 silent with color sequences version.

Phantom of the Opera, The. Claude Rains & Nelson Eddy. Directed by Arthur Lubin. 1943. Universal. 92 min. Sound. 16mm Color. *Rental:* Swank Motion & Twyman Films.

Phantom of the Opera, The. Herbert Lom & Heather Sears. Directed by Terence Fisher. 1962. Britain. 84 min. Sound. 16mm Color. *Rental:* Swank Motion.

Phantom of the Paradise, The. Paul Williams & Jessica Harper. Directed by Brian De Palma. 1974. Fox. 92 min. Sound. 16mm Color. *Rental:* Films Inc & Twyman Films.

Phantom of the Plains, The. Bill Elliott. Directed by Lesley Selander. 1945. Republic. 54 min. Sound. 16mm B&W. *Rental:* Ivy Films & Rep Pic Film. *Sale:* Rep Pic Film & Nostalgia Merchant.

Phantom of the Rue Morgue, The. Karl Malden, Claude Dauphin & Patricia Medina. Directed by Roy Del Ruth. 1954. Warners. 84 min. Sound. 16mm Color. *Rental:* Films Inc & Twyman Films.

Phantom Patrol, The. Kermit Maynard. Directed by Charles Hutchinson. 1936. Ambassador-Conn. 60 min. Sound. 16mm B&W. *Rental:* Modern Sound.

Phantom Plainsmen, The. Tom Tyler. Directed by John English. 1942. Republic. 57 min. Sound. 16mm B&W. *Rental:* Ivy Films. *Sale:* Rep Pic Film.

Phantom Planet, The. Dean Fredericks & Coleen Gray. Directed by William Marshall. 1962. American International. 82 min. Sound. 16mm B&W. *Rental:* Films Inc.

Phantom President, The. George M. Cohen & Claudette Colbert. Directed by Norman Taurog. 1932. Paramount. 80 min. Sound. 16mm B&W. *Rental:* Swank Motion.

Phantom Raiders, The. Walter Pidgeon & Joseph Schildkraut. Directed by Jacques Tourneur. 1940. MGM. 70 min. Sound. 16mm B&W. *Rental:* MGM United.

Phantom Ranger, The. Tim McCoy. Directed by Sam Newfield. 1938. Monogram. 55 min. Sound. 16mm B&W. *Rental:* Rep Pic Film. *Sale:* Cinema Concepts, Rep Pic Film & Reel Images. *Sale:* Video Comm, Videotape version.

Phantom Ship, The. Orig. Title: Mystery of the Mary Celeste, The. Bela Lugosi & Shirley Grey. Directed by Denison Clift. 1937. Guaranteed. 70 min. Sound. 16mm B&W. *Rental:* Budget Films, Em Gee Film Lib & Newman Film Lib. *Rental:* Ivy Films. *Sale:* Blackhawk Films & Ivy Films, Super 8 sound version.

Phantom Speaks, The. Richard Arlen & Lynne Roberts. Directed by John English. 1945. Republic. 54 min. Sound. 16mm B&W. *Rental:* Ivy Films. *Sale:* Rep Pic Film.

Phantom Stallion, The. Rex Allen. Directed by Harry Keller. 1953. Republic. 54 min. Sound. 16mm B&W. *Rental:* Ivy Films. *Sale:* Rep Pic Film.

Phantom Thunderbolt, The. Ken Maynard. Directed by Alan James. 1933. World Wide. 60 min. Sound. 16mm B&W. *Sale:* Cinema Concepts & Reel Images.

Phantom Tollbooth, The. Directed by Chuck Jones & Abe Levitov. 1970. MGM. (Animated). 90 min. Sound. 16mm Color. *Rental:* MGM United. *Rental:* MGM United, Videotape version.

Phase Four. Nigel Davenport. Directed by Saul Bass. 1974. Paramount. 86 min. Sound. 16mm Color. *Rental:* Films Inc.

Phedre. Marie Bell. Directed by Pierre Jourdan. 1968. France. 92 min. Sound. 16mm Color. subtitles. *Rental:* Films Inc.

Phenix City Story, The. John McIntyre & Kathryn Grant. Directed by Phil Karlson. 1955. Allied Artists. 100 min. Sound. 16mm B&W. *Rental:* Hurlock Cine.

Phenomena of Roots, The. Directed by Robert Guenette. 1978. Wolper. (Documentary). 52 min. Sound. 16mm Color. *Rental:* Films Inc. *Sale:* Films Inc.

Phffft. Judy Holliday & Jack Lemmon. Directed by Mark Robson. 1954. 91 min. Sound. 16mm B&W. *Rental:* Kit Parker.

Philadelphia Story, The. Cary Grant, Katharine Hepburn & James Stewart. Directed by George Cukor. 1940. MGM. 112 min. Sound. 16mm B&W. *Rental:* MGM United. *Rental:* MGM United, Videotape version.

Philip Guston. Directed by Michael Blackwood. 58 min. 16mm *Rental:* Blackwood. *Sale:* Blackwood.

Philippines, The. Directed by Arch Nicholson. 1976. Australia. 53 min. Sound. 16mm Color. *Rental:* Aust Info Serv.

Philo Vance Returns. Orig. Title: Infamous Crimes. William Wright & Terry Austin. Directed by William Beaudine. 1947. PRC. 64 min. Sound. 16mm B&W. *Sale:* Classics Assoc NY.

Philo Vance's Gamble. Alan Curtis & Terry Austin. Directed by Basil Wrangell. 1947. PRC. 62 min. Sound. 16mm B&W. *Sale:* Classics Assoc NY.

Philo Vance's Secret Mission. Alan Curtis & Sheila Ryan. Directed by Reginald Le Borg. 1947. PRC. 58 min. Sound. 16mm B&W. *Sale:* Classics Assoc NY.

Philosophy & Faith. 1977. Films Inc. (Documentary). 60 min. Videotape Color. *Sale:* Films Inc.

Philosophy & Moral Values. 1977. Films Inc. (Documentary). 60 min. Videotape Color. *Sale:* Films Inc.

Philosophy: Eastern-Western Consciousness. 1977. Films Inc. (Documentary). 60 min. Videotape Color. *Sale:* Films Inc.

Phoelix. Directed by Anna Ambrose. 1979. Britain. (Cast unlisted). 47 min. Sound. 16mm Color. *Rental:* Museum Mod Art.

Phoenix, The. Tatsuya Nakadai & Tomisaburo Wayakema. Directed by Kon Ichikawa. 1978. Japan. 137 min. Sound. Videotape Color. *Sale:* Tamarelles French Films.

Phone Call from a Stranger. Shelley Winters & Bette Davis. Directed by Jean Negulesco. 1952. Fox. 96 min. Sound. 16mm B&W. *Rental:* Films Inc.

Phoney American, The. William Bendix & Christine Kaufman. Directed by Akos Von Rathony. 1959. Signal. 72 min. Sound. 16mm B&W. *Rental:* Willoughby Peer.

Photographers, The. 1970. Time-Life. (Documentary). 52 min. Sound. 16mm Color. *Rental:* OK AV Ctr & Time-Life Multimedia. *Sale:* Time-Life Multimedia.

Photographers of the American Frontier: 1860-1880. Directed by Ray Witlin. 1979. Blackwood. (Documentary). 58 min. Sound. 16mm Color. *Rental:* Blackwood Films. *Sale:* Blackwood Films.

Photography. Directed by Pal Zolnay. 1973. Hungary. (Cast unlisted). 82 min. Sound. 16mm B&W. subtitles. *Rental:* Films Inc.

Physical Principles of Radiological Safety. 1952. Atomic Energy Commission. (Documentary). 51 min. Sound. 16mm B&W. *Rental:* Natl AV Ctr.

Physics of Underwater Sound. 3 pts. Canada. (Documentary). 56 min. Sound. 16mm B&W. *Rental:* Natl Film CN. *Sale:* Natl Film CN.

Piaf - the Early Years. Brigitte Ariel & Pascale Christophe. Directed by Guy Casaril. Fr. 1982. Fox. 104 min. Sound. 16mm Color. subtitles. *Rental:* Films Inc.

Picasso. 1954. API. (Documentary). 50 min. Sound. 16mm Color. *Rental:* McGraw-Hill Films & U Mich Media.

Picasso. 1972. Britain. (Documentary). 60 min. Sound. 16mm Color. *Rental:* Time-Life Multimedia. *Sale:* Time-Life Multimedia.

Picasso: A Painter's Diary. Directed by Perry Miller Adato. 1980. WNET. (Documentary). 94 min. Sound. 16mm Color. *Sale:* Perspect Film & Syracuse U Film. *Sale:* Perspect Film, Videotape version. *Sale:* Perspect Film, Videocassette version.

Picasso Is Ninety. 1971. CBS. (Documentary). 51 min. Sound. 16mm Color. *Rental:* Budget Films, Iowa Films, Kit Parker & U Mich Media. *Sale:* Carousel Films.

Picasso: War, Peace & Love. 1972. Museum Without Walls. (Documentary). 51 min. Sound. 16mm Color. *Rental:* U Mich Media.

Piccadilly. Anna May Wong, Gilda Gray, Charles Laughton & Cyril Ritchard. Directed by E. A. Dupont. 1929. Britain. 80 min. Silent. 16mm B&W. *Rental:* Em Gee Film Lib. *Sale:* Cinema Concepts, Silent 8mm version.

Piccadilly Jim. Robert Montgomery & Frank Morgan. Directed by Robert Z. Leonard. 1936. MGM. 97 min. Sound. 16mm B&W. *Rental:* MGM United.

Piccadilly Third Stop. Mai Zetterling & Terence Morgan. Directed by Wolf Rilla. 1960. Britain. 90 min. Sound. 16mm B&W. *Rental:* Liberty Co.

Pickpocket. Martin Lassalle. Directed by Robert Bresson. Fr. 1958. France. 75 min. Sound. 16mm B&W. subtitles. *Rental:* New Yorker Films.

Pickup. Beverly Michaels & Hugo Haas. Directed by Hugo Haas. 1951. Columbia. 78 min. Sound. 16mm B&W. *Rental:* Films Inc & Kit Parker.

Pickup Alley. Victor Mature. Directed by Trevor Howard & John Gilling. 1957. Britain. 76 min. Sound. 16mm B&W. *Rental:* Kit Parker.

Pickup on One Hundred One. Martin Sheen & Jack Albertson. Directed by John Florea. 1972. American International. 93 min. Sound. 16mm Color. *Rental:* Swank Motion.

Pickup on South Street. Richard Widmark & Jean Peters. Directed by Samuel Fuller. 1953. Fox. 80 min. Sound. 16mm B&W. *Rental:* Films Inc & Willoughby Peer.

Pickwick Papers. James Donald & Hermione Gingold. Directed by Noel Langley. 1950. Britain. 109 min. Sound. 16mm B&W. *Rental:* Budget Films, Kit Parker, Maljack, Roas Films, Video Comm, Westcoast Films & Wholesome Film Ctr. *Lease:* Video Comm. *Sale:* Cinema Concepts & Reel Images. *Rental:* Video Comm, *Lease:* Video Comm, Videotape version.

Picnic. William Holden & Kim Novak. Directed by Joshua Logan. 1956. Columbia. 115 min. Sound. 16mm Color. *Rental:* Arcus Film, Budget Films, Bosco Films, Charard Motion Pics, Film Ctr DC, Films Inc, Modern Sound, Natl Film Video, Swank Motion, Twyman Films, U of IL Film, Welling Motion Pictures, Wholesome Film Ctr & Willoughby Peer. *Rental:* Corinth Films & Kit Parker, Anamorphic version.

Picnic. Janine Gray, Glyn Houston & Dyson Lovell. 81 min. Sound. 16mm B&W. *Rental:* Bosco Films.

Picnic at Hanging Rock. Rachel Roberts & Dominic Guard. Directed by Peter Weir. 1975. Australia. 110 min. Sound. 16mm Color. *Rental:* Films Inc, Videotape version.

Picnic on the Grass. Paul Meurisse. Directed by Jean Renoir. Fr. 1959. France. 92 min. Sound. 16mm Color. subtitles. *Rental:* Corinth Films. *Lease:* Corinth Films.

Picture, The. Jacques Aubuchon. Directed by Lucian Peritelli. 1972. PBS. 58 min. Sound. 16mm Color. *Rental:* Grove. *Sale:* Grove.

Picture Mommy Dead. Don Ameche & Martha Hyer. Directed by Bert I. Gordon. 1966. Embassy. 88 min. Sound. 16mm Color. *Rental:* Films Inc.

Picture of Dorian Gray, The. Orig. Title: Dorian Gray. Hurd Hatfield & Angela Lansbury. Directed by Albert Lewin. 1945. MGM. 111 min. Sound. 16mm B&W. *Rental:* Films Inc & MGM United.

Picture Show Man, The. Rod Taylor, John Meillon & Patrick Cargill. 86 min. Sound. 16mm Color. *Rental:* Welling Motion Pictures.

Picture Snatcher, The. James Cagney & Ralph Bellamy. Directed by Lloyd Bacon. 1933. Warners. 77 min. Sound. 16mm B&W. *Rental:* MGM United.

Pictures That Moved, The. 45 min. 16mm B&W. *Rental:* Aust Info Serv.

Piece of Pleasure, A. Trans. Title: Partie de Plaisir, Une. Paul Gegauff & Daniella Gegauff. Directed by Claude Chabrol. Fr. 1976. France. 90 min. Sound. 16mm Color. subtitles. *Rental:* J Green Pics. *Sale:* Tamarelles French Film, Videotape version.

Piece of the Action, A. Sidney Poitier, Bill Cosby & James Earl Jones. Directed by Sidney Poitier. 1977. Warners. 133 min. Sound. 16mm Color. *Rental:* Swank Motion.

Piece of the Cake, A. 1969. NET. (Documentary). 58 min. Sound. 16mm B&W. *Rental:* Indiana AV Ctr. *Sale:* Indiana AV Ctr.

Pieces of Dreams. Robert Forster & Lauren Hutton. Directed by Daniel Haller. 1970. MGM. 100 min. Sound. 16mm Color. *Rental:* MGM United.

Pieces of Eight. 1973. American National. (Documentary). 85 min. Sound. 16mm Color. *Rental:* Video Comm.

Pied Piper, The. Monty Woolley & Anne Baxter. Directed by Irving Pichel. 1942. Fox. 87 min. Sound. 16mm B&W. *Rental:* Films Inc.

Pied Piper, The. Donovan. Directed by Jacques Demy. 1971. Paramount. 90 min. Sound. 16mm Color. *Rental:* Films Inc.

Pied Piper of Hamelin, The. Van Johnson & Claude Rains. Directed by Hal Stanley. 1957. Hal Stanley. 90 min. Sound. 16mm Color. *Rental:* Modern Sound, Welling Motion Pictures & Westcoast Films.

Pier Five Havana. Cameron Mitchell & Allison Hayes. Directed by Edward L. Cahn. 1959. United Artists. 67 min. Sound. 16mm B&W. *Rental:* MGM United.

Pier Thirteen *see* Me & My Gal.

Pier Twenty-Three. Hugh Beaumont & Richard Travis. Directed by William Berke. 1951. Lippert. 58 min. Sound. 16mm B&W. *Rental:* Mogulls Films.

Pierre of the Plains. John Carroll & Ruth Hussey. Directed by George B. Seitz. 1942. MGM. 66 min. Sound. 16mm B&W. *Rental:* MGM United.

Pig Pen. Trans. Title: Porcile. Jean-Pierre Leaud & Pierre Clementi. Directed by Pier Paolo Pasolini. Ital. 1972. New Line. 120 min. Sound. 16mm Color. subtitles. *Rental:* New Cinema & New Line Cinema. *Sale:* New Line Cinema.

Pigeon That Took Rome, The. Charlton Heston & Elsa Martinelli. Directed by Melville Shavelson. 1962. Paramount. 101 min. Sound. 16mm B&W. *Rental:* Films Inc.

Pigeon That Worked a Miracle, The. Directed by Walter Perkins. 1962. Disney. (Cast unlisted). 47 min. Sound. 16mm Color. *Rental:* Buchan Pic, Cine Craft, Disney Prod, Film Ctr DC, Films Inc, Iowa Films, Modern Sound, Roas Films, Syracuse U Film & U Mich Media.

Pigs vs. Freaks. Tony Randall & Eugene Roche. Directed by Dick Lowry. 1980. CBS. 105 min. Sound. 16mm Color. *Rental:* Twyman Films.

Pigskin Parade. Stuart Erwin & Patsy Kelly. Directed by David Butler. 1936. Fox. 95 min. Sound. 16mm B&W. *Rental:* Films Inc.

Pilgrim Adventure, The. 1964. ABC. (Documentary). 54 min. Sound. 16mm Color. *Rental:* McGraw-Hill Films, Syracuse U Film & U Of IL Film. *Sale:* McGraw-Hill Films, Syracuse U Film & U of IL Film.

Pilgrim Farewell. 1982. Films Inc.. (Cast unlisted). 110 min. Videotape Color. *Rental:* Films Inc. *Sale:* Films Inc.

Pilgrim Lady, The. Lynne Roberts & Alan Mowbray. Directed by Lesley Selander. 1947. Republic. 67 min. Sound. 16mm B&W. *Rental:* Ivy Films. *Sale:* Rep Pic Film.

Pilgrimage. Henrietta Crossman & Heather Angel. Directed by John Ford. 1933. Fox. 90 min. Sound. 16mm B&W. *Rental:* Films Inc.

Pilgrimage for Peace. 1965. Italy. (Documentary). 56 min. Sound. 16mm Color. narrated Eng. *Rental:* Films Inc.

Pilgrimage Play, The: The Life of Christ. Nelson Leigh. Directed by Frank Starger. 1951. 90 min. Sound. 16mm Color. *Rental:* Budget Films.

Pill for the People, A. 1977. 58 min. Sound. Videotape Color. *Rental:* PBS Video. *Sale:* PBS Video.

Pillar of Fire. Michael Shillo. Directed by Larry Frisch. 1963. Geva. 76 min. Sound. 16mm B&W. dubbed. *Rental:* Ivy Films.

Pillars of the Sky. Jeff Chandler & Dorothy Malone. Directed by George Marshall. 1956. Universal. 95 min. Sound. 16mm Color. *Rental:* Swank Motion.

Pillow Talk. Doris Day & Rock Hudson. Directed by Michael Gordon. 1959. Universal. 110 min. Sound. 16mm Color. *Rental:* Williams Films. *Rental:* Williams Films, Anamorphic version.

Pillow to Post. Ida Lupino & William Prince. Directed by Vincent Sherman. 1945. Warners. 96 min. Sound. 16mm B&W. *Rental:* MGM United.

Pilobolus. 1980. WNET. (Dance). 60 min. Sound. 16mm Color. *Rental:* Films Inc. *Sale:* Films Inc, Videotape version.

Pilobolus & Joan. 1973. WNET. (Ballet). 58 min. Videotape Color. *Sale:* Electro Art.

Pilobolus Dance Theater. 1976. WNET. (Documentary). 58 min. Videotape Color. *Rental:* WNET Media. *Sale:* WNET Media.

Pilot X. Orig. Title: Death in the Air. John Carroll & Lona Andre. Directed by Elmer Clifton. 1937. Puritan. 70 min. Sound. 16mm B&W. *Rental:* Mogulls Films.

Pimpernell Smith. Orig. Title: Mister V. Leslie Howard & Mary Morris. Directed by Leslie Howard. 1942. Britain. 121 min. Sound. 16mm B&W. *Rental:* Ivy Films. *Sale:* Rep Pic Film.

Pin Up Girl. Betty Grable, Joe E. Brown & Martha Raye. Directed by Bruce Humberstone. 1944. Fox. 83 min. Sound. 16mm Color. *Rental:* Films Inc.

Pinball Summer. Michael Zelniker & Carl Murotte. Directed by George Mikhalka. 1981. Canada. 92 min. Sound. 16mm Color. *Rental:* Williams Films.

Pincers: Aug. 1944 - March 1945. Directed by Hugh Raggett. (World at War Ser.). : Pt. 19.). 1973. Media Guild. (Documentary). 52 min. Sound. 16mm Color. *Rental:* Media Guild & U Cal Media. *Sale:* Media Guild. *Sale:* Media Guild, Videotape version.

Pinch Hitter, The. Charles Ray & Glen Hunter. Directed by Joseph Henabery. 1925. Associated Exhibitors. 50 min. Silent 16mm B&W. *Sale:* E Finney.

Pinch Hitter, The. Charles Ray & Sylvia Breamer. Directed by Victor Schertzinger. 1917. Triangle. 40 min. Silent. 16mm B&W. *Rental:* Budget Films, Em Gee Film Lib & Film Images.

Pinchcliffe Grand Prix, The. 1981. Clem William. (Animated). 78 min. Sound. 16mm Color. *Rental:* Williams Films.

Pink Angels, The. John Alderman. Directed by Lawrence Brown. 1971. Crown. 81 min. Sound. 16mm Color. *Rental:* Video Comm. *Lease:* Video Comm. *Rental:* Video Comm, *Lease:* Video Comm, Videotape version.

Pink Flamingos. Divine. Directed by John Waters. 1971. Saliva. 95 min. Sound. 16mm Color. *Rental:* New Line Cinema. *Sale:* New Line Cinema.

Pink Floyd. Directed by Adrian Maben. 1974. April Fools. (Documentary). 85 min. Sound. 16mm Color. *Rental:* B Raymond, Twyman Films & Westcoast Films.

Pink Floyd: The Wall. Directed by Alan Parker. 1982. MGM. (Experimental). 95 min. Sound. 16mm Color. *Rental:* MGM United. *Rental:* MGM United, Videotape version.

Pink Jungle, The. James Garner & George Kennedy. Directed by Delbert Mann. 1968. Universal. 104 min. Sound. 16mm Color. *Rental:* Swank Motion.

Pink Panther, The. Peter Sellers, Capucine & Claudia Cardinale. Directed by Blake Edwards. 1964. MGM. 113 min. Sound. 16mm Color. *Rental:* MGM United. *Rental:* MGM United, Videotape version.

Pink Panther Strikes Again, The. Peter Sellers & Herbert Lom. Directed by Blake Edwards. 1977. United Artists. 110 min. Sound. 16mm Color. *Rental:* Budget Films, Films Inc, MGM United, Swank Motion, Twyman Films & Welling Motion Pictures. *Rental:* MGM United, Anamorphic version. *Rental:* MGM United, Videotape version.

Pink Strings & Sealing Wax. Mervyn Johns & Googie Withers. Directed by Robert Hamer. 1950. Britain. 95 min. Sound. 16mm B&W. *Rental:* Film Classics.

Pinks & the Blues, The. 1980. WGBH. (Documentary). 57 min. Sound. 16mm Color. *Rental:* Iowa Films & U Cal Media, Videotape version.

Pinky. Jeanne Crain, Ethel Barrymore & Ethel Waters. Directed by Elia Kazan. 1949. Fox. 102 min. Sound. 16mm B&W. *Rental:* Films Inc.

Pinocchio. Directed by Ben Sharpsteen & Luske Hamilton. 1940. Disney. (Animated). 88 min. Sound. 16mm Color. *Rental:* Buchan Pic & Disney Prod.

Pinocchio. Alfred Muller. Directed by Walter Beck. 1967. Childhood. 70 min. Sound. 16mm Color. dubbed. *Rental:* Film Classics, Films Inc, Macmillan Films, Roas Films, Syracuse U Film, Video Comm & Wholesome Film Ctr. *Lease:* Macmillan Films.

Pinocchio in Outer Space. Directed by Ray Goossens. 1965. Universal. (Animated). 72 min. Sound. 16mm Color. *Rental:* Williams Films & Twyman Films.

Pinocchio's Birthday Party. 1974. (Anthology). 83 min. Sound. 16mm Color. *Rental:* Films Inc.

Pinocchio's Storybook Adventures. Directed by Ron Merk. 1979. First American. (Animated). 80 min. Sound. 16mm Color. *Rental:* Budget Films & Modern Sound. *Rental:* Westcoast Films, 90 mins. version.

Pinter People. Directed by Gerald Potterton. 1969. Grove Press. (Animated). 58 min. Sound. 16mm Color. *Rental:* Budget Films & Grove. *Sale:* Grove. *Rental:* Budget Films, 65 mins. version.

Pinto Bandit, The. Dave O'Brien. Directed by Elmer Clifton. 1944. PRC. 57 min. Sound. 16mm B&W. *Rental:* Mogulls Films.

Pinto Rustlers. Tom Tyler. Directed by Bernard B. Ray. 1936. Reliable. 60 min. Sound. 16mm B&W. *Rental:* Mogulls Films. *Sale:* Cinema Concepts & Reel Images.

Pioneer Builders. Ann Harding & Richard Dix. 1940. RKO. 86 min. Sound. 16mm B&W. *Rental:* RKO General Pics.

Pioneer Days. Jack Randall. Directed by Harry S. Webb. 1940. Monogram. 55 min. Sound. 16mm B&W. *Rental:* Hurlock Cine. *Sale:* Cinema Concepts & Reel Images.

Pioneer Justice. Lash LaRue & Al St. John. Directed by Ray Taylor. 1947. PRC. 54 min. Sound. 16mm B&W. *Sale:* Classics Assoc NY.

Pioneer Marshall. Monte Hale. Directed by Philip Ford. 1949. Republic. 60 min. Sound. 16mm B&W. *Rental:* Ivy Films. *Sale:* Rep Pic Film.

Pioneers, The. Tex Ritter. Directed by Al Herman. 1941. Monogram. 55 min. Sound. 16mm B&W. *Rental:* Hurlock Cine.

Pioneers, The. Directed by Christian Blackwood. 1977. Blackwood. (Documentary). 58 min. Sound. 16mm Color. *Rental:* Blackwood Films. *Lease:* Blackwood Films.

Pioneers of the West. Robert Livingston. Directed by Lester Orlebeck. 1940. Republic. 54 min. Sound. 16mm B&W. *Rental:* Ivy Films. *Sale:* Rep Pic Film.

Pipe Dreams. Gladys Knight. Directed by Stephen F. Verona. 1976. Embassy. 91 min. Sound. 16mm Color. *Rental:* Films Inc.

Pippi Goes on Board. Inger Nilsson. Directed by Olle Hellblom. 1975. Sweden. 84 min. Sound. 16mm Color. dubbed. *Rental:* Films Inc, Macmillan Films, Modern Sound & Williams Films. *Lease:* Macmillan Films.

Pippi in the South Seas. Inger Nilsson. Directed by Olle Hellblom. 1974. Sweden. 85 min. Sound. 16mm Color. dubbed. *Rental:* Films Inc, Macmillan Films, Modern Sound & Williams Films. *Lease:* Macmillan Films.

Pippi Longstocking. Inger Nilsson. Directed by Olle Hellblom. 1974. Sweden. 95 min. Sound. 16mm Color. dubbed. *Rental:* Films Inc, Macmillan Films, Modern Sound & Williams Films. *Lease:* Macmillan Films.

Pippi on the Run. Inger Nilsson. Directed by Olle Hellblom. 1973. Sweden. 97 min. Sound. 16mm Color. dubbed. *Rental:* Williams Films, Films Inc, Macmillan Films & Modern Sound. *Lease:* Macmillan Films.

Pippin. Ben Vereen & William Katt. Directed by David Sheehan. 1981. MGM. 108 min. Sound. 16mm Color. *Rental:* MGM United. *Rental:* MGM United, Videotape version.

Piranas, Las. Julio Aleman. Directed by Francisco Del Villar. Mexico. 97 min. Sound. 16mm Color. dubbed. *Rental:* Westcoast Films.

Piranha. Bradford Dillman & Kevin McCarthy. Directed by Joe Dante. 1978. New World. 92 min. Sound. 16mm Color. *Rental:* Films Inc.

Piranha, Piranha. Peter Brown & William Smith. 1972. American National. 96 min. Sound. 16mm Color. *Rental:* Video Comm. *Lease:* Video Comm. *Rental:* Video Comm, *Lease:* Video Comm, Videotape version.

Pirate, The. Judy Garland & Gene Kelly. Directed by Vincente Minnelli. 1948. MGM. 102 min. Sound. 16mm Color. *Rental:* MGM United. *Rental:* MGM United, Videotape version.

Pirate Movie, The. Kristy McNichol & Christopher Atkins. Directed by Ken Annakin. 1982. Fox. 100 min. Sound. 16mm Color. *Rental:* Films Inc.

Pirates of Blood River. Kerwin Matthews & Glenn Corbett. Directed by John Gilling. 1962. Britain. 87 min. Sound. 16mm Color. *Rental:* Charard Motion Pics, Films Inc & Film Ctr DC.

Pirates of Capri. Orig. Title: Captain Sirocco. Louis Hayward & Alan Curtis. Directed by Edgar G. Ulmer. 1949. Film Classics. 94 min. Sound. 16mm B&W. *Rental:* Buchan Pic & Mogulls Films.

Pirates of Penzance, The. 1974. Britain. (Operetta). 52 min. Sound. 16mm Color. *Rental:* B Raymond. *Sale:* B Raymond. *Sale:* B Raymond, Videotape version.

Pirates of Penzance, The. Kevin Kline & Angela Lansbury. Directed by Wilford Leach. 1983. Universal. 102 min. Sound. 16mm Color. *Rental:* Swank Motion. *Rental:* Swank Motion, Videotape version.

Pirates of the Prairie. Tim Holt & Cliff Edwards. Directed by Bert Gilroy. 1943. RKO. 57 min. Sound. 16mm *Rental:* RKO General Pics.

Pirates of Tripoli. Paul Henreid & Patricia Medina. Directed by Felix Feist. 1955. Columbia. 72 min. Sound. 16mm Color. *Rental:* Modern Sound.

Pirates on Horseback. William Boyd. Directed by Lesley Selander. 1941. Paramount. 54 min. Sound. 16mm B&W. *Sale:* Cinema Concepts.

Piri Knows Everything *see* Piri Mindent Tud.

Piri Mindent Tud. Trans. Title: Piri Knows Everything. Dajka Margit. Hungarian. Hungary. 80 min. Sound. 16mm B&W. subtitles. *Rental:* Mogulls Films.

Pirosmani. Avtandil Varazi & David Abashidze. Directed by Georgy Shengelaya. Rus. 1970. 85 min. Sound. 16mm Color. subtitles. *Rental:* Films Inc.

Pistol for Ringo, A. Montgomery Wood. Directed by Duccio Tessari. 1966. Embassy. 97 min. Sound. 16mm Color. dubbed. *Rental:* Films Inc.

Pistol Harvest. Tim Holt & Joan Dixon. Directed by Lesley Selander. 1952. RKO. 60 min. Sound. 16mm *Rental:* RKO General Pics.

Pistol Packin' Mama. Robert Livingston. Directed by Frank Woodruff. 1943. Republic. 64 min. Sound. 16mm B&W. *Rental:* Ivy Films. *Sale:* Rep Pic Film.

Pit & the Pendulum, The. Vincent Price & John Kerr. Directed by Roger Corman. 1961. American International. 85 min. Sound. 16mm Color. *Rental:* Arcus Film, Budget Films, Cine Craft, Film Ctr DC, Films Inc, Ivy Films, Twyman Films, Video Comm, Westcoast Films, Welling Motion Pictures, Wholesome Film Ctr, Williams Films & Willoughby Peer.

Pit of Loneliness, The. Edwige Feuillere & Simone Simon. Directed by Jacqueline Audry. Fr. 1954. France. 88 min. Sound. 16mm B&W. subtitles. *Rental:* Film Classics. *Rental:* Film Classics, Videotape version.

Pitfall. Dick Powell & Lizabeth Scott. Directed by Andre De Toth. 1948. MGM. 88 min. Sound. 16mm B&W. *Rental:* Ivy Films.

Pittsburgh. Marlene Dietrich & John Wayne. Directed by Lewis Seiler. 1942. Universal. 90 min. Sound. 16mm B&W. *Rental:* Swank Motion.

Pittsburgh Kid, The. Billy Conn & Jean Parker. Directed by Jack Townley. 1942. Republic. 76 min. Sound. 16mm B&W. *Rental:* Ivy Films.

Pixote. Marilia Pera & Jorge Juliao. Directed by Hector Babenco. Port. 1981. Brazil. 127 min. Sound. 16mm Color. *Rental:* New Yorker Films.

Place Called Glory, A. Orig. Title: Hell of Manitoba. Lex Barker. Directed by Sheldon Reynolds. 1966. Embassy. 92 min. Sound. 16mm Color. dubbed. *Rental:* Films Inc.

Place for Lovers, A. Marcelo Mastroianni & Faye Dunaway. Directed by Vittorio De Sica. 1969. MGM. 90 min. Sound. 16mm Color. *Rental:* MGM United.

Place for No Story, A. 1979. PBS. (Documentary). 59 min. Videotape Color. *Rental:* PBS Video. *Sale:* PBS Video.

Place in the Sun, A. Montgomery Clift, Elizabeth Taylor & Shelley Winters. Directed by George Stevens. 1951. Paramount. 120 min. Sound. 16mm B&W. *Rental:* Films Inc.

Place in the Sun, A. (Destination America Ser.). 1976. Media Guild. (Documentary). 52 min. Sound. 16mm Color. *Rental:* Media Guild. *Sale:* Media Guild. *Sale:* Media Guild, Videotape version.

Place of Dreams, A: The National Air & Space Museum. Directed by Peter S. Vogt. 1980. Learning Corp.. (Documentary). 59 min. Sound. 16mm Color. *Rental:* Learning Corp Am. *Sale:* Learning Corp Am. *Sale:* Learning Corp Am, Videotape version.

Place of One's Own, A. James Mason & Margaret Lockwood. Directed by Bernard Knowles. 1944. Britain. 91 min. Sound. 16mm B&W. *Rental:* Kit Parker.

Place to Be, A. 1979. PBS. (Documentary). 60 min. Videotape Color. *Rental:* PBS Video. *Sale:* PBS Video.

Plague of the Zombies. Andre Morell & Diane Clare. Directed by John Gilling. 1966. Britain. 90 min. Sound. 16mm Color. *Rental:* Films Inc.

Plague on Your Children, A. 1968. Britain. (Documentary). 72 min. Sound. 16mm B&W. *Rental:* Time-Life Multimedia. *Sale:* Time-Life Multimedia.

Plainsman, The. Gary Cooper & Jean Arthur. Directed by Cecil B. DeMille. 1936. Paramount. 113 min. Sound. 16mm B&W. *Rental:* Swank Motion & Williams Films.

Plainsman, The. Don Murray, Guy Stockwell & Abby Dalton. Directed by David Lowell Rich. 1966. Universal. 92 min. Sound. 16mm Color. *Rental:* Williams Films.

Plainsman & the Lady, The. Bill Elliott & Gail Patrick. Directed by Joseph Kane. 1946. Republic. 84 min. Sound. 16mm B&W. *Rental:* Ivy Films. *Sale:* Nostalgia Merchant.

Plaisir, Le. Danielle Darrieux & Claude Dauphin. Directed by Max Ophuls. Fr. 1951. France. 95 min. Sound. 16mm B&W. subtitles. *Rental:* Budget Films, Corinth Films, Images Film & Kit Parker. *Sale:* Festival Films, Glenn Photo, Natl Cinema, Reel Images & Images Film. *Sale:* Festival Films, Images Film & Tamarelles French Film, Videotape version.

Plan Nine from Outer Space. Orig. Title: Grave Robbers from Outer Space. Bela Lugosi & Vampira. Directed by Edward D. Wood Jr. 1956. Britain. 79 min. Sound. 16mm B&W. *Rental:* Budget Films, Films Inc, Ivy Films, Kit Parker & Video Comm. *Lease:* Video Comm. *Rental:* Video Comm, *Lease:* Video Comm. Videotape version.

Planet of Blood. Orig. Title: Queen of Blood. John Saxon, Basil Rathbone & Dennis Hopper. Directed by Curtis Harrington. 1966. American International. 81 min. Sound. 16mm Color. *Rental:* Budget Films & Films Inc.

Planet of Storms *see* Voyage to the Planet of Pre-Historic Women.

Planet of the Apes. Charlton Heston & Maurice Evans. Directed by Franklin Schaffner. 1968. Fox. (Anamorphic). 112 min. Sound. 16mm Color. *Rental:* Films Inc. *Rental:* Films Inc, Videotape version.

Planet of the Vampires. Orig. Title: Demon Planet, The. Barry Sullivan. Directed by Mario Bava. 1965. American International. 86 min. Sound. 16mm Color. dubbed. *Rental:* Films Inc.

Planet on the Prowl. Jack Stuart & Amber Collins. Directed by Antonio Margheriti. 1965. Italy. 80 min. Sound. 16mm Color. dubbed. *Rental:* Films Inc. *Rental:* Ivy Films, *Sale:* Ivy Films, Super 8 sound version.

Planet Outlaws. Buster Crabbe & Constance Moore. Directed by Ford Beebe & Saul A. Goodkind. 1939. Universal. 85 min. Sound. 16mm B&W. *Rental:* Em Gee Film Lib & Wholesome Film Ctr. *Sale:* Reel Images. *Sale:* Morcraft Films & Reel Images, Super 8 sound version. *Sale:* Reel Images, Videotape version.

Planets, The. 1976. Nova. (Documentary). 52 min. Sound. 16mm Color. *Rental:* Films Inc & U of IL Film. *Sale:* Films Inc. *Rental:* Films Inc, *Sale:* Films Inc, Videotape version.

Planets Against Us. Jany Clair & Michele Lemoin. 1961. France. 83 min. Sound. Super 8 B&W. dubbed. *Rental:* Ivy Films. *Sale:* Ivy Films.

Planets Nova, The. 1978. Britain. 52 min. Sound. 16mm Color. *Rental:* Syracuse U Film.

Plantation Boy. Trans. Title: Menino De Engenho. Savio Rolin. Directed by Walter Lima. Port. 1965. Brazil. 90 min. Sound. 16mm B&W. subtitles. *Rental:* New Yorker Films.

Plastic Prison. 1977. 58 min. Sound. Videotape *Rental:* PBS Video. *Sale:* PBS Video.

Plate Tectonics Theory. 1972. 58 min. Sound. 16mm Color. *Rental:* Iowa Films.

Platinum Blonde. Jean Harlow. Directed by Frank Capra. 1931. Columbia. 90 min. Sound. 16mm B&W. *Rental:* Budget Films, Films Inc, Inst Cinema, Kit Parker, Modern Sound, Swank Motion, Twyman Films, Westcoast Films, Welling Motion Pictures, Wholesome Film Ctr & Williams Films.

Platinum High School. Mickey Rooney & Terry Moore. Directed by Charles Haas. 1960. MGM. 95 min. Sound. 16mm B&W. *Rental:* Budget Films & Rep Pic Film. *Lease:* Rep Pic Film.

Play & Personality. 1962. 45 min. Sound. 16mm B&W. *Rental:* U Mich Media.

Play Championship Basketball. 1950. (Documentary). 60 min. Sound. 16mm B&W. *Rental:* U of IL Film.

Play Dirty. Michael Caine & Nigel Green. Directed by Andre De Toth. 1969. United Artists. 117 min. Sound. 16mm Color. *Rental:* MGM United. *Rental:* MGM United, Anamorphic version.

Play for Keeps. 1952. Gospel. (Documentary). 47 min. Sound. 16mm Color. *Rental:* Roas Films.

Play Girl. Loretta Young & Norman Foster. Directed by Ray Enright. 1932. Warners. 61 min. Sound. 16mm B&W. *Rental:* MGM United.

Play Girl. Kay Francis & James Ellison. Directed by Frank Woodruff. 1941. RKO. 75 min. Sound. 16mm *Rental:* RKO General Pics.

Play in the Hospital. 1969. 50 min. Sound. 16mm Color. *Rental:* Iowa Films.

Play it Again, Sam. Woody Allen & Diane Keaton. Directed by Herbert Ross. 1972. Paramount. 86 min. Sound. 16mm Color. *Rental:* Films Inc.

Play It As It Lays. Tuesday Weld & Anthony Perkins. Directed by Frank Perry. 1972. Universal. 102 min. Sound. 16mm Color. *Rental:* Swank Motion.

Play Misty for Me. Clint Eastwood & Jessica Walter. Directed by Clint Eastwood. 1971. Universal. 102 min. Sound. 16mm Color. *Rental:* Swank Motion. *Rental:* Swank Motion, Videotape version.

Playboy & the Christian, The. 1966. CBS. (Documentary). 56 min. Sound. 16mm B&W. *Rental:* Mass Media. *Sale:* Carousel Films.

Playboy of the Western World, The. Siobhan McKenna & Gary Raymond. Directed by Brian Desmond-Hurst. 1963. Britain. 99 min. Sound. 16mm Color. *Rental:* Films Inc & Janus Films.

Players. Ali McGraw & Dean-Paul Martin. Directed by Anthony Harvey. 1979. Paramount. 120 min. Sound. 16mm Color. *Rental:* Films Inc.

Playground in the Sky. Directed by Carl Boenish. 1981. (Documentary). 83 min. Sound. 16mm Color. *Rental:* Kino Intl. *Lease:* Kino Intl.

Playing Around. Alice White & Chester Morris. Directed by Mervyn LeRoy. 1930. Warners. 66 min. Sound. 16mm B&W. *Rental:* MGM United.

Playing Dead. Sidney Drew, Mrs. Sidney Drew. 1915. Vitagraph. 50 min. Silent. 16mm B&W. *Sale:* Morcraft Films.

Playmates. Peter Lind Hayes & John Barrymore. Directed by David Butler. 1942. RKO. 96 min. Sound. 16mm *Rental:* RKO General Pics.

Playtime. Jacques Tati. Directed by Jacques Tati. 1972. France. 108 min. Sound. 16mm B&W. *Rental:* Films Inc, Images Film & U Cal Media.

Plaza Suite. Walter Matthau & Maureen Stapleton. Directed by Arthur Hiller. 1971. Paramount. 114 min. Sound. 16mm Color. *Rental:* Films Inc. *Sale:* Tamarelles French Film, Videotape version.

Please Believe Me. Deborah Kerr & Robert Walker. Directed by Norman Taurog. 1950. MGM. 87 min. Sound. 16mm B&W. *Rental:* MGM United.

Please Don't Eat the Daisies. Doris Day, David Niven & Janis Paige. Directed by Charles Walters. 1960. MGM. 111 min. Sound. 16mm Color. *Rental:* MGM United. *Rental:* MGM United, Anamorphic version.

Please, Sir! John Alderton. Directed by Mark Stuart. Britain. 101 min. Sound. 16mm B&W. *Rental:* Cinema Five.

Pleasure Doing Business, A. Conrad Bain, Phyllis Diller & Tom Smothers. Directed by Steven Vagnino. 1979. TCA. 110 min. Sound. 16mm Color. *Rental:* Twyman Films.

Pleasure Drugs: The Great American High. 1982. NBC. (Documentary). 52 min. Sound. 16mm Color. *Rental:* Films Inc & U Cal Media. *Sale:* Films Inc.

Pleasure Garden, The. Virginia Valli & Carmelita Geraghty. Directed by Alfred Hitchcock. 1925. Britain. 75 min. Silent. 16mm B&W. *Rental:* A Twyman Pres, Classic Film Mus & Twyman Films. *Sale:* Classic Film Mus.

Pleasure of His Company, The. Fred Astaire & Debbie Reynolds. Directed by George Seaton. 1961. Paramount. 114 min. Sound. 16mm Color. *Rental:* Films Inc.

Pleasure Seekers, The. Ann Margret & Tony Franciosa. Directed by Jean Negulesco. 1964. Fox. (Anamorphic). 107 min. Sound. 16mm Color. *Rental:* Films Inc.

Plimpton: At the Wheel. 1974. Wolper. (Documentary). 52 min. Sound. 16mm Color. *Sale:* Films Inc.

Plimpton: Shootout at Rio Lobo. 1974. Wolper. (Documentary). 52 min. Sound. 16mm Color. *Rental:* Kent St U Film. *Sale:* Texture Film.

Plimpton: The Great Quarterback Sneak. 1974. Wolper. (Documentary). 52 min. Sound. 16mm Color. *Rental:* Films Inc. *Sale:* Films Inc.

Plisetskaya Dances. Directed by Vassili Katanyan. 1964. Russia. (Documentary). 70 min. Sound. 16mm B&W. narrated Eng. *Rental:* Corinth Films & Syracuse U Film. *Lease:* Corinth Films. *Rental:* Corinth Films, *Lease:* Corinth Films, Videotape version.

Plot Against Hitler, The. 1964. CBS. (Documentary). 52 min. Sound. 16mm B&W. *Rental:* Macmillan Films. *Sale:* Macmillan Films.

Plot Thickens, The. James Gleason & ZaSu Pitts. Directed by Ben Holmes. 1936. RKO. 69 min. Sound. 16mm *Rental:* RKO General Pics.

Plot to Murder Hitler, The. 1974. Wolper. (Documentary). 52 min. Sound. 16mm B&W. *Rental:* Films Inc, U of IL Film & Utah Media. *Sale:* Films Inc. *Rental:* Films Inc, *Sale:* Films Inc, Color version.

Plotters, The. Orig. Title: Primitives, The. Jane Holden & Bill Edwards. Directed by Alfred Travers. 1966. Britain. 80 min. Sound. 16mm B&W. *Rental:* Ivy Films. *Sale:* Classics Assoc NY.

Plough & the Stars, The. Barbara Stanwyck & Preston Foster. Directed by John Ford. 1936. RKO. 66 min. Sound. 16mm B&W. *Rental:* Films Inc. *Lease:* Films Inc.

Plunder Road. Gene Raymond & Wayne Morris. Directed by Hubert Cornfield. 1957. Fox. (Anamorphic). 72 min. Sound. 16mm B&W. *Rental:* Budget Films, Ivy Films & Kit Parker. *Sale:* Rep Pic Film.

Plunderers, The. Rod Cameron & Ilona Massey. Directed by Joseph Kane. 1948. Republic. 87 min. Sound. 16mm B&W. *Rental:* Ivy Films. *Sale:* Rep Pic Film.

Plunderers, The. Jeff Chandler & John Saxon. Directed by Joseph Pevney. 1960. Allied Artists. 94 min. Sound. 16mm B&W. *Rental:* Hurlock Cine.

Plunderers of Painted Flats. Corinne Calvet & John Carroll. Directed by Albert C. Gannaway. 1959. Republic. (Anamorphic). 77 min. Sound. 16mm B&W. *Rental:* Ivy Films. *Sale:* Rep Pic Film.

Plutocrats, The. 1970. Britain. (Documentary). 51 min. Sound. 16mm Color. *Rental:* Time-Life Multimedia. *Sale:* Time-Life Multimedia.

Plutonium: An Element of Risk. 1979. PBS. (Documentary). 59 min. Videotape Color. *Rental:* PBS Video. *Sale:* PBS Video.

Plutonium Connection, The. 1976. Nova. (Documentary). 59 min. Sound. 16mm Color. *Rental:* U Cal Media, U of IL Film & U Mich Media, Videotape version.

Plymouth Adventure, The. Spencer Tracy & Gene Tierney. Directed by Clarence Brown. 1952. MGM. 105 min. Sound. 16mm Color. *Rental:* MGM United.

Po Zakonu *see* By the Law.

Poachers *see* Furtivos.

Pocatello Kid, The. Ken Maynard. Directed by Phil Rosen. 1931. Tiffany. 60 min. Videotape B&W. *Sale:* Video Comm.

Pocket Money. Paul Newman & Lee Marvin. Directed by Stuart Rosenberg. 1972. National General. 102 min. Sound. 16mm Color. *Rental:* Swank Motion, Twyman Films & Williams Films.

Pocketful of Miracles, A. Glenn Ford & Bette Davis. Directed by Frank Capra. 1961. United Artists. 136 min. Sound. 16mm Color. *Rental:* MGM United, Roas Films, Welling Motion Pictures & Wholesome Film Ctr.

Poco. Chill Wills & Clint Ritchie. 1977. Cinema Shares. 88 min. Sound. 16mm Color. *Rental:* Budget Films & Films Inc.

Poem of Dances, A. 1973. Corinth. (Dance). 68 min. Sound. 16mm Color. *Rental:* Corinth Films. *Rental:* Corinth Films, *Lease:* Corinth Films, Videotape version.

Poet, The. Directed by Pip Benveniste. 1969. Benveniste. 49 min. Sound. 16mm B&W. *Rental:* Canyon Cinema.

Poetry in Motion. Directed by Ron Mann. 1983. Alimi. (Concert). Sound. 16mm Color. *Rental:* First Run.

Poetry: In Search of Hart Crane *see* In Search of Hart Crane.

Poil de Carotte. Harry Baur & Louis Gauthier. Directed by Julien Duvivier. Fr. 1932. France. 100 min. Sound. 16mm B&W. subtitles. *Rental:* Budget Films & Kit Parker. *Sale:* Natl Cinema, Festival Films & Reel Images. *Sale:* Festival Films & Tamarelles French Film, Videotape version.

Point, The. Directed by Fred Wolf. 1970. ABC. (Animated). 75 min. Sound. 16mm Color. *Rental:* Budget Films, Cine Craft, Film Ctr DC, Films Inc, Inst Cinems, Macmillam Films, Modern Sound, Newman Film Lib, Roas Films, Twyman Films, Video Comm, Welling Motion Pictures, Westcoast Films, Wholesome Film Ctr & Willoughby Peer. *Lease:* Macmillan Films, Videotape version.

Point Blank! Lee Marvin & Angie Dickinson. Directed by John Boorman. 1967. MGM. 92 min. Sound. 16mm Color. *Rental:* MGM United. *Rental:* MGM United, Anamorphic version.

Point of Order. Directed by Emile De Antonio. 1964. Continental. (Documentary). 97 min. Sound. 16mm B&W. *Rental:* New Cinema & New Yorker Films. *Sale:* New Yorker Films.

Point of Terror. Peter Carpenter. Directed by Alex Nichol. 1971. Gold Key. 83 min. Sound. 16mm Color. *Rental:* Video Comm. *Lease:* Video Comm. *Rental:* Video Comm, *Lease:* Video Comm, Videotape version.

Poisoned Air, The. 1966. CBS. (Documentary). 50 min. Sound. 16mm B&W. *Rental:* Syracuse U Film. *Sale:* Carousel Films. *Sale:* Carousel Films, Color version.

Poisoning of Michigan, The. 1974. Canada. (Documentary). 65 min. Sound. 16mm Color. *Rental:* Media Guild & U of IL Film. *Sale:* Media Guild.

Poisons, Pests & People. 1961. Canada. (Documentary). 60 min. Sound. 16mm B&W. *Rental:* Natl Film CN. *Sale:* Natl Film CN.

Poitin. Cyril Cusack, Cyril Cusak, Donal McCann & Niall Toibin. Directed by Bob Quinn. 1978. Ireland. 65 min. Sound. 16mm Color. subtitles. *Rental:* Museum Mod Art.

Poland: Communism's New Look. 1965. NET. (Documentary). 60 min. Sound. 16mm B&W. *Rental:* Indiana AV Ctr. *Sale:* Indiana AV Ctr.

Poland on a Tightrope. 1959. CBS. (Documentary). 52 min. Sound. 16mm B&W. *Rental:* Macmillan Films. *Sale:* Macmillan Films.

Poland: The Will to Be. Directed by Albert C. Waller. 1979. Readers Digest. (Documentary). 58 min. Sound. 16mm Color. *Rental:* Pyramid Film & U Cal Media. *Sale:* Pyramid Film. *Sale:* Pyramid Film, *Rental:* Pyramid Film, Videotape version.

Polar Bear Alert. 59 min. Sound. 16mm Color. *Rental:* Natl Geog. *Sale:* Natl Geog. *Sale:* Natl Geog, Videotape version.

Polaris Submarine: Journal of an Undersea Voyage. 1963. Navy. (Documentary). 56 min. Sound. 16mm Color. *Rental:* Natl AV Ctr.

Poletown Lives! Directed by George L. Corsetti, Richard Wieske & Jeanie Wylie. 1983. Information Factory. 52 min. Sound. 16mm Color. *Rental:* New Day Films & U Mich Media. *Sale:* New Day Films.

Police, The. Fred Gwynne & Murray Hamilton. Directed by Fielder Cook. 1972. KCET. 58 min. Sound. 16mm Color. *Rental:* Grove. *Sale:* Grove.

Police Academy. Steve Guttenberg & Bubba Smith. Directed by Hugh Wilson. 1985. Warners. 101 min. Sound. 16mm Color. *Rental:* Swank Motion.

Police Dog. 1972. Handel. (Documentary). 50 min. Sound. 16mm Color. *Rental:* Syracuse U Film.

Police Dog Story, The. James Brown & Merry Anders. Directed by Edward L. Cahn. 1960. United Artists. 62 min. Sound. 16mm B&W. *Rental:* MGM United.

Police Nurse. Ken Scott & Merry Anders. Directed by Maury Dexter. 1963. Fox. (Anamorphic). 64 min. Sound. 16mm B&W. *Rental:* Films Inc.

Police Power. 1965. NET. (Documentary). 55 min. Sound. 16mm B&W. *Rental:* Indiana AV Ctr.

Police Tapes. 1979. Motorola. (Documentary). 49 min. Sound. 16mm Color. *Rental:* Direct Cinema. *Sale:* Direct Cinema, Videotape version.

Police Tapes, The. Directed by Alan Raymond & Susan Raymond. 1976. Video Verite. (Documentary). 90 min. Videotape B&W. *Rental:* Macmillan Films. *Sale:* Macmillan Films.

Policewomen. Sondra Currie & Tony Young. Directed by Lee Frost. 1974. Crown. 99 min. Sound. 16mm Color. *Rental:* Films Inc.

Polish Flowers. 1978. Poland. (Documentary). 55 min. Sound. 16mm Color. *Rental:* Polish People.

Politics. Marie Dressler & Polly Moran. Directed by Charles Reisner. 1931. MGM. 73 min. Sound. 16mm B&W. *Rental:* MGM United.

Politics of Intimacy, The. Orig. Title: Ten Women Talk about Orgasm & Sexuality. 1974. Video Study Center. (Documentary). 50 min. Videotape B&W. *Rental:* Electro Art.

Politics of Poison, The. Directed by John David Rabinovitch. 1979. Corinth. (Documentary). 60 min. Sound. 16mm Color. *Rental:* Corinth Films. *Lease:* Corinth Films. *Lease:* Corinth Films, *Rental:* Corinth Films, Videotape version.

Politics of Torture, The. 1978. ABC. (Documentary). 50 min. Sound. 16mm Color. *Rental:* CA Newsreel. *Sale:* Ca Newsreel.

Pollution Is a Matter of Choice. 1970. NBC. (Documentary). 53 min. Sound. 16mm Color. *Rental:* Films Inc, Iowa Films, Syracuse U Film, U Cal Media, U Mich Media & Utah Media. *Sale:* Films Inc. *Sale:* Films Inc, Videotape version.

Polly of the Circus. Marion Davies & Clark Gable. Directed by Alfred Santell. 1932. MGM. 70 min. Sound. 16mm B&W. *Rental:* MGM United.

Pollyanna. Hayley Mills, Jane Wyman & Richard Egan. Directed by David Swift. 1960. Disney. 134 min. Sound. 16mm Color. *Rental:* Bosco Film, Buchan Pic, Cine Craft, Cousino Visual Ed, Ellliot Film Co, Film Ctr DC, Films Inc, Disney Prod, Elliot Film Co, MGM United, Modern Sound, Newman Film Lib, Roas Films Swank Motion, Twyman Films, Westcoast Films, Welling Motion Pictures & Williams Films.

Pollyanna. Mary Pickford & J. Wharton James. Directed by Paul Powell. 1920. United Artists. 60 min. Silent. 16mm B&W. *Rental:* Budget Films.

Polo Joe. Joe E. Brown & Carol Hughes. Directed by William McGann. 1936. Warners. 65 min. Sound. 16mm B&W. *Rental:* MGM United.

Poltergeist. Jobeth Williams, Craig T. Nelson & Beatrice Straight. Directed by Tobe Hooper. 1982. 115 min. Sound. 16mm Color. *Rental:* MGM United. *Rental:* MGM United, Videotape version.

Polynesian Adventure, The. 1968. National Geographic. (Documentary). 51 min. Sound. 16mm Color. *Rental:* McGraw-Hill Films. *Sale:* Natl Geog. *Sale:* Natl Geog, Videotape version.

Pom Pom Girls. Robert Carradine & Jennifer Ashley. Directed by Joseph Ruben. 1976. Crown International. 90 min. Sound. 16mm Color. *Rental:* Films Inc & Wholesome Film Ctr.

Pony Express. Ricardo Cortez. Directed by James Cruze. 1925. Paramount. 90 min. Silent. 16mm B&W. *Rental:* Budget Films, Em Gee Film Lib & Film Classics.

Pony Express. Charlton Heston & Rhonda Fleming. Directed by Jerry Hopper. 1953. Paramount. 101 min. Sound. 16mm Color. *Rental:* Films Inc.

Pony Express Rider. Stewart Petersen & Henry Wilcoxon. Directed by Robert Totten. 1979. Doty-Dayton. 100 min. Sound. 16mm Color. *Rental:* Swank Motion.

Pony Soldier. Orig. Title: McDonald of the Canadian Mounties. Tyrone Power & Cameron Mitchell. Directed by Joseph Newman. 1952. Fox. 82 min. Sound. 16mm Color. *Rental:* Films Inc.

Poor Cow. Carol White & Terence Stamp. Directed by Kenneth Loach. 1968. National General. 104 min. Sound. 16mm Color. *Rental:* Swank Motion.

Poor Little Rich Girl. Shirley Temple & Jack Haley. Directed by Irving Cummings. 1936. Fox. 77 min. Sound. 16mm B&W. *Rental:* Films Inc.

Poor Pay More, The. 1967. NET. (Documentary). 60 min. Sound. 16mm B&W. *Rental:* Indiana AV Ctr, Mass Media, U Cal Media, U of IL Film & U Mich Media. *Sale:* Indiana AV Ctr.

Pop Always Pays. Dennis O'Keefe & Leon Errol. Directed by Bert Gilroy. 1940. RKO. 67 min. Sound. 16mm B&W. *Rental:* RKO General Pics.

Pop Goes the Weasel *see* Lady Cocoa.

Popcorn: An Audio-Visual Rock Thing. Directed by Peter Clifton. 1969. Australia. (Documentary). 85 min. Sound. 16mm Color. *Rental:* Budget Films. *Rental:* Budget Films, Videotape version.

Pope of Greenwich Village, The. Eric Roberts & Mickey Rourke. Directed by Stuart Rosenberg. 1984. MGM-UA. Sound. 16mm Color. *Rental:* MGM United. *Rental:* MGM United, Videotape version.

Popes & Their Art: The Vatican Collections. 1983. NBC. (Documentary). 52 min. Sound. 16mm Color. *Rental:* Films Inc. *Sale:* Films Inc. *Sale:* Films Inc, Videotape version.

Popeye. Robin Williams & Shelley Duvall. Disney. 114 min. Sound. 16mm Color. *Rental:* Bosco Films, Elliot Film Co, Films Inc, MGM United, Roas Films, Swank Motion, Welling Motion Pictures, Westcoast Films & Williams Films.

Popeye Follies, The: His Times & Life. Directed by Max Fleischer. 1973. Max Fleischer. (Color sequences, Animated anthology). 85 min. Sound. 16mm B&W. *Rental:* MGM United.

Popi. Alan Arkin. Directed by Arthur Hiller. 1969. United Artists. 115 min. Sound. 16mm Color. *Rental:* Budget Films, MGM United & Westcoast Films.

Poppy. W. C. Fields & Lynne Overman. Directed by Edward Sutherland. 1936. Paramount. 74 min. Sound. 16mm B&W. *Rental:* Swank Motion.

Poppy. Norma Talmadge. Directed by Edward Jose. 1917. 16mm *Rental:* A Twyman Pres.

Poppy is Also a Flower, The. Orig. Title: Danger Grows Wild. Stephen Boyd, Trevor Howard & Omar Sharif. Directed by Terence Young. 1966. United Nations. 100 min. Sound. 16mm Color. dubbed. *Rental:* Budget Films, Bosco Films, Charard Motion Pics, Film Ctr DC, Wholesome Film Ctr & Willoughby Peer.

Poppy Is Also a Flower, The. Stephen Boyd, Omar Sharif & Rita Hayworth. 100 min. Sound. 16mm Color. *Rental:* Bosco Films.

Poprigunya *see* Gadfly.

Porcile *see* Pig Pen.

Pork Chop Hill. Gregory Peck & Harry Guardino. Directed by Lewis Milestone. 1959. MGM. 97 min. Sound. 16mm B&W. *Rental:* MGM United.

Porky's. Kim Cattrall & Kaki Hunter. Directed by Bob Clark. 1981. Fox. 98 min. Sound. 16mm Color. *Rental:* Films Inc.

Porky's Two, the Next Day. Dan Monahan & Wyatt Knight. Directed by Bob Clark. Fox. 95 min. Sound. 16mm Color. *Rental:* Films Inc.

Port of Call. Orig. Title: Hamnstad. Bengt Englund. Directed by Ingmar Bergman. Swed. 1948. Sweden. 100 min. Sound. 16mm B&W. subtitles. *Rental:* Films Inc, Janus Film & New Cinema. *Sale:* Tamarelles French Film, Videotape version.

Port of Forty Thieves. Stephanie Batchelor & Lynne Roberts. Directed by John English. 1944. Republic. 58 min. Sound. 16mm B&W. *Rental:* Ivy Films. *Sale:* Rep Pic Film.

Port of New York. Scott Brady & K. T. Stevens. Directed by Laslo Benedek. 1949. Eagle Lion. 79 min. Sound. 16mm B&W. *Rental:* Budget Films & Mogulls Films.

Port of Seven Seas. Wallace Beery & Frank Morgan. Directed by James Whale. 1938. MGM. 81 min. Sound. 16mm B&W. *Rental:* MGM United.

Port of Shadows. Orig. Title: Misty Wharf. Jean Gabin & Michele Morgan. Directed by Marcel Carne. Fr. 1938. France. 90 min. Sound. 16mm B&W. subtitles. *Rental:* Budget Films.

Portia on Trial. Orig. Title: Trial of Portia Merriman, The. Walter Abel & Neil Hamilton. Directed by George Nicholls Jr. 1937. Republic. 54 min. Sound. 16mm B&W. *Rental:* Ivy Films. *Sale:* Rep Pic Film.

Portnoy's Complaint. Richard Benjamin. Directed by Ernest Lehman. 1972. Warners. 101 min. Sound. 16mm Color. *Rental:* Films Inc.

Portrait de Marianne, Le. Claude Brasseur. Directed by Daniel Goldenbart. Fr. France. 95 min. Sound. 16mm Color. subtitles. *Rental:* French Am Cul. *Rental:* French Am Cul, Videotape version.

Portrait in Black. Lana Turner & Anthony Quinn. Directed by Michael Gordon. 1960. Universal. 112 min. Sound. 16mm Color. *Rental:* Swank Motion.

Portrait in Black & White. 1968. CBS. (Documentary). 54 min. Sound. 16mm B&W. *Rental:* U Mich Media & NYU Film Lib. *Sale:* Phoenix Films. *Sale:* Phoenix Films, Videotape version.

Portrait in Terror. Patrick McGee & William Campbell. 1965. Britain. 80 min. Sound. 16mm B&W. *Rental:* Video Comm.

Portrait of a Young Man. Directed by Henwar Rodakiewicz. 1931. Rodakiewicz. (Expermental). 48 min. Silent. 16mm B&W. *Rental:* Museum Mod Art. *Sale:* Museum Mod Art.

Portrait of an American Zealot, A. Directed by Alan Levin & Marc Levin. 1982. Levin. 55 min. Sound. 16mm Color. *Rental:* Museum Mod Art. *Sale:* Museum Mod Art.

Portrait of Jason, A. Directed by Shirley Clarke. 1967. Shirley Clarke. (Documentary). 105 min. Sound. 16mm B&W. *Rental:* New Yorker Films.

Portrait of Jennie, A. Jennifer Jones & Joseph Cotten. Directed by William Dieterle. 1948. Selznick. (Tinted Sequence). 94 min. Sound. 16mm *Rental:* Films Inc. *Sale:* ABC Film Lib, Super 8 sound version.

Portrait of Lenin, A. Trans. Title: Lenin v Polshe. Maxim Straukh. Directed by Sergei Yutkevich. 1965. Russia. 95 min. Sound. 16mm B&W. subtitles. *Rental:* Corinth Films.

Portrait of Maya Angelou, A. 58 min. Sound. Videotape Color. *Rental:* PBS Video. *Sale:* PBS Video.

Portrait of Moliere, A. Madeleine Renaud & Jean-Louis Barrault. Directed by Jean-Louis Barrault & G. Pansu. Fr. 1967. France. 62 min. Sound. 16mm Color. *Rental:* French Am Cul. *Rental:* Intl Film, *Sale:* Intl Film, Subtitled version.

Portrait of Teresa, A. Daisy Granados & Adolfo Llaurado. Directed by Pastor Vega. Span. 1979. Cuba. 115 min. Sound. 16mm Color. subtitles. *Rental:* Cinema Guild & New Yorker Films. *Sale:* Cinema Guild.

Portrait of the Artist As a Young Man, A. T. P. McKenna, Sir John Gielgud. Directed by Joseph Strick. 1978. Texture. 93 min. Sound. 16mm Color. *Rental:* Texture Film. *Sale:* Texture Film. *Sale:* Texture Film, Videotape version.

Portrait of Werner Herzog, A. Directed by Werner Herzog. Ger. 1978. Germany. 96 min. Sound. 16mm Color. subtitles. *Rental:* New Yorker Films.

Portraits of Women. Jorn Donner. Directed by Jorn Donner. Finnish. 1971. Finland. 84 min. Sound. 16mm Color. subtitles. *Rental:* Hurlock Cine.

Poseidon Adventure, The. Shelley Winters & Gene Hackman. Directed by Ronald Neame. 1972. Fox. 117 min. Sound. 16mm Color. *Rental:* Films Inc, Twyman Films & Williams Films. *Rental:* Films Inc, Anamorphic version.

Posse. Kirk Douglas & Bruce Dern. Directed by Kirk Douglas. 1975. Paramount. (Anamorphic). 94 min. Sound. 16mm Color. *Rental:* Films Inc.

Posse from Hell. Audie Murphy & John Saxon. Directed by Herbert Coleman. 1961. Universal. 89 min. Sound. 16mm Color. *Rental:* Swank Motion.

Possessed. Joan Crawford, Van Heflin & Raymond Massey. Directed by Curtis Bernhardt. 1947. Warners. 108 min. Sound. 16mm B&W. *Rental:* MGM United.

Possession of Joel Delaney, The. Shirley MacLaine. Directed by Waris Hussein. 1972. Paramount. 105 min. Sound. 16mm Color. *Rental:* Films Inc.

Possible Presidents, The: Vice Presidents & Third Parties. 1976. Post-Newsweek. (Documentary). 51 min. Sound. 16mm Color. *Rental:* U of IL Film. *Sale:* Lucerne Films. *Sale:* Lucerne Films, Videotape version.

Post Office Investigator. Warren Douglas & Jeff Donnell. Directed by George Blair. 1949. Republic. 60 min. Sound. 16mm B&W. *Rental:* Ivy Films. *Sale:* Rep Pic Film.

Postman Always Rings Twice, The. Lana Turner & John Garfield. Directed by Tay Garnett. 1946. MGM. 113 min. Sound. 16mm B&W. *Rental:* MGM United. *Rental:* MGM United, Videotape version.

Postman Always Rings Twice, The. Jack Nicholson & Jessica Lange. Directed by Bob Rafelson. 1981. Lorimar. 122 min. Sound. 16mm Color. *Rental:* Swank Motion. *Rental:* Swank Motion, Videotape version.

Postman Didn't Ring, The. Richard Travis & Brenda Joyce. Directed by Harold Schuster. 1942. Fox. 69 min. Sound. 16mm B&W. *Rental:* Films Inc.

Postman's Knock, The. Spike Milligan & Barbara Shelly. Directed by Robert Lyon. 1961. Britain. 88 min. Sound. 16mm B&W. *Rental:* MGM United.

Postmark for Danger. Terry Moore & William Sylvester. Directed by Guy Green. 1956. Britain. 78 min. Sound. 16mm B&W. *Rental:* Budget Films, Films Inc & Video Comm. *Lease:* Video Comm. *Rental:* Video Comm, Videotape version.

Posts, Il *see* Sound of Trumpets.

Postwar Hopes, Cold War Fears. 58 min. Sound. Videotape *Rental:* PBS Video. *Sale:* PBS Video.

Pot-o-Gold. James Stewart & Paulette Goddard. Directed by George Marshall. 1941. United Artists. 100 min. Sound. 16mm B&W. *Rental:* Classic Film Mus, Inst Cinema, Modern Sound, Mogulls Films, Newman Film Lib, Roas Films & Wholesome Film Ctr. *Sale:* Cinema Conceptsk. *Sale:* Blackhawk Films & Tamarelles French Film, Videotape version.

Potemkin. Vladimir Barsky, Grigori Alexandrou & Alexander Antonov. Directed by Sergei Eisenstein. 1925. Russia. (Musical score only). 67 min. Sound. 16mm B&W. *Rental:* Creative Film, Images Film, Ivy Films, Janus Films, Kino Intl, Kit Parker, Modern Sound, Utah Media, Natl Film Video, Twyman Films, U of IL Film, Westcoast Films & Wholesome Film Ctr. *Sale:* Blackhawk Film, Cinema Concepts, Morcraft Films & Images FIlm. *Lease:* Museum Mod Art. *Rental:* Budget Films, Creative Film, Em Gee Film Lib, Film Classics, Films Inc, Images Film, Kit Parker, Museum Mod Art, SD AV Ctr, U Mich Media, Video Comm, Wholesome Film Ctr & Willoughby Peer, *Sale:* Blackhawk Films, E Finney, Glenn Photo, Natl Cinema, Images Film, Morcraft Films & Reel Images, Silent 16mm version. *Sale:* Blackhawk Films, Super 8 sound version. *Sale:* Blackhawk Films, Glenn Photo & Reel Images, Super 8 silent version. *Rental:* Film Classics & Video Comm, *Sale:* Ivy Films, Maljack, Tamarelles French Film & Images Film, Videotape version. *Sale:* Images Film, Silent Videotape version.

Poto & Cabengo. Directed by Jean-Paul Gorin. 1979. New Yorker. (Documentary). 77 min. Sound. 16mm Color. *Rental:* New Yorker Films.

Potomok-Chingis Khan *see* Storm Over Asia.

Potters of Hebron. Directed by Robert Haber. 1976. Phoenix. (Documentary). 53 min. Sound. 16mm Color. *Rental:* Phoenix Films. *Sale:* Phoenix Films. *Sale:* Phoenix Films, Videotape version.

Pound. Joe Madden. Directed by Robert Downey. 1970. United Artists. 92 min. Sound. 16mm Color. *Rental:* MGM United.

Pour la Suite du Monde *see* Moontrap.

Pourquois Israel? Israel. (Documentary). 210 min. Sound. 16mm Color. *Rental:* Alden Films.

Poursuite, La. Claude Girard & Colette Renard. Directed by Francois Leterrier. 1963. France. 85 min. Sound. 16mm Color. *Rental:* French Am Cul. *Rental:* French Am Cul, Subtitled B&W version.

Poverty. 1973. Sterling. (Documentary). 56 min. Sound. 16mm Color. *Sale:* Sterling Ed Film.

Povo Organizado, O: The People Organized. Directed by Robert Van Lierop. 1976. Mozambique. (Documentary). 68 min. Sound. 16mm Color. *Rental:* Doc Assoc, U Mich Media & Tricontinental Film. *Sale:* Doc Assoc, Tricontinental Film & U of IL Film.

Powder Ridge. (Documentary). 70 min. Sound. 16mm Color. *Rental:* Video Comm.

Powder River. Rory Calhoun & Corinne Calvet. Directed by Louis King. 1953. Fox. 77 min. Sound. 16mm B&W. *Rental:* Films Inc.

Powder River Rustlers. Allan Lane. Directed by Philip Ford. 1949. Republic. 60 min. Sound. 16mm B&W. *Rental:* Ivy Films. *Sale:* Rep Pic Film & Nostalgia Merchant.

Powder Town. Edmond O'Brien & Victor MacLaglen. Directed by Rowland V. Lee. 1942. RKO General. 79 min. Sound. 16mm B&W. *Rental:* RKO General Pics.

Powdersmoke Range. Hoot Gibson, Harry Carey & Bob Steele. Directed by Wallace Fox. 1935. RKO. 72 min. 16mm RKO General Pics. B&W. *Rental:* Films Inc.

Power. William Boyd & Alan Hale. Directed by Howard Higgin. 1928. Pathe. 80 min. Silent. 16mm B&W. *Rental:* Em Gee Film Lib. *Sale:* E Finney.

Power, The. George Hamilton & Suzanne Pleshette. Directed by Byron Haskin. 1968. MGM. 100 min. Sound. 16mm Color. *Rental:* MGM United.

Power & the Glory, The. Spencer Tracy & Colleen Moore. Directed by William K. Howard. 1933. Fox. 76 min. Sound. 16mm B&W. *Rental:* Films Inc & Ivy Films.

Power & the Glory, The. Directed by Munroe Scott. 1971. Canada. (Documentary). 58 min. Sound. 16mm Color. *Rental:* Natl Film CN. *Sale:* Natl Film CN.

Power & the Prize, The. Robert Taylor & Burl Ives. Directed by Henry Koster. 1956. MGM. 89 min. Sound. 16mm B&W. *Rental:* MGM United. *Rental:* MGM United, Anamorphic version.

Power of Justice *see* Beyond the Sacramento.

Power of Matter, The. Canada. (Documentary). 58 min. Sound. 16mm B&W. *Rental:* Natl Film CN. *Sale:* Natl Film CN.

Power of the Market, The. 1980. Penn. (Documentary). 60 min. Videotape Color. *Rental:* Ency Brit Ed. *Sale:* Ency Brit Ed. *Rental:* Iowa Films, *Sale:* Ency Brit Ed, 2 pt. 16mm version version. *Sale:* Ency Brit Ed, 2 pt. videotape version version.

Power of the Press, The. Lionel Barrymore & Alan Hale. 1914. Klaw & Erlanger. 48 min. Silent. 16mm B&W. *Sale:* Glenn Photo. *Sale:* Glenn Photo, Super 8 silent version.

Power of the Press, The. Lee Tracy & Gloria Dickson. Directed by Lew Landers. 1943. Columbia. 63 min. Sound. 16mm B&W. *Rental:* Kit Parker.

Power of the Press, The. Douglas Fairbanks Jr. & Jobyna Ralston. Directed by Frank Capra. 1928. Columbia. 70 min. Silent. 16mm B&W. *Rental:* Kit Parker.

Power of the Resurrection, The. Richard Kiley & Jon Shepodd. 1960. Family. 65 min. Sound. 16mm Color. *Rental:* Roas Films.

Power Reactors: USA. 1958. Atomic Energy Commission. (Documentary). 55 min. Sound. 16mm Color. *Rental:* Natl AV Ctr.

Powers Girl. George Murphy & Carole Landis. Directed by Norman Z. McLeod. 1942. United Artists. 92 min. Sound. 16mm B&W. *Rental:* Ivy Films.

Powers That Be, The. Color. *Rental:* U Cal Media.

Practical Performance Examination for Emergency Medical Technicians. 1977. Public Health Service. (Documentary). 92 min. Videotape Color. *Sale:* Natl AV Ctr.

Practical Politics. 1966. Tufts U.. (Documentary). 65 min. Sound. 16mm B&W. *Rental:* Syracuse U Film.

Practical Procedures of Measurement. 1952. Atomic Energy Commission. (Documentary). 48 min. Sound. 16mm B&W. *Rental:* Natl AV Ctr.

Practically Yours. Claudette Colbert & Fred MacMurray. Directed by Mitchell Leisen. 1944. Paramount. 89 min. Sound. 16mm B&W. *Rental:* Swank Motion.

Practice Makes Perfect *see* Cavaleur.

Prairie, The. Alan Baxter & Lenore Aubert. Directed by Frank Wisbar. 1948. Screen Guild. 68 min. Sound. 16mm B&W. *Rental:* Film Classics, Film Ctr DC & Westcoast Films.

Prairie Badmen. Buster Crabbe. Directed by Sam Newfield. 1946. PRC. 55 min. Sound. 16mm B&W. *Sale:* Classics Assoc NY.

Prairie Law. George O'Brien & Virginia Vale. Directed by Bert Gilroy. 1940. RKO. 58 min. Sound. 16mm B&W. *Rental:* RKO General Pics.

Prairie Moon. Gene Autry. Directed by Ralph Staub. 1938. Republic. 54 min. Sound. 16mm B&W. *Rental:* Budget Films & Ivy Films. *Sale:* Blackhawk Films, Super 8 sound version.

Prairie Outlaws. Eddie Dean. Directed by Robert Tansey. 1945. Eagle Lion. 55 min. Sound. 16mm B&W. *Sale:* Classics Assoc NY.

Prairie Pals. Bill Boyd, Lee Powell & Art Davis. Directed by Peter Stewart. 1942. PRC. 60 min. Sound. 16mm B&W. *Rental:* Mogulls Films.

Prairie Pioneers. Robert Livingston & Bob Steele. Directed by Lester Orlebeck. 1941. Republic. 57 min. Sound. 16mm B&W. *Rental:* Ivy Films & Rep Pic Film. *Sale:* Rep Pic Film.

Prairie Pirate. Harry Carey. Directed by Edmund Mortimer. 1925. PDC. 50 min. Silent. 16mm B&W. *Rental:* Film Classics. *Sale:* Film Classics. *Sale:* Film Classics,

Prairie Rustlers. Buster Crabbe. Directed by Sam Newfield. 1945. PRC. 56 min. Sound. 16mm B&W. *Sale:* Classics Assoc NY.

Prairie Thunder. Dick Foran. Directed by B. Reeves Eason. 1937. Warners. 54 min. Sound. 16mm B&W. *Rental:* MGM United.

Pravda. Directed by Jean-Luc Godard. 1970. France. (Documentary). 58 min. Sound. 16mm Color. dubbed. *Rental:* Grove. *Sale:* Grove.

Predators, The. 1976. Stouffer. (Documentary). 50 min. Sound. 16mm Color. *Rental:* Iowa Films, U Mich Media, Stouffer Ent & Syracuse U Film. *Sale:* Stouffer Ent. *Sale:* Stouffer Ent, Videotape version.

Prehistoric Women. Martine Beswick. Directed by Michael Carreras. 1967. Britain. 91 min. Sound. 16mm Color. *Rental:* Films Inc.

Prejudice. David Bruce. Directed by Edward L. Cahn. 1949. Protestant Film Comm. 58 min. Sound. 16mm B&W. *Rental:* Newman Film Lib.

Prelude to Fame. Kathleen Ryan. Directed by Fergus McDonnell. 1950. Britain. 88 min. Sound. 16mm B&W. *Rental:* Em Gee Film Lib.

Prelude to War. Directed by Frank Capra. 1942. War Department. (Documentary). 53 min. Sound. 16mm B&W. *Sale:* Cinema Concepts, Museum Mod Art & Reel Images. *Sale:* Natl AV Ctr. *Rental:* Films Inc, Iowa Films, Natl AV Ctr & Video Comm, Videotape version.

Prelude to War. Walter Huston. 1965. Wolper. (Documentary). 50 min. Sound. 16mm B&W. narrated. *Rental:* Films Inc, Maljack Productions & Wholesome Film Ctr. *Sale:* Films Inc. *Sale:* Festival Films, 54 min. 1942 version.

Premature. 1981. Benchmark. (Documentary). 55 min. Sound. 16mm Color. *Sale:* Benchmark Films & Syracuse U Film. *Rental:* Iowa Films & Benchmark Films. *Sale:* Benchmark Films, 8mm version avail. version.

Premature Burial, The. Ray Milland & Hazel Court. Directed by Roger Corman. 1962. American International. 81 min. Sound. 16mm Color. *Rental:* Cine Craft, Ivy Films, Film Ctr DC, Twyman Films, Video Comm, Westcoast Films & Wholesome Film Ctr.

Premonition, The. Sharon Farrell. Directed by Robert Allen Schnitzer. 1976. Embassy. 95 min. Sound. 16mm Color. *Rental:* Films Inc.

Prescription for Life. 1967. American Heart Association. (Documentary). 48 min. Sound. 16mm Color. *Rental:* SD AV Ctr.

Present Past, The. Directed by Pat Patterson. 1976. Canada. (Documentary). 57 min. Sound. 16mm Color. *Rental:* Natl Film CN. *Sale:* Natl Film CN.

Presenting Lily Mars. Judy Garland & Van Heflin. Directed by Norman Taurog. 1943. MGM. 104 min. Sound. 16mm B&W. *Rental:* MGM United.

President Vanishes, The. Edward Arnold & Rosalind Russell. Directed by William A. Wellman. 1934. Paramount. 85 min. Sound. 16mm B&W. *Rental:* Museum Mod Art & Swank Motion.

President's Analyst, The. James Coburn & Godfrey Cambridge. Directed by Theodore J. Flicker. 1967. Paramount. 103 min. Sound. 16mm Color. *Rental:* Films Inc.

Presidents & Politics with Richard Strout. 58 min. Sound. Videotape *Rental:* PBS Video. *Sale:* PBS Video.

Presidents & Third Parties, The. 1976. Lucerne. (Documentary). 51 min. Sound. 16mm Color. *Sale:* Lucerne Films. *Sale:* Lucerne Films, Videotape version.

President's Lady, The. Charlton Heston & Susan Hayward. Directed by Henry Levin. 1953. Fox. 96 min. Sound. 16mm B&W. *Rental:* Films Inc.

President's Mystery, The. Orig. Title: One for All. Henry Wilcoxen & Betty Furness. Directed by Phil Rosen. 1936. Republic. 54 min. Sound. 16mm B&W. *Rental:* Ivy Films. *Sale:* Rep Pic Film.

Press for Time. Norman Wisdom. Directed by Robert Asher. 1966. Britain. 102 min. Sound. 16mm B&W. *Rental:* Cinema Five.

Pressure Point. Sidney Poitier & Bobby Darin. Directed by Hubert Cornfield. 1962. MGM. 89 min. Sound. 16mm B&W. *Rental:* MGM United.

Prestige. Melvyn Douglas & Adolphe Menjou. Directed by Tay Garnett. 1932. RKO. 71 min. Sound. 16mm B&W. *Rental:* RKO General Pics.

Presumed Innocent. 1980. PBS. (Documentary). 60 min. Sound. 16mm B&W. *Sale:* TVG Doc Art. *Sale:* TVG Doc Art, Videotape version.

Pretender, The. Albert Dekker & Catherine Craig. Directed by W. Lee Wilder. 1947. Republic. 68 min. Sound. 16mm B&W. *Sale:* Classics Assoc NY.

Pretty Baby. Brooke Shields & Keith Carradine. Directed by Louis Malle. 1978. Paramount. 109 min. Sound. 16mm Color. *Rental:* Films Inc.

Pretty Maids All in a Row. Rock Hudson & Angie Dickinson. Directed by Roger Vadim. 1971. MGM. 92 min. Sound. 16mm Color. *Rental:* MGM United.

Pretty Poison. Orig. Title: She Let Him Continue. Anthony Perkins & Tuesday Weld. Directed by Noel Black. 1968. Fox. 92 min. Sound. 16mm Color. *Rental:* Films Inc.

Preventing the Reality of Rape. 1983. Embassy. (Documentary). 53 min. Sound. 16mm Color. *Rental:* Films Inc. *Sale:* Films Inc. *Sale:* Films Inc, Videotape version.

Prezidido, El. Span. 1950. Mexico. (Cast unlisted). 90 min. Sound. 16mm B&W. *Rental:* Film Classics.

Price of a Union, The. Trans. Title: Rancon Dune Alliance, La. Directed by Sebastien Kamba. 1971. Zaire. 70 min. Sound. 16mm Color. subtitles. *Rental:* Museum Mod Art.

Price of Gold, The. 1982. Britain. (Documentary). 60 min. Sound. 16mm Color. *Rental:* Films Inc. *Sale:* Films Inc. *Sale:* Films Inc, Videotape version.

Priceless Treasures of Dresden, The. 1978. WNET. (Documentary). 59 min. Sound. 16mm Color. *Rental:* Indiana AV Ctr. *Sale:* Indiana AV Ctr. *Sale:* Indiana AV Ctr, Videotape version.

Pride & Prejudice. Greer Garson, Sir Laurence Olivier. Directed by Robert Z. Leonard. 1940. MGM. 118 min. Sound. 16mm B&W. *Rental:* MGM United. *Rental:* MGM United, Videotape version.

Pride & the Passion, The. Cary Grant, Sophia Loren & Frank Sinatra. Directed by Stanley Kramer. 1957. United Artists. 132 min. Sound. 16mm Color. *Rental:* MGM United.

Pride of Kentucky see Story of Sea Biscuit.

Pride of Maryland, The. Peggy Stewart & Stanley Clements. Directed by Philip Ford. 1950. Republic. 60 min. Sound. 16mm B&W. *Rental:* Ivy Films.

Pride of St. Louis, The. Dan Dailey & Joanne Dru. Directed by Harmon Jones. 1952. Fox. 93 min. Sound. 16mm B&W. *Rental:* Films Inc.

Pride of the Blue Grass, The. Edith Fellows & William Hopper. Directed by William McGann. 1939. Warners. 65 min. Sound. 16mm B&W. *Rental:* MGM United.

Pride of the Blue Grass, The. Vera Miles & Lloyd Bridges. Directed by William Beaudine. 1954. Allied Artists. 68 min. Sound. 16mm B&W. *Rental:* Ivy Films. *Sale:* Rep Pic Film.

Pride of the Bowery, The. Orig. Title: Here We Go Again. Bowery Boys. Directed by Joseph Lewis. 1941. Monogram. 61 min. Sound. 16mm B&W. *Rental:* Budget Films, Classic Film Mus, Ivy Films & Video Comm. *Lease:* Video Comm. *Sale:* Cinema Concepts, Videotape version.

Pride of the Marines, The. Orig. Title: Forever in Love. John Garfield & Eleanor Parker. Directed by Delmer Daves. 1945. Warners. 120 min. Sound. 16mm B&W. *Rental:* MGM United.

Pride of the Navy, The. James Dunn & Rochelle Hudson. Directed by Charles Lamont. 1939. Republic. 64 min. Sound. 16mm B&W. *Rental:* Ivy Films.

Pride of the Plains, The. Robert Livingston. Directed by Wallace Fox. 1943. Republic. 54 min. Sound. 16mm B&W. *Rental:* Ivy Films. *Sale:* Rep Pic Film.

Pride of the West, The. William Boyd. Directed by Lesley Selander & Gabby Hayes. 1938. Paramount. 60 min. Sound. 16mm B&W. *Lease:* Cinema Concepts. *Rental:* Budget Films.

Pride of the Yankees, The. Gary Cooper & Teresa Wright. Directed by Sam Wood. 1942. Goldwyn. 128 min. Sound. 16mm B&W. *Rental:* Films Inc, Syracuse U Films & Video Comm. *Lease:* Macmillan Films.

Priest & the Girl, The. Trans. Title: Padre e a Moca, O. Paolo Jose. Directed by Joaquin Pedro De Andrade. Port. 1966. Brazil. 89 min. Sound. 16mm B&W. subtitles. *Rental:* New Yorker Films.

Priest of Love, The. Ian McKellen, Janet Suzman & Ava Gardner. Directed by Christopher Miles. 1981. Britain. 125 min. Sound. 16mm Color. *Rental:* Images Film & Swank Motion.

Priest's Wife, The. Sophia Loren & Marcello Mastroianni. Directed by Dino Risi. 1971. Italy. 109 min. Sound. 16mm Color. *Rental:* Kerr Film.

Primal Man: Battle for Dominance. 1974. Films Inc. (Documentary). 52 min. Sound. 16mm Color. *Rental:* Films Inc. *Sale:* Films Inc.

Primal Man: Struggle for Survival. 1974. Films Inc. (Documentary). 52 min. Sound. 16mm Color. *Rental:* Films Inc. *Sale:* Films Inc.

Primal Man: The Human Factor. 1974. Films Inc. (Documentary). 52 min. Sound. 16mm Color. *Rental:* Films Inc. *Sale:* Films Inc.

Primal Man: The Killer Instinct. 1974. Films Inc. (Documentary). 52 min. Sound. 16mm Color. *Rental:* Films Inc. *Sale:* Films Inc.

Primal Mind, The. 58 min. Sound. 16mm Color. *Rental:* Cinema Guild.

Primary. 1960. Time-Life. (Documentary). 54 min. Sound. 16mm B&W. *Sale:* Direct Cinema. *Rental:* Direct Cinema.

Primate. Directed by Frederick Wiseman. 1973. Wiseman. (Documentary). 105 min. Sound. 16mm B&W. *Rental:* Zipporah Films. *Lease:* Zipporah Films, Videotape version.

Primavera de los Escorpions, La. Isela Vega & Enrique Alvarez Felix. Directed by Francisco Del Villar. Span. Mexico. 87 min. Sound. 16mm Color. subtitles. *Rental:* Westcoast Films.

Prime Cut. Lee Marvin & Gene Hackman. Directed by Michael Ritchie. 1972. National General. 91 min. Sound. 16mm Color. *Rental:* Films Inc & Swank Motion. *Rental:* Swank Motion, Anamorphic version.

Prime Minister, The. Sir John Gielgud & Diana Wynyard. Directed by Thorold Dickinson. 1941. Warners. 94 min. Sound. 16mm B&W. *Rental:* MGM United.

Prime of Miss Jean Brodie, The. Maggie Smith. Directed by Ronald Neame. 1969. Fox. 116 min. Sound. 16mm Color. *Rental:* Films Inc & Twyman Films.

Primitive Lover, The. Constance Talmadge & Harrison Ford. Directed by Sidney Franklin. 1922. First National. 65 min. Silent. 8mm B&W. *Sale:* Blackhawk Films.

Primitives, The see Plotters.

Primrose Path, The. Clara Bow. Directed by Harry Hoyt. 1925. Arrow. (Musical score only). 60 min. Sound. 16mm B&W. *Rental:* Film Classics. *Rental:* Film Classics, Silent 16mm version. *Sale:* Film Classics, Silent 8mm version. *Rental:* Film Classics, Videotape version.

Primrose Path, The. Ginger Rogers & Joel McCrea. Directed by Gregory La Cava. 1940. RKO. 93 min. Sound. 16mm B&W. *Rental:* Films Inc.

Prince & the Pauper, The. 1923. Austria. (Cast unlisted). 50 min. Silent. 16mm B&W. *Rental:* Film Classics.

Prince & the Pauper, The. Errol Flynn & Claude Rains. Directed by William Keighley. 1937. Warners. 120 min. Sound. 16mm B&W. *Rental:* MGM United.

Prince & the Pauper, The. Guy Williams, Donald Houston & Laurence Naismith. Directed by Don Chaffey. 1962. Disney. 93 min. Sound. 16mm Color. *Rental:* Buchan Pic, Cine Craft, Charard Motion Pics, Cousino Visual Ed, Williams Films, Bosco Films, Elliot Film Co, Films Inc, U of IL Films, MGM United, Newman Film Lib, Roas Films, Swank Motion, Film Ctr DC, Twyman Films, Westcoast Films & Welling Motion Pictures.

Prince Edward Island: The Development Plan. 2 pts. 1971. Canada. (Documentary). 113 min. Sound. 16mm B&W. *Rental:* Natl Film CN. *Sale:* Natl Film CN.

Prince Igor. Boris Khmelnitsky. Directed by Roman Tikhomirov. Rus. 1972. Russia. 105 min. Sound. 16mm Color. subtitles. *Rental:* Corinth Films. *Lease:* Corinth Films.

Prince of Foxes, The. Tyrone Power & Orson Welles. Directed by Henry King. 1949. Fox. 107 min. Sound. 16mm B&W. *Rental:* Films Inc.

Prince of Peace, The. 1962. Hearst. (Documentary). 50 min. Sound. 16mm B&W. *Sale:* King Features.

Prince of Pirates, The. John Derek & Barbara Rush. Directed by Sidney Salkow. 1953. Columbia. 80 min. Sound. 16mm Color. *Rental:* Modern Sound.

Prince of Players, The. Richard Burton & Raymond Massey. Directed by Philip Dunne. 1955. Fox. 105 min. Sound. 16mm Color. *Rental:* Films Inc, Inst Cinema & Willoughby Peer.

Prince of the City, The. Treat Williams & Jerry Orbach. Directed by Sidney Lumet. 1981. Orion. 167 min. Sound. 16mm Color. *Rental:* Films Inc.

Prince of the Plains, The. Monte Hale. Directed by Philip Ford. 1949. Republic. 60 min. Sound. 16mm B&W. *Rental:* Ivy Films. *Sale:* Rep Pic Film & Nostalgia Merchant.

Prince of Thieves, The. Jon Hall & Patricia Morison. Directed by Howard Bretherton. 1948. Columbia. 80 min. Sound. 16mm Color. *Rental:* Bosco Films & Kit Parker.

Prince Valiant. James Mason & Robert Wagner. Directed by Henry Hathaway. 1954. Fox. 100 min. Sound. 16mm Color. *Rental:* Williams Films & Films Inc. *Rental:* Films Inc, Anamorphic version.

Princess & the Pirate, The. Bob Hope & Virginia Mayo. Directed by David Butler. 1944. Goldwyn. 94 min. Sound. 16mm Color. *Rental:* Films Inc & Welling Motion Pictures.

Princess Cinderella. Roberto Villa. Directed by Sergio Tofano. 1955. Italy. 72 min. Sound. 16mm B&W. dubbed. *Rental:* Budget Films, Video Comm & Westcoast Films. *Sale:* Video Comm. *Rental:* Video Comm, Videotape version.

Princess of the Nile. Debra Paget & Jeffrey Hunter. Directed by Harmon Jones. 1954. Fox. 71 min. Sound. 16mm Color. *Rental:* Films Inc.

Princess Yang Kwei Fei. Trans. Title: Yang Kwei Fei. Machiko Kyo. Directed by Kenji Mizoguchi. Jap. 1955. Japan. 91 min. Sound. 16mm Color. subtitles. *Rental:* New Yorker Films.

Principal Enemy, The. Directed by Jorge Sanjines. Span. 1974. Peru. (Documentary). 100 min. Sound. 16mm B&W. subtitles. *Rental:* Cinema Guild. *Sale:* Cinema Guild.

Principles of Indexing. 1974. 86 min. Sound. Videotape Color. *Sale:* Natl AV Ctr.

Print Generation, The. Directed by J. J. Murphy. 1974. Murphy. (Experimental). 50 min. Sound. 16mm Color. *Rental:* Canyon Cinema & Museum Mod Art. *Sale:* Museum Mod Art.

Prison. 1971. NET. (Documentary). 59 min. Sound. 16mm B&W. *Rental:* Indiana AV Ctr. *Sale:* Indiana AV Ctr. *Sale:* Indiana AV Ctr, Super 8 sound version. *Sale:* Indiana AV Ctr, Videotape version.

Prison Nurse. Henry Wilcoxen & Marian Marsh. Directed by James Cruze. 1938. Republic. 54 min. Sound. 16mm B&W. *Rental:* Ivy Films. *Sale:* Rep Pic Film.

Prison: Reform or Revenge. 1973. WNET. (Documentary). 58 min. 16mm B&W. WNET Media., Videotape version.

Prison Train. Fred Keating, Linda Winters & Clarence Muse. Directed by Gordon Wiles. 1938. Equity. 64 min. Sound. 16mm B&W. *Rental:* Modern Sound & Museum Mod Art. *Sale:* Museum Mod Art. *Sale:* Blackhawk Films. *Sale:* Blackhawk Films, Super 8 sound version.

Prisoner, The. Sir Alec Guinness & Jack Hawkins. Directed by Peter Glenville. 1955. Britain. 91 min. Sound. 16mm B&W. *Rental:* Budget Films, Bosco Films, Films Inc, Kit Parker, Film Ctr DC, Twyman Films & Westcoast Films.

Prisoner of Second Avenue, The. Jack Lemmon & Anne Bancroft. Directed by Melvin Frank. 1974. Warners. 98 min. Sound. 16mm Color. *Rental:* Williams Films, Films Inc, Modern Sound, Swank Motion & Twyman Films.

Prisoner of Shark Island, The. Warner Baxter & Gloria Stuart. Directed by John Ford. 1936. Fox. 95 min. Sound. 16mm B&W. *Rental:* Films Inc.

Prisoner of War. Ronald Reagan & Steve Forest. Directed by Andrew Marton. 1954. MGM. 80 min. Sound. 16mm B&W. *Rental:* MGM United.

Prisoner of Zenda, The. Ronald Colman & Douglas Fairbanks Jr. Directed by John Cromwell. 1937. MGM. 100 min. Sound. 16mm B&W. *Rental:* MGM United.

Prisoner of Zenda, The. Stewart Granger & Deborah Kerr. Directed by Richard Thorpe. 1952. MGM. 100 min. Sound. 16mm Color. *Rental:* MGM United. *Rental:* MGM United, Videotape version.

Prisoner of Zenda, The. Peter Sellers & Lionel Jeffries. Directed by Richard Quine. 1979. Universal. 108 min. Sound. 16mm Color. *Rental:* Swank Motion.

Prisoners in Petticoats. Sue Noland & Anthony Caruso. Directed by Philip Ford. 1950. Republic. 60 min. Sound. 16mm B&W. *Rental:* Ivy Films. *Sale:* Rep Pic Film.

Prisoners of Hope: Multiple Sclerosis. 1980. Britain. (Documentary). 50 min. Sound. 16mm Color. *Rental:* U Cal Media & Films Inc. *Sale:* Films Inc. *Rental:* Films Inc, *Sale:* Films Inc, Videotape version.

Private Affairs. Robert Cummings, Hugh Herbert & Nancy Kelly. Directed by Albert S. Rogell. 1940. Universal. 80 min. Sound. 16mm B&W. *Rental:* Mogulls Films & Film Ctr DC.

Private Affairs of Bel Ami, The. George Sanders, Ann Dvorak & Angela Lansbury. Directed by Albert Lewin. 1947. MGM. 112 min. Sound. 16mm B&W. *Rental:* Budget Films, Ivy Films & Kit Parker. *Sale:* Rep Pic Film.

Private Battle, A. Jack Warden, Anne Jackson & Walter Cronkite. Directed by Robert Lewis. 1980. CBS. 105 min. Sound. 16mm Color. *Rental:* Twyman Films.

Private Benjamin. Goldie Hawn & Eileen Brennan. Directed by Howard Zieff. 1980. Warners. 100 min. Sound. 16mm Color. *Rental:* Swank Motion. *Rental:* Swank Motion, Videotape version.

Private Buckaroo. Andrews Sisters & Dick Foran. Directed by Edward Cline. 1942. Universal. 68 min. Sound. 16mm B&W. *Rental:* Budget Films, Classic Film Mus & Mogulls Films. *Sale:* Cinema Concepts.

Private Contentment. 1983. WNET. (Cast unlisted). 90 min. Sound. Videotape Color. *Rental:* Films Inc. *Sale:* Films Inc.

Private Detective. Jane Wyman & Dick Foran. Directed by Noel Smith. 1939. Warners. 55 min. Sound. 16mm B&W. *Rental:* MGM United.

Private Detective 62. Orig. Title: Man Killer. William Powell & Margaret Lindsay. Directed by Michael Curtiz. 1933. Warners. 67 min. Sound. 16mm B&W. *Rental:* MGM United.

Private Enterprise, A. Directed by Peter K. Smith. 1975. Britain. (Documentary). 78 min. Sound. 16mm Color. *Rental:* Films Inc. *Sale:* Films Inc. *Sale:* Films Inc, Videotape version.

Private Eyes, The. Tim Conway & Don Knotts. Directed by Lang Elliott. 1981. New World. 91 min. Sound. 16mm Color. *Rental:* Films Inc.

Private Hell Thirty-Six. Ida Lupino & Howard Duff. Directed by Don Siegel. 1954. Filmakers. 81 min. Sound. 16mm B&W. *Rental:* Ivy Films. *Sale:* Rep Pic Film.

Private Ivan Brovkin. Leonid Kharitonov. Directed by Ivan Lukinsky. Rus. 1955. Russia. 93 min. Sound. 16mm B&W. subtitles. *Rental:* Corinth Films.

Private Life, The. 1977. WNET. (Documentary). 60 min. Videotape Color. *Rental:* WNET Media. *Sale:* WNET Media.

Private Life of Don Juan, The. Douglas Fairbanks & Merle Oberon. Directed by Alexander Korda. 1934. Britain. 83 min. Sound. 16mm B&W. *Rental:* Budget Films, Classic FIlm Mus, Em Gee Film Lib, Films Inc, Ivy Films, Mogulls Films & Video Comm. *Sale:* Cinema Concepts & Reel Images. *Rental:* Video Comm, Videotape version.

Private Life of Henry the Eighth, The. Charles Laughton & Merle Oberon. Directed by Alexander Korda. 1933. Britain. 97 min. Sound. 16mm B&W. *Rental:* Budget Films, Classic Film Mus, Em Gee Film Lib, Films Inc, Images Film, Iowa Films, Ivy Films, Kit Parker, Maljack, Mogulls Films, Roas Films, Twyman Films, Video Comm, Westcoast Films & Wholesome Film Ctr. *Sale:* Cinema Concepts, Festival Films, Images Film, Morcraft Films, Natl Film Video & Reel Images. *Rental:* Ivy Films, *Sale:* Ivy Films, Morcraft Films & Reel Images, Super 8 sound version. *Sale:* Cinema Concepts, Festival Films, Ivy Films, Maljack, Reel Images, Tamarelles French Film, Video Comm & Images Film, Videotape version.

Private Life of Sherlock Holmes, The. Robert Stephens & Genevieve Page. Directed by Billy Wilder. 1970. United Artists. 125 min. Sound. 16mm Color. *Rental:* MGM United. *Rental:* MGM United, Anamorphic version.

Private Lives. Norma Shearer & Robert Montgomery. Directed by Sidney Franklin. 1931. MGM. 87 min. Sound. 16mm B&W. *Rental:* MGM United.

Private Lives of Elizabeth & Essex, The. Orig. Title: Elizabeth & Essex. Bette Davis & Errol Flynn. Directed by Michael Curtiz. 1939. Warners. 106 min. Sound. 16mm Color. *Rental:* MGM United.

Private Parts. Ayn Ruymen. Directed by Paul Bartel. 1973. MGM. 86 min. Sound. 16mm Color. *Rental:* MGM United.

Private President, The: The Man & His Family. 1976. Post-Newsweek. (Documentary). 51 min. Sound. 16mm Color. *Rental:* U of IL Film. *Sale:* Lucerne Films. *Sale:* Lucerne Films, Videotape version.

Private School. Phoebe Cates & Sylvia Kristel. Directed by Noel Black. 1983. Universal. 97 min. Sound. 16mm Color. *Rental:* Swank Motion. *Rental:* Swank Motion, Videotape version.

Private War of Major Benson, The. Charlton Heston & Tim Hovey. Directed by Jerry Hopper. 1955. Universal. 105 min. Sound. 16mm Color. *Rental:* Swank Motion.

Private Wore Skirts, The see Never Wave at a W. A. C..

Private Worlds. Claudette Colbert & Charles Boyer. Directed by Gregory La Cava. 1935. Paramount. 84 min. Sound. 16mm B&W. *Rental:* Swank Motion.

Private's Affair, A. Sal Mineo & Christine Carere. Directed by Raoul Walsh. 1959. Fox. (Anamorphic). 93 min. Sound. 16mm Color. *Rental:* Films Inc.

Private's Progress. Richard Attenborough & Ian Carmichael. Directed by John Boulting & Roy Boulting. 1956. Britain. 99 min. Sound. 16mm B&W. *Rental:* Budget Films.

Privilege. Paul Jones & Jean Shrimpton. Directed by Peter Watkins. 1967. Britain. 101 min. Sound. 16mm Color. *Rental:* Swank Motion.

Privileged. Directed by Michael Hoffman. 1982. 94 min. Sound. 16mm Color. *Rental:* New Yorker Films.

Prize, The. Paul Newman & Elke Sommer. Directed by Mark Robson. 1963. MGM. 135 min. Sound. 16mm Color. *Rental:* MGM United. *Rental:* MGM United, Anamorphic version.

Prize Fighter, The. Tim Conway & Don Knotts. Directed by Michael Preece. 1979. New World. 99 min. Sound. 16mm Color. *Rental:* Films Inc.

Prize of Gold, A. Richard Widmark & Mai Zetterling. Directed by Mark Robson. 1955. Columbia. 98 min. Sound. 16mm B&W. *Rental:* Inst Cinema.

Prizefighter & the Lady, The. Myrna Loy & Max Baer. Directed by W. S. Van Dyke. 1933. MGM. 103 min. Sound. 16mm B&W. *Rental:* MGM United.

Prizewinners, The. 1978. US Government. (Documentary). 59 min. Sound. 16mm Color. *Sale:* Natl AV Ctr.

Probability & Uncertainty: Quantum Mechanical View of Nature. 1964. Britain. (Documentary, kinescope). 56 min. Sound. 16mm B&W. *Rental:* U Cal Media.

Probable Passing of Elk Creek, The. Directed by Rob Wilson. Cinema Guild. (Documentary). 60 min. Sound. 16mm Color. *Rental:* Cinema Guild. *Sale:* Cinema Guild. *Rental:* Cinema Guild, *Sale:* Cinema Guild, Videotape version.

Probation Wife. Norma Talmadge. Directed by Sidney A. Franklin. 1919. 16mm *Rental:* A Twyman Pres.

Probe see Search.

Problem Girls. Helen Walker & Ross Elliott. Directed by E. A. Dupont. 1953. Columbia. 70 min. Sound. 16mm B&W. *Rental:* Kit Parker.

Problem of Being Georgie, The. Japan. (Cast unlisted). 50 min. Sound. 16mm B&W. *Sale:* Japan Society. *Sale:* Japan Society, Color version. *Sale:* Japan Society, Subtitled version. *Sale:* Japan Society, Videotape version.

Problem of Power, The. CC Films. 45 min. Sound. 16mm Color. *Rental:* Natl Council Of the Churches of Christ.

Problem: To Think of Dying. 1976. PBS. (Documentary). 59 min. Sound. 16mm Color. *Rental:* U Cal Media & Indiana AV Ctr.

Problems of the Aged: Part One. 52 min. Sound. 16mm Color. *Rental:* MTI Teleprograms Inc.

Proces, Le *see* Trial.

Process of Communication, The. 1967. 45 min. Sound. 16mm B&W. *Rental:* U Mich Media & Utah Media.

Prodigal, The. Lana Turner & Edmund Purdom. Directed by Richard Thorpe. 1955. MGM. 115 min. Sound. 16mm B&W. *Rental:* MGM United.

Prodigal, The. Lawrence Tibbett, Roland Young & Esther Ralston. 1931. MGM. 77 min. Sound. 16mm B&W. *Rental:* MGM United.

Producers, The. Zero Mostel & Gene Wilder. Directed by Mel Brooks. 1968. Embassy. 88 min. Sound. 16mm Color. *Rental:* Films Inc.

Prof. Erik Erikson. 2 pts. 1964. Association. (Documentary). 110 min. Sound. 16mm B&W. *Rental:* U Cal Media.

Professional Sweetheart. Ginger Rogers & Betty Furness. Directed by Merian C. Cooper. 1933. RKO. 70 min. Sound. 16mm *Rental:* RKO General Pics.

Professionals, The. Burt Lancaster, Lee Marvin & Robert Ryan. Directed by Richard Brooks. 1966. Columbia. 117 min. Sound. 16mm Color. *Rental:* Buchan Pic, Cine Craft, Corinth Films, Bosco Films, Images Film, Inst Cinema, U of IL Film, Ivy Films, Kerr Film, Modern Sound, Natl Film Video, Film Ctr DC, Twyman Films, Video Comm, Westcoast Films, Wholesome FIlm Ctr & Willoughby Peer. *Rental:* Corinth Films & Kit Parker, Anamorphic version.

Professor Beware. Harold Lloyd. Directed by Elliott Nugent. 1938. Paramount. 93 min. Sound. 16mm B&W. *Rental:* Swank Motion.

Professor Lettvin Tuned In. 1967. NET. (Documentary). 90 min. Sound. 16mm B&W. *Rental:* Indiana AV Ctr. *Sale:* Indiana AV Ctr.

Professor Mamlock. S. Mezhinsky. Directed by Adolf Minkin & Herbert Rappaport. Rus. 1938. Russia. 105 min. Sound. 16mm B&W. subtitles. *Rental:* Corinth Films.

Professor's Gamble, The. Roger Pryor & Cecilia Parker. Directed by Max Nosseck. 1941. PRC. 66 min. Sound. 16mm B&W. *Rental:* Mogulls Films.

Profile of Paul Robeson, A. 1979. PBS. (Documentary). 60 min. Videotape Color. *Rental:* PBS Video. *Sale:* PBS Video.

Profile of Terror. Orig. Title: Face of Terror. Richard Alden. Directed by James Landis. 1963. NTA. 91 min. Sound. 16mm B&W. dubbed. *Rental:* Ivy Films.

Profile of the Southern Moderate, A. NET. (Documentary). 59 min. Sound. 16mm B&W. *Rental:* Indiana AV Ctr. *Sale:* Indiana AV Ctr.

Program: A Chemical Society. Nancy Regan, Bill Bixby & Bruce Weitz. Pittsburgh/WQED. 58 min. Sound. 16mm Color. *Rental:* MTI Tele.

Program for Parents, A. 1983. Indiana U.. (Documentary). 90 min. Sound. 16mm Color. *Rental:* Indiana Av Ctr. *Sale:* Indiana Av Ctr. *Sale:* Indiana Av Ctr, Videotape version.

Program Two: Community Answers. Nancy Regan, Willie Stargell & Sandy Duncan. WQED/Pittsburgh. 58 min. Sound. 16mm Color. *Rental:* MTI & U Cal Media.

Project Moonbase. Donna Martell & Hayden Rorke. Directed by Richard Talmadge. 1953. Lippert. 90 min. Sound. 16mm B&W. *Rental:* Inst Cinema, Welling Motion Pictures & Willoughby Peer.

Project X. Christopher George & Henry Jones. Directed by William Castle. 1968. Paramount. 97 min. Sound. 16mm Color. *Rental:* Films Inc.

Projected Man, The. Bryant Halliday & Mary Peach. Directed by Ian Curteis. 1966. Britain. 76 min. Sound. 16mm Color. *Rental:* Swank Motion.

Projection of Australia, The. 1972. Australia. (Documentary). 59 min. Sound. 16mm Color. *Rental:* Aust Info Serv. *Sale:* Aust Info Serv.

Projection Privee. Bulle Ogier, Francoise Fabian & Jane Birkin. Directed by Francois Leterrier. Fr. 1973. France. 85 min. Sound. 16mm Color. subtitles. *Rental:* Speciality Films.

Projectionist, The. Chuck McCann, Rodney Dangerfield & Ina Balin. Directed by Harry Hurwitz. 1971. Maron. 87 min. Sound. 16mm Color. *Rental:* Images Film & New Cinema.

Prologue. Abbie Hoffman & Dick Gregory. Directed by Jean Genet & Robin Spry. 1970. Canada. 87 min. Sound. 16mm B&W. *Rental:* U Cal Media.

Prologue to Power. Directed by Munroe Scott. 1971. Canada. (Documentary). 58 min. Sound. 16mm Color. *Rental:* Natl Film CN. *Sale:* Natl Film CN.

Prom Night. Jamie Lee Curtis & Leslie Nielsen. Directed by Paul Lynch. 1980. Embassy. 91 min. Sound. 16mm Color. *Rental:* Films Inc.

Promessi Sposi, I. Gino Cervi. Directed by Valentino Brosio. Ital. 1938. Italy. 77 min. Sound. 16mm B&W. subtitles. *Rental:* Film Classics.

Promise, The. John Castle & Ian McKellen. Directed by Michael Hayes. 1969. Commonwealth. 95 min. Sound. 16mm Color. *Rental:* Rep Pic Film & Video Comm. *Lease:* Rep Pic Film.

Promise, The. Kathleen Quinlan & Stephen Collins. Directed by Gilbert Cates. 1979. Universal. 97 min. Sound. 16mm Color. *Rental:* Swank Motion.

Promise at Dawn, A. Melina Mercouri & Asaf Dayan. Directed by Jules Dassin. 1970. Embassy. 101 min. Sound. 16mm Color. *Rental:* Films Inc.

Promise Fulfilled *see* Wildcat of Tucson.

Promise Her Anything. Warren Beatty & Leslie Caron. Directed by Arthur Hiller. 1966. Paramount. 97 min. Sound. 16mm Color. *Rental:* Films Inc.

Promise of Love, The. Valerie Bertinelli & Jameson Parker. Directed by Don Taylor. 1980. CBS. 105 min. Sound. 16mm Color. *Rental:* Twyman Films.

Promised Land, The. 4 pts. 1959. Canada. (Documentary). 112 min. Sound. 16mm B&W. *Rental:* Natl Film CN. *Sale:* Natl Film CN.

Promised Land, The. Directed by Miguel Littin. Span. 1973. Chile. (Documentary). 110 min. Sound. 16mm Color. subtitles. *Rental:* Cinema Guild & New Yorker Films. *Sale:* Cinema Guild.

Promised Land, The. Directed by Carol Myers. 1979. Canada. (Documentary). 56 min. Sound. 16mm Color. *Rental:* Natl Film CN.

Promised Lands. Directed by Susan Sontag. 1973. France. (Documentary). 87 min. Sound. 16mm Color. narrated Eng. *Rental:* New Yorker Films.

Promises in the Dark. Marsha Mason & Ned Beatty. Directed by Jerome Hellman. 1979. Orion. 115 min. Sound. 16mm Color. *Rental:* Films Inc.

Promises! Promises! Jayne Mansfield & Marie McDonald. Directed by King Donovan. 1963. Weiss. 75 min. Sound. 16mm B&W. *Rental:* Budget Films.

Promoter, The. Alec Guiness & Glynis Johns. Directed by Ronald Neame. 1952. Janus. 88 min. Sound. 16mm B&W. *Rental:* Films Inc.

Properties of Radiation, The. 1952. Atomic Energy Commission. (Documentary). 68 min. Sound. 16mm B&W. *Rental:* Natl AV Ctr.

Property. Directed by Penny Allen. 1978. Cinema Perspectives. (Documentary). 93 min. Sound. 16mm Color. *Rental:* First Run & Icarus Films.

Prophecy, The. 1973. NBC. (Documentary). 83 min. Sound. 16mm Color. *Rental:* Films Inc. *Sale:* Films Inc.

Prophecy, The. Talia Shire & Robert Foxworth. Directed by John Frankenheimer. 1979. Paramount. Sound. 16mm Color. *Rental:* Films Inc.

Prophecy, A. Directed by Graham Coleman & David Lascelles. 54 min. 16mm Color. *Rental:* U Cal Media. *Sale:* U Cal Media. *Rental:* U Cal Media, *Sale:* U Cal Media, Videotape version.

Prophets & Promise of Classical Capitalism. 1976. Britain. (Documentary). 60 min. Sound. 16mm Color. *Rental:* U Cal Media, Films Inc, U of IL Film & Syracuse U Film. *Sale:* Films Inc. *Rental:* Films Inc, *Sale:* Films Inc, Videotape version.

Prosecutor, The. Barry Zoeller. 54 min. Sound. 16mm Color. *Rental:* Gospel Films.

Prosperity. Marie Dressler, Polly Moran & Norman Foster. Directed by Sam Wood. 1932. MGM. 90 min. Sound. 16mm B&W. *Rental:* MGM United.

Protection for Sale: Insurance Industry. 1983. Films Inc. 52 min. Sound. 16mm Color. *Rental:* Syracuse U Film.

Protest & Communication. 1968. Britain. (Documentary). 60 min. Sound. 16mm Color. *Rental:* Films Inc, Iowa Films, OK AV Ctr & Syracuse U Film. *Sale:* Films Inc. *Sale:* Films Inc, Videotape version.

Protestant Spirit U. S. A. 1977. Britain. (Documentary). 52 min. Sound. Videotape Color. *Rental:* U Cal Media, Iowa Films & U Mich Media.

Proud & the Beautiful, The. Michele Morgan & Gerard Philipe. Directed by Yves Allegret. 1956. France. 103 min. Sound. 16mm B&W. dubbed. *Rental:* Films Inc.

Proud & the Damned, The. Chuck Connors, Jose Greco & Cesar Romero. Directed by Ferde Grofe Jr. 1971. Gold Key. 96 min. Sound. 16mm Color. *Rental:* Budget Films, Video Comm, Welling Motion Pictures & Westcoast Films. *Sale:* Reel Images & Video Comm. *Rental:* Video Comm, *Lease:* Video Comm, Videotape version.

Proud & the Profane, The. William Holden & Deborah Kerr. Directed by George Seaton. 1956. Paramount. 111 min. Sound. 16mm B&W. *Rental:* Films Inc.

Proud Flesh, The. Eleanor Boardman & Patrick O'Malley. Directed by King Vidor. 1925. MGM. 63 min. Silent. 16mm B&W. *Rental:* MGM United.

Proud Ones, The. Robert Ryan & Virginia Mayo. Directed by Robert Webb. 1956. Fox. (Anamorphic). 94 min. Sound. 16mm Color. *Rental:* Films Inc.

Proud Stallion, The. Jorga Kotrbova. 1964. Czechoslovakia. 84 min. Sound. 16mm B&W. dubbed. *Rental:* Films Inc & Westcoast Films.

Proud Valley, The. Paul Robeson & Clifford Evans. Directed by Pen Tennyson. 1940. Britain. 77 min. Sound. 16mm B&W. *Rental:* Films Inc & Janus Films.

Proust. France. (Cast unlisted). 60 min. Sound. 16mm B&W. *Rental:* French Am Cul. *Rental:* French Am Cul, Videotape version.

Proust Tel Que Je L'Ai Connu. Directed by Gerard Herzog. France. (Documentary). 100 min. Sound. 16mm B&W. *Rental:* French Am Cul. *Rental:* French Am Cul, Videotape version.

Providence. Sir John Gielgud, Ellen Burstyn & Dirk Bogarde. Directed by Alain Resnais. 1977. France. 110 min. Sound. 16mm Color. *Rental:* Cinema Five & New Cinema.

Prowler, The. Van Heflin & Evelyn Keyes. Directed by Joseph Losey. 1951. United Artists. 90 min. Sound. 16mm B&W. *Rental:* Ivy Films.

Prudence & the Pill. Deborah Kerr & David Niven. Directed by Fielder Cook. 1968. Fox. (Anamorphic). 92 min. Sound. 16mm Color. *Rental:* Films Inc.

Prudence Crandall. Janice Rule. Directed by Alexander Singer. (Profiles in Courage Ser.). 1965. Saudek. 50 min. Sound. 16mm B&W. *Rental:* U of IL Film & Syracuse U Film. *Sale:* IQ Films. *Rental:* IQ Films, *Sale:* IQ Films, Spanish dubbed version.

Psychiatric Expert in the Case of an Emotionally Maltreated Child, The. 1978. 45 min. Sound. 16mm Color. *Rental:* Iowa Films.

Psychic Killer, The. Jim Hutton & Julie Adams. Directed by Ray Danton. 1975. Embassy. 90 min. Sound. 16mm Color. *Rental:* Films Inc.

Psycho. Anthony Perkins, Janet Leigh & Martin Balsam. Directed by Alfred Hitchcock. 1960. Paramount. 109 min. Sound. 16mm B&W. *Rental:* Budget Films & Swank Motion. *Sale:* Festival Films.

Psycho-Circus. Christopher Lee & Leo Genn. Directed by John Moxey. 1967. Britain. 65 min. Sound. 16mm Color. *Rental:* Ivy Films.

Psycho II. Tony Perkins, Vera Miles & Meg Tilly. Directed by Richard Franklin. 1983. Universal. 115 min. Sound. 16mm Color. *Rental:* Swank Motion. *Rental:* Swank Motion, Videotape version.

Psychology & Arthur Miller. 2 pts. 1969. Association. (Documentary). 110 min. Sound. 16mm B&W. *Rental:* Macmillan Films & Syracuse U Film. *Sale:* Macmillan Films.

Psychomania. George Sanders & Beryl Reid. Directed by Don Sharp. 1973. Scotia. 95 min. Sound. 16mm Color. *Rental:* Budget Films, Videotape version.

Psychopath, The. Patrick Wymark & Margaret Johnstone. Directed by Freddie Francis. 1966. Britain. (Anamorphic). 83 min. Sound. 16mm Color. *Rental:* Films Inc.

Psychotherapy Begins: The Case of Mr. Lin. 1955. Penn State. (Documentary). 56 min. Sound. 16mm B&W. *Rental:* U Mich Media & Utah Media.

Psychotherapy in Process: Case of Miss Mun. 1955. Pennsylvania State U.. (Documentary). 58 min. Sound. 16mm B&W. *Rental:* BYU Media & Utah Media.

Psycossissimo. Ugo Tognazzi. Directed by Steno. Ital. 1961. Italy. 88 min. Sound. 16mm B&W. subtitles. *Rental:* Films Inc.

Puberty Blues. Nell Schofield, Jad Capelja & Geoff Rhoe. Directed by Bruce Beresford. Australia. 87 min. Sound. 16mm Color. *Rental:* Swank Motion. *Rental:* Swank Motion, Videotape version.

Public Affair, A. Myron McCormick & Edward Binns. Directed by Bernard Girard. 1962. Parade. 75 min. Sound. 16mm B&W. *Rental:* Ivy Films, Super 8 sound version.

Public Cowboy Number One. Gene Autry. Directed by Joseph Kane. 1937. Republic. 54 min. Sound. 16mm B&W. *Rental:* Budget Films & Ivy Films. *Sale:* Blackhawk Films & Cinema Concepts, Super 8 sound version. *Sale:* Video Comm, Videotape version.

Public Deb Number One. George Murphy & Brenda Joyce. Directed by Gregory Ratoff. 1940. Fox. 80 min. Sound. 16mm B&W. *Rental:* Films Inc.

Public Defender. Boris Karloff & Richard Dix. Directed by Walter J. Ruben. 1931. RKO. 70 min. Sound. 16mm B&W. *Rental:* Mogulls Films.

Public Enemies *see* Gangs of the City.

Public Enemy. James Cagney & Jean Harlow. Directed by William A. Wellman. 1931. Warners. 84 min. Sound. 16mm B&W. *Rental:* Iowa Films & MGM United.

Public Enemy Number One: From Hiroshima to Hanoi. Directed by David Bradbury. 1981. Filmmakers. (Documentary). 55 min. Sound. 16mm Color. *Rental:* Film Makers & U Mich Media. *Sale:* Film Makers. *Sale:* Film Makers, Videotape version.

Public Enemy's Wife. Orig. Title: G-Man's Wife. Pat O'Brien & Margaret Lindsay. Directed by Nick Grinde. 1936. Warners. 69 min. Sound. 16mm B&W. *Rental:* MGM United.

Public Eye, The. Mia Farrow & Chaim Topol. Directed by Sir Carol Reed. 1972. Universal. 95 min. Sound. 16mm Color. *Rental:* Swank Motion.

Public Hero Number One. Lionel Barrymore & Jean Arthur. Directed by Walter J. Ruben. 1935. MGM. 91 min. Sound. 16mm B&W. *Rental:* MGM United.

Public Poison. 1972. Britain. (Documentary). 52 min. Sound. 16mm Color. *Rental:* Time-Life Multimedia. *Sale:* Time-Life Multimedia. *Rental:* Time-Life Multimedia, *Sale:* Time-Life Multimedia, Videotape version.

Public President, The: Wit & Warmth in the White House. 1976. Post-Newsweek. (Documentary). 51 min. Sound. 16mm Color. *Rental:* U of IL Film. *Sale:* Lucerne Films. *Sale:* Lucerne Films, Videotape version.

Public Sector Integrity Program, The. 1981. 50 min. Sound. Videotape Color. *Sale:* Natl AV Ctr.

Public Wedding. Jane Wyman & Dick Purcell. Directed by Nick Grinde. 1937. Warners. 58 min. Sound. 16mm B&W. *Rental:* MGM United.

Puddin' Head. Orig. Title: Judy Goes to Town. Judy Canova & Francis Lederer. Directed by Joseph Santley. 1940. Republic. 81 min. Sound. 16mm B&W. *Rental:* Ivy Films.

Pudovkin. 1960. Russia. (Documentary). 60 min. Sound. 16mm B&W. narrated Eng. *Rental:* Corinth Films.

Pueblo Affair, The. Hal Holbrook & Andrew Duggan. Directed by Anthony Page. 1976. Titus. 106 min. Sound. 16mm Color. *Rental:* Budget Films, Modern Sound & Welling Motion Pictures. *Sale:* Lucerne Films. *Sale:* Lucerne Films, Videotape version.

Puerto Rico. Directed by Jesus Diaz & Fernando Perez. Span. 1975. Cuba. (Documentary). 85 min. Sound. 16mm B&W. subtitles. *Rental:* Cinema Guild. *Sale:* Cinema Guild.

Puf N Stuf. Jack Wild & Martha Raye. Directed by Hollingsworth Morse. 1970. Universal. 98 min. Sound. 16mm Color. *Rental:* Williams Films.

Pulp. Michael Caine & Mickey Rooney. Directed by Mike Hodges. 1972. United Artists. 96 min. Sound. 16mm Color. *Rental:* MGM United.

Pumping Iron. Directed by George Butler & Robert Fiore. 1977. Cinema Five. (Documentary). 90 min. Sound. 16mm Color. *Rental:* Cinema Five, Videotape version.

Pumpkin Eater, The. Anne Bancroft & Peter Finch. Directed by Jack Clayton. 1964. Britain. 110 min. Sound. 16mm B&W. *Rental:* Budget Films, Cine Craft, CHarard Motion Pictures, Films Inc, Inst Cinema, Images Film, Kit Parker, Modern Sound, Welling Motion Pictures & Wholesome Film Ctr.

Punishment Park. Jim Bohan & Van Daniels. Directed by Peter Watkins. 1971. Sherpix. 88 min. Videotape Color. *Rental:* New Cinema. *Sale:* Video-Forum.

Puppet on a Chain. Barbara Parkins & Sven-Bertil Taube. Directed by Don Sharp & Geoffrey Reeve. 1971. Cinerama. 98 min. Sound. 16mm Color. *Rental:* Swank Motion.

Puppets & the Poet. 1979. PBS. (Cast unlisted). 59 min. Videotape Color. *Rental:* PBS Video. *Sale:* PBS Video.

Puppy, The. 1968. Japan. (Animated). Sound. 16mm Color. dubbed. *Rental:* MGM United.

Purchase Price, The. Barbara Stanwyck & George Brent. Directed by William A. Wellman. 1932. Warners. 68 min. Sound. 16mm B&W. *Rental:* MGM United.

Puritaine, Le *see* Puritan.

Puritan, The. Orig. Title: Puritaine, Le. Jean-Louis Barrault. Directed by Jeff Musso. 1938. 90 min. 16mm *Rental:* A Twyman Pres.

Purple Death from Outer Space. Buster Crabbe, Carol Hughes & Anne Gwynne. Directed by Ford Beebe & Ray Taylor. 1940. Universal. 87 min. Sound. 16mm B&W. *Rental:* Budget Films, Williams Films, Ivy Films, Kit Parker & Video Comm. *Rental:* Video Comm, Videotape version.

Purple Gang, The. Barry Sullivan & Robert Blake. Directed by Frank McDonald. 1960. Allied Artists. 85 min. Sound. 16mm B&W. *Rental:* Hurlock Cine.

Purple Haze. 1983. Thomas Fucci. 104 min. Sound. 16mm Color. *Rental:* Swank Motion.

Purple Heart, The. Dana Andrews & Richard Conte. Directed by Lewis Milestone. 1944. Fox. 99 min. Sound. 16mm B&W. *Rental:* Films Inc.

Purple Heart Diary. Frances Langford. Directed by Richard Quine. 1951. Columbia. 73 min. Sound. 16mm B&W. *Lease:* Time-Life Multimedia.

Purple Hearts. Ken Wahl, Cheryl Ladd & Stephen Lee. Directed by Sidney J. Furie. 1985. Warners. 115 min. Sound. 16mm Color. *Rental:* Swank Motion.

Purple Mask, The. Tony Curtis & Colleen Miller. Directed by Bruce Humberstone. 1955. Universal. 82 min. Sound. 16mm Color. *Rental:* Swank Motion.

Purple Monster Strikes, The. Dennis Moore & Linda Stirling. Directed by Spencer G. Bennett. 1945. Republic. 204 min. Sound. 16mm B&W. *Rental:* Ivy Films.

Purple Plain, The. Gregory Peck & Bernard Lee. Directed by Robert Parrish. 1955. United Artists. 100 min. Sound. 16mm Color. *Rental:* MGM United.

Purple Riders, The *see* Purple Vigilantes.

Purple Taxi, The. Charlotte Rampling & Fred Astaire. Directed by Yves Boisset. 1979. Quartet. 107 min. Sound. 16mm Color. *Rental:* Films Inc.

Purple V, The. Peter Lawford. Directed by George Sherman. 1943. Republic. 54 min. Sound. 16mm B&W. *Rental:* Ivy Films. *Sale:* Rep Pic Film.

Purple Vigilantes, The. Orig. Title: Purple Riders, The. Robert Livingston. Directed by George Sherman. 1938. Republic. 54 min. Sound. 16mm B&W. *Rental:* Ivy Films. *Sale:* Rep Pic Film.

Pursued. Robert Mitchum & Teresa Wright. Directed by Raoul Walsh. 1947. Warners. 101 min. Sound. 16mm B&W. *Rental:* Corinth Films. *Lease:* Corinth Films.

Pursuit. Chester Morris & Sally Eilers. Directed by Edwin L. Marin. 1935. MGM. 61 min. Sound. 16mm B&W. *Rental:* MGM United.

Pursuit Across the Desert. Pedro Armendariz. 1961. Mexico. 76 min. Sound. 16mm Color. dubbed. *Rental:* Ivy Films.

Pursuit of D. B. Cooper, The. Treat Williams & Robert Duvall. Directed by Roger Spottiswoode. 1981. Universal. 100 min. Sound. 16mm Color. *Rental:* Swank Motion. *Rental:* Swank Motion, Videotape version.

Pursuit of Happiness, The. 1968. Britain. (Documentary). 60 min. Sound. 16mm Color. *Rental:* Films Inc & Syracuse U Film. *Sale:* Films Inc. *Sale:* Films Inc, Videotape version.

Pursuit of Happiness, The. Michael Sarrazin & Barbara Hershey. Directed by Robert Mulligan. 1971. Columbia. 92 min. Sound. 16mm Color. *Rental:* Budget Films, Cine Craft, Kerr Film, Westcoast Films, Welling Motion Pictures & Willoughby Peer.

Pursuit of the Graf Spee, The. Orig. Title: Battle of the River Plate, The. John Gregson, Anthony Quayle & Peter Finch. Directed by Michael Powell & Emeric Pressburger. 1956. Britain. 119 min. Sound. 16mm Color. *Rental:* Budget Films, U of IL Film, Images Film, Kit Parker, Learning Corp Am, Modern Sound & Twyman Films. *Sale:* Learning Corp Am.

Pursuit to Algiers. Basil Rathbone. Directed by Roy William Neill. 1945. Universal. 65 min. Sound. 16mm B&W. *Rental:* Learning Corp Am & RKO General Pics. *Sale:* Learning Corp Am.

Pusher. Directed by Derek Roome. 1965. Caldwell. (Documentary). 60 min. Sound. 16mm B&W. *Rental:* Canyon Cinema.

Pushover. Fred MacMurray & Kim Novak. Directed by Richard Quine. 1954. Columbia. 110 min. Sound. 16mm B&W. *Rental:* Inst Cinema.

Puss 'n' Boots. Rafael Munoz. Directed by Roberto Rodriguez. 1961. Mexico. 91 min. Sound. 16mm Color. dubbed. *Rental:* Films Inc & Macmillan Films. *Lease:* Macmillan Films.

Pussycat, Pussycat, I Love You. Ian McShane & John Gavin. Directed by Rod Amateau. 1970. United Artists. 99 min. Sound. 16mm Color. *Rental:* MGM United.

Putney Swope. Arnold Johnson & Laura Greene. Directed by Robert Downey. 1969. Cinema Five. (Color sequences). 84 min. Sound. 16mm B&W. *Rental:* Cinema Five. *Lease:* Cinema Five.

Puttin' on the Ritz. Harry Richman & Joan Bennett. Directed by Edward Sloman. 1930. United Artists. 110 min. Sound. 16mm B&W. *Rental:* A Twyman Pres, Budget Films, Film Classics & Mogulls Films.

Puzzle, The. James Franciscus, Sir Robert Helpmann. Directed by Gordon Hessler. 1976. Sunrise. 91 min. Sound. 16mm Color. *Rental:* Modern Sound & Twyman Films.

Puzzle Children, The. 1976. WQED. (Documentary). 59 min. Sound. Videotape Color. *Rental:* U of IL Film & Indiana AV Ctr. *Sale:* Indiana AV Ctr.

Puzzle of a Downfall Child, The. Faye Dunaway, Barry Primus & Viveca Lindfors. Directed by Jerry Schatzberg. 1970. Universal. 104 min. Sound. 16mm Color. *Rental:* Swank Motion.

Pygmalion. Wendy Hiller & Leslie Howard. Directed by Anthony Asquith & Leslie Howard. 1938. Britain. 85 min. Sound. 16mm B&W. *Rental:* Films Inc, U of IL Film, Janus Films, New Cinema & Wholesome Film Ctr. *Sale:* Cinema Concepts. *Lease:* Learning Corp Am. *Rental:* Learning Corp Am, *Lease:* Learning Corp Am, Videotape version.

Pygmies, The. 1977. Films Inc. (Documentary). 46 min. Sound. 16mm Color. *Rental:* Syracuse U Film.

Pygmies of the Rain Forest, The. Directed by Kevin Duffy. 1976. Pyramid. (Documentary). 51 min. Sound. 16mm Color. *Rental:* Pyramid Film & Syracuse U Film. *Sale:* Pyramid Film. *Rental:* Pyramid Film, *Sale:* Pyramid Film, Videotape version.

Pygmy Island. Orig. Title: Jungle Jim on Pygmy Island. Johnny Weissmuller. Directed by William Berke. 1950. Columbia. 65 min. Sound. 16mm B&W. *Rental:* Cine Craft & Inst Cinema.

Pyro. Orig. Title: Thing Without a Face, The. Martha Hyer & Barry Sullivan. Directed by Julio Coll. 1964. American International. 99 min. Sound. 16mm Color. *Rental:* Films Inc.

Pyx, The. Karen Black & Christopher Plummer. Directed by Harvey Hart. 1973. Canada. 111 min. Sound. 16mm Color. *Rental:* Swank Motion.

Q Ships. Roy Travers & Douglas Herald. Directed by Geoffrey Barkas & Michael Barringer. 1928. Britain. 75 min. Sound. 16mm B&W. *Sale:* Blackhawk Films & Morcraft Films. *Sale:* Blackhawk Films & Morcraft Films, Super 8 silent version. *Sale:* Blackhawk Films, Silent 8mm version.

Qeros: The Shape of Survival. Directed by John Cohen. 1979. Films Inc. (Documentary). 50 min. Sound. 16mm Color. *Rental:* Films Inc & Syracuse U Film. *Sale:* Films Inc. *Sale:* Films Inc, Videotape version.

Quackser Fortune Has a Cousin in the Bronx. Gene Wilder & Margot Kidder. Directed by Waris Hussein. 1970. UMC. 90 min. Sound. 16mm Color. *Rental:* Budget Films.

Quadrophenia. Phil Daniels & Sting. Directed by Franc Roddam. 1979. World Northal. 115 min. Sound. 16mm Color. *Rental:* Corinth Films & WW Enter. *Rental:* WW Enter, Videotape version.

Quality Street. Katharine Hepburn & Franchot Tone. Directed by George Stevens. 1937. RKO. 85 min. Sound. 16mm B&W. *Rental:* Films Inc.

Quantrill's Raiders. Steve Cochran & Gale Robbins. Directed by Edward Bernds. 1958. Allied Artists. 71 min. Sound. 16mm Color. *Rental:* Hurlock Cine.

Quare Fellow, The. Patrick McGoohan & Sylvia Syms. Directed by Arthur Dreifuss. 1962. Britain. 85 min. Sound. 16mm B&W. *Rental:* Films Inc.

Quarry, The. 1978. Meredith Monk. 80 min. Sound. 16mm Color. *Rental:* Dance Film Archive.

Quartet. Directed by Ken Annakin, Arthur Crabtree, Harold French & Ralph Smart. 1949. Britain. (Anthology). 108 min. Sound. 16mm B&W. *Rental:* Budget Films, U of IL Film, Kit Parker, Learning Corp Am & Twyman Films. *Sale:* Learning Corp Am.

Quatermass & the Pit *see* Five Million Years to Earth.

Quatermass II: The Enemy from Space. Brian Donlevy & Sidney James. Directed by Val Guest. 1957. Britain. 85 min. Sound. 16mm B&W. *Rental:* Corinth Films.

Quatre Bassets Pour une Danois. Dean Jones & Suzanne Pleshette. Directed by Norman Tokar. 1966. Disney. 93 min. Sound. 16mm Color. dubbed Fr. *Rental:* Twyman Films.

Quatro Giornate Dì Napoli, Le *see* Four Days of Naples.

Que la Fete Commence *see* Let Joy Reign Supreme.

Quebec. John Barrymore Jr. & Corinne Calvet. Directed by Alan Le May. 1951. Paramount. 85 min. Sound. 16mm Color. *Rental:* Films Inc.

Queen, The. Directed by Frank Simon. 1968. Evergreen. (Documentary). 68 min. Sound. 16mm Color. *Rental:* Grove.

Queen & Prince Philip, The. 1981. Royal Heritage. (Documentary). 60 min. Sound. 16mm Color. *Rental:* Films Inc. *Sale:* Films Inc. *Rental:* Films Inc, *Sale:* Films Inc, Videotape version.

Queen Bee. Joan Crawford & Barry Sullivan. Directed by Ranald MacDougall. 1955. Columbia. 95 min. Sound. 16mm B&W. *Rental:* Cine Craft & Westcoast Films.

Queen Christina. Greta Garbo & John Gilbert. Directed by Rouben Mamoulian. 1933. MGM. 100 min. Sound. 16mm B&W. *Rental:* MGM United.

Queen Elizabeth. Sarah Bernhardt & Lou Tellegen. Directed by Louis Mercanton. 1912. France. 45 min. Silent. 16mm B&W. *Rental:* Em Gee Film Lib & Museum Mod Art. *Sale:* Glenn Photo. *Rental:* Ivy Films, *Sale:* Glenn Photo, Super 8 silent version. *Sale:* Glenn Photo, Silent 8mm version.

Queen Esther. 1968. Cathedral. (Cast unlisted). 50 min. Sound. 16mm B&W. *Rental:* Roas Films.

Queen for a Day. Phyllis Avery & Darren McGavin. Directed by Arthur Lubin. 1951. MGM. 107 min. Sound. 16mm B&W. *Rental:* Ivy Films. *Sale:* Rep Pic Film.

Queen for Caesar, A. Gordon Scott & Pascale Petit. 1962. Italy. 95 min. Sound. 16mm Color. dubbed. *Rental:* Ivy Films.

Queen Kelly. Gloria Swanson & Walter Byron. Directed by Erich Von Stroheim. 1928. United Artists. (Musical Score Only). 97 min. Sound. 16mm B&W. *Rental:* Kino Intl.

Queen of Babylon. Rhonda Fleming & Ricardo Montalban. Directed by Carlo Bragaglia. 1956. Fox. 98 min. Sound. 16mm Color. *Rental:* Films Inc.

Queen of Blood *see* Planet of Blood.

Queen of Burlesque. Evelyn Ankers. Directed by Sam Newfield. 1946. PRC. 70 min. Sound. 16mm B&W. *Sale:* Classics Assoc NY.

Queen of Outer Space. Zsa Zsa Gabor & Eric Fleming. Directed by Edward Bernds. 1958. Allied Artists. 80 min. Sound. 16mm Color. *Rental:* Hurlock Cine.

Queen of Sheba Meets the Atom Man, The. Jack Smith. Directed by Ron Rice. 1967. Ron Rice. 90 min. Silent. 16mm B&W. *Rental:* Canyon Cinema.

Queen of Spades, The. Dame Edith Evans & Anton Walbrook. Directed by Thorold Dickinson. 1949. Britain. 95 min. Sound. 16mm B&W. *Rental:* Janus Films.

Queen of Spades, The. Directed by Roman Tikhomirov. 1960. Russia. (Opera). 102 min. Sound. 16mm B&W. narrated Eng. *Rental:* Corinth Films.

Queen of Spades, The. Anton Walbrook & Dame Edith Evans. Directed by Thorold Dickinson. 1948. Janus. 95 min. Sound. 16mm B&W. *Rental:* Films Inc.

Queen of Spies *see* Joan of Ozark.

Queen of the Amazons. Robert Lowery & Patricia Morison. Directed by Edward Finney. 1947. Screen Guild. 61 min. Sound. 16mm B&W. *Rental:* Mogulls Films.

Queen of the Chorus. Virginia Brown Faire & Rex Lease. Directed by Charles Hunt. 1928. Anchor. 65 min. Silent. 16mm B&W. *Sale:* Cinema Concepts & Griggs Movie.

Queen of the Mob. Blanche Yurka & Ralph Bellamy. Directed by James Hogan. 1940. Paramount. 61 min. Sound. 16mm B&W. *Rental:* Swank Motion.

Queen of the Nile. Orig. Title: Nefertiti, Queen of the Nile. Jeanne Crain & Edmund Purdom. Directed by Fernando Cerchio. 1963. Fox. 92 min. Sound. 16mm B&W. *Rental:* Willoughby Peer.

Queen of the Stardust Ballroom. Maureen Stapleton & Charles Durning. 1974. CBS. 102 min. Sound. 16mm Color. *Rental:* Budget Films, Films Inc, U of IL Film, Kent St U Film, Kit Parker, Learning Corp Am, Mass Media, Syracuse U Film & Twyman Films. *Sale:* Learning Corp Am.

Queen of the Yukon. Irene Rich & Charles Bickford. Directed by Phil Rosen. 1940. Monogram. 70 min. Sound. 16mm B&W. *Rental:* Mogulls Films.

Quem Quaeritis, Abraham & Isaac, the Second Shepherd's Play. 1975. Films for the Humanities. (Documentary). 54 min. Sound. 16mm Color. *Rental:* Films Human & U of IL Film. *Sale:* Films Human.

Quentin Durward. Robert Taylor & Kay Kendall. Directed by Richard Thorpe. 1955. MGM. 101 min. Sound. 16mm Color. *Rental:* MGM United.

Querelle. Brad Davis, Franco Nero & Jeanne Moreau. Directed by Rainer Werner Fassbinder. 1983. Germany. 106 min. Sound. 16mm Color. subtitles. *Rental:* Swank Motion. *Rental:* Swank Motion, Videotape version.

Quest for Fire. Everett McGill & Ron Perlman. Directed by Jean-Jacques Annaud. 1982. Fox. 97 min. Sound. 16mm Color. *Rental:* Films Inc.

Question De la Vie *see* Matter of Life.

Question of Balance, A. 1977. Britain. (Documentary). 52 min. Sound. 16mm Color. *Rental:* U of IL Film, Iowa Films & U Mich Media.

Question of Survival, A. 1972. Britain. (Documentary). 52 min. Sound. 16mm Color. *Rental:* Time-Life Multimedia. *Sale:* Time-Life Multimedia.

Question of TV Violence, The. 1972. Canada. (Documentary). 56 min. Sound. 16mm Color. *Rental:* U Cal Media, Phoenix Films & Syracuse U Film. *Sale:* Phoenix Films. *Sale:* Phoenix Films, Videotape version.

Question Seven. Michael Gwynne. Directed by Stuart Rosenberg. 1961. DeRochement. 107 min. Sound. 16mm B&W. *Rental:* Budget Films, Films Inc, Lutheran Film, Newman Film Lib & Wholesome Film Ctr. *Sale:* Lutheran Film.

Quick & the Dead, The. Larry Mann. Directed by Robert Totten. 1962. Sam Altonian. 92 min. Sound. 16mm B&W. *Rental:* Westcoast Films.

Quick, Before It Melts. Robert Morse & George Maharis. Directed by Delbert Mann. 1964. MGM. 98 min. Sound. 16mm Color. *Rental:* MGM United. *Rental:* MGM United, Anamorphic version.

Quick Billy. Directed by Bruce Baillie. 1971. Bruce Baillie. (Experimental). 75 min. Sound. 16mm Color. *Rental:* Time-Life Multimedia.

Quick Gun, The. Audie Murphy & Merry Anders. Directed by Sidney Salkow. 1964. Columbia. 88 min. Sound. 16mm Color. *Rental:* Modern Sound.

Quick Millions. Spencer Tracy & Sally Eilers. Directed by Rowland Brown. 1931. Fox. 72 min. Sound. 16mm B&W. *Rental:* Films Inc.

Quick Money. Jack Carson & Fred Stone. Directed by Edward Killy. 1938. RKO. 59 min. Sound. 16mm B&W. *Rental:* RKO General Pics.

Quick, Let's Get Married *see* Seven Different Ways.

Quicksand. Mickey Rooney & Jeanne Cagney. Directed by Irving Pichel. 1950. MGM. 79 min. Sound. 16mm B&W. *Rental:* Budget Films & Video Comm. *Lease:* Video Comm. *Rental:* Video Comm, *Lease:* Video Comm, Videotape version.

Quiet American, The. Audie Murphy, Sir Michael Redgrave. Directed by Joseph L. Mankiewicz. 1958. United Artists. 120 min. Sound. 16mm B&W. *Rental:* MGM United.

Quiet Crisis, The. 1980. WCCO. (Documentary). 55 min. Sound. 16mm Color. *Rental:* Indiana AV Ctr. *Sale:* Indiana AV Ctr. *Rental:* Indiana AV Ctr, *Sale:* Indiana AV Ctr, Videotape version.

Quiet Duel, The. Toshiro Mifune & Takashi Shimura. Directed by Akira Kurosawa. Jap. 1949. Japan. 95 min. Sound. 16mm B&W. subtitles. *Rental:* Films Inc.

Quiet Gun, The. Forrest Tucker & Tom Brown. Directed by William Claxton. 1957. Fox. (Anamorphic). 78 min. Sound. 16mm B&W. *Rental:* Ivy Films & Westcoast Films. *Lease:* Rep Pic Film.

Quiet Man, The. John Wayne, Maureen O'Hara & Barry Fitzgerald. Directed by John Ford. 1952. Republic. 129 min. Sound. Color. *Rental:* Arcus Film, Budget Films, Cine Craft, Films Inc, Images Film, Ivy Films, Kit Parker, Modern Sound, Twyman Films, Welling Motion Pictures & Wholesome Film Ctr. *Lease:* Rep Pic Film. *Rental:* Ivy Films, *Sale:* Cinema Concepts & Ivy Films, Videotape version.

Quiet One, The. 1948. Mayer-Burstyn. (Documentary). 68 min. Sound. 16mm B&W. *Rental:* Budget Films, U Cal Media, Em Gee Film Lib, Films Inc, U of IL Film, Images Film, Kit Parker, Natl Cinema, U Mich Media, Mass Media, Mogulls Films, Syracuse U Film, Texture Film & Utah Media. *Sale:* Texture Film, Festival Films & Reel Images. *Sale:* Festival Films & Texture Film, Videotape version.

Quiet Please, Murder. Orig. Title: Rare Book Murder, The. George Sanders & Gail Patrick. Directed by John Larkin. 1942. Fox. 70 min. Sound. 16mm B&W. *Rental:* Films Inc.

Quiller Memorandum, The. George Segal & Sir Alec Guinness. Directed by Michael Anderson. 1966. Britain. 105 min. Sound. 16mm Color. *Rental:* Films Inc. *Rental:* Films Inc, Anamorphic version.

Quilt: Psychic Censor. 1976. Indiana Univ. 60 min. Sound. 16mm Color. *Rental:* Syracuse U Film.

Quincannon, Frontier Scout. Orig. Title: Frontier Scout. Tony Martin & Peggie Castle. Directed by Lesley Selander. 1956. United Artists. 83 min. Sound. 16mm Color. *Rental:* MGM United.

Quintet. Paul Newman & Fernando Rey. Directed by Robert Altman. 1979. Fox. 100 min. Sound. 16mm Color. *Rental:* Films Inc.

Quiver of Life, The. 1980. Canada. (Documentary). 57 min. Sound. 16mm Color. *Rental:* Time-Life Multimedia. *Sale:* Time-Life Multimedia. *Sale:* Time-Life Multimedia, Videotape version.

Quixote. 1965. 45 min. Sound. 16mm B&W Color. *Rental:* Filmmakers Coop.

Quo Vadis? Amleto Novelli & Gustavo Serena. Directed by Enrico Guazzoni. 1912. Italy. 116 min. Silent. 16mm B&W. subtitles Fr. subtitles Ger. *Rental:* Museum Mod Art.

Quo Vadis? Robert Taylor & Deborah Kerr. Directed by Mervyn LeRoy. 1951. MGM. 168 min. Sound. 16mm Color. *Rental:* MGM United. *Rental:* MGM United, Videotape version.

R. C. M. P. & the Treasure of Genghis Khan. Jim Bannon & Virginia Belmont. Directed by Fred C. Brannon & Yakima Canutt. 1948. Republic. 100 min. Sound. 16mm B&W. *Rental:* Ivy Films. *Sale:* Rep Pic Film.

R. D. Laing's Glasgow. 1978. Learning Corp. (Documentary). 50 min. Sound. 16mm Color. *Rental:* Kent St U Film & Learning Corp Am. *Sale:* Learning Corp Am.

R. D. 1, Box Ninety-Nine. 1978. Penn State. (Documentary). 59 min. Sound. 16mm Color. *Rental:* Penn St AV Serv. *Sale:* Penn St AV Serv. *Rental:* Penn St AV Serv, *Sale:* Penn St AV Serv, Videotape version.

R. P. M. Anthony Quinn & Ann-Margret. Directed by Stanley Kramer. 1970. Columbia. 91 min. Sound. 16mm Color. *Rental:* Cine Craft, Modern Sound & Welling Motion Pictures.

Ra Expeditions, The. Directed by Thor Heyerdahl. 1972. Universal. (Documentary). 93 min. Sound. 16mm Color. *Rental:* Swank Motion & Twyman Films.

Rabbit Hill. 1967. NBC. (Cast unlisted). 53 min. Sound. 16mm Color. *Rental:* McGraw-Hill Films, Syracuse U Film & Wholesome Film Ctr. *Sale:* McGraw-Hill Films.

Rabbit, Run. James Caan & Carrie Snodgress. Directed by Jack Smight. 1970. Warners. 94 min. Sound. 16mm Color. *Rental:* Westcoast Films, Anamorphic color version.

Rabbit Test. Billy Crystal & Charlotte Rae. Directed by Joan Rivers. 1978. Embassy. 88 min. Sound. 16mm Color. *Rental:* Films Inc.

Rabbit Trap, The. Ernest Borgnine & David Brian. Directed by Philip Leacock. 1959. Allied Artists. 75 min. Sound. 16mm B&W. *Rental:* MGM United.

Rabid. Marilyn Chambers & Joe Silver. Directed by David Cronenberg. 1977. Canada. 91 min. Sound. 16mm Color. *Rental:* Films Inc.

Race for Life. Richard Conte & George Coulouris. Directed by Terence Fisher. 1955. Lippert. 69 min. Sound. 16mm B&W. *Rental:* Budget Films.

Race for Number One, The. 1982. EBE. (Documentary). 54 min. Sound. 16mm Color. *Sale:* Ency Brit Ed & Syracuse U Film. *Rental:* Iowa Films & Ency Brit Ed. *Sale:* Ency Brit Ed, Videotape version.

Race for Space, The. 1960. McGraw-Hill. (Documentary). 55 min. Sound. 16mm B&W. *Rental:* U of IL Film, McGraw-Hill Films & Syracuse U Film. *Sale:* McGraw-Hill Films.

Race for Your Life, Charlie Brown! Directed by Bill Melendez. 1977. Paramount. (Animated). 76 min. Sound. 16mm Color. *Rental:* Films Inc.

Race, Intelligence & Education. 1971. Britain. (Lecture). 56 min. Sound. 16mm B&W. *Rental:* Time-Life Multimedia. *Sale:* Time-Life Multimedia.

Race Street. George Raft & William Bendix. Directed by Edwin L. Marin. 1948. RKO. 79 min. Sound. 16mm B&W. *Rental:* RKO General Pics.

Race to Extinction. 1966. Britain. (Documentary). 50 min. Sound. 16mm B&W. *Rental:* Time-Life Multimedia. *Sale:* Time-Life Multimedia.

Race to Oblivion, The. 1982. Physicians for Social Responsibility. (Documentary). 49 min. Sound. 16mm Color. *Rental:* U Cal Media & Mass Media Ministries.

Race with the Devil. Warren Oates & Peter Fonda. 1975. Fox. 88 min. Sound. 16mm Color. *Rental:* Films Inc.

Racers, The. Kirk Douglas & Bella Darvi. Directed by Henry Hathaway. 1955. Fox. (Anamorphic). 112 min. Sound. 16mm B&W. *Rental:* Films Inc.

Rachel & the Stranger. William Holden & Loretta Young. Directed by Norman Foster. 1948. RKO. 92 min. Sound. 16mm B&W. *Rental:* Films Inc. *Sale:* Tamarelles French Film, Videotape version.

Racing Blood. Bill Williams & Jean Porter. Directed by Wesley Barry. 1954. Fox. 75 min. Sound. 16mm Color. *Rental:* Willoughby Peer.

Racing Fool. Harry Brown & Reed Howes. Directed by Harry Joe Brown. 1927. Rayart. 60 min. Silent. 16mm B&W. *Rental:* Mogulls Films.

Racing Lady. Ann Dvorak & Harry Carey. Directed by Wallace Fox. 1937. RKO. 59 min. Sound. 16mm B&W. *Rental:* RKO General Pics.

Racing Luck *see* Red Hot Tires.

Rack, The. Paul Newman & Wendell Corey. Directed by Arnold Laven. 1956. MGM. 100 min. Sound. 16mm B&W. *Rental:* MGM United.

Racket, The. Robert Mitchum & Lizabeth Scott. Directed by John Cromwell. 1951. RKO. 88 min. Sound. 16mm B&W. *Rental:* Films Inc.

Racket Busters. Humphrey Bogart & George Brent. Directed by Lloyd Bacon. 1938. Warners. 71 min. Sound. 16mm B&W. *Rental:* MGM United.

Racketeer, The. Carole Lombard. Directed by Howard Higgin. 1931. Pathe. 70 min. Sound. 16mm B&W. *Rental:* Film Classics. *Sale:* Cinema Concepts & Natl Cinema.

Racketeers of the Range. Chill Wills & George O'Brien. Directed by Bert Gilroy. 1939. RKO. 62 min. Sound. 16mm B&W. *Rental:* RKO General Pics.

Racquet. Edie Adams, Bert Convy & Phil Silvers. Directed by David Winters. 1979. Cal-Am. 110 min. Sound. 16mm Color. *Rental:* Twyman Films.

Radar Men from the Moon. George Wallace & Aline Towne. Directed by Fred C. Brannon. 1951. Republic. 163 min. Sound. 16mm B&W. *Rental:* Ivy Films.

Radar Patrol vs. Spy King. Kirk Alyn & Jean Dean. Directed by Fred C. Brannon. 1949. Republic. 163 min. Sound. 16mm B&W. *Rental:* Ivy Films.

Radar Secret Service. John Howard & Adele Jergens. 1950. Lippert. 75 min. Sound. 16mm B&W. *Rental:* Mogulls Films.

Radiating the Fruit of Truth: Part Two. Directed by Graham Coleman & David Lascelles. 129 min. Sound. 16mm Color. *Rental:* U Cal Media. *Sale:* U CaL Media. *Rental:* U Cal Media, *Sale:* U Cal Media, Videotape version.

Radical Sex Styles. Directed by Armand Weston. 1973. Armand Weston. (Documentary). 50 min. Sound. 16mm B&W. *Rental:* Grove. *Sale:* Grove.

Radio City Revels. Bob Burns & Jack Oakie. Directed by Ben Stoloff. 1938. RKO. 90 min. Sound. 16mm B&W. *Rental:* Films Inc.

Radio Murder Mystery, The *see* Love Is on the Air.

Radio Ranch. Gene Autry & Frankie Darro. Directed by Otto Brower & B. Reeves Eason. 1934. Mascot. 80 min. Sound. 16mm B&W. *Rental:* Budget Films, Classic Film Mus, Em Gee Film Lib, Kit Parker & Film Ctr DC. *Sale:* Cinema Concepts. *Rental:* Ivy Films, *Sale:* Ivy Films, Super 8 Sound version.

Radio Star, The *see* Loudspeaker.

Radio Stars on Parade. Ralph Edwards & Frances Langford. Directed by Ben Stoloff. 1946. RKO. 69 min. Sound. 16mm *Rental:* RKO General Pics.

Rafer Johnson Story, The. 1963. Sterling. (Documentary). 55 min. Sound. 16mm Color. *Rental:* Syracuse U Film. *Sale:* Syracuse U Film.

Rafferty & the Gold Dust Twins. Alan Arkin & Sally Kellerman. Directed by Dick Richards. 1975. Warners. 91 min. Sound. 16mm Color. *Rental:* Films Inc & Swank Motion.

Raffles. David Niven & Olivia De Havilland. Directed by Sam Wood. 1940. Goldwyn. 72 min. Sound. 16mm B&W. *Rental:* Films Inc.

Rag Tag Champs, The. Larry B. Scott & Glynn Turman. Directed by Virgil Vogel. 1798. ABC. 48 min. Sound. 16mm Color. *Rental:* U of IL Film, MTI Tele & Roas Films. *Sale:* MTI Tele. *Sale:* MTI Tele, Videotape version.

Raga. Ravi Shankar & Yehudi Menuhin. Directed by Howard Worth. 1970. Apple. 96 min. Sound. 16mm Color. *Rental:* New Line Cinema. *Sale:* New Line Cinema.

Ragan. Ty Hardin & Antonella Lualdi. 1968. Italy. 92 min. Sound. 16mm Color. dubbed. *Rental:* Films Inc.

Rage. Glenn Ford & Stella Stevens. Directed by Gilberto Gazcon. 1966. Columbia. 103 min. Sound. 16mm Color. *Lease:* Time-Life Multimedia.

Rage. George C. Scott & Richard Basehart. Directed by George C. Scott. 1972. Warners. 104 min. Sound. 16mm Color. *Rental:* Cine Craft, Modern Sound, Video Comm & Welling Motion Pictures.

Rage at Dawn, A. Randolph Scott & Forrest Tucker. Directed by Tim Whelan. 1955. RKO. 86 min. Sound. 16mm Color. *Rental:* Ivy Films.

Rage in Heaven. Ingrid Bergman. Directed by W. S. Van Dyke. 1941. MGM. 85 min. Sound. 16mm B&W. *Rental:* MGM United.

Rage of Paris, The. Danielle Darrieux & Douglas Fairbanks Jr. Directed by Henry Koster. 1938. Universal. 78 min. Sound. 16mm B&W. *Rental:* Budget Films, Classic Film Mus, Kit Parker & Wholesome Film Ctr. *Sale:* Cinema Concepts & Festival Films. *Sale:* Festival Films, Videotape version.

Rage of the Vulture *see* Thunder in the East.

Rage to Live, A. Suzanne Pleshette, Bradford Dillman & Ben Gazzara. Directed by Walter Grauman. 1965. MGM. 102 min. Sound. 16mm B&W. *Rental:* MGM United.

Raggedy Ann & Andy. Directed by Richard Williams. 1977. Fox. (Anamorphic, Animated). 84 min. Sound. 16mm Color. *Rental:* Films Inc.

Raggedy Ann & Andy Holiday Special, The. 50 min. Sound. Videotape Color. *Rental:* Maljack Productions.

Raggedy Man, The. Sissy Spacek & Eric Roberts. Directed by Jack Fisk. 1981. Universal. 94 min. Sound. 16mm Color. *Rental:* Swank Motion. *Rental:* Swank Motion, Videotape version.

Raggedy Rose. Mabel Normand. 1926. Pathe. 58 min. Silent. 16mm B&W. *Rental:* Em Gee Film Lib.

Raging Bull, The. Robert DeNiro & Joe Pesci. Directed by Martin Scorsese. 1980. MGM. 129 min. Sound. 16mm B&W. *Rental:* MGM United. *Rental:* MGM United, Videotape version.

Ragman's Daughter, The. Simon Rouse. Directed by Harold Becker. 1974. Britain. 94 min. Sound. 16mm Color. *Rental:* Films Inc.

Rags to Riches. Alan Baxter & Mary Carlisle. Directed by Joseph Kane. 1941. Republic. 57 min. Sound. 16mm B&W. *Rental:* Ivy Films.

Ragtime. Howard E. Rollins Jr. & James Cagney. Directed by Milos Forman. 1981. Paramount. 155 min. Sound. 16mm Color. *Rental:* Films Inc.

Ragtime Cowboy Joe. Johnny Mack Brown. Directed by Ray Taylor. 1940. Universal. 60 min. Sound. 16mm B&W. *Rental:* Willoughby Peer.

Raid, The. Van Heflin & Anne Bancroft. Directed by Hugo Fregonese. 1954. Fox. 82 min. Sound. 16mm Color. *Rental:* Films Inc.

Raid on Rommel. Richard Burton. Directed by Henry Hathaway. 1971. Universal. 95 min. Sound. 16mm Color. *Rental:* Williams Films.

Raider, The. Orig. Title: Western Approaches. Directed by Patrick Jackson. 1946. Britain. (Documentary). 80 min. Sound. 16mm Color. *Rental:* Twyman Films.

Raiders, The. Richard Conte & Viveca Lindfors. Directed by Lesley Selander. 1952. Universal. 80 min. Sound. 16mm Color. *Rental:* Swank Motion.

Raiders from Beneath the Sea. Ken Scott & Merry Anders. Directed by Maury Dexter. 1965. Fox. 73 min. Sound. 16mm B&W. *Rental:* Films Inc.

Raiders of Red Gap. Bob Livingston. Directed by Sam Newfield. 1943. PRC. 56 min. Videotape B&W. *Sale:* Reel Images.

Raiders of Sunset Pass. Eddie Dew. Directed by John English. 1943. Republic. 56 min. Sound. 16mm B&W. *Rental:* Ivy Films.

Raiders of the Border. Johnny Mack Brown. Directed by J. P. McCarthy. 1944. Monogram. 55 min. Sound. 16mm B&W. *Rental:* Hurlock Cine.

Raiders of the Lost Ark. Harrison Ford & Karen Allen. Directed by Steven Spielberg. 1981. Paramount. 115 min. Sound. 16mm Color. *Rental:* Films Inc.

Raiders of the Range. Tom Tyler. Directed by John English. 1942. Republic. 53 min. Sound. 16mm B&W. *Rental:* Ivy Films. *Sale:* Rep Pic Film.

Raiders of the South. Johnny Mack Brown. Directed by Lambert Hillyer. 1946. Monogram. 55 min. Sound. 16mm B&W. *Rental:* Hurlock Cine.

Railroaded. John Ireland & Sheila Ryan. Directed by Anthony Mann. 1947. Eagle Lion. 80 min. Sound. 16mm B&W. *Sale:* Classics Assoc NY.

Rails Into Laramie. John Payne & Meri Blanchard. Directed by Jesse Hibbs. 1954. Universal. 81 min. Sound. 16mm Color. *Rental:* Swank Motion.

Railway Children, The. Dinah Sheridan & Jenny Agutter. Directed by Lionel Jeffries. 1971. Britain. 106 min. Sound. 16mm Color. *Rental:* Williams Films.

Rain. Joan Crawford & Walter Huston. Directed by Lewis Milestone. 1932. United Artists. 91 min. Sound. 16mm B&W. *Rental:* Budget Films, Em Gee Film Lib, Films Inc, Kit Parker, Learning Corp Am, Mogulls Films, Natl Film Video, Twyman Films, Video Comm, Westcoast Films & Wholesome Film Ctr. *Sale:* Festival Films & Learning Corp Am. *Rental:* Ivy Films, *Sale:* Cinema Concepts, Ivy Films & Morcraft Films, Super 8 sound version. *Sale:* Cinema Concepts, Festival Films, Tamarelles French Film & Video Comm, Videotape version. *Rental:* Classic Film Mus & Kit Parker, 78 mins. version.

Rain & Shine. Erzsi Pasztor. Directed by Ferenc Andras. Hungarian. 1977. Hungary. 98 min. Sound. 16mm Color. subtitles. *Rental:* New Yorker Films.

Rain Forest, The. 59 min. Sound. 16mm Color. *Rental:* National Geographic Society. *Rental:* National Geographic Society, Video version.

Rain or Shine. Joe Cook & Tom Howard. Directed by Frank Capra. 1930. Columbia. 90 min. Sound. 16mm B&W. *Rental:* Kit Parker.

Rain People, The. James Caan & Shirley Knight. Directed by Francis Ford Coppola. 1969. Warners. 102 min. Sound. 16mm Color. *Rental:* Films Inc.

Rainbow, The. Natalia Uzhvy. Directed by Mark Donskoi. Rus. 1944. Russia. 93 min. Sound. 16mm B&W. subtitles. *Rental:* Corinth Films & Mogulls Films.

Rainbow on the River. Orig. Title: It Happened In New Orleans. Bobby Breen & May Robson. Directed by Kurt Neumann. 1936. RKO. 100 min. Sound. 16mm B&W. *Rental:* Budget Films & Modern Sound.

Rainbow Over Texas. Roy Rogers & Dale Evans. Directed by Frank McDonald. 1946. Republic. 65 min. Sound. 16mm B&W. *Rental:* Ivy Films & Budget Films. *Sale:* Rep Pic Film.

Rainbow Over the Range. Tex Ritter. Directed by Al Herman. 1940. Monogram. 58 min. Sound. 16mm B&W. *Rental:* Hurlock Cine.

Rainbow Over the Rockies. Jimmy Wakely. Directed by Oliver Drake. 1947. Monogram. 54 min. Sound. 16mm B&W. *Rental:* Newman Film Lib.

Rainbow 'Round My Shoulder. Frankie Laine & Billy Daniels. Directed by Richard Quine. 1952. Columbia. 78 min. Sound. 16mm Color. *Rental:* Buchan Pic, Films Inc, Inst Cinema, Modern Sound, Newman Film Lib & Welling Motion Pictures.

Rainbow Valley. John Wayne. Directed by Robert N. Bradbury. 1935. Monogram. 60 min. Sound. 16mm B&W. *Rental:* Mogulls Film.

Rainbow's End. Hoot Gibson. Directed by Norman Spencer. 1934. First Division. 59 min. Sound. 16mm B&W. *Rental:* Classics Assoc NY, Ivy Films & Mogulls Films. *Sale:* Video Comm, Videotape version.

Rainmaker, The. Katharine Hepburn & Burt Lancaster. Directed by Joseph Anthony. 1956. Paramount. 121 min. Sound. 16mm Color. *Rental:* Films Inc.

Rainmakers, The. Bert Wheeler & Robert Woolsey. Directed by Fred Guiol. 1935. RKO. 75 min. Sound. 16mm B&W. *Rental:* Films Inc.

Rains of Ranchipur, The. Richard Burton & Lana Turner. Directed by Jean Negulesco. 1955. Fox. (Anamorphic). 104 min. Sound. 16mm Color. *Rental:* Films Inc.

Raintree County. Montgomery Clift & Elizabeth Taylor. Directed by Edward Dmytryk. 1957. MGM. (Anamorphic). 185 min. Sound. 16mm Color. *Rental:* MGM United.

Raise the Titanic! Jason Robards & Richard Jordan. Directed by Jerry Jameson. 1980. AFD. 112 min. Sound. 16mm Color. *Rental:* Swank Motion.

Raised in Anger. 1979. Media Guild. (Documentary). 54 min. Sound. 16mm Color. *Rental:* Media Guild & U Cal Media. *Sale:* Media Guild. *Sale:* Media Guild, Videotape version.

Raisin in the Sun, A. Sidney Poitier & Claudia McNeil. Directed by Daniel Petrie. 1961. Columbia. 128 min. Sound. 16mm B&W. *Rental:* Arcus Film, Budget Films, Cine Craft, Charard Motion Pics, Williams Films, Bosco Films, Films Inc, U Of IL Film, Images Film, Kit Parker, Modern Sound, Newman Film Lib, Natl Film Video, Roas Films, Swank Motion, Film Ctr DC, Twyman Films, Video Comm, Westcoast Films, Welling Motion Pictures, Wholesome Film Ctr & Willoughby Peer. *Rental:* Swank Motion, Videotape version.

Raising Children. 1979. PBS. (Documentary). 59 min. Videotape Color. *Rental:* PBS Video. *Sale:* PBS Video.

Raising the Wind *see* Roommates.

Raison Avant la Passion, La. Directed by Joyce Wieland. 1969. Joyce Wieland. (Experimental). 80 min. Sound. 16mm Color. *Rental:* Canyon Cinema.

Raj Gonds. 1982. Britain. 55 min. Sound. 16mm Color. *Rental:* Films Inc. *Sale:* Films Inc. *Sale:* Films Inc, Videotape version.

Rally 'Round the Flag, Boys. Paul Newman & Joanne Woodward. Directed by Leo McCarey. 1958. Fox. (Anamorphic). 106 min. Sound. 16mm Color. *Rental:* Films Inc.

Ramona. Ester Fernandez. Directed by Victor Urruchua. Span. 1948. Mexico. 93 min. Sound. 16mm B&W. subtitles. *Rental:* Trans-World Films.

Ramona. Loretta Young & Don Ameche. Directed by Henry King. 1936. Fox. 90 min. Sound. 16mm Color. *Rental:* Films Inc.

Ramparts of Clay. Directed by Jean-Louis Bertucelli. Arabic. 1971. Tunisia. (Native cast). 87 min. Sound. 16mm Color. subtitles. *Rental:* Cinema Five. *Sale:* Cinema Five. *Sale:* Tamarelles French Film, Videotape version.

Ramparts We Watch, The. 1943. DeRochemont. (Documentary). 60 min. Sound. 16mm B&W. *Rental:* Films Inc, MacMillan Films, U Mich Media & Syracuse U Film. *Sale:* MacMillan Films.

Ramrod. Joel McCrea & Veronica Lake. Directed by Andre De Toth. 1947. MGM. 94 min. Sound. 16mm B&W. *Rental:* Ivy Films. *Sale:* Rep Pic Film.

Ramsbottom Rides Again. Arthur Askey. Directed by John Baxter. 1956. Britain. 93 min. Sound. 16mm B&W. *Rental:* Charard Motion Pic.

Ranchers & Rascals. Leo Maloney. 1924. Steiner. 55 min. Silent. 16mm B&W. *Sale:* Blackhawk Films. *Sale:* Blackhawk Films, Super 8 silent version. *Sale:* Blackhawk Films, Silent 8mm version.

Rancho Deluxe. Jeff Bridges & Sam Waterston. Directed by Frank Perry. 1975. MGM. 93 min. Sound. 16mm Color. *Rental:* MGM United.

Rancho Grande. Gene Autry. Directed by Frank McDonald. 1940. Republic. 54 min. Sound. 16mm B&W. *Rental:* Ivy Films.

Rancho Notorious. Marlene Dietrich. Directed by Fritz Lang. 1952. RKO. 89 min. Sound. 16mm Color. *Rental:* Films Inc. *Lease:* Video Comm. *Rental:* Video Comm, *Lease:* Video Comm, Videotape version.

Rancon Dune Alliance, La *see* Price of a Union.

Random Harvest. Greer Garson & Ronald Colman. Directed by Mervyn LeRoy. 1942. MGM. 126 min. Sound. 16mm B&W. *Rental:* MGM United.

Randy Newman. 1980. Verve. (Concert). 58 min. Videotape Color. *Rental:* Films Inc.

Randy Rides Alone. John Wayne. Directed by Harry Fraser. 1934. Monogram. 59 min. Sound. 16mm B&W. *Rental:* Ivy Films & Mogulls Films. *Sale:* Cinema Concepts, Classics Assoc NY, Natl Cinema & Rep Pic Film. *Sale:* Video Comm, Videotape version.

Range Beyond the Blue. Eddie Dean. Directed by Ray Taylor. 1947. PRC. 55 min. Sound. 16mm B&W. *Sale:* Classic Assoc NY.

Range Busters, The. Ray Corrigan. Directed by S. Roy Luby. 1940. Monogram. 56 min. Sound. 16mm B&W. *Sale:* Films Inc.

Range Defenders. Robert Livingston. Directed by Mack V. Wright. 1937. Republic. 54 min. Sound. 16mm B&W. *Rental:* Ivy Films. *Sale:* Rep Pic Film.

Range Justice. Johnny Mack Brown. Directed by Ray Taylor. 1949. Monogram. 60 min. Sound. 16mm B&W. *Rental:* Budget Films.

Range Law. Johnny Mack Brown. Directed by Lambert Hillyer. 1944. Monogram. 60 min. Sound. 16mm B&W. *Rental:* Hurlock Cine & Mogulls Films. *Sale:* Video Comm, Videotape version.

Range Renegades. Jimmy Wakely. Directed by Lambert Hillyer. 1948. Monogram. 55 min. Sound. 16mm B&W. *Rental:* Hurlock Cine.

Range War. William Boyd. Directed by Lesley Selander. 1939. Paramount. 54 min. Sound. 16mm B&W. *Sale:* Cinema Concepts.

Rangeland Racket. George Houston. 1941. PRC. 60 min. Sound. 16mm B&W. *Rental:* Mogulls Films.

Ranger & the Lady, The. Roy Rogers. Directed by Joseph Kane. 1940. Republic. 54 min. Sound. 16mm B&W. *Rental:* Ivy Films. *Sale:* Cinema Concepts & Rep Pic Film.

Ranger Courage. Bob Allen. Directed by Spencer G. Bennett. 1936. Columbia. 60 min. Sound. 16mm B&W. *Rental:* Budget Films.

Ranger of Cherokee Strip. Monte Hale. Directed by Philip Ford. 1949. Republic. 60 min. Sound. 16mm B&W. *Rental:* Ivy Films. *Sale:* Rep Pic Film & Nostalgia Merchant.

Ranger's Code. Bob Steele. Directed by Robert N. Bradbury. 1933. Monogram. 60 min. Sound. 16mm B&W. *Rental:* Mogulls Films.

Rangers Ride, The. Jimmy Wakely. Directed by Derwin Abrahams. 1948. Monogram. 55 min. Sound. 16mm B&W. *Rental:* Hurlock Cine.

Rango. Directed by Ernest B. Schoedsack. 1931. Paramount. (Documentary, music & sound effects only). 67 min. Sound. 16mm B&W. *Rental:* Swank Motion.

Ransom. Glenn Ford & Donna Reed. Directed by Alex Segal. 1956. MGM. 104 min. Sound. 16mm B&W. *Rental:* Films Inc & MGM United.

Ransom Money. Broderick Crawford. 1976. Dimension. 90 min. Sound. 16mm Color. *Rental:* Williams Films, Modern Sound & Welling Motion Pictures. *Sale:* Salz Ent.

Rape. 2 pts. 1975. Aims. (Documentary). 60 min. Sound. 16mm Color. dubbed. *Rental:* U Mich Media.

Rape, The *see* Viol.

Rape, The. Zetta Apostolou & Zoras Tsapelis. Directed by Dino Dimopoulos. Gr. 1965. Greece. 86 min. Sound. 16mm B&W. subtitles Eng. *Rental:* Films Inc.

Rape-Crisis. Directed by Gary T. McDonald. Criminal Justice Center. (Documentary). 87 min. Sound. 16mm Color. *Rental:* Cinema Guild. *Sale:* Cinema Guild. *Sale:* Cinema Guild, Videotape version.

Rape of Love, The. Nathalie Mell & Alain Foures. Directed by Yannick Bellon. Fr. 1979. France. 115 min. Sound. 16mm Color. subtitles. *Rental:* Films Inc.

Rappaccini's Daughter. 1980. Perspective. (Cast unlisted). 57 min. Sound. 16mm Color. *Rental:* Iowa Films, Kent St U Film, U Mich Media & Utah Media. *Sale:* Perspect Film. *Sale:* Perspect Film, Videocassette version.

Rapteme Usted. Celia Gamez. Directed by Julio De Flechner. Span. Mexico. Sound. 16mm B&W. *Rental:* Film Classics.

Rapunzel, Let Down Your Hair. 1978. Britain. (Cast unlisted). 80 min. Sound. 16mm Color. *Rental:* Museum Mod Art.

Rare Book Murder, The *see* Quiet Please, Murder.

Rare Breed, The. James Stewart & Maureen O'Hara. Directed by Andrew V. McLaglen. 1966. Universal. 108 min. Sound. 16mm Color. *Rental:* Williams Films.

Rascal. Steve Forrest, Billy Mumy & Elsa Lanchester. Directed by Norman Tokar. 1969. Disney. 85 min. Sound. 16mm Color. *Rental:* Bosco Films, Cine Craft, Elliot Film Co, Film Ctr DC, Films Inc, MGM United, Modern Sound, Roas Films, Twyman Films, U of IL Film, Swank Motion, Swank Motion, Westcoast Films, Welling Motion Pictures & Williams Films.

Rascals. Jane Withers & Rochelle Hudson. Directed by Bruce Humberstone. 1938. Fox. 77 min. Sound. 16mm B&W. *Rental:* Films Inc.

Rashomon. Toshiro Mifune & Machiko Kyo. Directed by Akira Kurosawa. Jap. 1950. Japan. 83 min. Sound. 16mm B&W. subtitles. *Rental:* Films Inc & New Cinema. *Sale:* Tamarelles French Film, Videotape version. *Sale:* Natl Cinema, Dubbed version.

Rasputin. Orig. Title: Night They Killed Rasputin, The. John Drew Barrymore & Edmund Purdom. Directed by Pierre Chenal. 1960. Italy. 95 min. Sound. 16mm B&W. dubbed. *Rental:* Willoughby Peer.

Rasputin - the Mad Monk. Christopher Lee & Barbara Shelley. Directed by Don Sharp. 1966. Fox. (Anamorphic). 92 min. Sound. 16mm Color. *Rental:* Films Inc.

Rasputin & the Empress. John Barrymore & Ethel Barrymore. Directed by Richard Boleslawski. 1932. MGM. 125 min. Sound. 16mm B&W. *Rental:* MGM United.

Rasputin: Devil Or Saint?. Nikolai Malikoff. Directed by Martin Berger. 1928. Unusual. 53 min. Silent. 16mm B&W. *Sale:* Blackhawk Films. *Sale:* Blackhawk Films, Super 8 silent version. *Sale:* Blackhawk, Silent 8mm version.

Rat, The. Ivor Novello & Mae Marsh. Directed by Graham Cutts. 1925. Britain. 80 min. Silent. 16mm B&W. *Sale:* Cinema Concepts & Reel Images.

Rat Race, The. Tony Curtis & Debbie Reynolds. Directed by Robert Mulligan. 1960. Paramount. 105 min. Sound. 16mm Color. *Rental:* Films Inc.

Rationing. Wallace Beery & Marjorie Main. Directed by Willis Goldbeck. 1944. MGM. 93 min. Sound. 16mm B&W. *Rental:* MGM United.

Ratman. 1973. Britain. 53 min. Sound. 16mm Color. *Rental:* Time-Life Multimedia. *Sale:* Time-Life Multimedia.

Ratopolis. Directed by Gilles Therien. 1974. Canada. (Documentary). 57 min. Sound. 16mm Color. *Rental:* U Cal Media.

Rattle of a Simple Man, The. Diane Cilento & Harry H. Corbett. Directed by Muriel Box. 1965. Britain. 99 min. Sound. 16mm B&W. *Rental:* Liberty Co.

Ravagers, The. Richard Harris & Ann Turkel. Directed by Richard Compton. 1979. Columbia. 91 min. Sound. 16mm Color. *Rental:* Swank Motion.

Raven, The. Henry B. Walthall. Directed by Charles Brabin. 1915. Essanay. 50 min. Silent. 16mm B&W. *Rental:* Budget Films & Em Gee Film Lib. *Sale:* E Finney.

Raven, The. Vincent Price & Peter Lorre. Directed by Roger Corman. 1963. American International. 88 min. Sound. 16mm Color. *Rental:* Modern Sound.

Raven's End. Thommy Berggren. Directed by Bo Widerberg. Swed. 1964. Sweden. 99 min. Sound. 16mm B&W. subtitles. *Rental:* New Cinema & New Yorker Films.

Ravishing Idiot, The. Brigitte Bardot & Anthony Perkins. Directed by Edouard Molinaro. 1964. France. 105 min. Sound. 16mm B&W. dubbed. *Rental:* Modern Sound.

Raw Deal. Dennis O'Keefe & Claire Trevor. Directed by Anthony Mann. 1948. Eagle Lion. 78 min. Sound. 16mm B&W. *Rental:* Budget Films.

Raw Meat. Donald Pleasance & David Ladd. Directed by Gary Sherman. 1973. American International. 88 min. Sound. 16mm Color. *Rental:* Swank Motion.

Raw Timber. Tom Keene. Directed by Ray Taylor. 1937. Crescent. 70 min. Sound. 16mm B&W. *Rental:* Mogulls Films. *Sale:* Thunderbird Films.

Raw Wind in Eden. Esther Williams & Jeff Chandler. Directed by Richard Wilson. 1958. Universal. 93 min. Sound. 16mm Color. *Rental:* Swank Motion.

Rawhide. Smith Ballew & Lou Gehrig. Directed by Ray Taylor. 1938. Fox. 60 min. Sound. 16mm B&W. *Rental:* Modern Sound & Mogulls Films. *Sale:* Blackhawk Films. *Sale:* Blackhawk Films, Super 8 sound version. *Sale:* Blackhawk Films, Videotape version.

Rawhide. Orig. Title: Desperate Siege. Tyrone Power & Susan Hayward. Directed by Henry Hathaway. 1951. Fox. 86 min. Sound. 16mm B&W. *Rental:* Films Inc.

Rawhide Rangers. Johnny Mack Brown. Directed by Ray Taylor. 1941. Universal. 57 min. Sound. 16mm B&W. *Rental:* Budget Films.

Rawhide Years, The. Tony Curtis & Colleen Miller. Directed by Rudolph Mate. 1956. Universal. 85 min. Sound. 16mm Color. *Rental:* Swank Motion.

Raymie. David Ladd & Julie Adams. Directed by Frank McDonald. 1960. Allied Artists. 72 min. Sound. 16mm B&W. *Rental:* Hurlock Cine.

Razor's Edge, The. Tyrone Power & Gene Tierney. Directed by Edmund Goulding. 1946. Fox. 146 min. Sound. 16mm B&W. *Rental:* Williams Films, Films Inc & Twyman Films. *Sale:* Blackhawk Films, Golden Tapes, Magnetic Video & Video Lib, Videotape version.

Razumov. Pierre Fresnay & Jean-Louis Barrault. Directed by Marc Allegret. Fr. 1937. France. 97 min. Sound. 16mm B&W. subtitles. *Rental:* Film Classics.

Reach for Glory. Harry Andrews & Kay Walsh. Directed by Philip Leacock. 1962. Great Britain. 87 min. Sound. 16mm Color. *Rental:* Westcoast Films.

Reach for the Sky. Kenneth More & Muriel Pavlow. Directed by Lewis Gilbert. 1957. Britain. 104 min. Sound. 16mm B&W. *Rental:* Learning Corp Am. *Sale:* Learning Corp Am.

Reaching Back for Change: A Day of Transactional Analysis. 1974. Huron Valley Institute. (Documentary). 55 min. Sound. 16mm Color. *Rental:* U Mich Media.

Reaching for the Moon. Douglas Fairbanks & Eileen Percy. Directed by John Emerson. 1917. Artcraft. 78 min. Silent. 16mm B&W. *Rental:* Em Gee Film Lib & Museum Mod Art. *Sale:* Cinema Concepts, Griggs Movie, Glenn Photo & Natl Cinema. *Sale:* Glenn Photo, Super 8 silent version. *Sale:* Glenn Photo, Silent 8mm version. *Sale:* Tamarelles French Film, Videotape version.

Reaching for the Moon. Douglas Fairbanks & Bebe Daniels. Directed by Edmund Goulding. 1931. MGM. 62 min. Sound. 16mm B&W. *Rental:* A Twyman Pres, Budget Films, Classic Film Mus, Em Gee Film Lib, Film Ctr DC & Video Comm. *Sale:* Morcraft Films & Reel Images. *Sale:* Reel Images, Super 8 sound version.

Reaching from Heaven. Cheryl Walker & Hugh Beaumount. Directed by William Claxton. 1947. Concordia. 80 min. Sound. 16mm B&W. *Rental:* Newman Film Lib.

Reaction: A Portrait of a Society in Crisis. 1970. Canada. (Documentary). 58 min. Sound. 16mm Color. *Rental:* Natl Film CN. *Sale:* Natl Film CN.

Reading, Writing & Reefer. Directed by Robert Rogers. 1978. NBC. (Documentary). 52 min. Sound. 16mm Color. *Rental:* Films Inc, U of IL Film, Iowa Films & Syracuse U Film. *Sale:* Films Inc. *Sale:* Films Inc, Videotape version.

Ready, Willing & Able. Jane Wyman & Ruby Keeler. Directed by Ray Enright. 1937. Warners. 93 min. Sound. 16mm B&W. *Rental:* MGM United.

Reagan at Midterm. 1983. NBC. 52 min. Sound. Videotape Color. *Sale:* Films Inc.

Reagan: The First Hundred Days. 1981. NBC. (Documentary). 110 min. Videotape Color. *Rental:* Films Inc. *Sale:* Films Inc.

Real Glory, The. Gary Cooper & David Niven. Directed by Henry Hathaway. 1939. Goldwyn. 96 min. Sound. 16mm B&W. *Rental:* Films Inc.

Real Life. Albert Brooks & Charles Grodin. Directed by Albert Brooks. 1979. Paramount. 99 min. Sound. 16mm Color. *Rental:* Films Inc.

Real War in Space, The. 1983. Britain. 52 min. Sound. Videotape Color. *Sale:* Films Inc.

Real West, The. Directed by Donald B. Hyatt. 1961. NBC. (Documentary). 54 min. Sound. 16mm B&W. *Rental:* U Cal Media, U of IL Film, Images Film, Kit Parker, La Inst Res Ctr, McGraw-Hill Films, U Mich Media, SD AV Ctr, Syracuse U Film & Utah Media. *Sale:* McGraw-Hill Films.

Really Big Family, A. 1965. Wolper. (Documentary). 50 min. Sound. 16mm B&W. *Rental:* Films Inc. *Sale:* Films Inc. *Sale:* Films Inc, Videotape version.

Reap the Wild Wind. John Wayne & Susan Hayward. Directed by Cecil B. DeMille. 1942. Paramount. 124 min. Sound. 16mm Color. *Rental:* Williams Films.

Rear Window. James Stewart & Grace Kelly. Directed by Alfred Hitchcock. 1954. Universal. 112 min. Sound. 16mm Color. *Rental:* Swank Motion. *Rental:* Swank Motion, *Sale:* Tamarelles French Film, Videotape version.

Reason to Live, A Reason to Die, A. James Coburn & Telly Savalas. Directed by Tonino Valerii. 1974. K-Tel. 92 min. Sound. 16mm Color. *Rental:* Films Inc.

Rebecca. Sir Laurence Olivier & Joan Fontaine. Directed by Alfred Hitchcock. 1940. United Artists. 130 min. Sound. 16mm B&W. *Rental:* Festival Films. *Rental:* Festival Films, Videotape version.

Rebecca of Sunnybrook Farm. Shirley Temple & Randolph Scott. Directed by Allan Dwan. 1938. Fox. 80 min. Sound. 16mm B&W. *Rental:* Films Inc & Williams Films, videotape version.

Rebel, The see Call Me Genius. & Bushwackers.

Rebel City. Marjorie Lord & Bill Elliott. Directed by Thomas Carr. 1953. Allied Artists. 60 min. Sound. 16mm B&W. *Rental:* Hurlock Cine.

Rebel in the Ring. Bill Wellman Jr. & Arline Judge. 1964. Emerson. 85 min. 16mm B&W. *Rental:* Films Inc, Ivy Films & Rep Pic Film. *Lease:* Rep Pic Film.

Rebel Rousers. Cameron Mitchell, Jack Nicholson & Bruce Dern. Directed by Martin B. Cohen. 1970. Four-Star Excelsior. 78 min. Sound. Color. *Rental:* Films Inc & Wholesome Film Ctr. *Sale:* Cinema Concepts, Videotape version.

Rebel Without a Cause. James Dean & Natalie Wood. Directed by Nicholas Ray. 1955. Warners. 111 min. 16mm *Rental:* Arcus Film, Charard Motion Pics Cine Craft, Film Ctr DC, Kerr Film, Kit Parker, Modern Sound, Roas Films Swank Motion, Trans-World Films, Twyman Films, Video Comm, Westcoast Films, Wholesome Film Ctr, Williams Films & Willoughby Peer.

Rebellion. Tom Keene. Directed by Lynn Shores. 1936. Crescent. 60 min. Sound. 16mm B&W. *Rental:* Mogulls Films.

Rebellion, The. Toshiro Mifune. Directed by Masaki Kobayashi. Jap. 1975. Japan. (Anamorphic). 120 min. Sound. 16mm B&W. subtitles. *Rental:* Films Inc.

Rebellion in Patagonia. Directed by Hector Olivera. Span. 1974. Argentina. (Documentary).107 min. 16mm subtitles. *Rental:* Cinema Guild. *Sale:* Cinema Guild.

Rebels Against the Light. Tom Bell & Diane Baker. Directed by Alexander Ramati. 1966. Britain. 90 min 16mm B&W. *Rental:* Ivy Films & Video Comm.

Rebel's Son, A. Harry Baur, Patricia Roc & Roger Livesey. 1938. Britain. 80 min. 16mm B&W. *Rental:* Bosco Films.

Recent Advances in Neuromuscular Disease. 1968. US Government. (Documentary). 90 min. Sound. 16mm B&W. *Sale:* Natl AV Ctr.

Recital of Music & Dancing, A. 1973. Britain. 52 min. Sound. 16mm Color. *Rental:* Xerox Films. *Sale:* Xerox Films.

Reckless. Jean Harlow, William Powell & Franchot Tone. Directed by Victor Fleming. 1935. MGM. 96 min. Sound. 16 mm B&W. *Rental:* MGM United.

Reckless. Aidan Quinn & Daryl Hannah. Directed by James Foley Jr. 1984. MGM. 90 min. 16mm. *Rental:* MGM United *Rental:* MGM United, Videotape version

Reckless Hour, The. Dorothy Mackaill & Conrad Nagel. Directed by John Francis Dillon. 1931. Warners. 70 min. Sound. 16mm B&W. *Rental:* MGM United.

Reckless Moment, The. James Mason & Joan Bennett. Directed by Max Ophuls. 1949. Columbia. 84 min. 16mm B&W. *Rental:* Budget Films, U of IL Film, Images Film, Kit Parker & Learning Corp Am. *Sale:* Learning Corp Am.

Reckoning, The. Nicol Williamson Directed by Jack Gold. 1969. Columbia. 108 min. 16mm *Rental:* Modern Sound.

Reckoning: 1945 & After. Directed by Hugh Raggett. (World at War Ser.). : Pt. 25.). 1973. Media Guild. (Documentary). 52 min. Sound. 16mm Color. *Rental:* Media Guild & U Cal Media. *Sale:* Media Guild. *Sale:* Media Guild, Videotape version.

Record City. Ed Begley Jr. & Ruth Buzzi. Directed by Dennis Steinmetz. 1978. American International. 90 min. 16mm . *Rental:* Swank Motion.

Record Makers, The. 1977. Films Inc. (Documentary). 52 min. Sound. 16mm Color. *Rental:* Films Inc. *Sale:* Films Inc. *Sale:* Films Inc, Videotape version.

Record of a Tenement Gentleman, The. Trans. Title: Nagaya Shinshiroku. Choko Iida. Directed by Yasujiro Ozu. Jap. 1947. Japan. 72 min. Sound. 16mm B&W. subtitles. *Rental:* New Cinema & New Yorker Films.

Red & the Black, The. Danielle Darrieux & Gerard Philipe. Directed by Claude Autant-Lara. Fr. 1954. France. 125 min. 16mm B&W. subtitles. *Rental:* Ivy Films.

Red & the White, The. Jozsef Madaras & Tibor Molnar. Directed by Miklos Jancso. Rus. 1969. Russia. 92 min. Sound. 16mm B&W. subtitles. *Rental:* Films Inc.

Red Army, The. 1981. 58 min. Videotape *Rental:* PBS Video. *Sale:* PBS Video.

Red Badge of Courage, The. Audie Murphy & Bill Mauldin. Directed by John Huston. 1951. MGM. 69 min. 16mm B&W. *Rental:* MGM United. *Rental:* MGM United, Videotape version.

Red Ball Express, The. Jeff Chandler & Alex Nicol. Directed by Budd Boetticher. 1952. Universal. 83 min. Sound. 16mm B&W. *Rental:* Swank Motion.

Red Beard. Toshiro Mifune & Yuzo Kayama. Directed by Akira Kurosawa. Jap. 1965. Japan. 185 min. Sound. 16mm B&W. subtitles. *Rental:* Films Inc.

Red Blood. Art Hoxie. Directed by J. P. McGowan. 1926. Rayart. 50 min. Silent. 8mm B&W. *Rental:* Film Classics. *Sale:* Film Classics.

Red China. 1962. NBC. (Documentary). 54 min. Sound. 16mm B&W. *Rental:* McGraw-Hill Films & Syracuse U Film. *Sale:* McGraw-Hill Films.

Red China. 1970. Britain. (Documentary). 50 min. 16mm *Rental:* Time-Life Multi media. *Sale:* Time-Life Multimedia.

Red China Diary with Morley Safer. 1967. CBS. (Documentary). 54 min. Sound. 16mm Color. *Rental:* U Mich Media, Syracuse U Media & Phoenix Films. *Sale:* Phoenix Films. *Sale:* Phoenix Films, Videotape version.

Red China: Year of the Gun?. 1967. ABC. (Documentary). 51 min. Sound. 16mm Color. *Rental:* McGraw-Hill Film & Syracuse U Film. *Sale:* McGraw-Hill Film.

Red Danube, The. Walter Pidgeon & Ethel Barrymore. Directed by George Sidney. 1949. MGM. 119 min. Sound. 16mm B&W. *Rental:* MGM United. *Sale:* Reel Images, Super 8 sound version.

Red Deer of Rhum. 1978. 58 min. Sound. 16mm Color. *Rental:* U Mich Media.

Red Desert, The. Don Barry & Jack Holt. Directed by Ford Beebe. 1949. Lippert. 60 min. 16mm B&W. *Sale:* Morcraft Films & Reel Images. *Sale:* Morcraft Films & Reel Images, Super 8 sound version.

Red Desert. Monica Vitti & Richard Harris. Directed by Michelangelo Antonioni. Ital. 1964. Italy. 116 min. Sound. 16mm Color. subtitles. *Rental:* Films Inc.

Red Detachment of Women. 1971. China. (Cast Unlisted). 90 min. Sound. 16mm Color. *Rental:* CA Newsreel.

Red Dragon. Stewart Granger & Rosanna Schiaffino. Directed by Ernest Hoffbauer. 1967. Italy-Germany. 90 min. Sound. 16mm Color. dubbed. *Rental:* Video Comm & Willoughby Peer.

Red Dragon. Sidney Toler. Directed by Phil Rosen. 1945. Monogram. 60 min. Sound. 16mm B&W. *Rental:* Hurlock Cine & Video Comm.

Red Dust. Jean Harlow & Clark Gable. Directed by Victor Fleming. 1932. MGM. 83 min. Sound. 16mm B&W. *Rental:* MGM United.

Red Garters. Rosemary Clooney & Jack Carson. Directed by George Marshall. 1954. Paramount. 91 min. Sound. 16mm Color. *Rental:* Films Inc.

Red-Headed Woman. Jean Harlow & Chester Morris. Directed by Jack Conway. 1932. MGM. 74 min. Sound. 16mm B&W. *Rental:* Films Inc & MGM United.

Red Hot Romance. Basil Sydney. Directed by Victor Fleming. 1922. 16mm *Rental:* A Twyman Pres.

Red Hot Tires. Orig. Title: Racing Luck. Lyle Talbot & Mary Astor. Directed by D. Ross Lederman. 1935. Warners. 61 min. Sound. 16mm B&W. *Rental:* MGM United.

Red House, The see Casa Colorada.

Red House, The. Edward G. Robinson. Directed by Delmer Daves. 1947. 100 min. Sound. 16mm B&W. *Rental:* Budget Films, Classic Film Mus & Ivy Films. *Sale:* Festivals Films. *Sale:* Festival Films & Tamarelles French Film, Videotape version.

Red Inn, The. Fernandel & Francoise Rosay. Directed by Claude Autant-Lara. 1953. France. 100 min. Sound. 16mm B&W. subtitles. *Rental:* Film Classics.

Red Kimono, The. Priscilla Bonner & Theodore Von Eltz. Directed by Walter Lang. 1925. Vital. 70 min. Silent. 16mm B&W. *Rental:* Budget Films & Em Gee Film Lib. *Sale:* Morcraft Films. *Sale:* Morcraft Films, Super 8 version. *Sale:* Morcraft Films, Silent 8mm version.

Red Light. George Raft & Virginia Mayo. Directed by Roy Del Ruth. 1949. United Artists. 83 min. Sound. 16mm B&W. *Rental:* Hurlock Cine.

Red Lights Ahead. Andy Clyde & Lucille Gleason. Directed by Roland Reed. 1937. Chesterfield. 70 min. Sound. 16mm B&W. *Rental:* Modern Sound.

Red Line Seven Thousand. James Caan & Laura Devon. Directed by Howard Hawks. 1965. Paramount. 100 min. Sound. 16mm Color. *Rental:* Films Inc.

Red Menace, The. Orig. Title: Enemy Within, The. Robert Rockwell & Barbara Fuller. Directed by R. G. Springsteen. 1949. Republic. 87 min. Sound. 16mm B&W. *Rental:* Ivy Films & Rep Pic Film. *Lease:* Rep Pic Film.

Red Morning. Regis Toomey & Steffi Duna. Directed by Wallace Fox. 1935. RKO. 63 min. Sound. 16mm B&W. *Rental:* RKO General Pics.

Red Mountain. Alan Ladd & Lizabeth Scott. Directed by William Dieterle. 1951. Paramount. 84 min. Sound. 16mm Color. *Rental:* Films Inc.

Red Planet, The. 1977. 58 min. Sound. Videotape *Rental:* PBS Video. *Sale:* PBS Video.

Red Planet Mars. Peter Graves & Andrea King. Directed by Harry Horner. 1952. United Artists. 87 min. Sound. 16mm B&W. *Rental:* Budget Films & MGM United.

Red Pony, The. Robert Mitchum & Myrna Loy. Directed by Lewis Milestone. 89 min. Color. *Rental:* Arcus Film, Budget Films, Cine Craft, Williams Films, Ivy Films, Kit Parker, Modern Sound, Twyman Films, Westcoast Films, Welling Motion Pictures & Wholesome Film Ctr.

Red Pony, The. Henry Fonda & Maureen O'Hara. Directed by Robert Totten. 1974. Phoenix. 101 min. Sound. 16mm Color. *Rental:* Budget Films & Phoenix Films. *Sale:* Phoenix Films. *Sale:* Phoenix Films, Videotape version.

Red Psalm. Andrea Drahota. Directed by Miklos Jancso. Hungarian. 1972. Hungary. 88 min. Sound. 16mm Color. subtitles. *Rental:* Museum Mod Art.

Red Raiders. Ken Maynard & Paul Hurst. Directed by Albert S. Rogell. 1927. First National. 60 min. Silent. 16mm B&W. *Rental:* MGM United.

Red Red Dragon, The. Directed by Eric Porter. 1974. Solo Cup. (Animated). 85 min. Sound. 16mm Color. *Rental:* Budget Films, Williams Films, Film Pres & Westcoast Films.

Red River. John Wayne & Montgomery Clift. Directed by Howard Hawks. 1948. United Artists. 133 min. Sound. 16mm B&W. *Rental:* MGM United.

Red River Range. John Wayne & Ray Corrigan. Directed by George Sherman. 1938. Republic. 59 min. Sound. 16mm B&W. *Sale:* Rep Pic Film & Nostalgia Merchant.

Red River Renegades. Sunset Carson. Directed by Thomas Carr. 1946. Republic. 54 min. Sound. 16mm B&W. *Rental:* Ivy Films. *Sale:* Rep Pic Film.

Red River Robin Hood. Tim Holt & Cliff Edwards. Directed by Bert Gilroy. 1943. RKO. 57 min. Sound. 16mm B&W. *Rental:* RKO General Pics.

Red River Shore. Rex Allen & Slim Pickens. Directed by Harry Keller. 1953. Republic. 65 min. Sound. 16mm B&W. *Sale:* Rep Pic Film.

Red River Valley. Roy Rogers. Directed by Joseph Kane. 1941. Republic. 54 min. Sound. 16mm B&W. *Sale:* Rep Pic Film.

Red Rope, The. Bob Steele. Directed by S. Roy Luby. 1937. Monogram. 60 min. Sound. 16mm B&W. *Rental:* Ivy Films.

Red Shoes, The. Moira Shearer & Anton Walbrook. Directed by Michael Powell & Emeric Pressburger. 1948. Britain. 139 min. Sound. 16mm Color. *Rental:* Arcus Film, Budget Films, Films Inc, Un of IL Film, Images Film, Kit Parker, Learning Corp Am, Modern Sound, Twyman Films, Westcoast Films, Welling Motion Pictures & Wholesome Film Ctr. *Lease:* Learning Corp Am. *Rental:* Learning Corp Am, *Lease:* Learning Corp Am, Videotape version.

Red Signals. Earl Williams, Wallace McDonald & Eve Novak. Directed by J. P. McGowan. 1927. Sterling. 60 min. Silent. 16mm B&W. *Sale:* Blackhawk Films. *Sale:* Blackhawk Films, Super 8 silent version. *Sale:* Blackhawk Films, Silent 8mm version.

Red Skies of Montana. Richard Widmark & Richard Boone. Directed by Joseph Newman. 1952. Fox. 98 min. Sound. 16mm Color. *Rental:* Films Inc.

Red Sky at Morning. Richard Thomas & Catherine Burns. Directed by James Goldstone. 1971. Universal. 113 min. Sound. 16mm Color. *Rental:* Swank Motion.

Red Snow. Guy Madison & Carole Mathews. Directed by Boris L. Petroff. 1952. Columbia. 72 min. Sound. 16mm B&W. *Rental:* Inst Cinema.

Red Stallion. Robert Paige & Ted Donaldson. Directed by Lesley Selander. 1947. Eagle Lion. 82 min. Sound. 16mm Color. *Sale:* Classics Assoc NY.

Red Stallion in the Rockies. Jean Heather & Arthur Franz. Directed by Ralph Murphy. 1949. Eagle. 85 min. Sound. 16mm Color. *Sale:* Classics Assoc NY.

Red Star: The Soviet Union, 1941-1943. Directed by Hugh Raggett. (World at War Ser.). : Pt. 11.). 1973. Media Guild. (Documentary). 52 min. Sound. 16mm Color. *Rental:* Media Guild & U Cal Media. *Sale:* Media Guild. *Sale:* Media Guild, Videotape version.

Red Sun. Charles Bronson, Toshiro Mifune & Alain Delon. Directed by Terence Young. 1972. National General. 112 min. Sound. 16mm Color. *Rental:* Williams Films & Swank Motion.

Red Sundown. Rory Calhoun & Martha Hyer. Directed by Jack Arnold. 1956. Universal. 81 min. Sound. 16mm Color. *Rental:* Swank Motion.

Red Tent, The. Peter Finch & Sean Connery. Directed by Mikhail Kalatozov. 1971. Paramount. 121 min. Sound. 16mm Color. *Rental:* Films Inc.

Red Tomahawk, The. Howard Keel & Joan Caulfield. Directed by R. G. Springsteen. 1967. Paramount. 82 min. Sound. 16mm Color. *Rental:* Films Inc.

Red White & Black, The see Soul Soldier.

Redemption. John Gilbert & Renee Adoree. Directed by Fred Niblo. 1932. MGM. 67 min. Sound. 16mm B&W. *Rental:* MGM United.

Redevelopment: A Marxist Analysis. 1975. Resolution. (Documentary). 60 min. Sound. 16mm B&W. *Rental:* CA Newsreel. *Sale:* CA Newsreel.

Reds. Warren Beatty & Diane Keaton. Directed by Warren Beatty. 1981. Paramount. 199 min. Sound. 16mm Color. *Rental:* Films Inc.

Reducing. Marie Dressler, Polly Moran & Anita Page. Directed by Charles Reisner. 1931. MGM. 77 min. Sound. 16mm B&W. *Rental:* MGM United.

Redwood Forest Trail. Rex Allen & Jane Darwell. Directed by Leslie Fenton. 1949. Republic. 68 min. Sound. 16mm B&W. *Sale:* Rep Pic Film.

Reed: Insurgent Mexico. Claudio Obregon. Directed by Paul Leduc. Span. 1971. Mexico. (Sepia). 110 min. Sound. 16mm subtitles. *Rental:* New Cinema, New Yorker Films.

Reefer Madness. Orig. Title: Tell Your Children. Dave O'Brien. Directed by Louis Gasnier. 1936. New Line Cinema. 70 min. Sound. B&W. *Rental:* Budget Films, Classic Film Mus, Em Gee Film Lib, Films Inc, Images Film, Ivy Films, Kit Parker, New Cinema, New Line Cinema, Video Comm, Westcoast Films & Wholesome Film Ctr. *Sale:* Cinema Concepts, Festival Films, Glenn Photo & Morcraft Films. *Rental:* Films Inc, *Sale:* Festival Films, Videotape version.

Reel World of News, The. 58 min. Sound. Videotape *Rental:* PBS Video. *Sale:* PBS Video.

Reet, Petite & Gone. Louis Jordan. Directed by W. Crouch. 1947. 75 min. Sound. 16mm B&W. *Rental:* Budget Films & Em Gee Film Lib.

Reflection of Fear, A. Robert Shaw, Mary Ure & Sandra Locke. Directed by William Fraker. 1973. Columbia. 89 min. Sound. 16mm Color. *Rental:* Kit Parker.

Reflections: George Meany. Directed by Duncan Scott. 1979. ICA. (Interview). 52 min. Sound. 16mm Color. *Rental:* Natl AV Ctr. *Sale:* Natl AV Ctr. *Sale:* Natl AV Ctr, Videotape version.

Reflections: Samuel Eliot Morison. 1976. 58 min. Sound. 16mm Color. *Rental:* Natl AV Ctr. *Sale:* Natl AV Ctr.

Reflections in a Golden Eye. Elizabeth Taylor & Marlon Brando. Directed by John Huston. 1967. Warners. (Anamorphic). 109 min. Sound. 16mm Color. *Rental:* Films Inc, Twyman Film & Video Comm. *Sale:* Natl AV Ctr, Videotape version.

Reflections: Margaret Mead. 1979. National. (Interview). 52 min. Sound. 16mm Color. *Rental:* Natl AV Ctr. *Sale:* Natl AV Ctr. *Sale:* Natl AV Ctr, Videotape version.

Reflections on the Long Search. 1978. Britain. (Documentary). 52 min. Sound. 16mm Color. *Rental:* U Cal Media, U of IL Film, Iowa Films & U Mich Media, Videotape version.

Reflections on the News: No. 103. 1973. PBS. (Lecture). 60 min. Sound. 16mm B&W. *Sale:* WNET Media. *Sale:* WNET Media, Videotape version.

Reflections on the News: No. 107. 1973. PBS. (Lecture). 60 min. Sound. 16mm B&W. *Sale:* WNET Media. *Sale:* WNET Media, Videotape version.

Reflections on the News: No. 111. 1973. PBS. (Lecture). 60 min. Sound. 16mm B&W. *Sale:* WNET Media. *Sale:* WNET Media, Videotape version.

Reform School Girl. Gloria Castill & Ross Ford. Directed by Edward Bernds. 1957. 71 min. Sound. 16mm B&W. *Rental:* Budget Films.

Reformation, The. 1967. NBC. (Documentary). 52 min. Sound. 16mm Color. *Rental:* McGraw-Hill Films & Syracuse U Film. *Sale:* McGraw-Hill Films.

Reformer & the Redhead, The. June Allyson & Dick Powell. Directed by Norman Panama & Norman Frank. 1950. MGM. 90 min. Sound. 16mm B&W. *Rental:* MGM United.

Refugee, The *see* Three Faces West.

Regain *see* Harvest.

Regeneration. Rockliffe Fellows & John McCann. Directed by Raoul Walsh. 1915. 90 min. Silent. 16mm B&W. *Rental:* Budget Films.

Reggae. Count Prince Miller & Pyramids. Directed by Horace Ove. 1971. Impact. 70 min. Sound. 16mm Color. *Rental:* Icarus Films.

Reggie Mixes In. Douglas Fairbanks, Alma Rubens & Bessie Love. Directed by John Emerson. 1916. Fine Arts. 50 min. Silent. 16mm B&W. *Rental:* Em Gee Film Lib & Film Images. *Sale:* Blackhawk Films. *Rental:* Ivy Films, Super 8 silent version. *Sale:* Blackhawk Films, Silent 8mm version.

Regimentstochter. Aglaia Scmied, Gusti Wolf & Norbert Lindner. Ger. 1952. Austria. 90 min. Sound. Videotape Color. *Sale:* Tamarelles French Films.

Region Centrale, La. Orig. Title: Central Region, The. Directed by Michael Snow. 1971. Snow. (Experimental, two projectors required). 190 min. Sound. 16mm Color. *Rental:* Museum Mod Art.

Registered Nurse. Bebe Daniels & Lyle Talbot. Directed by Robert Florey. 1934. Warners. 63 min. Sound. 16mm B&W. *Rental:* MGM United.

Reg'lar Fellers. Roscoe Ates & Sara Padden. Directed by Arthur Dreifuss. 1941. PRC. 65 min. Sound. 16mm B&W. *Rental:* Alba House & Budget Films.

Regle du Jeu, Le *see* Rules of the Game.

Regrouping. Directed by Lizzie Borden. 1976. Borden. (Documentary). 77 min. Sound. 16mm B&W. *Rental:* Women Movies. *Sale:* Women Movies.

Regulators, The: Our Invisible Government. 1983. Learning Corp.. (Documentary). 50 min. Sound. 16mm Color. *Rental:* Budget Films, Iowa Film, Cal Media, Learning Corp Am & Utah Media. *Sale:* Learning Corp Am.

Rehearsal for D-Day. 1969. ABC. (Documentary). 53 min. Sound. 16mm B&W. *Rental:* McGraw-Hill Films. *Sale:* McGraw-Hill Films.

Reincarnate, The. Jack Creley. Directed by Don Haldane. 1971. Canada. 101 min. Sound. 16mm Color. *Rental:* Swank Motion.

Reincarnation of Peter Proud, The. Michael Sarrazin & Jennifer O'Neill. Directed by J. Lee Thompson. 1975. Cinerama. 104 min. 16mm Color. *Rental:* Swank Motion.

Reivers, The. Steve McQueen, Rupert Crosse & Clifton James. Directed by Mark Rydell. 1969. National General. 107 min. Sound. 16mm Color. *Rental:* Williams Films & Swank Motion.

Relation of Mathematics to Physics, The. 1964. Britain. (Documentary, kinescope). 55 min. Sound. 16mm B&W. *Rental:* U Cal Media.

Relations. Directed by Bill Fertik. 1975. Phoenix. (Documentary). Sound. 16mm Color. *Rental:* Phoenix Films. *Sale:* Phoenix Films. *Sale:* Phoenix Films, Videotape version.

Relax, Freddy. Morten Grunwald & Hanne Bork. Directed by Erik Balling. 1968. Denmark. 111 min. Sound. 16mm Color. dubbed. *Rental:* Ivy Films, Rep Pic Film & Video Comm. *Lease:* Rep Pic Film.

Religion in Indochina: The Way of the Ancestors. 1978. Britain. (Documentary). 52 min. Sound. 16mm Color. *Rental:* U Cal Media, Videotape version.

Religious Revolution & the Void, The. 1965. NET. (Documentary). 60 min. Sound. 16mm B&W. *Rental:* U of IL Film, Indiana AV Ctr & Mass Media.

Reluctant Astronaut, The. Don Knotts. Directed by Edward J. Montagne. 1967. Universal. 102 min. Sound. 16mm Color. *Rental:* Swank Motion & Welling Motion Pictures.

Reluctant Debutante, The. Rex Harrison & Kay Kendall. Directed by Vincente Minnelli. 1958. MGM. 96 min. Sound. 16mm Color. *Rental:* Films Inc & MGM United. *Rental:* Films Inc, Anamorphic version. *Rental:* MGM United, Videotape version.

Reluctant Dragon, The. Robert Benchley & Nana Bryant. Directed by Alfred M. Werker. 1941. Disney. 72 min. Sound. 16mm B&W. *Rental:* Williams Films, Disney Prod, Films Inc & MGM United.

Reluctant Saint, The. Maximilian Schell & Lea Padovani. Directed by Edward Dmytryk. 1962. Italy. 105 min. Sound. 16mm B&W. *Rental:* Cine Craft, Bosco Films, Films Inc, Inst Cinema, Modern Sound, Roas Films, Welling Motion Pictures & Wholesome Film Ctr.

Reluctant Stowaway, The. Billy Mumy. 1965. Fox. 60 min. Sound. 16mm B&W. *Sale:* Natl Cinema.

Remains to Be Seen. June Allyson & Van Johnson. Directed by Don Weis. 1953. MGM. 89 min. Sound. 16mm B&W. *Rental:* MGM United.

Remarkable Andrew, The. William Holden & Ellen Drew. Directed by Stuart Heisler. 1942. Paramount. 80 min. Sound. 16mm B&W. *Rental:* Swank Motion.

Remarkable Mr. Pennypacker, The. Dorothy McGuire & Clifton Webb. Directed by Henry Levin. 1959. Fox. (Anamorphic). 87 min. Sound. 16mm Color. *Rental:* Films Inc.

Remarkable Yamato Family, The. 2 pts. 1975. PBS. (Documentary). 120 min. Sound. 16mm B&W. *Rental:* WNET Media. *Sale:* WNET Media. *Sale:* WNET Media, Videotape version.

Rembetika: The Blues of Greece. 1982. Greece. (Documentary). 50 min. Sound. 16mm Color. narrated Eng. *Sale:* Wombat Productions. *Sale:* Wombat Productions, Videotape version.

Rembrandt. Charles Laughton & Elsa Lanchester. Directed by Alexander Korda. 1936. Britain. 83 min. Sound. 16mm B&W. *Rental:* Films Inc, Ivy Films & Welling Motion Pictures.

Remedy for Riches. Jean Hersholt & Edgar Kennedy. Directed by Erle C. Kenton. 1940. RKO. 70 min. Sound. 16mm B&W. *Rental:* Ivy Films & Mogulls Films.

Remember. Directed by Hugh Raggett. (World at War Ser.). : Pt. 26.). 1973. Media Guild. (Documentary). 52 min. Sound. 16mm Color. *Rental:* Media Guild & U Cal Media. *Sale:* Media Guild. *Sale:* Media Guild, Videotape version.

Remember My Name. Geraldine Chaplin & Anthony Perkins. Directed by Alan Rudolph. 1978. Columbia. 96 min. Sound. 16mm Color. *Rental:* Kit Parker.

Remember the Alamo. Rex Lease & Bruce Warren. Sound. 16mm B&W. *Rental:* Mogulls Films.

Remember the Day. Claudette Colbert & John Payne. Directed by Henry King. 1942. Fox. 86 min. Sound. 16mm B&W. *Rental:* Films Inc.

Remember the Night. Barbara Stanwyck & Fred MacMurray. Directed by Mitchell Leisen. 1940. Paramount. 94 min. Sound. 16mm B&W. *Rental:* Swank Motion.

Remnant, The. 1969. NBC. (Documentary). 56 min. Sound. 16mm Color. *Rental:* Films Inc. *Sale:* Films Inc.

Remote Control. William Haines & Charles King. Directed by Mal St. Clair. 1930. MGM. 75 min. Sound. 16mm B&W. *Rental:* MGM United.

Renaissance & the Resurrection, The. ABC. (Documentary). 55 min. Sound. 16mm Color. *Rental:* Iowa Films, McGraw-Hill Films & Syracuse U Film. *Sale:* McGraw-Hill Films.

Rendezvous. William Powell & Rosalind Russell. Directed by William K. Howard. 1935. MGM. 97 min. Sound. 16mm B&W. *Rental:* MGM United.

Rendezvous with Annie. Eddie Albert & Faye Marlowe. Directed by Allan Dwan. 1946. Republic. 89 min. Sound. 16mm B&W. *Rental:* Ivy Films. *Sale:* Rep Pic Film.

Rendezvous with Freedom. Directed by Marc Siegel. 1973. ABC. (Documentary). 56 min. Sound. 16mm Color. *Rental:* Films Inc.

Renegade Girl. Ann Savage & Alan Curtis. Directed by William Berke. 1948. Screen Guild. 70 min. Sound. 16mm B&W. *Rental:* Mogulls Films.

Renegade Ranger, The. Rita Hayworth & Tim Holt. Directed by Bert Gilroy. 1938. RKO. 59 min. Sound. 16mm *Rental:* RKO General Pics.

Renegade Trail. William Boyd. Directed by Lesley Selander. 1939. Paramount. 60 min. Sound. 16mm B&W. *Rental:* Budget Films. *Lease:* Cinema Concepts.

Renegades. Larry Parks & Edgar Buchanan. Directed by George Sherman. 1946. Columbia. 84 min. Sound. 16mm B&W. *Rental:* Films Inc.

Renegades of Sonora. Allan Lane. Directed by R. G. Springsteen. 1948. Republic. 60 min. Sound. 16mm B&W. *Rental:* Ivy Films. *Sale:* Rep Pic Film.

Renegades of the Rio Grande. Orig. Title: Bank Robbery. Rod Cameron & Fuzzy Knight. Directed by Howard Bretherton. 1945. Universal. 57 min. Sound. 16mm B&W. *Rental:* Budget Films.

Renegades of the West. Betty Furness & Tom Keene. Directed by Casey Robinson. 1933. RKO. 55 min. Sound. 16mm *Rental:* RKO General Pics.

Renewable Tree, The. 1976. Britain. (Documentary). 59 min. Sound. 16mm Color. *Rental:* U Mich Media & Syracuse U Film. *Rental:* U Cal Media, Videotape version.

Renfrew of the Royal Mounted. James Newell. Directed by Al Herman. 1937. Grand National. 70 min. Sound. 16mm B&W. *Rental:* Mogulls Films. *Sale:* Rep Pic Film.

Renfrew on the Great White Trail. Orig. Title: On the Great White Trail. James Newell. Directed by Al Herman. 1972. Grand National. 70 min. Sound. 16mm B&W. *Rental:* Mogulls Films. *Sale:* Morcraft Films.

Reno. Richard Dix & Anita Louise. Directed by John Farrow. 1940. RKO. 73 min. Sound. 16mm *Rental:* RKO General Pics.

Rentadick. James Booth & Julie Ege. Directed by Jim Clark. Britain. 85 min. Sound. 16mm B&W. *Rental:* Cinema Five.

Reou-Takh. Trans. Title: Big City. Alain Christian Plenet. Directed by Mahama Johnson Traore. Senegalese. 1972. Senegal. 60 min. Sound. 16mm Color. subtitles. *Rental:* Tricontinental Films.

Repeat Performance. Joan Leslie, Louis Hayward & Richard Basehart. Directed by Alfred M. Werker. 1947. Eagle Lion. 90 min. Sound. 16mm B&W. *Sale:* Classics Assoc NY.

Repent at Leisure. Kent Taylor & Wendy Barrie. Directed by Frank Woodruff. 1941. RKO. 66 min. Sound. 16mm *Rental:* RKO General Pics.

Replay. Marie Jose-Nat & Victor Lanoux. Directed by Michel Drach. Fr. 1978. France. 96 min. Sound. 16mm Color. subtitles. *Rental:* Films Inc.

Repo Man. Harry Dean Stanton, Emilio Estevez & Tracey Walter. Directed by Alex Cox. 1985. Universal. 92 min. Sound. 16mm Color. *Rental:* Swank Motion. *Rental:* Swank Motion, Videotape version.

Report, The. 1970. EMC. (Documentary). 53 min. Sound. 16mm B&W. *Rental:* U Cal Media. *Sale:* U Cal Media.

Report, Analyze, Evalute. 1976. Indiana U. (Documentary). 58 min. Color. *Sale:* Indiana AV Ctr. *Sale:* Indiana AV Ctr, Videotape version.

Report from Africa. 2 pts. 1956. CBS. (Documentary). 110 min. Sound. 16mm B&W. *Rental:* McGraw-Hill Films. *Sale:* McGraw-Hill Films.

Report from China. Directed by Toshio Tokiedo. 1970. Japan. (Documentary). 90 min. Sound. 16mm Color. narrated Eng. *Rental:* Film Images.

Report from Cuba. 1966. NET. (Documentary). 57 min. Sound. 16mm B&W. *Rental:* Indiana AV Ctr.

Report from the Aleutians. Directed by John Huston. 1943. US Government. 47 min. Sound. 16mm Color. *Rental:* Budget Films & Images Film. *Sale:* Natl AV Ctr.

Report on the Party & the Guests, A. Jan Klusak & Jiri Nemec. Directed by Jan Nemec. Czech. 1968. Czechoslovakia. 70 min. Sound. 16mm B&W. *Rental:* Films Inc.

Report to the Commissioner. Michael Moriarty & Yaphet Kotto. Directed by Milton Katselas. 1975. United Artists. 112 min. Sound. 16mm Color. *Rental:* Budget Films, Films Inc, MGM United & Westcoast Films.

Reporters, The. Catherine Deneuve & Richard Gere. Directed by Raymond Depardon. Fr. 1981. France. 101 min. Sound. 16mm Color. subtitles. *Rental:* Cinema Guild.

Reprieve. Ben Gazzara & Stuart Whitman. Directed by Millard Kaufman. 1962. 105 min. Sound. 16mm B&W. *Rental:* Hurlock Cine.

Reptile, The. Noel Willman. Directed by John Gilling. 1966. Britain. 90 min. Sound. 16mm Color. *Rental:* Films Inc.

Reptiles & Amphibians. 1968. National Geographic. (Documentary). 52 min. Sound. 16mm Color. *Rental:* McGraw-Hill Films & Natl Geog. *Sale:* Natl Geog. *Sale:* Natl Geog, Videotape version.

Reptilicus. Carl Ottoson. Directed by Sidney Pink. 1962. Denmark. 83 min. Sound. 16mm Color. dubbed. *Rental:* Budget Films, Charard Motion Pics, Kerr Film, Natl Serv, Westcoast Films, Welling Motion Pictures, Wholesome Film Ctr & Willoughby Peer.

Repulsion. Catherine Deneuve. Directed by Roman Polanski. 1965. France. 105 min. Sound. Videotape B&W. *Rental:* Budget Films, Cine Craft, Williams Films, Em Gee Film Lib, Films Inc, Inst Cinema, Images Film, Kit Parker, Swank Motion, Twyman Films, Westcoast Films, Welling Motion Pictures & Wholesome Film Ctr. *Sale:* Tamarelles French Film, Videotape version.

Requiem for a Gunfighter. Rod Cameron & Stephen McNally. Directed by Spencer G. Bennett. 1965. Embassy. 91 min. Sound. 16mm Color. *Rental:* Films Inc.

Requiem for a Heavyweight. Anthony Quinn & Jackie Gleason. Directed by Ralph Nelson. 1962. Columbia. 85 min. Sound. 16mm B&W. *Rental:* Arcus Film, Budget Films, Williams Films, Bosco Films, Films Inc, U of IL Film, Images Film, Kerr Film, Kit Parker, Modern Sound, Natl Film Video, Roas Films, Film Ctr DC, Twyman Films, Video Comm, Westcoast Films, Welling Motion Pictures & Wholesome Film Ctr, Videotape version.

Rescue at Entebbe. 1977. CBS. (Documentary). 55 min. Sound. 16mm Color. *Rental:* Alden Films.

Rescue Squad. Ralph Forbes. Directed by Spencer G. Bennett. 1936. Empire. 65 min. Sound. 16mm B&W. *Rental:* Film Classics.

Rescue Squad. Christopher Brett. Directed by Colin Bell. 1962. Britain. 54 min. Sound. 16mm B&W. *Sale:* Lucerne Films.

Rescue, The: The Search for Billy. 1970. Time-Life. (Documentary). 52 min. Sound. 16mm Color. *Rental:* Time-Life Multimedia. *Sale:* Time-Life Multimedia.

Rescuers, The. Directed by Wolfgang Reitherman. 1977. Disney. (Animated). 76 min. Sound. 16mm Color. *Rental:* Buchan Pic, Cine Craft, Bosco Films, Disney Prod, Elliot Film Co, Williams Films, Films Inc, Modern Sound, Newman Film Lib, Roas Films, Swank Motion, Film Ctr DC, Welling Motion Pictures & Westcoast Films.

Research Into Controlled Fusion. 1958. Atomic Energy Commission. (Documentary). 55 min. Sound. 16mm Color. *Rental:* Natl AV Ctr.

Resistance. Directed by Ken McMullen & Chris Rodrigues. 1976. Britain. 90 min. Sound. 16mm Color. *Rental:* Museum Mod Art.

Resolution of Saturn. 1982. 57 min. Sound. 16mm Color. *Rental:* Utah Media.

Restless Breed, The. Anne Bancroft & Scott Brady. Directed by Allan Dwan. 1957. Fox. 81 min. Sound. 16mm Color. *Rental:* Charard Motion Pics, Westcoast Films & Willoughby Peer.

Restless Earth, The: The Plate Tectonics Theory. 1972. WNET. (Documentary). 58 min. Sound. 16mm Color. *Rental:* Indiana AV Ctr & Syracuse U Film. *Sale:* Indiana AV Ctr.

Restoration of the Golden Shrine, The. Japan. (Documentary). 50 min. Sound. 16mm B&W. *Sale:* Japan Society. *Sale:* Japan Society, Color version. *Sale:* Japan Society, Videotape version.

Results of War, The: Are We Making a Good Peace?. 1976. Britain. (Documentary). 52 min. Sound. 16mm Color. *Rental:* Time-Life Multimedia. *Sale:* Time-Life Multimedia. *Rental:* Time-Life Multimedia, *Sale:* Time-Life Multimedia, Videotape version.

Resurgence: The Movement for Equality vs. The Ku Klux Klan. Directed by Peter Kinoy, Thomas Sigel & Pamela Yates. 1982. First Run. 54 min. Sound. 16mm Color. *Rental:* First Run. *Lease:* First Run.

Resurrection. Lupe Velez & John Boles. Directed by Edwin Carewe. 1931. Universal. 73 min. Sound. 16mm B&W. *Rental:* Swank Motion.

Resurrection. Ellen Burstyn & Sam Shepard. Directed by Daniel Petrie. 1980. Universal. 103 min. Sound. 16mm Color. *Rental:* Swank Motion.

Resurrection. Tamara Syomina & Yevgeni Matveyev. Directed by Mikhail Schweitzer. Rus. 1962. Russia. 155 min. Sound. 16mm B&W. subtitles. *Rental:* Corinth Films.

Resurrection of Zachary Wheeler, The. Angie Dickinson & Bradford Dillman. Directed by Bob Wind. 1972. Madison. 100 min. Sound. 16mm Color. *Rental:* Arcus Film, Budget Films, Ivy Films, Natl Film Video, Roas Films, Video Comm, Welling Motion Pictures & Westcoast Films. *Sale:* Video Comm. *Rental:* Video Comm, *Lease:* Video Comm, Videotape version.

Retik, the Moon Menace. Roy Barcroft & Aline Towne. Directed by Fred C. Brannon. 1966. Republic. 100 min. Sound. 16mm B&W. *Rental:* Bosco Films & Ivy Films. *Sale:* Rep Pic Film.

Retirement. Directed by Cinda Firestone. 1978. Cinema V. 50 min. Sound. 16mm Color. *Rental:* Cinema Five.

Retour d'Afrique, Le. Josee Destoop. Directed by Alain Tanner. Fr. 1973. Switzerland. 90 min. Sound. B&W. *Rental:* New Yorker Films. *Lease:* New Yorker Films. *Rental:* New Yorker Films, 109 version.

Retratos. Directed by Steward Bird. Puerto Rico. (Documentary). 53 min. Sound. 16mm Color. subtitles. *Rental:* Cinema Guild. *Sale:* Cinema Guild.

Retreat from Kiska. Toshiro Mifune & Seiji Maruyama. 1962. Japan. 90 min. Sound. 16mm B&W. *Rental:* Budget Films.

Retreat, Hell! Frank Lovejoy & Richard Carlson. Directed by Joseph Lewis. 1952. Warners. 95 min. Sound. 16mm B&W. *Rental:* Corinth Films. *Lease:* Corinth Films.

Retrospect. 1962. 55 min. Sound. 16mm B&W. *Rental:* Utah Media.

Return from the Ashes. Maximilian Schell & Ingrid Thulin. Directed by J. Lee Thompson. 1966. MGM. 107 min. Sound. 16mm B&W. *Rental:* MGM United.

Return from the Past. Lon Chaney Jr., Rochelle Hudson & John Carradine. 1967. Harold Goldman. 84 min. Sound. 16mm Color. *Rental:* Charard Motion Pics, Ivy Films & Video Comm.

Return from the Sea. Neville Brand & Jan Sterling. Directed by Lesley Selander. 1954. Allied Artists. 80 min. Sound. 16mm B&W. *Rental:* Hurlock Cine.

Return from Witch Mountain. Bette Davis & Christopher Lee. Directed by John Hough. 1978. Disney. 93 min. Sound. 16mm Color. *Rental:* Williams Films, Bosco Films, Disney Prod, Elliot Film Co, Films Inc, Film Pres, U of IL Film, MGM United, Modern Sound, Roas Films, Swank Motion, Film Ctr DC, Twyman Films, Westcoast Films & Welling Motion Pictures.

Return Journey. Directed by Ian Potts. 1981. Great Britain. (Documentary). 45 min. Sound. 16mm Color. *Rental:* Museum Mod Art. *Sale:* Museum Mod Art.

Return of a Man Called Horse, The. Richard Harris & Gale Sondergaard. Directed by Irwin Kershner. 1976. United Artists. 125 min. Sound. 16mm Color. *Rental:* Budget Films, Films Inc, MGM United, Westcoast Films & Welling Motion Pictures. *Rental:* MGM United, Videotape version.

Return of Billy the Kid, The see Billy the Kid Returns.

Return of Boston Blackie, The. Raymond Glenn & Strongheart the Dog. Directed by Harry Hoyt. 1927. First Division. 65 min. Silent. 16mm B&W. *Rental:* Mogulls Films.

Return of Casey Jones, The. Charles Starrett. Directed by J. P. McCarthy. 1933. Monogram. 75 min. Sound. 16mm B&W. *Rental:* Film Classics.

Return of Chandu, The. Bela Lugosi & Clara Kimball Young. Directed by Ray Taylor. 1943. Principal. 79 min. Sound. 16mm B&W. *Rental:* Budget Films, Film Ctr DC & Video Comm. *Rental:* Ivy Films, *Sale:* Ivy Films, Super 8 sound version. *Rental:* Video Comm, Videotape version.

Return of Count Yorga, The. Robert Quarry. Directed by Bob Kelljan. 1971. American International. 96 min. Sound. 16mm Color. *Rental:* Swank Motion.

Return of Daniel Boone, The. Trans. Title: Mayor's Nest, The. Bill Elliot & Dub Taylor. Directed by Lambert Hillyer. 1941. Columbia. 75 min. Sound. 16mm B&W. *Rental:* Alba House.

Return of Dr. Mabuse, The. Orig. Title: In the Steel Net of Dr. Mabuse. Trans. Title: Im Stahlnetz des Dr. Mabuse. Gert Frobe & Lex Barker. Directed by Harold Reinl. 1961. Germany. 88 min. Sound. 16mm B&W. dubbed. *Rental:* Budget Films.

Return of Dr. X, The. Humphrey Bogart & Dennis Morgan. Directed by Vincent Sherman. 1939. Warners. 63 min. Sound. 16mm B&W. *Rental:* MGM United.

Return of Don Camillo, The. Fernandel & Gino Cervi. Directed by Julien Duvivier. 1956. France-Italy. 115 min. Sound. 16mm B&W. dubbed. *Rental:* Inst Cinema.

Return of "Draw" Egan, The. William S. Hart. Directed by Thomas H. Ince. 1917. Ince. 55 min. Silent. 16mm B&W. *Rental:* Budget Films, Em Gee Film Lib, Film Images, Films Inc, Video Comm & Wholesome Film Ctr. *Sale:* Glenn Photo & Natl Cinema. *Sale:* Glenn Photo, Super 8 silent version. *Rental:* Westcoast Films, 115 mins. version. *Rental:* Video Comm, Videotape version.

Return of Frank James, The. Henry Fonda & Gene Tierney. Directed by Fritz Lang. 1940. Fox. 92 min. Sound. 16mm B&W. *Rental:* Video Comm.

Return of Jack Slade, The. Orig. Title: Texas Rose. John Ericson & Neville Brand. Directed by Harold Schuster. 1955. Allied Artists. 79 min. Sound. 16mm B&W. *Rental:* Ivy Films. *Sale:* Rep Pic Film.

Return of Jesse James, The. John Ireland & Ann Dvorak. Directed by Arthur Hilton. 1950. Lippert. 75 min. Sound. 16mm B&W. *Rental:* Budget Films & Mogulls Films. *Rental:* Westcoast Films, 60 mins. version.

Return of Martin Guerre, The. Nathalie Baye & Gerard Depardieu. Directed by Daniel Vigne. 1983. France. 111 min. Sound. Videotape Color. *Sale:* Tamarelles French Films.

Return of Master Killer, The. Liu Chia Hui. Hong Kong. 103 min. Sound. 16mm *Rental:* WW Enter. *Rental:* WW Enter, Videotape version.

Return of Mr. Moto, The. Henry Silva & Terence Longdon. Directed by Ernest Morris. 1965. Fox. 71 min. Sound. 16mm B&W. *Rental:* Films Inc.

Return of Monte Cristo, The. Louis Hayward & Barbara Britton. Directed by Henry Levin. 1946. Columbia. 91 min. Sound. 16mm B&W. *Rental:* Inst Cinema.

Return of October, The. Orig. Title: Date with Destiny, A. Glenn Ford & Terry Moore. Directed by Joseph Lewis. 1948. Columbia. 89 min. Sound. 16mm B&W. *Rental:* Inst Cinema.

Return of Peter Grimm, The. Lionel Barrymore & Helen Mack. Directed by George Nicholls. 1936. RKO. 82 min. Sound. 16mm *Rental:* RKO General Pics.

Return of Rin-Tin-Tin, The. Donald Woods & Robert Blake. Directed by Max Nosseck. 1947. Eagle Lion. 67 min. Sound. 16mm Color. *Rental:* Budget Films.

Return of Sabata, The. Lee Van Cleef. Directed by Frank Kramer. 1972. United Artists. 106 min. Sound. 16mm Color. dubbed. *Rental:* MGM United.

Return of the Ape Man, The. Bela Lugosi & John Carradine. Directed by Phil Rosen. 1944. Monogram. 65 min. Sound. 16mm B&W. *Rental:* Em Gee Film Lib. *Sale:* Rep Pic Film.

Return of the Badmen, The. Robert Ryan, Randolph Scott & Anne Jeffreys. Directed by Ray Enright. 1948. RKO. 90 min. Sound. 16mm B&W. *Rental:* RKO General Pics. *Sale:* Blackhawk Films, Videotape version.

Return of the Dragon, The. Bruce Lee. Directed by Bruce Lee. 1973. Hong Kong. 91 min. Sound. 16mm Color. *Rental:* Swank Motion.

Return of the Durango Kid, The. Charles Starrett. Directed by Derwin Abrahams. 1945. Columbia. 60 min. Sound. 16mm B&W. *Rental:* Westcoast Films.

Return of the Fly, The. Vincent Price & Brett Halsey. Directed by Edward Bernds. 1959. Fox. (Anamorphic). 78 min. Sound. 16mm B&W. *Rental:* Films Inc.

Return of the Giant Monsters, The. Kojiro Hongo. Directed by Noriaki Yuasa. 1967. Japan. 87 min. Sound. 16mm Color. dubbed. *Rental:* Films Inc.

Return of the Grey Wolf, The. Leader the Dog. 60 min. Silent. 16mm B&W. *Rental:* Mogulls Films.

Return of the Living Dead, The. Michael Greer & Marianna Hill. 90 min. Sound. 16mm Color. *Rental:* Ivy Films.

Return of the Pink Panther, The. Peter Sellers. Directed by Blake Edwards. 1975. United Artists. 113 min. Sound. 16mm Color. *Rental:* Budget Films, MGM United, Modern Sound, Roas Films, Swank Motion, Twyman Films, Welling Motion Pictures & Wholesome Film Ctr. *Rental:* MGM United, Anamorphic version. *Rental:* MGM United, Videotape version.

Return of the Scarlet Pimpernel, The. Barry K. Barnes & Sophie Stewart. Directed by Hans Schwartz. 1938. Britain. 84 min. Sound. 16mm B&W. *Rental:* Films Inc & Inst Cinema.

Return of the Sea Elephants, The. 1976. Metromedia. (Documentary). 52 min. Sound. 16mm Color. *Rental:* Churchill Films. *Rental:* Churchill Films, Videotape version.

Return of the Secaucus Seven, The. Mark Arnott, Maggie Renzi & Gordon Clapp. Directed by John Sayles. 1980. Specialty. 106 min. Sound. 16mm Color. *Rental:* Cinema Five.

Return of the Seven, The. Yul Brynner & Robert Fuller. Directed by Burt Kennedy. 1966. MGM. 95 min. Sound. 16mm Color. *Rental:* MGM United, Westcoast Films & Welling Motion Pictures.

Return of the Street Fighter, The. Sonny Chiba. Directed by Shigehiro Ozawa. 1975. Japan. 81 min. Sound. 16mm Color. dubbed. *Rental:* New Line Cinema.

Return of the Tall Blond Man with One Black Shoe, The. Pierre Richard. Directed by Yves Robert. Fr. 1975. France. 84 min. Sound. 16mm Color. subtitles. *Rental:* Specialty Films. *Sale:* Cinema Concepts & Video Lib, Videotape version.

Return of the Texan, The. Dale Robertson & Joanne Dru. Directed by Delmer Daves. 1952. Fox. 88 min. Sound. 16mm B&W. *Rental:* Films Inc.

Return of the Vampire, The. Bela Lugosi & Nina Foch. Directed by Lew Landers. 1943. Columbia. 70 min. 16mm B&W. *Rental:* Budget Films, Williams Films, Film Pres, Ivy Films, Modern Sound, Roas Films, Swank Motion, Twyman Films, Video Comm & Welling Motion Pictures.

Return of the Whistler, The. Michael Duane & Lenore Aubert. Directed by D. Ross Lederman. 1948. Columbia. 63 min. Sound. 16mm B&W. *Rental:* Bosco Films.

Return of Vassili Bortnikov, The. Orig. Title: Harvest. Sergei Lukyanov & Natalya Medvedeva. Directed by Vsevolod I. Pudovkin. Rus. 1953. Russia. 110 min. Sound. 16mm B&W. subtitles. *Rental:* Corinth Films.

Return of Wildfire, The. Orig. Title: Black Stallion. Richard Arlen & Patricia Morrison. Directed by Ray Taylor. 1948. Screen Guild. 81 min. Sound. 16mm B&W. *Rental:* Budget Films & Westcoast Films.

Return to Boggy Creek. Dawn Wells. 1977. Seven-Seven-Seven Distributors. 90 min. Sound. 16mm Color. *Rental:* Williams Films.

Return to Everest. 59 min. Sound. 16mm Color. *Rental:* National Geographic Society. *Rental:* National Geographic Society, Video version.

Return to Macon County. Nick Nolte & Don Johnson. Directed by Richard Compton. 1975. American International. 90 min. Sound. 16mm Color. *Rental:* Swank Motion.

Return to Oz. 1968. UPA. (Animated). 57 min. Sound. 16mm Color. *Rental:* Budget Films, Cine Craft, Charard Motion Pics, Films Inc, Inst Cinema, Newman Film Lib, Syracuse U Film, Twyman Films, Westcoast Films, Welling Motion Pictures & Willoughby Peer.

Return to Peyton Place. Carol Lynley & Eleanor Parker. Directed by Jose Ferrer. 1961. Fox. (Anamorphic). 122 min. Sound. 16mm Color. *Rental:* Films Inc.

Return to Poland. 1981. 58 min. Sound. Videotape *Rental:* PBS Video. *Sale:* PBS Video.

Return to Yesterday. Clive Brook & Anna Lee. Directed by Robert Stevenson. 1939. Britain. 72 min. Sound. 16mm B&W. *Rental:* Mogulls Films.

Reunion. Kevin Dobson & Joanna Cassidy. Directed by Russ Mayberry. 1980. CBS. 105 min. Sound. 16mm Color. *Rental:* Twyman Films.

Reunion in Vienna. Diana Wynyard & Frank Morgan. Directed by Sidney Franklin. 1933. MGM. 100 min. Sound. 16mm B&W. *Rental:* MGM United.

Reveille with Beverly. Ann Miller & Larry Parks. Directed by Charles Barton. 1943. Columbia. 78 min. Sound. 16mm B&W. *Rental:* Kit Parker.

Revelation of the Foundation. 1975. 68 min. Sound. 16mm Color. *Rental:* Canyon Cinema.

Revenge at Daybreak. Danielle Delorme & Henri Vidal. France. Sound. 16mm B&W. dubbed. *Rental:* Charard Motion Pics.

Revenge for Paco. Jean Servais & Robert Manuel. Directed by Jess Franco. 1965. France. 96 min. Sound. 16mm B&W. dubbed. *Rental:* Films Inc.

Revenge is My Destiny. Chris Robinson & Sidney Blackmer. Directed by Joseph Adler. 1971. Gold Key. 95 min. Sound. 16mm Color. *Rental:* Budget Films & Video Comm. *Sale:* Video Comm. *Rental:* Video Comm, *Lease:* Video Comm, Videotape version.

Revenge of Frankenstein, The. Peter Cushing & Francis Mathews. Directed by Terence Fisher. 1958. Britian. 94 min. Sound. 16mm Color. *Rental:* Arcus Film, Budget Films, Cine Craft, Charard Motion Pics, Williams Films, Bosco Films, Films Inc, Film Pres, Images Film, Ivy Films, Kit Parker, Modern Sound, Natl Film Video, Film Ctr DC, Twyman Films, Welling Motion Pictures, Westcoast Films & Wholesome Film Ctr.

Revenge of Ivanhoe, The. Clyde Rogers & Gilda Lousak. 1965. Italy. 100 min. Sound. 16mm Color. dubbed. *Rental:* Films Inc.

Revenge of the Cheerleaders, The. Carl Ballantine, Edra Gale & Rainbeaux Smith. Directed by Richard Lerner. 1977. Lerner/Dorsky. 88 min. Sound. 16mm Color. *Rental:* Corinth Films.

Revenge of the Creature, The. John Agar & Lori Nelson. Directed by Jack Arnold. 1955. Universal. 82 min. Sound. 16mm B&W. *Rental:* Swank Motion. *Rental:* Swank Motion, Three-D version.

Revenge of the Nerd, The. Chris Barnes & Manny Jacobs. 1982. CBS. 45 min. Sound. 16mm Color. *Sale:* Learning Corp Am. *Rental:* Learning Corp Am. *Sale:* Learning Corp Am, *Rental:* Learning Corp Am, Videotape version.

Revenge of the Pink Panther, The. Peter Sellers, Dyan Cannon & Herbert Lom. Directed by Blake Edwards. 1978. United Artists. (Anamorphic). 99 min. Sound. 16mm Color. *Rental:* MGM United. *Rental:* MGM United, Videotape version.

Revenge of the Virgins, The. Hank Delgado. 1962. 60 min. Sound. 16mm B&W. *Sale:* Morcraft Films. *Sale:* Morcraft Films, Super 8 sound version.

Revenge of the Zombies, The. John Carradine & Gale Storm. Directed by Steve Sekely. 1943. Monogram. 70 min. Sound. 16mm B&W. *Rental:* Mogulls Films & Westcoast Films.

Revenger of Zombies. 93 min. Sound. 16mm *Rental:* WW Enter. *Rental:* WW Enter, Videotape version.

Revengers, The. William Holden, Ernest Borgnine & Woody Strode. Directed by Daniel Mann. 1972. National General. 107 min. Sound. 16mm Color. *Rental:* Swank Motion.

Revenue Agent. Douglas Kennedy & Onslow Stevens. Directed by Lew Landers. 1951. Columbia. 72 min. Sound. 16mm B&W. *Rental:* Inst Cinema.

Revizor *see* Inspector General.

Revolt at Fort Laramie. John Dehner & Greg Palmer. Directed by Lesley Selander. 1957. United Artists. 73 min. Sound. 16mm Color. *Rental:* MGM United.

Revolt in Cananda. George Martin & Pamela Tudor. Directed by Mando De Ossurio. 1964. Spain. 107 min. Sound. 16mm Color. dubbed. *Rental:* Video Comm.

Revolt in the Big House. Gene Evans & Robert Blake. Directed by R. G. Springsteen. 1958. Allied Artists. 79 min. Sound. 16mm B&W. *Rental:* Hurlock Cine.

Revolt of Mamie Stover, The. Jane Russell & Richard Egan. Directed by Raoul Walsh. 1956. Fox. (Anamorphic). 93 min. Sound. 16mm Color. *Rental:* Films Inc.

Revolt of the Barbarians. Roland Caray & Mario Feliciani. 1964. Italy. 99 min. Sound. 16mm Color. dubbed. *Rental:* Films Inc.

Revolt of the Fisherman. Alexei Biky. Directed by Erwin Piscator. Rus. 1934. Russia. (Cast unlisted). 85 min. Sound. 16mm B&W. subtitles. *Rental:* Museum Mod Art.

Revolution. Directed by Jack O'Connell. 1968. Lopert. (Documentary). 87 min. Sound. 16mm Color. *Rental:* MGM United.

Revolution and the Three R's. 1966. Wolper. (Documentary). 50 min. Sound. 16mm B&W. *Rental:* Films Inc. *Sale:* Films Inc.

Revolution in Dhofar. 1973. Jimmy Vaughan. (Documentary). 55 min. Sound. 16mm Color. *Rental:* Tricontinental Film.

Revolution Until Victory. 1973. Third World Newsreel. (Documentary). 52 min. Sound. 16mm B&W. *Rental:* CA Newsreel. *Rental:* CA Newsreel, *Sale:* CA Newsreel, Spanish language version.

Revolutionary, The. Jon Voight. Directed by Paul Williams. 1970. United Artists. 101 min. Sound. 16mm Color. *Rental:* MGM United.

Revolutionists, The. Boris Shchukin. Directed by Vera Stroyeva. 1936. Russia. 107 min. Sound. 16mm B&W. subtitles. *Rental:* Corinth Films.

Revolving Teens. 60 min. Videotape Color. *Sale:* Videx Home LIb.

Reward, The. Max Von Sydow & Yvette Mimieux. Directed by Serge Bourguignon. 1965. Fox. 92 min. Sound. 16mm Color. *Rental:* Films Inc.

Rex, King of the Sierras. Hobart Bosworth. Directed by Samuel Diege. 1938. Grand National. 60 min. Sound. 16mm B&W. *Rental:* Budget Films.

Rex, King of the Wild Horses *see* King of the Wild Horses.

Rhapsody. Elizabeth Taylor & Vittorio Gassman. Directed by Charles Vidor. 1954. MGM. 116 min. Sound. 16mm B&W. *Rental:* MGM United.

Rhapsody in Blue. Robert Alda & Joan Leslie. Directed by Irving Rapper. 1945. Warners. 93 min. Sound. 16mm B&W. *Rental:* MGM United. *Rental:* MGM United, 139 version.

Rhino! Robert Culp & Harry Guardino. Directed by Ivan Tors. 1964. MGM. 91 min. Sound. 16mm Color. *Rental:* MGM United.

Rhinoceros. Zero Mostel & Gene Wilder. Directed by Tom O'Horgan. 1973. AFT. 101 min. Sound. 16mm Color. *Rental:* Films Inc.

Rhodes *see* Rhodes of Africa.

Rhodes of Africa. Orig. Title: Rhodes. Walter Huston & Oscar Homolka. Directed by Berthold Viertel. 1936. Britain. 90 min. Sound. 16mm B&W. *Rental:* Budget Films.

Rhubarb. Ray Milland & Jan Sterling. Directed by Arthur Lubin. 1951. Paramount. 94 min. Sound. 16mm B&W. *Rental:* Films Inc.

Rhythm & Blues Revue. Nipsey Russell & Mantan Moreland. Directed by Joseph Kohn. 1959. 90 min. Sound. 16mm B&W. *Rental:* Budget Films & Em Gee Film LIb.

Rhythm Hits the Ice. Orig. Title: Ice Capades. Ellen Drew & Jerry Colonna. Directed by Joseph Santley. 1942. Republic. 80 min. Sound. 16mm B&W. *Rental:* Ivy Films. *Sale:* Rep Pic Film.

Rhythm in the Clouds. Patricia Ellis & Warren Hull. Directed by John H. Auer. 1937. Republic. 54 min. Sound. 16mm B&W. *Rental:* Ivy Films. *Sale:* Rep Pic Film.

Rhythm Inn. Kirby Grant & Jane Frazee. Directed by Paul Landres. 1951. Monogram. 73 min. Sound. 16mm B&W. *Rental:* Hurlock Cine.

Rhythm of the Rio Grande. Tex Ritter. Directed by Al Herman. 1940. Monogram. 55 min. Sound. 16mm B&W. *Rental:* Hurlock Cine.

Rhythm of the Saddle. Gene Autry. Directed by George Sherman. 1938. Republic. 54 min. Sound. 16mm B&W. *Rental:* Ivy Films.

Rhythm on the Ranch *see* Rootin' Tootin' Rhythm.

Rhythm on the Range. Bing Crosby & Frances Farmer. Directed by Norman Taurog. 1936. Paramount. 85 min. Sound. 16mm B&W. *Rental:* Swank Motion.

Rhythm on the River *see* Freshman Love.

Rhythm on the River. Bing Crosby & Mary Martin. Directed by Victor Schertzinger. 1940. Paramount. 94 min. Sound. 16mm B&W. *Rental:* Swank Motion.

Rhythm Parade. Gale Storm & Robert Lowery. Directed by Howard Bretherton. 1942. Monogram. 80 min. Sound. 16mm B&W. *Rental:* Mogulls Film & Film Ctr DC.

Rich & Famous. Jacqueline Bisset, Candice Bergen & David Selby. Directed by George Cukor. 1981. 117 min. Sound. 16mm Color. *Rental:* MGM United. *Rental:* MGM United, Videotape version.

Rich & Strange. Orig. Title: East of Shanghai. Joan Barry & Percy Marmount. Directed by Alfred Hitchcock. 1931. Britain. 92 min. Sound. 16mm B&W. *Rental:* Janus Films.

Rich Are Always With Us, The. Ruth Chatterton, George Brent & Bette Davis. Directed by Alfred E. Green. 1932. Warners. 76 min. Sound. 16mm B&W. *Rental:* MGM United.

Rich Kids. Trini Alvarado & Jeremy Levy. Directed by Robert Young. 1979. United Artists. 97 min. Sound. 16mm Color. *Rental:* MGM United.

Rich Man, Poor Girl. Lana Turner & Robert Young. Directed by Reinhold Schunzel. 1938. MGM. 72 min. Sound. 16mm B&W. *Rental:* MGM United.

Rich Man, Poor Man. 6 pts. 1972. Britain. (Documentary). 300 min. Sound. 16mm Color. *Rental:* Time-Life Multimedia. *Sale:* Time-Life Multimedia. *Rental:* Time-Life Multimedia, *Sale:* Time-Life Multimedia, Videotape version

Rich, Young & Pretty. Jane Powell & Danielle Darrieux. Directed by Norman Taurog. 1951. MGM. 95 min. Sound. 16mm Color. *Rental:* MGM United.

Rich, Full Life, A *see* Cynthia.

Richard. Mickey Rooney & John Carradine. Directed by Lorees Yerby & Harry Hurwitz. 1973. Genesis. (Color Sequences). 75 min. Sound. 16mm B&W. *Rental:* Budget Films.

Richard Pryor Here & Now. Directed by Richard Pryor. 1983. Columbia. 94 min. Sound. 16mm Color. *Rental:* Swank Motion. *Rental:* Swank Motion, Videotape version.

Richard Pryor: Live in Concert. Richard Pryor. Directed by Jeff Margolis. 78 min. Sound. 16mm Color. *Rental:* Swank Motion.

Richard Pryor: Live on the Sunset Strip. Richard Pryor. Directed by Joe Layton. Columbia. 82 min. Sound. 16mm Color. *Rental:* Swank Motion. *Rental:* Swank Motion, Videotape version.

Richard T. Ely. Don O'Herlihy. Directed by Michael O'Herlihy. 1965. Saudek. 50 min. Sound. 16mm B&W. *Rental:* U Mich Media. *Sale:* IQ Film. *Rental:* IQ Film, *Sale:* IQ Film, Spanish dubbed version.

Richard Tauber Story, The. Trans. Title: Du Bist Die Welt Fur Mich. Richard Tauber. Directed by Ernst Marischka. Ger. 1953. Germany. 107 min. Sound. 16mm B&W. subtitles. *Rental:* Trans-World Films & Twyman Films.

Richard the Second. Derek Jacobi, Jon Finch, Sir John Gielgud. 1979. Britain. 157 min. Videotape Color. *Rental:* Iowa Films.

Richard the Third. Martin Shaw & Brian Protheroe. 1982. 230 min. Sound. Videotape Color. *Rental:* Iowa Films.

Richard the Third. Sir Laurence Olivier, Sir John Gielgud. Directed by Sir Laurence Olivier. 1955. Britain. 158 min. Sound. 16 mm Color. *Rental:* Films Inc & New Cinema.

Richard's Things. Liv Ullmann & Amanda Redman. Directed by Anthony Harvey. 1981. New World. 104 min. Sound. 16mm Color. *Rental:* Films Inc.

Richer Than the Earth *see* Whistle at Eaton Falls.

Richest Girl in the World, The. Joel McCrea & Miriam Hopkins. Directed by Pandro S. Berman. 1935. RKO. 76 min. Sound. 16mm *Rental:* RKO General Pics.

Richthofen, the Red Knight of Germany. 1929. Film Arts Guild. (Documentary). 75 min. Silent. 16mm B&W. *Rental:* Mogulls Films.

Riddle of the Sands. Michael York & Jenny Agutter. Directed by Tony Maylam. 102 min. Sound. Videotape Color. *Sale:* Vidamerica.

Riddles of the Sphinx. Directed by Laura Mulvey & Peter Wollen. 1977. Britain. (Experimental). 92 min. Sound. 16mm Color. *Rental:* Museum Mod Art & New Cinema.

Ride a Violent Mile. John Agar & Penny Edwards. Directed by Charles Marquis Warren. 1957. Republic. 79 min. Sound. 16mm B&W. *Rental:* Ivy Films. *Sale:* Rep Pic Film.

Ride a Wild Pony. Michael Craig, John Meillon & Robert Bettles. Directed by Don Chaffey. 1975. Disney. 90 min. Sound. 16mm Color. *Rental:* Buchan Pic, Williams Films, Bosco Films, Disney Prod, Elliot Film Co, Films Inc, Film Pres, U Of IL Film, MGM United, Modern Sound, Newman Film Lib, Roas Film, Twyman Films, Westcoast Films & Welling Motion Pictures.

Ride Back, The. Anthony Quinn & William Conrad. Directed by Allen H. Miner. 1957. United Artists. 79 min. Sound. 16mm B&W. *Rental:* MGM United.

Ride Beyond Vengeance. Chuck Connors & Michael Rennie. Directed by Bernard McEveety. 1966. Columbia. 100 min. Sound. 16mm Color. *Rental:* Modern Sound & Roas Films.

Ride Clear of Diablo. Audie Murphy & Dan Duryea. Directed by Jesse Hibbs. 1954. Universal. 80 min. Sound. 16mm Color. *Rental:* Swank Motion.

Ride, Cowboy, Ride. American Quarterhorse Association. 60 min. Sound. 16mm Color. *Rental:* OK AV Ctr.

Ride 'Em Cowboy. John Wayne & Henry B. Walthall. Directed by Fred Allen. 1932. Warners. 56 min. Sound. 16mm B&W. *Rental:* MGM United.

Ride 'Em Cowgirl. Dorothy Paige. Directed by Arthur Dreifuss. 1939. Grand National. 60 min. Sound. 16mm B&W. *Rental:* Grand National. *Rental:* Video Comm, *Lease:* Video Comm, Videotape version.

Ride in the Whirlwind. Cameron Mitchell, Millie Perkins & Jack Nicholson. Directed by Monte Hellman. 1967. Continental. 82 min. Sound. 16mm Color. *Rental:* Budget Films, Kit Parker & Kino Intl. *Sale:* Kino Intl.

Ride Lonesome. Randolph Scott & Pernell Roberts. Directed by Budd Boetticher. 1959. Columbia. (Anamorphic). 73 min. Sound. 16mm Color. *Rental:* Corinth Films, Bosco Films, Kit Parker, Modern Sound.

Ride Out for Revenge. Rory Calhoun & Gloria Grahame. Directed by Bernard Girard. 1958. United Artists. 79 min. Sound. 16mm B&W. *Rental:* MGM United.

Ride, Ranger, Ride. Gene Autry. Directed by Joseph Kane. 1936. Republic. 54 min. Sound. 16mm B&W. *Rental:* Budget Films & Ivy Films. *Sale:* Cinema Concepts & Reel Images.

Ride, Tenderfoot, Ride. Gene Autry. Directed by Frank McDonald. 1940. Republic. 54 min. Sound. 16mm B&W. *Rental:* Ivy Films.

Ride the High Country. Orig. Title: Guns in the Afternoon. Randolph Scott & Joel McCrea. Directed by Sam Peckinpah. 1962. MGM. 94 min. Sound. 16mm Color. *Rental:* MGM United. *Rental:* MGM United, Anamorphic color version.

Ride the High Iron. Don Taylor, Raymond Burr & Sally Forrest. Directed by Don Weis. 1956. Columbia. 74 min. Sound. 16mm B&W. *Rental:* Films Inc.

Ride the High Wind. Darren McGavin. Directed by David Millin. 1965. South Africa. 85 min. Sound. 16mm Color. *Rental:* Films Inc, Ivy Films & Rep Pic Film. *Lease:* Rep Pic Film.

Ride the Man Down. Brian Donlevy & Rod Cameron. Directed by Joseph Kane. 1953. Republic. 90 min. Sound. 16mm Color. *Rental:* Ivy Films. *Lease:* Rep Pic Film.

Ride the Pink Horse. Robert Montgomery & Wanda Hendrix. Directed by Robert Montgomery. 1947. Universal. 101 min. Sound. 16mm B&W. *Rental:* Swank Motion.

Ride the Tiger. George Montgomery & Victoria Shaw. Directed by Ferde Grofe Jr. 1971. Gold Key. 96 min. Sound. 16mm Color. *Rental:* Video Comm. *Lease:* Video Comm. *Rental:* Video Comm, *Lease:* Video Comm, Videotape version.

Ride the Wild Surf. Fabian & Tab Hunter. Directed by Don Taylor. 1964. Columbia. 101 min. Sound. 16mm Color. *Rental:* Arcus Film, Buchan Pic, Budget Films, Cine Craft, Films Inc, Modern Sound, Roas Films & Westcoast Films.

Ride to Hangman's Tree, The. Jack Lord & James Farentino. Directed by Alan Rafkin. 1967. Universal. 90 min. Sound. 16mm Color. *Rental:* Swank Motion.

Ride Vaquero. Robert Taylor & Ava Gardner. Directed by John Farrow. 1953. MGM. 91 min. Sound. 16mm Color. *Rental:* MGM United.

Rider in the Night. Annette De Villiers. Directed by Jan Perold. 1966. International. (Anamorphic). 103 min. Sound. 16mm Color. *Rental:* Mogulls Films. *Sale:* Mogulls Films.

Rider on a Dead Horse. John Vivyan & Lisa Liu. Directed by Herbert L. Strock. 1962. Allied Artists. 72 min. Sound. 16mm B&W. *Rental:* Hurlock Cine.

Rider on the Rain. Charles Bronson & Marlene Jobert. Directed by Rene Clement. 1970. France. 119 min. Sound. 16mm Color. dubbed. *Rental:* Cine Craft, Films Inc & Video Comm.

Riders for Justice. Tom Tyler & Bob Steele. Directed by John English. 1942. Republic. 56 min. Sound. 16mm B&W. *Rental:* Ivy Films. *Sale:* Rep Pic Film.

Riders from Nowhere. Jack Randall. Directed by Raymond K. Johnson. 1940. Monogram. 45 min. Sound. 16mm B&W. *Rental:* Hurlock Cine.

Riders from Tucson. Tim Holt & Richard Martin. Directed by Lesley Selander. 1950. RKO. 60 min. Sound. 16mm B&W. *Rental:* RKO General Pics.

Riders of Destiny. John Wayne. Directed by Robert N. Bradbury. 1933. Monogram. 60 min. Sound. 16mm B&W. *Rental:* Budget Films, Ivy Films & Mogulls Films. *Sale:* Classics Assoc NY & Rep Pic Film. *Sale:* Video Comm, Videotape version.

Riders of the Black Hills. Robert Livingston. Directed by George Sherman. 1938. Republic. 54 min. Sound. 16mm B&W. *Rental:* Ivy Films. *Sale:* Rep Pic Film.

Riders of the Dawn. Jack Randall. Directed by Robert N. Bradbury. 1937. Monogram. 53 min. Sound. 16mm B&W. *Rental:* Hurlock Cine.

Riders of the Deadline. William Boyd. Directed by Lesley Selander. 1943. United Artists. 65 min. Sound. 16mm B&W. *Lease:* Cinema Concepts.

Riders of the Dusk. Whip Wilson. Directed by Lambert Hillyer. 1949. Monogram. 55 min. Sound. 16mm B&W. *Rental:* Budget Films.

Riders of the Frontier. Tex Ritter. Directed by Spencer G. Bennett. 1939. Monogram. 55 min. Sound. 16mm B&W. *Rental:* Hurlock Cine.

Riders of the Law. Bob Steele. Directed by Robert N. Bradbury. 1935. Supreme. 60 min. Sound. 16mm B&W. *Rental:* Budget Films. *Sale:* Morcraft Films.

Riders of the Law. Jack Hoxie. Directed by Robert N. Bradbury. 1922. Sunset. 55 min. Silent. 16mm B&W. *Sale:* Film Classics & Morcraft Films.

Riders of the North. Bob Custer. Directed by J. P. McGowan. 1931. Syndicate. 57 min. Sound. 16mm B&W. *Sale:* Natl Cinema.

Riders of the Purple Sage. George Montgomery & Lynn Roberts. Directed by James Tinling. 1941. Fox. 56 min. Sound. 16mm B&W. *Rental:* Films Inc.

Riders of the Purple Sage. Tom Mix & Beatrice Burnham. Directed by Lynn Reynolds. 1925. Fox. (Musical score only, tinted). 56 min. Sound. 16mm B&W. *Rental:* Killiam Collect. *Sale:* Blackhawk Films, Super 8 Sound version. *Sale:* Blackhawk Films, Super 8 silent version.

Riders of the Purple Sage. George O'Brien & Marguerite Churchill. Directed by Hamilton MacFadden. 1931. Fox. 70 min. Sound. 16mm B&W. *Rental:* Films Inc.

Riders of the Range. Tim Holt & Martin Richard. Directed by Lesley Selander. 1950. RKO. 60 min. Sound. 16mm *Rental:* RKO General Pics.

Riders of the Rio Grande. Tom Tyler & Bob Steele. Directed by Howard Bretherton. 1943. Republic. 55 min. Sound. 16mm B&W. *Rental:* Ivy Films. *Sale:* Nostalgia Merchant.

Riders of the Rockies. Tex Ritter. Directed by Robert N. Bradbury. 1937. Grand National. 60 min. Videotape B&W. *Sale:* Video Comm.

Riders of the Sage. Bob Steele. Directed by Harry S. Webb. 1936. Aurora. 60 min. Sound. 16mm B&W. *Sale:* Morcraft Films.

Riders of the Timberline. William Boyd. Directed by Lesley Selander. 1941. Paramount. 54 min. Sound. 16mm B&W. *Sale:* Cinema Concepts.

Riders of the West. Buck Jones & Tim McCoy. Directed by Howard Bretherton. 1942. Monogram. 55 min. Sound. 16mm B&W. *Rental:* Hurlock Cine.

Riders of the Whistling Pines, The. Gene Autry. Directed by John English. 1949. Columbia. 70 min. Super 8 sound B&W. *Sale:* Reel Images.

Riders of the Whistling Skull. Orig. Title: Golden Trail, The. Robert Livingston. Directed by Mack V. Wright. 1937. Republic. 54 min. Sound. 16mm B&W. *Rental:* Ivy Films. *Sale:* Cinema Concepts & Rep Pic Film.

Riders to the Stars. William Lundigan & Richard Carlson. Directed by Richard Carlson. 1954. United Artists. 80 min. Sound. 16mm B&W. *Rental:* Cine Craft, Films Inc, MGM United & Westcoast Films.

Ridin' Down the Canyon. Roy Rogers. Directed by Joseph Kane. 1942. Republic. 54 min. Sound. 16mm B&W. *Rental:* Ivy Films & Budget Films. *Sale:* Cinema Concepts & Rep Pic Film.

Ridin' Down the Trail. Jimmy Wakely. Directed by Howard Bretherton. 1947. Monogram. 53 min. Sound. 16mm B&W. *Rental:* Hurlock Cine.

Ridin' Fool. Bob Steele. Directed by J. P. McCarthy. 1931. Tiffany. 60 min. Sound. 16mm B&W. *Rental:* Willoughby Peer. *Sale:* Cinema Concepts.

Ridin' On. Tom Tyler & Rex Lease. Directed by Bernard B. Ray. 1936. Reliable. 52 min. Sound. 16mm B&W. *Rental:* Budget Films & Mogulls Films. *Sale:* Morcraft Films.

Ridin' On a Rainbow. Gene Autry. Directed by Lew Landers. 1941. Republic. 54 min. Sound. 16mm B&W. *Rental:* Ivy Films. *Sale:* Blackhawk Films. *Sale:* Blackhawk Films, Super 8 sound version. *Sale:* Blackhawk Films, Videotape version.

Ridin' the Cherokee Trail. Tex Ritter. Directed by Spencer G. Bennett. 1941. Monogram. 55 min. Sound. 16mm B&W. *Rental:* Hurlock Cine.

Ridin' the Lone Trail. Bob Steele. Directed by Sam Newfield. 1937. Republic. 60 min. Sound. 16mm B&W. *Rental:* Ivy Films. *Sale:* Cinema Concepts & Reel Images.

Riding Avenger, The. Hoot Gibson. Directed by Harry Fraser. 1936. Division. 50 min. Sound. 16mm B&W. *Rental:* Video Comm. *Sale:* Morcraft Films & Reel Images. *Sale:* Morcraft Films & Reel Images, Super 8 sound version. *Rental:* Video Comm, *Sale:* Video Comm, Videotape version.

Riding High. Bing Crosby & Coleen Gray. Directed by Frank Capra. 1950. Paramount. 112 min. Sound. 16mm B&W. *Rental:* Films Inc.

Riding Mad. Yakima Canutt. Directed by Jacques Jaccard. 1924. Arrow. 60 min. Silent. 16mm B&W. *Rental:* Film Classics. *Sale:* Film Classics.

Riding on Air. Joe E. Brown & Guy Kibbee. Directed by Edward Sedgwick. 1937. RKO. 70 min. Sound. 16mm B&W. *Rental:* Classic Film Mus, Ivy Films & Mogulls Films. *Sale:* Cinema Concepts.

Riding Tall. Andrew Prine. Directed by Patrick J. Murphy. 1980. CBS. 92 min. Sound. 16mm Color. *Rental:* Twyman Films.

Riding the California Trail. Gilbert Roland. Directed by William Nigh. 1947. Monogram. 65 min. Sound. 16mm B&W. *Sale:* Video Comm. *Sale:* Video Comm, Videotape version.

Riding the Wind. Tim Holt & Ray Whitley. Directed by Bert Gilroy. 1950. RKO. 60 min. Sound. 16mm B&W. *Rental:* RKO General Pics.

Riding Tornado. Tim McCoy. Directed by D. Ross Lederman. 1932. Columbia. 59 min. Sound. 16mm B&W. *Rental:* Willoughby Peer.

Riding Wild. Kit Carson. Directed by Harry Harvey. 1919. Universal. 60 min. Silent. 16mm B&W. *Sale:* Mogulls Films.

Riel. Raymond Cloutier. Directed by George Bloomfield. 1978. Canada. 140 min. Sound. 16mm Color. *Rental:* Natl Film CN.

Rien Que Les Heures. Directed by Alberto Cavalcanti. 1926. France. 45 min. Silent. 16mm B&W. *Rental:* Museum Mod Art. *Sale:* Natl Cinema & Reel Images.

Riffraff. Jean Harlow & Spencer Tracy. Directed by Walter J. Ruben. 1936. MGM. 93 min. Sound. 16mm B&W. *Rental:* MGM United.

Riffraff. Pat O'Brien & Walter Slezak. Directed by Ted Tetzlaff. 1947. RKO. 80 min. Sound. 16mm B&W. *Rental:* Films Inc & RKO General Pics.

Rififi. Trans. Title: Du Rififi Chez les Hommes. Jean Servais & Carl Mohner. Directed by Jules Dassin. Fr. 1954. France. 115 min. Sound. 16mm B&W. subtitles. *Rental:* Budget Films & Kit Parker. *Sale:* Festival Films, Morcraft Films, Natl Cinema & Reel Images. *Sale:* Tamarelles French Film & Festival Films, Videotape version.

Rififi In Tokyo. Karl Boehm & Barbara Lass. Directed by Jacques Deray. 1963. France. 89 min. Sound. 16mm B&W. dubbed. *Rental:* Films Inc & MGM United.

Right Age to Marry, The. Frank Pettingell. Directed by Maclean Rogers. 1935. Britain. 60 min. Sound. 16mm B&W. *Rental:* Ivy Films. *Sale:* Rep Pic Film.

Right Approach, The. Frankie Vaughan & Juliet Prowse. Directed by David Butler. 1961. Fox. (Anamorphic). 92 min. Sound. 16mm B&W. *Rental:* Willoughby Peer.

Right Cross. June Allyson & Dick Powell. Directed by John Sturges. 1950. Fox. 90 min. Sound. 16mm B&W. *Rental:* MGM United. *Rental:* MGM United, Videotape version.

Right Man, The. Orig. Title: Her First Romance. Alan Ladd & Edith Fellows. 1940. Monogram. 80 min. Sound. 16mm B&W. *Rental:* Mogulls Films.

Right of Privacy, The. 1967. NET. (Documentary). 59 min. Sound. 16mm B&W. *Rental:* U Cal Media, U of IL Film & Indiana AV Ctr. *Sale:* Indiana AV Ctr.

Right of Way, The. Conrad Nagel & Loretta Young. Directed by Frank Lloyd. 1931. Warners. 65 min. Sound. 16mm B&W. *Rental:* MGM United.

Right On. Felipe Luciano. Directed by Herbert Danska. 1972. New Line. 85 min. Sound. 16mm Color. *Rental:* New Line Cinema. *Sale:* New Line Cinema. *Sale:* New Line Cinema, Videotape version.

Right Out of History: The Making of Judy Chicago's Dinner Party. Directed by Johanna Demetrakis. 1980. Demetrakas. (Documentary). 75 min. Sound. 16mm Color. *Rental:* Budget Films, Kit Parker & Phoenix Films. *Sale:* Phoenix Films. *Sale:* Phoenix Films, Videotape version.

Right Stuff, The. Sam Shepard, Scott Glenn & Dennis Quaid. Directed by Philip Kaufman. 1983. Warners. 192 min. Sound. 16mm Color. *Rental:* Swank Motion. *Rental:* Swnak Motion, *Sale:* Tamarelles French Film, Videotape version.

Right to Believe, The. 1975. ABC. (Documentary). 60 min. Sound. 16mm Color. *Rental:* Natl Churches Christ, U Cal Media, Roas Films & Xerox Films. *Sale:* Xerox Films.

Right to Die, The. 1974. ABC. (Documentary). 56 min. Sound. 16mm Color. *Rental:* Films Inc.

Right to Live, The. George Brent, Peggy Wood & Colin Clive. Directed by William Keighley. 1935. Warners. 69 min. Sound. 16mm B&W. *Rental:* MGM United.

Right to Romance, The. Robert Young & Ann Harding. Directed by Merian C. Cooper. 1934. RKO. 70 min. Sound. 16mm *Rental:* RKO General Pics.

Right to the Heart, A. Brenda Joyce & Stanley Clements. Directed by Eugene Forde. 1942. Fox. 74 min. Sound. 16mm B&W. *Rental:* Films Inc.

Rigoletto. 1975. Britian. (Opera). 56 min. Sound. 16mm Color. *Rental:* Centron Films. *Sale:* Centron Films.

Rigoletto. Tito Gobbi. Ital. Italy. Sound. 16mm Color. subtitles. *Rental:* Corinth Films.

Rikisha Man, The. Trans. Title: Muhymatsu. Toshiro Mifune. Directed by Hiroshi Inagaki. Jap. 1957. Japan. (Anamorphic). 106 min. Sound. 16mm Color. subtitles. *Rental:* Kit Parker.

Riley Family, The. 1967. EMC. (Kinescope). 59 min. Sound. 16mm B&W. *Rental:* U Cal Media. *Sale:* U Cal Media.

Rim of Disaster. Lassie. 1960. Wrather. 52 min. Sound. 16mm Color. *Rental:* Films Inc & Westcoast Films.

Rim of the Canyon. Gene Autry. Directed by John English. 1949. Columbia. 65 min. Sound. 16mm B&W. *Rental:* Budget Films & Roas Films.

Rimfire. Mary Beth Hughes & Henry Hull. Directed by B. Reeves Eason. 1949. Screen Guild. 64 min. Sound. 16mm B&W. *Rental:* Budget Films, Film Ctr DC & Westcoast Films.

Rimsky-Korsakov. Nikolai Cherkassov. Directed by G. Kazansky & Grigori Roshal. Rus. 1952. Russia. 113 min. Sound. 16mm Color. subtitles. *Rental:* Corinth Films.

Ring, The. Carl Brisson & Ian Hunter. Directed by Alfred Hitchcock. 1927. Britain. 85 min. Silent. 16mm B&W. *Rental:* Janus Films.

Ring of Bright Water. Bill Travers & Virginia McKenna. Directed by Jack Couffer. 1969. Cinerama. 107 min. Sound. 16mm Color. *Rental:* Films Inc.

Ring of Clay. 1980. PBS. (Documentary). 59 min. Sound. 16mm Color. *Rental:* PBS Video.

Ring of Fire. David Janssen & Joyce Taylor. Directed by Andrew Stone. 1961. MGM. 91 min. Sound. 16mm Color. *Rental:* MGM United.

Ring of Treason. Bernard Lee & William Sylvester. Directed by Robert Tronson. 1964. Paramount. 89 min. Sound. 16mm B&W. *Rental:* Films Inc.

Ring-A-Ding Rhythm *see* It's Trad Dad.

Ringo & His Golden Pistol. Mark Damon, Ettore Manni & Francesco De Rosa. 1966. Italy. 88 min. Sound. 16mm Color. dubbed. *Rental:* MGM United.

Ringo's World. 1974. (Documentary). 57 min. Sound. 16mm Color. *Rental:* Newman Film Lib.

Rings Around the World. 1967. Paramount. 95 min. Sound. 16mm Color. *Rental:* Films Inc.

Rings on Her Fingers. Henry Fonda & Gene Tierney. Directed by Rouben Mamoulian. 1942. Fox. 86 min. Sound. 16mm B&W. *Rental:* Films Inc.

Ringside. Don Barry & Tom Brown. Directed by Frank McDonald. 1949. Screen Guild. 70 min. Sound. 16mm B&W. *Rental:* Film Ctr DC.

Rio Bravo. John Wayne & Dean Martin. Directed by Howard Hawks. 1959. Warners. 141 min. Sound. 16mm Color. *Rental:* Williams Films, Films Inc, Swank Motion & Twyman Films. *Rental:* Swank Motion, Videotape version.

Rio Conchos. Richard Boone & Stuart Whitman. Directed by Gordon Douglas. 1964. Fox. 107 min. Sound. 16mm Color. *Rental:* Films Inc. *Rental:* Films Inc, Anamorphic version.

Rio Grande. John Wayne & Maureen O'Hara. Directed by John Ford. 1950. Republic. 105 min. Sound. 16mm B&W. *Rental:* Budget Films, Images Film, Ivy Films, Kit Parker, Modern Sound & Westcoast Films. *Lease:* Rep Pic Film. *Sale:* Cinema Concepts, Super 8 sound version.

Rio Grande Patrol. Tim Holt & Jane Nigh. Directed by Lesley Selander. 1951. RKO. 60 min. Sound. 16mm B&W. *Rental:* RKO General Pics.

Rio Grande Raiders. Sunset Carson. Directed by Thomas Carr. 1946. Republic. 54 min. Sound. 16mm B&W. *Rental:* Ivy Films. *Sale:* Rep Pic Film. *Sale:* Video Comm, Videotape version.

Rio Lobo. John Wayne & Jennifer O'Neil. Directed by Howard Hawks. 1971. National General. 114 min. Sound. 16mm Color. *Rental:* Williams Films, Films Inc & Swank Motion. *Rental:* Swank Motion, Videotape version.

Rio Rattler. Tom Tyler. Directed by Bernard B. Ray. 1935. Commodore. 60 min. Sound. 16mm B&W. *Rental:* Budget Films & Mogulls Films. *Sale:* Reel Images & Thunder Films. *Sale:* Reel Images, Super 8 sound version.

Rio Rita. Bud Abbott & Lou Costello. Directed by S. Sylvan Simon. 1942. MGM. 91 min. Sound. 16mm B&W. *Rental:* MGM United.

Riot. Gene Hackman & Jim Brown. Directed by Buzz Kulik. 1969. Paramount. 96 min. Sound. 16mm Color. *Rental:* Films Inc.

Riot in Cell Block Eleven. Neville Brand & Frank Faylen. Directed by Don Siegel. 1951. Allied Artists. 80 min. Sound. 16mm B&W. *Rental:* Budget Films & Ivy Films. *Sale:* Rep Pic Film.

Rip Roaring Buckaroo. Tom Tyler. Directed by Robert Hill. 1936. Puritan. 58 min. Sound. 16mm B&W. *Rental:* Budget Films. *Sale:* Cinema Concepts.

Rip Roaring Riley. Orig. Title: Mystery of Diamond Island, The. Lloyd Hughes & Grant Withers. Directed by Elmer Clifton. 1935. Puritan. 70 min. Sound. 16mm B&W. *Rental:* Mogulls Films.

Rip Van Winkle. Rufus Rose Co.. (Marionettes). 60 min. Sound. 16mm Color. *Rental:* Film Ctr DC.

Riptide. Norma Shearer, Robert Montgomery & Herbert Marshall. Directed by Edmund Goulding. 1934. MGM. 90 min. Sound. 16mm B&W. *Rental:* Films Inc.

Rise & Fall of D.D.T, The. Films Inc. (Documentary). 50 min. Sound. 16mm Color. *Sale:* Films Inc. *Sale:* Films Inc, Videotape version.

Rise & Fall of Money, The. 1976. Britain. (Documentary). 60 min. Sound. 16mm Color. *Rental:* U Cal Media, Films Inc, U of IL Film & Syracuse U Film. *Sale:* Films Inc. *Sale:* Films Inc, Videotape version.

Rise & Fall of the Third Reich, The. 1967. ABC. (Documentary). 58 min. Sound. 16mm B&W. *Rental:* Films Inc.

Rise & Shine. Milton Berle, Jack Oakie & Linda Darnell. Directed by Allan Dwan. 1941. Fox. 93 min. Sound. 16mm B&W. *Rental:* Films Inc.

Rise of English Socialism, The. 1966. Britain. (Documentary). 55 min. Sound. 16mm B&W. *Rental:* McGraw-Hill Films, U Mich Media & Syracuse U Film. *Sale:* McGraw-Hill Films.

Rise of Khrushchev, The. 1963. NBC. (Documentary). 54 min. Sound. 16mm B&W. *Rental:* U of IL Film, McGraw-Hill Films & Syracuse U Film. *Sale:* McGraw-Hill Films.

Rise of Louis the XIV, The. Jean-Marie Patte & Raymond Jourdan. Directed by Roberto Rossellini. Ital. 1965. Italy. 100 min. Sound. 16mm Color. subtitles. *Rental:* Films Inc, MacMillan Films & Museum Mod Art. *Lease:* MacMillan.

Rise of New Towns, The. Orig. Title: Cities, The Rise of New Towns. 1966. NET. (Documentary). 60 min. Sound. 16mm B&W. *Rental:* U of IL Film, Indiana AV Ctr, Iowa Films & Mass Media. *Sale:* Indiana AV Ctr.

Rise Of Soviet Power, The. 1966. Britain. (Documentary). 61 min. Sound. 16mm B&W. *Rental:* U of Il Film, McGraw-Hill Films, U Mich Media & Utah Media. *Sale:* McGraw-Hill Films.

Rise of the Dictators, The: Form! Riflemen, Form!. 1976. Britain. (Documentary). 52 min. Sound. 16mm Color. *Rental:* Time-Life Multimedia. *Sale:* Time-Life Multimedia. *Rental:* Time-Life Multimedia, *Sale:* Time-Life Multimedia, Videotape version.

Rise of the Mammals, The. 1980. Britain. (Documentary). 58 min. Videotape Color. *Rental:* Films Inc. *Sale:* Films Inc.

Rise of the Red Navy, The. Orig. Title: Rising of the Red Navy. 1980. Britain. (Documentary). 50 min. Sound. 16mm Color. *Rental:* Films Inc. *Sale:* Films Inc. *Rental:* Films Inc, *Sale:* Films Inc, Videotape version.

Rise Up & Walk. 1982. EMC. (Documentary). 55 min. Sound. 16mm Color. *Rental:* U Cal Media. *Sale:* U Cal Media. *Sale:* U Cal Media, Videotape version.

Rising of the Moon, The. Denis O'Dea & Noel Purcell. Directed by John Ford. 1957. Warners. 81 min. Sound. 16mm B&W. *Rental:* Films Inc & Twyman Films.

Rising of the Red Navy *see* Rise of the Red Navy.

Rising Tide, The. Directed by Boubaker Adjali. 1977. Africa. (Documentary). 58 min. Sound. 16mm Color. *Rental:* Icarus Films. *Sale:* Icarus Films.

Risky Business. Tom Cruise & Rebecca DeMornay. Directed by Paul Brickman. 1983. Warners. 96 min. Sound. 16mm Color. *Rental:* Swank Motion. *Rental:* Swank Motion, Videotape version.

Rite, The *see* Ritual.

Ritual, The. Orig. Title: Rite, The. Ingrid Thulin & Gunnar Bjornstrand. Directed by Ingmar Bergman. 1969. Sweden. 75 min. Sound. 16mm B&W. subtitles. *Rental:* Janus Films.

Ritz, The. Jack Weston & Rita Moreno. Directed by Richard Lester. 1976. Warners. 90 min. Sound. 16mm Color. *Rental:* Williams Films, Swank Motion & Twyman Films.

Rivals, The. Joan Hackett & Robert Klein. Directed by Krishna Shah. 1972. Embassy. 101 min. Sound. 16mm Color. *Rental:* Films Inc.

Rivals, The. 1976. Britain. 117 min. Videotape Color. *Rental:* Films Inc. *Sale:* Fims Inc.

Rivals, The. Stewart Petersen. Directed by Lyman Dayton. 1979. World Entertainment. 110 min. Sound. 16mm Color. *Rental:* Twyman Films & Welling Motion Pictures. *Rental:* Welling Motion Pictures, 86 mins. version.

River, The. Nora Swinburne & Arthur Shields. Directed by Jean Renoir. 1952. Britain. 90 min. Sound. 16mm Color. *Sale:* Budget Films & Films Inc. *Sale:* Salz Ent.

River, The. Jarmila Berankova. Directed by Josef Rovensky. Czech. 1933. Czechoslovakia. 86 min. Sound. 16mm B&W. *Rental:* Films Inc.

River & Death, The. Joaquin Cordero & Columba Dominquez. Directed by Luis Bunuel. Span. 1954. Spain. 90 min. Sound. 16mm B&W. subtitles Eng. *Rental:* Films Inc.

River Beat. Phyllis Kirk & John Bentley. Directed by Guy Green. 1954. Britain. 80 min. Sound. 16mm B&W. *Rental:* Ivy Films.

River Niger, The. Cicely Tyson & James Earl Jones. Directed by Krishna Shah. 1976. Columbia. 105 min. Sound. 16mm Color. *Rental:* Swank Motion.

River Nile, The. 1964. NBC. (Documentary). 54 min. Sound. 16mm Color. *Rental:* McGraw-Hill Films & Syracuse U Film. *Sale:* McGraw-Hill Films.

River of No Return. Robert Mitchum & Marilyn Monroe. Directed by Otto Preminger. 1954. Fox. (Anamorphic). 90 min. Sound. 16mm Color. *Rental:* Films Inc.

River Run. Louis Ober & Mark Jenkins. Directed by John Korty. 1970. Columbia. 87 min. Sound. 16mm Color. *Rental:* Swank Motion.

Riverboat Rhythm. Leon Errol & Frankie Carle. Directed by Leslie Goodwins. 1946. RKO. (Anamorphic). 65 min. Sound. 16mm B&W. *Rental:* Films Inc.

River's Edge, The. Ray Milland & Anthony Quinn. Directed by Allan Dwan. 1957. Fox. 87 min. Sound. 16mm Color. *Rental:* Films Inc.

River's End. Charles Bickford & Evalyn Knapp. Directed by Michael Curtiz. 1931. Warners. 74 min. Sound. 16mm B&W. *Rental:* MGM United.

River's End. Orig. Title: Double Identity. Dennis Morgan & Victor Jory. Directed by Ray Enright. 1940. Warners. 69 min. Sound. 16mm B&W. *Rental:* MGM United.

Rivers of Sand. Directed by Robert Gardner. 1974. Phoenix. (Documentary). 83 min. Sound. 16mm Color. *Rental:* Budget Films, U Cal Media & Phoenix Films. *Sale:* Phoenix Films. *Sale:* Phoenix Films, Videotape version.

RN Distinguished Leaders in Nursing: Mabel Keaton Stauper. 1977. US Government. (Documentary). 59 min. Sound. 16mm B&W. *Sale:* Natl AV Ctr.

Road Agent. Tim Holt & Noreen Nash. Directed by Lesley Selander. 1952. RKO. 60 min. Sound. 16mm *Rental:* RKO General Pics.

Road Back, The. Lassie. 1960. Wrather. 96 min. Sound. 16mm Color. *Rental:* Budget Films, Films Inc, Westcoast Films & Williams Films.

Road Games. Stacy Keach & Jamie Lee Curtis. Directed by Richard Franklin. 1981. Embassy. 100 min. Sound. 16mm Color. *Rental:* Films Inc.

Road Gang. Orig. Title: In Justice. Donald Woods & Kay Linaker. Directed by Louis King. 1936. Warners. 62 min. Sound. 16mm B&W. *Rental:* MGM United.

Road House. Ida Lupino & Cornel Wilde. Directed by Jean Negulesco. 1948. Fox. 95 min. Sound. 16mm B&W. *Rental:* Films Inc.

Road Hustlers. Jim Davis & Scott Brady. Directed by Larry E. Jackson. 1968. American International. 94 min. Sound. 16mm Color. *Rental:* Video Comm.

Road Show. Adolphe Menjou & Carole Landis. Directed by Hal Roach. 1941. United Artists. 86 min. Sound. 16mm B&W. *Rental:* Mogulls Films.

Road Signs on a Merry-Go-Round. 1967. CBS. (Documentary). 57 min. Sound. 16mm Color. *Rental:* U Cal Media, Syracuse U Film & Twyman Films. *Sale:* Carousel Films.

Road to Alcatraz. Robert Lowery & Grant Withers. Directed by Nick Grinde. 1945. Republic. 60 min. Sound. 16mm B&W. *Rental:* Ivy Films.

Road to Bali. Bob Hope, Dorothy Lamour & Bing Crosby. 1952. Paramount. 91 min. Sound. 16mm B&W. *Rental:* Films Inc. *Rental:* Ivy Films, *Sale:* Cinema Concepts, Ivy Films & Reel Images, Super 8 sound version.

Road to Denver. John Payne & Lee J. Cobb. Directed by Joseph Kane. 1955. Republic. 90 min. Sound. 16mm B&W. *Rental:* Ivy Films. *Lease:* Rep Pic Film.

Road to Eternity. Tatsuya Nakadai. Directed by Masaki Kobayashi. Jap. 1959. Japan. 181 min. Sound. 16mm B&W. subtitles. *Rental:* Films Inc.

Road to Fort Alamo. Ken Clark. Directed by John M. Old. 1966. Italy. 85 min. Sound. 16mm Color. dubbed. *Rental:* Ivy Films.

Road to Gettysburg. 2 Pts. 1968. ABC. (Documentary). 54 min. Sound. 16mm Color. *Rental:* McGraw-Hill Films & OK AV Ctr. *Sale:* McGraw-Hill Films.

Road to Glory, The. Fredric March & Warner Baxter. Directed by Howard Hawks. 1936. Fox. 101 min. Sound. 16mm B&W. *Rental:* Films Inc.

Road to Hollywood, The. 1948. Astor. (Anthology). 70 min. Sound. 16mm B&W. *Rental:* Willoughby Peer.

Road to Hong Kong, The. Bob Hope & Bing Crosby. Directed by Norman Panama. 1962. United Artists. 91 min. Sound. 16mm B&W. *Rental:* MGM United.

Road to Katmandu, The. 58 min. Sound. 16mm Color. *Rental:* OK AV Ctr.

Road to Life, The. Nikolai Batalov. Directed by Nikolai Ekk. 1931. Russia. 99 min. Sound. 16mm B&W. subtitles. *Rental:* Corinth Films & Museum Mod Art.

Road to Morocco, The. Bing Crosby & Bob Hope. Directed by David Butler. 1942. Paramount. 81 min. Sound. 16mm B&W. *Rental:* Williams Films.

Road to Nashville, The. Marty Robbins & Doodles Weaver. Directed by Will Zens. 1966. Crown. 110 min. Sound. 16mm Color. *Rental:* Video Comm. *Lease:* Video Comm. *Rental:* Video Comm, Videotape version.

Road to Paradise, The. Loretta Young & Jack Mulhall. Directed by William Beaudine. 1930. Warners. 76 min. Sound. 16mm B&W. *Rental:* MGM United.

Road to Reno, The. Randolph Scott & Hope Hampton. Directed by S. Sylvan Simon. 1938. Universal. 70 min. Sound. 16mm B&W. *Rental:* Mogulls Films & Film Ctr DC.

Road to Rio, The. Bing Crosby, Bob Hope & Dorothy Lamour. 1947. Paramount. 100 min. Sound. 16mm B&W. *Rental:* Arcus Film, Budget Films, Cine Craft, Films Inc, Inst Cinema, Modern Sound, Roas Films, Twyman Films, Video Comm, Westcoast Films, Welling Motion Pictures, Wholesome Film Ctr & Willoughby Peer.

Road to Ruin, The. Grant Withers. Directed by Norton S. Parker. 1928. True Life. 60 min. Silent. 16mm B&W. *Rental:* Budget Films & Em Gee Film Lib. *Sale:* Morcraft Films, Sound 16mm version.

Road to Salina, The. Robert Walker Jr., Mimsy Farmer, Rita Hayworth & Ed Begley. Directed by Georges Lautner. 1971. Embassy. (Anamorphic). 96 min. Sound. 16mm Color. *Rental:* Films Inc.

Road to Santiago, The. 1973. Media Guild. (Documentary). 52 min. Sound. 16mm Color. *Rental:* Media Guild. *Sale:* Media Guild. *Sale:* Media Guild, Videotape version.

Road to Singapore, The. William Powell & Louis Calhern. Directed by Alfred E. Green. 1931. Warners. 70 min. Sound. 16mm B&W. *Rental:* MGM United.

Road to Singapore, The. Bing Crosby & Bob Hope. Directed by Victor Schertzinger. 1940. Paramount. 85 min. Sound. 16mm B&W. *Rental:* Williams Films.

Road to the Big House, The. John Shelton & Ann Doran. Directed by Walter Colmes. 1947. Republic. 73 min. Sound. 16mm B&W. *Rental:* Ivy Films.

Road to Utopia, The. Bing Crosby & Bob Hope. Directed by Hal Walker. 1945. Paramount. 89 min. Sound. 16mm B&W. *Rental:* Williams Films.

Road to Wigan Pier, The. 1973. Britain. (Documentary). 60 min. Sound. 16mm Color. *Rental:* U of IL Film & Media Guild. *Sale:* Media Guild. *Sale:* Media Guild, Videotape version.

Road to Yesterday, The. William Boyd, Jetta Goudal & Joseph Schildkraut. Directed by Cecil B. DeMille. 1925. PDC. 105 min. Silent. 16mm B&W. *Rental:* EM Gee Film Lib, Kit Parker & Willoughby Peer. *Sale:* Blackhawk Films. *Sale:* Blackhawk Films, Super 8 silent version. *Sale:* Blackhawk Films, Silent 8mm version.

Road to Zanzibar, The. Bing Crosby & Bob Hope. Directed by Victor Schertzinger. 1941. Paramount. 92 min. Sound. 16mm B&W. *Rental:* Williams Films.

Road Warrior, The: Mad Max II. Mel Gibson. Directed by George Miller. 1981. Australia. 94 min. Sound. 16mm Color. *Rental:* Swank Motion. *Rental:* Swank Motion, Videotape version.

Roadblock. Charles McGraw & Joan Dixon. Directed by Harold Daniels. 1951. RKO. 73 min. Sound. 16mm B&W. *Rental:* Films Inc.

Roadhouse Murder. Bruce Cabot & Roscoe Karns. Directed by Walter J. Ruben. 1932. RKO. 73 min. Sound. 16mm *Rental:* RKO General Pics.

Roadie. Art Carney & Meatloaf. Directed by Alan Rudolph. 1980. United Artists. 101 min. Sound. 16mm Color. *Rental:* MGM United. *Rental:* MGM United, Videotape version.

Roads of Exile, The. Francois Simon & Dominique Labourier. Directed by Claude Goretta. Fr. 1978. France. 169 min. Sound. 16mm Color. subtitles. *Rental:* Corinth Films. *Lease:* Corinth Films. *Rental:* Corinth Films, *Lease:* Corinth Films, Videotape version.

Roald Amundsen: South Pole 1911. Directed by John Irvin. 1977. Britain. 49 min. Sound. 16mm Color. *Rental:* Time-Life Multimedia. *Sale:* Time-Life Multimedia. *Sale:* Time-Life Multimedia, Videotape version.

Roamin' Wild. Tom Tyler. Directed by Bernard B. Ray. 1936. Reliable. 60 min. 16mm B&W. *Rental:* Budget Films & Mogulls Films. *Sale:* Morcraft Films.

Roaming Lady. Fay Wray & Ralph Bellamy. Directed by Albert S. Rogell. 1936. Columbia. 70 min. Sound. 16mm B&W. *Rental:* Kit Parker.

Roar of the Crowd. Howard Duff. Directed by William Beaudine. 1953. Allied Artists. 77 min. Sound. 16mm B&W. *Rental:* Hurlock Cine.

Roar of the Dragon. Richard Dix & Edward Everett Horton. Directed by Wesley Ruggles. 1932. RKO. 70 min. Sound. 16mm B&W. *Rental:* Em Gee Film Lib. *Sale:* Glenn Photo.

Roarin' Lead. Robert Livingston. Directed by Mack V. Wright. 1937. Republic. 54 min. Sound. 16mm B&W. *Rental:* Ivy Films. *Sale:* Rep Pic Film.

Roaring City. Hugh Beaumont. Directed by William Berke. 1951. Lippert. 58 min. Sound. 16mm B&W. *Rental:* Mogulls Films.

Roaring Guns. Tim McCoy. Directed by Sam Newfield. 1936. Puritan. 60 min. Sound. 16mm B&W. *Rental:* Video Comm. *Sale:* Morcraft Films & Video Comm. *Sale:* Morcraft Films, Super 8 sound version.

Roaring Mountain. George O'Brien. 1938. Marcy. 70 min. Sound. 16mm B&W. *Rental:* Mogulls Films.

Roaring Rails. Buster Keaton & Marian Mack. Directed by Buster Keaton. 1926. Metro. 45 min. Silent. 16mm B&W. *Rental:* Mogulls Films.

Roaring Rangers. Charles Starrett. Directed by Ray Nazarro. 1946. Columbia. 60 min. Sound. 16mm B&W. *Rental:* Westcoast Films.

Roaring Road. Wallace Reid. Directed by James Cruze. 1919. Paramount. 55 min. Silent. 16mm B&W. *Rental:* Budget Films & Em Gee Film Lib. *Sale:* E Finney & Reel Images.

Roaring Six Guns. Kermit Maynard. Directed by J. P. McGowan. 1937. Ambassador. 60 min. Sound. 16mm B&W. *Sale:* Morcraft Films & Reel Images. *Sale:* Reel Images, Super 8 sound version.

Roaring Twenties, The. James Cagney & Humphrey Bogart. Directed by Raoul Walsh. 1939. Warners. 106 min. Sound. 16mm B&W. *Rental:* MGM United.

Roaring Westward. Jimmy Wakely. Directed by Oliver Drake. 1949. Monogram. 55 min. Sound. 16mm B&W. *Rental:* Hurlock Cine.

Robbers of the Range. Tim Holt & Virginia Vale. Directed by Bert Gilroy. 1941. RKO. 61 min. Sound. 16mm *Rental:* RKO General Pics.

Robbers, Rooftops & Witches. Tony Aldredge. 1982. 46 min. Sound. 16mm Color. *Rental:* Iowa Films & Learning Corp Am. *Sale:* Learning Corp Am. *Rental:* Learning Corp Am, *Sale:* Learning Corp Am, Videotape version.

Robbery. Stanley Baker & James Booth. Directed by Peter Yates. 1967. Britian. 113 min. Sound. 16mm Color. *Rental:* Films Inc & Wholesome Film Ctr.

Robby. Warren Raum & Ryp Siani. Directed by Ralph C. Bluemke. Britain. 60 min. Sound. Videotape Color. *Sale:* Tamarelles French Film.

Robe, The. Richard Burton & Jean Simmons. Directed by Henry Koster. 1953. Fox. 135 min. Sound. 16mm Color. *Rental:* Films Inc. *Rental:* Films Inc, Anamorphic version.

Robert A. Taft. Lee Tracy. Directed by Jose Quintero. 1965. Saudek. 50 min. Sound. 16mm B&W. *Rental:* U of IL Film. *Sale:* IQ Film. *Rental:* IQ Film, *Sale:* IQ Film, Spanish dubbed version.

Robert et Robert. Jacques Villeret & Charles Denner. Directed by Claude Lelouch. Fr. 1979. France. 95 min. Sound. 16mm Color. subtitles. *Rental:* Films Inc.

Robert Rauschenberg: Retrospective. Directed by Michael Blackwood. 45 min. 16mm Color. *Rental:* Blackwood. *Sale:* Blackwood.

Robert Scott & the Race for the South Pole. 1967. ABC. (Documentary). 55 min. Sound. 16mm Color. *Rental:* McGraw-Hill Films. *Sale:* McGraw-Hill Films.

Roberta. Fred Astaire, Ginger Rogers & Irene Dunne. Directed by William A. Seiter. 1936. RKO. 85 min. Sound. 16mm B&W. *Rental:* MGM United. *Rental:* MGM United, 105 min. version.

Robin & Marian. Sean Connery & Audrey Hepburn. Directed by Richard Lester. 1976. Columbia. 106 min. Sound. 16mm Color. *Rental:* Arcus Film, Budget Films, Williams Films, Bosco Films, Films Inc, Images Film, Modern Sound, Swank Motion, Twyman Films, Westcoast Films & Welling Motion Pictures.

Robin & the Seven Hoods. Dean Martin & Frank Sinatra. Directed by Gordon Douglas. 1964. Warners. 103 min. Sound. 16mm Color. *Rental:* Arcus Film.

Robin Hood. Douglas Fairbanks & Wallace Beery. Directed by Allan Dwan. 1922. United Artists. 120 min. Silent. 16mm B&W. *Rental:* A Twyman Pres, Museum Mod Art & Twyman Films.

Robin Hood. 1970. Australia. (Animated). 54 min. Sound. 16mm Color. *Rental:* Budget Films, Williams Films, Inst Cinema, Modern Sound, Roas Films, Twyman Films, Westcoast Films, Welling Motion Pictures & Willoughbly Peer. *Lease:* Inst Cinema.

Robin Hood. Directed by Wolfgang Reitherman. 1973. Disney. (Animated). 83 min. Sound. 16mm Color. *Rental:* Cine Craft, Williams Films, Disney Prod, Films Inc, MGM United, Swank Motion, Film Ctr DC & Twyman Films.

Robin Hood & the Pirates. Lex Barker. Directed by Giorgio Simoneli. 1960. Italy. 88 min. Sound. 16mm Color. dubbed. *Rental:* Modern Sound.

Robin Hood Jr. Frankie Lee. Directed by Clarence Bicker. 1923. East Coast. 48 min. Silent. 16mm B&W. *Rental:* Mogulls Films.

Robin Hood Jr. 1979. Britain. (Cast unlisted). 62 min. Sound. 16mm Color. *Sale:* Lucerne Films.

Robin Hood of El Dorado. Warner Baxter & Bruce Cabot. Directed by William A. Wellman. 1936. MGM. 86 min. Sound. 16mm B&W. *Rental:* MGM United.

Robin Hood of Monterey. Gilbert Roland. Directed by Christy Cabanne. 1947. Monogram. 70 min. Sound. 16mm B&W. *Rental:* Newman Film Lib. *Sale:* Video Comm, Videotape version.

Robin Hood of Sherwood Forest. API. (Animated). 55 min. Sound. 16mm Color. *Rental:* Twyman Films.

Robin Hood of Texas. Gene Autry. Directed by Lesley Selander. 1947. Republic. 54 min. Sound. 16mm B&W. *Rental:* Ivy Films. *Sale:* Blackhawk Films, Super 8 sound version.

Robin Hood of the Pecos. Roy Rogers. Directed by Joseph Kane. 1941. Republic. 54 min. Sound. 16mm B&W. *Rental:* Budget Films, Ivy Films & Westcoast Films. *Sale:* Cinema Concepts & Rep Pic Film.

Robin Hood: The Invincible Archer. 1974. (Animated). 80 min. Sound. 16mm Color. *Rental:* Films Inc.

Robin Hood with Mr. Magoo *see* Magoo in Sherwood Forest.

Robin, Peter & Darryl: Three to the Hospital. 1968. Center for Mass Communication. 53 min. Sound. 16mm B&W. *Rental:* NYU Film Lib.

Robin Williams, Off the Wall. 1980. Verve. 59 min. Videotape Color. *Rental:* Films Inc.

Robinson Crusoe. Fay Compton. Directed by M. A. Wetherell. 1927. Britain. 60 min. Silent. 16mm B&W. *Rental:* Film Classics. *Rental:* Film Classics & Mogulls Films, *Sale:* Film Classics, Silent 16mm version. *Rental:* Film Classics, Videotape version.

Robinson Crusoe. 1970. Australia. (Animated). 55 min. Sound. 16mm B&W. *Rental:* Budget Films, Williams Films, Films Inc, Inst Cinema, Modern Sound, Roas Films, Twyman Films, Westcoast Films & Wholesome Film Ctr.

Robinson Crusoe & the Tiger. Hugo Stiglitz. Directed by Rene Cardona Jr. 1972. Embassy. 109 min. Sound. 16mm Color. *Rental:* Films Inc.

Robinson Crusoe of Mystery Island. Mala, Rex & Buck. Directed by Mack V. Wright & Ray Taylor. 1936. Republic. 100 min. Sound. 16mm B&W. *Rental:* Ivy Films. *Sale:* Rep Pic Film.

Robinson Crusoe on Mars. Paul Mantee. Directed by Byron Haskin. 1964. Paramount. 110 min. Sound. 16mm Color. *Rental:* Films Inc.

Robot Monster. Orig. Title: Monster from Mars. George Nader. Directed by Phil Tucker. 1953. Astor. 60 min. Sound. 16mm B&W. *Sale:* Reel Images & Budget Films.

Robot vs. the Aztec Mummy, The. Trans. Title: La Monia Azteca Contra la Roboto Humano. Ramon Gay & Rosita Arenas. Directed by Rafael Portillo. 1959. Mexico. 65 min. Sound. 16mm dubbed. *Rental:* Budget Films.

Rocambole. Ramon Pereda. Directed by Ramon Peon. Span. 1962. Mexico. 103 min. Sound. 16mm B&W. *Rental:* Film Classics.

Rocco & His Brothers. Alain Delon & Annie Giradot. Directed by Luchino Visconti. Fr. & Ital. 1960. Italy/France. 150 min. Sound. 16mm B&W. subtitles. *Rental:* Corinth Films. *Lease:* Corinth Films.

Rock-a-Bye Baby. Jerry Lewis & Marilyn Maxwell. Directed by Frank Tashlin. 1957. Paramount. 103 min. Sound. 16mm Color. *Rental:* Films Inc.

Rock All Night. Dick Miller. Directed by Roger Corman. 1957. American International. 63 min. Sound. 16mm B&W. *Rental:* Films Inc & Westcoast Films.

Rock & Roll Revue. Duke Ellington & Mantan Moreland. Directed by Joseph Kohn. 1955. 70 min. Sound. 16mm B&W. *Rental:* Budget Films & Em Gee Film Lib. *Sale:* Morcraft Films. *Sale:* Morcraft Films, Super 8 sound version.

Rock & Soul '64. 1964. New Line Cinema. (Concert). 90 min. Videotape Color. *Sale:* New Line Cinema. *Rental:* New Line Cinema.

Rock Around the Clock. Bill Haley & the Comets & The Platters. Directed by Fred F. Sears. 1956. Columbia. 77 min. Sound. 16mm B&W. *Rental:* Budget Films, Cine Craft, Williams Films, Bosco Films, Films Inc, Inst Cinema, Kit Parker, Modern Sound, Swank Motion, Twyman Films, Westcoast Films, Welling Motion Pictures & Wholesome Film Ctr.

Rock City. 1973. Corinth. (Concert). 90 min. Sound. 16mm Color. *Rental:* Corinth Films.

Rock Gospel. 1979. PBS. (Concert). 58 min. Videotape Color. *Rental:* PBS Video. *Sale:* PBS Video.

Rock Island Trail. Orig. Title: Transcontinent Express. Forrest Tucker. Directed by Joseph Kane. 1949. Republic. 90 min. Sound. 16mm B&W. *Rental:* Ivy Films. *Sale:* Rep Pic Film.

Rock 'n' Roll High School. P. J. Soles & Vincent Van Patten. Directed by Allan Arkush. 1979. New World. 93 min. Sound. 16mm Color. *Rental:* Films Inc.

Rock Pretty Baby. Sal Mineo & John Saxon. Directed by Richard Bartlett. 1956. Universal. 89 min. Sound. 16mm B&W. *Rental:* Swank Motion.

Rock, Rock, Rock. Alan Freed. Directed by Will Price. 1957. DCA. 90 min. Sound. 16mm B&W. *Rental:* Castle Hill & Modern Sound.

Rock U.S.A. Directed by Christian Blackwood. 45 min. Sound. 16mm Color. *Rental:* Blackwood. *Sale:* Blackwood.

Rock You Sinners. Tony Crombie. Directed by Denis Kavanagh. 1958. Britain. 59 min. Sound. 16mm B&W. *Rental:* Budget Films.

Rockabilly Baby. Douglas Kennedy & Virginia Field. Directed by William Claxton. 1957. Fox. (Anamorphic). 82 min. 16mm B&W. *Rental:* Ivy Films. *Sale:* Rep Pic Film.

Rockaby. Samuel Beckett. 60 min. Sound. 16mm Color. *Rental:* Pennebaker. *Sale:* Pennebaker. *Sale:* Pennebaker, Videotape version.

Rockabye. Constance Bennett & Joel McCrea. Directed by George Cukor. 1932. RKO. 71 min. Sound. 16mm B&W. *Rental:* Films Inc.

Rockers. Leroy Wallace & Jacob Miller. Directed by Theodoros Bafaloukos. Jamaican. 1978. Jamaica. 99 min. Sound. 16mm Color. subtitles. *Rental:* New Yorker Films.

Rocket from Calabuch, The. Valentina Cortesa & Franco Fabrizi. Directed by Luis G. Berlanga. 1958. Italy. 81 min. Sound. 16mm B&W. dubbed. *Rental:* Ivy Films.

Rocket Man, The. Charles Coburn & Spring Byington. Directed by Oscar Rudolph. 1954. Fox. 79 min. Sound. 16mm B&W. *Rental:* Willoughby Peer.

Rocket to Nowhere, The. Orig. Title: Clown & the Kids in Outer Space, The. Jiri Vrstala. Directed by Jindrich Polak. 1957. Czechoslovakia. 79 min. Sound. 16mm B&W. dubbed. *Rental:* Budget Films, Films Inc & Macmillan Films. *Sale:* Macmillan Films.

Rocketship. Buster Crabbe & Jean Rogers. Directed by Ford Beebe. 1938. Universal. 79 min. Sound. 16mm B&W. *Rental:* Em Gee Film Lib, Newman Film Lib & Natl Film Video. *Rental:* Ivy Films, *Sale:* Cinema Concepts, Super 8 sound version. *Sale:* Cinema Concepts, Reel Images & Video Lib, Videotape version.

Rocketship X-M. Lloyd Bridges & Osa Massen. Directed by Kurt Neumann. 1951. Lippert. 77 min. Sound. 16mm B&W. *Rental:* Wade Williams. *Sale:* Reel Images, Super 8 sound version.

Rockin' in the Rockies. Mary Beth Hughes & Three Stooges. Directed by Vernon Keays. 1945. Columbia. 65 min. Sound. 16mm B&W. *Rental:* Cine Craft, Williams Films, Modern Sound, Twyman Films, Westcoast Films & Welling Motion Pictures.

Rocking Horse Winner, The. John Mills & Valerie Hobson. Directed by Anthony Pelissier. 1950. Britain. 91 min. Sound. 16mm B&W. *Rental:* Films Inc.

Rocky. Roddy McDowall & Edgar Barrier. Directed by Phil Karlson. 1948. Monogram. 76 min. Sound. 16mm B&W. *Rental:* Hurlock Cine & Bosco Films.

Rocky. Sylvester Stallone & Talia Shire. Directed by John G. Avildsen. 1976. United Artists. 120 min. Sound. 16mm Color. *Rental:* MGM United. *Rental:* MGM United, Videotape version.

Rocky Horror Picture Show, The. Tim Curry. Directed by Jim Sherman. 1975. Britain. 100 min. Sound. 16mm Color. *Rental:* Films Inc.

Rocky II. Sylvester Stallone, Talia Shire & Burgess Meredith. Directed by Sylvester Stallone. 1979. United Artists. 119 min. Sound. 16mm Color. *Rental:* MGM United. *Rental:* MGM United, Videotape version.

Rocky III. Sylvester Stallone, Talia Shire & Burt Young. Directed by Sylvester Stallone. 1001 min. Sound. 16mm Color. *Rental:* MGM United. *Rental:* MGM United, Videotape version.

Rocky Mountain. Errol Flynn & Patrice Wymore. Directed by William Keighley. 1950. Warners. 83 min. Sound. 16mm B&W. *Rental:* Swank Motion.

Rocky Mountain Mystery *see* Fighting Westerner.

Rocky Mountain Rangers. Robert Livingston. Directed by George Sherman. 1940. Republic. 54 min. Sound. 16mm B&W. *Rental:* Ivy Films. *Sale:* Rep Pic Film.

Rocky Mountain Reunion. 1979. Stouffer. 50 min. Sound. 16mm Color. *Rental:* Stouffer Ent. *Sale:* Stouffer Ent.

Rocky Rhodes. Buck Jones. Directed by Al Raboch. 1934. Universal. 60 min. Sound. 16mm B&W. *Rental:* Mogull's Films.

Rod Stewart & Faces in Concert. (Concert). 90 min. Videotape Color. *Sale:* Cinema Concepts. *Rental:* Ivy Films, 75 mins. version.

Rod Stewart In Concert. Britain. (Concert). 75 min. Sound. 16mm Color. *Rental:* Ivy Films.

Rodan. Kenji Sawara. Directed by Inoshiro Honda. 1957. Japan. 70 min. Sound. 16mm Color. dubbed. *Rental:* Ivy Films, Video Comm & Westcoast Films.

Rodeo. Jane Nigh & John Archer. Directed by William Beaudine. 1952. Monogram. 70 min. Sound. 16mm B&W. *Rental:* Hurlock Cine.

Rodeo King & the Senorita, The. Rex Allen. Directed by Philip Ford. 1951. Republic. 67 min. Sound. 16mm B&W. *Rental:* Ivy Films. *Sale:* Rep Pic Film.

Rodeo Red & the Runaway. Geraldine Fitzgerald. Directed by Bert Salzman. 1979. Learning Corp. 49 min. Sound. 16mm Color. *Rental:* Learning Corp Am. *Sale:* Learning Corp Am. *Sale:* Learning Corp Am, *Rental:* Learning Corp Am, Videotape version.

Roger Corman: Hollywood's Wild Angel. Directed by Ray Witlin. 1977. Blackwood. 58 min. Sound. 16mm Color. *Rental:* Blackwood Films. *Sale:* Blackwood Films.

Roger Toughy, Gangster. Preston Foster & Victor McLaglen. Directed by Robert Florey. 1944. Fox. 65 min. Sound. 16mm B&W. *Rental:* Films Inc.

Rogopag. Bruce Balaban & Alexandra Stewart. Directed by Jean-Luc Godard, Ugo Gregoretti, Pier Paolo Pasolini & Roberto Rossellini. Ital. 1962. Italy. 125 min. Sound. 16mm B&W. subtitles Eng. *Rental:* Films Inc.

Rogue, The. Richard Drake & Evelyn Winters. 1976. Group. 87 min. Sound. 16mm Color. *Rental:* Twyman Films.

Rogue Cop. Robert Taylor & Janet Leigh. Directed by Roy Rowland. 1954. MGM. 92 min. Sound. 16mm B&W. *Rental:* MGM United.

Rogue of the Range. Johnny Mack Brown. Directed by S. Roy Luby. 1936. Supreme. 60 min. Sound. 16mm B&W. *Sale:* Morcraft Films.

Rogue of the Rio Grande. Myrna Loy. Directed by Spencer G. Bennett. 1930. World Wide. 70 min. Sound. 16mm B&W. *Rental:* Video Comm. *Sale:* Video Comm, Videotape version.

Rogue River. Rory Calhoun & Peter Graves. Directed by John Rawlins. 1950. Eagle Lion. 84 min. Sound. 16mm Color. *Rental:* Ivy Films & Mogulls Films. *Sale:* Rep Pic Film.

Rogue's Gallery. Frank Jenks & H. B. Warner. Directed by Al Herman. 1944. PRC. 60 min. Sound. 16mm B&W. *Rental:* Ivy Films. *Sale:* Classics Assoc NY.

Rogue's March. Peter Lawford & Richard Greene. Directed by Allan Davis. 1952. MGM. 84 min. Sound. 16mm B&W. *Rental:* MGM United.

Rogues of Sherwood Forest. John Derek & Diana Lynn. Directed by Gordon Douglas. 1950. Columbia. 80 min. Sound. 16mm Color. *Rental:* Arcus Film, Cine Craft, Charard Motion Pics & Film Ctr DC.

Roland Garros. 1976. France. (Documentary). 55 min. Sound. 16mm Color. narrated Eng. *Rental:* French Am Cul. *Rental:* French Am Cul, French Language version.

Roll of Thunder, Hear My Cry. Claudia McNeil & Morgan Freeman. Directed by Jack Smith. 1978. Tomorrow Entertainment. 110 min. Sound. 16mm Color. *Rental:* Budget Films, Kit Parker, Learning Corp Am, Newman Film Lib, Roas Films, U of IL Film, Welling Motion Pictures & Wholesome Film Ctr. *Lease:* Learning Corp Am. *Rental:* Learning Corp Am, *Lease:* Learning Corp Am, Videotape version.

Roll On, Texas Moon. Roy Rogers. Directed by William Witney. 1946. Republic. 54 min. Sound. 16mm B&W. *Rental:* Ivy Films. *Sale:* Cinema Concepts, Rep Pic Film & Nostalgia Merchant.

Roll Thunder Roll. Jim Bannon. Directed by Lewis D. Collins. 1949. Eagle-Lion. 58 min. Sound. 16mm Color. *Rental:* Mogull's Films.

Roll, Wagons, Roll. Tex Ritter. Directed by Al Herman. 1939. Monogram. 70 min. Sound. 16mm B&W. *Rental:* Hurlock Cine. *Sale:* Cinema Concepts & Reel Images. *Sale:* Blackhawk Films, Videotape version.

Roller Boogie. Linda Blair, Jim Bray & Beverly Garland. Directed by Mark L. Lester. 1980. United Artists. 104 min. Sound. 16mm Color. *Rental:* MGM United.

Rollerball. James Caan & John Houseman. Directed by Norman Jewison. 1975. Universal. 128 min. Sound. 16mm Color. *Rental:* Budget Films, Films Inc, MGM United, Westcoast Films, Welling Motion Pictures & Wholesome Film Ctr. *Rental:* MGM United, Videotape version.

Rollercoaster. Richard Widmark & Timothy Bottoms. Directed by James Goldstone. 1977. Universal. 119 min. Sound. 16mm Color. *Rental:* Swank Motion. *Rental:* Swank Motion, Anamorphic version version.

Rollin' Home to Texas. Tex Ritter. Directed by Al Herman. 1941. Monogram. 55 min. Sound. 16mm B&W. *Rental:* Hurlock Cine.

Rollin' Plains. Tex Ritter. Directed by Al Herman. 1938. Grand National. 60 min. Sound. 16mm B&W. *Sale:* Cinema Concepts & Morcraft Films.

Rollin' Westward. Tex Ritter. Directed by Al Herman. 1939. Monogram. 55 min. Sound. 16mm B&W. *Rental:* Hurlock Cine.

Rolling Home. Jean Parker & Russell Hayden. Directed by William Berke. 1948. Screen Guild. 71 min. Sound. 16mm B&W. *Rental:* Buchan Pic, Budget Films, Mogull's Films & Newman Film Lib.

Rolling Stones at Hyde Park, The. (Concert). 55 min. Sound. 16mm Color. *Rental:* Ivy Films & Video Comm. *Rental:* Video Comm, Videotape version.

Rolling Thunder. William Devane & Tommy Lee Jones. Directed by John Flynn. 1978. American International. 99 min. Sound. 16mm Color. *Rental:* Swank Motion.

Rollover. Jane Fonda & Kris Kristofferson. Directed by Alan J. Pakula. 1981. Orion. 120 min. Sound. 16mm Color. *Rental:* Films Inc.

Roma, Citta Aperta *see* Open City.

Roman de la Louisiane, La. 3 pts. Directed by Jean Philippe Brunet. France. (Documentary). 165 min. Sound. 16mm Color. *Rental:* French Am Cul.

Roman Holiday. Gregory Peck & Audrey Hepburn. Directed by William Wyler. 1953. Paramount. 118 min. Sound. 16mm B&W. *Rental:* Films Inc & Wholesome Film Ctr.

Roman Scandals. Eddie Cantor. Directed by Frank Tuttle. 1933. Goldwyn. 92 min. Sound. 16mm B&W. *Rental:* Welling Motion Pictures.

Roman Spring of Mrs. Stone, The. Vivien Leigh & Warren Beatty. Directed by Jose Quintero. 1961. Warners. 104 min. Sound. 16mm Color. *Rental:* Films Inc & Twyman Films.

Romance. Greta Garbo & Lewis Stone. Directed by Clarence Brown. 1930. MGM. 76 min. Sound. 16mm B&W. *Rental:* Films Inc & MGM United.

Romance a la Carte. Anthony Hollis & Leslie Perrin. Directed by Maclean Rogers. 1938. Britain. 72 min. Sound. 16mm B&W. *Rental:* Mogull's Films.

Romance & Reality. (Civilization Ser.). 1968. Britain. (Documentary). 60 min. Sound. 16mm Color. *Rental:* Films Inc, OK AV Ctr, Syracuse U Film & Utah Media. *Sale:* Films Inc. *Sale:* Films Inc, Videotape version.

Romance & Rhythm. Ann Miller & Phil Silvers. Directed by John H. Auer. 1940. Republic. 86 min. Sound. 16mm B&W. *Rental:* Ivy Films. *Sale:* Rep Pic Film.

Romance in Manhattan. Ginger Rogers & Francis Lederer. Directed by Stephen Roberts. 1935. RKO. 78 min. Sound. 16mm *Rental:* RKO General Pics.

Romance of a Horsethief. Eli Wallach & Jane Birkin. Directed by Abraham Polonsky. 1971. Allied Artists. 101 min. Sound. 16mm Color. *Rental:* Hurlock Cine.

Romance of Happy Valley, The. Lillian Gish & Robert Harron. Directed by D. W. Griffith. 1919. Artcraft. 80 min. Silent. 16mm B&W. *Rental:* Museum Mod Art. *Lease:* Museum Mod Art.

Romance of Rosy Ridge, The. Van Johnson & Janet Leigh. Directed by Roy Rowland. 1947. MGM. 105 min. Sound. 16mm B&W. *Rental:* MGM United.

Romance of the Redwoods. Jean Parker & Charles Bickford. Directed by Charles Vidor. 1939. Columbia. 63 min. Sound. 16mm B&W. *Rental:* Inst Cinema.

Romance of the Rockies. Tom Keene. Directed by Robert N. Bradbury. 1937. Monogram. 55 min. Sound. 16mm B&W. *Rental:* Hurlock Cine.

Romance of the West. Eddie Dean & Chief Thundercloud. Directed by Robert Emmett. 1946. PRC. 58 min. Sound. 16mm Color. *Sale:* Classics Assoc NY.

Romance on the High Seas. Orig. Title: It's Magic. Doris Day & Jack Carson. Directed by Michael Curtiz. 1948. Warners. 99 min. Sound. 16mm B&W. *Rental:* MGM United.

Romance on the Range. Roy Rogers. Directed by Joseph Kane. 1942. Republic. 54 min. Sound. 16mm B&W. *Rental:* Budget Films & Ivy Films. *Sale:* Cinema Concepts & Rep Pic Film. *Sale:* Video Comm, Videotape version.

Romance on the Run. Donald Woods & Patricia Ellis. Directed by Gus Meins. 1938. Republic. 54 min. Sound. 16mm B&W. *Rental:* Ivy Films.

Romance Rides the Range. Fred Scott. 1936. Spectrum. 60 min. Sound. 16mm B&W. *Rental:* Mogull's Films.

Romanian Solution, The. 1978. Britain. (Documentary). 52 min. Sound. 16mm Color. *Rental:* U of IL Film, Iowa Films & U MIch Media, Videotape version.

Romanoff & Juliet. Peter Ustinov & Sandra Dee. Directed by Peter Ustinov. 1961. Universal. 112 min. Sound. 16mm Color. *Rental:* Swank Motion.

Romanovs, The. Directed by Victor Vicas. 1972. AIF. (Documentary). 60 min. Sound. 16mm B&W. *Sale:* Americas Films. *Sale:* Americas Films, Color version. *Sale:* Americas Films, Spanish version.

Romantic Age, The. Orig. Title: Naughty Arlette. Hugh Williams & Mai Zetterling. Directed by Edmond Greville. 1949. Britain. 86 min. 16mm B&W. *Rental:* Charard Motion Pics.

Romantic Ballet, The. 1981. 49 min. Sound. 16mm Color. *Rental:* Utah Media.

Romantic Comedy. Dudley Moore & Mary Steenburgen. Directed by Arthur Hiller. 1983. MGM-UA. 103 min. Sound. 16mm Color. *Rental:* MGM United. *Rental:* MGM United, Videotape version.

Romantic Englishwoman, The. Glenda Jackson & Michael Caine. Directed by Joseph Losey. 1975. New World. 116 min. Sound. 16mm Color. *Rental:* Films Inc.

Romantic Rebellion, The. Directed by Colin Clark. 1974. Readers Digest. 50 min. Sound. 16mm Color. *Rental:* Pyramid Film. *Sale:* Pyramid Film. *Sale:* Pyramid Film, *Rental:* Pyramid Film, Videotape version.

Rome Eleven O'Clock. Eva Vanicek & Carla Del Poggio. Directed by Giuseppe De Santis. Ital. 1953. Italy. 107 min. Sound. 16mm B&W. subtitles. *Rental:* Films Inc.

Rome Express. Conrad Veidt & Esther Ralston. Directed by Walter Forde. 1932. Britain. 82 min. Sound. 16mm B&W. *Rental:* Cinema Five.

Rome, Leeds & the Desert. 1977. Britain. (Documentary). 52 min. Sound. 16mm Color. *Rental:* U of IL Film, Iowa Films & U Mich Media, Videotape version.

Romeo & Jules. 60 min. Videotape Color. *Sale:* Vydio Philms.

Romeo & Juliet. Leslie Howard & Norma Shearer. Directed by George Cukor. 1936. MGM. 127 min. Sound. 16mm B&W. *Rental:* MGM United.

Romeo & Juliet. Laurence Harvey & Susan Shentall. Directed by Renato Castellani. 1954. Britain. 142 min. Sound. 16mm Color. *Rental:* Budget Films, Williams Films, Films Inc, U of IL Film, Images Film, Kit Parker, Learning Corp Am, Modern Sound, Roas Films, Twyman Films, Westcoast Films, Welling Motion Pictures & Wholesome Film Ctr. *Lease:* Learning Corp Am. *Rental:* Learning Corp Am, *Lease:* Learning Corp Am, Videotape version.

Romeo & Juliet. Royal Shakespeare Academy Players. 1965. Britain. 105 min. Sound. 16mm B&W. *Rental:* Syracuse U Film.

Romeo & Juliet. Rosemarie Dexter. Directed by Geronimo Meynier. 1967. Ivy. 105 min. Sound. 16mm Color. *Rental:* Ivy Films.

Romeo & Juliet. Leonard Whiting & Olivia Hussey. Directed by Franco Zeffirelli. 1968. Paramount. 138 min. Sound. 16mm Color. *Rental:* Films Inc.

Romeo & Juliet. John Gielgud. 1979. Britain. 167 min. Videotape Color. *Rental:* Iowa Films.

Romeo & Juliet. 1973. 47 min. Sound. 16mm Color. *Rental:* U Mich Media.

Romeo & Juliet Ballet. Rudolph Nureyev, Dame Margot Fonteyn. Directed by Paul Czinner. 1966. Britain. 126 min. Sound. 16mm Color. *Rental:* Corinth Films, Films Inc & Syracuse U Film.

Ronde, La. Simone Simon, Anton Walbrook & Simone Signoret. Directed by Max Ophuls. Fr. 1951. France. 109 min. Sound. 16mm B&W. subtitles. *Rental:* Films Inc & Janus Films.

Roof, The. Gabriella Pallotti. Directed by Vittorio De Sica. 1956. Italy. 95 min. Sound. 16mm B&W. subtitles. *Rental:* Budget Films & Kit Parker. *Sale:* Festival Films. *Sale:* Festival Films, Videotape version.

Roof of Japan, The. Directed by Sadoa Imamura. 1958. Japan. 90 min. Sound. 16mm Color. narrated Eng. *Rental:* Films Inc & Film Ctr DC.

Rookie, The. Tommy Noonan & Pete Marshall. Directed by George O'Hanlon. 1959. Fox. (Anamorphic). 84 min. Sound. 16mm B&W. *Rental:* Willoughby Peer.

Rookie Cop. Tim Holt & Virginia Weidler. Directed by Bert Gilroy. 1939. RKO. 60 min. Sound. 16mm *Rental:* RKO General Pics.

Rookie Fireman. Bill Williams & Marjorie Reynolds. Directed by Seymour Friedman. 1950. Columbia. 63 min. Sound. 16mm B&W. *Rental:* Inst Cinema & Newman Film Lib.

Rookie of the Year. Jodie Foster. 1975. ABC. 47 min. Sound. 16mm Color. *Rental:* D Wilson, Kent St U Film & U Mich Media.

Rookies in Burma. Alan Carney & Wally Brown. Directed by Leslie Goodwins. 1943. RKO. 62 min. Sound. 16mm B&W. *Rental:* Films Inc.

Rookies on Parade. Bob Crosby & Marie Wilson. Directed by Joseph Santley. 1941. Republic. 77 min. Sound. 16mm B&W. *Rental:* Ivy Films.

Room at the Top. Laurence Harvey, Simone Signoret, Sir Donald Wolfit. Directed by Jack Clayton. 1958. Britain. 116 min. Sound. 16mm B&W. *Rental:* Budget Films & Kino Intl. *Sale:* Kino Intl. *Lease:* Kino Intl.

Room Service. Marx Brothers & Lucille Ball. Directed by William A. Seiter. 1938. RKO. 78 min. Sound. 16mm B&W. *Rental:* Films Inc. *Sale:* Cinema Concepts, Super 8 sound version. *Sale:* Vidamerica, Videotape version.

Room to Let. Jimmy Hanley & Valentine Dyall. Directed by Godfrey Grayson. 1950. Britain. 69 min. Sound. 16mm B&W. *Rental:* Mogulls Films.

Roommates. Orig. Title: Raising the Wind. James Robertson Justice. Directed by Gerald Thomas. 1962. Britain. 91 min. Sound. 16mm B&W. *Rental:* Ivy Films.

Roosevelt, New Jersey: Visions of Utopia. Directed by Richard Kroehling. 52 min. Sound. 16mm Color. *Rental:* Cinema Guild.

Rooster Cogburn. John Wayne & Katharine Hepburn. Directed by Stuart Millar. 1975. Universal. 107 min. Sound. 16mm Color. *Rental:* Swank Motion & Twyman Films. *Rental:* Williams Films & Twyman Films, Anamorphic version.

Rootin' Tootin' Rhythm. Orig. Title: Rhythm on the Ranch. Gene Autry. Directed by Mack V. Wright. 1937. Republic. 54 min. Sound. 16mm B&W. *Rental:* Budget Films & Ivy Films. *Sale:* Cinema Concepts.

Roots. Orig. Title: African, The. 12 pts. Cicely Tyson & Edward Asner. Directed by Marvin J. Chomsky, David Greene, Gilbert Moses & John Erman. 1977. Wolper. 720 min. Sound. 16mm Color. *Rental:* Films Inc, U Mich Media & Syracuse U Film. *Sale:* Natl Churches Christ & Films Inc. *Rental:* Films Inc, *Sale:* Films Inc, Videotape version.

Roots of Evil. Christian Anders. 85 min. Sound. 16mm *Rental:* WW Enter. *Rental:* WW Enter, Videotape version.

Roots of Exile: A Moroccan Jewish Odyssey. Directed by Eugene Rosow. 1983. First Run. 90 min. Sound. 16mm Color. *Rental:* First Run. *Sale:* First Run.

Roots of Heaven, The. Errol Flynn & Trevor Howard. Directed by John Huston. 1958. Fox. 135 min. Sound. 16mm Color. *Rental:* Films Inc.

Rope. James Stewart, John Dall & Farley Granger. Directed by Alfred Hitchcock. 1948. Universal. 80 min. Sound. 16mm Color. *Rental:* Swank Motion. *Rental:* Swank Motion, Videotape version.

Rope Around the Neck. Dany Robin & Joan Richard. 1966. France. 85 min. Sound. 16mm B&W. dubbed. *Rental:* Ivy Films.

Rope Ladder to the Moon. 1970. Richard Price. (Documentary). 56 min. Sound. 16mm Color. *Rental:* Video Comm.

Rosalie. Nelson Eddy & Eleanor Powell. Directed by W. S. Van Dyke. 1937. MGM. 123 min. Sound. 16mm Color. *Rental:* Films Inc & MGM United.

Rose, The. Bette Midler & Alan Bates. Directed by Mark Rydell. 1979. Fox. 134 min. Sound. 16mm Color. *Rental:* Films Inc.

Rose Bowl Story, The. Marshall Thompson & Vera Miles. Directed by William Beaudine. 1952. Monogram. 73 min. Sound. 16mm B&W. *Rental:* Hurlock Cine. *Sale:* Rep Pic Film.

Rose Kennedy Remembers. 1975. Britain. (Documentary). 52 min. Sound. 16mm Color. *Rental:* Syracuse U Film & Time-Life Multimedia. *Sale:* Time-Life Multimedia, Videotape version.

Rose-Marie. Howard Keel & Ann Blyth. Directed by Mervyn LeRoy. 1954. MGM. 105 min. Sound. 16mm Color. *Rental:* Films Inc. *Rental:* Films Inc, Anamorphic version.

Rose-Marie: TV Title: Indian Love Call. Jeanette MacDonald, Nelson Eddy & Reginald Owen. Directed by W. S. Van Dyke. 1936. 110 min. Sound. 16mm B&W. *Rental:* MGM United.

Rose of Cimarron. Jack Beutel & Mala Powers. Directed by Harry Keller. 1952. Fox. 72 min. Sound. 16mm B&W. *Rental:* Charard Motion Pics, Westcoast Films & Wholesome Film Ctr.

Rose of the Rio Grande. Movita & John Carroll. Directed by William Nigh. 1938. Monogram. 60 min. Sound. 16mm B&W. *Rental:* Mogull's Films.

Rose of the Yukon. Steve Brodie & Lotus Long. Directed by George Blair. 1948. Republic. 61 min. Sound. 16mm B&W. *Rental:* Ivy Films.

Rose of Tralee. John Longden & Angela Clynne. Directed by Germain Burger. 1942. Britain. 80 min. Sound. 16mm B&W. *Rental:* Alba House.

Rose of Washington Square. Alice Faye & Tyrone Power. Directed by Gregory Ratoff. 1939. Fox. 86 min. Sound. 16mm B&W. *Rental:* Films Inc & Welling Motion Pictures.

Rose Tattoo, The. Anna Magnani & Burt Lancaster. Directed by Daniel Mann. 1955. Paramount. 117 min. Sound. 16mm B&W. *Rental:* Films Inc.

Roseanna McCoy. Charles Bickford & Raymond Massey. Directed by Irving Reis. 1949. Goldwyn. 89 min. Sound. 16mm B&W. *Rental:* Films Inc.

Rosebud. Peter O'Toole & Richard Attenborough. Directed by Otto Preminger. 1975. United Artists. 126 min. Sound. 16mm Color. *Rental:* MGM United, Westcoast Films & Wholesome Film Ctr.

Rosedale: The Way It Is. 1976. NET. (Documentary). 57 min. Sound. 16mm Color. *Rental:* Indiana AV Ctr. *Sale:* Indiana AV Ctr. *Sale:* Indiana AV Ctr, Videotape version.

Roseland. Christopher Walken & Geraldine Chaplin. Directed by James Ivory. 1977. Cinema Shares. 102 min. Sound. 16mm Color. *Rental:* Films Inc & New Yorker Films.

Rosemary's Baby. Mia Farrow & John Cassavetes. Directed by Roman Polanski. 1968. Paramount. 136 min. Sound. 16mm Color. *Rental:* Films Inc.

Roses Are Red. Orig. Title: Double Cross. Jeff Chandler & Don Castle. Directed by James Tinling. 1947. Fox. 66 min. Sound. 16mm B&W. *Rental:* Mogull's Films.

Roses in December: The Story of Jean Donovan. Directed by Ana Carrigan & Bernard Stone. 1982. First Run. (Documentary). 55 min. Sound. 16mm Color. *Rental:* First Run. *Lease:* First Run.

Rosie. Rosalind Russell & Sandra Dee. Directed by David Lowell Rich. 1967. Universal. 97 min. Sound. 16mm Color. *Rental:* Swank Motion.

Rosie the Riveter. Orig. Title: In Rosie's Room. Jane Frazee & Frank Albertson. Directed by Joseph Santley. 1944. Republic. 75 min. Sound. 16mm B&W. *Rental:* Ivy Films. *Sale:* Rep Pic Film.

Rosseau. France. (Cast unlisted). 60 min. Sound. 16mm B&W. *Rental:* French Am Cul. *Rental:* French Am Cul, Videotape version.

Rotation. Paul Esser & Irene Korb. Directed by Wolfgang Staudte. Ger. 1949. Germany. 83 min. Sound. 16mm B&W. subtitles. *Rental:* Films Inc.

Rothko Conspiracy, The. 1977. Films Inc. (Documentary). 90 min. Videotape Color. *Sale:* Films Inc.

Rotten to the Core. Anton Rodgers & Eric Sykes. Directed by John Boulting. 1965. Britain. 87 min. Sound. 16mm B&W. *Rental:* Twyman Films.

Rotten World About Us, The. 1981. Britain. (Documentary). 50 min. Sound. 16mm Color. *Rental:* Films Inc & Syracuse U Film. *Sale:* Films Inc. *Rental:* Films Inc, Videotape version. *Sale:* Films Inc,

Roue, La. Orig. Title: The Wheel. Severin Mars. Directed by Abel Gance. 1922. France. 153 min. Silent. 16mm B&W. *Rental:* Em Gee Film Lib.

Rough Cut. Burt Reynolds & David Niven. Directed by Don Siegel. 1980. Paramount. 111 min. Sound. 16mm Color. *Rental:* Films Inc.

Rough Magic. Directed by Timothy Knox. 1972. Knox. 91 min. Sound. 16mm Color. *Rental:* New Yorker Films.

Rough Night in Jericho, A. Dean Martin & George Peppard. Directed by Arnold Laven. 1967. Universal. 104 min. Sound. 16mm Color. *Rental:* Swank Motion.

Rough Riders of Cheyenne. Directed by Sunset Carson & Thomas Carr. 1945. Republic. 54 min. Sound. 16mm B&W. *Rental:* Ivy Films. *Sale:* Rep Pic Film.

Rough Riders of Durango. Allan Lane. Directed by Fred C. Brannon. 1950. Republic. 60 min. Sound. 16mm B&W. *Rental:* Ivy Films. *Sale:* Rep Pic Film.

Rough Riding Rangers. Rex Lease. Directed by Elmer Clifton. 1935. First Division. 60 min. Sound. 16mm B&W. *Sale:* Morcraft Films.

Roughly Speaking. Rosalind Russell & Jack Carson. Directed by Michael Curtiz. 1945. Warners. 117 min. Sound. 16mm B&W. *Rental:* MGM United.

Roughshod. Robert Sterling & Gloria Grahame. Directed by Mark Robson. 1945. RKO. 88 min. Sound. 16mm B&W. *Rental:* Films Inc.

Round-Up, The. Janos Gorbe & Andras Kozak. Directed by Miklos Jancso. Hungarian. 1965. Hungary. 89 min. Sound. 16mm B&W. subtitles. *Rental:* Films Inc.

Rounders, The. Henry Fonda & Glenn Ford. Directed by Burt Kennedy. 1965. MGM. 85 min. Sound. 16mm Color. *Rental:* MGM United, Anamorphic version.

Rounding Up the Law. Guinn Williams. 1922. Aywon. 50 min. Silent. 8mm B&W. *Rental:* Mogull's Films.

Roundup Time in Texas. Gene Autry. Directed by Joseph Kane. 1937. Republic. 54 min. Sound. 16mm B&W. *Rental:* Budget Films & Ivy Films. *Sale:* Cinema Concepts.

Roustabout. Elvis Presley & Barbara Stanwyck. Directed by John Rich. 1964. Paramount. 101 min. Sound. 16mm Color. *Rental:* Films Inc. *Sale:* Blackhawk Films, Cinema Concepts & Video Comm, Super 8 sound version, videotape version.

Routes of Exile: A Moroccan Jewish Odyssey. Directed by Eugene Rosow. 1982. First Run. (Documentary). 90 min. Sound. 16mm Color. *Rental:* First Run. *Lease:* First Run.

Roxie Hart. Ginger Rogers & Adolphe Menjou. Directed by William A. Wellman. 1942. Fox. 75 min. Sound. 16mm B&W. *Rental:* Films Inc.

Roy Lichtenstein. 1975. Blackwood. (Documentary). 52 min. Sound. 16mm Color. *Rental:* Blackwood Films. *Sale:* Blackwood Films.

Royal African Rifles. Orig. Title: Storm Over Africa. Louis Hayward & Veronica Hurst. Directed by Lesley Selander. 1953. Allied Artists. 75 min. Sound. 16mm Color. *Rental:* Ivy Films. *Sale:* Rep Pic Film.

Royal Archives of Elba, The: Syria. Directed by Mildred Alberg & Richard Ellison. 1980. Milberg. (Documentary). 58 min. Sound. 16mm Color. *Rental:* Films Inc & Syracuse U Film. *Sale:* Films Inc. *Rental:* Films Inc, *Sale:* Films Inc, Videotape version.

Royal Bed, The. Mary Astor & Lowell Sherman. Directed by Lowell Sherman. 1931. RKO. 74 min. Sound. 16mm *Rental:* RKO General Pics.

Royal Family of Broadway, The. Fredric March & Ina Claire. Directed by George Cukor & Cyril Gardner. 1930. Paramount. 82 min. Sound. 16mm B&W. *Rental:* Swank Motion.

Royal Flash. Malcolm MacDowell & Oliver Reed. Directed by Richard Lester. 1975. Britain. 98 min. Sound. 16mm Color. *Rental:* Films Inc.

Royal Heritage. 9 pts. 1980. Britain. (Documentary). 98 min. Sound. 16mm Color. *Rental:* Films Inc. *Sale:* Films Inc. *Sale:* Films Inc, Videotape version.

Royal Hunt of the Sun. Robert Shaw & Christopher Plummer. Directed by Irving Lerner. 1969. Cinema Center. 113 min. Sound. 16mm Color. *Rental:* Swank Motion.

Royal Scandal, A. Orig. Title: Czarina. Tallulah Bankhead & Charles Coburn. Directed by Otto Preminger. 1945. Fox. 94 min. Sound. 16mm B&W. *Rental:* Films Inc.

Royal Tour of Queen Elizabeth & Philip, The *see* Flight of the White Heron.

Royal Wedding. Orig. Title: Wedding Bells. Fred Astaire & Jane Powell. Directed by Stanley Donen. 1951. MGM. 92 min. Sound. 16mm B&W. *Rental:* Films Inc & MGM United. *Rental:* Films Inc, Color version. *Rental:* MGM United, Videotape version.

Rubber Racketeers. Ricardo Cortez & Rochelle Hudson. Directed by Harold Young. 1942. Monogram. 71 min. Sound. 16mm B&W. *Rental:* Hurlock Cine.

Rubber Tires. Bessie Love & May Robson. Directed by Alan Hale. 1925. P. D. C.. 90 min. Sound. 16mm B&W. *Rental:* Em Gee Film Lib, Film Classics & Modern Sound. *Sale:* Film Classics. *Rental:* Budget Films, *Sale:* Morcraft Films, Silent 16mm version. *Sale:* Morcraft Films, Super 8 silent version.

Rubens. 1947. BRF. Sound. 16mm B&W. *Rental:* U Mich Media.

Ruby. Piper Laurie & Stuart Whitman. Directed by Curtis Harrington. 1976. Dimension. 85 min. Sound. 16mm Color. *Rental:* Williams Films. *Sale:* Salz Ent.

Ruby Gentry. Jennifer Jones & Charlton Heston. Directed by King Vidor. 1952. Fox. 82 min. Sound. 16mm B&W. *Rental:* Films Inc. *Sale:* Tamarelles French Film, Videotape version.

Ruckus Manhattan. Directed by Peter Hutton. 1976. Hutton. 52 min. Sound. 16mm Color. *Rental:* Canyon Cinema.

Ruddigore. 1974. Britain. (Operetta). 52 min. Sound. 16mm Color. *Rental:* B Raymond. *Sale:* B Raymond. *Sale:* B Raymond, Videotape version.

Rude Boy. Directed by Jack Hazan, David Mingay & Clash. 1980. Britain. (Concert). 126 min. Sound. 16mm Color. *Rental:* Ivy Films & New Cinema.

Rudolph the Red-Nosed Reindeer. 1967. UPA. (Animated). 57 min. Sound. 16mm Color. *Rental:* Budget Films, Cine Craft, Films Inc, Roas Films, Film Ctr DC, Video Comm, Westcoast Films, Welling Motion Pictures & Willoughby Peer. *Sale:* Films Inc.

Rudolph the Red-Nosed Reindeer. Burl Ives. Coronet Films. 50 min. Sound. 16mm Color. *Rental:* MTI Teleprograms Inc.

Ruggles of Red Gap. Charles Laughton & Mary Boland. Directed by Leo McCarey. 1935. Paramount. 90 min. Sound. 16mm B&W. *Rental:* Museum Mod Art.

Rulers of the Sea. Douglas Fairbanks Jr. & Margaret Lockwood. Directed by Frank Lloyd. 1939. Paramount. 96 min. Sound. 16mm B&W. *Rental:* Swank Motion.

Rules of the Game, The. Trans. Title: Regle du Jeu, Le. Marcel Dalio. Directed by Jean Renoir. Fr. 1939. France. 110 min. Sound. 16mm B&W. *Rental:* Budget Films, Corinth Films, Em Gee Film Lib, Films Inc, Ivy Films, Janus Films, New Cinema, Kit Parker, Utah Media, Westcoast Films & Images Film. *Sale:* Cinema Concepts, Festival Films, Glenn Photo, Images Film, Natl Cinema & Reel Images. *Sale:* Glenn Photo, Super 8 sound version. *Sale:* Festival Films, Images Film & Tamarelles French Film, Videotape version.

Ruling Class, The. Peter O'Toole & Alastair Sim. Directed by Peter Medak. 1972. Embassy. 148 min. Sound. 16mm Color. *Rental:* Films Inc.

Ruling Houses, The: 1900-Day of Empires Has Arrived. 1976. Britain. (Documentary). 52 min. Sound. 16mm Color. *Rental:* Time-Life Multimedia. *Sale:* Time-Life Multimedia.

Ruling Voice, The. Walter Huston & Loretta Young. Directed by Rowland V. Lee. 1931. Warners. 74 min. Sound. 16mm B&W. *Rental:* MGM United.

Rumba. Carole Lombard & George Raft. Directed by Marion Gering. 1935. Paramount. 71 min. Sound. 16mm B&W. *Rental:* Swank Motion.

Rumba in Television. Julio Diaz. Span. Mexico. 70 min. Sound. 16mm B&W. subtitles. *Rental:* Mogulls Film.

Rumble Fish. Matt Dillon & Mickey Rourke. Directed by Francis Ford Coppola. 1983. 94 min. Sound. Videotape B&W. *Sale:* Tamarelles French Film.

Rumours of War. 1972. Britain. (Documentary). 60 min. Sound. 16mm Color. *Rental:* Time-Life Multimedia. *Sale:* Time-Life Multimedia.

Rumpelstiltskin. Clyde Tracy, Elizabeth Burbridge & Thomas H. Ince. 1915. New York. 57 min. Silent. 16mm B&W. *Rental:* Museum Mod Art. *Lease:* Museum Mod Art.

Rumpelstiltskin. Directed by Herbert Fredersdorf. 1955. Germany. (Cast unlisted). 81 min. Sound. 16mm Color. dubbed. *Rental:* Budget Films, Charard Motion Pics & Westcoast Films.

Rumpelstiltskin & The Golden Secret. (Cast unlisted). 80 min. Sound. 16mm Color. *Rental:* Films Inc.

Rumpo Kid, The. Orig. Title: Carry on, Cowboy. Sidney James, Kenneth Williams & Joan Sims. Directed by Gerald Thomas. 1965. Britain. 94 min. Sound. 16mm Color. *Rental:* Films Inc.

Run, Angel, Run. William Smith. Directed by Jack Starrett. 1969. Fanfare. 90 min. Sound. Videotape Color. *Sale:* Budget Films, Vidamerica & Westcoast Films.

Run, Appaloosa, Run. Directed by Larry Lansburg. 1966. Disney. (Documentary). 48 min. Sound. 16mm Color. *Rental:* Cine Craft, Disney Prod, Films Inc, Kent St U Film, Modern Sound, Roas Films, Film Ctr DC & Twyman Films.

Run, Cougar, Run. Stuart Whitman & Frank Aletter. Directed by Jerome Courtland. Disney. 87 min. Sound. 16mm Color. *Rental:* Cine Craft, Williams Films, Disney Prod, Films Inc, Film Pres, U of IL Film, Modern Sound, Newman Film Lib, Roas Films, Swank Motion, Film Ctr DC & Twyman Films.

Run for Cover. James Cagney & Viveca Lindfors. Directed by Nicholas Ray. 1955. Paramount. 92 min. Sound. 16mm B&W. *Rental:* Video Comm & Willoughby Peer.

Run for the Roses, A. Vera Miles & Stuart Whitman. 1978. Kodak. 93 min. Sound. 16mm Color. *Rental:* Films Inc & Modern Sound.

Run for Your Money, A. Sir Alec Guinness & Joyce Grenfell. Directed by Charles Frend. 1949. Britain. 83 min. Sound. 16mm B&W. *Rental:* Films Inc & Janus Films.

Run for Your Wife. Ugo Tognazzi & Marina Vlady. Directed by Gian Luigi Polidoro. 1966. Italy. 97 min. Sound. 16mm Color. dubbed. *Rental:* Hurlock Cine.

Run Home Slow. Mercedes McCambridge. 1965. Emerson. 75 min. Sound. 16mm B&W. *Rental:* Ivy Films.

Run Like a Thief. Kieron Moore & Ina Balin. Directed by Bernard Glasser. 1967. 98 min. Sound. 16mm Color. *Rental:* Films Inc.

Run of the Arrow. Rod Steiger, Brian Keith & Sarita Montiel. Directed by Samuel Fuller. 1957. Universal. 86 min. Sound. 16mm Color. *Rental:* Budget Films, Films Inc, Natl Film Video, Video Comm, Westcoast Films, Wholesome Film Ctr & Kit Parker. *Lease:* Video Comm. *Rental:* Video Comm, *Lease:* Video Comm, Videotape version.

Run Silent, Run Deep. Clark Gable & Burt Lancaster. Directed by Robert Wise. 1958. United Artists. 92 min. Sound. 16mm B&W. *Rental:* MGM United.

Run to the Sea. 1976. Gospel. (Cast Unlisted). 55 min. Sound. 16mm Color. *Rental:* Gospel Films.

Run Wild, Run Free. John Mills & Mark Lester. Directed by Richard C. Sarafian. 1969. Columbia. 100 min. Sound. 16mm Color. *Rental:* Arcus Film, Budget Films, Cine Craft, Bosco Films, Film Ctr DC, Film Pres, Films Inc, Inst Cinema, Modern Sound, Roas Films, Twyman Films, U of IL Film, Welling Motion Pictures, Westcoast Films, Wholesome Film Ctr & Williams Films.

Runaround, The. Ella Raines & Rod Cameron. Directed by Charles Lamont. 1946. Universal. 86 min. Sound. 16mm B&W. *Rental:* Swank Motion.

Runaway. 1981. Media Guild. (Documentary). 54 min. Sound. 16mm Color. *Rental:* Media Guild. *Sale:* Media Guild. *Sale:* Media Guild, Videotape version.

Runaway Bride, The. Mary Astor & Lloyd Hughes. Directed by Donald Crisp. 1930. RKO. 69 min. Sound. 16mm *Rental:* RKO General Pics.

Runaway Bus, The. Frankie Howerd, Margaret Rutherford & Petula Clark. 1955. Britain. 75 min. Sound. 16mm B&W. *Rental:* Budget Films, Charard Motion Pics, Liberty Co & Video Comm.

Runaway Express, The. Charles French & Blanche Mehaffey. Directed by Edward Sedgwick. 1926. Universal. 60 min. Silent. 16mm B&W. *Rental:* Mogulls Films.

Runaway Railway, The. Sidney Tafler. Directed by Jan Darnley-Smith. 1967. Britain. 60 min. Sound. 16mm B&W. *Rental:* Films Inc & Wholesome Film Ctr.

Runner Stumbles, The. Dick Van Dyke & Kathleen Quinlan. Directed by Stanley Kramer. 1979. Fox. 109 min. Sound. 16mm Color. *Rental:* Films Inc.

Running. Michael Douglas & Susan Anspach. Directed by Steven Hilliard Stern. 1980. Universal. 106 min. Sound. 16mm Color. *Rental:* Swank Motion.

Running Brave. Bobby Benson & Pat Hingle. Directed by D. C. Everett. 1983. Disney. 105 min. Sound. 16mm Color. *Rental:* Williams Films & Swank Motion.

Running Fence. Directed by David Maysles, Albert Maysles & Charlotte Zwerin. 1976. Maysles. 56 min. Sound. 16mm Color. *Rental:* Maysles Films. *Lease:* Maysles Films.

Running Man, The. Laurence Harvey & Lee Remick. Directed by Sir Carol Reed. 1963. Columbia. 103 min. Sound. 16mm B&W. *Rental:* Arcus Film, Charard Motion Pics, Films Inc, Inst Cinema, Modern Sound & Welling Motion Pictures. *Rental:* Corinth Films & Kit Parker, Anamorphic color version.

Running Target. Arthur Franz & Doris Dowling. Directed by Marvin R. Weinstein. 1956. United Artists. 83 min. Sound. 16mm B&W. *Rental:* MGM United.

Running Wild. W. C. Fields & Mary Brian. Directed by Gregory La Cava. 1927. Paramount. 68 min. Silent. 16mm B&W. *Rental:* Films Inc.

Rupture, La. Stephane Audran & Jean Pierre Cassel. Directed by Claude Chabrol. 1970. France. 125 min. Sound. 16mm Color. *Rental:* New Line Cinema.

Rush to Judgment. Directed by Emile De Antonio. 1967. Impact. 122 min. Sound. 16mm B&W. *Rental:* New Cinema & New Yorker Films. *Sale:* New Yorker Films.

Rushes. Directed by Barry Spinello. 1978. Direct Cinema. (Documentary). 56 min. Sound. 16mm Color. *Rental:* Direct Cinema. *Lease:* Direct Cinema.

Russia. Directed by Theodore Holcomb. 1972. Holcomb. (Documentary). 108 min. Sound. 16mm Color. *Rental:* Holcomb. *Sale:* Holcomb.

Russia Beneath the Sputniks. 1967. Britain. (Documentary). 52 min. Sound. 16mm B&W. *Rental:* Time-Life Multimedia. *Sale:* Time-Life Multimedia.

Russia: The Unfinished Revolution. 1967. Net. (Documentary). 60 min. Sound. 16mm B&W. *Rental:* U Cal Media, Indiana AV Ctr & U Mich Media. *Sale:* Indiana AV Ctr.

Russian Connection, The. 1982. Phoenix. 50 min. Sound. 16mm Color. *Rental:* Alden Films & Phoenix Films. *Sale:* Alden Films & Phoenix Films. *Sale:* Alden Films & Phoenix Films, Videotape version.

Russian Roulette. George Segal & Christina Raines. Directed by Lou Lombardo. 1975. Embassy. 103 min. Sound. 16mm Color. *Rental:* Films Inc.

Russians Are Coming, The Russians Are Coming, The. Alan Arkin & Eva Marie Saint. Directed by Norman Jewison. 1966. United Artists. 126 min. Sound. 16mm Color. *Rental:* MGM United. *Rental:* MGM United, Videotape version.

Russians Are Here, The. 58 min. Videotape *Rental:* PBS Video. *Sale:* PBS Video.

Russians: Insight Through Literature. 1953. 54 min. Sound. 16mm B&W. *Rental:* Iowa Films.

Russians, The: Insights Through Literature. Jo Van Fleet, Kim Hunter & Sam Wanamaker. 1963. CBS. 54 min. Sound. 16mm B&W. *Rental:* U of IL Film, U Mich Media & Syracuse U Film. *Sale:* McGraw-Hill Films.

Rustlers, The. Tim Holt & Richard Martin. Directed by Lesley Selander. 1949. RKO. 61 min. Sound. 16mm B&W. *Rental:* RKO General Pics.

Rustler's Hideout. Buster Crabbe. Directed by Sam Newfield. 1944. PRC. 60 min. Sound. 16mm B&W. *Sale:* Natl Cinema.

Rustlers of Devil's Canyon. Allan Lane. Directed by R. G. Springsteen. 1947. Republic. 54 min. Sound. 16mm B&W. *Rental:* Ivy Films.

Rustlers on Horseback. Allan Lane. Directed by Fred C. Brannon. 1950. Republic. 60 min. Sound. 16mm B&W. *Rental:* Ivy Films. *Sale:* Rep Pic Film & Nostalgia Merchant.

Rustler's Valley. William Boyd. Directed by Nate Watt. 1937. Paramount. 60 min. Sound. 16mm B&W. *Lease:* Cinema Concepts. *Sale:* Natl Cinema. *Sale:* Reel Images, Videotape version.

Rusty & the Falcon. Directed by Paul Kenworthy. 1958. Disney. (Cast unlisted). 47 min. Sound. 16mm Color. *Rental:* Buchan Pic, Cine Craft, Disney Prod, Films Inc, Iowa Films, Kent St U Film, U Mich Media, Modern Sound, Roas Films, Syracuse U Film & Film Ctr DC.

Rusty Leads the Way. Ted Donaldson & Ann Doran. Directed by Will Jason. 1948. Columbia. 59 min. Sound. 16mm B&W. *Rental:* Cine Craft, Films Inc & Inst Cinema.

Rusty Saves a Life. Ted Donaldson & John Litel. Directed by Seymour Freidman. 1949. Columbia. 68 min. Sound. 16mm B&W. *Rental:* Cine Craft, Films Inc & Inst Cinema.

Rusty's Birthday. Ted Donaldson & John Litel. Directed by Seymour Friedman. 1949. Columbia. 60 min. Sound. 16mm B&W. *Rental:* Cine Craft & Films Inc.

Ruth Page: An American Original. Directed by David Hahn. 1980. Films Inc. 59 min. Sound. 16mm Color. *Rental:* Syracuse U Film & Texture Film. *Sale:* Texture Film. *Sale:* Texture Film, Videotape version.

Ruthless. Zachary Scott & Diana Lynn. Directed by Edgar G. Ulmer. 1948. Eagle Lion. 104 min. Sound. 16mm B&W. *Rental:* Ivy Films & Westcoast Films. *Sale:* Rep Pic Film.

Ruy Blas. Jean Marais & Danielle Darrieux. Directed by Pierre Billon. 1944. France. 100 min. Sound. 16mm B&W. *Rental:* Film Classics, Videotape version.

Ryan's Daughter. Robert Mitchum & Sarah Miles. Directed by David Lean. 1970. MGM. 189 min. Sound. 16mm Color. *Rental:* MGM United. *Rental:* MGM United, Anamorphic version.

S-M. 1970. Grove. (Documentary). 50 min. Sound. 16mm B&W. *Rental:* Grove.

S. O. B. Julie Andrews & William Holden. Directed by Blake Edwards. 1981. Lorimar. 121 min. Sound. 16mm Color. *Rental:* Swank Motion. *Rental:* Swank Motion, Videotape version.

S. O. S. Quality X. 83 min. Videotape Color. *Sale:* Quality X Video.

S. O. S. Iceberg. Rod LaRocque & Leni Riefenstahl. Directed by Tay Garnett. 1933. Universal. 76 min. Sound. 16mm B&W. *Rental:* Swank Motion.

S. O. S. Tidal Wave. Ralph Byrd & George Barbier. Directed by John H Auer. 1939. Republic. 54 min. Sound. 16mm B&W. *Rental:* Ivy Films. *Sale:* Rep Pic Film.

S. P. Y. S. Elliot Gould & Donald Sutherland. Directed by Irwin Kershner. 1974. Fox. 87 min. Sound. 16mm Color. *Rental:* Williams Films, Films Inc & Welling Motion Pictures.

S.W.A.L.K. & To Love Somebody *see* Melody.

Saadia. Cornel Wilde & Rita Gam. Directed by Albert Lewin. 1954. MGM. 87 min. Sound. 16mm Color. *Rental:* MGM United.

Sabata. Lee Van Cleef & Frank Kramer. 1970. Italy. (Anamorphic). 106 min. Sound. 16mm Color. dubbed. *Rental:* MGM United.

Sabotage. Orig. Title: A Woman Alone. Sylvia Sidney & Oscar Homolka. Directed by Alfred Hitchcock. 1936. Britain. 79 min. Sound. 16mm B&W. *Rental:* Budget Films, Films Inc, Images Film, Kit Parker, Museum Mod Art, Video Comm, Westcoast Films & Wholesome Film Ctr. *Sale:* Cinema Concepts, Festival Films, Images Film & Reel Images. *Sale:* Festival Films & Tamarelles French Film, Videotape version.

Sabotage. Orig. Title: Spies at Work. Arleen Whelan & Joseph Sawyer. Directed by Harold Young. 1939. Republic. 71 min. Sound. 16mm B&W. *Rental:* Ivy Films & Westcoast Films.

Sabotage at Sea. Felix Aylmer & David Hutchison. Directed by Lesley Selander. 1943. Britain. 72 min. Sound. 16mm B&W. *Rental:* Ivy Films. *Sale:* Rep Pic Film.

Saboteur. Robert Cummings & Priscilla Lane. Directed by Alfred Hitchcock. 1942. Universal. 98 min. Sound. 16mm B&W. *Rental:* Swank Motion & Williams Films.

Sabre Jet. Robert Stack, Coleen Gray & Arlen Richard. Directed by Louis King. 1953. United Artists. 96 min. Sound. 16mm Color. *Rental:* Cine Craft, MGM United & United Artists Sixteen.

Sabrina. Humphrey Bogart, Audrey Hepburn & William Holden. Directed by Billy Wilder. 1954. Paramount. 113 min. Sound. 16mm B&W. *Rental:* Films Inc.

Sabu & The Magic Ring. Sabu & William Marshall. Directed by George Blair. 1957. Allied Artists. 61 min. Sound. 16mm B&W. *Rental:* Hurlock Cine.

SAC: Aloft & Below. 1963. CBS. (Documentary). 52 min. Sound. 16mm B&W. *Rental:* Macmillan Films. *Sale:* Macmillan Films.

Sacco & Vanzetti. Gian Maria Volonte & Riccardo Cucciolla. Directed by Guiliano Montaldo. 1972. Italy. 118 min. Sound. 16mm Color. dubbed. *Rental:* Films Inc, Inst Cinema, Tyman Films, Welling Motion Pictures & Budget Films.

Sacred Ground. 1976. (Documentary). 48 min. Sound. 16mm Color. *Rental:* SD AV Ctr.

Sad Horse, The. David Ladd & Chill Wills. Directed by James B. Clark. 1959. Fox. (Anamorphic). 78 min. Sound. 16mm Color. *Rental:* Films Inc.

Sad Sack, The. Jerry Lewis. Directed by George Marshall. 1957. Paramount. 98 min. Sound. 16mm B&W. *Rental:* Films Inc. *Rental:* Ivy Films, *Sale:* Blackhawk Films, Super 8 sound version, videotape version.

Sad Song of Yellow Skin, A. 1970. Canada. 60 min. Sound. 16mm Color. *Rental:* U Cal Media, Films Inc, U Mich Media, Syracuse U Film & Wholesome Film Ctr. *Sale:* Films Inc. *Sale:* Films Inc, Videotape version.

Sadat's Eternal Egypt with Walter Cronkite. 1980. CBS. 45 min. Sound. 16mm Color. *Rental:* Syracuse U Film. *Sale:* Carousel.

Saddle Aces. Rex Bell. Directed by Harry Fraser. 1935. Resolute. 57 min. Sound. 16mm B&W. *Rental:* Budget Films & Films Inc. *Sale:* Morcraft Films.

Saddle Buster, The. Tom Keene & Helen Foster. Directed by Fred Allen. 1932. RKO. 60 min. Sound. 16mm B&W. *Rental:* RKO General Pics.

Saddle Legion. Tim Holt & Dorothy Malone. Directed by Lesley Selander. 1952. RKO. 61 min. Sound. 16mm B&W. *Rental:* RKO General Pics.

Saddle Mountain Roundup. The Range Busters. Directed by S. Roy Luby. 1940. Monogram. 60 min. Sound. 16mm B&W. *Sale:* Cinema Concepts & Natl Cinema.

Saddle Pals. Gene Autry. Directed by Lester Orlebeck. 1947. Republic. 54 min. Sound. 16mm B&W. *Rental:* Ivy Films.

Saddle Serenade. Jimmy Wakely. Directed by Oliver Drake. 1945. Monogram. 55 min. Sound. 16mm B&W. *Rental:* Hurlock Cine.

Saddle the Wind. Robert Taylor & Julie London. Directed by Robert Parrish. 1958. MGM. 84 min. Sound. 16mm Color. *Rental:* MGM United. *Rental:* MGM United, Anamorphic version.

Saddle Tramp. Joel McCrea & Wanda Hendrix. Directed by Hugo Fregonese. 1950. Universal. 92 min. Sound. 16mm Color. *Rental:* Swank Motion.

Saddlemates. Robert Livingston & Bob Steele. Directed by Joseph Kane. 1941. Republic. 56 min. Sound. 16mm B&W. *Rental:* Ivy Films. *Sale:* Rep Pic Film & Nostalgia Merchant.

Sadie McKee. Joan Crawford & Franchot Tone. Directed by Clarence Brown. 1934. MGM. 88 min. Sound. 16mm B&W. *Rental:* MGM United.

Sadie Thompson. Gloria Swanson, Raoul Walsh & Lionel Barrymore. Directed by Raoul Walsh. 1928. United Artists. (Musical Score Only). 90 min. Sound. 16mm B&W. *Rental:* Kino Intl.

Sadko. Sergei Stolyarov. Directed by Alexander Ptushko. Rus. 1952. Russia. 88 min. Sound. 16mm B&W. subtitles. *Rental:* Corinth Films.

Safari. Victor Mature & Janet Leigh. Directed by Terence Young. 1956. Columbia. 91 min. Sound. 16mm Color. *Rental:* Charard Motion Pics, Films Inc, Inst Cinema, Modern Sound & Roas Films.

Safari Drums. John Sheffield & Douglas Kennedy. Directed by Ford Beebe. 1953. Monogram. 71 min. Sound. 16mm B&W. *Rental:* Hurlock Cine.

Safari Three Thousand. David Carradine & Stockard Channing. Directed by Harry Hurwitz. 1982. MGM. 91 min. Sound. 16mm Color. *Rental:* MGM United. *Rental:* MGM United, VIdeotape version.

Safe at Home. Mickey Mantle & Roger Maris. Directed by Walter Doniger. 1962. Columbia. 74 min. Sound. 16mm B&W. *Rental:* Buchan Pic, Cine Craft, Charard Motion Pics, Films Inc, Modern Sound, Natl Film Serv, Newman Film Lib, Roas Films, Welling Motion Pictures & Westcoast Films.

Safe in Hell. Orig. Title: Lost Lady, The. Donald Cook & Boris Karloff. Directed by William A. Wellman. 1931. Warners. 74 min. Sound. 16mm B&W. *Rental:* MGM United.

Safe Insect Control: No Silent Spring. 1970. EMC. 59 min. Sound. 16mm B&W. *Rental:* U Cal Media. *Sale:* U Cal Media.

Safe Place, A. Tuesday Weld, Orson Welles & Jack Nicholson. Directed by Henry Jaglom. 1971. BBS. 94 min. Sound. 16mm Color. *Rental:* Films Inc.

Safecracker, The. Ray Milland & Barry Jones. Directed by Ray Milland. 1958. MGM. 96 min. Sound. 16mm Color. *Rental:* MGM United.

Safety Factor, The. 1980. 58 min. Sound. Videotape *Rental:* PBS Video. *Sale:* PBS Video.

Safety in Numbers. Jed Prouty & Spring Byington. Directed by Mal St. Clair. 1938. Fox. 58 min. Sound. 16mm B&W. *Rental:* Films Inc.

Safety Last. Harold Lloyd. Directed by Fred Newmeyer & Sam Taylor. 1923. Pathe. (Musical Score Only). 60 min. Sound. 16mm B&W. *Rental:* Films Inc, Images Film, Janus Films, Kino Intl, Kit Parker & U Mich Media. *Sale:* Films Inc, Super 8 Sound version. *Sale:* Blackhawk Films, Super 8 Silent version.

Saga De Los Draculas, La. Narcusi Ibanez Mebta, Tina Sainz & Tony Isbert. Spain. 91 min. Sound. Videotape Color. subtitles. *Sale:* Tamarelles French Films.

Saga of Death Valley, The. Roy Rogers. Directed by Armand Schaefer. 1939. Republic. 54 min. Sound. 16mm B&W. *Rental:* Budget Films & Ivy Films. *Sale:* Rep Pic Film. *Sale:* Video Comm, Videotape version.

Saga of Hemp Brown, The. Rory Calhoun & Beverly Garland. Directed by Richard Carlson. 1958. Universal. 79 min. Sound. 16mm Color. *Rental:* Swank Motion.

Saga of William S. Hart, The. Em Gee. (Anthology). 63 min. Silent. 16mm B&W. *Rental:* Em Gee Film Lib. *Rental:* Westcoast Films, 50 min version.

Sagebrush Law. Tim Holt & Joan Barclay. Directed by Bert Gilroy. 1943. RKO. 56 min. Sound. 16mm B&W. *Rental:* RKO General Pics.

Sagebrush Rebellion. 1980. 58 min. Sound. 16mm Color. *Rental:* Utah Media.

Sagebrush Trail. John Wayne. Directed by Armand Schaefer. 1933. Monogram. 63 min. Sound. 16mm B&W. *Rental:* Budget Films & Ivy Films. *Sale:* Cinema Concepts, Classics Assoc NY, Rep Pic Film & Reel Images. *Sale:* Morcraft Films & Reel Images, Super 8 sound version. *Sale:* Video Comm, Videotape version.

Sagebrush Troubador. Gene Autry. Directed by Spencer G. Bennett. 1935. Republic. 54 min. Sound. 16mm B&W. *Rental:* Ivy Films.

Sahara. Humphrey Bogart & Bruce Bennett. Directed by Zoltan Korda. 1943. Columbia. 97 min. Sound. 16mm B&W. *Rental:* Arcus Film, Buchan Pic, Budget Films, Charard Motion Pics, Williams Films, Bosco Films, Films Inc, Images Film, Kit Parker, Modern Sound, Natl Film Video, Twyman Films, Video Comm, Westcoast Films, Welling Motion Pictures, Wholesome Film Ctr & Willoughby Peer.

Sahara. Brooke Shields & Lambert Wilson. Directed by Andrew V. McLaglen. 1983. Cannon. 105 min. Sound. 16mm Color. *Rental:* Swank Motion.

Sahara: La Caravane du Sel. 1969. NBC. (Documentary). 53 min. Sound. 16mm Color. *Rental:* Films Inc, Iowa Films, U Mich Media & Syracuse U Film. *Sale:* Films Inc. *Sale:* Films Inc, Videotape version.

Saigon. Alan Ladd & Veronica Lake. Directed by Leslie Fenton. 1948. Paramount. 94 min. Sound. 16mm B&W. *Rental:* Swank Motion.

Sail A Crooked Ship. Ernie Kovacs & Robert Wagner. Directed by Irving Brecher. 1961. Columbia. 88 min. Sound. 16mm B&W. *Rental:* Buchan Pic, Cine Craft, Bosco Films, Films Inc, Modern Sound, Film Ctr DC, Welling Motion Pictures & Wholesome Film Ctr.

Sail Into Danger. Dennis O'Keefe. Directed by Kenneth Hume. 1957. 72 min. 16mm *Rental:* A Twyman Pres.

Sailing. 1967. NET. (Documentary). 55 min. Sound. 16mm B&W. *Rental:* Indiana AV Ctr. *Sale:* Indiana AV Ctr.

Sailing Along. Jessie Matthews & Alastair Sim. Directed by Sonnie Hale. 1938. Britain. 94 min. Sound. 16mm B&W. *Rental:* Budget Films, Janus Films & Kit Parker.

Sailor Be Good. Jack Oakie & Vivienne Osborne. Directed by James Cruze. 1933. RKO. 54 min. Sound. 16mm B&W. *Rental:* Ivy Films.

Sailor Beware. Dean Martin & Jerry Lewis. Directed by Hal Walker. 1952. Paramount. 108 min. Sound. 16mm B&W. *Rental:* Films Inc.

Sailor from Gibraltar. Jeanne Moreau & Ian Bannen. Directed by Tony Richardson. 1967. Britain. 88 min. Sound. 16mm B&W. *Rental:* MGM United.

Sailor from the Comet. Trans. Title: Moryak iz Komety. Gleb Romanov. Directed by Isidore Annensky. Rus. 1958. Russia. 92 min. Sound. 16mm B&W. subtitles. *Rental:* Corinth Films.

Sailor-Made Man, A. Harold Lloyd. Directed by Harold Lloyd. 1921. Associated Exhibitors. (Musical Score Only). 83 min. Sound. 16mm B&W. *Rental:* Kino Intl.

Sailor of the King, The. Jeffrey Hunter & Michael Rennie. Directed by Roy Boulting. 1953. Fox. 83 min. Sound. 16mm B&W. *Rental:* Films Inc.

Sailor Takes a Wife, The. Robert Walker & June Allyson. Directed by Richard Whorf. 1945. MGM. 92 min. Sound. 16mm B&W. *Rental:* MGM United.

Sailor Who Fell from Grace with the Sea, The. Sarah Miles & Kris Kristofferson. Directed by Lewis John Carlino. 1976. Embassy. 105 min. Sound. 16mm Color. *Rental:* Films Inc.

Sailor's Holiday. Alan Hale & Sally Eilers. Directed by Fred Newmeyer. 1929. Pathe. 60 min. Silent. 16mm B&W. *Rental:* Mogulls Films.

Sailor's Lady. Nancy Kelly & Dana Andrews. Directed by Allan Dwan. 1940. Fox. 66 min. Sound. 16mm B&W. *Rental:* Films Inc.

Sailors on Leave. William Lundigan & Shirley Ross. Directed by Albert S. Rogell. 1941. Republic. 71 min. Sound. 16mm B&W. *Rental:* Ivy Films.

Sailors Three. Michael Wilding & Tommy Trindler. Directed by Walter Forde. 1940. Britain. 85 min. Sound. 16mm B&W. *Rental:* Mogulls Films.

St. Anthony of Padua. 1926. Portugal. (Music & sound effects, cast unlisted). 90 min. Sound. 16mm B&W. *Rental:* Film Classics.

Saint Benedict. Salesians. (Cast unlisted). 90 min. Sound. 16mm B&W. *Rental:* Bosco Films.

Saint Benny the Dip. Orig. Title: Escape If You Can. Dick Haymes, Nina Foch & Roland Young. Directed by Edgar G. Ulmer. 1951. United Artists. 90 min. Sound. 16mm B&W. *Rental:* Budget Films, MGM United & Mogulls Films.

St. Francis of Assisi. 1924. Spain. (Music & sound affects only, cast unlisted). 69 min. Sound. 16mm B&W. *Rental:* Film Classics.

Saint in London, The. George Sanders & Sally Grey. Directed by John Paddy Carstairs. 1939. RKO. 72 min. Sound. 16mm B&W. *Rental:* RKO General Pics.

Saint in New York, The. Louis Hayward, Jack Carson & Kay Sutton. Directed by Ben Holmes. 1938. RKO. 72 min. Sound. 16mm B&W. *Rental:* Films Inc & RKO General Pics.

Saint in Palm Springs, The. George Sanders & Wendy Barrie. Directed by Jack Hively. 1941. RKO. 66 min. Sound. 16mm B&W. *Rental:* RKO General Pics.

St. Ives. Charles Bronson, Maximilian Schell, Jacqueline Bisset & John Houseman. Directed by J. Lee Thompson. 1976. Warners. 94 min. Sound. 16mm Color. *Rental:* Williams Films, Swank Motion & Twyman Films.

Saint Jack. Ben Gazzara & Denholm Elliot. Directed by Peter Bogdanovich. 1979. New World. 112 min. Sound. 16mm Color. *Rental:* Films Inc.

St. Joan. Julie Harris. 1978. Films Inc. 60 min. Color. *Rental:* Films Inc. *Sale:* Films Inc.

St. Louis Blues. Nat King Cole & Eartha Kitt. Directed by Allen Reisner. 1958. Paramount. 93 min. Sound. 16mm B&W. *Rental:* Films Inc.

St. Louis Kid. Orig. Title: Perfect Weekend, The. James Cagney & Patricia Ellis. Directed by Ray Enright. 1934. Warners. 67 min. Sound. 16mm B&W. *Rental:* MGM United.

St. Martin's Lane. Orig. Title: Sidewalks of London. Charles Laughton, Rex Harrison & Vivien Leigh. Directed by Tim Whelan. 1940. 86 min. Sound. 16mm B&W. *Rental:* A Twyman Pres.

Saint Mary Mazzarello. Salesians. (Cast unlisted). 80 min. Sound. 16mm B&W. *Rental:* Bosco Films.

Saint Meets the Tiger, The. Hugh Sinclair & Jean Gillie. Directed by Paul L. Stein. 1942. RKO. 70 min. Sound. 16mm B&W. *Rental:* RKO General Pics.

St. Patrick's Day: Richard Brinsley Sheridan. 1973. Charles Playhouse. 54 min. Sound. 16mm B&W. *Sale:* Modern Mass. *Sale:* Modern Sound.

Saint-Simon. France. (Cast unlisted). 60 min. Sound. 16mm B&W. *Rental:* French Am Cul. *Sale:* French Am Cul, Videotape version.

Saint Strikes Back, The. George Sanders & Wendy Barrie. Directed by John Farrow. 1939. RKO. 69 min. Sound. 16mm *Rental:* Films Inc.

Saint Takes Over, The. George Sanders & Wendy Barrie. Directed by Jack Hively. 1940. RKO. 68 min. Sound. 16mm B&W. *Rental:* RKO General Pics.

St. Teresa of Lisieux. France. (Cast unlisted). Sound. 16mm B&W. *Rental:* Film Classics.

St. Valentine's Day Massacre, The. Jason Robards & George Segal. Directed by Roger Corman. 1968. Fox. 100 min. Sound. 16mm Color. *Rental:* Films Inc.

Sainted Sisters, The. Veronica Lake & Joan Caulfield. Directed by William D. Russell. 1948. Paramount. 90 min. Sound. 16mm B&W. *Rental:* Swank Motion.

Saintly Sinners. Don Beddoe & Ellen Corby. Directed by Jean Yarbrough. 1962. United Artists. 78 min. Sound. 16mm B&W. *Rental:* MGM United.

Saints & Sinners. Kieron Moore & Christine Norden. Directed by Leslie Arliss. 1949. Ireland. 100 min. Sound. 16mm B&W. *Rental:* Video Comm.

Saint's Double Trouble, The. George Sanders & Bela Lugosi. Directed by Jack Hively. 1940. RKO. 68 min. Sound. 16mm B&W. *Rental:* RKO General Pics.

Saint's Girl Friday, The. Louis Hayward & Diana Dors. Directed by Seymour Friedman. 1954. RKO. 68 min. Sound. 16mm B&W. *Rental:* Ivy Films.

Saint's Vacation, The. Hugh Sinclair & Leueen MacGrath. Directed by Leslie Fenton. 1941. RKO. 78 min. Sound. 16mm B&W. *Rental:* RKO General Pics.

Sakima & the Masked Marvel. William Forest & Louise Currie. Directed by John English. 1943. Republic. 100 min. Sound. 16mm B&W. *Rental:* Ivy Films. *Sale:* Rep Pic Film & Nostalgia Merchant.

Salamandre, La. Bulle Ogier. Directed by Alain Tanner. 1971. Switzerland. 125 min. Sound. 16mm B&W. subtitles. *Rental:* New Yorker Films.

Salammbo. 1914. Italy. (Tinted sequences). 75 min. Silent. 16mm B&W. *Rental:* Em Gee Film Lib. *Rental:* Em Gee Film Lib, Silent B&W 16mm version.

Salivation of Professor Bizarrov. 1978. 70 min. Sound. 16mm Color. *Rental:* Canyon Cinema.

Sallah. Haym Topol. Directed by Ephraim Kishon. Hebrew. 1965. Israel. 105 min. Sound. 16mm B&W. *Rental:* Budget Films, Charard Motion Pics, Modern Sound, Westcoast Films & Willoughby Peer.

Sally & St. Anne. Ann Blyth & Edmund Gwenn. Directed by Rudolph Mate. 1952. Universal. 90 min. Sound. 16mm B&W. *Rental:* Swank Motion.

Sally, Irene & Mary. Alice Faye & Tony Martin. Directed by William A. Seiter. 1938. Fox. 90 min. Sound. 16mm B&W. *Rental:* Films Inc.

Sally of the Sawdust. W. C. Fields. Directed by D. W. Griffith. 1925. United Artists. 92 min. Sound. 16mm B&W. *Rental:* A Twyman Pres, Budget Films & Killiam Collect. *Sale:* Blackhawk Films. *Sale:* Morcraft Films, Super 8 sound version. *Sale:* Blackhawk Films, Super 8 silent version.

Sally's Irish Rose. Julie Harris. Directed by George Pollack. 1958. 16mm *Rental:* A Twyman Pres.

Salo. Orig. Title: One Hundred & Twenty Days of Sodom. Paolo Bonacelli & Giorgio Cataldi. Directed by Pier Paolo Pasolini. Ital. 1977. Italy. 117 min. Sound. 16mm Color. subtitles. *Rental:* MGM United.

Salome. Alla Nazimova & Mitchell Lewis. Directed by Charles Bryant. 1923. Nazimova. 45 min. Sound. 16mm B&W. *Rental:* A Twyman Pres, Budget Films, Em Gee Film Lib, Kit Parker, Natl Film Video & Twyman Films. *Sale:* Cinema Concepts. *Sale:* Cinema Concepts, Griggs Movie & Select Film,

Salome. Rita Hayworth & Charles Laughton. Directed by William Dieterle. 1953. Columbia. 103 min. Sound. 16mm Color. *Rental:* Budget Films, Cine Craft, Bosco Films, Films Inc, Film Pres, Kit Parker, Westcoast Films & Welling Motion Pictures.

Salome, Where She Danced. Rod Cameron & Yvonne De Carlo. 1945. Universal. 90 min. Sound. 16mm Color. *Rental:* Classic Film Mus. *Sale:* Natl Cinema.

Salt & Pepper. Sammy Davis Jr. & Peter Lawford. Directed by Richard Donner. 1968. Britain. 101 min. Sound. 16mm Color. *Rental:* Budget Films, Films Inc & MGM United.

Salt for Svanetia. Directed by Mikhail Kalatozov. 1930. Russia. (Cast unlisted). 54 min. Silent. 16mm B&W. *Rental:* Museum Mod Art. *Lease:* Museum Mod Art.

Salt Lake Raiders. Allan Lane. Directed by Fred C. Brannon. 1950. Republic. 60 min. Sound. 16mm B&W. *Rental:* Ivy Films. *Sale:* Rep Pic Film.

Salt of the Earth. 1949. Cathedral. (Cast Unlisted). 50 min. Sound. 16mm B&W. *Rental:* Roas Films.

Salt of the Earth. Resaura Revueltas. Directed by Herbert Biberman. 1954. Independent. 94 min. Sound. 16mm B&W. *Rental:* Films Inc, Macmillan Films & Museum Mod Art.

Salty. Mark Slade & Nina Foch. Directed by Ricou Browning. 1974. Salt Water. 85 min. Sound. 16mm Color. *Rental:* Budget Films, Cine Craft, Williams Films, Films Inc, Roas Films, Video Comm & Wholesome Film Ctr.

Salty O'Rourke. Alan Ladd & Gail Russell. Directed by Raoul Walsh. 1945. Paramount. 99 min. Sound. 16mm B&W. *Rental:* Swank Motion.

Salut! J. W. Ian Ireland & Louise Lapare. Directed by Ian Ireland. 1978. Canada. 86 min. Sound. 16mm Color. subtitles. *Rental:* Natl Film CN. *Sale:* Natl Film CN.

Salut L'Artiste. Marcello Mastroianni & Francoise Fabian. Directed by Yves Robert. 1977. France. 102 min. Sound. 16mm Color. *Rental:* J Green Pics. *Rental:* J Green Pics, Dubbed version. *Sale:* Tamarelles French Film, Videotape version.

Salute John Citizen. Peggy Cummins & Stanley Holloway. Directed by Maurice Elvey. 1947. Britain. 74 min. Sound. 16mm B&W. *Rental:* Ivy Films.

Salute to Stan Laurel, A. 1965. (Kinescope). 60 min. Sound. 16mm B&W. *Sale:* Cinema Concepts.

Salvage Gang, The. Ali Allen & Amanda Coxell. Directed by John Krish. 1962. Britain. 52 min. Sound. 16mm B&W. *Rental:* Films Inc, Syracuse U Film & Wholesome Film Ctr. *Sale:* Lucerne Films.

Salvajes, Los. Orig. Title: Savages, The. Pedro Armendariz. Directed by Rafael Baledon. Span. 1955. Mexico. 83 min. Sound. 16mm B&W. subtitles. *Rental:* Trans-World Films.

Salvation Hunters. George K. Arthur & Georgia Hale. Directed by Josef Von Sternberg. 1925. United Artists. 60 min. Silent. 16mm B&W. *Rental:* Kit Parker.

Salvatore Giuliano. 1964. Italy. (Documentary). 123 min. Sound. 16mm B&W. narrated Eng. *Rental:* Swank Motion.

Salzburg Connection, The. Barry Newman & Anna Karina. Directed by Lee Katzin. 1972. Fox. 93 min. Sound. 16mm Color. *Rental:* Films Inc.

Sam Francis. 1975. Blackwood. (Documentary). 52 min. Sound. 16mm Color. *Rental:* Blackwood Films. *Sale:* Blackwood Films.

Sam Houston. J. D. Cannon. Directed by Sherman Marks. (Profiles in Courage Ser.). 1965. Saudek. 52 min. Sound. 16mm B&W. *Rental:* U of IL Film & U Mich Media. *Sale:* IQ Film. *Rental:* IQ Film, *Sale:* IQ Film, Spanish dubbed version.

Sam Whiskey. Burt Reynolds & Ossie Davis. Directed by Arnold Laven. 1969. United Artists. 96 min. Sound. 16mm Color. *Rental:* MGM United.

Samar. George Montgomery, Ziva Rodann & Gilbert Roland. Directed by George Montgomery. 1962. Philippines. 102 min. Sound. 16mm Color. *Rental:* Films Inc & Video Comm. *Lease:* Video Comm.

Sambizanga. Domingos Oliviera. Directed by Sarah Maldoror. 1972. Angola. 102 min. Sound. 16mm Color. *Rental:* New Yorker Films.

Same Time, Next Year. Ellen Burstyn & Alan Alda. Directed by Robert Mulligan. 1978. Universal. 119 min. Sound. 16mm Color. *Rental:* Swank Motion. *Rental:* Swank Motion, Videotape version.

Sammy, the Way-Out Seal. Jack Carson, Robert Culp & Patricia Barry. 1963. Disney. 86 min. Sound. 16mm Color. *Rental:* Buchan Films, Cine Craft, Cousino Visual Ed, Williams Films, Bosco Films, Disney Prod, Elliot Film Co, Films Inc, U of IL Film, MGM United, Modern Sound, Newman Film Lib, Roas Films, Swank Motion, Williams Films & Twyman Films.

Sammy's Super T-Shirt. 1979. Britain. (Cast unlisted). 59 min. Sound. 16mm Color. *Rental:* Lucerne Films. *Sale:* Lucerne Films.

Samourai, Le. Alain Delon & Nathalie Delon. Directed by Jean-Pierre Melville. Fr. 1967. France. 109 min. Sound. 16mm Color. subtitles. *Rental:* Films Inc.

Samskara: A Rite for A Dead Man. 1969. 120 min. Sound. 16mm B&W. *Rental:* Iowa Films.

Samson. Brad Harris. 1961. Italy. 100 min. Sound. 16mm B&W. *Rental:* Welling Motion Pictures.

Samson. Serge Merlin & Alina Janowska. Directed by Andrzej Wajda. Pol. 1961. Poland. 119 min. Sound. 16mm B&W. subtitles. *Rental:* Films Inc.

Samson & Delilah. Hedy Lamarr & Victor Mature. Directed by Cecil B. DeMille. 1949. Paramount. 120 min. Sound. 16mm Color. *Rental:* Films Inc, Modern Sound & Wholesome Film Ctr.

Samson & Delilah. Victor Jory & Ann Turkel. Directed by James L. Conway. 1979. NBC. 52 min. Sound. 16mm Color. *Sale:* Lucerne Films. *Rental:* Budget Films. *Sale:* Lucerne Films, Videotape version.

Samson & Gideon. Anton Geesink. 81 min. Sound. 16mm Color. *Rental:* Westcoast Films.

Samson & the Seven Miracles of the World. Gordon Scott & Yoko Tani. Directed by Riccardo Freda. 1962. Italy. 80 min. Sound. 16mm Color. dubbed. *Rental:* Charard Motion Pics, Films Inc, Westcoast Films & Willoughby Peer.

Samuel Beckett: Waiting for Godot-Contemporary Theater. Zero Mostel & Burgess Meredith. 1976. Films for the Humanities. 50 min. Sound. 16mm B&W. *Rental:* Films Human. *Sale:* Films Human. *Rental:* Films Human, *Sale:* Films Human, Color version.

Samurai: Part One. Toshiro Mifune. Directed by Hiroshi Inagaki. Jap. 1952. Japan. 92 min. Sound. 16mm B&W. subtitles. *Rental:* Films Inc.

Samurai: Part Three. Toshiro Mifune. Jap. 1956. Japan. 105 min. Sound. 16mm Color. subtitles. *Rental:* Films Inc.

Samurai: Part Two. Trans. Title: Musashi Miyamoto. Toshiro Mifune. Jap. 1954. Japan. 102 min. Sound. 16mm Color. subtitles. *Rental:* Films Inc.

Samurai Spy. Kohj Takahashi & Mutsuhiro Toura. Directed by Masahiro Shinoda. Jap. 1965. Shochiku. 99 min. Sound. 16mm B&W. subtitles. *Rental:* Films Inc.

San Antone. Rod Cameron & Forrest Tucker. Directed by Joseph Kane. 1952. Republic. 90 min. Sound. 16mm B&W. *Rental:* Ivy Films. *Sale:* Rep Pic Film.

San Antone Ambush. Monte Hale. Directed by Philip Ford. 1949. Republic. 60 min. Sound. 16mm B&W. *Rental:* Ivy Films. *Sale:* Rep Pic Film & Nostalgia Merchant.

San Antonio. Errol Flynn & Alexis Smith. Directed by David Butler. 1945. Warners. 111 min. Sound. 16mm Color. *Rental:* MGM United.

San Antonio Kid, The. Bill Elliott. Directed by Howard Bretherton. 1944. Republic. 54 min. Sound. 16mm B&W. *Rental:* Ivy Films & Rep Pic Film. *Sale:* Rep Pic Film & Nostalgia Merchant.

San Demetrio London. Walter Fitzgerald & Mervyn Johns. Directed by Charles Frend. 1943. Britain. 90 min. Sound. 16mm B&W. *Rental:* Liberty Co.

San Diego, I Love You. Jon Hall & Louise Albritton. Directed by Reginald Le Borg. 1944. Universal. 83 min. Sound. 16mm B&W. *Rental:* Swank Motion.

San Fernando Valley. Roy Rogers. Directed by John English. 1944. Republic. 54 min. Sound. 16mm B&W. *Rental:* Ivy Films. *Sale:* Rep Pic Film.

San Francisco. Clark Gable, Jeanette MacDonald & Spencer Tracy. Directed by W. S. Van Dyke. 1936. MGM. 115 min. Sound. 16mm B&W. *Rental:* MGM United.

San Francisco Good Times. Directed by Allan Francovich & Eugene Roscow. 1974. Unifilm. (Documentary). 60 min. Sound. 16mm B&W. *Sale:* Cinema Guild.

San Francisco Story, The. Joel McCrea & Yvonne De Carlo. Directed by Robert Parrish. 1952. Warners. 80 min. Sound. 16mm B&W. *Rental:* Modern Sound.

San Quentin. Humphrey Bogart & Ann Sheridan. Directed by Lloyd Bacon. 1937. Warners. 70 min. Sound. 16mm B&W. *Rental:* MGM United.

San Quentin. Lawrence Tierney & Barton MacLane. Directed by Gordon Douglas. 1946. RKO. 64 min. Sound. 16mm B&W. *Rental:* Films Inc.

Sanctuary. Lee Remick & Yves Montand. Directed by Tony Richardson. 1961. Fox. 90 min. Sound. 16mm B&W. *Rental:* Films Inc. *Rental:* Willoughby Peer, Anamorphic version.

Sanctuary. 58 min. Sound. Videotape *Rental:* PBS Video. *Sale:* PBS Video.

Sand. Mark Stevens & Rory Calhoun. Directed by Louis King. 1949. Fox. 88 min. Sound. 16mm B&W. *Rental:* Films Inc.

Sand Castle, The. Barry Cardwell. Directed by Jerome Hill. 1961. De Rochemont. 65 min. Sound. 16mm Color. *Rental:* Filmmakers Coop.

Sand Pebbles, The. Steve McQueen & Richard Attenborough. Directed by Robert Wise. 1966. Fox. 195 min. Sound. 16mm Color. *Rental:* Films Inc. *Rental:* Films Inc, Anamorphic version.

Sandakan Eight. Directed by Kei Kumai. Jap. 1977. Japan. (Cast unlisted). 120 min. Sound. 16mm Color. subtitles. *Rental:* Kino Intl. *Sale:* Kino Intl.

Sanders. Richard Todd. 1964. South Africa. 84 min. Sound. 16mm B&W. *Rental:* Ivy Films.

Sanders of the River. Orig. Title: Bosambo. Paul Robeson & Leslie Banks. Directed by Zoltan Korda. 1935. United Artists. 80 min. Sound. 16mm B&W. *Rental:* Budget Films & Em Gee Film Lib. *Sale:* Cinema Concepts & Classic Film Mus. *Sale:* Tamarelles French Film, Videotape version.

Sandino, Today & Forever. Directed by Jan Kees de Rooy. 1981. 55 min. 16mm Color. *Rental:* Icarus Films. *Sale:* Icarus Films, Videotape version.

Sandokan Fights Back. Ray Danton & Guy Madison. Directed by Luigi Capuano. 1964. Italy. 96 min. Sound. 16mm Color. *Rental:* Budget Films, Video Comm & Westcoast Films.

Sandokan the Great. Steve Reeves. Directed by Umberto Lenzi. 1965. MGM. 110 min. Sound. 16mm Color. *Rental:* MGM United.

Sandpiper, The. Richard Burton & Elizabeth Taylor. Directed by Vincente Minnelli. 1965. MGM. (Anamorphic). 116 min. Sound. 16mm Color. *Rental:* MGM United. *Rental:* MGM United, Videotape version.

Sandra. Trans. Title: Vaghe Stelle Dell'Orsa. Claudia Cardinale. Directed by Luchino Visconti. 1966. Italy. 100 min. Sound. 16mm B&W. *Rental:* Corinth Films & Swank Motion.

Sands of Iwo Jima, The. John Wayne & Forrest Tucker. Directed by Allan Dwan. 1949. Republic. 109 min. Sound. B&W. *Rental:* Budget Films, Ivy Films & Welling Motion Pictures. *Lease:* Rep Pic Film. *Sale:* Blackhawk Films, Cinema Concepts & Ivy Films, Videotape version.

Sands of the Kalahari, The. Stuart Whitman & Stanley Baker. Directed by Cy Endfield. 1965. Paramount. 119 min. Sound. 16mm Color. *Rental:* Films Inc.

Sandy Burke of U Bar U. Louis Bennison. Directed by Ira M. Lowry. 1919. Goldwyn. 55 min. Silent. 16mm B&W. *Sale:* E Finney.

Sangaree. Fernando Lamas & Arlene Dahl. Directed by Edward Ludwig. 1953. Paramount. 95 min. Sound. 16mm B&W. *Rental:* Video Comm & Willoughby Peer.

Sanjuro. Toshiro Mifune. Directed by Akira Kurosawa. Jap. 1962. Japan. 96 min. Sound. 16mm B&W. subtitles. *Rental:* Budget Films & Films Inc. *Sale:* Festival Films. *Sale:* Festival Films, Videotape version.

Sans Soleil. Directed by Chris Marker. 1982. 100 min. Sound. 16mm Color. *Rental:* New Yorker Films.

Sanshiro Sugata. Susuma Fujita & Denjiro Okoohi. Directed by Akira Kurosawa. Jap. 1943. Japan. 80 min. Sound. 16mm B&W. subtitles Eng. *Rental:* Films Inc.

Sansho the Bailiff. Directed by Kenji Mizoguchi. Jap. 1954. Japan. 119 min. Sound. 16mm B&W. subtitles. *Rental:* Budget Films, Films Inc & Kit Parker. *Sale:* Festival Films & Natl Cinema.

Santa & the Three Bears. 1977. Modern Sound. (Animated). 50 min. Sound. 16mm Color. *Rental:* Budget Films & Modern Sound. *Sale:* Modern Sound.

Santa Claus Action, The. Directed by Jon Bang Carlsen. 1979. Green Mountain Post. (Documentary). 45 min. Sound. 16mm Color. *Rental:* Green Mt.

Santa Claus Conquers the Martians. John Call & Leonard Hicks. Directed by Nicholas Webster. 1966. American International. 80 min. Sound. 16mm Color. *Rental:* Films Inc.

Santa Fe. Randolph Scott & Janis Carter. Directed by Irving Pichel. 1951. Columbia. 89 min. Sound. 16mm Color. *Rental:* Cine Craft.

Santa Fe Bound. Tom Tyler. Directed by Harry S. Webb. 1936. Reliable. 60 min. Sound. 16mm B&W. *Sale:* Morcraft Films.

Santa Fe Marshal. William Boyd. Directed by Lesley Selander. 1940. Paramount. 60 min. Sound. 16mm B&W. *Sale:* Cinema Concepts.

Santa Fe Passage. John Payne & Rod Cameron. Directed by William Witney. 1954. Republic. 90 min. Sound. 16mm B&W. *Rental:* Ivy Films. *Sale:* Rep Pic Film.

Santa Fe Saddlemates. Sunset Carson. Directed by Thomas Carr. 1945. Republic. 54 min. Sound. 16mm B&W. *Rental:* Ivy Films. *Sale:* Rep Pic Film & Nostalgia Merchant.

Santa Fe Satan. Richie Havens & Susan Tyrell. Directed by Patrick McGoohan. New Line Cinema. 100 min. Sound. 16mm Color. *Rental:* New Line Cinema.

Santa Fe Scouts. Tom Tyler & Bob Steele. Directed by Howard Bretherton. 1943. Republic. 55 min. Sound. 16mm B&W. *Rental:* Ivy Films. *Sale:* Rep Pic Film.

Santa Fe Stampede. John Wayne. Directed by George Sherman. 1938. Republic. 55 min. Sound. 16mm B&W. *Rental:* Ivy Films. *Sale:* Rep Pic Film & Nostalgia Merchant.

Santa Fe Trail. Errol Flynn & Olivia De Havilland. Directed by Michael Curtiz. 1940. Warners. 110 min. Sound. 16mm B&W. *Rental:* Budget Films, Kit Parker, MGM United, Modern Sound & Roas Films. *Sale:* Cinema Concepts, Festival Films & Morcraft Films, Super 8 sound version. *Rental:* Classic Film Mus, 90 mins version. *Sale:* Festival Films & Tamarelles French Film, Videotape version.

Santa Fe Uprising. Allan Lane. Directed by R. G. Springsteen. 1946. Republic. 54 min. Sound. 16mm B&W. *Rental:* Ivy Films. *Sale:* Nostalgia Merchant.

Santee. Glenn Ford & Dana Wynter. Directed by Gary Nelson. 1972. Vagabond. 93 min. Sound. 16mm Color. *Rental:* Films Inc.

Santiago's Ark. Ruben Figueroa. Directed by Albert C. Waller. 1972. ABC. 47 min. Sound. 16mm Color. *Rental:* Budget Films, Iowa Films & Syracuse U Film.

Saphead, The. Buster Keaton & Irving Cummings. Directed by Herbert Blache. 1921. Metro. (Tinted). 70 min. Sound. 16mm *Rental:* Twyman Films.

Sappho. 1979. 50 min. Sound. 16mm Color. *Rental:* Canyon Cinema.

Sapporo: Planned Growth. 1975. Canada. (Documentary). 57 min. Sound. 16mm Color. *Rental:* U Cal Media.

Saps at Sea. Stan Laurel & Oliver Hardy. Directed by Gordon Douglas. 1940. Hal Roach. 57 min. Sound. 16mm B&W. *Rental:* Budget Films, Williams Films, Em Gee Film Lib, Films Inc, Modern Sound, Film Images, Roas Films, Swank Motion, Film Ctr DC, Twyman Films, Welling Motion Pictures, Westcoast Films, Wholesome Film Ctr & Willoughby Peer. *Sale:* Blackhawk Films. *Sale:* Blackhawk Films, Super 8 sound version. *Sale:* Blackhawk Films, Super 8 silent version. *Rental:* Welling Motion Pictures, 70 mins. version.

Saracen Blade, The. Ricardo Montalban & Rick Jason. Directed by William Castle. 1954. Columbia. 76 min. Sound. 16mm Color. *Rental:* Modern Sound.

Sarah T: Portrait of a Teenage Alcoholic. Linda Blair & Verna Bloom. Directed by Richard Donner. 1975. NBC. 100 min. Sound. 16mm Color. *Rental:* Swank Motion.

Saratoga. Jean Harlow, Clark Gable & Walter Pidgeon. Directed by Jack Conway. 1937. MGM. 94 min. Sound. 16mm B&W. *Rental:* MGM United.

Sarge Goes to College. Alan Hale Jr. & Freddie Stewart. Directed by Will Jason. 1947. Monogram. 63 min. Sound. 16mm B&W. *Rental:* Hurlock Cine.

Sarumba. Doris Dowling & Michael Whalen. Directed by Marion Gering. 1950. Britain. 68 min. Sound. 16mm B&W. *Rental:* Film Classics.

Saskatchewan. Alan Ladd & Shelley Winters. Directed by Raoul Walsh. 1954. Universal. 87 min. Sound. 16mm Color. *Rental:* Swank Motion.

Saskatoon: Land & Growth Control. 1975. Canada. (Documentary). 57 min. Sound. 16mm Color. *Rental:* U Cal Media.

Sasquatch Amongst Us. 1973. 48 min. Sound. 16mm B&W. *Rental:* Canyon Cinema.

Sasquatch: The Legend of Bigfoot. 1978. American National. 94 min. Sound. 16mm Color. *Rental:* Westcoast Films, Videotape version.

Satan Bug, The. George Maharis & Richard Basehart. Directed by John Sturges. 1965. United Artists. 114 min. Sound. 16mm Color. *Rental:* Budget Films, Films Inc, MGM United, Westcoast Films & Welling Motion Pictures.

Satan Met a Lady. Bette Davis & Warren William. Directed by William Beaudine. 1936. Warners. 74 min. Sound. 16mm B&W. *Rental:* MGM United.

Satan Never Sleeps. William Holden & Clifton Webb. Directed by Leo McCarey. 1962. Fox. 126 min. Sound. 16mm Color. *Rental:* Films Inc. *Rental:* Films Inc, Anamorphic version.

Satanik. Magda Konopka. Directed by Piero Vivarelli. 1969. Allied Artists. 85 min. 16mm Color. dubbed. *Sale:* Blackhawk Films.

Satanis: The Devil's Mass. Directed by Ray Laurent. 1972. Sherpix. (Documentary). 70 min. Sound. 16mm Color. *Rental:* Budget Films.

Satan's Brew. Margit Carstensen & Kurt Raab. Directed by Rainer Werner Fassbinder. Ger. 1976. Germany. 110 min. Sound. 16mm Color. subtitles. *Rental:* New Cinema & New Yorker Films.

Satan's Cheerleaders. John Ireland & Yvonne De Carlo. Directed by Irving Pichel. 1977. 92 min. Sound. 16mm Color. *Rental:* Films Inc.

Satan's Cradle. Duncan Renaldo. Directed by Wallace Fox. 1949. United Artists. 16mm B&W. *Sale:* Video Comm.

Satan's Harvest. George Montgomery & Tippi Hedren. Directed by Ferde Grofe Jr. 1956. South Africa. 88 min. Sound. 16mm Color. *Rental:* Video Comm. *Lease:* Video Comm.

Satan's Satellites. Leonard Nimoy. Directed by Fred C. Brannon. 1958. Republic. 70 min. Sound. 16mm B&W. *Rental:* Ivy Films. *Sale:* Rep Pic Film.

Satellite in the Sky. Kieron Moore, Sir Donald Wolfit. Directed by Paul Dickson. 1956. Britain. 85 min. Sound. 16mm B&W. *Rental:* Charard Motion Pics.

Saturday Morning. Directed by Kent MacKenzie. 1971. Columbia. 89 min. Sound. 16mm Color. *Rental:* Churchill Films, Mass Media, Swank Motion & Twyman Films. *Rental:* Churchill Films, Videotape version.

Saturday Night & Sunday Morning. Albert Finney & Rachael Roberts. Directed by Karel Reisz. 1961. Britain. 90 min. Sound. 16mm B&W. *Rental:* Budget Films & Corinth Films. *Sale:* Morcraft Films. *Sale:* Morcraft Films, Super 8 sound version.

Saturday Night Fever. John Travolta & Karen Gorney. Directed by John Badham. 1977. Paramount. 118 min. Sound. Color. *Rental:* Films Inc. *Sale:* Cinema Concepts, Videotape version.

Saturday the Fourteenth. Richard Benjamin & Paula Prentiss. Directed by Howard R. Cohen. 1981. New World. 79 min. Sound. 16mm Color. *Rental:* Films Inc.

Saturday's Children. John Garfield & Anne Shirley. Directed by Vincent Sherman. 1949. Columbia. 101 min. Sound. 16mm B&W. *Rental:* MGM United.

Saturday's Hero. Orig. Title: Idols in the Dust. John Derek & Donna Reed. Directed by David Miller. 1951. Columbia. 111 min. Sound. 16mm B&W. *Rental:* Budget Films, Cine Craft, Films Inc & Newman Film Lib.

Saturday's Heroes. Van Heflin & Marian Marsh. Directed by Edward Killy. 1938. RKO. 66 min. Sound. 16mm B&W. *Rental:* RKO General Pics.

Saturn Three. Farrah Fawcett & Kirk Douglas. Directed by Stanley Donen. 1980. Britain. 111 min. Sound. 16mm Color. *Rental:* Swank Motion.

Satyajit Ray. 1978. American Film Institute. 55 min. 16mm Color. *Sale:* Am Film Inst.

Saudis, The. 1982. Phoenix. (Documentary). 49 min. Videotape Color. *Sale:* Phoenix Films.

Saul Alinsky Went to War. Orig. Title: Allinsky Went to War. 1969. 57 min. Sound. 16mm B&W. *Rental:* McGraw-Hill Films & U Mich Media. *Sale:* McGraw-Hill Films.

Savage, The. Charlton Heston & Susan Morrow. Directed by George Marshall. 1952. Paramount. 95 min. Sound. 16mm Color. *Rental:* Films Inc.

Savage Drums. Sabu & Lita Baron. Directed by William Berke. 1951. Lippert. 70 min. Sound. 16mm Color. *Rental:* Budget Films, Mogulls Films & Film Ctr DC.

Savage Eye, The. Barbara Baxley & Gary Merrill. Directed by Ben Maddow. 1959. 67 min. Sound. 16mm B&W. *Rental:* Films Inc.

Savage Frontier, The. Allan Lane. Directed by Harry Keller. 1953. Republic. 54 min. Sound. 16mm B&W. *Rental:* Ivy Films. *Sale:* Rep Pic Film & Nostalgia Merchant.

Savage Fury. Orig. Title: Call of the Savage. Noah Berry Jr. Directed by Lew Landers. 1935. Universal. 70 min. Sound. 16mm B&W. *Sale:* Morcraft Films.

Savage Gang, The. Ali Allen & Amanda Coxell. Directed by John Krish. 1962. Britain. 52 min. Sound. 16mm B&W. *Rental:* Films Inc.

Savage Guns. Richard Basehart & Don Taylor. Directed by Michael Carreras. 1962. MGM. 73 min. Sound. 16mm Color. *Rental:* MGM United. *Rental:* MGM United, Anamorphic version.

Savage Harvest. Tom Skerritt & Michelle Phillips. Directed by Robert Collins. 1981. Fox. 86 min. Sound. 16mm Color. *Rental:* Films Inc.

Savage Horde, The. Jim Davis & Adrian Booth. Directed by Joseph Kane. 1949. Republic. 90 min. Sound. 16mm B&W. *Rental:* Ivy Films. *Sale:* Rep Pic Film.

Savage Innocents. Anthony Quinn & Yoko Tani. Directed by Nicholas Ray. 1960. Paramount. 90 min. Sound. 16mm Color. *Rental:* Films Inc.

Savage Is Loose, The. George C. Scott & Trish Van Devere. Directed by George C. Scott. 1974. Campbell Devon. 114 min. Sound. 16mm Color. *Rental:* Twyman Films.

Savage Messiah, The. Dorothy Tutin & Scott Antony. Directed by Ken Russell. 1972. MGM. 100 min. Sound. 16mm Color. *Rental:* MGM United.

Savage Mutiny, The. Johnny Weismuller. Directed by Spencer G. Bennett. 1953. Columbia. 65 min. Sound. 16mm B&W. *Rental:* Inst Cinema.

Savage Pampas. Robert Taylor & Ty Hardin. Directed by Hugo Fregonese. 1966. Argentina. 97 min. Sound. 16mm Color. dubbed. *Rental:* Films Inc. *Rental:* Films Inc, Anamorphic version.

Savage Sam. Tommy Kirk, Marta Kristen & Brian Keith. Directed by Norman Tokar. 1963. Disney. 104 min. Sound. 16mm Color. *Rental:* Buchan Pic, Cine Craft, Cousino Visual Ed, Williams Films, Bosco Films, Disney Prod, Elliot Film Co, Films Inc, U of IL Film, MGM United, Modern Sound, Newman Film Lib, Roas Films, Swank Motion, Film Ctr DC, Twyman Films, Westcoast Films & Welling Motion Pictures.

Savage Season. Orig. Title: Dead Heat. Diane McBain & Victor Buono. 1970. Commonwealth. 96 min. Sound. 16mm Color. *Rental:* Ivy Films, Rep Pic Film & Video Comm. *Lease:* Rep Pic Film.

Savage Seven, The. Robert Walker. Directed by Richard Rush. 1968. American International. 96 min. Sound. 16mm Color. *Rental:* Video Comm & Westcoast Films.

Savage Sisters. Gloria Hendry & Cheri Caffaro. 1974. American International. 89 min. Sound. 16mm Color. *Rental:* Swank Motion.

Savage Splendor. Directed by Armand Denis & Lewis Cotlow. 1949. RKO. (Documentary). 61 min. Sound. 16mm Color. *Rental:* Films Inc.

Savage Wild, The. Directed by Gordon Eastman. 1970. American International. (Documentary). 103 min. Sound. 16mm Color. *Rental:* Budget Films & Films Inc.

Savages, The *see* Salvajes.

Savages. Louis J. Stadlen & Ultra Violet. Directed by James Ivory. 1972. Ismail Merchant. 110 min. Sound. 16mm Color. *Rental:* Corinth Films & New Yorker Films.

Savages of the Sea. Frank Merrill. Directed by Bruce Mitchell. 1973. Barsky. 75 min. Sound. 16mm B&W. *Rental:* Em Gee Film Lib. *Sale:* Glenn Photo. *Sale:* Glenn Photo, Super 8 silent version.

Savannah Smiles. Bridgette Andersen & Mark Miller. Directed by Pierre DeMaro. 1982. Embassy. 105 min. Sound. 16mm Color. *Rental:* Films Inc. *Sale:* Tamarelles French Film, Videotape version.

Save the Panda. 59 min. Sound. 16mm Color. *Rental:* National Geographic Society, Video version.

Save the Tiger. Jack Lemmon & Jack Gilford. Directed by John G. Avildsen. 1973. Paramount. 101 min. Sound. 16mm Color. *Rental:* Films Inc.

Saving Teeth for Lifetime Service: Foundations for Restorations & Cavity Liners. 1982. 58 min. Sound. Videotape Color. *Rental:* Natl AV Ctr.

Saving Teeth for Lifetime Service: Pin Retention of Amalgam Foundations & Restorations. 1982. 107 min. Sound. Videotape Color. *Sale:* Natl AV Ctr.

Saving Teeth for Lifetime Service: Prevention Is A Prerequisite To Dental Health. 1982. 59 min. Sound. Videotape Color. *Sale:* Natl AV Ctr.

Saving Teeth for Lifetime Service: Restoration & Maintenance of Class. 1982. 101 min. Sound. Videotape Color. *Sale:* Natl AV Ctr.

Say Amen, Somebody. Willie Mae & Ford Smith. Directed by George T. Nierenberg. 1983. MGM-UA. 100 min. Sound. 16mm Color. *Rental:* MGM United. *Rental:* MGM United, Videotape version.

Say Brother Special: The Nation of Islam. 1979. PBS. 60 min. Color. *Rental:* PBS Video. *Sale:* PBS Video.

Say Goodbye. 1970. Wolper. (Documentary). 52 min. Sound. 16mm Color. *Rental:* Films Inc, U of IL Film, U Mich Media & Syracuse U Film.

Say It With Music. 1975. Ken Anderson. (Cast unlisted). 50 min. Sound. 16mm Color. *Rental:* G Herne & Roas Films.

Say It With Music. Jack Payne Band. Directed by Jack Raymond. 1932. 16mm *Rental:* A Twyman Pres.

Say It With Sables. Francis X. Bushman & Helene Chadwick. Directed by Frank Capra. 1928. Columbia. 70 min. Sound. 16mm Color. *Rental:* Kit Parker.

Say It With Songs. Al Jolson & Marian Nixon. Directed by Lloyd Bacon. 1929. Warners. 87 min. Sound. 16mm B&W. *Rental:* MGM United.

Say One for Me. Bing Crosby & Debbie Reynolds. Directed by Frank Tashlin. 1959. Fox. 119 min. Sound. 16mm Color. *Rental:* Films Inc, Rep Pic Film, Swank Motion & Westcoast Films. *Rental:* Video Comm, Anamorphic color version.

Sayonara. Marlon Brando, Red Buttons & Myoshi Umeki. Directed by Joshua Logan. 1957. Warners. 147 min. 16mm Color. *Rental:* Films Inc & Twyman Films.

Scala, La. 1957. Warners. (Documentary). 60 min. Sound. 16mm Color. *Rental:* Corinth Films.

Scalawag. Kirk Douglas & Mark Lester. Directed by Kirk Douglas. 1974. Paramount. 93 min. Sound. 16mm Color. *Rental:* Films Inc.

Scalpel, The. Orig. Title: False Faces. Robert Lansing & Judith Chapman. Directed by John Grissmer. 1978. Embassy. 95 min. Sound. 16mm Color. *Rental:* Films Inc.

Scalphunters, The. Burt Lancaster & Shelley Winters. Directed by Sydney Pollack. 1968. United Artists. 102 min. Sound. 16mm Color. *Rental:* MGM United.

Scampolo. Romy Schneider & Paul Christian. Directed by Alfred Weidenmann. 1961. Germany. 95 min. Sound. 16mm Color. dubbed. *Rental:* Ivy Films.

Scamps *see* Strange Affection.

Scandal. Toshiro Mifune & Yoshiko Yamaguchi. Directed by Akira Kurosawa. Jap. 1950. Japan. 105 min. Sound. 16mm B&W. subtitles. *Rental:* Films Inc.

Scandal at Scourie. Greer Garson & Walter Pidgeon. Directed by Jean Negulesco. 1953. MGM. 89 min. Sound. 16mm B&W. *Rental:* MGM United. *Rental:* MGM United, Color version.

Scandal in Sorrento. Sophia Loren & Vittorio De Sica. Directed by Dino Risi. 1955. Italy. 92 min. Sound. 16mm Color. *Rental:* Ivy Films.

Scandal, Inc. Robert Hutton. Directed by Edward Mann. 1957. Republic. 80 min. Sound. 16mm B&W. *Rental:* Ivy Films. *Sale:* Rep Pic Film.

Scandal Sheet. Orig. Title: Dark Page, The. Broderick Crawford & Donna Reed. Directed by Phil Karlson. 1952. Columbia. 90 min. Sound. 16mm B&W. *Rental:* Inst Cinema & Kit Parker.

Scandalous Adventures of Buraikan, The. Tatsuya Nakadai. Directed by Masahiro Shinoda. Jap. 1970. Japan. (Anamorphic). 103 min. Sound. 16mm Color. subtitles. *Rental:* Corinth Films.

Scanners. Jennifer O'Neill & Stephen Lack. Directed by David Cronenberg. 1981. Embassy. 103 min. Sound. 16mm Color. *Rental:* Films Inc.

Scapegoat, The. Sir Alec Guinness & Nicole Maurey. Directed by Robert Hamer. 1959. Britain. 92 min. Sound. 16mm B&W. *Rental:* MGM United.

Scar, The. Orig. Title: Man Who Murdered Himself, The. Paul Henried & Joan Bennett. Directed by Steve Sekely. 1948. Eagle Lion. 83 min. Sound. 16mm B&W. *Rental:* Budget Films & Ivy Films. *Sale:* Rep Pic Film.

Scar of Shame, The. Harry Henderson & Lucia Moses. Directed by Oscar Micheaux. 1927. Colored Players Pictures. 69 min. Sound. 16mm B&W. *Rental:* Budget Films, Em Gee Film Lib & Standard Film.

Scaramouche. Stewart Granger & Eleanor Parker. Directed by George Sidney. 1952. MGM. 115 min. Sound. 16mm Color. *Rental:* MGM United.

Scarecrow. Gene Hackman & Al Pacino. Directed by Jerry Schatzberg. 1973. Warners. (Anamorphic). 112 min. Sound. 16mm Color. *Rental:* Films Inc, Swank Motion, Twyman Films & Williams Films.

Scarecrow in a Garden of Cucumbers, A. Holly Woodlawn. Directed by Robert Kaplan. 1972. New Line. 95 min. Sound. 16mm Color. *Rental:* New Line Cinema. *Sale:* New Line Cinema.

Scared Stiff. Orig. Title: Treasure of Fear. Jack Haley. Directed by Frank McDonald. 1945. Paramount. 65 min. Sound. 16mm B&W. *Sale:* Cinema Concepts.

Scared Straight. Directed by Arnold Shapiro. 1978. Golden West. 54 min. Sound. 16mm Color. *Rental:* Budget Films, U Cal Media, U of IL Film, Pyramid Film, Syracuse U Film & Viewfinders. *Sale:* Pyramid Film. *Rental:* Pyramid Film, *Sale:* Pyramid Film, Videotape version.

Scared to Death. Bela Lugosi & George Zucco. Directed by Christy Cabanne. 1947. Screen Guild. 65 min. Sound. 16mm Color. *Rental:* Mogulls Films & Westcoast Films. *Sale:* Cinema Concepts.

Scarface. Paul Muni & Ann Dvorak. Directed by Howard Hawks. 1932. MGM. 90 min. Sound. 16mm B&W. *Rental:* MGM United.

Scarface. Al Pacino & Steven Bauer. Directed by Brian De Palma. 1983. Universal. 170 min. Sound. 16mm Color. *Rental:* Swank Motion. *Rental:* Swank Motion, *Sale:* Tamarelles French Film, Videotape version.

Scarlet Claw, The. Basil Rathbone. Directed by Roy William Neill. 1944. Universal. 74 min. Sound. 16mm B&W. *Rental:* Learning Corp Am & Video Comm. *Sale:* Learning Corp Am.

Scarlet Clue, The. Sidney Toler & Manton Moreland. Directed by Phil Rosen. 1945. Monogram. 65 min. Sound. 16mm B&W. *Rental:* MGM United.

Scarlet Coat, The. Cornel Wilde & Michael Wilding. Directed by John Sturges. 1955. MGM. 110 min. Sound. 16mm Color. *Rental:* MGM United. *Rental:* MGM United, Anamorphic version.

Scarlet Dawn, The. Douglas Fairbanks Jr. & Lilyan Tashman. Directed by William Dieterle. 1932. Warners. 58 min. Sound. 16mm B&W. *Rental:* MGM United.

Scarlet Empress, The. Marlene Dietrich & Sam Jaffe. Directed by Josef Von Sternberg. 1934. Paramount. 109 min. Sound. 16mm B&W. *Rental:* Williams Films.

Scarlet Hour, The. Carol Ohmart & Tom Tryon. Directed by Michael Curtiz. 1956. Paramount. 110 min. Sound. 16mm B&W. *Rental:* Films Inc.

Scarlet Letter, The. Stuart Holmes. Directed by Carl Harbaugh. 1917. Fox. (Music & sound effects only). 79 min. Sound. 16mm B&W. *Rental:* Film Classics.

Scarlet Letter, The. Lillian Gish & Lars Hanson. Directed by Victor Seastrom. 1926. MGM. 98 min. Silent. 16mm B&W. *Rental:* MGM United.

Scarlet Letter, The. Colleen Moore, Henry B. Wathall & William Farnum. Directed by Robert Vignola. 1934. Majestic. 85 min. Sound. 16mm B&W. *Rental:* Budget Films, Em Gee Film Lib & Film Classics. *Sale:* Morcraft Films. *Sale:* Reel Images, Super 8 sound version. *Rental:* Film Classics, Videotape version.

Scarlet Letter, The. Senta Berger & Lou Castel. Directed by Wim Wenders. Ger. 1973. Germany. 94 min. Sound. 1973 Color. subtitles. *Rental:* Liberty Co..

Scarlet Pimpernel, The. Leslie Howard & Merle Oberon. Directed by Harold Young. 1935. Britain. 95 min. Sound. 16mm B&W. *Rental:* Buchan Pic, Budget Films, Classic Film Mus, Em Gee Film Lib, Films Inc, Kit Parker, Video Comm & Wholesome Film Ctr. *Sale:* Cinema Concepts, Festival Films & Reel Images. *Sale:* Morcraft Films & Reel Images, Super 8 sound version. *Sale:* Festival Films & Tamarelles French Film, Videotape version.

Scarlet River. Betty Furness & Tom Keene. Directed by Otto Brower. 1933. RKO. 57 min. Sound. 16mm B&W. *Rental:* RKO General Pics.

Scarlet Spear. John Bentley & Martha Hyer. Directed by George Breakston. 1955. Britain. 78 min. Sound. 16mm Color. *Rental:* Charard Motion Pics & Modern Sound.

Scarlet Street. Orig. Title: Bitch, The. Edward G. Robinson & Joan Bennett. Directed by Fritz Lang. 1954. Universal. 98 min. Sound. 16mm B&W. *Rental:* Budget Films, Classic Film Mus, Corinth Films, Em Gee Film Lib, Films Inc, Images Film, Ivy Films, Kit Parker & Welling Motion Pictures. *Sale:* Cinema Concepts, Festival Films, Glenn Photo, Reel Images & Images Film. *Sale:* Festival Films, Tamarelles French Film & Images Film, Videotape version.

Scatterbrain. Judy Canova & Alan Mowbray. Directed by Gus Meins. 1940. Republic. 72 min. Sound. 16mm B&W. *Rental:* Ivy Films.

Scattergood Pulls the Strings. Orig. Title: Hidden Crime. Guy Kibbee. Directed by Christy Cabanne. 1941. RKO. 70 min. Sound. 16mm B&W. *Rental:* Buchan Pic.

Scavenger Hunt. Richard Benjamin & Ruth Gordon. Directed by Michael Schultz. 1979. Fox. 116 min. Sound. 16mm Color. *Rental:* Films Inc.

Scavengers, The. Vincent Edwards & Carol Ohmart. Directed by John Cromwell. 1959. Republic. 79 min. Sound. 16mm B&W. *Rental:* Ivy Films.

Scene Changes. 1981. 49 min. Sound. 16mm Color. *Rental:* Utah Media.

Scene of the Crime. Van Johnson & Arlene Dahl. Directed by Roy Rowland. 1949. MGM. 95 min. Sound. 16mm B&W. *Rental:* MGM United.

Scenes from a Marriage. Liv Ullmann & Bibi Anderson. Directed by Ingmar Bergman. Swed. 1974. Sweden. 168 min. Sound. 16mm Color. subtitles. *Rental:* Cinema Five & New Cinema. *Lease:* Cinema Five.

Scenes from the Class Struggle in Portugal. Trans. Title: Cenas Da Luta De Classa Em Portugal. Directed by Robert Kramer & Phillip Spinelli. 1976. Barbara & David Stone. (Documentary). 80 min. Sound. 16mm Color. *Rental:* CA Newsreel.

Scenes from Under Childhood. Directed by Stan Brakhage. 1969. Stan Brakhage. 144 min. Silent. 16mm Color. *Rental:* Canyon Cinema & Films Inc.

Scenic Route. Directed by Mark Rappaport. 1978. New Line Cinema. (Cast unlisted). 76 min. Sound. 16mm Color. *Rental:* First Run & New Line Cinema. *Lease:* First Run.

Schatten see Warning Shadows.

Scheherazade. 1920. Czechoslovakia. (Cast unlisted). 60 min. Silent. 16mm B&W. *Rental:* Film Classics. *Sale:* Film Classics. *Rental:* Film Classics, *Sale:* Film Classics, Silent 8mm version.

Scheherazade. Orig. Title: One Thousand & One Nights. Anna Karina & Gerard Barray. Directed by Henri Gaspard-Huit. 1963. France/Italy. 110 min. Sound. 16mm Color. dubbed. *Rental:* Film Ctr DC & Films Inc.

Schizo. John Leyton & Lynn Frederick. Directed by Peter Walker. 1976. 109 min. Sound. 16mm Color. *Rental:* Budget Films.

Schizoid. Florinda Bolkan, Stanley Baker & Jean Sorel. Directed by Lucio Fulci. 1972. American International. 96 min. Sound. 16mm Color. *Rental:* Swank Motion.

Schizoid. Klaus Kinski, Marianna Hill & Craig Wasson. Directed by David Paulsen. 89 min. Sound. 16mm Color. *Rental:* Swank Motion. *Rental:* Swank Motion, Videotape version.

Schizophrenia: The Shattered Mirror. 1966. NET. (Documentary). 60 min. Sound. 16mm B&W. *Rental:* U Cal Media, U of IL Film, Indiana AV Ctr, U Mich Media, SD AV Ctr & Syracuse U Film. *Sale:* Indiana AV Ctr. *Sale:* Indiana AV Ctr, Videotape version.

Schloss Vogelod *see* Haunted Castle.

School Days: A Picture of Russian Education. 1957. University of Michigan. (Documentary). 70 min. Sound. 16mm Color. *Rental:* U Mich Media.

School District Experiences in Implementing Technology. 1982. 65 min. Sound. Videotape Color. *Sale:* Natl AV Ctr.

Schubert, the Melody Master. Orig. Title: Melody Master & New Wine. Ilona Massey & Alan Curtis. Directed by Reinhold Schunzel. 1941. United Artists. 81 min. Sound. 16mm B&W. *Rental:* Budget Films, Moguls Films & Welling Motion Pictures.

Schubert's Serenade. Louis Jouvet & Lillian Harvey. Directed by Jean Boyer. Fr. 1940. France. 98 min. Sound. 16mm B&W. subtitles. *Rental:* Film Classics.

Schulmeistre Contre Schulmeistre. Jacques Fabri. Directed by Jean-Pierre Decourt. Fr. 1975. France. 52 min. Sound. 16mm Color. subtitles. *Rental:* French Am Cul. *Rental:* French Am Cul, Videotape version.

Science & the Reality of Politics, The. 1973. WNET. 58 min. Sound. 16mm Color. *Rental:* WNET Media, Videotape version.

Science Fiction Collection, The. 70 min. Sound. 16mm Color. *Rental:* Budget Films.

Science in the Seventies. 1974. US Government. (Documentary). 52 min. Sound. 16mm Color. *Sale:* Natl AV Ctr. *Sale:* Natl AV Ctr, Videotape version.

Science of Murder, The. 1974. WGBH. (Documentary). 57 min. Sound. 16mm Color. *Rental:* Time-Life Multimedia. *Sale:* Time-Life Multimedia. *Sale:* Time-Life Multimedia, Videotape version.

Scorching Fury. Kirk Flamer. Sound. 16mm B&W. dubbed. *Rental:* Charard Motion Pics.

Scorn of Women, The. 1982. EBE. (Documentary). 52 min. Sound. 16mm Color. *Sale:* Ency Brit Ed. *Rental:* Iowa Films & Ency Brit Ed. *Sale:* Ency Brit Ed, Videotape version.

Scorpio. Burt Lancaster, Paul Scotfield & Alain Delon. Directed by Michael Winner. 1973. United Artists. 114 min. Sound. 16mm Color. *Rental:* MGM United & Wholesome Film Ctr.

Scotch on the Rocks. Orig. Title: Laxdale Hall. Ronald Squire & Raymond Huntley. Directed by John Eldridge. 1954. Britain. 77 min. Sound. 16mm B&W. *Rental:* Trans-World Film.

Scotland Yard. Nancy Kelly & John Loder. Directed by Norman Foster. 1941. Fox. 68 min. Sound. 16mm B&W. *Rental:* Willoughby Peer.

Scotland Yard. 1971. NBC. (Documentary). 51 min. Sound. 16mm Color. *Rental:* Films Inc. *Sale:* Films Inc. *Sale:* Films Inc, Videotape version.

Scotland Yard Inspector. Cesar Romero & Lois Maxwell. Directed by Sam Newfield. 1952. Lippert. 73 min. Sound. 16mm B&W. *Rental:* Budget Films.

Scotland Yard Investigator. Erich Von Stroheim & C. Aubrey Smith. Directed by George Blair. 1945. Republic. 68 min. Sound. 16mm B&W. *Rental:* Ivy Films.

Scott Joplin. Billy Dee Williams & Art Carney. 1977. Universal. 92 min. Sound. 16mm Color. *Rental:* Swank Motion.

Scott of the Antarctic. John Mills & Harold Warrender. Directed by Charles Frend. 1948. Britain. 110 min. Sound. 16mm Color. *Rental:* Budget Films.

Scott's Last Journey. 1960. Britain. (Documentary). 60 min. Sound. 16mm B&W. *Rental:* U Cal Media & U of IL Film.

Scoumone. Jean-Paul Belmondo & Claudia Cardinale. 1972. France. 87 min. Color. dubbed. *Sale:* Cinema Concepts & Video Lib.

Scoundrel, The. Noel Coward & Alexander Woollcott. Directed by Ben Hecht & Charles MacArthur. 1935. Paramount. 75 min. Sound. 16mm B&W. *Rental:* Swank Motion.

Scream & Scream Again. Vincent Price & Peter Cushing. Directed by Gordon Hessler. 1970. American International. 94 min. Sound. 16mm Color. *Rental:* Video Comm, Welling Motion Pictures & Westcoast Films.

Scream, Blacula, Scream. Pam Grier & William Marshall. Directed by Bob Kelljan. 1973. American International. 96 min. Sound. 16mm Color. *Rental:* Swank Motion.

Scream in the Dark, A. Robert Lowery & Marie McDonald. Directed by George Sherman. 1943. Republic. 54 min. Sound. 16mm B&W. *Rental:* Ivy Films.

Scream In The Streets, A. Frank Bannon, Linda York & John Kirkpatrick. 71 min. Sound. 16mm Color. *Rental:* Best Film & Video.

Scream of Fear, A. Susan Strasberg & Ann Todd. Directed by Seth Holt. 1961. Britain. 81 min. Sound. 16mm B&W. *Rental:* Arcus Film, Budget Films, Charard Motion Pics, Bosco Films, Films Inc, Modern Sound, Roas Films, Film Ctr DC & Twyman Films.

Scream of the Demon Lover. Jeffrey Chase & Jennifer Hartley. Directed by J. L. Merino. 1981. New World. 77 min. Sound. 16mm Color. *Rental:* Films Inc.

Screamers. Barbara Bach & Richard Johnson. Directed by Dan T. Miller. 1981. New World. 92 min. Sound. 16mm Color. *Rental:* Films Inc.

Screaming. Orig. Title: Carry on Screaming. Kenneth Williams & Charles Hawtrey. Directed by Gerald Thomas. 1966. Britain. 97 min. Sound. 16mm Color. *Rental:* Films Inc.

Screaming Eagles. Tom Tryon & Jan Merlin. Directed by Charles Haas. 1956. Allied Artists. 81 min. Sound. 16mm B&W. *Rental:* Hurlock Cine.

Screaming Mimi. Anita Ekberg, Gypsy Rose Lee & Philip Carey. Directed by Gerd Oswald. 1958. Columbia. 79 min. Sound. 16mm B&W. *Rental:* Kit Parker.

Screaming Skull, The. John Hudson & Peggy Webber. Directed by Alex Nichol. 1958. American International. 70 min. Sound. 16mm B&W. *Rental:* Films Inc & Video Comm.

Screaming Tiger, The. Wang Yu. Directed by Chein Lung. 1973. Hong Kong. 100 min. Sound. 16mm Color. dubbed. *Rental:* Swank Motion.

Scroll From a Son of a Star, A. Alden. 50 min. Sound. 16mm Color. *Rental:* Alden Films.

Scrooge. Sir Seymour Hicks & Donald Calthrop. Directed by Henry Edwards. 1935. Britain. 85 min. Sound. 16mm B&W. *Rental:* Buchan Pic, Budget Films, Film Classics, Kit Parker, Newman Film Lib, Film Ctr DC, Welling Motion Pictures & Willoughby Peer. *Sale:* Cinema Concepts, Kit Parker & Natl Cinema. *Rental:* Classic Film Mus, 59 mins. version.

Scrooge. Albert Finney, Sir Alec Guinness. Directed by Ronald Neame. 1971. National General. 111 min. Sound. 16mm Color. *Rental:* Swank Motion.

Scruggs: His Family & Friends. Earl Scruggs, Bob Dylan & Joan Baez. Directed by Amram Nowak. 1972. New Line. 95 min. Sound. 16mm Color. *Rental:* New Line Cinema. *Sale:* New Line Cinema.

Scudda Hoo-Scudda Hay. June Haver & Lon McCallister. Directed by F. Hugh Herbert. 1948. Fox. 98 min. Sound. 16mm B&W. *Rental:* Films Inc.

Scum. Ray Winstone & Phil Daniels. Directed by Alan Clarke. 1980. Britain. 95 min. Sound. 16mm Color. *Rental:* Corinth Films & WW Enter. *Rental:* WW Enter, Videotape version.

Sea Around Us, The. 1953. RKO. (Documentary). 61 min. Sound. 16mm Color. *Rental:* Films Inc. *Lease:* Films Inc. *Sale:* Blackhawk Films, Videotape version.

Sea Bat, The. Charles Bickford & Nils Asther. Directed by Wesley Ruggles. 1930. MGM. 69 min. Sound. 16mm B&W. *Rental:* MGM United.

Sea Beast, The. John Barrymore & Dolores Costello. Directed by Millard Webb. 1926. Warners. 114 min. Sound. 16mm B&W. *Rental:* MGM United.

Sea Behind the Dunes, The. 1980. Peace River. (Documentary). 57 min. Sound. 16mm Color. *Rental:* Time-Life Multimedia. *Sale:* Time-Life Multimedia. *Sale:* Time-Life Multimedia, Videotape version.

Sea Devils. Victor McLaglen, Preston Foster & Ida Lupino. 1937. RKO. 88 min. Sound. 16mm B&W. *Rental:* Films Inc. *Sale:* Cinema Concepts.

Sea Devils. Molly O'Day. 1931. 57 min. Sound. 16mm Color. *Rental:* Classic Film Mus.

Sea Gull, The. Trans. Title: Chaika. Alla Demidova. Directed by Yuri Karasik. Rus. 1971. Russia. (Anamorphic). 99 min. Sound. 16mm Color. subtitles. *Rental:* Corinth Films.

Sea Gypsies. Robert Logan. Directed by Stewart Rassil. 1978. Warners. 101 min. Sound. 16mm Color. *Rental:* Swank Motion.

Sea Hawk, The. Milton Sills & Wallace Beery. Directed by Frank Lloyd. 1924. Warners. 134 min. Sound. 16mm B&W. *Rental:* MGM United.

Sea Hawk, The. Errol Flynn & Brenda Marshall. Directed by Michael Curtiz. 1940. Warners. 130 min. Sound. 16mm B&W. *Rental:* MGM United. *Rental:* MGM United, 109 version.

Sea Hornet, The. Rod Cameron & Chill Wills. Directed by Joseph Kane. 1951. Republic. 84 min. Sound. 16mm B&W. *Rental:* Ivy Films. *Sale:* Rep Pic Film.

Sea Lion, The. Hobart Bosworth & Bessie Love. Directed by Rowland V. Lee. 1922. First National. 60 min. Silent. 16mm Color. *Rental:* Em Gee Film Lib & Film Classics. *Sale:* Film Classics & E Finney. *Sale:* Morcraft Films, Silent 8mm version.

Sea of Grass, The. Spencer Tracy & Katharine Hepburn. Directed by Elia Kazan. 1947. MGM. 131 min. Sound. 16mm B&W. *Rental:* MGM United.

Sea of Lost Ships, The. Walter Brennan & John Derek. Directed by Joseph Kane. 1953. Republic. 85 min. Sound. 16mm B&W. *Rental:* Ivy Films. *Sale:* Natl Telefim.

Sea Pirate, The. Gerald Barray. Directed by Roy Rowland. 1967. Italy. 85 min. Sound. 16mm Color. dubbed. *Rental:* Films Inc.

Sea Racketeers. Jeanne Madden & J. Carroll Naish. Directed by Hamilton MacFadden. 1937. Republic. 54 min. Sound. 16mm B&W. *Rental:* Ivy Films. *Sale:* Rep Pic Film.

Sea Shall Not Have Them, The. Sir Michael Redgrave & Dirk Bogarde. Directed by Lewis Gilbert. 1955. Britain. 90 min. Sound. 16mm B&W. *Rental:* Charard Motion Pics & Ivy Films. *Lease:* Rep Pic Film.

Sea Terror, The. 1954. France. (Cast unlisted). 70 min. Sound. 16mm B&W. *Rental:* Film Classics.

Sea Tiger, The. John Archer & Marguerite Chapman. Directed by Frank McDonald. 1952. Monogram. 75 min. Sound. 16mm B&W. *Rental:* Ivy Films. *Sale:* Rep Pic Film.

Sea Wife, The. Richard Burton & Joan Collins. Directed by Bob McNaught. 1957. Fox. (Anamorphic). 82 min. Sound. 16mm Color. *Rental:* Films Inc.

Sea Wolf, The. Edward G. Robinson & Ida Lupino. Directed by Michael Curtiz. 1941. Warners. 100 min. Sound. 16mm B&W. *Rental:* MGM United.

Seabirds of Isabella, The. 1977. Metromedia. 52 min. Sound. 16mm Color. *Sale:* Churchill Films. *Sale:* Churchill Films, Videotape version.

Seal Island. 1979. Britain. 55 min. Sound. 16mm Color. *Rental:* Lucerne Films. *Sale:* Lucerne Films.

Sealed Cargo. Dana Andrews & Carla Balenda. Directed by Alfred M. Werker. 1951. RKO. 90 min. Sound. 16mm B&W. *Rental:* Films Inc.

Sealed Lips. (Cast unlisted). 100 min. Sound. 16mm B&W. *Rental:* Alba House.

Sealed Soil. Directed by Marva Nabili. 1978. Iran. (Documentary). 90 min. Sound. 16mm Color. *Rental:* Icarus Films. *Sale:* Icarus Films.

Seals. 1971. Churchill Films. 52 min. Sound. 16mm Color. *Rental:* Churchill Films. *Rental:* Churchill Films, Videotape version.

Seance on a Wet Afternoon. Kim Stanley, Sir Richard Attenborough. Directed by Bryan Forbes. 1964. Britain. 52 min. Sound. Videotape B&W. *Sale:* Films Inc & VidAmerica.

Search, The. Montgomery Clift & Aline MacMahon. Directed by Fred Zinnemann. 1948. MGM. 103 min. Sound. 16mm B&W. *Rental:* MGM United.

Search, The. Trans. Title: Probe. Hugh O'Brien & Elke Sommer. Directed by Russ Mayberry. 1972. Warners TV. 97 min. Sound. 16mm Color. *Rental:* Video Comm.

Search & Destroy. Perry King & Don Stroud. Directed by William Fruett. 1979. Canada. 94 min. Sound. 16mm Color. *Rental:* Natl Film CN.

Search for a Century. 1983. Colonial Williamsburg. (Documentary). 59 min. Sound. 16mm Color. *Rental:* Colonial. *Sale:* Colonial. *Sale:* Colonial, Videotape version.

Search for a Mandate. Directed by Munroe Scott. 1971. Canada. 58 min. Sound. 16mm Color. *Rental:* Natl Film CN. *Sale:* Natl Film CN.

Search for Akhenaten, The. Trans. Title: Lost Pharaoh, The. Directed by Nicholas Kendell. 1980. 56 min. 16mm Color. *Rental:* Natl Film CN & U Cal Media.

Search for Alexander the Great, The. 4 pts. Nicholas Clay & Jane Lapotaire. 1980. Britain. 230 min. Sound. 16mm Color. *Rental:* Time-Life Multimedia. *Sale:* Time-Life Multimedia. *Sale:* Time-Life Multimedia, Videotape version.

Search for Bridey Murphy, The. Teresa Wright & Louis Hayward. Directed by Noel Langley. 1956. Paramount. 84 min. Sound. 16mm B&W. *Rental:* Films Inc.

Search for Danger. John Calvert & Albert Dekker. Directed by Jack Bernhard. 1949. Film Classics. 64 min. Sound. 16mm B&W. *Sale:* Classics Assoc NY.

Search for Life, The. 1979. PBS. (Documentary). 60 min. 16mm Color. *Rental:* PBS Video. *Sale:* PBS Video, Videotape version.

Search for Something Else, The. 1976. NBC. (Documentary). 51 min. Sound. 16mm Color. *Rental:* Films Inc. *Sale:* Films Inc. *Sale:* Films Inc, Videotape version.

Search for Survival, The. 1972. Gold Key. (Documentary). 94 min. Sound. 16mm Color. *Rental:* Budget Films, Films Inc, Modern Sound & Video Comm. *Lease:* Video Comm. *Rental:* Video Comm, *Lease:* Video Comm, Videotape version.

Search for the Great Apes, The. 1975. National Geographic. (Documentary). 52 min. Sound. 16mm Color. *Rental:* Natl Geog. *Sale:* Natl Geog. *Sale:* Natl Geog, Videotape version.

Search for the Lost Self, The. 1966. 60 min. Sound. 16mm B&W. *Rental:* U Mich Media.

Search for the Nile, The. 6 pts. Directed by Richard Marquand. 1972. Britain. (Cast unlisted). 360 min. Sound. 16mm Color. *Rental:* Time-Life Multimedia. *Sale:* Time-Life Multimedia.

Search for Ulysses, The. 1966. CBS. (Documentary). 53 min. Sound. 16mm B&W. *Rental:* Budget Films, Iowa Films & Syracuse U Film. *Sale:* Carousel Films. *Rental:* U Cal Media, U of IL Film & U Mich Media, *Sale:* Carousel Films, Color version.

Search for Unity, The: A European Idea. 1976. Britain. (Documentary). 52 min. Sound. 16mm Color. *Rental:* Time-Life Multimedia. *Sale:* Time-Life Multimedia. *Rental:* Time-Life Multimedia, *Sale:* Time-Life Multimedia, Videotape version.

Search for Vengeance, The. 1966. Wolper. (Documentary). 50 min. Sound. 16mm B&W. *Rental:* Films Inc. *Sale:* Films Inc. *Sale:* Films Inc, Videotape version.

Search in the Deep. 1970. Cousteau. (Documentary). 54 min. Sound. 16mm Color. *Rental:* Syracuse U Film.

Searchers, The. John Wayne & Jeffrey Hunter. Directed by John Ford. 1956. Warners. 119 min. Sound. 16mm Color. *Rental:* Swank Motion. *Rental:* Swank Motion, Videotape version.

Searching Wind, The. Robert Young & Sylvia Sidney. Directed by William Dieterle. 1946. Paramount. 108 min. Sound. 16mm B&W. *Rental:* Swank Motion.

Seas Beneath, The. George O'Brien & Marion Lessing. Directed by John Ford. 1931. Fox. 89 min. Sound. 16mm B&W. *Rental:* Films Inc.

Seas of Grass, The. 55 min. Color. *Rental:* EMC.

Seaside Swingers. Ron Moody & Liz Fraser. Directed by James Hill. 1965. Britain. 94 min. Sound. 16mm Color. *Rental:* Films Inc.

Season of Passion. Ernest Borgnine & Angela Lansbury. Directed by Leslie Norman. 1961. United Artists. 92 min. Sound. 16mm B&W. *Rental:* MGM United.

Sebastian. Dirk Bogarde & Susannah York. Directed by David Greene. 1968. Paramount. 100 min. Sound. 16mm Color. *Rental:* Films Inc.

Sebastiane. Leonard Treviglio. Directed by Paul Humfress & Derek Jarman. Latin. 1977. Cinema V. 89 min. Sound. 16mm Color. subtitles. *Rental:* Cinema Five.

Second American Revolution, The. 120 min. Sound. Videotape *Rental:* PBS Video. *Sale:* PBS Video.

Second Annual New Comedians Show, The. 1977. Verve. (Performance). 76 min. Color. *Rental:* Films Inc, Videotape version.

Second Battle of Britain, The. 1976. CBS. (Documentary). 49 min. Sound. 16mm Color. *Rental:* Budget Films, U Cal Media, Iowa Films, U Mich Media & Syracuse U Film. *Sale:* Carousel Films.

Second Best Secret Agent in the Whole Wide World, The. Orig. Title: Licensed to Kill. Tom Adams & Peter Bull. Directed by Lindsay Shonteff. 1966. Embassy. 96 min. Sound. 16mm Color. *Rental:* Films Inc.

Second Breath. Christine Fabrega & Paul Meurisse. Directed by Jean-Pierre Melville. Fr. 1966. France. 125 min. Sound. 16mm B&W. subtitles. *Rental:* Films Inc.

Second Chance. Ruth Warrick & John Hubbard. Directed by William Beaudine. 1950. Protestant Film Comm.. 80 min. Sound. 16mm Color. *Rental:* Newman Film Lib.

Second Chance. Robert Mitchum & Linda Darnell. Directed by Rudolph Mate. 1953. RKO. 82 min. Sound. 16mm Color. *Rental:* Films Inc.

Second Chance. 1966. NET. (Documentary). 60 min. Sound. 16mm B&W. *Rental:* Indiana AV Ctr. *Sale:* Indiana AV Ctr.

Second Chance. Catherine Deneuve, Anouk Aimee & Charles Denner. Directed by Claude Lelouch. Fr. 1976. France. 99 min. Sound. 16mm Color. subtitles. *Rental:* MGM United.

Second Chorus. Fred Astaire & Paulette Goddard. Directed by H. C. Potter. 1940. Paramount. 83 min. Sound. 16mm B&W. *Rental:* Budget Films, Classic Film Mus, Em Gee Film Lib, Ivy Films, Mogulls Films, Newman Film Lib, Rep Pic Film, Video Comm, Welling Motion Pictures & Wholesome Film Ctr. *Sale:* Rep Pic Film. *Sale:* Tamarelles French Film, Videotape version.

Second Erotic Film Festival, The. New Line Cinema. (Anthology). 95 min. Sound. 16mm Color. *Rental:* New Line Cinema.

Second Fiddle. Sonja Henie & Tyrone Power. Directed by Sidney Lanfield. 1939. Fox. 105 min. Sound. 16mm B&W. *Rental:* Films Inc.

Second Fiddle. Adrienne Corri & Lisa Gastoni. Directed by Maurice Elvey. 1958. Britain. 73 min. Sound. 16mm B&W. *Rental:* Video Comm.

Second Greatest Sex, The. Jeanne Crain & George Nader. Directed by George Marshall. 1955. Universal. 87 min. Sound. 16mm Color. *Rental:* Swank Motion.

Second Gun, The. Directed by Gerard Alcan. 1975. National General. (Documentary). 110 min. Sound. 16mm Color. *Rental:* Swank Motion.

Second Shepherd's Play, The. 1974. Films for the Humanities. (Cast unlisted). 52 min. Sound. 16mm Color. *Rental:* Films Human. *Sale:* Films Human.

Second Thoughts. Lucie Arnaz, Craig Wasson & Ken Howard. Directed by Lawerence Turman. 1983. Universal. 109 min. Sound. 16mm Color. *Rental:* Swank Motion.

Second Time Around, The. Debbie Reynolds & Steve Forrest. Directed by Vincent Sherman. 1961. Fox. 99 min. Sound. 16mm Color. *Rental:* Charard Motion Pics, Films Inc & Willoughby Peer. *Rental:* Willoughby Peer, Anamorphic version.

Second Transcontinental Nation, The. 1968. Canada. (Documentary). 58 min. Sound. 16mm B&W. *Rental:* U Cal Media.

Second Woman, The. Orig. Title: Ellen. Robert Young & Betsy Drake. Directed by James V. Kern. 1951. United Artists. 91 min. Sound. 16mm B&W. *Rental:* Budget Films & Video Comm. *Lease:* Video Comm. *Rental:* Video Comm, Videotape version.

Second World War, The. 3 parts. 1963. Encyclopaedia Britannica. (Documentary). 81 min. Sound. 16mm B&W. *Rental:* U Cal Media & Ency Brit Ed. *Sale:* Ency Brit Ed. *Sale:* Ency Brit Ed, Videotape version.

Seconds. Rock Hudson & John Randolph. Directed by John Frankenheimer. 1966. Paramount. 106 min. Sound. 16mm B&W. *Rental:* Films Inc.

Secret, The. Jean-Louis Trintignant & Philippe Noiret. Directed by Robert Enrico. 1974. France. 103 min. 16mm Color. dubbed. *Sale:* Cinema Concepts & Video Lib.

Secret Agent. Peter Lorre & Madeline Carroll. Directed by Alfred Hitchcock. 1936. Britain. 93 min. Sound. 16mm B&W. *Rental:* Budget Films, Em Gee Film Lib, Films Inc, Images Film, Kit Parker, Maljack, Natl Film Video, Video Comm & Westcoast Films. *Sale:* Cinema Concepts, Reel Images & Images Film. *Rental:* Ivy Films, *Sale:* Ivy Films & Reel Images, Super 8 sound version. *Sale:* Tamarelles French Film & Images Film, Videotape version.

Secret Agent, The. Directed by Jacki Ochs. 1983. (Documentary). 57 min. Sound. 16mm Color. *Rental:* First Run & Green Mt.

Secret Agent of Japan. Lynn Bari & Preston Foster. Directed by Irving Pichel. 1942. Fox. 72 min. Sound. 16mm B&W. *Rental:* Films Inc.

Secret Agent Superdragon. Ray Danton & Marisa Mell. Directed by Calvin Podgett. 1966. France. 99 min. Sound. 16mm Color. dubbed. *Rental:* Video Comm & Westcoast Films.

Secret Beyond the Door, The. Sir Michael Redgrave & Joan Bennett. Directed by Fritz Lang. 1948. Universal. 108 min. Sound. 16mm B&W. *Rental:* Budget Films, Ivy Films. *Sale:* Rep Pic Film.

Secret Boat, The. Xerox. (Cast unlisted). 77 min. Sound. 16mm Color. *Sale:* Xerox Films.

Secret Bowers, The. 1972. Britain. (Documentary). 50 min. Sound. 16mm Color. *Rental:* Time-Life Multimedia. *Sale:* Time-Life Multimedia.

Secret Bride, The. Orig. Title: Concealment. Barbara Stanwyck & Warren William. Directed by William Dieterle. 1935. Warners. 64 min. Sound. 16mm B&W. *Rental:* MGM United.

Secret Ceremony. Elizabeth Taylor, Mia Farrow & Robert Mitchum. Directed by Joseph Losey. 1969. Universal. 109 min. Sound. 16mm Color. *Rental:* Twyman Films.

Secret Conclave, The. Vittorio De Sica & Henri Vidal. Directed by Umberto Scarpelli. 1963. Italy. 90 min. Sound. 16mm B&W. dubbed. *Rental:* Films Inc & Roas Films.

Secret Door, The. Robert Hutton & Sandra Dorne. Directed by Gilbert Kay. 1964. Allied Artists. 72 min. Sound. 16mm B&W. *Rental:* Hurlock Cine.

Secret Enemies. Faye Emerson & Craig Stevens. Directed by Ben Stoloff. 1942. Warners. 58 min. Sound. 16mm B&W. *Rental:* MGM United.

Secret File-Hollywood. Robert Clarke & Francine York. Directed by Ralph Cushman. 1961. Crown. 85 min. Sound. 16mm B&W. *Rental:* Video Comm. *Lease:* Video Comm. *Rental:* Video Comm, *Lease:* Video Comm, Videotape version.

Secret Four, The see Kansas City Confidential.

Secret Fury, The. Claudette Colbert, Robert Ryan & Vivian Vance. Directed by Mel Ferrer. 1950. RKO. 86 min. Sound. 16mm B&W. *Rental:* Video Comm.

Secret Garden, The. Margaret O'Brien & Herbert Marshall. Directed by Fred M. Wilcox. 1949. MGM. 93 min. Sound. 16mm B&W. *Rental:* MGM United.

Secret Invasion, The. Stewart Granger & Raf Vallone. Directed by Roger Corman. 1964. United Artists. (Anamorphic). 98 min. Sound. 16mm Color. *Rental:* MGM United.

Secret Land, The. 1948. MGM. (Documentary). 71 min. Sound. 16mm Color. *Rental:* MGM United.

Secret Life of Adolph Hitler, The. Germany. (Documentary). 50 min. Sound. 16mm B&W. *Rental:* Budget Films & Em Gee Film Lib. *Sale:* Classic Film Mus.

Secret Life of an American Wife, The. Walter Matthau & Anne Jackson. Directed by George Axelrod. 1968. Fox. 50 min. Sound. 16mm Color. *Rental:* Films Inc.

Secret Life of Hernando Cortez, The. Taylor Mead & Ultra Violet. Directed by Leo Castelli. 1970. John Chamberlain. 69 min. Sound. 16mm Color. *Rental:* Canyon Cinema.

Secret Life of T. K. Dearing, The. Jodie Foster & Eduard Franz. Directed by Daniel Wilson. 1978. Time-Life. 47 min. Sound. 16mm Color. *Rental:* U of IL Film, Videotape version.

Secret Life of Walter Mitty, The. Danny Kaye & Virginia Mayo. Directed by Norman Z. McLeod. 1947. Goldwyn. 110 min. Sound. 16mm Color. *Rental:* Films Inc, Video Comm & Welling Motion Pictures.

Secret Man, The. Marshall Thompson & John Loder. Directed by Ronald Kinnoch. 1958. Britain. 78 min. Sound. 16mm B&W. *Rental:* Charard Motion Pics.

Secret of Convict Lake, The. Glenn Ford & Gene Tierney. Directed by Michael Gordon. 1951. Fox. 83 min. Sound. 16mm B&W. *Rental:* Films Inc.

Secret of Deep Harbor, The. Ron Foster & Merry Anders. Directed by Edward L. Cahn. 1961. United Artists. 70 min. Sound. 16mm B&W. *Rental:* MGM United.

Secret of Dr. Kildare, The. Lew Ayres, Lionel Barrymore & Larraine Day. Directed by Harold S. Bucquet. 1939. MGM. 87 min. Sound. 16mm B&W. *Rental:* Classic Film Mus & MGM United.

Secret of Dorian Gray, The. Orig. Title: Dorian Gray. Helmut Berger, Richard Todd & Herbert Lom. Directed by Massimo Dallamano. 1971. American International. 95 min. Sound. 16mm Color. *Rental:* Films Inc, Ivy Films, Rep Pic Film & Video Comm. *Lease:* Rep Pic Film.

Secret of Loving, The. Josh McDowell. 1976. Gospel. 51 min. Sound. 16mm Color. *Rental:* Gospel Films.

Secret of Madame Blanche, The. Irene Dunne & Lionel Atwill. Directed by Charles Brabin. 1933. MGM. 85 min. Sound. 16mm B&W. *Rental:* MGM United.

Secret of Magic Island, The. 1965. France. (Documentary). 63 min. Sound. 16mm Color. narrated Eng. *Rental:* Films Inc, Roas Films & Westcoast Films.

Secret of Michelangelo, The: Every Man's Dream. Directed by Milton Fruchtman. 1969. Capital Cities. (Documentary). 51 min. Sound. 16mm Color. *Rental:* Syracuse U Film.

Secret of Monte Cristo, The. John Gregson & Rory Calhoun. Directed by Monty Berman. 1961. MGM. 80 min. Sound. 16mm Color. *Rental:* Films Inc & MGM United.

Secret of My Success, The. Shirley Jones & Stella Stevens. Directed by Andrew Stone. 1965. MGM. (Anamorphic). 122 min. Sound. 16mm Color. *Rental:* MGM United.

Secret of NIMH, The. Directed by Don Bluth. 1982. 82 min. Sound. 16mm Color. *Rental:* MGM United. *Rental:* MGM United, Videotape version.

Secret of St. Ives, The. Richard Ney & Vanessa Brown. Directed by Phil Rosen. 1949. Columbia. 78 min. Sound. 16mm B&W. *Rental:* Cine Craft & Inst Cinema.

Secret of Santa Vittoria, The. Anthony Quinn & Anna Magnani. Directed by Stanley Kramer. 1969. United Artists. 139 min. Sound. 16mm Color. *Rental:* Budget Films, MGM United, Roas Films & Wholesome Film Ctr. *Rental:* MGM United, Anamorphic version.

Secret of the Blue Room, The. Paul Lukas & Edward Arnold. Directed by Kurt Neumann. 1932. Universal. 66 min. Sound. 16mm B&W. *Rental:* Swank Motion.

Secret of the Chateau, The. Claire Dodd & Jack LaRue. Directed by Richard Thorpe. 1935. Universal. 65 min. Sound. 16mm B&W. *Rental:* Swank Motion.

Secret of the Incas, The. Charlton Heston & Robert Young. Directed by Jerry Hopper. 1954. Paramount. 101 min. Sound. 16mm Color. *Rental:* Films Inc.

Secret of the Navajo Cave, The. (Cast unlisted). 100 min. Sound. 16mm Color. *Rental:* Budget Films & Bosco Films.

Secret of the Purple Reef, The. Peter Falk & Jeff Richards. Directed by William Witney. 1960. Fox. 80 min. Sound. 16mm Color. *Rental:* Budget Films & Inst Cinema. *Rental:* Willoughby Peer, Anamorphic version.

Secret of the Sacred Forest, The. Gary Merrill & Jon Provost. Directed by Michael Du Pont. 1970. Philippine Islands. 87 min. Sound. 16mm Color. *Rental:* Budget Films, Welling Motion Pictures & Westcoast Films.

Secret of the Sphinx, The. Tony Russell & Maria Perschy. 1964. Italy. 90 min. Sound. 16mm Color. *Rental:* Video Comm, Welling Motion Pictures & Westcoast Films.

Secret of the Wastelands. William Boyd. Directed by Derwin Abrahams. 1941. Paramount. 65 min. Sound. 16mm B&W. *Rental:* Westcoast Films.

Secret of the Whistler. Richard Dix. Directed by George Sherman. 1946. Columbia. 70 min. Sound. 16mm B&W. *Lease:* Time-Life Multimedia.

Secret Partner, The. Stewart Granger & Haya Harareet. Directed by Basil Dearden. 1961. Britain. 91 min. Sound. 16mm B&W. *Rental:* MGM United.

Secret Passion, The *see* Freud.

Secret Service. Richard Dix & Shirley Grey. Directed by Walter J. Ruben. 1931. RKO. 68 min. Sound. 16mm B&W. *Rental:* RKO General Pics.

Secret Service Investigator. Lloyd Bridges & Lynne Roberts. Directed by R. G. Springsteen. 1948. Republic. 60 min. Sound. 16mm B&W. *Rental:* Ivy Films.

Secret Service of the Air. Ronald Reagan & John Litel. Directed by Noel Smith. 1939. Warners. 61 min. Sound. 16mm B&W. *Rental:* MGM United.

Secret Seven, The. Tony Russell. Directed by Alberto De Martino. 1966. MGM. 94 min. Sound. 16mm Color. *Rental:* MGM United.

Secret Six, The. Clark Gable & Wallace Beery. Directed by Howard Bretherton. 1936. Fox. 70 min. Sound. 16mm B&W. *Rental:* MGM United.

Secret Valley, The. Richard Arlen & Jack Mulhall. Directed by Howard Bretherton. 1936. Fox. 70 min. Sound. 16mm B&W. *Rental:* Mogulls Films.

Secret Venture, The. Kent Taylor & Jane Hylton. Directed by R. G. Springsteen. 1957. Republic. 70 min. Sound. 16mm B&W. *Rental:* Ivy Films. *Lease:* Rep Pic Film.

Secret War of Harry Frigg, The. Paul Newman & Sylva Koscina. Directed by Jack Smight. 1968. Universal. 110 min. Sound. 16mm Color. *Rental:* Swank Motion.

Secret Ways, The. Richard Widmark & Sonja Ziemann. Directed by Phil Karlson. 1961. Universal. 112 min. Sound. 16mm B&W. *Rental:* Swank Motion.

Secret World, The. Jacqueline Bisset & Jean-Francois Maurin. Directed by Robert Freeman. 1969. France. 94 min. Sound. 16mm Color. dubbed. *Rental:* Films Inc.

Secrets. Norma Talmadge. Directed by Frank Borzage. 1924. 16mm *Rental:* A Twyman Pres.

Secrets of a Co-Ed. Tina Thayer & Otto Krueger. Directed by Joseph Lewis. 1942. PRC. 67 min. Sound. 16mm B&W. *Rental:* Mogulls Films.

Secrets of a Sorority Girl. Mary Ware & Rick Vallin. Directed by Lew Landers. 1946. PRC. 59 min. Sound. 16mm B&W. *Sale:* Classics Assoc NY.

Secrets of a Soul. Werner Krauss. Directed by G. W. Pabst. 1926. Germany. (Musical Score Only). 95 min. Sound. 16mm B&W. *Rental:* Film Images. *Sale:* Film Images. *Rental:* A Twyman Pres, 111 min. version.

Secrets of an Actress. Kay Francis & George Brent. Directed by William Keighley. 1938. Warners. 71 min. Sound. 16mm B&W. *Rental:* MGM United.

Secrets of Monte Carlo. June Vincent. Directed by George Blair. 1951. Republic. 61 min. Sound. 16mm B&W. *Rental:* Ivy Films.

Secrets of Scotland Yard. Edgar Barrier & C. Aubrey Smith. Directed by George Blair. 1944. Republic. 71 min. Sound. 16mm B&W. *Rental:* Ivy Films. *Sale:* Rep Pic Film.

Secrets of Sleep. 1976. Nova. (Documentary). 52 min. Sound. 16mm Color. *Rental:* U Cal Media, U of IL Film, U Mich Media & Syracuse U Film, Videotape version.

Secrets of the French Police. Gregory Ratoff & Frank Morgan. Directed by Edward Sutherland. 1933. RKO. 58 min. Sound. 16mm B&W. *Rental:* RKO General Pics.

Secrets of the Underground. John Hubbard & Virginia Grey. Directed by William Morgan. 1943. Republic. 71 min. Sound. 16mm B&W. *Rental:* Ivy Films.

Secrets of Women. Gunnar Bjornstrand & Eva Dahlbeck. Directed by Ingmar Bergman. 1952. Sweden. 108 min. Sound. 16mm B&W. *Rental:* Films Inc, Janus Films & New Cinema. *Sale:* Tamarelles French Film, Videotape version.

Security Risk. John Ireland & Dorothy Malone. Directed by Harold Schuster. 1954. Allied Artists. 69 min. Sound. 16mm B&W. *Rental:* Ivy Films. *Sale:* Rep Pic Film.

Seduced & Abandoned. Saro Urzi & Stefania Sandrelli. Directed by Pietro Germi. Ital. 1964. Italy. 118 min. Sound. 16mm B&W. subtitles. *Rental:* Budget Films, Images Film & Kit Parker. *Sale:* Festival Films. *Sale:* Festival Films, Tamarelles French Film & Images Film, Videotape version.

Seduction of Joe Tynan, The. Alan Alda & Melvyn Douglas. Directed by Jerry Schatzberg. 1979. Universal. 107 min. Sound. 16mm Color. *Rental:* Swank Motion. *Rental:* Swank Motion, Videotape version.

Seduction of Mimi, The. Giancarlo Giannini & Mariangela Melato. Directed by Lina Wertmuller. Ital. 1974. Italy. 92 min. Sound. 16mm Color. subtitles. *Rental:* New Cinema & New Line Cinema.

See America Thirst. Harry Langdon & Slim Summerville. Directed by William James Craft. 1930. Universal. 73 min. Sound. 16mm B&W. *Rental:* Swank Motion.

See Here, Private Hargrove. Robert Walker & Donna Reed. Directed by Wesley Ruggles. 1944. MGM. 100 min. Sound. 16mm B&W. *Rental:* Films Inc & MGM United.

See No Evil. Mia Farrow. Directed by Richard Fleischer. 1971. Columbia. 88 min. Sound. 16mm Color. *Rental:* Budget Films, Cine Craft, Williams Films, Films Inc, Film Pres, Kerr Film, Modern Sound, Roas Films, Film Ctr DC, Video Comm, Westcoast Films, Welling Motion Pictures, Wholesome Film Ctr & Willoughby Peer.

See You at Mao. Directed by Jean-Luc Godard. 1970. France. (Experimental). 54 min. Sound. 16mm Color. dubbed. *Rental:* Grove.

Seeds, The. 1975. ABC. 60 min. Sound. 16mm Color. *Rental:* Natl Churches Christ.

Seeds of a New Life. 1974. Perennial Education. 59 min. Sound. 16mm Color. *Rental:* U of IL Film.

Seeds of Self-Esteem, The. Dr. Kevin Leman. 45 min. Sound. 16mm Color. *Rental:* Gospel Films.

Seeking New Laws. 1964. Britain. (Documentary, kinescope). 58 min. Sound. 16mm B&W. *Rental:* U Cal Media.

Seeking the First American. 1979. Odyssey. Sound. Videotape Color. *Rental:* PBS Video. *Sale:* PBS Video.

Seems Like Old Times. Charles Grodin & Goldie Hawn. Directed by Jay Sandrich. 1980. Columbia. 101 min. Sound. 16mm Color. *Rental:* Swank Motion. *Rental:* Swank Motion, Videotape version.

Self-Portrait. Joby Baker. Directed by Maurice McEndree. 1973. Chile. 74 min. Sound. 16mm Color. *Sale:* Salz Ent.

Selling of the Pentagon, The. 1971. CBS. (Documentary). 52 min. Sound. 16mm B&W. *Rental:* Budget Films, U Cal Media, Iowa Films, U Mich Media, CA Newsreel, Syracuse U Film, Twyman Films & Welling Motion Pictures. *Sale:* Carousel Films. *Rental:* Kit Parker & Museum Mod Art, Color version.

Sellout, The. Walter Pidgeon & John Hodiak. Directed by Gerald Mayer. 1951. MGM. 83 min. Sound. 16mm B&W. *Rental:* MGM United.

Sellout, The. Richard Widmark & Oliver Reed. Directed by Peter Collinson. 1976. Britain/Italy. 89 min. Sound. 16mm Color. *Rental:* Welling Motion Pictures.

Selskaya Uchitelnitsa *see* Village Teacher.

Selznick Years, The. (Documentary). 74 min. Sound. 16mm Color. *Rental:* U of IL Film.

Semester of Discontent. 1967. NET. (Documentary). 60 min. Sound. 16mm B&W. *Rental:* U of IL Film, Indiana AV Ctr & SD AV Ctr.

Semi-Tough. Burt Reynolds, Kris Kristofferson & Jill Clayburgh. Directed by Michael Ritchie. 1977. United Artists. 108 min. Sound. 16mm Color. *Rental:* MGM United. *Rental:* MGM United, Videotape version.

Seminole. Rock Hudson & Barbara Hale. Directed by Budd Boetticher. 1953. Universal. 87 min. Sound. 16mm Color. *Rental:* Swank Motion.

Seminole Uprising. George Montgomery & Karin Booth. Directed by Earl Bellamy. 1955. Columbia. 74 min. Sound. 16mm Color. *Rental:* Modern Sound.

Senator Humphrey Subcommittee Hearing. 1971. Oklahoma State. 100 min. Sound. 16mm B&W. *Rental:* OK AV Ctr.

Senator Thomas Hart Benton *see* Thomas Hart Benton.

Senator Was Indiscreet, The. William Powell & Ella Raines. Directed by George S. Kaufman. 1948. Universal. 88 min. Sound. 16mm B&W. *Rental:* Budget Films, Ivy Films & Welling Motion Pictures. *Sale:* Rep Pic Film & Tamarelles French Film.

Send Me No Flowers. Rock Hudson & Doris Day. Directed by Norman Jewison. 1964. Universal. 100 min. Sound. 16mm Color. *Rental:* Williams Films.

Sender, The. Kathryn Harrold & Zeljko Ivanek. Directed by Roger Christian. 1982. Paramount. 91 min. Sound. 16mm Color. *Rental:* Films Inc.

Senechal the Magnificent. Fernandel & Nadia Gray. Directed by Jean Boyer. 1958. France. 78 min. Sound. 16mm B&W. dubbed. *Rental:* Ivy Films.

Senilita. Orig. Title: Careless. Claudia Cardinale & Anthony Franciosa. Directed by Mauro Bolognini. Ital. 1963. Italy. 110 min. Sound. 16mm B&W. subtitles. *Rental:* Kit Parker.

Senior Prom. Jill Corey & Louis Prima. Directed by David Lowell. 1958. Columbia. 82 min. Sound. 16mm B&W. *Rental:* Cine Craft, Inst Cinema & Modern Sound.

Senor Americano. Ken Maynard. Directed by Harry J. Brown. 1929. Universal. 60 min. Silent. 8mm B&W. *Sale:* Cinema Concepts.

Senora Du Tutti, La. Fr. 1934. Sound. 16mm Color. subtitles. *Sale:* Reel Images.

Sensation Hunters. Arline Judge & Preston Foster. Directed by Charles Vidor. 1934. Monogram. 80 min. Sound. 16mm B&W. *Rental:* Mogulls Films.

Sensations of Nineteen Forty-Five. Eleanor Powell & W. C. Fields. Directed by Andrew Stone. 1945. United Artists. 85 min. Sound. 16mm B&W. *Rental:* Budget Films, Ivy Films, Mogulls Films & Video Comm.

Sense of Loss, A. Directed by Marcel Ophuls. 1972. France. (Documentary). 135 min. Sound. 16mm Color. *Rental:* Cinema Five. *Sale:* Cinema Five. *Sale:* Tamarelles French Film, Videotape version.

Sense of Place, A. 1976. Canada. (Documentary). 57 min. Sound. 16mm Color. *Rental:* U Cal Media & Natl Film CN. *Sale:* Natl Film CN.

Sense of Wonder, A. 1968. ABC. (Documentary). 54 min. Sound. 16mm Color. *Rental:* McGraw-Hill Films & U Mich Media. *Sale:* McGraw-Hill Films.

Sense Perception. 2 pts. 1960. Moody. (Documentary). 55 min. Sound. 16mm Color. *Rental:* U of IL Film.

Senso. Alida Valli & Farley Granger. Directed by Luchino Visconti. Ital. 1954. Italy. 100 min. Sound. 16mm B&W Color. subtitles. *Rental:* Corinth Films. *Lease:* Corinth Films.

Sensory Deprivation & the Elderly. 2 pts. 1974. Penn State. 120 min. Videotape Color. dubbed. *Rental:* Penn St AV Serv. *Sale:* Penn St AV Serv.

Sentence, The. Marina Vlady & Robert Hossein. Directed by Jean Valere. France. 100 min. Sound. 16mm B&W. *Rental:* French Am Cul.

Sentenced to Success. 1977. Cine Information. (Documentary). 60 min. Sound. 16mm Color. *Rental:* Green Mt. *Sale:* Green Mt.

Sentiment & Song *see* Song of the Prairie.

Sentimental Bloke, A. Directed by Raymond Longford. 1918. Australia. (Cast unlisted). 73 min. Silent. 16mm B&W. *Rental:* MGM United.

Sentimental Journey. John Payne & Maureen O'Hara. Directed by Walter Lang. 1946. Fox. 94 min. Sound. 16mm B&W. *Rental:* Films Inc.

Sentinel, The. Chris Sarandon & Cristina Raines. Directed by Michael Winner. 1977. Universal. 92 min. Sound. 16mm Color. *Rental:* Swank Motion & Twyman Films.

Separate Peace, A. John Heyl & Parker Stevenson. Directed by Larry Peerce. 1972. Paramount. 104 min. Sound. 16mm Color. *Rental:* Films Inc. *Rental:* U of IL Film, Abridged 46-min. version.

Separate Realities. 1979. Penn State. (Documentary). 58 min. Sound. 16mm Color. *Rental:* Penn St AV Serv. *Sale:* Penn St AV Serv. *Rental:* Penn St AV Serv, *Sale:* Penn St AV Serv, Videotape version.

Separate Tables. David Niven & Deborah Kerr. Directed by Delbert Mann. 1958. United Artists. 98 min. Sound. 16mm B&W. *Rental:* MGM United.

Separate Ways. Karen Black & Tony LoBianco. Directed by Howard Avedis. 92 min. Sound. 16mm Color. *Rental:* Swank Motion.

Separation Trauma. 1981. 114 min. Sound. Videotape B&W. *Rental:* Iowa Films.

Sepia Cinderella. Sheila Geise. Directed by Arthur Leonard. 1947. Herald. 67 min. Sound. 16mm B&W. *Rental:* Em Gee Film Lib.

September Nineteen Thirty Nine. 1961. Zodiac. (Documentary). 60 min. Sound. 16mm B&W. *Rental:* Budget Films. *Sale:* Reel Images, Super 8 sound version.

September Storm. Joanne Dru & Mark Stevens. Directed by Byron Haskin. 1960. Fox. 99 min. Sound. 16mm Color. *Rental:* Willoughby Peer. *Rental:* Willoughby Peer, Anamorphic version.

September Thirtieth, Nineteen Fifty Five. Richard Thomas & Susan Tyrrell. Directed by James Bridges. 1978. Universal. 101 min. Sound. 16mm Color. *Rental:* Swank Motion.

Sequoia. Jean Parker & Russell Hardie. Directed by Chester M. Franklin. 1934. MGM. 73 min. Sound. 16mm B&W. *Rental:* MGM United.

Seraphita's Diary. Directed by Frederick Wiseman. 1983. Zipporah. (Documentary). 90 min. Sound. 16mm Color. *Rental:* Zipporah Films. *Sale:* Zipporah Films.

Serengeti Shall Not Die. Directed by Pierre-Dominique Gaisseau. 1959. Allied Artists. (Documentary). 83 min. Sound. 16mm Color. *Rental:* Budget Films.

Sergeant Deadhead. Frankie Avalon & Deborah Walley. Directed by Norman Taurog. 1965. American International. 89 min. Sound. 16mm Color. *Rental:* Westcoast Films.

Sergeant Jim. John Kitzmiller. Directed by France Stiglic. 1962. Yugoslavia. 82 min. Sound. 16mm B&W. *Rental:* Willoughby Peer.

Sergeant Madden. Wallace Beery & Tom Brown. Directed by Josef Von Sternberg. 1939. MGM. 82 min. Sound. 16mm B&W. *Rental:* MGM United.

Sergeant Matlovich vs. the USAF. Brad Dourif, Frank Converse & William Daniels. Directed by Paul Leaf. 1978. Tomorrow Entertainment. 98 min. Sound. 16mm Color. *Rental:* Budget Films, Kit Parker, Learning Corp Am, Twyman Films & Westcoast Films. *Lease:* Learning Corp Am. *Rental:* Learning Corp Am, *Lease:* Learning Corp Am, Videotape version.

Sergeant Murphy. Ronald Reagan & Donald Crisp. Directed by B. Reeves Eason. 1938. Warners. 57 min. Sound. 16mm B&W. *Rental:* MGM United.

Sergeant Ryker. Lee Marvin & Bradford Dillman. Directed by Buzz Kulik. 1968. Universal. 85 min. Sound. 16mm Color. *Rental:* Swank Motion.

Sergeant York. Gary Cooper, Walter Brennan & Joan Leslie. Directed by Howard Hawks. 1941. Warners. 134 min. Sound. 16mm B&W. *Rental:* MGM United.

Sergei Eisenstein. Orig. Title: Eisenstein. 1958. Russia. (Documentary). 50 min. Sound. 16mm B&W. narrated Eng. *Rental:* Budget Films, Corinth Films, Em Gee, Film Lib, Kent St U Film & Kit Parker. *Sale:* Cinema Concepts.

Serial. Martin Mull & Tuesday Weld. Directed by Bill Persky. 1980. Paramount. 91 min. Sound. 16mm Color. *Rental:* Films Inc.

Serpent, The. 1972. Open Theater. (Documentary). 80 min. Sound. 16mm B&W. *Rental:* A Cantor. *Sale:* A Cantor.

Serpent, The. Henry Fonda, Yul Brynner & Dirk Bogarde. Directed by Henri Verneuil. 1973. MGM. 115 min. Sound. 16mm Color. *Rental:* Budget Films, Film Ctr DC, Films Inc & Video Comm.

Serpent Island. Sonny Tufts. Directed by Bert I. Gordon. 1954. Gordon. 62 min. Sound. 16mm B&W. *Rental:* Charard Motion Pics.

Serpent of the Nile. Rhonda Fleming & William Lundigan. Directed by William Castle. 1953. Columbia. 81 min. Sound. 16mm B&W. *Rental:* Kit Parker.

Serpent's Egg, The. Liv Ullmann, David Carradine & Gert Froebe. Directed by Ingmar Bergman. 1977. Paramount. 110 min. Sound. 16mm Color. *Rental:* Films Inc.

Serpico. Al Pacino. Directed by Sidney Lumet. 1974. Paramount. 140 min. Sound. 16mm Color. *Rental:* Films Inc.

Servant, The. Dirk Bogarde & James Fox. Directed by Joseph Losey. 1963. Britain. 115 min. Sound. 16mm B&W. *Rental:* Films Inc & Janus Films.

Servant & Mistress, The. Victor Lanoux & Andrew Ferreol. Directed by Bruno Gantillon. New Line Cinema. 90 min. Sound. 16mm Color. *Rental:* New Line Cinema.

Servant in the House. Jean Hersholt & John Gilbert. Directed by Jack Conway. 1918. Triangle. 50 min. Silent. 16mm B&W. *Rental:* Film Classics. *Sale:* Film Classics. *Rental:* Film Classics, *Sale:* Film Classics, Silent 8mm version.

Servantes Du Bon Dieu, Les. Directed by Diane Letourneau. Fr. 1978. Canada. (Documentary). 90 min. Sound. 16mm Color. subtitles. *Rental:* Natl Film CN.

Service Deluxe. Constance Bennett & Vincent Price. Directed by Rowland V. Lee. 1938. Universal. 85 min. Sound. 16mm B&W. *Rental:* Swank Motion.

Sesame Street: No. 1. 1970. Children's TV Workshop. (Television program). 60 min. Sound. 16mm Color. *Rental:* Childrens Work. *Lease:* Childrens Work.

Sesame Street: No. 273. 1971. Children's TV Workshop. (Television program). 60 min. Sound. 16mm Color. *Rental:* Childrens Work. *Lease:* Childrens Work.

Sesame Street: No. 276. 1971. Children's TV Workshop. 60 min. Sound. 16mm Color. *Rental:* Childrens Work. *Lease:* Childrens Work.

Sesame Street: No. 319. 1971. Children's TV Workshop. 60 min. Sound. 16mm Color. *Rental:* Childrens Work. *Lease:* Childrens Work.

Sesenta Segundos de Vida. 1938. Spain. (Cast unlisted). 60 min. Sound. 16mm B&W. *Rental:* Film Classics.

Set-Up, The. Robert Ryan & Audrey Totter. Directed by Robert Wise. 1949. RKO. 72 min. Sound. 16mm B&W. *Rental:* Films Inc. *Lease:* Films Inc.

Seven. William Smith & Barbara Leigh. Directed by Andy Sidaris. 1979. American International. 100 min. Sound. 16mm Color. *Rental:* Swank Motion.

Seven Against the Sun. Gert Van Den Bergh. Directed by David Millin. 1965. Germany. 115 min. Sound. 16mm Color. dubbed. *Rental:* Films Inc.

Seven Alone. Dewey Martin & Aldo Ray. Directed by Earl Bellamy. 1976. Doty/Dayton. 100 min. Sound. 16mm Color. *Rental:* Swank Motion.

Seven Angry Men. Raymond Massey & Jeffrey Hunter. Directed by Charles Marquis Warren. 1955. Allied Artists. 90 min. Sound. 16mm B&W. *Rental:* Hurlock Cine.

Seven Beauties. Trans. Title: Pasqualino, Seven Beauties. Giancarlo Giannini, Fernando Rey & Shirley Stoller. Directed by Lina Wertmuller. 1976. Italy. 116 min. Sound. 16mm Color. *Rental:* Cinema Five, Videotape version.

Seven Brides for Seven Brothers. Jane Powell & Howard Keel. Directed by Stanley Donen. 1954. MGM. 102 min. Sound. 16mm Color. *Rental:* MGM United. *Rental:* MGM United, Anamorphic version. *Rental:* MGM United, Videotape version.

Seven Capital Sins, The. Eduardo De Filippo & Isa Miranda. 1952. 156 min. Sound. 16mm B&W. dubbed. *Rental:* Films Inc.

Seven Chances. Buster Keaton. Directed by Buster Keaton. 1925. Metro. 57 min. Silent. 16mm B&W. *Rental:* Films Inc. *Rental:* A Twyman Pres & Twyman Films, Sound version.

Seven Cities of Gold. Anthony Quinn & Richard Egan. Directed by Robert Webb. 1955. Fox. 103 min. Sound. 16mm Color. *Rental:* Films Inc.

Seven Days Ashore. Alan Carney & Wally Brown. Directed by John H. Auer. 1944. RKO. 74 min. Sound. 16mm B&W. *Rental:* Films Inc.

Seven Days in May. Burt Lancaster & Kirk Douglas. Directed by John Frankenheimer. 1964. Paramount. 120 min. Sound. 16mm B&W. *Rental:* Films Inc. *Sale:* Tamarelles French Film, Videotape version.

Seven Days in the Life of a President.
1965. Wolper. (Documentary). 50 min.
Sound. 16mm B&W. *Rental:* Films Inc.
Sale: Films Inc. *Sale:* Films Inc,
Videotape version.

Seven Days' Leave. Victor Mature &
Lucille Ball. Directed by Tim Whelan.
1942. RKO. 87 min. Sound. 16mm B&W.
Rental: Films Inc.

Seven Days to Remember. 1968.
Metromedia. 58 min. Sound. 16mm
B&W. *Rental:* Films Inc, Iowa Films, U
Mich Media & Wholesome Film Ctr.

Seven Different Ways. Orig. Title: Quick,
Let's Get Married. Ginger Rogers & Ray
Milland. Directed by William Dieterle.
1968. Commonwealth United. 102 min.
Sound. 16mm Color. *Rental:* Ivy Films.

Seven Doors to Death. June Clyde &
Chick Chandler. Directed by Elmer
Clifton. 1944. PRC. 70 min. Sound.
16mm B&W. *Rental:* Mogulls Films.

Seven Dwarfs to the Rescue. Rosanna
Podesta. Directed by P. W. Tamburella.
1965. Childhood. 84 min. Sound. 16mm
Color. dubbed. *Rental:* Roas Films, Film
Ctr DC, Westcoast Films, Wholesome
Film Ctr & Willoughby Peer.

Seven Eleven Ocean Drive. Edmond
O'Brien & Joanne Dru. Directed by
Joseph Newman. 1950. Columbia. 102
min. Sound. 16mm Color. *Rental:* Budget
Films & Inst Cinema.

Seven Faces of Dr. Lao, The. Tony
Randall & Arthur O'Connell. Directed by
George Pal. 1964. MGM. 100 min.
Sound. 16mm Color. *Rental:* MGM
United.

Seven Golden Men. Philippe Leroy.
Directed by Marco Vicario. 1969. Italy.
87 min. Sound. 16mm Color. dubbed.
Rental: Films Inc & Willoughby Peer.

Seven Guns to Mesa. Charles Quinlivan
& Lola Albright. Directed by Edward
Dein. 1958. Allied Artists. 69 min.
Sound. 16mm B&W. *Rental:* Ivy Films &
Rep Pic Film. *Sale:* Rep Pic Film.

Seven Hills to Rome. Mario Lanza &
Peggie Castle. Directed by Roy Rowland.
1958. MGM. 107 min. Sound. 16mm
Color. *Rental:* MGM United. *Rental:*
MGM United, Anamorphic version.

**Seven Hundred Eighty Four Days That
Changed America.** 1982. TCA.
(Documentary). 120 min. Videotape
Color. *Sale:* Films Inc.

Seven in a Barn. Brian. 60 min.
Videotape Color. *Sale:* Astro Video.

Seven Keys to Baldpate. Richard Dix &
Margaret Livingston. Directed by
Reginald Barker. 1929. RKO. 75 min.
Sound. 16mm B&W. *Rental:* Films Inc.

Seven Keys to Baldpate. Gene Raymond
& Walter Brennan. Directed by William
Hamilton & Edward Kelly. 1935. RKO.
80 min. Sound. 16mm B&W. *Rental:*
Films Inc.

Seven Keys to Baldpate. Philip Terry &
Jacqueline White. Directed by Lew
Landers. 1947. RKO. 68 min. Sound.
16mm B&W. *Rental:* Films Inc. *Lease:*
Films Inc.

Seven Little Foys, The. Bob Hope &
James Cagney. Directed by Melville
Shavelson. 1955. Paramount. 95 min.
Sound. 16mm Color. *Rental:* Arcus
Films, Budget Films, Cine Craft, Films
Inc, Modern Sound, Newman Film Lib,
Roas Films, Twyman Films, Video
Comm, Westcoast Films, Welling Motion
Pictures, Wholesome Film Ctr &
Willoughby Peer.

Seven Miles from Alcatraz. James Craig
& Bonita Granville. Directed by Edward
Dmytryk. 1942. RKO. 62 min. Sound.
16mm B&W. *Rental:* Films Inc.

Seven Minutes, The. Yvonne De Carlo.
Directed by Russ Meyer. 1971. Fox. 116
min. Sound. 16mm Color. *Rental:* Films
Inc.

Seven Per-Cent Solution, The. Alan
Arkin, Vanessa Redgrave & Robert
Duvall. Directed by Herbert Ross. 1977.
Universal. 113 min. Sound. 16mm Color.
Rental: Swank Motion.

Seven Samurai, The. Takashi Shimura,
Toshiro Mifune & Yoshio Inaba.
Directed by Akira Kurosawa. Jap. 1954.
Japan. 200 min. Sound. 16mm B&W.
subtitles. *Rental:* Budget Films, Films
Inc, Images Film & Syracuse U Film.
Sale: Images Film.

Seven Seas to Calais. Rod Taylor &
Keith Michell. Directed by Rudolph
Mate. 1963. MGM. 102 min. Sound.
16mm Color. *Rental:* MGM United.
Rental: MGM United, Anamorphic
version.

Seven Sinners. Edmund Lowe &
Constance Cummings. Directed by Albert
De Courville. 1936. Britain. 70 min.
Sound. 16mm B&W. *Rental:* Janus Films.

Seven Sinners. Marlene Dietrich & John
Wayne. Directed by Tay Garnett. 1940.
Universal. 87 min. Sound. 16mm B&W.
Rental: Swank Motion.

Seven Surprizes. 1964. Canada. (Color
sequences, Anthology). 77 min. Sound.
16mm B&W. *Rental:* Twyman Films.

Seven Sweethearts. Kathryn Grayson &
Van Heflin. Directed by Frank Borzage.
1942. MGM. 98 min. Sound. 16mm
B&W. *Rental:* MGM United.

Seven Thieves. Edward G. Robinson &
Rod Steiger. Directed by Henry
Hathaway. 1960. Fox. 102 min. Sound.
16mm B&W. *Rental:* Films Inc.

Seven Times Seven. Lionel Stander &
Terry-Thomas. 1972. Allied Artists. 100
min. Sound. 16mm B&W. *Rental:*
Hurlock Cine.

Seven Ups, The. Roy Scheider, Tony
LoBianco & Victor Arnold. Directed by
Philip D'Antoni. 1973. Fox. 103 min.
Sound. 16mm Color. *Rental:* Williams
Films.

Seven Ways from Sundown. Audie
Murphy & Barry Sullivan. Directed by
Harry Keller. 1960. Universal. 86 min.
Sound. 16mm Color. *Rental:* Swank
Motion.

Seven Wishes of a Rich Kid, The.
Butterfly McQueen. Directed by Larry
Elikann. 1979. Learning Corp. 46 min.
Sound. 16mm Color. *Rental:* Learning
Corp Am. *Sale:* Learning Corp Am. *Sale:*
Learning Corp Am, Videotape version.

Seven Women. Anne Bancroft & Sue
Lyon. Directed by John Ford. 1965.
MGM. 93 min. Sound. 16mm Color.
Rental: MGM United. *Rental:* MGM
United, Anamorphic version.

Seven Women from Hell. Patricia Owens
& Denise Darcel. Directed by Robert
Webb. 1961. Fox. (Anamorphic). 88 min.
Sound. 16mm B&W. *Rental:* Willoughby
Peer.

Seven Year Itch, The. Tom Ewell &
Marilyn Monroe. Directed by Billy
Wilder. 1955. Fox. (Anamorphic). 104
min. Sound. 16mm Color. *Rental:* Films
Inc & Williams Films.

Seven Years' Bad Luck. Max Linder.
Directed by Max Linder. 1921.
Robertson/Cole. 60 min. Sound. 16mm
B&W. *Rental:* Em Gee Film Lib. *Sale:*
Glenn Photo & Reel Images.

Seven Years in Tibet. Directed by Hans
Nieter. 1957. (Documentary). 76 min.
16mm Color. *Rental:* A Twyman Pres.

Seventeen Seventy Six. 1964. ABC.
(Documentary). 54 min. Sound. 16mm
Color. *Rental:* U of IL Film, McGraw-
Hill Films & Syracuse U Film. *Sale:*
McGraw-Hill Films.

Seventeen Seventy Six. William Daniels,
Howard Da Silva & Ken Howard.
Directed by Peter Hunt. 1972. Columbia.
148 min. Sound. 16mm Color. *Rental:*
Arcus Film, Budget Films, Bosco Films,
Cine Craft, Film Ctr DC, Films Inc,
Images Film, Inst Cinema, Modern
Sound, Natl Film Video, Swank Motion,
Twyman Films, Welling Motion Pictures,
Westcoast Films, Wholesome Film Ctr &
Williams Films. *Rental:* Swank Motion,
Anamorphic version. *Rental:* Images
Film, Videotape version.

Seventh Cavalry. Randolph Scott & Barbara Hale. Directed by Joseph Lewis. 1957. Columbia. 75 min. Sound. 16mm Color. *Rental:* Arcus Film, Charard Motion Pics, Inst Cinema, Kit Parker & Modern Sound.

Seventh Commandment, The. Jonathan Kidd. Directed by Irvin Berwick. 1961. Canada. 82 min. Sound. 16mm B&W. *Rental:* Video Comm. *Lease:* Video Comm. *Rental:* Video Comm, *Lease:* Video Comm, Videotape version.

Seventh Cross, The. Spencer Tracy & Hume Cronyn. Directed by Fred Zinnemann. 1964. United Artists. 123 min. Sound. 16mm Color. *Rental:* MGM United.

Seventh Dawn, The. William Holden & Susannah York. Directed by Lewis Gilbert. 1964. United Artists. 123 min. Sound. 16mm Color. *Rental:* MGM United.

Seventh Heaven. Janet Gaynor & Charles Farrell. Directed by Frank Borzage. 1927. Fox. 123 min. Sound. 16mm B&W. *Rental:* Films Inc, Killiam Collect & Museum Mod Art. *Sale:* Blackhawk Films, Super 8 sound version. *Sale:* Blackhawk Films, Super 8 silent version.

Seventh Seal, The. Max Von Sydow & Bibi Anderson. Directed by Ingmar Bergman. 1956. Sweden. 96 min. Sound. 16mm B&W. *Rental:* Films Inc, Janus Films, Images Film, New Cinema & Utah Media. *Sale:* Festival Films & Images Film. *Sale:* Festival Films, Videotape version.

Seventh Sin, The. Eleanor Parker & Bill Travers. Directed by Ronald Neame. 1957. MGM. (Anamorphic). 94 min. Sound. 16mm B&W. *Rental:* MGM United.

Seventh Step to Freedom, The. 1973. Canada. (Documentary). 58 min. Sound. 16mm Color. *Rental:* Natl Film CN. *Sale:* Natl Film CN.

Seventh Survivor, The. Austin Trevor & Jane Carr. Directed by Leslie Hiscott. 1943. Britain. 75 min. Sound. 16mm B&W. *Rental:* Ivy Films. *Sale:* Rep Pic Film.

Seventh Victim, The. Kim Hunter, Isabel Jewell & Tom Conway. Directed by Mark Robson. 1943. RKO. 71 min. Sound. 16mm B&W. *Rental:* Films Inc. *Lease:* Films Inc.

Seventh Voyage of Sinbad, The. Kerwin Mathews & Kathryn Grant. Directed by Nathan Juran. 1958. Columbia. 89 min. Sound. 16mm Color. *Rental:* Arcus Film, Buchan Pic, Bosco Films, Cine Craft, Charard Motion Pics, Film Ctr DC, Films Inc, Film Pres, Kit Parker, Kerr Film, Modern Sound, Natl Film CN, Newman Film Lib, Swank Motion, Twyman Films, Video Comm, Welling Motion Pictures, Westcoast Films, Wholesome Film Ctr, Williams Films & Willoughby Peer.

Seventh Year, The. Roy Scheider & Victor Arnold. Directed by Philip D'Antoni. Ger. 1969. 82 min. Sound. 16mm Color. subtitles Ger. *Rental:* Films Inc.

Seventy Deadly Pills, The. Gareth Robinson. Directed by Patrick Jackson. 1964. Britain. 55 min. Sound. 16mm B&W. *Sale:* Lucerne Films.

Severed Head, The. Lee Remick & Richard Attenborough. Directed by Dick Clement. 1970. Britain. 96 min. Sound. 16mm Color. *Rental:* Cine Craft, Welling Motion Pictures, Westcoast Films & Willoughby Peer.

Sevigne. France. (Cast unlisted). 60 min. Sound. 16mm B&W. *Rental:* French Am Cul. *Rental:* French Am Cul, Videotape version.

Sex. Louise Glaum. Directed by Fred Niblo. 1920. Hodkinson. 90 min. Silent. 16mm B&W. *Rental:* Em Gee Film Lib. *Sale:* Glenn Photo. *Rental:* Ivy Films, *Sale:* Glenn Photo, Super 8 silent version. *Sale:* Glenn Photo, Silent 8mm version.

Sex & the Single Girl. Tony Curtis & Natalie Wood. Directed by Richard Quine. 1964. Warners. 114 min. Sound. 16mm Color. *Rental:* Films Inc & Willoughby Peer.

Sex for Sale: The Urban Battle-Ground. Directed by Pamela Hill. 1977. ABC. (Documentary). 47 min. Sound. 16mm Color. *Rental:* Iowa Films, McGraw-Hill Films, Syracuse U Film & U of IL Film. *Sale:* McGraw-Hill Films.

Sex in the Comics. 70 min. Sound. 16mm Color. *Rental:* BF Video.

Sex in Today's World. 1968. Focus. (Documentary). 52 min. Sound. 16mm B&W. *Rental:* U Mich Media.

Sex Kittens Go to College. Mamie Van Doren & Tuesday Weld. Directed by Albert Zugsmith. 1960. Allied Artists. 94 min. Sound. 16mm B&W. *Rental:* Hurlock Cine.

Sex Madness. Orig. Title: They Must Be Told. 1934. Kent. (Cast unlisted). 57 min. Sound. 16mm B&W. *Rental:* Budget Films, Em Gee Film Lib, Ivy Films, Kit Parker, Maljack & Video Comm. *Sale:* Festival Films & Glenn Photo. *Rental:* Maljack & Video Comm, *Sale:* Festival Films, Videotape version.

Sex Shop, Le. Claude Berri & Nathalie Delon. Directed by Claude Berri. Fr. 1972. France. 90 min. Sound. 16mm Color. subtitles. *Rental:* New Line Cinema.

Sex Thief, The. David Warbeck. Directed by Martin Campbell. 1974. Britain. 89 min. Sound. 16mm Color. *Rental:* Films Inc.

Sextette. Mae West & Timothy Dalton. Directed by Ken Hughes. 1978. Crown. 91 min. Sound. 16mm Color. *Rental:* Films Inc.

Sextoons. New Line Cinema. (Animated, anthology). 90 min. Sound. 16mm Color. *Rental:* New Line Cinema.

Sexual Freedom in the Ozarks. (Documentary). 60 min. Videotape Color. *Sale:* Videx Home Lib.

Sexuality: The Human Heritage. 1975. PBS. (Documentary). 59 min. Sound. 16mm Color. *Rental:* U Cal Media, Indiana AV Ctr, Iowa Films & Syracuse U Film. *Sale:* Indiana AV Ctr.

Sgt. Pepper's Lonely Hearts Club Band. Peter Frampton, The Bee Gees & George Burns. Directed by Michael Schultz. 1978. Universal. 113 min. Sound. 16mm Color. *Rental:* Williams Films.

Sh! the Octopus. Allen Jenkins & Hugh Herbert. Directed by William McGann. 1937. Warners. 54 min. Sound. 16mm B&W. *Rental:* MGM United.

Shack Out on One Hundred One. Frank Lovejoy & Terry Moore. Directed by Edward Dein. 1955. Allied Artists. 80 min. Sound. 16mm B&W. *Rental:* Ivy Films. *Lease:* Rep Pic Film.

Shades of Gray. 1948. Army. 66 min. Sound. 16mm B&W. *Rental:* Natl AV Ctr.

Shadow, The. Henry Kendall & Felix Aylmer. Directed by George A. Cooper. 1940. Britain. 71 min. Sound. 16mm B&W. *Rental:* Ivy Films.

Shadow Catcher, The. Orig. Title: Edward S. Curtis, the Shadow. 1975. PBS. (Documentary). 83 min. Sound. 16mm Color. *Rental:* Budget Films, U Cal Media, U Mich Media, Phoenix Films & Syracuse U Film. *Sale:* Phoenix Films. *Sale:* Phoenix Films, Videotape version.

Shadow in the Sky. Ralph Meeker & Nancy Davis. Directed by Fred M. Wilcox. 1951. MGM. 78 min. Sound. 16mm B&W. *Rental:* MGM United.

Shadow in the Sun. Glenda Jackson. 1976. Britain. 90 min. Sound. 16mm Color. *Rental:* Films Inc. *Sale:* Films Inc. *Rental:* Films Inc, *Sale:* Films Inc, Videotape version.

Shadow Man. Cesar Romero & Kay Kendall. Directed by Richard Vernon. 1953. Lippert. 76 min. Sound. 16mm B&W. *Rental:* Budget Films.

Shadow of a Doubt. Teresa Wright & Joseph Cotten. Directed by Alfred Hitchcock. 1943. Universal. 108 min. Sound. 16mm B&W. *Rental:* Swank Motion & Williams Films.

Shadow of a Woman. Helmut Dantine & Andrea King. Directed by Joseph Santley. 1946. Warners. 78 min. Sound. 16mm B&W. *Rental:* MGM United.

Shadow of Doubt. Directed by Rolf Orthel. 1975. Holland. (Documentary, Color sequences). 90 min. Sound. 16mm B&W. narrated Eng. *Rental:* New Yorker Films.

Shadow of Doubt. Ricardo Cortez & Virginia Bruce. Directed by George B. Seitz. 1935. MGM. 75 min. Sound. 16mm B&W. *Rental:* MGM United.

Shadow of Terror. Dick Fraser. Directed by Lew Landers. 1945. PRC. 60 min. Sound. 16mm B&W. *Sale:* Classics Assoc NY.

Shadow of the Cat. Andre Morell & Barbara Shelley. Directed by John Gilling. 1961. Universal. 79 min. Sound. 16mm Color. *Rental:* Swank Motion.

Shadow of the Hawk. Jan-Michael Vincent & Marilyn Hassett. Directed by George McCowan. 1976. Columbia. 92 min. Sound. 16mm Color. *Rental:* Budget Films, Cine Craft, Modern Sound, Natl Film Video, Swank Motion & Westcoast Films.

Shadow of the Thin Man. William Powell & Myrna Loy. Directed by W. S. Van Dyke. 1941. MGM. 84 min. Sound. 16mm B&W. *Rental:* MGM United.

Shadow on the Wall. Ann Sothern & Zachary Scott. Directed by Patrick Jackson. 1950. MGM. 84 min. Sound. 16mm B&W. *Rental:* MGM United.

Shadow on the Window. John Drew Barrymore & Betty Garrett. Directed by William Asher. 1957. Columbia. 105 min. Sound. 16mm B&W. *Rental:* Inst Cinema.

Shadow Ranch. Buck Jones. Directed by Louis King. 1930. Columbia. 55 min. Sound. 16mm B&W. *Rental:* Em Gee Film Lib.

Shadow Strikes, The. Rod LaRocque & Lynn Anders. Directed by Lynn Shores. 1937. Grand National. 65 min. Sound. 16mm B&W. *Rental:* Budget Films, Classic Film Mus & Video Comm. *Rental:* Ivy Films, *Sale:* Ivy Films, Super 8 sound version. *Rental:* Video Comm, Videotape version.

Shadow Valley. Eddie Dean. Directed by Ray Taylor. 1947. Eagle Lion. 60 min. Sound. 16mm B&W. *Sale:* Classics Assoc NY.

Shadowed. Anita Louise & Lloyd Corrigan. Directed by John Sturges. 1946. Columbia. 70 min. Sound. 16mm B&W. *Rental:* Kit Parker.

Shadowman. Jacques Champreux & Gayle Hunnicut. Directed by Georges Franju. Fr. 1974. France. 105 min. Sound. 16mm Color. subtitles. *Rental:* New Line Cinema.

Shadows. Lon Chaney. Directed by Tom Forman. 1922. Lichtman. 70 min. Silent. 16mm B&W. *Rental:* Em Gee Film Lib & Film Classics. *Sale:* Blackhawk Films, Film Classics & E Finney. *Sale:* Blackhawk Films, Super 8 silent version. *Rental:* Film Classics, Videotape version.

Shadows of Chinatown. Bela Lugosi. 1936. Monogram. 60 min. Sound. 16mm B&W. *Rental:* Budget Films & Mogulls Films.

Shadows of Death. Buster Crabbe. Directed by Sam Newfield. 1945. PRC. 60 min. Sound. 16mm B&W. *Rental:* Ivy Films & Mogulls Films. *Sale:* Classics Assoc NY. *Sale:* Video Comm, Videotape version.

Shadows of Forgotten Ancestors. Ivan Nikolaichuk. Directed by Sergei Paradjhanov. Rus. 1964. Russia. 110 min. Sound. 16mm Color. subtitles. *Rental:* Films Inc, Janus Films & New Cinema.

Shadows of the Orient. Regis Toomey & Esther Ralston. Directed by Burt Lynwood. 1937. Monogram. 70 min. Sound. 16mm B&W. *Rental:* Mogulls Films.

Shadows of Tombstone. Rex Allen. Directed by William Witney. 1953. Republic. 54 min. Sound. 16mm B&W. *Rental:* Ivy Films. *Sale:* Rep Pic Film.

Shadows on the Range. Johnny Mack Brown. Directed by Lambert Hillyer. 1946. Monogram. 55 min. Sound. 16mm B&W. *Rental:* Hurlock Cine.

Shadows on the Sage. Tom Tyler & Bob Steele. Directed by Lester Orlebeck. 1943. Republic. 55 min. Sound. 16mm B&W. *Rental:* Ivy Films. *Sale:* Rep Pic Film.

Shadows on the Stairs. Frieda Inescort & Paul Cavanaugh. Directed by D. Ross Lederman. 1941. Warners. 63 min. Sound. 16mm B&W. *Rental:* MGM United.

Shadows Over Chinatown. Sidney Toler & Vanessa Brown. Directed by Terry Morse. 1946. Monogram. 66 min. Sound. 16mm B&W. *Rental:* Hurlock Cine.

Shaft. Richard Roundtree & Moses Gunn. Directed by Gordon Parks. 1971. MGM. 98 min. Sound. 16mm Color. *Rental:* MGM United. *Rental:* MGM United, Videotape version.

Shaft in Africa. Richard Roundtree. Directed by John Guillermin. 1973. MGM. 112 min. Sound. 16mm Color. *Rental:* MGM United.

Shaft's Big Score. Richard Roundtree & Moses Gunn. Directed by Gordon Parks. 1972. MGM. 16mm Color. *Rental:* MGM United.

Shaggy. Brenda Joyce & George Nokes. Directed by Robert Tansey. 1948. Paramount. 72 min. Sound. 16mm B&W. *Rental:* Films Inc.

Shaggy D. A., The. Dean Jones, Keenan Wynn & Tim Conway. 1978. Disney. 91 min. Sound. 16mm Color. *Rental:* Bosco Films, Disney Prod, Elliot Film Co, Films Inc, Film Pres, MGM United, Modern Sound, Roas Films, Swank Motion, Twyman Films, U of IL Film, Welling Motion Pictures, Westcoast Films & Williams Films.

Shaggy Dog, The. Fred MacMurray, Jean Hagen & Tommy Kirk. Directed by Charles Barton. 1959. Disney. 104 min. Sound. 16mm B&W. *Rental:* Bosco Films, Cine Craft, Disney Prod, Elliot Film Co, Film Ctr DC, Films Inc, MGM United, Modern Sound, Roas Films, Swank Motion, Twyman Films, U of IL Film, Welling Motion Pictures, Westcoast Films & Williams Films.

Shake Hands With the Devil. James Cagney & Don Murray. Directed by Michael Anderson. 1959. United Artists. 110 min. Sound. 16mm B&W. *Rental:* MGM United.

Shake, Rattle & Rock. Fats Domino. Directed by Edward L. Cahn. 1956. American International. 77 min. Sound. 16mm B&W. *Rental:* Films Inc & Welling Motion Pictures.

Shake, Rattle & Roll! Rock 'n' Roll Reunion. Verve. (Performance). 75 min. Videotape Color. *Rental:* Films Inc.

Shakedown. Lew Ayres & Joan Perry. Directed by David Selman. 1936. Columbia. 57 min. Sound. 16mm B&W. *Rental:* Kit Parker.

Shakespeare & His Stage: Approaches to Hamlet. 1975. Films for the Humanities. 46 min. Sound. 16mm B&W. *Rental:* Films Human & U of IL Film. *Sale:* Films Human.

Shakespeare & His Theatre. 1977. Media Guild. (Documentary). 52 min. Sound. 16mm Color. *Rental:* Media Guild. *Sale:* Media Guild. *Sale:* Media Guild, Videotape version.

Shakespeare in Perspective. 1983. Britain. (Lecture). 240 min. Videotape Color. *Sale:* Films Inc.

Shakespeare: Soul of an Age. 1963. NBC. (Documentary). 54 min. Sound. 16mm Color. *Rental:* McGraw-Hill Films, Syracuse U Film & U Mich Media. *Sale:* McGraw-Hill Films.

Shakespeare Wallah. Shashi Kapoor & Felicity Kendal. Directed by James Ivory. 1966. Britain. 115 min. Sound. 16mm B&W. *Rental:* Corinth Films, New Cinema & New Yorker Films.

Shakiest Gun in the West, The. Don Knotts, Jackie Coogan & Donald Barry. Directed by Alan Rafkin. 1968. Universal. 101 min. Sound. 16mm Color. *Rental:* Swank Motion.

Shakti: She Is Vital Energy. Directed by Dominique Crouillere. 1977. Canada. (Documentary). 57 min. Sound. 16mm Color. *Rental:* Natl Film CN. *Sale:* Natl Film CN. *Sale:* Natl Film CN, Videotape version.

Shakti with John McLaughlin. Verve. (Concert). 58 min. Color. *Rental:* Films Inc.

Shalako. Sean Connery & Brigitte Bardot. Directed by Edward Dmytryk. 1968. ABC. (Anamorphic). 113 min. Sound. 16mm Color. *Rental:* Films Inc.

Shall We Dance? Fred Astaire & Ginger Rogers. Directed by Mark Sandrich. 1937. RKO. 105 min. Sound. 16mm B&W. *Rental:* Films Inc.

Shalom. Directed by John Hackett. 1971. Israel. (Documentary). 74 min. Sound. 16mm Color. *Rental:* Films Inc, Macmillan Films, Phoenix Films & Syracuse U Film. *Sale:* Macmillan Films & Phoenix Films.

Shame. William Shatner & Frank Maxwell. Directed by Roger Corman. 1962. Filmgroup. 90 min. Sound. 16mm B&W. *Sale:* Morcraft Films. *Sale:* Morcraft Films, Super 8 sound version. *Sale:* Morcraft Films, Videotape version.

Shame. Max Von Sydow & Liv Ullmann. Directed by Ingmar Bergman. 1969. Sweden. 102 min. Sound. 16mm B&W. *Rental:* Em Gee Film Lib & MGM United. *Sale:* Reel Images. *Sale:* Tamarelles French Film, Videotape version.

Shameless Old Lady, The. Trans. Title: Vieille Dame Indigne, La. Sylvie. Directed by Rene Allio. Fr. 1966. France. 94 min. Sound. 16mm B&W. subtitles. *Rental:* Budget Films & New Yorker Films. *Sale:* Tamarelles French Film, Videotape version.

Shampoo. Warren Beatty & Julie Christie. Directed by Hal Ashby. 1975. Columbia. 110 min. Sound. 16mm Color. *Rental:* Films Inc, Images Film, Modern Sound, Swank Motion, Twyman Films, Westcoast Films, Wholesome Film Ctr & Williams Films.

Shamrock & the Rose, The. Mack Swain. Directed by Jack Nelson. 1927. Chadwick. 60 min. Silent. 16mm B&W. *Rental:* Em Gee Film Lib, E Finney & Willoughby Peer.

Shamrock Hill. Peggy Ryan & Ray McDonald. Directed by Arthur Dreifuss. 1949. Eagle Lion. 80 min. Sound. 16mm B&W. *Rental:* Alba House, Charard Motion Pics, Ivy Films & Mogulls Films. *Sale:* Rep Pic Film.

Shamus. John Francis Rooney. Directed by Eric Marquis. 1958. Ireland. 54 min. Sound. 16mm B&W. *Rental:* Films Inc.

Shamus. Burt Reynolds & Dyan Cannon. Directed by Buzz Kulik. 1973. Columbia. 99 min. Sound. 16mm Color. *Rental:* Arcus Film, Budget Films, Cine Craft, Films Inc, Modern Sound, Natl Film Video, Newman Film Lib, Roas Films, Swank Motion, Twyman Films, Welling Motion Pictures, Westcoast Films & Williams Films.

Shane. Alan Ladd & Jean Arthur. Directed by George Stevens. 1953. Paramount. 117 min. Sound. 16mm Color. *Rental:* Films Inc, Modern Sound, Syracuse U Film, Twyman Films & Wholesome Film Ctr.

Shane: The American Hero. Directed by George Stevens. 1979. Paramount. (Abridgement). 60 min. Sound. 16mm Color. *Rental:* Budget Films, La Inst Res Ctr, Modern Sound & U of IL Film.

Shanghai Chest, The. Roland Winters. Directed by William Beaudine. 1948. Monogram. 85 min. Sound. 16mm B&W. *Rental:* Hurlock Cine.

Shanghai Express, The. Marlene Dietrich & Clive Brook. Directed by Josef Von Sternberg. 1932. Paramount. 84 min. Sound. 16mm B&W. *Rental:* Swank Motion & Williams Films.

Shanghai Gesture, The. Gene Tierney & Walter Huston. Directed by Josef Von Sternberg. 1941. United Artists. 90 min. Sound. 16mm B&W. *Rental:* A Twyman Pres, Budget Films, Kit Parker & Willoughby Peer.

Shanghai Killers, The. Directed by Wang Tien Lin. 1973. Hong Kong. 90 min. Sound. 16mm Color. *Rental:* Swank Motion.

Shanghai Shadows. Directed by John David Rabinovitch. 1980. Corinth. (Documentary). 60 min. Sound. 16mm Color. *Rental:* Corinth Films. *Lease:* Corinth Films, *Rental:* Corinth Films, Videotape version.

Shanghai Story, The. Edmond O'Brien & Ruth Roman. Directed by William Beaudine Jr. 1954. Republic. 90 min. Sound. 16mm B&W. *Rental:* Ivy Films. *Sale:* Rep Pic Film.

Shanks. Marcel Marceau. Directed by William Castle. 1974. Paramount. 93 min. Sound. 16mm Color. *Rental:* Films Inc.

Shantytown. Mary Lee & John Archer. Directed by Joseph Santley. 1943. Republic. 66 min. Sound. 16mm B&W. *Rental:* Ivy Films.

Shao Lin Kung Fu Mystaogue. 93 min. Sound. 16mm Color. *Rental:* BF Video.

Shape of Things to Come, The. Jack Palance & Carol Lynley. Directed by George McCowan. 1979. Ventures. 105 min. Sound. 16mm Color. *Rental:* Twyman Films.

Shapes of Dissent, The. 1979. Britain. 52 min. Sound. 16mm Color. *Rental:* Time-Life Multimedia. *Sale:* Time-Life Multimedia. *Sale:* Time-Life Multimedia, Videotape version.

Shaping the Future. (Body in Question Series). 1979. (Documentary). 60 min. Sound. Color. *Rental:* Films Inc & Syracuse U Films. *Sale:* Films Inc.

Sharad of Atlantis. Ray Corrigan, Monte Blue & William Farnum. Directed by B. Reeves Eason & Joseph Kane. 1950. Republic. 100 min. Sound. 16mm B&W. *Rental:* Ivy Films. *Sale:* Rep Pic Film.

Shared Decision Making. 57 min. Sound. 16mm Color. *Rental:* U Mich Media.

Shark! Burt Reynolds & Arthur Kennedy. Directed by Samuel Fuller. 1968. Excelsior. 94 min. Sound. 16mm B&W. *Rental:* Ivy Films. *Lease:* Rep Pic Film.

Sharkey's Machine. Burt Reynolds & Rachel Ward. Directed by Burt Reynolds. 1981. Orion. 119 min. Sound. 16mm Color. *Rental:* Films Inc.

Sharks, The. 1970. (Documentary). 59 min. Sound. 16mm Color. *Rental:* Natl Geog. *Sale:* Churchill Films & Natl Geog. *Sale:* Natl Geog, *Rental:* Churchill Films, Videotape version.

Sharks' Treasure. Cornel Wilde & Yaphet Kotto. Directed by Cornel Wilde. 1975. United Artists. 95 min. Sound. 16mm Color. *Rental:* MGM United & Westcoast Films.

Shattered. Werner Krauss. Directed by Lupu Pick. 1921. Germany. 70 min. Silent. 8mm B&W. *Rental:* Ivy Films. *Sale:* Cinema Concepts.

Shattered Dreams. Miss Dupont & Bertram Grassby. Directed by Paul Scardon. 1921. Universal. 83 min. Silent. 16mm B&W. *Rental:* Budget Films & Em Gee Film Lib.

She. Betty Blythe & Carlyle Blackwell. Directed by Leander De Cordova. 1921. Britain. 85 min. Silent. 16mm B&W. *Rental:* Budget Films, Kerr Film & Video Comm. *Sale:* Blackhawk Films & Morcraft Films. *Sale:* Blackhawk Films, Super 8 silent version. *Rental:* Video Comm, Videotape version.

She. Helen Gahagan, Helen Mack & Randolph Scott. Directed by L. C. Holden & Irving Pichel. 1935. RKO. 94 min. Sound. 16mm B&W. *Rental:* A Twyman Pres & Twyman Films.

She. Ursula Andress & Peter Cushing. Directed by Robert Day. 1965. MGM. 106 min. Sound. 16mm Color. *Rental:* MGM United.

She & He. Sachiko Hidari & Kikuji Yamashita. Directed by Susumi Hani. Jap. 1963. Japan. 110 min. Sound. 16mm B&W. subtitles. *Rental:* Films Inc.

She Couldn't Say No. Eve Arden & Roger Pryor. Directed by William Clemens. 1940. RKO. 63 min. Sound. 16mm B&W. *Rental:* MGM United.

She Couldn't Say No. Robert Mitchum & Jean Simmons. Directed by Lloyd Bacon. 1954. RKO. 89 min. Sound. 16mm B&W. *Rental:* Films Inc.

She Couldn't Take It. Joan Bennett & George Raft. Directed by Tay Garnett. 1935. Columbia. 80 min. Sound. 16mm B&W. *Rental:* Kit Parker.

She Creature, The. Chester Morris, Marla English & Tom Conway. Directed by Edward L. Cahn. 1956. American International. 77 min. Sound. 16mm B&W. *Rental:* Films Inc.

She Dances Alone. Bud Cort & Max Von Sydow. Directed by Robert Fornheim. 1981. Kino. 87 min. Sound. 16mm Color. *Rental:* Kino Intl. *Sale:* Kino Intl.

She Demons. Irish McCalla & Tod Griffin. Directed by Richard Cunha. 1958. Astor. 80 min. Sound. 16mm B&W. *Rental:* Budget Films & Ivy Films. *Sale:* Morcraft Films & Reel Images.

She Devil, The. Jack Kelly & Mari Blanchard. Directed by Kurt Neumann. 1957. Fox. 79 min. Sound. 16mm B&W. *Rental:* Budget Films & Ivy Films. *Sale:* Rep Pic Film.

She Devil, The. 1940. (All black cast). 62 min. Sound. 16mm B&W. *Rental:* Kit Parker.

She Done Him Wrong. Mae West & Cary Grant. Directed by Lowell Sherman. 1933. Paramount. 68 min. Sound. 16mm B&W. *Rental:* Williams Films.

She Gods of Shark Reef. Don Durant & Bill Cord. Directed by Roger Corman. 1958. Filmways. 63 min. Sound. 16mm B&W. *Rental:* Westcoast Films.

She Goes to War. Eleanor Boardman & Alma Rubens. Directed by Henry King. 1929. United Artists. 50 min. Sound. 16mm B&W. *Rental:* Em Gee Film Lib. *Sale:* Glenn Photo.

She Had to Say Yes. Loretta Young & Lyle Talbot. Directed by Richard Wallace. 1933. Warners. 64 min. Sound. 16mm B&W. *Rental:* MGM United.

She Knew All the Answers. Joan Bennett & Franchot Tone. Directed by Richard Wallace. 1941. Columbia. 90 min. Sound. 16mm B&W. *Rental:* Kit Parker.

She Let Him Continue *see* Pretty Poison.

She Loved a Fireman. Ann Sheridan & Dick Foran. Directed by John Farrow. 1938. Warners. 57 min. Sound. 16mm B&W. *Rental:* MGM United.

She Married a Cop. Phil Regan & Jean Parker. Directed by Sidney Salkow. 1939. Republic. 54 min. Sound. 16mm B&W. *Rental:* Ivy Films. *Sale:* Rep Pic Film.

She Married Her Boss. Claudette Colbert & Melvyn Douglas. Directed by Gregory La Cava. 1935. Columbia. 90 min. Sound. 16mm B&W. *Rental:* Corinth Films & Swank Motion.

She Stoops to Conquer. 1976. Britain. (Cast unlisted). 119 min. Sound. Videotape Color. *Rental:* Films Inc. *Sale:* Films Inc.

She-Wolf of London, The. Don Porter & June Lockhart. Directed by Jean Yarbrough. 1946. Universal. 61 min. Sound. 16mm B&W. *Rental:* Swank Motion.

She Wore a Yellow Ribbon. John Wayne & Joanne Dru. Directed by John Ford. 1949. RKO. 103 min. Sound. Videotape Color. *Sale:* Arcus Film, Cine Craft, Film Ctr DC, Films Inc, Images Film, Macmillian Films, Modern Sound, RKO General Pics, Syracuse U Film, Twyman Films, Vidamerica, Video Comm, Welling Motion Pictures, Westcoast Films & Wholesale Film Ctr. *Lease:* Macmillan Films. *Rental:* RKO General Pics, 93 version.

She Wouldn't Say Yes. Rosalind Russell. Directed by Alexander Hall. 1945. Columbia. 87 min. Sound. 16mm B&W. *Rental:* Kit Parker.

Sheba Baby. Pam Grier. Directed by William Girdler. 1975. American International. 90 min. Sound. 16mm Color. *Rental:* Swank Motion.

Shed No Tears. Wallace Ford & June Vincent. Directed by Jean Yarbrough. 1948. Eagle Lion. 80 min. Sound. 16mm B&W. *Rental:* Mogulls Films.

Sheep Has Five Legs, The. Trans. Title: Mouton a Cinq Pattes, Le. Fernandel & Louis De Funes. Directed by Henri Verneuil. 1955. France. 95 min. Sound. 16mm B&W. *Rental:* Budget Films & Kit Parker. *Sale:* Reel Images. *Sale:* Tamarelles French Film, Videotape version.

Sheepman, The. Glenn Ford & Shirley MacLaine. Directed by George Marshall. 1958. MGM. 86 min. Sound. 16mm Color. *Rental:* MGM United. *Rental:* MGM United, Anamorphic version.

Sheer Sport. 1971. Canada. (Documentary). 50 min. Sound. 16mm Color. *Rental:* Natl Film CN. *Sale:* Natl Film CN.

Sheik Steps Out, The. Ramon Novarro & Lola Lane. Directed by Irving Pichel. 1937. Republic. 66 min. Sound. 16mm B&W. *Rental:* Ivy Films. *Sale:* Rep Pic Film.

Sheila Levine is Dead & Living in New York. Jeannie Berlin & Roy Scheider. Directed by Sidney J. Furie. 1975. Paramount. 112 min. Sound. 16mm Color. *Rental:* Films Inc.

Shenandoah. James Stewart & Rosemary Forsyth. Directed by Andrew V. McLaglen. 1965. Universal. 105 min. Sound. 16mm Color. *Rental:* Swank Motion. *Rental:* Swank Motion, Videotape version.

Shep Comes Home. Robert Lowery & Billy Kimbley. Directed by Ford Beebe. 1949. Screen Guild. 58 min. Sound. 16mm B&W. *Rental:* Budget Films, Charard Motion Pics & Film Ctr DC.

Shepherd of the Hills, The. John Wayne & Betty Field. Directed by Henry Hathaway. 1941. Paramount. 98 min. Sound. 16mm Color. *Rental:* Swank Motion.

Shepherd of the Night Flock. Directed by George Stoney. 1978. Museum of Modern Art. (Documentary). 57 min. Sound. 16mm B&W. *Rental:* Museum Mod Art.

Shepherd of the Ozarks. Orig. Title: Susanna. Weaver Brothers & Elviry. Directed by Frank McDonald. 1942. Republic. 70 min. Sound. 16mm B&W. *Rental:* Ivy Films.

Shepherds of Berneray, The. Directed by Allen Moore. 1981. Harvard U.. 55 min. Sound. 16mm Color. *Rental:* Museum Mod Art.

Sheriff of Cimarron. Sunset Carson. Directed by Yakima Canutt. 1945. Republic. 54 min. Sound. 16mm B&W. *Sale:* Rep Pic Film & Nostalgia Merchant.

Sheriff of Fractured Jaw, The. Kenneth Moore & Jayne Mansfield. Directed by Raoul Walsh. 1958. Fox. 102 min. Sound. 16mm Color. *Rental:* Films Inc.

Sheriff of Las Vegas. Bill Elliott. Directed by Lesley Selander. 1944. Republic. 54 min. Sound. 16mm B&W. *Rental:* Ivy Films & Rep Pic Film. *Lease:* Rep Pic Film.

Sheriff of Medicine Bow. Johnny Mack Brown. Directed by Lambert Hillyer. 1948. Monogram. 60 min. Sound. 16mm B&W. *Rental:* Budget Films.

Sheriff of Redwood Valley. Bill Elliott. Directed by R. G. Springsteen. 1946. Republic. 54 min. Sound. 16mm B&W. *Rental:* Ivy Films & Rep Pic Film. *Lease:* Rep Pic Film.

Sheriff of Sundown. Allan Lane. Directed by Lesley Selander. 1945. Republic. 55 min. Sound. 16mm B&W. *Rental:* Ivy Films. *Sale:* Rep Pic Film.

Sheriff of Tombstone. Roy Rogers. Directed by Joseph Kane. 1941. Republic. 54 min. Sound. 16mm B&W. *Rental:* Ivy Films. *Sale:* Rep Pic Film.

Sheriff of Wichita. Allan Lane. Directed by R. G. Springsteen. 1948. Republic. 60 min. Sound. 16mm B&W. *Rental:* Ivy Films. *Sale:* Rep Pic Film & Nostalgia Merchant.

Sherlock Holmes. Clive Brook & Ernest Torrance. Directed by William K. Howard. 1932. Fox. 68 min. Sound. 16mm B&W. *Rental:* Films Inc.

Sherlock Holmes & the Deadly Necklace. Christopher Lee & Senta Berger. Directed by Terence Fisher. 1964. Germany. 90 min. Sound. 16mm B&W. dubbed. *Rental:* Budget Films & Westcoast Films.

Sherlock Holmes & the Secret Weapon. Basil Rathbone. Directed by Roy William Neill. 1942. Universal. 68 min. Sound. 16mm B&W. *Rental:* Budget Films, Classic Film Mus, Learning Corp Am, Natl Film Video, Roas Films & Wholesome Film Ctr. *Sale:* Cinema Concepts, Festival Films & Learning Corp Am. *Sale:* Cinema Concepts, Super 8 sound version. *Sale:* Festival Films & Tamarelles French Films, Videotape version.

Sherlock Holmes & the Spider Woman. Orig. Title: Spider Woman, The. Basil Rathbone. Directed by Roy William Neill. 1944. Universal. 63 min. Sound. 16mm B&W. *Rental:* Learning Corp Am & Video Comm. *Sale:* Learning Corp Am.

Sherlock Holmes & the Voice of Terror. Basil Rathbone. Directed by John Rawlins. 1942. Universal. 65 min. Sound. 16mm B&W. *Rental:* Learning Corp Am & Video Comm. *Sale:* Learning Corp Am.

Sherlock Holmes Faces Death. Basil Rathbone. Directed by Roy William Neill. 1943. Universal. 68 min. Sound. 16mm B&W. *Rental:* Em Gee Film Lib, Learning Corp Am & Video Comm. *Sale:* Learning Corp Am.

Sherlock Holmes in Washington. Basil Rathbone. Directed by Roy William Neill. 1943. Universal. 71 min. Sound. 16mm B&W. *Rental:* Learning Corp Am & Video Comm. *Sale:* Learning Corp Am.

Sherlock, Jr. Buster Keaton. Directed by Buster Keaton. 1924. Metro. 75 min. Silent. 16mm B&W. *Rental:* A Twyman Pres & Films Inc.

Sherpas of Everest, The. 1970. Britain. (Documentary). 75 min. Silent. 16mm Color. *Rental:* Time-Life Multimedia. *Sale:* Time-Life Multimedia. *Rental:* Time-Life Multimedia, *Sale:* Time-Life Multimedia, Videotape version.

She's Got Everything. Ann Sothern & Jack Carson. Directed by Joseph Santley. 1938. RKO. 72 min. Sound. 16mm *Rental:* RKO General Pics.

She's My Weakness. Sue Carol & Arthur Lake. Directed by Melville Brown. 1931. RKO. 73 min. Sound. 16mm B&W. *Rental:* RKO General Pics.

She's Nobody's Baby: A History of American Women in the 20th Century. 1982. ABC. 55 min. Sound. 16mm Color. *Rental:* MTI Tele, Syracuse U Film & U Cal Media. *Sale:* MTI Tele.

Shield of Honor. Neil Hamilton & Thelma Todd. Directed by Emory Johnson. 1927. Universal. 72 min. Silent. 16mm B&W. *Rental:* Mogulls Films.

Shifting Sands. Orig. Title: Her Wanton Destiny. Gloria Swanson. Directed by Albert Parker. 1918. Triangle. 60 min. Silent. 16mm B&W. *Rental:* Em Gee Film Lib. *Sale:* E Finney. *Rental:* Cinema Concepts, Sound version.

Shinbone Alley. Directed by John D. Wilson. 1971. Allied Artists. (Animated). 99 min. Sound. 16mm Color. *Rental:* Hurlock Cine.

Shine on Harvest Moon. Roy Rogers. Directed by Joseph Kane. 1938. Republic. 54 min. Sound. 16mm B&W. *Rental:* Budget Films & Ivy Films. *Sale:* Rep Pic Film. *Rental:* Budget Films, 60 mins. version.

Shine on Harvest Moon. Ann Sheridan & Dennis Morgan. Directed by David Butler. 1944. Warners. 122 min. Sound. 16mm B&W. *Rental:* MGM United.

Shining, The. Jack Nicholson & Shelly Duvall. Directed by Stanley Kubrick. 1980. Warners. 120 min. Sound. 16mm Color. *Rental:* Swank Motion. *Rental:* Swank Motion, Videotape version.

Shining Hour, The. Joan Crawford, Melvyn Douglas, Robert Young & Margaret Sullavan. Directed by Frank Borzage. 1938. MGM. 76 min. Sound. 16mm B&W. *Rental:* MGM United.

Shining Mountains, The. 1970. NBC. 51 min. Sound. 16mm Color. *Rental:* Films Inc. *Sale:* Films Inc.

Shining Victory, The. Geraldine Fitzgerald & James Stephenson. Directed by Irving Rapper. 1941. Warners. 80 min. Sound. 16mm B&W. *Rental:* MGM United.

Shinto: Nature, Gods & Man in Japan. 1976. Japan. (Documentary). 48 min. Sound. 16mm Color. *Rental:* Iowa Films, Japan Society & U of IL Film. *Sale:* Japan Society. *Sale:* Japan Society, Videotape version.

Ship Comes In, A. Rudolph Schildkraut & Louise Dresser. Directed by William K. Howard. 1928. Pathe. 70 min. Silent. B&W. *Sale:* Cinema Concepts.

Ship from Shanghai, The. Conrad Nagel & Kay Johnson. Directed by Charles Brabin. 1930. MGM. 68 min. Sound. 16mm B&W. *Rental:* MGM United.

Ship of Fools, The. Vivien Leigh, Oskar Werner & Simone Signoret. 1965. Columbia. 130 min. Sound. 16mm B&W. *Rental:* Arcus Film, Bosco Films, Budget Films, Cine Craft, Charard Motion Pics, Films Inc, Images Film, Inst Cinema, Kit Parker, Modern Sound, Natl Film Video, Roas Films, Swank Motion, U of IL Film, Video Comm, Welling Motion Pictures, Westcoast Films, Wholesome Film Ctr & Williams Films.

Ship That Wouldn't Die, The. 1970. NBC. 51 min. Sound. 16mm Color. *Rental:* Films Inc. *Sale:* Films Inc. *Sale:* Films Inc, Videotape version.

Shipbuilders, The. Clive Brook. Directed by John Baxter. 1945. Britain. 86 min. Sound. 16mm B&W. *Rental:* Ivy Films. *Sale:* Rep Pic Film.

Shipmates. Robert Montgomery & Dorothy Jordan. Directed by Harry Pollard. 1931. MGM. 70 min. Sound. 16mm B&W. *Rental:* MGM United.

Shipmates Forever. Dick Powell & Ruby Keeler. Directed by Frank Borzage. 1935. Warners. 124 min. Sound. 16mm B&W. *Rental:* MGM United.

Ships of the Night. Jacqueline Logan & Sojin. Directed by Duke Worne. 1929. Rayart. 70 min. Silent. 16mm B&W. *Rental:* Em Gee Film Lib & Willoughby Peer.

Ships That Flew, The. 1974. Australia. (Documentary). 49 min. Sound. 16mm Color. *Rental:* Aust Info Serv. *Sale:* Aust Info Serv.

Shipwreck Island. Pablito Calvo. 1961. Spain. 93 min. Sound. 16mm Color. dubbed. *Rental:* Films Inc, Macmillan Films, Newman Film Lib & Westcoast Films. *Lease:* Macmillan Films.

Shirt Off Your Back, The. 1979. 58 min. Sound. Videotape Color. *Rental:* PBS Video. *Sale:* PBS Video.

Shock, The. Lon Chaney & Virginia Valli. Directed by Lambert Hillyer. 1923. Universal. 80 min. Silent. 16mm B&W. *Rental:* Budget Films & Em Gee Film Lib. *Sale:* Blackhawk Films. *Sale:* Blackhawk Films & Morcraft Films, Super 8 silent version.

Shock. Vincent Price & Lynn Bari. Directed by Alfred M. Werker. 1946. Fox. 70 min. Sound. 16mm B&W. *Rental:* Budget Films, Classic Film Mus & Willoughby Peer. *Sale:* Natl Cinema.

Shock. Alain Delon & Annie Giardot. Directed by Alain Jessua. Fr. 1974. France. 93 min. Sound. 16mm Color. subtitles. *Rental:* New Line Cinema.

Shock Corridor. Constance Towers & Peter Breck. Directed by Samuel Fuller. 1963. Allied Artists. 101 min. Sound. 16mm B&W. *Rental:* Budget Films, Hurlock Cine & Kit Parker.

Shock Treatment. Lauren Bacall & Stuart Whitman. Directed by Denis Sanders. 1964. Fox. 94 min. Sound. 16mm B&W. *Rental:* Films Inc.

Shock Troops. Trans. Title: Homme de Trop, Un. Bruno Cremer & Michel Piccoli. Directed by Costa-Gavras. Fr. 1968. France. 106 min. Sound. 16mm Color. subtitles. *Rental:* MGM United. *Rental:* MGM United, Dubbed version.

Shocking Miss Pilgrim, The. Betty Grable & Dick Haymes. Directed by George Seaton. 1947. Fox. 85 min. Sound. 16mm B&W. *Rental:* Films Inc.

Shockproof. Cornel Wilde & Patricia Knight. Directed by Douglas Sirk. 1949. Columbia. 79 min. Sound. 16mm B&W. *Rental:* Kit Parker.

Shoes of the Fisherman, The. Anthony Quinn & David Janssen. Directed by Michael Anderson. 1968. 162 min. Sound. 16mm Color. *Rental:* MGM United. *Rental:* MGM United, Anamorphic version.

Shoeshine. Rinaldo Smordoni. Directed by Vittorio De Sica. Ital. 1946. Italy. 93 min. Sound. 16mm B&W. subtitles. *Rental:* Films Inc & Janus Films.

Shogun Assassin. Tomisaburo Wakayama & Masahiro Tomikawa. Directed by Robert Houston. 1980. Japan. Sound. 16mm Color. dubbed. *Rental:* Films Inc.

Shoot First. Joel McCrea & Evelyn Keyes. Directed by Robert Parrish. 1953. United Artists. 88 min. Sound. 16mm B&W. *Rental:* MGM United.

Shoot Loud, Louder, I Don't Understand. Marcello Mastroianni & Raquel Welch. Directed by Eduardo De Filippo. 1967. Italy. 101 min. Sound. 16mm Color. dubbed. *Rental:* Cine Craft.

Shoot Out. Gregory Peck, Robert F. Lyons & Susan Tyrell. Directed by Henry Hathaway. 1971. Universal. 95 min. Sound. 16mm Color. *Rental:* Westcoast Films.

Shoot the Moon. Albert Finney, Diane Keaton & Karen Allen. Directed by Alan Parker. 1981. 124 min. Sound. 16mm Color. *Rental:* MGM United. *Rental:* MGM United, Videotape version.

Shoot the Piano Player. Trans. Title: Tirez Sur Le Pianiste. Charles Aznavour & Nicole Berger. Directed by Francois Truffaut. 1960. France. 84 min. Sound. 16mm B&W. subtitles. *Rental:* Budget Films, Em Gee Film Lib, Films Inc, Janus Films, New Cinema & Wholesome Film Ctr. *Sale:* Cinema Concepts, Natl Cinema & Reel Images. *Sale:* Tamarelles French Film, Videotape version.

Shoot to Kill. Russell Wade & Susan Walters. Directed by William Berke. 1946. Screen Guild. 63 min. Sound. 16mm B&W. *Rental:* Budget Films, Modern Sound, Mogulls Films & Video Comm.

Shoot to Kill. Frank Latimore & Fernando Sancho. Directed by Ramon Torrado. Spain. 87 min. Sound. 16mm B&W. dubbed. *Rental:* Modern Sound. *Rental:* Westcoast Films, 95 mins. version.

Shooting, The. Millie Perkins, Jack Nicholson, Wil Hutchins & Warren Oates. Directed by Monte Hellman. 1967. Continental. 82 min. Sound. 16mm Color. *Rental:* Budget Films & Kit Parker. *Sale:* Kino Intl.

Shooting Gallery Called America, A. 1975. NBC. (Documentary). 52 min. Sound. 16mm Color. *Rental:* Films Inc & Syracuse U Film. *Sale:* Films Inc. *Sale:* Films Inc, Videotape version.

Shooting High. Jane Withers & Gene Autry. Directed by Alfred E. Green. 1940. Fox. 65 min. Sound. 16mm B&W. *Rental:* Films Inc.

Shooting Irons. Orig. Title: West of Texas. James Newill & Dave O'Brien. Directed by Oliver Drake. 1943. Eagle Lion. 58 min. Sound. 16mm B&W. *Rental:* Video Comm.

Shooting Party, The. Gulina Belyayeva. Rus. 1977. Russia. 105 min. Sound. 16mm Color. subtitles. *Rental:* Corinth Films.

Shooting Straight. Richard Dix. Directed by Lowell Sherman. 1930. RKO. Sound. 16mm B&W. *Rental:* RKO General Pics.

Shootist, The. John Wayne, Lauren Bacall & Ron Howard. Directed by Don Siegel. 1976. Paramount. 99 min. Sound. 16mm Color. *Rental:* Films Inc.

Shop Around the Corner, The. James Stewart & Margaret Sullavan. Directed by Ernst Lubitsch. 1940. MGM. 97 min. Sound. 16mm B&W. *Rental:* MGM United.

Shop on Main Street, The. Ida Kaminska & Josef Kroner. Directed by Jan Kadar. 1965. Czechoslovakia. 128 min. Sound. 16mm B&W. subtitles. *Rental:* Films Inc & New Cinema.

Shop Talk. 83 min. Sound. 16mm Color. *Rental:* Cinema Guild.

Shopworn. Barbara Stanwyck & ZaSu Pitts. Directed by Nick Grinde. 1932. Columbia. 80 min. Sound. 16mm B&W. *Rental:* Kit Parker.

Shopworn Angel, The. Margaret Sullavan & James Stewart. Directed by Richard Wallace. 1938. MGM. 85 min. Sound. 16mm B&W. *Rental:* MGM United.

Shore Leave. William Shatner & Leonard Nimoy. Directed by Tobert Spaer. 1966. Star Trek. 50 min. Sound. 16mm Color. *Rental:* Roas Films & Westcoast Films.

Shores of the Cosmic Ocean, The. 1980. Cosmos. (Documentary). 60 min. Sound. 16mm Color. *Rental:* Films Inc. *Sale:* Films Inc. *Sale:* Films Inc, Videotape version.

Shors. Yevgeni Samoilov. Directed by Alexander Dovzhenko. Rus. 1939. Russia. 90 min. Sound. 16mm B&W. subtitles. *Rental:* Corinth Films.

Short Cut to Hell. Robert Ivers & Georgann Johnson. Directed by James Cagney. 1947. Paramount. 87 min. Sound. 16mm B&W. *Rental:* Films Inc.

Short Eyes. Bruce Davison & Jose Peres. Directed by Robert M. Young. 1977. Film League. 104 min. Sound. 16mm Color. *Rental:* Corinth Films & Images Film.

Short Grass. Rod Cameron & Cathy Downs. Directed by Lesley Selander. 1950. Monogram. 82 min. Sound. 16mm B&W. *Rental:* Hurlock Cine.

Short Happy Day from the Journey of A, A. Directed by Roderick Bradley. 1965. Roderick Bradley. 60 min. Sound. 16mm B&W. *Rental:* Canyon Cinema.

Short Memory, A. Britain. (Documentary). 60 min. Sound. 16mm B&W. *Rental:* Budget Films & Modern Sound. *Sale:* Modern Sound.

Shostakovich's Ninth Symphony. 1967. CBS. (Documentary). 54 min. Sound. 16mm B&W. *Rental:* McGraw-Hill Films, Syracuse U Film & U of IL Film. *Sale:* McGraw-Hill Films.

Shot in the Dark, A. William Lundigan & Ricardo Cortez. Directed by William McGann. 1941. Warners. 60 min. Sound. 16mm B&W. *Rental:* MGM United.

Shot in the Dark, A. Peter Sellers & Elke Sommer. Directed by Blake Edwards. 1964. United Artists. 101 min. Sound. 16mm Color. *Rental:* MGM United. *Rental:* MGM United, Videotape version.

Should Husbands Work? James Gleason & Marie Wilson. Directed by Gus Meins. 1939. Republic. 54 min. Sound. 16mm B&W. *Rental:* Ivy Films. *Sale:* Rep Pic Film.

Should Journalists Have the Right to Protect Their Sources? (Advocates Series). 1978. 59 min. Sound. Videotape *Rental:* PBS Video. *Sale:* PBS Video.

Should Ladies Behave? Lionel Barrymore & Alice Brady. Directed by Harry Beaumont. 1933. MGM. 90 min. Sound. 16mm B&W. *Rental:* MGM United.

Should Our Foreign Policy Include Covert Action by the CIA? (Advocates Ser.). 1978. 59 min. Sound. Videotape *Rental:* PBS Video. *Sale:* PBS Video.

Shout, The. Alan Bates & Susannah York. Directed by Jerzy Skolimowski. 1979. Britain. 86 min. Sound. 16mm Color. *Rental:* Films Inc.

Shout at the Devil. Lee Marvin & Roger Moore. Directed by Peter Hunt. 1976. American International. 128 min. Sound. 16mm Color. *Rental:* Swank Motion.

Shout for Joy. Erik Jacobson. 58 min. Sound. 16mm Color. *Rental:* Gospel Films.

Show, The. John Gilbert & Renee Adoree. Directed by Tod Browning. 1927. MGM. 75 min. Silent. 16mm B&W. *Rental:* MGM United.

Show Boat. Kathryn Grayson, Ava Gardner & Howard Keel. 1951. MGM. 108 min. Sound. 16mm Color. *Rental:* MGM United. *Rental:* MGM United, Videotape version.

Show Business. Eddie Cantor & Joan Davis. Directed by Edwin L. Marin. 1944. RKO. 92 min. Sound. 16mm B&W. *Rental:* Films Inc.

Show Girl, The. Mildred Harris & Mary Carr. Directed by Charles Hunt. 1927. Rayart. 65 min. Silent. 16mm B&W. *Rental:* Budget Films.

Show Girl in Hollywood. Alice White & Jack Mulhall. Directed by Mervyn LeRoy. 1930. Warners. 80 min. Sound. 16mm B&W. *Rental:* MGM United.

Show of Shows, The. John Barrymore & Beatrice Lillie. Directed by John Adolfi. 1929. Warners. 128 min. Sound. 16mm B&W. *Rental:* MGM United.

Show-Off, The. Red Skelton & Marilyn Maxwell. Directed by Harry Beaumont. 1946. MGM. 83 min. Sound. 16mm B&W. *Rental:* MGM United.

Show People. Marion Davies & William Haines. Directed by King Vidor. 1928. MGM. 106 min. Silent. 16mm B&W. *Rental:* MGM United.

Show Them No Mercy. Rochelle Hudson & Cesar Romero. Directed by George Marshall. 1935. Fox. 76 min. Sound. 16mm B&W. *Rental:* Films Inc.

Showboat. Irene Dunne, Allan Jones & Helen Morgan. Directed by James Whale. 1936. Universal. 110 min. Sound. 16mm B&W. *Rental:* MGM United.

Showboat Nineteen-Eighty-Four. Ed Nylund & Skip Covington. Directed by Richard R. Schmidt. New Line. 94 min. Sound. 16mm Color. *Rental:* New Line Cinema.

Showdown. William Boyd. Directed by Howard Bretherton. 1940. Paramount. 54 min. Sound. 16mm B&W. *Sale:* Cinema Concepts.

Showdown. Walter Brennan & Leif Ericson. Directed by Dorrell McGowan. 1950. Republic. 86 min. Sound. 16mm B&W. *Rental:* Ivy Films. *Sale:* Rep Pic Film & Nostalgia Merchant.

Showdown. Audie Murphy & Kathleen Crowley. Directed by R. G. Springsteen. 1963. Universal. 79 min. Sound. 16mm B&W. *Rental:* Swank Motion.

Showdown at Abilene. Jock Mahoney & Martha Hyer. Directed by Charles Haas. 1956. Universal. 80 min. Sound. 16mm Color. *Rental:* Swank Motion.

Showdown at Boot Hill. Charles Bronson & Robert Hutton. Directed by Gene Fowler. 1958. Fox. 76 min. Sound. 16mm B&W. *Rental:* Ivy Films.

Showdown at the Hoedown. 1979. Center for Southern Folklore. (Documentary). 60 min. Sound. Videotape Color. *Sale:* Ctr South Folklore.

Showdown at the O. K. Corral. 1974. Wolper. (Documentary). 52 min. Sound. 16mm B&W. *Rental:* Films Inc. *Sale:* Films Inc. *Rental:* Films Inc, *Sale:* Films Inc, Color version. *Sale:* Films Inc, Videotape version.

Showman, The. Directed by Albert Maysles & David Maysles. 1967. Maysles. (Documentary). 53 min. Sound. 16mm B&W. *Rental:* Maysles Films.

Shriek in the Night, A. Ginger Rogers & Lyle Talbot. Directed by Albert Ray. 1933. Allied. 74 min. Sound. 16mm B&W. *Rental:* Budget Films, Classic Film Mus, Em Gee Film Lib, Film Classics & Mogulls Films. *Sale:* Glenn Photo & Reel Images. *Sale:* Reel Images, Super 8 sound version.

Shrike, The. Jose Ferrer & June Allyson. Directed by Jose Ferrer. 1955. Universal. 88 min. Sound. 16mm B&W. *Rental:* Swank Motion.

Shut My Big Mouth. Joe E. Brown & Adele Mara. Directed by Charles Barton. 1942. Columbia. 80 min. Sound. 16mm B&W. *Rental:* Films Inc, Newman Film Lib, Roas Films & Welling Motion Pictures.

Shuttered Room, The. Gig Young & Carol Lynley. Directed by David Greene. 1968. Warners. 100 min. Sound. 16mm Color. *Rental:* Cine Craft, Films Inc, Video Comm, Westcoast Films & Willoughby Peer.

Siberia. 1967. NBC. (Documentary). 51 min. Sound. 16mm Color. *Rental:* U of IL Film & McGraw-Hill Films. *Sale:* McGraw-Hill Films. *Rental:* Budget Films, XB&W version.

Siberia: The Endless Horizon. 1969. National Geographic. (Documentary). 51 min. Sound. 16mm Color. *Rental:* Iowa Films, Natl Geog, Syracuse U Film, U Mich Media & Wholesome Film Ctr. *Sale:* Natl Geog. *Sale:* Natl Geog, Videotape version.

Siberian Lady Macbeth. Olivera Markovic & Ljuba Tadic. Directed by Andrzej Wajda. Rus. 1961. Russia. 90 min. Sound. 16mm B&W. subtitles. *Rental:* Films Inc.

Sicilian Clan, The. Jean Gabin & Alain Delon. Directed by Henri Verneuil. 1970. Fox. (Anamorphic). 121 min. Sound. 16mm Color. *Rental:* Films Inc.

Side Show. Winnie Lightner & Donald Cook. Directed by Roy Del Ruth. 1931. Warners. 64 min. Sound. 16mm B&W. *Rental:* MGM United.

Side Street. Farley Granger & Cathy O'Donnell. Directed by Anthony Mann. 1949. MGM. 81 min. Sound. 16mm B&W. *Rental:* MGM United.

Side Street. Tom Moore, Matt Moore & Owen Moore. Directed by Mal St. Clair. 1929. RKO. Sound. 16mm B&W. *Rental:* RKO General Pics.

Side Streets. Orig. Title: Woman in Her Thirties, A. Paul Kelly & Ann Dvorak. Directed by Alfred E. Green. 1934. Warners. 63 min. Sound. 16mm B&W. *Rental:* MGM United.

Sidecar Racers. Ben Murphy. Directed by Earl Bellamy. 1975. Britain. 100 min. Sound. 16mm Color. *Rental:* Twyman Films.

Sidehackers, The. Diane McBain & Ross Hagen. Directed by Gus Trikonis. 1969. Britain. 82 min. Sound. 16mm Color. *Rental:* Video Comm. *Lease:* Video Comm. *Rental:* Video Comm, *Lease:* Video Comm, Videotape version.

Sideshow. Don McGuire. Directed by Jean Yarbrough. 1950. Monogram. 67 min. Sound. 16mm B&W. *Rental:* Hurlock Cine.

Sidewalks of London. Charles Laughton & Vivien Leigh. Directed by Tim Whelan. 1940. Paramount. 86 min. Sound. 16mm B&W. *Rental:* Budget Films, Em Gee Film Lib, Film Classics, Kit Parker, Mogulls Films, Video Comm & Welling Motion Pictures. *Sale:* Glenn Photo. *Rental:* Video Comm, Videotape version.

Sidewalks of London see St. Martin's Lane.

Sidewalks of New York. Buster Keaton & Anita Page. Directed by Jules White. 1931. MGM. 71 min. Sound. 16mm B&W. *Rental:* MGM United.

Sidewinder One. Marjoe Gortner & Michael Parks. Directed by Earl Bellamy. 1977. Embassy. 97 min. Sound. 16mm Color. *Rental:* Films Inc.

Sidhartha. Shashi Kapoor & Simi Garewai. Directed by Conrad Rooks. 1973. India. 88 min. Sound. 16mm *Rental:* Budget Films.

Sidney Sheldon's Bloodline. Orig. Title: Bloodline. Audrey Hepburn, Ben Gazzara & James Mason. Directed by Terence Young. 1979. Paramount. 116 min. Sound. 16mm Color. *Rental:* Films Inc.

Siege at Red River, The. Van Johnson & Joanne Dru. Directed by Rudolph Mate. 1954. Fox. 87 min. Sound. 16mm Color. *Rental:* Films Inc.

Siege of Syracuse, The. Rossano Brazzi & Tina Louise. Directed by Pietro Francisci. 1962. Paramount. (Anamorphic). 97 min. Sound. 16mm Color. dubbed. *Rental:* Films Inc.

Siege of the Saxons, The. Orig. Title: King Arthur & the Siege of the Saxons. Janette Scott & Ronald Lewis. Directed by Nathan Juran. 1963. Britain. 85 min. Sound. 16mm Color. *Rental:* Arcus Film, Film Ctr DC, Films Inc, Modern Sound, Roas Films & Westcoast Films.

Siegfried. Orig. Title: Niebelungen. Margarete Schon & Margarete Schon. Directed by Fritz Lang. 1924. Germany. (Music & sound effects only). 86 min. Sound. 16mm B&W. *Rental:* Budget Films, Em Gee Film Lib, Film Images, Images Film, Iowa Films, Janus Films, Kit Parker & Museum Mod Art. *Sale:* Cinema Concepts & Film Images, *Rental:* A Twyman Pres, Silent 16mm version. *Rental:* Ivy Films, *Sale:* Blackhawk Films & Glenn Photo, Super 8 silent version. *Sale:* Tamarelles French Film, Videotape version. *Rental:* Westcoast Films, 130 mins. version.

Sierra. Audie Murphy & Wanda Hendrix. Directed by Alfred E. Green. 1950. Universal. 83 min. Sound. 16mm Color. *Rental:* Swank Motion.

Sierra Baron. Brian Keith & Mala Powers. Directed by James B. Clark. 1958. Fox. (Anamorphic). 80 min. Sound. 16mm Color. *Rental:* Films Inc.

Sierra Passage. Wayne Morris & Lola Albright. Directed by Frank McDonald. 1951. Monogram. 81 min. Sound. 16mm B&W. *Rental:* Hurlock Cine.

Sierra Stranger. Howard Duff & Dick Foran. Directed by Lee Sholem. 1957. Columbia. 82 min. Sound. 16mm B&W. *Rental:* Inst Cinema.

Sierra Sue. Gene Autry. Directed by William Morgan. 1941. Republic. 54 min. Sound. 16mm B&W. *Rental:* Ivy Films.

Siete de Copas, El. Antonio Aguila. Directed by Roberto Gavaldon. Mexico. 128 min. Sound. 16mm B&W. dubbed. *Rental:* Westcoast Films.

Siganme, Muchachos. Fred MacMurray. Directed by Norman Tokar. Span. 1966. Disney. 128 min. Sound. 16mm Color. dubbed. *Rental:* Twyman Films.

Sign of the Coyote. Fernando Casanova. 1966. Italy. 85 min. Sound. 16mm Color. dubbed. *Rental:* Ivy Films.

Sign of the Cross. Fredric March & Claudette Colbert. Directed by Cecil B. DeMille. 1932. Paramount. 120 min. Sound. 16mm B&W. *Rental:* Films Inc.

Sign of the Gladiator. Anita Ekberg & Jacques Sernas. Directed by Vittorio Glori. 1959. Italy. 89 min. Sound. 16mm Color. dubbed. *Rental:* Budget Films.

Sign of the Pagan. Jeff Chandler & Jack Palance. Directed by Douglas Sirk. 1954. Universal. 92 min. Sound. 16mm Color. *Rental:* Swank Motion.

Sign of the Ram. Susan Peters & Alexander Knox. Directed by John Sturges. 1948. Columbia. 84 min. Sound. 16mm B&W. *Rental:* Kit Parker.

Sign of the Virgin. Josef Cap & Jana Obermayerova. Directed by Zbynek Brynych. Czech. 1965. Czechoslovakia. 83 min. Sound. 16mm B&W. subtitles. *Rental:* Films Inc.

Sign of the Wolf. Michael Whalen & Grace Bradley. Directed by Howard Bretherton. 1941. Monogram. 80 min. Sound. 16mm B&W. *Rental:* Mogulls Films.

Sign of Zorro, The. Guy Williams. Directed by Norman Foster & Lewis R. Foster. 1960. Disney. 90 min. Sound. 16mm Color. *Rental:* Buchan Pic, Cine Craft, Cousino Visual Ed, Disney Prod, Film Ctr DC, Films Inc, MGM United, Modern Sound, Newman Film Lib, Roas Films, Twyman Films, U of IL Film & Williams Films.

Sign on the Door. Norma Talmadge. Directed by Herbert Brenon. 1921. 16mm *Rental:* A Twyman Pres.

Signal, The. Alexander Gavric & Maria Tosinski. 1962. Yugoslavia. 86 min. Sound. 16mm B&W. *Rental:* Ivy Films. *Sale:* Rep Pic Film.

Signals for Survival. Directed by Niko Tinbergen. 1970. Britain. 51 min. Sound. 16mm B&W. *Rental:* U Cal Media, McGraw-Hill Films & Syracuse U Film. *Sale:* McGraw-Hill Films.

Signpost to Murder. Joanne Woodward & Stuart Whitman. Directed by George Englund. 1964. MGM. 74 min. Sound. 16mm B&W. *Rental:* MGM United.

Signs of Life. Peter Brogle. Directed by Werner Herzog. Ger. 1968. Germany. 90 min. Sound. 16mm B&W. subtitles. *Rental:* New Yorker Films.

Silas Marner. Frederick Warde. 1916. Mutual. (Music & Narration). 50 min. Sound. 16mm B&W. *Rental:* Film Classics. *Sale:* Film Classics. *Rental:* Film Classics & Modern Sound, *Sale:* Film Classics, Silent 16mm version. *Rental:* Films Classics, Videotape version.

Silence, The. Will Geer & Ellen Geer. Directed by John Korty. 1974. CFA. 91 min. Sound. 16mm Color. *Rental:* Bosco Films, Budget Films, Film Pres, Welling Motion Pictures & Westcoast Films.

Silence, The. Ingrid Thulin & Gunnel Lindblom. Directed by Ingmar Bergman. Swed. 1963. Sweden. 95 min. Sound. 16mm B&W. subtitles. *Rental:* Films Inc, Janus Films & New Cinema.

Silence & Cry. Andras Kozak & Zoltan Latinovits. Directed by Miklos Jancso. Hungarian. 1968. Hungary. 79 min. Sound. 16mm B&W. subtitles. *Rental:* Films Inc.

Silence est d'Or, Le. Orig. Title: Man about Town. Maurice Chevalier. Directed by Rene Clair. Fr. 1943. France. 112 min. Sound. 16mm B&W. subtitles. *Rental:* Budget Films, Film Classics & Welling Motion Pictures.

Silence of the North. Ellen Burstyn & Tom Skerritt. Directed by Allan Winston King. 1981. Universal. 94 min. Sound. 16mm Color. *Rental:* Swank Motion. *Rental:* Swank Motion, Videotape version.

Silencers, The. Dean Martin & Stella Stevens. Directed by Phil Karlson. 1966. Columbia. 104 min. Sound. 16mm Color. *Rental:* Arcus Film, Budget Films, Cine Craft, Films Inc, Inst Cinema, Modern Sound, Video Comm, Welling Motion Pictures, Westcoast Films, Wholesome Film Ctr & Willoughby Peer.

Silent Army, The. 1980. PBS. (Documentary). 59 min. Sound. 16mm Color. *Rental:* PBS Video.

Silent Call, The. Gail Russell & David McLean. Directed by John Bushelman. 1961. Fox. 63 min. Sound. 16mm B&W. *Rental:* Inst Cinema.

Silent Conflict, The. William Boyd. Directed by George Archainbaud. 1941. United Artists. 61 min. Sound. 16mm B&W. *Sale:* Cinema Concepts.

Silent Enemy, The. 1929. Canada. 60 min. Silent. 16mm B&W. *Rental:* Em Gee Film Lib, Film Classics, Films Inc, Iowa Film, Modern Sound & Utah Media. *Sale:* Film Classics. *Sale:* Blackhawk Films, Super 8 sound version. *Sale:* Blackhawk Films, Super 8 silent version. *Rental:* Film Classics, Videotape version.

Silent Man, The. William S. Hart. Directed by William S. Hart. 1917. Artcraft. 70 min. Silent. 16mm B&W. *Rental:* Budget Films & Em Gee Film Lib. *Sale:* Natl Cinema, Em Gee Film Lib & Glenn Photo.

Silent Movie. Mel Brooks, Marty Feldman & Dom Deluise. Directed by Mel Brooks. 1976. Fox. 87 min. Sound. 16mm Color. *Rental:* Films Inc.

Silent Night, Bloody Night. Patrick O'Neal & James Patterson. Directed by Theodore Gershuny. 1973. Cannon. 87 min. Sound. 16mm Color. *Rental:* Swank Motion.

Silent Partner, The. Grant Withers & Joan Blair. Directed by George Blair. 1944. Republic. 54 min. Sound. 16mm B&W. *Rental:* Ivy Films. *Sale:* Rep Pic Film.

Silent Playground. Jean Anderson. Directed by Stanley Goulder. 1963. 16mm *Rental:* A Twyman Pres.

Silent Rage, The. Chuck Norris & Ron Silver. Directed by Michael Miller. 1982. Columbia. 105 min. Sound. 16mm Color. *Rental:* Swank Motion. *Rental:* Swank Motion, Videotape version.

Silent Raiders, The. Richard Bartlett. Directed by Richard Bartlett. 1954. Lippert. 65 min. Sound. 16mm B&W. *Rental:* Budget Films.

Silent Running. Bruce Dern & Cliff Potts. Directed by Douglas Trumbull. 1972. Universal. 90 min. Sound. 16mm Color. *Rental:* Swank Motion. *Rental:* Swank Motion, Videotape version.

Silent Scream. Rebecca Balding, Cameron Mitchell & Yvonne De Carlo. Directed by Denny Harris. 1979. American Cinema. 87 min. Sound. 16mm Color. *Rental:* Twyman Films, Westcoast Films & Wholesome Film Ctr.

Silent Speech. 1981. Britain. 50 min. Sound. 16mm Color. *Rental:* Films Inc. *Sale:* Films Inc. *Sale:* Films Inc, Videotape version.

Silent Spring of Rachel Carson, The. 1961. CBS. (Documentary). 54 min. Sound. 16mm B&W. *Rental:* U Cal Media. *Sale:* McGraw-Hill Films.

Silent Stranger, The. Tony Anthony. Directed by Vance Lewis. 1975. Italy. 92 min. Sound. 16mm Color. dubbed. *Rental:* MGM United.

Silent Valley, The. Tom Tyler. Directed by Bernard B. Ray. 1935. Commodore. 60 min. Sound. 16mm B&W. *Rental:* Mogulls Films. *Sale:* Cinema Concepts.

Silent Wilderness, The. American National. (Documentary). 92 min. Sound. 16mm Color. *Rental:* Westcoast Films & Williams Films.

Silent Witness, The. Directed by David W. Rolfe. 1978. Screenpro. (Documentary). 55 min. Sound. 16mm Color. *Rental:* Budget Films, Films Inc, Iowa Films, Mass Media, Modern Sound, Pyramid Film, Syracuse U Film, Twyman Films & U of IL Film. *Sale:* Pyramid Film. *Rental:* Pyramid Film, *Sale:* Pyramid Film, Videotape version.

Silent World, The. Directed by Jacques-Yves Cousteau. 1957. Columbia. (Documentary). 86 min. Sound. 16mm Color. *Rental:* Bosco Films.

Silk Express. Neil Hamilton & Sheila Terry. Directed by Ray Enright. 1933. Warners. 61 min. Sound. 16mm B&W. *Rental:* MGM United.

Silk Husbands & Calico Wives. House Peters. Directed by Alfred E. Green. 1920. Equity. 65 min. Silent. 16mm B&W. *Rental:* Em Gee Film Lib. *Sale:* Glenn Photo. *Sale:* Glenn Photo, Super 8 silent version.

Silk Stockings. Fred Astaire & Cyd Charisse. Directed by Rouben Mamoulian. 1957. MGM. 117 min. Sound. 16mm Color. *Rental:* MGM United. *Rental:* MGM United, Anamorphic version, Videotape version.

Silken Affair, A. David Niven & Genevieve Page. Directed by Roy Kellino. 1957. Britain. 96 min. Sound. 16mm B&W. *Rental:* Ivy Films.

Silks & Saddles. Orig. Title: College Racehorse. Toby Wing & Bruce Bennett. Directed by Robert Hill. 1938. Treo. 60 min. Sound. 16mm B&W. *Rental:* Mogulls Films.

Silkwood. Meryl Streep & Kurt Russell. Directed by Mike Nichols. 1983. Fox. 128 min. Sound. 16mm Color. *Rental:* Films Inc.

Silly Billies. Bert Wheeler & Robert Woolsey. Directed by Fred Guiol. 1936. RKO. 64 min. Sound. 16mm B&W. *Rental:* RKO General Pics.

Silver Bears, The. Michael Caine & Cybill Shepherd. Directed by Ivan Passer. 1978. Columbia. 113 min. Sound. 16mm Color. *Rental:* Budget Films, Modern Sound, Swank Motion, Welling Motion Pictures, Westcoast Films & Williams Films.

Silver Blaze, The. Orig. Title: Murder at the Baskervilles. Arthur Wonter & Ian Fleming. Directed by Thomas Bentley. 1941. Britain. 67 min. Sound. 16mm B&W. *Rental:* Bosco Films, Budget Films, Video Comm & Willoughby Peer. *Sale:* Blackhawk Films, Cinema Concepts & Glenn Photo. *Sale:* Blackhawk Films & Reel Images, Super 8 sound version. *Sale:* Tamarelles French Film, Videotape version.

Silver Box, The. Directed by Michael Wiese. 56 min. Sound. 16mm Color. *Rental:* Canyon Cinema.

Silver City. Edmond O'Brien & Yvonne De Carlo. Directed by Byron Haskin. 1951. Paramount. 90 min. Sound. 16mm Color. *Rental:* Films Inc.

Silver City Bonanza. Rex Allen. Directed by George Blair. 1950. Republic. 67 min. Sound. 16mm B&W. *Rental:* Ivy Films. *Sale:* Rep Pic Film.

Silver City Kid. Allan Lane. Directed by John English. 1945. Republic. 56 min. Sound. 16mm B&W. *Rental:* Ivy Films. *Sale:* Rep Pic Film.

Silver Cord, The. Irene Dunne & Joel McCrea. Directed by John Cromwell. 1933. RKO. 74 min. Sound. 16mm B&W. *Rental:* RKO General Pics.

Silver Dollar. Edward G. Robinson & Bebe Daniels. Directed by Alfred E. Green. 1932. Warners. 84 min. Sound. 16mm B&W. *Rental:* MGM United.

Silver Fox & Sam Davenport. 1962. Disney. (Documentary). 47 min. Sound. 16mm Color. *Rental:* Cine Craft, Disney Prod, Film Ctr DC, Films Inc, Modern Sound & Roas Films.

Silver Horde, The. Jean Arthur & Joel McCrea. Directed by George Archainbaud. 1931. RKO. 75 min. Sound. 16mm *Rental:* RKO General Pics.

Silver on the Sage. William Boyd. Directed by Lesley Selander. 1939. Paramount. 80 min. Sound. 16mm B&W. *Lease:* Cinema Concepts.

Silver Queen. Priscilla Lane & George Brent. Directed by Lloyd Bacon. 1942. United Artists. 80 min. Sound. 16mm B&W. *Rental:* Mogulls Films & Learning Corp Am. *Sale:* Learning Corp Am.

Silver Raiders. Whip Wilson. Directed by Wallace Fox. 1950. Monogram. 55 min. Sound. 16mm B&W. *Rental:* Hurlock Cine.

Silver Range. Johnny Mack Brown. Directed by Lambert Hillyer. 1946. Monogram. 55 min. Sound. 16mm B&W. *Rental:* Hurlock Cine.

Silver River. Errol Flynn & Ann Sheridan. Directed by Raoul Walsh. 1948. Warners. 110 min. Sound. 16mm B&W. *Rental:* MGM United.

Silver Skates. Belita & Kenny Baker. Directed by Leslie Goodwins. 1943. Monogram. 76 min. Sound. 16mm B&W. *Rental:* Film Ctr DC, Films Inc, Modern Sound, Mogulls Films & Wholesome Film Ctr.

Silver Spurs. Roy Rogers, John Carradine & Joyce Compton. Directed by Joseph Kane. 1943. Republic. 54 min. Sound. 16mm B&W. *Sale:* Cinema Concepts & Rep Pic Film.

Silver Stallion, The. David Sharpe & Chief Thundercloud. Directed by Edward Finney. 1941. Monogram. 57 min. Sound. 16mm B&W. *Rental:* Roas Films.

Silver Star, The. Edgar Buchanan & Marie Windsor. Directed by Richard Bartlett. 1956. 73 min. Sound. 16mm *Rental:* Budget Films.

Silver Streak, The. Arthur Lake & Sally Blane. Directed by Tommy Atkins. 1934. RKO. 80 min. Sound. B&W. *Sale:* Blackhawk Films Inc. *Rental:* Films Inc.

Silver Streak, The. Gene Wilder, Jill Clayburgh & Richard Pryor. Directed by Arthur Hiller. 1976. Fox. 113 min. Sound. 16mm Color. *Rental:* Films Inc.

Silver Trails. Jimmy Wakely. Directed by Christy Cabanne. 1948. Monogram. 55 min. Sound. 16mm B&W. *Rental:* Hurlock Cine.

Silver Whip, The. Dale Robertson & Rory Calhoun. Directed by Harmon Jones. 1953. Fox. 73 min. Sound. 16mm B&W. *Rental:* Films Inc.

Silver Wings & Santiago Blue. 1980. PBS. (Documentary). 59 min. Sound. 16mm Color. *Rental:* PBS Video.

Simon. Alan Arkin & Madeline Kahn. Directed by Marshall Brickman. 1980. Orion. 100 min. Sound. 16mm Color. *Rental:* Films Inc.

Simon Bolivar. Maximilian Schell & Rossana Schiaffino. 1972. Spain. 105 min. Sound. 16mm Color. dubbed. *Rental:* Films Inc & Video Comm. *Rental:* Video Comm, Videotape version.

Simon of the Desert. Silvia Pinal & Claudio Brook. Directed by Luis Bunuel. Span. 1965. Spain. 43 min. Sound. 16mm B&W. subtitles. *Rental:* Budget Films & Corinth Films. *Sale:* Cinema Concepts & Natl Cinema.

Simple Story, A. Romy Schneider & Bruno Cremer. Directed by Claude Sautet. Fr. 1979. France. 110 min. Sound. 16mm Color. subtitles. *Rental:* Films Inc & New Cinema.

Simultanes Circonstances 1976-1977. 3 pts. Directed by Patrick Delabre. 50 min. Silent. 16mm B&W. *Rental:* Canyon Cinema.

Sin of Harold Diddlebock, The. Harold Lloyd. 1950. RKO. 90 min. Sound. 16mm B&W. *Sale:* Festival Films, Glenn Photo, Images Film & Reel Images. *Rental:* Budget Films. *Rental:* Video Comm & Images Film, *Sale:* Cinema Concepts, Em Gee Film Lib, Festival Films & Images Film, Videotape version.

Sin of Harold Diddlebock, The *see* Mad Wednesday.

Sin of Madelon Claudet, The. Helen Hayes, Lewis Stone & Robert Young. Directed by Edgar Selwyn. 1931. 74 min. Sound. 16mm B&W. *Rental:* MGM United.

Sin Ship, The. Ian Keith & Mary Astor. Directed by Louis Wolheim. 1932. RKO. 65 min. Sound. 16mm B&W. *Rental:* RKO General Pics.

Sinai Field Mission. Directed by Frederick Wiseman. 1978. Zipporah. (Documentary). 127 min. Sound. 16mm B&W. *Rental:* Zipporah Films.

Sinbad & the Eye of the Tiger. Patrick Wayne & Taryn Power. Directed by Sam Wanamaker. 1977. Columbia. 114 min. Sound. 16mm Color. *Rental:* Arcus Film, Budget Films, Films Inc, Modern Sound, Newman Film Lib, Swank Motion, Twyman Films, Westcoast Films, Wholesome Film Ctr & Williams Films.

Sinbad the Sailor. Douglas Fairbanks Jr. & Maureen O'Hara. Directed by Richard Wallace. 1947. RKO. 117 min. Sound. 16mm Color. *Rental:* Films Inc.

Sinbad the Sailor. Orig. Title: Magic Adventures of Sinbad, the Sailor. 1963. Japan. 82 min. Sound. Videotape Color. dubbed. *Sale:* Budget Films, Cine Craft, Charard Motion Pics, Film Ctr DC, Newman Film Lib, Vidamerica, Video Comm, Welling Motion Pictures, Westcoast Films, Wholesome Film Ctr & Willoughby Peer.

Since the American Way of Death. 1979. PBS. (Documentary). 59 min. Sound. 16mm Color. *Rental:* PBS Video. *Sale:* PBS Video.

Since You Went Away. Claudette Colbert & Jennifer Jones. Directed by John Cromwell. 1944. United Artists. 150 min. Sound. 16mm B&W. *Rental:* Films Inc.

Sinful Davey. John Hurt & Pamela Franklin. Directed by John Huston. 1969. United Artists. (Anamorphic). 90 min. Sound. 16mm Color. *Rental:* MGM United.

Sing & Be Happy. Tony Martin & Leah Ray. Directed by James Tinling. 1937. Fox. 64 min. Sound. 16mm B&W. *Rental:* Films Inc.

Sing & Like It. ZaSu Pitts & Pert Kelton. Directed by William A. Seiter. 1934. RKO. 72 min. Sound. 16mm B&W. *Rental:* Films Inc & RKO General Pics.

Sing Another Chorus. Johnny Downs & Jane Frazee. Directed by Charles Lamont. 1941. Universal. 60 min. Sound. 16mm B&W. *Rental:* Film Ctr DC & Mogulls Films.

Sing Baby Sing. Alice Faye & Ritz Brothers. Directed by Sidney Lanfield. 1936. Fox. 87 min. Sound. 16mm B&W. *Rental:* Willoughby Peer.

Sing Boy Sing. Tommy Sands & Edmond O'Brien. Directed by Henry Ephron. 1958. Fox. 90 min. Sound. 16mm B&W. *Rental:* Willoughby Peer.

Sing, Cowboy, Sing. Tex Ritter. Directed by Robert N. Bradbury. 1937. Grand National. 60 min. Sound. 16mm B&W. *Sale:* Morcraft Films & Reel Images. *Sale:* Morcraft Films & Reel Images, Super 8 sound version.

Sing for Your Supper. Eve Arden & Buddy Rogers. Directed by Charles Barton. 1941. Columbia. 70 min. Sound. 16mm B&W. *Rental:* Kit Parker.

Sing Me a Love Song. Orig. Title: Come up Smiling. James Melton, Patricia Ellis & Ann Sheridan. 1936. Warners. 75 min. Sound. 16mm B&W. *Rental:* MGM United.

Sing, Neighbor, Sing. Roy Acuff & Ruth Terry. Directed by Frank McDonald. 1945. Republic. 70 min. Sound. 16mm B&W. *Rental:* Ivy Films. *Sale:* Rep Pic Film.

Sing Sing Thanksgiving. B. B. King. Directed by David Hoffman & Harry Wiland. 1974. Varied Directions. 78 min. Sound. 16mm Color. *Rental:* New Line Cinema.

Sing While You Dance. Ellen Drew & Robert Stanton. Directed by D. Ross Lederman. 1946. Columbia. 88 min. Sound. 16mm B&W. *Rental:* Kit Parker.

Sing While You're Able. Pinky Tomlin. Directed by Marshall Neilan. 1937. Melody. 70 min. Sound. 16mm B&W. *Sale:* Morcraft Films.

Sing Your Way Home. Jack Haley. Directed by Anthony Mann. 1945. RKO. 72 min. Sound. 16mm B&W. *Rental:* Films Inc.

Sing Your Worries Away. June Havoc & Buddy Ebson. Directed by Edward Sutherland. 1942. RKO. 71 min. Sound. 16mm *Rental:* RKO General Pics.

Singapore. Fred MacMurray & Ava Gardner. Directed by John Brahm. 1947. Universal. 79 min. Sound. 16mm B&W. *Rental:* Swank Motion.

Singapore Woman. Brenda Marshall & David Bruce. Directed by Jean Negulesco. 1941. Warners. 64 min. Sound. 16mm B&W. *Rental:* MGM United.

Singende Jugend *see* Orphan Boy of Vienna.

Singin' in the Corn. Judy Canova & Allen Jenkins. Directed by Del Lord. 1946. Columbia. 64 min. Sound. 16mm B&W. *Rental:* Kit Parker.

Singin' in the Rain. Gene Kelly & Debbie Reynolds. Directed by Gene Kelly & Stanley Donen. 1952. MGM. 103 min. Sound. 16mm Color. *Rental:* MGM United. *Rental:* MGM United, Videotape version.

Singing Buckaroo, The. Fred Scott. Directed by Tom Gibson. 1936. Spectrum. 60 min. Sound. 16mm B&W. *Rental:* Mogulls Films. *Sale:* Video Comm, Videotape version.

Singing Cowboy, The. Gene Autry. Directed by Mack V. Wright. 1936. Republic. 54 min. Sound. 16mm B&W. *Rental:* Ivy Films.

Singing Cowgirl, The. Dorothy Paige. Directed by Samuel Diege. 1939. Grand National. 59 min. Sound. 16mm B&W. *Rental:* Video Comm.

Singing Fool, The. Al Jolson. Directed by Lloyd Bacon. 1928. Warners. 100 min. Sound. 16mm B&W. *Rental:* MGM United.

Singing Guns. Vaughan Monroe & Ella Raines. Directed by R. G. Springsteen. 1949. Republic. 81 min. Sound. 16mm B&W. *Rental:* Ivy Films. *Sale:* Rep Pic Film.

Singing Hills, The. Gene Autry. Directed by Lew Landers. 1941. Republic. 54 min. Sound. 16mm B&W. *Rental:* Ivy Films.

Singing in the Dark. Moishe Oysher & Joey Adams. Directed by Max Nosseck. 1956. Israel. 80 min. Sound. 16mm B&W. *Rental:* Charard Motion Pics.

Singing Kid, The. Al Jolson & Claire Dodd. Directed by William Keighley. 1935. Warners. 84 min. Sound. 16mm B&W. *Rental:* MGM United.

Singing Marine, The. Dick Powell & Doris Weston. Directed by Ray Enright. 1937. Warners. 106 min. Sound. 16mm B&W. *Rental:* MGM United.

Singing Nun, The. Debbie Reynolds & Ricardo Montalban. Directed by Henry Koster. 1966. MGM. 98 min. Sound. 16mm Color. *Rental:* MGM United. *Rental:* MGM United, Anamorphic version.

Singing Princess, The. Julie Andrews. Pacific Films. 66 min. Sound. 16mm Color. *Rental:* BF Video.

Singing Vagabond, The. Gene Autry. Directed by Carl Pierson. 1936. Republic. 54 min. Sound. 16mm B&W. *Rental:* Ivy Films.

Singing Whale, The. 1975. Churchill Films. 52 min. Sound. 16mm Color. *Rental:* Churchill Films. *Rental:* Churchill Films, Videotape version.

Single Light, A. William Atherton. 1983. Learning Corp. 55 min. Sound. 16mm Color. *Rental:* Learning Corp Am. *Sale:* Learning Corp Am. *Sale:* Learning Corp Am, Videotape version.

Single Room Furnished. Jayne Mansfield. Directed by Matteo Ottaviano. 1967. Crown. 95 min. Sound. 16mm Color. *Rental:* Films Inc. *Rental:* Video Comm, Videotape version.

Sinister Journey. William Boyd. Directed by George Archainbaud. 1948. United Artists. 60 min. Sound. 16mm B&W. *Sale:* Cinema Concepts.

Sinister Monk, The. Karin Dor & Harald Leipnitz. Directed by Harold Reinl. 1965. Germany. 90 min. Sound. 16mm *Rental:* Budget Films.

Sinister Urge, The. Kenne Duncan & Carl Anthony. Directed by Edward D. Wood Jr. 1960. Mexico. 72 min. Sound. 16mm *Rental:* Budget Films.

Sink the Bismarck! Kenneth More & Dana Wynter. Directed by Lewis Gilbert. 1960. Britain. (Anamorphic). 97 min. Sound. 16mm B&W. *Rental:* Films Inc.

Sinner Take All. Bruce Cabot & Margaret Lindsay. Directed by Errol Taggart. 1936. MGM. 76 min. Sound. 16mm B&W. *Rental:* MGM United.

Sinners in Paradise. John Boles & Madge Evans. Directed by James Whale. 1938. Universal. 65 min. Sound. 16mm B&W. *Rental:* Swank Motion.

Sino-Indian Border Dispute. 1962. 45 min. 16mm B&W. *Rental:* Asian Film Lib.

Sino-Soviet Border Dispute: The New Tsar's Anti-China Atrocities. 1969. China. (Documentary). 67 min. Sound. 16mm B&W. *Rental:* Asian Film Lib.

Sins of Paris. Madeleine Lebeau. Directed by Henry Lepage. 1954. France. 77 min. Sound. 16mm B&W. *Rental:* Film Classics.

Sins of Rose Bernd, The. Maria Schell. Directed by Wolfgang Staudte. Ger. 1957. Germany. 85 min. Sound. 16mm B&W. subtitles. *Rental:* Films Inc.

Sins of the Children. Robert Montgomery & Leila Hyams. Directed by Sam Wood. 1930. MGM. 86 min. Sound. 16mm B&W. *Rental:* MGM United.

Sins of the Fleshapoids. Bob Cowan. Directed by Mike Kuchar. 1965. Mike Kuchar. 50 min. Sound. 16mm Color. *Rental:* Canyon Cinema.

Sioux City Sue. Gene Autry. Directed by Frank McDonald. 1946. Republic. 54 min. Sound. 16mm B&W. *Rental:* Ivy Films. *Sale:* Blackhawk Films. *Sale:* Blackhawk Films, Super 8 sound version.

Sir Arthur "Bomber" Harris. 1976. Britain. (Documentary). 52 min. Sound. 16mm Color. *Rental:* Time-Life Multimedia. *Sale:* Time-Life Multimedia. *Rental:* Time-Life Multimedia, *Sale:* Time-Life Multimedia, Videotape version.

Sir William Sim. 1976. Britain. (Documentary). 62 min. Sound. 16mm Color. *Rental:* Time-Life Multimedia. *Sale:* Time-Life Multimedia. *Rental:* Time-Life Multimedia, *Sale:* Time-Life Multimedia, Videotape version.

Siren of Atlantis, The. Jean-Pierre Aumont & Maria Montez. Directed by Gregg Tallas. 1948. United Artists. 75 min. Sound. 16mm B&W. *Rental:* Budget Films.

Siren of Bagdad, The. Patricia Medina & Paul Henried. Directed by Richard Quine. 1953. Columbia. 72 min. Sound. 16mm Color. *Rental:* Bosco Films & Kit Parker.

Sirius. Directed by Frantisek Vlacil. Czech. 1976. Czechoslovakia. (Cast unlisted). 53 min. Sound. 16mm Color. subtitles. *Rental:* Films Inc. *Sale:* Films Inc.

Sirocco. Humphrey Bogart, Lee J. Cobb & Zero Mostel. Directed by Curtis Bernhardt. 1951. Columbia. 98 min. Sound. 16mm B&W. *Rental:* Budget Films, Cine Craft, Films Inc, Images Film, Roas Films, Welling Motion Pictures & Westcoast Films.

Sis Hopkins. Judy Canova, Susan Hayward & Bob Crosby. Directed by Joseph Santley. 1941. Republic. 99 min. Sound. 16mm B&W. *Rental:* Ivy Films. *Sale:* Rep Pic Film.

Sister Beatrice. 1939. (Cast unlisted). 70 min. Sound. 16mm B&W. *Rental:* Film Classics.

Sister-in-Law, The. John Savage & Anne Saxon. Directed by Joseph Ruben. 1975. Crown. 85 min. Sound. 16mm Color. *Rental:* Films Inc.

Sister Kenny. Rosalind Russell & Alexander Knox. Directed by Dudley Nichols. 1946. RKO. 119 min. Sound. 16mm B&W. *Rental:* Films Inc. *Lease:* Films Inc.

Sister Streetfighter. Sonny Chiba & Sue Shiomi. Directed by Kazuhiko Yamaguchi. 1976. New Line. 86 min. Sound. 16mm Color. *Rental:* Films Inc.

Sister to Judas. Claire Windsor & Holmes Herbert. Directed by E. Mason Hopper. 1938. Mayfair. 80 min. Sound. 16mm B&W. *Rental:* Mogulls Films.

Sisters, The. Errol Flynn & Bette Davis. Directed by Anatole Litvak. 1938. Warners. 98 min. Sound. 16mm B&W. *Rental:* MGM United.

Sisters, The. Margot Kidder & Jennifer Salt. Directed by Brian De Palma. 1973. American International. 92 min. Sound. 16mm Color. *Rental:* New Line Cinema.

Sisters, The. Rufina Ninfontova. Directed by Grigori Roshal. Rus. 1957. Russia. 145 min. Sound. 16mm B&W. subtitles. *Rental:* Corinth Films.

Sisters of Satan, The. Anne Heywood. Britain. 91 min. Sound. 16mm Color. *Rental:* Films Inc & Maljack.

Sisters of the Gion. Yoko Umemura & Isuzu Yamada. Directed by Kenji Mizoguchi. Jap. 1936. Japan. 66 min. Sound. 16mm B&W. subtitles. *Rental:* Films Inc.

Sisters or the Balance of Happiness. Jutta Lampe. Directed by Margarethe Von Trotta. Ger. 1981. Germany. 95 min. Sound. 16mm Color. subtitles. *Rental:* Cinema Five.

Sit Down, Shut Up or Get Out. 1971. NBC. (Documentary). 58 min. Sound. 16mm Color. *Rental:* CC Films, Films Inc, Iowa Films, La Inst Res Ctr, Natl Churches Christ, Roas Films, Syracuse U Film, U Cal Media & Utah Media. *Sale:* Natl Churches Christ & Films Inc. *Sale:* Films Inc, Videotape version.

Sit-in. 1931. NBC. (Documentary). 54 min. Sound. 16mm B&W. *Rental:* Syracuse U Film. *Sale:* McGraw-Hill Films.

Sit Tight. Winnie Lightner & Joe E. Brown. Directed by Lloyd Bacon. 1931. Warners. 78 min. Sound. 16mm B&W. *Rental:* MGM United.

Sitting on the Moon. Roger Pryor & Grace Bradley. Directed by Ralph Staub. 1936. Republic. 54 min. Sound. 16mm B&W. *Rental:* Ivy Films. *Sale:* Rep Pic Film.

Sitting Pretty. Clifton Webb, Maureen O'Hara & Ossie Davis. Directed by Walter Lang. 1948. Fox. 84 min. Sound. 16mm B&W. *Rental:* Films Inc.

Sitting Target. Oliver Reed & Jill St. John. Directed by Douglas Hickox. 1972. MGM. 94 min. Sound. 16mm Color. *Rental:* MGM United.

Situation Hopeless-But Not Serious. Sir Alec Guinness, Robert Redford & Michael Connors. Directed by Gottfried Reinhardt. 1965. Paramount. 97 min. Sound. 16mm B&W. *Rental:* Films Inc.

Six Bears & a Clown. (Cast unlisted). 83 min. Sound. 16mm Color. *Rental:* Films Inc.

Six Bridges to Cross. Tony Curtis & Julie Adams. Directed by Joseph Pevney. 1955. Universal. 96 min. Sound. 16mm B&W. *Rental:* Swank Motion.

Six Characters in Search of an Author. Nikki Flacks. Directed by Ken Frankel. 1976. Britain. 58 min. Sound. 16mm Color. *Rental:* Films Human. *Sale:* Films Human. *Sale:* Films Human, Videotape version.

Six-Day Bike Rider. Joe E. Brown & Frank McHugh. Directed by Lloyd Bacon. 1934. Warners. 69 min. Sound. 16mm B&W. *Rental:* MGM United.

Six Days in Soweto. Anthony Thomas. 1978. California Newsreel. (Documentary). 55 min. Sound. 16mm Color. *Rental:* CA Newsreel & U Mich Media. *Sale:* CA Newsreel.

Six Foot Four. William Rusell. Directed by Henry King. 1919. Pathe. (Music & sound effects only). 50 min. Sound. 16mm B&W. *Rental:* Film Classics. *Sale:* Film Classics.

Six Great Ideas. Directed by Wayne Ewing. 1982. WNET. 360 min. Videotape Color. *Rental:* Films Inc. *Sale:* Films Inc.

Six-Gun Gold. Tim Holt & Ray Whitley. Directed by Bert Gilroy. 1941. RKO. 57 min. Sound. 16mm B&W. *Rental:* RKO General Pics.

Six-Gun Gospel. Johnny Mack Brown. Directed by Lambert Hillyer. 1943. Monogram. 55 min. Sound. 16mm B&W. *Rental:* Hurlock Cine.

Six-Gun Man. Bob Steele. Directed by Harry Fraser. 1946. PRC. 59 min. Sound. 16mm B&W. *Sale:* Classics Assoc NY.

Six-Gun Mesa. Johnny Mack Brown. Directed by Wallace Fox. 1950. Monogram. 55 min. Sound. 16mm B&W. *Rental:* Hurlock Cine.

Six-Gun Serenade. Jimmy Wakely. Directed by Ford Beebe. 1947. Monogram. 55 min. Sound. 16mm B&W. *Rental:* Hurlock Cine.

Six-Gun Trail. Tim McCoy. Directed by Sam Newfield. 1938. Victory. 60 min. Sound. 16mm B&W. *Rental:* Budget Films & Mogulls Films.

Six Hundred & Thirty Three Squadron. Cliff Robertson & George Chakiris. Directed by Walter Grauman. 1964. United Artists. (Anamorphic). 94 min. Sound. 16mm Color. *Rental:* MGM United.

Six Hundred Millennia: China's History Unearthed. 1979. PBS. (Documentary). 78 min. Sound. 16mm Color. *Rental:* PBS Video. *Sale:* PBS Video.

Six Hundred, Sixty-Six. 1976. Gospel. (Cast unlisted). 78 min. Sound. 16mm Color. *Rental:* Gospel Films.

Six in Paris. Directed by Jean-Luc Godard, Claude Chabrol, Jean Douchet, Jean Rouch, Jean-Daniel Pollet & Eric Rohmer. Fr. 1968. France. (Anthology). 90 min. Sound. 16mm Color. subtitles. *Rental:* New Yorker Films.

Six O'Clock & All's Well. Directed by Robert Spencer. 60 min. Sound. 16mm *Rental:* Cinema Guild.

Six of a Kind. W. C. Fields, George Burns & Gracie Allen. Directed by Leo McCarey. 1934. Paramount. 65 min. Sound. 16mm B&W. *Rental:* Swank Motion.

Six Pack. Kenny Rogers & Diane Lane. Directed by Daniel Petrie. 1982. Fox. 107 min. Sound. 16mm Color. *Rental:* Films Inc.

Six-Shootin' Sheriff. Ken Maynard. Directed by Harry Fraser. 1938. Grand National. 57 min. Sound. 16mm B&W. *Rental:* Budget Films, Super 8 sound version. *Sale:* Reel Images & Video Comm, *Rental:* Westcoast Films, Videotape version.

Six Weeks. Dudley Moore, Tyler Mary Moore & Katherine Healy. Directed by Tony Bill. 106 min. Sound. 16mm Color. *Rental:* Swank Motion. *Rental:* Swank Motion, Videotape version.

Six Wives of Henry VIII. Keith Michell. 1976. British. 540 min. Sound. 16mm Color. *Rental:* Films Inc. *Sale:* Films Inc. *Rental:* Films Inc, *Sale:* Films Inc, Videotape version.

Sixteen Candles. Molly Ringwald & Anthony Michael Hall. Directed by John Hughes. 1985. Universal. 93 min. Sound. 16mm Color. *Rental:* Swank Motion.

Sixteen Fathoms Deep. Lloyd Bridges & Arthur Lake. Directed by Irving Allen. 1948. Monogram. 85 min. Sound. 16mm B&W. *Rental:* Ivy Films. *Sale:* Rep Pic Film.

Sixteen in Webster Groves. 1967. CBS. (Documentary). 47 min. Sound. 16mm B&W. *Rental:* Mass Media, Roas Films, SD AV Ctr, Twyman Films, U Cal Media, U of IL Film & U Mich Media. *Sale:* Carousel Films.

Sixth Paul, The. 1969. NET. (Documentary). 58 min. Sound. 16mm B&W. *Rental:* Indiana AV Ctr.

Sixty-Eight. Directed by Norman Fruchter. 1968. Norman Fruchter. (Documentary). 60 min. Sound. 16mm B&W. *Rental:* CA Newsreel. *Sale:* CA Newsreel.

Sixty Glorious Years. Orig. Title: Victoria the Great. Anna Neagle & Anton Walbrook. Directed by Herbert Wilson. 1938. Britain. (Color sequences). 95 min. Sound. 16mm B&W. *Rental:* A Twyman Pres & Mogulls Films.

Sixty Minutes to Meltdown. 1983. Nova. (Documentary). 84 min. Sound. 16mm Color. *Rental:* U Cal Media.

Sizwe Banzi Is Dead. Ossie Davis & Ruby Dee. 1978. Films Inc. 60 min. Videotape Color. *Rental:* Films Inc. *Sale:* Films Inc.

Skabenga. Directed by George Michael. 1954. Allied Artists. (Documentary). 61 min. Sound. 16mm Color. *Rental:* Hurlock Cine.

Skateboard. Allen Garfield & Kathleen Lloyd. Directed by George Gage. 1977. Universal. 93 min. Sound. 16mm Color. *Rental:* Williams Films.

Skatetown U.S.A. Scott Baio & Flip Wilson. Directed by William A. Levey. 1979. Columbia. 98 min. Sound. 16mm Color. *Rental:* Budget Films, Swank Motion & Welling Motion Pictures.

Skating Spectacular, A. 1979. PBS. (Documentary). 59 min. Color. *Rental:* PBS Video. *Sale:* PBS Video, Videotape version, Color version.

Skezag. Wayne Shirley. Directed by Joel L. Freedman & Philip F. Messina. 1970. Cinnamon. 73 min. Sound. 16mm Color. *Rental:* Cinema Guild. *Sale:* Cinema Guild.

Ski Bum, The. Zalman King & Charlotte Rampling. Directed by Bruce Clark. 1970. Embassy. 94 min. Sound. 16mm Color. *Rental:* Films Inc.

Ski Champ, The. Tony Sailer. 1962. Comet. 90 min. Sound. 16mm Color. dubbed. *Rental:* Ivy Films.

Ski Fever. Martin Milner & Claudia Martin. Directed by Curt Siodmak. 1968. Allied Artists. 98 min. Sound. 16mm Color. *Rental:* Hurlock Cine.

Ski on the Wild Side. 1967. Warren Miller. (Documentary). 104 min. Sound. 16mm B&W. *Rental:* Budget Films & Films Inc.

Ski Party. Frankie Avalon & Deborah Walley. Directed by Alan Rafkin. 1965. American International. 90 min. Sound. 16mm Color. *Rental:* Cine Craft & Westcoast Films.

Skid Kids. A. E. Matthews & Lance Campbell. Directed by Don Chaffey. 1958. Britain. 65 min. Sound. 16mm B&W. *Sale:* Lucerne Films.

Skidoo. Jackie Gleason, Carol Channing & Groucho Marx. Directed by Otto Preminger. 1969. Paramount. (Anamorphic). 98 min. Sound. 16mm Color. *Rental:* Films Inc.

Skiff of Renald & Thomas, The. Directed by Bernard Gosselin. 1980. Canada. (Documentary). 57 min. Sound. 16mm Color. *Rental:* Museum Mod Art. *Sale:* Museum Mod Art.

Skill Demonstrations for Counseling Alcoholic Clients. 1977. 59 min. Sound. Videotape B&W. *Rental:* Natl AV Ctr. *Sale:* Natl AV Ctr.

Skin Game, The. Edmund Gwenn. Directed by Alfred Hitchcock. 1931. Britain. 88 min. Sound. 16mm B&W. *Rental:* Janus Films.

Skin of Our Teeth, The. 1968. Britain. (Documentary). 60 min. Sound. 16mm Color. *Rental:* Time-Life Multimedia. *Sale:* Time-Life Multimedia.

Skinny & Fatty. 1960. Japan. (Cast unlisted). 45 min. Sound. 16mm B&W. dubbed. *Rental:* McGraw-Hill Films & Syracuse U Film. *Sale:* McGraw-Hill Films.

Skipalong Rosenbloom. Orig. Title: Squareshooter, The. Maxie Rosenbloom & Hillary Brooke. Directed by Sam Newfield. 1951. Eagle Lion. 72 min. Sound. 16mm B&W. *Rental:* Mogulls Films.

Skipper Surprised His Wife, The. Robert Walker & Joan Leslie. Directed by Elliott Nugent. 1950. MGM. 85 min. Sound. 16mm B&W. *Rental:* MGM United.

Skiptracer. David Peterson, John Lazarus & Rudy Szabo. 90 min. Sound. 16mm Color. *Rental:* Williams Films.

Skirts Ahoy. Esther Williams & Vivian Blaine. Directed by Sidney Lanfield. 1952. MGM. 109 min. Sound. 16mm Color. *Rental:* MGM United.

Skull, The. Peter Cushing & Christopher Lee. Directed by Freddie Francis. 1965. Paramount. 83 min. Sound. 16mm Color. *Rental:* Films Inc.

Skull & Crown. Rin-Tin-Tin Jr. 1935. Reliance. 60 min. Sound. 16mm B&W. *Rental:* Mogulls Films. *Sale:* Morcraft Films.

Sky Above, the Mud Below, The. Directed by Pierre-Dominique Gaisseau. 1962. France. (Documentary). 90 min. Sound. 16mm Color. narrated Eng. *Rental:* Films Inc.

Sky Bandits, The. James Newill & Dave O'Brien. Directed by Ralph Staub. 1940. Monogram. 56 min. Sound. 16mm B&W. *Sale:* Cinema Concepts & Rep Pic Film.

Sky Bike, The. Britain. (Cast unlisted). 50 min. Sound. 16mm Color. *Rental:* Janus Films. *Sale:* Lucerne Films & Sterling Ed Film.

Sky Commando, The. Dan Duryea & Frances Gifford. Directed by Fred F. Sears. 1953. Columbia. 69 min. Sound. 16mm B&W. *Rental:* Cine Craft & Inst Cinema.

Sky Dragon, The. Roland Winters & Keye Luke. Directed by William Beaudine. 1949. Monogram. 64 min. Sound. 16mm B&W. *Rental:* Hurlock Cine.

Sky Full of Moon, A. Carleton Carpenter & Jan Sterling. Directed by Norman Foster. 1952. MGM. 75 min. Sound. 16mm B&W. *Rental:* MGM United.

Sky Giant. Joan Fontaine & Chester Morris. Directed by Lew Landers. 1938. RKO. 80 min. Sound. 16mm *Rental:* RKO General Pics.

Sky High. Tom Mix. Directed by Lynn Reynolds. 1922. Fox. 66 min. Silent. 16mm B&W. *Rental:* Em Gee Film Lib & Museum Mod Art.

Sky Is Falling, The. Carroll Baker, Richard Todd & Dennis Hopper. Italy. 91 min. Sound. 16mm Color. *Rental:* Films Inc.

Sky Is Gray, The. 1980. Perspective Films. 47 min. Sound. 16mm Color. *Rental:* Iowa Films, Kent St U Films, Syracuse U Film, U Mich Media & Utah Media. *Sale:* Perspect Film.

Sky Pilot, The. John Bowers & Colleen Moore. Directed by King Vidor. 1921. First National. 45 min. Silent. 16mm B&W. *Rental:* Em Gee Film Lib & Film Classics. *Sale:* Film Classics. *Sale:* Blackhawk Films, Super 8 silent version. *Rental:* Film Classics, Videotape version.

Sky Pirate, The. Michael McClanathan & Claudia Leacock. Directed by Andrew Meyer. 1970. Filmmakers. 105 min. Sound. 16mm Color. *Rental:* Canyon Cinema & New Line Cinema.

Sky Riders. James Coburn & Susannah York. Directed by Douglas Hickox. 1976. Fox. (Anamorphic). 91 min. Sound. 16mm Color. *Rental:* Films Inc, Welling Motion Pictures, Westcoast Films & Williams Films.

Sky Trap. Jim Hutton & Patricia Crowley. Disney. 96 min. Sound. 16mm Color. *Rental:* Films Inc.

Sky Without Stars. Horst Buchholz & Eva Kotthaus. Directed by Helmut Kautner. Ger. 1959. Germany. 105 min. Sound. 16mm B&W. subtitles. *Rental:* Budget Films.

Skybound. Lloyd Hughes & Eddie Nugent. Directed by Raymond K. Johnson. 1935. Puritan. 60 min. Sound. 16mm B&W. *Rental:* Mogulls Films.

Skydivers. Kevin Casey. Directed by Coleman Francis. 1963. Crown. 75 min. Sound. 16mm B&W. *Rental:* Video Comm. *Sale:* Video Comm. *Rental:* Video Comm, *Lease:* Video Comm, Videotape version.

Skyjacked. Charlton Heston & Yvette Mimieux. Directed by John Guillermin. 1972. MGM. 101 min. Sound. 16mm Color. *Rental:* MGM United.

Skylark. Claudette Colbert & Ray Milland. Directed by Mark Sandrich. 1941. Paramount. 94 min. Sound. 16mm B&W. *Rental:* Swank Motion.

Skyliner. Richard Travis & Pamela Blake. Directed by William Berke. 1949. Screen Guild. 60 min. Sound. 16mm B&W. *Rental:* Film Ctr DC.

Sky's the Limit, The. Jack Geddings, Jane Starr & Bruce Gordon. Directed by Harry Fraser. 1925. Aywon. 50 min. Silent. 16mm B&W. *Rental:* Film Classics. *Sale:* Reel Images, Videotape version.

Sky's the Limit, The. Fred Astaire & Joan Leslie. Directed by Edward H. Griffith. 1943. RKO. 89 min. Silent. 16mm B&W. *Rental:* Films Inc.

Sky's the Limit, The. 1980. Learning Corp.. (Documentary). 56 min. Sound. 16mm Color. *Rental:* Budget Films, Learning Corp Am & U Cal Media. *Sale:* Learning Corp Am. *Sale:* Learning Corp Am, *Rental:* Learning Corp Am, Videotape version.

Skyscraper Souls. Maureen O'Sullivan & Warren William. Directed by Edgar Selwyn. 1932. MGM. 100 min. Sound. 16mm B&W. *Rental:* MGM United.

Skyscraper Wilderness. Orig. Title: Big City. Luise Rainer & Spencer Tracy. Directed by Frank Borzage. 1937. MGM. 80 min. Sound. 16mm B&W. *Rental:* MGM United.

SL-1. 1984. C. Larry Roberts. 57 min. Sound. Color. *Sale:* Direct Cinema. *Sale:* Direct Cinema, Videotape version.

Slams, The. Jim Brown. Directed by Jonathan Kaplan. 1973. MGM. 97 min. Sound. 16mm Color. *Rental:* MGM United.

Slander. Van Johnson & Ann Blyth. Directed by Roy Rowland. 1956. MGM. 81 min. Sound. 16mm B&W. *Rental:* MGM United.

Slanderers, The. Johnnie Walker. Directed by Nat Ross. 1924. Universal. 55 min. Silent. 16mm B&W. *Sale:* E Finney.

Slap Shot. Paul Newman & Strother Martin. Directed by George Roy Hill. 1977. Universal. 121 min. Sound. 16mm Color. *Rental:* Swank Motion. *Rental:* Swank Motion, Videotape version.

Slattery's Hurricane. Richard Widmark & Linda Darnell. Directed by Andre De Toth. 1949. Fox. 83 min. Sound. 16mm B&W. *Rental:* Films Inc.

Slaughter. Jim Brown, Stella Stevens & Rip Torn. Directed by Jack Starrett. 1972. American International. 92 min. Sound. 16mm Color. *Rental:* Williams Films.

Slaughter Hotel. Klaus Kinski. Directed by Fernando Di Leo. 1971. Hallmark. 100 min. Sound. 16mm Color. dubbed. *Rental:* Maljack & Swank Motion.

Slaughter in San Francisco. Chuck Norris. 92 min. Sound. 16mm *Rental:* WW Enter. *Rental:* WW Enter, Videotape version.

Slaughter of the Innocents. 50 min. Sound. 16mm Color. *Rental:* Gospel Films.

Slaughter on Tenth Avenue. Richard Egan & Jan Sterling. Directed by Arnold Laven. 1957. Universal. 103 min. Sound. 16mm B&W. *Rental:* Swank Motion.

Slaughter Trail, The. Brian Donlevy & Gig Young. Directed by Irving Allen. 1951. RKO. 77 min. Sound. 16mm B&W. *Rental:* Films Inc.

Slaughterhouse-Five. Michael Sacks & Ron Liebman. Directed by George Roy Hill. 1972. Universal. 104 min. Sound. 16mm Color. *Rental:* Swank Motion. *Rental:* Swank Motion, Videotape version.

Slaughter's Big Ripoff. Jim Brown & Don Stroud. Directed by Ron Liebman. 1972. Universal. 104 min. Sound. 16mm B&W. *Rental:* Twyman Films.

Slave, The. Steve Reeves. Directed by Sergio Corbucci. 1963. Italy. 102 min. Sound. 16mm B&W. dubbed. *Rental:* MGM United.

Slave of Rome, The. Guy Madison & Rosanna Podesta. 1962. American International. 96 min. Sound. 16mm Color. dubbed. *Rental:* Westcoast Films.

Slave Ship. Warner Baxter & Wallace Beery. Directed by Tay Garnett. 1937. Fox. 92 min. Sound. 16mm B&W. *Rental:* Films Inc.

Slave Trade in the World Today. Directed by Roberto Malenotti. 1964. Continental. 86 min. Sound. 16mm Color. *Rental:* Budget Films.

Slaves. Ossie Davis & Stephen Boyd. Directed by Herbert Biberman. 1969. Continental. 102 min. Sound. 16mm Color. *Rental:* Budget Films.

Slaves of Babylon. Richard Conte & Linda Christian. Directed by William Castle. 1953. Columbia. 82 min. Sound. 16mm Color. *Rental:* Alba House & Inst Cinema.

Slaves of the Invisible Monster. Richard Webb, Aline Towne & George Meeker. Directed by Fred C. Brannon. 1951. Republic. 100 min. Sound. 16mm B&W. *Rental:* Ivy Films. *Sale:* Rep Pic Film.

Sleep My Love. Claudette Colbert, Robert Cummings & Don Ameche. Directed by Douglas Sirk. 1948. United Artists. 96 min. Sound. 16mm B&W. *Rental:* Ivy Films.

Sleep, the Fantastic Third of Your Life. 1968. ABC. (Documentary). 51 min. Sound. 16mm Color. *Rental:* McGraw-Hill Films, Syracuse U Film & U of IL Film. *Sale:* McGraw-Hill Film.

Sleeper. Woody Allen & Diane Keaton. Directed by Woody Allen. 1973. United Artists. 88 min. Sound. 16mm Color. *Rental:* MGM United. *Rental:* MGM United, Videotape version.

Sleepers West. Lloyd Nolan & Lynn Bari. Directed by Eugene Forde. 1941. Fox. 74 min. Sound. 16mm B&W. *Rental:* Films Inc.

Sleeping Beauty, The. Directed by Appolinari Dudko & Konstantin Sergeyev. 1964. Russia. (Anamorphic, dance). 92 min. Sound. 16mm Color. *Rental:* Corinth Films.

Sleeping Beauty, The. Carol Meier. Directed by Fritz Genschow. 1965. Childhood. 74 min. Sound. 16mm Color. dubbed. *Rental:* Budget Films, Cine Craft, Film Ctr DC, Roas Films & Westcoast Films.

Sleeping Car to Trieste. Jean Kent & Finlay Currie. Directed by John Paddy Carstairs. 1949. Britain. 95 min. Sound. 16mm B&W. *Rental:* Budget Films, Kit Parker, Learning Corp Am & Twyman Films. *Sale:* Learning Corp Am.

Sleeping Dogs. Sam Neill & Warren Oates. Directed by Roger Donaldson. 107 min. Sound. Videotape Color. *Sale:* Vidamerica.

Sleepy Lagoon. Judy Canova & Dennis Day. Directed by Joseph Santley. 1943. Republic. 65 min. Sound. 16mm B&W. *Rental:* Ivy Films. *Sale:* Rep Pic Film.

Sleepytime Gal. Judy Canova & Tom Brown. Directed by Albert S. Rogell. 1942. Republic. 84 min. Sound. 16mm B&W. *Rental:* Ivy Films.

Sleight of Hand. (Body in Question Series). 1979. (Documentary). 60 min. Videotape Color. *Rental:* Films Inc & Syracuse U Film. *Sale:* Films Inc.

Slender Thread, The. Anne Bancroft & Sidney Poitier. Directed by Sydney Pollack. 1965. Paramount. 100 min. Sound. 16mm B&W. *Rental:* Films Inc.

Sleuth. Sir Laurence Olivier & Michael Caine. Directed by Joseph L. Mankiewicz. 1972. Fox. 138 min. Sound. 16mm Color. *Rental:* Films Inc.

Slice of Death, A. David Chiang & Lo Lieh. Hong Kong. 86 min. Sound. 16mm Color. *Rental:* WW Enter. *Rental:* WW Enter, Videotape version.

Slight Case of Larceny, A. Mickey Rooney & Eddie Bracken. Directed by Don Weis. 1953. MGM. 71 min. Sound. 16mm B&W. *Rental:* MGM United.

Slight Case of Murder, A. Edward G. Robinson & Jane Bryan. Directed by Lloyd Bacon. 1938. Warners. 85 min. Sound. 16mm B&W. *Rental:* MGM United.

Slightly Dangerous. Robert Young & Lana Turner. Directed by Wesley Ruggles. 1943. MGM. 94 min. Sound. 16mm B&W. *Rental:* MGM United.

Slightly French. Orig. Title: Let's Fall in Love. Don Ameche & Dorothy Lamour. Directed by Douglas Sirk. 1949. Columbia. 81 min. Sound. 16mm B&W. *Rental:* Kit Parker.

Slightly Honorable. Pat O'Brien, Broderick Crawford & Eve Arden. Directed by Tay Garnett. 1940. United Artists. 88 min. Sound. 16mm B&W. *Rental:* U of IL Film, Learning Corp Am & Mogulls Films. *Sale:* Morcraft Films & Learning Corp Am.

Slightly Terrific. Leon Errol & Eddie Quillan. Directed by Edward Cline. 1944. Universal. 63 min. Sound. 16mm B&W. *Rental:* Inst Cinema & Mogulls Films.

Slim. Henry Fonda & Pat O'Brien. Directed by Ray Enright. 1937. Warners. 85 min. Sound. 16mm B&W. *Rental:* MGM United.

Slim Carter. Jock Mahoney & Julie Adams. Directed by Richard Bartlett. 1957. Universal. 82 min. Sound. 16mm Color. *Rental:* Swank Motion.

Slipper & the Rose, The. Richard Chamberlain & Gemma Craven. Directed by Bryan Forbes. 1976. Britain. 120 min. Sound. 16mm Color. *Rental:* Swank Motion.

Slippy McGee. Don Barry & Tom Brown. Directed by Albert J. Kelley. 1948. Republic. 65 min. Sound. 16mm B&W. *Rental:* Ivy Films. *Sale:* Rep Pic Film.

Slither. James Caan & Sally Kellerman. Directed by Howard Zieff. 1973. MGM. 96 min. Sound. 16mm Color. *Rental:* MGM United.

Slow Attack. Directed by Reinhard Hauff. Ger. 1981. Germany. 112 min. Sound. 16mm Color. subtitles *Rental:* New Yorker Films.

Slow Dancing in the Big City. Paul Sorvino & Anne Ditchburn. Directed by John G. Avildsen. 1978. United Artists. 101 min. Sound. 16mm Color. *Rental:* MGM United.

Slow Guillotine. 1970. NBC. (Documentary). 53 min. Sound. 16mm Color. *Rental:* Films Inc & U Cal Media. *Sale:* Films Inc. *Sale:* Films Inc, Videotape version.

Slow Run. Bruce Gordon & Jane Amsten. Directed by Larry Kardish. 1968. Film Makers Cooperative. 78 min. Sound. 16mm B&W. *Rental:* Canyon Cinema.

Slums of Berlin, The. Bernard Boetzke & Mady Christians. Directed by Gerhard Lamprecht. 1927. Germany. 120 min. Silent. 16mm B&W. *Sale:* Blackhawk Films. *Sale:* Blackhawk Films, Super 8 silent version.

Small Change. Georgy Desmouceaux. Directed by Francois Truffaut. 1976. France. 104 min. Sound. 16mm Color. *Rental:* Films Inc.

Small Circle of Friends, A. Brad Davis, Karen Allen & Jameson Parker. Directed by Rob Cohen. 1980. United Artists. 113 min. Sound. 16mm Color. *Rental:* MGM United.

Small Town Deb. Jane Withers & Jane Darwell. Directed by Harold Schuster. 1941. Fox. 72 min. Sound. 16mm B&W. *Rental:* Films Inc.

Small Town Girl. Jane Powell & Farley Granger. Directed by Leslie Kardos. 1953. MGM. 93 min. Sound. 16mm B&W. *Rental:* MGM United. *Rental:* MGM United, Color version.

Small Town in Texas, A. Timothy Bottoms & Susan George. Directed by Jack Starrett. 1976. American International. 95 min. Sound. 16mm Color. *Rental:* Swank Motion.

Small Town Story. Susan Shaw & Donald Houston. Directed by Montgomery Tully. 1953. Britain. 69 min. Sound. 16mm B&W. *Rental:* Charard Motion Pics.

Small Towns. 1981. 45 min. Sound. 16mm Color. *Rental:* Utah Media.

Smallest Show on Earth, The. Orig. Title: Big Time Operators, The. Bill Travers, Virginia McKenna, Peter Sellers & Margaret Rutherford. Directed by Basil Dearden. 1957. Britain. 80 min. Sound. 16mm B&W. *Rental:* Budget Films, Films Inc, Kit Parker & Video Comm.

Smart Alecs. East Side Kids. Directed by Wallace Fox. 1942. Monogram. 60 min. Sound. 16mm B&W. *Sale:* Cinema Concepts.

Smart Blonde. Glenda Farrell & Barton MacLane. Directed by Frank McDonald. 1936. Warners. 59 min. Sound. 16mm B&W. *Rental:* MGM United.

Smart Girls Don't Talk. Virginia Mayo & Bruce Bennett. Directed by Richard Bare. 1948. Warners. 81 min. Sound. 16mm B&W. *Rental:* MGM United.

Smart Money. Edward G. Robinson & James Cagney. Directed by Alfred E. Green. 1931. Warners. 83 min. Sound. 16mm B&W. *Rental:* MGM United.

Smart Politics. Freddie Stewart & June Preisser. Directed by Will Jason. 1948. Monogram. 67 min. Sound. 16mm B&W. *Rental:* Hurlock Cine.

Smart Woman. Constance Bennett & Brian Aherne. Directed by Edward A. Blatt. 1948. Allied Artists. 93 min. Sound. 16mm B&W. *Rental:* Hurlock Cine.

Smart Woman. Mary Astor & Edward Everett Horton. Directed by Gregory La Cava. 1932. RKO. 68 min. Sound. 16mm *Rental:* RKO General Pics.

Smartest Girl in Town, The. Ann Sothern & Gig Young. Directed by Joseph Santley. 1937. RKO. 58 min. Sound. 16mm *Rental:* RKO General Pics.

Smarty. Joan Blondell & Warren William. Directed by Robert Florey. 1934. Warners. 64 min. Sound. 16mm B&W. *Rental:* MGM United.

Smash Palace. Bruno Lawrence & Anna Jemison. Directed by Roger Donaldson. 1981. Atlantic. 100 min. Sound. 16mm Color. *Rental:* Films Inc.

Smash-Up: The Story of a Woman. Susan Hayward, Eddie Albert & Marsha Hunt. Directed by Stuart Heisler. 1947. Universal. 113 min. Sound. 16mm B&W. *Rental:* Budget Films, Kit Parker, Learning Corp Am & U of IL Film. *Sale:* Learning Corp Am.

Smashing of the Reich, The. Directed by Perry Wolff. 1962. France. 85 min. Sound. 16mm B&W. *Rental:* Budget Films. *Sale:* Festival Films.

Smashing the Money Ring. Ronald Reagan & Eddie Foy Jr. Directed by Terry Morse. 1939. Warners. 57 min. Sound. 16mm B&W. *Rental:* MGM United.

Smashing the Rackets. Chester Morris. Directed by Lew Landers. 1938. RKO. 60 min. Sound. 16mm *Rental:* RKO General Pics.

Smashing the Spy Ring. Ralph Bellamy & Fay Wray. Directed by Christy Cabanne. 1938. Columbia. 60 min. Sound. 16mm B&W. *Lease:* Time-Life Multimedia.

Smashing Time. Rita Tushingham & Lyn Redgrave. Directed by Desmond Davis. 1967. Britain. 96 min. Sound. 16mm Color. *Rental:* Films Inc.

Smile. Bruce Dern & Barbara Feldon. Directed by Michael Ritchie. 1975. United Artists. 113 min. Sound. 16mm Color. *Rental:* MGM United.

Smile of Reason, The. (Civilization Ser.). 1968. Britain. (Documentary). 60 min. Sound. 16mm Color. *Rental:* Films Inc, OK AV Ctr, Syracuse U Film & Utah Media. *Sale:* Films Inc. *Sale:* Films Inc, Videotape version.

Smile of the Walrus, The. 1977. Metromedia. (Documentary). 52 min. Sound. 16mm Color. *Rental:* Churchill Films. *Rental:* Churchill Films, Videotape version.

Smiles of a Summer Night. Eva Dahlbeck & Harriet Andersson. Directed by Ingmar Bergman. Swed. 1955. Sweden. 108 min. Sound. 16mm B&W. subtitles. *Rental:* Films Inc, Janus Films & New Cinema.

Smiley Gets a Gun. Dame Sybil Thorndike. Keith Calvert. Directed by Anthony Kimmins. 1959. Fox. 89 min. Sound. 16mm Color. *Rental:* Films Inc.

Smilin' Through. Jeanette MacDonald. Directed by Frank Borzage. 1941. MGM. 100 min. Sound. 16mm Color. *Rental:* MGM United.

Smiling Ghost, The. Alexis Smith & Wayne Morris. Directed by Lewis Seiler. 1941. Warners. 71 min. Sound. 16mm B&W. *Rental:* MGM United.

Smoke Signal. Dana Andrews & Piper Laurie. Directed by Jerry Hopper. 1955. Universal. 88 min. Sound. 16mm Color. *Rental:* Swank Motion.

Smokey & the Bandit. Burt Reynolds, Sally Field & Jackie Gleason. Directed by Hal Needham. 1977. Universal. 97 min. Sound. 16mm Color. *Rental:* Swank Motion. *Rental:* Swank Motion, Videotape version.

Smokey & the Bandit II. Burt Reynolds & Jackie Gleason. Directed by Hal Needham. 1980. Universal. 95 min. Sound. 16mm Color. *Rental:* Swank Motion. *Rental:* Swank Motion, Videotape version.

Smokey & the Bandit III. Jackie Gleason & Paul Williams. Directed by Dick Lowry. 1983. Universal. 88 min. Sound. 16mm Color. *Rental:* Swank Motion. *Rental:* Swank Motion, Videotape version.

Smokey Joe's Revenge. 1977. Britain. (Cast unlisted). 57 min. Sound. 16mm Color. *Rental:* Lucerne Films. *Sale:* Lucerne Films.

Smoking Guns. Orig. Title: Billy the Kid's Smoking Guns. Buster Crabbe. Directed by Sherman Scott. 1942. PRC. 63 min. Sound. 16mm B&W. *Rental:* Mogulls Films.

Smoking Spiral, The. 1967. NET. (Documentary). 60 min. Sound. 16mm B&W. *Rental:* Indiana AV Ctr.

Smooth Velvet, Raw Silk. 1976. Dimension. (Cast unlisted). 85 min. Sound. 16mm Color. *Rental:* Salz Ent.

Smouldering Fires. Pauline Frederick & Laura La Plante. Directed by Clarence Brown. 1924. Universal. 85 min. Silent. 16mm B&W. *Rental:* Film Images. *Sale:* Cinema Concepts, Silent 8mm version.

Smuggled Cargo. Rochelle Hudson & George Barbier. Directed by John H. Auer. 1939. Republic. 54 min. Sound. 16mm B&W. *Rental:* Ivy Films. *Sale:* Rep Pic Film.

Smuggler's Cove. Bowery Boys & William Beaudine. 1948. Monogram. 66 min. Sound. 16mm B&W. *Rental:* Mogulls Films.

Smuggler's Gold. Cameron Mitchell & Amanda Blake. Directed by William Berke. 1951. Columbia. 64 min. Sound. 16mm B&W. *Rental:* Inst Cinema & Newman Film Lib.

Snafu. Robert Benchley & Vera Vague. Directed by Jack Moss. 1946. Columbia. 82 min. 16mm B&W. *Rental:* Kit Parker.

Snake Pit, The. Olivia De Havilland & Mark Stevens. Directed by Anatole Litvak. 1948. Fox. 108 min. Sound. 16mm B&W. *Rental:* Films Inc, Twyman Films & Williams Films.

Snapshots. Directed by Mel Howard. 1975. Schwartz. (Experimental). 90 min. Sound. 16mm Color. *Rental:* Vision Quest. *Sale:* Vision Quest.

Snarl of Hate. Flash & The Wonder Dog. Directed by Noel Smith. 1926. Bischoff. 60 min. Silent. 16mm B&W. *Rental:* Film Classics. *Sale:* Film Classics.

Sniper, The. Arthur Franz & Adolphe Menjou. Directed by Edward Dmytryk. 1952. Columbia. 87 min. Sound. 16mm B&W. *Rental:* Budget Films, Charard Motion Pics, Films Inc & Kit Parker.

Snoopy Come Home. Directed by Lee Mendelssohn & Bill Melendez. 1972. National General. (Animated). 70 min. Sound. 16mm B&W. *Rental:* Cine Craft, Film Ctr DC, Films Inc, Newman Film Lib, Swank Motion & Williams Films.

Snow Country. Ryo Ikebe. Directed by Shiro Toyoda. Jap. 1957. Japan. 133 min. Sound. 16mm B&W. subtitles. *Rental:* Images Film & Iowa Films.

Snow Devils. Jack Stuart & Amber Collins. MGM. 92 min. Sound. 16mm Color. *Rental:* MGM United.

Snow Dog. Kirby Grant & Elena Verdugo. Directed by Frank McDonald. 1950. Monogram. 60 min. Sound. 16mm B&W. *Rental:* Budget Films, Hurlock Cine & Modern Sound.

Snow Job. Jean-Claude Killy & Vittorio De Sica. Directed by George Englund. 1972. France. 60 min. Sound. 16mm Color. *Rental:* Film Ctr DC, Films Inc & Willoughby Peer.

Snow Queen, The. Directed by Guenady Kanzansky. 1959. Russia. (Animated). 70 min. Sound. 16mm Color. dubbed. *Rental:* Kerr Film.

Snow Treasure. Trans. Title: Very Cold War, A. James Franciscus & Ilona Rodgers. Directed by Irving Jacoby. 1968. Allied Artists. 85 min. Sound. 16mm Color. *Rental:* Bosco Films, Budget Films, Westcoast Films & Willoughby Peer.

Snow White. Marguerite Clark. Directed by J. Searle Dawley. 1917. Paramount. 50 min. Silent. 8mm B&W. *Sale:* Film Classics.

Snow White. Diane Wagner. Directed by G. Kolditz. 1962. Childhood. 85 min. Sound. 16mm Color. dubbed. *Rental:* Budget Films, Cine Craft, Newman Film Lib & Roas Films.

Snow White & Rose Red. Rosemarie Seehofer. Directed by Emil Kobler. 1966. American International. 55 min. Sound. 16mm Color. narrated Eng. *Rental:* Cine Craft, Video Comm & Welling Motion Pictures.

Snow White & the Seven Dwarfs. Directed by David Hand. 1937. Disney. 83 min. Sound. 16mm Color. *Rental:* MGM United, Roas Films, Swank Motion, Welling Motion Pictures, Westcoast Films & Williams Films.

Snow White & the Three Stooges. Carol Heiss & the Three Stooges. Directed by Walter Lang. 1961. Fox. 107 min. Sound. 16mm Color. *Rental:* Films Inc. *Rental:* Willoughby Peer, Anamorphic version.

Snow White with Mr. Magoo. Orig. Title: Mister Magoo's Snow White. 1965. UPA. (Animated). 50 min. Sound. 16mm Color. *Rental:* Budget Films, Films Inc, Kerr Film, OK AV Ctr & Westcoast Films. *Sale:* Films Inc.

Snowball Express. Dean Jones, Nancy Olson & Harry Morgan. Directed by Norman Tokar. 1972. Disney. 93 min. Sound. 16mm Color. *Rental:* Bosco Films, Cine Craft, Elliot Film Co, Film Ctr DC, Films Inc, Film Pres, MGM United, Modern Sound, Newman Film Lib, Roas Films, Swank Motion, Twyman Films, U of IL Film, Welling Motion Pictures, Westcoast Films & Williams Films.

Snowbound. Directed by Andrew Young. 1978. Learning Corp. (Cast unlisted). 50 min. Sound. 16mm Color. *Rental:* Learning Corp Am & U Mich Media. *Sale:* Learning Corp Am. *Sale:* Learning Corp Am, *Rental:* Learning Corp Am, Videotape version.

Snowed Under. George Brent & Glenda Farrell. Directed by Ray Enright. 1936. Warners. 63 min. Sound. 16mm B&W. *Rental:* MGM United.

Snowfire. Don Megowan & Claire Kelly. Directed by Dorrell McGowan & Stuart McGowan. 1958. Allied Artists. 73 min. Sound. 16mm B&W. *Rental:* Hurlock Cine.

Snows of Kilimanjaro, The. Gregory Peck & Susan Hayward. Directed by Henry King. 1952. Fox. 117 min. Sound. 16mm Color. *Rental:* Films Inc.

So Dark the Night. Steven Geray. Directed by Joseph Lewis. 1946. Columbia. 72 min. Sound. 16mm B&W. *Rental:* Corinth Films & Inst Cinema.

So Darling, So Deadly. Brad Harris. 1967. Italy. 93 min. Sound. 16mm Color. dubbed. *Rental:* Westcoast Films.

So Dear to My Heart. Burl Ives, Beulah Bondi & Bobby Driscoll. Directed by Harold Schuster. 1948. Disney. 82 min. Sound. 16mm Color. *Rental:* Bosco Films, Buchan Pic, Cine Craft, Cousino Visual Ed, Disney Prod, Elliot Film Co, Film Ctr DC, Films Inc, MGM United, Modern Sound, Newman Film Lib, Roas Films, Swank Motion, Twyman Films, Welling Motion Pictures, Westcoast Films & Williams Films.

So Ends Our Night. Fredric March & Margaret Sullavan. Directed by John Cromwell. 1941. United Artists. 100 min. Sound. 16mm B&W. *Rental:* Ivy Films & Mogulls Films.

So Far From India. Directed by Nair Mira. (Documentary). 49 min. Sound. 16mm Color. *Rental:* Film Makers. *Sale:* Film Makers.

So Fine. Ryan O'Neal & Jack Warden. Directed by Andrew Bergman. 1982. Warners. 91 min. Sound. 16mm Color. *Rental:* Williams Films & Swank Motion. *Rental:* Swank Motion, Videotape version.

So Is This: Snow/Michael. 45 min. Silent. 16mm B&W. *Rental:* Canyon Cinema.

So Long Joey. Dave Boyer. 1973. Gospel. 63 min. Sound. 16mm Color. *Rental:* Gospel Films & Roas Films.

So Proudly We Hail. Claudette Colbert, Paulette Goddard & Veronica Lake. Directed by Mark Sandrich. 1943. Paramount. 125 min. Sound. 16mm B&W. *Rental:* Swank Motion.

So Red the Rose. Margaret Sullavan & Walter Connolly. Directed by King Vidor. 1935. Paramount. 83 min. Sound. 16mm B&W. *Rental:* Swank Motion.

So Soon to Die. Anne Bancroft & Richard Basehart. 1957. CBS. 60 min. Sound. 16mm B&W. *Rental:* Bosco Films.

So This Is Arizona. Wally Wales. 1931. Big Four. 60 min. Sound. 16mm B&W. *Rental:* Mogulls Films.

So This Is College. Elliot Nugent & Robert Montgomery. Directed by Sam Wood. 1929. MGM. 110 min. Sound. 16mm B&W. *Rental:* MGM United.

So This Is Love. Shirley Mason & William Collier Jr. 1928. Columbia. (Musical score only). 60 min. Sound. 16mm B&W. *Rental:* Kit Parker.

So This Is New York. Henry Morgan & Rudy Vallee. Directed by Richard Fleischer. 1948. United Artists. 79 min. Sound. 16mm B&W. *Rental:* Budget Films & Ivy Films. *Sale:* Rep Pic Film.

So This Is Paris. Monte Blue & Patsy Ruth Miller. Directed by Ernst Lubitsch. 1926. Warners. 68 min. Silent. 16mm B&W. *Rental:* Em Gee Film Lib & MGM United.

So This Is Paris. Tony Curtis & Gloria De Haven. Directed by Richard Quine. 1954. Universal. 96 min. Sound. 16mm Color. *Rental:* Swank Motion.

So This Is Washington. Lum & Abner & Alan Mowbray. Directed by Ray McCarey. 1943. RKO. 63 min. Sound. 16mm B&W. *Rental:* Inst Cinema.

So Well Remembered. John Mills & Martha Scott. Directed by Edward Dmytryk. 1947. RKO. 114 min. Sound. 16mm B&W. *Rental:* Kit Parker.

So You Won't Talk. Joe E. Brown. Directed by Edward Sedgwick. 1940. Columbia. 63 min. Sound. 16mm B&W. *Rental:* Westcoast Films.

Soak the Rich. Walter Connolly & John Howard. Directed by Ben Hecht & Charles MacArthur. 1936. Paramount. 87 min. Sound. 16mm B&W. *Rental:* Swank Motion.

Soapbox Derby. Michael Crawford & Keith Davis. Directed by Darcy Conyers. 1958. Britain. 64 min. Sound. 16mm B&W. *Sale:* Lucerne Films.

Social Classes - Nineteen Hundred: A World to Win. 1976. Britain. 52 min. Sound. 16mm Color. *Rental:* Time-Life Multimedia. *Sale:* Time-Life Multimedia. *Rental:* Time-Life Multimedia, *Sale:* Time-Life Multimedia, Videotape version.

Social Error, A. Orig. Title: Kidnapped. David Sharpe & Monte Blue. 1935. Commodore. 60 min. Sound. 16mm B&W. *Rental:* Mogulls Films.

Social Life of Small Urban Spaces, The. 1980. 55 min. Sound. 16mm Color. *Rental:* U Mich Media.

Social Register, The. Colleen Moore & Pauline Frederick. Directed by Marshall Neilan. 1934. Columbia. 74 min. Sound. 16mm B&W. *Rental:* Kit Parker.

Social Secretary, The. Norma Talmadge & Erich Von Stroheim. Directed by John Emerson. 1916. Fine Arts/Triangle. 50 min. Silent. 16mm B&W. *Rental:* Em Gee Film Lib.

Social Security: How Secure?. 1976. NBC. 52 min. Sound. 16mm Color. *Rental:* Films Inc, Syracuse U Film & U Mich Media. *Sale:* Films Inc.

Social Worker As Witness, The. 1981. 50 min. Sound. Videotape Color. *Rental:* Iowa Films.

Society Doctor. Chester Morris & Robert Taylor. Directed by George B. Seitz. 1935. MGM United. 68 min. Sound. 16mm B&W. *Rental:* MGM United.

Society Fever. Lois Wilson. Directed by Frank R. Strayer. 1935. Chesterfield. 75 min. Sound. 16mm B&W. *Rental:* Film Classics.

Sociobiology: The Human Animal. 1977. Nova. 57 min. Sound. 16mm Color. *Rental:* U Mich Media, Syracuse U Film & Time-Life Multimedia. *Sale:* Time-Life Multimedia. *Rental:* Time-Life Multimedia, *Sale:* Time-Life Multimedia, Videotape version.

Socrate, Le. Pierre Luzan & Martine Brochard. Directed by Robert Lapoujade. Fr. 1969. France. 90 min. Sound. 16mm Color. subtitles. *Rental:* New Yorker Films.

Socrates. Jean Sylvere. Directed by Roberto Rossellini. 1970. Italy. 154 min. Sound. 16mm B&W. *Rental:* New Yorker Films.

Sodom & Gomorrah. Stewart Granger & Pier Angeli. Directed by Geofredo Lombardo. 1963. Fox. 154 min. Sound. 16mm Color. *Rental:* Films Inc.

Sodom & Gomorrah. 1979. Lucerne. (Cast unlisted). 50 min. Sound. 16mm Color. *Sale:* Lucerne Films & Syracuse U Film. *Sale:* Lucerne Films, Videotape version.

Sofia. Gene Raymond & Sigrid Gurie. Directed by John Reinhardt. 1948. Film Classics. 80 min. Sound. 16mm B&W. *Rental:* Mogulls Films.

Soft Skin, The. Trans. Title: Peau Douce, La. Jean Desaily & Francoise Dorleac. Directed by Francois Truffaut. Fr. 1964. France. 120 min. Sound. 16mm B&W. subtitles. *Rental:* Janus Films.

Sol Madrid. David McCallum & Telly Savalas. Directed by Brian Hutton. 1968. MGM. 90 min. Sound. 16mm Color. *Rental:* MGM United.

Soldier, The. Ken Wahl & Alberta Watson. Directed by James Glickenhaus. 1982. Embassy. 87 min. Sound. 16mm Color. *Rental:* Films Inc.

Soldier Blue. Candice Bergen. Directed by Ralph Nelson. 1970. Embassy. 112 min. Sound. 16mm Color. *Rental:* Films Inc.

Soldier Girls. Directed by Nick Broomfield & Joan Churchill. 1980. Embassy. 87 min. Sound. 16mm B&W. *Rental:* Churchill Films, First Run & Syracuse U Film. *Rental:* Churchill Films, Videotape version.

Soldier in a Skirt. Orig. Title: Triple Echo. Oliver Reed & Glenda Jackson. Directed by Guy Green. 1973. Britain. 94 min. Sound. 16mm Color. *Rental:* New Line Cinema.

Soldier in the Rain. Jackie Gleason, Steve McQueen & Tuesday Weld. Directed by Ralph Nelson. 1963. Allied Artists. 96 min. Sound. 16mm B&W. *Rental:* Hurlock Cine.

Soldier of Fortune. Clark Gable & Susan Hayward. Directed by Edward Dmytryk. 1955. Fox. 96 min. Sound. 16mm Color. *Rental:* Films Inc.

Soldier of Orange, A. Rutger Hauer & Susan Penhaligon. Directed by Paul Verhoeven. 1979. Netherlands. 165 min. Sound. 16mm Color. subtitles. *Rental:* Twyman Films, Westcoast Films & Wholesome Film Ctr.

Soldier's Plaything, A. Ben Lyon, Jean Hersholt & Harry Langdon. Directed by Michael Curtiz. 1931. Warners. 57 min. Sound. 16mm B&W. *Rental:* MGM United.

Soldier's Prayer, A. Tatsuya Nakadai. Directed by Nakadai Kobayashi. Jap. 1961. Japan. 190 min. Sound. 16mm B&W. subtitles. *Rental:* Films Inc.

Soldiers Three. Stewart Granger & Walter Pidgeon. Directed by Tay Garnett. 1951. MGM. 95 min. Sound. 16mm B&W. *Rental:* MGM United.

Soleil Dans L'Oeil, Le. Anna Karina & Jacques Perrin. Directed by J. Bourdon. Fr. 1961. France. (Anamorphic). 80 min. Sound. 16mm B&W. *Rental:* French Am Cul. *Rental:* French Am Cul, Videotape version.

Solid Gold Cadillac, The. Judy Holliday & Paul Douglas. Directed by Richard Quine. 1956. Columbia. 99 min. Sound. 16mm Color. *Rental:* Arcus Film, Bosco Films, Buchan Pic, Budget Films, Cine Craft, Film Ctr DC, Films Inc, Kit Parker, Modern Sound, U of IL Film, Welling Motion Pictures & Wholesome Film Ctr.

Solitaire Man, The. Herbert Marshall & Mary Boland. Directed by Jack Conway. 1933. MGM United. 68 min. Sound. 16mm B&W. *Rental:* MGM United.

Solitary Child, The. Philip Friend & Barbara Shelley. Directed by Gerald Thomas. 1957. Britain. 63 min. Sound. 16mm B&W. *Rental:* Charard Motion Pics.

Solo. Jean-Pierre Mocky. Directed by Jean-Pierre Mocky. 1970. France. 90 min. Sound. 16mm Color. *Rental:* French Am Cul.

Solomon & Sheba. Yul Brynner & Gina Lollobrigida. Directed by King Vidor. 1959. United Artists. 139 min. Sound. 16mm Color. *Rental:* MGM United.

Solzhenitsyn's Children Are Making a Lot of Noise in Paris. Directed by Michael Rubbo. 1978. 87 min. 16mm Color. *Rental:* U Cal Media & Natl Film CN. *Sale:* Natl Film CN. *Rental:* Natl Film CN, *Sale:* Natl Film CN, Videotape version.

Sombra, the Spider Woman. Bruce Edwards, Virginia Lindley & Carol Forman. 1947. Republic. 100 min. Sound. 16mm B&W. *Rental:* Ivy Films. *Sale:* Rep Pic Film.

Sombrero. Ricardo Montalban & Pier Angeli. Directed by Norman Foster. 1953. MGM. 103 min. Sound. 16mm Color. *Rental:* Films Inc & MGM United.

Sombrero Kid, The. Don Barry & Lynn Merrick. Directed by George Sherman. 1942. Republic. 54 min. Sound. 16mm B&W. *Rental:* Ivy Films. *Sale:* Rep Pic Film.

Some American Feminists. Directed by Luce Guilbeault, Nicole Brossard & Margaret Wescott. 1977. Republic. 56 min. Sound. 16mm Color. *Rental:* A Mokin, Iowa Films & Natl Film CN. *Sale:* A Mokin.

Some Call It Greed. 1980. Learning Corp. 52 min. Sound. 16mm Color. *Rental:* Iowa Films, Learning Corp Am, Syracuse U Film, U Cal Media, U of IL Film & Utah Media. *Sale:* Learning Corp Am.

Some Came Running. Frank Sinatra & Shirley MacLaine. Directed by Vincente Minnelli. 1958. MGM. 137 min. Sound. 16mm Color. *Rental:* MGM United. *Rental:* Films Inc, Anamorphic version. *Rental:* MGM United, Videotape version.

Some Girls Do. Richard Johnson & Daliah Lavi. Directed by Ralph Thomas. 1970. United Artists. 91 min. Sound. 16mm Color. *Rental:* MGM United.

Some Kind of a Nut. Dick Van Dyke & Angie Dickinson. Directed by Garson Kanin. 1969. United Artists. 89 min. Sound. 16mm Color. *Rental:* MGM United.

Some Kind of Hero. Richard Pryor & Margot Kidder. Directed by Michael Pressman. 1982. Paramount. 95 min. Sound. 16mm Color. *Rental:* Films Inc.

Some Like It Hot. Tony Curtis & Jack Lemmon. Directed by Billy Wilder. 1959. 120 min. Sound. 16mm *Rental:* MGM United. *Rental:* MGM United, Videotape version.

Some of the Presidents' Men. 1978. Britain. 59 min. Sound. Videotape *Rental:* PBS Video. *Sale:* PBS Video.

Some People Have to Suffer. Christopher Pinney. 1976. Canada. (Documentary). 53 min. Sound. 16mm Color. *Rental:* Natl Film CN. *Sale:* Natl Film CN.

Some Won't Go. Directed by Gill Toff. 1968. American Documentary. 50 min. Sound. 16mm B&W. *Rental:* Creative Film.

Somebody Killed Her Husband. Farrah Fawcett & Jeff Bridges. Directed by Lamont Johnson. 1978. Columbia. 97 min. Sound. 16mm Color. *Rental:* Arcus Film, Budget Films, Cine Craft, Swank Motion, Welling Motion Pictures & Wholesome Film Ctr.

Somebody Loves Me. Betty Hutton & Ralph Meeker. Directed by Irving Brecher. 1952. Paramount. 97 min. Sound. 16mm Color. *Rental:* Films Inc.

Somebody Up There Likes Me. Paul Newman & Pier Angeli. Directed by Robert Wise. 1956. MGM. 113 min. Sound. 16mm B&W. *Rental:* MGM United. *Rental:* MGM United, Videotape version.

Somehow It Works. 1969. NBC. (Documentary). 52 min. Sound. 16mm Color. *Rental:* McGraw-Hill Films. *Sale:* McGraw-Hill Films.

Someone Must Govern Us. 1966. NET. (Documentary). 60 min. Sound. 16mm B&W. *Rental:* Indiana AV Ctr.

Someone to Remember. Mabel Paige & John Craven. Directed by Robert Siodmak. 1943. Republic. 80 min. Sound. 16mm B&W. *Rental:* Ivy Films. *Sale:* Rep Pic Film.

Something Big. Dean Martin & Brian Keith. Directed by Andrew V. McLaglen. 1972. Cinema Center. 108 min. Sound. 16mm Color. *Rental:* Swank Motion & Welling Motion Pictures.

Something for Everyone. Angela Lansbury & Michael York. Directed by Harold Prince. 1972. National General. 112 min. Sound. 16mm Color. *Rental:* Swank Motion.

Something for the Birds. Victor Mature & Patricia Neal. Directed by Robert Wise. 1952. Fox. 81 min. Sound. 16mm B&W. *Rental:* Films Inc.

Something for the Boys. Carmen Miranda & Michael O'Shea. Directed by Lewis Seiler. 1944. Fox. 87 min. Sound. 16mm Color. *Rental:* Films Inc.

Something in the Wind. Deanna Durbin & Donald O'Connor. Directed by Irving Pichel. 1947. Universal. 94 min. Sound. 16mm B&W. *Rental:* Swank Motion.

Something of Danger That Exists. 1978. US Government. 59 min. Sound. 16mm Color. *Sale:* Natl AV Ctr.

Something of Value. Rock Hudson & Sidney Poitier. Directed by Richard Brooks. 1957. MGM. 113 min. Sound. 16mm B&W. *Rental:* MGM United.

Something Short of Paradise. Susan Sarandon & David Steinberg. Directed by David Helpern Jr. 1979. American International. 91 min. Sound. 16mm B&W. *Rental:* Swank Motion.

Something to Live for. Mei Yu & Ching Kim. 1976. Gospel. 49 min. Sound. 16mm Color. *Rental:* Gospel Films.

Something to Sing About. Orig. Title: Battling Hoofer, The. James Cagney & William Frawley. Directed by Victor Schertzinger. 1936. Grand National. 84 min. Sound. 16mm B&W. *Rental:* Budget Films, Em Gee Film Lib, Maljack, Newman Film Lib & Video Comm. *Sale:* Cinema Concepts & Reel Images. *Sale:* Reel Images, Super 8 sound version.

Something Weird. Directed by Herschell G. Lewis. 1968. 80 min. Sound. 16mm Color. *Sale:* Festival Films. *Sale:* Festival Films, Videotape version.

Something Wicked This Way Comes. Jason Robards & Diane Ladd. Directed by Jack Clayton. 1983. Disney. 94 min. Sound. 16mm Color. *Rental:* Films Inc, MGM United, Swank Motion & Williams Films, videotape version.

Something Wild. Carroll Baker & Ralph Meeker. Directed by Jack Garfein. 1961. United Artists. 112 min. Sound. 16mm B&W. *Rental:* MGM United.

Sometimes a Great Notion. Paul Newman, Henry Fonda & Richard Jaeckel. 1972. Universal. 114 min. Sound. 16mm Color. *Rental:* Swank Motion. *Rental:* Swank Motion, Anamorphic version.

Somewhere in the Night. Richard Conte. Directed by Joseph L. Mankiewicz. 1946. Fox. 100 min. Sound. 16mm B&W. *Rental:* Films Inc.

Somewhere in Time. Christopher Reeve, Jane Seymour & Christopher Plummer. Directed by Jeannot Szwarc. 103 min. Sound. 16mm Color. *Rental:* Swank Motion. *Rental:* Swank Motion, Videotape version.

Son-Daughter. Ramon Novarro, Helen Hayes & Lewis Stone. Directed by Clarence Brown. 1932. MGM. 79 min. Sound. 16mm B&W. *Rental:* MGM United.

Son of a Gun. Bronco Billy Anderson & Joy Lewis. Directed by Richard Jones. 1919. Fox. 65 min. Sound. 16mm B&W. *Rental:* Budget Films, Em Gee Film Lib & Video Comm. *Sale:* Blackhawk Films. *Rental:* Ivy Films, Super 8 silent version.

Son of a Gunfighter. Russ Tamblyn & Kieron Moore. Directed by Paul Landres. 1966. MGM. 92 min. Sound. 16mm Color. *Rental:* MGM United. *Rental:* MGM United, Anamorphic version.

Son of a Sailor. Joe E. Brown & Frank McHugh. Directed by Lloyd Bacon. 1933. Warners. 73 min. Sound. 16mm B&W. *Rental:* MGM United.

Son of Ali Baba. Tony Curtis & Piper Laurie. Directed by Kurt Neumann. 1952. Universal. 75 min. Sound. 16mm Color. *Rental:* Swank Motion.

Son of Belle Starr. Keith Larsen & Peggie Castle. Directed by Frank McDonald. 1953. Allied Artists. 70 min. Sound. 16mm B&W. *Rental:* Hurlock Cine.

Son of Blob. Orig. Title: Beware! The Blob! Godfrey Cambridge & Robert Walker. Directed by Larry Hagman. 1972. Jack Harris. 91 min. Sound. 16mm Color. *Rental:* Budget Films, Films Inc, Film Pres, Video Comm, Welling Motion Pictures & Westcoast Films.

Son of Dr. Jekyll. Louis Hayward & Alexander Knox. Directed by Seymour Friedman. 1951. Columbia. 77 min. Sound. 16mm B&W. *Rental:* Film Ctr DC, Inst Cinema, Modern Sound & Williams Films.

Son of Dracula. Lon Chaney Jr. & Louise Albritton. Directed by Robert Siodmak. 1943. Universal. 80 min. Sound. 16mm B&W. *Rental:* Williams Films.

Son of Dracula. Ringo Starr & Harry Nilsson. Directed by Freddie Francis. 1974. Cinemation. 90 min. Sound. 16mm Color. *Rental:* Films Inc.

Son of El Cid. Mark Damon & Antonella Lualdi. 1965. Embassy. 100 min. Sound. 16mm Color. dubbed. *Rental:* Video Comm.

Son of Flubber. Fred MacMurray, Nancy Olson & Keenan Wynn. Directed by Robert Stevenson. 1963. Disney. 100 min. Sound. 16mm B&W. *Rental:* Bosco Films, Cine Craft, Elliot Film Co, Films Inc, MGM United, Modern Sound, Natl Film Serv, Roas Films, Swank Motion, Twyman Films, U of IL Film, Welling Motion Pictures, Westcoast Films & Williams Films.

Son of Football Follies: Super Bowl XIV. 46 min. Sound. Videotape Color. *Sale:* Vidamerica.

Son of Frankenstein. Basil Rathbone & Boris Karloff. Directed by Rowland V. Lee. 1939. Universal. 80 min. Sound. 16mm B&W. *Rental:* Williams Films.

Son of Fury. Tyrone Power. Directed by John Cromwell. 1942. Fox. 78 min. Sound. 16mm B&W. *Rental:* Films Inc.

Son of God's Country. Monte Hale. Directed by R. G. Springsteen. 1948. Republic. 60 min. Sound. 16mm B&W. *Rental:* Ivy Films. *Sale:* Rep Pic Film.

Son of Godzilla: Godzilla No Musuko. Tadao Takashima & Akira Kubo. Directed by Jun Fukuda. 1967. Japan. 86 min. Sound. 16mm Color. *Rental:* Budget Films.

Son of Hercules vs. the Medusa. Richard Harrison. 1967. Italy. 90 min. Sound. Color. dubbed. *Rental:* Budget Films & Modern Sound.

Son of Kong. Robert Armstrong & Helen Mack. Directed by Ernest B. Schoedsack. 1933. RKO. 61 min. Sound. 16mm B&W. *Rental:* Films Inc. *Lease:* Films Inc.

Son of Lassie. Peter Lawford & June Lockhart. Directed by S. Sylvan Simon. 1945. MGM. 100 min. Sound. 16mm Color. *Rental:* MGM United.

Son of Man. Colin Blakely. 1970. Britain. 96 min. Sound. 16mm B&W. *Rental:* Time-Life Multimedia. *Sale:* Time-Life Multimedia.

Son of Man. Fiorella Maria. Italy. 75 min. Sound. 16mm B&W. dubbed. *Rental:* Alba House.

Son of Monte Cristo. Louis Hayward. Directed by Rowland V. Lee. 1940. United Artists. 105 min. Sound. 16mm B&W. *Rental:* Budget Films & Kit Parker. *Sale:* Cinema Concepts & Reel Images. *Sale:* Morcraft Films & Reel Images, Super 8 sound version.

Son of Paleface. Bob Hope & Jane Russell. Directed by Frank Tashlin. 1952. Paramount. 95 min. Sound. 16mm Color. *Rental:* Budget Films, Cine Craft, Films Inc, Modern Sound, Roas Films, Twyman Films, Welling Motion Pictures, Westcoast Films, Wholesome Film Ctr & Willoughby Peer.

Son of Robin Hood. David Hedison & June Laverick. Directed by George Sherman. 1959. Britain. 81 min. Sound. 16mm Color. *Rental:* Charard Motion Pics & Films Inc. *Rental:* Willoughby Peer, Anamorphic version.

Son of Rusty. Ted Donaldson. Directed by Lew Landers. 1947. Columbia. 75 min. Sound. 16mm B&W. *Rental:* Cine Craft & Films Inc.

Son of Sinbad. Dale Robertson & Vincent Price. Directed by Ted Tetzlaff. 1955. RKO. 88 min. Sound. 16mm Color. *Rental:* Films Inc. *Lease:* Video Comm. *Rental:* Video Comm, *Lease:* Video Comm, Videotape version.

Son of the Border. Tom Keene & Julie Hayden. Directed by Lloyd Nosler. 1933. RKO. 55 min. Sound. 16mm B&W. *Rental:* RKO General Pics.

Son of the Navy. Orig. Title: Young Recruit. James Dunn & Jean Parker. Directed by William Nigh. 1940. Monogram. 72 min. Sound. 16mm B&W. *Rental:* Hurlock Cine & Roas Films.

Son of the Plains. Bob Custer. Directed by Robert N. Bradbury. 1931. Syndicate. 57 min. Sound. 16mm B&W. *Sale:* Natl Cinema.

Son of the Regiment. Yura Yankin. Directed by Vasili Pronin. Rus. 1949. Russia. 77 min. Sound. 16mm B&W. subtitles. *Rental:* Corinth Films.

Son of the Sheik. Rudolph Valentino & Vilma Banky. Directed by George Fitzmaurice. 1926. United Artists. 68 min. Sound. 16mm B&W. *Rental:* Em Gee Film Lib, Film Classics, Ivy Films, Kerr Film, Mogulls Films, Natl Film Video, Video Comm & Willoughby Peer. *Sale:* Blackhawk Films & E Finney. *Rental:* Killiam Collect, Sound 16mm tinted version. *Rental:* A Twyman Pres, Budget Films, Williams Films, Kit Parker, Film Images & Video Comm, *Sale:* Blackhawk Films, Silent 16mm, B&W version. *Sale:* Blackhawk Films, Super 8 sound version. *Sale:* Blackhawk Films, Super 8 silent version. *Sale:* Blackhawk Films, Videotape version. *Rental:* Film Classics, Videotape version.

Son of Zorro. George Turner & Peggy Stewart. Directed by Spencer G. Bennett. 1947. Republic. 163 min. Sound. 16mm B&W. *Rental:* Ivy Films.

Song at Twilight: An Essay on Aging. 1979. PBS. (Documentary). 59 min. B&W. *Rental:* PBS Video. *Sale:* PBS Video, Videotape version.

Song of Arizona. Roy Rogers. Directed by Frank McDonald. 1946. Republic. 54 min. Sound. 16mm B&W. *Rental:* Ivy Films. *Sale:* Rep Pic Film & Reel Images.

Song of Bernadette. Jennifer Jones & Charles Bickford. Directed by Henry King. 1943. Fox. 157 min. Sound. 16mm B&W. *Rental:* Films Inc, Twyman Films & Williams Films.

Song of Ceylon. Directed by John Grierson. 1934. Britain. 45 min. Sound. 16mm B&W. *Rental:* Films Inc & Syracuse U Film. *Sale:* Reel Images.

Song of China. Shang Kwahwu. Directed by Lo Ming Yau. Chinese. 1934. China. 60 min. Sound. 16mm B&W. subtitles. *Rental:* Budget Films & Trans-World Films.

Song of Freedom. Paul Robeson & Elizabeth Welch. Directed by J. Elder Wills. 1938. Treo. 70 min. Sound. 16mm B&W. *Rental:* A Twyman Pres, Budget Films, Em Gee Film Lib, Films Inc & Mogulls Films. *Sale:* Cinema Concepts & Film Images. *Sale:* Morcraft Films, Super 8 sound version. *Sale:* Cinema Concepts & Tamarelles French Film, Videotape version.

Song of India. Sabu & Gail Russell. Directed by Albert S. Rogell. 1949. Columbia. 77 min. Sound. 16mm B&W. *Rental:* Bosco Films, Films Inc, Inst Cinema & Mogulls Films.

Song of India. Conrad Nagel & Madge Evans. Directed by Jacques Feyder. 1931. MGM. 86 min. Sound. 16mm B&W. *Rental:* MGM United.

Song of Love. Katherine Hepburn & Robert Walker. Directed by Clarence Brown. 1947. MGM. 112 min. Sound. 16mm B&W. *Rental:* MGM United.

Song of Love. Norma Talmadge & Joseph Schildkraut. Directed by Chester M. Franklin & Frances Marion. 1923. 16mm *Rental:* A Twyman Pres.

Song of Mexico. Adele Mara & Edgar Barrier. Directed by Pablo Marin. 1945. Republic. 57 min. Sound. 16mm B&W. *Rental:* Ivy Films.

Song of My Heart. Sir Cedric Hardwicke & Audrey Long. Directed by Benjamin Glazer. 1948. Alllied Artists. 85 min. Sound. 16mm B&W. *Rental:* Film Ctr DC, Hurlock Cine & Swank Motion.

Song of Nevada. Roy Rogers. Directed by Joseph Kane. 1944. Republic. 54 min. Sound. 16mm B&W. *Rental:* Budget Films, Ivy Films & Roas Films. *Sale:* Rep Pic Film.

Song of Norway. Florence Henderson & Torald Maurstad. Directed by Andrew Stone. 1970. ABC. 110 min. Sound. 16mm Color. *Rental:* Films Inc.

Song of Old Wyoming. Eddie Dean & Lash LaRue. Directed by Robert Emmett. 1945. PRC. 65 min. Sound. 16mm B&W. *Sale:* Classics Assoc NY.

Song of Russia. Robert Taylor & Susan Peters. Directed by Gregory Ratoff. 1943. MGM. 107 min. Sound. 16mm B&W. *Rental:* MGM United.

Song of Scheherazade. Yvonne De Carlo & Brian Donlevy. Directed by Walter Reisch. 1947. Universal. 107 min. Sound. 16mm B&W. *Rental:* Swank Motion.

Song of Sister Maria. Dominique Blanchard. 1957. Italy. 81 min. Sound. 16mm B&W. dubbed. *Rental:* Films Inc.

Song of Songs. Marlene Dietrich & Brian Aherne. Directed by Rouben Mamoulian. 1933. Paramount. 88 min. Sound. 16mm B&W. *Rental:* Swank Motion.

Song of Summer. Max Adrian & Elizabeth Ercy. Directed by Ken Russell. 1968. Britain. 77 min. Sound. 16mm B&W. *Rental:* Images Film. *Sale:* Images Film.

Song of Texas. Roy Rogers. Directed by Joseph Kane. 1943. Republic. 54 min. Sound. 16mm B&W. *Rental:* Budget Films, Ivy Films & Roas Films. *Sale:* Cinema Concepts & Rep Pic Film. *Sale:* Morcraft Films, Super 8 sound version.

Song of the Canary. David Davis & Josh Hanig. 1978. New Day. 57 min. Sound. 16mm Color. *Rental:* New Day Films. *Sale:* New Day Films.

Song of the City. Margaret Lindsay & J. Carroll Naish. Directed by Errol Taggart. 1937. MGM. 68 min. Sound. 16mm B&W. *Rental:* MGM United.

Song of the Drifter. Jimmy Wakely. Directed by Lambert Hillyer. 1948. Monogram. 55 min. Sound. 16mm B&W. *Rental:* Hurlock Cine.

Song of the Gringo. Orig. Title: Old Corral, The. Tex Ritter. Directed by J. P. McCarthy. 1936. Grand National. 60 min. Sound. 16mm B&W. *Rental:* Em Gee Film Lib & Video Comm. *Sale:* Glenn Photo & Morcraft Films.

Song of the Islands. Betty Grable & Victor Mature. Directed by Walter Lang. 1942. Fox. 75 min. Sound. 16mm B&W. *Rental:* Films Inc.

Song of the Loon. Morgan Royce & John Iverson. Directed by Andrew Herbert. 1970. Hollywood Cinema. 80 min. Sound. 16mm Color. *Rental:* Kit Parker.

Song of the Open Road. Jane Powell & W. C. Fields. Directed by S. Sylvan Simon. 1944. United Artists. 94 min. Sound. 16mm B&W. *Rental:* Ivy Films & Rep Pic Film. *Lease:* Rep Pic Film.

Song of the Prairie. Orig. Title: Sentiment & Song. Ken Curtis & Jeff Donnell. Directed by Ray Nazarro. 1945. Columbia. 69 min. Sound. 16mm B&W. *Rental:* Budget Films.

Song of the Range. Jimmy Wakely. Directed by Wallace Fox. 1944. Monogram. 60 min. Sound. 16mm B&W. *Rental:* Hurlock Cine.

Song of the Saddle. Dick Foran. Directed by Louis King. 1936. Warners. 58 min. Sound. 16mm B&W. *Rental:* MGM United.

Song of the Shirt. 4 pts. Directed by Susan Clayton & Jonathan Curling. 1979. Britain. (Documentary). 135 min. Sound. 16mm B&W. *Rental:* Museun Mod Art.

Song of the Sierras. Jimmy Wakely. Directed by Oliver Drake. 1947. Monogram. 55 min. Sound. 16mm B&W. *Rental:* Hurlock Cine.

Song of the South. Ruth Warrick, Bobby Driscoll & James Bassett. Directed by Wilfred Jackson. 1946. Disney. 94 min. Sound. 16mm Color. *Rental:* Disney Prod, Film Ctr DC, Films Inc, MGM United & Swank Motion.

Song of the Thin Man. William Powell & Myrna Loy. Directed by Edward Buzzell. 1947. MGM. 86 min. Sound. 16mm B&W. *Rental:* MGM United.

Song of the Trail. Kermit Maynard. Directed by Russell Hopton. 1936. Ambassador. 60 min. Sound. 16mm B&W. *Rental:* Modern Sound. *Sale:* Morcraft Films & Reel Images. *Sale:* Reel Images, Super 8 sound version.

Song of the Wasteland. Jimmy Wakely. Directed by Thomas Carr. 1947. Monogram. 58 min. Sound. 16mm B&W. *Rental:* Hurlock Cine.

Song Parade, The. John Carroll & Marie McDonald. Directed by John H. Auer. 1950. Republic. 85 min. Sound. 16mm B&W. *Rental:* Ivy Films. *Sale:* Rep Pic Film.

Song Remains the Same, The. Led Zeppelin. Directed by Peter Clifton & Joe Massot. 1976. Warners. 136 min. Sound. 16mm Color. *Rental:* Swank Motion.

Song to Remember, A. Paul Muni, Merle Oberon & Cornel Wilde. Directed by Charles Vidor. 1945. Columbia. 112 min. Sound. 16mm B&W. *Rental:* Arcus Film, Bosco Films, Budget Films, Cine Craft, Charard Motion Pics, Film Ctr DC, Films Inc, Kit Parker, Modern Sound & Welling Motion Pictures.

Song Twenty-Three: Twenty-Third Psalm Branch. Directed by Stan Brakhage. 1966. Brakhage. 58 min. Sound. 8mm B&W. *Rental:* Canyon Cinema.

Song Without End. Dirk Bogarde & Capucine. Directed by Charles Vidor. 1960. Columbia. 130 min. Sound. 16mm Color. *Rental:* Arcus Film, Buchan Pic, Budget Films, Film Ctr DC, Films Inc, Kerr Film, Roas Films, Swank Motion & Welling Motion Pictures.

Song You Gave Me, The. Bebe Daniels & Victor Varconi. Directed by Paul L. Stein. 1934. Columbia. Sound. 16mm B&W. *Rental:* Kit Parker.

Sonnambula, La. Italy. (Opera). 92 min. Sound. 16mm B&W. narrated Eng. *Rental:* Corinth Films.

Sons & Lovers. Trevor Howard & Dean Stockwell. Directed by Jack Cardiff. 1960. Fox. 103 min. Sound. 16mm Color. *Rental:* Films Inc & Twyman Films. *Rental:* Films Inc, Anamorphic version.

Sons of Adventure. Russell Hayden & Lynne Roberts. Directed by Yakima Canutt. 1948. Republic. 60 min. Sound. 16mm B&W. *Rental:* Ivy Films & Westcoast Films.

Sons of Haji Omar. Directed by David Newman. 1978. 58 min. 16mm Color. *Rental:* National Film Serv & U Cal Media.

Sons of Katie Elder, The. John Wayne & Dean Martin. Directed by Henry Hathaway. 1965. Paramount. 122 min. Sound. 16mm Color. *Rental:* Films Inc.

Sons of Namatjira. 1982. EMC. (Documentary). 50 min. Sound. 16mm Color. *Rental:* U Cal Media.

Sons of the Anzacs: Nineteen Thirty Nine to Nineteen Forty Five. 1946. Australia. 79 min. Sound. 16mm B&W. *Rental:* Aust Info Serv. *Sale:* Aust Info Serv.

Sons of the Desert. Orig. Title: Fraternally Yours. Stan Laurel & Oliver Hardy. Directed by William A. Seiter. 1934. Hal Roach. 77 min. Sound. 16mm B&W. *Rental:* Budget Films, Em Gee Film Lib, Film Images, Films Inc, Ivy Films, Kit Parker, Roas Films, SD AV Ctr, Swank Motion, Welling Motion Pictures, Wholesome Film Ctr & Willoughby Peer. *Sale:* Blackhawk Films. *Sale:* Blackhawk Films, Super 8 sound version.

Sons of the Pioneers. Roy Rogers. Directed by Joseph Kane. 1942. Republic. 54 min. Sound. 16mm B&W. *Rental:* Ivy Films. *Sale:* Rep Pic Film.

Sons of the Sea. Sir Michael Redgrave & Valerie Hobson. Directed by Walter Forde. 1942. Britain. 91 min. Sound. 16mm B&W. *Rental:* MGM United.

Sons O'Guns. Joe E. Brown & Joan Blondell. Directed by Lloyd Bacon. 1936. Warners. 79 min. Sound. 16mm B&W. *Rental:* MGM United.

Sooky. Jackie Cooper & Jackie Coogan. Directed by Norman Taurog. 1931. Paramount. 85 min. Sound. 16mm B&W. *Rental:* Swank Motion.

Sophie's Choice. Meryl Streep, Kevin Kline & Peter MacNicol. Directed by Alan J. Pakula. 1985. Universal. 157 min. Sound. 16mm Color. *Rental:* Swank Motion.

Sophocles: Oedipus the King. 1975. Films for the Humanities. (Documentary). 45 min. Sound. 16mm Color. *Rental:* Films Human & U of IL Film. *Sale:* Films Human.

Sorcerer. Roy Scheider. Directed by William Friedkin. 1977. Paramount/Universal. 118 min. Sound. 16mm Color. *Rental:* Swank Motion.

Sorcerers, The. Boris Karloff & Susan George. Directed by Michael Reeves. 1967. Allied Artists. 87 min. Sound. 16mm Color. *Rental:* Hurlock Cine.

Sorceress, The. Marina Vlady. Directed by Andrew Michel. 1956. France. 62 min. Sound. 16mm B&W. *Rental:* Ivy Films.

Sorok Pervyi *see* Forty-First.

Sorority Girl. Susan Cabot & Dick Miller. Directed by Roger Corman. 1957. American International. 62 min. Sound. 16mm B&W. *Rental:* Budget Films & Films Inc.

Sorority House. Chill Wills & Ann Shirley. Directed by John Farrow. 1939. RKO. 64 min. Sound. 16mm *Rental:* RKO General Pics.

Sorrow & the Pity, The. Directed by Marcel Ophuls. 1972. France. (Documentary). 260 min. Sound. 16mm B&W. narrated Eng. *Rental:* Cinema Five. *Lease:* Cinema Five.

Sorrowful Jones. Bob Hope & Lucille Ball. Directed by Sidney Lanfield. 1949. Paramount. 88 min. Sound. 16mm B&W. *Rental:* Swank Motion.

Sorrows of Gin, The. Edward Herrmann & Sigourney Weaver. Directed by Jack Hofsiss. 1978. Miami Dade. 60 min. Sound. 16mm Color. *Sale:* Films Inc. *Sale:* Films Inc. *Sale:* Films Inc, Videotape version.

Sorrows of Satan, The. Adolphe Menjou, Ricardo Cortez & Carol Dempster. 1926. Paramount. 85 min. Silent. 16mm B&W. *Rental:* Museum Mod Art.

Sorry, Wrong Number. Barbara Stanwyck & Burt Lancaster. Directed by Anatole Litvak. 1948. Paramount. 89 min. Sound. 16mm B&W. *Rental:* Films Inc.

S.O.S. Coast Guard. Bela Lugosi & Ralph Byrd. Directed by William Witney & Alan James. 1942. Republic. 71 min. Sound. 16mm B&W. *Rental:* Ivy Films & Thunderbird Films. *Sale:* Rep Pic Film.

S.O.S. Tidal Wave. Ralph Byrd & George Barbier. Directed by John H. Auer. 1939. Republic. 54 min. Sound. 16mm B&W. *Rental:* Ivy Films. *Sale:* Rep Pic Film.

Soul-Fire. Richard Barthelmess & Bessie Love. Directed by John Robertson. 1925. First National. 90 min. Silent. 8mm B&W. *Rental:* Em Gee Film Lib. *Sale:* Glenn Photo.

Soul of Nigger Charley, The. Fred Williamson. Directed by Larry G. Spangler. 1973. Paramount. 109 min. Sound. 16mm Color. *Rental:* Films Inc.

Soul of the Beast, The. Madge Bellamy & Cullen Landis. Directed by John Griffith Wray. 1923. Metro. 55 min. Sound. 8mm B&W. *Rental:* Em Gee Film Lib & Ivy Films.

Soul Soldier. Orig. Title: Red White & Black, The. Rafer Johnson & Lincoln Kilpatrick. Directed by John Bud Cardos. 1972. Fanfare. 84 min. Sound. 16mm Color. *Rental:* Budget Films, Films Inc, Video Comm, Westcoast Films & Willoughby Peer.

Souls at Sea. Gary Cooper, George Raft & Frances Dee. Directed by Henry Hathaway. 1937. Paramount. 92 min. Sound. 16mm B&W. *Rental:* Swank Motion.

Souls to Soul. Ike Turner & Tina Turner. Directed by Denis Sanders. 1971. Cinerama. 96 min. Sound. 16mm Color. *Rental:* Swank Motion.

Sound & the Fury, The. Yul Brynner. Directed by Martin Ritt. 1959. Fox. 115 min. Sound. 16mm Color. *Rental:* Films Inc. *Rental:* Films Inc, Anamorphic version.

Sound of an Orchestra, The. 1966. CBS. (Documentary). 55 min. Sound. 16mm B&W. *Rental:* McGraw-Hill Films, U of IL Film & U Mich Media. *Sale:* McGraw-Hill Films.

Sound of Dolphins, The. 1976. Metromedia. 52 min. Sound. 16mm Color. *Rental:* Churchill Films. *Rental:* Churchill Films, Videotape version.

Sound of Laughter, The. Directed by John O'Shaughnesey. 1963. Union. 80 min. Sound. 16mm B&W. *Rental:* Films Inc, Roas Films, Wholesome Films Ctr & Willoughby Peer.

Sound of Music, The. Julie Andrews & Christopher Plummer. Directed by Robert Wise. 1965. Fox. (Anamorphic). 174 min. Sound. 16mm Color. *Rental:* Films Inc.

Sound of Trumpets, The. 1973. Ken Anderson. (Cast unlisted). 72 min. Sound. 16mm Color. *Rental:* G Herne & Roas Films.

Sound of Trumpets, The. Trans. Title: Post, Il. Sandro Panzeri. Directed by Ermanno Olmi. Ital. 1964. Italy. 90 min. Sound. 16mm B&W. subtitles. *Rental:* Films Inc & Janus Films.

Sound of Unsound, The. 1980. Canada. 57 min. Sound. 16mm B&W. *Rental:* Budget Films & Time-Life Multimedia. *Sale:* Time-Life Multimedia. *Sale:* Time-Life Multimedia, Videotape version.

Sound of Waves, The. Orig. Title: Surf, The. Kyoko Aoyama. Directed by Senkichi Taniguchi. 1954. Japan. 95 min. Sound. 16mm B&W. *Rental:* Film Images.

Sound Off. Mickey Rooney & Anne James. Directed by Richard Quine. 1952. Columbia. 83 min. Sound. 16mm B&W. *Rental:* Newman Film Lib & Welling Motion Pictures. *Rental:* Inst Cinema, Color version.

Sounder. Cicely Tyson & Paul Winfield. Directed by Martin Ritt. 1972. Fox. 105 min. Sound. 16mm Color. *Rental:* Budget Films, Films Inc, Welling Motion Pictures & Williams Films. *Sale:* Tamarelles French Film, Videotape version.

Sounds from the Mountains. Orig. Title: Echo, The. Setsuko Hara. Directed by Mikio Naruse. 1954. Japan. 96 min. Sound. 16mm B&W. *Rental:* Corinth Films.

Sounds of Anger, Echoes of Fear. 1979. 58 min. Sound. 16mm Color. *Rental:* Iowa Films.

Sounds of Love, The. 1983. 58 min. Sound. Videotape *Rental:* PBS Video. *Sale:* PBS Video.

South Africa. 1965. IU. 60 min. Sound. 16mm B&W. *Rental:* Syracuse U Film.

South Africa Belongs to Us. 1980. (Documentary). 57 min. Sound. 16mm Color. *Rental:* Icarus Films & U Mich Media. *Rental:* Icarus Films, *Sale:* Icarus Films, Videotape version.

South Africa: The Nuclear File. 1979. (Documentary). 54 min. Sound. 16mm Color. *Rental:* U Mich Media.

South Africa: The Riot That Won't Stop. 1979. PBS. (Documentary). 59 min. Sound. Videotape Color. *Rental:* PBS Video. *Sale:* PBS Video.

South Africa: The White Laager. 1977. 58 min. Sound. 16mm Color. *Rental:* Educ Media CA & U Mich Media.

South African Essay. 1965. NET. 120 min. Sound. 16mm B&W. *Sale:* Indiana AV Ctr & Syracuse U Film.

South Africa...Without Love. 1978. South Africa. 53 min. Sound. 16mm Color. *Rental:* U of IL Film.

South America-Voters or Violence? 1965. NET. (Documentary). 60 min. Sound. 16mm B&W. *Rental:* U Cal Media.

South-East Nuba, The. 1983. Britain. (Documentary). 60 min. Sound. 16mm Color. *Rental:* Films Inc. *Sale:* Films Inc. *Sale:* Films Inc, Videotape version.

South of Caliente. Roy Rogers. Directed by William Witney. 1951. Republic. 67 min. Sound. 16mm B&W. *Rental:* Ivy Films. *Sale:* Rep Pic Film.

South of Monterey. Gilbert Roland. Directed by William Nigh. 1947. Monogram. 63 min. B&W. *Sale:* Video Comm.

South of Rio. Monte Hale. Directed by Philip Ford. 1949. Republic. 60 min. Sound. 16mm B&W. *Rental:* Ivy Films. *Sale:* Rep Pic Film.

South of Santa Fe. Roy Rogers. Directed by Joseph Kane. 1942. Republic. 54 min. Sound. 16mm B&W. *Rental:* Budget Films & Ivy Films. *Sale:* Rep Pic Film. *Sale:* Cinema Concepts, Super 8 sound version.

South of Suez. George Brent & Brenda Marshall. Directed by Lewis Seiler. 1940. Warners. 85 min. Sound. 16mm B&W. *Rental:* MGM United.

South of Tahiti. Brian Donlevy & Broderick Crawford. Directed by George Waggner. 1941. Universal. 75 min. Sound. 16mm B&W. *Rental:* Film Ctr DC & Mogulls Films.

South of Texas. Gene Autry. Directed by George Sherman. 1939. Republic. 54 min. Sound. 16mm B&W. *Rental:* Ivy Films.

South of the Pago Pago. Victor McLaglen & Jon Hall. Directed by Alfred E. Green. 1940. United Artists. 96 min. Sound. 16mm B&W. *Rental:* Budget Films & Willoughby Peer.

South Pacific. Mitzi Gaynor & Rosanno Brazzi. Directed by Joshua Logan. 1958. Magna. 167 min. Sound. 16mm Color. *Rental:* Welling Motion Pictures & Westcoast Films.

South Pacific, The: End of Eden?. Directed by Julian Krainin. 1978. KCET. (Documentary). 58 min. Sound. 16mm Color. *Rental:* Pyramid Film & U of IL Film. *Sale:* Pyramid Film. *Rental:* Pyramid Film, *Sale:* Pyramid Film, Videotape version.

South Pacific Trail. Rex Allen. Directed by William Witney. 1952. Republic. 60 min. Sound. 16mm B&W. *Rental:* Ivy Films. *Sale:* Rep Pic Film.

South Riding. Sir Ralph Richardson & Edna Best. Directed by Victor Saville. 1938. Britain. 90 min. Sound. 16mm B&W. *Rental:* A Twyman Pres, Budget Films & Janus Films.

South to Karanga. Charles Bickford & James Craig. Directed by Harold Schuster. 1940. Universal. 60 min. Sound. 16mm B&W. *Rental:* Film Ctr DC & Mogulls Films.

Southeast Asia: The Other War. 1965. NET. 60 min. Sound. 16mm B&W. *Rental:* BYU Media, Indiana AV Ctr & Syracuse U Film.

Southern Accents, Northern Ghetto. 1967. ABC. (Documentary). 52 min. Sound. 16mm B&W. *Rental:* Syracuse U Film & U Mich Media. *Sale:* Benchmark Films.

Southern California. 1979. 70 min. Sound. 16mm Color. *Rental:* Canyon Cinema.

Southern Comfort. Keith Carradine & Powers Boothe. Directed by Walter Hill. 1981. Fox. 100 min. Sound. 16mm Color. *Rental:* Films Inc.

Southern Negro, The. 1967. KETC. (Documentary). 58 min. Sound. 16mm B&W. *Rental:* Indiana AV Ctr. *Sale:* Indiana AV Ctr.

Southern Star, The. George Segal, Orson Welles & Ursula Andress. Directed by Sidney Hayers. 1969. Columbia. 104 min. Sound. 16mm Color. *Rental:* Budget Films, Film Ctr DC, Inst Cinema, Modern Sound, Rep Pic Film, Welling Motion Pictures & Wholesome Film Ctr.

Southern Yankee, A. Orig. Title: My Hero. Red Skelton & Brian Donlevy. Directed by Edward Sedgwick. 1948. MGM. 90 min. Sound. 16mm B&W. *Rental:* Films Inc & MGM United.

Southerner, The. Zachary Scott & Betty Field. Directed by Jean Renoir. 1945. United Artists. 91 min. Sound. 16mm B&W. *Rental:* A Twyman Pres, Budget Films, Em Gee Film Lib, Films Inc, Images Film, Ivy Films, Kit Parker & Video Comm. *Sale:* Cinema Concepts, Festival Films, Glenn Photo, Reel Images & Images Film. *Sale:* Tamarelles French Film, Festival Films & Images Film, Videotape version.

Southie! 1979. PBS. (Documentary). 59 min. Sound. Color. *Rental:* PBS Video. *Sale:* PBS Video.

Southside One: One Thousand. Orig. Title: Forgery. Don Defore & Andrea King. Directed by Boris Ingster. 1950. Allied Artists. 83 min. Sound. 16mm B&W. *Rental:* Budget Films, Film Ctr DC & Hurlock Cine.

Southward Ho! Roy Rogers. Directed by Joseph Kane. 1939. Republic. 54 min. Sound. 16mm B&W. *Rental:* Ivy Films. *Sale:* Cinema Concepts & Rep Pic Film.

Southwest Passage. Orig. Title: Camels West. Rod Cameron & Joanne Dru. Directed by Ray Nazarro. 1954. United Artists. 75 min. Sound. 16mm Color. *Rental:* Inst Cinema & MGM United.

Soviet Woman, The. 1964. ABC. (Documentary). 53 min. Sound. 16mm B&W. *Rental:* McGraw-Hill Films. *Sale:* McGraw-Hill Films.

Soviets in Space. 1970. NBC. (Documentary). 51 min. Sound. 16mm Color. *Rental:* Films Inc. *Sale:* Films Inc.

Soweto: The Secret City. 1978. Britain. (Documentary). 53 min. Sound. 16mm Color. *Rental:* U of IL Film.

Soylent Green. Charles Heston & Edward G. Robinson. Directed by Richard Fleischer. 1973. MGM. (Anamorphic). 97 min. Sound. 16mm Color. *Rental:* MGM United. *Rental:* MGM United, Videotape version.

Space Academy. Filmation. (Cast unlisted). 66 min. Sound. 16mm Color. *Rental:* Williams Films.

Space Children, The. Adam Williams & Peggy Webber. Directed by Jack Arnold. 1958. Paramount. 69 min. Sound. 16mm B&W. *Rental:* Films Inc.

Space Flight IC-1. Bill Williams. Directed by Bernard Knowles. 1958. Paramount. 65 min. Sound. 16mm B&W. *Rental:* Films Inc.

Space for Man. 1979. PBS. (Documentary). 120 min. Color. *Rental:* PBS Video. *Sale:* PBS Video, Videotape version.

Space Master X-Seven. Bill Williams & Lyn Thomas. Directed by Edward Bernds. 1958. Fox. 87 min. Sound. 16mm B&W. *Rental:* Charard Motion Pics & Willoughby Peer.

Space Monster. Directed by Leonard Katzman. 80 min. Sound. 16mm B&W. *Rental:* Films Inc.

Space Seed. William Shatner & Ricardo Montalban. 1966. Star Trek. 52 min. Sound. 16mm Color. *Rental:* Roas Films, U of IL Film & Westcoast Films. *Sale:* Morcraft Films.

Space Shuttle, The: Mission to the Future. 80 min. Sound. Videotape Color. *Rental:* Maljack.

Space Soldiers Conquer the Universe *see* Flash Gordon Conquers the Universe.

Spaceship to the Unknown. Buster Crabbe & Jean Rogers. Directed by Frederick Stephani. 1938. Universal. 95 min. Sound. 16mm B&W. *Rental:* Ivy Films & Video Comm.

Spaceways. Howard Duff & Eva Bartok. Directed by Terence Fisher. 1953. Lippert. 80 min. Sound. 16mm B&W. *Rental:* Budget Films, Film Ctr DC & Willoughby Peer.

Spaniard's Curse, The. Lee Patterson & Tony Wright. Directed by Ralph Kemplen. 1958. Britain. 80 min. Sound. 16mm B&W. *Rental:* Charard Motion Pics.

Spanish Cape Mystery, The. Donald Cook & Jack La Rue. Directed by Lewis D. Collins. 1935. Republic. 76 min. Sound. 16mm B&W. *Rental:* Ivy Films. *Sale:* Rep Pic Film.

Spanish Dancer, The. Pola Negri & Antonio Moreno. Directed by Herbert Brenon. 1923. Paramount. 90 min. Silent. 16mm B&W. *Sale:* Cinema Concepts & Gleen Photo.

Spanish Earth, The. Directed by Joris Ivens. 1937. Spain. (Documentary). 54 min. Sound. 16mm B&W. narrated Eng. *Rental:* Films Inc & U Cal Media. *Lease:* Macmillan Films.

Spanish Gardener, The. Dirk Bogarde & Jon Whiteley. Directed by Philip Leacock. 1956. Britain. 97 min. Sound. 16mm Color. *Rental:* Kit Parker & Learning Corp Am. *Sale:* Learning Corp Am.

Spanish Main, The. Paul Henreid & Maureen O'Hara. Directed by Frank Borzage. 1945. RKO. 101 min. Sound. 16mm Color. *Rental:* Films Inc.

Spanish Turmoil, The. 1967. Britain. (Documentary). 64 min. Sound. 16mm B&W. *Rental:* Films Inc. *Sale:* Films Inc. *Rental:* Films Inc, *Sale:* Films Inc, Spanish language version. *Sale:* Films Inc, Videotape version.

Sparkle. Philip Thomas & Irene Cara. Directed by Sam O'Steen. 1976. Warners. 99 min. Sound. 16mm Color. *Rental:* Swank Motion.

Sparrows. Mary Pickford. Directed by William Beaudine. 1926. United Artists. 90 min. Silent. 16mm B&W. *Rental:* Budget Films, Em Gee Film Lib, Morcraft Films & Welling Motion Pictures. *Sale:* Natl Cinema. *Rental:* Killiam Collect, Tinted version. *Rental:* Blackhawk Films & Kit Parker, *Sale:* Blackhawk Films, Cinema Concepts & Natl Cinema, Music version 16mm version. *Sale:* Blackhawk Films, Super 8 sound version. *Rental:* Ivy Films, *Sale:* Blackhawk Films & Cinema Concept, Super 8 silent version. *Sale:* Blackhawk Films, Silent 8mm version. *Sale:* Blackhawk Films & Tamarelles French Film, Videotape version. *Sale:* Festival Films, 82 min 16mm & Videotape version.

Sparrows Can't Sing. Murray Melvin & Avis Bunnage. Directed by Joan Littlewood. 1963. Britain. 93 min. Sound. 16mm B&W. *Rental:* Janus Films.

Spartacus. Antonio Novelli. 1914. Italy. 60 min. Silent. 16mm B&W. *Rental:* Em Gee Film Lib & Film Classics. *Sale:* Film Classics. *Rental:* Film Classics, *Sale:* Film Classics, Silent 8mm version. *Rental:* Film Classics, Videotape version.

Spartacus. 1977. Russia. (Anamorphic, dance). 95 min. Sound. 16mm Color. *Rental:* Corinth Films. *Lease:* Corinth Films, *Rental:* Corinth Films, Videotape version.

Spartan Gladiators, The. Tony Russell & Massimo Serato. 1965. Italy. 78 min. Sound. 16mm Color. dubbed. *Rental:* MGM United.

Spawn of the North. George Raft & Henry Fonda. Directed by Henry Hathaway. 1938. Paramount. 110 min. Sound. 16mm B&W. *Rental:* Swank Motion.

Spawning, The. Tricia O'Neil & Steve Marachuk. 85 min. Sound. 16mm Color. *Rental:* Williams Films.

Speak Easy. Jimmy Durante & Buster Keaton. 1932. MGM. 82 min. Sound. 16mm B&W. *Rental:* MGM United.

Speaking of Love. 1979. PBS. (Documentary). 54 min. Videotape Color. *Rental:* PBS Video. *Sale:* PBS Video.

Spear of the Nation. Directed by Rigoberto Lopez. Span. 1977. Cuba. (Documentary). 55 min. Sound. 16mm Color. subtitles. *Rental:* Cinema Guild. *Sale:* Cinema Guild.

Spearman of Death. Kuo Chue & Chiang Cheng. 114 min. Sound. 16mm *Rental:* WW Enter. *Rental:* WW Enter, Videotape version.

Special Agent. George Brent & Bette Davis. Directed by William Keighley. 1935. Warners. 76 min. Sound. 16mm B&W. *Rental:* MGM United.

Special Court-Martial, The. Army. (Documentary). 56 min. Sound. 16mm B&W. *Rental:* Natl Av Ctr.

Special Day, A. Sophia Loren & Marcello Mastroianni. Directed by Ettore Scola. 1977. Italy. 110 min. Sound. 16mm Color. *Rental:* Cinema Five.

Special Delivery. Joseph Cotten & Eva Bartok. Directed by John Brahm. 1955. Columbia. 86 min. Sound. 16mm B&W. *Rental:* Films Inc & Inst Cinema.

Special Investigator. Richard Dix & J. Carrol Naish. Directed by Louis King. 1936. RKO. 61 min. Sound. 16mm B&W. *Rental:* RKO General Pics.

Special Jordan Program. 45 min. Sound. 16mm Color. *Rental:* Canyon Cinema.

Special Needs Adoption. 1981. 60 min. Sound. Videotape Color. *Rental:* Iowa Films.

Special Section. Louis Seigner & Michel Lonsdale. Directed by Costa-Gavras. Fr. 1975. France. 111 min. Sound. 16mm Color. subtitles. *Rental:* Swank Motion.

Special Treatment. Directed by Goran Paskaljevic. Serbo-Croatian. 1980. Yugoslavia. 90 min. 16mm Color. subtitles Eng. *Rental:* New Yorker Films.

Specialist, The. Adam West & John Alderson. Directed by Hikmet Avedis. 1975. Crown. 93 min. Sound. 16mm Color. *Rental:* Films Inc.

Specter of the Rose. Judith Anderson & Michael Chekhov. Directed by Ben Hecht. 1946. Republic. 90 min. Sound. 16mm B&W. *Rental:* Ivy Films. *Sale:* Rep Pic Film.

Spectre of Edgar Allan Poe, The. Robert Walker Jr. & Cesar Romero. Directed by Mohy Quandour. 1974. Cinerama. 87 min. Sound. 16mm Color. *Rental:* Swank Motion. *Sale:* Glenn Photo, Super 8 sound version.

Speed. James Stewart & Wendy Barrie. Directed by Edwin L. Marin. 1936. MGM. 72 min. Sound. 16mm B&W. *Rental:* MGM United.

Speed Crazy. Brett Halsey & Yvonne Lime. Directed by William J. Hole Jr. 1958. Allied Artists. 75 min. Sound. 16mm B&W. *Rental:* Hurlock Cine.

Speed Merchants, The. Directed by Michael Keyser. 1974. Toad Hall. (Documentary). 92 min. Sound. 16mm Color. *Rental:* Westcoast Films.

Speed Spook, The. Johnny Hines & Faire Binney. Directed by Charles Hines. 1924. East Coast. 100 min. Silent. 16mm B&W. *Sale:* Blackhawk Films. *Sale:* Blackhawk Films, Super 8 silent version.

Speedway. Elvis Presley. Directed by Norman Taurog. 1968. MGM. 107 min. Sound. 16mm Color. *Rental:* MGM United. *Rental:* MGM United, Anamorphic version.

Speedway. William Haines & Anita Page. Directed by Harry Beaumont. 1929. MGM. 80 min. Sound. 16mm B&W. *Rental:* MGM United.

Speedy. Harold Lloyd. Directed by Ted Wilde. 1928. Paramount. (Music & sound effects only). 72 min. Sound. 16mm B&W. *Rental:* Budget Films, Images Film, Janus Films, Kino Intl & Kit Parker. *Sale:* Blackhawk Films, Super 8 sound version. *Sale:* Blackhawk Films, Super 8 silent version. *Rental:* Budget Films, Silent version.

Spellbinder, The. Lee Tracy & Patric Knowles. Directed by Jack Hively. 1939. RKO. 69 min. Sound. 16mm B&W. *Rental:* RKO General Pics.

Spellbound. Ingrid Bergman & Gregory Peck. Directed by Alfred Hitchcock. 1945. 111 min. Sound. Videotape B&W. *Rental:* Festival Films.

SPFX: The Making of "The Empire Strikes Back". Directed by Robert Guenette. 1980. Films Inc. (Documentary). 52 min. Sound. 16mm Color. *Rental:* Films Inc. *Sale:* Films Inc. *Sale:* Films Inc, Videotape version.

Sphinx, The. Lesley-Anne Down & Frank Langella. Directed by Franklin Schaffner. 1981. Orion. 119 min. Sound. 16mm Color. *Rental:* Films Inc.

Spider, The. Richard Conte & Faye Marlowe. Directed by Robert Webb. 1945. Fox. 62 min. Sound. 16mm B&W. *Rental:* Films Inc.

Spider, The. Ed Kemmer & June Kennedy. Directed by Bert I. Gordon. 1958. American International. 77 min. Sound. 16mm B&W. *Rental:* Budget Films, Films Inc & Westcoast Films.

Spider Woman, The *see* Sherlock Holmes & the Spider Woman.

Spiderman. Nicholas Hammond & Lisa Eilbacher. Directed by E. W. Swackhamer. 1977. Columbia. 94 min. Sound. 16mm Color. *Rental:* Cine Craft & Williams Films.

Spiders. Carl De Vogy, Ressel Orla & Lil Dagover. Directed by Fritz Lang. 1919. Germany. (Tinted, music score). 137 min. Sound. 16mm *Rental:* Images Film. *Sale:* Images Film, Videotape version.

Spider's Strategem, The. Alida Valli. Directed by Bernardo Bertolucci. Ital. 1970. Italy. 97 min. Sound. 16mm Color. subtitles. *Rental:* New Yorker Films.

Spies. Willy Fritsch, Lupu Pick & Fritz Rasp. Directed by Fritz Lang. 1928. Germany. 85 min. Silent. 16mm B&W. *Rental:* Budget Films, Em Gee Film Lib, Film Images, Films Inc, Ivy Films, Janus Films, Kit Parker, Museum Mod Art & Video Comm. *Sale:* Blackhawk Films & Film Images. *Sale:* Blackhawk Films & New Cinema, Sound 16mm version. *Sale:* Blackhawk Films, Super 8 sound version. *Sale:* Blackhawk Films, Super 8 silent version. *Sale:* Tamarelles French Film, *Rental:* Video Comm, Videotape version. *Rental:* Westcoast Films, 127 mins. version.

Spies a-Go-Go. Orig. Title: Nasty Rabbit, The. Arch Hall Jr. Directed by James Landis. 1965. Fairway. 89 min. Sound. 16mm Color. *Rental:* Ivy Films & Video Comm.

Spies at Work *see* Sabotage.

Spies of the Air. Barry K. Barnes & Roger Livesey. Directed by David McDonald. 1939. Britain. 78 min. Sound. 16mm B&W. *Sale:* Rep Pic Film.

Spike, The. 1980. Britain. (Documentary). 50 min. Sound. 16mm Color. *Rental:* Films Inc & Syracuse U Film. *Sale:* Films Inc. *Sale:* Films Inc, Videotape version.

Spikes Gang, The. Lee Marvin & Gary Grimes. Directed by Richard Fleischer. 1974. United Artists. 96 min. Sound. 16mm Color. *Rental:* MGM United.

Spinal Tap. Christopher Guest & Michael McKean. Directed by Rob Reiner. 1983. Embassy. 90 min. Sound. 16mm Color. *Rental:* Films Inc.

Spinout. Elvis Presley. Directed by Norman Taurog. 1966. MGM. 90 min. Sound. 16mm Color. *Rental:* MGM United. *Rental:* MGM United, Anamorphic version.

Spiral Road, The. Rock Hudson & Burl Ives. Directed by Robert Mulligan. 1962. Universal. 140 min. Sound. 16mm Color. *Rental:* Swank Motion.

Spiral Staircase, The. Jacqueline Bisset & Christopher Plummer. Warners. 88 min. Sound. 16mm Color. *Rental:* Williams Films.

Spiral Staircase. Dorothy McGuire. Directed by Robert Siodmak. 1946. 83 min. Sound. Videotape B&W. *Rental:* Festival Films.

Spirit Catcher-The Art of Betye Saar, The. Directed by Suzanne Bavman. 1977. WNET. (Documentary). Sound. 16mm Color. *Rental:* Films Inc.

Spirit in a Landscape: The People Beyond. Directed by Carol Myers. 1975. Canada. (Documentary). 57 min. Sound. 16mm Color. *Rental:* Natl Film CN. *Sale:* Natl Film CN.

Spirit is Willing, The. Sid Caesar & Vera Miles. Directed by William Castle. 1967. Paramount. 100 min. Sound. 16mm Color. *Rental:* Films Inc.

"Spirit" of Punxsutawney, The. 1976. Penn State. (Documentary). 59 min. Sound. 16mm B&W. *Rental:* Penn St AV Serv. *Sale:* Pen St AV Serv. *Rental:* Penn St AV Serv, *Sale:* Pen St AV Serv, Videotape version.

Spirit of St. Louis. James Stewart & Bartlett Robinson. Directed by Billy Wilder. 1957. Warners. 135 min. Sound. 16mm Color. *Rental:* Films Inc, Modern Sound, Twyman Films & Williams Films. *Sale:* Tamarelles French Film, Videotape version.

Spirit of Stanford, The. Marguerite Chapman & Frankie Albert. Directed by Charles Barton. 1942. Columbia. 73 min. Sound. 16mm B&W. *Rental:* Newman Film Lib.

Spirit of the Beehive, The. Fernando Gomez. Directed by Victor Erice. Span. 1974. Spain. 95 min. Sound. 16mm Color. subtitles. *Rental:* Films Inc, Janus Films & New Cinema.

Spirit of the U.S.A., The Mary Carr & Johnny Walker. Directed by Emory Johnson. 1924. FBO. 60 min. Silent. 16mm B&W. *Rental:* Film Classics.

Spirit of the West. Hoot Gibson. Directed by Otto Brower. 1932. Allied. 60 min. Sound. Videotape B&W. *Sale:* Video Comm.

Spirit of West Point, The. Doc Blanchard & Glen Davis. Directed by Ralph Murphy. 1947. Film Classics. 77 min. Sound. 16mm B&W. *Sale:* Classics Assoc NY.

Spirit of Youth, The. Joe Louis & Mantan Moreland. Directed by Harry Fraser. 1937. Grand National. 70 min. Sound. 16mm B&W. *Rental:* Budget Films. *Sale:* Cinema Concepts & Morcraft Films.

Spirits of the Dead. Brigitte Bardot & Alain Delon. Directed by Roger Vadim, Louis Malle & Federico Fellini. 1969. American International. 117 min. Sound. 16mm Color. dubbed. *Rental:* Budget Films, Films Inc, Film Ctr DC, Video Comm, Welling Motion Picturesd, Westcoast Films & Wholesome Film Ctr.

Spite Marriage. Buster Keaton & Dorothy Sebastian. Directed by Edward Sedgwick. 1929. MGM. 95 min. Silent. 16mm B&W. *Rental:* MGM United.

Spitfire. Katherine Hepburn & Robert Young. Directed by John Cromwell. 1934. RKO. 88 min. Sound. 16mm B&W. *Rental:* Films Inc. *Lease:* Films Inc.

Spitfire. Leslie Howard & David Niven. Directed by Leslie Howard. 1942. Britain. 90 min. Sound. 16mm B&W. *Rental:* Budget Films & Classic Film Mus. *Sale:* Cinema Concepts & Reel Images.

Splash. Tom Hanks, Daryl Hannah & Eugene Levy. 1984. Disney. 111 min. Sound. 16mm Color. *Rental:* Bosco Films, Elliot Film Co, Roas Films, Swank Motion, Welling Motion Pictures, Westcoast Films & Williams Films.

Splendor. Miriam Hopkins & Joel McCrea. Directed by Elliott Nugent. 1935. Goldwyn. 77 min. Sound. 16mm B&W. *Rental:* Films Inc.

Splendour Undiminished. 1974. Canada. (Documentary). 57 min. Sound. 16mm Color. *Rental:* Natl Film CN. *Sale:* Natl Film CN.

Split, The. Jim Brown & Diahann Carroll. Directed by Gordon Flemyng. 1968. MGM. 90 min. Sound. 16mm Color. *Rental:* MGM United. *Rental:* MGM United, Anamorphic color version.

Split Second. Stephan McNally & Alexis Smith. Directed by Dick Powell. 1953. RKO. 85 min. Sound. 16mm B&W. *Rental:* Films Inc.

Spoiled Children. Trans. Title: Enfants Gates, Les. Michel Piccoli & Christine Pascal. Directed by Bertrand Tavernier. Fr. 1977. France. 113 min. Sound. 16mm Color. subtitles. *Rental:* Corinth Films & New Cinema.

Spoilers, The. William Farnum & Tom Santschi. Directed by Colin Campbell. 1914. Selig. 90 min. Silent. Super 8 B&W. *Sale:* Blackhawk Films.

Spoilers, The. Marlene Dietrich & John Wayne. Directed by Ray Enright. 1942. Universal. 84 min. Sound. 16mm B&W. *Rental:* Williams Films.

Spoilers of the Forest. Rod Cameron & Vera Ralston. Directed by Joseph Kane. 1956. Republic. 70 min. Sound. 16mm B&W. *Rental:* Ivy Films. *Sale:* Rep Pic Film.

Spoilers of the North. Paul Kelly & Adrian Booth. Directed by Richard Sale. 1947. Republic. 66 min. Sound. 16mm B&W. *Rental:* Ivy Films.

Spoilers of the Plains. Roy Rogers. Directed by William Witney. 1951. Republic. 68 min. Sound. 16mm B&W. *Rental:* Ivy Films. *Sale:* Rep Pic Film & Nostalgia Merchant.

Spoils of Poynton, The. 4 pts. 1976. Britain. (Cast unlisted). 180 min. Sound. 16mm Color. *Rental:* Films Inc. *Sale:* Films Inc. *Rental:* Films Inc, *Sale:* Films Inc, Videotape version.

Spoleto U. S. A: A Festival Discovers America. Directed by Michael Blackwood. 1977. Blackwood. 52 min. Sound. 16mm Color. *Rental:* Blackwood Films. *Sale:* Blackwood Films.

Spongers, The. Directed by Roland Joffe. 1978. Britain. (Documentary). 91 min. Sound. 16mm Color. *Rental:* Time-Life Multimedia. *Sale:* Time-Life Multimedia.

Spook Who Sat by the Door, The. Lawrence Cook & Paul Kelly. Directed by Ivan Dixon. 1973. MGM. 102 min. Sound. 16mm Color. *Rental:* MGM United.

Spooks Run Wild. Bowery Boys. Directed by Phil Rosen. 1941. Monogram. 60 min. Sound. 16mm B&W. *Rental:* Budget Films, Ivy Films, Newman Film Lib & Roas Films. *Sale:* Cinema Concepts & Reel Images. *Sale:* Reel Images, Super 8 sound version.

Sport As a Humanistic Activity. 1975. Penn State. (Documentary). 59 min. Videotape Color. *Rental:* Penn St AV Serv. *Sale:* Penn St AV Serv, Videotape version.

Sport Parade. Joel McCrea & Robert Benchley. Directed by Dudley Murphy. 1933. RKO. 65 min. Sound. 16mm B&W. *Rental:* RKO General Pics.

Sporting Blood. Clark Gable & Ernest Torrance. Directed by Charles Brabin. 1931. MGM. 82 min. Sound. 16mm B&W. *Rental:* MGM United.

Sporting Chance. John O'Malley & Edward Gargan. Directed by George Blair. 1945. Republic. 55 min. Sound. 16mm B&W. *Rental:* Ivy Films & Mogulls Films.

Spotlight Scandals. Billy Gilbert & Frank Fay. Directed by William Beaudine. 1943. Monogram. 65 min. Videotape B&W. *Sale:* Video Lib.

Spring & Port Wine. James Mason. Directed by Peter Hammond. 1971. Britain. 101 min. Sound. 16mm Color. *Rental:* Budget Films.

Spring Break. David Knell & Perry King. Directed by Sean Cunningham. 1982. Columbia. 104 min. Sound. 16mm Color. *Rental:* Swank Motion. *Rental:* Swank Motion, Videotape version.

Spring Fragrance. Choi Eun Hi & Kim Jin Kyoo. Directed by Shin San Okk. Korean. 1964. Korea. 90 min. Sound. 16mm Color. subtitles Eng. *Rental:* Films Inc.

Spring in Ethiopia. 1966. NET. (Documentary). 54 min. Sound. 16mm B&W. *Rental:* Indiana AV Ctr. *Lease:* Indiana AV Ctr.

Spring Is Here. Bernice Claire & Alexander Gray. Directed by John Francis Dillon. 1930. Warners. 79 min. Sound. 16mm B&W. *Rental:* MGM United.

Spring Madness. Maureen O'Sullivan & Lew Ayres. Directed by S. Sylvan Simon. 1938. MGM. 67 min. Sound. 16mm B&W. *Rental:* MGM United.

Spring Reunion. Betty Hutton & Dana Andrews. Directed by Robert Pirosh. 1957. United Artists. 79 min. Sound. 16mm B&W. *Rental:* MGM United.

Spring Song *see* Springtime.

Spring Tonic. ZaSu Pitts & Claire Trevor. Directed by Clyde Bruckman. 1935. Fox. 58 min. Sound. 16mm B&W. *Rental:* Films inc.

Springfield Rifle. Gary Cooper & Phyllis Thaxter. Directed by Andre De Toth. 1952. Warners. 93 min. Sound. 16mm Color. *Rental:* Films Inc, Twyman Films & Williams Films.

Springtime. Orig. Title: Spring Song. Carol Raye & Peter Graves. Directed by Montgomery Tully. 1947. Britain. 74 min. Sound. 16mm B&W. *Rental:* Ivy Films. *Sale:* Rep Pic Film.

Springtime in Texas. Jimmy Wakely. Directed by Oliver Drake. 1945. Monogram. 55 min. Sound. 16mm B&W. *Rental:* Hurlock Cine.

Springtime in the Rockies. Gene Autry. Directed by Joseph Kane. 1937. Republic. 54 min. Sound. 16mm B&W. *Rental:* Budget Films & Ivy Films. *Sale:* Reel Images. *Sale:* Morcraft Films & Reel Images, Super 8 sound version.

Springtime in the Sierras. Roy Rogers. Directed by William Witney. 1947. Republic. 54 min. Sound. 16mm B&W. *Rental:* Ivy Films. *Sale:* Cinema Concepts, Natl Cinema, Rep Pic Film & Reel Images.

Spurs. Hoot Gibson. Directed by B. Reeves Eason. 1930. Universal. 59 min. Sound. 16mm B&W. *Rental:* Swank Motion.

Spy Catcher, The. Frederick O'Brady & Colette Duval. 1964. 80 min. Sound. 16mm B&W. dubbed. *Rental:* Films Inc.

Spy in Black. James Mason & Valerie Hobson. Directed by Michael Powell. 1939. Britain. 82 min. Sound. 16mm B&W. *Rental:* Film Classics, Films Inc & Ivy Films.

Spy in the Green Hat, The. Robert Vaughan, David McCallum & Leo G. Carroll. Directed by Joseph Sargent. 1966. MGM. 78 min. Sound. 16mm Color. *Rental:* MGM United.

Spy in the Sky. Steve Brodie. Directed by W. Lee Wilder. 1958. Allied Artists. 70 min. Sound. 16mm B&W. *Rental:* Westcoast Films.

Spy Ship. Craig Stevens & Irene Manning. Directed by B. Reeves Eason. 1942. Warners. 63 min. Sound. 16mm B&W. *Rental:* MGM United.

Spy Smasher. Kane Richmond & Sam Flint. Directed by William Witney. 1942. Republic. 215 min. Sound. 16mm B&W. *Rental:* Ivy Films.

Spy Smasher Returns. Kane Richmond & Marguerite Chapman. Directed by William Witney. 1942. Republic. 100 min. Sound. 16mm B&W. *Rental:* Ivy Films. *Sale:* Rep Pic Film.

Spy Squad. Richard Miller & Dick O'Neill. Directed by Will Zens. 1963. Westhampton. 75 min. Sound. 16mm B&W. *Rental:* Ivy Films.

Spy Who Came in from the Cold, The. Richard Burton, Claire Bloom & Oskar Werner. Directed by Martin Ritt. 1965. Paramount. 110 min. Sound. 16mm B&W. *Rental:* Films Inc.

Spy Who Loved Me, The. Roger Moore, Barbara Bach & Richard Kiel. Directed by Lewis Gilbert. 1977. United Artists. 125 min. Sound. 16mm Color. *Rental:* MGM United. *Rental:* MGM United, Anamorphic version, Videotape version. *Rental:* MGM United,

Spy With a Cold Nose, The. Laurence Harvey & Lionel Jeffries. Directed by Daniel Petrie. 1966. Britain. 124 min. Sound. 16mm Color. *Rental:* Films Inc.

Spy With My Face, The. Robert Vaughan & David McCallum. Directed by John Newland. 1966. MGM. 88 min. Sound. 16mm Color. *Rental:* MGM United.

Squad Car. Paul Bryan & Don Marlowe. Directed by Ed Leftwich. 1960. Fox. 60 min. Sound. 16mm B&W. *Rental:* Willoughby Peer.

Squadron of Doom. John King, Jean Rogers & Noah Beery Jr. Directed by Ford Beebe & Clifford Smith. 1936. Universal. 70 min. Sound. 16mm B&W. *Rental:* Budget Films.

Square Dance Katy. Barbara Jo Allen & Warren Douglas. Directed by Jean Yarbrough. 1950. Monogram. 76 min. Sound. 16mm B&W. *Rental:* Hurlock Cine.

Square Deal Man. William S. Hart. Directed by Harley Knowles. 1917. Ince. 45 min. Silent. 16mm B&W. *Rental:* Em Gee Film Lib & Swank Motion. *Sale:* Blackhawk Films. *Rental:* Ivy Films, Super 8 silent version.

Square Deal Sanderson. William S. Hart. Directed by Lambert Hillyer. 1919. Artcraft. 60 min. Silent. 16mm B&W. *Rental:* Em Gee Film Lib. *Sale:* Em Gee Film Lib. *Sale:* Em Gee Film Lib, Silent 8mm version.

Squares. Andrew Prine. Directed by Patrick J. Murphy. 1972. Plateau. 92 min. Sound. 16mm Color. *Rental:* Budget Films & Video Comm.

Squareshooter, The see Skipalong Rosenbloom.

Squaw Man, The. Orig. Title: White Man, The. Warner Baxter, Charles Bickford & Lupe Velez. Directed by Cecil B. DeMille. 1931. Paramount. 107 min. Sound. 16mm B&W. *Rental:* Films Inc & MGM United.

Squeaker, The see Murder on Diamond Row.

Squibs Wins the Calcutta Sweep. Betty Balfour. Directed by George Pearson. 1922. Britain. 78 min. Silent. 16mm B&W. *Rental:* Museum Mod Art.

Squire of Gothos, The. William Shatner & Leonard Nimoy. Directed by Don Dougall. 1967. Star Trek. 50 min. Sound. 16mm Color. *Rental:* Roas Films & Westcoast Films.

Squirm. Don Scardino, Patricia Pearcy & Jean Sullivan. Directed by Jeff Lieberman. 1976. American International. 93 min. Sound. 16mm Color. *Rental:* Welling Motion Pictures.

Squizzy Taylor. (Cast Unlisted). Videotape *Sale:* Vidamerica.

SSSSSSSSS. Strother Martin & Dirk Benedict. Directed by Bernard Kowalski. 1973. Universal. 99 min. Sound. 16mm Color. *Rental:* Swank Motion.

Stage Door. Ginger Rogers & Katharine Hepburn. Directed by Gregory La Cava. 1937. RKO. 83 min. Sound. 16mm B&W. *Rental:* Films Inc. *Lease:* Films Inc. *Sale:* Blackhawk Films, Super 8 sound version. *Sale:* Blackhawk Films, Videotape version.

Stage Door Canteen. Alfred Lunt & Lynn Fontanne. Directed by Frank Borzage. 1943. United Artists. 126 min. Sound. 16mm B&W. *Rental:* Budget Films, Em Gee Film Lib, Inst Cinema, Mogulls Films, Video Comm & Willoughby Peer. *Sale:* Reel Images & Morcraft Films. *Sale:* Reel Images, Super 8 sound version.

Stage Fright. Jane Wyman & Marlene Dietrich. Directed by Alfred Hitchcock. 1950. Warners. 110 min. Sound. 16mm B&W. *Rental:* Films Inc, Swank Motion, Twyman Films & Vidamerica.

Stage from Blue River. Whip Wilson. Directed by Lewis D. Collins. 1951. Monogram. 55 min. Sound. 16mm B&W. *Rental:* Hurlock Cine.

Stage Mother. Franchot Tone & Alice Brady. Directed by Charles Brabin. 1933. MGM. 87 min. Sound. 16mm B&W. *Rental:* MGM United.

Stage Struck. Dick Powell & Joan Blondell. Directed by Busby Berkeley. 1936. Warners. 91 min. Sound. 16mm B&W. *Rental:* MGM United.

Stage Struck. Conrad Nagel. Directed by William Nigh. 1948. Monogram. 71 min. Sound. 16mm B&W. *Rental:* Hurlock Cine.

Stage Struck. Henry Fonda & Susan Strasberg. Directed by Sidney Lumet. 1958. RKO. 95 min. Sound. 16mm Color. *Rental:* Budget Films, Video Comm & Welling Motion Pictures. *Lease:* Video Comm.

Stage to Chino. George O'Brien & Virginia Vale. Directed by Bert Gilroy. 1940. RKO. 58 min. Sound. 16mm B&W. *Rental:* RKO General Pics.

Stage to Mesa City. Lash La Rue. Directed by Ray Taylor. 1948. Eagle Lion. 52 min. Sound. 16mm B&W. *Sale:* Classics Assoc NY.

Stage to Thunder Rock. Barry Sullivan & Marilyn Maxwell. Directed by William Claxton. 1964. Paramount. 82 min. Sound. 16mm Color. *Rental:* Films Inc.

Stagecoach. John Wayne & Claire Trevor. Directed by John Ford. 1939. United Artists. 96 min. Sound. B&W. *Rental:* Arcus Film, Budget Films, Em Gee Film Lib, Films Inc, Images Film, Ivy Films, Kit Parker, Learning Corp Am, Modern Sound, Mogulls Films, Newman Film Lib, Roas Films, Twyman Films, U of IL Film, Video Comm, Welling Motion Pictures, Westcoast Films & Williams Films. *Sale:* Learning Corp Am. *Sale:* Cinema Concepts & Glenn Photo, Videotape version.

Stagecoach. Bing Crosby & Ann-Margret. Directed by Gordon Douglas. 1966. Fox. 114 min. Sound. 16mm Color. *Rental:* Films Inc. *Rental:* Films Inc, Anamorphic version.

Stagecoach Driver. Whip Wilson. Directed by Lewis D. Collins. 1951. Monogram. 55 min. Sound. 16mm B&W. *Rental:* Hurlock Cine.

Stagecoach Express. Don Barry & Lynn Merrick. Directed by George Sherman. 1942. Republic. 54 min. Sound. 16mm B&W. *Rental:* Ivy Films. *Sale:* Rep Pic Film & Nostalgia Merchant.

Stagecoach Kid, The. Tim Holt. Directed by Lew Landers. 1949. RKO. 60 min. Sound. 16mm B&W. *Rental:* Films Inc.

Stagecoach Outlaws. Buster Crabbe. Directed by Sam Newfield. 1945. PRC. 59 min. Sound. 16mm B&W. *Sale:* Classics Assoc NY.

Stagecoach to Dancer's Rock. Warren Stevens & Martin Landau. Directed by Earl Bellamy. 1962. Universal. 70 min. 16mm B&W. *Rental:* Swank Motion.

Stagecoach to Denver. Allan Lane & Robert Blake. Directed by R. G. Springsteen. 1947. Republic. 54 min. Sound. 16mm B&W. *Rental:* Ivy Films. *Sale:* Natl Cinema & Reel Images.

Stagecoach to Fury. Forrest Tucker & Mari Blanchard. Directed by William Claxton. 1956. Fox. 76 min. Sound. 16mm B&W. *Rental:* Ivy Films & Willoughby Peer. *Sale:* Rep Pic Film.

Stagecoach to Monterey. Allan Lane & Peggy Stewart. Directed by Lesley Selander. 1945. Republic. 56 min. Sound. 16mm B&W. *Sale:* Rep Pic Film.

Stagecoach War. William Boyd. Directed by Lesley Selander. 1940. Paramount. 60 min. Sound. 16mm B&W. *Lease:* Cinema Concepts. *Rental:* Budget Films.

Stages: Houseman Directs Lear. Amanda C. Pope. 1982. Texture. 54 min. 16mm *Rental:* Texture Film. *Sale:* Texture Film. *Sale:* Texture Film, Videotape version.

Stahlnetz des Dr. Mabuse *see* Return of Dr. Mabuse.

Staircase, The. Rex Harrison & Richard Burton. Directed by Stanley Donen. 1969. Fox. (Anamorphic). 100 min. Sound. 16mm Color. *Rental:* Films Inc.

Stairway for a Star. 1948. Astor. (Anthology). 80 min. Sound. 16mm B&W. *Rental:* Mogulls Films.

Stairway to Heaven. Orig. Title: Matter of Life & Death, A. David Niven & Kim Hunter. Directed by Michael Powell. 1946. Britain. 108 min. Sound. 16mm Color. *Rental:* Budget Films, Films Inc, Images Film, Kit Parker, Learning Corp Am, Twyman Films & U of IL Film. *Sale:* Learning Corp Am.

Stakeout. Bing Russell & Eve Brent. Directed by James Landis. 1962. Crown. 81 min. Sound. 16mm B&W. *Rental:* Video Comm & Welling Motion Pictures. *Lease:* Video Comm. *Rental:* Video Comm, *Lease:* Video Comm, Videotape version.

Stalag Seventeen. William Holden & Don Taylor. Directed by Billy Wilder. 1953. Paramount. 120 min. Sound. 16mm B&W. *Rental:* Films Inc.

Stalin Era, The. 1967. KQED. (Documentary). 58 min. Sound. 16mm B&W. *Rental:* Indiana AV Ctr & Syracuse U Film.

Stalingrad. Directed by Hugh Raggett. 1973. Britain. (Documentary). 60 min. Sound. 16mm Color. *Rental:* Media Guild & U Cal Media.

Stalker, The. Alexander Kaidanovsky & Nikolai Grinko. Directed by Andrei Tarkovsky. Rus. 1980. Russia. 161 min. Sound. 16mm Color. subtitles. *Rental:* New Yorker Films.

Stalking Moon, The. Gregory Peck & Eva Marie Saint. Directed by Robert Mulligan. 1968. National General. 109 min. Sound. 16mm Color. *Rental:* Films Inc, Swank Motion & Williams Films.

Stallion Road. Ronald Reagan & Alexis Smith. Directed by James V. Kern. 1947. Warners. 97 min. Sound. 16mm B&W. *Rental:* MGM United.

Stamboul Quest. Myrna Loy & George Brent. Directed by Sam Wood. 1934. MGM. 88 min. Sound. 16mm B&W. *Rental:* MGM United.

Stampede. Texas Guinan. Directed by Francis Ford. 1921. Kramer. 50 min. Silent. 16mm B&W. *Rental:* Film Classics. *Sale:* Film Classics.

Stampede. Rod Cameron & Gale Storm. Directed by Lesley Selander. 1949. Allied Artists. 78 min. Sound. 16mm B&W. *Rental:* Hurlock Cine.

Stampeded *see* Big Land.

Stan Getz: A Musical Odyssey. 1980. Alden. (Concert). 52 min. Sound. 16mm Color. *Rental:* Alden Films.

Stand & Deliver. Lupe Velez, Warner Oland & Rod La Rocque. 1928. Pathe. 65 min. Silent. 16mm B&W. *Rental:* Film Classics. *Sale:* Film Classics. *Rental:* Film Classics, Silent 8mm version. *Rental:* Film Classics, Videotape version.

Stand at Apache River, The. Stephen McNally & Julie Adams. Directed by Lee Sholem. 1953. Universal. 77 min. Sound. 16mm B&W. *Rental:* Cousino Visual Ed.

Stand In. Leslie Howard, Joan Blondell & Humphrey Bogart. Directed by Tay Garnett. 1937. United Artists. 90 min. Sound. 16mm B&W. *Rental:* Budget Films, Films Inc, Kit Parker, Learning Corp Am, Roas Films & U of IL Film. *Sale:* Learning Corp Am & Tamarelles French Film.

Stand Together. 1977. London Newsreel Collective. (Documentary). 52 min. Sound. 16mm Color. *Rental:* CA Newsreel. *Sale:* CA Newsreel.

Stand Up & Be Counted. Jacqueline Bisset & Stella Stevens. Directed by Jackie Cooper. 1972. Columbia. 90 min. Sound. 16mm Color. *Rental:* Budget Films & Welling Motion Pictures.

Stand Up & Cheer. Shirley Temple & Warner Baxter. Directed by Hamilton McFadden. 1934. Fox. 80 min. Sound. 16mm B&W. *Rental:* Films Inc.

Standard First Aid Multimedia Course. 1978. 67 min. Sound. 16mm Color. *Rental:* Iowa Films.

Stanley. Chris Robinson & Alex Rocco. Directed by William Grefe. 1974. Crown. 105 min. Sound. 16mm Color. *Rental:* Budget Films, Films Inc, Roas Films & Video Comm. *Lease:* Video Comm. *Rental:* Video Comm, *Lease:* Video Comm, Videotape version.

Stanley & Livingstone. Spencer Tracy & Nancy Kelly. Directed by Henry King. 1939. Fox. 98 min. Sound. 16mm B&W. *Rental:* Films Inc & Twyman Films.

Star Chamber, The. Michael Douglas & Hal Holbrook. Directed by Peter Hyams. 1983. Fox. 105 min. Sound. 16mm Color. *Rental:* Films Inc.

Star Crash. Marjoe Gortner & Caroline Munro. Directed by Lewis Coates. 1979. New World. 91 min. Sound. 16mm Color. *Rental:* Films Inc.

Star Dust. Linda Darnell & John Payne. Directed by Walter Lang. 1940. Fox. 85 min. Sound. 16mm B&W. *Rental:* Films Inc & Willoughby Peer.

Star Eighty. Mariel Hemingway, Eric Roberts & Cliff Robertson. Directed by Bob Fosse. 1985. Warner. 102 min. Sound. 16mm Color. *Rental:* Swank Motion. *Rental:* Swank Motion, *Sale:* Tamarelles French Film, Videotape version.

Star for a Night. Claire Trevor & Jane Darwell. Directed by Lewis Seiler. 1936. Fox. 76 min. Sound. 16mm B&W. *Rental:* Films Inc.

Star Force. Wheeler Dixon. 1979. Gold Key. (Documentary). 96 min. Sound. 16mm Color. *Rental:* Gold Key.

Star is Born, A. Fredric March & Janet Gaynor. Directed by William A. Wellman. 1937. United Artists. 111 min. Sound. Color. *Rental:* Em Gee Film Lib, Films Inc, Images Film, Kit Parker, Mogulls Films, Roas Films & Welling Motion Pictures. *Sale:* Cinema Concepts, Festival Films, Glenn Photo & Images Film. *Sale:* Festival Films, Glenn Photo, Morcraft Films, Tamarelles French Film & Images Film, Videotape version.

Star Is Born, A. Barbara Streisand & Kris Kristofferson. Directed by Frank Pierson. 1976. Warners. 140 min. Sound. 16mm Color. *Rental:* Swank Motion. *Rental:* Swank Motion, Videotape version.

Star is Born, A. Judy Garland & James Mason. Directed by George Cukor. 1954. 181 min. Sound. Videotape Color. *Rental:* Festival Films.

Star Maker, The. Bing Crosby & Louise Campbell. Directed by Roy Del Ruth. 1939. Paramount. 94 min. Sound. 16mm B&W. *Rental:* Swank Motion.

Star of India - Gandhi. Directed by Louis Gainsborough. 1983. (Documentary). 90 min. 16mm *Rental:* A Twyman Pres.

Star of Midnight. William Powell & Ginger Rogers. Directed by Stephen Roberts. 1935. RKO. 90 min. Sound. 16mm B&W. *Rental:* RKO General Pics.

Star of Texas. Wayne Morris & Paul Fix. Directed by Thomas Carr. 1953. Monogram. 68 min. Sound. 16mm B&W. *Rental:* Hurlock Cine.

Star Over Texas *see* Stars Over Texas.

Star Packer, The. John Wayne. Directed by Robert N. Bradbury. 1934. Monogram. 59 min. Sound. 16mm B&W. *Rental:* Budget Films, Ivy Films & Mogulls Films. *Sale:* Classics Assoc NY & Rep Pic Film. *Sale:* Morcraft Films, Super 8 sound version.

Star Said No, The *see* Callaway Went Thataway.

Star-Spangled Girl, The. Sandy Duncan & Anthony Roberts. Directed by Jerry Paris. 1972. Paramount. 93 min. Sound. 16mm Color. *Rental:* Films Inc.

Star-Spangled Rhythm. Bing Crosby & Bob Hope. Directed by George Marshall. 1942. Paramount. 93 min. Sound. 16mm Color. *Rental:* Swank Motion.

Star Trek II: The Wrath of Khan. William Shatner & Leonard Nimoy. Directed by Nicholas Meyer. 1982. Paramount. 113 min. Sound. 16mm Color. *Rental:* Films Inc.

Star Trek: The Motion Picture. William Shatner & Leonard Nimoy. Directed by Robert Wise. 1979. Paramount. 130 min. Sound. 16mm Color. *Rental:* Films Inc.

Star Vehicle, The. 1972. Killiam. (Musical & Narration only). 60 min. Sound. 16mm B&W. *Rental:* Killiam Collect.

Star Wars. Mark Hamill & Harrison Ford. Directed by George Lucas. 1977. Fox. 121 min. Sound. 16mm Color. *Rental:* Films Inc.

Star Witness, The. Walter Huston, Frances Starr & Chic Sale. Directed by William A. Wellman. 1931. Warners. 68 min. Sound. 16mm B&W. *Rental:* MGM United.

Star! *see* Those Were the Happy Times.

Starbird & Sweet William. Don Haggerty & Skip Homeier. Directed by Jack Hively. 1976. Howco. 95 min. Sound. 16mm Color. *Rental:* Modern Sound, Roas Films & Westcoast Films.

Stardust. David Essex, Adam Faith & Larry Hagman. Directed by Michael Apted. 1973. Britain. 113 min. Sound. 16mm Color. *Rental:* Corinth Films & Swank Motion.

Stardust Memories. Woody Allen & Charlotte Rampling. Directed by Woody Allen. 1980. United Artists. 93 min. Sound. 16mm B&W. *Rental:* MGM United. *Rental:* MGM United, Videotape version.

Stardust on the Sage. Gene Autry. Directed by William Morgan. 1942. Republic. 54 min. Sound. 16mm B&W. *Rental:* Ivy Films.

Starfighters. Richard Jordahl & Robert Dornan. Directed by Will Zens. 1961. Westhampton. 84 min. Sound. 16mm Color. *Rental:* Ivy Films & Willoughby Peer.

Stark Fear. Beverly Garland & Skip Homeier. Directed by Ned Hockman. 1963. Ellis. 86 min. Sound. 16mm B&W. *Rental:* Films Inc & Ivy Films.

Starlight Night. (Cast unlisted). 50 min. Sound. 16mm B&W. *Rental:* Alba House.

Starry Messenger. (Ascent of Man Ser.). 1974. Britain. (Documentary). 52 min. Sound. 16mm Color. *Rental:* Iowa Films, U Cal Media, U Mich Media & Utah Media, Videotape version.

Stars. Sasha Kroushanshka & Jurgen Frorip. Directed by Konrad Wolf. Bulgarian. 1958. Bulgaria. 94 min. Sound. 16mm B&W. subtitles. *Rental:* Films Inc.

Stars & Stripes Forever. Orig. Title: Marching Along. Clifton Webb & Robert Wagner. Directed by Henry Koster. 1952. Fox. 89 min. Sound. 16mm B&W. *Rental:* Films Inc.

Stars are Singing, The. Rosemary Clooney & Lauritz Melchior. Directed by Norman Taurog. 1953. Paramount. 99 min. Sound. 16mm Color. *Rental:* Films Inc.

Stars in My Crown. Joel McCrea & Ellen Drew. Directed by Jacques Tourneur. 1950. MGM. 89 min. Sound. 16mm B&W. *Rental:* MGM United.

Stars Look Down, The. Sir Michael Redgrave, Margaret Lockwood & Emlyn Williams. Sir Directed by Sir Carol Reed. 1939. Britain. 104 min. Sound. 16mm B&W. *Rental:* Budget Films, Films Inc, Kit Parker & Museum Mod Art. *Sale:* Cinema Concepts & Reel Images. *Sale:* Cinema Concepts & Tamarelles French Film, Videotape version.

Stars of the Russian Ballet. Directed by G. Rappaport. 1953. Russia. (Ballet). 80 min. Sound. 16mm B&W. *Rental:* Corinth Films.

Stars Over Broadway. James Melton & Jane Froman. Directed by William Keighley. 1935. Warners. 89 min. Sound. 16mm B&W. *Rental:* MGM United.

Stars Over Texas. Orig. Title: Star Over Texas. Eddie Dean. Directed by Robert Tansey. 1946. PRC. 60 min. Sound. 16mm B&W. *Sale:* Classics Assoc NY.

Starship Invasions. Robert Vaughn & Christopher Lee. Directed by Ed Hunt. 1978. Warners. 90 min. Sound. 16mm Color. *Rental:* Swank Motion & Williams Films.

Starstruck. 1979. ABC. (Cast unlisted). 46 min. Sound. 16mm Color. *Rental:* Learning Corp Am. *Sale:* Learning Corp Am. *Sale:* Learning Corp Am, Videotape version.

Start Cheering. Jimmy Durante & Gertrude Niesen. Directed by Albert S. Rogell. 1938. Columbia. 63 min. Sound. 16mm B&W. *Rental:* Welling Motion Pictures.

Start the Revolution Without Me. Gene Wilder & Donald Sutherland. Directed by Bud Yorkin. 1970. Warners. 90 min. Sound. 16mm Color. *Rental:* Inst Cinema, Swank Motion, Twyman Films, Welling Motion Pictures & Willoughby Peer.

Starting Over. Jill Clayburgh, Burt Reynolds & Candice Bergen. Directed by Alan J. Pakula. 1979. Paramount. 105 min. Sound. 16mm Color. *Rental:* Films Inc.

State Dept. File Six Hundred Forty-Nine. Orig. Title: Assignment in China. William Lundigan & Virginia Bruce. Directed by Peter Stewart. 1949. Film Classics. 87 min. Sound. 16mm B&W. *Rental:* Film Ctr DC & Mogulls Films.

State Fair. Orig. Title: It Happened One Summer. Dana Andrews, Jeanne Crain & Vivian Blaine. Directed by Walter Lang. 1945. Fox. 100 min. Sound. 16mm Color. *Rental:* Charard Motion Pics, Films Inc, Roas Films, Twyman Films, Welling Motion Pictures & Willoughby Peer. *Sale:* Blackhawk Films, Magnetic Video & Video Lib, Videotape version.

State Fair. Will Rogers & Louise Dresser. Directed by Henry King. 1933. Fox. 97 min. Sound. 16mm B&W. *Rental:* Films Inc.

State Fair. Pat Boone & Ann-Margret. Directed by Jose Ferrer. 1962. Fox. (Anamorphic). 118 min. Sound. 16mm Color. *Rental:* Films Inc.

State of Siege. Yves Montand. Directed by Costa-Gavras. Fr. 1973. France. 120 min. Sound. 16mm Color. subtitles. *Rental:* Cinema Five. *Lease:* Cinema Five.

State of Siege, A. 1978. New Zealand. (Cast unlisted). 52 min. Sound. 16mm Color. *Rental:* Liberty Co.

State of the Union. Orig. Title: World & His Wife, The. Spencer Tracy & Katharine Hepburn. Directed by Frank Capra. 1948. MGM. 110 min. Sound. 16mm B&W. *Rental:* Williams Films.

State Police. John King & Constance Moore. Directed by John Rawlins. 1938. Universal. 70 min. Sound. 16mm B&W. *Rental:* Mogulls Films & Film Ctr DC.

State's Attorney. Orig. Title: Cardigan's Last Case. John Barrymore & Jill Esmond. Directed by George Archainbaud. 1932. RKO. 79 min. Sound. 16mm B&W. *Rental:* Mogulls Films.

Station Six Sahara. Carroll Baker & Peter Van Eyck. Directed by Seth Holt. 1964. Britain. 99 min. Sound. 16mm B&W. *Rental:* Corinth Films.

Station Ten. 1974. Canada. (Documentary). 58 min. Sound. 16mm Color. *Rental:* U Cal Media & Natl Film CN. *Sale:* Natl Film CN.

Station West. Dick Powell & Jane Greer. Directed by Sidney Lanfield. 1948. RKO. 92 min. Sound. 16mm B&W. *Rental:* Films Inc. *Sale:* Blackhawk Films, Super 8 sound version. *Rental:* RKO General Pics, 80 min. version.

Stations. 1974. Roger Hagan. (Documentary). 63 min. Sound. 16mm Color. *Rental:* U Mich Media.

Stations of the Elevated. Directed by Manny Kirchheimer. First Run. (Cast unlisted). 45 min. Sound. 16mm Color. *Rental:* First Run.

Statue of Shakshain, The. Japan. 50 min. Sound. 16mm B&W. narrated Eng. *Sale:* Japan Society. *Sale:* Japan Society, Color version. *Sale:* Japan Society, Videotape version.

Stavisky. Jean-Paul Belmondo & Charles Boyer. Directed by Alain Resnais. Fr. 1974. France. 117 min. Sound. 16mm Color. subtitles. *Rental:* Cinema Five. *Lease:* Cinema Five.

Stay As You Are. Trans. Title: Cosi Come Sei. Marcello Mastroianni. Directed by Alberto Lattuada. Ital. 1978. Italy. 105 min. Sound. 16mm Color. subtitles. *Rental:* New Line Cinema.

Stay As You Are *see* Stay the Way You Are.

Stay Away Joe. Elvis Presley. Directed by Peter Tewksbury. 1968. MGM. 102 min. Sound. 16mm Color. *Rental:* MGM United.

Stay Hungry. Jeff Bridges & Sally Field. Directed by Bob Rafelson. 1976. United Artists. 103 min. Sound. 16mm Color. *Rental:* Films Inc & MGM United.

Stay the Way You Are. Orig. Title: Stay As You Are. Trans. Title: Cosi Come Sei. Marcello Mastroianni. Directed by Alberto Lattuada. Ital. 1978. Italy. 105 min. Sound. 16mm Color. subtitles. *Rental:* New Line Cinema.

Staying Alive. John Travolta & Cynthia Rhodes. Directed by Sylvester Stallone. 1983. Paramount. 96 min. Sound. 16mm Color. *Rental:* Films Inc.

Steagle, The. Richard Benjamin, Chill Wills & Cloris Leachman. Directed by Paul Sylbert. 1971. Embassy. 91 min. Sound. 16mm B&W. *Rental:* Films Inc.

Steamboat Bill, Jr. Buster Keaton. Directed by Charles Reisner. 1928. United Artists. (Musical score only). Silent. *Rental:* A Twyman Pres, Budget Films, Creative Film, Em Gee Film Lib, Films Inc, Images Film, Kit Parker, Modern Sound, Video Comm & Welling Motion Pictures. *Sale:* Blackhawk Films, Cinema Concepts, E Finney & Natl Cinema. *Sale:* Tamarelles French Film, Videotape version. *Rental:* Killiam Collect, Tinted sound version. *Sale:* Blackhawk Films, Super 8 sound version. *Sale:* Blackhawk Films, Super 8 silent version. *Rental:* Bosco Films, *Rental:* Welling Motion Pictures & Westcoast Films, 71 mins version. *Rental:* Kit Parker, Music only version.

Steamboat 'Round the Bend. Will Rogers & Irwin S. Cobb. Directed by John Ford. 1935. Fox. 80 min. Sound. 16mm B&W. *Rental:* Films Inc.

Steel Against the Sky. Alexis Smith & Lloyd Nolan. Directed by Edward Sutherland. 1941. Warners. 67 min. Sound. 16mm B&W. *Rental:* MGM United.

Steel Claw, The. George Montgomery. Directed by George Montgomery. 1961. Philippines. 95 min. Sound. 16mm Color. *Rental:* Films Inc & Video Comm. *Lease:* Video Comm.

Steel Fist, The. Roddy McDowall & Kristine Miller. Directed by Wesley Barry. 1952. Monogram. 72 min. Sound. 16mm B&W. *Rental:* Hurlock Cine.

Steel Helmet, The. Gene Evans & Robert Hutton. Directed by Samuel Fuller. 1951. Lippert. 84 min. Sound. 16mm B&W. *Rental:* Budget Films, Inst Cinema & Willoughby Peer.

Steel Town. Ann Sheridan & John Lund. Directed by George Sherman. 1952. Universal. 84 min. Sound. 16mm B&W. *Rental:* Swank Motion.

Steel Trap, The. Joseph Cotten & Teresa Wright. Directed by Andrew Stone. 1952. Fox. 84 min. Sound. 16mm B&W. *Rental:* Budget Films.

Steelmakers, The. 1974. Korea. (Anamorphic, documentary). 140 min. Sound. 16mm B&W. *Rental:* Tricontinental Film.

Steeltown. 1966. Canada. (Documentary). 56 min. Sound. 16mm Color. *Sale:* Natl Film CN.

Stella. Ann Sheridan & Victor Mature. Directed by Claude Binyon. 1950. Fox. 83 min. Sound. 16mm B&W. *Rental:* Films Inc.

Stella Dallas. Barbara Stanwyck & John Boles. Directed by King Vidor. 1937. Goldwyn. 108 min. Sound. 16mm B&W. *Rental:* Films Inc.

Stella Maris. Mary Pickford & Conway Tearle. Directed by Marshall Neilan. 1918. Artcraft. 75 min. Silent. Super 8mm B&W. *Sale:* Cinema Concepts.

Step by Step. Lawrence Tierney & Anne Jeffreys. Directed by Phil Rosen. 1946. RKO. 62 min. Sound. 16mm B&W. *Rental:* Films Inc.

Step Lively. Frank Sinatra & George Murphy. Directed by Tim Whelan. 1944. RKO. 88 min. Sound. 16mm B&W. *Rental:* Films Inc.

Step Lively, Jeeves. Arthur Treacher & Patricia Ellis. Directed by Eugene Forde. 1937. Fox. 69 min. Sound. 16mm B&W. *Rental:* Films Inc & Swank Motion.

Step Over the Edge. 1975. Ken Anderson. (Cast unlisted). 70 min. Sound. 16mm Color. *Rental:* G Herne & Roas Films.

Stepchild. Brenda Joyce & Donald Woods. Directed by James Flood. 1947. PRC. 73 min. Sound. 16mm B&W. *Sale:* Classics Assoc NY.

Stepford Wives, The. Katherine Ross & Paula Prentiss. Directed by Bryan Forbes. 1974. Columbia. 114 min. Sound. 16mm Color. *Rental:* Budget Films, Films Inc, Inst Cinema, Kit Parker, Natl Film Video, Swank Motion, Twyman Films, Westcoast Films, Welling Motion Pictures, Wholesome Film Ctr & Williams Films.

Stephenses of Iowa, The. Directed by Arthur Barron & Mark Obenhaus. 1976. Group W. (Documentary). 59 min. Sound. 16mm Color. *Rental:* Iowa Films, Syracuse U Film, U Cal Media & U Mich Media. *Sale:* Carousel Films. *Sale:* Carousel Films, Videotape version.

Stepmother, The. Alejandro Rey. Directed by Hikmet Avedis. 1972. Crown. 94 min. Sound. 16mm Color. *Rental:* Budget Films & Video Comm. *Lease:* Video Comm.

Steppe, The. Marina Vlady. Directed by Alberto Lattuada. Fr. 1963. France-Italy. 110 min. Sound. 16mm B&W. subtitles. *Rental:* Liberty Co.

Steppenwolf. Max Von Sydow & Dominique Sanda. Directed by Fred Haines. 1974. D/R. 105 min. Sound. 16mm Color. *Rental:* Films Inc.

Steppin' in Society. Edward Everett Horton. Directed by Alexander Esway. 1945. Republic. 72 min. Sound. 16mm B&W. *Rental:* Ivy Films.

Stepping Out. Reginald Denny & Charlotte Greenwood. Directed by Charles Reisner. 1931. MGM. 73 min. Sound. 16mm B&W. *Rental:* MGM United.

Stepping Out: The Debolts Grow Up. 52 min. Sound. 16mm Color. *Rental:* Mass Media Ministries & Pyramid Film.

Sterile Cuckoo, The. Liza Minnelli & Wendell Burton. Directed by Alan J. Pakula. 1969. Paramount. 107 min. Sound. 16mm Color. *Rental:* Films Inc.

Steven Spielberg. 1978. American Film Institute. (Lecture). 55 min. Videotape Color. *Sale:* Am Film Inst.

Stevie, Samson & Delilah. Steven Hawkes Jr. 86 min. Sound. 16mm Color. *Rental:* Films Inc, Modern Sound & Westcoast Films.

Stick to Your Guns. William Boyd. Directed by Lesley Selander. 1941. Paramount. 54 min. Sound. 16mm B&W. *Sale:* Cinema Concepts.

Stigma. Philip M. Thomas. Directed by David E. Durston. 1973. Cinerama. 93 min. Sound. 16mm Color. *Rental:* Swank Motion.

Stiletto. Patrick O'Neal & Alex Cord. Directed by Bernard Kowalski. 1969. Embassy. 93 min. Sound. 16mm Color. *Rental:* Films Inc.

Still a Brother: Inside the Negro Middle Class. 1967. NET. (Documentary). 90 min. Sound. 16mm B&W. *Rental:* Indiana AV Ctr, McGraw-Hill Films, Syracuse U Film & U Mich Media. *Sale:* McGraw-Hill Films & Indiana AV Ctr.

Still of the Night. Meryl Streep & Roy Scheider. Directed by Robert Benton. 1982. MGM. 91 min. Sound. 16mm Color. *Rental:* MGM United.

Still Smokin'. Cheech Marin & Thomas Chong. Directed by Thomas Chong. 1983. Paramount. 92 min. Sound. 16mm Color. *Rental:* Films Inc.

Still Waters. 1978. Time-Life. (Documentary). 59 min. Sound. Color. *Rental:* Iowa Films, U of IL Film & U Mich Media, Videotape version.

Stillwell Road, The. 1947. US Government. (Documentary). 53 min. Sound. 16mm B&W. *Sale:* Budget Films, Images Film, Kit Parker, Natl AV Ctr, Reel Images & SD AV Ctr. *Sale:* Morcraft Films & Natl AV Ctr.

Sting, The. Paul Newman & Robert Redford. Directed by George Roy Hill. 1973. Universal. 129 min. Sound. 16mm Color. *Rental:* Swank Motion. *Rental:* Swank Motion, Videotape version.

Sting II, The. Jackie Gleason, Mac Davis & Teri Garr. Directed by Jeremy Paul Kagan. 1983. Universal. 103 min. Sound. 16mm Color. *Rental:* Swank Motion. *Rental:* Swank Motion, Videotape version.

Sting of the Dragon Masters, The. Angela Mas. Directed by Huang Feng. 1973. Hong Kong. 96 min. Sound. 16mm Color. dubbed. *Rental:* Budget Films, Films Inc & Westcoast Films.

Sting of the West. Jack Palance. 88 min. Sound. Videotape Color. *Rental:* Maljack.

Stingaree. Richard Dix. Directed by William A. Wellman. 1934. RKO. 80 min. Sound. 16mm B&W. *Rental:* Classic Film Mus.

Stingray. Christopher Mitchum & Sherry Jackson. 1978. Embassy. 100 min. Sound. 16mm Color. *Rental:* Films Inc.

Stitch in Time, A. 1979. PBS. (Documentary). 59 min. Videotape Color. *Rental:* PBS Video. *Sale:* PBS Video.

Stockcar! Richard Petty & Buddy Baker. Directed by John Holmstrom. 1977. Sunrise Entertainment. 95 min. Sound. 16mm Color. *Rental:* Twyman Films.

Stockyards: End of An Era. 1972. WTTW. (Documentary). 59 min. Sound. Color. *Rental:* Indiana AV Ctr. *Sale:* Indiana AV Ctr, Videotape version.

Stolen Airliner, The. Diana Day. Directed by Don Sharp. 1956. Britain. 59 min. Sound. 16mm B&W. *Sale:* Lucerne Films.

Stolen Face, The. Paul Henried & Lizabeth Scott. Directed by Terence Fisher. 1952. Lippert. 71 min. Sound. 16mm B&W. *Rental:* Mogulls Films.

Stolen Holiday. Kay Francis & Claude Rains. Directed by Michael Curtiz. 1937. Warners. 82 min. Sound. 16mm B&W. *Rental:* MGM United.

Stolen Hours. Susan Hayward & Michael Craig. Directed by Daniel Petrie. 1963. United Artists. 97 min. Sound. 16mm Color. *Rental:* MGM United.

Stolen Kisses. Trans. Title: Baiser Voles. Jean-Pierre Leaud & Delphine Seyrig. Directed by Francois Truffaut. Fr. 1969. France. 107 min. Sound. 16mm Color. *Rental:* Cinema Five & New Cinema. *Sale:* Tamarelles French Film, Videotape version.

Stolen Life, A. Bette Davis & Glenn Ford. Directed by Curtis Bernhardt. 1947. Warners. 107 min. Sound. 16mm B&W. *Rental:* MGM United.

Stolen Plans, The. Mavis Sage. Directed by James Hill. 1952. Britain. 57 min. Sound. 16mm B&W. *Sale:* Lucerne Films.

Stone Age Survivors, The. 1974. Explo Mundo. (Documentary). 57 min. Sound. 16mm Color. *Rental:* B Raymond. *Sale:* B Raymond.

Stone in the River, The. 1975. CBS. (Documentary). 60 min. Sound. 16mm Color. *Rental:* Natl Churches Christ. *Sale:* Natl Churches Christ.

Stone Killer, The. Charles Bronson. Directed by Michael Winner. 1973. Columbia. 89 min. Sound. 16mm Color. *Rental:* Arcus Film, Bosco Films, Budget Films, Cine Craft, Inst Cinema, Kerr Film, Modern Sound, Natl Film Video, Swank Motion, Welling Motion Pictures & Westcoast Films. *Sale:* Tamarelles French Film, Videotape version.

Stoned: An Anti-Drug Film. Scott Baio & Vinnie Bufano. 1980. Learning Corp. 50 min. Sound. 16mm Color. *Rental:* Learning Corp Am & Utah Media. *Sale:* Learning Corp Am. *Sale:* Learning Corp Am, *Rental:* Learning Corp Am, Videotape version.

Stones in the Park, The. 1969. Britain. 50 min. Sound. 16mm Color. *Rental:* Budget Films. *Sale:* Reel Images.

Stop at Nothing. Directed by Charles R. Seeling. 1924 Aywon. 50 min. Silent. 16mm B&W. *Sale:* Select Film.

Stop! Look! & Laugh! Three Stooges & Paul Winchell. Directed by Jules White. 1961. Columbia. 78 min. Sound. 16mm B&W. *Rental:* Arcus Films, Buchan Pic, Budget Films, Cine Craft, Film Ctr DC, Films Inc, Inst Cinema, Modern Sound, Natl Film Video, Newman Film Lib, Roas Films, Twyman Films, Welling Motion Pictures, Westcoast Films, Wholesome Film Ctr & Williams Films.

Stopover Tokyo. Robert Wagner & Joan Collins. Directed by Richard L. Breen. 1957. Fox. (Anamorphic). 100 min. Sound. 16mm Color. *Rental:* Films Inc.

Store, The. Directed by Frederick Wiseman. 1983. Zipporah. (Documentary). 90 min. Sound. 16mm Color. *Rental:* Zippprah Films.

Stork Bites Man. Jackie Cooper. Directed by Cy Endfield. 1947. United Artists. 69 min. Sound. 16mm B&W. *Rental:* Ivy Films.

Storm at Daybreak. Kay Francis & Walter Huston. Directed by Richard Boleslawski. 1933. MGM. 80 min. Sound. 16mm B&W. *Rental:* MGM United.

Storm Boy. Peter Cummins. Directed by Henry Safran. 1977. Australia. 90 min. Sound. 16mm Color. *Rental:* Budget Films, Learning Corp Am, Lewis Film, Modern Sound, Roas Films & Welling Motion Pictures. *Lease:* Learning Corp Am. *Sale:* Learning Corp Am, *Lease:* Learning Corp Am, Videotape version.

Storm Called Maria, A. 1959. Disney. (Documentary). 48 min. Sound. 16mm B&W. *Rental:* Buchan Pic, Cine Craft, Disney Prod, Films Inc, Iowa Films, Syracuse U Film & U Mich Media.

Storm Center. Bette Davis, Brian Keith & Kim Hunter. Directed by Daniel Taradash. 1956. Columbia. 87 min. Sound. 16mm B&W. *Rental:* Bosco Films & Kit Parker.

Storm Fear. Cornel Wilde, Jean Wallace & Lee Grant. Directed by Cornel Wilde. 1955. United Artists. 88 min. Sound. 16mm B&W. *Rental:* MGM United.

Storm in a Teacup. Rex Harrison & Vivien Leigh. Directed by Victor Saville. 1937. Britain. 86 min. Sound. 16mm B&W. *Rental:* A Twyman Pres, Budget Films, Em Gee Film Lib & Janus Films. *Sale:* Glenn Photo.

Storm Over Africa *see* Royal African Rifles.

Storm Over Asia. Trans. Title: Potomok-Chingis Khan. V. Inkizhinov & A. Dedintsev. Directed by Vsevolod I. Pudovkin. Rus. 1928. Russia. (Eng. title cards). 73 min. Silent. 16mm B&W. *Rental:* Budget Films, Images Film & Video Comm. *Sale:* Cinema Concepts, Festival Films & Images Film. *Rental:* Corinth Films, Em Gee Film Lib, Kit Parker, Museum Mod Art & Budget Films, *Sale:* Griggs Movie & Glenn Photo, 16mm silent version. *Rental:* Westcoast Films, 99 min. version. *Sale:* Festival Films, 102 min. version. *Sale:* Festival Films & Images Film, 102 min. Videotape version.

Storm Over Bengal. Patric Knowles & Rochelle Hudson. Directed by Sidney Salkow. 1938. Republic. 54 min. Sound. 16mm B&W. *Rental:* Ivy Films. *Sale:* Rep Pic Film.

Storm Over Lisbon. Vera Ralston & Richard Arlen. Directed by George Sherman. 1944. Republic. 86 min. Sound. 16mm B&W. *Rental:* Ivy Films. *Sale:* Rep Pic Film.

Storm Over the Supreme Court. 1963. CBS. (Documentary). 52 min. Sound. 16mm B&W. *Rental:* Syracuse U Film & U of IL Film. *Sale:* Carousel Films.

Storm Over Tibet. Rex Reason & Diana Douglas. Directed by Andrew Marton. 1952. Columbia. 87 min. Sound. 16mm B&W. *Rental:* Inst Cinema.

Storm Over Wyoming. Tim Holt & Richard Martin. Directed by Lesley Selander. 1950. RKO. 60 min. Sound. 16mm B&W. *Rental:* RKO General Pics.

Storm Rider. Scott Brady & Mala Powers. Directed by Edward Bernds. 1957. Fox. (Anamorphic). 70 min. Sound. 16mm B&W. *Rental:* Ivy Films. *Sale:* Rep Pic Film.

Stormy, the Thoroughbred. Robert Skene. Directed by Larry Lansburg. 1956. Disney. 46 min. Sound. 16mm Color. *Rental:* Buchan Pic, Cine Craft, Cousino Visual Ed, Disney Prod, Film Ctr DC, Films Inc, Modern Sound, Newman Film Lib, Roas Films & Twyman Films.

Stormy Weather. Lena Horne & Bill Robinson. Directed by Andrew Stone. 1943. Fox. 77 min. Sound. 16mm B&W. *Rental:* Films Inc.

Story About the Vistula River, A. 1978. Poland. (Documentary). 50 min. Sound. 16mm Color. narrated Eng. *Rental:* Polish People.

Story of a Love, The. Lucia Bose & Massimo Girotti. Directed by Michelangelo Antonioni. Ital. 1950. Italy. 102 min. Sound. 16mm B&W. subtitles. *Rental:* New Yorker Films.

Story of a Medieval City, The. 1977. 59 min. Sound. 16mm Color. *Rental:* Utah Media.

Story of a Woman, The. Bibi Andersson & Robert Stack. Directed by Leonardo Bercovicci. 1969. Universal. 110 min. Sound. 16mm Color. *Rental:* Swank Motion.

Story of Adele H., The Isabelle Adjani & Bruce Robinson. Directed by Francois Truffaut. 1975. New World. 97 min. Sound. 16mm Color. *Rental:* Films Inc.

Story of Alexander Graham Bell, The. Orig. Title: Modern Miracle, The. Don Ameche & Loretta Young. Directed by Irving Cummings. 1939. Fox. 97 min. Sound. 16mm B&W. *Rental:* Films Inc.

Story of Carl Gustav Jung, The. 3 pts. 1973. Britain. (Documentary). 90 min. Sound. 16mm Color. *Rental:* Time-Life Multimedia. *Sale:* Time-Life Multimedia.

Story of Danny Lester, The. Orig. Title: Bad Boy. Audie Murphy & Lloyd Noland. Directed by Kurt Neumann. 1949. Allied Artists. 87 min. Sound. 16mm B&W. *Rental:* Budget Films, Charard Motion Pics, Hurlock Cine & Inst Cinema.

Story of David, The. Orig. Title: David, the Outlaw. Jeff Chandler & Basil Sydney. Directed by Bob McNaught. 1960. Britain. 80 min. Sound. 16mm Color. *Rental:* Alba House.

Story of Destroyer Escort 733, The. Orig. Title: USS-VD: Ship of Shame. Keefe Brasselle & Esther Dale. 1943. US Navy/Paramount. 50 min. Sound. 16mm B&W. *Rental:* Budget Films & Kit Parker.

Story of Dr. Wassel, The. Gary Cooper & Laraine Day. Directed by Cecil B. DeMille. 1944. Paramount. 136 min. Sound. 16mm Color. *Rental:* Swank Motion.

Story of Dr. Ehrlich's Magic Bullet, The *see* Dr. Ehrlich's Magic Bullet.

Story of Esther, The. Victoria Principal & Michael Ansara. 1980. 50 min. Sound. 16mm Color. *Rental:* Budget Films, Modern Sound & Syracuse U Film. *Sale:* Lucerne Films. *Sale:* Lucerne Films, Videotape version.

Story of Esther Costello, The. Joan Crawford & Rossano Brazzi. Directed by David Miller. 1957. Britain. 103 min. Sound. 16mm B&W. *Rental:* Maljack. *Lease:* Maljack. *Lease:* Maljack, Videotape version.

Story of Floating Weeds, The. Takeshi Sakamoto. Directed by Yasujiro Ozu. Jap. 1934. Japan. 89 min. Sound. 16mm B&W. subtitles. *Rental:* New Cinema & New Yorker Films.

Story of G. I. Joe, The. Orig. Title: G. I. Joe. Burgess Meredith & Robert Mitchum. Directed by William A. Wellman. 1945. United Artists. 100 min. Sound. 16mm B&W. *Rental:* Budget Films & Mogulls Films.

Story of Gosta Berling, The. Orig. Title: Atonement of Gosta Berling. Trans. Title: Gosta Berling's Saga. Greta Garbo. Directed by Mauritz Stiller. 1924. Sweden. (Musical score only). 105 min. Sound. 16mm B&W. *Rental:* Budget Films & Kit Parker. *Sale:* Natl Cinema & Reel Images. *Sale:* Tamarelles French Film, Videotape version.

Story of Louis Pasteur, The. Paul Muni & Anita Louise. Directed by William Dieterle. 1935. Warners. 87 min. Sound. 16mm B&W. *Rental:* MGM United.

Story of O, The. Corinne Clery & Anthony Steel. Directed by Just Jaeckin. 1975. France. 97 min. Sound. 16mm Color. dubbed. *Rental:* Hurlock Cine.

Story of Pope Pius XII, The. Italy. (Documentary). 70 min. Sound. 16mm B&W. *Rental:* Budget Films.

Story of Robin Hood, The. Richard Todd, James Robertson Justice & Joan Rice. Directed by Ken Annakin. 1952. Disney. 84 min. Sound. 16mm Color. *Rental:* Bosco Films, Buchan Pic, Cine Craft, Cousino Visual Ed, Elliot Film Co, Film Ctr DC, Films Inc, MGM United, Modern Sound, Newman Film Lib, Swank Motion, Twyman Films, U of IL Film, Welling Motion Pictures, Westcoast Films & Williams Films.

Story of Ruth, The. Stuart Whitman & Tom Tryon. Directed by Henry Koster. 1960. Fox. 132 min. Sound. 16mm Color. *Rental:* Films Inc. *Rental:* Films Inc, Anamorphic version.

Story of San Michele, The. O. W. Fischer, Rosanna Schiaffino & Valentina Cortese. Germany/Italy. 120 min. Sound. 16mm Color. dubbed. *Rental:* Creative Film.

Story of SeaBiscuit, The. Orig. Title: Pride of Kentucky. Shirley Temple & Barry Fitzgerald. Directed by David Butler. 1949. Warners. 93 min. Sound. 16mm Color. *Rental:* MGM United.

Story of Sin, The. Directed by Walerian Borowczyk. Pol. 1976. Poland. 128 min. Sound. 16mm Color. subtitles. *Rental:* Cinema Five.

Story of the Blood Stream, The. 2 pts. 1957. Moody Institute. 53 min. Sound. 16mm Color. *Rental:* U Cal Media.

Story of the Last Chrysanthemum, The. Shotaro Hanayagi & Kakuko Mori. Directed by Kenji Mizoguchi. Jap. 1939. Japan. 115 min. Sound. 16mm B&W. subtitles. *Rental:* Films Inc.

Story of Three Loves, The. Leslie Caron & Kirk Douglas. Directed by Vincente Minnelli & Gottfried Reinhardt. 1953. MGM. 121 min. Sound. 16mm Color. *Rental:* MGM United.

Story of Vernon & Irene Castle, The. Fred Astaire & Ginger Rogers. Directed by H. C. Potter. 1939. RKO. 93 min. Sound. 16mm B&W. *Rental:* Films Inc.

Story of Will Rogers, The. Will Rogers Jr. & Jane Wyman. Directed by Michael Curtiz. 1952. Warners. 109 min. Sound. 16mm Color. *Rental:* Swank Motion.

Story on Page One, The. Rita Hayworth & Anthony Franciosa. Directed by Clifford Odets. 1959. Fox. (Anamorphic). 122 min. Sound. 16mm B&W. *Rental:* Films Inc.

Stowaway. Shirley Temple, Alice Faye & Robert Young. Directed by William A. Seiter. 1939. Fox. 87 min. Sound. 16mm B&W. *Rental:* Films Inc.

Strada, La. Anthony Quinn & Giulietta Masina. Directed by Federico Fellini. Ital. 1954. Italy. 107 min. Sound. 16mm B&W. subtitles. *Rental:* Films Inc & Janus Films.

Straight Is the Way. Franchot Tone & Karen Morley. Directed by Paul Sloane. 1934. MGM. 60 min. Sound. 16mm B&W. *Rental:* MGM United.

Straight, Place & Show. Orig. Title: They're Off. The Ritz Brothers. Directed by David Butler. 1938. Fox. 68 min. Sound. 16mm B&W. *Rental:* Films Inc.

Straight Shooter. Tim McCoy. Directed by Sam Newfield. 1939. Victory. 60 min. Sound. 16mm B&W. *Rental:* Budget Films.

Straight Shooting. Harry Carey & Mollie Malone. Directed by John Ford. 1917. Butterfly. 53 min. Silent. 16mm B&W. *Rental:* Film Images. *Sale:* Film Images, Silent 8mm version.

Straight Time. Dustin Hoffman. Directed by Ulu Grosbard. 1978. Warners. 114 min. Sound. 16mm Color. *Rental:* Swank Motion & Williams Films. *Rental:* Swank Motion, Videotape version.

Strait-Jacket. Joan Crawford & Diane Baker. Directed by William Castle. 1964. Columbia. 89 min. Sound. 16mm B&W. *Rental:* Bosco Films, Budget Films, Charard Motion Pictures, Modern Sound & Welling Motion Pictures.

Stranded. Kay Francis & George Brent. Directed by Frank Borzage. 1935. Warners. 72 min. Sound. 16mm B&W. *Rental:* MGM United.

Strange Adventure, A. Marla English & Nick Adams. Directed by William Witney. 1956. Republic. 70 min. Sound. 16mm B&W. *Rental:* Ivy Films. *Sale:* Rep Pic Film.

Strange Affection. Orig. Title: Scamps. Terrence Morgan, Richard Attenborough & Colin Peterson. Directed by Wolf Rilla. 1957. Britain. 90 min. Sound. 16mm B&W. *Rental:* Charard Motion Pics & Video Comm. *Rental:* Video Comm, Videotape version.

Strange Alibi. Arthur Kennedy & Joan Perry. Directed by D. Ross Lederman. 1941. Warners. 63 min. Sound. 16mm B&W. *Rental:* MGM United.

Strange & Terrible Times. 1973. NBC. (Documentary). 53 min. Sound. 16mm Color. *Rental:* Films Inc. *Sale:* Films Inc. *Sale:* Films Inc, Videotape version.

Strange Awakening, A. Lex Barker, Carole Matthews & Lisa Gastoni. Directed by Montgomery Tully. 1958. Britain. 69 min. Sound. 16mm B&W. *Sale:* Rep Pic Film.

Strange Bargain. Martha Scott & Jeffrey Lynn. Directed by Will Price. 1949. RKO. 68 min. Sound. 16mm B&W. *Rental:* Films Inc.

Strange Bedfellows. Rock Hudson & Gina Lollobrigida. Directed by Melvin Frank. 1965. Universal. 98 min. Sound. 16mm Color. *Rental:* Swank Motion.

Strange Behavior. Michael Murphy & Louise Fletcher. 93 min. Sound. 16mm *Rental:* WW Enter & Corinth Films. *Rental:* WW Enter & Corinth Films, Videotape version.

Strange Brew. Dave Thomas, Rick Moranis & Max Von Sydow. Directed by Rick Moranis & Dave Thomas. 1983. MGM-UA. 90 min. Sound. 16mm Color. *Rental:* MGM United. *Rental:* MGM United, Videotape version.

Strange Cargo. Joan Crawford, Clark Gable & Peter Lorre. Directed by Frank Borzage. 1940. MGM. 113 min. Sound. 16mm B&W. *Rental:* MGM United.

Strange Case of the Cosmic Rays, The. 1957. Bell Telephone. 60 min. Sound. 16mm Color. *Rental:* Utah Media.

Strange Case of the English Language, The. Directed by Andrew Rooney. 1967. CBS. 50 min. Sound. 16mm Color. *Rental:* Budget Films, Iowa Films, Phoenix Films, Syracuse U. Film, U Cal Media, U of IL Film, U Mich Media & Utah Media. *Sale:* Phoenix Films. *Sale:* Phoenix Films, Videotape version.

Strange Creatures of the Night. 1973. National Geographic. 52 min. Sound. 16mm Color. *Rental:* Natl Geog & U Cal Media. *Sale:* Natl Geog. *Sale:* Natl Geog, Videotape version.

Strange Death of Adolf Hitler, The. Ludwig Donath & Fritz Kortner. Directed by James Hogan. 1943. Universal. 72 min. Sound. 16mm B&W. *Rental:* Swank Motion.

Strange Door, The. Charles Laughton & Boris Karloff. Directed by Joseph Pevney. 1951. Universal. 81 min. Sound. 16mm B&W. *Rental:* Swank Motion.

Strange Fascination. Cleo Moore & Mona Barrie. Directed by Hugo Haas. 1952. Columbia. 80 min. Sound. 16mm B&W. *Rental:* Kit Parker.

Strange Gamble, The. William Boyd. Directed by George Archainbaud. 1948. United Artists. 61 min. Sound. 16mm B&W. *Sale:* Cinema Concepts.

Strange Holiday. Orig. Title: Day After Tomorrow, The. Claude Rains & Gloria Holden. Directed by Arch Oboler. 1946. PRC. 54 min. Sound. 16mm B&W. *Rental:* Films Inc & Ivy Films. *Sale:* Rep Pic Film.

Strange Illusion. Orig. Title: Out of the Night. James Lydon, Sally Eilers & Warren William. Directed by Edgar G. Ulmer. 1945. PRC. 85 min. Sound. 16mm B&W. *Rental:* Ivy Films & Mogulls Films. *Sale:* Classics Assoc NY & Rep Pic Film.

Strange Impersonation. Brenda Marshall & William Gargan. Directed by Anthony Mann. 1946. Republic. 68 min. Sound. 16mm B&W. *Sale:* Classics Assoc NY.

Strange Interlude. Norma Shearer, Clark Gable & Robert Young. Directed by Robert Z. Leonard. 1932. MGM. 112 min. Sound. 16mm B&W. *Rental:* MGM United.

Strange Intruder. Ida Lupino & Edmond Purdom. Directed by Irving Rapper. 1956. Allied Artists. 82 min. Sound. 16mm B&W. *Rental:* Ivy Films. *Lease:* Rep Pic Film.

Strange Invaders. Paul LeMat & Nancy Allen. Directed by Michael Laughlin. 1983. Orion. 94 min. Sound. 16mm Color. *Rental:* Films Inc.

Strange Justice. Reginald Denny. Directed by Victor Schertzinger. 1933. RKO. 69 min. Sound. 16mm B&W. *Rental:* RKO General Pics.

Strange Love of Martha Ivers, The. Barbara Stanwyck & Van Heflin. Directed by Lewis Milestone. 1946. Paramount. 117 min. Sound. 16mm B&W. *Rental:* Films Inc. *Sale:* Festival Films, Videotape version.

Strange Love of Molly Louvain, The. Ann Dvorak & Lee Tracy. Directed by Michael Curtiz. 1932. Warners. 74 min. Sound. 16mm B&W. *Rental:* MGM United.

Strange Mrs. Crane, The. Marjorie Lord & Robert Shayne. Directed by Sherman Scott. 1948. Republic. 62 min. Sound. 16mm B&W. *Rental:* Ivy Films. *Sale:* Rep Pic Film.

Strange One, The. Ben Gazzara, George Peppard & Pat Hingle. Directed by Jack Garfein. 1957. Columbia. 97 min. Sound. 16mm B&W. *Rental:* Kit Parker.

Strange Sleep, The. 1976. Nova. (Documentary). 59 min. Sound. Videotape Color. *Rental:* U Cal Media.

Strange Triangle. Signe Hasso & Preston Foster. Directed by Ray McCarey. 1946. Fox. 65 min. Sound. 16mm B&W. *Rental:* Films Inc.

Strange Vengeance of Rosalie, The. Ken Howard & Bonnie Bedelia. Directed by Jack Starrett. 1972. Fox. 107 min. Sound. 16mm Color. *Rental:* Films Inc.

Strange Victory. Directed by Leo Hurwitz. 1948. Brandon. (Documentary). 77 min. Sound. 16mm B&W. *Rental:* Films Inc & Museum Mod Art.

Strange Voyage. Eddie Albert & Elena Verdugo. Directed by Irving Allen. 1945. Monogram. 63 min. Sound. 16mm B&W. *Rental:* Budget Films & Hurlock Cine.

Strange Woman, The. Hedy Lamarr & George Sanders. Directed by Edgar G. Ulmer. 1946. United Artists. 101 min. Sound. 16mm B&W. *Rental:* Budget Films & Kit Parker.

Stranger, The. Edward G. Robinson & Loretta Young. Directed by Orson Welles. 1946. RKO. 95 min. Sound. 16mm B&W. *Rental:* Arcus Film, Budget Films, Em Gee Film Lib, Films Inc, Images Film, Ivy Films, Kit Parker, MGM United, Welling Motion Pictures, Video Comm & Westcoast Films. *Sale:* Cinema Concepts, Festival Films & Images Film. *Sale:* Tamarelles French Film, Festival Films & Images Film, Videotape version.

Stranger, The. Marcello Mastroianni & Anna Karina. Directed by Luchino Visconti. Ital. 1967. Italy. 104 min. Sound. 16mm Color. subtitles. *Rental:* Films Inc.

Stranger & the Gunfighter, The. Lee Van Cleef, Karen Yeh & Lo Lieh. 1976. Columbia. 107 min. Sound. 16mm Color. *Rental:* Cine Craft, Film Ctr DC, Modern Sound, Twyman Films, Welling Motion Pictures, Westcoast Films, Wholesome Film Ctr & Williams Films, R#Westcoast Films version.

Stranger at My Door. Macdonald Carey & Patricia Medina. Directed by William Witney. 1955. Republic. 85 min. Sound. 16mm B&W. *Rental:* Ivy Films. *Sale:* Rep Pic Film.

Stranger from Pecos. Johnny Mack Brown. Directed by Lambert Hillyer. 1943. Monogram. 55 min. Sound. 16mm B&W. *Rental:* Hurlock Cine & Lewis Film.

Stranger from Santa Fe. Johnny Mack Brown. Directed by Lambert Hillyer. 1945. Monogram. 55 min. Sound. 16mm B&W. *Rental:* Hurlock Cine.

Stranger from Venus. Patricia Neal & Helmut Dantine. Directed by Burt Balaban. 1954. Princess. 76 min. Sound. 16mm B&W. *Rental:* Wade Williams.

Stranger in My Arms. June Allyson & Jeff Chandler. Directed by Helmut Kautner. 1959. Universal. 88 min. Sound. 16mm B&W. *Rental:* Swank Motion.

Stranger in My Forest, A. 1975. Mark IV. (Cast unlisted). 70 min. Sound. 16mm Color. *Rental:* G Herne.

Stranger in Sacramento, A. Mickey Hargitay. Directed by Serge Bergonzelli. 1965. Italy. 94 min. Sound. 16mm Color. dubbed. *Rental:* Modern Sound.

Stranger in Town. Chic Sale & Ann Dvorak. Directed by Erle C. Kenton. 1932. Warners. 66 min. Sound. 16mm B&W. *Rental:* MGM United.

Stranger in Town, A. Alex Nichol & Colin Tapley. Directed by George Pollock. 1956. Astor. 74 min. Sound. 16mm B&W. *Rental:* Ivy Films & Video Comm.

Stranger in Town, A. Tony Anthony. Directed by Luigi Vanzi. 1968. Italy. 85 min. Sound. 16mm Color. dubbed. *Rental:* MGM United.

Stranger in Town, A. Frank Morgan & Richard Carlson. 1943. MGM. 67 min. Sound. 16mm B&W. *Rental:* MGM United.

Stranger is Watching, A. Kate Mulgrew, Rip Torn & James Naughton. Directed by Sean Cunningham. 1981. MGM-UA. 92 min. Sound. 16mm Color. *Rental:* MGM United. *Rental:* MGM United, Videotape version.

Stranger of the Hills. Ethel Ritchie & Edward Coxen. Directed by Bruce Mitchell. 1922. Anchor. 60 min. Silent. 16mm B&W. *Rental:* Mogulls Films.

Stranger on the Prowl. Paul Muni, Joan Lorring & Andrea Forzano. 1952. Italy. 82 min. Sound. 16mm B&W. dubbed. *Rental:* Ivy Films.

Stranger on the Third Floor, The. Peter Lorre & John MacGuire. Directed by Boris Ingster. 1940. RKO. 64 min. Sound. 16mm B&W. *Rental:* RKO General Pics.

Stranger Returns, The. Orig. Title: Man, a Horse & a Pistol, A. Tony Anthony & Dan Vadis. Directed by Luigi Vanzi. 1968. Italy. 90 min. Sound. 16mm Color. dubbed. *Rental:* MGM United.

Stranger Wore a Gun, The. Randolph Scott & Claire Trevor. Directed by Andre De Toth. 1953. Columbia. 83 min. Sound. 16mm Color. *Rental:* Modern Sound.

Strangers All. Preston Foster & Leon Ames. Directed by Charles Vidor. 1935. RKO. 69 min. Sound. 16mm B&W. *Rental:* RKO General Pics.

Strangers & Kin. Directed by Herb E. Smith. 1983. Appalshop. 58 min. Sound. 16mm Color. *Rental:* Appals. *Sale:* Appals. *Sale:* Appals, Videotape version.

Strangers at Sunrise. George Montgomery & Deana Martin. Directed by Percival Rubens. 1968. Commonwealth. 104 min. Sound. 16mm B&W. *Rental:* Ivy Films & Video Comm. *Lease:* Rep Pic Film.

Strangers in the City. Robert Gentile & Kenny Delmar. Directed by Rick Carrier. 1962. Embassy. 83 min. Sound. 16mm B&W. *Rental:* Films Inc.

Strangers in the Homeland. 1975. ABC. (Documentary). 60 min. Sound. 16mm Color. *Rental:* Natl Churches Christ.

Strangers in the Night. William Terry & Virginia Grey. Directed by Anthony Mann. 1944. Republic. 56 min. Sound. 16mm B&W. *Rental:* Ivy Films.

Strangers May Kiss. Norma Shearer & Robert Montgomery. Directed by George Fitzmaurice. 1931. MGM. 83 min. Sound. 16mm B&W. *Rental:* MGM United.

Strangers of the Night. Directed by Fred Niblo. 1923. Mayer. 80 min. Silent. 16mm B&W. *Rental:* MGM United.

Strangers on a Train. Farley Granger & Robert Walker. Directed by Alfred Hitchcock. 1951. Warners. 101 min. Sound. 16mm B&W. *Rental:* Swank Motion.

Strangers Return, The. Lionel Barrymore & Miriam Hopkins. Directed by King Vidor. 1933. MGM. 89 min. Sound. 16mm B&W. *Rental:* MGM United.

Strangers When We Meet. Kirk Douglas & Kim Novak. Directed by Richard Quine. 1960. Columbia. 117 min. Sound. 16mm Color. *Rental:* Budget Films, Cine Craft, Charard Motion Pics, Inst Cinema, Modern Sound & Welling Motion Pictures.

Strangler, The. Victor Buono. Directed by Burt Topper. 1963. Allied Artists. 80 min. Sound. 16mm B&W. *Rental:* Hurlock Cine.

Strangler of the Swamp, The. Robert Barrett & Rosemary La Planche. Directed by Frank Wisbar. 1946. PRC. 60 min. Sound. 16mm B&W. *Sale:* Classics Assoc NY.

Stranglers of Bombay. Guy Rolfe. Directed by Terence Fisher. 1960. Britain. 81 min. Sound. 16mm B&W. *Rental:* Kit Parker.

Strategic Air Command. James Stewart & June Allyson. Directed by Anthony Mann. 1955. Paramount. 114 min. Sound. 16mm Color. *Rental:* Films Inc.

Strategic Attack. 1951. U. S. Government. 50 min. Sound. 16mm Color. *Rental:* Natl AV Ctr. *Sale:* Natl AV Ctr.

Strategic Trust: The Making of Nuclear Free Palau. Directed by James Heddle. 58 min. Sound. 16mm Color. *Rental:* Cinema Guild.

Strategy, The. 1975. Idea. (Documentary). 70 min. Sound. 16mm B&W. *Rental:* NYU Film Lib.

Strategy of Terror. Hugh O'Brian & Barbara Rush. 1967. Universal. 90 min. Sound. 16mm Color. *Rental:* Swank Motion.

Stratton Story, The. James Stewart & June Allyson. Directed by Sam Wood. 1949. MGM. 106 min. Sound. 16mm B&W. *Rental:* MGM United. *Rental:* MGM United, Videotape version.

Strauss' Great Waltz *see* Waltzes from Vienna.

Stravinsky. 1966. Macmillan. (Documentary). 50 min. Sound. 16mm B&W. *Rental:* Dance Film Archive, Pennebaker, Syracuse U Film & Utah Media.

Stravinsky Portrait, A. Rolf Lieberman & Richard Leacock. 1965. Leacock. (Documentary). 58 min. Sound. 16mm B&W. *Rental:* Pennebaker. *Sale:* Pennebaker.

Straw Dogs. Dustin Hoffman & Susan George. Directed by Sam Peckinpah. 1971. Cinerama. 113 min. Sound. 16mm Color. *Rental:* Films Inc. *Sale:* ABC Film Lib, Super 8 sound version.

Strawberry Blonde, The. James Cagney & Olivia De Haviland. Directed by Raoul Walsh. 1941. Warners. 97 min. Sound. 16mm B&W. *Rental:* MGM United.

Strawberry Roan, The. Carol Raye & William Hartnell. Directed by Maurice Elvey. 1945. Britain. 70 min. Sound. 16mm B&W. *Rental:* Ivy Films. *Sale:* Rep Pic Film.

Strawberry Statement, The. Bruce Davison & Kim Darby. Directed by Stuart Hageman. 1970. MGM. 107 min. Sound. 16mm Color. *Rental:* MGM United.

Streamers. Matthew Modine & Michael Wright. Directed by Robert Altman. 1983. MGM-UA. 118 min. Sound. 16mm Color. *Rental:* MGM United. *Rental:* MGM United, Videotape version.

Street, The. Eugene Klopfer & Aud Egede Nissen. Directed by Karl Grune. 1923. Germany. 80 min. Silent. 16mm B&W. *Rental:* A Twyman Pres, Film Images & Museum Mod Art. *Sale:* Film Images.

Street Angel. Janet Gaynor & Charles Farrell. Directed by Frank Borzage. 1928. Fox. 102 min. Sound. 16mm B&W. *Rental:* Killiam Collect.

Street Bandits. Robert Clarke & Penny Edwards. Directed by R. G. Springsteen. 1951. Republic. 54 min. Sound. 16mm B&W. *Rental:* Ivy Films. *Sale:* Rep Pic Film.

Street Fighter, The. Sonny Chiba. Directed by Walter Hill. 1975. Japan. 90 min. Sound. 16mm Color. dubbed. *Rental:* New Line Cinema.

Street Girl. Jack Oakie & Betty Compson. Directed by Wesley Ruggles. 1930. RKO. 91 min. Sound. 16mm B&W. *Rental:* RKO General Pics.

Street Law. Franco Nero. 77 min. Sound. Videotape Color. *Sale:* Vidamerica.

Street of Chance. Burgess Meredith & Claire Trevor. Directed by Jack Hively. 1942. Paramount. 74 min. Sound. 16mm B&W. *Rental:* Swank Motion.

Street of Forgotten Women. Grace Fleming. 1925. 50 min. Silent. 16mm B&W. *Sale:* Morcraft Films.

Street of Missing Men. Charles Bickford & Harry Carey. Directed by Sidney Salkow. 1939. Republic. 64 min. Sound. 16mm B&W. *Rental:* Ivy Films.

Street of Shame. Machiko Kyo & Aiko Mimasu. Directed by Kenji Mizoguchi. Jap. 1956. Japan. 85 min. Sound. 16mm B&W. subtitles. *Rental:* Films Inc & Janus Films.

Street of Sorrow *see* Joyless Street.

Street of the Flower Boxes. 1972. NBC. (Documentary). 48 min. Sound. 16mm Color. *Rental:* Films Inc, U Mich Media & Utah Media. *Sale:* Films Inc. *Sale:* Films Inc, Videotape version.

Street of Women. Kay Francis & Roland Young. Directed by Archie Mayo. 1932. Warners. 60 min. Sound. 16mm B&W. *Rental:* MGM United.

Street Scene. Sylvia Sidney. Directed by King Vidor. 1931. United Artists. 80 min. Sound. 16mm B&W. *Rental:* Budget Films, Films Inc, Kit Parker, Mogulls Films, Video Comm & Wholesome Film Ctr. *Sale:* Cinema Concepts & Reel Images. *Sale:* Reel Images, Super 8 sound version.

Street Scenes-1970. Directed by Martin Scorsese. 1970. N.Y. Cinetracts. (Experimental). 75 min. Sound. 16mm Color. *Rental:* Images Film.

Street with No Name, The. Mark Stevens & Richard Widmark. Directed by William Keighley. 1948. Fox. 91 min. Sound. 16mm B&W. *Rental:* Films Inc.

Streetcar Named Desire, A. Vivien Leigh, Marlon Brando, Kim Hunter & Karl Malden. Directed by Elia Kazan. 1951. Charles K. Feldman. 122 min. Sound. 16mm B&W. *Rental:* MGM United & Swank Motion. *Rental:* Swank Motion, Videotape version.

Streets of Fire. Diane Lane & Michael Pare. Directed by Walter Hill. 1985. Universal. 98 min. Sound. 16mm Color. *Rental:* Swank Motion.

Streets of Laredo. William Holden & William Bendix. Directed by Leslie Fenton. 1949. Paramount. 75 min. Sound. 16mm B&W. *Rental:* Swank Motion.

Streets of New York. Orig. Title: Abe Lincoln of Ninth Avenue. Jackie Cooper & Marjorie Reynolds. Directed by William Nigh. 1939. Monogram. 73 min. Sound. 16mm B&W. *Rental:* Alba House, Hurlock Cine & Roas Films.

Streets of San Francisco. Robert Armstrong. Directed by George Blair. 1949. Republic. 60 min. Sound. 16mm B&W. *Rental:* Ivy Films. *Sale:* Rep Pic Film.

Streisand in Concert in Central Park. 1968. CBS. (Concert). 51 min. Videotape Color. *Sale:* Reel Images.

Strictly Dishonorable. Ezio Pinza & Janet Leigh. Directed by Melvin Frank. 1951. MGM. 95 min. Sound. 16mm B&W. *Rental:* MGM United.

Strictly Dynamite. Jimmy Durante & Lupe Velez. Directed by Pandro S. Berman. 1934. RKO. 74 min. Sound. 16mm B&W. *Rental:* RKO General Pics.

Strictly in the Groove. Ozzie Nelson & Leon Errol. Directed by Vernon Keays. 1943. Universal. 60 min. Sound. 16mm B&W. *Rental:* Mogulls Films, Newman Film Lib & Film Ctr DC.

Strike. Alexander Antonov & Grigori Alexandrou. Directed by Sergei Eisenstein. 1925. Russia. 97 min. Silent. 16mm B&W. *Rental:* Budget Films, Corinth Films, Em Gee Film Lib, Images Film & Utah Media. *Sale:* Glenn Photo, Reel Images & Images Film. *Rental:* Kit Parker, *Sale:* Glenn Photo, Music only version. *Rental:* Ivy Films, *Sale:* Glenn Photo & Reel Images, Super 8 silent version. *Sale:* Em Gee Film Lib & Images Film, Videotape version. *Rental:* Utah Media, 60 min. version.

Strike It Rich. Rod Cameron & Bonita Granville. Directed by Lesley Selander. 1948. Monogram. 81 min. Sound. 16mm B&W. *Rental:* Hurlock Cine.

Strike Me Deadly. Orig. Title: Crawling Hand, The. Gary Clarke. Directed by Herbert L. Strock. 1963. Medallion. 65 min. Sound. 16mm B&W. *Rental:* Westcoast Films.

Strike Up the Band. Mickey Rooney & Judy Garland. Directed by Busby Berkeley. 1940. MGM. 117 min. Sound. 16mm B&W. *Rental:* MGM United.

Strike Up the Band. 1977. Penn State. (Documentary). 59 min. Sound. 16mm Color. *Rental:* Penn St AV Serv. *Sale:* Penn St AV Serv. *Rental:* Penn St AV Serv, *Sale:* Penn St AV Serv, Videotape version.

Strip, The. Mickey Rooney & Sally Forrest. Directed by Leslie Kardos. 1951. MGM. 85 min. Sound. 16mm B&W. *Rental:* MGM United.

Strip Mining: Energy, Environment & Economics. Directed by Gene Du Bey & Frances Norton. 1979. Appalshop. (Documentary). 50 min. Sound. 16mm Color. *Rental:* Appals. *Sale:* Appals.

Strip Tease Murders, The *see* Lady of Burlesque.

Stripes. Bill Murray, Warren Oates & P. J. Soles. Directed by Ivan Reitman. 1981. Columbia. 105 min. Sound. 16mm Color. *Rental:* Swank Motion. *Rental:* Swank Motion, Videotape version.

Stripper, The. Joanne Woodward & Richard Beymer. Directed by Franklin Schaffner. 1963. Fox. (Anamorphic). 95 min. Sound. 16mm B&W. *Rental:* Films Inc.

Strohfeuer *see* Free Woman.

Stroke. Directed by Alan Jack Ruskin. 1972. New Line. (Exploitation). 95 min. Sound. 16mm Color. *Rental:* New Line Cinema. *Sale:* New Line Cinema.

Stroke. 1983. 60 min. Sound. Videotape Color. *Sale:* Natl AV Ctr.

Stroker Ace. Burt Reynolds & Loni Anderson. Directed by Hal Needham. 1983. Universal. 96 min. Sound. 16mm Color. *Rental:* Swank Motion. *Rental:* Swank Motion, Videotape version.

Stroll, The. Hawk Serpent. 53 min. Sound. 16mm Color. *Rental:* Filmmakers Coop.

Stromboli. Ingrid Bergman. Directed by Roberto Rossellini. 1950. Italy. 81 min. Sound. 16mm B&W. *Rental:* Budget Films, Films Inc, Kit Parker, Liberty Co, Video Comm & Westcoast Films. *Lease:* Video Comm. *Rental:* Video Comm, *Lease:* Video Comm, Videotape version.

Strong Man, The. Harry Langdon. Directed by Frank Capra. 1926. First National. 78 min. Silent. 16mm B&W. *Rental:* A Twyman Pres & Twyman Films.

Stronger Since the War? 1966. NET. (Documentary). 59 min. Sound. 16mm B&W. *Rental:* Indiana AV Ctr. *Lease:* Indiana AV Ctr.

Stronger Than Fear *see* Edge of Doom.

Stronger Than the Night. Wilhelm Koch-Hooge & Helgo Goring. Directed by Slatan Dudow. Ger. 1954. Germany. 112 min. Sound. 16mm B&W. subtitles. *Rental:* Films Inc.

Strongest Man in the World, The. Kurt Russell & Joe Flynn. Directed by Vincent McEveety. 1975. Disney. 92 min. Sound. 16mm Color. *Rental:* Disney Prod.

Strongheart. Henry B. Walthall, Lionel Barrymore & Blanche Sweet. 1914. Biograph. 45 min. Silent. 16mm B&W. *Rental:* Em Gee Film Lib. *Sale:* Blackhawk Films. *Rental:* Ivy Films, *Sale:* Blackhawk Films, Super 8 silent version.

Stronghold. Veronica Lake & Zachary Scott. Directed by Steve Sekely. 1952. Lippert. 70 min. Sound. 16mm B&W. *Rental:* Budget Films, Film Ctr DC, Mogulls Films & Westcoast Films.

Strongman Ferdinand. Heinz Herbert. Directed by Alexander Kluge. Ger. 1976. Germany. 98 min. Sound. 16mm Color. subtitles. *Rental:* Liberty Co.

Stroszek. Eva Mattes. Directed by Werner Herzog. Ger. 1977. Germany. 108 min. Sound. 16mm Color. dubbed. *Rental:* New Cinema & New Yorker Films.

Struggle, The. Hal Skelly & Zita Johann. Directed by D. W. Griffith. 1931. United Artists. 90 min. Sound. 16mm B&W. *Rental:* A Twyman Pres & Museum Mod Art.

Stuart Little. 1967. NBC. (Cast unlisted). 52 min. Sound. 16mm Color. *Rental:* McGraw-Hill Films & Syracuse U Film. *Sale:* McGraw-Hill Films.

Stuarts Restored, The. 1980. Royal Heritage. (Documentary). 60 min. Sound. 16mm Color. *Rental:* Films Inc. *Sale:* Films Inc. *Rental:* Films Inc, *Sale:* Films Inc, Videotape version.

Stud Farm, The. Directed by Andras Kovacs. Hungarian. 1978. Hungary. (Cast unlisted). 100 min. Sound. 16mm Color. subtitles. *Rental:* New Yorker Films.

Student As Interviewer, The. 1976. Indiana U. (Documentary). 53 min. Videotape Color. *Sale:* Indiana AV Ctr.

Student Bodies. Kristen Riter & Matt Goldsby. Directed by Mickey Rose. 1981. Paramount. 100 min. Sound. 16mm Color. *Rental:* Films Inc.

Student Nurses. Barbara Giftos & Karen Carlson. Directed by Stephanie Rothman. 1970. New World. 85 min. Sound. 16mm B&W. *Rental:* Films Inc.

Student of Prague, A. Paul Wegener. Directed by Stellan Rye. 1913. Germany. 56 min. Silent. 16mm B&W. subtitles. *Rental:* Budget Films, Em Gee Film Lib, Film Classics & Films Inc. *Sale:* Cinema Concepts, Film Classics, Glenn Photo & Reel Images. *Sale:* Cinema Concepts, Film Classics & Glenn Photo, Super 8 silent version. *Sale:* Tamarelles French Film, Videotape version.

Student Prince, The. Ann Blyth & Edmund Purdom. Directed by Richard Thorpe. 1954. MGM. 107 min. Sound. 16mm Color. *Rental:* MGM United. *Rental:* MGM United, Anamorphic version. *Rental:* MGM United, Videotape version.

Student Prince in Old Heidelberg, The. Norma Shearer & Ramon Navarro. Directed by Ernst Lubitsch. 1927. MGM. 103 min. Silent. 16mm B&W. *Rental:* Films Inc.

Student Teachers, The. Susan Damante & Brooke Mills. Directed by Jonathan Kaplan. 1973. New World. 84 min. Sound. 16mm Color. *Rental:* Films Inc.

Student Tour. Jimmy Durante & Betty Grable. Directed by Charles Reisner. 1934. MGM. 86 min. Sound. 16mm B&W. *Rental:* MGM United.

Studio Teacher, The. 1965. 47 min. Sound. 16mm B&W. *Rental:* U Mich Media.

Studs Lonigan. Christopher Knight & Frank Gorshin. Directed by Irving Lerner. 1960. United Artists. 95 min. Sound. 16mm B&W. *Rental:* MGM United.

Study in Scarlet, A. Reginald Owen & Alan Mowbray. Directed by Edwin L. Marin. 1934. World Wide. 77 min. Sound. 16mm B&W. *Rental:* Budget Films, Em Gee Film Lib & Video Comm. *Sale:* Glenn Photo.

Study in Terror, A. Anthony Quayle & John Neville. Directed by James Hill. 1966. Britain. 94 min. Sound. 16mm Color. *Rental:* Arcus Film, Bosco Films, Budget Films, Images Film, Modern Sound, Roas Films, Twyman Films, Welling Motion Pictures & Westcoast Films.

Stunt Man, The. Peter O'Toole & Steve Railsback. Directed by Richard Rush. 1980. Fox. 129 min. Sound. 16mm Color. *Rental:* Films Inc.

Stunts. Robert Forster & Fiona Lewis. Directed by Mark L. Lester. 1977. New Line. 90 min. Sound. 16mm Color. *Rental:* Films Inc & New Line Cinema.

Su Wa No Se, the Fourth World. Directed by Keiichi Ueno. 1978. Green Mountain Post. (Documentary). 75 min. Sound. 16mm Color. *Rental:* Green Mt. *Sale:* Green Mt.

Subida al Cielo: Mexican Bus Ride. Directed by Luis Bunuel. 73 min. Sound. 16mm B&W. *Rental:* Trans-World Films.

Subject Was Roses, The. Patricia Neal, Jack Albertson & Martin Sheen. Directed by Ulu Grosbard. 1968. MGM. 107 min. Sound. 16mm Color. *Rental:* MGM United.

Sublime & Anxious Eye, The. 1979. Britain. (Documentary). 52 min. Sound. 16mm Color. *Rental:* Films Inc. *Sale:* Films Inc. *Sale:* Films Inc, Videotape version.

Submarine. Jack Holt & Ralph Graves. Directed by Frank Capra. 1928. Columbia. (Musical score only). 80 min. Sound. 16mm B&W. *Rental:* Kit Parker.

Submarine Alert. Richard Arlen & Wendy Barrie. Directed by Frank McDonald. 1943. Paramount. 70 min. Sound. 16mm B&W. *Sale:* Morcraft Films. *Sale:* Morcraft Films, Super 8 sound version.

Submarine Command. William Holden & Nancy Olsen. Directed by John Farrow. 1951. Paramount. 87 min. Sound. 16mm B&W. *Rental:* Films Inc.

Submarine D-I. Pat O'Brien & George Brent. Directed by Lloyd Bacon. 1937. Warners. 98 min. Sound. 16mm B&W. *Rental:* MGM United.

Submarine Patrol. Richard Greene & Preston Foster. Directed by John Ford. 1938. Fox. 90 min. Sound. 16mm B&W. *Rental:* Films Inc.

Submarine Pirate, A. Syd Chaplin. Directed by Mack Sennett. 1915. Triangle. 45 min. Silent. 16mm B&W. *Sale:* Blackhawk Films. *Rental:* Ivy Films, Super 8 silent version.

Submarine X-I. James Caan. Directed by William Graham. 1965. United Artists. 89 min. Sound. 16mm Color. *Rental:* MGM United.

Subterfuge. Gene Barry & Joan Collins. Directed by Peter Graham Scott. 1968. Commonwealth United. 100 min. Sound. 16mm Color. *Rental:* Bosco Films, Charard Motion Pics, Films Inc, Ivy Films, Kerr Film, Video Comm, Welling Motion Pictures & Willoughby Peer.

Subterraneans, The. Leslie Caron & George Peppard. Directed by Ranald MacDougall. 1960. MGM. (Anamorphic). 89 min. Sound. 16mm Color. *Rental:* MGM United.

Suburban Living: Six Solutions. Orig. Title: Comparisons-Suburban Living. 1960. Canada. (Documentary). 60 min. Sound. 16mm B&W. *Rental:* Syracuse U Film.

Suburban Wall, The. 1974. Westinghouse. (Documentary). 50 min. Sound. 16mm Color. *Rental:* Edupac & NYU Film Lib. *Sale:* Edupac.

Subway in the Sky. Van Johnson & Hildegarde Neff. Directed by Muriel Box. 1959. United Artists. 86 min. Sound. 16mm B&W. *Rental:* MGM United.

Success: Alternate Title: American Success Co.. Jeff Bridges, Belinda Bauer & Ned Beatty. Directed by William Richert. 1979. Columbia. 94 min. Sound. 16mm Color. *Rental:* Kit Parker & Swank Motion. *Rental:* Swank Motion, Videotape version.

Success at Any Price. Douglas Jr. Fairbanks & Edward Everett Horton. Directed by Merian C. Cooper. 1934. RKO. 77 min. Sound. 16mm *Rental:* RKO General Pics.

Successful Calamity, The. George Arliss, Mary Astor & Randolph Scott. Directed by John Adolfi. 1932. Warners. 75 min. Sound. 16mm B&W. *Rental:* MGM United.

Successo, Il. Vittorio Gassman & Anouk Aimee. Directed by Mauro Morassi. Ital. 1963. Embassy. 103 min. Sound. 16mm B&W. *Rental:* Films Inc.

Such a Gorgeous Kid Like Me. Bernadette Lafont & Claude Brasseur. Directed by Francois Truffaut. Fr. 1973. France. 98 min. Sound. 16mm Color. subtitles. *Rental:* Corinth Films & Swank Motion.

Such Good Friends. Dyan Cannon, James Coco & Ken Howard. Directed by Otto Preminger. 1972. Paramount. 104 min. Sound. 16mm Color. *Rental:* Films Inc.

Such Is Life: So Ist das Lebanitakovy Je Zivot. Valeska Gert. Directed by Carl Junghans. 1929. Czechoslovakia-Germany. 74 min. Sound. 16mm B&W. *Rental:* Museum Mod Art.

Suckalo. Directed by Ron Taylor. 1971. Ron Taylor. (Documentary). 120 min. Sound. 16mm Color. *Rental:* Canyon Cinema & Film Images.

Sudden Danger. Bill Elliott & Beverly Garland. Directed by Hubert Cornfield. 1955. Allied Artists. 65 min. Sound. 16mm B&W. *Rental:* Hurlock Cine.

Sudden Death. Orig. Title: Fast on the Draw. Russell Hayden. Directed by Thomas Carr. 1950. Lippert. 60 min. Sound. 16mm B&W. *Rental:* Mogulls Films.

Sudden Impact. Clint Eastwood & Sondra Locke. Directed by Clint Eastwood. 1983. Warners. 115 min. Sound. 16mm Color. *Rental:* Swank Motion. *Rental:* Swank Motion, *Sale:* Tamarelles French Film, Videotape version.

Sudden Terror. Mark Lester & Lionel Jeffries. Directed by John Hough. 1971. National General. 95 min. Sound. 16mm Color. *Rental:* Swank Motion.

Sudden Wealth of the Poor People of Kombach, The. Directed by Volker Schlondorff. Ger. 1971. Germany. 94 min. 16mm B&W. subtitles. *Rental:* New Yorker Films.

Suddenly. Frank Sinatra & Sterling Hayden. Directed by Lewis Allen. 1954. United Artists. 77 min. Sound. 16mm B&W. *Rental:* Budget Films.

Suddenly an Eagle. 1976. Xerox. (Documentary). 52 min. Sound. 16mm Color. *Rental:* Kent St U Film & Xerox Films. *Sale:* Xerox Films.

Suddenly It's Spring. Paulette Goddard & Fred MacMurray. Directed by Mitchell Leisen. 1947. Paramount. 88 min. Sound. 16mm B&W. *Rental:* Swank Motion.

Suddenly, Last Summer. Elizabeth Taylor, Katharine Hepburn & Montgomery Clift. 1960. Columbia. 114 min. Sound. 16mm B&W. *Rental:* Arcus Film, Budget Films, Film Ctr DC, Films Inc, Images Film, Kerr Film, Kit Parker, Modern Sound, Natl Film Video, Twyman Films, U of IL Film, Welling Motion Pictures, Westcoast Films & Willoughby Peer. *Sale:* Tamarelles French Film, Videotape version.

Suds. Mary Pickford. Directed by John Francis Dillon. 1920. Pickford. 65 min. Silent. 8mm B&W. *Sale:* Cinema Concepts.

Sued for Libel. Kent Taylor & Linda Hayes. Directed by Leslie Goodwins. 1940. RKO. 69 min. Sound. 16mm B&W. *Rental:* RKO General Pics.

Sue's Leg: Remembering the Thirties. 1976. WNET. (Documentary). 60 min. Sound. 16mm Color. *Rental:* Indiana AV Ctr, U Cal Media & U of IL Film. *Sale:* Indiana AV Ctr.

Suez. Tyrone Power & Loretta Young. Directed by Allan Dwan. 1938. Fox. 105 min. Sound. 16mm B&W. *Rental:* Films Inc.

Suez. 1956. CBS. (Documentary). 55 min. Sound. 16mm B&W. *Rental:* McGraw-Hill Films & Syracuse U Film. *Sale:* McGraw-Hill Films.

Suffer the Little Children. 1971. NBC. (Documentary). 53 min. Sound. 16mm Color. *Rental:* Films Inc & U Mich Media. *Sale:* Films Inc. *Sale:* Films Inc, Videotape version.

Sugar Cane Alley. Garry Cadenat & Darling Legitimus. Directed by Euzhan Palcy. Fr. 1983. France. 103 min. Sound. 16mm Color. subtitles. *Rental:* New Yorker Films.

Sugar Cookies. (Cast unlisted). Sound. Videotape *Sale:* Vidamerica.

Sugar Film, The. 58 min. Sound. 16mm Color. *Rental:* Pyramid Film. *Sale:* Pyramid Film.

Sugar Hill. Marki Bey. Directed by Paul Maslansky. 1974. American International. 91 min. Sound. 16mm Color. *Rental:* Swank Motion.

Sugar Ray Robinson: Pound for Pound. 80 min. Sound. Videotape Color. *Rental:* Vidamerica.

Sugar Valley Sampler, A. 1979. Penn State. (Documentary). 58 min. Sound. 16mm Color. *Rental:* Penn St AV Serv. *Sale:* Penn St AV Serv. *Rental:* Penn St AV Serv, *Sale:* Penn St AV Serv, Videotape version.

Sugarland Express, The. Goldie Hawn & Ben Johnson. Directed by Steven Spielberg. 1974. Universal. 109 min. Sound. 16mm Color. *Rental:* Swank Motion. *Rental:* Swank Motion, Anamorphic version.

Suicide Commandos. Aldo Ray & Pamela Tudor. Directed by Camillo Bazzoni. 1968. Spain. 99 min. Sound. 16mm Color. dubbed. *Rental:* Video Comm & Westcoast Films.

Suicide Fleet. Ginger Rogers & Bill Boyd. Directed by Albert S. Rogell. 1932. RKO. 87 min. Sound. 16mm B&W. *Rental:* RKO General Pics.

Suicide's Wife, The. Angie Dickinson & Zohra Lampert. Directed by John Newland. 1980. CBS. 105 min. Sound. 16mm Color. *Rental:* Twyman Films.

Suite California. 1976. 46 min. Sound. 16mm Color. *Rental:* Canyon Cinema.

Sullivans, The. Anne Baxter & Thomas Mitchell. Directed by Lloyd Bacon. 1944. Fox. 111 min. Sound. 16mm B&W. *Rental:* Ivy Films.

Sullivan's Empire. Martin Milner & Clu Gulager. Directed by Thomas Carr & Harvey Hart. 1967. Universal. 85 min. Sound. 16mm Color. *Rental:* Swank Motion.

Sullivan's Travels. Joel McCrea & Veronica Lake. Directed by Preston Sturges. 1941. Paramount. 90 min. Sound. 16mm B&W. *Rental:* Williams Films.

Sultanat of Oman, The. Directed by Claude Deffarge & Gordian Troeller. Syria. (Documentary). 58 min. Sound. 16mm Color. *Rental:* Icarus Films. *Sale:* Icarus Films.

Summer & Smoke. Geraldine Page & Laurence Harvey. Directed by Peter Glenville. 1961. Paramount. 118 min. Sound. 16mm Color. *Rental:* Films Inc. *Rental:* Films Inc, Anamorphic version.

Summer Holiday. Mickey Rooney & Walter Huston. Directed by Rouben Mamoulian. 1948. MGM. 92 min. Sound. 16mm B&W. *Rental:* MGM United. *Rental:* MGM United, Color version. *Rental:* MGM United, Videotape version.

Summer Holiday. Cliff Richard & Lauri Peters. Directed by Peter Yates. 1963. Britain. 106 min. Sound. 16mm Color. subtitles. *Rental:* Charard Motion Pics.

Summer in the City. Wim Wenders. Ger. 1970. Germany. (Experimental). 101 min. Sound. 16mm B&W. subtitles. *Rental:* Liberty Co.

Summer Interlude. Orig. Title: Illicit Interlude. Maj-Britt Nilson. Directed by Ingmar Bergman. Swed. 1950. Sweden. 95 min. Sound. 16mm B&W. subtitles. *Rental:* Films Inc & Janus Films.

Summer Love. John Saxon & Molly Bee. Directed by Charles Haas. 1956. Universal. 85 min. Sound. 16mm B&W. *Rental:* Swank Motion.

Summer Lovers. Peter Gallagher, Daryl Hannah & Valerie Quennessen. Directed by Randal Kleiser. 1982. Orion. 98 min. Sound. 16mm Color. *Rental:* Swank Motion.

Summer Madness *see* Summertime.

Summer Magic. Hayley Mills, Burl Ives & Dorothy McGuire. 1963. Disney. 109 min. Sound. 16mm Color. *Rental:* Buchan Pic, Cine Craft, Cousino Visual Ed, Disney Prod, Film Ctr DC, Films Inc, Newman Film Lib, MGM United & U of IL Film.

Summer of My German Soldier, The. Kristy McNichol, Esther Rolle & Bruce Davison. 1978. Learning Corp. of America. 98 min. Sound. 16mm Color. *Rental:* Budget Films, Kit Parker, Learning Corp Am, Roas Films, Twyman Films, U of IL Film & Westcoast Films. *Lease:* Learning Corp Am. *Rental:* Learning Corp Am, *Lease:* Learning Corp Am, Videotape version.

Summer of Our Secrets. Videotape *Sale:* Vidamerica.

Summer Paradise. Brigitta Valberg & Sif Ruud. Directed by Gunnel Lindblom. Swed. 1978. Sweden. 113 min. Sound. 16mm Color. subtitles. *Rental:* Cinema Five.

Summer Sixty Eight. Directed by Norman Fruchter. 1968. Norman Fruchter. 60 min. Sound. 16mm B&W. *Rental:* CA Newsreel. *Sale:* CA Newsreel.

Summer Solstice. Henry Fonda & Myrna Loy. 1983. ABC. 55 min. Sound. 16mm Color. *Rental:* MTI Tele. *Sale:* MTI Tele.

Summer Stock. British. Title: If You Feel Like Singing. Judy Garland & Gene Kelly. Directed by Charles Walters. 1950. MGM. 109 min. Sound. 16mm Color. *Rental:* MGM United.

Summer to Remember, A. Borya Barkhatov. Directed by Grigor Daniela & Igor Talankin. Rus. 1961. Russia. 80 min. Sound. 16mm B&W. subtitles. *Rental:* Budget Films & Kit Parker. *Sale:* Festival Films & Reel Images. *Sale:* Tamarelles French Film, Videotape version.

Summer Wishes, Winter Dreams. Joanne Woodward, Martin Balsam & Sylvia Sidney. 1973. Columbia. 95 min. Sound. 16mm Color. *Rental:* Budget Films, Films Inc, Kerr Film, Kit Parker, Modern Sound, Natl Film Video, Swank Motion, Welling Motion Pictures & Wholesome Film Ctr.

Summerdog. Hobo. 1978. Film Foundry. 90 min. Sound. 16mm Color. *Rental:* Films Inc & Williams Films.

Summertime. Orig. Title: Summer Madness. Katharine Hepburn & Rossano Brazzi. Directed by David Lean. 1955. United Artists. 99 min. Sound. 16mm Color. *Rental:* Arcus Film, Budget Films, Films Inc, Kit Parker, Learning Corp Am, Modern Sound, New Cinema, Roas Films, Twyman Films & U of IL Film. *Sale:* Learning Corp Am.

Summertime Killer, The. Karl Malden & Olivia Hussey. Directed by Antonio Issai Isamendi. 1973. Embassy. 100 min. Sound. 16mm Color. *Rental:* Films Inc.

Summertree. Michael Douglas, Jack Warden & Barbara Bel Geddes. Directed by Anthony Newley. 1971. Columbia. 88 min. Sound. 16mm Color. *Rental:* Budget Films, Cine Craft, Films Inc, Inst Cinema, Welling Motion Pictures, Westcoast Films & Willoughby Peer.

Sun Also Rises, The. Tyrone Power & Ava Gardner. Directed by Henry King. 1957. Fox. (Anamorphic). 129 min. Sound. 16mm Color. *Rental:* Films Inc & Twyman Films.

Sun Comes Up, The. Jeanette MacDonald & Lloyd Nolan. Directed by Richard Thorpe. 1949. MGM. 95 min. Sound. 16mm Color. *Rental:* MGM United.

Sun Dagger, The. 1983. Bullfrog. (Documentary). 58 min. Sound. 16mm Color. *Rental:* Bullfrog Films & U Cal Media. *Sale:* Bullfrog Films. *Rental:* Bullfrog Films, Videotape version, 29 min. version.

Sun Never Sets, The. Douglas Fairbanks Jr. & Basil Rathbone. Directed by Rowland V. Lee. 1939. Universal. 98 min. Sound. 16mm B&W. *Rental:* Swank Motion.

Sun Shines Bright, The. Charles Winninger & Arleen Whelan. Directed by John Ford. 1954. Republic. 92 min. Sound. 16mm B&W. *Rental:* Ivy Films. *Sale:* Rep Pic Film.

Sun Valley Cyclone. Bill Elliott. Directed by R. G. Springsteen. 1946. Republic. 54 min. Sound. 16mm B&W. *Rental:* Ivy Films.

Sun Valley Serenade. Sonja Henie & John Payne. Directed by Bruce Humberstone. 1941. Fox. 85 min. Sound. 16mm B&W. *Rental:* Films Inc.

Sunbeam Solution, The. Films Inc. (Documentary). 52 min. Sound. 16mm Color. *Sale:* Films Inc. *Sale:* Films Inc, Videotape version.

Sunbonnet Sue. Gale Storm & Phil Regan. Directed by Ralph Murphy. 1945. Monogram. 89 min. Sound. 16mm B&W. *Rental:* Film Ctr DC, Hurlock Cine & Lewis Film.

Sunburn. Farrah Fawcett, Charles Grodin & Art Carney. Directed by Richard C. Sarafian. 1979. Paramount. 110 min. Sound. 16mm Color. *Rental:* Films Inc.

Sunday & Monday in Silence. 1973. Media Guild. (Documentary). 52 min. Sound. 16mm Color. *Rental:* Media Guild & U of IL Film. *Sale:* Media Guild. *Sale:* Media Guild, Videotape version.

Sunday, Bloody, Sunday. Peter Finch, Glenda Jackson & Murray Head. Directed by John Schlesinger. 1971. Britain. 110 min. Sound. 16mm Color. *Rental:* MGM United.

Sunday Dinner for a Soldier. Anne Baxter & John Hodiak. Directed by Lloyd Bacon. 1944. Fox. 86 min. Sound. 16mm B&W. *Rental:* Films Inc.

Sunday in New York. Cliff Robertson & Jane Fonda. Directed by Peter Tewksbury. 1963. MGM. 105 min. Sound. 16mm Color. *Rental:* MGM United.

Sunday Lovers. Roger Moore, Lynn Redgrave & Gene Wilder. Directed by Bryan Forbes, Gene Wilder & Edouard Molinaro. 1981. 127 min. Sound. 16mm Color. *Rental:* MGM United. *Rental:* MGM United, Videotape version.

Sunday Punch. William Lundigan & Jean Rogers. Directed by David Miller. 1942. MGM. 76 min. Sound. 16mm B&W. *Rental:* MGM United.

Sunday Sinners. Mamie Smith. Directed by Arthur Dreifuss. 1941. 65 min. Sound. 16mm B&W. *Rental:* Budget Films.

Sundays & Cybele. Hardy Kruger, Nicole Courcel & Patricia Gozzi. Directed by Serge Bourguignon. Fr. 1962. France. 110 min. Sound. 16mm B&W. subtitles. *Sale:* Budget Films, Corinth Films, Swank Motion, Twyman Films & Video Comm. *Sale:* Reel Images, Anamorphic version. *Rental:* Morcraft Films, Super 8 anamorphic version.

Sundown. Bruce Cabot & Gene Tierney. Directed by Henry Hathaway. 1941. United Artists. 105 min. Sound. 16mm B&W. *Rental:* Learning Corp Am & Video Comm. *Sale:* Cinema Concepts, Learning Corp Am & Reel Images.

Sundown Fury. Don Barry. Directed by George Sherman. 1942. Republic. 56 min. Sound. 16mm B&W. *Rental:* Ivy Films. *Sale:* Rep Pic Film.

Sundown in Santa Fe. Allan Lane. Directed by R. G. Springsteen. 1948. Republic. 60 min. Sound. 16mm B&W. *Rental:* Ivy Films. *Sale:* Rep Pic Film & Nostalgia Merchant.

Sundown Kid, The. Don Barry. Directed by Elmer Clifton. 1943. Republic. 55 min. Sound. 16mm B&W. *Rental:* Ivy Films. *Sale:* Rep Pic Film.

Sundown on the Prairie. Tex Ritter. Directed by Al Herman. 1939. Monogram. 55 min. Sound. 16mm B&W. *Rental:* Hurlock Cine.

Sundown Saunders. Bob Steele. Directed by Robert N. Bradbury. 1936. Supreme. 60 min. Sound. 16mm B&W. *Rental:* Budget Films.

Sundown Shindig. 1979. PBS. (Concert). 52 min. Sound. Videotape Color. *Rental:* PBS Video. *Sale:* PBS Video.

Sundown Trail. Tom Keene & Marion Shilling. Directed by Robert Hill. 1932. RKO. 55 min. Sound. 16mm B&W. *Rental:* RKO General Pics.

Sundowners, The. John Barrymore Jr. & Robert Preston. Directed by George Templeton. 1950. Eagle. 83 min. Sound. 16mm B&W. *Rental:* Budget Films & Film Classics. *Rental:* Ivy Films, Color version.

Sundowners, The. Deborah Kerr & Robert Mitchum. Directed by Fred Zinnemann. 1960. Warners. 133 min. Sound. 16mm Color. *Rental:* Charard Motion Pics, Films Inc, Inst Cinema, Twyman Films, Video Comm & Willoughby Peer.

Sunflower. Sophia Loren & Marcello Mastroianni. Directed by Vittorio De Sica. 1970. Italy. 101 min. Sound. 16mm Color. dubbed. *Rental:* Films Inc & Video Comm.

Sunken Treasure. 1972. Churchill Films. (Documentary). 52 min. Sound. 16mm Color. *Rental:* Churchill Films. *Rental:* Churchill Films, Videotape version.

Sunny. Marilyn Miller & Lawrence Gray. Directed by William A. Seiter. 1930. Warners. 80 min. Sound. 16mm B&W. *Rental:* MGM United.

Sunny. Ray Bolger & Dame Anna Neagle. Directed by Herbert Wilcox. 1940. RKO. 100 min. Sound. 16mm B&W. *Rental:* Budget Films. *Sale:* Cinema Concepts & Reel Images.

Sunny Side of the Street, The. Orig. Title: On the Sunny Side of the Street. Frankie Laine & Terry Moore. Directed by Richard Quine. 1951. Columbia. 71 min. Sound. 16mm Color. *Rental:* Welling Motion Pictures.

Sunny Side Up. Janet Gaynor & Charles Farrell. Directed by David Butler. 1929. Fox. 123 min. Sound. 16mm B&W. *Rental:* Killiam Collect.

Sunrise. Janet Gaynor & George O'Brien. Directed by F. W. Murnau. 1927. Fox. (Musical score only). 95 min. Sound. 16mm *Rental:* Killiam Collect & Museum Mod Art. *Sale:* Blackhawk Films, Super 8 sound version. *Sale:* Blackhawk Films, Super 8 silent version. *Rental:* Killiam Collect, Tinted version.

Sunrise Trail. Bob Steele. Directed by J. P. McCarthy. 1931. Tiffany. 60 min. Sound. 16mm B&W. *Rental:* Mogulls Films.

Sunscorched. Mark Stevens & Marianne Koch. Directed by Mark Stevens & Jesus Jaime Balcazar. 1965. Germany. 78 min. Sound. 16mm Color. dubbed. *Rental:* Ivy Films & Video Comm.

Sunset Boulevard. William Holden & Gloria Swanson. Directed by Billy Wilder. 1950. Paramount. 108 min. Sound. 16mm B&W. *Rental:* Films Inc.

Sunset Carson Rides Again. Sunset Carson. Directed by Oliver Drake. 1948. Astor. 62 min. Sound. 16mm B&W. *Rental:* Budget Films. *Sale:* Video Comm, Videotape version.

Sunset Cove. Jay B. Larson & Karen Fredrik. Directed by Al Adamson. 1978. Cal-AM. 87 min. Sound. 16mm Color. *Rental:* Films Inc.

Sunset in El Dorado. Roy Rogers. Directed by Frank McDonald. 1945. Republic. 54 min. Sound. 16mm B&W. *Rental:* Ivy Films. *Sale:* Rep Pic Film. *Sale:* Video Comm, Videotape version.

Sunset in the Desert. Roy Rogers. Directed by Joseph Kane. 1942. Republic. 54 min. Sound. 16mm B&W. *Rental:* Ivy Films. *Sale:* Rep Pic Film.

Sunset in the West. Roy Rogers. Directed by William Witney. 1950. Republic. 67 min. Sound. 16mm B&W. *Rental:* Ivy Films. *Sale:* Rep Pic Film.

Sunset in Wyoming. Gene Autry. Directed by William Morgan. 1941. Republic. 54 min. Sound. 16mm B&W. *Rental:* Ivy Films.

Sunset Range. Hoot Gibson. Directed by Ray McCarey. 1935. First Division. 59 min. Sound. 16mm B&W. *Rental:* Ivy Films. *Sale:* Classics Assoc NY & Rep Pic Film.

Sunset Serenade. Roy Rogers. Directed by William Morgan. 1942. Republic. 54 min. Sound. 16mm B&W. *Rental:* Ivy Films. *Sale:* Rep Pic Film.

Sunset Trail. William Boyd. Directed by Lesley Selander. 1938. Paramount. 60 min. Sound. 16mm B&W. *Rental:* Budget Films, Roas Films.

Sunshine Boys, The. Walter Matthau, George Burns & Richard Benjamin. Directed by Herbert Ross. 1975. MGM. 111 min. Sound. 16mm Color. *Rental:* MGM United. *Rental:* MGM United, Videotape version.

Sunshine's on the Way. Amy Wright & Scatman Crothers. 1981. Learning Corp. 47 min. Sound. 16mm Color. *Rental:* Learning Corp Am & Utah Media. *Sale:* Learning Corp Am.

Sunspot Mystery, The. 1976. Nova. (Documentary). 58 min. Sound. 16mm Color. *Rental:* U Cal Media, Videotape version.

Super, El. Trans. Title: Super, The. Raymundo Hidalgo-Gato & Reynaldo Medina. Directed by Leon Ichaso & Orlando Jimenez-Leal. 1979. New Yorker. 90 min. Sound. 16mm Color. subtitles. *Rental:* New Yorker Films.

Super, The see Super.

Super Cops. Ron Liebman & David Selby. Directed by Gordon Parks. 1973. MGM. 94 min. Sound. 16mm Color. *Rental:* MGM United.

Super Dude. William Elliott & Marki Bey. Directed by Henry Hathaway. 1976. Dimensions. 90 min. Sound. 16mm Color. *Sale:* Salz Ent.

Super Fly. Ron O'Neal. Directed by Gordon Parks Jr. 1972. Warners. 93 min. Sound. 16mm Color. *Rental:* Swank Motion, Twyman Films & Williams Films.

Super Fuzz. Terence Hill & Ernest Borgnine. Directed by Sergio Corbucci. 1981. Embassy. 97 min. Sound. 16mm Color. *Rental:* Films Inc.

Super Ninja. Cheing Tien Chi. Hong Kong. 109 min. Sound. 16mm *Rental:* WW Enter. *Rental:* WW Enter, Videotape version.

Super Plastic Elastic Goggles. Judy Carne, James Earl Jones & James Coco. 1971. NBC. 48 min. Sound. 16mm Color. *Rental:* Films Inc. *Sale:* Films Inc.

Super Seal. Foster Brooks & Sterling Holloway. Directed by Michael Dugan. 1975. Key International. 86 min. Sound. 16mm Color. *Rental:* Budget Films, Modern Sound & Westcoast Films.

Super Seven, The. Filmation. (Animated). 66 min. Sound. 16mm Color. *Rental:* Williams Films.

Super Show. Led Zeppelin & Eric Clapton. Directed by John Crone. 1969. Richard Price. 84 min. Sound. 16mm Color. *Rental:* Budget Films, Kit Parker & Video Comm.

Super Sleuth. Terry-Thomas & Margaret Lee. 1965. Britain. 84 min. Sound. 16mm Color. *Rental:* Video Comm.

Super Sleuth. Ann Sothern & Jack Oakie. Directed by Ben Stoloff. 1937. RKO. 70 min. Sound. 16mm B&W. *Rental:* RKO General Pics.

Super Stooges vs. the Wonder Woman. Nick Jordan. Directed by Al Bradley. 1975. Italy. 90 min. Sound. 16mm Color. dubbed. *Rental:* Swank Motion & Welling Motion Pictures.

Super Vixens. 1976. Meyer. (Exploitation). 85 min. Sound. 16mm Color. *Rental:* Corinth Films.

Superbug, Super Agent. Robert Mark & Heidi Hansen. Directed by Rudolf Zehetgruber. 1976. Central Park. 81 min. Sound. 16mm B&W. *Rental:* Swank Motion.

Superbug, the Wild One. Richard Lynn & Constance Siech. Directed by David Mark. 1976. Central Park. 81 min. Sound. 16mm Color. *Rental:* Swank Motion.

Superchick. Joyce Jillson. Directed by Ed Forsyth. 1973. Crown. 94 min. Sound. 16mm Color. *Rental:* Budget Films & Video Comm. *Lease:* Video Comm.

Superdad. Bob Crane & Barbara Rush. Directed by Vincent McEveety. 1974. Disney. 95 min. Sound. 16mm Color. *Rental:* Disney Prod & Films Inc.

Superfluous People. 1962. CBS. (Documentary). 54 min. Sound. 16mm B&W. *Rental:* McGraw-Hill Films, Mass Media, Syracuse U Film & U of IL Film. *Sale:* McGraw-Hill Films.

Superfly T. N. T. Ron O'Neal & Roscoe Lee Browne. Directed by Ron O'Neal. 1973. Paramount. 87 min. Sound. 16mm Color. *Rental:* Films Inc.

Superliners, The: Twilight of an Era. 59 min. Sound. 16mm Color. *Rental:* Natl Geog. *Sale:* Natl Geog. *Sale:* Natl Geog, Videotape version.

Superman II. Christopher Reeve & Margot Kidder. Directed by Richard Lester. 1980. Warners. 127 min. Sound. 16mm Color. *Rental:* Swank Motion. *Rental:* Swank Motion, Videotape version.

Superman III. Christopher Reeve, Richard Pryor & Margot Kidder. Directed by Richard Lester. 1983. Warners. 123 min. Sound. 16mm Color. *Rental:* Swank Motion. *Rental:* Swank Motion, Videotape version.

Superman: The Movie. Christopher Reeve, Gene Hackman, Glenn Ford & Margot Kidder. Directed by Richard Donner. 1978. Warners. 142 min. Sound. 16mm Color. *Rental:* Swank Motion. *Rental:* Swank Motion, Anamorphic version. *Rental:* Swank Motion, Videotape version.

Supernatural. Carole Lombard & Randolph Scott. Directed by Victor Halperin. 1933. Paramount. 67 min. Sound. 16mm B&W. *Rental:* Swank Motion.

Supersonic Race: Jet Planes. 1966. MCG-H. 60 min. Sound. 16mm B&W. *Rental:* Syracuse U Film. *Sale:* McGraw-Hill Films.

Supersonic Saucer, The. Marcia Monolescue. Directed by S. C. Fergusson. 1956. Britain. 50 min. Sound. 16mm B&W. *Sale:* Lucerne Films.

Support Your Local Gunfighter. James Garner & Suzanne Pleshette. Directed by Burt Kennedy. 1971. United Artists. 92 min. Sound. 16mm Color. *Rental:* MGM United.

Support Your Local Sheriff. James Garner & Joan Hackett. Directed by Burt Kennedy. 1969. United Artists. 92 min. Sound. 16mm Color. *Rental:* Arcus Film, Buchan Pic, MGM United, Modern Sound, Roas Films, Westcoast Films & Williams Films.

Suppose They Gave a War & Nobody Came? Tony Curtis & Brian Keith. Directed by Hy Averback. 1970. ABC. 111 min. Sound. 16mm Color. *Rental:* Films Inc.

Supreme Court & Civil Liberties, The: The Bank Secrecy Act of 1970. Henry Fonda, Burt Lancaster & John Saxon. 1979. PBS. 58 min. Sound. Videotape Color. *Rental:* PBS Video. *Sale:* PBS Video.

Supreme Secret, The. 1968. (Cast unlisted). 55 min. Sound. 16mm B&W. *Rental:* Roas Films.

Supresa Del Divorcio, La. 1950. Mexico. (Cast unlisted). 90 min. Sound. 16mm B&W. *Rental:* Film Classics.

Suprise Package. Yul Brynner & Mitzi Gaynor. Directed by Edward Sloman. 1960. Columbia. 100 min. Sound. 16mm B&W. *Rental:* Inst Cinema & Welling Motion Pictures.

Sur Faces. Directed by Ed Emschwiller. 1977. WNET. (Experimental). 59 min. Videotape Color. *Rental:* Electro Art. *Lease:* Electro Art.

Sur Vivre *see* There Are Others Worse Off Than Us....

Surf, The *see* Sound of Waves.

Surf Party. Bobby Vinton. Directed by Maury Dexter. 1964. Fox. 68 min. Sound. 16mm B&W. *Rental:* Films Inc.

Surgeon's Knife. Donald Houston. Directed by Gordon Parry. 1957. 83 min. 16mm *Rental:* A Twyman Pres.

Surrender. Mary Philbin & Ivan Mousjokine. Directed by Edward Sloman. 1927. Universal. 70 min. Silent. 16mm B&W. *Rental:* Em Gee Film Lib. *Sale:* Glenn Photo. *Sale:* Glenn Photo, Super 8 silent version.

Surrender. John Carroll, Walter Brennan & Vera Ralston. Directed by Allan Dwan. 1950. Republic. 90 min. Sound. 16mm B&W. *Rental:* Ivy Films. *Sale:* Rep Pic Film.

Surrender at Appomattox. 1974. Wolper. (Documentary). 52 min. Sound. 16mm B&W. *Rental:* Films Inc, Iowa Films, Syracuse U Film & U Mich Media. *Sale:* Films Inc. *Rental:* Films Inc, *Sale:* Films Inc, Color version.

Surrounded by Women. Franchot Tone & Virginia Bruce. Directed by George B. Seitz. 1937. MGM. 89 min. Sound. 16mm B&W. *Rental:* MGM United.

Surveillance: Who's Watching. 1972. NET. (Documentary). 60 min. Sound. 16mm B&W. *Rental:* Indiana AV Ctr & U Cal Media. *Sale:* Indiana Av Ctr. *Sale:* Indiana Av Ctr, Videotape version.

Survey of Black & White Attitudes. 1968. CBS. (Documentary). 55 min. Sound. 16mm B&W. *Rental:* Phoenix Films. *Sale:* Phoenix Films.

Survival. 1975. Mark IV. (Cast unlisted). 75 min. Sound. 16mm Color. *Rental:* G Herne.

Survival of Space Ship Earth. 1972. Warners. (Documentary). 60 min. Sound. 16mm Color. *Rental:* Swank Motion, Twyman Films & Wholesome Film Ctr.

Survival on the Prairie. 1969. NBC. (Documentary). 53 min. Sound. 16mm Color. *Rental:* Films Inc, Iowa Films, Syracuse U Film & U Mich Media. *Sale:* Films Inc. *Sale:* Films Inc, Videotape version.

Survive! Pablo Ferrel. Directed by Rene Cardona. 1976. Paramount. 85 min. Sound. 16mm Color. *Rental:* Films Inc.

Survivors, The. Directed by Steven Okazaki. 1982. First Run. (Documentary). 58 min. Sound. 16mm Color. *Rental:* First Run & U Mich Media. *Lease:* First Run.

Survivors, The. Walter Matthau & Robin Williams. Directed by Michael Ritchie. 1983. Columbia. 105 min. Sound. 16mm Color. *Rental:* Swank Motion. *Rental:* Swank Motion, Videotape version.

Susan & God. Joan Crawford, Fredric March, Rita Hayworth & Ruth Hussey. Directed by George Cukor. 1940. MGM. 117 min. Sound. 16mm B&W. *Rental:* MGM United.

Susan Lennox: Her Fall & Rise. Greta Garbo & Jean Hersholt. Directed by Robert Z. Leonard. 1931. MGM. 75 min. Sound. 16mm B&W. *Rental:* MGM United.

Susan Slept Here. Dick Powell & Debbie Reynolds. Directed by Frank Tashlin. 1954. RKO. 97 min. Sound. 16mm Color. *Rental:* Bosco Films, Budget Films, Video Comm, Westcoast Films & Wholesome Film Ctr. *Lease:* Video Comm.

Susan Starr. 1965. Time-Life. (Documentary). 54 min. Sound. 16mm B&W. *Rental:* Time-Life Multimedia. *Sale:* Time-Life Multimedia.

Susana. Directed by Luis Bunuel. Span. 1951. Spain. 82 min. Sound. 16mm B&W. subtitles. *Rental:* New Yorker Films.

Susanna *see* Shepherd of the Ozarks.

Susanna Pass. Roy Rogers. Directed by William Witney. 1949. Republic. 67 min. Sound. 16mm Color. *Rental:* Ivy Films. *Sale:* Rep Pic Film & Nostalgia Merchant.

Susannah of the Mounties. Shirley Temple & Randolph Scott. Directed by William A. Seiter. 1939. Fox. 73 min. Sound. 16mm B&W. *Rental:* Films Inc.

Susie Steps Out. David Bruce. Directed by Reginald Le Borg. 1946. United Artists. 67 min. Sound. 16mm B&W. *Rental:* Ivy Films.

Suspect, The. Charles Laughton & Ella Raines. Directed by Robert Siodmak. 1944. Universal. 85 min. Sound. 16mm B&W. *Rental:* Swank Motion.

Suspects, The. Mimsy Farmer & Paul Meurisse. Directed by Michel Wyn. 1978. France. 95 min. Sound. 16mm Color. dubbed. *Rental:* Modern Sound.

Suspense. Barry Sullivan & Bonita Granville. Directed by Frank Tuttle. 1946. Monogram. 101 min. Sound. 16mm B&W. *Rental:* Hurlock Cine & Mogulls Films.

Suspense Thriller Program: No. One. 70 min. Sound. 16mm *Rental:* Budget Films.

Suspense Thriller Program: No. Two. 70 min. Sound. 16mm *Rental:* Budget Films.

Suspicion. Cary Grant & Joan Fontaine. Directed by Alfred Hitchcock. 1941. RKO. 99 min. Sound. 16mm B&W. *Rental:* Films Inc. *Lease:* Films Inc, Super 8 sound version.

Suspira. Jessica Harper, Joan Bennett & Alida Valli. Directed by Dario Argento. 1977. International Classics. (Anamorphic). 92 min. Sound. 16mm Color. *Rental:* Films Inc.

Sutter's Gold. Edward Arnold & Lee Tracy. Directed by James Cruze. 1936. Universal. 94 min. Sound. 16mm B&W. *Rental:* Swank Motion.

Suzy. Jean Harlow & Cary Grant. Directed by George Fitzmaurice. 1936. MGM. 99 min. Sound. 16mm B&W. *Rental:* MGM United.

Svengali. John Barrymore & Marian Marsh. Directed by Archie Mayo. 1931. Warners. 81 min. Sound. 16mm B&W. *Rental:* Budget Films, Em Gee Film Lib, Films Inc, Kit Parker, MGM United, Standard Film, Video Comm, Wholesome Film Ctr & Willoughby Peer. *Sale:* Cinema Concepts, E Finney, Festival Films, Griggs Movie, Ivy Films, Tamarelles French Film & Video Comm. *Sale:* Festival Films, Videotape version.

Svengali. Hildegarde Neff & Donald Wolfit. Directed by Noel Langley. 1955. Britain. 82 min. Sound. 16mm Color. *Rental:* Budget Films & Video Comm.

Swamp Dwellers. 1973. Wole Soyinka. (Documentary). 58 min. Sound. 16mm B&W. *Rental:* Phoenix Films. *Sale:* Phoenix Films.

Swamp of Lost Monsters. Gaston Santos & Manola Savedra. Directed by Rafael Baledon. 1960. Mexico. 78 min. Sound. 16mm B&W. dubbed English. *Rental:* Budget Films.

Swamp Water. Walter Brennan, Walter Huston & Anne Baxter. Directed by Jean Renoir. 1941. Fox. 90 min. Sound. 16mm Color. *Rental:* Films Inc.

Swan, The. Adolphe Menjou & Ricardo Cortez. Directed by Dimitri Buchowetzski. 1925. Paramount. 90 min. Silent. 16mm B&W. *Sale:* Morcraft Films. *Rental:* A Twyman Pres.

Swan, The. Orig. Title: One Romantic Night. Lillian Gish & Rod La Rocque. Directed by Paul L. Stein. 1931. United Artists. 72 min. Sound. 16mm B&W. *Rental:* Film Classics & Twyman Films. *Rental:* Film Classics, Videotape version.

Swan, The. Sir Alec Guinness & Grace Kelly. Directed by Charles Vidor. 1956. MGM. 107 min. Sound. 16mm B&W. *Rental:* MGM United. *Rental:* Films Inc, Anamorphic version.

Swan Lake. Directed by Appolinari Dudko. 1968. Russia. (Dance). 90 min. Sound. 16mm Color. *Rental:* Corinth Films.

Swanee River. Don Ameche & Andrea Leeds. Directed by Sidney Lanfield. 1939. Fox. 84 min. Sound. 16mm B&W. *Rental:* Films Inc.

Swap, The: Sam's Song. Robert De Niro & Jennifer Warren. Directed by Jordan Leondopoulos. 1969. Cannon. 92 min. Sound. 16mm Color. *Rental:* Swank Motion.

Swarm, The. Michael Caine, Henry Fonda & Richard Widmark. Directed by Irwin Allen. 1978. Warners. 116 min. Sound. 16mm Color. *Rental:* Modern Sound, Swank Motion & Williams Films. *Rental:* Swank Motion, Anamorphic version.

Swarming, The. 1980. Britain. (Documentary). 58 min. Videotape Color. *Rental:* Films Inc. *Sale:* Films Inc.

Swashbuckler, The *see* Bedroom Bandit.

Swashbuckler, The. Robert Shaw & James Earl Jones. Directed by James Goldstone. 1976. Universal. 101 min. Sound. 16mm Color. *Rental:* Swank Motion. *Sale:* Tamarelles French Film, Videotape version.

Swastika. Directed by Philippe Mora. 1973. Black Inc. (Documentary). 100 min. Sound. 16mm Color. *Rental:* Films Inc.

Sweat of the Sun, The. 1975. Britain. (Documentary). 52 min. Sound. 16mm Color. *Rental:* Iowa Films, U Cal Media, U of IL Film & U Mich Media.

Sweden: Fire & Ice. 1973. Sweden. (Documentary). 54 min. Sound. 16mm B&W. narrated Eng. *Rental:* Modern Mass.

Sweden: Trouble in Paradise. 1961. CBS. (Documentary). 52 min. Sound. 16mm B&W. *Rental:* Macmillan Films. *Sale:* Macmillan Films.

Sweden, Waiting for the Spring. 1980. 58 min. Sound. Videotape *Rental:* PBS Video. *Sale:* PBS Video.

Swedish Wedding Night. Orig. Title: Assailant, The. Jarl Kulle. Directed by Ake Falck. Swed. 1964. Sweden. 101 min. Sound. 16mm B&W. subtitles. *Rental:* Swank Motion.

Sweeping Against the Winds. Theodore Von Eltz & Dorothy Lee. Directed by Victor Adamson. 1928. Adamson. 52 min. Sound. 16mm B&W. *Sale:* Morcraft Films.

Sweepings. Lionel Barrymore & William Gargan. Directed by John Cromwell. 1933. RKO. 80 min. Sound. 16mm B&W. *Rental:* RKO General Pics.

Sweepstakes. James Gleason & Eddie Quillan. Directed by Albert S. Rogell. 1932. RKO. 77 min. Sound. 16mm *Rental:* RKO General Pics.

Sweepstakes Winner. Marie Wilson & Allen Jenkins. Directed by William McGann. 1939. Warners. 60 min. Sound. 16mm B&W. *Rental:* MGM United.

Sweet Adeline. Irene Dunne & Donald Woods. Directed by Mervyn LeRoy. 1934. Warners. 87 min. Sound. 16mm B&W. *Rental:* MGM United.

Sweet Alyssum. Tyrone Power Sr. & Kathlyn Williams. Directed by Colin Campbell. 1915. Selznick. 45 min. Silent. 16mm B&W. *Rental:* Film Classics. *Sale:* Film Classics.

Sweet & Low Down. Benny Goodman & Linda Darnell. Directed by Archie Mayo. 1944. Fox. 75 min. Sound. 16mm B&W. *Rental:* Willoughby Peer.

Sweet & the Bitter, The. Paul Richards & Yoko Tani. 1965. 86 min. Sound. 16mm B&W. *Sale:* Rep Pic Film.

Sweet Bird of Youth. Paul Newman & Geraldine Page. Directed by Richard Brooks. 1962. MGM. 125 min. Sound. 16mm Color. *Rental:* MGM United. *Rental:* MGM United, Anamorphic version.

Sweet Charity. Shirley MacLaine & Ricardo Montalban. Directed by Bob Fosse. 1969. Universal. 157 min. Sound. 16mm Color. *Rental:* Swank Motion.

Sweet Hours. Directed by Carlos Saura. Span. 1982. Spain. 105 min. Sound. 16mm Color. subtitles. *Rental:* New Yorker Films.

Sweet Jesus, Preacher Man. Roger E. Mosley. Directed by Henning Schellerup. 1973. MGM. 103 min. Sound. 16mm Color. *Rental:* MGM United.

Sweet Kitty Bellairs. Claudia Dell & Walter Pidgeon. Directed by Alfred E. Green. 1930. Warners. 63 min. Sound. 16mm B&W. *Rental:* MGM United.

Sweet Love Bitter. Orig. Title: It Won't Rub Off, Baby. Dick Gregory, Robert Hooks, Don Murray & Herbert Danska. 1968. Film Two Associates. 92 min. Sound. 16mm B&W. *Rental:* Films Inc.

Sweet Mama. Alice White & David Manners. Directed by Edward Cline. 1930. Warners. 54 min. Sound. 16mm B&W. *Rental:* MGM United.

Sweet Music. Rudy Vallee, Ann Dvorak & Helen Morgan. Directed by Alfred E. Green. 1935. Warners. 100 min. Sound. 16mm B&W. *Rental:* MGM United.

Sweet Revenge. Orig. Title: Dandy, the All-American Girl. Stockard Channing & Sam Waterston. Directed by Jerry Schatzberg. 1977. MGM. 90 min. Sound. 16mm Color. *Rental:* MGM United. *Rental:* MGM United, Anamorphic version.

Sweet Ride, The. Tony Franciosa & Michael Sarrazin. Directed by Harvey Hart. 1968. Fox. 110 min. Sound. 16mm Color. *Rental:* Films Inc.

Sweet Rosie O'Grady. Betty Grable & Robert Young. Directed by Irving Cummings. 1943. Fox. 75 min. Sound. 16mm Color. *Rental:* Films Inc.

Sweet Smell of Sex, The. Directed by Robert Downey. Barnard L. Sackett. 72 min. Sound. 16mm Color. *Rental:* Filmmakers Coop.

Sweet Smell of Success, The. Burt Lancaster & Tony Curtis. Directed by Alexander Mackendrick. 1957. United Artists. 96 min. Sound. 16mm B&W. *Rental:* MGM United.

Sweet Sweetback's Baadasssss Song. Melvin Van Peebles. Directed by Melvin Van Peebles. 1971. Cinemation. 97 min. Sound. 16mm Color. *Rental:* Direct Cinema.

Sweet William. Sam Waterson. 86 min. Sound. Videotape *Rental:* WW Enter.

Sweetheart *see* Liebalala.

Sweetheart of Sigma Chi, The. Elyse Knox & Phil Regan. Directed by Jack Bernhard. 1946. Monogram. 72 min. Sound. 16mm B&W. *Rental:* Film Ctr DC.

Sweetheart of the Campus. Ruby Keeler, Ozzie Nelson & Harriet Hilliard. 1941. Columbia. 67 min. Sound. 16mm B&W. *Rental:* Bosco Films & Kit Parker.

Sweetheart of the Navy. Eric Linden & Cecilia Parker. Directed by Duncan Mansfield. 1937. Grand National. 70 min. Sound. 16mm B&W. *Rental:* Mogulls Films.

Sweethearts. Jeanette MacDonald, Nelson Eddy & Ray Bolger. Directed by W. S. Van Dyke. 1938. MGM. 114 min. Sound. 16mm B&W. *Rental:* MGM United.

Sweethearts on Parade. Ray Middleton & Lucille Norman. Directed by Allan Dwan. 1953. Republic. 90 min. Sound. 16mm Color. *Rental:* Ivy Films & Rep Pic Film. *Lease:* Rep Pic Film.

Swifty. Hoot Gibson. Directed by Alan James. 1936. Grand National. 61 min. Sound. 16mm B&W. *Rental:* Video Comm.

Swimmer, The. Burt Lancaster & Janice Rule. Directed by Frank Perry. 1968. Columbia. 94 min. Sound. 16mm Color. *Rental:* Budget Films, Cine Craft, Films Inc, Inst Cinema, Video Comm, Westcoast Films, Welling Motion Pictures, Wholesome Film Ctr & Willoughby Peer.

Swimming Pool, The. Alain Delon & Romy Schneider. Directed by Jacques Deray. 1970. France. 87 min. Sound. 16mm Color. dubbed. *Rental:* Films Inc.

Swindle, The. Trans. Title: Bidone, Il. Richard Basehart & Giulietta Masina. Directed by Federico Fellini. Ital. 1955. Italy. 92 min. Sound. 16mm B&W. subtitles. *Rental:* Ivy Films.

Swing High *see* Jive Junction.

Swing High, Swing Low. Carole Lombard & Fred MacMurray. Directed by Mitchell Leisen. 1936. Paramount. 96 min. Sound. 16mm B&W. *Rental:* Budget Films & Em Gee Film Lib. *Sale:* Morcraft Films & Reel Images. *Rental:* Ivy Films, *Sale:* Ivy Films & Reel Images, Super 8 sound version.

Swing Hostess. Martha Tilton. Directed by Sam Newfield. 1944. PRC. 80 min. Sound. 16mm B&W. *Rental:* Mogulls Films.

Swing It, Sailor. Wallace Ford & Isabel Jewell. Directed by Raymond Cannon. 1937. Grand National. 60 min. Sound. 16mm B&W. *Rental:* Mogulls Films.

Swing Parade. Gale Storm & Phil Regan. Directed by Phil Karlson. 1946. Monogram. 74 min. Sound. 16mm B&W. *Rental:* Film Ctr DC, Hurlock Cine & Film Ctr DC.

Swing Shift. Goldie Hawn & Kurt Russell. Directed by Jonathan Demme. 1985. Warners. 113 min. Sound. 16mm Color. *Rental:* Swank Motion.

Swing, Sister, Swing. Ken Murray & Johnny Downs. Directed by Joseph Santley. 1938. Universal. 70 min. Sound. 16mm B&W. *Rental:* Film Ctr DC & Mogulls Films.

Swing Time. Fred Astaire & Gingers Rogers. Directed by George Stevens. 1936. RKO. 103 min. Sound. 16mm B&W. *Rental:* Films Inc.

Swing Your Lady. Humphrey Bogart & Penny Singleton. Directed by Ray Enright. 1938. Warners. 77 min. Sound. 16mm B&W. *Rental:* MGM United.

Swing Your Partner. Vera Vague & Roger Clark. Directed by Frank McDonald. 1943. Republic. 72 min. Sound. 16mm B&W. *Rental:* Ivy Films.

Swinger, The. Ann-Margret & Tony Franciosa. Directed by George Sidney. 1966. Paramount. 81 min. Sound. 16mm Color. *Rental:* Films Inc.

Swingin' Along. Tommy Noonan & Peter Marshall. Directed by Charles Barton. 1962. Fox. 74 min. Sound. 16mm Color. *Rental:* Films Inc. *Rental:* Films Inc, Anamorphic version.

Swingin' on a Rainbow. Jane Frazee & Brad Taylor. Directed by William Beaudine. 1945. Republic. 72 min. Sound. 16mm B&W. *Rental:* Ivy Films. *Sale:* Rep Pic Film.

Swingin' Maiden, The *see* Iron Maiden.

Swinging Singing Years, The. 1962. 55 min. Sound. 16mm B&W. *Rental:* Budget Films & Em Gee Film Lib. *Sale:* Glenn Photo.

Swinging Summer, A. James Stacy & Martin West. Directed by Robert Sparr. 1965. United Screen Arts. 81 min. Sound. 16mm Color. *Rental:* Films Inc & Video Comm. *Lease:* Video Comm.

Swiss Conspiracy, The. David Janssen, John Saxon & Ray Milland. Directed by Jack Arnold. 1977. S.J. International. 92 min. Sound. 16mm Color. *Rental:* Arcus Film & Modern Films.

Swiss Family Robinson. Thomas Mitchell & Edna Best. Directed by Edward Ludwig. 1940. RKO. 84 min. Sound. 16mm B&W. *Rental:* Budget Films, Film Classics, Inst Cinema & Mogulls Films.

Swiss Family Robinson. John Mills & Dorothy McQuire. Directed by Ken Annakin. 1960. Disney. 126 min. Sound. 16mm Color. *Rental:* Disney Prod, Films Inc, Film Pres, MGM United, Swank Motion & Twyman Films.

Swiss Family Robinson. 1972. Australia. (Animated). 55 min. Sound. 16mm Color. *Rental:* Budget Films, Films Inc, Inst Cinema, Modern Sound, Roas Films, Westcoast Films, Welling Motion Pictures, Wholesome Film Ctr & Williams Films.

Swiss Miss. Stan Laurel & Oliver Hardy. Directed by John G. Blystone. 1938. MGM. 88 min. Sound. 16mm B&W. *Rental:* Alba House, Budget Films, Charard Motion Pics, Em Gee Film Lib, Film Images, Films Inc, Modern Sound, Roas Films, Swank Motion, Twyman Films, Welling Motion Pictures, Westcoast Films & Willoughby Peer. *Sale:* Blackhawk Films. *Sale:* Blackhawk Films, Super 8 sound version.

Switching On: Your Life in the Electronic Age. Filmmakers. (Documentary). 57 min. Videotape Color. *Sale:* Film Makers.

Switzerland. 1977. Bonaventure. (Documentary). 52 min. Sound. 16mm Color. *Rental:* U of IL Film. *Sale:* Bonaventure. *Sale:* Bonaventure, Videotape version.

Sword & the Dragon, The. Trans. Title: Ilya Mourmoretz. Boris Andreyev. Directed by Alexander Ptushko. 1956. Russia. 83 min. Sound. 16mm Color. dubbed. *Rental:* Film Ctr DC & Films Inc.

Sword & the Sorcerer, The. Lee Horsley & Kathleen Beller. Directed by Albert Pynn. 1985. Group I. 100 min. Sound. 16mm Color. *Rental:* Swank Motion. *Rental:* Swank Motion, Videotape version.

Sword in the Stone, The. Directed by Wolfgang Reitherman. 1963. Disney. 75 min. Sound. 16mm Color. *Rental:* Films Inc.

Sword of Ali Baba, The. Peter Mann & Jocelyn Lane. Directed by Virgil Vogel. 1965. Universal. 81 min. Sound. 16mm Color. *Rental:* Williams Films.

Sword of Doom, The. Tatsuya Nakadai & Toshiro Mifune. Directed by Kihachi Okamoto. Jap. 1967. Japan. 122 min. Sound. 16mm B&W Color. subtitles. *Rental:* Films Inc.

Sword of Lancelot, The. Orig. Title: Lancelot & Guinevere. Cornel Wilde & Jean Wallace. Directed by Cornel Wilde. 1963. Universal. 115 min. Sound. 16mm Color. *Rental:* Williams Films.

Sword of Monte Carlo, The. George Montgomery & Paula Corday. Directed by Maurice Geraghty. 1951. Fox. 80 min. Sound. 16mm B&W. *Rental:* Charard Motion Pics & Westcoast Films.

Sword of Sherwood Forest, The. Richard Greene & Peter Cushing. Directed by Terence Fisher. 1961. Columbia. 80 min. Sound. 16mm Color. *Rental:* Budget Films, Cine Craft, Charard Motion Pics, Film Ctr DC, Films Inc, Modern Sound, Roas Films & Welling Motion Pictures.

Sword of the Lord, The. 1976. Canada. (Documentary). 58 min. Sound. 16mm Color. *Rental:* U Cal Media.

Sword of Vengeance III *see* Lightning Swords of Death.

Sword of Venus. Orig. Title: Island of Monte Cristo. Robert Clarke. Directed by Harold Daniels. 1953. RKO. 77 min. Sound. 16mm B&W. *Rental:* Arcus Film.

Swordsman, The. Larry Parks & Ellen Drew. Directed by Joseph Lewis. 1948. Columbia. 81 min. Sound. 16mm Color. *Rental:* Buchan Pic, Cine Craft, Films Inc, Film Ctr DC & Modern Sound.

Swordsman of Siena. Stewart Granger & Christine Kaufman. Directed by Etienne Perier. 1962. MGM. 96 min. Sound. 16mm Color. *Rental:* MGM United. *Rental:* MGM United, Anamorphic version.

Sworn Enemy. Robert Young & Florence Rice. Directed by Edwin L. Marin. 1936. MGM. 74 min. Sound. 16mm B&W. *Rental:* MGM United.

Sylvia. Carroll Baker & George Maharis. Directed by Gordon Douglas. 1965. Paramount. 115 min. Sound. 16mm B&W. *Rental:* Films Inc.

Sylvia & the Phantom. Jacques Tati. Directed by Claude Autant-Lara. Fr. 1945. France. 88 min. Sound. 16mm B&W. subtitles. *Rental:* Films Inc & Janus Films.

Sylvia Scarlett. Katherine Hepburn & Cary Grant. Directed by George Cukor. 1935. RKO. 97 min. Sound. 16mm B&W. *Rental:* Films Inc. *Lease:* Films Inc.

Symbol Man, The *see* Mr. Symbol Man.

Symmetry in Physical Law. 1964. Britain. (Kinescope). 57 min. Sound. 16mm B&W. *Rental:* U Cal Media.

Sympathy for the Devil. Orig. Title: One Plus One. Rolling Stones. Directed by Jean-Luc Godard. 1968. Britain. 104 min. Sound. 16mm Color. *Rental:* New Cinema & New Line Cinema.

Symphonie Einer Welstadt. Ger. 1937. Germany. (Documentary). 79 min. Sound. 16mm B&W. *Rental:* Trans-World Films.

Symphonie Fantastique. 1948. Dance Films. (Dance). 51 min. Sound. 16mm B&W. *Rental:* Dance Film Archive. *Sale:* Dance Film Archive.

Symphonie Fantastique, La. Jean-Louis Barrault & Renee Saint-Cyr. Directed by Christian-Jaque. Fr. 1947. France. 97 min. Sound. 16mm B&W. *Rental:* Films Inc.

Symphonie Pastorale. Michele Morgan & Pierre Blanchar. Directed by Jean Delannoy. Fr. 1947. France. 105 min. Sound. 16mm B&W. subtitles. *Rental:* Trans-World Films. *Rental:* French Am Cul, R#Videotape version.

Symphony for a Massacre: The Corrupt. Michel Auclair & Claude Dauphin. Directed by Jacques Deray. 1965. France. 115 min. Sound. 16mm B&W. dubbed. *Rental:* Modern Sound.

Symphony for a Sinner. Directed by George Kuchar. 1979. 56 min. Sound. 16mm Color. *Rental:* Canyon Cinema.

Symphony of Six Million. Irene Dunne & Ricardo Cortez. Directed by Gregory La Cava. 1932. RKO. 94 min. Sound. 16mm B&W. *Rental:* RKO General Pics.

Symphony of the Don Basin *see* Enthusiasm.

Synanon. Chuck Connors, Eartha Kitt & Stella Stevens. Directed by Richard Quine. 1965. Columbia. 107 min. Sound. 16mm B&W. *Rental:* Kit Parker.

Syncopation. Jackie Cooper & Adolphe Menjou. Directed by William Dieterle. 1942. RKO. 88 min. Sound. 16mm B&W. *Rental:* Mogulls Films.

Szinbad. Zoltan Latinovits & Margit Dayka. Directed by Zoltan Huszariik. Hungarian. 1970. Hungary. 98 min. Sound. 16mm Color. subtitles. *Rental:* Films Inc.

T. A. M. I. Show. Supremes. Directed by Steve Binder. 1971. Electronovision. 90 min. Sound. 16mm B&W. *Rental:* Em Gee Film, New Line Cinema, Welling Motion Pictures, Westcoast Films & Willoughby Peer.

T-Men. Dennis O'Keefe & Wallace Ford. Directed by Anthony Mann. 1947. Eagle Lion. 91 min. Sound. 16mm B&W. *Rental:* Budget Films, Films Inc, Kit Parker, Mogulls Films & Willoughby Peer.

T. N. T. Jackson. Jeanne Bell. Directed by Cirio H. Santiago. 1975. New World. 75 min. Sound. 16mm Color. *Rental:* Films Inc.

T. N. T. Show, The. Donovan & Petula Clark. 90 min. Sound. 16mm Color. *Rental:* Budget Films, Films Inc, Westcoast Films & Willoughby Peer.

T. R. Baskin. Candice Bergen & James Caan. Directed by Herbert Ross. 1971. Paramount. 95 min. Sound. 16mm Color. *Rental:* Films Inc.

Table for Five. Jon Voight & Richard Crenna. Directed by Robert Lieberman. 1983. Warners. 122 min. Sound. 16mm Color. *Rental:* Swank Motion & Williams Films. *Rental:* Swank Motion, Videotape version.

Tabu. Anna Chevalier. Directed by F. W. Murnau. 1931. Paramount. (Musical score only). 78 min. Sound. 16mm B&W. *Rental:* Budget Films, Em Gee Film Lib, Images Film, Ivy Films, Janus Films & Kit Parker. *Sale:* Images Film. *Sale:* Em Gee Film Lib, Videotape version.

Tagenbuch Einer Verlorenin, Das *see* Diary of a Lost Girl.

Tahiti Honey. Simone Simon & Dennis O'Keefe. Directed by John H. Auer. 1943. Republic. 70 min. Sound. 16mm B&W. *Rental:* Ivy Films.

Tail Spin. Alice Faye & Constance Bennett. Directed by Roy Del Ruth. 1939. Fox. 84 min. Sound. 16mm B&W. *Rental:* Films Inc.

Tailor from Torzhok, The. Igor Ilinsky. Directed by Yakov Protazanov. Rus. 1925. Russia. (Musical score only). 64 min. Sound. 16mm B&W. *Rental:* Film Images. *Sale:* Film Images.

Tailor-Made Man, A. William Haines & Dorothy Jordan. Directed by Sam Wood. 1931. MGM. 80 min. Sound. 16mm B&W. *Rental:* MGM United.

Taira Clan Saga, The. Orig. Title: Tales of the Taira Clan. Raizo Ichikawa. Directed by Kenji Mizoguchi. Jap. 1953. Japan. 120 min. Sound. 16mm B&W. subtitles. *Rental:* New Line Cinema. *Sale:* New Line Cinema.

Take, The. Billy Dee Williams & Frankie Avalon. Directed by Robert Hartford-Davis. 1974. Columbia. 93 min. Sound. 16mm Color. *Rental:* Budget Films, Cine Craft, Swank Motion & Westcoast Films.

Take a Girl Like You. Oliver Reed & Hayley Mills. Directed by Jonathan Miller. 1970. Britain. 96 min. Sound. 16mm Color. *Rental:* Budget Films, Cine Craft, Films Inc & Welling Motion Pictures.

Take a Hard Ride. Jim Brown & Dana Andrews. Directed by Anthony Dawson. 1975. Fox. 103 min. Sound. 16mm Color. *Rental:* Films Inc.

Take a Letter, Darling. Rosalind Russell & Fred MacMurray. Directed by Mitchell Leisen. 1942. Paramount. 93 min. Sound. 16mm B&W. *Rental:* Swank Motion.

Take Care of My Little Girl. Jeanne Crain & Dale Robertson. Directed by Jean Negulesco. 1951. Fox. 93 min. Sound. 16mm Color. *Rental:* Films Inc.

Take Down. Lorenzo Lamas & Edward Herrmann. Directed by Kieth Merrill. 1979. Sunrise Entertainment. 107 min. Sound. 16mm Color. *Rental:* Modern Sound, Twyman Films & Williams Films.

Take Her, She's Mine. James Stewart & Sandra Dee. Directed by Henry Koster. 1963. Fox. 98 min. Sound. 16mm Color. *Rental:* Films Inc.

Take It All. Trans. Title: A Tout Prendre. Claude Jutra. Directed by Claude Jutra. Fr. 1966. Canada. 99 min. Sound. 16mm B&W. *Rental:* MGM United.

Take It Big. Ozzie Nelson & Harriet Hilliard. Directed by Frank McDonald. 1944. Paramount. 70 min. Sound. 16mm B&W. *Rental:* Mogulls Films.

Take It From the Top. Annie Girardot. 99 min. Sound. 16mm *Rental:* WW Enter. *Rental:* WW Enter, Videotape version.

Take It or Leave It. Phil Baker & Phil Silvers. Directed by Ben Stoloff. 1944. Fox. 75 min. Sound. 16mm B&W. *Rental:* Films Inc.

Take Me Back to Oklahoma. Tex Ritter. Directed by Al Herman. 1940. Monogram. 55 min. Sound. 16mm B&W. *Rental:* Video Comm. *Sale:* Cinema Concepts & Reel Images. *Rental:* Video Comm, *Lease:* Video Comm, Videotape version.

Take Me Out to the Ball Game. Frank Sinatra & Esther Williams. Directed by Busby Berkeley. 1949. MGM. 93 min. Sound. 16mm Color. *Rental:* MGM United.

Take Me to Paris. Albert Modley & Roberta Haley. Directed by Jack Raymond. 1938. Britain. 66 min. Sound. 16mm B&W. *Rental:* Mogulls Films.

Take Me to Town. Ann Sheridan & Sterling Hayden. Directed by Douglas Sirk. 1953. Universal. 81 min. Sound. 16mm Color. *Rental:* Swank Motion.

Take One False Step. William Powell & Shelley Winters. Directed by Chester Erskine. 1949. Universal. 94 min. Sound. 16mm B&W. *Rental:* Swank Motion.

Take the High Ground. Richard Widmark & Karl Malden. Directed by Richard Brooks. 1953. MGM. 100 min. Sound. 16mm Color. *Rental:* Films Inc & MGM United.

Take the Money & Run. Woody Allen & Janet Margolin. Directed by Woody Allen. 1968. ABC. 85 min. Sound. 16mm Color. *Rental:* Films Inc.

Take the World from Another Point of View. 1979. PBS. (Documentary). 60 min. 16mm Color. *Rental:* PBS Video. *Sale:* PBS Video, Videotape version.

Take This Job & Shove It. Robert Hays & Barbara Hershey. Directed by Gus Trikonis. 1981. Embassy. 100 min. Sound. 16mm Color. *Rental:* Films Inc.

Takeoff at Eighteen Hundred. Trans. Title: Despegue a las Diez y Ocho. Directed by Santiago Alvarez. 1970. Cuba. (Documentary). 90 min. Sound. 16mm B&W. *Rental:* CA Newsreel. *Rental:* CA Newsreel, Spanish language version.

Takeover. 1981. EMC. (Documentary). 90 min. Sound. 16mm Color. *Rental:* U Cal Media. *Sale:* U Cal Media.

Taking Back Detroit. Directed by Stephen Lighthill. 1980. Icarus. (Documentary). 55 min. Sound. 16mm Color. *Rental:* Icarus Films & U Mich Media. *Sale:* Icarus Films. *Sale:* Icarus Films, Videotape version.

Taking Care of Business. Robert Kaylor. 1971. Robert Kaylor. (Documentary). 50 min. Sound. 16mm Color. *Rental:* Time-Life Multimedia. *Sale:* Time-Life Multimedia.

Taking of Pelham One, Two, Three, The. Walter Matthau & Robert Shaw. Directed by Joseph Sergent. 1974. United Artists. (Anamorphic). 104 min. Sound. 16mm Color. *Rental:* Budget Films, MGM United, Westcoast Films & Welling Motion Pictures.

Taking Off. Lynn Carlin & Buck Henry. Directed by Milos Forman. 1971. Universal. 93 min. Sound. 16mm Color. *Rental:* Swank Motion & Twyman Films.

Tale of Five Women, A. Gina Lollobrigida & Eva Bartok. Directed by Romolo Marcellini. 1952. United Artists. 86 min. Sound. 16mm B&W. *Rental:* Ivy Films. *Lease:* Rep Pic Film.

Tale of Reliance & Hope, A. 1977. Penn State. (Documentary). 57 min. Sound. 16mm Color. *Rental:* Penn St AV Serv. *Sale:* Penn St AV Serv. *Rental:* Penn St AV Serv, *Sale:* Penn St AV Serv, Videotape version.

Tale of the Navajos, A. 1949. MGM. (Documentary). 58 min. Sound. 16mm Color. *Rental:* MGM United.

Tale of the Northern Lights, A. 1968. Radio-TV. (Animated). 51 min. Sound. 16mm Color. *Rental:* Films Inc.

Tale of the Woods, A. 1953. Russia. (Documentary). 60 min. Sound. 16mm Color. narrated Eng. *Rental:* Mogulls Films.

Tale of Two Cities, A. William Farnum & Florence Vidor. Directed by Frank Lloyd. 1917. Fox. 70 min. Silent. 16mm B&W. *Rental:* Killiam Collect.

Tale of Two Cities, A. Ronald Colman & Elizabeth Allen. Directed by Jack Conway. 1935. MGM. 121 min. Sound. 16mm B&W. *Rental:* Iowa Films & MGM United. *Rental:* MGM United, Videotape version.

Tale of Two Cities, A. Dirk Bogarde & Dorothy Tutin. Directed by Ralph Thomas. 1958. Britain. 107 min. 16mm B&W. *Rental:* Budget Films, Films Inc, Inst Cinema, Kit Parker, Learning Corp Am, Modern Sound, Roas Films, Twyman Films, U of IL Film, Welling Motion Pictures & Wholesome Film Ctr. *Lease:* Learning Corp Am. *Rental:* Learning Corp Am, *Lease:* Learning Corp Am, Videotape version.

Tale of Two Cities, A. Chris Sarandon, Barry Morse & Peter Cushing. Directed by Jim Goddard. 1980. Britain. 156 min. Sound. 16mm Color. *Rental:* Swank Motion.

Tale of Two Critters, A. Disney. (Animal cast). 47 min. Sound. 16mm Color. *Rental:* Disney Prod & Modern Sound.

Tale of Two Irelands, A. 1975. CBS. (Documentary). 52 min. Sound. 16mm Color. *Rental:* U Cal Media.

Tale of Two Worlds, A. Leatrice Joy & Wallace Beery. Directed by Frank Lloyd. 1921. Goldwyn. 75 min. Silent. Super 8 B&W. *Rental:* Ivy Films. *Sale:* Blackhawk Films.

Talent Scout. Donald Woods & Jeanne Madden. Directed by William Clemens. 1937. Warners. 62 min. Sound. 16mm B&W. *Rental:* MGM United.

Tales. Directed by Cassandra Gerstein. 1969. New Line Cinema. (Cast unlisted). 70 min. Sound. 16mm Color. *Rental:* New Line Cinema.

Tales from Beyond the Grave. Ian Bannen, Peter Cushing & Diana Dors. 1976. Britain. 98 min. Sound. 16mm B&W. *Rental:* Modern Sound.

Tales from the Crypt. Sir Ralph Richardson & Joan Collins. Directed by Freddie Francis. 1972. Cinerama. 92 min. Sound. 16mm Color. *Rental:* Images Film & Swank Motion.

Tales of Hoffman. Moira Shearer & Robert Rounseville. Directed by Michael Powell & Emeric Pressburger. 1951. Britain. 118 min. Sound. 16mm B&W. *Rental:* Budget Films & Twyman Films.

Tales of Hoffmann, The. 1975. Britain. (Opera). 56 min. Sound. 16mm Color. *Rental:* Centron Films. *Sale:* Centron Films.

Tales of Manhattan. Charles Boyer & Rita Hayworth. Directed by Julien Duvivier. 1942. Fox. 118 min. Sound. 16mm B&W. *Rental:* Films Inc.

Tales of Paris. Dany Saval & Dany Robin. Directed by Jacques Poitrenaud. Fr. 1962. France. 85 min. Sound. 16mm B&W. subtitles. *Rental:* Films Inc.

Tales of Robin Hood. Robert Clarke & Mary Hatcher. Directed by James Tinling. 1951. Lippert. 59 min. Sound. 16mm B&W. *Rental:* Budget Films, Cine Craft, Film Ctr DC & Westcoast Films.

Tales of Terror. Vincent Price & Peter Lorre. Directed by Roger Corman. 1962. American International. 90 min. Sound. 16mm Color. *Rental:* Arcus Film, Budget Films, Cine Craft, Film Ctr DC, Films Inc, Inst Cinema, Twyman Films, Video Comm, Westcoast Films, Welling Motion Pictures, Wholesome Film Ctr & Willoughby Peer.

Tales of the Taira Clan *see* Taira Clan Saga.

Tales of Washington Irving. 1970. Australia. (Animated). 60 min. Sound. 16mm Color. *Rental:* Budget Films, Inst Cinema, Modern Sound, Roas Films, Twyman Films, Westcoast Films, Wholesome Film Ctr & Willoughby Peer. *Lease:* Inst Cinema.

Tales That Witness Madness. Kim Novak & Jack Hawkins. Directed by Freddie Francis. 1973. Britain. 90 min. Sound. 16mm Color. *Rental:* Films Inc.

Talisman, The. Ned Romero & Linda Hawkins. Directed by John Carr. 1970. Universal. 89 min. Sound. 16mm B&W. *Rental:* Video Comm & Westcoast Films.

Talk About a Stranger. George Murphy & Nancy Davis. Directed by David Bradley. 1952. MGM. 65 min. Sound. 16mm B&W. *Rental:* MGM United.

Talk of the Devil. Margaret Rutherford & Ricardo Cortez. Directed by Sir Carol Reed. 1937. Britain. 86 min. Sound. 16mm B&W. *Rental:* Classic Film Mus.

Talk of the Town. Cary Grant, Jean Arthur & Ronald Colman. 1942. Columbia. 118 min. Sound. 16mm B&W. *Rental:* Budget Films, Films Inc, Images Film, Kit Parker, Modern Sound, Swank Motion, Twyman Films, U of IL Film & Welling Motion Pictures.

Talking Bear, The. Renato Rascal. Directed by Edmond Sechan. 1963. Italy. 86 min. Sound. 16mm Color. dubbed. *Rental:* Cine Craft & Films Inc.

Tall Blond Man with One Black Shoe, The. Pierre Richard & Mireille Darc. Directed by Yves Robert. Fr. 1973. France. 88 min. Sound. 16mm Color. dubbed Eng. *Rental:* Budget Films, Cinema Five & Inst Cinema. *Lease:* Cinema Five. *Sale:* Tamarelles French Film, Videotape version.

Tall, Dark & Handsome. Cesar Romero. Directed by Bruce Humberstone. 1941. Fox. 78 min. Sound. 16mm B&W. *Rental:* Films Inc.

Tall in the Saddle. John Wayne & Ella Raines. Directed by Edwin L. Marin. 1944. RKO. 86 min. Sound. 16mm B&W. *Rental:* Films Inc. *Lease:* Films Inc.

Tall Lie, The. Orig. Title: For Men Only. Paul Henried & Kathleen Hughes. Directed by Paul Henried. 1952. Lippert. 93 min. Sound. 16mm B&W. *Rental:* Budget Films.

Tall Men, The. Clark Gable & Jane Russell. Directed by Raoul Walsh. 1955. Fox. 121 min. Sound. 16mm B&W. *Rental:* Films Inc & Welling Motion Pictures. *Rental:* Films Inc, Anamorphic version.

Tall Story. Jane Fonda & Anthony Perkins. Directed by Joshua Logan. 1960. Warners. 91 min. Sound. 16mm Color. *Rental:* Films Inc, Inst Cinema, Welling Motion Pictures & Willoughby Peer.

Tall Stranger, The. Joel McCrea & Virginia Mayo. Directed by Thomas Carr. 1957. Allied Artists. 81 min. Sound. 16mm Color. *Rental:* Ivy Films. *Sale:* Rep Pic Film.

Tall T, The. Randolph Scott & Richard Boone. Directed by Budd Boetticher. 1956. Columbia. 78 min. Sound. 16mm Color. *Rental:* Bosco Films, Budget Films, Kit Parker, Modern Sound, Westcoast Films & Welling Motion Pictures.

Tall Target, The. Dick Powell & Paula Raymond. Directed by Anthony Mann. 1951. MGM. 78 min. Sound. 16mm B&W. *Rental:* MGM United.

Tall Texan, The. Lloyd Bridges & Lee J. Cobb. Directed by Elmo Williams. 1953. Lippert. 84 min. Sound. 16mm B&W. *Rental:* Budget Films, Film Ctr DC, Films Inc & Westcoast Films.

Tall Timber *see* Park Avenue Logger.

Talmage Farlow. 1981. 58 min. Sound. 16mm Color. *Sale:* Festival Films. *Sale:* Festival Films, Videotape version.

Tam-Lin. Ava Gardner. Directed by Roddy McDowall. 1971. American International. 104 min. Sound. 16mm Color. *Rental:* Ivy Films.

Tamahine. Nancy Kwan & John Fraser. Directed by Philip Leacock. 1964. MGM. 85 min. Sound. 16mm Color. *Rental:* MGM United. *Rental:* MGM United, Anamorphic version.

Tamarind Seed, The. Julie Andrews & Omar Sharif. Directed by Blake Edwards. 1975. Embassy. 123 min. Sound. 16mm Color. *Rental:* Films Inc.

Taming of the Shrew, The. Mary Pickford & Douglas Fairbanks Sr. Directed by Sam Taylor. 1929. United Artists. 80 min. Sound. 16mm B&W. *Sale:* Classic Film Mus.

Taming of the Shrew, The. Richard Burton & Elizabeth Taylor. Directed by Franco Zeffirelli. 1967. Columbia. 122 min. Sound. 16mm Color. *Rental:* Arcus Film, Bosco Films, Budget Films, Cine Craft, Corinth Films, Film Ctr DC, Films Inc, Images Film, Kit Parker, Modern Sound, Natl Film Video, Swank Motion, Twyman Films, U of IL Film, Westcoast Films, Welling Motion Pictures & Wholesome Film Ctr. *Rental:* Corinth Films, Films Inc, Images Film, Kit Parker & Twyman Films, Anamorphic version. *Rental:* Swank Motion, Videotape version.

Taming of the Shrew, The. John Cleese & Sarah Badel. 1980. Britain. 127 min. Sound. 16mm Color. *Rental:* Iowa Films.

Taming Sutton's Gal. John Lipton & Gloria Talbot. Directed by Lesley Selander. 1957. Republic. 71 min. Sound. 16mm B&W. *Rental:* Ivy Films. *Sale:* Rep Pic Film.

Tammy & the Bachelor. Debbie Reynolds & Leslie Nielsen. Directed by Joseph Pevney. 1957. Universal. 89 min. Sound. 16mm Color. *Rental:* Swank Motion. *Rental:* Swank Motion, Anamorphic version.

Tammy & the Doctor. Sandra Dee & Peter Fonda. Directed by Harry Keller. 1963. Universal. 88 min. Sound. 16mm Color. *Rental:* Swank Motion.

Tammy & the Millionaire. Debbie Watson. Directed by Sidney Miller, Ezra Stone & Leslie Goodwins. 1967. Universal. 87 min. Sound. 16mm Color. *Rental:* Swank Motion.

Tammy Tell Me True. Sandra Dee & John Gavin. Directed by Harry Keller. 1961. Universal. 97 min. Sound. 16mm Color. *Rental:* Swank Motion.

Tampico. Edward G. Robinson & Lynn Bari. Directed by Lothar Mendes. 1944. Fox. 75 min. Sound. 16mm B&W. *Rental:* Films Inc.

Tanganyika. Van Heflin & Ruth Roman. Directed by Andre De Toth. 1954. Universal. 81 min. Sound. 16mm Color. *Rental:* Swank Motion.

Tangier. Robert Preston & Maria Montez. Directed by George Waggner. 1946. Universal. 74 min. Sound. 16mm B&W. *Rental:* Swank Motion.

Tangier Incident. George Brent & Mari Aldon. Directed by Lew Landers. 1953. Monogram. 77 min. Sound. 16mm B&W. *Rental:* Hurlock Cine.

Tangled Fortunes. Francis X. Bushman. 1932. Big Four. 60 min. Sound. 16mm B&W. *Rental:* Mogulls Films.

Tank. James Garner & Shirley Jones. Directed by Marvin J. Chomsky. 1985. Universal. 113 min. Sound. 16mm Color. *Rental:* Swank Motion. *Rental:* Swank Motion, Videotape version.

Tank Commandoes. Don Kelly. Directed by Sherman Rose. 1958. American International. 80 min. Sound. 16mm B&W. *Rental:* Westcoast Films.

Tankerbomb. Directed by Mike Poole. 1978. Canada. (Documentary). 57 min. Sound. 16mm Color. *Rental:* Natl Film CN. *Sale:* Natl Film CN.

Tanks a Million. William Tracy & Joe Sawyer. Directed by Fred Guiol. 1941. Hal Roach. 60 min. Sound. 16mm B&W. *Rental:* Mogulls Films.

Tanned Legs. Ann Pennington & Arthur Lake. Directed by Marshall Neilan. 1930. RKO. 71 min. Sound. 16mm B&W. *Rental:* RKO General Pics.

Tantra of Gyuto, The. Directed by Sheldon Rochlin. New Line Cinema. (Cast unlisted). 50 min. Sound. 16mm Color. *Rental:* New Line Cinema.

Tanzania: The Quiet Revolution. 1965. NET. (Documentary). 60 min. Sound. 16mm B&W. *Rental:* Indiana AV Ctr & Syracuse U Film. *Sale:* Indiana AV Ctr.

Taoism: A Question of Balance. 1978. Britain. (Documentary). 52 min. Sound. 16mm Color. *Rental:* U Cal Media. *Rental:* U Cal Media, Videotape version.

Tap Dance Kid, The. Charles Honi Coles. Directed by Barra Grant. 1979. Learning Corp. 49 min. Sound. 16mm Color. *Rental:* Learning Corp Am. *Sale:* Learning Corp Am.

Tap Roots. Susan Hayward & Van Heflin. Directed by George Marshall. 1948. Universal. 109 min. Sound. 16mm Color. *Rental:* Video Comm.

Tapdancin'. Directed by Michael Blackwood. 58 min. 16mm *Rental:* Blackwood. *Sale:* Blackwood.

Taps. George C. Scott & Timothy Hutton. Directed by Harold Becker. 1981. Fox. 125 min. Sound. 16mm Color. *Rental:* Films Inc.

Tarantos, Los. Carmen Amaya. Directed by P. Rovira-Beleta. Span. 1963. Spain. 81 min. Sound. 16mm B&W. subtitles. *Rental:* Films Inc.

Tarantula. John Agar & Mara Corday. Directed by Jack Arnold. 1955. Universal. 80 min. Sound. 16mm B&W. *Rental:* Swank Motion.

Taras Bulba. Yul Brynner & Tony Curtis. Directed by J. Lee Thompson. 1962. United Artists. 123 min. Sound. 16mm Color. *Rental:* MGM United & Westcoast Films.

Tarawa Beachhead. Kerwin Matthews & Julie Adams. Directed by Paul Wendkos. 1958. Columbia. 77 min. Sound. 16mm B&W. *Rental:* Westcoast Films.

Target, The. Tim Holt & Richard Martin. Directed by Stuart Gilmore. 1952. RKO. 60 min. Sound. 16mm B&W. *Rental:* RKO General Pics.

Target for Scandal *see* Washington Story.

Target for Tonight. Directed by Harry Watt. 1941. Britain. (Documentary). 48 min. Sound. 16mm B&W. *Rental:* Budget Films, Em Gee Film Lib & Kit Parker. *Sale:* Festival Films.

Target Hong Kong. Richard Denning & Nancy Gates. Directed by Fred F. Sears. 1953. Columbia. 66 min. Sound. 16mm B&W. *Rental:* Films Inc & Inst Cinema.

Target: Sea of China. Harry Lauter, Aline Towne & Lyle Talbot. Directed by Franklin Adreon. 1953. Republic. 100 min. Sound. 16mm B&W. *Rental:* Ivy Films. *Sale:* Rep Pic Film.

Targets. Boris Karloff & Tim O'Kelly. Directed by Peter Bogdanovich. 1968. Paramount. 90 min. Sound. 16mm Color. *Rental:* Films Inc.

Tarka the Otter. Peter Bennett & Peter Ustinov. Directed by David Cobham. 1979. Britain. 91 min. Sound. 16mm B&W. *Rental:* Arcus Film & Twyman Films.

Tarnished. Dorothy Patrick, James Lydon & Arthur Franz. Directed by Harry Keller. 1949. Republic. 65 min. Sound. 16mm B&W. *Sale:* Rep Pic Film.

Tarnished Angel. Ann Miller & Lee Bowman. Directed by Leslie Goodwins. 1939. RKO. 68 min. Sound. 16mm B&W. *Rental:* RKO General Pics.

Tarnished Angels, The. Rock Hudson & Robert Stack. Directed by Douglas Sirk. 1957. Universal. 93 min. Sound. 16mm B&W. *Rental:* Swank Motion.

Tarnished Lady. Tallulah Bankhead & Clive Brook. Directed by George Cukor. 1931. Paramount. 83 min. Sound. 16mm B&W. *Rental:* Swank Motion.

Tars & Spars. Sid Caesar & Janet Blair. Directed by Alfred E. Green. 1946. Columbia. 88 min. Sound. 16mm B&W. *Rental:* Inst Cinema.

Tartar Invasion, The. Yoko Tani. 1963. Italy. 100 min. Sound. 16mm B&W. dubbed. *Rental:* Welling Motion Pictures.

Tartars, The. Orson Welles & Victor Mature. Directed by Richard Thorpe. 1962. Italy. (Anamorphic). 83 min. Sound. 16mm Color. dubbed. *Rental:* Films Inc & MGM United.

Tartuffe, the Hypocrite. Emil Jannings. Directed by F. W. Murnau. Ger. 1927. Germany. 70 min. Silent. 16mm B&W. *Rental:* A Twyman Pres, Em Gee Film Lib, Film Classics & Images Film. *Sale:* Film Classics & Images Film. *Rental:* Film Classics, Videotape version.

Tarzan & His Mate. Johnny Weissmuller & Maureen O'Sullivan. Directed by Cedric Gibbons & Jack Conway. 1934. MGM. 105 min. Sound. 16mm B&W. *Rental:* MGM United.

Tarzan & the Amazons. Johnny Weissmuller & Brenda Joyce. Directed by Kurt Neumann. 1945. RKO. 76 min. Sound. 16mm B&W. *Rental:* Charard Motion Pics. *Sale:* Cinema Concepts.

Tarzan & the Green Goddess. Bruce Bennett. Directed by Edward Kull. 1938. Principal. 70 min. Sound. 16mm B&W. *Rental:* Budget Films. *Sale:* Morcraft Films.

Tarzan Escapes. Johnny Weissmuller & Maureen O'Sullivan. Directed by Richard Thorpe. 1936. MGM. 89 min. Sound. 16mm B&W. *Rental:* MGM United.

Tarzan of the Apes. Elmo Lincoln & Enid Markey. Directed by Scott Sidney. 1918. First National. 60 min. Silent. 16mm B&W. *Rental:* Budget Films, Em Gee Film Lib, Film Classics & Kit Parker. *Sale:* Blackhawk Films, Cinema Concepts, Film Classics & Glenn Photo. *Rental:* Film Classics, Sound 16mm version. *Rental:* Ivy Films, *Sale:* Glenn Photo, Super 8 silent version. *Sale:* Reel Images, Videotape version.

Tarzan, the Ape Man. Johnny Weissmuller & Maureen O'Sullivan. Directed by W. S. Van Dyke. 1932. MGM. 100 min. Sound. 16mm B&W. *Rental:* Films Inc & MGM United. *Rental:* MGM United, Videotape version.

Tarzan, the Ape Man. Denny Miller & Joanna Barnes. Directed by Joseph Newman. 1959. MGM. 82 min. Sound. 16mm Color. *Rental:* MGM United.

Tarzan, the Ape Man. Bo Derek, Miles O'Keeffe & Richard Harris. Directed by John Derek. 1981. 112 min. Sound. 16mm Color. *Rental:* MGM United. *Rental:* MGM United, Videotape version.

Tarzan, the Fearless. Buster Crabbe & Julie Bishop. Directed by Robert Hill. 1933. Principal. 85 min. Sound. 16mm B&W. *Rental:* Budget Films, Syracuse U Film, Video Comm & Wholesome Film Ctr. *Sale:* Cinema Concepts.

Tarzan's Deadly Silence. Ron Ely & Woody Strode. Directed by Robert Friend. 1968. National General. 89 min. Sound. 16mm Color. *Rental:* Films Inc, Modern Sound, Swank Motion, Twyman Films & Williams Films.

Tarzan's Jungle Rebellion. Ron Ely & Sam Jaffe. Directed by William Witney. 1968. National General. 92 min. Sound. 16mm Color. *Rental:* Films Inc, Modern Sound, Swank Motion, Twyman Films & Williams Films.

Tarzan's Revenge. Glenn Morris & Eleanor Holm. Directed by D. Ross Lederman. 1938. Fox. 70 min. Sound. 16mm B&W. *Rental:* Budget Films. *Sale:* Cinema Concepts & Natl Cinema.

Task Force. Gary Cooper & Jane Wyatt. Directed by Delmer Daves. 1949. Warners. 117 min. Sound. 16mm B&W. *Rental:* MGM United.

Task Force South: The Battle for the Falklands. 1982. Britain. 120 min. Videotape Color. *Sale:* Films Inc.

Taste of Honey, A. Rita Tushingham, Dora Bryan & Robert Stephens. Directed by Tony Richardson. 1962. Britain. 100 min. Sound. 16mm B&W. *Rental:* Budget Films, Kino Intl & Twyman Films. *Sale:* Kino Intl. *Lease:* Kino Intl.

Taste the Blood of Dracula. Christopher Lee & Geoffrey Keen. Directed by Peter Sasdy. 1970. Britain. 91 min. Sound. 16mm Color. *Rental:* Films Inc, Film Ctr DC, Twyman Films & Williams Films.

Tattered Dress, The. Jeff Chandler & Jeanne Crain. Directed by Jack Arnold. 1957. Universal. 96 min. Sound. 16mm B&W. *Rental:* Swank Motion.

Tattoo. Bruce Dern & Maud Adams. Directed by Bob Brooks. 1981. Fox. 103 min. Sound. 16mm Color. *Rental:* Films Inc.

Tattoo Connection, The. Jim Kelly. 95 min. Sound. 16mm *Rental:* WW Enter. *Rental:* WW Enter, Videotape version.

Tattooed Dragon, The. Jimmy Wang Yu. Hong Kong. 83 min. Sound. 16mm *Rental:* WW Enter. *Rental:* WW Enter, Videotape version.

Tattooed Police Horse, The. 1964. Disney. (Documentary). 48 min. Sound. 16mm Color. *Rental:* Buchan Pic, Cine Craft, Disney Prod, Films Inc, Film Ctr DC, Modern Sound & Roas Films.

Tattooed Stranger, The. John Mills & Patricia White. Directed by Edward J. Montagne. 1950. RKO. 64 min. Sound. 16mm B&W. *Rental:* Films Inc.

Tattooed Tears. Directed by Joan Churchill & Nick Broomfield. 1978. Museum of Modern Art. (Documentary). 88 min. Sound. 16mm Color. *Rental:* Churchill Films & Museum Mod Art. *Sale:* Churchill Films, Videotape version.

Tawny Pipit. Bernard Miles & Rosamund John. Directed by Bernard Miles. 1944. Britain. 85 min. Sound. 16mm B&W. *Rental:* Budget Films & Kit Parker.

Taxi. James Cagney & Loretta Young. Directed by Roy Del Ruth. 1932. Warners. 85 min. Sound. 16mm B&W. *Rental:* MGM United.

Taxi. Dan Dailey & Constance Smith. Directed by Gregory Ratoff. 1953. Fox. 77 min. Sound. 16mm B&W. *Rental:* Willoughby Peer.

Taxi Driver. Robert De Niro & Cybill Shepherd. Directed by Martin Scorsese. 1976. Columbia. 112 min. Sound. 16mm Color. *Rental:* Swank Motion. *Rental:* Swank Motion, Videotape version.

Taxi, Mister! William Bendix & Joe Sawyer. Directed by Kurt Neumann. 1943. United Artists. 45 min. Sound. 16mm B&W. *Rental:* Budget Films.

Taza, Son of Cochise. Rock Hudson & Barbara Rush. Directed by Douglas Sirk. 1954. Universal. 79 min. Sound. 16mm Color. *Rental:* Swank Motion.

Tea & Sympathy. Deborah Kerr & Leif Erickson. Directed by Vincente Minnelli. 1956. MGM. 122 min. Sound. 16mm Color. *Rental:* MGM United. *Rental:* MGM United, Anamorphic version.

Teacher, The. Patricio Wood. Directed by Octavio Cortazar. Span. 1977. Cuba. 113 min. Sound. 16mm Color. subtitles. *Rental:* Cinema Guild. *Sale:* Cinema Guild.

Teacher, The. Angel Tompkins & Jay North. Directed by Hikmet Avedis. 1974. Crown. 98 min. Sound. 16mm Color. *Rental:* Films Inc.

Teacher & Technology, The. 1966. U. S. Government. (Documentary). 49 min. Sound. 16mm B&W. *Rental:* U Mich Media.

Teacher & the Miracle, The. Aldo Fabrizi. Directed by Aldo Fabrizi. 1961. Italy. 88 min. Sound. 16mm B&W. dubbed. *Rental:* Films Inc.

Teacher Gap, The. 1965. NET. (Documentary). 60 min. Sound. 16mm B&W. *Rental:* Indiana AV Ctr.

Teacher Training Experiences & Issues. 1983. 47 min. Sound. Videotape Color. *Rental:* Natl AV Ctr.

Teachers, The. 1966. San Fernando Valley State College. (Documentary). 49 min. Sound. 16mm B&W. *Rental:* U Cal Media.

Teacher's Pet. Clark Gable & Doris Day. Directed by George Seaton. 1958. Paramount. 120 min. Sound. 16mm B&W. *Rental:* Films Inc.

Teaching Basic Concepts. Anti-Defamation League. (Lecture). 52 min. Sound. 16mm B&W. *Rental:* ADL. *Sale:* ADL.

Teaching Basic Skills with Film. 1980. 83 min. Sound. 16mm Color. *Rental:* U Mich Media.

Teaching Interpersonal Skills to Health Professionals: Programs 2-7. 1978. 85 min. Sound. Videotape Color. *Rental:* Natl AV Ctr.

Teaching Sign Language to the Chimpanzee, Washoe. 1973. Penn State. (Documentary). 48 min. Sound. 16mm B&W. *Rental:* Iowa Films, Penn St AV Serv & Utah Media. *Sale:* Penn St AV Serv.

Teahouse of the August Moon, The. Marlon Brando & Glenn Ford. Directed by Daniel Mann. 1956. MGM. 125 min. Sound. 16mm Color. *Rental:* MGM United. *Rental:* MGM United, Anamorphic version.

Tear Gas Squad. John Payne & Dennis Morgan. Directed by Terry Morse. 1940. Warners. 55 min. Sound. 16mm B&W. *Rental:* MGM United.

Teatro Campesino, El. 1970. NET. (Documentary). 61 min. Sound. 16mm B&W. *Rental:* Indiana AV Ctr & U Mich Media. *Sale:* Indiana AV Ctr.

Teatro Espanol, El: El Villano En Su Rincon. Span. 1965. 46 min. Sound. 16mm Color. *Rental:* Utah Media.

Technique of Working with Addicts, The. 1973. US Government. (Documentary). 49 min. Sound. 16mm Color. *Sale:* Natl AV Ctr.

Teenage Caveman. Orig. Title: Out of the Darkness. Robert Vaughan. Directed by Roger Corman. 1958. American International. 66 min. Sound. 16mm B&W. *Rental:* Films Inc.

Teenage Doll: The Young Rebels. June Kenney & Fay Spain. Directed by Roger Corman. 1957. Allied Artists. 72 min. Sound. 16mm B&W. *Rental:* Hurlock Cine.

Teenage Frankenstein *see* I Was a Teenage Frankenstein.

Teenage Graffiti. Michael Driscoll & Jeannetta Arnette. Directed by Christopher G. Casler. 1977. Alllied Artists. 90 min. Sound. 16mm Color. *Rental:* Hurlock Cine.

Teenage Rebel. Ginger Rogers & Michael Rennie. Directed by Edmund Goulding. 1956. Fox. (Anamorphic). 94 min. Sound. 16mm B&W. *Rental:* Films Inc.

Teenage Revolution. 1965. Wolper. (Documentary). 50 min. Sound. 16mm B&W. *Rental:* Films Inc & Utah Media. *Sale:* Films Inc. *Sale:* Films Inc, Videotape version.

Teenagers. 1971. Family of Man. (Documentary). 50 min. Sound. 16mm B&W. *Rental:* Films Inc. *Sale:* Films Inc. *Rental:* Films Inc, *Sale:* Films Inc, Videotape version.

Teheran. Derek Farr. Directed by William Freshman. 1948. 86 min. 16mm *Rental:* A Twyman Pres.

Telefon. Charles Bronson & Lee Remick. Directed by Don Siegel. 1977. MGM. 103 min. Sound. 16mm Color. *Rental:* MGM United.

Telegraph Trail. John Wayne & Frank McHugh. Directed by Tenny Wright. 1933. Warners. 53 min. Sound. 16mm B&W. *Rental:* MGM United.

Telephone Operator. John Wayne & Frank McHugh. Directed by Scott Pembroke. Monogram. 60 min. Sound. 16mm B&W. *Rental:* Mogulls Films.

Television Around the World. Britain. (Documentary). 87 min. Sound. 16mm B&W. *Rental:* Time-Life Multimedia. *Sale:* Time-Life Multimedia.

Tell England. Orig. Title: Battle of Gallipoli. Carl Harbord. Directed by Anthony Asquith & Geoffrey Barkas. 1930. Britain. 85 min. Sound. 16mm B&W. *Rental:* Museum Mod Art.

Tell It to a Star. Robert Livingston & Adrian Booth. Directed by Frank McDonald. 1945. Republic. 67 min. Sound. 16mm B&W. *Rental:* Ivy Films.

Tell It to the Judge. Rosalind Russell, Robert Cummings & Gig Young. Directed by Norman Foster. 1949. Republic. 87 min. Sound. 16mm B&W. *Rental:* Kit Parker.

Tell It to the Marines. Lon Chaney & William Haines. Directed by George Hill. 1926. MGM. 90 min. Silent. 16mm B&W. *Rental:* Films Inc.

Tell Me a Riddle. Melvyn Douglas & Lila Kedrova. Directed by Lee Grant. 1980. Filmways. 90 min. Sound. 16mm Color. *Rental:* Swank Motion.

Tell Me Lies. Glenda Jackson & Stokely Carmichael. Directed by Peter Brook. 1968. Britain. (Color sequences). 118 min. Sound. 16mm B&W. *Rental:* Budget Films.

Tell Me My Name. Valerie Mahaffey, Barbara Barrie & Arthur Hill. Directed by Delbert Mann. 1977. Time-Life. 55 min. Sound. 16mm Color. *Rental:* U of IL Film, Videotape version.

Tell Me That You Love Me, Junie Moon. Liza Minnelli, Ken Howard & James Coco. Directed by Otto Preminger. 1971. Paramount. 112 min. Sound. 16mm Color. *Rental:* Films Inc.

Tell Me Where It Hurts. Maureen Stapleton. Directed by Paul Bogart. 1974. CBS. 78 min. Sound. 16mm Color. *Rental:* Budget Films, U Cal Media, Films Inc, Kent St U Film, Kit Parker, Learning Corp Am, U Mich Media, Modern Sound, Syracuse U Film, Twyman Films, U of IL Film, Westcoast Films & Wholesome Film Ctr. *Sale:* Learning Corp Am.

Tell No Tales. Melvyn Douglas & Louise Platt. Directed by Leslie Fenton. 1938. MGM. 69 min. Sound. 16mm B&W. *Rental:* MGM United.

Tell-Tale Heart, The. Laurence Payne & Adrienne Corri. Directed by Ernest Morris. 1960. Britain. 81 min. Sound. 16mm B&W. *Rental:* Films Inc, Welling Motion Pictures & Willoughby Peer. *Sale:* Morcraft Films. *Sale:* Morcraft Films, Super 8 sound version. *Sale:* Morcraft Films, Videotape version.

Tell Them Willie Boy Is Here. Robert Redford, Katherine Ross & Robert Blake. Directed by Abraham Polonsky. 1970. Universal. (Anamorphic). 98 min. Sound. 16mm Color. *Rental:* Swank Motion.

Tell Your Children *see* Reefer Madness.

Tembo. 1952. RKO. (Documentary). 80 min. Sound. 16mm Color. *Rental:* Budget Films.

Temiscaming, Quebec. 1975. Canada. (Documentary). 64 min. Sound. 16mm Color. *Rental:* CA Newsreel & U Cal Media.

Temperamental Wife. Constance Talmadge. Directed by John Emerson. 1919. 16mm *Rental:* A Twyman Pres.

Tempest. John Barrymore, Louis Wolheim & Sam Taylor. 1928. United Artists. 105 min. Silent. 16mm B&W. *Rental:* Em Gee Film Lib, Kerr Film, Kit Parker, Video Comm & Willoughby Peer. *Rental:* Killiam Collect, Tinted 16mm sound, musical score only version. *Rental:* Ivy Films, *Sale:* Blackhawk Films, Super 8 silent version.

Tempest. Silvana Mangano & Van Heflin. Directed by Alberto Lattuada. 1959. Paramount. 123 min. Sound. 16mm Color. *Rental:* Films Inc.

Tempest. Lassie. 1960. Wrather. 52 min. Sound. 16mm Color. *Rental:* Budget Films, Films Inc & Westcoast Films.

Tempest, The. 1979. Britain. (Cast unlisted). 150 min. Videotape Color. *Rental:* Iowa Films.

Tempest. Heathecote Williams & Toyah Wilcox. 95 min. Sound. Videotape *Rental:* WW Enter.

Temple of One Thousand Lights, The. Richard Harrison. 1965. Italy. 89 min. Sound. 16mm Color. dubbed. *Rental:* Bosco Films & Films Inc.

Temptation. Eva Novak. Directed by Edward Le Saint. 1923. Columbia. 72 min. Silent. 16mm B&W. *Rental:* Mogulls Films.

Temptress, The. Greta Garbo & Antonio Moreno. Directed by Mauritz Stiller & Fred Niblo. 1926. MGM. 95 min. Silent. 16mm B&W. *Rental:* MGM United.

Ten. Dudley Moore, Julie Andrews & Bo Derek. Directed by Blake Edwards. 1979. Orion. 123 min. Sound. 16mm Color. *Rental:* Films Inc. *Rental:* Films Inc, Anamorphic version.

Ten Cents a Dance. Barbara Stanwyck & Ricardo Cortez. Directed by Lionel Barrymore. 1931. Columbia. 79 min. Sound. 16mm B&W. *Rental:* Bosco Films & Kit Parker.

Ten Commandments, The. Charlton Heston & Yul Brynner. Directed by Cecil B. DeMille. 1956. Paramount. 219 min. Sound. 16mm Color. *Rental:* Films Inc.

Ten Commandments, The. John Marley & Kristoffer Tabori. 1979. Sunn. 50 min. Sound. 16mm Color. *Rental:* Budget Films & Modern Sound. *Sale:* Lucerne Films. *Sale:* Lucerne Films, Videotape version. *Rental:* Budget Films, 58 mins. version.

Ten Commandments, The. Theodore Roberts & Charles De Roche. Directed by Cecil B. DeMille. 1923. Paramount. 146 min. Silent. 16mm B&W. *Rental:* Films Inc.

Ten Days That Shook the World. Orig. Title: October. Directed by Sergei Eisenstein & Grigori Alexandrov. 1928. Russia. 107 min. Silent. 16mm B&W. *Rental:* Budget Films, Em Gee Film Lib, Film Images, Images Film, Inst Cinema, Kerr Film, Kit Parker, Macmillan Films, Museum Mod Art, Natl Film Video, Phoenix Films, Reel Images, U Mich Media, Video Comm, Westcoast Films & Willoughby Peer. *Sale:* Cinema Concepts, E Finney, Films Inc, Griggs Movie, Glenn Photo, Morcraft Films, Phoenix Films & Westcoast Films. *Lease:* Macmillan Films. *Sale:* Images Film, Natl Cinema & Reel Images, Sound 16mm, musical score only version. *Sale:* Glenn Photo & Reel Images, Super 8 silent version. *Sale:* Festival Films, Phoenix Films & Images Film, Videotape version.

Ten Days to Tulara. Sterling Hayden. Directed by George Sherman. 1958. United Artists. 77 min. Sound. 16mm B&W. *Rental:* MGM United.

Ten Day's Wonder. Orson Welles, Anthony Perkins & Marlene Jobert. Directed by Claude Chabrol. 1971. France. 108 min. Sound. 16mm Color. *Rental:* Films Inc.

Ten Dollar Raise, The. William V. Mong & Marguerite De La Motte. Directed by Edward Sloman. 1921. Fox. 71 min. Silent. 16mm B&W. *Rental:* Films Inc.

Ten from Your Show of Shows. Sid Caesar & Imogene Coca. Directed by Max Liebman. 1973. 92 min. Sound. 16mm B&W. *Rental:* Swank Motion.

Ten from Your Shows of Shows. 1973. Continental. (Kinescope, anthology). 92 min. Sound. 16mm B&W. *Rental:* Films Inc, Swank Motion & Twyman Films.

Ten Gentlemen from West Point. Maureen O'Hara & George Montgomery. Directed by Henry Hathaway. 1942. Fox. 105 min. Sound. 16mm B&W. *Rental:* Films Inc.

Ten Little Indians *see* And Then There Were None.

Ten Little Indians. Hugh O'Brian & Stanley Holloway. Directed by George Pollock. 1965. Souvaine. 92 min. Sound. 16mm B&W. *Rental:* Films Inc, Film Ctr DC, Westcoast Films & Williams Films.

Ten Little Indians. Oliver Reed & Elke Sommer. Directed by Peter Collinson. 1975. Britain. 98 min. Sound. 16mm Color. *Rental:* Films Inc.

Ten Minutes of Love. Lawrence Chenault. Directed by Oscar Micheaux. 1932. Micheaux. 65 min. Sound. 16mm B&W. *Rental:* Budget Films.

Ten Nights in a Barroom. William Farnum. Directed by William A. O'Connor. 1931. Roadshow. 75 min. Sound. 16mm B&W. *Rental:* Budget Films, Em Gee Film Lib, Mogulls Films & Video Comm. *Sale:* Cinema Concepts & Griggs Movie.

Ten North Frederick. Gary Cooper & Suzy Parker. Directed by Philip Dunne. 1958. Fox. (Anamorphic). 102 min. Sound. 16mm B&W. *Rental:* Films Inc.

Ten Rillington Place. Sir Richard Attenborough & Judy Geeson. Directed by Richard Fleischer. 1971. Britain. 109 min. Sound. 16mm Color. *Rental:* Arcus Film, Cine Craft, Films Inc, Images Film, Kerr Film, Kit Parker, Modern Sound, Welling Motion Pictures, Westcoast Films & Willoughby Peer.

Ten Seconds That Shook the World. 1963. Wolper. (Documentary). 55 min. Sound. 16mm B&W. *Rental:* Films Inc, U Mich Media, Syracuse U Film & Wholesome Film Ctr. *Sale:* Films Inc, Videotape version.

Ten Seconds to Hell. Jeff Chandler & Jack Palance. Directed by Robert Aldrich. 1959. United Artists. 93 min. Sound. 16mm B&W. *Rental:* MGM United.

Ten Tall Men. Burt Lancaster & Jody Lawrence. Directed by Willis Goldbeck. 1951. Columbia. 97 min. Sound. 16mm B&W. *Rental:* Arcus Film, Bosco Films, Buchan Pic & Charard Motion Pics.

Ten Thirty P. M. Summer. Melina Mercouri & Peter Finch. Directed by Jules Dassin. 1966. United Artists. 85 min. Sound. 16mm Color. *Rental:* MGM United.

Ten Thousand Bedrooms. Dean Martin & Anna Maria Alberghetti. Directed by Richard Thorpe. 1957. MGM. 113 min. Sound. 16mm Color. *Rental:* MGM United. *Rental:* MGM United, Anamorphic version.

Ten to Midnight. Charles Bronson & Andrew Stevens. Directed by J. Lee Thompson. 1983. Cannon. 100 min. Sound. 16mm Color. *Rental:* Swank Motion.

Ten Wanted Men. Randolph Scott & Richard Boone. Directed by Bruce Humberstone. 1955. Columbia. 80 min. Sound. 16mm Color. *Rental:* Kit Parker.

Ten Who Dared. Orig. Title: Colorado Pioneers, The. Brian Keith & John Beal. Directed by William Beaudine. 1960. Disney. 92 min. Sound. 16mm Color. *Rental:* Buchan Pic, Cine Craft, Cousino Visual Ed, Disney Prod, Elliot Film Co, Film Ctr DC, Films Inc, Modern Sound, Newman Film Lib, Twyman Films & U of IL Films.

Ten Women Talk about Orgasm & Sexuality *see* Politics of Intimacy.

Tenant, The. Roman Polanski, Isabelle Adjani, Melvyn Douglas & Shelley Winters. Directed by Roman Polanski. 1976. Paramount. 124 min. Sound. 16mm Color. *Rental:* Films Inc.

Tender Comrade. Ginger Rogers & Robert Ryan. Directed by Edward Dmytryk. 1943. RKO. 102 min. Sound. 16mm B&W. *Rental:* Films Inc.

Tender is the Night. Jennifer Jones & Jason Robards. Directed by Henry King. 1962. Fox. (Anamorphic). 146 min. Sound. 16mm Color. *Rental:* Films Inc.

Tender Mercies. Robert Duvall & Tess Harper. Directed by Bruce Beresford. 1982. Universal. 93 min. Sound. 16mm Color. *Rental:* Swank Motion. *Rental:* Swank Motion, Videotape version.

Tender Sharks. Anna Karina & Mario Adorf. France/Italy. 90 min. Sound. 16mm Color. dubbed. *Rental:* Modern Sound.

Tender Trap, The. Frank Sinatra & Debbie Reynolds. Directed by Charles Walters. 1955. MGM. 111 min. Sound. 16mm Color. *Rental:* MGM United. *Rental:* MGM United, Anamorphic version. *Rental:* MGM United, Videotape version.

Tender Years, The. Joe E. Brown. Directed by Harold Schuster. 1948. Fox. 80 min. Sound. 16mm B&W. *Rental:* Bosco Films & Films Inc.

Tenderfoot, The. Joe E. Brown & Ginger Rogers. Directed by Ray Enright. 1932. Warners. 70 min. Sound. 16mm B&W. *Rental:* MGM United.

Tendres Cousines. Thierry Tevini & Anja Shute. Directed by David Hamilton. Fr. 1980. France. 90 min. Sound. Videotape Color. *Sale:* Tamarelles French Films.

Tennessee Champ. Dewey Martin & Shelley Winters. Directed by Fred M. Wilcox. 1954. MGM. 73 min. Sound. 16mm B&W. *Rental:* MGM United.

Tennessee Johnson. Orig. Title: Man on America's Conscience, The. Van Heflin & Ruth Hussey. Directed by William Dieterle. 1942. MGM. 100 min. Sound. 16mm B&W. *Rental:* MGM United.

Tennessee Newsreels. Directed by David L. Van Vactor. 1968. David L. Van Vactor. (Documentary, Color sequences). 50 min. Silent. 16mm B&W. *Rental:* Canyon Cinema.

Tennessee's Partner. Ronald Reagan & John Payne. Directed by Allan Dwan. 1955. RKO. 87 min. 16mm Color. *Rental:* Films Inc.

Tension. Richard Basehart & Audrey Totter. Directed by John Berry. 1949. MGM. 95 min. Sound. 16mm B&W. *Rental:* MGM United.

Tension at Table Rock. Richard Egan & Dorothy Malone. Directed by Charles Marquis Warren. 1956. RKO. 93 min. Sound. 16mm Color. *Rental:* Budget Films, Video Comm & Westcoast Films. *Lease:* Video Comm.

Tentacles. John Huston & Shelley Winters. Directed by Oliver Hellman. 1977. American International. 90 min. Sound. 16mm Color. *Rental:* Welling Motion Pictures & Williams Films.

Tenth Avenue Angel. Margaret O'Brien & Angela Lansbury. Directed by Roy Rowland. 1948. MGM. 74 min. Sound. 16mm B&W. *Rental:* MGM United.

Tenth Avenue Kid. Horace MacMahon. Directed by Bernard Vorhaus. 1938. Republic. 54 min. Sound. 16mm B&W. *Rental:* Ivy Films. *Sale:* Rep Pic Film.

Tenth International Tournee of Animation. Orig. Title: International Tournee of Animation. 1975. Film Wright. (Anthology). 100 min. Sound. 16mm Color. *Rental:* Film Wright.

Tenth Maccabiah Games. (Documentary). 48 min. Sound. 16mm Color. *Rental:* Alden.

Tenth Victim, The. Marcello Mastroianni & Ursula Andress. Directed by Elio Petri. 1965. Embassy. 92 min. Sound. 16mm Color. *Rental:* Films Inc.

Teorema. Terence Stamp & Sylvana Mangano. Directed by Pier Paolo Pasolini. Ital. 1968. Italy. 98 min. Sound. 16mm Color. subtitles. *Rental:* Budget Films & Kino Intl. *Sale:* Kino Intl. *Lease:* Kino Intl.

Tercera Palabra, La. Pedro Infante & Marga Lopez. Directed by Julian Soler. Span. 1955. Mexico. 110 min. Sound. 16mm B&W. subtitles. *Rental:* Trans-World Films.

Teresa. Pier Angeli & John Erickson. Directed by Fred Zinnemann. 1951. MGM. 105 min. Sound. 16mm B&W. *Rental:* MGM United.

Teresa Venerdi. Trans. Title: Doctor Beware. Vittorio De Sica & Anna Magnani. Directed by Vittorio De Sica. Ital. 1941. Italy. 90 min. Sound. 16mm B&W. subtitles. *Rental:* Cinema Guild.

Term of Trial. Sir Laurence Olivier & Sarah Miles. Directed by Peter Glenville. 1963. Warners. 113 min. Sound. 16mm B&W. *Rental:* Swank Motion & Twyman Films.

Termites & Telescopes. 1979. (Documentary). 58 min. Sound. Videotape *Rental:* PBS Video. *Sale:* PBS Video.

Terms of Endearment. Shirley MacLaine & Debra Winger. Directed by James Brooks. 1983. Paramount. Sound. 16mm *Sale:* Films Inc. *Sale:* Tamarelles French Film, Videotape version.

Terra Trema, La. Citizens of Aci-Trezza. Directed by Luchino Visconti. 1948. 162 min. Sound. 16mm B&W. subtitles. *Rental:* Films Inc.

Terrace, The. Graciela Borges. Directed by Leopoldo Torre-Nilsson. Span. 1965. Argentina. 90 min. Sound. 16mm B&W. subtitles. *Rental:* Swank Motion.

Terre Em Transe. Jardel Filho & Paulo Autran. Directed by Glauber Rocha. 1966. Brazil. 115 min. Sound. 16mm B&W. subtitles. *Rental:* Hurlock Cine & New Cinema.

Terrible Secret, The. 1979. Daniel Wilson. 47 min. Sound. 16mm Color. *Rental:* D Wilson. *Rental:* D Wilson, Videotape version.

Terrified. Rod Lauren & Steve Drexel. Directed by Lew Landers. 1963. Crown. 70 min. Sound. 16mm B&W. *Rental:* Budget Films, Video Comm, Westcoast Films & Welling Motion Pictures. *Lease:* Video Comm.

Territory of Others, The. 93 min. Sound. 16mm Color. *Rental:* Films Inc & Video Comm. *Lease:* Video Comm. *Rental:* Video Comm, *Lease:* Video Comm, Videotape version.

Terror, The. Pearl White. Directed by Clifford Smith. 1924. Universal. 60 min. Silent. 16mm B&W. *Rental:* Film Classics. *Sale:* Film Classics.

Terror, The. Boris Karloff & Jack Nicholson. Directed by Roger Corman. 1963. American International. 81 min. Sound. 16mm Color. *Rental:* Budget Films, Film Ctr DC, Films Inc, Natl Film, Twyman Films, Video Comm, Westcoast Films, Wholesome Film Ctr, Williams Films & Willoughby Peer. *Sale:* Cinema Concepts & Natl Cinema. *Sale:* Reel Images, Super 8 sound version.

Terror, The. John Nolan & James Aubrey. Directed by Norman J. Warren. 1979. Britain. 86 min. Sound. 16mm Color. *Rental:* Films Inc.

Terror see Perils of Paris.

Terror & the Time, The. 1978. Victor Jara Collection. (Documentary). 75 min. Sound. 16mm Color. *Rental:* CA Newsreel. *Sale:* CA Newsreel.

Terror at Midnight. Orig. Title: And Suddenly You Run. Scott Brady & Joan Vohs. Directed by Franklin Adreon. 1955. Republic. 72 min. Sound. 16mm B&W. *Rental:* Ivy Films.

Terror Beneath the Sea. Peggy Neal & Eric Nielson. Directed by Hajime Sato. 1966. Japan. 85 min. Sound. 16mm Color. dubbed. *Rental:* Films Inc. *Rental:* Ivy Films, *Sale:* Ivy Films, Super 8 sound version.

Terror by Night. Basil Rathbone. Directed by Roy William Neill. 1946. Universal. 60 min. Sound. 16mm B&W. *Rental:* Budget Films, Classic Film Mus, Em Gee Film Lib, Learning Corp Am, Natl Film Video, Newman Film Lib, Video Comm & Westcoast Films. *Sale:* Cinema Concepts, Festival Films, Glenn Photo, Learning Corp Am & Reel Images. *Sale:* Glenn Photo, Super 8 sound version. *Sale:* Festival Films & Tamarelles French Film, Videotape version.

Terror from the Crypt. Christopher Lee. Directed by Freddie Francis. 1960. Britain. 90 min. Sound. 16mm Color. *Rental:* Video Comm & Westcoast Films.

Terror from the Year Five Thousand: Cage of Doom. Joyce Holden. Directed by Robert J. Gurney. 1958. American International. 74 min. Sound. 16mm B&W. *Rental:* Films Inc.

Terror in a Texas Town. Sterling Hayden & Sebastian Cabot. Directed by Joseph Lewis. 1958. United Artists. 80 min. Sound. 16mm B&W. *Rental:* MGM United.

Terror in the Crypt. Christopher Lee. Directed by Thomas Miller. 1960. Spain. 84 min. Sound. 16mm Color. dubbed. *Rental:* Budget Films & Westcoast Films.

Terror in the Jungle. Robert Burns. Directed by Tom DeSimone, Andy Janzack & Alexander Grattan. 1968. Crown. 85 min. Sound. 16mm Color. *Rental:* Video Comm. *Lease:* Video Comm.

Terror in the Wax Museum. Ray Milland & Elsa Lanchester. Directed by George Fenady. 1973. Cinerama. 90 min. Sound. 16mm Color. *Rental:* Swank Motion & Welling Motion Pictures.

Terror of Rome Against the Son of Hercules. Mark Forrest. Directed by Mario Caiano. 1960. Italy. 100 min. Sound. 16mm Color. dubbed. *Rental:* Films Inc.

Terror of the Plains. Tom Tyler. 1934. Steiner. 60 min. Sound. 16mm B&W. *Rental:* Mogulls Films. *Sale:* Cinema Concepts.

Terror of Tiny Town, The. Jed Buell's Midgets. Directed by Sam Newfield. 1933. Columbia. 65 min. Sound. 16mm B&W. *Rental:* Budget Films, Film Ctr DC, Ivy Films & Kit Parker. *Sale:* Cinema Concepts. *Sale:* Morcraft Films, Super 8 sound version.

Terror on a Train. Glenn Ford & Anne Vernon. Directed by Ted Tetzlaff. 1953. MGM. 72 min. Sound. 16mm B&W. *Rental:* MGM United.

Terror on the Britannia *see* Juggernaut.

Terror Street. Dan Duryea. Directed by Montgomery Tully. 1954. Lippert. 84 min. Sound. 16mm B&W. *Rental:* Budget Films.

Terror Strikes *see* War of the Colossal Beast.

Terror: To Confront or Concede?. 1978. Britain. (Documentary). 52 min. Sound. 16mm Color. *Rental:* Films Inc & U of IL Film. *Sale:* Films Inc. *Rental:* Films Inc, *Sale:* Films Inc, Videotape version.

Terror Train. Ben Johnson & Jamie Lee Curtis. Directed by Roger Spottiswoode. 1980. Fox. 97 min. Sound. 16mm Color. *Rental:* Films Inc.

Terrorism: The World at Bay. 1979. PBS. (Documentary). 97 min. Sound. 16mm Color. *Rental:* PBS Video. *Sale:* PBS Video.

Terrorists, The. Sean Connery & Ian McShane. Directed by Casper Wrede. 1975. Fox. 97 min. Sound. 16mm Color. *Rental:* Films Inc.

Terrornauts, The. Simon Oates, Zena Marshall & Charles Hawtrey. 1967. Britain. 75 min. Sound. 16mm Color. *Rental:* Films Inc & Video Comm.

Terrors on Horseback. Buster Crabbe. Directed by Sam Newfield. 1946. PRC. 55 min. Sound. 16mm B&W. *Sale:* Classics Assoc NY.

Tess. Nastassja Kinski & Peter Firth. Directed by Roman Polanski. 1979. Columbia. 170 min. Sound. 16mm Color. *Rental:* Swank Motion. *Rental:* Swank Motion, Videotape version.

Tess of the Storm Country. Diane Baker & Lee Philips. Directed by Paul Guilfoyle. 1960. Fox. 85 min. Sound. 16mm Color. *Rental:* Films Inc. *Rental:* Willoughby Peer, Anamorphic version.

Test, The. Rin-Tin-Tin. Directed by Bernard B. Ray Jr. 1936. Reliable. 60 min. Sound. 16mm B&W. *Rental:* Film Classics.

Test of Donald Norton, The. Tyrone Power Sr. Directed by B. Reeves Eason. 1926. Chadwick. 75 min. Silent. 16mm B&W. *Rental:* Willoughby Peer, Silent 8mm version.

Test Pilot. Clark Gable, Spencer Tracy & Myrna Loy. Directed by Victor Fleming. 1938. MGM. 118 min. Sound. 16mm B&W. *Rental:* MGM United.

Testament. Jane Alexander & William Devane. Directed by Lynne Littman. 1983. Paramount. 89 min. Sound. 16mm Color. *Rental:* Films Inc.

Testament of Dr. Cordelier, The. Orig. Title: Experiment in Evil. Jean-Louis Barrault. Directed by Jean Renoir. Fr. 1959. France. 95 min. Sound. 16mm B&W. subtitles. *Rental:* Corinth Films. *Lease:* Corinth Films.

Testament of Dr. Mabuse, The. Rudolph Klein-Rogge. Directed by Fritz Lang. 1932. Germany. 120 min. Sound. 16mm B&W. *Rental:* Films Inc & Janus Films.

Testament of Dr. Mabuse, The *see* Crimes of Dr. Mabuse.

Testament of Orpheus, The. Jean Cocteau, Edouard Dermithe & Henri Cremieux. Directed by Jean Cocteau. Fr. 1959. France. 83 min. Sound. 16mm B&W. subtitles. *Rental:* Budget Films & Images Film. *Sale:* Reel Images & Images Film.

Teton: Decision & Disaster. 1979. PBS. (Documentary). 58 min. Sound. Color. *Rental:* PBS Video. *Sale:* PBS Video, Videotape version.

Tex. Matt Dillion, Jim Metzler & Meg Tilly. Directed by Tim Hunter. 103 min. Sound. 16mm Color. *Rental:* Films Inc, MGM United & Swank Motion.

Tex Rides with the Boy Scouts. Tex Ritter. Directed by Ray Taylor. 1937. Grand National. 60 min. Sound. 16mm B&W. *Sale:* Cinema Concepts, Morcraft Films & Reel Images.

Texas. William Holden & Glenn Ford. Directed by George Marshall. 1941. Columbia. 94 min. Sound. 16mm B&W. *Rental:* Welling Motion Pictures.

Texas Across the River. Dean Martin & Alain Delon. Directed by Michael Gordon. 1966. Universal. 101 min. Sound. 16mm Color. *Rental:* Swank Motion.

Texas Carnival. Esther Williams & Red Skelton. Directed by Charles Walters. 1951. MGM. 76 min. Sound. 16mm Color. *Rental:* MGM United.

Texas Chainsaw Massacre, The. Marilyn Burns. Directed by Tobe Hooper. 1974. Bryanston. 91 min. Sound. 16mm Color. *Rental:* New Line Cinema & Swank Motion.

Texas City. Johnny Mack Brown. Directed by Lewis D. Collins. 1952. Monogram. 54 min. Sound. 16mm B&W. *Rental:* Hurlock Cine.

Texas Cowboy. Bob Steele. Directed by Robert N. Bradbury. 1929. FBO. 55 min. Silent. 16mm B&W. *Sale:* Blackhawk Films. *Rental:* Ivy Films, *Sale:* Blackhawk Films, Super 8 silent version.

Texas Gunfighter. Ken Maynard. Directed by Phil Rosen. 1932. Tiffany. 60 min. Sound. 16mm B&W. *Sale:* Cinema Concepts, Natl Cinema & Reel Images.

Texas Jack. Jack Perrin. 1935. Commodore. 60 min. Sound. 16mm B&W. *Rental:* Mogulls Films.

Texas Kid. Johnny Mack Brown. Directed by Lambert Hillyer. 1943. Monogram. 55 min. Sound. 16mm B&W. *Rental:* Budget Films & Hurlock Cine. *Sale:* Cinema Concepts.

Texas Lady. Claudette Colbert & Barry Sullivan. Directed by Tim Whelan. 1955. RKO. 86 min. Sound. 16mm B&W. *Rental:* Ivy Films. *Lease:* Rep Pic Film.

Texas Lawmen. Johnny Mack Brown. Directed by Lewis D. Collins. 1951. Monogram. 54 min. Sound. 16mm B&W. *Rental:* Hurlock Cine.

Texas Legionnaires. Roy Rogers. 1938. Republic. 54 min. Sound. 16mm B&W. *Rental:* Ivy Films. *Sale:* Rep Pic Film.

Texas Manhunt. Bill Boyd, Lee Powell & Art Davis. 1941. PRC. 60 min. Sound. 16mm B&W. *Rental:* Mogulls Films.

Texas Masquerade. William Boyd. Directed by George Archainbaud. 1944. United Artists. 61 min. Sound. 16mm B&W. *Lease:* Cinema Concepts.

Texas Pioneers: The Blood Brother. Bill Cody. Directed by Harry Fraser. 1932. Monogram. 60 min. Sound. 16mm B&W. *Rental:* Mogulls Films.

Texas Rangers. George Montgomery & Gale Storm. Directed by Phil Karlson. 1951. Columbia. 74 min. Sound. 16mm Color. *Rental:* Cine Craft, Roas Films & Twyman Films.

Texas Rangers, The. Fred MacMurray & Jean Parker. Directed by King Vidor. 1936. Paramount. 98 min. Sound. 16mm B&W. *Rental:* Swank Motion.

Texas Rose *see* Return of Jack Slade.

Texas Serenade *see* Old Corral.

Texas Terror. John Wayne & Gabby Hayes. Directed by George Sherman. 1940. Republic. 54 min. Sound. 16mm B&W. *Rental:* Ivy Films. *Sale:* Classics Assoc NY & Rep Pic Film.

Texas to Bataan: The Long Trail. Range Busters. Directed by Robert Tansey. 1942. Monogram. 58 min. Sound. 16mm B&W. *Rental:* Budget Films.

Texas Trail. William Boyd. Directed by David Selman. 1937. Paramount. 60 min. Sound. 16mm B&W. *Lease:* Cinema Concepts.

Text of Light, The. Directed by Stan Brakhage. 1974. Brakhage. (Experimental). 67 min. Silent. 16mm Color. *Rental:* New Cinema.

Thames, The. (Documentary). 59 min. Sound. 16mm Color. *Rental:* National Geographic Society. *Rental:* National Geographic Society, Video version.

Thank God & the Revolution. 1980. Icarus. (Documentary). 55 min. Sound. 16mm Color. *Rental:* Icarus Films & CC Films. *Sale:* Icarus Films, Videotape version.

Thank God It's Friday. Donna Summer & Andrea Howard. Directed by Robert Klane. 1978. Columbia. 101 min. Sound. 16mm Color. *Rental:* Budget Films, Swank Motion & Williams Films.

Thank You All Very Much. Sandy Dennis & Ian McKellen. Directed by Waris Hussein. 1969. Columbia. 106 min. Sound. 16mm Color. *Rental:* Budget Films & Charard Motion Pics.

Thank Your Lucky Stars. Dennis Morgan & Joan Leslie. Directed by David Butler. 1943. Warners. 127 min. Sound. 16mm B&W. *Rental:* MGM United.

Thanks a Million. Dick Powell & Fred Allen. Directed by Roy Del Ruth. 1935. Fox. 87 min. Sound. 16mm B&W. *Rental:* Films Inc.

Thanks a-Plenty, Boss. 1973. Roundtable. (Documentary). 48 min. Sound. 16mm Color. *Rental:* BYU Media.

Thanks for Everything. Jack Haley & Jack Oakie. Directed by William A. Seiter. 1938. Fox. 72 min. Sound. 16mm B&W. *Rental:* Films Inc.

Thanks for the One Time. 1981. 45 min. Sound. 16mm Color. *Rental:* Iowa Films & Learning Corp Am. *Sale:* Learning Corp Am. *Rental:* Learning Corp Am, *Sale:* Learning Corp Am, Videotape version.

Thanos & Despina. Olga Carlatos. Directed by Nico Papatakis. Gr. 1967. Greece. 96 min. Sound. 16mm B&W. subtitles. *Rental:* Grove.

That Brennan Girl. James Dunn & Mona Freeman. Directed by Alfred Santell. 1946. Republic. 97 min. Sound. 16mm B&W. *Rental:* Ivy Films. *Sale:* Rep Pic Film.

That Certain Feeling. Bob Hope & Eva Marie Saint. Directed by Norman Panama & Melvin Frank. 1956. Paramount. 102 min. Sound. 16mm Color. *Rental:* Films Inc.

That Certain Thing. Ralph Graves & Viola Dana. Directed by Frank Capra. 1928. Columbia. (Musical score only). 70 min. Sound. 16mm B&W. *Sale:* Kit Parker.

That Certain Woman. Bette Davis & Henry Fonda. Directed by Edmund Goulding. 1937. Warners. 93 min. Sound. 16mm B&W. *Rental:* MGM United.

That Championship Season. Bruce Dern, Stacy Keach & Robert Mitchum. Directed by Jason Miller. 1985. Cannon. 108 min. Sound. 16mm Color. *Rental:* Swank Motion. *Rental:* Swank Motion, Videotape version.

That Cold Day in the Park. Sandy Dennis & Michael Burns. Directed by Robert Altman. 1969. Commonwealth. 106 min. Sound. 16mm Color. *Rental:* Budget Films, Cine Craft, Charard Motion Pics, Ivy Films, Kit Parker, Rep Pic Film, Video Comm & Willoughby Peer. *Lease:* Rep Pic Film.

That Darn Cat. Hayley Mills & Dean Jones. Directed by Robert Stevenson. 1965. Disney. 116 min. Sound. 16mm Color. *Rental:* Cine Craft, Williams Films, Bosco Films, Disney Prod, Elliot Film Co, Films Inc, Film Pres, U of IL Film, MGM United, Modern Sound, Natl Serv, Newman Film Lib, Roas Film, Swank Motion, Film Ctr DC, Twyman Films, Westcoast Films & Welling Motion Pictures.

That Ever-Lovin' Babe. 1963. Hearst. (Documentary). 50 min. Sound. 16mm B&W. *Sale:* King Features.

That Forsyte Woman. Orig. Title: Forsyte Saga, The. Errol Flynn & Greer Garson. Directed by Compton Bennett. 1949. MGM. 112 min. Sound. 16mm Color. *Rental:* MGM United. *Rental:* MGM United, Videotape version.

That Funny Feeling. Sandra Dee & Bobby Darin. Directed by Richard Thorpe. 1965. Universal. 93 min. Sound. 16mm Color. *Rental:* Swank Motion.

That Gang of Mine. East Side Kids. Directed by Joseph Lewis. 1940. Monogram. 62 min. Sound. 16mm B&W. *Rental:* Budget Films.

That Girl from Paris. Lily Pons & Lucille Ball. Directed by Leigh Jason. 1936. RKO. 110 min. Sound. 16mm B&W. *Rental:* Films Inc.

That Hamilton Woman. Orig. Title: Lady Hamilton. Vivien Leigh & Sir Laurence Olivier. Directed by Alexander Korda. 1941. United Artists. 128 min. Sound. 16mm B&W. *Rental:* Films Inc & Ivy Films.

That I May See. Jeffrey Lynn & Ruth Hussey. 1951. Father Peyton. 60 min. Sound. 16mm B&W. *Rental:* Roas Films.

That Kind of Woman. Sophia Loren & Tab Hunter. Directed by Sidney Lumet. 1959. Paramount. 92 min. Sound. 16mm B&W. *Rental:* Films Inc.

That Lady. Olivia De Haviland & Paul Scotfield. Directed by Terence Young. 1955. Fox. 100 min. Sound. 16mm Color. *Rental:* Films Inc & Willoughby Peer.

That Lady from Peking. Carl Betz & Nancy Kwan. Directed by Eddie Davis. 1970. Commonwealth United. 100 min. Sound. 16mm Color. *Rental:* Ivy Films, Rep Pic Film & Video Comm. *Lease:* Rep Pic Film.

That Lady in Ermine. Betty Grable & Douglas Fairbanks Jr. Directed by Ernst Lubitsch. 1948. Fox. 89 min. Sound. 16mm Color. *Rental:* Films Inc.

That Long Night in Forty-Three. Belinda Lee, Gabriele Ferzetti & Gino Cervi. Directed by Florestano Vancini. 1960. Italy. 110 min. Sound. 16mm B&W. dubbed. *Rental:* Cinema Guild.

That Mad Mr. Jones *see* Fuller Brush Man.

That Man Bolt. Fred Williamson. Directed by Henry Levin & David Lowell Rich. 1973. Universal. 102 min. Sound. 16mm Color. *Rental:* Swank Motion.

That Man from Rio. Jean-Paul Belmondo & Francoise Dorleac. Directed by Philippe De Broca. Fr. 1964. France. 114 min. Sound. 16mm Color. subtitles. *Rental:* MGM United.

That Man in Istanbul. Horst Bucholtz & Sylva Koscina. Directed by Antonio Issai Isamendi. 1966. Germany. 117 min. Sound. 16mm Color. dubbed. *Rental:* Cine Craft, Charard Motion Pics, Films Inc, Modern Sound, Westcoast Films & Wholesome Film Ctr.

That Man's Here Again. Hugh Herbert & Tom Brown. Directed by Louis King. 1937. Warners. 58 min. Sound. 16mm B&W. *Rental:* MGM United.

That Midnight Kiss. Kathryn Grayson & Mario Lanza. Directed by Norman Taurog. 1949. MGM. 98 min. Sound. 16mm B&W. *Rental:* MGM United.

That Nazty Nuisance *see* Last Three.

That Night in Rio. Alice Faye & Don Ameche. Directed by Irving Cummings. 1941. Fox. 94 min. Sound. 16mm Color. *Rental:* Films Inc & Williams Films.

That Obscure Object of Desire. Fernando Rey, Carole Bouquet & Angela Molina. Directed by Luis Bunuel. Span. 1977. First Artists. 100 min. Sound. 16mm Color. subtitles. *Rental:* Films Inc.

That Other Woman. Virginia Gilmore & James Ellison. Directed by Ray McCarey. 1942. Fox. 75 min. Sound. 16mm B&W. *Rental:* Films Inc.

That Tennessee Beat. Minnie Pearl & Merle Travis. Directed by Richard Brill. 1966. Fox. 84 min. Sound. 16mm B&W. *Rental:* Films Inc.

That Touch of Mink. Cary Grant & Doris Day. Directed by Delbert Mann. 1962. Universal. 99 min. Sound. 16mm B&W. *Rental:* Budget Films, Ivy Films, Video Comm & Welling Motion Pictures. *Lease:* Rep Pic Film & Arcus Films.

That Uncertain Feeling. Merle Oberon & Melvyn Douglas. Directed by Ernst Lubitsch. 1941. United Artists. 86 min. Sound. 16mm B&W. *Rental:* Budget Films, Ivy Films & Willoughby Peer.

That Uncertain Paradise. 1975. WGTV. (Documentary). 60 min. Sound. 16mm Color. *Rental:* WNET Media. *Sale:* WNET Media. *Rental:* WNET Media, *Sale:* WNET Media, Videotape version.

That War in Korea. 1963. NBC. (Documentary). 79 min. Sound. 16mm B&W. *Rental:* Films Inc, Iowa Films, Syracuse U Film, U Cal Media, U of IL Film & Wholesome Film Ctr. *Sale:* Films Inc. *Sale:* Films Inc, Videotape version.

That Way with Women. Dane Clark & Sydney Greenstreet. Directed by Frederick De Cordova. 1947. Warners. 84 min. Sound. 16mm B&W. *Rental:* MGM United.

That Wonderful Urge. Tyrone Power & Gene Tierney. Directed by Robert B. Sinclair. 1948. Fox. 81 min. Sound. 16mm B&W. *Rental:* Films Inc.

That's the Way It Is see Elvis-That's the Way It Is.

That'll Be the Day. Directed by Claude Whatham. 90 min. Sound. 16mm Color. *Rental:* New Line Cinema.

That's Entertainment. 1974. MGM. (Color sequences, anthology). 131 min. Sound. 16mm B&W. *Rental:* MGM United. *Rental:* MGM United, Videotape version.

That's Entertainment II. Gene Kelly & Fred Astaire. Directed by Gene Kelly. 1976. 133 min. Sound. 16mm Color. *Rental:* MGM United. *Rental:* MGM United, Videotape version.

That's My Baby. Richard Arlen & Ellen Drew. Directed by William Berke. 1944. Republic. 67 min. Sound. 16mm B&W. *Rental:* Ivy Films. *Sale:* Classics Assoc NY & Rep Pic Film.

That's My Boy. Dean Martin & Jerry Lewis. Directed by Hal Walker. 1951. Paramount. 98 min. Sound. 16mm B&W. *Rental:* Films Inc.

That's My Girl. Lynne Roberts & John Hamilton. Directed by George Blair. 1947. Republic. 67 min. Sound. 16mm B&W. *Rental:* Ivy Films.

That's My Man. Orig. Title: Will Tomorrow Ever Come? Don Ameche & Catherine McLeod. Directed by Frank Borzage. 1947. Republic. 99 min. Sound. 16mm B&W. *Rental:* Ivy Films. *Sale:* Rep Pic Film.

That's Right, You're Wrong. Lucille Ball, Dennis O'Keefe & Kay Kayser. Directed by David Butler. 1939. RKO. 88 min. Sound. 16mm *Rental:* Films Inc & RKO General Pics.

That's Your Funeral. Bill Fraser. Directed by John Robins. Britain. 85 min. Sound. 16mm B&W. *Rental:* Cinema Five.

Theatre Girls. Directed by Kim Longinotto & Claire Poliak. 1978. Britain. (Documentary). 80 min. Sound. 16mm B&W. *Rental:* Women Movies. *Sale:* Women Movies.

Theatre of Blood. Vincent Price & Diana Rigg. Directed by Douglas Hickox. 1973. United Artists. 104 min. Sound. 16mm B&W. *Rental:* MGM United, Roas Films, Westcoast Films & Wholesome Film Ctr.

Theatre of Death. Christopher Lee & Lelia Goldoni. Directed by Samuel Gallu. 1966. Britain. 101 min. Sound. 16mm Color. *Rental:* Budget Films & Video Comm. *Lease:* Video Comm. *Rental:* Video Comm, *Lease:* Video Comm, Videotape version.

Theatre Royal. Flanagan & Allen. Directed by John Baxter. 1949. Britain. 68 min. Sound. 16mm B&W. *Rental:* Ivy Films. *Sale:* Rep Pic Film.

Their Big Moment. ZaSu Pitts & Slim Summerville. Directed by James Cruze. 1934. RKO. 70 min. Sound. 16mm B&W. *Rental:* Films Inc. *Lease:* Films Inc.

Their Own Desire. Norma Shearer & Robert Montgomery. Directed by E. Mason Hopper. 1929. MGM. 80 min. Sound. 16mm B&W. *Rental:* MGM United.

Theirs Is the Glory. Directed by Brian Desmond-Hurst. 1945. Britain. (Documentary). 75 min. Sound. 16mm B&W. *Rental:* Budget Films.

Them! James Whitmore & Edmund Gwenn. Directed by Gordon Douglas. 1954. Warners. 75 min. Sound. 16mm B&W. *Rental:* Films Inc, Twyman Films, Video Comm & Williams Films.

Them Nice Americans. Bonar Colleano & Vera Day. Directed by Anthony Young. 1958. Britain. 63 min. Sound. 16mm B&W. *Rental:* Budget Films.

Theme & Variations. 1980. Britain. (Documentary). 58 min. Videotape Color. *Rental:* Films Inc. *Sale:* Films Inc.

Then There Were Three. Frank Lattimore & Alex Nichol. Directed by Alex Nichol. 1961. Italy. 83 min. Sound. 16mm B&W. dubbed. *Rental:* Ivy Films & Westcoast Films.

Theodora Goes Wild. Irene Dunne & Melvyn Douglas. Directed by Richard Boleslawski. 1936. Columbia. 95 min. Sound. 16mm B&W. *Rental:* Corinth Films & Swank Motion.

Therapy. Directed by Laurence Schwab. 1968. Laurence Schwab. (Experimental). 48 min. Sound. 16mm B&W. *Rental:* Films Inc.

There Are Others Worse Off Than Us... Trans. Title: Sur Vivre. 1973. Canada. (Documentary). 58 min. Sound. 16mm B&W. *Rental:* Natl Film CN. *Sale:* Natl Film CN.

There But for Fortune. Directed by John Chapman & Julio Moline. 1982. First Run. (Documentary). 60 min. Sound. 16mm Color. *Rental:* First Run. *Lease:* First Run.

There Goes Kelly. Jackie Moran & Wanda McKay. Directed by Phil Karlson. 1945. Monogram. 60 min. Sound. 16mm B&W. *Rental:* Mogulls Films.

There Goes My Girl. Ann Sothern & Gene Raymond. Directed by Ben Holmes. 1937. RKO. 74 min. Sound. 16mm *Rental:* RKO General Pics.

There Goes My Heart. Fredric March & Virginia Bruce. Directed by Norman Z. McLeod. 1938. United Artists. 85 min. Sound. 16mm B&W. *Rental:* Inst Cinema.

There Goes the Groom. Ann Sothern & Burgess Meredith. Directed by Joseph Santley. 1938. RKO. 65 min. Sound. 16mm *Rental:* RKO General Pics.

There Is No God But God. 1977. Britain. (Documentary). 52 min. Sound. 16mm Color. *Rental:* Iowa Films, U of IL Film & U Mich Media.

There Was a Crooked Man. Norman Wisdom & Renee Houston. Directed by Sidney J. Furie. 1961. Britain. 106 min. Sound. 16mm B&W. *Rental:* MGM United.

There Was a Father. Chishu Ryu. Directed by Yasujiro Ozu. Jap. 1942. Japan. 87 min. Sound. 16mm B&W. subtitles. *Rental:* Films Inc.

There's a Girl in My Heart. Lee Bowman & Elyse Knox. Directed by Arthur Dreifuss. 1949. Allied Artists. 81 min. Sound. 16mm B&W. *Rental:* Hurlock Cine & Film Ctr DC.

There's a Girl in My Soup. Peter Sellers & Goldie Hawn. Directed by Roy Boulting. 1970. Columbia. 95 min. Sound. 16mm Color. *Rental:* Arcus Film, Budget Films, Cine Craft, Charard Motion Pics, Williams Films, Films Inc, Modern Sound, Natl Film Video, Roas Films, Swank Motion, Film Ctr DC, Video Comm, Westcoast Films, Welling Motion Pictures, Wholesome Film Ctr & Willoughby Peer.

There's a New Wind Blowing. 1954. Fox. (Documentary). 50 min. Sound. 16mm Color. *Rental:* G Herne & Newman Film Lib.

There's Always Tomorrow. Robert Taylor & Binnie Barnes. Directed by Edward Sloman. 1934. Universal. 84 min. Sound. 16mm B&W. *Rental:* Swank Motion.

There's Always Tomorrow. Barbara Stanwyck, Joan Bennett & Fred MacMurray. Directed by Douglas Sirk. 1956. Universal. 84 min. Sound. 16mm B&W. *Rental:* Swank Motion.

There's No Business Like Show Business. Ethel Merman, Donald O'Connor & Marilyn Monroe. Directed by Walter Lang. 1954. Fox. 117 min. Sound. 16mm Color. *Rental:* Films Inc, Twyman Films & Williams Films. *Rental:* Films Inc, Anamorphic version.

There's Someone for Everyone. 1979. 55 min. Sound. 16mm Color. *Rental:* U Mich Media.

Therese Desqueroux. Emmanuelle Riva. Directed by Georges Franju. Fr. 1963. France. 97 min. Sound. 16mm B&W. subtitles. *Rental:* French Am Cul.

Thermidor. Trans. Title: Ca Ira. Directed by Tinto Brass. 1964. Italy. (Documentary). 97 min. Sound. 16mm B&W. narrated Eng. *Rental:* Films Inc.

These Are the Damned. MacDonald Carey, Viveca Lindfors & Shirley Ann Field. Directed by Joseph Losey. 1961. Britain. 87 min. Sound. 16mm B&W. *Rental:* Corinth Films & Swank Motion. *Rental:* Corinth Films, Anamorphic version.

These Glamour Girls. Lew Ayres & Lana Turner. Directed by S. Sylvan Simon. 1939. MGM. 80 min. Sound. 16mm B&W. *Rental:* MGM United.

These States. 3 pts. Directed by Andre De la Varre. 1975. Bicentennial Council. (Documentary). 90 min. Sound. 16mm Color. *Rental:* Films Inc & Macmillan Films. *Sale:* Macmillan.

These Thousand Hills. Don Murray & Lee Remick. Directed by Richard Fleischer. 1959. Fox. (Anamorphic). 96 min. Sound. 16mm Color. *Rental:* Films Inc.

These Three. Miriam Hopkins & Merle Oberon. Directed by William Wyler. 1936. Goldwyn. 92 min. Sound. 16mm B&W. *Rental:* Films Inc.

These Wilder Years. James Cagney & Barbara Stanwyck. Directed by Roy Rowland. 1956. MGM. 91 min. Sound. 16mm B&W. *Rental:* MGM United.

Thetford au Milieu de Notre Vie. Theo Gagne. Directed by Fernand Dansereau & Iolande Rossignol. Fr. 1978. Canada. 83 min. Sound. 16mm Color. subtitles. *Rental:* Natl Film CN. *Sale:* Natl Film CN.

They All Come Out. Rita Johnson & Tom Neal. Directed by Jacques Tourneur. 1939. MGM. 69 min. Sound. 16mm B&W. *Rental:* MGM United.

They All Kissed the Bride. Joan Crawford & Melvyn Douglas. Directed by Alexander Hall. 1942. Columbia. 87 min. Sound. 16mm B&W. *Rental:* Kit Parker.

They Are Their Own Gifts. 3 pts. Directed by Lucille Rhodes & Margaret Murphy. 1978. New Day. (Documentary). 52 min. Sound. 16mm Color. *Rental:* New Day Films. *Sale:* New Day Films.

They Call It Sin. Loretta Young & George Brent. Directed by Thornton Freeland. 1932. Warners. 70 min. Sound. 16mm B&W. *Rental:* MGM United.

They Call Me Mr. Tibbs. Sidney Poitier & Barbara McNair. Directed by Gordon Douglas. 1970. United Artists. 105 min. Sound. 16mm Color. *Rental:* MGM United, Westcoast Films & Welling Motion Pictures.

They Call Me Trinity. Terence Hill & Bud Spencer. Directed by E. B. Clucher. 1971. Italy. 108 min. Sound. 16mm Color. *Rental:* Films Inc, Roas Films, Video Comm & Welling Motion Pictures.

They Called Him Amigo. Ernst-Georg Schwiller & Erich Franz. Directed by Heiner Carow. Ger. 1959. Germany. 62 min. Sound. 16mm B&W. subtitles Eng. *Rental:* Films Inc.

They Called Us les Filles Du Roy. Directed by Anne-Claire Poirier. 1975. Canada. (Documentary). 57 min. Sound. 16mm Color. *Rental:* Natl Film CN. *Sale:* Natl Film CN.

They Came from Beyond Space. Robert Hutton. Directed by Freddie Francis. 1967. Britain. 85 min. Sound. 16mm Color. *Rental:* Films Inc & Video Comm.

They Came to Blow Up America. George Sanders & Anna Sten. Directed by Edward Ludwig. 1943. Fox. 73 min. Sound. 16mm B&W. *Rental:* Films Inc.

They Came to Cordura. Gary Cooper & Rita Hayworth. Directed by Robert Rossen. 1959. Columbia. 123 min. Sound. 16mm Color. *Rental:* Bosco Films, Budget Films, Cine Craft, Corinth Films, Films Inc, Modern Sound, Video Comm & Welling Motion Pictures. *Rental:* Corinth Films & Kit Parker, Anamorphic version.

They Came to Rob Las Vegas. Gary Lockwood & Lee J. Cobb. Directed by Antonio Issai Isamendi. 1969. Warners. 127 min. Sound. 16mm Color. *Rental:* Arcus Film.

They Died With Their Boots On. Errol Flynn & Olivia De Havilland. Directed by Raoul Walsh. 1942. Warners. 138 min. Sound. 16mm B&W. *Rental:* MGM United.

They Don't Wear Black Tie. Fernanda Montenegro & Gianfrancesco Guarnieri. Directed by Leon Hirszman. Port. 1981. Brazil. 120 min. Sound. 16mm Color. subtitles. *Rental:* New Yorker Films.

They Drive by Night. George Raft, Humphrey Bogart & Ida Lupino. Directed by Raoul Walsh. 1940. Warners. 97 min. Sound. 16mm B&W. *Rental:* MGM United.

They Gave Him a Gun. Spencer Tracy, Franchot Tone & Gladys George. Directed by W. S. Van Dyke. 1937. MGM. 93 min. Sound. 16mm B&W. *Rental:* MGM United.

They Got Me Covered. Bob Hope & Dorothy Lamour. Directed by David Butler. 1943. RKO. 95 min. Sound. 16mm B&W. *Rental:* Films Inc.

They Knew What They Wanted. Charles Laughton & Carole Lombard. Directed by Garson Kanin. 1940. RKO. 80 min. Sound. 16mm B&W. *Rental:* Films Inc. *Lease:* Films Inc.

They Learned About Women. Joe Schenk & Gus Van. Directed by Jack Conway & Sam Wood. 1936. MGM. 97 min. Sound. 16mm B&W. *Rental:* MGM United.

They Live by Night. Orig. Title: Twisted Road, The. Farley Granger & Cathy O'Donnell. Directed by Nicholas Ray. 1948. RKO. 95 min. Sound. 16mm B&W. *Rental:* Films Inc.

They Made Her a Spy. Sally Eilers & Allan Lane. Directed by Jack Hively. 1939. RKO. 80 min. Sound. 16mm *Rental:* RKO General Pics.

They Made Me a Criminal. John Garfield & Ann Sheridan. Directed by Busby Berkeley. 1939. Warners. 92 min. Sound. B&W. *Rental:* Budget Films, Em Gee Film Lib, Kit Parker, MGM United & Wholesome Film Ctr. *Sale:* Festival Films. *Rental:* Em Gee Film Lib, Ivy Films & Video Comm, *Sale:* Cinema Concepts, Festival Films, Ivy Films & Morcraft Films, Videotape version.

They Meet Again. Jean Hersholt. Directed by Erle C. Kenton. 1941. RKO. 69 min. Sound. 16mm B&W. *Rental:* Budget Films, Ivy Films & Mogulls Films.

They Met in Argentina. Maureen O'Hara & Gene Raymond. Directed by Lou Brock. 1941. RKO. 77 min. Sound. 16mm B&W. *Rental:* RKO General Pics.

They Might Be Giants. George C. Scott & Joanne Woodward. Directed by Anthony Harvey. 1971. Universal. 88 min. Sound. 16mm Color. *Rental:* Swank Motion.

They Must Be Told *see* Sex Madness.

They Only Kill Their Masters. James Garner & Katharine Ross. Directed by James Goldstone. 1972. MGM. 97 min. Sound. 16mm Color. *Rental:* MGM United.

They Raid by Night. Paul Kelly & Lyle Talbot. Directed by Spencer G. Bennett. 1942. PRC. 90 min. Sound. 16mm B&W. *Rental:* Inst Cinema.

They Rode West. Robert Francis & Donna Reed. Directed by Phil Karlson. 1954. Columbia. 84 min. Sound. 16mm Color. *Rental:* Kit Parker.

They Saved Hitler's Brain. Orig. Title: Madman of Mandoras. Walter Stocker & Audrey Caire. Directed by David Bradley. 1964. Crown. 81 min. Sound. 16mm B&W. *Rental:* Ivy Films & Video Comm. *Lease:* Video Comm. *Rental:* Video Comm, *Lease:* Festival Films & Video Comm, Videotape version.

They Shoot Horses, Don't They? Jane Fonda & Gig Young. Directed by Sydney Pollack. 1969. ABC. 129 min. Sound. 16mm Color. *Rental:* Films Inc, Anamorphic version.

They Wanted to Marry. Betty Furness & Gordon Jones. Directed by Lew Landers. 1937. RKO. 68 min. Sound. 16mm B&W. *Rental:* RKO General Pics.

They Went That-a-Way & That-a-Way. Tim Conway, Chuck McCann & Dub Taylor. Directed by Edward J. Montagne & Stuart McGowan. 1978. Sunrise. 106 min. Sound. 16mm Color. *Rental:* Films Inc, Modern Sound & Twyman Films.

They Were Expendable. Robert Montgomery & John Wayne. Directed by John Ford. 1945. MGM. 136 min. Sound. 16mm B&W. *Rental:* MGM United.

They Were Ten. Ninette Teomi & Leo Filer. Directed by Baruch Diener. 1961. Universal. 105 min. Sound. 16mm B&W. *Rental:* Swank Motion.

They Who Tread on the Tiger's Tail *see* Men Who Tread on the Tiger's Tail.

They Won't Believe Me. Robert Young & Susan Hayward. Directed by Irving Pichel. 1947. RKO. 95 min. Sound. 16mm B&W. *Rental:* Films Inc.

They Won't Forget. Claude Rains & Lana Turner. Directed by Mervyn LeRoy. 1937. Warners. 94 min. Sound. 16mm B&W. *Rental:* MGM United.

They're Off *see* Straight, Place & Show.

They'll Never Surrender. Directed by Heinz Paul. 1935. Germany. 80 min. Sound. 16mm B&W. dubbed. *Rental:* Alba House.

They're a Weird Mob. Chips Rafferty. Directed by Michael Powell. 1966. Australia. 112 min. Sound. 16mm B&W. *Rental:* Cinema Five.

They've Killed President Lincoln! 1971. Wolper. (Documentary). 52 min. Sound. 16mm Color. *Rental:* Films Inc, Iowa Films & Wholesome Film Ctr. *Sale:* Films Inc.

Thief, The. James Caan & Tuesday Weld. Directed by Michael Mann. 1981. United Artists. 120 min. Sound. 16mm Color. *Rental:* MGM United. *Rental:* MGM United, Videotape version.

Thief, The. Ray Milland & Rita Gam. Directed by Russell Rouse. 1952. United Artists. (No dialog). 85 min. Sound. 16mm B&W. *Rental:* Budget Films, Films Inc, Kit Parker, Video Com & Willoughby Peer. *Lease:* Video Comm.

Thief in the Night, A. 1973. Mark IV. (Cast unlisted). 73 min. Sound. 16mm Color. *Rental:* G Herne.

Thief of Bagdad, The. Douglas Fairbanks & Anna May Wong. Directed by Raoul Walsh. 1924. United Artists. (Musical score only). 135 min. Sound. 16mm B&W. *Rental:* Budget Films, Em Gee Film Lib, Films Inc, Images Film, Kit Parker, Twyman Films, Utah Media, Video Comm, Westcoast Films & Willoughby Peer. *Sale:* Blackhawk Films, Cinema Concepts, Festival Films, Griggs Movie & Natl Cinema. *Rental:* U Cal Media, Twyman Films, Video Comm & Welling Motion Pictures, *Sale:* Blackhawk Films, Natl Cinema & See-Art Films, Sound 16mm version. *Rental:* Killiam Collect & New Cinema, Tinted version. *Rental:* Ivy Films, *Sale:* Blackhawk Films, Super 8 sound version. *Sale:* Blackhawk Films, Super 8 silent version. *Sale:* Festival Films & Tamarelles French Film, Videotape version. *Rental:* Bosco Films, 50 mins. version.

Thief of Bagdad, The. Sabu & Conrad Veidt. Directed by Zoltan Korda. 1940. United Artists. 109 min. Sound. 16mm B&W. *Rental:* Films Inc & Ivy Films. *Rental:* Ivy Films, Color version.

Thief of Bagdad, The. Steve Reeves & Georgia Moll. Directed by Arthur Lubin. 1961. Italy. 89 min. Sound. 16mm Color. dubbed. *Rental:* Cine Craft, Films Inc, Westcoast Films & Welling Motion Pictures.

Thief of Bagdad, The. Roddy McDowall & Peter Ustinov. Directed by Clive Donner. 1978. Palm. 101 min. Sound. 16mm Color. *Rental:* Films Inc.

Thief of Paris, The. Jean-Paul Belmondo & Charles Denner. Directed by Louis Malle. Fr. 1967. France. 119 min. Sound. 16mm Color. subtitles. *Rental:* MGM United.

Thief Who Came to Dinner, The. Ryan O'Neal & Jacqueline Bisset. Directed by Bud Yorkin. 1973. Warners. 105 min. Sound. 16mm Color. *Rental:* Cine Craft, Film Ctr DC & Williams Films.

Thieves. Marlo Thomas & Charles Grodin. Directed by John Berry. 1977. Paramount. 103 min. Sound. 16mm Color. *Rental:* Films Inc.

Thieves Fall Out. Eddie Albert & Joan Leslie. Directed by Ray Enright. 1941. Warners. 72 min. Sound. 16mm B&W. *Rental:* MGM United.

Thieves' Highway. Richard Conte & Valentina Cortesa. Directed by Jules Dassin. 1949. Fox. 94 min. Sound. 16mm B&W. *Rental:* Films Inc.

Thieves Like Us. Keith Carradine & Shelley Duvall. Directed by Robert Altman. 1974. United Artists. 123 min. Sound. 16mm Color. *Rental:* MGM United.

Thin Air. Orig. Title: Body Stealers, The. George Sanders & Maurice Evans. Directed by Gerry Levy. 1968. Sagitarius. 95 min. Sound. 16mm Color. *Rental:* Hurlock Cine, Bosco Films & Willoughby Peer. *Sale:* Video Comm.

Thin Ice. Sonja Henie & Tyrone Power. Directed by Sidney Lanfield. 1937. Fox. 78 min. Sound. 16mm B&W. *Rental:* Films Inc.

Thin Man, The. William Powell & Myrna Loy. Directed by W. S. Van Dyke. 1944. MGM. 100 min. Sound. 16mm B&W. *Rental:* MGM United.

Thin Man Goes Home, The. William Powell & Myrna Loy. Directed by Richard Thorpe. 1944. MGM. 100 min. Sound. 16mm B&W. *Rental:* MGM United.

Thin Red Line, The. Keir Dullea & Jack Warden. Directed by Andrew Marton. 1963. Allied Artists. 99 min. Sound. 16mm B&W. *Rental:* Hurlock Cine.

Thine Is the Power: A Citizen's Guide to the Nuclear Energy Debate. 1977. (Documentary). 87 min. Sound. 16mm Color. *Rental:* U of IL Film.

Thing, The. Kenneth Tobey & James Arness. Directed by Christian Nyby. 1951. RKO. 87 min. Sound. 16mm B&W. *Rental:* Films Inc.

Thing, The. Kurt Russell & Wilford Brimley. Directed by John Carpenter. 1982. Universal. 127 min. Sound. 16mm Color. *Rental:* Swank Motion. *Rental:* Swank Motion, Videotape version.

Thing That Couldn't Die, The. William Reynolds & Andrea Martin. Directed by Will Cowan. 1958. Universal. 69 min. Sound. 16mm B&W. *Rental:* Swank Motion.

Thing With Two Heads, The. Ray Milland & Roosevelt Grier. Directed by Lee Frost. 1972. American International. 93 min. Sound. 16mm Color. *Rental:* Swank Motion.

Thing Without a Face, The *see* Pyro.

Things I Cannot Change. Directed by Tanya Ballantyne. 1966. Canada. (Documentary). 54 min. Sound. 16mm B&W. *Rental:* Films Inc & Museum Mod Art. *Sale:* Films Inc & Museum Mod Art. *Sale:* Films Inc, Videotape version.

Things in Their Season. Patricia Neal. 1974. Tomorrow Entertainment. 79 min. Sound. 16mm Color. *Rental:* Budget Films, Kent St U Film, Kit Parker, Learning Corp Am, Mass Media, Syracuse U Film, Twyman Films & U of IL Film. *Sale:* Learning Corp Am.

Things to Come. Raymond Massey & Sir Ralph Richardson. Directed by William Cameron Menzies. 1936. Britain. 92 min. Sound. B&W. *Rental:* Budget Films, Em Gee Film Lib, Films Inc, Images Film, Inst Cinema, Kit Parker, Mogulls Films, Natl Film Video, Film Ctr DC, Video Comm, Westcoast Films & Wholesome Film Ctr. *Sale:* Cinema Concepts, Festival Films, Glenn Photo, Images Film, Reel Images & Video Comm. *Sale:* Cinema Concepts, Festival Films, Glenn Photo & Images Film, Videotape version.

Think Dirty. Marty Feldman & Shelley Berman. 1978. Quartet. 94 min. Sound. 16mm Color. *Rental:* Films Inc.

Thinking in Action. 1983. DeBano. 75 min. Videotape Color. *Rental:* U Cal Media.

Thinking Machines, The. 1960. CBS. (Documentary). 54 min. Sound. 16mm B&W. *Rental:* U Mich Media. *Sale:* Carousel Films.

Third Alarm, The. Ralph Lewis & Johnnie Walker. Directed by Emory Johnson. 1922. FBO. 75 min. Silent. 16mm B&W. *Sale:* E Finney.

Third Generation, The. Eddie Constantine & Hanna Schygulla. Directed by Rainer Werner Fassbinder. Ger. 1979. Germany. 111 min. Sound. 16mm Color. subtitles. *Rental:* New Cinema & New Yorker Films.

Third Generation Making Dances, The: Seven Post-Modern Choreographers. Directed by Michael Blackwood. 89 min. 16mm *Rental:* Blackwood. *Sale:* Blackwood.

Third Man, The. Joseph Cotten, Orson Welles & Alida Valli. Directed by Sir Carol Reed. 1950. Selznick. 93 min. Sound. B&W. *Rental:* Arcus Film, Budget Films, Em Gee Film Lib, Inst Cinema, Kit Parker, La Inst Res Ctr, Natl Film Video, Newman Film, Utah Media, Twyman Films, Westcoast Films, Welling Motion Pictures & Wholesome Film Ctr. *Sale:* Reel Images. *Rental:* Images Film, Morcraft Films & Twyman Films, *Sale:* Cinema Concepts & Images Film, 105 min. version. *Sale:* Cinema Concepts, Morcraft Films, Reel Images & Tamarelles French Film, Videotape version. *Rental:* Utah Media, 101 min. version.

Third Man on the Mountain, The. Michael Rennie & Janet Munro. Directed by Ken Annakin. 1959. Disney. 107 min. Sound. 16mm Color. *Rental:* Buchan Pic, Cine Craft, Cousino Visual Ed, Elliot Film Co, Films Inc, U of IL Film, Modern Sound, Newman Film Lib & Film Ctr DC.

Third Millenium, The. Directed by Jorge Bodanzky. 95 min. Sound. 16mm Color. *Rental:* Cinema Guild.

Third Secret, The. Stephen Boyd & Jack Hawkins. Directed by Charles Crichton. 1964. Britain. (Anamorphic). 103 min. Sound. 16mm B&W. *Rental:* Films Inc.

Third Testament, The. 1976. Britain. (Documentary). 330 min. Sound. 16mm Color. *Rental:* Time-Life Multimedia. *Sale:* Time-Life Multimedia. *Rental:* Time-Life Multimedia, *Sale:* Time-Life Multimedia, Videotape version.

Third Voice, The. Edmond O'Brien & Julie London. Directed by Hubert Cornfield. 1960. Fox. (Anamorphic). 80 min. Sound. 16mm B&W. *Rental:* Willoughby Peer.

Third World, Third World War. 1970. Cuba. (Documentary). 90 min. Sound. 16mm B&W. *Rental:* Tricontinental Film.

Thirsty Dead, The. John Carradine & Jennifer Billingsley. Directed by Terry Becker. 1974. Mitan. 90 min. Sound. 16mm Color. *Rental:* Films Inc.

Thirteen *see* Eye of The Devil.

Thirteen Days to Die. Thomas Alder & Horst Frank. 1965. Germany. 100 min. Sound. 16mm B&W. dubbed. *Rental:* Westcoast Films.

Thirteen Fighting Men. Grant Williams & Brad Dexter. Directed by Harry Gerstad. 1960. Fox. (Anamorphic). 96 min. Sound. 16mm B&W. *Rental:* Willoughby Peer.

Thirteen Frightened Girls. Murray Hamilton & Joyce Taylor. Directed by William Castle. 1963. Columbia. 89 min. Sound. 16mm Color. *Rental:* Films Inc & Westcoast Films.

Thirteen Ghosts. Charles Herbert & Jo Morrow. Directed by William Castle. 1960. Columbia. (Three-D, Special glasses required). 88 min. Sound. 16mm Color. *Rental:* Kit Parker.

Thirteen Hours by Air. Fred MacMurray & Joan Bennett. Directed by Mitchell Leisen. 1936. Paramount. 80 min. Sound. 16mm Color. *Rental:* Swank Motion.

Thirteen Rue Madeleine. James Cagney & Richard Conte. Directed by Henry Hathaway. 1946. Fox. 95 min. Sound. 16mm B&W. *Rental:* Films Inc.

Thirteen West Street. Alan Ladd & Rod Steiger. Directed by Philip Leacock. 1962. Columbia. 80 min. Sound. 16mm B&W. *Rental:* Modern Sound.

Thirteen Women. Irene Dunne & Myrna Loy. Directed by George Archainbaud. 1933. RKO. 73 min. Sound. 16mm B&W. *Rental:* RKO General Pics.

Thirteenth Chair, The. Conrad Nagel & Leila Hyams. Directed by Chester M. Franklin. 1929. MGM. 80 min. Sound. 16mm B&W. *Rental:* MGM United.

Thirteenth Chair, The. Directed by George B. Seitz. 1937. MGM. (Cast unlisted). 70 min. Sound. 16mm B&W. *Rental:* MGM United.

Thirteenth Guest, The. Ginger Rogers & Lyle Talbot. Directed by Albert Ray. 1932. Monogram. 70 min. Sound. 16mm B&W. *Rental:* Hurlock Cine.

Thirteenth Hour, The. Lionel Barrymore & Polly Moran. Directed by Chester M. Franklin. 1927. MGM. 57 min. Silent. 16mm B&W. *Rental:* MGM United.

Thirteenth International Tournee of Animation, The. 1978. Film Wright. (Animated, anthology). 90 min. Sound. 16mm Color. *Rental:* Film Wright.

Thirty-Day Princess, The. Sylvia Sidney & Cary Grant. Directed by Marion Gering. 1934. Paramount. 76 min. Sound. 16mm B&W. *Rental:* Swank Motion.

Thirty-Foot Bride of Candy Rock, The. Lou Costello & Dorothy Provine. Directed by Sidney Miller. 1959. Columbia. 73 min. Sound. 16mm B&W. *Rental:* Buchan Pic, Budget Films, Cine Craft, Charard Motion Pics, Bosco Films, Films Inc, Inst Cinema, Modern Sound, Roas Films, Film Ctr DC, Welling Motion Picture & Westcoast Films.

Thirty Is a Dangerous Age, Cynthia. Dudley Moore & Suzy Kendall. Directed by Joseph McGrath. 1968. Britain. 85 min. Sound. 16mm Color. *Rental:* Films Inc, Modern Sound, Welling Motion Pictures & Westcoast Films. *Sale:* Tamarelles French Film, Videotape version.

Thirty Nine Hundred Million & One. 1974. Britain. (Documentary). 50 min. Sound. 16mm Color. *Rental:* U Mich Media.

Thirty-Nine Steps, The. Robert Donat & Madeleine Carroll. Directed by Alfred Hitchcock. 1935. Britain-Janus. 80 min. Sound. B&W. *Rental:* Budget Films, Cine Craft, Em Gee Film Lib, Film Classics, Films Inc, Images Film, Ivy Films, Iowa Films, Janus Films, Kit Parker, Maljack, Mogulls Films, Newman Film Lib, Natl Film Video, Roas Films, Utah Media, Video Comm, Welling Motion Pictures & Wholesome Film Ctr. *Sale:* Reel Images. *Rental:* Ivy Films, *Sale:* Cinema Concepts, Ivy Films & Tamarelles French Film, Videotape version.

Thirty-Nine Steps, The. Robert Powell & David Warner. Directed by Don Sharp. 1978. Britain. 102 min. Sound. 16mm Color. *Rental:* Arcus Film & Twyman Films.

Thirty-Nine Steps, The. Kenneth Moore & Taina Elg. Directed by Ralph Thomas. 1959. Britain. 93 min. Sound. 16mm Color. *Rental:* Cinema Five.

Thirty Seconds Over Tokyo. Spencer Tracy, Robert Walker & Van Johnson. Directed by Mervyn LeRoy. 1944. MGM. 135 min. Sound. 16mm B&W. *Rental:* MGM United.

Thirty Seven-Seventy Three. Directed by Richard Myers. 1974. 60 min. Sound. 16mm B&W. *Rental:* Canyon Cinema.

Thirty-Six Hours. Eva Marie Saint, Rod Taylor & James Garner. Directed by George Seaton. 1965. MGM. 115 min. Sound. 16mm B&W. *Rental:* Films Inc. *Rental:* MGM United, Anamorphic version.

Thirty Winchester for El Diablo. Carl Mohner. Directed by Frank G. Carrol. 1965. Germany. 91 min. Sound. 16mm Color. dubbed. *Rental:* Video Comm.

Thirty Years of Fun. Directed by Robert Youngson. 1963. Fox. (Anthology). 85 min. Sound. 16mm B&W. *Rental:* Budget Films, Films Inc, Kit Parker, Modern Sound, Newman Film Lib, Roas Films, U of IL Film & Wholesome Film Ctr.

This Above All. Tyrone Power & Joan Fontaine. Directed by Anatole Litvak. 1942. Fox. 110 min. Sound. 16mm B&W. *Rental:* Films Inc.

This Britain: Heritage of the Sea. 1975. National Geographic. (Documentary). 53 min. Sound. 16mm Color. *Rental:* Natl Geog. *Sale:* Natl Geog. *Sale:* Natl Geog, Videotape version.

This Child Is Rated X. 2 pts. 1971. NBC. (Documentary). 52 min. Sound. 16mm Color. *Rental:* Films Inc, Iowa Films, U Mich Media, OK AV Ctr, Syracuse U Film, Twyman Films & Utah Media. *Sale:* Films Inc. *Sale:* Films Inc, Videotape version.

This Could Be The Night. Jean Simmons & Paul Douglas. Directed by Robert Wise. 1957. MGM. 104 min. Sound. 16mm B&W. *Rental:* MGM United. *Rental:* MGM United, Anamorphic version.

This Day & Age. Charles Bickford & Judith Allen. Directed by Cecil B. DeMille. 1933. Paramount. 85 min. Sound. 16mm B&W. *Rental:* Swank Motion.

This Earth Is Mine. Rock Hudson & Jean Simmons. Directed by Henry King. 1959. Universal. 125 min. Sound. 16mm Color. *Rental:* Swank Motion.

This England. Constance Cummings & Emlyn Williams. Directed by David McDonald. 1943. Britain. 77 min. Sound. 16mm B&W. *Rental:* Ivy Films. *Sale:* Rep Pic Film.

This Generation Has No Future. 1975. Britain. (Documentary). 52 min. Sound. 16mm Color. *Rental:* U of IL Film.

This Gun for Hire. Alan Ladd & Veronica Lake. Directed by Frank Tuttle. 1942. Paramount. 81 min. Sound. 16mm B&W. *Rental:* Swank Motion.

This Happy Breed. Celia Johnson & Robert Newton. Directed by David Lean. 1947. Britain. 114 min. Sound. 16mm Color. *Rental:* Janus Films.

This Happy Feeling. Debbie Reynolds & Curt Jurgens. Directed by Blake Edwards. 1958. Universal. 92 min. Sound. 16mm Color. *Rental:* Swank Motion.

This Is a Hijack. Adam Roarke & Neville Brand. Directed by Barry Pollack. 1973. 90 min. Sound. 16mm Color. *Rental:* Budget Films.

This is Elvis. David Scott. Directed by Andrew Solt & Malcolm Leo. 1981. Warners. 101 min. Sound. 16mm B&W. *Rental:* Williams Films & Swank Motion.

This Is Marshall McLuhan: The Medium Is the Massage. 2 pts. 1967. NBC. (Documentary). 53 min. Sound. 16mm Color. *Rental:* U Cal Media, U of IL Film, Iowa Films, McGraw-Hill Films, U Mich Media, OK AV Ctr, Syracuse U Film & Utah Media. *Sale:* McGraw-Hill Films.

This is My Affair. Robert Taylor & Barbara Stanwyck. Directed by William A. Seiter. 1969. Fox. 51 min. Sound. 16mm B&W. *Rental:* Films Inc.

This Is My Love. Linda Darnell & Rick Jason. Directed by Stuart Heisler. 1954. RKO. 91 min. Sound. 16mm Color. *Rental:* Ivy Films. *Sale:* Rep Pic Film.

This Is My Son. 1977. Family. (Cast unlisted). 125 min. Sound. 16mm Color. *Rental:* Wholesome Film Ctr. *Sale:* Natl Churches Christ.

This Is Noel Coward. Noel Coward & Richard Burton. Directed by Charles Castle. 1974. Cantor. 60 min. Sound. 16mm Color. *Rental:* A Cantor. *Sale:* A Cantor.

This Is Robert. 1942. New York University. (Documentary). 80 min. Sound. 16mm B&W. *Rental:* U Cal Media. *Sale:* NYU Film Lib.

This is Sholem Aleichem. Jack Gilford, David Burns & Nancy Walker. 51 min. Sound. 16mm Color. *Rental:* Films Inc.

This Is the Army. Kate Smith, Frances Langford & Joe Louis. Directed by Michael Curtiz. 1943. Warners. 120 min. Sound. Color. *Rental:* Budget Films, Em Gee Film Lib, Kit Parker & Video Comm. *Sale:* Cinema Concepts, Glenn Photo & Natl Cinema. *Sale:* Glenn Photo, Videotape version.

This Island Earth. Jeff Morrow & Faith Domergue. Directed by Joseph Newman. 1955. Universal. 86 min. Sound. 16mm Color. *Rental:* Williams Films.

This Land. 1969. Canada. (Documentary). 57 min. Sound. 16mm B&W. *Sale:* Natl Film CN. *Rental:* Natl Film CN.

This Land is Mine. Charles Laughton & Maureen O'Hara. Directed by Jean Renoir. 1943. RKO. 103 min. Sound. 16mm B&W. *Rental:* Films Inc. *Lease:* Films Inc.

This Man Is Mine. Irene Dunne & Ralph Bellamy. Directed by John Cromwell. 1934. RKO. 76 min. Sound. 16mm B&W. *Rental:* RKO General Pics.

This Man Must Die. Jean Yanne. Directed by Claude Chabrol. Fr. 1970. France. 115 min. Sound. 16mm Color. subtitles. *Rental:* Hurlock Cine.

This Man's Navy. Wallace Beery & Tom Drake. Directed by William A. Wellman. 1945. MGM. 100 min. Sound. 16mm B&W. *Rental:* MGM United.

This Marriage Business. Jack Carson & Victor Moore. Directed by Christy Cabanne. 1938. RKO. 71 min. Sound. 16mm B&W. *Rental:* RKO General Pics.

This Modern Age. Joan Crawford & Pauline Frederick. Directed by Nick Grinde. 1931. MGM. 68 min. Sound. 16mm B&W. *Rental:* MGM United.

This Nude World. 1930. (Documentary). 60 min. Sound. 16mm B&W. *Sale:* Morcraft Films.

This Property is Condemned. Natalie Wood & Robert Redford. Directed by Sydney Pollack. 1966. Warners. 110 min. Sound. 16mm Color. *Rental:* Films Inc.

This Question of Color. 1965. NET. (Documentary). 60 min. Sound. 16mm B&W. *Rental:* Indiana AV Ctr.

This Question of Violence. 1968. NET. (Documentary). 59 min. Videotape *Sale:* Indiana AV Ctr & Phoenix Films.

This Savage Land. Barry Sullivan & Glenn Corbett. Directed by Vincent McEveety. 1968. Universal. 98 min. Sound. 16mm Color. *Rental:* Swank Motion.

This Side of Heaven. Lionel Barrymore & Fay Bainter. Directed by William K. Howard. 1934. MGM. 78 min. Sound. 16mm B&W. *Rental:* MGM United.

This Sporting Life. Richard Harris & Rachel Roberts. Directed by Lindsay Anderson. 1963. Britain. 114 min. Sound. 16mm B&W. *Rental:* Budget Films & Films Inc.

This Strange Passion. Arturo De Cordova & Delia Garces. Directed by Luis Bunuel. Span. 1952. Spain. 82 min. Sound. 16mm B&W. subtitles Eng. *Rental:* Films Inc.

This Time for Keeps. Robert Sterling & Irene Rich. Directed by Charles Reisner. 1942. MGM. 73 min. Sound. 16mm B&W. *Rental:* MGM United.

This Was Paris. Ben Lyon, Ann Dvorak & Robert Morley. Directed by John Harlow. 1942. Warners. 77 min. Sound. 16mm B&W. *Rental:* MGM United.

This Week-Eighteen Forty-Four. 1975. Britain. (Documentary). 60 min. Sound. 16mm Color. *Rental:* B Raymond. *Sale:* B Raymond.

This'll Make You Whistle. Jack Buchanan. Directed by Herbert Wilcox. 1938. Britain. 75 min. Sound. 16mm B&W. *Rental:* A Twyman Pres & Ivy Films. *Sale:* Rep Pic Film.

Thomas Corwin. George Rose. Directed by Michael Ritchie. (Profiles in Courage Ser.). 1965. Saudek. 50 min. Sound. 16mm B&W. *Rental:* IQ Film & Syracuse U Film. *Sale:* IQ Film. *Rental:* IQ Film, *Sale:* IQ Film,

Thomas Crown Affair, The. Steve McQueen & Faye Dunaway. Directed by Norman Jewison. 1968. United Artists. 102 min. Sound. 16mm Color. *Rental:* MGM United. *Rental:* MGM United, Videotape version.

Thomas Edison: Lightning Slinger. David Huffman & Rosemary DeCamp. Directed by Henning Schellerup. 1979. NBC. 51 min. Sound. 16mm Color. *Sale:* Lucerne Films & Welling Motion Pictures. *Sale:* Lucerne Films, Videotape version.

Thomas Graal's Best Child. Victor Seastrom. Directed by Mauritz Stiller. 1918. Sweden. 105 min. Silent. 16mm B&W. *Rental:* Em Gee Film Lib & Kit Parker. *Sale:* Cinema Concepts, Natl Cinema & Reel Images. *Sale:* Festival Films, 70 min. version. *Sale:* Tamarelles French Film, Videotape version.

Thomas Graal's Best Film. Orig. Title: Wanted, an Actress. Victor Seastrom. Directed by Mauritz Stiller. 1916. Sweden. 55 min. Silent. 16mm B&W. *Rental:* Budget Films, Em Gee Film Lib & Kit Parker. *Sale:* Reel Images & Festival Films.

Thomas Hart Benton. Orig. Title: Senator Thomas Hart Benton. Brian Keith. Directed by Lamont Johnson. (Profiles in Courage Ser.). 1965. Saudek. 50 min. Sound. 16mm B&W. *Rental:* IQ Film, U Mich Media, Syracuse U Film & U Mich Media. *Sale:* IQ Film. *Rental:* IQ Film, *Sale:* IQ Film, Spanish dubbed version.

Thomas the Imposter. Emmanuelle Riva & Fabrice Rouleau. Directed by Georges Franju. Fr. 1965. France. 94 min. Sound. 16mm B&W. subtitles +. *Rental:* New Yorker Films.

Thomasine & Bushrod. Max Julien & Vonetta McGee. Directed by Gordon Parks Jr. 1974. Columbia. 95 min. Sound. 16mm Color. *Rental:* Williams Films, Films Inc, Modern Sound, Swank Motion, Westcoast Films & Welling Motion Pictures.

Thoroughbred, The. Pauline Garon. Directed by Oscar Apfel. 1925. Truart. 50 min. Silent. 8mm B&W. *Rental:* Film Classics. *Sale:* Film Classics.

Thoroughbred, The. Helen Twelvetrees. Directed by Richard Thorpe. 1930. Tiffany. 60 min. Sound. 16mm B&W. *Sale:* Reel Images.

Thoroughbreds. Tom Neal & Adele Mara. Directed by George Blair. 1945. Republic. 55 min. Sound. 16mm B&W. *Rental:* Ivy Films.

Thoroughbreds Don't Cry. Judy Garland & Mickey Rooney. Directed by Alfred E. Green. 1937. MGM. 80 min. Sound. 16mm B&W. *Rental:* MGM United.

Thoroughly Modern Millie. Julie Andrews, Mary Tyler Moore, Carol Channing & Beatrice Lillie. Directed by George Roy Hill. 1967. Universal. 138 min. Sound. 16mm Color. *Rental:* Films Inc & Swank Motion.

Those Calloways. Brian Keith & Vera Miles. Directed by Norman Tokar. 1964. Disney. 131 min. Sound. 16mm Color. *Rental:* Cine Craft, Films Inc, U of IL Film, MGM United & Film Ctr DC.

Those Daring Young Men in Their Jaunty Jalopies. Tony Curtis & Terry-Thomas. Directed by Ken Annakin. 1969. Paramount. (Anamorphic). 125 min. Sound. 16mm Color. *Rental:* Films Inc.

Those Endearing Young Charms. Robert Young & Laraine Day. Directed by Lewis Allen. 1945. RKO. 82 min. Sound. 16mm B&W. *Rental:* Films Inc & RKO General Pics.

Those Fantastic Flying Fools. Orig. Title: Jules Verne's Rocket to the Moon. Burl Ives & Troy Donahue. Directed by Don Sharp. 1967. American International. 92 min. Sound. 16mm Color. *Rental:* Arcus Film, Budget Films, Films Inc, Roas Films, Video Comm, Westcoast Films, Welling Motion Pictures & Willoughby Peer.

Those High Gray Walls. Walter Connolly & Onslow Stevens. Directed by Charles Vidor. 1939. Columbia. 82 min. Sound. 16mm B&W. *Rental:* Kit Parker.

Those Incredible Diving Machines. 1971. Churchill Films. 52 min. Sound. 16mm Color. *Rental:* Churchill Films. *Rental:* Churchill Films, Videotape version.

Those Kids from Town. Percy Marmont. Directed by Lance Comfort. 1944. Britain. 82 min. Sound. 16mm B&W. *Rental:* Ivy Films.

Those Lips, Those Eyes. Frank Langella & Glynnis O'Connor. Directed by Michael Pressman. 1980. United Artists. 106 min. Sound. 16mm Color. *Rental:* MGM United.

Those Magnificent Men in Their Flying Machines. Orig. Title: Magnificent Men in Their Flying Machines. Terry-Thomas & Stuart Whitman. Directed by Ken Annakin. 1966. Fox. (Anamorphic). 131 min. Sound. 16mm Color. *Rental:* Films Inc, Twyman Films & Williams Films, Videotape version.

Those Redheads from Seattle. Rhonda Fleming & Gene Barry. Directed by Lewis R. Foster. 1953. Paramount. 90 min. Sound. 16mm Color. *Rental:* Films Inc.

Those Three French Girls. Fifi D'Orsay & Reginald Denny. Directed by Harry Beaumont. 1930. MGM. 75 min. Sound. 16mm Color. *Rental:* MGM United.

Those Were the Days. William Holden & Bonita Granville. Directed by Theodore Reed. 1940. Paramount. 76 min. Sound. 16mm B&W. *Rental:* Swank Motion.

Those Were the Happy Times. Orig. Title: Star! Julie Andrews & Daniel Massey. Directed by Robert Wise. 1968. Fox. (Anamorphic). 120 min. Sound. 16mm Color. *Rental:* Films Inc.

Thou Shalt Honor Thy Wife *see* Master of the House.

Thou Shalt Not Kill. Charles Bickford & Owen Davis Jr. Directed by John H. Auer. 1940. Republic. 66 min. Sound. 16mm B&W. *Rental:* Ivy Films. *Sale:* Rep Pic Film.

Thousand & One Hands, A. Directed by Souhel Ben Barka. African Dialect. 1973. Africa. (Documentary). 80 min. Sound. 16mm Color. subtitles. *Rental:* Cinema Guild. *Sale:* Cinema Guild.

Thousand & One Nights, A. Cornel Wilde & Evelyn Keyes. Directed by Alfred E. Green. 1945. Columbia. 93 min. Sound. 16mm B&W. *Rental:* Newman Film Lib.

Thousand & One Nights, A. Jeff Cooper & Raf Vallone. Directed by Ellchi Yanase. 1968. Italy. 90 min. Sound. 16mm Color. dubbed. *Rental:* Films Inc & Video Comm.

Thousand Clowns, A. Jason Robards & Barbara Harris. Directed by Fred Coe. 1966. United Artists. 118 min. Sound. 16mm B&W. *Rental:* MGM United. *Rental:* MGM United, Videotape version.

Thousand Eyes of Dr. Mabuse, The. Trans. Title: Die Tausand Augen des Dr. Mabuse. Dawn Addams & Peter Van Eyck. Directed by Fritz Lang. 1960. Germany. 103 min. Sound. 16mm B&W. *Rental:* Budget Films, Em Gee Film Lib & Inst Cinema.

Thousands Cheer. Kathryn Grayson & Gene Kelly. Directed by George Sidney. 1943. MGM. 126 min. Sound. 16mm Color. *Rental:* MGM United.

Thread of Life, The. 1960. MGM. (Documentary). 50 min. Sound. 16mm Color. *Rental:* BYU Media & Utah Media.

Threat, The. Michael O'Shea & Virginia Grey. Directed by Felix Feist. 1949. RKO. 66 min. Sound. 16mm B&W. *Rental:* Films Inc.

Three. Velimir-Bata Zivojinovic. Directed by Aleksander Petrovic. Serbo-Croatian. 1965. Yugoslavia. 70 min. Sound. 16mm B&W. subtitles. *Rental:* New Yorker Films.

Three: A Trilogy for Today's Youth. 1973. Ken Anderson. (Cast unlisted). 75 min. Sound. 16mm Color. *Rental:* G Herne.

Three Ages, The. Buster Keaton & Wallace Beery. Directed by Buster Keaton. 1923. Metro. 62 min. B&W. *Sale:* Festival Films. *Rental:* A Twyman Pres & Budget Films. *Rental:* Budget Films, Color version. *Sale:* Festival Films, Videotape version.

Three-&-a-Half Musketeers, The. Tin-Tan. 1961. Italy. 85 min. Sound. 16mm Color. dubbed. *Rental:* Ivy Films.

Three Approaches to Psychotherapy. 1964. Psychological. (Lecture). 117 min. Sound. 16mm B&W. *Rental:* Iowa Films, SD AV Ctr & U Mich Media. *Rental:* U of IL Film, Color version.

Three Avengers, The. Bruce Li. Hong Kong. 95 min. Sound. 16mm Color. *Rental:* WW Enter. *Rental:* WW Enter, Videotape version.

Three Bad Men. George O'Brien & Olive Borden. Directed by John Ford. 1926. Fox. 92 min. Silent. 16mm B&W. *Rental:* Killiam Collect.

Three Bites of the Apple. David McCallum & Sylva Koscina. Directed by Alvin Janzer. 1967. MGM. 105 min. Sound. 16mm Color. *Rental:* MGM United. *Rental:* MGM United, Anamorphic version.

Three Blind Mice. Loretta Young. Directed by William A. Seiter. 1938. Fox. 75 min. Sound. 16mm B&W. *Rental:* Films Inc.

Three Blondes in His Life. Jock Mahoney & Greta Thyssen. Directed by Leon Shoolock. 1960. Westhampton. 81 min. Sound. 16mm B&W. *Rental:* Ivy Films.

Three Boys on a Safari. 1973. Africa. (Cast unlisted). 57 min. Sound. 16mm Color. *Rental:* Lucerne Films & Modern Sound. *Sale:* Lucerne Films.

Three Brave Men. Ernest Borgnine & Ray Milland. Directed by Philip Dunne. 1957. Fox. (Anamorphic). 88 min. Sound. 16mm B&W. *Rental:* Films Inc.

Three Brothers. Philippe Noiret & Charles Vanel. Directed by Francesco Rosi. Ital. 1982. New World. 113 min. Sound. 16mm Color. subtitles. *Rental:* Films Inc.

Three Bullets for a Long Gun. Beau Brummell. Directed by Peter Henkel. 1972. Italy. 106 min. Sound. 16mm Color. dubbed. *Rental:* Films Inc.

Three by Hitchcock: Champagne, Manxman & The Ring. Orig. Title: Alfred Hitchcock Trilogy. Directed by Alfred Hitchcock. Britain. (Anthology). 85 min. Silent. 16mm B&W. *Rental:* Em Gee Film Lib & Images Film. *Sale:* Glenn Photo.

Three by Martha Graham. Directed by John Houseman. 1970. Pyramid. (Dance). 85 min. Sound. 16mm Color. *Rental:* Pyramid Film. *Sale:* Pyramid Film. *Sale:* Pyramid Film, *Rental:* Pyramid Film, Videotape version.

Three by Straub: Bridegroom, The Comedienne & The Pimp. Directed by Jean-Marie Straub. Fr. 1963. France. (Experimental). 92 min. Sound. 16mm B&W. subtitles. *Rental:* New Yorker Films.

Three Caballeros, The. Directed by Norman Ferguson. 1944. Disney. (Animated). 72 min. Sound. 16mm Color. *Rental:* Bosco Films, Buchan Pic, Cine Craft, Cousino Visual Ed, Disney Prod, Elliot Film Co, Films Inc, U of IL Film, MGM United, Modern Sound, Newman Film Lib, Roas Films, Swank Motion, Roas Film, Swank Motion, Film Ctr DC, Twyman Films, Westcoast Films, Welling Motion Pictures & Williams Films.

Three Came Home. Claudette Colbert & Patric Knowles. Directed by Jean Negulesco. 1950. Fox. 106 min. Sound. 16mm B&W. *Rental:* Films Inc.

Three Came to Kill. Cameron Mitchell & John Lupton. Directed by Edward L. Cahn. 1960. United Artists. 70 min. Sound. 16mm B&W. *Rental:* MGM United.

Three Cheers for the Irish. Thomas Mitchell & Dennis Morgan. Directed by Lloyd Bacon. 1940. Warners. 100 min. Sound. 16mm B&W. *Rental:* MGM United.

Three Coins in the Fountain. Jean Peters & Louis Jourdan. Directed by Jean Negulesco. 1954. Fox. 102 min. Sound. 16mm Color. *Rental:* Films Inc. *Rental:* Films Inc, Anamorphic color version.

Three Comrades. Margaret Sullavan, Robert Taylor & Franchot Tone. Directed by Frank Borzage. 1937. MGM. 98 min. Sound. 16mm B&W. *Rental:* MGM United.

Three Cubans. 1969. Robert Cohen. (Documentary). 57 min. Sound. 16mm Color. *Rental:* Syracuse U Film. *Sale:* Phoenix Films.

Three Dangerous Ladies. Glynis Johns, Ronee Blakely & John Hurt. 1979. Learning Corp. (Anthology). 83 min. Sound. 16mm Color. *Rental:* Learning Corp Am. *Lease:* Learning Corp Am.

Three Daring Daughters. Jeanette MacDonald & Jane Powell. Directed by Fred M. Wilcox. 1948. MGM. 115 min. Sound. 16mm Color. *Rental:* MGM United.

Three Days of the Condor. Robert Redford. Directed by Sydney Pollack. 1975. Paramount. (Anamorphic). 118 min. Sound. 16mm Color. *Rental:* Films Inc.

Three Desperate Men. Preston Foster & Virginia Grey. Directed by Sam Newfield. 1950. Lippert. 69 min. Sound. 16mm B&W. *Rental:* Film Ctr DC & Mogulls Films.

Three Evil Masters. Chen Kuan Tai. Hong Kong. 98 min. Sound. 16mm *Rental:* WW Enter. *Rental:* WW Enter, Videotape version.

Three Faces East. Constance Bennett & Erich Von Stroheim. Directed by Roy Del Ruth. 1930. Warners. 72 min. Sound. 16mm B&W. *Rental:* MGM United.

Three Faces of Eve, The. Joanne Woodward & David Wayne. Directed by Nunnally Johnson. 1957. Fox. 95 min. Sound. 16mm B&W. *Rental:* Films Inc & Williams Films. *Rental:* Films Inc, Anamorphic version.

Three Faces West. Orig. Title: Refugee, The. John Wayne & Sigrid Gurie. Directed by Bernard Vorhaus. 1940. Republic. 83 min. Sound. 16mm B&W. *Rental:* Ivy Films. *Lease:* Rep Pic Film.

Three for Jamie Dawn. Laraine Day & Richard Carlson. Directed by Thomas Carr. 1956. Allied Artists. 81 min. Sound. 16mm B&W. *Rental:* Ivy Films. *Sale:* Rep Pic Film.

Three for the Money *see* Win, Place or Steal.

Three for the Show. Betty Grable, Marge Champion & Gower Champion. Directed by H. C. Potter. 1955. Columbia. 91 min. Sound. 16mm Color. *Rental:* Arcus Film, Bosco Films, Films Inc & Welling Motion Pictures.

Three from Illinois. 1969. NBC. (Documentary). 53 min. Sound. 16mm Color. *Rental:* Films Inc. *Sale:* Films Inc. *Sale:* Films Inc, Videotape version.

Three Girls About Town. Joan Blondell, Binnie Barnes & Janet Blair. Directed by Leigh Jason. 1941. Columbia. 73 min. Sound. 16mm Color. *Rental:* Kit Parker.

Three Godfathers. John Wayne, Ward Bond & Mae Marsh. Directed by John Ford. 1948. MGM. 106 min. Sound. 16mm Color. *Rental:* MGM United.

Three Guns for Texas. Orig. Title: Laredo. Neville Brand & Peter Brown. Directed by David Lowell Rich. 1967. Universal. 99 min. Sound. 16mm Color. *Rental:* Williams Films.

Three Guys Named Mike. Jane Wyman & Van Johnson. Directed by Charles Walters. 1951. MGM. 90 min. Sound. 16mm B&W. *Rental:* MGM United. *Rental:* MGM United, Videotape version.

Three Hearts for Julia. Ann Sothern & Lee Bowman. Directed by Richard Thorpe. 1943. MGM. 90 min. Sound. 16mm B&W. *Rental:* MGM United.

Three Horsemen. 1983. EMC. 55 min. Sound. 16mm Color. *Rental:* U Cal Media. *Sale:* U Cal Media.

Three Hundred & Seventeenth Platoon, The. Jacques Perrin & Bruno Cremer. Directed by Pierre Schoendorffer. Fr. 1965. France. 100 min. Sound. 16mm B&W. subtitles. *Rental:* Films Inc.

Three Hundred & Thirty Million Gods. 1977. Britain. (Documentary). 52 min. Sound. 16mm Color. *Rental:* Iowa Films, U of IL Film & U Mich Media.

Three-Hundred from Stephanie. Tony Orlando & Peter Graves. Directed by Clyde Ware. 1980. Telepictures. 96 min. Sound. 16mm Color. *Rental:* Twyman Films.

Three Hundred Spartans, The. Richard Egan & Diane Baker. Directed by Rudolph Mate. 1962. Fox. 114 min. Sound. 16mm Color. *Rental:* Films Inc. *Rental:* Films Inc, Anamorphic version.

Three "I". 1971. Canada. (Documentary). 59 min. Sound. 16mm B&W. *Rental:* Natl Film CN. *Sale:* Natl Film CN.

Three in the Attic. Yvette Mimieux & Christopher Jones. Directed by Richard Wilson. 1968. American International. 90 min. Sound. 16mm Color. *Rental:* Budget Films, Film Ctr DC, Films Inc & Video Comm.

Three in the Cellar. Orig. Title: Up in the Cellar. Joan Collins, Larry Hagman & Wes Stern. Directed by Theodore J. Flicker. 1970. American International. 92 min. Sound. 16mm Color. *Rental:* Film Ctr DC & Films Inc.

Three in the Saddle. Tex Ritter. Directed by Harry Fraser. 1945. PRC. 60 min. Sound. 16mm B&W. *Rental:* Ivy Films & Mogulls Films. *Sale:* Classics Assoc NY.

Three Into Two Won't Go. Rod Steiger & Claire Bloom. Directed by Peter Hall. 1969. Britain. 110 min. Sound. 16mm Color. *Rental:* Swank Motion.

Three Invincible Sergeants. Richard Harrison. 1964. Italy. 88 min. Sound. 16mm Color. dubbed. *Rental:* Films Inc.

Three Is a Family. Charlie Ruggles. Directed by Edward Ludwig. 1944. United Artists. 85 min. Sound. 16mm B&W. *Rental:* Film Classics, Mogulls Films & Welling Motion Pictures.

Three Little Girls in Blue. June Haver & George Montgomery. Directed by Bruce Humberstone. 1946. Fox. 90 min. Sound. 16mm Color. *Rental:* Films Inc.

Three Little Sisters. Mary Lee & William Shirley. Directed by Joseph Santley. 1944. Republic. 68 min. Sound. 16mm B&W. *Rental:* Ivy Films. *Sale:* Rep Pic Film.

Three Little Words. Fred Astaire & Red Skelton. Directed by Richard Thorpe. 1950. MGM. 102 min. Sound. 16mm Color. *Rental:* MGM United. *Rental:* MGM United, Videotape version.

Three Live Ghosts. Richard Arlen & Beryl Mercer. Directed by Bruce Humberstone. 1936. MGM. 62 min. Sound. 16mm B&W. *Rental:* MGM United.

Three Live Ghosts. Joan Bennett, Charles Laughton & Robert Montgomery. Directed by Thornton Freeland. 1936. 16mm *Rental:* A Twyman Pres.

Three Lives. Directed by Kate Millet. 1971. Impact. (Documentary). 75 min. Sound. 16mm Color. *Rental:* Icarus Films. *Sale:* Icarus Films.

Three Lives of Thomasina, The. Patrick McGoohan, Susan Hampshire & Karen Dotice. Directed by Don Chaffey. 1963. Disney. 97 min. Sound. 16mm Color. *Rental:* Bosco Films, Cine Craft, Cousino Visual Ed, #Elliot Film Co, Film Ctr DC, Films Inc, MGM United, Modern Sound, Newman Film Lib, Roas Films, Swank Motion, Twyman Films, U of IL Film, Westcoast Films, Welling Motion Pictures & Williams Films.

Three Looms Waiting. 1971. Britain. (Documentary). 50 min. Sound. 16mm Color. *Rental:* Iowa Films, U Cal Media & U Mich Media.

Three Maxims, The. Anna Neagle. Directed by Herbert Wilcox. 1937. 16mm *Rental:* A Twyman Pres.

Three Men. 1965. Net. (Documentary). 60 min. Sound. 16mm B&W. *Rental:* Indiana AV Ctr. *Sale:* Indiana AV Ctr.

Three Men from Texas. William Boyd. Directed by Lesley Selander. 1940. Paramount. 54 min. Sound. 16mm B&W. *Sale:* Cinema Concepts.

Three Men on a Horse. Frank McHugh & Joan Blondell. Directed by Archie Mayo. 1936. Warners. 85 min. Sound. 16mm B&W. *Rental:* MGM United.

Three Mesquiteers, The. John Wayne & Robert Livingston. Directed by Ray Taylor. 1936. Republic. 54 min. Sound. 16mm B&W. *Rental:* Ivy Films. *Sale:* Cinema Concepts, Rep Pic Film & Reel Images.

Three Musketeers, The. Orig. Title: Valiant Three, The. Ritz Brothers. Directed by Allan Dwan. 1939. Fox. 72 min. Sound. 16mm B&W. *Rental:* Films Inc.

Three Musketeers, The. Douglas Fairbanks. Directed by Fred Niblo. 1921. United Artists. 172 min. Silent. 16mm B&W. *Rental:* A Twyman Pres, Em Gee Film Lib, Twyman Films & Museum Mod Art.

Three Musketeers, The. Jack Mulhall, Raymond Hatton & John Wayne. Directed by Armand Schaefer & Colbert Clark. 1933. Mascot. 75 min. Sound. 16mm B&W. *Rental:* Budget Films.

Three Musketeers, The. Gene Kelly & Lana Turner. Directed by George Sidney. 1948. MGM. 126 min. Sound. 16mm Color. *Rental:* MGM United.

Three Musketeers, The. Robert Clarke & John Hubbard. Directed by Budd Boetticher. 1951. Britain. 60 min. Sound. 16mm B&W. *Rental:* Budget Films, Cine Craft & Films Inc.

Three Musketeers, The. Michael York & Raquel Welch. Directed by Richard Lester. 1974. Fox. 107 min. Sound. 16mm Color. *Rental:* Films Inc. *Rental:* Films Inc, Anamorphic version.

Three Musketeers, The. Directed by John Halas. 1976. Britain. (Animated). 72 min. Sound. 16mm Color. *Rental:* Budget Films & Film Pres.

Three Musketeers, The. Paul Lukas & Walter Abel. Directed by Rowland V. Lee. 1935. RKO. 96 min. Sound. 16mm *Rental:* RKO General Pics.

Three Nuts in Search of a Bolt. Mamie Van Doren. Directed by Tommy Noonan. 1964. Harlequin. 90 min. Sound. 16mm Color. *Rental:* Budget Films.

Three of a Kind. Orig. Title: Cooking up Trouble. Billy Gilbert, Maxie Rosenbloom & June Lang. Directed by D. Ross Lederman. 1944. Monogram. 65 min. Sound. 16mm B&W. *Rental:* Budget Films, Ivy Films, Rep Pic Film & Video Comm. *Lease:* Rep Pic Film.

Three On a Couch. Jerry Lewis & Janet Leigh. Directed by Jerry Lewis. 1966. Columbia. 109 min. Sound. 16mm Color. *Rental:* Arcus Film, Budget Films, Cine Craft, Charard Motion Pics, Film Ctr DC, Films Inc, Film Pres, Inst Cinema, Modern Sound, Newman Film Lib, Roas Films, Twyman Films, Welling Motion Pictures & Westcoast Films.

Three On a Match. Bette Davis, Joan Blondell & Ann Dvorak. Directed by Mervyn LeRoy. 1933. Warners. 64 min. Sound. 16mm B&W. *Rental:* MGM United.

Three On a Spree. Jack Watling & Renee Houston. Directed by Sidney J. Furie. 1961. Britain. 83 min. Sound. 16mm B&W. *Rental:* MGM United.

Three On a Ticket. Hugh Beaumont & Cheryl Walker. Directed by Sam Newfield. 1947. PRC. 64 min. Sound. 16mm B&W. *Sale:* Classics Assoc NY.

Three On the Heights. 58 min. Sound. 16mm Color. *Rental:* Alden Films.

Three On the Trail. William Boyd. Directed by Howard Bretherton. 1936. Paramount. 65 min. Sound. 16mm B&W. *Lease:* Cinema Concepts.

Three Outlaw Samurai. Tetsuro Tamba. Directed by Hideo Gosha. Jap. 1975. Japan. 120 min. Sound. 16mm B&W. subtitles. *Rental:* Films Inc.

Three Outlaws. Neville Brand & Bruce Bennett. Directed by Sam Newfield. 1956. Associated. 75 min. Sound. 16mm B&W. *Rental:* Ivy Films. *Sale:* Rep Pic Film.

Three Ring Circus. Dean Martin & Jerry Lewis. Directed by Joseph Pevney. 1954. Paramount. 103 min. Sound. 16mm Color. *Rental:* Films Inc.

Three R's of Sex Education, The. 1970. NET. (Documentary). 60 min. Sound. 16mm B&W. *Rental:* Indiana AV Ctr. *Sale:* Indiana AV Ctr.

Three Secrets. Eleanor Parker, Patricia Neal & Ruth Roman. Directed by Robert Wise. 1949. Warners. 98 min. Sound. 16mm B&W. *Rental:* Corinth Films.

Three Sisters, The. Lyubov Sokolva & Margarita Volodina. Directed by Samson Samsonov. Rus. 1964. Russia. 115 min. Sound. 16mm B&W. subtitles. *Rental:* Corinth Films.

Three Sisters, The. Geraldine Page, Sandy Dennis & Kim Stanley. Directed by Paul Bogart. 1966. Actors Guild. 168 min. Sound. 16mm B&W. *Rental:* Budget Films, Ivy Films, Kit Parker & Video Comm. *Lease:* Video Comm.

Three Sisters, The. Alan Bates. Directed by Sir Laurence Olivier. 1973. AFT. 165 min. Sound. 16mm Color. *Rental:* Films Inc.

Three Sisters, The. Janet Suzman. 1976. Britain. 136 min. Videotape Color. *Rental:* Films Inc. *Sale:* Films Inc. *Rental:* Films Inc, 60 mins version.

Three Smart Girls. Deanna Durbin & Nan Gray. Directed by Henry Koster. 1937. Universal. 84 min. Sound. 16mm B&W. *Rental:* Swank Motion.

Three Smart Girls Grow Up. Deanna Durbin & Charles Winninger. Directed by Henry Koster. 1939. Universal. 73 min. Sound. 16mm B&W. *Rental:* Swank Motion.

Three Songs About Lenin. Directed by Dziga Vertov. Rus. 1934. Russia. (Documentary). 68 min. Sound. 16mm B&W. subtitles. *Rental:* Corinth Films.

Three Sons. Edward Ellis. Directed by Jack Hively. 1939. RKO. 72 min. Sound. 16mm B&W. *Rental:* Films Inc.

Three Sons O' Guns. Wayne Morris, Irene Rich & Marjorie Rambeau. Directed by Ben Stoloff. 1941. Warners. 65 min. Sound. 16mm B&W. *Rental:* MGM United.

Three Steps to the Gallows *see* White Fire.

Three Stooges Follies, The. Directed by Jules White. 1974. Columbia. (Anthology). 106 min. Sound. 16mm B&W. *Rental:* Cine Craft, Williams Films, Films Inc, Film Pres, Inst Cinema, Kit Parker, Modern Sound, Natl Film Video, Roas Films, Swank Motion, Twyman, Twyman Films, Westcoast Films, Welling Motion Pictures, Wholesome Film Ctr & Budget Films. *Rental:* Bosco Films, 85 mins. version. *Rental:* Welling Motion Pictures, 116 mins. version.

Three Stooges Go Around the World in a Daze, The. The Three Stooges. Directed by Norman Maurer. 1963. Columbia. 94 min. Sound. 16mm B&W. *Rental:* Bosco Films, Budget Films, Cine Craft, Charard Motion Pics, Film Ctr DC, Films Inc, Film Pres, Inst Cinema, Modern Sound, Natl Video, Roas Films, Twyman Films, Westcoast Films, Welling Motion Pictures & Wholesome Film Ctr.

Three Stooges in Orbit, The. The Three Stooges. Directed by Edward Bernds. 1962. Columbia. 87 min. Sound. 16mm B&W. *Rental:* Arcus Film, Budget Films, Cine Craft, Films Inc, Film Pres, Inst Cinema, Modern Sound, Natl Film Video, Roas Films, Twyman Films, Westcoast Films, Welling Motion Pictures, Wholesome Film Ctr & Williams Films.

Three Stooges Meet Hercules, The. The Three Stooges. Directed by Edward Bernds. 1962. Columbia. 89 min. Sound. 16mm B&W. *Rental:* Arcus Film, Cine Craft, Charard Motion Pics, Williams Films, Film Pres, Films Inc, Inst Cinema, Modern Sound, Natl Film Video, Film Ctr DC, Twyman Films, Westcoast Films, Welling Motion Pictures & Wholesome Film Ctr.

Three Stooges Parade, The. 6 pts. 1934-45. Columbia. Sound. 16mm B&W. *Rental:* Films Inc.

Three Strange Loves. Birgit Tengroth. Directed by Ingmar Bergman. 1949. Sweden. 84 min. Sound. 16mm B&W. *Rental:* Films Inc, Janus Films & New Cinema.

Three Strangers. Geraldine Fitzgerald, Sydney Greenstreet & Peter Lorre. Directed by Jean Negulesco. 1946. Warners. 92 min. Sound. 16mm B&W. *Rental:* MGM United.

Three Stripes in the Sun. Orig. Title: Gentle Sergeant, The. Aldo Ray & Phil Carey. Directed by Richard Murphy. 1955. Columbia. 93 min. Sound. 16mm B&W. *Rental:* Buchan Pic, Charard Motion Pics, Cine Craft, Films Inc, Modern Sound & Westcoast Films.

Three Swords of Zorro. Guy Stockwell. 1960. Spain. 88 min. Sound. 16mm B&W. dubbed. *Rental:* Ivy Films & Westcoast Films.

Three Tales Dark & Dangerous. 1979. Learning Corp. (Anthology). 84 min. Sound. 16mm Color. *Rental:* Learning Corp Am. *Lease:* Learning Corp Am.

Three Ten to Yuma. Glenn Ford & Van Heflin. Directed by Delmer Daves. 1957. Columbia. 92 min. Sound. 16mm B&W. *Rental:* Arcus Film, Bosco Films, Budget Films, Cine Craft, Film Ctr DC, Films Inc, Kit Parker, Modern Sound, Twyman Films, U of IL Film, Video Comm & Westcoast Films.

Three Texas Steers. Orig. Title: Danger Rides the Range. John Wayne & Carole Landis. Directed by George Sherman. 1939. Republic. 56 min. Sound. 16mm B&W. *Rental:* Ivy Films. *Sale:* Rep Pic Film & Nostalgia Merchant.

Three the Hard Way. Fred Williamson & Jim Brown. Directed by Gordon Parks. 1974. Allied Artists. 92 min. Sound. 16mm Color. *Rental:* Hurlock Cine.

Three Tough Guys. Isaac Hayes & Lino Ventura. Directed by Duccio Tessari. 1974. Paramount. 92 min. Sound. 16mm Color. *Rental:* Films Inc.

Three Violent People. Charlton Heston & Anne Baxter. Directed by Rudolph Mate. 1956. Paramount. 100 min. Sound. 16mm Color. *Rental:* Films Inc.

Three Who Care. 1979. Penn State. (Documentary). 58 min. Sound. 16mm Color. *Rental:* Penn St AV Serv. *Sale:* Penn St AV Serv. *Rental:* Penn St AV Serv, *Sale:* Penn St AV Serv, Videotape version.

Three Who Loved. Conrad Nagel & Betty Compton. Directed by George Archainbaud. 1931. RKO. 78 min. Sound. 16mm B&W. *Rental:* RKO General Pics.

Three Wise Fools. Margaret O'Brien & Lionel Barrymore. Directed by Edward Buzzell. 1946. MGM. 90 min. Sound. 16mm B&W. *Rental:* Films Inc & MGM United.

Three Wise Girls. Jean Harlow. Directed by William Beaudine. 1931. Columbia. 70 min. Sound. 16mm B&W. *Rental:* Films Inc & Welling Motion Pictures.

Three Wishes for Cinderella. (Cast unlisted). 46 min. Sound. 16mm Color. dubbed. *Rental:* Films Inc.

Three Women. Sissy Spacek, Shelley Duvall & Janice Rule. Directed by Robert Altman. 1977. Fox. (Anamorphic). 123 min. Sound. 16mm Color. *Rental:* Films Inc.

Three Word Brand. William S. Hart & Jane Novak. Directed by Lambert Hillyer. 1921. Hart. 55 min. Silent. 16mm B&W. *Rental:* Em Gee Film Lib. *Sale:* Reel Images. *Sale:* Reel Images, Super 8 silent version.

Three Worlds of Bali, The. 58 min. Sound. Videotape *Rental:* PBS Video. *Sale:* PBS Video.

Three Worlds of Gulliver. Kerwin Mathews & Jo Morrow. Directed by Jack Sher. 1960. Columbia. 100 min. Sound. 16mm Color. *Rental:* Arcus Film, Budget Films, Cine Craft, Charard Motion Pics, Williams Films, Bosco Films, Films Inc, Film Pres, U of IL Film, Kerr Film, Kit Parker, Modern Sound, Newman Film Lib, Natl Film Video, Roas Films, Swank Motion, Syracuse U Film, Twyman Films, Video Comm, Westcoast Films, Welling Motion Pictures, Wholesome Film Ctr & Willoughby Peer.

Three Young Americans in Search of Survival. 1973. (Documentary). 103 min. Sound. 16mm Color. *Rental:* Utah Media.

Three Young Texans. Jeffrey Hunter & Mitzi Gaynor. Directed by Henry Levin. 1954. Fox. 77 min. Sound. 16mm Color. *Rental:* Films Inc, Welling Motion Pictures & Willoughby Peer.

Threepenny Opera, The. Orig. Title: Dreigroschenoper, Die. Lotte Lenya & Rudolph Forster. Directed by G. W. Pabst. Ger. 1931. Germany. 112 min. Sound. 16mm B&W. subtitles. *Rental:* Films Inc, Janus Films & New Cinema. *Sale:* Reel Images.

Three's a Crowd. Harry Langdon. Directed by Harry Langdon. 1927. First National. 80 min. Silent. 16mm B&W. *Rental:* A Twyman Pres & Twyman Films.

Three's a Crowd. Pamela Blake. Directed by Lesley Selander. 1945. Republic. 58 min. Sound. 16mm B&W. *Rental:* Ivy Films.

Threshold. Donald Sutherland & John Marley. Directed by Richard Pearce. 1983. Fox. 97 min. Sound. 16mm Color. *Rental:* Films Inc. *Sale:* Tamarelles French Film, Videotape version.

Threshold of Liberty, The. 1979. Britain. (Documentary). 52 min. Sound. 16mm Color. *Rental:* Time-Life Multimedia & U Cal Media. *Sale:* Time-Life Multimedia. *Sale:* Time-Life Multimedia, Videotape version.

Thrill of Brazil, The. Ann Miller, Evelyn Keyes & Kennan Wynn. Directed by S. Sylvan Simon. 1946. Columbia. 91 min. Sound. 16mm B&W. *Rental:* Bosco Films.

Thrill of It All, The. Doris Day & James Garner. Directed by Norman Jewison. 1963. Universal. 108 min. Sound. 16mm Color. *Rental:* Swank Motion.

Thrill of Youth, The. June Clyde & Dorothy Peterson. Directed by Richard Thorpe. 1932. Invincible. 70 min. Sound. 16mm B&W. *Rental:* Mogulls Films.

Throne of Blood. Toshiro Mifune. Directed by Akira Kurosawa. Jap. 1957. Japan. 105 min. Sound. 16mm B&W. subtitles. *Rental:* Films Inc. *Lease:* Macmillan Films.

Through a Glass Darkly. Harriet Andersson. Directed by Ingmar Bergman. Swed. 1961. Sweden. 91 min. Sound. 16mm B&W. subtitles. *Rental:* Films Inc, Janus Films & New Cinema.

Through All Time. 1979. PBS. (Documentary). 58 min. Videotape Color. *Rental:* PBS Video. *Sale:* PBS Video.

Through the Breakers. Holmes Herbert & Margaret Livingston. Directed by Joseph C. Boyle. 1928. Gotham. 60 min. Silent. 16mm B&W. *Sale:* Morcraft Films.

Through the Looking Glass Darkly. 1973. WKY. (Documentary). 59 min. Sound. 16mm Color. *Rental:* OK AV Ctr.

Thumbs Up. Elsa Lanchester, Gertrude Neisen & Brenda Joyce. Directed by Joseph Santley. 1943. Republic. 67 min. Sound. 16mm B&W. *Rental:* Ivy Films.

Thunder Afloat. Wallace Beery & Chester Morris. Directed by George B. Seitz. 1939. MGM. 95 min. Sound. 16mm B&W. *Rental:* MGM United.

Thunder & Lightning. David Carradine & Kate Jackson. Directed by Corey Allen. 1977. Fox. (Anamorphic). 94 min. Sound. 16mm Color. *Rental:* Films Inc & Welling Motion Pictures.

Thunder Bay. James Stewart & Joanne Dru. Directed by Anthony Mann. 1953. Universal. 102 min. Sound. 16mm Color. *Rental:* Swank Motion.

Thunder in God's Country. Rex Allen. Directed by George Blair. 1951. Republic. 67 min. Sound. 16mm B&W. *Rental:* Ivy Films. *Sale:* Rep Pic Film.

Thunder in the City. Edward G. Robinson & Nigel Bruce. Directed by Marion Gering. 1937. Columbia. 76 min. Sound. 16mm B&W. *Rental:* Budget Films & Mogulls Films. *Sale:* Morcraft Films & Reel Images. *Sale:* Morcraft Films & Reel Images, Super 8 sound version.

Thunder in the Desert. Bob Steele. Directed by Sam Newfield. 1937. Republic. 60 min. Sound. 16mm B&W. *Rental:* Ivy Films & Mogulls Films. *Sale:* Rep Pic Film.

Thunder in the East. Orig. Title: Rage of the Vulture. Alan Ladd & Deborah Kerr. Directed by Charles Vidor. 1953. Paramount. 98 min. Sound. 16mm B&W. *Rental:* Films Inc.

Thunder in the Pines. George Reeves & Denise Darcel. Directed by Robert Edwards. 1949. Lippert. 62 min. Sound. 16mm B&W. *Rental:* Film Ctr DC & Westcoast Films.

Thunder in the Skies. 1978. Britain. (Documentary). 51 min. Sound. 16mm Color. *Rental:* Iowa Films, Kent St U Film, U Cal Media, U of IL Film & U Mich Media.

Thunder in the Sun. Susan Hayward & Jeff Chandler. Directed by Russell Rouse. 1959. Paramount. 81 min. Sound. 16mm Color. *Rental:* Films Inc.

Thunder in the Valley. Lon McCallister & Peggy Ann Garner. Directed by Louis King. 1947. Fox. 103 min. Sound. 16mm Color. *Rental:* Films Inc.

Thunder of Drums, A. Richard Boone & George Hamilton. Directed by Joseph Newman. 1961. MGM. 97 min. Sound. 16mm Color. *Rental:* Films Inc & MGM United. *Rental:* Films Inc, Anamorphic version.

Thunder On the Hill. Claudette Colbert & Ann Blyth. Directed by Douglas Sirk. 1951. Universal. 84 min. Sound. 16mm B&W. *Rental:* Swank Motion.

Thunder Over Arizona. Skip Homeier & Jack Elam. Directed by Joseph Kane. 1956. Republic. 75 min. Sound. 16mm B&W. *Rental:* Ivy Films. *Sale:* Rep Pic Film.

Thunder Over Mexico. Directed by Sergei Eisenstein & Grigori Alexandrov. 1933. Mexico. (Documentary, musical score only). 70 min. Sound. 16mm B&W. *Rental:* A Twyman Pres, Museum Mod Art & Twyman Films.

Thunder Pass. Dane Clark & Dorothy Patrick. Directed by Frank McDonald. 1954. Lippert. 65 min. Sound. 16mm B&W. *Rental:* Ivy Films. *Sale:* Rep Pic Film.

Thunder River Feud. Ray Corrigan & Max Terhune. Directed by S. Roy Luby. 1942. Monogram. 60 min. Sound. 16mm B&W. *Sale:* Morcraft Films. *Sale:* Morcraft Films, Super 8 sound version.

Thunder Road. Robert Mitchum & Gene Barry. Directed by Arthur Ripley. 1958. United Artists. 92 min. Sound. 16mm B&W. *Rental:* MGM United.

Thunder Town. Bob Steele. Directed by Harry Fraser. 1946. PRC. 57 min. Sound. 16mm B&W. *Sale:* Rep Pic Film.

Thunderball. Sean Connery & Adolfo Celi. Directed by Terence Young. 1965. United Artists. 132 min. Sound. 16mm Color. *Rental:* MGM United. *Rental:* MGM United, Videotape version.

Thunderbirds. John Drew Barrymore & John Derek. Directed by John H. Auer. 1952. Republic. 98 min. Sound. 16mm B&W. *Rental:* Ivy Films. *Sale:* Rep Pic Film.

Thunderbirds. Gene Tierney & Preston Foster. Directed by William A. Wellman. 1942. Fox. 78 min. Sound. 16mm B&W. *Rental:* Films Inc.

Thunderbolt. Richard Arlen & George Bancroft. Directed by Josef Von Sternberg. 1929. Paramount. 94 min. Sound. 16mm B&W. *Rental:* Museum Mod Art & Swank Motion.

Thunderbolt. Directed by William Wyler & John Sturges. 1945. USA. (Documentary). 42 min. Sound. 16mm Color. *Rental:* Budget Film & Images Film.

Thunderbolt & Lightfoot. Clint Eastwood & Jeff Bridges. Directed by Michael Cimino. 1974. United Artists. 115 min. Sound. 16mm Color. *Rental:* Budget Films, MGM United, Westcoast Films & Wholesome Film Ctr. *Rental:* MGM United, Videotape version.

Thundergap Outlaws. James Newill & Dave O'Brien. 1947. PRC. 61 min. Sound. 16mm B&W. *Rental:* Video Comm.

Thunderhead, Son of Flicka. Roddy McDowall & Preston Foster. Directed by Louis King. 1945. Fox. 78 min. Sound. 16mm Color. *Rental:* Films Inc, Twyman Films & Williams Films.

Thunderhoof. Preston Foster & Mary Stewart. Directed by Phil Karlson. 1948. Columbia. 77 min. Sound. 16mm B&W. *Rental:* Kit Parker.

Thundering Caravans. Eddy Waller, Richard Crane & Allan Lane. Directed by Harry Keller. 1952. Republic. 54 min. Sound. 16mm B&W. *Sale:* Rep Pic Film & Nostalgia Merchant.

Thundering Gunslingers. Buster Crabbe. Directed by Sam Newfield. 1944. PRC. 61 min. Sound. 16mm B&W. *Rental:* Mogulls Films.

Thundering Hoofs. Fred Thompson & Peggy O'Day. Directed by Albert S. Rogell. 1924. Aywon. 61 min. Silent. 16mm B&W. *Rental:* Mogulls Films.

Thundering Hoofs. Tim Holt & Ray Whitley. Directed by Lesley Selander. 1942. RKO. 61 min. Sound. 16mm B&W. *Rental:* RKO General Pics.

Thundering Jets. Rex Reason & Audrey Dalton. Directed by Helmut Dantine. 1958. Fox. 73 min. Sound. 16mm B&W. *Rental:* Ivy Films. *Sale:* Rep Pic Film.

Thundering Trail. Tom Tyler & Bob Steele. Directed by John English. 1943. Republic. 56 min. Sound. 16mm B&W. *Rental:* Ivy Films. *Sale:* Rep Pic Film.

Thunderstorm. Linda Christian & Carlos Thompson. Directed by John Guillermin. 1956. Allied Artists. 81 min. Sound. 16mm B&W. *Rental:* A Twyman Pres & Hurlock Cine.

Thus Spake Richard Strauss. 1972. CBS. (Documentary). 48 min. Sound. 16mm B&W. *Rental:* Phoenix Films & Syracuse U Film. *Sale:* Phoenix Films. *Sale:* Phoenix Films, Videotape version.

THX Eleven Thirty Eight. Robert Duvall & Donald Pleasance. Directed by George Lucas. 1971. Warners. 88 min. Sound. 16mm Color. *Rental:* Cine Craft, Film Ctr DC, Films Inc, Inst Cinema, Modern Sound, Swank Motion, Twyman Films & Williams Films. *Rental:* Twyman Films, Anamorphic version. *Rental:* Swank Motion, Videotape version.

Tiberius. Abbe Lane. 1966. Italy. 101 min. Sound. 16mm B&W. dubbed. *Rental:* Ivy Films.

Tibet. Directed by Felix Greene. 1977. Britain. (Documentary). 60 min. Sound. 16mm Color. *Rental:* Cinema Guild.

Tibet: A Buddhist Trilogy. 3 pts. 1982. EMC. 233 min. Sound. 16mm Color. *Rental:* U Cal Media. *Sale:* U Cal Media, Videotape version.

Ticket to Heaven, A. Nick Mancuso, Saul Rubinek & Meg Foster. Directed by Ralph Thomas. 1981. 107 min. Sound. 16mm Color. *Rental:* MGM United.

Ticket to Paradise, A. Roger Pryor & Wendy Barrie. Directed by Aubrey Scotto. 1936. Republic. 67 min. Sound. 16mm B&W. *Rental:* Ivy Films.

Ticket to Tomahawk, A. Dan Dailey & Anne Baxter. Directed by Richard Sale. 1950. Fox. 91 min. Sound. 16mm B&W. *Rental:* Films Inc.

Tickle Me. Elvis Presley & Julie Adams. Directed by Norman Taurog. 1965. Allied Artists. 90 min. Sound. 16mm Color. *Rental:* Hurlock Cine.

Ticklish Affair, A. Shirley Jones & Gig Young. Directed by George Sidney. 1963. MGM. 89 min. Sound. 16mm Color. *Rental:* MGM United. *Rental:* MGM United, Anamorphic version.

Ticktaban. Minda Moro. 1949. Monogram. 56 min. Sound. 16mm B&W. *Rental:* Hurlock Cine.

Tick...Tick...Tick. Jim Brown, Fredric March & George Kennedy. Directed by Ralph Nelson. 1970. MGM. 100 min. Sound. 16mm Color. *Rental:* MGM United.

Tidikawa & Friends. 1971. Vision Quest. (Documentary). 80 min. Sound. 16mm Color. *Rental:* U Cal Media, U Mich Media & Vision Quest. *Sale:* Vision Quest.

Tiefland. Directed by Leni Riefenstahl. Ger. 1954. Germany. (Opera). Sound. 16mm Color. *Rental:* Janus Films.

Tiempo Es el Viento, El. Cuba. (Documentary). 60 min. Sound. 16mm Color. *Rental:* Tricontinental Film.

Ties That Bind. Directed by John Labow. 1973. Canada. (Documentary). 58 min. Sound. 16mm Color. *Rental:* Natl Film CN. *Sale:* Natl Film CN.

Tiffany Jones. Anouska Hempel. Directed by Peter Walker. 1976. Cineworld. 90 min. Sound. 16mm Color. *Rental:* Williams Films.

Tiger Attacks, The. Lino Ventura & Estelle Blaine. 1963. France. 100 min. Sound. 16mm B&W. dubbed. *Rental:* Films Inc.

Tiger Bay. Horst Buchholz & Hayley Mills. Directed by J. Lee Thompson. 1959. Britain. 105 min. Sound. 16mm B&W. *Rental:* Budget Films, Films Inc, Images Film, Learning Corp Am, Twyman Films & U of IL Film. *Sale:* Learning Corp Am.

Tiger by the Tail. Christopher George & Dean Jagger. Directed by John Gilling. 1968. American International. 68 min. Sound. 16mm Color. *Rental:* Ivy Films, Rep Pic Film, Video Comm, Welling Motion Pictures & Willoughby Peer. *Lease:* Rep Pic Film.

Tiger Fangs. Frank Buck. Directed by Sam Newfield. 1943. PRC. 54 min. Sound. 16mm B&W. *Rental:* Mogulls Films.

Tiger Force. 1975. Hong Kong. (Cast unlisted). 86 min. Sound. 16mm Color. dubbed. *Rental:* Budget Films, Films Inc & Modern Sound.

Tiger in the Smoke. Donald Sinden & Muriel Pavlow. Directed by Roy Ward Baker. 1956. Britain. 85 min. Sound. 16mm B&W. *Rental:* Cinema Five.

Tiger Makes Out, The. Eli Wallach & Anne Jackson. Directed by Arthur Hiller. 1967. Columbia. 95 min. Sound. 16mm Color. *Rental:* Cine Craft, Films Inc, Inst Cinema, Welling Motion Pictures & Wholesome Film Ctr.

Tiger Man *see* Lady & the Monster.

Tiger on the Loose. Army. (Documentary). 56 min. Sound. 16mm B&W. *Rental:* Natl AV Ctr.

Tiger Shark. Edward G. Robinson & Richard Arlen. Directed by Howard Hawks. 1932. Warners. 80 min. Sound. 16mm B&W. *Rental:* MGM United.

Tiger Town. Roy Scheider & Justin Henry. Disney. 76 min. Sound. 16mm Color. *Rental:* Williams Films, Bosco Films, Elliot Film Co, Roas Film, Westcoast Films & Welling Motion Pictures.

Tiger Woman, The. Adele Mara & Kane Richmond. Directed by Philip Ford. 1945. Republic. 57 min. Sound. 16mm B&W. *Rental:* Ivy Films.

Tiger Woman, The *see* Perils of the Darkest Jungle.

Tight Little Island. Orig. Title: Whiskey Galore. Joan Greenwood & Basil Radford. Directed by Alexander Mackendrick. 1949. Britain. 82 min. Sound. 16mm B&W. *Rental:* Budget Films, Images Film, Janus Films, Kit Parker, Learning Corp Am, Twyman Films & U of IL Film. *Sale:* Learning Corp Am.

Tight Packers & Loose Packers. 1977. Britain. (Documentary). 57 min. Sound. 16mm Color. *Rental:* U of IL Film & U Mich Media.

Tight Spot. Ginger Rogers & Edward G. Robinson. Directed by Phil Karlson. 1955. Columbia. 97 min. Sound. 16mm B&W. *Rental:* Budget Films, Bosco Films, Inst Cinema, Kit Parker, Roas Films & Welling Motion Pictures.

Tighten Your Belts, Bite the Bullet. 1980. City Crisis Film Group. (Documentary). 48 min. Sound. 16mm Color. *Rental:* Icarus Films. *Sale:* Icarus Films. *Sale:* Icarus Films, Videotape version.

Tightrope. Clint Eastwood & Genevieve Bujold. Directed by Richard Tuggle. 1985. Warner. 114 min. Sound. 16mm Color. *Rental:* Swank Motion.

Tightrope to Terror. 1983. 52 min. Color. *Sale:* Lucerne Films.

Tigris. 1911. Italy. (Cast unlisted). 51 min. Silent. 16mm B&W. *Rental:* Em Gee Film Lib.

Tigris Expedition, The. 1978. National Geographic. (Documentary). 59 min. Sound. 16mm Color. *Rental:* Natl Geog & Syracuse U Film. *Sale:* Natl Geog. *Sale:* Natl Geog, Videotape version.

Tiki-Tiki. Russia. (Animated). 75 min. Sound. 16mm Color. *Rental:* Ivy Films & Video Comm. *Rental:* Video Comm, Anamorphic version.

Tiko & the Shark. Marlene Among. Directed by Folco Quilici. 1966. MGM. 100 min. Sound. 16mm Color. dubbed. *Rental:* MGM United.

Till Marriage Do Us Part. Laura Antonelli & Jean Rochefort. Directed by Luigi Comencini. Ital. 1979. Cinema Five. 97 min. Sound. 16mm Color. subtitles. *Rental:* Cinema Five.

Till the Clouds Roll By. June Allyson & Judy Garland. Directed by Richard Whorf. 1946. MGM. 136 min. Sound. 16mm Color. *Rental:* Arcus Film, Budget Films, Bosco Films, Em Gee Film Lib, Films Inc, Kit Parker, Maljack, MGM United, Natl Film Video, Roas Films, Video Comm, Welling Motion Pictures & Westcoast Films. *Sale:* Cinema Concepts, Glenn Photo, Natl Cinema & Reel Images. *Sale:* Reel Images, Super 8 sound version. *Rental:* MGM United, Videotape version.

Till the End of Time. Dorothy McGuire & Guy Madison. Directed by Edward Dmytryk. 1946. RKO. 105 min. Sound. 16mm B&W. *Rental:* Films Inc.

Till We Meet Again. Merle Oberon, George Brent & Pat O'Brien. Directed by Edmund Goulding. 1940. Warners. 99 min. Sound. 16mm B&W. *Rental:* MGM United.

Till We Meet Again. Ray Milland & Barbara Britton. Directed by Frank Borzage. 1944. Paramount. 88 min. Sound. 16mm B&W. *Rental:* Swank Motion.

Tillie & Gus. W. C. Fields & Alison Skipworth. Directed by Francis Martin. 1933. Paramount. 61 min. Sound. 16mm B&W. *Rental:* Swank Motion.

Tillie Wakes Up. Marie Dressler. Directed by Harry Davenport. 1917. Peerless/World. (Music & sound effects only). 41 min. Sound. 16mm B&W. *Rental:* Film Classics. *Sale:* Film Classics & E Finney. *Rental:* Film Classics, *Sale:* Blackhawk Films & Film Classics, Silent 16mm version. *Rental:* Ivy Films, *Sale:* Blackhawk Films, Super 8 silent version.

Tillie's Punctured Romance. Marie Dressler, Charlie Chaplin & Mabel Normand. Directed by Mack Sennett. 1914. Keystone. (Musical score & sound effects only). 50 min. Sound. 16mm B&W. *Rental:* A Twyman Pres, U Cal Media, Films Inc, Images Film, Ivy Films, Kit Parker, Mogulls Films, Film Images, Roas Films, Film Ctr DC, Video Comm & Welling Motion. *Sale:* Blackhawk Films, Cinema Concepts, E Finney, Griggs Movie, Morcraft Films, Natl Cinema, See-Art Films & Video Comm. *Rental:* Budget Films, Creative Film, Em Gee Film Lib, Ivy Films, Modern SoundTwyman Films, Video Comm, Welling Motion Pictures, Wholesome Film Ctr & Willoughby Peer, *Sale:* Blackhawk Films, Film Classics & Reel Images, Silent 16mm version. *Rental:* Killiam Collect, Tinted version. *Sale:* Blackhawk Films, Super 8 sound version. *Sale:* Blackhawk Films, Griggs Movie & Reel Images, Super 8 silent version. *Rental:* Ivy Films, *Sale:* Tamarelles French Film, Videotape version.

Tim Driscoll's Donkey. David Coote. Directed by Terry Bishop. 1955. Britain. 56 min. Sound. 16mm B&W. *Sale:* Lucerne Films.

Timber Fury. David Bruce. Directed by Bernard B. Ray. 1950. Eagle Lion. 63 min. Sound. 16mm B&W. *Rental:* Budget Films, Film Ctr DC, Lewis Film & Westcoast Films.

Timber Stampede. Chill Wills & George O'Brien. Directed by Bert Gilroy. 1939. RKO. 59 min. Sound. 16mm B&W. *Rental:* RKO General Pics.

Timber Trail, The. Monte Hale. Directed by Philip Ford. 1947. Republic. 67 min. Sound. 16mm B&W. *Rental:* Ivy Films. *Sale:* Rep Pic Film.

Timber War. Kermit Maynard. Directed by Sam Newfield. 1936. Ambassador/Conn. 56 min. Sound. 16mm B&W. *Rental:* Modern Sound.

Timberjack. Sterling Hayden & Vera Ralston. Directed by Joseph Kane. 1955. Republic. 94 min. Sound. 16mm B&W. *Rental:* Ivy Films. *Lease:* Rep Pic Film.

Timbuctoo. Alastair Sim. Directed by Walter Summers. 1933. Britain. 74 min. Sound. 16mm B&W. *Rental:* Film Classics.

Timbuktu. Victor Mature & Yvonne De Carlo. Directed by Jacques Tourneur. 1959. United Artists. 91 min. Sound. 16mm B&W. *Rental:* MGM United.

Time. 1946. US Government. (Documentary). 57 min. Sound. 16mm B&W. *Sale:* Natl AV Ctr.

Time After Time. Malcolm McDowell & David Warner. Directed by Nicholas Meyer. 1979. Warners. 112 min. 16mm Color. *Rental:* Swank Motion. *Rental:* Swank Motion, Videotape version.

Time & Dreams. Directed by Morton Jordan. 1976. Temple U.. 55 min. Sound. 16mm B&W. *Rental:* Museum Mod Art. *Sale:* Museum Mod Art.

Time Bandits, The. John Cleese & Sean Connery. Directed by Terry Gilliam. 1981. Embassy. 116 min. Sound. 16mm Color. *Rental:* Films Inc.

Time for Building, A. 1967. Lutheran. (Documentary). 58 min. Sound. 16mm B&W. *Rental:* Budget Films.

Time for Burning, A. 1966. Quest. (Documentary). 58 min. Sound. 16mm B&W. *Rental:* Budget Films, Iowa Films, Lutheran Film, U Mich Media, Mass Media, Twyman Films & U Nev AV Ctr. *Sale:* Lutheran Film.

Time for Dying, A. Richard Lapp & Audie Murphy. Directed by Budd Boetticher. 1969. USA. 73 min. Sound. 16mm Color. *Rental:* Corinth Films.

Time for Every Season, A. 1972. Gold Key. (Documentary). 95 min. Sound. 16mm Color. *Rental:* Budget Films, Films Inc & Video Comm. *Lease:* Video Comm. *Rental:* Video Comm, *Lease:* Video Comm, Videotape version.

Time for Killing, A. Glenn Ford & George Hamilton. Directed by Phil Karlson. 1967. Columbia. 88 min. Sound. 16mm Color. *Lease:* Time-Life Multimedia.

Time in the Sun, A. Directed by Sergei Eisenstein & Marie Seton. 1939. Mexico. (Documentary). 59 min. Sound. 16mm B&W. narrated Eng. *Rental:* Corinth Films, Films Inc & Museum Mod Art.

Time Is Running Out. Simone Signoret & Dane Clark. 1955. France. 90 min. Sound. 16mm B&W. dubbed. *Rental:* Ivy Films & Video Comm. *Rental:* Video Comm, Videotape version.

Time Limit. Richard Widmark & Richard Basehart. Directed by Karl Malden. 1957. United Artists. 96 min. Sound. 16mm B&W. *Rental:* MGM United.

Time Machine, The. Rod Taylor & Yvette Mimieux. Directed by George Pal. 1960. MGM. 103 min. Sound. 16mm Color. *Rental:* Williams Films & MGM United. *Rental:* MGM United, Videotape version.

Time Machine, The. Directed by Terence McCarthy. 1973. Canada. 52 min. Sound. 16mm Color. *Rental:* Films Inc. *Sale:* Films Inc. *Sale:* Films Inc, Videotape version.

Time Machine, The. Andrew Duggan, Whit Bissell & John Beck. Directed by Henning Schellerup. 1979. Viacom. 105 min. Sound. 16mm Color. *Rental:* Modern Sound & Williams Films. *Sale:* Lucerne Films. *Sale:* Lucerne Films, Videotape version.

Time of His Life, The. Richard Hearne. Directed by Leslie Hiscott. 1955. Britain. 74 min. Sound. 16mm B&W. *Rental:* Inst Cinema.

Time of Man, The. 1970. BFA. (Documentary). 50 min. Sound. 16mm Color. *Rental:* U Cal Media, U Mich Media, OK AV Ctr & Syracuse U Film. *Sale:* Phoenix Films.

Time of the Jackals, The. Directed by Les Rose. 1976. CTV. 50 min. Sound. 16mm Color. *Rental:* Films Inc, U of IL Film & Syracuse U Film. *Sale:* Films Inc. *Sale:* Films Inc, Videotape version.

Time of Their Lives, The. Lou Abbott & Bud Costello. Directed by Charles Barton. 1946. Universal. 82 min. Sound. 16mm B&W. *Rental:* Swank Motion.

Time Out for Rhythm. Ann Miller, Rudy Vallee & Three Stooges. Directed by Sidney Salkow. 1941. Columbia. 75 min. Sound. 16mm B&W. *Rental:* Kit Parker.

Time to Die, A. 1983. CBS. (Documentary). 49 min. Sound. 16mm Color. *Rental:* MTI Tele. *Sale:* MTI Tele.

Time to Kill. Lloyd Nolan & Heather Angel. Directed by Herbert I. Leeds. 1942. Fox. 61 min. Sound. 16mm B&W. *Rental:* Films Inc.

Time to Live with Leo Buscaglia, A. 1982. 50 min. Sound. Videotape *Rental:* PBS Video. *Sale:* PBS Video.

Time to Love & a Time to Die, A. John Gavin & Lilo Pulver. Directed by Douglas Sirk. 1958. Universal. 132 min. Sound. 16mm Color. *Rental:* Williams Films.

Time to Sing, A. Hank Williams Jr. & Shelley Fabrares. Directed by Arthur Dreifuss. 1968. MGM. 91 min. Sound. 16mm Color. *Rental:* MGM United. *Rental:* MGM United, Anamorphic version.

Time Travelers, The. Preston Foster & Philip Carey. Directed by Ib Melchior. 1964. American International. 82 min. Sound. 16mm Color. *Rental:* Budget Films, Charard Motion Pics, Westcoast Films, Welling Motion Pictures & Wholesome Film Ctr.

Time Without Pity. Sir Michael Redgrave & Ann Todd. Directed by Joseph Losey. 1957. Janus. 88 min. Sound. 16mm B&W. *Rental:* Films Inc.

Timerider. Fred Ward & Belinda Bauer. Directed by William Dear. 1983. Simcom. 93 min. Sound. 16mm Color. *Rental:* Swank Motion. *Rental:* Swank Motion, Videotape version.

Times For. Carole Schneemann & Carmel Court. Directed by Stephen Dwoskin. 1970. Britain. 80 min. Sound. 16mm Color. *Rental:* Canyon Cinema.

Times Square. Tim Curry, Trini Alvarado & Robin Johnson. Directed by Alan Moyle. 1980. AFO. 111 min. Sound. 16mm Color. *Rental:* Swank Motion.

Times Square Lady. Robert Taylor & Virginia Bruce. Directed by George B. Seitz. 1935. MGM. 69 min. Sound. 16mm B&W. *Rental:* MGM United.

Timetable. Mark Stevens & Felicia Farr. Directed by Mark Stevens. 1956. United Artists. 79 min. Sound. 16mm B&W. *Rental:* MGM United.

Timing Reels Nos. One & Two. 87 min. Sound. 16mm *Rental:* Filmmakers Coop.

Timon of Athens. 1980. Britain. (Cast unlisted). 120 min. Color. *Rental:* Iowa Films.

Timothy's Quest. Joseph Depew. Directed by Sidney Olcott. 1922. American. 75 min. Silent. 16mm B&W. *Rental:* Em Gee Film Lib & Film Classics. *Sale:* Cinema Concepts & Film Classics.

Tim's Choice. Swank. (Documentary). 52 min. Sound. 16mm Color. *Rental:* Swank Motion.

Tin Drum, The. David Bennent & Mario Adorf. Directed by Volker Schlondorff. Ger. 1979. Germany. 142 min. Sound. 16mm Color. subtitles. *Rental:* Films Inc. *Rental:* Festival Films, Videotape version.

Tin Lizzie Tycoon. 1963. Swank. (Documentary). 50 min. Sound. 16mm B&W. *Sale:* Killiam Collect.

Tin Man, The. Directed by Michal Bat Adam. Hebrew. 1980. Israel. 90 min. Sound. 16mm Color. subtitles. *Rental:* New Yorker Films.

Tin Pan Alley. Jack Oakie & Alice Faye. Directed by Walter Lang. 1940. Fox. 94 min. Sound. 16mm B&W. *Rental:* Films Inc.

Tin Star, The. Henry Fonda & Anthony Perkins. Directed by Anthony Mann. 1957. Paramount. 93 min. Sound. 16mm B&W. *Rental:* Films Inc.

TinderBox, The. Rolf Ludwig. Directed by Siegfried Hartmann. 1968. Childhood. 70 min. Sound. 16mm Color. dubbed. *Rental:* Films Inc.

Tingler, The. Vincent Price & Judith Evelyn. Directed by William Castle. 1959. 85 min. Sound. 16mm B&W. *Rental:* Kit Parker.

Tintorera, La. Susan George & Fiona Lewis. Directed by Rene Cardona Jr. 1977. UFD. 91 min. Sound. 16mm B&W. *Rental:* Films Inc.

Tioga Kid, The. Eddie Dean. Directed by Ray Taylor. 1948. Eagle Lion. 60 min. Sound. 16mm B&W. *Sale:* Classics Assoc NY.

Tip Off, The. Ginger Rogers & Robert Armstrong. Directed by Albert S. Rogell. 1932. RKO. 75 min. Sound. 16mm B&W. *Rental:* RKO General Pics.

Tip on a Dead Jockey. Robert Taylor & Dorothy Malone. Directed by Richard Thorpe. 1957. MGM. 109 min. Sound. 16mm B&W. *Rental:* MGM United. *Rental:* MGM United, Anamorphic version. *Rental:* MGM United, Videotape version.

Tirando a Matar. Angel Infante. Directed by Rafael Baledon. Mexico. 83 min. Sound. 16mm B&W. *Rental:* Westcoast Films.

Tirez Sur Le Pianiste *see* Shoot the Piano Player.

Tis a Pity She's a Whore. Trans. Title: Addio Fratello Crudele. Charlotte Rampling & Oliver Tobias. Directed by Guiseppe Patroni Griffi. 1971. Italy. 91 min. Sound. 16mm Color. dubbed. *Rental:* Films Inc.

Titan: The Story of Michangelo. 1950. Pandora. (Documentary). 67 min. Sound. 16mm B&W. *Rental:* Budget Films, U Cal Media, Kit Parker, U Mich Media & Syracuse U Film. *Sale:* Master Monica.

Titanic. Barbara Stanwyck & Clifton Webb. Directed by Jean Negulesco. 1953. Fox. 98 min. Sound. 16mm B&W. *Rental:* Films Inc.

Titans-USA. Britain. (Documentary). 61 min. Sound. 16mm B&W. *Rental:* Time-Life Multimedia. *Sale:* Time-Life Multimedia. *Rental:* Time-Life Multimedia, *Sale:* Time-Life Multimedia, Spanish language version. *Sale:* Time-Life Multimedia, Videotape version.

Titfield Thunderbolt, The. Stanley Holloway. Directed by Charles Crichton. 1953. Britain. 84 min. Sound. 16mm B&W. *Rental:* Janus Films.

Titicut Follies, The. Directed by Frederick Wiseman. 1967. (Documentary). Zipporah. 89 min. Sound. 16mm B&W. *Rental:* U Mich Media & Zipporah Films. *Lease:* Zipporah Films.

TNT Show, The. 90 min. Sound. 16mm B&W. *Rental:* Budget Films.

To Be a Crook. Trans. Title: Fille Des Fusil, Une. Jean-Pierre Kalfon & Amidou. Directed by Claude Lelouch. Fr. 1967. France. 95 min. Sound. 16mm B&W. subtitles. *Rental:* Swank Motion. *Rental:* Swank Motion, Dubbed version.

To Be a Doctor. 1980. NBC. (Documentary). 52 min. Sound. 16mm Color. *Rental:* Films Inc. *Sale:* Films Inc. *Sale:* Films Inc, Videotape version.

To Be a Jew In Arab Lands. 46 min. Sound. 16mm Color. *Rental:* Alden Films.

To Be Black. 1970. McGraw/Hill. (Documentary). 52 min. Sound. 16mm B&W. *Rental:* McGraw-Hill Films. *Sale:* McGraw-Hill Films.

To Be Indian. Canada. (Documentary). 56 min. Sound. 16mm B&W. *Rental:* CBC. *Sale:* CBC.

To Be or Not to Be. Carole Lombard & Jack Benny. Directed by Ernst Lubitsch. 1942. United Artists. 90 min. Sound. 16mm B&W. *Rental:* Budget Films, Films Inc, U of IL Film, Images Film, Kit Parker, Learning Corp Am, Mogulls Films, Roas Films, Twyman Films, Video Comm, Welling Motion Pictures, Westcoast Films, Wholesome Film Ctr & Willoughby Peer. *Sale:* Learning Corp Am. *Sale:* Cinema Concepts & Glenn Photo, Super 8 sound version. *Sale:* Tamarelles French Film, Videotape version.

To Be Young, Gifted & Black. Ruby Dee, Barbara Barrie & Al Freeman Jr. 1972. NET. 90 min. Sound. 16mm Color. *Rental:* Indiana Ctr, U Mich Media, Twyman Films & U Cal Media. *Sale:* Indiana Ctr. *Sale:* Indiana AV Ctr, Videotape version.

To Beat the Band. Johnny Mercer & Hugh Herbert. Directed by Ben Stoloff. 1936. RKO. 67 min. Sound. 16mm B&W. *Rental:* RKO General Pics.

To Build a Fire. Ian Hoag. Directed by David Cobham & Anthony Short. 1970. United. 54 min. Sound. 16mm Color. *Rental:* Budget Films, Films Inc, Kit Parker, Video Comm, Westcoast Films & Wholesome Film Ctr. *Lease:* Video Comm.

To Build a Future. 54 min. Sound. 16mm Color. *Rental:* Budget Films.

To Build Our Future. 58 min. Sound. Videotape *Rental:* PBS Video. *Sale:* PBS Video.

To Catch a Thief. Cary Grant & Grace Kelly. Directed by Alfred Hitchcock. 1955. Paramount. 106 min. Sound. 16mm Color. *Rental:* Films Inc.

To Commit a Murder. Louis Jourdan, Senta Berger & Edmond O'Brien. Directed by Edouard Molinaro. 1970. Cinerama. 91 min. Sound. 16mm Color. dubbed. *Rental:* Swank Motion.

To Die in Madrid. Directed by Frederic Rossif. 1963. Audio. (Documentary). 90 min. Sound. 16mm B&W. *Rental:* Films Inc.

To Die of Love. Trans. Title: Mourir D' Aimer. Annie Giradot & Bruno Pradal. Directed by Andre Cayatte. Fr. 1972. France. 110 min. Sound. 16mm Color. subtitles. *Rental:* MGM United.

To Die, To Live: The Survivors of Hiroshima. 1982. Britain. (Documentary). 63 min. Sound. 16mm Color. *Rental:* Films Inc. *Sale:* Films Inc & Syracuse U Film. *Sale:* Films Inc, Videotape version.

To Die Today. 1971. Canada. (Documentary). 50 min. Sound. 16mm B&W. *Rental:* U Cal Media, Film Makers & U Mich Media. *Sale:* Film Makers. *Sale:* Film Makers, Videotape version.

To Each His Own. Olivia De Havilland & John Lund. Directed by Mitchell Leisen. 1946. Paramount. 122 min. Sound. 16mm B&W. *Rental:* Swank Motion.

To Every Creature. Moody. (Documentary). 48 min. Sound. 16mm Color. *Rental:* G Herne.

To Expect to Die: A Film About Living. 1979. PBS. (Documentary). 59 min. Videotape Color. *Rental:* PBS Video. *Sale:* PBS Video.

To Feed the Hungry. 1969. 45 min. Sound. 16mm Color. *Rental:* U Mich Media.

To Find a Man. Pamela Sue Martin & Lloyd Bridges. Directed by Buzz Kulik. 1972. Columbia. 93 min. Sound. 16mm Color. *Rental:* Swank Motion.

To Find a Rainbow. 1973. American National. (Documentary). 96 min. Sound. 16mm Color. *Rental:* Budget Films & Video Comm. *Lease:* Video Comm. *Rental:* Video Comm, *Lease:* Video Comm, Videotape version.

To Find Our Life: The Peyote Hunt of the Huichols of Mexico. 1970. Univ. of California. (Documentary). 65 min. Sound. 16mm Color. *Rental:* Syracuse U Film, U Cal Media & U Mich Media.

To Forget Venice. Erland Josephson & Eleanora Giorgi. Directed by Franco Brusati. Ital. 1979. Italy. 108 min. Sound. 16mm Color. subtitles. *Rental:* Films Inc.

To Have & Have Not. Humphrey Bogart & Lauren Bacall. Directed by Howard Hawks. 1944. Warners. 100 min. Sound. 16mm B&W. *Rental:* MGM United.

To Hell & Back. Audie Murphy & Charles Drake. Directed by Jesse Hibbs. 1955. Universal. 106 min. Sound. 16mm Color. *Rental:* Williams Films.

To Hex with Sex. Paula Shaw. Directed by Simon Nuchtern. 1975. RAF Industries. 86 min. Sound. 16mm Color. *Rental:* Video Comm.

To Kill a Clown. Alan Alda & Blythe Danner. Directed by George Bloomfield. 1972. Fox. 82 min. Sound. 16mm Color. *Rental:* Films Inc.

To Kill a Man. Gary Lockwood & James Shigeta. Directed by Vincent McEveety. 1964. MGM. 86 min. Sound. 16mm B&W. *Rental:* MGM United.

To Kill a Mockingbird. Gregory Peck & Mary Badham. Directed by Robert Mulligan. 1962. Universal. 129 min. Sound. 16mm B&W. *Rental:* Swank Motion. *Rental:* Swank Motion, Videotape version.

To Kill a Rover. Chang Chung. Directed by Wang Ping. 1965. China. 114 min. Sound. 16mm Color. *Rental:* Westcoast Films.

To Live *see* Ikiru.

To Live in Freedom. Hebrew. 1974. Palestine-Israel. (Documentary). 54 min. Sound. 16mm Color. subtitles. *Rental:* Icarus Films. *Sale:* Icarus Films.

To Live Till You Die. 1965. NET. (Documentary). 60 min. Sound. 16mm B&W. *Rental:* Indiana AV Ctr. *Sale:* Indiana AV Ctr.

To Live Until You Die. 1983. Nova. (Documentary). 57 min. Sound. 16mm Color. *Rental:* U Cal Media.

To Live with Herds. Directed by David MacDougall. African Dialect. 1973. Uganda. (Documentary). 68 min. Sound. 16mm B&W. subtitles. *Rental:* U Cal Media & Film Images. *Sale:* U Cal Media & Film Images. *Rental:* U Cal Media, *Sale:* U Cal Media, Color version. *Sale:* U Cal Media, Videotape version.

To Love. Harriet Andersson & Zbigniew Cybulski. Directed by Jorn Donner. Swed. 1964. Sweden. 90 min. Sound. 16mm B&W. subtitles. *Rental:* Films Inc.

To Love a Vampire. Ralph Bates. Directed by Jimmy Sangster. 1970. Britain. 95 min. Sound. 16mm Color. *Rental:* Corinth Films.

To Mary With Love. Warner Baxter & Myrna Loy. Directed by John Cromwell. 1936. Fox. 86 min. Sound. 16mm B&W. *Rental:* Films Inc.

To Paris With Love. (Cast unlisted). Videotape *Sale:* Vidamerica.

To Please a Lady. Clark Gable & Barbara Stanwyck. Directed by Clarence Brown. 1950. MGM. 92 min. Sound. 16mm B&W. *Rental:* MGM United.

To Reach the Dawn. 1966. Reynolds. (Documentary). 48 min. Sound. 16mm Color. *Rental:* Modern Talking.

To Remember or To Forget. Ludmilla Chursina & Girt Yakoviev. Directed by Ian Streich. Rus. 1982. Russia. 90 min. Sound. 16mm Color. subtitles. *Rental:* IFEX.

To Sing Our Own Song. 1983. Britain. (Documentary). 50 min. Sound. 16mm Color. *Rental:* Films Inc. *Sale:* Films Inc. *Sale:* Films Inc, Videotape version.

To Sir With Love. Sidney Poitier & Judy Geeson. Directed by James Clavel. 1967. Columbia. 105 min. Sound. 16mm Color. *Rental:* Arcus Film, Budget Films, Cine Craft, Charard Motion Pics, Williams Films, Bosco Films, Films Inc, Film Pres, Images Film, Inst Cinema, U of IL Film, Kerr Film, Modern Sound, Natl Film Video, Roas Films, Swank Motion, Film Ctr DC, Twyman Films, Video Comm, Westcoast Films, Welling Motion Pictures, Wholesome Film Ctr & Willoughby Peer.

To the Ends of the Earth. Dick Powell & Signe Hasso. Directed by Robert Stevenson. 1948. Columbia. 109 min. Sound. 16mm B&W. *Rental:* Budget Films, Cine Craft, Films Inc, Inst Cinema & Film Ctr DC.

To the South Pole with Peter Scott. 1967. Britain. (Documentary). 52 min. Sound. 16mm B&W. *Rental:* Time-Life Multimedia. *Sale:* Time-Life Multimedia.

To Think of Dying. 1976. PBS. (Documentary). 59 min. Sound. 16mm Color. *Rental:* Indiana AV Ctr. *Sale:* Indiana AV Ctr.

To Trap a Spy. Robert Vaughan & David McCallum. Directed by Don Medford. 1966. MGM. 92 min. Sound. 16mm Color. *Rental:* MGM United.

Toast, A. Directed by Jan Lomnicki. 1966. Poland. (Documentary). 70 min. Sound. 16mm Color. narrated Eng. *Rental:* Polish People.

Toast of New Orleans, The. Mario Lanza & Kathryn Grayson. Directed by Norman Taurog. 1950. MGM. 97 min. Sound. 16mm Color. *Rental:* MGM United.

Toast of New York, The. Cary Grant & Edward Arnold. Directed by Rowland V. Lee. 1937. RKO. 109 min. Sound. 16mm B&W. *Rental:* RKO General Pics.

Toast to Vienna in Three-Quarter Time, A. 1966. CBS. (Documentary). 51 min. Sound. 16mm Color. *Rental:* McGraw-Hill Films. *Sale:* McGraw-Hill Films.

Tobor the Great. Charles Drake & Karin Booth. Directed by Lee Sholem. 1954. Republic. 77 min. Sound. 16mm B&W. *Rental:* Charard Motion Pics & Ivy Films. *Sale:* Rep Pic Film.

Toby Tyler. Kevin Corcoran, Henry Calvin & James Drury. Directed by Charles Barton. 1960. Disney. 96 min. Sound. 16mm Color. *Rental:* Bosco Films, Cine Craft, Disney Prod, Elliot Film Co, Films Inc, U of IL Film, MGM United, Modern Sound, Roas Films, Twyman Films, Westcoast Films, Welling Motion Piction & Williams Films.

Tocqueville's America. 1971. Canada. (Documentary). 60 min. Sound. 16mm B&W. *Rental:* U Cal Media & Indiana AV Ctr. *Sale:* Indiana AV Ctr.

Today in the Land of the Bible. 1977. Bonaventure. (Documentary). 50 min. Sound. 16mm Color. *Rental:* U of IL Film. *Sale:* Bonaventure. *Sale:* Bonaventure, Videotape version.

Today We Live. Joan Crawford, Gary Cooper & Robert Young. Directed by Howard Hawks. 1933. MGM. 115 min. Sound. 16mm B&W. *Rental:* MGM United.

Todos Los Dias, Un Dia. Julio Iglesias & Isa Lorenz. Directed by Orlando Jimenez-Leal. Span. Spain. 89 min. Sound. Videotape Color. subtitles. *Sale:* Tamarelles French Films.

Together. Directed by Sean Cunningham. 1972. New Line. (Documentary). 72 min. Sound. 16mm Color. *Rental:* New Line Cinema. *Sale:* New Line Cinema.

Together? Jacqueline Bisset & Maximilian Schell. Directed by Armenia Balducci. 1981. QFI. 91 min. Sound. 16mm Color. *Rental:* Films Inc.

Together Again. Charles Boyer & Irene Dunne. Directed by Charles Vidor. 1944. Columbia. 100 min. Sound. 16mm B&W. *Rental:* Bosco Films & Kit Parker.

Together Brothers, The. Ahmad Narradin. Directed by William Graham. 1974. Fox. 94 min. Sound. 16mm Color. *Rental:* Films Inc.

Together with Leo Buscaglia. 1981. 52 min. Sound. Videotape *Rental:* PBS Video. *Sale:* PBS Video.

Togetherness. George Hamilton & Peter Lawford. Directed by Arthur Marks. 1970. Cerberus. 101 min. Sound. 16mm Color. *Rental:* Video Comm, Wholesome Film Ctr & Willoughby Peer.

Toklat. 1971. Sunn International. (Documentary). 90 min. Sound. 16mm Color. *Rental:* Budget Films, Cine Craft, Films Inc, Roas Films, Video Comm & Westcoast Films. *Lease:* Video Comm. *Rental:* Video Comm, *Lease:* Video Comm, Videotape version.

Tokyo After Dark. Richard Long & Michi Kobi. Directed by Norman Herman. 1959. Paramount. 80 min. Sound. 16mm B&W. *Rental:* Films Inc.

Tokyo Joe. Humphrey Bogart, Alexander Knox & Sessue Hayakawa. Directed by Stuart Heisler. 1949. Columbia. 88 min. Sound. 16mm B&W. *Rental:* Budget Films, Films Inc, Welling Motion Pictures & Westcoast Films.

Tokyo Olympiad. Directed by Kon Ichikawa. 1965. Japan. (Documentary). 95 min. Sound. 16mm Color. narrated Eng. *Rental:* Films Inc, Anamorphic version.

Tokyo Senso Sengo Hiwa *see* Man Who Left His Will on Film.

Tokyo Story, The. Chishu Ryu. Directed by Yasujiro Ozu. Jap. 1953. Japan. 139 min. Sound. 16mm B&W. subtitles. *Rental:* Budget Films, New Cinema & New Yorker Films.

Tokyo: The Fifty First Volcano. 1972. Britain. (Documentary). 51 min. Sound. 16mm Color. *Rental:* Films Inc. *Sale:* Films Inc.

Tol'able David. Richard Barthelmess. Directed by Henry King. 1921. Inspiration. (Tinted). 109 min. Sound. 16mm *Rental:* Film Images, Iowa Films, Twyman Films & Willoughby Peer. *Sale:* E Finney & Film Images. *Rental:* Budget Films, Em Gee Film Lib, Kit Parker, Museum Mod Art, Modern Sound, SD AV Ctr & Video Comm, *Sale:* Blackhawk Films, Cinema Concepts, Griggs Movie, Museum Mod Art, Natl Cinema & Reel Images, Silent 16mm B&W version. *Sale:* Video Comm, Super 8 silent version. *Sale:* Tamarelles French Film, Videotape version. *Rental:* Iowa Films, 84 min. version. *Sale:* Festival Films, 79 min. version. *Sale:* Festival Films, 79 min. Videotape version.

Tol'able David. Richard Cromwell & Noah Beery. Directed by John G. Blystone. 1930. Paramount. 78 min. Sound. 16mm B&W. *Rental:* Films Inc.

Toll Gate, The. William S. Hart. Directed by Lambert Hillyer. 1920. Paramount. 55 min. Silent. 16mm B&W. *Rental:* Budget Films, Em Gee Film Lib, Ivy Films, Iowa Films, Kit Parker, Museum Mod Art, Film Images & Video Comm. *Sale:* Blackhawk Films. *Rental:* Killiam Collect, Tinted sound 16mm, musical score only version. *Sale:* Blackhawk Films, Super 8 silent version.

Tolstoy: From Riches to Rags. 1972. Britain. (Documentary). 70 min. Sound. 16mm Color. *Rental:* Kent St U Film.

Tolstoys, The. Directed by Victor Vicas. 1972. AIF. (Documentary). 60 min. Sound. 16mm B&W. *Sale:* Americas Films. *Sale:* Americas Films, Spanish version.

Tom Brown of Culver. Tom Brown & Tyrone Power Sr. Directed by William Wyler. 1932. Universal. 82 min. Sound. 16mm B&W. *Sale:* ank Motion.

Tom Brown's Schooldays. Freddie Bartholomew & Sir Cedric Hardwicke. Directed by Robert Stevenson. 1940. RKO. 81 min. Sound. 16mm B&W. *Rental:* Budget Films, Charard Motion Pics, Film Classics, Films Inc, Ivy Films, Mogulls Films, Video Comm & Wholesome Film Ctr. *Lease:* Video Comm. *Sale:* Cinema Concepts & Natl Cinema.

Tom Brown's Schooldays. Robert Newton. Directed by Gordon Parry. 1951. Britain. 94 min. Sound. 16mm B&W. *Rental:* Liberty Co, Natl Film Video, Rep Pic Film, Liberty Co & Video Comm. *Lease:* Rep Pic Film & Video Comm.

Tom Brown's Schooldays. Anthony Murphy. 1976. Britain. 240 min. Sound. 16mm Color. *Rental:* Films Inc. *Sale:* Films Inc. *Rental:* Films Inc, Videotape version.

Tom, Dick & Harry. Ginger Rogers, George Murphy & Burgess Meredith. Directed by Garson Kanin. 1941. RKO. 86 min. Sound. 16mm B&W. *Rental:* Films Inc.

Tom Edison: The Boy Who Lit Up the World. Videotape *Rental:* Vidamerica.

Tom Horn. Steve McQueen, Linda Evans & Richard Farnsworth. Directed by William Wiard. 1980. Warners. Sound. 16mm Color. *Rental:* Swank Motion & Williams Films. *Rental:* Swank Motion, Videotape version.

Tom Jones. Albert Finney & Susannah York. Directed by Tony Richardson. 1963. United Artists. 127 min. Sound. 16mm Color. *Rental:* MGM United. *Rental:* MGM United, Videotape version.

Tom Sawyer. Johnny Whittaker & Celeste Holm. Directed by Don Taylor. 1973. United Artists. (Anamorphic). 99 min. Sound. 16mm Color. *Rental:* MGM United, Modern Sound, Roas Films, Westcoast Films, Wholesome Film Ctr & Williams Films.

Tom Sawyer. Jackie Coogan & Mitzi Green. Directed by John Cromwell. 1930. Paramount. 86 min. Sound. 16mm B&W. *Rental:* Arcus Film & Swank Motion.

Tom Sawyer, Detective. Donald O'Connor & Billy Cook. Directed by Louis King. 1938. Paramount. 68 min. Sound. 16mm B&W. *Rental:* Swank Motion.

Tom Thumb. Russ Tamblyn & Alan Young. Directed by George Pal. 1958. MGM. 98 min. Sound. 16mm Color. *Rental:* MGM United & Westcoast Films.

Tom, Tom, the Piper's Son. Directed by Ken Jacobs. 1969. Ken Jacobs. (Experimental). 100 min. Silent. 16mm Color. *Rental:* Museum Mod Art.

Tomahawk Trail, The *see* Iroquois Trail.

Tomahawk Trail, The. Orig. Title: Mark of the Apache. Chuck Connors & John Smith. Directed by Robert Parry. 1957. United Artists. 60 min. Sound. 16mm B&W. *Rental:* MGM United.

Tomb of Ligeia, The. Vincent Price & Elizabeth Shepherd. Directed by Roger Corman. 1965. American International. 79 min. Sound. 16mm Color. *Rental:* Arcus Film, Budget Films, Cine Craft, Charard Motion Pics, Film Ctr DC, Films Inc, Inst Cinema, Twyman Films, Video Comm, Welling Motion Pictures, Westcoast Films, Wholesome Film Ctr & Willoughby Peer, Anamorphic color version.

Tomb of Torture, The. Orig. Title: Metempsycho. Annie Albert & Mark Marion. Directed by Anthony Kristye. 1963. Italy. 80 min. Sound. 16mm B&W. dubbed. *Rental:* Modern Sound.

Tomboy & the Champ, The. Candy Moore & Ben Johnson. Directed by Francis D. Lyon. 1961. Universal. 92 min. Sound. 16mm Color. *Rental:* Video Comm.

Tombstone Canyon. Ken Maynard. Directed by Alan James. 1932. World Wide. 60 min. Sound. Super 8mm B&W. *Sale:* Cinema Concepts & Morcraft Films.

Tomcats, The. Chris Mulkey & Polly King. Directed by Harry E. Kerwin. 1977. Dimension. 84 min. Sound. 16mm Color. *Sale:* Salz Ent.

Tommy. Ann-Margret & Roger Daltrey. Directed by Ken Russell. 1975. Columbia. 110 min. Sound. 16mm Color. *Rental:* Swank Motion. *Rental:* Swank Motion, Videotape version.

Tomorrow. William Faulkner & Robert Duvall. Directed by Joseph Anthony. 1972. 102 min. Sound. Videotape B&W. *Sale:* Tamarelles French Film.

Tomorrow at Seven. Chester Morris & Frank McHugh. Directed by Ray Enright. 1934. RKO. 61 min. Sound. 16mm B&W. *Rental:* Ivy Films.

Tomorrow at Ten. John Gregson & Robert Shaw. Directed by Lance Comfort. 1964. Britain. 80 min. Sound. 16mm B&W. *Rental:* Films Inc, Welling Motion Pictures & Willoughby Peer.

Tomorrow Came Much Later: A Journey of Conscience. 1981. WVIZ. 58 min. Sound. 16mm Color. *Rental:* Centron Films & U of IL Film. *Sale:* Centron Films, Videotape version.

Tomorrow Is Maybe. 1970. NET. (Documentary). 60 min. Sound. 16mm Color. *Rental:* Indiana AV Ctr, Videotape version.

Tomorrow is My Turn. Charles Aznavour & Nicole Courcel. Directed by Andre Cayatte. Fr. & Ger. 1960. France-Germany. 117 min. Sound. 16mm B&W. subtitles. *Rental:* Films Inc.

Tomorrow Is Yesterday. William Shatner & Leonard Nimoy. Directed by Michael O'Herlihy. 1967. Star Trek. 50 min. Sound. 16mm Color. *Sale:* Reel Images.

Tomorrow Man, The. Don Francks. Directed by Tibor Takacs. 1978. Canada. 80 min. Sound. 16mm Color. *Rental:* Natl Film CN. *Sale:* Natl Film CN.

Tomorrow Mexico *see* Jutro Meksyk.

Tomorrow the World. Betty Field & Skip Homeier. Directed by Leslie Fenton. 1944. United Artists. 85 min. Sound. 16mm B&W. *Rental:* Film Classics.

Tomorrow We Live. Orig. Title: Man Without a Conscience, The. Ricardo Cortez & Jean Parker. Directed by Edgar G. Ulmer. 1942. PRC. 67 min. Sound. 16mm B&W. *Rental:* Mogull's Films.

Tomorrow's Children. Sterling Holloway. Directed by Bryan Foy Jr. 1934. Bryan Fox. 55 min. Sound. 16mm B&W. *Rental:* Budget Films & Kit Parker. *Sale:* Am Mut Bio & Reel Images. *Sale:* Morcraft Films, Super 8 sound version.

Tomorrow's Television: Get What You Want or Like What You Get. 1969. NET. (Documentary). 62 min. Sound. 16mm B&W. *Rental:* Indiana AV Ctr. *Sale:* Indiana AV Ctr.

Tomorrow's World: Feeding the Billions. 1968. NBC. (Documentary). 53 min. Sound. 16mm Color. *Rental:* McGraw-Hill Films. *Sale:* McGraw-Hill Films.

Tomorrow's World: Feeding the Billions. 1967. 54 min. Sound. 16mm Color. *Rental:* Iowa Films & Utah Media.

Tong Man, The. Sessue Hayakawa & Helen Jerome Eddy. 1919. Robertson-Cole. 75 min. Silent. 16mm B&W. *Rental:* Budget Films & Em Gee Film Lib. *Sale:* Blackhawk Films, MGM United & Morcraft Films. *Sale:* Blackhawk Films, Super 8 silent version.

Tongpan. 1977. Thailand. (Native cast). 60 min. Sound. 16mm B&W. *Rental:* Icarus Films. *Sale:* Icarus Films.

Tongues of Man: Part One-Diaster at Babel. 1977. 58 min. Sound. Videotape *Rental:* PBS Video. *Sale:* PBS Video. *Sale:* PBS Video, 16mm version.

Tongues of Man: Part Two-A World Language?. 1977. 58 min. Sound. Videotape *Rental:* PBS Video. *Sale:* PBS Video. *Sale:* PBS Video, 16mm version.

Toni. Charles Blavette. Directed by Jean Renoir. Fr. 1934. France. 90 min. Sound. 16mm B&W. subtitles. *Rental:* New Yorker Films. *Sale:* Cinema Concepts, Natl Cinema & Reel Images.

Tonight & Every Night. Rita Hayworth & Janet Blair. Directed by Victor Saville. 1945. Columbia. 92 min. Sound. 16mm B&W. *Rental:* Bosco Films & Kit Parker.

Tonight at Eight Thirty *see* Meet Me Tonight.

Tonight Show, The. Jerry Lewis, Ed McMahon & Patrice Munsel. 1969. NBC. 78 min. Videotape Color. *Sale:* Reel Images.

Tonight We Raid Calais. Annabella & John Sutton. Directed by John Brahm. 1943. Fox. 70 min. Sound. 16mm B&W. *Rental:* Films Inc.

Tonight We Sing. David Wayne & Ezio Pinza. Directed by Mitchell Leisen. 1953. Fox. 109 min. Sound. 16mm Color. *Rental:* Films Inc.

Tonight's the Night. David Niven & Yvonne De Carlo. Directed by Mario Zampi. 1954. Allied Artists. 88 min. Sound. 16mm Color. *Rental:* Hurlock Cine.

Tonio Kroger. Jean-Claude Brialy & Nadja Tiller. Directed by Rolf Thiele. Ger. Germany. 88 min. 16mm B&W. subtitles. *Rental:* Trans-World Films.

Tonta Tonta, Pero No Tanto. Maria Elena Velasco. Directed by Fernando Cortes. Mexico. 91 min. Sound. 16mm Color. *Rental:* Westcoast Films.

Tonto Basin Outlaws. Ray Corrigan & John King. Directed by S. Roy Luby. 1941. Republic. 62 min. Sound. 16mm B&W. *Sale:* Cinema Concepts & Rep Pic Film.

Tonto Kid, The. Rex Bell. Directed by Harry Fraser. 1935. Resolute. 56 min. Sound. 16mm B&W. *Rental:* Em Gee Film Lib. *Sale:* Glenn Photo & Morcraft Films.

Tony Draws a Horse. Cecil Parker & Anne Crawford. Directed by John Paddy Carstairs. 1950. Britain. 91 min. Sound. 16mm B&W. *Rental:* Charard Motion Pics.

Tony Rome. Frank Sinatra & Jill St. John. Directed by Gordon Douglas. 1967. Fox. (Anamorphic). 110 min. Sound. 16mm Color. *Rental:* Films Inc.

Too Bad She's Bad. Sophia Loren & Vittorio De Sica. Directed by Alessandro Blasetti. 1955. Italy. 95 min. Sound. 16mm B&W. dubbed. *Rental:* Ivy Films.

Too Early, Too Late. Directed by Jean-Marie Straub. Ger. 1981. Germany. 105 min. Sound. 16mm Color. subtitles. *Rental:* New Yorker Films.

Too Hot to Handle. Clark Gable, Myrna Loy & Walter Pidgeon. Directed by Jack Conway. 1938. MGM. 105 min. Sound. 16mm B&W. *Rental:* MGM United.

Too Late Blues. Bobby Darin & Stella Stevens. Directed by John Cassavetes. 1962. Paramount. 100 min. Sound. 16mm B&W. *Rental:* Films Inc.

Too Late for Tears. Lizabeth Scott, Dan Duryea & Don DeFore. Directed by Byron Haskin. 1949. United Artists. 99 min. Sound. 16mm B&W. *Rental:* Budget Films.

Too Late the Hero. Cliff Robertson & Michael Caine. Directed by Robert Aldrich. 1970. Cinerama. 93 min. Sound. 16mm Color. *Rental:* Films Inc. *Sale:* ABC Film Lib, Super 8 sound version.

Too Many Cooks. Bert Wheeler & Dorothy Lee. Directed by William A. Seiter. 1932. RKO. 77 min. Sound. 16mm B&W. *Rental:* RKO General Pics.

Too Many Girls. Lucille Ball & Richard Carlson. Directed by George Abbott. 1940. RKO. 108 min. Sound. 16mm B&W. *Rental:* Films Inc.

Too Many Husbands. Jean Arthur, Fred MacMurray & Melvyn Douglas. Directed by Wesley Ruggles. 1940. Columbia. 84 min. Sound. 16mm B&W. *Rental:* Kit Parker.

Too Many Winners. Hugh Beaumont & Trudy Marshall. Directed by William Beaudine. 1947. Eagle Lion. 60 min. Sound. 16mm B&W. *Sale:* Classics Assoc NY.

Too Many Wives. Anne Shirley & Gene Lockhart. Directed by Ben Holmes. 1937. RKO. 61 min. Sound. 16mm B&W. *Rental:* RKO General Pics.

Too Much Harmony. Bing Crosby & Jack Oakie. Directed by Edward Sutherland. 1933. Paramount. 76 min. Sound. 16mm B&W. *Rental:* Swank Motion.

Too Young to Kiss. June Allyson & Van Johnson. Directed by Robert Z. Leonard. 1951. MGM. 89 min. Sound. 16mm B&W. *Rental:* MGM United.

Toolbox Murders, The. Cameron Mitchell. Directed by Dennis Donnelly. 1979. Cal-Am. 93 min. Sound. 16mm Color. *Rental:* Budget Films & Films Inc.

Tootsie. Dustin Hoffman, Jessica Lange & Teri Garr. Directed by Sydney Pollack. 1985. Columbia. 116 min. Sound. 16mm Color. *Rental:* Swank Motion. *Rental:* Swank Motion, Videotape version.

Top Banana. Phil Silvers & Rose-Marie. Directed by Alfred E. Green. 1954. United Artists. 100 min. Sound. 16mm Color. *Rental:* MGM United.

Top Gun. Sterling Hayden & William Bishop. Directed by Ray Nazarro. 1955. United Artists. 73 min. Sound. 16mm B&W. *Rental:* MGM United.

Top Hat. Fred Astaire & Ginger Rogers. Directed by Mark Sandrich. 1935. RKO. 108 min. Sound. 16mm B&W. *Rental:* Films Inc & RKO General Pics. *Sale:* Nostalgia Merchant & Vidamerica, Videotape version.

Top of the Form. Harry Fowler & Alfie Bass. Directed by John Paddy Carstairs. 1953. Britain. 75 min. Sound. 16mm B&W. *Rental:* Cinema Five.

Top of the World. Dale Robertson, Frank Lovejoy & Evelyn Keyes. Directed by Lewis R. Foster. 1955. United Artists. 90 min. Sound. 16mm B&W. *Rental:* MGM United.

Top Speed. Joe E. Brown & Jack Whiting. Directed by Mervyn LeRoy. 1930. Warners. 74 min. Sound. 16mm B&W. *Rental:* MGM United.

Topaz. Frederick Stafford & John Forsyth. Directed by Alfred Hitchcock. 1969. Universal. 125 min. Sound. 16mm Color. *Rental:* Swank Motion.

Topaze. John Barrymore & Myrna Loy. Directed by Harry D'Arrast. 1933. RKO. 80 min. Sound. 16mm B&W. *Rental:* Films Inc.

Topaze. Fernandel. 1938. France. Sound. 16mm B&W. *Sale:* Cinema Concepts & Festival Films.

Topeka. William Elliott & Phyllis Coates. Directed by Thomas Carr. 1953. Allied Artists. 69 min. Sound. 16mm B&W. *Rental:* Hurlock Cine.

Topeka Terror. Allan Lane. Directed by Howard Bretherton. 1945. Republic. 55 min. Sound. 16mm B&W. *Rental:* Ivy Films. *Sale:* Rep Pic Film.

Topele. Gedi Yagil. Directed by Leo Filler. 1970. Israel. 82 min. Sound. 16mm Color. *Rental:* Films Inc.

Topkapi. Melina Mercouri & Maximilian Schell. Directed by Jules Dassin. 1964. United Artists. 120 min. Sound. 16mm Color. *Rental:* MGM United.

Topper. Cary Grant & Roland Young. Directed by Norman Z. Mcleod. 1937. MGM. 96 min. Sound. 16mm B&W. *Rental:* Images Film & Willoughby Peer.

Topper Returns. Roland Young & Carole Landis. Directed by Roy Del Ruth. 1941. United Artists. 85 min. Sound. 16mm B&W. *Rental:* Budget Films, Cine Craft, Em Gee Film Lib, Inst Cinema, Kit Parker, Roas Films, Video Comm, Wholesome Film Ctr & Willoughby Peer. *Sale:* Cinema Concepts, Festival Films & Reel Images. *Rental:* Ivy Films & Morcraft Films, *Sale:* Ivy Films & Reel Images, Super 8 sound version. *Sale:* Festival Films, Videotape version.

Topper Takes a Trip. Constance Bennett & Roland Young. Directed by Norman Z. McLeod. 1939. United Artists. 72 min. Sound. 16mm B&W. *Rental:* Inst Cinema & Willoughby Peer.

Tora! Tora! Tora! Martin Balsam, Joseph Cotten & E. G. Marshall. Directed by Richard Fleischer & Toshiro Masuda. 1970. Fox. (Anamorphic). 143 min. Sound. 16mm Color. *Rental:* Films Inc, Twyman Films, Welling Motion Pictures, Westcoast Films & Williams Films, Anamorphic version. *Rental:* Films Inc,

Torch, The. Orig. Title: Bandit General. Paulette Goddard & Pedro Armendariz. Directed by Emilio Fernandez. 1950. Eagle Lion. 90 min. Sound. 16mm B&W. *Rental:* Budget Films & Ivy Films.

Torch Song. Joan Crawford & Michael Wilding. Directed by Charles Walters. 1953. MGM. 90 min. Sound. 16mm Color. *Rental:* MGM United.

Torchy Blane in Chinatown. Glenda Farrell & Barton MacLane. Directed by William Beaudine. 1939. Warners. 58 min. Sound. 16mm B&W. *Rental:* MGM United.

Torchy Blane in Panama. Lola Lane & Paul Kelly. Directed by William Clemens. 1938. Warners. 58 min. Sound. 16mm B&W. *Rental:* MGM United.

Torchy Gets Her Man. Glenda Farrell & Barton MacLane. Directed by William Beaudine. 1938. Warners. 62 min. Sound. 16mm B&W. *Rental:* MGM United.

Torchy Plays with Dynamite. Jane Wyman & Allen Jenkins. Directed by Noel Smith. 1939. Warners. 59 min. Sound. 16mm B&W. *Rental:* MGM United.

Torchy Runs for Mayor. Glenda Farrell & Barton MacLane. Directed by Ray McCarey. 1939. Warners. 60 min. Sound. 16mm B&W. *Rental:* MGM United.

Torero! Luis Procuna & Manolete. Directed by Carlos Velo. 1957. Columbia. 75 min. Sound. 16mm B&W. narrated Eng. *Rental:* Films Inc.

Torment. Mai Zetterling & Alf Kjellin. Directed by Alf Sjoberg. Swed. 1944. Sweden. 90 min. Sound. 16mm B&W. subtitles. *Rental:* Films Inc, Janus Films & New Cinema.

Tormented. Richard Carlson & Susan Gordon. Directed by Bert I. Gordon. 1960. Allied Artists. 75 min. Sound. 16mm B&W. *Rental:* Hurlock Cine.

Torn Curtain. Paul Newman & Julie Andrews. Directed by Alfred Hitchcock. 1966. Universal. 128 min. Sound. 16mm Color. *Rental:* Films Inc & Swank Motion.

Tornado. Directed by George Murray. 1975. NBC. (Documentary). 52 min. Sound. 16mm Color. *Rental:* Films Inc. *Sale:* Films Inc. *Sale:* Films Inc, Videotape version.

Toronado Range. Eddie Dean. Directed by Ray Taylor. 1948. Eagle Lion. 58 min. Sound. 16mm B&W. *Sale:* Classics Assoc NY.

Torpedo Alley. Mark Stevens & Dorothy Malone. Directed by Lew Landers. 1953. Allied Artists. 84 min. Sound. 16mm B&W. *Rental:* Ivy Films.

Torpedo Bay. James Mason & Lilli Palmer. Directed by Charles Frend. 1964. Filmways. 91 min. Sound. 16mm B&W. *Rental:* Films Inc & Westcoast Films.

Torpedo of Doom, The. Lee Powell & Herman Brix. Directed by William Witney. 1939. Republic. 100 min. Sound. 16mm B&W. *Rental:* Ivy Films. *Sale:* Rep Pic Film.

Torpedo Run. Glenn Ford & Ernest Borgnine. Directed by Joseph Pevney. 1958. MGM. 96 min. Sound. 16mm Color. *Rental:* MGM United. *Rental:* MGM United, Anamorphic version.

Torpedoed. Orig. Title: Our Fighting Navy. H. B. Warner & Richard Cromwell. Directed by Norman Walker. 1937. Britain. 70 min. Sound. 16mm B&W. *Rental:* Mogulls Films.

Torre Bella. Directed by Thomas Harlan. Port. 1977. Portugal. (Documentary). 140 min. Sound. 16mm Color. subtitles. *Rental:* Tricontinental Film.

Torrent. Orig. Title: Ibanez' Torrent. Greta Garbo. Directed by Monta Bell. 1926. MGM. 80 min. Silent. 16mm B&W. *Rental:* MGM United.

Torrid Zone. James Cagney & Ann Sheridan. Directed by William Keighley. 1940. Warners. 88 min. Sound. 16mm B&W. *Rental:* MGM United.

Torse. 1977. Merce Cunningham. (Dance). 60 min. Sound. 16mm Color. *Sale:* M Cunningham.

Torse. Karole Armitage. Directed by Charles Atlas. 1977. (Left & Right Screen). 55 min. Sound. 16mm Color. *Rental:* M Cunningham. *Sale:* M Cunningham.

Torso Murder Mystery, The. Orig. Title: Traitor Spy. Bruce Cabot. Directed by Walter Summers. 1939. Britain. 67 min. Sound. 16mm B&W. *Rental:* Film Classics.

Tortilla Flat. Spencer Tracy & Hedy Lamarr. Directed by Victor Fleming. 1942. MGM. 106 min. Sound. 16mm B&W. *Rental:* MGM United.

Torture Garden. Jack Palance & Burgess Meredith. Directed by Freddie Francis. 1967. Columbia. 93 min. Sound. 16mm Color. *Rental:* Cine Craft, Modern Sound, Westcoast Films, Welling Motion Pictures & Budget Films.

Torture of Silence, The. Mrs. Emmy Lyn. Directed by Abel Gance. 1917. France. 50 min. Silent. 16mm B&W. *Rental:* Em Gee Film Lib. *Sale:* Festival Films & Reel Images. *Sale:* Reel Images, Super 8 silent version.

Torture Ship. Lyle Talbot & Sheila Bromley. Directed by Victor Halperin. 1939. PRC. 57 min. Sound. 16mm B&W. *Rental:* Video Comm.

Tosca. Franca Duval & Franco Corelli Directed by Carmine Gallone. Ital. 1960. Italy. (Opera). 111 min. Sound. 16mm B&W. narrated Eng. *Rental:* Corinth Films.

Total Health. 1980. Broadcasting & Film Comm.. (Documentary). 60 min. Videotape Color. *Lease:* Natl Churches Christ.

Toto & the Poachers. John Aloisi. Directed by Brian Salt. 1958. Britain. 50 min. Sound. 16mm Color. *Sale:* Lucerne Films.

Touch, The. Elliott Gould, Bibi Anderson & Max Von Sydow. Directed by Ingmar Bergman. Swed. 1971. Sweden. 112 min. Sound. 16mm Color. dubbed. *Rental:* Films Inc.

Touch & Go. (Cast unlisted). Videotape *Sale:* Vidamerica.

Touch of Class, A. George Segal & Glenda Jackson. Directed by Melvin Frank. 1973. Embassy. 105 min. Sound. 16mm Color. *Rental:* Swank Motion.

Touch of Evil. Orson Welles, Charlton Heston & Janet Leigh. Directed by Orson Welles. 108 min. Sound. 16mm Color. *Rental:* Swank Motion.

Touch of Larceny, A. James Mason, George Sanders & Vera Miles. Directed by Guy Hamilton. 1960. Paramount. 93 min. Sound. 16mm B&W. *Rental:* Films Inc.

Touch of Sensitivity, A. 1981. Britain. (Documentary). 50 min. Sound. 16mm Color. *Rental:* Films Inc, U Mich Media & Syracuse U Film. *Sale:* Films Inc. *Rental:* Films Inc, *Sale:* Films Inc, Videotape version.

Touchables, The. Judy Huxtable. Directed by Robert Freeman. 1968. Fox. 97 min. 16mm Color. *Rental:* Films Inc.

Touched by Love. Deborah Raffin, Diane Lane & Michael Learned. Directed by Gus Trikonis. 1980. Columbia. 97 min. Sound. 16mm Color. *Rental:* Swank Motion. *Rental:* Swank Motion, Videotape version.

Tough Guy. Jackie Cooper & Jean Hersholt. Directed by Chester M. Franklin. 1936. MGM. 77 min. Sound. 16mm B&W. *Rental:* MGM United.

Tough Kid. Frankie Darro & Mantan Moreland. Directed by Howard Bretherton. 1940. Monogram. 59 min. Sound. 16mm B&W. *Rental:* Hurlock Cine.

Tough Men. Skyline Productions. 58 min. Sound. 16mm Color. *Rental:* Gospel Films.

Tough Old Gut: Italy, Nov. 1942 - June 1944. Directed by Hugh Raggett. (World at War Ser.). : Pt. 13.). 1973. Media Guild. (Documentary). 52 min. Sound. 16mm Color. *Rental:* Media Guild & U Cal Media. *Sale:* Media Guild. *Sale:* Media Guild, Videotape version.

Tougher They Come, The. Wayne Morris & Preston Foster. Directed by Ray Nazarro. 1950. Columbia. 90 min. Sound. 16mm B&W. *Rental:* Inst Cinema.

Toughest Man in Arizona, The. Vaughan Monroe & Joan Leslie. Directed by R. G. Springsteen. 1952. Republic. 90 min. Sound. 16mm B&W. *Rental:* Ivy Films. *Sale:* Rep Pic Film.

Tour En l'Air. Directed by Grant Munro. 1973. Canada. (Documentary). 50 min. Sound. 16mm Color. *Rental:* U Mich Media & Natl Film CN. *Sale:* Natl Film CN. *Sale:* Natl Film CN, *Rental:* Natl Film CN, Videotape version.

Tour of the White House with Mrs. John F. Kennedy, A. 1962. CBS. (Documentary). 58 min. Sound. 16mm B&W. *Rental:* McGraw-Hill Films. *Sale:* McGraw-Hill Films.

Tourist Trap. Jon Van Ness. Directed by David Schmoeller. 1979. Compass. 85 min. Sound. 16mm Color. *Rental:* Films Inc.

Tournament Tempo. Orig. Title: Gay Blades. Alian Lane & Jean Rogers. Directed by George Blair. 1946. Republic. 71 min. Sound. 16mm B&W. *Rental:* Ivy Films. *Sale:* Rep Pic Film.

Tout Va Bien. Jane Fonda & Yves Montand. Directed by Jean-Luc Godard & Jean-Paul Gorin. Fr. 1972. France. 95 min. Sound. 16mm Color. subtitles. *Rental:* New Cinema & New Yorker Films.

Tovarich. Charles Boyer & Claudette Colbert. Directed by Anatole Litvak. 1937. Warners. 98 min. Sound. 16mm B&W. *Rental:* MGM United.

Toward Poetic Realism: 1936-1938. Directed by Armand Panigel. Fr. France. (Documentary). 70 min. Sound. 16mm B&W. subtitles. *Rental:* French Am Cul.

Toward Reconciliation. CC Films. 60 min. Sound. Videotape Color. *Rental:* Natl Churches Christ.

Towards Baruya Manhood. 9 pts. 1973. Australia. (Documentary). 505 min. Sound. 16mm Color. *Rental:* Aust Info Serv. *Sale:* Aust Info Serv.

Tower of Babel, The. Ron Palillo & Vince Edwards. Directed by Jack Hively. 1979. 51 min. Sound. 16mm *Rental:* Budget Films, Lucerne Films & Syracuse U Film. *Sale:* Lucerne Films, Videotape version.

Tower of London, The. Vincent Price & Michael Pate. Directed by Roger Corman. 1962. United Artists. 79 min. Sound. 16mm B&W. *Rental:* MGM United.

Tower of London, The. Basil Rathbone & Boris Karloff. Directed by Rowland V. Lee. 1939. Universal. 92 min. Sound. 16mm B&W. *Rental:* Swank Motion.

Towering Inferno, The. Paul Newman, Steve McQueen & Faye Dunaway. Directed by John Guillermin. 1974. Fox/Warners. 165 min. Sound. 16mm Color. *Rental:* Films Inc, Swank Motion, Twyman Films & Williams Films. *Rental:* Films Inc, Anamorphic version.

Towers of Silence. Directed by Jamil Dehlavi. Urdu. 1975. Pakistan. (Cast unlisted). 54 min. Sound. 16mm B&W. subtitles. *Rental:* Texture Film. *Sale:* Texture Film.

Town Bloody Hall. Directed by Chris Hegedus & D. A. Pennebaker. 1978. Pennebaker. (Documentary). 88 min. Sound. 16mm Color. *Rental:* Pennebaker. *Sale:* Pennebaker.

Town Called Hell, A. Robert Shaw, Stella Stevens & Martin Landau. Directed by Robert Parrish. 1971. Scotia International. 97 min. Sound. 16mm Color. *Rental:* Budget Films, Video Comm, Welling Motion Pictures & Westcoast Films.

Town on Trial, A. Charles Coburn & John Mills. Directed by John Guillermin. 1957. Columbia. 96 min. Sound. 16mm B&W. *Rental:* Kit Parker.

Town Tamer, A. Dana Andrews & Terry Moore. Directed by Lesley Selander. 1965. Paramount. 89 min. Sound. 16mm Color. *Rental:* Films Inc.

Town That Cried Terror!, The Oliver Reed & Stuart Whitman. Directed by Richard Compton. 1977. New World. 86 min. Sound. 16mm Color. *Rental:* Films Inc.

Town Went Wild, The. Freddie Bartholomew & James Lydon. Directed by Ralph Murphy. 1944. PRC. 70 min. Sound. 16mm B&W. *Rental:* Budget Films & Ivy Films. *Sale:* Classics Assoc NY & Rep Pic Film.

Town Without Pity. Kirk Douglas & E. G. Marshall. Directed by Gottfried Reinhardt. 1961. United Artists. 104 min. Sound. 16mm B&W. *Rental:* MGM United.

Toy, The. Richard Pryor, Jackie Gleason & Scott Schwartz. Directed by Richard Donner. 1985. Columbia. 102 min. Sound. 16mm Color. *Rental:* Swank Motion. *Rental:* Swank Motion, Videotape version.

Toy Wife, The. Trans. Title: Frou Frou. Luise Rainer & Robert Young. Directed by Richard Thorpe. 1938. MGM. 90 min. Sound. 16mm B&W. *Rental:* MGM United.

Toys Are Not for Children. Marcia Forbes & Frank Warren. Directed by Stanley H. Brasslof. 1972. Maron. 85 min. Sound. 16mm B&W. *Rental:* Budget Films.

Toys in the Attic. Dean Martin & Geraldine Page. Directed by George Roy Hill. 1963. United Artists. 90 min. Sound. 16mm B&W. *Rental:* Charard Motion Pics & MGM United.

TR & His Times. 58 min. Sound. Videotape *Rental:* PBS Video. *Sale:* PBS Video.

Track of the Jaguar. Lassie. 1960. Wrather. 52 min. Sound. 16mm Color. *Rental:* Films Inc, Kerr Film & Westcoast Films.

Track of the Moonbeast, The. Chase Cordell & Donna Leigh Drake. 1976. Cinema Shares. 90 min. Sound. 16mm Color. *Rental:* Films Inc.

Track of the Vampire. Orig. Title: Blood Bath. William Campbell. Directed by Stephanie Rothman & Jack Hill. 1966. American International. 80 min. Sound. 16mm B&W. *Rental:* Films Inc.

Track the Man Down. Kent Taylor & Petula Clark. Directed by R. G. Springsteen. 1957. Republic. 73 min. Sound. 16mm B&W. *Rental:* Ivy Films. *Sale:* Rep Pic Film.

Track Two. Gordon Keith & Jack Lemmon. Directed by Harry Sutherland. 1982. Canada. 90 min. Sound. 16mm Color. *Rental:* First Run. *Lease:* First Run.

Trackdown. Jim Mitchum & Karen Lamm. Directed by Richard T. Heffron. 1976. United Artists. 98 min. Sound. 16mm Color. *Rental:* MGM United.

Tracking the Killer, or Call of the Wilderness. Sound. 16mm B&W. *Sale:* Blackhawk Films. *Sale:* Blackhawk Films, Super 8 sound version. *Sale:* Blackhawk Films, Super 8 silent version.

Tracy Rides. Tom Tyler. Directed by Harry S. Webb. 1934. Steiner. 60 min. Sound. 16mm B&W. *Rental:* Mogull's Films.

Trade Winds. Joan Bennett & Fredric March. Directed by Tay Garnett. 1938. United Artists. 94 min. Sound. 16mm B&W. *Rental:* Budget Films, Film Classics, Learning Corp Am & U of IL Film. *Sale:* Learning Corp Am. *Sale:* Glenn Photo, Super 8 sound version.

Trader Horn. Harry Carey & Edwina Booth. Directed by W. S. Van Dyke. 1931. MGM. 102 min. Sound. 16mm B&W. *Rental:* MGM United.

Trader Horn. Rod Taylor, Anne Heywood & Jean Sorel. Directed by Reza S. Badiyi. 1973. MGM. 105 min. Sound. 16mm Color. *Rental:* MGM United.

Trading Places. Dan Aykroyd & Eddie Murphy. Directed by John Landis. 1983. Paramount. 117 min. Sound. 16mm Color. *Rental:* Films Inc.

Tradition of Justice, A. 1979. PBS. (Documentary). 59 min. Videotape Color. *Rental:* PBS Video. *Sale:* PBS Video.

Traffic. Jacques Tati. Directed by Jacques Tati. 1973. France. 89 min. Sound. 16mm Color. *Rental:* Films Inc, Swank Motion & Twyman Films.

Traffic in Crime. Kane Richmond & Adele Mara. Directed by Lesley Selander. 1946. Republic. 56 min. Sound. 16mm B&W. *Rental:* Ivy Films.

Traffic in Souls. Matt Moore. 1913. Universal. 50 min. Silent. 16mm B&W. *Rental:* Budget Films. *Sale:* Reel Images. *Rental:* Ivy Films, Super 8 silent version.

Traffic Snarl, The. 1967. NET. (Documentary). 60 min. Sound. 16mm B&W. *Rental:* Indiana AV Ctr.

Tragedy at Midnight, A. John Howard & Margaret Lindsay. Directed by Joseph Santley. 1942. Republic. 54 min. Sound. 16mm B&W. *Rental:* Ivy Films. *Sale:* Rep Pic Film.

Tragedy of the Red Salmon, The. 1975. Churchill Films. (Documentary). 52 min. Sound. 16mm Color. *Rental:* Churchill Films. *Rental:* Churchill Films, Videotape version.

Tragic Diary of Zero the Fool, The. Gerald S. Cogan. Directed by Morley Markson. 1972. New Line. 84 min. Sound. 16mm B&W. *Rental:* New Cinema & New Line Cinema. *Sale:* New Line Cinema.

Trail Beyond, The. John Wayne. Directed by Robert N. Bradbury. 1934. Monogram. 79 min. Sound. 16mm B&W. *Rental:* Ivy Films. *Sale:* Classics Assoc NY & Rep Pic Film.

Trail Blazers, The. Robert Livingston & Bob Steele. Directed by George Sherman. 1940. Republic. 54 min. Sound. 16mm B&W. *Rental:* Ivy Films. *Sale:* Rep Pic Film.

Trail Dust. William Boyd. Directed by Nate Watt. 1936. Paramount. 60 min. Sound. 16mm B&W. *Lease:* Cinema Concepts.

Trail Guide. Tim Holt & Linda Douglas. Directed by Lesley Selander. 1952. RKO. 60 min. Sound. 16mm B&W. *Rental:* RKO General Pics.

Trail of Kit Carson, The. Allan Lane. Directed by Lesley Selander. 1945. Republic. 56 min. Sound. 16mm B&W. *Rental:* Ivy Films. *Sale:* Rep Pic Film.

Trail of Robin Hood, The. Roy Rogers. Directed by William Witney. 1950. Republic. 54 min. Sound. 16mm Color. *Rental:* Ivy Films & Modern Sound. *Sale:* Rep Pic Film & Nostalgia Merchant.

Trail of Tears. 1970. NET. (Documentary). 100 min. Sound. 16mm B&W. *Rental:* Indiana AV Ctr. *Sale:* Indiana AV Ctr.

Trail of Terror. James Newill & Dave O'Brien. Directed by Oliver Drake. 1944. PRC. 64 min. Sound. 16mm B&W. *Rental:* Westcoast Films. *Sale:* Morcraft Films.

Trail of the Apache, Chance. Christopher Clarke & Bruce M. Fischer. 85 min. Sound. 16mm Color. *Rental:* Best Film & Video Corp..

Trail of the Hawk. Yancey Lane & Dickie Jones. Directed by Edward Dmytryk. 50 min. Sound. 16mm B&W. *Sale:* Morcraft Films. *Sale:* Morcraft Films, Super 8 sound version.

Trail of the Lonesome Pine, The. Fred MacMurray, Sylvia Sidney & Henry Fonda. Directed by Henry Hathaway. 1936. Paramount. 102 min. Sound. 16mm Color. *Rental:* Swank Motion.

Trail of the Mounties, The. Russell Hayden. Directed by Howard Bretherton. 1948. Screen Guild. 42 min. Sound. 16mm B&W. *Rental:* Film Ctr DC, Mogulls Films & Westcoast Films.

Trail of the Pink Panther, The. Peter Sellers & David Niven. Directed by Blake Edwards. 1982. United Artists. 97 min. Sound. 16mm Color. *Rental:* MGM United. *Rental:* MGM United, Videotape version.

Trail of the Silver Spurs, The. Range Busters. Directed by S. Roy Luby. 1941. Monogram. 58 min. Sound. 16mm B&W. *Rental:* Budget Films & Films Inc.

Trail of the Vigilantes. Franchot Tone & Peggy Moran. Directed by Allan Dwan. 1940. Universal. 78 min. Sound. 16mm B&W. *Rental:* Swank Motion.

Trail of the Wild. Directed by Gordon Eastman. 1974. Gold Key. (Documentary). 92 min. Sound. 16mm Color. *Rental:* Video Comm. *Lease:* Video Comm.

Trail of the Yukon. Kirby Grant. Directed by William Crowley. 1949. Monogram. 69 min. Sound. 16mm B&W. *Rental:* Cine Craft & Hurlock Cine.

Trail of Vengeance. Johnny Mack Brown. Directed by Sam Newfield. 1937. Republic. 60 min. Sound. 16mm B&W. *Rental:* Mogulls Films. *Sale:* Rep Pic Film.

Trail Riders. Orig. Title: Overland Trail. The Range Busters. Directed by Robert Tansey. 1942. Monogram. 57 min. Sound. 16mm B&W. *Rental:* Budget Films & Modern Sound. *Sale:* Cinema Concepts.

Trail Street. Randolph Scott & Robert Ryan. Directed by Ray Enright. 1947. RKO. 84 min. Sound. 16mm B&W. *Rental:* Films Inc.

Trail to Mexico. Jimmy Wakely. Directed by Oliver Drake. 1946. Monogram. 56 min. Sound. 16mm B&W. *Rental:* Hurlock Cine.

Trailblazers of Modern Dance. 1976. WNET. (Documentary). 58 min. Sound. 16mm Color. *Rental:* U Cal Media, Indiana AV Ctr & WNET Media. *Sale:* Indiana AV Ctr & WNET Media. *Sale:* Indiana AV Ctr, Videotape version.

Trailin' Trouble. Ken Maynard. Directed by Arthur Rosson. 1937. Grand National. 60 min. Sound. 16mm B&W. *Rental:* Budget Films. *Sale:* Video Comm, Videotape version.

Trailing Double Trouble. Range Busters. Directed by S. Roy Luby. 1940. Monogram. 60 min. Sound. 16mm B&W. *Rental:* Films Inc.

Trail's End. Dave O'Brien. Directed by Al Herman. 1935. Beaumont. 60 min. Sound. 16mm B&W. *Sale:* Natl Cinema.

Train, The. Burt Lancaster & Paul Scofield. Directed by John Frankenheimer. 1965. United Artists. 132 min. Sound. 16mm B&W. *Rental:* MGM United.

Train Robbers, The. Ann-Margret & John Wayne. Directed by Burt Kennedy. 1973. Warners. 92 min. Sound. 16mm Color. *Rental:* Williams Films, Film Ctr DC & Films Inc. *Sale:* Tamarelles French Film, Videotape version.

Train to Alcatraz, The. Milburn Stone & Jane Darwell. Directed by Philip Ford. 1948. Republic. 60 min. Sound. 16mm B&W. *Rental:* Ivy Films. *Sale:* Rep Pic Film.

Traitor, The. Tim McCoy. Directed by Sam Newfield. 1936. Puritan. 60 min. Sound. 16mm B&W. *Sale:* Video Comm.

Traitor Spy see Torso Murder Mystery.

Traitor Within, A. Don Barry & Ralph Morgan. Directed by Frank McDonald. 1942. Republic. 61 min. Sound. 16mm B&W. *Rental:* Ivy Films.

Traitors, The. Span. 1973. Argentina. (Documentary). 114 min. Sound. 16mm Color. subtitles. *Rental:* Cinema Guild. *Sale:* Cinema Guild.

Tramp, Tramp, Tramp. Harry Langdon & Joan Crawford. Directed by Harry Edwards. 1926. MGM. 65 min. Silent. 16mm B&W. *Rental:* A Twyman Pres & Twyman Films.

Trampa Para un Cadaver. Guillermo Murray. Directed by Francisco Del Villar. Mexico. 83 min. Sound. 16mm Color. *Rental:* Westcoast Films.

Tramplers, The. Joseph Cotten & Gordon Scott. Directed by Albert Band. Ital. 1966. Italy. 105 min. Sound. 16mm Color. *Rental:* Films Inc.

Trans-Europ Express. Jean-Louis Trintignant & Daniel Emilfork. Directed by Alain Robbe-Grillet. Fr. 1968. France. 105 min. Sound. 16mm B&W. subtitles. *Rental:* Video Comm & Westcoast Films.

Transatlantic Merry-Go-Round. Jack Benny & Patsy Kelly. Directed by Ben Stoloff. 1934. United Artists. 90 min. Sound. 16mm B&W. *Rental:* Mogulls Films.

Transatlantic Tunnel. Richard Dix, Walter Huston & George Arliss. Directed by Maurice Elvey. 1935. Britain. 94 min. Sound. 16mm B&W. *Rental:* Budget Films, Em Gee Film Lib, Janus Films, Kit Parker, Mogulls Films & Video Comm. *Sale:* Cinema Concepts. *Rental:* Ivy Films, *Sale:* Cinema Concepts & Ivy Films, Super 8 sound version.

Transcontinent Express see Rock Island Trail.

Transcontinental Limited. Johnny Hines & Alec B. Francis. Directed by Nat Ross. 1926. Chadwick. 65 min. Silent. 16mm B&W. *Rental:* Mogulls Films. *Sale:* Willoughby Peer, Silent 8mm version.

Transgression. Kay Francis & Ricardo Cortez. Directed by Herbert Brenon. 1931. RKO. 69 min. Sound. 16mm B&W. *Rental:* RKO General Pics.

Transplant Experience, The. 1976. Nova. (Documentary). 50 min. Sound. 16mm Color. *Rental:* Kent St U Film & U of IL Film.

Transport from Paradise. Zdenek Stepenek. Directed by Zbynek Brynych. Czech. 1963. Czechoslovakia. 93 min. Sound. 16mm B&W. subtitles. *Rental:* Icarus Films.

Transportation. 1973. Sterling. (Documentary). 56 min. Sound. 16mm Color. *Rental:* Sterling Ed Film. *Sale:* Sterling Ed Film.

Transuranium Elements. 2 pts. 1968. Atomic Energy Commission. (Documentary). 129 min. Sound. 16mm B&W. *Rental:* Natl AV Ctr.

Trap, The. Lon Chaney. Directed by Robert Thornby. 1919. Universal. 60 min. Silent. 16mm B&W. *Rental:* Em Gee Film Lib. *Sale:* Em Gee Film Lib.

Trap, The. Orig. Title: Murder at Malibu Beach. Sidney Toler. Directed by Howard Bretherton. 1947. Monogram. 70 min. Sound. 16mm B&W. *Rental:* Hurlock Cine & Mogulls Films.

Trap, The. Richard Widmark & Lee J. Cobb. Directed by Norman Panama. 1959. Paramount. 84 min. Sound. 16mm Color. *Rental:* Films Inc.

Trap of Solid Gold, The. Cliff Robertson, Dina Merrill & Dustin Hoffman. Directed by Paul Bogart. 1967. ABC. 51 min. Sound. 16mm B&W. *Rental:* Trans-World Films & Utah Media. *Sale:* Intl Films.

Trapeze. Burt Lancaster & Gina Lollobrigida. Directed by Sir Carol Reed. 1956. United Artists. 105 min. Sound. 16mm Color. *Rental:* Budget Films, Films Inc & MGM United.

Trapp Family, The. Hans Holt. Directed by Wolfgang Liebeneiner. 1961. Germany. 113 min. Sound. 16mm Color. dubbed. *Rental:* Alba House.

Trapped. Lloyd Bridges & John Hoyt. Directed by Richard Fleischer. 1949. Eagle Lion. 78 min. Sound. 16mm B&W. *Rental:* Mogulls Films.

Trapped by Boston Blackie. Chester Morris & June Vincent. Directed by Seymour Friedman. 1948. Columbia. 67 min. Sound. 16mm B&W. *Rental:* Maljack. *Lease:* Maljack.

Trapped by the Mormons. Evelyn Brent. Directed by H. B. Parkinson. 1922. Britain. 70 min. Silent. 16mm B&W. *Rental:* Em Gee Film Lib. *Sale:* Glenn Photo & Morcraft Films. *Rental:* Ivy Films, Super 8 Silent version.

Trapped in Tangiers. Edmund Purdom & Genevieve Page. Directed by Antonio Cervi. 1960. Italy. (Anamorphic). 74 min. Sound. 16mm B&W. dubbed. *Rental:* Westcoast Films & Willoughby Peer.

Trapped in the Badlands. George Houston. 1941. PRC. 60 min. Sound. 16mm B&W. *Rental:* Mogulls Films.

Trash. Joe Dallesandro & Holly Woodlawn. Directed by Paul Morrissey. 1970. Cinema V. 103 min. Sound. 16mm Color. *Rental:* Cinema Five. *Lease:* Cinema Five.

Trauma. John Conte & Lynn Bari. Directed by Malcolm Young. 1963. Parade. 92 min. Sound. 16mm B&W. *Rental:* Ivy Films.

Trauma: It's an Emergency. 1975. WNET. (Documentary). 90 min. Sound. 16mm Color. *Rental:* WNET Media. *Sale:* WNET Media. *Sale:* WNET Media, Videotape version.

Traumatic Injuries. 1978. 50 min. Sound. Videotape Color. *Sale:* Natl AV Ctr.

Travelers' Tales. 1980. Cosmos. (Documentary). 60 min. Sound. 16mm Color. *Rental:* Films Inc. *Sale:* Films Inc. *Rental:* Films Inc, *Sale:* Films Inc, Videotape version.

Traveling Executioner, The. Stacy Keach & Bud Cort. Directed by Jack Smight. 1970. MGM. (Anamorphic). 94 min. Sound. 16mm sound Color. *Rental:* MGM United.

Traveling Saleslady, The. Joan Blondell & Glenda Farrell. Directed by Ray Enright. 1935. Warners. 65 min. Sound. 16mm B&W. *Rental:* MGM United.

Traveling Saleswoman, The. Joan Davis & Andy Devine. Directed by Charles Reisner. 1950. Columbia. 109 min. Sound. 16mm B&W. *Rental:* Kit Parker.

Travelling Husbands. Frank Albertson & Hugh Herbert. Directed by Paul Sloane. 1932. RKO. 74 min. Sound. 16mm *Rental:* RKO General Pics.

Travels With My Aunt. Maggie Smith & Alec McCowen. Directed by George Cukor. 1972. MGM. 109 min. Sound. 16mm Color. *Rental:* MGM United.

Traviata, La. Tito Gobbi & Massimo Serato. Directed by Carmine Gallone. Ital. 1948. Italy. 82 min. Sound. 16mm B&W. subtitles. *Rental:* Kerr Film.

Traviata, La. Anna Moffo & Gino Bechi. Directed by Mario Lafranchi. Ital. 1967. Italy. 100 min. Sound. 16mm Color. subtitles. *Rental:* Films Inc.

Traviata, La. Lucia Evangelista & Giulio Gari. 1952. Astor. 55 min. Sound. 16mm B&W. *Rental:* Budget Films & Video Comm.

Traviata, La. 1975. Britain. (Opera). 57 min. Sound. 16mm Color. *Rental:* Centron Films. *Sale:* Centron Films.

Traviata, La. Teresa Stratas & Placido Domingo. Directed by Franco Zeffirelli. 1983. Universal. 112 min. Sound. 16mm Color. subtitles. *Rental:* Swank Motion. *Rental:* Swank Motion, *Sale:* Tamarelles French Film, Videotape version.

Tread Softly Stranger. Diana Dors & Terence Morgan. Directed by Gordon Parry. 1958. Britain. 91 min. Sound. 16mm B&W. *Rental:* Video Comm. *Rental:* Video Comm, Videotape version.

Treason & Transition. Directed by Munroe Scott. 1971. Canada. (Documentary). 57 min. Sound. 16mm Color. *Rental:* Natl Film CN. *Sale:* Natl Film CN.

Treasure, The. Jon Provost & Lassie. 1956. Wrather. 52 min. Sound. 16mm B&W. *Rental:* Films Inc & Westcoast Films.

Treasure! 1976. National Geographic. (Documentary). 59 min. Sound. 16mm Color. *Rental:* Natl Geog & Syracuse U Film. *Sale:* Natl Geog, Videotape version.

Treasure, The. Albert Steinruck & Ilka Gruning. Directed by G. W. Pabst. 1932. 51 min. Silent. 16mm B&W. *Rental:* Films Inc.

Treasure at the Mill. Richard Palmer. Directed by Max Anderson. 1957. Britain. 60 min. Sound. 16mm B&W. *Sale:* Lucerne Films.

Treasure Island. Wallace Beery & Lionel Barrymore. Directed by Victor Fleming. 1934. MGM. 110 min. Sound. 16mm B&W. *Rental:* MGM United & OK AV Ctr. *Rental:* MGM United, Videotape version.

Treasure Island. Bobby Driscoll & Robert Newton. Directed by Byron Haskin. 1950. Disney. 96 min. Sound. 16mm Color. *Rental:* Buchan Pic, BYU Media, Cine Craft, Cousino Visual Ed, Williams Films, Bosco Films, Disney Prod, Elliot Film Co, Films Inc, U of IL Film, MGM United, Newman Film Lib, Roas Films, Swank Motion, Film Ctr DC, Twyman Films Westcoast Films & Welling Motion Pictures.

Treasure Island. Orig. Title: Mister Magoo's Treasure Island. 1965. UPA. (Animated). 50 min. Sound. 16mm Color. *Rental:* Inst Cinema, Films Inc, Kerr Film, Macmillan Films, Film Ctr DC, Westcoast Films, Welling Motion Pictures & Willoughby Peer.

Treasure Island. 1970. Australia. (Animated). 54 min. Sound. 16mm Color. *Rental:* Budget Films, Inst Cinema, Roas Films, Swank Motion, Syracuse U Film & Wholesome Film Ctr. *Lease:* Inst Cinema.

Treasure Island. Orson Welles, Walter Slezak & Lionel Stander. Directed by John Hough. 1972. Warners. 92 min. Sound. 16mm Color. *Rental:* Twyman Films.

Treasure Island Revisited. 1973. (Animated). 81 min. Sound. 16mm Color. *Rental:* Films Inc, Westcoast Films & Wholesome Film Ctr.

Treasure of Arne, The. Hjalmar Selander. Directed by Mauritz Stiller. 1919. Sweden. 83 min. Silent. 16mm B&W. *Rental:* Em Gee Film Lib & Museum Mod Art.

Treasure of Bruce Li. Bruce Li. 86 min. Sound. 16mm Color. *Rental:* BF Video.

Treasure of Fear *see* Scared Stiff.

Treasure of Jamaica Reef, The. Stephen Boyd, David Ladd & Roosevelt Grier. Directed by Virginia Stone. 1975. Lighthouse. 88 min. Sound. 16mm Color. *Rental:* Budget Films & Westcoast Films.

Treasure of Lake Titicaca, The. 1970. Cousteau. (Documentary). 54 min. Sound. 16mm Color. *Rental:* Syracuse U Film.

Treasure of Lost Canyon, The. William Powell & Julie Adams. Directed by Ted Tetzlaff. 1952. Universal. 82 min. Sound. 16mm Color. *Rental:* Williams Films.

Treasure of Matecumbe, The. Robert Foxworth, Joan Hackett & Peter Ustinov. 1976. Disney. 116 min. Sound. 16mm Color. *Rental:* Disney Prod, Films Inc & Twyman Films.

Treasure of Monte Cristo, The. Glenn Langan & Adele Jergens. Directed by William Berke. 1949. Screen Guild. 70 min. Sound. 16mm B&W. *Rental:* Budget Films & Film Ctr DC.

Treasure of Pancho Villa, The. Rory Calhoun & Shelley Winters. Directed by George Sherman. 1955. RKO. 96 min. Sound. 16mm Color. *Rental:* Budget Films, Video Comm & Westcoast Films. *Lease:* Video Comm. *Rental:* Video Comm, *Lease:* Video Comm, Videotape version.

Treasure of San Gennaro, The. Senta Berger & Harry Guardino. Directed by Dino Risi. 1968. Paramount. 102 min. Sound. 16mm Color. *Rental:* Films Inc.

Treasure of the Aztecs, The. Lex Barker & Gerald Barry. Directed by Robert Siodmak. 100 min. Sound. 16mm Color. *Rental:* Westcoast Films.

Treasure of the Golden Condor, The. Cornel Wilde & Constance Smith. Directed by Delmer Daves. 1953. Fox. 93 min. Sound. 16mm B&W. *Rental:* Films Inc.

Treasure of the Sierra Madre, The. Humphrey Bogart & Walter Huston. Directed by John Huston. 1948. Warners. 126 min. Sound. 16mm B&W. *Rental:* MGM United. *Sale:* Tamarelles French Film, Videotape version.

Treasures from the Valley of the Kings. 1974. Explo Mundo. (Documentary). 52 min. Sound. 16mm Color. *Rental:* B Raymond. *Sale:* B Raymond.

Treasures of Jasna Gora, The. 1978. Poland. (Documentary). 50 min. Sound. 16mm Color. narrated Eng. *Rental:* Polish People.

Treasures of the Golden Cobra. David Warbek. 95 min. Sound. 16mm *Rental:* WW Enter. *Rental:* WW Enter, Videotape version.

Treatment of Cardiac Arrhythmias by Drugs & Electricity, The. 1968. US Government. (Documentary). 90 min. Sound. 16mm B&W. *Sale:* Natl AV Ctr.

Tree Grows in Brooklyn, A. Dorothy McGuire, James Dunn & Peggy Ann Garner. Directed by Elia Kazan. 1945. Fox. 128 min. Sound. 16mm B&W. *Rental:* Films Inc, Twyman Films, Video Comm, Willoughby Peer & Williams Films.

Tree of Liberty, The *see* Howards of Virginia.

Tree of Life, The. Alden. (Documentary). 55 min. Sound. 16mm Color. *Rental:* Alden Films.

Tree of the Wooden Clogs, The. Luigi Ornaghi & Francesca Moriggi. Directed by Ermanno Olmi. Ital. 1979. Italy. 185 min. Sound. 16mm Color. subtitles. *Rental:* New Yorker Films.

Tree of Thorns, The. 1981. Britain. (Documentary). 50 min. Sound. 16mm Color. *Rental:* Films Inc. *Sale:* Films Inc. *Rental:* Films Inc, *Sale:* Films Inc, Videotape version.

Tree That Put the Clock Back, The. 1972. Britain. (Documentary). 50 min. Sound. 16mm Color. *Rental:* Time-Life Multimedia. *Sale:* Time-Life Multimedia. *Sale:* Time-Life Multimedia, Spanish language version. *Sale:* Time-Life Multimedia, Videotape version.

Trelawney of the "Wells". Elaine Taylor. 1976. Britain. 124 min. Videotape Color. *Rental:* Time-Life Multimedia. *Sale:* Time-Life Multimedia.

Trenchcoat. Margot Kidder & Robert Hays. Directed by Michael Tuchner. 1983. Disney. 91 min. Sound. 16mm Color. *Rental:* Films Inc, Swank Motion, Williams Films & MGM United.

Tres Claves, Los. Span. 1950. Mexico. (Cast unlisted). 90 min. Sound. 16mm Color. *Rental:* Film Classics.

Tres Perfectas Casadas, Los. Mauricio Garces. Directed by Benito Alazraki. Span. Mexico. 90 min. Sound. 16mm Color. *Rental:* Westcoast Films.

Tretya Meshchanskaya *see* Bed & Sofa.

Trial. Glenn Ford & Dorothy McGuire. Directed by Mark Robson. 1955. MGM. 105 min. Sound. 16mm B&W. *Rental:* MGM United.

Trial, The. Trans. Title: Proces, Le. Anthony Perkins & Jeanne Moreau. Directed by Orson Welles. 1962. France. 118 min. Sound. 16mm B&W. dubbed. *Rental:* Budget Films, Corinth Films, Em Gee Film Lib, Films Inc, Images Film, Kit Parker & Natl Film Video. *Sale:* Festival Films, Natl Cinema, Reel Images & Images Film. *Sale:* Festival Films & Images Film, Videotape version.

Trial & Error. Peter Sellers & Sir Richard Attenborough. Directed by James Hill. 1962. Britain. 99 min. Sound. 16mm B&W. *Rental:* MGM United.

Trial at Nuremberg, The. 1964. Wolper. (Documentary). 50 min. Sound. 16mm B&W. *Sale:* Syracuse U Film & Wholesome Film Ctr. *Sale:* Films Inc. *Sale:* Films Inc, Videotape version.

Trial: First Day. 1970. 89 min. Sound. 16mm B&W. *Rental:* Utah Media.

Trial for Rape, The. Directed by Maria Grazia Belmonti. Ital. 1979. Italy. (Documentary). 60 min. Sound. 16mm B&W. subtitles. *Rental:* Women Movies. *Sale:* Women Movies.

Trial: Fourth & Final Day. 1970. 89 min. Sound. 16mm B&W. *Rental:* Utah Media.

Trial Lawyers, The. 1968. CBS. 54 min. Sound. 16mm B&W. *Rental:* Phoenix Films. *Sale:* Phoenix Films, Color version.

Trial of Billy Jack, The. Tom Laughlin. Directed by T. C. Frank. 1974. Warners. 173 min. Sound. 16mm Color. *Rental:* Films Inc, Swank Motion, Twyman Films & Williams Films.

Trial of Denton Cooley, The. 1978. 59 min. Sound. Videotape *Rental:* PBS Video. *Sale:* PBS Video.

Trial of Joan of Arc, The. Florence Zarrez. Directed by Robert Bresson. Fr. 1962. France. 63 min. Sound. 16mm B&W. subtitles. *Rental:* Films Inc & Icarus Films.

Trial of Louis Pasteur, The. Sacha Guitry. Directed by Sacha Guitry. Fr. 1935. France. 79 min. Sound. 16mm B&W. subtitles. *Rental:* Film Classics. *Rental:* Film Classics, Videotape version.

Trial of Mary Dugan, The. Norma Shearer & Lewis Stone. Directed by Bayard Veiller. 1929. MGM. 120 min. Sound. 16mm B&W. *Rental:* MGM.

Trial of Mary Dugan, The. Laraine Day. Directed by Norman Z. McLeod. 1940. MGM. 90 min. Sound. 16mm B&W. *Rental:* MGM United.

Trial of Portia Merriman, The *see* Portia on Trial.

Trial of the Catonsville Nine, The. Directed by Gordon Davidson. 1972. Cinema V. 85 min. Sound. 16mm Color. *Rental:* Cinema Five.

Trial of Xavier Solorzano, The. 1980. PBS. (Documentary). 90 min. Sound. 16mm Color. *Rental:* PBS Video.

Trial: The First Day. 1970. NET. (Documentary). 90 min. Sound. 16mm B&W. *Rental:* Indiana AV Ctr. *Sale:* Indiana AV Ctr. *Sale:* Indiana AV Ctr, Videotape version.

Trial: The Fourth & Final Day. 1970. NET. (Documentary). 90 min. Sound. 16mm B&W. *Rental:* Indiana AV Ctr & Syracuse U Film. *Sale:* Indiana AV Ctr. *Sale:* Indiana AV Ctr, Videotape version.

Trial: The Second Day. 1970. NET. (Documentary). 90 min. Sound. 16mm B&W. *Rental:* Indiana AV Ctr. *Sale:* Indiana AV Ctr & Utah Media. *Sale:* Indiana AV Ctr, Videotape version.

Trial: The Third Day. 1970. NET. (Documentary). 90 min. Sound. 16mm B&W. *Rental:* Indiana AV Ctr. *Sale:* Indiana AV Ctr & Utah Media. *Sale:* Indiana AV Ctr, Videotape version.

Trial Without Jury. Robert Rockwell & Barbara Fuller. Directed by Philip Ford. 1950. Republic. 60 min. Sound. 16mm B&W. *Rental:* Ivy Films. *Sale:* Rep Pic Film.

Trials of Alger Hiss, The. Directed by John Lowenthal. 1980. Corinth. (Documentary). 166 min. Sound. 16mm Color. *Rental:* Corinth Films. *Sale:* Direct Cinema. *Rental:* Direct Cinema, *Sale:* Direct Cinema, Videotape version.

Trials of Charles De Gaulle, The. 1964. CBS. (Documentary). 54 min. Sound. 16mm B&W. *Rental:* McGraw-Hill Films & Syracuse U Film. *Sale:* McGraw-Hill Films.

Trials of Oscar Wilde, The. Peter Finch, James Mason & Nigel Patrick. Directed by Ken Hughes. 1960. 123 min. Sound. 16mm Color. *Rental:* MGM United.

Triangle. Dana Wynter & Ray Danton. 1970. Commonwealth. 95 min. Sound. 16mm Color. *Rental:* Budget Films, Ivy Films, Rep Pic Film & Video Comm. *Lease:* Rep Pic Film.

Tribal Eye, The. 7 pts. 1976. Britain. (Documentary). 385 min. Sound. 16mm Color. *Rental:* Iowa Films. *Rental:* Iowa Films, Videotape version.

Tribe That Hides from Man, The. Directed by Adrian Cowell. 1972. NET. (Documentary). 62 min. Sound. 16mm Color. *Rental:* U Cal Media, Indiana AV Ctr & Human Issues. *Sale:* Human Issues.

Tribulations of a Chinese in China *see* Up to His Ears.

Tribute to a Bad Man, A. James Cagney & Irene Papas. Directed by Robert Wise. 1956. MGM. 95 min. Sound. 16mm Color. *Rental:* MGM United.

Tribute to John Cage, A. 1973. WGBH. (Documentary). 60 min. Videotape Color. *Sale:* Electro Art.

Tricetjedna Vestinu *see* Ninety Degrees in the Shade.

Trick Baby. Mel Stewart. Directed by Larry Yust. 1972. Universal. 98 min. Sound. 16mm Color. *Rental:* Swank Motion.

Tried by Fire. 2 pts. 1945. Army. (Documentary). 56 min. Sound. 16mm B&W. *Rental:* Natl AV Ctr.

Trigger Effect, The. 1978. Britain. (Documentary). 53 min. Sound. 16mm Color. *Rental:* U Cal Media, U of IL Film, Iowa Films, Kent St U Film & U Mich Media, Videotape version.

Trigger Fingers. Tim McCoy. Directed by Sam Newfield. 1939. Victory. 60 min. Sound. 16mm B&W. *Rental:* Roas Films.

Trigger Fingers. Johnny Mack Brown. Directed by Lambert Hillyer. 1946. Monogram. 55 min. Sound. 16mm B&W. *Rental:* Hurlock Cine.

Trigger, Jr. Roy Rogers. Directed by William Witney. 1950. Republic. 68 min. Sound. 16mm Color. *Rental:* Ivy Films. *Sale:* Rep Pic Film & Nostalgia Merchant. *Sale:* Nostalgia Merchant, Color version.

Trigger Pals. Art Jarrett & Lee Powell. Directed by Sam Newfield. 1939. Grand National. 55 min. Sound. 16mm B&W. *Rental:* Modern Sound.

Trigger Smith. Jack Randall. Directed by Alan James. 1939. Monogram. 55 min. Sound. 16mm B&W. *Rental:* Hurlock Cine.

Trigger Tom. Tom Tyler. Directed by Harry S. Webb. 1935. Reliable. 60 min. Sound. 16mm B&W. *Rental:* Mogulls Films.

Trigger Trail. Rod Cameron & Fuzzy Knight. Directed by Lewis D. Collins. 1944. Universal. 59 min. Sound. 16mm B&W. *Rental:* Budget Films.

Trigger Trio, The. John Wayne. Directed by William Witney. 1937. Republic. 54 min. Sound. 16mm B&W. *Rental:* Ivy Films. *Sale:* Cinema Concepts & Rep Pic Film.

Trilby. Clara Kimball Young & Wilton Lackaye. Directed by Maurice Tourneur. 1915. World. 65 min. Silent. 16mm B&W. *Rental:* Em Gee Film Lib & Kit Parker. *Sale:* Blackhawk Films & Cinema Concepts. *Sale:* Blackhawk Films, Super 8 silent version. *Sale:* Festival Films, 50 min. version.

Trillion Dollars for Defense, A. 1982. WNET Media. (Documentary). Sound. 16mm Color. *Sale:* Films Inc.

Trilogy *see* Truman Capote's Trilogy.

Trilogy of Terror. Karen Black. 78 min. Sound. Videotape Color. *Rental:* Maljack Productions.

Trinity is Still My Name. Terence Hill & Bud Spencer. Directed by E. B. Clucher. 1972. Italy. 101 min. Sound. 16mm Color. dubbed. *Rental:* Films Inc.

Trio. 1963. Hearst. (Documentary). 50 min. Sound. 16mm B&W. *Sale:* King Features.

Trio Infernal, Les. Michel Piccoli & Romy Schneider. Directed by Francis Girod. 1974. France. 106 min. Sound. 16mm Color. dubbed. *Rental:* Films Inc.

Trip, The. Peter Fonda & Susan Strasberg. Directed by Roger Corman. 1967. American International. 85 min. Sound. 16mm Color. *Rental:* Cine Craft, Films Inc, Video Comm, Welling Motion Pictures, Westcoast Films, Wholesome Film Ctr & Willoughby Peer.

Trip Through Purgatory, A *see* Voyage to Grand Tartarie.

Trip to Nowhere, A. 1970. NBC. (Documentary). 53 min. Sound. 16mm Color. *Rental:* Films Inc & U Mich Media. *Sale:* Films Inc. *Sale:* Films Inc, Videotape version.

Trip to Paris, A. Jed Prouty & Spring Byington. Directed by Mal St. Clair. 1938. Fox. 63 min. Sound. 16mm B&W. *Rental:* Films Inc.

Trip to Where?, A 1968. Navy. (Documentary). 50 min. Sound. 16mm Color. *Rental:* Kit Parker.

Trip With the Teacher, A. Zalman King & Brenda Fogarty. Directed by Earl Barton. 1975. Crown. 91 min. Sound. 16mm Color. *Rental:* Films Inc.

Triple Cross. Joe Kirkwood Jr. & James Gleason. Directed by Reginald Le Borg. 1951. Monogram. 60 min. Sound. 16mm B&W. *Rental:* Inst Cinema.

Triple Echo *see* Soldier in a Skirt.

Triple Justice. George O'Brien & Virginia Vale. Directed by Bert Gilroy. 1940. RKO. 66 min. Sound. 16mm B&W. *Rental:* RKO General Pics.

Triple Threat. Sammy Baugh & Sid Luckman. Directed by Jean Yarbrough. 1948. Columbia. 70 min. Sound. 16mm B&W. *Rental:* Inst Cinema.

Tripoli. John Payne & Maureen O'Hara. Directed by Will Price. 1950. Paramount. 100 min. Sound. 16mm B&W. *Rental:* Video Comm & Willoughby Peer.

Tristana. Catherine Deneuve, Fernando Rey & Franco Nero. Directed by Luis Bunuel. Span. 1970. Spain. 95 min. Sound. 16mm Color. subtitles. *Rental:* A Twyman Pres & Films Inc.

Triumph in Stone: Gothic Cathedrals in France. Directed by Derek Stewart. 1979. (Documentary). 42 min. Sound. 16mm Color. *Rental:* A Cantor. *Sale:* A Cantor.

Triumph of a Genius *see* Friedrich Schiller.

Triumph of Christy Brown, The. 1971. NET. (Documentary). 60 min. Sound. 16mm B&W. *Rental:* Indiana AV Ctr.

Triumph of Hercules, The. Orig. Title: Hercules vs.the Giant Warriors. Dan Vadis. Directed by Alberto De Martino. 1964. Italy. 100 min. Super 8 sound B&W. dubbed. *Rental:* Ivy Films & Modern Sound. *Rental:* Ivy Films, Color version.

Triumph of Michael Strogoff, The. Curt Jurgens & Capucine. 1964. France-Germany. 118 min. Sound. 16mm Color. dubbed. *Rental:* Westcoast Films. *Rental:* Video Comm & Westcoast Films, Anamorphic version.

Triumph of Sherlock Holmes, The. Arthur Wonter & Lyn Harding. Directed by Leslie Hiscott. 1935. Britain. 84 min. Sound. 16mm B&W. *Rental:* Budget Films & Willoughby Peer. *Sale:* Cinema Concepts, Festival Films & Reel Images. *Sale:* Festival Films & Tamarelles French Film, Videotape version.

Triumph of the Will. Directed by Leni Riefenstahl. 1934. Germany. (Documentary). 120 min. Sound. 16mm B&W. *Rental:* Budget Films, Inst Cinema, Iowa Films, Kit Parker, La Inst Res Ctr, U Mich Media, Museum Mod Art, Natl Film Video, U IL Film & Utah Media. *Sale:* Cinema Concepts, Natl Cinema, Phoenix Films, Images Film & Reel Images. *Rental:* Museum Mod Art, Abridged 42-min. version. *Rental:* Corinth Films, Images Film, Janus Films, Twyman Films & Westcoast Films, Subtitled version. *Rental:* Images Film, *Sale:* Images Film, Abridged 52 min. version. *Sale:* Phoenix Films, *Sale:* Images Film, Videotape version. *Sale:* Images Film, 111 min. subtitled videotape version.

Triumphant Hour, The. Don Ameche, Ann Blyth & Pat O'Brien. 1952. Father Peyton. 60 min. Sound. 16mm B&W. *Rental:* Roas Films.

Triumphant Union & the Canadian Confederation. 1968. Canada. (Documentary). 59 min. Sound. 16mm B&W. *Rental:* U Cal Media.

Trobriand Cricket, The: An Ingenious Response to Colonialism. Directed by Jerry W. Leach. 1976. EMC. (Documentary). 53 min. Sound. 16mm Color. *Rental:* U Cal Media, Iowa Films & U Mich Media. *Sale:* U Cal Media. *Sale:* U Cal Media, Videotape version.

Trobriand Islanders, The. 1950. Britain. (Documentary). 66 min. Sound. 16mm Color. *Rental:* U Cal Media.

Trog. Joan Crawford. Directed by Freddie Francis. 1970. Britain. 91 min. Sound. 16mm Color. *Rental:* Films Inc.

Troilus & Cressida. Anton Lesser. 1981. Britain. 190 min. Sound. Videotape Color. *Rental:* Iowa Films.

Trois Mousquetaires, Les. Georges Marchal, Bourvil & Gino Cervi. Directed by Andre Hunebelle. 1953. France. 120 min. Sound. 16mm Color. *Rental:* French Am Cul, B&W version.

Trojan Brothers, The *see* Murder in the Footlights.

Trojan Horse, The. Steve Reeves & John Drew Barrymore. Directed by Giorgio Ferroni. 1962. Italy. 105 min. Sound. 16mm Color. dubbed. *Rental:* Arcus Film, Budget Films, Charard Motion Pics, Film Ctr DC, Modern Sound & Willoughby Peer. *Rental:* Willoughby Peer, Anamorphic color version.

Trojan Women, The. Katharine Hepburn, Vanessa Redgrave & Irene Papas. Directed by Michael Cacoyannis. 1971. Cinerama. 105 min. Sound. 16mm Color. *Rental:* Williams Films & Swank Motion. *Rental:* Swank Motion, Anamorphic version.

Trojan Women, The: The Euripides. 1973. Alley Theater. (Documentary). 54 min. Sound. 16mm B&W. *Rental:* Modern Mass. *Sale:* Modern Mass.

Trollenberg Terror, The *see* Crawling Eye.

Trollstenen. Directed by Gunvor Nelson. 1976. Serious Business. (Documentary). 125 min. Sound. 16mm Color. *Rental:* Canyon Cinema & Serious Bus. *Sale:* Serious Bus.

Tron. Jeff Bridges, Bruce Boxleitner & David Warner. Disney. 96 min. Sound. 16mm Color. *Rental:* Bosco Films, Elliot Film Co, Films Inc, Roas Films, MGM United, Swank Motion, Westcoast Films, Welling Motion Pictures & Williams Films, Videotape version.

Trooper Hook. Joel McCrea & Barbara Stanwyck. Directed by Charles Marquis Warren. 1957. MGM. 82 min. Sound. 16mm B&W. *Rental:* MGM United.

Troopship *see* Farewell Again.

Tropic Zone. Ronald Reagan & Rhonda Fleming. Directed by Lewis R. Foster. 1953. Paramount. 89 min. Sound. 16mm B&W. *Rental:* Video Comm & Willoughby Peer.

Tropical Heat Wave. Estelita Rodriguez & Robert Hutton. Directed by R. G. Springsteen. 1952. Republic. 74 min. Sound. 16mm B&W. *Rental:* Ivy Films. *Sale:* Rep Pic Film.

Tropici. Joel Barcelos & Janira Santiago. Directed by Gianni Amico. Ital. 1969. Italy. 87 min. Sound. 16mm B&W. subtitles. *Rental:* New Yorker Films.

Trou Normand, Le *see* Crazy for Love.

Trouble Busters. Jack Hoxie. Directed by Lewis D. Collins. 1933. Majestic. 51 min. Sound. 16mm B&W. *Sale:* Cinema Concepts & Rep Pic Film.

Trouble for Two. Robert Montgomery & Rosalind Russell. Directed by Walter J. Ruben. 1936. MGM. 75 min. Sound. 16mm B&W. *Rental:* MGM United.

Trouble in Coal Country. Directed by Fred Flamenhaft. 1977. NBC. (Documentary). 52 min. Videotape Color. *Sale:* Films Inc.

Trouble in Paradise. Miriam Hopkins & Herbert Marshall. Directed by Ernst Lubitsch. 1932. Paramount. 86 min. Sound. 16mm B&W. *Rental:* Williams Films.

Trouble in Store. Norman Wisdom. Directed by John Paddy Carstairs. 1953. Britain. 85 min. Sound. 16mm B&W. *Rental:* Cinema Five.

Trouble in Sundown. George O'Brien & Rosalind Keith. Directed by Bert Gilroy. 1939. RKO. 60 min. Sound. 16mm B&W. *Rental:* RKO General Pics.

Trouble in Texas. Tex Ritter & Rita Hayworth. Directed by Robert N. Bradbury. 1937. Grand National. 60 min. Sound. 16mm B&W. *Rental:* Mogulls Films & Video Comm. *Sale:* Cinema Concepts & Morcraft Films. *Sale:* Glenn Photo, Super 8 sound version.

Trouble in the Family. 1965. NET. (Documentary). 90 min. Sound. 16mm B&W. *Rental:* U Cal Media, U of IL Film, Indiana AV Ctr, Iowa Films, U Mich Media, Mass Media, NYU Film Lib & Syracuse U Film. *Sale:* Indiana AV Ctr.

Trouble in the Glen. Orson Welles & Margaret Lockwood. Directed by Herbert Wilcox. 1954. Britain. 91 min. Sound. 16mm B&W. *Rental:* Ivy Films. *Lease:* Rep Pic Film.

Trouble in Utopia. (Shick of the New Ser.). 1979. Britain. (Documentary). 52 min. Sound. 16mm Color. *Rental:* U Cal Media, Videotape version.

Trouble Man. Robert Hooks & Paul Winfield. Directed by Ivan Dixon. 1972. Fox. 99 min. Sound. 16mm Color. *Rental:* Films Inc.

Trouble on Fashion Avenue. 60 min. Sound. 16mm Color. *Rental:* Cinema Guild.

Trouble That Truth Makes, The. 1977. WNET. (Documentary). 60 min. Videotape Color. *Rental:* WNET Media. *Sale:* WNET Media.

Trouble With Angels, The. Rosalind Russell & Hayley Mills. Directed by Ida Lupino. 1966. Columbia. 105 min. Sound. 16mm Color. *Rental:* Arcus Film, Buchan Pic, Budget Films, Cine Craft, Charard Motion Pics, Williams Films, Bosco Films, Films Inc, Film Pres, Inst Cinema, U of IL Film, Modern Sound, Natl Film Video, Roas Films, Swank Motion, Film Ctr DC, Twyman Films, Westcoast Films, Welling Motion Pictures & Wholesome Film Ctr. *Rental:* Bosco Films & U of IL Film, 112 mins version.

Trouble With Girls, The. Elvis Presley. Directed by Peter Tewksbury. 1969. MGM. (Anamorphic). 104 min. Sound. 16mm Color. *Rental:* MGM United.

Trouble With Harry, The. Shirley MacLaine, John Forsyth & Edmund Gwenn. Directed by Alfred Hitchcock. 1955. Universal Classics. 99 min. Sound. 16mm Color. *Rental:* Swank Motion.

Trouble With Miss Switch, The. 1980. ABC. (Animated). 48 min. Sound. 16mm Color. *Rental:* MTI Tele & U of IL Film. *Sale:* MTI Tele. *Sale:* MTI Tele, Videotape version.

Trouble With Tribbles, The. William Shatner. Directed by Joseph Pevney. 1967. Star Trek. 52 min. Sound. 16mm Color. *Rental:* Em Gee Film Lib, U of IL Film, OK AV Ctr, Roas Films & Westcoast Films, Super 8 sound version.

Trouble With Women, The. Ray Milland & Teresa Wright. Directed by Sidney Lanfield. 1947. Paramount. 80 min. Sound. 16mm B&W. *Rental:* Swank Motion.

Troubled Cities. 1966. NET. (Documentary). 60 min. Sound. 16mm B&W. *Rental:* Indiana AV Ctr. *Sale:* Indiana AV Ctr.

Troublemaker, The. The Premise Troupe. Directed by Theodore J. Flicker. 1964. Janus. 80 min. Sound. 16mm B&W. *Rental:* Films Inc.

Troublemakers, The. Directed by Robert Machover & Norman Fruchter. 1966. Robert Machover. (Documentary). 54 min. Sound. 16mm B&W. *Rental:* Cinema Guild. *Sale:* Cinema Guild.

Troubles, The: Conquest. 1982. Media Guild. (Documentary). 54 min. Sound. 16mm Color. *Rental:* Media Guild. *Sale:* Media Guild. *Sale:* Media Guild, Videotape version.

Troubles, The: Deadlock. 1982. Media Guild. 54 min. Sound. Videotape Color. *Rental:* Media Guild. *Sale:* Media Guild.

Troubles, The: Intervention. 1982. Media Guild. (Documentary). 54 min. Sound. 16mm Color. *Rental:* Media Guild. *Sale:* Media Guild, Videotape version.

Troubles, The: Partition. 54 min. Sound. 16mm Color. *Rental:* Media Guild.

Troubles, The: Rebellion. 1982. Media Guild. (Documentary). 54 min. Sound. 16mm Color. *Rental:* Media Guild. *Sale:* Media Guild. *Sale:* Media Guild, Videotape version.

Troubles, The: Rising. 1982. Media Guild. (Documentary). 54 min. Sound. 16mm Color. *Rental:* Media Guild. *Sale:* Media Guild. *Sale:* Media Guild, Videotape version.

Trout, The. Trans. Title: Truite, La. Isabelle Huppert & Jean-Pierre Cassel. Directed by Joseph Losey. Fr. 1982. France. 105 min. Sound. 16mm Color. subtitles. *Rental:* Swank Motion. *Sale:* Tamarelles French Film, Videotape version.

Truck Stop Women. Lieux Dressler & Claudia Jennings. Directed by Mark L. Lester. 1974. Britain. 88 min. Sound. 16mm Color. *Rental:* New Line Cinema.

Truck Turner. Isaac Hayes & Yaphet Kotto. Directed by Jonathan Kaplan. 1974. American International. 91 min. Sound. 16mm Color. *Rental:* Swank Motion.

True As A Turtle. John Gregson & Cecil Parker. Directed by Wendy Toye. 1957. Britain. 85 min. Sound. 16mm B&W. *Rental:* Cinema Five.

True Confession. Carole Lombard & Fred MacMurray. Directed by Wesley Ruggles. 1937. Paramount. 84 min. Sound. 16mm B&W. *Rental:* Swank Motion.

True Confessions. Robert De Niro & Robert Duvall. Directed by Ulu Grosbard. 1981. MGM. 107 min. Sound. 16mm Color. *Rental:* MGM United. *Rental:* MGM United, Videotape version.

True Friends. Trans. Title: Veriye Druzya. Boris Churkov. Directed by Mikhail Kalatozov. Rus. 1954. Russia. 105 min. Sound. 16mm B&W. subtitles. *Rental:* Corinth Films.

True Glory, The. Directed by Sir Carol Reed & Garson Kanin. 1945. Columbia. (Documentary). 85 min. Sound. 16mm B&W. *Rental:* Budget Films, Films Inc, IFEX, Images Film, Kit Parker, U Mich Media & Natl AV Ctr. *Sale:* Natl AV Ctr & Reel Images. *Sale:* Natl AV Ctr, Videotape version.

True Grit. John Wayne & Kim Darby. Directed by Henry Hathaway. 1969. Paramount. 128 min. Sound. 16mm Color. *Rental:* Films Inc.

True Heart Susie. Lillian Gish & Robert Harron. Directed by D. W. Griffith. 1919. Artcraft. 86 min. Silent. 16mm B&W. *Rental:* Budget Films, Em Gee Film Lib, Films Inc, Kit Parker & Museum Mod Art. *Lease:* Museum Mod Art. *Sale:* Reel Images & Glenn Photo. *Rental:* Ivy Films, *Sale:* Glenn Photo & Reel Images, Super 8 silent version.

True Story of an Election, The. 1962. Churchill. (Documentary). 60 min. Sound. 16mm Color. *Rental:* U Mich Media, Syracuse U Film & Churchill Films.

True Story of Jesse James, The. Orig. Title: James Brothers, The. Robert Wagner & Jeffrey Hunter. Directed by Nicholas Ray. 1957. Fox. (Anamorphic). 93 min. Sound. 16mm Color. *Rental:* Films Inc.

True to Life. Mary Martin & Dick Powell. Directed by George Marshall. 1943. Paramount. 93 min. Sound. 16mm B&W. *Rental:* Swank Motion.

Truite, La *see* Trout.

Truman. 1962. McGraw Hill. (Documentary). 52 min. Sound. 16mm B&W. *Rental:* Syracuse U Film. *Sale:* McGraw-Hill Films.

Truman Capote's "The Glass House". Orig. Title: Glass House, The. Alan Alda, Vic Morrow & Billy Dee Williams. Directed by Tom Gries. 1972. CBS. 94 min. Sound. 16mm Color. *Rental:* Budget Films, Films Inc, Kent St U Film, Kit Parker, Learning Corp Am, U Mich Media, Mass Media, Syracuse U Film, Twyman Film, U of IL Film, Welling Motion Pictures & Wholesome Film Ctr. *Lease:* Learning Corp Am.

Truman Capote's Trilogy. Orig. Title: Trilogy. Geraldine Page & Maureen Stapleton. Directed by Frank Perry. 1969. Allied Artists. 99 min. Sound. 16mm Color. *Rental:* Hurlock Cine.

Trusted Outlaw. Bob Steele. Directed by Robert N. Bradbury. 1937. Republic. 60 min. Sound. 16mm B&W. *Rental:* Ivy Films & Mogulls Films.

Truth, The. Clayton Moore. 1960. Wrather. 75 min. Sound. 16mm Color. *Rental:* Video Comm.

Truth About Communism, The. (Documentary). 78 min. Sound. 16mm B&W. *Rental:* Modern Sound.

Truth About Murder, The. Orig. Title: Lie Detector, The. Bonita Granville & Morgan Conway. Directed by Lew Landers. 1946. RKO. 63 min. Sound. 16mm B&W. *Rental:* Films Inc.

Truth About Spring, The. Hayley Mills & John Mills. Directed by Richard Thorpe. 1965. Universal. 102 min. Sound. 16mm Color. *Rental:* Swank Motion.

Truth About Women, The. Laurence Harvey, Julie Harris & Eva Gabor. Directed by Muriel Box. 1957. Britain. 106 min. Sound. 16mm Color. *Rental:* Kit Parker.

Truth About Youth, The. Loretta Young & Myrna Loy. Directed by William A. Seiter. 1930. Warners. 68 min. Sound. 16mm B&W. *Rental:* MGM United.

Truth & History. 50 min. Sound. 16mm Color. *Rental:* Gospel Films.

Try a Little Tenderness. (Body in Question Sr.). 1979. (Documentary). 60 min. Videotape Color. *Rental:* Films Inc & Syracuse U Film. *Sale:* Films Inc.

Try & Get Me. Frank Lovejoy & Lloyd Bridges. Directed by Cy Endfield. 1951. MGM. 85 min. Sound. 16mm B&W. *Rental:* Budget Films.

Trygon Factor, The. Stewart Granger & Robert Morley. Directed by Cyril Frankel. 1967. Warners. 88 min. Sound. 16mm Color. *Rental:* Willoughby Peer.

Tsetse Trap, The. 1978. Britain. (Documentary). 53 min. Sound. 16mm Color. *Rental:* Iowa Films & Kent St U Film.

Tu Moisonneras la Tempete. Directed by R. L. Bruckberger. France. (Documentary). 95 min. Sound. 16mm B&W. *Rental:* French Am Cul.

Tu Seras Terriblement Gentille. Karen Blanguernon & Victor Lanoux. Directed by Dirk Sanders. Fr. 1968. France. 90 min. Sound. 16mm Color. subtitles. *Rental:* French Am Cul.

Tucson Raiders. Bill Elliott. Directed by Spencer G. Bennett. 1944. Republic. 54 min. Sound. 16mm B&W. *Rental:* Ivy Films.

Tudor Rose. Orig. Title: Nine Days a Queen. Nova Pilbeam. Directed by Robert Stevenson. 1936. Britain. 80 min. Sound. 16mm B&W. *Rental:* Budget Films & Mogulls Films.

Tudors, The. 1980. Royal Heritage. (Documentary). 60 min. Sound. 16mm Color. *Rental:* Films Inc. *Sale:* Films Inc. *Rental:* Films Inc, *Sale:* Films Inc, Videotape version.

Tuesday Morning Workout. Brian. 60 min..Videotape Color. *Sale:* Astro Video.

Tugboat Annie. Marie Dressler & Wallace Beery. Directed by Mervyn LeRoy. 1933. MGM. 85 min. Sound. 16mm B&W. *Rental:* MGM United.

Tugboat Annie Sails Again. Jane Wyman & Ronald Reagan. Directed by Lewis Seiler. 1940. Warners. 77 min. Sound. 16mm B&W. *Rental:* MGM United.

Tulips. Gabe Kaplan & Bernadette Peters. Directed by Rex Bromfield. 1982. Embassy. 91 min. Sound. 16mm Color. *Rental:* Films Inc.

Tulsa. Susan Hayward & Robert Preston. Directed by Stuart Heisler. 1949. Eagle Lion. 90 min. Sound. 16mm Color. *Rental:* Budget Films, Films Inc & Roas Films. *Sale:* Festival Films. *Sale:* Festival Films & Tamarelles French Film, Videotape version.

Tulsa Kid, The. Don Barry. Directed by George Sherman. 1940. Republic. 54 min. Sound. 16mm B&W. *Rental:* Ivy Films. *Sale:* Rep Pic Film & Nostalgia Merchant.

Tumbledown Ranch in Arizona. Range Busters. Directed by S. Roy Luby. 1941. Monogram. 60 min. Sound. 16mm B&W. *Rental:* Films Inc.

Tumbleweed Trail. Eddie Dean. Directed by Robert Tansey. 1946. PRC. 59 min. Sound. 16mm B&W. *Sale:* Classics Assoc NY.

Tumbleweeds. William S. Hart. Directed by King Baggott. 1925. United Artists. (Music & sound effects only). 80 min. Sound. 16mm B&W. *Rental:* Budget Films, Em Gee Film Lib, Kit Parker, Utah Media & Willoughby Peer. *Sale:* Cinema Concepts & Griggs Movie. *Rental:* Film Images, Silent 16mm version. *Rental:* Killiam Collect, Tinted version. *Sale:* Morcraft Films, Super 8 sound version. *Rental:* Ivy Films, Super 8 silent version. *Sale:* Tamarelles French Film, Videotape version.

Tumblin' Tumbleweeds. Gene Autry. Directed by Joseph Kane. 1935. Republic. 54 min. Sound. 16mm B&W. *Rental:* Ivy Films.

Tuna Clipper. Roddy McDowall & Elena Verdugo. Directed by William Beaudine. 1949. Monogram. 77 min. Sound. 16mm B&W. *Rental:* Hurlock Cine.

Tundra. 1936. Borroughs/Tarzan. (Documentary). 87 min. Sound. 16mm B&W. *Rental:* Film Ctr DC.

Tunes of Glory. Sir Alec Guinness & John Mills. Directed by Ronald Neame. 1960. Britain. 106 min. Sound. 16mm Color. *Rental:* Budget Films, U of IL Film, Images Film, Kit Parker, Learning Corp Am, Modern Sound, New Cinema & Roas Films. *Sale:* Learning Corp Am.

Tunisian Victory. 1944. MGM. (Documentary). 76 min. Sound. 16mm B&W. *Rental:* Budget Films.

Tunnel of Love, The. Richard Widmark & Doris Day. Directed by Gene Kelly. 1958. MGM. (Anamorphic). 98 min. Sound. 16mm B&W. *Rental:* MGM United.

Tunnelvision. Directed by Neil Israel. 1976. World Wide. (Anthology). 75 min. Videotape Color. *Sale:* Cinema Concepts.

Tupamaros! Directed by Jan Lindqvist. 1972. Sweden. (Documentary). 50 min. Sound. 16mm Color. *Rental:* U Cal Media & Cinema Guild. *Sale:* Cinema Guild.

Turandot. 1983. Germany. (Opera). 138 min. Sound. Videotape Color. *Sale:* Tamarelles French Film.

Turbulence. Missonary Enterprise Co.. 51 min. Sound. 16mm Color. *Rental:* Gospel Films.

Turf Boy. Orig. Title: Mister Celebrity. Buzzy Henry & James Seay. Directed by William Beaudine. 1941. PRC. 75 min. Sound. 16mm B&W. *Rental:* Alba House.

Turksib. Victor Turin. Directed by Victor Turin. 1929. Russia. 99 min. Silent. 16mm B&W. *Rental:* Corinth Films & Film Images. *Sale:* Film Images.

Turn Back the Clock. Otto Kruger & Lee Tracy. Directed by Edgar Selwyn. 1933. MGM. 80 min. Sound. 16mm B&W. *Rental:* MGM United.

Turn of the Tide, The. Geraldine Fitzgerald. Directed by Norman Walker. 1935. Britain. 80 min. Sound. 16mm B&W. *Rental:* Ivy Films & Rep Pic Film. *Lease:* Rep Pic Film.

Turnabout. Carole Landis & John Hubbard. Directed by Hal Roach. 1940. MGM. 85 min. Sound. 16mm B&W. *Rental:* Willoughby Peer.

Turning Point, The. William Holden & Edmond O'Brien. Directed by William Dieterle. 1952. Paramount. 85 min. Sound. 16mm B&W. *Rental:* Films Inc.

Turning Point, The. Anne Bancroft, Shirley MacLaine & Tom Skerritt. Directed by Herbert Ross. 1977. Fox. 119 min. Sound. 16mm Color. *Rental:* Williams Films & Films Inc.

Turning Wind, The *see* Barravento.

Turtle On Its Back. Jean-Francois Stevenin & Bernadette Lafont. Directed by Luc Beraud. Fr. 1977. France. 110 min. Sound. 16mm Color. subtitles. *Rental:* New Line Cinema.

Tut: The Boy King. Directed by William Kronick. 1977. Wolper. (Documentary). 52 min. Sound. 16mm Color. *Rental:* U Cal Media, Films Inc, U of IL Film & Syracuse U Film. *Sale:* Films Inc. *Sale:* Films Inc, Videotape version.

Tuttles of Tahiti, The. Charles Laughton & Jon Hall. Directed by Charles Vidor. 1942. RKO. 92 min. Sound. 16mm B&W. *Rental:* Films Inc. *Lease:* Films Inc.

Tutto A Posto E Niente In Ordine see All Screwed Up.

Tuxedo Junction. Orig. Title: Gang Made Good, The. Sally Payne & Thurston Hall. Directed by Frank McDonald. 1941. Republic. 70 min. Sound. 16mm B&W. *Rental:* Ivy Films.

TV on Trial. 1979. PBS. (Documentary). 119 min. Color. *Rental:* PBS Video. *Sale:* PBS Video, Videotape version.

Twelfth International Tournee of Animation. Orig. Title: International Tournee of Animation. 1977. Film Wright. (Animated anthology). 90 min. Sound. 16mm Color. *Rental:* Film Wright.

Twelfth Night. 3 pts. Westinghouse. (Cast unlisted). 84 min. Sound. 16mm B&W. *Rental:* Macmillan Films, OK AV Ctr. *Lease:* Macmillan Films.

Twelfth Night. Alec McCowen & Trevor Peacock. 1979. Britain. 124 min. Videotape Color. *Rental:* Iowa Films.

Twelfth Night. Klara Luchko & Alla Larionova. Directed by Yan Fried. 1956. Russia. 88 min. Sound. 16mm Color. dubbed. *Rental:* Corinth Films.

Twelve Angry Men. Henry Fonda & E. G. Marshall. Directed by Sidney Lumet. 1957. United Artists. 95 min. Sound. 16mm B&W. *Rental:* MGM United.

Twelve Chairs, The. Orig. Title: Fifth Chair, The. Archil Gomiashvili. Directed by L. Gaidai. Rus. 1971. Russia. (Anamorphic). 160 min. Sound. 16mm Color. subtitles. *Rental:* Corinth Films.

Twelve Chairs, The. Ron Moody, Frank Langella & Dom DeLuise. Directed by Mel Brooks. 1970. UMC. 94 min. Sound. 16mm Color. *Rental:* Modern Sound.

Twelve Crowded Hours. Lucille Ball & Richard Dix. Directed by Lew Landers. 1939. RKO. 64 min. Sound. 16mm *Rental:* RKO General Pics.

Twelve Hours to Kill. Barbara Eden & Grant Richards. Directed by Edward L. Cahn. 1960. Fox. (Anamorphic). 83 min. Sound. 16mm B&W. *Rental:* Willoughby Peer.

Twelve O'Clock High. Gregory Peck & Gary Merrill. Directed by Henry King. 1949. Fox. 133 min. Sound. 16mm B&W. *Rental:* Films Inc.

Twelve to the Moon. Ken Clark & Michi Kobi. Directed by David Bradley. 1960. Columbia. 74 min. Sound. 16mm B&W. *Rental:* Cine Craft, Charard Motion Pics, Films Inc & Westcoast Films.

Twenties, The. 58 min. Sound. Videotape *Rental:* PBS Video. *Sale:* PBS Video.

Twentieth Century. John Barrymore & Carole Lombard. Directed by Howard Hawks. 1934. Columbia. 93 min. Sound. 16mm B&W. *Rental:* Budget Films, Williams Films, Films Inc, U of IL Film, Images Film, Kit Parker, Modern Sound, Swank Motion, Twyman Films, Westcoast Films, Welling Motion Pictures & Wholesome Film Ctr.

Twenty-Fifth Hour, The. Anthony Quinn & Virna Lisi. Directed by Henri Verneuil. 1967. MGM. 134 min. Sound. 16mm Color. *Rental:* MGM United. *Rental:* MGM United, Anamorphic version.

Twenty-Five Fireman's Street. Rita Beekees. Directed by Istvan Szabo. Hungarian. 1973. Hungary. 97 min. Sound. 16mm Color. subtitles. *Rental:* Films Inc.

Twenty Four Eyes. Hideko Takamine. Directed by Keisuke Kinoshita. Jap. 1954. Japan. 116 min. Sound. 16mm B&W. subtitles. *Rental:* Films Inc.

Twenty Four Hours in Czechoslovakia. 1971. Canada. (Documentary). 58 min. Sound. 16mm Color. *Rental:* Natl Film CN. *Sale:* Natl Film CN.

Twenty Million Miles to Earth. William Hopper & Joan Taylor. Directed by Nathan Juran. 1957. Columbia. 82 min. Sound. 16mm B&W. *Rental:* Budget Films, Cine Craft, Charard Motion Pics, Films Inc, Kit Parker, Modern Sound, Roas Films, Film Ctr DC & Video Comm.

Twenty Million Sweethearts. Dick Powell & Ginger Rogers. Directed by Ray Enright. 1934. Warners. 89 min. Sound. 16mm B&W. *Rental:* MGM United.

Twenty Plus Two. David Jansen & Jeanne Crain. Directed by Joseph Newman. 1961. Allied Artists. 100 min. Sound. 16mm B&W. *Rental:* Hurlock Cine.

Twenty-Seventh Day, The. Gene Barry & Valerie French. Directed by William Asher. 1957. Columbia. 75 min. Sound. 16mm B&W. *Rental:* Films Inc, Inst Cinema & Roas Films.

Twenty-Third Cease Fire. Directed by Jean-Francois Dars, Marc Kravetz & Marc Mourani. 1976. Icarus. (Documentary). 52 min. Sound. 16mm Color. *Rental:* Icarus Films. *Sale:* Icarus Films.

Twenty-Thousand Leagues Under the Sea. Alan Holubar & Jane Gail. Directed by Alan Holubar. 1917. Universal. 93 min. Silent. 16mm B&W. *Rental:* Bosco Films, Budget Films, Elliot Film, Video Comm & Westcoast Films. *Rental:* Ivy Films, Super 8 silent version. *Sale:* Blackhawk Films, Silent 8mm version. *Rental:* Video Comm,

Twenty-Thousand Leagues Under the Sea. Kirk Douglas, James Mason & Peter Lorre. Directed by Richard Fleischer. 1954. Disney. (Anamorphic). 127 min. Sound. 16mm Color. *Rental:* Cine Craft, Williams Films, Disney Prod, Elliot Film Co, Films Inc, Film Pres, U of IL Film, MGM United, Newman Film Lib, Roas Film, Swank Motion, Film Ctr DC & Twyman Films. *Rental:* Swank Motion, Videotape version.

Twenty-Thousand Years in Sing Sing. Spencer Tracy & Bette Davis. Directed by Michael Curtiz. 1933. Warners. 78 min. Sound. 16mm B&W. *Rental:* MGM United.

Twenty-Three Paces to Baker Street. Van Johnson & Vera Miles. Directed by Henry Hathaway. 1956. Fox. 103 min. Sound. 16mm Color. *Rental:* Films Inc & Video Comm.

Twenty Years of Rock & Roll. (Color sequences, anthology). 60 min. Videotape *Sale:* Cinema Concepts.

Twice Blessed. Preston Foster & Gail Patrick. Directed by Harry Beaumont. 1945. MGM. 76 min. Sound. 16mm B&W. *Rental:* MGM United.

Twice-Promised Land, The: Israel. 1963. Hearst. (Documentary). 50 min. Sound. 16mm B&W. *Sale:* King Features.

Twice Told Tales. Vincent Price & Sebastian Cabot. Directed by Sidney Salkow. 1963. United Artists. 119 min. Sound. 16mm Color. *Rental:* MGM United, Westcoast Films, Welling Motion Pictures & Wholesome Film Ctr.

Twice Upon a Time. Jack Hawkins & Elizabeth Allen. Directed by Emeric Pressburger. 1953. Britain. 100 min. Sound. 16mm B&W. *Rental:* Inst Cinema.

Twilight for the Gods. Rock Hudson & Cyd Charisse. Directed by Joseph Pevney. 1958. Universal. 119 min. Sound. 16mm Color. *Rental:* Swank Motion.

Twilight in the Sierras. Roy Rogers & Dale Evans. Directed by William Witney. 1950. Republic. 67 min. Sound. 16mm Color. *Rental:* Ivy Films. *Sale:* Rep Pic Film. *Sale:* Nostalgia Merchant, Color version.

Twilight in Tokyo. Setsuko Hara & Isuzu Yamada. Directed by Yasujiro Ozu. Jap. 1957. Japan. 141 min. Sound. 16mm B&W. subtitles. *Rental:* films Inc.

Twilight of Honor. Richard Chamberlain & Joey Heatherton. Directed by Boris Sagal. 1963. MGM. (Anamorphic). 104 min. Sound. 16mm B&W. *Rental:* MGM United.

Twilight on the Rio Grande. Gene Autry & Adele Mara. Directed by Frank McDonald. 1947. Republic. 60 min. Sound. 16mm B&W. *Rental:* Ivy Films.

Twilight on the Trail. William Boyd. Directed by Howard Bretherton. 1941. Paramount. 60 min. Sound. 16mm B&W. *Rental:* Budget Films. *Sale:* Glenn Photo.

Twilight Time. Karl Malden. Directed by Goran Paskaljevic. 1982. MGM. 102 min. Sound. 16mm Color. *Rental:* MGM United. *Rental:* MGM United, Videotape version.

Twilight Zone: The Movie. Dan Aykroyd & Albert Brooks. Directed by Joe Dante, John Landis, George Miller & Steven Spielberg. 1983. Warners. 120 min. Sound. 16mm Color. *Rental:* Swank Motion. *Rental:* Swank Motion, Videotape version.

Twilight's Last Gleaming. Burt Lancaster & Paul Winfield. Directed by Robert Aldrich. 1977. Allied Artists. 144 min. Sound. 16mm Color. *Rental:* Hurlock Cine.

Twinkle in God's Eye, The. Mickey Rooney & Hugh O'Brian. Directed by George Blair. 1955. Republic. 73 min. Sound. 16mm B&W. *Rental:* Ivy Films.

Twins of Evil, The. Peter Cushing. Directed by John Hough. 1972. Britain. 85 min. Sound. 16mm Color. *Rental:* Swank Motion.

Twist All Night. Louis Prima & June Wilkinson. Directed by William J. Hole Jr. 1962. American International. 78 min. Sound. 16mm B&W. *Rental:* Budget Films & Westcoast Films.

Twist Around the Clock. Chubby Checker & Dion. Directed by Oscar Rudolph. 1962. Columbia. 86 min. Sound. 16mm B&W. *Rental:* Williams Films, Bosco Films & Kit Parker.

Twist of Fate, A. Ginger Rogers, Jacques Bergerac & Herbert Lom. 1954. United Artists. 89 min. Sound. 16mm B&W. *Rental:* MGM United.

Twist of Sand, A. Richard Johnson & Honor Blackman. Directed by Don Chaffey. 1968. Britain. 90 min. Sound. 16mm Color. *Rental:* MGM United.

Twisted Brain, The. Pat Cardi. Directed by Larry Stouffer. 1974. Crown. 85 min. Sound. 16mm Color. *Rental:* Films Inc & Video Comm. *Lease:* Video Comm.

Twisted Cross. 1958. NBC. (Documentary). 55 min. Sound. 16mm B&W. *Rental:* U Cal Media, McGraw-Hill Films, U Mich Media, Syracuse U Film & Utah Media. *Sale:* McGraw-Hill Films.

Twisted Detective, The. Klaus Kinski & Alain Delon. 123 min. Sound. Videotape *Rental:* WW Enter.

Twisted Nerve, The. Hayley Mills & Hywel Bennett. Directed by Roy Boulting. 1969. National General. 116 min. Sound. 16mm Color. *Rental:* Williams Films & Swank Motion.

Twisted Road, The *see* They Live by Night.

Twisted Trails. Tom Mix. Directed by Tom Mix. 1916. Selig. 45 min. Sound. 16mm B&W. *Rental:* Em Gee Film Lib & Film Classics. *Sale:* Film Classics. *Rental:* Film Classics, *Sale:* Film Classics, Silent 8mm version. *Rental:* Film Classics, Videotape version.

Twitch of the Death Nerve, The. Claudine Auger. Directed by Mario Bava. 1972. Italy. 91 min. Sound. 16mm Color. dubbed. *Rental:* Video Comm.

Two Against the Law. Alain Delon & Jean Gabin. Directed by Jose Giovanni. Fr. 1975. France. 100 min. Sound. 16mm Color. subtitles. *Rental:* J Green Pics. *Rental:* J Green Pics, Dubbed version. *Sale:* Tamarelles French Film, Videotape version.

Two Against the World. Orig. Title: Case of Mrs. Pembrooke, The. Humphrey Bogart & Beverly Roberts. Directed by William McGann. 1936. Warners. 57 min. Sound. 16mm B&W. *Rental:* MGM United.

Two Against the World. Constance Bennett & Neil Hamilton. Directed by Archie Mayo. 1932. Warners. 71 min. Sound. 16mm B&W. *Rental:* MGM United.

Two Alone. Beulah Bondi & Jean Parker. Directed by Merian C. Cooper. 1934. RKO. 74 min. Sound. 16mm B&W. *Rental:* RKO General Pics.

Two Are Guilty. Tony Perkins & Jean-Claude Brialy. Directed by Andre Cayatte. 1964. France. 131 min. Sound. 16mm B&W. dubbed. *Rental:* MGM United.

Two Ballet Birds. 1969. CBS. (Documentary). 51 min. Sound. 16mm B&W. *Rental:* McGraw-Hill Films. *Sale:* McGraw-Hill Films.

Two Before Zero. 1962. Ellis. (Documentary). 78 min. Sound. 16mm B&W. *Rental:* Films Inc.

Two Black Sheep *see* Two Sinners.

Two Champions of Death. 105 min. Sound. 16mm *Rental:* WW Enter. *Rental:* WW Enter, Videotape version.

Two Daughters. Anil Chatterjee & Chandana Bannerjee. Directed by Satyajit Ray. Bengali. 1964. India. 114 min. Sound. 16mm B&W. subtitles. *Rental:* Films Inc, Janus Films & New Cinema.

Two Deaths of Adolf Hitler, The. 1974. Media Guild. 52 min. Sound. 16mm Color. *Rental:* Media Guild. *Sale:* Media Guild. *Sale:* Media Guild, Videotape version.

Two-Edged Sword, A. 58 min. Sound. Videotape *Rental:* PBS Video. *Sale:* PBS Video.

Two English Girls. Jean-Pierre Leaud. Directed by Francois Truffaut. Fr. 1972. France. 108 min. Sound. 16mm Color. subtitles. *Rental:* Films Inc & Janus Films.

Two-Faced Woman. Greta Garbo, Melvyn Douglas & Constance Bennett. Directed by George Cukor. 1941. MGM. 94 min. Sound. 16mm B&W. *Rental:* MGM United.

Two Faces of China, The. 1969. Pictura. (Documentary). 50 min. Sound. 16mm Color. *Rental:* U Cal Media.

Two-Fisted Justice. The Range Busters. Directed by Robert Tansey. 1943. Monogram. 55 min. Sound. 16mm B&W. *Rental:* Modern Sound.

Two-Fisted Law. Tim McCoy. Directed by D. Ross Lederman. 1932. Columbia. 56 min. Sound. 16mm B&W. *Rental:* Willoughby Peer.

Two Flags West. Joseph Cotten & Linda Darnell. Directed by Robert Wise. 1950. Fox. 92 min. Sound. 16mm B&W. *Rental:* Films Inc.

Two for the Road. Audrey Hepburn & Albert Finney. Directed by Stanley Donen. 1967. Fox. (Anamorphic). 111 min. Sound. 16mm Color. *Rental:* Films Inc & Twyman Films.

Two for the Seesaw. Robert Mitchum & Shirley MacLaine. Directed by Robert Wise. 1962. MGM. 120 min. Sound. 16mm B&W. *Rental:* MGM United.

Two for Tonight. Bing Crosby & Joan Bennett. Directed by Frank Tuttle. 1935. Paramount. 61 min. Sound. 16mm B&W. *Rental:* Swank Motion.

Two Gals & a Guy. Janis Paige & Robert Alda. Directed by Alfred E. Green. 1951. MGM. 90 min. Sound. 16mm B&W. *Rental:* Mogulls Films.

Two Gentlemen of Verona. John Hudson & Joanne Pearce. 1983. 137 min. Sound. Videotape Color. *Rental:* Iowa Films.

Two Girls & a Sailor. June Allyson, Gloria De Haven & Van Johnson. Directed by Richard Thorpe. 1944. MGM. 126 min. Sound. 16mm B&W. *Rental:* MGM United.

Two-Gun Justice. Tom Keene. Directed by Alan James. 1938. Monogram. 50 min. Sound. 16mm B&W. *Rental:* Hurlock Cine.

Two-Gun Lady. Peggie Castle, William Talman & Marie Windsor. Directed by Richard Bartlett. 1956. Associated. 75 min. Sound. 16mm B&W. *Sale:* Rep Pic Film.

Two-Gun Man, The. Ken Maynard. Directed by Phil Rosen. 1931. Tiffany. 60 min. Sound. 16mm B&W. *Rental:* Budget Films. *Sale:* Cinema Concepts, Reel Images & Video Comm.

Two-Gun Man from Harlem, The. Herb Jeffries & Mantan Moreland. Directed by Richard C. Kahn. 1938. Grand National. 60 min. Sound. 16mm B&W. *Rental:* Budget Films.

Two-Gun Sheriff, The. Don Barry. Directed by George Sherman. 1941. Republic. 54 min. Sound. 16mm B&W. *Rental:* Ivy Films. *Sale:* Rep Pic Film.

Two-Gun Troubador, The. Orig. Title: Lone Troubador, The. Fred Scott. Directed by Raymond K. Johnson. 1939. Spectrum. 60 min. Sound. 16mm B&W. *Rental:* Mogulls Films.

Two Guns & a Badge. Wayne Morris. Directed by Lewis D. Collins. 1954. Allied Artists. 70 min. Sound. 16mm B&W. *Rental:* Hurlock Cine.

Two Guys From Milwaukee. Dennis Morgan & Jack Carson. Directed by David Butler. 1946. Warners. 85 min. Sound. 16mm Color. *Rental:* MGM United.

Two Guys from Texas. Orig. Title: Two Texas Knights. Dennis Morgan & Jack Carson. Directed by David Butler. 1948. Warners. 86 min. Sound. 16mm Color. *Rental:* MGM United.

Two-Headed Spy, The. Jack Hawkins & Gia Scala. Directed by Andre De Toth. 1958. Britain. 93 min. Sound. 16mm B&W. *Rental:* Kit Parker.

Two Heroic Sisters of the Grasslands. 1965. 45 min. Sound. 16mm Color. *Rental:* Asia Film Library.

Two Hours to Doom *see* Dr. Strangelove.

Two-Hundred Motels. Frank Zappa. Directed by Frank Zappa & Tony Palmer. 1971. MGM. 99 min. Sound. 16mm Color. *Rental:* MGM United. *Rental:* MGM United, Videotape version.

Two in Revolt. Louise Latimer & John Arledge. Directed by Glenn Tryon. 1936. RKO. 65 min. Sound. 16mm B&W. *Rental:* RKO General Pics.

Two in the Dark. Walter Abel & Margot Grahame. Directed by Ben Stoloff. 1936. RKO. 74 min. Sound. 16mm B&W. *Rental:* Films Inc. *Lease:* Films Inc.

Two Kennedys, The. 115 min. Sound. Videotape B&W. *Rental:* Maljack Productions.

Two Kingdoms. 1948. Cathedral. (Cast unlisted). 60 min. Sound. 16mm B&W. *Rental:* Newman Film Lib.

Two Korean Families. Directed by Patricia Lewis Jaffe. 1979. Macmillan. (Documentary). 59 min. Sound. 16mm Color. *Rental:* Films Inc. *Sale:* Films Inc.

Two-Lane Blacktop. James Taylor & Warren Oates. Directed by Monte Hellman. 1972. Universal. 102 min. Sound. 16mm Color. *Rental:* Swank Motion.

Two Little Bears, The. Eddie Albert & Jane Wyatt. Directed by Randall Hood. 1961. Fox. 81 min. Sound. 16mm B&W. *Rental:* Charard Motion Pics, Films Inc & Swank Motion. *Rental:* Willoughby Peer, Anamorphic B&W version.

Two Living, One Dead. Bill Travers & Virginia McKenna. Directed by Anthony Asquith. 1966. Britain. 92 min. Sound. 16mm B&W. *Rental:* Films Inc.

Two Lost Worlds. James Arness & Bill Kennedy. Directed by Norman Dawn. 1950. Eagle Lion. 61 min. Sound. 16mm B&W. *Sale:* Classics Assoc NY.

Two Loves. Shirley MacLaine & Laurence Harvey. Directed by Charles Walters. 1961. MGM. 100 min. Sound. 16mm Color. *Rental:* MGM United. *Rental:* MGM United, Anamorphic version.

Two Marines & a General *see* War, Italian Style.

Two Masks: One Face. 1977. Films Inc. (Documentary). 60 min. Videotape Color. *Sale:* Films Inc.

Two Men & a Girl *see* Honeymoon.

Two-Minute Warning. Charlton Heston & John Cassavetes. Directed by Larry Peerce. 1976. Universal. 115 min. Sound. 16mm Color. *Rental:* Swank Motion.

Two Minutes to Play. Bruce Bennett & Fuzzy Knight. Directed by Robert Hill. 1937. Victory. 71 min. Sound. 16mm B&W. *Rental:* Film Classics. *Rental:* Film Classics, Videotape version.

Two Mrs. Carrolls, The. Humphrey Bogart & Barbara Stanwyck. Directed by Peter Godfrey. 1947. Warners. 99 min. Sound. 16mm B&W. *Rental:* MGM United.

Two Mules for Sister Sara. Clint Eastwood & Shirley MacLaine. Directed by Don Siegel. 1970. Universal. 113 min. Sound. 16mm Color. *Rental:* Swank Motion.

Two O'Clock Courage. Tom Conway & Ann Rutherford. Directed by Anthony Mann. 1945. RKO. 66 min. Sound. 16mm B&W. *Rental:* Films Inc. *Lease:* Films Inc.

Two of a Kind. Lizabeth Scott & Edmond O'Brien. Directed by Henry Levin. 1951. Columbia. 75 min. Sound. 16mm B&W. *Rental:* Films Inc & Kit Parker.

Two of Us, The. Michel Simon & Alain Cohen. Directed by Claude Berri. Fr. 1968. France. 86 min. Sound. 16mm B&W. subtitles. *Rental:* New Yorker Films.

Two on a Guillotine. Dean Jones & Connie Stevens. Directed by William Conrad. 1965. Warners. 107 min. Sound. 16mm B&W. *Rental:* Films Inc.

Two or Three Things I Know About Her. Marina Vlady. Directed by Jean-Luc Godard. Fr. 1966. France. 85 min. Sound. 16mm Color. subtitles. *Rental:* New Cinema & New Yorker Films.

Two People. Peter Fonda & Lindsay Wagner. Directed by Robert Wise. 1973. Universal. 100 min. Sound. 16mm Color. *Rental:* Swank Motion.

Two Rode Together. James Stewart & Richard Widmark. Directed by John Ford. 1961. Columbia. 109 min. Sound. 16mm Color. *Rental:* Budget Films, Cine Craft, Charard Motion Pics, Corinth Films, Bosco Films, Films Inc, Film Pres, Inst Cinema, U of IL Film, Images Film, Kerr Film, Kit Parker, Modern Sound, Natl Film Video, Film Ctr DC, Twyman Films, Westcoast Films, Welling Motion Pictures & Wholesome Film Ctr.

Two Seconds. Edward G. Robinson & Preston Foster. Directed by Mervyn LeRoy. 1932. Warners. 68 min. Sound. 16mm B&W. *Rental:* MGM United.

Two Senoritas from Chicago. Joan Davis & Jinx Falkenburg. Directed by Frank Woodruff. 1943. Columbia. 70 min. Sound. 16mm B&W. *Rental:* Kit Parker.

Two Sinners. Orig. Title: Two Black Sheep. Otto Krueger & Martha Sleeper. Directed by Arthur Lubin. 1935. Republic. 72 min. Sound. 16mm B&W. *Rental:* Ivy Films.

Two Sisters from Boston. June Allyson & Kathryn Grayson. Directed by Henry Koster. 1946. MGM. 112 min. Sound. 16mm B&W. *Rental:* MGM United.

Two Smart People. Lucille Ball & John Hodiak. Directed by Jules Dassin. 1946. MGM. 93 min. Sound. 16mm B&W. *Rental:* MGM United.

Two Texas Knights *see* Two Guys from Texas.

Two Thoroughbreds. Joan Leslie. Directed by Jack Hively. 1939. RKO. 62 min. Sound. 16mm B&W. *Rental:* Films Inc.

Two Thousand Maniacs! Connie Mason & Thomas Wood. Directed by Herschell G. Lewis. 1964. Boxoffice Spectaculars. 88 min. Sound. 16mm Color. *Rental:* Films Inc.

Two Thousand One: A Space Odyssey. Keir Dullea & Gary Lockwood. Directed by Stanley Kubrick. 1968. MGM. 138 min. Sound. 16mm Color. *Rental:* MGM United. *Sale:* Festival Films, Videotape version.

Two Tickets to Broadway. Tony Martin & Janet Leigh. Directed by James V. Kern. 1951. RKO. 106 min. Sound. 16mm Color. *Rental:* Films Inc.

Two-Way Stretch. Peter Sellers & Wilfred Hyde-White. Directed by Robert Day. 1961. Britain. 87 min. Sound. 16mm B&W. *Rental:* Budget Films & Corinth Films.

Two Weeks. Constance Talmadge. Directed by Sidney Franklin. 1920. 16mm *Rental:* A Twyman Pres.

Two Weeks in Another Town. Kirk Douglas & Cyd Charisse. Directed by Vincente Minnelli. 1962. MGM. (Anamorphic). 107 min. Sound. 16mm Color. *Rental:* MGM United. *Rental:* MGM United, Videotape version.

Two Weeks to Live. Lum & Abner. Directed by Mal St. Clair. 1943. RKO. 76 min. Sound. 16mm B&W. *Rental:* Budget Films & Inst Cinema. *Sale:* Morcraft Films. *Sale:* Morcraft Films, Super 8 sound version.

Two Weeks with Love. Jane Powell & Ricardo Montalban. Directed by Roy Rowland. 1950. MGM. 92 min. Sound. 16mm Color. *Rental:* MGM United. *Rental:* MGM United, Videotape version.

Two Wise Maids. Polly Moran & Donald Cook. Directed by Phil Rosen. 1937. Republic. 54 min. Sound. 16mm B&W. *Rental:* Ivy Films. *Sale:* Rep Pic Film.

Two Women. Sophia Loren & Jean-Paul Belmondo. Directed by Vittorio De Sica. Ital. 1961. Italy. 105 min. Sound. 16mm B&W. subtitles. *Rental:* Films Inc.

Two Worlds of Angelita, The. Directed by Jane Morrison. Span. 1982. Spain. 73 min. Sound. 16mm Color. subtitles. *Rental:* First Run.

Two-Year-Old Goes to the Hospital, A. Britain. (Documentary). 50 min. Sound. 16mm B&W. *Rental:* U Cal Media. *Sale:* NYU Film Lib.

Two Years Before the Mast. Alan Ladd & Brian Donlevy. Directed by John Farrow. 1946. Paramount. 98 min. Sound. 16mm B&W. *Rental:* Swank Motion.

Twyla Tharp: Making Television Dance. Directed by Don Mischer. 1980. 58 min. Sound. 16mm Color. *Rental:* Budget Films.

Tycoon. John Wayne & Laraine Day. Directed by Richard Wallace. 1947. RKO. 129 min. Sound. 16mm Color. *Rental:* Films Inc. *Lease:* Films Inc.

Tyranny of Control, The. 1980. Penn. 60 min. Videotape Color. *Rental:* Iowa Films. *Sale:* Ency Brit Ed. *Sale:* Ency Brit Ed, 2 pt. 16mm version. *Sale:* Ency Brit Ed, 2 pt. Videotape version.

Tyrant of the Sea. Rhys Williams & Ron Randall. Directed by Lew Landers. 1950. Columbia. 70 min. Sound. 16mm B&W. *Rental:* Inst Cinema.

U-Sixty Seven. Alan Hale & Laura La Plante. 1936. Astor. 70 min. Sound. 16mm B&W. *Rental:* Budget Films.

U-Two Affair, The. 1962. McGraw Hill. (Documentary). 54 min. Sound. 16mm B&W. *Rental:* Syracuse U Film.

U-Two Thirty Eight & the Witch Doctor. Clayton Moore & Phyllis Coates. Directed by Fred C. Brannon. 1952. Republic. 100 min. Sound. 16mm B&W. *Rental:* Ivy Films. *Sale:* Rep Pic Film.

U. S. S. Teakettle *see* You're in the Navy Now.

Ubangi. 1931. Pizor. (Documentary). 75 min. Sound. 16mm B&W. *Rental:* Film Classics.

Ubu Roi. Directed by Jean-Christophe Averty. France. (Cast unlisted). 97 min. Sound. 16mm B&W. *Rental:* French Am Cul.

Ubu Roi. 1977. Miami-Dade. (Cast unlisted). 60 min. Videotape Color. *Sale:* Films Inc.

U.F.O. *see* Unidentified Flying Objects.

U.F.O. Directed by Wheeler Dixon. 1979. Gold Key. (Documentary). 96 min. Sound. 16mm Color. *Rental:* Gold Key.

U.F.O. Target Earth. Nick Plakias. Directed by Michael D. DeGaetano. 1974. Maron. 82 min. Sound. 16mm Color. *Rental:* Budget Films.

Ugetsu. Trans. Title: Ugetsu Monogatari. Machiko Kyo. Directed by Kenji Mizoguchi. Jap. 1953. Japan. 96 min. Sound. 16mm B&W. subtitles. *Rental:* Budget Films, U Cal Media, Em Gee Film Lib, Films Inc, Inst Cinema, Images Film, Janus Films, Kit Parker, New Cinema, Liberty Co & Utah Media. *Sale:* Reel Images, Festival Films, Natl Cinema & Images Film. *Sale:* Tamarelles French Film, Festival Films & Images Film, Videotape version.

Ugetsu Monogatari *see* Ugetsu.

Ugly American, The. Marlon Brando & Sandra Church. Directed by George Englund. 1963. Universal. 120 min. Sound. 16mm Color. *Sale:* Films Inc & Swank Motion.

Ugly Dachshund, The. Dean Jones, Suzanne Pleshette & Charles Ruggles. Directed by Norman Tokar. 1966. Disney. 93 min. Sound. 16mm Color. *Rental:* Buchan Pic, Cine Craft, Cousino Visual Ed, Bosco Films, Disney Prod, Elliot Film Co, Films Inc, U of IL Film, MGM United, Modern Sound, Roas Films, Swank Motion, Film Ctr DC, Twyman Films, Westcoast Films, Welling Motion Pictures & Williams Films.

Ugly Ones, The. Richard Wyler & Thomas Milan. Directed by Eugenio Martin. 1968. Italy-Spain. 96 min. Sound. 16mm Color. dubbed. *Rental:* MGM United.

Ukigusa *see* Floating Weeds.

Ukraine in Flames, The. Directed by Alexander Dovzhenko. 1945. Russia. 56 min. Sound. 16mm B&W. narrated Eng. *Rental:* Corinth Films.

Ultimate Risk, The. 1970. Time-Life. (Documentary). 52 min. Sound. 16mm Color. *Rental:* Time-Life Multimedia. *Sale:* Time-Life Multimedia. *Sale:* Time-Life Multimedia, Spanish language version. *Sale:* Time-Life Multimedia, Videotape version.

Ultimate Warrior, The. Yul Brynner & Max Von Sydow. Directed by Robert Clouse. 1975. Warners. 92 min. Sound. 16mm Color. *Rental:* Swank Motion.

Ultimo Dia de la Guerra, El *see* Last Day of the War.

Ulysses. Orig. Title: James Joyce's Ulysses. Milo O'Shea & Barbara Jefford. Directed by Joseph Strick. 1967. Continental. 140 min. Sound. 16mm B&W. *Rental:* Budget Films, Films Inc & Texture Film. *Sale:* Texture Film. *Sale:* Texture Film, Videotape version.

Ulysses. Kirk Douglas & Sylvana Mangano. Directed by Mario Camerini. 1955. Paramount. 104 min. Sound. 16mm Color. dubbed. *Rental:* Charard Motion Pics, Films Inc, Williams Films, Kerr Film, Modern Sound, Film Ctr DC, Twyman Films, Video Comm, Westcoast Films & Willoughy Peer.

Ulysses Against the Son of Hercules. Georges Marchal. Directed by Mario Caiano. 1963. Italy. 87 min. Sound. 16mm Color. dubbed. *Rental:* Films Inc.

Ulzana's Raid. Burt Lancaster & Bruce Davison. Directed by Robert Aldrich. 1972. Universal. 103 min. Sound. 16mm Color. *Rental:* Swank Motion.

Umberto D. Carlo Battisti & Marie Pia Casilio. Directed by Vittorio De Sica. Ital. 1951. Italy. 89 min. Sound. 16mm B&W. subtitles. *Rental:* Budget Films, Films Inc, Janus Films, Natl Cinema & New Cinema.

Umbrellas of Cherbourg, The. Catherine Deneuve & Nino Castelnuovo. Directed by Jacques Demy. Fr. 1964. France. Sound. 16mm Color. subtitles. *Rental:* Films Inc.

Umealit the Whale Hunters. 1980. 58 min. Sound. Videotape *Rental:* PBS Video. *Sale:* PBS Video.

Unashamed. Helen Twelvetrees & Robert Young. Directed by Harry Beaumont. 1932. MGM. 77 min. Sound. 16mm B&W. *Rental:* MGM United.

Unbelievable Varan, The *see* Varan, the Unbelievable.

Uncertain Death: La Morte Incerta. Mary Maude & Yelena Samarina. Mexico. Sound. 16mm B&W. dubbed. *Rental:* MGM United.

Uncertain Glory. Errol Flynn & Paul Lukas. Directed by Raoul Walsh. 1944. Warners. 102 min. Sound. 16mm B&W. *Rental:* MGM United.

Unchained Goddess, The. 1958. Bell Telephone. (Documentary). 60 min. Sound. 16mm Color. *Rental:* Utah Media.

Unchastened Woman, The. Theda Bara. Directed by James Young. 1925. Chadwick. 75 min. Silent. 16mm B&W. *Rental:* Ivy Films.

Uncle Harry. George Sanders & Geraldine Fitzgerald. Directed by Robert Siodmak. 1945. Universal. 81 min. Sound. 16mm B&W. *Rental:* Budget Films, Ivy Films & Kit Parker. *Sale:* Rep Pic Film.

Uncle Joe Shannon. Burt Young & Doug McKeon. Directed by Joe Hanwright. 1978. MGM. 99 min. Sound. 16mm Color. *Rental:* MGM United.

Uncle Sam Magoo. 1970. UPA. (Animated). 55 min. Sound. 16mm Color. *Rental:* Arcus Film, Budget Films, Williams Films, Inst Cinema, Modern Sound, Roas Films, Film Ctr DC, Twyman Films, Westcoast Films, Welling Motion Pictures & Willoughby Peer.

Uncle Tom's Cabin. James B. Lowe & Sam Lucas. Directed by William Robert Daly. 1914. World. 75 min. Silent. 16mm B&W. *Rental:* Budget Films.

Uncle Tom's Cabin. Mona Ray. Directed by Harry Pollard. 1926. Universal. 60 min. Silent. 16mm B&W. *Rental:* Mogulls Films. *Sale:* Reel Images. *Rental:* Ivy Films, Super 8 silent version.

Uncle Tom's Cabin. 1983. 55 min. Sound. 16mm Color. *Rental:* U Mich Media.

Uncle Vanya. Innokenty Smoktunovsky. Directed by Andrei Mikhalkov-Konchalovsky. Rus. 1972. Russia. (Color sequences). 110 min. Sound. 16mm Color. subtitles. *Rental:* Corinth Films.

Uncle Vanya. Sir Laurence Olivier & Joan Plowright. Directed by John Dexter. 1976. Britain. 47 min. Sound. 16mm B&W. *Rental:* Films Human. *Rental:* Arcus Film & Films Human.

Uncle Was a Vampire. Christopher Lee & Renato Rascel. Directed by Pio Angeletti. 1959. Italy. 95 min. Sound. 16mm dubbed. *Rental:* Budget Films.

Uncommon Valor. Gene Hackman. Directed by Ted Kotcheff. 1983. Paramount. 100 min. Sound. Videotape Color. *Sale:* Tamarelles French Film.

Unconquered. Gary Cooper & Paulette Goddard. Directed by Cecil B. DeMille. 1947. Paramount. 148 min. Sound. 16mm Color. *Rental:* Williams Films.

Unconquered Bandit, The. Tom Tyler. Directed by Harry S. Webb. 1935. Reliable. 60 min. Sound. 16mm B&W. *Rental:* Mogulls Films.

Undead, The. Pamela Duncan. Directed by Roger Corman. 1957. American International. 76 min. Sound. 16mm B&W. *Rental:* Westcoast Films.

Undefeated, The. John Wayne & Rock Hudson. Directed by Andrew V. McLaglen. 1969. Fox. (Anamorphic). 118 min. Sound. 16mm Color. *Rental:* Films Inc.

Under Age. Nan Grey & Alan Baxter. Directed by Edward Dmytryk. 1941. Columbia. 60 min. Sound. 16mm B&W. *Rental:* Kit Parker.

Under Arizona Skies. Johnny Mack Brown. Directed by Lambert Hillyer. 1946. Monogram. 55 min. Sound. 16mm B&W. *Rental:* Hurlock Cine & Lewis Film.

Under Arrest *see* Blazing Across the Pecos.

Under California Stars. Roy Rogers. Directed by William Witney. 1948. Republic. 54 min. Sound. 16mm B&W. *Rental:* Budget Films, Ivy Films & Modern Sound. *Sale:* Rep Pic Film & Nostalgia Merchant. *Sale:* Nostalgia Merchant, Color version.

Under Capricorn. Ingrid Bergman & Joseph Cotten. Directed by Alfred Hitchcock. 1949. Warners. 117 min. Sound. 16mm Color. *Rental:* Budget Films, Films Inc, Museum Mod Art, Video Comm & Wholesome Film Ctr. *Lease:* Video Comm. *Sale:* Vidamerica, Videotape version.

Under Colorado Skies. Monte Hale. Directed by R. G. Springsteen. 1947. Republic. 65 min. Sound. 16mm B&W. *Rental:* Ivy Films. *Sale:* Rep Pic Film.

Under Cover of Night. Edmund Lowe & Florence Rice. Directed by George B. Seitz. 1937. MGM. 71 min. Sound. 16mm B&W. *Rental:* MGM United.

Under Eighteen. Warren William & Marian Marsh. Directed by Archie Mayo. 1932. Warners. 80 min. Sound. 16mm B&W. *Rental:* MGM United.

Under Fiesta Stars. Gene Autry. Directed by Frank McDonald. 1941. Republic. 54 min. Sound. 16mm B&W. *Rental:* Ivy Films.

Under Fire. Rex Reason & Henry Morgan. Directed by James B. Clark. 1957. Fox. 78 min. Sound. 16mm B&W. *Rental:* Ivy Films. *Sale:* Rep Pic Film. *Rental:* Westcoast Films & Willoughby Peer, Anamorphic version.

Under Fire. Nick Nolte & Gene Hackman. Directed by Roger Spottiswoode. 1983. Orion. 100 min. Sound. 16mm Color. *Rental:* Films Inc.

Under Mexicali Stars. Rex Allen. Directed by George Blair. 1950. Republic. 67 min. Sound. 16mm B&W. *Rental:* Ivy Films.

Under Milk Wood. Richard Burton, Peter O'Toole & Elizabeth Taylor. Directed by Andrew Sinclair. 1971. Britain. 90 min. Sound. 16mm Color. *Rental:* Films Inc.

Under My Skin. John Garfield & Micheline Prelle. Directed by Jean Negulesco. 1950. Fox. 86 min. Sound. 16mm B&W. *Rental:* Films Inc.

Under Nevada Skies. Roy Rogers. Directed by Frank McDonald. 1946. Republic. 54 min. Sound. 16mm B&W. *Rental:* Ivy Films. *Sale:* Rep Pic Film.

Under Secret Orders. Erich Von Stroheim & Dita Parlo. Directed by Edmond Greville. 1933. France. 65 min. Sound. 16mm B&W. dubbed. *Rental:* Budget Films.

Under Strange Flags. Tom Keene. Directed by Lynn Shores. 1936. Crescent. 70 min. Sound. 16mm B&W. *Rental:* Mogulls Films.

Under Sunny Skies. Trans. Title: Dalyokaya Nevesta. A. Karlyev. Directed by E. Ivanov-Barkov. Rus. 1949. Russia. 87 min. Sound. 16mm B&W. subtitles. *Rental:* Corinth Films.

Under Ten Flags. Van Heflin & Charles Laughton. Directed by Julio Coll. 1960. Paramount. 92 min. Sound. 16mm B&W. *Rental:* Films Inc.

Under Texas Skies. Bob Custer. Directed by J. P. McGowan. 1930. Syndicate. 58 min. Sound. 16mm B&W. *Sale:* Natl Cinema.

Under Texas Skies. Robert Livingston & Bob Steele. Directed by George Sherman. 1940. Republic. 54 min. Sound. 16mm B&W. *Rental:* Ivy Films. *Sale:* Rep Pic Film.

Under the Clock *see* Big Clock.

Under the Rainbow. Chevy Chase & Carrie Fisher. Directed by Steve Rash. 1981. Orion. 97 min. Sound. 16mm Color. *Rental:* Films Inc.

Under the Red Robe. Raymond Massey, Annabella & Conrad Veidt. Directed by Alan Crosland. 1937. Fox. 82 min. Sound. 16mm B&W. *Rental:* A Twyman Pres & Em Gee Film Lib.

Under the Roofs of Paris. Albert Prejean. Directed by Rene Clair. Fr. 1930. France. 95 min. Sound. 16mm B&W. subtitles. *Rental:* Budget Films, Corinth Films, Em Gee Film Lib, Films Inc, Images Film & Kit Parker. *Lease:* Corinth Films. *Sale:* Cinema Concepts, Glenn Photo, Reel Images & Images Film. *Sale:* Cinema Concepts, Tamarelles French Film & Images Film, Videotape version.

Under the Volcano. Albert Finney, Jacqueline Bisset & Anthony Andrews. Directed by John Huston. 1985. Universal. 109 min. Sound. 16mm Color. *Rental:* Swank Motion.

Under the Yum Yum Tree. Jack Lemmon & Carol Lynley. Directed by David Swift. 1963. Columbia. 110 min. Sound. 16mm Color. *Rental:* Arcus Film, Charard Motion Pics, Cine Craft, Films Inc, Modern Sound, Film Ctr DC & Welling Motion Pictures.

Under Two Flags. Ronald Colman & Claudette Colbert. Directed by Frank Lloyd. 1936. Fox. 110 min. Sound. 16mm B&W. *Rental:* Films Inc & Willoughby Peer.

Under Western Stars. Roy Rogers. Directed by Joseph Kane. 1938. Republic. 54 min. Sound. 16mm B&W. *Rental:* Ivy Films. *Sale:* Cinema Concepts & Rep Pic Film.

Undercover. John Clements & Michael Wilding. Directed by Sergei Nolbandov. 1942. Britain. 90 min. Sound. 16mm B&W. *Rental:* Mogulls Films.

Undercover Agent. Russell Gleason & Shirley Deane. Directed by Howard Bretherton. 1939. Republic. 56 min. Sound. 16mm B&W. *Rental:* Ivy Films & Mogulls Films.

Undercover Maisie. Ann Sothern & Barry Nelson. Directed by Harry Beaumont. 1947. MGM. 90 min. Sound. 16mm B&W. *Rental:* MGM United.

Undercover Man. Johnny Mack Brown. Directed by Albert Ray. 1936. Republic. 60 min. Sound. 16mm B&W. *Rental:* Ivy Films. *Sale:* Rep Pic Film.

Undercover Man. William Boyd. Directed by Lesley Selander. 1942. MGM. 80 min. Sound. 16mm B&W. *Rental:* Budget Films.

Undercover Man. Glenn Ford & Nina Foch. Directed by Joseph Lewis. 1949. Columbia. 81 min. Sound. 16mm B&W. *Rental:* Budget Films, Inst Cinema & Kit Parker.

Undercover Woman. Robert Livingston. Directed by Thomas Carr. 1946. Republic. 56 min. Sound. 16mm B&W. *Rental:* Ivy Films.

Undercovers Hero. Peter Sellers & Lila Kedrova. Directed by Roy Boulting. 1975. MGM. 95 min. Sound. 16mm Color. *Rental:* MGM United.

Undercurrent. Katharine Hepburn & Robert Taylor. Directed by Vincente Minnelli. 1946. MGM. 116 min. Sound. 16mm B&W. *Rental:* MGM United.

Underground. Jeffrey Lynn & Philip Dorn. Directed by Vincent Sherman. 1941. Warners. 94 min. Sound. 16mm B&W. *Rental:* MGM United.

Underground. Directed by Emile De Antonio, Mary Lampson & Haskell Wexler. 1978. Action Twenty-Seven. (Documentary). 88 min. Sound. 16mm Color. *Rental:* Action Film Lib, Cinema Guild, First Run & New Cinema. *Sale:* Cinema Guild & First Run.

Undersea Kingdom. Ray Corrigan. Directed by B. Reeves Eason. 1950. Republic. 240 min. Sound. 16mm B&W. *Rental:* Ivy Films.

Undertaker & His Pals, The. Robert Lowery & Rad Fulton. Directed by David C. Graham. 1967. Howco. 60 min. Sound. 16mm B&W. *Rental:* Budget Films, Films Inc, Modern Sound & Video Comm.

Underwater! Jane Russell & Richard Egan. Directed by John Sturges. 1955. RKO. 99 min. Sound. 16mm Color. *Rental:* Films Inc. *Sale:* Tamarelles French Film, Videotape version.

Underwater City. William Lundigan & Julie Adams. Directed by Frank McDonald. 1962. Columbia. 78 min. Sound. 16mm B&W. *Rental:* Buchan Pic, Cine Craft, Inst Cinema, Kerr Film & Modern Sound.

Underwater Warrior, The. Dan Dailey. Directed by Andrew Marton. 1958. MGM. 90 min. Sound. 16mm B&W. *Rental:* MGM United. *Rental:* MGM United, Anamorphic version.

Underworld. Clive Brook, George Bancroft & Evelyn Brent. Directed by Josef Von Sternberg. 1927. Paramount. 83 min. Sound. 16mm B&W. *Rental:* Museum Mod Art.

Underworld Story, The. Orig. Title: Whipped, The. Dan Duryea & Herbert Marshall. Directed by Cy Endfield. 1950. Allied Artists. 90 min. Sound. 16mm B&W. *Rental:* Hurlock Cine.

Underworld U.S.A. Cliff Robertson & Dolores Dorn. Directed by Samuel Fuller. 1961. Columbia. 99 min. Sound. 16mm B&W. *Rental:* Budget Films, Images Film, Kit Parker, Swank Motion & Welling Motion Pictures.

Undying Monster, The. Orig. Title: Hammond Mystery, The. James Ellison & John Howard. Directed by John Brahm. 1942. Fox. 60 min. Sound. 16mm B&W. *Rental:* Films Inc.

Une Vie. Maria Schell & Christian Marquand. Directed by Alexandre Astruc. Fr. 1958. Janus. 88 min. Sound. 16mm Color. subtitles. *Rental:* Films Inc.

Unearthly, The. John Carradine & Allison Hayes. Directed by Brooke L. Peters. 1957. Republic. 73 min. Sound. 16mm B&W. *Rental:* Ivy Films.

Unearthly Stranger, The. John Neville. Directed by John Krish. 1964. Britain. 80 min. Sound. 16mm B&W. *Rental:* Films Inc.

Uneasy Borders: Rhodesia. 1978. Britain. (Documentary). 53 min. Sound. 16mm Color. *Rental:* U of IL Film.

Uneasy Terms. Michael Rennie & Nigel Patrick. Directed by Vernon Sewell. 1948. Britain. 91 min. Sound. 16mm B&W. *Rental:* Ivy Films. *Sale:* Rep Pic Film.

Unexpected, The. 53 min. Sound. 16mm Color. *Rental:* Ency Brit Ed & Iowa Films. *Sale:* Ency Brit Ed. *Sale:* Ency Brit Ed, Videotape version.

Unexpected Guest, The. William Boyd. Directed by George Archainbaud. 1947. MGM. 60 min. Sound. 16mm B&W. *Sale:* Cinema Concepts.

Unexpected Uncle. Charles Coburn & Anne Shirley. Directed by Peter Godfrey. 1942. RKO. 67 min. Sound. 16mm B&W. *Rental:* RKO General Pics.

Unexpected Voyage of Pepito & Cristobal, The. 1970. Cousteau. (Documentary). 54 min. Sound. 16mm Color. *Rental:* Syracuse U Film.

Unexplained, The. 1970. NBC. (Documentary). 52 min. Sound. 16mm Color. *Rental:* Films Inc & Syracuse U Film. *Sale:* Films Inc. *Sale:* Films Inc, Videotape version.

Unfaithful, The. Ann Sheridan & Lew Ayres. Directed by Vincent Sherman. 1947. Warners. 106 min. Sound. 16mm B&W. *Rental:* MGM United.

Unfaithful Wife, The *see* Femme Infidele.

Unfaithfully Yours. Rex Harrison & Linda Darnell. Directed by Preston Sturges. 1948. Fox. 105 min. Sound. 16mm B&W. *Rental:* Films Inc.

Unfinished Business. Irene Dunne & Robert Montgomery. Directed by Gregory La Cava. 1941. Universal. 96 min. Sound. 16mm B&W. *Rental:* Swank Motion.

Unfinished Journey of Robert F. Kennedy, The. 1970. (Documentary). 74 min. Sound. 16mm Color. *Rental:* Modern Sound.

Unfinished Piece for Player Piano. Alexander Kalyagin & Elena Solovei. Directed by Nikita Mikhalkov. Rus. 1977. Russia. 105 min. Sound. 16mm Color. subtitles. *Rental:* Corinth Films.

Unfinished Story, An. Sergei Bondarchuk. Directed by Friedrich Ermler. Rus. 1955. Russia. 93 min. Sound. 16mm B&W. subtitles. *Rental:* Corinth Films.

Unfinished Task, The. Ray Collins & Angie Dickinson. Directed by William Claxton. 1956. Concordia. 72 min. Sound. 16mm B&W. *Rental:* Roas Films.

Unforgiven, The. Burt Lancaster & Audrey Hepburn. Directed by John Huston. 1960. United Artists. 120 min. Sound. 16mm Color. *Rental:* MGM United.

Unguarded Hour, The. Franchot Tone & Loretta Young. Directed by Sam Wood. 1936. MGM. 87 min. Sound. 16mm B&W. *Rental:* MGM United.

Unguarded Moment, The. Esther Williams & George Nader. Directed by Harry Keller. 1956. Universal. 95 min. Sound. 16mm Color. *Rental:* Swank Motion.

Unheard Cry, The. 1969. 45 min. Sound. 16mm B&W. *Rental:* Natl AV Ctr.

Unholy Garden, The. Ronald Colman & Fay Wray. Directed by George Fitzmaurice. 1931. Goldwyn. 75 min. Sound. 16mm B&W. *Rental:* Films Inc.

Unholy Night, The. Roland Young & Boris Karloff. Directed by Lionel Barrymore. 1929. MGM. 94 min. Sound. 16mm B&W. *Rental:* MGM United.

Unholy Rollers, The. Claudia Jennings. Directed by Vernon Zimmerman. 1972. American International. 89 min. Sound. 16mm Color. *Rental:* Swank Motion.

Unholy Three, The. Lon Chaney. Directed by Tod Browning. 1925. MGM. 73 min. Silent. 16mm B&W. *Rental:* MGM United.

Unholy Wife, The. Diana Dors & Rod Steiger. Directed by John Farrow. 1957. RKO. 94 min. Sound. 16mm Color. *Rental:* Budget Films & Video Comm. *Lease:* Video Comm.

Unidentified Flying Objects. Orig. Title: U.F.O. Directed by Winston Jones. 1956. United Artists. (Cast unlisted). 92 min. Sound. 16mm B&W. *Rental:* MGM United.

Unidentified Flying Oddball. Ron Moody, Kenneth More & Jim Dale. Directed by Russ Mayberry. 1979. Disney. 93 min. Sound. 16mm Color. *Rental:* Williams Films, Bosco Films, Disney Prod, Elliot Film Co, Films Inc, Film Pres, U of IL Film, MGM United, Modern Sound, Roas Films, Swank Motion, Film Ctr DC, Twyman Films & Welling Motion Pictures.

Uninvited, The. Ray Milland & Ruth Hussey. Directed by Lewis Allen. 1944. Paramount. 89 min. Sound. 16mm B&W. *Rental:* Williams Films.

Union City. Deborah Harry & Dennis Lipscomb. Directed by Mark Reichert. 1980. Kinesis. 85 min. Sound. 16mm Color. *Rental:* Corinth Films.

Union Depot. Orig. Title: Gentleman for a Day. Douglas Fairbanks Jr. & Joan Blondell. Directed by Alfred E. Green. 1932. Warners. 68 min. Sound. 16mm B&W. *Rental:* MGM United.

Union Maids. Directed by Julia Reichert & James Klein. 1976. New Day. (Documentary). 50 min. Sound. 16mm B&W. *Rental:* U Mich Media & New Day Films. *Sale:* New Day Films.

Union Man. 1966. NET. (Documentary). 60 min. Sound. 16mm B&W. *Rental:* Indiana AV Ctr.

Union Pacific. Barbara Stanwyck & Joel McCrea. Directed by Cecil B. DeMille. 1939. Paramount. 135 min. Sound. 16mm B&W. *Rental:* Williams Films.

Union Station. William Holden & Nancy Olson. Directed by Rudolph Mate. 1950. Paramount. 80 min. Sound. 16mm B&W. *Rental:* Films Inc.

U. S. Armed Forces Bicentennial Band & Chorus, The. 1979. PBS. (Concert). 59 min. Videotape Color. *Rental:* PBS Video. *Sale:* PBS Video.

U. S. Food Machine, The. Canada. (Documentary). 57 min. Sound. 16mm Color. *Rental:* CBS Inc. *Sale:* CBS Inc.

United States vs. Aaron Burr. 1977. US Government. (Documentary). 76 min. Sound. 16mm Color. *Rental:* Iowa Films, Kent St U Film, LA Inst Res Ctr & U Mich Media. *Sale:* Natl AV Ctr. *Sale:* Natl AV Ctr, *Rental:* Natl AV Ctr, Videotape version.

University. 1961. Canada. (Documentary). 59 min. Sound. 16mm B&W. *Rental:* McGraw-Hill Films. *Sale:* McGraw-Hill Films.

Unknown, The. Lon Chaney, Joan Crawford & Norman Kerry. Directed by Tod Browning. 1927. MGM. 65 min. Silent. 16mm B&W. *Rental:* MGM United.

Unknown Chaplin: The Mutual Period 1916-1917. 1983. Britain. (Documentary). 60 min. Sound. 16mm Color. *Rental:* U Cal Media & Media Guild. *Sale:* Media Guild. *Sale:* Media Guild, Videotape version.

Unknown Chaplin: Unshown Chaplin. 52 min. Sound. 16mm Color. *Rental:* Media Guild. *Sale:* Media Guild. *Sale:* Media Guild, Videotape version.

Unknown Chaplin, The: 1918-1931. 1983. Britain. (Documentary). 60 min. Sound. 16mm Color. *Rental:* U Cal Media & Media Guild. *Sale:* Media Guild. *Sale:* Media Guild, Videotape version.

Unknown Guest, The. Victor Jory & Pamela Blake. Directed by Kurt Neumann. 1943. Monogram. 64 min. Sound. 16mm B&W. *Rental:* Hurlock Cine & Bosco Films.

Unknown Island, The. Barton McLane & Virginia Grey. Directed by Jack Bernhard. 1948. Film Classics. 75 min. Sound. 16mm B&W. *Sale:* Classics Assoc NY.

Unknown Man, The. Walter Pidgeon & Ann Harding. Directed by Richard Thorpe. 1951. MGM. 86 min. Sound. 16mm B&W. *Rental:* MGM United.

Unknown Ranger. Rex Ray. 1924. 45 min. Silent. 16mm B&W. *Rental:* Mogulls Films.

Unknown Soldier. Henry B. Walthall. Directed by D. W. Griffith. 1917. Griffith. 60 min. Silent. 16mm B&W. *Rental:* Em Gee Film Lib.

Unknown Terror, The. John Howard & Mala Powers. Directed by Charles Marquis Warren. 1957. Fox. 79 min. Sound. 16mm B&W. *Rental:* Film Ctr DC & Westcoast Films. *Sale:* Rep Pic Film.

Unknown Wilderness, The. 1972. Gold Key. (Documentary). 90 min. Sound. 16mm Color. *Rental:* Films Inc & Video Comm. *Lease:* Video Comm.

Unknown World, The. Jim Bannon & Victor Killian. Directed by Terry Morse. 1951. Lippert. 74 min. Sound. 16mm B&W. *Rental:* Budget Films.

Unman, Wittering & Zigo. David Hemmings. Directed by John MacKenzie. 1971. Paramount. 100 min. Sound. 16mm Color. *Rental:* Films Inc.

Unmarried Woman, An. Jill Clayburgh & Alan Bates. Directed by Paul Mazursky. 1978. Fox. 124 min. Sound. 16mm Color. *Rental:* Films Inc, Twyman Films & Williams Films.

Unmasked. Raymond Burr & Barbara Fuller. Directed by George Blair. 1949. Republic. 60 min. Sound. 16mm B&W. *Rental:* Ivy Films. *Sale:* Rep Pic Film.

Unquiet Death of Ethel & Julius Rosenberg, The. 1973. Nat. Public Affairs. (Documentary). 90 min. Sound. 16mm Color. *Rental:* U Cal Media.

Unremarkable Birth, An. Directed by Diane Beaudry. 1978. 52 min. 16mm Color. *Rental:* National Film & U Cal Media.

Unseen, The. Joel McCrea & Gail Russell. Directed by Lewis Allen. 1945. Paramount. 80 min. Sound. Videotape B&W. *Sale:* Swank Motion & VidAmerica.

Unseen, The. Barbara Bach & Sidney Lassick. 89 min. Sound. Videotape *Rental:* WW Enter.

Unseen World, The. 1971. ABC. (Documentary). 49 min. Sound. 16mm Color. *Rental:* U Cal Media, McGraw-Hill Films & Syracuse U Film. *Sale:* McGraw-Hill Films.

Unsinkable Molly Brown, The. Debbie Reynolds & Harve Presnell. Directed by Charles Walters. 1964. MGM. 128 min. Sound. 16mm Color. *Rental:* MGM United. *Rental:* MGM United, Anamorphic version.

Unsinkable Sea Otter!, The 1975. Churchill Films. (Documentary). 52 min. Sound. 16mm Color. *Rental:* Churchill Films. *Rental:* Churchill Films, Videotape version.

Unstrap Me! Directed by George Kuchar. 1968. George Kuchar. (Exploitation). 79 min. Sound. 16mm Color. *Rental:* Canyon Cinema.

Unsuspected, The. Claude Rains & Joan Caulfield. Directed by Michael Curtiz. 1947. Warners. 103 min. Sound. 16mm B&W. *Rental:* MGM United.

Untamed. Tyrone Power & Susan Hayward. Directed by Henry King. 1955. Fox. (Anamorphic). 111 min. Sound. 16mm Color. *Rental:* Films Inc.

Untamed. Joan Crawford & Robert Montgomery. Directed by Jack Conway. 1929. MGM. 88 min. Sound. 16mm B&W. *Rental:* MGM United.

Untamed Africa. Directed by Wyant D. Hubbard. 1933. Warners. (Documentary). 56 min. Sound. 16mm B&W. *Rental:* MGM United.

Untamed Breed, The. Sonny Tufts & Barbara Britton. Directed by Charles Lamont. 1948. Columbia. 75 min. Sound. 16mm B&W. *Rental:* Newman Film Lib.

Untamed Fury. Mikael Conrad & Leigh Whipper. Directed by Ewing Scott. 1947. PRC. 65 min. Sound. 16mm B&W. *Rental:* Inst Cinema.

Untamed Heiress. Judy Canova & Don Barry. Directed by Charles Lamont. 1954. Republic. 70 min. Sound. 16mm B&W. *Rental:* Ivy Films. *Sale:* Rep Pic Film.

Untamed Lands. American National. (Documentary). 93 min. Sound. 16mm Color. *Rental:* Westcoast Films.

Until September. Karen Allen & Thierry L'hermite. Directed by Richard Marquand. 1984. MGM. Sound. 16mm Color. *Rental:* MGM United.

Until She Talks. Pamela Reed. Directed by Mary Lampson. 1980. First Run. 45 min. Sound. 16mm Color. *Rental:* First Run.

Until They Get Me. Pauline Stark. Directed by Frank Borzage. 1917. Triangle. 55 min. Silent. 16mm B&W. *Rental:* Budget Films. *Sale:* Morcraft Films.

Until They Sail. Paul Newman & Jean Simmons. Directed by Robert Wise. 1957. MGM. 95 min. Sound. 16mm B&W. *Rental:* MGM United. *Rental:* MGM United, Anamorphic version.

Untouched, The. Ricardo Montalban. 1956. Excelsior. 80 min. Sound. 16mm B&W. *Rental:* Mogulls Films.

Unwed Mother Interview. 1965. USC. 68 min. Sound. 16mm B&W. *Rental:* Iowa Films.

Unwritten Code, The. Ann Savage & Tom Neal. Directed by Herman Rosten. 1944. Columbia. 61 min. Sound. 16mm B&W. *Rental:* Kit Parker.

Up! Margo Winchester. Directed by Russ Meyer. 1976. Meyer. 80 min. Sound. 16mm Color. *Rental:* Corinth Films.

Up From the Beach. Cliff Robertson & Red Buttons. Directed by Robert Parrish. 1965. Fox. 99 min. Sound. 16mm B&W. *Rental:* Films Inc. *Rental:* Films Inc, Anamorphic version.

Up Front. David Wayne & Tom Ewell. Directed by Alexander Knox. 1951. Universal. 92 min. Sound. 16mm B&W. *Rental:* Swank Motion.

Up in Central Park. Deanna Durbin & Dick Haymes. Directed by William A. Seiter. 1946. Universal. 84 min. Sound. 16mm B&W. *Rental:* Swank Motion.

Up in Smoke. Cheech Marin & Thomas Chong. Directed by Lou Adler. 1978. Paramount. 86 min. Sound. 16mm Color. *Rental:* Films Inc.

Up in the Air. 1982. Britain. (Cast unlisted). 43 min. Sound. 16mm Color. *Rental:* Janus Films. *Sale:* Lucerne Films.

Up in the Cellar *see* Three in the Cellar.

Up in the World. Norman Wisdom. Directed by John Paddy Carstairs. 1956. Britain. 90 min. Sound. 16mm B&W. *Rental:* Cinema Five.

Up Pompeii. Frankie Howard & Michael Hordern. Directed by Bob Kellett. 1971. Britain. 90 min. Sound. 16mm Color. *Rental:* Video Comm. *Lease:* Video Comm. *Rental:* Video Comm, Videotape version.

Up the Down Staircase. Sandy Dennis & Patrick Bedford. Directed by Robert Mulligan. 1967. Warners. 123 min. Sound. 16mm Color. *Rental:* Modern Sound.

Up the Junction. Suzy Kendall & Dennis Waterman. Directed by Peter Collinson. 1968. Britain. (Anamorphic). 119 min. Sound. 16mm Color. *Rental:* Films Inc.

Up the Ladder. Virginia Valli. Directed by Edward Sloman. 1925. Universal. 75 min. Silent. 16mm B&W. *Rental:* Em Gee Film Lib.

Up the River. Spencer Tracy & Claire Luce. Directed by John Ford. 1930. Fox. 85 min. Sound. 16mm B&W. *Rental:* Films Inc.

Up the Sandbox. Barbra Streisand & David Selby. Directed by Irwin Kershner. 1973. National General. 88 min. Sound. 16mm Color. *Rental:* Williams Films, Films Inc, Swank Motion & Twyman Films.

Up to His Ears. Orig. Title: Tribulations of a Chinese in China. Jean-Paul Belmondo & Ursula Andress. Directed by Philippe De Broca. Fr. 1966. France. 92 min. Sound. 16mm Color. subtitles. *Rental:* MGM United.

Up to His Neck. Ronald Shiner. Directed by John Paddy Carstairs. 1954. Britain. 85 min. Sound. 16mm B&W. *Rental:* Cinema Five.

Update: Adult Learning & the New Technologies. PBS. (Documentary). 120 min. Videotape Color. *Rental:* PBS Video. *Sale:* PBS Video.

Upper Hand, The. Jean Gabin & Gert Frobe. Directed by Denys De la Patelliere. 1967. France. (Anamorphic). 86 min. Sound. 16mm Color. dubbed. *Rental:* Films Inc.

Upper World, The. Warren William & Ginger Rogers. Directed by Roy Del Ruth. 1934. Warners. 75 min. Sound. 16mm B&W. *Rental:* MGM United.

Uprising, The. Directed by Peter Lilienthal. 1981. West Germany-Costa Rica. (Documentary). 96 min. Sound. 16mm Color. narrated Span. subtitles. *Rental:* Kino Intl. *Lease:* Kino Intl.

Uptight. Raymond St. Jacques & Ruby Dee. Directed by Jules Dassin. 1969. Paramount. 104 min. Sound. 16mm Color. *Rental:* Films Inc.

Uptown New York. Jack Oakie & Raymond Hatton. Directed by Victor Schertzinger. 1932. World Wide. 85 min. Sound. 16mm B&W. *Sale:* Cinema Concepts, Morcraft Films & Natl Cinema.

Uptown Saturday Night. Sidney Poitier & Bill Cosby. Directed by Sidney Poitier. 1974. Warners. 104 min. Sound. 16mm Color. *Rental:* Swank Motion & Williams Films. *Rental:* Swank Motion, Viceotape version.

Uranium Boom. Dennis Morgan & Patricia Medina. Directed by William Castle. 1956. Columbia. 67 min. Sound. 16mm B&W. *Lease:* Time-Life Multimedia.

Urban Cowboy. John Travolta & Scott Glenn. Directed by James Bridges. 1980. Paramount. 135 min. Sound. 16mm Color. *Rental:* Films Inc.

Urban Insurrection in Northern Ireland. 1970. Ireland. (Documentary). 50 min. Sound. 16mm B&W. *Rental:* CA Newsreel.

Urgh! a Music War. The Police & The Go-Go's. Directed by Derek Burbidge. 1981. Britain. 124 min. Sound. 16mm Color. *Rental:* Corinth Films.

Urubu. 1946. United Artists. (Documentary). 66 min. Sound. 16mm B&W. *Rental:* Ivy Films.

U.S. Route One: American Profile. 1965. NBC. (Documentary). 54 min. Sound. 16mm Color. *Rental:* McGraw-Hill Films, U Mich Media & Syracuse U Film. *Sale:* McGraw-Hill Films.

U.S.A: A Time for Decision. 1967. NET. (Documentary). 60 min. Sound. 16mm B&W. *Rental:* Indiana AV Ctr.

Use of Audiovisual Media for Improvement of Student Teaching & Related Experiences, The. 1970. 52 min. Sound. 16mm B&W. *Rental:* Utah Media.

Used Cars. Kurt Russell & Jack Warden. Directed by Robert Zemeckis. 1980. Columbia. 111 min. Sound. 16mm Color. *Rental:* Swank Motion. *Rental:* Swank Motion, Videotape version.

Using the Journal. 2 pts. 1976. Indiana U.. (Documentary). 94 min. Videotape Color. *Sale:* Indiana AV Ctr.

USS-VD: Ship of Shame *see* Story of Destroyer Escort 733.

Utah. Roy Rogers. Directed by John English. 1945. Republic. 54 min. Sound. 16mm B&W. *Rental:* Budget Films, Em Gee Film Lib & Ivy Films. *Sale:* Cinema Concepts & Rep Pic Film.

Utah Blaine. Rory Calhoun & Susan Cummings. Directed by Fred F. Sears. 1957. Columbia. 75 min. Sound. 16mm B&W. *Rental:* Cine Craft.

Utah Ground Zero Health Effects of Nuclear War. 1982. 58 min. Sound. 16mm Color. *Rental:* Utah Media.

Utah Kid. Hoot Gibson. Directed by Vernon Keays. 1944. Monogram. 60 min. Sound. 16mm B&W. *Rental:* Mogulls Films.

Utah Trail. Tex Ritter. Directed by Al Herman. 1938. Grand National. 57 min. Sound. 16mm B&W. *Rental:* Video Comm. *Sale:* Natl Cinema.

Utah Wagon Train. Rex Allen. Directed by Philip Ford. 1951. Republic. 67 min. Sound. 16mm B&W. *Rental:* Ivy Films. *Sale:* Rep Pic Film.

Utamaro & His Five Women. Minnosulee Bando. Directed by Kenji Mizoguchi. Jap. 1946. Japan. 95 min. Sound. 16mm B&W. subtitles. *Rental:* New Yorker Films.

Utopia. Orig. Title: Atoll K. Stan Laurel & Oliver Hardy. Directed by Leo Johannon. 1952. France. 80 min. Sound. 16mm B&W. dubbed. *Rental:* Budget Films. *Sale:* Cinema Concepts, New Cinema & Reel Images. *Rental:* Ivy Films & Morcraft Films, Super 8 sound version.

V. D. Blues. Dick Cavett, James Coco & Robert Drivas. 1973. NET. 60 min. Sound. 16mm Color. *Rental:* Modern Talking.

Vacances de Monsieur Hulot, Les *see* Mr. Hulot's Holiday.

Vacation Days. Freddie Stewart & June Preisser. Directed by Arthur Dreifuss. 1947. Monogram. 68 min. Sound. 16mm B&W. *Rental:* Hurlock Cine.

Vacation from Love. Dennis O'Keefe & Florence Rice. Directed by George Fitzmaurice. 1938. MGM. 66 min. Sound. 16mm B&W. *Rental:* MGM United.

Vacation from Marriage. Robert Donat & Deborah Kerr. Directed by Alexander Korda. 1945. MGM. 94 min. Sound. 16mm B&W. *Rental:* MGM United.

Vacation in Reno. Jack Haley & Anne Jeffreys. Directed by Leslie Goodwins. 1946. RKO. 60 min. Sound. 16mm B&W. *Rental:* Films Inc.

Vado, l'Ammazzo E Torno *see* Any Gun Can Play.

Vagabond King, The. Oreste & Kathryn Grayson. Directed by Michael Curtiz. 1956. Paramount. 88 min. Sound. 16mm Color. *Rental:* Films Inc.

Vagabond Lady, The. Robert Young, Evelyn Venable & Reginald Denny. Directed by Sam Taylor. 1935. MGM. 75 min. Sound. 16mm B&W. *Rental:* MGM United.

Vagabond Lover, The. Rudy Vallee. Directed by Marshall Neilan. 1929. RKO. 80 min. Sound. 16mm B&W. *Rental:* Budget Films. *Sale:* Cinema Concepts & Reel Images.

Vagabond Prince, The. H. B. Warner & Dorothy Dalton. 1916. Triangle. 60 min. Sound. 16mm B&W. *Sale:* Natl Cinema.

Vaghe Stelle Dell'Orsa *see* Sandra.

Valachi Papers, The. Charles Bronson & Lino Ventura. Directed by Terence Young. 1972. Columbia. 125 min. Sound. 16mm Color. *Rental:* Bosco Films, Budget Films, Films Inc, Kerr Films, Natl Film Video, Swank Motion, Westcoast Films, Welling Motion Pictures, Wholesome Film Ctr & Williams Films.

Valdez is Coming. Burt Lancaster & Susan Clark. Directed by Edwin Sherin. 1971. United Artists. 90 min. Sound. 16mm Color. *Rental:* MGM United & Westcoast Films.

Valentine, The. Jack Albertson & Mary Martin. 1980. Time-Life. 92 min. Sound. 16mm Color. *Rental:* Time-Life Multimedia. *Sale:* Time-Life Multimedia.

Valentino. Anthony Dexter & Eleanor Parker. Directed by Lewis Allen. 1951. Columbia. 105 min. Sound. 16mm Color. *Rental:* Kit Parker.

Valentino. Rudolph Nureyev & Michelle Phillips. Directed by Ken Russell. 1977. MGM. 128 min. Sound. 16mm Color. *Rental:* MGM United.

Valerie. Sterling Hayden & Anita Ekberg. Directed by Gerd Oswald. 1957. United Artists. 84 min. Sound. 16mm B&W. *Rental:* MGM United.

Valerie & Her Week of Wonders. Jaroslava Schallerova. Directed by Jaromil Jires. Czech. 1971. Czechoslovakia. 75 min. Sound. 16mm Color. subtitles. *Rental:* Films Inc & Janus Films.

Vali, the Witch of Positano. Vali Meyers. Directed by Sheldon Rochlin. 1966. Diane & Sheldon Rochlin. 65 min. Sound. 16mm Color. *Rental:* New Line Cinema.

Valiant Hombre. Duncan Renaldo. Directed by Wallace Fox. 1949. MGM. 60 min. Videotape B&W. *Sale:* Video Comm.

Valiant Three, The *see* Three Musketeers.

Valley, The. Bulle Ogier & Micheal Gothard. Directed by Barbet Schroeder. 100 min. Sound. 16mm Color. *Rental:* Direct Cinema.

Valley Fever. 1980. 60 min. Sound. Videotape Color. *Rental:* Natl AV Ctr. *Sale:* Natl AV Ctr.

Valley Girl. Nicolas Cage & Deborah Foreman. Directed by Martha Coolidge. 1982. MGM. 95 min. Sound. 16mm Color. *Rental:* MGM United. *Rental:* MGM United, Videotape version.

Valley of Death. Lex Barker & Pierre Brice. Germany. 90 min. Sound. 16mm Color. dubbed. *Rental:* Westcoast Films.

Valley of Decision. Gregory Peck & Greer Garson. Directed by Tay Garnett. 1945. MGM. 120 min. Sound. 16mm B&W. *Rental:* MGM United.

Valley of Fear. Johnny Mack Brown. Directed by Lambert Hillyer. 1947. Monogram. 55 min. Sound. 16mm B&W. *Rental:* Hurlock Cine.

Valley of Fury *see* Chief Crazy Horse.

Valley of Hunted Men. Tom Tyler & Bob Steele. Directed by John English. 1942. Republic. 56 min. Sound. 16mm B&W. *Rental:* Ivy Films. *Sale:* Rep Pic Film & Nostalgia Merchant.

Valley of Mystery. Richard Egan & Peter Graves. Directed by Joseph Leytes. 1966. Universal. 94 min. Sound. 16mm Color. *Rental:* Swank Motion.

Valley of Terror. Kermit Maynard. Directed by Al Herman. 1937. Ambassador. 59 min. Sound. 16mm B&W. *Rental:* Modern Sound. *Sale:* Blackhawk Films. *Sale:* Blackhawk Films, Super 8 sound version.

Valley of the Dinosaurs, The. James Franciscus & Gila Golan. Columbia. 95 min. Sound. 16mm Color. *Rental:* Williams Films.

Valley of the Dolls. Barbara Parkins & Patty Duke. Directed by Mark Robson. 1967. Fox. (Anamorphic). 120 min. Sound. 16mm Color. *Rental:* Films Inc.

Valley of the Dragons. Sean McClory & Cesare Danova. Directed by Edward Bernds. 1961. Columbia. 79 min. Sound. 16mm B&W. *Rental:* Roas Films & Film Ctr DC.

Valley of the Eagles. Jack Warner & Nadia Gray. Directed by Terence Young. 1952. Britain. 83 min. Sound. 16mm B&W. *Rental:* Budget Films, Inst Cinema, Modern Sound, Mogulls Films, Video Comm & Westcoast Films.

Valley of the Giants. Wayne Morris & Claire Trevor. Directed by William Keighley. 1938. Warners. 79 min. Sound. 16mm Color. *Rental:* MGM United.

Valley of the Head Hunters. Johnny Weissmuller. Directed by William Berke. 1953. Columbia. 67 min. Sound. 16mm B&W. *Rental:* Inst Cinema.

Valley of the Kings. Robert Taylor & Eleanor Parker. Directed by Robert Pirosh. 1954. MGM. 86 min. Sound. 16mm Color. *Rental:* MGM United.

Valley of the Sun. Lucille Ball & James Craig. Directed by George Marshall. 1942. RKO. 79 min. Sound. 16mm B&W. *Rental:* Films Inc.

Valley of the Zombies. Robert Livingston & Adrian Booth. Directed by Philip Ford. 1946. Republic. 56 min. Sound. 16mm B&W. *Rental:* Ivy Films. *Sale:* Rep Pic Film.

Valley of Vengeance. Orig. Title: Vengeance. Buster Crabbe. Directed by Sam Newfield. 1944. PRC. 57 min. Sound. 16mm B&W. *Rental:* Bosco Films & Mogulls Films.

Valparaiso Mi Amor. Directed by Aldo Francia. Span. 1970. Chile. 85 min. Sound. 16mm B&W. subtitles. *Rental:* Cinema Guild. *Sale:* Cinema Guild.

Valparaiso, Valparaiso. Alain Cuny. Directed by Pascal Aubier. Fr. 1971. France. 97 min. Sound. 16mm Color. subtitles. *Rental:* New Line Cinema. *Sale:* New Line Cinema.

Vampire, The. John Beal & Colleen Gray. Directed by Paul Landres. 1957. United Artists. 74 min. Sound. 16mm B&W. *Rental:* MGM United.

Vampire Bat. Melvyn Douglas, Fay Wray & Lionel Atwill. 1933. Majestic. 67 min. Sound. 16mm B&W. *Rental:* Kit Parker & Lewis Film. *Rental:* Budget Films, Em Gee Film Lib & Video Comm, Condensed 48 min. version.

Vampire Circus. Adrienne Corri & John Moulder Brown. Directed by Robert Young. 1972. Fox. 87 min. Sound. 16mm Color. *Rental:* Films Inc.

Vampire Lovers, The. Ingrid Pitt & Peter Cushing. Directed by Roy Ward Baker. 1971. Britain. 86 min. Sound. 16mm Color. *Rental:* Images Film & Video Comm.

Vampire Men of the Lost Planet. John Carradine. Directed by Al Adamson. 1969. Independent International. 85 min. Videotape Color. *Sale:* Blackhawk Films.

Vampire's Coffin, The. German Robles & Ariadne Welter. Directed by Fernando Mendez. 1958. Mexico. 85 min. Sound. 16mm B&W. dubbed. *Rental:* Budget Films.

Vampire's Ghost, The. Charles Gordon & Adele Mara. Directed by Lesley Selander. 1945. Republic. 54 min. Sound. 16mm B&W. *Rental:* Ivy Films. *Sale:* Rep Pic Film.

Vampire's Night Orgy, The. Jack Taylor. Directed by Leon Klimovsky. 1974. International Amusements. (Anamorphic). 86 min. Sound. 16mm Color. *Rental:* Films Inc.

Vampiro Sangriento *see* Bloody Vampire.

Vampyr. Orig. Title: Castle of Doom. Julian West & Henriette Gerard. Directed by Carl Th. Dreyer. 1931. Denmark. (Music & sound effects only). 66 min. Sound. 16mm B&W. *Rental:* A Twyman Pres, Budget Films, Em Gee Film Lib, Film Classics, Images Film, Kit Parker, U Cal Media & Video Comm. *Sale:* Festival Films & Reel Images. *Rental:* Twyman Films & Video Comm, German dialog with subtitles version. *Sale:* Cinema Concepts & Reel Images, Super 8 sound version. *Rental:* Film Classics, *Sale:* Festival Films, Images Film & Tamarelles French Film, Videotape version.

Van, The. Stuart Getz & Deborah White. Directed by Sam Grossman. 1977. Crown International. 86 min. Sound. 16mm Color. *Rental:* Films Inc & Wholesome Film Ctr.

Van Gogh: A Self Portrait. 1961. NBC. (Documentary). 55 min. Sound. 16mm Color. *Rental:* U of IL Film, Iowa Films & McGraw-Hill Films. *Sale:* McGraw-Hill Films.

Vanessa, Her Love Story. Helen Hayes & Robert Montgomery. Directed by William K. Howard. 1935. MGM. 76 min. Sound. 16mm B&W. *Rental:* MGM United.

Vanina Vanini. Sandra Milo & Laurent Terzieff. Directed by Roberto Rossellini. Ital. 1961. Italy. 125 min. Sound. 16mm Color. subtitles. *Rental:* Corinth Films.

Vanishing American, The. Scott Brady & Audrey Totter. Directed by Joseph Kane. 1955. Republic. 90 min. Sound. 16mm B&W. *Rental:* Ivy Films.

Vanishing American, The. Richard Dix, Lois Wilson & Noah Beery. Directed by George B. Seitz. 1926. Paramount. (Musical score only). 110 min. Sound. 16mm B&W. *Rental:* Killiam Collect. *Sale:* Cinema Concepts, Festival Films, Griggs Movie & Natl Cinema. *Rental:* Em Gee Film Lib, Silent 16mm version. *Sale:* Film Classics, Super 8 silent version. *Sale:* Festival Films & Tamarelles French Film, Videotape version.

Vanishing Cornwall. 1967. Sterling. (Documentary). 60 min. Sound. 16mm Color. *Sale:* Sterling Ed Film.

Vanishing Land, The. 1972. Gold Key. (Documentary). 90 min. Sound. 16mm Color. *Rental:* Budget Films, Films Inc, Video Comm & Westcoast Films. *Lease:* Video Comm. *Rental:* Video Comm, *Lease:* Video Comm, Videotape version.

Vanishing Point. Barry Newman & Cleavon Little. Directed by Richard C. Sarafian. 1971. Fox. 107 min. Sound. 16mm Color. *Rental:* Films Inc.

Vanishing Westerner, The. Monte Hale. Directed by Philip Ford. 1950. Republic. 60 min. Sound. 16mm B&W. *Rental:* Ivy Films. *Sale:* Rep Pic Film.

Vanity Fair. Minnie Maddern Fiske. Directed by Eugene Nowland. 1916. Edison-Kleine. 75 min. Silent. 8mm B&W. *Sale:* Film Classics.

Vanity Fair. Myrna Loy & Conway Tearle. Directed by Chester M. Franklin. 1932. Hollywood. 80 min. Sound. 16mm B&W. *Rental:* Mogulls Films. *Rental:* Film Classics, Videotape version.

Vanquished, The. John Payne & Jan Sterling. Directed by Edward Ludwig. 1953. Paramount. 84 min. Sound. 16mm B&W. *Rental:* Video Comm & Willoughby Peer.

Varan, the Unbelievable. Orig. Title: Unbelievable Varan, The. Myron Healey. Directed by Inoshiro Honda & Jerry A. Baerwitz. 1962. Japan. 70 min. Sound. 16mm B&W. dubbed. *Rental:* Video Comm. *Lease:* Video Comm. *Rental:* Video Comm, *Lease:* Video Comm, Videotape version.

Variations V. 1965. Cunningham. (Dance). 50 min. Sound. 16mm B&W. *Rental:* M Cunningham.

Varieties on Parade. Jackie Coogan. Directed by Ron Ormond. 1951. Lippert. 56 min. Sound. 16mm B&W. *Rental:* Budget Films & Mogulls Films.

Variety. Emil Jannings & Lya De Putti. Directed by E. A. Dupont. 1925. Germany. 57 min. Silent. 16mm B&W. *Rental:* A Twyman Pres, Budget Films, Creative Film, Em Gee Film Lib, Images Film, Janus Films, Kit Parker, Museum Mod Art & Film Images. *Sale:* Cinema Concepts, Festival Films, Griggs Movie, Glenn Photo, Natl Cinema, Film Images & Images Film. *Sale:* Festival Film & Images Film, *Sale:* Festival Films, Videotape version.

Variety Girl. Bing Crosby & Bob Hope. Directed by George Marshall. 1947. Paramount. 93 min. Sound. 16mm B&W. *Rental:* Swank Motion.

Variety Time. Jack Paar & Leon Errol. Directed by Hal Yates. 1948. RKO. 59 min. Sound. 16mm *Rental:* Films Inc & RKO General Pics.

Varsity Show. Dick Powell, Priscilla Lane & Rosemary Lane. 1937. Warners. 80 min. Sound. 16mm B&W. *Rental:* MGM United.

Vatican, The. 1963. ABC. (Documentary). 54 min. Sound. 16mm B&W. *Rental:* McGraw-Hill Films. *Sale:* McGraw-Hill Films. *Rental:* McGraw-Hill Films & Syracuse U Film, *Sale:* McGraw-Hill Films, Color version.

Vatican, The. 1970. Britain. (Documentary). 52 min. Sound. 16mm Color. *Rental:* Time-Life Multimedia. *Sale:* Time-Life Multimedia. *Rental:* Time-Life Multimedia, *Sale:* Time-Life Multimedia, Spanish language version. *Rental:* Time-Life Multimedia, *Sale:* Time-Life Multimedia, Videotape version.

Vault of Horror, The. Terry-Thomas, Michael Craig & Glynis Johns. Directed by Roy Ward Baker. 1973. Cinerama. 86 min. Sound. 16mm Color. *Rental:* Modern Sound & Swank Motion.

Veils of Baghdad, The. Victor Mature & Mari Blanchard. Directed by George Sherman. 1953. Universal. 82 min. Sound. 16mm Color. *Rental:* Swank Motion.

Veinte Docenas De Hijos. Fred MacMurray & Vera Miles. Directed by Norman Tokar. 1966. Disney. 128 min. Sound. 16mm Color. dubbed. *Rental:* Twyman Films.

Velvet Touch, The. Rosalind Russell & Leo Genn. Directed by John Gage. 1948. RKO. 97 min. Sound. 16mm B&W. *Rental:* Films Inc.

Vendetta. Faith Domergue. Directed by Mel Ferrer. 1950. RKO. 84 min. Sound. 16mm B&W. *Sale:* ank Motion.

Venetian Affair, The. Robert Vaughn & Elke Sommer. Directed by Jerry Thorpe. 1966. MGM. 92 min. Sound. 16mm Color. *Rental:* MGM United. *Rental:* MGM United, Anamorphic version.

Venetian Twins, The. 1977. Miami-Dade. (Cast unlisted). 60 min. Videotape Color. *Sale:* Films Inc.

Venezuela: Last Chance for Democracy. 1966. NET. (Documentary). 55 min. Sound. 16mm B&W. *Rental:* Indiana AV Ctr.

Venezuela: Making of a Government. 1965. IU. 59 min. Sound. 16mm B&W. *Rental:* Syracuse U Film.

Vengeance see Valley of Vengeance.

Vengeance. William Thourlby. Directed by Dene Hilyard. 1964. Crown. 80 min. Sound. 16mm B&W. *Rental:* Video Comm. *Lease:* Video Comm.

Vengeance. Richard Harrison. Directed by Anthony Dawson. 1971. Italy. 100 min. Sound. 16mm Color. dubbed. *Rental:* Films Inc. *Rental:* Films Inc, Anamorphic version.

Vengeance in the Saddle see Bullets & Saddles.

Vengeance of Gregory Walters, The see Feud of the West.

Vengeance of Kali, The. Lex Barker, Senta Berger & Ian Hunter. 1965. Teleworld. 105 min. Sound. 16mm Color. dubbed. *Rental:* Films Inc.

Vengeance of Pancho Villa, The. John Ericson & Gustavo Rojo. 1967. Spain. 87 min. Sound. 16mm Color. dubbed. *Rental:* Films Inc & Willoughby Peer.

Vengeance of Rannah, The. Rin-Tin-Tin Jr. & Bob Custer. Directed by Franklin Shamray. 1936. Reliable. 50 min. Sound. 16mm B&W. *Rental:* Mogulls Films.

Vengeance of She, The. John Richardson & Olinka Berova. Directed by Cliff Owen. 1968. Fox. 101 min. Sound. 16mm Color. *Rental:* Films Inc.

Vengeance of the Deep. Lloyd Hughes & Shirley Anne Richards. 70 min. Sound. 16mm B&W. *Rental:* Bosco Films.

Vengeance of the Zombies. Paul Nashy. Directed by Leon Klimovsky. 1972. Spain. 91 min. Sound. 16mm Color. *Rental:* Films Inc.

Vengeance Valley. Burt Lancaster & Robert Walker. Directed by Richard Thorpe. 1951. MGM. 82 min. Sound. 16mm Color. *Rental:* MGM United.

Venice Be Damned. 1971. NBC. (Documentary). 52 min. Sound. 16mm Color. *Rental:* Films Inc. *Sale:* Films Inc. *Sale:* Films Inc, Videotape version.

Venice: City in Danger. Directed by Helen Jean Rogers. 1968. ABC. (Documentary). 52 min. Sound. 16mm Color. *Rental:* Kit Parker & McGraw-Hill Films. *Sale:* McGraw-Hill Films.

Venom. Sterling Hayden & Klaus Kinski. Directed by Piers Haggard. 1982. Paramount. 93 min. Sound. 16mm Color. *Rental:* Films Inc.

Venom & Eternity. Jean Cocteau & Jean-Louis Barrault. Directed by Jean Isidore Isou. Fr. 1953. France. (Experimental). 90 min. Sound. 16mm B&W. subtitles. *Rental:* A Twyman Pres & Twyman Films.

Vent de l'Est, Le *see* Wind From the East.

Venus in Furs. James Darren & Barbara McNair. Directed by Jess Franco. 1970. American International. 86 min. Sound. 16mm Color. *Rental:* Ivy Films & Rep Pic Film. *Lease:* Rep Pic Film.

Venus of Love. Constance Talmadge. Directed by Marshall Neilan. 1927. 16mm *Rental:* A Twyman Pres.

Vera Cruz. Gary Cooper & Burt Lancaster. Directed by Robert Aldrich. 1954. MGM. 94 min. Sound. 16mm Color. *Rental:* MGM United.

Verboten. James Best & Susan Cummings. Directed by Samuel Fuller. 1959. Columbia. 93 min. Sound. 16mm B&W. *Rental:* Budget Films, Kit Parker, Westcoast Films & Video Comm. *Lease:* Video Comm.

Verdict, The. Sydney Greenstreet & Peter Lorre. Directed by Don Siegel. 1946. Warners. 86 min. Sound. 16mm B&W. *Rental:* MGM United.

Verdict, The. Paul Newman & Charlotte Rampling. Directed by Sidney Lumet. 1982. Fox. 120 min. Sound. 16mm Color. *Rental:* Films Inc.

Verdugo, El *see* Not on Your Life.

Veriye Druzya *see* True Friends.

Vernon Florida. Directed by Errol Morris. 1981. 60 min. Sound. 16mm Color. *Rental:* New Yorker Films.

Veronika Voss. Rosel Zech & Hilmar Thate. Directed by Rainer Werner Fassbinder. Ger. 1982. 105 min. 16mm B&W. subtitles. *Rental:* MGM United. *Rental:* MGM United, Videotape version.

Versailles: Palace Temple of the Sun King. Fr. 1975. France. (Documentary). 51 min. Sound. 16mm Color. *Rental:* French Am Cul. *Rental:* French Am Cul, Dubbed version.

Verse Person Singular. 1982. Films Inc.. (Performance). 60 min. Videotape Color. *Rental:* Films Inc. *Sale:* Films Inc.

Vertigo. James Stewart & Kim Novak. Directed by Alfred Hitchcock. 1958. Universal. 120 min. Sound. 16mm Color. *Rental:* Swank Motion. *Rental:* Swank Motion, *Sale:* Tamarelles French Film, Videotape version.

Very Brief Romance of Barbara Frietchie & Stonewall Jackson, The. 55 min. Sound. 16mm Color. *Rental:* Filmmakers Coop.

Very Cold War, A *see* Snow Treasure.

Very Curious Girl, A. Bernadette Lafont & Georges Geret. Directed by Nelly Kaplan. Fr. 1969. Janus. 107 min. Sound. 16mm Color. subtitles. *Rental:* Films Inc.

Very Delicate Matter, A. 1982. ABC. 46 min. Sound. 16mm Color. *Rental:* Learning Corp Am. *Sale:* Learning Corp Am. *Sale:* Wombat Productions & Learning Corp Am, *Lease:* Learning Corp Am, Videotape version.

Very Honorable Guy, A. Joe E. Brown & Alice White. Directed by Lloyd Bacon. 1934. Warners. 64 min. Sound. 16mm B&W. *Rental:* MGM United.

Very Idea, The. Frank Craven & Sally Blane. Directed by William LeBaron. 1930. RKO. Sound. 16mm B&W. *Rental:* RKO General Pics.

Very Natural Thing, A. Robert Joel & Bo White. Directed by Christopher Larkin. 1974. New Line Cinema. 85 min. Sound. 16mm Color. *Rental:* New Line Cinema.

Very Private Affair, A. Brigitte Bardot & Marcello Mastroianni. Directed by Louis Malle. 1962. MGM. 95 min. Sound. 16mm Color. dubbed. *Rental:* MGM United. *Rental:* MGM United, Videotape version.

Very Remarkable Yamato Family, The. 2 pts. 1975. WNET. (Documentary). 118 min. Sound. 16mm Color. *Rental:* Indiana AV Ctr, Syracuse U Film & U Cal Media. *Sale:* Indiana AV Ctr. *Sale:* Indiana AV Ctr, Videotape version.

Very Thought of You, The. Dennis Morgan, Faye Emerson & Eleanor Parker. Directed by Delmer Daves. 1944. Warners. 99 min. Sound. 16mm B&W. *Rental:* MGM United.

Very Young Lady, A. Jane Withers. Directed by Harold Schuster. 1941. Fox. 79 min. Sound. 16mm B&W. *Rental:* Films Inc.

Vessel of Wrath. Orig. Title: Beachcomber, The. Charles Laughton. Directed by Erich Pommer. 1937. 16mm *Rental:* A Twyman Pres.

Viaccia, La. Jean-Paul Belmondo & Claudia Cardinale. Directed by Mauro Bolognini. Ital. 1960. Embassy. 103 min. Sound. 16mm B&W. subtitles. *Rental:* Films Inc. *Rental:* Films Inc, Dubbed version.

Vicar of Bray, The. Stanley Holloway. Directed by Henry Edwards. 1937. Britain. 64 min. Sound. 16mm B&W. *Rental:* Ivy Films.

Vicar of Wakefield, The. Sir John Hare. Directed by Fred Paul. 1917. Thanhouser. 50 min. Silent. 16mm B&W. *Rental:* Film Classics. *Sale:* Film Classics. *Rental:* Film Classics, *Sale:* Film Classics, Silent 8mm version.

Vice & Virtue. Annie Giradot & Robert Hossein. Directed by Roger Vadim. 1965. MGM. 108 min. Sound. 16mm B&W. dubbed. *Rental:* MGM United.

Vice Presidency, The. 1956. CBS. (Documentary). 51 min. Sound. 16mm B&W. *Rental:* U Mich Media. *Sale:* McGraw-Hill Films.

Vice Squad. Orig. Title: Girl in Room Seventeen, The. Edward G. Robinson & Paulette Goddard. Directed by Arnold Laven. 1953. MGM. 88 min. Sound. 16mm B&W. *Rental:* MGM United.

Vicious Breed. 1956. 85 min. 16mm *Rental:* A Twyman Pres.

Vicious Circle *see* Woman in Brown.

Vicious Years, The. Orig. Title: Gangster We Made, The. Tommy Cook. Directed by Robert Florey. 1950. Film Classics. 81 min. Sound. 16mm B&W. *Rental:* Film Classics.

Vicki. Jeanne Crain & Jean Peters. Directed by Harry Horner. 1953. Fox. 85 min. Sound. 16mm B&W. *Rental:* Films Inc.

Victim! Dirk Bogarde, Sylvia Sims & Dennis Price. Directed by Basil Dearden. 1961. Britain. 100 min. Sound. 16mm B&W. *Rental:* Films Inc & Janus Films.

Victims, The. 1966. Anti-Defamation League. (Documentary). 48 min. Sound. 16mm B&W. *Rental:* ADL. *Sale:* ADL.

Victor de la Brigade Mondaine. George Descrieres. Directed by Jean-Pierre Decourt. Fr. 1971. France. 55 min. Sound. 16mm Color. *Rental:* French Am Cul.

Victor-Victoria. Julie Andrews, James Garner & Robert Preston. Directed by Blake Edwards. 1982. 133 min. Sound. 16mm Color. *Rental:* MGM United. *Rental:* MGM United, Videotape version.

Victoria & Albert. 1980. Royal Heritage. (Documentary). 60 min. Sound. 16mm Color. *Rental:* Films Inc. *Sale:* Films Inc. *Rental:* Films Inc, *Sale:* Films Inc, Videotape version.

Victoria, Queen & Empress. 1980. Royal Heritage. (Documentary). 60 min. Sound. 16mm Color. *Rental:* Films Inc. *Sale:* Films Inc. *Rental:* Films Inc, *Sale:* Films Inc, Videotape version.

Victoria the Great *see* Sixty Glorious Years.

Victors, The. Vincent Edwards & Albert Finney. Directed by Carl Foreman. 1963. Columbia. 147 min. Sound. 16mm B&W. *Rental:* Budget Films, Cine Craft, Charard Motion Pics, Bosco Films, Films Inc, Modern Sound & Twyman Films. *Rental:* Kit Parker, Anamorphic version.

Victors of the Dry Land, The. 1980. Britain. (Documentary). 58 min. Videotape Color. *Rental:* Films Inc. *Sale:* Films Inc.

Victory. Frederic March & Betty Field. Directed by John Cromwell. 1940. Paramount. 78 min. Sound. 16mm B&W. *Rental:* Swank Motion.

Victory. Sylvester Stallone & Michael Caine. Directed by John Huston. 1981. Lorimar. 117 min. Sound. 16mm Color. *Rental:* Swank Motion. *Rental:* Swank Motion, Videotape version.

Victory at Sea. 1954. NBC. 84 min. Sound. 16mm B&W. *Rental:* Films Inc & Wholesome Film Ctr. *Sale:* Films Inc. *Sale:* Films Inc, Videotape version.

Vida Provisoria, La. Directed by Mauricio Gomes Leite. Port. 1969. Brazil. 80 min. Sound. 16mm B&W. subtitles. *Rental:* New Yorker Films.

Vidas Secas. Antonio Sampaio. Directed by Nelson Pereira. Port. 1963. Brazil. 115 min. Sound. 16mm B&W. subtitles. *Rental:* New Yorker Films.

Video Guide to Wine, A. Winevision. (Documentary). 60 min. Videotape Color. *Rental:* Time-Life Multimedia. *Sale:* Time-Life Multimedia.

Video Variations. Directed by Fred Barzyk. 1972. Boston Symphony. (Experimental). 50 min. Videotape Color. *Sale:* Electro Art.

Videodrome. James Woods & Deborah Harry. Directed by David Cronenberg. 1983. Universal. 90 min. Sound. 16mm Color. *Rental:* Swank Motion. *Rental:* Swank Motion, Videotape version.

Videotrivia. Worldwide Sports. 60 min. Videotape Color. *Rental:* Best Film & Video Corp.

Videotrivia. Movies & Television. 60 min. Videotape Color. *Rental:* Best Film & Video Corp..

Vie Continue, La. Trans. Title: Life Goes On. Annie Girardot, Jean Pierre Cassel & Moshe Dux. Directed by Moshe Mizrahi. Fr. 93 min. Sound. 16mm Color. subtitles. *Rental:* Swank Motion.

Vie d'Ange, La. Paule Baillargeon. Directed by Pierre Harel. Fr. 1978. Canada. 98 min. Sound. 16mm Color. subtitles. *Rental:* Natl Film CN. *Sale:* Natl Film CN.

Vie de Chateau, La see Matter of Resistance.

Vie Passionnee De Georges Clemenceau, La. France. (Documentary). 80 min. Sound. 16mm B&W. *Rental:* French Am Cul. *Rental:* French Am Cul, Videotape version.

Vieille Dame Indigne, La see Shameless Old Lady.

Vienna Waltzes. Anton Walbrook. Directed by Emile Edwin Reinart. 1961. Hoffberg. 83 min. Sound. 16mm B&W. dubbed. *Rental:* Budget Films.

Viet Cong, The. 1968. CBS. (Documentary). 54 min. Sound. 16mm B&W. *Rental:* Phoenix Films. *Sale:* Phoenix Films. *Rental:* Phoenix Films, *Sale:* Phoenix Films, Color version.

Vietnam: A Television History. 13 pts. 1983. WGBH. (Documentary). 780 min. Sound. 16mm Color. *Rental:* Films Inc, Iowa Films & Syracuse U Film. *Sale:* Films Inc. *Sale:* Films Inc, Videotape version.

Vietnam: An American Journey. Directed by Robert Richter. 1980. First Run. (Documentary). 85 min. Sound. 16mm Color. *Rental:* Films Inc & First Run.

Vietnam: An Historical Document. 1975. CBS. (Documentary). 56 min. Sound. 16mm Color. *Rental:* U Cal Media, Iowa Films, U Mich Media & Syracuse U Film. *Sale:* Carousel Films.

Vietnam & the Aftermath: A Conversation with Clark Clifford. 1976. PBS. (Documentary). 60 min. Sound. 16mm Color. *Rental:* WNET Media, Videotape version.

Vietnam: Journal of a War. 1968. Britain. (Documentary). 52 min. Sound. 16mm B&W. *Rental:* Time-Life Multimedia. *Sale:* Time-Life Multimedia.

Vietnam Memorial. 1983. 52 min. Sound. Videotape *Rental:* PBS Video. *Sale:* PBS Video.

Vietnam: Picking up the Pieces. Directed by Jon Alpert, Keiko Tsuno & Karen Ranucci. 1977. Downtown Community TV. (Documentary). 60 min. Videotape Color. *Rental:* Electro Art, Sound 16mm version.

Vietnam Requiem, A. Directed by Bill Couturie & Jonas McCord. 1983. 58 min. Sound. Color. *Rental:* Direct Cinema. *Sale:* Direct Cinema. *Sale:* Direct Cinema, Videotape version.

View from Pompey's Head, The. Richard Egan & Dana Wynter. Directed by Philip Dunne. 1955. Fox. (Anamorphic). 97 min. Sound. 16mm Color. *Rental:* Films Inc.

View from the Edge, A. (Shock of the New Ser.). 1980. Time-Life. (Documentary). 52 min. Sound. 16mm Color. *Rental:* U Cal Media & Time-Life Multimedia. *Sale:* Time-Life Multimedia.

Vigil in the Night. Carole Lombard & Brian Aherne. Directed by George Stevens. 1940. RKO. 96 min. Sound. 16mm *Rental:* RKO General Pics.

Vigil in the Night. Carole Lombard & Brian Aherne. Directed by George Stevens. 1940. RKO. 96 min. Sound. 16mm B&W. *Rental:* Films Inc.

Vigilante Force. Kris Kristofferson & Jan-Michael Vincent. Directed by George Armitage. 1976. MGM. 89 min. Sound. 16mm Color. *Rental:* MGM United.

Vigilante Hideout. Allan Lane. Directed by Fred C. Brannon. 1950. Republic. 60 min. Sound. 16mm B&W. *Rental:* Ivy Films. *Sale:* Rep Pic Film.

Vigilante Terror. Bill Elliott & Fuzzy Knight. Directed by Lewis D. Collins. 1954. Allied Artists. 60 min. Sound. 16mm B&W. *Rental:* Hurlock Cine.

Vigilantes of Boomtown, The. Allan Lane. Directed by R. G. Springsteen. 1947. Republic. 54 min. Sound. 16mm B&W. *Rental:* Ivy Films.

Vigilantes of Dodge City, The. Bill Elliott. Directed by Wallace Grissell. 1944. Republic. 54 min. Sound. 16mm B&W. *Rental:* Ivy Films & Rep Pic Film. *Lease:* Rep Pic Film.

Vigny. France. (Cast unlisted). 60 min. Sound. 16mm B&W. *Rental:* French Am Cul. *Rental:* French Am Cul, Videotape version.

Viking, The. Charles Starrett. Directed by Varick Frissel & George Melford. 1931. Canada. 70 min. Sound. 16mm B&W. *Rental:* Budget Films.

Viking Queen. Don Murray & Adrienne Corri. Directed by Don Chaffey. 1967. Fox. 91 min. Sound. 16mm Color. *Rental:* Films Inc.

Viking Women & the Sea Serpent, The. Abby Dalton. Directed by Roger Corman. 1957. American International. 66 min. Sound. 16mm Color. *Rental:* Westcoast Films.

Vikings, The. Kirk Douglas & Tony Curtis. Directed by Richard Fleischer. 1958. United Artists. 114 min. Sound. 16mm Color. *Rental:* MGM United.

Villa! Brian Keith & Cesar Romero. Directed by James B. Clark. 1958. Fox. (Anamorphic). 72 min. Sound. 16mm Color. *Rental:* Films Inc.

Villa Rides. Yul Brynner & Robert Mitchum. Directed by Buzz Kulik. 1968. Fox. 125 min. Sound. 16mm Color. *Rental:* Films Inc.

Village, The. Directed by Mark McCarty. 1969. University of California. (Documentary). 70 min. Sound. 16mm B&W. *Rental:* U Cal Media & U Mich Media. *Sale:* U Cal Media.

Village Barn Dance, The. Richard Cromwell. Directed by Frank McDonald. 1940. Republic. 72 min. Sound. 16mm B&W. *Rental:* Ivy Films.

Village Dances of Yugoslavia, The. 1982. IFA. (Dance). 60 min. Sound. 16mm Color. *Rental:* U Cal Media.

Village of the Damned, The. George Sanders & Barbara Shelley. Directed by Wolf Rilla. 1960. Britain. 78 min. Sound. 16mm B&W. *Rental:* MGM United. *Rental:* MGM United, Videotape version.

Village of the Daughters, The. Eric Sykes & Gregoire Aslan. Directed by George Pollock. 1961. Britain. 88 min. Sound. 16mm B&W. *Rental:* MGM United.

Village of the Giants, The. Beau Bridges & Tommy Kirk. Directed by Bert I. Gordon. 1965. Embassy. 80 min. Sound. 16mm Color. *Rental:* Films Inc.

Village Sleuth, The. Charles Ray & Winifred Westover. Directed by Jerome Storm. 1920. Paramount. 65 min. Silent. 16mm B&W. *Rental:* Em Gee Film Lib. *Sale:* Blackhawk Films. *Sale:* Blackhawk Films, Super 8 silent version.

Village Tale, A. Randolph Scott & Kay Johnson. Directed by John Cromwell. 1935. RKO. 80 min. Sound. 16mm B&W. *Rental:* RKO General Pics.

Village Teacher. Trans. Title: Selskaya Uchitelnitsa. Vera Maretskaya. Directed by Mark Donskoi. Rus. 1947. Russia. 99 min. Sound. 16mm B&W. subtitles. *Rental:* Corinth Films.

Village That Refused to Die, The. 1960. 55 min. Sound. 16mm *Rental:* Budget Films.

Villain. Richard Burton & Ian McShane. Directed by Michael Tuchner. 1971. MGM. 97 min. Sound. 16mm Color. *Rental:* Cine Craft, MGM United, Modern Sound & Swank Motion. *Rental:* MGM United, Anamorphic version.

Villain, The. Kirk Douglas, Ann-Margret & Arnold Schwarzenegger. Directed by Hal Needham. 1979. Columbia. 93 min. Sound. 16mm Color. *Rental:* Swank Motion, Westcoast Films & Williams Films. *Rental:* Westcoast Films, 97 min. Modern sound version.

Villain Still Pursued Her, The. Orig. Title: Drunkard, The. Alan Mowbray & Anita Louise. Directed by Edward Cline. 1941. RKO. 67 min. Sound. 16mm B&W. *Rental:* Budget Films, Ivy Films, Rep Pic Film & Wholesome Film Ctr. *Sale:* Rep Pic Film & Reel Images. *Rental:* Ivy Films, *Sale:* Ivy Films & Reel Images, Super 8 sound version.

Villano En Su Rincon, El. 1970. 46 min. Sound. 16mm Color. *Rental:* Syracuse U Film & U Mich Media.

Vincent, Francois, Paul & the Others. Yves Montand. Directed by Claude Sautet. Fr. 1974. France. 113 min. Sound. 16mm Color. subtitles. *Rental:* J Green Pics. *Sale:* Tamarelles French Film, Videotape version.

Vincent Massey. 1959. Canada. (Documentary). 59 min. Sound. 16mm B&W. *Rental:* Natl Film CN. *Sale:* Natl Film CN.

Vinoba Bhave: Walking Revolution. 1964. International Film Bureau. (Documentary). 49 min. Sound. 16mm Color. *Rental:* Syracuse U Film.

Vintage, The. Pier Angeli & Michele Morgan. Directed by Jeffrey Hayden. 1957. MGM. 92 min. Sound. 16mm Color. *Rental:* MGM United. *Rental:* MGM United, Anamorphic version.

Vintage W. C. Fields. W. C. Fields. (Compilation). 95 min. 16mm *Rental:* A Twyman Pres.

Viol, Le. Orig. Title: Rape, The. Bibi Andersson. Directed by Jacques-Doniol Valcroze. Fr. 1969. France. 78 min. Sound. 16mm Color. subtitles. *Rental:* Budget Films, Ivy Films & Video Comm.

Violence. Nancy Coleman & Michael O'Shea. Directed by Jack Bernhard. 1947. Monogram. 72 min. Sound. 16mm B&W. *Rental:* Hurlock Cine.

Violent Earth, The. Directed by Robert Kitts. 1973. ITC. (Documentary). 60 min. Sound. 16mm Color. *Rental:* Natl Geog & Syracuse U Film. *Sale:* Natl Geog. *Sale:* Natl Geog, Videotape version.

Violent Enemy, The. Tom Bell & Ed Begley. Directed by Don Sharp. 1969. 92 min. Sound. 16mm Color. *Rental:* Budget Films.

Violent Four, The. Gian-Maria Volonte & Thomas Milian. Directed by Carlo Lizzani. 1968. Paramount. 98 min. Sound. 16mm Color. dubbed. *Rental:* Films Inc.

Violent Hour, The see Dial Eleven Nineteen.

Violent Men, The. Glenn Ford & Barbara Stanwyck. Directed by Rudolph Mate. 1955. Columbia. 96 min. Sound. 16mm Color. *Rental:* Films Inc, Modern Sound & Welling Motion Pictures.

Violent Ones, The. Fernando Lamas & Aldo Ray. Directed by Fernando Lamas. 1967. Feature Film Corp. 87 min. Sound. 16mm Color. *Rental:* Ivy Films & Rep Pic Film. *Lease:* Rep Pic Film.

Violent Saturday. Victor Mature & Richard Egan. Directed by Richard Fleischer. 1955. Fox. (Anamorphic). 91 min. Sound. 16mm Color. *Rental:* Films Inc.

Violent Stranger, The. Zachary Scott & Faith Domergue. 1958. Britain. 83 min. Sound. 16mm B&W. *Rental:* Charard Motion Pics.

Violent Universe, The. 5 pts. 1970. NET. (Documentary). 150 min. Sound. 16mm B&W. *Rental:* Indiana AV Ctr & U Cal Media. *Sale:* Indiana AV Ctr. *Sale:* Indiana AV Ctr, Videotape version.

Violent Years, The. Jean Moorhead & Barbara Weeks. Directed by Franz Eichorn. 1958. 65 min. Sound. 16mm *Rental:* Budget Films.

Violetera, La. Sarita Montiel & Raf Vallone. Directed by Luis Cesar Amadori. Span. 1960. Mexico. 116 min. Sound. 16mm B&W. subtitles. *Rental:* Trans-World Films.

Violette. Isabelle Huppert & Stephane Audran. Directed by Claude Chabrol. Fr. 1978. France. 123 min. Sound. 16mm Color. subtitles. *Rental:* New Yorker Films.

Violons du Bal, Les. Marie-Jose Nat. Directed by Michel Drach. Fr. 1974. France. 110 min. Sound. 16mm Color. subtitles. *Rental:* Films Inc.

V.I.P: My Brother Superman. Directed by Bruno Bozzetto. 1968. Italy. (Animated). 85 min. Sound. 16mm Color. dubbed. *Rental:* Distribution Sixteen.

V.I.P.'s, The. Elizabeth Taylor & Richard Burton. Directed by Anthony Asquith. 1963. MGM. 119 min. Sound. 16mm Color. *Rental:* MGM United. *Rental:* Films Inc, Anamorphic color version.

Virgil Thomson: Composer. Directed by John Huszar. 1979. Cantor. (Documentary). 60 min. Sound. 16mm Color. *Rental:* A Cantor. *Sale:* A Cantor.

Virgin & the Gypsy, The. Joanna Shimkus & Franco Nero. Directed by Christopher Miles. 1970. Britain. 85 min. Sound. 16mm Color. *Rental:* Budget Films, Films Inc, Kerr Film, Kit Parker, Video Comm & Westcoast Films.

Virgin of Guadelupe, The. Ramon Navarro. Mexico. 111 min. Sound. 16mm B&W. *Rental:* Trans-World Films.

Virgin President, The. Severn Darden. Directed by Graeme Ferguson. 1969. New Line Cinema. 73 min. Sound. 16mm B&W. *Rental:* New Cinema & New Line Cinema.

Virgin Queen, The. Bette Davis & Richard Todd. Directed by Henry Koster. 1955. Fox. (Anamorphic). 92 min. Sound. 16mm Color. *Rental:* Films Inc.

Virgin Soldiers, The. Hywel Bennet & Lynn Redgrave. Directed by John Dexter. 1969. Britain. 96 min. Sound. 16mm Color. *Rental:* Corinth Films & Kit Parker.

Virgin Spring, The. Max Von Sydow & Gunnel Lindblom. Directed by Ingmar Bergman. Swed. 1959. Sweden. 88 min. Sound. 16mm B&W. subtitles. *Rental:* Films Inc, Janus Films & New Cinema.

Virginia City. Errol Flynn & Miriam Hopkins. Directed by Michael Curtiz. 1940. Warners. 121 min. Sound. 16mm B&W. *Rental:* MGM United.

Virginia City. 1979. PBS. (Documentary). 54 min. Videotape Color. *Rental:* PBS Video. *Sale:* PBS Video.

Virginia Hill Story, The. Dyan Cannon & Harvey Keitel. Directed by Joel Schumacher. 1976. Rosenberg. 77 min. Sound. 16mm Color. *Rental:* Lucerne Films. *Sale:* Lucerne Films. *Sale:* Lucerne Films, Videotape version.

Virginian, The. Kenneth Harlan & Florence Vidor. Directed by Tom Forman. 1923. Preferred. 60 min. Silent. 16mm B&W. *Sale:* Blackhawk Films. *Sale:* Blackhawk Films, Super 8 silent version.

Virginian, The. Gary Cooper & Walter Huston. Directed by Victor Fleming. 1929. Paramount. 90 min. Sound. 16mm B&W. *Rental:* Williams Films.

Viridiana. Silvia Pinal & Francisco Rabal. Directed by Luis Bunuel. Span. 1961. Spain. 90 min. Sound. 16mm B&W. subtitles. *Rental:* Budget Films, Corinth Films, Em Gee Film Lib, Films Inc, Images Film & Utah Media. *Sale:* Festival Films, Natl Cinema & Images Film. *Lease:* Corinth Films. *Sale:* Em Gee Film Lib, Festival Films & Images Film, Videotape version.

Virtue. Carole Lombard. Directed by Edward Buzzell. 1932. Columbia. 70 min. Sound. 16mm B&W. *Rental:* Welling Motion Pictures.

Virtue's Revolt. Edith Thornton & Crawford Kent. Directed by James Chapin. 1924. Steiner. 55 min. Silent. 16mm B&W. *Sale:* Thunderbird Films. *Sale:* Thunderbird Films, Super 8 sound version.

Virtuous Sin, A. Walter Huston & Kay Francis. Directed by George Cukor & Louis Gasnier. 1930. Paramount. 81 min. Sound. 16mm B&W. *Rental:* Swank Motion.

Vision of the Blind. 1978. Britain. (Documentary). 48 min. Sound. 16mm Color. *Rental:* Films Inc & U of IL Film. *Sale:* Films Inc. *Rental:* Films Inc, *Sale:* Films Inc, Videotape version.

Visions of Eight. Directed by Milos Forman, John Schlesinger, Juri Ozerov, Claude Lelouch, Kon Ichikawa, Michael Pfleghar, Mai Zetterling & Arthur Penn. 1973. Wolper. (Documentary). 110 min. Sound. 16mm Color. *Rental:* Cinema Five. *Lease:* Cinema Five.

Visit, The. Ingrid Bergman & Anthony Quinn. Directed by Bernhard Wicki. 1964. Fox. (Anamorphic). 100 min. Sound. 16mm B&W. *Rental:* Films Inc.

Visit to a Chief's Son, A. Richard Mulligan. Directed by Lamont Johnson. 1974. MGM. 92 min. Sound. 16mm Color. *Rental:* MGM United.

Visit to a Small Planet, A. Jerry Lewis. Directed by Norman Taurog. 1960. Paramount. 101 min. Sound. 16mm B&W. *Rental:* Films Inc. *Rental:* Ivy Films, *Sale:* Blackhawk Films, Super 8 sound version, Videotape version.

Visit to Washington with Mrs. Lyndon B. Johnson, A. 1966. ABC. (Documentary). 60 min. Sound. 16mm Color. *Rental:* McGraw-Hill Films. *Sale:* McGraw-Hill Films.

Visiteurs du Soir, Les. Orig. Title: Night Visitors. Trans. Title: Devil's Envoys. Alain Cuny. Directed by Marcel Carne. Fr. 1942. France. 118 min. Sound. 16mm B&W. subtitles. *Rental:* Films Inc & Janus Films.

Visiting Artists. 2 Pts. 1979. PBS. (Documentary). 109 min. Videotape Color. *Rental:* PBS Video. *Sale:* PBS Video.

Visiting Hours. Lee Grant & William Shatner. Directed by Jean-Claude Lord. 1982. Fox. 103 min. Sound. 16mm Color. *Rental:* Films Inc.

Visitor, The. Glenn Ford, Mel Ferrer, John Huston & Shelley Winters. Directed by Michael J. Paradise. 1980. International Picture Show. 103 min. Sound. 16mm Color. *Rental:* Twyman Films.

Visitors, The. Patrick McVey. Directed by Elia Kazan. 1972. MGM. 88 min. Sound. 16mm Color. *Rental:* MGM United.

Vital Spark, The. 1981. Britain. (Documentary). 50 min. Sound. 16mm Color. *Rental:* Films Inc. *Sale:* Films Inc. *Rental:* Films Inc, *Sale:* Films Inc, Videotape version.

Vitelloni, I. Franco Fabrizi & Alberto Sordi. Directed by Federico Fellini. Ital. 1956. Italy. 104 min. Sound. 16mm B&W. subtitles. *Rental:* Corinth Films. *Lease:* Corinth Films.

Viva Knievel! Evel Knievel & Gene Kelly. Directed by Gordon Douglas. 1977. Warners. 104 min. Sound. 16mm Color. *Rental:* Swank Motion & Williams Films. *Rental:* Swank Motion, Anamorphic version.

Viva la Muerte *see* Don't Turn the Other Cheek.

Viva La Muerte. Nuria Espert & Anouk Ferjac. Directed by Fernando Arrabal. Fr. 1974. France. 90 min. Sound. 16mm Color. subtitles. *Rental:* New Line Cinema.

Viva la Republica. Orig. Title: Long Live the Republic. Directed by Pastor Vega. Span. 1975. Cuba. (Documentary). 100 min. Sound. 16mm B&W. subtitles. *Rental:* Cinema Guild. *Sale:* Cinema Guild.

Viva Las Vegas. Elvis Presley & Ann-Margret. Directed by George Sidney. 1964. MGM. 86 min. Sound. 16mm Color. *Rental:* Films Inc & MGM United. *Rental:* MGM United, Videotape version.

Viva Maria. Brigitte Bardot & Jeanne Moreau. Directed by Louis Malle. Fr. 1966. France. 114 min. Sound. 16mm Color. subtitles. *Rental:* MGM United.

Viva Max! Peter Ustinov & Pamela Tiffin. Directed by Jerry Paris. 1969. Commonwealth. 93 min. Sound. 16mm Color. *Rental:* Films Inc, Budget Films, Cine Craft, Charard Motion Pics, Bosco Films, Film Pres, Inst Cinema, Ivy Films, Kerr Film, Lewis Film, Rep Pic Film, Roas Films, Film Ctr DC, Video Comm, Westcoast Films, Welling Motion Pictures , Wholesome Film Ctr & Willoughby Peer. *Lease:* Rep Pic Film.

Viva Portugal. Directed by Christiane Gerhards. 1975. Portugal. (Documentary). 80 min. Sound. 16mm Color. narrated Eng. *Rental:* Cinema Guild. *Sale:* Cinema Guild.

Viva Villa. Wallace Beery. Directed by Howard Hawks. 1934. MGM. 114 min. Sound. 16mm B&W. *Rental:* MGM United.

Viva Zapata! Marlon Brando & Anthony Quinn. Directed by Elia Kazan. 1952. Fox. 113 min. Sound. 16mm B&W. *Rental:* Films Inc.

Vivacious Lady. James Stewart & Ginger Rogers. Directed by George Stevens. 1938. RKO. 90 min. Sound. 16mm B&W. *Rental:* Films Inc.

Vivir un Instante. Span. 1950. Mexico. (Cast unlisted). 90 min. Sound. 16mm B&W. *Rental:* Film Classics.

Vivre Sa Vie *see* My Life to Live.

Vixen. Erica Gavin. Directed by Russ Meyer. 1968. Eve. 71 min. Sound. 16mm Color. *Rental:* Corinth Films. *Sale:* Cinema Concepts & Video Lib, Videotape version.

Vo Imya Zhizni *see* Miracle of Dr. Petrov.

Vogues of 1938. Joan Bennett & Warner Baxter. Directed by Irving Cummings. 1937. United Artists. 113 min. Sound. 16mm B&W. *Rental:* Learning Corp Am. *Sale:* Learning Corp Am.

Voice in the Mirror, A. Richard Egan & Julie London. Directed by Harry Keller. 1958. Universal. 102 min. Sound. 16mm B&W. *Rental:* Swank Motion.

Voice in the Night, A *see* Wanted for Murder.

Voice of Bugle Ann, The. Lionel Barrymore & Eric Linden. Directed by Richard Thorpe. 1936. MGM. 70 min. Sound. 16mm B&W. *Rental:* MGM United.

Voice of Change, The. 1962. Hearst. (Documentary). 50 min. Sound. 16mm B&W. *Sale:* King Features.

Voice of Hollywood, The. Buster Keaton & Ken Maynard. 1929. 60 min. Sound. 16mm Color. *Sale:* Festival Films. *Sale:* Festival Films, Videotape version.

Voice of Scandal, The *see* Here Comes Carter.

Voice of the City, The. Willard Mack & Robert Ames. Directed by Willard Mack. 1939. MGM. 83 min. Sound. 16mm B&W. *Rental:* MGM United.

Voice of the Whistler, The. Richard Dix. Directed by William Castle. 1945. Columbia. 60 min. Sound. 16mm B&W. *Lease:* Time-Life Multimedia.

Voices. Directed by Richard Mourdant. 1969. Britain. (Documentary). 60 min. Sound. 16mm Color. *Rental:* New Cinema & New Line Cinema.

Voices. Michael Ontkean & Amy Irving. Directed by Robert Markowitz. 1979. MGM. 106 min. Sound. 16mm Color. *Rental:* MGM United.

Voices from the Russian Underground. 1970. CBS. (Documentary). 52 min. Sound. 16mm B&W. *Rental:* U Mich Media.

Voices of Spirit. 1976. Green Mountain Post. (Documentary). 60 min. Sound. 16mm B&W. *Rental:* Green Mt. *Sale:* Green Mt.

Voie Lactee, La *see* Milky Way.

Volcanic Landscape. 1973. Martin Moyer. (Documentary). 58 min. Sound. 16mm Color. *Rental:* OK AV Ctr.

Volcano. Bebe Daniels & Ricardo Cortez. Directed by William K. Howard. 1926. Paramount. 70 min. Silent. 16mm B&W. *Rental:* Films Inc.

Volcano. 1975. Canada. (Documentary). 59 min. Sound. 16mm Color. *Rental:* Natl Film CN. *Sale:* Natl Film CN.

Volcano. Directed by Donald Brittain & John Kramer. 1977. Cinema V. 110 min. Sound. 16mm Color. *Rental:* Cinema Five & Natl Film CN.

Volga, The. 1966. CBS. (Documentary). 49 min. Sound. 16mm Color. *Rental:* McGraw-Hill Films, Syracuse U Film & U Mich Media. *Sale:* McGraw-Hill Films & Natl Geog. *Sale:* Natl Geog, Videotape version.

Volga-Volga. Tolya Shalaev. Directed by Grigori Alexandrov. Rus. 1938. Russia. 95 min. Sound. 16mm B&W. subtitles. *Rental:* Corinth Films.

Volpone. Harry Baur & Louis Jouvet. Directed by Maurice Tourneur. Fr. 1939. France. 95 min. Sound. 16mm B&W. subtitles. *Rental:* Budget Films, Corinth Films, Images Film, Kit Parker & French Am Cul. *Sale:* Festival Films, Natl Cinema & Images Film. *Lease:* Corinth Films. *Sale:* Tamarelles French Film, Videotape version.

Volpone by Ben Jonson. 3 pts. 1967. Britain. (Cast unlisted). 90 min. Sound. 16mm B&W. *Rental:* U Mich Media.

Voltaire. George Arliss & Doris Kenyon. Directed by John Adolfi. 1933. Warners. 72 min. Sound. 16mm B&W. *Rental:* MGM United.

Volunteer Jam. Charlie Daniels Band. Britain. 75 min. Sound. 16mm Color. *Rental:* Ivy Films. *Rental:* Ivy Films, 120 mins. version.

Volunteer Jam. Allman Brothers. 90 min. Videotape Color. *Sale:* Cinema Concepts.

Volunteers, The. 1967. NET. (Documentary). 55 min. Sound. 16mm B&W. *Rental:* Indiana AV Ctr.

Voluptuous Vixens '76. EVR. 72 min. Videotape Color. *Sale:* Enter Video.

Von Richthofen & Brown. John Phillip Law & Don Stroud. Directed by Roger Corman. 1971. United Artists. 98 min. Sound. 16mm Color. *Rental:* MGM United.

Von Ryan's Express. Frank Sinatra & Trevor Howard. Directed by Mark Robson. 1965. Fox. (Anamorphic). 117 min. Sound. 16mm Color. *Rental:* Williams Films, Films Inc & Twyman Films. *Rental:* Films Inc, Videotape version.

Voodoo Man. Bela Lugosi & John Carradine. Directed by William Beaudine. 1944. Monogram. 65 min. Sound. 16mm B&W. *Rental:* Budget Films, Ivy Films, Mogulls Films & Video Comm.

Voodoo Tiger. Johnny Weissmuller. Directed by Spencer G. Bennett. 1952. Columbia. 67 min. Sound. 16mm B&W. *Rental:* Maljack. *Lease:* Maljack. *Lease:* Maljack, Videotape version.

Voodoo Woman. Marla English & Tom Conway. Directed by Edward L. Cahn. 1957. American International. 77 min. Sound. 16mm B&W. *Rental:* Films Inc & Video Comm.

Vortex, The. James Russo, Lydia Lunch & Bill Rice. 1982. 87 min. Sound. 16mm Color. *Rental:* First Run.

Vote for Huggett. Jack Warner & Petula Clark. Directed by Ken Annakin. 1949. Britain. 85 min. Sound. 16mm B&W. *Rental:* Cinema Five.

Voulkos & Company. 1973. EMC. (Documentary). 65 min. Sound. 16mm Color. *Rental:* U Cal Media.

Voyage, The. Sophia Loren & Richard Burton. Directed by Vittorio De Sica. 1974. MGM. 102 min. Sound. 16mm Color. *Rental:* MGM United.

Voyage Du Pere, La. Fernandel & Lilli Palmer. Directed by Denys De La Patelliere. Fr. 1966. France. 93 min. Sound. 16mm Color. *Rental:* French Am Cul.

Voyage en Ballon, La. Pascal Lamourisse. Directed by Albert Lamourisse. Fr. 1960. France. 85 min. Sound. 16mm Color. subtitles. *Rental:* French Am Cul.

Voyage en Douce, La. Directed by Michel Deville. Fr. 1980. 97 min. Sound. 16mm Color. subtitles Eng. *Rental:* New Yorker Films.

Voyage Imaginaire, Le. Trans. Title: Imaginary Voyage, The. Jean Birlin. Directed by Rene Clair. 1925. France. 67 min. Silent. 16mm B&W. *Rental:* Em Gee Film Lib. *Sale:* Glenn Photo, Super 8 silent version.

Voyage into Space. Akio Tito. 1965. Japan. 98 min. Sound. 16mm Color. dubbed. *Rental:* Films Inc.

Voyage of the Brigantine Yankee. 1967. National Geographic. (Documentary). 52 min. Sound. 16mm Color. *Rental:* U Cal Media, U Mich Media, Syracuse U Film, Wholesome Film Ctr & Natl Geog. *Sale:* Natl Geog. *Sale:* Natl Geog, Videotape version.

Voyage of the Damned. Faye Dunaway & Max Von Sydow. Directed by Stuart Rosenberg. 1976. Embassy. 158 min. Sound. 16mm Color. *Rental:* Films Inc.

Voyage Surprise. Maurice Baquet & Martine Carol. Directed by Pierre Prevert. Fr. 1946. France. 108 min. Sound. 16mm B&W. subtitles. *Rental:* Images Film. *Lease:* Images Film. *Sale:* Festival Films. *Sale:* Festival Films, Videotape version.

Voyage to a Pre-Historic Planet. Basil Rathbone & Faith Domergue. Directed by John Sebastian. 1965. American International. 80 min. Sound. 16mm Color. *Rental:* Films Inc.

Voyage to Grand Tartarie, The. Orig. Title: Trip Through Purgatory, A. Micheline Lanctot & Jean-Louis Bideau. Directed by Jean-Charles Tacchella. Fr. 1974. France. 100 min. Sound. 16mm Color. subtitles. *Rental:* New Line Cinema.

Voyage to Italy, A. Ingrid Bergman & George Sanders. Directed by Roberto Rossellini. 1953. Italy. 75 min. Sound. 16mm B&W. dubbed. *Rental:* Films Inc & Images Film. *Sale:* Festival Films, Images Film & Reel Images. *Sale:* Festival Films, Videotape version.

Voyage to the Bottom of the Sea, The. Walter Pidgeon & Joan Fontaine. Directed by Irwin Allen. 1961. Fox. 107 min. Sound. 16mm Color. *Rental:* Charard Motion Pics, Films Inc, Inst Cinema, Twyman Films, Video Comm & Willoughby Peer. *Rental:* Williams Films & Willoughby Peer, Anamorphic version.

Voyage to the Enchanted Isles, The. 1968. CBS. (Documentary). 54 min. Sound. 16mm Color. *Rental:* Budget Films, U Mich Media, U of IL Film & Syracuse U Film. *Sale:* Phoenix Films.

Voyage to the End of the Universe, The. Dennis Stephens. Directed by Jindrich Polak. 1962. American International. 81 min. Sound. 16mm B&W. dubbed. *Rental:* Video Comm & Westcoast Films.

Voyage to the Planet of Pre-Historic Women. Orig. Title: Planet of Storms. Mamie Van Doren. Directed by Peter Bogdanovich. 1966. American International. 81 min. Sound. 16mm Color. *Rental:* Films Inc.

Voyou, Le *see* Crook.

Vreden's Dag *see* Day of Wrath.

Vrooder's Hooch *see* Crazy World of Julius Vrooder.

Vulture, The. Robert Hutton & Akim Tamiroff. Directed by Lawrence Huntington. 1967. Paramount. 91 min. Sound. 16mm B&W. *Rental:* Films Inc.

W. Twiggy & Michael Witney. Directed by Richard Quine. 1974. Cinerama. 95 min. Sound. 16mm Color. *Rental:* Swank Motion.

W. C. Fields & Me. Rod Steiger & Valerie Perrine. Directed by Arthur Hiller. 1976. Universal. 112 min. Sound. 16mm Color. *Rental:* Swank Motion.

W. C. Fields Festival. Rohauer. (Anthology). 108 min. Sound. 16mm B&W. *Rental:* Janus Films.

W. C. Fields Film Festival: No. One. 68 min. Sound. 16mm *Rental:* Budget Films.

W. C. Fields Film Festival: No. Two. 60 min. Sound. 16mm *Rental:* Budget Films.

W. W. & the Dixie Dancekings. Burt Reynolds. Directed by John G. Avildsen. 1975. Fox. 94 min. Sound. 16mm Color. *Rental:* Films Inc, Twyman Films, Welling Motion Pictures & Williams Films.

Wabash Avenue. Betty Grable & Victor Mature. Directed by Henry Koster. 1950. Fox. 92 min. Sound. 16mm Color. *Rental:* Films Inc.

Wac from Walla Walla, The. Judy Canova & Stephen Dunne. Directed by William Witney. 1952. Republic. 82 min. Sound. 16mm B&W. *Rental:* Ivy Films. *Sale:* Rep Pic Film.

Wacki Taxi. John Astin. 90 min. Sound. 16mm Color. *Rental:* Bosco Films.

Wackiest Ship in the Army, The. Jack Lemmon & Ricky Nelson. Directed by Richard Murphy. 1960. Columbia. 99 min. Sound. 16mm Color. *Rental:* Arcus Film, Buchan Pic, Budget Films, Cine Craft, Charard Motion Pics, Williams Films, Bosco Films, Films Inc, Modern Sound, Newman Film Lib, Natl Film Video, Roas Film, Film Ctr DC, Twyman Films, Westcoast Films, Welling Motion Pictures & Wholesome Film Ctr.

Wacky World of Mother Goose, The. 1967. Embassy. (Animated). 82 min. Sound. 16mm Color. *Rental:* Films Inc.

Waco. William Elliott. Directed by Lewis D. Collins. 1958. Allied Artists. 68 min. Sound. 16mm B&W. *Rental:* Hurlock Cine.

Waco. Howard Keel & Jane Russell. Directed by R. G. Springsteen. 1966. Paramount. 85 min. Sound. 16mm Color. *Rental:* Films Inc.

Wages of Fear, The. Yves Montand & Vera Clouzot. Directed by Henri-Georges Clouzot. Fr. 1953. France. 138 min. Sound. 16mm B&W. subtitles. *Rental:* Budget Films, Corinth Films, Em Gee Film Lib, Films Inc, Images Film, Kit Parker, Natl Film Video, Roas Films, Video Comm & Wholesome Film Ctr. *Sale:* Festival Films, Natl Cinema & Reel Images. *Lease:* Corinth Films. *Sale:* Festival Films & Tamarelles French Film, Videotape version.

Wagon Tracks. William S. Hart & Jane Novak. Directed by Lambert Hillyer. 1919. Paramount. 60 min. Silent. 16mm B&W. *Rental:* Em Gee Film Lib & Film Images. *Sale:* Blackhawk Films & Film Images. *Rental:* Ivy Films, Super 8 silent version.

Wagon Tracks West. Bill Elliott. Directed by Howard Bretherton. 1943. Republic. 55 min. Sound. 16mm B&W. *Rental:* Ivy Films. *Sale:* Rep Pic Film & Nostalgia Merchant.

Wagon Train. Tim Holt & Martha O'Driscoll. Directed by Bert Gilroy. 1941. RKO. 59 min. Sound. 16mm B&W. *Rental:* RKO General Pics.

Wagon Wheels. Orig. Title: Caravans West. Randolph Scott & Gail Patrick. Directed by Charles Barton. 1934. Paramount. 54 min. Sound. 16mm B&W. *Rental:* Budget Films.

Wagon Wheels Westward. Bill Elliott. Directed by R. G. Springsteen. 1945. Republic. 54 min. Sound. 16mm B&W. *Rental:* Ivy Films & Rep Pic Film. *Sale:* Rep Pic Film & Nostalgia Merchant.

Wagonmaster. Ben Johnson & Joanne Dru. Directed by John Ford. 1950. RKO. 85 min. Sound. 16mm B&W. *Rental:* Films Inc.

Wagons Roll at Night, The. Humphrey Bogart & Sylvia Sidney. Directed by Ray Enright. 1941. Warners. 86 min. Sound. 16mm B&W. *Rental:* MGM United.

Wagons West. Rod Cameron & Peggie Castle. Directed by Ford Beebe. 1952. Monogram. 68 min. Sound. 16mm Color. *Rental:* Hurlock Cine.

Wagons Westward. Chester Morris & Anita Louise. Directed by Lew Landers. 1940. Republic. 54 min. Sound. 16mm B&W. *Rental:* Ivy Films. *Sale:* Rep Pic Film.

Wait Till the Sun Shines, Nellie. David Wayne & Jean Peters. Directed by Henry King. 1952. Fox. 109 min. Sound. 16mm B&W. *Rental:* Films Inc.

Waiting for Fidel. Directed by Michael Ruddo. 1974. Canada. (Documentary). 58 min. Sound. 16mm Color. *Rental:* Museum Mod Art & Natl Film CN. *Sale:* Museum Mod Art & Natl Film CN.

Waiting for Godot. Zero Mostel, Burgess Meredith & Kurt Kasznar. Directed by Alan Schneider. 1975. PBS. 102 min. Sound. 16mm B&W. *Rental:* Films Human, Grove & New Cinema. *Sale:* Films Human & Grove.

Waiting for Love. Ludmila Gurchenko. Directed by Pyotr Todorovsky. 1982. Russia. 80 min. Sound. 16mm Color. subtitles. *Rental:* IFEX.

Wajda Trilogy *see* Ashes & Diamonds.

Wajda Trilogy *see* Kanal.

Wajda Trilogy *see* Generation.

Wake Island. Robert Preston & Brian Donlevy. Directed by John Farrow. 1942. Paramount. 87 min. Sound. 16mm B&W. *Rental:* Swank Motion.

Wake Me When It's Over. Ernie Kovacs & Dick Shawn. Directed by Mervyn LeRoy. 1960. Fox. 126 min. Sound. 16mm Color. *Rental:* Films Inc. *Rental:* Films Inc, Anamorphic color version.

Wake of the Red Witch, The. John Wayne & Gail Russell. Directed by Edward Ludwig. 1948. Republic. 106 min. Sound. 16mm B&W. *Rental:* Budget Films & Ivy Films. *Lease:* Rep Pic Film.

Wake of Thirty-Eight, The. 1979. PBS. (Documentary). 59 min. Videotape Color. *Rental:* PBS Video. *Sale:* PBS Video.

Wake Up & Dream. June Haver & John Payne. Directed by Lloyd Bacon. 1946. Fox. 92 min. Sound. 16mm Color. *Rental:* Films Inc.

Wake Up & Kill. Robert Hoffman & Lisa Gastoni. Directed by Carlo Lizzani. 1966. Italy. 126 min. Sound. 16mm Color. dubbed. *Rental:* MGM United.

Wake Up, Mes Bons Amis. Trans. Title: Pays Sans Son Sens, Un. 1972. Canada. (Documentary). 118 min. Sound. 16mm B&W. narrated Eng. *Rental:* Natl Film CN. *Sale:* Natl Film CN.

Walden *see* Diaries, Notes & Sketches.

Walk a Crooked Mile. Louis Hayward & Dennis O'Keefe. Directed by Gordon Douglas. 1948. Columbia. 91 min. Sound. 16mm B&W. *Rental:* Budget Films, Bosco Films & Films Inc.

Walk a Tightrope. Dan Duryea & Patricia Owens. Directed by Frank Nesbitt. 1964. Paramount. 69 min. Sound. 16mm B&W. *Rental:* Films Inc.

Walk, Don't Run. Cary Grant & Jim Hutton. Directed by Charles Walters. 1966. Columbia. 117 min. Sound. 16mm Color. *Rental:* Buchan Pic, Budget Films, Cine Craft, Charard Motion Pics, Bosco Films, Films Inc, Inst Cinema, Modern Sound, Newman Film Lib, Roas Films, Film Ctr DC, Westcoast Films, Welling Motion Pictures & Wholesome Film Ctr.

Walk East on Beacon. Orig. Title: Crime of the Century, The. George Murphy & Virginia Gilmore. Directed by Alfred M. Werker. 1952. Columbia. 98 min. Sound. 16mm B&W. *Rental:* Buchan Pic, Cine Craft, Charard Motion Pics, Films Inc, Newman Film Lib, Film Ctr DC & Budget Films.

Walk in My Shoes. 1963. ABC. (Documentary). 54 min. Sound. 16mm B&W. *Rental:* Mass Media & Utah Media. *Sale:* McGraw-Hill Films.

Walk in the Spring Rain, A. Ingrid Bergman & Anthony Quinn. Directed by Guy Green. 1969. Columbia. 100 min. Sound. 16mm Color. *Rental:* Cine Craft, Films Inc, Modern Sound, Roas Films, Film Center DC, Welling Motion Pictures & Wholesome Film Ctr.

Walk in the Sun, A. Dana Andrews & Richard Conte. Directed by Lewis Milestone. 1945. Fox. 117 min. Sound. 16mm B&W. *Rental:* Budget Films, Em Gee Film Lib, Films Inc, Images Film, Kit Parker, Roas Films, Video Comm, Westcoast Films & Wholesome Film Ctr. *Sale:* Cinema Concepts, Festival Films & Glenn Photo, Super 8 sound version. *Sale:* Images Film, Videotape version.

Walk Into Hell, A. Chips Rafferty. Directed by Lee Robinson. 1957. Australia. 93 min. Sound. 16mm Color. *Rental:* Films Inc & Kerr Films.

Walk Like a Dragon. Jack Lord & Nobu McCarthy. Directed by James Clavel. 1960. Paramount. 95 min. Sound. 16mm B&W. *Rental:* Films Inc.

Walk on the Wild Side, A. Laurence Harvey & Jane Fonda. Directed by Edward Dmytryk. 1962. Columbia. 114 min. Sound. 16mm B&W. *Rental:* Budget Films, Charard Motion Pictures, Films Inc, Inst Cinema, Kerr Film, Kit Parker, Modern Sound & Welling Motion Pictures.

Walk Proud. Robby Benson & Sarah Holcomb. Directed by Robert Collins. 1979. Universal. 102 min. Sound. 16mm Color. *Rental:* Williams Films.

Walk Softly, Stranger. Joseph Cotten & Alida Valli. Directed by Robert Stevenson. 1950. RKO. 81 min. Sound. 16mm B&W. *Rental:* Films Inc.

Walk Tall. Willard Parker & Joyce Meadows. Directed by Maury Dexter. 1960. Fox. (Anamorphic). 60 min. Sound. 16mm B&W. *Rental:* Willoughby Peer.

Walk the Proud Land. Anne Bancroft & Audie Murphy. Directed by Jesse Hibbs. 1956. Universal. 88 min. Sound. 16mm Color. *Rental:* Swank Motion. *Rental:* Swank Motion, Anamorphic version.

Walk with Love & Death, A. Anjelica Huston & Assaf Dayan. Directed by John Huston. 1969. Fox. 90 min. Sound. 16mm Color. *Rental:* Films Inc.

Walkabout. Jenny Agutter & Lucien John. Directed by Nicolas Roeg. 1971. Fox. 95 min. Sound. 16mm Color. *Rental:* Films Inc.

Walkaround Time. 1973. Merce Cunningham. (Dance). 48 min. Sound. 16mm Color. *Rental:* Dance Film Archive. *Sale:* M Cunningham. *Sale:* M Cunningham, *Rental:* M Cunningham, Videotape version.

Walking Back. Sue Carol & Robert Edeson. Directed by Rupert Julian. 1928. Pathe. 60 min. Silent. 16mm B&W. *Rental:* Film Classics. *Sale:* Film Classics.

Walking Dead, The. Boris Karloff & Ricardo Cortez. Directed by Michael Curtiz. 1936. Warners. 66 min. Sound. 16mm B&W. *Rental:* MGM United.

Walking Down Broadway *see* Hello, Sister.

Walking Hills, The. Randolph Scott & Arthur Kennedy. Directed by John Sturges. 1949. Columbia. 78 min. Sound. 16mm B&W. *Rental:* Kit Parker.

Walking My Baby Back Home. Donald O'Connor & Janet Leigh. Directed by Lloyd Bacon. 1953. Universal. 95 min. Sound. 16mm Color. *Rental:* Swank Motion.

Walking Nightmare *see* Living Ghost.

Walking on Air. Ann Sothern & Gene Raymond. Directed by Joseph Santley. 1936. RKO. 69 min. Sound. 16mm B&W. *Rental:* RKO General Pics.

Walking Stick, The. Samantha Eggar & David Hemmings. Directed by Eric Till. 1970. Britain. 101 min. Sound. 16mm Color. *Rental:* MGM United.

Walking Tall. Joe Don Baker & Elizabeth Hartman. Directed by Phil Karlson. 1973. Cinerama. 125 min. Sound. 16mm Color. *Rental:* Modern Sound, Swank Motion, Welling Motion Pictures, Westcoast Films, Wholesome Film Ctr & Williams Films.

Walking Tall: The Final Chapter. Bo Swenson & Forrest Tucker. Directed by Jack Starrett. 1977. American International. 112 min. Sound. 16mm Color. *Rental:* Swank Motion & Welling Motion Pictures.

Walking Tall: Part Two. Bo Swenson, Richard Jaeckel & Luke Askew. Directed by Earl Bellamy. 1975. American International. 109 min. Sound. 16mm Color. *Rental:* Welling Motion Pictures.

Walking Target, The. Ron Foster & Joan Evans. Directed by Edward L. Cahn. 1960. United Artists. 74 min. Sound. 16mm B&W. *Rental:* MGM United.

Walkover. Jerzy Skolimowski. Directed by Jerzy Skolimowski. Pol. 1965. Poland. 77 min. Sound. 16mm B&W. subtitles. *Rental:* New Yorker Films.

Wall in Jerusalem, A. Directed by Frederic Rossif. 1971. France. (Documentary). 90 min. Sound. 16mm B&W. *Rental:* Budget Films, Icarus Films, Images Film, U Mich Media, Modern Sound, Twyman Films, Willoughby Peer & Alden. *Sale:* Images Film & Alden. *Sale:* Images Film, Videotape version.

Wall of Death, The. Laurence Harvey & Susan Shaw. Directed by Lewis Gilbert. 1951. Britain. 82 min. Sound. 16mm B&W. *Rental:* Film Classics.

Wall Street Cowboy. Roy Rogers. Directed by Joseph Kane. 1939. Republic. 54 min. Sound. 16mm B&W. *Rental:* Ivy Films. *Sale:* Rep Pic Film.

Wall Street: Where the Money Is. 1969. Metromedia. (Documentary). 82 min. Sound. 16mm B&W. *Rental:* Films Inc. *Sale:* Films Inc. *Sale:* Films Inc, Videotape version.

Wallaby Jim of the Islands. George Houston. Directed by Charles Lamont. 1937. Grand National. 70 min. Sound. 16mm B&W. *Rental:* Mogulls Films.

Wallflower. Robert Hutton & Joyce Reynolds. Directed by Frederick De Cordova. 1948. Warners. 77 min. Sound. 16mm B&W. *Rental:* MGM United.

Walls of Fire. 1973. RBC. (Documentary). 82 min. Sound. 16mm Color. *Rental:* U Cal Media.

Walls of Jericho, The. Cornel Wilde & Kirk Douglas. Directed by John M. Stahl. 1948. Fox. 106 min. Sound. 16mm B&W. *Rental:* Films Inc & Willoughby Peer.

Walls of Malapaga, The. Trans. Title: Au Dela Des Grilles. Jean Gabin & Isa Miranda. Directed by Rene Clement. Fr. 1949. France. 91 min. Sound. 16mm B&W. subtitles. *Rental:* Film Classics.

Waltz of the Toreadors. Peter Sellers & Margaret Leighton. Directed by John Guillermin. 1962. Britain. 110 min. Sound. Videotape Color. *Sale:* Budget Films, Films Inc, U of IL Film, Janus Films, Kit Parker, Learning Corp Am, Modern Sound, Twyman Films & VidAmerica. *Sale:* Learning Corp Am.

Waltz Time. Patricia Medina & Peter Graves. Directed by Paul L. Stein. 1946. Britain. 91 min. Sound. 16mm B&W. *Rental:* Ivy Films.

Waltzes from Vienna. Orig. Title: Strauss' Great Waltz. Jessie Matthews & Edmund Gwenn. Directed by Alfred Hitchcock. 1933. Britain. 80 min. Sound. 16mm B&W. *Rental:* Classic Film Mus.

Wan: Rice Bowl. 1962. 48 min. Sound. 16mm Color. *Rental:* Filmmakers Coop.

Wanda & the Wicked Princess. (Animated). 55 min. Sound. 16mm Color. *Rental:* Films Inc.

Wanderer, The. Japan. (Cast unlisted). 90 min. Sound. 16mm B&W. *Sale:* Japan Society.

Wanderer, The: Trans. Title: Grand Meaulnes, Le. Brigitte Fossey & Jean Blaise. Directed by Jean- Gabriel Albicocco. Fr. 1969. France. 103 min. Sound. 16mm Color. *Rental:* Kit Parker. *Rental:* Kit Parker, Anamorphic version. *Sale:* Kit Parker, Videotape version.

Wanderers, The. Ken Wahl & Karen Allen. Directed by Philip Kaufman. 1979. Orion. 113 min. Sound. 16mm Color. *Rental:* Films Inc.

Wandering Through Winter. 1970. Xerox. (Documentary). 50 min. Sound. 16mm Color. *Rental:* Cinema Guild, Syracuse U Film & Xerox Films. *Sale:* Xerox Films.

Wanderlust see Mary Jane's Pa.

Wanted By the Law. H. B. Warner. Directed by Robert N. Bradbury. 1924. Sunset. 50 min. Silent. 16mm B&W. *Rental:* Willoughby Peer.

Wanted By the Police. Frankie Darro & Mantan Moreland. Directed by Howard Bretherton. 1940. Monogram. 50 min. Sound. 16mm B&W. *Rental:* Hurlock Cine.

Wanted: Dead or Alive. Whip Wilson. Directed by Thomas Carr. 1951. Monogram. 55 min. Sound. 16mm B&W. *Rental:* Hurlock Cine.

Wanted for Murder. Trans. Title: Voice in the Night, A. Eric Portman & Dulcie Gray. Directed by Lawrence Huntington. 1946. Britain. 91 min. Sound. 16mm B&W. *Rental:* A Twyman Pres & Twyman Films.

Wanted: Jane Turner. Lee Tracy & Paul Guilfoyle. Directed by Edward Killy. 1936. RKO. 69 min. Sound. 16mm B&W. *Rental:* RKO General Pics.

Wanted, an Actress see Thomas Graal's Best Film.

War & Peace. Audrey Hepburn & Henry Fonda. Directed by King Vidor. 1956. Paramount. 208 min. Sound. 16mm Color. *Rental:* Films Inc.

War Arrow. Maureen O'Hara & Jeff Chandler. Directed by George Sherman. 1953. Universal. 78 min. Sound. 16mm Color. *Rental:* Swank Motion.

War at Home, The. Directed by Alexander Brown & Glenn Silber. First Run. (Documentary). 100 min. Sound. 16mm Color. *Rental:* First Run. *Lease:* First Run.

War Between Men & Women, The. Jack Lemmon & Barbara Harris. Directed by Melville Shavelson. 1972. National General. 110 min. Sound. 16mm Color. *Rental:* Roas Films & Swank Motion.

War Between the Planets, The see War of the Planets.

War Between the Tates, The. Richard Crenna & Elizabeth Ashley. Directed by Lee Philips. 1976. Susskind. 99 min. Videotape Color. *Sale:* Time-Life Multimedia.

War Comes to America. Directed by Frank Capra. 1945. War Department. (Documentary). 67 min. Sound. 16mm B&W. *Rental:* Budget Films, Images Film, Iowa Films, Kit Parker, La Inst Res Ctr, Maljack Productions, Museum Mod Art, Natl AV Ctr, Syracuse U Film & Twyman Films. *Sale:* Festival Films & Reel Images. *Lease:* Museum Mod Art. *Sale:* Festival Films & Natl Av Ctr, Videotape version.

War Drums. Lex Barker, Joan Taylor & Ben Johnson. Directed by Reginald Le Borg. 1957. MGM. 75 min. Sound. 16mm Color. *Rental:* MGM United.

War from the Air. 1975. 58 min. Sound. Videotape *Rental:* PBS Video. *Sale:* PBS Video.

War Game, The. Michael Aspel. Directed by Peter Watkins. 1966. Britain. 47 min. Sound. Videotape B&W. *Sale:* Tamarelles French Film.

War Games. Matthew Broderick & Dabney Coleman. Directed by John Badham. 1983. MGM. 114 min. Sound. 16mm Color. *Rental:* MGM United. *Rental:* MGM United, Videotape version.

War Goddess, The. Alena Johnston & Luciana Paluzzi. Directed by Terence Young. 1975. Italy. 89 min. Sound. 16mm Color. dubbed. *Rental:* Swank Motion.

War Gods of the Deep. Orig. Title: City Under the Sea. Vincent Price & Tab Hunter. Directed by Jacques Tourneur. 1965. American International. 85 min. Sound. 16mm Color. *Rental:* Westcoast Films & Wholesome Film Ctr.

War Hunt. John Saxon & Robert Redford. Directed by Denis Sanders. 1962. MGM. 81 min. Sound. 16mm B&W. *Rental:* MGM United.

War in the Pacific. (Documentary). Sound. 16mm B&W. *Rental:* Film Classics. *Rental:* Film Classics, Videotape version.

War Is Hell. Tony Russell. Directed by Burt Topper. 1963. Allied Artists. 81 min. Sound. 16mm B&W. *Rental:* Hurlock Cine.

War Is Over, The see Guerre Est Finie.

War, Italian Style. Orig. Title: Two Marines & a General. Buster Keaton & Martha Hyer. Directed by Luigi Scattini. 1967. Italy. 130 min. Sound. 16mm Color. dubbed. *Rental:* Films Inc, Kerr Film, Welling Motion Pictures & Westcoast Films. *Rental:* Welling Motion Pictures, 84 mins. version.

War Lord, The. Charlton Heston & Richard Boone. Directed by Franklin Schaffner. 1965. Universal. 130 min. Sound. 16mm Color. *Rental:* Williams Films.

War Lover, The. Steve McQueen & Robert Wagner. Directed by Philip Leacock. 1963. Columbia. 105 min. Sound. 16mm B&W. *Rental:* Charard Motion Pics, Films Inc, Modern Sound, Wholesome Film Ctr & Budget Films.

War Machine, The. 1981. 50 min. Sound. 16mm Color. *Rental:* U Mich Media.

War Nurse, The. Robert Montgomery & June Walker. Directed by Edgar Selwyn. 1930. MGM. 81 min. Sound. 16mm B&W. *Rental:* MGM United.

War of Eighteen-Twelve, The. 1968. Canada. (Documentary). 58 min. Sound. 16mm B&W. *Rental:* U Cal Media.

War of the Colossal Beast, The. Orig. Title: Terror Strikes. Sally Fraser & Roger Pace. Directed by Bert I. Gordon. 1958. American International. 69 min. Sound. 16mm B&W. *Rental:* Films Inc.

War of the Fools, The. Peter Kostka & Miroslav Holub. Directed by Karel Zeman. 1964. Czechoslovakia. 90 min. Sound. 16mm B&W. dubbed. *Rental:* Films Inc.

War of the Gargantuas, The. Russ Tamblyn. Directed by Henry G. Saperstein. 1970. Japan. 89 min. Sound. 16mm Color. dubbed. *Rental:* Budget Films, Cine Craft, Films Inc, Kerr Film, Roas Films, Film Ctr DC, Video Comm, Westcoast Films, Welling Motion Pictures & Wholesome Film Ctr.

War of the Gods, The. 1972. Britain. (Documentary). 66 min. Sound. 16mm Color. *Rental:* U Mich Media.

War of the Planets, The. Orig. Title: War Between the Planets. Lisa Gastoni & Franco Nero. Directed by Anthony Dawson. 1970. Italy. 92 min. Sound. 16mm Color. dubbed. *Rental:* MGM United.

War of the Wildcats, The. Orig. Title: In Old Oklahoma. John Wayne & Martha Scott. Directed by Albert S. Rogell. 1943. Republic. 102 min. Sound. 16mm B&W. *Rental:* Ivy Films. *Lease:* Rep Pic Film.

War of the Worlds, The. Gene Barry & Ann Robinson. Directed by Byron Haskin. 1953. Paramount. 85 min. Sound. 16mm Color. *Rental:* Films Inc.

War of the Zombies, The. John Drew Barrymore. Directed by Giuseppe Vari. 1965. American International. 80 min. Sound. 16mm Color. dubbed. *Rental:* Films Inc & Westcoast Films.

War Party, The. Michael T. Mikler. Directed by Lesley Selander. 1965. Fox. 72 min. Sound. 16mm B&W. *Rental:* Films Inc.

War Story, A. Directed by Anne Wheeler. 1981. 81 min. 16mm Color. *Rental:* National Film & U Cal Media.

War Wagon, The. John Wayne & Kirk Douglas. Directed by Burt Kennedy. 1967. Universal. 104 min. Sound. 16mm Color. *Rental:* Swank Motion. *Rental:* Swank Motion, Anamorphic color version.

Warao, The. 1978. U. of California. (Documentary). 57 min. Sound. 16mm Color. *Rental:* U Cal Media. *Sale:* U Cal Media. *Sale:* U Cal Media, Videotape version.

Warlock. Richard Widmark & Henry Fonda. Directed by Edward Dmytryk. 1959. Fox. (Anamorphic). 122 min. Sound. 16mm Color. *Rental:* Films Inc.

Warlords of Atlantis. Doug McClure, Peter Gilmore & Cyd Charisse. 1978. Columbia. 96 min. Sound. 16mm Color. *Rental:* Arcus Film, Budget Films, Williams Films, Modern Sound, Newman Film Lib, Swank Motion, Twyman Films, Westcoast Films & Wholesome Film Ctr.

Warlords of Crete *see* Minotaur.

Warm December, A. Sidney Poitier & Esther Anderson. Directed by Sidney Poitier. 1973. National General. 100 min. Sound. 16mm Color. *Rental:* Williams Films & Swank Motion.

Warning Shadows. Orig. Title: Schatten. Fritz Kortner. Directed by Arthur Robison. 1923. Germany. 96 min. Silent. 16mm B&W. *Rental:* A Twyman Pres, Budget Films, Em Gee Film Lib, Museum Mod Art & Kit Parker. *Sale:* Glenn Photo, Morcraft Films & Reel Images. *Sale:* Glenn Photo, Super 8 version.

Warning Shot! David Janssen & Ed Begley. Directed by Buzz Kulik. 1966. Paramount. 100 min. Sound. 16mm Color. *Rental:* Films Inc.

Warpath. Edmond O'Brien & Dean Jagger. Directed by Byron Haskin. 1951. Paramount. 95 min. Sound. 16mm Color. *Rental:* Films Inc.

Warrendale. John Brown & Terry Adler. Directed by Allan King. 1966. Janus. 100 min. Sound. 16mm B&W. *Rental:* Films Inc.

Warrior, The. 1974. Media Guild. (Documentary). 52 min. Videotape Color. *Rental:* Media Guild. *Sale:* Media Guild.

Warrior & the Slave Girl, The. Gianna Maria Canale & Georges Marchal. Directed by Vittorio Cottafavi. 1960. Italy. 89 min. Sound. 16mm B&W. dubbed. *Rental:* Cine Craft, Film Ctr DC & Inst Cinema.

Warrior Empress, The. Tina Louise & Kerwin Mathews. Directed by Pietro Francisci. 1961. Columbia. 97 min. Sound. 16mm Color. *Lease:* Time-Life Multimedia.

Warriors, The. Errol Flynn & Joanne Dru. Directed by Henry Levin. 1955. Allied Artists. 85 min. Sound. 16mm Color. *Rental:* Hurlock Cine.

Warriors, The. Michael Beck & James Remar. Directed by Walter Hill. 1979. Paramount. 94 min. Sound. 16mm Color. *Rental:* Films Inc.

Warsaw Ghetto, The. 1967. Britain. (Documentary). 51 min. Sound. 16mm B&W. *Rental:* Alden Films, Budget Films, Images Film & U Mich Media.

Warsaw-Quebec: How Not to Destroy a City. 1975. Canada. (Documentary). 57 min. Sound. 16mm Color. *Rental:* Natl Film CN. *Sale:* Natl Film CN.

Warsaw Story, The. 1978. Poland. (Documentary). 50 min. Sound. 16mm Color. narrated Eng. *Rental:* Polish People.

Washington Irving's Spain. 1974. National Geographic. (Documentary). 50 min. Sound. 16mm Color. *Rental:* Modern Talking & Natl Geog. *Sale:* Natl Geog. *Sale:* Natl Geog, Videotape version.

Washington Melodrama. Frank Morgan & Lee Bowman. Directed by S. Sylvan Simon. 1941. MGM. 80 min. Sound. 16mm B&W. *Rental:* MGM United.

Washington Merry-Go-Round. Lee Tracy & Walter Connolly. Directed by James Cruze. 1932. Columbia. 80 min. Sound. 16mm B&W. *Rental:* Kit Parker.

Washington Story, The. Orig. Title: Target for Scandal. Van Johnson & Patricia Neal. Directed by Robert Pirosh. 1952. MGM. 82 min. Sound. 16mm B&W. *Rental:* MGM United.

Washington: The Last Plantation. 1973. American Educational. (Documentary). 50 min. Sound. 16mm Color. *Rental:* Am Ed Films. *Sale:* Am Ed Films.

Washoe. Western Artists. (Documentary). 56 min. Sound. 16mm B&W. *Sale:* McGraw-Hill Films.

Wasp Woman, The. Susan Cabot. Directed by Roger Corman. 1959. Allied Artists. 72 min. Sound. 16mm B&W. *Rental:* Hurlock Cine. *Sale:* Reel Images.

Watashi Wa Nakanai *see* I'll Never Cry!.

Watashi Wa Nisai *see* Being Two Isn't Easy.

Watch, The. Japan. (Cast unlisted). 50 min. Sound. 16mm B&W. *Sale:* Japan Society.

Watch on the Rhine. Bette Davis & Paul Lukas. Directed by Herman Shumlin. 1943. Warners. 114 min. Sound. 16mm B&W. *Rental:* MGM United.

Watch on the Ruhr. 1958. McGraw-Hill. (Documentary). 54 min. Sound. 16mm B&W. *Rental:* U Mich Media.

Watch Out - We're Mad. Bud Spencer & Terence Hill. Directed by Marcello Fondato. 1979. Italy. 102 min. Sound. 16mm Color. dubbed. *Rental:* Films Inc, Modern Sound & Williams Films.

Watch the Birdie. Red Skelton. Directed by Jack Donohue. 1951. MGM. 71 min. Sound. 16mm B&W. *Rental:* MGM United.

Watch Your Stern. Kenneth Connor & Leslie Phillips. Directed by Gerald Thomas. 1961. Britain. 88 min. Sound. 16mm B&W. *Rental:* Film Ctr DC.

Watch Your Wife. Pat O'Malley & Virginia Valli. Directed by Sven Gade. 1926. Universal. 75 min. Silent. 16mm B&W. *Rental:* Mogulls Films.

Watcher in the Woods, The. Bette Davis, Jane Alexander & Glynnis O'Connor. Directed by John Hough. 1980. Disney. 106 min. Sound. 16mm Color. *Rental:* Swank Motion & Williams Films.

Water Crisis, The. 1980. McGraw-Hill. (Documentary). 57 min. Sound. Videotape Color. *Rental:* U Mich Media.

Water Famine, The. 1961. CBS. (Documentary). 54 min. Sound. 16mm B&W. *Rental:* U Mich Media & Syracuse U Film. *Sale:* Carousel Films.

Water: More Precious Than Oil. 1980. 58 min. Sound. Videotape *Rental:* PBS Video. *Sale:* PBS Video.

Water Planet, The. 1976. Metromedia. (Documentary). 52 min. Sound. 16mm Color. *Rental:* Churchill Films. *Rental:* Churchill Films, Videotape version.

Water Rustlers. Dorothy Paige. Directed by Samuel Diege. 1939. Grand National. 60 min. Sound. 16mm B&W. *Rental:* Video Comm. *Sale:* Morcraft Films. *Sale:* Morcraft Films, Super 8 sound version.

Waterfront. Dennis Morgan & Ward Bond. Directed by Terry Morse. 1939. Warners. 59 min. Sound. 16mm B&W. *Rental:* MGM United.

Waterfront Lady. Ann Rutherford & Barbara Pepper. Directed by Joseph Santley. 1935. Mascot. 70 min. Sound. 16mm B&W. *Rental:* Budget Films.

Waterhole Number Three. James Coburn & Joan Blondell. Directed by William Graham. 1968. Paramount. 95 min. Sound. 16mm Color. *Rental:* Films Inc.

Waterloo. Rod Steiger & Christopher Plummer. Directed by Sergei Bondarchuk. 1971. Paramount. (Anamorphic). 123 min. Sound. 16mm Color. *Rental:* Films Inc.

Waterloo Bridge. Vivien Leigh & Robert Taylor. Directed by Mervyn LeRoy. 1940. MGM. 100 min. Sound. 16mm B&W. *Rental:* MGM United.

Waterloo Road. John Mills, Stewart Granger & Alastair Sim. Directed by Sidney Gilliat. 1944. Britain. 74 min. Sound. 16mm B&W. *Rental:* Budget Films.

Watermelon Man, The. Godfrey Cambridge & Estelle Parsons. Directed by Melvin Van Peebles. 1970. Columbia. 100 min. Sound. 16mm Color. *Rental:* Budget Films, Cine Craft, Films Inc, Kit Parker, Modern Sound, Natl Film Video, Roas Films, Swank Motion, Twyman Films, Welling Motion Pictures, Westcoast Films, Wholesome Films Ctr & Williams Films.

Watermen. Directed by Roman V. Slezas & Holly Fisher. 1972. Odeon. (Documentary). 53 min. Sound. 16mm Color. *Rental:* Odeon Films. *Sale:* Odeon Films.

Watership Down. Directed by Martin Rosen. 1978. Embassy. (Animated). 87 min. Sound. 16mm Color. *Rental:* Films Inc.

Wattstax. Directed by Mel Stuart. 1973. Columbia. (Documentary). 100 min. Sound. 16mm Color. *Rental:* Budget Films, Cine Craft, Corinth Films, Swank Motion & Westcoast Films.

Watusi. George Montgomery & Taina Elg. Directed by Kurt Neumann. 1959. MGM. 85 min. Sound. 16mm Color. *Rental:* MGM United.

Wave, a Wac & a Marine, A. Elyse Knox & Henny Youngman. Directed by Phil Karlson. 1944. Monogram. 73 min. Sound. 16mm B&W. *Sale:* Classics Assoc NY.

Wavelength. 1967. 45 min. Sound. 16mm Color. *Rental:* Canyon Cinema.

Waves, The: Redes. Directed by Fred Zinnemann. 1936. Mexico. (Documentary). 60 min. Sound. 16mm B&W. *Rental:* Museum Mod Art.

Waxworks. Conrad Veidt, Emil Jannings & Werner Krauss. Directed by Paul Leni. 1924. Germany. 56 min. Silent. 16mm B&W. *Rental:* A Twyman Pres, Budget Films & Twyman Films.

Way Back Home. Orig. Title: Old Greatheart. Bette Davis & Phillips Lord. Directed by William A. Seiter. 1932. RKO. 81 min. Sound. 16mm B&W. *Rental:* Mogulls Films.

Way Down East. Lillian Gish & Richard Barthelmess. Directed by D. W. Griffith. 1920. United Artists. 110 min. Sound. 16mm B&W. *Rental:* A Twyman Pres, Images Film, Iowa Films, Kerr Film, Kit Parker, Museum Mod Art, Twyman Films, U Cal Media, Video Comm, Welling Motion Pictures & Wholesome Film Ctr. *Sale:* Cinema Concepts, E Finney, Festival Films, Glenn Photo, Morcraft Films, Natl Cinema, See-Art Films & Images Film. *Rental:* Budget Films, Films Inc, Swank Motion & Video Comm, *Sale:* Glenn Photo, Morcraft Films & Reel Images, Silent 16mm version. *Rental:* Killiam Collect, *Sale:* Glenn Photo, Silent tinted 16mm version. *Rental:* Ivy Films & Morcraft Films, *Sale:* Glenn Photo, Super 8 silent version. *Sale:* Cinema Concepts, Em Gee Film Lib, Festival Films, Ivy Films, Morcraft Films, Video Comm & Images Film, Videotape version. *Rental:* Westcoast Films, 135 mins version. *Rental:* Westcoast Films, 90 mins version.

Way For a Sailor, The. John Gilbert & Wallace Beery. Directed by Sam Wood. 1930. MGM. 83 min. Sound. 16mm B&W. *Rental:* MGM United.

Way It Is, The. 1967. NET. (Documentary). 60 min. Sound. 16mm B&W. *Rental:* Indiana AV Ctr, U Cal Media & U Mich Media. *Sale:* Indiana AV Ctr.

Way of a Gaucho, The. Rory Calhoun & Gene Tierney. Directed by Jacques Tourneur. 1952. Fox. 91 min. Sound. 16mm Color. *Rental:* Films Inc.

Way of All Flesh, The. Akim Tamiroff & Gladys George. Directed by Louis King. 1940. Paramount. 86 min. Sound. 16mm B&W. *Rental:* Swank Motion.

Way of Music, The. 1977. Miami-Dade. (Documentary). 60 min. Videotape Color. *Sale:* Films Inc.

Way of the Ancestors, The. 1978. 52 min. Sound. 16mm Color. *Rental:* Iowa Films & U Mich Media.

Way of the Artist, The. 1977. Miami-Dade. (Documentary). 60 min. Videotape Color. *Sale:* Films Inc.

Way of the Cross, The. 1966. NBC. (Documentary). 54 min. Sound. 16mm Color. *Rental:* Films Inc. *Sale:* Films Inc. *Sale:* Films Inc, Videotape version.

Way of the Strong, The. Mitchell Lewis & Alice Day. Directed by Frank Capra. 1928. Columbia. (Musical score only). 60 min. Sound. 16mm B&W. *Rental:* Kit Parker.

Way of the West, The. Wally Wales & Art Mix. Directed by Robert Tansey. 1935. 52 min. Sound. 16mm B&W. *Rental:* Budget Films.

Way of the Wind, The. Charles Tobias & Maynardo Ackerman. Directed by Charles Tobias. 1976. USA. 112 min. Sound. 16mm Color. *Rental:* BF Video & Budget Films.

Way of the World, The. 1977. Miami-Dade. (Cast Unlisted). 60 min. Videotape Color. *Sale:* Films Inc.

Way Out, The. Gene Nelson & Mona Freeman. Directed by Montgomery Tully. 1956. RKO. 90 min. Sound. 16mm B&W. *Rental:* Video Comm.

Way Out Men. 1966. Wolper. (Documentary). 50 min. Sound. 16mm B&W. *Rental:* Films Inc. *Sale:* Films Inc.

Way Out West. Stan Laurel & Oliver Hardy. Directed by James W. Horne. 1936. Hal Roach. 77 min. Sound. 16mm B&W. *Rental:* Alba House, Budget Films, Cine Craft, Em Gee Film Lib, Film Ctr DC, Film Images, Films Inc, Film Pres, Iowa Films, Ivy Films, Images Film, Kit Parker, Maljack, Modern Sound, Newman Film Lib, Roas Films, Swank Motion, Twyman Films, Video Comm, Welling Motion Pictures, Westcoast Films, Willoughby Peer & Williams Films. *Sale:* Blackhawk Films. *Sale:* Blackhawk Films, Super 8 sound version. *Rental:* Maljack & Video Comm, *Sale:* Blackhawk Films, Videotape version.

Way Out West. William Haines & Leila Hyams. Directed by Fred Niblo. 1930. MGM. 80 min. Sound. 16mm B&W. *Rental:* MGM United.

Way to the Gold, The. Jeffrey Hunter & Sheree North. Directed by Robert Webb. 1957. Fox. (Anamorphic). 95 min. Sound. 16mm B&W. *Rental:* Films Inc.

Way We Were, The. Barbra Streisand & Robert Redford. Directed by Sydney Pollack. 1973. Columbia/USA 118 min. Sound. 16mm Color. *Rental:* Arcus Films, Bosco Films, Budget Films, Cine Craft, Films Inc, Images Film, Modern Sound, Newman Film Lib, Swank Motion, Twyman Films, Welling Motion Pictures, Westcoast Films, Wholesome Film Ctr & Williams Films. *Rental:* Swank Motion, Anamorphic version. *Rental:* Images Film, Videotape version.

Way West, The. Kirk Douglas, Robert Mitchum & Richard Widmark. Directed by Andrew V. McLaglen. 1967. United Artists. 122 min. Sound. 16mm Color. *Rental:* MGM United.

Wayfarers, The. Lassie. 1955. Wrather. 76 min. Sound. 16mm B&W. *Rental:* Films Inc & Westcoast Films.

Ways of Women, The. Sven Johansen. Directed by Gabriel Axel. 1971. Sweden. 89 min. Sound. 16mm Color. dubbed. *Rental:* Hurlock Cine.

Wayward Bus, The. Jayne Mansfield & Joan Collins. Directed by Victor Vicas. 1957. Fox. (Anamorphic). 89 min. Sound. 16mm B&W. *Rental:* Films Inc.

Wayward Girl, The. Marcia Henderson & Barbara Eden. Directed by Lesley Selander. 1957. Republic. 72 min. Sound. 16mm B&W. *Rental:* Ivy Films. *Sale:* Rep Pic Film.

Wayward Wife, The: La Provinciale. Gina Lollobrigida. Directed by Mario Soldati. 1953. Italy. 115 min. Sound. 16mm B&W. dubbed. *Rental:* Cinema Guild.

Way...Way Out. Jerry Lewis. Directed by Gordon Douglas. 1966. Fox. (Anamorphic). 101 min. Sound. 16mm Color. *Rental:* Films Inc.

We All Came to America. 1976. Gould. (Documentary). 53 min. Sound. 16mm Color. *Rental:* Budget Films. *Sale:* Lucerne Films. *Sale:* Lucerne Films, Videotape version.

We All Loved Each Other So Much. Vittorio Gassman, Nino Manfredi & Stefania Sandrelli. Ital. 1977. Italy. 124 min. Sound. 16mm Color. subtitles. *Rental:* Cinema Five.

We Are All Arab Jews in Israel. Orig. Title: We Are All Jewish Arabs. Directed by Igaal Niddam. 1977. Israel. (Documentary). 120 min. Sound. 16mm Color. *Rental:* New Yorker Films. *Sale:* New Yorker Films.

We Are All Jewish Arabs see We Are All Arab Jews in Israel.

We Are All Picasso! Orig. Title: Bozarts. Directed by Jacques Giraldeau. 1974. Canada. (Documentary). 59 min. Sound. 16mm Color. dubbed. *Rental:* Natl Film CN. *Sale:* Natl Film CN.

We Are from Kronstadt. V. Zaichikov. Directed by Yefim Dzigan. 1936. Russia. 93 min. Sound. 16mm B&W. subtitles. *Rental:* Corinth Films.

We Are the Palestinian People. 1972. Cine News. (Documentary). 52 min. Sound. 16mm B&W. *Rental:* Canyon Cinema & Tricontinental Film. *Sale:* Tricontinental Film.

We Came to Ann Arbor. 1979. 50 min. Sound. 16mm Color. *Rental:* U Mich Media.

We Can Decide. 58 min. Sound. Videotape Color. *Rental:* PBS Video. *Sale:* PBS Video.

We Can Help: Specialized Training for Law Enforcement Professionals. 1976. 112 min. Sound. 16mm Color. *Rental:* Iowa Films.

We Demand Freedom. 1974. Third World Newsreel. (Documentary). 55 min. Sound. 16mm B&W. *Rental:* CA Newsreel.

We Dig Coal: A Portrait of Three Women. 58 min. Sound. 16mm Color. *Rental:* Cinema Guild.

We Live Again. Anna Sten & Fredric March. Directed by Rouben Mamoulian. 1934. Goldwyn. 82 min. Sound. 16mm B&W. *Rental:* Films Inc.

We of the Never Never. 1982. Australia. (Cast unlisted). 136 min. Sound. 16mm Color. *Rental:* Swank Motion.

We Saw It Happen. 1954. U. S. Government. (Documentary). 58 min. Sound. 16mm B&W. *Rental:* U Mich Media.

We Still Kill the Old Way. Gian Maria Volonte & Irene Papas. Directed by Elio Petri. Ital. 1968. Italy. 92 min. Sound. 16mm Color. subtitles. *Rental:* MGM United.

We Went to College. Walter Abel & Una Merkel. Directed by Joseph Santley. 1936. MGM. 69 min. Sound. 16mm B&W. *Rental:* MGM United.

We Were German Jews. Directed by Michael Blackwood. 58 min. 16mm Color. *Rental:* Blackwood. *Sale:* Blackwood.

We Were One Man. Serge Avedikian & Piotr Stanislas. Directed by Phillippe Valois. Fr. 1980. France. 90 min. Sound. Videotape Color. subtitles. *Sale:* Tamarelles French Film.

We Were Strangers. Jennifer Jones & John Garfield. Directed by John Huston. 1949. Columbia. 105 min. Sound. 16mm B&W. *Rental:* Bosco Films & Kit Parker.

We Who Are About to Die. Preston Foster & John Beal. Directed by Christy Cabanne. 1936. RKO. 82 min. Sound. 16mm B&W. *Rental:* RKO General Pics.

We Will Freeze in the Dark. 1977. McGraw-Hill. (Documentary). 45 min. Sound. 16mm Color. *Rental:* U of IL Film & McGraw-Hill Films. *Sale:* McGraw-Hill Films.

We're in the Army Now see Pack Up Your Troubles.

Weapon, The. Steve Cochran & Lizabeth Scott. Directed by Val Guest. 1957. Republic. 80 min. Sound. 16mm B&W. *Rental:* Ivy Films. *Sale:* Rep Pic Film.

Weather Machine, The. 1977. PBS. (Documentary). 117 min. Sound. 16mm Color. *Rental:* U Cal Media & Indiana AV Ctr. *Sale:* Indiana AV Ctr. *Sale:* Indiana AV Ctr, Videotape version.

Weavers, Wasn't That a Time, The. Pete Seeger & Lee Hays. Directed by Jim Brown. 1982. Jim Brown/ United Artists. Films Inc. 78 min. Sound. Videotape Color. *Rental:* Direct Cinema & Films Inc.

Web, The. Ella Raines & Edmond O'Brien. Directed by Michael Gordon. 1947. Universal. 87 min. Sound. 16mm B&W. *Rental:* Swank Motion.

Web of Danger. Bill Kennedy & Adele Mara. Directed by Philip Ford. 1947. Republic. 58 min. Sound. 16mm B&W. *Rental:* Ivy Films. *Sale:* Rep Pic Film.

Web of Evidence. Orig. Title: Beyond This Place. Van Johnson & Vera Miles. Directed by Jack Cardiff. 1959. Allied Artists. 88 min. Sound. 16mm B&W. *Rental:* Ivy Films. *Sale:* Rep Pic Film.

Web of Fear. Michele Morgan & Dany Saval. Directed by Francois Villiers. 1964. France-Spain. 90 min. Sound. 16mm B&W. dubbed. *Rental:* Ivy Films.

Web of the Spider. Anthony Franciosa. Directed by Anthony Dawson. 1970. Cinema Shares. 90 min. Sound. 16mm Color. *Rental:* Budget Films & Films Inc.

Webs of Steel. Helen Holmes. Directed by J. P. McGowan. 1925. Anchor. 50 min. Silent. 16mm B&W. *Rental:* Mogulls Films. *Rental:* Willoughby Peer, Silent 8mm version.

Webster Groves Revisited. 1966. CBS. (Documentary). 53 min. Sound. 16mm B&W. *Rental:* Twyman Films, U Cal Media & U Mich Media. *Sale:* Carousel Films.

Wedding, A. Carol Burnett & Geraldine Chaplin. Directed by Robert Altman. 1978. Fox. 125 min. Sound. 16mm Color. *Rental:* Films Inc.

Wedding, The. Daniel Olbrychski & Emilia Krakowska. Directed by Andrzej Wajda. Pol. 1975. Poland. 110 min. Sound. 16mm Color. subtitles. *Rental:* Amerpol Ent.

Wedding, The. 1973. Milwaukee Rep. Theater. (Cast unlisted). 54 min. Sound. 16mm B&W. *Rental:* Modern Mass. *Sale:* Modern Mass.

Wedding Bells *see* Royal Wedding.

Wedding Breakfast *see* Catered Affair.

Wedding Camels, The. Directed by David MacDougall & Judith MacDougall. 1978. Extension Media Center. (Documentary). 108 min. Sound. 16mm Color. *Rental:* U Cal Media. *Sale:* U Cal Media. *Sale:* U Cal Media, Videotape version.

Wedding in Blood. Stephane Audran & Michel Piccoli. Directed by Claude Chabrol. Fr. 1974. France. 98 min. Sound. 16mm Color. subtitles. *Rental:* New Line Cinema.

Wedding in White. Donald Pleasance & Carol Kane. Directed by William Fruett. 1972. Canada. 103 min. Sound. 16mm Color. *Rental:* Museum Mod Art.

Wedding Night. Gary Cooper & Anna Sten. Directed by King Vidor. 1935. Goldwyn. 85 min. Sound. 16mm B&W. *Rental:* Films Inc.

Wedding of Palo, The. Directed by F. Dalsheim & Knud Rasmussen. Icelandic. 1934. Denmark. (Documentary). 72 min. Sound. 16mm B&W. subtitles. *Rental:* Em Gee Film Lib & Museum Mod Art. *Sale:* Glenn Photo.

Wedding Party, The. Robert DeNiro & Jill Clayburgh. Directed by Wilford Leach, Brian De Palma & Cynthia Munroe. 1969. Ondine. 90 min. Sound. Videotape B&W. *Sale:* Vidamerica.

Weddings & Babies. Viveca Lindfors & John Myhers. Directed by Morris Engel. 1958. Engel. 81 min. Sound. 16mm B&W. *Rental:* Films Inc.

Weddings Are Wonderful. June Clyde & Rene Day. Directed by Maclean Rogers. 1941. Britain. 72 min. Sound. 16mm B&W. *Rental:* Ivy Films. *Sale:* Rep Pic Film.

Wednesday's Child. Edward Arnold & Frankie Thomas. Directed by Pandro S. Berman. 1935. RKO. 69 min. Sound. 16mm B&W. *Rental:* RKO General Pics.

Wee Willie Winkie. Shirley Temple & Victor McLaglen. Directed by John Ford. 1937. Fox. 75 min. Sound. 16mm B&W. *Rental:* Films Inc.

Week-End in Havana. Alice Faye & John Payne. Directed by Walter Lang. 1941. Fox. 80 min. Sound. 16mm Color. *Rental:* Films Inc.

Week-End a Zuydcote *see* Weekend at Dunkirk.

Weekend. Mireille Darc & Jean Yanne. Directed by Jean-Luc Godard. Fr. 1968. France. 105 min. Sound. 16mm Color. subtitles. *Rental:* New Cinema & New Yorker Films.

Weekend at Dunkirk. Orig. Title: Week-End a Zuydcote. Jean-Paul Belmondo & Catherine Spaak. Directed by Henri Verneuil. 1964. France-Italy. 101 min. Sound. 16mm B&W. dubbed. *Rental:* Films Inc.

Weekend at the Waldorf. Ginger Rogers, Lana Turner & Van Johnson. Directed by Robert Z. Leonard. 1945. MGM. 120 min. Sound. 16mm B&W. *Rental:* MGM United.

Weekend Athletes, The. 1978. Best. (Documentary). 48 min. Sound. 16mm Color. *Rental:* Best Films & U of IL Film. *Sale:* Best Films.

Weekend for Three. Dennis O'keefe & Jane Wyatt. Directed by Tay Garnett. 1942. RKO. 66 min. Sound. 16mm B&W. *Rental:* RKO General Pics.

Weekend in Vermont. 1976. Britain. (Documentary). 150 min. Sound. 16mm Color. *Rental:* Films Inc & U Cal Media. *Sale:* Films Inc. *Sale:* Films Inc, Videotape version.

Weekend Marriage. Orig. Title: Working Wives. Loretta Young & George Brent. Directed by Thornton Freeland. 1932. Warners. 66 min. Sound. 16mm B&W. *Rental:* MGM United.

Weekend Murders, The. Anna Moffo & Lance Percival. Directed by Michele Lupo. 1972. Italy. 98 min. Sound. 16mm Color. dubbed. *Rental:* MGM United.

Weekend with Father. Van Heflin & Patricia Neal. Directed by Douglas Sirk. 1951. Universal. 83 min. Sound. 16mm B&W. *Rental:* Swank Motion.

Weekend with the Babysitter. Susan Romen. Directed by Don Henderson. 1970. Britain. 93 min. Sound. 16mm Color. *Rental:* Video Comm. *Lease:* Video Comm. *Rental:* Video Comm, *Lease:* Video Comm, Videotape version.

Week's Vacation, A. Nathalie Baye & Gerard Lanvin. Directed by Bertrand Tavernier. Fr. 1980. France. 102 min. Sound. 16mm Color. subtitles. *Rental:* Films Inc.

Weird, Wicked World! 1965. ABC. (Documentary). 82 min. Sound. 16mm Color. *Rental:* Films Inc.

Welcome Home. Erik Jacobson. 54 min. Sound. 16mm Color. *Rental:* Gospel Films.

Welcome Home, Soldier Boys. Joe Don Baker. Directed by Richard Compton. 1972. Fox. 91 min. Sound. 16mm Color. *Rental:* Films Inc.

Welcome, Mr. Marshall! Lolita Sevilla & Manolo Moran. Directed by Luis G. Berlanga. Span. 1953. Spain. 86 min. Sound. 16mm B&W. subtitles. *Rental:* Films Inc. *Rental:* Films Inc, Dubbed version.

Welcome Mr. Washington. Peggy Cummins & Donald Stewart. Directed by Leslie Hiscott. 1945. Britain. 88 min. Sound. 16mm B&W. *Rental:* Ivy Films. *Sale:* Rep Pic Film.

Welcome Stranger. Bing Crosby & Barry Fitzgerald. Directed by Elliott Nugent. 1947. Paramount. 107 min. Sound. 16mm B&W. *Rental:* Swank Motion.

Welcome to Britain. Directed by Ben Lewin. 1975. Britain. (Documentary). 72 min. Sound. 16mm Color. *Rental:* Museum Mod Art.

Welcome to Clinton County. 1979. Penn State. (Documentary). 58 min. Sound. 16mm Color. *Rental:* Penn St AV Serv. *Sale:* Penn St AV Serv. *Rental:* Penn St AV Serv, *Sale:* Penn St AV Serv, Videotape version.

Welcome to Hard Times. Henry Fonda & Janice Rule. Directed by Burt Kennedy. 1967. MGM. 103 min. Sound. 16mm Color. *Rental:* MGM United.

Welcome to L. A. Keith Carradine & Sally Kellerman. Directed by Alan Rudolph. 1978. United Artists. 106 min. Sound. 16mm Color. *Rental:* MGM United.

Welcome to Pepperland. (Concert). 52 min. Sound. 16mm Color. *Rental:* Video Comm.

Welcome to Yap. 1980. 58 min. Sound. Videotape *Rental:* PBS Video. *Sale:* PBS Video.

Welfare. Directed by Frederick Wiseman. 1975. Zipporah. (Documentary). 167 min. Sound. 16mm B&W. *Rental:* Zipporah Films. *Lease:* Zipporah Films, Videotape version.

Welfare Revolt, The. Directed by Herbert Krosney. 1968. NET. (Documentary). 60 min. Sound. 16mm B&W. *Rental:* Indiana AV Ctr & U Cal Media. *Sale:* Indiana AV Ctr.

Well, The. Richard Rober & Harry Morgan. Directed by Leo Popkin & Russell Rouse. 1951. United Artists. 85 min. Sound. 16mm B&W. *Rental:* Budget Films, Films Inc, Kit Parker & Video Comm. *Lease:* Video Comm.

We'll Bury You! 1963. Columbia. (Documentary). 74 min. Sound. 16mm B&W. *Rental:* Kit Parker.

Well-Digger's Daughter, The. Trans. Title: Fille Du Puisatier, La. Raimu, Fernandel & Josette Day. Directed by Marcel Pagnol. Fr. 1946. France. 120 min. Sound. 16mm B&W. subtitles. *Rental:* Budget Films, Corinth Films & Kit Parker.

Well-Groomed Bride, The. Olivia De Havilland & Ray Milland. Directed by Sidney Lanfield. 1946. Paramount. 75 min. Sound. 16mm B&W. *Rental:* Swank Motion.

Well of Love. Lassie & Bruce Bennett. Wrather. 76 min. Sound. 16mm Color. *Rental:* Modern Sound.

We'll Smile Again. Flanagan & Allen. Directed by John Baxter. 1948. Britain. 59 min. Sound. 16mm B&W. *Rental:* Ivy Films. *Sale:* Rep Pic Film.

Wells Fargo. Joel McCrea & Frances Dee. Directed by Frank Lloyd. 1937. Paramount. 94 min. Sound. 16mm B&W. *Rental:* Swank Motion.

Wells Fargo Gunmaster. Allan Lane. Directed by Philip Ford. 1951. Republic. 60 min. Sound. 16mm B&W. *Rental:* Ivy Films. *Sale:* Rep Pic Film.

Wellsprings. 1976. WPBT. (Documentary). 58 min. Sound. 16mm Color. *Rental:* U Mich Media.

We're Alive. 1974. Iris. (Color sequences, documentary). 50 min. Sound. 16mm B&W. *Rental:* New Cinema.

We're Fighting Back. Kevin Mahon, Paul McCrane & Ellen Barkin. Directed by Lou Antonio. 1981. Highgate. 93 min. Sound. 16mm Color. *Rental:* Learning Corp Am. *Sale:* CBS Inc & Learning Corp Am.

We're in the Money. Joan Blondell & Glenda Farrell. Directed by Ray Enright. 1935. Warners. 65 min. Sound. 16mm B&W. *Rental:* MGM United.

We're in the Navy Now. Wallace Beery & Raymond Hatton. Directed by Edward Sutherland. 1926. Paramount. 70 min. Silent. 16mm B&W. *Rental:* Film Classics & Mogulls Films. *Sale:* Film Classics. *Rental:* Film Classics, *Sale:* Film Classics, Silent 8mm version.

We're Moving Up: The Hispanic Migration. 1980. NBC. (Documentary). 80 min. Videotape Color. *Rental:* Films Inc. *Sale:* Films Inc.

We're No Angels. Humphrey Bogart & Peter Ustinov. Directed by Michael Curtiz. 1955. Paramount. 103 min. Sound. 16mm Color. *Rental:* Films Inc.

We're Not Dressing. Bing Crosby & Carole Lombard. Directed by Norman Taurog. 1934. Paramount. 63 min. Sound. 16mm B&W. *Rental:* SWank Motion.

We're Not Married. Ginger Rogers & Marilyn Monroe. Directed by Edmund Goulding. 1952. Fox. 85 min. Sound. 16mm B&W. *Rental:* Films Inc.

We're Not the Jet Set. B. A. Peterson Family. Directed by Robert Duvall. 1977. Chekuee. 85 min. Sound. 16mm Color. *Rental:* Films Inc.

We're on the Jury. Victor Moore & Helen Broderick. Directed by Ben Holmes. 1937. RKO. 71 min. Sound. 16mm B&W. *Rental:* RKO General Pics.

We're Only Human. Preston Foster & Jane Wyatt. Directed by James Flood. 1936. RKO. 80 min. Sound. 16mm *Rental:* RKO General Pics.

We're Rich Again. Buster Crabbe & Billie Burke. Directed by Pandro S. Berman. 1934. RKO. 72 min. Sound. 16mm B&W. *Rental:* RKO General Pics.

Werewolf, The. Joyce Holden & Don Megowan. Directed by Fred F. Sears. 1956. Columbia. 80 min. Sound. 16mm B&W. *Rental:* Modern Sound.

Werewolf of London, The. Henry Hull & Valerie Hobson. Directed by Stuart Walker. 1935. Universal. 75 min. Sound. 16mm B&W. *Rental:* Swank Motion.

West & Soda. Directed by Bruno Bozzetto. 1965. Italy. (Animated). 90 min. Sound. 16mm Color. dubbed. *Rental:* Distribution Sixteen.

West Eleven. Eric Portman & Diana Dors. Directed by Michael Winner. 1963. Britain. 93 min. Sound. 16mm B&W. *Rental:* Liberty Co.

West Meets East. 1977. Britain. (Documentary). 52 min. Sound. 16mm Color. *Rental:* Iowa Films, U of IL Film & U Mich Media.

West of Broadway. John Gilbert, Lois Moran & El Brendel. Directed by Harry Beaumont. 1931. MGM. 66 min. Sound. 16mm B&W. *Rental:* MGM United.

West of Charles Russell, The. 2 pts. 1969. NBC. (Documentary). 53 min. Sound. 16mm Color. *Rental:* Films Inc, OK AV Ctr, Syracuse U Film & U Mich Media. *Sale:* Films Inc. *Sale:* Films Inc, Videotape version.

West of Cheyenne. Tom Tyler. Directed by Sam Nelson. 1931. 55 min. Sound. 16mm B&W. *Sale:* Natl Cinema.

West of Cimarron. Tom Tyler & Bob Steele. Directed by Lester Orlebeck. 1942. Republic. 56 min. Sound. 16mm B&W. *Rental:* Ivy Films. *Sale:* Rep Pic Film & Nostalgia Merchant.

West of Nevada. Rex Bell. Directed by Robert Hill. 1936. Colony. 60 min. Sound. 16mm B&W. *Rental:* Em Gee Film Lib & Mogulls Films. *Sale:* Glenn Photo.

West of Pinto Basin. The Range Busters. Directed by S. Roy Luby. 1940. Monogram. 56 min. Sound. 16mm B&W. *Rental:* Films Inc.

West of Shanghai. Boris Karloff & Beverly Roberts. Directed by John Farrow. 1937. Warners. 64 min. Sound. 16mm B&W. *Rental:* MGM United.

West of Texas *see* Shooting Irons.

West of the Alamo. Jimmy Wakely. Directed by Oliver Drake. 1946. Monogram. 60 min. Sound. 16mm B&W. *Rental:* Hurlock Cine.

West of the Badlands. Roy Rogers. 1940. Republic. 54 min. Sound. 16mm B&W. *Rental:* Ivy Films. *Sale:* Rep Pic Film.

West of the Divide. John Wayne. Directed by Robert N. Bradbury. 1934. Monogram. 60 min. Sound. 16mm B&W. *Rental:* Budget Films, Ivy Films & Mogulls Films. *Sale:* Classics Assoc NY, Rep Pic Film, Reel Images & Morcraft Films. *Sale:* Cinema Concepts, Reel Images & Thunderbird Films, Super 8 sound version.

West of the Law. Buck Jones & Tim McCoy. Directed by Howard Bretherton. 1942. Monogram. 60 min. Sound. 16mm B&W. *Rental:* Hurlock Cine. *Sale:* Reel Images.

West of the Rio Grande. Johnny Mack Brown. Directed by Lambert Hillyer. 1944. Monogram. 55 min. Sound. 16mm B&W. *Rental:* Hurlock Cine.

West of Wyoming. Johnny Mack Brown. Directed by Wallace Fox. 1950. Monogram. 55 min. Sound. 16mm B&W. *Rental:* Hurlock Cine.

West of Zanzibar. Lon Chaney. Directed by Tod Browning. 1929. MGM. 75 min. Silent. 16mm B&W. *Rental:* MGM United.

West Point of the Air. Robert Young & Wallace Beery. Directed by Richard Rosson. 1935. MGM. 90 min. Sound. 16mm B&W. *Rental:* MGM United.

West Side Kid, The. Don Barry & Peter Lawford. Directed by George Sherman. 1943. Republic. 58 min. Sound. 16mm B&W. *Rental:* Ivy Films.

West Side Story. Natalie Wood, Richard Beymer & Rita Moreno. Directed by Jerome Robbins & Robert Wise. 1961. United Artists. 155 min. Sound. 16mm Color. *Rental:* MGM United. *Rental:* MGM United, Videotape version.

West to Glory. Eddie Dean. Directed by Ray Taylor. 1947. PRC. 61 min. Sound. 16mm B&W. *Sale:* Classics Assoc NY.

West Virginia: Life, Liberty, & the Pursuit of Coal. 1973. 52 min. Sound. 16mm Color. *Rental:* Utah Media.

Westbound Limited. Ralph Lewis. Directed by Emory Johnson. 1923. FBO. 60 min. Silent. 16mm B&W. *Rental:* Budget Films & Em Gee Film Lib.

Westbound Stage. Tex Ritter. Directed by Spencer G. Bennett. 1940. Monogram. 55 min. Sound. 16mm B&W. *Rental:* Hurlock Cine.

Western Approaches *see* Raider.

Western Heritage. Tim Holt. Directed by Wallace Grissell. 1948. RKO. 61 min. Sound. 16mm B&W. *Rental:* Films Inc.

Western Jamboree. Gene Autry. Directed by Ralph Staub. 1938. Republic. 54 min. Sound. 16mm B&W. *Rental:* Ivy Films.

Western Justice. Bob Steele. Directed by Robert N. Bradbury. 1935. Commodore. 60 min. Sound. 16mm B&W. *Rental:* Budget Films. *Sale:* Morcraft Films.

Western Pacific Agent. Kent Taylor & Sheila Ryan. Directed by Sam Newfield. 1951. Lippert. 65 min. Sound. 16mm B&W. *Rental:* Bosco Films, Budget Films & Film Ctr Dc.

Western Terror. Orig. Title: Buzzy Rides the Range. Dave O'Brien. Directed by Richard C. Kahn. 1940. Astor. 57 min. Sound. 16mm B&W. *Rental:* Budget Films. *Sale:* Video Comm.

Western Union. Robert Young & Randolph Scott. Directed by Fritz Lang. 1941. Fox. 95 min. Sound. 16mm Color. *Rental:* Films Inc.

Westerner, The. Gary Cooper & Walter Brennan. Directed by William Wyler. 1940. Goldwyn. 100 min. Sound. 16mm B&W. *Rental:* Films Inc.

Westerplatte. Directed by Stanislaw Rozewicz. Pol. 1967. Poland. (Documentary). 85 min. Sound. 16mm B&W. subtitles. *Rental:* Polish People.

Westfront Nineteen Eighteen. Orig. Title: Four from the Infantry. Gustav Diessel. Directed by G. W. Pabst. Ger. 1930. Germany. 89 min. Sound. 16mm B&W. subtitles. *Rental:* Janus Films & Museum Mod Art.

Westland Case, The. Preston Foster & Barbara Pepper. Directed by Christy Cabanne. 1937. Universal. 70 min. Sound. 16mm B&W. *Rental:* Mogulls Films.

Westward Bound. Buffalo Bill Jr. Directed by Harry S. Webb. 1930. Syndicate. 58 min. Sound. 16mm B&W. *Sale:* Natl Cinema.

Westward Bound. Ken Maynard, Hoot Gibson & Bob Steele. Directed by Robert Tansey. 1944. Monogram. 60 min. Sound. 16mm B&W. *Rental:* Lewis Film.

Westward Ho! John Wayne. Directed by Robert N. Bradbury. 1935. Republic. 55 min. Sound. 16mm B&W. *Rental:* Ivy Films. *Sale:* Rep Pic Film.

Westward Movement, The. 5 pts. 1962. Encyclopaedia Britannica. (Documentary). 90 min. Sound. 16mm Color. *Rental:* Ency Brit Ed. *Sale:* Ency Brit Ed. *Sale:* Ency Brit Ed, Videotape version.

Westward Passage. Laurence Olivier & Bonita Granville. Directed by Robert Milton. 1932. RKO. 73 min. Sound. 16mm B&W. *Rental:* RKO General Pics.

Westward the Women. Robert Taylor & Denise Darcel. Directed by William A. Wellman. 1951. MGM. 118 min. Sound. 16mm B&W. *Rental:* MGM United.

Westward Trail. Eddie Dean. Directed by Ray Taylor. 1948. Eagle Lion. 60 min. Sound. 16mm B&W. *Sale:* Classics Assoc NY.

Westworld. Richard Benjamin & Yul Brynner. Directed by Michael Crichton. 1973. MGM. (Anamorphic). 88 min. Sound. 16mm Color. *Rental:* MGM United. *Rental:* MGM United, Videotape version.

Wet Earth & Warm People. 1973. Canada. (Documentary). 59 min. Sound. 16mm Color. *Rental:* Films Inc, Natl Film CN & Utah Media. *Sale:* Natl Film CN. *Rental:* Natl Film CN, *Sale:* Natl Film CN, Videotape version.

Wet Parade, The. Lewis Stone, Walter Huston & Jimmy Durante. Directed by Victor Fleming. 1932. MGM. 120 min. Sound. 16mm B&W. *Rental:* MGM United.

Wetbacks. Lloyd Bridges & Nancy Gates. Directed by Henry McCune. 1956. Banner. 80 min. Sound. 16mm B&W. *Rental:* Newman Film Lib.

We've Always Done It This Way. 1978. ATV. (Documentary). 52 min. Sound. 16mm Color. *Rental:* CA Newsreel & U Mich Media.

Whale of a Tale, A. William Shatner & Marty Allen. Directed by Erving M. Brown. 1975. Lukris. 90 min. Sound. 16mm Color. *Rental:* Films Inc.

Whale Watch. 1983. Nova. 57 min. Sound. 16mm Color. *Rental:* U Cal Media.

Whales. 1976. Metromedia. (Documentary). 52 min. Sound. 16mm Color. *Rental:* Churchill Films. *Rental:* Churchill Films, Videotape version.

Whales, Dolphins & Men. 1972. Nova. (Documentary). 51 min. Sound. 16mm Color. *Rental:* Films Inc & U Mich Media. *Sale:* Films Inc. *Rental:* Films Inc, *Sale:* Films Inc, Videotape version.

What a Blonde! Leon Errol & Richard Lane. Directed by Leslie Goodwins. 1945. RKO. 71 min. Sound. 16mm B&W. *Rental:* Films Inc.

What a Carve-Up *see* No Place Like Homicide.

What a Chassis! *see* Belle Americaine, La.

What a Man! *see* Never Give a Sucker an Even Break.

What a Way to Go! Shirley MacLaine & Paul Newman. Directed by J. Lee Thompson. 1964. Fox. (Anamorphic). 111 min. Sound. 16mm Color. *Rental:* Films Inc.

What a Woman! Rosalind Russell & Brian Aherne. Directed by Irving Cummings. 1943. Columbia. 100 min. Sound. 16mm B&W. *Lease:* Time-Life Multimedia.

What Are We Doing to Our Children?: Locked Up, Locked Out. 1973. CBS. 45 min. Sound. 16mm Color. *Rental:* Syracuse U Film & U Mich Media.

What Are We Doing to Our World? 2 pts. 1967. CBS. (Documentary). 54 min. Sound. 16mm Color. *Rental:* McGraw-Hill Films, Syracuse U Film, U Mich Media & Utah Media. *Sale:* McGraw-Hill Films.

What Became of Jack & Jill? Vanessa Howard & Mona Washburne. Directed by Bill Bain. 1972. Fox. 93 min. Sound. 16mm Color. *Rental:* Films Inc.

What Can I Tell You? 1980. Centre. (Documentary). 55 min. Sound. 16mm Color. *Rental:* Centre Co. *Sale:* Centre Co. *Sale:* Centre Co, Videotape version.

What Could You Do With a Nickel? Directed by Carla DeVito. 1982. Sound. 16mm Color.

What Did You Do in the War, Daddy? James Coburn & Dick Shawn. Directed by Blake Edwards. 1966. United Artists. 105 min. Sound. 16mm Color. *Rental:* MGM United.

What Did You Learn in School Today? 1972. WNET. (Documentary). 48 min. Sound. 16mm B&W. *Rental:* Indiana AV Ctr & U Cal Media. *Sale:* Indiana AV Ctr.

What Do You Say to a Naked Lady? Directed by Allen Funt. 1970. United Artists. (Documentary). 92 min. Sound. 16mm Color. *Rental:* Budget Films, MGM United & Welling Motion Pictures.

What Does Classical Music Mean? 1959. CBS. (Documentary). 59 min. Sound. 16mm B&W. *Rental:* McGraw-Hill Films, U of IL Media & U Mich Media. *Sale:* McGraw-Hill Films.

What Does Music Mean? 1962. CBS. (Documentary). 58 min. Sound. 16mm B&W. *Rental:* #McGraw-Hill Films, Syracuse U Film & U of IL Film. *Sale:* McGraw-Hill Films.

What Does Orchestration Mean? 2 pts. 1964. CBS. (Documentary). 55 min. Sound. 16mm B&W. *Rental:* OK AV Ctr, Syracuse U Film, U of IL Film & U Mich Media. *Sale:* McGraw-Hill Films.

What Ever Happened to Aunt Alice? Geraldine Page & Ruth Gordon. Directed by Lee Katzin. 1969. ABC. 101 min. Sound. 16mm Color. *Rental:* Films Inc. *Sale:* ABC Film Lib, Super 8 sound version.

What Every Woman Knows. Helen Hayes, Madge Evans & Brian Aherne. Directed by Gregory La Cava. 1934. MGM. 92 min. Sound. 16mm B&W. *Rental:* MGM United.

What Happened to Rosa? Mabel Normand & Tully Marshall. Directed by Victor Schertzinger. 1921. Goldwyn. 55 min. Silent. 16mm B&W. *Rental:* Em Gee Film Lib. *Sale:* Morcraft Films.

What Happens in a One Week T Group. 1974. 45 min. Sound. 16mm Color. *Rental:* U Mich Media.

What Harvest for the Reaper? 1967. NET. (Documentary). 59 min. Sound. 16mm B&W. *Rental:* Indiana AV Ctr & U Cal Media. *Sale:* Indiana AV Ctr.

What Is a Concerto? 1966. CBS. (Documentary). 61 min. Sound. 16mm B&W. *Rental:* McGraw-Hill Films, Syracuse U Film & U of IL Film. *Sale:* McGraw-Hill Films.

What Is a Melody? 1962. CBS. (Documentary). 53 min. Sound. 16mm B&W. *Rental:* U of IL Film, McGraw-Hill Films, U Mich Media, SD AV Ctr & Syracuse U Film. *Sale:* McGraw-Hill Films.

What Is a Mode? 1966. CBS. (Documentary). 59 min. Sound. 16mm B&W. *Rental:* U of IL Film. *Sale:* McGraw-Hill Films. *Rental:* Budget Films & McGraw-Hill Films, *Sale:* McGraw-Hill Films, Color version.

What Is American Music? 1967. CBS. (Documentary). 59 min. Sound. 16mm B&W. *Rental:* McGraw-Hill Films, SD AV Ctr, Syracuse U Film & U of IL Film. *Sale:* McGraw-Hill Films.

What Is Impressionism? 1967. CBS. (Documentary). 54 min. Sound. 16mm B&W. *Rental:* McGraw-Hill Films, Syracuse U Film & U of IL Film. *Sale:* McGraw-Hill Films.

What Is New? 1981. 49 min. Sound. 16mm Color. *Rental:* Utah Media.

What Is Sonata Form? 1967. CBS. (Documentary). 54 min. Sound. 16mm B&W. *Rental:* McGraw-Hill Films, Syracuse U Film & U of IL Film. *Sale:* McGraw-Hill Films.

What is This Thing Called Food? Directed by Thomas Tomizawa. 1976. NBC. (Documentary). 52 min. Sound. 16mm Color. *Rental:* Films Inc, U of IL Film & U Mich Media. *Sale:* Films Inc. *Sale:* Films Inc, Videotape version.

What Makes a Good Father? 1979. PBS. (Documentary). 60 min. Videotape Color. *Rental:* PBS Video. *Sale:* PBS Video.

What Makes Music Symphonic? 1958. CBS. (Documentary). 60 min. Sound. 16mm B&W. *Rental:* McGraw-Hill Films & Syracuse U Film. *Sale:* McGraw-Hill Films.

What Man Shall Live & Not See Death? 1971. NBC. (Documentary). 57 min. Sound. 16mm Color. *Rental:* Films Inc, Iowa Films, U Mich Media, OK AV Ctr & Syracuse U Film. *Sale:* Films Inc. *Sale:* Films Inc, Videotape version.

What! No Beer? Jimmy Durante & Buster Keaton. Directed by Edward Sedgwick. 1933. MGM. 66 min. Sound. 16mm B&W. *Rental:* MGM United.

What Parents Should Know About Drugs. ABC. 55 min. Sound. 16mm Color. *Rental:* MTI Tele.

What Price Coal? 1979. Nova. (Documentary). 60 min. Videotape Color. *Rental:* PBS Video. *Sale:* PBS Video.

What Price Crime? Charles Starrett. Directed by Al Herman. 1935. Beacon. 60 min. Sound. 16mm B&W. *Rental:* Mogulls Films.

What Price Glory? Victor McLaglen, Edmund Lowe & Dolores Del Rio. Directed by Raoul Walsh. 1926. Fox. (Musical score only, tinted). 122 min. Sound. 16mm *Rental:* Killiam Collect. *Sale:* Blackhawk Films, Super 8 sound version. *Sale:* Blackhawk Films, Super 8 silent version. *Rental:* Museum Mod Art, Silent 16mm version.

What Price Health? 1972. NBC. (Documentary). 53 min. Sound. 16mm Color. *Rental:* Films Inc, Iowa Films & U Mich Media. *Sale:* Films Inc.

What Price Hollywood? Constance Bennett & Lowell Sherman. Directed by George Cukor. 1932. RKO. 88 min. Sound. 16mm B&W. *Rental:* Films Inc. *Lease:* Films Inc.

What Price Valor. Lassie. 1960. Wrather. 52 min. Sound. 16mm Color. *Rental:* Budget Films & Films Inc.

What Shall We Do About Mother? 1980. CBS. (Documentary). 49 min. Sound. 16mm Color. *Rental:* Carousel Films, Iowa Films, Kent St U Film, Syracuse U Film, U Cal Media & U Mich Media. *Sale:* Carousel Films. *Sale:* Carousel Films, Videotape version.

What the Peeper Saw. Mark Lester & Britt Ekland. Directed by James Kelly. 1972. Embassy. 97 min. Sound. 16mm Color. *Rental:* Films Inc.

What Time Is Your Body? 1975. Britain. (Documentary). 50 min. Sound. 16mm Color. *Rental:* Films Inc. *Sale:* Films Inc. *Sale:* Films Inc, Videotape version.

What You Are is Where You Were When. 1976. Films Inc. (Lecture). 90 min. Videotape Color. *Rental:* Films Inc & Roas Films. *Sale:* Films Inc. *Rental:* U of IL Film, Kinescope version.

What You Are Isn't Necessarily What You Will Be. 1980. Films Inc. (Lecture). 60 min. Sound. 16mm Color. *Rental:* Films Inc. *Sale:* Films Inc. *Rental:* Films Inc, *Sale:* Films Inc, Videotape version.

Whatever Happened to Baby Jane? Bette Davis & Joan Crawford. Directed by Robert Aldrich. 1962. Warners. 132 min. Sound. 16mm B&W. *Rental:* Charard Motion Pics, Films Inc, Modern Sound, Swank Motion, Twyman Films, Video Comm, Williams Films & Willoughby Peer. *Sale:* Morcraft Films, Super 8 sound version. *Rental:* Swank Motion, Videotape version.

Whatever Happened to Childhood? 1970. Churchill Films. 52 min. Sound. 16mm Color. *Rental:* Churchill Films. *Rental:* Churchill Films, Videotape version.

Whatever Happened to El Salvador? 1982. NBC. (Documentary). 52 min. Sound. 16mm Color. *Sale:* Films Inc.

Whatever Lola Wants *see* Damn Yankees.

What's Buzzin' Cousin? Ann Miller. Directed by Charles Barton. 1943. Columbia. 80 min. Sound. 16mm B&W. *Lease:* Time-Life Multimedia.

What's Good for G.M. 1981. 45 min. Sound. 16mm Color. *Rental:* Iowa Films.

What's Happening: The Beatles in the U.S.A.. Directed by Albert Maysles & David Maysles. 1969. Maysles. 55 min. Sound. 16mm B&W. *Rental:* Maysles Films.

What's Happening to Television? 1966. NET. (Documentary). 60 min. Sound. 16mm B&W. *Rental:* Indiana AV Ctr. *Sale:* Indiana AV Ctr.

What's in a Face? 1974. Britain. (Documentary). 52 min. Sound. 16mm Color. *Rental:* Time-Life Multimedia. *Sale:* Time-Life Multimedia. *Rental:* Time-Life Multimedia, *Sale:* Time-Life Multimedia, Videotape version.

What's New at School? 1972. CBS. 45 min. Sound. 16mm Color. *Rental:* U Mich Media.

What's New, Pussycat? Peter Sellers & Peter O'Toole. Directed by Clive Donner. 1965. United Artists. 108 min. Sound. 16mm Color. *Rental:* MGM United. *Rental:* MGM United, Videotape version.

What's So Bad About Feeling Good? George Peppard & Mary Tyler Moore. Directed by George Seaton. 1968. Universal. 94 min. Sound. 16mm Color. *Rental:* Williams Films.

What's the Matter With Helen? Debbie Reynolds & Shelley Winters. Directed by Curtis Harrington. 1971. United Artists. 101 min. Sound. 16mm Color. *Rental:* Budget Films, MGM United, Welling Motion Pictures, Westcoast Films & Wholesome Film Ctr.

What's Up Doc? Barbra Streisand & Ryan O'Neal. Directed by Peter Bogdanovich. 1972. Warners. 94 min. Sound. 16mm Color. *Rental:* Swank Motion. *Rental:* Swank Motion, Videotape version.

What's Up, Josh? John McDowell. 1975. Gospel. 54 min. Sound. 16mm Color. *Rental:* Gospel Films & Roas Films.

What's Up, Tiger Lily? Woody Allen. Directed by Senkichi Taniguchi & Woody Allen. 1966. Japan. 78 min. Sound. 16mm Color. dubbed. *Rental:* Budget Films, Cine Craft, Charard Motion Pics, Films Inc, Ivy Films, Twyman Films, Video Comm, Welling Motion Pictures, Westcoast Films, Wholesome Film Ctr & Willoughby Peer, Super 8 Sound version.

What's Wrong with Our Schools? 1980. Penn. (Documentary). 60 min. Videotape Color. *Rental:* Iowa Films. *Sale:* Ency Brit Ed. *Sale:* Ency Brit Ed, 2 pt. 16mm version. *Sale:* Ency Brit Ed, 2 pt. Videotape version.

What's Wrong with the Social Sciences? 1971. Britain. (Lecture). 56 min. Sound. 16mm B&W. *Rental:* Time-Life Multimedia. *Sale:* Time-Life Multimedia.

Wheel, The *see* Roue.

Wheel of Ashes. Directed by Peter Emmanuel Goldman. 1968. Peter Emmanuel Goldman. (Documentary). 92 min. 16mm B&W. *Rental:* Canyon Cinema.

Wheel of Fortune. John Wayne & Ward Bond. Directed by John H. Auer. 1942. Republic. 83 min. Sound. 16mm B&W. *Rental:* Ivy Films. *Lease:* Rep Pic Film.

Wheel of Fortune, The. 1978. Britain. (Documentary). 52 min. Sound. 16mm Color. *Rental:* Iowa Films, Kent St U Film, U Cal Media, U of IL Film & U Mich Media, Videotape version.

Wheeler Dealers, The. James Garner & Lee Remick. Directed by Arthur Hiller. 1963. MGM. 106 min. Sound. 16mm Color. *Rental:* MGM United. *Rental:* MGM United, Anamorphic version.

Wheels of Destiny, The. Ken Maynard. Directed by Alan James. 1934. Universal. 64 min. Sound. 16mm B&W. *Rental:* Swank Motion.

When a Feller Needs a Friend. Jackie Cooper & Ralph Graves. Directed by Harry Pollard. 1932. MGM. 76 min. 16mm B&W. *Rental:* MGM United.

When a Man Rides Alone. Tom Tyler. Directed by J. P. McGowan. 1933. Freuler. 60 min. Sound. 16mm B&W. *Sale:* Cinema Concepts.

When a Man's a Man. John Bowers. Directed by Edward Cline. 1924. First National. 55 min. Silent. 16mm B&W. *Rental:* Mogulls Films.

When a Man's a Man. George O'Brien & Paul Kelly. Directed by Edward Cline. 1935. Fox. 70 min. Sound. 16mm B&W. *Rental:* Mogulls Films.

When a Stranger Calls. Charles Durning & Carol Kane. Directed by Fred Walton. 1979. Columbia. 97 min. Sound. 16mm Color. *Rental:* Swank Motion. *Rental:* Swank Motion, Videotape version.

When a Woman Fights Back. 1979. PBS. (Documentary). 59 min. Videotape Color. *Rental:* PBS Video. *Sale:* PBS Video.

When a Woman Loves. Ineko Arima. Directed by Heinosuki Gosho. Jap. 1960. Japan. 97 min. Sound. 16mm Color. subtitles. *Rental:* Video Comm. *Rental:* Budget Films, Anamorphic version.

When Chicago Was Hollywood. 1969. NBC. (Documentary, Tinted). 54 min. Sound. 16mm *Rental:* Films Inc & Kent St U Film. *Sale:* Films Inc.

When Comedy Was King. 1960. Fox. (Anthology). 81 min. Sound. 16mm B&W. *Rental:* Budget Films, Films Inc, Ivy Films, Kit Parker, Modern Sound, Newman Film Lib, Roas Films, Twyman Films, U Cal Media, Video Comm, Viewfinders, Welling Motion Pictures, Wholesome Film Ctr & Willoughby Peer. *Lease:* Carousel Films.

When Dinosaurs Ruled the Earth. Angela Dorian & Robin Hawdon. Directed by Val Guest. 1970. Warners. 96 min. Sound. 16mm Color. *Rental:* Films Inc.

When Eight Bells Toll. Anthony Hopkins & Jack Hawkins. Directed by Etienne Perier. 1971. Cinerama. 94 min. Sound. 16mm Color. *Rental:* Swank Motion.

When Gangland Strikes. Ray Greenleaf & Anthony Caruso. Directed by R. G. Springsteen. 1955. Republic. 70 min. Sound. 16mm B&W. *Rental:* Ivy Films. *Sale:* Rep Pic Film.

When Hell Broke Loose. Charles Bronson & Richard Jaeckel. Directed by Kenneth G. Crane. 1958. Paramount. 78 min. Sound. 16mm B&W. *Rental:* Films Inc.

When I Grow Up. Bobby Driscoll & Robert Preston. Directed by Michael Kanin. 1951. Eagle Lion. 90 min. Sound. 16mm B&W. *Rental:* Film Ctr DC, Films Inc, Ivy Films, Lewis Film & Wholesome Film Ctr.

When in Rome. Van Johnson & Paul Douglas. Directed by Clarence Brown. 1952. MGM. 78 min. Sound. 16mm B&W. *Rental:* MGM United.

When Irish Eyes Are Smiling *see* Irish Eyes Are Smiling.

When Joseph Returns. Directed by Zsolt Kezdi-Kovacs. Hungarian. 1976. Hungary. (Cast unlisted). 92 min. Sound. 16mm Color. subtitles. *Rental:* New Cinema & New Yorker Films.

When Knights Were Bold. Jack Buchanan & Fay Wray. Directed by Jack Raymond. 1936. Britain. 70 min. Sound. 16mm B&W. *Sale:* Cinema Concepts.

When My Baby Smiles at Me. Dan Dailey & Betty Grable. Directed by Walter Lang. 1948. Fox. 98 min. Sound. 16mm Color. *Rental:* Charard Motion Pics, Video Comm & Welling Motion Pictures.

When Strangers Marry *see* Betrayed.

When Taekwondo Strikes. Jhoon Rhee & Angela Mao. 101 min. Sound. 16mm Color. *Rental:* WW Enter. *Rental:* WW Enter, Videotape version.

When the Bough Breaks. Patricia Roc & Rosamund John. Directed by Lawrence Huntington. 1947. Britain. 81 min. Sound. 16mm B&W. *Rental:* Cinema Five.

When the Boys Meet the Girls. Connie Francis & Harve Presnell. Directed by Alvin Ganzer. 1965. MGM. 110 min. Sound. 16mm Color. *Rental:* MGM United.

When the Cat Comes *see* Cassandra Cat.

When the Clouds Roll By. Douglas Fairbanks & Kathleen Clifford. Directed by Victor Fleming. 1919. United Artists. 93 min. Silent. 16mm B&W. *Rental:* A Twyman Pres, Em Gee Film Lib & Museum Mod Art.

When the Daltons Rode. Randolph Scott & Kay Francis. Directed by George Marshall. 1940. Universal. 80 min. Sound. 16mm B&W. *Rental:* Swank Motion.

When the Girls Take Over. Jackie Coogan & Robert Lowery. Directed by Russell Hayden. 1962. Parade. 80 min. Sound. 16mm B&W. *Rental:* Ivy Films.

When the Legends Die. Richard Widmark. Directed by Stuart Millar. 1972. Fox. 105 min. Sound. 16mm Color. *Rental:* Films Inc & Twyman Films.

When the Mountains Tremble. Rigoberta Menchu. Directed by Pamela Yates & Thomas Sigel. Eng. & Span. 1983. 83 min. Sound. 16mm Color. subtitles Eng. *Rental:* New Yorker Films.

When the North Wind Blows. Dan Haggerty & Henry Brandon. Directed by Stewart Raffil. 1979. Viacom. 113 min. Sound. 16mm Color. *Rental:* Modern Sound & Williams Films. *Sale:* Lucerne Films. *Sale:* Lucerne Films, Videotape version.

When the People Awake. Directed by Alfonso Beato. Span. 1972. Chile. (Documentary). 60 min. Sound. 16mm Color. subtitles. *Rental:* Cinema Guild. *Sale:* Cinema Guild.

When the West Was Young. Orig. Title: Heritage of the West. Randolph Scott & Sally Blane. Directed by Henry Hathaway. 1933. Chile. 70 min. Sound. 16mm B&W. *Sale:* Morcraft Films & Reel Images. *Sale:* Morcraft Films & Reel Images, Super 8 sound version.

When Thief Meets Thief. Charles Boyer. Directed by Raoul Walsh. 1937. United Artists. 87 min. Sound. 16mm B&W. *Rental:* Classic Film Mus.

When Thief Meets Thief *see* Jump for Glory.

When Time Ran Out. Paul Newman, Jacqueline Bisset & William Holden. Directed by James Goldstone. 1980. Warners. 108 min. Sound. 16mm Color. *Rental:* Modern Sound, Swank Motion, Twyman Films & Williams Films.

When We First Met. Amy Linker & Andrew Sabiston. 1983. 54 min. Sound. 16mm Color. *Rental:* Learning Corp Am. *Sale:* Learning Corp Am. *Sale:* Learning Corp Am, Videotape version.

When Were You Born? Jeffrey Lynn, Margaret Lindsay & Anna May Wong. Directed by William McGann. 1938. Warners. 65 min. Sound. 16mm B&W. *Rental:* MGM United.

When Will the Birds Return? 1975. Australia. 52 min. Sound. 16mm Color. *Rental:* Aust Info Serv. *Sale:* Aust Info Serv.

When Willie Comes Marching Home. Dan Dailey & Corinne Calvet. Directed by John Ford. 1950. Fox. 82 min. Sound. 16mm B&W. *Rental:* Films Inc.

When Worlds Collide. Richard Derr & Barbara Rush. Directed by Rudolph Mate. 1951. Paramount. 82 min. Sound. 16mm Color. *Rental:* Films Inc.

When You Reach December. 1974. Westinghouse. (Documentary). 50 min. Sound. 16mm Color. *Rental:* Edupac & NYU Film Lib. *Sale:* Edupac.

When You're in Love. Grace Moore & Cary Grant. Directed by Robert Riskin. 1937. Columbia. 104 min. Sound. 16mm B&W. *Rental:* Kit Parker.

When You're Smiling. Jerome Courtland & Lola Albright. Directed by Joseph Santley. 1950. Columbia. 75 min. Sound. 16mm B&W. *Rental:* Inst Cinema & Welling Motion Pictures.

When's Your Birthday? Joe E. Brown. Directed by Harry Beaumont. 1937. RKO. 77 min. Sound. 16mm B&W. *Rental:* Inst Cinema & Ivy Films. *Sale:* Cinema Concepts, Super 8 sound version.

Where Angels Go - Trouble Follows! Rosalind Russell & Stella Stevens. Directed by James Neilson. 1968. Columbia. 95 min. Sound. 16mm Color. *Rental:* Arcus Film, Bosco Films, Budget Films, Film Ctr DC, Films Inc, Film Pres, Modern Sound, Natl Film Video, Newman Film Lib, Roas Films, Twyman, Twyman Films, Video Comm, Welling Motion Pictures, Westcoast Films & Wholesome Film Ctr.

Where Are Your Children? Gale Storm & Jackie Cooper. Directed by William Nigh. 1944. Monogram. 73 min. Sound. 16mm B&W. *Rental:* Hurlock Cine.

Where Danger Lives. Robert Mitchum & Faith Domergue. Directed by John Farrow. 1950. RKO. 84 min. Sound. 16mm B&W. *Rental:* Films Inc.

Where Did the Colorado Go? 1976. Nova. (Documentary). 59 min. Sound. 16mm Color. *Rental:* Iowa Films, Kent St U Film, Syracuse U Film, U Cal Media, U of IL Film & U Mich Media, Videotape version.

Where Do Teenagers Come From? 1980. Depatie-Freling. (Cast unlisted). 47 min. Sound. 16mm Color. *Rental:* Time-Life Multimedia. *Sale:* Time-Life Multimedia. *Sale:* Time-Life Multimedia, Videotape version.

Where Do We Go from Here? Fred MacMurray & June Haver. Directed by Gregory Ratoff. 1945. Fox. 77 min. Sound. 16mm Color. *Rental:* Films Inc.

Where Does It Hurt? Peter Sellers & Jo Ann Pflug. Directed by Rod Amateau. 1972. Cinerama. 95 min. Sound. 16mm Color. *Rental:* Swank Motion.

Where Eagles Dare. Richard Burton & Clint Eastwood. Directed by Brian Hutton. 1969. MGM. 158 min. Sound. 16mm Color. *Rental:* MGM United. *Rental:* MGM United, Anamorphic version.

Where Eagles Fly. Heinz Fussle. 58 min. Sound. 16mm Color. *Rental:* Gospel Films.

Where East Is East. Lon Chaney. Directed by Tod Browning. 1929. MGM. 75 min. Silent. 16mm B&W. *Rental:* MGM United.

Where Have All the Germans Gone? (Destination America Ser.). 1976. Media Guild. 52 min. Sound. 16mm Color. *Rental:* Media Guild. *Sale:* Media Guild. *Sale:* Media Guild, Videotape version.

Where Is Doc Robbin? *see* Who Killed Doc Robbin?.

Where Is Prejudice? 1967. NET. (Documentary). 60 min. Sound. 16mm B&W. *Rental:* Indiana AV Ctr, U Cal Media & U Mich Media.

Where It's At. David Janssen & Robert Drivas. Directed by Garson Kanin. 1969. United Artists. 104 min. Sound. 16mm Color. *Rental:* MGM United.

Where Love Has Gone. Susan Hayward & Bette Davis. Directed by Edward Dmytryk. 1964. Paramount. (Anamorphic). 114 min. Sound. 16mm Color. *Rental:* Films Inc.

Where No Man Has Gone Before. William Shatner & Leonard Nimoy. Directed by James Goldstone. 1966. Star Trek. 50 min. Sound. 16mm Color. *Rental:* Westcoast Films.

Where the Boys Are. Connie Francis & Dolores Hart. Directed by Henry Levin. 1960. MGM. 99 min. Sound. 16mm Color. *Rental:* MGM United. *Rental:* MGM United, Anamorphic version. *Rental:* MGM United, Videotape version.

Where the Buffalo Roam. Tex Ritter. Directed by Al Herman. 1938. Monogram. 55 min. Sound. 16mm B&W. *Rental:* Hurlock Cine.

Where the Buffalo Roam. Bill Murray, Peter Boyle & Bruno Kirby. Directed by Art Linson. 1985. Universal. 98 min. Sound. 16mm Color. *Rental:* Swank Motion. *Rental:* Swank Motion, Videotape version.

Where the Bullets Fly. Tom Adams & Dawn Addams. Directed by John Gilling. 1966. Britain. 88 min. Sound. 16mm Color. *Rental:* Films Inc.

Where the Lilies Bloom. Julie Gholson. Directed by William Graham. 1974. United Artists. 97 min. Sound. 16mm Color. *Rental:* MGM United.

Where the North Begins. Russell Hayden. Directed by Howard Bretherton. 1947. Screen Guild. Sound. 16mm B&W. *Rental:* Budget Films, Film Ctr DC & Mogulls Films.

Where the Red Fern Grows. James Whitmore & Beverly Garland. Directed by Norman Tokar. 1975. Doty-Dayton. 100 min. Sound. 16mm Color. *Rental:* Buchan Pic, Modern Sound, Swank Motion & Westcoast Films.

Where the River Bends *see* Bend of the River.

Where the Sidewalk Ends. Dana Andrews & Gene Tierney. Directed by Otto Preminger. 1950. Fox. 100 min. Sound. 16mm B&W. *Rental:* Films Inc.

Where the Spies Are. David Niven. Directed by Val Guest. 1965. MGM. 110 min. Sound. 16mm Color. *Rental:* MGM United.

Where the West Begins. Jack Randall. Directed by J. P. McGowan. 1938. Monogram. 55 min. Sound. 16mm B&W. *Rental:* Hurlock Cine.

Where There's a Will. Hartley Power & Gina Malo. Directed by William Beaudine. 1936. Britain. 80 min. Sound. 16mm B&W. *Rental:* Cinema Five.

Where There's Smoke. Annie Giradot. Directed by Andre Cayatte. Fr. 1973. France. 112 min. Sound. 16mm Color. subtitles. *Rental:* Cinema Five.

Where Time Began. Kenneth More. Directed by J. Piquer Simon. 1978. International Picture Show. 90 min. Sound. 16mm Color. *Rental:* Films Inc, Modern Sound & Twyman Films.

Where Trails End. Tom Keene. Directed by Robert Tansey. 1942. Monogram. 55 min. Sound. 16mm B&W. *Sale:* Reel Images.

Where Were You When the Lights Went Out? Doris Day & Robert Morse. Directed by Hy Averback. 1968. MGM. 94 min. Sound. 16mm Color. *Rental:* MGM United. *Rental:* MGM United, Anamorphic version.

Where's Jack? Tommy Steele & Stanley Baker. Directed by James Clavel. 1969. Paramount. 119 min. Sound. 16mm Color. *Rental:* Films Inc.

Where's Poppa? Ruth Gordon & George Segal. Directed by Carl Reiner. 1970. United Artists. 87 min. Sound. 16mm Color. *Rental:* Films Inc & MGM United. *Sale:* Tamarelles French Film, Videotape version.

Wherever We Lodge. 1977. CC Film. (Documentary). 60 min. Sound. 16mm Color. *Sale:* Natl Churches Christ.

Which Way Is Up? Richard Pryor. Directed by Michael Schultz. 1977. Universal. 93 min. Sound. 16mm Color. *Rental:* Swank Motion. *Rental:* Swank Motion, Videotape version.

Which Way to the Front? Jerry Lewis & Jan Murray. Directed by Jerry Lewis. 1970. Warners. 96 min. Sound. 16mm Color. *Rental:* Films Inc.

Whiffs. Elliott Gould. Directed by Ted Post. 1975. Fox. (Anamorphic). 90 min. Sound. 16mm Color. *Rental:* Films Inc.

While the City Sleeps. Dana Andrews & Rhonda Fleming. Directed by Fritz Lang. 1956. RKO. 100 min. Sound. 16mm B&W. *Rental:* Budget Films, Kit Parker, Video Comm, Welling Motion Pictures, Westcoast Films & Wholesome Film Ctr. *Lease:* Video Comm. *Rental:* Kit Parker & Video Comm, *Lease:* Video Comm, Anamorphic version.

While the Patient Slept. Aline MacMahon & Guy Kibbee. Directed by Ray Enright. 1935. Warners. 66 min. Sound. 16mm B&W. *Rental:* MGM United.

Whip, The. Directed by Maurice Tourneur. 1917. Paragon. (Cast unlisted). 50 min. Silent. 16mm B&W. *Rental:* Em Gee Film Lib. *Sale:* Glenn Photo. *Sale:* Glenn Photo, Super 8 silent version.

Whip Hand, The. Raymond Burr & Elliott Reed. Directed by William Cameron Menzies. 1952. RKO. 82 min. Sound. 16mm B&W. *Rental:* RKO General Pics.

Whiplash. Dane Clark & Alexis Smith. Directed by Lewis Seiler. 1949. Warners. 91 min. Sound. 16mm B&W. *Rental:* MGM United.

Whipped, The *see* Underworld Story.

Whipsaw. Myrna Loy & Spencer Tracy. Directed by Sam Wood. 1935. MGM. 83 min. Sound. 16mm B&W. *Rental:* MGM United.

Whirlpool. Jean Arthur & Jack Holt. Directed by Roy William Neill. 1934. France. Sound. 16mm B&W. subtitles. *Rental:* Kit Parker.

Whirlpool. Gene Tierney & Richard Conte. Directed by Otto Preminger. 1949. Fox. 105 min. Sound. 16mm B&W. *Rental:* Films Inc.

Whirlpool. Alain Delon. Fr. France. 106 min. Sound. 16mm B&W. subtitles. *Rental:* WW Enter. *Rental:* WW Enter, Videotape version.

Whirlpool of Life, The *see* Fille de L'Eau.

Whirlwind Bombing Germany, Sept. 1939 - April 1944. Directed by Hugh Raggett. (World at War Ser.). : Pt. 12.). 1973. Media Guild. (Documentary). 52 min. Sound. 16mm Color. *Rental:* Media Guild. *Sale:* Media Guild & U Cal Media. *Sale:* Media Guild, Videotape version.

Whirlwind Horseman, The. Ken Maynard. Directed by Robert Hill. 1938. Grand National. 60 min. Sound. 16mm B&W. *Rental:* Roas Films. *Sale:* Morcraft Films. *Sale:* Cinema Concepts, Super 8 sound version.

Whiskey & Sofa *see* Operation Moonlight.

Whiskey Galore *see* Tight Little Island.

Whiskey Mountain. Christopher George. Directed by Charlie Daniels. 1978. Celestial. 90 min. Sound. 16mm Color. *Sale:* Salz Ent. *Rental:* BF Video. *Sale:* Salz Ent, Super 8 silent version.

Whisper from Space, A. 1979. 57 min. Sound. 16mm Color. *Rental:* Utah Media.

Whisperers, The. Dame Edith Evans. Eric Portman. Directed by Bryan Forbes. 1967. Britain. 105 min. Sound. 16mm B&W. *Rental:* Films Inc & MGM United.

Whispering City. Paul Lukas & Mary Anderson. Directed by Fedor Ozep. 1947. Canada. 95 min. Sound. 16mm B&W. *Rental:* Mogulls Films & Westcoast Films.

Whispering Footsteps. John Hubbard & Rita Quigley. Directed by Howard Bretherton. 1944. Republic. 54 min. Sound. 16mm B&W. *Rental:* Ivy Films. *Sale:* Rep Pic Film.

Whispering Ghosts. Milton Berle & Brenda Joyce. Directed by Alfred M. Werker. 1942. Fox. 75 min. Sound. 16mm B&W. *Rental:* Films Inc.

Whispering Skull. Tex Ritter. Directed by Elmer Clifton. 1944. PRC. 60 min. Sound. 16mm B&W. *Rental:* Ivy Films & Mogulls Films. *Sale:* Classics Assoc NY & Rep Pic Film.

Whispering Smith. Alan Ladd & Brenda Marshall. Directed by Leslie Fenton. 1948. Paramount. 88 min. Sound. 16mm Color. *Rental:* Swank Motion.

Whispering Smith Speaks. George O'Brien & Irene Ware. Directed by David Howard. 1935. Fox. 70 min. Sound. 16mm B&W. *Rental:* Lewis Film & Mogulls Films.

Whispering Smith vs. Scotland Yard. Richard Carlson & Greta Gynt. Directed by Francis Searle. 1952. RKO. 77 min. Sound. 16mm B&W. *Rental:* Ivy Films.

Whispering Winds. Theodore Von Eltz & Dorothy Lee. Directed by James Flood. 1928. Tiffany-Stahl. 70 min. Silent. 16mm B&W. *Sale:* Morcraft Films.

Whistle, The. William S. Hart. Directed by Lambert Hillyer. 1921. Paramount. 90 min. Silent. 16mm B&W. *Rental:* Em Gee Film Lib & Video Comm. *Sale:* Blackhawk Films. *Rental:* Ivy Films, Super 8 silent version.

Whistle at Eaton Falls, The. Orig. Title: Richer Than the Earth. Lloyd Bridges & Ernest Borgnine. Directed by Robert Siodmak. 1951. De Rochemont. 95 min. Sound. 16mm B&W. *Rental:* Cine Craft, Films Inc & Ivy Films.

Whistle Down the Wind. Hayley Mills & Alan Bates. Directed by Bryan Forbes. 1960. Britain. 98 min. Sound. 16mm B&W. *Rental:* Films Inc & Janus Films.

Whistler, The. Richard Dix & J. Carrol Naish. Directed by William Castle. 1944. 59 min. Sound. 16mm B&W. *Rental:* Budget Films.

Whistling Bullets. Kermit Maynard. Directed by John English. 1936. Ambassador. 60 min. Sound. 16mm B&W. *Sale:* Morcraft Films. *Rental:* Budget Films.

Whistling Dan. Ken Maynard. Directed by Phil Rosen. 1932. Tiffany. 60 min. Sound. 16mm B&W. *Sale:* Natl Cinema.

Whistling Hills, The. Johnny Mack Brown. Directed by Derwin Abrahams. 1951. Monogram. 58 min. Sound. 16mm B&W. *Rental:* Hurlock Cine.

Whistling in Brooklyn. Red Skelton & Ann Rutherford. Directed by S. Sylvan Simon. 1943. MGM. 87 min. Sound. 16mm B&W. *Rental:* MGM United.

Whistling in the Dark: Scared. Una Merkel & Ernest Truex. Directed by Elliott Nugent. 1933. MGM. 80 min. Sound. 16mm B&W. *Rental:* MGM United.

White Angel, The. Kay Francis & Ian Hunter. Directed by William Dieterle. 1936. Warners. 75 min. Sound. 16mm B&W. *Rental:* MGM United.

White Bird with a Black Spot, The. Larisa Kadochnikova. Directed by Yuri Ilyenko. Rus. 1972. Russia. (Anamorphic). 102 min. Sound. 16mm Color. subtitles. *Rental:* Corinth Films.

White Bondage. Gordon Oliver & Jean Muir. Directed by Nick Grinde. 1937. Warners. 59 min. Sound. 16mm B&W. *Rental:* MGM United.

White Bridge, The. 45 min. Sound. 16mm Color. *Rental:* Alden Films.

White Buffalo, The. Charles Bronson, Jack Warden & Kim Novak. Directed by J. Lee Thompson. 1977. United Artists. 98 min. Sound. 16mm B&W. *Rental:* MGM United.

White Cargo. Walter Pidgeon & Hedy Lamarr. Directed by Richard Thorpe. 1942. MGM. 90 min. Sound. 16mm B&W. *Rental:* MGM United.

White Cliffs of Dover, The. Irene Dunne & Alan Marshall. Directed by Clarence Brown. 1944. MGM. 130 min. Sound. 16mm B&W. *Rental:* MGM United.

White Cockatoo, The. Ricardo Cortez & Jean Muir. Directed by Robert Florey. 1935. Warners. 70 min. Sound. 16mm B&W. *Rental:* MGM United.

White-Collar Rip-off, The. 1975. NBC. (Documentary). 52 min. Sound. 16mm Color. *Rental:* Films Inc & Syracuse U Film. *Sale:* Films Inc. *Sale:* Films Inc, Videotape version.

White Comanche, The. Joseph Cotten & William Shatner. Directed by Gilbert Kay. 1967. RKO. 90 min. Sound. 16mm Color. *Rental:* Budget Films & Video Comm. *Lease:* Video Comm.

White Corridors. Petula Clark. Directed by Patrick Jackson. 1951. 102 min. 16mm *Rental:* A Twyman Pres.

White Dawn, The. Warren Oates & Timothy Bottoms. Directed by Philip Kaufman. 1974. Paramount. 110 min. Sound. 16mm Color. *Rental:* Films Inc.

White Eagle, The. Buck Jones. Directed by Lambert Hillyer. 1932. Columbia. 60 min. Sound. 16mm B&W. *Rental:* Willoughby Peer.

White Fang. Franco Nero & Virna Lisi. Directed by Lucio Fulci. 1976. Italy. 91 min. Sound. 16mm Color. dubbed. *Rental:* Films Inc & Westcoast Films.

White Feather. Robert Wagner & John Lund. Directed by Robert Webb. 1955. Fox. (Anamorphic). 100 min. Sound. 16mm Color. *Rental:* Films Inc.

White Fire. Orig. Title: Three Steps to the Gallows. Scott Brady & Mary Castle. Directed by John Gilling. 1954. Lippert. 80 min. Sound. 16mm B&W. *Rental:* Budget Films & Charard Motion Pics.

White Gods. 1937. Trekalog. (Documentary). 60 min. Sound. 16mm B&W. *Rental:* Mogulls Films.

White Gorilla, The *see* Nabonga.

White-Haired Girl, The. 1972. China. (Ballet). 120 min. Sound. 16mm Color. *Rental:* China People.

White Heat. James Cagney & Virginia Mayo. Directed by Raoul Walsh. 1949. Warners. 114 min. Sound. 16mm B&W. *Rental:* MGM United.

White Hell of Pitz Palu, The. Orig. Title: White Ice. Leni Riefenstahl. Directed by G. W. Pabst & Arnold Fanck. 1929. Germany. (Musical & sound effects only). 75 min. Sound. 16mm B&W. *Rental:* Museum Mod Art & Swank Motion.

White House Red Carpet with Julia Child, The. 1968. NET. (Documentary). 49 min. Sound. 16mm B&W. *Rental:* Indiana AV Ctr. *Sale:* Indiana AV Ctr. *Rental:* Indiana AV Ctr, *Sale:* Indiana AV Ctr, Color version.

White House Story, The. 1967. Jensen. (Documentary). 56 min. Sound. 16mm B&W. *Rental:* McGraw-Hill Films & Syracuse U Film. *Sale:* McGraw-Hill Films.

White Ice *see* White Hell of Pitz Palu.

White Lightning. Stanley Clements & Steve Brodie. Directed by Edward Bernds. 1953. Allied Artists. 61 min. Sound. 16mm B&W. *Rental:* Hurlock Cine.

White Lightning. Burt Reynolds. Directed by Joseph Sargent. 1973. United Artists. 101 min. Sound. 16mm Color. *Rental:* Arcus Film, MGM United, Modern Sound, Roas Films, Westcoast Films, Wholesome Film Ctr & Williams Films. *Rental:* MGM United, Videotape version.

White Line Fever. Jan-Michael Vincent. Directed by Jonathan Kaplan. 1975. Columbia. 90 min. Sound. 16mm Color. *Rental:* Arcus Film, Budget Films, Films Inc, Kit Parker, Modern Sound, Natl Film Video, Swank Motion, Welling Motion Pictures, Westcoast Films & Wholesome Film Ctr.

White Man, The *see* Squaw Man.

White Man's Country. 1973. Anthony-David. (Documentary). 51 min. Sound. 16mm Color. *Rental:* Films Inc & U Mich Media. *Sale:* Films Inc. *Sale:* Films Inc, Videotape version.

White Orchid, The. William Lundigan & Peggie Castle. Directed by Reginald Le Borg. 1954. United Artists. 90 min. Sound. 16mm Color. *Rental:* Mogulls Films & Willoughby Peer.

White Outlaw, The. Art Acord. Directed by Robert J. Horner. 1928. Exhibitors. 55 min. Super 8 silent B&W. *Rental:* Ivy Films. *Sale:* Blackhawk Films.

White Pongo. Richard Fraser & Maris Wrixon. Directed by Sam Newfield. 1945. PRC. 73 min. Sound. 16mm B&W. *Rental:* Budget Films, Ivy Films & Mogulls Films. *Sale:* Classics Assoc NY & Rep Pic Film.

White Poodle, The. Volodva Polyakov. Directed by Grigori Roshal & V. Shredal. 1956. Russia. 70 min. Sound. 16mm B&W. narrated Eng. *Rental:* Corinth Films.

White Reindeer, The. Mirjami Kuosmanen. Directed by Erik Blomberg. 1956. Finland. 75 min. Sound. 16mm B&W. *Rental:* A Twyman Pres & Twyman Films.

White Rose, The. Mae Marsh, Carol Dempster & Neil Hamilton. Directed by D. W. Griffith. 1923. United Artists. 136 min. Silent. 16mm B&W. *Rental:* Museum Mod Art.

White Search, The. Directed by Dick Barrymore. 1970. Dick Barrymore. (Documentary). 90 min. Sound. 16mm Color. *Rental:* Budget Films, Cine Craft, Film Ctr DC, Films Inc, Kerr Film, Modern Sound, Roas Films, Swank Motion, Twyman Films & Westcoast Films.

White Shadows of the South Seas. Directed by W. S. Van Dyke. 1928. MGM. (Documentary, music & sound effects only). 85 min. Sound. 16mm B&W. *Rental:* Film Inc.

White Sheep, The. Glenn Tryon. Directed by Hal Roach. 1924. Pathe. 90 min. Silent. 16mm B&W. *Rental:* Em Gee Film Lib. *Sale:* Glenn Photo.

White Sheik, The. Alberto Sordi & Giulietta Masina. Directed by Federico Fellini. Ital. 1952. Italy. 86 min. Sound. 16mm B&W. subtitles. *Rental:* Films Inc & New Cinema.

White Sin, The. Madge Bellamy. Directed by William A. Seiter. 1924. FBO. 60 min. Silent. 16mm B&W. *Rental:* Em Gee Film Lib. *Sale:* Cinema Concepts, Em Gee Film Lib & Griggs Movie.

White Sister, The. Lillian Gish & Ronald Colman. Directed by Henry King. 1923. MGM. 113 min. Silent. 16mm B&W. *Rental:* MGM United.

White Sister, The. Helen Hayes & Clark Gable. Directed by Victor Fleming. 1933. MGM. 101 min. Sound. 16mm B&W. *Rental:* MGM United.

White Stallion, The. Orig. Title: Harmony Trail. Ken Maynard. Directed by Robert Tansey. 1946. Astor. 60 min. Videotape B&W. *Sale:* Video Comm.

White Tiger, The. Priscilla Dean & Wallace Beery. Directed by Tod Browning. 1925. Universal. 88 min. Silent. 16mm B&W. *Rental:* Budget Films & Video Comm. *Sale:* Cinema Concepts & Select Film, Silent 8mm version. *Rental:* Video Comm, Videotape version.

White Tower, The. Glenn Ford & Claude Rains. Directed by Ted Tetzlaff. 1950. RKO. 98 min. Sound. 16mm Color. *Rental:* Films Inc.

White Wilderness. Directed by James Algar. 1958. Disney. (Documentary). 73 min. Sound. 16mm Color. *Rental:* Bosco Films, Buchan Pic, Cine Craft, Cousino Visual Ed, Elliot Film Co, Film Ctr DC, Films Inc, MGM United, Modern Sound, Newman Film Lib, Roas Films, Swank Motion, Twyman Films, U of IL Film, Welling Motion Pictures, Westcoast Films & Williams Films.

White Witch Doctor. Susan Hayward & Robert Mitchum. Directed by Henry Hathaway. 1953. Fox. 96 min. Sound. 16mm Color. *Rental:* Films Inc.

White Zombie. Bela Lugosi. Directed by Victor Halperin. 1932. United Artists. 92 min. Sound. 16mm B&W. *Rental:* A Twyman Pres & Kit Parker. *Sale:* Festival Films. *Rental:* Budget Films, Em Gee Film Lib, Films Inc, Swank Motion, Video Comm, Westcoast Films & Wholesome Film Ctr, *Sale:* Reel Images & Video Comm, 68 mins. version. *Rental:* Ivy Films, *Sale:* Cinema Concepts & Ivy Films, Super 8 sound version. *Sale:* Natl Cinema, 74 mins. version. *Sale:* Festival Films, Videotape version.

Whitewater. 1980. PBS. (Documentary). 59 min. Sound. 16mm Color. *Rental:* PBS Video.

Who? Elliott Gould & Trevor Howard. Directed by Jack Gold. 1973. Britain. 93 min. Sound. 16mm Color. *Rental:* Hurlock Cine.

Who Are the Debolts? John Korty. 1977. Korty. (Documentary). 72 min. Sound. 16mm Color. *Rental:* Budget Films, Iowa Films, Mass Media, Pyramid Film, Syracuse U Film, U of IL Film & U Mich Media. *Sale:* Pyramid Film. *Rental:* Pyramid Film, *Sale:* Pyramid Film, Abridged 54 min. version. *Rental:* Pyramid Film, *Sale:* Pyramid Film, Videotape version.

Who Decides Disability? 58 min. Sound. Videotape *Rental:* PBS Video. *Sale:* PBS Video.

Who Do You Kill? Diana Sands & George C. Scott. 1964. Talent Associates-Paramount. 51 min. Sound. 16mm B&W. *Rental:* U Cal Media & U Mich Media. *Sale:* Carousel Films.

Who Done It? Bud Abbott & Lou Costello. Directed by Erle C. Kenton. 1942. Universal. 75 min. Sound. 16mm B&W. *Rental:* Swank Motion.

Who Goes There?: A Primer on Communism. 1963. NBC. (Documentary). 54 min. Sound. 16mm B&W. *Rental:* McGraw-Hill Films, Syracuse U Film & U of IL Film. *Sale:* McGraw-Hill Films.

Who Has Seen the Wind? Maria Schell, Stanley Baker & Edward G. Robinson. 1965. Xerox. 90 min. Sound. 16mm B&W. *Rental:* U Mich Media. *Sale:* Xerox Films.

Who in Sixty-Eight? 1967. 51 min. Sound. 16mm Color. *Rental:* Utah Media.

Who Invited Us? 1969. NET. (Documentary). 60 min. Sound. 16mm B&W. *Rental:* Indiana AV Ctr, U Cal Media & U Mich Media. *Sale:* Indiana AV Ctr. *Sale:* Indiana AV Ctr, Videotape version.

Who Is Dr. Goddard? 1961. Hearst. (Documentary). 50 min. Sound. 16mm B&W. *Sale:* King Features.

Who Is Harry Kellerman & Why Is He Saying Those Terrible Things About Me? Dustin Hoffman & Barbara Harris. Directed by Ulu Grosbard. 1971. National General. 108 min. Sound. 16mm Color. *Rental:* Swank Motion.

Who Is Havin' Fun? 1980. Inst. for Study of Human Issues. (Documentary). Sound. 16mm Color. *Rental:* Human Issues.

Who Is Killing the Great Chefs of Europe? George Segal, Jacqueline Bisset & Robert Morley. Directed by Ted Kotcheff. 1978. Warners. 112 min. Sound. 16mm Color. *Rental:* Modern Sound, Swank Motion, Twyman Films & Williams Films.

Who is My Sister? 1979. PBS. (Documentary). 88 min. Videotape Color. *Rental:* PBS Video. *Sale:* PBS Video.

Who Killed Aunt Maggie? Wendy Barrie & Edgar Kennedy. Directed by Arthur Lubin. 1940. Republic. 54 min. Sound. 16mm B&W. *Rental:* Ivy Films. *Sale:* Rep Pic Film.

Who Killed Doc Robbin? Orig. Title: Where Is Doc Robbin? Larry Olsen & Don Castle. Directed by Bernard Carr. 1948. United Artists. 55 min. Sound. 16mm B&W. *Rental:* Budget Films, Newman Film Lib & Roas Films. *Rental:* Budget Films, Color version. *Sale:* Morcraft Films, Super 8 sound version.

Who Killed Gail Preston? Rita Hayworth & Don Terry. Directed by Leon Barsha. 1938. Columbia. 61 min. Sound. 16mm B&W. *Rental:* Kit Parker.

Who Killed Lake Erie? 1969. NBC. (Documentary). 51 min. Sound. 16mm Color. *Rental:* Films Inc, Iowa Films, Syracuse U Film, Twyman Films, U Cal Media & U Mich Media. *Sale:* Films Inc & Utah Media. *Sale:* Films Inc, Videotape version.

Who Killed the Cat? Mervyn Johns & Vanda Godsell. Directed by Montgomery Tully. 1966. Britain. 87 min. Sound. 16mm B&W. *Rental:* Modern Sound.

Who Might As Well Say That I See What I Eat Is the Same What I See? Directed by Michael Chanan. 1972. Oxford U.. (Interview). 60 min. Sound. 16mm Color. *Rental:* New Yorker Films.

Who Protects the Consumer? 2 pts. 1980. Penn. 60 min. Sound. 16mm Color. *Rental:* Iowa Films. *Sale:* Ency Brit Ed. *Sale:* Ency Brit Ed, Videotape version. *Sale:* Ency Brit Ed, 2 pt. Videotape version.

Who Protects the Worker? 2 pts. 1980. Penn. 60 min. Sound. 16mm Color. *Sale:* Ency Brit Ed. *Sale:* Ency Brit Ed, Videotape version. *Sale:* Ency Brit Ed, 2 pt. Videotape version.

Who Remembers Mama? Directed by Allen Mondell & Cynthia Salzman Mondell. 1980. New Day. (Documentary). 58 min. Sound. 16mm Color. *Rental:* New Day Films & U Mich Media. *Sale:* New Day Films. *Rental:* New Day Films, *Sale:* New Day Films, Videotape version.

Who Shall Live & Who Shall Die? Directed by Laurence Jarvik. 1982. USA. (Documentary). 90 min. Sound. 16mm B&W. *Rental:* Kino Intl. *Lease:* Kino Intl.

Who Slew Auntie Roo? Shelley Winters & Mark Lester. Directed by Curtis Harrington. 1972. Britain. 91 min. Sound. 16mm Color. *Rental:* Swank Motion & Welling Motion Pictures.

Who Speaks for Birmingham? 1961. CBS. (Documentary). 58 min. Sound. 16mm B&W. *Rental:* CBS Inc.

Who Speaks for Earth? 1980. Cosmos. (Documentary). 60 min. Sound. 16mm Color. *Rental:* Films Inc. *Sale:* Films Inc. *Rental:* Films Inc, *Sale:* Films Inc, Videotape version.

Who Speaks for Man? 1969. NET. (Documentary). 56 min. Sound. 16mm B&W. *Rental:* Indiana AV Ctr & U Cal Media. *Rental:* Indiana AV Ctr, Color version.

Who Was That Lady? Tony Curtis & Dean Martin. Directed by George Sidney. 1960. Columbia. 115 min. Sound. 16mm B&W. *Rental:* Cine Craft, Film Ctr DC, Films Inc, Modern Sound & Welling Motion Pictures.

Who Will Fight for America? 1981. NBC. (Documentary). 52 min. Videotape Color. *Rental:* Films Inc. *Sale:* Films Inc.

Whole Shootin' Match, The. Directed by Eagle Pennell. 1980. Cinema Perspectives. (Documentary). 108 min. Sound. 16mm Color. *Rental:* First Run & New Line Cinema. *Lease:* First Run.

Whole Town's Talking, The. Edward G. Robinson & Jean Arthur. Directed by John Ford. 1935. Columbia. 86 min. Sound. 16mm B&W. *Rental:* Budget Films, Films Inc, Kit Parker, Swank Motion, Twyman Films, Welling Motion Pictures & Wholesome Film Ctr.

Whole World Is Watching, The. 1968. PBS. (Documentary). 55 min. Sound. 16mm B&W. *Rental:* Indiana AV Ctr & U Cal Media. *Sale:* Indiana AV Ctr.

Who'll Stop the Rain? Nick Nolte, Tuesday Weld & Michael Moriarty. Directed by Karel Reisz. 1978. United Artists. 126 min. Sound. 16mm Color. *Rental:* MGM United. *Sale:* Tamarelles French Film, Videotape version.

Wholly Moses. Dudley Moore, Richard Pryor & Madeline Kahn. Directed by Gary Weis. 1980. Columbia. 102 min. Sound. 16mm Color. *Rental:* Arcus Film, Films Inc, Swank Motion, Welling Motion Pictures & Williams Films. *Rental:* Swank Motion, Videotape version.

Who's Afraid of Opera? 240 min. Sound. 16mm Color. *Rental:* Phoenix Films. *Sale:* Phoenix Films. *Sale:* Phoenix Films, Videotape version.

Who's Afraid of Virginia Woolf? Elizabeth Taylor & Richard Burton. Directed by Mike Nichols. 1966. Warners. 129 min. Sound. 16mm B&W. *Rental:* Swank Motion. *Rental:* Swank Motion, Videotape version.

Who's Been Sleeping in My Bed? Dean Martin & Carol Burnett. Directed by Daniel Mann. 1963. Paramount. 103 min. Sound. 16mm Color. *Rental:* Films Inc. *Rental:* Films Inc, Anamorphic version.

Who's Got a Right to Rhodesia? 1977. CBS. (Documentary). 53 min. Sound. 16mm Color. *Rental:* Syracuse U Film & U Mich Media. *Sale:* Carousel Films.

Who's Got the Action? Dean Martin & Lana Turner. Directed by Daniel Mann. 1962. Paramount. 93 min. Sound. 16mm Color. *Rental:* Films Inc.

Who's Got the Horse? Xerox. (Cast unlisted). 64 min. Sound. 16mm B&W. *Sale:* Xerox Films.

Who's Keeping Score?: Hearing Day One. 3 pts. 1981. 59 min. Sound. Videotape Color. *Rental:* Natl AV Ctr. *Sale:* Natl AV Ctr.

Who's Minding the Mint? Jim Hutton & Dorothy Provine. Directed by Howard Morris. 1967. Columbia. 97 min. Sound. 16mm Color. *Rental:* Arcus Film, Buchan Pic, Budget Films, Cine Craft, Charard Motion Pics, Film Ctr DC, Films Inc, Film Pres, Modern Sound, Roas Films, Twyman Films, Video Films, Video Comm, Welling Motion Pictures, Westcoast Films & Wholesome Film Ctr.

Who's Minding the Store? Jerry Lewis. Directed by Frank Tashlin. 1963. Paramount. 90 min. Sound. 16mm Color. *Rental:* Films Inc.

Who's Out There? 60 min. Sound. Videotape Color. *Rental:* Maljack Productions.

Whose Life Is It Anyway? Directed by Richard Everitt. 1974. Britain. (Cast unlisted). 53 min. Sound. 16mm Color. *Rental:* U Mich Media.

Whose Life Is It Anyway? Richard Dreyfuss, John Cassavetes & Christine Lahti. Directed by John Badham. 1981. MGM. 118 min. Sound. 16mm Color. *Rental:* MGM United. *Rental:* MGM United, Videotape version.

Why Are Team-Teaching & Non-Grading Important? 1966. 49 min. Sound. 16mm B&W. *Rental:* OK AV Ctr.

Why Can't I Learn? 1974. Capac. (Documentary). 54 min. Sound. 16mm Color. *Rental:* U of IL Film.

Why Can't I Learn? 1978. Media Five. (Documentary). 51 min. Sound. 16mm Color. *Rental:* Films Inc. *Sale:* Films Inc. *Sale:* Films Inc, Videotape version.

Why Do Birds Sing? 1979. PBS. (Documentary). 60 min. Videotape Color. *Rental:* PBS Video. *Sale:* PBS Video.

Why Do I Feel This Way?: Profiles Of Depression. 1979. Boston Broadcasters. (Documentary). 48 min. Sound. 16mm Color. *Rental:* U of IL Film & MTI Tele. *Rental:* MTI Tele, Videotape version.

Why Does Herr R. Run Amok? Kurt Raab. Directed by Rainer Werner Fassbinder. Ger. 1969. Germany. 87 min. Sound. 16mm Color. subtitles. *Rental:* New Cinema & New Yorker Films.

Why Girls Leave Home. Lola Lane & Sheldon Leonard. Directed by William Berke. 1945. PRC. 69 min. Sound. 16mm B&W. *Sale:* Classics Assoc NY.

Why I Sing. 1973. Canada. (Documentary). 58 min. Sound. 16mm Color. *Rental:* Natl Film CN. *Sale:* Natl Film CN.

Why Me? 1975. KNXT. (Documentary). 57 min. Sound. 16mm Color. *Rental:* Budget Films & Syracuse U Film.

Why Rock the Boat? Stuart Gillard. Directed by John Howe. 1974. Canada. 112 min. Sound. 16mm Color. *Rental:* Natl Film CN. *Sale:* Natl Film CN. *Sale:* Natl Film CN, Videotape version.

Why Sailors Go Wrong. Sammy Cohen & Nick Stuart. Directed by Henry Lehrman. 1928. Fox. 60 min. Silent. 16mm B&W. *Rental:* Mogulls Films.

Why Save Florence? 1970. NET. (Documentary). 59 min. Sound. 16mm Color. *Rental:* Indiana AV Ctr. *Sale:* Indiana AV Ctr.

Why Shoot the Teacher. 1978. Canada. (Cast unlisted). 99 min. Sound. 16mm Color. *Rental:* Films Inc.

Why Work? 2 pts. Directed by Alan Levin. 1976. WNET. (Documentary). 120 min. Sound. 16mm Color. *Rental:* CA Newsreel & WNET Media. *Sale:* WNET Media.

Why Worry? Harold Lloyd. Directed by Fred Newmeyer & Sam Taylor. 1923. Pathe. (Music & sound effects only). 55 min. Sound. 16mm B&W. *Rental:* Janus Films, Kino Intl & Kit Parker. *Sale:* Films Inc, Videotape version.

Wichita. Joel McCrea & Vera Miles. Directed by Jacques Tourneur. 1955. Allied Artists. 81 min. Sound. 16mm Color. *Rental:* Hurlock Cine.

Wicked As They Come. Herbert Marshall & Arlene Dahl. Directed by Ken Hughes. 1957. Columbia. 94 min. Sound. 16mm B&W. *Rental:* Kit Parker.

Wicked Dreams of Paula Schultz, The. Elke Sommer & Bob Crane. Directed by George Marshall. 1968. United Artists. 113 min. Sound. 16mm Color. *Rental:* MGM United.

Wicked Lady, The. Faye Dunnaway, Sir John Gielgud & Alan Bates. Directed by Michael Winner. 1983. Cannon. 98 min. Sound. 16mm Color. *Rental:* Swank Motion.

Wicked, Wicked. David Bailey & Tiffany Bolling. Directed by Richard Bare. 1973. MGM. (Anamorphic). 95 min. Sound. 16mm Color. *Rental:* MGM United.

Wicked Woman, A. Mady Christians & Jean Arthur. Directed by Charles Brabin. 1934. MGM. 74 min. Sound. 16mm B&W. *Rental:* MGM United.

Wide Boy. Ronald Howard & Susan Shaw. Directed by Ken Hughes. 1952. Britain. 80 min. Sound. 16mm B&W. *Sale:* Morcraft Films. *Sale:* Morcraft Films, Super 8 sound version.

Wide Open. Edward Everett Horton & Patsy Ruth Miller. Directed by Archie Mayo. 1930. Warners. 69 min. Sound. 16mm B&W. *Rental:* MGM United.

Wide Open Faces. Joe E. Brown & Jane Wyman. Directed by Kurt Neumann. 1938. Columbia. 67 min. Sound. 16mm B&W. *Rental:* Ivy Films & Mogulls Films.

Wide Open Town. William Boyd. Directed by Lesley Selander. 1941. Paramount. 54 min. Sound. 16mm B&W. *Sale:* Cinema Concepts.

Widow, The. Michael Learned & Farley Granger. Directed by J. Lee Thompson. 1976. Lorimar. 102 min. Sound. 16mm Color. *Sale:* Lucerne Films. *Sale:* Lucerne Films, Videotape version.

Widow Couderc, The. Alain Delon & Simone Signoret. Directed by Pierre Granier-Deferre. Fr. 1971. France. 92 min. Sound. 16mm Color. subtitles. *Rental:* J Green Pics. *Rental:* J Green Pics, Dubbed version. *Sale:* Tamarelles French Film, Videotape version.

Widow from Chicago, The. Edward G. Robinson & Alice White. Directed by Edward Cline. 1930. Warners. 64 min. Sound. 16mm B&W. *Rental:* MGM United.

Wife Among Wives, A. Directed by David MacDougall & Judith MacDougall. 1982. EMC. (Documentary). 72 min. Sound. 16mm Color. *Rental:* U Cal Media. *Sale:* U Cal Media. *Sale:* U Cal Media, Videotape version.

Wife for a Night. 1974. Italy. (Cast unlisted). 90 min. Sound. 16mm B&W. dubbed. *Rental:* Ivy Films.

Wife, Husband & Friend. Loretta Young & Warner Baxter. Directed by Gregory Ratoff. 1939. Fox. 80 min. Sound. 16mm B&W. *Rental:* Films Inc.

Wife of Monte Cristo, The. Lenore Aubert & John Loder. Directed by Edgar G. Ulmer. 1946. PRC. 80 min. Sound. 16mm B&W. *Sale:* Classics Assoc NY.

Wife Takes a Flyer, The. Joan Bennett & Franchot Tone. Directed by Richard Wallace. 1942. Columbia. 86 min. Sound. 16mm B&W. *Rental:* Kit Parker.

Wife vs. Secretary. Myrna Loy, Clark Gable & Jean Harlow. Directed by Clarence Brown. 1936. MGM. 85 min. Sound. 16mm B&W. *Rental:* MGM United.

Wife Wanted. Kay Francis & Veda Ann Borg. Directed by Phil Karlson. 1946. Monogram. 70 min. Sound. 16mm B&W. *Rental:* Hurlock Cine & Mogulls Films.

Wifemistress. Laura Antonelli & Marcello Mastroianni. Directed by Marco Vicario. Ital. 1979. Italy. 101 min. Sound. 16mm Color. subtitles. *Rental:* Films Inc. *Sale:* Tamarelles French Film, Videotape version.

Wife's Relations, The. Orig. Title: Lost Heiress, The. Shirley Mason & Ben Turpin. Directed by Maurice Marshall. 1928. Columbia. 70 min. Silent. 16mm B&W. *Rental:* Mogulls Films.

Wilbur & Orville: The Air Devils. James Carroll Jordan & Chris Beaumont. Directed by Henning Schellerup. 1979. NBC. 52 min. Sound. 16mm Color. *Sale:* Lucerne Films & Welling Motion Pictures. *Sale:* Lucerne Films, Videotape version.

Wilbur & Orville: The First to Fly. Videotape *Sale:* Vidamerica.

Wilby Conspiracy, The. Sidney Poitier & Michael Caine. Directed by Ralph Nelson. 1975. United Artists. 105 min. Sound. 16mm Color. *Rental:* MGM United & Welling Motion Pictures.

Wild & the Innocent, The. Audie Murphy & Joanna Dru. Directed by Jack Sher. 1959. Universal. 84 min. Sound. 16mm Color. *Rental:* Swank Motion.

Wild & Wonderful. Tony Curtis & Christine Kaufmann. Directed by Michael Anderson. 1964. Universal. 88 min. Sound. 16mm Color. *Rental:* Swank Motion.

Wild & Woolly. Douglas Fairbanks & Eileen Percy. Directed by John Emerson. 1917. Douglas Fairbanks Pictures. 67 min. Silent. 16mm B&W. *Rental:* A Twyman Pres, Em Gee Film Lib, Museum Mod Art & Kit Parker. *Sale:* Learning Corp Am & Natl Cinema. *Rental:* Ivy Films, *Sale:* Blackhawk Films, Super 8 silent version. *Rental:* Kit Parker, 60 min version version.

Wild & Woolly. Jane Withers & Walter Brennan. Directed by Alfred M. Werker. 1937. Fox. 64 min. Sound. 16mm B&W. *Rental:* Willoughby Peer.

Wild Angels, The. Peter Fonda & Nancy Sinatra. Directed by Roger Corman. 1966. American International. 93 min. Sound. 16mm Color. *Rental:* Cine Craft, Films Inc, Video Comm, Welling Motion Pictures, Wholesome Film Ctr & Willoughby Peer.

Wild Beauty. Rex the Wonder Horse. Directed by Henry MacRae. 1927. Universal. 60 min. Silent. 8mm B&W. *Sale:* E Finney.

Wild Beauty. Don Porter & Lois Collier. Directed by Wallace Fox. 1946. Universal. 59 min. Sound. 16mm B&W. *Rental:* Swank Motion.

Wild Blue Yonder, The. Wendell Corey & Vera Ralston. Directed by Allan Dwan. 1952. Republic. 98 min. Sound. 16mm B&W. *Rental:* Ivy Films. *Sale:* Rep Pic Film.

Wild Boys of the Road. Orig. Title: Dangerous Age. Frankie Darro & Rochelle Hudson. Directed by William A. Wellman. 1933. Warners. 68 min. Sound. 16mm B&W. *Rental:* MGM United.

Wild Brian Kent. Ralph Bellamy & Mae Clark. Directed by Howard Bretherton. 1936. RKO. 60 min. Sound. 16mm B&W. *Rental:* Mogulls Films.

Wild Bunch, The. William Holden & Ernest Borgnine. Directed by Sam Peckinpah. 1969. Warner. (Anamorphic). 135 min. Sound. 16mm Color. *Rental:* Films Inc. *Rental:* Festival Films, Videotape version.

Wild Cargo. Directed by Armand Denis. 1934. RKO. (Documentary). 96 min. Sound. 16mm B&W. *Rental:* Films Inc.

Wild Child, The. Francois Truffaut & Jean-Pierre Cargol. Directed by Francois Truffaut. Fr. 1970. France. 85 min. Sound. 16mm B&W. subtitles. *Rental:* MGM United.

Wild Country. Eddie Dean. Directed by Ray Taylor. 1947. PRC. 59 min. Sound. 16mm B&W. *Rental:* Ivy Films. *Sale:* Classics Assoc NY & Rep Pic Film.

Wild Country. Steve Forrest, Vera Miles & Ron Howard. Directed by Robert Totten. 1971. Disney. 100 min. Sound. 16mm Color. *Rental:* Bosco Films, Cine Craft, Elliot Film Co, Film Ctr DC, Film Pres, Films Inc, MGM United, Modern Sound, Newman Film Lib, Roas Films, Swank Motion, Twyman Films, U of IL Film, Welling Motion Pictures, Westcoast Films & Williams Films.

Wild Dakotas, The. Jim Davis & Bill Williams. Directed by Sam Newfield. 1956. Associated. 75 min. Sound. 16mm B&W. *Rental:* Willoughby Peer. *Sale:* Rep Pic Film.

Wild Dogs of Africa, The see Miss Goodall & the Wild Dogs of Africa.

Wild Duck, The. 1976. Britain. (Cast unlisted). 109 min. Videotape Color. *Rental:* Films Inc. *Sale:* Films Inc.

Wild Duck, The. Peter Kern & Jean Seberg. Directed by Hans W. Geissendorfer. Ger. 1976. Germany. 100 min. Sound. 16mm Color. subtitles. *Rental:* New Yorker Films.

Wild Fire! 1970. MGM. (Documentary). 50 min. Sound. 16mm Color. *Rental:* Films Inc, Syracuse U Film & Wholesome Film Ctr. *Sale:* Films Inc. *Sale:* Films Inc, Videotape version.

Wild Frontier, The. Allan Lane. Directed by Philip Ford. 1948. Republic. 59 min. Sound. 16mm B&W. *Rental:* Ivy Films. *Sale:* Rep Pic Film.

Wild Geese, The. Richard Burton & Roger Moore. Directed by Andrew V. McLaglen. 1978. Britain. 120 min. Sound. 16mm Color. *Rental:* Hurlock Cine.

Wild Geese Calling. Henry Fonda & Joan Bennett. Directed by John Brahm. 1941. Fox. 78 min. Sound. 16mm B&W. *Rental:* Films Inc.

Wild Girl. Eva Tanguay. Directed by Howard Estabrook. 1917. Select. 60 min. Silent. 16mm B&W. *Rental:* Twyman Films.

Wild Goose Jack. Jack Miner & Jim Bawden. 1983. 57 min. Sound. Color. *Rental:* Direct Cinema. *Sale:* Direct Cinema. *Sale:* Direct Cinema, Videotape version.

Wild Guitar. Arch Hall Jr. Directed by Ray Dennis Steckler. 1962. Fairway. 89 min. Sound. 16mm Color. *Rental:* Ivy Films.

Wild Harvest. Alan Ladd & Dorothy Lamour. Directed by Tay Garnett. 1947. Paramount. 92 min. Sound. 16mm B&W. *Rental:* Swank Motion.

Wild Heritage. Will Rogers Jr. & Maureen O'Sullivan. Directed by Charles Haas. 1958. Universal. 78 min. Sound. 16mm Color. *Rental:* Swank Motion.

Wild Horse. Hoot Gibson. Directed by Sidney Algier & Richard Thorpe. 1931. Hoffman. 60 min. Sound. 16mm B&W. *Rental:* Mogulls Films.

Wild Horse Ambush. Michael Chapin & Eilene Janssen. Directed by Fred C. Brannon. 1951. Republic. 60 min. Sound. 16mm B&W. *Rental:* Ivy Films. *Sale:* Rep Pic Film.

Wild Horse Canyon. Yakima Canutt. 1925. 60 min. Silent. 16mm B&W. *Sale:* Reel Images.

Wild Horse Canyon. Jack Randall. Directed by Robert Hill. 1938. Monogram. 60 min. Sound. 16mm B&W. *Rental:* Budget Films.

Wild Horse Phantom. Buster Crabbe. Directed by Sam Newfield. 1944. PRC. 56 min. Sound. 16mm B&W. *Rental:* Ivy Films & Mogulls Films. *Sale:* Classics Assoc NY & Rep Pic Film.

Wild Horse Range. Jack Randall. Directed by Raymond K. Johnson. 1940. Monogram. 55 min. Sound. 16mm B&W. *Rental:* Hurlock Cine.

Wild Horse Rodeo. Robert Livingston. Directed by George Sherman. 1937. Republic. 54 min. Sound. 16mm B&W. *Rental:* Ivy Films & Rep Pic Film. *Sale:* Reel Images.

Wild Horse Rustlers. Bob Livingston. Directed by Sam Newfield. 1943. PRC. 58 min. Sound. 16mm B&W. *Rental:* Mogulls Films.

Wild Horses. (Cast unlisted). 88 min. Sound. Videotape Color. *Sale:* Vidamerica.

Wild Horses, Broken Wings. Directed by D. B. Jones. 1979. Learning Corp. (Documentary). 58 min. Sound. 16mm Color. *Rental:* Learning Corp Am. *Sale:* Learning Corp Am. *Sale:* Learning Corp Am, Videotape version.

Wild in the Country. Elvis Presley. Directed by Philip Dunne. 1961. Fox. 114 min. Sound. 16mm Color. *Rental:* Willoughby Peer. *Rental:* Willoughby Peer, Anamorphic version.

Wild in the Streets. Hal Holbrook, Shelley Winters, Christopher Jones & Diane Varsi. Directed by Barry Shear. 1968. American International. 96 min. Sound. 16mm Color. *Rental:* Cine Craft, Charard Motion Pics, Film Ctr DC, Video Comm, Welling Motion Pictures, Westcoast Films, Wholesome Film Ctr & Willoughby Peer.

Wild Innocence. Chut the Kangaroo. Directed by Ken J. Hall. 1937. Australia. 70 min. Sound. 16mm B&W. *Rental:* Budget Films & Film Classics. *Rental:* Film Classics, Videotape version.

Wild is the Wind. Anna Magnani & Anthony Quinn. Directed by George Cukor. 1957. Paramount. 111 min. Sound. 16mm B&W. *Rental:* Films Inc.

Wild Little Bunch, The. Jack Wild. Directed by David Hemmings. Bryanston. 86 min. Sound. 16mm Color. *Rental:* Swank Motion.

Wild Man of Borneo, The. Frank Morgan & Mary Howard. Directed by Robert B. Sinclair. 1941. MGM. 78 min. Sound. 16mm B&W. *Rental:* MGM United.

Wild Mustang. Harry Carey. Directed by Harry Fraser. 1935. William Berke. 60 min. Sound. 16mm B&W. *Rental:* Mogulls Films. *Sale:* Reel Images. *Sale:* Morcraft Films & Reel Images, Super 8 sound version.

Wild Ninety. Norman Mailer. Directed by Norman Mailer. 1972. New Line. 90 min. Sound. 16mm B&W. *Rental:* New Line Cinema. *Sale:* New Line Cinema.

Wild North, The. Stewart Granger & Cyd Charisse. Directed by Andrew Marton. 1952. MGM. 97 min. Sound. 16mm Color. *Rental:* MGM United.

Wild on the Beach. Frankie Randall. Directed by Maury Dexter. 1965. Fox. 77 min. Sound. 16mm B&W. *Rental:* Films Inc.

Wild One, The. Marlon Brando & Lee Marvin. Directed by Laslo Benedek. 1954. Columbia. 79 min. Sound. 16mm B&W. *Rental:* Arcus Film, Budget Films, Cine Craft, Films Inc, Images Film, Inst Cinema, Kerr Film, Kit Parker, Modern Sound, Swank Motion, Twyman Films, Video Comm, Welling Motion Pictures, Westcoast Films, Wholesome Film Ctr & Williams Films.

Wild Oranges. Virginia Valli & Ford Sterling. Directed by King Vidor. 1924. MGM. 74 min. Silent. 16mm B&W. *Rental:* MGM United.

Wild Orchids. Greta Garbo & Lewis Stone. Directed by Sidney Franklin. 1929. MGM. 100 min. Silent. 16mm B&W. *Rental:* MGM United.

Wild Party, The. Anthony Quinn & Carol Ohmart. Directed by Harry Horner. 1957. United Artists. 81 min. Sound. 16mm B&W. *Rental:* MGM United.

Wild Party, The. Clara Bow & Fredric March. Directed by Dorothy Arzner. 1929. 76 min. Sound. 16mm B&W. *Rental:* Swank Motion.

Wild Rapture. Orig. Title: Congolaise. 1940. Film Classics. (Native cast). 78 min. Sound. 16mm B&W. *Rental:* Ivy Films.

Wild Rebels, The. Steve Alaimo. Directed by William Grefe. 1967. Crown. 90 min. Sound. 16mm Color. *Rental:* Video Comm. *Lease:* Video Comm.

Wild Riders, The. Alex Rocco & Elizabeth Knowles. Directed by Richard Kanter. 1971. Tudor. 91 min. Sound. 16mm Color. *Rental:* Video Comm. *Lease:* Video Comm.

Wild River. Montgomery Clift, Lee Remick & Jo Van Fleet. Directed by Elia Kazan. 1960. Fox. (Anamorphic). 105 min. Sound. 16mm Color. *Rental:* Films Inc & Wholesome Film Ctr.

Wild River. 1974. National Geographic. (Documentary). 52 min. Sound. 16mm Color. *Rental:* Syracuse U Film, U Mich Media & Natl Geog. *Sale:* Natl Geog. *Sale:* Natl Geog, Videotape version. *Rental:* Films Inc, Anamorphic version.

Wild Rovers, The. William Holden & Ryan O'Neal. Directed by Blake Edwards. 1971. MGM. 110 min. Sound. 16mm Color. *Rental:* MGM United. *Rental:* MGM United, Anamorphic version.

Wild Science. 1976. EBE. (Documentary). 51 min. Sound. 16mm Color. *Rental:* Ency Brit Ed, La Inst Res Ctr & Syracuse U Film. *Sale:* Ency Brit Ed. *Sale:* Ency Brit Ed, Videotape version.

Wild Season, The. Gert Van Den Bergh. Directed by Emil Nofal. 1968. South Africa. 92 min. Sound. 16mm Color. *Rental:* Cine Craft & Swank Motion.

Wild Seed. Michael Parks. Directed by Brian Hutton. 1965. Universal. 99 min. Sound. 16mm B&W. *Rental:* Swank Motion.

Wild Stallion. Ben Johnson & Edgar Buchanan. Directed by Lewis D. Collins. 1952. Monogram. 70 min. Sound. 16mm B&W. *Rental:* Hurlock Cine.

Wild Stampede, The. Luis Aguilar & Christiane Martel. 1962. NTA. 90 min. Sound. 16mm Color. *Rental:* Ivy Films.

Wild Strawberries. Victor Sjostrom & Ingrid Thulin. Directed by Ingmar Bergman. Swed. 1957. Sweden. 90 min. Sound. 16mm B&W. subtitles. *Rental:* Films Inc, Janus Films, Images Film & New Cinema. *Sale:* Festival Films & Images Film. *Sale:* Festival Films & Tamarelles French Film, Videotape version.

Wild Style. Directed by Charlie Ahearn. 1983. 83 min. Sound. 16mm Color. *Rental:* First Run.

Wild Swans, The. 1972. (Animated). 52 min. Sound. 16mm Color. *Rental:* Films Inc.

Wild West, The. Eddie Dean & Lash La Rue. Directed by Robert Tansey. 1946. PRC. 73 min. Sound. 16mm B&W. *Sale:* Classics Assoc NY.

Wild, Wild Planet. Orig. Title: Galaxy Criminals, The. Tony Russell & Franco Nero. Directed by Anthony Dawson. 1967. Italy. 93 min. Sound. 16mm Color. dubbed. *Rental:* MGM United.

Wildcat, The. Gordon Clifford. Directed by Harry Fraser. 1926. Aywon. 50 min. Silent. 16mm B&W. *Rental:* Mogulls Films.

Wildcat. Richard Arlen & Buster Crabbe. Directed by Frank MacDonald. 1942. Paramount. 80 min. Sound. 16mm B&W. *Sale:* Morcraft Films. *Sale:* Morcraft Films, Super 8 sound version.

Wildcat Bus. Fay Wray & Paul Guilfoyle. Directed by Frank Woodruff. 1940. RKO. 63 min. Sound. 16mm B&W. *Rental:* RKO General Pics.

Wildcat of Tucson. Orig. Title: Promise Fulfilled. William Elliott. Directed by Lambert Hillyer. 1941. Columbia. 60 min. Sound. 16mm B&W. *Rental:* Newman Film Lib.

Wildcat Saunders. Jack Perrin. Directed by Harry Fraser. 1935. World Wide. 57 min. Sound. 16mm B&W. *Sale:* Natl Cinema.

Wildcat Trooper, The. Kermit Maynard. Directed by Elmer Clifton. 1936. Ambassador-Conn. 59 min. Sound. 16mm B&W. *Rental:* Modern Sound.

Wilder Summer, A. Nancy Kulp & Paul Dooley. 1983. Learning Corp.. 54 min. Sound. 16mm Color. *Rental:* Learning Corp Am. *Sale:* Learning Corp Am. *Rental:* Learning Corp Am, *Sale:* Learning Corp Am, Videotape version.

Wilderness Journey. Jimmy Cane. 1971. American National. 94 min. Sound. 16mm Color. *Rental:* Budget Films, Video Comm, Westcoast Films & Williams Films. *Lease:* Video Comm.

Wilderness Journey. Tony Tucker Williams. 94 min. Sound. 16mm Color. *Rental:* Films Inc.

Wildfire. Bob Steele. Directed by Robert Tansey. 1946. Screen Guild. 60 min. Sound. 16mm Color. *Rental:* Mogulls Films & Willoughby Peer.

Wildfire! 1971. MGM. (Documentary). 50 min. Sound. 16mm Color. *Rental:* Films Inc & U Mich Media. *Sale:* Films Inc.

Will Any Gentleman? George Cole & Joan Sims. Directed by Michael Anderson. 1952. Britain. 84 min. Sound. 16mm B&W. *Rental:* Mogulls Films.

Will B. Able's Baggy Pants & Co. Burlesque. Will B. Able. HBO. 75 min. Videotape Color. *Rental:* Films Inc.

Will Penny. Charlton Heston & Donald Pleasance. Directed by Tom Gries. 1968. Paramount. 100 min. Sound. 16mm Color. *Rental:* Films Inc.

Will Rogers: Champion of the People. Robert Hays, Jack Elam & Gene Evans. Directed by Jack Hively. 1977. NBC. 49 min. Sound. 16mm Color. *Rental:* Williams Films & Welling Motion Pictures. *Sale:* Lucerne Films. *Sale:* Lucerne Films, Videotape version.

Will Shakespeare - Gent. 1967. Britain. (Documentary). 50 min. Sound. 16mm B&W. *Rental:* Time-Life Multimedia. *Sale:* Time-Life Multimedia.

Will Success Spoil Rock Hunter? Orig. Title: Oh! for a Man. Jayne Mansfield & Tony Randall. Directed by Frank Tashlin. 1957. Fox. 95 min. Sound. 16mm Color. *Rental:* Films Inc. *Rental:* Films Inc, Anamorphic version.

Will the Fishing Have to Stop? 1979. Nova. (Documentary). 60 min. Videotape Color. *Rental:* PBS Video. *Sale:* PBS Video.

Will to Be Free, The. Louis Jourdan & Morris Carnovsky. 1975. ABC. 60 min. Sound. 16mm Color. *Rental:* Natl Churches Christ & Films Inc. *Sale:* Films Inc.

Will Tomorrow Ever Come? *see* That's My Man.

Willa Cather's America. Directed by Richard Schickel. 1977. WNET. (Documentary). 60 min. Sound. 16mm Color. *Rental:* Films Human. *Sale:* Films Human.

Willamsburg File, The. 1976. 58 min. Sound. Videotape *Rental:* PBS Video. *Sale:* PBS Video.

Willard. Bruce Davison & Ernest Borgnine. Directed by Daniel Mann. 1971. Cinerama. 95 min. Sound. 16mm Color. *Rental:* Arcus Film, Buchan Pic, Modern Sound, Swank Motion, Westcoast Films, Wholesome Film Ctr & Williams Films.

Willi Busch Report, Der. Tilo Pruchner & Dorothea Moritz. Directed by Niklaus Schilling. Ger. 1979. Germany. 118 min. Sound. 16mm Color. subtitles. *Rental:* Cinema Five.

William Faulkner: A Life on Paper. Directed by Robert Squier. 1980. Mississippi ETV. (Documentary). 120 min. Sound. 16mm Color. *Rental:* Films Inc. *Sale:* Films Inc. *Sale:* Films Inc. *Rental:* Films Inc, *Sale:* Films Inc, Videotape version.

William Faulkner's Mississippi. 1966. Metromedia. (Documentary). 49 min. Sound. 16mm B&W. *Rental:* Benchmark Films, Iowa Films, Syracuse U Film, U Cal Media & U Mich Media. *Sale:* Benchmark Films. *Sale:* Benchmark Films, 8mm version avail. version.

William Tell. Conrad Veidt. Directed by Heinz Paul. Ger. 1935. Germany. 70 min. Sound. 16mm B&W. subtitles. *Rental:* Film Classics.

Williamsburg File, The. 1982. Colonial Williamsburg. (Documentary). 45 min. Sound. 16mm Color. *Rental:* Colonial.

Willie & Joe Back at the Front. Tom Ewell & Harvey Lembeck. Directed by George Sherman. 1952. Universal. 87 min. Sound. 16mm B&W. *Rental:* Swank Motion.

Willie & Phil. Michael Ontkean & Paul Sharkey. Directed by Paul Mazursky. 1980. Fox. 116 min. Sound. 16mm Color. *Rental:* Films Inc.

Willie Dynamite. Roscoe Orman & Diana Sands. Directed by Gilbert Moses. 1973. Universal. 102 min. Sound. 16mm Color. *Rental:* Williams Films.

Willie McBean & His Magic Machine. Directed by Arthur Rankin Jr. 1965. Magna. (Animated). 94 min. Sound. 16mm Color. *Rental:* Buchan Pic, Budget Films, Cine Craft, Charard Motion Pics, Twyman Films, Video Comm, Westcoast Films & Wholesome Film Ctr.

Willie Wonka & the Chocolate Factory. Gene Wilder & Jack Albertson. Directed by Mel Stewart. 1971. Paramount. 98 min. Sound. 16mm Color. *Rental:* Films Inc.

Willmar Eight, The. Directed by Lee Grant. 1980. California Newsreel. (Documentary). 55 min. Sound. 16mm Color. *Rental:* CA Newsreel, Frist Run, Iowa Films & U Mich Media.

Wilson. Alexander Knox & Geraldine Fitzgerald. Directed by Henry King. 1944. Fox. 120 min. Sound. 16mm Color. *Rental:* Films Inc & Twyman Films.

Win, Place or Steal. Orig. Title: Three for the Money. Alex Karras, McLean Stevenson & Dean Stockwell. Directed by Richard Bailey. 1972. Cinema National. 93 min. Sound. 16mm Color. *Rental:* Budget Films & Welling Motion Pictures.

Winchester for Hire. Edd Byrnes & Guy Madison. Directed by E. G. Rowland. 1968. Italy. 90 min. Sound. 16mm Color. dubbed. *Rental:* Cine Craft, Inst Cinema, Kerr Film, Modern Sound, Welling Motion Pictures & Westcoast Films.

Winchester Seventy-Three. James Stewart & Shelley Winters. Directed by Anthony Mann. 1950. Universal. 92 min. Sound. 16mm B&W. *Rental:* Swank Motion & Williams Films.

Wind, The. Lillian Gish & Lars Hanson. Directed by Victor Seastrom. 1928. MGM. 120 min. Silent. 16mm B&W. *Rental:* MGM United.

Wind Across the Everglades. Burl Ives & Christopher Plummer. Directed by Nicholas Ray. 1958. Warners. 93 min. Sound. 16mm Color. *Rental:* Films Inc.

Wind & the Lion, The. Sean Connery & Candice Bergen. Directed by John Milius. 1975. MGM. (Anamorphic). 119 min. Sound. 16mm Color. *Rental:* MGM United.

Wind From the East. Trans. Title: Vent de l'Est, Le. Gian-Maria Volonte. Directed by Jean-Luc Godard. Fr. 1970. France. 95 min. Sound. 16mm Color. subtitles. *Rental:* Films Inc, New Cinema & New Line Cinema.

Wind is Driving Him Toward the Open Sea, The. 52 min. Sound. 16mm Color. *Rental:* Filmmakers Coop.

Wind Raiders of the Sahara. 1974. National Geographic. (Documentary). 52 min. Sound. 16mm Color. *Rental:* Natl Geog. *Sale:* Natl Geog. *Sale:* Natl Geog, Videotape version.

Windflowers. Pola Chapelle. Directed by Adolfas Mekas. 1968. Adolfas Mekas. 64 min. Sound. 16mm B&W. *Rental:* Kit Parker.

Windjammer. George O'Brien. Directed by Ewing Scott. 1937. RKO. 59 min. Sound. 16mm B&W. *Rental:* Mogulls Films.

Windom's Way. Peter Finch & Mary Ure. Directed by Ronald Neame. 1957. Britain. 108 min. Sound. 16mm Color. *Sale:* Learning Corp Am. *Rental:* Vidamerica. *Rental:* Vidamerica, Videotape version.

Window, The. Bobby Driscoll & Barbara Hale. Directed by Ted Tetzlaff. 1949. RKO. 73 min. Sound. 16mm B&W. *Rental:* Films Inc. *Lease:* Films Inc.

Windows. Talia Shire & Elizabeth Ashley. Directed by Gordon Willis. 1980. United Artists. 94 min. Sound. 16mm Color. *Rental:* MGM United.

Windows of Heaven. 1963. Brigham Young. (Documentary). 50 min. Sound. 16mm Color. *Rental:* BYU Media. *Rental:* BYU Media, Subtitled version.

Winds of the Wasteland. John Wayne. Directed by Mack V. Wright. 1936. Republic. 54 min. Sound. 16mm B&W. *Rental:* Budget Films & Ivy Films. *Sale:* Rep Pic Film & Reel Images. *Sale:* Reel Images, Super 8 sound version.

Windsplitter, The. Paul Lambert & Joyce Taylor. Directed by Julius D. Feigelson. 1971. Futurama. 95 min. Sound. 16mm Color. *Rental:* Budget Films & Video Comm. *Lease:* Video Comm.

Windwalker, The. Trevor Howard, James Remar & Nick Ramus. Directed by Keith Merrill. 1985. Pacific International. 106 min. Sound. 16mm Color. *Rental:* Swank Motion.

Wine of Youth, The. Eleanor Boardman, James Morrison & Zasu Pitts. Directed by King Vidor. 1924. MGM. 70 min. Silent. 16mm B&W. *Rental:* MGM United.

Wine, Women & Horses. Ann Sheridan & Barton MacLane. Directed by Louis King. 1937. Warners. 64 min. Sound. 16mm B&W. *Rental:* MGM United.

Wing & a Prayer, A. Don Ameche & Dana Andrews. Directed by Henry Hathaway. 1944. Fox. 97 min. Sound. 16mm B&W. *Rental:* Films Inc.

Winged Colt, The. Slim Pickens & Jane Withers. Directed by Larry Elikann. 1978. ABC. 66 min. Sound. 16mm Color. *Rental:* Roas Films. *Sale:* MTI Tele, Videotape version.

Winged Victory. Lon McCallister & Jeanne Crain. Directed by George Cukor. 1944. Fox. 98 min. Sound. 16mm B&W. *Rental:* Films Inc.

Winged World, The. 1967. National Geographic. (Documentary). 52 min. Sound. 16mm Color. *Rental:* Natl Geog, Syracuse U Film, Wholesome Film Ctr & U Cal Media. *Sale:* Natl Geog. *Sale:* Natl Geog, Videotape version.

Wings. Clara Bow & Gary Cooper. Directed by William A. Wellman. 1927. Paramount. (Music & sound effects only). 130 min. Sound. 16mm B&W. *Rental:* Films Inc. *Rental:* Films Inc, Silent 16mm version.

Wings & the Woman. Robert Newton & Anna Neagle. Directed by Herbert Wilcox. 1943. RKO. 94 min. Sound. 16mm B&W. *Rental:* RKO General Pics.

Wings for the Eagle. Dennis Morgan & Ann Sheridan. Directed by Lloyd Bacon. 1942. Warners. 85 min. Sound. 16mm B&W. *Rental:* MGM United.

Wings in the Dark. Cary Grant & Myrna Loy. Directed by James Flood. 1935. Paramount. 77 min. Sound. 16mm B&W. *Rental:* Swank Motion.

Wings of an Eagle. American National. (Documentary). 94 min. Sound. 16mm Color. *Rental:* Westcoast Films.

Wings of Eagles, The. John Wayne & Dan Dailey. Directed by John Ford. 1957. MGM. 111 min. Sound. 16mm Color. *Rental:* MGM United.

Wings of Mystery. Judy Geeson & Hennie Scott. Directed by Gilbert Gunn. 1960. Britain. 55 min. Sound. 16mm B&W. *Sale:* Lucerne Films.

Wings of the Hawk. Van Heflin & Julie Adams. Directed by Budd Boetticher. 1953. Universal. 81 min. Sound. 16mm Color. *Rental:* Swank Motion.

Wings of the Morning. Henry Fonda & Annabella. Directed by Harold Schuster. 1936. Britain. 87 min. Sound. 16mm Color. *Rental:* A Twyman Pres & Budget Films.

Wings of the Navy. George Brent, John Payne & Olivia De Havilland. Directed by Lloyd Bacon. 1939. Warners. 89 min. Sound. 16mm B&W. *Rental:* MGM United.

Wings Over Honolulu. Ray Milland & Wendy Barrie. 1937. Universal. 78 min. Sound. 16mm B&W. *Rental:* Swank Motion.

Wings Over the Pacific. Inez Cooper & Edward Norris. Directed by Phil Rosen. 1943. Monogram. 65 min. Sound. 16mm B&W. *Rental:* Mogulls Films.

Wings Over Wyoming. Orig. Title: Hollywood Cowboy. George O'Brien. Directed by Ewing Scott. 1937. RKO. 65 min. Sound. 16mm B&W. *Sale:* Morcraft Films & Reel Images. *Sale:* Reel Images, Super 8 sound version.

Winifred Wagner. Directed by Hans Jurgen Syberberg. Ger. 1975. Germany. (Documentary). 104 min. Sound. 16mm Color. subtitles. *Rental:* Liberty Co.

Winner Take All. James Cagney, Marion Nixon & Virginia Bruce. Directed by Roy Del Ruth. 1932. Warners. 66 min. Sound. 16mm B&W. *Rental:* MGM United.

Winners & Losers: Poverty in California. 1979. PBS. (Documentary). 59 min. Sound. Videotape Color. *Rental:* PBS Video. *Sale:* PBS Video.

Winner's Circle, The. Jean Willes & Morgan Farley. Directed by Felix Feist. 1948. Fox. 74 min. Sound. 16mm B&W. *Rental:* Learning Corp Am. *Sale:* Learning Corp Am.

Winners of the Wilderness. Tim McCoy & Joan Crawford. Directed by W. S. Van Dyke. 1927. MGM. 80 min. Silent. 16mm B&W. *Rental:* MGM United.

Winning. Paul Newman & Joanne Woodward. Directed by James Goldstone. 1969. Universal. 123 min. Sound. 16mm Color. *Rental:* Swank Motion.

Winning Of the West. Gene Autry. Directed by George Archainbaud. 1953. Columbia. 70 min. Sound. 16mm B&W. *Sale:* Blackhawk Films. *Sale:* Blackhawk Films, Videotape version.

Winning Ticket, The. Leo Carrillo & Irene Hervey. Directed by Charles Reisner. 1935. MGM. 70 min. Sound. 16mm B&W. *Rental:* MGM United.

Winslow Boy, The. Robert Donat, Margaret Leighton & Sir Cedric Hardwicke. Directed by Anthony Asquith. 1950. Britain. 97 min. Sound. 16mm B&W. *Rental:* Budget Films, Films Inc & Kit Parker.

Winstanley. Miles Halliwell & Jerome Willis. Directed by Kevin Brownlow & Andrew Mollo. 1975. Britain. 96 min. Sound. 16mm B&W. *Rental:* Images Film.

Winston Churchill. 1964. Wolper. (Documentary). 52 min. Sound. 16mm B&W. *Rental:* Budget Films & Syracuse U Film.

Winter a-Go-Go. James Stacy & Beverly Adams. Directed by Richard Benedict. 1965. Columbia. 90 min. Sound. 16mm Color. *Rental:* Modern Sound & Newman Film Lib.

Winter Carnival. Ann Sheridan & Richard Carlson. Directed by Charles Reisner. 1939. United Artists. 105 min. Sound. 16mm B&W. *Rental:* Film Classics, Inst Cinema, Learning Corp Am & Mogulls Films. *Lease:* Learning Corp Am.

Winter Comes Early. Art Hindle & Trudy Young. 1974. Cannon. 112 min. Sound. 16mm Color. *Rental:* Williams Films.

Winter Kept Us Warm. John Labow. Directed by David Sector. 1965. Canada. 80 min. Sound. 16mm B&W. *Rental:* Canyon Cinema.

Winter Kills. Jeff Bridges & John Huston. Directed by William Richert. 1979. Embassy. 97 min. Sound. 16mm Color. *Rental:* Films Inc.

Winter Light. Ingrid Thulin & Gunnar Bjornstrand. Directed by Ingmar Bergman. Swed. 1962. Sweden. 80 min. Sound. 16mm B&W. subtitles. *Rental:* Films Inc, Janus Films & New Cinema. *Sale:* Tamarelles French Film, Videotape version.

Winter Lilies. 1979. PBS. (Documentary). 59 min. Sound. Videotape Color. *Rental:* PBS Video. *Sale:* PBS Video.

Winter Meeting. Bette Davis & Jim Davis. Directed by Bretaigne Windust. 1948. Warners. 104 min. Sound. 16mm B&W. *Rental:* MGM United.

Winter Soldier. 1980. Twyman. (Documentary, Tinted). 90 min. Sound. 16mm Color. *Rental:* Twyman Films.

Winter Wind. Jacques Charrier & Marina Vlady. Directed by Miklos Jancso. Fr. 1969. France-Hungary. (Anamorphic). 80 min. Sound. 16mm B&W. subtitles. *Rental:* Grove.

Winter Wonderland. Charles Drake & Lynne Roberts. Directed by Bernard Vorhaus. 1947. Republic. 71 min. Sound. 16mm B&W. *Sale:* Classics Assoc NY.

Winterhawk. Michael Dante & Leif Erickson. Directed by Charles B. Pierce. 1976. American International. 98 min. Sound. 16mm Color. *Rental:* Wholesome Film Ctr.

Winter's Tale, A. Jeremy Kemp & Anna Calder Marshall. 1980. Britain. 173 min. Videotape Color. *Rental:* Iowa Films.

Winterset. Burgess Meredith & Margo. Directed by Alfred Santell. 1936. RKO. 80 min. Sound. 16mm B&W. *Rental:* Budget Films, Em Gee Film Lib, Film Classics, Films Inc, Kit Parker & Video Comm. *Sale:* Cinema Concepts, Festival Films & Glenn Photo. *Sale:* Glenn Photo, Super 8 sound version. *Sale:* Festival Films, Videotape version.

Wintertime. Sonja Henie & Jack Oakie. Directed by John Brahm. 1943. Fox. 82 min. Sound. 16mm B&W. *Rental:* Films Inc.

Wise Girl. Ray Milland & Walter Abel. Directed by Leigh Jason. 1938. RKO. 70 min. Sound. 16mm B&W. *Rental:* RKO General Pics.

Wise Girls. Elliott Nugent. Directed by E. Mason Hopper. 1930. MGM. 92 min. Sound. 16mm B&W. *Rental:* MGM United.

Wishing Machine, The. Xerox. (Cast unlisted). 75 min. Sound. 16mm Color. *Sale:* Xerox Films.

Wishing Ring, The. Directed by Maurice Tourneur. 1914. World. (Cast unlisted). 60 min. Silent. 16mm B&W. *Rental:* Em Gee Film Lib. *Sale:* Festival Films.

Witch, The. Mirja Mane. Directed by Roland Hallstrom. Swed. 1955. Sweden. 70 min. Sound. 16mm B&W. subtitles. *Rental:* A Twyman Pres & Films Inc.

Witch, The. Rosanna Schiaffino & Richard Johnson. Directed by Damiano Damiani. 1969. Italy. 98 min. Sound. 16mm B&W. dubbed. *Rental:* Budget Films, Kerr Film & Video Comm.

Witchcraft. Lon Chaney Jr. Directed by Don Sharp. 1964. Britain. 79 min. Sound. 16mm B&W. *Rental:* Films Inc.

Witchcraft Among the Azande. 1982. Britain. 52 min. Videotape Color. *Rental:* Film Makers. *Sale:* Film Makers.

Witchcraft Seventy. Directed by Luigi Scattini. 1970. Filmways. 82 min. Sound. 16mm Color. *Rental:* Films Inc.

Witchcraft Through the Ages. Orig. Title: Haxan. Directed by Benjamin Christiansen. 1920. Sweden. (Musical score only) (Cast unlisted). 75 min. Sound. 16mm B&W. *Sale:* Films Inc & Reel Images. *Rental:* Budget Films, Em Gee Film Lib, Janus Films & Kit Parker, Silent 16mm version. *Sale:* Reel Images, Super 8 sound version. *Sale:* Tamarelles French Film, Videotape version.

Witches: New Fashion, Old Religion. 1972. Media Guild. 52 min. Sound. 16mm Color. *Rental:* Media Guild. *Sale:* Media Guild. *Sale:* Media Guild, Videotape version.

Witchfinder General *see* Conqueror Worm.

Witchmaker, The. Anthony Eisley & John Lodge. Directed by William O. Brown. 1969. Excelsior. 101 min. Sound. 16mm Color. *Rental:* Budget Films, Films Inc, Kerr Film, Video Comm & Westcoast Films.

Witch's Hammer, The. Directed by Otakar Vavra. Czech. 1971. Czechoslovakia. (Cast unlisted). 100 min. Sound. 16mm B&W. *Rental:* New Line Cinema. *Sale:* New Line Cinema.

Witch's Mirror, The. Rosita Arenas & Armando Calvo. Directed by Chano Urueta. Span. 1961. Mexico. 75 min. Sound. 16mm B&W. subtitles. *Rental:* Budget Films.

With a Song in My Heart. Susan Hayward & Rory Calhoun. Directed by Walter Lang. 1952. Fox. 117 min. Sound. 16mm Color. *Rental:* Films Inc & Twyman Films.

With Babies & Banners: The Story of the Women's Emergency Brigade. Directed by Lorraine Gray. 1978. 45 min. Sound. 16mm Color. *Rental:* Cinema Guild & Iowa Films.

With Custer at Little Big Horn. Orig. Title: General Custer at Little Big Horn. Ray Stuart. Directed by Harry Fraser. 1926. Sunset. 70 min. Silent. 16mm B&W. *Rental:* Film Classics & Mogulls Films. *Sale:* Film Classics.

With God on Our Side. 1982. Phoenix. 59 min. Sound. 16mm Color. *Rental:* U Cal Media, Iowa Films & Phoenix Films. *Sale:* Phoenix Films. *Sale:* Phoenix Films, Videotape version.

With Hardship Their Garment. 1975. Britain. (Documentary). 52 min. Sound. 16mm Color. *Rental:* U of IL Film.

With Liberty & Justice for All. 1956. Saudek. (Documentary, Kinescope). 60 min. Sound. 16mm B&W. *Rental:* U of IL Film. *Sale:* IQ Films.

With Love & Kisses. Pinky Tomlin & Toby Wing. Directed by Leslie Goodwins. 1936. Melody. 71 min. Sound. 16mm B&W. *Rental:* Budget Films.

With Sitting Bull at Spirit Lake Massacre. Bryant Washburn. Directed by Robert N. Bradbury. 1925. Sunset. 72 min. Silent. 16mm B&W. *Rental:* Mogulls Films.

With Six You Get Egg Roll. Doris Day & Brian Keith. Directed by Howard Morris. 1968. National General. 95 min. Sound. 16mm Color. *Rental:* Films Inc, Swank Motion & Williams Films.

With the Cuban Women *see* Con los Mujeres Cubanas.

With These Hands: The Rebirth of the American Craftsman. Directed by Daniel Wilson. 1970. Daniel Wilson. (Documentary). 53 min. Sound. 16mm Color. *Rental:* D Wilson & U Mich Media. *Sale:* D Wilson.

With Words & Music. Irene Hervey & Robert Armstrong. Directed by Milton Carruth. 1937. Universal. 60 min. Sound. 16mm B&W. *Rental:* Mogulls Films.

Within America. 3 pts. 1980. Centre. (Documentary). 100 min. Sound. 16mm Color. *Rental:* Centre Co. *Sale:* Centre Co. *Sale:* Centre Co, Videotape version.

Within the Law. Norma Talmadge. Directed by Frank Lloyd. 1923. 16mm *Rental:* A Twyman Pres.

Within These Walls. Thomas Mitchell & Mary Anderson. Directed by Bruce Humberstone. 1945. Fox. 71 min. Sound. 16mm B&W. *Rental:* Films Inc.

Without a Trace. Kate Nelligan & Judd Hirsch. Directed by Stanley R. Jaffe. 1983. Fox. 121 min. Sound. 16mm Color. *Rental:* Films Inc.

Without Anesthesia. Ewa Dalkowska. Directed by Andrzej Wajda. Pol. 1978. Poland. 116 min. Sound. 16mm Color. subtitles Eng. *Rental:* New Yorker Films.

Without Apparent Motive. Jean-Louis Trintignant. Directed by Philippe Labro. Fr. 1972. France. 102 min. Sound. 16mm Color. subtitles. *Rental:* Films Inc.

Without Honor. Laraine Day, Dane Clark & Franchot Tone. Directed by Irving Pichel. 1949. United Artists. 69 min. Sound. 16mm B&W. *Rental:* Budget Films.

Without Love. Spencer Tracy & Katharine Hepburn. Directed by Harold S. Bucquet. 1945. MGM. 111 min. Sound. 16mm B&W. *Rental:* MGM United.

Without Onion. Beverly Washburn. Directed by Dan Dunkelberger. 1966. Ken Anderson. 70 min. Sound. 16mm Color. *Rental:* Roas Films.

Without Orders. Ward Bond & Robert Armstrong. Directed by Lew Landers. 1937. RKO. 69 min. Sound. 16mm *Rental:* RKO General Pics.

Without Reservations. Claudette Colbert & John Wayne. Directed by Mervyn LeRoy. 1946. RKO. 101 min. Sound. 16mm B&W. *Rental:* Bosco Films, Budget Films, Video Comm & Welling Motion Pictures. *Lease:* Video Comm.

Without Warning. Jack Palance & Martin Landau. Directed by Greydon Clark. 1980. Filmways. 89 min. Sound. 16mm Color. *Rental:* Swank Motion.

Witness Chair, The. Ann Harding & Walter Abel. Directed by George Nicholls. 1936. RKO. 64 min. Sound. 16mm *Rental:* RKO General Pics.

Witness for the Prosecution. Tyrone Power & Charles Laughton. Directed by Billy Wilder. 1957. United Artists. 114 min. Sound. 16mm B&W. *Rental:* MGM United.

Witness to Murder. Barbara Stanwyck & George Sanders. Directed by Roy Rowland. 1954. United Artists. 83 min. Sound. 16mm B&W. *Rental:* MGM United.

Witnesses, The. Directed by Frederic Rossif. 1961. 81 min. Sound. 16mm B&W. *Rental:* Films Inc.

Wives & Lovers. Janet Leigh & Van Johnson. Directed by John Rich. 1963. Paramount. 103 min. Sound. 16mm B&W. *Rental:* Films Inc.

Wives' Tale, A. 73 min. Sound. 16mm Color. *Rental:* Cinema Guild.

Wives Under Suspicion. Warren William & Gail Patrick. Directed by James Whale. 1938. Universal. 75 min. Sound. 16mm B&W. *Rental:* Swank Motion.

Wiz, The. Diana Ross & Lena Horne. Directed by Sidney Lumet. 1978. Universal. 133 min. Sound. 16mm Color. *Rental:* Swank Motion. *Rental:* Swank Motion, Videotape version.

Wizard of Babylon, The. Directed by Rainer Werner Fassbinder. Eng. & Ger. 1982. 83 min. Sound. 16mm Color. subtitles Eng. *Rental:* New Yorker Films.

Wizard of Baghdad. Dick Shawn & Diane Baker. Directed by George Sherman. 1960. Fox. 93 min. Sound. 16mm Color. *Rental:* Charard Motion Pics & Inst Cinema. *Rental:* Willoughby Peer, Anamorphic version.

Wizard of Mars, The. John Carradine & Roger Gentry. Directed by David L. Hewitt. 1964. Goldman. 84 min. Sound. 16mm Color. *Rental:* Films Inc, Ivy Films, Rep Pic Film & Video Comm. *Lease:* Rep Pic Film.

Wizard of Menlo Park, The. 1963. Hearst. (Documentary). 50 min. Sound. 16mm B&W. *Sale:* King Features.

Wizard of Oz, The. Larry Semon & Oliver Hardy. Directed by Larry Semon. 1925. Chadwick. 80 min. Silent. 16mm B&W. *Rental:* Budget Films, Em Gee Film Lib, Kit Parker & Standard Film. *Sale:* Glenn Photo. *Sale:* Glenn Photo, Super 8 silent version.

Wizard of Oz, The. Judy Garland & Frank Morgan. Directed by Victor Fleming. 1939. MGM. (B&W Sequences). 100 min. Sound. 16mm Color. *Rental:* MGM United. *Rental:* MGM United, Videotape version.

Wizard of Waukesha, The. Directed by Susan Brockman & Catherine Orentreich. First Run. (Documentary). 59 min. Sound. 16mm Color. *Rental:* Direct Cinema & First Run. *Sale:* Direct Cinema. *Sale:* Direct Cinema, Videotape version.

Wizard Who Spat on the Floor, The. 1974. Britain. (Documentary). 60 min. Sound. 16mm Color. *Rental:* Time-Life Multimedia. *Sale:* Time-Life Multimedia. *Rental:* Time-Life Multimedia, *Sale:* Time-Life Multimedia, Videotape version.

Wizards. Directed by Ralph Bakshi. 1977. Fox. (Animated). 81 min. Sound. 16mm Color. *Rental:* Films Inc.

Wobblies, The. Directed by Steward Bird & Deborah Shaffer. First Run. (Documentary). 89 min. Sound. 16mm Color. *Rental:* First Run. *Lease:* First Run.

Wolf Call. John Carroll & Movita. Directed by George Waggner. 1939. Monogram. 70 min. Sound. 16mm B&W. *Rental:* Hurlock Cine.

Wolf Dog. Jim Davis. Directed by Sam Newfield. 1958. Fox. (Anamorphic). 69 min. Sound. 16mm B&W. *Rental:* Willoughby Peer.

Wolf Hunters. Kirby Grant & Jan Clayton. Directed by Budd Boetticher. 1949. Monogram. 60 min. Sound. 16mm B&W. *Rental:* Budget Films, Hurlock Cine, Lewis Film & Modern Sound.

Wolf Larsen. Barry Sullivan & Peter Graves. Directed by Harmon Jones. 1958. Allied Artists. 83 min. Sound. 16mm B&W. *Rental:* Ivy Films. *Sale:* Rep Pic Film.

Wolf Man, The. Claude Rains & Warren William. Directed by George Waggner. 1941. Universal. 75 min. Sound. 16mm B&W. *Rental:* Swank Motion.

Wolf of New York, The. Edmund Lowe & Jerome Cowan. Directed by William McGann. 1940. Republic. 67 min. Sound. 16mm B&W. *Rental:* Ivy Films.

Wolf Pack: U-Boat In the Atlantic, 1939-1944. Directed by Hugh Raggett. (World at War Ser.). : Pt. 10.). 1973. Media Guild. (Documentary). 52 min. Sound. 16mm Color. *Rental:* Media Guild & U Cal Media. *Sale:* Media Guild. *Sale:* Media Guild, Videotape version.

Wolf Tracks. Jack Hoxie. Directed by Mack V. Wright. 1920. Universal. 50 min. Silent. 8mm B&W. *Rental:* Budget Films. *Sale:* Film Classics.

Wolf Woman, The. Anne Borel & Fred Stafford. Directed by R. D. Silver. 1976. Dimension. 84 min. Sound. 16mm Color. *Sale:* Salz Ent.

Wolfen. Albert Finney & Diane Venora. Directed by Michael Wadleigh. 1981. Orion. 115 min. Sound. 16mm Color. *Rental:* Films Inc.

Wolfheart's Revenge. Guinn Williams. 1924. Aywon. 55 min. Silent. 16mm B&W. *Sale:* Morcraft Films.

Wolves & the Wolf Men. 1970. MGM. (Documentary). 52 min. Sound. 16mm Color. *Rental:* Films Inc, Syracuse U Film, U Cal Media, U of IL Film, U Mich Media & Wholesome Film Ctr. *Sale:* Films Inc. *Sale:* Films Inc, Videotape version.

Wolves Of the Range. Robert Livingstone. Directed by Sam Newfield. 1943. PRC. 61 min. Sound. 16mm B&W. *Sale:* Cinema Concepts.

Woman, a Family, A. Directed by Joris Ivens & Marceline Loridan. 1978. China. (Documentary). 108 min. Sound. 16mm Color. *Rental:* Cinema Arts.

Woman Against Woman. Herbert Marshall, Virginia Bruce & Mary Astor. Directed by Robert B. Sinclair. 1938. MGM. 61 min. Sound. 16mm B&W. *Rental:* MGM United.

Woman Alone, A. Anna Sten. Directed by Eugene Frenke. 1937. 79 min. 16mm *Rental:* A Twyman Pres.

Woman & the Hunter. Ann Sheridan, David Farrar & John Loder. Directed by George Breakston. 1957. Britain. 79 min. Sound. 16mm B&W. *Rental:* Ivy Films. *Sale:* Rep Pic Film.

Woman & the Puppet. Geraldine Farrar. Directed by Reginald Barker. 1920. 16mm *Rental:* A Twyman Pres.

Woman Between, The. Anita Louise & Lily Damita. Directed by Victor Schertzinger. 1932. RKO. 73 min. Sound. 16mm *Rental:* RKO General Pics.

Woman Chases Man. Miriam Hopkins & Joel McCrea. Directed by John G. Blystone. 1937. Goldwyn. 69 min. Sound. 16mm B&W. *Rental:* Films Inc.

Woman Disputed, The. Norma Talmadge & Gilbert Roland. Directed by Henry King & Sam Taylor. 1928. 16mm *Rental:* A Twyman Pres.

Woman Doctor. Henry Wilcoxen & Claire Dodd. Directed by Sidney Salkow. 1939. Republic. 54 min. Sound. 16mm B&W. *Rental:* Ivy Films. *Sale:* Rep Pic Film.

Woman Eater, The. George Coulouris & Vera Day. Directed by Charles Saunders. 1959. Britain. 75 min. Sound. 16mm B&W. *Rental:* Budget Films, Modern Sound & Video Comm.

Woman for Charlie, A *see* Cockeyed Cowboys of Calico County.

Woman for Joe, A. Diane Cilento & George Baker. Directed by George More O'Ferrall. 1955. Britain. 91 min. Sound. 16mm B&W. *Rental:* Cinema Five.

Woman from Headquarters, The. Virginia Houston & Barbara Fuller. Directed by George Blair. 1950. Republic. 60 min. Sound. 16mm B&W. *Rental:* Ivy Films. *Sale:* Rep Pic Film.

Woman Gives, The. Norma Talmadge. Directed by Roy William Neill. 1920. 16mm *Rental:* A Twyman Pres.

Woman Hunt. Steven Piccaro. Directed by Maury Dexter. 1962. Fox. (Anamorphic). 60 min. Sound. 16mm B&W. *Rental:* Films Inc.

Woman I Stole, The. Jack Holt & Fay Wray. Directed by Irving Cummings. 1933. Columbia. Sound. 16mm B&W. *Rental:* Kit Parker.

Woman in Blue, The *see* Femme en Bleu.

Woman in Brown, The. Orig. Title: Vicious Circle. Conrad Nagel. Directed by W. Lee Wilder. 1948. Britain. 70 min. Sound. 16mm B&W. *Rental:* Inst Cinema.

Woman in Green, The. Basil Rathbone & Nigel Bruce. Directed by Roy William Neill. 1945. Universal. 68 min. Sound. 16mm B&W. *Rental:* Budget Films, Classic Film Mus, Em Gee Film Lib, Learning Corp Am, Newman Film Lib, Natl Film Video, Roas Films, Video Comm & Westcoast Films. *Sale:* Cinema Concepts, Festival Films, Glenn Photo & Learning Corp Am. *Sale:* Blackhawk Films & Glenn Photo, Super 8 sound version. *Sale:* Festival Films & Tamarelles French Film, Videotape version.

Woman in Her Thirties, A *see* Side Streets.

Woman in Red, The. Barbara Stanwyck & Gene Raymond. Directed by Robert Florey. 1935. Warners. 68 min. Sound. 16mm B&W. *Rental:* MGM United.

Woman in the Dark, The. Penny Edwards & Ross Elliott. Directed by George Blair. 1951. Republic. 60 min. Sound. 16mm B&W. *Rental:* Ivy Films. *Sale:* Rep Pic Film.

Woman in the Dunes, The. Kyoko Kishida. Directed by Hiroshi Toshigahara. Jap. 1964. Japan. 130 min. Sound. 16mm B&W. subtitles. *Rental:* Budget Films, Corinth Films, Images Film, Kit Parker, Natl Film Video & Wholesome Film Ctr. *Sale:* Cinema Concepts, Festival Films & Natl Cinema. *Lease:* Corinth Films. *Rental:* Corinth Films, *Sale:* Festival Films, Videotape version.

Woman in the Moon, The. Trans. Title: Die Frau Im Mond. Willy Fritsch & Fritz Rasp. Directed by Fritz Lang. 1929. Germany. 115 min. Silent. 16mm B&W. *Rental:* A Twyman Pres, Budget Films, Em Gee Film Lib, Films Inc, Images Film & Kit Parker. *Sale:* Cinema Concepts, Festival Film, Reel Images & Images Film. *Rental:* Budget Films, *Sale:* Cinema Concepts, Sound 16mm version. *Sale:* Cinema Concepts, Super 8 sound version. *Sale:* Reel Images, Super 8 silent version. *Rental:* Kit Parker, Music Version version. *Sale:* Festival Films & Images Film, Videotape version.

Woman in the Suitcase, The. Enid Bennett & William Conklin. Directed by Fred Niblo. 1920. Paramount. 65 min. Silent. 16mm B&W. *Sale:* Blackhawk Films. *Sale:* Blackhawk Films, Super 8 silent version.

Woman in the Window, The. Joan Bennett & Edward G. Robinson. Directed by Fritz Lang. 1944. RKO. 99 min. Sound. 16mm B&W. *Rental:* MGM United.

Woman in White, The. Alexis Smith & Eleanor Parker. Directed by Peter Godfrey. 1948. Warners. 109 min. Sound. 16mm B&W. *Rental:* MGM United.

Woman is a Woman, A. Trans. Title: Femme Est Une Femme, Une. Jean-Paul Belmondo & Anna Karina. Directed by Jean-Luc Godard. Fr. 1964. France. 88 min. Sound. 16mm B&W. subtitles. *Rental:* New Yorker Films. *Rental:* New Yorker Films, Anamorphic version.

Woman Next Door, The. Gerard Depardieu & Fanny Ardant. Directed by Francois Truffaut. Fr. 1981. 106 min. 16mm Color. subtitles. *Rental:* MGM United.

Woman Obsessed, A. Susan Hayward & Stephen Boyd. Directed by Henry Hathaway. 1959. Fox. 102 min. Sound. 16mm Color. *Rental:* Charard Motion Pics. *Rental:* Willoughby Peer, Anamorphic color version.

Woman of Affairs, A. Greta Garbo, John Gilbert & Douglas Fairbanks Jr. Directed by Clarence Brown. 1929. MGM. 100 min. Silent. 16mm B&W. *Rental:* MGM United.

Woman of Distinction. Rosalind Russell & Ray Milland. Directed by Edward Buzzell. 1950. Columbia. 85 min. Sound. 16mm B&W. *Rental:* Kit Parker.

Woman of Experience. ZaSu Pitts & H. B. Warner. Directed by Harry J. Brown. 1932. RKO. 76 min. Sound. 16mm *Rental:* RKO General Pics.

Woman of Paris, A. Edna Purviance, Adolphe Menjou & Carl Miller. Directed by Charles Chaplin. 1923. United Artists. (Musical score only). 85 min. Sound. 16mm B&W. *Rental:* Films Inc.

Woman of Straw, A. Sean Connery & Gina Lollobrigida. Directed by Basil Dearden. 1964. MGM. 117 min. Sound. 16mm Color. *Rental:* MGM United.

Woman of the North Country. Ruth Hussey & Rod Cameron. Directed by Joseph Kane. 1952. Republic. 90 min. Sound. 16mm B&W. *Rental:* Ivy Films. *Sale:* Rep Pic Film.

Woman of the Town. Claire Trevor & Albert Dekker. Directed by George Archainbaud. 1943. MGM. 88 min. Sound. 16mm B&W. *Rental:* Budget Films, Kit Parker & Learning Corp Am. *Sale:* Learning Corp Am. *Sale:* Magnetic Video, Videotape version.

Woman of the Year. Katharine Hepburn & Spencer Tracy. Directed by George Stevens. 1942. MGM. 105 min. Sound. 16mm B&W. *Rental:* MGM United. *Rental:* MGM United, Videotape version.

Woman on Pier Thirteen, The. Orig. Title: I Was a Communist. Laraine Day & Robert Ryan. Directed by Robert Stevenson. 1949. RKO. Sound. 16mm B&W. *Rental:* Films Inc.

Woman on the Beach. Joan Bennett & Robert Ryan. Directed by Jean Renoir. 1947. RKO. 71 min. Sound. 16mm B&W. *Rental:* Films Inc. *Lease:* Films Inc.

Woman Racket, The. Tom Moore & Blanche Sweet. Directed by Albert J. Kelley. 1930. MGM. 70 min. Sound. 16mm B&W. *Rental:* MGM United.

Woman Rebel, The. 1976. 58 min. Sound. Videotape *Rental:* PBS Video. *Sale:* PBS Video. *Sale:* PBS Video, 16mm version.

Woman Rebels, A. Katharine Hepburn & Herbert Marshall. Directed by Mark Sandrich. 1936. RKO. 88 min. Sound. 16mm B&W. *Rental:* Films Inc. *Lease:* Films Inc.

Woman They Almost Lynched, The. Joan Leslie & Brian Donlevy. Directed by Allan Dwan. 1952. Republic. 90 min. Sound. 16mm B&W. *Rental:* Ivy Films. *Lease:* Rep Pic Film.

Woman Times Seven. Shirley MacLaine & Peter Sellers. Directed by Vittorio De Sica. 1967. Embassy. 99 min. Sound. 16mm Color. *Rental:* Films Inc.

Woman to Woman. Directed by Donna Deitsch. 1975. Serious Business. (Experimental). 48 min. Sound. 16mm Color. *Rental:* Serious Bus. *Sale:* Serious Bus.

Woman Wanted. Joel McCrea & Maureen O'Sullivan. Directed by George B. Seitz. 1935. MGM. 68 min. Sound. 16mm B&W. *Rental:* MGM United.

Woman Who Came Back, The. John Loder & Nancy Kelly. Directed by Walter Colmes. 1945. Republic. 69 min. Sound. 16mm B&W. *Sale:* Classics Assoc NY.

Woman-Wife. Directed by Gary Galsworth. 1967. Gary Galsworth. 48 min. Silent. B&W. *Rental:* Canyon Cinema.

Woman Without a Face *see* Mister Buddwing.

Woman Without Love, A. Directed by Luis Bunuel. Span. 1951. Spain. 85 min. Sound. 16mm B&W. subtitles *Rental:* New Yorker Films.

Womanhouse. Directed by Johanna Demetrakis. 1975. Insight. (Documentary). 50 min. Sound. 16mm Color. *Rental:* New Cinema.

Woman's Decision, A. Maja Komorowska. Directed by Krzysztof Zanussi. Pol. 1977. Poland. 99 min. Sound. 16mm Color. subtitles. *Rental:* Cinema Five.

Woman's Face, A. Joan Crawford & Melvyn Douglas. Directed by George Cukor. 1941. MGM. 105 min. Sound. 16mm B&W. *Rental:* MGM United.

Woman's Faith, A. Alma Rubens, Jean Hersholt & ZaSu Pitts. Directed by Edward Laemmle. 1925. Universal. 84 min. Silent. 16mm B&W. *Rental:* Mogulls Films.

Woman's Man. John Halliday & Wallace Ford. Directed by Edward Ludwig. 1934. Monogram. 80 min. Sound. 16mm B&W. *Rental:* Mogulls Films.

Woman's Place, A. 1974. ABC. (Documentary). 52 min. Sound. 16mm Color. *Rental:* Iowa Films, U Cal Media & U Mich Media. *Sale:* Xerox Films.

Woman's Secret, A. Maureen O'Hara & Melvyn Douglas. Directed by Nicholas Ray. 1949. RKO. 83 min. Sound. 16mm B&W. *Rental:* Films Inc.

Woman's Vengeance, A. Jessica Tandy & Charles Boyer. Directed by Zoltan Korda. 1947. Universal. 96 min. Sound. 16mm B&W. *Rental:* Swank Motion.

Woman's World, A. Clifton Webb & June Allyson. Directed by Jean Negulesco. 1954. Fox. (Anamorphic). 94 min. Sound. 16mm Color. *Rental:* Films Inc.

Women, The. Norma Shearer & Joan Crawford. Directed by George Cukor. 1939. MGM. 134 min. Sound. 16mm B&W. *Rental:* MGM United.

Women Are Like That. Pat O'Brien & Kay Francis. Directed by Stanley Logan. 1938. Warners. 78 min. Sound. 16mm B&W. *Rental:* MGM United.

Women Are Trouble. Paul Kelly & Stuart Erwin. Directed by Errol Taggart. 1936. MGM. 59 min. Sound. 16mm B&W. *Rental:* MGM United.

Women in a Changing World. 1974. Fieldstaff. (Documentary). 48 min. Sound. 16mm Color. *Rental:* Syracuse U Film, U Cal Media, U of IL Film, U Mich Media & Utah Media.

Women in Bondage. Gail Patrick & Nancy Kelly. Directed by Steve Sekely. 1943. Monogram. 70 min. Sound. 16mm B&W. *Rental:* Mogulls Films.

Women in Cuba: Buenos Dias, Companeras. Directed by Aviva Slesin. Span. 1975. Cuba. (Documentary). 58 min. Sound. 16mm Color. subtitles. *Rental:* U of IL Film & Phoenix Films. *Sale:* Phoenix Films. *Sale:* Phoenix Films, Videotape version.

Women in His Life, The. Otto Kruger & Ben Lyon. Directed by George B. Seitz. 1933. MGM. 76 min. Sound. 16mm B&W. *Rental:* MGM United.

Women in Love. Alan Bates, Oliver Reed & Glenda Jackson. Directed by Ken Russell. 1970. United Artists. 132 min. Sound. 16mm Color. *Rental:* MGM United. *Rental:* MGM United, Videotape version.

Women in Prison. 1974. CBS. (Documentary). 54 min. Sound. 16mm Color. *Rental:* Budget Films, Iowa Films, Syracuse U Film, U Cal Media & U Mich Media. *Sale:* Carousel Films.

Women in Revolt. Candy Darling & Holly Woodlawn. Directed by Andy Warhol. 1972. New Line. 97 min. Sound. 16mm Color. *Rental:* New Line Cinema. *Sale:* New Line Cinema.

Women in Sports. 1980. Pyramid. (Documentary). 58 min. Sound. 16mm Color. *Rental:* U Cal Media & Pyramid Film. *Sale:* Pyramid Film. *Rental:* Pyramid Film, *Sale:* Pyramid Film, Videotape version.

Women in the Wind. Kay Francis & William Gargan. Directed by John Farrow. 1939. Warners. 65 min. Sound. 16mm B&W. *Rental:* MGM United.

Women in War. Wendy Barrie & Patric Knowles. Directed by John H. Auer. 1940. Republic. 71 min. Sound. 16mm B&W. *Rental:* Ivy Films.

Women Inside, The. 1980. Indiana U. (Documentary). 60 min. Sound. 16mm Color. *Rental:* U Cal Media & Indiana AV Ctr. *Sale:* Indiana AV Ctr.

Women Like Us. Directed by Marvin Einhorn. 1979. NBC. (Documentary). 52 min. Sound. 16mm Color. *Rental:* Films Inc. *Sale:* Films Inc. *Rental:* Films Inc, *Sale:* Films Inc, Videotape version.

Women Men Marry, The. George Murphy & Claire Dodd. Directed by Errol Taggart. 1937. MGM. 61 min. Sound. 16mm B&W. *Rental:* MGM United.

Women of Glamour. Virginia Bruce & Melvyn Douglas. Directed by Gordon Wiles. 1937. Columbia. 69 min. Sound. 16mm B&W. *Rental:* Kit Parker.

Women of Pitcairn Island. James Craig & Lynn Bari. Directed by Jean Yarbrough. 1956. Fox. (Anamorphic). 77 min. Sound. 16mm B&W. *Rental:* Ivy Films. *Sale:* Rep Pic Film.

Women of Sin. France. (Cast unlisted). Sound. 16mm B&W. dubbed. *Rental:* Mogulls Films.

Women of the Night. Kinuyo Tanaka & Sanae Takasugi. Directed by Kenji Mizoguchi. Jap. 1948. Japan. 75 min. Sound. 16mm B&W. subtitles. *Rental:* Films Inc.

Women On the March. 1958. Canada. (Documentary). 60 min. Sound. 16mm B&W. *Rental:* Natl Film CN & Syracuse U Film. *Sale:* Natl Film CN. *Rental:* Natl Film CN, *Sale:* Natl Film CN, Videotape version.

Women Without Men *see* Blonde Bait.

Women Without Names. Simone Simon & Valentina Cortesa. Directed by Geza Radvanyi. Fr. & Ital. 1950. France-Italy. 91 min. Sound. 16mm B&W. subtitles. *Rental:* Kit Parker.

Women's Happy Time Commune, The. Directed by Sheila Paige. 1972. Women Make Movies. (Cast unlisted). 50 min. Sound. 16mm Color. *Rental:* Women Movies.

Women's Health: A Question of Survival. Directed by Marlene Sanders. 1976. ABC. (Documentary). 49 min. Sound. 16mm Color. *Rental:* U Cal Media & McGraw-Hill Films. *Sale:* McGraw-Hill Films. *Sale:* McGraw-Hill Films, Videotape version.

Women's Prison. Ida Lupino & Howard Duff. Directed by Lewis Seiler. 1955. Columbia. 80 min. Sound. 16mm B&W. *Rental:* Kit Parker.

Won Ton Ton, the Dog Who Saved Hollywood. Bruce Dern, Madeline Kahn & Art Carney. Directed by Michael Winner. 1976. Paramount. 92 min. Sound. 16mm Color. *Rental:* Films Inc.

Wonder Bar. Al Jolson, Kay Francis & Dick Powell. Directed by Lloyd Bacon. 1934. Warners. 84 min. Sound. 16mm B&W. *Rental:* MGM United.

Wonderful Country, The. Robert Mitchum & Julie London. Directed by Robert Parrish. 1959. United Artists. 96 min. Sound. 16mm Color. *Rental:* MGM United.

Wonderful Crook, The. Gerard Depardieu & Marlene Jobert. Directed by Claude Goretta. Fr. 1975. Switzerland. 112 min. Sound. 16mm Color. subtitles. *Rental:* New Yorker Films.

Wonderful Land of Oz, The. Joy Webb. Directed by Barry Mahon. 1969. Childhood. 72 min. Sound. 16mm Color. *Rental:* Westcoast Films.

Wonderful Tale of Namu see Namu, the Killer Whale.

Wonderful Thing. Norma Talmadge. Directed by Herbert Brenon. 1921. 16mm *Rental:* A Twyman Pres.

Wonderful to Be Young. Cliff Richard & Robert Morley. Directed by Sidney J. Furie. 1962. Paramount. 92 min. Sound. 16mm Color. *Rental:* Films Inc.

Wonderful World of Hans Christian Andersen, The see World of Hans Christian Andersen.

Wonderful World of Puss'n Boots, The. Directed by Kimio Yabuki. 1961. Japan. (Animated). 91 min. Sound. 16mm Color. dubbed. *Rental:* Budget Films & Welling Motion Pictures.

Wonderful World of the Brothers Grimm, The. Laurence Harvey & Karl Boehm. Directed by Henry Levin & George Pal. 1962. MGM. 135 min. Sound. 16mm Color. *Rental:* MGM United. *Rental:* MGM United, Anamorphic version.

Wonderful World of Those Cuckoo Crazy Animals, The see It's Showtime.

Wonders of Aladdin, The. Donald O'Connor & Vittorio De Sica. Directed by Henry Levin. 1961. Embassy. 93 min. Sound. 16mm Color. *Rental:* Films Inc.

Woodcutters of the Deep South. Directed by Lionel Rogosin. 1973. Tricontinental. (Documentary). 90 min. Sound. 16mm Color. *Rental:* Icarus Films. *Sale:* Icarus Films.

Woodrow Wilson. 2 pts. Whit Bissell. Directed by Alexander Singer. (Profiles in Courage Ser.). 1965. Saudek. 50 min. Sound. 16mm B&W. . *Rental:* IQ Films. *Rental:* IQ Films, *Rental:* IQ Films, Spanish version.

Woodstock! Directed by Michael Wadleigh. 1970. Warners. (Documentary, Anamorphic). 184 min. Sound. 16mm Color. *Rental:* Swank Motion. *Rental:* Swank Motion, Videotape version.

Woolloomooloo. 1978. Australia. (Documentary). 75 min. Sound. 16mm Color. *Rental:* Icarus Films. *Sale:* Icarus Films.

Word, The see Ordet.

Word Is Out. 1978. Mariposa. (Documentary). 130 min. Sound. 16mm Color. *Rental:* New Cinema & New Yorker Films.

Words & Music. Judy Garland & Lena Horne. Directed by Norman Taurog. 1948. MGM. 100 min. Sound. 16mm Color. *Rental:* MGM United.

Words & Music. 1968. CBS. (Documentary). 54 min. Sound. 16mm B&W. *Rental:* McGraw-Hill Films. *Sale:* McGraw-Hill Films.

Words & Music. Sammy Cahn. 1977. Video Corp. of America. 110 min. Videotape Color. *Sale:* Video Corp.

Work & Fulfillment. 1979. PBS. (Documentary). 59 min. Videotape Color. *Rental:* PBS Video. *Sale:* PBS Video.

Work of Gomis. Directed by Yvonne Hannemann. 1973. Yvonne Hannemann. (Documentary). 50 min. Sound. 16mm Color. *Rental:* Serious Bus. *Sale:* Serious Bus.

Work, Work, Work. 1979. PBS. (Documentary). 59 min. Videotape Color. *Rental:* PBS Video. *Sale:* PBS Video.

Working. Barbara Barrie, Eileen Brennan & Rita Moreno. 1982. WNET. 90 min. Videotape Color. *Rental:* Films Inc. *Sale:* Films Inc.

Working Class Goes to Heaven, The. Trans. Title: Classe Operaia Va in Paradiso, La. Gian Maria Volonte. Directed by Elio Petri. Ital. 1972. Italy. 105 min. Sound. 16mm Color. subtitles. *Rental:* New Line Cinema.

Working for the Lord. 1976. Gould. (Documentary). 52 min. Sound. 16mm Color. *Rental:* Syracuse U Film. *Sale:* Lucerne Films. *Rental:* Lucerne Films, Videotape version.

Working Girls. Sarah Kennedy, Laurie Rose & Mary Beth Hughes. Directed by Stephanie Rothman. 1975. Dimension. 80 min. Sound. 16mm Color. *Sale:* Salz Ent.

Working Man, The. George Arliss & Bette Davis. Directed by John Adolfi. 1933. Warners. 78 min. Sound. 16mm B&W. *Rental:* MGM United.

Working Wives see Weekend Marriage.

World & His Wife, The see State of the Union.

World According to Garp, The. Robin Williams, Mary Beth Hurt & Glenn Close. Directed by George Roy Hill. 1983. Warners. 136 min. Sound. 16mm Color. *Rental:* Swank Motion. *Rental:* Swank Motion, Videotape version.

World at War, The. 1980. (Documentary). 44 min. Sound. 16mm B&W. *Rental:* Budget Films, Mongulls Films & Natl AV Ctr. *Sale:* Natl AV Ctr. *Sale:* Natl AV Ctr, Videotape version.

World at War, The. 26 pts. 1982. Media Guild. 1352 min. Sound. 16mm Color. *Rental:* Iowa Films. *Sale:* Media Guild. *Sale:* Media Guild & Tamarelles French Film, Videotape version.

World Changes, The. Paul Muni & Mary Astor. Directed by Mervyn LeRoy. 1933. Warners. 91 min. Sound. 16mm B&W. *Rental:* MGM United.

World for Ransom, A. Dan Duryea & Gene Lockhart. Directed by Robert Aldrich. 1954. Allied Artists. 82 min. Sound. 16mm B&W. *Rental:* Ivy Films. *Sale:* Rep Pic Film.

World Gone Mad, A. Orig. Title: The Public Be Hanged. Pat O'Brien, Evelyn Brent & Mary Brian. Directed by Christy Cabanne. 1933. Majestic. 80 min. Sound. 16mm B&W. *Rental:* Budget Films. *Sale:* Reel Images. *Sale:* Reel Images, Super 8 sound version.

World Hunger! Who Will Survive? 1979. PBS. (Documentary). 90 min. Videotape Color. *Rental:* PBS Video. *Sale:* PBS Video.

World I See, The. 1962. Hearst. (Documentary). 50 min. Sound. 16mm B&W. *Sale:* King Features.

World in His Arms, The. Gregory Peck & Anthony Quinn. Directed by Raoul Walsh. 1952. Universal. 104 min. Sound. 16mm Color. *Rental:* Swank Motion.

World in My Corner, The. Audie Murphy & Barbara Rush. Directed by Jesse Hibbs. 1956. Universal. 82 min. Sound. 16mm B&W. *Rental:* Swank Motion.

World Is Round, The. Directed by Ian McLaren. 1976. Canada. (Documentary). 54 min. Sound. 16mm Color. *Rental:* Natl Film CN. *Sale:* Natl Film CN.

World Moves On, The. Madeleine Carroll & Franchot Tone. Directed by John Ford. 1934. Fox. 90 min. Sound. 16mm B&W. *Rental:* Films Inc.

World of Abbott & Costello, The. 1965. Universal. (Anthology). 75 min. Sound. 16mm B&W. *Rental:* Swank Motion.

World of Apu, The. Orig. Title: Apu Trilogy, The. Soumitra Chaterjee. Directed by Satyajit Ray. 1960. India. 103 min. Sound. 16mm B&W. *Rental:* Budget Films, Em Gee Film Lib, Films Inc & Images Film. *Sale:* Festival Films, Natl Cinema & Images Film. *Sale:* Festival Films, Videotape version.

World of Buckminster Fuller, The. Directed by Robert Snyder. 1975. Cornerstone. (Documentary). 90 min. Sound. 16mm Color. *Rental:* Arcus Film.

World of Carl Sandburg, The. Uta Hagen & Fritz Weaver. 1967. NET. 59 min. Sound. 16mm B&W. *Rental:* Budget Films, Indiana AV Ctr, Phoenix Films, Syracuse U Film & U of IL Film. *Sale:* Indiana AV Ctr & Phoenix Films. *Sale:* Phoenix Films, Videotape version.

World of Gilbert & George, The. Directed by George Passmore & Gilbert Proesch. 1980. Britain. (Experimental). 69 min. Sound. 16mm Color. *Rental:* Museum Mod Art. *Sale:* Museum Mod Art.

World of Hans Christian Andersen, The. Orig. Title: Wonderful World of Hans Christian Andersen, The. 1973. United Artists. (Animated). 80 min. Sound. 16mm Color. *Rental:* Films Inc, Kerr Film, Video Comm, Westcoast Films & Wholesome Film Ctr.

World of Henry Orient, The. Peter Sellers & Paula Prentiss. Directed by George Roy Hill. 1964. United Artists. 106 min. Sound. 16mm Color. *Rental:* MGM United.

World of Jacques-Yves Cousteau, The. 1967. Wolper. (Documentary). 48 min. Sound. 16mm Color. *Rental:* Syracuse U Film, U Cal Media, U Mich Media & Natl Geog. *Sale:* Films Inc & Natl Geog. *Sale:* Natl Geog, Videotape version.

World of Mother Teresa, The. Directed by Ann Petrie. 1980. Films Inc. (Documentary). 58 min. Sound. 16mm Color. *Rental:* U Cal Media & Films Inc. *Sale:* Films Inc. *Rental:* Films Inc, *Sale:* Films Inc, Videotape version.

World of Mystery. Directed by Wheeler Dixon. 1979. Gold Key. (Documentary). 96 min. Sound. 16mm Color. *Rental:* Gold Key.

World of Piri Thomas, The. 1968. NET. (Documentary). 60 min. Sound. 16mm B&W. *Rental:* Indiana AV Ctr, U Cal Media & U Mich Media. *Rental:* U Mich Media, Color version. *Sale:* Indiana AV Ctr, Videotape version.

World of Suzie Wong, The. William Holden & Nancy Kwan. Directed by Richard Quine. 1960. Paramount. 128 min. Sound. 16mm Color. *Rental:* Films Inc.

World of the Beaver, The. 1973. CBS. (Documentary). 50 min. Sound. 16mm Color. *Rental:* Phoenix Films. *Sale:* Phoenix Films.

World of the Vampires, The. Trans. Title: Mundo de los Vampiros, El. Mauricio Garces & Erna Martha Bauman. Directed by Alfonso Corona Blake. 1960. Mexico. 83 min. Sound. 16mm B&W. dubbed. *Rental:* Budget Films.

World of Tomorrow, The. Directed by Tom Johnson & Lance Bird. 1984. Tom Johnson. 78 min. Sound. 16mm Color. *Rental:* Direct Cinema.

World of Yaacov Agam, The. Directed by Adrian Mayben. France. (Documentary). 60 min. Sound. 16mm Color. *Rental:* A Cantor. *Sale:* A Cantor.

World of Yukar, The. 2 Pts. 1964. NHK. (Documentary). 60 min. Sound. 16mm Color. dubbed. *Rental:* U Mich Media.

World Owes Me a Living, The. David Farrar & Judy Campbell. Directed by Vernon Sewell. 1946. Britain. 89 min. Sound. 16mm B&W. *Rental:* Ivy Films. *Sale:* Rep Pic Film.

World Safari. 1971. American National. (Documentary). 100 min. Sound. 16mm Color. *Rental:* Budget Films, Films Inc & Video Comm. *Lease:* Video Comm. *Rental:* Video Comm, *Lease:* Video Comm, Videotape version.

World, the Flesh & the Devil, The. Harry Belafonte, Inger Stevens & Mel Ferrer. Directed by Ranald MacDougall. 1959. MGM. 95 min. Sound. 16mm B&W. *Rental:* MGM United. *Rental:* MGM United, Anamorphic version.

World to Win, A. 1975. Britain. (Documentary). 52 min. Sound. 16mm Color. *Rental:* U of IL Film, Videotape version.

World Turned Upside Down, The. 1966. Britain. (Documentary). 80 min. Sound. 16mm B&W. *Rental:* Films Inc & U Mich Media. *Sale:* Films Inc. *Rental:* Films Inc, *Sale:* Films Inc, Videotape version.

World Turned Upside Down, The. 1974. Wolper. (Documentary). 52 min. Sound. 16mm Color. *Rental:* Films Inc, Syracuse U Film & U Mich Media. *Sale:* Films Inc.

World War II Battles. 3 pts. 1971. Britain. (Documentary). 150 min. Sound. 16mm Color. *Rental:* Time-Life Multimedia. *Sale:* Time-Life Multimedia.

World War II: The Pacific Theater. 1978. Fox. (Documentary). 55 min. Videotape B&W. *Sale:* Blackhawk Films.

World War II: The Propaganda Battle. 58 min. Sound. Videotape *Rental:* PBS Video. *Sale:* PBS Video.

World Was His Jury, The. Edmond O'Brien & Mona Freeman. Directed by Fred F. Sears. 1958. Columbia. 82 min. Sound. 16mm B&W. *Rental:* Inst Cinema.

World West Bank Story, The. 1981. 58 min. Sound. Videotape Color. *Rental:* PBS Video. *Sale:* PBS Video.

World Within World. (Ascent of Man Ser.). 1974. Britain. (Documentary). 52 min. Sound. 16mm Color. *Rental:* U Cal Media, U Mich Media & Utah Media, Videotape version.

World Without End. Hugh Marlowe & Nancy Gates. Directed by Edward Bernds. 1956. Allied Artists. 80 min. Sound. 16mm Color. *Rental:* Hurlock Cine.

World Without Sun. Trans. Title: Monde Sans Soleil, Le. Directed by Jacques-Yves Cousteau. 1964. France. (Documentary). 91 min. Sound. 16mm Color. narrated Eng. *Rental:* Arcus Film, Buchan Pic, Cine Craft, Films Inc, Kerr Film, Kit Parker, Twyman Films, Welling Motion Pictures, Westcoast Films, Wholesome Film Ctr & Willoughby Peer.

Worldly Madonna, The. Clara Kimball Young. Directed by Harry Garson. 1922. Equity. 45 min. Silent. 16mm B&W. *Sale:* Blackhawk Films. *Rental:* Blackhawk Films, Super 8 silent version.

Worlds Apart. Lynn Borden. Directed by Jan Sadlo. 1967. Gospel. 89 min. Sound. 16mm Color. *Rental:* Educ Media CA & Roas Films.

World's Greatest Athlete, The. Jan-Michael Vincent. Directed by Robert Scheerer. 1973. Disney. 92 min. Sound. 16mm Color. *Rental:* Bosco Films, Disney Prod, Elliot Film Co, Films Inc, Modern Sound, Roas Films, Swank Motion, Welling Motion Pictures, Westcoast Films & Williams Films.

World's Greatest Lover, The. Gene Wilder, Carol Kane & Dom DeLuise. Directed by Gene Wilder. 1977. Fox. 89 min. Sound. 16mm Color. *Rental:* Films Inc, Twyman Films & Williams Films, Videotape version.

World's Greatest Photography Course. (Cast unlisted). Videotape *Rental:* Vidamerica.

Worlds in Collision. 1978. Time-Life. (Documentary). 48 min. Sound. 16mm Color. *Rental:* Films Inc & U of IL Film. *Sale:* Films Inc. *Sale:* Films Inc, Videotape version.

World's Largest Television Studio, The. 1972. (Documentary). 60 min. Videotape B&W. *Sale:* Electro Art.

World's Young Ballet, The. Mikhail Baryshnikov. Directed by Arkadi Tsineman. 1970. Russia. 70 min. Sound. 16mm B&W. narrated Eng. *Rental:* Corinth Films. *Lease:* Corinth Films.

Worship of Nature, The. (Civilization Ser.). 1968. Britain. (Documentary). 60 min. Sound. 16mm Color. *Rental:* Films Inc, Syracuse U Film & Utah Media. *Sale:* Films Inc. *Rental:* Films Inc, *Sale:* Films Inc, Videotape version.

Would-Be Gentleman, The. Trans. Title: Bourgeois Gentilhomme, Le. Comedie Francaise. Directed by Jean Meyer. Fr. 1958. France. 95 min. Sound. 16mm Color. subtitles. *Rental:* Films Inc.

Woven Gardens. 1975. Britain. (Documentary). 52 min. Sound. 16mm Color. *Rental:* Iowa Films, Kent St U Film, U Cal Media & U of IL Film.

Woyzeck. Jose Ferrer. 1978. Britain. 60 min. Videotape Color. *Rental:* Films Inc. *Sale:* Films Inc.

Woyzeck. Klaus Kinski. Directed by Werner Herzog. Ger. 1978. Germany. 82 min. Sound. 16mm Color. subtitles. *Rental:* New Yorker Films.

Wozzeck. Kurt Meisel & Helga Zulch. Directed by Georg Klaren. Ger. 1947. Germany. 96 min. Sound. 16mm B&W. subtitles Eng. *Rental:* Films Inc.

WR, Mysteries of Organism. Milena Dravic. Directed by Dusan Makavejev. Serbo-Croatian. 1971. Yugoslavia. 84 min. Sound. 16mm Color. subtitles. *Rental:* Cinema Five. *Lease:* Cinema Five.

Wrangler's Roost. The Range Busters. Directed by S. Roy Luby. 1941. Monogram. 57 min. Sound. 16mm B&W. *Rental:* Budget Films & Films Inc. *Sale:* Morcraft Films.

Wrath of God, The. Robert Mitchum & Rita Hayworth. Directed by Ralph Nelson. 1972. MGM. (Anamorphic). 111 min. Sound. 16mm Color. *Rental:* MGM United.

Wreck of the Hesperus, The. William Parker. Directed by John Hoffman. 1948. Columbia. 70 min. Sound. 16mm B&W. *Rental:* Bosco Films, Films Inc & Inst Cinema.

Wreck of the Mary Deare, The. Gary Cooper & Charlton Heston. Directed by Michael Anderson. 1959. MGM. 105 min. Sound. 16mm Color. *Rental:* MGM United. *Rental:* MGM United, Anamorphic version. *Rental:* MGM United, Videotape version.

Wrecker, The. Carlyle Blackwell & Benita Hume. Directed by G. M. Bolvary. 1929. Tiffany. 60 min. Silent. 16mm B&W. *Rental:* Em Gee Film Lib.

Wrecking Crew. Richard Arlen & Chester Morris. Directed by Frank McDonald. 1942. Paramount. 70 min. Sound. 16mm B&W. *Rental:* Mogulls Films.

Wrecking Crew. Dean Martin, Elke Sommer & Sharon Tate. Directed by Phil Karlson. 1968. Columbia. 104 min. Sound. 16mm Color. *Rental:* Arcus Film, Cine Craft, Charard Motion Pics, Film Ctr DC, Films Inc, Inst Cinema, Modern Sound, Roas Films, Video Comm, Welling Motion Pictures, Westcoast Films & Wholesome Film Ctr.

Wrestler, The. Edward Asner & Elaine Giftos. Directed by Jim Westman. 1974. Entertainment Ventures. 95 min. Sound. 16mm Color. *Rental:* Budget Films.

Wrestler & the Clown, The. S. Chekan. Directed by Konstantin Yudin & Boris Barnet. Rus. 1957. Russia. 99 min. Sound. 16mm B&W. subtitles. *Rental:* Corinth Films.

Wrestling Women vs. the Aztec Mummy. Trans. Title: Luchadoras Contra la Momia, Las. Armande Silvestre & Elizabeth Campbell. Directed by Rene Cardona. 1964. Mexico. 88 min. Sound. 16mm B&W. dubbed. *Rental:* Budget Films & Kit Parker.

Writing Forceful Sentences. 1956. Indiana University. (Kinescope, Lecture). 58 min. Sound. 16mm B&W. *Rental:* Indiana AV Ctr & U Cal Media. *Sale:* Indiana AV Ctr.

Writing on the Wall, The. 1978. Britain. (Documentary). 50 min. Sound. 16mm Color. *Rental:* Films Inc, U Cal Media, U of IL Film & U Mich Media. *Sale:* Films Inc. *Rental:* Films Inc, *Sale:* Films Inc, Videotape version.

Writings of the Nazi Holocaust, The. Anti-Defamation League. (Lecture). 60 min. Sound. 16mm B&W. *Rental:* ADL. *Sale:* ADL.

Written on the Wind. Rock Hudson & Lauren Bacall. Directed by Douglas Sirk. 1956. Universal. 99 min. Sound. 16mm Color. *Rental:* Swank Motion & Williams Films.

Wrong Box, The. Peter Sellers, John Mills, Sir Ralph Richardson. Directed by Bryan Forbes. 1966. Britain. 105 min. Sound. 16mm Color. *Rental:* Arcus Film, Bosco Films, Budget Films, Charard Motion Pictures, Film Ctr DC, Film Inc, Images Film, Kit Parker, Modern Sound, Natl Film Video, Roas Films, Swank Motion, Twyman Films, U of IL Film, Welling Motion Pictures, Westcoast Films, Wholesome Film Ctr & Willoughby Peer.

Wrong Is Right. Sean Connery & George Grizzard. Directed by Richard Brooks. 1982. Columbia. 117 min. Sound. 16mm Color. *Rental:* Swank Motion. *Rental:* Swank Motion, Videotape version.

Wrong Kind of Girl *see* Bus Stop.

Wrong Man, The. Henry Fonda & Vera Miles. Directed by Alfred Hitchcock. 1957. Warners. 105 min. Sound. 16mm B&W. *Rental:* Films Inc, Swank Motion & Twyman Films.

Wrong Move, The. Directed by Wim Wenders. Ger. 1976. Germany. (Cast Unlisted). 103 min. Sound. 16mm Color. subtitles. *Rental:* Liberty Co.

Wrong Road, The. Helen Mack & Lionel Atwill. Directed by James Cruze. 1937. Republic. 54 min. Sound. 16mm B&W. *Rental:* Ivy Films. *Sale:* Rep Pic Film.

W.U.S.A. Paul Newman, Joanne Woodward & Anthony Perkins. Directed by Stuart Rosenberg. 1970. Paramount. (Anamorphic). 115 min. Sound. 16mm Color. *Rental:* Films Inc.

Wuthering Heights. Sir Laurence Olivier & Merle Oberon. Directed by William Wyler. 1939. Goldwyn. 104 min. Sound. 16mm B&W. *Rental:* Films Inc, Syracuse U Film & Video Comm.

Wuthering Heights. Anna Calder-Marshall & Timothy Dalton. Directed by Robert Fuest. 1971. American International. 105 min. Sound. 16mm Color. *Rental:* Arcus Film, Images Film, Video Comm, Welling Motion Pictures & Wholesome Film Ctr.

Wuthering Heights. Directed by Luis Bunuel. Span. 1953. Spain. 90 min. Sound. 16mm B&W. subtitles Eng. *Rental:* New Yorker Films.

Wuxing People's Commune. Directed by Boyce Richardson. 1980. 56 min. 16mm Color. *Rental:* Natl Film CN.

WX Uns Hopp. 60 min. Sound. 16mm B&W. *Rental:* Canyon Cinema.

Wyoming. Wallace Beery & Leo Carillo. Directed by Richard Thorpe. 1940. MGM. 85 min. Sound. 16mm B&W. *Rental:* MGM United.

Wyoming. William Elliott & Vera Ralston. Directed by Joseph Kane. 1947. Republic. 95 min. Sound. 16mm B&W. *Rental:* Ivy Films. *Sale:* Rep Pic Film.

Wyoming Bandit. Allan Lane. Directed by Philip Ford. 1949. Republic. 60 min. Sound. 16mm B&W. *Rental:* Ivy Films. *Sale:* Rep Pic Film & Nostalgia Merchant.

Wyoming Kid, The *see* Cheyenne.

Wyoming Outlaw. John Wayne. Directed by George Sherman. 1939. Republic. 56 min. Sound. 16mm B&W. *Rental:* Ivy Films. *Sale:* Rep Pic Film.

Wyoming Roundup. Whip Wilson. Directed by Thomas Carr. 1952. Monogram. 53 min. Sound. 16mm B&W. *Rental:* Hurlock Cine.

Wyoming Wildcat. Don Barry. Directed by George Sherman. 1941. Republic. 54 min. Sound. 16mm B&W. *Rental:* Ivy Films. *Sale:* Rep Pic Film.

X-Fifteen. Charles Bronson & Mary Tyler Moore. Directed by Richard Donner. 1961. United Artists. (Anamorphic). 106 min. Sound. 16mm Color. *Rental:* MGM United.

X From Outer Space. Eiji Okada. Directed by Kazui Nihonmatsu. 1966. Japan. 89 min. Sound. 16mm Color. dubbed. *Rental:* Films Inc.

X Marks the Spot. Neil Hamilton & Anne Jeffreys. Directed by George Sherman. 1942. Republic. 54 min. Sound. 16mm B&W. *Rental:* Ivy Films. *Sale:* Rep Pic Film.

X: The Man with X-Ray Eyes. Ray Milland. Directed by Roger Corman. 1963. American International. 80 min. Sound. 16mm Color. *Rental:* Budget Films, Film Ctr DC, Films Inc, Welling Motion Pictures, Westcoast Films, Wholesome Film Ctr & Willoughby Peer.

X, Y & Zee. Elizabeth Taylor, Michael Caine & Susannah York. Directed by Brian Hutton. 1971. Columbia. 110 min. Sound. 16mm Color. *Rental:* Cine Craft, Films Inc, Kerr Film, Welling Motion Pictures & Willoughby Peer.

Xala. Seun Samb. Directed by Ousmane Sembene. 1974. New Yorker. 123 min. Sound. 16mm Color. *Rental:* New Yorker Films. *Lease:* New Yorker Films.

Xanadu. Newton Olivia John, Gene Kelly & Michael Beck. Directed by Robert Greenwald. 93 min. Sound. 16mm Color. *Rental:* Swank Motion. *Rental:* Swank Motion, Videotape version.

Xian. Directed by Sue Yung Li & Shirley Sum. 58 min. 16mm Color. *Rental:* U Cal Media. *Sale:* U Cal Media. *Sale:* U Cal Media, Videotape version.

Xica. Zeze Motta & Walmor Chagas. Directed by Carlos Diegues. Port. 1976. Brazil. 120 min. Sound. 16mm Color. subtitles. *Rental:* New Yorker Films.

Y el Cielo Fue Tomado Por Asalto. Trans. Title: And the Heavens Were Taken by Storm. Directed by Santiago Alvarez. Span. 1975. Cuba. (Documentary). 120 min. Sound. 16mm Color. *Rental:* Cinema Guild. *Sale:* Cinema Guild.

Y Otra Vez, Una. Directed by Eduardo Maldonado. Span. 1974. Mexico. (Cast unlisted). 90 min. Sound. 16mm B&W. subtitles. *Rental:* Tricontinental Film. *Rental:* Tricontinental Film, Unsubtitled version.

Yakuza, The. Robert Mitchum. Directed by Sydney Pollack. 1975. Warners. 112 min. Sound. 16mm Color. *Rental:* Films Inc, Swank Motion & Twyman Films. *Rental:* Films Inc, Anamorphic version.

Yamaba: Old Woman of the Mountains. 1978. 90 min. Sound. Videotape Color. *Rental:* Iowa Films.

Yamamba: Act Two. 1979. 45 min. Sound. 16mm Color. *Rental:* U Mich Media.

Yanco. Ricardo Ancona. Directed by Rogelio A. Gonzalez. 1964. Mexico. 85 min. Sound. 16mm B&W. *Rental:* Bosco Films, Budget Films, Em Gee Film Lib, Films Inc & Kit Parker. *Sale:* Reel Images, Inst Cinema, Natl Cinema & Reel Images. *Sale:* Festival Films, 91 min. version. *Sale:* Festival Films & Tamarelles French Film, Videotape version.

Yang Kwei Fei *see* Princess Yang Kwei Fei.

Yangtse Incident. Richard Todd. Directed by Michael Anderson. 1957. 16mm *Rental:* A Twyman Pres.

Yank at Oxford, A. Robert Taylor & Lionel Barrymore. Directed by Jack Conway. 1938. MGM. 102 min. Sound. 16mm B&W. *Rental:* MGM United.

Yank in Ermine, A. Peter Thompson & Harold Lloyd Jr. Directed by Gordon Parry. 1952. Britain. 84 min. Sound. 16mm Color. *Rental:* Ivy Films.

Yank in Korea, A. Lon McCallister. Directed by Lew Landers. 1951. Columbia. 73 min. Sound. 16mm B&W. *Lease:* Time-Life Multimedia.

Yank in Libya, A. H. B. Warner & Joan Woodbury. Directed by Al Herman. 1942. PRC. 69 min. Sound. 16mm B&W. *Rental:* Mogulls Films.

Yank in London, A. Orig. Title: I Live in Grosvenor Square. Anna Neagle & Rex Harrison. Directed by Herbert Wilcox. 1946. Britain. 106 min. Sound. 16mm B&W. *Rental:* Mogulls Films.

Yank in the R. A. F., A Tyrone Power & Betty Grable. Directed by Henry King. 1941. Fox. 97 min. Sound. 16mm B&W. *Rental:* Films Inc.

Yank in Vietnam, A. Marshall Thompson. Directed by Marshall Thompson. 1964. Allied Artists. 81 min. Sound. 16mm B&W. *Rental:* Hurlock Cine.

Yank on the Burma Road, A. Barry Nelson & Laraine Day. Directed by George B. Seitz. 1942. MGM. 66 min. Sound. 16mm B&W. *Rental:* Films Inc & MGM United.

Yankee Buccaneer. Jeff Chandler & Scott Brady. Directed by Frederick De Cordova. 1952. Universal. 86 min. Sound. 16mm Color. *Rental:* Swank Motion.

Yankee Clipper. William Boyd & Elinor Faire. Directed by Rupert Julian. 1927. PDC. 75 min. Silent. 16mm B&W. *Rental:* Em Gee Film Lib & Film Classics. *Sale:* Cinema Concepts. *Rental:* Killiam Collect, *Sale:* Blackhawk Films, Sound 16mm version. *Sale:* Blackhawk Films, Super 8 sound version. *Sale:* Festival Films, 60 min. silent 16mm version.

Yankee Doodle Dandy. James Cagney & Walter Huston. Directed by Michael Curtiz. 1942. Warners. 126 min. Sound. 16mm B&W. *Rental:* MGM United.

Yankee Doodle in Berlin. Ford Sterling & Ben Turpin. Directed by Mack Sennett. 1919. Sennett. 50 min. Silent. 16mm B&W. *Rental:* Budget Films & Iowa Films. *Sale:* Blackhawk Films. *Sale:* Blackhawk Films, Super 8 silent version.

Yankee Fakir. Douglas Fowley & Joan Woodbury. Directed by W. Lee Wilder. 1947. Republic. 70 min. Sound. 16mm B&W. *Sale:* Classics Assoc NY.

Yankee Sails Across Europe. 1969. National Geographic. (Documentary). 51 min. Sound. 16mm Color. *Rental:* Natl Geog, U Mich Media, Wholesome Film Ctr & Natl Geog. *Sale:* Natl Geog. *Sale:* Natl Geog, Videotape version.

Yanks. Richard Gere & Vanessa Redgrave. Directed by John Schlesinger. 1979. Universal. 139 min. Sound. 16mm Color. *Rental:* Swank Motion, 141 version.

Yanks Ahoy. William Tracy & Joe Sawyer. Directed by Kurt Neumann. 1943. Hal Roach. 60 min. Sound. 16mm B&W. *Rental:* Budget Films.

Yanks Are Coming, The. Mary Healy & Maxie Rosenbloom. Directed by Alexis Thurn-Taxis. 1942. PRC. 72 min. Sound. 16mm B&W. *Rental:* Mogulls Films.

Yanks Are Coming, The. 1964. Wolper. (Documentary). 55 min. Sound. 16mm B&W. *Rental:* Films Inc, U of IL Film, U Mich Media, Syracuse U Film, Utah Media & Wholesome Film Ctr. *Sale:* Films Inc. *Sale:* Films Inc, Videotape version.

Yaqui Drums. Rod Cameron & J. Carrol Naish. Directed by Jean Yarbrough. 1957. Republic. 70 min. Sound. 16mm B&W. *Rental:* Ivy Films. *Sale:* Rep Pic Film.

Year Of Living Dangerously, The. Mel Gibson & Sigourney Weaver. Directed by Peter Weir. 1982. Australia. 115 min. Sound. 16mm Color. *Rental:* MGM United. *Rental:* MGM United, Videotape version.

Year of the Communes, The. 1970. Association. (Documentary). 52 min. Sound. 16mm Color. *Rental:* U Mich Media.

Year of the Mayors, The. 1969. NBC. (Documentary). 53 min. Sound. 16mm Color. *Rental:* Films Inc. *Sale:* Films Inc.

Year of the Polaris, The. 1960. Navy. (Documentary). 55 min. Sound. 16mm B&W. *Rental:* Natl AV Ctr.

Year of the Tiger, The. Directed by David Davis, Deirdre English & Steve Talbot. 1974. Vietnam. (Documentary). 62 min. Sound. 16mm Color. *Rental:* Odeon Films. *Sale:* Odeon Films.

Year of the Wildebeest, The. 1976. Benchmark. (Documentary). 55 min. Sound. 16mm Color. *Rental:* Benchmark Films, U Cal Media, Iowa Films, U Mich Media & Syracuse U Film. *Sale:* Benchmark Films. *Sale:* Benchmark Films, 8mm version avail. version.

Year of the Woman, The. Directed by Sandra Hochman. 1974. Rugoff. (Documentary). 80 min. Sound. 16mm Color. *Rental:* New Line Cinema.

Yearling, The. Gregory Peck & Jane Wyman. Directed by Clarence Brown. 1946. MGM. 135 min. Sound. 16mm B&W. *Rental:* MGM United. *Rental:* MGM United, Color version.

Years After, The. Harry Belafonte & Joan Baez. 1976. ABC. 60 min. Sound. 16mm Color. *Rental:* Natl Churches Christ.

Years Between, The. 1975. ABC. (Documentary). 60 min. Sound. 16mm Color. *Rental:* Films Inc. *Sale:* Films Inc.

Years of the Beast, The. 98 min. Sound. 16mm Color. *Rental:* Gospel Films.

Years Without Days *see* Castle on the Hudson.

Years 1904-1914, The: Drums Begin to Roll. 1976. Britain. (Documentary). 52 min. Sound. 16mm Color. *Rental:* Time-Life Multimedia. *Sale:* Time-Life Multimedia. *Rental:* Time-Life Multimedia, *Sale:* Time-Life Multimedia, Videotape version.

Yellow Cab. 1978. Britain. (Documentary). 48 min. Sound. 16mm Color. *Rental:* Time-Life Multimedia. *Sale:* Time-Life Multimedia. *Sale:* Time-Life Multimedia, Videotape version.

Yellow Cab Man, The. Red Skelton & Gloria De Haven. Directed by Jack Donohue. 1950. MGM. 85 min. Sound. 16mm B&W. *Rental:* MGM United.

Yellow Canary, The. Anna Neagle & Richard Greene. Directed by Herbert Wilcox. 1944. RKO. 98 min. Sound. 16mm B&W. *Rental:* Films Inc.

Yellow Canary, The. Pat Boone & Barbara Eden. Directed by Buzz Kulik. 1963. Fox. (Anamorphic). 93 min. Sound. 16mm B&W. *Rental:* Films Inc.

Yellow Dust. Richard Dix & Leila Hyams. Directed by Wallace Fox. 1936. RKO. 68 min. Sound. 16mm B&W. *Rental:* RKO General Pics.

Yellow Fin. Wayne Morris & Adrian Booth. Directed by Frank McDonald. 1951. Monogram. 74 min. Sound. 16mm B&W. *Rental:* Hurlock Cine.

Yellow Jack. Robert Montgomery & Lewis Stone. Directed by George B. Seitz. 1938. MGM. 85 min. Sound. 16mm B&W. *Rental:* MGM United.

Yellow Rolls-Royce, The. Ingrid Bergman, Rex Harrison & Shirley MacLaine. Directed by Anthony Asquith. 1965. MGM. 122 min. Sound. 16mm Color. *Rental:* MGM United. *Rental:* MGM United, Anamorphic color version.

Yellow Rose of Texas, The. Roy Rogers. Directed by Joseph Kane. 1944. Republic. 54 min. Sound. 16mm B&W. *Rental:* Ivy Films. *Sale:* Rep Pic Film. *Sale:* Reel Images & Video Comm, Videotape version.

Yellow Sky. Gregory Peck & Richard Widmark. Directed by William A. Wellman. 1948. Fox. 99 min. Sound. 16mm B&W. *Rental:* Films Inc.

Yellow Slippers, The. 1961. Poland. (Cast unlisted). 45 min. Sound. 16mm Color. *Sale:* McGraw-Hill Films. *Rental:* McGraw-Hill Films.

Yellow Submarine, The. Directed by George Dunning. 1968. United Artists. (Animated). 85 min. Sound. 16mm Color. *Rental:* Budget Films, Films Inc, Ivy Films, Kit Parker, Modern Sound, Twyman Films, Welling Motion Pictures, Westcoast Films, Wholesome Film Ctr & Williams Films. *Lease:* Ivy Films & King Features.

Yellow Trail from Texas, The. 1978. Britain. (Documentary). 50 min. Sound. 16mm Color. *Rental:* Films Inc & U of IL Film. *Sale:* Films Inc. *Rental:* Films Inc, *Sale:* Films Inc, Videotape version.

Yellowbeard. Graham Chapman & John Cleese. Directed by Mel Damski. 1983. Orion. 101 min. Sound. 16mm Color. *Rental:* Films Inc.

Yellowstone Cubs. 1965. Disney. (Documentary). 47 min. Sound. 16mm Color. *Rental:* Cine Craft, Cousino Visual Ed, Disney Prod, Film Ctr DC, Films Inc, Kent St U Film, Modern Sound, Roas Films, Twyman Films & Utah Media.

Yentl. Barbara Streisand, Mandy Patinkin & Amy Irving. Directed by Barbra Streisand. 1983. MGM-UA. 134 min. Sound. 16mm Color. *Rental:* MGM United. *Rental:* MGM United, Videotape version.

Yeomen of the Guard, The. 1974. Britain. (Operetta). 52 min. Sound. 16mm Color. *Rental:* B Raymond. *Sale:* B Raymond. *Sale:* B Raymond, Videotape version.

Yes. 1967. Northwestern University. (Color sequences, Experimental). 54 min. Sound. 16mm B&W. *Rental:* Northwest Film Lib.

Yes, Giorgio. Luciano Pavarotti & Kathryn Harrold. Directed by Franklin Schaffner. 1982. MGM-UA. 110 min. Sound. 16mm Color. *Rental:* MGM United. *Rental:* MGM United, Videotape version.

Yes, My Darling Daughter. Roland Young, Priscilla Lane & Fay Bainter. Directed by William Keighley. 1939. Warners. 86 min. Sound. 16mm B&W. *Rental:* MGM United.

Yes or No? Norma Talmadge. Directed by Roy William Neill. 1920. 16mm *Rental:* A Twyman Pres.

Yes, Sir, Mr. Bones. Sally Anglin & Pete Daley. Directed by Ron Ormond. 1951. Lippert. 55 min. Sound. 16mm B&W. *Rental:* Budget Films.

Yes, Sir, That's My Baby. Donald O'Connor & Gloria De Haven. Directed by George Sherman. 1949. Universal. 83 min. Sound. 16mm Color. *Rental:* Swank Motion.

Yessongs. (Concert). 90 min. Videotape Color. *Sale:* Cinema Concepts.

Yesterday Girl. Directed by Alexander Kluge. Ger. 1966. Germany. (Cast Unlisted). 90 min. Sound. 16mm Color. subtitles. *Rental:* Liberty Co.

Yesterday the Coyote Sang. 1964. NET. (Documentary). 60 min. Sound. 16mm B&W. *Rental:* U of IL Media & Indiana AV Ctr. *Sale:* Indiana AV Ctr.

Yesterday, Today & Tomorrow. Sophia Loren & Marcello Mastroianni. Directed by Vittorio De Sica. Ital. 1964. Italy. 120 min. Sound. 16mm B&W. subtitles. *Rental:* Films Inc & U Mich Media.

Yesterday, Tomorrow & You. 1979. Connections. (Documentary). 53 min. Sound. 16mm Color. *Rental:* Iowa Films, Kent St U Film, U Cal Media, U of IL Film & U Mich Media, Videotape version.

Yesterday's Hero see Hoosier Schoolboy.

Yesterday's Witness: A Tribute to the American Newsreel. Directed by Christian Blackwood. 1976. Blackwood. (Documentary). 52 min. Sound. 16mm Color. *Rental:* Blackwood Films. *Lease:* Blackwood Films.

Yiddle with His Fiddle. Molly Picon. Directed by Joseph Green. Yiddish. 1937. Poland. 90 min. Sound. 16mm B&W. subtitles. *Rental:* Budget Films & Films Inc.

Yin & Yang of Mr. Go, The. Burgess Meredith, Jeff Bridges & James Mason. Hong Kong. 98 min. Sound. 16mm Color. *Rental:* Films Inc.

Yo Contemple Su Gloria see I Beheld His Glory.

Yo Soy Chicano. Dolores Huerta & Reies Lopez Tijerina. Directed by Jesus Trevino. Span. 1972. Tricontinental. 60 min. Sound. 16mm Color. subtitles. *Rental:* Cinema Guild, Indiana AV Ctr, Iowa Films, Natl Film CN, U Cal Media, U Mich Media & Utah Media. *Sale:* Indiana AV Ctr, Cinema Guild & Natl Film CN.

Yo Soy el Criminal. Span. 1950. Mexico. (Cast unlisted). 90 min. Sound. 16mm B&W. *Rental:* Film Classics.

Yo Soy Satanas. 90 min. Sound. Videotape Color. *Sale:* Tamarelles French Film.

Yodelin' Kid from Pine Ridge, The. Orig. Title: Hero of Pine Ridge, The. Gene Autry. Directed by Joseph Kane. 1937. Republic. 54 min. Sound. 16mm B&W. *Rental:* Ivy Films. *Sale:* Video Comm, Videotape version.

Yog, Monster from Space. Akira Kubo. Directed by Inoshiro Honda. 1971. Japan. 84 min. Sound. 16mm Color. dubbed. *Rental:* Swank Motion.

Yojimbo. Toshiro Mifune. Directed by Akira Kurosawa. Jap. 1961. Japan. 110 min. Sound. 16mm B&W. subtitles. *Rental:* Budget Films, Em Gee Film Lib, Films Inc & Utah Media. *Sale:* Natl Cinema & Reel Images. *Sale:* Tamarelles French Film, Videotape version.

Yokel Boy. Albert Dekker & Eddie Foy Jr. Directed by Joseph Santley. 1942. Republic. 68 min. Sound. 16mm B&W. *Rental:* Ivy Films.

Yol: The Trek Of Life. Tarik Akan & Halil Ergun. Directed by Serif Goren. Turkish. 1983. Turkey. 111 min. Sound. 16mm Color. subtitles. *Rental:* Swank Motion. *Rental:* Swank Motion, Videotape version.

Yolanda & the Thief. Fred Astaire & Lucille Bremer. Directed by Vincente Minnelli. 1945. MGM. 108 min. Sound. 16mm Color. *Rental:* MGM United.

Yongary, Monster from the Deep. Nam Chung Im. Directed by Kim Ki-Duk. 1968. China. 79 min. Sound. 16mm Color. dubbed. *Rental:* Films Inc.

Yor: The Hunter from the Future. Reb Brown & Corinne Clery. Directed by Anthony Dawson. 1983. Columbia. 105 min. Sound. 16mm Color. *Rental:* Swank Motion. *Rental:* Swank Motion, Videotape version.

You & Me. Sylvia Sidney & George Raft. Directed by Fritz Lang. 1938. Paramount. 90 min. Sound. 16mm B&W. *Rental:* Swank Motion.

You Are At the Bargaining Table. 1955. American Management Association. (Documentary). 50 min. Sound. 16mm B&W. *Rental:* OK, AV Ctr & U Cal Media.

You Are Not Alone. Ernst Johansen & Anders Agenso. Directed by Lasse Nielsen. Denmark. 90 min. Sound. Videotape Color. *Sale:* Tamarelles French Film.

You Are Old, Father William. 1980. Britain. (Documentary). 50 min. Sound. 16mm Color. *Rental:* Films Inc, Syracuse U Film & U Cal Media. *Sale:* Films Inc. *Sale:* Films Inc, Videotape version.

You Are What You Eat. Directed by Barry Feinstein. 1968. Commonwealth. (Documentary). 75 min. Sound. 16mm Color. *Rental:* Budget Films, Films Inc, Ivy Films & Video Comm.

You Belong to Me. Orig. Title: Good Morning, Doctor. Barbara Stanwyck & Henry Fonda. Directed by Wesley Ruggles. 1941. Columbia. 97 min. Sound. 16mm B&W. *Rental:* Bosco Films & Kit Parker.

You Can't Sleep Here see I Was a Male War Bride.

You Can't Beat Love. Joan Fontaine & Preston Foster. Directed by Christy Cabanne. 1937. RKO. 82 min. Sound. 16mm B&W. *Rental:* RKO General Pics.

You Can't Buy Everything. May Robson & Lewis Stone. Directed by Charles Reisner. 1934. MGM. 83 min. Sound. 16mm B&W. *Rental:* MGM United.

You Can't Buy Luck. Vinton Haworth & Hedda Hopper. Directed by Lew Landers. 1937. RKO. 61 min. Sound. 16mm B&W. *Rental:* RKO General Pics.

You Can't Cheat an Honest Man. W. C. Fields. Directed by George Marshall. 1939. Universal. 74 min. Sound. 16mm B&W. *Rental:* Swank Motion.

You Can't Escape Forever. George Brent & Brenda Marshall. Directed by Jo Graham. 1942. Warners. 77 min. Sound. 16mm B&W. *Rental:* MGM United.

You Can't Fool Your Wife. Lucille Ball & James Ellison. Directed by Ray MacCarey. 1940. RKO. 68 min. Sound. 16mm *Rental:* RKO General Pics.

You Can't Get Away with Murder. Humphrey Bogart, Gale Page & John Litel. Directed by Lewis Seiler. 1939. Warners. 78 min. Sound. 16mm B&W. *Rental:* MGM United.

You Can't Grow a Green Plant in a Closet. 1970. Roy Nolan. (Documentary). 54 min. Sound. 16mm B&W. *Rental:* U Cal Media & OK AV Ctr.

You Can't Have Everything. Alice Faye & Don Ameche. Directed by Norman Taurog. 1937. Fox. 99 min. Sound. 16mm B&W. *Rental:* Films Inc.

You Can't Take It With You. James Stewart, Jean Arthur & Lionel Barrymore. Directed by Frank Capra. 1938. Columbia. 127 min. Sound. 16mm B&W. *Rental:* Arcus Film, Budget Films, Cine Craft, Williams Films, Bosco Films, Films Inc, Inst Cinema, U of IL Film, Images Film, Kit Parker, Modern Sound, Natl Film Video, Roas Films, Twyman Films, Westcoast Films, Welling Motion Pictures & Wholesome Film Ctr.

You Can't Win 'Em All. Tony Curtis & Charles Bronson. Directed by Peter Collinson. 1970. Columbia. 97 min. Sound. 16mm Color. *Rental:* Charard Motion Pics, Films Inc, Inst Cinema, Kerr Film, Modern Sound, Welling Motion Pictures & Westcoast Films.

You for Me. Peter Lawford & Jane Greer. Directed by Don Weis. 1952. MGM. 71 min. Sound. 16mm B&W. *Rental:* MGM United.

You Gotta Stay Happy. James Stewart & Joan Fontaine. Directed by H. C. Potter. 1948. Universal. 100 min. Sound. 16mm B&W. *Rental:* Swank Motion.

You Have Seen Nothing at Hiroshima 1956-1961. Directed by Armand Panigel. Fr. France. (Documentary). 75 min. Sound. 16mm B&W. subtitles. *Rental:* French Am Cul.

You Have to Run Fast. Craig Hill & Elaine Edwards. Directed by Edward L. Cahn. 1961. United Artists. 71 min. Sound. 16mm B&W. *Rental:* MGM United.

You Light Up My Life. Didi Conn & Joe Silver. Directed by Joseph Brooks. 1977. Columbia. 90 min. Sound. 16mm Color. *Rental:* Arcus Film, Budget Films, Films Inc, Modern Sound, Newman Film Lib, Swank Motion, Twyman Films, Westcoast Films & Williams Films.

You Must Be Joking! Terry-Thomas & Lionel Jeffries. Directed by Michael Winner. 1965. Columbia. 100 min. Sound. 16mm B&W. *Rental:* Twyman Films.

You Never Can Tell. Dick Powell & Peggy Dow. Directed by Lou Breslow. 1951. Universal. 78 min. Sound. 16mm B&W. *Rental:* Swank Motion.

You Only Live Once. Henry Fonda & Sylvia Sidney. Directed by Fritz Lang. 1937. United Artists. 79 min. Sound. 16mm B&W. *Rental:* Budget Films, Films Inc, Images Film, Kit Parker, Learning Corp Am, Welling Motion Pictures & Westcoast Films. *Sale:* Learning Corp Am. *Sale:* Tamarelles French Film, Videotape version.

You Only Live Twice. Sean Connery & Donald Pleasence. Directed by Lewis Gilbert. 1967. United Artists. 115 min. Sound. 16mm Color. *Rental:* MGM United. *Rental:* MGM United, Videotape version.

You Said a Mouthful. Joe E. Brown & Ginger Rogers. Directed by Lloyd Bacon. 1932. Warners. 70 min. Sound. 16mm B&W. *Rental:* MGM United.

You Were Meant for Me. Jeanne Crain & Dan Dailey. Directed by Lloyd Bacon. 1948. Fox. 92 min. Sound. 16mm B&W. *Rental:* Films Inc.

You Were Never Lovelier. Fred Astaire & Rita Hayworth. Directed by William A. Seiter. 1942. Columbia. 98 min. Sound. 16mm B&W. *Rental:* Budget Films, Films Inc, Inst Cinema, Kit Parker, Swank Motion, Twyman Films & Welling Motion Pictures.

You'll Find Out. Kay Kayser. Directed by David Butler. 1940. RKO. 97 min. Sound. 16mm B&W. *Rental:* Films Inc.

You'll Get Yours When You're Sixty-Five. 1973. CBS. (Documentary). 49 min. Sound. 16mm Color. *Rental:* U Mich Media. *Sale:* Carousel Films.

You'll Like My Mother. Patty Duke, Rosemary Murphy & Richard Thomas. Directed by Lamont Johnson. 1972. Universal. 93 min. Sound. 16mm Color. *Rental:* Williams Films & Swank Motion.

You'll Never Get Rich. Fred Astaire & Rita Hayworth. Directed by Sidney Lanfield. 1941. Columbia. 89 min. Sound. 16mm B&W. *Rental:* Budget Films, Films Inc, Inst Cinema, Kit Parker, Swank Motion, Twyman Films, Welling Motion Pictures, Westcoast Films & Wholesome Film Ctr.

You'll Never See Me Again. Ben Gazzara & Leo Genn. 1959. Britain. 62 min. Sound. 16mm B&W. *Rental:* Ivy Films. *Sale:* Rep Pic Film.

Young Abe Lincoln. Allen Williams, Brock Peters & Andrew Prine. Sunn. 50 min. Sound. 16mm Color. *Rental:* Williams Films, Videotape version.

Young America. Jane Withers & Jane Darwell. Directed by Louis King. 1942. Fox. 73 min. Sound. 16mm B&W. *Rental:* Willoughby Peer.

Young Americans. 1965. NET. (Documentary). 60 min. Sound. 16mm B&W. *Rental:* Indiana AV Ctr & Mass Media.

Young Americans. Milton C. Anderson. Directed by Alexander Grasshoff. 1967. Columbia. 104 min. Sound. 16mm Color. *Rental:* Budget Films, Film Ctr DC, Films Inc, Inst Cinema, Modern Sound, Video Comm, Welling Motion Pictures & Westcoast Films.

Young & Dangerous. Edward Binns & Mark Damon. Directed by William Claxton. 1957. Fox. (Anamorphic). 78 min. Sound. 16mm B&W. *Rental:* Ivy Films. *Sale:* Rep Pic Film.

Young & Innocent. Orig. Title: Girl Was Young, The. Percy Marmont & Nova Pilbeam. Directed by Alfred Hitchcock. 1937. Britain. 80 min. Sound. 16mm B&W. *Rental:* Budget Films, Em Gee Film Lib, Films Inc, Janus Films, Kit Parker, Images Film & Video Comm. *Sale:* Cinema Concepts, Festival Films, Images Film, Reel Images & Video Comm. *Sale:* Cinema Concepts, Festival Films, Tamarelles French Film & Images Film, Videotape version.

Young & the Brave, The. Rory Calhoun & William Bendix. Directed by Francis D. Lyon. 1963. MGM. 84 min. Sound. 16mm B&W. *Rental:* MGM United.

Young & the Damned, The. Trans. Title: Olvidados, Los. Estele Inda. Directed by Luis Bunuel. Span. 1951. Mexico. 81 min. Sound. 16mm B&W. subtitles. *Rental:* Budget Films, Corinth Films, Films Inc, Images Film, Kit Parker, Macmillan Films, Utah Media, Wholesome Film Ctr & Westcoast Films. *Sale:* Cinema Concepts, Images Film, Natl Cinema & Reel Images. *Lease:* Corinth Films. *Sale:* Festival Films, 88 min. version. *Sale:* Festival Films & Images Film, 88 min. Videotape version.

Young & Wild. Scott Marlowe & Gene Evans. Directed by William Witney. 1958. Republic. 69 min. Sound. 16mm B&W. *Rental:* Ivy Films. *Sale:* Rep Pic Film.

Young & Willing. William Holden & Susan Hayward. Directed by Edward H. Griffith. 1943. United Artists. 81 min. Sound. 16mm B&W. *Rental:* Inst Cinema, Learning Corp Am & Mogulls Films. *Sale:* Learning Corp Am. *Sale:* Tamarelles French Film, Videotape version.

Young Aphrodites. Takis Emmanouel. Directed by Nikos Koundiuros. Gr. 1964. Greece. 87 min. Sound. 16mm B&W. subtitles. *Rental:* Films Inc & Janus Films.

Young April. Joseph Schildkraut & Bessie Love. Directed by Donald Crisp. 1926. PDC. 65 min. Silent. 16mm B&W. *Rental:* Em Gee Film Lib, Film Classics & Mogulls Films. *Sale:* Film Classics. *Rental:* Film Classics & Mogulls Films, *Sale:* Film Classics, Silent 8mm version.

Young at Art: New York High School for Performing Arts. 59 min. Sound. Videotape *Rental:* PBS Video. *Sale:* PBS Video.

Young at Heart, The. Frank Sinatra & Doris Day. Directed by Gordon Douglas. 1954. Warners. 117 min. Sound. 16mm B&W. *Rental:* Arcus Film, Bosco Films, Budget Films, Charard Motion Pics, Film Ctr DC, Welling Motion Pictures & Willoughby Peer. *Lease:* Rep Pic Film.

Young Bess. Jean Simmons & Stewart Granger. Directed by George Sidney. 1953. MGM. 112 min. Sound. 16mm Color. *Rental:* MGM United.

Young Bill Hickock. Roy Rogers. Directed by Joseph Kane. 1940. Republic. 54 min. Sound. 16mm B&W. *Rental:* Ivy Films. *Sale:* Rep Pic Film.

Young Billy Young. Robert Mitchum & Angie Dickinson. Directed by Burt Kennedy. 1969. United Artists. 88 min. Sound. 16mm Color. *Rental:* MGM United.

Young Bride, The. Arline Judge & Cliff Edwards. Directed by William A. Seiter. 1932. RKO. 76 min. Sound. 16mm B&W. *Rental:* RKO General Pics.

Young Buffalo Bill. Roy Rogers. Directed by Joseph Kane. 1940. Republic. 54 min. Sound. 16mm B&W. *Rental:* Ivy Films & Westcoast Films. *Sale:* Rep Pic Film.

Young Caruso, The. Gina Lollobrigida. Directed by Giacomo Gentilomo. 1953. Italy. 80 min. Sound. 16mm B&W. dubbed. *Rental:* Inst Cinema.

Young Cassidy. Rod Taylor & Maggie Smith. Directed by Jack Cardiff. 1965. MGM. 110 min. Sound. 16mm Color. *Rental:* MGM United.

Young Daniel Boone. David Bruce. Directed by Reginald Le Borg. 1950. Monogram. 71 min. Sound. 16mm Color. *Rental:* Hurlock Cine & Inst Cinema.

Young Dillinger. Nick Adams & Victor Buono. Directed by Terry Morse. 1965. United Artists. 102 min. Sound. 16mm B&W. *Rental:* Hurlock Cine.

Young Dr. Freud. Ger. 1977. Austria. (Cast unlisted). 73 min. Sound. 16mm B&W. subtitles. *Rental:* Films Human & U of IL Films. *Sale:* Films Human. *Sale:* Films Human, Videotape version.

Young Dr. Freud. 1977. Austria. (Cast unlisted). 73 min. Sound. 16mm B&W. *Rental:* Films Human & U of IL Films.

Young Dr. Kildare. Lew Ayres & Lionel Barrymore. Directed by Harold S. Bucquet. 1938. MGM. 82 min. Sound. 16mm B&W. *Rental:* MGM United.

Young Doctors, The. Fredric March & Eddie Albert. Directed by Phil Karlson. 1961. United Artists. 100 min. Sound. 16mm B&W. *Rental:* MGM United.

Young Doctors in Love. Michael McKean & Sean Young. Directed by Garry Marshall. 1982. Fox. 96 min. Sound. 16mm Color. *Rental:* Films Inc.

Young Don't Cry, The. Sal Mineo & James Whitmore. Directed by Alfred M. Werker. 1957. Columbia. 89 min. Sound. 16mm B&W. *Rental:* Films Inc & Inst Cinema.

Young Dynamite. Frankie Darro. Directed by Leslie Goodwins. 1937. Conn. 60 min. Sound. 16mm B&W. *Rental:* Film Classics.

Young Eagles. Buddy Rogers & Jean Arthur. Directed by William A. Wellman. 1930. Universal. 68 min. Sound. 16mm B&W. *Rental:* Swank Motion.

Young Eagles. 12 episodes. Bobby Cox, Jim Vance & Carter Dixon. 1934. First Division. Sound. 16mm B&W. *Rental:* Films Ctr DC, Mogulls Films & Williams Films. *Sale:* Video Comm, Videotape version.

Young Frankenstein. Gene Wilder, Marty Feldman & Madeline Kahn. Directed by Mel Brooks. 1975. Fox. 109 min. Sound. 16mm B&W. *Rental:* Films Inc.

Young Fury. Rory Calhoun & Virginia Mayo. Directed by Christian Nyby. 1965. Paramount. (Anamorphic). 80 min. Sound. 16mm Color. *Rental:* Films Inc.

Young Girl *see* Caraba.

Young Graduates, The. Patricia Wymer. Directed by Robert Anderson. 1971. Tempo. 100 min. Sound. 16mm Color. *Rental:* Video Comm. *Lease:* Video Comm. *Rental:* Video Comm, *Lease:* Video Comm, Videotape version.

Young Guns. Russ Tamblyn & Gloria Talbott. Directed by Albert Band. 1956. Allied Artists. 84 min. Sound. 16mm B&W. *Rental:* Hurlock Cine.

Young Guns of Texas. James Mitchum, Jody McCrea & Alan Ladd Jr. Directed by Maury Dexter. 1962. Fox. (Anamorphic). 78 min. Sound. 16mm Color. *Rental:* Films Inc.

Young Hannah, Queen of the Vampires. Andrew Prine & Mark Damon. Directed by Ray Danton. 1973. Atlas. 81 min. Sound. 16mm Color. *Rental:* Budget Films.

Young Hero, The. Bruce Li. 91 min. Sound. 16mm Color. *Rental:* BF Video.

Young in Heart, The. Douglas Fairbanks Jr. & Janet Gaynor. Directed by Richard Wallace. 1938. United Artists. 86 min. Sound. 16mm B&W. *Rental:* Budget Films, Film Classics, Mogulls Films & Willoughby Peer.

Young Jesse James. Ray Stricklyn & Willard Parker. Directed by William Claxton. 1960. Fox. (Anamorphic). 73 min. Sound. 16mm B&W. *Rental:* Willoughby Peer.

Young Killers, The *see* High School Confidential.

Young Land, The. Patrick Wayne & Dennis Hopper. Directed by Ted Tetzlaff. 1959. Columbia. 89 min. Sound. 16mm Color. *Rental:* Films Inc & Williams Films.

Young Lions, The. Marlon Brando, Montgomery Clift & Dean Martin. Directed by Edward Dmytryk. 1958. Fox. (Anamorphic). 167 min. Sound. 16mm B&W. *Rental:* Films Inc.

Young Lovers, The. Orig. Title: Never Fear. Sally Forrest & Keefe Brasselle. Directed by Ida Lupino. 1950. Eagle Lion. 75 min. Sound. 16mm B&W. *Rental:* Inst Cinema.

Young Lovers, The. Peter Fonda & Nick Adams. Directed by Samuel Goldwyn Jr. 1964. MGM. 105 min. Sound. 16mm Color. *Rental:* MGM United.

Young Man with a Horn. Kirk Douglas, Doris Day & Lauren Bacall. Directed by Michael Curtiz. 1950. Warners. 111 min. Sound. 16mm B&W. *Rental:* Films Inc.

Young Man with Ideas. Glenn Ford & Ruth Roman. Directed by Mitchell Leisen. 1952. MGM. 84 min. Sound. 16mm B&W. *Rental:* MGM United.

Young Man with Opinions. 2 Pts. Canada. (Documentary). 60 min. Sound. 16mm B&W. *Rental:* Natl Film CN.

Young Mr. Lincoln. Jane Fonda & Marjorie Weaver. Directed by John Ford. 1938. Fox. 100 min. Sound. 16mm B&W. *Rental:* Films Inc, Ivy Films & Twyman Films.

Young Mr. Pitt. Robert Donat & Phyllis Calvert. Directed by Sir Carol Reed. 1942. Britain-Fox. 118 min. Sound. 16mm B&W. *Rental:* Films Inc.

Young Nun, The. Laura Efrikian & Jonathan Elliot. Directed by Bruno Paolinelli. 1964. 93 min. Sound. 16mm B&W. *Rental:* Films Inc.

Young Paul Baroni *see* Kid Monk Baroni.

Young People. Shirley Temple & Jack Oakie. Directed by Allan Dwan. 1940. Fox. 78 min. Sound. 16mm B&W. *Rental:* Films Inc.

Young Philadelphians, The. Orig. Title: City Jungle, The. Paul Newman & Barbara Rush. Directed by Vincent Sherman. 1959. Warners. 136 min. Sound. 16mm B&W. *Rental:* Charard Motion Pics, Films Inc, Inst Cinema & Video Comm.

Young Racers, The. Mark Damon & William Campbell. Directed by Roger Corman. 1963. American International. 84 min. Sound. 16mm Color. *Rental:* Cine Craft, Charard Motion Pics, Westcoast Films & Wholesome Film Ctr.

Young Ranger, The. Spain. (Cast unlisted). 90 min. Sound. 16mm B&W. dubbed. *Rental:* Bosco Films.

Young Rebel-Cervantes *see* Cervantes.

Young Recruit *see* Son of the Navy.

Young Runaways, The. Kevin Coughlin & Patty McCormack. Directed by Arthur Dreifuss. 1968. MGM. 91 min. Sound. 16mm Color. *Rental:* MGM United.

Young Savages. Burt Lancaster & Shelley Winters. Directed by John Frankenheimer. 1961. United Artists. 100 min. Sound. 16mm B&W. *Rental:* MGM United.

Young Stranger, The. James MacArthur, Kim Hunter & James Daly. Directed by John Frankenheimer. 1957. RKO. 84 min. Sound. 16mm B&W. *Rental:* Budget Films, Kit Parker, Video Comm, Westcoast Films & Wholesome Film Ctr. *Lease:* Video Comm.

Young Swingers, The. Rod Lauren & Molly Bee. Directed by Maury Dexter. 1964. Fox. 71 min. Sound. 16mm B&W. *Rental:* Films Inc.

Young Tom Edison. Mickey Rooney & Fay Bainter. Directed by Norman Taurog. 1940. MGM. 86 min. Sound. 16mm B&W. *Rental:* MGM United.

Young Torless. Matthieu Carriere & Barbara Steele. Directed by Volker Schlondorff. Ger. 1966. Germany. 87 min. Sound. 16mm B&W. subtitles. *Rental:* New Yorker Films.

Young Warriors, The. James Drury & Steve Carlson. Directed by John Peyser. 1966. Universal. 93 min. Sound. 16mm Color. *Rental:* Swank Motion. *Rental:* Swank Motion, Anamorphic version.

Young Winston. Robert Shaw, Anne Bancroft & Simon Ward. Directed by Sir Richard Attenborough. 1973. Columbia. 145 min. Sound. 16mm Color. *Rental:* Budget Films, Films Inc, Images Film, Kit Parker, Modern Sound, Swank Motion, Twyman Films, Welling Motion Pictures & Westcoast Films. *Rental:* Swank Motion, Anamorphic version.

Young World, A. Christine Delaroche & Nino Castelnuovo. Directed by Vittorio De Sica. Fr. 1966. France. 84 min. Sound. 16mm B&W. subtitles. *Rental:* MGM United.

Youngblood Hawke. James Franciscus & Suzanne Pleshette. Directed by Delmer Daves. 1964. Warners. 137 min. Sound. 16mm B&W. *Rental:* Films Inc.

Younger Generation, The. Jean Hersholt & Ricardo Cortez. Directed by Frank Capra. 1929. Columbia. 80 min. Sound. 16mm B&W. *Rental:* Kit Parker.

Youngest Profession, The. Virginia Weidler & John Carroll. Directed by Edward Buzzell. 1943. MGM. 82 min. Sound. 16mm B&W. *Rental:* MGM United.

Your Cheatin' Heart. George Hamilton & Susan Oliver. Directed by Gene Nelson. 1964. MGM. (Anamorphic). 99 min. Sound. 16mm B&W. *Rental:* MGM United.

Your Erroneous Zones. 1980. Films Inc. (Lecture). 97 min. Sound. 16mm Color. *Rental:* Films Inc. *Sale:* Films Inc. *Rental:* Films Inc, *Sale:* Films Inc, Videotape version.

You're a Sweetheart. George Murphy & Alice Faye. Directed by David Butler. 1937. Universal. 96 min. Sound. 16mm B&W. *Rental:* Swank Motion.

You're in the Army Now. Phil Silvers & Jimmy Durante. Directed by Lewis Seiler. 1941. Warners. 79 min. Sound. 16mm B&W. *Rental:* MGM United.

You're in the Navy Now. Orig. Title: U. S. S. Teakettle. Gary Cooper & Jane Greer. Directed by Henry Hathaway. 1951. Fox. 92 min. Sound. 16mm B&W. *Rental:* Films Inc.

You're My Everything. Dan Dailey & Anne Baxter. Directed by Walter Lang. 1949. Fox. 94 min. Sound. 16mm B&W. *Rental:* Films Inc. *Rental:* Films Inc, Color version.

You're Never Too Young. Dean Martin & Jerry Lewis. Directed by Norman Taurog. 1955. Paramount. 102 min. Sound. 16mm Color. *Rental:* Films Inc.

You're Not So Tough. Dead End Kids. Directed by Joe May. 1940. Universal. 72 min. Sound. 16mm B&W. *Rental:* Swank Motion.

You're Out of Luck. Frankie Darro & Mantan Moreland. Directed by Howard Bretherton. 1941. Monogram. 61 min. Sound. 16mm B&W. *Rental:* Hurlock Cine.

You're Telling Me. W. C. Fields & Buster Crabbe. Directed by Erle C. Kenton. 1934. Paramount. 66 min. Sound. 16mm B&W. *Rental:* Swank Motion.

You're Too Fat. 1974. NBC. (Documentary). 52 min. Sound. 16mm Color. *Rental:* Films Inc & U Mich Media. *Sale:* Films Inc. *Sale:* Films Inc, Videotape version.

Yours, Mine & Ours. Lucille Ball & Henry Fonda. Directed by Melville Shavelson. 1968. United Artists. 111 min. Sound. 16mm Color. *Rental:* Arcus Film, MGM United, Modern Sound, Roas Films, Welling Motion Pictures & Williams Films.

Youth & the Quarter Horse. American Quarterhorse Association. (Documentary). 54 min. Sound. 16mm Color. *Rental:* U of IL Film.

Youth Drug Ward, The. 1972. KQED. (Documentary). 60 min. Sound. 16mm Color. *Rental:* Film Wright. *Sale:* Film Wright.

Youth in Revolt. Sweden. (Documentary). 77 min. Sound. 16mm B&W. *Rental:* Film Classics.

Youth of Maxim, The. Boris Chirkov. Directed by Grigori Kozintsev & Leonid Trauberg. Rus. 1935. Russia. 85 min. Sound. 16mm B&W. subtitles. *Rental:* Corinth Films.

Youth of Peter the Great, The. Dmitry Zolotukhin. Directed by Sergei Gerassimov. Rus. 1981. Russia. 140 min. Sound. 16mm Color. subtitles. *Rental:* Corinth Films. *Rental:* Corinth Films, Videotape version.

Youth on Parade. John Hubbard & Ruth Terry. Directed by Albert S. Rogell. 1942. Republic. 63 min. Sound. 16mm B&W. *Rental:* Inst Cinema & Ivy Films.

Youth on Parole. Marian Marsh & Gordon Oliver. Directed by Phil Rosen. 1937. Republic. 54 min. Sound. 16mm B&W. *Rental:* Ivy Films. *Sale:* Rep Pic Film.

Youth Runs Wild. Bonita Granville & Kent Smith. Directed by Mark Robson. 1944. RKO. 67 min. Sound. 16mm B&W. *Rental:* Films Inc.

Youth Terror: The View from Behind the Gun. 1978. ABC. 48 min. Sound. 16mm Color. *Rental:* McGraw-Hill Films & Syracuse U Film. *Sale:* McGraw-Hill Films.

You've Come a Long Way, Maybe? 1981. 55 min. Sound. 16mm Color. *Rental:* U Mich Media.

Yue E. 1978. 60 min. Sound. Videotape Color. *Rental:* Iowa Films.

Yuki, the Snow Girl. 1972. Japan. 60 min. Sound. 16mm B&W. narrated Eng. *Rental:* Japan Society.

Yukon Flight. James Newill & Dave O'Brien. Directed by Ralph Staub. 1940. Monogram. 57 min. Sound. 16mm B&W. *Rental:* Budget Films & Mogulls Films.

Yukon Gold. Kirby Grant & Martha Hyer. Directed by Frank McDonald. 1952. Monogram. 63 min. Sound. 16mm B&W. *Rental:* Hurlock Cine.

Yukon Manhunt. Kirby Grant. Directed by Frank McDonald. 1951. Monogram. 60 min. Sound. 16mm B&W. *Rental:* Hurlock Cine & Modern Sound.

Yukon Passage. 1977. National Geographic. (Documentary). 59 min. Sound. 16mm Color. *Rental:* Natl Geog. *Sale:* Natl Geog. *Sale:* Natl Geog, Videotape version.

Yukon Vengeance. Kirby Grant. Directed by William Beaudine. 1954. Allied Artists. 68 min. Sound. 16mm B&W. *Rental:* Ivy Films. *Sale:* Rep Pic Film.

Yulya's Diary. 1980. 58 min. Sound. Videotape *Rental:* PBS Video. *Sale:* PBS Video.

Yumi Yet: Independence for Papua New Guinea. Directed by Dennis O'Rourke. 1979. Australia. (Documentary). 54 min. Sound. 16mm Color. subtitles. *Rental:* Films Inc & Syracuse U Film. *Sale:* Films Inc.

Z. Yves Montand & Irene Papas. Directed by Costa-Gavras. Fr. 1969. France. 128 min. Sound. 16mm Color. subtitles. *Rental:* Cinema Five. *Lease:* Cinema Five.

Z. P. G. Orig. Title: Zero Population Growth. Oliver Reed & Geraldine Chaplin. Directed by Michael Campus. 1972. Paramount. 95 min. Sound. 16mm Color. *Rental:* Films Inc.

Zabriskie Point. Mark Frechette & Daria Halprin. Directed by Michelangelo Antonioni. 1970. MGM. 112 min. Sound. 16mm Color. *Rental:* MGM United. *Rental:* MGM United, Anamorphic version. *Sale:* Tamarelles French Film, Videotape version.

Zachariah. John Rubenstein & Pat Quinn. Directed by George Englund. 1971. Cinerama. 92 min. Sound. 16mm Color. *Rental:* Films Inc.

Zack & the Magic Factory. 1983. ABC. (Cast unlisted). 50 min. Sound. 16mm Color. *Rental:* MTI Tele. *Sale:* MTI Tele.

Zagreb Festival. 1971. Yugoslavia. (Animated, anthology). 90 min. Sound. 16mm Color. *Rental:* Film Images. *Sale:* Film Images.

Zalmen or the Madness of God. Joseph Wiseman. 1973. NET. 120 min. Sound. 16mm Color. *Rental:* WNET Media. *Sale:* WNET Media. *Sale:* WNET Media, Videotape version.

Zamba. Jon Hall & June Vincent. Directed by William Berke. 1949. Eagle Lion. 75 min. Sound. 16mm B&W. *Rental:* Ivy Films & Mogulls Films.

Zandy's Bride. Gene Hackman & Liv Ullmann. Directed by Jan Troell. 1974. Warners. 97 min. Sound. 16mm Color. *Rental:* Westcoast Films.

Zanzabuku. Directed by Lewis Cotlow. 1956. Republic. (Documentary). 67 min. Sound. 16mm B&W. *Rental:* Ivy Films & Rep Pic Film. *Sale:* Rep Pic Film.

Zapatillas Coloradas. Alfredo Barbieri. Directed by Juan Sires. 1953. Spain. 85 min. Sound. 16mm B&W. *Rental:* Film Classics. *Rental:* Film Classics, Videotape version.

Zapped! Scott Baio & Willie Aames. Directed by Robert J. Rosenthal. 1982. Embassy. 90 min. Sound. 16mm Color. *Rental:* Films Inc.

Zarak. Victor Mature, Michael Wilding & Anita Ekberg. Directed by Terence Young. 1957. Columbia. 99 min. Sound. 16mm Color. *Rental:* Bosco Films & Kit Parker.

Zardoz. Sean Connery & Charlotte Rampling. Directed by John Boorman. 1974. Fox. 102 min. Sound. 16mm Color. *Rental:* Films Inc. *Sale:* Tamarelles French Film, Videotape version.

Zaza. Claudette Colbert & Bert Lahr. Directed by George Cukor. 1938. Paramount. 83 min. Sound. 16mm B&W. *Rental:* Swank Motion.

Zazie. Catherine Demongeot & Philippe Noiret. Directed by Louis Malle. Fr. 1960. France. 90 min. Sound. 16mm Color. subtitles. *Rental:* New Cinema & New Yorker Films.

Zebra Force. Mike Lane & Richard X. Slattery. Directed by Joe Tornatore. 1976. 83 min. Sound. 16mm Color. *Rental:* Films Inc.

Zebra in the Kitchen. Jay North & Martin Milner. Directed by Ivan Tors. 1965. MGM. 93 min. Sound. 16mm Color. *Rental:* MGM United.

Zelig. Woody Allen & Mia Farrow. Directed by Woody Allen. 1983. Warners. 84 min. Sound. 16mm B&W. *Rental:* Films Inc & Swank Motion. *Rental:* Swank Motion, *Sale:* Tamarelles French Film, Videotape version.

Zem Spieva. Orig. Title: Earth Sings, The. Directed by Karel Plicka. 1932. Czechoslovakia. (Documentary, musical score only). 68 min. Sound. 16mm B&W. *Rental:* Museum Mod Art.

Zemlya *see* Earth.

Zen in Ryoko-In. 1972. Total Communications. (Documentary). 71 min. Sound. 16mm Color. *Rental:* Films Inc, Macmillan Films & Syracuse U Film. *Sale:* Macmillan Films.

Zenobia. Orig. Title: Elephants Never Forget. Oliver Hardy & Harry Langdon. Directed by Gordon Douglas. 1939. Hal Roach. 73 min. Sound. 16mm B&W. *Rental:* Mogulls Films, Wholesome Film Ctr & Willoughby Peer.

Zeppelin. Michael York & Elke Sommer. Directed by Etienne Perier. 1971. Britain. 97 min. Sound. 16mm Color. *Rental:* Cine Craft, Films Inc, Natl Film, Video Comm & Willoughby Peer.

Zerbrochene Krug, Der. Trans. Title: Broken Jug, The. Emil Jannings & Paul Dahlke. Directed by Gustav Ucicky. Ger. 1937. Germany. 86 min. Sound. 16mm B&W. subtitles. *Rental:* Trans-World Films.

Zerda's Children. 1980. Phoenix. (Documentary). 53 min. Sound. 16mm Color. narrated Eng. *Rental:* Phoenix Films & U Cal Media. *Sale:* Phoenix Films. *Sale:* Phoenix Films, Videotape version.

Zero for Conduct. Jean Daste. Directed by Jean Vigo. Fr. 1933. France. 44 min. Sound. 16mm B&W. subtitles. *Rental:* Budget Films, Em Gee Film Lib, Images Film & Kit Parker. *Sale:* Cinema Concepts, Festival Films, Glenn Photo, Images Film & Reel Images. *Sale:* Festival Films & Tamarelles French Film, Videotape version.

Zero Hour. Otto Krueger & Jane Darwell. Directed by Hall Bartlett. 1939. Republic. 54 min. Sound. 16mm B&W. *Rental:* Ivy Films. *Sale:* Rep Pic Film.

Zero in the Universe. Jock Livingston. Directed by George Moorse. 1967. Jock Livingston. 85 min. Sound. 16mm B&W. *Rental:* Canyon Cinema.

Zero Population Growth *see* Z. P. G..

Ziegfeld Follies. William Powell, Fred Astaire & Judy Garland. Directed by Vincente Minnelli. 1946. MGM. 110 min. Sound. 16mm Color. *Rental:* MGM United. *Rental:* MGM United, Videotape version.

Ziegfeld Girl. Lana Turner, Hedy Lamarr & Judy Garland. Directed by Busby Berkeley. 1941. MGM. 130 min. Sound. 16mm B&W. *Rental:* MGM United.

Zig Zag. George Kennedy & Anne Jackson. Directed by Richard A. Colla. 1970. MGM. 104 min. Sound. 16mm Color. *Rental:* MGM United. *Rental:* MGM United, Anamorphic version.

Ziggy Stardust. David Bowie. Directed by D. A. Pennebaker. 1983. Fox. 91 min. Sound. 16mm Color. *Rental:* Corinth Films.

Zita. Joanna Shimkus & Katina Paxinou. Directed by Robert Enrico. 1968. France. 94 min. Sound. 16mm Color. *Rental:* Swank Motion.

Ziz, Boom, Bah. Orig. Title: College Days. Peter Lind Hayes & Mary Healy. Directed by William Nigh. 1941. Monogram. 70 min. Sound. 16mm B&W. *Rental:* Budget Films & Video Comm. *Lease:* Video Comm. *Rental:* Video Comm, Videotape version.

Zola. France. (Cast unlisted). 60 min. Sound. 16mm B&W. *Rental:* French Am Cul. *Rental:* French Am Cul, Videotape version.

Zombies of the Stratosphere. Judd Holdren & Aline Towne. Directed by Fred C. Brannon. 1952. Republic. 163 min. Sound. 16mm B&W. *Rental:* Ivy Films.

Zombies on Broadway. Orig. Title: Loonies on Broadway. Alan Carney & Wally Brown. Directed by Gordon Douglas. 1945. RKO. 68 min. Sound. 16mm B&W. *Rental:* Films Inc.

Zoo in Budapest. Loretta Young & Gene Raymond. Directed by Rowland V. Lee. 1933. Fox. 85 min. Sound. 16mm B&W. *Rental:* Films Inc.

Zoos of the World. 1970. National Geographic. (Documentary). 52 min. Sound. 16mm Color. *Rental:* Natl Geog, SD Av Ctr, Syracuse U Film, U Mich Media & Wholesome Film Ctr. *Sale:* Natl Geog. *Sale:* Natl Geog, Videotape version.

Zoot Suit. Daniel Valdez & Tyne Daly. Directed by Luis Valdez. 1981. Universal. 103 min. Sound. 16mm Color. *Rental:* Swank Motion.

Zorba the Greek. Anthony Quinn, Alan Bates & Lila Kedrova. Directed by Michael Cacoyannis. 1964. Fox. 146 min. Sound. 16mm B&W. *Rental:* Films Inc.

Zorns Lemma. Directed by Hollis Frampton. 1970. Hollis Frampton. (Experimental). 60 min. Sound. 16mm Color. *Rental:* Canyon Cinema.

Zorro. Alain Delon & Stanley Baker. Directed by Duccio Tessari. 1975. France. 90 min. Sound. 16mm Color. dubbed. *Rental:* Hurlock Cine.

Zorro. Filmation. 66 min. Sound. 16mm Color. *Rental:* Williams Films.

Zorro Rides Again. John Carroll & Duncan Renaldo. Directed by William Witney. 1958. Republic. 217 min. Sound. 16mm B&W. *Rental:* Ivy Films. *Sale:* Rep Pic Film. *Rental:* Ivy Films, Min. 70 version.

Zorro: The Gay Blade. George Hamilton, Lauren Hutton & Ron Leibman. Directed by Peter Medak. 1981. Fox. 97 min. Sound. 16mm Color. *Rental:* Films Inc.

Zorro's Black Whip. George J. Lewis & Linda Stirling. Directed by Spencer G. Bennett. 1944. Republic. 177 min. Sound. 16mm B&W. *Rental:* Budget Films & Ivy Films.

Zorro's Fighting Legion. Reed Hadley & Sheila Darcy. Directed by William Witney. 1939. Republic. 215 min. Sound. 16mm B&W. *Rental:* Ivy Films.

Zotz! Tom Poston & Julia Meade. Directed by William Castle. 1962. Columbia. 105 min. Sound. 16mm B&W. *Rental:* Buchan Pic, Cine Craft, Films Inc, Modern Sound, Roas Films, Swank Motion, Welling Motion Pictures & Westcoast Films.

Zoya. Galina Vodianitskaya. Directed by Lev Arnchtam. 1944. Russia. 86 min. Sound. 16mm B&W. subtitles. *Rental:* Corinth Films.

Zulu. Stanley Baker, Jack Hawkins & Michael Caine. Directed by Cy Endfield. 1965. Embassy. 138 min. Sound. 16mm Color. *Rental:* Films Inc.

Zulu Dawn. Burt Lancaster & Peter O'Toole. Directed by Douglas Hickox. 1979. Britain. 98 min. Sound. 16mm Color. *Rental:* Twyman Films, Westcoast Films & Wholesome Film Ctr.

Zulu Zion. 1977. Britain. (Documentary). 52 min. Sound. 16mm Color. *Rental:* U of IL Film, Iowa Films & U Mich Media.

Zvenigora. Mikola Nedemsky & Polina Otava. Directed by Alexander Dovzhenko. 1928. Russia. 73 min. Silent. 16mm B&W. *Rental:* Budget Films, Corinth Films, Em Gee Film Lib, Kit Parker & Westcoast Films. *Sale:* Festival Films, Glenn Photo & Reel Images. *Lease:* Corinth Films.

SERIALS INDEX

Ace Drummond. 13 episodes. John King & Jean Rogers. Directed by Ford Beebe & Clifford Smith. 1936. Universal. Sound. 16mm B&W. *Rental:* Budget Films, Morcraft Films & Willoughby Peer. *Sale:* Morcraft Films.

Adams Chronicles, The. 13 episodes. 1976. Britain. (Cast unlisted). Sound. 16mm Color. *Rental:* Indiana AV Ctr & U of IL Film. *Sale:* Indiana AV Ctr.

Adventures of Batman & Robin, The. 15 episodes. Robert Lowery. Directed by Spencer G. Bennett. 1948. Columbia. Sound. 16mm B&W. *Rental:* Westcoast Films. *Sale:* Cinema Concepts, Super 8 sound version.

Adventures of Captain Marvel, The: Return of Captain Marvel. 12 episodes. Tom Tyler & Louise Currie. Directed by William Witney & John English. 1941. Republic. Sound. 16mm B&W. *Rental:* Budget Films & Ivy Films. *Rental:* Ivy Films, *Sale:* Ivy Films, Super 8 sound version. *Sale:* Cinema Concepts, Videotape version.

Adventures of Dusty Bates, The. 5 episodes. Britain. (Cast unlisted). Sound. 16mm B&W. *Rental:* Roas Films.

Adventures of Frank & Jesse James, The. 13 episodes. Clayton Moore, Noel Neill & Steve Darrell. Directed by Fred C. Brannon & Yakima Canutt. 1948. Republic. Sound. 16mm B&W. *Rental:* Ivy Films.

Adventures of Frank Merriwell, The. 12 episodes. Don Briggs & Jean Rogers. Directed by Clifford Smith. 1936. Universal. Sound. 16mm B&W. *Rental:* Welling Motion Pictures.

Adventures of Rex & Rinty, The. 12 episodes. Kane Richmond, Harry Woods & Rin-Tin-Tin Jr. 1935. Universal. Sound. 16mm B&W. *Rental:* Budget Films & Williams Films.

Adventures of Sir Galahad, The. 15 episodes. George Reeves & Lois Hall. Directed by Spencer G. Bennett. 1949. Columbia. Sound. 16mm B&W. *Rental:* Williams Films.

Adventures of Smiling Jack. Tom Brown & Rose Hobart. Directed by Ray Taylor & Lewis D. Collins. 1943. Universal. Sound. 16mm B&W. *Rental:* Classic Film Mus.

Adventures of Tarzan, The. 13 episodes. Elmo Lincoln. Directed by Robert Hill. 1928. Artclass. Silent. 16mm B&W. *Rental:* Em Gee Film Lib. *Sale:* Glenn Photo. *Sale:* Glenn Photo, Super 8 silent version. *Sale:* Glenn Photo, Silent 8 mm version.

Adventures of the Flying Cadets, The. 13 episodes. Robert Armstrong, Johnny Downs & Jennifer Holt. Directed by Ray Taylor & Lewis D. Collins. 1943. Universal. Sound. 16mm B&W. *Rental:* Budget Films, Film Classics, Film Ctr DC, Mogulls Films & Westcoast Films.

Ali & His Baby Camel. 15 Episodes. Mohamed Rifai. Directed by Henry Geddes. 1960. Britain. Sound. 16mm Color. *Sale:* Lucerne Films.

Ambush at Devil's Gap. 6 episodes. Chris Barrington. Directed by David Eastman. 1966. Britain. Sound. 16mm B&W. *Sale:* Lucerne Films.

Around the World in Eighty Days. 16 episodes. 1972. API. (Animated). Sound. 16mm Color. *Rental:* Westcoast Films. *Sale:* Inst Cinema.

Batman. 6 episodes. Lewis Wilson & J. Carrol Naish. Directed by Lambert Hillyer. 1943. Columbia. Silent. 8mm B&W. *Rental:* Westcoast Films.

Belphegor. 13 episodes. Juliette Greco. 1964. France. Sound. 16mm B&W. subtitles. *Rental:* French Am Cul.

Black Arrow, The. 15 episodes. Robert Scott & Adele Jergens. Directed by B. Reeves Eason. 1944. Columbia. Sound. 16mm B&W. *Rental:* Inst Cinema, Newman Film Lib & Williams Films.

Black Coin, The. 15 episodes. Dave O'Brien, Constance Bergen & Snub Pollard. Directed by Al Herman. 1936. Stage & Screen. Sound. 16mm B&W. *Sale:* Morcraft Films. *Sale:* Morcraft Films, *Rental:* Budget Films, Super 8 sound version.

Blake of Scotland Yard. 12 episodes. Ralph Byrd, Herbert Rawlinson, Joan Barclay & Lloyd Hughes. Directed by Robert Hill. 1937. Victory. 73 min. Sound. 16mm B&W. *Rental:* Budget Films, Film Classics & Mogulls Films. *Sale:* Cinema Concepts.

Bruce Gentry. 15 episodes. Tom Neal & Judy Clark. Directed by Spencer G. Bennett & Thomas Carr. 1949. Columbia. Sound. 16mm B&W. *Rental:* Williams Films.

Buck Rogers. 12 Episodes. Buster Crabbe, Constance Moore & Jackie Moran. 1939. Universal. Sound. 16mm B&W. *Rental:* Budget Films, Ivy Films & Video Comm. *Sale:* Ivy Films, Morcraft Films & Reel Images, Super 8 sound version.

Burn 'em Up Barnes. 12 episodes. Frankie Darro & Lola Lane. Directed by Colbert Clark & Armand Schaefer. 1934. Mascot. Sound. 16mm B&W. *Rental:* Video Comm. *Sale:* Cinema Concepts, Morcraft Films & Natl Cinema. *Sale:* Morcraft Films, Super 8 sound version.

Captain America. 15 episodes. Dick Purcell & Lorna Gray. Directed by John English & Elmer Clifton. 1943. Republic. Sound. 16mm B&W. *Rental:* Budget Films & Ivy Films. *Sale:* Cinema Concepts, Videotape version.

Captain Celluloid vs. the Film Pirates. 4 episodes. Adventure. (Cast unlisted). Silent. 16mm B&W. *Rental:* Em Gee Film Lib. *Sale:* Blackhawk Films, Silent 8mm version.

Captain Marvel. Tom Tyler. Directed by William Witney & John English. 1941. Columbia. Sound. 16mm B&W. *Rental:* Kit Parker.

Captain Video. 15 episodes. Judd Holdren & Larry Stewart. Directed by Spencer G. Bennett & Wallace Grissell. 1951. Columbia. Sound. 16mm B&W. *Rental:* Inst Cinema & Film Ctr DC.

Chimp Mates. 5 episodes. 1976. Britain. (Cast unlisted). Sound. 16mm Color. *Sale:* Lucerne Films.

Clutching Hand, The. 15 episodes. Jack Mulhall & William Farnum. Directed by Al Herman. 1936. Stage & Screen 65 min. Sound. 16mm B&W. *Rental:* Video Comm. *Sale:* Morcraft Films. *Sale:* Morcraft Films, Super 8 sound version.

Cody of the Pony Express. 12 Episodes. Jock O'Mahoney, Dickie Moore & Peggy Stewart. Directed by Spencer G. Bennett. 1950. Columbia. Sound. 16mm B&W. *Rental:* Inst Cinema & Williams Films.

Congo Bill. 15 Episodes. Don McGuire, Cleo Moore & Jack Ingram. Directed by Spencer G. Bennett & Thomas Carr. 1948. Columbia. Sound. 16mm B&W. *Rental:* Inst Cinema.

Crimson Ghost, The. 12 Episodes. Charles Quigley, Linda Stirling & Clayton Moore. Directed by William Witney & Fred C. Brannon. 1946. Republic. Sound. 16mm *Rental:* Ivy Films. *Sale:* Cinema Concepts, Videotape version.

Dangers of the Canadian Mounted. 12 episodes. Jim Bannon & Virginia Belmont. Directed by Fred C. Brannon & Yakima Canutt. 1948. Republic. Sound. 16mm B&W. *Rental:* Ivy Films.

Daredevils of the Red Circle. 12 episodes. Gene Townley & Tiny Dawson. Directed by William Witney & John English. 1939. Republic. Sound. 16mm *Rental:* Ivy Films, Videotape version.

Daughter of Don Q, The. 12 episodes. Adrian Booth, Kirk Alyn & Roy Barcroft. Directed by Spencer G. Bennett & Fred C. Brannon. 1946. Republic. 163 min. Sound. 16mm B&W. *Rental:* Ivy Films & Video Comm.

Desperadoes of the West. 12 episodes. Richard Powers, Judy Clark & Roy Barcroft. Directed by Fred C. Brannon. 1950. Republic. Sound. 16mm B&W. *Rental:* Ivy Films.

Devil Horse, The. Harry Carey & Edwina Booth. Directed by Otto Brower. 1932. Mascot. Sound. 16mm B&W. *Rental:* Video Comm. *Sale:* Morcraft Films. *Sale:* Video Comm, Videotape version.

Dick Tracy. 15 episodes. Ralph Byrd & Smiley Burnette. Directed by Ray Taylor. 1937. Republic. Sound. 16mm B&W. *Rental:* Em Gee Film Lib, Films Inc, Ivy Films, Video Comm, Westcoast Films & Wholesome Film Ctr. *Lease:* Video Comm. *Rental:* Video Comm, *Lease:* Reel Images & Video Comm, Videotape version.

Dick Tracy Returns. 15 episodes. Ralph Byrd & Charles Middleton. Directed by William Witney. 1938. Republic. 100 min. Sound. 16mm B&W. *Rental:* Budget Films, Films Inc & Video Comm. *Lease:* Video Comm. *Rental:* Video Comm, *Lease:* Video Comm, Videotape version.

Dick Tracy vs. Crime Inc. 15 episodes. Ralph Byrd & Ralph Morgan. Directed by William Witney. 1941. Republic. Sound. 16mm B&W. *Rental:* Films Inc, Ivy Films, Video Comm & Westcoast Films. *Lease:* Video Comm. *Rental:* Video Comm, *Lease:* Video Comm, Videotape version.

Dick Tracy's G-Men. Ralph Byrd & Irving Pichel. Directed by William Witney & John English. 1939. Republic. 100 min. Sound. 16mm B&W. *Rental:* Budger Films, Films Inc, Ivy Films & Video Comm. *Lease:* Video Comm. *Rental:* Video Comm, *Sale:* Video Comm, Videotape version.

Don Daredevil Rides Again. 12 episodes. Ken Curtis, Aline Towne & Roy Barcroft. Directed by Fred C. Brannon. 1951. Republic. Sound. 16mm B&W. *Rental:* Ivy Films.

Don Winslow of the Coast Guard. 13 episodes. Don Terry & Elyse Knox. Directed by Ray Taylor & Lewis D. Collins. 1943. Universal. Sound. 16mm B&W. *Rental:* Budget Films, Modern Sound, Welling Motion Pictures & Willoughby Peer.

Don Winslow of the Navy. 12 episodes. Don Terry, John Litel & Claire Dodd. 1942. Universal. Sound. 16mm B&W. *Rental:* Budget Films, Film Ctr DC, Inst Cinema, Welling Motion Pictures & Willoughby Peer. *Sale:* Morcraft Films. *Sale:* Reel Images, Videotape version.

Drums of Fu Manchu. 15 episodes. Henry Brandon. Directed by William Witney & John English. 1940. Republic. Sound. 16mm B&W. *Rental:* Video Comm.

Federal Agents vs. Underworld Inc. 12 episodes. Kirk Alyn & Rosemary LaPlanche. Directed by Fred C. Brannon. 1949. Republic. Sound. 16mm B&W. *Rental:* Ivy Films.

Federal Operator Ninety Nine. 12 episodes. Marten Lamont & Helen Talbot. Directed by Spencer G. Bennett & Wallace Grissell. 1945. Republic. Sound. 16mm B&W. *Rental:* Ivy Films.

Fighting Devil Dogs, The. 12 episodes. Lee Powell & Herman Brix. Directed by William Witney & John English. 1939. Republic. Sound. 16mm B&W. *Rental:* Ivy Films & Video Comm.

Fighting Marines. 12 episodes. Grant Withers & Ann Rutherford. Directed by B. Reeves Eason & Joseph Kane. 1935. Mascot. Sound. 16mm B&W. *Sale:* Cinema Concepts & Natl Cinema.

Fighting with Kit Carson. 12 episodes. Johnny Mack Brown & Noah Beery Jr. Directed by Armand Schaefer & Colbert Clark. 1933. Mascot. Sound. 16mm B&W. *Rental:* Budget Films, Kerr Film & Video Comm.

Five Clues to Fortune. 8 episodes. John Rogers & David Hemmings. Directed by Joe Mendoza. 1957. Britain. Sound. 16mm B&W. *Sale:* Lucerne Films.

Five on a Treasure Island. 8 episodes. Rel Grainer & Richard Palmer. Directed by Gerald Landau. 1957. Britain. Sound. 16mm B&W. *Rental:* Films Inc. *Sale:* Lucerne Films.

Flame Fighters, The. 12 episodes. Herbert Rawlinson. Directed by Duke Worne & Robert Dillon. 1925. Rayart. Silent. 16mm B&W. *Rental:* Mogulls Films.

Flaming Frontiers. 15 episodes. Johnny Mack Brown. Directed by Ray Taylor & Alan James. 1938. Universal. Sound. 16mm B&W. *Rental:* Budget Films. *Sale:* Morcraft Films, Videotape version.

Flash Gordon. 13 episodes. Buster Crabbe, Jean Rogers & Charles Middleton. Directed by Frederick Stephani. 1936. Universal. Sound. 16mm B&W. *Rental:* Budget Films, Ivy Films, Kerr Film, Video Comm & Welling Motion Pictures.

Flash Gordon Conquers the Universe. 12 episodes. Buster Crabbe, Carol Hughes & Charles Middleton. Directed by Ford Beebe & Ray Taylor. 1940. Universal. Sound. 16mm B&W. *Rental:* Budget Films, Em Gee Film Lib, Ivy Films, Kerr Film, Video Comm & Welling Motion Pictures. *Sale:* Morcraft Films. *Sale:* Morcraft Films, Super 8 sound version. *Rental:* Video Comm, *Lease:* Video Comm, Videotape version.

Flash Gordon's Trip to Mars. 15 episodes. Buster Crabbe, Jean Rogers & Charles Middleton. Directed by Ford Beebe & Robert Hill. 1939. Universal. Sound. 16mm B&W. *Rental:* Budget Films, Ivy Films & Video Comm.

Flying Disc Man from Mars. 12 episodes. Walter Reed & Lois Collier. Directed by Fred C. Brannon. 1950. Republic. Sound. 16mm B&W. *Rental:* Ivy Films.

G-Men Never Forget. 12 episodes. Clayton Moore, Roy Barcroft & Ramsey Ames. Directed by Fred C. Brannon & Yakima Canutt. 1948. Republic. Sound. 16mm B&W. *Rental:* Ivy Films.

G-Men vs. the Black Dragon. 15 episodes. Rod Cameron & Constance Worth. Directed by William Witney. 1943. Republic. Sound. 16mm B&W. *Rental:* Ivy Films.

Galloping Ghost, The. 12 episodes. Red Grange. Directed by B. Reeves Eason. 1931. Mascot. Sound. 16mm B&W. *Rental:* Em Gee Film Lib. *Sale:* Cinema Concepts, Natl Cinema & Select Film.

Gang Busters. 13 episodes. Kent Taylor & Irene Hervey. Directed by Noel Smith & Ray Taylor. 1942. Universal. Sound. 16mm B&W. *Sale:* Natl Cinema.

Ghost of Zorro, The. 12 episodes. Clayton Moore, Pamela Blake & Roy Barcroft. Directed by Fred C. Brannon. 1949. Republic. Sound. 16mm B&W. *Rental:* Ivy Films.

Ghost Riders of the West. 12 episodes. Robert Kent & Peggy Stewart. Directed by Spencer G. Bennett. 1946. Republic. Sound. 16mm B&W. *Rental:* Ivy Films.

Government Agents vs. Phantom Legion. 12 episodes. Walter Reed & Mary Ellen Kay. Directed by Fred C. Brannon. 1951. Republic. Sound. 16mm B&W. *Rental:* Ivy Films.

Great Alaskan Mystery, The. 13 episodes. Ralph Morgan & Marjorie Weaver. Directed by Ray Taylor & Lewis D. Collins. 1944. Universal. Sound. 16mm B&W. *Sale:* Classic Film Mus.

Green Archer, The. 15 episodes. Victor Jory & Iris Meredith. Directed by James W. Horne. 1940. Columbia. Sound. 16mm B&W. *Rental:* Newman Film Lib & Williams Films. *Sale:* Reel Images. *Rental:* Williams Films & Newman Film Lib, Videotape version.

Hawk of the Wilderness. 12 episodes. Herman Brix. Directed by John English & William Witney. 1938. Republic. Videotape B&W. *Sale:* Cinema Concepts.

Holt of the Secret Secret Service. 15 episodes. Jack Holt & Evelyn Brent. Directed by James W. Horne. 1932. Mascot. Sound. 16mm B&W. *Sale:* Natl Cinema.

Hop Harrigan. 15 episodes. William Bakewell & Jennifer Holt. Directed by Derwin Abrahams. 1946. Columbia. Sound. 16mm B&W. *Rental:* Westcoast Films.

Hurricane Express. 12 episodes. John Wayne & Joseph Girard. Directed by Armand Schaefer & J. P. MacGowan. 1932. Mascot. Sound. 16mm B&W. *Rental:* Budget Films, Ivy Films, Kerr Film, Video Comm & Westcoast Films. *Sale:* Natl Cinema, Select Film & Cinema Concepts. *Rental:* Budget Films, Super 8 sound version.

Invisible Monster, The. 12 episodes. Richard Webb, Aline Towne & George Meeker. Directed by Fred C. Brannon. 1951. Republic. Sound. 16mm B&W. *Rental:* Ivy Films.

James Brothers of Missouri, The. 12 episodes. Keith Richards, Noel Neill & Roy Barcroft. Directed by Fred C. Brannon. 1949. Republic. Sound. 16mm B&W. *Rental:* Ivy Films.

Jesse James Rides Again. 13 episodes. Clayton Moore, Linda Stirling & Roy Barcroft. Directed by Fred C. Brannon & Thomas Carr. 1947. Republic. Sound. 16mm B&W. *Rental:* Ivy Films.

Jungle Drums of Africa. 12 episodes. Clayton Moore & Phyllis Coates. Directed by Fred C. Brannon. 1952. Republic. Sound. 16mm B&W. *Rental:* Ivy Films.

Jungle Menace. 15 episodes. Frank Buck & Reginald Denny. Directed by Harry Fraser & George Melford. 1937. Columbia. Sound. 16mm B&W. *Rental:* Roas Films & Video Comm.

Jungle Queen. 13 episodes. Ruth Roman, Lois Collier & Eddie Quillan. 1945. Universal. Sound. 16mm B&W. *Rental:* Inst Cinema, Mogulls Films & williams Films.

Jungle Raiders. 15 episodes. Kane Richmond, Eddie Quillan & Veda Ann Borg. Directed by Lesley Selander. 1945. Columbia. Sound. 16mm B&W. *Rental:* Inst Cinema.

Junior G-Men. 12 episodes. Billy Halop & Huntz Hall. Directed by Ford Beebe & John Rawlins. 1940. Republic. Sound. 16mm B&W. *Rental:* Film Ctr DC & Westcoast Films. *Sale:* Morcraft Films.

King of the Carnival. 12 episodes. Harry Lauter, Frank Bennett & Robert Shayne. Directed by Franklin Adreon. 1946. Republic. Sound. 16mm B&W. *Rental:* Ivy Films.

King of the Forest Rangers. 12 episodes. Larry Thompson & Helen Talbot. Directed by Spencer G. Bennett & Fred C. Brannon. 1946. Republic. Sound. 16mm B&W. *Rental:* Ivy Films.

King of the Jungleland. 15 episodes. Clyde Beatty & Elaine Shephard. Directed by B. Reeves Eason & Joseph Kane. 1949. Republic. Sound. 16mm B&W. *Rental:* Ivy Films.

King of the Rocket Men. 12 episodes. Tristram Coffin & Mae Clarke. Directed by Fred C. Brannon. 1949. Republic. Sound. 16mm B&W. *Rental:* Ivy Films & Video Comm.

King of the Wild. 12 episodes. Boris Karloff & Walter Miller. Directed by B. Reeves Eason. 1931. Mascot. Sound. 16mm B&W. *Rental:* Inst Cinema & Mogulls Films.

Last Frontier, The. 12 episodes. Lon Chaney Jr., Dorothy Gulliver & Francis X Bushman Jr. Directed by Spencer G. Bennett. 1932. RKO. Sound. 16mm B&W. *Rental:* Film Classics, Mogulls Films & Video Comm.

Last of the Mohicans, The. 12 episodes. Harry Carey. Directed by Ford Beebe & B. Reeves Eason. 1932. Mascot. Sound. 16mm B&W. *Rental:* Film Classics.

Lightning Warrior, The. 12 episodes. Rin-Tin-Tin, Frankie Darro & George Brent. Directed by Armand Schaefer & Ben Kline. 1931. Mascot. Sound. 16mm B&W. *Rental:* Newman Film Lib & Video Comm.

Lone Defender, The. 12 episodes. Rin-Tin-Tin. Directed by Richard Thorpe. 1930. Mascot. Sound. 16mm B&W. *Rental:* Mogulls Films.

Lone Ranger, The. 15 episodes. Lee Powell. Directed by William Witney & John English. 1938. Republic. Sound. Videotape B&W. *Sale:* Reel Images.

Lost City, The. 12 episodes. Kane Richmond, Claudia Dell & Ralph Lewis. 1935. Krellberg. Sound. 16mm B&W. *Rental:* Williams Films, Mogulls Films & Video Comm.

Lost City of the Jungle, The. 13 episodes. Russell Hayden, Lionel Atwill & Key Luke. Directed by Ray Taylor & Lewis D. Collins. 1946. Universal. Sound. 16mm B&W. *Rental:* Budget Films, Mogulls Films & Roas Films.

Lost Jungle, The. 12 episodes. Clyde Beatty. Directed by Armand Schaefer & David Howard. 1934. Mascot. Sound. 16mm B&W. *Rental:* Budget Films, Em Gee Film Lib, Kerr Film, Mogulls Films, Video Comm & Westcoast Films. *Sale:* Natl Cinema & Cinema Concepts. *Sale:* Reel Images & Video Comm, Videotape version.

Lost Planet, The. 15 episodes. Forrest Taylor & Judd Holdren. Directed by Spencer G. Bennett. 1953. Columbia. Sound. 16mm B&W. *Rental:* Williams Films.

Man with a Steel Whip, The. 12 episodes. Richard Simmons & Barbara Bestar. Directed by Franklin Adreon. 1954. Republic. Sound. 16mm B&W. *Rental:* Ivy Films.

Manhunt of Mystery Island. 15 episodes. Richard Bailey & Linda Sterling. Directed by Spencer G. Bennett, Wallace Grissell & Yakima Canutt. 1945. Republic. Sound. 16mm B&W. *Rental:* Ivy Films.

Masked Marvel, The. 12 Episodes. William Forrest & Louise Currie. Directed by Spencer G. Bennett. 1943. Republic. Sound. 16mm B&W. *Rental:* Ivy Films. *Sale:* Nostalgia Merchant. *Sale:* Cinema Concepts, Videotape version.

Master Key, The. 13 episodes. Milburn Stone, Jan Wiley & Dennis Moore. Directed by Ray Taylor & Lewis D. Collins. 1945. Universal. Sound. 16mm B&W. *Rental:* Inst Cinema, Roas Films, Video Comm & Willoughby Peer.

Master Spy, The. 12 episodes. (Cast unlisted). Sound. 16mm B&W. *Rental:* Mogulls Films.

Masters of Venus, The. 8 episodes. Amanda Coxwell & Robin Stewart. Directed by Ernest Morris. 1962. Britain. Sound. 16mm B&W. *Rental:* Films Inc. *Sale:* Lucerne Films.

Miracle Rider, The. 15 episodes. Tom Mix & Joan Gale. Directed by Armand Schaefer & B. Reeves Eason. 1935. Mascot. Sound. 16mm B&W. *Rental:* Budget Films, Cine Craft, Em Gee Film Lib, Kerr Film, Video Comm & Westcoast Films. *Sale:* Natl Cinema & Cinema Concepts. *Sale:* Reel Images, Videotape version.

Mysterious Doctor Satan. 15 episodes. Eduardo Cianneli & Robert Wilcox. Directed by William Witney & John English. 1940. Republic. Sound. 16mm B&W. *Rental:* Ivy Films & Video Comm.

Mystery of the Double Cross, The. 5 episodes. Philippa Brewster & Peter Hale. Pathe. Silent. 16mm B&W. *Sale:* Blackhawk Films. *Sale:* Blackhawk Films, Silent 8mm version.

Mystery of the River Boat. 13 episodes. Robert Lowery & Lyle Talbot. Directed by Lewis D. Collins & Sam Taylor. 1944. Universal. Sound. 16mm B&W. *Rental:* Film Classics, Film Ctr DC & Westcoast Films.

Mystery Squadron. Bob Steele & Jack Mulhall. Directed by Colbert Clark & David Howard. 1933. Mascot. Sound. 16mm B&W. *Rental:* Budget Films. *Sale:* Natl Cinema. *Sale:* Reel Images & Video Comm, Videotape version.

New Adventures of Tarzan, The. 12 episodes. Herman Brix & Frank Baker. Directed by Edward Kull. 1935. Burroughs-Tarzan. Sound. 16mm B&W. *Rental:* Em Gee Film Lib. *Sale:* Budget Films, Glenn Photo & Morcraft Films.

Nyoka & the Tigermen. 15 episodes. Kay Aldridge & Clayton Moore. Directed by William Witney. 1942. Republic. Sound. 16mm B&W. *Rental:* Ivy Films. *Sale:* Nostalgia Merchant.

Officer Four-Four-Four. 12 episodes. Walter Miller. Directed by Ben Wilson. 1926. Davis. Sound. 16mm B&W. *Rental:* Em Gee Film Lib. *Sale:* Glenn Photo.

Oregon Trail, The. 15 episodes. Johnny Mack Brown. Directed by Ford Beebe. 1939. Universal. Sound. 16mm B&W. *Rental:* Film Classics, Roas Films, Video Comm & Willoughby Peer.

Overland Mail. 15 episodes. Lon Chaney & Helen Parrish. Directed by Ford Beebe & John Rawlins. 1941. Universal. Sound. 16mm B&W. *Sale:* Classic Film Mus.

Overland with Kit Carson. 15 episodes. Bill Elliott, Frankie Darro & Chief Thundercloud. Directed by Sam Nelson & Norman Deming. 1939. Columbia. 16mm B&W. *Rental:* Inst Cinema, Modern Sound & Williams Films.

Painted Stallion. 12 episodes. Ray Corrigan & Hoot Gibson. Directed by Alan James & Ray Taylor. Rel. 1937. Republic. Sound. 16mm B&W. *Rental:* Ivy Films. *Sale:* Morcraft Films. *Sale:* Reel Images, Videotape version.

Panther Girl of the Kongo, The. 12 episodes. Phyllis Coates & Myron Healey. Directed by Franklin Adreon. 1954. Republic. 16mm B&W. *Rental:* Ivy Films.

Perils of the Darkest Jungle. 12 episodes. Allan Lane, Linda Stirling & Duncan Renaldo. Directed by Wallace Grissell. 1951. Republic. Sound. 16mm B&W. *Rental:* Ivy Films.

Perils of the Royal Mounted. 15 episodes. Robert Stevens, Nell O'Day & Herbert Rawlinson. Directed by James W. Horne. 1942. Universal. Sound. 16mm B&W. *Rental:* Inst Cinema & Newman Film Lib.

Phantom Creeps, The. 12 episodes. Bela Lugosi, Robert Kent & Regis Toomey. Directed by Ford Beebe & Saul A. Goodkind. 1939. Universal. Sound. 16mm B&W. *Rental:* Budget Films, Em Gee Film Lib, Kerr Film & Video Comm. *Sale:* Natl Cinema & Select Film. *Rental:* Video Comm, Videotape version.

Phantom Empire. 12 episodes. Gene Autry & Frankie Darro. Directed by Otto Brower. Rel. 1935. Mascot. Sound. 16mm B&W. *Rental:* Budget Films, Kerr Film, Williams Films & Video Comm. *Sale:* Cinema Concepts, Morcraft Films, Natl Cinema & Westcoast Films. *Rental:* Video Comm, *Sale:* Video Comm, Videotape version.

Pirate's Harbor. 12 episodes. Kane Richmond & Kay Aldridge. Directed by Spencer G. Bennett. 1944. Republic. Sound. 16mm B&W. *Rental:* Video Comm.

Power God, The. 15 episodes. Ben Wilson & Neva Gerber. 1926. Davis. Silent. 16mm B&W. *Rental:* Em Gee Film Lib. *Sale:* Glenn Photo. *Sale:* Glen Photo, Silent 8mm version.

Purple Monster Strikes, The. 15 Episodes. Dennis Moore, Linda Stirling & Roy Barcroft. Directed by Spencer G. Bennett. 1945. Republic. Sound. 16mm B&W. *Rental:* Ivy Films. *Sale:* Cinema Concepts, Videotape version.

Radar Men from the Moon. 12 episodes. George Wallace & Aline Towne. Directed by Fred C. Brannon. 1951. Republic. 16mm B&W. *Rental:* Ivy Films. *Sale:* Cinema Concepts, Videotape version.

Radar Patrol vs. Spy King. 12 episodes. Kirk Alyn & Jean Dean. Directed by Fred C. Brannon. 1949. Republic. Sound. 16mm B&W. *Rental:* Ivy Films.

Radio Patrol. 13 episodes. Grant Withers. Directed by Ford Beebe & Clifford Smith. 1937. Universal. Sound. 16mm B&W. *Rental:* Willoughby Peer.

Raiders of Ghost City. 13 episodes. Dennis Moore & Wanda McKay. Directed by Ray Taylor & Lewis D. Collins. 1944. Universal. Sound. 16mm B&W. *Sale:* Classic Film Mus.

Raiders of the River. 8 episodes. Richard O'Sullivan. Directed by John Haggarty. 1956. Britain. Sound. 16mm B&W. *Sale:* Lucerne Films.

Red Barry. 13 episodes. Buster Crabbe & Frances Robinson. Directed by Ford Beebe & Alan James. 1938. Universal. Sound. 16mm B&W. *Rental:* Welling Motion Pictures & Willoughy Peer.

Return of Chandu. 12 episodes. Bela Lugosi & Clara Kimball Young. Directed by Ray Taylor. Rel. 1934. Principal. Sound. 16mm B&W. *Rental:* Video Comm. *Sale:* Reel Images. *Sale:* Reel Images, Super 8 sound version. *Sale:* Reel Images, Videotape version.

Riders of Death Valley. 15 episodes. Dick Foran, Buck Jones, Leo Carillo & Charles Bickford. Directed by Ford Beebe & Ray Taylor. 1941. Universal. Sound. 16mm B&W. *Rental:* Budget Films, Kerr Film & Video Comm.

Robinson Crusoe of Clipper Island. 14 episodes. Mala, Rex, Buck & Herbert Rawlinson. Directed by Mack V. Wright & Ray Taylor. 1936. Republic. Sound. 16mm B&W. *Rental:* Ivy Films. *Sale:* Natl Cinema & Morecraft Films.

Royal Mounted Rides Again, The. 13 episodes. Bill Kennedy & Milburn Stone. Directed by Ray Taylor & Lewis D. Collins. 1945. Universal. Sound. 16mm B&W. *Rental:* Roas Films.

Scarlet Horseman, The. 13 episodes. Peter Cookson, Janet Shaw, Paul Guilfoyle & Virginia Christine. Directed by Ray Taylor & Lewis D. Collins. 1946. Universal. Sound. 16mm B&W. *Rental:* Budget Films & Roas Films.

Sea Hound, The. 15 Episodes. Buster Crabbe, Jimmy Lloyd & Pamela Blake. Directed by Mack V. Wright & B. Reeves Eason. 1947. Columbia. Sound. 16mm B&W. *Rental:* Williams Films.

Sea Raiders. 12 episodes. Dead End Kids. Directed by Ford Beebe & John Rawlins. 1941. Universal. Sound. 16mm B&W. *Sale:* Classic Film Mus.

Secret of Treasure Island, The. 15 episodes. Don Terry, Grant Withers & Hobart Bosworth. 1938. Columbia. Sound. 16mm B&W. *Rental:* Williams Films.

Shadow of the Eagle. 12 episodes. John Wayne. Directed by Ford Beebe. 1932. Mascot. Sound. 16mm B&W. *Rental:* Budget Films, Em Gee Film Lib, Kerr Film, Video Comm & Westcoast Films. *Sale:* Natl Cinema & Cinema Concepts. *Rental:* Video Comm, *Lease:* Video Comm, Videotape version.

Sky Raiders. 12 episodes. Donald Woods & Billy Halop. Directed by Ford Beebe & Ray Taylor. 1941. Universal. Sound. 16mm B&W. *Sale:* Classic Film Mus.

Son of the Sahara. 8 episodes. Darryl Read. Directed by Frederic Goode. 1967. Britain. Sound. 16mm B&W. *Sale:* Lucerne Films.

Son of Zorro. 13 episodes. George Turner, Peggy Stewart & Roy Barcroft. Directed by Spencer G. Bennett & Fred C. Brannon. 1947. Republic. Sound. 16mm B&W. *Rental:* Ivy Films.

Spy Smasher. 12 episodes. Kane Richmond & Marguerite Chapman. Directed by William Witney. 1942. Republic. Sound. 16mm B&W. *Rental:* Budget Films, Ivy Films & Video Comm.

Tank Crew & the Dog, The. 8 episodes. F. Pieczka & J. Gajos. Directed by Konrad Nalecki. Pol. Poland. Sound. 16mm B&W. subtitles. *Rental:* Polish People.

Three Musketeers, The. John Wayne, Raymond Hatton & Jack Mulhall. Directed by Armand Schaefer & Colbert Clark. 1933. Mascot. Sound. 16mm B&W. *Rental:* Budget Films & Video Comm. *Sale:* Natl Cinema, Select Film & Cinema Concepts. *Sale:* Reel Images & Video Comm, Videotape version.

Tim Tyler's Luck. 13 episodes. Frankie Thomas & Jack Mulhall. Directed by Ford Beebe. 1937. Universal. Sound. 16mm B&W. *Rental:* Select Film & Willoughby Peer. *Sale:* Select Film.

Trader Tom of the China Seas. 12 episodes. Harry Lauter, Aline Towne & Lyle Talbot. Directed by Franklin Adreon. 1953. Republic. Sound. 16mm B&W. *Rental:* Ivy Films.

Treasure of Malta, The. 6 episodes. Mario Debono. Directed by Derek Williams. 1963. Britain. Sound. 16mm B&W. *Sale:* Lucerne Films.

Unbroken Arrow, The. 6 episodes. 1976. Britain. (Cast unlisted). Sound. 16mm Color. *Sale:* Lucerne Films.

Undersea Kingdom. Ray Corrigan, Monte Blue & William Farnum. Directed by B. Reeves Eason & Joseph Kane. 1950. Republic. Sound. 16mm B&W. *Rental:* Budget Films, Em Gee Film Lib, Ivy Films, Westcoast Films & Wholesome Film Ctr. *Sale:* Video Comm, Videotape version.

Vanishing Legion, The. 15 episodes. Harry Carey. Directed by B. Reeves Eason. 1931. Mascot. Sound. 16mm B&W. *Rental:* Video Comm. *Sale:* Natl Cinema. *Sale:* Video Comm, Videotape version.

Vigilante, The. 15 episodes. Ralph Byrd & Ramsey Ames. Directed by Wallace Fox. 1947. Columbia. Sound. 16mm B&W. *Rental:* Westcoast Films.

Vigilantes Are Coming, The. 12 episodes. Robert Livingston & Kay Hughes. Directed by Mack V. Wright. 1936. Republic. 230 min. Sound. 16mm B&W. *Rental:* Ivy Films.

Whispering Shadow, The. 13 episodes. Bela Lugosi. Directed by Al Herman. 1933. Mascot. Sound. 16mm B&W. *Rental:* Budget Films, Em Gee Film Lib, Kerr Film, Mogulls Films, Video Comm & Westcoast Films. *Sale:* Cinema Concepts & Natl Cinema. *Rental:* Video Comm, *Sale:* Video Comm, Videotape version.

Winners of the West. 13 episodes. Dick Foran & Anne Nagel. Directed by Ford Beebe & Ray Taylor. 1940. Universal. Sound. 16mm B&W. *Rental:* Budget Films, Film Classics, Film Ctr DC, Inst Cinema & Mogulls Films. *Sale:* Morcraft Films.

Wolf Dog. 12 episodes. Rin-Tin-Tin Jr., Frankie Darro & Boots Mallory. Directed by Harry Fraser & Colbert Clark. 1933. Mascot. Sound. 16mm B&W. *Rental:* Inst Cinema.

Wolves of Kultur, The. 7 episodes. Leah Baird. Directed by Joseph A. Golden. 1918. Pathe. Silent. 16mm B&W. *Sale:* Blackhawk Films. *Sale:* Blackhawk Films, Silent 8mm version.

Woman in Grey, The. Arlene Pretty & Henry G. Sell. 1919. Silent. 16mm B&W. *Sale:* Blackhawk Films. *Sale:* Blackhawk Films, Super 8 sound version. *Sale:* Blackhawk Films, Super 8 silent version. *Sale:* Blackhawk Films, Silent 8 mm version.

Zombies of the Stratosphere. 12 chapters. Judd Holdren, Aline Towne & Leonard Nimoy. Directed by Fred C. Brannon. 1952. Republic. Sound. 16mm B&W. *Rental:* Ivy Films.

Zorro Rides Again. 12 episodes. John Carroll, Reed Howes & Duncan Renaldo. Directed by William Witney. 1937. Republic. Sound. 16mm B&W. *Rental:* Ivy Films & Video Comm. *Rental:* Video Comm, Videotape version.

Zorro's Black Whip. 12 episodes. George J. Lewis & Linda Stirling. Directed by Spencer G. Bennett & Wallace Grissell. 1944. Republic. Sound. 16mm B&W. *Rental:* Budget Films, Ivy Films & Video Comm. *Sale:* Cinema Concepts.

Zorro's Fighting Legion. 12 episodes. Reed Hadley, Sheila Darcy & Carleton Young. Directed by William Witney & John English. 1939. Republic. Sound. 16mm B&W. *Rental:* Budget Films, Ivy Films, Video Comm & Westcoast Films. *Sale:* Cinema Concepts & Morcraft Films, Super 8 sound version. *Sale:* Morcraft Films, Videotape version.

DIRECTORS INDEX

607

SHINSUKE OGAWA
Peasants of the Second Fortress, The
pg. 383

KOHEI OGURI
Muddy River pg. 339

GEORGE O'HANLON
Rookie, The pg. 427

GERRY O'HARA
All the Right Noises pg. 11
Maroc Seven pg. 316

NOBUHIKO OHBAYASHI
Confession, The pg. 99

MICHAEL O'HERLIHY
One & Only Genuine Original Family
 Band, The pg. 367
Richard T. Ely pg. 417
Tomorrow Is Yesterday pg. 516

TOM O'HORGAN
Futz pg. 182
Rhinoceros pg. 417

KIHACHI OKAMOTO
Kill! pg. 266
Sword of Doom, The pg. 490

STEVEN OKAZAKI
Survivors, The pg. 487

DENNIS O'KEEFE
Angela pg. 17

SHIN SAN OKK
Spring Fragrance pg. 472

SIDNEY OLCOTT
Claw, The pg. 94
From the Manger to the Cross pg.
 179
Monsieur Beaucaire pg. 334
Only Woman, The pg. 370
Timothy's Quest pg. 513

JOHN M. OLD
Road to Fort Alamo pg. 422

JOEL OLIANSKY
Competition, The pg. 99

HECTOR OLIVERA
Rebellion in Patagonia pg. 410

SIR LAURENCE OLIVIER
Hamlet pg. 209
Henry V pg. 218
Richard the Third pg. 418
Three Sisters, The pg. 508

ERMANNO OLMI
Fiances, Les pg. 161
Man Named John, A pg. 310
One Fine Day pg. 367
Sound of Trumpets, The pg. 468

Tree of the Wooden Clogs, The pg.
 522

RALPH OLSEN
Legend of a Gunfighter pg. 282

ROLF OLSEN
Journey Into the Beyond pg. 260

DANIEL O'MALLEY
Mountain Man pg. 338

RON O'NEAL
Superfly T. N. T. pg. 486

ROBERT O'NEIL
Angel pg. 17
Blood Mania pg. 55

MARCEL OPHULS
Banana Peel pg. 32
Memory of Justice, The pg. 322
Sense of Loss, A pg. 444
Sorrow & the Pity, The pg. 468

MAX OPHULS
Caught pg. 82
Earrings of Madame de ..., The pg.
 142
Exile, The pg. 153
Letter from an Unknown Woman, A
 pg. 285
Liebelei pg. 285
Lola Montes pg. 292
Plaisir, Le pg. 391
Reckless Moment, The pg. 410
Ronde, La pg. 427

CATHERINE ORENTREICH
Wizard of Waukesha, The pg. 565

RON ORIEUX
Fort Good Hope pg. 174

LESTER ORLEBECK
Gauchos of Eldorado pg. 185
Outlaws of the Cherokee Trail pg.
 375
Pals of the Pecos pg. 377
Pioneers of the West pg. 389
Prairie Pioneers pg. 396
Saddle Pals pg. 431
Shadows on the Sage pg. 448
West of Cimarron pg. 550

RON ORMOND
Black Lash pg. 50
Kentucky Jubilee pg. 265
Mesa of Lost Women, The pg. 324
Outlaw Women pg. 375
Varieties on Parade pg. 537
Yes, Sir, Mr. Bones pg. 572

ALAN ORMSBY
Deranged pg. 122

DENNIS O'ROURKE
Yumi Yet pg. 576

ROLF ORTHEL
Shadow of Doubt pg. 448

WALLACE ORTON
Old Mother Riley's Ghosts pg. 364

JOHN O'SHAUGHNESEY
Sound of Laughter, The pg. 468

JOHN O'SHEA
Broken Barrier pg. 66

ABE OSHEROFF
Dreams & Nightmares pg. 139

NAGISA OSHIMA
Boy pg. 61
Ceremony, The pg. 83
Cruel Story of Youth, The pg. 108
Death by Hanging pg. 119
Diary of a Shinjuku Thief pg. 128
Empire of Passion, The pg. 147
In the Realm of the Senses pg. 243
Man Who Left His Will on Film, The
 pg. 311
Merry Christmas, Mr. Lawrence pg.
 323

SAM O'STEEN
Brand New Life, A pg. 63
I Love You, Goodbye pg. 237
Sparkle pg. 470

THADDEUS O'SULLIVAN
On a Paving Stone Mounted pg. 365

GERD OSWALD
Agent from H.A.R.M. pg. 7
Brass Legend, The pg. 63
Bunny O'Hare pg. 70
Crime of Passion pg. 107
Fury at Showdown pg. 182
Kiss Before Dying, A pg. 269
Screaming Mimi pg. 439
Valerie pg. 536

RICHARD OSWALD
Captain from Kopenick pg. 76
Isle of Missing Men pg. 250
Lovable Cheat, The pg. 297
My Song Goes Round the World pg.
 344

MATTEO OTTAVIANO
Single Room Furnished pg. 457

GERARD OURY
Brain, The pg. 62
Delusions of Grandeur pg. 122
Gentle Art of Murder, The pg. 186
Mad Adventures of "Rabbi" Jacob,
 The pg. 302

DAVID OUTERBRIDGE
Art of the Potter, The pg. 24

HORACE OVE
Reggae pg. 412

CLIFF OWEN
Bawdy Adventures of Tom Jones, The
 pg. 36

ENRICO SALERNO
Gentlemen Marry Brunettes pg. 187
Girl Next Door, The pg. 191
Half Angel pg. 208
I'll Get By pg. 240
Let's Make It Legal pg. 284
Meet Me After the Show pg. 321
My Wife's Best Friend pg. 344
Spoilers of the North pg. 472
Ticket to Tomahawk, A pg. 510

ENRICO SALERNO
Anonymous Venetian, The pg. 19

SOHRAB SHAHID SALES
Diary of a Lover pg. 128

SIDNEY SALKOW
Adventures of Martin Eden, The pg. 5
Big Night, The pg. 46
Blood on the Arrow pg. 55
Bulldog Drummond at Bay pg. 69
Cafe Hostess pg. 73
Chicago Confidential pg. 87
City Without Men pg. 93
Faithful in My Fashion pg. 155
Fighting Throughbreds pg. 163
Flight at Midnight pg. 169
Flight Lieutenant pg. 169
Girl from God's Country, The pg. 190
Golden Hawk, The pg. 196
Great Sioux Massacre, The pg. 202
Iron Sheriff, The pg. 249
Last Man on Earth, The pg. 277
Lone Wolf Strikes, The pg. 293
Murder Game, The pg. 340
Night Hawk, The pg. 353
Pathfinder, The pg. 381
Prince of Pirates, The pg. 398
Quick Gun, The pg. 404
She Married a Cop pg. 450
Storm Over Bengal pg. 478
Street of Missing Men pg. 481
Time Out for Rhythm pg. 512
Twice Told Tales pg. 527
Woman Doctor pg. 566

BRIAN SALT
Toto & the Poachers pg. 518

JAIME SALVADOR
Castillos en el Aire pg. 80

BERT SALZMAN
Rodeo Red & the Runaway pg. 425

ABABACAR SAMB
Jom pg. 259

SALVATORE SAMPERI
Malicious pg. 307

BILL SAMPSON
Ace Eli and Rodger of the Skies pg. 2

EDWARD SAMPSON
Fast & the Furious, The pg. 158

SAMSON SAMSONOV
Grasshopper, The pg. 200

Three Sisters, The pg. 508

LUIS SAN ANDRES
Joey pg. 257

HELKE SANDER
All Round Reduced Personality, The pg. 11

DENIS SANDERS
Crime & Punishment U. S. A. pg. 107
Elvis-That's the Way It Is pg. 146
Invasion of the Bee Girls, The pg. 248
One Man's Way pg. 368
Shock Treatment pg. 452
Souls to Soul pg. 468
War Hunt pg. 545

DIRK SANDERS
Tu Seras Terriblement Gentille pg. 526

MARLENE SANDERS
Women's Health pg. 568

MARTHA SANDLIN
Lady Named Baybie, A pg. 273

JAY SANDRICH
Seems Like Old Times pg. 444

MARK SANDRICH
Aggie Appleby pg. 8
Buck Benny Rides Again pg. 68
Carefree pg. 78
Cockeyed Cavaliers, The pg. 95
Follow the Fleet pg. 171
Gay Divorcee, The pg. 185
Hips Hips Hooray pg. 223
Man About Town pg. 307
Melody Cruise pg. 321
Shall We Dance? pg. 449
Skylark pg. 460
So Proudly We Hail pg. 463
Top Hat pg. 517
Woman Rebels, A pg. 567

JIMMY SANGSTER
Fear in the Night pg. 160
To Love a Vampire pg. 514

JORGE SANJINES
Blood of the Condor, The pg. 55
Courage of the People pg. 104
Principal Enemy, The pg. 398

ALFRED SANTELL
Aloma of the South Seas pg. 12
Beyond the Blue Horizon pg. 43
Breakfast for Two pg. 64
Daddy Long Legs pg. 111
Having Wonderful Time pg. 213
Internes Can't Take Money pg. 247
Jack London pg. 253
Mexicana pg. 324
Orchids & Ermine pg. 371
Patent Leather Kid, The pg. 381
Polly of the Circus pg. 393
That Brennan Girl pg. 499
Winterset pg. 564

GIANCARLO SANTI
Grand Duel, The pg. 199

CIRIO H. SANTIAGO
Ebony, Ivory & Jade pg. 143
Firecracker pg. 165
Muthers, The pg. 342
T. N. T. Jackson pg. 490

JOSEPH SANTLEY
Behind the News pg. 39
Blond Cheat pg. 53
Brazil pg. 63
Call of the Canyon pg. 74
Chatterbox pg. 86
Cocoanuts, pg. 95
Dancing Feet pg. 112
Down Mexico Way pg. 137
Earl Carroll's Vanities pg. 142
Good Night, Sweetheart pg. 197
Harmony Lane pg. 212
Here Comes Elmer pg. 219
Hitch-Hike to Happiness pg. 224
Jamboree pg. 254
Joan of Ozark pg. 257
Laughing Irish Eyes pg. 279
Loudspeaker, The pg. 297
Meet the Missus pg. 321
Melody & Moonlight pg. 321
Melody Ranch pg. 322
Million Dollar Baby pg. 326
Music in My Heart pg. 341
Puddin' Head pg. 402
Rhythm Hits the Ice pg. 417
Rookies on Parade pg. 427
Rosie the Riveter pg. 428
Shadow of a Woman pg. 448
Shantytown pg. 449
She's Got Everything pg. 451
Sis Hopkins pg. 458
Sleepy Lagoon pg. 461
Smartest Girl in Town, The pg. 462
Swing, Sister, Swing pg. 489
There Goes the Groom pg. 500
Three Little Sisters pg. 507
Thumbs Up pg. 509
Tragedy at Midnight, A pg. 519
Walking on Air pg. 544
Waterfront Lady pg. 547
We Went to College pg. 548
When You're Smiling pg. 554
Yokel Boy pg. 573

JESUS FERNANDEZ SANTOS
Goya pg. 199

NELSON PEREIRA DOS SANTOS
Alienist, The pg. 10
How Tasty Was My Little Frenchman pg. 232

ROBERTO SANTOS
Hour & Time of Augusto Matraga, The pg. 231

HENRY G. SAPERSTEIN
War of the Gargantuas, The pg. 546

RICHARD C. SARAFIAN
Fragment of Fear pg. 176
Lolly Madonna XXX pg. 292

FOREIGN-LANGUAGE FILMS INDEX

AFRICAN DIALECT
Harder They Come, The
Harvest, Three Thousand Years
To Live with Herds

ARABIC
Clouds Over Israel
Night of Counting the Years, The
Ramparts of Clay

BENGALI
Adversary, The
Aparajito
Company Limited
Kanchenjungha
Mahanagar
Music Room, The
Two Daughters

BULGARIAN
Goat Horn, The
Last Summer, The
Peach Thief, The
Stars

CHINESE
Black Panther, The
Guerillas on the Plains
My Heart Flies
Song of China

CZECHOSLOVAKIAN
Adrift
Case for a Young Hangman, A
Cassandra Cat
Closely Watched Trains
Competition, The
Daisies
Divine Emma, The
Ecstasy
End of a Priest, The
End of August at the Hotel Ozone,
   The
Fabulous Baron Munchausen, The
Fifth Horseman Is Fear, The
Fireman's Ball, The
Fruit of Paradise, The
Goalkeeper Also Lives on Our Street,
   The
Intimate Lighting
Joke, The

Krakatit
Loves of a Blonde, The
Man Who Lies, The
Martyrs of Love
Most Beautiful Age, The
Report on the Party & the Guests, A
River, The
Sign of the Virgin
Sirius
Transport from Paradise
Valerie & Her Week of Wonders
Witch's Hammer, The

DANISH
Day of Wrath
Dear Irene
Doktor Glas
Gertrud
Ordet

DUTCH
Girl with Red Hair, The
Mariken
Max Havelaar

FINNISH
Portraits of Women

FRENCH
A Nous la Liberte
Abysses, Les
Act of Agression, An
Adieu Philippine
Adorable Julia
Adorable Menteuse
Adventures of Mr. Wonderbird, The
Affaire Est Dans le Sac, L'
Age d'Or, L'
Agence Barnett, L'
Alexander: Very Happy Alexander
Alphaville
And Now My Love
Anderson Platoon, The
Angel & Sinner
Angele
Anges du Peche, Les
Animals, The
Annapurna
Apprenti Salaud, L
Arrestation d'Arsene Lupin, Le
Arsene Lupin Contre Sherlock
   Holmes

Atalante, L'
Atalante, L'
Au Hasard Balthazar
Au Pays de l'Eau Tranquille
Aussi Longue Absence, Une
Aviator's Wife, The
Babette Goes to War
Bad Company
Baker's Wife, The
Balearic Caper, The
Ballerina
Ballot Blackmail: Gangs, Inc.
Balzac
Banana Peel
Band of Outsiders
Barres
Basket of Crabs, A
Bay of Angels
Beau Serge, Le
Beauty & the Beast
Bed & Board
Bedroom Bandit, The
Beethoven
Belle
Belle Americaine, La
Belle Apparence, La
Belle de Jour
Berenice
Bete Humaine, La
Bigorne, Caporal de France, La
Biquefarre
Birgitt Hass Must Be Killed
Bizarre, Bizarre
Black Moon
Black Thursday
Blood of a Poet
Blow for Blow
Blue Country
Bon Anniversaire
Bonaparte & the Revolution
Bonjour Amour
Bonne Soupe, La
Bonnes Causes, Les
Boucher, Le
Boudu Saved from Drowning
Bride Wore Black, The
By the Blood of Others
Bye, See You Monday: Au Revoir, A
   Lundi
Cage aux Folles, La
Cage Aux Folles II, La
Camisards, Les
Carabiniers, Les
Carmen
Carnival in Flanders

Caroline Cherie
Casque d'Or
Cavalcade des Heures
Ce Soir Ou Jamais
Certain Tradition of Quality, A: 1945-1955
Cesar
Cesar & Rosalie
Chamade, La
Chambre, La
Champs Elysees
Charles-Dead or Alive
Chat, Le
Chateaubriand
Chienne, La
Children of Paradise
Chinoise, La
Chloe in the Afternoon
Chocolate Eclair, Le
Chronicle of a Summer: Paris 1960
Cinema du Diable
Cite de l'Indicible Peur, La
Clair de Femme: Womanlight
Claire's Knee
Classical Art Under the Occupation & the Liberation
Claudel
Cleo from Five to Seven
Clockmaker, The
Cloportes
Club de Femmes
Cocktail Molotov
Colonel Durand, Le
Confession, The
Conformist, The
Conspiration Malet, La
Contempt
Corbeau, Le
Coup de Tete: Hothead
Coup de Torchon
Cousin, Cousine
Cow & I, The
Crazy for Love
Crime & Punishment
Crook, The
Day for Night
Daydreamer, The
Days of Our Years
December
Delusions of Grandeur
Dernieres Vacances, Les
Desire
Destroy, She Said
Diary of a Chambermaid
Diary of a Country Priest
Dirty Hands
Discreet Charm of the Bourgeoisie, The
Disorder & Afterwards
Disparus de Saint Agil, Les
Don Quixote
Donkey Skin
Dossier Fifty-One
Dreams of Love
Drole de Paroissien, Un
Drugstore Romance
Du Guesclin
Dupont Lajoie
Earrings of Madame de ..., The
Emilienne & Nicole
Enfant Dans la Foule, Un
Enfants Terribles, Les
Entre Nous
Eternal Return, The

Etoiles Du Midi, Les
Every Man for Himself
Exhibition, The
Eyes Without a Face
Fanny
Fantastic Night, The
Farrebique
Faute de L'abbe Mouret, La
Femme Douce, La
Femme Infidele, La
Femmes Fatales
Femmes Savantes, Les
Fire Within, The
First Age of the French Cinema 1895-1914, The
First Time, The
Five-Day Lover
Forbidden Games
Four Hundred Blows
Four Nights of a Dreamer
Francois Villon
Frantic
French Provincial
Friend of the Family, A
From Munich to the Funny War
Gai Savoir, Le
Galia
Game Is Over, The
Gates of Paris, The
Gauloises Bleues, Les
Gentle Art of Murder, The
Gervaise
Get Out Your Handkerchiefs
Gide
Give Her the Moon
Godelureaux, Les
Going Places
Golden Age of the Silent Film, The: 1915-1928
Golgotha
Goto L'Ile d'Amour
Goulaleuse, La
Goupi-Main's Rouges, Les
Grain De Sable, Le: Circular Triangle
Grand Amour, Un
Grand Illusion
Grand Illusions, The: 1939-1941
Grand Ocean, The
Grand Remue-Menage, Le
Grande Breteche, La
Grande Illusion, La
Green Room, The
Guerre Est Finie, La
Happy New Year Caper, The
Harvest
Heart of Paris, The
Heart to Heart
Hiroshima, Mon Amour
Homme Au Chapeau Noir, L'
Hotel-Chateau
Huit Coups de l'Horloge, Les
I Sent a Letter to My Love
Icy Breasts
Idiot, The
Immortelle, L'
Improper Conduct
Intrepide, L'
Invitation, The
It's Raining in Santiago
J'Accuse
Jacques le Fataliste
Jaguar
Jeanne Dielman: Twenty Three Quai Du Commerce, Ten Eighty Bruxelles

Jeunes Filles de Paris
Joeur D'Echec, Le
Joli Mai, Le
Josepha
Jour de Fete
Jour Se Leve, Le
Journal d'un Fou, Le
Judex
Judge & the Assassin, The
Jules & Jim
Julie the Redhead
Jupiter's Thigh
Jusqu'Au Coeur
Just Before Nightfall
King of Hearts
Koumiko Mystery, The
Lac du Dames, La
Lacemaker, The
Lacombe, Lucien
Lady Chatterley's Lover
L'Amour Fou
Lancelot of the Lake
Last Chance, The
Last Metro, The
Last Woman, The
Last Year at Marienbad
Late Matthew Pascal, The
Leda
Let Joy Reign Supreme
L'Etoile du Nord
Letter from Siberia, A
Letter to Jane, A
Letters from My Windmill
Liaisons Dangereuses, Les
Liberte Une
Life, Love & Death
Life Upside Down
Light Years Away
Line of Demarcation
Little Theatre of Jean Renoir, The
Lit...Ze Bawdy Bed, Le
Live for Life
Lola Montes
Loneliness of the Long Distance Singer, The: The Yves Montand Story
Loulou
Love & the Frenchwoman
Love of Life
Love on the Run
Lovers, The
Lower Depths, The: Underground
Lucrece Borgia
Lumiere
Lumiere d'Ete
Lys Blancs, Les
Mad Adventures of "Rabbi" Jacob, The
Madame Bovary
Madame Rosa
Mademoiselle
Mado
Magnifique, Le
Maitre de Santiago, Le
Maitre d'Ecole, Le
Male of the Century
Man & a Woman, A
Man Escaped, A
Man in the Raincoat, The
Man Who Loved Women, The
Man Without a Face, The
Mandabi
Marie-Louise
Marius

Aguirre, the Wrath of God
Akrobat Scho-o-on
Alexander the Second of Russia
Ali, Fear Eats the Soul
Alice in the Cities
All Round Reduced Personality, The
Almost Angels
Alte und der Junge Konig, Der
American Friend, The
American Soldier, The
Andreas Schluter
Atlantide, L'
Backstairs
Bandit & the Princess, The
Baron Munchhausen
Berlin Alexanderplatz
Bettelstudent, Der
Beware of a Holy Whore
Bitter Tears of Petra Von Kant, The
Blue Angel, The
Blue Light, The
Blumen Aus Nizza
Brutalization of Franz Blum, The
Buddenbrooks
Calm Prevails Over the Country
Captain from Koepenick, The
Castle, The
Cat & Mouse
Charm of La Boheme, The
Chinese Roulette
Chronicle of Anna Magdalena Bach,
   The
Chronicle of Gray House, The
Class Relations
Confess, Dr. Corda!
Coup de Grace
Daughter of the Regiment
Daughters of Eve
Despair
Diary of a Lover
Dr. Robert Koch
Effi Briest
Eine Nacht in Venedig
Eternal Mask, The
Every Man for Himself & God
   Against All
Fabian
Fidelio
Fliegende Klassenzimmer, Das
Flying Dutchman, The
Fox & His Friends, The
Free Woman, A
From the Cloud to the Resistance
Gasparone
Germany Awake!
Germany in Autumn
Germany Pale Mother
Germany, Year Zero
Gleiwitz Case, The
Goalie's Anxiety at the Penalty Kick,
   The
Gods of the Plague
Golem, The
Great Ecstasy of the Sculptor Steiner,
   The
Heart of Glass, The
History Lessons
Hitlerjunge Quex
Hunters Are the Hunted, The
I Am My Films: A Portrait of
   Werner Herzog
In a Year of Thirteen Moons
Italiano Brava Gente
Jacob the Liar

Jail Bait
Kameradschaft
Karamazov
Katzelmacher
King in Shadow, A
Knife in the Head
Komodianten
Kuhle Wampe
Land of Silence & Darkness
Last Ten Days, The
Left-Handed Woman, The
Liebelei
Lissy
Lola
Lost Honor of Katharina Blum, The
Ludwig Van Beethoven
M
Maedchen in Uniform
Malou
Man Who Walked Through the Wall,
   The
Marianne & Juliane
Marriage of Maria Braun, The
Merchant of Four Seasons, The
Merry-Go-Round
Moses & Aaron
Mother Kusters Goes to Heaven
Murderers Are Among Us
Nosferatu the Vampire
Not Reconciled
Orphan Boy of Vienna, The
Portrait of Werner Herzog, A
Regimentstochter, Die
Richard Tauber Story, The
Rotation
Satan's Brew
Scarlet Letter, The
Seventh Year, The
Signs of Life
Sins of Rose Bernd, The
Sisters or the Balance of Happiness
Sky Without Stars
Slow Attack
Stronger Than the Night
Strongman Ferdinand
Stroszek
Sudden Wealth of the Poor People of
   Kombach, The
Summer in the City
Symphonie Einer Welstadt
Tartuffe, the Hypocrite
They Called Him Amigo
Third Generation, The
Threepenny Opera, The
Tiefland
Tin Drum, The
Tomorrow is My Turn
Tonio Kroger
Too Early, Too Late
Veronika Voss
Westfront Nineteen Eighteen
Why Does Herr R. Run Amok?
Wild Duck, The
Willi Busch Report, Der
William Tell
Winifred Wagner
Wizard of Babylon, The
Woyzeck
Wozzeck
Wrong Move, The
Yesterday Girl
Young Dr. Freud
Young Torless
Zerbrochene Krug, Der

GREEK

Antigone
Electra
Iphigenia
Rape, The
Thanos & Despina
Young Aphrodites

HEBREW
Clouds Over Israel
Daughters Daughters!
Dreamer, The
Hero's Wife
House on Chelouche St., The
I Love You, Rosa
Kazablan
Lupo
Margo
Sallah
Tin Man, The
To Live in Freedom

HINDI
Boot Polish
Calcutta
Charulata
Chess Players, The
Days & Nights in the Forest
Devi
Distant Thunder
Middleman, The
Nayak
Pather Panchali

HUNGARIAN
Adoption
Age of Daydreaming, The
Angi Vera
Dialogue
Father
Just Like at Home
Madame Dery
Nine Months
Piri Mindent Tud
Rain & Shine
Red Psalm
Round-Up, The
Silence & Cry
Stud Farm, The
Szinbad
Twenty-Five Fireman's Street
When Joseph Returns

ICELANDIC
Wedding of Palo, The

ITALIAN
Accattone
Adventurer of Tortuga, The
Adventures of Scaramouche, The
Aida
Al Fateh
Alfredo, Alfredo
All Screwed Up
All the Way, Boys
Allegro Non Troppo
Alone in the Streets
Amarcord
Amore, L'
Angelo
Angels of Darkness
Any Gun Can Play
Ape Woman, The
Avventura, L'

Samurai: Part Three
Samurai: Part Two
Samurai Spy
Sandakan Eight
Sanjuro
Sanshiro Sugata
Sansho the Bailiff
Scandal
Scandalous Adventures of Buraikan,
   The
Seven Samurai, The
She & He
Sisters of the Gion
Snow Country
Soldier's Prayer, A
Story of Floating Weeds, The
Story of the Last Chrysanthemum,
   The
Street of Shame
Sword of Doom, The
Taira Clan Saga, The
There Was a Father
Three Outlaw Samurai
Throne of Blood
Tokyo Story, The
Twenty Four Eyes
Twilight in Tokyo
Ugetsu
Utamaro & His Five Women
When a Woman Loves
Woman in the Dunes, The
Women of the Night
Yojimbo

KOREAN
Fate of Gum Hui & Un Hui, The
Spring Fragrance

LATIN
Sebastiane

MAYAN
Chac

NORWEGIAN
Edvard Munch

PERSIAN
Cow, The

POLISH
Akropolis
Aria for an Athlete
Ashes & Diamonds
Barrier
Camera Buff
Camouflage
Constant Factor, The
Contract, The
Direction: Berlin
Dybbuk, The
Eve Wants to Sleep
Everything for Sale
Family Life
Generation, A
Homo Varsoviensis
Hunting Flies
Identification Marks: None
Innocent Sorcerers
Kanal
Knife in the Water

Landscape After Battle
Man of Iron
Man of Marble
Passenger, The
Pearl in the Crown, The
Peasants, The
Samson
Story of Sin, The
Tank Crew & the Dog, The
Walkover
Wedding, The
Westerplatte
Without Anesthesia
Woman's Decision, A

PORTUGUESE
Alienist, The
All Nudity Shall Be Punished
Bahia
Barravento
Bravo Guerreiro, O
Cabezas Cortadas
Deceased, The
Free People in Guinea-Bissau
Gabriela
Gaijin
Ganga Zumba
Gods & the Dead, The
Grande Cidade, El
Heirs, The
Hour & Time of Augusto Matraga,
   The
How Tasty Was My Little
   Frenchman
I Love You
Killed the Family & Went to the
   Movies
Margin, The
Os Fuzis
Pixote
Plantation Boy
Priest & the Girl, The
They Don't Wear Black Tie
Torre Bella
Vida Provisoria, La
Vidas Secas
Xica

ROMANIAN
Codine

RUSSIAN
Admiral Ushakov
Aelita
Aerograd: Frontier
Aleko
Alexander Nevsky
And Quiet Flows the Don
Andrei Rublev
Anna Karenina
Anna Karenina
Arsenal
Asya
Ballad of a Soldier
Baltic Deputy
Battle for Siberia, The
Belated Flowers
Boris Godunov
Brothers Karamazov, The
Chapayev
Childhood of Maxim Gorky, The
Cinderella
Cossacks Beyond the Danube

Cossacks of the Kuban
Cranes Are Flying, The
Crime & Punishment
Dimka
Don Quixote
Dream of a Cossack, The
End of St. Petersburg, The
Eugene Onegin
Extraordinary Adventures of Mr.
   West in the Land of the Bolsheviks,
   The
Farewell, Doves
Fate of a Man
Father of a Soldier
Father Sergius
First Swallow, The
Flames on the Volga
Gambler, The
General Line, The: Old & New
Girl with the Hatbox, The
Grand Concert, The
Grasshopper, The
Great Battle of the Volga, The
Great Glinka, The
Gypsy Camp Vanishes into the Blue,
   The
Happiness
Heroes of Shipka
House That I Live In, The
Hunting Accident, The
Idiot, The
Inside Russia
Inspector General, The
Italiano Brava Gente
Ivan Pavlov
Ivan the Terrible
Ivan the Terrible: Part One
Ivan the Terrible: Part Two
Jamilya
King Lear
Lady With a Dog, The
Lenin in October
Lesson in Life, A
Letter That Was Never Sent, The
Mashenka
Maximka
May Night
Mechanics of the Brain
Miracle of Dr. Petrov, The
Mumu
My Apprenticeship
My Beloved
Mysterious Discovery, The
Nest of Gentry
Nineteen-Eighteen
Once There Was a Girl
Orphans, The
Overcoat, The
Peace to Him Who Enters
Pedagogical Poem, A
Peter the First
Peter the Great: Part Two
Pirosmani
Prince Igor
Private Ivan Brovkin
Professor Mamlock
Rainbow, The
Red & the White, The
Resurrection
Return of Vassili Bortnikov, The
Revolt of the Fisherman
Rimsky-Korsakov
Sadko
Sailor from the Comet

Dear John
Devil's Eye, The
Devil's Wanton, The
Doll, The
Duet for Cannibals
En Natt
Face to Face
Fanny & Alexander
Four Ninety-One
Girls, The
Gladiators, The
Gorilla, The
Great Adventure, The
Hour of the Wolf
Hugs & Kisses
I Am Curious: Blue
I Am Curious: Yellow
Lesson in Love, A
Loving Couples
Magic Flute, The
Magician, The
Man on the Roof, The
Miss Julie

Monika
Naked Night, The
Near & Far Away
Night Is My Future
One Summer of Happiness
Persona
Port of Call
Raven's End
Scenes from a Marriage
Silence, The
Smiles of a Summer
  Night
Summer Interlude
Summer Paradise
Swedish Wedding Night
Through a Glass Darkly
To Love
Torment
Touch, The
Virgin Spring, The
Wild Strawberries
Winter Light
Witch, The

TURKISH
Baba
Father, The
Kambur
Yol: The Trek Of Life

URDU
Towers of Silence

VIETNAMESE
Devil's Island
First Rice, The

WOLOF
Jom: The Story of a People

YIDDISH
Brivele der Mamen, A
Cantor's Son, The
Laughter Thru Tears
Lies My Father Told Me
Yiddle with His Fiddle

FILM REFERENCE WORKS

This section is composed of two parts, a bibliography and a classified list. The classified list categorizes by subject those titles in the bibliography that can provide further information on the films in this book, as well as being helpful in programming and developing festivals. Most of the works listed in the bibliography can be found in major library collections. (Full addresses are given for publishers of periodicals to facilitate subscription.) An * preceding a periodical title denotes that the periodical has been indexed in *Media Review Digest* since 1970.

Bibliography

Academy Awards Oscar Annual. La Habra, CA: ESE California, 1971–

American Film Institute Catalog of Motion Pictures: Feature Films. 1961–70. 2 vols. Edited by Richard P. Krafsur. New York: R. R. Bowker, 1976.

American Film Institute Catalog of Motion Pictures: Feature Films. 1921–30. 2 vols. Edited by Kenneth W. Munden. New York: R. R. Bowker, 1971.

British Film Catalogue. Edited by Denis Gifford. New York: McGraw-Hill, 1973.

Classic Images. 301 E. Third St., Muscatine, IA 52761. 1962–

Educational Film Locator. 2nd ed. New York: R. R. Bowker, 1980.

L'Encyclopédie du Cinéma (in French). Edited by Roger Boussinot. Paris, France: Bordas, 1967.

Film Buff's Bible. Edited by D. Richard Baer. Hollywood Film Archive, 1979.

Film Evaluation Guide. 3 vols. New York: Educational Film Library Assn., 1965, 1968, and 1972.

Film Directors: A Guide to Their American Films. James Robert Parish and Michael R. Pitts. Metuchen, NJ: Scarecrow Press, 1974.

Film Music: From Violins to Video. Edited by James L. Limbacher. Metuchen, NJ: Scarecrow Press, 1974.

Forty Years of Screen Credits. Edited by John T. Weaver. Metuchen, NJ: Scarecrow Press, 1970.

Haven't I Seen You Somewhere Before? Edited by James L. Limbacher. Ann Arbor, MI: Pierian Press, 1979.

International Film Guide. Edited by Peter Cowie. New York: NY Zoetrope, 1983.

International Index to Film Periodicals. Edited by Karen Jones. New York: R. R. Bowker, 1972 and 1973; New York: St. Martin's Press, 1974–1978.

International Motion Picture Almanac. Edited by Martin Quigley. New York: Quigley Publications, 1929–

Keeping Score. Edited by James L. Limbacher. Metuchen, NJ: Scarecrow Press, 1981.

Library of Congress Catalog of Films and Other Projected Materials. Washington, DC: Library of Congress, 1951–

Media Review Digest. Pierian Press, 931 S. State St., Ann Arbor, MI 48106. 1970–

Monthly Film Bulletin. British Film Institute, 81 Dean St., London, England. 1934–

The Motion Picture Film Editor. Edited by Rene L. Ash. Metuchen, NJ: Scarecrow Press, 1974.

Motion Pictures, 1894–1912, 1912–1939, 1940–1949, 1950–1959, 1960–1969, and *1970–1979.* 6 vols. with supplements. Washington, DC: Library of Congress, 1951, 1953 (2 vols.), 1960, 1971, 1981.

Movies Made for Television. Edited by Alvin H. Marill. New York: Da Capo, 1981.

Movies on TV. Edited by Steven H. Scheuer. New York: Bantam Books, 1983.

New York Times Film Reviews, 1913–1982. 13 vols. New York: Times Bks. (new volume every two years).

Reference Guide to Fantastic Films. 3 vols. Edited by Walt Lee. Los Angeles, CA: Chelsea-Lee Books, 1974.

Screen World. Crown Publishers, 419 Park Ave. S., New York, NY 10016. 1949–

TV Feature Film Source Book. Edited by Avra Fliegelman. New York: Broadcast Information Bureau, 1959–

TV Movies. Edited by Leonard Maltin. New York: New Am. Library, 1983.

A Title Guide to the Talkies, 1927–1963. Edited by Richard B. Dimmit. Metuchen, NJ: Scarecrow Press, 1965.

A Title Guide to the Talkies, 1964–1974. Edited by Andrew A. Aros, Metuchen, NJ: Scarecrow Press, 1977.

Twenty Years of Silents, 1908–1929. Edited by John T. Weaver. Metuchen, NJ: Scarecrow Press, 1971.

Variety. 154 West 46 St., New York, NY 10036. 1905–

The Videotape and Disc Guide to Home Entertainment. National Video Clearinghouse. New York: New American Library, 1982.

Who Was Who on Screen. 3rd ed. Edited by Evelyn Mack Truitt, New York: R. R. Bowker, 1983.

Who Wrote the Movie and What Else Did He Write? 1936–1969. Edited by Leonard Spigelgass. Los Angeles, CA: Academy of Motion Picture Arts and Sciences and The Writers Guild of America, 1970

Classified by Subject

ACTOR'S FILM CREDITS (Deceased)
Who Was Who on Screen

ACTOR'S SILENT FILM CREDITS
Twenty Years of Silents, 1908–1929

ACTOR'S SOUND FILM CREDITS
Forty Years of Screen Credits
L'Encyclopédie du Cinéma

AUTHOR'S CREDITS
Who Wrote the Movie and What Else Did He Write? 1936–1969

AWARDS (Academy)
Academy Awards Oscar Annual
International Film Guide
Media Review Digest

AWARDS (N.Y. Film Critics, etc.)
International Motion Picture Almanac

BRITISH FILMS
British Film Catalogue

COMPOSERS OF FILM SCORES
Film Music: From Violin to Video

Keeping Score

COPYRIGHT INFORMATION
Motion Pictures, 1894–1912, 1912–1939, 1940–1949, 1950–1959, *and* 1960–1969

CREDITS (Complete)
American Film Institute Catalog of Motion Pictures
British Film Catalogue
Film Buff's Bible
Monthly Film Bulletin

Reference Guide to Fantastic Films
Screen World
Variety

DIRECTOR'S CREDITS
Film Directors: A Guide to Their American Films

EDITOR'S CREDITS
The Motion Picture Film Editor

FILM DESCRIPTIONS
Educational Film Locator
Film Evaluation Guide
Library of Congress Catalog of Films and Other Projected Materials
Movies on TV
TV Movies

LITERARY SOURCES
Haven't I Seen You Somewhere Before?

A Title Guide to the Talkies

PLOT OUTLINES
American Film Institute Catalog of Motion Pictures
New York Times Film Review, 1913–1980

PRICES (Rental, Sale, and Lease)
Consult individual distributor's catalog for latest prices

REMAKES
Haven't I Seen You Somewhere Before?

REVIEWS
Classic Images
Film Evaluation Guide
International Index to Film Periodicals
Media Review Digest
Monthly Film Bulletin

New York Times Film Reviews, 1913–1980

SEQUELS
Haven't I Seen You Somewhere Before?

SERIES FILMS
Haven't I Seen You Somewhere Before?

TELEVISION AVAILABILITY
TV Feature Film Source Book
Movies on TV
TV Movies

TELEVISION FILMS
Movies Made for Television

VIDEOTAPE
Classic Images
The Videotape and Disc Guide to Home Entertainment

NAME AND ADDRESS
DIRECTORY

A Cantor, *(Cantor, Arthur, Inc.),* 33 W. 60th St., New York, NY 10023 Tel 212-664-1290 (SAN 653-1903).

A Mokin, *(Mokin, Arthur, Prod.),* 17 W. 60th St., New York, NY 10023 Tel 212-757-4868 (SAN 653-4880).

A Twyman Pres, *(Twyman, Alan, Presents, The Rohauer Collection, Inc.),* 592 S. Grant Ave., Columbus, OH 43206 Tel 614-469-0720 (SAN 695-6386).

ABC Film Lib, *(ABC Film Library),* 560 Main St., Ft. Lee, NJ 07063 (SAN 653-1814).

ABC Learn, *(ABC Wide World of Learning),* 1330 Ave. of the Americas, New York, NY 10019 Tel 212-581-7777 (SAN 653-1806).

Action Film Lib, *(Action 27 Film Library),* P.O. Box 315, Franklin Lakes, NJ 07417 Tel 201-891-8240 (SAN 653-1822).

ADL, *(Anti-Defamation League of B'nai B'rith; 0-88464),* 823 United Nations Plaza, New York, NY 10017 Tel 212-490-2525 (SAN 204-7616).

Alba-House, *(Alba House (Don Bosco)),* 7050 Pinehurst, Box 40, Dearborn, MI 48126 Tel 313-582-2033 (SAN 653-1865).

Alden Films, *(Alden Films),* 7820 20th Ave., Brooklyn, NY 11214 (SAN 653-1873).

Am Ed Films, *(American Educational Films, Inc.),* 162 Fourth Ave. N., Suite 123, Nashville, TN 37219 Tel 615-242-3330 (SAN 653-1830).

Am Film Inst, *(American Film Institute, The; 0-931282),* Kennedy Ctr., Washington, DC 20566 (SAN 223-6044).

Am Mut Bio, *(American Mutoscope & Biograph Co. of Milwaukee),* 3802 E. Cudahy Ave., Cudahy, WI 53110 (SAN 653-1881).

Americas Films, *(America's Films),* 1735 N. W. Seventh St., Miami, FL 33125 Tel 305-643-0250 (SAN 653-1857).

Amerpol Ent, *(Amerpol Enterprises),* 11601 Joseph Campeau, Hamtramck, MI 48212 Tel 313-365-6780 (SAN 653-189X).

Appals, *(Appalshop),* P.O. Box 743, Whitesburg, KY 41858 (SAN 217-6270).

Arcus Film, *(Arcus Films, Inc.),* 1225 Broadway, New York, NY 10001 Tel 212-686-2216 (SAN 653-1911).

Asia Soc, *(Asia Society, Inc.; 0-87848),* 725 Park Ave., New York, NY 10021 Tel 212-288-6400 (SAN 281-2916); Dist. by: Charles E. Tuttle, Co., P.O. Box 419, Rutland, VT 05701 Tel 802-773-8930 (SAN 213-2621).

Asia Soc Inc
See Asia Soc

Asian Film Lib, *(Asian Film Library),* 609 Columbus Ave., New York, NY 10024 Tel 212-877-3732 (SAN 653-1849).

Aust Info Serv, *(Australian Information Service),* 636 Fifth Ave., New York, NY 10111 Tel 212-245-4000 (SAN 653-1997).

Auteur Films, *(Auteur Films),* 1042 Wisconsin Ave., NW, Washington, DC 20007 Tel 202-333-6966 (SAN 653-1989).

B Raymond, *(Raymond, Bruce. A., Prod.),* 353 St. Clair Ave. E., Toronto, Ont. M4Y 1P3, .

BC *Imprint of* **Grove**

Benchmark Films, *(Benchmark Films),* 145 Scarborough Rd., Briarcliff Manor, NY 10510 Tel 914-762-3838 (SAN 653-2012).

Best Films, *(Best Films),* Box 725, Del Mar, CA 92014 Tel 714-755-9327 (SAN 653-2055).

BF Video, *(Best Film & Video Corp.),* 98 Cutter Mill Rd., Great Neck, NY 11021 Tel 516-487-4515 (SAN 686-6255).

Blackhawk Films, *(Blackhawk Films),* Davenport, IA 52808 Tel 319-323-9736 (SAN 653-2098).

Blackwood Films, *(Blackwood Films),* 251 W. 57th St., New York, NY 10019 Tel 212-688-0930 (SAN 653-2071).

Bosco Films, *(Don Bosco Films),* 48 Main St., Box T, New Rochelle, NY 10802 Tel 914-632-6562 (SAN 653-2527).

Brazos Films, *(Brazos Films; 0-933797),* 10341 San Pablo Ave., El Cerrito, CA 94530 Tel 415-525-7471 (SAN 653-2101); Dist. by: Flower Films, 10341 San Pablo Ave., El Cerrito, CA 94530 Tel 415-525-0942 (SAN 653-2748).

Buchan Pic, *(Buchan Pictures),* 254 Delaware Ave., Buffalo, NY 14202 Tel 716-853-1805 (SAN 653-211X).

Budget Films, *(Budget Films),* 4590 Santa Monica Blvd., Los Angeles, CA 90029 Tel 213-660-0187 (SAN 653-2128).

Bullfrog Films, *(Bullfrog Films),* Oley, PA 19547 Tel 215-779-8226 (SAN 653-2136).

BYU Media, *(Young, Brigham, Univ.),* 290 Herald R. Clark Bldg., Provo, UT 84601 Tel 801-374-1211 (SAN 653-2144).

C Starr, *(Starr, Cecile),* 50 W. 96th St., New York, NY 10025 Tel 212-749-1250 (SAN 653-2357).

CA Newsreel, *(California Newsreel/Media at Work/Resolution),* 630 Natoma, San Francisco, CA 94103 Tel 415-621-6196 (SAN 653-5097).

Cambridge Doc, *(Cambridge Documentary Films),* Box 385, Cambridge, MA 02139 Tel 617-354-3677 (SAN 653-2225).

Canyon Cinema, *(Canyon Cinema Cooperative),* 2325 Third St., San Francisco, CA 94107 Tel 415-626-2255 (SAN 653-337X).

Carman Ed Assoc, *(Carman Educational Assoc.),* Box 205, Youngstown, NY 14174 (SAN 653-2330).

Carousel Films, *(Carousel Films),* 241 E. 49th St., New York, NY 10036 Tel 212-683-1660 (SAN 653-2241).

Castle Hill, *(Castle Hill Production),* 1700 Broadway, New York, NY 10019 Tel 212-399-0362 (SAN 671-8191).

CBC, *(Canadian Broadcasting Corp.; 0-88794),* Box 500 Terminl A, Toronto Ont. M5W 1E6, .

CBS Inc, *(CBS, Inc.),* 51 W. 52 St., New York, NY 10019 Tel 212-765-4321 (SAN 653-2284).

Centre CO, *(Centre Prod.),* 1327 Spruce St., Suite 3, Boulder, CO 80302 Tel 303-444-1166 (SAN 653-2365).

Centron Films, *(Centron Educational Films/Esquire Communications Group),* 1621 W. Ninth St., Lawrence, KS 66044 Tel 913-843-0400 (SAN 653-2349).

Charard Motion Pics, *(Charard Motion Pictures),* 2110 E. 24 St., Brooklyn, NY 11229 Tel 718-891-4339 (SAN 653-2381).

Childrens Work, *(Children's Television Workshop),* One Lincoln Plaza, New York, NY 10023 Tel 212-595-3456 (SAN 268-9081).

China Peoples, *(U. S.-China Peoples Friendship Assn. of New York),* 41 Union Square W., No. 1228, New York, NY 10003 Tel 212-736-7355 (SAN 218-1347).

Churchill Films, *(Churchill Films),* 622 N. Robertson Blvd., Los Angeles, CA 90069 (SAN 653-2411).

Cine Craft, *(Cine-Craft Co.),* 1720 W. Marshall, P.O. Box 4126, Portland, OR 79209 Tel 503-228-7484 (SAN 653-2314).

Cine Info, *(Cine Information),* 419 Park Ave. S. 19th flr., New York, NY 10016 Tel 212-686-9897 (SAN 653-2454).

Cinema Arts, *(Cinema Arts Associates/Cinema Perspectives),* 200 Park Ave. S., Suite 1319, New York, NY 10003 Tel 212-254-8778 (SAN 653-2179).

Cinema Concepts, *(Cinema Concepts/Cinema 8),* 2461 Berlin Turnpike, Newington, CT 06111 Tel 203-667-1251 (SAN 653-242X).

Cinema Five, *(Cinema 5),* 1585 Broadway, New York, NY 10036 Tel 212-975-0550 (SAN 653-2446).

Cinema Guild, *(Document Assocs./Cinema Guild),* 1697 Broadway, Suite 802, New York, NY 10019 Tel 212-246-5522 (SAN 653-2551).

Classic Film Mus, *(Classic Film Museum),* 6 Union Sq., Dover-Foxcroft, ME 04426 Tel 207-564-8371 (SAN 653-2373).

Classics Assoc NY, *(Classics Assocs., Inc.),* 236 W. 27th St., 14th flr., New York, NY 10001 Tel 212-989-9546 (SAN 695-6378).

Colonial, *(Colonial Williamsburg Foundation),* P.O. Box Drawer C, Williamsburg, VA 23185 Tel 804-229-1000 (SAN 278-4971); Dist. by: University Press of Virginia, P.O. Box 3608, Univ. Sta., Charlottesville, VA 22903 Tel 804-924-3468 (SAN 202-5361).

Concern Dying, *(Concern for Dying),* 250 W. 57th St., Suite 831, New York, NY 10107 Tel 212-246-6962 (SAN 225-9346).

Corinth Films, *(Corinth Films),* 410 E. 62 St., New York, NY 10021 Tel 212-421-4770 (SAN 653-2500).

Cousino Visual Ed, *(Cousino Visual Ed. Serv.),* 1945 Franklin Ave., Toledo, OH 43624 Tel 419-246-3691 (SAN 653-2462).

Creative Film, *(Creative Film Society),* 8435 Geyser Ave., Northridge, CA 91324 Tel 818-885-7288 (SAN 217-698X).

Crystal, *(Crystal Prod.),* Box 12317, Aspen, CO 81612 (SAN 653-2489).

Ctr South Folklore, *(Center for Southern Folklore; 0-89267),* 1216 Peabody Ave., P.O. Box 40105, Memphis, TN 38104 Tel 901-726-4205 (SAN 209-2247).

D Wilson, *(Wilson, Daniel, Production),* 300 W. 55 St., New York, NY 10019 Tel 212-765-7148 (SAN 653-2586).

Dance Film Archive, *(Dance Film Archive),* Rochester, NY 14627 (SAN 653-2535).

Direct Cinema, *(Direct Cinema, Ltd.),* Box 69589, Los Angeles, CA 90069 Tel 213-656-4700 (SAN 653-256X).

Disney Prod, *(Disney, Walt, Prod.),* 6904 Tujunga Ave., Hollywood, CA 91605 Tel 800-423-2200 (SAN 653-2543).

Distribution Sixteen, *(Distribution 16),* 32 W. 40th St., 2L, New York, NY 10018 Tel 212-730-0280 (SAN 653-5364).

E Finney, *(Finney, Edward),* 1578 Queens Blvd., Hollywood, CA 90069 Tel 213-656-0200 (SAN 653-273X).

Educ Dev Ctr, *(Education Development Ctr., Inc.; 0-89292),* Orders to: EDC Publishing Ctr., 55 Chapel St., Newton, MA 02160 Tel 617-969-7100 (SAN 207-821X).

Educ Media CA, *(Educational Media Corp./UEVA),* 6930 Tujunga Ave., N. Hollywood, CA 91605 Tel 213-985-3921 (SAN 653-2616).

Edupac, *(Edupac),* 231 Norfolk St., Walpole, MA 02081 Tel 617-668-7746 (SAN 653-2594).

Electro Art, *(Electronic Arts Intermix, Inc.),* 84 Fifth Ave. Room 403, New York, NY 10011 (SAN 278-7113).

Elliot Film Co, *(Elliot Film Co.),* 2635 Nicollet Ave., Minneapolis, MN 55408 Tel 612-870-3750 (SAN 653-2608).

Em Gee Film Lib, *(Em Gee Film Library),* 6924 Canby Ave., Suite 103, Reseda, CA 91335 Tel 818-981-5506 (SAN 653-2640).

Emb Ireland, *(Embassy of Ireland),* 2234 Massachusetts Ave., SW, Washington, DC 20008 Tel 202-483-7639 (SAN 653-3841).

Embassy Calif, *(Embassy Pictures),* 1901 Ave. of the Stars, Los Angeles, CA 90067 (SAN 656-3872).

Ency Brit Ed, *(Encyclopaedia Britannica Educational Corp.; 0-87827),* Affil. of Encyclopaedia Britannica, Inc., 425 N. Michigan Ave., Chicago, IL 60611 Tel 312-321-6800 (SAN 201-3851).

Enter Video, *(Entertainment Video Releasing),* 1 E. 57th St., New York, NY 10022 Tel 212-752-2240 (SAN 653-2683).

Ever *Imprint of Grove*

EverBC *Imprint of Grove*

Festival Films, *(Festival Films),* 2841 Irving Ave., South Minneapolis, MN 55408 Tel 612-870-4744 (SAN 653-2691).

Film Classics, *(Film Classic Exchange; 0-9610916),* P.O. Box 77568 Dockweiler Stn., Los Angeles, CA 90007 Tel 213-731-3854 (SAN 265-1351).

Film Ctr DC, *(Film Center),* 938 K St., NW, Washington, DC 20001 Tel 202-393-1205 (SAN 653-5461).

Film Images, *(Film Images/Radim Films),* 1034 Lake St., Oak Park, IL 60301 Tel 312-386-4826 (SAN 653-5259).

Film Makers, *(Film-Makers Library),* 133 E. 58th St., New York, NY 10022 (SAN 653-3388).

Film Pres, *(Film Presentation Co.),* 514 Rt. 27, Box 232, Iselin, NJ 08830 Tel 201-283-1700 (SAN 653-3418).

Film Wright, *(Film Wright),* 4530 18th St., San Francisco, CA 94114 Tel 415-863-6100 (SAN 653-3515).

Filmmakers Coop, *(Filmmakers Cooperative),* 175 Lexington Ave., New York, NY 10016 Tel 212-889-3820 (SAN 670-6142).

Films Human, *(Films Humanities; 0-89113),* Box 2053, Princeton, NJ 08540 Tel 201-329-6912 (SAN 653-2705); P.O. Box 378, Princeton, NJ 08540 (SAN 680-1145).

Films Inc, *(Films, Inc.),* 733 Wilmette Ave. (Suite 202), Wilmette, IL 60091 Tel 312-256-6600 (SAN 653-3396) Tel 800-323-1406.

First Run, *(First Run Features),* 144 Bleecker St., New York, NY 10012 Tel 212-673-6881 (SAN 653-3469).

Flower Films, *(Flower Films/Les Blank),* 10341 San Pablo Ave., El Cerrito, CA 94530 Tel 415-525-0942 (SAN 653-2748).

Fremontia, *(Fremontia Films),* Box 315, Franklin Lakes, NJ 07417 (SAN 653-3442).

French Am Cul, *(Society for French American Cultural Services & Educational Aid),* 972 Fifth Ave., New York, NY Tel 212-570-4400 (SAN 275-4509).

G Herne, *(Herne, Gary L., Sales),* 910 Hilton Rd., Ferndale, MI 48220 Tel 313-398-4144 (SAN 653-3620).

Glenn Photo, *(Glenn Photo Supply),* 6924 Canby Ave., Suite 103, Reseda, CA 91335 (SAN 653-3590).

Gold Key, *(Gold Key Entertainment),* 855 N. Cahuenga Blvd., Los Angeles, CA 90067 (SAN 653-3523).

Golden Tapes, *(Golden Tapes Videotape Library),* 336 Foothill Rd., Beverley Hills, CA 90213 Tel 213-550-8156 (SAN 653-3574).

Gospel Films, *(Gospel Films),* Box 455, Muskegon, MI 49443 Tel 616-773-3361 (SAN 653-3582).

Graphic Curr, *(Graphic Curriculum),* 699 Madison Ave., New York, NY 10021 Tel 212-688-0033 (SAN 653-3604).

Great Plains, *(Great Plains National Instructional Television Library; 0-9614949),* Box 80669, Lincoln, NE 68501 Tel 800-228-4630 (SAN 213-0696).

Green Mt, *(Green Mountain Post Films),* Box 229, Turners Falls, MA 01376 Tel 413-863-4754 (SAN 653-3566).

Griggs Movie, *(Griggs-Moviedrome),* 263 Harrison St., Nutley, NJ 07110 (SAN 653-3558).

Grove, *(Grove Pr., Film Div.; 0-8021; 0-394),* 196 W. Houston St., New York, NY 10014 Tel 212-242-4900 (SAN 201-4890). *Imprints:* BC (Black Cat Books); Ever (Evergreen Books); EverBC (Evergreen-Black Cat Books); Zebra (Zebra Books).

Human Issues
See ISHI PA

Hurlock Cine, *(Hurlock Cine-World),* 13 Arcadia Rd.(P.O. Box W), Old Greenwich, CT 06870 Tel 203-637-4319 (SAN 653-2438).

Icarus Films, *(Icarus Films/Cinema Perspectives),* 200 Park Ave. S., Suite 1319, New York, NY 10003 Tel 212-674-3375 (SAN 653-3736).

IFEX, *(International Film Exchange),* 201 W. 52nd St., New York, NY 10019 Tel 212-582-4318 (SAN 672-7859).

Images Film, *(Images Film Archive),* 300 Phillips Pk. Rd., Mamaroneck, NY 10543 Tel 914-381-2993 (SAN 653-3760).

Indiana AV Ctr, *(Indiana Univ., Audio-Visual Ctr.),* Bloomington, IN 47405 Tel 812-332-0211 (SAN 653-3779).

Inst Cinema, *(Institutional Cinema, Inc.),* 10 First St., Saugerties, NY 12477 Tel 914-246-2848 (SAN 653-3744).

Intl Film, *(International Film Bureau, Inc.; 0-8354),* 332 S. Michigan Ave., Chicago, IL 60604 Tel 312-427-4545 (SAN 207-4931).

Iowa Films, *(University of Iowa),* C-5 Seashore Hall, Iowa City, IA 52242 Tel 319-353-5885 (SAN 671-8140).

IQ Film, *(I.Q. Films),* Box 326, Wappingers Falls, NY 12590 Tel 914-297-0070 (SAN 653-3787).

ISHI PA, *(Institute for the Study of Human Issues; 0-89727; 0-915980),* 210 S. 13th St., Philadelphia, PA 19107 Tel 215-732-9729 (SAN 207-6608); P.O. Box 2367, Philadelphia, PA 19103 (SAN 669-1102).

Ivy Films, *(Ivy Films),* 165 W. 46th St., New York, NY 10036 Tel 212-382-0111 (SAN 653-3876).

J Green Pics, *(Green, Joseph, Pictures Co.),* 200 W. 58th St., New York, NY 10019 Tel 212-246-9343 (SAN 653-3612).

Janus Films, *(Janus Films),* 1213 Wilmette Ave., Wilmette, IL 60091 Tel 312-256-3200 (SAN 653-3892).

JER Pictures, *(JER Pictures),* 165 W. 46th St., New York, NY 10036 Tel 212-247-4220 (SAN 653-3914).

Kent St U Film, *(Kent State Univ., Film Rental Ctr.),* Kent, OH 44242 Tel 216-672-3456 (SAN 653-3949).

Kerr Film, *(Kerr Film Exchange),* 3034 Canon St., San Diego, CA 92106 Tel 619-224-2406 (SAN 653-3981).

Killiam Collect, *(Killiam Collection, Rental Div.),* 6 E. 39th St., New York, NY 10016 Tel 212-684-3920 (SAN 653-4007).

King Features, *(King Features Prod.),* 235 E. 45th St., New York, NY 10017 Tel 212-682-5600 (SAN 653-4015).

Kino Intl, *(Kino International Corp.),* 250 W. 57th St., New York, NY 10019 Tel 212-586-8720 (SAN 672-7816).

Kit Parker, *(Parker, Kit, Films),* 1245 Tenth St., Monterrey, CA 93940 Tel 408-649-5573 (SAN 653-404X) Tel 800-538-5838.

La Inst Res Ctr, *(Louisiana State Univ., Instructional Resources Ctr.),* Himes Hall, Rm. 118, Baton Rouge, LA 70803 Tel 504-388-1135 (SAN 653-421X).

Lat Amer Film, *(Latin-American Film Project),* 419 Park Ave. S., 19th Fl., New York, NY 10016 Tel 212-686-9897 (SAN 653-4082).

Learning Corp Am, *(Learning Corp. of America),* 1350 Ave. of the Americas, New York, NY 10019 Tel 212-397-9330 (SAN 653-4147).

Lewis Film, *(Lewis Film Services),* 1425 E. Central, Witchita, KS 67214 Tel 316-263-6991 (SAN 653-4171).

Liberty Co, *(Liberty Co., The),* 695 W. Seventh St., Plainfield, NJ 07060 Tel 201-757-1450 (SAN 653-550X).

Lucerne Films, *(Lucerne Films),* 37 Ground Pine Rd., Morris Plains, NJ 07950 (SAN 653-4759).

Lutheran Film, *(Lutheran Film Associates),* One Main Place, Dallas, TX 75250 Tel 214-747-8048 (SAN 653-4198).

M Cunningham, *(Cunningham, Merce, Dance Foundation),* 463 West St., New York, NY 10014 Tel 212-691-9751 (SAN 653-2322).

McGraw-Hill Films, *(CRM/McGraw-Hill Films),* 110 15th St., Del Mar, CA 92014 Tel 714-453-5000 (SAN 653-4821).

Macmillan Films, *(Macmillan Films),* 34 MacQuestern Pkwy. S., Mt. Vernon, NY 10550 Tel 914-664-5051 (SAN 653-4767).

Magnetic Video, *(Magnetic Video Corp.),* 23705 Industrial Pk. Dr., Farmington Hills, MI 48018 Tel 313-477-6066 (SAN 653-4775).

Malaysia Emb, *(Embassy of Malaysia),* 2401 Massachusetts Ave., NW, Washington, DC 20008 Tel 202-234-7600 (SAN 653-4783).

Maljack, *(Maljack Productions VCI),* P.O. Box 153, Tinley Park, IL 60477 Tel 312-687-7881 (SAN 653-4848).

Mass Media, *(Mass Media Assocs.),* 2116 N. Charles St., Baltimore, MD 21218 Tel 301-727-3270 (SAN 653-4856).

Master Monica, *(Master & Masterworks),* 1431 Ocean Ave., Suite 1400, Santa Monica, CA 90401 Tel 213-393-8337 (SAN 653-4791).

Maysles Films, *(Maysles Films),* 250 W. 54th St., New York, NY 10019 Tel 212-582-6050 (SAN 653-4805).

Media Guild, *(Media Guild),* 11526 Sorrento Valley Road, San Diego, CA 92121 Tel 619-755-9191 (SAN 678-3201).

Merco Intl, *(Merco International Films),* Box B, Somis, CA 93066 Tel 805-484-2213 (SAN 653-4813).

MGM United, *(MGM/United Artists Entertainment),* 1350 Ave. of the Americas, New York, NY 10019 Tel 800-223-0933 (SAN 670-610X).

Modern Mass, *(Modern Mass Media),* Box 950, Chatham, NJ 07928 Tel 210-635-6000 (SAN 653-4910).

Modern Sound, *(Modern Sound Pictures),* 1402 Howard St., Omaha, NE 68102 Tel 800-228-9584 (SAN 653-4864).

Modern Talking, *(Modern Talking Picture Service),* 5000 Park St. N, St. Petersburg, FL 33709 Tel 813-541-7571 (SAN 656-2043).

Mogulls Films, *(Mogull's Films),* 1280 North Ave., Plainfield, NJ 07062 Tel 201-753-6004 (SAN 653-4872).

Morcraft Films, *(Morcraft Films/Penguin Video),* Formerly: Thunderbird Films, P.O. Box 65157, Los Angles, CA 90065 (SAN 682-0395).

MTI Tele, *(MTI Teleprograms Inc./A Simon & Schuster Communications Company; 0-916070),* 108 Wilmot Rd., Deerfield, IL 60015 Tel 312-940-1260 (SAN 211-0350).

Natl AV Ctr, *(National Audio-Visual Ctr., General Services Administration),* Washington, DC 20409 Tel 310-763-1896 (SAN 653-4937).

Natl Cinema, *(National Cinema Service),* Box 43, Ho-Ho-Kus, NJ 07423 Tel 201-445-0776 (SAN 653-5038).

Natl Film CN, *(National Film Board of Canada),* 1251 Ave. of the Americas, New York, NY 10020 Tel 212-586-5131 (SAN 653-5062).

Natl Film Video, *(National Film & Video Center),* 1425 Liberty Rd., Eldersburg, MD 21784 Tel 800-638-1688 (SAN 653-5070).

Natl Geog, *(National Geographic Society; 0-87044),* 17th & "M" Sts., NW, Washington, DC 20036 Tel 202-857-7000 (SAN 202-8956).

New Cinema, *(New Cinema, Ltd.),* 35 Britain St., Toronto, Ont. M5A 1R7, .

New Day Films, *(New Day Films),* 1697 Broadway, New York, NY 10019 Tel 212-247-0511 (SAN 217-9660).

New Front, *(New Front Films),* 1409 Willow St., Minneapolis, MN 55403 Tel 612-872-0805 (SAN 672-1745).

New Line Cinema, *(New Line Cinema),* 575 Eighth Ave., New York, NY 10018 Tel 212-674-7460 (SAN 653-5089).

New Time Films, *(New Time Films),* 74 Varick Street, New York, NY 10013 Tel 212-226-8097 (SAN 672-0366).

New Yorker Films, *(New Yorker Films),* 16 W. 61st St., New York, NY 10023 Tel 212-247-6110 (SAN 653-5127).

Newman Film Lib, *(Aument Film Library),* Formerly, Newman Film Library, 1444 Michigan Ave. NE, Grand Rapids, MI 49508 Tel 616-454-8157 (SAN 653-5054).

Northwest Film Lib, *(Northwestern Univ., Film Library),* Box 1665, Evanston, IL 60204 Tel 312-869-0600 (SAN 653-5119).

Nostalgia Merchant, *(Nostalgia Merchant, The),* 6255 Sunset Blvd., Suite 1019, Hollywood, CA 90028 Tel 800-421-4495 (SAN 653-5518).

NYU Film Lib, *(New York Univ., Film Library),* 26 Washington Pl., New York, NY 10003 Tel 212-777-2000 (SAN 653-5135).

Odeon Films, *(Odeon Films),* Box 315, Franklin Lakes, NJ 07417 (SAN 653-5143).

OK AV Ctr, *(Oklahoma State Univ., Audio-Visual Ctr.),* Stillwater, OK 74078 Tel 405-372-6211 (SAN 653-516X).

Open Circle, *(Open Circle Cinema),* Box 315, Franklin Lakes, NJ 07417 Tel 201-891-8240 (SAN 653-5186).

PBS Video, *(PBS Video),* 475 L'Enfant Plaza SW, Washington, DC 20024 Tel 202-488-5220 (SAN 653-5194).

Penn St AV Serv, *(Pennsylvania State Univ., Audio-Visual Services),* Special Services Bldg., University Park, PA 16802 Tel 814-865-6314 (SAN 653-5216).

Pennebaker, *(Pennebaker Assocs.),* 21 W. 86th St., New York, NY 10024 Tel 212-469-9195 (SAN 653-4155).

Perspect Film, *(Perspective Films/Esquire Communications Group; 0-89611),* 369 W Erie St., Chicago, IL 60610 (SAN 221-007X).

Phoenix Films, *(Phoenix/BFA Films & Video),* 470 Park Ave. South, New York, NY 10016 Tel 212-684-5910 (SAN 653-5224).

Polish People, *(Embassy of the Polish People's Republic),* 2640 16th St. NW, Washington, DC 20009 Tel 202-234-3800 (SAN 653-5232).

Pyramid Film, *(Pyramid Films),* Box 1048, Santa Monica, CA 90406 (SAN 218-2807).

Red Ball, *(Red Ball Films, Inc.),* 41 Union Sq., New York, NY 10003 Tel 212-924-4368 (SAN 218-303X).

Red Fox Ent, *(Red Fox Enterprises),* Rt. 209 E., Elizabethville, PA 17023 (SAN 653-5267).

Reel Images, *(Reel Images),* P.O. Box C, Sandy Hook, CT 06482 Tel 203-426-2574 (SAN 653-5275).

Rep Pic Film, *(Republic Pictures Film),* Div. of Republic Pictures Corp., 12636 Beatrice St., Los Angeles, CA 90066-0930 Tel 213-306-4040 (SAN 695-4413).

RKO General Pics, *(RKO Radio Pictures),* 1440 Broadway, New York, NY 10018 Tel 212-764-7108 (SAN 653-5283).

Roas Films, *(Roa's Films),* 1696 N. Astor St., Milwaukee, WI 53202 Tel 414-271-0861 (SAN 653-5291).

S Goldwyn, *(Goldwyn, Samuel),* 200 W. 57th St., New York, NY 10019 Tel 212-315-3030 (SAN 695-6793).

Salz Ent, *(Salzburg Enterprises),* Atrium Bldg., 98 Cutter Mill Rd., Great Neck, NY 11001 Tel 516-487-4515 (SAN 653-5348).

Schoenfeld, *(Schoenfeld Film Dist.),* 241 E. 34th Street, New York, NY 10016 Tel 212-532-5210 (SAN 671-8299).

SD AV Ctr, *(South Dakota State Univ., Audio Visual Ctr.),* University Station, Brookings, SD 57006 Tel 605-688-5115 (SAN 653-5313).

See-Art Films, *(See-Art Films),* Box 638, Ardsley-on-Hudson, NY 10503 Tel 914-591-9207 (SAN 653-533X).

Southern Chroniclers, *(Southern Chroniclers),* Box 9925, Savannah, GA 31412 Tel 912-236-7757 (SAN 653-5372).

Special Purpose Films, *(Special Purpose Films),* 26740 Latigo Shore Dr., Malibu, CA 90265 (SAN 653-5380).

Specialty Films, *(Specialty Films),* 911 NE 50th, Seattle, WA 98105 Tel 206-634-3834 (SAN 653-5399).

Standard Film, *(Standard Film Service),* P.O. Box 52, Frankenmuth, MI 48734 Tel 517-652-8881 (SAN 653-5402).

Step Ahead Films, *(Step Ahead Films),* 1800 Ave. of the Stars, Suite 900, Los Angeles, CA 90067 (SAN 653-5305).

Sterling Ed Film, *(Sterling Educational Films),* 241 E. 34th St., New York, NY 10016 Tel 212-683-6300 (SAN 653-5410).

Stouffer Ent, *(Stouffer Enterprises),* P.O. Box 4740, Aspen, CO 81611 Tel 303-925-9227 (SAN 653-5429).

Swank Motion, *(Swank Motion Pictures),* 201 S. Jefferson Ave., St. Louis, MO 63166 Tel 314-534-6300 (SAN 653-5437) Tel 800-325-3344.

Syracuse U Film, *(Syracuse Univ., Film Rental Ctr.),* 1455 E. Colvin St., Syracuse, NY 13210 Tel 315-423-2452 (SAN 653-5445).

T Holcomb, *(Holcomb, Theodore),* 11 E. 90th St., New York, NY 10028 Tel 212-861-6293 (SAN 653-3728).

Tamarelles French Film, *(Tamarelle's French Film House),* 110 Cohasset Stage Rd., Chico, CA 95925 Tel 916-895-3429 (SAN 653-5453).

Texture Film, *(Texture Film Collection),* P.O. Box 1337, Skokie, IL 60076 Tel 312-256-4436 (SAN 218-1037).

Threshold Films, *(Threshold Films),* 2025 N. Highland Ave., Hollywood, CA 90068 Tel 213-874-8413 (SAN 653-547X).

Trans-World Films, *(Trans-World Films),* 332 S. Michigan Ave., Chicago, IL 60604 Tel 312-922-1530 (SAN 653-5542).

Tricontinental, *(Tricontinental Film Center/Unifilm),* 419 Park Ave. S., New York, NY 10016 Tel 212-686-9877 (SAN 695-6807).

TVG Doc Art, *(TVG Documentary Arts Project),* Box 315, Franklin Lakes, NJ 07417 Tel 201-891-8240 (SAN 653-5526).

Twyman Films, *(Twyman Films),* 4700 Wadsworth Rd. P.O. Box 605, Dayton, OH 45414 Tel 513-276-5941 (SAN 653-5550).

U Cal Media, *(University of California, Extension Media Center),* 2223 Fulton St., Berkeley, CA 94720 Tel 415-845-6000 (SAN 653-2195).

U Col Media Ctr, *(University of Colorado, Educational Center, Bureau of Audio-Visual Instruction),* P.O. Box 379, Boulder, CO 80309 Tel 303-443-2211 (SAN 653-5607).

U Comm Video, *(University Community Video),* Studio A, Rarig Ctr., University of Minnesota, 330 21st Ave. S., Minneapolis, MN 55455 (SAN 218-141X).

U Mich Media, *(University of Michigan, Media Resources Center),* 416 Fourth St., Ann Arbor, MI 48109 Tel 313-764-5360 (SAN 653-483X).

U Nev AV Ctr, *(Univ. of Nevada, Audio-Visual Ctr.),* Education Bldg., Reno, NV 89507 (SAN 653-5615).

U of IL Film, *(University of Illinois, Film Center),* 1325 S. Oak St., Champaign, IL 61820 Tel 217-333-1360 (SAN 653-3752).

U of SD Film Lib, *(Univ. of South Dakota, Film Library),* Educational Media Ctr., Vermillion, SD 57069 Tel 605-677-5411 (SAN 653-5321).

United Doc Film, *(United Documentary Films),* Box 315, Franklin Lakes, NJ 07417 Tel 201-891-8240 (SAN 653-5593).

United Meth Comm, *(United Methodist Communications),* 810 12th Ave. South, Nashville, TN 37203 Tel 615-256-0530 (SAN 653-5585).

Utah Media, *(Univ. of Utah, Educational Media Ctr.),* Milton Bennion Hall 207, Salt Lake City, UT 84110 Tel 801-322-6112 (SAN 653-5623).

Vidamerica, *(Vidamerica),* 235 East 55th St., New York, NY 10022 Tel 212-355-1600 (SAN 670-6444).

Video Comm, *(Video Communications, Inc.),* 6555 E. Skelly Dr., Tulsa, OK 74145 Tel 918-662-6460 (SAN 653-564X) Tel 800-331-4077.

Video-Forum, *(Video-Forum; 0-88432),* Div. of Jeffrey Norton Pubs., 96 Broad St., Guilford, CT 06437 Tel 203-453-9794 (SAN 217-4707).

Viewfinders, *(Viewfinders),* Box 1665, Evanston, IL 60204 Tel 312-869-0600 (SAN 653-5658).

Vision Quest, *(Vision Quest),* Box 206, Lawrenceville, NJ 08648 Tel 609-896-1359 (SAN 653-5674).

W Ewing Films, *(Ewing, Wayne, Films),* Box 32269, Washington, DC 20007 (SAN 653-5712).

W Greaves, *(Greaves, William, Prod.),* 1776 Broadway, Suite 1802, New York, NY 10019 Tel 212-586-7710 (SAN 653-5747).

Wade Williams, *(Williams, Wade, Prod.),* 5500 Ward Parkway, Kansas City, MO 64113 Tel 816-523-2699 (SAN 653-5801).

Welling Motion Pictures, *(Welling Motion Pictures),* 454 Meacham Ave., Elmont, NY 11003 Tel 516-354-1066 (SAN 653-5720).

Westcoast Films, *(Westcoast Films),* 25 Lusk St., San Francisco, CA 94107 Tel 415-362-4700 (SAN 653-5704) Tel 800-227-3058.

Weston Woods Studios, *(Weston Woods Studios),* Weston, CT 06680 Tel 203-226-0600 (SAN 653-5739).

Wholesome Film Ctr, *(Wholesome Film Center),* 20 Melrose St., Boston, MA 02116 Tel 617-426-0155 (SAN 653-5755).

Williams Films, *(Williams, Clem, Films),* 2240 Noblestown Rd., Pittsburgh, PA 15205 Tel 412-921-5810 (SAN 653-2519) Tel 800-245-1146.

Willoughby Peer, *(Willoughby-Peerless),* 115 W. 31st St., New York, NY 10001 Tel 212-929-6477 (SAN 654-9640).

WNET Media, *(WNET/13 Media Service),* 356 W. 58th. St., New York, NY 10019 Tel 212-262-4940 (SAN 653-5771).

Wombat Productions, *(Wombat Productions, Inc.),* Little Lake, Glendale Rd., Box 70, Ossining, NY 10562 Tel 914-762-0011 (SAN 653-578X).

Women Movies, *(Women Make Movies),* 100 Fifth Ave., Rm. 1208, New York, NY 10011 Tel 212-929-6477 (SAN 276-7236).

World Northal, *(World Northal Corp.),* 1 Dag Hammarskjold Plaza, New York, NY 10017 Tel 212-223-8181

(SAN 653-5763).

WW Enter, *(WW Entertainment),* 205 E. 42nd St., New York, NY 10014 Tel 212-661-3350 (SAN 688-9581).

Young People Media, *(Young People's Specials, Multimedia Program Prod.),*

140 W. Ninth St., Cincinnati, OH 45202 (SAN 653-5828).

Zebra *Imprint of* **Grove**

Zipporah Films, *(Zipporah Films),* 1 Richdale Ave., Cambridge, MA 02140 Tel 617-576-3603 (SAN 653-5836).

NAMES AND ADDRESSES
BY AREA

NEW YORK

ABC Wide World of Learning, 1330 Ave. of the Americas, New York, NY 10019 Tel 212-581-7777 (SAN 653-1806).

Alden Films, 7820 20th Ave., Brooklyn, NY 11214 (SAN 653-1873).

Anti-Defamation League of B'nai B'rith, *(0-88464),* 823 United Nations Plaza, New York, NY 10017 Tel 212-490-2525 (SAN 204-7616).

Arcus Films, Inc., 1225 Broadway, New York, NY 10001 Tel 212-686-2216 (SAN 653-1911).

Asia Society, Inc., *(0-87848),* 725 Park Ave., New York, NY 10021 Tel 212-288-6400 (SAN 281-2916); Dist. by: Charles E. Tuttle, Co., P.O. Box 419, Rutland, VT 05701 Tel 802-773-8930 (SAN 213-2621).

Asian Film Library, 609 Columbus Ave., New York, NY 10024 Tel 212-877-3732 (SAN 653-1849).

Australian Information Service, 636 Fifth Ave., New York, NY 10111 Tel 212-245-4000 (SAN 653-1997).

Benchmark Films, 145 Scarborough Rd., Briarcliff Manor, NY 10510 Tel 914-762-3838 (SAN 653-2012).

Best Film & Video Corp., 98 Cutter Mill Rd., Great Neck, NY 11021 Tel 516-487-4515 (SAN 686-6255).

Blackwood Films, 251 W. 57th St., New York, NY 10019 Tel 212-688-0930 (SAN 653-2071).

Buchan Pictures, 254 Delaware Ave., Buffalo, NY 14202 Tel 716-853-1805 (SAN 653-211X).

Canadian Broadcasting Corp., 245 Park Ave., New York, NY 10017 Tel 212-687-8600 (SAN 670-6304).

Cantor, Arthur, Inc., 33 W. 60th St., New York, NY 10023 Tel 212-664-1290 (SAN 653-1903).

Carman Educational Assoc., Box 205, Youngstown, NY 14174 (SAN 653-2330).

Carousel Films, 241 E. 49th St., New York, NY 10036 Tel 212-683-1660 (SAN 653-2241).

Castle Hill Production, 1700 Broadway, New York, NY 10019 Tel 212-399-0362 (SAN 671-8191).

Charard Motion Pictures, 2110 E. 24 St., Brooklyn, NY 11229 Tel 718-891-4339 (SAN 653-2381).

Cine Information, 419 Park Ave. S. 19th flr., New York, NY 10016 Tel 212-686-9897 (SAN 653-2454).

Cinema Arts Associates/Cinema Perspectives, 200 Park Ave. S., Suite 1319, New York, NY 10003 Tel 212-254-8778 (SAN 653-2179).

Cinema 5, 1585 Broadway, New York, NY 10036 Tel 212-975-0550 (SAN 653-2446).

Classics Assocs., Inc., 236 W. 27th St., 14th flr., New York, NY 10001 Tel 212-989-9546 (SAN 695-6378).

Corinth Films, 410 E. 62 St., New York, NY 10021 Tel 212-421-4770 (SAN 653-2500).

Cunningham, Merce, Dance Foundation, 463 West St., New York, NY 10014 Tel 212-691-9751 (SAN 653-2322).

Dance Film Archive, Rochester, NY 14627 (SAN 653-2535).

Direct Cinema, Ltd., Box 69589, Los Angeles, CA 90069 Tel 213-656-4700 (SAN 653-256X).

Distribution 16, 32 W. 40th St., 2L, New York, NY 10018 Tel 212-730-0280 (SAN 653-5364).

Document Assocs./Cinema Guild, 1697 Broadway, Suite 802, New York, NY 10019 Tel 212-246-5522 (SAN 653-2551).

Don Bosco Films, 48 Main St., Box T, New Rochelle, NY 10802 Tel 914-632-6562 (SAN 653-2527).

Electronic Arts Intermix, Inc., 84 Fifth Ave. Room 403, New York, NY 10011US (SAN 278-7113).

Entertainment Video Releasing, 1 E. 57th St., New York, NY 10022 Tel 212-752-2240 (SAN 653-2683).

Film-Makers Library, 133 E. 58th St., New York, NY 10022 (SAN 653-3388).

Filmmakers Cooperative, 175 Lexington Ave., New York, NY 10016 Tel 212-889-3820 (SAN 670-6142).

Films Incorporated, 440 Park Ave. S., New York, NY 10016 Tel 212-889-7910 (SAN 670-6169) Tel 800-223-6246.

First Run Features, 144 Bleecker St., New York, NY 10012 Tel 212-673-6881 (SAN 653-3469).

Goldwyn, Samuel, 200 W. 57th St., New York, NY 10019 Tel 212-315-3030 (SAN 695-6793).

Graphic Curriculum, 699 Madison Ave., New York, NY 10021 Tel 212-688-0033 (SAN 653-3604).

Greaves, William, Prod., 1776 Broadway, Suite 1802, New York, NY 10019 Tel 212-586-7710 (SAN 653-5747).

Green, Joseph, Pictures Co., 200 W. 58th St., New York, NY 10019 Tel 212-246-9343 (SAN 653-3612).

Holcomb, Theodore, 11 E. 90th St., New York, NY 10028 Tel 212-861-6293 (SAN 653-3728).

I.Q. Films, Box 326, Wappingers Falls, NY 12590 Tel 914-297-0070 (SAN 653-3787).

Icarus Films/Cinema Perspectives, 200 Park Ave. S., Suite 1319, New York, NY 10003 Tel 212-674-3375 (SAN 653-3736).

Images Film Archive, 300 Phillips Pk. Rd., Mamaroneck, NY 10543 Tel 914-381-2993 (SAN 653-3760).

Institutional Cinema, Inc., 10 First St., Saugerties, NY 12477 Tel 914-246-2848 (SAN 653-3744).

International Film Exchange, 201 W. 52nd St., New York, NY 10019 Tel 212-582-4318 (SAN 672-7859).

Ivy Films, 165 W. 46th St., New York, NY 10036 Tel 212-382-0111 (SAN 653-3876).

JER Pictures, 165 W. 46th St., New York, NY 10036 Tel 212-247-4220 (SAN 653-3914).

Killiam Collection, Rental Div., 6 E. 39th St., New York, NY 10016 Tel 212-684-3920 (SAN 653-4007).

King Features Prod., 235 E. 45th St., New York, NY 10017 Tel 212-682-5600 (SAN 653-4015).

Kino International Corp., 250 W. 57th St., New York, NY 10019 Tel 212-586-8720 (SAN 672-7816).

Latin-American Film Project, 419 Park Ave. S., 19th Fl., New York, NY 10016 Tel 212-686-9897 (SAN 653-4082).

Learning Corp. of America, 1350 Ave. of the Americas, New York, NY 10019 Tel 212-397-9330 (SAN 653-4147).

Liberty Co., The, 695 W. Seventh St., Plainfield, NJ 07060 Tel 201-757-1450 (SAN 653-550X).

Macmillan Films, 34 MacQuestern Pkwy. S., Mt. Vernon, NY 10550 Tel 914-664-5051 (SAN 653-4767).

Maysles Films, 250 W. 54th St., New York, NY 10019 Tel 212-582-6050 (SAN 653-4805).

MGM/United Artists Entertainment, 1350 Ave. of the Americas, New York, NY 10019 Tel 800-223-0933 (SAN 670-610X).

Mokin, Arthur, Prod., 17 W. 60th St., New York, NY 10023 Tel 212-757-4868 (SAN 653-4880).

National Film Board of Canada, 1251 Ave. of the Americas, New York, NY 10020 Tel 212-586-5131 (SAN 653-5062).

New Line Cinema, 575 Eighth Ave., New York, NY 10018 Tel 212-674-7460 (SAN 653-5089).

New Time Films, 74 Varick Street, New York, NY 10013 Tel 212-226-8097 (SAN 672-0366).

New York Univ., Film Library, 26 Washington Pl., New York, NY 10003 Tel 212-777-2000 (SAN 653-5135).

New Yorker Films, 16 W. 61st St., New York, NY 10023 Tel 212-247-6110 (SAN 653-5127).

Pennebaker Assocs., 21 W. 86th St., New York, NY 10024 Tel 212-469-9195 (SAN 653-4155).

Phoenix/BFA Films & Video, 470 Park Ave. South, New York, NY 10016 Tel 212-684-5910 (SAN 653-5224).

RKO Radio Pictures, 1440 Broadway, New York, NY 10018 Tel 212-764-7108 (SAN 653-5283).

Red Ball Films, Inc., 41 Union Sq., New York, NY 10003 Tel 212-924-4368 (SAN 218-303X).

Salzburg Enterprises, Atrium Bldg., 98 Cutter Mill Rd., Great Neck, NY 11001 Tel 516-487-4515 (SAN 653-5348).

Schoenfeld Film Dist., 241 E. 34th Street, New York, NY 10016 Tel 212-532-5210 (SAN 671-8299).

See-Art Films, Box 638, Ardsley-on-Hudson, NY 10503 Tel 914-591-9207 (SAN 653-533X).

Select Audio Visual, 902 Broadway, New York, NY 10010 Tel 212-598-9800 (SAN 653-5356).

Starr, Cecile, 50 W. 96th St., New York, NY 10025 Tel 212-749-1250 (SAN 653-2357).

Sterling Educational Films, 241 E. 34th St., New York, NY 10016 Tel 212-683-6300 (SAN 653-5410).

Swank Motion Pictures, 393 Front St., Hempstead, NY 11550 Tel 516-538-6500 (SAN 670-6320); 60 Bethpage Rd., Hicksville, NY 11801 Tel 516-931-7500 (SAN 670-6339).

Syracuse Univ., Film Rental Ctr., 1455 E. Colvin St., Syracuse, NY 13210 Tel 315-423-2452 (SAN 653-5445).

Tricontinental Film Center/Unifilm, 419 Park Ave. S., New York, NY 10016 Tel 212-686-9877 (SAN 695-6807).

Twyman Films, 1035 Beach Road, Buffalo, NY 14225 Tel 716-631-8578 (SAN 670-6150).

Twyman Films, 45 W.45 St.(Rm. 503), New York, NY 10036 Tel 800-543-9594 (SAN 670-6223).

U. S.-China Peoples Friendship Assn. of New York, 41 Union Square W., No. 1228, New York, NY 10003 Tel 212-736-7355 (SAN 218-1347).

Vidamerica, 235 East 55th St., New York, NY 10022 Tel 212-355-1600 (SAN 670-6444).

WNET/13 Media Service, 356 W. 58th. St., New York, NY 10019 Tel 212-262-4940 (SAN 653-5771).

Welling Motion Pictures, 454 Meacham Ave., Elmont, NY 11003 Tel 516-354-1066 (SAN 653-5720).

Willoughby-Peerless, 115 W. 31st St., New York, NY 10001 Tel 212-929-6477 (SAN 654-9640).

Wilson, Daniel, Production, 300 W. 55 St., New York, NY 10019 Tel 212-765-7148 (SAN 653-2586).

Wombat Productions, Inc., Little Lake, Glendale Rd., Box 70, Ossining, NY 10562 Tel 914-762-0011 (SAN 653-578X).

Women Make Movies, 100 Fifth Ave., Rm. 1208, New York, NY 10011 Tel 212-929-6477 (SAN 276-7236).

World Northal Corp., 1 Dag Hammarskjold Plaza, New York, NY 10017 Tel 212-223-8181 (SAN 653-5763).

WW Entertainment, 205 E. 42nd St., New York, NY 10014 Tel 212-661-3350 (SAN 688-9581).

EAST

ABC Film Library, 560 Main St., Ft. Lee, NJ 07063 (SAN 653-1814).

Action 27 Film Library, P.O. Box 315, Franklin Lakes, NJ 07417 Tel 201-891-8240 (SAN 653-1822).

American Film Institute, The, (0-931282), Kennedy Ctr., Washington, DC 20566 (SAN 223-6044).

Auteur Films, 1042 Wisconsin Ave., NW, Washington, DC 20007 Tel 202-333-6966 (SAN 653-1989).

Bullfrog Films, Oley, PA 19547 Tel 215-779-8226 (SAN 653-2136).

Cambridge Documentary Films, Box 385, Cambridge, MA 02139 Tel 617-354-3677 (SAN 653-2225).

Cinema Concepts/Cinema 8, 2461 Berlin Turnpike, Newington, CT 06111 Tel 203-667-1251 (SAN 653-242X).

Classic Film Museum, 6 Union Sq., Dover-Foxcroft, ME 04426 Tel 207-564-8371 (SAN 653-2373).

Disney, Walt Prod., 11 Quine St., Cranford, NJ 07016 Tel 201-272-3150 (SAN 670-6177) Tel 800-631-7345.

Education Development Ctr., Inc., (0-89292), Orders to: EDC Publishing Ctr., 55 Chapel St., Newton, MA 02160 Tel 617-969-7100 (SAN 207-821X).

Edupac, 231 Norfolk St., Walpole, MA 02081 Tel 617-668-7746 (SAN 653-2594).

Embassy of Ireland, 2234 Massachusetts Ave., SW, Washington, DC 20008 Tel 202-483-7639 (SAN 653-3841).

Embassy of Malaysia, 2401 Massachusetts Ave., NW, Washington, DC 20008 Tel 202-234-7600 (SAN 653-4783).

Embassy of the Polish People's Republic, 2640 16th St. NW, Washington, DC 20009 Tel 202-234-3800 (SAN 653-5232).

Ewing, Wayne, Films, Box 32269, Washington, DC 20007 (SAN 653-5712).

Film Center, 938 K St., NW, Washington, DC 20001 Tel 202-393-1205 (SAN 653-5461).

Film Presentation Co., 514 Rt. 27, Box 232, Iselin, NJ 08830 Tel 201-283-1700 (SAN 653-3418).

Fremontia Films, Box 315, Franklin Lakes, NJ 07417 (SAN 653-3442).

Green Mountain Post Films, Box 229, Turners Falls, MA 01376 Tel 413-863-4754 (SAN 653-3566).

Griggs-Moviedrome, 263 Harrison St., Nutley, NJ 07110 (SAN 653-3558).

Hurlock Cine-World, 13 Arcadia Rd.(P.O. Box W), Old Greenwich, CT 06870 Tel 203-637-4319 (SAN 653-2438).

Lucerne Films, 37 Ground Pine Rd., Morris Plains, NJ 07950 (SAN 653-4759).

Mass Media Assocs., 2116 N. Charles St., Baltimore, MD 21218 Tel 301-727-3270 (SAN 653-4856).

Modern Mass Media, Box 950, Chatham, NJ 07928 Tel 210-635-6000 (SAN 653-4910).

Mogull's Films, 1280 North Ave., Plainfield, NJ 07062 Tel 201-753-6004 (SAN 653-4872).

National Audio-Visual Ctr., General Services Administration, Washington, DC 20409 Tel 310-763-1896 (SAN 653-4937).

National Cinema Service, Box 43, Ho-Ho-Kus, NJ 07423 Tel 201-445-0776 (SAN 653-5038).

National Film & Video Center, 1425 Liberty Rd., Eldersburg, MD 21784 Tel 800-638-1688 (SAN 653-5070).

New Day Films, 7 Harvard St., Brookline, MA 02145 Tel 617-566-5914 (SAN 653-5046).

Odeon Films, Box 315, Franklin Lakes, NJ 07417 (SAN 653-5143).

Open Circle Cinema, Box 315, Franklin Lakes, NJ 07417 Tel 201-891-8240 (SAN 653-5186).

PBS Video, 475 L'Enfant Plaza SW, Washington, DC 20024 Tel 202-488-5220 (SAN 653-5194).

Pennsylvania State Univ., Audio-Visual Services, Special Services Bldg., University Park, PA 16802 Tel 814-865-6314 (SAN 653-5216).

Red Fox Enterprises, Rt. 209 E., Elizabethville, PA 17023 (SAN 653-5267).

Reel Images, P.O. Box C, Sandy Hook, CT 06482 Tel 203-426-2574 (SAN 653-5275).

TVG Documentary Arts Project, Box 315, Franklin Lakes, NJ 07417 Tel 201-891-8240 (SAN 653-5526).

United Documentary Films, Box 315, Franklin Lakes, NJ 07417 Tel 201-891-8240 (SAN 653-5593).

Video-Forum, Div. of Jeffrey Norton Pubs., (0-88432), 96 Broad St., Guilford, CT 06437 Tel 203-453-9794 (SAN 217-4707).

Vision Quest, Box 206, Lawrenceville, NJ 08648 Tel 609-896-1359 (SAN 653-5674).

Weston Woods Studios, Weston, CT 06680 Tel 203-226-0600 (SAN 653-5739).

Wholesome Film Center, 20 Melrose St., Boston, MA 02116 Tel 617-426-0155 (SAN 653-5755).

Williams, Clem, Films, 2240 Noblestown Rd., Pittsburgh, PA 15205 Tel 412-921-5810 (SAN 653-2519) Tel 800-245-1146.

Williams, Clem Films, 10 High St. (Suite 10), Medford, MA 02155 Tel 617-391-1600 (SAN 670-624X) Tel 800-225-4456.

Zipporah Films, 1 Richdale Ave., Cambridge, MA 02140 Tel 617-576-3603 (SAN 653-5836).

SOUTH

American Educational Films, Inc., 162 Fourth Ave. N., Suite 123, Nashville, TN 37219 Tel 615-242-3330 (SAN 653-1830).

America's Films, 1735 N. W. Seventh St., Miami, FL 33125 Tel 305-643-0250 (SAN 653-1857).

Appalshop, P.O. Box 743, Whitesburg, KY 41858 (SAN 217-6270).

Films Inc., 476 Plasamour Dr. NE, Atlanta, GA 30324 Tel 404-873-5101 (SAN 695-6890).

Louisiana State Univ., Instructional Resources Ctr., Himes Hall, Rm. 118, Baton Rouge, LA 70803 Tel 504-388-1135 (SAN 653-421X).

Modern Talking Picture Service, 5000 Park St. N, St. Petersburg, FL 33709 Tel 813-541-7571 (SAN 656-2043).

Southern Chroniclers, Box 9925, Savannah, GA 31412 Tel 912-236-7757 (SAN 653-5372).

Swank Motion Pictures, 7926 Jones Branch Dr., McLean, VA 22101 Tel 703-821-1040 (SAN 670-6193) Tel 800-336-1000.

United Methodist Communications, 810 12th Ave. South, Nashville, TN 37203 Tel 615-256-0530 (SAN 653-5585).

MIDWEST

Alba House (Don Bosco), 7050 Pinehurst, Box 40, Dearborn, MI 48126 Tel 313-582-2033 (SAN 653-1865).

American Mutoscope & Biograph Co. of Milwaukee, 3802 E. Cudahy Ave., Cudahy, WI 53110 (SAN 653-1881).

Amerpol Enterprises, 11601 Joseph Campeau, Hamtramck, MI 48212 Tel 313-365-6780 (SAN 653-189X).

Argosy Films Inc., 1939 Central St., Evanston, IL 60513 Tel 312-485-3925 (SAN 670-6347).

Aument Film Library, Formally, Newman Film Library, 1444 Michigan Ave. NE, Grand Rapids, MI 49508 Tel 616-454-8157 (SAN 653-5054).

Blackhawk Films, Davenport, IA 52808 Tel 319-323-9736 (SAN 653-2098).

Centron Educational Films/Esquire Communications Group, 1621 W. Ninth St., Lawrence, KS 66044 Tel 913-843-0400 (SAN 653-2349).

Cousino Visual Ed. Serv., 1945 Franklin Ave., Toledo, OH 43624 Tel 419-246-3691 (SAN 653-2462).

Disney, Walt Prod., 666 Busse Hgwy., Park Ridge, IL 60068 Tel 312-825-0155 (SAN 670-6207) Tel 800-323-0128.

Elliot Film Co., 2635 Nicollet Ave., Minneapolis, MN 55408 Tel 612-870-3750 (SAN 653-2608).

Festival Films, 2841 Irving Ave., South Minneapolis, MN 55408 Tel 612-870-4744 (SAN 653-2691).

Film Images/Radim Films, 1034 Lake St., Oak Park, IL 60301 Tel 312-386-4826 (SAN 653-5259).

Films, Inc., 733 Wilmette Ave., Suite 202, Wilmette, IL 60091 Tel 312-256-6600 (SAN 653-3396).

Gospel Films, Box 455, Muskegon, MI 49443 Tel 616-773-3361 (SAN 653-3582).

Great Plains National Instructional Television Library, (0-9614949), Box 80669, Lincoln, NE 68501 Tel 800-228-4630 (SAN 213-0696).

Herne, Gary L., Sales, 910 Hilton Rd., Ferndale, MI 48220 Tel 313-398-4144 (SAN 653-3620).

Indiana Univ., Audio-Visual Ctr., Bloomington, IN 47405 Tel 812-332-0211 (SAN 653-3779).

Janus Films, 1213 Wilmette Ave., Wilmette, IL 60091 Tel 312-256-3200 (SAN 653-3892).

Kent State Univ., Film Rental Ctr., Kent, OH 44242 Tel 216-672-3456 (SAN 653-3949).

Lewis Film Services, 1425 E. Central, Witchita, KS 67214 Tel 316-263-6991 (SAN 653-4171).

MTI Teleprograms Inc./A Simon & Schuster Communications Company, (0-916070), 108 Wilmot Rd., Deerfield, IL 60015 Tel 312-940-1260 (SAN 211-0350).

Magnetic Video Corp., 23705 Industrial Pk. Dr., Farmington Hills, MI 48018 Tel 313-477-6066 (SAN 653-4775).

Maljack Productions VCI, P.O. Box 153, Tinley Park, IL 60477 Tel 312-687-7881 (SAN 653-4848).

Modern Sound Pictures, 1402 Howard St., Omaha, NE 68102 Tel 800-228-9584 (SAN 653-4864).

New Front Films, 1409 Willow St., Minneapolis, MN 55403 Tel 612-872-0805 (SAN 672-1745).

Northwestern Univ., Film Library, Box 1665, Evanston, IL 60204 Tel 312-869-0600 (SAN 653-5119).

Perspective Films/Esquire Communications Group, (0-89611), 369 W Erie St., Chicago, IL 60610 (SAN 221-007X).

Roa's Films, 1696 N. Astor St., Milwaukee, WI 53202 Tel 414-271-0861 (SAN 653-5291).

Standard Film Service, P.O. Box 52, Frankenmuth, MI 48734 Tel 517-652-8881 (SAN 653-5402).

Swank Motion Pictures, 201 S. Jefferson Ave., St. Louis, MO 63166 Tel 314-534-6300 (SAN 653-5437) Tel 800-325-3344.

Swank Motion Pictures, 2777 Finley Rd., Downers Grove, IL 60515 Tel 312-629-9004 (SAN 670-6290).

Texture Film Collection, P.O. Box 1337, Skokie, IL 60076 Tel 312-256-4436 (SAN 218-1037).

Trans-World Films, 332 S. Michigan Ave., Chicago, IL 60604 Tel 312-922-1530 (SAN 653-5542).

Twyman, Alan, Presents, The Rohauer Collection, Inc., 592 S. Grant Ave., Columbus, OH 43206 Tel 614-469-0720 (SAN 695-6386).

Twyman Films, 4700 Wadsworth Rd. P.O. Box 605, Dayton, OH 45414 Tel 513-276-5941 (SAN 653-5550).

University Community Video, Studio A, Rarig Ctr., University of Minnesota, 330 21st Ave. S., Minneapolis, MN 55455 (SAN 218-141X).

University of Illinois, Film Center, 1325 S. Oak St., Champaign, IL 61820 Tel 217-333-1360 (SAN 653-3752).

University of Iowa, C-5 Seashore Hall, Iowa City, IA 52242 Tel 319-353-5885 (SAN 671-8140).

University of Michigan, Media Resources Center, 416 Fourth St., Ann Arbor, MI 48109 Tel 313-764-5360 (SAN 653-483X).

Viewfinders, Box 1665, Evanston, IL 60204 Tel 312-869-0600 (SAN 653-5658).

Williams, Clem Films, 146 W. Harrison St., Oak Park, IL 60304 Tel 312-525-1505 (SAN 670-641X).

Williams, Wade, Prod., 5500 Ward Parkway, Kansas City, MO 64113 Tel 816-523-2699 (SAN 653-5801).

Young People's Specials, Multimedia Program Prod., 140 W. Ninth St., Cincinnati, OH 45202 (SAN 653-5828).

WEST

Award Films, 525 North Laurel Ave., Los Angeles, CA 90048 (SAN 696-0030).

Best Films, Box 725, Del Mar, CA 92014 Tel 714-755-9327 (SAN 653-2055).

Brazos Films, (0-933797), 10341 San Pablo Ave., El Cerrito, CA 94530 Tel 415-525-7471 (SAN 653-2101); Dist. by: Flower Films, 10341 San Pablo Ave., El Cerrito, CA 94530 Tel 415-525-0942 (SAN 653-2748).

Budget Films, 4590 Santa Monica Blvd., Los Angeles, CA 90029 Tel 213-660-0187 (SAN 653-2128).

CRM/McGraw-Hill Films, 110 15th St., Del Mar, CA 92014 Tel 714-453-5000 (SAN 653-4821).

California Newsreel/Media at Work/Resolution, 630 Natoma, San Francisco, CA 94103 Tel 415-621-6196 (SAN 653-5097).

Canyon Cinema Cooperative, 2325 Third St., San Francisco, CA 94107 Tel 415-626-2255 (SAN 653-337X).

Centre Prod., 1327 Spruce St., Suite 3, Boulder, CO 80302 Tel 303-444-1166 (SAN 653-2365).

Churchill Films, 622 N. Robertson Blvd., Los Angeles, CA 90069 (SAN 653-2411).

Cine-Craft Co., 1720 W. Marshall, P.O. Box 4126, Portland, OR 79209 Tel 503-228-7484 (SAN 653-2314).

Creative Film Society, 8435 Geyser Ave., Northridge, CA 91324 Tel 818-885-7288 (SAN 217-698X).

Crystal Prod., Box 12317, Aspen, CO 81612 (SAN 653-2489).

Disney, Walt, Prod., 6904 Tujunga Ave., Hollywood, CA 91605 Tel 800-423-2200 (SAN 653-2543).

Educational Media Corp./UEVA, 6930 Tujunga Ave., N. Hollywood, CA 91605 Tel 213-985-3921 (SAN 653-2616).

Em Gee Film Library, 6924 Canby Ave., Suite 103, Reseda, CA 91335 Tel 818-981-5506 (SAN 653-2640).

Embassy Pictures, 1901 Ave. of the Stars, Los Angeles, CA 90067 (SAN 656-3872).

Film Classic Exchange, *(0-9610916),* P.O. Box 77568 Dockweiler Stn., Los Angeles, CA 90007 Tel 213-731-3854 (SAN 265-1351).

Film Wright, 4530 18th St., San Francisco, CA 94114 Tel 415-863-6100 (SAN 653-3515).

Films Inc., 5625 Hollywood Blvd., Hollywood, CA 90028 Tel 213-466-5481 (SAN 695-6904) Tel 800-421-0612.

Finney, Edward, 1578 Queens Blvd., Hollywood, CA 90069 Tel 213-656-0200 (SAN 653-273X).

Flower Films/Les Blank, 10341 San Pablo Ave., El Cerrito, CA 94530 Tel 415-525-0942 (SAN 653-2748).

Glenn Photo Supply, 6924 Canby Ave., Suite 103, Reseda, CA 91335 (SAN 653-3590).

Gold Key Entertainment, 855 N. Cahuenga Blvd., Los Angeles, CA 90067 (SAN 653-3523).

Golden Tapes Videotape Library, 336 Foothill Rd., Beverley Hills, CA 90213 Tel 213-550-8156 (SAN 653-3574).

Kerr Film Exchange, 3034 Canon St., San Diego, CA 92106 Tel 619-224-2406 (SAN 653-3981).

Lutheran Film Associates, One Main Place, Dallas, TX 75250 Tel 214-747-8048 (SAN 653-4198).

Master & Masterworks, 1431 Ocean Ave., Suite 1400, Santa Monica, CA 90401 Tel 213-393-8337 (SAN 653-4791).

Media Guild, 11526 Sorrento Valley Road, San Diego, CA 92121 Tel 619-755-9191 (SAN 678-3201).

Merco International Films, Box B, Somis, CA 93066 Tel 805-484-2213 (SAN 653-4813).

MGM/United Artists Entertainment, 5890 W. Jefferson Blvd., Culver City, CA 91230 Tel 213-838-2148 (SAN 669-7518) Tel 800-847-4119.

Morcraft Films/Penguin Video, Formerly: Thunderbird Films, P.O. Box 65157, Los Angles, CA 90065 (SAN 682-0395).

Nostalgia Merchant, The, 6255 Sunset Blvd., Suite 1019, Hollywood, CA 90028 Tel 800-421-4495 (SAN 653-5518).

Oklahoma State Univ., Audio-Visual Ctr., Stillwater, OK 74078 Tel 405-372-6211 (SAN 653-516X).

Parker, Kit, Films, 1245 Tenth St., Monterrey, CA 93940 Tel 408-649-5573 (SAN 653-404X) Tel 800-538-5838.

Pyramid Films, Box 1048, Santa Monica, CA 90406 (SAN 218-2807).

Republic Pictures Film, Div. of Republic Pictures Corp., 12636 Beatrice St., Los Angeles, CA 90066-0930 Tel 213-306-4040 (SAN 695-4413).

South Dakota State Univ., Audio Visual Ctr., University Station, Brookings, SD 57006 Tel 605-688-5115 (SAN 653-5313).

Special Purpose Films, 26740 Latigo Shore Dr., Malibu, CA 90265 (SAN 653-5380).

Specialty Films, 911 NE 50th, Seattle, WA 98105 Tel 206-634-3834 (SAN 653-5399).

Step Ahead Films, 1800 Ave. of the Stars, Suite 900, Los Angeles, CA 90067 (SAN 653-5305).

Stouffer Enterprises, P.O. Box 4740, Aspen, CO 81611 Tel 303-925-9227 (SAN 653-5429).

Tamarelle's French Film House, 110 Cohasset Stage Rd., Chico, CA 95925 Tel 916-895-3429 (SAN 653-5453).

Threshold Films, 2025 N. Highland Ave., Hollywood, CA 90068 Tel 213-874-8413 (SAN 653-547X).

University of California, Extension Media Center, 2223 Fulton St., Berkeley, CA 94720 Tel 415-845-6000 (SAN 653-2195).

University of Colorado, Educational Center, Bureau of Audio-Visual Instruction, P.O. Box 379, Boulder, CO 80309 Tel 303-443-2211 (SAN 653-5607).

Univ. of Nevada, Audio-Visual Ctr., Education Bldg., Reno, NV 89507 (SAN 653-5615).

Univ. of South Dakota, Film Library, Educational Media Ctr., Vermillion, SD 57069 Tel 605-677-5411 (SAN 653-5321).

Univ. of Utah, Educational Media Ctr., Milton Bennion Hall 207, Salt Lake City, UT 84110 Tel 801-322-6112 (SAN 653-5623).

Video Communications, Inc., 6555 E. Skelly Dr., Tulsa, OK 74145 Tel 918-662-6460 (SAN 653-564X) Tel 800-331-4077.

Westcoast Films, 25 Lusk St., San Francisco, CA 94107 Tel 415-362-4700 (SAN 653-5704) Tel 800-227-3058.

Young, Brigham, Univ., 290 Herald R. Clark Bldg., Provo, UT 84601 Tel 801-374-1211 (SAN 653-2144).

CANADA

Canadian Broadcasting Corp., *(0-88794),* Box 500 Terminl A, Toronto Ont. M5W 1E6, CN .

New Cinema, Ltd., 35 Britain St., Toronto, Ont. M5A 1R7, CN .

Raymond, Bruce. A., Prod., 353 St. Clair Ave. E., Toronto, Ont. M4Y 1P3, CN .